AF352587

Muiwlanej kikamaqki –
Honouring Our Ancestors

STUDIES IN ATLANTIC CANADA HISTORY

Editors: John G. Reid, Heidi MacDonald,
and Peter L. Twohig

This monograph series focuses on the history of Atlantic Canada, interpreting the scope of this field in a way that is deliberately inclusive and accommodating. As well as studies that deal wholly with any aspect of the history of the Atlantic region (or part thereof), the series extends to neighbouring geographical areas that are considered in conjunction with or in parallel with a portion of Atlantic Canada. Atlantic Canada's oceanic or global relationships are also included, and studies from any thematic or historiographical perspective are welcome.

Books in the Series

Meaghan Elizabeth Beaton, *The Centennial Cure: Commemoration, Identity, and Cultural Capital in Nova Scotia during Canada's 1967 Centennial Celebrations*

Jeffers Lennox, *Homelands and Empires: Indigenous Spaces, Imperial Fictions, and Competition for Territory in Northeastern North America, 1690–1763*

Lachlan MacKinnon, *Closing Sysco: Industrial Decline in Atlantic Canada's Steel City*

Margaret Conrad, *At the Ocean's Edge: A History of Nova Scotia to Confederation*

S. Karly Kehoe, *Empire and Emancipation: Scottish and Irish Catholics at the Atlantic Fringe, 1780–1850*

Harvey Amani Whitfield, *Biographical Dictionary of Black Slaves in the Maritimes*

Janet E. Chute et al., *Muiwlanej kikamaqki – Honouring Our Ancestors: Mi'kmaq Who Left a Mark on the History of the Northeast, 1680 to 1980*

Muiwlanej kikamaqki – Honouring Our Ancestors

Mi'kmaq Who Left a Mark on the History of the Northeast, 1680 to 1980

Edited by Janet E. Chute

Foreword by Donald M. Julien

Authors:
B.A. Balcom, Diane Chisholm, Janet E. Chute, Carrie Gloade, Anne Marie Lane Jonah, Doris Labradore, Bunny McBride, Mora Dianne O'Neill, Nik Phillips, Travis Pinn, and Heather Sutherland

Research And Editing Assistance:
Victor Alex, Marie Anne Battiste, Vernon Cope, Courtney Brooks-Monteith, Richard Denny, Mary-Ellen Googoo, Marjorie Gould, James Howe Sr., Allison Lloy, Lillian Marshall, Charles A. Martijn, Natalie McConnell, Brittany Pennel, Nicholas Prisk, Gregory Solomon, Mary Wells, and Sherise Williams

University of Toronto Press
Toronto Buffalo London

ISBN 978-1-4875-4613-7 (cloth)   ISBN 978-1-4875-4614-4 (EPUB)
ISBN 978-1-4875-4615-1 (PDF)

Library and Archives Canada Cataloguing in Publication

Title: Muiwlanej kikamaqki – honouring our ancestors : Mi'kmaq who left a mark on the history of the northeast, 1680 to 1980 / edited by Janet E. Chute ; foreword by Donald M. Julien ; authors: B.A. Balcom [and ten others] ; research and editing assistance: Victor Alex [and sixteen others].
Other titles: Honouring our ancestors
Names: Chute, Janet Elizabeth, editor.
Description: Includes bibliographical references and index.
Identifiers: Canadiana (print) 20230205984 | Canadiana (ebook) 20230206123 | ISBN 9781487546137 (hardcover) | ISBN 9781487546144 (EPUB) | ISBN 9781487546151 (PDF)
Subjects: LCSH: Canada, Eastern – History. | CSH: Mi'kmaq – Canada, Eastern – History. | CSH: First Nations leadership – Canada, Eastern – History.
Classification: LCC E99.M6 M85 2023 | DDC 971.3004/97343 – dc23

Cover design: Louise OFarrell
Cover image: Chief Joseph Julian from a postcard courtesy of Madeline Martin

All author royalties for *Muiwlanej kikamaqki – "Honouring Our Ancestors"* are being donated directly to the Confederacy of Mainland Mi'kmaq in Truro to support a prize for Mi'kmaw students who are graduating high school and attending university or another institution of higher learning. The award is named the Dr. Elsie Charles Basque Prize in honour of the remarkable woman to whom this work is dedicated.

We wish to acknowledge the land on which the University of Toronto Press operates. This land is the traditional territory of the Wendat, the Anishnaabeg, the Haudenosaunee, the Métis, and the Mississaugas of the Credit First Nation.

This book has been published with the help of a grant from the Federation for the Humanities and Social Sciences, through the Awards to Scholarly Publications Program, using funds provided by the Social Sciences and Humanities Research Council of Canada.

University of Toronto Press acknowledges the financial support of the Government of Canada, the Canada Council for the Arts, and the Ontario Arts Council, an agency of the Government of Ontario, for its publishing activities.

*To Elsie Charles Basque, author, activist, educator, and humanitarian
(12 May 1916–11 April 2016)*

I cannot cross the Great Lake to talk to you for my canoe is too small and I am too old and weak. Cannot look upon you for my eyes not see so far. You cannot hear my voice across the Great Waters. I therefore send you this Wampum and Paper talk to tell the Queen I am in trouble. My people are in trouble. I have seen upwards of a Thousand Moons. When I was young I had plenty. Now I am old, poor, and sickly too. My people are poor. No hunting grounds … Our fathers possessed them all. Now we cannot cut a tree to warm our Wigwam in Winter unless the White Man please … We look to you the Queen. The White Wampum tell that we hope in You … My Head and my Heart shall go to the One above for you.

Louis-Benjamin Peminout Paul to Queen Victoria, 1841

Contents

Foreword

It is an honour, privilege, and pleasure to provide this foreword to *Muiwlanej kikamaqki – Honouring Our Ancestors: Mi'kmaq Who Left a Mark on the History of the Northeast, 1680 to 1980* by Janet E. Chute and her colleagues. This volume is a compilation of painstaking research and documentation completed through the collaboration of Mi'kmaw and non-Mi'kmaw scholars, including Aboriginal university students who have worked under the guidance of Dr. Chute. It is an intriguing collection of factual historical information about Aboriginal leadership across Mi'kma'ki (the Atlantic Provinces, southern Quebec, and Maine) and the seven Mi'kmaw districts.

From a Mi'kmaw perspective, this book is useful because it highlights historical genealogical issues by focusing on kinship connections among our families and these families' interrelationships with early settlers: Acadian, Planter, Germanic, and Loyalist. It gives the reader a clear view of the importance of family connections between the Mi'kmaq and the Acadians, as well as later settlers within Mi'kma'ki. It also provides an overview of the leadership of each district and attests to the consistent diplomacy that Mi'kmaw leaders practised with colonial officials.

Dr. Elsie Charles Basque, to whom this book is dedicated, was the first Mi'kmaw person to graduate from the Nova Scotia Teachers College. She devoted her long life to education and community service, for which she received numerous honours and accolades. As a researcher myself into Mi'kmaw history and land and resource rights for over fifty years, I highly recommend that this volume, written in Elsie's memory, be read by all wanting to learn more about the Aboriginal history of the Northeast. And to the authors and students responsible for the almost unbelievable amount of historical investigatory work undertaken in researching and writing this book – congratulations!

Dr. Donald M. Julien, CM, ONS, DCL, DHumL
Executive Director of CMM
Keptin of the Grand Council of Mi'kmaq for the Sipekne'katik District

Preface

Welcome to *Muiwanalej Kikmanaqik*: "Let's Honour Our Ancestors"

This volume explores the lives of noteworthy Mi'kmaw individuals whose thoughts, actions, and aspirations had an impact on the history of the Northeast, but whose activities were too often relegated to the shadows of history. In this work, these persons' achievements hold centre stage. This is essentially a reference book; providing a lengthy index so that information pertaining to these persons may be retrieved and used as basis for further research. There is much to admire in Mi'kmaw leaders' past community and emigration policies, organizational and negotiating skills, diplomatic endeavours, and stewardship of land and resources. This is matched today by important new insights furnished by excellent Mi'kmaw scholars who successfully re-centre Indigenous nationhood and lifeways and so have "an impact on the way we understand the field itself."[1] It is hoped that, in providing new information and perspectives, this volume too will engage the interest of Indigenous and non-Indigenous readers alike, engender pride in Mi'kmaw leadership legacies, and encourage Mi'kmaw youth and others to probe more deeply into the history of the Northeast.

The project was instigated with a threefold purpose: to encourage senior scholars to submit works on noted or interesting individuals, to enable Aboriginal university students to research and write Mi'kmaw biographies, and to confirm Mi'kmaw history as an integral part of Canadian and American history. It progressed through two stages, with these goals remaining paramount throughout.

During stage one, from the spring of 1990 to the fall of 1991, the project received assistance from the Social Sciences and Humanities Research Council of Canada (SSHRC) under postdoctoral grants 456-89-0192 and 457-90-0153. Owing to SSHRC's generous support the recipient of these grants, Janet E. Chute, was able to hire two industrious Aboriginal university students, Doris Labradore and Natalie McConnell, as her assistants. All three toured the Northeast conducting research in archives and museums and meeting local historians. Doris and Natalie remained part of the project until late 2008.

The project also gained the valuable support of Gillian Allen, B.A. Berton, Marie Battiste, Patti Doyle-Bedwell, Joan Dawson, Olive Patricia Dickason, Marjorie Gould, Father

Clarence-J. d'Entremont,[2] Donald M. Julien, Cathy Martin, and Charles Martijn. These persons soon became friends; their generosity in sharing knowledge and support for the project won them a lasting place in the hearts of the principal investigator and her students. Scholarly direction was provided by Leslie Jane McMillan, John Reid, Fred Wien, and William C. Wicken. Editing assistance was offered by A.J.B. Johnston. Others helped with the collection and interpretation of data, among them Bernard Amiro, Jerry Bartlett, Joan Dawson, Alex Denny, Richard Denny, Sarah Denny, Alden Francis, Mary Francis, Frank Jeremy, Sandy Julien, Doug Knockwood, Florence Marie Knockwood, Henry Knockwood, Isabelle Knockwood, William Labrador, Greg McEwan, Richard McEwan, Wallis Nevin, Charlie Paul, Daniel N. Paul, Lawrence Paul, Peter Partington, Kenny Prosper, Lillian Pictou, Viola Robinson, David Schmidt, Helen Sylliboy, Ruth Holmes Whitehead, and Max Zwicker. Caroline and Roddy Gould graciously opened their home at Waycobah, Cape Breton, to visiting academics and students alike. The proprietors of Milford House, established around 1900 as a wilderness lodge along Highway 8 between Annapolis Royal and Liverpool and with a history of employing Mi'kmaw guides, made the Mi'kmaw students feel especially welcome. Early stages of the study also benefitted from the assistance of Donald Marshall Sr. and his son Donald Marshall Jr., as well as from Alex Denny and John Joe Sark.[3]

Stage two followed the launch of SSHRC's Aboriginal Research Strategic Programs, an initiative guided by Craig McNaughton, SSHRC's director of knowledge mobilization and program integration. Principal investigator Janet E. Chute and co-applicant Mora Dianne O'Neill obtained their first grant from this source in 2004, an Aboriginal Research Development Grant (no. 856-2009-0045) in 2009, and an extension of the 2009 grant until the end of September 2012. Attainment of this SSHRC funding allowed for the convening in 2005 of a conference at the Membertou Trade Centre in Cape Breton with invited guests from the Cape Breton Mi'kmaw community. Members of this conference anticipated the production of Mi'kmaw biographies of a standard equal to those appearing in the *Dictionary of Canadian Biography,* though a departure from *DCB* stylistic guidelines would be permitted to allow for copious and often lengthy endnotes. Endnotes, it was felt, could provide insights into interpretative processes that guided students and authors, especially as some of the research was expected to break new ground. During the conference, Elders Margaret Johnson and Murdena Marshall dispensed with the project's original title, "Empowering the Mi'kmaw Voice in the Creation of Personal Histories," and Lillian Marshall suggested *Muiwanalej Kikmanaqik,* "Let's Honour Our Ancestors," as an alternative.[4] Their reasoning was based on two premises: first, that the student researchers would prefer the title change, and second, that the initial title underestimated the power "now and forever" resident in the Mi'kmaw voice. The Aboriginal students agreed, and the second title was adopted. It also was not long before the student participants demonstrated a vital spirit of enquiry that lent this new title credence. Their desire to honour the memory of cherished ancestors permeated their research activities and lent acuity and insight to their academic findings.

At this point Marjorie Gould, Joe B. Marshall, Mary-Ellen Googoo, and Donald M. Julien generously agreed to serve as project partners. Student researchers benefitted immensely from Ruth Holmes Whitehead's labours in setting up the Nova Scotia Museum's online Mi'kmaw Portraits Collection as well as from two of her books, *The Old Man Told Us* and *Niniskamijinaqik/Ancestral Images: The Mi'kmaq in Art and Photography.* Both these works drew on documentary and pictorial evidence to provide windows into the Mi'kmaw past.[5] Since Darlene A. Ricker's *L'sitkuk: The Story of the Bear River Mi'kmaw Community* already offered comprehensive information on the Lewis, Meuse, and Pictou families of southwestern Nova Scotia, our project only touched upon these Mi'kmaw families in order to avoid duplication of information.[6]

Scholars Carol Ann (Bunny) McBride, Harald E.L. Prins, B.A. Balcom, Anne Marie Lane Jonah, Mora Dianne O'Neill, and Diane Chisholm contributed biographical entries based on years of investigative research. Though Bunny McBride and Harald Prins's entry on Donald Sanipass (1928–2007) contravenes the temporal parameters of this project, it retains special significance because it demonstrates how a traditional Elder contributed significantly to changes within modern Aboriginal society.[7] Berton A. ("Sandy") Balcom, a retired senior historian at Fortress Louisbourg Historical Park, submitted chapters 15 to 21 on early Cape Breton leaders Capisto, Isidore, François N'8gin'tok, Jacques Padanuques, Jean Michau, Michel Michau, and Denis Michau. Anne Marie Lane Jonah, currently a senior historian with the Regional Office of Parks Canada in Halifax, investigates the life of the aristocratic Marie Joseph le Borgne de Belisle, outlines how a young *métis* woman from Merliguèche (now Lunenburg) named Marguerite Guedry ran afoul of the Louisbourg establishment when she married a French ensign, and provides a haunting portrayal of Marguerite, a domestic who served in a Louisbourg household. Mora Dianne O'Neill, associate curator of historical prints and drawings at the Art Gallery of Nova Scotia in Halifax, furnishes an account of the enigmatic nineteenth-century figure John W. Johnson, who eschewed his non-Indigenous origins to join Northeastern Abenaki society. The volume concludes with Diane Chisholm's sensitive perspective on Mi'kmaw spirituality, which she developed while working with Aboriginal Elders, academic associates, and students as coordinator of the Mi'kmaq Resource Centre at the University of Cape Breton in Sydney.

The students and university graduates who joined the project during stage two were Carrie Gloade, Doris Labradore, Alison Lloy, Natalie McConnell, Courtney Brooks-Monteith, Brittany Pennel, Nik Phillips, Travis Pinn, Ray Sewell, Gregory Solomon, Heather Sutherland, Mary Wells, and Sherise Williams. Most, but not all, claim Aboriginal heritage. Though these persons often faced competing interpretations arising from the evidence at hand, they usually settled on one, while proffering alternative interpretations in endnotes. Those who directed student researchers to relevant data included Carla Asprey, Don Awalt, Elsie Charles Basque, Kevin Boucher, Ruth Randall Cann, Vernon Cope, Dwight Dorey, Bob Gloade, Daniel Gloade, Gordon Gloade, Steve Gloade, Debbie Gloade, Debora Gloade, Frances Gray-Godin, Linda Green, James Howe, Dora Jones, Willa Kaiser, Marguerite Labrador, Gerald Lavigne, Ian Lawrence, Roger Lewis, Mary-Frances Lynch, Maxine Townsend, Lillian Marshall, Nancy Morgan, Delbert Muise, John Muise, Sylvestre Muise, Stephen Pennel, David Peter-Paul, Basil Peters, Fred Phillips Sr., Bill Partridge, Nicholas Prisk, Brian Purdy, Rose Purdy, Linda Rafuse, Mary Sanipass, Trevor Sanipass, Garry Shutlak, Gilbert Sewell, Heather Stevens, Mary Jane Stevens, Maxine Townsend, and Anjali Vohra. Every voice proved uniquely significant. Nathan Sowry graciously sent a photograph of William Thomas Gloade of Millbrook and Shubenacadie from the photographic collection of the Smithsonian's National Museum of the American Indian in Washington, DC. Craig McNaughton and Anna Torgerson of SSHRC, in cooperation with Mount Saint Vincent University, ably administered funding and monitored the course of research. Under Craig McNaughton's auspices three students, Courtney Brooks-Monteith, Brittany Pennel, and Mary Wells, also became guests of the director and staff of Aboriginal Research Strategic Programs at SSHRC's headquarters in Ottawa.

Special gratitude is extended to the late Patrick O'Neill, vice president of research at Mount Saint Vincent University, who in 2004 encouraged Janet E. Chute and Mora Dianne O'Neill to embark on stage two of the project. Patrick understood that biographical work constitutes a never-ending story as new information comes to light. A.J.B. Johnson, Debora Pollock, Dorothy Anne Snyder, and Janet Forrest read over early versions of chapters. Marlene Martin of Millbrook near Truro in Nova Scotia kindly supplied a photograph of Chief Joseph Julien. University of Toronto acquisitions editor Len Husband brought together knowledgeable and insightful readers to assist with the manuscript in its early stages, as well as amiably shepherded the work along to its final form. Freelance editor Terry Teskey admirably shouldered the lion's share of copy-editing, and did so with great care, determination, and incisiveness. Finally, the principal investigator acknowledges the assistance of her mother, Mary Elizabeth (Betty) Chute, as well as her husband, Richard Haugen, who aided in so many ways with research and travel, and who kept the home fires burning while she and her students conducted fieldwork.

Introduction

This volume presents biographies of Mi'kmaw individuals living between 1680 and 1970 who left indelible positive imprints on Atlantic Provinces history. The project that guided this work began as an initiative launched in 2004 by the Social Science and Humanities Research Council of Canada (SSHRC) designed to bring seasoned scholars and Aboriginal university students together to produce novel insights into the Mi'kmaw past by examining events through the eyes of the Mi'kmaw individuals experiencing them.[1] The parameters of the study reach back into the late seventeenth century. Until the 1770s, the sphere of Mi'kmaw community thought and action had a significant impact on the course of history in the Northeast. Though muted and marginalized under policies implemented during the British colonial regime, the Mi'kmaq in the late twentieth century began once again to influence the Canadian social mainstream, a trend that has grown stronger in recent years.

Scarcity of autobiographical and other personal papers pertaining to the individuals chosen for biographical treatment entailed adopting a broad community approach to provide context for a person's life story. This meant extending a personal history to include the legacy that a subject left to their families and to society. Originally it was intended that the biographical entries would adhere to the format set down in the *Dictionary of Canadian Biography* (DCB).[2] This goal was altered because the scarcity of autobiographical and personal records pertaining to the Mi'kmaq prior to 1900 required greater reliance on community oral traditions. Documentary sources rarely did more than touch upon the life of an individual under investigation; cross-referencing of documentary information with oral evidence was needed to form a rounded portrayal. This required that the audience be kept abreast of how information was accessed and used, which in turn gave rise to copious endnotes. Some of the longer biographies, furthermore, examine a person's family, community, and descendants, so that the number of individuals subject to biographical treatment in this volume is large. Chapters 1, 2, 3, 6, 7, 9, 11, 12, 15, and 19 are full-length articles rather than relatively brief biographical entries, which have been researched and in some cases written by students exploring the lives of their Aboriginal ancestors.

In shorter entries the reference section uses the abbreviated format that appears in the *Dictionary of Canadian Biography*; in longer entries citations appear sequentially throughout the text. As two major goals of this project were to introduce students to the practice of writing Aboriginal biography and to have them identify areas for future research, students were instructed to ensure that the sources they used were clearly set out in endnotes, and some of these became lengthy. It is hoped that future scholars will employ such information to begin new research that will build upon, confirm, or correct the present narratives. The approach taken towards biographical writing varies from entry to entry, depending on the subject and the nature of the information available. Some entries cover an individual's life story from birth to death, others focus on the high points of an individual's personal history, and still others examine lasting influences that a person had on their community.

Research was conducted by Aboriginal students who often chose to investigate their own ancestors, who were well known to their families. Their desire to interview parents, close family members, and local historians to glean oral traditions provided a fresh "insider" approach to information gathering. And as they progressed, their inquiries invariably gave rise to new understandings. Where the writing of a personal history owes a major debt to such dedicated work undertaken by Aboriginal student researchers, students' names are given in an acknowledgment section at the end of the entry.

Like gems gleaming in parent rock, most of the oral traditions shared by community members led to deeper seams of valuable knowledge. And stories emerged from unexpected quarters as well. Though some in their retelling had crossed cultural and social boundaries, most oral traditions retained an authentic vitality.[3] Hearing such stories proved a heady experience for Indigenous students, who initially felt that gaining reputable information on the Aboriginal past constituted a challenge. Historian William C. Wicken has argued that the "colonization of Mi'kmaw history and memory" has veiled genuine understandings of what happened historically within Mi'kmaw communities.[4] Yet the ability to access Mi'kmaw oral traditions first-hand allowed students to do their research without worrying about non-Mi'kmaw obfuscations or distortions of the historical record.

Essays on the individuals selected by student researchers for biographical treatment were placed on a par with the contributions by seasoned scholars B.A. Balcom, Diane Chisholm, Anne Marie Lane Jonah, Harald Prins, Bunny McBride, and Mora Dianne O'Neill, all of whom are academics whose careers have included writing detailed personal histories of Mi'kmaw individuals. B.A. Balcom and Anne Marie Lane Jonah worked for many years as historians with Fortress Louisbourg Historic Park in Cape Breton. Their entries provide novel insights into late seventeenth- and eighteenth-century Mi'kmaw life in what is now Cape Breton. Diane Chisholm, coordinator of the Mi'kmaw Resource Centre at the University of Cape Breton in Sydney, Nova Scotia, provides sensitive understandings of Mi'kmaw spirituality and world view. Husband-and-wife team Bunny McBride and Harald Prins, who until recently were both on the faculty of the Department of Anthropology at the University of Kansas, have published numerous books and articles on Indigenous peoples in the Northeast.[5] Their entry on Donald Sanipass arose from years of dedicated supportive work they offered Chief Sanipass and his council, work that eventually gave rise to Washington's recognition of the Aroostook Mi'kmaw community of Maine as a legal Aboriginal entity. Mora Dianne O'Neill, an author and a curator with the Art Gallery of Nova Scotia in Halifax, developed an interest in John W. Johnson (1829–1907) during her years researching historic prints and paintings on Indigenous subjects for other publications. John W. Johnson rejected his European origins to follow an Eastern Abenaki way of life. The works of each of these authors do much to restore the sphere of Mi'kmaw experience to an integral place in the history of the Northeast.

The student researchers were initially recruited from Dalhousie University and were later joined by undergraduate and graduate students from Mount Saint Vincent University and Saint Mary's University. In 1990 and 1991 two Aboriginal undergraduate students from Dalhousie University, Doris Labradore and Natalie McConnell, set out with the principal investigator to conduct archival investigations in southwestern Nova Scotia, Prince Edward Island, and Cape Breton. They also interviewed Mi'kmaw persons who were knowledgeable about their own history. This early research was a wonderful initiation into the complexities of Mi'kmaw history, since Mi'kmaw community historians went out of their way to share their knowledge and perceptions. Sadly, many of the older well-informed keepers of community memory the trio interviewed are now departed from this life, among them Charlie Paul of Yarmouth, who was the first person to take the reins of administrating the Acadia First Nation; Lillian Pictou (née Alexis) of Yarmouth; Sandy Julien of Millbrook; Grand Chief Donald Marshall Sr.; and Grand Captain Alex Denny. Doris Labradore, whose paternal Mi'kmaw ancestors hailed from Bridgewater along Nova Scotia's South Shore, and Natalie McConnell, who was of Anishinaabe ancestry, also wanted to learn about the Mi'kmaw experience from Marie Battiste, who was then working as an educational administrator at Eskasoni, Cape Breton.[6]

The biographical project gained a sudden and welcome boost in 2004 when Craig McNaughton of the Social Sciences and Humanities Research Council (SSHRC) announced an initiative that allowed hiring of additional Aboriginal university students and expanded the sphere of research. Monies became available to travel to archives and museums throughout the Atlantic Provinces, Maine, and Ottawa; to convene forums where collected information could be discussed with members of the Mi'kmaw community; to attend academic conferences and give introductory papers; and to visit and share ideas with Mi'kmaw Elders. One highlight of this phase of research was an invitation from Craig McNaughton and his team in Ottawa to students Brittany Pennel, Courtney Brooks-Monteith, and Mary Wells to travel to SSHRC's headquarters to discuss their work. Over the course of research eleven students did the lion's share of work on the entries not prepared by academics. These were Caroline (Carrie) Gloade, Doris Labradore, Allison Lloy, Natalie McConnell, Courtney Brooks-Monteith, Brittany Pennel, Nik Phillips, Travis Pinn, Gregory Solomon, Heather Sutherland, and Mary Wells – the majority of whom are of Aboriginal heritage and four of whom – Carrie Gloade, Nik Phillips, Travis Pinn, and Heather Sutherland – are also co-authors.

This volume contains thirty-seven chapters, with thirty-six being biographical in nature. These biographies are organized into five parts, with each part corresponding to a geographic district within the Mi'kmaq's homeland of Mi'kma'ki. Part 1, consisting of chapters 1 to 9, relates to southwestern Nova Scotia, known to the Mi'kmaq as Kespukwitk, or "land's end." Individuals examined in these initial nine chapters regarded Kespukwitk as their home. Chapter 1 follows the life of Charles Alexis (c.1730–c. 1799) and provides an overview of his legacy in the Cape Sable region. Chapter 2 looks at the descendants – the Glodes or Gloades – of a seventeenth-century chief named Jehan Grand Claude (c.1650–c.1730) who resided in the vicinity of Port Royal. Carrie Gloade is a co-author with Janet Chute on this entry. Chapter 3, researched by Doris Labradore, focuses on Paul Guédry *dit* Labrador (1701–c.1780) and the emergence by the end of the Seven Years' War of the Mi'kmaw Labrador family. Chapter 4 by Anne Marie Lane Jonah investigates another member of the Guedry family, Marguerite Guedry (c.1730–?), a *métis*[7] woman from Merliguéche (now Lunenburg) who ran afoul of the French authorities by marrying a man from the upper echelons of Louisbourg's military establishment. Chapter 5 looks at an early eighteenth-century Minas head chief, Pierre Momcharret (1686–c.1745), while chapter 6 focuses on a La Have chief named François Mius, a grandson of a French baron, Philippe I Mius d'Entremont of Pobomcoup. Chapter 7 examines the lives of Jean-Baptist Thoma, or Thomas (c.1700–c.1785), who was a friend of the British during the Seven Years' War, and Phillip Bernard (c.1710–c.1825), who in 1786 became a landholder at the Head of St. Margaret's Bay. Both of these leaders were associated at different times with a sizable Mi'kmaw community on Panuke Lake, near Piziquid (now Windsor, Nova Scotia).[8] Nik Phillips, co-author with Janet E. Chute of this chapter, is a descendant of Phillip Bernard. Chapter 8, researched by

Brittany Pennel, on Pennel Argomartin (c. 1722–1817), focuses on the founding and development of the Gold River Mi'kmaw community in Lunenburg County. Chapter 9 provides insights into the life of Stephen Knockwood Jr. (1834–1938), whose ancestral roots lay with the Minas Band but who resided most of his life in Kings County, Nova Scotia. An active, industrious individual, he was reputed to have lived to the age of 104.

Part 2 pertains to lands at Cobequid, along the Shubenacadie, Stewiacke, and upper Musquodoboit rivers and along Nova Scotia's Eastern Shore. The Shubenacadie district is known as *Sipekne'katik* or "the place where the wild potatoes or groundnuts grow," and the Eastern Shore is *Eskikewa'tik*, which may mean "the skin dressers' country," though this is not certain. Part 2 contains three chapters: chapter 10 on Paul Peminout (or Peminuit, c.1720–c.1812) and his descendants; chapter 11 by Dianne O'Neill on John W. Johnson (1829–1907), who though of European ancestry by preference turned Aboriginal; and chapter 12 containing a lengthy discussion of the life of Joseph Julien (1872–1957). Chief Julien is referred to in this chapter as "The Man at the Centre" since he interacted extensively with other leaders throughout the Northeast. The historic framework of Part 2 spans three centuries, from 1760 to 1960. During the American Revolution, Paul Peminout forged an amiable relationship with Nova Scotia's lieutenant-governor, Michael Francklin, and as a result Peminout and his son Jacques received land grants within the *Sipekne'katik* district. In the early twentieth century Joseph Julien settled at Millbrook near Truro, where he encouraged Mi'kmaq living in Halifax County to move to the Millbrook community to escape the cataclysmic effects of Nova Scotia's Mi'kmaw centralization policy: by government fiat all Mi'kmaq in Nova Scotia were to settle at one of two growth centres, Shubenacadie or Eskasoni. Those who chose instead to relocate to Millbrook included members of the Cope and the east coast Paul families.[9] Chapter 12 also touches on the lives of Mi'kmaw relocatees who originally lived either in Annapolis County or in the Northumberland Strait area, known in Mi'kmaq as *Piktuk aqq Epexiwitk*. *Piktuk* refers to the stretch of Nova Scotia mainland directly opposite Prince Edward Island and translates as "the place of the explosions," while *Epexiwitk*, meaning "lying on or hovering over the water like a mirage," is the Mi'kmaw term for Prince Edward Island.

Part 3 investigates Mi'kmaw activities in the district known as *Siknikt* or *Sikniktewaq*, translatable as "the drainage area." *Siknikt* is the Mi'kmaw term from which the English place name "Chignecto" is derived, although the Mi'kmaw district extends northward as far as the lower Miramichi River area and into interior Maine. It overlaps with the district of *Kespuk*, or *Kespe'kewaq* (northeastern New Brunswick and southern Quebec, known during the French era as Gaspé). Part 3 is fairly lengthy, containing four chapters that span from 1680 to the 1980s. Chapter 13 provides an in-depth look at the life and times of Joseph Argimault, who in the mid-1750s, along with Paul Laurent and the missionary Jean-Louis Le Loutre, tried to persuade the British to reserve a vast tract of land for the exclusive use of the Mi'kmaq, extending inland from the Northumberland Strait to the north bank of the Shubenacadie River. Chapter 14 follows the life story of Jean Battist Bouta, who was born at Annapolis Royal, entered the fur trade, and finally settled near the Acadian village of Pomquet in what is now Antigonish County, where he established the precursor of the First Nation. Marie Ann Battist, a descendant on her paternal side of Bouta, helped the students with this chapter. Chapter 15, by Bunny McBride and Harald E.L. Prins, focuses on the life of Donald Joseph Sanipass, a chief and noted basketmaker. Sanipass was born at Shediac in the *Siknikt* district but spent most of his adult life in the Aroostook Mi'kmaw community, near Houlton, Maine. Mi'kmaq from *Siknikt*, *Kespek*, and Cape Breton historically entered Maine to hunt and trade and more recently to harvest potatoes, berries, and other crops. Some became permanent residents of Aroostook County. McBride and Prins stress how cherished traditional Mi'kmaw values endowed Chief Sanipass with the resilience and strength to lead the Aroostook community, with McBride's and Prins's help, through a campaign to achieve a new federal legal identity, which it acquired under the Aroostook Band of Micmacs Settlement Act in 1991.

Part 4 focuses on the district of *Kespek* (or *Kespe'kewaq*), which means "last land." *Kespek* extends from the Miramichi River region northward to the tip of the Gaspé Peninsula in southern Quebec. Chapter 17, the only biographical entry in this part, examines the life of Nicholas Prisk II Ouiouche (c.1769–c.1859) of the Nepisiguit River region of northeastern New Brunswick. Chief Prisk rebuilt the Nepisiguit Mi'kmaw group after most of the Mi'kmaw population evacuated the Nepisiguit area following the Battle of Restigouche in 1760. The chapter traces how the band's growth was influenced by Prisk's marriage to a daughter of John Young, a British trader. Young was an employee of Commodore George Walker's trading establishment at Nepisiguit prior to the onset of the American Revolution. The collapse of Walker's trading enterprise under privateer onslaughts set Walker's employees adrift. Several, including Young, intermarried with local Mi'kmaq and Acadians, whose *métis* offspring established a distinctive multi-ethnic community at what is now Bathurst. The Youngs and the Prisks formed a vital interconnected group whose ranks were swelled by intermarriages with incomers. Prisk encouraged these families to remain as members of his band, much to the chagrin of British administrators, who wanted to reduce the number of Mi'kmaq in the Bathurst area.

Part 5 relates to the district of *Unama'ki* (or *Unama'kik*), which until the late nineteenth century extended eastward from Antigonish to embrace all of Cape Breton Island, the isles of St. Pierre and Miquelon, and southern Newfoundland. This broad definition of the term is employed in a chapter that examines the activities of the eighteenth-century chief Jeannot Peguidalouet, using the word as it was employed in the eighteenth and early nineteenth centuries. Currently, however, the term is restricted to Cape Breton Island, while *K'Taqmkuk*, or "the land across the water," denotes Newfoundland. *Unama'ki* has been translated as "the land of fog," although a recent interpretation holds it to be a variant of *Mi'kma'ki*, or the "Mi'kmaw land."[10]

Part 5 contains twenty chapters, more than any other section, though all but one are relatively short. Seven of these, chapters 17 to 23, are written by B.A. Balcom and focus on seventeenth- and eighteenth-century *Unama'ki* chiefs whose personal histories appear in chronological order, except when members of a single family are grouped together. The chapters examine the lives of Capisto (c.1600–c.1658), Isidore (c.1664–c.1720), Francis N'8gin'tok (? –c.1740), Jacques Padanuques (c.1700–c.1745), Jean Michau (?–c.1730), Michel Michau (c.1700–c.1750), and Denis Michau (c. 1700–1751). Chapters 23 and 24 by Anne Marie Lane Jonah, by contrast, consider the lives of two Mi'kmaw women who occupied polar ends of the social spectrum in eighteenth-century French society. Chapter 25 explores the life of Marie-Joseph le Borgne de Belisle (c.1711–1754), a granddaughter on her mother's side of Baron Vincent d'Abbadie de Saint-Castin and his Malecite wife Mathilde, also known as Pidianske, while chapter 24 introduces the reader to Marguerite (1713–c.1746), an orphan Mi'kmaw girl who became a domestic servant at Fortress Louisbourg, while chapter.

Chapters 26 to 32 continue the biographical investigation of *Unama'ki* leaders. Aside from Jeannot Peguidalouet (1705–c.1792), the individuals chosen for biographic treatment are Thoma Denny (c.1665–c.1767), Michel Thoma Denny Sr. (c.1753–1834), Michel Thoma Denny Jr. (1768–1852), Francis Thoma Denny (c.1770–c.1868), John Denny Sr. (c.1810–1887), and John Denny Jr. (1841–1918). The lengthy article that comprises chapter 26 traces *Unama'ki* district chief Jeannot Peguidalouet's diplomatic ventures with both the French and English regimes, his treaty-making, his encouragement of Mi'kmaw emigration to Newfoundland, and his peacekeeping endeavours among Mi'kmaq and Acadians along the Northumberland Strait.

Chapter 33 departs from an emphasis on prominent leaders associated with the Thoma-Denny family by introducing Beloni Thoma Denny (c.1800–1849), educated to read and write by a teacher named Stephen Lawlor at Eskasoni, but who died from cold and starvation in April 1849 after failing to receive aid from Sydney townspeople. The following chapter looks at the resource and land campaigns led by Chief Peter Googoo (1771– c.1860) of Whycocomagh. Chapter 35 presents a life history of Andrew Alex (1849–1930), who became a respected *putu's*, or record-keeper, of the Mi'kmaw Grand Council, while Chapter 36 focuses on the activities of Grand Chief Gabriel Sylliboy (1874–1964).

The volume concludes with a discussion in chapter 37 of Mi'kmaw spirituality and world view written by Diane Chisholm, who draws upon knowledge gained while working at the Mi'kmaq Resource Centre at Cape Breton University.

Since the range of historical topics that arose during preparation of these biographies was too great to address within the parameters of this project, it was felt that four areas in particular – Mi'kmaw leadership in the Northumberland shore region,[11] the exercise of Mi'kmaw resource protocols, the identity of Mi'kmaw-*métis*, and life histories of Mi'kmaw women – could be presented as fields for future research. Regarding the first research area, two leaders from the Northumberland Strait area, Paul Chachegonouet ("Vieau à Paul") of Merigomish[12] and Anthony Eury of Remsheg (now Wallace),[13] owing to their friendship with the British during the American Revolution, were accorded licences of occupation to land in 1783.[14] Chief Chachegonouet was succeeded by his son Assem Paul, who died at the age of eighty-six in 1847 from a virulent fever. Assem's successor was Peter Toney, most likely a grandson of Captain Toney.[15] Peter Toney remained chief at Merigomish until his band moved to Pictou Landing. Peter Wilmot (1824–1932), born at Pictou Landing, would become Toney's successor. Remaining in the Cobequid area for several years, he was instrumental in laying the foundations of the Millbrook Reserve near Truro. His successor was Mathew Francis, who became a prayer chief, a member of the Mi'kmaw Grand Council, an affiliate of both Grand Chief John Denny Jr. and his successor, Grand Chief Gabriel Sylliboy, and a friend and colleague of Chief Joseph Julien.[16]

A second intriguing field for future research concerns Mi'kmaw leaders' aegis over resources and the traditional respect protocols paid to chiefs by users of these resources. This subject is first raised in chapter 1 on Charles Alexis and revisited in chapter 10 on Nicholas Prisk II Ouiouche. In the past, Acadians at Cape Sable acknowledged the territorial prerogatives of Mi'kmaw leaders, especially relating to riverine fish such as salmon and eel. Evidence for such protocols emerged during study of the lives of the Alexis chiefs and from examination of proprietary rights claimed by head chiefs residing on the Nepisiguit and Restigouche rivers in New Brunswick. During the French era the Mi'kmaw were regarded as wielding a degree of proprietary discretion over the distribution of resources, a fact that an elderly Listuguj (Restigouche) head chief, Joseph Claude, endeavoured to impress on British commissioners who visited his community in 1786. Claude's claims subsequently were ridiculed by officials bent on securing Britain's unobstructed right to the salmon fishery,[17] yet it is likely the men belonging to Commodore George Walker's trading station at Nepisiguit prior to 1780 respected Native resource protocols to a degree. In the final years of the American Revolution, after American privateers razed Walker's Nepisiguit establishment, Walker's employees were set adrift, and many joined the bands of their Mi'kmaw spouses. British fishing enterprises that arrived at Nepisiguit and Listuguj following the close of the Revolutionary War usurped the Mi'kmaw fishery in a series of events that Chief Claude denounced in 1786.[18]

The third area for future research lies with the question: Who exactly are the Mi'kmaw-*métis*? As noted above, the word *métis* with a lowercase *m* denotes anyone of both Indigenous and non-Indigenous ancestry, whereas *Métis* with a capital *m* describes a person who belongs to a recognized politicized group, such as the "New Nation" of western Canada. Within the Maritimes, the term *métis* was rarely used by missionaries and government officials to define either individuals or populations, although the word appears once or twice in the registers of Abbé Sigogne of southwestern Nova Scotia. Sigogne, however, exhibited a racial bias against persons he designated as *sang mêlé* (mixed blood), and tried during the nineteenth century to categorize his French-speaking Roman Catholic parishioners as *sang pur* (pure blood) Acadien and his Mi'kmaq-speaking parishioners as simply *Indien*. Yet he knew that a constituency had existed since the seventeenth century who spoke both French and Mi'kmaq, and who drew upon the cultural potentials of both sides of their ancestral heritage.[19] Today, whether a *Métis* nation able to be legally and politically recognized under section 35 of the Canadian Constitution Act of Canada exists in the Atlantic Provinces and southern Quebec remains a highly controversial issue, despite determined advocacy groups' demands since the 1980s for such recognition. The authors of this work consider this one for the courts to decide.[20] Meanwhile, the term *métis*, where it appears in this work, relates to individuals and groups throughout the Atlantic Provinces who exhibit both Mi'kmaw and (mainly) European biological and cultural traits.

The fourth and final area identified for future research centres on Mi'kmaq women. While women do appear throughout this volume, only three form the focus of in-depth biographical treatment, and these women all lived in the eighteenth century. One problem with providing comprehensive profiles of women stemmed from the lack of relevant documentary evidence left by the patriarchal French and British colonial regimes. This situation only marginally improved until the 1960s, when Mi'kmaw women began making a significant mark in the fields of education, business, law, film, politics, social work, administration, book authorship, poetry writing, cultural studies, and medicine. Some have proven to be exceptionally creative thinkers, winning accolades from their own communities as well as academe, provincial governments, and the country. Although this florescence began prior to 1960, it was decided during the course of this project that a focus on Mi'kmaw women would demand new models as well as copious consecrated research, and was best left to a separate study. This work has benefitted from the guidance of many senior Mi'kmaq female academics, among them Marie Battiste and Marjorie Gould, as well as respected female local historians Most of the students who worked on this project, moreover, have been women and have shown exceptional scholarship in their research, ways of discussing issues, and presentation of ideas on paper. It is hoped that a study devoted to the biographical treatment of Mi'kmaw women will appear before long.

A remarkable Mi'kmaw woman whose personal history certainly deserves biographical treatment in the near future is Dr. Elsie Charles Basque (1916–2016), a descendent though her paternal grandmother, Henrietta Bartlett (or Henrietta Bartholomew-Alexis), of Chief Charles Alexis of Cape Sable (c.1730–c.1799). Elsie stood with her sister Lucy on a Yarmouth dock at the age of eight watching as her mother departed on a steamer for Boston. She was raised by a single-parent father, was temporarily placed in foster care with an Acadian family until her father recovered from tuberculosis, briefly entered and braved the residential school system long enough to despise it, and became the class valedictorian for her high school graduating class in Meteghan, Digby County. She graduated from the Nova Scotia Teacher's College, became the first Mi'kmaw individual to teach in the public school system, and as a dedicated humanitarian argued in both Canada and the United States for the rights of the elderly. Last but certainly not least, she was a wife and mother who wished to preserve for posterity what she had learned to cherish over her long and eventful lifetime.[21] In her later years she engaged in historical and genealogical research that resulted in her writing poignant personal stories, several of which she posted online with accompanying photographs for the world to share. This volume is dedicated to Elsie Charles Basque (1916–2016), teacher, historian, genealogist, writer, social activist – and inspiration to us all.

– Janet E. Chute

Part One

Kespukwitk – Southwestern Nova Scotia

1

Charles Alexis and the Bartlett and Charles Families

At The Forks of the Tusket River

Charles Alexis was born around 1730 to Jacques Alexis (c.1690–c.1773) and Angélique.[1] According to René-Charles de Breslay, a Roman Catholic priest at Port Royal, both Jacques and his wife were Mi'kmaq from Cape Sable, although it is possible Jacques was born into the Penobscot nation and as a young man moved to southwestern Nova Scotia.[2] Charles, who was Jacques's second son, would prove to be many things to many people. He started out as a fur trade middleman with the help of the prominent Cape Sable Tecouramart family. In 1754 he wed an Acadian woman from Annapolis Upper River named Anne Hébert, which strengthened his trading and diplomatic ties with the Acadian community. He arose as head chief of Cape Sable in 1776, and in the 1780s and 1790s engaged in diplomatic proceedings with the British at Halifax on behalf of the greater Mi'kmaw community. In the 1790s he joined with the Mi'kmaw Charles family, who fished and farmed near the upper reaches of the Tusket River. In his final years he organized a drive to acquire a grant of land from the Crown embracing an ancient Mi'kmaw eel fishery and planting ground at Eel Brook, in what now is Yarmouth County.

Handsome, daring, and intelligent – his nickname "Caboche" in Acadian French means "big head" or "smart"[3] – he cut a romantic figure within southwestern Mi'kmaw society around 1754 by marrying the youngest daughter of Antoine Hébert and his second wife, Anne Orillon.[4] Anne Hébert, born on 14 February 1741, would have been around fourteen years of age when she married Charles Alexis. She would die on 20 September 1831 at the advanced age of ninety at Les Fourches, or "The Forks" of the Tusket River, now known as Quinan.[5] Charles's marriage to Anne drew the attention of both local Acadians and French officials at the Fortress of Louisbourg. A French gentleman at Louisbourg named Monsieur de la Varenne remarked on 8 May 1756 in a letter to his friend at Rochelle, France, that "it is not many years since a very pretty French girl ran away into the woods with a handsome young Indian, who married her after his country fashion." Though the girl's relations and friends followed her and begged her to come back with them to their village, "no persuasions, or instances, could prevail on her to return." Though neither Charles's nor Anne's name was specifically mentioned in de la Varenne's letter, the passage almost certainly referred to their union. De la Varenne focused on the notoriety a marital union between a Mi'kmaw man and an Acadian girl elicited at a time when such marriages were extremely rare, although ultimately the French administration, for fear of angering their Mi'kmaw allies, decided to support the union and let the two live "happily together."[6]

De la Varrene's sentimental perspective contrasted sharply with the pragmatic view of the marriage held in 1793 by George Henry Monk, Nova Scotia's Indian commissioner, who suggested that the union, initially sanctioned by Mi'kmaw custom, was merely an expedient alternative to deportation for the young Anne Hébert.[7] Yet the date of de la Varenne's account implies that the marriage occurred at least a year and a half prior to the spring of 1756, which would suggest it was based more on affection than expediency on Anne's part, since British removals of Acadians from Cape Sable did not begin until 1756. Charles and Anne's marriage over the years proved a sound and lasting one, with Anne outliving her husband by thirty-two years. When she died at Quinan in 1831, her body was brought down from The Forks to Eel Brook and interred in the Roman Catholic cemetery of Ste. Anne du Ruisseau in Argyle Township, Yarmouth County.[8]

The fact that the surname "Alexis" existed among the Penobscot of what is now Maine prior to 1700, but was not found among the Mi'kmaq before 1720, suggested that Charles's father, Jacques, permanently left the Penobscot nation upon marrying into the Cape Sable band. Jacques was a long-distance middleman trader, whose eldest son, François-Joseph Alexis, was baptized at sea shortly after his birth in March of 1727 by Guillaume Blanchard Jr., an Acadian shipowner residing across the Bay of Fundy on the Petitcodiac River.[9] Since Jacques and his family were intimately connected with Acadian fur trade society, they sometimes relied upon Acadian vessels to travel between Cape Sable and other trading stations along the Atlantic coast.

In his youth Charles Alexis joined his father as a member of fur brigades that crossed the Bay of Fundy and pressed past Petitcodiack en route to Quebec. With time, this gave him access to some degree of personal portable wealth in terms of silken turbans, silver ornaments, fine woolen blanket coats, and linen shirts. Had Charles Alexis and his wife married in 1754, as de la Varenne's account suggests, their first two years together as a wedded couple might well have proven relatively prosperous and peaceful, especially compared with what was to follow. The middle to late 1750s were tumultuous and frightening years for young Acadians and Mi'kmaw youths alike in the Cape Sable region. Many already had fought shoulder to shoulder and had their bravery tested in confrontations with the English during King George's War (1744–48).[10] Anne Hébert's half brother, Louis Hébert *dit* Baguette, joined the Acadian resistance fighters led by Joseph Broussard *dit*

Beausoleil, and skirmished with the British during the 1755 Acadian deportations from Grand Pré before leaving for Quebec in 1756.[11] Acadians who, with the help of the Mi'kmaq, escaped being forcibly removed in 1755 believed they might find refuge from English vitriol in southwestern Nova Scotia. Yet with the onset of the Seven Years' War (1756–63), most found they had to continue to resist English aggression by joining with Cape Sable Acadian leaders such as Eustache Corporan, who resided at Ouikmakagan, a Mi'kmaw, *métis*, and Acadian community located near present-day Ste. Anne du Ruisseau.[12]

Governor Charles Lawrence felt the Cape Sable Acadians encouraged Indigenous raids on the Lunenburg settlers, so in April 1756 he instructed Major Jedidiah Preble, a New England battalion leader, to muster 167 soldiers in two vessels, the *Vulture* and the *Mary*, to capture and deport as many Acadians from the Cape Sable area as they could find. On 14 May of the same year he intensified his campaign to curtail Indigenous raids on the fledgling British and German South Shore settlements by placing a bounty on Mi'kmaw scalps.

Fear of the scalp bounty failed to cool the military ardour of the Cape Sable Mi'kmaq, who continued to help their Acadian neighbours. Though seventy-two Acadians were rounded up by Preble's men and taken to Boston, close to two hundred Acadians escaped along with their priest, Abbé Jean-Baptiste Gay Desenclaves. These individuals met up with the Cape Sable Mi'kmaq at a site on the Tusket River later known as Reynard's Bridge, or Reynardton.[13] The two groups coordinated their movements with strategic precision. Three months after Preble's raid, Eustache Corporan, who had recently returned to Ouikmakagan from Boston, volunteered to pilot an expedition commanded by Captain Joseph Gorham to locate and arrest the remainder of the Acadians, but instead led the British astray on the banks of the Abuptic River.[14] According to one New England source, at least six of Gorham's men were killed when his contingent was suddenly ambushed by a combined Acadian and Indigenous party waiting in the woods.[15]

Following this incident, the Cape Sable Mi'kmaq and Acadians enjoyed relative peace for over a year. Though Charles Alexis and Anne Hébert had married previously according to Mi'kmaw customary practice, once Abbé Desenclaves took refuge with them they would have solemnized their wedding vows according to the rites of the Roman Catholic Church. But this respite would not last. On 11 September 1758 four ships under the command of Major Roger Morris left Halifax bound for Cape Sable with orders to deport the remaining Acadians. Joseph Gorham's rangers were aboard, along with 325 members of the 35th Regiment under the command of Major Henry Fletcher. Learning of the vessels' progress along the coast, a party of frightened Acadians sent a letter four days later to Thomas Pownell, the governor of Massachusetts Bay, calling for assistance in halting the British attempt to deport them, but their plea to Boston came too late.[16] The English soon dropped anchor at the mouth of the Argyle River and scoured the surrounding landscape for evidence of their elusive quarry. Though the Acadians initially managed to evade their pursuers, the British finally located a cluster of Acadians and Mi'kmaq on the first Sunday in October. While Abbé Desenclaves was presiding over a service in a small wooden chapel along the Cheggogin River, he and his congregation were suddenly surrounded and captured.[17]

After rounding up the Acadian congregants and torching all the Acadian buildings they could find, the British attackers compelled Desenclaves to reveal the whereabouts of other Acadians. Meanwhile Mi'kmaq who were hiding in the woods near the chapel immediately set off to warn the Acadians sequestered in the interior.[18] In consequence, twenty-one Acadian households and six Mi'kmaw families, among them the household of Charles Alexis, were able to flee to safety further up the Tusket River. Acadians who later approached the coast were rounded up in 1758 up by Gorham's rangers, brought to George's Island in Halifax, and eventually deported. After this incident, journeys to the shoreline could prove perilous for the Mi'kmaq, as an oral tradition about a surprise ranger attack on an unsuspecting Mi'kmaw encampment in what is now Digby County outlined all too clearly.[19] Anne Hébert and her husband, though doubtless grieving the loss of their Acadian kin, sought a less precarious life removed from intercolonial warfare by remaining at The Forks, along the middle reaches of the Tusket River.

Charles Alexis and Anne Hébert hunted, trapped, picked berries, and fished at stone fish weirs. Drawing on the cultural legacy of Anne's Acadian relatives, they planted potatoes, corn, and other vegetables at Les Fourches and tended a small orchard of apple and pear trees.[20] The Forks was an ancient habitation site for the Mi'kmaq's ancestors, who had inscribed pictoglyphs on local rocks, and it still supported a sizeable Mi'kmaw community.[21] Within two decades Charles and his wife raised six boys and at least one girl, Marie, along the middle reaches of the Tusket. Michel Alexis was their eldest son, followed by Joseph.[22] Three other sons arrived in short order: Samuel, Abraham, and Bartholomew. When Charles's brother François-Joseph died around 1773, Charles adopted François-Joseph's son, Jean-Baptiste Alexis, whom he raised as one of his own offspring. Acadian friends and kinfolk who had escaped deportation assisted Charles and Anne in erecting a bark-roofed log home similar to the dwellings found in pre-1758 French and *métis* communities along the Atlantic coast. Several log outbuildings, which stored furs and smoked and dried meat and fish, completed the Alexis homestead.

Living in a Resource-Rich Environment

In the final years of the Seven Years' War the Cape Sable head chief, Michel Argomartin, sent a Mi'kmaw delegation to Halifax to extend peace overtures to the British, although there is no firm evidence that Argomartin himself ever signed a formal peace treaty in 1760 or 1761.[23] Argomartin's actions, however, elicited an exemption from Governor Charles Lawrence's 1756 scalp bounty for members of his band, so Charles Alexis and his family were free once again to come and go over the Cape Sable landscape. Following spring weir fishing for gaspereau and salmon, Charles, Anne, and their children would travel from The Forks through a series of lakes, streams, and portages to Great Pubnico Lake,[24] where he would meet with other Mi'kmaq who canoed with him down the Barrington River to the Atlantic coast. Prior to the British embargo of 1748 on the trans-shipment of fur and fish out of Pobomcoup (also spelled Poubomcoup),[25] now East Pubnico, as well as from the Saint John River, Charles Alexis had acted as a fur trade middleman similar to his father Jacques. Crossing the Bay of Fundy with a load of furs and then following the river and portage system lying between the upper Saint John River and the St. Lawrence River proved a lucrative enterprise for Cape Sable Mi'kmaq, intent on obtaining French trade goods from Montreal. When not involved with brigades to the region north of the St. Lawrence, Mi'kmaw trappers traded furs locally with the Acadian French at

Pobomcoup, Ministiguèsche (now Barrington Head) and Port Razoir (now the town of Shelburne). Local chiefs and head men regulated the local hunting territory system and joined with neighbouring leaders to discuss points of Mi'kmaw policy, land usage, and trade at assemblies held at ancient council grounds at Eel Brook and near present-day Middle Ohio, Shelburne County. Visiting Mi'kmaw participants encamped on the lower reaches of the Roseway River.[26] Long Island, situated ten miles, or sixteen kilometres, upstream on the Roseway River from the town of Shelburne, was one such encampment. Another site lay at "Indian Gardens" on the neighbouring Clyde River.[27]

Until the Acadian deportations in the middle to late 1750s, there were ample resources for both the Mi'kmaw and Acadian communities in southwestern Nova Scotia, known in Mi'kmaq as *Kespukwitk* or "the last land."[28] Caribou, moose, bear, beaver, smaller fur bearers, and berries provided nourishment depending on the season. Scrubby, esker-strewn moraine lands lying northeast of the Cheboque River were prime habitat for caribou and moose. Inland forests also provided peltry for trade, wood for building and manufacturing, and medicinal plants. Rivers teemed seasonally with anadromous fish, particularly gaspereau – also known as alewife or kayak – and salmon. Along the coast, headlands became rich birding grounds during the spring and fall migration, as did offshore islands, which also attracted seals and walrus. Porpoise, sturgeon, and small whales could be taken in St. Mary's Bay. Shellfish abounded in tidal flats. Estuarine weirs captured cod, mackerel, pollock, and sea bass. The Alexis family would also have maintained a stone or brush riverine weir, known in the Mi'kmaw language as a *nijigan*. Pole and brush weirs were erected at points along the Salmon, Tusket, Roseway, and Clyde rivers where brackish tidal water met fresh water coming from inland. Large stone weirs, spanning watercourses in a V- or W-shaped formation, were used to corral migrating salmon and gaspereau on the higher reaches of rivers. Eels were collected at these same weirs in woven eel pots. After drying or smoking their catch, Charles Alexis and his family would return to The Forks to harvest their potatoes and other crops, as well as pick fruit from their orchard. By late fall they pressed further inland to pursue their winter hunt, which provided not only meat but furs for trade.

Extended family members visiting for social, diplomatic, and trade purposes figured highly in the Alexis family's seasonal round. After a spell on the coast, the family ascended the Barrington River, passed through Great Pubnico Lake, and returned by way of Madashack, Great Barren, and Quinan lakes to The Forks. From there they accessed the headwaters of the Tusket River, where there was a portage route heading west to a level forested terrain, which would be punctuated in the early nineteenth century by the settler communities of Carleton, Forest Glen, and Gardner's Mills.[29] This region lay close to the upper reaches of the Salmon River, especially Hectanooga, which today lies in the District of Clare, Digby County.[30] From Hectanooga they travelled down the Salmon River to the Gulf of Maine, where clams, crustaceans, and other shellfish abounded on coastal mudflats. An old tote road that existed until 1811 led east through Chebogue, or *Tebok* in the Mi'kmaw language, to the mouth of the Tusket River, by which they once again ascended to The Forks, fishing as they went.[31]

Campsites along the Roseway and Clyde rivers, easily accessible from the upper Tusket, provided rest stops where parties could camp and fish en route to the coast. The Roseway, Clyde, Barrington, and Tusket rivers followed convoluted valleys etched into the glacially scarred landscape of the Cape Sable interior before reaching the Atlantic Ocean. By contrast, the Salmon, Meteghan, and Sissaboo rivers to the southwest flowed directly into the Gulf of Maine. Yet all radiated out, like spokes of a huge wheel, from a hub-like watershed bounded by what is now the Tobeatic Wilderness Area.[32] The Cape Sable Mi'kmaq knew each facet of their landscape intimately, and the watershed area in particular was vested with special cosmological significance as the fountainhead from which all riverine waters sprang.

The entire Cape Sable district band met at least once a year at Eel Brook. In the months prior to an assembly, Mi'kmaw parties would pitch their wigwams in the vicinity of what in 1762 became Lockeport in Shelburne County, and would spear tuna from canoes.[33] They then travelled to the Barrington River, ascended to Great Pubnico Lake, pressed westward overland to Pobomcoup, and finally arrived by canoe at Eel Brook, now the centre of the Roman Catholic parish of Ste. Anne du Ruisseau. After 1722 the French missionary, Abbé Antoine Gaulin, who began journeying regularly to Cape Sable as part of his annual itinerant labours,[34] met with these Mi'kmaq. Mi'kmaw visitors to Eel Brook pitched their dwellings at nearby Ouikmakagan, whose name translates from the Mi'kmaw language as "Place of Eels."[35] Once a Mi'kmaw summer village site, by the 1740s Ouikmakagan developed into a small but bustling fur trade community with Acadian, Mi'kmaw, and *métis* residents.[36] Acadian families formed the permanent core of this village, with each household having a bark-roofed log dwelling, while the Mi'kmaw population swelled and waned with the seasons. In the late eighteenth century the locality of Eel Brook was subsumed by the village and parish of Ste. Anne du Ruisseau, belonging to the District of Argyle, Yarmouth County.

Prior to the Seven Years' War, Eel Brook in the late spring provided more than enough eels for all visitors. Not only was the flesh of eels high in calories, and so a welcome dietary addition after the sparse diet of the early spring, but to Algonquian speakers throughout the Northeast, eels were considered spiritual entities endowed with medicinal properties. Ingestion of eel flesh linked the individual eater as well as the group to the cosmological whole and was treated as a ritual act requiring the observance of respect protocols.[37] Festivities also punctuated eel-spearing season at Eel Brook; it was a time of reunion and celebration. Until the death in 1762 of Abbé Pierre Maillard, the last of the French missionaries to serve under the French colonial regime, the Mi'kmaq considered Rocco Point, a small peninsula near Eel Brook that jutted out into Tusket Bay, as a sacred site where they met with their priest and received the sacraments.[38]

Cape Sable Mi'kmaw Leadership Prior to 1771

During the French era, the place name "Cap Sable" referred to the coast of Shelburne and Yarmouth counties, though the territory of the Cape Sable Mi'kmaq included southern Digby County and ran inland to the watersheds of the district's major rivers. Cape Sable was a region with deep historic roots, being associated with the seventeenth-century governor of Acadia, Charles de Saint-Étienne de la Tour (1593–1666),[39] as well as Philippe I Mius d'Entremont (1609–c.1700), La Tour's *procurer du roi* who was vested with a barony in 1653. The Cape Sable Mi'kmaq formed a regional band whose numbers fluctuated between 90 and 150 individuals. This group established close diplomatic and fur-trading ties with La Tour's establishments at Cheboque and

on Cape Sable Island, as well as d'Entremont's seigneury at Pobomcoup. Baron d'Entremont built a stone manor, storehouses, and wharves and maintained regular trading connections with the French and *métis* communities of Port Razoir, La Have, and Merliguèche, which was situated where the town of Lunenburg now stands.[40]

Unique to this part of Nova Scotia were the respect protocols shown by the local Acadian population towards Mi'kmaw territorial and resource rights. Acadians made payments in goods or money to Mi'kmaw leaders for the right to fish at certain weirsites, or to hunt in crucial Mi'kmaw resource locales.[41] The origin of these protocols is obscure, though it doubtless had roots in the integral role the Mi'kmaq played early on in the fur trade. The French were disinclined to offend chiefs upon whom the local economy depended. By the late 1670s the Cape Sable Mi'kmaq also acquired a reputation for vigorously defending their territorial prerogatives. Prior to this they were on generally peaceable terms with European visitors of many nationalities, Portuguese, French, Spanish, Basque, and English. As time passed however, Cape Sable's exposed position at the southwestern tip of the Nova Scotian peninsula made its Mi'kmaw inhabitants vulnerable to raids from crews of vessels passing up the seacoast from New England. One of the worst such raids occurred early in the spring of 1676 during King Philip's War when a Cape Sable chief and sixteen members of his band were lured aboard a New England ketch, owned by Boston shipping merchant and land speculator Simon Lynde and leased by Jean (or John) Melanson *dit* Lavadure, an Acadian man whom the Mi'kmaq knew well and who spoke their language. Lavadure inveigled the chief and his men onto his vessel with the promise of a hospitable meal, but instead of enjoying a repast, the Mi'kmaq were seized, secured below deck, and forced to sail to Faial Island in the Azores, where they were sold as slaves.[42]

The perpetrator of this ruse was a New England sea captain named Henry Lawson, who counted on Jean Lavadure, as well as William Waldron, one of his close relatives, to be his accomplices in crime.[43] Lawson, Waldron, Lavadure, and several others eventually were arrested in Boston, though Lavadure, released on bail raised by his mother at Port Royal, skipped trial and returned to Acadia. The fact that Lavadure had participated for years in the fur trade, spoke Mi'kmaq as well as French and English, and even had kin connections to the d'Entremont family at Pobomcoup must have set Mi'kmaw sensibilities severely on edge.[44]

According to the Mi'kmaw customary code, serious insults and injuries of this nature demanded either revenge or restitution, and at first the Cape Sable leaders sought revenge. Little is known of the Mi'kmaq's attitudes or actions towards the Acadian residents of Pobomcoup at this time, but it is recorded that a party of Cape Sable Mi'kmaq, along with a number of Penobscot affiliates, in July of 1677 waylaid twenty-seven men belonging to the crews of six New England vessels fishing at Port La Tour, including a schooner belonging to Robert Roules named the *William and Mary*. The Mi'kmaq's plans to inflict vengeance went awry, however, when the perpetrators themselves were captured by Roules's men, taken aboard the *William and Mary*, and carried to Marblehead. When they disembarked, a grisly scenario unfolded. A number of Marblehead women, smarting from repeated Indigenous raids on their community during the war, fell upon the Mi'kmaq and their Eastern Abenaki associates and began stripping living flesh from their bones.[45] This incident in turn sparked a string of Mi'kmaw reprisals against New England vessels. The originally peaceful Cape Sable Mi'kmaw leaders thus became swept up in a maelstrom of conflict that by the early 1700s thrust them into the centre of Indigenous–New England hostilities.

Back in Nova Scotia, the Cape Sable Acadian community made overtures to the local Indigenous leaders to atone for the heinousness of Lavadure's crime. It must have been challenging at first, for the 1676 incident underscored how deceptive even persons of French extraction might be towards the Mi'kmaq. To restore and maintain Mi'kmaw trust, the d'Entremonts at Pobomcoup found it expedient to observe a system of respect protocols that prioritized Mi'kmaw rights to weirsites and other riverine resources over those of the French. These new measures helped to allay Mi'kmaw distrust of the French. Yet ever afterwards Cape Sable leadership involved two distinct functions, the first a diplomatic one to deal effectively with outside agencies and the second a defensive one to ensure the collective weal of the group. At times these separate tasks were divided between two leaders, though the district's head chief retained primary responsibility for protecting his people's territorial aegis and critical resources from molestation.

By 1727, a twenty-seven-year-old Mi'kmaw leader named Pierre Chegau, whose family's roots went back in the Cape Sable region to the 1650s,[46] often acted as a delegate for his group's head chief, Paul Tecouramart.[47] Paul Tecouramart, born at Cheboque in 1663, had four sons, Antoine, Jean-Baptiste Philippe, Anathase, and Eustache, the eldest of which, Antoine, born in 1684, became his father's diplomatic aide.[48] Antoine Tecouramart in turn had two sons, Antoine *fils* (Antoine Jr.) and Charles. These Tecouramarts forged close ties with the Alexis family, first through their common association with trading brigades to Quebec and second around 1745 when Eustache married Marie Alexis, one of Charles Alexis's sisters.[49]

The Tecouramarts' proprietary rights to specific fishing locales were respected by the Acadian population. In 1751 Jacques II Mius d'Entremont *dit* Pobomcoup and his *métis*-Mi'kmaq cousin from Merliguèche, François Mius, bought a *nijigan*, or fish weir, from Eustache Tecouramart for seventy French livres – a goodly sum at the time. This weirsite was located near Ministiguèche, or present-day Barrington Head, though negotiations occurred at Pobomcoup. The transaction elicited a formal deed of purchase signed by several witnesses, including Baron Charles Mius d'Entremont of Pobomcoup, son of Jacques I Mius d'Entremont *dit* Pobomcoup and Charles La Tour's daughter, Anne; Charles Mius's brother-in-law Pierre Landry; Jacques II Mius d'Entremont; and Joseph Mius d'Entremont.[50] The signing of this contract was a clear instance of how recognition of prior Indigenous right to resources came to govern much of Acadian life at Cape Sable.

Paul Tecouramart had been preceded as Cape Sable district leader by Jean-Baptiste Medosgnel, formally recognized as chief of Cape Sable by the French in 1722 and the British at Annapolis Royal in 1726.[51] Chief Medosgnel was probably in his forties in the early 1720s, since he and his wife Madelaine had a seventeen-year-old daughter, Marguerite Baptiste, who married Pierre Chegua at Port Royal on 25 June 1726.[52] Soon after this date Paul Tecouramart became the district chief, to be succeeded in turn by Pierre Chegua. Antoine Tecouramart, Paul Tecouramart's son, acted as Chegua's negotiator until at least 1750.[53]

Little is known about the nature of Cape Sable leadership prior to chiefs Medosgnel, Tecouramart, and Chegua. Scattered Mi'kmaw names gleaned from early documentary sources provide tantalizing glimpses, but they do not steer the researcher towards any clear genealogical connections among Cape Sable leaders prior to 1700.[54] Charles de Saint Étienne de la Tour, governor of Acadia from 1631 to 1642 and, following his rival Charles de Menou d'Aulnay Charnisay's death in 1650 by drowning, from 1653 to 1657, wed an Indigenous woman in the the mid 1620s.[55] Though this woman may have been the daughter of a Cape Sable leader, she was more likely of the Etchemin nation, since La Tour had operated a trading post on the Penobscot River. La Tour remarried twice following his first wife's death; both of these women were French.

Philippe I Mius d'Entremont (1609–c.1700), a Norman who came to Acadia in 1651 as La Tour's lieutenant major, was awarded the barony of Pobomcoup. In 1653 his lands extended west from Forchu, or present-day Yarmouth, to Cap-Nègre, or Cape Negro, on the east.[56] Mi'kmaw traders visited Pobomcoup regularly from the early 1650s to the early 1750s. In the 1690s warriors from Cape Sable met at Jemseg and later at a fort on the Saint John River, with the French governor of Acadia, Joseph Robineau de Villebon, who sent them to attack outlying New England settlements.[57] During Queen Anne's War from 1702 until 1713, Mi'kmaw leaders, as well as chiefs of the Malecite and Penobscot nations, rallied to the call of Bernard-Anselm d'Abbadie de Saint-Castin to defend Port Royal against the English. Bernard-Anselm Saint-Castin was a son of Baron Jean-Vincent d'Abbadie de Saint-Castin and an Etchemin woman, Marie-Marthe Pidiĕmiskoa, daughter of an Etchemin chief named Madockawando, whom the baron had married according to Indigenous custom in 1652.[58] Port Royal fell, for the last time, on 2 October 1710 to a formidable New England force commanded by Sir Francis Nicholson. The town was then renamed Annapolis Royal. Bernard-Anselm and his Indigenous guerilla fighters, however, inflicted one last devastating blow on the Annapolis Royal garrison commanded by Governor Samuel Vetch the following June in what would become known as the Battle of Bloody Creek.[59]

Not all southwestern Nova Scotian Mi'kmaw leaders remained hostile to the English in 1710. Indigenous fur trade middlemen, in particular, felt that by extending peace overtures to Annapolis Royal they might open up new avenues for trade. In February of 1711 a Cape Sable Mi'kmaw delegation proved ready to negotiate peace if favourable trade terms could be secured.[60] These negotiators, however, had no intention of severing their previous commercial ties with the Acadians and adopting the English as their exclusive trading partner. In 1713, when the Treaty of Utrecht bestowed an uneasy peace on Acadia, the d'Entremonts at Pobomcoup retained their kin and commercial linkages with Saint-Castin's trading station in the Penobscot Valley.[61] Since the barony of Pobomcoup was the hub of trade in southwestern Acadia for over a century, Bernard-Anselm's Penobscot associates would have brought their furs there to trade.[62] Pobomcoup's founder, Baron Philippe I Mius d'Entremont, died at Grand Pré around 1700,[63] after which his third and youngest son, Philippe II Mius *dit* d'Azy, figured prominently in the life of Charles Alexis, since two of Philippe's grandchildren, Jacques Mius and Hélène Mius, married two of Charles Alexis's siblings.[64]

Philippe II Mius *dit* d'Azy consorted with two Mi'kmaw women in succession. By his first Mi'kmaw spouse, whose name remains unknown, he had five children. The eldest, Joseph I Mius *dit* d'Azy, prior to his marriage to Marie Amirault *dit* Tourangeau of Ouikmakagan, lived at Port Razoir with his uncle, Abraham Mius d'Entremont *dit* Pleinmarais. He was a farmer, but two of his younger brothers, Mathieu and Maurice, entered fur trade society. Laurent Mius, a grandchild of Joseph Mius and Marie Amirault, would wed one of Charles Alexis and Anne Hébert's daughters, Marie, in 1780.[65] When Philippe Mius *dit* d'Azy's first spouse died he went to Ministiguèsche, where he associated with a second Mi'kmaw woman named Marie. Their union produced seven more children, all of whom entered fur trade society. Their daughters married Acadian traders or Mi'kmaq middlemen, while their sons became active in the fur trade in their own right.[66]

With the final transfer of the suzerainty of Nova Scotia from the French to the British in 1713, resulting trade disruptions caused new political splits within the Acadian and Mi'kmaw communities. Acadians reliant on fur commerce feared that the English might woo the Mi'kmaq as economic partners and then redirect furs to Annapolis Royal. A few Mi'kmaq leaders felt that extending the hand of friendship to the British might bring trade benefits, but others proved determinedly hostile. From spring to fall parties of Cape Sable Mi'kmaq lay in wait along with their Acadian associates at river mouths where New England fishing crews were apt to take on fresh water. When vessels were sighted, the Mi'kmaq rebuffed the intruders with threats and demands that their territorial aegis be respected.

The Mi'kmaw's widespread trading and diplomatic contacts brought them into frequent contact with Eastern Abenaki residing south and west of the Gulf of Maine. As New England settlers pressed north of the Kennebec River, Eastern Abenaki leaders rose in anger at the disrespect these incomers showed towards their traditional resource prerogatives, such as rights to wood and traditional fishing locales. At this time the Cape Sable group began sending delegates to Indigenous councils in Maine and elsewhere in the Northeast, with resulting fruitful exchanges of both people and ideas.[67]

Trials, Treaties, and Trips to Quebec

Little direct military aid could be expected from the French authorities, who in 1715 were stationed at Louisbourg on Isle Royale, though the French offered the southwestern Mi'kmaq supplies and ammunition. Following the Treaty of Utrecht of 1713 French officialdom had invited the mainland Mi'kmaq to move to Cape Breton, but the Cape Sable band ignored such overtures. Instead, armed with French ammunition, supplies, and moral support from the newly established Fortress of Louisbourg, the Mi'kmaw grew more daring. When New England fishermen refused to respect Indigenous territorial prerogatives, vessels were boarded and crews taken for ransom. By 1715 New England was beginning to feel its commerce had come up against an incorrigible impediment along the northeastern seaboard and, worse, that any attempt to negotiate with the Cape Sable leaders would prove futile, since the chiefs had retorted that the "lands are theirs and they can make Warr and peas [*sic*, peace] when they please."[68]

Swelling Indigenous anger in the Kennebec River region eventually led to reprisal raids against outlying northern New England settlements; in response, in 1722 Massachusetts declared war against the Eastern Abenaki. The Cape Sable band was swept into the forum of hostilities along with its southern Indigenous neighbours. This conflict, known variously in New England as Dummer's War, Lovewell's War, and Rale's War, lasted from 1722 to 1725. After two years of hostilities, Penobscot diplomats, most prominently Chief Loron Alexis, also known as Loron Sagourrab, were the first to sue for peace.[69] Yet it appears that the Mi'kmaq were also weary of the war, mainly owing to its harmful effects on Indigenous trade.[70]

These developments did not occur soon enough to prevent several devastating New England attacks on Mi'kmaw communities. In 1724 the Massachusetts government commissioned Captain Joseph Marjory of the sloop *Lark* to cruise off Cape Sable to prevent Mi'kmaw raids on the New England fishing fleet, as well as to harass French transshipments of furs and fish obtained from Indigenous and Acadian sources.[71] Massachusetts saw Marjory as uniquely qualified to fulfil this role since in July 1723 the captain had captured seven persons at Merliguèche whom he believed to be Mi'kmaq and sent them to Boston. Among this number were François Mius, the twenty-three-year-old son of Philippe II Mius *dit* d'Azy, and two sons of Jean-Baptiste Guedry, an Acadian trader who pursued the fur and fish trade. In 1725, when New England finally extended overtures of peace and friendship to the Mi'kmaq, Massachusetts promised to secure the release of these captives. In consequence, in June 1726 ten head men from Cape Sable, including head chief Jean-Baptiste Medogsnel, Medogsnel's future son-in-law Pierre Chegua, and Paul Tecouramart, with his sons Antoine and Jean-Baptiste Philippe, arrived at Annapolis Royal to sign a ratification of a peace treaty made at Boston with the Eastern Abenaki the preceding year. All expected an immediate return of the prisoners to Nova Scotia.[72]

What they anticipated failed to happen. The British viewed the treaty signing of 1726 as only a way station on the path to continued peace proceedings, not as the conclusion of the conflict.[73] When further so-called peace negotiations dragged on for over a year, the Mi'kmaq grew impatient. On 26 August 1726 four members of the Mius and Guedry families – Jean-Baptiste Guedry *dit* Labrador and his son, Jean-Baptiste Guedry *fils*, Jacques (or James) Mius, and Jacques's brother Philippe III Mius – plus a few Mi'kmaw associates, including a man from Chignecto named John Missel, commandeered a New England fishing sloop that had put in to Merliguèche to take on supplies. Their intention was to employ the sloop and its crew as ransom to force Boston to release its prisoners, but their plan failed miserably. The Mi'kmaw and Acadian party were themselves overpowered, confined, placed on trial in Boston, and hanged for committing robbery on the high seas.[74] When one Mi'kmaw prisoner, François

Mius (1700–c.1765), the youngest son of Philippe II Mius *dit* d'Azy, was released and arrived back at Merliguèche, he felt little affection for the English or New Englanders and increasingly aligned his interests with the French at Louisbourg.

Hardly the last word on the subject of preserving the peace, the 1726 treaty signed at Annapolis Royal nevertheless obligated Paul Tecouramart and Pierre Chegua to act as informers for the British regarding any activities involving the Cape Sable Mi'kmaw community that the British considered suspicious. Tecouramart proved willing to assist the British as long as they did not interfere in his trading affairs. Until his death around 1730, his activities apparently were viewed by the British as above reproach.[75] His son Antoine Tecouramart, however, became the target of suspicion in the early spring of 1735 when a brigantine called the *Baltimore* heading for Annapolis, Maryland, foundered on the Cheboque salt marshes, not far from where Antoine and his brother Anathase had a camp. The only occupants of the vessel were a middle-aged woman claiming to be Susannah Buckler, the wife of the captain, and two indentured servants, one a young girl named Margaret McDonnell. Rescued by the Mi'kmaq and brought to Pobomcoup, the older woman tried to account for her circumstances by stating that the vessel's captain, along with all his crew, recently had died aboard ship of thirst, hunger, and an unspecified illness. She then accused Antoine and his brother of robbing her of valuables and threatening her with violence. Antoine and Anathase later were cleared of these charges when it was found that the woman, whose real surname was Wilson, was actually a convict who was being shipped with other convicts from Ireland to Annapolis in Maryland. As the ship passed Cape Sable, the other prisoners had mutinied, killed the captain and crew, and fled, leaving Wilson to fend for herself. Pierre Chegua not long afterward noted a number of freshly dug graves on an island he passed as he journeyed by canoe along the coast from La Hève to Cape Sable.[76]

During the period of relative peace that characterized the 1730s, the main thrust of Mi'kmaw resistance to British intrusion on their lands switched from Cape Sable to the Minas region. Pierre Chegua, who had assumed the Cape Sable head chieftainship following his father-in-law Jean-Baptist Medogsnel's death, retained amiable relationships not only with Acadians living along the Atlantic coast but also with

the British at Annapolis Royal. His band meanwhile retained its strength of numbers: in 1735 Cape Sable had a Mi'kmaw population of between 158 and 166 people.[77] Mi'kmaw brigades, as before the Mi'kmaw War, now travelled unobstructed to Quebec, and if anything, trade intensified. Some Mi'kmaw middlemen continued to wed Huron and Algonkin women, and one such marriage occurred in the mid-1720s between Antoine Tecouramart and Marie Magdelaine, a Huron from Lorette near Montreal. On 29 November 1727 this couple brought their firstborn son, thirteen-month-old Antoine Tecouramart *fils*, to Annapolis Royal to be baptized.[78] In 1733 they had a second son, Charles. Yet the Tecouramarts continued visiting Lorette, for as late as 1780 one of Charles's daughters, Rose Tecouramart, married a Huron man and remained in the province of Quebec.[79]

Such ties among trading partners, reinforced by kinship, endured the vicissitudes of intercolonial warfare and, later, settler intrusions. Commercial and friendship ties with the Acadians who pursued the fur trade were restored. Yet the relationship with French officialdom began to change. By 1730 the intimacy characteristic of Acadian-Indigenous interrelations along the Atlantic coast contrasted sharply with the distancing policies of Louisbourg's elite. Louisbourg wanted to keep the Mi'kmaq socially at arm's length while preserving Indigenous willingness to provide military assistance to the French when needed. To maintain this state of affairs, the French distributed provisions, clothing, blankets, guns, ammunition, and honorifics such as commissions, medals, and military dress. For example, Philippe II d'Azy's son, François Mius, on 25 July 1742 received a parchment commission at Fortress Louisbourg appointing him "Chef de Merligueshe" from the French commandant, Jean-Baptiste-Louis Le Prévost Duquesnel.[80]

The consequences of this new French policy were immediately apparent to the British and New Englanders. As early as 9 July 1739, Captain Peter Warren, returned from patrolling the eastern Acadian seaboard in the warship *Squirrel* out of Boston, warned that the governor of Canada and the French at Louisbourg were giving out "new guns" and vesting prominent Indigenous leaders with parchment commissions to encourage them to harass English and New England shipping. Each Mi'kmaw leader holding a commission, Warren explained, was expected "to command a particular district" and bore the "Title of Captain of the Port to which he belonged."[81] Though a Cape Sable head chief may have received a French commission similar to that obtained in 1742 by François Mius of Merliguèche, it is more probable that Pierre Chegua and later the Tecouramarts were passed over by the French since they, under the terms of the 1726 treaty, still had to inform the English, whenever asked, of the activities of their Mi'kmaw fellows. Such differential treatment from Louisbourg would not, however, have affected the nature of interrelationships within the kin-based Mi'kmaw community extending from La Hève to Cape Sable. Each spring and often in the fall, many Mi'kmaw families came in canoe brigades to meet with their itinerant missionary and participate in ritual ceremonies at what is now Rocco Point, near present-day Ste. Anne du Ruisseau. The Cape Sable head chief personally welcomed each party arriving at the shoreline and attended to his guests' sustenance and comfort. The copious eels found in the spring and fall at Eel Brook fed the burgeoning population, and these visits became seasons of song, dance, courtship, marriage, general festivities, and meetings of diplomatic import.

Chief François Mius *dit* d'Azy wed a Mi'kmaw woman, Marie, according to Mi'kmaw custom, and the pair had a son named Jacques, who around 1745 wed Charles Alexis's sister Bridget Alexis. Another of Charles's sisters, Marie, wed Eustache Tecouramart. Charles's brother, Pierre-Paul Alexis, meanwhile married Helen Mius, Jacques Mius's sister. Such marital alliances, some involving brother-sister exchanges, led to the Mius, Alexis, and Tecouramart families becoming close friends and business partners. On 2 June 1751, for instance, when François Mius of Merliguéche and Jacques II Mius d'Azy bought a fish weir from Eustache Tecouramart for seventy livres, Charles and Joseph d'Entremont of Pobomcoup acted as witnesses to the transaction.[82] Over time, auspicious kin alliances ushered members of the Alexis family directly into the upper echelons of fur trade society in southwestern Nova Scotia. Marriages between the offspring of Philippe Mius II *dit* d'Azy and leading Acadian, *métis*, and Mi'kmaw individuals forged a stable community embracing southwestern Nova Scotia and extending across the Bay of Fundy to the Saint John River region.[83] Kin alliances granted the resilience needed to endure the vicissitudes of intercolonial wars and trade disruptions. Great travellers, the fur trade middlemen regularly voyaged to Montreal and the Upper Great Lakes country. They crossed the Bay of Fundy, often using shallops rather than canoes though some, like the Alexis family, also travelled in Acadian vessels, then pressed up the Saint John River and beyond to the St. Lawrence River, and from there to Quebec and Montreal. Such travels became annual events, engaged in for diplomatic and social reasons as well as trade. They also coursed along the shores of the Gulf of Maine to the Penobscot River Valley, or plied the waters of the Gulf of St. Lawrence towards Prince Edward Island, known by the French as Île St. Jean, and Cape Breton, or Île Royale. Some voyaged to the Magdalene Islands, the Isles of St. Pierre and Miquelon, and Newfoundland.

These institutional aspects of the fur trade had their roots in the late seventeenth century. After 1690 the English kept only a skeleton military presence in Acadia, which did little to stem the tide of fur brigades proceeding past Port Royal towards Quebec and Montreal. The French had been routed from Port Royal by Sir William Phips's expedition in 1690, but Joseph Robineau de Villebon, the French commandant in Acadia from 1690 to 1700, located his headquarters in Acadia at Jemseg and later on the Saint John River. Jemseg and the mouth of the Saint John River were major trade depots, as well as mustering points during the intercolonial wars.[84] After the Treaty of Ryswick of 1697 returned Acadia to France, the French proved jealous overseers of the fur trade, with French vessels patrolling the waters of the Bay of Fundy to prevent Cape Sable Mi'kmaq from stealing away to trade at Boston, as well as to keep New Englanders from intercepting furs destined for France. In consequence, by 1700 many Cape Sable Mi'kmaw fur trade middlemen like the Tecouramarts focused on gaining access to markets along the north shore of the St. Lawrence. They also interacted with the Algonkins of Odanak living near Quebec and the Lorette Huron-Wyandot community near Montreal. Cape Sable men married Algonkin and Huron women, and vice versa.

By contrast to this traditional Aboriginal spirit of inclusiveness, the contractual world of French-Indigenous relations at Fortress Louisbourg by the early 1750s had become formalistic and austere. Though supplies and gifts given out by the French each year lent an air of stability and cohesion to this transactional world, the French had little interest in forging closer ties with the Mi'kmaq. The social divide between the residents of Pobomcoup, Ministiguèche, Ouikmakagan, and Merliguèche and French officialdom at Louisbourg grew ever wider. The marriage in February 1709 of Louis Du Pont Duchambon de Verger (1680–1775) and Marie-Jeanne Mius d'Entremont (1688–1745) of Pobomcoup, a granddaughter of Baron Philippe I Mius d'Entremont and a daughter of Jacques I Mius d'Entremont *dit* Pobomcoup and Anne La Tour, caused hardly a stir within French official circles. Yet in 1754, when a young second ensign of French aristocratic background named Jules César Félix de la Noüe de Bogard without his superiors' permission married Marguerite Guedry, a daughter of Paul Guedrey *dit* Labrador and Anne Mius of Merliguèche, the Superior Council at Louisbourg set out to have the union annulled.[85] By this time the paramount intermediaries between French officialdom and the Mi'kmaw population were the French missionaries, particularly Abbé Jean-Louis Le Loutre and Abbé Pierre Maillard. As these Frenchmen had greater contact with the chiefs than most of Louisbourg's elite, they proved more willing than French officialdom to address pressing Mi'kmaw concerns. These missionaries, however, were forbidden to bring their Indigenous followers to the fortress, and marriages between their congregants and French officialdom were prohibited.

Charles Alexis's Early Years

Charles Alexis was around ten years of age at the outbreak of the War of the Austrian Succession in 1740 and so would have been too young to seek French honorifics and accolades in battle accorded prominent Mi'kmaw-*métis* leaders, such as Chief François Mius. The conflict, which lasted until 1748, resulted in the capture of Louisbourg by the English in 1745 and the fortress's return to the French under the Treaty of Aix-la-Chapelle in 1748. Members of Charles Alexis's family, if not Charles himself, may have participated in the Siege of Grand Pré on 11 February 1747, in which 140 British soldiers were killed in a single night along with their commander, Colonel Arthur Noble, by a combined French, Acadian, and Indigenous force. In response, the British outlawed twelve Acadian resistance fighters, including Charles Alexis's future brother-in-law Louis Hébert *dit* Baguette, and offered a reward of eighty pounds sterling to anyone who could deliver one

of the outlaws to the British authorities within six months.[86]

This proclamation struck at the heart of the Acadian population, but the greatest blow to the Mi'kmaq came when the British levied an embargo on trade entering or leaving the Cape Sable area in 1748. As this meant the end of Pobomcoup as a major French fur transshipment centre in southwestern Nova Scotia, its economic impact proved devastating to the Cape Sable band. The establishment of Halifax the following year ensured that the embargo would be rigidly maintained. Tensions worsened in the fall of 1749 when the Mi'kmaq, who resented a large British settlement being erected in their midst without any consultation between their chiefs and the British, launched a series of raids on Halifax and Dartmouth. This chain of events prompted Governor Edward Cornwallis to levy a scalp bounty on Mi'kmaw heads, an act that underscored the status of the Mi'kmaq as enemies of the British regime until the Mi'kmaw leaders of their own accord could prove otherwise. Even in the face of Cornwallis's draconian proclamation, some Mi'kmaw leaders still sought to gain British trust by making peace overtures. Circumstances surrounding the signing of a peace and friendship treaty on 22 November 1752 between Cornwallis's successor as governor, Sir Peregrine Thomas Hopson, and a Mi'kmaw party from the Shubenacadie and Musquodoboit areas led by Major Jean-Baptiste Cope went awry, however, when a party of Englishmen seeking scalp bounty killed a group of Cape Sable Mi'kmaq at Mocodome, near Country Harbour. The Mi'kmaq along the eastern Atlantic coast exacted vengeance for this crime by killing all but one of the crew of a government schooner moored at Jeddore, east of Halifax. Anthony Casteel alone was spared because he could speak French.[87]

Despite the tumult of Mi'kmaq-British political relations, the Cape Sable leadership kept trying to seek a viable peace treaty with the English. The deleterious effect on their economy of the embargo on furs and trade goods, let alone Cornwallis's scalp bounty, were enough in November of 1753 to prompt a council representing a band of Cape Sable Mi'kmaq to send two delegates to meet with yet another governor, Charles Lawrence, and his council. The two Mi'kmaw delegates who visited Halifax were both fur trade middlemen who previously had been on friendly terms with the British. One of these men, Baptist Thomas, was almost certainly a brother-in-law of Chief François

Mius named Jean-Baptist Thomas (or Thoma), who was born at Cape Sable and had been espousing peace with the British for several years.[88] The other was a head man named François Jean de Perisse, who like Chief Thoma hailed originally from Annapolis and claimed to be acting on behalf of an unnamed Cape Sable chief – most likely Pierre Chegua – who could not be present. Evidently the Chegua and Tecouramart families felt their people's cause might best be served by men associated with Annapolis who already enjoyed favourable standing with British authorities. Moreover, Antoine Tecouramart's younger brother, Jean-Baptiste Philippe Tecouramart, recently had joined forces with Abbé Jean-Louis Le Loutre at Beaubassin, and Antoine probably knew that if the British got wind of this development, his own reception in Halifax would be a cool one.[89]

Thoma and de Perisse declared that the band of sixty individuals they represented from Cape Sable had never joined with other Mi'kmaq in harrying the British, had returned any deserters they had met with, and had assisted New England vessels in distress. Their constituents had upheld the stipulations of the 1726 treaty with the British and so deserved consideration for their faithfulness. And since their group had refused to join in any violent acts against the British, they had received no presents from the French.[90] The delegates' words proved persuasive enough to convince the governor-in-council that, despite serious recent altercations with certain parties of Mi'kmaq, "it might be of great advantage to support and encourage such of them as should come in and be willing to remain friends with us." Acts of friendship and kindness over time might even convince "the whole of them that it would be more for their interest to be our friends than enemies."[91] Along with this far more positive appraisal of the future of Mi'kmaw-British relations, there was the incentive of knowing that these two Indigenous leaders who stood before them might provide lucrative trading opportunities for the Halifax merchant community.[92] The governor deemed the occasion worthy of a present distribution, so he and his council concluded their audience with the Mi'kmaw delegates by furnishing them with sufficient bread, blankets, pork, powder, shot, and tobacco for their families, "being as they say twenty in number."[93]

Thoma and de Perisse represented the relatively few Mi'kmaq from southwestern Nova Scotia who chose not to accompany the fiery French missionary

Abbé Le Loutre to Beaubassin, near the Isthmus of Chignecto. Many Cape Sable Mi'kmaw fur trade middlemen, facing imminent economic destitution from the 1748 embargo and hounded by English scalp hunters, left southwestern Nova Scotia in the spring of 1750 to follow Le Loutre's suggestion that they take their furs to Beaubassin, and from there to French posts along the Northumberland Strait. The abbé further persuaded them to remain for protracted periods of time in the Beaubassin region, where they could obtain supplies from both Louisbourg and Quebec. Several of François Mius's sons rallied to the missionary's call, as well as the chief's nephew, Antoine Mius, who at Beaubassin rose to become a chief in his own right.[94] These men joined Le Loutre soon after Governor Cornwallis's destruction of the Mi'kmaw village of Merliguèche in October 1749, where François Muis had been chief. By 1753 Jean-Baptiste Philippe Tecouramart and his wife, Madame Le Songeur, who was either an Acadian or a Huron woman, and Antoine Tecouramart *père's* two sons, Antoine *fils* who was twenty-five years old and Charles who had just reached twenty, also were residing at Beaubassin.[95] While at Le Loutre's mission these men, under the auspices of Joseph Argimault of Chignecto and Paul Laurent, the leader from La Hève, began to develop a new policy to guide Mi'kmaw interactions with the British.[96]

Joseph Argimault and Paul Laurent became the most vocal proponents of the Mi'kmaq's acquiring a large chunk of Nova Scotia for the Mi'kmaw community's exclusive use.[97] With Le Loutre's help, they devised a scheme that involved getting the English to consent to the Mi'kmaq's retention of a vast tract lying northeast of the Shubenacadie River. Their main challenge, however, lay in getting the Halifax council to take their plan seriously. Though from 1749 to 1755 Le Loutre mustered Mi'kmaw warriors and Acadians for forays against the British in what has been called "Le Loutre's War," he also became involved in a far more pacific aspect of Mi'kmaw strategizing. The tract his Mi'kmaw associates wished reserved for their exclusive use extended over the eastern part of present-day New Brunswick, the shore of the Northumberland Strait as far east as Canso, the eastern Atlantic coastline as far south as Chezzetcook, and all the interior region lying north of the Shubenacadie River. Major Jean-Baptiste Cope of Shubenacadie and Musquodoboit, who with his associates signed a peace treaty with the British in 1752, favoured this scheme. But Cope's instrumental role in the revenge killing of a government party at Jeddore in 1753 in retaliation for the murder of Cape Sable Mi'kmaq by several Englishmen precluded him from participating in any further peace negotiations with the British.[98]

The Cape Sable Mi'kmaw peace overtures of 1753 faltered as, egged on by Le Loutre, Mi'kmaw parties from southwestern Nova Scotia resumed raids on English and New England shipping.[99] An oral tradition that circulated among settlers in Queens County held that the "Pigtow" (Pictou) family, assigned to defend the command of Port Joli, around 1750, captured the crew of a New England schooner and killed its members by degrees by making them lie on a rock previously heated by a large fire. Four years later some of these Pictous, caught tampering with the rudder of an American fishing craft anchored at Port Joli, were sunk when the vessel's crew hurled down large stones into their canoe. All in the canoe died except one woman named Molly Pictou, who was carried to United States.[100] Even Charles Alexis, as a youth during Le Loutre's War, waited with his companions at the mouth of the Barrington River to raid any New England vessels that ventured close to shore.[101]

With time, however, younger members of the Mius and Tecouramart families, including Jean-Baptiste Philippe Tecouramart and Antoine Mius, began to join with Joseph Argimault and Paul Laurent in backing a scheme to let the English develop Halifax peaceably in return for the Mi'kmaq's exclusive right to the tract northeast of the Shubenacadie River. When they heard of it, the Lords of Trade and Plantations in London, England, ridiculed the idea. Not only was it associated with Le Loutre, whom they distrusted deeply, but it also allowed French vessels unobstructed passage along the Northumberland Strait to Quebec and interfered with British control of the Canso fishery. The plan nevertheless remained in circulation within the Mi'kmaw community long after Le Loutre fled Nova Scotia for France in 1755. After the second fall of Fortress Louisbourg in 1758 it gained the backing of Abbé Pierre Maillard, who switched his attachment from France to Britain and by 1760 had begun working for the colonial government in Halifax. Maillard's support of the concept of a Mi'kmaw homeland in the northeastern part of the province must have exerted a strong influence on the political will of the Mi'kmaw nation, for as

early as April 1760 chiefs were approaching the British in Halifax in order to sign treaty. No members of the Alexis family were among them, however, nor, as far as is known, were chiefs Pierre Chegua or Antoine Tecouramart *père*. Abbé Jean Manach, who laboured in the missionary field alongside Maillard, informed the British commander at Fort Cumberland, Colonel Joseph Frye, that the paramount Cape Sable leader was a man named Michel Argomartin.[102]

There is, however, no document that actually confirms that Michel Argomartin signed a treaty with the British in 1760. Instead, the district chief Michel Argomartin sent a delegate, a member of the Chegua family named François Shagwaough, who was probably one of Chief Pierre Chegua's sons, to Halifax.[103] Shagwaough arrived before the governor-in-council on 24 April 1760 and declared not only that he was willing to make a submission to the British government, but that his chief, Michel Argomartin, also planned "speedily to appear in person."[104] Argomartin may never have arrived, though Francis Keehosgeith of Cape Sable came soon afterwards to make a personal submission and receive a pass.[105] The only chiefs from southwestern Nova Scotia known definitely to have signed a treaty with the British, however, were Paul Laurent and François Mius.[106] Chiefs Argimault and Laurent's bid for a homeland did not fall on completely deaf ears in Halifax, for on 4 May 1762 Lieutenant Governor Jonathon Belcher incorporated the substance of the Mi'kmaw proposal into a Royal Proclamation. Though reputedly not circulated widely, the proclamation had the backing of Maillard, who undoubtedly assured the Mi'kmaq that their campaigning for a reserve may not have been entirely in vain.[107] Belcher's proclamation met its demise, however, when the Lords of Trade and Plantations in December the same year denounced its terms as "impudent and absurd."[108] Faced with such opposition overseas, Belcher and his council immediately dropped the idea of reserving such a tract in Nova Scotia.

Charles Alexis remained aloof from the diplomatic forum during and immediately following the Seven Years' War. After the deportation of many of his close Acadian kin and associates, he and Anne Hebért pressed inland and remained at The Forks. From there he joined fur brigades to Quebec until the 1780s, and he sat in councils with chiefs Argomartin and Chegua and other head men. The fur trade remained viable economically at the close of the Seven Years' War, and for several years the British operated a government truckhouse at Cape Sable. Each family head had his own hunting and trapping territory and exercised a proprietary aegis over the animals and fish on his tract. When the truckhouse closed in 1764, trappers took most of their hides, furs, and feathers to merchants at Liverpool or Halifax. But local markets also arose, a development that took a less than a decade. When Sylvanus Cobb approached Cape Sable in 1759 in a vessel laden with New England passengers intent on making the region their home, they were fired on by Mi'kmaq and Acadians.[109] By contrast, in the mid-1760s the Cape Sable band had gained a reputation for succouring early settlers by bringing them wild game and fish when they went hungry, and for their honesty in dealing with the newcomers.[110]

Yet the settlers' coming still sent shock waves throughout the Mi'kmaw community. In the late 1750s plans had been laid in Britain and New England to import numerous "proprietors" who it was hoped would turn the Cape Sable countryside into a mosaic of prosperous farms and fishing villages. The Acadian deportation of the mid-1750s had resulted in acres of vacant cleared fields and meadows that were quickly taken up by these newcomers. Without sufficient farm produce for sustenance, these new residents at first competed with the Mi'kmaq for game, riverine fish, and wood. They eyed the shore for stands of good timber and sites on which to establish saw mills. The newly established Barrington Township, superimposed on countryside where formerly only twelve French families had pursued the fur trade and cod fishery, now was subdivided among two hundred proprietors from Cape Cod, Plymouth, and Nantucket. Each had been promised fifty acres to establish a new home in Nova Scotia. By June of 1762 the Planter population of Barrington, Argyle, and Yarmouth townships numbered around five hundred. The first actual division of land in Yarmouth Township in 1763 also reserved all offshore islands for fishermen, who simply transferred northward the skills and experience they had gained in the New England fishery. Protestant churches were erected at Forchu (later the town of Yarmouth) and Cheboque, while roads were cut along both banks of the Cheboque River. Within a decade the Cape Sable coastal landscape had been completely and irrevocably transformed.[111]

The Mi'kmaq also faced other challenges. The treaties they had signed in 1760 and 1761 promised to supply them with Roman Catholic clergy, but since the death of Maillard in 1762 Roman Catholicism had been overshadowed by the strongly Protestant leanings of the incoming New England settlers. As late as 1767 no Catholic priests had been supplied.[112] Chief François Mius, who was a devoted Roman Catholic, became incensed.[113] Anger at the British unwillingness to provide priests mingled with the grief many Mi'kmaw leaders felt at the failure of their heartfelt campaign to secure a sizeable reserve north of the Shubenacadie River. Maillard's death only compounded their problems, since the missionary had furnished a vital link with the past and had provided words of hope and guidance for the future. Now the Mi'kmaq had few friends from outside their own community. To make matters worse, apprehensions arose within certain settler communities that the Mi'kmaq might act on their discontent by attacking farms at Lunenburg.[114] As a last-ditch campaign to gain justice for their people, Joseph Argimault and Jean-Baptiste Philippe Tecouramart, both of whom had been deeply involved in the campaign to gain a reserve as well as to acquire a Roman Catholic missionary, decided to try to lay their people's grievances in person before the British monarch. So, on 30 September 1763 "Joseph Shickakett, Captain of the Tribe of Cumberland" (Joseph Argimault) and "John [or Jean] Baptiste of Cape Sable" applied for and received a pass at Halifax to "depart from thence for England, Ireland by any conveyance that may offer."[115] The fate of their projected expedition remains unknown. Neither man's name ever appeared in the documentary record again.

In the Face of Settler Incursions, 1763 Onward

After Michel Argomartin's death around 1763, François Chegua assumed the Cape Sable leadership. Chegua was so esteemed by the Acadians who began returning to the vicinity of the Eel Brook about 1767 that they left an ancient Mi'kmaw encampment ground near the shores of Eel Brook vacant for the chief and his group to use each spring and fall. "Sheshaw Park," known to the French-speaking community as "Parc à Sheshaw," lies within the bounds of the village of Ste. Anne du Ruisseau and has never been settled upon. The word "Sheshaw" derives from the surname "Chegua." Though Chegua died about 1768, the Acadians retained, and still retain, the campground in memory of the Mi'kmaw chief and his descendants who frequented it seasonally.[116] This is another example of a respect protocol that has endured among the Acadians of Ste. Anne du Ruisseau into recent times.[117] When Charles Alexis's elder brother, François-Joseph Alexis, assumed the status of Cape Sable head chief in 1768 or 1769, he too, as protector of the Mi'kmaq's territorial aegis, became the recipient of such shows of respect from the local Acadian population.

Incoming waves of settlers from 1759 to 1771 usurped much of the Mi'kmaq's former territory along the Cape Sable coast. New England Planters, Irish, Scots, and English, as well as Acadian returnees, established orchards and began to till the soil of the Mi'kmaq's prime caribou-and moose-hunting grounds. Members of the Halifax administrative elite, among them Charles Morris, the superintendent general of the province's Crown Lands department, and the Reverend John Breynton, the rector of St. Anglican Paul's Church in Halifax, coveted the cleared patches containing Mi'kmaw dwellings and gardens in the vicinity of Eel Brook.[118]

Eel Brook, which in the French language is known as "Ruisseau-aux-Anguilles," contained the most crucial Mi'kmaw eel fishery within the Cape Sable district. Currently located within the Parish of Ste. Anne de Ruisseau, its shores contained the encampment grounds of the chiefs of Cape Sable. On 22 June 1771 François-Joseph Alexis acquired a commission from Governor William Campbell and his council that included official assurances that the Cape Sable Mi'kmaq would retain unmolested access to their gardens, hunting grounds, and fishery at Eel Brook. Alexis evidently had caught the attention of Lieutenant Governor Michael Francklin, Campbell's second-in-command, who had been on the lookout for reliable Mi'kmaw leaders to keep the peace in the face of the new settler influxes. News of Alexis's acts of kindness to new settlers may have reached Francklin either in Halifax or at the lieutenant governor's residence in Windsor. It would have been on Francklin's recommendation that Campbell extended Alexis a right to "hunt fish, and Improve lands under the usual instructions, particularly in the Creek known as Eel Creek [almost certainly Eel Brook], without hindering or molesting any other subjects."[119] So, in a somewhat paradoxical fashion, on 22 June 1771 François-Joseph Alexis attained a commission to keep using the resources of a locale that the Cape Sable Mi'kmaq had occupied since time immemorial, and over which their chiefs had exercised territorial prerogatives, recognized not only by Mi'kmaq of other districts but also by the Acadians.[120]

Under this new government fiat, the Cape Sable Mi'kmaq theoretically could fish alongside settlers at Eel Brook, but henceforth could wield no special territorial aegis over the ancient eel fishery. It seemed that all that Chief François-Joseph Alexis actually acquired from his commission was a red coat and some honorifics, since the governor had granted him "the honour to wear the Glorious Colours of our Gracious Sovereign King George the Third." One can envision François-Joseph Alexis decked out for the occasion in red regimentals, with epaulets, wearing a hat laced with gold braid, sporting a new medal about his neck and carrying a Union Jack. Yet he also faced the thinly veiled threat that unless he acted "as a good, faithful overseer" by ordering the Cape Sable Mi'kmaq "to keep themselves always in subjection and obedience" to the British monarch, his commission as well as his people's rights to Eel Brook would be revoked. From this point onward it seemed that Chief Alexis's ability to keep the peace would form the crux upon which everything the Mi'kmaq cherished at Eel Creek would depend. Campbell made this point clear by emphasizing that "only upon this condition I do grant unto you the said Francis Alexis leave to hunt, fish and Improve lands."[121]

The government in 1771 expected the Mi'kmaq to abide by the same laws as other inhabitants at Cape Sable.[122] Under British common law they could participate with others in harvesting tidewater fish resources by peacefully negotiating with their settler neighbours for a share of the catch. Yet there was an oddity in the mode of early grant allotment in the District of Argyle that suggests Michael Francklin, who became lieutenant governor of Nova Scotia in 1766, may have had a hand in ensuring that seven hundred acres surrounding the Mi'kmaw fishery and village at Eel Brook remained exempt from the granting process for at least another decade. Ranald MacKinnon, an émigré Highland Scot who had assisted the British regime with the expulsion of the Acadians, was rewarded for his services in 1766 by being given a grant of two thousand acres theoretically covering the entire District of Argyle. Yet MacKinnon's grant did not seriously impinge on the Eel Brook Mi'kmaw community.[123] MacKinnon, along with Reverend John Breynton, in 1773 presented a memorial to the executive council asking expressly for the seven hundred acres around Eel Brook occupied by the Mi'kmaq, which he claimed he possessed despite "an exclusive right to Said rivulet being Claimed by the Indians."[124] For reasons that are still unclear, the governor and council in Halifax hedged in making an immediate decision regarding Mackinnon's petition. Not only had the Lords of Trade and Plantations in England temporarily placed a prohibition in April of 1773 on the allocation of new grants in Nova Scotia, but Lieutenant Governor Francklin doubtless wished to placate François-Joseph Alexis by respecting the chief's wish that his people remain at Eel Brook undisturbed.[125] With the onset of the American Revolution, any further official consideration of MacKinnon's and Breynton's memorial ceased until the end of the war. [126]

The Anatomy of the Alexis Family: 1757 to 1800

Charles Alexis had at least seven siblings. His father and mother, Jacques Alexis and Angélique, raised at least five sons, François-Joseph[127] – who received baptism in 1727 in the absence of a priest at the hands of Guillaume Blanchard Jr. – Jacques, Charles, Pierre-Paul, and Thomas; and three daughters, Marie, Bridget, and Geneviève. By the mid-1740s the Alexis and Tecouramart families were allied, since Eustache Tecouramart, one of Antoine Tecouramart's younger sons, wed Jacques's daughter Marie.[128] Two of François Mius's family followed suit in the early 1760s by marrying into the Alexis family.

The only documentary sources that shed light on the anatomy of Jacques Alexis's family between 1727 and 1770 are the registers of Abbé Charles-François Bailly. Lieutenant Governor Michael Francklin, who recognized the right of returning Acadians to remain in southwestern Nova Scotia, also sought to assuage the Mi'kmaq's anger at not having a Roman Catholic missionary by appointing Abbé François-Charles Bailly de Messein in 1768 to minister to the spiritual needs of both the Mi'kmaq and Acadians.[129] During his itinerant travels around the province, Bailly discovered that many members of the former Cape Sable band were scattered over the landscape at the close of the Seven Years' War. As the first Roman Catholic missionary to labour among the Mi'kmaq since the death of Abbé Pierre Maillard in 1762, he also faced a huge backlog of baptisms and marriages to perform or confirm. In the absence of a priest,

baptisms, marriages, and funeral rites had been presided over by Mi'kmaw chiefs and Acadian leaders, as Maillard shortly before his death had instructed these men to do.[130] Yet, although these men had been diligent in conforming to Maillard's last wishes, news of a new missionary's arrival brought Acadian and Mi'kmaw families flocking to Bailly's side. Some of the first Mi'kmaq Abbé Bailly encountered in Nova Scotia were members of the closely kin-related Alexis, Tecouramart, and Mius families.

The Tecouramarts had drifted back to the Atlantic coast from Beaubassin in the late 1750s. Bailly met Antoine Tecouramart's eldest son, Antoine d'Ekounemat (Tecouramart) *fils*, at Piziquid, now Windsor, on 4 June 1769. Antoine *fils* and his wife Cecile brought four-year-old twins, Isidore and Marie Jeanne, to the missionary to be baptized.[131] They were accompanied by Paul Toutou (Chegua), who, like Antoine *fils*, was slowly wending his way back to Cape Sable from the Isthmus of Chignecto. On 29 June at Chezzetcook east of Halifax, Bailly also located Antoine *fils*'s brother Charles Tecouramart, along with Bernard Argomartin of La Have, Pierre-Paul Alexis, and Jacques Mius, a son of Chief François Mius and a great-grandson of Baron Philippe I Mius d'Entremont of Pobomcoup. In the early 1760s Jacques Mius married "Brigid [*sic*, Bridget] Alexis," while Bridget's brother Pierre-Paul Alexis wed Jacques Mius's sister, Hélène Mius.[132] Jacques Mius and Bridget introduced their four-year-old daughter, Marie, as well as a one-year-old, Marie-Jeanne Mius, to Bailly for baptism. The missionary also baptized three of Pierre-Paul Alexis and Hélène Mius's children: Germain who was five, Hierome who was four, and Noel, two.[133]

Following the close of the Seven Years' War, this kin-related group lived at La Héve – renamed "La Have" by the British – where François Mius remained chief until his death around 1765. In the late spring of 1769, five members of the Alexis family in toto had travelled eastward along the Atlantic coast to meet with Bailly at Chezzetcook: Bridget and Pierre-Paul Alexis, who were married and accompanied by children, and three others, Paul, Thomas, and Geneviève Alexis, who acted as sponsors at the children's baptisms.[134]

In early August of 1769 Bailly travelled by sea to Eel Brook, where he met the Cape Sable head chief, François-Joseph Alexis. The locale where the missionary disembarked, at the southeastern extremity of Comeau's Hill, is still known today as "La Pointe á Monsieur Bailly." On 6 August the abbé held mass in the shadow of a huge boulder, which for years had a distinctive white cross inscribed on its face known as La Roche de Saint-Pierre or "St. Peter's Rock." When a sizeable crowd gathered for the service, François-Joseph Alexis and his wife Marie Anne pressed to the fore to present their four-year-old son, Jean-Baptiste Alexis, for baptism.[135] François-Joseph was accompanied by his brother, Jacques Jaco, who was present with his wife, Marguerite.[136] Jacques Jaco and Marguerite had brought two sons, five-year-old Simon and three-year-old Jerome Alexis, to be baptized.[137] Bailly stayed at Eel Brook for several weeks, but by mid-September he made his way north to Baie Sainte-Marie, or St. Mary's Bay, where he met Eustache Tecouramart, the man who had sold the fishweir to Jacques Mius d'Entremont and François Mius in 1751. On 21 September, Eustache and his wife Marie Alexis asked Bailly to baptize two of their daughters, Anne and Marie.[138]

Abbé Bailly only remained in Nova Scotia three years. Feeling isolated in the face of an intolerant Protestant campaign against his missionary labours that arose at Halifax, he left the east coast in 1772 and eventually became coadjutor bishop of Quebec. His registers of 1768–72, however, remained at Caraquet to provide a brief window into what was happening within the Mi'kmaw and Acadian communities after the end of the Seven Years' War. Though the names of Charles Alexis and Anne Hébert do not appear in their pages, Charles and his wife may have ventured down from The Forks to participate in the sacraments Bailly conducted at Eel Brook in August 1769. The Forks, called *Machoudiak* in the Mi'kmaw language and meaning a "coming together" or "meeting,"[139] was still exclusively Mi'kmaw territory at the time; the first Acadian families would not enter the area until the late 1770s. The Mi'kmaw encampment ground at Machoudiak was an ancient one located near large stone weirs that spanned the river at intervals, each weir shaped like a V or a W. The points of the Vs had openings where woven containers could be inserted to collect migrating fish and eels. To underscore the antiquity of the Mi'kmaq's occupation of this area, an ancient Mi'kmaw burial ground lay at Koucougôke, east of The Forks.[140]

Between 1757 and 1790 Charles Alexis and Anne Hébert raised a sizeable family of five sons and at least one daughter. Michel (c.1757–1803) was the eldest

son, followed by Joseph (c.1758–c.1852),[141] Samuel (c.1759–c.1820), Bartholomew (c.1760–c.1830), and André (c.1762–c.1825).[142] The daughter was named Marie Alexis *dit* Michaud (c.1766–1807). Michel, Joseph, and Marie, like their parents, lived much of their time in the interior, both at The Forks and in the vicinity of present-day Kemptville on the upper Tusket River. Bartholomew and Andre, meanwhile, frequented the Salmon River area. Following the death of Chief François-Joseph Alexis about 1775, Charles assumed responsibility for raising his brother's son, Jean-Baptiste Alexis. Born in 1769, Jean-Baptiste was treated by Charles's sons and daughters as their sibling, since sibling and cousin relationships were viewed almost identically among the Mi'kmaq.

Each spring Charles Alexis and his family travelled to the coast to encamp at Eel Brook in the District of Argyle. By 1793 he also began to establish a summer encampment on Long Island in the Roseway River, Shelburne County. Around this time Bartholomew and his brother Abraham began pitching their camps on the lower reaches of the Salmon River in Digby County. Marie Alexis *dit* Michaud, meanwhile, lived with her parents at The Forks until 1780, when she married Laurent Mius, a grandson of Joseph I Mius *dit* d'Azy and Marie Amirault *dit* Tourangeau and a great-grandson of Philippe Muis dit d'Azy and his first Mi'kmaw country wife.[143] Marie and Laurent had a son named Jean-Baptist Mius, and at least two daughters, Ozithe and Marguerite. A third girl, Marie Mius, born before 1780 and who later married Olivier Frontain at The Forks, was more likely a child Laurent fathered before he met Marie, or else was a foster daughter.[144]

Bartholomew Alexis, born circa 1760, married a woman whose identity remains unknown, though it has been suggested that she was an Acadian from Digby County. He had a son, Étienne Bartholomew-Alexis *dit* Wisow, around 1780; a second son, Joseph, born about 1785; and a daughter, Bridget, who was probably the youngest of the family. Étienne Bartholomew-Alexis married an Acadian woman from Digby County and in 1819 had a son and namesake, Étienne (or Ekien) Bartholomew-Alexis *dit* Wisow *fils*, who in 1875 became leader of the Cape Sable band and was better known as Stephen Wisow Jr. Étienne Bartholomew-Alexis *père* and his wife had a second son Abraham, born about 1825. Bartholomew Alexis and his descendants all retained close connections with the Acadian communities that arose in the 1780s at Salmon River, Eel Brook, and The Forks.

Charles Alexis as Cape Sable District Chief

François-Joseph Alexis remained Cape Sable head chief only for a few years before he died around 1775, after which his younger brother Charles assumed the office during the American Revolution and for two decades thereafter. Charles Alexis's term of leadership coincided with the end of the fur trade era in southwestern Nova Scotia; the return and settlement of the former Acadian exiles; the arrival of numerous New Englanders and British settlers who would fish, farm, and establish grist mills and sawmills; and the Loyalist incursions of 1783 and 1784. Political deftness and diplomatic skill in upholding Cape Sable Mi'kmaw interests became the hallmarks of his leadership during this era of radical change. Throughout his life Charles remained faithful to Britain, despite numerous incidents that would test his fidelity.

British recognition of an existing temporary moratorium on infringements on Mi'kmaw rights to Eel Brook militated against Alexis's support for the rebel cause during the American Revolution, even though John Allan, a Nova Scotian who represented Cumberland Township in the House of Assembly in 1775 and 1776, sought to bring both the Mi'kmaq and Malecite into George Washington's camp. When Allan stated he had heard that chiefs of four Abenaki nations had shown some interest in helping the Americans, Washington appointed him superintendent of the Indians in the Eastern Department and commander of the American militia stationed at Machias, Maine. On 11 July 1776 Washington also urged the Continental Congress to engage warriors from the Penobscot, Malecite, and Mi'kmaq nations, if necessary, at full continental pay. The Congress responded by sanctioning the mustering of five hundred Eastern Abenaki soldiers under the joint command of Indigenous field officers, and commissioned officers, half of whom would be non-Indigenous and the rest of Indigenous extraction. Soon afterwards ten Mi'kmaq and several Malecite (*Wolastoqiyik* or *Wᵊlastᵊkwiyik*)[145] leaders, including the Mi'kmaw chiefs John Battis and Sabbatis Netobcobroit, travelled to Watertown, the seat of the Massachusetts government in exile during the war. This party wanted to find out whether the truckmaster at Machias could offer their

people better prices and longer credit for their furs than the British firm of Simonds and White on the Saint John River or Charles Jadis's trading station at nearby Grimcross Creek.[146]

Persuaded by General Washington and his emissaries, the ten Indigenous delegates signed a treaty at Watertown on 19 July 1776 by which they swore to acknowledge the independence of the United States and assist the fledging republic by urging other Indigenous groups to join the rebel cause. The Mi'kmaw nation as a whole, however, remained aloof from these treaty negotiations. Influenced by his peers' reluctance to give support to the treaty, one of the Mi'kmaw signers, John Battis, later stated that he had not realized the document bound him to fight alongside the revolutionaries, and so claimed immunity from the force of those specific conditions.[147]

In response to this split in Indigenous ranks, Allan held a conference on 19 September 1776 at Cocagne, lying north of Shediac in present-day New Brunswick, with seven Mi'kmaw head chiefs, including Charles Alexis. The chiefs were courteous but bluntly honest. They would not fight for the revolutionary cause. They intended to show a copy of the American treaty to the British at Fort Cumberland before returning it to Boston. They also wanted Allan to transcribe the essentials of their conversation with him so they could furnish the officials at Fort Cumberland written proof of their continued good intentions towards Britain. Not surprisingly, Allan refused, and instead directed the Aboriginal leaders to write to the Massachusetts government themselves explaining their refusal to fight. The Mi'kmaq then sent their own missive to Watertown expressing their polite regrets.[148]

The most severe test of Chief Alexis's fidelity to Britain arose immediately after the revolutionary war, when incipient political tussles between the Alexis family and the province flared into a heated controversy. A major reversal for the Mi'kmaw cause ensued when the Halifax council dispensed with any serious consideration of the Mi'kmaq's claim to Eel Brook. On 4 September 1778 Ranald MacKinnon, equipped with a commission as colonel of the Queens County Militia[149] and accompanied by light infantry composed of Highland emigrants, had attacked and repelled American privateers who were threatening communities on Cape Sable Island.[150] This event, which made MacKinnon a local hero, prompted Halifax to pay the militia colonel heed.

In the changed political climate following the reinstitution of land granting as a result of the Loyalist migrations, the council re-examined MacKinnon and Breynton's earlier application for seven hundred acres at Eel Brook. On 21 January 1785 its members confirmed the desired grant under Reverend Breynton's name.[151] Other than the Mi'kmaq, few contested this decision, since Michael Francklin, the main supporter of Cape Sable Mi'kmaw land interests, had died in 1782.

In response to this new development, Charles Alexis journeyed to Halifax in mid-June 1786 to meet with Lieutenant Governor John Parr and discuss the state of Mi'kmaw land issues at Cape Sable. Parr explained to Alexis that the Cape Sable Mi'kmaq were the ones to choose the location to be granted, although it is fairly certain that the seven hundred acres at Eel Brook constituted the main topic of conversation. Earlier in February of the same year, Parr had allotted a five-hundred-acre freehold grant to Chief Philip Bernard of St. Margaret's Bay, a transaction Charles Alexis certainly would have heard about and that may well have prompted his visit to Halifax.[152]

After the chief's audience with him, Parr had six lines of instructions, dated 22 June 1786, drafted and sent to Charles Morris, the superintendent general of Crown Lands, requesting Morris to "[b]e so good to accommodate the Bearers for [a] Grant of Land near Cape Sable, agreeable to their wishes." The memo bore the signature "Charles Alexis," along with Parr's initials.[153] Morris was also told to furnish the provincial secretary, Richard Bulkeley, with a clear description of the tract.[154] The surveyor general of Crown Lands definitely received these instructions, since a brief undated statement signed by Morris was filed later with the memo. But there was no plan or description attached to this document, which simply read "A License for the Indian bearers to occupy their lands and usual Hunting Grounds unmolested."[155]

The question remains: Had Parr in June of 1786 intended to allocate a freehold grant to the Cape Sable Mi'kmaq, as he previously had to Chief Philip Bernard? Charles Alexis certainly thought so, and this formed the basis of his future correspondence and actions with regard to the Halifax council. Yet Charles Morris did not interpret Parr's words in such a light, for he later contended that Alexis and his people, at best, might receive a licence "to occupy their lands and usual Hunting Grounds unmolested."[156]

Few situations could have been fraught with more ambiguity. Neither Parr nor Morris had delineated any territorial bounds that could be used to allocate either a grant or a licence. The interpretation that Crown Lands department accorded to Parr's memo and the meaning the Mi'kmaq ascribed to it were diametrically at odds. To Alexis, Parr's memo signified the English administration's recognition of the Mi'kmaq's prior right to land and resources, a right already respected by the Acadians. Each year the chief invited his kin and Indigenous visitors to travel to Eel Brook and camp at Sheshaw Park, which the Acadians left vacant for the Mi'kmaw visitors. At the peak of the eeling season, when there was sufficient food for all, the Cape Sable head chief and certain Acadian leaders, foremost among them a respected head man named Pierre Mius, administered baptisms, marriages, and last rites to the assembly in the absence of a priest. At such times the number of Indigenous and Acadian visitors to Eel Brook could reach several hundred. Among these were Mi'kmaq from La Hève, who came to renew their social, political, and kin ties with the Cape Sable group.[157]

The coming of the Planters had posed problems for the Mi'kmaq, but none as serious as the challenges that arose following the arrival of the Loyalists. The Mi'kmaq expected the Planters, who arrived from New England between 1759 and 1761, to treat what they saw as their prior rights to land and fisheries in a fashion similar to the Acadian French. And some Planters did at first, to preserve the peace.[158] But this situation radically changed as the Mi'kmaq became overwhelmed demographically by Loyalist influxes. Given the sheer number of Loyalists entering southwestern Nova Scotia by 1783, English-speaking residents of Yarmouth, Tusket, Barrington, and Shelburne felt they could safely ignore any Indigenous petitions for them to recognize Mi'kmaw rights. The Cheboque and Tusket areas had contained traditional Mi'kmaw encampment sites, but with an incursion onto these lands of cliquish Loyalists of Dutch extraction from New York in 1785, the Mi'kmaq permanently vacated these locales.

Charles Alexis doubtless had relayed these circumstances to the lieutenant governor in great detail in1786. But when the Halifax council refused to assist the Mi'kmaq, members of the Cape Sable Mi'kmaw community simply began ignoring the lines that surveyors were drawing over their territory at Eel Brook. They seasonally continued to reside near their eel fishery, even though large game and fur bearers in the surrounding woods were diminishing with the building of roads and the clearing of fields. When the Mi'kmaq eventually were forced to abandon cherished sites along the coast, their tolerance changed to impatience, though never to outright anger. The Acadian returnees, while sympathetic to the Mi'kmaq's plight, were in a poor position to help during these early years. For although Michael Francklin originally promised eighteen arpents of land to each Acadian family head, following his death the administration in Halifax took quite a different tack:[159] the absentee landlords McKinnon and Breynton, who had secured title to the land surrounding Eel Brook, now compelled all Acadians in the vicinity to pay them rent. For years afterwards these Acadians were not allowed to possess land freehold, nor were they able to hold public office. Even faced with such prejudicial treatment and with accompanying new stresses, seven Acadian family heads – Joseph Babin, Jean Bourque, Pierre LeBlanc, Pierre Mius, Louis Mius, Dominique Pothier, and Pierre Surette – continued to respect Mi'kmaw resource rights, as had their ancestors. As far as is known, no evidence of ill will ever arose between these men and Charles Alexis's people.

Until the end of the American Revolution, Charles Alexis and Anne Hébert remained at The Forks, to avoid the increasing population pressure along the coast. After their daughter Marie married Laurent Mius in 1780, they may have participated to a greater degree in local Acadian affairs. In the early 1780s, however, they pressed higher up the Tusket River system to the vicinity of modern-day Kemptville, as incoming Acadians to The Forks were clearing large fields and appropriating ancient weirsites. By contrast, Laurent Mius and Marie chose to dwell permanently at The Forks.[160] Laurent was an orchard farmer, and as there was little fog in the interior, the area was good for growing fruit. There were grassy meadows for livestock, vast blueberry fields, and the stone weirs, built generations before by the Mi'kmaq. Laurent, born around 1739, was at least forty years old when he married Marie Alexis, who was around twenty years his junior. Yet after seventeen years of marriage Marie died first, in 1807.[161] After her body was discovered on 4 October 1807 in the *"millieux des bois,"* perhaps as the result of an accident while out trapping in the forest, her son Jean-Baptiste and "several of her daughters" carried her remains to Eel

Brook, where they were interred in the Ste. Anne du Ruisseau cemetery. At her funeral, Marie was referred to for the first time as "Marie Alexis *dit* Michaud," an oddity since no other persons named Michaud lived at The Forks.[162]

The numerous Muise *dit* Gaspereau family living today at Quinan regard Laurent Mius's son, Jean-Baptiste Mius, as an ancestor.[163] These Acadians retained close attachments to the Mi'kmaw families who passed through The Forks in the spring and fall, and in expectation of the Mi'kmaq's appearances they reserved a plot called the *cabano* site to the east of their village where the Mi'kmaq could set up their wigwams and lean-tos.[164] Charles Alexis and Anne Hébert likely encamped near Laurent Mius's family whenever they visited The Forks.

In contrast to the interior, where riverine fish and game were still abundant, such resources quickly depleted along the coast. During the years when settlers were still establishing farms or marine fishing industries, many had to rely temporarily for basic necessities on the riverine fish trade as well as hunting big game and trapping peltries for sale. This brought them into direct economic competition with the local Mi'kmaq and by 1790 had drastically reduced the game population. Though many reports exist of the Mi'kmaq succouring settlers in the wintertime by bringing them gifts of game and fish, with time it became obvious that the settlers' reduction of game would affect even Mi'kmaq residing in the interior.[165] To address this serious situation, Charles Alexis called for a series of all-Mi'kmaw councils to be convened, with representatives attending from groups throughout the province, beginning in late December 1793 until the late spring of 1794 at Gaspereau Lake, a scenic body of water nestled in a trough on the side of the South Mountain in Kings County about ten miles (or sixteen kilometres) south of Kentville.

Charles Alexis and his colleagues chose the timing of their assembly with care. On 1 February 1793 France and Britain declared war. When news of the ensuing conflict reached Nova Scotia a month later, fears arose among the settler population of a possible invasion from a French naval force, especially since most of the Halifax garrison had been dispatched to the West Indies. To offset the lack of regular soldiers, the Halifax establishment expected the Mi'kmaq to figure in the defence of the colony. Lieutenant Governor John Wentworth wrote to Henry Dundas on

3 May suggesting that a militia unit be raised of between sixty and one hundred Mi'kmaw warriors, who would be supplied with provisions and clothing during their term of service.[166] The Mi'kmaq, Wentworth argued, would need little persuading to enlist since most had been reduced to extreme want owing to the impact of settlement and road building on the game population, and the relative mildness of the two previous winters. In July of the same year a far more parsimonious model for an Indigenous militia was drafted by Brigadier General James Ogilvie, who at the same time dispensed with any notions of paying the Mi'kmaw recruits, granting them supplies, or incurring any other than "unavoidable contingent expenses."[167]

Olgivie's emissaries contacted Charles Alexis at Cape Sable in late July to muster a party of able-bodied men to send to Halifax. Accordingly, the chief set out to gain his people's views on what should be done. He may even have hoped, given the state of alarm throughout the province, to be able to use his influence as a potentially valuable military ally of the British – with strong young men under his command – to bargain for a Crown grant at Eel Brook. But those he met chose to reserve judgment on Ogilvie's proposals until they and other leaders had met in council. Of far greater import to the Mi'kmaw constituency was the rapid decline of fish, game, and fur bearers owing to settler trapping practices, usurpation of fishing locales, road building, and destruction of forest land. There also had been blatant discrepancies in the way the government had allotted land to certain chiefs and not to others. Most leaders had received licences of occupation that were held merely at the pleasure of the Crown, whereas a few others had been allocated large freehold grants.[168] As he felt responsible for bringing his people's grievances to the attention of the government, Charles Alexis and his two eldest sons, Michel and Joseph, set out in August 1793 in a canoe for the Head of St. Margaret's Bay. There they spent two months with Chief Philip Bernard, who in 1786 had received a Crown grant for five hundred acres from Governor John Parr. Evidently the trio wanted to find out from Chief Bernard about of the advantages and liabilities of acquiring a freehold grant versus obtaining a licence of occupation.[169]

None of the chiefs were particularly interested in rallying to the British banner and serving in a militia unit that offered them no promises of pay, supplies, presents, or commissions. Instead they decided not

to act on the government's summons until a course of action was determined in the upcoming councils. In the interim, Charles would visit Halifax and try to find a government agent who proved sympathetic enough to Mi'kmaw interests to embody the grievances and other issues that might arise at these councils in a petition, to be directed to the lieutenant governor's office.

Charles Alexis Directs a Petition to Lieutenant Governor Wentworth

In 1783 George Henry Monk had been appointed provincial Indian commissioner in order to oversee the allocation in December of that year of licences of occupation to the heads of six Mi'kmaw groups throughout the province.[170] Upon completion of these licensing tasks Monk's duties as Indian commissioner ceased for a decade, until the crisis of 1793 called him back into operation. And despite the straightened circumstances within which Brigadier General Ogilvie's scheme to recruit a Mi'kmaw militia would operate, Monk patriotically agreed not only to superintend Indian Affairs in the province, but, if necessary also lead the Mi'kmaw combatants into battle.[171]

After meeting with Chief Bernard, Charles Alexis honed the approach he would take in meeting with the executive council. In 1786 he thought that Governor John Parr had accorded him a grant at Eel Brook, but later was told that he had been mistaken. Still, he felt fairly optimistic that if he could explain his unusual land case to Parr or one of his council members, the colossal administrative error that allowed settlers onto Mi'kmaw land at Eel Brook would be rectified by government fiat. Parr, however, had died in 1791, and when the chief arrived in Halifax in early December he faced Sir John Wentworth, who had never heard of Chief Alexis's land problems and manifested no interest in discussing them. Instead, Wentworth immediately redirected Alexis to Windsor to meet with George Henry Monk.

Monk heard ahead of time that Charles was on his way, and the idea worried him. He distrusted the chief, since he had been told that Alexis's wife Anne was a daughter of "Anthony Ebere [*sic*, Hébert] of Annapolis … who was an active man at the time of the removal of the Acadians from this province; + during the disturbances among them at that time."[172] Chief Alexis could cause serious problems if he ever encouraged his Acadian kinsmen to rebel against the government, a disturbing thought, especially as Monk had recently learned of depredations wrought by disaffected Mi'kmaq on settler properties in the Windsor area.[173] Lieutenant Governor Wentworth had proclaimed that any Mi'kmaq engaged in rebellious acts should be incarcerated in Fort Edward, yet Monk hesitated to act on Wentworth's instructions until he had firm proof that Charles Alexis was actually involved in seditious activities.[174]

When Charles and his two sons arrived at Monk's Windsor office on 10 December 1793, Monk's attitude towards his visitors was at first chilly and reserved. Seemingly undeterred, Charles congenially introduced his sons Michel and Joseph, and added that he and his wife had six children. He then stated that he was responsible for twenty-two families at Cape Sable, and apologized for his lateness in responding to the official summons given him in July. His tardiness, he explained, stemmed from "contrary winds" that had "slowed the progress of his canoe along the coast."[175]

Monk knew perfectly well that it would take more than unfavourable weather conditions to delay Charles' arrival in Halifax for five months, and suspected that the chief's procrastination arose from his lack of interest in volunteering to fight when he would receive neither pay nor provisions. The commissioner also correctly surmised from a few things the chief said that Cape Sable leader soon would be participating in an all-Mi'kmaw council, to be held along the Gaspereau River Valley, near Melanson, the site of an ancient Mi'kmaw meeting ground.[176] However, when this subject was broached with Charles, the chief refused to divulge the location, scope, and nature of the council, which whetted Monk's suspicions[177]

Charles decided to apprise Monk, cautiously and by degrees, of the nature of the Mi'kmaq's predicament when it came to land and resources. To gain the commissioner's trust, he stated that he had supported the British cause during the American Revolution and had been assured by Lieutenant Governor John Parr in 1786 that his traditional territorial lands at Cape Sable would in consequence be secured to him. Subsequently, however, Mi'kmaw land interests had been ignored by the government and abused by the settlers. Monk had a daily journal in which he jotted down what Charles Alexis told him. "[He] complains that the French people (formerly the

French neutrals), + some English have taken away the Lands that he has cleared and make a garden of," Monk recorded. "[He] had on former complaint to Govr. Parr recd. a promise that his land should be restored to him, but was deceived." The Mi'kmaq felt they had been lulled into "complacency" by the British, who gave them "every thing they asked for + continuing to give them supplies till all their Land, Rivers, and Hunting Places were taken up and settled in Townships and then stopping all supplies + leaving them deprived and destitute of every means of subsistence."[178]

When Charles perceived that Monk was going to take what he said seriously by recording his words in a journal, he decided at last to ask the commissioner to draft a petition to Wentworth acquainting the lieutenant governor with the perfidious treatment his people had received since the British came among them.[179] By this time Monk was feeling less anxious about his visitors, but he still felt he needed to know more about the Indigenous councils scheduled to take place in the province. One way he felt he might get the Mi'kmaq to talk was to offer them provisions. Though he observed that the chief and his sons, whom he described as "stout young men," did not need government handouts to sustain them, he decided to offer the party a small quantity of powder and shot, seven yards of cloth, some thread, and two loaves of bread.[180]

Faced with what he felt was a parsimonious assortment of goods, Chief Alexis enquired if regular distributions of government supplies, similar to those given out by Michael Francklin prior to 1782, would ever be resumed. He meant to proceed carefully in order not to offend the commissioner. Yet, on hearing that Monk had been instructed to provide provisions only to the ill and aged, Michel, who was conversant in broken English, retorted "with marked + significant exaculations [sic, vocal ejaculations]" that the Mi'kmaq "regretted having peacefully suffered the English to possess the whole country before they were made secure of a continuance of supplies."[181] To Michel, the thought of having a powerful political entity in his midst with which he could establish no reciprocal relationship was anathema, since it contradicted traditional northeastern Algonquian conceptions about the proper workings of power. The Cape Sable band had always formed an integral part of their region's economy and polity. During the French era they had traded furs and offered military assistance to the French Crown. Later, they aided the Planter settlers and the returning Acadians when they needed it and pledged their loyalty to Britain during the American Revolution, all for little or no return from the new establishment that had taken root at Halifax. Most recently the Loyalists, many of whom retained a collective memory of Aboriginal raids on New England settlements during the French and Indian Wars, regarded the Mi'kmaq with a mixture of suspicion, fear, and disdain. And through it all, their chiefs, who had aided and remained at peace with their new neighbours, received no honours, provisions, or land from a government grateful for their continued cooperation.

Michel's desire for ongoing government supplies was rooted not only in the Mi'kmaq's need for practical necessities such as food and clothing, but also in their traditional ideological need to be vital participants in the cosmological functioning of the world around them. Monk's replies to their questions told of a new order that threatened to leave the Mi'kmaq powerless and functionless as well as physically destitute. While Charles and Michel complained about the scarcity of game and the depredations of settlers, they also voiced chagrin at having been treated so shamefully when they had tolerated so much from the British for so long. Fearing he would not be understood, Michel gave vent to his frustrations by declaring, "What Country [or place in the world order]" was left for the Mi'kmaq "now the English give no more provisions or cloaths [*sic*, clothes]?"[182] As the British had grown powerful, they should be willing to share their largess with those who over the years had assisted them, and not regard the Mi'kmaq like beggars.

After his three visitors left his office, Monk reflected on Michel's barrage of heated words. He realized now that the Mi'kmaw party were expounding an integrated policy stance that was strongly informed by Indigenous cultural values, and not merely spouting disjointed grievances. He felt embarrassed about the way the government allocated land grants to some Mi'kmaw leaders and not to others who were probably just as deserving. Since the Mi'kmaw party had come by way of St. Margaret's Bay, he further suspected that chiefs Alexis and Bernard had compared notes on their respective treatment from the government on land issues.[183] Not only were the Alexis party shrewd, well informed, and influential within the broader Mi'kmaw

community, but they also operated outside his sphere of control. The Mi'kmaq "appear more restless + dissatisfied with their situation than I have ever known them to be," he confided to Wentworth. "Some of the more intelligent among them make circuitous visits with different Tribes and give false reasons for such long and unusual excursions."[184] Though less worried about Chief Alexis than he had been initially, Monk still decided for the sake of caution to employ a peddler named Job Ross as a spy, to ferret out any signs of seditious activity associated with the Indigenous councils at Gaspereau Lake.[185]

He also monitored Charles Alexis's activities by asking Mi'kmaq visitors to his office if they had met with the Cape Sable leader and, if so, inquiring what he was up to. Two incidents in particular confirmed that Charles was bringing Mi'kmaw leaders together to share ideas. The first involved a visit on 12 January 1794 from James (or Jacques) Peminout Paul and his son John, who were en route from Gaspereau Lake to Newport in East Hants County. Accompanying them were the elderly Minas chief Barthélèmy Quarred (or Batholomew Momcharret) and Louis Anthony (Toney), who acted as James's interpreter.[186] All proved extremely reluctant to talk about Charles Alexis. When the commissioner asked if they had met the Cape Sable chief, they made odd facial gestures before replying in the negative, which led Monk to suspect the "truth of the reply," especially when James made an allusion to two loaves of bread, the exact quantity Monk had given Charles Alexis.[187]

The second incident occurred on 20 February 1794 when Monk was approached by Francis Emable, who held the synonymous names "François Jannot" or "François Peguidalouet." Francis was a nephew of a former head chief of Cape Breton, Jannot Peguidalouet, who had signed treaty with the British in 1761. In 1783 Monk also had provided Chief Peguidalouet with a licence of occupation for land at East Bay, now Eskasoni in Cape Breton. Francis stated that his uncle had died and that he had left Cape Breton to hunt between Canso and Antigonish, a remark that made the commissioner wonder why he had come so far out of his way to visit Windsor. When asked if he knew Chief Alexis, Francis hedged, though he admitted that the Cape Sable group were "better off than most." A taciturn man who was not easily flustered, Francis decided to reveal to Monk that he was actually on his way to attend one of the Mi'kmaw councils presided over by Chief Alexis. Lighting his pipe and getting comfortable before speaking, he casually averred that he would welcome any provisions Monk might give him, since the Mi'kmaq at "Gaspero Lake … would be glad of little flour."[188]

That Charles Alexis had been presiding over Indigenous councils throughout the winter and spring was further confirmed when the Peminouts and Bartholomew Momcharret returned to Windsor on 31 March 1794.[189] According to Chief Momquarret, Charles had camped at a site "between Windsor and Annapolis," where he "had seen all the other Indians who wished him to speak for them."[190] The Cape Sable leader had informed his listeners that he intended to meet with Monk to discuss the matters that had arisen in the Indigenous assemblies. Monk knew then that his fears had been unfounded. The peddler, Job Ross, returned to Windsor soon afterwards with little news to report and received ten dollars for his counter-insurgency activities. The Mi'kmaq had remained peaceable throughout the early spring.[191]

Charles Alexis returned to Windsor several times during the spring of 1794 to provide Monk with ideas to include in the petition the commissioner had promised to Wentworth. He demanded that the promises made to his people be "honoured,"[192] which would mean sustaining a workable spirit of reciprocity so that avenues of communication could be kept open between the Mi'kmaq and the colonial authorities. Distribution of government supplies had formed an integral part of this ongoing conversation prior to 1782. The Mi'kmaq still expected the British monarch to treat them as a caring father would a faithful son and, in return, they would keep the peace and supply military assistance when needed. Chief Alexis's failure to appear to the government's summons in the early summer of 1793 had not been an act of insubordination. Instead, it embodied a protest that the spirit of reciprocity that informed relations between the British and Mi'kmaq during Michael Francklin's term as provincial Indian commissioner had been swept away by an emphasis on parsimony and strategic manipulation of supplies. To the Cape Sable leader, this alone constituted a crisis of immense proportions warranting a round of serious discussions with other chiefs.

During his discussions with Charles Alexis, Monk often found himself caught between what his superiors expected of him as Indian commissioner and what Chief Alexis hoped he would accomplish on behalf of the Mi'kmaq. The Mi'kmaq claimed they were starving.[193] In the fall of 1793 Monk had departed radically from the policy guidelines set out for him by Sir John Wentworth, who wanted him to focus on pacifying the Mi'kmaq without "pandering" to their wants. Wentworth worried far more about the likelihood of external agents stirring the Indigenous people to question and resist English rule than he did about the hardships the Mi'kmaq faced. Monk, by contrast, not only grasped the desperation felt by many Indigenous leaders by 1794, but also had some appreciation of the Mi'kmaw world view, so he listened. And, as he did, his distrust was replaced by admiration for the Cape Sable leader's devotion to and determination to assist his people.[194]

The chief also contacted Monk's kinsman and former business partner George Deschamps, whom he apprised that, owing to the government's reluctance to grant his people land at Eel Brook, his group had ceased to plant. The Mi'kmaq "cannot go to work on their lands without it being made their own," he charged.[195] Deschamps, who had traded with the Mi'kmaq for many years and was conversant with Mi'kmaw culture and language, sympathized with Charles's position, so he assisted Monk early in 1794 in completing the petition based on the ideas the chief had dictated to the commissioner. This document reiterated the hardships the Mi'kmaw people had experienced since the time of Michael Francklin's death in 1782. It also spoke of their continued willingness to fight for King George even though the promise that they should always have provisions had subsequently been broken. The petition concluded "[t]hat nine years ago when the Superintendent was settling English Towns he told the Indians they must live as Brothers to the English who came to settle … and Governor Parr told the Indians they should always be taken care of and have relief when they were in distress – but now the Mikmacks have little or no hunting Ground – no regular supplies – no Brothers except among themselves, and know not where to go or what to do."[196] Having placed the burden of responding to this plaint squarely on the lieutenant governor, Monk signed the document and delivered it on 24 January 1794 to Wentworth.[197]

Even after the petition was sent, Charles Alexis continued sporadically to visit the commissioner's office. In November 1797 Monk recorded in his letterbook that Alexis believed the Cape Sable Mi'kmaq "were restless + distressed at the settlements making in places that were formerly their best hunting +

fishing country." The commissioner also learned that the chief was continuing to hold conferences with other Mi'kmaw leaders; during the preceding summer he had left Cape Sable and passed by Windsor to travel to the South Mountain and Annapolis – "an uncommon route of very great distance compared with the usual + direct way by St. Marys Bay + Digby."[198] Chief Alexis was not a regular visitor at Monk's office, however, and his name appears infrequently in Monk's requisitions for Mi'kmaw supplies. The Cape Sable band was able to maintain a sufficient degree of economic autonomy to eschew reliance on government relief.[199]

Lieutenant Governor Wentworth must have ignored the Mi'kmaw petition, since no reply to it could be found, but subsequent events suggest that the Indigenous leaders participating in the Gaspereau Lake councils held in 1793 and 1794 agreed to remain peaceful while launching a series of petitions for grants to their major fishing sites, gardens, and other crucial resource areas. In 1794 Solomon Jeremy, whose first name "Solomon" was rendered as "Sulno" in Mi'kmaq, and Joseph Glode directed a memorial to Halifax for a parcel of land inland from the La Have settlement in Lunenburg County.[200] Though some of Sulno's descendants continued to live at La Have and New Germany well into the 1830s, others left La Have after the government ignored their request and moved to Cape Sable.[201]

Louis Anthony (or Toney), who had acted as Jacques Peminout Paul's interpreter in December 1793 and January 1794, was the father of several sons and daughters who lived along the shore of the Annapolis Basin. A son of Captain Anthony Ury, a Pictou chief well known at Halifax for his support of the British cause during the American Revolution,[202] Louis was fluent in English and French as well as Mi'kmaq, and frequently was employed as an interpreter by government officials as well as Mi'kmaw leaders.[203] Two of Louis's sons, Peter and Daniel, in the early 1800s joined a group at the Gut of Annapolis led by Andrew James Meuse, while around 1819 one of his daughters, Madeline, became Meuse's wife.[204] Chief Meuse and his Toney in-laws set out to secure a reserve in Annapolis County, as well as gain protection for their local porpoise hunt.

These Mi'kmaq soon joined forces with Abbé Jean-Mandé Sigogne (1763–1844), who had been appointed Roman Catholic missionary to the Mi'kmaq and Acadians in southwestern Nova Scotia in June

1799.[205] Sigogne was a classical scholar, choir director, and social activist as well as a cleric and, once he grew to know his congregants, an advocate of Mi'kmaw and Acadian land and resource rights. He also became well acquainted with Jacques Mius, a son of François Mius of La Have, who in turn was Andrew James Meuse's father. Jacques Mius camped near Sigogne's clerical headquarters in the District of Clare in Digby County. When Sigogne in 1812 expressed an interest in Mi'kmaw history, Jacques produced his father's French commission of 1742, a silver medal, and a parchment copy of the peace and friendship treaty his father had signed with the British in November of 1761. Jacques relinquished the commission and treaty to Sigogne's care, but kept the medal to wear in church on special occasions.[206]

Sigogne persuaded Jacques Mius and his son Andrew James Meuse to press for the establishment of a farming community at Bear River spanning the Digby–Annapolis County line. In 1825 Andrew James Meuse travelled to England with the Protestant humanitarian Walter Bromley to obtain a land grant with the assistance of King William IV. Through Bromley's auspices, Mius gained an audience with the British monarch, though he did not obtain a freehold grant – his primary aim. Instead, the combined efforts of Sigogne and Peleg Wiswall, a judge from Digby, helped him secure a reserve at Bear River in 1827.[207]

Though several families of Mi'kmaq immediately moved to the reserve, none had the surname "Alexis," probably because Andrew James Meuse's mother Bridget was an Alexis. The Mi'kmaw kinship system traditionally proscribed cousin marriage to the third descending generation, so at least two generations would pass before members of the Alexis family could marry into the Bear River band, formed principally of Meuse's extended family.[208] By the 1860s, however, several of the Alexis family who became guides made Bear River their headquarters, and marriage between the Meuse and Alexis families resumed.

The Cape Sable band similarly wanted secure title to lands where they could fish and raise crops. As early as 1798, when a severe storm decimated forests along the Atlantic coast from Halifax to Shelburne County, and wildfires burning the deadfall the following year drove away game, many Mi'kmaq from Halifax and Lunenburg Counties traversed the charred countryside to Cape Sable.[209] So many of the Mi'kmaq's former haunts lay vacant that a surveyor named Titus Smith, who was cruising the landscape in 1801, wondered at first if all the Mi'kmaw population had left the province to avoid starvation. Smith saw few moose or caribou, and it was not until he entered the Cape Sable district that he saw any signs of beaver activity.[210] Despite Smith's concerns, members of the executive council in Halifax proved unsympathetic. Despite Charles Alexis's determination in 1794 to inform the lieutenant governor of the hardships the Mi'kmaq already faced from settler incursions, the government did nothing, even when the situation for Indigenous people worsened dramatically four years later. Economic hardship, Lieutenant Governor Wentworth proclaimed in 1798, would render the Aboriginal population more malleable in times of military crisis, since a starving population would prove "vigorously Faithful" once they were afforded government relief.[211]

As petitions recounting Mi'kmaw grievances obviously were not going to engender any long-term solutions, Charles Alexis spearheaded a new Indigenous land acquisition campaign.[212] He held that cultivation of crops would have to compensate for losses in the trapping and hunting sector, and instructed his sons to settle on and then apply to the government for grants to their main fishing, hunting, and planting sites. Accordingly, Michel, Joseph, Jean-Baptiste, and Samuel Alexis began farming on a tract on almond-shaped Long Island, lying in the Roseway River, sixteen kilometres inland from the town of Shelburne.[213] The same year another of Charles Alexis's sons, Bartholomew, set up an encampment on property in southern Digby County belonging to George Ring, a Planter who had emigrated from New England in the 1770s and was sympathetic to Mi'kmaw interests. Ring's land lay on the eastern bank of the lower Salmon River.[214] In the early 1790s a meandering tote road cut through the forest from Digby to Yarmouth town and beyond to Cheboque, Tusket, Pubnico, and Eel Brook. The proximity of Bartholomew's camp to this road gave him foot access to markets in both directions. Bartholomew gardened and maintained a weirsite, and though relatively secure from molestation on the Ring property, he still set out, in accordance with his father's wishes, to acquire a grant of his own fronting on the Salmon River.

In the late 1790s Charles Alexis drafted one last petition asking for a grant to his people's meeting ground at Eel Brook. The Court of Quarter Sessions for the Yarmouth and Argyle Districts of Shelburne County[215] delayed a long time before refusing his request. Finally, in April 1800, they fell back on the same excuse that the surveyor general, Charles Morris, had used in 1786: that the Mi'kmaq possessed the same privileges as the settlers to fish in streams in the Cape Sable district, provided they followed the fishery regulations.[216] As far as they were concerned, the Mi'kmaq did not need land along the river to exercise these rights.

Charles Alexis died late in 1798 or early in 1799, before he had the opportunity to rebut this ruling. His demise certainly occurred before Sigogne's arrival in July 1799, since the abbé's parish registers for Ste. Anne du Ruisseau make no mention of it. In his last days he had been in the care of his wife Anne Hèbert at The Forks. After his death, his body was taken to Eel Brook and interred in a small, consecrated gravesite nearby at Rocco Point, next to a wooden chapel built by the Spiritan priest and missionary Joseph-Mathurin Bourg, who briefly visited Cape Sable in 1784.[217] Michel Alexis, his eldest son, who married Marie Mius of The Forks around the same time Laurent Mius wed Michel's sister Marie Alexis, succeeded his father as leader of Cape Sable.[218] Halifax's decision to deny the Mi'kmaq a secure foothold at Eel Brook undoubtedly discouraged Michel, for though he continued to preside over special gatherings at Eel Brook, he joined his brother Joseph for most of the year on Long Island in the Roseway River. The remainder of his band's population scattered out over the Cape Sable landscape.

Abbé Sigogne Meets the Alexis Family

Abbé Jean-Mandé Sigogne set sail from Halifax for Cape Sable on 1 July 1799. Disembarking at Eel Brook on 4 July, he remained three weeks in the Acadian and Mi'kmaw settlement before riding on horseback an uncomfortable fifty miles north through the wilderness over the stone-strewn tote road leading to his second parish, Ste. Marie, in the District of Clare.[219] Sigogne's original instructions were to labour mainly among the Acadian population of St. Mary's Bay. But though he made Pointe-de-l'Église (or "Church Point") his headquarters, from 1805 to 1824 he travelled twice a year to Ste. Anne du Ruisseau, once in summer and once in winter, to stay three months at a time in the lower parish.[220] The journey took three days each way, with overnight stops at Salmon River and Yarmouth. To facilitate matters, in 1809 he erected a wooden church consecrated to Ste. Anne. During the months Sigogne was unavailable to administer the sacraments in his church at Eel Brook, Pierre Mius or François Gilis, who were literate in French and could speak the Mi'kmaw language, would perform these rites.[221]

One of the first Cape Sable Mi'kmaq to meet with Sigogne was Pierre Alexis *dit* Eptemec (c.1730–1820). Pierre, who was over sixty years old, was likely the same Pierre Alexis *dit* Eptemec who had lived at La Hève in the late 1760s with his first wife, Hélène Mius.[222] Sigogne's predecessor, Abbé Charles-François Bailly, met Pierre and Hélène at Chezzetcook in 1769. Pierre enjoyed an elevated status within the Cape Sable Mi'kmaw community as the only remaining son of Jacques Alexis and Angélique. At an elaborate ceremony hosted by the local Mi'kmaw and Acadian communities, Sigogne confirmed Pierre's second marriage to Marie-Agnès Antoine (Toney) on 26 April 1800. Pierre Mius had presided over the couple's marriage on 10 August 1795, but the two wanted Sigogne to renew their vows before a large gathering at Eel Brook. Witnesses to the celebration included André Alexis, who had come across country from Salmon River, Laurent Mius from The Forks, and several prominent Acadians: Hippolite Babin, Charles Le Blanc, François Gilis, and Jacques Le Roy. Doubtless André Alexis's brother Bartholomew Alexis was among the invited guests, as well as Laurent Mius's wife, Marie Alexis, who was Pierre's niece.[223]

Sigogne had only been at Eel Brook four days when Pierre Alexis *dit* Eptemec and his second wife Marie-Agnès brought their three-year-old daughter, Magdalene, to him for baptism.[224] Four days later, on 12 July, the couple also presented three more of their daughters for baptism: Anastasie, who was five years old, born in July 1795; Cecile, two, born in January 1797; and an infant, Charlotte, born in March 1799. Accompanying this party was a middle-aged man named Pierre Alexis, who along with his wife Anne wanted Sigogne to baptize their young daughter, Marie-Charlotte. This second Pierre was almost certainly an older son of Pierre Alexis Sr. and his first wife, Hélène Mius. Fabien Alexis, who accompanied Pierre Alexis Jr., would have been Pierre Jr.'s brother.[225] Following the birth of several daughters, in 1805 Pierre Alexis *dit* Eptemec and Marie-Agnès

finally had a son, Jacques Alexis, who later dwelt on Long Island near the town of Shelburne.[226]

The second family group intent on meeting Sigogne at Eel Brook was headed by Jean-Baptiste Alexis (1765–c.1825), the son of Chief François-Joseph Alexis who, following his father's death, had been raised by Charles Alexis. Jean-Baptiste and his wife Marie Amquarette (Momcharret) brought an infant daughter, Anne, on 7 November 1799 to Sigogne for baptism. Another daughter, Marie-Françoise, was born to this couple in 1806. On 10 April the following year Jean-Baptiste and Marie's eldest son, François Alexis, married a Mi'kmaw woman from West Pubnico named Isabelle Beliard.[227] Jean-Baptiste was probably the father of Honore Alexis, who later married Paul Williams (c.1770–c.1856), a head man from Great Pubnico Lake, inland from West Pubnico, Yarmouth County.[228] Jean-Baptiste and his family seasonally resided on Long Island in Shelburne County.

The third family to arrive at Eel Brook was that of the Cape Sable head chief Michel Alexis (c.1757–c.1803) and his wife Marie Muis, whose infant son Michel *fils* was baptized on 12 November 1799.[229] Michel's younger brother Joseph did not seek Sigogne's services until 28 July 1805, when he and his wife Marie-Joseph Muis brought a two-year-old son, Joseph Alexis *dit* Makaq, to the abbé for baptism. Sigogne noted that during St. Anne's Day festivities in 1805 Bartholomew Alexis from Salmon River, his daughter Bridget, his brother André Alexis, and a member of the Charles family who had recently arrived from Prince Edward Island were all camped near Michel and Joseph Alexis at Eel Brook.[230]

Out of the twenty or so Mi'kmaw families that lived at Cape Sable, only members of the Alexis family asked Abbé Sigogne to perform baptisms, marriages, and burials. No other Mi'kmaq, except for the occasional few who acted as witnesses or godparents, appear in the Ste. Anne du Ruisseau registers during these early years. One exception was Pierre Chishaw Jr. (*sic*, Chegua) who along with his wife Agnès brought a daughter, Eusebe, to Eel Brook to be baptized on 15 December 1800.[231] A possible explanation is that the Cape Sable head chief felt a lingering sense of entitlement about presiding over ceremonial rites at Eel Brook.[232] As the paramount Indigenous power-holder, he would be the first to request services from any new missionary. Pierre Chegua Jr. also presided at ceremonies as a head man, but others rarely entered the ritual forum.

Sigogne had his work cut out for him. Except for a few marriages and baptisms registered years before by Abbé Bailly, virtually no written records existed on which the missionary could base any judgements concerning his new Mi'kmaw parishioners. This must have proven taxing, especially when Chief Michel Alexis and others of the Alexis family began to pressure him to petition Halifax for land grants along major rivers. Michel, Joseph, Samuel, Bartholomew, and André Alexis set their sights on preserving their people's access to traditional riverine resources. The most vital arteries were those whose fish fed the occupants of Mi'kmaw encampments lying far up the Tusket River. Michel, Joseph, Samuel, Jean-Baptiste and the elderly Pierre-Paul Alexis camped near the mouths of the Roseway, Barrington, and Clyde rivers during the summers. In the fall they journeyed to the upper reaches of the Tusket River where they fished at stone weirs, hunted, trapped, and harvested the produce of gardens they had planted in the spring.[233] Bartholomew Alexis and his brother André occasionally joined their close kin in Shelburne County by journeying across from the upper Salmon River to the upper Tusket and its tributaries, and then canoeing down the Roseway River to Long Island. These Mi'kmaq regularly importuned Sigogne to back their ongoing campaign to regain Mi'kmaw control over lands along the Salmon River and at Eel Brook.[234]

Carving Footholds on the Cape Sable Landscape: A Mi'kmaw Foothold on the Salmon River

Bartholomew Alexis's goal in 1800 was to acquire a government grant on the banks of the lower Salmon River. Even though George Ring had permitted him since 1792 to maintain a large weir on his property, Bartholomew still found his fishing was hampered by landowners downriver blocking the stream.[235] He complained to local officials of his non-Indigenous neighbours' lack of compliance with the fishery regulations, but when these efforts failed to stop injury to his weir fishery, he resorted to stronger measures. Around this time, he began to refer to himself as "Bartlett" rather than "Bartholomew," perhaps because "Bartlett" sounded the way a Mi'kmaw speaker pronounced "Bartholomew." Many of his descendants also came to refer to themselves as "Bartletts" rather than as members of the "Bartholomew-Alexis" family.[236]

Though confronted by settlers at Tusket who opposed the Mi'kmaq's right to participate in the riverine fishery, Bartlett Alexis was certainly not friendless or defenceless. He was respected by Acadians who lived at Salmon River, among them members of the Commeau, Thibeault, Deveau, and Guedry families. As noted above, in the past these Acadians and the Mi'kmaq had interacted on a friendly basis and occasionally intermarried. When Bartholomew was a young man in the 1760s his people had provided fish, game, berries, and shellfish for the Acadian returnees during their first harsh winters, and the Mi'kmaq's kindness had not been forgotten.[237]

Certain Planters, among them George Ring and Joshua Frost, also took a genuine interest in Mi'kmaw concerns.[238] The Mi'kmaq grew to trust and to some degree rely on their Planter friends, who occasionally backed the Mi'kmaw Bartletts in their political tussles with a cliquish group of Loyalists living at Yarmouth and Tusket who resented the Mi'kmaq's fishing wherever they wished. When Bartlett Alexis found settlers interfering in his fishery in 1801, he sought out Joshua Frost, a justice of the peace, who agreed to draft a complaint for Bartlett and send it to Sir John Wentworth in Halifax. The resulting petition informed the lieutenant governor that "Bartlett Elixe" and six of his band were being molested on their fishing grounds at Salmon River and demanded government protection.[239]

When Wentworth did not reply right away to this petition, Bartlett's brother Samuel Alexis took up the torch in 1802 by once again pressing for a grant of land at Eel Brook. As no written request by Samuel Alexis exists in the documentary record, he must have travelled to Halifax and met with the lieutenant governor face to face. Wentworth gleaned considerable information about Mi'kmaw land and resource problems from this exchange, for in December of 1802 he wrote Michael Wallace, the provincial treasurer,[240] stating that the Cape Sable Mi'kmaq "by their own account" were "a sober and industrious people" who planted and fished for subsistence on lands their ancestors had inhabited for generations. Their main grievance, he continued, "concerned the settlers' practice of blocking streams by nets that impeded fish from reaching the upper reaches of the watercourses." Wentworth then directed Wallace to contact the Shelburne County magistrates, whose jurisdiction at that time embraced modern-day Yarmouth and Shelburne Counties, and instruct them to have lands laid out for the Mi'kmaw people "suitable to their needs." [241] They also were to take measures to prevent further depredations on the Mi'kmaw fishery.

Even Wentworth's instructions failed to dispel magisterial lethargy when the Court of Quarter Sessions in the spring of 1803 turned to the question of allocating river frontage to the Mi'kmaq who asked for it. Finally, in April, the Sessions informed Wentworth that the parcel at Eel Brook asked for by Samuel Alexis had already been granted. Reluctant to revisit the fishery issue, they also argued that as far as they knew only one settler had ever interfered with a Mi'kmaw weirsite, and deemed Bartlett Alexis's "complaint unworth [sic] of further notice."[242] Not only was Bartlett's grievance far from "being well founded," they contended, but the Mi'kmaq "ever enjoy and exercise as great if not a greater share of privilege claimed Than any of His Majesty's natural born Subjects resident in the District."[243] This last statement suggests that some were familiar with the respect protocols towards the Mi'kmaq, which still lingered on in certain Acadian communities, but in the end Samuel Alexis's and Bartlett Alexis's land and resource campaign foundered in a welter of apathy and opposition at the local level.

Wentworth had his own reason for supporting certain Mi'kmaw causes. His goals differed radically from the Mi'kmaq's own. In the years leading up to the War of 1812 the lieutenant governor wanted to placate the Indigenous population lest the Mi'kmaq be persuaded by French emissaries to attack outlying English settlements.[244] Given the expediency that motivated Wentworth's support, and the callous disdain manifested by magistrates who deliberately misconstrued the Mi'kmaq's memorials as asking for special fishing privileges, it was surprising that the Mi'kmaw campaign actually got as far as it did. Much of the positive impetus derived from Frost's support. Joshua Frost was not afraid to confront the deep-seated prejudices that led his magisterial peers to stymie the Mi'kmaq's land and resource campaign.[245] Frost was, more often than not, at odds with the political constituency of Dutch Loyalist émigrés who, brought from New York to southwestern Nova Scotia by Captain John Van Norden, had rapidly assumed official positions at Tusket and Yarmouth. Van Norden, who first took up land on the Roseway River near Shelburne, was among this number, for by 1800

he had moved to Tusket where he established a grist mill and became the local fisheries inspector.[246]

Frost's lone support for the Mi'kmaq was not enough to change official attitudes. Added to the opposing mix were absentee landlords like Ranald MacKinnon, whose successful petitions for vast tracts of territory had deprived the Mi'kmaq in the mid-1780s of their traditional hunting, fishing, and planting grounds. Similar to the Loyalist émigrés of Dutch extraction, MacKinnon disdained his Planter neighbours for what he considered their pro-American leanings. When in the summer of 1775 Frost's father, the Reverend John Frost, went so far as to preach a sermon stating that he hoped the British some day would return to England "confuted and confused," MacKinnon cut off any further relations with the Frost family until the day he died. He even wrote one of his daughters, Penelope, out of his will just a few months before his death in 1804, on the grounds that she had disobeyed his wishes and married a Frost.[247]

As fisheries inspector, John Van Norden had no interest in promoting Mi'kmaw resource claims, and others of the Dutch Loyalist community went even further, by treating the Mi'kmaq as unwelcome intruders wherever they went. When Miner Vander Horn and his son were arraigned at Tusket in October 1807 on charges that Bartlett Alexis raised against them "of accosting the body of one Jane Alexis" – who likely was one of Bartlett's daughters – the majority of the magistrates turned a blind eye to the Mi'kmaq's pleas for justice. Though Alexis was called upon to provide evidence before the court, none of his testimony was ever recorded. The actual events that took place were so glossed over in the written record that the nature and seriousness of the crime, let alone the motive behind it, cannot be reconstructed from the evidence at hand.[248] It has been suggested that the incident may have been a settler bid to quash Bartlett Alexis's resource campaign by targeting and sexually threatening female members of his household.[249] While the crime may have been more serious than the court would acknowledge, when Miner Vander Horn begged to have his case "thrown on the mercy of the court," he and his son were simply fined sixpence and released without further ado.[250]

At about the same time an even a worse tragedy befell the Alexis family. Michel Alexis, the Cape Sable head chief, drowned when his canoe suddenly foundered in strong currents off the seaward extremity of Cape Sable Island. Upon his death his younger brother Joseph immediately assumed the Cape Sable leadership. Given the extent of factional strife within the local magisterial body and the fact that many Loyalist settlers still distrusted the Mi'kmaq's protestations of loyalty to the British Crown, the new chief could do little to further his people's land and resource campaign in the years surrounding the War of 1812.[251]

At the close of the war many of the Mi'kmaw Bartletts still resided at Salmon River, while the Cape Sable district chief Jean-Baptiste Alexis and his family remained on Long Island. When Sigogne stayed overnight in 1813 at Salmon River en route to Ste. Anne du Ruisseau, he held his first Catholic mass at the home of Jean Deveau, with many of the Bartletts and Alexis in attendance.[252] Bartlett Alexis's descendants later attended church services at Meteghan and, after 1849, at the newly built St. Vincent de Paul Church at Salmon River. If the Vander Hornes had sought to dislodge the Bartletts from their traditional riverine weirsite by threatening vulnerable members of their household, their ploy was a miserable failure. The Bartletts continued fishing on the Ring property until 1816, when George Ring died and his estate was subdivided among his heirs. The plot on which the Bartletts encamped became parcel 1 of Lot no. 40, bequeathed to Ring's daughter, Louisa.

Louisa and her siblings acknowledged that the Bartletts retained certain rights stemming from long occupation, so on 4 October 1816 Bartholomew Alexis Sr. was asked to state the length of time he had occupied Lot 40, and to register his mark confirming this information on the deed of transfer. He replied that he first had settled on Ring's property twenty-four years before, in 1792, and his words were recorded. His eldest son, Étienne, or Stephen Bartlett-Alexis (c.1780–c.1865), whose name was pronounced "Ekien" by the Mi'kmaq,[253] along with Paul Pictou and Samuel Mius witnessed this transaction by placing their marks near the elderly Bartlett's on the deed document.[254] It turned out the 1816 subdivision did not affect the Mi'kmaq substantially, since most of Bartholomew Alexis Sr.'s descendants continued living at their encampment on the Salmon River until the 1880s.

Bartholomew Alexis Sr. hunted and trapped north of Hectanooga during the winter and after the spring fish run travelled to the eastern Atlantic coast. During the summers he and his family often visited his close kin on Long Island in the Roseway River. In 1824 Sigogne recorded Bartholomew as being elderly and infirm, dwelling in a camp in the District of Argyle, probably at Sheshaw Park at Eel Brook, with two boys. His son Ekien Bartlett Sr. lived in a nearby camp with two adult women but no children. Ekien, who was born at Salmon River around 1780, had been given the nickname *Wisow*,[255] which in Mi'kmaq means "green" or "yellow-green,"[256] and several of his descendants also used the sobriquet *Wisow*. Some who lived at Salmon River even chose to use the English surname "Green" in preference to "Bartholomew-Alexis" or "Bartlett."[257]

Ekien Wisow Sr.'s younger brothers, Philippe, Joseph, and John Bartlett, were born in the 1780s. In 1820 Philippe lived at Annapolis Royal,[258] while Joseph camped with Ekien Wisou, Pierre Chegua Jr., and Pierre's brother, Gabriel Chegua, at Sheshaw Park near Eel Brook.[259] John Bartholomew-Alexis moved to Lunenburg County where he died before 1850. He had a son Joseph, born between 1812 and 1814, who lived in Summerside, now Dayspring, Lunenburg County. Joseph married and had two sons: Tom, born in 1851, and Joseph Jr., born in 1853. After his wife died in about 1865, Joseph Sr. by 1871 consorted with Mahalia Frank, a twenty-five-year-old widow of German descent and Church of England denominational background who bore him a third son, Simon, as well as several daughters.[260]

Joseph Bartlett's son Tom, twenty years old in 1871, married Emeline Crowell, also known as Amelia Moore, the daughter of an English Planter named Mason Moore and his consort, Marie Crowell of Argyle.[261] Tom and Emeline were raising a six-year-old girl, Agnès, and an eleven-month-old infant, Mary E. Bartlett. Tom's eighteen-year-old brother Joseph was still unmarried at this time.[262] Ten years later, Tom and Emeline were still living in Joseph Bartlett Sr.'s household while raising two more children, William, who was six, and Hannah, who was two months old. In 1888 their family had grown to include four more children, Henry, John, Simon, and Mary Caroline. By this time Tom's younger brother Joseph had left Summerside and lived at Tusket.

Joseph Bartlett Sr. and Mahalia's household in Lunenburg County was a culturally diverse one, as Mahalia Frank was of Protestant Germanic ancestry, Emeline Moore (Crowell) was English and in 1871 Joseph also was raising a twelve-year-old girl of African descent named Esther Barbon or Burbon. His household contained two more boys, George, born in 1868, who was probably born to Mahalia before his mother's marriage to Joseph Bartlett Sr., and Stephen, born in 1871.[263] In 1881, George was thirteen years old. Like his mother, Mahalia, he was listed as "German." Stephen, by contrast, was Joseph and Mahalia's son. While Joseph Sr.'s family was the only household in Summerside reported as having members of Mi'kmaw ancestry, the Bartletts resided near Christopher Carver and John Awalt, farmers who had close connections with the Mi'kmaq of Lunenburg County.[264] When Joseph Bartlett Sr. died about 1885, Mahalia in 1891 married John Charles of Cape Sable.[265]

Bartholomew Alexis Sr. died at Salmon River about 1830 and was succeeded as patriarch of the Bartlett family by his eldest son Ekien Wisow Sr. Ekien Sr. wed an Acadian *métis* woman whose name was either Susan Michaud or Susan Michael. The couple had seven children: Ekien Bartlett *dit* Wisow Jr., also known as Stephen Bartlett *dit* Wisow Jr. or Stephen Wisow Jr. (c.1807–1901);[266] Joseph (c.1812–c.1885); Abraham (c.1815–65); James; John; and two daughters. According to church registers housed at St. Jerome parish in West Caledonia, Ekien Bartlett Sr. and Susan Michaud also raised a foster child, Philip Sayers (Siah, Cyr, or Josiah).[267]

Ekien Wisow Sr.'s eldest son, Stephen Wisow Jr., lived most of his life at Salmon River, though after 1885 he moved seasonally to the Tusket Lakes region and died on the outskirts of Yarmouth. Around 1835 Stephen Wisow Jr. married Mary Ellen Brooks. The couple raised at least ten children: Mary Anne, born in 1832; Joseph, born about 1836; Frances, born in 1842; Nancy or Anastasia, born in the late 1840s; Mary Rose, born about 1850; Madeline, born in the early 1850s; James, born in 1855 or 1856; Harriet, born in 1860; Rosalie, born around 1863; and Francis or "Frank," born in 1864. John Bartlett, who became a guide and lumberman and died unmarried on 14 September 1937 at age of seventy-six at Elmswood, Lunenburg County, was probably another son.[268] Though Joseph stayed in Digby County, most of Stephen Wisow Jr. and Mary Ellen's offspring moved around southwestern Nova Scotia, returning to Salmon River only during hard times to seek support and solace from close kin.[269]

Following Ekien Wisow Sr.'s death at Salmon River about 1865, Peter Charles Sulno became Cape Sable district chief. He would be succeeded in turn by Stephen Wisow Jr. about 1875. Two of Stephen Wisow Jr.'s daughters, Mary Anne and Madeline, married into the Charles family. Mary Anne wed John Charles, and the couple in 1855 had a daughter Susan Charles at Cornwallis, Kings County. Madeline in her late middle age in 1883 became the second wife of John's brother, Jim Charles, of gold prospecting fame.[270] Widowed soon after the birth of her only child, Philip, Madeline married Frank Bernard of Liverpool on 2 September 1888.[271] Another of Stephen Wisow Jr.'s daughters, Nancy, wed a fourth cousin, François Alexis, who worked as a cooper at West Pubnico. François was a son of Francois-Joseph Alexis, a grandson of Joseph Alexis of Long Island in Shelburne County, and a great grandson of Chief Charles Alexis. François and Nancy had a son, Samuel Alexis, in 1873. When François died a few years later, Nancy lived at Salmon River with her father until her death, at age thirty-five, in 1880.[272]

Another of Stephen Wisow Jr.'s daughters, Frances, born at Church Point, Digby County, first married Noel Pictou in 1866 at Meteghan, and after Noel's death wed Joseph Labrador of Bear River in 1912 when she was sixty years of age. In 1876 her sister Mary Rose married Peter Labrador of Bear River, a son of James and Madeline Labrador, at Ste. Anne du Ruisseau. At the same time and place Mary Rose's brother, James, married Mary Ann Labrador, Peter Labrador's sister – another example of brother-sister exchange between two families.[273] When Mary Ann Labrador died a few years later, James Bartlett, still in his twenties, returned to Salmon River.[274] While there he met and wed a woman named Christie, whose surname is unknown. James and Christie lived in the Tusket Lakes area for many years before moving to Yarmouth, where James took care of his aging father. James's brother, François or Frank Bartlett, married Susan Jerome of Millbrook near Truro in 1896.[275]

In addition to Stephen Bartlett *dit* Wisow Jr., Ekien Wisow Sr. had a second son, Joseph Bartlett, born about 1815, who wed Hannah Bobbiei of Caledonia in 1840. The couple had a son, Stephen, soon after they were married. Following Hannah's death, Joseph wed Catherine Peters, who bore him twins, Joseph and Peter, in 1860. Catherine may have died in childbirth, for in 1862 Joseph married a third time, to Julia Pictou. Joseph and Julia had at least six children: Joseph-Matthew, baptized at Plympton in 1863; Hilaire, baptized at St. Vincent de Paul Church, Salmon River, in 1866; Henriette (or Henrietta) Christina, born at Salmon River in 1867;[276] Stephen Oliver in 1870; James Sullivan (or "Solin"), born at

Ohio, Shelburne County, in 1873; and Benjamin Bartlett, born at Salmon River in 1880.[277]

Ekien Sr.'s third son, Abraham (or Abram) Bartlett-Alexis, known as "Abraham *Musi Wisow*" ("Abraham Mr. Wisow"), was born about 1815 at Ohio near Long Island, Shelburne County.[278] Abraham married Mary Ann Phillips in the early 1850s and had four children: Germain (Jeremiah or "Jerry") in 1854, who married a Malecite woman named Elizabeth Paul; Sarah, born about 1856, who wed Abraham Michael of Bear River; and two boys who both died before they reached twelve years of age.[279] Germain became a well-known Mi'kmaw showman and took the stage name "Jerry Lonecloud."[280]

John Bartlett, Ekien Sr.'s fourth son, born about 1816, married a woman who remained unnamed in the historic record, with whom he had a son Joseph at Yarmouth in 1831. This Joseph Bartlett, who married but had become a widower by the mid-1860s, married a second time to Anne Morris of Chester in 1867, and the couple lived most of their lives in Bridgewater, Lunenburg County.[281] Ekien Sr.'s fifth and youngest son, James Bartlett, born in 1819, lived at Mill Village in Queens County before moving around 1860 to Great Pubnico Lake in Yarmouth County, where he lived close to his niece Nancy and her husband, François Alexis.[282]

One Last Attempt to Acquire Land at Eel Brook

The various branches of the Bartlett family, all of whom shared a sense of attachment to Salmon River, and the Alexis contingent, whose representatives had spread out over Yarmouth and Shelburne Counties, recognized Joseph Alexis, better known by this time as Joseph Luxey of Long Island, as a local chief. Joseph had a reputation among both the Mi'kmaq and many local settlers for being a sober, hard-working man and devoted to his Roman Catholic faith. Each Sunday Chief Luxey "gathered his little company together for prayer and exhortation. Every morning and evening he performed his religious exercise. He was never known to have been intoxicated."[283] In the years following the War of 1812 he considered reviving his father's earlier campaign to obtain a Crown grant of the land fronting his group's most important riverine fishing site at Eel Brook.

While some Mi'kmaw leaders were willing to aid the British, Joseph Alexis still resented the way the British colonial regime had treated his father Charles

Alexis. During the War of 1812 his attachment to the Halifax establishment was barely lukewarm. Unlike Chief François Mius, who signed a friendship treaty with the British in 1761, Joseph's father had made no similar pacts with the British. From the mid-1780s until the turn of the eighteenth century, as we saw above, all of Charles's petitions to Halifax for land were given lip service and then dismissed. Even Jacques Mius, François Mius's eldest son and one of Charles Alexis's brothers-in-law, by 1812 had come to regard the colonial administration with suspicion. Like other Mi'kmaq who possessed treaty parchments and medals bequeathed to them from a past era, Jacques viewed such items as conferring personal status.[284]

For the same reason that Sigogne encouraged the Acadians to profess loyalty to Britain – so their leaders would cease to be regarded with suspicion by colonial administrators – he sought to establish a working relationship between the Cape Sable chief and the Halifax officialdom. He began to integrate the Mi'kmaq into a calendrical round of Roman Catholic ritual activities. Twice a year he held high mass at the new parish church of Ste. Anne du Ruisseau, whose construction he had overseen in 1809.[285] In preparation for these special ceremonies, he recruited Mi'kmaw men with good singing voices to learn Latin anthems so they could join his choir on 1 November for Toussaint, or All Saint's Day, and on 26 July for St. Anne's Day. Since St. Anne was the Mi'kmaq's patron saint, the week around 26 July became a time of reunion and festivity that contrasted strikingly with the more formal rituals associated with the rest of the ceremonial round.[286] As many as two hundred individuals from neighbouring Mi'kmaw communities congregated annually at Eel Brook for the St. Anne's festivities. Mi'kmaw visitors who travelled from as far away as Gold River and La Have usually met at Barrington Harbour, before proceeding in a brigade of canoes to Eel Brook.[287]

Mi'kmaq canoeing past Shelburne County often stopped overnight at Long Island, so Joseph Alexis decided to petition for a grant of land containing his family's encampment, which lay near a productive fishery, reserves of good timber, and the ancient Mi'kmaw sacred site and council ground at Middle Ohio. The colonial government had recognized a Mi'kmaw presence on Long Island as early as 1807, though nothing had been done to secure Indigenous possession of the tract. After the close of the War of 1812, land competition in Shelburne County waned as Loyalists who had settled around Shelburne town quitted tracts they felt were too rocky and inhospitable for farming.

Joseph also joined with others in trying to obtain land at Eel Brook. Lacking a deed to their campground near Ste. Anne du Ruisseau, each year they encountered settlers usurping their fields and harvesting their crops. When the Mi'kmaq told their concerns to their missionary, whom they now affectionately addressed as *Mussikonn* ("Mr. Sigogne"),[288] Sigogne relayed their grievances to Bishop Joseph-Octave Plessis, who in 1815 came down from Quebec to visit Nova Scotia. Plessis immediately addressed the problems Sigogne related to him, and consequently Lieutenant Governor John Coape Sherbrooke had two letters appear on his desk, the first written by Sigogne on 1 March 1815 asking on behalf of the Mi'kmaq for a grant at Eel Brook, and a second one from Bishop Plessis in August requesting that Sherbrooke make a thorough investigation into Mi'kmaw land issues in Nova Scotia.[289]

Sigogne wanted to know why the Mi'kmaq, after supposedly receiving a licence of occupation for land at Eel Brook in 1786, had lost the right to occupy the tract and what the government intended to do about it. Although Sigogne's actual letter has not survived, the abbé evidently did not mince words. Sherbrook handed a letter to the surveyor general, Charles Morris III (1759–1831), directing him to deal with the Mi'kmaw land matter as soon as possible.[290] Morris reviewed the situation with some embarrassment. Droves of erstwhile settlers were vacating their former grants in Shelburne and Yarmouth Counties to seek more fertile farming properties elsewhere in the province or were returning to the United States. In the wake of their departure the Crown Lands office was faced with a plethora of inquiries from landless hopefuls wanting to attain escheated land. The status of the vacated lands was in limbo, however, and worse still, survey records were in disarray. The boundaries of the parcels that had been granted often overlapped, a legacy of the late 1780s when grants were being allocated to incoming Loyalists so quickly that record keeping at the provincial land office failed to keep up and became disorganized.

Charles Morris's father, Charles Morris II (1731–1802), moreover, had procured a Crown grant to Morris Island, close to Eel Brook. His son Charles III, who had succeeded his father as provincial surveyor general of Crown Lands, would be in a conflict of interest if Mi'kmaw claims threatened his own family's land holdings.[291] Although his father when surveyor general had signed the licence of occupation given Charles Alexis in 1786, in 1815 the son claimed to have no knowledge of this prior land transaction. "I have not heard of those Indians since untill [*sic*] now," he declared.[292]

The land at Eel Brook that the Mi'kmaq had pressed Sigogne to write to Sherbrooke about was already granted, Morris concluded, and even if after an arduous search of the records a tract through escheat did fortuitously become available nearby, he had no funds at his disposal to "pay for the hire of a Deputy [Surveyor], Chainbearers, axe men or Flags or Clerk, Draftsmen or any incidental expense whatever."[293] The best thing that could happen to the Mi'kmaq was for the lieutenant governor over the next five years to permit the Crown Lands Office to try to locate and set aside a reserve, rather than a freehold grant, for the Cape Sable group.[294] In the interim the Cape Sable group were to look for land in other situations, "nearer their hunting grounds."[295]

By the time Morris again conferred with the Mi'kmaq, the chief and his people had been casting around for alternate locales to claim as their own. They argued that the Roseway and Clyde rivers formed important stopping points in their seasonal round of travels from the interior to the Atlantic coast.[296] Though a small point of land called "Rabraduce" or "Labraduce" had been set aside for them as a landing place by the early settlers of Barrington Township, they needed much larger tracts on which to raise crops.[297] As a result of his audience with them, in 1820 Morris presided over the formation of a one-thousand-acre reserve at the forks of the Clyde River. Though not as fertile as the land at Eel Brook, this allocation fulfilled the terms of a new government policy by which the Mi'kmaq would receive a thousand acres in each county of the province.[298] Morris knew that the Mi'kmaq had occupied the Eel Brook area "from a very antient [*sic*, ancient] date," but by 1820 he considered the area lost to them. The best he could suggest was that some sort of law might be passed to protect them "in their Burial ground at the spot where their cross is placed."[299]

Acquiring a Grant on the Roseway River

Long Island, Shelburne County, lay just east of Middle Ohio, where according to Mi'kmaw oral tradition the Mi'kmaq in the 1700s had maintained a council forum, shaped like a stone amphitheater.[300] The Roseway River site therefore retained ceremonial as well as economic importance. When Charles Alexis's second son, Joseph Alexis (c.1758–1852), realized that the island's previous grantees had vacated the site and the land was subject to escheat, he immediately set out to contact the new lieutenant governor, Lord Dalhousie – only this time, fortuitously, the lieutenant governor came to him.

Joseph Alexis bided his time awaiting an appropriate occasion to present his claim to a parcel on Long Island directly to George Ramsey, ninth Earl of Dalhousie. An opportunity suddenly arose on 17 July 1817 while Dalhousie was visiting Shelburne. "I received today a great many Memorials from … people claiming the protection of government and licenses of occupation to sit free on these deserted lands," Dalhousie wrote in his journal for that day. "Also [a memorial] from a small tribe of Indians that is said to be settled and industriously fixed on Long Island in the Roseway River."[301] News had spread far and wide that land was now available, and Joseph found himself jostling in a crowd composed of "new settlers, old soldiers, sailors, [and] Black & colour people from New York" to present his petition.[302] Yet, while admitting his sympathies lay with the Mi'kmaq's interests, Dalhousie relied on Charles Morris, the surveyor general, to respond to the Mi'kmaw memorial. Morris did nothing.

No action was taken by the government with regard either to the 1817 memorial or to protecting the Mi'kmaw burial ground at Eel Brook. Consequently Pierre-Paul Alexis *dit* Eptemec and his son Jacques Alexis, Joseph Alexis, Jean-Baptiste Alexis, Jean-Baptiste's son François, and Samuel Alexis chose a new tack. In 1819 they ceased their campaign for land at Eel Brook, went to Halifax, and petitioned the executive council for a grant of two hundred acres on Long Island. The five petitioners "have dwelt on the Island for twenty five years as permanent inhabitants," their memorial stated, "and are the fathers of twenty four children, all of whom reside on the Island." Though they had never received assistance from the government, they claimed that "by their own industry and exertions in cultivating the island … [they had] made many improvements" and hoped the lieutenant governor would "encourage them to continue their exertions" by awarding them their grant.[303]

This time Dalhousie showed more than interest; he ensured that the group received 225 acres on the Roseway River.[304] These Mi'kmaq "shall have my encouragement + I will pay immediate attention to this memorial," he wrote across the top of Joseph's petition.[305] Though at the time they received no document confirming their title to land on Long Island, the Mi'kmaq began treating the tract on which they planted and logged timber as a freehold grant. It was not long, however, before they faced a new problem, one that Lord Dalhousie unwittingly created in 1818 by encouraging Welsh emigrants to settle on Long Island.[306] Two Welsh families immediately began to encroach on the land claimed by the Mi'kmaq. The Welshmen's cattle knocked down the Mi'kmaw farmers' fences and trampled their gardens, but Joseph had the fences repaired and even entered into a transaction where the family at fault leased pasturage from him. Yet with time these incidences of trespass grew more severe, and the government proved reluctant to intervene. In the 1820s only ten Mi'kmaw families, or thirty-four persons, many of them belonging to the Alexis family,[307] resided in Shelburne County, but they proved to have a strong sense of proprietorship over their tract on Long Island.

In the spring of 1827 Chief Joseph Alexis's group on Long Island numbered just thirteen persons, with several elderly and not a few infirm.[308] Around 1824 Abbé Sigogne had listed Joseph and Jacques Alexis, Jean-Baptist Alexis's son, as the only Mi'kmaw family heads belonging to the Alexis family living in Shelburne County.[309] Owing to lack of game, the late 1820s and the 1830s were punctuated by seasons of hardship, and many Mi'kmaq moved out of province.[310] One of Jean-Baptist Alexis's daughters, Honore, who about 1812 had married Paul Williams from West Pubnico, also occasionally stayed with the Alexis family on Long Island. As he grew older, Joseph's hopes for the secure economic future of his family in Shelburne County rested on the industriousness shown by his sons Lewis, born in 1812, and John, who was younger, in hunting, fishing, trapping, farming the land, and cutting timber. When nearby logging companies called for men to work in the woods, Lewis and John headed for the logging camps. Lewis also exhibited an entrepreneurial knack.

In the early 1830s Joseph Alexis was again facing settlers who grazed cattle on his fields and illicitly harvested his hay, so he applied to Halifax for a confirmation of his parcel as a freehold grant.[311] In response, he received 325 acres from the government in 1834, though no survey of the plot's boundaries was made until February 1839.[312] Now Joseph had a paper and survey plan he could wave in the face of trespassers on his property. Though Joseph vested the deed with the force of a freehold grant, some government officials referred in their correspondence to his Long Island property as a "reserve."[313] Joseph at times benefitted from this ambiguity surrounding his property's status, since the province protected his land as it would a bona fide reserve. For instance, when a settler from Barrington named John D. Pinkham contacted the Crown Lands office in 1835 and asked for a reassignment of the Mi'kmaw property to him on the grounds that the Mi'kmaq so often vacated the island, the government paid him no heed.[314]

Selling a Foothold on the Upper Tusket River

Although these encroachments on the Roseway River were annoying, they were nothing compared to the threat of settler usurpation that in 1822 loomed over the Alexis's interior encampment and fishing grounds on the Upper Tusket. The twenty or so families that composed the Mi'kmaw community under Joseph Alexis's leadership had a spring, fall, and winter headquarters on the east bank of the upper Tusket River, within what is now the rural community of Kemptville. By 1822 they had built at least one frame house, constructed a number of outbuildings, and raised "one hundred Bushells of potatoes, Indian corn and other garden stuff."[315] The presence of the house suggests that Joseph had relocated his elderly mother, Anne Hébert, who was eighty-two years old, to this spot. Her daughter Marie and Marie's husband Laurent Mius at The Forks both were dead by 1811, and Anne's remaining sons and daughters probably wished her to spend her last years under their care.

The upper Tusket furnished an agreeable locale for the elderly matriarch of the Alexis family to rendezvous with her offspring both from Salmon River and the Roseway River area. Meanwhile, Chief Peter Charles Sulno and his brother Francis Charles I (or Sr.) maintained an encampment lower down on the Tusket River, in an area of virgin forest that would later give rise to the settlements of Carleton, Gardiner's Mills, and Forest Glen. They lived with members of the Pictou, Peters, and Michael families, while members of the Mius (or Meuse) family drifted north into Digby and Annapolis Counties and settled by 1821 at Bear River. In the 1830s at least two of Francis Charles I's sons, including Francis Charles II (or Jr.) and James ("Jim") Charles – both grandsons of Charles Snow (or Sulno), the patriarch of the Mi'kmaw Charles family – moved to the Kejimkujik Lake area.[316] (The Charles family genealogy may be found in note 394.) Individuals bearing the surnames "Argomartin" and "Chegua" also still inhabited the Tusket area, though there was no mention by the 1840s of the Tecouramarts, who had intermarried with the Alexis in the past. Some Tecouramarts may have departed for the Huron community at Lorette in the province of Quebec, where Charles Tecouramart's daughter Rose took up residence well before 1800.[317] Others may have adopted a different surname.

For part of the year the Mi'kmaq occupied a tract that straddled a hill in the interior of Yarmouth County lying between Saint Andrew's Lake (now Beaverhouse Lake) and the upper reaches of the Tusket River. This parcel contained an ancient portage trail between the two water bodies, and its rise is still known as "Indian Hill." By the early 1820s the trail had become a tote road, and an unpaved roadway now follows this early path. It formed part of the route by which the Cape Sable Mi'kmaq, for generations, had accessed the interior from the Atlantic coast, by following a chain of lakes, rivers, and portages connecting the upper Clyde and Roseway rivers with the upper Tusket.[318] The Mi'kmaw ground contained an important weirsite on the east side of the Tusket River, at what is now known as School Cove, as well as valuable beaver meadows. The same area also contained a prehistoric sacred site, probably a burial mound. Early settlers reported an earthen feature "10 feet wide by 10 feet long and 4 feet high."[319] Stone artefacts taken from this mound in 1863 were placed in the safekeeping of Dr. Joseph B. Bond of Yarmouth, though their whereabouts today are unknown.[320]

Incomers to the upper Tusket in the 1820s were mainly retired military personnel or descendants of Loyalists. Two distinct groups of Loyalists settled along the lower Tusket River and at The Forks at the close of the American Revolution. The first consisted of one hundred families from New Jersey, New York, and adjacent colonies, and most of these soon left. The second wave came a year or two later, from North Carolina. One of the best known of these persons was Major Samuel Andrews. Andrews had a large family and three of his adult sons, David, Alexander, and Abner, along with James Hulbert and Heman Gardner, petitioned the government for farmland further up the river.

The Alexis family extended the hand of friendship to these men. Oral traditions still circulating around Kemptville praise the Mi'kmaq for helping the Andrews find pasturage for their cattle on the east bank of the river. Yet when Joseph and Jean-Baptiste Alexis learned in 1823 that Major Andrew's sons were staking claims to the very parcel on which their house and gardens stood, they contacted the lieutenant governor, Sir James Kempt, and asked for a deed to their plot. Jean-Baptiste, now fifty-eight years old, also expressed indignation that his people had had to shift their garden plots three times already, undoubtedly a reference to the provinces' lack of protection for Mi'kmaw land interests at Eel Creek, The Forks, and on Long Island, and specified that the Mi'kmaq's present house and gardens lay inland, "twenty two miles from the sea."[321] Despite his family's making a clearing, maintaining a weir at the site, and harvesting over one hundred bushels of potatoes the previous year, he continued, "three men had come on their land with the intention of taking possession." He concluded with the hope that, as his group had been "so frequently removed," Kempt would take up their case and grant them their parcel, "or such other Lands as you Your Excellency may think proper."[322]

In response, the government on 20 November 1824 granted Jean-Baptiste Alexis and his family a freehold grant to a fifty-acre strip, wedged between Lot 1, a two-hundred-acre farm grant allocated to David Andrews to the north, and Lot 2, Abner Andrews's two-hundred-acre parcel lying immediately to the south of the Alexis's plot.[323] The strip was marked as plot "A," and labelled as being "for the accommodation of the Indians," on a survey plan of the thousand-acre grant made to the Andrews brothers and their associates. The growing settler community on both sides of the river was called "Kemptville" in honour of Lieutenant Governor Sir James Kempt, who gave out the land grants. Its inhabitants were predominately Baptist and Methodist, and early on engaged in the logging trade. As logs were rafted downstream, they broke the Mi'kmaq's weirs, which as early as 1811 had been prohibited on the lower Tusket because they obstructed the flow of timber downstream. Some land was obtained mainly for speculative purposes. David Andrews held his

property only one year before selling it in May 1825 to Seth Tinkham, who later married Mary Hulbert.[324] As the forest retreated before the axe and weir fishing became difficult owing to the growing logging industry, the Mi'kmaq, within three years of acquiring their grant, removed their interior base to The Forks, especially as Roman Catholic services were held in that community. On 7 April 1826 Joseph and Samuel Alexis sold their fifty acres and improvements at Kemptville to Daniel Nickerson of Argyle for five pounds. As Jean-Baptiste Alexis's name does not appear on the deed of sale, he may have died prior to the mid-1820s.[325]

Joseph Howe Visits West Pubnico

During the 1830s Mi'kmaq living near West Pubnico in Yarmouth County also sought help in their quest to secure land. Following the lifting of a prohibition on Acadians holding public office in 1791, these Mi'kmaq found a sympathetic ear for their problems in Benoni d'Entremont (1744–1841), who in 1818 became Nova Scotia's first Acadian magistrate. Benoni's son, Simon d'Entremont (1788–1886), mastered the fundamentals of the Mi'kmaw language well enough to discuss land problems with the local Mi'kmaw population in clear terms.[326] When Simon d'Entremont became the first Acadian MPP in 1836, he was approached by Paul Williams, a head man who about 1812 had married Honore Alexis, a daughter of Jean-Baptist Alexis and granddaughter of Chief François-Joseph Alexis.[327] Williams wanted to obtain a plot on Great Pubnico Lake, back of West Pubnico, where his group planted crops and grew orchards, so d'Entremont directed his attention to the land department in Halifax.[328] When Joseph Howe, the political reformer, assumed the office of provincial Indian commissioner in the spring of 1842, he visited Barrington in October that same year and found Williams and four other Mi'kmaw family heads, Freeman Francis, Joe Francis, John Paul, and a widow named Molly Paul, prepped and ready to push for the land they desired at Great Pubnico Lake. Paul Williams was by this time an elderly man who had recently lost his first wife, Honore Alexis, and was preparing to wed Molly Paul. His son John Williams (c.1815–c.1890) had married Betsy Ann Peminout Paul from Stewiacke, and the couple settled on the Preston Road near Dartmouth where John was embarking on a career as a guide.[329] Since Paul

Williams no longer had any immediate family members living near him, he doubtless looked forward to marrying Molly.

The Great Pubnico Lake Mi'kmaw group in 1842 numbered around forty individuals.[330] Paul Williams informed Howe that though the Mi'kmaq pitched their camps in a dozen places over the countryside in the course of a season, they claimed Great Pubnico Lake, "seven miles long above the Barrington River, as their favourite residence." He continued that if the government would see fit to provide land and building materials he would build a house and set an example to the rest by expanding his farming endeavours. Accordingly, Howe instructed the nearest surveyor to lay off seven hundred acres for Williams's party.[331]

Howe had little inkling of the influence wielded throughout the Cape Sable district by Chief Joseph Alexis and his son Lewis. While passing through Shelburne County he had bypassed Joseph's farming community on Long Island, though he was aware that the settlement had at least one log house, fields, and an orchard.[332] "As to Roseway River, about 10 miles above Shelburne," he jotted down in his diary, "a family … have been settled for many years on a portion of an Island that appears to have been granted to them, as I do not find it among the Reserves [in my folio]. They are popularly called Luxies, though Alexis appears to be the true name."[333] Howe had been informed by local settlers that the Alexis family continuously moved around the countryside and that these "erratic habits" had retarded their agricultural progress. He also noted that Chief Joseph Alexis had died by this time, as had his son Joseph Alexis *dit* Makaq, while Lewis and John alone remained. Lewis Alexis had three children at the time; John had two.[334]

Howe was dissuaded in October 1842 from going to Long Island by a sawmill owner who told him that the Mi'kmaw men were part of a lumbering party working on the Jordan River so far back in the woods that it might "be difficult if not impossible to find them."[335] Howe later felt a pang of conscience over his hasty decision, especially when Cornelius White, a settler who knew the Alexis family well, wrote that "Lewis Luxey raised black cattle and tried to imitate some of the habits and pursuits" of the settlers around him.[336] Howe would have known that in the fall of 1842 Lewis Alexis and his brother had other family members who would have stayed behind on

Long Island to take care of the farm, and would have shown him around their property if he had gone to see it. Lewis Alexis was considered intelligent, hard-working, and honest. "I should have visited the place," Howe reminisced, and "I shall take steps to ascertain the nature of their title and to protect them in their quiet possession of their property."[337]

Before passing by Long Island, Howe and a Mi'kmaw guide, Cobliel (or Gabriel) Glode, had visited a fledgling Indigenous farming settlement on Cecumgega Lake, also known as Fairy Lake or Kejimkujik Lake,[338] which today lies within the parameters of Kejimkujik National Park in Queens County. The settlement was led by John Jeremy, who had visited Howe in Halifax the previous year with a petition for land. It consisted of six families, with members of the Charles and Glode families being prominent, though Howe noted that Chief Joseph Alexis's son, Lewis Alexis, expressed interest in joining the settlement. The commissioner also had a surveyor rerun the boundaries of a thousand-acre reserve on the Wildcat River, known as Reserve No. 12, near Brookfield, Queens County, and subdivide the tract into ten lots of one hundred acres each.[339]

When Howe arrived back in Halifax his researches showed that the Luxey family's land was a grant, but he decided to treat it like a reserve. He immediately contacted an overseer of the poor living in the locality, Philip Bower, to report on the condition of the Alexis's landholdings. Bower was close to the Mi'kmaq, and remembered the size of the parcel originally occupied by them.[340] He contended that the Mi'kmaw leaders had approached him to enforce a recent act gauged to prevent trespass on reserves. The chief especially wanted the government to protect his upland on the east side of the island from further encroachment.[341] A substantial fence had subsequently been built in response to Luxey's request, but Samuel Irwin's cattle still knocked it down. In the end, despite Luxey's opposition, the upland became a common, available for all to graze cattle.

Bower once again drove off Irwin's cattle and helped Luxey mend his fence. When Bower charged Irwin with stealing logs and staves off the same property the following December however, Irwin countered that "not one stick had been taken without the Indian's consent." This led Bower to approach Lewis Alexis about the matter. Lewis sidestepped any discussion of Irwin's infractions and argued that, while he had leased timber and pasture land to another of his Welsh neighbours, John Quinlan, Quinlan had failed to pay him any rent for several years.[342] As way of proof of his contentions, Luxey produced an affidavit signed by John Quinlan and dated 24 May 1840 that read "I promise to pay Louie Aley [*sic*, Alexis] twelve shillings for a price of wild grass on the island."[343]

From 1843 to 1846 Lewis Alexis, now better known as "Lewey Luxey Sr.," seemed to have given up the struggle to protect his eastern meadow, as he left the Roseway parcel in the care of the younger members of his family and moved temporarily to Fairy Lake in Queens County, where he had an allotment of 119 acres on the lakeshore, next to John Pictou's and Francis Charles II's parcels, and close to a Mi'kmaw petroglyph site, popularly known at the time as the "Fairy Rocks."[344] His decision to move to this new locale was probably guided by the fact that his sister, Sally Alexis, had married Joseph Peters, one of the Mi'kmaw farmers.[345] The mid-1840s were difficult years for members of this farming community, however. A potato blight devastated crops in 1845 and 1846, accompanied by an outbreak of virulent fever that severely affected the Indigenous settlers. Despite the heady prospects promulgated by Howe in 1842 for Mi'kmaq who took up agricultural pursuits, within three years many of those who farmed marginal lands found themselves worse off than their contemporaries who retained a more traditional way of life. Lewis Luxey in consequence left Kejimkujik Lake to live on one hundred acres with his brother, John Luxey, at the Wildcat reserve near Brookfield. Lewis Luxey's Lot 1 was one of ten such parcels surveyed at Wildcat under Howe's auspices in 1843.[346] Lewis and John went to work with a will, cutting timber and framing barns for their livestock.[347]

In 1849, Joseph Bartlett, Stephen Wisow Jr.'s younger brother, born about 1815, travelled from Salmon River to reside temporarily near his relative Lewis Luxey at Mill Village, on the Port Medway River in Queens County.[348] By this time Lewis Luxey Sr. had risen as a local chief in his father Joseph Alexis's stead. He had close connections to the Bear River, since he led sportsmen on moose hunting and fishing expeditions and Bear River was the major rendezvous for Mi'kmaw guides in southwestern Nova Scotia. While at Bear River, Luxey associated with Gabriel Toney, a relative of Chief Meuse's wife, Magdalene Toney. Gabriel, who had travelled widely throughout Newfoundland and the Maritime region

before settling for a while in southwestern Nova Scotia, directed a petition to the House of Assembly in January 1846 in which he declared he was writing on behalf of Mi'kmaq suffering economic hardship in Annapolis, Digby, Yarmouth, Shelburne, and Queens counties. There were 125 families, or 500 people, living in the five counties, he declared, who desperately needed blankets to survive the winter cold. Toney further requested a government commission to bolster his status as a *Kespukwitk* district chief, as well as a small sum to defray costs he had incurred while travelling around visiting various families.[349]

Gabriel became spokesperson for the Cape Sable and Annapolis group after the death of Bartholomew Alexis Sr. in 1830, but he did not hold his position for long. He died in Dartmouth near Sullivan's Pond in 1846, evidently as a result of a fever that had spread to Halifax and Dartmouth by that year, and was buried in the graveyard of St. Patrick's Roman Catholic Church. A few years before, while still living in Yarmouth County, Gabriel Toney associated with the family of a girl named Santu (c.1840–c.1917) who claimed that her father had Beothuk ancestry.[350] He may have brought Santu with him from Yarmouth County; she later married twice and lived out her latter days at Shubenacadie.[351] To fill the political vacuum left by Gabriel Toney's death, Lewis Alexis and his distant kinsman, the elderly Chief James Andrew Meuse Sr. of Bear River, and eight other prominent Mi'kmaw leaders banded together to carry a petition, dated 8 February 1849, to Halifax.

One of these petitioners, Peter Toney, may have been Meuse's brother-in-law, but he could just as easily have been the Peter Toney who was chief of Cumberland County at the time. Alternatively, he might have been the Peter Toney who was a well-known chief of the Merigomish band.[352] All things considered, it is most likely that the Peter Toney who went to Halifax in 1849 was the Merigomish chief, who had been in Halifax on similar missions before.

The document carried by Toney and his associates, which was placed directly in the hands of Lieutenant Governor John Harvey, called for supplies for Mi'kmaq still suffering from the ravages of the potato blight and the fever epidemic of 1846–48. It denounced the erection of dams that destroyed valuable salmon and alewife fisheries, as well as the actions of settlers who drove Mi'kmaq off their farmlands and reduced them to peddling wooden manufactures to make ends meet. They also requested an exemption from a new law that only allowed the Mi'kmaq to spear fish five days a week.[353] Abraham Gesner, the provincial Indian commissioner, organized not only these chiefs' conveyance to and accommodation while in Halifax but also their return transportation. Yet Lewis Luxey eschewed the return travel arrangements to stay longer in Halifax and investigate the possibly of acquiring more property on Long Island.[354]

Perceiving a unique opportunity while in the capital, Lewis located the Crown Lands office and presented John Spry Morris, Charles Morris III's successor to the office of provincial surveyor general of Crown Lands,[355] with a memorial listing eleven points relating to injuries he had suffered at the hands of non-Indigenous neighbours. He also gave Morris eleven pounds to stake his claim to the upriver end of Long Island. His father, Joseph Luxey, had occupied this area for wood and wild hay for forage long before the Welsh immigrants arrived, and Lewis wanted it back. There also was money owing him, he complained. The Irwins and Quinlans had recognized the Mi'kmaq's prerogative right to the upland meadow jutting out into the Roseway River on the east side of the island. Between 1823 and 1845, Samuel and John Irwin had paid the Mi'kmaq rent for the use of it. Yet after that date Luxey was only able to collect half of the rent owed, and though one of the Irwins promised to pay the remainder, no money was ever forthcoming. Finally, Samuel Irwin, Robert Quinlan, and Thomas Quinlan, "finding that no legal steps had been taken to enforce payment," commenced trespassing freely on the meadow. Having his patience tried and needing the rent money to support his growing family, Luxey decided to bolster his claim at least to the upriver end of the island by securing it directly from the Crown Lands Department.[356]

When he returned to Brookfield, Luxey took the precaution of contacting Whitman Freeman, the deputy surveyor who in 1843 had subdivided the Wildcat reserve under Joseph Howe's auspices into ten lots, to check in periodically with the Crown Lands Department to see how Morris was coming along with his land request. "Please place the application before the government and let him know the result," Freeman appealed to Morris on 15 June 1849, in response to Luxey's persistence. "He is seeking all the land from where his fence crosses the Island to the Eastern extremity of the same." Freeman admitted that he sympathized with the chief and already had advanced him money to buy his parcel. He also would run the lines of the property when the time proved appropriate. Lewis Luxey, always vigilant, "wants to be present at the survey," Freeman added.[357] Luxey eventually received his request, for around 1852 he consolidated his gains and sold all his property on Long Island to Colin C. Bowers for between seventy and seventy-five pounds.[358] Though he did not lose contact with members of either or the Bowers or Quinlan families, Luxey nevertheless retreated to Lot No.1 at Wildcat where, with his brother John, he began to clear five or six acres of the forest.[359]

After this date money arrived in the Luxey household in dribs and drabs. Colin Bowers had arranged with the chief to pay off the price of the Long Island parcel in instalments of roughly five pounds yearly. John Spry Morris felt ambivalent about this since Luxey still would retain considerable control over the land until Bowers completely paid up. The surveyor general demanded that the Quinlans and Irwins formally take out their grants in Shelburne County lower down on Long Island from the Bowers-Luxey's plot and then sent a curt letter to the non-Mi'kmaw settlers telling them to vacate all portions of the former "reserve" once and for all.[360] But the Crown Lands Department did not have to retain this protective stance over Bowers's and Luxey's land for long, since in a private deal with Bowers, Luxey on 31 July 1863 repurchased one hundred acres of the land he had formerly owned, excluding the meadow, for forty-four dollars. Two years later he bought the whole north end of the island for another forty-four dollars. Though this parcel was too sterile for agricultural purposes, it held valuable stands of timber.[361] Lewis Luxey, who continued to engage in private consultations with potential buyers and local surveyors before contacting the land office directly, also became an expert timber cruiser and logger. For several years he focused on taking timber off the 115 acres at the north end of the island, leaving the Irwins and Quinlans to figure out among themselves who might exercise rights over the meadow jutting out eastward into the Roseway River.

Lewis Luxey's Wheelin' and Dealin' from Wildcat, Queens County

Caribou and moose were returning to Cape Sable, and by 1850 Chief Lewis Luxey built up a clientele of sportsmen who regarded him as a skilled hunting and fishing guide. Guiding in the fall for at least a dollar a day and working in the woods during the winter brought in money, so the chief could purchase more land on the Roseway River at the standard rate. Alexander Hamilton, the deputy surveyor assigned to run the lines in response to Luxey's land transactions, argued in 1862 that no new survey might be needed since Luxey intended to use the same western line as the one originally laid out for his father. The Crown Lands Department demurred, however, and compelled Hamilton to run a survey the following year. While working over the ground, Hamilton admitted he found Luxey's activities perplexing. Between 1857 and 1862 Luxey focused on convincing the government that he was his father Joseph Alexis's main heir.[362] Hamilton knew that Chief Joseph Alexis had "2 surviving heirs besides Lewis + 3 children of a sister who died," and argued that he failed to comprehend how Lewis could appropriate all the proceeds of land and timber sales from a tract that once belonged to everyone in Joseph's family.[363]

Had Lewis allowed his entrepreneurial penchant to overrule his responsibilities to others as an Indigenous leader, as Hamilton suggested? Oral traditions stress his unselfishness and concern for others. Given the Mi'kmaw social and political network within which he operated as a local chief, it would have been difficult, if not impossible, for Luxey to flout Mi'kmaw social conventions relating to land and resources. The two heirs that Hamilton referred to in 1862 were one of Lewis Luxey's sisters and his younger brother John. John, who had a wife and two children, continued to live near Lewis until the 1880s.[364] It is difficult to determine which one of Luxey's many sisters Hamilton felt should be counted as an heir. Molly Luxey had died in 1857.[365] Carey Anne Luxey, who had married Joseph Francis around 1835, was still living at Great Pubnico Lake. Carey Ann and her husband had adopted an orphan named Stephen Murree who later took "Francis" as his surname and became the father of Louisa Francis, the wife of the First World War hero Samuel Freeman Glode (or Gloade),), who was born on 20 April 1880.[366] Glode, from Milton, Queens County, in his memoirs stated that in 1888, when he was eight years old, his parents temporarily exchanged their residence at Milton for a dwelling at Shelburne belonging to Francis Luxey, a son of Lewis Luxey Sr. and his second wife, Mary Ann Cobliel.[367] Another of Lewis's sisters, Sally

Peters, lived at Fairy Lake until she and her husband, Joseph Peters, moved to Bear River.

By the 1850s, Chief Lewis Luxey had nine children. He wed his first wife Elizabeth Glode about 1830 while he lived at Long Island, and the couple had four children: John, the eldest, Joseph in 1833, Eliza Rose in 1836, and Mary around 1837.[368] Since all of these children were born prior to 1840, they would have grown up at the Roseway River settlement. When Elizabeth Glode died in 1843, Lewis Luxey Sr. married Mary Ann Cobliel, the daughter of Cobliel (Gabriel) Glode, who had guided Joseph Howe over the Queens County landscape in 1842.[369] From then on, Lewis Luxey Sr. lived primarily in Queens County where he and Mary Ann had five children: Catherine or Kate in 1844, Francis-Joseph in 1846, Étienne (nicknamed "Eggy" or "Heggy") around 1850, Mary Anne in 1853, Lewis Jr. in 1854, and John around 1855.[370] These sons and daughters became more adept at traversing the clearings and woods along the Wildcat River than navigating the Roseway River. Two of Lewis and Mary Ann's sons, Étienne and Lewis Luxey Jr., became well-known hunting and fishing guides near Paradise, Annapolis County.

The social and religious sphere of Mi'kmaw life was changing radically during these years. Mi'kmaq were frequenting churches in their neighbourhoods rather than gathering in large assemblages to receive the sacraments at Eel Brook. Abbé Sigogne died in 1844, during a time of immense change for the Cape Sable Mi'kmaw community. The brigades of bark canoes that once had plied the waters along the Atlantic coast to Ste. Anne du Ruisseau had vanished. Ekien Wisow Sr.'s descendants now attended churches at Salmon River, Meteghan, Wedgeport, or Bear River, while Lewis Luxey and his family had their children baptized at St. Jerome's Church in Caledonia, St. Gregory's Church in Liverpool, or St. Louis Church at Annapolis Royal. Along with his uncles and siblings, Lewis likely would have been present at Eel Brook on 20 September 1831 to pay his last respects to his grandmother, Anne Hébert, before her body was laid to rest in the cemetery at Ste. Anne du Ruisseau. She would be buried in auspicious company. Only the bodies of a few other prominent Mi'kmaq, such as Chief Peter Charles Sulno around 1875, would be ritually conveyed from the interior to be interred in the cemetery at Ste. Anne du Ruisseau. While by 1870 most burials occurred in local Roman Catholic graveyards, some were still performed by traditional leaders of a Mi'kmaw community and so remained unrecorded in the pages of any church register.

The land at Roseway River in Shelburne County was resurveyed in the 1850s, but Lewis's problems did not go away. According to Samuel Prescott Fairbanks, appointed provincial Crown Lands commissioner in 1857, the soil was so poor at the north end of the island that once the timber was gone, all that remained was "an almost useless fragment."[371] By 1865 Lewis Luxey Sr. was also embroiled in boundary disputes with his brother-in-law, Newell Cobliel, at Wildcat near Brookfield.[372] The growth of jobs nearby in the logging industry had drained people away from Fairy Lake, and the Wildcat settlement had become overcrowded. Samuel Fairbanks, having shouldered the office of provincial Indian commissioner as well as his duties in the land office, had little time to focus on Long Island or Lewis Luxey. He wanted most reserves sold and the money put in an Indian Affairs trust fund. Luxey's property could not be disposed of for such purposes, so Fairbanks either ignored it or, through carelessness, misrepresented it. On 25 February 1893 he wrote a letter to Joseph Howe in which he confused the Roseway River with the Salmon River of Digby County. In it the commissioner stated that he had investigated "the case of Lewis Alexis, who claimed to be protected in his right to a lot of land situate on the Salmon River, in the County of Shelburne."[373] Having to tend to his affairs at Brookfield, Luxey, however, had little time to focus on the muddles government was getting itself into with his Long Island property, and in December of 1866 sold all his holdings on the Roseway River for two hundred dollars to Colin Bowers.[374]

From this time on into the late 1880s Lewis Luxey maintained a small farm at Brookfield,[375] where he resided near his sons-in-law Matthew Pictou and Joseph Jeremy.[376] Another of his daughters, Eliza Rose Luxey, married Alex (or Alec) Jeremy in 1855 and lived near her father on the four-hundred-acre Ponhook Lake reserve, but when Alex died she married Noel Paul and in 1872 moved to the Annapolis area.[377] After Confederation in 1867 the newly formed Department of Indian Affairs held that the former population of Cape Sable had either pressed eastward into Queens County or northward into Digby County on the Gulf of Maine. Twenty family heads had been allocated blankets in coastal Shelburne County, in contrast with thirty adults who had received blankets in Queens County.[378] An Indian Affairs census drawn up in 1871 enumerated twenty-eight Mi'kmaq of all ages in Shelburne County while listing eighty-three in Queens County. Yet the Mi'kmaw population for Shelburne and Yarmouth Counties together, according to Ottawa, only came to forty-eight individuals. Even when seven individuals residing at Salmon River were added to the list, the Cape Sable group from the federal government's perspective only numbered fifty-five, less than half the size it was a century earlier.[379]

The 1871 census, however, on closer inspection proves very incomplete. Five years earlier, in 1866, when the province was in the grip of a scare that Fenians might invade its borders from the United States, Ekien Bartlett *dit* Wisow Sr.'s successor as Cape Sable district chief, Peter Charles Sulno (c.1788–c.1875) – whose name "Sulno" seems to have arisen from the Mi'kmaw pronunciation of the surname "Snow"[380] – at nearly eighty years of age travelled down from Carleton Lake to Tusket to send a petition and a census of his band to the House of Assembly. Sulno called himself the "Chief of Yarmouth County" and stated that he could muster thirteen "good marksmen from 16 to 45 years of age" to assist the British cause, provided they received four or five light muskets from the government. Manifesting a striking command of protocol when addressing royalty and its representatives, Charles claimed to hope that the recipient of his missive in Halifax would tender the services he offered "to his Great Brother Sir W.J. Williams, Governor and Commander in Chief," adding that he had seen the son of the "Great and Good Mother Queen Victoria" at Halifax in 1860.[381]

The census that Chief Sulno attached to his petition listed fifteen family heads, numbering in all twenty-seven adults, if one included married women who were not identified by name. The chief meanwhile categorized children by gender. There were sixty-three boys and fifty-three girls, which totalled 116 persons under the age of fourteen. According to Sulno's estimation, 143 individuals of all ages fell under his aegis, a number that would have been higher had he included Lewis Luxey Sr.'s family at Brookfield, but whom he evidently omitted. Peter Charles also pointed out that he and his family encamped on the middle reaches of the Tusket River while the majority of his group resided at Pubnico, where there was work in the woods.[382] This was a far cry from the mere fifty-five persons recorded for the Cape Sable band by the Indian Affairs Department. Peter

Charles Sulno was raising eight children, three girls and five boys, along with one orphan boy. Stephen Wisow Jr. and his younger brother Joseph Bartlett were both living in Sulno's encampment in 1866.[383] Joseph and his wife had three young girls living with them at the time, while Stephen Wisow Jr. and Mary Brooks were raising a family of ten sons and eight daughters, as well as an adopted son.[384] Ekien Bartlett Sr.'s third son, Abraham, had died the previously year in Vermont, and his three sons and daughter had not yet arrived back from the United States.[385]

The disparity between population numbers presented by government lists at the time and those tendered by the head chief of the Cape Sable district is not surprising. Few officials, if any, penetrated into the interior around Carlton Lake or around Pubnico Great Lake during the 1860s and 1870s to gather census data about Mi'kmaq residence patterns and family size. In 1842 John Ryder, the member for Argyle who had defeated Simon d'Entremont at the polls in 1840, dissuaded Howe from locating Mi'kmaq with farm plots along the Tusket River. For a staunch political reformer, Howe was naive in 1842 when it came to gauging the degree of hostility Ryder and his associates harboured towards Mi'kmaw land and resource interests. Unlike his political rival d'Entremont, Ryder manifested no interest in Mi'kmaw welfare, and may have intended to discourage the Indian commissioner at the start from setting aside lands for the Mi'kmaq along the Tusket River, as Howe already had done in the vicinity of Great Pubnico Lake.[386] Ryder nevertheless provided Howe with a list of Mi'kmaq living on the Tusket that included the names of Peter Charles Sulno and Francis Charles II. Ryder, like Howe, was a Reformer, and this doubtless led the commissioner to take his words seriously. Yet Ryder's disparaging comments about the Mi'kmaw families on the list denigrated the character of the robust group that the Cape Sable district chief, Peter Charles Sulno, considered under his leadership auspices from 1830 to 1870. Worse, it prevented Howe from getting to know and understand a portion of a dynamic Indigenous community that later would play an important role in the development of the Acadia First Nation.

A Focus on the Mi'kmaw Charles Family

Peter Charles Sulno remained Cape Sable district chief from roughly 1830 until his death around 1870. An intriguing oral tradition, passed down through four generations in the Mi'kmaw Charles family, holds that Peter Charles Sulno and his brother, Francis Charles I, were both sons of a man named Charles Snow (c.1755–1800), called "Sulno" by the Mi'kmaq. One of Charles Snow's great-grandsons – and co-author Travis Pinn's ancestor – named Joseph Charles in 1939 wrote a letter outlining the origins of the Mi'kmaw Charles family, which was preserved by his daughter, Elsie Charles Basque.[387] According to this document, Charles Snow voyaged by ship from Scotland to Pictou County in the late eighteenth century and married a Mi'kmaw woman from the District of Clare in Digby County. Snow and his wife, who may have attached themselves for a while to Chief Jacques Mius's band at Clare, lived at Cape Sable for several years before returning to Pictou County, where Snow's eldest sons remained.[388] Following Snow's death, his widow came back to Clare with her youngest sons, who married local Mi'kmaq women and joined the Cape Sable band. Joseph Charles's grandfather, Francis Charles I, born in 1794, was eighteen years old at the onset of the War of 1812, and was said to have been "placed at Argyle with 80 other warriors to repel attacks of pirates along the east coast." This force destroyed two ships at the Head of Argyle harbour, which must have been American privateers, akin to those rebuffed by Ranald MacKinnan and his corps of Scottish émigrés.[389]

Travis cautions, however, that this oral tradition "comes solely from an oral history which is fleshed out by its teller, Joe Charles, and his descendants. That Charles Sulno had Scottish origins lacks any documentary support, despite an extensive search to find such evidence."[390]

While no contemporary documentary evidence exists to confirm that the patriarch of the Charles family at Cape Sable was indeed a man named Charles Snow, Abbé Sigogne noted in 1803 that an Antoine Charles from the Northumberland Strait area acted as godparent to Joseph Alexis, an infant son of Joseph Alexis and Marie-Joseph Muice (Mius).[391] Antoine Charles may have been a son of Charles Snow, and his acting as a godparent of an Alexis child suggests that members of the Charles Sulno and Alexis families were already interacting by the early 1800s. Charles Snow's sons, Chief Peter Charles Sulno and Francis Charles I., camped near the present-day communities of Carleton Lake and Forest Glen.[392] Peter Charles Sulno had two wives, the second one being surnamed "Peters." He had at least three children, Gabriel, Frank, and Louise.[393] Peter Charles Sulno's brother, Francis Charles I, whose second wife was Magdalene Peters, had five children, Francis Charles II, James ("Jim"), Joseph, Job, and John. John Charles, the youngest, was born in 1836 and married four times.[394] He and his first wife, Mary Ann Bartlett, had one daughter, Susan Charles, born around 1855. With his second wife, Elizabeth Labrador, he had two daughters, Anne, born about 1861, and Mary, born about 1863.[395] Marriage to his third wife, an Englishwoman named Mary Jane Firth (also known as Jane Crowell), the daughter of Maria Crowell and Thomas Firth of Jordan River, who was another of Maria Crowell's consorts,[396] produced three children: Joseph, born on 8 March 1873 at Woods Harbour near Barrington Passage in Shelburne County, Clara born circa 1875, and Matthew born 6 June 1877.[397] John's fourth wife was Mahalia Frank.

Joseph, John Charles's son, was literate since he attended the school at Pubnico Head taught by a schoolteacher named John I. Brand. He also listened to stories told by his father about his paternal ancestor, Charles Snow, and in the summer of 1939 shared this information with his cousin Mary Rose Charles, who was then living at Kennebunkport in Maine.[398] Joseph's letter to Mary Rose, written in a fine cursive hand, still exists.[399] In it, Joseph held that the Mi'kmaw Charles family of Cape Sable were descended from a Scottish émigré who arrived in Pictou County around the time the first Scots settlers disembarked from the *Hector* in 1773. Though the name "Charles Snow" does not appear on the *Hector*'s passenger list, Joseph Charles's daughter, Elsie Charles Basque, mused that her great-great-grandfather might have been a crewman who "jumped ship" and whose decision to remain in Nova Scotia went unrecorded."[400]

Fighting for a Foothold at West Pubnico

The Mi'kmaq living at West Pubnico, who regarded Chief Peter Charles Sulno as their district chief, purposely kept quiet about their lands on Great Pubnico Lake. Unlike in Queens and Digby counties, where government demarcation of reserves alerted opportunists to Mi'kmaw timber reserves and rendered these reserves vulnerable to timber plundering, no illicit logging had occurred either at Great Pubnico Lake or on the Clyde River. Most West Pubnico Mi'kmaq figured out "that what the government did not know, they would not tell them."[401] The existence of the seven acres set out for them by Joseph Howe at Great Pubnico Lake had become a best-kept secret, since Howe had somehow failed to confirm the tract as a reserve, and Ottawa had no records in its office that indicated it had ever been reserved by order-in-council.

This secret remained hidden until the late 1880s. Then, in 1890, a logging interest, Whitman and Barnaby, petitioned the Crown Lands Department for a licence to harvest timber from the Great Pubnico Lake tract. Alerted to this development, the Cape Sable Mi'kmaq were not long in defending their interests. In January 1891 Matthew Francis approached John I. Brand, the Pubnico Head schoolteacher whose students included several Mi'kmaw children, to lodge a complaint for him. His father Joseph Francis, Matthew Francis declared, along with Paul Williams and several other Mi'kmaq had received seven hundred acres in 1843 on the east side of Great Pubnico Lake fifty years earlier. The land had been surveyed under Howe's orders to belatedly make up for the previous absence of a reserve in Yarmouth County, and then forgotten about by both the province and Ottawa. As far as Matthew Francis was concerned, the land still belonged to the Mi kmaq.

Brand passed along Francis's grievance to William Law, a local merchant and the Yarmouth County MPP, who in turn contacted James H. Austin, the commissioner of Crown Lands in Halifax. Law wrote to Austin that he could find no record of any order-in-council confirming the reserve, even though he had a title searcher examine the local grant books dating from 1847 through to 1849. Had Law known the actual date when Howe set out the reserve, he would have realized that the title search should have run much earlier than 1847 in order to find the grant. Law added that he and his associates were complacent about the status of this plot for many years, since they thought that originally the land around Great Pubnico Lake had been granted to Alexander McNutt in 1759.[402] He further remarked that Samuel Freeman, a timber merchant and boatbuilder in Liverpool, as well as a former Liberal MPP for Queens County, was also interested in obtaining the tract.[403]

Brand, a firm supporter of the Mi'kmaq's interests, stressed to Law that in 1840 Paul Williams and Matthew Francis had approached Simon d'Entremont and Obed Homes, then the MPP for Barrington, to secure a tract for them in the vicinity of Great Pubnico Lake. He emphasized that the Mi'kmaq had "cleared up land, planted orchards and … some of them had considerable stock."[404] He further stressed that "both [the] French and English are highly indignant since the Mi'kmaq have occupied the land so long that everyone knew about and respected their rights to the tract."[405] Brand concluded that he wasn't surprised by the bungling going on around him; he had heard of copious mistakes made by the Crown Lands office, and demanded that the office send someone down to investigate.[406]

The Acadian community also came to the Mi'kmaq's aid, perhaps to reciprocate for the assistance the Mi'kmaq had given them surrounding the Seven Years' War. Though the Mi'kmaq's presence prior to 1894 had failed to leave any permanent mark in bureaucratic files, the Indigenous group obviously had become regarded as a valuable and vital part of the West Pubnico community, with many supporters. An elderly Jean Marie, better known as "Johnny Muree Jr." of Bell Neck, Argyle, son of Jean-Marie Blanchard and Claire Muise, declared that he had been an axeman on the reserve's original survey in 1843. Not only could he testify to helping run the lines, but he also could locate the old markers. Copies of passages from Joseph Howe's journal of his "western tour" of 1842 as well as documents dating from 1843 that pertained to the reserve and its survey were circulated around West Pubnico. In the face of such a unified campaign, Indian Affairs could do little else but comply with Mi'kmaw demands. The reserve's boundaries were re-run and a survey plan was registered. Deputy land surveyor James A. McKay admitted to Austin on 18 September 1894 that though he had trouble marking boundaries since most of the axemen and chainbearers who had accompanied the original survey had died, the survey was complete.[407] The Mi'kmaw community at Great Pubnico Lake at least now had some official recognition, even though William Law continued to proclaim that if the land were not formally granted to the Mi'kmaq, then Freeman should get his grant.[408] The whole incident elicited surprise from Indian Affairs officials in Ottawa, who thought the Cape Sable Mi'kmaq were all but extinct. Only fifteen years previously a local Yarmouth historian had stated, "we see but little of them and that serves to convince us that before long, we shall see less."[409] It was hardly a prophetic pronouncement. During the 1890s Ottawa saw and

heard more of them than it had in a long time. Those at Great Pubnico Lake remained on their lands, and several eventually purchased lots for farming.

In September 1894 Ottawa also arranged a resurvey of the Clyde River reserve, noting that a few Mi'kmaq also associated with West Pubnico, among them James Francis, Joseph Francis, and James Luxey and their families, returned seasonally to the area. A small clearing on the right bank of the river known as Indian Gardens attested to antiquity of the Mi'kmaw people's possession.[410] This reserve had been bypassed by timber thieves and so had become a favourite resort of the Mi'kmaq for fishing in the spring and fall and for holding summer social gatherings.

Chief Lewis Luxey Sr.'s Final Years

Lewis Luxey Sr. from 1875 to 1895 regularly travelled to the Clyde River tract in Shelburne County to visit with Cape Sable band members encamped in the area.[411] He also engaged in timber deals on the Wildcat reserve, Queens County. In 1878 he and his son John leased timber rights to over three hundred acres near Brookfield, for thirty dollars per annum, to their neighbour Ephraim Hunt.[412] Even in his late seventies he was still buying and selling land and dealing in timber. In 1894, when he was eighty-two years old, he also supported the West Pubnico Mi'kmaq in their campaign to regain their Great Pubnico Lake reserve so they could farm and cut wood on it. In his twilight years Lewis had learned to be cautious in his business transactions and so avoided pitfalls that ensnared others. For example, one of his sons-in-law, Alex Jeremy, fell into a dubious deal in 1854 when he leased for next to nothing all the timber rights on the four-hundred-acre Ponhook reserve in Queens County for ninety-nine years to the wily merchant, shipbuilder, justice of the peace, and politician Samuel Freeman of Liverpool.[413]

Louis Luxey Sr. was now fairly economically secure. His guiding expertise had gained him a professional clientele. Until the early 1870s he lived at Bear River where he guided sportsmen from throughout eastern Canada and the northeastern United States.[414] Aware of the dangers of placing too much reliance on marginal agricultural pursuits, he had diversified economically and as a result had by the 1890s put away some money. He embarked on regular trips to Annapolis Royal where he sold farm produce in the fall and bought supplies. He worked in the woods during the winters, for which he kept a horse.

In his early eighties Lewis Luxey Sr. left Shelburne County and settled on the Wildcat reserve in Queens County. From there, his family members who lived with him visited with their cousins, the Bartletts of Salmon River, and both families maintained close kin ties with the Charles family.[415] Luxey even briefly became swept up in a mining venture begun by Jim Charles, a son of Francis Charles I of the Tusket River area. Jim Charles's foray into prospecting and mining proved colourful, transiently lucrative, finally disappointing, and ultimately tragic. Around 1870 he located alluvial gold back of Kemptville and sold his takings for a good return to Judge John William Ritchie at Annapolis Royal and to buyers in Boston. For a while he and his first wife, Lizzie Glode, owned a pair of fine horses, drove an elegant carriage, and wore clothes that were the height of Boston fashion. But Charles's prosperity was short lived. During an altercation with a neighbour, Ben Hamilton, who had been pressuring him to reveal his lode's location, Jim struck Hamilton a fatal blow to the head. With the help of friends, Charles eventually was legally exonerated for his part in Hamilton's death on the grounds of extenuating circumstances. He was eager to regain control of his lode and made preparations with members of Louis Luxey Sr.'s family at Brookfield to do so.[416] Owing to a miasma of mystique and suspicion that dogged him after Hamilton's death, he had trouble staking claim to his mine. Jim's lode was rediscovered in 1881 by two brothers, Charles and James Reeves from Kemptville, who in 1886 sold their claim to the Kempt Gold Mining Company.[417]

In 1883 Madeline Bartlett wed Jim Charles, and Lewis Luxey allowed the pair to take over Lot No. 1 at Wildcat so they could begin farming. The marriage proved to be a short and rocky one, however, and Lewis Luxey Sr. and his family learned a valuable lesson from Charles's experiences concerning the perils surrounding the search for gold. They refrained from any further mining ventures. The elderly chief retired to live out his final days peacefully, though modestly, on the Wildcat reserve.

Lewis Luxey Sr.'s eldest son Joseph married Marguerite Wallace, a great granddaughter of Chief Philip Bernard of St. Margaret's Bay, and the couple lived at Brookfield with Joseph's parents, whom they cared for into their senior years. After Lewis's death about 1890 his widow, Mary Ann Cobliel, went to live with her Glode relatives at Milton and died at Liverpool at the age of eighty-eight in 1917.[418] As adults, Mary Ann and Lewis Luxey Sr.'s children spread throughout southwestern Nova Scotia. Francis-Joseph Luxey moved to Shelburne County and then West Pubnico, while Étienne (or Stephen) married Margaret Brooks and became a well-known guide around Paradise in the Annapolis Valley. Eggy Luxey died at Middleton, Annapolis County, in 1941, reputedly at 105 years of age. This would have made him born in 1835, although this date is highly controversial. Far more likely, Eggy was born around 1850.[419] Eggy's younger brother, Lewis Luxey Jr. (1854–1939), married Mary Catherine Lucy Michael (1855–1938) in 1871 at St. Croix Roman Catholic Church in Plymouth, Digby County. Afterwards the pair lived at Bear River, where Lewis Jr. became a guide.[420] In their late forties, around 1900, they moved to Yarmouth to live near the elderly Cape Sable chief Stephen Bartholomew Alexis *dit* Wisow Jr., who had left most members of his immediate family at Salmon River. Accompanying Lewis and Mary were their son Benoni – better known as "Ben" (c.1880–1930) – and their daughter Josephine (1887–1990). Another of Lewis Luxey Jr.'s brothers, named James Luxey (c.1856–c.1958), also moved to Yarmouth. Meanwhile, following her husband Joseph Jeremy's death, Lewis Luxey Jr.'s sister Kate Luxey for many years travelled by canoe with others of her family along the Atlantic coast to Maine, Massachusetts, and upstate New York.[421]

Like his sister Kate, Lewis Luxey Jr. also travelled extensively throughout the Northeast. In the mid 1920s he told Halifax journalist Clara Archibald Dennis, daughter of Senator William Dennis who owned the *Halifax Herald*, that he had guided in four counties; Shelburne, Queens, Annapolis, and Yarmouth, and in four separate journeys he and three Mi'kmaw companions had paddled a canoe for eight hours across the Bay of Fundy to reach Saint John, New Brunswick, and parts beyond. Lewis further explained that as guiding, hunting, and fishing around Bear River no longer provided a viable livelihood for his family, he was forced to move to the Yarmouth reserve, which Chief Stephen Wisow Jr. had been instrumental in establishing in 1887. Despite lingering environmental problems with the Yarmouth site – it was boggy and stony – Lewis proudly acknowledged his group's vital role in securing the reserve. "We chose it," he exclaimed to Dennis. Owing to the Cape Sable Mi'kmaq's patience and persistence. "We got 25 acres [for a reserve] in Yarmouth here … [and] no white people can settle on it."[422]

Moving from Bear River to Yarmouth was challenging. Since the big game population had declined in southwestern Nova Scotia, strict bag limits had been introduced by the province, and fewer hunters ventured into the woods. Guiding became so competitive that Lewis Jr.'s son Ben decided not to follow his father's economic lead, but relied for his livelihood on trapping furs around Yarmouth, making baskets and other wooden items, and gardening. He viewed the Gravel Pit reserve as a good place to manufacture baskets and wooden implements, with copious stands of ash and maple nearby. Ben died, a single man, at age forty-six in 1930.[423]

Ben's sister Josephine kept the memories of her grandfather, Chief Lewis Luxey Sr., alive among her children by telling them stories about the chief's activities. Consequently, her grandfather's reputation as a land negotiator, power holder, and district chief developed into an oral legacy that has been handed down through generations of Luxey's descendants to the present day.[424] Luxey's activities had spanned the end of an era in which prominent Mi'kmaw leaders were expected to act on decisions made in Mi'kmaw councils with little or no interference from government agencies. These decisions often had major impacts on the Mi'kmaw constituency, but such consequences usually eluded the observation of provincial authorities. And not all stories of events about Chief Lewis Luxey were handed down by his direct descendants. One such story alleges that Luxey killed a man, Tom Wallace, to avenge Wallace's murder of Tom Phillips's wife. Tom Phillips was a grandson of Chief Philip Bernard of St. Margaret's Bay, who in the early 1790s was an associate of Charles Alexis and supported the Cape Sable head chief in his land and resource campaigns.

This incident, which allegedly occurred around 1852, was kept hidden from mainstream society by members of Lewis Luxey Sr.'s immediate family. It came to light about 1927 in a conversation between Abraham Bartholomew-Alexis's son Jeremiah Bartlett, also known as "Jerry Lonecloud," and Harry Piers, the curator of the Nova Scotia Museum of Natural History in Halifax. While Lonecloud condemned Tom Wallace for killing Phillips's wife at the head of St. Margaret's Bay, he did not cast any

moral aspersions on Chief Luxey for avenging this act, for he knew that Luxey's actions had not been construed as murder by the Mi'kmaw community. They had not occurred in isolation, unbeknownst to others of the Mi'kmaw nation, but would have been guided by a decision made in a Mi'kmaw council. In 1823 Judge Thomas Chandler Haliburton noted that the Mi'kmaq still retained a "code of traditionary and customary laws among themselves," and Chief Luxey's alleged act proved that this code still obtained over a quarter of a century later.[425]

According to Lonecloud, Tom Wallace, who had married one of Tom Phillips's daughters named Mary Ann, became involved in a heated argument with his mother-in-law because he threatened to leave the St. Margaret's Bay area and take several of her grandchildren with him. When she persisted in preventing him from leaving with his children, Wallace turned on her in a rage and shot her as she climbed over a fence in an attempt to flee from him. Chief Lewis Luxey, who retained close associations with the St. Margaret's Bay Mi'kmaq group, vowed vengeance on Wallace, whom he later tracked down and shot at South Wallace Lake, Yarmouth County.[426]

Luxey's actions had been sanctioned by the broader Mi'kmaw community under the code of which Haliburton wrote, and therefore he suffered no severe punitive consequences either from his Mi'kmaw peers or from representatives of the legal mainstream – who likely knew nothing of the incident in any case. After Wallace's death his widow, Mary Ann Phillips, married Jerry Lonecloud's father, Abraham Bartholomew-Alexis *dit* Wisow, and in 1854 gave birth to Jerry. Abraham Wisow had been born in 1815 at Ohio, near Long Island on the Roseway River,[427] which attests to the fact that the Bartholomew-Alexis (or Bartlett) family and the "Luxies" of the Roseway River area remained closely connected well into the late nineteenth century. Kin ties bound them to the Phillips family of St. Margaret's Bay as well, since not only did Abraham Wisow marry Tom Wallace's widow, but in the 1870s one of Wallace and Mary Ann Phillips's daughters, Margaret, married Joseph Luxey, Chief Lewis Luxey Sr.'s eldest son.[428]

Although Luxey suffered no legal consequences in the case of Tom Wallace's death, there still may have been a negative reaction within the South Shore Mi'kmaw community to Luxey's action that compelled Chief Luxey in the 1850s to move away from the Roseway River area and live at Bear River. In the aftermath of Wallace's killing, Abraham Wisow and his new bride also set out for Belfast, Maine, where their son Jeremiah, best known as "Jerry," was born on 4 July 1854.[429]

Jerry Bartlett and his parents nevertheless returned to Salmon River soon afterwards. There, Abraham Wisow and Mary Ann Phillips would have three more children: Sarah, born in 1856, and two boys who would die in childhood.[430] The Mi'kmaw encampment ground along the Salmon River during these years remained a site for fishing, festivities, and welcoming visitors. Traditional activities predominated. The group's leader, Ekien Bartholomew-Alexis Sr., who until his death about 1865 was also the chief medicine man, periodically bade youths sit about him in a circle and listen to his teachings.[431] Ideological life at Salmon River was a syncretistic blend of traditional Mi'kmaw belief overlain by a veneer of Roman Catholic ritual and precept. Jerry could remember his father Abraham and his uncle Stephen Bartlett Jr. *dit* Wisow singing in churches at Salmon River and Eel Brook.

The Showman of the Bartlett-Alexis Family: "Jerry Lonecloud" (1854–1930)

Jerry Bartholomew-Alexis throughout his life held several names: Germain, Jeremiah Bartholomew-Alexis, Jerry Bartlett, Jerry Lonecloud, and "Haselmah Laksi" (where "Selmah" = Jeremiah and "Laski" = Alexis or Luxey). Jerry was a showman, guide, and local chief, a traditional medicine practitioner with an extensive knowledge of Mi'kmaw lore and herbal remedies, and an amateur ethnologist and historian. From the late nineteenth century to the 1920s he had many conversations with Harry Piers, curator of the Nova Scotia Museum, and Halifax journalist Clara Archibald Dennis about his career as a showman, his activities with the Halifax County band, and his guiding adventures.[432]

Piers's and Dennis's writings reveal that Jerry believed both in the powers of solely spiritual curing and the ameliorative effects of herbal remedies. When he was a very young boy his parents travelled throughout eastern Canada and the United States selling traditional Mi'kmaw medicines. In 1856, after he was cured of a bout of convulsions at aged two, his parents brought him to be baptized at the Basilica of Sainte-Anne-de-Beaupré, about thirty kilometres

east of Quebec, probably under the name "Germain Bartholomew-Alexis." His family lodged for a time at Kahnawake near Montreal and then camped on the shores of Lake Champlain. Around 1860 his father Abraham travelled to New York where he enlisted for two terms of service in the Union Army during the Civil War. In 1865 Abraham, who was recognized for his role as a marksman in the party that had captured John Wilkes Booth, the man who shot President Abraham Lincoln, went to collect his portion of a substantial monetary reward. But he never returned. Jerry and his siblings assumed that their father had been murdered for his share of the money. Their mother Mary Ann also died around the same time and was buried at Waterbury in Vermont. Jerry now was left alone to shepherd two younger brothers and a sister home to Nova Scotia.

Memories of stories their mother used to tell them about a grant of land belonging to the Phillips family at the Head of St. Margaret's Bay, where one day they might settle, gave Jerry and his siblings strength to keep going.[433] But when they reached New Brunswick, they were met by several of Mary Ann Phillip's relatives, who squired them not to St. Margaret's Bay but to Cape Sable, where they were taken under the wing of the district chief, Peter Charles Sulno. Sulno had assumed leadership of the Cape Sable band about 1865, upon the death of Ekien Bartlett Sr.[434] Born in the early 1790s, he was around eighty years of age in 1870. He still occupied his encampment at Carleton Lake as he had in 1866. Jerry described it as being located "between Parr's and Ogden's Lakes [on the] west branch of the Tusket River, about 4 miles north of Carleton." Jerry adored the elderly chief, who magnanimously agreed to teach the orphan boy his knowledge of medicine, legends, and other lore. In return, Jerry cared for the elderly man during his final years, and around 1875 he accompanied Chief Sulno's body to the cemetery at Ste. Anne du Ruisseau at Eel Brook for burial.[435]

Jerry then moved to Bear River to live with his relative James Meuse, a son of Chief Andrew James Meuse.[436] Jerry's two young brothers died of unknown causes around this time, while his sister Sara wed Abraham Michael. Jerry lived with Meuse until they both were recruited by John E. Healey, of Healey and Bigelow's Wild West Show. Not long after, both journeyed to Boston to join Healey's Kickapoo Medicine Company.[437] The Kickapoo Medicine Company made and sold patent medicines, and it was during his stint in Boston with this company that Jerry gained his stage name, "Doctor Jerry Lonecloud."[438] For a while there was an intriguing possibility that Healey and Bigelow's Wild West Show might perform at the Crystal Palace in London, England, but when this did not pan out, Jerry broke away from Healy's organization and formed his own company, The Kiowa Indian Company. By this time he had earned a widespread reputation as a medicine man and legend keeper.[439] When his company petered out, he travelled to New Brunswick where he recruited a young Malecite woman by the name of Elizabeth Paul to play the role of Pocahontas in a show featuring Pocahontas and John Smith. Jerry and Elizabeth soon became romantically involved and were formally married on 18 June 1889 at St. Joseph's Church in Bridgewater, though they were informally married previous to this date, by Mi'kmaw custom, in Kentville.[440]

The couple raised six children: Rosie, Mary Anne, Jerry, Hannah, Elizabeth, and Louis Abraham.[441] Each fall and winter Jerry returned to the woods to hunt, fish, and trap. A deft businessman, he also maintained a clientele of American sportsmen whom he guided, and from 1882 to 1910 he operated a guiding business at Liscomb in Guysborough County.[442] For a while Jerry and Elizabeth separated, since while at Liscomb he had an affair with a married woman and by her had a son.[443] He also shared ethnographic information, artefacts, and natural curiosities with Harry Piers, the curator of the Nova Scotia Museum. He lived for a while at Enfield, and later he travelled between Elmsdale and a cabin he had built on an island in Lake Thomas, near Fall River, while he worked to secure property rights for Mi'kmaq being displaced from their encampment sites by government fiat or by local landowners.[444] One of his main goals was to secure a permanent title for the Mi'kmaq of Tufts Cove, Dartmouth. He further sought to compel the government to direct monies from timber sales on the Ship Harbour reserve towards buying a tract for the Elmsdale Mi'kmaq, who were being evicted by a local landowner from an encampment ground they had occupied for generations.[445]

Then, on 6 December 1917, while Jerry was visiting Kentville, tragedy struck. Two of his daughters – Rosie, who had married a Mi'kmaw man from Shubenacadie named Jim MacDonald and gone to live at Tuff's Cove, and Hannah, who lived near Rosie – died in the Halifax Explosion. It was an especially sad time, for another of his daughters, Mary Anne, had died earlier during the First World War. Resilient to the core, Jerry continued to advocate for Mi'kmaw land and resource interests. He served as sub-chief and then chief of the Halifax County band, and adopted the title "Chief Medicine Man for Halifax County." During this time he and Elizabeth were temporarily reunited, although they drifted apart again. And despite his best efforts, which included persuading Harry Piers to draft numerous letters to Ottawa, the government expropriated the Halifax County reserves, after which many Mi'kmaq affected by this action, including Lonecloud's wife Elizabeth, his daughter Libby, and son Louis, relocated to the Millbrook reserve.[446]

As he approached his late seventies, Jerry Lonecloud continued to share information and artefacts with his friend Harry Piers, ply his medicinal remedies, and manufacture articles out of wood for sale. He became an easily recognizable figure at the Halifax market with his lanky physique, cane in one hand and his other arm encircled with baskets. His long, greying hair was "tied in neat little pigtails ... with gay ribbons woven into the end of the braids."[447] Though blind in one eye and losing his sight in the other, he regularly walked from his residence on Mumford Road to the market. He died on 15 April 1930 from heart disease at age seventy-nine. According to his death certificate, his body lies in St. Patrick's Cemetery in Dartmouth, though no grave marker with his name on it exists there.[448]

The "Gravel Pit" Community at Yarmouth

As far as is known, none of Jerry Bartlett's descendants ever returned to settle in southwestern Nova Scotia, so a number of Mi'kmaw persons today bearing the surname "Bartlett" descend from Ekien Bartlett *dit* Wisow Sr.'s two eldest sons, Chief Stephen Wisow Jr. and Joseph Bartlett. Others are descendants of Ekien Wisow Sr.'s nephew, Joseph Bartlett of Summerside, now Dayspring in Lunenburg County.[449] When Joseph died in Lunenburg County, his son Tom and his wife, Emeline Crowell, moved to Tusket in Yarmouth County, where by 1900 their children formed a core group within the Cape Sable Mi'kmaw community. Tom's brother, Stephen Bartlett, wed Christie Toney and the couple had a son Abraham at Tusket in 1906.[450] Following Christie's death, Stephen Bartlett married Rose Labrador in 1933 when he was sixty-two.[451] James Sullivan Bartlett, born in 1873 to Joseph Bartlett and Julia Pictou, also lived his early life at Tusket, although in his teenage years he moved to Yarmouth where he married Mary Rose Charles in 1894. The couple and their children lived at Yarmouth until 1924, when they departed for the United States.

Though Chief Stephen Wisow Jr. had eight boys and ten girls living in his household at Salmon River in 1866, only a few members of his family moved with him to Yarmouth twenty years later.[452] In the mid-1880s Wisow began to reside seasonally in a log dwelling along the extreme east end of Starr's Road in Yarmouth, near the headwaters of the Cheboque River. Despite its unglamorous name of "The Gravel Pit," the land was flat, lay close to markets two miles away, and had a depth of soil for small gardens. With time the Mi'kmaq accorded it a more sonorous name, "The Arcadia reserve," drawn from the nearby village of Arcadia. In the 1940s this was shortened to "Acadia." Its name in the Mi'kmaw language was *Malikiaq*.

At first, Stephen Bartlett Jr. *dit* Wisow and a few family members stayed at Yarmouth only for short periods of time, selling baskets and other wares before returning in the fall to the woods north of Hectanooga to hunt, fish, guide, and join logging camps.[453] The chief also travelled each spring and summer to visit members of the Cape Sable band at various coastal encampments in Digby, Yarmouth, and Shelburne Counties. As he aged and became less mobile, however, Stephen Wisow Jr. realized he needed secure title to the land on which his dwelling stood, and began to send persistent appeals to Ottawa for a reserve at Yarmouth. In response, the federal government finally agreed to purchase 68 acres, or 27.7 hectares, lying 3.2 kilometres east of Yarmouth, which included property on which Wisow had planted his garden. Ottawa also promised to build Wisow a frame house.

The property formerly had belonged to Thomas Willett, who had used it to mine gravel – hence the name "The Gravel Pit." Upon Willett's death, the plot fell to his son George and his daughter Annie, who were all too ready to enter into negotiations to sell the land to Ottawa in December 1887.[454] The tract was low lying and swampy, and in the early years before infilling began, the dampness of the ground gave rise to disease. Adults and children died of the scourges of pulmonary tuberculosis, pneumonia,

diphtheria, and cholera. Families who suffered economically owing to the drain on their health caused by such diseases also dealt with the consequences of acute malnutrition, such as children being born with rickets.

Chief Stephen Wisow Jr., by contrast, retained good health to an advanced age. On the federal census for 1891 the elderly Cape Sable chief was listed as being eighty-four years of age, which put his date of birth as 1807.[455] Classified at this time as an illiterate basketmaking widower, he was living in the frame house the government had built for him and was still recognized as the Cape Sable head chief. Each spring and fall he met with prominent Acadians from Ste. Anne du Ruisseau to receive salt and other gifts for granting members of the Acadian community the right to fish eels in Eel Brook.[456] Until his death in 1901 both the Mi'kmaw and the Acadian communities regarded him as a traditional power-holder with knowledge of historic protocols and northeastern Algonquian medicine and ritual.

Stansbury Hagar, an American ethnologist who interviewed the chief between 1875 and 1894, claimed that the Cape Sable leader was the only man he ever met who had seen a medicinal plant known as *Mededeskooï*, associated with the spirit of the rattlesnake and used to make both a healing salve and a love potion. Designated the "rattling plant," *Mededeskooï* remained invisible. The only people who could see and use the plant had to possess knowledge of special rituals, to be undertaken before one could access its powers. Stephen Wisow Jr. stated to Hagar he had once seen a *Mededeskooï*, but added that he had not performed the proper rituals. Hagar therefore presumed the chief was not one of the most skilled medicine practitioners. However, Wisow Jr. might have been expressing characteristic northeastern Algonquian reticence about any special medicine powers he had, especially as Hagar was an outsider to his culture.[457]

In 1891 Stephen Wisow Jr.'s son, James Bartlett, who was thirty-six at the time, was living in a frame shanty located near his father's dwelling on Starr's Road in Yarmouth. At the same time, Tom Bartlett (1851–96) and his wife Emeline Moore (Crowell), now thirty, occupied a shanty with six children: Mary, aged ten; Hannah, aged eight; Henry, seven; John, six; Simon, four; and Mary Caroline, who was ten months old. Stephen Wisow Jr.'s grandson, James Sullivan Bartlett, born on 20 February 1873 to Joseph Bartlett and

Julia Pictou, was also living at Yarmouth.[458] In 1891 only five adults – Stephen Wisow Jr., James Bartlett, Tom Bartlett, Tom's wife Emeline, and James Sullivan Bartlett – were living on the Gravel Pit reserve. Tom and Emeline had six children with them: Hannah (eight), Henry (seven), Henry (six), John (five), Simon (four), and Mary, who was six months old.[459]

Two years later the Cape Sable chief's son, James Bartlett, had remarried and was living at Yarmouth with his new wife, Christie.[460] Near him dwelt James Sullivan Bartlett, who was still unmarried. Two other men, Samuel Bartlett and Solomon Bartlett, living at the Gravel Pit reserve, do not appear in the documentary record again after this date, and may have been sons of Chief Stephen Bartlett. At this time C.P. Smith, the local Indian agent, proffered a surprising and undoubtedly erroneous population estimate, given its extremely asymmetrical sex ratio: that the Mi'kmaw population of Yarmouth County consisted of twenty-eight adult male heads and only four adult women, two of whom were widows. He added that these persons could be found scattered anywhere over the landscape from Hectanooga to West Pubnico.[461]

Still seasonally mobile, parties of Mi'kmaq regularly camped at what was known as "the *cabano* site" at The Forks before descending to Great Pubnico Lake and from there canoeing down the Barrington River into Shelburne County. During the late nineteenth century, the encampment ground at Labraduce (or Rabraduce), Shelburne County, provided convenient bivouacs for Mi'kmaq who were logging in the nearby woods. Tom Bartlett and Emeline Crowell often camped at Labraduce, where their sons James, William Henry, John Berton, and Simon were born. In the mid-1880s Tom and his family moved to Tusket where they had two more daughters, Mary Elizabeth in 1889 and Mary Caroline in 1890. They also visited Salmon River frequently and were often accompanied on these travels by Tom's brother Joseph.

When Tom Bartlett suddenly died in 1896, just before the birth of his youngest child Joseph, Emeline moved to the Gravel Pit reserve at Yarmouth, where during the winters she occupied a shanty near Stephen Wisow Jr., since the chief assisted widows in times of hardship.[462] Although illiterate herself, Emeline knew the value of education in the rapidly changing world at the beginning of the twentieth century and worked tirelessly to ensure her children

received the schooling that would allow them to take an integral place in the Canadian or American mainstream as well as Mi'kmaw society. To provide for her family she made baskets and performed domestic labour around Tusket and Yarmouth.[463]

In 1901, following Chief Stephen Jr. *dit* Wisow's death at Yarmouth, Emeline joined her eldest son James Bartlett's household on Starr's Road.[464] James was likely the man described in one account as dignified and honest, who by the 1940s had become an itinerant peddler, selling his baskets and wooden items such as butter tubs and clothesline poles around the Yarmouth area, and often receiving a meal from his buyers.[465] Emeline's brother-in-law, Stephen Bartlett, meanwhile kept a frame dwelling at Tusket large enough to house not only his wife Christie Toney and two pre-teenage children but also two lodgers, John Charles and a woman named "Mary E. Williams." John at this time was married to Mary Jane Firth.[466]

Each of Tom Bartlett's and Emeline Moore's adult children followed a distinctive path. In 1936 Mary Elizabeth Bartlett, known as "Lizzie," born at The Forks in 1889, married Herbert Arthur Goudey, son of Arthur Goudey and Madeline Smith of Yarmouth. Neither the bride nor the groom was young at the time: Lizzie was forty-six and Herbert, a trucker, was a sixty-one-year-old widower. The extensive Goudey family of Yarmouth and Tusket retained kin relations with the Churchill family of Yarmouth, so Connie and Lizzie Churchill stood as Mary and Herbert's witnesses.[467] In 1909 Lizzie Bartlett's younger sister Mary Caroline wed Stephen Glode, born in 1885 to James Glode and Sarah Toney, at West Pubnico, after which the couple lived near James's parents at the Tusket Lakes.[468] When disease and malnutrition dogged the minuscule Tusket Mi'kmaw community during the Great Depression, several of Mary Caroline and Stephen's children succumbed to pneumonia, tuberculosis, and exposure.[469] In a story that made headlines, in February 1933 their thirteen-year-old son Clarence Glode died while trying to rescue his eight-year-old brother Gordon, who had fallen through the ice on the Tusket River and later also died from the effects of hypothermia.[470] Hard times dogged the Glode family even following the Depression years. When Mary Caroline succumbed to tuberculosis in 1948, Stephen Glode supported himself by basketmaking and marginal farming. He chose not to remarry and in 1957, when he was seventy-two years old, he burned to death at Yarmouth in a tragic accidental house fire.[471]

Tom and Emeline's sons faced many serious challenges from sickness, discrimination, and poverty. James, the eldest, remained at Yarmouth and seems to have lived to a relatively old age. William Henry Bartlett, the second eldest, died at age eighty on 25 June 1954 of heart disease. Henry outlived his wife and children, who all succumbed to tuberculosis.[472]

Tom and Emeline's youngest son, Simon Thomas Bartlett, born on 4 September 1886 either at West Green Harbour or at Labraduce near the town of Shelburne, was a veteran of the First World War. Around 1913 he married Mary (also Margaret or "Maggie") Shaw Paul, the daughter of Alexander Paul and Mary Pictou of Sheburne County, and by the war's onset had two infant children, Dean and Louise. Not long afterwards Simon enlisted in the army and served in France during the remainder of the war. His homecoming in 1919 was a bitter one. Not only was he wounded in action, leaving him a partial invalid for the rest of his life, but in his absence his wife Mary and his two young children had experienced hunger and poverty so pressing that all three finally succumbed to malnutrition, exhaustion, and exposure.[473]

The best that many Mi'kmaw veterans like Simon could do after their return to civilian life was to seek work in the woods and become lumbermen, river drivers, and mill workers. Since the opportunities for employment in the woods after the war were slightly better in southern Digby than at Yarmouth or Shelburne, Simon moved north to Hectanooga, where he married Eva Labrador, a daughter of Samuel Labrador and Frances Murree, in 1920.[474] Hard work was out of the question, however, for Simon was very ill. He only lived for six more years. Though he constantly travelled back and forth between Weymouth in Digby County and Tusket in Yarmouth County, he was severely hampered by tuberculosis, which he held he had contracted overseas in the trenches of Europe. Two of the Bartlett's children also contracted this disease.[475] One bright spot in Simon and Eva's life was the birth at Kentville of Joseph Simon Bartlett in 1923. Like his father, Joseph Simon joined the military, served in the Second World War and the Korean War, and became a staunch member of the Royal Canadian Legion, Clare Branch 52. He died aged eighty-five at what was to become the headquarters of the Acadian First Nation at Yarmouth.[476] Joseph Simon had little time to get to know his father,

however, as Simon Thomas Bartlett died of tuberculosis at Kentville in Kings County when his youngest son was only two, on 4 September 1925 at the age of only thirty-four years and five months.[477]

Chief Stephen Wisow Jr.'s son James Bartlett *dit* Wisow, who was born at Salmon River around 1855, maintained seasonal encampments at Sheshaw Park, on the Tusket Lakes, at Eel Brook, and at Great Pubnico Lake. On 9 February 1876 James Wisow wed Mary Anne Labrador from Bear River, while his sister Rose married Mary Anne's brother, Peter Labrador, in a double wedding at Ste. Anne du Ruisseau.[478] Though Mary Anne Labrador died in 1879,[479] she and James likely were the parents of John Bartlett, who was born at Jordan Branch in Shelburne County in May 1876.[480] About 1890 James married again to a woman named Christie and soon afterwards moved to the Gravel Pit reserve at Yarmouth.

John Bartlett, recorded as a single man living in Shelburne County in the early 1890s, in 1895 wed his third wife, Julia Labrador from Jordan River, and the pair lived at Barrington Passage until 1928. Julia had been married before and had two sons from her first marriage, Albert and Henry. The couple had five children living with them in 1921: James Albert, who was fifteen; Mary Emma, nine; John Simon, six; John George, four; and Mary Catherine, four months old. Julia's seventy-one-year-old mother-in-law from her first marriage lived in the same household. The 1921 federal census lists John as forty-eight years of age, which would make him three years older than the John Bartlett born to James Wisow in 1876, though the date on the census may be erroneous. John and Julia had several more children between 1921 and 1928, so they had a large family, though Mary Catherine, John George, and two children born after 1921, John William and Mary Lucy, later died of tuberculosis. On 16 February 1944 John and Julia also lost their eighteen-year-old son Thomas Vincent Bartlett, who died of exposure when the steamship on which he worked as a seaman was wrecked off the coat of Digby County during the First World War.[481]

The Bartletts and Luxeys, despite their dispersed settlement pattern, in the early 1900s focused on retaining access annually to their traditional meeting ground at Eel Brook. Between 1786 and 1820 they had been deprived of all legal title to it, despite Charles Morris III's allegedly good intentions to set a small parcel aside for them in 1815. They had even had lost their claim to their ancient burial ground at Rocco

Point, as Morris never instigated the legislation necessary to reserve it. Yet the Mi'kmaq refused to be bitter, and most began adapting to life at the dawn of a new century. They still camped regularly at Sheshaw Park and attended the Ste. Anne du Ruisseau church for baptisms, weddings, burials, and St. Anne's Day ceremonies. Over time, members of the Bartlett and Alexis families from Hectanooga, Tusket, Barrington, and Shelburne areas wed individuals of the Charles, Labrador, Michael, Williams, Pictou, and Toney families. Bartletts worked in the woods alongside Labradors from Jordan Falls, Shelburne County, who had already acquired reputations as skilled lumbermen and river drivers.

Many of the Bartletts and Charles, among them Joseph Charles and James Sullivan Bartlett, were ambitious for the upcoming generation. Whenever possible, they encouraged their children to attend school to learn to read and write. In 1894 James Sullivan Bartlett, son of Joseph Bartlett Sr. and Julia Pictou, wed Mary Rose Charles, a young, attractive woman born at Yarmouth in 1880, and the two lived for thirty years in Yarmouth. James Sullivan, who was literate, was a guide, carpenter, and furniture manufacturer. He also could move houses on skids – a skill he probably learned from his Acadian neighbours at Salmon River during his youth. Mary Rose Charles, who was fifteen at the time of her marriage, had attended grade school for several years at Meteghan and so could read, write, and do basic arithmetic.[482] She manufactured fancy baskets that she sold in Yarmouth. Each summer the two went to New England at harvest season to pick potatoes, berries, and other fruit for commercial landowners; over time, in no small part owing to Mary Rose's business acumen, they accumulated enough money to buy a small house on Starr's Road.[483] Yet their early years of marriage were difficult ones. Their first son, Joseph Elia Bartlett, died shortly after birth in 1895. A second son, born in 1899 and also named Joseph, like his namesake also died in infancy, while a third son, James Henry, born in 1911, died of cholera in 1915.[484] The loss of three sons was followed by the births of four daughters: Frances Viola was born in 1898, Louise Mary Margaret in 1903, Dorothy in 1906, and Marguerite Julia in 1913.[485]

Despite their frequent hardships, James Sullivan Bartlett and Mary Rose Charles formed a striking couple wherever they went. James stood just under average height at five feet, five inches and sported

shiny black hair and arresting brown eyes. In the early 1900s he earned good money as a carpenter. It is rumoured that he helped to construct Bartlett's wharf in Yarmouth and for a while owned a house on King Street. Since she herself was educated, Mary Rose encouraged her daughters to go to school and work hard academically. Their good looks and education soon made the Bartlett daughters sought after by Mi'kmaw and non-Mi'kmaw suitors alike. It was not long before nineteen-year-old Louise Bartlett caught the eye of twenty-one-year-old James A. Maher, an Irishman who had immigrated a few years before to Brooklyn, New York. The two may first have met while Louise and her family were visiting New England during the summer.

For years, James Sullivan, Mary Rose, and their daughters stayed in New England for only a few months before returning to Cape Sable in the fall. But this pattern of life was to be radically disrupted. Soon after Louise Bartlett and James Mahar were married at St. Ambrose Church in Yarmouth on 27 November 1922, James took his new bride to Hartford, Connecticut.[486] Despite the distance, Louise kept in regular touch with her parents and siblings, and when economic conditions worsened in Yarmouth and her family members began to show signs of malnutrition, Louise prevailed on them to move to the United States. In response, James Sullivan Bartlett, now sixty-one years old, sold his remaining house on Starr's Road for a dollar to Tom Bartlett's widow Emeline, and embarked with Mary Rose and his three unmarried daughters in 1924 on the *Prince George* out of Yarmouth bound for Boston. Though the steamer's manifest identified the purpose of their voyage as an opportunity to visit family, the Bartletts decided en route to take up residence permanently in New England. The party arrived in Boston on 1 July and immediately set out for Hartford.[487]

Louise's education enabled her to participate in many parts of New England society, and her attractive mother Mary Rose likely fitted into her daughter's social circle. Mary Rose was undoubtedly relieved to have her husband and younger family members escape the ravages of contagious disease that had hounded their family in Nova Scotia, particularly the scourge of pulmonary tuberculosis so common on Starr's Road. James Sullivan Bartlett eventually earned a stable living as a carpenter and hunting and fishing guide at North Kennebunkport (now Arundel), Maine, where he died on 28 July

1938.[488] All of James Sullivan Bartlett and Mary Rose's daughters wed Americans, with only one, Frances Viola (1908–44), marrying an Indigenous man of Penobscot ancestry from Oldtown, Maine. None of these Bartletts ever returned to Cape Sable other than for brief visits. Yet even after 1924, when James Sullivan and his wife moved to the United States, their daughters communicated regularly with their cousins, the children and grandchildren of their father's sister, Henriette Christina Bartlett, who had married Samuel Labrador in 1886.[489] James Sullivan also kept in touch with Tom Bartlett's widow, Emeline Moore (Crowell), who continued to live on Starr's Road until she died at age seventy-eight in 1935.[490]

In her final years Emeline's nephew Abraham Bartlett, the son of Stephen Bartlett of Tusket, cared for her. Abraham's mother Christie Toney died in 1932, and the following year his father Stephen wed Rose Labrador.[491] Rose was a sister of Maggie Labrador, Joseph Charles's wife, as well as of Eva Labrador, Simon Bartlett's wife. During the final years of his life Stephen Bartlett frequently camped at Sheshaw Park at Eel Brook, the site that for so many years had held a special sacred significance to the Alexis family. Stephen was sixty years old at the time of his second marriage, while Rose Labrador was only twenty-four. Rose's father Samuel Labrador, who had been born in Yarmouth in 1867 to Stephen Labrador and Mary Rose Maffre, encouraged his daughters to acquire the essentials of reading and writing.[492] And it was a trait Samuel shared with his second wife, Frances Murree, who was Rose's mother. Consequently, their daughter Rose was literate and fairly well travelled.

The Great Pubnico Lake Settlement, 1870–1910

Two years prior to his father's second marriage, Abraham Bartlett of Tusket at age twenty-four also married for a second time, to twenty-one-year-old Ella Gertrude Muree, daughter of John Muree and Unica McGray of West Pubnico.[493] Ella was a cousin of Stephen Bartlett's second wife Rose. Following Ella's death in 1934 Abraham wed a third time to Annie Emily Pictou from Jordan Falls, and the pair settled along the Great Pubnico Lake Road.[494] Until the late 1940s, tuberculosis, pneumonia, influenza, diphtheria, cholera, and malnutrition took a toll on the Mi'kmaq population at Yarmouth and Tusket, but Abraham Bartlett and his new wife benefitted from life in the healthier and often more prosperous community near West Pubnico.

The Great Pubnico Lake Road settlement was ethnically diverse. In the early 1800s a road referred to by the Acadians as "Le Chemin du Lac" had been cut through four miles – or 6.4 kilometres – of scrubland to join West Pubnico with Great Pubnico Lake. The community that soon formed consisted of Mi'kmaq, Acadians, British, some Black Loyalists, and a few individuals of African ancestry from the Caribbean.[495] By the late 1800s a local lumber mill provided a more stable mode of living than was available at either the Tusket Lakes or Yarmouth. One of the best-known and historically intriguing families, the Murrees, descended from Jean-Marie *dit* Blanchard, a French-speaking individual of African descent who was born in Bayonne, France. By hiring himself out as a sailor, Jean-Marie lived for several years in Santo Domingo, the capital of what is now the Dominican Republic, but later found his way to Cape Sable. At Ste. Anne du Ruisseau in 1806 he married Claire Mius, daughter of Charles-Amand II Mius, a descendant of Baron Philippe I Mius d'Entremont, the first seigneur of Pobomcoup. Though he remained at Abbot's Harbour, in the Cape Sable district, Jean-Marie's descendants spread to West Pubnico and The Forks. As his first name was Jean-Marie, locals called him "Johnny Murree." In 1843 one of his sons, Johnny Murree Jr., assisted in the first survey of the seven-hundred-acre Great Pubnico Lake reserve, and one of his granddaughters, Ella Gertrude Murree, was Abraham Bartlett's first wife.

Stephen Wisow Jr.'s son James Bartlett and James's second wife Christie joined the small settlement formed of members of the Murree, Pictou, Gloade, and Charles families lying at the eastern end of the Great Pubnico Lake Road. This community was far less peripatetic than the Mi'kmaq at Tusket, Eel Brook, Yarmouth, and Salmon River. A lumber mill, built at "The Landing," or where the road met the southeastern shore of Great Pubnico Lake, ushered in a period of prosperity in the lumber business during the late 1860s, when a free trade agreement with the United States fueled wooden shipbuilding in the fisheries sector. The work attracted Mi'kmaw men from as far away as Queens and Lunenburg Counties. The first proprietor of the mill was a man named Sutherland, but after changing hands several times, in the 1880s it operated under the auspices of the Seeley family from Argyle. George Seeley lived along the

Pubnico Lake Road and knew its Mi'maw residents well, so a sense of comradeship developed over the years between the mill's owners and the workers.[496] In 1881 Seeley's closest neighbours were John Charles and his wife, Mary Jane Firth, whose son Joseph was seven years old at the time. Joseph attended the school taught by John I. Brand, who also acted as census taker for Pubnico district in 1881.[497]

By the early 1880s most of the local Mi'kmaw children attended school, and some families could afford to buy the land on which they had built their small houses, root cellars, and outbuildings. They represented a diversity of talents. Men of the Francis, Glode, Labrador, Paul, Pictou, and Williams families were noted for their river driving skills. Other men and women excelled as artisans, making ornate baskets as well as containers and wooden implements. Still others, among them John Charles and John Pictou, were hunters, fishers, and trappers and manufactured baskets and birchbark- and canvas-covered canoes. In consequence, the seven-hundred-acre so-called Pubnico Lake reserve was dotted for a number of years with hunting camps interspersed with garden plots, small apple orchards, and productive blueberry and cranberry fields.[498] Those with some Acadian ancestry, such as the Labradors who came from the Jordan River area, were trilingual, speaking Mi'kmaq, French, and English.

One of the largest families living along the Great Pubnico Lake Road was headed by Matthew Glode (c.1825–1913) and his wife Victoire Francis. About 1856 Matthew had moved to Yarmouth County from Queens County, and was later joined by his brother, John. Two of Matthew's and Victoire's sons, John William Newel Glode and Samuel, were hunting and fishing guides. About 1860 John William Newel Glode married Mary Elizabeth Murree (1834–1918), a granddaughter of Claire Mius and Jean-Marie *dit* Blanchard.[499] Their son, John Newel Glode, better known as "Young Johnny Glode," also took up guiding.[500] John Newel married Margaret Robbins and worked as a guide until the mid-1950s, when he retired to Yarmouth, where several of his descendants live today.[501] Near the Glodes' plot on the Pubnico Lake Road lay the small frame dwelling of Joe Pictou, a lumberman who had been born at Caledonia in Queens County in 1876 to John Pictou and Mary Jane Muise, but who preferred working in the woods of Yarmouth County. Joe Pictou never married, and like his neighbour John Newel Glode eventually

retired to Yarmouth in the mid-1950s.[502] A respected traditional healer, Maria Elizabeth Charles, who was married to Stephen Carty, also lived along the Great Pubnico Lake Road in the middle to late 1800s.[503]

By the early 1900s many of the Labradors of the Jordan River area in Shelburne County had moved to Barrington Passage looking for work. The same was true for members of Joseph Bartlett Sr.'s family, hailing originally from Summerside in Lunenburg County. Both families produced skilled lumbermen and river drivers, and when members of the families intermarried cousins often worked together. John Charles meanwhile moved back and forth between Barrington Passage and Tusket, where he lodged with Tom Bartlett's son Stephen Bartlett and his wife Christie Toney. Mahalia Frank, whom he married in 1891, travelled with him.[504] John's son Joseph Charles, a carpenter, lumberman, hunter, trapper and, according to a photograph that exists of him, likely a manufacturer of canoes, no longer lived at Tusket by this time. Joseph had struck up a friendship with Samuel Labrador, a lumberman from the West Pubnico area. Facing a dearth of jobs in Yarmouth County – the shipbuilding boom at West Pubnico, fostered by the Liberal government's free trade agreement with the United States, had ended, and many mills in Yarmouth County shut down in the wake of the 1878 Conservative National Policy, which favoured central Canadian manufacturers – Samuel left for Hectanooga to pursue employment in the woods of Digby County, and Joseph Charles followed. In 1902 Joseph Charles wed Samuel Labrador's and Henriette Christina Bartlett's daughter, "Maggie" Labrador, at St. Vincent de Paul Church at Salmon River.[505] The following year the couple settled down in Hectanooga, where Joseph secured work at the local Harrington Mill.[506] Despite their tendency to disperse widely over the landscape, many of the Charles family, including Joseph Charles and Maggie's renowned daughter Elsie Charles, traced roots back to the closely kin-knit community at Barrington Passage and Great Pubnico Lake.

After suffering through two stillbirths early in her marriage, in 1904 and 1908, Maggie delivered two daughters: Lucy Marie Celeste, born in 1905, and Elsie, born at Hectanooga, Digby County, in 1916, who would become a well-known activist, educator, and humanitarian.[507] Even with two young daughters, however, Maggie did not stay in Nova Scotia. She was bright and ambitious, and her husband Joseph had taught her the fundamentals of reading and writing. To Maggie, southwestern Nova Scotia represented hardship and social restriction without the kind of opportunities she felt awaited her south of the international border. She was one of the first Cape Sable Mi'kmaw women to wrench herself away from her community and on her own terms seek new prospects in New England. Evidently driven an expanded outlook on life, she longed to try out her talents and skills in a large city. Accordingly, she departed by steamer for Boston in late 1921, leaving her elder daughter Lucy and a bewildered five-year-old Elsie "alone on the Yarmouth docks as she left." Following her departure, Lucy and Elsie lived for a while with other families of Bartletts on the Yarmouth reserve and then for a while with their father, although in 1922 a childless couple at Salmon River, Edmond Deveau ("á Edmond á Luc") and his wife Lizzie took Elsie in when Joseph temporarily fell ill.

The same year, Joseph sent Lucy to New England to find his wife. Lucy located her mother in Boston, but instead of returning to Nova Scotia in the fall she met and married Carl Pinn.[508] Elsie stayed on in Cape Sable, and when she reached fourteen years of age in 1930 she was briefly placed in the Shubenacadie residential school – the school's first year of operation – purportedly because her father had read an article that made the school sound "grand." The Shubenacadie school proved to be anything but grand, yet Elsie's early experiences there fostered her wellsprings of courage and determination. When she rebelled against the school's strictures by branding them antithetical to true scholarly pursuits, her father helped her gain entrance to a school in Meteghan. Owing to her exceptional academic abilities, in her graduating year she was appointed class valedictorian.[509] She became the first Mi'kmaw person to graduate from the Nova Scotia Teacher's College. In addition to a productive career teaching in the mainstream school system, and marriage to Isaac Basque of Shubenacadie and child rearing, she worked in the field of Indigenous elder care and community services in Boston. She had experience in this field, for she cared for her father Joseph Charles in his final years, and when he died in 1940 at age sixty-seven in the Victoria General Hospital in Halifax, it was she who ensured his body was transported to Hectanooga to be buried there, in accordance with his last wishes. After receiving numerous honours and accolades for her long-standing devotion to education

and community service, and after travelling widely as a humanitarian and educator, Elsie spent her final years in the Cape Sable area where she was born, and passed away at age ninety-nine in April of 2016.[510]

Maggie Labrador and her daughters Lucy and Elsie Charles had in their youths rebelled against the restrictive social norms and unpredictable economic environment confronting the Mi'kmaw community in southwestern Nova Scotia in the early to middle twentieth century, and sought wider horizons. These independent-minded women inspired others to overcome economic and social problems by showing alternative vistas for both contemplation and action.

Passed Over and Ignored, 1901–1958

Although there was dynamism within the Cape Sable Mi'kmaw population in the late nineteenth and early twentieth centuries, following Chief Stephen Wisow Jr.'s death in 1902 the federal Department of Indian Affairs and the province of Nova Scotia regarded the Mi'kmaw population of Yarmouth and southern Digby Counties as a leaderless scattering of people, lacking any political representation, and thus easily ignored. An Indian agent had been appointed for each county along the southwestern Nova Scotian coastline, with the mandate to submit an approximate census of the Indigenous population in each precinct, and to dispense meagre monetary aid where there were cases of infectious disease or where special relief was needed. Agent William H Whalen estimated in the fall of 1903 that there were seventy Mi'kmaq living in Yarmouth County, but made no attempt to determine if these persons had kinship ties with the seventy-seven individuals enumerated by agent R.G. Irvin in the spring of 1903 for Shelburne County. There were, of course. Population exchanges between the two areas were frequent. On 6 October 1907 Whalen told Frank Pedley, the deputy superintendent of Indian Affairs in Ottawa, that only two families resided on the Yarmouth reserve. The rest would "not reside on the reserve" and remained "scattered all over the country, some at Salmon River, Tusket, at the Forks, Pubnico Head and Hectanooga." He added that the health of many Mi'kmaq in Yarmouth County was "poor" but did not specify in what way.[511]

According to Indian agents' reports during the first decade of the twentieth century, most Mi'kmaw men in southwestern Nova Scotia acted as guides, worked as hands in saw mills or on log drives, made baskets, and fashioned mast hoops for the schooner fishing fleet and carved axe handles. Children attended school when they could. Houses consisted of log or frame structures that were often liberally whitewashed. Most Mi'kmaq were considered "sober and law-abiding." But being an Indian agent was a poorly paid, part-time position. The brevity and inconclusiveness of reports submitted to Ottawa suggested that few agents actually spent time trying to get to know their Mi'kmaw constituents well, though there were a few exceptions.[512] For instance, though he had few monetary resources at his disposal to assist the Mi'kmaq, Gordon L. Cann, the Indian agent for Yarmouth County in the late 1920s and early 1930s, regularly saved flattened cartons from his primary job as a tobacco jobber and used them to line the walls of the Mi'kmaq's otherwise poorly insulated frame dwellings.[513]

Indian agents in Nova Scotia were expected to act as front-liners in brokering government policies, especially those associated with centralization around and after the First World War and with recruitment of children into Indian residential school.[514] The scattered nature of the Mi'kmaw population and its frequent mobility within the old Cape Sable region, however, precluded these agents from easily finding and pressuring parents into releasing their children to the residential school system. The minuscule reserve at Yarmouth, moreover, was too insignificant for Ottawa to consider asking for its surrender, though it encouraged inhabitants to move en masse to Shubenacadie, as occurred in many other parts of southwestern Nova Scotia in the early 1940s. Much of the Yarmouth reserve's soil was gravelly glacial moraine, poor for farming, so it served mainly as a refuge and retirement settlement for elderly Mi'kmaq, including Lewis Luxey Jr. and his wife Mary Lucy Michael.[515] Luxey Jr., who moved to the Gravel Pit about 1900, relied on his unmarried son Ben to assist him with hunting and trapping until Ben grew too ill to enter the woods; he died at the age of forty-six on 3 March 1930 in Yarmouth. Lewis was away at the time, so Emeline Moore, identified on Ben's death certificate as his "aunt" – though her husband Tom Bartlett was actually Ben's father Louis's third cousin – had to inform the local authorities of Ben's passing.[516]

The acreage on Starr's Road also served as a manufacturing centre for industrious basketmakers like Lewis Luxey's daughter Josephine, born at Bear River on 17 April 1888. Josephine was a courageous and feisty woman who excelled at basketmaking, quillworking, and related fancy work. She travelled about the Maritimes as well as the New England states selling her wares at markets or from door to door on foot. Though she was unable to hear or speak as the result of a serious childhood ailment she contracted at the age of seven, she married twice and had seven children. Her first husband, James Pictou, whom she married in 1906, worked in the wintertime in the woods with his kin at Jordan River, and during the summer often travelled with her to sell baskets.[517] He and Josephine passed their skills in basketry and woodworking on to their children Clifford, Marguerite, Mary Rose, and John.[518] In his later years John Pictou Jr. and his wife Lillian would run a well-known basket and handcraft shop along Starr's Road.[519] When James Pictou died in 1919 Josephine married a second time, to Wilfred Robinson, whose parents hailed from Meteghan. The couple had three sons, Louis Bernard, Peter, and James Albert. [520] Louis Bernard married Viola Hood, and the couple had eight children. Most of these, upon reaching adulthood, would retain close connections with the Acadia band. For over seven decades Josephine Luxey's industry and artistry gave a positive spirit of continuity to the Yarmouth reserve despite its unglamorous name of the "Gravel Pit." Josephine, who regarded the Starr's Road settlement as her home base throughout her adult life, died at Yarmouth Regional Hospital in 1990, reputedly soon after celebrating her 102nd birthday. (A site on Ancestry.com, however, has her living to 103 years, from 1887 to 1990.)[521]

Despite its small resident population, the Starr's Road community continued as the hub of the Cape Sable band, which in the early decades of the twentieth century was only a shadow of its former self. After Chief Stephen Wisow Jr.'s death in c.1902, the band had neither chief nor council and was viewed as politically impotent by Ottawa, and even by some members of the broader Mi'kmaw community. In 1891 Chief John Noel at Shubenacadie proclaimed that the jurisdiction of the Bear River leader included Yarmouth and Shelburne Counties, a claim voiced by other Mi'kmaw leaders into the 1920s.[522] During these years there were no Mi'kmaw advocates in the Yarmouth area calling for better living conditions in the frigid shanties of the logging camps. And only one or two from further east along the Atlantic coast pressed for rights to hunt and fish at sites frequented by their people for generations, but now usurped by government fiat for the use of others. William Labrador of Wildcat launched a campaign at Bridgewater in support of Mi'kmaw salmon fishing rights, and was arrested for his efforts.[523] Labrador acted courageously and alone, for the lives of most Mi'kmaq had become tied to the rhythms of the seasonal harvest cycles, fall guiding and trapping activities, and the winter and spring requirements of the logging industry in the woods and on the rivers. They had little time or energy to pursue any major Indigenous rights campaign.

In 1914, American anthropologist Frank Gouldsmith Speck, conducting research on Mi'kmaw family hunting territories in southwestern Nova Scotia, failed to distinguish tracts belonging to hunters and trappers of the Cape Sable band from hunting territories maintained by families of the Bear River band.[524] And since Speck contended that the constellations of neighbouring family hunting territories spread out over the landscape might reflect land use patterns going back a hundred or more years, the results of his study suggested that the Cape Sable group had become defunct well before 1900. A hunting territory on Medway Lake, Annapolis County, identified as belonging in the 1850s to "Stephen Bartlett (Wisa'n, 'yellow')" was, by virtue of its geographic location, classified as part of the Bear River band's territorial holdings.[525] Though in the eyes of academia and Ottawa officialdom the Cape Sable band by 1900 had been reduced by force of circumstances into a political nonentity, a residual dynamism still lingered within the Cape Sable community. Over the next three decades this group would weather, not in small part because of its population's highly dispersed settlement pattern, the challenges of outmigration, government-sponsored centralization, and agents seeking Mi'kmaw children for the residential school system.

The scattered populace of Yarmouth and Shelburne Counties proved especially inaccessible to prying external agencies, and in this its experiences differed radically from those of the neighbouring Bear River band, who lost residents to centralization and the residential school at Shubenacadie. Other than at Yarmouth, where rarely fewer than three families lived on a permanent basis during these years, Indian agents lacked the means to track down even a small cross-section of the Cape Sable Mi'kmaw community in order to access its children's

educational status. Yet children attended school when they could, as learning to read, write, and do arithmetic remained a high priority among certain Mi'kmaw families. This stood some Mi'kmaw individuals in good stead when they negotiated to buy freehold property, which happened fairly frequently around West Pubnico and near Meteghan in Digby County. Such transactions, however, occurred beneath the radar of Indian Affairs. In 1990 a local historian named Jerry Bartlett, son of John Bartlett and Marguerite Bartlett and who hailed originally from Shelburne County, informed Janet Chute and her field assistant Doris Labradore that the Bartlett and Alexis families in particular wanted secure title to their land and resources in the face of settler intrusions onto their traditional territory.[526]

The number of Mi'kmaw property owners in the Cape Sable area was always small. The greatest number clustered along the Pubnico Lake Road en route to Great Pubnico Lake. In the mid 1950s the government jettisoned its earlier centralization policy and began compiling a schedule of reserves that would be officially retained within the province. To facilitate the administrative reorganization, in July of 1957 Indian Affairs' regional supervisor F. Bart McKinnon and his associate D. R. Cassie contacted Mi'kmaq living in Yarmouth, Shelburne, and Queens counties to find out, among other things, what aspirations they might have for the future. They encountered only three families on the Yarmouth reserve, but these residents, who occupied two frame houses along Starr's Road, proved fiercely loyal to what they viewed as their group's distinctive Mi'kmaw identity. They wanted a political entity to be established in the Cape Sable area, capable of representing their specialized interests, though also attached to the broader framework of administrative structures being established by the government throughout the Atlantic Provinces. One resident, Charlie Paul, was exasperated at having been urged during the centralization era to move to Shubenacadie. He had been born at West Pubnico, relocated his family to Yarmouth in 1932, and had no intention of ever moving anywhere else again.[527]

Further east on the Wildcat reserve in Queens, eighty-six-year-old John Jeremy, a grandson on his maternal side of Chief Lewis Luxey Sr.,[528] impressed upon government investigators that the local Mi'kmaq's mobile and highly dispersed settlement pattern arose from the lack of steady employment in any one area for any stretch of time. He explained that most men in Yarmouth. Shelburne, and Queens Counties worked in the woods during the winters, fished in the spring, travelled to New England to harvest potatoes in the summer months, and picked blueberries in the fall. Any political structure designed to represent these people would have to consider these realities.[529] But John Jeremy's words went unheeded. McKinnon and Cassie submitted a plan to Ottawa, dated 4 December 1956, gauged to divide the mainland Nova Scotia Mi'kmaq into six separate Indian Act bands. The Cape Sable band was not one of them.[530] Instead, residents of scattered Mi'kmaw communities stretching eastward from Yarmouth to Gold River in Lunenburg County unilaterally were placed on a "general list" and allocated only a spokesperson, rather than a chief and council, to voice their interests and grievances. No consideration whatsoever was given to the continuing integrity of the Cape Sable group.[531] Despite being once again ignored by officialdom, the Cape Sable's Mi'kmaw population retained its social cohesiveness. Since its male members had not been recruited into the banks schooner fishing industry or the building trades, the Mi'kmaw population still manifested little hierarchy according to income and class.[532] In lieu of such distinctions, webs of family ties predominated. Within the Alexis family alone, members of the Luxey and Bartlett branches recognized and exercised bonds between cousins until the third descending generation, and sometimes even beyond.[533]

Birth of the Acadia First Nation

The latent dynamism at the core of the Cape Sable group and its political associates was not dormant for long after 1960. Spurred on in part by the growth of Aboriginal rights campaigns elsewhere in the mid-1960s, a new generation of local leaders convened meetings to discuss and further the distinctive interests of Mi'kmaq residing along the Atlantic coast from southern Digby County to Lunenburg County. In 1968 these meetings culminated in the formation of a new Mi'kmaw political entity, called the "Acadia band." Charlie Labrador of Queens County and Charlie Paul of Yarmouth County were vocal advocates for this body, which originally was to follow a system that embodied life chiefs responsible for a scattered constituency, loyal to its core no matter where in the region its members resided. Charlie

Labrador was proud of his ancestral connections to the Alexis chiefs of the Cape Sable district, as his mother Beatrice Jeremy had been a granddaughter of Joseph Jeremy and Kate Luxey of Molega and Wildcat. In 1968 he was installed as the Acadia band's first chief.[534]

Charlie only headed this new political entity for two years, from 1968 to 1971. Without government economic assistance, he could not carry out his administrative duties as chief in town and still earn enough from his labours in the woods to support his family. In consequence, the leadership succession policy that guided the formation of the Acadia band had to be revised. The original goal of maintaining a sequence of life chiefs, whose initial appointments would be determined by a council developed for the purpose, was dropped. It proved unworkable in the twentieth-century economic and political context. Instead, the Acadia band opted to adopt a triennial elective system, similar to other Maritime bands. When Charlie Labrador stepped down, Charlie Paul became the first chief elected under the new system.[535]

Chief Paul and his councillors in the early 1970s assumed jurisdiction over six reserve communities spanning four counties. Running from east to southwest, these were Gold River in Lunenburg County, Wildcat and the small Medway River and Ponhook reserves in Queens County, one thousand acres on the Clyde River in Shelburne County, and the reserve on Starr's Road in Yarmouth County.[536] Ottawa meanwhile contended that the seven hundred acres set aside for the Mi'kmaq by Joseph Howe in 1843 at Great Pubnico Lake could not be considered as one of the Acadia band's holdings since, it was argued, Howe had failed to confirm this tract as a reserve prior to Confederation. But what the band retained from its traditional mandate that distinguished it from most other Mi'kmaw administrative structures was its focus on providing adequate political representation for the interests of a widely scattered populace, the greater part of which lived off reserve.

By the early 1980s what became known as the Acadia First Nation began an innovative policy of enabling a sizeable dispersed population to retain vital links with its group's headquarters on the Yarmouth reserve. The Yarmouth reserve's land base comprised only 3 per cent of the Acadia band, making it the second smallest reserve in the band, though it has a greater population than all the other component reserves combined. The sense of cohesion within the Cape Sable group attached to this entity has been born out of great political, economic, and social struggle, for it is a community that, though widely dispersed geographically, remained for generations held together by close-knit, reticulate webs of kinship ties and threads of common interest in preserving certain cherished territorial tracts. Many persons belonging to the Acadia First Nation still can and do trace lines of descent either on their father's or mother's side – and sometimes both – to past Cape Sable chiefs. The inclusion of persons of Acadian, British, German, African, American, and First Nations ancestry other than Mi'kmaq within the mix has only enriched the matrix and imbued it with diverse skills and talents.

Major changes that affected the community in positive ways followed in relatively short order. Bill C-31, passed by the federal government in 1986, allowed individuals who had lost their Mi'kmaw legal status either because their father was not Mi'kmaq or because of superior educational achievements to reclaim their status on the basis of their mother's and, in many instances, their grandparents' status.[537] The younger Robinsons – grandchildren of Josephine Alexis (Luxey) and great-grandchildren of Lewis Luxey Jr. – fell into this category, and upon regaining their Aboriginal status soon occupied a number of vital leadership roles. At time of writing (2019), Louis Bernard Robinson and Viola Robinson's daughter, Deborah Robinson, has occupied the office of chief at the Acadia First Nation for over thirty years.[538]

Today the Acadia First Nation embraces five reserve communities, as well as a sizeable off-reserve Mi'kmaw population that remains dispersed throughout Digby, Yarmouth, Shelburne, Queens, Lunenburg, and parts of Annapolis counties.[539] The Yarmouth reserve occupies 27.57 hectares of land lying off a busy stretch of road adjacent to the Yarmouth airport, about three kilometres east of the town of Yarmouth.[540] The reserve has three roads, each named after a specific branch of the Alexis family. A recent road extension called "Luxey's Lane" leads to the modern First Nation Band Office and Health Service Centre.[541] Bartlett's Lane, a tributary road, intersects this thoroughfare, and Robinson Road, a residential street, lies not far away. The Acadia First Nation in 1993, furthermore, acquired twenty-three hundred acres of land in Gardeners Mill, near Kemptville in Yarmouth County, as a gift from its previous owner, John Cook.[542] While offering many opportunities for future economic development, this tract in the interior of Yarmouth County is also of major historical importance to the Cape Sable Mi'kmaw population.

Two prominent leaders who once pitched their camps in the Carleton Lake area were Bartholomew Alexis Sr. and Peter Charles Sulno. Their wisdom and determination guided the Cape Sable group during the difficult years after the American Revolution when waves of settlers threatened to overwhelm the Mi'kmaw population. In the 1780s and 1790s, when prospects for the group looked bleak, Chief Charles Alexis's refusal to allow the government to continue to dispute the validity of his people's agency inspired other Mi'kmaw leaders to follow his example and stand up for their interests. Until the late 1800s this led generation after generation of Alexis leaders to become involved to some degree in pressing for Mi'kmaw land and resource rights. Their determination was fueled by traditional beliefs regarding how Mi'kmaw leaders should act on behalf of their people. This era terminated with the death of Stephen Bartlett Jr. *dit* Wisow in 1901. Following the death of this last "traditional chief," Ottawa refused to recognize any form of Cape Sable chief and council, or to provide additional property to supplement the minuscule reserve at Yarmouth.

During the early twentieth century government administrators, and even the well-known anthropologist Frank Gouldsmith Speck, who specialized in investigating Northeastern Algonquian culture, subsumed what remained of the Cape Sable band under the jurisdiction of Bear River. As a historic entity, the Cape Sable band might warrant academic scrutiny for its interaction with French administrators and fur traders, the integral roles it played during eighteenth-century intercolonial conflicts, and even for the Mi'kmaw rights campaign launched in 1793 by Charles Alexis. Yet by 1914 Speck evinced no interest in seeking any vestigial traditional practices that might be associated with the Cape Sable group.[543] Like the Ottawa bureaucrats, he believed its demise began with the Loyalists' coming to southwestern Nova Scotia, between 1783 and 1785.

Despite this short-sighted, erroneous view that dominated governmental and academic perspectives from 1871 to 1967, in less than seventy years the Cape Sable band has risen like a phoenix from the ashes to regain much of its former political stature and independence. The Cape Sable band historically constituted one of the most prominent Mi'kmaw entities in the Northeast. Its warriors participated in intercolonial wars, its diplomats participated in peacemaking councils, and its economic middlemen in the late seventeenth and eighteenth centuries grew prosperous traversing trade routes west to Montreal and beyond.

By the first decades of the twentieth century, however, it had grown invisible to those who occupied the corridors of power. In 1967, to gain official recognition from Ottawa, it joined forces with several smaller Mi'kmaw communities along the Atlantic coast, from Gold River in Lunenburg County to Wildcat in Queens County. Though this concerted action is sometimes portrayed as a marriage of convenience fostered mainly by outside government intervention, these component communities had in the past produced leaders who supported the district leader, Charles Alexis, in his appeals on behalf of a broad Mi'kmaw constituency. Together they succeeded in preserving a distinctive Indigenous identity in southwestern Nova Scotia. Their legacy embraces a story of a population besieged for generations by formidable political, economic, and social challenges thrust upon them by the growth of the British colonial regime in the Northeast. Yet, by retaining strong bond of kinship within a widespread populace, they refused to become socially fragmented, but rather were sustained by the activities of chiefs of outstanding fortitude, determination, and resilience. Several present-day leaders of the Acadia First Nation trace ancestral ties back over the generations to Chief Charles Alexis, either through the Luxeys or through the Bartletts. And it can be stated with confidence that if Charles Alexis were alive today, they would be making their collective patriarch proud.

– Janet E. Chute and Travis Pinn

Acknowledgments: The authors are grateful for assistance, dating back to the early 1990s, from Bernard Amiro, Jean Babin, Jerry Bartlett, Tim Bernard, Ruth Randall Cann, Father Clarence-J. d'Entremont, Bernie Doucet, Riel d'Entremont and other employees of the Musée des Acadiens and Archives, Mrs. Barney Francis, Carrie Gloade, Deborah Gloade, Doris Labradore, Ian Lawrence, Frank Jeremy, Donald M. Julien, John Muise *dit* "Le Dude," Charlie Paul, Peter Partington, Philip Partington, Lillian Pictou, Travis Pinn, Jeff Purdy, Rose Purdy, Melanie Robinson-Purdy, Linda Rafuse – who is curator of the Simeon Perkins Museum and a great-great granddaughter of Johnny Muree and Unica McGray – and Viola Robinson.

2

Jehan Grand Claude: Patriarch of the Claude/Glode/Gloade Family of Southwestern Nova Scotia

The Grand Claudes

The Claude/Glode/Gloade family is one of the oldest and largest of the Mi'kmaw families of southwestern Nova Scotia, a region known to the Indigenous population as *Kespukwitk*, or *Gespugwitg*, meaning "last land." The surname "Glode" arose in the late eighteenth century from the French word "Claude" and has gone through variant spellings. "Gloade" was adopted in the 1880s in central Nova Scotia, while "Glode" remained how the surname was, and still is, spelled in parts of Digby and Yarmouth Counties.[1]

During the seventeenth and early eighteenth centuries the family's ancestor, Jehan Grand Claude (1640–c.1730), in the spring and fall camped at Lequille, near a riverine eel and salmon fishery at the base of an escarpment east of Annapolis Royal.[2] The headwaters of the Mersey-Medway river system took their rise just east of Lequille.[3] In late fall Jehan and other members of the Port Royal band, numbering just over one hundred persons in 1708, travelled down the upper reaches of the Mersey River to their winter hunting territories in the interior of present-day Annapolis and Queens counties.[4] The Glode hunting and fishing territory was extensive, flanking the Mersey-Medway river system, extending from the Annapolis Basin to present-day Liverpool and east along the Atlantic coast to the La Have River.[5] What is now Liverpool in the seventeenth century was called "Port Rossignol" by the French

and *Ogomkigeak*, meaning "dry sandy place," by the Mi'kmaq. *Ogomkigeak* was a summer encampment lying near headlands where hunters could take water fowl.

After spring fishing at Lequille, Mi'kmaw families journeyed to series of ancient raised beaches along the Bear River, which runs along the Annapolis County–Digby County border. From a coastal camping ground, which later was given the name "Bear River," they set out in canoes to the shores of an inlet of the Annapolis Basin called, in French, the *Ranquet* or *Ranquette*, just west of the modern town of Digby, to hunt sea mammals.[6] Seasonally Mi'kmaw fur trade middlemen left from either Port Rossignol or Port Royal, canoed to Lake Kejimkujik, and then followed a water and portage route to present-day Weymouth in Digby County where they accessed the Gulf of Maine. They then followed the coast to where they could cross the Bay of Fundy and continue north to Quebec or south to New England. Mi'kmaq who remained in *Kespukwitk* travelled up and down the Atlantic coast, pitching their wigwams at traditional encampment sites. It was an ancient pattern of movement that relied heavily on the availability of riverine fish.[7]

The Mi'kmaq knew the interior of *Kespukwitk* intimately, a fact recognized by the French intendant Jacques de Muelles in 1685 when he accompanied Mi'kmaw guides on an arduous canoe trip across the province from the Annapolis Basin to Port

Rossignol.[8] In the late seventeenth century the river abounded in salmon, gaspereau, and eels while lands on either side had caribou, moose, and copious fur bearers. One of the most productive eeling weirsites, later known as Indian Gardens, lay in present-day Queens County. Since the territory was also rich in furs, Jehan Grand Claude and his trading contemporaries at times enjoyed considerable affluence. One can imagine Jehan attending festivities at Port Royal garbed in a fine cotton shirt, satin turban, and silver trade ornaments, all obtained from the French.

The Mersey-Medway River system, whose headwaters took their rise just east of Lequille, was central to the Claude/Glode family's travel in the interior. In the vicinity of present-day Kentville, Kings County, a well-worn trail also ascended the South Mountain to Gaspereau Lake in Kings County, pressed over the divide, and then traced a line of lakes, streams, and portages to the headwaters of the La Have River. Jehan Grand Claude fished, hunted, and trapped inland in a tract that lay between Annapolis Royal and the Atlantic coast, and that formed his main hunting territory, until his death around 1730. The Glode/Gloade family today still regards this vast region as a kind of spiritual homeland, as it formed the hunting grounds of their ancestors.

Jehan Claude as an Elderly Peacekeeper and Diplomat, 1722 to 1730

In 1708 Jehan Grand Claude, also known as "Jackish," was sixty-eight years old and his wife, Marie Medosset, was fifty-five.[9] The couple had five sons and one daughter: René was born in 1685, Claude in 1687, Marie Catherine in 1689, Joseph in 1691, Martin in 1693, and François in 1703. René Grand Claude, the eldest son, was married by 1708 and he and his wife Marie had a one-year-old daughter, Cecille.[10] Though his father was a prominent member of the Port Royal band he was not its leader; that position was occupied from 1700 to 1768 by Jean-Baptiste Thomas Albiston, also known as Thomas Albissou or Chief Thoma.[11] Rather than focusing on political matters, Jehan directed his attention to new trading opportunities opening up within Acadian communities at La Have and elsewhere along the Atlantic coast.

Though Jehan Grand Claude knew that peace and political stability were good for trade, prior to the British conquest of Port Royal in 1710 he manifested little interest in acting as a spokesperson on behalf of his people. This suddenly changed in 1722, when he, at age eighty-two, was thrust into a lead negotiator role by a set of unique circumstances. Influenced by their Algonquian-speaking neighbours the Eastern Abenaki, who denounced New England's appropriation of their hunting and fishing grounds, the Annapolis group resisted British usurpation of their weirsites along the Annapolis River. In response the English, fearing attacks on their garrison at Fort Anne, in 1714 engaged Mohawk warriors to repel any hostile advances from those they viewed as "enemy Indians." The Mi'kmaw population consequently drained away from Annapolis Royal. Where in 1708 there had been 102 Mi'kmaq at Port Royal, by 1722 there were ten families, numbering in all only 43 individuals.[12]

The Mi'kmaq also grew incensed at English settler intrusions onto lands at Minas, now Horton, without any consultation with the Mi'kmaw proprietors. By the spring of 1720 this discontent had reached a crescendo and, encouraged by the French at Louisbourg, the Minas band spearheaded a devastating attack on the British fishing depot at Canso.[13] It was the preamble of a conflict known in New England as "Dummer's War," which spread to Nova Scotia. The perpetrators then harassed New England shipping along the Atlantic coast and in the Bay of Fundy. Soon after the Canso attack, eleven Mi'kmaw warriors under a Minas chief, Pierre Nunquadden (now Knockwood), raided a vessel belonging to John Alden, a New England merchant, and carried away valuable merchandise. In October of the same year, Pierre Couaret (Momcharret) *dit* Cellier and his brother Antoine delivered a letter to Fort Anne declaring that the British had no right to enter the Minas district without their consent. God had given them their lands, they proclaimed, to which they had as much right as the trees and grass had to grow in the field, and they would remain masters of it, independent of the British or the French.[14]

Despite growing tensions elsewhere, throughout 1721 the Annapolis band upheld a fragile peace with the British. Chief Jean-Baptiste Thoma tried to calm English fears by asserting that those under his immediate aegis would not take up arms, though he failed to persuade neighbouring chiefs to commence talks with the governor and council at Fort Anne.[15] When Governor Richard Philipps began to exhibit periodic bouts of paranoia, usually elicited by successive reports of Eastern Abenaki attacks on outlying New

England settlements, he instructed Lieutenant Governor John Doucett and Major Paul Mascarene of the Governor's Council in 1722 to secure and impound Mi'kmaw hostages in order to secure the good behaviour of Mi'kmaq living around the fort. It could not have been too difficult for the English to round up Jehan Grand Claude's sixty-nine-year-old wife Marie Medosset, thirty-three-year-old daughter Marie Catherine, and nineteen-year-old son François, who at the time were likely focused on the Lequille weir fishery. Marie Catherine and François joined nineteen other Mi'kmaw men, women, and children being retained as hostages and for several months endured life in Fort Anne's gloomy, dank dungeon.[16] Meanwhile the elderly Jehan Grand Claude, now exclusively referred to in British accounts as "Jackish" ("Jack-*ech*" or "Little Jack"), and his sons René, Joseph, Claude, and Martin escaped detection.

On Friday, 19 October 1722, Jehan Grand Claude approached Fort Anne and asked for the release of his wife, daughter, and son.[17] This the council agreed to do, but on one condition –that he submit to the last clause of a proclamation drafted at Canso by Governor Philipps by which Jehan had to swear not to do "anything in prejudice to the Government & that he would give himself Information of any who might have any evil Designe against it."[18] Even if he agreed, however, he would not get his wish immediately. Instead, he was told to stay near the fort until ordered to come to the negotiating table at an undetermined future date.

A directive finally reached Jehan the last week of October instructing him to make an appearance before the Annapolis council. Accompanied this time by his sons Claude and Martin, he arrived at the fort on 2 November 1722, only to be told that the council members had to deliberate further on his case. It was possible that too much time had elapsed between the issuing of Philipps's proclamation and Jehan's request to be included under its provisions. This doubtless came as a surprise to the elderly Mi'kmaq, given the amount of time he had already had to wait, but eventually the council determined that "as the Proclamation had been so long in coming to this Place," he might, after all, "Embrace the Benefit of said Clause." The British commended Jehan's family on their tranquility and good behaviour, and added that "they or Others who have Demean'd themselves Peaceably during these Troubles, or not acted Violently against his Majesty's subjects, should be Admitted upon such

Tarmes (*sic*, Terms) as aforesaid, the 19th of October Last prescribed to them."[19] The actual signing of the treaty by Jehan Grand Claude, whose three family members had to suffer for months in prison as the result of English fears, took place on 5 November 1722, after which his wife, son, and daughter were finally freed.[20]

The terms of the 1722 pact forbade Jehan to keep company with "enemy Indians" such as the Momcharrets, seen as fallen under French sway.[21] Such sanctions held little weight within the Mi'kmaw community, however, and failed to drive a wedge between Jehan and his trading associate Pierre Momcharret *dit* Cellier. The two men continued to interact amiably, as did their children and grandchildren. Since Jehan emerged from the treaty proceedings of November 1722 politically unscathed, other Mi'kmaq could not have construed his willingness to sign as an act of abject submission to British authority or wholly as an expedient ploy to liberate his wife, son, and daughter from Fort Anne's dungeon.

A close reading of the Annapolis Council minutes for 5 November 1722 reveals that Jehan actually exercised a degree of agency within the negotiating forum. First, the council, after talking with him, made several minor amendments to the original terms of Philipps's proclamation that were then translated into French for his "better Understanding the Same."[22] Second, the provisions were read aloud before they were proffered to Jehan for signing, and the elderly Mi'kmaq and the few associates who accompanied him were furnished with copies of the treaty to take away with them.[23] Finally and most important, Jehan wielded sufficient influence to bring other Mi'kmaq to the negotiating table who, like him, wanted a politically stable environment in which to pursue their entrepreneurial goals.[24] On 12 November 1722 three other Mi'kmaw leaders, among them the Annapolis head chief, Jean-Baptiste Thoma, arrived at Fort Anne to embrace the protection of the British government, and they, too, received the terms of the agreement translated into French.[25] Those who signed treaty and received British passports could pass unmolested throughout the province to meet with fur buyers, and presumably also travel to trade with New England merchants.

In 1726 Jehan's third son Joseph inscribed his mark on a peace and friendship treaty made between the English and the Mi'kmaq at Annapolis Royal. The document was a ratification of a treaty signed between New England and the Eastern Abenaki the preceding year in Boston and heralded the end of Dummer's War. René, Claude, and François signed after him, although their father's name does not appear, which suggests he had transferred his duties as chief to Joseph by this time. Joseph may have been specially delegated by the eighty-six-year-old Jehan to represent him at the treaty proceedings. Joseph distinguished himself from his brothers by signing his name "Joseph Le Grand," rather than "Grand Glode." He also, unlike most Mi'kmaw leaders at the time, accompanied his signature mark with a totemic representation. Joseph's totem did not depict an animal or plant entity, as was usually the case among Algonquian speakers, but was wholly abstract in character: a rectangle set on edge to look like a diamond, with a cross inside. The cross's lines emanated from the four corners, similar to the cross of St. Andrews of Scotland. This flag-like mark may also have been used by Jehan.[26] Interestingly, of several signed copies of the treaty that have been preserved, the treaty document bearing the totemic marks is the only one on which the Grand Claudes's names appear. Evidently the English made some effort to track them down and ensure their presence at the final signing.[27]

For years Jehan Grand Claude had encouraged his sons, principally for trade purposes, to forge close ties with French and *métis* in the fur-trading and fishing communities along the eastern Atlantic seaboard. But there also was a religious component to these connections. In 1722 Abbé Antoine Gaulin was appointed by the French regime at Louisbourg to serve the Mi'kmaq and Acadians along the Atlantic coast. Though Jehan's sons continued to attend sacraments in the Roman Catholic parish of St. Jean-Baptiste at Annapolis Royal, after 1738 they also travelled to the coast to meet with the itinerant French missionary to the Mi'kmaq, Abbé Le Loutre.[28]

During his long life Jehan Grand Claude remained on peaceful terms with the British. His sons followed his pacific bent by remaining neutral during the 1722–25 conflict and in subsequent intercolonial conflicts. Jehan died around 1730 at about ninety years of age. He had weathered the effects of the trade rivalries between Charles La Tour and d'Aulnay Charnisay, seen the British occupy Port Royal from 1657 to 1667, stood by as the fort was returned to France under the Treaty of Breda, retreated from Sir William Phips's attack on Port Royal in 1690, and watched as a French governor of Acadia, Joseph Robineau (also

Robinau) de Villebon, set up his headquarters on the Saint John River from which he deployed warriors to raid New England.

French control of the lands flanking the Annapolis Basin ended in 1710 with the capture of Port Royal by a New England force led by Sir Francis Nicholson, followed by the consolidation of British suzerainty over peninsular Nova Scotia under the terms of the Treaty of Utrecht of 1713. Despite the waves of unrest that swept over the countryside from 1722 to 1730, the Annapolis band retained its territories inviolate. Jehan Grand Claude advocated the need for political and economic stability in southwestern Nova Scotia so that the harvesting and marketing of resources from these lands could continue unabated. Other than Intendant de Muelles and a few intrepid traders who followed in the wake of Captain Pierre Rossignol, the interior fastnesses of present-day Annapolis, Queens, and Lunenburg counties remained unpenetrated by Europeans. The integrity of the Mi'kmaq's land and resources, especially the riverine fisheries, in this area would not be compromised until the mid-1780s, with the coming of Loyalists following the American Revolution.

Marriage Alliances within Atlantic Coast Fur-Trading Society

Following the death of his first wife about 1720, Jehan's eldest son René (1685–c.1730) wed Françoise Mius, a daughter of Philippe II Mius d'Entremont *dit* d'Azy and Marie, Mius's second Mi'kmaq consort.[29] Philippe II d'Azy, who was a son of Baron Philippe I Mius d'Entremont of the seigneury of Pobomcoup, now East Pubnico in Yarmouth County, maintained a trading post at Chichimichecady on Second Peninsula, near the present-day town of Lunenburg. René's second marriage brought him into close contact with *métis* and Mi'kmaw trade middlemen throughout southwestern Nova Scotia, since the barony of Pobomcoup constituted a major transshipment station for furs to France. After their marriage, René and Françoise lived at La Hève, eastward of Françoise's father's trading centre on Second Peninsula. Following René's death about 1734, Françoise Mius on 26 August 1735 married Chief Pierre Momcharret *dit* Cellier of Minas. Momcharret recently had lost his first wife, Louise Innocent.[30] René's brother Joseph Grand Claude also died before he could exercise a significant influence on fur trade affairs. After her release from Fort Anne in 1722, his sister Marie Catherine also fails to appear again in the documentary record.

The case was different for Claude Grand Claude (1687–c.1760), whose offspring continued to live around Annapolis Royal. Claude married a *métis* woman, Marie Pierre, and the names of three of their children – Marie, born in the early 1720s, Denis, born in 1728, and Charles, born in 1732 – appear in the registers of the Parish of St. Jean-Baptiste, Annapolis Royal.[31] Though it is not known whom Denis and Charles later married, on 25 August 1735 their sister Marie wed Charles de Perisse, son of Guillaume de Perisse of Annapolis and Anne Eptemec of La Hève (an Indigenous and *métis* coastal community renamed "La Have" after 1760. Claude's wife Marie may have been French.[32] It has also been argued that the de Perisse family may have descended from Semcoudech, a Port Royal Mi'kmaq who early in the seventeenth century took the name "Paris" (or "Perisse") after visiting Paris, France.[33]

Martin Grand Claude (1693–c.1760) became the best known of Jehan Grand Claude's sons. The second-youngest son, Martin, in his youth travelled from Lequille to La Hève and back again on a seasonal basis. To do this he followed the route from Gaspereau Lake to the upper reaches of the La Have River, since the Mersey River route involved canoeing for a stretch along the Atlantic coast. It was a practice followed by many Port Royal Mi'kmaw youth, since it introduced them to *métis* women from coastal fur-trading families as well as to new trading prospects. On 25 February 1727, when he was thirty-four, Martin married Marguerite Lejeune at Annapolis Royal.[34] Marguerite was the daughter of François Lejeune *dit* Briart (or Briard), an Acadian, and Marie Egighighes, the daughter of a prominent La Hève Mi'kmaw family.[35] Martin and Marguerite spent most of the year at La Hève, though the couple brought their infant son, Paul Martin Grand Claude (1735–c.1820), to be baptized at Annapolis Royal on 25 August 1735, the same day that Claude's daughter Marie wed Charles de Perisse.[36] Martin Grand Claude and his wife had two other sons, Martin Jr. and Nicolas, whose names do not appear in the documentary record until 1769.[37] Meanwhile, Jehan Grand Claude's youngest son, François Grand Claude, born in 1703, married Marie Cellier *dit* Boitou (or Bouta), a daughter of Pierre Momcharret *dit* Bouta, a fur trade middleman and brother of Chief

Pierre Momcharret of Minas. François and Marie had a son François, baptized in 1735.[38]

The Grand Claudes at La Hève: 1727–1760

After their marriage in 1727, Martin Grand Claude and his wife Marguerite Lejeune joined the French coastal settlement of La Hève. The couple established close ties with neighbouring Mi'kmaq and *métis* who formed a tightly knit Mi'kmaq social entity, having frequently relied on one another for support in the past. The Acadian and *métis* living at La Point at the mouth of the La Hève River (known as "Fleuve La Hève" by the Acadian population) by the 1730s included the descendants of Pierre Lejeune *dit* Briart and his brother, Martin Lejeune *dit* Briart, although Martin later moved to Port Maltois (now Port Medway, in Queens County).[39] Their sister Jeanne Lejeune was the paternal grandmother of Martin Grand Claude's wife, Marguerite Lejeune. Pierre Lejeune *dit* Briart Sr., the paternal ancestor of all three, had first arrived in at La Hève in 1632.

Like Port Royal, La Hève had a tumultuous history. The settlement's founder, Isaac de Razilly, envisioned the small community on the point as the future capital of Acadia. Not long afterwards La Hève became a farming centre and port of call for fishing vessels, with a chapel, a fort, and a school run by the Capuchin friars for local Mi'kmaq children. Southward, at Port Rossignol, Nicolas Denys operated a shore fishery and relied on Mi'kmaw labour to supply riverine fish, especially salmon.

Following de Razilly's sudden death in 1636, La Hève experienced a series of severe disruptions that caused the Lejeune family to turn to the Mi'kmaq for support. Charles de Menou d'Aulnay Charnissay, who kept a watchful eye on potential trading rivals, tried to remove the entire La Hève Acadian population to Port Royal in the late 1640s. Several families of French and *métis*, among them the Lejeunes, escaped at this time with their Mi'kmaw kin into the interior, from which they only emerged only after d'Aulnay's death in 1650. Shortly after they returned, their settlement was destroyed a second time in 1653 by d'Aulnay's creditor, Emmanuel LeBorgne. Since LeBorgne's men razed all the buildings, not even sparing the chapel, the French and *métis* again had to flee temporarily into the woods.[40]

La Hève's displaced inhabitants returned within two years and resumed fishing, farming, and trading.

They built log cabins with pole and bark roofs within the confines of fenced garden lots. In 1684 Governor François-Marie Perrot provided a measure of defence for the small settlement by restoring Fort Sainte-Marie de Grace at the mouth of the river and establishing a small local garrison. He also erected a chapel and solicited priests to conduct the sacraments for the Acadians, *métis*, and Mi'kmaq.[41] Except for a brief need to escape from a party of hostile New Englanders in 1705, the predominately *métis* population remained until the late 1750s, when the British ransacked La Hève and deported what Acadians they could find. Between 1705 and 1758 some La Hève Mi'kmaq launched retaliatory raids against New England and British shipping, a practice encouraged by the French. After Fortress Louisbourg was completed by 1720, the French authorities took a keen interest in the La Hève community, since they saw it as a potential recruiting ground for warriors in the event of an outbreak of war between the French and English crowns.[42] They further noted that the La Hève Mi'kmaq seasonally visited the Annapolis area and in 1739 even claimed that La Hève and Annapolis Royal "forment une village," owing to the regularity of population flow between the two settlements. From La Hève Mi'kmaq could travel to either Minas or Annapolis Royal in just three days, giving the small coastal community strategic significance.[43]

When Martin Grand Claude transferred his entrepreneurial focus from Port Royal/Annapolis Royal to La Hève, it meant shifting his market from the trading centre at the seigneury of Pobomcoup (now East Pubnico), established in 1653 by Baron Philippe Mius d'Entremont and carried on by the baron's sons, to localized exchanges with Acadian and *métis* buyers. Throughout King George's War (1744–48) and the Seven Years' War (1756–63), Martin Grand Claude, like most of his Acadian associates, sought to retain a neutral stance *vis à vis* the British, even though in 1749 the British devastated their community's economic prospects by placing an embargo on French coastal trade.

In 1753, to avoid Governor Edward Cornwallis's scalp bounty levied in the fall of 1749, as well as to initiate trade with the British in lieu of the French, Chief Claude Gisigash (Egighighes) of La Hève extended peace overtures to Halifax, a policy likely supported by Martin Grand Claude as well, who was related to Gisigash through his wife.[44] While Abbé Le Loutre urged the Mi'kmaq to participate in attacks on Lunenburg settlers, both Egighighes and Martin Grand Claude left raiding to their more bellicose neighbours, among them François Mius and the related Labrador family who resided in the woods between Merliguèche (now Lunenburg) and the upper reaches of the La Hève River.[45]

The final blow to La Hève's trading community accompanied the Acadian Grand Dérangement between 1755 and 1759. Many of the Lejeunes, experienced with these sudden disruptions, proved prescient and moved in the early 1750s to a remote northern sector of the Bras d'Or Lake in Cape Breton or to New Brunswick, and so avoided deportation by the English.[46] Martin Grand Claude did not follow his *métis* kin to Cape Breton, however, but likely stockpiled furs and other commodities to be marketed in Halifax or Liverpool once the Seven Years' War ended and peace returned.

From 1754 to 1760, Chief Paul Laurent of La Hève, like his predecessor Claude Egighighes, sought peaceful accommodations with the British without compromising Mi'kmaw interests. On 10 March 1760 Laurent, in company with two other chiefs, signed a peace and friendship treaty with the British. On 28 April the same year Charles Grand Claude, the son of Claude Grand Claude and Marie Pierre, along with seven other southwestern Mi'kmaq leaders including Jean and Joseph Ball (Paul) of the Chester area, Pierre Momcharret *dit* Cellier's son Barthélèmy (or Bartholomew) Momcharret of Minas, and François Cope of Sheet Harbour along the Eastern Shore also signed treaty and received passports enabling them to travel freely throughout the province.[47] While in Halifax these leaders were consulted on such matters as fixing prices for furs and other trade commodities, since Governor Jonathan Belcher had instructed that the Mi'kmaq be consulted prior to the launching of a new British fur trade system. Always attentive to new trade opportunities, Martin Grand Claude and his three sons Paul Martin, Martin Jr., and Nicolas doubtless journeyed from La Hève to take advantage of a new trading post established in 1765 by the Liverpool merchant Simeon Perkins on the Mersey River. Perkins's station, as had Nicolas Denys's fishery during the French era, lay near Potomac, a traditional Mi'kmaw

Anatomy of the Claude/Glode/Gloade Family, 1640–1910

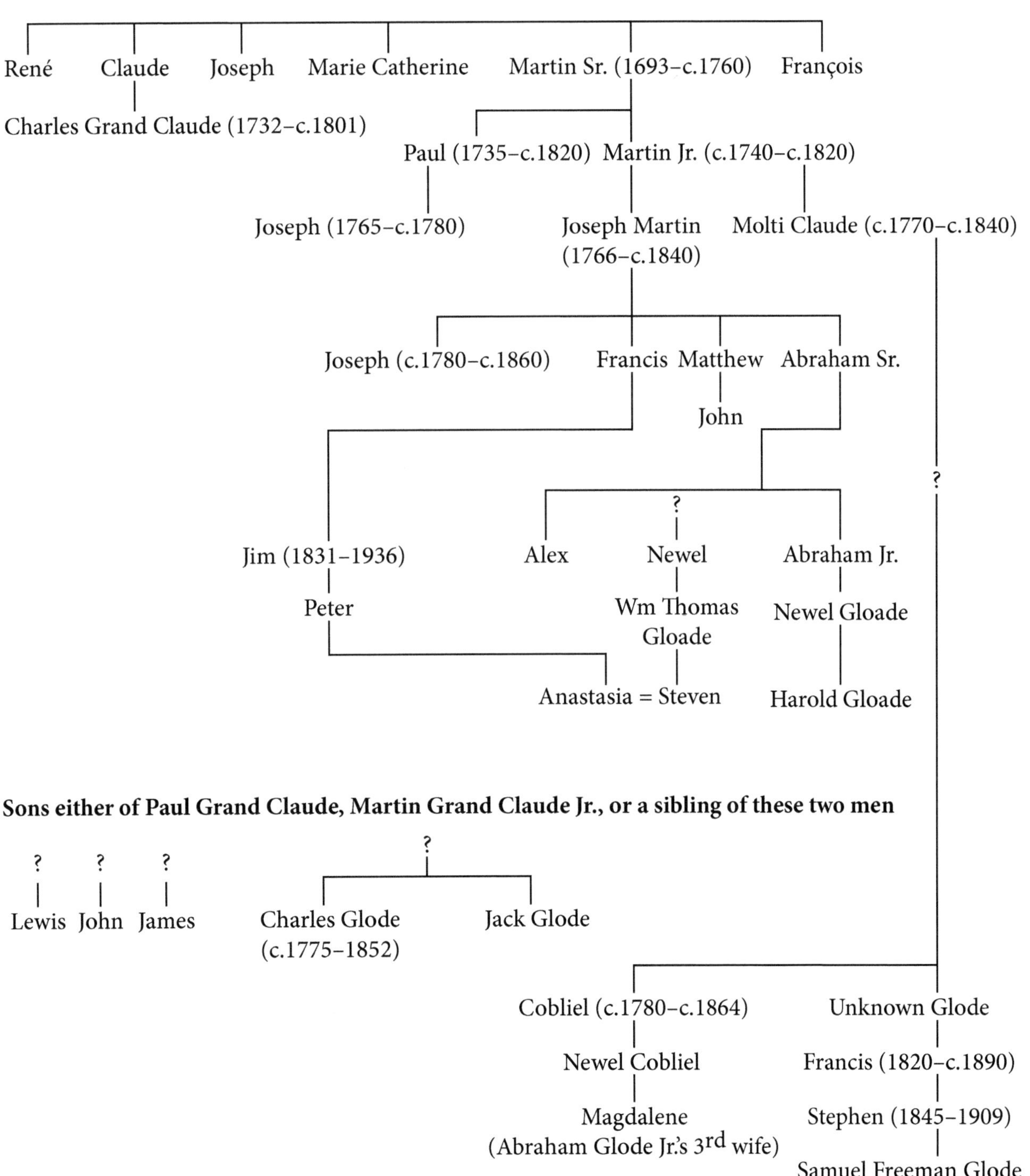

encampment ground located across the Rossignol (or Mersey) River from present-day Milton.[48]

François Mius meanwhile refused to sign treaty, along with his neighbouring chiefs, until persuaded to do so on 9 November 1761 by Abbé Pierre Maillard. Following the fall of Quebec in 1759, Maillard facilitated peaceful reconciliation between the Mi'kmaq and British. The abbé's significant efforts lessened British fears of the Mi'kmaq. After the scalp bounties of 1749 and 1756 were repealed, Martin Grand Claude was able to travel freely up and down the Atlantic coast with three other head men, Bernard Argomartin, Jean Ball (Paul), and Philip Bernard, all prominent members of the sizable La Hève band.[49] Chief Argomartin (c.1722–1817) and his son John Pennel Sr. had fought alongside General James Wolfe against the French on the Plains of Abraham in 1759. For this they eventually received land after the end of the War of 1812 at the mouth of the Gold River, in Lunenburg County. Chief Philip Bernard (c.1710–c.1825) entered British good graces during the American Revolution when he and his band drove off an American privateer that was harassing settlers along the shores of St. Margaret's Bay. For this action Bernard attained a freehold land grant at the Head of St. Margaret's Bay in 1786. Jean Ball (c.1710–c.1830) acquired a similar grant at East Chester in 1793. These prominent Atlantic coast leaders looked forward to viable trade contacts with the British, similar to those they had experienced prior to 1756 with the Acadians and *métis* living along the Atlantic seaboard.

Reintegrating into a Changed Post-war World, 1763–1801

The Seven Years' War ended in 1763 with the signing of the Peace of Paris. Until his death around 1765, François Mius held that certain La Hève leaders such as Martin Grand Claude acted far too compliantly with the interests of the new British regime. Mius was particularly incensed by Halifax's reluctance to supply a Roman Catholic missionary to replace Abbé Pierre Maillard, who had died in 1762. The British under the treaties of 1760 and 1761 had promised that the Mi'kmaq would always have a Roman Catholic priest to attend to their spiritual affairs. The Halifax establishment, however, backed by the Society for the Propagation of the Gospel in Foreign Parts, hoped in vain up until 1768 that the Mi'kmaq might be wooed from Roman Catholicism to Anglicanism. Though Grand Claude's descendants remained loyal

to Abbé Pierre Maillard's final instructions to remain on good terms with the new British regime, there is no evidence that they, unlike the Annapolis chief Jean-Baptist Thoma, ever toyed with Anglicanism. Instead their family heads conducted prayer sessions in their dwellings and, guided by their cherished prayer books written in hieroglyphic script, presided over births, marriages, and burial ceremonies in the absence of a priest. Finally in 1768, Lieutenant Governor Michael Francklin, in response to the plethora of Mi'kmaw grievances spearheaded by François Mius (who did not live long enough to see the consummation of his campaign), appointed Abbé Charles-François Bailly de Messein to serve among the Mi'kmaq, as well as Acadians returning from exile, in peninsular Nova Scotia and Cape Breton.[50]

Bailly only remained in Nova Scotia from 1768 to 1773, after which he left for Quebec. On 21 June 1769 he met with an assemblage of Mi'kmaq and Acadians at Chezzetcook, east of Halifax. The gathering included Martin Grand Claude Sr.'s sons Paul Martin, Martin Jr., and Nicolas. Bailly was the last missionary or government official to use the surname "Grand Claude" in his register entries, although he did so inconsistently. For instance, he used both "Paul Grand Claude" and simply "Paul Claude" in his registers. Paul Martin and his wife, Marie Anne Nebenne, had brought two children, René who was six and Joseph who was four, to the missionary for baptism. Martin Jr. and his wife, Anne Marie, meanwhile presented Bailly with twins, Joseph and Anne, aged three, for the same purpose.[51] The third brother, Nicolas, was evidently single, but he stood as a godparent for Paul Martin's one-year old son Nicolas. The Grand Claudes formed part of a small Mi'kmaq delegation to Chezzetcook composed of Paul Martin Grand Claude, Paul Pictou, Jacques Mius (François Mius's son), and Pierre-Paul Alexis – all of whom hailed from the La Have area. They were accompanied by Pierre Momcharret *dit* Cellier's son and successor, Chief Bartholomew Momcharret of Minas. Four days later, on 25 June 1769, Momcharret confirmed his marriage to Marie Joachim in front of the Grand Claudes and Jacques Mius, who was witness to the ceremony.[52]

Over the next fifteen years the Grand Claudes assisting in reconstructing a community on the La Have River based closely on the *métis* settlement that had been destroyed by the British in the late 1750s. Though the coastline around La Have had been appropriated by Planters and Germanic settlers, the

Grand Claudes, the Jeremy family, and the Martins erected neat log cabins with bark roofs, fenced in their gardens and fields, grew potatoes, corn, and root crops, and planted apple orchards on the upper reaches of the La Have River, near the head of navigation where Bridgewater now stands. Their community shrank when Jacques Mius and Pierre-Paul Alexis moved to Cape Sable. Those who remained wanted secure title to their tract and had Solomon Jeremy and Joseph Claude petition Lieutenant Governor John Parr's office in 1784 for a land grant "to the rear of the English settlement at La Have where they had made improvements."[53] Joseph Claude, was almost certainly the nineteen-year-old son of Paul Martin Grand Claude and Marie Anne Nebenne.

Solomon Jeremy and Joseph (Grand) Claude acquired a licence of occupation to this parcel the same year, but the government failed to provide any protection against avaricious settlers who in a few years usurped the Mi'kmaq's gardens and fields.[54] Loyalists vied with the Mi'kmaq for scarce fisheries and game resources, so that by the early 1790s not only had the Mi'kmaw lost their traditional fishing locales, but moose and beaver populations had also fallen to levels incapable of sustaining a primarily hunting population. Consequently Solomon Jeremy, Michael Jeremy, Joseph Grand Claude, and Peter Martin, who had now pushed inland as far as the shores of New Germany Lake, approached John Christopher Rudolph of Lunenburg to petition Halifax for them on 1 May 1793 stating their wish to re-establish their farming community further upriver from their English and Germanic neighbours. Impressed with the Mi'kmaq's desire to retain their independence rather than relying on government relief, the lieutenant governor, Sir John Wentworth, directed the surveyor general, Charles Morris, to lay out five hundred acres for the band on the shores of New Germany Lake.[55]

Leaving La Have, 1800–1820

The Grand Claudes who lived at La Have often went to Liverpool to trade their furs and visit close kin, whose band along the Mersey River system rarely numbered less than ninety persons. In 1794 Liverpool merchant Simeon Perkins claimed that twenty-one Mi'kmaw families lived in Queens County, "with 3 single men, besides some youths."[56] It appears that, despite movements in and out of the Liverpool area, Mi'kmaw population numbers in Queens County

from the 1790s to the first decades of the nineteenth century remained fairly stable.

Owing to the opportunities for trade offered by Perkins and other Liverpool merchants, Martin Claude Jr. (c.1740–c.1820) regularly visited the lower Mersey River area. He relied more on hunting and fishing than his slightly older brother Paul who, along with his son Joseph, advocated a more settled form of existence based on farming and cultivation of orchards, like that of the Acadians. Yet despite the size of the land grant allotted to them, the La Have band suffered from settler intrusions and game scarcities that made self-sufficiency difficult.[57] The government, in response to petitionings from the Mi'kmaq during years of major hardship, set out a supply depot at Halifax to furnish bands with relief. On 18 November 1796 George Henry Monk, the provincial Indian commissioner, who had been directed by Lieutenant Governor John Wentworth to alleviate the worst instances of poverty and suffering among the Mi'kmaq population,[58] met with Paul Grand Claude's son Joseph, who had journeyed from La Have to Halifax to ask for enough clothing, supplies, and ammunition to last his family through the winter.[59]

On 2 July the following year, Monk further recorded that the Halifax merchant Joseph Davis supplied Paul Grand Claude's younger brother, "Old Martin Claude," as well as Martin's wife and nine other family members with clothing, provisions, and ammunition worth £17.2.6.[60] In 1797 Martin Grand Claude Jr. still cared for a large family. And in January 1808 the firm of Hartshorne and Tremain issued supplies and repaired a gun belonging to Martin's older brother, "Paul Martyn Grove" (or Paul Martin Grand Claude, 1735–c.1820, who like Martin Jr. was a son of Martin Grand Claude Sr. of La Have).[61]

Years Following 1800

The two Joseph Grand Claudes whom Abbé Bailly had baptized in 1769 grew to manhood at La Have, married, and raised families.[62] Paul Grand Claude's son Joseph, who petitioned John Parr in 1784, remained farming the longest of all the Grand Claudes at La Have. Joseph likely cared for his father until Paul Martin Grand Claude's death around 1820. By contrast, Martin Grand Claude Jr.'s son Joseph Martin by 1790 had begun to overwinter in the interior of Queens County with kin belonging to the Annapolis band. Hunting in the late 1790s had grown very poor throughout southwestern Nova Scotia. In March of 1798, a Mi'kmaw party composed of Joseph Martin Claude, aged thirty-two, Joseph's brother Andrew Claude, a Cape Sable head man named Paul Williams, Joseph Alexis, son of the Cape Sable district chief Charles Alexis, and Peter Argomartin, also from Cape Sable, approached Thomas Walker, an Annapolis Royal merchant, for provisions to last them through to spring. The Mi'kmaq party claimed to represent the interests of twenty-two Cape Sable families. Walker apprised Sir John Wentworth that the group arrived at his store "in extreme distress," so he had provided them with corn, herring, potatoes, and molasses. In response to Williams's request for farming equipment, Walker also furnished the Mi'kmaq with axes and hoes to assist them with their spring planting.[63]

Walker's encouragement of Mi'kmaw agriculture bore fruit. Joseph Martin Claude, his brother Andrew, and his father Martin Grand Claude Jr. settled at present-day Greenfield, Queens County, where they could fish as well as plant. In 1795 Joseph Martin began guiding settlers on hunting and fishing excursions into the interior of Queens County. Paul Williams, who lived at West Pubnico in present-day Yarmouth County, persuaded several Cape Sable Mi'kmaw families to plant potatoes, root vegetables, corn, and apple orchards on the shores of Great Pubnico Lake, at the head of the Barrington River. Meanwhile Joseph Alexis established a Mi'kmaw farming community on Long Island in the Roseway River, Shelburne County.[64]

Not long afterwards two natural catastrophes occurred between Jeddore, east of Halifax, and Shelburne County. The first was the Great Storm of 1798, which flattened forests and left deadwood to be consumed by forest fires. The second was an outbreak of smallpox in the spring of 1801 that spread along the coast from Halifax to Lunenburg County, compelling many of the Grand Claudes still living at La Have to congregate at Liverpool by the fall of 1801.[65] The forest fires, exacerbated by a series of hot, dry summers, denuded large swathes of forest all the way from Halifax County to Shelburne County.[66] Such conditions would have required Joseph, Paul Grand Claude's son, to hunt on the Mersey River until his hunting territory lying nearer to La Have became repopulated with game and fur-bearing animals.

Two census documents, the first for Lunenburg County drawn up about 1800 and the second for Queens County compiled by William Barss in 1801 in response to a government circular asking for numbers of Mi'kmaq to be recorded in each county, give useful insights into the anatomy and movements of the Grand Claude family in the early nineteenth century. The only Mi'kmaq listed at La Have in the spring of 1801 were three family heads, "Sulno Jeremy" (Solomon Jeremy) – the same man who led the campaign to attain a government land grant at La Have – Sulno's close relative Gabriel Jeremy, and "Joseph Cloud" (Joseph Paul Claude). Joseph Claude was listed as a widower, with three children.[67] His father, Paul Grand Claude Sr., undoubtedly would have been present, since he was still alive in 1808 according to Monk's account book, but may not have been listed because he lived with his son and so was not considered by the census taker to be a family head.

The 1801 census compiled by Barss of the Mi'kmaq of Queens County lists Paul Williams and John Williams, who was probably Paul's brother, as camped at Liverpool.[68] Molti (Matthew) Pictou was also enumerated with his wife,[69] as was a man named Newel and two members of the Peters family. But by far the majority were surnamed Claude or a variant thereof. Twelve men were descendants of Martin Grand Claude and Marguerite Lejeune of La Have. These were (1) Joseph Paul Claude, a widower, who also appeared on the 1800 list for Lunenburg County; (2) Martin or Molti Claude Jr., now in his early sixties, along with his wife; (3) Martin's son Molti, with a wife and six children; (4) Sollon (Jerome) Claude, with a wife and three children; (5) Pelig Claude, with a wife and six children; (6) Joseph Martin Claude, with a wife and six children; (7) Nicholas Claude, likely the person whom Bailly met at Chezzetcook in 1769 and who was single; (8) Andrew Claude, who had accompanied his brother Joseph Martin Claude to Annapolis in 1798 and who had a wife and six children; (9) another Joseph Claude with a wife and four children who was likely a sibling of Molti Claude; two unmarried youths, (10) Francis Claude and (11) Peter Claude; and (12) Charles Claude with a wife and three children. The band at Liverpool numbered ninety-four.[70]

The first man listed on the Queens County census, Joseph Paul Claude, later returned to La Have where he remained for another decade. By contrast, several of his close kin, among them Martin Grand Claude Jr. and his sons Joseph Martin and Molti, left La Have permanently to camp and plant on the lower reaches of the Mersey River. In 1807 a committee of colonial administrators in Halifax responsible for Mi'kmaw affairs divided mainland Nova Scotia into twelve administrative districts and appointed a correspondent in each district to report back on the state of the Mi'kmaq within his jurisdiction. Since the Claudes circulated within three of these districts, those of Chester, Liverpool, and Annapolis, the government agents had little chance to get to know individual members of the Claude family well. Government distributions of guns, ammunition, and provisions were restricted to Mi'kmaq only in extreme need, which did not include the Claude family. And despite the fact that the Claudes were on amiable terms with incoming settlers, the government committee – composed of Charles Morris, George Henry Monk, Edward Mortimer, and William Cottnam Tonge – ignored them, focusing instead on leaders they felt might foment political unrest among the Mi'kmaw population prior to the onset of the War of 1812.[71]

After leaving La Have, the aging patriarch Martin Grand Claude (c.1740–c.1820) situated his family at Potamoc (or Potomac, also known as Potanoc or Potanoc Falls) on the lower Mersey River, the ancient Mi'kmaw encampment and trading site across the river from present-day Milton. Martin likely chose Potamoc for economic reasons since Simeon Perkins ran a trading post and sawmill nearby.[72] "Potamoc" or "Potomac" derives from an Eastern Algonquian term meaning "trading place." Martin's sons could find employment in the commercial riverine fishery and mill as well as in the fur trade. By the late eighteenth century several sawmills had sprung up across from Potamoc, but seasonal logging drives had not yet infringed on the integrity of the Mi'kmaq's major fishing locales or their hunting territories. Mill owners later would hire the Mi'kmaq as river drivers, an occupation at which some became especially skilled.

Most of Martin Grand Claude Jr.'s children were born at La Have during the American Revolution from 1775 to 1783 when there were no Roman Catholic clergy circulating among the Mi'kmaq to record births. Abbé Sigogne, the first missionary to return to the Mi'kmaw after Bailly left in 1773, did not commence his labours in southwestern Nova Scotia until 1799. For this reason, while it is probable that Martin Grand Claude Jr. was either the father or grandfather of a local head man named Cobliel (Gabriel) Claude (c.1790–1857) who lived along the lower Mersey River, one cannot point to any register entry to confirm either contention. What is known is that Martin Grand Claude Jr.'s eldest son, Joseph Martin Claude (1766–c.1835), moved into the Caledonia district of interior Queens County while several of his male siblings and cousins camped on lands nearer to the Annapolis Basin.[73] These men together comprised a generational cohort formed of Joseph Martin Claude, Joseph Paul Claude (1765– c.1830, who had left La Have permanently after his father Paul Grand Claude's death around 1820), Charles Claude whose name also appears on the 1801 Liverpool census, Charles's brother Jacques (or "Jack") Claude, Lewis Claude, John Claude, and other two men both named "James Claude." Most, if not all, of these members of the Claude family would have spent their earliest years along the La Have River.[74] Several of these men in 1820 showed Charles Morris, the provincial surveyor general, a tract they wished to have reserved for their band that lay along the Wildcat River, near Molega Lake in interior Queens County. The thousand-acre reserve that Morris laid out the same year was first known as the Brookfield reserve and later as Wildcat Reserve No. 12. It was not settled upon, however, until the early 1840s.

Much of the problem was that forest fires in the interior had so reduced game levels that planting crops and guiding settlers in this region proved untenable for several years. Joseph Martin Claude, whom local settlers called "Joseph Glode" rather than "Joseph Claude," remained at Potamoc, fishing and acting as an intermediary between his people and groups of settlers who were slowly advancing up the Mersey River from Liverpool. His services were much in need. Titus Smith, a surveyor whose team in 1801 was tracing a rough trail hacked through the woods from Liverpool to Annapolis Royal by William Burke, a settler who occasionally employed Joseph Martin Glode as guide, found that most of the Mi'kmaq he met en route were suspicious of strangers and recoiled in anger when Smith suggested they cultivate the land. They "would use every means" to disengage a Mi'kmaq individual disposed to farm "from their new occupation ... and seem to have as strong a prejudice against our way of living as we have against theirs," Smith averred.[75] But given the fact that many Mi'kmaq in the past had cultivated crops and orchards at La Have and Barrington, among other areas, only to have their fields usurped by avaricious settlers, their reluctance to farm, despite the new hardships they faced in hunting, does not seem surprising.

Some non-Indigenous hunters, both local and visiting, shot moose and caribou in large quantities only for their antlers and left the carcasses to rot. Settlers appropriated fisheries used by the Mi'kmaw people for generations. By contrast, the Mi'kmaq maintained a system of traditional cultural protocols that respected family hunting territory boundaries and required that no hunter take more than he needed. The settlers' complete lack of such monitoring practices had laid the countryside open to the consequences of wastefulness – declining game and fish stocks. In lieu of furs or hides to trade, families at Potamoc and elsewhere along the Mersey River began catching and barrelling fish for commercial exchange.[76] For many years farming seemed risky since no government protections prevented settler trespasses on Mi'kmaw fields. Provincial authorities failed to acknowledge that land had been granted to the La Have Mi'kmaq in 1793, even though Solomon Jeremy's descendants in 1829 petitioned the lieutenant governor, Sir Peregrine Mailtland, for redress for what they had endured over the preceding decade on their grant.[77] In the late 1820s some members of Jeremy's family, formerly settled at La Have and known as the "Sulnos" (or "Solomons'), moved to Queens County and joined the band along the Mersey River. These Mi'kmaq, owing to their past relationship with Acadian *métis* society, respected farming as long as it enhanced the diverse traditional Mi'kmaw economy and was not pursued intensively to the detriment of hunting, fishing, and trapping. In welcoming these Mi'kmaw newcomers, Joseph Martin Glode paved the way for other members of his band to reconsider farming as a complementary subsistence strategy to hunting and so incorporate it as part of their seasonal round.

After Paul Martin Grand Claude died at La Have, his son Joseph Paul gave up investing time and effort in the La Have grant and moved to the lower Mersey River area.[78] Yet not all of the Claudes who had formerly lived at La Have relocated further south along the coast. Meanwhile, those that moved to the Liverpool area continued to intermarry with families further east, nearer La Have. For instance, in the late 1840s Peter Claude (or Glode, as the surname came to be written) from the lower Mersey River region married Fanny Pennel, a daughter of Chief Joseph Pennal of Gold River, and raised a family at Bridgewater.[79] All of these Claudes/Glodes continued to exercise their family's traditional territorial prerogatives to the vast tract lying between the Atlantic coast and the Annapolis Basin.

Joseph Martin Glode Becomes Queens and Annapolis District Chief

Despite the hardships confronting the Mi'kmaq at the turn of the eighteenth century, Martin Grand Claude Jr.'s son Joseph Martin Glode (1766–c.1840) gained a lasting reputation as a wise and diplomatic leader among both the local settler population and his Mi'kmaw kin and colleagues.[80] By accompanying William Burke and other non- Mi'kmaw newcomers on hunting expeditions from Port Medway – now Mill Village – to Lake Kejimkujik between 1795 and 1830, he represented the vanguard of Mi'kmaw commercial guides in Queens County. Titus Smith, while surveying in 1801, lodged temporarily with William Burke who, with his wife Marie Foster, had erected a cabin on a knoll just south of the Medway River, at what would become South Brookfield. By this time Joseph Martin Glode had guided Burke on several hunting expeditions, though Smith, surprisingly, does not mention this fact despite his familiarity with Burke. By contrast, Halifax journalist Clara Dennis as late as 1937 heard stories about Joseph Glode piloting Burke into the interior of Queens County.[81]

Joseph Martin Glode watched over those for whom he felt responsible, whether Mi'kmaq or non-Mi'kmaq. Following William Burke's and Mary Foster's decision in the late 1790s to establish a pioneer homestead in the midst of the forest, the chief kept an eye on the couple and their children, caring for their needs in emergencies. This spirit of concern proved reciprocal. A member of Mary Foster's birth family named John Foster, along with his wife Dorcas Smith of Port Medway, raised an infant Mi'kmaw boy, Allan Foster. Allan was born into the Glode family in 1799 but his father either was unable to raise him or died before his birth.[82] And Allan was not the only settler with close ties to the Glodes. After 1811, John Mehlman (Mailman) Jr. of New Dublin Township in

Lunenburg County, who claimed Mi'kmaw in addition to German ancestry, interacted closely with Glodes at Caledonia and Milford. A woman descended from John Mehlman was even rumoured to have been the second wife, or consort, of Charles Glode of Annapolis, a man whose life will be discussed at length in the following pages.[83]

Prior to 1790 Joseph Martin Glode married Sarah Phillips, a daughter of Chief Philip Bernard of St. Margaret's Bay. The two raised a sizeable family. One of their sons, Francis Glode (c.1790–c.1890), later married Madeleine Knockwood and moved to the shores of Kejimkujik Lake where he reputedly lived to be one hundred years old.[84] Another son, Joseph Glode Jr. (c.1800–c.1880), in 1834 married Mary Ann Stephens at a festive and well-attended wedding ceremony held at Caledonia in Queens County. This couple's main place of residence was at Lequille.[85] A third son, Abraham Glode Sr., born about 1814, married three times and died at Bear River at age ninety-six in 1910.[86] According to oral traditions gleaned from the Yarmouth Mi'kmaw community, Joseph also had two more sons in his final years, Matthew Glode (c.1825–1913)[87] and John Glode (1834–c.1900). Born in Caledonia, Matthew married Victoire Francis on 2 July 1854 at Plympton in Digby County, and the couple lived between Barrington and West Pubnico, while John, born at Bear River, joined Matthew at West Pubnico about 1870.

Although Caledonia was a traditional Mi'kmaw rendezvous and encampment area, it was not as heavily populated by Mi'kmaq as other regions of Queens County, so Joseph readily welcomed newcomers into this part of his peoples' territory.[88] Lack of good roads retarded extensive settlement into the interior for many years, although between 1800 and 1822 a few settlers struggled along a rough trail cut through the woods to take up lands at Caledonia, Harmony Mills, Kempt, and Northfield. The chief's amiable attitude towards newcomers at times elicited an equally warm response from early settlers. On 10 March 1822 Joseph cordially introduced himself to members of a pioneer work camp who were clearing ground preparatory to planting crops among the stumps. The camp's heads, Patrick Lacey and Thomas Jones, offered the chief a hearty breakfast that he ate with relish, after which he left for the woods where he reputedly killed fifteen moose not more than thirteen miles from where Lacey and Jones had pitched their tents. As Joseph doubtless offered much of this meat to his new friends, his hunting feat of 10 March 1822 was long remembered in Queens County settler circles.[89]

Joseph's visits to settler enclaves in the interior provided opportunities for him, as a hunting and fishing guide, to scout out potential clients. Moose levels slowly recovered in Queens County after 1820 and winter fur trapping continued to bring a measure of independence. As farms arose, and settlers turned from eating game to consuming farm-raised meat and produce, moose and caribou rebounded in regions of the countryside dominated by barrens and eskers. As a guide, Joseph Martin Glode represented a long-standing tradition that harked back to the French era. Ever since 1685, when Mi'kmaq escorted French intendant Jacques de Meulles across the province from Port Royal to Port Rossignol, Indigenous inhabitants of the Mersey River area had been noted for their guiding acumen. After 1710 English traders also depended on Mi'kmaq to find fur sellers, while British military officers, looking to bag fine sets of antlers to bolster their reputations as good shots, avidly sought out Mi'kmaw guides at Liverpool, Mill Village, and Annapolis Royal.

Chief Joseph Martin Glode assumed the duties of organizing, instructing, and encouraging members of hunting expeditions, whose safety and success in the interior principally lay in his hands, at the cost to his clients of anywhere from half a dollar to a dollar a day. Securing provisions, guns, and ammunition for the hunting party were a client's responsibility, while the Mi'kmaq supplied water transportation. Guiding was an occupation that required strength and stamina, but it required less "wheeling and dealing" than the sphere of fur trade negotiations. Because of his amiable and diplomatic manner as well as his skill as a hunter, Joseph built up a sizeable clientele and so could depend seasonally on a fairly stable income from this source to supplement his family's intake from hunting, fishing, trapping, and planting. Though the chief died around 1835, before the rise of "guide meets" where guides could demonstrate their skills competitively, he attracted attention and admiration from a wide constituency and laid the foundation for several of his sons and grandsons to follow in his footsteps.

Though an excellent woodsman, Joseph was not opposed to farming at a time when many Mi'kmaq around him eschewed European-introduced agricultural practices. Joseph traded his furs with Liverpool merchants, and as a farmer he also became well known to Roman Catholic clergy associated with St. Jerome's parish in Caledonia.[90] He grew potatoes and other crops, which many of his Mi'kmaw countrymen felt promoted assimilation into settler society and the consequent jettisoning of facets of traditional culture that had sustained the Mi'kmaq for generations. According to settlers and clergy, however, who were among those who received meat and produce from him, Claude kept an open mind on the subject as long as farming was not imposed on the Mi'kmaq without their input and consent. With time, since their chief accepted farming as one of his occupations, his band's distrust of and animosity towards agriculture gradually waned.

When Chief Joseph Martin Glode died either late in 1834 or early in 1835, his younger brother Molti (or Martin) Glode assumed responsibility for the welfare of band members living primarily by hunting and fishing along the lower reaches of the Mersey River. The elderly Molti and his wife Geneviève, who may have been Acadian, had several married sons living near them at Potamoc by this time, one of whom almost certainly was Cobliel (or Gabriel) Glode, born about 1780. Another was likely François-Joseph, who wed Magdaleine Alexis in 1832.[91] A third, Paul Glode, born in 1805, lived with his wife at Potamac and probably cared for his parents in their later years. Molti, ever since his years at La Have, had maintained close ties with the Alexis family, and Jean-Baptiste Alexis and Bridget Alexis stood as godparents at Molti's son Paul's baptism at Ste. Anne du Ruisseau, in the Argyle District of Yarmouth County, on 31 March 1807.[92] In November 1835 Molti directed a petition to the lieutenant governor, Sir Colin Campell, stating that while he, as chief, was elderly and lame, he still had around twenty family heads under his aegis who required supplies for the upcoming winter.[93] The following January he contacted Campbell again, listing sixteen fellow Mi'kmaw petitioners who needed blankets and provisions.[94]

Though 113 individuals had collected at Caledonia in 1836 for a Mi'kmaw council meeting and feast to install Molti as their new district chief following Joseph Martin Glode's death, Molti did not retain the office for long.[95] In 1837 he joined Joe Jeremy in petitioning once again for supplies and provisions, but

as it was the last document on which his name appears, he may have died shortly afterwards.[96] Molti's death left a power vacuum in band ranks that was filled by two contenders to the chiefship: Jack Glode (c.1770–c.1860), a quiet, sagacious man who was a brother of Charles Glode (c.1775–1852) and probably Joseph Martin Glode as well.

Jack planted potatoes and other root vegetables on an old mill site at Lequille, near the General's Bridge spanning the Lequille River, but his economic round also included weir fishing, taking water fowl in the spring and fall, porpoise shooting in the summer, and hunting and trapping during the winter. Lequille was positioned so that a man could readily engage in all these activities and still easily access markets at Annapolis Royal. Long before the French built the first grist mill at Lequille in 1605, the locale had furnished a rendezvouz for Mi'kmaq living along the Mersey River and throughout the Annapolis Valley. The headwaters of Mersey River could be reached from the Annapolis Basin by a series of short portages. Nestled at the base of rocky cliffs, the Mi'kmaw encampment where Jack lived was sheltered from inclement winds. The river supported salmon, sturgeon, smelts, eels, and herring. Local mudflats provided shellfish and attracted shorebirds and ducks. Jack felt at home in the area and had no intention of leaving it. When pressured to do so by his people, he accepted the office of chief, but always left the more high-profile speaking duties to his brother Charles when the band interacted with government authorities. Prior to 1820 Jack and Charles Glode both lived at Lequille and shared a family hunting territory that lay between Lequille and Caledonia. (By the 1840s their surname was always spelled "Glode" rather than "Claude," and though today most descendants of Jehan Grand Claude spell their surname "Gloade," there are some, particularly in Queens, Digby, and Yarmouth counties, who prefer to keep the older spelling "Glode." Where such a preference has been maintained, a person's surname is spelled accordingly.)

Charles Glode and the "Glode Settlement" along the Liverpool-Annapolis Road

As a young man Charles Glode struck up a relationship with several English-speaking families at Annapolis Royal. Around 1795 he married an English woman named Frances Tobias, and by 1801 he and his wife had four young children. "Tobias" was the surname of a relatively affluent Annapolis Royal family descended from Jacob Tobias, a medical doctor who lived at Digby during the late eighteenth century. While some of Jacob's descendants later moved to Lequille, no specific information could be found regarding Frances Tobias's immediate parentage.[97] Frances's family seem to have welcomed Charles into their ranks, however. And it is even possible that members of the branch of the Tobias family living at Lequille, recognizing Charles's natural talents as a speaker, groomed him for the public podium and ensured he wore suitable clothes on his speaking tours. They may have encouraged him to advocate farming among his people, though Charles never felt entirely comfortable with this role. For years he would waver between urging his Mi'kmaw associates to farm in order to assimilate into settler society, and promoting the preservation of Mi'kmaw lands for traditional purposes under a system that involved licences of occupation, land grants, and land purchases.

Charles's role as a campaigner for a Mi'kmaw farming settlement near Lequille developed further under the tutelage of Abbé Jean-Mandé Sigogne, who strongly impressed upon him the value of establishing Mi'kmaw agricultural communities in a rapidly changing world. Sigogne further challenged Charles to have the "courage of the French people" by building himself a frame house.[98] This Charles ignored, preferring to live in a dwelling of logs with a pole and bark roof, although he allowed his Mi'kmaq in-laws to build him a sizeable barn on a clearing he had made about seventeen kilometres inland from Lequille. With the abbé's support, Charles in 1822 acquired some basic agricultural tools and went to work chopping trees along the eastern side of the Annapolis-Liverpool Road, where today the highway runs between Graywood and Milford.[99] In among the tree stumps he planted a few acres of potatoes.

Not long after this, Charles and his brother Jack suddenly realized that a public highway was going to replace the old trail cut by William Burke through the woods between the Atlantic coast and Annapolis Royal. This road would cut right through the middle of their hunting territory.[100] So, on Charles's recommendation, Jack Glode, Francis Glode, and Molti (Malti or Martin) Paul petitioned the lieutenant governor, Sir James Kempt, for four tracts to plant on just west of "Liverpool Head," now called Milford. They all stressed that the road, then under construction,

would bring in settlers who would dramatically disturb the wildlife they depended upon for survival. In the face of this threat they needed secure title to their lands, much of which was suitable for raising crops to supplement returns from hunting, should animals grow scarce.[101]

Sigogne drafted a memorial for the four Mi'kmaw petitioners and contacted Judge Thomas Ritchie at Annapolis Royal. He stressed to Ritchie, the member of the Legislative Assembly for Annapolis County, that the proposed settlement might serve as a useful example to other Mi'kmaq within the province.[102] Though members of the Board of Land Commissioners for the District of Eastern Annapolis County were sceptical and resisted the idea, Sigogne's persuasive skills and Lieutenant Governor Kempt's personal interest in fostering Mi'kmaw agricultural communities won out. In 1823 each of the four petitioners received a location ticket for a long rectangular strip of land containing between 183 and 200 acres. The three lots accorded to Charles and Jack Glode and Molti Paul were situated on the north side of the road and stretched back through the woods to a stream connected to the watershed of the Mersey-Medway river system.[103] Francis Glode obtained a lot on the opposite side of the road.

These four tracts were laid out in 1824,[104] but before the survey occurred, Molti Paul's son Peter Paul joined the settlement in Molti's place.[105] Sigogne initially hoped that all the Mi'kmaw properties would converge around a common centre, but an allotment in the immediate area previously laid out for Jasper Williams, who was not Mi'kmaq, precluded this arrangement.[106] Williams's lot cut off Charles's parcel from the others, but from his semi-isolated homestead flanking Williams's lot, Charles promoted causes dear to him, the foremost being the welfare of the somewhat dispersed Mi'kmaw community lying along the Annapolis-Liverpool Road.

Oratorical skill has always been a distinctive leadership trait among Algonquian-speaking peoples, and in many ways Charles Glode was the epitome of the Mi'kmaw orator. A showman as well as a speaker, Charles early on attracted the attention of Judge Ritchie by speaking at minor social events in Annapolis Royal. When Ritchie informed his legal and political colleague, Judge Thomas Chandler Haliburton, about Charles's farming abilities and remarkable speaking talents, Haliburton, who succeeded Ritchie as Annapolis County's representative in the House in 1826, invited the Mi'kmaw orator and campaigner to accompany him to Halifax in March 1827. In Halifax the lieutenant governor refunded Charles any expenses he had incurred in securing his grant and provided him with funds to purchase additional agricultural implements.[107]

Perhaps seeing Charles not only as a "yeoman" but as a kindred spirit, since the judge too had a penchant for oratory, Haliburton invited Charles to speak on 12 February 1828 to the House of Assembly on the evils of strong drink. Charles cut a striking figure in Halifax.[108] The substance of his speech was derived from a petition that Chief James Andrew Meuse of Bear River had drafted with the assistance of Abbé Sigogne, but that Haliburton had deemed inappropriate for a "frequent inebriate" such as Meuse to present to the House.[109] Despite Charles's imperfect English, his audience showered the forceful, handsome, and impeccably dressed advocate of prohibition with accolades. The Speaker of the House treated him with special respect and attention.[110] Joseph Howe, who kept apace of such events through his friends Abbé Sigogne and Haliburton,[111] urged in the newspaper the *Novascotian* that the public "allow the eye to rest on such men as Gload." Charles even gained a measure of international renown when the noted British anti-slave and prison reformer and Quaker philanthropist Samuel Gurney praised his talents as a speaker.[112] Charles's willingness to farm also attracted favourable reviews. William Bowman, a friend of Gurney's, proclaimed, "I have always undertaken that he was amongst the foremost in this new line of business."[113] Unlike many of his Mi'kmaw kin, Charles proved so well versed in agricultural practices that it causes one to wonder if he had been taken in by a settler family in his youth and taught to farm.[114] Charles also could write in English, and Joseph Howe became one of his correspondents.

From the 1820s to the early 1840s Charles still rode fairly high on the success of his farming campaign. Sheriff Edward H. Cutler, who had presided over the registration at the Mi'kmaq's allotments at the Annapolis Royal Lands Office, commended his tenacity in bringing his plans to fruition. "Charles," he wrote in 1841 to the provincial secretary, Sir Rupert George, is "a sober, industrious man" who has "made such improvements as to render himself comfortable."[115] This information was passed along to the lieutenant governor, Lord Falkland, who described

Charles to the Colonial Office as a good farmer with twenty or thirty acres under cultivation and several head of livestock. Farming as well as hunting and trapping, Falkland claimed, had brought economic security to Charles's household.[116]

By contrast, Charles Glode's Mi'kmaw associates proved far more interested in preserving their traditional lands inviolate from settler trespass than in labouring to establish a permanent agricultural village. Peter Paul moved to Lequille near Jack Glode, while Francis Glode, after desultorily chopping a few acres of timber, settled at Kejimkujik Lake.[117] By the 1840s Charles was cultivating his plot in solitude, deserted by all the others who had been allotted location tickets with him in 1824. It must have piqued him, for Charles still cherished the traditional Mi'kmaw way of life. He had no intention of giving up hunting and guiding and he had sought ways to encourage Mi'kmaq and settlers to appreciate value in each other's culture. He refused to embrace the settlers' housing preferences, and the cattle he kept were oxen, able to work rather than produce meat or milk for consumption. Charles preferred his potatoes fried in caribou fat rather than butter. Milk was required only in small quantities for porridge, or to whiten tea, and the main value of a cow would be to increase the size of one's herd.

By the mid-1830s Charles was no longer content to be merely a spokesperson for the southwestern Mi'kmaq, but wished to be their district chief. Yet in order to secure his wish he had to vie with his brother Jack, and face even stiffer competition from Chief Andrew James Meuse of Bear River. In 1823 Charles and Jack had acted together quickly and forcefully because their traditional lands were threatened. They had sought to promote Mi'kmaq-controlled communities, based not only on farming but also on fishing, hunting, and guiding. It was a facet of his role Charles sometimes forgot or ignored, and so was branded as politically presumptuous by others of his group who chose to remain fishers and hunters.

Jack meanwhile, asthmatic and afflicted with either an eye affliction or, blindness as he wore a patch over his left eye, increasingly tried to relinquish his authority as a traditional district chief to Charles, who embraced it enthusiastically. Though Sigogne and the Halifax officialdom directed Jack to replace Andrew James Meuse as chief owing to the latter's frequent intemperance, and especially after Meuse pawned a medal given to him in 1821 by

Queen Adelaide, Jack preferred to keep a low profile and continued on as district leader only after his own people asked him to retain the office. Though he had lost some of the confidence of the Mi'kmaw constituency, Charles continued to act as liaison between the Mi'kmaq and the provincial government. In 1835 he asked not only for seed for Lewis Alexis (also known as "Lewis Luxey"), John Jeremy, and others at Kejimkujik but also for five pounds to build himself a house, though no monies for house construction arrived.[118] In 1838 Charles Glode informed Sigogne that 415 "souls" in the counties of Lunenburg, Queens, Shelburne, and Annapolis lay under his chiefly aegis, information that was sent to the British Colonial Office.[119] On 20 April 1841 he petitioned for seed potatoes for seven Mi'kmaw family heads, including his brother Jack.[120]

If he could not be the district chief, Charles, now the only remaining resident of the original "Glode settlement," more than anything wanted freehold land. When Jasper Williams sold his lot to Francis William Pickman in 1835, Charles waited for Pickman to place his property on the market again. The opportunity to buy arose on 1 November 1839 when Pickman divided his tract in half and offered the bottom section to Charles for fifteen pounds.[121] Once Charles had made his purchase, he petitioned the legislature on 10 February 1840 for freehold title to the land he acquired in 1824 as well, so he might transfer the whole three hundred acres to his heirs. Though meeting some resistance in the legislature, his request was granted on 22 February of the same year.[122] Yet, oddly, Charles continued to petition Halifax with the same request, which suggests that the government neglected to inform him that his request for a freehold grant actually had been approved.[123]

The government, eager to make the Mi'kmaq into farmers, was quick to reply to his requests for seeds and tools. On 20 April 1841 Charles contacted Lord Falkland to explain that although few Mi'kmaq remained at the Glode settlement, the situation would be temporary. It was challenging enough for European newcomers to become pioneer farmers, let alone Mi'kmaq "accustomed to roam at large in the Forest." Yet four family heads – John Glode, Joseph Glode, Joe Peter, and an elderly widow named Molly Knockwood – still wanted to farm so that the "blessing of civilized life may be realized."[124] On 17 March the following year Charles asked Andrew

Henderson, the schoolmaster at Albion Vale in Annapolis Royal, to draft a second petition to Falkland asking for seed potatoes and tools for six families, which he held still lived along the Liverpool-Annapolis Road. Three more families, he added, were expected to join later the same year. The family heads named in this document were John Jeremy, Francis Charles, Joseph Peters, Abraham Peters, Francis Meuse, and his brother Jack Glode. All these men had some experience farming since five of them had been planting for at least a year on the shores of Kejimkujik Lake, while Jack had been doing the same at Lequille. At the bottom of the petition, Charles instructed Henderson to write "Charles Glode, Governor of the Micmac Tribe of Indians, residing in the County of Annapolis."[125]

There is no evidence that any Mi'kmaw council ever appointed Charles to such a status within his group. Andrew James Meuse, Charles's neighbour at Bear River, occasionally referred to himself as a "governor" because to do so symbolized continuity with the type of chiefship manifested by his grandfather, François Mius of La Hève. François Mius's status had been embedded in an eighteenth-century French practice that recognized Mi'kmaw head chiefs as leaders of territorial "commands." Such persons acted as political middlemen between their groups and the French authorities, who viewed them as recruiting agents, able to muster military support for the French cause during intercolonial wars with England. "Chefs," as they were called during the French era, received military commissions, medals, and presents to distribute to their people.[126]

François Mius had been granted a "Chef's Commission" by the French at Louisbourg in 1742, and Chief Claude Egighighes of La Have had "Anglicized" his leadership office by referring to himself in 1753 as the "governor of La Have." By the close of the Seven Years' War, the English term "governor" had supplanted the older French appellation "chef." Though not all district leaders employed "governor" in referring to their office, as late as 1860s chiefs Charles Alexis and Francis Charles Sulno of Cape Sable still considered themselves to be in a reciprocal relationship with the Crown where they were expected to supply military aid if needed.[127] Owing to the radically changed relationship between the Mi'kmaq and the provincial government by the mid-nineteenth century, the term "governor," unless it referred directly to a district chief recognized by a band, had little concrete meaning in either the traditional Mi'kmaq or the broader colonial context. With the assistance of Abbé Sigogne, Judge Peleg Wiswal of Digby, and the Halifax humanitarian Walter Bromley, François Mius's grandson Andrew James Meuse had been instrumental in securing a thousand-acre reserve at Bear River near the Annapolis-Digby County border.[128] Meuse used the title "governor" in his correspondence with the government, probably basing it on his grandfather's practice during the eighteenth century, but for Charles to use the term as he did in 1842 seems to have been mainly a form of status mongering.

On receiving the Glode's petition Falkland passed it on to Joseph Howe, whom he had recently appointed as provincial Indian commissioner. Howe, in turn, wrote on 6 March 1842 to Andrew Henderson, Albion Vale's schoolmaster, to find out about the Glode settlement. He also requested that Henderson act as a local agent to keep an eye on matters along the Liverpool-Annapolis Road. Charles evidently that felt his efforts should be rewarded with increased status in the eyes of the government. To test his standing in this respect, he argued that John Jeremy, Francis Charles, Joe Peters, and Abraham Peters should also have a hoe and a spade each, which accordingly were provided to the Mi'kmaq by Andrew Henderson, a merchant living at Annapolis, with Howe's permission.[129] Henderson nevertheless confided to Howe on 27 May 1842 that Charles Glode's posturing had caused him to be regarded by others with a certain degree of suspicion. Jack may have reassigned much of his authority to his brother, but this was "done without the consent of the people, and consequently Jack, who is much respected by his Tribe, is still considered their rightful Chief." Henderson concluded by stating that while Charles was the "more active and intelligent," Jack proved the "more sagacious and manly."[130]

Charles Glode found himself in an awkward situation, as the Mi'kmaw constituency was coming to view him as an agent of assimilation into settler society.[131] Because of this Charles never became a chief "regularly recognized by his Tribe."[132] He may have felt he had done everything he could to better his own lot and that of his people. He had chosen the site of the Glode farming settlement with care. It not only contained flat land with good soil and timber, but offered strategic opportunities for those who still

wished to combine their planting with a more traditional lifestyle. It was near Lequille, up to this point the headquarters of the Glode leadership in Annapolis County. The shores of nearby Grand Lake contained weir sites and an ancient burial ground, and lay athwart two watersheds, one that supplied the Allain River running towards the Annapolis Basin and a second that fed the much larger Mersey-Medway river system draining towards the Atlantic. The Milford area lay in the midst of a network of traditional Indigenous water routes and trails running in all four directions.[133] When the Virginia Road to Bear River was constructed, which branched off the Liverpool-Annapolis Road at Milford, handcarts and horse-drawn wagons became useful means of moving heavy loads from one settlement to another. Charles Glode could not be faulted for his attempts to blend the old with the new. But his tendency to favour government incentives and objectives over Mi'kmaw decision-making protocols won him few plaudits from his own people.

Joseph Howe, who became Nova Scotia's Indian commissioner in 1842, set out in October of that year to meet with as many Mi'kmaq in southwestern Nova Scotia as he could reach by horse and wagon. Charles Glode ranked high on Howe's list of persons to visit. In the late spring of 1842 Charles Glode and John Jeremy had travelled to Halifax to inform Howe of what was happening along the Liverpool-Annapolis Road and to tell of a second farming experiment Jeremy and several other Mi'kmaq were beginning at Kejimkujik Lake on the Queens-Annapolis County boundary.[134] Howe found Jeremy's words about the prospects for the Kejimkujik settlement intriguing, but hardly listened to Charles. Charles acted as though the Kejimkujik farming experiment was merely an extension of his own cherished Annapolis-Liverpool Road community, and apparently Howe refused to countenance any suggestion that the new settlement be politically contingent on the old.

From then on, when it came to matters concerning the Kejimkujik Mi'kmaw settlement, Joseph Howe dealt solely with John Jeremy and left Charles out of the conversation. It thus appears that Howe had reservations about Charles from this very first meeting. Had Howe accepted an invitation from Charles's brother Jack to participate in a conference that the Mi'kmaq of Queens and Annapolis Counties were convening at "the Annapolis Gut" in June, he might have been better informed about the Mi'kmaq's views of both the Glode and Kejimkujik settlements, but he either could not or did not wish to attend this meeting.[135] In the interim Henderson warned him of Charles Glode's political difficulties with his own people, which doubtless further coloured Howe's estimation of the situation.

When Howe failed to meet with Jack and his constituency in the spring, he also missed a valuable opportunity to let the Mi'kmaq know about his intention to visit their communities the following autumn. As things stood, none of the Mi'kmaq realized that Howe was planning to visit them. And since the Indian commissioner began his western tour of the province so late in the season, men had begun their fall moose hunting and so were unreachable in the woods.

When Howe visited the Lequille Mi'kmaw encampment in late October 1842, he met only "two to three families." The Mi'kmaq were occupying the same locale as that romantically depicted in a steel engraving of General's Bridge by artist and engraver W.H. Bartlett, who visited Lequille shortly before Howe.[136] Coopering as well as manufacturing baskets and other wooden items for sale had replaced hunting as principal occupations, for most members of the community were elderly. Howe noted that several of the aged persons accompanying Jack Glode seemed to have been "cast upon him by the honorary rank which he held." To the commissioner, Jack was the rightful chief, a "stout and apparently respectable man, bearing among his own people and among the whites a very high character." Yet because he was "somewhat advanced in years" and troubled with asthma, Howe considered Jack unsuitable for spearheading any farming experiment he might propose. Jack's group, moreover, was too far from Annapolis Royal for children regularly to attend school. Howe decided at last to give the chief a small sum of money to be distributed among his elderly charges. But before Howe left, Jack pressed the commissioner to try and secure a few acres of cultivatable land for him on the mill site at Lequille. Howe ruminated over this request, realizing that lands around had already been granted and to purchase additional property could prove costly, but so importunate was the old chief that he promised that if a tract could be obtained on moderate terms

he "would recommend a compliance" with Jack's wish.[137]

Feeling he had done all he could at Lequille for the time being, Howe left the community and drove his horse and wagon down the Liverpool-Annapolis Road. The road, flanked by struggling pioneer farms, proved "very indifferent," and as it approached Milton it devolved into little more than a winding path through the woods.[138] Howe was carrying a survey plan, to which he frequently referred, which showed the location of the four Mi'kmaw tracts as set out in the series of 1824 grants to the Mi'kmaq. Although on 26 February 1840 Kempt's successor as lieutenant governor, Sir Colin Campbell, had complied with Glode's wishes and ordered Surveyor General John Spry Morris to resurvey Glode's tract as a freehold grant,[139] Howe failed to distinguish between Charles's lot and those of Charles's Mi'kmaw associates. And evidently Campbell failed to inform either Howe or Glode about the change.

The trip to Glode's farm took Howe longer than he expected. It was necessary at the end to leave the main road and follow a lane through the woods the last mile or so.[140] As night had fallen, he found himself, in the absence of neighbouring houses, in the rather embarrassing predicament of having to cast himself on the good will of Charles's two daughters, one twelve and the other fifteen, for food and lodging for the night. There was no mother present, and their father was away on a hunting expedition, so it took all of Howe's persuasive capabilities to get them to lift the latch and let him in. Once they recognized their father's associate, however, they stabled Howe's horse and provided him with a warm supper of herrings, potatoes, and tea. Later in the evening, to pass the time, as the girls and their guest had so few "topics in common," the commissioner fell to writing down, by birch bark torchlight, "Indian nouns with their corresponding English words, an exercise," Howe noted, "which seemed to interest my young friends very much."[141]

The next morning the commissioner surveyed the premises for two hours and then left for Annapolis Royal, as Charles had not returned. Over thirty acres of land had been cleared. Howe found the barn roomy and commodious, with good stalls, a clean threshing floor, a loft filled with hay, a plough, a harrow, and yokes for oxen. Two head of cattle stood in the stalls. Charles had secured his potatoes in a root cellar. The farm's fences were adequate, especially as there was no neighbouring livestock to test them. Yet Howe also found much to criticize. While the commissioner had welcomed the comforts provided by Glode's camp the previous night, in the morning light he contended that Charles was remiss in not building himself a proper frame house. While he recognized that the absence of neighbours, furthermore, might in part be due to the bad condition of the road, the distance from town, and the rocky soil, he also remembered that Charles's own people accused him of "selfishness." To Howe this was not always "a bad trait" in a Mi'kmaq individual. Howe held that strong notions of and attachment to property protected a person from constantly having their person and possessions subordinated to the wishes of the group. Yet an inconsistent attitude towards Mi'kmaq property also ultimately led Howe to be contradictory in his appraisals of Charles Glode and his household, for while he referred to Charles's girls as guileless "perfect children of nature," he had come to see their father as shrewd and calculating.[142]

This perception of Charles's character gained prominence after Charles wrote to him on 12 November 1842 offering to sell the government one of his three yokes of oxen for the use of the Bear River settlement. Howe had been looking for a yoke for this purpose since the beginning of November, and Charles leapt at the chance to prove himself equal to any settler in the cattle-selling forum.[143] A sale, moreover, would comply with a suggestion the commissioner had made to Charles earlier regarding the need to change stock regularly. Though Charles gave no indication by what standards he priced his animals, he informed Howe that the government could have a six-year-old yoke for twenty-one pounds, an eight-year-old yoke for twenty pounds, and a four-year-old yoke for eighteen pounds.[144] Glode added that the sale of oxen would allow him to keep the cow the commissioner had promised him in October, as well as erect a frame house, according to specifications that Howe set out.[145] Evidently completely unaware that the commissioner would consider his prices excessive and so snub his offer, Charles concluded his missive on a cordial, even whimsical note: "P.S. I was very sorry that I was away when you staid at my Wig-wam. A fortnights' good hunting in the *Nebookt* [woods] among the *teyam* [moose] or *copete* [beaver], would not please me so well as a sight of

the *Netap* [friend] so *wilmadock* [good] to our *elnook* [people].[146]

Charles desperately needed the money. Howe bluntly had declared his displeasure with the fact that Charles had failed to construct a frame house. A small frame house was not something Charles really wanted; his camp was comfortable enough, but he did not want to lose Howe as an associate. His status largely depended on being seen as the Indian commissioner's friend. As no money for a house-building enterprise seemed forthcoming from the government, Charles banked on the sale of his oxen to contribute towards something the commissioner, more than he, wanted. At the Kejimkujik settlement John Jeremy, who had a house build and paid for him by the government, declared that he considered his new frame house far less commodious than his log camp.[147] Jeremy's complaint may have displeased Howe and his associates, but it echoed what Charles was feeling at the time.

In trying his best to raise the funds for the house to satisfy the commissioner, however, Charles only ended up displeasing Howe, as Howe considered Charles's asking prices for the oxen preposterous and made no secret of his feelings. The same day Charles approached the government purchasing agent, William Nicholls, to offer his oxen for sale, Nicholls apprised Howe that he knew a person who had bought a good team for only twelve pounds.[148] "Don't take Glode's cattle unless you can get as good and as cheap as elsewhere," Howe barked back at Nicholls.[149]

When he discovered that the government, without even negotiating for his cattle, had purchased a yoke elsewhere,[150] Charles Glode was devastated. If the house was ever to be completed, he had no other option but to petition for money to build it. On 8 May 1843 Charles approached William Nicholls for sufficient funding to complete his house building. He doubtless felt abandoned and fearful, since Howe had recently not only refused his brother Jack money to purchase property at Lequille, but had denied him provisions owing to the fact that Jack did not plant extensively.[151] Still, Howe proved willing to negotiate, if only to get Charles "out of his Wigwam." The money promised in the fall of 1842 for a cow, around four pounds, could be spent on frame house construction, on condition that Charles built and furnished his dwelling properly, with a fire-proof cellar.[152] Howe then recanted and allowed Charles ten pounds in June 1843 to help with his house.[153] This amount, though welcome, was still not enough. Charles by this time had fallen into debt. Either he impoverished himself building the house according to government standards, or he could sell part of his land and try to make ends meet with the proceeds of the sale. Worse, Howe retired in 1843 from the position of Nova Scotia's Indian commissioner, so Charles lost his closest government contact.

For a while he toyed with the idea of selling the property. On 1 March 1845, unaware that his two-hundred-acre lot already had been granted to him in 1840, Glode petitioned Lieutenant Governor Falkland for freehold title to his land so he could sell it. He only knew that he had obtained a licence of occupation – and the date he gave for this, 1831, was incorrect. Charles then recounted a number of terrible tragedies that had beset him over the preceding two years. "At the time of issue of the licence your petitioner had a family of 7 children," he explained, "the two elder ones being sons, all of whom, with the exception of the youngest (a girl) are now dead and having lost their assistance your petitioner is unable to improve further or manage so large a farm." He wanted his grant of two hundred acres confirmed so he could farm on a smaller portion of it and sell the rest, since his "advancing age" would not admit of his working more property.

Charles' "X" on this petition was followed by signatures of most of the most prominent men in Annapolis Royal: Thomas Ritchie, the Reverend Edward Gilpin, T.B. Gilpin, George Runciman, Bernard Gilpin, James Cowling, James Gray J.P., James Ritchie, George Millidge, W. Ruggles, and Joseph Norman. Faced with this array of prominent citizens of Annapolis, an astonished surveyor general, John Spry Morris, quickly clarified matters by explaining that the lot applied for had been granted in 1840.[154] Yet Charles now hesitated to place his land on the market. The fact that it was isolated and would not fetch a good price in what by 1844 was a minor economic recession precluded its sale.

Charles's problems worsened further. In the autumn of 1845, a devastating "bilious fever" struck the Mi'kmaq of Annapolis and Queens Counties. It continued into 1846, when it spread to Mi'kmaq in Halifax and Dartmouth, leaving many families desolate.[155] Dr. Robert Leslie, MD, who also acted as Indian agent for the Lequille and Milford areas, wrote in the fall of 1845 that Charles continued "well," as

did Jack, Joseph, and Peter Paul, though Charles was experiencing hard economic times. The following year, however, his report changed. In spring 1846 he listed the health of both Charles Glode's wife and Peter Paul as "poor," though Jack and Joseph Glode, both living at Lequille, were "comfortable." Jack still had four children and Joseph had six, while Paul's family numbered ten. In the fall, Molly Knockwood, Francis Glode's elderly mother-in-law whom Francis, Charles, and Jack Glode had been caring for since 1841, succumbed to the disease.[156] Then on 21 December 1846, Alfred Spurr, who owned a tract abutting Charles's property, apprised Alfred Whitman, a local farmer and land surveyor, that Charles and his wife were very ill.[157] Charles survived the bout of fever, but his wife Frances did not. Though no date of death is given for her, she probably died in 1847.

Yet Charles's physical constitution must have been weakened by the attack of illness, for he found it increasingly difficult to farm without the support of a family about him. He had not only lost a wife who had been his companion for many years, but also had no sons to help him on the land.[158] In a cruel reversal of fate, Charles's fortunes had sunk beneath those of his more traditional contemporaries who had proven more inured to the pull of government influence and interference. He briefly consorted with a Mehlman woman from Queens County, but this relationship did not last long. As the elderly Charles's health declined, he fell under the care of his sole remaining daughter, Mary, at Lequille.

In 1852 Charles Glode died intestate. He had previously named his brother Jack as his executor, but Jack had died soon after he acquired his own plot of land in 1845, so Edward W. Cutler, the sheriff of Annapolis Royal, administered all arrangements pertaining to Charles's estate. On 8 April 1852 Cutler was given a year to dispose of enough of Charles's property to settle any outstanding debts.[159] Accordingly, the one hundred acres Charles had bought from Jasper Williams in 1839 was placed on the block and sold to John Carter for £25.10s, but this still left the two-hundred-acre grant in Charles's heir Mary's hands.[160]

Mary, who remained unmarried, sold the tract in 1889 after subdividing it into two equal halves the same way John Williams's grant had been split in 1839. On 13 July 1889 Albert Hubley, a farmer and employment of the Harnish mill in Graywood, purchased the upper half of the lot for twenty-five dollars, while the lower, improved portion went to Enos D. Hubley, Albert's brother, for forty dollars.[161] Thus ended Charles's family's freehold tenure at Milford, an experiment driven by Mi'kmaw tenacity, yet doomed owing to lingering Mi'kmaw prejudices against agriculture, a severe disease epidemic, and inconsistent government practices.

In 1883 the Department of Indian Affairs initiated an investigation into the status of the eight hundred acres belonging to the Glode settlement that were still held by Mi'kmaq under tickets of location. The department instructed George Wells, the local Indian agent, to secure a surrender of the remaining acreage from the former holders' heirs, but in December Wells replied that the Mi'kmaq had no intention of relinquishing their land.[162] He further related that, in 1861, Francis Glode and two of his sons, Jacob and Simon, had wanted to sell their two-hundred-acre parcel at Milton but had been forbidden to do so by the government as Francis did not hold a freehold lot.[163] Peter Glode in 1867 for an annual payment of twenty dollars had leased his father Jack's (or John's) parcel for a term of ninety-nine years.[164] And on 1 July 1894 Peter Paul for a consideration of ten pounds had placed his father Molti Paul's parcel under a ninety-nine-year lease.[165] Peter's family members had signed the lease agreement with a series of "Xs" before Jack Glode, whose name was written "John," Alexander Easson, the local Indian agent Robert Leslie, and an elderly judge, William Ritchie, who acted as witnesses to the transaction.[166] In the end Ottawa imposed its own definition on the confused land situation. The parcels belonging to the Glode settlement, it held, were to be treated like small reserves whose underlying title at Confederation had passed to the Department of Indian Affairs. On these grounds the department in 1926 disposed of the remaining eight hundred acres by a land surrender obtained from the Annapolis band.[167]

Charles Glode's endeavours to establish the Glode settlement along the Liverpool-Annapolis Road have not been forgotten. Milford residents still view him as one of the pioneer farmers of their community. Yet the success of his farming settlement relied greatly on sustained government support, and when he no longer had a steady flow of government goods to distribute, he lost his Mi'kmaw following. In the end the province abandoned him to his fate, misunderstanding the tragic consequences for a man who was continually confronted and pulled apart by conflicting expectations from various quarters.

Landholding among other Annapolis County Glodes

Joseph Glode Jr. (c.1780–c.1880), the son of Chief Joseph Martin Glode of Caledonia, moved to Lequille after his marriage in 1834 to Mary Ann Stephens. There, he became the "captain" of the Annapolis County Mi'kmaq. In the early 1840s he backed a campaign launched by John Smith, a settler from Newport, West Hants County, to ban the use of snares in moose hunting. Moose snares, the two argued, entangled cattle in their lines as well as wild game, and injured the Mi'kmaw hunt as much as farmers' livestock.[168] Smith and Glode made an effective team, for not long after their petition on the subject reached Halifax in 1843, the House of Assembly passed legislation banning the use of snares.[169]

Energized by this positive response from the House, Joseph mustered the support of other Mi'kmaq, including his uncles Jack and Charles Glode as well as several prominent Annapolis Royal citizens,[170] and directed a second petition to Halifax calling for closed seasons on settler moose hunting. This directive, too, accomplished its aim. In 1844 the House empowered the Courts of General Sessions to impose closed seasons on moose hunting and regulate the selling of moosemeat.[171] A large number of the signees to this petition were Mi'kmaq heads of families. Joseph Glode, Charles Glode, and John (Jack) Glode placed their names first on the document, followed by Peter (Toney) Bobiei, Francis Jeremy, Jim Jeremy, John Jeremy, Lewis Luxey (or Alexis), James Muse (Meuse), James Muse Jr., Stephen Muse, Abraham Peter (or Peters), Joseph Peter, Francis Charles, Joseph Peurnall (*sic*, Pennel), Samuel Pictou, Abraham Toney, Joseph Toney, Newel Toney, and Thomas Salome.[172] At the bottom of this list, and separate from the cluster of names belonging to the Annapolis Royal settler elite, stood the name "T.C. Tobias."[173] Yet all that could be found about T.C. Tobias was that he was born in Annapolis Royal in 1801 and went as a young man to Rio de Janeiro, from which he returned to Nova Scotia via New York in

1835, married a woman named Augusta, and in his later years became a collector of customs at Annapolis Royal.[174] His rationale for setting off his signature to the 1844 petition remains a mystery.[175]

The petitioners claimed that settlers' "rapacity" had left few moose "to afford sustenance to the Former Lords of the Soil." Pregnant moose were especially vulnerable during March when deep snow made them easy prey for settlers' dogs, out hunting with their masters. Large numbers of moose had been known to have been killed in this manner by "a single party." To rectify this slaughter, petitioners proposed that March be recognized as a closed season for settler moose hunting, since it was at that season that the Mi'kmaq relied most heavily on moose for their survival.[176] In 1847 Joseph Glode and Louis Alexis (regularly known as Lewis Luxey) called for the lifting of restrictions that prevented Mi'kmaq from fishing more than five days a week.[177] Unlike the former two petitions with which Jospeh was associated, this one did not gain its goal. The Mi'kmaw for many years afterwards had to abide by the five-day limitation on their fishing activities, and though Joseph's descendants rarely acknowledged their feeling on this matter to outsiders,[178] among themselves they deeply resented the impositions that the government placed on their traditional and still cherished way of life.

In the late 1840s Chief Jack Glode, Captain Joseph's uncle, was still was caring for three of his own children as well as the elderly individuals whom Howe had noted as being part of his band in 1842. As Annapolis district chief, Jack was responsible for the orphaned, aged, and infirm. Yet he lacked resources to shelter even himself comfortably, and as he grew older he increasingly insisted that the government help him build a frame house. In 1845 his settler friends at Annapolis Royal encouraged him to take advantage of lowered land prices during a temporary economic recession, informing him that a widow named Elizabeth Ritchie had placed the lot he wanted at Lequille on the market. Jack then set out to raise the two pounds purchase price by petitioning Lord Falkland, first on 26 June and a second time on 2 October.[179] He explained to the lieutenant governor that he had timber cut and was ready to build so that he could practise "husbandry and assimilation to the Habits of the White Man." Jack's pleas for money to erect a frame house had been

ignored by Commissioner Howe in 1843, but in 1845 Jack felt confident that Lord Falkland would help him obtain the "certain land" where he had already cultivated a sizable garden.[180] When the lieutenant governor forwarded him the necessary purchase money in the fall of 1845, Jack bought the Ritchie lot on 12 February 1846. The property comprised three acres of the old mill site that the chief had occupied for years.[181]

Jack's son, Peter Glode, lived at Cecumgega or Fairy Lake (today known as Kejimkujik Lake), which lay on the Annapolis-Queens County border. Mi'kmaw farming near them included the farming allotments of John Jeremy and his wife Sally Tony, Joseph Peters and his wife Sally Alexis, and Francis Charles, who had wed Molly Peters.[182] The Fairy Lake farming settlement had been initiated in 1841 by John Jeremy, but Jeremy, by treating his allotment as freehold, sold his plot to Jim Charles. Charles kept some cows and made butter that he sold to local settlers, an unusual activity for a Mi'kmaq at that time.[183] After Mi'kmaw departures in the late 1840s from Cecumgega Lake to Brookfield in Queens County, Peter Glode (c.1800–1884), his wife Hannah Labrador, and Jim Charles remained the last of the original Mi'kmaw farmers who took up plots at Kejimkujik. The Fairy Lake settlement had suffered in 1845 and 1846 from a severe potato blight, the damming of rivers by mill owners, trespasses from land- and timber-hungry settlers, and competition from hunting parties formed of men from surrounding milltowns and mining camps. Around 1860 one of Peter Glode's daughters took up with a local "ne'er-do-well" named Jim Hamilton who one day physically accosted Jim Charles, knowing that Charles had a gold mine whose location he refused to disclose. In self-defence, Jim Charles hit Hamilton with a gun butt and killed him. When Peter and Jim informed a local merchant and magistrate named John Harlow of the affair, Harlow called a magistrate's court where Peter Glode's testimony helped secure Jim Charles's freedom.[184]

For several years Peter and Jim were neighbours of Francis Glode (c.1770–c.1870), likely a son of Joseph Martin Glode of Caledonia. Francis reputedly died at Kejimkujik around one hundred years of age.[185] During the 1850s he, his wife Madeleine Knockwood, and their sons Simon, Joseph, and Jim lived in Queens County in a cabin on a peninsula jutting out into

Kejimkujik Lake, while Peter Glode, their close relative, farmed on an island offshore, still called "Piel's Island." In 1843 Joseph Howe had instructed a surveyor, Whitman Freeman, to set out one hundred acres for each Mi'kmaq belonging to the Kejimkujik farming settlement, but as neither Peter's nor Francis's parcels approached this size, they later acquired location tickets to small plots on the opposite shore of the Lake, in Annapolis County.[186]

Jack Glode's son Peter Glode, and Peter's wife Hannah Labrador, both born in 1829, had at least three sons, John, Peter Jr., and Francis, as well as two daughters, Marie and Kate.[187] Peter Jr., born in 1851, produced a stage show that he took on tour in the early 1900s to supplement his income from farming, hunting, and fishing. Accompanied by his wife and a daughter, he gave musical concerts throughout eastern Canada and New England in which he played the violin, sang, demonstrated the Snake Dance, Tomahawk Dance, and Step Dance, and spoke about Mikmaw culture.[188] Peter Jr. and his family eventually moved permanently to the United States. On 11 May 1876 his sister Marie married Jacques (or James) Glode, a son of Matthew Gloade and Victoire Glode of Pubnico. Kate, born in 1858, though she was listed as married on the 1881 census, had no husband with her but did have three children: Mary Anne, who was twelve, Annie, six, and John, one. After Jim Charles sold his plot on the lake in 1864 and Francis Glode died about 1870, Peter and Hannah became the sole residents of the Fairy Lake farming settlement.[189] Peter and Hannah both died in June of 1884, though Kate lived on at Kejimkujik Lake for several years after her parents' death. A report written in 1884 by Thomas J. Butler, the Indian agent at Caledonia, praised Peter Sr.'s self-sufficiency and reminisced that he had been "a man of an industrious nature, and had made a very comfortable home for himself and family." He also alerted the Department of Indian Affairs that "bad neighbours" had frightened Peter's daughter Kate from her family's homestead in order to cut timber on her land.[190]

Captain Joseph Glode, who had petitioned the government in 1844, was, like Francis, probably a son of Chief Joseph Martin Claude, and following Jack Glode's death he arose as the Annapolis district leader. The Mi'kmaw captain lived at Lequille and retained strong kin ties with Mi'kmaq from the Newport and Windsor area. He and his wife Mary Ann Stephens both had been raised near Annapolis Royal, a point noted by the priest who married them in 1834.[191] Joseph also was "Captain Joseph Glode" from whom the Baptist missionary Silus Tertius Rand elicited several legends, including "The Magical Coat, Shoes, and Sword," and "The Boy That was Transformed into a Horse." Both stories involved a syncretistic blending of French folklore, introducing kings, queens, and princesses, with a distinctly Mi'kmaw emphasis on power-holders being able to overcome formidable odds though viewed by others as physically small, weak, and insignificant.[192] Joseph must have had imbibed French folklore from his grandfather, Martin Grand Claude Jr. (c.1740–c.1820), who had spent his youth among the French *métis* and Acadians of La Have.

In 1898 Indian agent James Farrell noted that, while no Mi'kmaq lived on farms in Milford or Maitland, some held lands at Lequille, Paradise, and Middleton.[193] Several of these were freehold grants. There were special festivities held at Lequille, such as St. Anne's Day ceremonies in late July and an Easter "flag raising."[194] Community members also showed courage and resilience in the face of tragedy. James Edward Beckwith, Indian agent at Kentville in 1886, marvelled at the stoicism with which Chief Joseph Glode's widow faced her lot in life after the death of her husband. She cultivated an acre of land, which Beckwith erroneously presumed belonged to the government.[195] It was "not overly productive," he noted, but she persevered in cultivating it. "She is the same patient, preserving, industrious woman that she ever was within the past ten years," he wrote. "I have known her to nurse and bury her husband, her son, her two daughters and a grandson, and never saw her shed a tear but upon one occasion, when she called upon me to enable her to get something from the doctor to ease the pain and hacking cough, when a tear came forth unbidden, but turning for a moment, as if ashamed, she became herself again."[196]

Benjamin Pictou succeeded Chief Joseph Glode at Lequille as Annapolis district chief around 1880. Benjamin, born at a fishing site called "Eel Weir" near Lake Kejimkujik on 7 September 1830, was the son Matthew Pictou (c.1811–c.1890) and an Acadian woman named Henriette Guillet (Juillehaut or Gehue). On 21 January 1851 Bejamin married Mary Ellen Glode (1824–55), who hailed from Lequille. But when Mary Ellen died giving birth to their first child, Joseph, Benjamin Pictou married again, to Madeline Paul on 11 February 1857, and the couple had eight children who survived infancy. The chief died at Lequille at 101 years of age on 30 March 1931.[197] Several of Benjamin Pictou and Madeline Paul's descendants live at Lequille today.

Despite strong leadership shown by Chief Benjamin Pictou, the government administratively split up the Mi'kmaw Annapolis district constituency, which traditionally had formed a seamless district polity from Lequille extending eastward across the province from the Annapolis Basin to Liverpool. While the Annapolis band, at least on paper, had fallen in 1807 under the aegis of three distinct jurisdictions set up by a committee responsible for Indian matters in the province, the Mi'kmaq experienced little government intervention in their internal affairs until after Confederation in 1867. After that date, however, the band became politically divided by external fiat into distinct Mi'kmaw communities, with Bear River reserve regarded as the administrative hub of Mi'kmaw communities in Annapolis and Digby Counties, and the Wildcat reserve serving as the main jurisdictional centre for groups in Queens and Shelburne Counties.

A major consequence of the growth of the Bear River community was the draining away of the political importance of Lequille, which for generations had been the headquarters of Glode leadership. By 1850 Lequille was an ethnically diverse community of around 420, composed not only of English, Irish, and Mi'kmaq but also descendants of Black Loyalists having the surnames "Bailey," "Burill," "Cromwell," "Cuff," "Currie," "Francklin," "Francis," "Jackson," "Moses," "Mott," "Ruggles," and "Stevenson." Some of these Loyalists had intermarried with the Mi'kmaq.[198] The Mi'kmaw community held various festivities, particularly at and around St. Anne's Day, at which all were welcome. These included dances where Lequille's residents heard fiddle playing performed by men such as Joseph Penall (or Pennel), whose skill at rendering intricate step-dance tunes on his violin was legendary throughout southwestern Nova Scotia. In 1898 James Farrell, Dr. Robert Leslie's successor as the Annapolis County Indian agent, wrote to Ottawa that the Mi'kmaq at Lequille, as well as around neighbouring Paradise and Middleton, were in good health, temperate, and law abiding. Most made their living by guiding, lumbering, river driving, coopering, fishing, hunting, and basket making.[199]

From the 1850s onward, families bearing the surname "Glode" (or "Gloade") were referred to in census and church records, and even by the Mi'kmaq themselves, as Annapolis County Glodes, Bear River Glodes, Milford Glodes, Milton Glodes, Greenfield Glodes, and Yarmouth County Glodes. During the same years the once internally kin-related and socially and politically unified Glode family of southwestern Nova Scotia consequently lost much of its representational strength within provincial and federal corridors of power. Yet Glode/Gloade memories of past linkages to specific geographical areas continued to be strong until the turn of the nineteenth century, and still linger to some degree today.

Glodes on the Lower Mersey and Medway Rivers: *Ogomkigeak* (Liverpool), *Potamoc/Potanoc* (Milton), and *Ponhook* (Indian Gardens) and Greenfield

If Charles and Jack Glode were well-known Mi'kmaw leaders on the upper Mersey River system, even more Glodes were noted for their political and other publicly recognized activities on the lower Mersey. Peter Glode and his wife Hannah were successful long-time farmers in Queens County, while Samuel Freeman Glode from Potamoc was a noted First World War hero.[200] Mi'kmaq had congregated seasonally on the lower reaches of the Mersey and Medway Rivers to take salmon and gaspereau – which locally is known as alewife or kayak – by spear and weir for countless generations.[201] The occupation sites of Potamoc and Cowie's Falls near Milton, though irrevocably altered in recent years by the dredging of a canal and the erection of a hydroelectric dam and powerhouse, were ancient Mi'kmaw weirsites. Between 1820 and 1840 Molti (or Martin) Glode (c.1770–c.1840) was head man in this area, and after his death Cobliel (Gabriel, Cobbeyall, Cablael, c.1790–c.1864) became local chief. Molti most likely was a son of "old Martyn Claude" (c.1740–c.1820) of La Have whose name appeared in Indian commissioner George Henry Monk's account books in the 1790s.

While there is insufficient documentary evidence to show degrees of relationship existing between Molti Glode and Cobliel Glode, it is probably safe to suggest that Molti was either Cobliel's father or one of his uncles. Meanwhile, Francis Glode, born circa 1820, who was the grandfather of Sam Glode and who succeeded Cobliel as chief, was probably one of Cobliel's older sons.[202] Local settlers recounted how Francis in the 1880s presided over Mi'kmaw council meetings in the Molega Lake area.[203] All three men followed Joseph Martin Claude's lead by escorting sportsmen on hunting and fishing expeditions out of Liverpool and Port Medway, now Mill Village. Francis succeeded Joseph Martin Glode as leader on the lower Medway River, and when Francis grew elderly one of his sons, Stephen, continued to guide with his sons in the Kejimkujik Lake region.

With the erection of numerous mills at Milton by 1835, Molti Glode petitioned Halifax each year for blankets and provisions to assist the twenty families he had under his aegis through the winter.[204] The head men of Molti's band included an elderly man named Francis Glode, born about 1804;[205] Francis-Joseph Glode, born about 1805;[206] and Molti's son Paul, born in 1807, who later moved to Caledonia.[207] Other families in the group included members of the Alexis, Francis, Labrador, Martin, Michael, Paul, and Pictou families. In their youth, these Mi'kmaq would have borne the brunt of the temporary collapse of the Mi'kmaw economy based on fur trading. During years that fur-bearing animals were scarce, local family heads came to rely instead on trading salmon with local merchants for blankets, flour, and kettles. However, log driving, river dredging, and sawmills had by the 1830s caused salmon stocks to drop dramatically. Though guiding provided alternative income, during the years Molti Glode was chief the Milton band experienced some very lean years.

Cobliel Glode (c.1780–c.1864), Molti Glode's successor as local chief, like his ancestors hunted and fished along the Medway River. Cobliel and his wife Mary Anne Bobbiei (or Bobieye) had at least one son, Newel, born in 1838, and five daughters: Mary Ann, born about 1829; Bridget, born in 1840; Mary, born in 1847; and Alicia and Magdalene, both born in 1850.[208] Mary Ann Cobliel (Glode) became the wife of Chief Lewis Luxey (or Alexis) Sr. of Brookfield in Queens County.[209]

Cobliel Glode is best known to modern-day historians for guiding Joseph Howe, the reform politician, writer, and newspaper editor, through Queens County in 1842. Howe, during his brief stint as provincial Indian commissioner in 1842–43, was winding his way by horse and wagon around the southwestern Nova Scotian coastline, aiming to end his journey at the Glode settlement in Annapolis County, when he realized that if he went into the interior of

Queens County on his own he would get lost. When he explained that he needed Mi'kmaw assistance to locate the Mi'kmaw farming community on Kejimkujik Lake, which he had been hearing about since the spring, settlers at Liverpool recommended that he hire Cobliel Glode as his guide.

Cobliel and his family occupied an encampment ground where Ponhook Lake drains into the Medway River.[210] There was no Greenfield in 1842, just a straggling row of logging shanties and mills along the trail leading to William Burke's Brookfield settlement. After hearing on October 15 that Cobliel was a reliable, sober individual "of a good character," Howe invited him to find both the Kejimkujik settlement and the thousand-acre tract reserved for the Mi'kmaw by Charles Morris in 1820.[211] Cobliel accepted the commissioner's offer and took a seat in Howe's horse-drawn wagon, although he warned that the final lap of the journey would have to be made on foot. From 16–21 October the two made a circuit from Liverpool to the Mi'kmaw settlement on Kijimkujik Lake and then back to Ponhook again. "Gaby," as Howe addressed Cobliel, was in his element, for his ancestors had hunted and fished over the terrain for generations. Incoming settlers recognized this, for place names like "Big Glode Island" and "Little Glode Island" in Molega Lake testified to the Glode family's long-standing presence in this area.[212]

Howe soon found out, however, that despite Cobliel's fine-grained knowledge of the countryside, he had never heard of any Mi'kmaw reserve laid off by the government in 1820 on the Medway River system. Instead, the chief took the opportunity of being alone with the commissioner to apprise Howe of problems he had with mill owners trying to appropriate his people's traditional encampment ground as a mill yard. Earlier on in their journey, Howe accidently left his book of survey plans at "Morton's," a residence belonging to Sylvanus Morton, a well-known timber merchant. Howe thus had no referents to ascertain the reserve's location, and only on his return from the interior, when he had the plans before him, did he find it lay ten miles further north than he anticipated, nearer to Brookfield. The whole fiasco proved fortunate for Cobliel, who had the commissioner's undivided attention for his own problems. He pointed out settler depredations on the Mi'kmaq's two-acre encampment ground on the Mersey River known as "Indian Gardens," as well as at the Mi'kmaw fishery near Lake Rossignol.[213] He further asked Howe to protect his people's ancient cemetery at Ponhook on the Mersey, where a number of stones were set in the ground as markers on individual graves.

Lacking his survey plans, Howe admitted the strength and antiquity of the Mi'kmaq's attachment to the Ponhook and Medway locales from what he was hearing, and promised to reserve the fishery and burial ground. Had he the plans, he would have seen that Gabriel's encampment was not on the reserve set out in 1820. Once back at Morton's place, Howe retrieved his plans, recognized his mistake, and braced himself for conflicts not only with the settlers who wanted to develop the Mi'kmaw site as mill yard, but with the Mi'kmaq themselves who did not want to move. Yet the commissioner kept such thoughts to himself, for he had to rely on Cobliel's assistance in getting to Kejimkujik Lake. Part of the way was accessible by horse and wagon, but the final portion had to be covered on foot over rough and often boggy terrain. The ranks of Howe's party, moreover, had swelled in size with the addition of interested local settlers who wanted to see the interior of the county for themselves. Unfazed by these changes in plan, Cobliel led Howe's party down "rather blind paths, [and] through swamps and wild meadows" for about five miles before reaching the shore of Kejimkujik Lake.[214] Here they had to launch canoes. By this time dusk had fallen and, worse, a cold, drenching rain had begun to fall. Later that evening, in the safety and warm comfort of John Jeremy's camp, the commissioner penned his gratitude in his diary for the hospitality of John Jeremy's wife, who supplied his party with lodging, fried moosemeat, potatoes, and tea.

Her husband, who was away at Annapolis Royal purchasing supplies at the time of Howe's visit, had visited Howe's office in the spring to secure title for his group's clearings on the lake.[215] As usual, owing to the lateness of the year, the men of the settlement were either out hunting or at Annapolis Royal, so the commissioner had to be satisfied with talking with the women and children.[216] He worried about facing the settler population on his return, after promising Cobliel the lands he wanted, and Cobliel's shooting of the rapids on the way down the Mersey did nothing to steady his nerves. Going back by way of Brookfield, Howe and his party visited what would become Wildcat Reserve No. 12 before meeting

with Cobliel's people at the encampment site below Ponhook Lake. Things did not go as badly with the settlers as Howe had feared. He was able to make arrangements to have the Mi'kmaw burial ground reserved and fenced. He also bargained with Barnabus Miles, a local settler, to purchase one-third of an acre of riverbank near the Mi'kmaw fishing site "to be held for the use and benefit of Coblial (*sic*, Cobliel) Glode and his people." Howe then wrote Whitman Freeman, a local surveyor, to lay off ten acres around the burial plot – now Medway River Reserve No. 11 – and an additional four hundred acres on the east side of the Liverpool (now Mersey) River at "Liverpool Ponhook" or "First Lake" to include a "Burial Ground and improvements there."[217] This tract is now known as Ponhook Reserve No. 10.

Doubtless Cobliel Glode had a hand in getting the commissioner to reserve this second tract as well. In 1837, when the site was surveyed, the tract's occupants were Malti (Molti or Martin) Glode, Peter Bobiei, Alex Davis, Francis Labrador, Alex Jeremy, Joseph Jeremy, and Sally Maltai (or Molti). The reserve, set out in 1843 by Howe, was for Joseph Molti, Ellick (Alex) Davis, Ellick (Alex) Jeremy, and Peter Toney, so a few of the original group remained on the Ponhook Lake site.[218] This parcel originally sat at the foot of First Lake, but the contours of the landscape were changed by the Mersey Pulp and Paper Company in the 1920s building Power Dam No. 1 that flooded First Lake, Second Lake, Rossignol Lake, Yeaton Lake, Fourth Lake, Fifth Lake, and Lowe's Lake into one massive body of water called "Lake Rossignol."

Cobliel Glode guided Howe for five days into the interior Queens County, and received one pound for his services.[219] Though Howe continued to refer affably to the chief in his later correspondence, Cobliel and Howe clashed briefly at an impromptu council meeting. The commissioner had just learned that the chief's encampment at what later became Greenfield was not on a reserve, and doubtless the Mi'kmaq feared that they would not only have to leave their traditional land base but that once Howe realized he did not have to regard the settlers who occupied the site as trespassers he might even renege on his promise to provide government protection for their fishery and graveyard.

According to one contemporary newspaper account, Cobliel and his people sat "sphinx-like" until the commissioner finished speaking. Howe delineated how the chief must move to the reserve on the Wildcat River at once, promising him "aid in proportion to his exertions" in convincing other Mi'kmaq to follow him there.[220] Howe then concluded by affirming that the local burial site would be safe from desecration, and sat down. At this, Cobliel, exhibiting a "splendid physique and dignified bearing," rose "and intoned with great deliberation and emphasis … Howe, I believe you lie."[221]

Cobliel did not deeply distrust Howe as a person, but he suspected that Howe's ideological proclivities would not permit the Mi'kmaq to pursue their seasonal exploitation of their crucial traditional resource areas. The chief still carried on personable correspondence with Howe after 1843 when Howe ceased to be provincial Indian commissioner. Howe's reversal of attitude, however, would have been offensive to the Mi'kmaq and likely sent shock waves through the Mi'kmaw community along the Mersey-Medway river system, all the way to Annapolis. Cobliel's experience with Howe underlined the dangers of too close relations with officials whose actions might prove unpredictable and exclusionary if one did not have secure title to one's land. When a mill was built at Ponhook Bridge in 1846, Cobliel moved from Greenfield to "Lamoony Island" (Big La Mouna Island) in Ponhook Lake on the upper Mersey River system. By contrast, others of Cobliel's group remained living at present-day Greenfield, where Roman Catholic itinerant priests encouraged them to attend mass and sacraments at a small chapel erected at Bangs Falls.

Cobliel preferred to spend his final years in relative isolation with his family on the shores of Molega Lake.[222] In 1856 he petitioned the government for money to construct a frame house, for which he received five pounds from the government. He also wanted freehold title to his forty-acre farming plot, for settlers were vying for land on the Mersey and Medway Rivers and were not afraid to petition for land already occupied by the Mi'kmaq.[223] In February 1857 the surveyor Whitman Freeman, speaking on Cobliel's behalf, wrote to Halifax that "Cobleale [*sic*, Cobliel] is an old inhabitant of this Country, has a Family, [and] He has been a considerable portion of time during the last ten years living upon an island situate in Malaga [*sic*, Molega] Lake." He "entertains a strong desire and attachment to the Island, to be perpetuated in his family and their descendents." No

other person, Whitman continued, "had any claim to his Island. Unable to obtain a grant in the usual way by purchase, he asks for a reserve of the Island."[224] Yet no freehold grant was ever issued to him. In 1858 Cobliel was suffering from a serious illness from which the doctor who visited him twice and bled him with leeches did not expect him to recover. He did, however, recover sufficiently to live a few more years, since his name appears on a list drawn up in 1862 of Mi'kmaq living in Queens County.[225] He died at Molega Lake about 1864.

Newel (or Noel) Cobliel (c.1838–1901), Cobliel Glode's son, hunted and guided along the lower Medway River, but after his father's death he left Molega Lake and lived on the west side of Big Bon Mature Lake, which flows into the Mersey River about twelve miles above Liverpool.[226] He kept a small farm at this locale until his death in 1901, though for a short period in the early 1890s he lived with Abraham Glode Jr. and Madeline at Greenfield. When Thomas H. Raddall visited this farmsite in 1923, it been stripped of its timber but still retained the name, "Cobleal's Beach."[227] Newel Cobliel and his wife, Mary Anne Molti, had seven children: Madeline, John, Anne, Joseph, James Solomon, Paul David, and Mary Charlotte.[228] Born in 1865, Madeline Cobliel at age nineteen became the third wife of Abraham Glode Jr. of Bear River in 1885, and the pair were married for twenty-two years. Her father Newel Glode farmed at Greenfield, and his new son-in-law Abraham Glode Jr. lived for several years on his father-in-law's farm. Abraham, who moved to Greenfield to be with his wife, and Madeline had ten children: Abraham on 21 July 1885, Benjamin in 1886, Joseph in 1888, Mary Jane (or "Janie") at Mill Village on 20 October 1889, Isaac on 18 April 1893, Bridget at Milton on 19 May 1895, Henry in 1900, Bonaparte in 1901, Janet about 1906, and Elizabeth in 1907. After Abraham Glode Jr.'s death in 1907, Madeline at age forty-four had yet another son, Clarence, born in 1909. The identity of Clarence's father remains unknown.[229] Mi'kmaw kin connections in such instances often proved complicated, but they provided a frame for working relationships, family and community integration, and, during times of sadness, avenues of support and consolation. From the 1930s to the 1950s, Clarence Glode was well known to chandlers and shipping merchants at Lunenburg, as he was a skilled woodworker and made mast hoops and items of rigging for fishing schooners. In 1957 he and his family were the only

Mi'kmaq living on the Gold River reserve, laid out in 1818 in coastal Lunenburg County. Later he moved to Bear River, where several of his descendants live today.

Clarence's maternal grandfather, Newel Cobliel (Glode) of Greenfield, was one of the last of the Glode family to guide on the lower Medway River. Some of the most noted guides in Queens County in the the early decades of the twentieth century were sons of Stephen Glode, the son in turn of Chief Francis Glode of Potamoc and Madeline Molti. In their early years, Stephen's sons stayed near Del Thomas's Milford House on the Annapolis-Liverpool Highway. One unexpected attraction for sportsmen and tourists alike at the lodge must have been Stephen's son Samuel Freeman's Glode's pet moose, Niggly.[230] Samuel's brothers Jim, Louis, John, Mike, Peter, and Steve Jr. all guided at Lake Kejimkujik.[231] A major employer in the area was the Kedgemakooge Rod and Gun Club, which established a hunting and fishing lodge on Kejimkujik Lake not far from the Annapolis-Queens County boundary in 1909, the same year as the formation of the Nova Scotia Guides' Association.[232]

When Newel Cobliel's father Cobliel Glode died about 1864, the latter's office as sub-chief of the lower Mersey-Medway river system was assumed by Francis Glode (c.1820–c.1900). In the 1940s Francis's grandson Samuel Freeman Glode shared what he knew of the history of his immediate family with Queens County historian and novelist Thomas H. Raddall. His grandfather Francis Glode, he recounted, had been born about 1820 at Cowies Falls near Milton and later married Madeline Molti (or Martin), who apparently was his second wife.[233] Francis was sometimes called by his nickname "Uglass" (*Aglass* or *Aglasieo*), which Thomas Raddall recognized as a Mi'kmaw rendition of the word "English person."[234] Around 1858, Francis Glode, Madeline Molti, and their eldest son Stephen travelled by bark canoe from Milton to Montreal following an ancient waterway and portage. They stayed the winter at Montreal at a camp with others they knew and returned the next spring.[235]

Sam maintained that his paternal grandparents circulated among three major encampment grounds, one being Potamoc at Milton, another situated on the Pleasant River draining into Molega Lake, and a third at the juncture of Ponhook Lake and the Medway River, near present-day Greenfield. Most of the

year, however, Francis and his family remained at Potamoc.

Francis and Madeline had at least five children. One son, Newel, drowned at Jordan River in Shelburne County during a river drive. Two other sons, Stephen and Francis Jr., married daughters of James Michael and Catherine Helen Labrador.[236] Stephen Glode (1845–December 15, 1909)[237] wed Mary Michael, while Francis Glode Jr. (1846–71) married Mary's sister Kate Boudreau, a widow.[238] Francis Jr., not long after the birth of his only child, also named Francis, died of consumption and was buried in the Mi'kmaw graveyard at Ponhook, on the shore of the Mersey River below Lake Rossignol.[239] The infant Francis was then adopted by Stephen Francis of Milton, Kate Boudreau's third husband. A fourth son of Francis Glode and Madeline, Peter, born in 1852, wed Fanny Pennel, a daughter of Joseph Pennel of Gold River. During the 1920s, Peter and Fanny lived near Bridgewater in Lunenburg County.[240] Peter's sister, Mary Ann Glode, also wed into the Pennel family by marrying James Pennel, a son of Joseph Pennel and Sophia Rafuse of New Germany, on 19 May 1870.[241]

Guiding and river driving were the reason why many of these Glodes continued to travel to Shelburne, Milford, and Kejimkujik Lake into the early years of the twentieth century.[242] Several were hired as guides at Milford House, a vacationing lodge situated on the upper end of the Annapolis-Liverpool Road specializing in hunting and fishing that its owner, Del Thomas, had refurbished from an older halfway house hotel owned by Thomas's family.[243] The establishment consisted of a lodge and cabins made internationally famous by Albert Bigelow Paine's publication in 1908 of *The Tent Dwellers*.[244]

Francis Glode Sr.'s eldest son Stephen was one of the first Mi'kmaq to guide out of Thomas's establishment. Most of the time Stephen lived at Milton, where he wed twice.[245] His first wife, Mary Michael, was born at Brookfield in 1853 and was sixteen years old at the time of her marriage to Stephen on 3 October 1869. In 1870 the couple had a daughter, Mary Anne, and on 7 May 1872 a son, James, in Shelburne County.[246] Mary died in 1874 giving birth to an infant who died the following day.[247] Stephen later married Sarah Jane Labrador, daughter of a medicine woman named Polly Labrador, who was born at Tusket Forks – now Quinan – and later lived near Great Pubnico Lake in Yarmouth County. Sarah Jane Labrador gave birth to thirteen children: Samuel Freeman on 20 April 1878; Michael on 10 March 1880; Mary Madeline on 1 April 1882, who died three days later on 4 April; Annie on 1 September 1884; Francis – best known as "Frank" – on 20 August 1886; James Michael on 16 January 1888;[248] Stephen Jr. on 16 June 1888; Maria Katherine around 1890;[249] Maria on 19 August 1891; a second son named Stephen on 24 November 1894;[250] twins Peter Newell and Elizabeth on 20 August 1897; and John on 2 November 1898. Sarah Jane Labrador died in 1904 and her husband, Stephen Glode Sr., in 1909.[251]

Disease and the deleterious effects of trench warfare during the First World War on those who served overseas thinned the family's ranks. Elizabeth died in 1911 of tuberculosis and Maria died at age twenty of the same disease. The Stephen Glode who was born in 1888, as well as John and Anne, disappear early from the documentary record, so they too must have died young. Frank Glode married Mary Paul of Bear River and had three daughters. Michael (1880–1944), better known as "Mike Glode," married Bessie Carver, "lived in Milton all his days, and was a boss on the log drives down the Mersey River."[252] During the first decades of the twentieth century he appeared in tourist brochures as a guide for hire.[253] An excellent hunter, fisherman, and guide, he died suddenly of a heart attack in 1944. His brother James Albert, born at Milton on 16 January 1888, wed Anastasia Lafford in 1912. A captain of the Halifax County Mi'kmaw band, James lived before the war in Dartmouth, where he gained public attention on 10 March 1916 as the first Mi'kmaq to enlist in the conflict in Europe. He joined the 219th Highland Battalion of the Highland Brigade, as did his brother Peter Newell Glode a year later.[254] James was gassed overseas and, after his return, lived at Londonderry, Colchester County, where he suffered from serious breathing problems. He died of pneumonia at age thirty-four on 4 August 1922. Peter Newell on his return from overseas lived in Annapolis, Shelburne, Lunenburg, and Colchester Counties before moving back to Milton in 1953, where he died in 1954.[255] The younger Stephen Glode, born in 1894, did not go to war, but moved from Milton to the Millbrook reserve near Truro. He suffered from spasms and died, unmarried, in 1958.[256] James Glode and his wife Anastasia lived most of their lives at Londonderry, near Truro.[257]

A Mi'kmaw War Hero. During the First World War Samuel Freeman Glode became a decorated war hero owing to his bravery in saving the lives of twenty men in a collapsed tunnel under No Man's Land. Though illiterate, he became the main storyteller and historian of his immediate family. Author Thomas Raddall described him as tall and handsome, with striking black hair and eyes and an exceptional intelligence. In 1944 Glode recounted to Raddall stories about his early life and adventures overseas. Further information was gathered from Sam Glode in 1953 by T.B. Smith. Sam's memory proved so acute that he could remember meeting an elderly woman named Bella McCoy whose husband, Robert McQuhue, had belonged to the Liverpool garrison before the barracks were deserted by the British military in 1794.

When Sam was eight or nine years old he moved with his family to Shelburne, where they traded living quarters with Francis Alexis (or Luxey) and Mary Anne Paul, who then moved into the Glode's house at Milton.[258] Sam's father Stephen walked the entire sixty miles to Shelburne dragging a little handcart with a few blankets, pots, and tools. When they stopped, Sam's mother made baskets while Sam and his father shot partridges and fished. Game wardens had banned the use of leister spears to take salmon at Milton, but spear fishing was still practised by Mi'kmaq in the Cape Sable district, and was an activity Sam enjoyed. En route an old piece of sail canvas made a covering for the family lean-to at night. Sam lived for a while along the Great Pubnico Lake Road, back of West Pubnico in Yarmouth County, with Matthew Glode, who was related to him. He also visited his mother's mother, Polly Labrador, who lived near Matthew. Molly Labrador hailed originally from The Forks (now Quinan), and in her later years was regarded at West Pubnico as a medicine woman by Mi'kmaq and non-Mi'kmaq alike.[259]

Since the Alexis (or Luxey) family wanted to remain at Milton a few years longer, the Glodes stayed in Shelburne County and did not return to Queens County until 1891. The following summer Sam's father led his family to New Germany in Lunenburg County, travelling by way of Petite Rivière and across the La Have River by ferry, where they camped with one of Sam's father's uncles from Shubenacadie. Drawing upon his wide repertoire of woods skills, Sam as he grew older wintered alone in the solitude of his hunting territory on Pebbelogitch Lake in interior Queens County, trapping and otherwise living off the land. He lamented the disappearance of the caribou that used to migrate in numbers through the area. One reason Sam was given for their demise was that "the building of the railways between Bridgewater and Middleton and between New Germany and Caledonia … stopped the caribou moving."[260]

In 1900 Sam married Louisa Francis, a daughter of Stephen Francis and Katherine ("Katy") Michael from Barrington Head, Shelburne County, in a well-attended wedding ceremony at St. Gregory's Church in Liverpool.[261] (Sam's father-in-law Stephen actually had been born into the Murree family in 1845 but, orphaned early in life and raised by Louisa's grandparents, Joseph Francis and Katherine [or Kate] Anne Alexis, he eventually took "Francis" rather than "Murree" as his surname. His adoptive father, Joseph Francis, was part of a Mi'kmaw party that asked Joseph Howe in 1842 to lay out a reserve at Great Pubnico Lake, near the Shelburne County-Yarmouth County border.) The union produced only one child, Lewis Walter Glode, on 10 March 1900.[262] When just shy of his sixteenth birthday, Lewis lied about his age, claiming he was born on 11 March 1898 so he could enlist in the army during the First World War and be sent overseas. Upon his return he guided and found employment as a labourer building new roads and dams. After 1929 he worked at the Liverpool pulp mill. At one point he claimed he had found an outcropping of gold, though he proved reluctant to share knowledge of his findings.[263] Lewis remained all his life at Milton where he married Minnie Carver Lowe, daughter of Henry Carver and Catherine Cowie, in 1921.[264] Some of his descendants still live in the Milton area.

When his wife Louisa died in 1905, Sam Glode did not marry again. The same year as his wife's death he guided at Milford House and the following year was invited by one of his cousins, John Glode from Caledonia, to participate in a logging drive down the Exploits River in central Newfoundland.[265] John worked for an American logging firm that exported wood to Germany, married a local white woman, and settled permanently in Newfoundland.[266]

Guiding at Milton House in 1908 introduced Sam to Dr. A.C. Fales, an ophthalmologist practising in Boston who originally hailed from Nova Scotia.[267]

Fales encouraged Sam to visit him in Boston. Other wealthy Americans also invited him to their homes and introduced him to theatre productions and other forms of urban entertainment. When he was not guiding or visiting patrons he retreated to spend solitary winter months on his trapline. Versatile to the extreme, Sam displayed pluck, equanimity, courage, and creativity in a range of environments, though he was most at home in the woods.

In 1909 Fales asked Sam to serve as a guide on an expedition to Alaska with him and a New York real estate tycoon, H.Q. French. The trip, which included a cook named R.G. Thomas and a second guide, George Ritchie, involved a steamer voyage to Skagway, the train to Whitehorse, and a laborious canoe paddle up the Pelly River to where it flows into the Yukon. It took forty-six days to get to the Yukon River and only five days to descend the Pelly. With the onset of winter hard upon them, they paddled day and night. Fales and French focused on bagging caribou and moose that carried a gigantic spread of antlers, suitable for trophy mounting. If Sam Glode felt any cultural proclivity as a Mi'kmaq to question the wanton wastage of animals (carcasses of animals with inferior racks were simply discarded and left to rot), he never voiced criticism. His goal was to cater to the needs of those he guided, for which he earned one dollar and a half per day.

In Queens County, Sam also cut timber. He worked hard as a lumberman, but he also played hard. He could step dance and square dance to fiddle music all night long.[268] Yet when cutting wood for local companies became an arduous, year-round activity, Sam decided to quit. In 1915 he was chopping hemlocks along Highway 8 in the blistering summer heat when his brother-in-law John Francis announced, "Let's go to war – it can't be no worse than this."[269] The $1.10 the army paid a day proved enticing, so Sam, at age thirty-seven, went to New Brunswick where he enlisted in and trained with the 64th Battalion at Sussex Camp. He was sent overseas to Shorncliff and then transferred to West Sandling in England.

At West Sandling, John Francis became a sniper in the 25th Expeditionary Force, while Sam, after training in the 8th Battalion, was placed in the No. 1 Tunneling Company of the Royal Canadian Engineers. Sam did not know it, but at the same time his fifteen-year-old son Lewis Walter Glode lied about his age to the authorities in order to fight overseas with the 246th Battalion of the Nova Scotia Highlanders. Father and son later met overseas, when Sam exhibited considerable anxiety over his son's welfare. Lewis, though wounded superficially by shrapnel, arrived home safely.

As a sapper during the war, Sam dug trenches below Vimy Ridge, worked on troop transport highways, and defused mines. He joined the La Clytte Camp, close to Ypres in Belgium, for over a year and participated in the Battle of Passchendaele late in 1917 and the Battle of Amiens in 1918. Between 17 April and 7 May 1915, at the famous Hill 60, southwest of Ypres, Sam demonstrated exceptional courage and tenacity. As a corporal in charge of twenty men tunnelling towards the German lines at Messines in 1915, he single-handedly dug through to the surface in No Man's Land, and restored pure air for his comrades in a collapsed section of tunnel until a rescue party released them.[270]

Sam's party were digging shallow service tunnels or "saps," to camouflage work on the main tunnels that could penetrate as far as thirty-five kilometres down, when the party was called to work on a main tunnel. They knew the Germans were counter-mining the area, but during a spell when no ominous sounds could be heard they were instructed to work deep underground. According to T. B. Smith, "Sam organized his crew and was sitting down in a position where he could control the operation, when there was a terrific concussion and Sam came to himself to find the air stifling, the air line to them cut, the sap closed."[271] At this point his detailed memory of the surface landscape aided him. "You look at a piece of country and it's like a picture in your mind," he explained.[272] Lacking this visual image, his companions – mostly miners from Cape Breton – had lost their will to dig until Sam directed them to a place where they could tunnel successfully towards the surface. For his fortitude and clear thinking, Sam was promoted to the rank of sergeant and received the Distinguished Conduct Medal, an honour reserved for non-commissioned officers who performed valiant acts of courage.[273] Until 1993 it, along with the Distinguished Service Order awarded to commissioned officers, ranked only one level below the Victoria Cross.[274]

Sam remained humble about his accomplishments at the Front. He had not expected any honours. After his return from the war he lived for a while quietly at Bear River, and was surprised when he was called upon to travel to Halifax and receive his medal. For the remainder of his life Sam continued sporadically to guide at Milford House, while several of his brothers and nephews, as well as his son Lewis, worked for the Bowater Mersey pulp and paper mill. He finally built a humble cabin at Two Mile Hill at Potamoc, close to where he had been born and near his brother-in-law John Francis. Today, Milford House claims Sam as its most famous guide, though after the war he had to reduce the amount of time he devoted to guiding.[275] During the war he fell gravely ill at Cologne, Germany, before he was shipped home, and he complained as he grew older that the war "took a lot offa me."[276] He no longer possessed the stamina to trap and hunt for an entire winter in the woods but instead preferred to spend the colder months drinking a few beers and sharing stories with companions at the Liverpool Legion, where he met Thomas Raddall. Being a high-profile figure at Milton, he was involved in many community events. He helped search for two missing boys, Floyd and Victor Laing, who disappeared in the woods northwest of Liverpool in December 1941 and were suspected of being killed by a Mi'kmaw man whom Sam knew. Sam visited this man and asked him directly if he was responsible for the boys' deaths, but the man "reportedly turned his head to the wall, and kept his silence."[277]

Sam Glode died at seventy-nine years of age in Camp Hill Hospital in Halifax on 25 October 1957. His body was transported to Queens County and buried with full Royal Canadian Legion honours in St. Gregory's Roman Catholic cemetery on College Street in Liverpool.[278] To Thomas Raddall, who attended the war hero's funeral, Sam Freeman Glode was an exceptional man whom he felt honoured to have known.[279]

The Yarmouth County Glodes

Until the 1950s, Glodes lived along a gravel road cut from West Pubnico to Great Pubnico Lake (also called "Sabine Lake") lying inland from West Pubnico. Local church records suggest that no Glodes settled permanently in this area until the 1840s.

The countryside, which embraced Barrington, Great Pubnico Lake, and the Tusket Lakes, fell under the territorial auspices of the district chief of the Cape Sable band.[280] Paul Williams, whose name appears on the 1801 Barss census of Queens County Mi'kmaq, was a sub-chief in this area, which was separate from the traditional jurisdiction of the Glode leadership. The watershed feeding the Clyde, Roseway, and Tusket rivers was distinct from that of the Mersey River, whose watershed lay near Milton in Annapolis County, the core of Glode territory. To reach Great Pubnico Lake, Mi'kmaq hailing from Queens County travelled along the Atlantic coast to Barrington and then proceeded inland up the Barrington River, with its series of rapids. An alternate route led from Kejimkujik Lake to the headwaters of the Sissaboo River in Digby County and from there to Weymouth. To cut across county in other places was arduous since the terrain was rocky and boggy. The last lap of the journey from Weymouth involved coasting past the town of Yarmouth and around the Tuskets to West Pubnico. Either way, getting to Great Pubnico Lake meant a long journey from Lequille, Bear River, Milton, or Liverpool.

Descendants of Jehan Grand Claude nevertheless had used both routes for generations, since they carried furs to a trading centre at what is now East Pubnico established in the seventeenth century by Baron Philippe I Mius d'Entremont, seigneur of Pobomcoup. When the English destroyed this station during the Acadian deportations, several of the Grand Claudes joined Philippe I Mius d'Entremont's *métis* grandson, François Mius, in escaping from the English into the woods back of Mahone Bay.[281] Much later, after Abbé Jean-Mandé Sigogne's appointment in 1799 to serve among the Mi'kmaq and Acadians of southwestern Nova Scotia, the first Grand Claude to visit Sigogne in what is now Yarmouth County was "Molti Grand Claude" or Molti Glode (c.1770–c.1840). Molti and his wife, "Geneviève á Louis," brought their four-month-old son Paul to be baptized at Ste. Anne du Ruisseau on 30 March 1807. A Cape Sable leader, Jean-Baptist Alexis, and "Bridgette Alexis," a daughter of Jean-Baptist's first cousin Bartholomew Alexis, acted as the infant's sponsors.[282] Following this ceremony Molti Glode and Geneviève did not remain in the Cape Sable district, though they formed the vanguard of other members of their family who visited and decided to stay longer.

The extended family of Matthew Glode and Victoire Francis. The second wave of Glodes into the Cape Sable district was led by Matthew Glode, who was born at Caledonia in Queens County in

1824 or 1825 and died at Pubnico Head on 30 April 1913 at around the age of eighty-four. Matthew likely was one of the youngest sons of Chief Joseph Martin Claude of Caledonia, though he might also have been a son of Francis Glode Sr. (c.1790–c.1890) and Magdalene Knockwood, and thus an older brother of Francis's son Jim Glode.[283] Matthew used the surname "Glode," and some of his descendants continue today to use this spelling, while others by 1920 adopted the surname "Gloade."[284] A short, stocky fellow, Matthew was always addressed by his Mi'kmaw companions as "Matteo."[285]

Matthew was close enough in age to Jim Glode (1831–1936) that the two, as boys, became close friends and hunted together in the woods between Caledonia and Kejimkujik Lake. He also had a younger brother, John, born at Bear River around 1834. Following Chief Joseph Martin Glode's death around 1840, Matthew moved from Caledonia with Francis and Jim Glode to Bear River, where he obtained sufficient schooling to be listed as "literate" on census returns.[286] On 2 July 1854 he married Victoire Francis by banns at St. Croix Roman Catholic Church in Plympton, Digby County, and afterwards moved with his new bride to Great Pubnico Lake, where Victoire's parents lived. There he constructed a small house and planted a garden and apple orchard as other Mi'kmaq in the area had done for generations. He also fished at weirsites at Barrington Head and along the neighbouring Clyde River.[287]

According to a census compiled in 1866 by the Cape Sable district chief, Peter Charles Sulno, Matthew Glode and his wife Victoire were the only members of the Glode family living in Yarmouth County at the time, but this would soon change.[288] Around 1870 Matthew's younger brother John moved from Bear River with his wife Victoria to settle on a lot next to Matthew at West Pubnico. Mi'kmaw claims to land parcels in this area were tenuous. In 1843 Joseph Howe ordered seven hundred acres to be surveyed as a reserve for Paul Williams, James Francis, Philip Francis, Joseph Francis, and James Luxey east of Great Pubnico Lake where the Mi'kmaq had planted potatoes and a fruit trees for many years.[289] After trespassers settled on these fields in the early 1890s, the Mi'kmaq asked the Indian Affairs Department to eject them, but were informed that Howe had forgotten to confirm the acreage as a reserve; therefore it was not transferred to the federal government on the Mi'kmaq's behalf at the time of Confederation in 1867.[290] As a result, the local Mi'kmaw community moved to lands on either side of a road cut between the lake and West Pubnico, where they built cabins atop small stone cellars and planted potato gardens and apple orchards. Their frame houses were sparsely furnished with some cots, a chair or two, and a metal stove for boiling water. Once the Mi'kmaq had settled along the Great Pubnico Road, no further land squabbles arose. Matthew and Victoire raised six children in their small cabin.

Their eldest son, James or Jacques Glode, was born on 20 August 1853. In 1876 James married Mary Anne Glode, a daughter of Peter and Hannah Glode of Kejimkujik, at the Church of St. Pierre de Pubnico. When Mary Anne died about 1881, James two years later wed Sarah Toney, daughter of James Toney and Catherine Molti of Caledonia. James Glode and his second wife Sara had a son Stephen on 25 June 1885 and a daughter Victoria Jane in November 1886.[291] Victoria Jane remained at Pubnico, while in 1903 Stephen Glode began consorting with twelve-year-old Mary Caroline Bartlett, born in July 1891 to Thomas Bartlett (or Bartlett-Alexis) and Emeline Moore (or Crowell) of Tusket; he subsequently married her, and the couple moved to Tusket to live with Mary Caroline's family.[292]

In 1916 Matthew Glode's son Stephen enlisted at Halifax in the 246th Battalion of the Nova Scotia Highlanders and served overseas in the First World War. Although he came back from the war physically unscathed, several of his and Mary Caroline's children took ill soon after his return and died at a young age. Pulmonary tuberculosis, diphtheria, influenza, measles, cholera, and malnutrition repeatedly plagued the small Mi'kmaw community at Tusket. In February 1933 Stephen and Mary Caroline's son Clarence, who was only thirteen, died trying to save his younger brother Gordon, who had fallen through the ice on the Tusket River. Gordon afterwards died of hypothermia.[293] Despite these hardships Stephen's family remained a close-knit one, with ties to the Great Pubnico Lake Road community, local Acadian families, and Mi'kmaq living in Lunenburg County. In 1939 Stephen and Mary Caroline's daughter Evangeline wed Charles Daurie (or Dorey) of New Germany at a ceremony at Ste. Anne du Ruisseau, Eel Brook, Yarmouth County.[294] Evangeline's mother, Mary Caroline,

succumbed to tuberculosis at age fifty-four in 1948, and nine years later Stephen Glode, living alone on Main Street in Yarmouth, died at age seventy-two in a house fire.[295]

Matthew and Victoire's second-eldest son, Sam Glode, born in 1859, wed Molly Murree in the early 1870s and worked as a guide. Sam and Molly had at least one son, John, before Sam died at West Pubnico on 14 February 1935.[296] Pierre Glode, Matthew and Victoire's third son, was born on 29 March 1863 and baptized at Ste. Ann du Ruisseau on the 31st of the same month.[297] This date is very close to the birthdate – 9 February 1863 – sometimes erroneously accorded to Matthew's fourth son, John William Glode, even though Pierre's birth is confirmed by an entry in a church register and there is no evidence that Pierre and John William were twins. Instead, John William was probably born on 9 Febuary 1866, the birthdate ascribed to him in the 1911 federal census. Matthew and Victoire Francis also had three daughters, Mary Ann Catherine Glode born on 2 May 1860, Christine Glode baptized at St. Pierre de Pubnico on 25 April 1864, and Victoire Jean Glode baptized at West Pubnico on 11 October 1875.[298]

John William Glode wed Mary Elizabeth Murree, a daughter of Joseph Muree of The Forks (now Quinan) and Marie-Jeanne, a Mi'kmaw woman. Samuel Freeman Glode, who during his teen years lived with Matthew Glode and his wife Victoire at West Pubnico, always treated John William Glode as his close kin relation.[299] Like other members of the Murree family, John's mother Mary Elizabeth Murree was a descendant of Jean-Marie *dit* Blanchard, a French-speaking Black mercenary who fled to Nova Scotia from the Caribbean during slave uprisings in the late eighteenth century in Santo Domingo, now the capital of the Dominican Republic. Jean-Marie's name was later changed to "Murree," while "Blanchard" was a surname given him by the local Acadian community. On 18 February 1806 Jean-Marie *dit* Blanchard married Claire Muise, a *métis* descendant of a Mi'kmaw woman and a son of Baron Philippe I d'Entremont of Pobomcoup named Philippe II Mius d'Entremont *dit* d'Azy, at Ste. Anne du Ruisseau.[300] Abbé Sigogne noted in his registers at the time of their wedding that Jean-Muree was a "native of Bayonne, France" and "a sailor."[301] Jean-Marie and Claire Muise had two sons, Joseph Muree and Jean-Baptiste Casimer Muree *dit* Blanchard.

Jean-Baptiste, also known as "John Murray," married Cecile Betrand *dit* Maffre, a daughter of a runaway solder and a *métis* woman. Sons and daughters of both brothers lived along the Atlantic coast in Yarmouth County and at The Forks.

John William Newel Glode Sr. and Elizabeth Muree had a son, John Newel, who became known as Young Johnny Glode. John Newel Jr. was born at West Pubnico on 4 December 1887. On 10 April 1910 John Newel married Margaret (or Mary) E. Robbins, a daughter of Henry and Eliza Connolly Robbins of Argyle in Yarmouth County. John Newel became a noted guide and river driver. He also became a freehold property owner, for in June of 1904 he purchased the land around the cabin of Albert E. Carland and his wife along the Great Pubnico Lake Road.[302] Following John Newel's death, his heirs sold this parcel, except for a rectangular piece measuring 260 x 165 feet that John had conveyed to Ray S. Skinner on 17 April 1947.[303]

One of his property transactions was confusing. On 8 May 1929 Leo G. d'Entremont of West Pubnico gifted John Newel two hundred acres on the eastern shore of Great Pubnico Lake, which John immediately reconveyed six days later, for the nominal sum of a dollar, to Bourneff Lovitt, a land broker from Massachusetts.[304] Possibly, while he was grateful for d'Entremont's generosity, John Newel may not have wanted the responsibilities of maintaining extensive acreage that others might put to better use. He did not need the money from a land sale, and it is unlikely the parcel could have been turned into a Mi'kmaw reserve. Since he retained freehold title to his small property from Albert Carland and his wife, John differed from his neighbours, several of whom lacked any formal deed or title to the plots they occupied along the road. John could buy, sell, and even give away land because he commanded a steady wage.

In the early 1920s John Newel became a river driver for the Scott family's lumbering business, established by Thomas Scott on the Barrington River in the early 1900s. According to Hilton Scott, Thomas Scott's grandson, "Glode was the chief river driver." Scott admired John Newal and the other Mi'kmaq who lived along the Great Pubnico Lake Road. "They were good people, all of 'em," he stated. "You could trust them with anything."[305] Some Mi'kmaq travelled from a small Mi'kmaw

community known as the "Gravel Pit," lying just east of the town of Yarmouth, to work in the woods and rivers back of West Pubnico. During their stay, these men boarded with kin living along the Great Pubnico Lake Road.[306] Mi'kmaw log drivers had to send logs past Whistler Point, Wabei, Mushquash, Big Falls, and Little Lake, and there were several sets of rapids on the way down.[307] It was rigorous, dangerous work, but it paid.

Matthew Glode, the patriarch of the West Pubnico Glodes, had numerous younger family members caring for him until his death at eighty-eight years on 30 April 1913. His slightly younger brother John Glode, who married Victoria Murree, died about 1891.[308] John and Victoria raised a son, John Jr., who married Elizabeth Labrador and worked in the fishing industry at Barrington. They also had two daughters, Mary Catherine born in 1860, and Victory Jane born on 7 October 1875. On 21 August 1886 Mary Catherine Glode wed William James Carty, the son of Stephen Carty, an Englishman who with his Mi'kmaw wife Maria Elizabeth Charles lived along the Great Pubnico Lake Road.[309] After his father-in-law John's death, William James Carty and his wife lived for a few years with Matthew Glode's household, although he regularly visited his mother Maria Elizabeth Charles, who preferred to live alone in her own house. Maria, highly regarded for her basket weaving, also concocted and dispensed efficacious medicinal remedies. In her later years she was called the "Vieille Gaigue" – a term no one today seems able to translate, other than to state that Gaigue is a place in Ireland.[310] William James Carty fell through the ice and drowned at age forty-five in 1915, and his widow Mary Catherine moved in with her widowed mother, Victoria Muree Glode.[311] Victoria was a skilled artisan. Hilton Scott, owner of a local lumber mill, said of her, "The Old Glode, Victoria, that was Johnnie [Jr.]'s mother, she was older than Methuselah's goat. She was the chief basket maker and you should have seen her with the drawknife."[312] Victoria died at seventy-four years of age on 27 December 1918.[313]

Matthew and John Glode both were literate, having been educated at Bear River before coming to Yarmouth County. They encouraged their children to attend school at West Pubnico, which opened up opportunities for the younger generation to work at various careers elsewhere in the province. Land tenure was always an issue in this community. Except for John Newel Glode and a few others, most of the dozen or so residents of the Great Pubnico Lake Road community lacked freehold tenure. Yet as late as the mid-1940s a straggling row of small dispersed cabins, beginning roughly midway between the highway and the lake, flanked the road at intervals. The stone foundations of these cabins were very small, about six metres in length and somewhat less in width. For those who enjoyed hunting and guiding, it proved a rewarding life and they did not want to move. John Newel Glode Jr. remained on his property, renewing his guiding licence each year, until the early 1950s, when he retired to live in the town of Yarmouth.

No families live along the Great Pubnico Lake Road today, but one can still observe the ruins of the small stone foundations gradually being obliterated by scrub growth. The first basement, close to the road on the south side, marks the spot where John Newel Glode's dwelling once stood. Near to it lies the foundation of a cabin that belonged to Harvey Nelson.[314] A little further on the same side is a stone foundation built by John Pictou, and still further up lies John Glode Sr.'s old dwelling site.[315] These stone cellars allowed for storage of potatoes and other root crops. As one approaches Great Pubnico Lake, there are lots that belonged to others in the Great Pubnico Lake community, including Annie Surette, John Murree, William Mius *dit* Billock, Eliza Robbins, and George Seeley.

No foundations of barns can be found, for no domesticated animals were kept other than a few chickens and, rarely, a pig. The land was unsuitable for pasture, being boggy scrub, and the men spent months away guiding or working in the woods. Small fields were cleared for potatoes. If needed, oxen could be borrowed from farmers in the Pubnicos or Tusket, since horses were unsuited for work in such terrain. The community abruptly ended near the shore of the lake, as the Scott family and Acadians from the Pubnicos held title to property in this area. At one time the old road from West Pubnico to Shelburne cut across the Old Pubnico Lake Road at right angles, just above the straggling line of houses. Now overgrown but still observable, traces of this road indicate that community members might have chosen their site because it lay at a crossroad.

Moose had again grown scarce by the 1930s, but until 1950 John Newel Glode Jr. renewed his

provincial guiding licence each year. When log driving ended on the Barrington River in 1957, the community disappeared, but by this time John Newel Jr. was sixty years old and living at Yarmouth. He died on 10 October 1960 at the age of seventy-two.[316] His seven children, since they had attended school, gained employment in fields completely unrelated to their father's former work in the woods. Today only a few crumbling basements testify to the many years that the Glodes, among them "Young Johnie," lived near West Pubnico.

The Bear River Glodes

The Bear River reserve, straddling the Annapolis-Digby County line, exhibits naturally terraced hillsides formed from ancient raised shorelines that provided encampment sites for the Indigenous population for thousands of years. It was occupied at the time of the coming of the first French settlers. Andrew James Mius, a great-grandson of Chief François Mius of La Have, became a chief in the Annapolis Basin area in about 1815, though his territorial aegis was restricted by Glode prerogatives to the countryside flanking the Mersey-Medway system. Between 1800 and 1880 the Glode district chief mainly lived at Lequille, though he moved around seasonally to St. Mary's Bay on the Gulf of Maine, Bear River, the Gut of Annapolis, and across the Bay of Fundy to the Parrsboro shore in Cumberland County. Another member of the Glode family, Molti Glode Sr., meanwhile acted as a sub-chief of the lower Mersey and Medway river area.

The history of the Bear River Glode family was inexorably intertwined with that of the Mi'kmaw Mius family. After François Mius died at La Have around 1765, his son Jacques Mius moved to the Cape Sable district and by 1812 lived near Abbé Sigogne's headquarters in Clare District, Digby County. Sigogne came to know the elderly Jacques and his son André James well, and encouraged them to sponsor a Mi'kmaw farming community at Bear River. Both were reluctant at first. Immediately after his father Jacques's death, André James and his brother, Jean (or John), lived for several years near the Gut of Annapolis. While there, André James married Madeline Toney, a daughter of Louis Toney, whose father Anthony (or Toney) Eury (Ury) in Pictou County had supported the British cause during the American Revolution.[317] Madeline invited her brothers,

Peter and Daniel Toney, to live near her. André James's group grew when John (or Jack) Glode, James Glode, and Lewis Glode from Lequille as well as Stephen and Francis Knockwood from Minas joined it at the Gut of Annapolis. Lewis Glode, John Mius, and several others also annually travelled to obtain the sacraments from Father Power, a Roman Catholic priest stationed at Minudie, Cumberland County.[318]

The Mi'kmaq from the Gut of Annapolis group crossed the Bay of Fundy to the Parrsboro Shore to hunt, and by the mid-1850s several Glodes originally from the Annapolis Basin area had settled permanently in Cumberland County. For instance, Abraham Glode, who was born on 1 April 1867 to parents from Lequille who later joined the Cumberland County band, was left an orphan in 1875 and was raised by John Logan, a Mi'kmaw head man living near Amherst. Abraham married twice. His first wife was a Mi'kmaw woman named Mary, and the couple travelled frequently to New Brunswick and Maine. His second wife was Annie Jane McGrath, daughter of an Irish-Acadian family headed by Michael McGrath of Parrsboro, and the couple raised two daughters and two sons on a small but thriving farm at Newville.[319] The Annapolis County Glodes continued to have close ties with their kin living in Cumberland County, and at least one Glode born in the Parrsboro area, Noel Glode, returned to Bear River in the early 1930s to marry.[320]

After 1820 members of the Glode, Toney (or Tony), and Knockwood families who had begun to regard André James Mius as their chief reluctantly gave up their headquarters at the Gut of Annapolis in the face of settler encroachments. Around 1818 Abbé Sigogne again pressured André James Mius, better known as "Andrew James Meuse," to sponsor a Mi'kmaw farming settlement, and Meuse's eventual concurrence with Sigogne's wishes led to a schism within the Annapolis band. One camp was composed of those who left Annapolis County for the Parrsboro Shore where they could continue their hunting and fishing way of life unimpeded, and on the other side a small group willing to experiment with agriculture. In 1821 Meuse, with the support of Sigogne, Judge Peleg Wiswal of Digby, and a Halifax humanitarian named Walter Bromley, had the government survey and confirm a thousand-acre reserve at Bear River to promote farming near the Annapolis-Digby County border. Lewis, John, Joseph, and

James Glode immediately moved to Bear River with the few Toneys and Knockwoods who had chosen not to cross the Bay of Fundy. But the early years at Bear River were often difficult, since food shortages and disease epidemics plagued the fledgling farming settlement. Lewis Glode and his brother John both died before 1828, with an elderly Francis Knockwood marrying John's young widow and fostering her four children.[321]

Though his headquarters as district chief was at Lequille, in his last years Chief Joseph Martin Claude also resided for months at a time at Bear River. In 1829 one of his sons, Francis Glode (c.1785–c.1880), was listed along with his younger brothers Abraham, Joseph, and John Glode as occupants of the Bear River Mi'kmaw settlement.[322] Francis, who with his wife Magdalene Knockwood was briefly involved in Charles Glode's farming venture near Milford in the 1820s and lived at Kejumkujik Lake in the 1830s, joined the Bear River community permanently in 1841. At this time the government provided him with an axe, hoe, spade, and some other farm equipment. He farmed one of the thirty-acre allotments into which the reserve in 1828 had been subdivided under the auspices of Judge Peleg Wiswall. In 1842 the provincial Indian commissioner, Joseph Howe, who visited Bear River in the fall of that year, observed that he was doing "well."[323] Yet it soon became obvious that the government authorities had far underestimated Francis's capacities. He not only could farm but also had carpentry skills that he likely learned from Acadian artisans. Francis proved an "ingenious woodworker," skilled in manufacturing yokes and sleds as well as building frame dwellings. According to William Nicholls, a magistrate and merchant appointed by Howe in 1842 to oversee Mi'kmaw affairs at Bear River, Francis had been given permission to take as much timber off the reserve as he needed for house construction.[324]

Four years later Francis further gained a reputation for having a "generous, disinterested" nature. In the fall of 1846, a contagious onslaught of "remittent bilious fever" struck the Bear River Mi'kmaw community and prostrated most of its population. Nicholls arranged for the erection of a makeshift hospital while Francis, although himself still convalescent, attended unstintingly to his fellow sufferers.[325] He travelled from camp to camp sharing his food and other supplies until he nearly impoverished himself. Only his abilities as an excellent hunter and trapper kept him going. The Annapolis Indian agent, Dr. Robert Leslie, referred to Francis as a man "of great humanity and intellect" and recommended he be given a freehold grant.[326]

Following his recovery from the lingering effects of the fever of 1846–47, Francis became a guide at Bear River, an occupation at which his son Jim Glode, born at Kejimkujik on 25 July 1831, soon surpassed his father.[327] By the 1870s Jim was considered one of best guides in Nova Scotia. In his boyhood he hunted with his father's brother, Matteo (Matthew) Glode, but after marrying Victoire Francis in 1854 Matthew moved to be near his in-laws at Pubnico Head, Yarmouth County. Jim's next hunting companion was his cousin Abraham Glode Jr. (c.1851–c.1907), and the two remained close until Abraham, after marrying Madeline Glode in 1885, moved away to live at Greenfield, Queens County, with his wife's parents. Jim set out to make a mark in the guiding world. A well-dressed, handsome, and wiry man sporting a bushy mustache and dark hair until an advanced age, when his hair suddenly turned white, Jim Glode appears in photographs dating from the late nineteenth to the early twentieth century.[328] Harry Piers, curator of the Nova Scotia Museum in Halifax from 1899 to 1940, made a point in 1921 of tracking down information about Jim's guiding exploits.[329] Piers learned that Jim, along with Paul Williams's son John, had gone hunting with Prince Arthur in 1869,[330] and that he and Matteo Glode had guided Lord Dunraven around what became known as Dunraven Bay, Queens County, in 1876.[331] Jim also travelled with the Quebec politician, businessman, and humanitarian the Honourable Charles Alexander, on a hunting expedition to the foothills of the Rocky Mountains.[332]

Jim moved from Bear River to Shubenacadie in 1910 after he started going blind, and lived with his son, Peter, who had married four times and who with his fourth wife, Anne (or Annie) Toney Maloney, cared for Jim in his final years.[333] Peter, like his father, was a recent arrival at Shubenacadie, having previously lived for several years at Elmsdale, on the Halifax-Hants County line. On 26 July, St. Anne's Day 1929, Halifax journalist Clara Archibald Dennis interviewed and took several photographs of the ninety-eight-year-old retired guide.[334] Jim told Dennis that his parents had been "Francis Glode and Magdalene Knockwood," while his grandfather, "Joseph Glode, had been French from Liverpool."[335]

Just previous to this interview, Dennis had spoken with another elderly member of the Glode family, Joseph Glode, born in 1830 or 1831, since the journalist claimed he was ninety-eight or ninety-nine in 1929. Joseph was likely one of Jim Glode's brothers, or may have been Jim's twin.[336] Joseph held that he had moved around during his lifetime from Bear River to Pubnico Head and Windsor, and claimed to have crossed the Bay of Fundy twice by canoe. Since he hunted on the Tusket River and near Lake Rossignol, he could point out sites of mythic and historic interest.[337] At Gabriel's Falls three miles from Tusket Village, he pointed out, was a granite spirit rock associated in Mi'kmaw lore with a "mermaid," while on Second Lake in Queens County a boulder was addressed reverently as "Grandmother" and offered gifts of tobacco. The Mi'kmaw word *Gayesquack*, Joseph continued, roughly translatable as "voices in the sky," referred to the "Screechies," ghostly noises and sometimes piercing screeches reputedly heard emanating from a bog near an ancient Mi'kmaq cemetery close to Lake Rossignol. Joseph further mentioned that frequent disease epidemics desecrated the ranks of many Mi'kmaw families. In the late 1840s around only eighty Mi'kmaq lived in Queens County and fewer in Annapolis County, which made finding spouses within the southwestern Mi'kmaw community difficult. It had not been so in the distant past, when sickness was less prevalent and people lived longer. "My father was 104 years old when he died," Joseph proclaimed, "and my mother was 100."[338]

On the basis of what Joseph Glode had told her, Clara Dennis drew up a few questions that she hoped Jim Glode would answer. These included "Who was the great Simon Glode, the Mi'kmaw prophet who foretold of the end of the world?" and "What were the Screechies?"[339] Jim at first tried to ignore the question relating to his brother Simon, who had made some prognostications regarding the future of the Mi'kmaq.[340] In the end, Jim replied to Dennis's question obliquely by stating that a person named Simon might be a "Glode who belonged to Indian gardens or Kejimkujik or Glode's Island," but that most people thought "he's telling them crazy stories." He added that his father Francis had been a "great prophet" and could predict the weather.[341] Regarding the Screechies, he explained they were shrill disembodied voices that could be heard underwater and in the air.

Dennis next tried to get Jim to speak about sacred sites where hunters laid down tobacco as gifts to spiritual agencies, but Jim sidelined her question and described a small Roman Catholic chapel that lay along a Mi'kmaw trail towards Pictou. He next explained that Charles Alexander and his brother, while he was guiding them, had mainly been interested in acquiring specimens of animals and birds to take to England. Jim had first gone west in 1872 or 1873 and had been present in 1876 when General George Armstrong Custer was defeated at the Battle of Little Bighorn. Without elaborating to Dennis how he became associated with the conflict, he stated ambiguously, "I was a guide and Captain of a Regiment ... I did not fight."[342] He also claimed to have been to Montana and California.[343] Jim concluded by stating that he had married several times, but of the eleven children born to his wives only two were still living, Peter Glode and a daughter Mary.[344]

Harold Gloade, whose father, Newel Gloade, was Jim's first cousin (Jim and Newel's fathers being brothers), as a boy in the late 1920s used to visit Jim Glode at Shubenacadie and listen for hours to his stories.[345] In so doing Harold, who always spelled Jim's surname "Gloade" rather than "Glode," attained a far more comprehensive understanding than Clara Dennis of Jim's adventures out west. "James Gloade," Harold noted, "was scout for a survey party in the State of Wyoming in 1876, when the party was raided by Crazy Horse. Nobody had been hurt, but Crazy Horse had taken all their horses, and most of their food, and when James Gloade's party had finally reached a settlement, they got word of the battle [of Little Bighorn] and wondered whether perhaps their horses had been instrumental in the outcome of that fight."[346]

Jim Glode died at Shubenacadie of acute bronchitis at the age of 104 years and 7 months on 29 February 1936. Other than his blindness at an advanced age, Jim had been relatively healthy most of his life. In his final years, however, he suffered from dementia. He would sit on his bed for hours and make paddling movements, get off his bed and move it around as though he were portaging a canoe, and then sit down again and resume "paddling." As ethnohistorian Ruth

Holmes Whitehead has written, only death released him from his "endless dream of travelling the rivers and forests of the mind, hunting and guiding."[347]

Jim's paternal uncle Abraham Glode Sr. – who was Harold Gloade's grandfather – was also long lived. A well-known hunter, trapper, and guide as well as a dispenser of woods lore, Abraham died at Bear River at age ninety-six on 8 August 1910 from bronchitis.[348] A younger son of Chief Joseph Martin Claude, Abraham Glode Sr. preferred a traditional Mi'kmaw way of life. After moose and caribou populations recovered somewhat in southwestern Nova Scotia during the 1850s, the guiding life offered Abraham a reprieve from repeated government admonitions that he, like his much older brother Francis, should settle down and farm. Around age seventeen Abraham began living with Mary Ann Meuse (c.1818–c.1850), a daughter of Chief Andrew James Meuse and Madeline Toney, in a union sanctioned by Mi'kmaw custom rather than Roman Catholic rite.[349] During the summers they would travel eastward from Lequille to Windsor, or go to Liverpool to peddle baskets and other wooden manufactures along the Atlantic coast. Between 1832 and 1848 Abraham Glode Sr. and Mary Ann had five children: Alexander, born at Liverpool on 5 May 1832; Newel, born at Windsor in 1836; Annie, born in 1843; Sarah, born about 1845; and Louis, born at Bear River in November 1848. Abraham Sr.'s second son, Newel, later lived at Halifax and in Colchester County, where his sister Annie lived with him.[350]

When Abraham Glode Sr.'s first wife Mary Ann died, about 1850, Abraham wed Margaret Knockwood, a daughter of Stephen Knockwood Sr. of Bear River, at St. Croix Roman Catholic Church in Plympton, Digby County, on 31 December 1851. The couple had only one son, Abraham Glode Jr., born in 1851. Following Margaret's death in 1853, Abraham married a third time, to Nellie (or Helen) Peters at Plympton on 28 October 1854. Abraham Glode Sr. and Nellie had a daughter Isabella around 1864, but Isabella may have died young as she does not appear in the 1881 census.

Abraham Sr. and Nellie Peters then focused on raising Abraham Glode Jr., Abraham's son by his second wife Margaret. Abraham Jr. married three times, first to Nancy Jeremy at Plympton, Digby County, on 9 January 1871;[351] second at Annapolis Royal on 16 September 1878 to Nancy Siah (or Cyr), a daughter of a Mi'kmaw traditional power holder named Solomon Siah;[352] and third at Caledonia on 15 January 1885 to Madeline Glode, a daughter of Newel Cobliel Glode and Mary Ann Molti of Greenfield, Queens County. Madeline was Abraham Jr.'s third or fourth cousin.[353] When Abraham Jr. remarried, his son Newel, born on 14 October 1870 to Abraham and Nancy Jeremy, so disliked his stepmothers – first Nancy Siah and then Madeline Glode – that he preferred until he was twenty years of age to live with his grandfather, Abraham Glode Sr.[354]

Despite this arrangement, Abraham Glode Jr. did not completely relinquish paternal control over Newel. He held some strong views on how Newel should be brought up and sought to enforce them, though Newel occasionally rebelled against his father's directives.[355] Abraham Jr., who felt schooling was unnecessary for his son, had himself attended the schoolhouse at Bear River for a few years in the 1840s, but he must have disliked his classroom experience for he discouraged Newel from attending.[356] Newel's son Harold once noted that Abraham went to the school one day and "found Newel standing in a corner with a yardstick between his teeth to prevent him from resting against the wall." Since Abraham failed to see "where that would serve in any future endeavour," he promptly removed Newel from the class.[357] Though Abraham Jr.'s actions in this instance may have been a welcome relief to the young boy, as they spared him continued chagrin and embarrassment, Newel still preferred the wise and loving guidance his grandfather could offer when the two were in the woods or together on porpoise-hunting expeditions. Abraham Sr., moreover, had no qualms about his grandson attaining the rudiments of reading and writing, and Newel was listed as "literate" on the 1891 federal census return.

In 1892 Newel, who went by the surname "Gloade" rather than "Glode," wed Mary Ann Peters at St. Louis Church in Annapolis Royal.[358] The couple had eleven children: Joseph Newel in 1893, Simeon in 1894, Sylvester in 1895, Mary Elizabeth in 1897, Mary Nancy in 1899, Joseph Malti (Joseph Martin) on 9 April 1901 (who later lied about his age to serve overseas in World War I and died shortly upon his return to Bear River),[359] Mary Ellen in 1910 (who died at age five of cholera), Mary Louise in 1907, Michael Joseph on 1 February 1909, John in 1910, and Thomas Louis in 1913.

Even as a married man Newel still remained close to his grandfather, and accompanied the elderly man planting potatoes in the spring, travelling and porpoise hunting in the summer, birding and guiding in the fall, and hunting and trapping during the winter.[360] Since Abraham was intelligent and informative, he was approached by journalists and ethnographers interested in Mi'kmaw culture.[361] In the mid 1870s ethnographer Stansbury Hagar began interviewing him at Digby to learn as much as possible about Mi'kmaw "intelligence and knowledge of the Native lore." Hagar blamed the Roman Catholic missionaries for Abraham Sr.'s inability to read or write English, though he noted that some Mi'kmaq read hieroglyphics rather than Roman script, words that implied that Abraham was one of these persons. Over time, Hagar collected detailed information from Abraham and his grandson Newel on the serpent dance, performed principally at an installation of a new chief; recorded starlore and legends and stories, including one about a man who made himself small enough to hide in a water lily in order to successfully woo a woman, and then lived underwater; and on Mi'kmaw games such as *woltesakun*, or *waltes*, a dice game.[362]

At ninety years of age in 1904, Abraham Glode Sr. was still spry enough to go moose hunting back of St. Margaret's Bay. At the time he admitted he had not been in Halifax for forty years, though he stated that as a younger man he had made many trips to the city each year on foot to sell furs to a trader named Kaiser.[363] After enjoying good health for most of his life, on 8 August 1910 he died suddenly of bronchitis brought on by "exposure."[364] His wife Nellie Peters died the following year.[365] His grandson Newel missed him tremendously, having spent so many enjoyable seasons with him in the woods and on the water.[366] After Newel's wife Mary Ann Peters died on 5 January 1917, Newel married Beatrice Rose McKay de Long, daughter of Eli McKay and Maria Fiendell of Upper Northfield, Lunenburg County, at Annapolis Royal on 7 June 1920.[367]

Prior to his marriage Newel Gloade worked as a guide and river driver. He and Rose had met at Elmwood, near New Germany, Lunenburg County, when Newel was forty-eight and Rose was forty. Rose brought four children from a previous marriage with her to Lequille, and she and Newel went on to have Harold on 11 September 1920, whom they raised along with Newel's sons and daughters from his marriage to Mary Anne Peters.[368] About the time of Harold's birth, Frank Barnjman hired Newel to monitor the antics of an old water-driven sawmill located at Graywood, on a brook running from Lamb's Lake, inland from Lequille.[369] Built in 1868, the sawmill had been operated by three brothers, George, Alexander, and Joseph Isaac Harnish. When Alexander Harnish eventually took over the mill from his brothers, he erected a mansion on a hill on the opposite side of the millstream. This house had fallen vacant by 1920, and the Barnjmans, seeing Newel and Rose as trustworthy people, offered them accommodations in the old Harnish mansion. Newel also arranged for Ella, one of Rose's daughters, to marry Denny Brooks, a relative of his, and he secured living quarters for the new couple in another house on the Barnjman estate.[370]

Newel's duties as property caretaker also included minor carpentry work and launching boats on Lamb's Lake, while Rose found employment as an upstairs maid for the Barnjman family. But Newell's main responsibility was the mill. It was driven by a submerged wooden turbine that, even when the mill was not in operation, would turn on its own during heavy rains if extra water pressure built up behind it. Newel had to put a long plank under the flywheel to prevent the water pressure from destroying the turbine apparatus, and then secure the workings with a plug.

The mill lay idle most of the time that Newel worked as its caretaker, except for a brief period of operation in 1925 when a million board feet of lumber was sawn.[371] This proved an easier and more satisfying time for the Gloade family, since it provided wage employment near at hand. Newel no longer had to be away for months during the winter working on the Clyde River, at Bloody Creek, or on Tusket or Sissaboo rivers as he had in the past, cutting timber and driving logs after the spring thaw. The local economy of the 1920s, which required Mi'kmaw individuals to compete with settlers for scarce positions in order to make ends meet, had replaced the earlier Mi'kmaq one, guided by the seasons and the ebb and flow of nature's abundance. This new state of affairs isolated the worker from the wider economy and often left him at the mercy of forces beyond his control. "I remember that few of us, if any, were aware of trade balances or whether the dollar was shrinking or growing on the world markets," Harold Gloade explained, "we just

knew there was work at a wage a man could feed his family on."[372]

With the mill working in 1925 and Newel at home most evenings, young Harold enjoyed listening to his father's stories about guiding, hunting, fishing, porpoise hunting, and logging. Little did he know that he was storing fodder for his creativity; much later, after attending school and working in the wider world, he began to write short stories about his boyhood. His book *From My Vantage Point* is a continuation into modern times of the lively Mi'kmaw narrative tradition exhibited by so many of the Gloade family, as it illustrates the rewards, challenges, and changes facing the Mi'kmaq at Graywood and Lequille. Newel and his family visited six or seven Mi'kmaw families living at the General's Bridge fairly regularly, so Harold in writing about his youth could pen delightful portrayals of Joe Penall playing his fiddle while his brother-in-law Dennis Brooks step danced, or the many ways in which his "Aunt" Lucy Pictou shared her hospitality with others.

Any hopes Newel Gloade may have had for continued stable employment were dashed, however, when the Graywood mill suddenly closed permanently in 1926. In a chapter aptly entitled "The Final Bow," Harold Gloade tells how his father abruptly "packed up" his family in 1927 and moved to Truro. The "Final Bow" referred to the closure of the mill but also to the Gloade's final adieu to Lequille and Bear River. In moving eastward, Newel and his family followed earlier Gloades who had passed through the Annapolis Valley towards Paradise and Middleton, Nine Mile River and Elmsdale, before finally settling in Cambridge, Kentville, Newport, Hantsport, Windsor, Truro, or across the Bay of Fundy in Cumberland County.[373]

Owing to the development of electricity, which did away with the need for oil lanterns, and the appearance of mineral-based lubricating oils, the Mi'kmaw porpoise hunt became redundant.[374] Many smaller mills were shutting down, and there were fewer opportunities in the guiding industry. Men who remained guides cultivated the art of showmanship, which complemented the traditional Mi'kmaw emphasis on poise and strong delivery when speaking. These same qualities made them engaging companions on guiding expeditions and at guides' meets. Mi'kmaq who had engaging personal skills still behaved in a manner reminiscent of the heyday of guiding, when men such as Jim Glode were widely known for their guiding expertise. Guides' meets, moreover, provided forums for socializing, where individuals shared their hunting expertise and woods lore and engaged in friendly competition.[375] Guiding was not as dangerous as river driving, and though demanding, it allowed for respectful and long-lasting relationships to develop between guides and their clientele.

When the famous guide Jim Glode moved to Shubenacadie, his place was filled by Mi'kmaw guiding notables such as Louis Peters, John McEwan, and Louis Harlow, who recruited their clients by travelling to international guides' meets and sportsman shows throughout eastern Canada, New England, and the central United States.[376] With the incorporation of the Nova Scotian Guides Association in 1920 came new guidelines requiring all guides to have a licence from the provincial government. Yet guiding only offered a short-lived economic reprieve from an otherwise faltering traditional economy. Caribou had disappeared from the province by this time, and the bag limit on moose had fallen to one moose per hunter, dimming the interest of many formerly avid American sportsmen. Many of those whose parents once had been guides at Bear River already had moved away to live at points east, particularly Truro and Shubenacadie.

Movement East

Some Glodes/Gloades from Annapolis Queens and Lunenburg counties temporarily joined small, scattered Mi'kmaq encampments at Prospect, Portuguese Cove, Chocolate Lake, Rockingham, Waverly, and Dartmouth Crossing for commercial, social, and religious reasons. In 1846 Thomas Glode, who probably had been born at La Have in the 1780s and who in the 1820s used to regularly visit the Roman Catholic church at Prospect, south of Halifax, moved with his twenty-year-old son Joseph and a younger boy named Peter Glode to the outskirts of Dartmouth. Perhaps he hoped to escape the onslaught of a bilious fever affecting Mi'kmaq in the southwestern part of the province. Though Thomas contracted the disease when it spread eastward, he survived and by the mid 1860s he and Joseph were settled with twenty-seven other Mi'kmaw families near Dartmouth at Red Bridge, situated at the fork of the Preston and Guysborough roads.[377] Joseph joined the Halifax County

band and by his mid-forties he was a captain of the Halifax County Mi'kmaw district council. One of his duties was to participate in meetings convened by the *Sipekne'katik* district chief, Jacques-Pierre Peminout Paul, to discuss possible effects Confederation might have on Mi'kmaw treaty rights.[378] Glodes like Joseph, Halifax County chief Joseph C. Cope averred, were called *Pickinag*.[379]

Newel (or Noel) Gloade (1836–c.1900), the second-eldest son of Abraham Glode Sr. (c.1814–1910) and Mary Ann Meuse of Bear River, also moved east. Newel was born in Windsor, West Hants County, during one of his parents' peddling jaunts through the Annapolis Valley. Raised at Lequille and Bear River, he left his father's household to go to New Brunswick where circa 1860 he met and married Anatasia Vicaire, who hailed from Restigouche in southern Quebec.[380] He brought his bride back to Nova Scotia and the couple spent several years living on the outskirts of Halifax, probably near Chocolate Lake at the head of the Northwest Arm. Their first child, Louis, was born in 1861, followed by William Thomas in 1866, James in 1871, and Sarah around 1873.[381] By 1878 Newel and Anastasia had moved to Nine Mile River in Hants County, where two more daughters, Annie and Katherine, were born. They also adopted a girl named Mary Helen Maccan, born about 1872, who may have been an abandoned white child.[382]

Their son Louis, who remained illiterate all his life, worked as a cooper. By contrast, Louis's brother William Thomas, usually known as "Tom," not only attended school but while at Acadia Mines in Colchester County acquired apprentice papers as an industrial bricklayer and plasterer. For a while in the 1930s Tom worked constructing chimneys for the Mersey Bowater Paper Company's mill.[383] When both brothers married, however, they continued to live most of the time near their parents. In 1884 Louis wed Mary Noel, and not long afterwards Tom married Mary Cope. Louis and his Mary did not have children for a number of years, while Tom and Mary had a son James in 1890.

Louis and Mary Noel eventually had a daughter Mary in 1897, but Mary Noel must have died shortly afterwards, since in 1900 Louis wed Susan Bernard from Cape Breton[384] and the couple had a son, Noel Andrew Gloade, in 1901.[385] Louis's father, Newel Gloade, also died, since his name does not appear on the 1901 federal census. After his death his widow Anastasia, or Nancy, moved to the Millbrook reserve, near Truro. She assisted her son Tom for a few years with a small farm on the new reserve, though by 1920 she had remarried, to a man surnamed Paul. She died a widow in 1925.[386] A slightly younger woman named Annie Gloade, born in 1843, who was likely Newel's younger sister, joined the Millbrook community at the same time as Anastasia. Annie had two young children in her care, Joe Laffert (or Lafford), nine years old, and Annie, Joe's sister, who was four. Joe and Annie's parents had been Frank Lafford and Sarah Gloade, another of Newel Gloade's sisters.[387]

Tom did not immediately move to Millbrook. In 1891 he and Mary Cope had a daughter Annie at Londonderry Station[388] and a second son, Daniel Thomas, at Acadia Mines early in 1903.[389] Until 1903 Tom shunted back and forth between Acadia Mines and Millbrook looking for work. In 1904 Tom and Mary had a third son, Stephen Anthony, who was also born in Londonderry. They also retained custody of Mary Helen Maccan, Tom's parents' adopted daughter.[390] When the mine works shut down soon afterwards, Tom searched for work in and around Truro, as little employment could be found on the Millbrook reserve in its fledgling years. The Mi'kmaq were still getting used to being reoriented away from the Salmon River, now deflected underground beneath the town of Truro, and making the Truro Hilton upland, near the rail line, their permanent headquarters.[391] Millbrook had plenty of wild game and ash trees for making baskets, but it was the opportunity for wage employment in Truro that attracted Tom Gloade and others qualified to make the best out of the new situation. Tom proved to be a dependable worker and soon built up a steady clientele in the plastering business. When Mary, his first wife and the mother of his children, suddenly died in 1909, he married Christiana, or "Chrissie," Snow, a daughter of John Snow and Nancy Noel of Canso.[392]

Tom became very politically active after 1909. He was persuaded to assist with a Mi'kmaw drive to attain more land for the reserve, a campaign that ended successfully when Millbrook received an additional 120 acres in 1910. Between 1909 and 1911 he also became swept up in discussions about the fate of Mi'kmaw lands in Annapolis and Queens Counties once inhabited by Mi'kmaw farming settlements, but now lying deserted. Peter Gloade and his wife Hannah, the last Mi'kmaq to remain at the Kejimkujik farming settlement, must have spread word shortly before their deaths in 1884 that the government was eyeing their tract at Kejimkujik with the goal of selling it. Millbrook became a hub for discussions on this and related subjects.

The Mi'kmaw land and resource campaign reached a climax in 1909. Preoccupation with financial retrenchment had caused the province to join forces with Ottawa in obtaining leases or surrenders of reserves considered to be underpopulated or vacant. From his headquarters in Cape Breton, the Mi'kmaw grand chief, John Denny Jr., launched a major campaign to stem such leases or surrenders.[393] Denny countered that that the Mi'kmaq Grand Council could direct Mi'kmaq from communities lacking wood to Kejimkujik, where they could cut timber and manufacture wooden items needed in the mines, such as pick handles, posts, beams, and wooden tubs. To the grand chief, the government simply was taking advantage of an unfortunate situation since, after Jim Charles moved away and Peter and Hannah Gloade died in 1884, no Mi'kmaw "watchdogs" remained on the Kejimkujik tract to monitor government goings-on.[394]

As time was of the essence, Chief Denny immediately contacted six chiefs, including Chief Joseph Gould of Millbrook, and asked them to petition Ottawa denouncing the projected lease as well as any further surrenders of land. He then personally wrote Frank Oliver, the federal minister of the interior, asking that the Mi'kmaq be allowed to retain their land for their own unique development purposes. Ottawa received these petitions, dated between 11 March and 24 April 1909, but because they countered government goals to have the area surrendered, permanently archived them.[395] It is possible the Mi'kmaq did not even receive an official answer to their petitions.

Undaunted, Chief Denny in 1913 recruited Frank Gouldsmith Speck, a University of Pennsylvania anthropologist, to record the locations of Mi'kmaw hunting territories in Nova Scotia. Both Denny and Speck felt this to be valuable work as it directed public attention away from the reserves towards the Mi'kmaw's traditional land use system.[396] Mi'kmaw historians knowledgeable about Mi'kmaw hunting practices, among them the Gloades of the Mersey-Medway river system, proved happy to assist, and Speck felt energized by their support. Denny and Speck were joined in their campaign by a dynamic chief named Joseph Julien, who at the time was living along Kings Road in Sydney.[397] The *Sydney Record*, a Cape Breton newspaper, in 1914 even quoted Speck as saying "the Micmacs are very interesting … as their knowledge of the ancient matters is quite extensive; and with the help of Chief Julien and Grand Chief John Denny Jr. of Eskasoni, it will be possible to reconstruct the entire family divisions of Nova Scotia and Cape Breton."[398]

Chiefs Denny and Julien, who were both then living in Cape Breton, doubtless appreciated having the camaraderie and assistance of the well-connected and seasoned leader Tom Gloade as a *keptin* in the Mi'kmaw Grand Council, of which all three were members. In 1916 and for at least two years afterwards, he was both a prayer leader and a captain of the Mi'kmaw Grand Council, duties that caused him to become a close associate of William "Daoi" Peminout Paul, a traditional *Sipekne'katik* leader and spiritual guide. A community-minded person, Tom Gloade also officiated at ceremonies in Millbrook, at the new Sacred Heart Church on the reserve. During the war years he served in the reserve infantry, as a member of the 1st Battalion of the Royal Nova Scotia Highlanders.[399]

Yet despite the climate of cautious optimism that taken root around Denny's scheme to develop the Kejimkujik tract in 1909, following the grand chief's death in 1918 Ottawa successfully pressed for a surrender of the Kejimkujik lands, the parcels associated with the old Glode settlement, and whatever Mi'kmaw freehold property still remained at Lequille.[400] These land cessions occurred during the height of the First World War, when many Mi'kmaw men were away serving overseas.[401]

News of these land surrenders must have come as a blow to Tom Gloade, given his and the others' efforts to explain to the government how the traditional Mi'kmaw land use system operated and how crucial its maintenance was to the Mi'kmaq's continued existence in Queens and Annapolis counties. And as soon as these surrenders occurred, a host of new associated land issues arose. Joseph Julien, who was elected as chief at Truro in 1917, sought to make the Millbrook reserve into a haven for Mi'kmaw migrants from Halifax, Hants,

and Annapolis counties who either had been driven from their traditional lands by government fiat or had found it necessary to seek new economic opportunities elsewhere in the province.[402] Tom immediately assumed a seat on Chief Julien's council and supported the new chief in his quest to establish a strong Mi'kmaw political and economic base at Truro.

Post-war Years at Millbrook and Hantsport

Soon after Grand Chief John Denny Jr.'s death, John Denny Paul arose as a Halifax County chief, with Jeremiah Bartlett-Alexis, or "Jerry Lonecloud," as his spokesperson. Tom and Louis Gloade forged political ties with this new leader, and Louis's son Noel Andrew married one of Chief Paul's daughters, Mary.[403] While Jerry Lonecloud's Malecite wife, Elizabeth Paul, resided at Millbrook with one of her sons, Louis Bartlett-Alexis, Jerry in his mid-seventies consorted with a young woman named Annie Gloade from Millbrook, likely a descendant of Newel Gloade and Anastasia Vicaire.[404]

During the early post-war years, the Department of Indian Affairs launched a concerted drive to rid the federal government of its jurisdiction over reserves in Halifax, Queens, and Annapolis counties. Scattered reserves with few Mi'kmaw occupants were viewed as burdens on public coffers. Chief Joseph Julien countered this new policy by viewing any form of centralization directed solely by government fiat as an anathema. He, Tom Gloade, and Chief Paul began to work tirelessly to turn Millbrook into a homeland for Mi'kmaq uprooted as a result of these political, economic, and social changes.[405] During the early stages of the government centralization campaign, as reserves along Nova Scotia's Eastern Shore were surrendered and absorbed into the mainstream landholding system, a number of Mi'kmaw families, driven from lands east of Halifax, settled with Chief Julien's assistance along a road at Millbrook nostalgically and "affectionately known as Halifax County."[406]

The mid-1920s brought a brief political and economic reprieve from the strains and stresses of the first decade of the twentieth century. A feeling of prosperity was in the air, and a few Mi'kmaw individuals owned cars. Most children attended the local day school, at least for the early grades, and the adult population was beginning to exhibit a diversity of skills.

Many families manufactured hockey sticks, baskets, axe and pick handles, and wooden tubs. Charles Wilmot, Chief Peter Wilmot's son, and Tom Gloade's brother-in-law Alex Cope still trapped on the land, though Alex also maintained a small fur farm. Tom's son Stephen Anthony Gloade (1903–62) helped Alex snare breeding foxes for his fur farm. Other people worked at local mills or entered the trades, and many families farmed a few acres. Tom Gloade owned a cow, pigs, and some chickens; his mother, Anastasia Vicaire, tended to these animals' needs while he pursued the plastering trade, made wooden items for sale and, in the winter, often worked in the woods. Yet the mid-1920s were also difficult years. Tom's wife, Chrissie Snow, died in November 1925.[407] Earlier the same year his son Daniel Thomas (1886–1931) married sixteen-year-old Lavinia Brooks, and in succeeding years Dan and his wife had a succession of stillborn children. Only one child lived into adulthood, and Dan himself died in 1931.[408] A bright spot, however, was Tom's son Stephen Anthony's marriage to Anastasia Gloade, a daughter of Peter Gloade and Jeanette Prosper Toney of Shubenacadie.[409]

In 1927 things further improved. Newel Gloade, Newel's second wife Rose Beatrice McKay, and the couple's seven-year-old son Harold turned up at Tom's door looking for accommodation. One of Newel's older sons, Michael-Joseph, better known as "Mike," also toyed with the idea of moving from Lequille to Millbrook, but after he secured employment with a mill in Digby County, only Newel, Beatrice, and Harold moved in with Tom, whom Harold affectionately referred to as his "uncle," although Tom was actually Harold's father's first cousin.[410] (Harold's father's father and Tom's father were brothers.)

Tom graciously received the trio into his commodious home. He was a widower, his wife Chrissie having died two years earlier, leaving him with his son Stephen Anthony and his adopted sister Mary Helen Maccan. His mother Anastasia had also died in 1925, so he likely appreciated having kin join his household and help out with cooking, cleaning, and farm chores. With time he became young Harold's mentor. "His house was large and so was the goodness of his heart," Harold wrote, "for he made us welcome. Very welcome. He was one of the gentlemen who taught me the finer points of the Micmac language, and if I wanted to know about anything at all, I would generally ask him."[411]

In his later years Harold Gloade provided an astonishingly detailed portrayal of his parents' and "Uncle" Tom's lives at Millbrook during the late 1920s. Newel's reputation was enhanced within the local Mi'kmaw community when it was discovered he was blessed with "second sight" – a mysterious trait that enabled him to find things that were lost or to determine what direction to walk in the woods. It was a trait the Mi'kmaq believed was passed down through the generations in certain families.[412] Harold recalled that Tom had all his close relatives living around him. Next door to him lived his sister Kate, while his brother Louis had a house three doors away. His son, Thomas Daniel Gloade, lived just beyond Louis where the road bent to the left, as did Michael Thomas and his wife Annie Gloade, who was Tom's daughter. Louis's son Noel Andrew Gloade lived close to Michael and Annie.[413]

Tom Gloade was still employed as an industrial mason and plasterer in Truro, though he and his son Stephen, who at various times worked as a carpenter and game warden, soon opened the only store on the reserve; otherwise people had to walk to Truro for supplies.[414] Even when the Depression hit in October 1929, "Tom Gloade, a mason of some renown, was able to find a house that needed some plaster, if the owner could afford to have the work done."[415] He left Millbrook for a prolonged period in 1930, when he built brick chimneys for the Mersey Paper Company's plant at Brooklyn, on the north shore of Liverpool Bay.[416]

When his brother Louis died at age sixty-eight on 23 October 1929, Tom took Louis's son, Charles Louis Gloade, under his wing until Charles was old enough in 1931 to marry Annie Jane Sylliboy at Millbrook.[417] By this time his cousin Newel Gloade and his family had moved to Hantsport to find work. Lacking the buffer that Tom Gloade's skill as a mason and plasterer offered against economic vicissitudes, Newel Gloade was hit particularly hard by the onset of the Great Depression in October 1929, when he often lacked employment. When he was sixty-two, Tom Gloade married a forty-four-year-old widow from Shubenacadie, Bridget Anne Sack, on 22 June 1931.[418] Bridget, Isaac Sack and Ann Cope's daughter, was an attractive woman elegant in dress and manner. Tom lived at Shubenacadie with his new wife only three years before he died of heart disease at sixty-eight and was buried in the Church of St. Catherine Cemetery, Indianbrook, on 24 October 1934.

Figure 2.1. Kin Connections between Thomas William Gloade and Harold Gloade

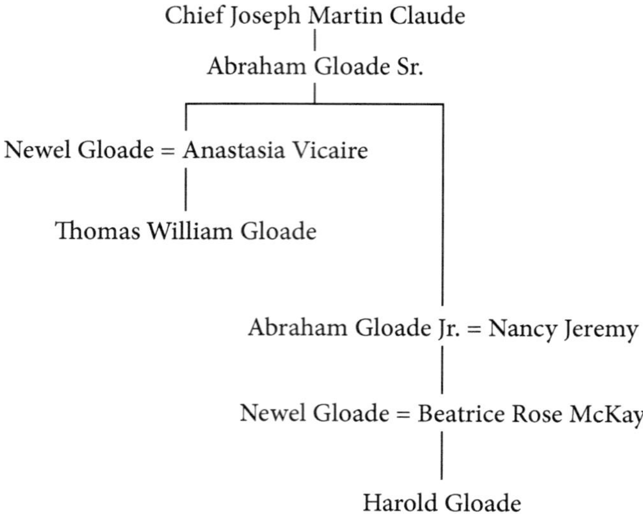

Following Tom's marriage and then his death, Newel Gloade had to look elsewhere than his cousin for economic security for his family. As mills closed down and unskilled labourers lost their jobs, Newel and his family moved around once again, looking for work. One of Harold's most prominent memories before his family left Millbrook was of the earthquake of 18 November 1929, which struck while he and his father were visiting their relative Jim Glode and Jim's son Peter at Shubenacadie.[419] Harold enjoyed being in the company of elderly Mi'kmaq like Jim who had made their living from guiding and river driving.[420] At guide meets, and particularly at an annual event held at Lake William in Lunenburg County, both Newel and Harold sought opportunities to talk with Mi'kmaw guides from Milton, Milford, Bear River, Paradise, and Lequille. But by the late 1920s guiding as means of earning a livelihood had declined radically in importance in southwestern Nova Scotia. When Harold informed Joseph Penall (or Pennel) of Lequille that he wanted to become a guide, Penall dissuaded him from the idea by warning that "guiding would not be held too much longer."[421]

During the mid-1930s Harold and his parents lived at the Crossroads outside Hantsport. Their house lay on the road leading to a Mi'kmaw community that in 1907 was designated the "Horton Reserve 35" and today forms the headquarters of the Glooscap First Nation, or *Pesikitk*.[422] Here Newel, Rose Beatrice, and Harold lived with Mary Nancy Stephens, one of Newel's daughters from his first marriage to Mary Ann Peters.[423] Nancy's husband, Louis Mulchie Stephens, worked at the Minas Basin Pulp and Paper Company, established in 1933 by Roy Jodrey and continued by his son John.[424] It was one of the first companies to hire Mi'kmaq on a full-time basis, and it provided Louis Mulchie with a stable income.[425] While living at the Crossroads, Newel and his wife made baskets for the apple trade, but for Harold millwork and the construction industry offered far higher monetary returns than guiding or basketry.[426] A pedlar in his early teens and later a carpenter, Harold at age seventeen married Irene Agnes MacDonald at Enfield on 8 June 1938.[427] His mother, Rose Beatrice, died at Hantsport on 15 April 1939, but his father Newel would live another twenty-six years in the same town and would maintain a home base for Harold's wife and children while Harold travelled with the construction business. With longevity equal to that of his grandfather Abraham Gloade Sr., Newel died at age ninety-six in 1966 and was buried at St. John's Cemetery in Windsor.[428] By this time Harold had journeyed to "Windsor, Ontario, in Canada, and as far west as Texas in the United States." In his later years he would become the Mi'kmaw Grand Council captain for the Glooscap community.[429]

Harold knew about the grand chief and council's previous land and resource campaigns, as well as Joseph Julien's and Tom Gloade's determined efforts to ensure that the Mi'kmaq would have sufficient land

and resources to survive into the future. To leaders of insight and political acumen such as these men, the government's draconian imposition in 1930 of the Indian residential school system on the Mi'kmaw community, followed by the brunt of Mi'kmaw centralization policy in the early 1940s, must have come as colossal insults. The residential school system and centralization revealed the worst facets of a government policy driven by cultural insensitivity and a narrow focus on retrenchment. In the face of such blatant disregard for human rights, community residents often had to take matters into their own hands. Mike Gloade, an electrician, claimed that when agents came to Millbrook to collect children for the residential school, his mother "drove them off with a mop."[430]

Though Ottawa at first tried to draw vague parallels between government centralization policy and the goals of Mi'kmaw leaders such as Peter Wilmot, Joseph Julien, and Tom Gloade, who wanted to establish a refuge and homeland in central Nova Scotia, the problematic consequences of government policy admitted no such comparison. In 1917 Chief Julien and counsellor Tom Gloade carefully monitored the carrying capacity of resources in the Truro area in relation to the numbers of Mi'kmaw being invited to join the Millbrook community. The government engaged in no such monitoring. As early as 1943, the Indianbrook settlement at Shubenacadie, regarded by the government as a growth centre, was overcrowded. With the local resources depleted, a negligible local job market, and most of the timber chopped down to build sub-standard housing, some of the most recent newcomers wound their way back to their former haunts. Harold Gloade remembered constructing "four shells of shacks on the Horton reserve" in 1942 for a dollar a day.[431] He further observed that one Mi'kmaw man, who was determined to keep his old house rather than move into government housing, thought he lived in a "mansion" when compared to the Gloade family's small, ramshackle dwelling, built under government directives.[432]

In the aftermath of the Great Depression, Millbrook, with its tradition of sound leadership, "bounced back after the long hard struggle with hard times."[433] The nearby Debert army base built during the war offered employment, and "from all this there emerged a new brand of tradesman, keen, adaptable, and above all, capable."[434] Gordon Gloade of Millbrook stressed that being a carpenter in the 1950s and 1960s also allowed for freedom of movement, since in the United States "a good carpenter could readily find a job."[435] It was the dawn of a new era as young Gloades expanded their social and economic horizons well beyond Atlantic Canada and, though few ever forgot their roots, began to make their mark on Canadian society as a whole.

Conclusion

Descended from a Mi'kmaw leader named Jehan Grand Claude and his wife Marie Medosset whose ancestral roots lay deep in the early French era at Port Royal, the Glodes/Gloades over time have participated in fur trading, treaty making, farming, commercial fishing, guiding, both local band and Mi'kmaw Grand Council politics, independent businesses, the trades and, most recently, a host of professional careers.[436] In 1722 Jehan Claude signed a treaty of neutrality with the English administration at Port Royal that likely enhanced his trading opportunities in southwestern Nova Scotia and doubtless allowed him to amass a degree of wealth. His descendants have interacted and intermarried with persons of diverse backgrounds. Some were noted war veterans. Leaders such as he were always on the lookout for new economic opportunities for their people. He demonstrated a resilient spirit in the face of economic and political hardships that led his family to become one of the most dynamic and sizable in southwestern Nova Scotia. One distinguishing characteristic of this group is their lasting adherence to maintaining their richly endowed lands in southwestern Nova Scotia in the face of settler incursions. Yet they did not resort when pressured to violence, but instead relied on diplomatic means to retain their territorial access and control.

The district band to which the Gloades belonged traditionally exercised territorial aegis over a vast tract in interior Annapolis, Queens, and Lunenburg counties. The countryside along the Mersey-Medway river system was so well known to male members of this family that they could describe its features in intimate physical detail, and several could imbue it with mythic qualities born of their ancestors' three hundred years of close attachment to the land.[437] The ingenuity and adaptability that marked the lives of Glodes/Gloades from Lequille to Liverpool, and from Yarmouth to the Cobequids, left an indelible mark in the realm of political leadership, and many of this family hold leadership offices today.[438] Since 1960 several Glode/Gloade women have fostered cutting-edge developments in Indigenous social work and education, among other professional fields.[439] Finally, members of the family have contributed immeasurably to our understanding of the Nova Scotian past. Nineteenth-century writers like Silus Tertius Rand and Stansbury Hagar and, in the twentieth century, Clara Dennis, Thomas H. Raddall, and Frank Gouldsmith Speck relied heavily on historical information supplied by knowledgeable descendants of the eighteenth-century head man Jehan Grand Claude for their investigations into Mi'kmaw society and culture. Yet these recorded stories only touch on the tremendous reservoir of cultural and historical knowledge maintained within the family's many branches. Since there is so much yet to learn, let us hope that future generations belonging to this family will take up the torch.

– Janet E. Chute and Carrie Gloade

Acknowledgments: We are grateful to Daniel Gloade, Deborah Gloade of Bear River, Debora Gloade of Yarmouth, Gordon Gloade, Mike Gloade, Steve Gloade, Muriel Gloade-Barr, Bruce Jodrey, Martha Jodrey, Donald Julien, Alan Knight, Basil Peters, Dan Ramsay, and Linda Rafuse for their assistance with sections of this chapter. Carrie Gloade was the principal research assistant and helped in innumerable other ways by contacting people to interview and sharing personal stories from her family's past.

3

Paul Guédry dit *Labrador and the Mi'kmaw Labrador Family of Nova Scotia*

The Mi'kmaq and the Guédrys along the Atlantic Coast

Paul Guédry *dit* Labrador (3 January 1701–c.1767), nicknamed the *Grivois* or "the jovial," was a fur trader, fisherman, provisioner and coastal pilot at Merliguèche (also spelled Mirliguèche), located on the site of the present-day town of Lunenburg along Nova Scotia's South Shore.[1] Silus Tertius Rand, a well-known nineteenth-century Baptist missionary to the Mi'kmaq, held that "Merliguèche" derived from the Mi'kmaw word *melegech*, "milk," and referred to the foamy, milky billows that appeared on the surface of seawater during a windstorm.[2] The Mi'kmaq did not use the word to denote a specific bay or the land around it; its use as an identifier for what became Lunenburg Harbour began with the French. The French also bestowed the name "Merliguèche" on a nearby Mi'kmaw summer village.

While Paul Guédry likely lacked Indigenous ancestry, his father, Claude Guédry, prior to his marriage to his Acadian mother Margaret Petitpas traded for years at the mouth of the Saint John River and had at least one Indigenous consort. Furthermore, Paul's wife, Nannette Anne-Marie Mius d'Azy (1705–c.1767), whom Paul married in 1722, was the daughter of an Acadian father, Philippe Mius II d'Entremont *dit* d'Azy (1660–c.1730), and a Mi'kmaw mother, Marie. After his father's death in 1723, Paul became proprietor of his family's fur trading and fishing station at Merliguèche known by the British as the "Labrador Farm." When the British in 1749 began routing Acadians, *métis*, and Mi'kmaq from their villages along the Atlantic coast, he, Nanette Anne-Marie, and their three youngest children – Paul *fils* ("son" or "Jr."), Jean Petit-Jean, and François, all born between 1742 and 1749 – left Merliguèche for Île St. Jean (now Prince Edward Island). In 1752 they accepted land, seed, and farming supplies at Baie des Espagnols, Île Royale (present-day North Sydney, Cape Breton) from the French administration at Fortress Louisbourg.

While in Cape Breton Paul missed the trading life, so within two years he, his wife, and Paul fils, Jean Petit-Jean, and François, who were still living with them, returned to Merliguèche. Since they soon faced harassment from British officials, who were fearful of their close relations with the neighbouring Mi'kmaq, they sought to escape British detection. Within a year they pressed into the interior of Lunenburg County along with Nanette Anne-Marie's brother, François Mius, who was head chief of the nearby Mi'kmaw village. By adopting a Mi'kmaw way of life at Mushamush Lake, which lay inland from Mahone Bay, they were able to avoid deportation by the British between 1755 and 1760. During these years Paul *fils*, and perhaps Jean Petit-Jean and François as well, married Mi'kmaw women and remained at Mushamush, where their descendants joined the local Mi'kmaw community.[3] After 1754 Paul Guédry *dit* Labrador's movements and activities, and those of his close kin, thus had a major bearing on the lives of several of the younger generation of Labradors, who became the ancestors of men and women bearing the surname "Labrador" among the Mi'kmaw population today.

Paul Guédry's Parents, Siblings, In-Laws, and Cousins

Paul's paternal grandfather, Charles Guédry, immigrated from Rochelle, France, to Port Royal around 1671, likely aboard the *L'Oranger*. Upon his arrival in Acadia Charles began trading with the Mi'kmaq and Malecite (Wolastoqiyik),[4] so his son, Claude Guédry *dit* Lavadure (c.1648–1723),[5] from an early age was familiar with Northeastern Algonquian language and culture. When Claude married Marguerite Petitpas (c.1660–1730) at Beaubassin in 1683, she was a widow and Claude had three years earlier ended a liaison with a woman named Kesk8a[6] who lived at Menagoneche, an Indigenous village and French trade depot situated on the Saint John River where the city of Saint John, New Brunswick, stands today.[7] Kesk8a, who was either Malecite or Mi'kmaq, lived with Claude between 1672 and 1680 and bore him a daughter, Jeanne.[8]

Claude had lived openly with Kesk8a, and it is even possible the two wed according to the rites of the Roman Catholic Church, although this is uncertain. During early seventeenth century it was considered good geopolitical strategy on the part of the French administration of Acadia to encourage unions between French men and Indigenous women.[9] Not only were French women scarce in the early years of Acadian settlement, but for men involved in fur trading, Indigenous women provided valuable kin linkages to bands, possessed a knowledge of the country, exhibited useful technological and survival skills, and understood Indigenous cultural protocols. Jeanne Guédry's exact birth date is unknown, since she was not baptized until several years later. In the absence of a priest on the frontier, a child's baptism could be delayed for years. By the time Claude brought Jeanne on 2 June 1681 to be baptized by Claude Moireau, a Recollect priest stationed at Menagoneche, which recently had become part of the Parish of Beaubassin, Kesk8a had either died or deserted Guédry.[10] Jeanne La Tour, a *métis* daughter of Charles de Saint-Etienne de La Tour, stood as Jeanne's godmother at the baptism, which suggests Guédry was accepted by the

upper echelons of Acadia's fur trading elite.[11] Claude Petitpas *fils* (c.1663–c.1731), a coastal pilot who soon was to become Claude Guédry's brother-in-law, was Jeanne's godfather.

Paul Guédry's maternal grandfather, Claude Petitpas *père*, Sieur de La Fleur (1624–c.1690), was strikingly different from Paul's father, the "rough and ready" frontier trader. Claude Petitpas *père* was a well-educated man, born in Gascony, France. During the 1680s he was a *greffier* – a justice official and administrative secretary – at Port Royal. Sieur de la Fleur's wife, Catherine Briand Bugaret (1630–c.1695), was the daughter of a Basque shipbuilder, Bernard Bugaret, who before he moved to Port Royal in 1638 worked for two years as a hunting expedition leader with Nicolas Denys's lumbering teams at La Hève and Merliguèche. Catherine was an educated, politically active woman who, after her husband Claude's death in 1690, married Charles Chevalier *dit* La Tourasse, first sergeant to Governor Joseph Robinau de Villebon at Jemseg. La Tourasse had political dealings with both the French and English, and following the Massachusetts Bay Colony's victory arising from the Battle of Port Royal on 16 May 1690, he moved to Port Royal to become president of Sir William Phips's council. Five years later, his wife Catherine died at sea en route to Boston, after volunteering to help Abraham Boudrot, another member of the Acadian elite, negotiate an exchange of prisoners between New England and the French.

Claude Petitpas *père* and Catherine Bugaret's daughter Margaret was, at the time of her marriage to Claude Guédry, the widow of Martin Dugas (1656–79), son of Abraham Dugas, a skilled Port Royal gunsmith. Margaret and Martin had two children, Abraham and Marie, who along with their mother joined Claude Guédry's household at Merliguèche in 1683. Although Marguerite and her second husband hailed from radically different social backgrounds, Claude exhibited special strengths owing to his knowledge of Indigenous society and his deep roots in the Acadian fur trade. For a number of years, he invited his new brother-in-law, Claude Petitpas *fils*, the third of Claude Petitpas *père*'s fifteen children, to assist him with the Merliguèche trade.[12] Over time, neighbouring Acadian commercial fish and fur-trading communities along the South Shore – at La Hève, Petit Rivière, and Port Maltois (now Port Medway) – that initially had contained only from one to three families grew and became increasingly interconnected with each other and with the surrounding Mi'kmaq through a web of kin ties and other social affiliations.[13]

Claude Guédry and Marguerite Petitpas's family grew rapidly.[14] In 1688, the French governor Menneval's secretary, Gargas, recorded that twenty-one persons – ten Europeans and eleven Mi'kmaq – lived at Merliguèche. The Guédrys had a log house and outbuildings surrounded by half an acre under cultivation, while the Mi'kmaq camped nearby in two wigwams.[15] Claude Petitpas *fils*, who in 1685 wed a Mi'kmaw woman named Marie-Thérèze at Port Royal, erected his dwelling close by, so Claude Guédry *père*'s children for a few years had regular contact with their younger *métis* first cousins, Barthélèmy Petitpas (1687–c.1745) and Judith Petitpas (1693–?).

Claude Guédry temporarily moved to Port Royal in 1694, during the War of the League of Augsburg (1688–97). With a prudent pragmatism characteristic of Acadians who traded with the British and New Englanders as well as the French, he and fifty-eight eight other Acadians at Port Royal signed an oath of allegiance to King William III of England delivered to them in August of 1695 by Emes Fleetwood, captain of the English frigate *Sorling*.[16] This action protected Guédry's entitlement to his lands and trading rights at Port Royal during the years the Massachusetts's provisional government was in power.

Claude Guédry lived fairly comfortably at Port Royal. A year after the Treaty of Ryswick returned Acadia to France in 1697, Claude and his wife Marguerite possessed eight arpents of cultivated land, ten head of cattle, two sheep, eight pigs, and one gun.[17] Abraham Dugas still lived with his mother and step-father, while Abraham's sister Marie had wed Joseph Guyon *dit* Dion the previous year. Claude's *métis* daughter Jeanne did not appear on the census, and may have died. Between 1683 and 1697 Claude *père* and his wife had nine children: Claude in 1683, Jean-Baptiste in 1684, Charles in 1686, Alexis in 1688, Augustin in 1690, Marie-Josephe around 1692, Claude *fils* in 1694, Joseph in 1695, and Pierre in 1697. But despite the fact that Claude had land and livestock at Port Royal, he chose to return to the fishing and fur trading way of life at Merliguèche once hostilities between the French and English were over. His youngest son, Paul Guédry *dit* Labrador, was born at Merliguèche on 3 January 1701. In the absence of a priest, Paul was baptized by Marie Dugas's husband,

Joseph Guyon, while Paul's godparents – his elder brother Jean-Baptist Guédry and Marie Tibodeau – looked on.[18] Paul's baptism was followed in 1703 by the birth of his youngest sibling, Françoise, in 1703.[19]

Unlike his older siblings who had spent much of their early lives at Port Royal, Paul Guédry regarded Merliguèche as home. Three of his brothers, Claude, Charles, and Alexis, left their father's household by 1701. Claude Jr., born in 1683, reputedly remained unmarried and died relatively early in life. Charles Guédry married a Mi'kmaw woman known as Kesha or "Morning Star" and for a year lived near Piziquid, which the British would later rename "Windsor." In 1703 he left Piziquid to be with his brother Alexis, who with his Mi'kmaw spouse had moved to Cobequid, near present-day Truro.[20] Paul's closest companions were the siblings closest to him in age, as well as his *métis* second cousin Barthélèmy Petitpas (1687–1747) at Musquodoboit on Nova Scotia's Eastern Shore, where Claude Petitpas *fils* from the late 1690s to the early 1700s managed a trading post.[21]

Like Claude Guédry, Claude Petitpas remained on good terms with visiting New Englanders. He sheltered New England fishermen from Mi'kmaw attacks during Dummer's War (1722–25), for which he received a monetary reward from the legislative council in Boston. Since Barthélèmy Petitpas and his younger brother, Louis-Benjamin Petitpas, born around 1726, spoke fluent Mi'kmaw as well as French, they later played prominent roles as Mi'kmaw interpreters and negotiators. Barthélèmy in the 1740s interpreted for the French regime at Fortress Louisbourg, while Louis-Benjamin, between 1759 and 1762 assisted Abbé Pierre Maillard, who during those years served the Mi'kmaq and Acadians from a Roman Catholic mission headquarters in Halifax.[22]

Paul in his youth also associated with the *métis* sons and daughters of Philippe Mius I d'Entremont *dit* d'Azy, who was the son of Baron Philippe Mius I d'Entremont of Pobomcoup (now East Pubnico), and he eventually married one of Philippe II's daughters.[23] These connections would aid him immeasurably in his trading ventures. Prior to 1749, when the British placed an embargo on French commerce in southwestern Nova Scotia, Merliguèche and neighbouring coastal Acadian communities relied on the French trans-shipment centre at Pobomcoup to send furs and fish to France. In 1670 the French governor, Hector d'Andigné de Grandfontaine, had appointed Philippe II's father as *procurer du roi*, a prestigious position the baron held for twenty-eight years. The baron's other two sons, Jacques Mius d'Entremont *dit* Pobomcoup and Abraham Mius d'Entremont de Pleinmarais, both wed daughters of Charles La Tour, and after the death of their father around 1699 maintained the Pobomcoup trading station.[24] Jacques and Abraham occupied the upper ranks of French colonial society,[25] while their younger brother Philippe entered the fur trade, consorted with two Mi'kmaw women in succession, and had a large family whose members associated closely with the Mi'kmaq.[26]

Following the death around 1688 of Philippe II's first Mi'kmaw consort, his children fell under the care of his brother Abraham at Ministiguèshe (now Barrington Head, Shelburne County). Philippe II at this time moved his trading operations to a post at Chichimichecady[27] (on present-day Second Peninsula, Lunenburg County) where he joined the local band, adopted much of the Mi'kmaw way of life, and consorted with a second Mi'kmaw woman, Marie. While collecting census information in this area in 1707, Père Pierre La Chasse divided the local population into those he regarded as Mi'kmaq and those he held to be strictly French. Since he based his judgments on considerations of occupation and lifestyle rather than biological connection, the census he completed in 1708 listed Philippe II and his family at Chichimichecady as "*sauvage.*"[28]

Paul Guédry also was a close friend of the families of the two brothers Pierre Lejeune *dit* Briard (c.1684–c.1750) and Martin Lejeune *dit* Briard (c.1661–1740). Pierre Lejeune and his wife Marie Tibodeau (or Thibaudeau) settled at Petit Rivière in 1708, and in 1725 Paul's sister Françoise wed their son Jean.[29] Martin Lejeune, who resided at Port Maltois (now Port Medway), married a Mi'kmaw woman, Marie-Jeanne Kaygonias, and following Marie-Jeanne's death around 1702 wed a second time to Jean Godet. Like Claude Guédry *père*, Pierre and Martin Lejeune moved to Port Royal around 1694 and at the end of the War of the League of Augsburg returned to the Atlantic coast.[30] Their sister, Jeanne Lejeune, married a Mi'kmaq from La Hève named François Joseph, and the couple had a son, François *fils* (c.1682–c.1760) who later wed Marie, a daughter of Chief Claude Egighighes of La Hève.[31] In contrast to Philippe Mius II at Chichimichecady, who opposed the British, Claude Egighighes remained neutral, a stance that encouraged neutrality among the Lejeunes as well.

A Focus on the Merliguèche Community in the Early 1700s

The Guédry, Petitpas, Mius d'Entremont, and Lejeune families spaced themselves out along the Atlantic coast to avoid commercial competition and gain access to different Mi'kmaw groups. They cultivated small gardens and grazed livestock on clearings in the thick woods back of their log habitations. Houses near them generally belonged to their in-laws. In the 1680s Claude Guédry *père* had erected a commodious house with a stone chimney and pole-and-bark roof for his family at Merliguèche. He also built a barn, although farming remained marginal in nature. Less than three acres were under cultivation at Merliguèche in 1687, much to the chagrin of French administrators at Port Royal who knew that fertile soil flanked a creek that ran into the ocean just south of the Merliguèche post.[32] Wharves for shallops and other small trading vessels dotted the coastline. The Mi'kmaq frequented this waterfront and occasionally accompanied members of the Guédry family when they sailed to Musquodoboit, Petit Rivière, or Pobomcoup.

The Mi'kmaq and their Acadian neighbours also assembled at Merliguèche for religious celebrations, since both adhered to the calendrical rites of the Roman Catholic Church. Prior to 1654 a chapel, fort, and school had existed at nearby La Hève, but these structures had been razed to the ground in a struggle between rival French factions. Merliguèche lacked a chapel, so the community erected makeshift structures to accommodate visiting clerics and host services and festivities. The rare visit from an itinerant priest gave rise to a flurry of activity; local Acadians, Acadian-*métis*, and Mi'kmaq laboured to prepare a feast for all who attended services. Mass would be held either in the Guédry homestead or, if the weather cooperated, outdoors in the makeshift chapel. Visitors converged in droves from outlying communities, travelling either by shallop or by canoe brigade. Bark canoes were drawn up on the sandy beach, while larger Acadian vessels were secured at the wharf or anchored offshore. A religious service might be conducted in Mi'kmaw, which both the Mi'kmaq and the Acadian *métis* understood. If a death occurred in the community the body, after proper burial rites, was interred at a site still known today as the "Old French Cemetery."

New dwellings arose at Merliguèche as persons married and families grew. At age twenty-four in 1708 Paul Guédry's elder brother Jean-Baptiste wed fourteen-year-old Madeleine, who was almost certainly the *métis* daughter of Philippe II Mius and his second consort, Marie.[33] Jean-Baptiste Guédry and Madeleine Mius lived for twelve years at Merliguèche before leaving around 1720 with their four children, Paul, Marie, Jean-Baptiste *fils*, and Joseph, to assist Jean-Baptiste *père's* aging father-in-law at the Chichimichecady post, south of Merliguèche.[34] Paul Guédry married Madeleine's sister, Nannette Anne-Marie Mius, two years later. Paul's brother, Pierre Guédry *dit* Grivois, a noted coastal pilot, dwelt near him and encouraged him to learn to pilot vessels as well. It was not long before Paul was guiding vessels around the southwestern tip of Nova Scotia to Pobomcoup and Port Royal, and at times on trading trips to Boston. New commercial opportunities also arose. While markets in Boston had begun to rely more on locally produced goods than on Acadian products, crews of New England fishing vessels seeking fresh water and provisions at Merliguèche before departing for the Sable Island Bank brought potential trading partners literally to the Guédry family's front doorstep.

For the rest of his life Claude Guédry *père* sought to remain on affable terms with these New Englanders, since the exigencies of commerce favoured neutrality, even in times of war. His establishment also gained a reputation of being a safe haven whenever danger threatened. When a hostile Mi'kmaw party boarded a New England vessel near Merliguèche in1715, the ship's master, Captain Odoiorn, appealed to Claude Guédry to save his crew and vessel. In response, Guédry immediately sent for Pierre Walker, the Minas head chief better known as Pierre Momcharret, who used "Walker" as one of his surnames. On arriving at Merliguèche, Momcharret successfully negotiated the release of both Odoiorn's men and ship.[35] Massachusetts afterwards argued that since Merliguèche comprised part of Britain's territorial acquisitions under the terms of the Treaty of Utrecht of 1713, the Mi'kmaq's actions in taking over Odoiorn's vessel constituted a serious infringement of New England's territorial right. Meanwhile the Mi'kmaq, who considered themselves a free-acting, unconquered constituency, viewed New England's use of their coastline as unsanctioned trespass, worthy of redress.

Dummer's War of 1722–1725 and Its Aftermath

When Paul Guédry was only fifteen years of age, the French completed their fortress at Louisbourg in Cape Breton and set about encouraging Mi'kmaw leaders to defend sections of the Acadian coastline – which they dubbed "commands" – against New England encroachment. Though many chiefs complied with these orders, the Indigenous people also had their own ways of addressing unwelcome intrusions on their lands. Each year delegates were sent to attend a council forum, which Frank Speck, a twentieth-century anthropologist, has called "The Eastern Wabanaki Confederacy."[36] The Mi'kmaq were latecomers to these councils, although during the 1720s Wolastoqiyik (Malecite), Penobscot, Passamaquoddy, Eastern Abenaki, and Ottawa attendees discussed issues and formulated ideas that later were rapidly disseminated throughout the Northeast. But while the Mi'kmaq may not have been full-fledged members of this Confederacy until late, they still were allies of the organization. On occasion, they sent representatives and, following the close of Dummer's War, joined the Confederacy.[37]

A contentious issue raised in these councils was Massachusetts's decision to permit settlers to hunt and fish in locales the Eastern Abenaki delegates held had been reserved to them by treaty. As members of the Eastern Wabanaki Confederacy, the Mi'kmaq felt obliged to join their allies in their contest with New England. In 1720 Mi'kmaw warriors mounted a protest against the attempts by New England fishers to wrest the Canso fishery away from Mi'kmaw and French control. In a surprise attack, they took Canso, captured eighteen New England fishing vessels, and threatened to kill twenty or so crew members.[38] They eventually transported many of these captives to Merliguèche, where it was only through the shrewd negotiating skill of a New England sloop's captain named Blin, who once had been held captive by the Mi'kmaq long enough to grasp certain Indigenous protocols regarding exchange and ransom, that these men's lives were saved. A New England and British raid two years later on the mission village of Nanrantsouak (Norridgewock), in what is now the state of Maine, prompted Indigenous retaliations on outlying New England settlements and led Governor Shirley of Massachusetts to declare war on the Eastern Abenaki on 25 July 1724. Closer to home at Merliguèche, Mi'kmaw leaders strenuously opposed liquor sales to their people by crews of the New England fishing fleet.[39] Louisbourg also prevailed upon an itinerant missionary, Abbé Antoine Gaulin, to muster the Mi'kmaq living on the shores of Mahone Bay at Merliguèche so that the French authorities could determine the number of young, able-bodied men forming their constituency and, if need be, call upon them to fight.[40]

During Dummer's War,[41] New Englanders setting out to capture Aboriginal persons drew few distinctions between Acadian-*métis*, who often looked Aboriginal, and members of Mi'kmaw bands, and took both indiscriminately. When Captain Blin was ordered by Boston to capture Aboriginal prisoners at Merliguèche, he apprehended only persons associated either by birth or marriage with the Claude Guédry *pere* family.[42] Those listed were Paul Guédry and his wife Nanette Anne-Marie Mius, Claude Guédry *fils*, Augustin Guédry and his wife Jeanne Hébert, and a sixth man Blin identified as "Philippe Guédry" (although, as far as is known, Claude Guédry *père* and Marguerite Petitpas did not have a son named Philippe).[43] The six prisoners were first taken to New Hampshire, then to Boston.[44]

At the time of their capture, both Nanette Anne-Marie and Jeanne Hébert were pregnant. Nanette gave birth to a daughter, Judith (Judique), in Boston, while Jeanne Hébert gave birth to twin girls, Marie-Hélène and Marie-Joseph.[45] The twins' grandfather, Claude Guédry *père*, presided over the conditional baptism of these infants on 9 January 1723, having travelled to Boston specifically for this purpose. Known in French as *ondoye*, this conditional baptism usually was followed by confirmation of the earlier rite by a priest, but the elderly Claude did not live to see the performance of this second rite. Baptizing his grandchildren was likely the last public act he performed on behalf of his family, as he died later the same year.

Blin's taking of prisoners constituted the first of two major depredations committed by New England on the Acadian-*métis* of Merliguéche during the war years. On 18 July 1723, the crew of a vessel under the command of Captain Joseph Marjory, commissioned to protect the New England fishery, captured, according to a declaration made by Marjory in Boston on 18 December 1724, Philippe II Mius's twenty-three-year-old son François Mius *dit* d'Azy and Jean Baptiste Guédry's son Paul.[46] Paul Guédry and

François Mius, who were close in age, were confined to prison in Boston for over three years, even though a ratification of a peace and friendship treaty, signed at Annapolis Royal in 1726 between the Indigenous population and the British Crown, specifically stipulated in its terms that all Mi'kmaw prisoners would be released.[47]

A Plan Gone Awry

After his father's death in 1723 Jean-Baptiste Guédry grew increasingly impatient with Boston's reluctance to release his son and François Mius. Finally, assisted by Captain Decoy, the master of a French vessel that put in to Merliguèche on 24 September 1726 to trade cattle, he, his fourteen year-old son Jean-Baptiste Guédry *fils*, and two of his brothers-in-law, James (or Jacques) Mius and Philippe Mius *fils*, devised a hasty and risky venture to force Boston to return the prisoners.[48] Their plot involved luring a New England ship into Merliguéche harbour, boarding the vessel, taking most of the crew captive, and then dispatching a few crew members to sail to Boston with orders to secure a release of the captives. Seven members of the local Mi'kmaw band – John Missell, Salmon (or Solomon, who was also called "Ferman"), Salmon's son Louis, Marsel (or Marcel), and Marsel's wife and his two children – also agreed to take part in this endeavour.

The party did not have to wait long. The next day the *Tryal*, a New England fishing sloop with five crewmen, sailed into Merliguèche harbour looking for water and provisions. At first the vessel's company was hailed congenially by those on shore. Claude Guédry's widow, Marguerite Petitpas, ignorant of her son's and his companions' motivations, invited the vessel's captain, Samuel Doty (or Daley) and some of his crew up to her house to enjoy a convivial glass of punch. Doty and several of his men gratefully accepted Marguerite's offer by joining her in the Guédry homestead.

With the captain temporarily absent from his vessel, Jean-Baptiste, his son, and James and Philippe Mius put their plan into action. James and Philippe boarded the *Tryal* and caught and bound Philip Sachimus, the ship's Aboriginal watchman, to the masthead. They then approached Doty, who was told that two crewmen would be released to sail to Boston and spread the word that the other three men would only be freed once Massachusetts agreed to release Paul Guédry and François Mius. Once Marguerite Petitpas realized what was about to transpire, she and her son Augustin pleaded with Jean-Baptist to jettison his plans, but Jean-Baptiste ignored their pleas. The captain was bound with ropes to prevent him from escaping, while Jean-Baptiste defiantly tore down the ship's red ensign and tied the colours around his waist as a holster for a pistol he had taken from a crewman. The following morning, he declared, he would order the sloop to sail to the village of Chichimichecady, on Second Peninsula, where the *Tryal*'s crew would be held hostage until his son and François Mius were safely returned to Merliguéche.

This plot collapsed early the next day. When the vessel's steersman was unbound in order to guide the ship, he suddenly overwhelmed his captors. Salmon, Louis, and Marsel at this point escaped out a cabin window into the sea and, rescued by a passing vessel, told stories of their adventure that eventually reached the ears of Louisbourg's governor, Joseph Broullian de Saint-Ovide.[49] The *Tryal* proceeded on to Boston, where the vessel's captain and crew turned over the Acadian and Mi'kmaw party to the colonial authorities. Jean Baptist and his teenage son, the two Mius brothers, and John Missel were given the opportunity to explained the reasons for their actions before a special session of the Massachusetts Admiralty Court convened on 4 and 5 October 1726. During these proceedings the Guédrys spoke in French, while the Mius brothers and John Missel stated their case in the Mi'kmaw language. John Gyles, who had been a former captive among the Mi'kmaq and Malecite, interpreted during the Mius brothers' and John Missel's testimonies. Their goal, the three stressed, was to secure the release of prisoners held at Boston, although the strength of their words was undermined by their penchant to blame Jean-Baptiste for involving them in such a dangerous undertaking in the first place. Despite the defending arguments of George Hughes, the advocate for the prisoners,[50] when the members of the court discerned that goods belonging to the ship, such as rings, pistols, and provisions, had been pilfered they charged Jean-Baptiste, his son, Philippe and James Mius, and John Missel with piracy on the high seas. Despite the fact that no one had been killed or injured, the court decided to levy the harshest of punishments, probably because the *Tryal* had been an unarmed fishing vessel operating in peacetime.[51] All

five men, after being charged and found guilty of piracy on 2 November 1726, were hanged at Boston on 13 November 1726.[52]

New England's decision to hang several Acadians and Mi'kmaq as an example to the Mi'kmaq of what would happen if such incidents continued did little in the end to stop Indigenous attacks on the New England fishery. Instead, a new spirit of resistance arose, fueled by a desire to avenge the Boston deaths. In 1727 attacks on ships occurred at Jeddore and Liscombe along Nova Scotia's Eastern Shore, while a party of thirty Mi'kmaq, identified as "Indians of Labrador" (or the Bras d'Or Lake region of Cape Breton),[53] commandeered a vessel at Port au Basque and sailed it back to Merliguèche.[54] French officials at Louisbourg rejoiced that the Mi'kmaq had not been cowed by the recent events in Boston, since they feared that the cessation of hostilities in 1725 between the Eastern Abenaki and New England threatened to leave the "southwestern flank of Canada dangerously exposed."[55] With French incentives added to the mix, the Boston affair had the power to rekindle widespread Indigenous bitterness against New England. But to avoid suggestions of complicity in fomenting hostility, Governor Ovide purchased the ship's cargo from the Merliguèche Mi'kmaq and informed the ship's owner of his vessel's whereabouts. Yet this innocent facade was difficult for the French to maintain, since the Mi'kmaw party who boarded the vessel near Port au Basque had hoisted French colours.[56] Massachusetts threatened to punish Mi'kmaw raids on shipping with the full force of the law,[57] while Nova Scotia's governor Lawrence Armstrong pursued a placatory course. Unnerved by the thought of the Indigenous community intensifying its depredations, and concerned about the safety of his poorly fortified garrison at Annapolis Royal, Armstrong sought to mollify Mi'kmaw resentments by sending presents to the Merliguèche leaders and disavowing any personal participation in the harsh punishment meted out by New England to the Merliguèche community in the fall of 1726.[58]

Despite the tumultuous times, Paul Guédry publicly avowed neutrality, and as a result of his diplomatic endeavours retained possession of the Guédry homestead at Merliguèche for twenty-eight more years. In addition to Judith, born in Boston in 1722, he and Nanette Anne-Marie Mius had five more children between 1723 and 1733: Jacques in 1724; Claude about 1726, Jean-Anselm in 1730, Marguerite in 1732, and Joseph-Thomas in 1733. Nine years later the couple had three more children, Paul *fils* in 1742, Jean Petit-Jean in 1743, and François in 1749.

A Brief Retreat to Piziquid

In the years leading up to the onset of King George's War (1744–48) the Merliguèche population through natural increase grew and became increasingly productive. Between 350 and 400 acres of cropland and pasture were cleared and cultivated, since the community's cattle, wheat, and vegetables found ready markets at Louisbourg.[59] Rather than forming one vast field, this acreage lay over the landscape in scattered parcels, divided from one another by bush. Paul Guédry was regarded as the community patriarch. He became known far and wide for his hospitality towards others, whether French from Louisbourg, British from Annapolis Royal, or members of New England fishing crews. He regularly entertained his Mi'kmaw relatives in his home, despite the fact that his brother-in-law François Mius derided his commitment to neutrality and pressed him to harass the British. The French at Louisbourg, meanwhile, rewarded Mius for his loyalty to the French cause. Governor Baptist Louis Le Prevost Duquesnel on 25 July 1742 supplied him with a medal and presents, and vested him with a *brevet de commission* recognizing Mius as "Chef de Mikmaq de Mirliguèche."[60] In return, Duquesnel expected the Mi'kmaw leader to defend a "command" extending along the eastern Atlantic coast from Chichimichecady to La Hève.

In the early to middle 1740s, Paul Guédry's household became a comfortable retreat for several of his nephews. Paul was particularly fond of Nicolas Joseph Deschamps *dit* La Cloche (c.1710–c.1758), who had wed a daughter of his sister Marie-Thérèse Guédry. Two other frequent guests were his brother Pierre Guédry *dit* LaBine's sons Jean-Baptiste (or Jean) Guédry *dit* Grivois and Joseph Guédry *dit* LaBine.[61] At this time Merliguèche's population began to decline. A report, commissioned by the governor of New France and drafted in 1745 by intendant Gilles Hocquart and the Marquis de Beauharnois, noted that "[a]t Merliguèche, a small harbour five leagues east of La Hève, are only eight settlers, among the rest Paul Guidry, alias Grivois, jovial or jolly, a good coast pilot."[62]

Though this document presumably referred principally to a decline in the number of male family heads, late in 1749 the settlement's population dropped radically after soldiers from Halifax destroyed nearby Chichimichecady. Paul Guédry moved his family to Île St. Jean, while Pierre Guédry *dit* LaBine went to Chignecto and joined Joseph Broussard *dit* Beausoleil's corps of Acadian and Aboriginal resistance fighters. Broussard toured Acadia from Beaubassin to Cape Sable recruiting Aboriginal support for the French, as well as encouraging defections of British soldiers from the garrison at Annapolis Royal. His activities aroused so much consternation in New England that on 21 October 1747 Governor William Shirley of Massachusetts issued a proclamation declaring Beausoleil and twelve others – including Pierre Guédry *dit* LaBine and Pierre's slightly older brother Joseph Guédry – to be "guilty of treason and outlaws."[63]

A reward of 50 pounds sterling was offered for each man who was delivered up within six months, and any of the outlaws could turn in one of his fellows to claim not only the fifty pounds but also an unconditional pardon. Despite these incentives to have Pierre apprehended and turned over to the British authorities, he remained at large until after the close of the war. In 1750 a second charge was laid against him and three of his companions, Jacques Le Blanc, J.P. Pitre, and Pierre Rembour, for encouraging nine soldiers to desert from Richard Philipp's regiment at Port Royal. (The keystone of the British garrison of Nova Scotia in the 1740s was the 40th Regiment of Foot whose colonel, Richard Phillips [1661–1750], was governor from 1717 to 1749.) Though a trial date was set for August 1750, Pierre eluded capture and arraignment. He died at Port Toulouse, Île Royale (now St. Peter's, Cape Breton) on 30 August 1751, still a free man.[64]

At this time both Pierre Guédry and Pierre Guédry *dit* LaBine often referred to themselves simply as "Labrador," as did Pierre Guédry *dit* LaBine's two sons, Jean-Baptiste and Joseph. Paul Guédry remained neutral during the Seven Years' War, though others of his family did not.[65] "Labrador" was a corruption of his father's name "Lavadure," which means "greenness" and alludes to farmers and farming. As well, it pinpointed the geographical locale in Cape Breton where the Guédrys often traded; it was a Mi'kmaw custom to address persons by the place name of the locality they frequented.[66] As coastal pilots and traders, Paul and his brother Pierre often travelled to Bras d'Or Lake in Cape Breton. The word "Labrador," with its variant spelling "La Bras d'Or," translates as "labourer." "Labrador" is a

Spanish surname, while "Lavrador" and "Lavradure" are Portuguese.[67] Yet Portuguese sailors engaged in the early whaling industry in North America were called "Labradors," as was the coastline off which they ventured.[68] Yet there is much to suggest that the appearance by the mid-1740s of "Labrador" as a sobriquet among the Acadians and Acadian-*métis* at Merliguèche and Piziquid owes as much to Aboriginal tradition as to European naming practices.

Since his brother Pierre and his brother-in-law François Mius both avidly supported the French cause during the war, Paul, who continued to remain neutral, moved to Piziquid in the fall of 1746 in order to avoid being tarred by the British with the same brush as his kinsmen. It was at Piziquid that Paul and his family nearly died the following spring in a flash flood. The incident might have spelled tragedy for the entire Guédry household had it not been for the heroic action of a large dog belonging to Paul's friend, Joseph Cope.[69] Cope had named his dog "Duc" because he rescued the animal from a ship belonging to the plague-ridden Duc d'Anville's fleet that limped into Chebucto Harbour in September 1746. Paul, his wife, and their three youngest children were welcome at Cope's camp "at the fording place," but they wanted to select their own spot on which to settle over the course of the winter. Their choice to build and occupy a dwelling on a narrow earthen promontory jutting out into the Piziquid River – now the Avon River – was not a good one. One winter's day the tide rose unusually high and water and ice cut off their dwelling from the mainland. Waves tore at the house and threatened to send it as well as what was left of the promontory drifting away on the turn of the tide.

No human being dared venture out into the turbulent waters, but Duc three times plunged into the torrent and crossed over to the Guédry's house, on each return swim carrying a person. He first rescued the Guédry children, who were strapped by ropes to his back, and deposited them safely on the mainland. Cope next dispatched his dog with a long rope that Paul Guédry tied to the front of a toboggan in which Nanette Anne-Marie was pulled to safety. Finally, in "a similar manner, Paul Labrador was brought ashore."[70]

Peace, When There Is No Peace

News of signing of the Treaty of Aix-La-Chapelle in 1748 ending King George's War did not reach Annapolis Royal until May 1749. At Piziquid, Paul Guédry *dit* Labrador heard of the onset of peace the following spring and returned to his family homestead on the Atlantic coast in early July. In his absence the British scrutinized Merliguèche for its potential as a haven for new settlers.[71] In June Governor Edward Cornwallis ordered his sixth-rate warship *Sphinx* to put into Merliguèche for fresh provisions and then sent men ashore to explore. On their return they praised the fertility of the soil but claimed that the local inhabitants failed to make the best use of the countryside's natural assets. "The families they found there," Cornwallis noted, "have very comfortable wooden houses covered with bark, a good many Cattle and Sheep, and clear more ground than serves themselves." Upwards of fifty Acadian and *métis* families, he added, claimed that they had "always looked upon themselves as English subjects; have their grants from [Lieutenant] Colonel Mascarene, the Governor of Annapolis, and showed an unfeigned joy to hear of the new settlement."[72]

Paul Guédry had liked Paul Mascarene when he first met him. Guédry had forged a pact with the lieutenant colonel back in 1740 when he swore to remain neutral, in large part to protect his lands at Merliguèche from British molestation.[73] When Guédry left Piziquid to return to his homestead in 1749 he anticipated that the terms and spirit of the earlier arrangement would continue to govern British-Acadian relations. However, subsequent events disabused him of this expectation. After 1748 Merliguèche's residents had to elude a British embargo levied on French goods destined for the Saint John River area or Louisbourg. The "unfeigned joy" that, according to Cornwallis, the Acadians and *métis* expressed on first hearing about the projected British settlement at Merliguèche turned to dismay when they found that Germanic and Huguenot families would take up all their lands and they would receive no compensation. Other equally discouraging events followed. Late in the summer of 1749 the Mi'kmaq retaliated with anger when the British founded Halifax without first consulting them. At the same time Cornwallis charged Paul Guédry's brother-in-law, François Mius, with participating in raids on Halifax and sent troops to raze Mius's village and trading post at Chichimichecady. When Paul found that he, too, was beginning to be eyed with suspicion, he left for Île St. Jean, accompanied by his wife, his youngest children, and his daughter Judith and her husband

Jean Cousins. His youngest son, François, was baptized at Port-La-Joye, Île St. Jean, on 20 November 1749.[74]

In August 1750 Paul, now forty-nine years of age, relocated once again, this time to Bras du Sud, Baie des Espagnols, Île Royale (now Sydney, Cape Breton). After the British pressured the Acadians on the mainland to take an oath of allegiance, requiring them to bear arms in the service of the British king, tensions arose between the British and French, leading Paul to seek a less politically charged milieu, where he also was given a house and rations by the French at Louisbourg. During the summer of 1751 he lived with his family aboard one of his trading vessels off Louisbourg, where he traded with the local Mi'kmaq. In the fall he moved ashore and the following spring planted fields of cabbage, turnips, and beans and tended livestock he purchased at Louisbourg.

The members of the Acadian-*métis* community at Baie des Espagnols were closely kin related. In 1752 Paul and his wife Nannette Anne-Marie Mius lived with their twenty-three-year-old son Jean, their twenty-year-old daughter Marguerite, and their three youngest sons Paul *fils*, Jean Petit-Jean, and François, who all were under ten.[75] Paul's daughter Françoise and her husband Jean Lejeune lived nearby. Paul's brother Augustin Guédry and his wife Jeanne Hébert had seven adult children living near them. Augustin and Jeanne had three sons: Jean-Baptiste, twenty-four; Joseph, seventeen; and Pierre, eleven.[76] There were also their twin daughters, Marie-Joseph and Marie-Hélène, who were born in Boston in 1722, along with two younger married daughters, Jeanne and Ursule. Augustin's daughter Marie-Joseph around 1746 married Charles Boutin, a son of Joseph Boutin and Marie-Margaret Lejeune *dit* Briart, who welcomed her unwed twin, Marie-Hélène, into his household.[77] Jeanne Guédry and her husband Julian Borneuf, who had resided briefly at Mira before moving to Baie des Espagnols, had Jeanne's younger brother Pierre living with them.[78] Ursule meanwhile was married to Charles Boutin's brother Paul. Marie Guédry – a daughter of Jean-Baptiste Guédry *dit* Labrador, Paul's older brother who was hanged in Boston in 1726 – and her husband Germain Lejeune also lived at Baie des Espagnols.[79]

Germain Lejeune had a close associate, Charles Le Roy, whom Governor Shirley of Massachusetts during King George's War had outlawed along with Pierre Guédry *dit* LaBine. Roy had become the spokesperson of the Baie des Espagnols community.[80] Paul Guédry, while greatly respected in the farming settlement, had declined to take on extra responsibilities since he continued to busy himself with affairs at Merliguèche and frequently was absent from Baie des Espagnols. During the harsh winters of 1751–52 and 1752–53 he returned to Merliguèche to tend to livestock that he had left in the care of others. He was at Merliguèche most of 1753, where he traded in fish, furs, provisions, and cattle as before, even though it was a risky business owing to the British embargo. In 1753, when the French at Louisbourg suddenly cut off relief to the Baie des Espagnols settlement, families suffered from hunger. Charles Le Roy and the families with him mulled over a return to the vicinity of the Labrador farm in a desperate hope that the new settlers the British reportedly were sending to the Merliguèche area might revitalize local markets.

These settlers arrived in the spring. A flotilla of hired New England vessels crammed with Germanic and Huguenot passengers left Halifax for Lunenburg County in early June 1753, led by the flagship *Albany* carrying Colonel Charles Lawrence, the commander of the new Lunenburg settlement. The passengers, still bitter about the squalid accommodations provided for them in Halifax, and fearful of Indigenous raids and Acadian resentment since the farmland they would occupy had been cleared by the Acadian-*métis* community, proved a disgruntled lot. As well, after disembarking at Merliguèche on 8 June several men under Lawrence's charge immediately declared their intention to desert. In consequence, Lawrence began casting about for a local person familiar with the countryside and its inhabitants who could assist him. Not long afterwards an Acadian, who was almost certainly Paul Guédry's nephew Nicolas Joseph Deschamps *dit* La Cloche, adopted the name "Joseph Deschamps *dit* Cloverwater" and stepped forward to offer his services to the colonel as an aide, guide, and coastal pilot. He revealed very little about himself to Lawrence, other than that he was a nephew of Paul Guédry, whom he referred to as "Vieux Labrador."[81] Cloverwater's use of "Vieux" in this context denoted Paul's status as Merliguèche's patriarch rather than his age, since in 1753 Paul was fifty-two years old and Joseph was only nine years younger. He also bent the truth in informing Lawrence that he had a Mi'kmaw mother, and thus was of *métis* ancestry. He must have felt that these ploys increased his worth as an informant to the British. Paul Guédry reciprocated the respect his nephew accorded him by not revealing Joseph's French name or his lack of Indigenous ancestry to the British authorities.

During the summer of 1753 Lawrence regarded Cloverwater as his principal informant. The commander felt no need to question the truthfulness of anything his new and accommodating aide said, and even contemplated what rewards he might bestow on him in order to retain his services. "Deschamps alias Cloverwater (the son of an Acadian by an Indian woman), behaves very faithfully and is very useful to us," he noted in his journal on 16 June 1753. "He expects (as he tells me) that he shall get notice if ye Indians come down to disturb us, and he offers, as no Frenchman ever did yet, to go with a party of our people to a proper place for cutting them off on their passage … He goes on shore & comes on board when he pleases, and sleeps, sometimes with his Uncle Labrador, & sometimes on ye Albany. His whole behaviour seems to be without disguise insomuch that I wish he would indulge in a request that he makes of a spot of garden ground for his family. For – I think I am certain of his being both capable & willing to render some services to ye settlement."[82]

Between 28 June and 2 July 1753, Lawrence made arrangements to relocate Joseph Deschamps's wife, Marie-Therese, and children from Piziquid to Lunenburg, where he anticipated granting them a sizeable tract of land in the new settlement.[83] Joseph was not party to these proceedings: he was assisting Joseph Gorham and his rangers track some settlers who had deserted Lunenburg and proceeded thirty miles up a woods trail between Mahone Bay and Piziquid – for which he received pay of twelve pence per day.[84] The settlers had hatched their daring escape plan after hearing about the cleared land, livestock, and provisions the French might offer them if they went to Île St. Jean (Prince Edward Island).[85] They ultimately eluded their pursuers, so they must have had guidance from persons familiar with the terrain.[86] This incident made Lawrence more determined than ever to convince Paul's nephew to join the Lunenburg settlement. "Deschamps has been with Capt. Gorham & two whale boats in ye river at ye head of Mahone Bay, by which ye Indians pass from Pisiquid to this part of the country," Lawrence penned in his journal on 2 July. "They strictly examined ye Indian paths, but could find no signs of anybody having passed lately

that way. The poor fellow seems very uneasy about his wife & children, which, if he could get hither, I believe he would sit down contently 'among us' & be useful, having fewer prejudices & more understanding than any inhabitant I have yet seen in ye Country."[87]

Despite Lawrence's almost unbridled faith in Deschamps early in the summer of 1753, by September the same year several British officials had determined that Cloverwater was not *métis*. The provincial surveyor general, Charles Morris, who was laying out farm lots contiguous to the town of Lunenburg, on 15 September held that Deschamps was "neutral French," while Governor Peregrine Thomas Hopson in a communication to the London Board of Trade dated 22 October described him as a "French Pilot and Guide."[88] Cloverwater furthermore was not the only one of Paul's nephews who in 1753 sought to ingratiate himself with the British. In 1753 Pierre Guédry *dit* LaBine's thirty-two-year-old son Jean-Baptiste also lived at Merliguèche and similarly hoped to gain land and provisions in return for certain services rendered. There were many risks attendant on such a role, however. After he warned a New England fishing captain of an imminent Indigenous attack upon his crew, the Mi'kmaq, angry that he had foiled their plans, fired thirty pellets of buckshot at him that pierced his topcoat and lodged permanently in his back.[89]

Jean-Baptiste Guédry *dit* LaBine, who also went by "Grivois," may have offended the local Mi'kmaq, but he suffered far worse anxiety on another head. His deceased father, Pierre Guédry *dit* LaBine, had been outlawed for participating in the Acadian resistance movement, and his son feared that if the British learned this fact about his parentage, he might be driven from Merliguèche.[90] Lawrence was eventually bound to discover his real identity, and he did not want the future safety of his family, who still remained at Piziquid, to be jeopardized by relocating them to Merliguèche. In the interim, he hoped the British would allow him the freedom to stay at his uncle Paul Guédry's homestead whenever he visited the Atlantic coast.

The serious situation in Cape Breton meanwhile forced groups to return to their own haunts on the South Shore. In August 1745, twenty-five Acadians and *métis* arrived at Lunenburg claiming they were all kin of Paul Labrador and former inhabitants of Merliguèche.[91] Nine were male family heads, of which two, "Joseph Guedri" (Guédry) and his brother Pierre, were Augustin Guédry's sons.[92] The seven others were Charles Boutin, Paul Boutin, Julian Bourneuf, Francis Lucas, Sebastian Bourneuf, Pierre Erio, and Claude Eriot.[93] Sixteen women and their children accompanied these men. Since all were willing to take the oath of allegiance to the British Crown, William Cotterell, the provincial secretary, was willing to offer them land, tools, and provisions and to recommend that they be treated kindly. Lawrence agreed to place them on the victualling list, optimistically adding that the tales they brought with them about the grim conditions on Île Royale might dissuade further desertions.[94] Despite Cotterell's and Lawrence's assistance, however, most left in the fall of 1754 for Piziquid where the following year they, including Augustin's two sons Joseph and Pierre, were deported by the British to Pennsylvania and Maryland.[95]

In a strange quirk of fate, the timing of their departure to Piziquid coincided with the arrival in October 1745 of a second group of twenty-seven individuals from Baie des Espagnols led by Charles Le Roy. Le Roy, who was born at Port Royal around 1698, was the son of Jean Le Roy and Marie Aubois, a *métis* woman. Charles's son, Charles Le Roy *fils*, married Marguerite Lejeune, a granddaughter of Martin Lejeune *dit* Briart and Marie Jeanne Kagijonias. Most of the descendants of Martin Lejeune and his brother Pierre chose to return to Île Royale. Those who evaded deportation settled in a concealed community at Little Bras d'Or (now Grand Narrows, Cape Breton). Most of these persons were members of the Lejeune family.

Though this group's decision to return to Merliguèche was born more of fear and hunger than informed planning, Charles Roy – who sometimes anglicized his name to "Charles King" in an attempt to make his presence at Lunenburg more palatable – promised to make proper arrangements for his followers with the British authorities. Lawrence immediately sent four of this party overland to Piziquid to lodge with relatives there, while the rest he temporarily placed on the victualling list until he decided what to do with them. He knew Le Roy, no matter what he called himself, had been branded an outlaw for being a resistance fighter, and watched this new arrival particularly closely.[96] King, he contended, was "an artful fellow" who could not be trusted.[97]

Early in spring 1755 Lawrence dispensed with the services of Nicolas Joseph Deschamps and

Jean-Guédry Baptiste *dit* LaBine *dit* Grivois, and in their place hired John Steinfort, a former lieutenant of a British privateer and an overseer at Lunenburg. When Steinfort in April tendered a "rather evil account" of Charles Le Roy, Lawrence ordered that Le Roy and his associates be struck off the provisioning list, citing what he held to be their "incorrigible sloth and idleness."[98] Doubtless the uncertainty about their fate caused their reluctance to work; seeing their future prospects blighted owing to British suspicions towards them, most left for Cape Breton.[99] A few were captured by the British in 1758 after the fall of Louisbourg and taken to France, but the majority joined an Acadian-*métis* settlement at Petit Bras d'Or (now Grand Narrows, Cape Breton).[100]

Meanwhile, Paul's nephew Jean-Baptiste Guédry realized his worst fears. In August 1754 Cotterell, the provincial secretary, informed Lawrence that Paul Guédry's paternal nephew "Jean" was actually a son of the outlawed Pierre *dit* LaBine.[101] Jean-Baptiste could no longer hide behind an assumed name in the hope of preventing his father's outlaw status from adversely affecting his relations with the British. He remained at Merliguèche until early September, and when his uncle Paul could no longer provide him with sanctuary he returned to Piziquid. On 21 September 1754 Cotterell pronounced Jean *persona non grata* at Lunenburg and directed Captain Alexander Murray, commander at Piziquid (also Pisiquid), to warn "Grivoir [*sic*, Grivois] that if he ever goes to Lunenburg without a pass, he will be taken up."[102]

Acting under deportation orders from Colonel Lawrence, on 5 September 1755 Captain Murray corralled 184 Acadians at Piziquid, including Jean-Baptiste Guédry and his family, and held them in close custody until ships arrived to carry them to Massachusetts.[103] Jean-Baptiste later penned two letters to the governor of Massachusetts; the first dated 26 December 1757 and a second, dated 27 June 1766, bearing the signature "Jn. Labardor [*sic*, Labrador]."[104] In both missives he described how prior to 1754 he saved the crew of a New England vessel off Nova Scotia's Atlantic coast and afterwards was forced to flee Merliguèche at great cost to his family and himself. In October 1766, using the surname "LaBine," he gained passage to Montreal. He and his family settled near Montreal at St. Alexis and remained in the province of Quebec, where they became the ancestors of the LaBine family in North America.[105]

Humiliation from the French at Louisbourg

Despite being distressed by the deportation of his kinfolk from Piziquid and Grand Pré in 1755, Paul Guédry stayed at Merliguèche for at least another year.[106] Deportations of Acadians living along the Atlantic coast did not begin until 1756. Paul, however, was facing a crisis of some magnitude in Cape Breton that concerned his daughter Marguerite. Marguerite had wed Jules César Félix de la Noüe de Bogard, a second ensign at Fortress Louisbourg, and the French authorities were doing everything in their power to force an annulment. This debacle stood as a striking testament to the widening social distance between French imperial designs at Louisbourg and Acadian *métis* interests.

Marguerite and de la Noüe had met after the ensign assumed charge of the Acadian-*métis* community at Baie des Espagnols.[107] Knowing that de la Noüe's superiors would oppose their marriage, Margaret and her fiancé married clandestinely in 1754. When discovered, their union elicited a storm of protest from the members of the Superior Council at Louisbourg, who claimed that Marguerite was an unfit spouse for the likes of the aristocratic de la Noüe. They argued that Marguerite's maternal grandparents, Philippe II Mius d'Entremont *dit* d'Azy and his Mi'kmaw consort Marie, had never been married so that Marguerite's rights to property succession were tenuous at best. They further pointed out the serious breach in military protocols ensuing from the secret marriage. And, finally, they stressed that as Marguerite was a *métis* woman, a "fille de sang mêlé" – she and her family belonged to an inferior class that lay beyond the pale of the Louisbourg military elite. Fearing that other officers might follow de la Noüe's lead, the Superior Council unilaterally annulled the marriage in 1755 and sent de la Noüe and the priest who married the couple back to France in disgrace.[108] During the whole affair, Paul Guédry and his family were placed in an unpredictable and humiliating position by the French regime they had formerly looked to for protection and sustenance. Not only had a marriage been torn asunder, but the entire Labrador family had been cast into social limbo, caught between the rising power of the British elite at Halifax and the disdainful treatment accorded them by the French at Louisbourg. Not surprisingly, some Labradors began to identify more closely with the Mi'kmaw population

Flight into the Interior

In 1753, a naval draftsman, Robert Walter, drew a nautical chart of Lunenburg Harbour that depicted "Labrador's Farm" as a strip of land wedged between Lunenburg's West Common and the Mahone Bay shoreline. The parcel straddled a small brook running into the head of the harbour. The Labrador homestead, strategically positioned to the north of the brook, had for years served as a landmark for ships entering port.[109]

Unlike Acadian homes at Cape Sable and Pobomcoup, the homestead escaped burning by the British prior to 1762. After being vacated by the Guédrys, it likely was occupied for a few years by a settler family. When the property increased in value, it was confiscated by the British without any compensation being offered to the Guédry family. In 1762, the parcel was included in a grant made to Lieutenant Colonel Patrick Sutherland upon his retirement. The tract embraced "about seven acres … formerly in the possession of Paul Labrador."[110]

Paul Guédry and his family were now landless. They had little desire, especially following the forced annulment of Marguerite and de la Noüe's marriage, to once again attempt farming at Baie des Espagnols. When the British began deporting Acadians living along the Atlantic coast, Paul and his family retreated to the interior of Lunenburg County. Since several of his close kin on the threshold of the Seven Years' War had become leaders in the Acadian-Indigenous resistance movement, it was impossible for him to remain a neutral trader and property holder. The lands that once belonging to the old Merliguèche community, now renamed "Lunenburg," were transformed by the British into township lots, garden lots, and common. After Sutherland tore the old Guédry house down, the only vestige of the past that remained was the old French graveyard where generations of Guédrys and their kinsmen had been buried.[111]

Since most of his Acadian and *métis* kin had been rounded up and deported by the British from Piziquid, Cape Breton, and Prince Edward Island, and transported to points south or to France, Paul in 1757 turned to the Mi'kmaq for refuge. At risk of being deported, he, his wife, and his three youngest sons Paul *fils*, Jean Petit-Jean, and François joined his brother-in-law François Mius on lands near Mushamush Lake, lying inland from Mahone Bay. They remained in the interior until the autumn of 1761, when

François Mius signed a peace and friendship treaty with the British. Since the names of Paul, his wife, Jean Petit-Jean, and François do not appear again in the documentary record, they must have died in the interior. Paul Labrador *fils*, born in 1742, may have survived the Seven Years' War, since the name "Paul Labrador" appears on an 1801 government census of the Mi'kmaw population of Mushamush.[112] Alternatively, this Paul Labrador may have been a son of a resistance fighter known simply as "Labrador," who was likely Paul's nephew Joseph Guédry *dit* LaBine, son of Paul's deceased brother Pierre Guédry *dit* LaBine

The years between 1755 and 1760 were as precarious for members of the Labrador family hiding in the interior as they were for the settlers, who were repeatedly subject to raids by resistance fighters. Around Lunenburg, La Hève (now renamed La Have), Blockhouse, and the Western Shore, professional rangers as well as scouting parties formed of local settlers scoured woodland trails for evidence of combined Acadian-*métis* and Mi'kmaw encampments. To elude their scrutiny, the Mi'kmaq and their kin penetrated the back country, where they knew settlers rarely ventured, and fished in sheltered coves to gather enough food to live.

Today, place names on modern maps of the region of East Chester, Lunenburg County, and near the southern base of Aspotogan Mountain, such as "Labrador Lake" and "Labrador Castle" – a rocky peak near the East River that may once have served as a lookout point – still stand as testaments to the movements of the Labrador family during the Seven Years' War. The Labradors and their Mi'kmaw kin camped between East Chester, the Head of St. Margaret's Bay, and inland to Panuke Lake, on the headwaters of the St. Croix River, back of Windsor.[113] At the height of the war, the lands with which they were most familiar became far too dangerous for them to occupy for any length of time, owing to nightly patrols that protected the new settlements.[114]

"Labrador": Nemesis of the Lunenburg County Settlers

During the Seven Years' War a member of the Labrador family, referred to in historical accounts only as "Labrador," emerged as a daring and fearsome Acadian-Mi'kmaw resistance fighter. Labrador raided and killed numerous settlers between 1756 and 1758,

but he is best known for participating in two sudden and devastating attacks on unsuspecting individuals along the Atlantic coast, first at Rous and Covey Islands in Mahone Bay and then near Bridgewater.

The first and most notorious raid occurred in the spring of 1756. The governor of New France, Pierre François de Rigaud, had ordered the intrepid French officer Charles Deschamps de Boishébert et de Raffetot to muster an Indigenous militia at Ste. Anne's Point, on the Saint John River, specifically to harass the Lunenburg settlements. The majority of these raiders were Malecite from Aukpaque, but a few Mi'kmaq and Acadian resistance fighters were invited to join en route. According to French accounts, Boishebert's recruits killed twenty settlers and took five prisoners, actions that gave rise to several first-hand renditions of events by settlers who survived the attacks.[115] One particularly poignant story, referred to as the "Raid on Lunenburg," concerned an attack made during the evening of 8 May 1756 on the Payzant family of Covey's Island. According to the nineteenth-century Lunenburg County historian Mather Byles Desbrisay, five persons died in this raid.[116] A body of Indigenous militia, formed of Malecite, Mi'kmaq and *métis*, killed a man living on nearby Rous Island and then forced the man's young son to guide them to Covey's Island, where Lewis Payzant had a house and a store. On their arrival at the store, the militia first killed and scalped Lewis Payzant's oldest son, then Lewis Payzant and, finally, a female servant and her child.[117]

After setting the Payzant's house alight, the attackers captured Lewis's wife Marie Anne Payzant, her three sons John, Lewis Jr., and Philip, and her daughter. These persons were conveyed by the attacking party to East Chester and then forced to march overland to Panuke Lake, at the head of the St. Croix River. They passed Windsor the following night in canoes.[118] After a long and arduous journey during the evening hours, the next day they reached the French settlement at Cape Chignecto, from where they journeyed to the Jesuit mission of Ste. Anne's at Aukpaque, near Ste. Anne's Point (present-day Fredericton).

Marie Anne Payzant was sent on to Quebec, where she bore a child in captivity in December 1756. Her other children were held at Aukpaque until the summer of 1757; they were released after she petitioned the Roman Catholic Bishop of Quebec and paid a ransom to secure her children's freedom.

Charles Germain, the Jesuit missionary at Aukpaque, then had the children transferred to Quebec, where mother and children remained three years in captivity. They were not freed until after the British took that city in 1759.[119]

Though several Lunenburg settlers later claimed that the main motive behind this raid was to rob goods from Lewis Payzant's store, far more likely it arose from vengefulness against the British establishment, egged on by French gifts and other incentives distributed to Malecite warriors and *métis* resistance fighters. Labrador likely joined in the fray and complied with French aims because of the British dispossession of the Labrador family's landholdings at Merliguèche.[120] During King George's War – part of the Seven Years' War – members of the Indigenous militia also received presents and monetary rewards for bringing English-speaking captives as well as scalps to Quebec.[121] But for Labrador, the fight was intensely personal.

Labrador played the leading role in the second attack two years later, where he used tracking dogs to stalk his victims. On 13 July 1758 two settlers, John Wagner and his companion John Tanner, were swimming along with some boys in the La Have River close to Hartlin's Mill, located not far from present-day Bridgewater. Hearing a dog bark and then seeing Labrador approaching clad in Mi'kmaq garb, one of the boys dressed quickly and fled. Labrador shot and killed Wagner and fired a musket ball through Tanner's waistcoat and shirt. Tanner survived, but he afterwards harboured a deep bitterness towards Labrador for killing his friend. At first, Labrador did little to assuage this anger. According to Desbrisay, "Years afterwards, when Tanner lived on Heckman's Island, Labrador encamped there for the purpose of catching mink, and went to Tanner's house, where he boasted of the large number of men he had killed. Unable to forget what had occurred near Hartlin's Mill, Tanner went several times to shoot Labrador, but failed to do so, 'his conscience never allowing the deed.' Tanner however referred to Labrador as 'Teufel,' 'Devil.'"[122]

Labrador, whether he was Joseph Guédry *dit* La Bine *dit* Labrador or another member of the Guédry family, for years incited terror along the Lunenburg County frontier. Mi'kmaw oral tradition holds that Labrador's full name was Joseph Labrador, which tends to support the suggestion that Labrador was Joseph Guédry *dit* Labrador, the fourth-eldest son

of Pierre Guédry *dit* LaBine.[123] Joseph would have dressed like a Mi'kmaq and spoken the Mi'kmaw language. His zeal in pursuing his quest posed serious problems for the leaders who advocated neutrality, yet near the close of the Seven Years' War he jettisoned his championship of resistance and seemed to show a genuine desire for reconciliation with the Lunenburg settlers. In this he was undoubtedly influenced by Abbé Pierre Maillard, who counselled peace with the British. When Chief François Mius, at Maillard's behest, signed a peace treaty in November of 1761.[124] Labrador too laid down his arms. Peace demanded a new code of behaviour. Once, in a chance encounter in a country store, when one of Lewis Payzant's sons asked him if he were the one who killed his father, he without demur answered, "I am, but it was war then." Perhaps partially to atone for the fear and loss he had caused during the Seven Years' War, he then presented John Tanner with a "finely made and decorated brass and steel tomahawk."[125]

Labrador undoubtedly was a grandson of Claude Guédry *père* and Marguerite Petitpas, but who were his parents? He could not have been a son of Paul Guédry. Paul's youngest sons, Paul *fils*, Jean Petit-Jean, and François, were all under age fourteen in 1756, Two other of Paul's sons, Jean-Anselm (1730–c.1808) and Joseph-Thomas (1730–c.1815), were deported by the British in 1755.[126] Instead, Labrador was likely a son of Pierre Guédry *dit* LaBine, with Pierre's twenty-four-year-old son Joseph Guédry *dit* Labrador being the most likely candidate.[127]

Joseph's father Pierre died at Port Toulouse, Île Royale, in the fall of 1751. Two of his sons, Jean-Baptiste and Augustin, could not possibly have been Labrador. The older, Jean-Baptiste, born in 1721, in 1754 left for Piziquid, from where he was deported by the British the following year. Augustin, born in 1740, meanwhile was too young to be Labrador. He was only fourteen or fifteen in 1755 when a British ship overtook the vessel in which he was journeying down Nova Scotia's Eastern shore en route to Merliguèche. He jumped overboard, swam to shore, and fled with the Mi'kmaq. Following the close of the Seven Years' War, he emerged from the interior and reintegrated into Acadian society, becoming both a merchant and farmer, and manifested little interest in sustaining relationships with the Mi'kmaq who had previously sheltered him.[128] This, however, was not true of Augustin's brother Joseph. In 1752 Joseph was twenty, still unwed, and living in the household of his older brother Charles at Pointe-a-la Jeunesse, Île Royale. He even may have been with his brother Augustin on the vessel heading to Merliguèche when it was boarded by British intent on taking captives. Like Augustin, he also may have reached shore safely and lived among the Mi'kmaq, but unlike his brother he later did not reappear among the Acadians. Instead, he wed an Indigenous woman and chose to reside with the Mi'kmaq permanently.

Out from Hiding

Even after peace treaties were signed between the British and two chiefs from La Have, it took years for the Lunenburg settlers to lay aside their fears of the Mi'kmaq. When Paul Guédry, who now went exclusively by the name "Paul Labrador," ventured out from Mushamush after 1760 to trade furs and wooden manufactures at the surrounding settlements of Lunenburg, Clearland, Blockhouse, La Have, and Chester, he tried to dispel settler fears of the Mi'kmaw and Acadian population by interacting cordially with all parties he met on his travels. The Chester Congregationalist minister, the Reverend John Seccombe, remarked in his diary on 16 September 1761 that Paul Labrador, whom Seccombe regarded as Mi'kmaq, brought Mr. Bridges, Seccombe's host, five partridges.[129] Yet when rumours circulated the following summer of a possible French invasion near Lunenburg, Lieutenant Governor Jonathan Belcher admitted that the settlers' lingering concerns were "too well founded" to be taken lightly.[130] Tensions within the town of Lunenburg could escalate suddenly, as happened when a settler incensed the local Mi'kmaw population by stealing a keg of rum out of a Mi'kmaw canoe, and when a Mi'kmaw woman stole a minor item belonging to a settler. When no French invasion occurred and the Mi'kmaw chiefs, particularly Paul Laurent, the head chief of La Have, maintained their peace, the trepidation subsided.[131] Abbé Pierre Maillard, now seriously ill, cautioned the Mi'kmaq and Acadian-*métis* from Lunenburg and Cape Sable against any rash acts, while Paul Labrador's cousin Lewis-Benjamin Petitpas, an interpreter and Maillard's assistant, promised his employer that he, too, would remind chiefs to adhere strictly to the terms of the treaties.[132]

Until the fall of 1770 Paul Guédry and other Labradors who had been hiding in the interior tended to stay close to Mushamush.[133] Not until 23 December

1770 would a member of the Labrador family – Philippe Labrador, along with his wife, Mary Bisk8n– travel to Halifax to meet with Abbé Charles François Bailly de Messein, an itinerant missionary who baptized their son, François-Noel.[134] Philippe would have been a close relative of Paul Labrador, and it is even conceivable that he was Joseph Labrador's eldest son.[135] Abbé Bailly considered Philippe's entire family to be Mi'kmaq.

Joseph Labrador Sr.'s name appears in letterbooks and accounts kept by George Monk, Nova Scotia's Indian commissioner from 1783 to 1808. On 21 November 1796 Labrador Sr. arrived in Halifax, accompanied by five women and seven infants.[136] On 1 January 1797 "Capt. Jo Labradore" – who, if he was Jospeh LaBine, was born in 1732 and so was sixty-five years of age – was sufficiently esteemed by Halifax's officialdom to warrant receiving a "Blue Coat, Scarlet waistcoat & Pantaloons & Dress Compleat [*sic*, Complete]," worth £8.3.4.[137] He must have cut a dashing figure. No other Mi'kmaw recipient on Monk's list received items like these in the late 1790s; such honorifics and ceremonial dress were gifts more in keeping with an earlier era. In the late 1770s Joseph Labrador Sr. may have attracted the attention of Michael Francklin, Nova Scotia's Indian commissioner during the American Revolution. Had Joseph employed his martial skills in apprehending an American privateer off Nova Scotia's coast during the American Revolution, or performed some other successful, albeit unrecorded, foray in support of the British cause, it very well could have erased the government's formerly negative estimation of him and made him an ally of the British Crown.

In 1801 three Mi'kmaw Labradors, "Joseph Labradore, wife & 2 children; Ball [Paul] Labradore, wife and 1 child; and Newell Labradore and his mother," were officially enumerated at Mushmush, which lay only sixteen kilometres east of the site of the old Labrador Farm. The government supplied these Mi'kmaq with guns, ammunition, blue cloth, blankets, axes, salt, fish, meal, and tobacco.[138] Joseph was accorded the status of "captain" by the British, owing to his friendship towards them. Though only forty years old, he was the eldest of the party (and hence born in 1761). This would make him too young to be Joseph LaBine *dit* Labrador, but he could have been LaBine's son.[139] Joseph, Paul, and Newel all may have been sons of the former resistance fighter, or they may have been a mix of brothers and cousins.

In this case Ball (Paul) Labrador may have been Paul *fils*, Paul Guédry's second-eldest son. Yet the fact that Newell Labrador had his mother residing with him suggests that Paul's wife, Nanette Ann-Marie Mius, was not the "mother" referred to on the 1801 census. Nanette in 1801 would have been ninety-six years old.[140] More likely Newel's mother was Marie Cope, the widow of Joseph Labrador Sr. (in turn probably Joseph Guédry *dit* LaBine), who may have died in a smallpox outbreak that struck Mi'kmaw communities along the Atlantic coast earlier the same year.

These Labradors hunted and fished with their Cope relatives on lands lying between Musquodoboit and Sheet Harbour, although they periodically returned to their family's traditional lands in Lunenburg County. Merchants and officials who dealt with Joseph at Musquodoboit continued to deem him a person of "good character," whereas they often distrusted Francis Cope, the local chief.[141] When smallpox broke out along the Eastern Shore in the spring of 1801, the Labradors and Copes fled to the area around Mushamush, Lunenburg County, to escape the disease's ravages. While they were there, a quarrel between two women led to a serious rift between the two families. At Clearland, which lay only a few kilometres from Mushamush, Francis Labrador's wife and another woman began to argue. Hoping to settle the fight amiably, Captain François Cope tried to intervene but was stabbed by Labrador's wife and later died of his wounds. Cope would have been a nephew of Joseph Cope, whose dog Duc had saved Paul Labrador and his family. Furthermore, Francis Labrador may have been François-Noel Labrador, the person now thirty-one years of age who as a child was baptized by Abbé Bailly in December 1770. When Captain Cope's sons Joseph and Thomas Cope returned from hunting, they tracked Labrador's wife to a house belonging to a settler named Boutilier, but failed to locate and apprehend the woman.[142] Not long afterwards a solemn procession conveyed Captain Cope's remains for burial in the ancient Mi'kmaw cemetery at Indian Point near Oakland, on Mahone Bay.

The Copes left Mushamush almost immediately, while the Labradors stayed on their traditional lands. In 1808 Paul Labrador joined members of the Jeremy and Bernard families at La Have, but on the whole throughout the early 1800s the Labradors remained concentrated around Mushamush in Lunenburg County.[143] After the government the same year set up eight agencies to monitor Mi'kmaw activities throughout the province, agents Akins and Thompson at Liverpool and Chester assured Halifax that in the event of any future war, the Mi'kmaq in their district – presumably including the Labradors – "would cheerfully come forward" and "promise their assistance."[144]

Movement to Queens and Shelburne Counties

No Labradors lived in Queens or Shelburne counties prior to 1820. The first family group to move to Shelburne County was headed by Bernard (Penall or Pennel) Labrador, whose wife was from Barrington. One drawing factor was the Roman Catholic services and sacraments performed by Abbé Jean-Mandé Sigogne at Ste. Anne du Ruisseau in the neighbouring District of Argyle, Yarmouth County.[145] A smallpox outbreak in 1817 in Lunenburg County also may have prompted initial movement south along the coast.[146] Sigogne noted in 1824 that three Labrador brothers – Penall Labrador, who had a wife, two sons, and a daughter; Eusebe Labrador, who had a daughter; and François Labrador, who had a wife and two daughters – were camped with two Cape Sable head men, Jacques and Joseph Alexis, at Ste. Anne du Ruisseau.[147] Not far away two younger men, François and Paul Labrador, who had no children living with them at the time, and Bartholomew Alexis and his son Étienne Alexis *dit* Wisow occupied a second camp.[148] All were waiting for Sigogne's arrival.

These Labradors fished and hunted at Jordan River, Port Hébert, and Barrington, and during the summer travelled east to trade furs at Liverpool or Halifax, socialize with kin in other communities, and visit the Roman Catholic priest at the Church of Our Lady of Mount Carmel at Prospect, just south of Halifax. Penall Labrador's son, Joseph Penall (or Pennel) Labrador, married Molly Williams, a daughter of Paul Williams of Barrington and his wife Honore Alexis (Luxey), in 1826 at Prospect. Joseph and Molly afterwards lived at Port Hébert, Shelburne County, but in 1834 returned again to Prospect to have their son, François, baptized.[149] By this time Penall Labrador had developed a peripatetic basket trade, to compensate for an increasing lack of game. Many Nova Scotia officials regarded the Mi'kmaq as indigent dependents on government relief, but they had to praise the Labradors for their industry. Owing to their *métis* roots the Labradors cleared fields, raised crops, constructed log cabins, built wooden fishing boats, wove nets, coopered barrels, and net-fished for cod. Joseph Howe, the provincial Indian commissioner, also noted that unlike other Mi'kmaw families, they steeped fish in brine and barrelled it for commercial sale.[150]

By the early 1840s Penall Labrador's sons were logging, guiding, and manufacturing wooden implements for sale to local settlers. When he was Indian commissioner in the fall of 1842, Joseph Howe intended to meet with Joseph Penall Labrador and his wife at Port l'Hebert, but by the time Howe reached their farm Joseph and his family had left for Jordan River to work in the woods. After surveying the Labradors' property, Howe jotted down in his travel journal that "they are in possession of a 200 acre lot, have a log house, and live mainly by the fishery." The commissioner then continued on to Sable River to meet Joseph's brother Francis, who lived with his wife Mary Ellen Alexis (or Luxey) and six children.[151] When Howe arrived Francis was barrelling fish while four of his children looked on. Mary Ellen immediately offered Howe a room for the night, which he accepted gratefully, for he had travelled a long way and the autumn wind was cold. That night, finding himself enveloped in a warm, comfortable bed, he praised the Labrador brothers for their penchant to construct "snug camps."

The next morning François told Howe he wanted to obtain a parcel of land alongside Joe and Molly's farm, to which Howe answered that little or no ungranted land existed at Port l'Hebert.[152] The best he could promise was to instruct a surveyor, Donald McKay, to run the lines of Joseph's lot at Port Hébert.[153] It is doubtful whether Joseph or François ever received a deed to property as a result of their meeting with Howe. Instead, for years they were deemed squatters on their Shelburne County lands at Port Hébert, Jordan River, and Sable River. Their children and close Labrador relatives, mainly through marriage, joined Mi'kmaw communities at Gold River and New Germany, Lunenburg County, and at West Pubnico and Tusket, Yarmouth County.[154]

In the mid-nineteenth century François Labrador (whose name in church records appears as "François La Bras d'Or") lived much of the time at Sable River, although he assisted with Roman Catholic sacraments conducted in Queens County, at St. Gregory's Church in Liverpool and St. Jerome's Church in Caledonia. François and his wife Mary Ellen Alexis were close to the local Acadian population, as were

their children and grandchildren. In 1898 one of their granddaughters, Marguerite, or "Maggie," married Alphée Babin, a descendant of Joseph Babin *dit* Carino, an Acadian who gave his name to Carino's Island in Argyle Township, Yarmouth County.[155] After working for a spell in the United States, Alphée anglicized his surname to "Burbine" and became the ancestor of the *métis* Burbine family of southwestern Nova Scotia.

François Labrador's descendants exhibited several distinctive Acadian kinship traits, one of which was cousin marriage. Although unions among even distant cousins traditionally were rare among the Mi'kmaq, the Labradors practised marriage between third cousins. For instance, Benjamin Labrador, born in 1868 at Jordan Falls, Shelburne County, to Thomas Labrador and Hannah Glode, married Charlotte Covey and the couple had a daughter named Anne Marion who in turn married Alphée Burbine and Marguerite Labrador's son Frank.[156] In the late 1950s Frank Burbine and Anne Marion ran a trailer park in Shelburne County.[157]

Steven Labrador, who was likely François Labrador and Mary Ellen Alexis's eldest son, wanting a parcel on which to farm, joined a Mi'kmaw farming settlement on Cegumega Lake, also known as Kejimkujik Lake, on the Queens County-Annapolis border.[158] Stephen began improvements on the one hundred acres given him by the government, but a series of harsh winters and hot, dry summers made farming in the interior impractical.[159] He moved to Bear River for a number of years, and then camped at the forks of the Clyde and Shelburne rivers.

Most of Stephen's children later moved to the Wildcat reserve, near South Brookfield, Queens County. Their tenure to land at Clyde River in Shelburne County had come into question, although they were aware that one thousand acres in the area had been laid out for the Mi'kmaq in 1820. Despite Mi'kmaw testimony to the contrary, as late as 1893 the Nova Scotia Crown Lands Office still debated with them whether or not a reserve ever existed.[160] In response to Mi'kmaw appeals, Ottawa finally demanded that Nova Scotia resurvey both the Wildcat and Clyde River reserves and ensure that both were properly confirmed. This meant that members of the Labrador family in Queens and Shelburne Counties no longer had to fear they might be deemed squatters and evicted from their lands. Other Labradors lived at Bear River in Annapolis County, at Lequille near

Annapolis Royal, at Kentville in Kings County, and near Bridgewater in Lunenburg County.[161] Several living in Queens County became well-known hunting and fishing guides, and by the 1930s two in particular, John Labrador and Peter Labrador, competed regularly in guides' tournaments.[162]

Past Meets Present

Today, many Mi'kmaw Labradors still regard the countryside around Mushamush, Lunenburg County, as their traditional "heartland." Children of Labrador families who after 1820 moved south along the Atlantic coast married into Mi'kmaw families living at Gold River and New Germany.[163] Other Labradors travelled back and forth regularly between kin in Shelburne County and in Lunenburg County. By the mid-1850s at least two Labrador families lived at Bridgewater. Whenever a visiting Roman Catholic priest arrived in Bridgewater in 1851 and began conducting mass in a family home belonging to John and Mary Tobin, they joined the services. Weddings and funerals, however, were almost always performed in a Roman Catholic church in either Queens or Shelburne counties.[164] It was not until after the construction in 1889 of St. Joseph Church in Bridgewater that marriages were conducted locally and the dead were buried locally, in St. Joseph's churchyard. The abundant fish in the upper La Have River and the proximity of regular Roman Catholic services encouraged Francis and Hannah's children to make Bridgewater their home. One of them, Louis Labrador, and his wife Mary Arenburg had a large family. In 1883 two of their sons, John and Louis Labrador Jr., discovered gold near Bridgewater and had their proprietary rights as mineral explorers "acknowledged and recorded."[165]

In the early twentieth century, rumours circulated that a reserve had been laid out at Bridgewater for Tom Labrador and his son Louis. Tom was the local head man in the Bridgewater area, so in 1916 he "received an invitation to take part in an election at Shubenacadie of a Grand Chief for the counties of Halifax, Lunenburg, Queens, Kings, Hants, Colchester and Cumberland."[166] Eleven years later, William Labrador (1877–1931),[167] Tom Labrador's son, prompted an early test case on the question of the existence of Aboriginal fishing rights when he, in defiance of prevailing game laws, took salmon out of season in the La Have River at Bridgewater. William pleaded not guilty under the terms of the 1752 Peace and Friendship Treaty and, in 1928, lost his case. His arguments nevertheless furnished precedents for the better-known case relating to Indigenous rights launched in 1928 by Mi'kmaw Grand Chief Gabriel Sylliboy, and for the Simon case of 1985, which finally recognized Mi'kmaw rights to hunt and fish under the terms of the 1752 treaty.[168]

Louis Labrador and his wife Mary Arenburg still maintained a traditional family hunting tract on the upper La Have River.[169] Louis and Mary's youngest son, Louis Francis Labrador, born in 1892, was as a blacksmith in Bridgewater who in 1930 wed Beatrice Jeremy, a daughter of Chief Joseph Jeremy of Clyde River, Shelburne County.[170] When Louis Francis Labrador suddenly died at Bridgewater in 1934, his son Charles Labrador (1932–2002) – best known as "Charlie" – left his paternal family's traditional haunts along the La Have River and went to live at Wildcat in Queens County with his mother's family.[171]

Charlie Labrador was instrumental in negotiations leading up to the formation of the Acadia Band (now the Acadia First Nation), and in 1969 became the new band's first chief. Until the late 1960s, Mi'kmaw communities along the Atlantic coast from Halifax to Yarmouth were placed on a "General List," which meant they lacked representatives who could deal directly with the federal Department of Indian Affairs. Charlie, during his two years as chief, worked hard to have the Acadia Band placed on equal footing with other Mi'kmaw political constituencies. He acted as community ombudsman, defusing potentially volatile situations that could have damaged the public image of the Acadia Band. When a party of Mi'kmaq at Gold River, Lunenburg County, was accused of taking timber off their reserve without a permit, Charlie proved a perceptive and efficient mediator, since he knew and was respected by all parties concerned.[172] He also saw a future for Native teachers and guides in the ecotourism field, and on 1 October 1997 received the Grand Chief Donald Marshall Memorial Elder Award for assiduously promoting important aspects of Mi'kmaw culture. While today members of the Labrador family may be found in all walks of life, Charlie Labrador particularly encouraged his kin to become teachers of the knowledge he had learned under the mentorship of his grandfather, Joseph Jeremy.[173]

In the mid-eighteenth century the Labradors had to leave Merliguèche, where for over half a century they had operated an important fur-trading, fishing, farming, and supply station on the Atlantic coast. Today, many Labradors still have not forgotten this fact.[174] During and after the Seven Years' War, until the first decade of the nineteenth century, they lived near Mushamush, Lunenburg County, until several families moved into the Caledonia region of Queens County, and finally into Shelburne County. With time they relinquished their family's Acadian practice of reckoning genealogical connections principally by means of lineal descent and adopted the Mi'kmaw kin system, which involves a lateral emphasis on sibling and cousin relationships. The Labradors of Nova Scotia nevertheless share a common early history with the Guédrys, Guidrys, and LaBines of Maryland, Louisiana, and Texas. Historians Mather Byles Desbrisay and Winthrop P. Bell developed a monolithic stereotype of what they believe an Indigenous man named "Labrador" to be like in the past, and for many years this has coloured the view of the reading public. Only recently have Indigenous and non-Indigenous scholars begun to focus on the vital and diverse historical roles played by members of the Guédry *dit* Labrador family from the early eighteenth century to the present.

For instance, a novel and intriguing recent study by Nicole Dannielle Gilhuis claims that the Labradors were viewed by the pre-1713 colonial French administration as "Acadian" but after this date became increasing invisible in the colonial record owing to their distance from Port Royal and their close interactions with the Indigenous community. Eventually they almost disappeared from the record altogether, and colonial scholars and administrators, among them J. Bernard Gilpin, suggested that the Labrador name might simply have been a temporary "territorial designation."[175] But as Gilhuis points out, the Labradors were "found" and then reintroduced in the colonial record – but as "Indians" rather than "Acadians." Because of this, she refers to them as "revenants" (meaning "the returned") or "colonial ghosts."[176] Although the biographical treatment of the Labradors in this volume examines the impact on this family of colonial wars, colonial policies, and imposed ethnic boundaries, it is careful not to undermine the validity of the Labradors as a distinctive family throughout history who proudly regarded themselves as denizens of a land to which they, owing to their complex culture and historic past, had definite rights and responsibilities. This view of themselves has elevated many of their members to leadership positions within both the Indigenous and non-Indigenous communities in southwestern Nova Scotia, and makes them wary of being ethnically pigeonholed in ways that might socially and politically limit their future potential.[177]

– Janet E. Chute and Doris Labradore

4

Marguerite Guédry

The daughter of an Acadian and a *métis* woman, Marguerite Guédry (c.1730–date unknown) had facets of her life carefully recorded by the French at Louisbourg because of her marriage to a French officer in 1754. Her husband's commanding officer opposed the marriage, which resulted in a hearing and court records that provided details of parts of her life as well as testified to powerful prejudices in French colonial society.

Marguerite's mother, Anne Mius d'Entremont *dit* Azy or d'Azy, was the daughter of Philippe Mius d'Azy and a Mi'kmaw woman identified in French records as "Marie." Anne, Philippe and Marie's youngest child, was a member of a French/Mi'kmaw family with European noble status and an important role in the history of Acadia/Nova Scotia. In the mid-seventeenth century the French crown granted her grandfather, Philippe Mius d'Entremont, the barony of Poubomcoup (Pubnico, in southwestern Nova Scotia) in a traditional Mi'kmaw location for trade. There he engaged in the fur trade and fishery, while French traders in Port Royal and La Hève struggled for control of the colony. This household adapted and remained in Acadia, although isolated from France and even the Acadian capital of Port Royal much of the time. Philippe's son, Anne's father, was one of several young men of the founding generation of Acadians who married into the Mi'kmaw community.

Mirliguèche (or Merliguèche), where Marguerite was born, was a traditional Mi'kmaw community.

The neighbouring community, La Hève (previously La Have) had been home to a small number of Acadians and combined Acadian/Mi'kmaw families after 1634, when a French settlement was established at the site. Marguerite's father, Paul, the son of Claude Guedry and Marguerite Pettipas, had grown up in the Mirliguèche/La Hève region. In the summer of 1722 New Englanders captured Paul, his father, and four of his brothers during a war between the British and the Mi'kmaq of the region. They also took Anne's half-brother, François Mius, who by this time lived exclusively with the Mi'kmaq at Merliguèche. Paul and the others were identified as Mi'kmaq, as they lived in a predominantly Mi'kmaw community.[1] Paul's older brother, Jean Baptiste, was one of a group of five Acadians and Mi'kmaq who were hanged in Boston for acts of piracy related to the capture at Mirliguèche of a New England fishing vessel after a peace was concluded between the British and the Mi'kmaq in 1726.[2] These incidents illustrate how closely the Guédrys were tied to their Mi'kmaw neighbours. Paul's father's first wife, Kesk8a, the mother of Marguerite's half-sister, Jeanne, was also a Mi'kmaq.[3]

Marguerite's family was among the many Acadians who chose to leave British-ruled Acadia after the War of the Austrian Succession (1744–48). During this war some Acadians and Mi'kmaq cooperated with French efforts to retake Acadia, and so the position of both Acadians and Mi'kmaq in British territory was much more difficult than it had been prior to 1744. This situation was intensified by the ill will among New Englanders resulting from the treaty terms that returned Louisbourg, captured in 1745 by a New England force, to French control. In this political climate, Marguerite's family and many others chose to abandon their homes and resettle in the French territory of Île Royale (Cape Breton).

The French had encouraged both Mi'kmaq and Acadians to relocate to Île Royale after the island fell to French control under the terms of the Treaty of Utrecht in 1713. Relatively few made the move until after 1749, when several new Acadian communities, including the Baie des Espagnols (Sydney), were established for the refugees. When a French official took a census in 1752 of the Acadians, he recorded Paul Guédry and Anne Mius at the head of a family of five boys, ranging in age from two to twenty-two years, and one daughter, Marguerite, twenty. They had been receiving rations since their arrival in 1750 and owned two cows and seven pigs. They were doing well in comparison with many of the refugees. They also had many extended family members in the community: siblings, cousins, and nephews. The community of Baie des Espagnols was optimistic that the land they had been granted was "suited to the production of all kinds of grain, vegetables, and roots."[4]

In the new village, Marguerite met and was courted by the French officer in command of the tiny outpost, Chevalier Jules César Félix de la Noüe de Bogard. Their marriage was celebrated in the middle of a February night in 1754.[5] Two years after the census the village still had no parish church, so the marriage took place in her father's house. The wedding party consisted of Marguerite's family and a few neighbours. Following the ceremony, Marguerite's father fired a few shots from his musket into the winter night sky, expressing his joy at the new marriage and alerting his neighbours. Two aspects of the wedding indicated that this marriage was out of the ordinary: that the wedding took place in a private home, and that musket shots were fired, an act that resembled contemporary Mi'kmaw practice for marriages, as described by Abbé Maillard. De la Noüe had no family or friends to tell his genealogy, but his noble status and his being an officer could have functioned as equivalents. Marguerite's family indicated that they valued this marriage by paying a wedding gift to de la Noüe of two thousand livres. Such payments by a bride's parents were a European practice, not a Mi'kmaw one.[6]

The commanding officer of the groom did not share Paul Guédry's pleasure at the wedding. Enseigne de la Noüe's request to marry had been refused twice by his commandant in Louisbourg; he had only been allowed to return to the Baie des Espagnols after giving his "word of honour" that he would not marry Marguerite Guédry, a promise he had no intention of keeping. Immediately upon his return he sent a small fishing boat to the commandant at Port Dauphin (Englishtown) requesting that the Recollect chaplain, Père Hyacinth Lefebvre, be sent to administer last rites, a ruse to lure the chaplain. Lefebvre would not have known that de la Noüe had been forbidden to marry, so after his arrival in the Baie des Espagnols the chaplain willingly presided over the commandant's and his new bride's wedding.

Lefebvre almost certainly would have thought that the marriage had received official sanction from Louisbourg. Officers in the French colonial troops, and in fact all French soldiers, had to have their commanding officer's permission in order to marry. And commanders in colonial settings would have been more concerned about the marriages of young noblemen from France, as their far-distant parents relied upon commanders to prevent their sons from entering into a colonial marriage that would advance neither their personal interests nor their careers. Marriage to Marguerite Guédry did not offer de la Noüe any advantages, other than the dowry payment, that would be appreciated by his European parents. Consequently, his commandant forbade it. The young officer's insistence on getting married resulted in his being tried for insubordination; the rationale for the trial hinged on Marguerite's obscure origins contrasted with his auspicious ones. A ruling breaking the marriage was sought, and the gist of the proceedings to annul the marriage before the conseil superieur (the highest court of Louisbourg) focused on Marguerite's *métis* parentage.

All of Marguerite's neighbours, including her aunt and uncle and her close friends, were called upon to provide statements of their knowledge of events. Before each witness gave his or her deposition, the court usher read the crown prosecutor's complaint, which charged de la Noüe with insubordination for disobeying his commanding officer's directive not to marry "the named Guédry, daughter of Paul Guédry *dit* Grivois and a *sauvagesse*, his wife,

Acadians."[7] Most of the witnesses stated with precision the Mi'kmaw connection in Marguerite's mother's family, a detail that was common knowledge to her neighbours; only three of twenty witnesses did not describe her heritage, and only one stated that he knew her mother's name but nothing about her parentage. Her father's connection to the Mi'kmaq was never mentioned in the charges or the witnesses' depositions. The three witnesses who said nothing of Marguerite's parentage were her closest relatives in the community.[8] None of her relatives and family friends who had witnessed the marriage appeared before the hearing, even though some of them were called.[9]

The prosecutor addressed Marguerite's mother's mixed heritage by describing her as a *sauvagesse* and an Acadian in the same sentence. Metropolitan French regularly distinguished colonials from metropolitans by describing the former as "Creole" or "Acadian." They suggested some of the behaviours they considered typical of Acadians as derived from associations with the Mi'kmaq.[10] These metropolitan prejudices contributed to de la Noüe's commandant's charges and complaints. In fact, statements from the trial provide evidence that practices related to patterns of the seasons, part of Mi'kmaw traditions, had developed in this Acadian community. Two of the Acadians called by the court had not attended the wedding in February as they were then wintering, *hivernant*, in the woods, a practice that was common in Mi'kmaw society but not among the French.[11]

In warmly expressing his feelings about his marriage in two letters to his superior, de la Noüe claimed that he wrote with tears streaming down his cheeks, begging that his marriage be allowed to stand. Nonetheless he said that he would return to Louisbourg if his commander persisted. He did return, accepted his discipline, and continued his career as a colonial officer, later serving in Louisiana.[12] Marguerite did not write or have the chance to express her feelings about her husband and her broken marriage, so we cannot know her reasons for her actions. Whether she shared de la Noüe's feelings or, in addition to her sentiments, aspired to the social status in Louisbourg society that some of her cousins already had achieved cannot be determined from the record of her marriage.[13] She was not called upon to give testimony at the hearing. Witnesses described her father's joyous outburst, firing his rifle in the middle of the night, and her brothers' proud boasting of her marriage, but nothing was said of Marguerite's behaviour. Later her brother Thomas came forward to defend her rights and demand the return of the two thousand livres the family had paid to de la Noüe, based on his promise to marry Marguerite.[14]

In January 1755 Jean Huet, the court usher of the conseil superieur of Louisbourg, travelled overland for two days, from Louisbourg to Baie de Espagnols, to summon Marguerite to appear before the court to hear its ruling on her marriage. De la Noüe, who was also summoned, had already been sent back to France. The court usher recorded that he spoke to Marguerite directly at her father's house. In February the usher was sent to make the two-day journey again, as Marguerite had not appeared before the court. He wrote in his statement that he read the summons directly to Marguerite at her father's house, but he did not record if she said anything in reply. She did not appear before the council to hear their ruling of the breaking of her marriage and the declaration that any children thereof would be bastards. The regime that rejected Marguerite and ended her marriage only endured a few more years in North America. In fall 1755 the conflict that would escalate into the Seven Years' War began as the British administration expelled the Acadian population from Nova Scotia. Marguerite's family and the community of Baie des Espagnols were dispersed after the fall of Louisbourg in 1758. Marguerite's cousins found their way to Saint Pierre and Miquelon and Cayenne,[15] but as yet we do not know where Marguerite found refuge.

– Anne Marie Lane Jonah

5

Pierre Momcharret, Chief of Minas

The Momcharret Family of Annapolis Royal and Minas

Pierre Momcharret (1686–c.1740) (Anecouaret, Anquarret, Couaret, Quarret, Nimquaret) *dit* Cellier (also known as Pierre Cellier)[1] was one of the first Mi'kmaw leaders to launch a campaign for Mi'kmaw territorial rights. Appearing as "Pierre Anecouaret" on a 1708 French census for the Mines (Minas) district, Pierre by 1720 was leader of a band of around sixty individuals who fished and hunted along the Gaspereau River in what is now eastern Kings County, Nova Scotia.[2] His father was a Mi'kmaw leader named Momcharret while his mother, Marie Cellier, born around 1663, was likely an Acadian or *métis* woman from Port Royal.[3]

Chief Momcharret and Marie Cellier had five sons who all became prominent figures within the Mi'kmaw community of southwestern Nova Scotia. Their oldest sons, Jean (1678–c.1745) and Antoine (1678–c.1740), who were twins, belonged to the Minas band, while Jacques Momcharret (1683–c.1745) at Port Royal looked after his widowed mother and her two youngest sons who, for some undetermined reason, were both named "Pierre."[4] These two Pierres in their later years became fur trade middlemen; with the older Pierre of the two (1687–c.1745) taking the name "Pierre Momcharret *dit* Cellier" and becoming a district chief, and the younger Pierre (1692–c.1760) calling himself "Pierre Momcharret

dit Bouta."[5] Around 1710 Pierre Momcharret *dit* Cellier wed Marie Innocente and raised a large family at Annapolis Royal, though the couple lost several children due to disease.[6] When Marie died in 1727, Cellier in 1735 married Françoise Mius, a daughter of Philippe II Mius d'Azy, the youngest son of Baron Philippe I Mius d'Entremont of Pobomcoup (now East Pubnico) and a Mi'kmaw woman named Marie.[7] Pierre Cellier and François Mius's union proved commercially and socially advantageous to the entire Momcharret family, as it gave them ready access to the Seigneury of Pobomcoup and its trans-shipment station, which sent furs directly to France.

Defending Mi'kmaw Territorial Rights

Pierre Momcharret *dit* Cellier, in addition to being a chief, was a fur trade middleman, who in the early eighteenth century visited French, English, and New England merchants to exchange goods for furs. At this time, he occasionally used the name "Peter Walker."[8] His familiarity with several New England traders led at least one ship's master to appeal to him for help after hostile Mi'kmaw parties boarded a trading vessel and captured its crew. At Merliguèche, now Lunenburg, Captain Odoiorn in 1715 prevailed upon an Acadian merchant, Claude Guedry, to fetch "Pierre Walker" from Minas. The chief then obligingly negotiated with the leaders of the Merliguèche band to secure the lives of Odoiorn's men.[9]

By 1720, however, Chief Momcharret's interests focused more on protecting his people's land and resource rights than external trading interests, especially when British and New England military and mining interests entered the Minas region. Using the surname "Couraret," Pierre and his older brother Antoine in October 1720 wrote to the British governor at Annapolis Royal claiming that the Mi'kmaq were the rightful owners of the soil:

[C]ete terre, icy que Dieu nous a donné dont nous pouvons conté estre ausy tot que les arbres y sont né ne pouvez nous estre disputé part personne … Nous sommes Maistre independente de personne et vouolons avoir notre pays libre. (This land here, which God has given us, which we can tell is as early [*sic*, ancient] as the trees [that] were born [there] cannot be disputed by anyone … We are Masters independent of everyone and wish to have our country free.)[10]

The metaphor comparing the Mi'kmaq to trees and grass growing naturally out of the earth that God had given them figured prominently in a number of later Mi'kmaw communications directed to colonial authorities between 1720 and 1755, not only from Minas but also from Cape Breton and Chignecto.[11] While the Minas Mi'kmaq adamantly denied that their words were influenced by the French at Louisbourg, their statements probably had the support of French Roman Catholic priests, most notably the Recollect Félix Pain who during the 1720s was stationed at Minas. They also boarded New England merchant vessels in the Minas Basin, while calling for "rent payment" to be paid them as long as unsolicited trading took place on their lands.[12]

The Momcharrets' letter raised British fears which led to the capture of several Mi'kmaw men and women who were then held at Annapolis Royal for security purposes; British fears were particularly aroused because they had failed to establish viable ties with the Mi'kmaq through either trade or sporadic gift-giving. Governor Lawrence Armstrong called the Momcharret's petition an "insolent letter" and thought "it advisable to arm in case of a rupture with them."[13] Among the Mi'kmaq imprisoned at Annapolis Royal were Chief Jehan Grand Claude's sixty-nine-year-old wife Marie Medosset, his thirty-three-year-old daughter Marie Catherine, and his nineteen-year-old son François. These three along with several others were incarcerated in the dungeon

at Fort Anne for several months, an act that did nothing to stem Mi'kmaw anger at the overrunning of Annapolis and Minas areas with British soldiers, settlers, and New Englanders seeking sites to launch commercial ventures.

To avenge the British capture of their associates at Annapolis Royal, Pierre and Antoine Momcharret joined a group of Mi'kmaw and Penobscot warriors in attacking Canso in 1720. They later participated in other forays against the British during Dummer's War of 1722–25. After the close of this conflict, Pierre Nimquaret (Momcharret) and "Antoine Nimquaret" of Minas, as well as their brother Jean and their two youngest brothers named Pierre, met at Annapolis Royal in June 1726 to sign a ratification of a Treaty of Peace and Friendship made between the British and Eastern Abenaki at Boston the previous year. Despite this, the brothers held fast to their intention to protect their people from injury and their lands against incursions from alien mining interests and military installations.[14]

In 1731 Pierre and Antoine Momquarret joined in a Mi'kmaw raid that destroyed a house and a store at a colliery owned by Henry Cope of Boston. To prevent the coal mine from operating throughout the following winter, they and their companions camped on the mine site and refused to move until they had been paid rent for the use of the land. Whether the Mi'kmaq ever received any rent remains unclear, although from the tenor of British official reports pertaining to the event, one would suspect not.[15] The Minas band also resisted English attempts to build an armament magazine and soldiers' quarters and reported on English activities in their area to the French authorities at Louisbourg.

It is not known exactly when Pierre Momcharret died, though his name ceases to be found in the documentary record after 1740, and possibly he died about this time. Without his stabilizing influence at Minas, relations between the Mi'kmaq and the English establishment fell into a turmoil that lasted until the threshold of King George's War in 1744. On 9 April 1742, the council at Annapolis Royal reported a raid at Minas on a sloop belonging to William Trefry. A Mi'kmaw party had cut the cables to the vessel's anchors, on "deferred loan" from the brigantine *Baltimore*, which ran aground on salt marshes near Cheboque, now Acadia in Yarmouth County.[16] They then took control of the sloop, plundered the vessel's hold, and sold some of its cargo to neighbouring Acadians. On orders from Annapolis Royal, Alexandre Bourg *dit* Bellehumeur circulated a petition declaring that the Mi'kmaq, in accordance with the terms of the treaty they had signed in 1726, had to compensate Trefry for his losses. In response, Jacques Momcharret, who by this time had moved from Annapolis Royal to Minas, and another Minas leader named Thomas Wouito called their band members together to apprise them of the problem they faced, retrieved as much of the stolen property as they could, and ensured that satisfaction was made. The Mi'kmaw captains then assured Governor Paul Mascarene at Annapolis Royal that no members of their band at Minas had taken part in the heist. They further expressed concern that war might soon be declared between the English and French Crowns, and declared that they wanted to keep the peace until they knew how the future would lie. The perpetrators of the heist, they concluded, must have come from outside the Minas area. "Glad to see that the Indians here had no share in the robbery, and that you are well disposed to procuring satisfaction," Mascarene wrote back approvingly.[17] The Council at Annapolis then issued a severe warning that any Acadians abetting Mi'kmaw parties in pillaging traders or buying goods "so piratically taken" would be "deemed rebels."[18]

Chief Pierre Momcharret's sons, closer to the French than the English, participated in King George's War (1744–48) by joining in two sieges of Annapolis Royal, though their paternal uncle Jacques Momcharret, who by this time who was over sixty years old, may not have participated. The younger generation also would have fought on the side of the French in the Seven Years' War. After the fall of Quebec, however, Abbé Jean Manach recommended one of Chief Pierre's sons, Bartélèmy (Bartholomew) Momcharret, to the commander of Fort Cumberland as a Mi'kmaq who might be willing to enter a peace pact with the British.[19] Manach was right, for in April of the same year Bartélèmy, in company with Charles Grand Claude, Thomas Ball, and five other Mi'kmaw leaders, came to Halifax and signed a peace and friendship treaty with the British.[20]

In 1763 Isaac Deschamps, a judge of Huguenot ancestry living at Fort Edward, Piziquid (now Windsor), noted that fifty-three persons belonging to the "Tribe of Amquaret" were hunting along the shores of the Piziquid River (now the Avon River) and the Gaspereau River.[21] Barthélèmy remained a head man, though by 1763 the chief of the Minas group was Joseph Bernard. The band had been displaced from most of their original hunting and fishing ground by incoming Planters and, after 1785, by Loyalist settlers.

On 28 August 1769 Pierre's son Bartélèmy Momcharret and his wife Marie Joachim brought two daughters – one-year-old Marie Agnes and two-year old Marie Monique – to be baptized by Abbé Charles-François Bailly at Piziquid.[22] Between 1763 and 1769 Bartélèmy had risen to become, once again, the head chief of Minas band. The next twenty years would be difficult ones for his people, however, and when he appeared, an elderly man, at the door of Indian commissioner George Henry Monk's office in 1794 he appeared sick and dispirited.[23] His band had dwindled in size until in 1800 it numbered only twenty members. The family heads belonging to his group in this year included his son "Bartholomy Amquaret *fils*, Pierre Amquaret, Paul Amquaret, Philippe Amquaret, Simon Amquaret, Blaize Amquaret, Joseph Dugas, François Michel, Jean Argoumartine [Argomartin], Joseph Argoumartine [Argomartin] and Joseph Denis."[24] Prior to the end of the American Revolutionary War, Marie Joachim died and Bartholomew Momcharret wed Magdalene Argomartin, who invited several of her Argomartin kin, including her brother Peter from Cape Sable, to join her at Minas.[25] Persons with the Momcharret surname later married members of the Bernard, Knockwood, Glode, and Labrador families. Individuals bearing this surname could still be found in Annapolis and Kings counties until the 1860s, after which time the Momcharret surname died out.[26]

– Janet E. Chute, assisted by Doris Labradore

6

François Mius dit *d'Azy: Forest Aristocrat*

François Mius[1] (c.1700–1765) was one of the best-known eighteenth-century chiefs in Nova Scotia. His father, Philippe II Mius d'Entremont *dit* d'Azy, was the third and youngest son of Baron Philippe I Mius d'Entremont (1609–c.1700) and Madeleine Hélie du Tillet of the Seigneury of Pobomcoup.[2] Philippe I, his wife, and their daughter came to Acadia from Cherbourg, Normandy, in 1651. In 1653 the governor of Acadia, Charles de Saint-Étienne de la Tour (1593–1666), granted Philippe I the seigneury of Pobomcoup, which extended from the present-day town of Yarmouth to the Clyde River in Shelburne County.[3] The baron built a stone manor house and a trading and trans-shipment station at what now is East Pubnico, and sent furs and fish to France. In addition to their eldest child, Marie-Marguerite (1749–14), the baron and his wife had a daughter Madeleine (b.1669) and three sons, Jacques Mius d'Entremont de Pobomcoup (1654–1736), Abraham Mius d'Entremont de Pleinmarais (also Plemazais or Plemarch; 1658–1702), and François's father, Philippe II Mius d'Entremont *dit* d'Azy (1660–c.1730).[4]

Philippe II Mius *dit* d'Azy entered the fur trade at a young age. He settled first at Ouikmakagan, a French and *métis* settlement located near what is now Ste. Anne du Ruisseau, Yarmouth County, and later maintained a fur post at the Mi'kmaw village of Chichimichecady on present-day Second Peninsula, Lunenburg County.[5] While at Ouikmakagan Philippe II between 1679 and 1685 consorted with an unidentified Mi'kmaw woman with whom he had five children, Joseph, Marie, Maurice, Mathieu, and Françoise. Joseph, reputedly the patriarch of the "Acadian branch" of the Mius family, was born about 1673 and married Marie Amirault, a daughter of François Amirault *dit* Tourangeau and Marie Pitre of Ouikmakagan; he farmed and fished for a living.[6] His descendants took the surname "Muise." Not all of Philippe II Mius d'Azy's sons by his first consort became farmers: Mathieu and Maurice married Indigenous women and entered the fur trade, Mathieu at Cape Sable and Maurice at Musquodoboit.[7]

As the youngest son, Philippe II Mius *dit* d'Azy had little chance of inheriting his father's title and lands. When his brother Jacques and his wife Ann La Tour inherited the seigneury in 1700, Philippe II visited his elder brother to trade furs and socialize. Following his first Mi'kmaw consort's death about 1685, Philippe II lived for a year at Ministiguesche, now Barrington Head, with Abraham *dit* Pleinmarais and then moved to La Hève (now La Have). In the 1690s he established the trading post at Chichimichecady (or Chichimiscadie), where he lived with a second Mi'kmaw spouse, whom he probably wed by Mi'kmaw custom, named Marie.[8] By 1708 he and Marie had nine children: Jacques in 1688, Jean-Baptiste about 1689, Pierre in 1691, Madeleine in 1694, Françoise in 1697, Marie about 1698, François in 1700, Philippe III in 1703, and Nanette Anne-Marie in 1705. Priest, historian, and genealogist Clarence-J.

d'Entremont distinguished these individuals from the children born to Philippe II d'Azy's first Indigenous spouse, since all members of the second group immersed themselves in fur trade society. François Mius, the third youngest,[9] remained close to his father, and after Philippe II's death around 1730 assumed charge of the Chichimichecady post.

When François Mius was twenty-three years old the captain and crew of a New England vessel apprehended him and several of his companions at Merliguèche, or present-day Lunenburg, and held them captive in Boston. Massachusetts failed to set Mius and his associates free in accord with the provisions of a treaty the Mi'kmaq signed at Annapolis Royal in the spring of 1726, and so François's thirty-eight-year-old brother Jacques (or James) Mius, his twenty-two-year-old brother Philippe III Mius, his brother-in-law Jean-Baptiste Guedry, and Guedry's son and namesake Jean-Baptiste Guedry Jr. joined four of their Indigenous companions at Merliguèche, now Lunenburg, in commandeering a New England fishing sloop with the intention of ransoming the vessel and its captain, Samuel Doty (or Daley), to secure François's and the others' release. The plan went awry. Jacques, Jean-Baptiste, and Philippe were captured and along with their Mi'kmaw companions were taken to Boston, tried, found guilty of piracy on the high seas, and hanged on 13 November 1726. At the outset of the Seven Years' War, one of Jacques's sons, Antoine Mius, a minor La Hève chief, went to Beaubassin on the Chignecto Isthmus, where Abbé Jean-Louis Le Loutre encouraged him to fight for the French cause. Antoine asserted that his father had been killed in Boston.[10] His brother, Paul Laurent, at the time was the head chief of La Have.

Late in 1726 or early in 1727, François Mius was freed by the Massachusetts government and returned to Merliguèche. He spoke Mi'kmaq and French, and had also learned some English while in Boston. This stood him in good stead as a trading chief, since he could negotiate trade deals in three languages. Around 1728 he married a Mi'kmaw woman named Marie from La Hève (also known as La Have by this time)[11] who was referred to in one Mi'kmaw oral tradition as "Marie Coyoteblanc." The couple had several children, two of whom, Jacques Mius and Hélène Mius, married into the Alexis family of Cape Sable.[12] Jacques wed Bridget Alexis, a daughter of Jacques Alexis and Angelique, while Hélène married Pierre-Paul Alexis, Jacques's brother. It was a form of

Mi'kmaw kin exchange that could forge close ties between two families for several generations.[13]

When François assumed charge of the Chichimichecady post, he and his family lived in a nearby Mi'kmaw village. Owing to his widespread kin and trade contacts throughout southwestern Nova Scotia, he became an influential and fairly prosperous man. He travelled to trade in Montreal and may have visited New England for the same purpose. François also had a close relationship with his brother, Jean-Baptist Mius d'Azy, who was a year younger than the ill-fated Jacques, hanged in Boston. Around 1700 Jean-Baptist wed a Mi'kmaw woman named Marie and the two raised a sizeable family at Merliguèche.[14] Another brother, Pierre Mius, left Merliguèche at an early age and afterwards moved around, trading in various places along the Atlantic coast. Pierre wed Marguerite LaPierre *dit* Laroche and for several years he and his wife lived in the Saint John River area. The couple had a son, Pierre *fils*, who died at Grand Pré on 3 May 1727.

François Mius's four sisters married Acadian traders or Indigenous fur trade middlemen. His eldest sister, Madeleine, at age fourteen married Jean-Baptist Guedry, who was ten years her senior. Jean-Baptiste was hanged in Boston in 1726 for piracy, along with his brother-in-law Jacques Mius. The second-eldest sister, Françoise, as a young girl married a Mi'kmaw man who died relatively young. Françoise next wed René Grand Claude of Annapolis Royal, and when René died in about 1734 she married a third time, to Chief Pierre Momcharret *dit* Cellier of Annapolis.[15] Marie, François's third sister, wed Chief Jean Baptist Thoma and lived most of her life at Annapolis Royal and at Panuke Lake, near Windsor. His youngest sister, Nanette Anne-Marie, married Paul Guedry *dit* Labrador, a coastal pilot, fur trader, fishing merchant, and farmer at Merliguèche.[16] In 1754, at Baie des Espagnols, Île Royale, one of Paul Guedry and Anne's daughters, Marguerite, wed Chevalier Jules César Félix de la Noüe de Bogard. De la Noüe deliberately did not tell his superior officer about the union, but he could not keep his marriage secret. When De la Noüe's commandant at Fortress Louisbourg found out, he annulled the union.[17]

François Mius was devoted to the Roman Catholic faith as it was professed by the itinerant French missionaries Abbé Jean-Louis Le Loutre and Abbé Pierre Maillard, both graduates of the Séminaire des Missions Étrangères in Paris. Le Loutre and Maillard ensured that Mi'kmaw loyalty to the French was rewarded with presents and commissions. François Mius would have been far too young to fight under the command of Bernard-Anselme d'Abbadie de Saint-Castin against the English in 1710, and after the Treaty of Utrecht of 1713 ushered in an uneasy peace he had no opportunities to prove his prowess as a warrior in the field. He did not sign the treaty of 1726 at Annapolis Royal, and after 1726 he was in a position to muster warriors at short notice should conflict between the French and British Crowns break out. Unlike many of the chiefs who did sign the 1726 treaty, Mius had no intention of remaining peaceful towards the British if circumstances did not favour such a position.[18]

The French at Fortress Louisbourg sought Indigenous "captains" whose lands flanked river mouths and bays and who would watch for and repel British and Bostonians from their shores. On 25 July 1742, on the eve of the day celebrating the Mi'kmaq's patron saint, St. Anne, the French governor at Louisbourg, Jean-Baptiste Louis Le Prevost, Chevalier Seigneur Duquesnel, vested François Mius with a *brevet de commission*, naming him "Chef de Mikmaq de Mirliguèche." One of Francois's sons, Jacques Mius, retained this document in his safe keeping until the early nineteenth century.[19] Even though François was in his mid-forties at the outset of King George's War in 1844, he and some of his sons may have followed Abbé Pierre Maillard in 1744 and 1745 in joining two failed French sieges of the British garrison at Fort Anne, Annapolis Royal.

Even before the British deported his Acadian kin between 1755 and 1759, he had been incensed by a trade embargo imposed in 1748 on French and Indigenous trans-shipments out of Pobomcoup, with the British settling Halifax in 1749 without consulting with the local Mi'kmaq, and with the imposition of Governor Cornwallis's scalp bounty the same year. Yet perhaps the greatest insult of all was Cornwallis's destruction and burning of his village and trading post at Chichimichecady in the fall of 1749. At fifty-five years of age François likely joined raids that the French missionary Abbé Jean-Louis Le Loutre directed against outlying Lunenburg settlements.[20] Such attacks, which occurred suddenly, proved devastating to those who experienced them. Even today, the author found descendants of Germanic settlers living on Second Peninsula in Lunenburg County who could explain why their ancestral homesteads were constructed with small windows facing the landward side and large windows towards the front, facing the water: the small windows discouraged human entry, while larger front windows gave a clear view of any attackers approaching in canoes or boats.[21]

By 1760, François Mius was back at La Hève. Having seen his relations deported from Pobomcoup and Ouikmakagan, and finding both villages razed and burned to the ground, he not surprisingly remained extremely suspicious of the British. François's son Jacques in 1812 told Abbé Jean-Mandé Sigogne that he still possessed his father's French *brevet de commission*, his medal, and copy of a 1761 treaty; Sigogne immediately wrote Lieutenant Governor John Coape Sherbrook and apprised him of the fact. The abbé added that he had "demanded of him his Father's credential letters, which he willingly delivered." But Jacques refused to part with his father's French medal, since he wore it to church, and he later bequeathed it to his son, André Jacques Mius. He also shared interesting particulars with Sigogne concerning his father's reluctance to comply on 9 November 1761 with British treaty-making proceedings in Halifax. Maillard, deserted by the French following the second fall of Louisbourg, encouraged the Mi'kmaq to capitulate peacefully to the British, yet François, despite the affection he felt for the missionary, doggedly refused to comply. He continuously danced, with a tomahawk in his hand, around the hole into which he was expected to drop his weapon. When Maillard asked him why he baulked at relinquishing his tomahawk and signing the treaty, François replied that he feared the British might fail to honour their promises to uphold and defend Mi'kmaw rights. According to Jacques Mius's account, Maillard, in blatant defiance of British treaty-making protocols, assured the chief that if he or his people were ever left defenceless they might again take up the hatchet. Only then did Mius agree to bury the hatchet and sign the treaty.[22]

The British, under the provisions of the treaty that Mius signed in 1761, had promised to ensure that a Roman Catholic missionary would always be available to serve the Mi'kmaq. When approached by a Mi'kmaw delegation headed by Muis on 22 August 1762, Lieutenant Governor Belcher promised to fill the vacancy, left by Maillard's death on the 12th of the same month, by providing a priest "as soon as one could be obtained."[23] Belcher's successor, Lieutenant Governor Montague Wilmot, similarly promised to find priests, but later reneged on his promise. When the Lords of Trade and Plantations in London,

England, did not agree to Wilmot's suggestions that two or three French-speaking Roman Catholic priests might be sent from the King's German possessions, Wilmot fell back on a policy calculated to convert the Mi'kmaq to Anglicanism. The missionaries to do so were to be hired under the auspices of the Society for the Propagation of the Gospel in Foreign Parts. When the Mi'kmaq returned to Halifax in frustration, since to them nothing had transpired, Wilmot was instructed to tell them that "the king would attend to the situation" and to remain silent about the fact that Protestants had been considered as suitable replacements. When such missionaries failed to arrive in Nova Scotia, two Anglican clerics already labouring in the province, the Reverend Thomas Wood at Annapolis Royal and J.B. Moreau at Lunenburg, spent almost a decade fruitlessly trying to convert the Mi'kmaq to Anglicanism.

The situation grew particularly tense during the summer of 1763. On 22 August of that year François Mius and four of his Mi'kmaw associates came to Halifax and delivered a petition to Lieutenant Governor Wilmot, demanding a priest.[24] The Mi'kmaq proved both obdurate and importunate. François was a stalwart adherent of the Roman Catholic faith who conducted his religious devotions daily. Those who knew him remembered him as a devoted Catholic, who eschewed alcohol, could read Mi'kmaw syllabics, and conducted baptisms, weddings, and funerals in the absence of a priest. He spearheaded the movement calling for a Roman Catholic priest. This Indigenous campaign reached a crescendo around the time of François's death in about 1765. Michael Francklin, who became Nova Scotia's lieutenant governor the following year, viewed the denial of priests to the Mi'kmaq as a serious breach of faith, and set out to find a suitable replacement for Maillard. Yet François Mius never saw the fruit of Francklin's efforts, for by the time Maillard's replacement, Abbé Charles-François Bailly, arrived in 1768, François Mius had died.

The chief's son Jacques, born about 1740, married Bridget Alexis of Cape Sable around 1760. The couple faced droves of settlers entering the La Have district and usurping the Mi'kmaq's crucial resource areas along the Atlantic coast. After Abbé Bailly returned to Quebec in 1772, Jacques and his group moved to Cape Sable, where they settled near Abbé Jean-Mandé Sigogne's headquarters at Church Point in Clare District, Digby County. Jacques, unlike his father François, who disdained alcoholic beverages, was frequently inebriated, although he continued to be highly respected by the Mi'kmaw community. Jacques and Bridget Alexis had a large family. One son, André Jacques, who following his father's death referred to himself as "Governor Meuse," rose to be an important Mi'kmaw leader in the Annapolis Royal area. André Jacques Mius, whose name later was Anglicized to "Andrew James Meuse," was a politician, orator, and diplomat. He also was deeply devoted to the Roman Catholic religion, as his father and grandfather had been before him. He promoted several Mi'kmaw land and resource campaigns, beginning with a movement in January 1821 to counter a settler drive to ban Mi'kmaw porpoise hunting in the Annapolis Basin.[25]

More than anything else, however, Andrew James Meuse wanted a freehold Crown grant in Annapolis County, and he petitioned Lieutenant Governor James Kempt for a tract on 3 March 1820. Sigogne along with Halifax humanitarian Walter Bromley supported him in his quest. The chief received a licence of occupation for acreage encompassing an ancient Mi'kmaw encampment at Bear River but, evidently distrusting the permanence of licences, he continued to press for freehold title. Kempt hedged at giving Meuse and his people a freehold grant since he thought the Mi'kmaq might transfer their allotments to settlers, so in 1825 Meuse and Bromley went together to England to solicit a permanent grant of land on which Mius and his group might farm. But even though the pair held an audience with King William and Queen Adelaide, the chief could not secure a Crown grant.[26] When he paid a second visit to London in 1831–32 Meuse became acquainted with the noted London banker and humanitarian Samuel Gurney as well as the Quaker philanthropist Elizabeth Fry. Both Gurney and Frye proved sympathetic to the chief's quest for land. Meuse also later visited the United States, on fundraising drives.

Though Chief Andrew James Meuse failed to obtain the freehold grant he wanted, with the backing of Sigogne, Bromley, and Judge Peleg Wiswall, who lived at Digby, he was able to get the government to confirm the sixteen-hundred-acre Bear River Reserve near the Annapolis-Digby County boundary. His descendants today, who all have assumed the surname "Meuse," remain prominent members of the Bear River, or *L'sitkuk*, Mi'kmaw community.

– Janet E. Chute, assisted by Brittany Pennel

7

The Panuke Lake-St. Margaret's Bay Connection: The Thoma/Thomas and Phillips Families of Southwestern Nova Scotia

Jean-Baptiste Thoma (1670–c.1769) and Philip Bernard (c.1710–c.1825)

The Panuke Lake Mi'kmaw community near Windsor, headed in the mid-eighteenth century by Jean-Baptiste Thoma, and the Mi'kmaq of St. Margaret's Bay, which in the late eighteenth century recognized Philip Bernard as chief, belonged to the same Mi'kmaw organizational entity, the Minas regional band. Panuke Lake, situated at the headwaters of the St. Croix River flowing into the Minas Basin, was a safe interior headquarters for Mi'kmaw leaders during the Seven Years' War, which lasted from 1756 to 1763.[1] The Panuke Lake band accessed the coast of St. Margaret's Bay by following by a series of rivers, lakes, and streams that drained eastward from Panuke Lake into the Atlantic Ocean.

Chief Thoma's full name was Jean-Baptiste Thomas Albiston. Although his descendants living today at Millbrook, near Truro, use the surname "Thomas," "Thoma" was the way the chief's surname was written and pronounced during the eighteenth century. In 1722 Thoma was hailed as chief of the Annapolis River district by both the French and the British. Born in 1670 at Port Royal, Thoma in 1745 moved his group to an ancient Indigenous encampment ground at Panuke Lake and began to extend peace overtures to the English.[2] Around 1760 he persuaded the much younger Philip Bernard to cast his lot in with the British, and owing to the bonds of peace and friendship Chief Bernard later forged with the Halifax establishment during the American Revolution, Bernard received freehold title in 1786 to a tract on St. Margaret's Bay. His descendants adopted a modified form of his first name as their surname (adding an extra "l" to become "Phillips"), and members of the Phillips family currently living at Millbrook, Cole Harbour in Dartmouth, and Cambridge in Kings County still remember that their ancestor had connections to St. Margaret's Bay. In the 1830s several of Bernard's sons held family hunting territories over lands between St. Margaret's Bay and Panuke Lake that extended east into the Rawdon Hills. This region previously had been the hunting preserve of Chief Thoma and his band.

Mi'kmaw oral traditions focusing on Thoma and Bernard warrant careful scrutiny, since both leaders acted as diplomatic intermediaries between their people and the British. Chief Thoma, who signed a friendship pact with the British at Annapolis in 1722 and 1726 – and possibly 1728 as well – championed peacemaking even in 1749 and 1750 when the British colonial establishment was extending bounties to rangers and settlers who collected Mi'kmaw scalps. Thoma's diplomatic overtures attracted attention. During the closing years of the Seven Years' War Joseph Gorham, who had commanded a formidable ranger company, heralded Thoma as a model chief. Influenced by Thomas, Philip Bernard later retained a close connection with the British at Halifax. And when British fears of the Mi'kmaq surfaced once again during the American Revolution, Bernard inspired confidence by confronting and repelling American privateers in St. Margaret's Bay. As a reward for his services, the colonial government granted Bernard five hundred acres at the Head of St. Margaret's Bay. Yet despite the fact that Thoma and Bernard both acquired territory as a reward for allying their interest and activities with the British Crown, their descendants had to struggle to retain these lands.

An Intriguing Oral Tradition

Mi'kmaw oral traditions passed down for over 250 years in the Thoma/Thomas family maintain that Jean-Baptiste Thoma's father, or even Thoma himself, was born an Englishman named Thomas Albiston who deserted a naval ship, escaped with the help of the Mi'kmaq, and married a Mi'kmaw woman. This story has been traced to Louis Thoma or Thomas (born c.1790), a storyteller who Chief Thoma's grandson (although sometimes erroneously identified as Thoma's son).[3] That Thoma himself was English is problematic, however, since there are no accounts of him ever speaking English, only Mi'kmaq and imperfect French. Around 1810 Louis Thomas wed Mary Morris, the daughter of Paul Morris, whose hunting and trapping grounds in the mid-eighteenth century embraced the present-day Halifax Commons and Public Gardens. Louis and Mary had at least three children, Michael (c.1810–c.1875), Neil (c.1815–c.1880), and Marie-Antoinette (1822–1912).[4] Michael travelled between the Rawdon Hills and Shubenacadie, while Neil remained for a decade or more in the Northumberland Strait region. All were familiar with the oral tradition concerning the sailor named Thomas Albiston who had jumped ship.

In the early 1850s Michael Thomas began encouraging his Mi'kmaw associates at Rawdon to farm. His efforts in this direction won him the confidence of Provincial Indian Commissioner William Chearnley, who depended on him to purchase and distribute ten pounds of seed to Mi'kmaq at Shubenacadie who had cleared land. Among those who received a portion of this seed was Peter Sack, who had married Michael's sister, Marie-Antoinette. Peter Sack and Marie-Antoinette Thomas had four children: Francis in 1840, Louis in 1845, Catherine in 1849, and Isaac (the grandfather of a well-known Shubenacadie resident named Max Basque) in 1855.[5] In the 1840s the

Sacks moved seasonally between Rawdon and Shubenacadie, before settling around 1855 at the forks of the Preston and Truro roads, near Dartmouth, where Marie-Antoinette regaled her family with stories of her paternal ancestor who deserted the navy. Peter and Marie-Antoinette also travelled seasonally to visit kin at Elmsdale, on the Halifax-Hants County boundary. Following Peter Sack's death, Marie-Antoinette, known affectionately by this time as "Marlnan-ette ... our old great mother," in 1870 wed a widower, Chief John Noel of Shubenacadie,[6] and in consequence her son Isaac Sack also joined the Shubenacadie community to which his mother's second husband belonged.[7]

After Michael Thomas's first wife, named Sarah (surname unknown), died, he wed Mary Jeremy (or Jerome). Michael and Mary had at least two children, Adelaide (sometimes called "Madeleine")[8] in 1844 and Josiah in 1862. Michael's brother Neil lived for several years near the town of Pictou, where he met his wife, Mary Ann Toney, with whom he raised three children, Abraham, Francis, and Madeleine. When Abraham, born on Prince Edward Island in 1844, wed Marie Loolan (Lulan) in 1865, Adelaide Thomas, his first cousin, stood as a witness.[9] Adelaide lived with a small Mi'kmaw community at Bedford near Halifax until 1874, when she became the second wife of John Williams, a widower and well-known guide, born around 1819 near Great Pubnico Lake in Yarmouth County.[10] Adelaide's younger brother, Josiah Thomas, in 1885 wed fifteen-year-old Rosie Gooley (who sometimes used the surname "Jeremy") at Halifax, and the couple had two sons, Frank and Michael, and a daughter, Mary.[11]

In the 1890s these Thomases left Dartmouth and Bedford to settle at Elmsdale, and later Shubenacadie. Two of Josiah Thomas's sons, Frank (c.1885–c.1950) and Michael (1887–1960), lived at Shubenacadie. Frank wed Matilda Lena Sack and raised a family,[12] while Michael married twice. The name of his first wife is not known,[13] but his second wife, whom he wed in 1908, was Annie Gloade, a daughter of William Thomas Gloade and Mary Cope of Millbrook, near Truro. Following his marriage to Annie, Michael lived with his in-laws at Millbrook.[14] Between 1867 and 1924, Michael had at least ten children by his two wives, but all his offspring died young[15] except for two daughters, Edith Jane born in 1911 and Clare Agnes born in 1914.

Wisps of the story concerning Thomas Albiston eventually became wider known, for in 1984 Max

Basque, who obtained his family's history from his maternal grandfather Isaac Sack – who in turn had heard it from his wife, Marie-Antoinette Thomas – recounted it to ethnohistorian Ruth Holmes Whitehead:

> Well, the original Thomas was a deserter from Cornwallis' outfit … I guess when Halifax was founded, round about 1749 – and there were a lot of Indians, quite a settlement up on – now they call 'em Dartmouth Lakes, different name. But the Indian name was Panu'k.[16]

Max also knew that two of the deserter's children, whom he called "Clara" and "Absalom," had been kept hostage by the British, although he was unsure where or when.[17] His account nevertheless bore resemblances to journal entries written in the mid-eighteenth century by Captain John Knox that describe the detention of two Mi'kmaw youths, Anselm and Clare Thomas, from April 1757 to October 1758 at Annapolis Royal, and later at Halifax, where both died of smallpox.[18] Basque gleaned only the most minimal temporal or geographical referents from what his grandfather Isaac Sack had told him, so he assumed that the original Chief Thoma had lived on Lake Banook in Dartmouth rather than on Panuke Lake, back of Windsor. He also assumed that "Clara" and "Absalom" were siblings of his great-great-grandfather, Louis Thomas, when they would have been a generation or two older.[19] Louis Thomas and his wife were raising children in the 1820s, which suggests Louis was born between 1770 and 1780. Chief Thoma died around 1769, so Louis would have been a grandson or even a great-grandson, not a son, of the Panuke chief.

Another version of the story came from Edith Jane Thomas (1911–2004), a daughter of Michael Thomas and Annie Gloade. Edith Jane in 1939 married Henry Louis Peters,[20] lived at Millbrook near Truro, and like Max Basque was vitally interested in family history. Around 1980 she compiled a unique genealogical chart of the Thoma family (see chapter 17, plate 33), with lines branching out in all directions from a central personage whom she dubbed "Thomas [the] sailor." This "sailor" was obviously the same as Max Basque's "naval deserter." On her chart Edith surrounded the core "sailor" figure with the names of her paternal relatives. She made no attempt to establish a time line, since one line branching out

from "Thomas [the] sailor" connected directly with the name of Michael Thomas, her father.[21] Evidently, more than anything she wanted to depict all her paternal relatives that she knew about on one page.[22]

Lacking access to census records, church registers, and vital statistics, Max Basque and Edith Thomas Peters relied wholly on what had been transmitted to them orally through many generations. In so doing, they both compressed events into a time frame beginning in 1749 and ending around 1800, even though Chief Thoma lived from 1670 to around 1769. Yet their determination to have the stories formally recorded, either on paper or on tape, preserved a valuable oral tradition that might otherwise have been lost. For this, modern historians owe them a debt of gratitude. Common elements in their stories confirm beyond question that Jean-Baptiste Thomas Albiston, an eighteenth-century Mi'kmaw leader, negotiator, and peacemaker, was not only ancestral to them both but one of the most interesting figures of the 1750s and 1760s in the Windsor area (known at the time as "Piziquid").

Louis Thomas and His Descendants, Recreated with the Help of Edith Jane Thomas's Geneaology:

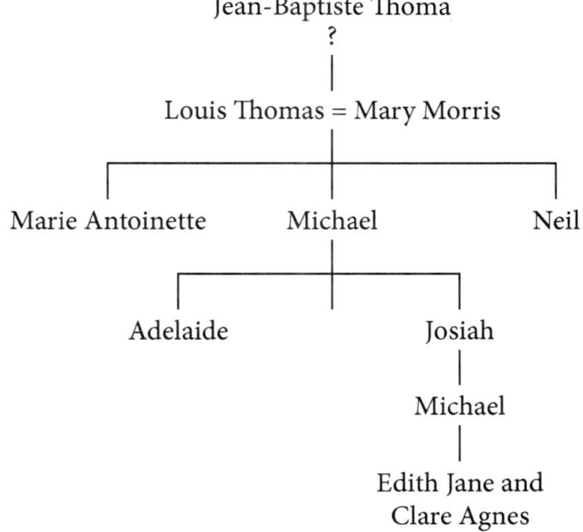

Documentary Evidence Relating to Jean-Baptiste Thomas Albiston at Annapolis Royal, 1700–1745

For the first four decades of the eighteenth century, Jean-Baptiste Thoma was district chief of the Annapolis River district. According to a French census compiled in 1708 by Père Pierre La Chasse, "[Jean-Baptiste] Thomas Albaston [Albiston]," born in 1670, was thirty-eight years old, living at Port Royal with his thirty-one-year-old wife Catherine Ann and their three children, Ann, twelve, Marie-Josephte (or -Josephe), nine, and Pierre, one. Little could be determined about his youth. Some stories circulating within the Mi'kmaw community claim that he was the *métis* son of an Englishman named Thomas Albiston and a Mi'kmaw woman. Père La Chasse encountered two orphan boys at Cape Sable with the surname "Albissou," or Albiston. The first was fifteen-year-old "Claude *fils* dalbasou" (Claude *fils* d'Albiston) and the second was thirteen-year-old "Denis d'Albasou" (Denis [*fils*] d'Albiston). Furthermore, a ten-year-old orphan boy, "Marcel fils d'Albissou," lived at Port Royal in 1708, and a nine-year-old orphan girl, "Marie dalbasou," at Musquodoboit.[23] Based on this data, as well as oral evidence, Thomas Albiston was likely an impressed naval crewman who in the early years of the English occupation of Port Royal deserted his ship and fled into the woods with the Mi'kmaq.[24] At Cape Sable he consorted with a Mi'kmaw woman and, between 1670 and 1698, had at least four children, with Jean-Baptiste Thoma Albiston being was the eldest, followed by Claude, Denis, and Marcel.[25]

In 1722 Abbé Antoine Gaulin identified "Thomas Albaston [Albiston]" as chief of ten families, or forty-three individuals, at Port Royal (as he persisted in calling it; the English had renamed it "Annapolis Royal" in 1713).[26] The same year, both Thoma and Jehan Grand Claude received medals and commissions, since both leaders had entered into personal pacts of peace and friendship with British Executive Council at Annapolis Royal.[27] On 4 June 1726, "Baptist Tomus" signed a peace and friendship treaty with the British at Annapolis Royal on behalf of the Mi'kmaq living along the Annapolis River.[28] In August of the same year Thoma, an unmarried widower, appeared as a witness at a wedding for René Nectab8 and Catherine Anorgin.[29] That fall he began courting Marie Mius, a daughter of Philippe II Mius *dit* d'Azy and his second Mi'kmaw spouse, Marie. Philippe d'Azy was the third and youngest son of Baron Philippe I Mius d'Entremont, Seigneur of Pobomcoup, so Marie was the baron's granddaughter.

Since in 1708 Pierre La Chasse in drawing up his census made no mention of Marie Mius when enumerating Philippe dit d'Azy's family members at La Hève (formerly La Have), Marie must have been born after 1708.[30] But no marriage according to Roman Catholic rite could have taken place before 1730, since it appears until that time Jean-Baptiste Thoma was already married: his first wife Catherine Ann was still alive when Marie began cohabiting with the chief. It may have been that Catherine Ann was gravely ill in 1726, which might explain the tolerance the Roman Catholic clergy showed for Thoma's bigamous behaviour. Catherine Ann, identified as the "wife of Jean B. Thomas, chief of the Mikmak of this River," died at age fifty on 29 March 1730, and her body was interred in the St. Jean-Baptiste parish cemetery.[31] Catherine Anne's grown children, Ann, Marie-Josephe, and Pierre, continued to live at Annapolis Royal. Between 1726 and 1732, Thoma and Marie had at least four children, Gabriel in 1727, Clare in 1732, Anselm c.1735, and Jacques c.1740.[32]

A Kin-Based Political and Trading Universe

By 1720 Thoma, renowned as an orator and diplomat, frequently spoke on behalf of local leaders from the Cape Sable, Annapolis, Minas, and Le Have bands. He moved throughout southwestern Nova Scotia visiting Indigenous political and trading associates, among them the Momcharret family of Annapolis and Minas and the Cape Sable leaders Jean-Baptiste Medosgnel, Paul Tecouramart, and by the 1730s Pierre Chegua. He also kept abreast of political changes in British circles that might affect his people. In spring 1719, he visited Richard Philipps and plied the British governor with questions concerning relations between the British and French Crowns. He especially wanted to know, now that the British controlled Annapolis Royal, if his people would be able to continue to practise their Roman Catholic religion. Philipps assured the chief that Roman Catholic clergy would remain in the province, and encouraged him to invite other Mi'kmaw leaders to meet with him at Fort Anne, Annapolis Royal, to discuss the matter. The chief agreed to sign a pact, and went away "satisfied" with Philipps's replies to his queries, but balked at bringing in other leaders until he knew whether or not the British had presents to distribute.[33] He afterwards kept a low profile at Annapolis Royal and remained neutral during Dummer's War from 1722 to 1725. He realized that the ultimate disposition of territory in Acadia was decided in overseas political forums, where little or no attention was paid to Indigenous interests. He was certain, however, that the British were at Annapolis Royal to stay.

The British in 1713 had razed the second Port Royal the French had erected and with which Thoma would have been familiar, and constructed Fort Anne on its former site. At this time, many members of Thoma's group living along the Annapolis River, among them the Copes, the Momcharrets, and several members of the Grand Claude family, who all formerly had traded with the French at Port Royal, began to move eastward towards the Shubenacadie River Valley or dwell near Acadian and *métis* settlements along the eastern Atlantic coast.[34] The Grand Claudes and Momcharrets were fur trade middlemen, whose activities involved a large kin-based Indigenous trade network focused on the trans-shipment station at the Barony of Pobomcoup. It incorporated smaller trading villages, among these Musquodoboit and Merliguèche, with the latter located where the town of Lunenburg now stands. As a result of this population redistribution, the old Port Royal band, which in 1708 had numbered 102, by 1722 had dwindled to a mere 43 persons.[35]

Thoma, who also was a middleman trader, was a central figure in this kin-based trade network, since his wife Marie Mius, whom he likely wed according to Mi'kmaw custom, was closely connected with the owner of the trans-shipment station on the barony of Pobomcoup.[36] She also belonged to a reticulate web of kin relations that spanned the Kespukwitk district, since her father had fourteen children by his two Mi'kmaw consorts, with Marie being the youngest child of Philippe's second union.[37] Many of Philippe's sons and in-laws were fur and fish traders, while a few of his daughters, among them Marie, wed prominent Mi'kmaw middlemen traders and political leaders. Marie Mius doubtless proved crucial to Thoma's maintenance of his widespread trading alliances, which included numerous Acadian, *métis*, and Mi'kmaw brothers-in-law. Affinal connections were also important in this society, given the Mi'kmaw kinship system's generational bias and its emphasis on treating brothers-in-law and cousins similar to siblings. Through his wife, Thoma was related not only to the immediate family of Philippe Mius d'Entremont *dit* Azy but also to the Guèdrys, the Grand Claudes, and after 1735 the Momcharrets.[38]

Yet few of Thoma's brothers-in-law shared his desire to foster peaceful intercourse with the British. Some of the Grand Claudes supported his stance, because they, too, traded with Annapolis Royal and occasionally expanded their commercial ventures to Boston. The patriarch of the Grand Claude family, Jehan Grand Claude, in 1722 personally entered a peace pact with the British to obtain the release of his wife and daughter who were being held at Fort Anne as a warning to Mi'kmaq who provoked the English. When Thoma and Jehan (or "Jackish") refrained from taking up arms during Dummer's War, they received British medals and passports to ensure their safe passage throughout the province.[39] Yet Thoma's father-in-law Phillipe Mius d'Azy until his death around 1730 and the Momcharrets of Minas favoured their kin-based attachments to the French Crown and the denizens of the French trading station at Pobomcoup. Philippe Mius *dit* d'Azy and his son François traversed the countryside collecting furs that he carried to the Seigneury of Pobomcoup for shipment to France. It was a profitable relationship. Seagoing vessels docked at Pobomcoup unloaded a diverse array of French goods; tomahawks, axes, guns, and ammunition; utilitarian household articles, such as kettles, knives, and cloth for shirts, skirts, and blankets; luxury textiles such as fine cotton and silk for turbans; edible delicacies such as tea, sugar, raisins, and almonds; and silver ornaments. A portion of these goods was loaded on canoes or shallops by Mi'kmaw middlemen and taken across the Bay of Fundy to the mouth of the Petitcodiack River. From there the goods were transported by a river and portage route to the St. Lawrence River Valley and exchanged for furs. These furs were then traded for more goods at Montreal.

By remaining in the vicinity of Annapolis Royal, when so many other leaders had left for Minas and points east, Thoma and Grand Claude shouldered almost the whole diplomatic burden of maintaining good relations with the British.[40] British officialdom, to reward them, provided them with written requisitions so they could obtain supplies on the governor's tab from the local Acadian inhabitants, promised to offer a listening ear when they wished to speak with representatives of the colonial government, and encouraged them to bring their furs, fish, and feathers to Annapolis Royal. By contrast, Mi'kmaw leaders who had not submitted to British authority were prohibited from trading at Fort Anne and were classified as "enemy Indians."[41] The British policy of dispensing requisitions and offering trading benefits to specific chiefs soon proved very hard to monitor, and if contravened extremely difficult to enforce by sanction. Further problems arose because the inhabitants of Annapolis Royal remained unsure about who was and was not an "enemy Indian." Members of the Robichaud family in particular tended to welcome chiefs of every political stripe. Rumours soon circulated that Thoma had fraternized with – and even passed on British trade goods to – Mi'kmaw leaders who had not signed any pacts with Annapolis Royal. Early in the spring of 1723, William Cook, Lewis Frontain, John Pipper, and John Rolph swore under oath that they had seen Prudent Robichaud, an Acadian delegate friendly with the Mi'kmaq and who spoke the Mi'kmaw language fluently, sitting in company with a party of "enemy Indians who had provisions & a bottle of Rum."[42] Robichaud in consequence was summoned to the parish chapel of Saint Jean-Baptiste on 26 April 1723 and interrogated as to his recent activities by several officials from Fort Anne, as well as the four men who had accused him. Robichaud calmly replied to the charges by claiming that the Mi'kmaw man with whom he had been socializing was no other than Thoma, a friend of the British. What his accusers had presumed to be a sack with rum inside was only a bag with a "Hatt, a Shirt and a pair of Stockings which belonged to … Toma who was there and had the *Governor's* Passport & had sent to him for the Same." He denied giving Thoma "Liquor or Provisions of any Sort." He knew that the chief had requisitions to obtain "Bread, Beef & Butter" from the Acadians and "supposed that Toma & some others … being under the Protection of the Government and having the *Governour's* Pass, had got said provisions Some Where up the River amongst the Inhabitants." As for the so-called enemy Indians, he retorted, they were a small Mi'kmaw party who visited Thoma and asked him to send a letter to Lieutenant Governor John Doucett expressing their willingness "to make their Submission and be Received as friends" by the British. Robichaud concluded his testimony by stating that he had apprised the lieutenant governor of the Mi'kmaq's desire to make peace on the same evening they first met Thoma and had expected Thoma to act as their intermediary. Faced with Robichaud's ingenious counter-defence, Doucett and his council could do little else than waive all charges against him and, after offering Robichaud a warning reminder not to hold "correspondence with any of the Enemy Indians in the future," dismissed him.[43]

Thoma also directed his peacemaking appeals to chiefs Pierre and Antoine Momcharret, but in the early 1720s the Momcharrets were set on protecting Mi'kmaw territorial prerogatives against British intrusion in the Minas region.[44] Far more concerned than Thoma about British expansionist aspirations in the Minas region, which they feared would deleteriously impact their people's lands, resources, and lucrative trading networks, they chose to lay their views directly before the British Executive Council. They declared that their decision-making powers operated independently of pressures exerted by French missionary priests or officials at Louisbourg, but the council were not so sure. For a while the executive council considered stationing twenty soldiers at Minas, but later decided against this course since it might endanger the lives of Thoma, Grand Claude, and others who remained on good terms with the British Crown.[45]

Following the close of Dummer's War in 1725, in 1726 "Piere Amquarett" (Pierre Momcharret) nevertheless signed a treaty of peace and friendship with the British at Annapolis Royal that posed as a ratification of a similar treaty made at Boston the previous year between the British and the Eastern Abenaki.[46] Prudent Robichaud translated the treaty's terms into Mi'kmaw. The Mi'kmaw chiefs and head men, the majority of which hailed from the Kespukwitk district, promised to keep the peace and arrange for payment of reparation should any of their people living within their respective jurisdictions commit crimes involving property against the British. The British laid plans for further treaty-making, during which time an uneasy peace reigned for five years. Like the other chiefs, Pierre Momcharret in 1726 had agreed to right any wrongs committed against British and New England traders at Minas. At the same time, younger members of the Minas group, vehemently opposed to any English military presence in their midst, declared that New England traders should pay rent for the privilege of using their local resources and landing goods on their shores. Yet, perhaps because of the furore that British punitive action provoked within the Kespukwitk Indigenous community in the early 1720s, the council at Annapolis Royal avoided offending the Minas band. Unlike the French at Louisbourg, they also had few presents to distribute to whet Mi'kmaw compliance, and they lacked close Indigenous contacts at Minas with whom they could open up negotiations. In the absence of two-way consultation and mutual understanding, the Mi'kmaq at Minas practised a policy of containment, using subterfuge and scare tactics to keep the British behind their garrison walls at Annapolis Royal.

Mi'kmaw Opposition to British Expansion at Minas

A few members sitting on the Executive Council at Annapolis Royal nevertheless entertained hopes that the Minas Mi'kmaq might respond positively to the construction of barracks, magazine, and blockhouse in their district if they were told the structure would double as a supply depot for Mi'kmaw trade goods and presents – should such gifts ever become available to distribute.[47] But when it became blatantly obvious that the Mi'kmaq would deeply resent having British soldiers billeted their midst, Lieutenant Governor Lawrence Armstrong embarked on a course of a hasty and ill-conceived deception. The buildings being erected at Grand Pré, he told the Mi'kmaw leaders, comprised a granary and supply shelter, both slated merely for emergency use. Fully aware of the governor's ruse, the Minas Mi'kmaq denounced the King's Council for being disrespectful of their territorial prerogatives and for not being honest with them.

A party of volatile Mi'kmaw youths began to hurl threats at René LeBlanc, the Acadian carpenter overseeing the construction of the barracks, magazine, and blockhouse, whom they saw as abetting the English expansionist scheme.[48] Then, on 13 July 1732, violence erupted when Jacques and Antoine, two sons of Winaguadesh,[49] along with their cousin Andress (Andreas), burst into René LeBlanc's Piziquid dwelling and assaulted LeBlanc at dagger-point while he was conversing with Ensign Samuel Cottnam[50] and Major Henry Cope, a New England military officer and Boston merchant.[51] According to Cope, the Mi'kmaq strongly opposed the construction proceedings and declared that the land was theirs, since "King George had Conquered Annapolis, But not Menis."[52] To drive home these allegations, another Mi'kmaw party afterwards violently dispossessed a colliery, house, and store owned by Cope and occupied the site throughout the winter of 1732–33 to prevent any further mining operations.[53] René LeBlanc also was found dead in his house in 1733, the victim of mysterious foul play.[54]

Despite the turmoil evoked at Annapolis Royal by knowledge of these events, the Momcharrets managed to retain the Minas leadership for another decade. This was a major feat, given the seriousness of allegations brought against them, beginning with LeBlanc's death and escalating though time as the number of attacks on trading vessels at Minas increased. Despite the Momcharret's desire to remain aloof, they often were thrust into the fray. In 1737 six young men – Claude Nicoute; Claude's brother François Nicoute; Barthelomy (Barthélèmy) Momcharret, who "was the Chief's wife's Son";[55] Jacques Ashe; Biscaroon (or Biskerone); and Biscaroon's son "Paule Biskerone" – raided *The Friend's Adventure*, a sloop belonging to Stephen Jones anchored in the Piziquid River (now the Avon River).[56] According to Jones, at midnight on 1 June the Mi'kmaw party boarded his sloop and forced him to hoist sail and steer towards Cobequid. While passing Cape Tendue, or Cape Split, they robbed him "of £800 and upwards worth of goods."[57] Jones also claimed that while the Minas head chief, whom he called "Honik," was not present at the scene of the heist, it was done by the chief's "Order & also that he assisted in dividing the Plunder."[58] In the end, the British had difficulty identifying the instigators of the raid and so failed to lay charges. The only chief they could corner at Minas, Thomas Wonito, who signed the 1726 treaty under the name "Thomas Outine," pleaded innocence of the entire affair.

Pierre Momcharret died about 1740, since thereafter no mention of him appears in the documentary record. He was succeeded by his brother Jacques Momcharret, who even more than Pierre disassociated himself from depredations on traders committed by younger members of his band.[59] When Jacques Momcharret found himself under intense British scrutiny in the spring of 1742 following an attack at Grand Pré on a sloop belonging to William Trefry, he went to Annapolis Royal and renewed his allegiance to the terms of the 1726 treaty. Under this pact he was bound to exact restitution from the perpetuators of a raid; accordingly, on 13 April 1742 the British sent a letter to Jacques and his second-in-command, "Captain Thomas Wouits" (Thomas Wonito or Outine) instructing them to collect and return Trefry's goods. All that remained of Trefry's belongings, aside from the sloop, which later drifted into the Annapolis Basin, were a few goods recovered by two Acadian deputies. The British immediately furnished one of these deputies, Alexander Bourg *did* Bellehumeur (1671–1760), with a copy of the 1726 treaty to keep on hand to remind the chiefs of their duties. But though Jacques Momcharret seems to have sincerely set out to recover the missing goods, the restitution process dragged on for over a year, with only partial success as far as Trefry was concerned.[60]

Thoma, the Peace Negotiator

Chief Thoma remained neutral during King George's War from 1744 to 1748. Around 1745, when he was in his mid-seventies, he and his family moved from Annapolis Royal to the ancient Mi'kmaw campground at Panuke Lake, not far from the present-day community of Three Mile Plains, east of Windsor. From here he interacted with the Acadian and *métis* population at Piziquid. His continuing desire to seek peaceful accommodation with the British likely inspired a letter, drafted by Pierre Landry on 24 August 1745 and directed to Annapolis Royal, on behalf of the Mi'kmaq and *métis* of Piziquid. The letter stated that certain Mi'kmaw leaders "desired to make Peace" and wished time to "consult with the rest of their people" on the subject. During the early years of King George's War, however, the governor's council was disinclined to trust Mi'kmaw professions of friendship and loyalty to the British Crown, "unless a security could be obtained for them." As a result, the council cursorily reviewed and then promptly forgot about the letter.[61] Far from extending the hand of friendship to the Mi'kmaw community of Piziquid, the British summoned a force of rangers to Minas under the command of Captain John Gorham and his brother Joseph. Gorham's Rangers, who were mainly Wampanoag and Nauset from the Cape Cod area of Massachusetts, immediately set about indiscriminately attacking Mi'kmaw encampments wherever they could be found.[62]

During this tumultuous time Chief Jacques Momcharret of Minas died, and Bartholomew Momcharret, the new Minas head chief, faced an uncertain future. The uneasy peace that ensued following the signing, in 1748, of the Treaty of Aix-la-Chapelle brought little relief to the Mi'kmaw community. The kin-based fur trading network centred on the seigneury of Pobomcoup collapsed under an English embargo on Indigenous and Acadian trade. The following year, Governor Edward Cornwallis countered Indigenous raids on newly established Halifax by placing a bounty on Mi'kmaw scalps and burning François Mius's trading post near Lunenburg. In 1750, the British finally established a barracks and blockhouse, Fort Edward, at the junction of the St. Croix and Piziquid Rivers, in the heart of the Acadian and Mi'kmaw community at Piziquid.[63] The Minas Mi'kmaq, confronted with this local assault on their territorial integrity, and faced with large numbers of troops stationed at Halifax and Lunenburg, realized that continued efforts to contain the British would be fruitless – within a very short time the British had grown too strong for them. With British regulars in the province, the most vocal Indigenous advocates of the campaign for Mi'kmaw land and resource integrity left for the Chignecto Isthmus area. Yet despite the fear and concern that these events fomented among his people, Thoma continued to hold to the path of peace and neutrality rather than countenance confrontation.

From 1749 to 1753, Thoma joined with a few other chiefs, most notably Jean-Baptiste Cope from Shubenacadie and Musquodoboit, and Paul Laurent of La Have, in seeking opportunities to open peacemaking negotiations with Halifax. Cope, whom Thoma would have known because Cope's parents had lived at Port Royal prior to 1713, signed a peace and friendship treaty at Halifax on 22 November 1752. The subsequent killing of a party of Mi'kmaq by Englishmen at Mocodome on the eastern Atlantic coast in the spring of 1753 caused Cope to renounce his former pact with the English, but this did not halt the flow of peace overtures from other quarters. In November of 1753 a Cape Sable chief, most likely Pierre Chegua, contacted Thoma at Panuke Lake and asked him to approach the executive council in Halifax with a peace offer.[64] Thoma agreed, and in company with François Jean de Perisse, whose family, like Cope's, originally hailed from the Annapolis district, travelled to Halifax to forge a peace pact with the British. During these negotiations, Thoma received a gold-laced hat, as well as provisions, blankets, and ammunition for twenty families, though he signed no peace accords.[65] The composition of bands at Minas and at Cape Sable also changed as the result of the British deportation of Acadians from Grand Pré in 1755, and later from the Atlantic coast between 1756 and 1759. By exercising kin ties to the Mi'kmaw community, a number of Acadians found refuge among their Mi'kmaw kin, though these newcomers increased the size of bands at a time when getting enough to eat and wear, let alone acquiring trade goods, was extremely difficult. Meanwhile, any aspirations that Thoma or his Mi'kmaw associates may have entertained of ushering in an era of peaceful co-existence between the Annapolis and Cape Sable bands and the Halifax establishment were swept away in 1756, with the onset of the Seven Years' War.

Paul Laurent, a La Hève chief, left for the Chignecto Isthmus, so Thoma, now in his early eighties, remained the main peacemaking advocate in the southwestern part of the province. The chief now considered all the countryside extending across the province from Panuke Lake to St. Margaret's Bay, as well as the Rawdon Hills, as falling under his proprietary aegis.[66] Panuke Lake was of strategic importance to the Mi'kmaq, since it stood near the province's watershed divide. It fed the St. Croix River to the west and also stood first in a line of lakes and streams that drained east to the Atlantic Ocean. One branch of this system drained into St. Margaret's Bay, while a second one met up with the East River, at East Chester in Lunenburg County.[67] The Mi'kmaq plied these routes so frequently between the Atlantic coast and the Minas Basin that the land they traversed formed one large Indigenous hunting territory.[68] Sheltered by forests east of Lake Panuke, where rangers rarely penetrated and where hunters could still find caribou, moose, fish, and migrating birds, Thoma waited patiently.[69] The size of his family also increased: at the advanced age of eighty-seven, he and his wife Marie Mius, forty-eight, had another son, Joachim, in 1757. Within the following six years, the chief also accepted an orphaned infant, Pierre Martyn Thomas, the son of an Acadian *métis* named André Martin, into his household.[70]

Hostage Giving in Hopes of Peace: 1757–1758

In the late 1750s Thoma cast about, once again, for ways to extend peace overtures to the British without compromising vital Indigenous interests. Not long after, the chief was again called to act as a peace advocate by some of his people, since many Mi'kmaw leaders living at Minas and along the Atlantic coast were weary of the stresses and disruptions of war.[71] From his forest retreat back of Windsor, Thoma embarked in 1757 on a major peacemaking mission. After meeting in council with political associates from the Minas regional band, the chief sent a small party to Annapolis Royal that included two of his sons,

Gabriel and Anselm, and his daughter Clare.[72] Gabriel was thirty years of age, Anselm was in his teens, while Clare was an attractive woman of twenty-five. On approaching Fort Anne, the young Mi'kmaw delegates beckoned to the officers to come to them. An interpreter was sent, who explained to Captain John Knox that the youthful delegation "belonged to a settlement at Pan-nook, in the county of Lunenburg (which lies to the eastward ... about three or four and twenty leagues)."[73] (In 1750, the Piziquid area, which included Panuke Lake, present-day Windsor, and Falmouth, was considered part of the Lunenburg district.) Clare and Anselm agreed to remain as hostages at the fort to secure safe passage across the province for their elderly father, who wanted to travel from Panuke Lake to the Atlantic coast to hold a council meeting in Lunenburg County. Possibly, in so doing Thoma hoped to parley with Colonel Patrick Sutherland, the commanding officer at Lunenburg.[74] He likely also wished to persuade his brothers-in-law, Paul Guedry *dit* Labrador and François Mius, who both were at odds with the British and hiding in the woods back of Mahone Bay, to come to the negotiating table.

Clare and Anselm informed the officers they met at Fort Ann that they were willing to become hostages of the Annapolis Royal garrison, and added that if the British "did not choose to trust and employ them as allies, [they] prayed that they may be reputed and treated hereafter at least as neutrals." Once Clare and Anselm had been taken into custody in the fort, their other brother promised to return in October with his father and the other chiefs to retrieve his siblings and "to convince the English of their sincerity."

Captain John Knox, an officer who conversed twice with Clare, wrote in his journal that she was "not taller than five feet five inches; somewhat Dutch-built, but very sprightly, and had much of the French in her manner and behaviour ... [S]he is comely and not disagreeable; her complexion was not so fair as the British, nor yet so dark as the French in general are; her features are large, with sprightly black eyes, hair of the same colour, thin lips and a well-shaped nose."[75] All that Clare possessed of her original Mi'kmaw garb was a turban about her head, pendants that hung from her ears, and an array of beads around her neck from which was suspended a silver cross. Anselm, meanwhile, was dressed in clothing gleaned from the officers of the garrison, except for a wooden cross that was suspended by a leather thong from the buttonhole of his coat. He was younger, shorter, and darker complexioned than his sister and, to Knox, surly and uncommunicative during his stay at Fort Anne. While shaking Knox's hand at their first meeting, however, he unleashed an emotional torrent of words, none of which Knox understood. Clare, by contrast, saluted Knox "in the French manner." Like her brother she spoke a mixture of Mi'kmaq and French that, in Knox's estimation, was so "low and thick" that the officer could grasp little of what she said. If Knox knew that Clare's mother, Marie Mius, was a granddaughter of Baron Mius d'Entremont of Pobomcoup, many of whose descendants recently had been deported from the Cape Sable area, he did not record this fact in his journal. On his second visit with Clare, she asked him for a pen, ink, and paper, which she soon filled with Mi'kmaw hieroglyphics that were even less comprehensible to Knox than the French she spoke.[76] Oddly, though Fort Anne had an official interpreter, Knox had no one to assist him in communicating with Clare.

By bringing one or two Minas leaders with him, it is likely Thoma planned to spread word to the Lunenburg Mi'kmaq and *métis*, among them Paul Labrador and his children, to try to come to some sort of peaceful understanding with the British, who were proving too powerful for them to resist. Yet the chief was unable to fulfil his objective. Instead of being guaranteed safe passage by the British as he expected, Thoma and his contingent were fired upon by rangers or settlers as they reached the outskirts of Lunenburg. The old chief, already suspecting something was amiss, slipped behind the English-speaking party who were escorting him, and narrowly escaped with his life by falling down and lying prone on the ground until it was safe for him to creep away into the shelter of the forest. Fearful of Mi'kmaq who might be lurking in the woods, the English party did not pursue the elderly man. As a result of this incident several Mi'kmaw leaders not surprisingly suspected British treachery, and late in October of 1757 chose not to extend peaceful overtures to the British at Annapolis Royal and Lunenburg, as they had earlier promised Thoma they would.[77]

The Panuke Lake chief nevertheless continued his determined appeals for the forging of a peace pact between the English and the Mi'kmaq. On 1 April 1758 Thoma, whom Captain Knox referred to as "the Old Sachem," appeared at Fort Anne with one of his sons, who may have been either Gabriel

or Jacques, and several other Mi'kmaq. In contrast to his son, who wore a turban on his head "extravagantly adorned with feathers and beads," Thoma dressed "not at all like an Indian" – which suggests his garb approximated that of his Acadian and *métis* brothers-in-law. To Knox, he appeared "an honest, cheerful, well-looking old man much resembling his daughter." The Mi'kmaw party, after firing two shots from Mayass-Hill and raising a flag of truce, came forward and sought to exchange four of the men they had with them for the two young hostages at the fort. In reply, the officers explained that no exchange of hostages could be made as, once it appeared that their father was not returning in the fall, Clare and Anselm had departed with the old garrison in October and were "both well at Halifax." The Mi'kmaq then withdrew to Panuke Lake to await another opportunity to collect the hostages, an occasion that would never arise, for not long afterwards Knox heard that Clare and Anselm, while at Halifax, had succumbed to smallpox.[78]

Since the countryside along the St. Croix River and at Panuke Lake was not considered particularly arable, Thoma's group escaped the cutting edge of agricultural development that took place on the Acadian dykelands, vacated by the Acadians during *le Grand Dérangement*. Another major advantage of the area was its proximity to the new town of Windsor, established on the foundations of the Acadian community of Piziquid. Windsor furnished trading opportunities for the Mi'kmaq to sell game and fish, baskets, and wooden implements to farmers.[79] It also became the headquarters for a series of provincial Indian commissioners, beginning with Joseph Gorham, who occupied the office from 1766 to1772.[80]

King Thoma's Final Years: A Teacher and Model Chief

Although "Beleban Quarrie" (Bartholomew Momcharret) signed a treaty of peace and friendship with the British on behalf of the Minas Mi'kmaq in the spring of 1760, officials at Halifax, Windsor, and Annapolis Royal continued to favour Thoma while studiously ignoring Chief Momcharret.[81] Representatives of the British establishment had come to know and trust the elderly Panuke Lake leader, who was a visitor to their homes at Windsor and Annapolis Royal. From 1763 to 1768 Thoma was elevated above all other Mi'kmaw leaders in central Nova Scotia as a model chief, whom others ought to emulate.[82] Thoma congenially and diplomatically accepted this new role thrust upon him, despite the tragedies and setbacks he encountered during the Seven Years' War in dealing with the British.[83] Now, in a sudden turnaround from the apathy and neglect he had encountered in the late 1750s, he found himself and his family members courted with feasting and celebration. He was pressed to join the Church of England and to encourage other Mi'kmaq to do so.

Thoma also mentored officials and clergymen in the Mi'kmaw language. His most astute student was the Reverend Thomas Wood, an Anglican clergyman who first arrived in Halifax in 1752 under the auspices of the Society for the Propagation of the Gospel in Foreign Parts.[84] Wood, a competent linguist, had studied the Mi'kmaw language from 1759 to 1762 with Abbé Pierre Maillard and later Maillard's assistant, Jean-Baptiste Roma. He had, moreover, been at the Roman Catholic missionary's bedside during his final illness in 1762 at Halifax and had administered last rites as set down in the Anglican prayer book. His final service to Maillard elevated Wood above all other Anglican clergy in the chief's eyes, for Thoma had been a devotee of Maillard's quest after 1758 to establish and maintain peace between the Indigenous population and the British colonial government. In 1764 Wood moved to Annapolis Royal and soon began travelling to Minas to meet with Thoma. Recognizing yet another language teacher in the elderly Mi'kmaw leader, whom he referred to as "King Thoma," Wood prevailed on the chief to help him with his studies, using some of Maillard's writings in Mi'kmaq as study texts.[85]

Thoma also was invited to be a guest at the Windsor home of Joseph Gorham (1725–90), commander of Gorham's Rangers who, during the Seven Years' War, had hunted down the Mi'kmaq, but who from 1766 to 1772 was Nova Scotia's deputy Indian agent. In the mid-1760s Gorham also hosted Anglican religious services that Thoma and his Mi'kmaw associates from the Annapolis district, Minas, and Panuke Lake attended. Wood enjoyed offering simple sermons in Mi'kmaw on these occasions, since he realized that while some of the Mi'kmaw population "know French and a very few English [words] ... most of them know no other Language but Mickmack." A highlight of Wood's linguistic as well as theological career occurred when in July 1767 he was asked to

read prayers in the Mi'kmaw language to a number of assembled chiefs and their followers at a service at St. Paul's Church, Halifax, presided over by Governor William Campbell, Lieutenant Colonel William Dalrymple, other leading officers of the army and navy, and numerous local inhabitants.[86] Later the same summer, Wood arranged an Anglican wedding service for Pierre Jacques (or Pierre Sack) and "Marie-Joseph Thomas," also known as Marie-Josephe Thoma, who, being born in 1699, was "the eldest daughter of old King Thoma, who looks on himself as the hereditary King of the Mickmacks for many generations past." "[S]ome time ago," the reverend confided further to his superiors in London, "I prevailed on him to drink our Great King George's health in a Bumper of Wine, and acknowledge him to be their lawful King." After the wedding service, which was attended by "Sir Thomas Rich, an English Baronet and several other Gentlemen" in addition to Thoma's Mi'kmaw relatives, Wood continued to wine and dine the Mi'kmaw couple and their guests at his home.[87]

Thoma's life was marked by adventure and mystery until his final years. Although he had not fled "from [Edward] Cornwallis' outfit" in 1749, as Max Basque claimed, he might well have been the son of an English naval deserter.[88] Throughout his later years he expressed a desire to bring peace, under English rule, to the Northeast. It is noteworthy that Thoma persisted in this quest despite the English ruination in 1749 of his brother-in-law's trading post,[89] deportations of his Acadian kin, and being shot at by Lunenburg settlers while on his mission of peace. Something unique and resilient in his psyche kept him loyal to the English Crown even before Abbé Maillard in 1758 agreed to encourage the Mi'kmaq to sign treaty, and while Gorham's Rangers and mercenary settlers still scoured the Nova Scotian landscape seeking Mi'kmaw scalps.[90]

By the late 1760s Thoma only left the Panuke Lake area to attend to pressing business.[91] Despite Wood's proselytism, when an opportunity arose for Thoma to return to the Roman Catholic fold, he took it. On 28 August 1768, he and his fifty-eight-year-old wife Marie Mius had their youngest son, Joachim, baptized at Piziquid by Abbé Charles-François Bailly, a missionary sent to serve the Mi'kmaq and Acadians.[92] Chief Thoma was ninety-eight when he attended his son's ceremony, and he lived at least another year, dying around one hundred years of age.

Thoma's Protégé: Chief Philip Bernard of St. Margaret's Bay

Chief Thoma's descendants are not alone in sharing recollections of a deserter joining the Mi'kmaq in times past. In 2013 Fred Phillips Sr., a member of the Annapolis Valley First Nation, claimed that his Phillips's ancestors, living at the Head of St. Margaret's Bay, sheltered "deserters" or "pirates" who eventually joined their group.[93] Phillips's contention is sound, as it is well documented that Mi'kmaq at times provided refuge for military deserters.[94] Mary Barbara Catherine Mason (née Knickle), the wife of George Fréderic Mason, an early Montebéliard immigrant to settle on Margaret's Bay, around 1813 hid a naval deserter brought to her by John Penall Sr. (or Pennel) of Gold River. The Masons at the time lived opposite Todd's Island in St. Margaret's Bay, and not only came to know Chief Philip Bernard and his group well, but also probably spoke the Mi'kmaw language. With Bernard's permission, Mason built a roomy log cabin at the Head of St. Margaret's Bay, on land granted by the government to Bernard in 1786. With time, this log dwelling became internationally known as a retreat for sports hunters and anglers, with the local Mi'kmaq employing their expertise in the woods by becoming fishing and hunting guides. The lodge was even visited by royalty, for shortly before 1800 Edward, the Duke of Kent, George III's fourth son and the builder of Prince's Lodge just outside of Halifax, overnighted in this cabin before returning to England.[95]

The Anatomy of the Phillips Family

The Phillips family of southwestern Nova Scotia descend from Chief Philip Bernard (c.1735–c.1820). Bernard, a member of the "Amquarret" (or "Momcharret") regional band centred at Minas, later lived at La Have and St. Margaret's Bay. In his youth he hunted, fished, and trapped along the Gaspereau River Valley. He also probably attended peacemaking councils convened by Chief Thoma at Panuke Lake in the mid-1750s. Over time Philip Bernard's sons and daughters adopted the surname "Phillips" (or "Philip"). Chief Bernard accessed the Atlantic coast from Minas either by travelling down a drainage system, taking its rise east of Panuke Lake, or by following a water and portage route from Gaspereau Lake, Kings County, to the La Have River. While

Judge Isaac Deschamps of Windsor listed the heads of families belonging in 1763 to the Momcharret Minas band led by Captain Joseph Bernard, he did not mention Philip Bernard.[96] By this time Philip Bernard probably had moved to the Panuke Lake settlement, from which he travelled to the Atlantic coast to weir fish. This was a common Mi'kmaw practice for members of Chief Thoma's band. A quarter of a century after Thoma's death, two of Captain Joseph Bernard's sons, Joseph and Francis Bernard, accompanied by Pierre Martyn Thomas, Chief Thoma's foster son, were hunting and fishing in 1794 "in the woods, between Windsor and Chester."[97]

Around 1770, Philip Bernard joined a large Mi'kmaw community at La Have, which included members of the Argomartin, Jeremy, and Martin families as well as descendants of the well-known eighteenth-century Annapolis fur trade middleman Martin Grand Claude. Any pirate or deserter who joined Bernard's group probably would have done so at this time, since deserters, pirates, and privateers occasionally sheltered in Mahone Bay. The very term "Mahone" comes from the French *mahonne*, which refers to a type of boat favoured by privateers and pirates.[98] These Mi'kmaq either boarded or repelled American privateer vessels during the American Revolution. For instance, in 1808 John Umlah, a retired soldier who farmed on the eastern side of St. Margaret's Bay, reported that in the mid-1770s he and four others, two of whom were Mi'kmaq, captured "an American privateer of Seven Guns and 24 men" lying in anchor in Dover Harbour, adjoining St. Margaret's Bay.[99] According to Barbara (Mason) Peart, a direct descendant in the paternal line of George Fréderic Mason, oral traditions passed down in her family hold that Philip Bernard was given land in the early 1780s in return for assisting the British militarily. "Apparently they had rendered services to George III, the third Hanoverian king," she avers, "who reigned … from 1760 to 1820."[100]

Owing to Thoma's influence on him in his youth, Chief Bernard remained a firm ally of the British Crown. On the strength of the military assistance he provided the British during the American Revolution, he drew the attention of Michael Francklin, provincial Indian commissioner in the late 1770s with the government of Lieutenant Governor Sir Richard Hughes. Bernard's closest associates at the time were Solomon Bescoloon (Biscaroon, Biskerone) and Thomas Ambroise, originally members of the

Momcharret band at Minas, and likely sons-in-law of the chief.[101] When the large La Have band began to split up and its members disperse by 1781, Chief Bernard and his kin forged east towards St. Margaret's Bay and, like other head men, sought ways of gaining secure title to the land they came to occupy after the American Revolution.[102]

While Philip Bernard's star remained ascendant in British circles, the Minas head chief, Bartholomew Momcharret (c.1715–c.1797) and his kin, having lost their French missionaries, Acadian allies, lucrative trading empire, and lands to incoming Planters, faced a difficult and uncertain future. Their activities were closely monitored by the garrison stationed at Fort Edward, and after the close of the Seven Years' War there were reports of Minas band members, and even their chief, suffering physical abuse from settlers.[103] Despite signing a peace treaty with the British in 1760, Momcharret also received little respect from British officialdom. This must have been a source of deep concern to the elderly chief. In 1760 the Minas leaders still retained vestiges of their earlier autonomy, but with the arrival of settlers intent on farming their land, the Mi'kmaq had to adapt to radically different circumstances within a few years.[104]

Most of the time, Bartholomew Momcharret assumed a low political profile. He tried briefly in January 1794 to exercise a degree of chiefly authority before the Indian commissioner, George Henry Monk, but without much success. Though in poor health, he had journeyed to Windsor with Jacques Peminout Paul, Jacques's son John, and Louis Toney to find out if goods, supplies, and services formerly distributed under Michael Francklin's auspices might be resumed. Monk ignored the words of the Minas chief, whom he described as "an old man & very poorly covered with rags."[105] The meeting instead became dominated by a clash of wills between Monk and Jacques Paul. Monk, fearful of a Mi'kmaw uprising, demanded to know why the Mi'kmaq had been convening at Gaspereau Lake, to which Jacques Paul answered he would say nothing until he heard the British might extend provisions. When Momcharret, adopting a gentler tone, tried to rephrase Jacques Paul's enquiry about supplies in the Mi'kmaw language, Monk again abruptly brushed his words aside. After being admonished to remain quiet, the Minas leader faltered, fell silent, and "appeared unwell."[106] Chief Bartholomew Momcharret died soon after this incident. A younger Bartholomew Momcharret,

born around 1737, who appears in the documentary record after 1794, was a son of the old Minas chief.[107]

While travelling seasonally between Minas, La Have, and St. Margaret's Bay, Philip Bernard and his wife Marie-Joseph raised six sons and several daughters, born between 1755 and 1780. From 1793 to 1809 John, Joseph, Paul, William, and Catherine Phillips appear in merchant supply lists furnished to George Henry Monk. In accord with a custom first developed by the French missionaries and later adopted by the Mi'kmaq, sons took their father's first name as their surname. Another youthful member of the family, Peter Phillips, was living in 1801 at Stewiacke with a wife and four young children. Interestingly James Fulton, a Stewiacke merchant, recorded that Peter was a "seaman," which suggests that Peter crewed on vessels sailing out of La Have and St. Margaret's Bay. This practice was not unusual for Mi'kmaq by 1800, for Fulton added that several Mi'kmaw individuals he knew had "shiped [shipped] on board of Vefsels [vessels] and was [sic] good Hands."[108]

Members of the Argomartin, Basque, Momcharret, Morris, and Paul families accompanied Philip Bernard to obtain supplies from a merchant named Joseph Davies and the mercantile firm of Hartshorne and Boggs.[109] On 6 May 1796, Davies noted that only three families, those of Chief Bernard, Ambroise, and Bescoloon, lived at St. Margaret's Bay.[110] Chief Bernard's extended family grew rapidly. One of his oldest sons, Joseph Phillips (c.1757–c.1830), born at either Minas or Panuke, married Molly, a daughter of Peter Argomartin, and the couple had five children at Minas.[111] Joseph Sr. became a guide in the Annapolis Valley.

A second, younger Joseph Phillips, probably Joseph Sr.'s grandson, a handsome and agile man, became a noted – if somewhat colourful – hunting and fishing guide from roughly 1830 to 1860.[112] In an age lacking modern transport conveyances, Joseph Phillips could travel with surprising speed from one end of the province to the other, sometimes going from Yarmouth to the Gut of Canso in a matter of days. Though he engaged in legitimate guiding, he possessed a rogue streak. His trickster-like antics, and those of his companion Tall Peter Pennel or Penall (Argomartin) from New Germany, astounded William Chearnley, the Indian commissioner from 1853 to 1862, for their daring and originality.[113] But like his maternal great-grandfather Peter Argomartin, Joseph had a dark side. He was known to steal, even stooping to pilfering his companions' hunting equipment, a practice almost unheard of within the Mi'kmaw community. Despite his usual high spirits he could become surly and even violent when drinking heavily.[114] When middle-aged, he froze to death along a roadside after a drinking bout. Harry Piers, curator of the Nova Scotia Museum, learning of his demise, wrote, "I have a vivid recollection of his perfectly formed body, His small feet, His prepossessing Countenance, His light steps and His Magnificent crop of jet black Hair (alas poor rogue Joe)."[115]

Joseph Phillips Sr. had a younger brother, Thomas Phillips (c.1765–c.1850), probably born at La Have. Thomas accompanied his father to the Head of St. Margaret's Bay in the mid-1780s, and on 2 February 1797 visited Davies's trading establishment with seven of his children.[116] He lived briefly in the Antigonish area, and around 1830 moved to an old Mi'kmaw encampment site at Elmsdale, along the Shubenacadie Valley.[117] Thomas Phillips had four sons: Thomas Phillips Jr. (c.1795–1864), born at St. Margaret's Bay, who worked as a guide at Panuke Lake and Rawdon and died at Panuke Lake in 1764; Francis Phillips (c.1820–90), who along with Louis Paul maintained a fish weir at Ingraham's (now Ingram's) River in Halifax County; Newel (or Noel) Phillips (1830–1912) of Elmsdale; and Louis Phillips (c.1835–c.1915), who moved between Elmsdale and a Mi'kmaw community at the forks of the Old Guysborough and Preston roads.

The Mi'kmaw name for all these Phillips was *Doodoo*, a term that no one can translate today.[118] On 20 March 1929, a Joseph C. Cope, a well-informed local historian, told Harry Piers that "Philip" or "Phillips" was an English appellation adopted by members of a family who, among their own people, went by the name *Dodo* or *Tutuis*.[119] Newel Phillips of Elmsdale and his brother Louis Phillips were called "the Doodoos." By the mid-1800s, Doodoos lived in Halifax, Guysborough, Hants, and Colchester counties. In 1860 a smallpox outbreak in Guysborough County caused a Mi'kmaw group to seek refuge at Pope's Harbour on Nova Scotia's eastern shore.[120] Afterwards, Isabel Dodo (*Doodoo*), an elderly Mi'kmaw medicinal practitioner, settled on lands she previously had occupied in the early 1850s, closer to Halifax. For several years she lived in the Chain Lakes area (near what is now Bayers Lake Industrial Park in Halifax) before returning to Country Harbour, Guysborough County, where she died at an advanced age. Born around 1780, Isabel was probably a granddaughter of Chief Philip Bernard. Her remains were buried in a traditional Mi'kmaw burial ground on an island in the St. Mary's River.[121]

Land in Return for Allegiance

Prior to 1780, whenever Philip Bernard came from Minas to the Atlantic coast he lived with the La Have band. At the close of the American Revolution, however, he set his sights on land on St. Margaret's Bay, which had abundant resources to ensure his family's future. Since he assisted the British capture of American privateers along the Atlantic coast during the recent war, he knew he had supporters within the ranks of colonial officialdom, and felt confident in petitioning for a land grant.[122] Philip Bernard, Solomon Bescoloon, and Thomas Ambroise carried their petition directly to Lieutenant Governor Richard Hughes who, like Michael Francklin (who died in 1782), offered gifts to Mi'kmaw leaders to induce them to remain loyal to the British cause.[123] Their first memorial, although treated with a degree of respectful consideration, did not bear fruit, so following Hughes's departure from Nova Scotia on 31 July 1781, they contacted Hughes's successor, Sir Andrew Snape Hamond, with a similar request.[124]

This time they were more successful. On 24 June 1782 Hamond gave them a licence of occupation to 550 acres on the eastern shore of St. Margaret's Bay, lying just south of present-day Whynaught's Point. The tract, rhomboid in shape and deeper than it was long, lay north of a large grant previously accorded to Benjamin Green.[125] The parcel contained a large Mi'kmaw encampment ground, a council forum, and a traditional Mi'kmaw cemetery.[126] It also had served over the years as a lookout point for espying European vessels approaching Mi'kmaw territory. Near Big Indian Island (also called Micou's Island), a Mi'kmaq party during the eighteenth century had surprised a Spanish galleon, killed its crew, and reputedly hid its cargo of gold in a cleft in the rock on an island off Ingramport.[127]

Though Chief Bernard, and Bescoloon and Ambroise, received written confirmation from Lieutenant Governor Hamond in 1782 of their right to occupy 550 acres on St. Margaret's Bay, along with a detailed description of their property's "metes and bounds," it soon turned out that Brook Watson, an influential British merchant and politician, had already secured the tract on which they wished to settle, had it surveyed, and through his agents in Nova Scotia was selling off lots.[128] In consequence, Chief Bernard's group were dispossessed of their parcel within four years. With dogged determination, on 1 February 1786 they petitioned Hamond's successor, Lieutenant Governor John Parr, stating their grievances and asking for another tract of roughly the same size at the Head of St. Margaret's Bay. They pointedly added that they had been promised a secure grant by Hughes and Hamond, and expected the same assurances from Parr.[129]

In 1786 time was of the essence for the Mi'kmaq. The government no longer needed Mi'kmaw military allies to fight its enemies, and the province was filling up with Loyalist settlers. Sir Andrew Snape Hamond had overseen the cutting of a road from Birch Cove in Rockingham through to the Head of St. Margaret's Bay, and had granted nine thousand acres in lots to forty-five proprietors. In 1783 Parr established French Village on the eastern shore of St. Margaret's Bay as a settlement for French-speaking pioneers from Lunenburg County. Many of these, such as the Bouteliers, Dauphinees, Hubleys, and Masons, were of Montébeliard ancestry. Former Lunenburgers of Germanic extraction, among them the Slaughenwhites and Whynaughts, soon joined them. Without a grant of their own in the midst of this influx, the Mi'kmaq's gardening plots at St. Margaret's Bay and their crucial Indian River fishery would be overrun with competitors.

In response to the Mi'kmaq's demands, a grant of five hundred acres was set out at the Head of St. Margaret's Bay by order-in-council on 2 February 1786. On 28 February, Parr issued a warrant to survey to the provincial surveyor general, Charles Morris, who on 3 March reported on his activities in this line to Sir John Wentworth, surveyor general of the King's Woods. On 3 March 1786 Parr issued the grant, an allocation confirmed on 6 March by John Wentworth and registered formally on 10 March 1786. The grant's description read: "Beginning at a Spruce standing in a Cove on the Western side near where the River [Indian River] discharges itself into the Bay; thence to run North 19° W 46 chains; thence N 32°E 80 chains; thence S 49° E 93 chains; or until it comes to Lands laid out to Simon Gowen and others; thence to be bounded by said Gowen's land untill it comes to the sea shore of Saint Margaret's Bay aforesaid; thence to be bounded by the several Courses of the said Shoar

[*sic*, shore] untill it meets the Bounds first mentioned containing Five Hundred acres."[130] By this document the Mi'kmaq secured permanent title to five hundred acres at the Head of St. Margaret's Bay, provided they made the necessary improvements.

While researching the history of St. Margaret's Bay, Barbara (Mason) Peart found that the tract specified in Bernard's grant lay across the water from "Slaughenwhite Point," now called "Allen's Heights," on a site where British barracks once stood.[131] The chief's band occupied an encampment ground on Indian Hill that the Mi'kmaq had used for many generations, maintaining weir fishing stations along the Northeast River and Indian River.[132] "The sparkling body of water between Sheep's (Todd's) Island and Slaughenwhite Point (today near Allen Heights)," Peart explains, "received its name from the local chief" and is still known as "Bernard's Cove.'"[133]

Bernard's, Biscoloon's, and Ambroise's grant was given in "free and common soccage."[134] This meant the holders were subject to conditions that required them after two years to pay a quit rent "at the rate of two shillings for every hundred acres" due annually on the Feast of St. Michael, and by three years to clear and cultivate at least three acres out of every fifty acres of "plantable land."[135] Unlike under a licence of occupation, they were able freely to sell part or all of their holdings. The 10 March 1786 property allocation was the first recorded grant of land title to a Mi'kmaw group, and it provided impetus for the creation of the reserve system in Nova Scotia in 1820.[136]

Bernard and his two associates proved far more fortunate than their neighbour Paul Morris at Pendant Bay (now Pennant Creek, near Sambro), who two years earlier had received a tract of land to occupy "only during His Majesty's pleasure." Morris and his group were soon driven off their plot by settlers employing harsh and even violent means to gain control over the local riverine fishery.[137] The dispossessed Mi'kmaq moved to areas where resources seemed more assured and more safely accessed. A few, including members of the Phillips family, pursued a productive eel and alewife[138] weir fishery on Ingraham's River, lying just south of St. Margaret's Bay. Though they met settler competition here as well, they tenaciously defended their fishery by sending complaints to Halifax.

Surveyor General Morris, noting the settlers' rapacity regarding Mi'kmaw property and resources at St. Margaret's Bay as well as at neighbouring locales, argued that henceforth Mi'kmaw land should be reserved in perpetuity rather than be granted outright, a practice that almost always led to its being sold "by fair means or foul."[139] Morris's arguments eventually led to a three-hundred-acre reserve being set aside for the Mi'kmaq at Ingraham's River, though the parcel was not properly surveyed for many years. It lay inland, above a large grant laid out for "Charles Ingraham and others," situated on the lower reaches of Ingraham's River.[140]

In addition to settler intrusions, Chief Bernard soon faced other challenges that led several members of his band to retreat up the Panuke Lake drainage system towards Panuke, Windsor, and Minas. Between 1792 and 1801 a series of cold winters, dry summers, and resultant forest fires reduced the numbers of game animals.[141] Neighbouring settlers tried to alleviate the Mi'kmaq's hardship, though many also sought reimbursement for their efforts from the government. In 1799 George Pike spent £1 17s supplying emergency victuals and board for eight Mi'kmaq belonging to a single camp on the shores of St. Margaret's Bay.[142] These persons were almost certainly Chief Bernard and his immediate family members. The situation grew worse as one approached Halifax. Titus Smith, who surveyed the interior of southwestern Nova Scotia in 1800 and 1801, reported that severe fires had denuded most of the interior except for the mountainous region lying north of St. Margaret's Bay and eastward to Rawdon, where one could still find good mast timber.[143] Moose, caribou, and beaver populations dropped to drastically low levels, owing not only to the ravages of fire but also to settlers' overhunting. A final devastating blow came in the fall of 1800. When reports arrived that smallpox was spreading down the coast from points on the Eastern Shore, Philip Bernard and his family fled to the interior.[144]

Conditions during winter of 1800–1801 were exceedingly harsh. Despite the terror elicited by news of the smallpox outbreak, in the early spring Philip Bernard's group needed to come to the coast to prepare their weirs for the alewife fishery. They were in destitute condition. In March 1801 John Wooden, a settler at St. Margaret's Bay who sometimes distributed potatoes to Mi'kmaw families, informed the colonial government that Chief Bernard and his "Distrist [*sic*, distressed] Family" have been "back in the woods all winter without any Provisions or Gun or powder." Usually the chief remained determinedly

independent of government handouts, Wooden continued, but this winter had proven so cold, resources so scanty, and sickness so prevalent that hunting had been difficult. Extenuating weather conditions, coupled with the chief's insistence, Wooden stressed, induced him to put pen to paper.[145] After over a century of exposure to the use of guns and ammunition, Chief Bernard had needed to rely on his reserves of knowledge about how to fashion and use traditional Indigenous hunting technology. This enabled the Mi'kmaw leader and his family to survive the desperate winter and re-establish their territorial aegis over the Head of St. Margaret's Bay the following spring.[146]

Land Sales at St. Margaret's Bay

Wooden's assistance exemplified how well Philip Bernard had come to know several of the settlers living near them. These men, when asked, spoke favourably of the old chief. They also seem to have monitored each other's relations with the chief and his group, to keep any settler transactions with the Mi'kmaw community honest and so ensure the continuance of good relations between the Mi'kmaq and families living at French Village and Mason's Point. Over the next three decades many complaints would be filed about settler encroachments on reserves along the South Shore, particularly the reserve at Ingraham's River, but at St. Margaret's Bay any loss of Mi'kmaw land occurred only by sale. While to the Mi'kmaq these sales may have been rooted in necessity rather than choice, the head chief of St. Margaret's Bay always retained some degree of leverage over the terms of sale.

The first sale involved land for a road allowance. With the arrival of the new settlers, traffic had dramatically increased along the narrow road that circumvented the base of the ridge of hills back of the shoreline. Alterations to this route were needed, so in the summer of 1815 Chief Bernard found road workers digging up his fields, which lay on a flat, fertile interval between the old road and the shoreline. He soon put a stop to such undertakings and demanded five pounds for injury to his potato crop.[147]

James Walker, the commissioner from Lunenburg County in charge of the road work, showed enough presence of mind to interview a few local settlers to find out if Philip Bernard did indeed warrant compensation. Although he lived in Chester, he had never heard of the chief and was surprised to find how much the Mi'kmaw leader was liked and respected by those living around him. Still, he was not inclined to be generous when it came to compensation, and consequently depreciated Bernard's farming efforts. Eight or ten dollars, he suggested to Henry H. Cogswell, the deputy provincial secretary on 7 March 1815, should be sufficient to solve the problem, for Bernard's crop, he added disparagingly, probably would only yield around a peck of potatoes.[148] The establishment at Halifax disagreed. Apparently Chief Bernard still carried enough weight with the Provincial Secretary's Office to overrule consideration of such a paltry sum, and the chief received the five-pound compensation for which he had asked on 27 May 1816.[149] The long-lasting consequences of the road building proved serious. The route of the road had been altered at Indian River Bridge and brought lower down towards the shore. When Walker finally agreed to the five pounds compensation it was only on condition that Bernard allow the alienation of a road allowance that traversed the flattest, most arable, and most accessible part of the chief's property. A survey of the altered boundaries of the reserve was made in 1818.[150]

The widening of the road destroyed the most fertile portion of the Mi'kmaq's tract. What remained of the grant remained principally valuable for its fishery on the Indian River, which during fish runs was crowded with anglers staying at George Mason's hunting and fishing cabin, first known as "Fisherman's Cottage" but by this time renamed "Willow Cottage." Mason had built this roomy log cabin, with Chief Bernard's permission, on a section of Bernard's grant, lying across from Todd's Island. Willow Cottage became a resort for sportsmen from Halifax, and prior to 1800 once accommodated Edward the Duke of Kent while he was on a moose-hunting expedition.[151] As the cabin stood on Bernard's grant, Mason, who by this time was a blacksmith as well as farmer, and the cabin's caretaker, may have paid Bernard an annual rent until he bought the property. Another advantage to the Mi'kmaq of having Mason's lodge on their property was the opportunity it afforded them to guide its guests, for a daily fee, on hunting and fishing expeditions up the Indian River.

Yet because the future of farming at Indian River had been compromised by the road construction, Bernard and his wife Marie-Joseph decided to sell Mason sixty acres around Willow Cottage for thirty pounds. The deed of sale, dated 29 September 1817, simply stated that the parcel alienated lay on the "west side of the North River" and that as its bounds had previously been determined by the various parties involved, they did not need to be recapitulated in the deed document.[152] By the fall of 1817 the elderly Philip Bernard, no longer able to hunt or plant as he had in past years, may have appreciated having the sale money, simply as income to enhance his quality of life in his final days.

Chief Philip Bernard and his wife Marie-Josephte acted alone in deciding to sell; neither Biskaroon's nor Ambroise's names were on the 1817 deed of sale.[153] Though Biskaroon and Ambroise were probably still alive, Bernard and his wife were in a position to appropriate sole ownership of the freehold grant. Most likely, Biskaroon and Ambroise had moved away from St. Margaret's Bay. Over the next twenty years most of Bernard's sons, daughters, sons-in-law, and grandchildren moved to other parts of the province. Often an announcement of a projected exodus caused serious friction between those who wanted to leave and those who resisted the others leaving. An oral tradition related by Jerry Lonecloud, a grandson of Thomas Phillips Jr., recounts how Thomas Phillip Jr.'s wife, an Acadian, was shot at the Head of St. Margaret's Bay by "her Mohawk son-in-law Sunislars."[154] This so-called "Mohawk" was actually a British settler from the Cape Sable district named Tom Wallace, who according to St. Gregory's Roman Catholic parish church records wed Tom's daughter, Mary Ann Phillips, at Liverpool around 1840. Wallace's mother-in-law did not want Wallace to take her daughter and grandchildren away, presumably to Cape Sable. A heated argument arose between the two, during which Wallace shot his mother-in-law with a rifle as she was attempting to flee from him by climbing over a fence. According to Lonecloud, "Sunislars" (Wallace) was apprehended and tried at Halifax, but the judgment, if any, proved ineffectual. Wallace was also brought before a Mi'kmaw judge, and afterwards released.[155] Chief Lewis Alexis (or Luxey) Sr. of Shelburne later located Wallace in the interior of Yarmouth County and shot him, evidently with the concurrence of Bernard's and the Cape Sable bands, to avenge the killing of Thomas Phillip's wife.[156] Wallace's widow, Mary Ann Phillips, then wed Abraham (or Abram) Bartholomew-Alexis, a relation of Louis Alexis Sr. born at Salmon River, Digby County. In 1854 Mary Ann Phillips and Abraham Bartholomew-Alexis had a son, Jerry Lonecloud.

Certain aspects of this case sound suspiciously like another criminal case tried twenty years earlier in Halifax by Judge Brenton Halliburton of the Supreme Court of Nova Scotia. Around 1830 Peter Paul, wanting to leave his in-laws' encampment on Hammonds Plains with his wife and children but thwarted by his mother-in-law Mary Phillips, fatally shot Mary in the face with buckshot as she was climbing over a fence. Mary likely was the wife of Thomas Phillips Sr., who seasonally travelled between St. Margaret's Bay, Ingram's River, and Hammonds Plains. On the premise that Peter Paul fell under the laws of the province "no matter where he might rove," Halliburton found him guilty of murder.[157] Lonecloud might have mixed up aspects of the two cases, or borrowed elements from each to embellish his own story.

After Chief Bernard's death, with a sudden rise in the numbers of settlers moving into St. Margaret Bay's as a result of the improved shore road, the spirit of mutual respect that had governed Chief Bernard's interrelations with surrounding settlers dissipated, and land trespasses began to occur. Many of his sons and daughters, finding the most fertile land at the head of the bay taken up and unable to protect the rest of their tract from external insult, drifted across the province to Panuke River system, or crossed over to Rawdon and into the Shubenacadie Valley.[158] In 1854 William Chearnley, Nova Scotia's Indian commissioner, lamented on the basis of somewhat dubious evidence that the grant on St. Margaret's Bay, once valued at "six hundred pounds," had been parted with "for a few gallons of rum."[159] Yet for at least two decades after the land sale of 1819, Thomas Phillips Sr., his son Thomas Jr., and others of their kinsfolk seasonally visited whatever remained of the acreage belonging to the Bernard grant at the Head of St. Margaret's Bay. The increasing density of settlement on either side of the grant had led to timber plunder and illicit expansion of fields and meadows, and had even threatened a graveyard, much to the chagrin of the Crown Lands Department.[160] Settler families who had initially been on good terms with the Mi'kmaq became increasingly disrespectful of Mi'kmaw property rights as land and resources around St. Margaret's Bay grew scarcer. In 1854 Commissioner Chearnley also reported that "the desecration of their ancient burial grounds" remained "a source of great annoyance" to the Mi'kmaq. "Upon the grant that I have instanced in St. Margaret's Bay," he continued, "one of these are [sic] situated;

for many years it was duly honored, but lately it has been ploughed up."[161] Consequently, traditional burial practices at the Head of St. Margaret's Bay and at the ancient cemetery near French Village gave way to rites administered by the priest at the Church of Our Lady of Mount Carmel, at Prospect.[162] Chearnley further noted that mills built at St. Margaret's Bay destroyed "the fish that frequented the streams," while a scarcity of fur-bearing animals not only raised prices and enhanced the marketability of peltry but also led settlers to take up trapping as an occupation in competition with the local Mi'kmaq.

Owing to these outsiders constantly vying with them for land and resources at Indian River, the group at the Head of Saint Margaret's Bay began to scatter.[163] Some band members revisited areas around Minas that their parents had vacated in the late eighteenth century. The younger Phillips hunted and fished at Panuke Lake, in the Rawdon Hills, along the Gaspeareau River Valley as far as Gaspereau Lake, and around Lequille, near Annapolis Royal.[164] During the late eighteenth century they had travelled with Philip Bernard to trade furs at Halifax and Windsor. After Bernard's death, they combined trapping with guiding sportsmen on fishing and big game hunting expeditions. Their earliest clients hailed from the ranks of the Halifax military elite – which ensured that they became well known to members of the garrison community. As their reputation as excellent trackers and woodsmen grew and spread, their clientele became more diverse, including members of the rising professional class at Halifax and Windsor.

A small Mi'kmaw community arose on the three-hundred-acre Ingram's River reserve laid out by Surveyor General Charles Morris in 1820.[165] The core members of this group were Thomas Phillips Sr.'s son Francis and three of Francis's sisters, Rosy, Sally, and Mary Phillips. Rosy and her husband, Christopher Paul, and well as two of Christopher Paul's brothers, Louis [Lewis] and Francis Caninic (or Kininick) Paul, lived at Ingram's River.[166] Peter Paul, who shot his mother-in-law Mary Phillips (Thomas Phillip Sr.'s wife), was a sibling of Christopher, Louis, and Francis Caninic Paul. Sally Phillips married Peter Toney, while Mary Phillips married Joseph Cope of Sheet Harbour[167] The men who guided military officers on moose hunts and fishing expeditions would have developed their initial clientele of sportsmen during their younger years, while George Mason's Willow

Cottage resort was still in operation at St. Margaret's Bay.

Land Disputes in Coastal Halifax County

On 7 May 1842 Titus Smith, who surveyed the Ingraham's River (now Ingram River) reserve in 1834, recommended to John Spry Morris, the provincial surveyor general, that the tract be subdivided into six lots of fifty acres each for the six families who lived there semi-permanently. Each parcel, Morris added, should retain some frontage on the river.[168] But though the reserve was resurveyed in 1852, no such subdivision was ever made.[169]

The Phillips and their Paul relatives fished and farmed at Ingram's River until the mid-1850s, when they moved to the Panuke Lake settlement back of Windsor. During the early 1830s Chief Bernard's grandsons, Thomas Jr. and Francis Phillips, who lived much of the time at the Head of St. Margaret's Bay, journeyed each fall to Ingraham's River to meet with Christopher, Francis, and Louis Paul to fish for eels. The reserve, rectangular in shape, spanned the river and flanked the interior boundary of a sizeable waterfront grant allocated to Charles Ingraham and his associates in 1765, as well as a smaller lot owned by Robert Markam. The best eeling locale lay upstream from the river's mouth. There were rarely a large number of families operating the weir at any one time. Joseph Howe, who visited the reserve on 9 October 1842 in his capacity as provincial Indian commissioner, found but a single family, whom he did not identify, engaged in the fishery.[170]

Howe revisited the site on 29 April 1843, during the spring alewife fishery. Here the commissioner encountered Francis Phillips, whom Howe described as an energetic one-eyed man, as well as Christopher and Louis Paul busily constructing bark wigwams and setting up a brush weir. These three stated that Joseph Cope, Mary Phillips's husband, as well as Sally Phillips's husband Peter Toney[171] also had claims upon the land. "These people consider themselves proprietors, and reside here every summer," Howe noted. "Their land lies on both sides of Ingraham's River, a stream which rises about the neighbourhood of Ardoise [near Newport Corner, West Hants County], and draining a chain of lakes, falls into the long inlet at the head of St. Margaret's Bay."[172]

Four small farming lots had been cleared and fenced on the flats skirting the river, about a quarter of a mile from the main shore road. In 1843 the residents numbered sixteen: three husbands, three wives, and ten children. The commissioner spent most of his visit imparting advice to the farmers on fence construction and modes of preserving the potato crop, which had rotted the previous winter because the tubers had been buried too shallowly in an earthen hillside. Once the lecture was over, Howe's audience peppered him with questions and complaints. Howe felt that the greatest problems stemmed from the fact that neither the Mi'kmaq nor the neighbouring settlers had a clear idea where the lines of the reserve lay. With the Mi'kmaq "not knowing what to protect," he posited, "the latter [i.e., settlers] trespass without knowledge as often as from intention." Yet despite his willingness to give some trespassers the benefit of the doubt, Howe denounced attempts by others to deny the Mi'kmaq access to local resources lying within their reserve's boundaries. "An absurd idea" prevailed, he declared, that the Mi'kmaq "had no right to cut or sell wood off their own land, and had not a common right with the whites to the river fishery." [173]

The litany of grievances on both sides did not stop there. The Mi'kmaq complained that the settlers turned cattle onto their clearings, while the settlers deemed the Mi'kmaq's fences "unlawful." Despite what had escalated into a hotbed of contention, Howe tried "to set all parties right" as best he could. He explained to the Mi'kmaw farmers and fishermen "in the presence of their neighbours what were their rights," while endeavouring "to make them sensible of their duties also." Feeling that some progress had been made, he supplied each Mi'kmaw family with a pick, a hoe, and ten bushels of seed potatoes and then went on his way.[174]

Even after the reserve's boundaries became clearly marked in 1852, instances of trespass only worsened. On 25 July 1853 Francis Phillips and Louis Paul complained to Colonel William Chearnley, who had recently been installed as provincial Indian commissioner, that the logging firm of Webber and Company had built a dam on the section of river lying below their reserve that had flooded their potato fields and prevented any fish from reaching their weir traps.[175] Chearnley, an enthusiastic fisherman and big game hunter as well as a founder of the Nova Scotia Fish and Wildlife Protection Society, responded energetically to these men's complaints about the loss of their fishery.[176] The commissioner's reports describing the situation eventually reached the desk of James B. Uniacke, who in April of 1854 had been appointed commissioner of Crown Lands.

Uniacke sent a letter to the company's president, Webber, threatening him with legal action if he did not permit at least half the river to be open at all times, but when Webber refused to remove his dam, the Crown Lands commissioner, by this time elderly and unwell, lost interest in the matter. Once it became known that no legal consequences would follow from the continued obstruction of the river, the reserve became increasingly subject to timber pillage and seasonal incursions of anglers who usurped the best fishing locales.[177]

Around the time of Confederation in 1867, the Indian Affairs Department in Ottawa cursorily reviewed the state of the Ingraham's River reserve, and then ignored its existence for over ten years.[178] In 1886 the Indian agent stationed at Enfield, the Reverend A.P. Desmond, faced with an application from Caleb F. Hubley to purchase six acres of the reserve for a mill site, suggested to Indian Affairs that an inspection be made of the tract and a council be held with the Mi'kmaw proprietors to determine their feelings on the matter. The inspector furnished for this task, James Lane, tendered a damming report. The forest had been plundered, leaving only a bleak landscape of stumps and bog totally unfit for agricultural purposes. No Mi'kmaw person, he continued, had lived at the site for fifty years. The document further held that the stretch of river passing through the reserve yielded only salmon and trout, much prized by the hundreds of anglers who regularly took up positions along its banks each spring and fall. No mention was made of the runs of eels and alewife so valued by the Mi'kmaq in years past.[179]

Father Desmond also served as the Roman Catholic priest at St. Bernard's Church in Enfield and made itinerant rounds to the Mi'kmaw communities of Elmsdale, Enfield, Grand Lake, the forks of Preston and Guysborough roads, and Shubenacadie. Owing to his spiritual duties, he likely was, of all non-Aboriginal persons who expressed an interested in these settlements, the most accurate at reading the pulse of Mi'kmaw opinion regarding land surrenders. Desmond felt he had to sharply counter Lane's report. Lane not only had underestimated the size and worth of the reserve and its resources, but had failed to charge the sports fishers with trespass and deny them access to the tract. He also stated that the

paltry sum offered for the mill site "was no temptation to destroy the fishing" since he knew that on occasion persons from Dartmouth Elmsdale and Cole Harbour still resorted there in the spring and fall.[180] Finally, no surrender could be taken without a meeting at which the majority of the Mi'kmaq possessing an interest in the reserve were present to express their views. Yet Desmond's assertions provided only a temporary bulwark against the tide of government aspirations to obtain a land surrender.[181] The province eventually overruled Desmond's contention that it was necessary to seek out and negotiate with the original proprietors and their descendants before any cession could be proposed. In 1919 a small pool of Mi'kmaw signatories, whose connections with the reserve on St. Margaret's Bay remained somewhat nebulous, was hastily mustered and pressed into service to sign a series of surrender documents, after which the tract at Ingraham's River, along with several other parcels that had been reserved along the Atlantic coast for the Mi'kmaq, reverted to the province.[182]

As happened with the grant at the Head of St. Margaret's Bay twenty years before, the permanent Mi'kmaw population of the Ingraham's River reserve by the mid-1855s drained away, with the dispersal of Chief Bernard's grandsons, granddaughters, in-laws, and great-grandchildren to other parts of the province. The Mi'kmaq continued to make seasonal use of both locales, however. Mi'kmaw oral traditions hold that Phillips residing at Rockingham and Birch Cove on the Bedford Basin, Elmsdale, Cole Harbour, and Cambridge seasonally visited both sites to cut ash and maple withes for baskets, as late as the 1940s.[183] In 1820 the surveyor general, Charles Morris, obscured the status of Mi'kmaw title to the plot at the Head of St. Margaret's Bay by sometimes referring to the parcel as a grant and sometimes a reserve. This ambiguity made it difficult to alienate, either by sale or through reversion to the province.[184] Beginning in the 1840s, the simplest administrative course before Confederation in 1867 was to let "sleeping dogs lie" by treating the land left unsold at the Head of St. Margaret's Bay as a reserve.[185]

Leases at times were conveyed for mill sites and hunting camps, but after the sale of 1817 no further parcels of land were alienated until a series of expropriations for public works occurred in the early 1900s. Barbara (Mason) Peart provides detailed information about the erection of mills along the Indian River, the Prince of Wales Hotel, and her family home – known as Saraquay House – in the area around the time of Confederation, but remains much more cautious about discussing the division and parcelling out of the Bernard grant after 1820. She merely observes that a chart prepared in 1962 by the Nova Scotia Power Commission shows that 166 acres of the tract was sold much later to James Croucher and the remainder divided among George Mason and James Boutellier. The grantor in these transactions was the Crown.[186]

In 1895 Indian Affairs in Ottawa had briefly shaken the province out of its lethargy by asking for an enquiry into Crown grants held by the Mi'kmaq throughout Nova Scotia, and specifically noted this tract among them.[187] Once it was revealed that the grant had been awarded in free and common soccage, giving the owners freedom to covey the property to whom they wished, the Crown Lands Department furnished Ottawa with a sketch of the tract, and there the matter stood, indefinitely. Today the majority of the tract is marked as Crown property, except for sections on the shoreline and along the lake and river drainage that have been occupied for many years by the Nova Scotia Power Commission for a generating station.[188]

But if the province forgot that the land once belonged to Chief Philip Bernard and his family, the Mi'kmaq did not. Memories of the grant at the Head of St. Margaret's Bay lingered on among the chief's descendants. One of them, Jerry Lonecloud, informed Harry Piers, the curator of the Nova Scotia Museum, that his mother Mary Ann Phillips, the daughter of Thomas Phillips Jr., had been born at a "camping ground at the foot of Big Indian Lake, head of St. Margaret's Bay."[189] Thomas Jr. was the son of Thomas Phillips Sr., who was likely *Tomeag*, Lonecloud's maternal great-grandfather, who, according to Père Paul Pacifique, lent his name to Lake Thomas, near Fall River, west of Halifax.[190]

Thomas Jr.'s daughter, Mary Ann Phillips, was raised at the Head of St. Margaret's Bay. Mary Ann and her first husband, Tom Wallace, lived on the St. Margaret's Bay grant, but following her marriage to her second husband, Abraham Bartlett-Alexis, she travelled extensively throughout the Northeast. At Waterbury, Vermont, in the 1860s, while Abraham was away collecting prize money for the role he played in capturing Abraham Lincoln's assassin John Wilkes Booth, she promised her children that someday they all would return to a tract her father possessed at the Head of St. Margaret's Bay.[191] According to Clara Dennis, a reporter with the *Halifax Herald*, Lonecloud in the 1920s also maintained that his mother was the sole heir to this property.[192] His grounds for this assertion were ill founded, however, since Mary Ann had a number of paternal cousins. While speaking with Dennis, Lonecloud ignored the territorial claims of others belonging to the Phillips family, among them Thomas Phillips Sr.'s son Newel (Noel) Phillips at Elmsdale.[193] Newel also passed on information about the grant to his children who in turn relayed the knowledge to Newel's grandchildren and great-grandchildren. As late as October 2013, Newel Phillips's great-grandson, Fred Phillips of Cambridge, Nova Scotia, knew full well that his paternal ancestors once had been proprietors of land at St. Margaret's Bay.[194]

Thomas Phillips of Panuke Lake

Thomas Phillips Jr. (c.1795–1864) was thirty-five years older than his brother Newel (1830–1912). He was born at St. Margaret's Bay before his father Thomas Phillips Sr. left for Elmsdale. A note in Harry Piers's handwriting, in the margin of an 1855 edition of the first volume of Campbell Hardy's book *Sporting Adventures in The New World*, housed in the library of the Nova Scotia Museum, says that "Tom Philips [Jr.] was born at the foot of Big Indian Lake, head of St. Margaret's Bay, and died (circa 1864) at Three Mile Plains, Windsor, about 45 years before 1919."[195] Pier's brief inscription also states that a gravestone was erected in Thomas Phillips's honour at the Old Parish Burying Chapel at Windsor by judge and author Thomas Chandler Haliburton.[196] Piers likely received this information from Lonecloud, who was mistaken about Haliburton raising a grave marker, since by the time of Thomas Phillips Jr.'s death Haliburton had retired to England.[197]

Around 1830 Thomas Phillips Jr. moved from the Head of St. Margaret's Bay to Panuke, the Aboriginal community mentioned by Jean-Baptiste Thoma's son and daughter Anselm and Clare Thoma to Captain John Knox in 1758. The Panuke Lake area was scarcely populated in the 1830s, since most of Thoma's descendants had moved to Rawdon or to lands along the Shubenacadie River Valley.[198] Big game in the interior had dwindled, and during the winter of 1834 fell to such a low that Thomas Phillips joined Charles Lewis, Peter Mews [Mius or Meuse],

Noel Morris, John Simons, and Paul Joseph Stevens in petitioning the government for relief.[199] Similar conditions prevailed in 1836.[200] Moose and caribou populations, overhunted by the first influxes of settlers into the Minas area, were so devastated that moose did not begin to recover until the mid-1840s, and the caribou never did. By the 1850s, however, the moose population had re-established sufficiently to support a small Mi'kmaw settlement at Panuke Lake, provided that hunting was supplemented by gardening and that residents went weir fishing each spring and fall on the Atlantic coast.

Major problems soon arose at the fisheries along the coast. In the 1850s, as mentioned above, the logging enterprise Webber and Company constructed a dam on Ingram's River and drove logs downstream that destroyed the Mi'kmaq's weir. After fruitlessly petitioning the province for assistance against the company's trespasses, Francis Phillips, his wife Mary Paul, and Christopher Paul with his wife Rosey Phillips and their two sons Abraham and Noel Paul joined Thomas Phillips Jr. at Panuke Lake in the late 1850s.[201] Christopher Paul's brother Francis and his wife and children as well as members of the Bernard, Jeremy, Morris, Simon, and Stevens families soon followed. In 1852 this group successfully petitioned for a four-hundred-acre reserve at Panuke Lake, but as the Mi'kmaw population fluctuated at Panuke Lake from year to year, only Thomas Phillips, Christopher Paul, and the latter's two sons received surveyed lots, of one hundred acres each. Since Noel Paul was still only a boy, he lived with his parents while his plot was held by the others in trust until he reached the age of majority. The government supplied the adults of the community who farmed their lots with agricultural equipment and lumber and tools to build log houses.

Revitalization at Panuke Lake, 1850–1863

Thomas Phillips Jr., perhaps drawing on his earlier memories of the popularity of Mason's Willow Cottage at the Head of St. Margaret's Bay, set out to establish a resort-like environment at the Panuke Lake settlement where sportsmen could rest after their journey in from Windsor and enjoy some of the gastronomic delicacies of the local fields and forest, among these berries, wild fish, and game, before leaving in the transportation provided by their guides to hunt and fish further afield. Because

Phillips's mother was Acadian, he also may have had a better idea than some of his Mi'kmaw contemporaries about how to grow and present garden produce in a way that appealed to the European palate. Phillips's residence at the foot of Panuke Lake represented "a sort of half-way house."[202] The services it offered catered to military officers, professionals from the Atlantic Provinces and New England, and even British royalty. Lonecloud held that his maternal grandfather guided Albert Edward, the Prince of Wales, during the prince's four-month tour of North America in 1860.[203] The prince entered "Ponhook Lake from Windsor," at which point Tom Phillips, Frank Caninic, and Newel Jeremy "led the royal moose-hunting expedition from the Panuke Lake settlement into the Rawdon Hills.[204]

Thomas Phillips, though he spoke English, was a man of few words. Captain Campbell Hardy, a retired military officer, nevertheless found the guide to be a competent tracker and an innovative and responsible provider of services to his clients. En route home from a fishing trip in New Brunswick in September 1853, Hardy decided to embark on a two-day moose hunt in the Panuke Lake region. After experiencing what he described as a "tortuous" wagon ride over a corduroy road lying between Windsor and Panuke Lake, he was surprised, after the road swung sharply east and crossed a bridge, to find a cluster of neat log cabins surrounded by gardens.

Hardy immediately sought out Thomas Phillips, who had been highly recommended to him as a guide. Thomas was hoeing a potato field when the officer arrived, and stooped silently to whittle a piece of wood while Hardy spoke to him. The captain later declared him to be the "most taciturn [man] I ever met with." Instead of giving Hardy any promises, Thomas simply pointed him in the direction of Christopher Paul's cabin and asked him to enquire there about acquiring a guide.[205] Though Hardy immediately understood that a strong bond existed between Paul and Phillips, he failed to recognize that they were brothers-in-law – a kin relation among the Mi'kmaq charged with reciprocal respect and mutual obligation.

In contrast to the reticent Tom Phillips, Christopher Paul was extremely enthusiastic about the prospect of an upcoming moose hunt, though he stressed that Phillips would have to be the principal guide. With his daughter away with her husband, Abraham Bartholomew-Alexis, in the United States, Phillips had been managing his gardening and guiding on his own, which attracted much respect from his neighbouring in-laws. According to Hardy, Christopher Paul insisted that "Old Phillips would have to accompany us, as a worthy old man, a widower, all along with his dog. He had been one the smartest Indians in the province, and was still a good hunter."[206]

Hardy praised the "tight little canoe" that Phillips and Paul had fashioned together the previous summer, declaring that "[i]t was one of the prettiest models and best goers I ever saw."[207] Awed by the beauty of the autumnal colours and the majesty of the gleaming bodies of lake water stretching away to the southwest in the direction of the Atlantic, the captain ensconced himself "comfortably" in the bottom of the canoe, while Phillips and Paul paddled for three hours against a strong headwind. The party finally beached their canoe on the western shore of Long Lac, and Tom and Christopher made a bivouac to shelter their client for the night out of discarded poles and bark from one of Tom's previous camps.[208]

The following day, sightings of fresh tracks and grunting noises heard in the distance in response to the guides' calls revealed that animals were definitely in the area, but the wily quarry kept retreating at the men's approach. The damp and rough terrain wore out Hardy's footwear, which hampered him from moving about quickly, so Paul had to improvise a pair of moccasins out of a spare piece of hide just to enable Hardy to walk around. When rain began to pour down in torrents, preventing any further hunting, two hours of solid paddling by the guides brought Hardy back to the Panuke Lake settlement. Though Hardy mused that Phillips and Paul must have felt disgruntled by their lack of success in having their client bag a moose, the captain appreciated the concern for his comfort and the ingenuity and resourcefulness his guides had shown. Although Tom Phillips was continually referred to as "old" by Christopher Paul, this designation would have been one mainly of respect, as Tom in 1853 proved an extremely fit person who could weather driving wind and rain while enduring hours of strenuous physical labour.

Thomas Phillips Jr. and the Pauls together shouldered responsibility for the success of the Panuke guiding establishment, which remained a well-known destination for sports throughout the 1850s. As early as 1832 Phillips petitioned Surveyor General John Spry Morris to have a large rectangular reserve surveyed on Panuke Lake. Though he kept receiving assurances from the government that a reserve would be laid out and confirmed, the boundaries of a tract would not be surveyed until 1852, and then very sketchily. After each receiving one hundred acres, Tom and his brothers-in-law went to work with a will, planting potatoes and other crops, including corn.[209] For over twenty years they guided sportsmen through forests and over barrens. Yet by the late 1850s increasingly stringent game laws, involving reduced bag limits for big game, hastened the end of their once popular guiding enterprise. The death of Thomas Phillips Jr., one of the most famous guides in eastern Canada, at Three Mile Plains in 1864 marked the end of the heyday of big game hunting in the Panuke Lake and Rawdon regions.

Three Mile Plains drew persons of diverse ethnicities. There were Mi'kmaq from the Panuke Lake, Rawdon, and Windsor Junction areas, including Copes, Brooks, Hoods, Stevens, Thomases, and members of the Phillips, Paul, and Morris families. Ben Morris, a blind and respected elder who moved from Halifax County to be near his sons, occupied a cabin overlooking the Panuke Lake watershed until his death in 1918.[210] There were descendants of Black Loyalists and people of Caribbean extraction. During the 1860s, miners, quarry workers, and railway employees from continental Europe settled at Three Mile Plains. In 1865 German-speaking immigrants came to the region, some veterans of continental wars, others drawn by the lure of gold. The community consequently exhibited a range of cultures, social mores, and religious attachments. The Mi'kmaq were Roman Catholic, the Blacks were Baptist, and many of the labourers of German extraction were Lutheran. Intermarriage occurred, and the resultant intermingling of ethnicities and ideas fostered the growth of a unique cultural crucible in southwestern Nova Scotia. In time this gave rise to new, in-depth understandings of the nature of Mi'kmaw and Black struggles to gain freedom and recognition within the Canadian milieu.[211]

The seeds of this movement were just being sown when the Panuke Lake Mi'kmaw community had to face new and extremely daunting challenges. Since large-circumference paper birch trees had dwindled in numbers by 1870, canoe bark became scarce.[212] Non-Mi'kmaw hunters and trappers took any remaining animals that could be found in woods that were rapidly being clear-cut by loggers. The St. Croix Lumber Company acquired timber licences over swaths of surrounding woodland and built a series of rolling dams from Panuke Lake through the chain of lakes and rivers towards the Atlantic coast, blocking access to the ancient water and portage route to St. Margaret's Bay. Francis von Ellershausen, a German mining engineer, who founded nearby Ellershouse in 1865, constructed a rail line and built thirty-two houses for the German immigrant families who worked in his mines. Blasting and train traffic drove game away from the Panuke Lake area.

By 1865, only one Mi'kmaw cabin remained occupied at Panuke Lake, that of Christopher Paul, whose sons were away working in New Brunswick.[213] Illicit logging had drastically reduced the monetary value of the land around Panuke Lake. In 1905 R.W. Mackenzie, a surveyor from Enfield, claimed that had less timber been plundered from the reserve, it would have been worth in excess of $2,500, a fairly large sum for the time, but given its denuded state it would fetch at sale only a fraction of that sum.[214] Moreover, the St. Croix Lumber Company purchased two large parcels, originally granted in 1827 to John Todd and John Stark of Windsor, which later were found, owing to an improper survey, to encroach deeply into the side of the Mi'kmaq's reserve facing away from the St. Croix River. The ensuing large triangular bite cutting into the backside of the reserve reduced the size of the Mi'kmaw tract from 400 acres to 268.3 acres.[215] As a result, the reserve lost valuable hardwood timber and hemlock that might have gone into band coffers, and caused Christopher Paul in the 1870s to seek compensation from the government. This call for redress remained on file at Ottawa for a century, ignored by both the province and the Department of Indian Affairs until 1975, when renewed Mi'kmaw inquiries on the subject prompted the provincial Crown Lands Department to lay the burden of rectifying the situation on the federal government and Scott Paper, then operating on the lands formerly held by the St. Croix Lumber Company.[216]

The Mi'kmaw economy at Panuke Lake collapsed, since only subsistence farming was feasible on the shallow rocky soil, and no Mi'kmaq at that time felt inclined to join the ranks of the mine labourers at Ellershouse. Yet memories of the Panuke area as a prime hunting region lingered on among Mi'kmaq living around Windsor. As late as 1914, anthropologist Frank Gouldsmith Speck gained enough information to plot the outlines of Tom Phillips's old hunting territory around Panuke Lake, vacant since

the late 1850s.[217] In hunting, fishing, and planting at Lake Panuke, Tom and his kin repopulated an area that was deserted when Chief Thoma's descendants moved to Rawdon and Shubenacadie. After 1865, however, the Phillips too vacated the Panuke Lake area. Members of the family meanwhile lived near Dartmouth, at Elmsdale along the Shubenacadie river valley, and on lands in the Annapolis Valley.

Newel Phillips of Elmsdale

Newel (Noel) Philips (1830–1916), a son of Thomas Phillips Sr., was probably born at the Head of St. Margaret's Bay. He spent his youth at Elmsdale, situated along the boundary shared by Halifax and Colchester Counties. Like many other young, single Mi'kmaq men, in his twenties Newel travelled to New England looking for work.[218] In 1868, when he was thirty-eight, he returned to Nova Scotia and wed Martha Comeau (1854–85), a fifteen-year-old girl of Acadian and Aboriginal descent from Meteghan, Digby County. The couple raised their family at Elmsdale.[219]

Though he often visited his relatives at St. Margaret's Bay, Newel became a core member of the small Elmsdale Mi'kmaw community, composed of three or four families. He and Martha had three children, Isaac in 1869, Lewis Jacob in 1880, and Charles Joseph in 1882.[220] Others at Elmsdale included Newel's sister, a widow named Ann, and a younger couple, "Noel Bennar [Bernard]" and his wife "Jeannet [Janet]."[221] Joseph and Louis Phillips, also Newel's siblings, were seasonal visitors. Despite the fact that Martha Comeau, born in 1854, was twenty-four years younger than her husband, she died at age thirty in 1885. Around this time, Isaac married Elizabeth Phillips and went to live with his father-in-law and mother in-law, Francis E. Phillips and Mary Paul,[222] at Lawrencetown, Annapolis County. His father, Newel, appears on the 1891 federal census living with his eight-year-old son Charles Joseph.[223] His neighbours were Joseph "Jerime" (or Joseph Jeremy, also known as "Joseph Howe Sr.") and his wife Jane and five children; Louis Peters – newly arrived from Bear River – his wife Susan, and a three-year-old daughter; and Newel Hammond and his wife Jasmine, a couple in their thirties from New Germany, Lunenburg County, who so far remained childless.[224]

Isaac's wife's father, Francis, was related to Isaac's father, Newel, since both were sons of Thomas Phillips Sr. of St. Margaret's Bay and Panuke Lake. Isaac and his wife Elizabeth thus were second cousins. Prior to moving to Lawrencetown, Francis Phillips had lived on the Ingram's River reserve, but depredations to his weir fishing grounds by logging interests forced him to relocate, first to Gold River, Lunenburg County, and then to Lawrencetown in Annapolis County.[225] Francis manufactured split baskets and wooden items for sale as well as working as a wage labourer on nearby farms. He gathered ash and maple withes and fished for trout, salmon, and gaspereau. Laden with baskets and wooden items they had fashioned during the winter, Isaac and Elizabeth each spring travelled from the Annapolis Valley to Elmsdale to visit with Isaac's elderly father and to peddle their manufactures to local farmers. In the summer they camped on the Cole Harbour reserve, located on the east side of Morris Lake, near to markets in Dartmouth and Halifax.[226] By fall, Isaac and his wife were at St. Margaret's Bay, fishing in the river and cutting ash and maple withes on his ancestors' lands. Winter found them back at Lawrencetown. In 1906, Isaac and Elizabeth, along with their eight-year-old daughter Theresa and five-year-old son Thomas, dwelt for five years on the Cole Harbour reserve, where their youngest son Charles was born on 4 June 1907.[227] In 1911, they left Cole Harbour to settle permanently on the Cambridge reserve, a tract of land in Kings County that a sizeable group formed of members of the Brooks, Jeremy, Francis, Knockwood, Pictou, and Toney families had received from the government in 1880.[228]

Charles Joseph Phillips and his wife, Margaret Cope, a daughter of Alexander ("Sandy") Cope and Mary Paul,[229] stayed for over a year at Cole Harbour but by the spring of 1911 had left for Elmsdale to live with Newel Phillips. Newel Phillips's household soon was one of the largest in the Elmsdale community, since 1911 Charles and Margaret had five children, James, Joseph, Margaret, Lilley, and Mary, ranging in ages from three to eight years of age.[230] Each spring the Mi'kmaw settlement swelled in size to embrace from thirty-eight to forty persons.[231] Most were transients, whereas Newel Phillips had occupied the site for over thirty years. Newel also was interested in political events and, even at an advanced age, participated in meetings focusing on treaties and Mi'kmaw land rights. In 1912 he and two of his sons, Joe and Jacob, supported Charles Big Peter Peminout Paul's campaign for election as Shubenacadie district chief.[232]

When Jacob Gilby, the proprietor of the Elmsdale encampment site, sought to evict the Mi'kmaq from his property in 1916, Newel Phillips and Joseph Howe Sr. became witnesses in the ensuing land dispute. The number of Mi'kmaq in Halifax and Hants Counties had increased, owing to a decline in guiding opportunities and a desire to be close to Halifax markets. Farmers like Gilby feared that their lands soon would become dotted with Mi'kmaw encampments.[233] In the midst of this dispute, Jerry Lonecloud, whose mother was one of Newel Phillips's sisters, took a leading role in an ensuing government enquiry in 1916 that revealed, among other things, that the Elmsdale settlement was not a reserve, despite its being marked as such on a geological survey of Canada map.[234] Since Newel Phillips, his brother Louis, and Joseph Howe Sr. had maintained houses and gardens at Elmsdale for decades, Lonecloud took depositions from the three men and sent the information to Ottawa in July 1916. He anticipated the documents would attest to the Mi'kmaq's long residency in the area. "Old Newel," he stressed, had been born at Elmsdale in 1830 and still resided on the same plot his father (whom Lonecloud did not identify by name) had tended before him.[235]

Lonecloud on 6 July 1916 also wrote a disgruntled letter to the deputy-superintendent of Indian Affairs, charging A.J. Boyd, the nearest Indian agent, who lived at River Bourgeois in Cape Breton, with withholding from the Mi'kmaq monies that had accrued from timber sales on the Ship Harbour reserve. He had discovered that Marks Brothers, the logging company operating at Ship Harbour, had paid over $4,500 in stumpage and timber dues that the Elmsdale Mi'kmaq would need if forced to move to Grand Lake or Cole Harbour in Halifax County.[236] Lonecloud stressed that the Mi'kmaq resented being cast as "squatters," since the "whole land of the Province we once called our own." "However," he continued, "failing other recognized rights, we feel that we can at least clearly claim this particular property by what you term squatters rights, and we urge and expect you to see that our rights, of whatever kind, are duly respected."[237]

Newel died of pneumonia at Camp Hill Hospital, part of the Victoria General Hospital in Halifax, at age eighty-six in 1916, but the claims case persisted for another three years before the Mi'kmaw community finally decided to abandon the old Elmsdale settlement.[238] Though the Mi'kmaq lost the case, the inquiry surrounding it had led to the collection of valuable data. Owing to the efforts of Martin Sack, a councillor who "was very factual and added no hearsay,"[239] information tendered under oath by "Newel and Elewie [Louis] Doodoo" was placed on file in Ottawa, where it became accessible to lawyers and academics interested in cases predicated on the existence of Aboriginal right attending long possession.

Following Newel's death, Charles Joseph moved to Cole Harbour, where his wife Margaret, known as "Meggie" or "Maggie," wanted her husband to put down permanent roots. Together they built a sturdy frame farmhouse and a barn on the Cole Harbour reserve and raised seven children to adulthood: James, Joseph, Margaret, Charles Alexander, Lillian, Mary, and Catherine.[240] In subsequent years the Phillips family would dodge the brunt of a government's centralization scheme, gauged to concentrate the province's Mi'kmaw population at just two locales, Shubenacadie and Eskasoni. Meanwhile, Charles engaged in a seasonal round of farming, fishing, and hunting. Paying little attention to provincial game laws, he maintained a hunting territory at all seasons in the Rawdon Hills and kept his family stocked with meat and fish. He and Meggie, who could read and write, sent their children to school, grew hay and vegetables, raised a cow and a few chickens, and played host to relatives from the Cambridge area who seasonally visited their homestead en route to Dartmouth and Halifax to sell their baskets and other wares.

Campaign to Preserve the Cole Harbour Reserve

Charles, like his father Newel before him, made baskets and wooden items for sale, trapped furs to trade in Halifax, and supplied fresh meat by taking deer, which had moved in to replace moose on his hunting grounds in the Rawdon Hills. During the summer he Margaret travelled from Dartmouth to join a small cluster of lean-tos and wooden shacks at Birch Cove near Rockingham, along the Bedford Highway.[241] At a prearranged time he would meet his first cousin, Isaac Phillip, from Cambridge in Kings County, and the two often would travel together around Rockingham and Bedford peddling baskets and other wares. Jerry Lonecloud, exercising his kin ties with his mother's kin, also joined the small community.[242] The encampment site was an old one, dating back

before the 1800s. For many years it remained hidden from traffic in a grove of trees lying along the shore road. A crystalline stream, which formed a small waterfall as it flowed over a rocky ridge near the Birch Cove encampment, supplied the Mi'kmaq with drinking water.[243]

Birch Cove developed into a rendezvous site where residents shared ideas with Mi'kmaw visitors from other parts of the province. Between 1930 and 1945 much of this discussion centred on the issue of Mi'kmaw hunting rights. Charles and his wife, now almost always affectionately referred to as "Meggie," were often approached for suggestions and advice. Charles had successfully extended his fields, tended his buildings, made and repaired farming machinery, and kept a small herd of cattle. All of these demonstrations of independent enterprise made it difficult for government officials to ease him off his land and force him to go to Shubenacadie, especially after 1945, when it became blatantly obvious that the centralization scheme was not working.

Charles Joseph Phillips and Meggie Cope, owing to their vehement opposition to government centralization policy in the early 1940s, became targets of government scrutiny. When Charles was apprehended by provincial game wardens in 1950 on a charge of deer-jacking, Meggie viewed the incident primarily as another opportunity to defend the traditional aspects of Mi'kmaw life that she and her husband cherished. Following Phillips's arrest, Meggie directed several cogent letters to the Department of Indian Affairs in Ottawa, not only on behalf of her husband but also to promote a campaign for resource and treaty rights in support of the entire Mi'kmaw community. According to Meggie, her husband had been exercising his treaty rights by hunting for subsistence for his family on traditional Mi'kmaw territory. "I don't want my husband to pay that fine," she declared; "if he does that settles the matter for all Indians forever, hereafter. He has shot a deer every year since we have been here for last 35 years before his arrest. Some new Mounties [are] trying to make [a] name and fame for themselves. We try to be as self supporting as we can, and we Indians have Millions of Dollars in Hands in Ottawa. So why cannot we be supported by those funds to help us pay to have the matter taken up in Court and have a Supreme Court ruling? If my husband is arrested then I want full support while he is locked up because he is all the help mate I have."[244]

Meggie and Charles braced themselves to challenge government penetration into those distinctive facets of their lives that to them were the very essence of what it was to be Mi'kmaq. They had been able to hunt, fish, and plant for years without any hindrance from agencies associated with the increasingly commercialized governance over Crown lands and resources, but no longer.[245] Both were well aware of the 1928 Gabriel Sylliboy decision that brought the existence of treaty rights into contention before the law, and both felt it was time for another test case to come before the courts that might overturn the Sylliboy ruling and uphold the existence of Aboriginal right.

The opportunity never arose. A series of tragedies struck the Phillips household and made any thought of pursuing a court battle untenable. In July 1957 two government investigators, Bart McKinnon and D.R. Cassie, turned up at Margaret Cope's house at Cole Harbour to interview the seventy-year-old householder. While they admired the "lovely, clean, well-finished" frame abode, the well-tended animals, including a horse, and some horse-drawn farming implements, they soon learned about the numerous difficulties the Phillips family faced. Margaret explained that her husband Charles had died from pneumonia on 21 April the same year, and that most of her time the previous winter had been spent caring for him during his illness.[246] As well, the previous year her son Charles Alexander Phillips, born in 1912, was found dead on 28 April 1956 along the railway tracks near Fairview, back of Africville.[247] According to information given on his official death certificate, Charles Alexander, at times somewhat of a prodigal, had been carousing with buddies from Rockingham on the day in question and had tripped and fallen in front of a moving train. His mother and siblings, however, suspected that foul play may have occurred, with Charles Alexander having been beaten unconscious by unknown persons before he was hit by the train.[248]

McKinnon and Cassie knew that Meggie had withstood vicissitudes that would have devasted a soul with less pluck and determination. She was beginning to transition into the tasks of maintaining a forty-acre farm on her own; her children had all moved away upon marriage or had died, with only one son living in a nearby community left to help her. Her son Charles Alexander's death had left her with "five fatherless grandchildren" as well as his young widow Florence Mae Pippy, born and raised in Newfoundland, to watch over, all of whom, she stressed, would be counted among her heirs.[249]

Meggie struggled to remain economically independent. Other than her Old Age Security pension, she did not rely on the government for any monetary assistance. If times proved hard, she stated she would take on outside work whenever the occasion arose to do so. She wanted title to her farm but feared it might fall under the provincial taxing scheme. Obviously deeply moved by her courage, enterprise, and determination, McKinnon and Cassie promised to see that the land at Cole Harbour remained on a general reserve list, and so would not be subject to property taxes. With her husband and her son gone, Meggie felt she had a right to be feisty when it came to protecting her land. Though born at Sheet Harbour, the investigatory team noted, she had "lived at Cole harbour for 41 years and does not intend to leave it until she goes out feet first."[250]

With an air of determination, Meggie single-handedly prevented the dissolution of the Cole Harbour reserve. Meanwhile, on the Cambridge reserve Isaac Phillips, a craftsman and farm labourer, paved the way for the development of reciprocal relations with local farmers advantageous to both parties. Though work could be arduous on farms or in the woods, midsummer was often a time for travel. Isaac and his son Charles worked for wages during planting and harvest seasons, and manufactured potato and apple hampers, fruit boxes, domestic baskets, butter moulds, clotheslines, and ornamented containers. In return for producing these items, much needed by the farming community, a tradition arose among the more established farmers of Kings County of allowing Mi'kmaq free access to stands of ash and maple on their properties.[251] Knowledge of the value of the Mi'kmaw community to the Cambridge area further prompted a landholder, Albert A. Webster, in the late nineteenth century to release 34.8 acres of his farmland along the Cornwallis River for sale to Ottawa, a tract that officially became recognized as the Cambridge reserve on 9 February 1880.[252]

From the 1940s to the 1960s families seasonally left by train to harvest berries or pick potatoes in Maine. Abundant stands of ash and maple around Cambridge also brought Mi'kmaw visitors from as far away as Cape Breton to harvest wood, which is how Isaac's son Charles met his wife, Natalie Poulette, from Eskasoni. Isaac acted as the community's unofficial spokesperson and, with time, these leadership duties were assumed by Charles, who in 1968 became the first chief of the *Kampalijek*, Cambridge, Nova Scotia, Mi'kmaw community.[253] During the years the government tried to implement its centralization scheme, Charles temporarily joined his in-laws at Castle Bay, Eskasoni, but by the late 1940s he was back at Cambridge. His son, Fred Phillips, remembered his parents, his sisters and himself piling into the family's green pick-up truck with baskets and other items for sale in Halifax. Since rust spots on the truck's green chassis had been daubed over with yellow paint, the vehicle had been dubbed "The Green Hornet." The truck stopped at Shubenacadie, Enfield, and Cole Harbour before proceeding to Halifax, where wares were sold at the market as well as door to door.[254] The highway – and less frequently the train – now furnished transportation to the Atlantic coast; the ancient portage routes from Panuke Lake to Chester and St. Margaret Bay lay abandoned. The drastic reduction of big game that led to the end of guiding at Panuke Lake prompted a redistribution of Mi'kmaw population, with the loss of population at Panuke Lake fuelling a concurrent rise in numbers at Cambridge in Kings County. Owing to their conjoined histories, these two locales, albeit in different counties, today form one administrative unit.

As late as the 1920s, Thomas Phillips Jr.'s grandson, Jerry Lonecloud, knew he was descended from a chief who held a grant of land at the Head of St. Margaret's Bay. Exactly the same tradition was conveyed to Newel Phillips of Elmsdale, who told it to his son Isaac, who in turn passed it on to his children. It is an orally transmitted legacy that spans well over two centuries. Fred Phillips of Cambridge reported that his father Charles also used to take his family on visits to the Head of St. Margaret's Bay when he was a boy. Mainstream society has forgotten that this land ever lay under Aboriginal title. Since Confederation in 1867 the Department of Indian Affairs ignored the presence of this grant and eventually considered it completely sold or forfeited to the Crown. Today, the portion of the tract not used for hydroelectric purposes is registered on PID maps as Crown Land.[255]

Fallow Ground

Many Mi'kmaq today at Millbrook, Shubenacadie, and Cambridge trace their ancestry back to members of the old Minas regional band that once ranged along the Gaspereau River. A few also know that Thomas Phillips Jr. rescued the old Aboriginal Panuke Lake settlement from obscurity in the 1850s. Since the mid-1930s, however, the Panuke tract has suffered neglect. The original shores of Panuke Lake, visited by Captain Campbell Hardy in 1853, are flooded by waters restrained by the Salmon Hole Dam, built in 1938 at the Windsor end of Panuke Lake to carry the lake's waters by culvert to power the Hantsport Mill.[256] No traces remain of the wooden bridge that once spanned the easternmost end of the lake, or of the road that once led into the heart of the Mi'kmaw settlement. The only access to the western side of the St. Croix River is by an earthen track for trucks servicing the dam. The reserve on the other side is virtually inaccessible by car and, except for some small camps lying along woods trails, currently lies vacant. In 1957 a government interviewing and research team recommended that no roads be built or services be offered to the reserve, since the area offered so few local employment opportunities.[257] For a century, survey maps have depicted the large triangular bite, discussed above, that reduced the size of the reserve from 400 to less than 269 acres. After 1975, however, the Scott Paper Company relinquished rights to the triangular piece of land and so restored the reserve to much of its original acreage.

During the mid-eighteenth century, Panuke Lake offered a refuge from the storms of war for Chief Jean-Baptist Thoma and family. Later, from the 1830s to the early 1860s, it gave Thomas Phillips, who remained a hunter and guide at heart, a place to pursue his guiding profession with pride. After his death, popular attitudes lauded farmers' inroads upon the forest and denigrated the Mi'kmaw community. Hunting, fishing, and guiding were viewed as backward and old-fashioned modes of existence that brought only poverty and ultimately despair to those who persisted in clinging to them. The "function of the [Mi'kmaw] hunter," it was claimed, "was to exalt, by his very distress, the agriculturalist."[258] But the very branding of the Panuke Lake region as agriculturally unviable has proved to be its salvation, for it still remains Mi'kmaw land. Though presently no one permanently lives on the Panuke Lake reserve, it remains administratively under the jurisdiction of the Annapolis First Nation, *Kampalijek*, located along the Cornwallis River near Cambridge Station in Kings County. Since the government has deemed the Panuke Lake region southeast of Windsor economically unviable, what is presently one of the most attractive geographic areas along the watershed divide of peninsular Nova Scotia remains in the hands of descendants of members of the Phillips, Thomas, Paul, and Toney families who invested over two centuries of time and energy in protecting it and stewarding its forested reserves. Though it currently stands as a wilderness of recovering cut-over timber lands and corralled lake waters, it is rich in history and gives every indication of rebounding after its fallow period with new possibilities for the future.

– Nik Phillips and Janet E. Chute, assisted by Carrie Gloade

Acknowledgments: Nik Phillips was responsible for the part of this entry concerning Chief Philip Bernard. The authors thank Walter Comeau, Vernon Cope, Marguerite Labrador, Basil Peters, and Fred Phillips Sr. for their valuable contributions to the oral history of the Thomas, or Thoma, and Phillips families. Carrie Gloade's father, Mike Gloade, a relative of Edith Jane Thomas Peters, supplied a genealogical chart of the Thomas family that Peters compiled, showing the "sailor" named "Thomas" at the chart's core.

8

Bernard Argomartin and the Pennel/Pennell and Hammond Families of Southwestern Nova Scotia

Mi'kmaw Fighters at the Fall of Quebec

In the 1830s lawyer and historian Beamish Murdoch (1800–76) conversed with an elderly Mi'kmaw man near Chester, Nova Scotia, who told him that as a boy he had joined General James Wolfe's expedition in 1759 and been at the fall of Quebec. The man even made gestures with his fingers to show how closely together the bodies of the dead had lain on the Plains of Abraham:

> His name was Captain Penall. He said he was born at St. Margaret's Bay, Nova Scotia, and that he went as a boy of about 14 years with the English expedition to the capture of Quebec. He was taken great care of by his people and nicely dressed with clean linen and blue cloth dress. He said the dead lay closely together in the battle, holding up his fingers to express how close and thick the bodies lay there. I was told that in his manhood he was affluent – had built a brick house in the bay, and used to get his wine by the pipe or hogshead from Halifax.[1]

This "Captain Penall" was John Pennel Sr. (c.1745–c.1843), son of Chief Bernard Argomartin (c.1722–1817). "Pennel" derives from the pronunciation of "Bernard" by a Mi'kmaw speaker."[2] Born around 1722, Bernard Argomartin was one of several chiefs living in southwestern Nova Scotia who supported the British during the final years of the Seven

Years' War.[3] The chief probably joined his young son John on the expedition to Quebec, as a guide and warrior. Both father and son may have been recruited by Michael Francklin, who in the early to middle 1750s traded among the Mi'kmaq, spoke the Mi'kmaw language, became lieutenant governor of Nova Scotia in the 1760s, and during the American Revolution was the provincial Indian commissioner. Murdoch remained sceptical that the chief ever owned a brick residence: "This may have been somewhat exaggerated," he reflected, "as I never saw any traces in the place of brick or stone building." He was willing to concede, however, that "the fish and fur trade in those days was extensive, and Penall may have also had some gratuities from the government," grateful for his past military service.[4]

Possible Origins of "Argomartin"

In the 1920s a well-known Mi'kmaw storyteller, Jerry Lonecloud, told Harry Piers, curator of the Nova Scotia Museum, that Bernard Argomartin had two names, "El-go-mard-dinip" (Argomartin) and "André Martin," the name of an Indigenous interpreter who in 1749 lived at Cobequid. Lonecloud pointed out that "André Martin," when spoken by a Mi'kmaq person, sounds similar to "Argomartin."[5] He also recounted an intriguing tale about El-go-mard-dinip, who in his earlier years camped on Indian Point, near French Village on St. Margaret's Bay. When a Spanish

170

ship sailed too close to the Mi'kmaw encampment, El-go-mard-dinip and his band captured, ransacked, and burned the vessel, killed its crew, and buried its cargo of gold bullion in a crevice on a nearby island.[6] Lonecloud failed to specify whether the gold was ever retrieved.

A second suggestion regarding the origin of the Argomartin name comes from ethnohistorian Ruth Holmes Whitehead, who posits that "Argomartin" may be a variant of "Argim8" ("Argimeau," "Argimault"), which she holds derives from *L'kimu*, meaning "he sends" (implying that the name's bearer had aptitude as a visionary and spiritual messenger).[7] Joseph Argimault was a noted late-seventeenth-century head chief from the Chignecto Isthmus area. A third possibility is that "Argomartin" derives from "Talgoumatique," a Mi'kmaw surname found at Cape Sable in the early 1700s. Louis Talgoumatique and his wife Marie Agathe appear on a 1708 French census and their son, Michel Argomartin, who was born in 1708, became a Cape Sable chief.[8] In 1760 Michel sent a delegate, François Shagwaough (or Chegua), to Halifax to engage the British in peace making negotiations.[9] That Bernard Argomartin had kin connections to André Martin of Cobequid or to Chief Argimault of Chignecto cannot be confirmed by documentary evidence. It seems likely, however, that Bernard and Michel Argomartin were related, with Michel possibly being Bernard Argomartin's father.

The End of the Seven Years' War to the Close of the War of 1812

During the spring and fall, Bernard Argomartin and his group occupied salmon, gaspereau, and eel fishing sites along the Gould River – renamed the Gold River in 1800 – and known to the Mi'kmaq as Amagapslegek, or "Rocky River."[10] During the summer, they either camped at La Have, Lunenburg County, or on the shores of St. Margaret's Bay, in Halifax County. The upper reaches of the La Have River gave them access to portage routes and trails, by which they reached Annapolis Royal in a matter of days. Their winter hunting territories lay between Hammonds Plains, near Halifax, and St. Margaret's Bay.[11]

They also made periodic trips to Halifax and the Eastern Shore. On 28 June 1769 Chief Argomartin and his wife, Isabelle Angelique Nankout (Knockwood), brought an infant son, Joseph, to be baptized by Abbé Charles-François Bailly at Chezzetcook, east of Halifax.[12] Bailly recently had been appointed to serve the Mi'kmaq and Acadians returning from exile. Pennel (Bernard) and Isabelle had been waiting six years to participate in Roman Catholic sacraments, as the Mi'kmaq's previous missionary, Abbé Pierre Maillard, died in 1762 and, despite official promises, was not replaced until 1768. The couple already had a son, John Pennel, born in 1746 and thus twenty-three years older than Joseph. They also had a son named Francis (c.1750–c.1840) as well as several daughters, one of whom was named Mary.[13]

When big game declined dramatically in the late eighteenth century, Bernard and his family had to seek ammunition and provisions at Windsor or Halifax to tide them over the winter. Chief Argomartin's name appears in requisition books kept during the mid-1790s by the provincial Indian commissioner, George Henry Monk.[14] Though the Mi'kmaq still regarded the articles they received from the government as tokens of continued appreciation for their past military service, Britain had begun to view its former Indigenous military allies to little more than tiresome dependents upon the provincial purse.[15] The elderly chief often travelled to Windsor with a younger associate, Philip Bernard of St. Margaret's Bay. After 1796, however, his son John obtained goods under his own name.[16] John's independence in this respect suggests that Chief Argomartin had transferred some of his leadership duties to his oldest son, who probably cared for his elderly father. John's brother Francis appears in the documentary record in the early 1800s, although Joseph, baptized in 1769, does not appear on requisition lists, and may have died at a young age.[17]

John and Francis dropped "Argomartin" as their surname and replaced it with their father's first name, "Pennel." A nominal census taken in this year at Gold River described Chief Argomartin as the leader of a group of twenty-one Mi'kmaw individuals, most with the surname "Penall" (Pennel). There were five family heads: Penall Halgomartin (Argomartin), John Penall, Francis Penall, Joseph Quarrett (Momquarret or Momcharret), and Peter Docomaw. The last two men presumably were sons-in-law of the chief.[18] When a virulent smallpox epidemic spread along the Atlantic coast in 1801, this group obtained supplies and medical assistance from the government.[19] Six years later, the province appointed Major Thompson of Chester, as well as several local merchants, to provide supplies to the Mi'kmaq whenever the government deemed it necessary, though it appears that Argomartin's band only ever received minimal help from these sources.[20]

By 1800, an influx of settlers of Loyalist and Germanic extraction into coastal Lunenburg County compelled the chief and his sons to petition for secure title to their fishing grounds at the mouth of the Gold River. Since Bernard Argomartin's travelling companion, Philip Bernard, had received a large freehold grant at the Head of St. Margaret's Bay in 1786 from Lieutenant Governor John Parr, Argomartin and his son John decided to petition the government for land at Gold River on the same terms.[21]

They found their initial efforts thwarted for over a decade, since the land they wanted lay within the compass of a vast grant extending from Chester to Gold River allocated in 1765 to a Congregationalist minister, the Reverend John Seccombe, and his associates. As long as the land forming the Seccombe grant lacked settlers, the Mi'kmaq were free to pursue the same seasonal economic round they had since the early 1700s. In 1810, however, the Seccombe tract came up for forfeiture, owing to its unimproved state and to circulating allegations that Seccombe, at the height of the American Revolution, had shown sympathy for the rebel cause.[22] After this series of revelations the Mi'kmaq's situation radically changed. Settlers from Lunenburg and Chester jockeyed for tracts along the west, or seaward, side of the Gold River. In consequence, Chief Argomartin and his son John began lobbying the government in Halifax. In 1810 the chief petitioned Charles Morris, the surveyor general of Crown lands, for a tract "up the Gold River" on which to begin a farm. They asked that the land be secured "wholly and exclusively" for the benefit of "their posterity in perpetuity."[23] This request apparently landed on deaf ears in Halifax, despite Chief Bernard's earlier success at acquiring five hundred acres on the shores of St. Margaret's Bay. By contrast, Argomartin's people were told that no land in their quarter remained ungranted.[24] Even after Reverend Seccombe and his associates relinquished their proprietary rights to the vast tract extending to the Gold River area, Morris remarked somewhat desultorily in 1810 to Joseph Crandle, a Baptist reverend located at Chester, that a Mi'kmaq named "Panhorne" had "made an application for lands near where they are settled at Chester [sic, Gold River]." Morris doubted if much would come of it, but stated

he would pass on the application to the lieutenant governor, Sir George Prevost.[25] The Mi'kmaq would not receive a response to their petition from the Crown Lands Department for eight more years.

While they waited, Chief Argomartin and John Pennel launched a campaign to obtain farm equipment and building materials so they could begin farming. They first approached Abbé Jean-Mandé Sigogne, a Roman Catholic missionary headquartered in the District of Clare, Digby County. Sigogne had arrived in Nova Scotia in 1799 but since then had become so involved in assisting the Shubenacadie band with their farming endeavours that the Pennels next turned to Captain Walter Bromley, former paymaster of the 23rd Regiment of the Welsh Fusiliers, who devoted his retirement years to humanitarian objectives.[26] In 1813 Bromley envisioned developing what he called "settlement asylums" for the Mi'kmaq and Malecite, where the Indigenous peoples could learn to plant and harvest, become educated, and pursue training in the trades.[27] The Gold River community felt they might find a sympathetic ear in Bromley, and invited him to survey the tract they hoped to obtain. The intensification of the War of 1812, however, precluded executive action respecting the granting of land or the provision of seeds and farming equipment.

By this time John Pennel Sr. had three sons: a married son named Joseph; a younger still-unwed son, John Jr.; and James, who was around two years of age. Pennel also had several daughters, one of whom, Magdalene, married a *métis* man from the Gaspé named Thomas Hammond at the close of the war.

A Tale of a *Métis* Deserter

The story of how Magdalene Pennel's family first met Thomas Hammond on Hammonds Plains has all the trappings of a storybook romance. Early in the War of 1812 two youths, Thomas Cotton and one of Cotton's relatives,[28] were conscripted at the Gaspé into the service of the British navy to serve as crew aboard the captured American brig, *Jane*.[29] When this brig anchored in Lunenburg Harbour in 1813, both men escaped and fled east along the coast. Near Blockhouse, Cotton fled into the woods and later, after changing his surname to "Hallamore," lived out the rest of his days at New Cornwall, Lunenburg County, where he married and raised a family.[30] The other deserter continued walking until, in the early dawn hours, he reached Chief John Pennel's camp on Hammonds Plains. The Mi'kmaw leader, seeing two men from the distant warship running to catch up with the deserter, immediately told him to hide beneath a pile of blankets at the back of Pennel's wigwam while he devised a clever bluff to put the pursuers off the track of their quarry. When the two men from the ship arrived, they and the chief conversed briefly in French.[31] Pennel declared that he would feel gravely insulted if the search party searched his dwelling, and to lend emphasis to his words he took up his tomahawk and brandished it. Finally, he "struck the ground and said, "Well, you may search the camp, – but if you find he is not here – and I can tell you he is not – I will kill you both with my tomahawk for not believing me.""[32]

Pennel's ruse worked, and the members of the search party set off towards the east. After their departure, John led the man who had been hiding under his pile of furs to a house belonging to "Mrs. Mason located near the French village, at the Head of St. Margaret's Bay." This woman was the wife of George Frédéric Mason, one of the original settlers at what is now Mason's Point.[33] Mrs. Mason thought it best to conceal the deserter's identity by giving him the name "Thomas Hammond," appropriate since he had been found on "Hammonds Plains." While Hammond complied with this directive, he wanted it known than that he was of *métis* descent, being the son of an Englishman from Marlow in Buckinghamshire, England, and a woman of Mi'kmaw and French ancestry from the Gaspé region. Hammond and Magdalene Pennel were married around 1815.[34] Hammond was an intelligent person, fluent in French, English, and Mi'kmaq and likely also literate to some degree. He was to prove an invaluable assistant to Chief Pennel in his father-in-law's later campaigns to secure land from the government.[35]

The Gold River Farming and Fishing Community

Following the resumption of peace in 1814, the colonial government for six years was sympathetic to the Indigenous land campaign. Since the Pennel family was claiming territorial aegis over the entire Gold River system, they at first objected to the settlement in 1816 of New Ross, a community lying thirty kilometres upriver from the Atlantic coast. Their opposition ebbed, however, when Captain William Ross, the settlement's founder, welcomed them into his home and regaled them with tunes on his violin. According to a story that folklorist Helen Creighton recorded in 1949 from Captain Burt Ross, William Ross's grandson, when William Ross died suddenly in 1822, leaving his widow Mary and her children on the brink of destitution, the Gold River Mi'kmaq brought them food. One particular day, as Mary Ross wondered how she could continue to feed her children, she heard a knock on the window. It was the Pennels, carrying "four or five salmon" for her family's dinner.[36]

When Bernard Argomartin died at age ninety-five in 1817, his seventy-two-year-old son John Pennel Sr. succeeded him as Gold River chief.[37] More determined than ever, Pennel sought to establish a claim to his family's traditional fishing and hunting territory along the Gold River. In 1813, deeming the time ripe for yet another petition to Halifax, John Pennel Sr., Thomas Hammond, and thirty-nine other Mi'kmaw family heads drafted a document asking for acreage along the Gold River and directed it to Lord Dalhousie, the lieutenant-governor.[38] Appeals from both Sigogne and Bromley on behalf of the Gold River Mi'kmaq also crossed Dalhousie's desk. All these memorials received executive attention, for once Bromley had assured the Mi'kmaq that any assistance would not be contingent on their conversion to Protestantism, the government allocated £250, a substantial sum at the time, to foster Mi'kmaw farming settlements at both Gold River and Shubenacadie. It also began to consider carving a parcel for the Mi'kmaq out of a corner of the Seccombe grant, which since 1765 had been only minimally improved. Bolstered by this encouraging news from Halifax, the Mi'kmaq went to work with a will. Bromley noted with satisfaction that, with his encouragement, the Gold River group by the end of 1818 had cleared and planted six acres of cropland.

The legislative grant provided monies to erect two wooden frame houses, each with a loft that functioned as an attic for storage. The first house, built for John Pennel Sr., his wife, two sons, and several daughters, was situated on the interval between the Atlantic shoreline and the east bank of the Gold River. At the time John Sr. and his wife had two sons, Joseph (c.1814–c.1876, nicknamed "Joe Goose") and John Jr. (c.1820–c.1860), living with them. One of the chief's grown daughters, Magdalene, who as mentioned above was Thomas Hammond's wife, had temporarily moved to Shubenacadie with her husband. Another, Elizabeth, wed John Newel and

Main Family Heads Examined in This Chapter

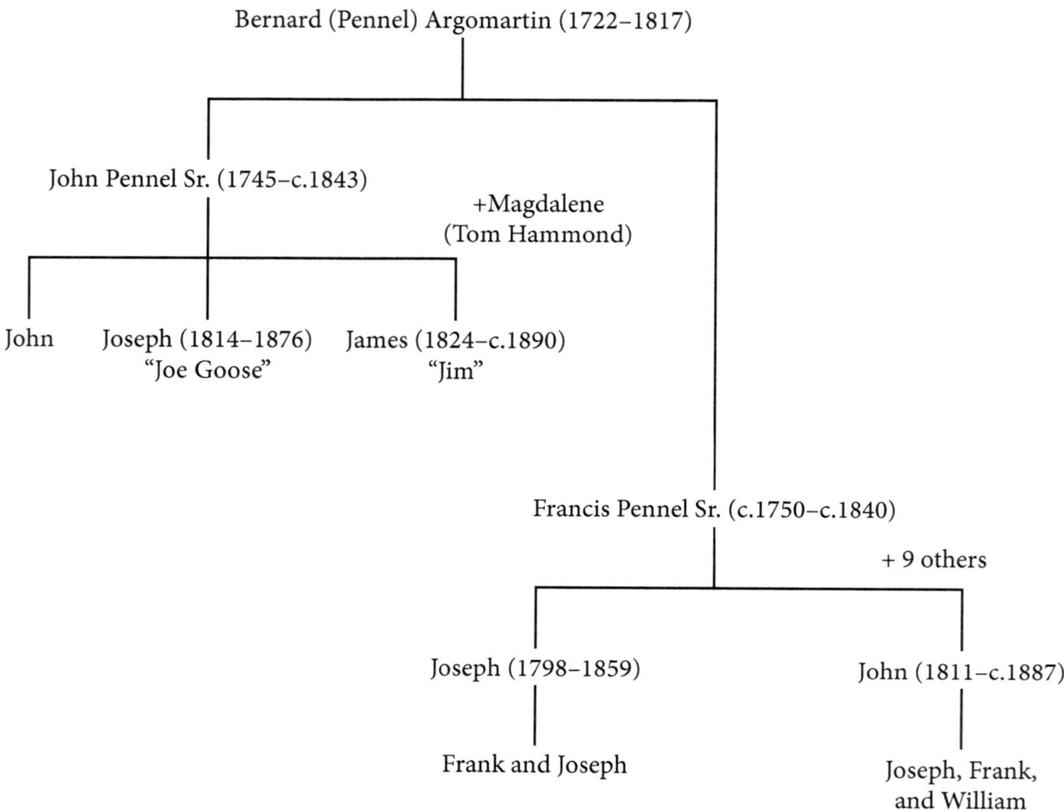

lived nearby. A third daughter, Catherine, though unwed in 1818, would marry Francis Paul Caninic (or Kininick) of East River, near Chester, in the 1830s.[39]

The second frame house was erected upland of the Gold River for Francis Pennel, his wife, and their large family, including Joseph (1798–1859), Newel (c.1790–c.1860), "Tall Peter" (c.1800–c.1865), and seven-year-old John (1811–87). Their structure was the more elaborate of the two, with a stone chimney and a central iron stove.[40] Francis's wife, who was either Acadian or Germanic, kept the house well swept and organized and proudly displayed a china set when guests came to visit.[41]

New Germany, 1850–1870

The chief received a plough, spades, hoes, equipment to harvest hay, and seed potatoes. Though John

Pennel Sr. much preferred living in a bark wigwam, he tried to placate Bromley and his humanitarian associates by moving into his house, clearing a few acres of land on the interval, and planting hay and potatoes. The interval was the only spot at the mouth of Gold River where the soil had much depth. The upland, where Francis's house stood on the west side of the river, was hilly, rocky, and covered with scrub bush. In response to the chief's and Thomas Hammond's repeated, importunate requests, part of the Seccombe grant was made available near the mouth of the Gold River and returned to the province for the use of the Mi'kmaq. In 1820 a plan of a thousand-acre reserve was drafted on paper, in keeping with a government directive to put aside one thousand acres of land in each county for the Mi'kmaw population. Originally intended to encompass land on both sides of the Gold River, this reserve was confirmed by an order-in-council designating it the possession of Chief John Pennel and his band.[42] It was not the freehold grant for which Pennel and Hammond had petitioned, and its boundaries would not be run on the ground until 1852.[43] Consequently, for years its lines and extent remained ambiguous. Joseph Howe, provincial Indian commissioner in 1842 and 1843, believing that the government had acted on its 1820 intention to reserve one thousand acres in Lunenburg County, held that the tract covered "960 acres [of upland] on the west side of the Gold River, with an additional 41 acres forming the interval, lying near the post road bridge," on the river's east bank. According to Howe, the reserve was 1,001 acres in size.[44]

With Chief John Pennel's encouragement, the Gold River Mi'kmaq tried to work the land. When the government provided a few head of cattle, they built two barns and harvested six acres of hay each year to be stored during the winter to feed their livestock. It was not long, however, before Tom Hammond, feeling slighted at not receiving government aid like his in-laws, and having to wrestle a living from the stony, unforgiving soil near the mouth of Gold River, moved to Shubenacadie, where Bromley was also establishing a farming settlement.[45] Following his marriage to Magdalene Penall (Pennel) around 1815, he stayed away until the spring of 1823 when, perhaps because his wife missed her kinfolk, he returned to Lunenburg County. After eleven years of raising crops along the Atlantic coast, he began farming in 1832 at New Germany. Soon afterwards he persuaded the provincial surveyor general, Charles Morris, to lay out fifty acres of farmland for him along the east branch of the La Have River. From then on, he and Magdalene only went to Gold River for short periods to visit her kin.[46] When he discovered that the Crown Lands Office had failed to confirm the surveyed plot as a land grant, for over four years he fruitlessly petitioned the government to rectify the situation. Meanwhile, he built a house and outbuildings on his plot, cleared additional land, and raised hay, potatoes, and garden produce, some of which he sold. Seeing Hammond's accomplishments, several of his sons-in-law settled alongside him and also established farms, so by the 1850s the locale boasted a small but flourishing farming community. For over thirty years the land it was situated on was known informally as the New Germany Reserve. Finally, long after Tom Hammond's death, a tract of 953 acres was officially set off in 1880 by Charles Morris's son, Surveyor General

John Spry Morris, for the community's members and confirmed as Indian Reserve 19A.[47]

Commissioner Howe's Visit

The political reformer and journalist Joseph Howe, who was provincial Indian commissioner in 1842 and 1843, visited Gold River in fall 1842. Almost immediately after arriving, he learned that all the Pennels he met were sons and daughters of Chief Bernard Argomartin, who had died in 1817. He also was told that one of Argomartin's sons, Francis, had recently died.[48] John, Francis's older brother, meanwhile was rivalling his father's longevity. Born in 1745, he was now in his late eighties. Of Argomartin's daughters, only one, Mary, was still alive, though "blind and helpless." Mary's husband and children were dead.[49]

Howe had been informed that the Gold River settlement comprised the only Mi'kmaw farming community between Halifax and Liverpool, and that houses had been built for two of Chief Argomartin's sons. He noted with chagrin, however, that only Francis's house was still occupied. Chief John Pennel Sr. and his family were camped at "a very productive eel weir" on the Gold River.[50] Three of John Sr.'s sons – Joseph (c.1814–c.1876), John Jr. (c.1820–c.1860), and James (1824–90) – lived with him, though as it was the fall season Joseph was away hunting when the commissioner arrived. James, a youth of eighteen, was also absent, and may have joined Joseph in the woods. John Jr. was assisting his elderly father at the fish weir. In conversing with John Jr., who spoke some English, Howe learned that the chief's house had been turned into a hay barn. Its foundation was severely damaged in an attempt to move it on skids from the interval to the upland on the opposite side of the river. The chief probably decided to relocate his dwelling when settlers encroached on his fields near the river's mouth and along the ocean front. He still grazed a few cattle and put up hay each fall to feed them, which he stored in the attic of his old house. He, by choice, lived in a wigwam.

Howe felt this was a retrograde step, so as an incentive to John Sr. and his family, he promised to furnish monies to make the chief's damaged house habitable once again. Whether these repairs encouraged the elderly chief to move back into the frame structure remains doubtful, however, since after his death around 1843 his sons vacated the reserve and moved upriver to New Germany to join Tom Hammond and his family. The only intact frame house in 1842 belonged to Francis's widow. Her son, John, occupied the dwelling after her death around 1856 and, according to historian M.B. Desbrisay, still lived in it in 1868.[51]

In autumn 1842 Francis Pennel's widow invited Howe to spend a night at her abode and to have breakfast with her the next morning. Her house stood in the midst of cabins and wigwams built by her sons Joseph (1798–1859), Newel (c.1800–c.1865), "Tall Peter" (c.1810–65), and John (1811–87). Howe praised her home's "cheerful, obliging and hospitable atmosphere." As she was elderly, her house was not as tidy as it had been when her husband was alive, but Howe still remarked on its cleanliness, which he felt surpassed many a settler's abode. He especially enjoyed talking with her sons Joseph and John and was particularly taken with "Joe," whom he considered a "smart young fellow, neatly dressed."[52] When Joseph told Howe he wanted to build a new barn, the commissioner promised to supply him with nails and hinges.[53] Joseph and John had mastered the art of fly fishing and ran a guiding operation. Howe recognized that the two men had carved out a unique entrepreneurial niche for themselves, by blending their traditional Mi'kmaw salmon-fishing knowledge with the latest fly-fishing techniques. Sportspeople flocked to the Pennels' community each year owing to their adeptness at fly fishing, which, Howe stressed, was practised by the Mi'kmaq inhabitants of Gold River and "nowhere else."[54]

Although the commissioner noted that attention to agricultural pursuits had waned at Gold River, since only an acre of potatoes was cultivated by the community in 1842, he also journeyed to New Germany, where he praised the farming practices carried on by Tom Hammond and his sons. "With some exertion, and some occasional aid this settlement may be enlarged, and much improved," he mused, "especially given the good many children and young people about it." Despite appearances, he also hoped that agriculture might be revived at Gold River, and suggested a monetary infusion to get things moving in that direction. "About £25 laid out judiciously at Gold River would lead to greater shows of industry and enterprise," he proclaimed. Before he left Lunenburg County, Howe sought out the Reverend Joseph Dimock, a Baptist minister at Chester, whom he appointed to act as a liaison between the local Mi'kmaw community and the Indian Affairs commissioner's

office.[55] He also contacted David Killiard, a Chester schoolmaster, whom he directed to go to Gold River and teach the Mi'kmaw children "the importance of acquiring the rudiments of our language and some acquaintance with arithmetic."[56]

Years of Change, 1845–1870

Howe's interest in preserving the Aboriginal land base and his infusion of money beneficially affected the Gold River Mi'kmaw settlement for a few years, since agricultural efforts increased and small cabins and barns came to dot the west side of the river.[57] In 1845 a Wesleyan missionary by the name of Charles Churchill described passing over the bridge at Gold River to find a few Mi'kmaw "cottages surrounded by small patches of cultivated ground."[58] Yet this impetus to farm would not last. Beginning late in 1845, a blight destroyed the potato crop, followed by a virulent disease epidemic that devastated fledging Mi'kmaw farming communities throughout the province. After Chief John Pennel Sr.'s death around 1843, just prior to the onslaught of these scourges, his sons Joseph and James gave up trying to wrest a living from the land and relied exclusively on hunting, fishing, guiding, harvesting logs for sale, and making and peddling baskets and other wooden items.

There were other major changes as well. The younger generation of Pennels and their relatives, the Hammonds, faced a shrinking pool of marriageable partners. Until the late 1820s the Gold River Mi'kmaq had drawn their spouses from a sizable band near La Have. In 1784 two head men belonging to this group, "Soulnow Geremy" (Solomon Jeremy) and Joseph Glode, petitioned Halifax for a land grant for their people on the upper La Have River. Despite the government's allocation of a licence of occupation to these men soon afterwards, as late as 1830 the La Have band still lacked secure title to their land, and most of its members moved south into Queens and Shelburne Counties.[59]

On 26 December 1850 John Pennel Sr.'s son Joseph, or Joe Goose, wed Sophia Rafuse (1825–c.1876) of Gold River.[60] Sophia was a daughter of Johannes George Rafuse (1795–1875) and Maria Elizabeth Louisa Kaiser.[61] In 1851 John Hammond, Joseph's brother-in-law, wed Sophia's sister, Susanna Rafuse (1828–c.1860).[62] In December of the same year, when he was forty years of age, Francis Pennel's son John wed Marion Barbara Rafuse, a daughter of Johannes

Daniel Rafuse and Margaret Adams of Martin's River.[63] Johannes Daniel Rafuse (1788–c.1877) was the older brother of Johannes George Rafuse.[64] John Pennel Jr. endeavoured to farm similar to his in-laws, who were early settlers along the South Shore.[65] Though he faced economic challenges, his hard work usually paid off, and his and Barbara's union proved to be a stable and long lasting one.

John and Barbara raised their family in Francis Pennel's old house on the Gold River Reserve. By contrast, John's first cousin Joe Goose and his wife Sophia, sometimes accompanied by John Hammond and Sophia's sister Susanna, embarked on a peripatetic lifestyle, peddling baskets and other wooden manufactured items along the road between Bridgewater and New Germany.[66] Joseph and Sophia returned each fall to New Germany, where many of their sons and daughters, as well as their grandchildren, married non-Indigenous settlers.[67] Some remained at New Germany; others settled on the Wildcat River Reserve in Queens County, and others went to Shelburne County.[68]

New Challenges from Timber and Mining Interests

Until the late 1850s the Pennels' angling operations brought a degree of affluence to the Mi'kmaw community. After this date commercial interests vied with one another to strip the Gold River reserve of its valuable marketable resources. Gold miners found gold-bearing seams along the river, and loggers eyed the area's rich timber reserves. Both interests looked at harnessing the river's water power. One local entrepreneur, E. Macdonald, even contended that Seccombe's heirs had never deeded their father's grant back to the province, so essentially the Mi'kmaw people remained squatters.[69] Tension between the Indigenous population and Macdonald came to a head when Macdonald built a dam and sawmill on the west side of Gold River, and a small party of Mi'kmaq threatened to burn the mill down.

Francis Pennel's son Joseph (1798–1859) rose as chief at Gold River following John Pennel Sr.'s death around 1843. Joseph was apprehensive about the violence that might erupt should Macdonald and his associates continue to ignore Mi'kmaw rights to local lands and resources. John Pennel Sr.'s youngest son, James, one of the Mi'kmaw camp vehemently opposed to Macdonald, blatantly defied Joseph's

leadership by wanting to take matters into his own hands. In frustration, Joseph directed a petition to the lieutenant governor, Major General John Gaspard Le Marchant, asking for clarification regarding his people's tenure to the reserve and its resources. "The sounds of whites are [heard] in every direction," he complained. "I take my pen in hand to let you know that the people about Gold River are cutting wood and destroying it … I have the right to the land I live on; now I want to ask you if I have a right or any possession to live on that land, and … please see the Member of the House of Assembly about it. Some [commercial interests] say they have a grant of this land, but we have not seen it and we want to know if it is true."[70]

Pennel's inquiries prompted the first actual survey of the Gold River Reserve.[71] Conducted by John Spry Morris in 1852, it replicated the dimensions contained in Joseph Howe's 1843 description of the reserve, rather than in Charles Morris's 1820 account of the tract. Howe had maintained that the reserve embraced 960 acres on the west side of the river and 41 acres on the east side.[72] The resultant survey therefore enclosed a parcel of 1,001 acres.[73] In 1843 Howe also had estimated that the entire reserve tract was not worth more than £350, but with the discovery of gold its value soared. In June 1861 prospectors Daniel Dimock and David Whitfield from Chester confirmed the presence of gold in quartz-bearing rocks along the river, precipitating a local gold rush. Tailings from stamp mills soon polluted the river, while the incessant pounding drove away animals. Moose and other big game also grew scarce owing to logging parties working in the woods. Faced with these challenges, Joseph Pennel contemplated two lines of action: he mainly wanted to escape the onerous burdens of leadership and live apart on his farm on the upper reaches of the Gold River, but he also felt he could not relinquish his responsibility towards his people.

The situation grew particularly severe for members of the Pennel family who still lived primarily by hunting and fishing. Lack of food ushered in disease, especially tuberculosis. Two of Joseph's brothers, Tall Peter and Newel, died, and their bodies were interred around 1865 in the ancient Mi'kmaw cemetery on Indian Point, near Oakland on Mahone Bay.[74] By this time the local salmon fishery had also failed, as sawmills and gold mining sheds, at the while pouring toxic effluents into the river, jockeyed for space along the shoreline. To escape the dismal economic prospects that faced him, since guiding no longer proved a viable option, John Pennel Sr.'s son Joseph (Joe Goose) drank heavily, and inebriation and hunger made him vulnerable to illness.

Once an integral part of Gold River's guiding business, Joseph Pennel by the mid-1860s was reduced to relying on the proceeds of the peripatetic basketmaking industry. He and his wife Sophia Rafuse watched helplessly as, one by one, their youngest children succumbed to pulmonary tuberculosis. When Joseph himself contracted tuberculosis around 1870, he displayed a bittersweet sense of humour in the face of his difficulties. According to Jerry Lonecloud, Joseph, on being arrested for public drunkenness in Yarmouth, once asked the local magistrate, Nathan Hilton, to give him a chit showing he had paid the required fine. He needed the receipt, Joe said, since he might die and he needed to prove he had paid his debt. Otherwise, St. Peter at the Pearly Gates might say, "You have to go get a receipt from Judge Hilton, and how could a poor Indian go all over Hell to find Judge Hilton!"[75]

A far grimmer account, describing Joseph's and his wife's demise, was told to Harry Piers of the Nova Scotia Museum by an elderly woman who had attended Joseph's funeral in 1876. Joseph and his wife must have collapsed, owing to a combination of illness, fatigue, and exposure, after walking for miles peddling their wares. Their bodies were found, lying side by side, near the foundation of an old church about four miles below Conquerall Bank, "on the south side, near Bridgewater." Their kin carried their remains to West La Have, where the interment of their bodies constituted the first burials in the recently consecrated soil of St. Peter's Parish cemetery.[76]

The Pennel Reserve on Wallabeck Lake

Joseph Pennel, Gold River's chief in the early 1850s, and his younger brother John had derived income for over two decades from their mastery of the sport of angling. By the time of their father Francis Pennel's death around 1840, they were the two most sought after fishing guides in Lunenburg County,[77] escorting government officials, military personal, and prominent Halifax merchants on fishing expeditions up the Gold River.[78] Joseph personally guided Captain William Chearnley, Nova Scotia's Indian commissioner

from 1853 to 1862. He also accompanied Joseph Howe and two brothers, George and Henry Piers, members of the Halifax merchant family to which Harry Piers, the curator of the Nova Scotia Museum, also belonged.[79] All four sportsmen viewed Joseph as a trusted and respected associate on the water and in the woods.[80] Guiding granted Joseph a measure of economic stability, and in difficult times he could retreat to the woods, where he subsisted on fish and potatoes grown on small plots in the bush.[81] Solitude provided respite from the strains and stresses of leading fishing and hunting expeditions and renewed his energies. When he died in 1859, Joseph's reputation as a noted fishing and moose-hunting guide outlasted him for over half a century.[82]

As early as 1853, however, Joseph suffered deaths of close family members as well as other personal losses, and his family had begun to feel the pinch of poverty.[83] He had lost his first wife, Mary Alexis, and only one child, a daughter, remained living. Several of his brothers also had died.[84] His earlier aspirations to establish a strong economic base for Gold River founded on the guiding industry were dashed in the mid-1850s when a swarm of commercial interests set out to extract the reserve's most marketable resources.[85] The provincial government lacked the muscle to prosecute persons and businesses that encroached on the reserve after 1852, even though a legal survey of the reserve's boundaries had been completed. Chearnley suggested that trespassers should pay for the plots on which they encroached, but this option was deemed too difficult and costly for the government to enforce. James B. Uniacke, the superintendent of Crown lands, wanted to eject squatters by having a special law passed for the purpose. Yet despite Uniacke's recommendations, no punitive action for infringements on Aboriginal lands and resources at Gold River was undertaken prior to 1860.[86]

The chief toyed with the two lines of action open to him – escaping the burdens of chiefship vs. maintaining his responsibility to his people – but discovered he could pursue neither satisfactorily. Whenever he became disillusioned in the late 1830s and 1840s with life at the mouth of the Gold River, he moved upriver to a projection of land lying between the west end of Wallabeck Lake and Camp Lake, not far from New Ross.[87] He stayed at this locale for nine years, during which time he built a log house, cleared land, and grew potatoes and other crops. The insecurity of his tenure to his farm became blatantly clear, however, when in 1845 he temporarily returned to Gold River to see to problems his people wanted him to address, and a man named Hiscock trespassed by planting on his fields.[88] In February 1853 he wrote Halifax to have Hiscock removed, adding despondently that, as all his adult children were dead, it was difficult for him to confront the trespasser on his own. He further stressed that since logging had destroyed the salmon fishery on the reserve that his people had been "given forty years ago," the Mi'kmaq needed additional land further up the La Have River, at New Germany.[89]

In the late 1830s Joseph Pennel had dreamt of saving enough money by guiding to buy one hundred acres at Wallabeck Lake, where he could live out his last days. The land around Wallabeck Lake had wood for making baskets, axe handles, and other wooden implements, an occupation he could pursue in addition to farming as he grew older.[90] Fifty-five years old in 1853, he wanted to retire from continuously contacting the provincial authorities for one thing or another on behalf of his group. When he recognized that he could not amass sufficient funds to purchase the property he wanted, he, with the assistance of Lieutenant Colonel George Bayers, whom he had guided on hunting and fishing expeditions, petitioned Lieutenant Governor John Gaspard Le Marchant for a Crown grant.[91] Joseph drew on what he knew of Pennel family history to bolster his application. His grandfather, he contended, had "settled at Gold River nearly one hundred years ago." He implied that Bernard Argomartin had been vested by the British with some sort of entitlement to land at the mouth of the Gold River as early as 1760.[92] Then, in a different vein, he explained that his second wife, Marian Louisa Labrador, wanted "to live like a white" and had pressed him to gain freehold control of his Wallabeck Lake property. His youngest children, he continued, "were anxious to adopt the same pursuits of life as that formerly engaged in by their mother."[93]

The executive council in Halifax agreed to give Pennel land but not in the form of a freehold grant. Instead, Joseph's importunate appeal to the lieutenant governor resulted in the survey and confirmation on 3 March 1854 of a 107-acre tract on Wallabeck Lake, later designated as Pennel Indian Reserve No. 19.[94] As soon as the reserve was surveyed, Joseph and two of his sons, Frank and James, both under twelve years of age, began cutting timber so rapidly that by 1855 a rectangular clear-cut swath extended back from the lakeshore into the surrounding forest. By that time Joseph's best guiding days lay far behind him. In 1855 he fell ill and continued to suffer ill health until his death four years later. William Chearnley, who had accompanied Joseph on numerous hunting expeditions, erected a gravestone over Joseph's gravesite in St. Augustine's Roman Catholic cemetery in Chester. In a vein both laudatory and humorous, Chearnley's inscription on the stone, which adopted the nineteenth-century spelling of Joseph's surname, purported to assuage the fears of local wildlife by announcing the death of the famous hunter and guide:

In Memory of Joseph Penall, Indian,
by William Chearnley, A.D. 1859.
Gone to death's call is Indian Joe.
Moose-deer, rejoice
Here buried, rests your deadliest foe.[95]

The Hammonds and Pennels of New Germany

The original occupants of the New Germany tract, Thomas Hammond (c.1772–c.1860) and Magdalene Pennel (c.1800–c.1846), raised five children: John, Tom Jr., Frank, Hannah, and Lewis.[96] Many of the younger generation of Hammonds married non-Indigenous spouses. For instance, John Hammond (1824–1918) wed Susanna Rafuse and raised four daughters: Angeline (1848–1915), Agnes (1850–1919), Mary Ellen (1852–1931), and Teresa (1854–1937). Angeline in 1872, married Charles Foster, who according to oral tradition was raised by a Mi'kmaw woman from Annapolis County named Molly Glode, who afterwards lived with the Fosters at New Germany until her death. John and Susanna's second daughter, Agnes, around 1873 wed Ozias Beeler from Annapolis County.[97] Mary Ellen married Samuel Dorey (or Dares) from Newburne, Lunenburg County, in 1875,[98] and in 1872 Teresa wed Abenego (or Adelbriezo) Penny from Midville Branch, also in Lunenburg County.[99] These persons' non-Mi'kmaw spouses settled down with their wives on the East Branch of the La Have River. John Hammond himself lived to an advanced age, dying at Gold River in 1918 when he was ninety-four years old.[100]

Thomas Hammond and Magdalene Pennel's second son, Tom Jr., married a Phillips from the Head of St. Margaret's Bay. Their third son, Frank, in 1873 married Cassie Meisner from Baker Settlement in Lunenburg County,[101] while Frank's sister Hannah wed Lewis Phillips and had a son, Lewis Phillips Jr. Louis in turn wed a Mi'kmaw woman and had a son, Noel Phillips, who lived at New Ross.[102] When Tom Hammond's wife Magdalene died around 1846, Tom married a second time to Marie Paul, a woman of Mi'kmaw and French ancestry with whom he had two children, James and Margaret. James married a Paul woman from Shubenacadie whom he brought back to live at New Germany, while Margaret married James Steven Charles from Cape Sable.[103] After Tom Hammond's second wife Marie's death, he wed a third time around 1854 to a woman of Germanic ancestry named Elizabeth Frank, or Franck, and had a daughter Selina and a son Henry.[104] By the time Tom died in his late eighties around 1860, his children had either become core members of or were frequent visitors to a community that in the early twentieth century would be named "Elmwood."[105] Commissioner William Chearnley supported their desire to have secure title to their land along the East Branch of the La Have River by instructing the deputy surveyor, John Spry Morris, to survey a parcel in 1853 of roughly 960 acres for them near Lake Peter.[106]

No attempt was made in 1853 to subdivide this new reserve into farm plots, and not long afterwards, as many of the residents were pursuing agriculture, land disputes arose. John Pennel Sr.'s youngest son, James or "Jim" Pennel (c.1824–c.1890), and his nephews John Hammond (1814–1918) and Lewis Hammond (c.1817–c.1870), opposed subdivision and were often at the centre of community disputes on the subject.[107] James, who was in his thirties during the early 1850s, and John Hammond built log cabins on their plots at New Germany. James wed May Anne Toney (also known as Mary Anne Paul), and one of their daughters, Anne, was born in the farming community in 1856.[108] Yet in 1861, at just over fifty years of age, James decided he no longer wanted to be a farmer and abandoned his homestead and potato field. He tried to log but got into disputes with his neighbours when he cut on their land. To access forests further away, he persuaded his nephews John and Lewis Hammond, their half-brother James Hammond (c.1850–1935), and Tall Peter Pennel[109] to move to an encampment on the upper Gold River, near New Ross, and cut timber for sale.[110] Their decision to live in the woods distressed Commissioner Chearnley, for he felt, as Joseph Howe had before him, that any desire to dwell in bark camps, after living for years in wooden houses, was regressive. After

casting about for an explanation for James's behaviour, Chearnley traced it to the province's reluctance to eject trespassers and supervise a proper division of allotments.[111] On 3 March 1862 the commissioner complained to the provincial secretary's office that at least "three families were about to abandon their grounds from the Boundary line not having been properly defined years ago." The Mi'kmaq felt frustrated by official inaction on the issue and believed they had no option but to move, subject as they were "to all kinds of annoyances by trespassers." Chearnley concluded with a pointed admonition: "This matter was brought to the notice of the proper authorities and still remains unsettled."[112]

In 1862, however, James Hammond suddenly changed his mind and campaigned against moving to New Ross area.[113] Instead, he claimed that a subdivision of the reserve would vest each farmer with a legal title so each could defend his plot against intrusion. That James was pressuring Chearnley to countenance a subdivision brought him into conflict with his half-brothers James and Lewis, but the majority of the residents at New Germany agreed to allow a subdivision of their reserve into ten allotments, from thirty-five to one hundred acres in size. Samuel Dorey's son Pius (or Pyas) Dorey settled on Lot 1, Mary Dorey held Lot 2, and Lots 3, 4, and 5 belonged respectively to Ozias Beeler, Frank Penny, and Abednego Penny. Lot 6 belonged to Bertha McIsaac and George Zink, while John Bartlett (Alexis), originally from Cape Sable, held Lot 7. James Hammond resided on Lot 8. T. Beeler and E. Joudrey shared Lot 9, while Howard Beeler and T. Joudrey settled on Lot 10.[114]

Since James Pennel, John Hammond, and Lewis Hammond had opposed the subdivision, they failed to receive any acreage. Though they could camp in wooded areas or reside with propertied kin, they now were considered landless. James and his nephews apparently were unsuccessful in their logging venture, since they returned to New Germany in 1862. James's Mi'kmaw wife from Shubenacadie died in 1861, and, upon taking up his new allotment at New Germany in 1862, he married Elizabeth Dorey of Newburne, Lunenburg County.[115] Owing to its more tranquil atmosphere, the New Germany farming community underwent a minor revitalization in the late 1860s. Residents engaged in agriculture, hunting, fishing, trapping, guiding, basketmaking, and harvesting timber as before but, intent on having their children educated, they got together and for several years paid a schoolteacher's salary out of their meagre earnings. Lessons were conducted in various people's homes, and not until 1885 did Ottawa supply funds to build a schoolhouse and hire Josephine Wiles as the new school's first teacher. This occurred at the same time the community's land base was officially recognized as New Germany Reserve No.19 A.

After 1862 James Pennel and Mary Anne began travelling up and down the South Shore between Liverpool, in Queens County, and New Germany, pitching their wigwam wherever they could find sufficient fish and game for food and wood for basketmaking. They would return to New Germany for a season, generally in the winter, but since their former garden plot had lain vacant so long, it became assimilated into a neighbouring parcel worked by the Dorey family. When the Pennels stayed at New Germany, they camped on fringe land not used for agricultural purposes. In their late years, they lacked the resources to contribute to paying for the local schoolteacher, so it is doubtful if their youngest children learned to read or write. Several of their older children, however, attended school and were literate.

When Mary Anne Toney died, James Pennel wed a second time, to Elizabeth Dorey. James and his two wives had at least ten children: Anne in 1856, Mary Ellen in 1865, James Jr. in 1867, Marteen (or Mary Magdalene) around 1870, Joseph ("Joe") in 1872 – who became a celebrated fiddler throughout southwestern Nova Scotia – and, between 1873 and 1888, "Tall Peter," Mary, Catherine, Nancy, and Thomas. James and his wife attempted to have their infants baptized soon after their birth at Bridgewater, but this was not always possible. Despite their devotion to the Roman Catholic faith, their peripatetic lifestyle prevented them from readily accessing a priest who could perform the proper sacraments. Though most of their children died young from tuberculosis, several married and had children. Catherine, for instance, married Henry Carver and had two daughters, Josephine and Minnie Naomi.[116] But Joseph Pennel (1872–1950) was the only one who lived to a relatively advanced age. In 1905, at Plympton, Digby County, he wed Mary Christine (or "Kate") Pictou, a daughter of Chief Benjamin Pictou of Lequille, Annapolis County. Joseph and Mary Christine raised three daughters who all died relatively young of tuberculosis.[117]

Luther Roth, an itinerant Lutheran minister sent to serve among the Icelandic settlers of Lunenburg County from 1876 to 1890, devoted an entire chapter of a book that he wrote, entitled *Acadie and the Acadians*, to James Pennel, whom he called "Jim." Roth admired Jim for his dignified bearing, sense of the aesthetic, graciousness towards guests, deep attachment to his Christian faith, love of children and animals, woodworking skills, and hunting and fishing expertise. He described his Mi'kmaw acquaintance as "tall and graceful" and noted that Jim's wife, who likely was Elizabeth Dorey, in her younger days "had been once, no doubt, a beauty."[118] Roth met the Pennels in the spring of 1888, when the Mi'kmaw hunter, basketmaker, and peddler was in his sixties, accompanied by his wife and three children. The Pennels' baby was sick; its parents lovingly tended to the child's needs. Their clean and tidy wigwam displayed a whimsical mix of incongruity and innovation, since Jim had inserted two windows, each "eight inches by ten," in the opposing walls of the dwelling by "securing the glass to the bark with tacks."[119] There also was a camp chest, on which visitors could sit in comfort.

Jim displayed so many unique and diverse facets of character and skill that Roth wanted to get to know him better. He knew from reading Desbrisay's *History of the County of Lunenburg* that the Pennels were descended from a noted late-eighteenth-century chief. There was in Jim's politeness, he mused, a "hauteur that showed the blue blood of the Algonquian chieftain, for he was an Agdamonton and the Agdamonctons had royal blood."[120] Roth asked Pennel to make him a splint basket, which he would collect at a later date. The minister looked forward to spending more time with his Mi'kmaq acquaintance, but when he returned he found that the Pennels' ill baby had died. This event cast such a pall over the family that Roth knew it was out of the question to insist on having a basket made. He also realized that when personal tragedy struck, Jim and his wife were often very much alone.

When their baby died, the Pennels were camped a considerable distance from St. Joseph's parish cemetery in Bridgewater, and Jim had to carry the dead infant in his arms the entire way. As often happened, when he arrived at the parish yard there was no priest to conduct the funeral service. In 1889 St. Joseph's parish, which was still in the process of building a church, was served by an itinerant priest who visited Bridgewater only on occasion.[121] Jim had to dig a hole in the consecrated ground to bury his own child "while his wife repeated over such parts of the burial service as she could."[122]

Following this interment, the Pennels abandoned the campground where Roth used to visit them. The minister met Jim only once more, in 1889. He was driving a gaunt horse pulling a springless, two-wheeled wooden cart with five women crammed together so tightly in the back that they had to wrap their arms around each other to keep from falling out. A few Mi'kmaw men walked on either side of the cart. Roth thought at first that they, like many other people in the vicinity, had been attending an inauguration ceremony for the Nova Scotia Central Railway, which had just completed its line from Middleton in the Annapolis Valley through to Lunenburg by way of Bridgewater. Upon further inquiry, however, he found it was a funeral procession.[123] One of Jim Pennel's brothers, unnamed by Roth, had died, and the mourners were on their way home to New Germany following the funeral service in Bridgewater. Roth knew from Jim's hollow cheeks and his "sunken and bright" eyes that he had consumption. The disease progressed rapidly, and when Jim died a few months later, the minister vented his frustration at mainstream society's inability to prevent such a tragedy. "Is he better off than he was of old?" he fumed; "… It does not look so. And if he be worse now than then, somebody must be to blame."[124]

What Roth did not fathom was the depth of Jim's discouragement at having so many of his dreams destroyed, owing to the radical environmental changes that happened after 1860 at Gold River. Before Jim's final battle with tuberculosis, his increasing despondency stemmed from his inability to become a noted fisher, hunter, and guide like his grandfather, his father, and his paternal first cousin, Joseph. He could not have foreseen that, during the minor gold rush between 1861 and 1885, miners would vie for locations on which to erect stamp mills whose tailings destroyed the angling fishery and whose noise drove away game.[125] Logging camps meanwhile operated further upriver, and dams were built to keep water levels high so that logs could be driven downstream to a steam sawmill that Alexander Chisholm, Alexander Anderson, Ezra Ernest, and Albert H. Zwicker built in 1887 at the mouth of the Gold River. The entry of the resource industries meant the end of a way of life that Jim cherished, and unlike others of his kinsmen, he lacked the means and education effectively to counter these industries and the environmental depredation they caused.

Land and Resource Disputes, 1869–1933

Despite the numerous disruptions caused after 1861 by miners and loggers, Francis Pennel Sr.'s son John Pennel (1811–1887) and his wife Marion Barbara Rafuse stayed at Gold River. Their three sons Joseph Pennel (c.1851–c.1890), Frank Pennel (1853–1920), and William Pennel (1865–1920) sought ways of earning a living without acquiescing to the demands of the formidable commercial interests that often opposed their activities. All three men lived at Gold River where they worked in the local logging industry, maintained small gardens, made wooden manufactures, and continued some fishing and trapping. The salmon and other fish they caught they traded in Chester or at Indian Point on Mahone Bay.[126] Mining pits were being sunk into gold-bearing seams close to their properties, but none of the brothers seemed interested in becoming prospectors, or in trying their own hand at mining, as was the case with some members of the Mi'kmaw Cope and Charles families. The minuscule Mi'kmaw community located on the eastern side of Beech Hill at Gold River, over which John Pennel presided until the late 1880s as unofficial head, by the mid-1890s was little more than a cluster of two or three frame houses, each sheltering one of John Pennel's sons. The old family homestead, built in 1818, was no longer standing. Frank Pennel and his wife, Mary Edna Veinotte, occupied another, smaller frame house and kept up the kitchen garden begun decades before by Frank's grandmother, Mrs. Francis Pennel.[127] Mary Edna cared for her husband's aging parents, and when John Pennel died, aged seventy-six, on 29 March 1887, she and Frank took responsibility for his funeral arrangements. Meanwhile Frank Pennel's two unwed brothers, Joseph and William, resided in separate houses.

Joseph, who had attained an elementary education in his earlier years, spearheaded a campaign upbraiding the federal government for its neglectful attitude towards the Gold River Mi'kmaq since Confederation, and the resulting case ended up at the Supreme Court.[128] Years before, in 1869, the Gold River Mi'kmaw community had directed a petition to the House of Assembly complaining about William Sutherland illicitly cutting timber on their reserve, though the Department of Indian Affairs refused to investigate Sutherland's logging practices for another twenty-six years, and then only when faced with Mi'kmaw legal action. In 1895 Joseph Pennel, angered at the numerous encroachments that had taken place on the reserve without the Mi'kmaq's consent, resorted to legal counsel. Joseph had saved sufficient money from working in logging camps in the United States to hire a Bridgewater lawyer, V.J. Paton, to examine the nature and history of Mi'kmaw land and resource rights on the reserve from a legal perspective. Paton soon found that, while Section 91 of the British North America Act (BNA Act), enacted at Confederation in 1867, vested responsibility for the protection of Indigenous lands and resources in the federal government, Ottawa in 1869 had permitted the province, unbeknownst to the Mi'kmaq, to allocate two mining locations as well as a host of timber tracts to external commercial interests.

A 160-acre parcel on the west bank of the Gold River that once belonged to a part of the old Seccombe grant known as the "old Althorpe location" was allocated to William Sutherland in 1868, who afterwards sold his grant to George A. Heisler.[129] Amos Heisler and his heirs meanwhile received a licence of occupation to the approximately 40 acres covering the interval between the shoreline and the highway where John Pennel Sr.'s house originally stood on the east side of the river in 1818. Sutherland's presence on the reserve proved particularly damaging to the Mi'kmaw seasonal round of activities, as he restricted Mi'kmaw access to the western river bank for fishing and logging. Undoubtedly, Joseph Pennel's campaign was spurred on in part by the untimely deaths of some his older Pennel relatives, among them his father's paternal cousin Jim, who succumbed in 1890 to hunger, cold, and disease brought on by hardships stemming from lack of access to his people's crucial traditional resource sites.

Joseph Pennel showed considerable daring in his responses to encroachments on his group's lands. His lawyer, Paton, legally dislodged one unwanted occupant of the reserve, William Mosher, who in an attempt to harness the river's water power had become embroiled in a controversy over riparian rights. Paton backed Pennel's drive for return of lands taken from the reserve, yet it also was apparent that the interests arrayed against him were extremely aggressive and experienced political lobbyists. Even Joseph Howe, who since the 1840s had known the Pennels personally after he assumed the combined office of minister of the interior and superintendent general of Indian Affairs, seemed powerless by 1871 to stem the tide of land alienation arising from miners willing to fight in

both the public forum and the courts for what they wanted. The Chester businessman E. Macdonald demanded that Howe initiate an inquiry into the viability of Ottawa keeping the Gold River reserve. To back his contentions, Macdonald cited population statistics from an 1852 Indian Affairs report stating that only three Mi'kmaw families, or twelve individuals, lived at Gold River at the time John Spry Morris had conducted his survey. Macdonald claimed the reserve should be extinguished on the basis of these numbers alone; for the federal government to continue maintaining a landholding system that had long ago outlived its usefulness constituted a grave impediment to the future of commercial enterprise along Nova Scotia's South Shore.[130]

Macdonald derided Commissioner Chearnley's willingness in the 1850s to listen sympathetically to Mi'kmaw complaints that they had received no rent from timber mill owners who built on their property. With the rise of the mining boom in the Gold River area, any interest in Mi'kmaw rights was sidelined as miners began poring over the pages of the *Gold Gazette*, published in Halifax, anxious to make their fortunes in the newly opened goldfields. Macdonald countered that it was the Mi'kmaq who should pay rent, something they would be forced to do anyway once they lost their reserve. No part of the Gold River tract they occupied, he claimed, had ever "been deeded back to the government for the use of the Indians by Secomb [*sic*, Seccombe], who held the whole place under a grant 40 years ago." With the Aboriginal title proving so faulty, why need Ottawa spend any time at all considering the claims of men like the Pennels?[131]

In response, Joseph Pennel added another facet to his campaign agenda. In the early 1900s, the Halifax and South Western Railway was in the process of constructing a railway between Halifax and Yarmouth. Pennel wanted to ensure the Mi'kmaq received a monetary return for any reserve property expropriated for the rail line's right of way.[132] His bid for compensation meant that the reserve's boundaries had to be resurveyed, though Charles Starratt, the surveyor hired locally by the Department of Indian Affairs in 1902 for this purpose, baulked at undertaking a task associated with so little consistent evidence and so many unresolved conflicting claims. Though repeatedly goaded by Ottawa for his inaction, Staratt hedged by claiming that the markers associated with John Spry Morris's 1852 survey had been moved deliberately by outside parties in many places, which made running any new lines extremely difficult. When the federal government finally insisted in 1905 that he begin work, he caved in to pressures exerted by Ottawa and omitted the contentious Heisler tract lying east of the river as part of the reserve.[133] For this he was criticized by Charles Harlow, the Indian agent who lived in Caledonia in Queens County, who, like Chearnley before him, held that the interval belonged to the reserve. Also, Harlow favoured a subdivision of the reserve as a possible solution to the land disputes.[134]

Frank Pennel and his younger brother William (1864–1920) carried on the Mi'kmaw land and resource campaign after Joseph left in 1910 for Maine to find work. Ottawa soon dubbed the two "the heirs of John Penall" and "defenders of old Argomartin lands."[135] Only six persons remained at Gold River, two families and an elderly woman who lived alone. Frank Pennel and his wife, Mary Edna, headed one family. The couple had numerous children, but owing to disease many had died young. In 1910 they only had one son remaining, Frank, born in 1909, but over the following four years they would have three more: Annie in 1911, Joseph in 1912, and Barbara in 1914.[136] The second family was headed by William Pennel, who in 1889 wed Catherine Eisnor, and when Catherine died in 1896 he married again in 1905 to Emma Zwicker.[137] The elderly resident was Barbara Rafuse, John Pennell Jr.'s widow, who lived by herself in her own dwelling.

Starratt completed his survey in November 1910 but felt uncomfortable about the results of his work, since he had a nagging feeling that the eastern portion once had formed part of the reserve. For this reason, as early as 1907 he suggested that the Department of Indian Affairs employ V.J. Paton to look into the validity of the Heisler claims to land at Gold River, since Paton had acted for the band in the past and had access to all the old documents.[138] When contacted by Ottawa, Paton was not long in replying: as far as he was concerned, the two parties had little claim on the reserve. Paton was engaged by Indian Affairs in 1907 but, like the surveyor Starratt, he must have felt some trepidation regarding his duties, for years passed before he submitted his final report on 8 August 1912. He contended, in points 7 and 8 of his submission, that neither external party had any rights to the lands they claimed to possess:

7. The Dominion Government has perfect title to the land as against everybody but the Indians themselves, except possibly that portion of the Indian reserve covered by the Rev. John Secum [*sic*, Seccombe] grant passed before Confederation, which grant covers the land claimed by Amos Heisler and a very small triangular part of the land claimed by George Heisler.

8. So far as I can ascertain, the Heislers have not been able to trace the title back to Secum and I understand that there has been no possession under the Secum grant by any person having a paper title going back to that grant.[139]

The same year, Frank and William faced an especially daunting and irritating challenge as a group of Chester entrepreneurs publicly derided the Pennels for lacking sufficient "Indigenous character" to be considered truly Mi'kmaq. Such racially inspired taunts, unfortunately, proved all too common at the time, fuelled as they were by intense competition for Aboriginal land and resources. As a by-product of their slur campaign, the businessmen hoped to extinguish the Lunenburg County reserves for once and all.[140] Under the brunt of these painful attacks, William wrote Indian Affairs soliciting information on the nature of differences between land tenure on a reserve and freehold property holding.[141] Not long afterwards, he petitioned the province for, and received, twenty-five acres on the shore of Chester Basin, where he continued farming until his death in 1920.[142]

Despite being a property owner, William Pennel continued to fight for Mi'kmaw rights. When Paton asked him if he would act as a plaintiff for his band should a legal case arise in the future, William readily agreed to do so.[143] Paton proved prescient: in due course a legal dispute arose between George Heisler and one Robert C. Stewart, a Chester Basin miner and developer to whom William Mosher, despite his ejection from the Sutherland location in 1895, had been able to transfer his alleged riparian rights. Stewart immediately sunk shafts, built bunkhouses, and erected a stamp mill on the west side of the river. He also sought to control local water power. In response, George Heisler, who held rights, which he argued stemmed from Ottawa, to the Sutherland grant, erected trespassing signs and threatened to charge Stewart $150 per year for the privilege of remaining on what he claimed was his exclusive property.[144] Stewart countered by conducting a search into Heisler's title and found an affidavit, dated 1869, stating that the grant on the west side of the river had been made to William Sutherland purely on a conditional basis, and that Nova Scotia would refuse to become involved in any dispute should Sutherland's title ever be challenged by Ottawa. This condition, Stewart boasted, invalidated George Heisler's title, and since the Pennels had agreed to let him continue mining on the Sutherland tract, he should be regarded as the location's rightful occupant. He further offered to pay Indian Affairs ten dollars annually for a perpetual lease of the Sutherland property, according to an arrangement that he attested had been agreed upon by Ottawa when he first purchased Mosher's rights.[145] George Heisler meanwhile vehemently debunked Stewart's assertions.

On 16 December 1912, the legal case *His Majesty the King and George J. Heisler et al.* was launched in Nova Scotia's Supreme Court, with the Department of Indian Affairs, along with William Pennel, acting as plaintiff.[146] Ottawa had dispensed with V.J. Paton for these proceedings and hired another lawyer from Bridgewater, Arthur Roberts, to act on its behalf. The case had not progressed very far before William Pennel himself was apprehended on charges of taking 375 logs without a permit and selling them to the Kent Lumber company.[147] He still stood as a witness in the Heisler case, but the presiding judge, by the name of Benjamin J. Russell, proved far more favourable to the evidence marshalled by George Heisler.[148] Pennel was charged under Section 128 of the Indian Act, while his assistant in the woods, John Walker, who was not Mi'kmaq, was charged with trespassing on a reserve under Section 127 of the Indian Act, which carried a harsher penalty.[149]

The same spring William's brother, Frank Pennel, was apprehended on a charge of timber trespass. Frank had made 527 railway ties from trees located near his house west of the main thoroughfare through the reserve, Beech Hill Road, and had already hauled 162 down to the rail line for transport and sale to Messrs. Oxner and Hennigar at Chester Basin.[150] He protested that he had even approached the new Indian agent, N.P. Freeman, for permission to cut.[151] Whatever the case, his ties were seized.[152] These two cases of what the Indian Department and Crown Lands branded as "timber theft" shed a dark cloud over the Mi'kmaq's claims in the eyes of the Ottawa authorities. In November Judge Benjamin Russell dismissed the Mi'kmaw claims, and he ruled in August 1913 that George Heisler and Amos Heisler's

heirs owned the lands they occupied.[153] Owing to this judgment, the Gold River reserve was immediately reduced to 735 acres.[154]

Insult was soon added to injury. On 9 April 1914 Charles Harlow's successor as Indian agent, N.P. Freeman, claimed that the Mi'kmaq might be willing to surrender their reserve, an assertion that lacked much foundation but may have been prompted by William Pennel's sending a petition to Ottawa in March 1914 asking to buy a piece of reserve property and subsequently having his request denied.[155] William had hoped to be able to earn a living from logging, without outside interference, and contended that his right to log harked back to the early years of the nineteenth century when Chief John Pennel Sr. claimed that the Gold River site appealed to him since it furnished an abundance of fish, game, and wood. But in 1914 Ottawa was in the process of allocating timber leases on the reserve and did not wish to deal with complicating factors. Powerful interests, moreover, were interested in the water power on these lands.[156] To reduce competition from enterprising Mi'kmaw individuals, agent Freeman began discouraging companies from hiring Mi'kmaw labour in the woods.[157]

Band members came to understand that the federal Indian Act allowed for the sale of marketable timber off a reserve by external interests, but denied the reserve's occupants much control over harvesting and disposing of wood. It was a realization that radically altered Mi'kmaw perceptions of the economic opportunities available to their community and compelled many to move away from Gold River. Things continued to look bleak for many years. Pollution from mine tailings had destroyed the once-famed local salmon fishery, and timber poachers had left the surrounding forest almost denuded. The Mi'kmaq who remained on the reserve eked out a meagre living making baskets and articles of rigging for Lunenburg County's schooner fleet. Younger members of William's and Frank's families left to find work in Halifax, the Annapolis Valley, Digby County, and the eastern United States. Ottawa would eventually put an end to the province's unilaterally granting of land and resource rights to outsiders, and the Mi'kmaq would in consequence gain greater control over their lands and resources.[158] Though demonstrating remarkable business acumen in the 1830s in developing Mi'kmaw guiding and angling industries at Gold River, and in learning on their own to prepare railway ties from squared timber, until 1914 Chief

Argomartin's descendants faced accusations of resource theft and fines they could rarely pay by conducting these new activities on lands they held to be their own.

The Termination of New Germany Reserve No. 19 A

The small Mi'kmaw farming community located near Lake Peter on the East Branch of the La Have River existed until 1928. After that date, proponents of a federal-provincial centralization policy gauged to extinguish as many reserves as possible along the Atlantic coast to cut costs, free up resources for development, and have acreage revert to the province withdrew monetary support of the Mi'kmaw agricultural settlement. The community at New Germany, they deemed, failed to exhibit sufficient "Indianness," owing to its economic sufficiency and emphasis on education, to warrant Ottawa's continuing to maintain either a reserve or a schoolhouse for them. To be educated, informed, and enterprising simply did not jibe with the "public view" of the "Indian" as "uneducated, uninformed and unprogressive." The manner in which federal support was cut back was insidious, occurring unilaterally and in stages, beginning in 1928 with the government retracting funding for the school. The following year the community was renamed "Elmwood," and residents were told they had to buy their farms and schoolhouse from the government. During the height of the Great Recession documents were circulated promising monetary return for a surrender agreement.

In the end, the policy instigators got what they wanted. Surrender papers were signed on 5 June 1933; the cession of New Germany Reserve No. 19 was confirmed by order-in-council on 29 August 1933.[159] Some Mi'kmaw residents later would hold that the pressure they felt to surrender in 1933 constituted a travesty and betrayal of trust by Ottawa at a time when they and their neighbours were feeling economically vulnerable. The cession immediately stripped Chief Argomartin's and Tom Hammond's descendants of their legal "Indian" status and, following the reserve tract's reversion to the province, compelled them to take out freehold property and pay land taxes. Yet despite the official affronts to their Indigenous identity and rights in early 1933, Mi'kmaw families at Elmwood continued to nurture a social hub within their community that hosted a variety of distinctive Mi'kmaw events and activities.[160]

Threats to the Continuance of the Lunenburg County Reserves

Government centralization policy also threatened the continued existence of the Gold River Reserve and the Wallabeck Lake or Pennel Reserve. In 1934 the Mi'kmaq nearly lost the Wallabeck Lake Reserve because H.J. Bury, the supervisor of timber lands for the Department of Indian Affairs, claimed that the tract conferred on Joseph Pennel in the early 1850s had been viewed solely as a private woodlot by Joseph and his son Frank, who had shorn the tract of its valuable timber. Bury continued that once Joseph died, and his son Frank had harvested the best wood, Frank in the early 1900s conveyed a written deed of some description for the parcel to the Kent Lumber Company. This document was transferred in 1930 to the Gold River Pulpwood Company, which built a warehouse on the property. Try as he might, however, Bury could find no evidence that the parcel had ever legally been conveyed away from the Mi'kmaq. In 1932, realizing their tenure to the reserve was tentative, the Gold River Pulpwood Company proposed to buy the land outright, which in turn forced Indian Affairs to review whether or not such a sale should be allowed.

For a year, the federal government wavered back and forth between surrendering the Wallabeck Lake parcel and leasing it to the Gold River Pulpwood Company, which claimed it would harvest timber in ways that would benefit the Gold River band by providing them with jobs.[161] Then suddenly, without any consultation with the Mi'kmaq, on 10 May 1933 Ottawa called for the surrender and sale of the Pennel Reserve. A cession paper for the tract was drawn up by Indian Affairs at the same time a document was prepared that called for the surrender of the New Germany Reserve. The New Germany reserve was subsequently ceded, but the proceedings set in motion towards surrender of the Pennel Reserve went no further. Ottawa reconsidered leasing the land, as well as levying a penalty on trespassers of anywhere from twenty to eighty dollars for each year of illegal occupancy. At this point, the Gold River Pulpwood Company upped its ante, pressing for a surrender, and offered three hundred dollars to purchase the property; but Ottawa continued to vacillate. In the end, on 21 July 1934 Ottawa agreed to lease the reserve for twenty years, at a rate of ten dollars per annum, an amount based on agreements made years before to Robert Stewart and the Gold River Pulpwood Company. It does not appear that the Mi'kmaq were ever formally consulted regarding any of Ottawa's decisions on this matter, though behind the scenes it is likely that when they got wind of events they registered strong enough disapproval to compel Ottawa, in 1934, to back down and permit the tract to remain a reserve.[162]

Ottawa had already contemplated surrendering the Gold River Reserve. The earlier gold rush was becoming a memory, though the Lacey Mine continued operating in the Chester Basin area until 1940.[163] In the shadow of decaying mills, warehouses, wharves, silent stamp mills, and tailing heaps that leeched pollutants and surrounded by abandoned mining pits, the population of the Gold River Reserve community dwindled to less than ten people. After the reserve was resurveyed in 1910 to reflect its diminished size, Ottawa prevented the Mi'kmaq from cutting squared timber for railway and building suppliers. Frank Pennel's descendants, the only persons who still remained permanently on the reserve, continued to log, reportedly illegally, while scratching out a living fashioning baskets, axe handles, butter tubs, laundry poles, and articles of rigging for Lunenburg County's schooner fleet. William Pennel's offspring, by contrast, retained William's parcel of land at Chester Basin where they engaged in farming for a number of years. But within a decade, Pennels from both families had left to find work in Halifax and would not return to Gold River for many years.

Given the small size of the reserve population, the Department of Indian Affairs hoped to dispense with the problems of monitoring resource use and defending against encroachers by dispensing with the Gold River Reserve altogether. On 14 March 1927 a document circulated in Indian Affairs offices in Ottawa that erroneously claimed the Gold River Reserve had been surrendered, and that the cession had afterwards been approved by order-in-council. What happened next is unclear, but evidently Mi'kmaw antagonism to the government's unilateral decision halted the progression towards any final recognition of the surrender by Ottawa's legal branch, and both the cession and the order-in-council were abrogated at the very last minute. In 1910 a second survey was undertaken of the Gold River reserve, and on 14 March 1927 an enigmatic document, termed "Surrender No. 1011" in Ottawa's files, stated that the reserve, as surveyed, had been "surrendered for sale

or lease." This transaction was actually approved by order-in-council no. 746 on 14 April 1927. But unlike the previous scenario with the New Germany Reserve, the transaction was suddenly rescinded and the tract, in 1959, was simply deemed "not sold."[164]

Mi'kmaq living at Gold River today still remember this confusing incident, along with the frustration felt when the various economic enterprises in which they had invested hope and energy had to be abandoned. They knew that between 1818 and 1850 their ancestors had tried their hand at agriculture, although the soil on the reserve was shallow and rocky and at best allowed only marginal farming. To gain an alternative source of income, they demonstrated remarkable business acumen by the 1840s in developing a unique Mi'kmaw angling operation along the Gold River; but by the mid-1860s the salmon fishery had been destroyed and leeching from mine tailings and refuse from lumber mills polluted the local drinking water. They also knew that their Mi'kmaw kin and neighbours at New Germany, by learning to farm successfully and fending economically for themselves, had established a solid base for the community of Elmwood but had also been shorn of their reserve land and their legal Indigenous status. Not surprisingly, some, like William Pennel, who prior to his death in 1920 resided with his family on his farming grant at Chester Basin, began wondering if continuing to publicly identify as an Aboriginal, let alone fight for his people's rights, was worth it. When William died in Halifax in 1920, he was identified on his death certificate as a fifty-five-year-old "English farmer" from Chester Basin.[165]

Post–Second World War Years

Frank Pennel's son Frank Jr. continued living on the Gold River after the Second World War until the early 1970s. Frank was periodically charged with resource theft and fined for taking resources off lands the Mi'kmaq considered their own. In 1969, he was pursuing a scheme to harvest wood and build log cabins for a commercial venture he had planned for the reserve but soon met with opposition from Indian Affairs. When Gold River became part of the newly founded Acadia Band (now the Acadia First Nation) later the same year, the chief of the new band, Charles (or "Charlie") Labrador, intervened to settle the dispute. The Pennels, however, vacated the reserve for several decades, frustrated at what they felt were limited economic opportunities open to them at Gold River.

None of Frank Pennel Jr.'s descendants would return to Gold River prior to the year 2000. A few other Mi'kmaq who retained close kin ties with the neighbouring Indigenous community, many of whom were partly of Germanic descent, eked out a living in the 1950s and 1960s basketmaking and, when possible, working in the woods. In 1957 only Steve Labrador and Clarence Glode lived on the reserve. Glode, who had been living at Gold River for 22 years, made his living by manufacturing axe handles and mast hoops for sailboats and yachts. He remained relatively economically secure, since he had found a market for his wares with several suppliers in the Mahone Bay area.[166] Meanwhile, the only resident of the Pennel Reserve was Spurgeon Knockwood, a son of Stephen Knockwood Jr. and Laura Butler (née Paul) from Blue Mountain, Kings County. (Spurgeon was a logger and also cut pulpwood.)[167] Another fifty years would pass before the population at either of these reserves increased.

Today the Gold River Reserve and the Pennel Reserve are administered by the Acadia First Nation.[168] The unilateral extinguishment in 1928–29 of the New Germany Reserve by government fiat has left many descendants of the Pennels and Hammonds, who were deprived of their legal Indigenous status, with a lingering sense of chagrin and loss. It is therefore not surprising that staunch advocates of the Native Council of Nova Scotia hail from their ranks. The abundance of resources to be found along the shores of the Gold River has attracted Mi'kmaq to the locale for countless generations. Yet in the early 1990s the environmental degradation inflicted on the Gold River landscape by logging and mining over the preceding years made it difficult for the casual observer ever to imagine that fisheries and forests of the Gold River area once attracted sizable Mi'kmaw populations on an annual basis.[169]

The Gold River Reserve presently occupies 667 acres or 270.2 hectares flanking Trunk 3 Highway on the west and is entered by the Beech Hill Road. Since 2000, there has been a return of Mi'kmaw families to the area, among them Pennels, encouraged by an influx of government monies elicited by the proactive activities of the Acadia First Nation to which the Gold River community now belongs. Increased educational attainment has resulted in more residents of the reserve who are employed in professions or in skilled trades; many of these individuals look upon the reserve as a "bedroom community" and work in Halifax.

Along with these changes, there has been a revival of interest in Gold River's history, accompanied by a strong desire – particularly among younger residents – to preserve, perpetuate, and celebrate the distinctiveness of being Indigenous, through powwows and other local festivities. Such events not only attract Mi'kmaw individuals from throughout the Atlantic region, but also the Mi'kmaq's non-Indigenous neighbours, who are always warmly invited to participate in the events and learn more about Mi'kmaw culture. Like a phoenix rising from the ashes, the Gold River Mi'kmaw community is once again beginning to make a significant mark not only on the Mi'kmaw constituency but on society at large.

– Janet E. Chute and Brittany Pennel

Acknowledgments: Special thanks are extended to Don Awalt, Dwight Dorey, Deborah Gloade, Willa Kaiser (née Rafuse), Doris Labradore, William Labrador, Dora Jones, Don Julien, Cheryl MacDonald, Stephen Pennel, Walter and Janet Piers, and members of the Eisener, Kaiser, and Hatt families of Gold River and Indian Point for their aid with this chapter. Brittany Pennel, the student research assistant for this essay, is a descendant of Frank Pennel Jr. and Mary Edna Veinotte of Gold River. She was invaluable in tracking down historic sources, finding persons to interview, and organizing this chapter. Britanny's uncle, Frank Pennel of Gold River, also shared his knowledge and insights. Tragically, while working with his niece on this project, Frank, a roofer, died following a fall at a construction site in Halifax.

9

Stephen Knockwood Jr. of Kings County, Nova Scotia

The Kentville Farmer

Stephen Knockwood Jr. (c.1834–26 October 1938), a determined, hard-working person, lived all his life in two cultural worlds.[1] He bought a farm, sent his children to be educated at a one-room schoolhouse built in 1865 at Brooklyn Corner near Kentville, Nova Scotia, and aspired to the material comforts of his non-Indigenous neighbours. Yet he also understood and appreciated beliefs and practices whose roots lay deep in Mi'kmaw traditional culture. Throughout his long life – he reputedly was 104 years old when he died in 1938 – he embraced various facets of these two worlds and made them uniquely his own.[2] For his first fifty years he followed the hunting way and trapping way of life of his Mi'kmaw forbears, during which time he gained a reputation as an excellent hunting guide. He later joined Abraham Pineo Gesner (1792–1864), a medical practitioner, a geologist who invented kerosene, and a collector of ethnological and natural history specimens, as Gesner's guide and collecting protégé on expeditions along the Parrsboro Shore and throughout the Annapolis Valley.[3]

Inspired by Gesner, who during his term as Nova Scotia's Indian commissioner from 1847 and 1853 advocated the development of agriculture among the Mi'kmaq, Knockwood in 1868 took a labouring job with the Windsor and Annapolis Railway, a branch of the Dominion Atlantic Railway headquartered in Kentville, in order to earn enough money to buy a small farm along Brooklyn Street in Kings County. In 1877 he finally accumulated eighty dollars – a hefty sum in those days – to buy four acres of land from Gesner's brother-in-law, the Honourable Samuel Chipman, in the "Pine Woods" on the northwest side of the Cornwallis River, back of the town of Kentville.[4] Since Knockwood's farm lay within the parameters of the area over which his ancestors had wielded territorial aegis, his land purchase may have incorporated a wish to reclaim a minuscule part of his family's ancient heritage, after his grandfather's people were driven out of the area by settlers intent on clearing forest for fields. In keeping with his faith in the benefits of Western education, Knockwood enrolled his children in school, where they were the only Mi'kmaw children attending the small Brooklyn Street schoolhouse.

A hard worker, Knockwood succeeded at farming his small sector of the Kings County landscape. His four acres, located on a projection of land jutting out into the Cornwallis River, like neighbouring farms had sandy soil, but Knockwood made it prosper. To its north lay the "Pine Woods community," formed of around twenty Mi'kmaw families, many of whom were Knockwood's relatives, and whose forbears had also been dispossessed of their haunts along the Kennecook and Gaspereau Rivers by incoming settlers. There also were a few Black families with the surnames "James" and "Jarvis" who had immigrated into the area following the War of 1812.[5] Members of the Knockwood family had seasonally occupied the Pine Woods since at least 1800. Though Stephen Knockwood Jr. was born in Digby County and raised near Bear River, he retained ties with his extended kin near Kentville, among them John Knockwood Sr., born in 1812, who was almost certainly Stephen's paternal uncle.[6] Others included John Knockwood Jr. and his wife Catherine Darrie or Dorey, and Peter Knockwood Sr. and his wife Mary.[7] Members of the Paul family, among them John Paul and his wife Adelaide Bobbiei, Francis Paul and his wife Elizabeth Jeremy, and Newel Paul and his wife Mary Pictou, were relatives of Stephen's wife, Sarah Ann Paul. These Pauls were descendants of Paul Peminout, a noted eighteenth-century district chief who lived at Stewiacke along the Shubenacadie River Valley.[8] This diverse population occupied the Pine Woods for more than seventy years before the government in 1904 appropriated the land on which their dwellings stood to establish a British army training facility, Camp Aldershot.[9]

Owing to his connections with Gesner, who owned a farm at Chipman's Corner, Knockwood acquired a penchant for property management, gaining respect from the Planter as well as the Pine Woods population. In the years around 1880, he directed the Pine Woods community's volunteer fire brigade whenever accidental bush fires broke out along the north bank of the Cornwallis River.[10] He and Sarah Ann, who had married in Kentville around 1873, also began to attract attention on their visits to town.[11] Knockwood acquired two wagons and a spirited team of horses of which he was inordinately proud, and he often paraded them through the Kentville streets. "Knockwood," the local Indian agent James Edward Beckwith proclaimed, "was the first here to own a fine horse and riding wagon and a good harness" in addition to his utilitarian farm wagon.[12]

By 1886 Stephen Knockwood proved more ready than ever to explore any opportunity that might increase his assets. "Stephen Knockwood Jr.," Beckwith attested in that year, "stands above all the rest as an industrious, enterprising and ambitious man. Not content with four acres of land and house and barn which he always had as private property, he has within the last year purchased 50 acres of land further up the river, and, although owing for the most of it, if his health continues for a few years, I think he will pay for it."[13] Beckwith was right: though Stephen

temporarily went into debt after buying the fifty acres on the south side of Brooklyn Street, he quickly paid off what he owed and continued to purchase and sell properties, almost always at a profit.

Stephen often was away from home, selling furs, guiding, working on logging teams, river driving, hunting porpoise, and engaging in various labouring jobs so he could save money and retain his independence as a freehold farmer. He also was proud of his Mi'kmaw heritage, and his knowledge of woodlore became legendary at Kentville and Cambridge, where he generously passed on what he knew to others. He and his wife in the early years of their marriage always conversed in the Mi'kmaw language in their home, and since both were descendants of chiefs, they each transmitted leadership skills to their children, skills that would hold up well under many challenges.

These challenges began almost immediately. Since there was little free land left after the descendants of the Planters expanded out over the Annapolis Valley floor, Samuel Chipman had been able to drive a hard bargain for the four acres he sold Knockwood.[14] Agent Beckwith claimed that Knockwood in 1877 had paid Chipman three times what his lot was actually worth. Yet despite this inauspicious start, Knockwood received clear title to his property and by 1881 had built a "respectable house," raised a barn, kept horses and a pair of steers, owned a good farm wagon and other agricultural equipment, and had "plans to seed about one and a quarter acres in the spring."[15]

Undaunted by setbacks, in the early 1880s Knockwood had gone to work with a will, and his industry and careful saving paid off. Despite Stephen's haughty spurning of government interference in his affairs, Beckwith, eager to reward such frugality, agricultural acumen, and ingenuity, decided to grant him enough free seed to cover one and a half acres, a quarter of an acre more than Knockwood originally had intended to sow.[16] Yet there were indications that, in his heart, Knockwood preferred the traditional Mi'kmaw occupations of hunting, fishing, and guiding over laborious farming endeavours. During his lengthy absences in the bush, or while he was out porpoise hunting, the well-being of his farm relied wholly on the labours of his wife and children. In 1882 Knockwood left for several months, relying on his wife and children "to take care of his home while he himself has gone porpoise hunting for the summer."[17] Beckwith noted that Sarah Ann soldiered on under these circumstances, coping with numerous farm chores while tending to her children. He presciently surmised that this unusual division of labour might lead to family stress, since most Mi'kmaw women and children accompanied their male family head to the shores of the Annapolis Basin during the porpoise-hunting season and helped to render down porpoise oil. It must have been hard for Sarah Ann to watch her neighbours leave each summer and know she must remain behind.

By 1885 Stephen and Sarah Ann had eight children: Katherine (or Katia) around 1874, Joseph in 1875, Stephen John (John) in 1878, Benjamin in 1879, Madeline around 1880, Rachael in 1883, Harry in 1884, and Henry in November 1885.[18] They would later have Marie. For a while Stephen and his wife embraced their newfound wealth and status by taking great pride in their possessions and their children's accomplishments at school. But Sarah Ann also was an independent and pious woman, well known for her services as a midwife and dedicated to raising her family according to the values of the distinctive brand of Roman Catholicism that, by the late nineteenth century, was a deeply entrenched facet of Mi'kmaw national identity.[19] Her husband focused more on earning money and ensuring that his children worked hard at their studies, and his aspirations to gain items and services that only money and education could buy gradually caused a rift between him and his wife. The two parted company in 1894. Stephen moved temporarily to Cambridge Station in Kings County, while Sarah Ann remained on the farm in the Pine Woods.[20]

Stephen experienced lengthy periods of separation from his children. Sarah Ann, now forty-eight years old, passed control of the family farm to her son, Stephen John Knockwood, though Stephen retained the title to the property. The 1890s brought years of financial hardship, and ideological and social challenges that tested Stephen's loyalty to the Roman Catholic faith. For a while he left the Roman Catholic Church altogether and joined a Baptist congregation at Blue Mountain on the South Mountain, not far from Gaspereau Lake, Kings County. Before his death, however, he recouped his financial losses and returned to his original faith. He died a fairly affluent man for a South Mountain farmer. His final will and testament shows he had accumulated over one thousand dollars in assets, much of which he placed in an endowment fund for St. Joseph's Roman Catholic parish, to contribute to the construction of St. Bernadette's church on land situated near the Cambridge Reserve.[21]

Learning at a Young Age to Surmount Obstacles

Ever since he was a boy, Stephen Knockwood Jr. exhibited a boldness of spirit, a daunting intellect, and an ability to barter and get what he wanted, despite the fact that he could neither read nor write. He was born either as early as 1834 or as late as 1847 at Sandy Cove, Digby County, not far from the Mi'kmaw community of L'sitkuk at Bear River, on the Annapolis County-Digby County line.[22] His father, Stephen Knockwood Sr., trapped, hunted, and guided in the fall and winter, took porpoise in the Bay of Fundy during the summer, and engaged in some marginal farming. Though a member of the Bear River Band, the elder Knockwood rarely resided for long periods of time at L'sitkuk, even though Abbé Jean-Mandé Sigogne, the local Roman Catholic missionary, and Sigogne's good friend from Digby, Judge Peleg Wiswall, had a thirty-acre lot flanking St. Anne's Church on the thousand-acre L'sitkuk Reserve expressly surveyed in 1828 for him to occupy. When provincial Indian commissioner Joseph Howe made a tour of southwestern Nova Scotia in the autumn of 1842, he met Stephen Knockwood Sr. at an encampment two miles away from Sigogne's mission headquarters in the Township of Clare, Digby County.[23] Knockwood's slab camp was one of three such dwellings sheltering, in all, twenty-one persons of various ages who had travelled from the Bear River area to meet the missionary. Four of the men, including Knockwood, were heads of families.[24] On arriving at Bear River a few days later, Howe noted with some chagrin that farming was obviously not a high priority for Stephen Sr., who had leased his plot on the reserve to a white neighbour.[25]

Yet Stephen Sr. was canny enough to realize that there was wisdom in the counsel Howe offered the Bear River Mi'kmaq – become educated and diversify your economic options – and it was a message he impressed on his children. Stephen Jr. failed to receive any formal education since his youth was spent hunting, trapping, and guiding with his father, but he strove to speak passable English while retaining his fluency in the Mi'kmaw language. Endowed with a canny business sense, he could juggle numbers in his head despite not being able to read mathematical notation. He also attained a sound knowledge of traditional medicine, skills in the negotiating forum, and last but not least, the knowledge of how to farm. His early years spanned one of the most daunting times for fledging Mi'kmaw agriculturalists. After several southwestern Mi'kmaq, among them Charles Glode along the Liverpool-Annapolis Road and John Jeremy at Kejimkujik Lake, had devoted time and effort to farming, a blight akin to that which gave rise to the Irish potato famine destroyed their potato crops from 1845 to 1847. At the same time a series of dry summers precipitated forest fires in the interior and dampened their resolve to replant. Fortunately, Stephen Knockwood Sr. supplemented his minimal agricultural ventures by working as a fishing and hunting guide, and thus kept economic hardship at bay. Determined to follow in his father's footsteps, Stephen Knockwood Jr. became "one of the best-known guides in western Nova Scotia, and he enjoyed a very high reputation among sportsmen." During his lifetime he was said to have "killed over five hundred bears and … was unequalled in moose and deer hunting."[26]

Brief History of the Neocout (Knockwood) Family of Minas

Much of Stephen Knockwood Jr.'s resilience and determination stemmed from hearing oral traditions of deeds performed by one of his influential early-eighteenth-century ancestors, Chief Jacques Neocout.[27] All Mi'kmaw individuals bearing the Knockwood surname stem by descent, adoption, or fosterage from Jacques Neocout and his Mi'kmaw wife, Marie. According to a French nominal census compiled by Father Pierre La Chasse in 1708, Jacques Neocout, born in 1663, and Marie had three sons, Claude (thirteen), René (nine), and Jacques (six), as well as three daughters, Marie (eighteen), Louise (sixteen), and Jeanne (2). Jacques, heralded by the French in 1722 as leader of the entire Minas Mi'kmaw community, travelled annually to Port Toulouse, Île Royale (now Cape Breton), to receive medals and other honorifics from the French government.[28]

Losses of young Mi'kmaw men in confrontations with New England forces during the Mi'kmaw War (1722–25) depleted the Minas group's population. The Minas band, which in 1708 numbered fifty-nine individuals, by 1722 stood at forty-four, which suggests that its able-bodied men and youths had become warriors and had assumed the risks involved.[29]

Although chiefs Pierre and Antoine Momcharret, living along the nearby Gaspereau River, declared to the British in 1720 that "[w]e are masters independent of everyone and wish to have our country free," it was Neocout who put up the staunchest resistance to British incursions on his territory.[30] The virulence of the Neocout band's attacks on British and New England targets made British officialdom reluctant to parley with the leaders of this group. On 4 June 1726 "Jacques Nughquit" signed a Treaty of Peace and Friendship with the British at Fort Anne, Annapolis Royal, but not as the paramount Minas chief – the British reserved that honour for Pierre Momcharret. Instead, Nughquit's name appears almost at the end of the list of signatories.[31]

Within the Mi'kmaw constituency, however, Jacques Neocout was still leader of a distinct Mi'kmaw group residing along the Kennetcook River, which takes its rise near the present-day town of Douglas and empties into the Avon River.[32] Following 1726, anywhere the British attempted to gain a foothold, Neocout and his people demanded rent from the intruders for the privilege of staying. In fall 1732 they attacked a partially built magazine the British had erected in the Minas area and took possession of a colliery owned and operated by a Boston businessman, Henry Cope. Cope could only watch helplessly throughout the winter months as the Mi'kmaq continued to occupy his coal mine, since the garrison at Annapolis Royal lacked the capacity to effectively oppose the Mi'kmaq and the Acadians refused to get involved. Meanwhile Chief Neocout and his people called loudly for compensation for any future mining ventures undertaken on their traditional territories.[33]

Jacques Neocout's sons and grandsons harassed New England merchant shipping at Piziquid and Minas. On 4 June 1737 two members of the Minas band, Paul Biscaroon and Jacques Ashe, encouraged five youths among whom were including Claude and François Neocout to board the sloop *Friends Adventure* trading at Minas.[34] The attacking party cut the vessel's cables and compelled its crew to sail to Cape Tendue (now Cape Split) where, according to ship's master Stephen Jones, they plundered the vessel of goods amounting to £1,546.[35] Not long afterward, Jacques Neocout either died or stepped down as a Minas leader and Joseph Neocout emerged as head chief, with Claude Neocout as the band's first captain and Claude's younger brother, François, as its second captain.[36]

The 1737 raid was an embarrassment to the British since it was carried out in peacetime by a handful of Mi'kmaw youths. After a sloop belonging to William Trefry and trading in 1742 at Grand Pré was also robbed, the British decided to send circular letters complaining of these actions to the Minas chiefs.[37] A Minas head man, Thomas Wouito (Ouytau, Outine), promised to try to curb any excesses caused by youngsters plundering traders in the basin.[38] Yet his words conveyed no real intent to curb illicit boarding of New England or British trading ships; to the Mi'kmaw leaders such acts were protests against unwarranted trespass on their land.

Acadians at Minas, caught in the middle between British and Mi'kmaw interests and yet expected to act as informers for the British, often paid a high price. Alexandre Bourg was suspended from his post as a notary public for failing to prevent the Mi'kmaw raids;[39] Bourg's successor, René LeBlanc, while attempting to keep his activities in line with British wishes, was mysteriously killed.[40] The years leading up to and during King George's War (1744–48) were fraught with tension and fear on all sides. A letter drafted in 1745 by Pierre Landry at the insistence of the Mi'kmaq claimed that the local leaders desired peace, but that they still had to consult with the wider Mi'kmaw community on the subject. The British, chagrined at what they viewed as evidence of Mi'kmaw intransigence, imposed an embargo on Acadian trade with the Mi'kmaq and voiced an empty threat that "no vessel would go up the Bay" to Minas until the Mi'kmaq "be brought to terms."[41] Undeterred by these threats, the Neocouts and their associates continued their raids, while the British fumed from behind the ramparts of their badly undermanned and crumbling fortress at Annapolis Royal.

Despite the turmoil caused in 1755 when the British deported their Acadian neighbours from Grand Pré during the Grand Dérangement, the Minas Mi'kmaq held on to their traditional hunting territories. Isaac Deschamps, who since 1760 had run a truckhouse at Piziquid (now Windsor) to trade with the local Mi'kmaq,[42] noted that two distinct bands still resided in the Minas area: the "Tribe of Nocoot," comprising seventy-eight persons holding hunting territories along the Kennetcook River, and the "Tribe of Amquaret [Momcharret]," living on the Gaspereau River. The Acadians called the Kennetcook River area "Quenetcou," which derived from a

Mi'kmaw place name meaning "the place ahead" or "the place further on."[43] In 1760 an elderly Joseph Neocout was still chief of the Kennetcook River band, whose members remained attached to the French until the close of the Seven Years' War in 1763.[44]

Joseph Neocout's final years as chief would see the end of the Neocout family's defiant bids for territorial independence. After 1759, waves of Planters from New England moved into the Minas area to populate the newly established townships of Windsor, Falmouth, and Newport, and in so doing demographically overwhelmed the indigenous population. Evidently British authorities during these years were inclined to take any altercations between the local Mi'kmaq and incoming Planters very seriously, to preserve the newly minted peace. When two men from Cornwallis Township, Jeheil Dewolf and John Arnold Hammond, in 1763 assaulted Bartholomew Neocout, the local chief's son, both assailants were tried, charged, and fined by the Hants County Court of Quarter Sessions, with the fines exacted from the perpetrators going directly to Neocout. Dewolf, who pleaded guilty to hitting Neocout with a stick while the latter was allegedly intoxicated, was fined forty shillings, while Hammond, who refused to admit guilt other than for hitting Neocout with a stick in a manner that he claimed did not hurt his victim, faced a much stiffer fine of three pounds. At the conclusion of this matter, the court proceedings held that the Mi'kmaq were "well satisfied" with the arrangement and in consequence "promised they would do everything in their power to maintain a good understanding between them and us."[45] One can almost hear, embodied in these words, a collective sigh of relief from the settlers of Cornwallis Township that the incident did not elicit any Mi'kmaw retaliatory action.

Only months before, the Neocouts had joined other Mi'kmaq throughout the province in calling for the appointment of a Roman Catholic missionary, since no priests remained in Nova Scotia after Abbé Pierre Maillard's death in 1762. Their demands finally met with a response from Lieutenant Governor Michael Francklin, who appointed Abbé Charles-François Bailly missionary to the Mi'kmaq and Acadians in 1768. Bailly met with members of the Neocout family at Chezzetcook, east of Halifax, in June 1769. The Mi'kmaw party was composed of siblings and cousins from the Kennetcook River area, among them Francis-Xavier Neocout, Joseph

Neocout, Françoise Neocout, and Isabelle Angelique Pennel (née Neocout), who had brought several children to be baptized.[46]

Entries in Abbé Bailly's baptismal registers for 1769–70 show the wide network of marriage alliances that the Neocout group had forged with neighbouring bands. Françoise Neocout was married to Joseph Momcharret of Minas and Isabelle Angelique to Bernard (Pennel) Argomartin, who lived in Lunenburg County. Magdalene Neocout's husband, Hippolite Argimault, came from the Chignecto Isthmus region.[47] Finally, François Neocout, born in 1725, and who by 1769 was his band's chief, dwelt part of the year in Kings County and in the fall crossed over the Bay of Fundy to hunt and fish along the Parrsboro Shore.[48]

During the 1760s, the British continued to favour Bartholomew Momcharret over other Minas leaders.[49] The elderly Joseph Neocout seemed to have played no role in peacemaking proceedings between the Mi'kmaq and the British Crown, although it is possible that Neocout refused to parley, owing to his lingering allegiance to the defeated French regime. Even under the leadership of François Neocout, resentment over land losses and fears of settler hostility ran deep. To assuage matters, Michael Francklin, Nova Scotia's Indian commissioner during the American Revolution, hired Charles Neocout, a Minas head man, as an emissary to carry messages for the government from the mouth of the Saint John River inland to Aukpaque. He regularly travelled among the British forts on the frontier.[50] This bid to ease tensions between the Neocouts and the British government must have worked, for in the fall of 1778 Charles Neocout earned accolades for playing a major role in a "spirited attempt to surprise a Rebell whale boat crew."

Until the close of the American Revolution the Neocouts group remained on territory back of the Newport Township, although living off the land had become exceedingly difficult owing to the settlers' ravaging of the local forest and the consequent decrease in game. Jean Barthélèmy (or John Bartholomew) Neocout, who succeeded François Neocout as band chief, found he had to petition Governor John Wentworth during the winter of 1784 for provisions and other supplies to feed and clothe his people.[51] As a result of the economic distresses of the 1780s, Neocouts began to spall off their original group and press towards the Chignecto region.

François-Xavier Neocout (c.1755–1832), after marrying Marie-Madeleine Peminout Paul, a daughter of Chief Paul Peminout of Stewiacke, left for Bay Verte. The couple dwelt at Grand Barachois, New Brunswick, for several years, and by 1816 resided at Aboujane, where Francois-Xavier died on 17 April 1832. Some of their descendants became members of the Fort Folly band near Dorchester.[52] Other Neocouts went further afield, to Lennox Island in the northern part of Prince Edward Island, to the Îles of Saint-Pierre and Miquelon, or to the west coast of Newfoundland.[53]

Neocouts who stayed in southwestern Nova Scotia began to travel seasonally to Parrsboro or into Digby County, especially after smallpox outbreaks in 1801 and 1802 caused bands living along the eastern Atlantic seaboard to flee to the Minas Basin area.[54] In consequence, some of those already at Minas, feeling the pressure of increased numbers, in March 1801 joined Thomas Neocout, who had joined forces with Louis Toney, the son of a noted late eighteenth-century leader from Pictou named Captain Anthony Ury, and began looking for lands to inhabit away from Minas.[55] Not long afterwards, this group joined a small band living at the Gut of Annapolis, from where they seasonally set out for Bear River and Digby. Owing to Thomas Neocout's choice of locale to raise his family, it is very possible that he was Stephen Knockwood Sr.'s father, as well as the father of several other Knockwoods who came to live in the Bear River area.[56]

Since Mi'kmaq at this time travelled considerable distances in a single season, it is likely Thomas Neocout (or Knockwood) frequently ventured east along the Annapolis Valley floor to visit family members still living at Kentville. In 1808 Jonathan Crane, the Indian agent for Cornwallis Township, noted that Mi'kmaw visitors regularly passed through the Minas district en route to Minudie and the Parrsboro Shore in Cumberland County to meet Roman Catholic priests, visit with relatives, and celebrate special occasions.[57] Knockwoods who lived at Shediac and Petitcodiac crossed over to Prince Edward Island for the same purpose, and by the 1840s members of the same extended family participated in St. Anne's Day celebrations in Cape Breton.[58] Not all reunions and festivities proved joyous, however, since many settlers were still distrusted and any unexplained, untoward occurrences could give rise to suspicion. As late as September 1849, an elderly chief, "Joseph Nokut [Neocout or Knockwood] of Shediac" – charged that English-speaking farmers had caused thirty-four Mi'kmaw deaths by poisoning flour and butter offered to a Mi'kmaw assemblage at Nappan, Cumberland County.[59] Though the number of such grave allegations diminished over the next two decades, many Knockwoods, Stephen Knockwood Jr. among them, suspected – and with good reason – that the government's chief motive was to take the last of their traditional lands and marginalize them on reserves.

Property Dealings

For three years Stephen Knockwood Jr. lived near Cambridge. Although the Mi'kmaq of Kings County received an 18.7-hectare reserve near Cambridge Station on 3 March 1880 known as Cambridge Reserve No. 32, he disliked the thought of being under the thumb of the federal Department of Indian Affairs, so he refused to move onto the tract.

His wife Sarah Ann continued to live on the Pine Woods property. She struggled to make ends meet; her farm was often dubbed "Hungry Hill" by Kentville residents.[60] After the farm's expropriation in 1904, Sarah Ann moved to Upper Dyke Village and then occupied a small frame house at the extreme east end of Brooklyn Street. She still sent her children to school, as did her son Stephen John, who with his wife Rosie Gooley lived with Sarah Ann. According to a student register for the Brooklyn Street School, dated 1897, twelve-year-old Henry, Sarah Ann's youngest son, sporadically attended classes. He evidently felt little motivation to study: English was not his first language, his parents had been living apart for three years, and the one-room schoolhouse he had to attend was hardly a milieu that appreciated cultural diversity. This pattern was not true of all of the Knockwood children, however. Stephen John and Rosie had a son Stephen John Jr., who in 1913 at age eleven was in grade five and had an excellent school report and a good attendance record.[61]

In addition to still taking care of several of her children and one grandchild on her own, Sarah Ann was raising a foster child, Charlotte Kathleen (or Katie) Tonbarge, born in 1901, who was probably white.[62] As time passed she relied heavily for basic necessities on Stephen John and Rosie. Her husband Stephen Jr. not only failed to provide for her, but had taken up with another woman from the South Mountain named Laura Butler.

The steps leading to this development are unclear. For a number of years Stephen was more interested in buying and selling real estate than in caring for his wife and family. Between 1886 and 1924 he bought and sold at least four properties. But other, unknown circumstances may have prevailed as well. Sarah Ann may at one point have grown sickly and needed more time and care than her energetic husband was willing to offer, though that this constituted a permanent condition seems unlikely, given the duties she had to shoulder to care for her children and foster child. The two also may have experienced irreconcilable differences, owing to Stephen Knockwood's seemingly greater interest in acquiring material wealth than in sharing his assets with the Mi'kmaw community to which Sarah Ann was intimately connected. When Knockwood received monetary compensation for his farm from the government in 1904, there was no record of his sharing any of these proceeds with his wife and family. Yet as both he and his wife were baptized Roman Catholics, Knockwood and his wife never formally separated. They simply stopped living together and resided in separate dwellings for the rest of their lives. In 1897 Stephen left Cambridge and bought fifty acres at Blue Mountain in Kings County, Nova Scotia, a small, mainly Baptist community lying just under twenty-four kilometres from Kentville. In November of the following year he acquired three additional acres at Blue Mountain from James Lockhart and his wife, Sarah Ann Lockhart.[63] These land purchases constituted major turning points in his life.

For one, they initiated his close friendship with the Lockhart family of Blue Mountain, particularly William Lockhart, whose land abutted Stephen's own three acres. More significantly, they heralded his open admission of his romantic attachment, at sixty-four years of age, to Laura Butler, a Mi'kmaw widow who shared the house he constructed on the three acres he bought in 1898. Laura hailed from Kentville and her maiden name was Paul.[64] Over successive years he and Laura had two daughters, Lily May in 1904 and Annie Laura Louise in 1908, and two sons, William in 1909 and Spurgeon Leander in 1913.[65]

Though he kept title to the three acres at Blue Mountain in his own name until his death, Knockwood relinquished his usufructuary right to the parcel so that Laura and their children might use the resources on it as they saw fit for their support should he die. When it turned out that William

Lockhart did not hold a clear right to dispose of the three acres he had sold Knockwood in November 1898, Knockwood had to make further arrangements with Watson O'Leary of Marlboro in the State of Massachusetts, who held residual rights by means of a life lease. In consideration of one dollar a year rent paid to O'Leary during O'Leary's lifetime, the matter was resolved, and after O'Leary's death the parcel was finally placed in Knockwood's two-year-old daughter Lily May's name on 21 March 1906.[66] Looking forward to a respectable, comfortable retirement from farming, he had begun to dispose of some of his landholdings to increase his monetary savings. As he was seventy-two years of age, he wanted to provide a measure of future security for his youngest children.

Farming at Blue Mountain

To this end, on 7 March 1901 he sold the fifty acres he had bought at Blue Mountain in 1897 to his friend William Lockhart's son, James Lockhart, for a dollar, provided that Lockhart allowed Knockwood to continue pasturing his two head of cattle on the property.[67] His generosity likely stemmed from James Lockhart's unwritten promise to help with farming tasks that the elderly Knockwood felt incapable of tackling by himself. Though still physically fit, Knockwood devised an arrangement with his nearest neighbours where, in return for their being able to plant on part of his land, they would share a portion of the harvest with him. This reduced his farming workload and provided for basic necessities. But he still had heavy family responsibilities, and Laura had given birth to a son William in 1909.[68] So, to increase the yield of his fields, he turned for assistance to one of his sons-in-law, Arthur Dorey, whom his daughter Annie Laura Louise, then twenty-four years of age, had married in 1932. Dorey, a farmer from Lunenburg County nineteen years her senior, proved willing to sow seed, harvest crops, and perform other duties on his father-in-law's farm.[69] Knockwood still retained eighty acres of land at Blue Mountain, though by this time he and Laura Butler were living quietly in a small cabin at Forest Home, on the south shore of Gaspereau Lake.

Despite his age, Knockwood was hardly through dealing in land. On 18 June 1912 he had bought considerable acreage on the south side of Brooklyn Street in Cornwallis Township from John H. Bowles, which he sold twelve years later, on 24 August 1924, to Willard Ells for 500 dollars.[70] A second profitable land deal, made with George Chase concerning lands at Blue Mountain and Port Williams, followed in 1932.[71] On 23 May of the same year Knockwood sold eighty-eight acres at Blue Mountain to William Lockhart's son, Thomas Lockhart, for 350 dollars on condition that the seller first removed all buildings from the property.[72] That land too fetched a good price, and showed that even at age eighty-nine Knockwood was adept in property dealing. All proceeds from these sales Knockwood carefully banked.

While participating in such transactions Knockwood usually kept the nature of his and Laura Butler's relationship cloaked in ambiguity. In only one land deed, that arising from the 1924 sale of five hundred acres to Willard Ells, is Laura referred to as Knockwood's "wife" – though he treated her in all other respects as his spouse.[73] In the end, convention prevented him from acknowledging her as his wife in his final property dispositions.[74] Instead, shortly before his death, he legally conveyed the three acres at Blue Mountain to his "housekeeper" Laura Butler, in trust for his and her sons William and Spurgeon Knockwood, who sold the parcel in 1943.[75] Both sons made their living by lumber trade and had little interest in farming.

Stephen Knockwood Jr. died at Blanchard-Fraser Memorial Hospital on 26 October 1938, aged 104 years, and was buried in the cemetery of St. Joseph's Parish in Kentville. In his last will and testament, which he had drawn up on 21 April 1936, he left Stephen John, Benjamin, and Joseph – his and his first wife Sarah Ann's sons – the sum of a dollar each. He left his daughters a similar amount. This bequest gave the executor of his estate, Barry W. Roscoe, no end of trouble after Stephen's death, since while John still lived in Nova Scotia, Benjamin and Joseph, along with one of their sisters, Marie, had moved near Farmington, Maine, and proved hard to reach (which was particularly vexing when the matter concerned the paltry amount of one dollar).[76] For whatever reason, in the midst of the Great Depression when a sizeable bequest would doubtless have been welcome, Knockwood bypassed his eldest sons by dividing the bulk of his assets between his Forest Home family and a major charitable donation to St. Joseph's Roman Catholic Parish, centred in Kentville.

Stephen Knockwood's Legacy

Knockwood left his so-called "housekeeper," Laura Butler, fifty dollars. Also, his homestead, farm outbuildings, farming equipment, and all his personal effects at Blue Mountain would remain hers for "the term of her natural life." Upon her death, these assets would devolve upon William and Spurgeon Knockwood, in equal shares. In all, Knockwood's estate grossed a little over one thousand dollars, a sizable sum in 1938.[77] Once dues and other matters were deducted, the remnant of the estate would go as a gift to St. Joseph's Parish headquartered in Kentville. After wrestling with a few minor matters regarding this final disbursement, executor Roscoe on 23 September 1940 handed a check for $570.45 to the St. Joseph's parish priest, Father J.W. Brown.[78]

During his lifetime, Stephen had lived in two worlds and had done relatively well in both in terms of material success. His legacy had strongly altruistic components. His gift to St. Joseph's Parish was his way of giving back unselfishly to the Mi'kmaw community, and was regarded as such by the Mi'kmaq at Cambridge and the local clergy. It also elicited generosity in others. Not long afterwards, another bequest of six hundred dollars was added to Knockwood's amount by a former member of the parish, who had died in the United States. The combined funds gave Father Brown and his assistant, J.P. Hayes, the means to erect St. Bernadette's Church on an acre of land flanking the Cambridge Reserve. No longer would elderly Mi'kmaw parishioners each week have to trek to St. Joseph's church in Kentville, seven miles away. Community members helped with the church's construction, while private donors provided pews and a bell for the steeple. Fittingly, the bell had once belonged to Engine 32 of the Dominion Atlantic Railway, the line for which Knockwood had worked in the early 1870s.[79]

During the last fifty years of his life, Stephen Knockwood Jr. cut a figure that defied easy categorization. He was listed simply as an "Indian" on the deed for his Pine Woods property in 1877, but as he grew proficient in agriculture, others saw him as a farmer. By 1901 census enumerators had taken to leaving blank columns after his name where his religion and marital status were concerned. There can be no doubt he felt that to be regarded as an "Indian," in the way the Canadian government defined the term

after Confederation, severely compromised one's occupational and educational opportunities.[80] He, by contrast, excelled in everything he did, whether it required a grasp of Mi'kmaw traditional knowledge or belonged to the sphere of agriculture and business negotiation. With a determined character, a strong physical constitution, and a family tendency to longevity, Knockwood remained in good health until the final years of his life. Though at times it seemed he placed personal status and occupational imperatives above the needs of family and community, the reality may have been far more complex. He understood the cultural tenets of Mi'kmaw responsibility and leadership, for he was descended from an ancient line of influential chiefs. His final gift to the parish and the Cambridge Mi'kmaw community suggests he wanted his last act to be in line with Mi'kmaq and not western European leadership values.

Oral traditions show that his descendants approached Knockwood's disposal of assets per his will, as well as his familial relationships, philosophically. Spurgeon Knockwood's wife, Florence May Knockwood (née Corkum), in 1990 readily admitted to the author that not only did Knockwood have two families but, as evidenced by her fairly comprehensive knowledge of Knockwood's children by his first wife Sarah Ann (née Paul), members of Stephen Knockwood's two families after 1870 did have periodic reunions.[81] It was clear that all of Knockwood's descendants belonged to the same Mi'kmaw community and shared the same desire to preserve their cherished heritage.

Stephen Knockwood Jr. appeared larger than life in all he did, a person whose intelligence, canny business acumen, breadth of vision, and physical constitution befitted one destined to become a centenarian. And his descendants have played, and continue to play, high-profile roles in both Mi'kmaw and mainstream society. His youngest son, Spurgeon Knockwood, became a well-known logger in Lunenburg County, and by 1950 had moved to the Pennel Reserve near New Ross where he lived until his death. He and Florence May remained Baptists, and he was buried in the Baptist graveyard at New Ross.[82] Spurgeon's sister Annie Laura Louise followed the lead of her husband, Arthur Dorey, in becoming Anglican, while his other sister Lily May married Hollis Dunham C. Durham and remained Baptist.[83] The elderly Stephen Knockwood Jr. proved remarkably open to letting his children follow the religion of their choice, but in his heart of hearts he remained committed to Roman Catholicism.

Back at Kentville and Points East

By 1916 Stephen Knockwood Jr.'s son, Stephen John Knockwood, was an important Mi'kmaw community leader, along with Michael Thomas from Rawdon, and both men wanted their status as Mi'kmaw leaders and their activities on behalf of their people to be recognized by the government.[84] Yet in the early 1900s Ottawa sought to consolidate the Mi'kmaq on a few reserves, Cambridge not being one of them, and refused to recognize leaders of non-reserve communities.[85] Consequently, both men watched the development of the Millbrook community near Truro in Colchester County with interest, and in April 1920 petitioned for leave to move there.[86] Millbrook's chief, Joseph Julien, invited them both to join him at Truro, but the Indian agent, A.P. Boyd, blocked their appeal, stating that, unlike the families the government slated to settle at Millbrook, neither man hailed from Halifax County. Michael Thomas contested Boyd's judgment and finally was admitted to Millbrook, but Stephen John decided instead to move his family to Indian Brook, where he found ample scope for his leadership abilities by serving three terms as the community's chief in the 1940s and 1950s.[87]

Stephen John Knockwood and his first wife, Rosie Gooley, had four children: Stephen John Jr. in 1902, Benjamin around 1903, Lucy in 1904, and in 1907, Mary, who died young. He and his second wife, Mary Theresa Eunice Simons, a well-known basketmaker, had Joseph, Henry, Roseanne (or Rose Ann), Isabelle, and Noel Raymond. Like his father Stephen Knockwood Jr., he valued traditional knowledge. He could recite or sing stories, legends, prayers, hymns, and songs by heart, feats recorded by Dartmouth folklorist Helen Creighton in the 1940s.[88] But notwithstanding his special skills and leadership abilities, he faced many challenges. Despite his support of education for Mi'kmaw youth, three of his children, beginning in the mid-1930s, were taken and sent without his permission to the Shubenacadie Residential School, which was the antithesis of the kind of education he espoused. He also charged that most of the promises offered to encourage Mi'kmaw families to relocate to Shubenacadie under the government centralization scheme failed to be honoured.

Stephen John Knockwood's sons and daughter by Theresa Simons travelled widely. Joseph left Shubenacadie for Maine. Henry, a residential school survivor and later a decorated World War II veteran, could provide poignant insights on life in the Canadian Services as a Mi'kmaw individual.[89] Rose Ann Knockwood, an author, poet, and welfare officer, earned her bachelor of social work from Dalhousie University in 1991, at the age of sixty-five. Isabelle, who attended residential school from the age of four in 1936 until she was eleven, participated as an activist in the American Indian Movement (AIM) and was a political activist in Boston during the 1960s until pursuing university studies and her later career as a writer. She wrote of her early experiences at residential school in *Out of the Depths*, a book she wrote with Gillian Thomas while a student at Saint Mary's University in Halifax.[90] While working on her master's thesis in 2013, she received an honorary doctorate from St. Mary's University. And Noel Raymond Knockwood (1932–2014) was a residential school survivor, a veteran of the Korean War, a Native Studies instructor during the 1970s in the Transition Year Programme at Dalhousie University, a director of the Native Friendship Centre in Halifax, and an addictions counsellor. He won a National Aboriginal Achievement Award and in his later years assumed the office of sergeant-at-arms in the Nova Scotia Legislature. Noel Raymond's early education only extended to grade six, but after his years in the military he finished high school and earned a bachelor of arts degree from St. Mary's University and a diploma from the Cody Institute at St. Francis Xavier University in Antigonish. He spoke Mi'kmaq fluently, and from 1975 until his death in April 2014 he was an active member of the Mi'kmaw Grand Council, during which time he acted as an advisor and spiritual leader by blending his family's deep interest in knowledge and learning with the leadership tradition of his ancestors.[91] It is a testament to human resilience and the human spirit that, given Stephen Knockwood Jr.'s desire to have his descendants succeed in both the Mi'kmaw and non-Indigenous worlds, they – despite major challenges – have done as he wished and admirably so, carving themselves important niches in Nova Scotian history by showing how cherished Mi'kmaw cultural values can contribute to bettering Canada's cultural, educational, social, and political life.

– Janet E. Chute, assisted by Doris Labradore

Acknowledgments: The author is grateful to her field assistant, Doris Labradore, a graduate of Dalhousie University, for collecting information in 1990 relating to Stephen Knockwood's life. Though Doris Labradore's father, John Labrador, hailed from Bridgewater, her mother, a member of the Bent family, lived in Kentville near the site of the old Pine Woods settlement and knew the history of the area. Florence May Knockwood, Spurgeon Knockwood's widow, received us graciously at her home near New Ross and shared valuable historical information. Many other people over the years also provided information for this essay, among them Stephen Knockwood's granddaughter Isabelle and grandsons Henry and Noel Raymond. The author is also grateful to Mohamed and Theeby Elkateb and Florence May Knockwood. The author's grandfathers, John Chute, in the late nineteenth century lived near the Knockwood homestead in the Pine Woods, near Kentville, and respected Stephen Knockwood Jr. as an intelligent and energetic community leader.

Part Two

Wagobagitk, Sipekne'katik aqq Eskikewa'kik – Cobequid, the Shubenacadie District, and Nova Scotia's Eastern Shore

10

Paul Peminout and the Peminout Pauls of the Sipekne'katik District

A British Supporter

Paul Peminout[1] (c.1725–c.1812) was an eighteenth-century Mi'kmaw head man living along the Stewiacke River in central Nova Scotia until he emerged during the American Revolution as district chief of the Shubenacadie River Valley region, known in Mi'kmaq as Sipekne'katik, or "the place of the wild potatoes or groundnuts."[2] His early life is shrouded in mystery, except for occasional insights about him revealed in oral traditions. One such oral tradition portrays him as an ally, friend, and possibly a confidante of Michael Francklin (1733–82), who was a member of the province's merchant and official elite. Peminout and Francklin likely came to know one another during one of Francklin's hunting expeditions along the Shubenacadie River Valley in the early 1750s, or during trade transactions.[3]

Francklin was lieutenant governor of Nova Scotia from March 1766 until the spring of 1776, and he assumed the office of role of acting governor during four of Governor William Campbell's absences. In 1777 he became provincial Indian commissioner, a position he held until his death in November 1782.[4] Legend has it that during the Seven Years' War, Peminout, with Francklin's encouragement, accompanied General James Wolfe in September 1759 to fight the French on the Plains of Abraham, and afterwards received a bright red cloak from General Jeffrey Amherst in recognition of the value of his service in persuading other

Mi'kmaw leaders to fight with the British in 1758 and 1759.[5] Peminout was reputed to have cut a striking figure with his red cloak swirling behind him.[6]

Though one of the first, Peminout was not the only Mi'kmaw leader to support the British in the 1750s. As early as 1745, during King George's War, several Mi'kmaw head men near Piziquid (now Windsor, Nova Scotia), among them Jean-Baptiste Thoma of Panuke Lake, extended peace overtures to the British at Annapolis Royal. Tired of the disruptive impact of war on their communities, they persuaded Pierre Landry, a Mi'kmaq-speaking Acadian, to write down their wishes and convey them in a letter to the British governor. It soon became obvious, however, that Mi'kmaw peacemaking missions would be rebuffed by the British authorities as long as open conflict existed between England and France.[7]

Immediately following the signing of the Treaty of Aix-la-Chapelle in 1748, a few leaders resumed their calls for peace, but they jettisoned these initiatives after the British established a fort near Grand Pré and established Halifax without any recognition whatsoever of prior Aboriginal claims to either area.[8] In response, a Mi'kmaw council at Port Toulouse, Île-Royale (now St. Peter's, Cape Breton) directed a letter to Governor Edward Cornwallis in September 1749 warning that if their claims were not recognized, their warriors would harass any colonists who dared leave the protection of their palisades. While their missive was less a declaration of war than an expression of extreme exasperation with the British for ignoring their territorial rights,[9] Governor Edward Cornwallis, despite pleas for caution from the London Colonial Office, decided to overawe the Mi'kmaq by force rather than commence diplomatic negotiations. It was a policy that prompted the very Mi'kmaw reprisals Cornwallis dreaded.[10]

True to their word, the Mi'kmaq, along with Acadian resistance fighters, began raids on Halifax and Dartmouth in the fall and winter of 1749–50.[11] Owing to the terror these forays caused among local townsfolk, Cornwallis in October 1749 placed a bounty of ten guineas on Mi'kmaw scalps.[12] While it is unlikely that this proclamation fostered the cessation of hostilities that occurred in the spring of 1752, the Mi'kmaq nevertheless agreed to lay down their arms. The Mi'kmaw council in Cape Breton evidently had revised its strategies in favour of renewed peace overtures.

The Mi'kmaq contended that an enduring peace would only ensue once the British recognized prior Indigenous rights to the land. They also expected payment in return for permitting the British to settle at Halifax.[13] The Mi'kmaq considered these stipulations timely and just, as they drew on long-standing northeastern Algonquian cultural practices that called for compensation whenever an outside party used land or resources.[14] Major Jean-Baptiste Cope, at that time the Sipekne'katik district chief, or *bun*, agreed to convey these messages to Halifax.[15] Cope's territorial aegis embraced an important Acadian and Mi'kmaw religious site, St. Anne's mission, established in 1722 by Abbé Antoine Gaulin, a graduate of the seminary of the Société des Missions Étrangères de Paris, based in Quebec.[16] Standing near the juncture of the Stewiacke and Shubenacadie Rivers, this mission lay five French leagues upstream from where the mouth of the Shubenacadie River emptied into Cobequid Bay. It served both the Sipekne'katik Mi'kmaq and Acadian-*métis* from settlements along the eastern Atlantic coast.[17]

Despite the fact that Shubenacadie leaders like Cope interacted with French missionaries within their midst, they still found it practical to agree to certain accommodations with the British, to ensure the safety of their community.[18] During peacetime this required negotiations and a degree of compromise with agents of both the French and British Crowns, but in time of war, head men faced difficult challenges. Often they had to make choices that, if

unsuccessful, undermined their authority and led to their political downfall.

The Mi'kmaq in the eighteenth century lacked the numbers, organizational strength, and technical capacity to affect the balance of power between the imperial contenders in the Northeast. Even the influence that the French missionaries, residing at the Roman Catholic mission of St. Anne on the banks of the Shubenacadie River, wielded over their Indigenous congregants had a deleterious effect on the stability of Sipekne'katik district leadership, by introducing role conflicts. Mi'kmaw chiefs tried to heed the directives of the French clergy, but they also had to address the growing political influence of the British at Annapolis Royal and, later, Halifax. Consequently, chiefs at Shubenacadie replaced one another with surprising frequency.[19] Between 1722 and 1750 the Sipekne'katik Mi'kmaq experienced a succession of four district chiefs, and it soon appeared that Jean-Baptiste Cope would face similar stresses and strains.

A Peace Overture Made and Then Jettisoned

A seasoned political leader of forty-six years of age, Major Cope was appointed late in the summer of 1752 as a peacemaking delegate by Mi'kmaw councils at Chignecto and Cape Breton, as well as by the Sipekne'katik community.[20] After being apprised by the British authorities that he would be cordially received at Halifax,[21] Cope arrived at the governor's council chambers on 12 September bearing a memorial pointedly stating that Mi'kmaq expected to be paid for insults to their territorial rights. Should such remuneration be forthcoming, then further peace proposals might be considered.[22]

Though Cope endeavoured to bring his people's demands to the negotiating table, he soon found himself outmaneuvered by the executive council. Council members ignored his call for compensation and encouraged him to sign a treaty of peace and friendship, similar to a treaty the British made with the Eastern Abenaki in 1725. Under this treaty's terms, the Mi'kmaq would keep the peace, return military deserters, and succour British and New Englanders who were shipwrecked or in distress. Rather than paying the Mi'kmaq for British contravention of rights, the British promised not to molest them on their hunting and fishing grounds and to establish a truckhouse at Shubenacadie.[23] However, each year on 1 October the Sipekne'katik band, as well as other groups who chose to sign treaty, would receive gifts to renew the ongoing agreement. A provision was also included that any Mi'kmaw grievances could be brought to the attention of the executive council, to be settled fairly in the courts of British jurisprudence.[24]

After consulting with his people, Cope and three of his head men, Andrew Handley (André) Martin, Gabriel Martin, and Francis Jeremiah, arrived in Halifax on 22 November 1752 and signed a peace agreement on behalf of around ninety Mi'kmaw men, women, and children.[25] Throughout the following winter Cope tried, with limited success, to bring other Mi'kmaw leaders to the peacemaking table.[26] Then things rapidly soured.

Louisbourg's officialdom and the missionaries, especially Abbé Le Loutre, who had just returned from a visit to France, denounced Cope's action.[27] Faced with strident opposition from the French, Cope sought to regain as much of his former political autonomy as possible, in case the recent treaty fell through and the British insulted his people. An incident of the latter order arose in February 1753 when James Grace and John Connor of Halifax killed six Mi'kmaq at Mocodome (now County Harbour), along Nova Scotia's Eastern Shore.[28] The investigation that ensued at Halifax was biased and inconclusive. Bitter and seeking vengeance, Cope concocted an elaborate ruse to punish his betrayers. He invited a government sloop to anchor in Jeddore Harbour, and on 21 April 1753 joined several others in killing the vessel's captain and crew, except for one man, Anthony Casteel. Casteel, who survived by passing himself off as a Frenchman, learned the genuine story of what ensued at Mocodome in February 1753 from a Mi'kmaw woman he met while he was being transported by the Mi'kmaq to Cobequid.[29] Cope never parleyed with the British again, and until his death around 1758 remained an inveterate opponent of the British regime.[30]

The office of Sipekne'katik district chief fell to Claude René, who signed treaty with the British in 1760 on behalf of the Shubenacadie Mi'kmaq.[31] Chief René lived for at least another decade, to be succeeded by Paul Peminout. The 1760s and 1770s constituted an era of unprecedented change along the Shubenacadie River Valley. Settler influxes overwhelmed the Mi'kmaq numerically. Rapid population growth in the new townships of Falmouth, Cornwallis, Newport, and Horton fueled Indigenous anxieties, and

tensions between the settlers and Mi'kmaq arose whenever colonists heedlessly pressed onto territory containing resources crucial to Mi'kmaw survival.

A few British officials pointed to the Shubenacadie River region as a locale where Mi'kmaq might be induced to settle and farm.[32] On the eve of the Seven Years' War, however, it was feared that the Shubenacadie River would serve as a Mi'kmaw war road, since it constituted "the most considerable of all the Indian Passes, from the Eastward and Northward, to the Parts adjacent to Halifax."[33] To destroy St. Anne's mission's value as a Mi'kmaw mustering site for French and Indigenous resistance fighters, in 1755 British soldiers burned the mission to the ground.[34]

Indigenous and Acadian reprisal was swift. A party of Mi'kmaq and Acadians living along the Stewiacke River counter-attacked and killed thirty British soldiers. In this conflict's aftermath, the Sipekne'katik chief, occasionally assisted by the itinerant French missionary Abbé Pierre Maillard, held religious services the best they could at their desecrated mission site.[35] Maillard sought to make the Mi'kmaq as religiously self-sufficient as possible. Chiefs were given leave to perform rites of marriage, burial, and baptism in the absence of an ordained cleric, as well as preside over yearly religious festivities, such as St. Anne's Day on 26 July.[36] After the mission site was granted to Lieutenant Colonel Frederick Hamilton in 1763, Mi'kmaw and Acadians continued to visit it to hold religious ceremonies.

The Sipekne'katik Mi'kmaq and Michael Francklin

Michael Francklin, who arrived in Halifax from England in 1752, learned of the 1752 treaty proceedings as well as the 21 April 1753 debacle at Jeddore directly from John Connors, since the ferryman owned the premises Francklin rented for his first dram shop.[37] Despite fearsome stories Francklin must have heard of Indigenous raids and reprisals, he had sufficiently ingratiated himself with the Sipekne'katik Mi'kmaq by the spring of 1754 that they agreed to escort him on hunting expeditions along the Shubenacadie River valley. The youthful merchant dealt in spirituous liquors, but he also traded valuable practical articles with band members such as clothing, blankets, guns, and ammunition. His genuine interest in and respect for Mi'kmaw culture, as well as his stores of welcome merchandise, caused the Sipekne'katik Mi'kmaq to welcome him as a friend.

Owing to his connections with the Shubenacadie Mi'kmaw constituency and his ability to speak French fluently, Francklin escaped harm after being captured by a travelling Indigenous party and taken to the Gaspé, where he remained from June to October of 1754. During these months the Sipekne'katik Mi'kmaq negotiated with his captors for his continued safety. He was well enough treated by the Mi'kmaq that he deliberately delayed returning home, and instead had monies forwarded by friends in Halifax to him at the Gaspé so he could spend more time learning about the Mi'kmaw language and customs.[38]

Francklin also attended Mi'kmaw councils held near Halifax and encouraged Peminout and his associates to uphold the British cause. Peminout afterwards staunchly defended his support of the British, despite enmity from chiefs who favoured the French. His son Phillip followed his father's lead, and allegedly was killed around 1758 in what is now Point Pleasant Park after declaring that he would fight for the British during the Seven Year War. His political opponents, among them Jean-Baptiste Cope, are reported to have chased him to the Halifax palisades and shot him down in a hail of bullets.[39] Another of the chief's sons, François, was later said to have killed Cope to avenge his brother's death.[40]

When Francklin became lieutenant governor, his superiors at the Colonial Office sent him a set of ambiguous instructions that claimed most "settlement [in Nova Scotia] was made beyond the Limits prescribed by the Royal Proclamation [of 1763]."[41] Perhaps owing to this lack of clarity, Francklin ignored the proclamation's provisions, which declared that in order for the British to acquire Aboriginal land, negotiations first had to be opened with Mi'kmaw leaders, compensation agreed upon, and a surrender made. Instead, the lieutenant governor began to secure large land grants throughout the province, which he placed in his own name but which he intended later to transfer to specific leaders.

Francklin also distributed gifts to chiefs and their head men. His predecessor in office, Lieutenant Governor Montague Wilmot, in 1764 was told to seek out chiefs of "such rank and consideration [as] to render it prudent to allow them regular presents – for the safety of incoming settlers to the province," and Francklin continued this practice. He also lent an ear to Mi'kmaw grievances. When the Sipekne'katik Mi'kmaq apprised him of their lack of clergy and the dilapidated state of their mission, he arranged in 1767 for the appointment of two Roman Catholic missionaries, and in 1770 had a small chapel built on the St. Anne's mission site.[42]

In 1777 Francklin, finding himself bypassed for a continued term as lieutenant governor owing to the actions of political rivals, successfully argued his fitness for the role of superintendent of Indian Affairs on the grounds that he knew the Mi'kmaq and in 1754 had lived as a captive with them. By this time Peminout had been the Sipekne'katik district leader for several years, having succeeded to the office on Claude René's death around 1772. Peminout had received gifts and even the promise of a land grant from Francklin in the early 1770s,[43] but the two men's mutual respect for one another increased during the American Revolutionary years, when Peminout was in his early fifties and Francklin in his forties. While he was Indian commissioner, Francklin secured stipends for Mi'kmaw emissaries employed by the government, defended Mi'kmaq who suffered abuse from settlers, and rewarded feats of Indigenous heroism.[44] Peminout's close association with Francklin meanwhile gave him access to British corridors of power in Halifax and Windsor and raised him in the esteem of the Mi'kmaw community at large. It so changed the nature of Sipekne'katik leadership that the formerly rapid turnover of district leaders along the Shubenacadie River Valley ceased.

The Peminout Land Grants: Stewiacke and Shubenacadie Grand Lake

In the late eighteenth century, Paul Peminout's territorial aegis was extensive and untrammelled by settlement. Until 1810, his group occupied an ancient encampment ground on the lower reaches of the Stewiacke River known in Mi'kmaq as *Esiktaweak*,[45] but the lands under his jurisdiction extended east to the Atlantic coast, west to the watershed of the Kennetcook River, northwest to the Cobequid Basin, and up the Stewiacke River into Pictou County. Remembering Francklin's promise in 1772 to protect his proprietary rights, and faced in the late 1770s with a community of disbanded soldiers at Fort Ellis, which stood at the juncture of the Shubenacadie and Stewiacke rivers, Chief Peminout appealed in the spring of 1779 for a land grant similar to one accorded the

Malecite in 1767 on the Saint John River.[46] His appeal was successful. Francklin supported his claims, and on 28 June 1779 the executive council accorded the chief a two-mile-square tract on the middle reaches of the Stewiacke River, adjoining Lord Egmont's lands. The allotment was to be "made to Mr. Francklin and Paul Pemmeywicte, One of the Principal Indians, in Trust to and for the said Indians."[47]

Francklin may have intended to later transfer the trust deed solely into the chief's name, but at age forty-nine he suddenly died, probably of a heart attack, on 8 November of 1782 while handing out blankets to the Mi'kmaq at his Buckingham Street resident in Halifax. Consequently the tract was neither formally registered nor surveyed prior to the arrival of Loyalists in the Stewiacke River area. Peminout likely joined the ranks of the two hundred Mi'kmaq who attended Francklin's funeral and, voicing a death chant, solemnly followed his coffin to its place of burial in the crypt of St. Paul's Church.[48]

Hearing no more about his property, Peminout in 1783 travelled to Windsor where he demanded that George Henry Monk, Francklin's successor as Indian superintendent, ensure that his grant was recognized by the government.[49] Monk referred the matter to Governor John Parr, noting that "Paul Bemeneault prays for a Grant of Land on the River Schediach [*sic*, Stewiacke] applied for him & his tribe by the late Superintendent Mr. Francklin."[50] At the time Peminout represented four families holding a joint interest in the Stewiacke tract: Peminout's own immediate family, his grown son Pierre's family, and the families of two of Pierre's sons.

Monk lumped Peminout's property in with eight other tracts throughout Nova Scotia accorded to the Mi'kmaq.[51] On 17 December 1782 he drafted a licence of occupation for this land, which read:

A License for Paul Pemmenwick [Peminout] and the Indians in the District of Shubenacadie & Cobequid. To Occupy a Tract of Land Situate laying and being on the River called Stewyack, to the Eastward and Adjoining land granted to the late Earl of Egmont and others extending One Mile Back on each side of the said River, and Two Miles in a right line up the said River Measuring from the Eastern Bound of said Egmont's Land containing Two Thousand Five hundred and Sixty Acres.[52]

Although Monk prepared a licence of occupation for Peminout's tract, it ultimately was treated as an outright grant and sold by its proprietors. By contrast, the other eight were held only "at the pleasure of His Majesty" and made into reserves or else expropriated by the powers that be for settlement purposes.[53] On 18 December 1783, the provincial surveyor-general, Charles Morris (1759–1831), accorded a second grant to the Sipekne'katik chief's son, Jacques-Pierre (Jacques or James) and nine of his sons. Morris's description of Jacques's tract, which lay in Halifax County at the head of Shubenacadie Grand Lake, which formed the headwaters of the Shubenacadie River, was unusual in that it lacked both areal boundaries and estimated acreage:

A License for Jack or James Pemmenwick [Peminout],[54] son of the Chief of the Tribe of the Shubenaccadie Indians, of land sufficient for nine families (being his children) on the Northern side of the River Shubenaccadie at the Point where the great Lake Discharges Itself, and extending on the Great Lake, and the said River, with Liberty of Hunting and Fishing in the Woods, Lakes and Rivers of that Vicinity."[55]

This allotment was also treated by the Peminouts as a freehold grant, capable of alienation by its owners. The vague description of its boundaries and the ambiguous nature of the Mi'kmaq's tenure of the land (was it merely a licence of occupation or an outright grant?) would cause problems in the future, though at the time land in the area was not in high demand, and no survey was undertaken of the parcel for another twenty years.

Chief Peminout's Family: 1790–1810

Throughout his lifetime Paul Peminout, whose wife remains unknown,[56] had at least nine sons and three daughters. Two sons, Phillip and François, died before 1760, while two others, Joseph[57] and Simon, appear infrequently in the documentary record.[58] By contrast, the chief's youngest sons, Pierre Sr. (c.1740–c.1830), Jacques (c.1745–c.1810),[59] and Louis-Benjamin (1762–1842),[60] figure prominently in the history of the Sipekne'katik district. And, although the evidence is scanty for such a contention, another of the chief's sons may have been Hobblewest (Ambroise?) Paul of Stewiacke, the father of Mary Christiana Peminout Paul Morris (c.1804–1886), a striking woman who excelled as a barkworker, quillworker, basketmaker, and seamstress and was sought out in the 1850s and 1860s as an artist and photographer's model.[61]

Pierre Sr., Chief Peminout's third-youngest son, remained on the Stewiacke grant for most of his life and took care of his father in his final years. Under his leadership the Stewiacke Mi'kmaw community briefly flourished economically in the early 1800s, with trade being carried on with several local merchants.[62] Pierre Sr. and his wife Marie had at least five sons: Pierre Jr. (c.1763–c.1850), Nestus (b.1764), Abluis (b.c1768), James (b.c.1869), and Joseph (b.1770).[63] In 1801 James Fulton, a merchant and justice of the peace living at Stewiacke, responded to a government circular requesting information on the Colchester County Mi'kmaq, by reporting on Nestus, Abluis, and Joseph's coopering and farming activities. He did not, however, mention Pierre Jr., who had left the Stewiacke area by 1801.[64]

Pierre Sr.'s younger brother Jacques-Pierre Peminout Paul lived at Nelegakumik, or "[the place of] broken snowshoes," in Newport Township.[65] A devout Roman Catholic, in the 1790s Jacques aided Jean Baptist Roma, who prior to 1762 had been one of Abbé Maillard's assistants. The two during the summer conducted Roman Catholic services in the Mi'kmaw language at Chezzetcook and, more occasionally, at St. Anne's mission along the Shubenacadie River.[66] Jacques, who lived near Newport Station in Hants County, had nine sons: John (also known as Jean Lucien, c. 1766–c.1815),[67] Samuel (c.1770–c.1844), Francis (1778–1861), Gorham (c.1779–c.1860), Peter, Thomas, Claude, Alexis, and James.[68]

Chief Peminout's youngest son, Louis-Benjamin, whose Mi'kmaw name was "Passimaugh Pemmineweet [Peminout]," was a hunter, fisher, cooper, and farmer. The Colchester County justice of the peace James Fulton referred to him as "the son of old Capt. Paul of Stewiack," while British officials in Halifax, Joseph Howe among then, addressed him as "Sam," most likely derived from the Mi'kmaw pronunciation of "Louis-Ben."[69] In 1802 Louis-Benjamin lived north of Shubenacadie Great Lake, "up Near the Nine Mile River," with his wife, Madelaine Ball, three sons "over thirteen years of age," and a two-year old named Jacques-Pierre. A year before he had sent Louis, one of his older sons who later became a Mi'kmaw judge, to live with a farmer named Paul Woodworth and learn how to cultivate the soil.[70] Louis-Benjamin usually hunted at Stewiacke with his brother Pierre, whose sons received a bounty of ten shillings from their settler neighbours for every bear they killed.[71]

Forcing An Official Acknowledgement of Mi'kmaw Grievances

Francklin's successor George Henry Monk held the office of Indian superintendent for sixteen years, from 1783 to 1799, during which time he drew up and registered licences of occupation for Mi'kmaw hunting and fishing tracts throughout the province. After 1799, the office of Indian superintendent lapsed for seven years, until 1807, when Monk resumed his former duties until 1809.

The change of Indian superintendent in 1783 meant the onset of a radically new order. Monk was the antithesis of Francklin in both his attitudes towards and his treatment of the Mi'kmaq. He knew that his predecessor had rewarded chiefs with generous presents and promises of land for their fidelity to the British during the American Revolution. But being by nature a parsimonious person and associated with some of Francklin's political rivals,[72] Monk viewed the practice of annually dispensing presents and honorifics as an extravagant waste of government largesse, gauged to foster Mi'kmaw idleness and indigence. Since Indigenous military allies were not as crucial to the British as formerly, Monk's superiors, moreover, circumscribed the amount of money he had available for food, blankets, clothing, and ammunition.

Monk's primary course of action was to deny any able-bodied Mi'kmaq access to government supplies. When Jacques Peminout Paul (whom Monk identified as "James … the son of Paul Emannit"), Jacques's eldest son John, Bartholomew Momquarret [or Momcharret] the elderly Minas head chief, and Louis Anthony (or Toney), who acted as Jacques's interpreter,[73] appeared at the commissioner's door in Windsor on 12 January 1794, Monk steeled himself to refuse his visitors' requests. Once inside Monk's office, Jacques immediately embarked on a lengthy speech in Mi'kmaq, which Louis Toney translated into English.[74] He had come, he explained, to inform Monk that big game hunting and fishing had failed the previous fall owing to competition from settlers. In consequence, his people were reduced to subsisting on hares, partridges, and small pond fish.

Despite Jacques's animated appeal, Monk at first proved unsympathetic and abrupt. He suspected Jacques's speech had been "concerted" the previous fall by Mi'kmaw leaders such as Charles Alexis of Cape Sable, whom he feared would spread anti-British sentiments should the annual government present distributions not be restored. To hasten Jacques's party on its way, he attempted to mollify his visitors by handing out meagre supplies of cloth, powder, and ammunition and then bid them adieu. Jacques was not so easily placated. He retorted that he construed the Indian superintendent's lack of generosity as an insult, since the pittance of cloth he received would not "cover all his nine children if they were laid together on the ground." It would be better for the Mi'kmaq his people "to suffer as they had done till they were all dead," he concluded, than to take trifles that barely allowed them to exist.

To diffuse the tension, Monk resorted to a tactic of divide-and-conquer to win over Louis Toney by minor bribery, and so separate him from his companions. Louis was given extra cloth, thread, and buttons and invited to act on occasion as Monk's interpreter. The commissioner also tried to get Louis to reveal the reason why Charles Alexis passed through Windsor on 10 December, less than a month before.[75] The Cape Sable leader had married a daughter of Antoine Hébert, an Acadian who had opposed the Acadian removals of the mid-1750s, and Monk wanted to determine if Alexis resented British authority.[76]

Louis Toney was able to dodge the commissioner's question because at that moment Jacques, who hitherto had spoken only Mi'kmaq, asked Monk in clear English if he would give him two loaves of bread. It was a tactical coup on Jacques's part, for Monk remembered giving Charles Alexis two loaves on 10 December, and it piqued him that Jacques knew of this. His Mi'kmaw visitors were far more informed and politically sophisticated than he had given them credit for. Both Jacques and Louis were capable of engaging him in a game of wits in which he, if he were not careful, might come out the loser.

They also made it clear that no matter how hard Monk might try to pry information from either of them, they would tell him only what they had been delegated to relay by others of their nation, and no more. Seeing little use in prolonging the meeting, Monk became impatient and urged the Mi'kmaq to leave. When Bartholomew Momcharret turned to speak, the commissioner abruptly silenced the elderly Minas chief on the grounds he was reiterating the same message Jacques had delivered. Louis Toney stated pointedly that the Mi'kmaq expected Monk to report the contents of Jacques's speech to Lieutenant Governor John Wentworth. Monk countered that

Wentworth offered only what the King ordered and, as the King's servant, lacked to the authority to restore annual present distributions. At this, Jacques exclaimed in Mi'kmaq, while his son John translated, that if "King George was so poor that he could give no more to the Indians, the Indians better take nothing."[77] While Monk saw the discontinuance of presents as a savings to the provincial treasury, Jacques viewed it as an abrogation of a long-standing pact forged between the British Crown and the Mi'kmaw people. When Monk showed him the door, John as he went out muttered, "I won't trouble you again. The Indians must take care of themselves."[78]

The incident left Monk feeling uneasy. He was certain that every word uttered in his office would be repeated to other Mi'kmaw leaders, especially Charles Alexis. He even wondered if he might face a Mi'kmaw uprising of some kind, engendered in the back country around Gaspereau Lake in Kings County, where Alexis had been headed. He also hired a petty merchant, Job Ross, to find out what he could about Mi'kmaw meetings and movements. Ross reported back a week later that the Mi'kmaq intended to remain peaceful, and since they were experiencing severe hardship, wanted their grievances to be laid before the lieutenant governor.[79] After reflecting on this new information, Monk had to admit that Mi'kmaw pleas for provisions and supplies might prove hard to ignore. Settlers around Newport, Falmouth, and Rawdon overhunted the game reserves, drove the Mi'kmaq from their fishing locales, and burned the forest so that animals of any kind had grown extremely scarce. In the weeks following, Monk encountered even more disturbing news concerning the extent of Mi'kmaw distress from hunger and cold. Letters sent to him by military personnel and several concerned settlers at Newport told of such terrible suffering among the Mi'kmaq that even the few who might harbour militant intentions had to subordinate such thoughts to the struggle simply to keep alive.[80] In the end, Monk took pen in hand and set down the main points of Jacques's speech, adding clauses supplied to him by Charles Alexis, who sporadically visited his office. These he organized into a petition to send to Lieutenant Governor Wentworth in Halifax.

Jacques's son John met with Monk again on 6 February and expressed despair at forgoing charity he could no longer live without. At first, the commissioner considered turning him away empty handed as punishment for his impertinence, but on second thought decided to invite him back the following day. After arranging for Michael Francklin's widow, Susannah Boutineau, and a Windsor merchant named George Deschamps, who during the American Revolution had been the shipping agent at Fort Howe, to be present at the meeting, he gave John a chance to make amends and offered him some provisions for his wife and child.[81]

Before he left, John asked Monk for confirmation that the petition his father had requested had been sent to the lieutenant governor. Monk replied in the affirmative. On 24 January a courier, D. Rudolph, had left Windsor for Halifax with a memorial for Wentworth that explained that the coasts and river valleys once frequented by the Mi'kmaw population had been settled by Europeans, roads had been carved into the interior, and settlers pursued the same dwindling stocks of game and fish as the original proprietors of the land. Settlers often prevented Mi'kmaq from cutting wood on their properties, and where wood was still accessible, basket manufacturing usually provided insufficient income for clothes and provisions. The memorial further pointed out that, since "no back country" existed in Nova Scotia – as it did in the Canadas – to which the Mi'kmaw people might flee, the Mi'kmaq feared that without government supplies they would perish in their own country. Until Francklin's death in 1782, they could count on receiving regular distributions of articles that kept them from want. But now they received no more presents or supplies. Nine years previously, when townships were being settled, they had been told by Lieutenant Governor John Parr that they and the new settlers could live together as brothers. "But now the Mickmacks have little or no hunting ground – no regular supplies, no Brothers except among themselves and know not where to go or what to do."[82] The petition closed by hoping Sir John Wentworth would recognize the Mi'kmaq as loyal to the British Crown and grant them relief.

On 5 March John returned to Windsor with Samuel, one of his brothers. After expressing relief that the petition was sent, the two stated they had been hunting back of Horton and Falmouth and were in need of supplies. They also asked for additional provisions for their father, Jacques. To this Monk replied he had implemented a new rule. Having failed to quash gift distributions once and for all, he made it mandatory for any individual wishing assistance to be present in person in order to receive food or goods. For years Jacques had been in the habit of deputing his sons to fetch government provisions, a practice Monk was determined to stop.[83] Their request denied, John and Samuel announced they would immediately travel to Halifax, but refused to elaborate on their reasons for going there.[84] Despite their distress in the midst of a harsh winter, they resisted being reduced to beggars. In the past, their father Jacques had been welcomed at Halifax by provincial officials, military personnel, and dignitaries, and they were optimistic that their trip, too, would bear fruit.

Jacques's two sons returned to Monk's office a week later. In the interim Monk was kept abreast of their activities by Francis Penard (Bernard), a friend of the Peminouts from Minas, who informed him that the two had attained an audience with the lieutenant governor. After meeting with Wentworth, John and Samuel also contacted Richard Bulkeley (1717–1800), who had accompanied Governor Cornwallis to Halifax in 1749 and overseen the delivery of government supplies and allocation of land grants to the Mi'kmaq, until his retirement as provincial secretary in 1792. Willing to assist grandsons of a chief who served the British Crown, the elderly Bulkeley directed his son and successor, James Michael Freke Bulkeley, to draft an order demanding that the Mi'kmaq's requests be promptly and properly addressed. This document read:

> I am to inform you that upon a presentation of distress by the Indians who are the Bearers hereof, His Excy. the Lt. Govr. has given to them 2 muskets, 2 lbs. powder, 8 lb. of shot, with 8 lbs. pork and 10 lbs. bread to each. His Excel. also desires that if you find the Family to which they belong requires further assistance, you will give them a week's or fortnight's allowance according to the system proposed in your last letter to him. J.M.F. Bulkeley[85]

After John and Samuel, with two of their younger brothers in tow, returned to Windsor on 11 March, they immediately handed Bulkeley's document to the commissioner. Monk still felt compelled to refuse Jacques provisions, but as a compromise agreed to supply Jacques with food and goods if he agreed to come to Windsor in person. And once again he appealed to Francklin's widow to assist in securing a harmonious resolution to an awkward situation. Fortunately for the commissioner, Jacques was disposed to be conciliatory when he arrived on 31

March. Standing before Monk, Mrs. Francklin, and members of his family, Jacques apologized for his former conduct. He next declared that, as the representative of the Mi'kmaq living at Cobequid, Windsor, Cornwallis, Annapolis, and the South Mountain, his aim had been to strengthen his peoples' ties with the Crown, not undermine those that existed. He further acknowledged that he had seen Charles Alexis, who had visited all the other Mi'kmaq who had asked Jacques to speak for them. He expected that several of Chief Alexis's deputies would arrive in Windsor shortly and speak on behalf of the Cape Sable band, who formed a separate constituency from his own. He would not join them and for the rest of the winter intended to hunt around Shubenacadie. His hesitancy in coming to see Monk arose from his fears that he would not be hospitably received. It was his wife and sons who eventually persuaded him to visit Windsor. Then, with the friendly face of Mrs. Francklin before him, recalling what he held to be an older and more congenial order, Jacques reconfirmed his loyalty to King George.

Monk then released 120 rations of supplies to his Mi'kmaw visitors. He also warned that if any member of the Peminout family engaged in conversation derogatory to the king, he would hold Jacques personally responsible. He closed the meeting by stressing that he would monitor Jacques's and his sons' activities and remain in close contact with the lieutenant governor regarding them – an empty threat, since Sir John Wentworth was fond of the Peminouts, especially after he received a pair of warm mittens whose wool had been carded, dyed, and knitted by Jacques's wife.[86]

Lands Sales and Lingering Claims

Hard pressed for money to buy food and clothing, the Peminouts began alienating portions of their land along the Stewiacke River. In January 1794, Henry McClellan and John Bonnell, acting through an agent named Charles Dickson,[87] pressured Paul Peminout and his son Pierre to sell them one square mile on either side of the Stewiacke River. Dickson was a familiar figure to the Peminouts, since he along with two other Windsor merchants, Job Ross and George Deschamps, in the past distributed government supplies to the Mi'kmaq. As soon as McClellan and Bonnell's intentions became publicly known, three other settlers also vied to acquire portions of the Stewiacke tract.

Once Lieutenant Governor Wentworth gave his approval, "Pemmewick Paul" and his son Pierre on 31 March 1794 sold the portion of their grant lying furthest upstream along the Stewiacke River. Their return for this sale was not large: McClellan and Bonnell received 1,280 acres for £25.[88] Not long afterwards, Robert Kennedy bought 200 acres on the river's north side for £7,[89] Henry McClellan and William Kennedy purchased 200 more acres for £6.5, and John Bonnell obtained 24 acres on the south side of the river for £3.[90] *In toto*, the Mi'kmaq in 1794 received only £41.5 for 1,704 acres. This left 856 acres of the Stewiacke grant, originally 2,560 acres, in Peminout hands.

Eleven years later, the Peminouts sold two further parcels, one of which may not even have been within the bounds of the Stewiacke grant. On 31 May 1801, Joseph "Pemmewit" (Peminout) agreed within six months to sell Richard Upham 150 acres on the north side of the Stewiacke River for £100.[91] This land was fertile, for £100 was a fair sum at the time, and included an "unimproved farm" on which the Mi'kmaq settled after the 1794 purchases had been made.[92] While this farm lay outside the bounds of the Peminout grant, John Harris, the farm's original grantee, may have decided not to continue on the land and instead relinquished it at some point to the Mi'kmaq.[93] The second plot, sold by Peter Peminout Paul Sr. to John Bonnell on 25 June 1805 for £2, definitely lay within the original grant, but it remained unsurveyed and lacked areal definition. The deed of sale, signed by Samuel Smith and Benjamin Goodwin, the witnesses to the transaction, simply defined the plot's inner boundary "as running from Henry McClellan's lower line of land" along the course of the river until it "strikes the lower line of the Indian grant."[94] If the land surveyed by Harris lay within the Indian grant, the Peminouts' 1801 sale of 150 acres would have reduced the Mi'kmaq's holdings to about 100 acres. But there is no way of telling, given the imprecise nature of the description on the 1805 deed docket, whether the sale of 1805 was for 100 acres or not. Given that Joseph and Jacques Peminout Paul had received £100 for 150 acres four years previously, £2 for 100 acres constituted a poor bargain.

The land sales made between 1794 and 1805 left a host of questions in their wake. Had the whole of the original Peminout grant at Stewiacke been alienated, or did a small portion still remained unsold?[95] Had all the Peminouts who had a claim to the Stewiacke tract agreed to the sales? Mi'kmaw families continued seasonally to hunt and fish along the Stewiacke River, and several Peminouts still occupied small parcels of land in the Stewiacke area.[96] The nebulous character of these land sales, coupled with the possibility that an Aboriginal lien still lingered within the "Indian grant," would arise as bones of contention within the Mi'kmaw community in the late twentieth century.[97]

During the first decade of the nineteenth century, Louis-Benjamin Peminout Paul lived on the Shubenacadie Grand Lake grant, where he built two log cabins and cleared fifty acres on either side of Lewey's Brook, which emptied into the head of the lake. He also planted on an offshore island, dubbed "Paul's Island" by local settlers. He felt obliged to cultivate the soil, since settlers had so overhunted game in the area that beaver, moose, and caribou, and even partridge and rabbits, had grown scarce."[98] Farming was unpredictable at Lewey's Brook, but his brothers Jacques and Pierre and their families at Stewiacke were faring far worse. In January 1803, James Fulton and other justices of the Colchester Court of Sessions informed James Brenton, Charles Morris, and Michael Wallace, members of a newly established commission responsible for the distribution of Mi'kmaw relief, that Jacques, John, Peter, Claude, Abluis, Joseph, and Nestus were suffering from hunger and cold, and needed food and blankets.[99] The commissioners at first hesitated, claiming in contradistinction to Fulton and his associates that most of the Peminouts were "strong, likely young men." In the end, however, they agreed to provide monies from the provincial relief fund because of outbreaks of sickness at Stewiacke and the fact that "one old man" (undoubtedly Paul Peminout) still lived with the group. Their hesitancy in acting sooner, they continued, arose from the fact that Jacques's son John and Peter Sr.'s son Peter Jr. had been "mis-spending the summer in idle journeys to Quebec, when they ought to have been providing for the support of their aged relatives."[100] The magistrates were instructed to discourage such wanderings and impress upon the Mi'kmaq "the necessity of trusting to their own exertions for bread."[101]

Still faced with shortages of funds, in April 1808 the Peminouts allowed a survey of the 104 acres containing Louis-Benjamin's clearing and made arrangements to sell at least part of their land at Shubenacadie Grand Lake.[102] Jacques, who since 1893 had held principal title to this grant, must have died

soon afterwards, for on 6 June 1812 his father, Paul "Pemmineau," sold the plot for sixty pounds to Richard John Uniacke, the provincial attorney general.[103] In August 1812 the parcel came to form a minuscule portion of a vast four-thousand-acre grant awarded to Norman Fitzgerald Uniacke, who divided it among seven proprietors.[104]

The surveyor general, Charles Morris (1759–1831), viewed this sale as an unmitigated disaster for the Sipekne'katik Mi'kmaq, since the property contained important fisheries and its soil was fertile.[105] To Morris, the transaction was a prime example of why reserves should be established for the Mi'kmaw in perpetuity, without right of extinguishment. Later, in 1820, Morris would lay out Shubenacadie Reserve No. 13, a thousand-acre tract on Shubenacadie Grand Lake disposable only by formal surrender, but by this time the best land in the area had been purchased, so the reserve lacked good soil and productive weir sites.[106]

To compensate for their territorial losses owing to their recent land sales, the Peminouts decided to apply for a grant of land surrounding the old St. Anne's mission site. The chapel Michael Francklin had built for them in 1770 had fallen into disrepair, and a landlord was trying to prevent their access to the property. The time seemed opportune to appeal to Halifax for more land, since in the face of warnings of a possible outbreak of war with the United States, the colonial government leaned towards being more receptive to Indigenous needs and grievances.[107] Three of Jacques's sons, Samuel, Francis, and Gorham, wasted no time in petitioning for 2,100 acres, or 200 acres for each of eleven family heads living at Shubenacadie. This tract, they added, should be fertile, close to markets and, most important, embrace their cherished mission site on the west bank of the Shubenacadie River.[108]

Wentworth and Charles Morris refused to countenance any negotiations with the farmer who owned the mission site, and slashed the amount of land the Mi'kmaq could acquire down to 100 acres per family. The resultant 1,100-acre tract lay "four miles east of Parker's bridge" and roughly four kilometers away from the Shubenacadie River. The Peminouts viewed this land, designated "Shubenacadie Reserve No. 14" in 1820,[109] with considerable disappointment, since it failed to encompass the mission site, lay a considerable distance from markets, lacked good soil, and suffered from settler infringement: in 1812 the Ellis family had built a dam for a grist mill and a saw mill on neighbouring property that backed up a local stream and turned a trough in the reserve landscape into a bog that still exists today.[110]

Louis-Benjamin as Sipekne'katik District Chief

Paul Peminout died around 1812. No accounts have been left of his funeral, other than a Mi'kmaw oral tradition holding that on his deathbed the chief requested his body be transported to Halifax and interred alongside Jean Baptist Cope's grave in Point Pleasant Park. His burial site, reputedly selected as a posthumous gesture of reconciliation to the Cope family, lay east of the Martello Tower on the shores of the North West Arm.[111]

Following the chief's burial, the Shubenacadie group began to prepare the way for the installation of a new chief. Louis-Benjamin Peminout Paul was the leading candidate for the office, but certain protocols had to be followed before his appointment could be broadcast throughout the Mi'kmaw community. Louis-Benjamin, along with his nephews Francis, Samuel, and Gorham, left in June 1813 with their wives and eleven children for New Brunswick, and on 1 July arrived on the doorstep of Lieutenant Governor George Stracey Smythe's residence in Saint John. Their business in New Brunswick, they told Smythe, concerned "the choice of a Chief according to the custom of their Tribe."[112] In accordance with the tenets of the Eastern Wabanaki Confederacy, representatives of neighbouring Abenaki nations, among them the Malecite, were invited to ratify the appointment of a new Mi'kmaw district chief. Being unfamiliar with the Peminouts and learning they were from Newport, Nova Scotia, Smythe contacted Lieutenant Colonel Robertson, a senior officer who assured him that the "Pauls were well known to him and several of the officers of the King's residence."[113] When the Mi'kmaq cannily compared the poor treatment they often received from officials in the Northeast with what Indigenous populations in the Canadas might expect from their governments, they received some flour and a barrel of pork for their journey.[114]

The following day the Mi'kmaw party, carrying their supplies, left for Fredericton to visit with a local Roman Catholic priest. They then attended a council meeting near Saint John on 5 July 1813 with Malecite leaders from the Saint John River Valley. At this event, delegates from neighbouring northeastern nations, among them the Penobscot and Passamaquoddy, met with Louis-Benjamin Peminout Paul to appraise his fitness for leadership. Successive councils continued to examine the candidate. Ratification of a chiefly appointment by other nations in the Northeast constituted a lengthy process, often taking over a year to complete.[115]

Louis-Benjamin, his three nephews, and their families returned to Nova Scotia by February 1814, their mission accomplished. The representatives of the Eastern Wabanaki Confederacy had accepted Louis-Benjamin as a new district leader, so they embarked on the next step, confirmation of their choice by heads of government and the Roman Catholic Church in Halifax. Claiming that their sales of baskets during the previous winter had been poor, John Peminout Paul, his brother Samuel, and Joseph Barss petitioned the government for money and provisions, almost certainly with the intention of contributing both towards hosting a feast to celebrate Louis-Benjamin's final installation as Sipekne'katik head chief.[116]

Samuel also met with Abbé Jean-Mandé Sigogne, a Roman Catholic missionary who since 1799 had ministered to the Mi'kmaw and Acadians of Yarmouth and Digby, and in 1814 extended his itinerant travels to Shubenacadie. Impressed by Louis-Benjamin's deep concern for the welfare of his people, the abbé agreed to write a petition to the lieutenant governor, Sir John Coape Sherbrooke, calling for government recognition of Louis-Benjamin's appointment. After promising to express the same loyalty towards George III "which they had formerly kept to and had for the French Kings," Louis-Benjamin, Samuel, Francis, Pierre, and Jean Lucien appended their signatures to Sigogne's memorial. The tenor of their pledges harked back to the reciprocal relationship their people had maintained with the monarch during the French regime, one that made them allies rather than subjects of the French king.[117]

In the aftermath of the War of 1812, Sherbrooke expressed pleasure at encountering an influential chief who was willing to ensure peace and stability among his people. The lieutenant governor responded to Sigogne's petition by preparing a commission, dated 28 April 1814, that proclaimed Louis-Benjamin as leader, not only of the Shubenacadie district but of all the Mi'kmaq in Nova Scotia. The new chief was instructed to use his "utmost endeavours to keep all persons belonging to the Tribe, Loyal, Industrious and Sober and to render them good Subjects and Christians." In turn, the Mi'kmaq of the province were "required to obey you as their chief." The chief at a special installation ceremony then received both the commission and a gilt medal engraved with the head of King George III.[118]

Louis-Benjamin then turned to renewing his people's campaign to obtain the St. Anne's mission site. He had heard of the American Indian Institution headed by Sir Thomas Saumarez, having as its secretary Walter Bromley, a retired paymaster of the 23rd Regiment, the Welch Fusiliers.[119] Bromley lived in Halifax, and when he delivered a public address in late March on possible ways of ameliorating the hardships faced by the Indigenous population of the province, he found he had three very attentive Mi'kmaq, Louis-Benjamin, Samuel, and Gorham Peminout Paul, sitting in his audience.

Bromley advocated the establishment of a farming settlement at Shubenacadie, and the Peminouts carefully tailored Bromley's scheme to fit their own purposes. On 18 May 1814 they approached Charles Morris to help them secure the "place of the old Mass House and Burial Ground [of St. Anne's] on the western side [of the] Shubenaccadie River," construction materials for a new chapel to replace the one built by Francklin, and monies to travel to Maine. Morris drafted a memorial to Sherbrooke calling for the purchase of the mission site, and had all nine of Jacques's sons – John, Francis, Samuel, Gorham, Peter, Thomas, Claude, Alexis, and James – sign the document. In 1814 St. Anne's mission site was owned by a farmer named James Ellis, who had built a sawmill and grist mill on the property. Morris suggested that the government ask Ellis if he would consider selling fifty acres surrounding the chapel. Knowing that the Peminouts also wanted to attend meetings of the Eastern Wabanaki Confederacy, he wrote to Henry Cogswell, the provincial secretary, explaining that the Mi'kmaq needed "a pass to go to Passamaquoddy to be signed by His Excellency the Governor which will give them consequence with the other tribes."[120] Morris then directed both the memorial and letter to Cogswell, for delivery to the lieutenant governor.

In response to an appeal in 1814 from Sigogne, between twenty-two and twenty-eight Mi'kmaw families collected at Shubenacadie, only to find that the Roman Catholic diocese could not sustain a Mi'kmaw farming community. The following year, Sigogne introduced Louis-Benjamin to Bishop Joseph-Octave Plessis, the Roman Catholic vicar general of the Diocese of Quebec, whose jurisdiction at the time extended to Nova Scotia.[121] Plessis, who was touring Nova Scotia in 1815, listened to a speech presented by Louis-Benjamin on 15 July and afterwards admitted he was moved to the point of tears by the chief's account of the hardships besetting his people. He had few resources at his disposal to help, but he promised to approach the lieutenant governor for aid to begin a Mi'kmaw farming experiment at Shubenacadie.[122]

Help also arose from Protestant humanitarian circles. When Bromley declared that twenty-two Mi'kmaw families at Shubenacadie had begun farming, and that Louis-Benjamin, Francis, and Gorham were promoters of this undertaking, he received six hundred pounds in two instalments from the New England Company, as well as monies from the North American Indian Institution and a London-based missionary society.[123] After Sherbrooke's successor, Lord Dalhousie, declared his willingness to assist, Bromley in 1817 received a further twenty-five pounds from the Legislative Assembly to build a road to the Shubenacadie reserve.[124] Bromley purchased seed and six head of cattle, had a log house built for the chief and two frame houses for Gorham and Francis, and in the fall of 1818 he enthusiastically reported that the settlement had taken root.[125] Fifty acres had been cleared, with twenty-three fenced and sown with grain and vegetables. Although only twelve of the original twenty-two families remained on the land, all were planting crops and caring for livestock.[126]

Louis-Benjamin's solicitation of Protestant humanitarian aid nevertheless led some Mi'kmaq to denounce his practice of accepting assistance from what they deemed "inappropriate" sources. Father Vincent de Paul, appointed by Bishop Plessis to serve the Mi'kmaq and Acadians along the Eastern Atlantic coast, was shocked to learn at St. Anne's Day festivities at Chezzetcook in July 1817 that a faction plotted to kill the chief for undermining the primacy of Roman Catholicism among the Mi'kmaq. These men felt that Louis-Benjamin's acceptance of help from other than Roman Catholic prelates and representatives of the British Crown was detrimental to the Roman Catholic mission to the Mi'kmaq, and could not be tolerated without bringing serious Mi'kmaw identity issues to the fore.[127] A leader who forged cordial linkages with "Methodist dissenters" simply was not to be trusted.

Despite the seriousness of the challenge, Louis-Benjamin rose to the occasion. After his nephew Francis Paul delivered a brief speech claiming that the chief wished only to be a benefactor to his people, he rose and announced that, though he appreciated the seed, tools, and cattle provided by Bromley, such would never cause him to renounce the religion of his people. "The potatoes, cows and other provisions," he declared, "are good. I have taken and made use of them, but his religion is worthless, I will have none of it." Moving to the front of the church, the chief then professed his faith before the altar, winning over the Mi'kmaw congregation and impressing Father Vincent with his courage and fortitude.[128]

Louis-Benjamin emerged from this contest stronger than ever. He had demonstrated his ability to establish a reciprocal relationship with the colonial government in the interests of his people and affirmed his religious faith, which as a chief he was expected to uphold. His detractors may have been members of the Cope family, who lived along the Eastern Shore. If so, this would make Peminout's responses even more remarkable, for it would have healed any rift lingering between the Copes and Peminouts once and for all. After this incident, there is no further mention of friction arising between the Eastern Shore Mi'kmaw constituency and the Sipekne'katik district chief.[129]

Not long after this incident Gorham, who occupied the rank of second chief in the Sipekne'katik leadership hierarchy, launched a campaign against the consumption of spirituous liquors. In March 1821 he encouraged Francis Peminout Paul, Chief Louis-Benjamin Peminout Paul, the chief's son Louis, and Francis Toney to petition the General Assembly to prohibit liquor sales on the Shubenacadie reserve. By 1829 he also called for legislative changes to allow children to attend school on their reserve, and for teachers who could help the Mi'kmaq learn to read the Bible in English. Styling himself the "Governor and Chief of the Indians of Nova Scotia," he demanded that his voice be heard, since his people had defended the province during the American Revolution. Yet little came of these appeals. The General Assembly replied that, if the Mi'kmaq chose, they could send their children to publicly funded schools, and left it up to the discretion of local magistrates to curtail liquor sales, which they rarely did.[130] The

government's lack of interest in his educational initiatives particularly frustrated Gorham, who was aware that government assistance for education was being provided to several Indigenous communities in Upper Canada.[131]

Even more pressing problems soon demanded the Peminouts' attention. During the winter of 1830–31 an outbreak of bilious fever forced families to remain in the interior where they lacked the means to purchase warm clothes, blankets, and provisions. In early January, Louis-Benjamin moved onto the Anglican glebe ground at Windsor, where he met with Reverend George William Morris, the local Anglican minister who was also a son of Charles Morris, the provincial surveyor general.[132] The chief informed the reverend, who claimed to speak some Mi'kmaq, that he represented two hundred individuals at Windsor, Rawdon, Newport, and Kennetcook who were suffering from cold, hunger, and disease.[133]

On 17 January the minister incorporated the chief's grievances into a petition that he later personally conveyed to Lieutenant Governor Peregrine Maitland in Halifax. It stated that fifty men, women, and children at Rawdon shared ten worn-out blankets among them, and "sometimes the children are crying the whole night on account of the cold." Fires set by settlers and "the sound of the axe" in the woods scared away game. Good land contiguous to markets belonged to proprietors who refused to allow the Mi'kmaq to camp, cut withes for basket making, or take firewood for fuel. After leaving their accustomed haunts to travel to distant markets to sell their wares, families often returned with very little to show for their effort. Several tried to farm, but sedentary life provided them with few of the material, cultural, and spiritual supports that their earlier ways had done. They found it hard to adopt alien habits, "as it would no doubt be difficult for those accustomed to civilized life to reconcile themselves to the Indian manner of living." Reverend Morris added that it was the government's responsibility, and not the duty of his parish, to relieve the Mi'kmaq's distress, since if he personally distributed funds or food his Mi'kmaw visitors, they might come to view him as the local almoner.[134] The memorial struck a responsive chord with the members of the General Assembly, who granted Louis-Benjamin a portion of the public fund of one hundred pounds budgeted for Mi'kmaw relief.[135] Most of it he distributed to persons engaged in farming activities, though all members of his group found it difficult to remain at Shubenacadie the year round, since peddling wooden manufactures and hunting and trapping and still provided most of their income during these lean years.[136]

Gorham recovered from his disappointment at not getting a local school built and instead focused on acquiring a new chapel. On 20 November 1837 he petitioned Halifax one last time for the St. Anne's mission site to be returned to the Mi'kmaq, but when this proved a fruitless task, in 1839 he obtained twenty pounds to erect a church on the 1,100-acre Shubenacadie reserve.[137] Gorham, assisted by Louis-Benjamin's son Louis, ordered building materials and volunteered their own labour during all phases of construction.[138] Upon the building's completion, Gorham became steward of the new church, a role of which he was particularly fond.

Louis-Benjamin's Petition to Queen Victoria

In May 1840 Louis-Benjamin Peminout Paul, by this time in his late seventies, appeared in a parade celebrating the wedding of Queen Victoria to Prince Albert of Saxe-Coburg-Gotha, which had been held in London three months earlier.[139] The chief and his wife, Madelaine,[140] rode through the streets of Halifax in a "gentleman's carriage, decked in evergreens" drawn by a horse "decorated with blue and white ribbons." The procession, with the chief's carriage at its head, "moved along Hollis Street, past Hon. M. Tobin's and to Government House," then to the dockyard where "the artillery fired a salute, three cheers were given, and the march was re-commenced through Dutch Town." At the end of the route, on the Grand Parade, members of charitable societies offered the Mi'kmaq "fish, fish pies, bread, butter, cheese, cake, and porter," while Thomas Forrester, president of The Philanthropic Society, "presented a scarf to the old Chief." No meat was served to the Roman Catholic guests, it being a Friday. The Philanthropic Society earlier had provided funds for cloth and beads so that Mi'kmaw seamstresses could manufacture cloth coats, with elegant beaded double-curve designs on their fronts, cuffs, and epaulets, for the men to wear, while the women donned peaked beaded caps and displayed double-curve designs and geometric motifs worked in beads and appliqué along the hems of their skirts.[141]

Despite the gaiety and pomp accompanying the occasion, newspaper accounts adopted a melancholic

strain in their portrayals of Louis-Benjamin and the other Mi'kmaw participants. The *Acadian Recorder* cast the "venerable chief," plagued by blindness, suffering from an undetermined illness, and who ate in "dignified silence" at the feast held on the Grand Parade, as a symbol of an entire people who were passing away before the rise of a new "civilizing order."[142] This doleful observation with romanticized notions of the disappearance of the "Noble Savage" is found in many poems and essays of this era.

The thought of his people being in decline deeply affected the old chief, who that fall dictated an eloquent appeal to Queen Victoria regarding the difficulties facing his people. Under his Mi'kmaw name, Pausaumigh Pemmenauweet, he addressed the queen with a traditional welcoming phrase, reflective more of a warm greeting between equals than an obeisant salutation of a subject for his monarch. "Our good friend Sir John Coape Sherbrooke" had vested him with a commission to speak "on behalf of the Mi'kmaq of Nova Scotia," he began, and he had matters on his mind that he wished he and the Queen could discuss face to face, were he not too elderly and ill to travel to London.

> I cannot cross the Great Lake to talk to you for my canoe is too small and I am too old and weak. Cannot look upon you for my eyes not see so far. You cannot hear my voice across the Great Waters. I therefore send you this Wampum and Paper talk to tell the Queen I am in trouble. My people are in trouble. I have seen upwards of a Thousand Moons. When I was young I had plenty. Now I am old, poor, and sickly too. My people are poor. No hunting grounds – no beaver or otter – no nothing. Indians poor – poor forever. No Store, no Chest, no Clothes, all these Woods once ours. Our fathers possessed them all. Now we cannot cut a tree to warm our Wigwam in Winter unless the White Man please. The Micmacs now receive no presents, but one small blanket for a whole family. The Governor [Viscount Falkland] is a good man but he cannot help us now. We look to you the Queen. The White Wampum tell that we hope in you. Pity your poor Indians in Nova Scotia … Let us not perish. Your Indian Children love you, and will fight for you against all your enemies … My Head and my Heart shall go to the One above for you.[143]

He added that he had met the Duke of Kent, the queen's father, many years before in Nova Scotia.[144]

At the bottom of the document he placed an "X" beside the inscription "Pausaumigh Pemmenauweet, Chief of the Micmac Tribe of Indians in Nova Scotia." "Gorcum [Gorham Paul], Second Chief of the Micmacs" and "François, first Captain of the Micmac Warriors," signed as witnesses.[145]

The poignancy of Louis-Benjamin Peminout Paul's petition arguably makes it the most quoted of all Mi'kmaw memorials, yet its purport was the same as the speech directed over fifty years previously by Jacques Peminout Paul to Commissioner George Henry Monk. The Mi'kmaq had been displaced from lands that were once theirs. So as not to perish, they needed to regain access to resources they had lost: lands, wood for manufacturing, animals to pursue in the forest, and fish to take in the rivers. Embodied in the chief's address was a hope that his attempt to forge reciprocal ties with the British monarch would allow the Mi'kmaq to continue as a distinct people.

The London Colonial Office received the chief's petition on 1 January 1841, examined it for its stylistic form and content since its drafter was anonymous, and forwarded it to the queen, who was deeply moved by its message.[146] Officials in the British Colonial Office, however, still laboured under the erroneous impression that the Mi'kmaq, en masse, had opposed the British in various colonial wars.[147] Despite the fact that at least one chief fought with Wolfe on the Plains of Abraham and the Peminouts had participated in the Seven Years' War and the American Revolution, officials held that Mi'kmaq claims could not be based on any bond with the Crown other than that accorded ordinary subjects. The imperial government owed them no debt of gratitude for past military service, as it did for many groups in the Canadas. At best, all the Mi'kmaq warranted was some sort of compensation for land loss – a vague proposition, since Nova Scotia had never recognized the provisions of the Royal Proclamation of 1763. Regarded as a specialist in matters affecting the Mi'kmaq, Anthony Blackwood of the Colonial Office cautioned against Britain's shouldering any obligations of a fiduciary nature in Nova Scotia that might mean additional expense to British taxpayers.[148] By the early 1840s, Britain was divesting itself of its obligations to its overseas colonies under the new tenets of "Little Englandism." Instead, Nova Scotia's lieutenant governor, Viscount Falkland, was instructed to amass what funds he could and do something "at home" to relieve the Mi'kmaq's distress.

Joseph Howe and the Peminouts, 1842–1843

Louis-Benjamin doubtless felt deeply disappointed by Britain's refusal to acknowledge his ongoing reciprocal bond with the Crown, set out in his commission from Sherbrooke in 1814. Lord Falkland recoiled at the thought of having to address the chief's grievances, since funds were short: the House of Assembly would not pay a provincial Indian superintendent a salary, only travelling expenses, making it unlikely that they would respond benevolently to the Mi'kmaq's plight. Joseph Howe, who assumed the office of Indian commissioner in the spring of 1842, nevertheless was intrigued by the opportunity to establish Mi'kmaw farming communities in Nova Scotia.[149] A political reformer and journalist, Howe saw the Mi'kmaw community of Nova Scotia as a landscape on which to foster an experiment in Indigenous community living. He knew that during the French regime, Mi'kmaw leaders had been given commissions over "commands," which recognized them as responsible to both their people and the French government, a historical precedent that Howe felt could be modified to serve his own ends.[150] Otherwise his plans drew upon the New England township model. Each farming community would be led by a chief and council answerable to the colonial government, and have a church and, if possible, a school. Reserves would be subdivided into farm concessions and chiefs groomed to act as semi-governmental agents, who would relay provincial policy decisions downward to their bands as well as funnel ideas and grievances upward from their Mi'kmaw constituents to the Indian commissioner.

At first, Howe held a jaundiced view of chiefs' political capabilities and their relationship with the Roman Catholic Church. A Mi'kmaw person, he argued, neither "knows nor cares what changes convulse the political world, and perhaps the whole extent of his connexions with his own church amount to a letter of friendship now and then from the Bishops of Nova Scotia or Quebec."[151] He only met Louis-Benjamin Peminout Paul, whom he referred to colloquially as "Sam," after the ailing and elderly Sipekne'katik district leader had taken to his bed for the last time.[152] In April 1842 Howe sent the chief, who at the time was almost completely blind, a gift of five shillings.[153] Louis-Benjamin's death likely occurred within a month, yet, oddly, the commissioner made no reference to it in either his letters or his reports.[154]

Howe had to resolve a dispute regarding a parcel of land at East Chester, Lunenburg County, in which Louis-Benjamin's widow, Madelaine Ball – whom Howe called "Margaret" – held one-third interest.[155] The patriarch of the Ball family, Jean Ball, like his contemporary Paul Peminout, had supported the British during the Seven Years' War. In April 1760 Jean also was one of the first Mi'kmaw chiefs to sign a peace treaty with the British and secure a British passport.[156] In 1788 three of his sons, John Jr., Joseph, and Thomas Ball, jointly obtained a grant of land near the mouth of the East River at Indian Point, East Chester. This grant, accorded to the Ball family in freehold, in 1793 was subdivided into lots 31 and 32 of Chester Township, and in the early 1820s one lot was purchased by a man named Booth who subdivided it and sold his land to others.[157] These buyers occupied the tract continuously for twenty-six years, which, as far as Howe was concerned, "shut out Indian title." The Indian commissioner, however, felt that the Ball family still retained an interest in the other half, which contained a valuable limestone quarry.

In 1799 this quarry, with Sir John Wentworth's approval, was leased to a Halifax interest for a term of fourteen years at five shillings per annum.[158] Not long afterwards a local settler, Tobias Cook, offered one of Chief Ball's sons, Joseph, ten pounds for the quarry. Cook later drew up a deed of sale and registered it at the Lunenburg County Deeds Office on 21 May 1823, even though the quarry's boundaries remained undefined and Joseph received no money. Howe figured that, by this sale, at least a third more of the grant had been lost to the Mi'kmaq. He evaluated the worth of the remainder of the land and retrieved what money for it he could, which included factoring in the value of the stone taken from the quarry site since 1823.[159] He then set out to locate heirs whom he felt deserved a share of the compensation money.

It was a difficult task. Jean Ball's sons John Jr., Joseph, and Thomas and two daughters Mary Ann and Molly had died by 1842. One heir who was still living was Louis-Benjamin's widow, Madelaine, who deserved one-third of the estate.[160] A great-grandchild of Jean Ball, Madelaine, born around 1775, was a daughter of Thomas Ball's son Francis.[161] Howe finally met up with Madelaine at Rawdon, near Windsor, and paid her £2 5s 7p "as her share of the balance of thirty pounds received from Tobias Cook."[162]

Shortly after Louis-Benjamin's death, Madelaine wed Pierre Thomas of Rawdon, who for many years had been a close companion of the chief's nephew, Francis Peminout Paul. In mid-May 1842 Francis, who at the time had assumed a probationary position as acting chief of the Sipekne'katik district, joined Howe and Pierre Thomas on a jaunt through the Shubenacadie River Valley. Howe enjoyed Francis's and Pierre's company, since his two Mi'kmaw companions kept pointing out natural phenomena and interpreting them in ways that, today, would be recognized as insights of Indigenous ethnoscience. At one point, Francis informed Howe that his father, Jacques Paul Peminout, had once spoken about ancient "whale bones" that had been found in freshwater shallows at Shubenacadie Grand Lake. So detailed was Francis's description of these fossils that the bones were later identified as mastodon vertebrae, some of them large enough to be used as chairs.[163]

After traversing the upland back of Shubenacadie village, Howe arrived at Parker's Bridge and was surprising to find only Gorham Peminout Paul, Gorham's Malecite wife, and the couple's two foster children living on the reserve. Gorham had abandoned his frame house, built in 1817 under Bromley's supervision, in favour of a commodious wigwam, sporting doors at either end. The frame dwelling had been turned into a barn. On observing this, Howe fumed that Bromley's initiatives in 1817 and 1818 to promote settlement, animal husbandry, and cultivation of crops among the Mi'kmaq at Shubenacadie had imploded into a colossal waste of money, which he as Indian commissioner was determined not to replicate. Cows and other livestock that Bromley had introduced into the community had been poorly cared for and were slaughtered for feasts, or when families left the area. Gorham one spring had killed all his livestock before moving for a year to New Brunswick to visit his wife's family.[164]

Gorham's wigwam was comfortable, and large enough to serve as a public council forum as well as a family domicile. Howe, however, who viewed any return to wigwam life as a retrograde step, had Gorham's frame house put in order and a new barn built alongside it.[165] This dwelling stood near the church, which had been built with the government monies Gorham had received from Halifax in 1839, though there had been insufficient funds to complete the chapel's interior.[166] Since Howe intended to install chiefs as intermediaries between the provincial government and the local community, he focused on examining the Sipekne'katik band's leadership structure. At first its complexity confounded him, as he had not expected to encounter an elaborate hierarchy of offices among the Mi'kmaq, but he eventually identified a head chief, two captains, and at least one Mi'kmaw judge.[167] Howe claimed that Gorham's status of second chief paralleled the European rank of "major," which lay just above the office of first captain.

Francis and Gorham's congeniality, coupled with their acumen in the diplomatic forum, made Howe less critical than he had initially been of Mi'kmaw political structures and attitudes. He also recognized the genuineness of Peminout grievances concerning land and resource loss. Howe wondered why a farmer could be allowed to construct a mill dam lying just off the Mi'kmaw tract that flooded a large portion of the reserve. He also felt it was wrong that band members had to walk two and a half miles to access the Shubenacadie River, when most of their summer travel was still by bark canoe. When Francis and Gorham told the commissioner that their family had for many years cherished the hope that they could attain bottomland around St. Anne's mission site, Howe petitioned the government to review the matter. In response, the Mi'kmaq received 650 acres, in addition to the 1,100 acres already in their possession, which still lay at a considerable distance from the river.[168]

Howe then ordered a local deputy land surveyor, William Faulkner, to subdivide the enlarged reserve, now containing 1,760 acres, into 100-acre farm lots and locate individual families on specific plots.[169] When Gorham, warning that individual ownership could lead to land alienation as happened at East Chester, contested Howe's right to subdivide the reserve, the commissioner chastised the second chief for wanting to "own the entire reserve." Yet the commissioner remained wary of Gorham's close connections with the Roman Catholic Church, and dreaded resistance from religious prelates, who might prove even more determined than Gorham to thwart what he saw as necessary for "civilizing" the Shubenacadie community.

Even as he fumed over what he perceived as Gorham's narrow-minded self-interest in preventing the subdivision of the reserve, Howe expressed admiration and even awe at the generosity of spirit Gorham displayed in fostering two children. The first child was a *métis* youth named John Jadis (c.1827–c.1925), a grandson of Gorham's Malecite wife.[170] The second

was an attractive twenty-two-year-old girl, "Mary Ann McHenery" (McHenry), born to an Irish mother and a Scottish father.[171] "Within the humble wigwams," Howe reflected, "there may often be found the higher feelings of benevolence and steadfast fidelity, which, in the dwellings of our [European] race, are sometimes wanting."[172]

The emphasis Howe placed on subdividing the Shubenacadie reserve prompted Gorham to threaten to launch out on his own and form a new agricultural community. In July 1842 Gorham petitioned Viscount Falkland, claiming to have a number of Mi'kmaw families under his aegis who all pledged to abstain from spirituous drink and required at least sixteen hundred acres of land where they could grow crops, "fortified by their religion and safe from temptations held out by liquor traders."[173] Members of this pledging community dispersed, however, when Falkland refused Gorham's request.

Owing to Gorham's vigilance in caring for the new chapel on the reserve and acting as its prayer leader in the absence of a priest, it provided a sanctuary to Mi'kmaw visitors throughout the year. A large gathering attended the chapel at Christmas and on St. Anne's Day, July 26. The acting chief, Francis Peminout Paul, attended by his captains and the judges, read prayers and sacred passages from bound pages of hieroglyphic writings, painstakingly copied many years before from Abbé Maillard's original texts. The chief also hosted a feast for all present. This feasting was most pronounced at Christmas, although after the formation of the independent Archdiocese of Nova Scotia on 15 February 1842, many Sipekne'katik Mi'kmaq participated in services and Roman Catholic calendrical festivities at St. Mary's Cathedral Basilica in Halifax.[174] This practice soon elicited concern in official circles about the expense of maintaining those who stayed behind in the province's capital following the close of ceremonies.[175]

Though they often participated in religious events in Halifax, the Peminouts were rarely a financial burden on provincial coffers. Instead, prior to the election and installation of a new chief, Francis and Gorham vied with each other to demonstrate their ability to provide for the welfare of their people. When Gorham in the spring of 1844 lost the community-based election for district chief, he at first threatened to leave Shubenacadie permanently. He had hoped to win because of the energy he put into his land campaigns, his attempts to ban spirituous liquors, and his contributions to his people's religious life. His defeat left him with a simmering resentment towards his victorious brother, an anger the Reverend William Walsh successfully subdued on 4 May 1844 during a special service held in Halifax at St. Mary's Basilica.[176]

Francis Peminout Paul Becomes Chief

Francis Peminout Paul (1778–1861) succeeded his uncle Louis-Benjamin as Sipekne'katik district chief during an unusual installation service. On 4 May, both Francis and Gorham's claims were examined and weighed by the assembled Mi'kmaw congregants, and a decision made "before the altar," after which Walsh gave a short speech and invested Francis with the insignia of office. Francis was then led to a platform so that "homage" could be "tendered him by all the Mi'kmaw men present."[177] The newly chosen leader and his Mohawk wife[178] then joined a parade that proceeded a short distance along Pleasant Street (now Barrington Street) to Government House, where Francis and his retinue paid their respects to the queen's representative, Viscount Falkland, and performed a dance.

This ceremony represented a major departure from earlier succession protocols since, instead of deciding in an all-Mi'kmaw council who would succeed to office, the Sipekne'katik Mi'kmaq left the final decision-making stages in the hands of a prelate of the Roman Catholic Church. Francis's appointment did not prompt Mi'kmaw delegations to attend from New Brunswick or Maine so that neigbouring eastern Algonquian leaders could ratify the appointment. Walsh's blessing was deemed sufficient.

Francis Peminout Paul was a hard worker and highly politically active. Contemporary accounts portray him as an articulate, courageous, energetic, and wise leader esteemed by his constituents. When avenues opened up for him to do so, he presented informed, well-organized, and forceful views on the sad state of Mi'kmaw rights in the province. Francis felt it was wrong that Louis-Benjamin's petition of 1841 had been sidelined, and early in spring 1844 tried to secure funding from the Legislative Assembly in order to visit Queen Victoria in London and explain the Mi'kmaq's concerns to her in person.[179] When his request was denied, Francis temporarily turned his attention to the declining vitality of religious ceremonialism in his community.[180]

On 23 December 1845 the sixty-seven-year-old chief informed both Lieutenant Governor Falkland and the Roman Catholic priest at Shubenacadie, Father Kennedy, that he had no money to buy provisions for the annual Christmastide feast at Shubenacadie. The best he could offer guests were a few potatoes. Since it was important to have periodic renewals of trust and friendship between a leader and his people, Francis stressed that his people "would starve" both emotionally and physically if he were not granted resources to make Christmas a time of sharing and festivity for all concerned. Kennedy in particularly grasped the positive psychological – and even cosmological – implications that an immediate gesture of kindness and understanding on the part of the government and church would convey to the Mi'kmaq. Francis's request received an immediate response when Father Kennedy presented the chief with a gift of a barrel of rye flour and four dollars in cash.[181]

December was followed by a harsh January. On 31 January the chief wrote Falkland that since Howe's resignation in 1843 as Indian commissioner, his people tottered on the brink of starvation. It was an unjust fate, since their forefathers had been "comfortable, happy, and independent, being the rightful owners of the country and all that appertained thereto." If someone soon did not dispense relief, he cautioned, this "ancient Tribe ... will become extinct." Practical requests followed. The Mi'kmaq needed wearing apparel and "a good stock of warm blankets." To ensure the continuation of farming "in the Township of Douglas ... given by government to his late Father [Jacques],"[182] Francis also requested that the lieutenant governor, before spring, send him "a pair of oxen, a few sheep and a supply of seed potatoes and wheat."[183]

Worse even than the imminent starvation Francis described was a virulent fever that prostrated inhabitants of encampments from Pictou to Digby County and left many dead.[184] In February 1847 William Walsh, who was now archbishop of Halifax, sent a medical practitioner named Edward Jennings, along with an infantry medic with the 60th Rifles named Dr. Richardson whom the Mi'kmaq especially requested to attend to their needs, to ascertain whether the sickness was still making inroads in central Nova Scotia.[185] Jennings and Richardson braved snowdrifts, sleigh upsets, and cutting winds to visit three Mi'kmaw communities: the Indian Road, which lay two and a half miles back of the village of Shubenacadie; a cluster of wigwams at Maitland, fifty-seven miles from Halifax; and Salt House Head, located on the Bay of Fundy approximately five miles beyond the Maitland. By this time the disease had run its course and the doctors found few instances of fever. On his return to Halifax, however, Dr. Jennings performed a delicate operation at Shubenacadie on Judge Christopher Paul's jaw, which had become ulcerated owing to two infected teeth.

In September of the same year Abraham Pineo Gesner, the newly appointed provincial Indian commissioner, asked chiefs and captains to meet with him to determine "timely means" of addressing future cases of Mi'kmaw distress.[186] At the same time, Gesner praised Louis-Benjamin's promotion of farming and urged Francis Peminout Paul to continue his uncle's legacy. Yet by the early spring of 1849 the commissioner realized the futility of expecting the Mi'kmaq to effect a radical change in their circumstances on their own. They faced too many severe challenges. During the previous winter an outbreak of smallpox in the Annapolis Valley had forced families to scatter to avoid contagion.[187] Fourteen family heads at Shubenacadie clung to the hope that the government would provide them with tools and seed to continue farming, despite the fact that for two summers a potato blight had destroyed their crops. Others, seeing no future in farming, simply wandered over the landscape, looking for places to pitch their wigwams and take a few fish, partridges, and rabbits.[188]

Ten Mi'kmaw leaders, including Chief Francis Peminout Paul from mainland Nova Scotia, harkened to Gesner's call to find a means of rectifying the hardships the Mi'kmaq faced. Following several meetings with the commissioner during the winter of 1849, in February they addressed a petition to Lieutenant Governor John Harvey asking that representatives of the British Crown formally recognize their rights as a distinct people, as enshrined in treaties of peace and friendship signed in the past by their chiefs. Promises made at the time of the most recent treaty were still fresh in their minds:

Tired of a war that destroyed many of our people, almost ninety years ago our Chief made peace and buried the hatchet forever. When that peace was made, the English Governor promised us [legal] protection, as much land as we wanted, and the preservation of our fisheries and game. These we now very much want.[189]

Wrongs dealt them included the damming of rivers that destroyed their fisheries, their expulsion from ancient camping sites, the desecration of their burial grounds, the passing of restrictive game laws, and inadequate access to markets for their baskets and other manufactures. Yet despite the blight borne on "the poison wind," they had not given up farming and, if provided with tools and seed, would try again.[190]

Francis, Gorham, and Louis Paul from Sipekne'katik and seven other leaders from mainland Nova Scotia – Andrew James Meuse Sr. from Bear River near the Digby County line, Gabriel Bonus (or Bonis) from the Annapolis Valley, Louis Luxey from Shelburne County, Peter Morris from central Nova Scotia, and Peter Toney, Xavier Paul, and Francis Paul from Pictou County – met Gesner in Halifax on the cloudy, cold morning on 8 February 1849.[191]

Each of these chiefs inscribed a special mark, such as a cross, a pipe or a heart, on the petition beside their name. Gesner had arranged for these leaders to assemble first at Dalhousie College before proceeding to Government House to hand their document to the Lieutenant Governor, John Harvey. After this they were to return to the legislative building to meet with the House of Assembly.[192]

At Dalhousie College, the Mi'kmaq formed into an orderly column and this parade of Mi'kmaw pageantry proceeded through the streets, with Francis Peminout Paul and the other leaders in their traditional dress, resplendent with medals and other honorifics. The sight drew admiration from the press. Younger participants were described as "fine stalwart fellows," while "old *Saagauch* Paul" – the "*Winjeet Sagamore*" (high chief) – was portrayed as a "truly venerable and respectable man, remarkable for his wisdom and sagacity."[193] Though in their petition the Mi'kmaq expressed the fear that they would soon "pass away from neglect like a withering leaf in a summer's sun," Gesner hoped that a warm welcome from members of the Assembly and the lieutenant governor, along with the favourable press coverage, would revive their flagging spirits.[194]

Francis Peminout Paul's Petition of 1853

The chiefs' rendezvous with the Assembly and Lieutenant Governor Harvey was widely publicized, so doubtless it caught the attention of the Reverend Silus Tertius Rand (1810–89), a Baptist cleric and missionary living in Cornwallis Township, Kings County. Earlier in 1847 Rand had contemplated moving to a mission station in Burma, but as his wife refused to leave Nova Scotia, he decided instead to serve among the Mi'kmaq.[195] He had begun learning Mi'kmaq, and within a few years could converse in the language with fair fluency. In 1849 he and the Reverend James Twining, an Anglican with an evangelical bent and Baptist leanings, solicited monies to establish the Halifax-based Micmac Missionary Society.[196] Knowing Rand was able to speak Mi'kmaq, Francis approached the Baptist missionary in the fall of 1852 and asked if he would write a petition for him to Queen Victoria. That Francis's request to Rand occurred exactly one hundred years after Jean-Baptiste Cope signed a peace treaty with the British, on 22 November 1752, was probably not mere coincidence. However, Francis directed Rand to wait until 25 July 1853, the day before St. Anne's Day, to draft the petition to the Queen so that the memorial might be imbued with the special spiritual energy the Mi'kmaq felt emanated from the festivity's observance. This power, the chief hoped, would attract royal favour and elicit a sense of obligation towards the Mi'kmaq.

When the time came, the process of drafting the memorial occurred in two stages. Francis first dictated what he wanted to say to his spokesperson Louis Paul, and Louis then repeated to Rand what the chief told him, which the missionary copied down verbatim. Rand penned two copies of the petition, one in Mi'kmaq, using Roman script, and another in English. The chief stressed that he wanted both versions to be as widely publicized as possible.

The memorial began by forcefully arguing that the Mi'kmaq felt "this whole Peninsula belongs of right to us, it having been bestowed upon our forefathers by the Great Creator Himself, and having never been voluntarily disposed of either by them or by us their descendants, nor was it ever wrested from us by force of arms." Then, echoing Jean-Baptist Cope's words of 1752, it called for payment for tracts of land for which the Mi'kmaq had "never received … any adequate remuneration." As a consequence of this wholesale appropriation of land and resources arising from the denial of Mi'kmaw rights, European settlers flourished while the Mi'kmaw population found it "entirely impossible" to obtain a livelihood in ways they understood and cherished.[197]

Rand emphasized to a newly appointed lieutenant governor, Sir John Gaspard Le Marchant, that Francis Peminout Paul would not hear of the word "subject" being used when it came to the nature of the relationship he wanted preserved between his people and the Crown:

It may be proper to state that the Indians do not consider themselves subjects to Queen Victoria. I had written this expression at the close of the Petition. The venerable old chief – Francis Paul – shook his head. That expression could not be admitted. "We treated as an independent nation" said he, "and no steps had ever been taken to alter this relation." I must say I admired the independent Spirit of the old man. I dashed my pen thro the offensive expression.[198]

After striking out the words "your obedient subject" in the final line of the petition, he substituted the phrase your "faithful and dutiful children."[199] This satisfied the elderly chief because it harked back to the paternal relation the French Crown once held towards its Mi'kmaw allies, and which the Mi'kmaw saw as continuing into the British regime under the terms of the peace and friendship treaties signed in 1752, 1760, and 1761.

Francis declared that when peace was made between the Shubenacadie Mi'kmaq and the British near the close of the Seven Years' War, "the sword and tomahawk had been buried by mutual consent" and the treaty ratified with all the "solemnities of an oath." The Mi'kmaq remembered that at the time "it was stipulated we should be left in the quiet and peaceable possession of far the greater portion of this Peninsula."[200] It was not surprising that many Mi'kmaq returned to older ways of life with which they were most accustomed. But these ways were yearly becoming more difficult to pursue, owing to the spread of farms, the destruction of Mi'kmaw fisheries, and farmers' denying Mi'kmaw families the wood needed for their manufactures.

The Mi'kmaq suffered from poverty, but who had made them poor? They held no legal title to their lands and so could not obtain credit, drawing upon their reserves as security. Worse, their best efforts were impeded by racism. They were not expected to succeed, and so were given government handouts rather than sustained assistance. "But," the petitioners stressed, "in the light of that great bright sun which shines upon us all alike; and in the presence of that Great Creator who made us all, we would ask whose fault is it that we are Indians? And who gave the white man a right to deceive and despise and oppress us simply on the ground that the color of our skin is somewhat different from his own? If this be a crime, certainly we are not the perpetrators of it."[201]

The Creator, the memorial continued, would not make mistakes or desert his children. The Mi'kmaq, who loved and heeded God's commands, deserved to be respected as a distinct people. The invisible shackles of racism, moreover, were not hampering Indigenous aspirations equally everywhere in British North America. Indigenous groups in the Canadas were signing treaties that provided them with resources for the future; so why were not the same things happening in Nova Scotia? Chief Francis Peminout Paul then answered his own rhetorical question by stating that treaties his people signed with the Crown may have granted them rights, but these rights had not been honoured. Most important, the Mi'kmaq's lands had never been surrendered by any treaty. They had been given to the Mi'kmaq by the Creator Himself, and still belonged to his people, despite the fact that settlers occupied them and were trying to dispossess the Mi'kmaw people of the rights God gave to them. Aware of the terms of the Royal Proclamation of 1763 relating to surrenders of Indigenous territory, Francis charged that "we have never received for them any adequate compensation." The terms of the proclamations and the treaties have never been violated by the Indian, but the white man has not fulfilled his engagements."[202]

Rand summed up his views on Francis's petition in his letter to Sir John Gaspard Le Marchant. "I cannot vouch for the truth of the statements contained in the Petition, tho I fear they are all too true," he confided. "I have read the Petition publicly at Charlottetown, St. John, Fredericton and many other places, and intend to publish it here and in England … to call attention to the claims of the Indians."[203] Since Francis lived most of his time in 1853 along the Eastern Road (now Main Street) in Dartmouth, Rand referred to him as "Chief of Cheebookt [Chebucto]" rather than as the Shubenacadie district chief.[204] He admired the nerve of the old leader, who claimed that the Mi'kmaq knew the terms of the treaty they signed with the Crown in 1760 and wanted a proper search to be made for it. Rand then took the two versions of the memorial, the one in the Mi'kmaw

language and the other in English, and sent both to England in the care of the Reverend James Twining.

The recipients of the petition in London, however, branded the Mi'kmaw petition "a white fabrication," and it may not have ever reached the queen. Despite the fact that it employed Mi'kmaw turns of phrase and presented ideas that chiefs at the time were discussing throughout the Northeast,[205] Rand was charged with concocting the document for his own purposes.[206] Rather than an English translation of ideas spoken in Mi'kmaq, as Rand represented it to be, the memorial was held to have been "written and conceived in English" and only later translated into Mi'kmaq.[207] Statements contained in the petition had touched a sensitive nerve at the British Colonial Office, and questionable tactics were resorted to in order to stanch their impact. The accusations directed at him – that he had spoken for the Mi'kmaw without consulting them, and had engaged in deceitful practices in writing the memorial – were untrue and unjustifiable. The ideas found in the 1853 petition formed tenets of a vital Mi'kmaw land and resource rights campaign that has continued to the present day.[208]

The lack of attention paid to this petition, compared to the widespread interest in the formal petition of Louis-Benjamin Peminout two years earlier, suggested that the Colonial Office valued style over substance when it came to weighing what the Mi'kmaq had to say. No official analysis of its content was undertaken, nor was any action taken in response. The Sipekne'katik district leaders had nurtured an optimistic hope that a positive response from London would compel the provincial government to sit up and take notice of their complaints and claims like never before, but Francis Paul and his associates began to suspect that their appeal had gone astray when it took almost a year for a reply to reach them from London. Since the response they received gave no indication that the Colonial Office had even investigated the matter behind the document, let alone wrestled with its contents, the chief could only lament the lack of assistance for or understanding of his Indigenous rights campaign.[209]

By this time Francis, Gorham, and Louis Paul were pursuing yet another tack: trying to achieve government recognition of residual Mi'kmaw rights on Crown Lands. Weary from dictating, signing, and sending petitions that, after months of waiting, bore little fruit, the elderly chief launched his last request.

In a memorial to the Legislative Council, dated 21 February 1854, Chief Francis Peminout Paul and his two associates argued that many stands of valuable vacant forested lands, "called Crown Lands," should be placed at the disposal of the Mi'kmaq, so they could develop them in a manner compatible with their own economic and cultural goals. They "begged to submit to the conscientious and candid judgment of your Honourable House whether these lands at least are not upon every principle of truth and justice the property of our tribe."[210]

Francis Peminout Paul received no reply from London to his appeal, though its substance would remain part of his nation's collective memory and inspired policies upheld in the early twentieth century by Grand Chief John Denny Jr. as well as providing, in 1985, the grounds for *Simon v. The Queen,* which finally recognized Mi'kmaw hunting rights on Crown Land.[211] But in the 1850s the ideas set out in the petition were considered radical and inflammatory by colonial administrators, and so were given short shrift in governmental circles.

Land Disputes at Shubenacadie and Middle Stewiacke

The chief faced other trying situations in the early 1850s. Early in the spring of 1851 he had to mediate a land dispute on the Shubenacadie reserve. The boundaries of the one-hundred-acre farm lots laid out by William Faulkner in 1843 had been ignored by community members, and in consequence some farmers had large tracts while other families, who wanted to farm, could only attain small plots. With the assistance of a neighbouring settler, Francis R. Parker, Francis met with and addressed the complaints of the aggrieved parties and by May 1851 effected a land redistribution, seemingly to the satisfaction of all parties.[212]

Another problem, much harder to resolve, involved a remnant of land allegedly still belonging to the Mi'kmaq at Stewiacke.[213] The Crown Lands commissioner, James B. Uniacke, who in 1852 administered all the reserves in the province,[214] called for a new survey of the Stewiacke tract, an action that may have been prompted by a Mi'kmaw request. William Faulkner, the same man who surveyed the Shubenacadie farm lots in 1843, was ordered to investigate whether or not all of the Stewiacke had been sold. When his task included overseeing a migration and

a valuation of improvements regarding the tract, he baulked at the prospect. Faulkner knew that Governor Parr in 1783 had granted a licence of occupation to the Mi'kmaq for two miles square along the Stewiacke River, but the only plan that he could find relating to this particular tract was one attached to an award of 360 acres made on 18 August 1815 to Joseph Marshall.[215] Several local settlers claimed to know the grant's boundaries, especially its southwest corner, which formed a reference point for them when ascertaining the areal extent of their own properties.

Faulkner faced a difficult dilemma. He did not want to rely on the word of the settlers, but he lacked firm documentary grounds on which to proceed. In 1842 Joseph Howe had reported that Mi'kmaw land remained at Stewiacke, and wondered whether it might serve as a suitable locale for a Mi'kmaw farming settlement.[216] Yet ten years later a Crown Lands "Memorandum of Indian Reserves" stated that all reserve land in Colchester county had been "sold by the Indians."[217] Faulkner was so daunted by the contradictory data at his disposal that he tried to duck the whole issue by proposing instead to survey two thousand acres on the south side of the river – which included a portion of the old Peminout grant – and lay it out in lots.[218]

When his superiors rejected this option, he examined the Colchester County deed books and focused on a sale made in 1794 by Paul Peminout and Peter (Pierre) Paul (Sr.) to Henry McClellan and John Bonnell, of one square mile on either side of the Stewiacke River – the only sale that had been undertaken with government approval. Yet he was unable to find the root of the title to associated property, that belonging to George Taylor, which extended back before 1826. He also complained to Uniacke that local settlers tried to prevent his survey, since they feared the Mi'kmaq might "imagine that they had gained a possession."[219] In the end, the matter proved too much for him. In 1857 he drafted a short, incomplete report on what he had found, and bowed out of surveying the tract. Uniacke, possibly on Faulkner's advice, then contacted Samuel Fairbanks to continue the survey, using plans furnished to Fairbanks by William A. Hendry, the deputy commissioner of Crown Lands.[220]

Fairbanks had no easier time completing his task than Faulkner, and he too, left the project unfinished. In 1861, the members of a farming community at Middle Stewiacke collectively raised money and paid for Deputy Surveyor Isaac Archibald to run the bounds, as best he could, of the old Peminout grant.[221] By this time, it had become clear that certain early settlers, among them John Bonnell, had been encouraged by the province to stake claims in localities where the grant's original boundaries remained ambiguous. Though Archibald drafted a rough plan of the original Peminout tract, he floundered when he tried to determine property lines lying within the grant. No further government surveys were undertaken in the area during the nineteenth century.[222]

While Francis Peminout Paul, prior to his retirement as Sipekne'katik leader in 1855, was unable to rekindle government interest in the Middle Stewiacke land matter, Pierre Paul Peminout Sr.'s descendants continued to claim a remnant of the tract. In 1864 they asked Andrew James Meuse Jr. of Bear River, whose father had joined Francis in petitioning the lieutenant governor in 1849, to present a petition to the House of Assembly on behalf of "Peter Paul's heirs" whose lands had been "unfairly arrested [wrested]" from them by "certain inhabitants of Stewiac."[223] Their petition received no response, and not until the early twentieth century would the Mi'kmaq once again raise the issue of Indigenous residual rights at Stewiacke.

In 1855, Francis transferred his leadership responsibilities to his first cousin, Jacques-Pierre Peminout Paul, the youngest son of Louis-Benjamin Peminout Paul, and moved to Dartmouth, where he retired from public life to live a quiet, somewhat secluded existence. Though his life was brightened by small consolations, like the province's flickering interest in the late 1850s in the Stewiacke claim, the leader wanted respite from his earlier years of toil and travel. Francis's earlier courageous struggles on behalf of his people's treaty and land rights did not go unnoticed, however. In February 1855 a petition arrived in Halifax signed by numerous Sipekne'katik band members, several settlers, and the Reverend James Twining, requesting that a permanent pension be accorded Francis out of the provincial treasury, owing to his years of dedication to his peoples' welfare.[224] When he died, aged eighty-three, on 16 May 1864 at his house on the Eastern Road (Main Street, Dartmouth), the province provided free train transport for the chief's remains from Dartmouth to Shubenacadie, for burial in the cemetery at Indian Brook.[225]

A *Kinap* at the Helm: Jacques-Pierre Peminout Paul as District Chief

Following Francis's retirement as Sipekne'katik chief, his many responsibilities fell to his successor Jacques-Pierre Peminout Paul (1800–95), known to the Mi'kmaq community as *Sä'kéj-Piel* and to the English-speaking community as "James Paul." In 1855 Jacques-Pierre assumed the office of acting chief for a year, before being formally installed by the Roman Catholic archbishop William Walsh at St. Mary's Basilica in Halifax on 15 September 1856.[226] At this occasion, Walsh vested the new chief with a gilt medal from Pope Pius IX bearing the image of the pontiff. Lieutenant Governor John Gaspard Le Marchant presented Jacques-Pierre with a written endorsement of his appointment at a ceremony at Government House later the same day.[227]

The youngest son of Louis-Benjamin Peminout Paul and Madeline, Jacques-Pierre was born on 5 January 1800 at Rocky Lake, Halifax County, not far from Bedford.[228] He was a tall, slender man with a mustache, beard, and wavy hair.[229] He was an excellent hunter and capable of feats of great physical strength, to the degree that he was considered a *kinap*, a Mi'kmaw person of power. Legend had it that he single-handedly destroyed a dam that was impeding fish migrations near Windsor, and in advanced years stopped the turning of a windmill's apparatus by grasping one of the windmill's blades in his hand.[230] His shamanic propensities included transforming solid objects, such as a pipestem or a teacup, into malleable matter whose shape he could manipulate with his fingers.[231]

He married twice. His first marriage, to a woman named Sally, produced a daughter and at least three sons, but in 1847 an outbreak of what may have been typhus struck his encampment at Maitland Chapel (now South Maitland), and Sally and several of his children died. The following year he was reported as living with only two children.[232] Around 1852 he wed a widow named Madeleine, who had at least three children by her first husband, Louis Noel of Pictou.[233] Though he and his second wife had no biological children of their own, Jacques-Pierre was close to Madeleine's son, John Noel (1829–1911), who upon reaching adulthood acted as Jacques-Pierre's spokesperson and eventually succeeded him as chief.[234]

Jacques-Pierre presented a study in contrasts. In public he appeared as a grave, dignified figure. He was easily spotted at councils and religious ceremonies because of his lanky figure, beard, traditional beaded coat, beaded leggings, and chief's regalia that included the George III medal presented to his father, Louis-Benjamin Peminout Paul, in 1814; he also possessed the gilt medal from the pope given to his father by Bishop William Walsh in 1856. He was a *kinap,* yet he also had a whimsical, warm side; he regularly visited kin and friends and was regarded as a kindly, protective, fatherly type, especially to young children.[235]

The chief's reputation as an orator suffered severely, however, because he disliked giving public speeches. When asked to deliver a welcoming address to Albert Edward, Prince of Wales (who later became Edward VII) in May 1860, he turned the composition and delivery of the speech over to an Englishman, John Thomas Lane, known locally as "Paddy Lane." Lane served as a clerk in the Customs House, but on occasion also administrated medicines to Mi'kmaq. He dubbed himself the Shubenacadie band's "Medicine Man," partly because he supplied this medical care to the Mi'kmaq and partly from what can only be termed a streak of eccentricity. Lane enjoyed donning traditional Mi'kmaw costume and relished the opportunity to address the prince in person.

As spokesperson, Lane proved a poor choice. Nothing could have been further in spirit and tone from Francis Peminout Paul's feisty petition to Queen Victoria of 1853 than the anaemic speech Lane delivered, on behalf of Francis's successor, to the queen's son seven years later. Lane referred to the Sipekne'katik chief and his retinue as humble subjects of her Majesty who had learned to accept that they and what they stood for would pass away before the forces of "civilization." While the Mi'kmaq's skill in constructing emergency camps might have proven of utility during the Crimean War, Lane averred, little else associated with their culture contributed to the province's vitality and growth. "[All] that remains to them now is in their hearts and memories, to feel and remember that they once were a people," Lane stated, before digressing somewhat presumptuously to claim that one of his own ancestors had rescued Charles the Second, following the king's defeat at the Battle of Worcester. He made no references to Mi'kmaq military service during the Seven Years' War and the American Revolution, when leaders like Paul Peminout were viewed by Michael Francklin as valuable allies of the British Crown. All in all, Lane's

presentation was gauged to make the Mi'kmaq look as politically innocuous as possible.[236]

Local newspapers took up the theme of Mi'kmaw poverty and powerlessness by stressing that, prior to the festivities in July, the Mi'kmaq had been too impoverished to afford cloth and beads to fashion articles of their traditional dress. Instead, they had to rely on charitable subscriptions in order to rise to the sartorial requirements of public sensibilities.[237] This fact was not lost on the young prince, who offered Jacques-Pierre fifty pounds sterling.[238] The money was presented to the chief by William Chearnley, the provincial Indian commissioner, at a ceremony in the orderly room of the Chebucto Greys on 11 August 1860, before a large crowd. The chief had camped for two weeks at Tufts Cove in Dartmouth in anticipation of this event.[239]

Despite his reluctance to speak in public, Jacques-Pierre could express himself clearly enough in English when he wanted. As the winter of 1860–61 proved exceedingly harsh, Jacques-Pierre and Captain Joseph Cope, who both were camped in Newport Township, decided to petition the House of Assembly for relief.[240] In February Jacques-Pierre dictated a speech in English to the Reverend John M. McLeod, a Presbyterian minister living at Newport, calling for education for his people and the recognition of Aboriginal land and resource rights. He argued that the Mi'kmaq should receive day schools on their reserves, similar to educational institutions found in many Indigenous communities in Upper Canada and parts of the United States. Money was especially needed, he continued, "sufficient to erect a suitable school house at Shubenacadie, to furnish it with school apparatus, and to support a teacher." He also wanted the school placed under the control of the school commissioners of the province, with the superintendent of education to be consulted in the selection of the teacher. Thirty-one Mi'kmaq signed the document, which McLeod afterwards directed to the House of Assembly.[241] Like his cousin Gorham before him, Jacques-Pierre had previously spoken out on behalf of Mi'kmaw youth. The chief's interest in youth likely stemmed from his deep affection for his foster son, John Noel, who following Gorham's death became second chief at Shubenacadie. Jacques-Pierre delegated so many of his leadership responsibilities to John that John's status within the Sipekne'katik community began to approximate Jacques-Pierre's own.

Around this time a new face appeared on the Shubenacadie council, a captain who hailed originally from Cape Breton by the name of Andrew Paul.[242] There also were a number of new, up-and-coming Mi'kmaw political voices arising within the Halifax County sub-district of the Sipekne'katik Grand Council. Around the time of Confederation in 1867, Captain Joseph Cope and Captain Peter Cope Jr. represented the Halifax County band. Peter Cope Jr.'s sturdy Cape Cod–style house at Red Bridge, near the junction of the Preston and the Old Guysborough roads, became the centre of political discussions that Chief Jacques-Pierre Peminout Paul and John Noel frequently attended. The Indian Road settlement – which at the time was little more than a line of wooden houses flanking a dirt avenue on the Shubenacadie reserve – remained Jacques-Pierre's headquarters, but he liked to spend several weeks during the summer at Red Bridge, listening to his constituents' problems and addressing their concerns.

Political discussions at Cope's house became animated in the months prior to Confederation, as fears arose that Indigenous rights might evaporate with the rise of a radically different order. To learn what the Mi'kmaq might expect after 1867, John Noel and Peter Cope Jr. mustered funds and passports to travel to London and discuss the matter with the queen. After Noel reneged on going to Britain, Cope sailed for London alone, and though he failed to secure an audience with Queen Victoria he met with members of the Colonial Office. On his return passage, Cope had the rare opportunity of receiving first-hand information on what was transpiring from Joseph Howe and Charles Tupper, who discussed the Confederation process with the Mi'kmaw delegate. After his arrival home Cope assured his audience at Red Bridge that their rights would not be jettisoned in the early stages of Canada's journey towards nationhood.[243]

In 1878, the Shubenacadie reserve was resurveyed at the Mi'kmaq's insistence and deemed to contain 1,750 acres.[244] That same year Jacques-Pierre, John Noel, and Christopher Paul led a Mi'kmaw delegation to welcome the Marquis of Lorne to Nova Scotia.[245] Yet the chief otherwise increasingly focused on the past. In 1883 he relinquished all his public duties to John Noel so that he could focus in his later years on receiving visitors and attending to religious duties, which he preferred.[246] He especially enjoyed storytelling and, endowed with a prodigious memory, earned respect as a local historian.[247] Sitting on his

cot, covered with caribou hide, and tucked in between his Waterloo stove and the cabin wall, Jacques-Pierre would toss chunks of wood in the fire while entertaining his listeners with stories of the past and, occasionally, subtle but still startling demonstrations of his shamanic prowess.[248]

New political dynamisms, by contrast, were emerging from discussions in council forums held at Red Bridge. The rise of new ideas elicited a host of petty political rivalries. In 1878 Peter Cope Jr. suspected that Captain Andrew Paul had been directed by Mi'kmaw grand chief John Denny Sr., headquartered at Eskasoni in Cape Breton, to monitor and intervene in land issues in Halifax County, which Cope considered under his exclusive territorial aegis. Peter Cope's son, Joseph Charles Cope, continued to nurture this rivalry until the younger Cope and Andrew Paul learned to work together harmoniously as members of the Sipekne'katik council.[249]

The temporary schism between the Copes and Andrew Paul, however, paled in significance with a heated controversy that arose in 1883 between John Noel and John Denny Jr., John Denny Sr.'s son and successor as grand chief. Despite lack of support from his foster father or other members of the Shubenacadie council, John Noel set out to have the jurisdiction of the Sipekne'katik leader eclipse the political aegis of the grand chief. Lieutenant Governor Sherbrook in 1814, he declared, had recognized Jacques-Pierre's father, Louis-Benjamin Peminout Paul, as chief of the Mi'kmaq population of Nova Scotia. He overlooked the fact that in 1814 Nova Scotia did not include Cape Breton, which at the time formed a separate colony with its own lieutenant governor and executive council.[250]

John Noel's "presumptions" prompted a number of family heads at Shubenacadie in 1883 to draft to two petitions to Lieutenant Governor Adams George Archibald. Both documents pointed out Noel's historical inaccuracies and stressed that most Sipekne'katik Mi'kmaq opposed his exalted claims. The first memorial, dated 5 February 1883 and signed by Jacob Brooks, Abraham Hood, Joseph Hood, Stephen Hood, Christopher Peminout Paul, and Peter Paul, explained that John Noel was not the Shubenacadie chief, and even if he were, the office of grand chief of the Mi'kmaw nation properly belonged to John Denny Jr. of Cape Breton.[251] When Lieutenant Governor Archibald replied on 29 March, asking for additional information, Judge Christopher Peminout

Paul, Stephen Hood,[252] and fifty-nine others wrote that "about one hundred and thirty four years ago" the grand chieftainship had been placed "in the family of Denas [*sic*, Denny or Denys], and it has continued to descend from father to son, following the blood until the present time – John Denas [John Denny] being now the regular chief – he being a resident of the County of Cape Breton."[253] The content of these two petitions, along with Father Pacifique's endorsement of John Denny Jr. as grand chief, cooled Noel's ambitions, and the contentious issue did not arise again.[254]

During his final years, the chief remained aloof from fractious political currents, and in 1895, aged nine-five, he died and was buried at Shubenacadie.[255] On 12 May 1897 his foster son John Noel, despite the brief uproar he engendered in 1883, won the election for new chief held on the Shubenacadie reserve, by this time known by two names, "the Spring Brook Reserve" and "Indian Brook." On hearing the news, his supporters gave a loud three cheers and waved their hats. This event differed from earlier elections at Shubenacadie in that it was the first to follow electoral mandates set out in the 1885 Indian Act. After promising to uphold ritual duties and precedents marking the Sipekne'katik leadership's long and distinctive association with the Roman Catholic Church, Chief Noel, wearing the gilt medallion bearing the image of Pope Pius IX, travelled to Halifax to receive the blessing of Archbishop Cornelius O'Brien.[256]

John Noel, the successor to Jacques Pierre Peminout Paul, cut an impressive figure in public.[257] A handsome, clean-shaven, and rather heavy-set man with thick black hair and dark penetrating dark eyes, he provided a striking contrast to the tall, lanky, and bearded Peminout leaders. Usually accompanied by his wife, Marie-Antoinette Thomas, he attended many public occasions, among them the unveiling of the fountains at Halifax's Public Gardens during celebrations for Queen Victoria's Diamond Jubilee of 1897.[258] When John Noel died at eighty-two years of age on 20 May 1911, Louis Noel McDonald Jr. acted as interim chief for a year.[259]

Big Peter as Sipekne'katik Chief, and William *Daoi* Peminout Paul, "a Holy Man"

On 27 July 1912 Stephen Peter Peminout Paul (1850–1930), a son of Judge Christopher Peminout Paul and Margaret Barbaire, was elected chief by a large majority. Stephen Peter was usually called by the nickname "Big Peter," to differentiate him from one of Andrew Paul's sons named Peter Paul.[260] As with John Noel's election, his victory failed to involve the round of ratifications by neighbouring Eastern Wabanaki nations that had characterized installations of Sipekne'katik chiefs in the past. Confirmation of his appointment by a Roman Catholic prelate remained the only vestige of the earlier ritual order.

Big Peter was sixty-three years old when he became chief. Born on the Shubenacadie reserve, at age twenty-five he was second captain under Chief Jacques-Pierre Peminout Paul, and rose to be first captain under Chief John Noel.[261] He was ceremonially installed as district chief at Halifax on 15 March 1912 by Archbishop Edward Joseph McCarthy. Flanked by his three captains John McDonald, Jeremiah Bartlett-Alexis (Jerry Lonecloud), and Martin Sack, the leader arrived at the archbishop's residence on Dresden Row at ten o'clock in the morning, where McCarthy lit candles and bestowed a blessing on his Indigenous visitors, who knelt before the him. The archbishop then vested Big Peter with the gilt medallion that had formerly been worn by Chief John Noel, and instructed him to uphold the tenets and ceremonies of the Roman Catholic Church. At 10:20 a.m., after shaking hands in farewell with the archbishop, the chief, shaded by a large umbrella, and his retinue walked along Spring Garden Road to the Provincial Museum of Nova Scotia, where they met with Harry Piers, the museum's curator.[262]

Piers observed that none of his visitors wore Mi'kmaw ceremonial dress, but appeared in "homespun clothes." The curator also noted that the silver King George III medal, which Lieutenant Governor Sherbrook had bestowed on Louis-Benjamin Peminout in 1814, had not yet been given to Peter Paul.[263] This prompted a quick search that revealed that, in addition to the 1814 medal, some early documents and a set of stone wampum beads known to have been in the possession of Jacques-Pierre Paul were missing. A large silver medallion, reputedly older than the medal given by Sherbrooke to Louis-Benjamin Peminout, also could not be found. The Mi'kmaq pressed Piers to contact the Reverend William L. Young, who was believed to have borrowed these items around 1893 from Chief John Noel and not yet returned them. Piers later retrieved some papers from Young, but the stone beads and medallion appeared to be irrevocably lost.[264]

For over 130 years the Mi'kmaq of the Sipekne'katik district had recognized a member of the Peminout family as their district chief. By 1912, however, the Sipekne'katik leadership had changed to embrace three divisions based on geography, in addition to its earlier hierarchy of chief, captains, and judges. During Big Peter's term as leader, there was a captain for Hants and Kings Counties, a captain for Halifax and Lunenburg Counties, and a captain for Cumberland and Colchester Counties.[265] On 28 August 1911 Joseph Jeremy was elected as the captain for Halifax County, although after Big Peter's electoral victory in July of 1912, Ottawa, without any stated reason, called both Big Peter's and Jeremy's elections into question and declared both to be invalid. Undoubtedly Big Peter and Jeremy posed challenges to the government, since they both opposed the alienation of certain reserve lands the government intended to expropriate but that the Sipekne'katik Mi'kmaq, particularly those living in Halifax County, wanted to retain.[266]

A major land dispute erupted at Elmsdale, lying on the Hants-Halifax County boundary, when Jacob Gilby, a farmer, found that a geological survey map showed a reserve on a tract he regarded as his private property.[267] An investigation of land records in Halifax and Ottawa, prompted by Gilby's complaints, revealed that the drafters of the geological survey map had erred. No reserve had ever been laid out at Elmsdale. The Mi'kmaq at Elmsdale countered that their rights to the parcel they occupied stemmed from Jacques Peminout Paul's grant of 1783, which covered much of what later became Elmsdale. Martin Sack, who assumed the role of community advocate and historian, also held that they possessed rights by virtue of long possession and set about collecting documents and oral traditions to confirm that the parents of three of his associates, Noel Phillips, Louis Phillips, and Joseph Howe Sr., lived at Elmsdale prior to 1812, when the first surveys took place. Despite the evidence Sack amassed in support of the Mi'kmaw claim, Gilby was unrelenting.[268] The Mi'kmaq had no option but to make arrangements to move.

Ottawa's refusal to recognize Big Peter as the Sipekne'katik chief undermined his political credibility in the eyes of those threatened with eviction from Elmsdale. During band elections, many members of the Elmsdale Mi'kmaw community instead voted for other leaders whom they thought better qualified to help with their difficulties. In consequence, after only one year in office, on 28 July 1913 Big Peter, who had

no descendants who might enter later election races, lost an election held to Maximus Simon Basque.[269] Basque, owing to his own experience in providing for his family, was well aware of the stresses and strains caused by forced removals, through either landowner evictions or the need to seek wage employment.[270]

Simon Basque was re-elected on 26 July 1915.[271] During his terms in office, Jeremiah Bartholomew-Alexis joined him in petitioning Ottawa for funds they knew had accrued from the Mi'kmaq's sale of timber on the Ship Harbour reserve. The money, they proposed as Big Peter and others had, might go towards purchasing a tract at Sand Point on Shubenacadie Grand Lake, where the families who were being evicted from Elmsdale might settle. As a captain of the Halifax County Band, Bartholomew-Alexis lobbied Ottawa on behalf of the Mi'kmaq at Elmsdale, Tuft's Cove, Ship Harbour, Sheet Harbour, and Quoddy.[272] Despite the Mi'kmaq's long occupation of all these areas and, in many instances, their possession of grants or licences of occupation to lands, when they complained of settler trespasses they often were treated as squatters. Frustrated by these occurrences, individuals and families emigrated to central Canada or the United States to seek wage employment.[273]

In the midst of this political and economic turmoil, Simon Basque stepped down in November 1915 and Peter Paul, Andrew Paul's son, was elected in his stead. It appeared that a more forceful leader was needed, and Peter Paul temporarily fulfilled expectations upon winning the election at Shubenacadie on 24 February 1916. Peter Paul and his brother, John Denny Paul – who was first captain of the Halifax County band – immediately opened negotiations with Ottawa regarding the content of treaties signed in the past with their people.[274] Despite this initiative to examine and uphold treaty rights, Jerry Bartholomew-Alexis, frustrated with being ejected from the council since Big Peter's defeat in 1913, politically opposed Andrew Paul's sons and longed for the stability and traditional knowledge represented by the Peminout chiefs. Though in 1915 he hoped for a return of Big Peter Peminout Paul as chief, he had to concede that traditional skills and knowledge alone were no match for the challenges facing the Mi'kmaq on the threshold of the twentieth century.[275] An election held in June 1917 returned a new leader, Isaac Sack (1855–1930), as "the grand chief of Shubenacadie."[276] Isaac, born on 15 June 1855, was the son of

Peter Sack and Marie Antoinette Thomas.[277] After his father's death, Isaac was treated like a son by his mother's second husband, John Noel – who was the foster son in turn of Jacques-Pierre Peminout Paul. From Chief Noel, Isaac learned about and came to admire the leadership legacy established by Paul Peminout and his sons.

One of the major challenges facing Isaac Sack in 1917 was the government's intent to implement a centralization policy calculated to force the Mi'kmaq to live in a restricted number of "growth centres," and to return their reserves to the status of Crown Lands or have them sold to industrialists and land developers. The scheme was predicated on a great deal of misinformation. The Mi'kmaq were deemed to have abandoned two reserves lying south of Halifax, at Ingraham's River and Pendant Cove, and three others, Ship Harbour, Sheet Harbour, and Quoddy, along the Eastern Shore. Although the Mi'kmaq seasonally visited these tracts for the purposes of fishing, hunting, and harvesting wood, Ottawa's timber inspector Henry J. Bury in 1912 held that all five parcels were "vacant" and should be expropriated. Any Mi'kmaw individuals who still claimed attachment to them, he continued, should be relocated to Shubenacadie. Both the province and Ottawa acted upon his directives, and not long afterwards all five reserves were ceded and extinguished.[278] Land cessions and government expropriations continued over the following years, until only one small reserve remained in Halifax County, Cole Harbour Reserve No. 4, lying on the east side of Morris Lake in Dartmouth.[279]

At the same time, as we saw above, the parcel at Sand Point on Shubenacadie Grand Lake, once proposed as a refuge for Mi'kmaq evicted from Elmsdale, was never was purchased. Elmsdale's former residents settled at Indian Brook or joined the Millbrook settlement near Truro. Monies from the sales of timber at Ship Harbour were used to construct houses at Millbrook for those relocating. In 1887 Mi'kmaq at Truro had insisted that the Department of Indian Affairs purchase 135 acres to form Millbrook Reserve No. 27. Between 1904 and 1910, this land base was expanded, through the purchase of three additional parcels of 40 acres each, to 760.48 acres.[280] Although Millbrook initially presented a "ragtag" appearance, since many families moved in at the same time and houses had to be put up quickly, by 1919 it boasted thirty-five frame dwellings sheltering a thriving, close-knit community.[281]

Joseph Julien, Millbrook's chief, at this time called for reinvestigation of the ambiguities surrounding the fate of the old 1779 Francklin-Peminout tract on the Stewiacke River. In July 1919 he wrote to the Crown Lands Office in Ottawa, demanding a copy of Archibald's 1861 plan of the Middle Stewiacke tract.[282] Having secured this plan, he sent it to Indian Affairs timber inspector Henry J. Bury with a request that the Indian Affairs Department find out whether the Mi'kmaq still had any claim to land in the area.[283] Though affecting to pursue the matter, J.D. MacLean, the deputy superintendent of Indian Affairs, fell back on the faulty and incomplete information provided in William Faulkner's 1857 report. On 13 February 1920 Ottawa informed Chief Julien that, prior to Confederation, the Mi'kmaq living "in that portion of the province had deeded away the whole of the Reserve."[284]

The efforts of Francis Peminout Paul and Joseph Julien to elicit a thorough investigation into Mi'kmaw residual land rights at Middle Stewiacke were not forgotten at either Shubenacadie or Millbrook, near Truro.[285] Preparations for a twentieth-century claim benefitted from the oral traditions gleaned over the years by the last member of the Peminout family to assume leadership office. William Peminout Paul, born on 19 July 1858 to Joseph Peminout Paul and his wife while they were living in South Cambridge, Massachusetts, spent his early years in Dorchester, New Brunswick.[286] He served two terms as an elected chief at Indian Brook, from 26 July 1921 to 28 August 1933 and from 28 December 1936 to 9 February 1942.[287] William was especially familiar with the old Indigenous and Acadian trail between Salmon River, Colchester County, and Merigomish in Pictou County, as he frequently visited Maligomish (known to the settler population as "Indian Island'), situated in Merigomish Harbour, which the Mi'kmaq considered a sacred site. As late as the 1960s, Harold Gloade in his autobiographical work *From My Vantage Point* could still pinpoint exactly where the house of "Mister Daoi Paul" stood in 1929 on the Indian Brook landscape.[288] According to Gloade, Paul was "a holy man." He led prayers both at church and in his home, held important meetings in his front room, presided over fundraising campaigns, and became recognized for the remainder of his life, doubtless without the knowledge of the Department of Indian Affairs, as the "grand chief" of the Sipekne'katik district. "It was common knowledge he could recite the entire

Passion of Christ, in hymn, without looking at a book," Gloade maintained. "He had a good voice, strong and clear, making it easy to follow, especially if you had a tendency to sing a little off-key, because you felt you wouldn't be heard." Because of his continuing broad and intense involvement with Mi'kmaw affairs in Nova Scotia, he retained the office of Sipekne'katik grand chief until his death.[289]

Even in his advanced years, Daoi Paul could remember a host of oral traditions, songs, and stories, several of which he shared with author Thomas Raddall and folklorist and ethnomusicologist Helen Creighton.[290] In 1944 he told Creighton, "I spent nearly all of my time by getting my living out of the forest," and felt he had a special gift for calling animals.[291] Like his Peminout predecessors, he travelled widely for political and ceremonial purposes, working closely with other leaders, among them Matthew Francis of Pictou Landing, Stephen John Knockwood Sr. of Shubenacadie, Joseph Julien of Millbrook, and Ben Christmas of Membertou.[292]

Revival of a Valuable Leadership Legacy

Memories of the political activities of the Peminout leaders faded in the early decades of the twentieth century, commensurate with the decline of traditional Sipekne'katik district leadership protocols. Following the close of the First World War, young men returning from overseas embraced new ideas and pursued new goals. Issues and events that had engrossed the Peminout leaders meant less to later generations than to their ancestors. There were exceptions: as late as 1989, Max Basque, elected Shubenacadie chief in 1913, could recount incidents of Chief Jacques-Pierre Peminout's shamanic prowess to Ruth Holmes Whitehead, an ethnohistorian with the Nova Scotia Museum. Yet Basque failed to touch on vital land and resource campaigns that dominated so much of Jacques-Pierre's and other Peminout leaders' political lives.[293]

Scholars consequently have to reconstruct these facets of the Peminout leaders' lives mostly from documentary sources. Since the 1980s there has been a renewed interest in Mi'kmaw petitions and speeches targeting land and resource rights. The words and political activities of Paul Peminout and his descendants are being researched and reviewed, with new attention being given to specific phrases. In some quarters, Paul Peminout, Louis-Benjamin Peminout Paul, and Francis Peminout Paul have come to represent the epitome of the traditional northeastern Algonquian leader, who employs their political, financial, oratorical, spiritual, and diplomatic acumen to act on behalf of their constituency. Their goal was to ensure the welfare of all who placed themselves under their care and protection. They resolved disputes, healed grudges before they developed into long-standing hatreds, and propounded on rights they held were enshrined in treaties and commissions obtained from the Crown's representatives. Because of their hard work and courage, the rights and principles that they struggled to publicize in the public forum passed into the collective memory of the Sipekne'katik First Nation, and are capable of being examined once again in the legal and constitutional forum. Even their most frustrating struggles have borne fruit, since study of them reveals a tenacious quest for justice and the recognition of the Mi'kmaq as a distinct people.

– Janet E. Chute, assisted by Courtney Brooks-Monteith, Brittany Pennel, and Mary Wells

Acknowledgments: Thanks are extended to Tim Bernard of the Mainland Confederacy of Mi'kmaq and to Wallis Stevens, who for several years worked for TARR (Treaty and Aboriginal Rights Research), for tracking down elusive documentary sources. Ruth Holmes Whitehead graciously provided access to the Nova Scotia Museum's materials, including photographs, of Sipekne'katik leaders.

11

John W. Johnson

The Life of John W. Johnson, published by Johnson himself in Maine in 1861, is classified as a captivity narrative, but the only fears and feelings of captivity Johnson experienced followed his reconnection as a youth to his original birth family. After his return John's biological father would hire three strong men to catch and imprison him in a room in a building in Portland, Maine, whenever Penobscot or Mi'kmaw persons were in the neighbourhood of Limerick Academy where John attended school.[1] His father's rationale for so doing was to prevent his son from running away and joining the Penobscot or Mi'kmaw community, since John made it clear that he preferred residing among his Indigenous companions to living within white settler society.[2]

Once he was legally independent of his birth family, John would visit Oldtown, the largest Penobscot community in Maine, and in 1855 at the age of twenty-six he married Susan Newell, a Penobscot doctor with whom he lived in Biddeford, Maine.[3] Nicknamed "Indian John" by those around him, he became an outsider to settler society, a wanderer, loyal to his Abenaki and Mi'kmaw families. His autobiography, written shortly before 1861, provides fascinating portrayals of Mi'kmaq daily life. Following Susan's death, in 1869 he wed Mary A. (McGillicuddy) Hendley, had two sons,[4] and by the early 1880s worked in a cotton mill in Taunton, Massachusetts. He died at Trull Hospital in Biddeford at age seventy-seven in 1907.[5]

While living with the Mi'kmaq in his youth he became familiar with Indigenous life in Nova Scotia, particularly along the Shubenacadie River, in the Pictou region, and in Cape Breton during the 1830s and 1840s. He also described the unfortunate predicament he found himself in after he returned to settler society:

> I had lived with them so long that they seemed to be my people. I had hunted with them for the deer, I had chased with them on the hunting grounds, with them I had passed twenty years of life, and so strong had the attachment become that their people seemed my people, and I felt like one of their number. I could with them be free to rove the forest, or paddle upon the beautiful lakes, but with the whites I thought that I must content myself to live forever in a house that covered a small piece of ground, and there caged up, pass my days.[6]

John W. Johnson, known to Eastern Algonquian speakers as "John Lawshian" or "John Glossian," was born in Hollis, Maine, most probably on 7 October 1829.[7] Found wandering lost in the Maine woods on 16 May 1833 at the age of four by a party of Mi'kmaq, Johnson was encouraged by his Indigenous rescuers to follow them to an open area near Halifax, Nova Scotia, which the Mi'kmaq referred to as "the Great Hunting Ground." Here, John played "snow snakes" with the other children:

[T]he "snake," so called, is a piece of maple some two feet in length, about four inches wide, and like a sled runner, being flat and turned up at one end. The children would dig out a very narrow path in the snow, upon some hill side, quite long, and then standing at the top set the "snakes" down, and let them run down the path; sometimes they would jump out at the side of the path into the snow, other times stop, and ones behind would often jump over them and bound on. The owner of the "snake" that went the greatest distance in the path would be entitled to the others.[8]

By age five he had successfully learned to use a bow and arrow and went on salmon-spearing expeditions.[9] His account provides details of the great distances regularly travelled by "tribes," or family groups, who spent their summers "hunting, fishing, and trapping," and when winter came, pitched their dwellings "upon some good place to hunt, or upon the edge of some settlement" where they made baskets, and thus passed the winter.[10] During the winter of 1836–37, in order to trade furs, his group went north to the Labrador Coast where he "lived in a stone hut, a kind of one that they usually inhabit, lined with moss, and in the top a hole for the smoke to go out. This hut was a very comfortable one, much more so than many that I have since lived in. To get into it we had to crawl some distance through a narrow passage."[11]

He next recalled travelling on lakes and rivers by canoe, but stronger memories began about 1840 when he was living in the Amherst area with James Paul and his wife, whom he called his mother and father. A local farmer's wife taught him the alphabet and he began to learn to read from a primer. He writes that his "tribe" used to make money "repairing tubs, &c., and they also made some very nice fancy boxes out of porcupine quills, dyed different colours."[12] His family spent the next winter at Aristigooch,[13] then moved to Prince Edward Island, "a great resort for fishing vessels and therefore a good trading place to sell baskets, furs, and fancy articles to the sailors," before going to Miramichi for the winter months. After making baskets, coopering, and hunting for the winter, they moved back to the Londonderry area, near Truro, in 1842. Because James Paul was cruel when drunk, Johnson ran away first to Truro and then to Dartmouth in 1843, where he "fell in with an Indian doctor named Tomah, and who had quite a large family, having sons and daughters married, who with their children were living with him, making in all,

with myself, thirty in number."[14] The family, along with Johnson, soon moved on to Digby for the winter, where the doctor practised medicine, some made baskets, and the others hunted and fished. After two or three months at Annapolis Royal selling baskets and other fancy articles, they progressed to Old Barns on the Bay of Fundy for fishing and hunting. When winter approached the family went to Brookfield and pitched a camp forty feet in diameter in a grove of rock maples.

> We cut first six long spruce poles, and stacked them together in the form of a cone, tying the top ends, and allowing the other ends to be about twenty feet from each other in the form of a circle. Between these poles we placed numerous smaller ones, running both ways, and upon these poles we placed our strips of birch bark, each piece nicely lapping over others, and neatly stitched together with spruce roots. These were tied to the poles, and when thus covered, it was perfectly tight, excepting a hole in the top through which the smoke passed. The fire was built in the middle of the tent, around which when very cold, we would all gather, and pass the time very comfortably.[15]

In 1844 they moved to Truro and from there northeast to Aristigooch and Ishcomich, before camping at Pictou for the winter where they traded and manufactured different kinds of baskets. In 1846, after camping on the John's River (River John in Pictou County), where they caught shad, alewives, smelts, and other fish and traded off quite a number of baskets in the spring, they went on to Wallace and stopped there all the summer to hunt, fish, and make baskets. The following winter they camped on Cape Breton Island, where they spent most of their time making baskets and porcupine quill boxes. At the Gut of Canso in the spring, they sold their winter goods and continued slowly along the eastern Atlantic coast to Halifax.

Tomah and his family, including Johnson, continued to travel and, at eighteen, Johnson revealed an entrepreneurial bent. When Tomah's group moved to Halifax in 1847 and camped near "Halifax Hill" (Citadel Hill), making baskets and quill work, Johnson saved the money he made selling his own baskets and other goods, and turned to buying baskets and fancy work from the others. He and a nephew of Tomah than took the steamer to Boston in March 1847 and sold their goods either at a stand on the Common or by going from house to house. Later Johnson stopped at towns throughout New England before going to New York. Because the quill boxes stacked efficiently within each other, he was able to carry five or six hundred dollars' worth of goods. He noted that "the fancy quill boxes are very pretty, and make a beautiful ornament, and sell from one to fifteen dollars."[16] Since the purchasing power of six hundred dollars in 1848 is roughly equivalent to fifteen thousand dollars today, Johnson obviously enjoyed a successful two month's work.[17] Equally obvious is the respect accorded to the time and skill involved in making a quilled box: at about this time in Halifax, the artist William Valentine[18] charged one pound for an 11" x 13" profile in oil and five pounds for a 16" x 19" portrait,[19] so the market value of a quill box could exceed that of a small portrait in oils.

In May he took a steamer back to Halifax. Since Tomah and his family now had a considerable stockpile of fancy work, twenty of the family went with Johnson back to New York about the first of August, where they sold about half their supply before moving on to Philadelphia. They made cloth tents in Philadelphia that Johnson found inferior to the birchbark wigwams. Some of the Mi'kmaq manufactured goods while others in the group sold them for about three months, before moving on to Pine Woods, a locale near Springfield, Massachusetts, for the winter, adding boards to their cloth tents to make them more comfortable.

In the spring of 1848 they all moved to Newport, Rhode Island, and did well making fancy baskets and other small articles. Moving back to New Bedford, Roxbury, and Lowell, Massachusetts, they were bothered by parties of roving Irish, who tried to provoke trouble. After a winter in Boston, where Tomah practised medicine, the others took a steamer back to Halifax in 1849, but Johnson remained in the United States.

During the next decade, he worked as an actor, a millworker, and a sailor, studied medicine, and made baskets to sell whenever his funds were low:

> Before the ash can be worked, or before it will strip, it
> has to be pounded very hard, striking about two blows

in the same place, until every part has been pounded, and then each year's growth becomes somewhat separated and can be stripped off, and these parts can also be stripped, if desired, into pieces as thin as a ribbon. The strips are usually about seven feet long, and smoothed by placing the strip upon the knee, and then gauging the knife upon it, drawing the strip through, giving to it an equal thickness, which requires some little practice.[20]

After 1855, when he wed Susan Newell, the doctor from the Penobscot settlement at Oldtown, he formed a theatrical company with her brothers Thomas and Loring. Eventually Johnson and his wife settled at Biddeford, Maine, where she practised medicine and he sold baskets. His birth-brother was the train station agent there and recognized a scar on Johnson's forehead. The story of a white man who had been raised by Indians was already circulating in the town when his birth father arrived to meet him. The initial meeting did not go well, since Johnson was irritated by the mob of local citizens threatening to "hang up every red-skin in the State of Maine."[21] Eventually he bought an ambrotype salon from which his wife also practised medicine. After Susan's death he married a white woman but continued his peripatetic life, practising medicine himself and later joining the Kickapoo Indian Medicine show. To the end of his life he was considered one of their own by his Penobscot relatives. His acquisition of the Sable Island ponies used in his act suggests a continuing connection with Nova Scotia as well.

Johnson's story reveals that the travelling patterns followed by the Mi'kmaq before the middle of the nineteenth century stretched from Labrador to Massachusetts, and that their manufactured goods – baskets, quill boxes, and other wood products – competed successfully in the marketplace. His story offers a contrast to the usual depiction in much of the literature of the time, and subsequent to it, of Indigenous destitution and despair.

– Mora Dianne O'Neill

12

The Man at the Centre: Chief Joseph Julien, the Halifax County Band, and the Development of the Millbrook Community

Early Childhood

Chief Joseph Julien, who was born in Thorburn, Pictou County, on 31 October 1872 and died on 6 February 1957, surmounted family tragedy and poverty in his early years to become one of the most politically astute Mi'kmaw leaders of the twentieth century. Orphaned at a very young age when his mother, Madeline, died in childbirth and his father, Noel, drowned in a river-driving accident in New Brunswick, he was sent to Cape Breton, where he had to rely on the charity of people at Eskasoni and North Sydney for basic necessities such as food and clothing. As he grew older he became the responsibility of several prominent Mi'kmaw community leaders in Cape Breton. For a while he resided with Gabriel Sylliboy at Whycocomagh (*Waycobah* or *We'koqma'q*), later he lived at Eskasoni with the elderly Grand Chief John Denny Sr. (c.1810–87), and after Denny's death he joined the household of John Denny Jr. (1841–1918), John Denny Sr.'s son and successor as grand chief who also lived at Eskasoni. Gabriel Sylliboy succeeded the latter as grand chief.

The Denny household was a politically active one; upon becoming grand chief in 1881 John Denny Jr. countered attempts to do away with what the Department of Indian Affairs in Ottawa deemed to be "unoccupied reserves." Denny argued that reserves with few occupants, such as a tract on Kejimkujik Lake in Queens County, Nova Scotia, confirmed by order-in-council in 1843, should be preserved as refuges or homelands for the benefit of the Mi'kmaw nation at large.[1] The grand chief and Grand Council had the authority to send surplus Mi'kmaw labour from Cape Breton and elsewhere in the Maritime Provinces to harvest timber, which then would be shipped by the Atlantic Province's developing rail transit system to centres where the wood would be made into manufactured goods. Denny, who invested considerable thought, study, and energy in his scheme, targeted a specialized market, the Northumberland Strait and Cape Breton mining industry, which needed beams, tubs, and pickaxe and shovel handles. To the grand chief, an economic strategy that entailed distributing populations relative to available lands and resources not only made good economic sense, it also drew upon resource strategies employed by his people in their traditional hunting territory system for generations.

Introduced at an early age to the principles on which the grand chief founded his land and resource campaign, Joseph Julien upheld and applied them when he became chief of Millbrook, near Truro, in 1919. Despite challenges he faced from 1910 to the mid-1940s from government centralization policy, which sought to relocate all of the Nova Scotian Mi'kmaq to either Shubenacadie (the headquarters of the *Sipekne'katik* First Nation, also known as Indian Brook) or Eskasoni, he stood by his belief that chiefs and councils should be the only ones to regulate entry into a Mi'kmaw community by exercising control over band membership. He also endeavoured to balance local populations relative to the carrying capacity of the land and, when circumstances warranted it, learned how to effectively secure additional territory as well as monetary resources from the government.[2]

His success in carrying out many of his political goals owed much to his congenial and inclusive nature. These character traits, coupled with his intelligence and capacity for hard work, gained him praise from the Mi'kmaw and non-Indigenous community alike. They also won him a far greater degree of co-operation from Indian Affairs administrators, who otherwise might have been disposed to undermine what he was trying to accomplish: increased band council powers that placed land purchase, resource protection and use, and community resource development principally in Mi'kmaw hands. To Julien, Ottawa should remain in a facilitating rather than a controlling role. Throughout his leadership career he evinced diplomatic tact and an almost uncanny knack of getting people to like him, traits born from his rare equanimity of spirit, sense of humour, and a spiritual dimension to his life that imbued even his most mundane dealings with others. He worked closely and effectively with other Mi'kmaw leaders as well as with government agents. While congenial and interested in other points of view, he was strongly disciplined and stood his ground firmly under fire on matters of principle that were important to him.

The Julien Family's Miramichi and Cape Breton Roots

Despite the fact he had lost his parents early in life, Joseph Julien retained a lively interest in his family history, which he gleaned from relatives and close associates at Eskasoni. The parents of his father, Noel Julien, hailed from the Miramichi River region of New Brunswick.[3] Joseph found he could trace his ancestry back four generations on both his maternal and paternal sides to a chief named "King John Julien" who lived in the late 1770s along the Northwest Miramichi River, and John's brother, Chief Francis Julien of the Little Southwest Branch of the Miramichi, known in Mi'kmaq as *Metepenagiag*.

These two Julien chiefs played an important role during the American Revolution in neutralizing what threatened to be a volatile era in Mi'kmaw-settler relations along the Miramichi River. After a trader named John Cort in the early summer of 1779 had his storehouses raided and burned by unknown perpetrators, British fears escalated that rebel sympathies among the Miramichi Indigenous population might have fuelled the attacks. A warship, *HMS Viper*, was sent to the spot and seized sixteen Mi'kmaw suspects, but when John Julien assured the British that his family and followers would remain quiet, the *Viper's* captain, Augustus Harvey, concluded a treaty of peace and friendship with the two chiefs and their captains on 28 July 1779. Later the same year, in September 1779, John and Francis Julien joined eight other "consequential leaders" in travelling to Windsor, Nova Scotia, to ask the provincial Indian commissioner, Michael Francklin, to release the Mi'kmaw prisoners, who were being held in custody at Quebec. Francklin demurred; instead, he asked the Juliens and their associates to sign another pact on 22 September 1779 disavowing any dealings with George Washington and his emissary, John Alan. This the chiefs did, after which all the prisoners except two of the ringleaders were released by the governor of Quebec, Frederick Haldimand.[4] King John Julien used his shrewd negotiating powers in 1783 to acquire a licence of occupation to a twenty-thousand-acre reserve along the Northwest Miramichi – the largest tract ever allotted to Mi'kmaq in the Northeast – though by 1808 government agents had reduced the reserve to half its original acreage.[5]

As the Miramichi reserve became smaller, in the 1820s some young male members of the Julien family sought wage work elsewhere in the Maritimes.[6] While these persons rarely severed kin ties completely with their original band, they met and married individuals from other groups and joined the communities of their in-laws.[7] Band lists from Cape Breton show Juliens living permanently in Cape Breton as early as 1830. In 1841 there were two Juliens, Noel and Thomas, in Cape Breton, who may have been brothers; at that time only Thomas was married and had children. Noel moved around in the 1840s, but by 1851 he was also married and camping with Grand Chief John Denny Sr. and others at North Sydney. In 1857 Noel Julien's wife was living on her own at Barra Head (present-day Potlotek), while Noel worked elsewhere.[8] In the summer of 1862 Noel, Grand Chief John Denny Sr., John Gold (or Gould), and members of the Benoit, Bernard, Googoo, and Poulett families lived in a small settlement at North Sydney to take advantage of wage labour in the nearby town.[9] On 22 August 1865 Noel, accompanied by his son Peter Julien, joined other Mi'kmaq at Chapel Island (Potlotek) near St. Peter's in signing a petition to Lieutenant Governor Richard Graves MacDonnell for funds for a bridge to span a stream near the local mission church.[10] Owing to geographical factors and chronology, it is highly probable that this Noel Julien was Joseph Julien's grandfather.

In the late 1860s Joseph Julian's father, a young bachelor named Noel, moved to Afton (or Paqtnkek), Antigonish County, where he married a local woman, Madeline (or Magdalene) Benoit.[11] The couple's eldest son, Steven, was born around 1870. Joseph Julien, who was their second son, arrived on 31 October 1872 and was baptized at St. Ann's Roman Catholic Church in Thorburn, Pictou County. A daughter, Mary Nancy, followed.[12] Following Nancy's birth, Noel and Madeline moved to North Sydney where Noel took labouring jobs, but he soon left for New Brunswick to river drive and work on ships, leaving his young family at Eskasoni. It was at this point that tragedy struck. In 1877 Madeline died in childbirth, Steven took sick and died in the same summer, and Noel drowned in the Saint John River soon afterwards.[13] Relatives at Burnt Church (or Esgenoopetitj), New Brunswick, offered to take Mary Nancy into their home, but Joseph was left unclaimed at the age of five: he "didn't have a permanent residence; he wandered from house to house as he was growing up in Eskasoni."[14] Though he had to go about seeking food and clothing, he never went completely without, for Mi'kmaw values do not allow an orphan to ask for sustenance and not receive it.

When Gabriel Sylliboy of Whycocomagh took him in, he taught the young boy how to track and hunt game, trap, fish, and construct wooden implements like buckets and axe handles for sale. For a year Joseph also lived in the household of John Denny Sr. at Eskasoni, and when the grand chief died in 1881, he lived with John Denny Jr., Denny Sr.'s son and successor. Aware of the young boy's penchant for learning and his reflective, spiritually imbued nature, Denny Jr. taught the young Joseph to read and write hieroglyphic characters so he could lead, as well as participate in, traditional Mi'kmaq religious ceremonies. Since many hieroglyphic texts pertained to religious matters, Joseph also learned prayers, chants, responses, and hymns. Possessing a sonorous voice, he joined with the grand council prayer leaders in reciting religious texts and singing hymns. Denny thus inducted the youth by degrees into a body of religious material passed down orally and by means of hieroglyphic script since the early eighteenth century. Joseph's gentle responses to others' spiritual questionings, as well as compassion and care for others, soon made him a welcome visitor at family prayer meetings and at sick people's bedsides.

New Friends, Associates, and In-Laws

Joseph Julien was determined to make a mark on mainstream society that would benefit his people. He admired, though he could not emulate, John Denny Jr.'s ability to speak Gaelic and French as well as Mi'kmaq and English. Instead he set out to hone his speaking skills in Mi'kmaq and English and improve his writing abilities, and embarked on studies at the small one-room day school at Eskasoni.[15] The schoolhouse was a short walk from his residence, since the grand chief's frame house stood on a small peninsula jutting out into East Bay, close to the centre of the village where the school house was. Denny meanwhile groomed Joseph for an increasingly active role in Mi'kmaw community affairs, and was rewarded by his protégé's progress in learning how to effectively address Mi'kmaw political, social, and economic needs. Joseph in his early years also was encouraged to develop a range of sincere friendships that became a wellspring of valuable social capital he could draw upon later in his life.

Upon turning seventeen, he met a young widow named Louise Morris, and after a brief courtship presided over by elders of the Denny family, the two married in 1889 and set up housekeeping at Eskasoni.[16] Little is known about their six-year relationship other than that in 1895 Louise suddenly died from complications of childbirth. Aside from the stillborn infant, the couple had no children. Learning of a need for workers on a section of the Intercolonial Railway line passing through Rockingham into Halifax, Joseph soon after became a railway labourer, and when this work ended he took a job at Oland & Son Brewery in Dartmouth.[17] In his spare time, he also made baskets and axe handles to sell at the Halifax Market.[18]

The knowledge and experience he gained while a boy out hunting, fishing, and tracking in Cape Breton came into play when he was called upon in 1907 to guide George W.C. Oland, president of Oland &

Son Brewery, and his twenty-two-year-old son Sidney C. Oland on a hunting and fishing trip in Halifax County. Sidney Oland admired Joseph's engaging congeniality and honest, hard-working demeanour, and though Joseph was seven years older than Sidney, the relation between the two men grew from its simple patron-client beginnings into a genuine camaraderie, based partly on both men's love of hockey.[19] Like the friendships he had earlier cultivated as a youth, his friendship with Oland later proved of inestimable value when he became chief of a growing Mi'kmaw community on the outskirts of Truro. When the Oland's brewery in Dartmouth was destroyed in the Halifax Explosion of 6 December 1917, however, Joseph lost an important source of paid employment, since the Dartmouth brewery was not rebuilt.

While living in Dartmouth in 1897 Joseph also married a second time, to Mary Jane Paul, who was raised in Nyanza, Cape Breton. The same year the couple had a son, John Julien, who later served overseas in the First World War.[20] For two years Joseph and his wife lived on the Cole Harbour reserve, during which time Joseph heard stories of the past from his friends and neighbours as he sat by stoves in their frame houses or at their hunting camps. A favourite was Andrew Paul, a farmer who arrived in Dartmouth from Whycocomagh, Cape Breton, about 1840. In 1879 Paul lobbied Ottawa for a reserve on the shores of Morris Lake in Cole Harbour, and in August 1880 his efforts secured approximately twenty-three acres extending from "Minister's [now Morris'] Lake towards Eastern Passage" as a refuge for Mi'kmaq displaced from their traditional lands along the eastern Atlantic coast. Settlers already had cleared fields and erected a number of houses and outbuildings on the site, and the government provided lumber and shingles to build additional frame dwellings. The tract, owned by Judge William Almon Johnstone of Windsor before it was purchased by the Department of Indian Affairs, was fertile, wooded in spots, and lay close to Dartmouth and Halifax markets.[21] Since Andrew Paul also promoted Grand Chief Denny Jr.'s land campaign, Joseph's own close personal attachment to the grand chief doubtless strengthened his relationship with the elderly Cole Harbour community leader. In 1899 Joseph and Mary Jane moved to a small Mi'kmaw community on the east side of the Narrows at Tufts Cove, to be closer to the brewery where Joseph worked. There tragedy struck Joseph again, for Mary Jane became ill within a year and died in 1900.

Richer for the friends he had made and the stories he had been told at Cole Harbour and Tufts Cove, Joseph Julien moved the following year to Millbrook near Truro. From there he commuted to work as a labourer at Elmsdale, situated on the Hants-Halifax County boundary. Millbrook's acting chief, Joseph Gould, was a *keptin* (captain) of the grand council and, like Andrew Paul, was born at Whycocomagh and supported Grand Chief John Denny Jr.'s land and resource policies. In 1887 the Department of Indian Affairs purchased a rectangular, thirty-five-acre parcel after two leaders, Peter Wilmot and Sandy Cope Sr., stressed that land was needed for Mi'kmaq in the Cobequid area. Millbrook, while established seven years later than the Cole Harbour reserve, arose for much the same reason – to provide a refuge and a centre for development for Mi'kmaw families displaced from their traditional lands by government fiat.

Peter Wilmot and Sandy Cope Sr., Millbrook's Founders

The development in the 1880s of a Mi'kmaw community in the Cobequid area owed much to the determination and insight of a chief from Pictou County named Peter Wilmot. *We'kopekwitk*, the Mi'kmaw word from which the name "Cobequid" derives, means "as far as the water will flow," and originally encompassed a vast region lying between Stewiacke and the Cobequid Mountains. Under Wilmot's auspices, *We'kopekwitk* also designated the new settlement he founded near Truro. In the early 1900s, Wilmot was not well known to Joseph Julien. Yet owing to Wilmot's political associations with Sandy Cope Sr., and his participation in the Mi'kmaw grand council of which Joseph later also became a member, the two once they settled near each other at Millbrook became firm friends.

There were few Mi'kmaq living in the Cobequid region prior to the late 1880s, though transients from Pictou County seasonally camped along the Salmon River to take fish in the stream that ran through Cobequid village.[22] A Mi'kmaw band inhabited the Stewiacke River area, but Cobequid was practically deserted by the Mi'kmaq following the Acadian deportations of 1755. During the French regime, the area had been home to a thriving Acadian community boasting five churches. French settlements spread inland from Cobequid Bay as far as Stewiacke, leaving the lower reaches of the Shubenacadie River under Mi'kmaw territorial control. Mi'kmaw families from the Pictou area accessed the region by travelling south down the Stewiacke River and then travelling west, while Mi'kmaq from the eastern Atlantic coast reached Cobequid by ascending either the Shubenacadie or Musquodoboit rivers. The Shubenacadie River, which cuts across the "shoulder" of the province like a bandolier, also was the route by which Mi'kmaw groups reached Cobequid Bay and, from there, the North River, which flowed past the town of Cobequid and extended inland towards Tatamagouche on the shore of the Northumberland Strait.[23]

Cobequid had provided a central meeting place for Acadians and Mi'kmaq alike. Yet British scorched-earth tactics left all five of Cobequid's churches, including the old landmark chapel at Point de l'Église (now Masstown) and the Mi'kmaw mission at the juncture of the Stewiacke and Shubenacadie Rivers, in charred ruins. One family that at the end of the eighteenth century had annually visited Cobequid to fish was headed by Francis Wilmot from Pictou. Though Francis originally hailed from Antigonish, around 1800 he joined the Merigomish band led by Paul Chachegonout, also known as "Vieaux à Paul."[24] In 1783 Chief Chachegonout secured a licence of occupation from the colonial government for a large tract on "the southeast side of the East Branch of the Harbour or River Margomish [Merigomish], or Port Luttrell."[25] As no reserve was surveyed in the area, the Mi'kmaq ranged over lands granted to British incomers while trying to protect the integrity of their ancient ceremonial and burial sites on Indian Island (now Merigomish Harbour Indian Reserve No. 31) and along the east shore of Pictou Harbour.[26]

Francis Wilmot's grandson, Peter Wilmot (1826–1932), was born in July 1826 to Joseph Wilmot and Madeline Dinian and baptized soon afterwards at Merigomish on 26 July, St. Anne's Day. In his younger years Peter belonged to the band at Merigomish, where he married three or four times in succession, the second time to an Acadian woman, Marie Landry, with whom he had a daughter named Sarah in 1880.[27] In all, he had around nine children.[28] Perhaps to escape the ravages of a disease epidemic in Pictou County that began in 1846, in 1852 Peter, his wife and children, and his mother pitched their wigwam for over a year on the banks of the Salmon River at present-day Hilden, near Bible Hill, where his mother died.[29] In 1862 Wilmot, along with a few family heads who had joined him from points further east – James

Cope from Hantsport, Michael Allan, Ann Morris, Tom Noel, and Tom Thomas from Shubenacadie – moved to a site on King Street in Truro known as "Christmas Crossing," since a family from Cape Breton named Christmas had camped there.[30] This land subsequently was sold and in 1885 became the campus of Nova Scotia's School of Agriculture.[31]

Alexander or Sandy Cope Sr. (1853–1930), who later would become Joseph Julien's father-in-law, began to camp at Christmas Crossing prior to its sale. Born at Sheet Harbour on the eastern Atlantic coast, Sandy Cope Sr. hunted north of Truro, near Debert. Like other Eastern Shore Mi'kmaq, he reached Cobequid by ascending the Musquodoboit River, which took its rise ninety-seven kilometres south of the Cobequid Mountains. When he was not on his hunting grounds Cope often accompanied Wilmot, who had begun to cruise the countryside looking for new land on which to found a Mi'kmaw settlement. When the two in 1885 discovered a tract near McCuller's Mill Brook that abounded in game, firewood, and ash trees for wooden manufactures, they encouraged the others to leave Christmas Crossing for this new location. In December 1886 Wilmot, who had become spokesperson for his small group, launched a vigorous campaign to persuade the Department Indian Affairs to attain the Mill Brook property as a reserve. His efforts bore fruit, for exactly a year later, in December 1887, Ottawa bought a thirty-five-acre roughly rectangular parcel, which was traversed by the old post road to Halifax and bordered on the Intercolonial Railway allowance, from John Waller Jr. of Truro for $350. Wilmot and Cope were not long in broadcasting throughout the Mi'kmaw community the news that a new permanent land base had been secured for Mi'kmaq from Pictou, Hants, and Halifax counties who might wish to settle there.[32]

Wilmot was unanimously elected as the first chief of the new Millbrook community in 1887, though he soon faced opposition from Indian agents who likely felt threatened by this elderly but still politically astute leader.[33] Within two years he left for Cumberland County, where he also was elected chief, though he spent increasingly more time at his hunting camp at Sunny Brae in Pictou County. He did not return to Millbrook until 1919, when, at the age of 93, he moved into a humble wooden shanty belonging to his son Charles. He would die at 106 years of age on 27 December 1932 at Millbrook, the community he had helped found.[34]

Joseph Julien and the Copes from the Eastern Shore

After Wilmot left Truro in 1889 Millbrook's residents went about establishing a community infrastructure. With the financial backing of an elderly cooper named "Soolian Bill" – or William Prosper – who offered his life savings to benefit the rest, the Mi'kmaw community obtained enough lumber in 1897 to build Sacred Heart Roman Catholic Church.[35] Mi'kmaw carpenters provided the labour to build the church, and soon after constructed a day school. At this time Newel Gloade, who had been working at Acadia Mills at Londonderry, retired with his wife Anastasia Vicaire to Millbrook with their two grown sons, Louis and William Thomas Gloade.[36] Under the direction of Sandy Cope Sr., Louis and Tom helped the community to acquire three small additional parcels, amounting altogether to 120 acres, as firewood reserves between 1904 and 1910.[37] After the office of Millbrook chief had remained vacant for over a decade, Joseph Gould from Whycocomagh, who may have been directed to go to Truro by Grand Chief John Denny Jr., finally became acting chief in 1906 for two years and was succeeded in 1908 by Abraham Gould, though the Department of Indian Affairs refused to recognize either man's election.

There thus was no chief at Millbrook in 1901 when Joseph Julien first moved to the community. Joseph had not got to know Chief Wilmot well prior to Wilmot's leaving, though in later years, through his connections with the grand council, he would participate in many ceremonies where Peter Wilmot was also in attendance, and came to view the older man as a close friend. Millbrook's affairs in Wilmot's absence were running smoothly, however, owing to the unofficial leadership exercised by Sandy Cope Sr. Sandy, the eldest son of Frank Cope and Mary Ann Quigley, was born on 4 November 1853 at Sheet Harbour, 114 kilometres east of Halifax.[38] He was a hunter, trapper and guide par excellence who escorted officers into the Cobequid Hills on hunting and fishing expeditions. Sandy and his second wife, Mary Paul from Newdy Quoddy on Nova Scotia's Eastern Shore, had three sons and three daughters whom Joseph Julien enjoyed visiting. Sandy Cope Sr. and his sons could tell engaging stories about their ancestor Major Jean-Baptiste Cope (1698–c.1758) who signed a treaty at Halifax in 1752, but the following year regretted his decision and joined the resistance movement against the English.[39] Sandy also knew that Cope was killed by his political opponents near Halifax around 1758, after which the chief's eldest sons, François (c.1720–c.1770) and Joseph (c.1725–1784), moved to Sheet Harbour to become leaders of the Mi'kmaq living along the Eastern Shore.

Joseph Julien, who was twenty-nine years old in 1901, also enjoyed visiting other members of Sandy Cope Sr.'s household at Millbrook. Sandy Sr.'s younger brother, Henry Cope, lived with him, as did his younger sister Libby who would eventually move to Edmonton. Another of Sandy Sr.'s sisters, Annie, wed Isaac Sack and lived in Elmsdale.[40] Sandy Cope Sr., who married three times, had four sons and three daughters: Sandy Cope Jr. in 1885, Margaret or "Meggie" Nancy in 1886, Susan Jane in 1889, Bridget in 1891, Frank in 1894, Joseph in 1895, and John Edwin (or Edward) in 1899.[41] The attractive and vivacious fifteen-year-old Bridget Cope particularly caught Joseph's eye.

Joseph's visits to the Cope household at Millbrook became more frequent during the summer of 1905, and on 19 June 1905 he married Bridget Cope at St. Bernard's Church in Enfield.[42] Sandy Sr. and Mary had encouraged Bridget to dress stylishly and learn how to read and write. In many ways Bridget was an ideal mate for Joseph, since she shared his love of learning and had a host of kin connections because she had so many older siblings. After their wedding Joseph and Bridget settled on the original thirty-five acres that Peter Wilmot had obtained in 1887 from the federal government.[43] The history Joseph learned at this time about his father-in-law's people, the Copes, and his mother-in-law's relatives, the East Coast Pauls, would prove immensely valuable to him, since the Copes and Pauls formed the core of the "Halifax County Band," the constituency on whose behalf Joseph would act in future years.

The Copes of Sheet Harbour

From his new in-laws, Joseph Julien doubtless learned that near the end of the Seven Years' War one of Jean-Baptiste Cope's sons, François (c.1720–c.1770), made peace with the British. François, who also went by the name "Blanchois (François) *Wyegawook*" (the Mi'kmaw name for Sheet Harbour),[44] in company with seven other Mi'kmaw leaders signed a peace and friendship treaty with the British at Halifax on 28 April 1760. François's younger brother Joseph lived with

The Copes of Jeddore, Musquodoboit, and Wyegawook (Sheet Harbour)

Some members of the Cope family and their relation to Joseph Julien's wife, Bridget Cope:

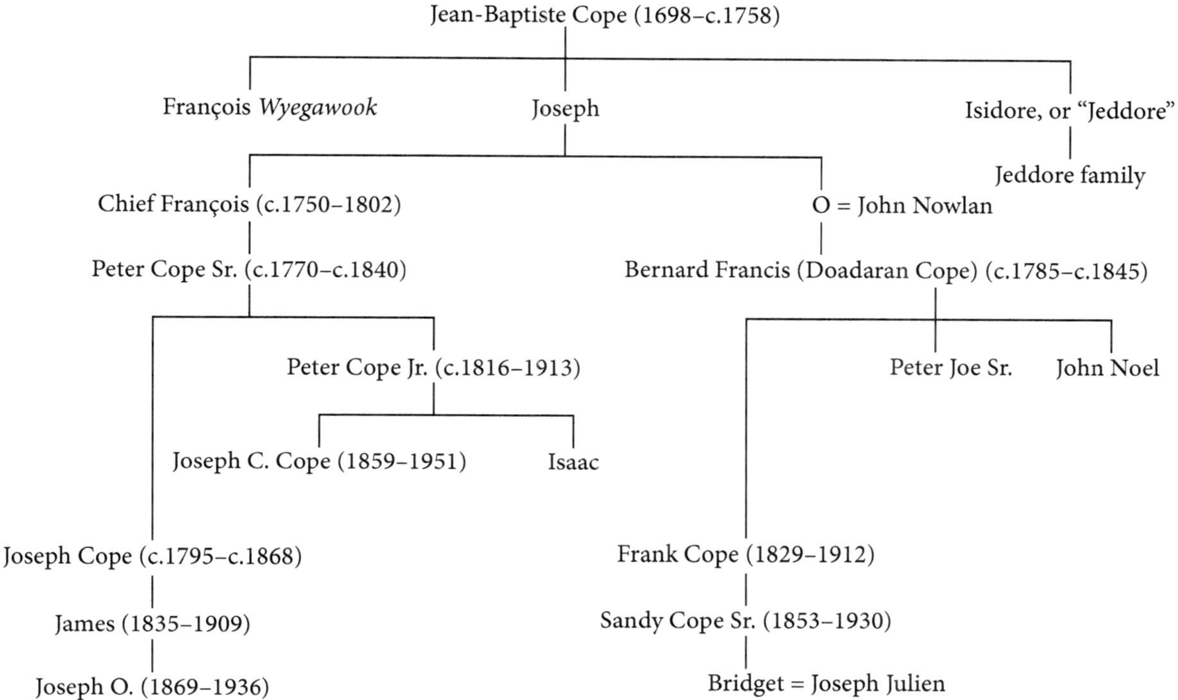

Paul Labrador's family at Piziquid (now Windsor) in 1747, but after his father's death moved permanently to Sheet Harbour to be near François.[45] François and Joseph also had a brother, Isidore (c.1727–c.1840) who lived between Jedddore and Musquodoboit, and two sisters, Margaret and Anne. François Cope probably died around 1770, since his name does not appear in the documentary record after this date. Joseph meanwhile had a son named François Cope (c.1750–1802) and several daughters, one of whom in the 1770s began living with an Irish trader, John Nowlan, who maintained a post at Newdy Quoddy.[46] Nowlan and his wife had at least twelve children.[47] The best known, Bernard François Nowlan (c.1785–c.1845), who also went by the name Bernard François or Francis Doadaran Cope or simply Doadaran Cope,[48] and his wife Molly had at least three children by 1840, one of whom, Frank, was Sandy Cope Sr.'s father.

About the time of the trader John Nowlan's first appearance on the Eastern Shore, the colonial government allocated vast tracts in the Sheet Harbour region to absentee landowners. In 1773 Jonathon Belcher (1710–76) received a Crown grant of five thousand acres at the head of Sheet Harbour. To protect his people's resource area, Joseph Cope approached Michael Francklin, the provincial Indian commissioner, to request that his hunting territory at Sheet Harbour be made a Mi'kmaw reserve, but Francklin died in 1782 before any such action might be taken. The following year the province contemplated bringing Loyalists to Sheet Harbour, so Joseph again pressed for land. To avoid friction between the Mi'kmaq and the new settlers, the government offered the chief a licence of occupation to land flanking Belcher's grant "running up both sides of the eastern branch of the river, including the salmon fishery." An agreement made in September 1783 allocated "eleven thousand five hundred & twenty Acres" to the chief and his group. There were two stages to the drafting of this document, however. The first result of negotiations recognized Mi'kmaw prerogatives to hunting and fishing locales, and granted the Mi'kmaq the right to contest settler intrusions on their grounds. After being revised by the executive council, however, the final wording of what turned out to be a licence of occupation reneged on the former promise to allow the Mi'kmaq to occupy their land in perpetuity: occupancy of the land was now contingent on "the pleasure of the Crown." This stipulation made it impossible for the Mi'kmaq on their own to restrict outsiders' access to their resource areas, and ultimately limited the duration of their occupancy to a term laid down by government fiat.[49] Since no effort was ever made to survey or to protect the tract against trespass, Mi'kmaq occupation of this land at Sheet Harbour proved short.

After his father Joseph died in 1784, François Cope hoped to secure a smaller parcel that fronted the harbour. George Henry Monk, Nova Scotia's newly appointed Indian commissioner, relayed Cope's wishes to the lieutenant governor. "Francis Cope, Chief (or Capt.) of a Tribe of Ten Families ... at Wigawick" (*sic*, Wyegawook), Monk reported to John Parr, "solicit[s] for a Grant of Land at the Head of Sheet Harbour beginning at the Forks of the River & running two miles on each side [of] the main River, from thence north two miles so as to include both branches of the River & to comprehend 2400 acres – which tract was first granted to John Greere & became again liable to Forfeiture."[50] But neither Cope nor Monk received any reply to this petition.

The arrival of the Loyalists in the area, though initially disruptive, did not totally dislodge the Mi'kmaq from their traditional fishing sites on the Musquodoboit River and at Sheet Harbour. One prominent Mi'kmaw head man who remained in the Musquodoboit River area was Isidore Cope (c.1727–c.1840), also known as "Captain Isidore," Jeddore Cope, and *Wedge-it-doo* (*We'jitu*), which may mean "I found it" and possibly relates to a vision he experienced in his youth.[51] Isidore was remembered as a *kinap*, supernaturally endowed with great physical strength and longevity. During the 1790s Isidore hunted at Jeddore, along the Musquodoboit River, and near his seasonal campground on First Dartmouth Lake.[52] He had ten sons, among them Philip, Peter, John, and Ned, who took the surname "Jeddore" rather than "Cope."[53] In 1796 a Halifax merchant, Joseph Davis, wrote Monk that "Isidore Cope, Capt. Paul Bonico [Bonis or Bonus] and Matthew Paul [had] settled on [the] Musquodoboit River,"

while François Cope, Molly Cope, Lewis Cope, Paul Cope, and Joseph Labrador (who was likely François Cope's brother-in-law) lived at Sheet Harbour. Davis regarded Isidore and François Cope as the heads of what he called "the Eastward Tribe."[54] From 1783 to 1802 François Cope remained chief, while Isidore, Paul Bonis, and Joseph Labrador were captains.

In the late 1790s, Chief François Cope traded with John Nowlan's establishment at Newdy Quoddy as well as a private merchant at Sheet harbour named Peter McConachie, so his name appeared infrequently in Monk's government requisition lists. François and his family did not escape official scrutiny altogether, however. In 1800 James Fulton, who was a merchant at Stewiacke, a justice of the peace, and an unofficial appendage of Commissioner Monk's office, reported to Monk that Cope was fifty years old and Labrador forty. Both were married and each man had four children.[55] Captain Labrador was favoured by government officials over Chief Cope, for in June 1796 Labrador was given a "Blue Coat, Scarlet Waistcoat, Scarlet Pantaloons, and Dress complete," whereas Cope received no such emoluments. Government unfairness shown to the Copes, including broken promises regarding land, lack of protection for the Mi'kmaw salmon fishery, and the tendency to turn a blind eye to settler desecration of Mi'kmaw gravesites, haunted John Sprott, an itinerant Anglican minister at Musquodoboit.[56] According to Sprott, the Copes harboured a sense of betrayal that sporadically caused them to denounce what they felt was the government's perfidious treatment of their rights. Isidore once stressed that he retained "sovereignty of the soil, for the land of Musquodoboit belonged to him, and we [the settlers] were all intruders."[57] Yet despite the many challenges they faced, lands near them still had moose, caribou, and salmon, which were scarce elsewhere in the province, and so they could maintain an independence of spirit and action that Halifax officialdom grudgingly admired.[58]

The leadership of the Eastward Tribe changed radically during the summer of 1802 when Chief François Cope was fatally stabbed by the wife of François Labrador after he tried to quell an argument between two women at Clearland in Lunenburg County.[59] A solemn procession conveyed Cope's remains to Oakland for burial in an ancient cemetery at Indian Point on Mahone Bay. Doadaran Cope, who would have been in his thirties at the time, assumed responsibility for caring for François

Cope's widow and her youngest children. Two of the chief's sons, Louis (c.1780–c.1854) and Peter Cope Sr. (c.1785–c.1840), were grown men with families of their own in 1804, but Joseph and Thomas were youths, born after 1785.[60] Though they also joined the elderly Isidore Cope on his hunting expeditions, these boys regarded Doadaran as a father figure.[61] Isidore in the late 1830s retreated more and more to his camp on the Musquodoboit River, where he was reputed to have died at age 97 around 1840, although one account held he was as old as 113 years of age.[62]

Peter Cope Sr. also died around this time. Peter was born too early in the eighteenth century to be a son of Doadaran Cope, and though it is possible he was a son of John Nowlan, most likely his father was Chief François Cope, who died in 1802.[63] Peter's grandson Joseph C. Cope stated that his father occasionally used the surname "Nowlan," but it is possible that Peter Cope Jr. was "borrowing" a name from his cousins with whom he hunted and guided sportsmen.[64] In the 1790s Peter Cope Sr., who hunted and travelled to acquire supplies with Captain Isidore Cope in the 1790s, married Mollie Salome (b.c.1782), and was living in Cape Breton in 1816 when his youngest son, Peter Jr., was born.[65] But except for social and trading journeys to Cape Breton, he lived along the Eastern Shore. Like his uncle Isidore, he gained the reputation of being a *kinap*, or strongman. Around 1835 he also assumed leadership of the Eastward Tribe. What little is known about him comes from a few notes jotted down by his educated grandson, Joseph Charles Cope (1859–1951), better known as Joseph C. Cope, who on occasion turned his hand to writing local history. One story tells about a grueling wrestling contest in which Joseph's grandfather strangled a bear to death by grasping the base of its tongue, revealing him to be a large, strong, quick-thinking, and courageous man.[66]

Peter Cope Sr. and his wife had three sons, Joseph (c.1795–c.1868), Louis (c.1815–c.1854), and Peter Jr. (1816–1913). By 1840 all three had left the Sheet Harbour area to settle elsewhere, although they periodically returned to the Atlantic coast. His eldest son Joseph joined a Mi'kmaw encampment located on private lands at Shubenacadie Grand Lake known as King's Siding or Sand Point. Louis Cope, who wed Mary Thomas of Panuke Lake near Windsor, moved to the outskirts of Dartmouth where he guided sportsmen and participated in canoe regattas on the Dartmouth Lakes. Peter Jr. built a house at Second Red Bridge, on Red Bridge Pond, located near Dartmouth at the junction of the Waverley Road and the old Preston Road.[67] Their father, except for occasional journeys to Cape Breton for trade and social purposes, remained on the Eastern Shore, and after his death around 1840 his mantle of leadership fell first to Doadaran Cope, next to his eldest son, Joseph Cope (c.1800–c.1868), and finally to Peter Cope Jr. (c.1816–c.1913).

With fishing and logging settlements expanding along the coast, a small semi-permanent Mi'kmaw community arose at Beaverdam Lake (also written as Beaver Dam Lake), forty-seven kilometres southeast of Truro and lying along the Sheet Harbour Road constructed in 1817 between Upper Musquodoboit and Sheet Harbour. This community furnished a refuge in the interior. It was composed first of wigwams and log cabins and later of frame houses with stone basements, the remains of which could still be seen well into the twentieth century.[68] From his headquarters at Beaverdam Lake Doadaran Cope, immediately following Peter Cope Sr.'s death, assumed the leadership for the Eastward Tribe for about five years. From the 1820s to the 1840s, Peter Cope Sr.'s responsibilities had been particularly challenging, since moose numbers radically declined owing to overhunting. Once the settler population established farming and fishing settlements along the shore, however, their reliance on hunting waned, and by 1840 herds had rebounded. Doardoran shot the first moose in many years, prompting a major celebration at his camp in lower Sackville, located at the juncture of the Beaverbank and Old Cobequid Roads, which Mi'kmaq attended "from all over the province."[69]

With the spread of farms and fishing communities along the coast, Doadaran and his family moved inland to the Mi'kmaw settlement at Beaverdam Lake. There Doadaran and Molly raised Frank Cope (1828–1912),[70] who was Sandy Cope Sr.'s father; Peter Joe Cope Sr. (1834–1912);[71] and John Noel Cope (1847–1918), also known as "John Bolmoltie."[72] Doadaran and Molly also had several daughters. One was Nancy, or Anastastia Molly Cope, who married a man known simply as "Charles," probably a local fisherman. This couple's daughter, Susan, later had a daughter Anastasia, or Nancy, by a fisherman surnamed Wessel from Sober Island.[73]

Doadaran Cope suffered from seizures, and not long after his triumphal moose hunt, around 1845, he and a young boy drowned when, during one of his epileptic episodes, he upset their canoe on Ship Harbour Lake, now Lake Charlotte.[74] Following his death, his widow Molly supported her family by her special knack of capturing and taming bear cubs, which she sold at high prices as novelties to officers of the Halifax garrison. In 1852 the government, in response to petitions from Doadaran and Molly's heirs, accorded them acreage at Beaverdam Lake for a reserve. In 1861 Molly married a second time, to the elderly widower Joseph Paul, who was a brother of Francis Paul, a boat builder and a patriarch of the East Coast Paul family. She died at Sheet Harbour in 1900 at the advanced age of 104.[75]

After the deaths of his close companions Isidore, Peter Cope Sr., and Doadaran, Captain Paul Bonis (Bonus, Bonice) decided to leave the Musquodoboit area for Cumberland County. One reason for his removal may have been a rise in sickness among the Mi'kmaq of the Eastern Shore. There were several outbreaks of smallpox in the Musquodoboit Valley, and by the 1850s at least four families living in the area had lost all their members.[76] Isidore may have fallen victim to smallpox, which was a severe loss, since in the 1830s he had taught young men skills in hunting and tracking, among them Peter Joe Cope Sr., one of Peter Cope Sr.'s sons, and John Williams, who all became noted guides.[77]

In the fall of 1869 Peter Joe Cope Sr., John Williams, and Louis Noel accompanied Queen Victoria's son, the nineteen-year-old Prince Arthur, Duke of Connaught and Strathearn, on a hunting expedition near Caledonia in Queens County. Peter Joe Sr. also guided in Newfoundland. These men were expert hunters and guides, and followed the practice of dividing up the landscape into hunting territories. Peter Joe Cope Sr. maintained a hunting territory up the Sheet Harbour River between Fifteen Mile and Rocky lakes, while his brother John Noel Cope hunted along the Musquodoboit River. His son Peter Joe Cope Jr. (1857–1917) had a tract north of Sheet Harbour, though he also had close connections with the local settler community and worked in the fishing industry. On 10 May 1878 Peter Joe Jr. married Mary Alexandria Farnell, the daughter of a fisherman named James Farnell, and the couple had Mary Sarah Cope, who in 1902 wed Thomas E. Logan, a Sheet Harbour fisherman.[78] Doadaran's sons and grandsons also accorded hunting rights to their relatives from Millbrook who ventured to the coast by way of the Shubenacadie and Musquodoboit valleys. Sandy Cope

Sr. retained a hunting territory around Tangier and Scraggy Lakes.[79] Abraham Gould from Cape Breton and later Millbrook,[80] who married into the Cope family, had a territory back of Sheet Harbour.[81]

Following their father's death, Doadaran Cope's sons supported Peter Cope Sr.'s son Joseph Cope (c.1795–c.1868) as the new leader of the Eastward Tribe. Born just before the turn of the eighteenth century, Joseph had an engaging, lively demeanour and was a favourite of the sportsmen he guided. He lived at Sheet Harbour until the early 1830s, when he wed Mary Phillips of Panuke Lake at Windsor, and later moved to Indian Point on Shubenacadie Grand Lake. A traditionalist at heart, Joseph followed aspects of ancient Mi'kmaw hunting ideology, which included laying offerings of tobacco at the base of a Grandmother Rock situated on the western shore of Shubenacadie Grand Lake.[82]

Upon being told of Joe Cope's hunting and guiding prowess, Joseph Howe, the provincial Indian commissioner, in the spring of 1842 made a special trip to Indian Point by horse and wagon to visit with Cope and his family. Though Cope's wife Mary was ill, Howe stayed long enough to ask the couple if they would let two of their sons, James and John, be educated at government expense at the Roman Catholic seminary at Halifax until they could read and write.[83] John Cope may have died while at the seminary, but his brother James left with at least the fundamentals of reading, writing, and arithmetic. He rarely used these skills when he returned to Shubenacadie Grand Lake; for around twenty years thereafter he assisted his father as a camp boy on hunting excursions with officers of the Halifax garrison.[84]

Among the persons Joseph Cope guided in the 1850s were William Chearnley, commissioner of Indian Affairs for Nova Scotia from 1853 to 1862, and Lieutenant Campbell Hardy. Joseph on these excursions was almost always accompanied by his son James, whom he called "Jem," and at times by another son, Peter Cope Jr.[85] In 1867, on one of his last visits to see the Cope family, Hardy, now a captain of the Halifax garrison, noted that Joseph had moved his family to a site near the newly constructed Intercolonial Railway line, and about half an hour's paddle along the lake by canoe from Wellington Station in Halifax County. The Copes had taken over a "substantial frame house," which Hardy called "Cope's Castle," on a lot that had a barn and a water-driven sawmill built by a settler who afterwards abandoned the place. The house embraced a family living space, a workshop, and a storage site for Joseph's woodworking, farming, and fur-trapping equipment. Hardy noted its walls were gaily decorated with religious pictures and illustrations cut out of *Punch*.[86]

While he was chief Joseph Cope assumed responsibility for the welfare of Mi'kmaq living in the environs of Dartmouth and Halifax, as well as those along the Eastern Shore. He convened councils, hosted feasts, and conversed with local authorities about Mi'kmaw individuals who had strayed from their community's constraints, grown derelict, and fallen into tragic circumstances, among them Annie Glode, found dead in the winter of 1848 in an abandoned barn on the outskirts of Halifax.[87] He petitioned for government monetary relief and medicines for the hungry, aged, and infirm.[88] His camp in the Rawdon Hills offered him a respite from these duties. Campbell Hardy claimed that Cope jealously guard his hunting territory as his personal preserve "and private property."[89] Despite his reputation as an expert guide, as he grew older he preferred the solitude of his interior woodlands. On his own land he was no longer a mere dollar-a-day employee of the officers he escorted, but was free to act in accord with his stores of ancient knowledge of the countryside and its resources. In 1867 the elderly hunter refused to guide sportsmen owing to his increasing bow-leggedness and declining hearing and eyesight, and he died within a year.

Joseph's son James (1835–1909) worked as a cooper, guide, trapper, and farmer. He wed Margaret Paul, and after her death in 1864 he married Magdalene Thomas from Panuke Lake, back of Windsor, in 1865 when he was thirty years old, though his marriage certificate states he was only twenty-two.[90] The pair first lived at Wellington Station, where they cared for James's aging father, but after Joseph's death they went to Windsor. They also occasionally visited the Atlantic coast, as their son Joseph O. Cope was born in 1869 at Ship Harbour.[91] James had a family hunting territory in the foothills of the Cobequid Hills near the Economy River, north of the Cobequid Basin, and from 1862 onwards frequently visited the Truro region.[92] He also prospected for gold in the Rawdon Hills, and in 1886 was credited with finding the ore lode known locally as the "Cope vein." This find sparked the development of the Rawdon Gold Mines, and Joe received six thousand dollars for his finder's rights from the Central Rawdon Gold Mining Company.[93]

Joseph O. Cope (1869–1936), Joseph's son, married Sarah Tracy in Windsor, later moved to Hantsport, and eventually settled on the Mines Road in Falmouth.[94] Joseph during the winters hunted near Economy in the Cobequid Hills and in the spring and fall fished at Carr's Brook on the Parrsboro Shore, where several of his children were born.[95] Joseph and Sarah raised nine children, all of whom were educated.[96] One of their sons, William, lived in Kentville. Two others, James and John, enlisted to fight overseas in the First World War. Even Joseph offered his services to the war effort and was accepted for local duty, although at the mature age of forty-five, and with only one arm, he was not sent overseas. The years surrounding the First World War were hard on these Copes. Joseph and Sarah's eldest son, James, who enlisted in the 76th Regiment of the Canadian Militia and was sent to France to serve with the 106th Battalion of the 76th Regiment, died in action at eighteen years of age.[97] He later received military distinction for his conduct in uniform. His younger brother John, who lied about his age in order to serve overseas, survived the war but succumbed to the effects of mustard gas after arriving back in Nova Scotia.[98] Then, on 13 October 1918, Sarah Tracy suddenly died within one week of contracting the Spanish flu.[99] News of the Copes' trials prompted former Indian commissioner William Chearnley, in 1930 retired from government service and living in Ireland, to reminiscence about James and Joseph O. Cope.[100] The following year Mary Agnes, one of Joseph O. Cope and Sarah Tracy's daughters, married Michael G. Martin, a son of John Martin and Madeline Benoit of Conne River, Newfoundland, at Millbrook.[101] Madeline was related to Joseph Julien's mother Madeline Benoit, a kin connection that prompted John and his new wife to settle at Millbrook, where many of their descendants live today.[102] Mary Agnes's father Joseph O. Cope briefly settled at Millbrook, although he died at 68 years in 1936 while working as a labourer at Gold River, Lunenburg County.[103]

Peter Cope Jr., chief of the Eastward Tribe from the mid-1860s until his death, was said to have been the last member of the Cope family to be formally addressed as "Captain" by the government authorities in Halifax. His father Peter Sr.'s penchant for camping on the eastern side of First Dartmouth Lake, now Lake Banook, inspired Peter to return to the same area. Peter Jr. wed Louisa Paul and the couple had two sons, Joseph Charles Cope on Easter

Day 1859 and Isaac Cope in 1863.[104] He was a trapper and guide, and in the 1850s and 1860s hunted with Commissioner William Chearnley for five seasons.[105] He and Louisa lived for several years along the Beaverbank Road in Lower Sackville, but in the early 1860s moved to the Dartmouth Lakes area where, at Second Red Bridge, he and his wife built a frame house.[106] Like many fishermen's houses found along the Eastern Shore, the Copes' house was a one-and-a-half-storey saltbox-style dwelling, with a hipped roof, summer kitchen, and a chimney at one end. Since Peter did some farming, his property included a barn and several outbuildings.[107]

For generations the Second Red Bridge site had been a stopping point for Mi'kmaq travelling by canoe down the Shubenacadie River to the lower Dartmouth Lakes. The Copes' house flanked the Dartmouth-to-Truro Road, completed in 1827, which meant visitors could approach on foot as well as by water. Cope's saltbox, which furnished a landmark on the countryside, remained standing until the turn of the twentieth century. From 1867 to the mid 1870s it was a focal point in a Mi'kmaw community composed of twenty-seven heads of families.[108] In 1866 Peter Cope Jr. invited Mi'kmaw leaders to his home to discuss the subject of treaty rights and the dangers Confederation could pose to the terms of the treaties. Since they could express their people's wishes clearly in English, Peter Cope Jr. and John Noel of Shubenacadie, who was Chief Jacques-Pierre Peminout Paul's adopted son, were delegated to travel to England to meet with Queen Victoria. Noel pulled out of the arrangement shortly before embarkation, but Cope soldiered on. While in London, he stressed the need to preserve and enhance Mi'kmaw treaty rights under the new federation, topics of discussion he continued on shipboard with Charles Tupper and Joseph Howe, who travelled home across the Atlantic on the same Inman Line steamer, *City New York*.[109]

Though let down by John Noel's refusal to accompany him to London, Peter Cope Jr. nonetheless remained fiercely loyal to the Shubenacadie leadership of which John Noel was part, seeing himself as a sub-chief of the Sipekne'katik district leadership hierarchy, presided over by Chief Jacques-Pierre Peminout Paul. As his father aged and he shouldered more duties, he faced an increasingly challenging slate of responsibilities. Except for a few Copes and the hardy members of the Eastern Paul family, who

clung heroically to their ancestral lands by diversifying their economic base, the years between 1870 and 1890 saw the final stages of dispersal of the Eastward Tribe. This band, who in the late seventeenth century had met with French fur traders at Musquodoboit, interacted with Acadians and their priests at Chezzetcook, and forged such a close alliance with the trader John Nowlan that he by 1796 became a member of their group, was rapidly diminishing in numbers.[110] According to an Indian Affairs report, by 1871 the Mi'kmaw population of the Musquodoboit area, which at the time included Jeddore, Musquodoboit, Ship Harbour, and Sheet Harbour, had dwindled to around thirty persons, many of them elderly.[111]

The East Coast Paul family

Sandy Cope Sr.'s wife, and Joseph Julien's mother-in-law, was Mary Paul (1868–c.1925), a daughter of Joseph Paul and Jane Kegan (also Kauchen, Kachen, or Keagan) of East Quoddy along the Easter Shore.[112] The Eastern Shore of Nova Scotia had given rise to an ethnically diverse community, as Mi'kmaw men often married daughters of nearby settlers, and Mi'kmaw women married men from settler communities. The members of the East Coast Paul family entrenched in the Ship Harbour area by the late eighteenth century were known as the *Eskekagooah Joguns*, or *Soguns* (literally, the "East Coast *Joguns*").[113] Ship Harbour was home to a cluster of closely related families, with many bearing the surname "Paul."[114] Matthew Paul was a member of Isidore Cope and Paul Bonis's group at Musquodoboit in the 1790s, but after Isidore died and Bonis left for Cumberland County, Matthew relocated to Ship Harbour. The Mi'kmaw community at Ship Harbour gradually grew until, in 1848, two brothers, Francis and Joseph Paul Sr. – likely both sons of Matthew Paul, who had died by this time – petitioned Abraham Gesner, Nova Scotia's Indian commissioner from 1846 to 1853, for acreage at Fish Lake at the Head of Ship Harbour. Fish Lake was an ancient Mi'kmaw rendezvous spot; even during the late 1840s, in the autumn the Fish Lake encampment ground might host as many as sixty Mi'kmaw individuals at one time.[115]

Gesner was sympathetic to the Mi'kmaq's position, but he had to play his cards carefully, as the province was unwilling to increase the acreage already allocated to the Mi'kmaw population within Nova Scotia. After 1842, the upper limit of acreage agreed upon by the province amounted to 22,050 acres.[116] It thus was necessary for the commissioner to arrange for another reserve to be ceded first, before a new reserve could be created.[117] This task was eased by the fact that the Pauls were still in contact with the Bonis family in Cumberland County. Although Captain Paul Bonis had died by 1848, his two sons Noel and Tom Bonis belonged to a group headed by a Parrsboro chief named John Logan.[118] Chief Logan admitted his group had no intention whatsoever of settling along the Shinimicas River in Cumberland County where a thousand-acre reserve had been set out for them by order-in-council in 1820.[119] In consequence, the Pauls camped during the winter of 1848–49 on the east side of Ship Harbour and waited expectantly for both the surrender of the Shinimicas tract and the establishment of their own reserve.[120]

Owing to the Pauls' importunity, the abandoned Shinimicas reserve was ceded in 1862, after which seven hundred acres at the Head of Ship Harbour, designated Reserve No. 18, was laid out for the petitioners. The tract was subdivided into seven lots of one hundred acres each, with Francis Paul (c.1800–c.1895), his wife, and six children taking one lot and his brother Joseph Paul Sr. (c.1810–c.1916) with his wife and five children taking a second lot.[121] One of Francis Paul's sons, Joseph Paul (1826–c.1900), occupied a third lot. The other four lots belonged to Louis Paul,[122] James Paul,[123] Louis Brooks, and Louis Noel – who had come from the Martinque Beach area and married into the Paul family.[124] Joseph Paul Sr., although he had lost an eye in an accident, and Francis Paul were hunters and guides whose hunting territories extended as far inland as the Stewiacke River Valley. Younger members of the Mi'kmaw community either hunted back of Ship Harbour or along the upper reaches of the Musquodoboit River.[125]

Younger Pauls, among them Francis's son Joseph Paul Jr., built frame houses, wharves, and barns. They started a woodworking industry making oars, wooden tubs, mast hoops, and ship's knees for the fishing industry; they trapped, guided, made barrels, and manufactured baskets; and they farmed and sold their produce and wooden wares at the Ship Harbour market. Their diversity of occupations brought year-round income. They also engaged in mineral prospecting. Gold fever in California in 1849 had its repercussions in Nova Scotia. After 1855 the Ship Harbour Pauls kept their eyes open for indications of the yellow metal as they hunted for moose over the Tangier barrens. Joseph Paul Sr., while out hunting

along the Tangier River with two companions, Frank Cope and Louis Noel *dit Plowitch,* was the first to spot a ridge of laurels that he knew grew in association with gold-bearing parent rock. The Mi'kmaw party were guiding Champagne L'Estrange, a lieutenant with the Royal Artillery, and Gilbert Elliot of the H.M.S. *Indus* on an autumn moose hunt. L'Estrange later told several persons who were reputedly knowledgeable geologists about the quartz veins Joseph Paul had shown him, but since he failed to produce rock specimens indicating the presence of gold, he "was discouraged about prosecuting the discovery by the ridicule of the *savan[t]s* in mineralogy."[126] Paul's finds conjured up sufficient excitement locally, however, that in May 1860 a Musquodoboit farmer named John Pulsivar set out on a mineral-exploring expedition with Joseph Paul Sr., Francis Paul, and James Paul to Mooseland, inland from Tangier. The party found a chunk of quartz in a nearby brook that, when broken open, contained flecks of gold.[127] One discovery led to another, and in October of the same year a settler named Peter Mason found a vein of gold at the head of Tangier Harbour. Owing to the ensuing flood of amateur prospectors into Mooseland and Tangier tramping the countryside early the next spring, the province registered Mooseland and Tangier as official gold districts in April 1861.[128]

During the height of the east coast gold mining frenzy, which did not last past 1885, the Pauls along with Francis Doadaran Cope's sons supplied moose and fish meat to various mining camps. Both prospecting and provisioning brought income, but Francis Paul Sr. went further. Well known and liked by the local settlers, Francis learnt carpentry and the craft of wooden boatbuilding. In 1853 he had erected a large frame shed for his boatbuilding and coopering activities, which had an internal chamber that doubled as a "wayside inn" for Mi'kmaw visitors to Ship Harbour. The mid-1850s were the golden age of wooden boatbuilding as well as mineral prospecting along the eastern shore, and both industries absorbed a wide range of wooden items made by Francis and his family, who for a while found their enterprises profitable. Disaster struck, however, on the night of 16 December 1857 when fire consumed the "framed building ... with all its contents – hay, staves, and coopering and boatbuilding tools." Francis, in his late fifties and with a large family to feed and shelter, doubted he could regain his livelihood after this setback without government assistance.[129]

Francis failed to secure the help from the government he so badly needed, while other challenges loomed on the horizon for the Ship Harbour community in general. As moose once again grew scarce the province severely restricted bag limits on big game, and opportunities for guiding diminished. Families continued to have large numbers of children, but the futures of these children became uncertain.[130] Some families felt that, in the face of radical changes taking place along the eastern shore, the younger generation should be introduced to the fundamentals of writing and reading in English. The Pauls and Copes touted education and sent their children to local schools, but this meant less labour was available on the farm and in the forest. And there were unexpected bouts of severe sickness. In March 1858 a few of the Pauls, as well as Peter Cope Jr. and Peter Joe Cope Sr., were taken seriously ill at Sheet Harbour, though they recovered.[131] In 1861 smallpox appeared at Pope's Harbour, east of Ship Harbour, and travelled down the coast towards Halifax.[132] This outbreak may have been responsible for the death of Joseph Paul Sr.'s first wife, for in the same year he married Doadaran's widow, Molly Cope, who had been living alone since her husband drowned. Joseph's marriage to the elderly but youthful-acting and energetic widow earned him a new nickname, "Joe Molly."[133]

The Mi'kmaw lands at Ship Harbour reserve also became a target for timber poachers, who plundered large swaths of the forest close to the shoreline. In response, Joseph Paul Jr. and his new sixteen-year-old Germanic bride, Johanna Kauchen (or Kachen) – who around 1900 took the name Jane Kegan (or Keagan) and claimed at times to be Scottish, though her name change preceded the anti-German feeling that arose during the First World War years – decided soon after their marriage in 1865 to vacate Ship Harbour. On 9 November 1866 they drew up a petition for a grant of land further east along the coast and sent it to Halifax, where it was presented by provincial Indian commissioner Samuel Fairbanks to Lieutenant Governor Sir William Fenwick Williams, who at the time refused to support it. Joseph meanwhile built a house on a nearby island, which today is still known as "Joseph Paul's Island," and, after a determined struggle to gain the grant in the Quoddy area, during which time he received several disparaging and humiliating missives from Halifax, in 1868 he obtained his desired land in the form of a lease both to the island and to one hundred acres on the

mainland at Newdy Quoddy (now East Quoddy) from Williams's successor, Lieutenant Governor Charles Hastings Doyle.[134] This tract lay near where John Nowlan had his trading post in the late eighteenth century. Joseph Paul and his wife farmed and Joseph also prospected, guided, and hunted. Cultivation of crops on what proved to be stony ground in often damp, foggy weather was challenging, but the couple persisted and raised a large family. Between 1866 and 1888 they had twelve children: Francis Thomas in 1866, Mary in 1868, John Abram in 1869, John Edward in 1870, twins Joseph Daniel and Gabriel in 1872, Sara Anne in 1876, Bridget Ellen or "Lily" in 1878, Susan Jane in 1881, Margaret in 1882, Elizabeth in 1885, and Katie in 1888.[135]

Illicit settler hunting and trapping and timber robbery continued on the Pauls' East Quoddy property, but Joseph and Jane, despite mounting problems, fought tenaciously to retain their one hundred acres. Ottawa felt uneasy about levying the same sanctions against trespass on a grant given to Mi'kmaw proprietors as on a reserve, confirmed by order-in-council. In the 1880s, following her husband's death around 1899, and into the first two decades of the twentieth century, Jane Kegan repeatedly lobbied the Department of Indian Affairs for protection from trespass;[136] when she finally received a response in 1921, Ottawa explained that the federal government's hesitancy in acting arose from the Pauls' having received their land, not as a reserve, but in "free and common soccage." Eventually, however, the Department of Indian Affairs agreed to initiate special action to protect their property that they had farmed long before they officially received a grant to it.[137]

Jane Kegan Paul stayed on the Quoddy property after her husband died, but her children gradually moved away. The last to leave was her son John Paul. In 1905 John Edward, now in his late thirties, and his wife Emily had four young children: Susan Jane born in 1895; William Gabriel in 1896, John Edward Jr. in 1900, and Rupert in 1901.[138] One of John's cousins, Peter Paul, who was a farmer, cooper, carpenter, guide, and prospector, visited John at Quoddy occasionally, though he maintained a dwelling on a ten-acre lot at Beaverdam Lake, which he helped secure as a reserve.[139] Farming at East Quoddy had so grown precarious owing to settler trespasses and spates of bad weather that John and Peter Paul cleared land in 1906 at Sheet Harbour. In 1910 they persuaded Indian Affairs to survey a reserve for them at that locale. The tract, known as Indian Reserve no. 36, subsumed the five acres they had already cleared, and was laid out in two sections. The first parcel, of 150 acres, formed a narrow strip extending from the southwest side of Sheet Harbour to Grand Lake. The other tract, on the opposite side of the harbour, was small and roughly rectangular in size. Estimated to be from thirty to fifty acres in size in a hilly area, it contained two acres of cleared land.[140]

As soon as they received the reserve at Sheet Harbour, the Pauls and their associates entered into negotiations with the Department of Indian Affairs to lease the timber on the Ship Harbour reserve, which they saw as a potential source of continuing income. In 1910 they secured an agreement from Ottawa stating that Marks Brothers Lumbering Company could harvest timber on the reserve provided all lease monies and stumpage dues accrued over time to the Mi'kmaq.[141] Over the next three decades, the younger generation of Mi'kmaq left the Eastern Shore for extended periods to seek work in other parts of the Atlantic Provinces or in New England. Some left permanently. Joseph Paul Jr. and Jane Kegan's grandson, William Gabriel Paul (born to Joseph's third son, John Edward Paul) moved to the Millbrook Band, but following the onset of the Great Depression worked in the New Brunswick logging industry and for a while chose to take employment as a stevedore at the dockyards in Saint John, New Brunswick.[142] He and his family later returned to live at Indian Brook. William Gabriel's sons Lawrence Alexander and Daniel N. Paul have arisen as important political and cultural leaders both at Millbrook near Truro and within the Mi'kmaw community as a whole.[143]

A Leadership Clash and the Rise of the "Halifax County Band"

When timber harvesting began at Ship Harbour and Ottawa offered the Mi'kmaq no way of monitoring the accumulation or distribution of timber revenue, the Pauls began casting around for a leader who would keep an eye on their financial interests. Their sights soon fell on Joseph C. Cope, the eldest son of Peter Cope Jr. of Second Red Bridge, who could read and write well in English and demonstrated an affinity for their concerns. Joseph was also a kinsman, since Cope's mother Louisa Paul belonged to the East Coast Paul family. The group that Joseph C. Cope championed in the late 1800s was held together by a complicated network of kinship relations, with a time depth of several generations. It included the Copes, the East Coast Pauls, members of the Jadis family, the Noels and McDonalds, Louis Morris, Louis Morris's brothers John and Ben Morris of Dartmouth, and various in-marrying newcomers. Joseph intended to work in close cooperation with the Sipekne'katik head chief, Jacques-Pierre Peminout Paul, as long as the Shubenacadie leadership regarded him as a valuable district sub-chief.

For this reason, Joseph expressed considerable chagrin when Andrew Paul, who was not one of the *Joguns* or East Coast Pauls but came from Cape Breton – and was therefore considered by Cope to be an outsider – suddenly took the lead in 1879 in successfully negotiating with Ottawa for a reserve at Cole Harbour.[144] Andrew Paul was responding to a situation in which over sixty Mi'kmaq seasonally encamped at various sites in and around Dartmouth without secure title to the lands they occupied. Descendants of "Old Paul Morris," who received a licence of occupation in the 1780s to a tract at Sambro, just south of Halifax, had pulled back from the coast when settlers contested their rights to the local fishery. They resided for a while along the Prospect Road and later moved to Dartmouth. The grandfather of Louis, John, and Ben Morris maintained a camp at the outlet of Morris Lake, named after him, so his grandchildren knew the Cole Harbour area well.[145] Meanwhile an elderly Tom Morris, who belonged to the same family, and his wife Mary Christiana Paul Morris left Dartmouth to farm near the head of the North West Arm.[146] An extended family of Toneys, who first camped on the east side of Sullivan's Pond in Dartmouth, settled near the Shubenacadie canal along a waterfront lane that local residents dubbed "Toney Street."[147] Other families were scattered along the shores of the Bedford Basin. While some had long association with a particular locale, others were newcomers from other parts of the province, so a land base near Halifax and Dartmouth was very much needed.

Andrew Paul's immediate response to this situation was to have acreage at Cole Harbour set aside for those who wished, or had, to move there. In 1880 Joseph C. Cope, his wife Rebecca Jadis, four of his children, his father Peter Cope Jr., his mother Louisa Paul, and his brother Isaac were among those who had to move to Cole Harbour, since a large lumber mill occupied the Copes' former farm tract at Second

Red Bridge.[148] Owing to his kin connections with past leaders of the old Eastward Tribe, he expected to lead the Cole Harbour Mi'kmaw community. What he failed to realize in 1880 was that out of the ashes of the Eastward Tribe a new politicized entity, which Cope himself a decade later would name the "Halifax County Band," was already emerging.[149] The Cole Harbour reserve community formed the administrative core, but it did not constitute the geographic circumference of this new constituency. In Cape Breton, the newly installed Grand Chief John Denny Jr. realized what was happening along the Eastern Shore and sent Andrew Paul a bevy of instructions about the importance of working with government agents to forward a land and resource campaign that would embrace the whole of Halifax County.

Andrew Paul's ongoing duties as a captain of the Mi'kmaw Grand Council included preventing loss of reserve land and trying to secure more for the Halifax County Mi'kmaw population. By contrast, Cope viewed the establishment of the Cole Harbour reserve community as an opportunity to exercise his leadership capabilities over what was left of the old Eastward Tribe in much the same manner as his father and grandfather had done before him. He immediately invited many of his relatives to join him. But though he was surrounded by supportive kin, he soon found that his mantle of leadership continuously had to be shared with Andrew Paul, who had the ear of the grand chief, the local agent, and several government authorities in Ottawa. Cope in his early years as a leader – he was only thirty-two years old in 1880 – was zealous in what he felt were his duties, but he lacked the diplomatic acumen that might have lessened his constant bickering with Paul. He also clashed with the local Indian agent, the Reverend A.P. Desmond. This became so apparent that the Department of Indian Affairs found it necessary to conduct an investigation into Cope's assertions that he be recognized as the sole "Vice Chief of Cow Bay" (or Cole Harbour reserve) under the Shubenacadie district leadership. One of the persons Ottawa contacted, the elderly Thomas William Ritchie (1808–90), who had provided legal counsel when the Cole Harbour reserve was purchased, admitted he vaguely remembered that Joseph C. Cope's father, Peter Cope Jr., was once chief of Halifax County, while the Peminout Pauls were leaders of the Shubenacadie Mi'kmaq, but as to the status of the son in 1883, he could not rightly say.[150]

Desmond upheld Andrew Paul as the rightful chief, as Andrew was the individual who regularly informed the agent about events and matters at Cole Harbour. Desmond suspected that Cope and John Noel of Shubenacadie were in cahoots against Paul, but in 1883 he could not put his finger directly on the cause of his uneasiness. Cope always preferred to bypass the local agent by communicating directly with Ottawa, a practice of which Desmond was well aware.[151] In his letters, Cope contended that Paul failed to uphold the lines of the original 1880 survey of the reserve and that consequently individuals were infringing on each other's property rights.[152] Desmond preferred interrelating only with Paul. He knew that Paul and the Reverend Desmond C. O'Connor, Desmond's predecessor as agent, had worked together harmoniously during their efforts in 1879 and 1880 to secure the reserve.[153] As Desmond had the spiritual charge of St. Bernard's Church in Enfield as well as his responsibilities to the Department of Indian Affairs to consider, he almost always tried to take the most congenial route towards solving problems. He already had experienced some notable successes in preserving reserves under his charge from trespass from outsiders.[154] Yet in the spring of 1888 he faced a new and unforeseen challenge: a deep and bitter rift between Joseph C. Cope and Andrew Paul that reverberated throughout the entire Sipekne'katik district.

Cope became aggressively insistent in his demands to Ottawa, but most of his aims were commendable. He called for lumber slated for houses on the reserve to be equally distributed to all community residents, for a school to be built and a teacher hired, and for specific measures to be agreed upon to prevent persons from encroaching on each other's farm plots. Despite his importunity, the two goals he most valued – the construction of a school and a means for enforcing respect for property lines – failed to materialize in the early 1880s.[155] Boundaries continued to go unheeded and remained a chronic source of contention. Despite this, his letters to Indian Affairs merely netted him innocuous, unhelpful responses. Finally, he was informed that though the reserve would be held "for all time to come for the benefit of the Indians," any matters concerning its administration would have to be referred to the local agent.[156] Cope then reluctantly turned to Desmond, but when the agent failed to respond to his grievances, Cope wrote Ottawa and charged Desmond with incompetence.[157]

Desmond was shocked, and his initial perturbation worsened in May 1888 when he discovered that an election had been held from which Cope had emerged victorious, and he had not even been notified. Assuming it to have been conducted under the Indian Act's electoral provisions of 1880, he wrote to Ottawa asking for clarification. What constituency, he queried, had done the voting? Had it been restricted to just the Cole Harbour Mi'kmaw community, or did it embrace the Mi'kmaw population of the whole county? Finally, he noted that as "Andrew Paul was head of the community when it was first given by the government," why had Cope arisen so quickly as its chief?[158] Andrew Paul meanwhile penned his own brief note to Ottawa. On 17 December 1888 he informed Lawrence Vankoughnet, the deputy superintendent of Indian Affairs, that he felt he temporarily had to abandon Cole Harbour. Though he had tried hard to "Bleas [sic, Bless] My own Indians," the word around Cole Harbour was that if he left, sufficient government money might accrue "to buy a Bbl. of flour for each family." This made others in the Cole Harbour community anxious to see him go; in consequence, his fences had been smashed and he had to flee with his family, cattle in tow, to Upper Stewiacke.[159]

While it is doubtful that Cope would ever resort to bribery to force Andrew Paul's departure, there can be no question that he stooped to questionable tactics early in 1888 to win his way. Suspecting that the election had been staged independently of Indian Affairs and involved a voting constituency whose parameters remained undefined, Ottawa questioned Cope about his part in the proceedings, at the same time asking him to step down. Cope rather ingeniously replied that he was only trying to ensure affairs at Cole Harbour were run with promptness and efficiency. Only he held the reins that could ensure good order. Andrew Paul could not settle the numerous disputes that kept cropping up, and as for the local agent, he could be dispensed with. "[W]e will no longer bother or depend on father Desmond," he averred. "[W]e have written and begged often enough to know that he is not the man for us. As a priest we love him and would do anything to please him, but as an Indian Agent he is rather careless, [as] perhaps [he has] too much other work to do."[160]

At this point Desmond began his own investigation, something he had considered doing in 1883. This time he learned that Cope had prevailed on John Noel, the adopted son of Shubenacadie district chief Jacques-Pierre Paul Peminout, to use his influence in Cope's favour during the election campaign. Noel allegedly had spread a rumour that "Andrew Paul [had] never contributed towards the church at Shubenacadie, Hants Co., [and] on the strength of that he induced the Indians to vote for Cope."[161] Since the Shubenacadie chapel was the central gathering point for the entire Shubenacadie Valley religious and political community, references to it wielded a powerful symbolic charge capable of conjuring up images of past continuity and stability.[162] Desmond realized that Cope viewed himself as a catalytic agent, capable of forging new linkages between the Cole Harbour group and the Peminout leadership at Shubenacadie. Yet the priest felt that, even under Cope, the sub-chieftainship headquartered at Cole Harbour would remain little more than a relic of an earlier time, when the Eastward Tribe under its Cope leaders exercised its own independence.

Desmond felt there was only one solution, and that lay in politically neutralizing the Halifax group. There was simply no necessity "for a vice-chief of Halifax County," he wrote Vankoughnet, and the office must be abolished once and for all.[163] Before making any major moves, however, Ottawa had the sense to appeal directly to the wider Shubenacadie Mi'kmaw population for advice, and it was this constituency that finally put an end to the feud between the two Cole Harbour leaders. The Sipekne'katik Mi'kmaq construed Cope's clashes with Andrew Paul as a part of an ongoing effort by certain Shubenacadie leaders, who were supported by Cope, to eclipse the Mi'kmaw grand chief, John Denny Jr., who was represented locally in Dartmouth by Andrew Paul. John Noel, it was averred, already had been severely chastised for trying to elevate his status as Shubenacadie head chief above that of the grand chief in Cape Breton in two petitions, the first instigated by Judge Christopher Paul Peminout and the second by Jacob Brooks, both sent to the lieutenant governor in 1883.[164] This was serious business, and Cope, not wanting to be targeted as the person responsible for resurrecting this earlier dispute, retreated with his wife Rebecca Jadis, their several daughters, and two young sons Joseph and Frank to Windsor Junction to live with his brother Isaac Cope until the situation cooled.[165]

Cope made no secret of the fact that he felt the leadership of the Halifax County band should be restricted to descendants of the old Eastward Tribe, especially families who had joined Captain Peter Cope Jr. at Second Red Bridge around the time of Confederation. To him, Grand Chief John Denny Jr. was "interfering" by mandating persons for leadership roles who came from areas outside of the Eastern and Shubenacadie districts. Denny then supported these "outsiders" over local chiefly candidates.[166] Such a practice, he thundered, contradicted the way leaders in the Shubenacadie and Musquodoboit regions had retained control over membership within their bands' ranks for centuries. He also knew that his own leadership prospects would be in jeopardy if he could no longer exercise this discretion.

In the end, Cope chose not to run for Cole Harbour chief again. He came to accept that the Cole Harbour reserve had been designated as a place where Mi'kmaq living in or around Dartmouth might settle on land set apart for their exclusive use, regardless of where they originally came from. Cope also proved correct in noting that chiefs of Cole Harbour would continue to have problems with internal control because of the nebulous nature of their constituency. The Grand Council's instructions to Andrew Paul in 1880 had been to attain a land base for scattered families, but neither Grand Chief Denny nor Paul could figure out a way to preserve harmony in the face of Cole Harbour's diversity of families, which in 1888 lacked any integrating core. Yet the reserve functioned as a valuable entry point for Mi'kmaq from other parts of the province hoping to gain a foothold in Dartmouth's employment world, and in 1896 Joseph Julien would make use of the Cole Harbour reserve for that exact purpose.

Once he eschewed the trials and tribulations of being the Halifax County "vice chief," Cope seemed happier. He also was given a second opportunity to assist his people. In 1890 he was appointed a captain of the Shubenacadie district council, under Chief John Noel. Andrew Paul also took a seat on this council, and he and Cope, their past animosities towards one another forgotten, worked together until Chief John Noel's death in 1911.[167] Cope briefly left for Ontario in the fall of 1891, perhaps to conduct some business in Ottawa on behalf of his people. He did not stay away long. In July 1892 he wrote to Indian Affairs thanking Ottawa for providing monetary support for his trip, but stressed that as the experience had taught him the value of family and friends in Nova Scotia, he henceforth would better his condition "nearer home and

read Ontario papers less."[168] He also remained deeply loyal to the Shubenacadie leadership, and when John Noel was installed as Shubenacadie district chief on 12 May 1897, he participated in the ceremony.[169] At thirty-eight years of age, he no longer proved jealously ambitious, bristling with the zealous angst of a young man not yet out of his twenties. Instead, he exhibited a more serene, studious, and philosophical side, juxtaposed with a wry sense of humour. His one major sadness during these years was the loss in 1909 of his wife Rebecca.

Cope mellowed still further during the first decades of the twentieth century. On Saint Valentine's Day 1910 Cope, now a fifty-year-old widower, married Catherine Muise, a forty-year-old widow, in a formal wedding ceremony at St. Louis Church in Annapolis Royal.[170] The couple first lived at Enfield, where Catherine helped Joseph care for his elderly father Peter Cope Jr., who remained a widower after his wife Louisa's death in 1905. After Peter Cope Jr. died in 1913 at the advanced age of ninety-seven,[171] Joseph experimented with a variety of occupations and hobbies. He wrote about Mi'kmaw culture and recounted oral traditions, and because he was an accomplished storyteller he became known throughout the province as a raconteur.[172] He was tall, erect, and dapper, with a bushy mustache and a lively eye. His engaging sense of humour made it hard for others not to like him. Around 1916 he struck up a friendship with Harry Piers (1870–1940), curator of the Nova Scotia Museum in Halifax.[173] Since he could write in English better than many of his non-Mi'kmaw contemporaries of the time, he jotted down facts, stories, and memories of the past in his breezy copperplate handwriting to share with Piers. In scanning his letters, one finds that in his spare time he perused histories that touched on the lives of Indigenous people, among them works by Francis Parkman and Beamish Murdoch. Intelligent, a hard worker, and a clever inventor with a strong artistic bent, he constantly explored new avenues of expression, becoming with time a local historian, taxidermist, professional photographer, inventor, woodworker, hunter, prospector, trapper, and guide.[174]

At the onset of the First World War, Joseph moved with Catherine to the outskirts of Bridgewater in Lunenburg County, where he tinkered with his various inventions. Like other Mi'kmaw leaders, he wanted to ally with the Crown in the war effort, but since he was fifty-seven years old, too old to shoulder arms, he invented a device to allow aerial bombs to glide onto their targets. Piers helped him submit his plans to the Ministry of Munitions in London, England. Though the comptroller of munitions ultimately decided not to put Cope's device into production, he nevertheless expressed his appreciation and thanks that "in such a far away spot as Mossman's Grant, the call is heard to do something for the good of the Empire."[175]

After the war Joseph and Catherine returned to Enfield. During these years Joseph liked to visit Halifax and share stories he had been told by his father and other Mi'kmaw elders with Harry Piers.[176] He told Piers that the Copes traditionally were called *Obsquooch,* and when he wrote stories down on paper for the museum curator, he would sign them with his Mi'kmaw name "*Sesep Obsquooch.*"[177] He also liked to regale Piers with updates on his latest inventions. In 1924 he was working on a rat trap – one that "will destroy from one Rat to 1,000 a night." He intended to test his contraption near his home, since "Enfield Station House is full of them," he remarked wryly.[178]

Joseph and his brother Isaac sat on the Shubenacadie district band council well into the 1920s. Joseph became a captain, while John Denny Paul, a son of his former political rival Andrew Paul, rose as sub-chief of the Halifax County Band. Joseph's children were the only heirs of the leadership legacy established in the eighteenth century by the Cope leaders of the old Eastward Tribe. Isaac Cope, who died at Windsor Junction at age eighty-six in 1949, had no living children at the time of his death. His only son, fourteen-year-old Louis Cope, was killed in the Halifax Explosion of 6 December 1917 while attending school at Tuft's Cove.[179] Joseph C. Cope, who outlived his brother by only two years, died at age ninety-three at Indian Brook, Shubenacadie, on 7 March 1951. He was buried in Indian Brook's St. Catherine's Cemetery, respected and honoured by his people.[180]

Despite formidable odds, both the Mi'kmaw Grand Council and the Shubenacadie leadership had weathered the first decades of the twentieth century. Piers noted that following the disappearance of the old Minas band around 1830, the jurisdiction of the Shubenacadie head chief and council had expanded to cover Kings, Lunenburg, and Cumberland counties in addition to Colchester, Hants, and Halifax counties, which encompassed the Shubenacadie, Stewiacke, and Musquodoboit river systems.[181] Prior to Confederation, county boundaries held little importance to Mi'kmaw leaders, as their traditional constituencies lay along major river drainages. In 1871 the Department of Indian Affairs established seven administrative districts within the province of Nova Scotia, with one of the largest of them being the Shubenacadie agency. During Joseph Julien's term as a leader at Millbrook, however, Shubenacadie's jurisdiction radically constricted, with the Cole Harbour community acting as an independent community before finally falling in 1960 under Millbrook's aegis.

Ottawa's Assault on "Unoccupied Reserves"

Grand Chief John Denny Jr. knew perfectly well that the government was trying to force the Mi'kmaq off Nova Scotia's landscape, but he refused to be intimidated. In response to government intentions, he had devised his own land and resource policy. He expected Indigenous leaders throughout Nova Scotia to unite and hold on to the tracts they had, and also try to enhance their lands' resource potential. In the late nineteenth century, Mi'kmaw leaders were not particularly concerned about their land being taken away from them; their concerns mostly lay with keeping at bay trespassers who coveted their timber, fish, and big game. Indian Affairs' protocols demanded that all the Mi'kmaw inhabitants of an agency be notified and be present at the negotiating table before any land surrender could take place. When instructed in 1886 to look into ceding the Ingraham's (or Ingram's) River reserve in Halifax County, agent Desmond baulked at what seemed to him to be insurmountable difficulties in contacting all Mi'kmaq, twenty years and older, who retained an interest in the tract.[182] Descendants of the original land holders had spread out over the landscape. Consequently, in the early 1900s all the reserves in Halifax County were mostly intact.

Throughout the leadership disputes at Cole Harbour in the 1880s there was never any suggestion of terminating the Cole Harbour reserve. From a vital, bustling independent community, the Cole Harbour Mi'kmaw settlement shrank until its land lay virtually vacant in 1906, when Joseph Julien's feisty sister-in-law Margaret Cope, affectionately known as "Meggie" or "Mag," persuaded her husband Charles Phillips to begin farming on the unoccupied tract. A.P. Boyd, the only full-time Indian agent for all of Nova Scotia, at this time resided at River Bourgeois in Richmond County, Cape Breton, and thus was hard to reach. Boyd was also slow in replying to letters, but when he did respond he shared Desmond's viewpoint. The situation would shift, however, under the administrative aegis of Henry P. Bury, the Department of Indian Affairs' inspector of timber reserves for Nova Scotia. As early as 1909 Bury had aspirations of dispensing with all unoccupied or "unnecesssary" reserves and concentrating the Mi'kmaw at three centres within the province, and, ideally just two, Shubenacadie and Eskasoni.

In 1909 Grand Chief John Denny Jr. alerted other Mi'kmaw leaders to Bury's scheme and its impending threat to their reserve lands. After reading a newspaper article about the government's intention to place the Kejimkujik reserve in Queens County under a timber lease, Denny responded with a counterplan to turn unoccupied Mi'kmaw lands into resource hinterlands for the use of unemployed Mi'kmaq in the northeastern parts of the province. The relocated families could harvest wood to manufacture beams, railway ties, tubs, carts, and pick handles, which then could be shipped by rail for use in the mines. His scheme also had a covert intent. It would deprive the government of an excuse to terminate a reserve simply because it was unoccupied. Between 12 March and 24 April 1909 Denny sent out letters to several leaders residing north of the Shubenacadie River drainage, among them Chief Joseph Gould of Millbrook and Chief Solomon Morris of Kings Road reserve in Sydney, Cape Breton, asking them to contact Indian Affairs denouncing the leasing of the Kejimkujik land. Those he approached immediately complied. Denny also upheld the continuance of reserve communities on the outskirts of towns and cities, such as Cole Harbour or the Kings Road settlement, to furnish Mi'kmaq families with a stable base while seeking employment opportunities. Ultimately the grand chief's and his supporters' heroic efforts to prevent the surrender of the Kejimkujik parcel, as well as the relocation of the populace of Kings Road, were quashed by coercive government fiats during the First World War years. The Kings Road settlement was expropriated under an order of the Exchequer Court in 1915, and the Kejimkujik reserve was ceded in 1918.[183]

Joseph Julien was living with his third wife, Bridget Cope, at Millbrook when the grand chief asked the acting Millbrook chief, Joseph Gould, to help prevent the Kejimkujik tract from being alienated. Doubtless at the time Joseph mused on what his foster father had instructed him regarding the perils of letting the population under one's charge demographically exceed the carrying capacity of one's land base. He also knew that an ability to secure new lands helped avoid the political pitfalls of having to mete out diminishing resources within a restricted space. These were valuable lessons he would draw on when he later became Millbrook's chief. From his father-in-law Sandy Cope Sr. he learned of the deep sense of betrayal felt by leaders of the old Eastward Tribe, who had lost their territorial prerogatives over a vast landscape along the eastern seacoast. This knowledge, drawn from persons who had first-hand experience with the chiefs about whom they spoke, as well as with the challenges that these leaders' people faced, gave him an insightful overview of the past.[184] It informed his cogmpassionate and understanding way of dispensing advice as a prayer leader, and enabled him when he became a chief to devise innovative policies at Truro that won him the esteem of Mi'kmaw leaders throughout the province. By the early 1920s it would raise him to the status of the "man at the centre" by investing his words with a force that would bring others throughout Nova Scotia to be with him, and so swell Millbrook's population and its potentialities.

But that would not occur for another decade. In 1909 he had a wife to care for, and a baby on the way. Bridget gave birth to a daughter whom the couple named Rachel Mary Julien, but Joseph's joy at this birth was followed by sorrow, for in January 1910 Bridget died. Kindly neighbours offered assistance. Realizing that Joseph would face problems properly caring for the infant as well as working, Ben Brooks and his wife agreed to take Rachel Mary and raise her at Millbrook while Joseph temporarily sought employment in Sydney, Cape Breton.

The Cape Breton Years

Joseph Julien lived in the Kings Road Mi'kmaw community in Sydney for five years, from February 1910 to January 1915. He was already familiar with the North Sydney Mi'kmaw community located about thirty kilometres away, since John Denny Sr. had stayed there when Joseph was a boy and still under the elderly grand chief's care. In the mid-1840s a Mi'kmaw satellite settlement arose on two-and-a-half acres along the Kings Road, which was set aside as a reserve in 1846 and eventually drew labourers from Eskasoni who worked at Sydney in the summer and left for home during the winter. John Isaac, who settled on the Kings Road in 1879, was the community's first permanent resident, and when more year-round wage labour became available the Kings Road settlement grew, its population fluctuating in keeping with the vicissitudes of the local steel industry.

After Confederation Ottawa recognized this community's minuscule land base as Kings Road Indian Reserve No. 28a, although the parcel grew even smaller in 1888 after the expropriation of two-thirds of an acre for the Intercolonial Railway allowance, which traced the shoreline of the Sydney River. Most Mi'kmaq living on the parcel worked at odd jobs rather than with the steel town's coke ovens and blast furnaces, but their numbers rose steadily as the prosperity of the city of Sydney as a whole increased. The Department of Indian Affairs built a school and constructed a two-compartment concrete public privy, which connected to the nearby river by a single sewer pipe that repeatedly clogged and caused the sanitary system to malfunction. Community residents, who lacked funds of their own to rectify the problem, became a target for the barbs of their mainstream neighbours in the business and political community. The naysayers, having invested in lands in the immediate vicinity, latched onto the difficulties the Mi'kmaq were having with their public toilets to launch a campaign for the settlement's removal.

Foremost among the lobbyists in for the dismantlement of the Kings Road settlement was J.A. Gillies, a Parliamentarian who in 1877 had bought property adjoining what two years later became the reserve. Gillies's motives for casting aspersions on the Kings Road settlement in 1899 sprang from his hope that if the Mi'kmaq were removed property prices in the area would soar, and he could profitably place his land on the market.[185]

Joseph Julien wed soon after his arrival in the community and this time fortune smiled, for Joseph and his family remained healthy throughout their five years in Cape Breton. His marriage on 17 July 1910 to sixteen-year-old Annie Louise Googoo of Whycocomagh, within only seven months of Bridget Cope's death, suggests that the union may have been arranged by Grand Chief John Denny Jr. To all appearances, Joseph and Annie Louise's marriage was a happy one.[186] Annie Louise was a diminutive woman with pleasantly rounded features who wore her long dark hair in thick braids on either side of her face.

Her husband, who at age thirty-eight had developed into a handsome, slender, middle-aged man with a neatly clipped mustache, towered head and shoulders above her.

Owing to his engaging personality Joseph soon made new friends and acquaintances. Soon after his arrival in Sydney he met Joe Christmas, a former chief of the Kings Road settlement and a strong supporter, like Joseph, of Grand Chief John Denny Jr.'s land and resource campaign. Joe Christmas was a descendant of Christmas Thoma, a son in turn of Chief Thoma Denny (1669–c.1770) who lived during the French colonial regime. Joe and his son Ben wanted to preserve their community despite its overcrowding.[187] Christmas felt that an important step was to seek more land and funding from the Department of Indian Affairs. Since Joseph and Joe both supported education for Mi'kmaw youth that enhanced rather than undermined Mi'kmaw culture and called for radical improvements in local living conditions, the two men became close associates. Joseph also was nominated to run for chief, and in October 1912 he succeeded Solomon Morris, the former incumbent. After his wife gave birth to a son Noel on 24 May 1912, Joseph had to look for paid employment to support his growing family, since the chief's office was unremunerated. He accepted an offer from the Department of Indian Affairs to become a provincial Indian constable, and as such was responsible for assisting in the apprehension and delivery of Mi'kmaw prisoners to provincial authorities.[188] But when community members complained that his role as constable, answerable to Ottawa, constituted a conflict of interest with his role as chief, Joseph resigned his leadership position and Joe Christmas stepped in as acting chief for the remainder of the three-year term.[189] Though Joseph's work as a provincial constable provided a stable income, it proved so stressful and demanding that he retained it for only two years, during which he and Annie Louise welcomed a new daughter, Mary, on 4 February 1914.

Though he was less financially secure, Joseph's resignation as Indian constable left him time to engage in local politics. J.A. Gillies was calling for the surrender and sale of the reserve, claiming it still posed a health hazard to its neighbours. Joseph, Joe Christmas, and Grand Chief John Denny Jr. anticipated that a proposal for a land cession would have to go before the entire Mi'kmaw constituency of Cape Breton, which they thought would almost certainly reject it. But in 1915 Gillies and his supporters levelled a new and more formidable legislative weapon against the Mi'kmaw position. An amendment to the Indian Act, passed by Laurier's Liberal government in 1911 but delayed in its implementation for four years by Laurier's Conservative successor Robert Borden, suddenly was passed in late August 1915. Under the terms of this amendment the governor in council, upon the recommendation of the superintendent general of Indian Affairs, might dispose of any "surplus Indian land" if such a course of action received the approval of the judge of the Exchequer Court.[190]

A hearing was convened at Sydney in September 1915 before Mr. Justice L.A. Audette of the Exchequer Court. Thirty-four witnesses were called, with Gillies representing the City of Sydney, and Joseph Julien, Joe Christmas, and Joe's son Ben –at the time only nineteen years old – speaking on behalf of the residents of the Kings Road settlement. When his turn came to take the witness stand, Joseph stressed that overcrowding and whatever unsanitary conditions might exist were not the fault of the community, but arose because of Ottawa's failure to overhaul the faulty sanitation system. As the settlement's proximity to the river constituted one of its most vital assets, what was needed to ameliorate matters was more land next to the current reserve to allow for proper community development. Joe and Ben Christmas echoed these sentiments and pressed the government for funding to improve their settlement's infrastructure. Yet the testimony of the Mi'kmaw witnesses and their supporters could not prevail against the determined campaign of Gillies and his associates. The Kings Road's Mi'kmaw residents were compelled without their consent to move, and settled on a tract later called Membertou.[191]

The enquiry proceedings had been an ordeal but, as he had with other trials he had faced in life, Joseph Julien gleaned insights from the experience that strengthened him in the future. In 1915 he demonstrated that he not only possessed a deliberate and kindly manner, as befitted a diplomatic, articulate, generous, and spiritually astute individual, but that he could be a disciplined, trenchant, and fast thinker on his feet when occasion demanded it. His time in Sydney, furthermore, had introduced him to the young Ben Christmas, who became a pioneer activist in regional Aboriginal affairs, and with whom Joseph would work closely for the benefit of the Mi'kmaw people in future years.[192]

Joseph Julien as Millbrook's Leader

At the end of his five years in Sydney, Joseph Julien, Annie Louise, and their children Noel and Mary moved back to Truro in January 1915. As part of the Grand Council's ongoing outreach program, Grand Chief John Denny Jr. had requested that Joseph become the Grand Council prayer leader for the Millbrook community.[193] Though their arrival at Truro should have been a happy experience, with Joseph reuniting with his daughter Rachael and Annie Louise expecting the birth of another child, three-year-old Noel suddenly died, and the family grieved his unexpected loss. Annie Louise gave birth to a son Edward on 21 May 1915, but then Edward also died, in 1916. Between 1915 and 1929 Joseph and Annie Louise had five more children, Alexander ("Sandy"), Steven, Mary Catherine, Frank, and Madeline, of whom only Sandy, Frank, and Madeline would live to adulthood. Sandy Julien (1917–2012), named after Sandy Cope Sr., was born on 31 August 1917.[194] Steven, born in 1921 and named after Joseph's older brother Steven who died in 1877, only lived to age fifteen before dying in 1936.[195] A daughter, Mary Catherine, arrived in March of 1924 but only lived for seven days. On 6 May 1926 another son, Frank Michael, was born. But then tragedy interrupted, for in July 1928 fourteen-year-old Mary, who had been born in Sydney, died. Over a year later, on 27 September 1929, Joseph and Annie Louise welcomed their last child, Madeline, named after Joseph's mother.[196]

Millbrook residents rejoiced that Joseph had returned, since he could replace Joseph Gould, who agreed only to be an acting chief. In 1917 Joseph was elected chief, along with one councillor, William Thomas Gloade, for a two-year term. The Department of Indian Affairs refused to sanction the election, however, and it was only after the Millbrook community "without hesitation" on 2 January 1919 elected Joseph to a three-year term as chief that Ottawa proved willing to recognize his appointment.[197] Following this official confirmation, Joseph Julien could show his true colours as a negotiator, diplomat, and campaigner for Mi'kmaw land and resource rights.

What struck Joseph most forcefully on his return to Colchester County was the furore that had broken out between leaders of the Halifax County Band and several settlers. Shortly before the outbreak of the First World War, property owners at Grand Lake, Elmsdale, and Tuft's Cove had sought

Ottawa's assistance in ejecting clusters of Mi'kmaw families who occupied their lands. One of the most persistent lobbyists was a farmer named Jacob Gilby, who wanted around thirty Mi'kmaq evicted from his property at Elmsdale. Assisted by Harry Piers, the curator of the Nova Scotia Museum who drafted petitions on their behalf, Martin Sack and Jeremiah Bartlett-Alexis collected depositions between 1916 and 1919 from the oldest living residents of Elmsdale and sent them to Ottawa, hoping to acquire the Elmsdale site by virtue of long possession.[198] When their bid proved legally untenable, they pressed the Department of Indian Affairs to purchase the land.[199] A.P. Boyd, the provincial Indian agent, knowing that Gilby refused to sell, began a desultory search for other parcels around Shubenacadie Grand Lake and Windsor that might be purchased, though little came of his efforts, since landowners were reluctant to sell to Indian Affairs. Gilby's strident voice, moreover, was soon joined by others of the same ilk. In 1917 a man surnamed Farnell launched a campaign to persuade Ottawa to relocate the Tuft's Cove Mi'kmaw settlement, while the following year C. Musgrave called for eight Mi'kmaw families to be removed from his lands at Shubenacadie Grand Lake. These families only narrowly escaped being ejected from lands they had occupied for generations by entering into a contract with a neighbouring landowner, A.P. King, who allowed them to live on his property as long as they supplied him with firewood.[200]

On 10 March 1916 a new and dynamic politicized body, calling itself the "Micmac Tribe of Indians of Halifax County," petitioned Indian Affairs demanding that the five thousand dollars that they understood had accrued from their leasing of timber lands on their Ship Harbour reserve in 1913 to the Marks Lumbering Company be placed at their disposal for the "benefit of their tribe."[201] Monies were required by their people to build houses at either Shubenacadie Grand Lake or Indian Brook.[202] Then, on 27 April 1916, Louis Paul, the acting chief for this new constituency, called for Ottawa to purchase 350 acres for a new reserve at Sandy Cove on Shubenacadie Grand Lake for families who were being evicted from Elmsdale and Tufts Cove.[203] Jeremiah Bartlett-Alexis added that older families at Tufts Cover wanted "compensation if they leave the place."[204] In November this group's new leader, John Denny Paul, a grandson of the late Andrew Paul of Cole Harbour, charged Indian Affairs to lay out lots at Sandy Cove

as well as send him a copy of his commission as chief of Halifax County.[205] Ottawa did neither. In early December Paul declared that given the impasse, he required funds from Indian Affairs to send a delegation to Ottawa to review "certain old treaties which the said delegation will bring with it, and to discuss other matters."[206] This petition, too, elicited no response.

For the next five years, the thought of a large sum ensuing from the lease of Ship Harbour's timber lands pervaded Halifax Band council discussions like the proverbial ship due to come in. Equipped with such funds, the Mi'kmaq felt, they would be lifted out of their former status as supplicants. No longer would they continually have to beg for money from Indian Affairs, but instead would enjoy a degree of discretionary spending power. Such hopes would be dashed, however, as Ottawa refused to reveal the manner in which it disposed of the timber monies, or even if it disposed of them at all. As late as 1921, Jeremiah Bartlett-Alexis still could declare that if he got elected as a chief, he would ensure that "proper consideration" be given "to the payment of monies for the Timber Lands."[207]

The East Coast Paul family were particularly frustrated during these years. The Ship Harbour reserve, formed in response to their petitioning in the late 1840s, for sixty years had suffered from external trespasses over which they had no control. Joseph Paul Jr. and Jane Kegan faced the same problems at East Quoddy. Their sons and daughters had left to reside on the seventy-seven-acre reserve accorded the Mi'kmaq at Sheet Harbour in 1915. In early December 1917 they were preparing yet another petition requesting the Ship Harbour timber monies when, suddenly, their campaign was swallowed up by the horror of the Halifax Explosion. On 6 December 1917, Mi'kmaw occupants of seven shanties at Tufts Cove were caught up in the blast.[208] Nine were killed,[209] while amazingly twelve survived, among them several of the Nevin family employed at the Halifax Armory or working on vessels in the harbour. The explosion left many on both sides of the harbour wounded and suffering. A tenement house in Halifax was hastily set up by the Department of Indian Affairs to shelter Mi'kmaq, mostly from Tufts Cove, who had been injured. It was a devastating blow to families who were already experiencing anxiety, especially as many had members fighting overseas at the front.

Chief Joseph Julien acted quickly. In a manner characteristic of a traditional leader who offered protection to his people, he reached out to Mi'kmaq at Dartmouth, Halifax, Wellington Station, Elmsdale, Enfield, Windsor Junction – wherever individuals and families had been deleteriously affected. Millbrook would become a place of refuge for the displaced, suffering, and wounded, and where they could begin to build new futures. Following a number of petitions sent to Millbrook from eastern sub-chief John Denny Paul on behalf of his constituency at Enfield, Halifax, and Dartmouth, Chief Julien and his council on 18 June 1919 not only officially accepted but warmly welcomed any members of the Halifax County Band who wished to resettle at Millbrook.[210] Joseph set out immediately to acquire more land for his community, to ensure that no problems with overcrowding – the effects of which he remembered all too well from his years along the Kings Road in Sydney – would ever happen at Millbrook.

In April and May of 1919, the chief and three band councillors, William Thomas Gloade, William J. Stephens,[211] and Frank Gould, negotiated with Henry J. Bury, the Department of Indian Affairs' timber inspector, to purchase the one-hundred-acre Henry Creelman property that had come up for sale for $2,500 on the eastern flank of the reserve. Bury readily agreed, despite his reluctance to support the formation of new reserves elsewhere. The Creelman property lay on level ground along the old post road, had at least 60 per cent of its acreage cleared for planting, and boasted a sizeable farm house.[212] Indian Affairs asked Chief Julien to move into the house in order to keep it in good repair. Its former owner had ties with the local Mi'kmaq, for members of the Creelman family of Colchester County had been in close contact with the Stewiacke Mi'kmaq for generations.[213] Samuel and his relative Henry Creelman always had allowed the Mi'kmaq to harvest wood for their manufactures and for firewood off the Creelman property outside Truro. There was only one minor problem: the Creelman estate was separated physically from the older sector of the reserve by a road allowance that remained in the possession of the Intercolonial Railway. This strip would not be acquired by Millbrook until 1952.

Joseph Julien Addresses the Grievances of the Halifax County Band

Henry J. Bury stated that any funds reserved in trust for the Mi'kmaq would be deposited into a single account, to be withdrawn when needed. The leaders of the Halifax County Band thus expected that Ottawa would exercise its fiduciary responsibility and release their funds from the timber lease for their use. At a forum convened by Indian Affairs at Truro on 18 June 1919, leaders of the Halifax County Band at first consented to the release of $5,000 of the held amount in Ottawa's coffers to facilitate the purchase of the Creelman estate.[214] But that was as far as their unanimity extended, for Bury stipulated that the release would be contingent on the Mi'kmaq's surrendering three reserves in Halifax County. John Denny Paul, Louis Paul, Martin Sack, and Jeremiah Bartlett-Alexis had been petitioning for monies from the Ship Harbour timber lease for years, but none of them expected receipt of the funds to become conditional on their cession of the Sambro tract, reserved in 1784 for Paul Morris and his family,[215] the Ingraham's River reserve confirmed in 1852 for Louis Paul and Francis Phillips, and the Ship Harbour reserve attained through the efforts of the East Coast Pauls and which, presumably, still remained a revenue source for the Mi'kmaq.[216] Not aware of what was coming, the Pauls and Martin Sack sat dumbfounded while clauses of the surrender document were read and then passed to them to sign. Martin Sack's name led the list of signatories.[217] He doubtless came to the meeting expecting to hear that the Ship Harbour monies would finally be released, and instead was bowled over by Ottawa's machinations.[218] After the surrender was pushed through, the three tracts involved were sold for $2,500. No mention was made of the timber revenue. Martin Sack and the other Halifax County Band leaders gradually realized that sizeable losses in land and resources had been foisted on them by Indian Affairs in order to cut back on departmental administrative costs and escape the burdens of Indigenous land and resource protection. There was no alternative but for families to press on and prepare for a move to Millbrook. To assuage their anxieties, Chief Julien on 18 August 1919 – two months to the day after the fateful events of June – extended a warm welcome to fifteen families setting out to begin life anew in Truro.[219]

Grand Chief John Denny Jr. had died the previous year. Had he been alive in 1919 he probably would have lamented the loss of these tracts as sorrowfully as he grieved the loss of the Kejimkujik reserve and the Kings Road parcel. Chief Joseph Julien, being in many respects Denny's protégé when it came to land and resource issues, felt shocked and saddened by the Mi'kmaw land losses that occurred in the negotiating arena within his own community, yet he was forced to stand aloof. Whereas Denny had successfully claimed a special immunity from the political vicissitudes accompanying the workings of the triennial electoral system Ottawa imposed on bands in 1899,[220] Joseph lacked such autonomy. His ability to attain more land for firewood and settlement purposes at Millbrook depended to great measure on timber inspector Bury's support. While Bury and other officials did not intimidate him, they forced him to play his hand shrewdly and diplomatically. With the help of these men, the chief was well prepared for the arrival of the new families, with cleared land, good soil, firewood, clean water sources, a road for transport into Truro, and the promise of markets for their wares in town. The newly acquired tract, like the original thirty-five acres, was surveyed into long strip lots, each with either frontage on or easy access to the road and sufficient room at the back for outbuildings, gardens, and livestock. For his part, Bury viewed the chief's willingness to welcome Mi'kmaq from Halifax County and thoroughly prepare for their arrival as a panacea that would lure between eighty-five and one hundred Mi'kmaq off private property, stem the tide of landowners' complaints, and hasten a trend towards opening up "unoccupied reserves" to tourism, timber leases, and mining exploitation.[221]

It has been argued that Millbrook's response to the devastation wrought by the Halifax Explosion prompted Indian Affairs officials, foremost among them Bury, to consider centralization as a viable way to slash the Department of Indian Affairs' administrative costs. Though what happened at Millbrook from 1919 to 1927 has sometimes been erroneously viewed as the first phase of a conjoint governmental and Mi'kmaw-directed centralization scheme, instituted under Chief Julien's and Bury's aegis, if examined from a Mi'kmaw perspective it might far better be described as a quest to construct a secure homeland within the greater Mi'kmaw polity.[222] During the turmoil of the First World War, people needed a secure refuge where they could make their own decisions and relate them to a council that listened to their needs. Chief Julien set parameters by retaining the traditional rights of a Mi'kmaw leader to accept or deny anyone wishing to become part of his band, thus reserving to himself and his council enough control to prevent overcrowding on their

reserve.[223] He also worked tirelessly to attain land and resources for their support. He disagreed with Bury's ideas about land cessions, but he knew that his effectiveness as a leader in the long run depended on keeping an open avenue of communication with the timber inspector. The later centralization scheme, imposed by Ottawa's coercive fiat between 1932 and 1945, would be anathema to him, since he adhered to Grand Chief John Denny Jr.'s land and resource tenets.[224] But in 1919 and 1920 the government did not use extremely severe coercive tactics, such as burning Mi'kmaw houses as they had at Whycocomagh, Cape Breton, to compel Mi'kmaw families to relocate. Those that journeyed to Millbrook in response to Chief Joseph Julien's invitation came of their own free will, and worked hard to establish a vital settlement. Bury showered both Chief Julien and his community with accolades. To Bury, the chief showed leadership acumen in 1934 in supervising the erection of thirty houses and ensuring that the Millbrook community had an adequate supply of firewood to last for many years into the future. Meanwhile Millbrook had access to both road and railway transportation, and nearby Truro provided employment opportunities and markets for Mi'kmaw wares. Bury concluded that Ottawa's best interests could only be served by promoting Millbrook's continued success, since the community, so far, had proven a "credit to the province."[225]

Despite Millbrook's assets, Julien was not able to persuade members of the Halifax County Band to move en masse to Truro. In 1921 there were still fifty individuals residing at Bedford, twenty-nine at Elmsdale, and twenty-eight at Enfield.[226] One person resistant to moving to Millbrook was Martin Sack, who lived at Elmsdale with his brother-in-law Albert Noel Howe Jr. (better known as Bert Howe) until both men were forced by government fiat in 1930 to move to Shubenacadie.[227] Bert's stay at Shubenacadie was brief; he, his wife Mary Jane, and their three children – Annie, Flossie, and Pauline – soon left for the Atlantic coast, where they built a house on the part of Reserve No. 36 lying nearest to Church Point, which jutted out into Sheet Harbour.[228] Sole occupants of the Sheet Harbour reserve for many years, Bert and Mary Jane had eleven more children – fourteen children in all – who as they grew up and married occupied sectors of the reserve on both sides of the harbour. Following the First World War, Joseph C. Cope retained several years at Enfield with his son Joseph Cope Jr. and his daughter-in-law Josephine Howe.

He later moved to Lunenburg County. Sack, Howe, and Cope displayed a feisty, independent streak when it came to choosing their places of residence, a trait also manifested by Sandy Cope Sr.'s daughter, Meggie Phillips, who preferred living with her husband on the Cole Harbour reserve to living anywhere else.

If employment opportunities existed where they lived, families proved hesitant to heed Joseph Julien's call and move to Millbrook. Several of Joseph Cope and Sarah Tracey's sons and daughters from the Hantsport area joined the Millbrook community prior to 1935 – among them Leo Cope who later became a Second World War casualty – but others with stable jobs preferred to remain around Falmouth or in Cumberland County.[229] Descendants of Doadaran Cope and the East Coast Pauls still lived at Beaverdam Lake, while a few Mi'kmaq, mostly around Halifax and Dartmouth, chose to pass as mainstream citizens. Some of the latter were skilled labourers who could find work as carpenters, mechanics, longshoremen, railway labourers, specialized woodworkers, farmers, dressmakers, and tailors.

The arrival of incomers to Millbrook prompted a succession of sudden spurts of activity. Usually families arrived in kin-related clusters, and most members of these could trace lineal or collateral kin ties to others already living at Millbrook. In late June 1919 five families, numbering twenty-two individuals, moved from Windsor Junction to Truro.[230] By the first week of July they were joined by five more families, this time from Elmsdale.[231] The largest migration of people occurred on 18 August 1919 when Joseph Julien and his council accepted the members of five large families, consisting of between fifty-three and fifty-five individuals formerly belonging to the Halifax County Band.[232] Among them was William G. Paul, an East Coast Paul who was born at Sheet Harbour in 1896.[233] Other incomers travelled from Cape Breton. A cousin of Joseph Julien's wife Annie Louise named Peter Googoo, who had a wife and five children, petitioned Millbrook's council. The chief accepted the Googoo family on 21 June 1920, but only after making sure that sufficient land could be secured for them in the older part of the reserve.[234] Several Goulds, originally from Cape Breton, who had lived along the Eastern Shore before going to Millbrook, for years after their move to Millbrook returned each year to Senora, east of Quoddy, to visit graves of their family members buried on the Atlantic coast.[235] Peter Wilmot also left Pictou County around this time to live with his son Charles at Millbrook.

Ottawa did not initially concur with Chief Julien's control of Millbrook's membership, but Joseph usually got his way in the long run. In April 1920 Michael Thomas and Stephen John Knockwood from the Kentville-Windsor area both applied to join Millbrook.[236] While Joseph Julien agreed to accept them, A.P. Boyd held that neither man was a member of the Halifax County Band and sought to prevent their entry. Michael Thomas nevertheless persisted and was settled by the chief and council in the older sector of the reserve.[237] Stephen Knockwood meanwhile decided to join the Shubenacadie Band and later served three terms as its chief.[238]

Chief Julien's gracious demeanour ensured that his relations with Indian Affairs officials during these years remained cordial. Though Bury's and Julien's aims for the Nova Scotia Mi'kmaw population were to diverge radically in the future, Joseph in 1919 felt that he and the timber inspector could productively consider the possibilities of attaining still more land for the Millbrook community. To this end he began an enquiry into the prevailing status of a large tract on the Stewiacke River promised during the American Revolution by Michael Francklin to a Cobequid chief named Paul Pemmenwick, or Peminout. He learned that the executive council on 28 June 1779 had agreed to the survey of a two-mile square tract on the middle Stewiacke, adjoining Lord Egmont's lands. This grant was "made to Mr. Francklin and Paul Pemmeywicte, One of the Principal Indians, in Trust to and for the said Indians."[239] Finally, on 17 December 1783 the Shubenacadie head chief, Paul Pemmenwick or Peminout, received a licence of occupation – though at times it also was treated like a grant – to a "Tract of Land, Situate on the River called Stewyack."[240] Joseph doubtless had access to far more information than historians can reconstruct today from remaining oral traditions and historical documents, since the chief had first-hand contact with men and women who remembered the past clearly.

To pursue this quest, he needed copies of documents and survey maps. Well aware of the importance of having authenticated documents in hand, in July 1919 he wrote to the Crown Lands Office in Ottawa asking for a copy of a survey plan of the old Stewiacke grant drawn up in 1861 by a Truro surveyor named Isaac Archibald.[241] Once the plan arrived, he immediately sent it to Bury, asking the timber inspector to review it to see if the Mi'kmaq still had claims to land.[242] He knew there had been disputes over the placement of property boundaries within the grant, and rumours had been circulating that not all of the tract had been alienated by the Peminouts. On 13 February 1920 J.D. MacLean, the deputy superintendent of Indian Affairs, after perusing an incomplete and inconclusive report on the boundaries and sale of the Stewiacke grant written in 1857 by a Colchester County surveyor, William Faulkner, rather presumptuously informed Joseph that prior to Confederation the Mi'kmaq living "in that portion of the province had deeded away the whole of the Reserve."[243] Chief Julien's seemingly futile appeal for Ottawa to probe ambiguities surrounding the old 1779 Francklin-Peminout tract have not been forgotten by the Mi'kmaw community, however.[244]

In addition to his historical research and focus on data collection, Chief Joseph Julien also strictly organized and monitored internal matters within the community. Joseph refused to countenance any form of sub-leadership at Millbrook. Even former leaders of the Halifax County Band like Louis Paul and John Denny Paul had to abide by decisions made by the Colchester County chief and his council. John Denny Paul's son Stephen, meanwhile, became a respected prayer leader in Pictou County who retained possession of two nineteenth-century Mi'kmaw Bibles, the oldest one written in hieroglyphics.[245] Right from the beginning Joseph sought to forge Millbrook into a unified political entity, free of the kind of divisiveness that had wracked the Cole Harbour reserve by 1888. Though the two Pauls expressed initial chagrin, their resistance cooled once they understood that leadership offices would be open to newcomers under the prevailing system. Upon Millbrook's adoption of the triennial electoral system on 2 January 1919, Louis Paul, former acting chief of the Halifax County Band, was elected to a seat on council.[246]

Joseph's constituency appreciated his methodical approach to political, land, and resource matters during Millbrook's years of trial, but then temporarily rejected him, as least formally, as their leader when things became easier. With the advent of relatively prosperous years from 1925 to 1934, Joseph – the tireless organizer and political innovator – was not returned as chief, though he was still referred to as "the chief" – a disjunction between overt and more covert leadership during these years that warrants greater exploration. William Thomas Gloade was chief from January 1925 to January 1928 and was succeeded by Louis Paul from January 1928 to January 1931. For the next twelve years, from 1931 to 1943, for some reason no chief was elected, though doubtless Joseph remained a vital force in community leadership circles. Joseph then was re-elected chief on 2 January 1934, a position he retained until his death in 1957.[247]

While he was leader, Joseph maintained tight controls over internal land allocation. Although he lived in the Creelman farm house,[248] in accordance with Ottawa's wishes he reserved the rest of the Creelman property exclusively for former members of the Halifax County Band. Since the parcel had been purchased with their monies, they alone would reap the benefits of their expenditure. With time the Creelman property came to be known affectionately as "Halifax County" by the rest of Millbrook's residents.[249] Substantial houses soon arose, since William G. Paul and several others from the Eastern Shore were carpenters, among them John Denny Paul and his brothers Louis and Peter Paul. Jerry Lonecloud and his Malecite wife, Elizabeth Paul, had parted company several years previously, so she lived as a single woman on the Creelman tract with her son Louis.

The mid-1920s brought a reprieve from the economic distress of the past years. A feeling of prosperity was in the air, and a few people even drove cars. The Millbrook population exhibited a diversity of skills and occupations. William Thomas Gloade worked throughout the province as a mason and plasterer, as well as in Millbrook as the local store keeper. Charles Wilmot and Alex Cope Sr. trapped furs, though Alex also maintained a fox farm. Others worked at mills in Truro, and families maintained small farms, made wooden items, and worked in the woods during the winter. Some women worked as domestics in town. Most children attended school and so were being educated, at least in the early grades.

Basketmaking was common, though several artisans who sold baskets at shops along the highway raised the craft to a fine art. Men continued to manufacture axe handles, pick handles, and tubs. One distinctly Mi'kmaw occupation that thrived at Millbrook from 1890 to 1930 was the production of wooden hockey sticks. The Starr Manufacturing Company, originally established in Dartmouth in 1860 to make ice skates, by 1890 was commissioning Mi'kmaw families to furnish hockey sticks that these families shipped by train to Dartmouth. The sticks were sold across Canada under the "Mic Mac" brand label. Made of hornbeam wood, cut with a square saw from that part of the tree where the roots branched out at the base, the earliest sticks had a curved blade, somewhat like shinny sticks, though by the 1870s these had been completely replaced by sticks with a straight blade whose edge hugged the ice.[250] Through-out the 1920s Joseph Julien made large numbers of these sticks, which he carefully hand-fashioned out of hornbeam templates with a crooked knife, dried over a fire, baled, and then readied for shipment to Starr Manufacturing. When his friend Sidney C. Oland realized the extent of Joseph's trade, he instructed the drivers of his delivery trucks – once they had off-loaded their beer in Truro – to stop at Millbrook, pick up Joseph's supply of sticks, and convey them, gratis, to Dartmouth for his friend.[251] Years later, in 1971, Sidney Oland's son, Lieutenant Governor Victor de Bedia Oland, would present Millbrook with two tro-phies in memory of his father's long-term friendship with Chief Joseph Julien.[252]

Millbrook in the 1920s was not large but, ow-ing to Chief Julien's planning and hard work, it was well laid out. Newel Gloade, his wife Rose Beatrice McKay, and his seven-year-old son Harold were relative latecomers when they arrived in 1927 from Lequille in Annapolis County to live with Newel's relative, Grand Council captain William Thomas Gloade.[253] According to Harold, who in his later life wrote books in which he shared boyhood memories, from the right vantage point one could survey the entire Millbrook community. If one walked along the old post road from "the Truro end, on the right-hand side," one first came to the house of Sandy Cope Sr., "then Frank Gould, then Alex Cope, son of Sandy, then Tom [William Thomas] Gloade's."[254] William Thomas Gloade's sister, Kate, had the house next to her brother, and then "there were the houses of Char-lie Henry Brooks, Madeline Silliboy [or Sylliboy], Louis Gloade and Ben Knockwood. The pasture was next to that." Where the dirt road bent to the left, one could find the "house of Dan, son of Tom Gloade, and just a little beyond that lived Jochi Silliboy. There was a little hill beyond Jochi's house, and Michael Thomas lived there." These houses all belonged to the original reserve. Just beyond that, there was a road to the right that led to the "homes of Peter Paul and Johnny Brooks, then over a bridge, across the tracks and up a hill to where John Martin and Michael Ber-nard lived in those days."[255]

Back on the highway one could view the Creel-man property and the "vast expanse of Chief Julian's

[sic, Julien's] property," beyond which "was a vacant house that would be occupied by Joseph [Jeremy] Howe and his family the following year. Farther along the highway, over a little bridge, another road led to the right to the homes of Ben Brooks and Joseph, son of Ben. They lived opposite each other. Farther along this road and to the left lived Elizabeth Paul, Jerry Lonecloud's wife, and her son Louis. Dick Louis Paul's house stood at the end of this road, which was the one dubbed 'Halifax County.'" What was known as the "Mackenzie farm" lay near the Millbrook schoolhouse, and not far away was the house of the elderly Newel Gloade, William Thomas Gloade's fa-ther. Church Road, which intersected with the old post road, "served as a long lane to where John Abram and Henry Sack had their respective houses. Charlie Wilmot's house was on the Church Road corner, and his father, Peter, lived next to him. Peter was ninety-nine years old at that time … Next, and back from the highway, lived Jim Francis, and Stephen Paul's house was last."[256] Millbrook under Chief Julien's leadership remained a cohesive community where "when someone enjoyed good fortune, his neigh-bour smiled a little. If someone experienced sadness of one kind or another, his neighbour would stop for a moment and silently weep."[257]

Chief Julien's task of allotting land to newcomers ceased following William Thomas Gloade's election as chief in 1925. The main work in this line had been done anyway. In 1919 and 1920 Joseph had welcomed over ninety new residents into the Millbrook com-munity, but by 1925 this inflow had subsided to a trickle. What has been termed the "first phase" of Mi'kmaw centralization in Nova Scotia "virtually halted."[258] Reserve population stabilized at around 125 persons, with the few new arrivals tending to balance out those who died or left. John Denny Paul died at age sixty-three in 1924, leaving behind his brothers Peter and Louis Paul who continued to contribute substantially to community life into the 1940s.[259] William Gabriel Paul, a grandson of Joseph Paul and Jane Kegan of Quoddy, married Mary Agnes Noel of Millbrook and the couple set out for Saint John, New Brunswick, where they lived for several years. An-other loss to the political life of the community oc-curred in 1931 when William Thomas Gloade moved to Shubenacadie upon marrying Bridget Anne Sack, a daughter of Isaac Sack and Annie Cope, who had been widowed the previous year.[260] Most residents stayed, however, as they appreciated the safety and stability Millbrook offered in the mid-1920s. It enabled them to transition into a lifestyle that broadened their social and occupational horizons while still letting them hold older, cherished values and practices.

While chief, Joseph Julien continued to act as a Grand Council prayer leader and choir member. According to his wife Annie Louise Googoo, Joseph was known to be a "sort of a deacon" whose duties included praying in the Mi'kmaw language over sick and dying community members. He also sang Mi'kmaw hymns "at celebrations, funerals and at high mass" at Millbrook's Church of the Sacred Heart.[261] Sad occasions included the deaths of Sandy Cope Sr. in 1930 and Peter Wilmot in 1932.[262] At Peter Wilmot's funeral ceremony on 27 December, Joseph joined in a choir along with Matthew Francis from Pictou Landing, Francis's brothers Tom Francis and Steve Francis, Chief William Paul of Shubenacadie, and Alex Cope Jr.[263] Both Sandy Cope Sr. and Peter Wilmot had been indispensable to Millbrook's founding and development. They also had been the most skilled trackers, hunters, trappers, and guides on the reserve, so when they died a valuable store of traditional Mi'kmaw knowledge and lore was gone forever. Four years later, Joseph Julien and Annie Louise Googoo's fifteen-year-old son Steven died on 3 August 1936. Yet even in the wake of community funerals and the harsh economic setbacks of the Great Depression, people looked back on Millbrook history and found occasion to celebrate. Annie Louise noted that at a large party held in honour of her husband's sixty-fifth birthday on October 1937, at which individuals wore traditional costumes, participated in dances, "and sang native folk songs," Joseph stood up and made a speech in which he reviewed the preceding years "as satisfactory ones for Millbrook."[264]

The Challenges of Betrayal: Resisting Government Centralization Policy

A recent work by Emma Battell Lowman and Adam J. Barker entitled *Settler: Identity and Colonialism in 21st Century Canada* addresses the devastation wrought by settler colonization on Indigenous societies. It states that "[s]ettler colonization seeks to transfer land from Indigenous people to settler control. Land, in this sense, refers to something akin to 'place': territories imbued with resources that give rise to opportunities, and form the basis of social life, sustaining political economies and informing cultural and community practices."[265] The government in the early twentieth century viewed the Mi'kmaq as incapable of permeating the landscape with such meaning, while, ironically, Grand Chief John Denny Jr. and Chief Joseph Julien spent considerable time and energy proposing systems and policies to sustain viable Aboriginal economies, which might have worked, had Indigenous land dispossession not have taken place.

Instead, government centralization promised the Mi'kmaq houses and services which it could not deliver, on limited land bases which proved too small to accommodate large populations. Millbrook's population was 124 in 1931. Fifteen years later it had about the same number of residents. Not so at Indian Brook, at Shubenacadie. By 1946, 816 people resided at Indian Brook where only 41 had dwelt before. Many of the 40 or so persons recorded as living at Indian Brook before implementation of the centralization policy d not even lived on the reserve, but on neighbouring land owned by a farmer surnamed Snyder. Crowding into one community was the result of Ottawa's implementation of a disastrous removal policy imposed on a poorly informed people under threat of enfranchisement and consequent loss of Aboriginal status.

Centralization meant the forced migration, by government fiat, of all Nova Scotian Mi'kmaq to just two locales, Shubenacadie and Eskasoni. Basically, it was founded on a bid to get as much Mi'kmaw land as possible for settlement and resource development, and promote governmental retrenchment.[266] When what was supposed to be only a temporary wartime income tax became a permanent fixture after the war, it exposed Ottawa in the late 1920s and 1930s to charges of overspending taxpayers' money on Indian Affairs administration. With the onset of the Great Depression in 1929 and with many Mi'kmaq on relief, the calls for government to reduce such burdens on the public purse became increasing insistent. A report drafted by W.S. Arneil in 1941 narrowed the designated destination communities to just two, Shubenacadie and Eskasoni, while maintaining that any Mi'kmaw family that could demonstrate self-sufficiency could remain where they were, provided they assumed the full duties of citizenship by becoming enfranchised.[267] In the mid-1920s H.P. Bury had pointed to Millbrook as a glowing example of what should be replicated elsewhere in the province. Now he now bowed to Ottawa's lead in jettisoning the Millbrook reserve in favour of nearby Shubenacadie, which would be provided with a lumber mill to furnish jobs for the unemployed. As with the Indian residential school system, the pecuniary, paternalistic ideology that drove centralization policy dealt a colossal insult to the intelligence and accomplishments of Mi'kmaw leaders like Joseph Julien. Both schemes showed the worst the government could offer when driven by cultural insensitivity and a narrow focus on retrenchment.

What Ottawa did not bank on in the midst of its land grab was the insightfulness and resilience of leaders like Joseph Julien. During the 1930s he had to face the inevitable layoffs of Millbrook's residents as employment opportunities drastically shrank. For many, applying for relief seemed the only option for survival. Mi'kmaw manufacturing of hockey sticks petered out as hockey stick production became industrialized. Those who had earlier left the community to find work elsewhere in the Maritimes found that in hard economic times the government frowned upon their returning to anywhere other than one of the two designated growth centres. When William G. Paul, a carpenter and lumberman as well as a stevedore, lost his position at the Saint John dockyards, he and his family were shipped unceremoniously back to Indian Brook, rather than to Millbrook where they had previously resided, and told to farm.[268] Only three families left Millbrook for Indian Brook in the early 1940s after hearing of promises of work at the Shubenacadie lumber mill. One of them was headed by Michael Isaac Sack, a son of Henry Sack and Susan Jerome of Millbrook, who had numerous kin at Indian Brook and so had many social as well as economic reasons for leaving.[269] According to Annie Louise Googoo, Indian Affairs "tried to trick the people into moving to Shubenacadie. They promised work and new homes. They managed to get a few people moved, but the majority stood behind Chief Julien."[270]

In 1940 and 1941, then, Joseph Julien faced the most critical challenge of his leadership career: Ottawa had decided, based on a modification of various centralization models furnished them in the 1930s by H.P. Bury, to *compel* Millbrook residents to move to Shubenacadie. The government's far-reaching scheme called for all Nova Scotian Mi'kmaq to relocate to either Shubenacadie or Eskasoni. The immediate consequence of centralization's implementation was overcrowding, coupled with Ottawa's complete disregard of either land's inability to sustain large population increases. The much-touted jobs in Shubenacadie's logging industry and sawmill terminated once the forests surrounding Indian Brook were cut down. Efforts at farming and even the maintenance of kitchen gardens suffered from lack of open land. Poorly insulated houses made of green lumber, hastily erected to shelter the incomers, buckled and warped in warm weather and were freezing inside during the winter.[271] The relative substantiality of the residential and administrative compounds built for government staff at Indian Brook underscored the prevailing social inequality between persons attached to government-sponsored institutions and the rest of the reserve populace. With the main resources depleted and a negligible alternative job market in the Shubenacadie area, incomers sought to drift back to their old haunts, even though in many instances their former homes and even their local schools had been razed by fire in the early 1940s.

Joseph Julien, who was now firmly back "in the saddle" as chief, was horrified by what he saw happening at Shubenacadie. At Millbrook, he had carefully monitored the ability of local resources to support population increases; at Shubenacadie the government did no such monitoring. In a manner similar to Grand Chief John Denny Jr. before him, Joseph contacted his many friends and associates across the province to assist him in denouncing the new policy. Chief Ben Christmas of Membertou immediately joined with Joseph in sending a flurry of letters and petitions to Ottawa opposing the scheme. Ben Christmas, who had become president of the United General Indian Council of Nova Scotia, had been involved since his youth with regional Indigenous organizations. He was intelligent, focused, and direct in his assertions. For three straight years, from 1940 to 1943, the two sniped away at what they held to be Ottawa's presumptuous, draconian plan, for neither leader had any intention of ever again relinquishing their people's lands or removing people from their respective jurisdictions. Grand Chief John Denny Jr. would have been proud.

By 1942 other leaders' voices began to rise in a crescendo to join the refrain already launched by the Truro and Membertou chiefs. On 29 January 1943 the eighty-three-year-old Joseph C. Cope sent a scathing letter to Ottawa with his own views on the disastrous effects centralization was having on the Mi'kmaw community.[272] Matthew Francis of Pictou Landing directed a grievance to the Department of Indian

Affairs denouncing the scheme. The Cumberland County Mi'kmaq sent a petition with eighty-three names, while an even longer document, with one hundred signatures, arrived from Middle River. Chief Noel Marshall at Barra Head, Cape Breton, directed his many concerns about the policy to the office of Prime Minister William Lyon Mackenzie King. At Cole Harbour, "Meggie" Cope Phillips – Joseph's second wife Bridget's sister – tried everything she could think of to keep the government from uprooting her community. Grand Chief Gabriel Sylliboy and Grand Captain Simon Denny wrote the superintendent of Indian Affairs and minister of mines, Thomas Alexander Crerar, in March of 1944 stating that they felt the government had deluded their people and unjustly taken their land, after which Grand Chief Sylliboy left Eskasoni in protest, to return to his former home at Whycocomagh.[273]

Victory at Last

In the summer of 1942 Joseph Julien, finding that Ottawa was ignoring his petitions, embarked on a more determined, two-pronged course of resistance. First, he explained the situation existing on the Millbrook reserve to Wilfred Burchell, a well-known Truro lawyer, who promised to help the chiefs launch a strong resistance to any government attempts to remove the Millbrook population.[274] In addition to preparing a petition, which was signed by the residents of Millbrook and sent to Ottawa, Burchell drafted a legal letter to Thomas Alexander Crerar, superintendant of Indian Affairs, informing him that Burchell had been retained by Chief Julien to correspond with Ottawa regarding "an intended move" of the Mi'kmaq at Millbrook to Shubenacadie. The chief objected to the move and wished him to relay seven points why the relocation should not take place. He argued: "First, of the 43 families on the reserve, only a minority were receiving government support; second, around fifty percent of the women were steadily employed in Truro in restaurants or as domestics; third, the men were employed in Truro as carpenters or day labourers, taking care of lawn work or gardening; fourth, moving these people to Shubenacadie would only place more of them on government allowance; fifth, not only were the men not a burden on the town of Truro, but a number of them were enlisted in the local Reserve Army from which they would be forced to resign if they had to move; sixth, all baskets made on the reserve were sold

in Halifax through an organization that sent the sale proceeds back to the artisans in Millbrook who then spent the money in Truro; and finally the heads of the families on the reserve felt very contented, and are better off financially where they are, than if they should be moved."[275]

Burchell reiterated that Chief Julien felt relocation would cause "discontent and uneasiness." Former members of the Halifax County Band in particular had come to Truro with the government's blessing, were "promised good homes, and [were told] that there was a sum of money set aside to build these homes." According to the chief, this money had "never materialized," so the Millbrook leadership still optimistically awaited "any further intended moves" in this direction "on the part of the government." Burchell concluded with an appeal to Ottawa's patriotism in the midst of the ongoing war effort: Chief Joseph Julien and his committee had suggested "that the cost incurred by the Government in moving these people could at the present time be used to a better advantage, if used for the furtherance of the war Cause."[276]

Next, Chief Julien travelled to Halifax to meet personally with his long-time friend Colonel Sidney C. Oland. After listening to Joseph complain that Ottawa was luring families away from Millbrook by vacuous promises of long-term jobs in Shubenacadie, Sidney Oland agreed to fund the chief's way to Ottawa so that he could represent his community's case against centralization in person. Once in the nation's capital, Julien declared that it was impolitic for Ottawa to try to dissolve a reserve that in the 1920s had been extolled by the government's own agents as a credit to the province: Henry J. Bury not only had encouraged him to develop Millbrook resources but also had upheld the community as an example of what other reserves might accomplish. A review of these facts revealed the hypocrisy at the heart of the centralization scheme. Millbrook was still a vital, functioning entity.[277] It had weathered the depression years of the 1930s because it had farmland and small businesses, and with time it would flourish again economically, as it had in the mid-1920s, as young people learned new trades.[278] Before he left for home, Chief Julien's impassioned speeches, backed by obvious support from Colonel Oland, Wilfred Burchell, and Membertou chief Ben Christmas, had persuaded Ottawa to leave Millbrook to its own devices.

The chief had won a major victory. Upon returning to Millbrook, he immediately convened a special meeting to tell the community's residents that Ottawa had agreed at last to continue assisting the Millbrook community and that no one had to relocate.[279] His listeners, who had placed their trust in their chief's efforts and refused to move, were exuberant. During his later years he enjoyed the company of his family and friends and regularly attended and participated in Grand Council gatherings, often leading the hymn singing. His success as a negotiator in Ottawa won him recognition within the province, and he was asked to preside over special ceremonies, among these the christening of the tribal-class destroyer *HMCS MicMac* in 1944.[280]

Slowing down to enjoy the fruits of victory was not part of Chief Julien's itinerary. In 1946 he sent a comprehensive report on the state of the Millbrook band to a Commission on Indian Affairs in order to assist Ottawa in defining its role in the future of Mi'kmaw reserve communities. His views were sought a second time in 1949, when along with councillors Michael Martin and John T. Brooks he directed another report to the head of another Commission on Indian Affairs.[281] Such information helped change government attitudes, for in 1950 a new superintendent general of Indian Affairs, F.B. McKinnon, announced that in Nova Scotia "smaller reserves are here to stay." In 1959 Ottawa officially recognized the integrity of smaller Mi'kmaw bands throughout the province, acknowledged their chiefs and councils, and assisted with the extent of their jurisdictions.[282] The Sheet Harbour, Beaverdam Lake, and Cole Harbour reserves now fell under Millbrook's administration.[283] Owing to Chief Julien's efforts to provide a homeland for Mi'kmaq from east of Dartmouth, his legacy included endowing Millbrook with the three small reserve parcels still remaining along Nova Scotia's eastern shore – all that was left of the once vast domain under the territorial aegis of the "Eastward Tribe."

Under Joseph Julien's direction, Millbrook in 1952 acquired the railway allowance that in the past had impeded access from the Creelman property to the rest of the Truro reserve. And beginning in 1954, the chief, Sandy Cope Jr., and Henry Peters set out to persuade Ottawa to transfer to their community 625.48 acres of a rifle range belonging to the Department of National Defence, in order to gain additional space and firewood and to further consolidate Millbrook's land base.[284] The acquisition of this sizeable property in 1955 marked another momentous achievement in Chief Julien's lengthy leadership career. This property, which today hosts the Truro Power Centre, expanded Millbrook's land base to a little over 1,110 acres.[285]

Joseph Julien continued as chief until his death on 6 February 1957 from a heart complaint at the age of eighty-five years, three months, and six days. Following a large community funeral, his remains were buried in the graveyard of the Church of the Sacred Heart.[286] During his final years he had warned his daughter and sons of the long, often frustrating, and rarely well-remunerated hours of hard work that accompanied a leadership office, but two of his offspring, Rachel Marshall and Sandy Julien, refused to be dissuaded. Both became band councillors, with Rachel serving a term as Millbrook's chief.[287] Other members of his family have gone on to excel in administration, education, economics, historical research, public and military service, writing and, not surprisingly, athletics – especially the game of hockey.

Joseph Julien provided a shining example of how to run a modern reserve community, since he made certain he and his counsellors were involved in decision-making processes at every stage. Had government officials, while they were praising Millbrook, noted that one of Chief Julien's strongest suits was never to allow population numbers to overwhelm local resources, they might have been able to prevent some of the devastating consequences of centralization, which threw such cautions to the wind and for years retarded Indian Brook's economic viability. With time bureaucrats came to respect his trenchant criticisms of Ottawa's poorly conceived and ill-fated centralization scheme, and changes were put in place. Shortly after his death in 1957, Order-in-Council PC 1960-61 officially ended the centralization era by establishing eleven bands throughout Nova Scotia, as well as a General List of Mi'kmaq in southwestern Nova Scotia not recognized as forming an organized band.[288]

Throughout his career, he respected the integrity of the efforts of others in his community – no matter how menial some of their economic activities might have seemed to others, especially during the Great Depression. He defended their rights and ensured they had the means to continue working, and did all with a good-natured diplomacy that alienated few and won many admirers both within and without the

Millbrook community. After his death certain prominent individuals (among them the sons of William G. Paul) who left Millbrook in the late 1920s returned as seasoned leaders to build upon the strong community foundations Chief Julien had established during his lifetime.[289]

Julien's voice in the 1920s, through speeches, letters, and petitions, called out to individuals and families from east, west, north, and south – to assist with land and resource issues and to provide for a Mi'kmaw community that functioned outside the narrow parameters set by government policy. Many responded to his call to help establish a vital, integrated Mi'kmaw settlement at Millbrook, and to ensure that Mi'kmaw people after 1957 had a controlling interest in their communities. Despite trial and hardship, the community survived owing to Joseph's ability to forge lasting relationships with other Mi'kmaw leaders, government officials, mainstream professionals, industrialists and politicians, as well as clergy and members of the local athletic community – persons from all social and economic stations – who admired his diplomacy, intelligence, honesty, practicality, organizational acumen and, certainly not least, his spiritual resoluteness. He had endured poverty and tragedy himself, and sought to heal the wounded spirit in others, often putting others' needs above his own. Kinsfolk, friends, and acquaintances, appreciating his genuineness, responded to his pleas for assistance in tumultuous times and gave what they had to offer to aid his campaigns. His ability to orchestrate this convergence of human talents, resources, and skills from all points of the compass made him truly a "man at the centre" – bent on preserving and enhancing a community whose strong organizational foundations and solid values would ensure its continued progress and future success, educationally, politically, socially, and in the fields of business and development.[290]

– Janet E. Chute, assisted by Vernon Cope, James Howe Sr., Donald M. Julien, and Heather Sutherland

Acknowledgments: Gratitude is extended to Courtney Brooks-Monteith, Brittany Pennel, and Mary Wells, student investigators on this entry, for their research, insights, and hard work. Their participation in this project included a trip for all three to work at the National Archives of Canada in Ottawa and to meet with Dr. Craig McNaughton, founder of the Social Sciences and Humanities Research Council's Aboriginal Strategic Grants program, and his team in that city. Dr. Donald M. Julien shared interesting stories and valuable knowledge of the past. The principal author and her assistants also owe a large debt to Roddy Gould and his wife Caroline Gould (née Paul, 1919–2011), well-known artist, artisan, businessperson, and linguist at Waycobah in Cape Breton, who helped them gather information. Caroline and Roddy's Gould's daughter, Dr. Marjorie Gould, an educational administrator, supported the biographical project from its inception. Daniel N. Paul graciously allowed reproduction of a photograph in his possession of his great-grandfather, Joseph Paul of East Quoddy. Heather Sutherland, a descendant of a Cope woman from Sober Island, who graduated from the Atlantic Canadian Studies program at Saint Mary's University, helped immeasurably with the chapter's content and editing. Donald M. Julien, director of the Mainland Confederacy of Mi'kmaq, who is the grandson of Chief Joseph Julien, shared stories about his ancestor as well as offering encouragement to the principal investigator and students alike. Vernon Cope, a direct descendant of Joseph C. Cope, helped locate persons to interview and provided personal recollections. Gillian Allen, senior legal and historical consultant for Kwilmu'kw Maw-klusuagn (the Mi'kmaw Rights Initiative), provided invaluable information and editing assistance. Thanks are also due to Carla Asprey of the Native Council of Nova Scotia, Tim Bernard, Carrie Gloade, Linda Green, Florella Howe, James Howe, Lillian Marshall, Cathy Martin, James Michael, Wallace Nevin, the late Bruce Oland, Richard Oland, Basil Peters, and Mary Jane Stevens.

Part Three

Siknikt, Ulustuk, Piktuk aqq Epexiwitk – Chignecto District, Northern Maine, the Northumberland Strait Area, and Prince Edward Island

13

The Times, Policies and Legacy of Joseph Argimault, Chief of Siknikt (Chignecto)

A Negotiator and Policymaker

Joseph Argimault (Argimou, Argim8, Ulgîmoo)[1] was a seventeenth-century Mi'kmaw diplomat and leader. Born to Philippe Argimault and his wife Anne in 1698, he was the son and grandson of chiefs and traditional power holders.[2] His territorial prerogatives extended from the Petitcodiac River – the *Petgotgoiag* or "bent stream"[3] – northward to the Richibucto River and across the Isthmus of Chignecto (Siknik) into what is now Cumberland County, Nova Scotia. The Petitcodiac River was of strategic significance to both the Mi'kmaq and French, since it formed the lower reaches of a river and portage route between the Atlantic coast and the St. Lawrence River.[4] The broader area formed the Mi'kmaw district of *Siknikt*, or *Sikniktewaq*, which means "drainage area."[5] Chief Argimault's activities were interwoven with the Acadian experience in this region, and during the 1750s he maintained close relationships with officials, traders, missionaries, and Acadian resistance fighters. Around 1750 he became one of the foremost proponents of a Mi'kmaq peacemaking campaign in the Northeast that focused on the establishment of a Mi'kmaw homeland.

Favoured by the French for agricultural settlement and by the English as a buffer zone between Quebec and northern New England, the Chignecto district became the focus of a heated territorial dispute between England and France that continued unabated until the Treaty of Paris of 1763. During these tumultuous years, Joseph Argimault devised a unique policy to govern the division of land into Mi'kmaw and European areas of use. Though he and his band joined with Indigenous and Acadian resistance forces against English expansion into Minas, Chebucto (now Halifax), and Beaubassin, his commitment to neutrality and peacemaking during the Seven Years' War propelled him to prominence in the eyes of British and well as French officialdom. On 8 August 1761 he signed a treaty of peace and friendship with the British on behalf of the Sikniktewaq Mi'kmaw community.[6] Yet his exercise of a distinctive Mi'kmaw brand of leadership predated this treaty-signing by a decade and continued afterwards for another two years, until 1763.

Though Père Claude Morreau, the Recollect priest at Beaubassin, baptized Joseph Argimault's father Philippe in 1785, Christianity in the late seventeenth century lay like a thin veneer over what still remained a vital traditional Mi'kmaw belief system in the Chignecto district.[7] During the late seventeenth century, the Chignecto band had two chiefs, Pierre Argim8 (or Argimault, 1616–c.1716), who was Joseph's grandfather, and Agigigab8it, who died before 1708.[8] Although the exact ranking between the chiefs remains unknown, the Chignecto band continued to have two chiefs until the mid-nineteenth century. Pierre Argim8 was a shaman, playing distinctive roles in band rituals as well as in the broader diplomatic forum. He and his wife, Nemegermi, had four sons: Etienne Mokabo in 1660, François N8dajal in 1668, Anthoine in 1673, and Philippe – who was Joseph's father – in 1676. They also had three daughters: Anne Teb8da8k8w around 1659, Yarenbouch in 1668, and Agnes in 1675. François, Anthoine, and Philippe were still living at Chignecto in 1708 when Père Pierre LaChasse compiled a nominal census of the Beaubassin Mi'kmaw band, though Étienne was not listed and may have died. Pierre Argim8, born in 1618, was ninety years old in 1708, living in the household of forty-year-old Jean Anquestoute. Madelaine Jean, Anquestoute's thirty-five-year-old wife, was likely another of Pierre's daughters.[9] Although Pierre was elderly and under the care of close kin, as a shaman he still would have wielded considerable authority within his band.

Relations with French Officials, Settlers, Traders, and Priests, 1675–1710

During the 1670s and 1680s the Chignecto Mi'kmaq operated fairly independently of the French at Beaubassin. Band members ranged widely over the countryside throughout the year. During the winter they hunted and trapped on family hunting territories along the Petitcodiac River and in the spring fished and took migrating water fowl on the Tantramar Marsh, on the Isthmus of Chignecto. When the Recollect friar Père Claude Moreau (or Moireau) arrived at Beaubassin in 1675, he encouraged the Mi'kmaq to sow potatoes, pumpkin, and corn at Petitcodiac and at their major village, *Mejagouech*, situated on the edge of the Tantramar Marsh near present-day Amherst. In the summer most of the band crossed to the coast of the Northumberland Strait to fish, collect berries, and trade with fledging Acadian settlements. Many spent several months on Île Saint Jean, now Prince Edward Island, collecting shellfish and making voyages into the Gulf of St. Lawrence where they hunted sea mammals off the Magdalene Islands.[10] On their return to Île St. Jean, these hunters traded their surplus meat and seal oil with the French at Port La Joye. Late summer and early fall found the band members fishing and harvesting crops on the lower Petitcodiac River, getting ready to leave for their hunting territories in the interior, and the cycle would begin again.

Though the Mi'kmaq had interacted for generations with European traders and French officials,

between 1675 and 1690 little of this intercourse in the Beaubassin area was cordial. In the early 1660s, Michel Le Neuf de la Vallière, a French military commander and somewhat unscrupulous entrepreneur, associated with Nicolas Denys, an older, more established merchant and official living on Île Royale, and around 1666 married Denys's daughter Marie.[11] When Denys's post at Saint-Pierre, Île Royale, burned to the ground during the winter of 1668–69, he moved his trading ventures and those of his son, Richard Denys de Fronsac, to Nepisiguit (now Bathurst) and Miramichi. In 1672 la Vallière established his own trading station at Chignecto and in 1676 obtained a grant, ten leagues in extent, on the Chignecto Isthmus from Governor Louis de Buade de Frontenac, which became the seigneury of Beaubassin. In accordance with Frontenac's instructions La Valliere set about attracting settlers, and by 1676 his small trading outpost had grown into a community of 127 French inhabitants.[12] While his father-in-law Nicolas Denys struggled at Nepisiguit to recover his losses from the Île Royale fire, La Vallière grew affluent enough to build a military post and church at Beaubassin. Over the next decade a steady trickle of settlers arrived and took up lands along the Petitcodiac. La Vallière, promoted to commandant of Acadia in 1678, imposed rules and regulations conducive mainly to his own interests on the inhabitants and local Mi'kmaq.[13] Owing to his presumptuous attitude, it was not long before a land dispute arose between the commandant and Jacques Bourgeois, a surgeon, whose claims to land at Chignecto preceded those of La Vallière. The disagreement was finally settled, in Bourgeois's favour, in 1705. During the proceedings leading up to this decision, the surgeon contended that the seigneur had appropriated land to which he felt he had prior right – yet neither La Vallière nor Bourgeois thought to include the Mi'kmaq, who truly held prior right, in the discussion.[14]

If the appropriation of their land aggravated the Mi'kmaq, they were even more chagrined by the commandant's trade policies. La Vallière, like his predecessor as governor, Jacques de Chambly, lined his pockets by selling licences to captains of New England trading vessels rather than attempting to impose any beneficial order on French commerce. The licences gave New Englanders the right to land fish and trade with the Indigenous people, despite the Mi'kmaq's reluctance to deal with some New England parties whose trading practices they had good reason to believe were unscrupulous.[15] Although these newcomers came ashore to take on water, build temporary shelters, and dry fish, no prior consultation ever took place with the Mi'kmaw leaders, who contended that they still exercised proprietary aegis over the landscape. The French traders at Beaubassin were no better. Sieur Michel Le Neuf de la Vallière, the seigneur of Beaubassin, not only ignored Indigenous land and resource rights but was notorious for his mistreatment of Indigenous middlemen traders, referred to as "captaines" in the documents. The commandant expected his employees to pillage brigades that traded with his rivals and rob any individual hunters they encountered of their furs and hides.[16] Owing to the abuse they faced from La Vallière's men, the Mi'kmaq began clandestinely exchanging furs, feathers, and fish with certain inhabitants whom they trusted. Given the climate of trade reciprocity that La Vallière sought to maintain with Simon Bradstreet, the last governor of the Massachusetts Bay colony, they also may have traded at Boston, though there is no concrete evidence of this. While they were often distrustful of the commandant, the Mi'kmaq respected their local priest, Père Claude Moreau, and when at Beaubassin attended religious services at the chapel of Notre-Dame du Bon Secours built by La Vallière in 1686.[17] When La Vallière left for Quebec in 1687, his son-in-law Sebastien de Villieu assumed control over the local fur commerce, along with the network of Mi'kmaw trade relations associated with it.[18]

Affairs briefly worsened for the Chignecto Mi'kmaq after 1687. Père Moreau left Beaubassin to be replaced by Jean Baudoin, a Sulpician priest with a military background who had little respect for the Mi'kmaq and was harsh, dictatorial, manipulative, and at times physically abusive to them. When contacted about Mi'kmaw individuals allegedly killing some settlers' cattle, Joseph Robineau de Villebon, La Vallière's successor as governor of Acadia, left Baudoin to his own devices to administer punishment to his Mi'kmaw congregants – a decision he regretted afterwards. "If the priest tolerates such disorder as cattle killing among the Micmac, it is that he may constrain them in regard to other matters," Villebon reflected. "Last year he beat one of them, [and] left him for dead."[19] Not surprisingly, the Mi'kmaq avoided the Beaubassin area; Only twenty-one individuals were recorded as living at Chignecto in 1688. While the onset of the War of the League of

Augsburg in 1688 drew Indigenous warriors away to conduct raids on northern New England settlements, it appears that many other members of the Chignecto group simply left the region for other parts. Even with the resumption of peace in 1697, the Chignecto band remained small and fluctuated in size, as Mi'kmaw fur trade middlemen were often away.[20]

The long-distance Indigenous trade to Montreal, Quebec, and the Great Lakes flourished following the end of the Iroquois Wars in 1701.[21] Strategically positioned so as to wield influence over the flow of trade, Mi'kmaw leaders along the Petitcodiac River forged alliances with Cape Sable leaders, who acquired French trade goods directly from the Seigneury of Pobomcoup, where until 1699 Baron Philippe Mius d'Entremont and, later, his sons operated a trans-shipment station.[22] The vital trade network that Mi'kmaw leaders forged with Pobomcoup, as well as smaller Acadian-*métis* fur and fishing settlements along the Atlantic coast, distanced them from the vicissitudes of trading with self-interested French officials at Beaubassin. Jean Baudoin's willingness by the late 1690s to accompany them on their military forays to New England may have mitigated their bitter dislike of the priest, but it never made them adherents of his harsh policies.[23] The Chignecto Mi'kmaq made it clear that they would tolerate neither being regarded as pawns of French commercial interests nor being treated as fodder for the wiles of manipulative officials and priests. And though they appreciated and used European trade goods, they were not abjectly dependent on them, as some historians have contended.[24] Their lives had been changed by the presence of the French, but not in ways they felt they could not handle and alter in some ways to suit their purposes.

A practice that had its inception during Villebon's term in office was the offering of gifts and honorifics to Indigenous leaders who during periods of intercolonial warfare mustered warriors to assist the French cause. Gift giving became more systematized and ritualized when the governor located his headquarters at Jemseg on the Saint John River, and doubtless Beaubassin's chiefs participated in these ceremonies. Nevertheless, the chequered experiences the Mi'kmaq had with the French at Beaubassin prior to 1700 likely bolstered their determination to retain a high degree of autonomy within the council forum. Though at least two Chignecto head men would have been present at French present distributions during

Queen Anne's War from 1702 to 1713, the leaders continued to be wary of unwarranted interference in their lives from either the French or British.

Philippe Argimault: Shaman and Chief

Philippe Argimault (1676–c.1750) assumed leadership of the Chignecto district following his father Pierre's death around 1710. In this year a large New England force led by Sir Francis Nicholson wrested Port Royal from the French, after which the Treaty of Utrecht of 1713 transferred mainland Acadia to the British Crown. At this time, Philippe was in his mid-thirties, with a wife named Anne and at least seven children: Charles, Joseph, Guillaume, Jeanne, Michel, Françoise, as well as a second son named Joseph.[25] The older Joseph Argimault, born in 1698 and his father's successor as a leader, was ten when his father became a chief at Chignecto. After 1715 only this Joseph and his brother, Michel, born in 1704, appear again in the documentary record. Like his father Pierre Argim8, Philippe was both a shaman and a chief. The Chignecto band continued to have two leaders, one being Philippe and the other Joseph Pedoujaeolet.[26] In his early years, Philippe was a formidable warrior and also undoubtedly a member of what Frank Gouldsmith Speck, a twentieth-century anthropologist, has termed the "Eastern Wabanaki Confederacy."[27] The Confederacy represented an alliance of northeastern Indigenous nations whose leaders met to address ways of responding to European appropriations of their lands and resources. Northeastern Algonquian diplomatic and negotiating protocols were marked in its forums by exchanges of wampum.

Once the French established Fortress Louisbourg on Île Royale, accorded to the French Crown under the terms of the Treaty of Utrecht, gift giving to chiefs became regularized at special ceremonies held for the purpose.[28] By 1720, councils where the Mi'kmaq were harangued to support France in upcoming wars were held annually mainly at Port Toulouse on Île Royale and at Port-La-Joye, Île Saint Jean, located on the present-day Hillsborough River near Charlottetown, Prince Edward Island, although they also occurred sporadically at Port Dauphin (now St. Anne's, Cape Breton) and at Fortress Louisbourg. During the conflict in the Northeast, often called Dummer's War or Father Rale's War, from 1722 to 1725, the English tried to thwart this French influence by administrating a degree of selective control, under a licensing system, over the activities of French Roman Catholic priests in Acadia. The executive council of Annapolis Royal denounced what they viewed as "seditious activities" of the Recollect Félix Pain among the Mi'kmaq of Chignecto, and early in the spring of 1725 had the "Incendiary Félix" replaced by the more moderate Père Isidore.[29] Likely in response to a call to distress New England shipping issued by the Eastern Wabanaki Confederacy, Mi'kmaw parties in June 1722 captured two New England trading vessels in the Bay of Fundy, one of them taken very near Chignecto.[30] Philippe, who organized raids during the conflict, was undoubtedly the "formidable and stalwart … Algimoosh" ("Little Argim8") or "Great Witch" that New Brunswick historian Robert Cooney in 1832 identified as leading a contingent of Mi'kmaq and Penobscot against the British at Canso in 1724.[31]

At the close of the 1722–25 hostilities, "Philippe Eargomot, Chief of Chicanickto [Philip Argimault, Chief of Chignecto]" and his twenty-two-year-old brother Michel signed a peace and friendship treaty on 4 June 1726 with the British at Annapolis Royale.[32] Joseph Pedoujaeolet was not present, and may have died during the previous war, so Michel acted as second chief. (According to Mi'kmaw oral tradition, Michel later took the name "Michel Augustine" and became the head chief of the Richibucto band.)[33] By 1840, two graduates of the Séminaire des Missions Étrangères in Paris came to wield considerable influence with Philippe Argimault and his people. Abbé Pierre Maillard came to Île Royale in the spring of 1735 and, after concentrated study, learned to speak Mi'kmaq well enough to teach it in 1737 to a new arrival, Abbé Jean-Louis Le Loutre. From the late 1730s to the mid 1750s, Maillard and Le Loutre focused on their missionary labours among the Mi'kmaq and Acadians, Maillard in Cape Breton and Le Loutre on the Acadian mainland.

Le Loutre, headquartered by the spring of 1738 twelve leagues from Cobequid near the junction of the Shubenacadie and Stewiacke Rivers, soon extended his itinerant rounds as far west as Beaubassin. Recruitment of warriors from Argimault's band for French military purposes escalated under his direction, since the missionary proved to be at least as zealous in his promotion of French military aims and interests as he was in his commitment to God. Maillard, who was less bellicose and able to speak Mi'kmaq with great facility, displayed a lively interest in ethnographic matters and wrote insightfully about Mi'kmaw culture. He held conversations with Indigenous leaders, among them Chief Philippe Argimault, whom he met around 1743 at Port-La-Joye on Île Saint-Jean. Philippe, who was around sixty-seven years old at that time, visited the French at Port-La-Joye each year. Maillard called Argimault the "*vieux jongleur*" (old shaman)," which indicated that the Mi'kmaq leader, although baptized by Père Moreau in 1685, retained merely a superficial attachment to Christianity. Despite this, Maillard admired the chief's breadth of traditional knowledge and the spirit of sincerity with which he answered the missionary's many questions.

Argimault evinced great pride in the fact that many of the old ways were still alive. They constituted a store of knowledge upon which his people could draw should goods or gifts from European sources fail. The chief described many aspects of Mi'kmaw life prior to European contact, elements of material culture and social organization, including leadership and ranking, rituals, and attitudes.[34] He further stressed that the greatest of all *Manidoo* (spirits of the Algonquian cosmology) was the all-pervading Sun Spirit (*Niskam*), to whom the Mi'kmaq turned for guidance in their everyday actions. Those in distress prayed to the animating power of the sun, which renewed mind and body. The Sun also was the focus of annual ritual, for the Mi'kmaq performed a ceremony that centred on a holy woman, or "chief's woman," guarding a sacred fire during the last days of the third moon. At the end of the female fire keeper's vigil, and on an appointed day, she, representing the earth, would mate with the band chief, representing the sun, in a way that allegedly released the revitalizing powers of the universe and set the cosmological forces on a course towards spring. Women who faithfully tended the sacred fire were highly honoured. If a woman previously had been a concubine, she was accorded her freedom and could select a husband of her choice.[35]

Maillard learned from Argimault that in the Mi'kmaw religion human beings played an integral role in the balance and perpetuation of cosmic forces. Based on what the chief told him about the Sun Spirit, the missionary tailored his presentation of Christian rituals to make them more palatable to his Mi'kmaw audience. Maillard selected the Roman Catholic ceremony of St. Anne's Day, 26 July, as an appropriate date for a revitalization ceremony that blended the

Mi'kmaq's respect for the revitalizing powers of the Sun with a reverence for St. Anne, the patron saint of childbirth and regeneration.[36] The symbolism of the monstrance, the vessel that holds the Host during Eucharistic rites, was also slightly changed. In the eighteenth-century mission field the monstrance was often referred to as *soleil* rather than *ostensior*, which reinforced a distinctly Mi'kmaq rather than Roman Catholic interpretation of its value and purpose. In this way, Argimault's influence remained alive for many years within the Roman Catholic Mi'kmaw mission movement. As late as the 1930s, the Capuchin Father Pacifique at St. Anne de Restigouche in Quebec observed that Mi'kmaw attitudes towards the monstrance were "somewhat unorthodox."[37]

The Power of Metaphor

Equally important, Argimault's words gave Maillard special insight into the unifying power inherent in Mi'kmaw tradition and legend. On being asked what Mi'kmaw life was like prior to the coming of the Europeans, Argimault replied, "Mon Pere, avant votre arrive [arrivée] dans ces countrees – cy [ce] qui sont cette terre ou le Grand Dieu nous a fait naitre et ou nous sommes crus commes les herbes et les arbres. (My Father, before you arrived in these regions, this was a land where the Great Spirit gave us birth and where we are rooted like the grass and the trees which you see.)"[38]

Maillard by the early 1740s recognized the central importance of this belief to Mi'kmaw thought and action. A strong sense of community could quickly be conjured up through comparison of the *Elnu'k*, or Mi'kmaw people, to the grass and trees of the field. Because the Mi'kmaq had arisen from the womb of the soil under the Sun Spirit's beneficent rays, Argimault argued, his people bore a special and exclusive relationship to their territory, akin to the vegetation that grew naturally about them.[39] Such symbolically charged phrases, appearing in Mi'kmaw speeches, explanations, and threats, inspired action each time the Mi'kmaw polity was confronted by European encroachment. In June 1720 chiefs at Fronsac Passage (now the Strait of Canso) chastised the governor of Île Royale, Joseph de Monbeton de Brouillan *dit* Saint-Ovide, for presumptuously suggesting that they had only two options, to swear allegiance to the English king or move to Cape Breton and live under French rule. "[L]earn from us that we were born on this earth upon which you march even before the trees that you see beginning to grow," they cautioned.[40] As far as they were concerned, Saint-Ovide's dismissive attitude towards their professions of strong attachment to the soil had potentially forfeited his right to consider them as allies of the French Crown. Yet the French were not the only recipients of such protestations. Several months later, in a letter, dated 2 October 1720 directed to Governor Philipps at Annapolis Royal, two Minas chiefs, Pierre and Antoine Momcharret, lambasted the English and New Englanders for trespassing on their territorial prerogatives by declaring that "this land that God gave to us, on which we could be counted even before the trees were born" belonged undisputedly to their people.[41] These metaphorical comparisons of people to grass and trees exclusively characterized Mi'kmaw oratory. They did not arise in forums presided over by speakers of other Eastern Abenaki nations. As they were central to their campaign to retain land and resource rights, the Mi'kmaq used such words for over thirty years as a rallying cry and for their unifying force.[42]

Conjoined Acadian and Indigenous Resistance, 1730–1748

Petitcodiac became a haven for fugitive Acadians following the British conquest of Acadia in 1710. Disgruntled Acadians left their former lands lying between Annapolis Royal and Minas to settle on tidewater tracts flanking the Shepody, Memramcook, and Petitcodiac rivers. Small Acadian settlements sprang up in what became known as Acadia's "Trois Rivières" or "Three Rivers" region. Though little is known about initial contacts between these Acadians and Philippe Argimault's people, the two constituencies soon came to realize that they both opposed English expansionist aspirations.[43]

The Acadians of the Chignecto district had endured cultural discrimination and oppression. In 1710, while still living in the Annapolis Valley, they were forced to work as free labourers for the English, as well as sell their agricultural produce to the Annapolis Royal garrison at a lower price than they could get elsewhere. Once they moved to the Beaubassin area, some of them, nourishing a lively hope that France might once again gain control of Acadia, attacked British officials and traders. As early as 1711, Abraham Gaudet and his Acadian and *métis*

associates from Beaubassin captured Pierre Capon, a Huguenot commissary officer from Annapolis Royal, and held him for ransom. Small parties of disaffected Acadians gradually coalesced into a formidable resistance movement, bent on acts of militancy even when the French and British Crowns were at peace.[44] In the 1730s two future famous Acadian resistance fighters, Joseph Broussard *dit* Beausoleil and his elder brother Alexandre Broussard, moved from the shores of the Annapolis River to Chipoudy (Shepody) Bay, to escape the overbearing English and to live near kin and close companions, most notably Pierre II Surrette. In 1740 the two Broussards set up an extended family compound, the Village des Beausoleils, on the upper Petitcodiac River at present-day Boundary Creek near Moncton.[45] This site became a mustering ground for participants in Acadian resistance campaigns. When not fighting in campaigns, the Acadians and Mi'kmaq traded with one another. (A few Acadians and members of Chief Argimault's band also undoubtedly intermarried at the small chapel at Village des Beausoleils, although how many is unknown, since all of Le Loutre's registers later were lost.)

Joseph Broussard *dit* Beausoleil and his Acadian companions, who spoke Mi'kmaq and understood Mi'kmaw culture, encouraged their Indigenous neighbours to join them on guerrilla raids on Annapolis Royal and other British outposts during King George's War, which lasted from 1744 to 1748. While relatively cordial in the late 1730s towards the British at Annapolis Royal, Abbé Le Loutre during King George's War developed into a fiery militant, with the blessings of the governor of New France, the Marquis Beauharnois, and the Abbé de L'Isle-Dieu, Quebec's vicar general in Paris.[46] At the onset of war in 1744, Le Loutre moved his mission headquarters from Shubenacadie to Pointe-à-Beauséjour on Missiguash Creek, near present-day Sackville, New Brunswick. He then acted as an agent of the French government, intent on employing Mi'kmaw fighters for French geopolitical ends while adopting, for charismatic ends, the trappings of a *buoin*, or unpredictable shaman. Missionaries among the Acadians elsewhere in Acadia were cautioned by the British to uphold a doctrine of neutrality, but this did not apply to missionaries among the Mi'kmaq and Acadians at Chignecto.[47] Le Loutre preached to Acadian and Mi'kmaq alike of the constant need to fight British expansionist proclivities by containing the garrison at Annapolis

Royal behind its palisades. The English consequently put a price on his head, yet he felt that living off the Acadian peninsula made him less of a target. He also held that a combined force of French regulars and Mi'kmaw warriors might drive the British out of Acadia altogether. Such a victory would not only redound to the glory and honour of France and the Roman Catholic Church, but also foster a safe and peaceful future habitation for Mi'kmaq and Acadian alike. Le Loutre's and Beausoleil's admonitions to the Mi'kmaq, to rally to the call and fight for Acadia's freedom from British rule, brought Mi'kmaw leaders and the French the closest together they had been in over three decades.

As soon as King George's War[48] began, warriors from Chief Argimault's group joined the two Broussards, Pierre II Surrette, and several other Acadian resistance fighters from Petitcodiac, Shepody, and Memramcook. Mustering at Village des Beausoleils, they proceeded to Beaubassin where they were joined by more Acadians and Mi'kmaq, and then travelled east to the Atlantic coast. At Baie Verte they met up with François Dupoint Duvivier, a French officer and merchant, and a force of two hundred Frenchmen to launch a successful siege from 13 to 24 May 1744 on the English military and fishing station at Canso.[49] Within a month Duvivier was planning an assault on Annapolis Royal, and he expected Abbé Le Loutre, the Acadian resistance fighters, and the Mi'kmaq to join in the attack.

In early June Le Loutre received orders from Jean-Baptiste-Louis Le Prévost Duquesnel, the governor of Île Royale, to muster three hundred Mi'kmaw and Malecite warriors, along with the Broussards and their companions, and proceed overland from Beaubassin to Cobequid. From Cobequid they were to press along the floor of the Annapolis Valley and descend on the British garrison at Annapolis Royal. After setting up camp outside Fort Anne at Annapolis Royal, on 1 July they laid siege to a nearby blockhouse, though the soldiers inside were soon rescued by a detachment of British regulars led by Captain Edward How. The Mi'kmaq then waited. They had been told that French reinforcements would arrive, but when August arrived and Duvivier did not appear, many left in disgust.[50] It was only after Joseph-Nicolas Gautier, a wealthy merchant from Lequille near Annapolis Royal, revealed his partisan sympathies for the French by bringing 170 Mi'kmaw and Malecite warriors, 50 French marines, and Abbé

Maillard, now the vicar general of Isle Royale, by ship to the Annapolis Basin that another siege of Fort Anne could be mounted.

Duvivier eventually appeared but proved to be a poor military strategist. When he rallied his French and Indigenous forces to attack Fort Anne in August, Colonel John Gorham and his corps of rangers formed of approximately fifty Mohawk and ten Wampanoag prepared to go to Annapolis Royal, to try to force Duvivier's men to disperse. On 6 September Duvivier defiantly marched his men up to the British palisades, where they stood until a cannon ball aimed at them caused their quick retreat. The next day, under a flag of truce, the French officer offered Colonel Paul Mascarene the opportunity of surrendering, to which Mascarene responded by barricading his troops inside Fort Anne's walls until two vessels carrying seventy soldiers arrived from Boston on 26 September.[51] Being outmanned and outmanoeuvred, Duvivier left the Annapolis Royal area early in October. Not long after, the government of Massachusetts officially declared war on the Mi'kmaq by offering a bounty for the head of any Mi'kmaw man, woman, or child. The ill-planned siege of Annapolis Royal not only cost the French the respect of the Indigenous warriors who had joined Duvivier's expedition, but also unleashed John Gorham and his rangers to hunt down Mi'kmaq throughout the province.[52]

One fact became very clear during the summer and fall of 1744. While members of the Acadian resistance movement proved determined to fight on almost regardless of circumstances, this was not going to be the case with the Mi'kmaq. Despite the French provision of food, guns, ammunition, and more specialized presents, if matters seemed to be going awry or their distinctively Indigenous goals failed to be met the Mi'kmaq left the field of battle. This left the French in a quandary, since they realized they could not rely on the Acadians left in mainland Acadia to take up arms against the English. A successful French campaign would have to depend heavily on Indigenous leaders and members of the Acadian resistance, particularly Joseph Broussard *dit* Beausoleil, to muster needed guerilla warriors to continue the fight.

Weighing Options, 1745–1748

A number of chiefs from the Minas and Piziquid (now Windsor, Nova Scotia) areas began to watch the war's progression with interest, and when the course of events weighed against the French, they began reviewing their options for the future. After a siege lasting forty-seven days, the successful capture of Louisbourg on 28 June 1745 by a naval expedition led by Commodore Peter Warren of the British Royal Navy[53] and two New England naval commanders, William Pepperrell and Edward Tyng, brought matters to a head within the Minas Mi'kmaw community. The Minas chiefs had expected the collapse of the French regime at Louisbourg weeks before it happened. A Mi'kmaw party travelling with Abbé Maillard had observed the combined British and New England fleet at Canso, where it had taken on provisions before continuing on to Louisbourg, and news spread quickly to Minas. An English embargo, which had been set at Tatamagouche on 15 June, prevented French supply ships from reaching Louisbourg, and the French, hemmed within their fortress walls, found themselves both under-provisioned and unable to call for military assistance from the Indigenous constituency.

Concerned lest in future years the British drive the French entirely from the Northeast, on 24 August 1745, less than a month after the fall of Louisbourg, Mi'kmaw leaders from the Annapolis River region, Minas, Shubenacadie, and Cobequid acted boldly. They extended a peace overture, drafted in French by Pierre Landry of Piziquid, to the executive council at Annapolis Royal.[54] Failing to receive an answer to their first letter, they sent a second, more pointed missive by way of a Mi'kmaw courier named François Courmarse. This campaign for peace was restricted wholly to the Mi'kmaq, as the two letters' originators argued that they could not answer for the activities of Indigenous "strangers," even if the peace was signed. This time executive council responded that it could not act until a similar bid for peace emanated from all the Mi'kmaw chiefs in the country, when a "security could be obtained from them" that the peace would be lasting.[55]

In the face of this localized Mi'kmaw movement favouring peace with the English, Le Loutre's superiors in Quebec appointed him the Mi'kmaq's military leader in Acadia.[56] Similar instructions were issued to Maillard in Cape Breton, though late in 1745 Maillard was captured by the British, taken to Boston, and deported temporarily to France.[57] In the aftermath of the Mi'kmaw peace overtures, Le Loutre was told to watch for, and intercept, any communications

between the Mi'kmaq population and the garrison at Annapolis Royal. Presents of guns, ammunition, clothing, knives, and medals were also placed at his disposal to woo the Mi'kmaq back to the French cause.[58] Warming to his new role, the missionary spent the winter of 1745 and 1746 at Minas specifically for this purpose. Early in 1746 he received additional orders, to act as a privileged liaison between the Mi'kmaq, Acadians, and a French naval expedition under the command of Admiral Jean-Baptiste Louis Frédéric de La Rochefoucauld de Roye, the Duc d'Anville, planning to retake Louisbourg.

News of the coming of the Duc d'Anville expedition revived flagging Mi'kmaw interest in supporting the French. In late June 1746, Lieutenant Jean-Baptiste-Nicolas-Roch de Ramezay sailed from Quebec to Beaubassin with over seven hundred Canadian and Indigenous fighters, while Le Loutre went to Three Rivers and the Saint John river valley to recruit warriors.[59] Maillard returned to Acadia from France to join Le Loutre in mustering warriors. Ramezay also sent his nephew, Charles Deschamps de Boishébert et de Raffetot, to scout out an encampment of New England militia near Port-La-Joye.[60] Soon afterwards, two hundred Mi'kmaq and three hundred Malecite and Eastern Abenaki, who previously had been mustered at Beaubassin, joined French seigneur and officer Joseph-Michel Legardeur de Croisille et de Montesson and his men in a surprise attack on 11 July 1746 on two hundred militiamen belonging to the Massachusetts 29th Regiment, stationed on Île Saint-Jean since July the previous year.[61]

Ramezay aborted his plans for a siege of Annapolis Royal in August, since the Duc d'Anville's fleet did not arrive until September, and in disarray. The French flotilla was buffeted by storms at sea and, worse, its men and crew were ravaged by a typhus epidemic that, when the vessels landed at Chebucto, spread with deleterious consequences among the Mi'kmaq waiting with Le Loutre on the shore.[62] The Duc d'Anville died suddenly and was buried at Chebucto, after which Jacques-Pierre de Taffanel de la Jonquière, who took over command of the vestiges of the fleet, dismissed all thoughts of attacking Annapolis Royal and sailed immediately for France. Le Loutre followed in his wake the same fall, embarking from Chebucto on the *La Sirène*, not to return to Beaubassin until after the close of the war.[63]

In Le Loutre's absence, around fifty Mi'kmaq from Beaubassin participated in a major winter military engagement gauged to thwart British plans to occupy the head of the Bay of Fundy. In January 1747 a land expedition including Boishébert, Maillard, and the Mi'kmaq and led by three French officers, Nicholas-Antoine Coulon de Villiers, Captain Louis-Luc la Corne, and Joseph Marin de La Malgue, surprised and defeated five hundred Massachusetts militia commanded by Colonel Arthur Noble, quartered at Grand Pré.[64] The victory would be short lived, however, for the following March one hundred New England volunteers under the leadership of Captain John Rous reclaimed Grand Pré for the English.[65]

Raids on English outposts, shipping, and Cape Breton mining installations continued under Maillard's directives until the close of hostilities between France and Britain.[66] There were still significant numbers of persons within the Indigenous community who questioned which side, British or French, would prove the winner once hostilities ceased. It was only with the return of Île Royale to the French in 1748, under the terms of the Treaty of Aix-la-Chapelle, that the Beaubassin Mi'kmaq showed renewed support for the French cause.

In July 1749 Le Loutre arrived back in Beaubassin, having crossed the Atlantic on the *Chabanne* in company with Charles Des Herbiers de la Ralière, Île Royale's new governor.[67] His orders were to abandon Shubenacadie and take up permanent quarters on the Chignecto Isthmus. He further was to persuade the Mi'kmaw parishioners of his former Shubenacadie mission, as well as "others dependent on it," living between Cobequid and Cape Sable to join him at Chignecto.[68] The overseas treaty of 1748 failed to quell outbreaks of hostilities in Acadia. By late July Le Loutre was again recruiting warriors from the upper Petitcodiac and the Three Rivers district, despite the fact that peace reigned, at least on paper, between the French and English Crowns.

Initial Mi'kmaw Responses to the Founding of Halifax

While Le Loutre was gaining his bearings at Beaubassin, the Mi'kmaq along the eastern Atlantic seaboard sought to satisfy their curiosity about the new English governor, Edward Cornwallis, who landed at Chebucto on 21 June 1749 with twenty-five hundred settlers to establish Halifax. A least one Mi'kmaw group met with Cornwallis, and Mi'kmaw individuals mingled peacefully with newcomers.[69] Some

brought the settlers gifts of meat and fish. Mi'kmaw leaders elsewhere, including the chiefs of Chignecto, meanwhile adopted a "wait and see" attitude until August, until further events provided guidance on how they should respond to this new phenomenon in their midst.

The British had expansionist aspirations. The celebratory atmosphere that pervaded New England following the fall of Louisbourg had been replaced by disappointment and rage when, at the stroke of a pen, the fortress was handed back in 1748 to the French. Cornwallis set out to placate and impress New England by making Halifax into a military stronghold, with palisades, five forts, several blockhouses, and two Regiments of Foot.[70] During the summer of 1749 he constructed a road to Minas that he fortified by building Fort Vieux Logis at its terminus, and laid out plans for further fortified settlements at Windsor, Whitehead near Canso, La Have, and Baye Verte.[71] He retained a company of sixty rangers under John Gorham at the head of the Bedford Basin, where he constructed Fort Sackville in 1750. His broader mandate included the settlement and fortification of Lunenburg, Chezzetcook, and lands on the Bay de Chaleurs.

The Mi'kmaq, who had many and varied channels for obtaining information about British strategic plans, were appalled. The treaty they had signed at Annapolis Royal in 1726 implied that they would be consulted on any future British settlements "lawfully to be made." Yet Cornwallis held that the fact many Mi'kmaq had sided with the French during King George's War revealed the weakness of the 1726 pact and left him with only one option, to garrison new British settlements against an unpredictable and dangerous Mi'kmaw presence. To the governor, if something were to be "lawfully made" it must follow the dictates of British law; no Indigenous involvement in the process would be tolerated. The Mi'kmaq felt that, ideally, their relationship with a European monarch should approximate that of cherished children watched over by a beneficent father, while to the British administrators the authority of government resided in the king's person, the apex of law, to which all dutiful subjects must submit.[72] The Mi'kmaq acted on the basis of their own distinctive cultural understanding of their land and resource rights. Ensuing hostilities between 1749 and 1755 have been dubbed "Abbe Le Loutre's War," although such a designation diminishes the independent role played by the Mi'kmaq, who used force to gain recognition from both the English and French for their land and re-source campaign.

While the Mi'kmaw constituency bided its time before acting either pacifically or with hostility to the new settlement at Chebucto, Cornwallis, in keeping with his instructions from the Lords of Trade and Plantations in London, extended peace overtures to Mi'kmaw and Malecite chiefs living west of the Missiguash River, to strengthen Britain's bid to the tract north of the Isthmus of Chignecto, still claimed by France.[73] He foresaw no problems, as he had been welcomed cordially by local Mi'kmaw delegations and he expected similar responses from Indigenous leaders elsewhere.

Le Loutre, moreover, had only just returned from France and had not yet begun a recruiting campaign for warriors among the Mi'kmaq at Beaubassin. In the interim, Cornwallis focused on making peace solely with the Chignecto Mi'kmaq and the Malecite on the Saint John River. Philippe Argimault, however, did not attend and, having reached age seventy-three, may have been ill, since his son Joseph succeeded him as head chief of Chignecto the following year. Instead, a man named Johannes Pedousaghtigh represented the Chignecto band.[74] Early in August 1749 Cornwallis sent Captains Edward How and John Rous to the mouth of the Saint John River to summon the thirteen Indigenous delegates he had invited, among them four Malecite leaders, François Arondawish (also known as Aurodowish and Francis des Salles) from Aupukque (now Apohaqui on the Kennebacasis River), Noellobig from Medoctic, and Simon Sactawino and Jean Battiste Maddouanhook from the lower Saint John River area.[75] How and Rous also collected a Penobscot leader, Neptune Abbodouallette, and Johannes Pedousaghtigh, the only Mi'kmaw representative.[76] These men attended a two-day ceremony, held on 14 and 15 August, aboard the British naval transport ship *Beaufort*, which lay at anchor in Chebucto Harbour. The climax of the occasion was the renewal of the 1726 peace and friendship treaty, previously signed at Annapolis Royal. A few of the Mi'kmaw delegates stated they still possessed copies of the 1726 treaty and, as they had heard about the 1748 peace between France and England, wished to be included under the terms of the latter pact as well.[77] The signed treaty parchment later was carried by Edward How to the mouth of Saint John River for ratification by several other Malecite chiefs.[78]

Keeping the British East of the Missaguash River

The strategic nature of Cornwallis's peace-making appeals immediately raised suspicions west of the Missiguash River. The British governor's rationale for favouring Mi'kmaq who lived in the disputed territory was so strikingly transparent that it discouraged other chiefs from approaching the treaty table. The Missiguash River remained the temporary boundary line between English and French territory until such time as the European boundary commission, composed of French and English commissioners with a mandate to examine the claims of both sides in the land dispute, could settle on a more permanent border. Under the terms of the Treaty of Aix-la-Chapelle, Britain had obtained Acadia "according to its ancient limits" – a definition the French and British could not agree upon. The French initially were willing to concede the English a small parcel of land in southwestern Nova Scotia, though the founding of Halifax made such a concession redundant. "Ancient Acadia," the French argued, neither covered the entire Nova Scotian peninsula nor extended northwest beyond the Isthmus of Chignecto.[79] Le Loutre argued that "ancient Acadia" related only to the small area around Annapolis Royal, though he was willing to concede that if for diplomatic purposes more land needed to be accorded the British, the boundary line could be drawn from Cobequid to Canso. By contrast, the British considered Acadia to extend across the Isthmus of Chignecto and then southward to the Kennebec River of present-day Maine and northward to Quebec.

In August of 1749 Le Loutre began harassing the British into staying east of the Missaguash River by promoting attacks on any English who ventured near Beaubassin. In August 1749 a Mi'kmaw war party unsuccessfully tried to capture two English warships with orders to prevent Acadians from fleeing to Prince Edward Island.[80] Several deaths occurred on both sides, among them a Chignecto head chief, a Shubenacadie leader who had followed Le Loutre to Beaubassin, and Tom Daniel, a ship's captain.[81] The Chignecto leader who died was not named although, owing to the timing of the event, he may have been the seventy-three-year-old chief Philippe Argimault, whose name does not appear again in the documentary record. On 18 September Mi'kmaq and Malecite killed three more Englishmen at Chignecto.[82] Le Loutre later wrote that the Chignecto Mi'kmaq met in council late in the summer of 1749 to decide how to respond to what they held were "unjust invasions of the English" on their territory. Their first step was to send beaded war wampum belts and necklaces to the Malecite and Penobscot, their colleagues in the Eastern Wabanaki Confederacy, to persuade them to break the treaty they recently signed at Halifax.[83] Councils convened in Cape Breton under Maillard's auspices manifested the same warlike posturing, while the French at Louisbourg strove to keep Indigenous bellicosity at a fever pitch by supplying arms and ammunition to be used in raids against the English.[84]

In November 1749 Chevalier Louis de La Corne, a captain in the French regular army, arrived at Beaubassin and elicited oaths of allegiance to the French king from Acadian farmers living west of the Missiguash River, on the tract France claimed as its own. He also strengthened the area militarily by erecting an earthenwork redoubt at Beauséjour, and built fortifications and organized militia companies at Memramcook and on the Petitcodiac River, near the modern-day village of Hillsborough, New Brunswick.[85] A militia quarters was established at Shepody. Le Loutre meanwhile persuaded Acadians living in bone fide British territory to relocate westward onto lands falling under La Corne's protection, and called for Mi'kmaw raids on Halifax and other outposts to counter British expansionism. His first station was at Missaguash Creek, although in November he entrenched himself near La Corne's camp at Pointe-a-Beauséjour overlooking the Tantramar Marshes. At this second locale, the site of present-day Sackville, New Brunswick, he apprised the Chignecto Mi'kmaq of a new plan to compel the English to acknowledge Mi'kmaw rights to land and resources. The English, he stressed, would not capitulate without a strong show of military force. For this reason, Le Loutre recommended that a steady barrage of raids be kept up until the British realized that their containment behind their palisades could only be ended by coming to mutually agreeable terms with the French and the original occupiers of the soil.

The lack of strong French civil government in Acadia placed both Le Loutre and Maillard at the centre of this Indigenous movement. Since they were expected to promote French military goals among the Mi'kmaq even in peacetime, they had to listen carefully and understand Indigenous goals and aspirations if they were to retain any position of influence.[86] Maillard, who had assumed responsibility for Le Loutre's former mission at Shubenacadie after Le Loutre went to Chignecto, was the better of the two at achieving a syncretic blend of Indigenous aspirations with French goals. Le Loutre's forte was sending strident appeals to leaders of the Abenaki community, as well as other nations in the Northeast, for warriors to counter what he considered England's grandiose territorial presumptions.

The Mi'kmaq viewed the establishment of Halifax as an illegal invasion of their territory and by the end of September 1749 had devised an integrated plan that they expected would be coordinated by Le Loutre and Maillard, who would also be their scribes and interpreters. First, the Mi'kmaq remembered treaty promises made to them by the English in 1726 that no infringements on their lands or hunting would occur. Mi'kmaw leaders at the time promised not to molest English in "their *Settlements* already *made* or *lawfully to be made*." They assumed that the word "lawfully" in this context meant they would be consulted before the English established any new settlements. Second, since British settlement had spread without their consent, they agreed with Le Loutre that the British should be restricted to southwestern Nova Scotia, through diplomatic measures if possible but by armed resistance if not.[87] Third, they called for a neutral buffer zone to be recognized between the lands claimed by the French west of the Missiguash River and the tract under British aegis in southwestern Nova Scotia, embracing both Annapolis Royal and Halifax. The idea of buffer zones, which would lie exclusively under Indigenous auspices, had been discussed for years in Eastern Wabanaki Confederacy councils. Aboriginal representatives to these forums knew that in 1720 three members of the Massachusetts council, Jonathan Belcher, Samuel Sewall, and Edmund Quincy, advised that a boundary be drawn along the Kennebec River marking the northern extremity of New England settlement. Territory lying north of this line would form a buffer zone between New England and southwestern peninsular Acadia.[88] Though inspired by past debates in the Massachusetts council, the scheme for a buffer zone in Nova Scotia, with no European forts allowed within its parameters, revealed ideological characteristics that were distinctly Mi'kmaq in form and conception, as we will see below.

On 24 September 1749 the Mi'kmaw community invited Maillard to attend a major council at Port Toulouse, a French military outpost located near

Saint-Pierre, now St. Peter's, Cape Breton. Chiefs attended from throughout *Mi'kma'ki*, the Mi'kmaq's domain in the Northeast.[89] They expected the missionary to write down their speaker's words and fashion them into a letter that could be conveyed to Governor Cornwallis in Halifax. Maillard, using Roman script, wrote down the speech in its original Mi'kmaw and then translated the words into French. Four months later it was translated into English at the office of the *Gentleman's Magazine* in London, England, and gained international attention when it appeared in print in 1750 under the heading "A letter said to be sent by the Indian Prince of Nova Scotia, to the English governor of Chebucto."[90] In Mi'kmaq, the proclamation read:

Chagmau: Oülà éimen, oülà edli oüikademenkik, oülá edli éli doûn, oüjagaloujan, oülà paoüe demen néguèch ktélikichkatpachin, oülà néguèch kedoüi mechtayajou demen magamiguéou, nân nai, nân anuchema edli ougichkaliei, nân nil elnoüi telei, nân n'magamiiquen, kedélbana nân kijoûlk ignemouich n'oüémtaguin yapchiou.

(*Governor*: The place where you are, where you are building dwellings, where you are now building a fort, where you want, as it were, to enthrone yourself, this land of which you wish to make yourself now absolute master, this land belongs to me, I have come from it as certainly as the grass, it is the very place of my birth and of my dwelling, this land belongs to me, the Elnoüi, yes, I swear, it is God who has given it to me to be my country forever.)[91]

Incorporating a powerful metaphor similar to the one likening the Mi'kmaq to the grass that Philippe Argimault had shared with Maillard on Île St. Jean eight years previously, this declaration maintained that the Mi'kmaq had an incontestable right to the land and its resources. No peace could arise as long as the British destroyed any middle ground for understanding and negotiation by presenting the Mi'kmaw community with a fait accompli, an invasion on lands it considered its own. The lowliest of creatures would fight to save its life,[92] and though the document embodied a call to arms, the Mi'kmaq had been driven to take this course. The perception that the Mi'kmaq (referred to in the declaration by their proper national designation, the *Elnoüi* or *L'nuk*), although small in number and military strength compared to the British, had inherent worth emanating from the Great Spirit

was decidedly northeastern Algonquian in tone and spirit. "My King and thy king over the great waters," the message continued, "have agreed upon a certain distribution of lands, therefore they are at peace ... It is you who drives me away. Show me a place where you would that I could take refuge."[93] The declaration concluded with the veiled warning: "I am going to go and see you very soon, yes, I shall certainly see you soon."[94]

The British, the Mi'kmaq averred, in taking over Chebucto without negotiation or consultation had committed an offence that demanded restitution. The *Gentleman's Magazine* regarded this charge as more than an exotic curiosity: it showed that the Mi'kmaq could speak with a single voice in support of their claims, a fact that took precedence over even the veiled threat directed towards British settlement overseas. Meanwhile Maillard, who until just a few months previously had been espousing a more moderate course of action, manifested few qualms about supporting the declaration's militant aspects.[95] After participating in the council at Port Toulouse, he admitted to the Abbé Du Fau, one of the directors of the Séminaire des Missions Étrangères, that he was becoming increasingly sympathetic towards the Mi'kmaw cause. Since the French regular army could not intervene in peacetime, he explained to his superior in Paris, the Mi'kmaw population were left wholly to themselves to defend what they had as best they could, "to prevent the British from becoming entirely the master of the interior of Acadia."[96]

Indigenous Raids and English Counterattacks

The Mi'kmaq took great risks in attacking English fortifications and settlements, even though their knowledge of the landscape, rivers, and forest trails was far superior to that of the British. By November 1749 both Halifax and Annapolis Royal had reinforced their defences and were in "fairly good shape" to deal with sporadic raids.[97] Warriors and their comrades in arms, the Acadian resistance fighters, consequently sought out vulnerable targets that they approached stealthily and attacked with cunning precision. On 30 September 1749 thirty warriors, mostly from Beaubassin, attacked six men cutting trees at a saw mill in Dartmouth. They killed four – two were scalped and two decapitated – and took one prisoner, while a sixth person escaped. Rangers afterwards caught three of the Mi'kmaq perpetrators and beheaded two and scalped one.[98] Cornwallis prevented any negotiations between the British and the Mi'kmaq, since he held the Mi'kmaw declaration to embody an all-out proclamation of war. Yet he also refused to declare war in response to the Mi'kmaw attacks, for to do so, he apprised the British Colonial Office in London, would "be in some sort to own them as a free people whereas they ought to be looked on as Rebels to His Majesty, or as so many Banditti Ruffians and treated accordingly."[99]

Instead, on 2 October 1749 Cornwallis issued a proclamation offering ten guineas for a Mi'kmaw scalp and the same amount for each Mi'kmaw person brought in alive. Any individual found aiding the Mi'kmaq, moreover, would be treated as if he were one.[100] The same month soldiers under the governor's orders razed the Mi'kmaw village of Chichimichecady, near Merliguèche (now Lunenburg) on Nova Scotia's South Shore, an act that impelled several sons of the Merliguèche head chief François Mius as well as Mius's nephews Paul Laurent and Antoine Mius to join the resistance fighters already stationed at Beaubassin.[101] The governor raised two additional companies of rangers, one commanded by Captain Francis Bartelo and the other by Captain William Clapham, to serve alongside John Gorham's men. Cornwallis also instigated what he hoped would prove a "divide and conquer" strategy by offering generous inducements to the Malecite to remain loyal to Britain. Major Ezekiel Gilman, a veteran of the 1745 fall of Louisbourg, accordingly was sent with Captain Clapham to the Saint John River region with one thousand bushels of corn and other provisions, with lesser amounts to be sent to Cape Sable in southwestern Nova Scotia.[102] The governor also laid plans to fortify the Chignecto region and again set a price on Le Loutre's head. Once there is "a good fort at Chignecto," he proclaimed, it "will be possible to harass & hunt them by Sea & Land" until they sue for peace or vacate the colony.[103]

Despite Cornwallis's bounty proclamation, Mi'kmaq from Chignecto, Eastern Abenaki warriors, and Acadian militia from Three Rivers participated in late November 1749 in an attack on the English at Fort Vieux Logis, in what later became known as the "Siege of Grand-Pré."[104] Their aim was to blockade the fort and free the Acadians to leave Minas and move to the Chignecto district. Cornwallis had been restricting the Acadians' movements to compel them to take an unconditional oath of allegiance to the British Crown. Le Loutre, who prompted the raid, wanted the Minas inhabitants to swell the population of his own projected settlement at Three Rivers, and to this end he threatened the Minas Acadians with Indigenous reprisals if they did not move to lands west of the Missiguash River. Not every Acadian family in the Minas district wanted to leave, but this did not stop Le Loutre from taking measures to ensure that Indigenous warriors would be on hand for whatever purposes he needed. In November he travelled to Piziquid and sent out a call for all "Micmacs, Mariches, Cinabres, Hurons, Abenaquis, Esquimaux" to come to the Minas district.[105] Those he could muster launched a second surprise raid on Fort Vieux Logis on 8 December 1749, at which time Lieutenant John Hamilton, an Acadian notary named Le Blanc and eighteen soldiers were taken hostage. The captives were led from Grand Pré to Baie Verte, then to Canada, where they were ransomed back to the British several years later.[106]

Cornwallis responded to the siege of Fort Vieux Logis by ordering John Gorham and his rangers to scour the countryside on either side of the newly constructed road from Halifax to Minas for Mi'kmaq intent on intercepting English land communications. He also seized the property of Acadians who had participated in the siege. Gorham left Fort Sackville on 18 March 1750 and reached the Acadian village of Five Houses on the St. Croix River two days later.[107] Not long after, a skirmish with a Mi'kmaw party deteriorated into a siege, in which Gorham and two other rangers were wounded. Their calls for assistance elicited reinforcements from Halifax which forced the Mi'kmaq to retreat. Gorham stationed his rangers in the parish church of L'Assomption at Piziquid, which he pulled down to construct Fort Edward, and urged his men to continue to search for and destroy any Mi'kmaq they encountered.[108]

Cornwallis next turned his attention to Chignecto. In April he dispatched Colonel Charles Lawrence and Captains John Rous and Joseph Gorham to roust La Corne from his earthenwork redoubt at Pointe-à-Beauséjour.[109] Indigenous scouts monitored Lawrence's progress up the Cumberland Basin. Warned of Lawrence's coming, Charles Boishébert, stationed at Nerepis on the upper Saint John River, sent Malecite warriors to join the Mi'kmaq at Beaubassin, where a large Indigenous workforce dug trenches in preparation for Lawrence's arrival. By the time the British party landed, the trenches and earthenworks were finished and Beaubassin was in flames.

Le Loutre had ordered the burning of the Acadian village, along with its ornate cathedral and its newly planted fields, to prevent any Acadian property from falling into English hands. (This would prove an ill-advised move, since it failed to deter the English and caused hunger and hardship among the local Acadians the following winter.) When confronted on 1 May 1750 by an unexpected hail of gunfire from Acadian and Indigenous resistance fighters ensconced in their trenches, Lawrence and his three hundred men withdrew to Minas.

The Chignecto Indigenous and Acadian fighters threw their full energies into resisting what they viewed as an English intrusion into their very heartland. They shot Captain Bartello, the leader of one of the ranger companies, and repulsed Joseph Gorham and thirty of his rangers when they descended on the village of Petitcodiac. By mid-September 1750 Lawrence was back at the isthmus with seven hundred men, a force that far outnumbered the Acadian and Indigenous contingent that briefly opposed it.[110] After gaining the ground, Lawrence razed the ancient Mi'kmaw village of Mejagouech, which had been located on high ground east of the Missiguash River, and began constructing Fort Lawrence.[111] In reprisal, Chignecto resistance fighters on 30 September launched another lightening raid on Dartmouth, which resulted in five settler deaths.[112]

Following the completion of the British fort, a brief and uneasy lull in hostilities occurred that allowed for an exchange of ideas across the lines. Captain How, a British commissary officer who spoke Mi'kmaq and in the past had acted as a negotiator with the Eastern Abenaki, received orders from Halifax to determine if the Chignecto Mi'kmaq might be amenable to making a peace treaty. At an informal meeting at Fort Lawrence, How broached the subject to Le Loutre, who replied that if the Mi'kmaq were to take the English offer seriously, they must be granted a "quarter of the Country to themselves, unsurrounded by any forts of ours."[113] The missionary added that his Shubenacadie mission had to be included in the tract. Their discussions did not progress far, however, for on 15 October 1750 a concealed sniper, rumoured to have been a Mi'kmaq from Miramichi named Étienne Bâtârd, shot and fatally wounded How.[114] Rumours circulated that it may have been because of How's ideological views or his participation in the French provisioning trade.[115] But whether How was killed over a religious matter, competition in the commercial sphere, or because his peacemaking efforts offended certain individuals, one thing was certain: the English would not instigate any more peacemaking negotiations at Chignecto. Henceforth all Mi'kmaw peacemaking parties had to make the long trek to Halifax.

Though How had not reported formally to the governor regarding the Mi'kmaq's demands, information on them filtered down to Cornwallis, for on 7 November 1750 the governor railed to the Colonial Office: "Their demands, or rather their Priests, are so preposterous and ridiculous that they can't be in earnest, such as abandoning Chignecto, not making a Fort, Giving them half the Country." Cornwallis ignored such appeals and chose to rely on strong-arm tactics to force the Mi'kmaq to capitulate to British wishes. "Since the establishment [of the fort] at Chignecto, no Indians have appeared in these parts," Cornwallis averred to his superiors, and "I flatter myself they will come to a Peace."[116]

Captain Charles Morris, who had been hired in 1748 by Governor Shirley of Massachusetts to survey the shores of the Cumberland Basin and since then had kept abreast of events in the area, was not so sure. He felt that since Le Loutre's return from France in 1749, the missionary had almost exclusively directed his energies to making the Three Rivers area a hive of anti-British partisan activity and Aboriginal resistance. To Morris, the answer lay in razing the Acadian settlements in the Petitcodiac region and replacing them with Protestant farming communities.[117] A fort mounted at Cape Maringuoin, he added, would prevent French supply vessels from accessing Shepody Bay and the Cumberland Basin, and so would starve the Acadians out.[118]

Le Loutre favoured the establishment of a neutral buffer zone, since it would prevent policies such as Morris's from being implemented. Without a British military presence at Chignecto he could have French supplies shipped to Baie Verte and then transported across the isthmus to the Petitcodiac region. He also hoped that the European boundary commission, which had been reviewing territorial matters in the Northeast since 1748, would settle on a line granting France clear title to lands surrounding the Cumberland Basin and west of the Missiguash River. He had spent over a year persuading, cajoling, and prodding Acadians from Grand Pré, Minas, Piziquid, and Beaubassin to move to Three Rivers.[119] The settlement project was a massive undertaking and difficult to initiate without copious financial assistance, since the carrying capacity of the un-dyked land around Three Rivers was low. Dykes had to be built to support large numbers of people.[120] As things stood, Acadian population numbers were already too high, since many of Le Loutre's Acadian congregants from his former missions at Shubenacadie and Cobequid had followed him to Chignecto. To support these newcomers, log and earthen dykes fitted with *aboiteaux*, or sluice gates, had to be built along the entire length of the tidemarsh to ensure that local fields yielded their full potential.

In early spring 1751 Le Loutre faced a host of problems. His burning of croplands at Beaubassin the previous year had caused a famine to arise during the cold and harsh winter of 1750–51. The British came to refer to the beleaguered inhabitants, rendered landless and propertyless by the missionary's impulsive actions of 1749 and 1750, as "Acadian refugees." Arrivals of French supply ships were unpredictable, and Le Loutre distrusted British provisioners. Just prior to the construction of Fort Lawence, an English merchant vessel trading at Majagouech reputedly had distributed contaminated foodstuffs to an assembly of Mi'kmaq, Malecite, and Eastern Abenaki, and upwards of two hundred Indigenous persons had died of food poisoning.[121] When French supplies failed to appear on time, the missionary had to divert food meant for the garrison, or slated for the Mi'kmaq, to feed the local inhabitants. Finally, certain French officials implicated him in How's death, though no charges were ever laid against him.[122] Yet despite these challenges, the missionary remained optimistic. He planned fundraising ventures to Quebec and France to acquire monies for his extensive *aboiteau* project, and intended to keep promoting attacks against English settlements until the English conceded to his boundary preferences simply to restore the peace.

Following a winter hiatus from hostilities, Acadian resistance fighters and Mi'kmaq warriors mustered at Joseph Broussard *dit* Beausoleil's call for another raid on Dartmouth. After crossing the Minas Basin and proceeding down the Shubenacadie River to the Dartmouth area, they set up camp at Eastern Passage, across the harbour from Halifax. On 26 March they slipped through the forest to kill fifteen Dartmouth settlers, and two days later took two prisoners. While popular notions often assume that Indigenous persons alone carried out these attacks, most raids were conjoint forays by Acadians and Indigenous warriors acting together, with a common goal of containing the British within a restricted geographical compass. Another surprise raid on Dartmouth, again led by Beausoleil, occurred at four in the morning on 13 May 1751, when sixty Mi'kmaq and thirty-two Acadians killed twenty settlers and took numerous hostages. Though the foray took place close to a blockhouse, the late hour and the swiftness and cunning employed in the attack must have mesmerized the inexperienced soldiers into inactivity, for the victims' cries elicited little response.[123] The May incident was the last major raid of 1751. A few soldiers were captured near Fort Lawrence in the fall of 1751, but no large parties later went against British settlements.[124]

The following spring and summer also were peaceful. Anxious to obtain money for dyking the tidal lands at Three Rivers, Le Loutre set out for Quebec in 1752 and left the responsibilities of his missionary charge to Abbé Jean Manach, a graduate of the Séminaire des Missions Étrangères who had arrived at Chignecto in 1751.[125] When Le Loutre found few backers for his settlement project in Quebec, he crossed the Atlantic Ocean to France, hoping to gain an audience with the French court. His expectations were more than fulfilled, for not only was he able to collect 150,000 livres for his *aboiteau* project, but Antoine Louis Rouillé, the French minister of marine, in January 1753 asked the missionary to collaborate with him in writing a report to be submitted to the international boundary commission.[126]

Le Loutre was away from Beaubassin from August 1752 until spring 1753. After the usual winter lull in fighting, it soon seemed in spring 1752 that the Mi'kmaq intended to halt hostilities.[127] No mustering of men occurred at Chignecto for raiding parties.[128] Partly this was because French incentives were lacking. The wily missionary was not on hand to award money or presents for British scalps, urge men on to militant action, and withhold or give absolution depending on whether or not the applicant was willing to fight the British.[129] The winter of 1751–52 proved harsh, and many at Chignecto suffered from famine, were war weary, and longed for security for their families.[130] As the ceasefire continued, the leaders of the Chignecto band adopted a wait-and-see attitude and tentatively began to discuss ways to extend peace overtures to the British while still protecting Mi'kmaw interests.

In the spring of 1751 the territorial dispute between the French and English Crowns prompted French fort building. Fort Beauséjour arose on the west bank of the Missisguash River, on the site of La Corne's former earthen redoubt. There were also two French satellite military installations; Fort Gaspereau at the mouth of the Gaspereau River running into Baye Verte (now the site of Port Elgin, New Brunswick) and Fort Mengoneche, built by Boishébert on the site of an Indigenous village on the lower Saint John River where the city of Saint John stands today. To avoid the formidable presences of forts Lawrence and Beauséjour, which glowered at each other from opposite banks of the Missaguash River, Joseph Argimault, the new Chignecto district chief, camped beside Fort Gaspereau near an old portage route cutting across the isthmus.[131]

A Ceasefire, a New Chignecto District Chief, and Preparations for Treaty Making

Philippe Argimault, who died around 1749, was succeeded as district chief of Chignecto by his son Joseph, who in 1752 was fifty-four years old. Joseph and his wife Marie had a large family, and Pierre, their eldest son, was now thirty-one.[132] Joseph was a moderate leader, skilled in diplomacy and capable of confronting thorny issues arising in the council forum. He presided over an encampment located on a point extending into Baie Verte, across from Fort Gaspereau,[133] where he was visited by French officials and traders from Louisbourg who used Baie Verte as a trans-shipment base for furs and livestock.[134]

Joseph Argimault advocated the establishment of a neutral Indigenous buffer zone between the north shore of the Shubenacadie River and Chignecto, and shared his views on this subject with other Mi'kmaw leaders throughout Nova Scotia. Traditional Algonquian power holders were expected to maintain a balance among forces seen and unseen, and the land and resource campaign Argimault upheld was an extension of his cosmology, which saw the material world animated by many and diverse sources of power, not just the two imperial contenders France and Britain. Argimault, already an esteemed religious figure and warrior, felt no need to enhance his political prowess by pursuing self-interested schemes. His band's chequered relationship in the past with French officialdom at Beaubassin vested them with a will to retain, as much as possible, their

autonomy from European interference of any kind. For Argimault, the Chignecto area was not only a headquarters for militancy but also a crucible for independent thought and action.

During 1751 and 1752 Chief Argimault met in council with two other district chiefs, Jean-Baptiste Cope of Shubenacadie and Musquodoboit and Claude Gagiosh (or Gisigash) of La Have.[135] Cope spoke French and on occasion wore European clothes, characteristics that caused speculation that he was the person who, dressed in an officer's regimentals "with his hair curled, powdered and in a bag," had lured How to his death.[136] Cope and Gagiosh, who were around Argimault's age, both recognized their political colleague as a member of a highly ranked family whose counsels carried weight.[137] Cope travelled regularly from the Atlantic coast to Cobequid, Chignecto, and Cape Breton to attend councils and as a courier of messages.[138] By 1752 he was to assume another role, that of treaty maker with the British. His actions, however, remained highly strategic, which suggests they were worked out in councils that drew upon the ideas and interests of the entire Mi'kmaw nation.[139]

Paul Laurent, a leader from La Have in his early thirties in 1752, by the mid 1750s became Argimault's assistant and possibly his confidante when some of Argimault's other supporters were left destitute by British desecration of their villages.[140] Paul was captured as a boy and sent to Boston, where he learned to speak English. After his return he lived at Chichimichecady, but when Cornwallis destroyed his village in 1749, he moved to La Have and then to Chignecto. While at Chignecto, Laurent confided to the interpreter Anthony Casteel that his father had been hanged in Boston, which suggests he was a son of Jacques Mius, convicted by the Court of Massachusetts of piracy and hanged on 2 November, 1726.[141] In 1752 Laurent joined the Mi'kmaw encampment near Fort Gaspereau and supported Joseph Argimault's land and resource claim. Two other La Have leaders accompanied him to Chignecto: his brother Antoine Mius[142] and Chief Jean-Baptiste Philippe Tecouramart, son of an eighteenth-century Cape Sable leader named Paul Tecouramart. Best known as "Jean-Baptiste of Cape Sable," Chief Tecouramart would become Joseph Argimault's closest companion.

Argimault and his political colleagues wanted to achieve greater prosperity and stability for their people during a time when the French and British Crowns were at peace. Living the closest to Halifax,

Cope likely had accompanied the first Mi'kmaw delegations that met with Cornwallis, since early in 1749 Abbè Maillard had noted the Shubenacadie band's peaceful demeanour towards the British.[143] Yet in 1752 Cope had to proceed cautiously, knowing his intent to extend peace overtures to the English would not bode well with the French. Jean-Louis, le Comte de Raymond, the new governor of Île Royale, regarded the disputed territory west of the Missisguash River as a hotbed of suspicious activity. Soon after his arrival at Louisbourg on 3 August 1751, Raymond sent René La Morue (or René Lamoureux), a chief at Antigonish, to pressure the Malecite along the Saint John River to renege on the treaty they signed in 1749 with the English.[144] He also acquired a report, dated July 1751, by Captain Louis La Vallière revealing that even Étienne Bâtârd covertly socialized with soldiers from Fort Lawrence and had received presents to induce him to make peace with the British. La Corne's successor as commandant at Fort Beauséjour, Pierre-Roch de Saint-Ours Deschaillons, had done little to prevent these exchanges, for Bâtârd and his companions had left Fort Lawrence unimpeded, carrying their presents with them.[145] But Raymond particularly worried about the steep reduction in the number of French supply ships reaching Beaubassin, owing to British embargos operating in Baie Verte and the Cumberland Basin. As far as the French were concerned, the Mi'kmaq had an insatiable desire for gifts, and the governor feared that the Chignecto band might use the diminishment of presents as an excuse to begin negotiating with the British.[146] Raymond had a right to be worried, though for different reasons, for the Chignecto group were devising a policy that required a degree of independence from the French.[147]

While the French complained about lack of presents, the British Board of Trade criticized Cornwallis's harsh treatment of the Mi'kmaw population. The Lords of Trade and Plantations in London cautioned Cornwallis that a peace with the Mi'kmaq would allow farming settlement to expand across the province, reduce costs, and enable the colony to be more self-supporting. They hinted further that Gorham's rangers might be disbanded, as a retrenchment measure.[148] A British regular officer, Captain George Scott, also suggested to the governor that if peace were secured, a government-regulated system of truck houses might be built near Mi'kmaw villages, which would be profitable for the British and foster permanent economic ties with the Aboriginal people. And, like Morris, Scott saw replacing the Acadians at Chignecto with Protestant settlers as a way of countering further Mi'kmaw hostilities.[149] But as long as Fort Beauséjour remained standing and the French retained their fortifications at Three Rivers, English settlement at Chignecto was stymied.[150]

Cornwallis heeded what the Board of Trade had said. On 17 July 1752 he convened his council to discuss ways of retracting his earlier harsh and intolerant policy towards the Mi'kmaw population.[151] Suggestions at this meeting included promising yearly gifts to win Mi'kmaq loyalty and acknowledge their prior claim to soil and, in keeping with Scott's proposal, constructing truckhouses to encourage Mi'kmaw trade with the English. The following day the governor issued a new slate of orders forbidding hostilities against Mi'kmaw groups that made peace with the British, a document that radically altered the scope and intent of the 1749 bounty proclamation.[152]

The Treaty of 1752

Governor Cornwallis and his council were probably the first to commence negotiations, although this is controversial. Anthony Casteel, a linguist and interpreter for the government in Halifax, informed Île Royale's governor, Jean-Louis Raymond, that Cope extended the first peacemaking overtures to Halifax in a "letter Cope sent himself to Governor Cornwallis."[153] In July 1752, Cornwallis asked a Halifax merchant and coffee house owner named William Piggott to seek out a Mi'kmaw chief amenable to opening negotiations with the British while Piggott was visiting Port Toulouse.[154] This Indigenous leader, it was hoped, would sign a treaty and then initiate a cumulative peacemaking process, whereby one chief after another would come to Halifax and place their marks on the treaty parchment.[155]

Piggott was going to Cape Breton anyway, to collect on a debt owed him by Joseph Maurice, an Acadian merchant from Chignecto, so Cornwallis loaded his trading vessel with government presents for the purposes of his new peacemaking mission.[156] Piggott likely met Cope at the annual St. Anne's Day celebrations at Port Toulouse, and urged the chief to come to Halifax. After that, Piggott encountered a steady stream of problems. He was sailing in French waters off Port Toulouse when he was suddenly apprehended by a Mi'kmaw party, who seized his vessel, doubtless confiscated the presents in its hold, and sailed to Petit de Grat on Île Madam to collect a ransom for their prize from the French. Peregrine Thomas Hopson, who succeeded Cornwallis as governor of Nova Scotia on 3 August 1752, learned of Piggott's difficulties from the Comte de Raymond.[157] Though Raymond did not demand a ransom for the release of Piggott's boat, difficulties arose when Piggott tried to retrieve the vessel from the Mi'kmaq. So, in addition to extracting the monies owed him by Maurice, which proved taxing enough, he now had to seek alternative conveyance back to Halifax. Cope later boasted to the interpreter Casteel that he gained control of "Picket's vessel and went to Chebuctoe."[158]

Whether Cope made his way south along the Atlantic coast in Piggott's vessel or not, the chief arrived in Halifax in early September and set up camp on the harbour side of a large knoll, which during the American Revolutionary War would become the site of Fort Needham. For several weeks he had been consulting with other chiefs in council before acting on the English offer.[159] Now feeling some degree of confidence in the support of his peers, Cope attended a meeting with Hopson and his council on 14 September. In response to a question concerning what measures might prompt the Mi'kmaq to agree to a peace, he emphasized that the Mi'kmaq must be paid for the lands occupied by the British. This answer echoed the northeastern Algonquian mandate that compensation must be extended to an Indigenous power holder for the use of land and resources that lay under his territorial aegis. Cope at this time was advocating establishment of a buffer zone between French and British territories that would remain under Indigenous control. Argimault and Paul Laurent, as we have seen, would propose such a course of action later, in 1754 and 1755. The governor and council at Halifax, by contrast, wanted to avoid the confusion and pitfalls that officially unauthorized sales of land between settlers and the Eastern Abenaki had caused the government of Massachusetts.[160]

On 16 September, the chief further explained that the Mi'kmaq wanted to exercise their own jurisdictional protocols in their own territory, while the British could do the same in their domain, provided they first "paid" for the privilege. Since the *Sipekne'katik* district leader's territorial prerogatives traditionally encompassed the Chebucto peninsula, Cope also sought to define a firm geographical boundary between the two jurisdictions, an issue being

mulled over, as he spoke, within Indigenous councils throughout the Northeast. While no treaty was signed in September, before Cope left Halifax he was promised unmolested occupation of his hunting and fishing grounds, a truckhouse on the Shubenacadie River, annual presents for as long as he remained a friend of the English, a golden belt, a laced hat, and another laced hat for his son Joseph. Yet no progress had been made towards identifying a boundary between Mi'kmaq and British domains, and likely because of this, Cope proved slow in returning to Halifax.[161]

First, he had to consult with the other leaders. Joseph Argimault and the chiefs assembled at Baie Verte had been monitoring Cope's progress – or rather, lack of it – towards establishing boundaries between Mi'kmaw and English territorial jurisdictions. Had Cope succeeded in getting the British to recognize the Shubenacadie River as the line of demarcation between his territories to the north and British lands to the south, then Argimault and his associates could have moved on to the next phase of their plan: negotiating with the British for a neutral buffer zone having the Shubenacadie River as its southern boundary. That Cope could not persuade the English to address Mi'kmaw boundary aspirations was a disappointment, but Argimault and his associates still hoped that Cope could inject enough distinctly Indigenous diplomatic devices into the negotiating process to serve as useful precedents for the Mi'kmaw constituency in the future.

With this new mandate from his peers, Cope arrived back in Halifax in early November. He came alone, not an unusual practice for a chief acting on behalf of an Indigenous political vanguard on a controversial issue. For three weeks he ruminated over the possible consequences of his actions before placing his sole signature on the treaty document handed him on 22 November 1752. After promising to bring other chiefs to the negotiating table, he directed Piggott to go with the treaty to Indian Harbour, near Liscomb, to meet with three of his principal men, Andrew (or André) Handley Martin, Gabriel Martin, and François Jeremy.[162] Many of Cope's band had left for their hunting territories, but Piggott found the two Martins and Jeremy waiting for him on the shore. They accompanied the merchant to Halifax and, during an elaborate ceremony at Fort Needham Hill presided over by the governor and his council, placed their marks after Cope's signature on the treaty parchment.[163] A hatchet and sword afterwards were ritually buried near Cope's camp overlooking the Narrows.[164] Piggott then returned the three men to Beaver Harbour, just east of modern-day Sheet Harbour, where they left for their hunting grounds.[165]

The pact, dated 22 November 1752, was essentially the same treaty the Mi'kmaq had signed at Annapolis Royal in 1726, though with a few significant changes. It omitted any mention of settlements "lawfully to be made,"[166] but like the earlier agreement, it offered rewards to Aboriginal persons who rescued shipwrecked sailors, promised satisfaction in British courts of law if disputes arose or if the Mi'kmaq were molested in any way "by His Majesty's subjects," and claimed to respect Mi'kmaw rights to hunt and fish, though no mention was made where such practices would continue. Emphasis was placed on Cope and his men persuading other chiefs to sign treaty while denouncing those who refused to come to Halifax. Provisions also were drawn up for a truckhouse to be built at Shubenacadie; the delivery of six months of foodstuffs to Cope's group at Jeddore, east of Halifax; and presents to be distributed every 1 October for as long as the Mi'kmaq remained in friendship with the British.[167] Hopson had elaborate broadsheets printed in English and French and bearing the British royal coat of arms posted throughout the colony, giving the terms of the treaty, and warning British subjects to "forbear all acts of Hostilities against the aforesaid Major Jean-Baptiste Cope" and his group.[168] Hearing of the pact and seeing the broadsheets, New Englanders "jubilantly announced the treaty in their newspapers."[169]

The Lords of Trade and Plantations in London also announced their pleasure at hearing of the treaty's signing, but added that they trusted other Mi'kmaw bands "would soon follow their Example," since one treaty alone would "be forever ineffectual untill [sic] a General Peace is made." Once this occurred a new era of colonial prosperity would begin; settlers would move freely throughout the province, farms would arise on fertile soil, fisheries would expand, colonial deficits would be reduced, and trade would increase. Mi'kmaw commerce would become an appendage of the colonial budget. Hopson's instructions were to keep an exact account of what trade is "carried with the Indians you are already at peace with, that we may be the better able to judge of the advantage to be derived to the publick [sic] from it."[170]

During the winter of 1752–53 Cope shouldered a heavy burden. Hopson had him promise that he would bring other leaders to Halifax within a month of the treaty signing. Yet because he had failed in his mission to get the English to recognize the existence of geographical boundaries, a matter of concern to the entire Mi'kmaw community, many chiefs refused to follow him. By the beginning of December no Mi'kmaq had appeared in Halifax, and Hopson was getting worried. On 6 December 1752 he cautioned the Lords of Trade and Plantations that Cope was leader of a band of ninety individuals, and while the Mi'kmaw leader promised to "bring over the rest," this eventuality was "more to be hoped for than trusted to."[171] Unbeknownst to Hopson, Cope was doing his best to bring leaders in. In his travels about the province the Shubenacadie leader found other chiefs interested in learning whether some sort of diplomatic middle ground might accrue from treaty making with the British. Most agreed it would be good to have a forum in Halifax sympathetic to Mi'kmaw interests, where they might discuss land boundaries and protections for Indigenous persons and their resources. Since the headquarters of the Mi'kmaw land and resource rights campaign lay at Chignecto, Cope, his son Joseph Cope, and Claude Gagiosh approached Joseph Argimault at Baie Verte. Always cautious, and not yet sure of the tack he would take before the executive council, Argimault only reluctantly agreed to join the other two in late December. An accident that befell him en route gave him an excuse not to proceed farther. On 4 January Hopson had to apprise the Lords of Trade and Plantations that Cope and his party had left the isthmus with the Chignecto chief, who "on his way ... burnt his arm and this day returned."[172] Cope next visited bands along the Atlantic coast as far south as Cape Sable, an arduous and time-consuming task: travelling on foot in winter was difficult, and once the chief arrived at his destination he had to initiate council discussions, listen to speeches, and record results.

Perfidious Agents of Albion

Despite Cope's hard work, a few high-ranking British officials viewed his peacemaking efforts with scepticism. The executive council's registrar, John Salusbury, branded the pact he had signed as "a foolish bit of formality."[173] By contrast, Governor Hopson and Charles Morris (1711–81), the latter of whom was at the time surveying the Lunenburg settlement, remained tentatively hopeful.[174] Over the winter, Morris claimed, "chiefs of every tribe in the Peninsula … sent in messages of friendship."[175] But suddenly, in the early spring while many Mi'kmaq were still on their hunting territories in the interior, all such missives stopped.

Louisbourg officialdom naturally evinced deep concern over Cope's activities. Jacques Prévost de la Croix, the financial commissary at Louisbourg, directed a steady stream of letters on the subject to Antoine-Louis Rouillé, the French minister of marine. As early as 10 September 1752, Prévost branded Cope's band as "tous mauvais subjets" (all bad subjects).[176] Yet he dismissed the notion that the chief's actions posed a threat to France's control over its Indigenous militia corps, since he felt Cope's interests focused almost exclusively on the attainment of English presents.[177] The treaty, he held, would founder for lack of widespread Mi'kmaw support. Raymond, more removed from the French-Aboriginal transactional forum than Prévost, since the commissary was responsible for dispensing annual gifts to the Indigenous population, echoed the commissary's words. Cope, the French governor proclaimed, was "un ivrogne et mauvais sujet" (an unruly and bad subject).[178] Rouillé meanwhile tried to lessen Raymond's fears by arguing thatany Mi'kmaw leanings towards the British were a temporary aberration, stemming from the unpredictability of French gift distributions.

In the spring, Prévost sent Rouillé three more letters containing news, gleaned from Mi'kmaw sources, of shocking events that had occurred in February and April along Nova Scotia's Eastern Shore. Two Cape Sable men had been murdered, an incident the local Indigenous population attributed to a party of Englishmen. Since the Mi'kmaw accounts were confusing and contradictory with regard to details, the best Rouillé could determine was that an English schooner crew, after raiding stores the government had given to the Mi'kmaq of Jeddore, proceeded east along the coast, killed the Cape Sable couple in a small bay, and then accidently ran their vessel aground. Two of the schooner's four-man crew died in the shipwreck or were killed by the Mi'kmaq. Prévost suspected that the Mi'kmaq were not involved in the killings, although when asked, his Indigenous informants refused to admit to a French official that some of their nation might have assisted Englishmen. The schooner's hold contained little

except apples and onions, undoubtedly stolen from the band at Jeddore. Hunters from Cape Breton had stumbled on the bodies of Joseph, a Cape Sable man, and his pregnant wife that were so badly hacked they were identifiable only by the dagger and tobacco pouch Joseph wore. Six more Mi'kmaw individuals were killed at Mocodome, now Country Harbour, including a mother and child.[179]

These revelations were to take on an even more sinister tone. By mid-April the executive council in Halifax heard from French sources that four Englishmen in early February went to Jeddore where they robbed Cope's band of forty barrels of provisions. The four then killed two Mi'kmaw persons near Liscomb and mutilated their bodies, atrocities that the perpetrators clearly intended as a hate crime, to compel the Mi'kmaq to break off peaceful relations with the British. Running into heavy fog and winds, their vessel foundered on the beach at Mocodome, now Country Harbour, Guysborough County, near where Cope's principal men had waited for Piggott the previous November. Two of the Englishmen died in the shipwreck, while the others were rescued by members of a Mi'kmaw camp consisting of four adult men and a woman and her infant.[180] The Englishmen, on regaining their strength, murdered and scalped the Mi'kmaq, beginning with the woman and child, stole their canoe, and paddled to Halifax.[181]

On 15 April 1753 Captain John Connor and James Grace, carrying six Mi'kmaw scalps, arrived in Halifax in a bark canoe. Connor, well known around Halifax as "the one-eyed bargemen," for years had operated a ferry across Halifax Harbour's narrows. The two men signed a deposition under oath stating that their schooner, *Dunk*, and its four-man crew, composed of Connor, Grace, Michael Haggerty, and John Poor, had been captured by Mi'kmaq from the Antigonish area. Four Mi'kmaq men, while standing on a point of land between Country Harbour and Torbay, had beckoned to them. In response, they steered towards shore and were approached by nine Mi'kmaq in two canoes who boarded their vessel, dispatched Haggerty and Poor by blows to the head, ran the schooner aground, and took Connor and Grace inland, where the two waited seven weeks for an opportunity to escape. Connor held that the attack on their vessel occurred west of Torbay on 21 February. On 8 April, in an effort to regain their liberty, they killed a Mi'kmaw woman, her child, and four Mi'kmaw men before making their escape in a canoe.[182]

When Charles Morris, who in addition to being a surveyor was a justice of the Inferior Court of Common Pleas for Halifax, asked Connor and Grace to state the object of their voyage down the Eastern Shore so early in February, they replied ingeniously that they "had been putting into various inlets." The vagueness of this reply disturbed Morris. He also felt it odd that on 8 April the Mi'kmaw men left Connor and Grace alone with a Mi'kmaw mother and her child at a camp where there were guns, ammunition, and axes.[183] Connor and Grace admitted they killed the woman and child first, and then the men on their return.

Additional evidence suggested that the Englishmen were more likely perpetrators than victims. Early in March, Joseph Cope arrived in Halifax and asked for a government vessel to visit Jeddore and remove the last vestiges of the government's gift of provisions. Little was left of the foodstuffs, he maintained, because his people had been robbed of forty barrels of supplies by the crew of a ship whose description matched that of the schooner *Dunk*. Anthony Casteel, the government's interpreter and coastal pilot, also met a Mi'kmaq who claimed that "the English began [hostilities] first; that they [the Mi'kmaq] had done no manner of harm for a long time and that the English had been killing people."[184] Morris could not shake the suspicion that Connor and Grace had cold-bloodedly killed their Mi'kmaw victims, brought their scalps back to Halifax – perhaps hoping for a scalp payment – and then devised a fanciful tale about how they had suffered a Mi'kmaw attack at Mocodome.[185] John Connor had lost his wife in one of the Mi'kmaw raids on Dartmouth and was still bitter enough to exact revenge, so no one asked for a more thorough investigation, and no charges were laid. Morris at least saw that, under the terms of an order-in-council, Connor and Grace would be required to "give security to answer any charges the Indians might possibly prefer [*sic*, proffer]."[186] Connor returned to being Halifax's ferryman, and on his death in 1757 was interred under a gravestone bearing his name in what is now the Old Burying Ground, at the corner of Barrington Street and Spring Garden Road.

The Mi'kmaq, however, did not forget what had transpired, nor did they intend to let the matter drop. After Hopson agreed to Joseph Cope's request to have barrels of provisions removed from Isidore (Jeddore) on 16 May, Joseph Cope, François Jeremy, and

another Mi'kmaw man named Bernard joined Anthony Casteel, the interpreter, aboard a sloop crewed by eight government employees under the command of Captain Bannerman.[187] Jeddore was only a day's sail from Halifax and, as soon as the vessel arrived its crew began loading into its hold barrels that the Mi'kmaq wanted returned to Halifax. The loading was continuing the next day, 17 May, when Anthony Casteel, owing to his familiarity with the Mi'kmaw language, realized something was terribly wrong. Jean-Baptiste Cope took him aside and emphasized the enormity of the crime that the earlier schooner captain and his men had perpetrated against his people, who had sincerely desired peace. Even as they spoke, relatives of the Cape Sable couple whose bodies were found in the early spring, and Cape Breton Mi'kmaq with kin ties to the six persons killed at Mocodome, were sitting in a council at Jeddore presided over by Paul Laurent and Étienne Bâtârd (whom Casteel erroneously referred to as "Anthony Bâtârd") trying to determine what should be done. The bereaved thirsted for revenge and blamed Cope for the fate that befell their relatives. The British were duplicitous, they maintained; Cope had been unwise to trust them. It was not enough that the Englishmen had broken their promise to protect the Mi'kmaq against molestation. An innocent babe, who had not yet been christened, had been brutally murdered by settlers, while the Halifax jurisprudence system favoured the word of the men who had committed the crime. Chief Cope's peacemaking with the British at Halifax, furthermore, elicited sharp censure from the governor of Île Royale and brought Cope into conflict with the French clergy.[188] Cope confided to Castell that he was experiencing mental torment, since he doubted the missionaries would grant him absolution to save his soul, and there were some chiefs who challenged his leadership and wished his death. He intimated he wanted Casteel to take him to Halifax and, while there, write a letter to the English governor asking for a priest to visit him. "[A]fter he had made confession," he declared, "his people could do to him as they would, he would not be afraid."[189]

After the government sloop had ridden at anchor for two days, it became blatantly clear to Casteel that he and his companions would be in dire straits if they did not leave.[190] When he tried to warn the others, however, a crew member named Samuel Cleaveland ignored him. Instead, displaying an avaricious streak, Cleaveland, without consulting the Mi'kmaq, on 19 May revisited the Mi'kmaq's cache of supplies at the head of Jeddore and collected several barrels of peas for his pigs in Halifax. The other crew members waited two days for Cleaveland to return to their vessel, which by this time was wedged in the narrow upper end of Jeddore Harbour. On the second day, 21 May, several canoes approached carrying Mi'kmaq individuals; the Mi'kmaq boarded the vessel, apprehended the crew, and carried them to shore. At West Jeddore, all the vessel's men were killed and scalped, except for Casteel. Captain Bannerman was the first to be dispatched, so the Mi'kmaq may have thought he and Cleaveland meant to rob them. The crew members' scalps were distributed to the bereaved to assuage their sorrow for their losses, after which the Mi'kmaq burned the government sloop.[191]

When asked about his Christian beliefs, Casteel replied to the Mi'kmaq that he was a French Roman Catholic, and to prove his sincerity kissed a cross suspended on a chain about the neck of one of the chiefs.[192] He then was placed under the guard and protection of a man he simply referred to as "my master."[193] Casteel travelled with the Mi'kmaq to Cobequid, where Jean-Baptiste Cope had cached his copy of the treaty with an Acadian family. He later was handed the treaty document and told to read it out loud to the others in the group, but while he was reading one man sitting near him suddenly snatched the document out of his hand and threw it in the fire.[194]

Casteel was embroiled in a second disconcerting incident on 12 June, when Paul Laurent told him he would pay his ransom, kill him, and take his scalp, in order to avenge the death of his father, who had been hanged in Boston years before.[195] Jacques Maurice, the brother of Joseph Maurice with whom Piggott had dealings, diffused this potentially violent situation by offering Casteel's master money, so the interpreter could be sent immediately to Louisbourg. As soon as he arrived at the fortress, Le Loutre, who had arrived back from France on the *Bizarre* at the beginning of May and was resting at Louisbourg before returning to Beaubassin, met and grilled him about matters of major concern to the Mi'kmaq, especially the settlement of Merliguèche, or Lunenburg, by foreign Protestants.[196] According to the missionary, neither the Mi'kmaq nor the Acadians could continue be tossed back and forth between two contending imperial powers, but needed to have leaders strong enough to be able to establish permanent homelands in the

Northeast for both groups. He further stressed that no peace pact would be binding unless it included the council at Chignecto, presided over by Chief Joseph Argimault. If the British really wanted peace, Cornwallis – whom the missionary denounced as the "scum of the earth" – should have waited until Le Loutre returned from France and then have written to him for advice on how to proceed.[197] The peacemaking proceedings had gone awry since the British governor had unwisely begun negotiations with Cope, whom the missionary deemed "the tail of one of the least of the tribes."[198]

Charles Morris in Halifax wondered if the treaty of 1752 would be completely undone by the circumstances surrounding the murders of the Mi'kmaw persons at Mocodome. He believed the Mi'kmaq "would have signed articles of peace this spring," he wrote to Cornwallis in England, "if this accident [involving the deaths at Mocodome] does not prevent them."[199] Yet two leaders from southwestern Nova Scotia, Claude Gagiosh of La Have and Jean-Baptiste Thoma of Panuke Lake, near Windsor, remained unfazed in their determination to make peace with the English. Both leaders' bands had suffered economically from British trade embargos along the Atlantic coast, though Thoma in particular had retained friendly relations with the English at Annapolis Royal since the 1720s. In April 1753 Gagiosh, styling himself "the governor of Lahéve," went to Halifax and placed his mark on a document similar to the one Cope had signed the preceding November.[200] Not long after, Baptiste Thoma and François Jean de Perisse, representing the intentions of Chief François Shagwaough (or Chegua) of Cape Sable, also asked for peacemaking negotiations to commence. In consequence, Colonel Patrick Sutherland, who at the time was overseeing the settlement of Lunenburg, sent a schooner down to Cape Sable to bring the two leaders up to Halifax.

Once in Halifax, Thoma and de Perisse declared before the executive council on 16 November that, as they had never joined in raids on any British settlements, the French denied their band supplies and presents. Worse, some Mi'kmaq along the Eastern Shore had "renewed hostilities by killing some of your people," which so tarnished their own reputation that they could no longer trade with the English. Meanwhile, British embargos on Indigenous commerce between Cape Sable and the Saint John River Valley had reduced them "to great extremes for want of both provisions and clothing." They asked for an "authentic written instrument" that they might show to traders from Halifax and other English subjects, if need arose. Although the members of the executive council did not specifically mention furnishing a "written instrument," they gave the Mi'kmaw leaders provisions, blankets, ammunition, tobacco, and headwear indicative of their rank. They also expressed the hope that the entire Mi'kmaw nation "might at length be convinced that it would be more for their interest to be our friends than enemies."[201]

Despite the peace treaty signed with Gagiosh at La Have, the British failed to consult the leaders of the Indigenous population before locating Germanic settlers at Merliguèche. Though Gagiosh's people remained peaceful, this was not true for others, particularly members of the *métis* Mius and Labrador families.[202] Raids on the Lunenburg settlers were initiated by Acadians and *métis* who were angry at having been displaced by the English from their lands at Merliguèche.Only later did reinforcements come from Chignecto and the Saint John's River area. The French missionaries were only tangentially involved and poorly informed. Le Loutre had to approach Casteel about the situation in Lunenburg County, since in France neither he nor Rouillé could attain a clear picture of what was transpiring along Nova Scotia's South Shore.[203] Rather than being cast adrift in a sea of turbulent and unsettling events fostered by French and British machinations, the Mi'kmaq were beginning to be more autonomous in their thoughts and actions. While they welcomed assistance from Acadian resistance fighters bent on containing British expansionism, chiefs of Chignecto sought new ways of structuring the field of Mi'kmaw relations with both the French and British authorities.[204]

Charles Lawrence, who succeeded Hopson as governor of Nova Scotia in November 1753, felt he could subdue the Mi'kmaq and Acadians. By promoting British settlement throughout the countryside, he would overwhelm the Indigenous population through sheer numbers. Blockhouses would be built near the new settlements and along major transportation routes. The first targets for settlement would be east of Halifax, La Have on the South Shore, Tatamagouche on the Northumberland Strait, and Cobequid, all sites frequented by Acadians and Mi'kmaq. Since Chignecto was the mustering ground for attacks on Lunenburg, he also vowed to take stern measures against Acadian partisans from Three Rivers and fill their area with settlers.[205] In this he was supported by Charles Morris, George Scott, and the Lords of Trade and Plantations. All three abhorred raids, which were expensive to counter, retarded settlement, and hindered resource development. In March 1754 the Board of Trade called for a census to be taken of Mi'kmaw numbers, the locations of their villages, their sources of provisions, and their "ways of passage, in order to mount a stern offensive against them."[206]

Armed with his instructions from London, Lawrence, without any consultation with the local Mi'kmaq, founded a new settlement east of Halifax, which the twenty families to whom the governor gave grants named "Lawrencetown."[207] As a means to overwhelm the Mi'kmaq and the French it proved a dismal failure, for despite the presence of a blockhouse, a large party of Acadians and Mi'kmaq from Chignecto descended on Lawrencetown in May 1754 led by Joseph Broussard *dit* Beausoleil, who personally killed and scalped four settlers and two soldiers. In August the governor had to withdraw what settlers remained to Halifax to protect them from further forays.[208] Mi'kmaq and Acadian resistance fighters continued to hem in British expansion from 1754 to 1760, during which time any spirit of conciliation within the local English community, or among the Lords of Trade and Plantations in London, fell to a very low ebb.

Peacemaking Activities at Chignecto, 1754–1755

In the early spring of 1754 there were between fifty-seven and sixty warriors camping at the mouth of the Gaspereau River. When one includes women and children, this suggests an Indigenous population at Chignecto of close to 350 persons.[209] Many of the visitors present were from southwestern Nova Scotia. As long as the French and British Crowns were at peace, Mi'kmaw leaders wanted to negotiate a settlement focusing on the English agreeing to acknowledge and respect their lands, resources, and trading rights. When Le Loutre agreed to their wishes for a second ceasefire, Joseph Argimault also persuaded the missionary to help with his campaign to get the British to set aside a vast tract of land north of the Shubenacadie River for the Mi'kmaq. Inspired by their district chief's courage and forthrightness, and anticipating that their leader's aspirations might actually become a reality, the assemblage at Chignecto evinced considerable hope for the future.

Argimault held that all European forts north of the Shubenacadie River should be razed and the countryside between Halifax and Chignecto be recognized as neutral territory by both French and British. The Mi'kmaq living on this tract could then choose their own markets for their furs, feathers, sea mammal oil, and wooden manufactures. Argimault's scheme owed much to a bid, raised in 1720 in the Massachusetts Council, which called for a neutral territory north of the Kennebec River.[210] Although such a neutral buffer zone had never been realized by the French and British in the Northeast, notions associated with the Massachusett's council proposal percolated northward, likely carried by representatives of the Eastern Wabanaki Confederacy, to be resuscitated at Chignecto. In the Chignecto context, the ideas were shaped into a Mi'kmaw-directed campaign focusing on the attainment of a tract to be held exclusively under Mi'kmaw territorial jurisdiction.

Though Le Loutre had to countenance the Mi'kmaq's plan if he were to continue to hold their esteem, he also genuinely felt that a neutral buffer zone would serve the ends of his cherished Acadian settlement at Three Rivers by providing a hedge against British expansion into the Chignecto district. In May 1754 Le Loutre contacted Captain John Hamilton, the same man who had been captured by the Mi'kmaq in November 1749 at Fort Vieux Logis in Grand Pré and taken to Canada, where Le Loutre secured his ransom. Upon his release, Hamilton married Mary Handfield, the daughter of Captain John Handfield, his commanding officer at Annapolis Royal, and rose in military rank and in the estimation of British colonial society both at Annapolis Royal and Halifax. While in captivity, Hamilton grew to appreciate many facets of Mi'kmaw culture – and he was not the only British official at the time to do so. Michael Francklin, Nova Scotia's lieutenant governor from 1766 to 1776 and afterwards superintendent of Indian Affairs during the American Revolution, wanted to learn as much as he could about Mi'kmaw language and culture while he was held captive by Mi'kmaq at Chignecto and Gaspé from late summer 1754 to early winter 1755.[211]

Hamilton realized that Le Loutre, for all his controlling ways, was genuinely interested in helping the Mi'kmaq, so he agreed to open up avenues of communication with Annapolis Royal and Beaubassin.[212] At the end of May he also wrote Governor Lawrence,

stating that the Mi'kmaq at Chignecto would like to tender a peace agreement. While this letter has not been preserved, one can get an idea of the letter's contents by the response it elicited from Captain William Cotterell, the provincial secretary. After Lawrence shared Hamilton's letter with Cotterell, Cotterell set out on 3 June to dissuade Hamilton from having any further dealings with Le Loutre. The missionary, Cotterell cautioned, duped people into thinking he was sincere and well intentioned. The scheme the missionary attributed to the Mi'kmaq was probably only part of a ploy to draw in unsuspecting Englishmen and work his "iniquity and mischief." With regard to that plan alone, Cotterell continued, "I can for my own part assure you, that he made the very same proposal almost *verbatim*, that you have now transmitted, to captain How and me at Chignecto about three days before he caused that horrible treachery to be perpetrated against poor How, who was drawn into it under a pretense of conferring with Le Loutre upon this very subject."[213]

In July of 1754 Hamilton was posted to Fort Lawrence, commanded by Captain George Scott. At Chignecto, Hamilton and Le Loutre continued their discussions face to face. Since the Mi'kmaq promised not to attack the English at Fort Lawrence (and the most militant of the Acadia resistance fighters were away harassing Lawrencetown), Hamilton safely crossed the Missiguash River by the Buot Bridge to visit Le Loutre at Fort Beauséjour. One evening he and Le Loutre even shared a dinner prepared by the missionary. At Fort Beauséjour, the two fleshed out a second letter for Hamilton to send to Lawrence.[214] On receiving it, Lawrence instructed Hamilton to inform his commanding officer, Scott, to tell any chiefs who wished to extend peace overtures to the British that they must go to Halifax. The governor also expected Hamilton to keep on meeting with Le Loutre, "not to assume [an] authority to negotiate, but if anything material is said, to report it to his commanding officer."[215]

The Mi'kmaq at Chignecto knew they needed Le Loutre to help them define the vast tract in the northeastern part of the province that would serve as a homeland for both them and the Acadian refugees. It would be a neutral reserve for all who were disinherited from their lands by British expansionism, open to Mi'kmaq, *métis*, and Acadians in southwestern Nova Scotia as well as those who lived north of the Shubenacadie River. No one knew this better than Thomas Pichon, a French official who worked for the French at Chignecto and also acted as an intelligent and witty spy for the British.[216] At times Pichon also wrote letters for Le Loutre, whom he regarded as a cunning manipulator of French colonial policy and the tenets of the Roman Catholic faith. In his letters to Captain Scott and, later, Captain John Hussey, who succeeded Scott as commanding officer at Fort Lawrence in July, Pichon referred to Le Loutre as "Moses," owing to the missionary's penchant to view himself as leading Acadian refugees to a "promised land" west of the Missiguash River. The Mi'kmaq were to be his aides in this quest. Yet Pichon did not believe the Mi'kmaq were simple dupes of the missionary. "Their laws and customs are imprinted upon their hearts, and always flow from the dictates of good sense," he stressed. "[T]hey will never confide in a person for whom they have not a value."[217]

Le Loutre had given up waiting for the verdict on the submission he and Antoine-Louis Rouillé had sent in 1753 to the international boundary commission, which was still embroiled in trying to define the limits of Acadia.[218] Direct negotiation with the British now seemed to him to be the only way to secure a buffer zone between Three Rivers and Halifax. Owing to Hamilton's efforts, an opportunity soon presented itself. On 17 August Captain Hussey, in keeping with instructions from Lawrence, wrote asking Le Loutre to accompany a delegation of Mi'kmaw chiefs to Halifax and aid the leaders in presenting their claims. The commander would prepare passports of safe conveyance for them all. Yet Le Loutre delayed in responding. In a long letter written in French on 27 August 1754, he apologized for his tardiness, stating that religious duties had intervened and that he had had to speak with Joseph Argimault. The chief had given him a list of six propositions to convey to the English governor. First, however, the Indigenous council had delegated Joseph Argimault and Paul Laurent to consult with Hussey, and the British commander had agreed to meet with them. On the appointed day, the chiefs convened at Fort Beauséjour, crossed over to the British side of the river with Le Loutre in a small canoe, and then waited for Hussey, who was late appearing. When Hussey finally arrived, he refused to step down from his wagon and greet the chiefs, who were offended by his haughty behaviour. The commander emphasized to his Mi'kmaw audience, standing below him, that he could not act as a go-between with Halifax with regard to any Aboriginal

land and resource scheme, but that the chiefs would have to make their concerns known directly to the governor and council in Halifax.[219]

Le Loutre continued that Hussey had promised to carry a letter to the governor for him, and while the missionary was in the process of writing it, Jean-Baptiste Cope appeared at his door. Cope stated that on 8 August an English surveying team of over one hundred men under the command of Captain Mathew Floyer had cut through the woods past Le Loutre's former mass house at Shubenacadie, and continued on to Cobequid.[220] Despite the ceasefire, the missionary warned, as chief of the Shubenacadie district Cope would not tolerate flagrant territorial trespasses. Floyer and his men had not consulted with the Mi'kmaq before they left the main route of communication. If they did that again they would be attacked, which would be an unfortunate occurrence at a time when the Chignecto Mi'kmaq were trying to secure a durable peace. Le Loutre further chastised Lawrence for regarding any Acadian refugees who previously took oaths of allegiance to the British Crown as criminals if they ever shouldered arms against Britain. Cope took responsibility for controlling the movements of the Acadian refugees.[221] The previous Sunday after high mass at Fort Beauséjour, the Shubenacadie district chief, another French-speaking Mi'kmaw man,[222] and a Malecite, or Wolastoqiyik, named Toubik from Meductic had stood up and threatened the Acadian refugees that if they ever ventured back across the Missiguash, they would be treated as enemies by the Indigenous population.[223]

Le Loutre explained that Argimault had revealed the deliberations of a Mi'kmaw council held that very day – Monday, 27 September – and had made the missionary promise to write them down and convey them to Halifax. There were six propositions. First, Argimault and his council resolved not to carry out any further acts of hostility until the British governor and his council replied to their proposals. Hoping to exert as much pressure as possible on British officialdom, the missionary added that the Mi'kmaw fully expected a respectful, positive answer in writing from Halifax. Second, they agreed to allow British subjects to travel the main roads across the province. Third and most important, they wanted to have the British establishment acknowledge their right to a sizable territory in northeastern Nova Scotia that would include the site of their mission at Shubenacadie.

Fourth, the Mi'kmaw council had decided on the exact extent of this tract, which would extend

> south of Baye Verte, taking in Fort Lawrence and the land around it as far as the entrance to Minas, and from the entrance to Minas into Cobequit as far as and including Chigabenakady, and from this last place, formerly my mission, going on and next descending as far as the Mouskedabouck [Musquodoboit] River, and from this place, which on the east bank [lies] approximately eight leagues from Halifax, passing by the Bay, all islands, Baye Sainte-Marie, and Moukoudorme [Mocodome] as far as Canceau [Canso] and from Canceau through the strait of Fronsac [the Canso Strait] to the aforementioned Baye Verte.[224]

Le Loutre did not mention the Three Rivers region, even though Argimault maintained traditional territorial aegis over this area, since as far as Le Loutre was concerned it lay within French territory. Fifth, the Mi'kmaq wanted "no manner of forts or fortresses, either French or English," within the limits of their tract, a demand they felt was "très modique, et fort bornèc eu égard à l'immensité de terres qui'ils ont possede[e]s" (very modest, and quite limited in regard to the size of the lands that they have possessed). Finally, they wanted a reply from Halifax between St. Michael's Day (29 September) and All Saint's Day (1 November).[225] Le Loutre concluded his letter by arguing that since it was the British, not the Mi'kmaq, who wanted negotiations to take place in Halifax, it would only be fair to first send someone here "with whom they could at least lay down preliminary conventions."[226] The Mi'kmaw delegates did not want to make the long journey to Halifax without some idea of what they might expect once they arrived. The Mi'kmaq had already chosen their delegates: Joseph Argimault and Paul Laurent. In keeping with northeastern Algonquian protocols, these men would ensure that the "treaty which will be made as a consequence, will be communicated to their allies, who will have to sign and approve [it], as well as their missionaries, to cover it with all the formalities required, and make it more authentic in order that it might be that much more solid and durable." The tenor of these aspirations and intentions was distinctly Mi'kmaq in tone, untinged by external missionary intervention, and Le Loutre, exhibiting a rare selfless attitude for once, revealed that it was his "essential duty" to contribute to their success.[227]

Despite his earlier invitation to have Mi'kmaw delegates come to Halifax, Lawrence was in no mood to take the six Mi'kmaw proposals seriously. He saw Le Loutre as the sole and self-interested perpetrator of what he considered a ridiculous scheme. To the governor, the missionary had duped Joseph Argimault into recommending the destruction of Fort Lawrence so that Beaubassin could be returned to the refugee Acadians. He branded the contents of Le Loutre's letter "insolent and absurd," and directed Le Loutre to acquaint the Mi'kmaq that "that if they had any serious thoughts of making peace" they must endeavour, without their missionary, to make their own way to Halifax, "where they will be Treated with on reasonable Conditions."[228]

As early as 12 January 1755 Captain Hussey, in response to instructions from Halifax, requested that François Arcenault, who spoke the Mi'kmaw language, and Jacques Maurice, the Beaubassin merchant, contact Joseph Argimault and have him come to Fort Lawrence. Hussey hoped that with Arcenault agreeing to act as interpreter, Le Loutre could be excluded from the upcoming negotiations. It did not take the missionary long to get wind of Hussey's intentions, however, and on 15 January Le Loutre wrote the English commander warning that, while the chiefs were "very well disposed" to make peace, they wanted any proposals made by the English in writing, as they were "not amused with words and speeches."[229] Le Loutre handed his letter to Argimault who, accompanied by Paul Laurent and François Arcenault, approached Fort Lawrence under a flag of truce.[230] After reading the letter, Hussey immediately apprised Le Loutre that he would only communicate with the chiefs by themselves, who would find that "the government, far from intending to amuse them as you pretend, is ready to enter into a firm and lasting peace with them upon reasonable conditions."[231]

There matters stood for three days. Then on 18 January, wanting to bypass Le Loutre, Hussey quickly drafted a document for Argimault to take to the other chiefs at Baie Verte. It proclaimed that the British Crown wished for a lasting peace, and that Hussey's instructions were to persuade a delegation of leaders to go to Halifax and make a treaty. The delegates would be furnished with passports to ensure their safety on their journey.[232] The following day Hussey received back a pithy note from Alkimou (Argimault) at Fort Gaspereau, written with François Arcenault's assistance. The district chief told the commander that Mi'kmaw delegates were preparing to leave for Halifax, but they required a letter stating that Hussey knew of the Mi'kmaq's peacemaking plan and, at the very least, was not opposed to it. We are "sending François Arsenault [or Arcenault] to get from you a letter which you promised us," Argimault stressed. This document "should be your assurance that the Government will grant us a domain for hunting and fishing, that neither fort not fortress shall be built upon it, that we shall be free to come and go whenever we please. Moreover, we know what we have told you; we have said the same thing in the Council, and it would be vexatious for us to undertake this journey, if you do not give us some reason to hope."[233]

Around the same time, Argimault, Laurent, and Arcenault, with Jacques Maurice in tow, appeared at Fort Lawrence for a half-hour consultation with Captain Hussey, who tried to explain to Argimault why he considered Le Loutre's participation in the peacemaking process entirely self-interested. When the Mi'kmaq changed the subject by asking the commander to explain Governor Lawerence's views on their proposals, Hussey told them once again to separate from the missionary and go to Halifax to speak to the governor personally.[234] The commander knew full well he could not give Argimault any guarantees to any demands, and he had no authority to negotiate. All he could do was what he had done before: offer ambiguous promises that he trusted would compel the chief to go to Halifax. Once Argimault was in Halifax, "which in my opinion is the only proper place to treat of a peace," he claimed, "you may be assured of obtaining from [Lawrence] everything that you can in reason ask."[235]

On 20 January Hussey also drafted a carefully worded letter to Governor Lawrence stating that the Mi'kmaw delegates would be willing to travel to Halifax "could they believe that the Government would grant them a piece of land to hunt and fish on, which they might enjoy as their own property and on which no Fort or Fortress is to be built, and that they may have complete liberty to go and trade where and with whom they think proper."[236] This letter was placed in an unsealed envelope, as Argimault had requested, and handed to the chief to carry to Halifax. In following the chief's directives so exactly, Hussey knew he was overstepping his orders, but he probably felt that a chance at making peace with the Chignecto Mi'kmaq was worth the risk. He further knew from

Pichon that the Mi'kmaq were aware of the numbers of warriors they could at any time put into the field.[237] As they could negotiate from a position of strength, they deserved a listening ear.

Had Hussey access to information Pichon acquired four days later from Le Loutre regarding the military strength of the Mi'kmaq at Gaspereau, he might have shown even more concern. While dining with Le Loutre in his quarters at Fort Beauséjour the evening of 24 January 1755, Pichon learned that the Chignecto Mi'kmaw council, to give their proposals "teeth," had contacted the Mi'kmaw Grand Council of Cape Breton to be on the alert should negotiations in Halifax fail. "Everything is ready for an attack," Pichon confided. Abbé Manach was stationed at Cobequid to intercept British land correspondence passing along the Shubenacadie River Valley, while Henri Daudin promised to keep Le Loutre abreast of what was happening within the Mi'kmaw community at Annapolis Royal. Should an attack happen, the Mi'kmaq had decided to spare Mejagouech (Fort Lawrence) until the British could be evacuated, but if the British refused to leave, the warriors would "no longer spare them [from serious harm]."[238]

Knowing that a great deal rode on the manner in which they were received in Halifax, four chiefs, with François Arcenault as their interpreter, set out for Halifax around the first of February. Joseph Argimault and Paul Laurent were the party's main spokespersons, and another man, referred to simply as "François," was probably one of Argimault's sons. The fourth Mi'kmaw delegate was unidentified. Pichon, on the basis of Le Loutre's communications to him, expected Argimault to arrive at the Cobequid church the following Sunday for mass, and to reach Halifax within a week. Yet on 9 February Pichon revealed to Hussey that the previous night François Arcenault had returned to his home at Baie Verte, having left Argimault at Cobequid with Abbé Manach.[239] Restructuring had taken place within the delegation's ranks, since after some reflection Joseph Argimault, and possibly his son, decided to leave Laurent and the fourth delegate to press on alone to Halifax with the list of Mi'kmaw demands. Laurent later informed the Halifax council that Argimault, having fallen sick at Cobequid, could not complete the journey. But given that Argimault was soon afterwards well enough to travel back to Chignecto, his illness could not have been severe and may even have been used as an excuse to avoid going to Halifax. He likely sensed British reluctance to address his proposals, and felt it more dignified and diplomatic to keep out of the line of fire. Laurent would carry the torch for the land and resource campaign, and at the same time make an excuse for the Chignecto district chief's absence.[240]

Pressing on by snowshoe, Paul Laurent and his companion reached Halifax in a matter of days. At a meeting with the governor's council on 12 February he immediately informed the assembly – probably in French since he was conversant in that language – that the "Chief of the Mickmac tribe called Algamond [sic, Argimault] had set out with him from Beauséjour to come to Halifax, in order to treat of a Peace, but having fallen sick at Cobequid [and] not being able to proceed further," he had sent Laurent on with the proposals from the Mi'kmaw council. Laurent then presented a document proposing that the Mi'kmaq "have a tract of Land given them for Fishing, shooting and Hunting, which tract should extend from Baye Verte along the Coast to Canso Bay to a place within three Leagues of the New Eastern settlements [at Chezzetcook], from thence in a right line to the Indian mass house on the Chibenacadie River, from thence to the head of the Minas Basin, and thence to the western part of Cobequid and from thence to Beaubassin, including the English Fort at Chignecto which first should be demolished and that no other fort should be erected within the limits of the said tract."[241]

Already fairly familiar with this request, the Halifax council members began to cautiously bat some ideas around and ask some minor questions, while avoiding conclusive comments. On being asked what security the Mi'kmaq "would give to keep the peace, in case such a Tract of Land should be allowed them," Paul Laurent replied that "he could say nothing to that, he being desired to bring in these proposals and to carry back an answer which he desired might be in Writing, and that the Council would specify therein the quantity of land that they would allow them," especially if it were felt that the amount of land for which the delegates asked "was too much." This last comment – evincing a power-of-the-powerless approach commonly used in northeastern Algonquian diplomatic forums – threw the burden of decision-making on the executive council.[242] Paul Laurent controlled the parameters of the discussion, but he admitted he was not authorized to sign a treaty on behalf of his people, only to report back on the

reception the Mi'kmaw requests received. The Halifax council decided at that point to halt any further discussion on the subject. "[A]fter much conversation with the said Paul on the subject of the Peace and the unreasonableness of the demands made them by the Tribes," the executive council promised to provide Laurent an answer in writing the following morning at ten o'clock.[243]

On 13 February, the council tendered a convoluted, fundamentally negative response to Laurent's address. There was no mention of removal of forts, trading arrangements, or any acknowledgment of Indigenous rights to land.[244] "The demands you make in our opinion are so extremely exorbitant," the reply began, "it appears impossible for his Majesty's Council to gain any other positive answer thereto than that they are Perfectly disposed to an allowance of such a tract of country for your hunting, fishing etc. as will be abundantly sufficient for you, and what we doubt not you yourselves will like and approve, and may be easily adjusted here if you send the Chiefs of your Tribes to this place to treat with us." This statement's only unambiguous facet was the charge for Paul Laurent to ensure other chiefs came to Halifax to make peace.[245] The discussion ended with a cautionary note: "You are sensible that certain captains of your Tribes (at least persons styling themselves such) made Peace under promises of bringing in the other Tribes, and instead of bringing in those Tribes, the Treaties have been perfidiously broken."[246] The members of the executive council made it clear they would not have a repetition of the troubling treaty-making experience they had faced with Jean-Baptiste Cope.

Back at Beaubassin, Pichon meanwhile became intrigued by Le Loutre's two-pronged and ultimately contradictory approach to the Mi'kmaq peacemaking campaign. The missionary sincerely supported Aboriginal land and resource rights, but in a roundabout way. The Mi'kmaq, he charged, were "the owners of all the land, and, owing to the methods employed by the English, these poor wretches find themselves hemmed in, with insufficient territory for their own use."[247] He held the Indigenous cause secondary to his own interest in establishing an Acadian homeland west of the Missiguash, but if the Mi'kmaq succeeded in obtaining their tract, it would act as a convenient buffer for his Acadian refugee settlement. Though Pichon felt Le Loutre overestimated the hardships Mi'kmaq faced as a result of settlement, he also knew that the Mi'kmaq had few to state their case before the English authorities. Le Loutre gave voice to their land and resource interests.[248] Pichon also realized, however, that as Le Loutre grew to doubt that the neutral buffer zone would ever emerge, his loyalties towards the Indigenous peacemaking campaign wavered. Instead, he seemed to get a perverse satisfaction in holding that a rejection of their claims would drive the Mi'kmaq to commit further hostilities against the English. "Moses does not want peace," Pichon confided to Hussey on 31 January 1755. "Let it be made elsewhere, he says: his Indians will join those of [the Jesuit missionary to the Malecite] Father Charles Germain and the Kennebecs and attack the English in the neighbourhood of Pentagoet."[249] The missionary had even informed the governor of Canada that he did "not consider the ... peace seriously, because the English would not give up Mejagouech and their fort."[250]

These series of exchanges between Hussey and Pichon show how dependent the British had become on such seepages of information from the French side. Paul Laurent returned to Chignecto late in February 1755 with news that the British might consider discussing land matters before an assemblage of chiefs at Halifax. Yet he received no final reply to the Mi'kmaw land scheme, no mention of the possibility of renegotiating earlier treaties, and no follow-up invitation to come to Halifax to discuss peace.[251] The Mi'kmaw campaign to have their six propositions accepted at Halifax suffered because of Le Loutre's association with them, but there was also the fact that in 1755, on the threshold of the Seven Years' War, the British were not going to allow French vessels to proceed unobstructed along their northern coast, dismantle Fort Lawrence to provide for a neutral buffer zone, or put their fisheries at Canso in jeopardy.[252] In the wake of Paul Laurent's journey to Halifax, the campaign and the proposals went "underground," to arise in modified form in the final years of the Seven Years' War.[253]

The Seige of Fort Beauséjour and the Second Fall of Louisbourg

The three months following Paul Laurent's return to Chignecto in late February proved to be the calm before the storm. Le Loutre and the French commandant, Louis Du Pont Duchambon de Vergor, started arming settlers near the French fort, while the missionary bombastically lambasted certain refugee Acadians from the pulpit for refusing to bear arms even for the French.[254] Le Loutre also instructed his Mi'kmaw parishioners to intercept land communications between Chignecto and Halifax. Boishébert received orders to assemble Malecite warriors, though he temporarily found himself in a quandary, since after he stated that furs could be sold only to him, the Malecite "threatened to treat him as an enemy."[255] By early June, however, Boishébert had mustered around two hundred Malecite and Mi'kmaw warriors, just in time to see thirty-one transports carrying two thousand New England militia, as well as three British warships under General Robert Monckton's command, sail into the Cumberland Basin and anchor near Cape Maringouin.[256] The siege of Fort Beauséjour lasted two weeks, with Vergor surrendering to the British on 16 June 1755.[257] During the siege, numbers of Wolastokiyik and Mi'kmaq warriors dwindled. Boishébert pleaded for the safe departure of the few Aboriginal militia who remained.[258] The British renamed the French stronghold on the Missiguash River "Fort Cumberland" and the French fort on Baie Verte, which capitulated soon afterwards, "Fort Monckton." Boishébert used explosives to blow up Fort Menagouèche on the Saint John River before the British arrived, and escaped to Shepody with around six hundred Acadian refugees.[259]

Le Loutre fled in disguise from Fort Beauséjour in the final stages of the siege. He made his way to Quebec, where he met with a cool reception from the bishop of Quebec. Returning to Louisbourg, he boarded a ship for France but was captured on the high seas and detained by the British for eight years on the Isle of Jersey. Without a missionary at Chignecto to conduct the sacraments, Mi'kmaq could choose one of three courses of action. The first, amenable to those associated with Le Loutre's former mission at Shubenacadie, was to return to Shubenacadie, or travel to Cape Breton and join Maillard's mission centre on Île de Saint Famille (Island of the Holy Family, or Chapel Island), near Port Toulouse.[260] Close to two hundred individuals choose this option.[261] A second alternative, one more daring and dangerous, was to join with Acadian resistance leaders like Joseph Broussard *dit* Beausoleil, who, despite the hardships their activities exacted on their families and followers, kept up their guerilla warfare against the British. Jean-Baptiste Cope seems to have followed this course of action.[262]

A final choice, one that the Chignecto band under Chief Joseph Argimault opted for, was to return to their hunting and fishing grounds and try as far as possible to resume their traditional way of life. Warriors from the group were called out to fight the English, at first sporadically and later more frequently, as the Petitcodiac region became the arena for a series of turbulent and ultimately tragic events. Governor Lawrence wanted all Acadians, including those at Three Rivers, deported from the colony as quickly as possible in order to repopulate their lands with Protestant settlers, a determination confirmed by the executive council on 28 July 1755. In early August 1755 Robert Monckton, acting under Lawrence's orders, ordered the Acadians to swear an oath to the British Crown, and although almost four hundred agreed to do so, as soon as they reached Fort Cumberland they were charged with insincerity and rebellious practices and thrown into prison camps.[263] Lawrence next sent a force under Captain Joseph Frye (1712-1794) to seek out and capture additional Acadians residing at Petitcodiac and Shepody. Beginning on 1 August, Frye's men burned 253 Acadian buildings. When they set fire to the Shepody mass house on 3 August, Boishébert and one hundred of his Acadian and Indigenous resistance fighters raised a cry and burst out of the woods. Frye's contingent fled before this unexpected onslaught, with a loss of twenty-two men. Another major expedition under Frye later in August followed.[264] Not wanting to be delayed longer in his Acadian deportation scheme, Lawrence pressed Monckton to be faster in loading Acadian captives on ships waiting for them in Cumberland Basin. In response to these instructions, the first Acadians were placed aboard ship on 10 September, and just over a month later, on 13 October, Captain John Rous led a fleet of ten transports out of Cumberland Basin, filled with Acadians taken from lands west of the Missiguash River and bound for new and unknown lands in South Carolina and Georgia. As Rous's ships progressed down the Bay of Fundy, they met with other transports bearing Acadians from the Minas region.[265] The English burned Acadian villages in the Three Rivers area throughout September, until all that was left of the settlement to which Le Loutre had devoted his hard work and money were blackened foundations and ashes.[266]

Acadians who fled into the woods with the Mi'kmaq were pursued by the British. A few, among them Joseph Broussard *dit* Beausoleil and his brother Alexandre Broussard, were extraordinarily courageous in staging a spectacular escape from British confinement at Chignecto.[267] They afterwards joined Boishébert's new headquarters at Shediac on the Northumberland Strait, where they recruited guerilla warriors from local Mi'kmaw bands to carry on the struggle. The Broussard brothers had had left Village des Beausoleils on the Petitcodiac River when it became too dangerous to maintain a headquarters there. It stood vacant for three years until burned by the British shortly after the second fall of Louisbourg. At this time, over two hundred Acadian refugee families relocated to land lying between Shediac and Cocagne.[268] During the winter of 1755–56 Broussard fitted out a schooner as a privateer and raided British shipping in the Bay of Fundy, not only as resistance but also to obtain provisions for the refugee camps, which were chronically short of food, ammunition, and other supplies.[269]

The Chignecto Mi'kmaq and the Second Fall of Louisbourg

The possibly of a formal war between England and France had been on the minds of English and French officials for some time.[270] After Le Loutre's departure, Joseph Broussard *dit* Beausoleil became the main leader of the Acadian resistance movement and began to encourage Mi'kmaq and Malecite to mount a series of raids on Fort Cumberland and Fort Monckton beginning the following January.[271] After April these hostilities spread province wide. On 8 May 1756 Malecite from Aukpaque and a smaller party of Mi'kmaq from Chignecto, joined by bitterly disgruntled Acadians, *métis*, and Mi'kmaq from the Merliguèche area – mustered by Boishébert under orders from the governor of Canada, Pierre-François de Rigaud, Marquis de Vaudreuil[272] – combined in a major attack on Lunenburg that left twenty settlers dead, including members of the well-known Payzant family.[273] In August, two farming families, the Hatts and the Lays, perished in a second raid on Lunenburg. Additional blockhouses were erected at Mahone Bay and along the Western Shore, but despite such protections five more raids on Lunenburg occurred over the next three years. In response to the first raid, of 8 May, Governor Lawrence issued a proclamation on 14 May 1756 offering a twenty-five-pound reward for each scalp of a male Mi'kmaq or Malecite person, and the same amount for each Mi'kmaw individual, male or female, brought in alive.[274] Three days later Britain formally declared war on France, although the onset of the war was not publicly announced at Halifax until 9 August.[275] Boishébert mustered his Indigenous militia to take Fort Monckton, but when his men arrived at Baie Verte on 12 October 1756 they found that the British had heard of their coming and burned their fort to the ground.

By 1 January 1757 Charles Deschamps de Boishébert et de Raffetot had moved seven hundred Acadian refugees, along with the Indigenous warriors attached to his cause, to a site he called "Camp d'Espérance," or "Camp Hope," on Beaubears Island in the Miramichi River. Only a few Mi'kmaq remained at this site over the winter. For the most part the Indigenous people who resided at the camp were Malecite, whom Boishébert the preceding fall had persuaded along with their missionary to accompany him. Conditions there rapidly deteriorated owing to overcrowding, cold, lack of provisions, and sickness, though Father Germain tried to parcel out the meagre foodstuffs as best he could by giving equal shares to Acadian and Indigenous alike.[276]

Mi'kmaq from Chignecto, Malecite from the Saint John River region, and the Canibas, who were Abenaki from the present-day Waterville area of Maine, rallied early in the summer of 1757 at news that the French would provide provisions and other supplies to Indigenous warriors who aided them in protecting the fortress of Louisbourg. The Chignecto Mi'kmaq were already ensconced at Abbé Maillard's near Port Toulouse when Boishébert arrived with the Malecite and Canibas in late June. On 10 July 1757, Maillard officiated at an elaborate ritual war dance performed by the Mi'kmaq and Malecite before French squadron commander Emmanuel-Auguste de Cahideuc, Comte du Bois de la Motte.[277] When the French and their Indigenous and Acadian militia successfully withstood Lord Loudoun's and Admiral Francis Holburne's naval siege of Louisbourg in late summer 1757, 250 Indigenous fighters camped near Louisbourg took part in the hostilities.[278] Over the following winter, the Mi'kmaq and Malecite went back to their hunting territories, to return the following spring. Conditions were difficult on the Miramichi River, but the Acadian and Mi'kmaq resistance forces made one successful foray against a wood-cutting party near Annapolis Royal on 6 December 1757. Finding that one soldier had been killed and seven taken captive, Captain Peter Pigou, with a

detachment of 130 men from Fort Anne, pursued the attackers. When the Mi'kmaq and Acadians staged a second successful ambush, the British suffered a high number of casualties, including the loss of Pigou.[279]

The following summer, the number of Indigenous militia assembled in Cape Breton had grown to between five and seven hundred warriors.[280] They were joined by about a thousand French militia and three thousand regulars.[281] For more than two years the French had been involved in preparing for a major British attack. Reinforcements had been brought from neighbouring groups, and chiefs had been posted at sites along the coast as lookouts.[282] Boishébert's arrival on 28 May, with his corps of 230 Mi'kmaq and Acadians – some from Chignecto and the rest drawn from Maillard's Mi'kmaw and Acadian parishioners – was greeted with jubilation at Louisbourg. Though Governor Drucour feasted the Mi'kmaq and welcomed them with speeches and present distributions, he soon had to curb his fellow officers' high expectations. The Malecite and their Abenaki allies refused to join Boishébert, reputedly because he had again imposed a disadvantageous trading monopoly on them. By the time Boishébert and his Mi'kmaw militia approached, moreover, the British fleet had arrived and taken up position. This made it impossible to approach the fortress directly, so Boishébert, Maillard, and the Mi'kmaw and Acadian militiamen set up camp to the north of Louisbourg, on the Mira River.

The second and final siege of Louisbourg began on 8 June 1758, with the British landing at Anse de la Cormorandière (now Kennington Cove), a short distance west of Louisbourg. The governor of Île Royale, Augustine Boschenry de Drucour, three days into the siege had urged Maillard to press Boishébert to launch an immediate attack on the British landing proceedings, but Boishébert ignored the abbe's appeals and let a pivotal opportunity pass, much to Maillard's chagrin. The Mi'kmaq, as had the Malecite previously, chaffed at Boishebert's roughshod behaviour towards them and, in the face of their reluctance to engage in hostilities, Boishebert withdrew to the Mira.[283] This allowed the British an entire week to land their guns, equipment, and supplies, almost unopposed.[284] To Maillard, Boishébert's breach of duty proved fatal to French fortunes, for once the British had their artillery in position the French were overwhelmed by British firepower.[285] The British prime minister, William Pitt, who did not want to see another failure like Loudoun's and Holburne's expedition of the previous year, provided ample men, ships, and funding for the siege. Major General Jeffrey Amherst, the expedition's leader, could draw on a force of 27,000 men on 157 British warships under the naval command of Admiral Edward Boscawen, whereas Drucour had only 3,500 regulars, augmented by the Aboriginal and Acadian militia, and 3,800 crewmen on 11 vessels.[286]

Louisbourg fell to the British for the last time on 26 July 1758. Maillard, who had maintained an encampment at Mira Bay during the siege, withdrew to Port Toulouse, to be followed by Boishébert and the Indigenous militia, with the British tracking behind them. The French officer eluded his pursuers, while some of the Mi'kmaw warriors travelled to the South Shore of Nova Scotia, where they again raided Lunenburg.[287] Colonel Monckton was ordered to take command of the French posts on the Saint John River, so Maillard, Germain, and Boishébert removed to what they hoped would the quieter environs of Beaubears Island, located on the old seventeenth-century seigneury of Richard Denys de Fronsac (1641–91) at Miramichi.[288] There they were joined by a large number of Acadian refugees from Port Toulouse. Boishébert, with four hundred militia, left in August 1758 to lay unsuccessful siege to Fort St. George on the Kennebec River and to participate in several other minor raids in Maine. With Boishébert and his men away, three ranger commanders, Joseph Gorham, Benoni Danks, and Sylvanus Cobb, embarked on what has been called "The Petitcodiac River Campaign" – a series of British military operations beginning in earnest in June 1750 and lasting until November. In late June, Danks's rangers began hunting down the Acadian resistance leaders, and on 1 July they ambushed Joseph Broussard *dit* Beausoleil and thirty other Acadians, scalped three of the company, and captured the others. Beausoleil, though wounded, escaped and gradually recovered at Boishébert's camp on the Miramichi.[289]

Revival of the Mi'kmaw Land and Resource Campaign

Chief Joseph Argimault's bid for a large Mi'kmaw reserve in the northeastern part of the province – a proposal ridiculed by the British in the mid-1750s – came to be accepted by the executive council in Halifax for a brief spell between fall 1760 and spring 1762.

Abbé Pierre Maillard was likely the driving force behind Lieutenant Governor Jonathan Belcher's decision. The British found Maillard an amenable and far less manipulative person than Le Loutre.[290] He was sincerely devoted to the well-being of both the Mi'kmaq and Acadians, and his willingness to assist the British came at a time when both Mi'kmaq and Acadian resistance fighters were facing formidable challenges.

During the first weeks of November 1758, British rangers cruised up and down the Petitcodiac River, specifically looking for Joseph Broussard *dit* Beausoleil's house.[291] When Dank's men found it at Village des Beausoleils it was deserted, so Danks wasted no time killing Broussard's livestock, burning his house, and destroying his crops. Captain Sylvanus Cobb also destroyed many Acadian houses, though he and his forces met opposition from local Acadians and Mi'kmaq. On 13 November Beausoleil's men, supported by warriors from Chief Argimault's band, suddenly attacked Cobb's party. Danks came to Cobb's rescue, and together their rangers took a dozen Acadian men and women hostage. Gorham's Rangers burned over one hundred Acadian homes and then returned to Fort Frederick at the mouth of the Saint John River with their prisoners.[292] Between fall 1758 and summer 1760 the British continued to raid villages and acquire Acadian hostages in the Three Rivers area, along the Gulf of St. Lawrence, and on the Gaspé Peninsula. No structures escaped destruction, for in 1758 the oldest Acadian stone church was set afire at a site that still bears the name "Burnt Church."[293] Soon after the fall of Louisbourg, General James Wolfe with a force of 1,500 men sought out the Miramichi refugee camp and razed houses and burned fields. In consequence, on 12 September 1758 a party of 190 Miramichi Acadians, many hungry and ill, surrendered to Colonel Joseph Frye at Fort Cumberland.[294]

The rangers' presence made Mi'kmaq occupation of the Petitcodiac River region hazardous, at least during the summer and fall months.[295] From late 1758 to late 1759, the Chignecto Mi'kmaq sought protection from the Acadian resistance leaders, Beausoleil and Pierre II Surrette. As long as they lived near their allies, they could share meagre supplies and provisions. Provisioning ships no longer appeared from Canada, owing to a British blockade in the Gulf of St. Lawrence. The Acadians' main hope lay in capturing British supply ships. Despite such hardships, the resistance fighters were as ready to fight as ever, for "the fight was all they knew, and they were determined to see it through to the end."[296] Donning war paint, the Mi'kmaq and Acadians in January of 1759 ambushed five English soldiers who were crossing the bridge over the Missiguash River, and scalped them. The site today is still known as "Bloody Bridge."[297] Later the same spring several dozen Mi'kmaq and Acadians followed Beausoleil to the Dartmouth area where they raided a battery built on a knoll opposite Cornwallis Island – now McNab's Island – and killed five soldiers.[298] By April, they had renewed their attacks on Lunenburg.[299] Tenacious Acadians also began to trickle back into the Petitcodiac Valley from their former hiding places in the woods and plant crops for the following year's subsistence. With the aid of the local Mi'kmaq, they captured a provision vessel in the Bay of Fundy and, while they released the crewmen, they took the boat far up the Petitcodiac River where they absconded with the contents of its hold: desperately needed food, ammunition, and other supplies.[300]

During summer 1759 Maillard set up a camp, including Mi'kmaq and Acadians, at *Malogomish* (now Merigomish, Pictou County). The towering pines of the surrounding forest provided little browse for big game, so the inhabitants planted crops to supplement their returns from fishing and trapping. They also raided English vessels proceeding along the Northumberland Strait from a small privateer, constructed within the Acadian and Mi'kmaw community.[301] Brigadier-General Edward Whitmore, who had taken over command at Louisbourg, could not believe the speed and efficiency with which the Acadian and Mi'kmaw community racked up successful heists. Between 9 and 25 August, alone, the crew of their privateer had captured seven ships.[302] While Maillard was still at Malogomish (Merigomish), Quebec fell to the British on 13 September 1759, an event that must have shaken the abbé and his companions. For twenty-three years he had served France's religion and its cause, and now he feared being abandoned by the French governor, Pierre-François de Rigaud de Vaudreuil-Cavagnial. Owing to the British blockade in the Gulf of Saint Lawrence, French assistance of any kind for the resistance campaign at Merigomish was sporadic at best. No longer would Maillard's parishioners receive provisioning from a French government grateful for their military services, nor would they gain protection from

the harshness of British punitive policies under the shelter of French law. Maillard lacked the diehard fighting spirit of Beausoleil and feared what the future might hold for the Mi'kmaq. Mi'kmaq leaders, among them Joseph Argimault, still longed for a homeland where the Mi'kmaw nation might continue to grow and develop away from the buffeting tides of French and British intercolonial conflict, European settlement, and European resource development. In this role he could arise as a beacon of stability and consistency within the Mi'kmaw polity, traits that must have attracted Maillard to him just as they had to his shamanic father, Philippe Argimault, at Port-La-Joye around 1745.

Maillard soon had an opportunity to discuss peacemaking with the British. Chagrined at the loss of so many British provisioning vessels in such a short space of time, Whitmore sent Major Henry Schomberg to Merigomish between September 29 and mid-October 1759 to investigate.[303] Schomberg was not Whitmore's first choice, for Schomberg was beginning to fall into puzzling moods that made him outspoken and defiant. Yet Whitmore had already dispatched several officers who failed to halt the activities of those he deemed a horde of "unruly pirates." Shomberg was his last resort.[304] Until the fall of 1759, Maillard and his associates evaded detection by hiding in coves and behind islands. Though some vessels were retaken and delivered to their owners, the perpetrators of the raids remained at large. Schomberg, the last officer Whitmore could count on to go out so late in the season, found that instead of his having to scour the coastline quarry, the Acadians and Mi'kmaq came down to the shore on 26 October 1759 and hailed his ship. Under a flag of truce, they stated they had heard that Quebec had fallen. The Acadians then "agreed to Surrender Themselves" and the Mi'kmaq expressed a wish "to enter into Terms of Peace."[305] In all, there were about four hundred Mi'kmaw warriors and an even greater number of French.[306]

When Schomberg compared the large size of this community with his own relatively small force, he was taken aback. Feeling he had to adopt a conciliatory attitude, he affirmed in Whitmore's name that Quebec had indeed fallen, but that those before him could keep their possessions, liberty, property, and Roman Catholic religion if they agreed to a peace with Britain. As he seemed to be avoiding making any unilateral demands, the Mi'kmaq or the Acadians responded favourably to the terms that Schomberg claimed he had "the honour" of proffering. A similar strain of respect permeated his discussions with Maillard, whom he hoped would come to trust him. With this in mind, he wrote the abbé, beginning his letter with the words, "If[,] my Reverend father, you doubt the sincerity of my heart, I am ready to exchange hostages and I would be delighted to have the honour of seeing you aboard my frigate."[307] And he was evidently successful, for over the course of several weeks he entered into amiable discussions with Maillard and other leaders of the community, and hostages were exchanged. Eventually a formal truce was signed on 26 November by the British officer and the missionaries, who acted on behalf of their respective constituencies. Schomberg then arranged for seven Mi'kmaq to visit Louisbourg and confer further with General Whitmore. As a surety for their safe return, two or three British soldiers were constrained to remain at Malagomich.[308]

Hearing of the truce made under Maillard's auspices, and of the Acadians taking oaths of allegiance to the British Crown, Boishébert expressed his indignation.[309] Not long afterwards Jean-François Bourdon de Domberg, a high-ranking French military officer, denounced Maillard as a traitor to France. Maillard responded that his situation and that of the Mi'kmaq with him were well-nigh hopeless, and the only way they could alleviate their lot was to encourage a peace with the British. It was a pivotal decision on his part, and by it he granted the Mi'kmaw chiefs an honourable way to again approach the British negotiating table. At Louisbourg, the new governor of Cape Breton, Edward Whitmore, did not treat the chiefs as rebels; he instead had them sign a document in December 1759 by which they swore oaths of allegiance to the British Crown and promised to maintain the peace.[310] Though this document has been lost, and Whitmore seemingly failed to forward copies to his superiors, it must have given the Mi'kmaq at the Merigomish encampment enough encouragement to discuss and plan to make further peace overtures in the spring of 1760.[311] They had hardly returned from their winter hunting before they sent delegates to Halifax for this purpose. Maillard, wholly supporting their intentions, and grateful to the British for providing an opportunity for them to make peace, wrote poignantly to one British officer, "I love my chains because you have made them seem agreeable to me, to the point that I wish that you would not break them for a good while."[312]

Treaty Signing during the Final War Years

In either the fall of 1759 or the early spring of 1760, Maillard accepted Charles Lawrence's invitation to to come to Halifax as a government agent on a salary of £150 per annum to persuade the Mi'kmaq to sign treaties of peace and friendship.[313] As provincial Indian commissioner, he had three French- and Mi'kmaw-speaking assistants: Louis-Benjamin Petitpas, who travelled with him, secured food, and cared for him when he fell ill; Louis-Benjamin's half-brother, Joseph Petitpas; and Jean-Baptist Roma.[314] One of the abbé's first requests to the executive council was that he be allowed to maintain an oratory in a barnlike building at the foot of what is now Tobin Street in Halifax.[315] Here he held services for Mi'kmaq and Acadians who visited the town. Although he now worked for the British, he found he also still maintained the esteem of his religious superiors, for in 1760 he was appointed vicar general of Nova Scotia.[316] In this capacity he set out on itinerant journeys to Shubenacadie, Chignecto, Pictou, Cape Breton, La Have, Lunenburg, and Cape Sable.

Following Quebec's fall, the Jesuit missionary Charles Germain, who served among the Passamaquoddy and Malecite, and Abbé Jean Manach at Miramichi encouraged their Indigenous congregants to extend peace overtures to the British. During fall 1759 Indigenous leaders throughout the Northeast held councils to discuss the relative strength of the French and British positions. Many chiefs wanted to open up commercial negotiations with the British, since no viable opportunities for trade with either the French or British had existed for almost five years, and the British were promising to construct truckhouses in their regions. Some Mi'kmaq openly supported Britain by this time, others wished to remain attached to France, while still others, among them Chief Argimault, retained a wait-and-see stance. As in 1749, the British focused first on securing the neutrality of Passamaquoddy of the Kennebec River region and the Malecite of the Saint John River area. When the British opened peacemaking negotiations in November 1759 at Fort Frederick (present-day Saint John, New Brunswick), Germain urged compliance with the British terms.[317] Mi'kmaw delegates later proceeded to Halifax, where on 23 February

1760 a peace and friendship treaty, essentially a re-newal of the pact signed at Annapolis Royal in 1726, was signed between the British Crown and the Passamaquoddy and Malecite.[318] The two Eastern Abe-naki nations received promises from the British that truckhouses would be established among them, and in return pledged their neutrality. As well, they sent hostages, as surety, to Fort Frederick.[319]

The Mi'kmaq also held numerous councils throughout the province. Word spread quickly about the British interest in the Malecite and Passamaquoddy. In fall 1759 the Shubenacadie group set out to ensure that their people would receive equal attention in the British diplomatic forum. Accordingly, Roger Morris, a delegate of the Shubenacadie district chief, Claude René, arrived with four associates in Halifax on 9 January 1760, and presented the governor and council with overtures of peace. Their band, the five men explained, were waiting for the council's reply at Jeddore. Governor Lawrence welcomed Morris's party and sent the delegates back to their people "with assurances of friendship and a readiness to make a peace."[320]

In the middle of one of the council's negotiation sessions with the Malecite and Passamaquoddy on 13 January, the importunate Morris appeared again, with three Frenchmen from Pictou and the Shubenacadie leader, Claude René, whom Abbé Maillard commended for both his bravery and his piety.[321] The party stressed that seventy persons at Jeddore needed moose meat to live, but since their hunters could not leave their women and children alone in the coldest month of the year to hunt, they needed government provisions to sustain their families while they were away. Eager to have them agree to a treaty, Lawrence gave them a rowboat equipped with a barrel of flour, a barrel of pork, and two barrels of bread to tow back to Jeddore.[322]

To the north, at Chignecto, Paul Laurent and Michel Augustine, the chief of Richibucto,[323] pressed Abbé Jean Manach to assist them in gaining an audience with Colonel Joseph Frye, the British commander at Fort Cumberland, the old Fort Beauséjour.[324] Manach had already decided to visit Frye in January, to plea for British protection for Acadians still living in the northeastern part of the colony, so he invited chiefs Laurent and Augustine to accompany him. The three arrived at Fort Cumberland on 30 January 1760. Since Paul Laurent could speak English, he recapitulated that the Chignecto

council wanted the opportunity to resume negotiations with the governor. When Frye expressed his surprise at Laurent's fluency in English, the La Have chief told him that as a youth he had been captured and imprisoned in Boston, where he lived with a Mr. Henshaw, a blacksmith, in whose household he learned English. Frye accepted their professions of friendship with the British Crown and directed them to go to Halifax to meet with Governor Lawrence.[325]

Before he left, Manach provided Frye with a list of fourteen chiefs who wanted to meet with him and discuss peacemaking in the near future. Frye expressed his amazement at the number.[326] Realizing how ignorant the British officer was about the Mi'kmaq, Manach explained that the chiefs belonged to a people "by the name of Mickmacks" who numbered around three thousand persons. Eleven of their chiefs, including Joseph Argimault, mentioned on his list represented Mi'kmaw communities either on or north of the Shubenacadie River, while only three, Paul Laurent of La Have, Bartholomew Momcharret of Minas, and Michel Argomartin of Cape Sable, lived in southwestern Nova Scotia.[327] The missionary further stressed that most of the chiefs would be coming to Fort Cumberland once spring hunting was over. The Mi'kmaw language, he added, had "so much excellence" to it that if the fact were known in Europe, "there would be seminaries erected for the propagation of it." Unmoved by Manach's enthusiasm for Mi'kmaw culture and language, Frye reflected woefully that, once Fortress Louisbourg was reduced "to a pile of rubble," he would be left alone to deal with this flood of Indigenous petitioners.[328]

Ten other southwestern Nova Scotian chiefs, none of whom were mentioned in Manach's list, visited Halifax in April. In late April two Cape Sable leaders expressed an interest in effecting a peace, although if they signed an actual pact, the treaty document has not survived.[329] On 28 April 1760 eight more Mi'kmaw leaders, representing the Chester area, Minas, La Have, and the Eastern Shore, followed suit.[330] Jean-Baptiste Cope's son or grandson, "Blanchois Wyegawook [François of Sheet Harbour]," joined this party on behalf of the Eastern Shore Mi'kmaq.[331] Unfortunately, only the passes and not the treaties have survived, so it can only be assumed that the pact made on 28 April was the same as the one signed the following month by Paul Laurent and his associates.

Knowing that several southwestern Mi'kmaq had expressed their readiness to make peace, Paul

Laurent and Michel Augustine swiftly sent couriers to Jeddore to apprise Roger Morris and Claude René of their coming. Laurent went first to Lunenburg in early March to meet with Colonel Sutherland, where a government schooner then picked him up and conveyed him to Halifax.[332] Then on 10 March 1760 Paul Laurent, accompanied by Michel Augustine and Claude René, entered the council chambers, handed Governor Lawrence the letters Frye had sent by him, and declared that the whole Mi'kmaw nation had decided to make peace on the terms granted already to the Malecite and Passamaquoddy. The executive council then resolved to make peace with each Mi'kmaw chief who came in, and "afterwards to have a general treaty signed at Chignecto." They also promised to ensure that government-sponsored truck-houses would be established, one of which would operate at Fort Cumberland.[333] Paul Laurent, the successor of Claude Gagiosh, who apparently had died by this time, then signed treaty on behalf of the La Have band, Claude René placed his mark on the document as the Shubenacadie leader, while Michel Augustine signed as chief of Richibucto.[334] (The general treaty-signing that the government promised to hold at Chignecto was never staged, and the truckhouse operations only ran for three years until, owing to fiscal mismanagement, the system gave way to a licensing structure for traders from specific communities.) Following the treaty-signing ceremony, each of the three chiefs left with gifts and a copy of the treaty.

At the time of these signings, a British victory in North America was far from certain. French forces remained in New France in large numbers, and an increase in French strength, coupled with assistance from Acadian and Indigenous milita, could still undermine British control of the Gulf of St. Lawrence, penetrate the British blockade in the gulf, and pave the way for the French recapture of Quebec. On 28 April 1760 Louis-Joseph de Montcalm's successor as commander of the French forces in North America, François Gaston, the Chevalier de Lévis, defeated a British force led by General James Murray at Sainte-Foy near Quebec. Buoyed by this victory, Lieutenant François La Giraudais, commanding four hundred troops, sailed from Bordeaux with an armed frigate, *Le Machault*, and five transport ships laden with provisions. As they tried to run the British blockade, however, two transport ships were seized and another was shipwrecked. On 15 May 1760 the remaining French vessels, a frigate and two merchant ships, entered the Gulf of St. Lawrence and anchored near the Mi'kmaw community of Listuguj (Restigouche).

Boishébert, with the Acadian and Indigenous resistance fighters, assisted the French in return for arms and provisions. After several Royal Navy ships under the command of Captain John Byron on 22 June blocked La Giraudais's vessels in the estuary of the Restigouche River, the French tried to escape by sailing upstream, turning their frigate broadside, and setting up cannon on the shore. The Indigenous and Acadian militia covered their movements with protective gunfire. In the end the French scuttled their frigate and one transport vessel and turned over the second merchant ship to Byron, as it held British prisoners. The French camped at Listuguj on the Restigouche River throughout the summer of 1760, but when they heard of Chevalier de Lévis's capitulation to General Amherst's army at Montreal on 6 September, followed by Pierrre-François de Rigaud Vaudreuil-Cavagnial's formal surrender of Canada two days later, they too capitulated to the British, on 29 October 1760.[335] The Battle of Restigouche of 1760 signalled not only the formidable nature of the British blockade, but also the end of the Acadian resistance movement. Without adequate provisioning, Acadians hiding in the woods at Three Rivers faced such a harsh winter that Beausoleil felt obliged to ask the British at Fort Cumberland to supply food and shelter for sixty-three people. But many Acadians fled into the woods. Joseph and Alexandre Broussard and their companions were taken prisoners of war, sent to St. George's Island in Halifax, and eventually deported.[336]

Mi'kmaw and Malecite groups in the northeastern part of the province before and during the Battle of Restigouche remained internally divided in their loyalties, some favouring the French and others desiring to placate the British, until the French cause lost much of its appeal for all following La Giraudais's failure to run the British blockade. Over a year passed between the 1760 treaty signings and Joseph Argimault's appearance in Halifax on 8 July 1761 to sign the peace pact. With Maillard acting as his interpreter, Argimault promised to relinquish his former allegiance to the French king and acknowledge the newly installed British monarch, George III, as "his only lawful Sovereign."[337] Belcher, Lawrence's successor,[338] must have given the Chignecto leader assurances regarding the British legal system's ability to uphold Indigenous rights, since Argimault also declared he "would always esteem King George III as his good Father and Protector." The Chignecto chief then placed his mark on the treaty, laid his hatchet in a hole dug for the purpose, and along with others about him drank to the king's health and raised three loud cheers.[339]

This ceremony was followed on 25 August 1761 by a visit to Halifax of four chiefs from the northeastern sector of the province: Joseph Shabecholouet from Miramichi, Étienne Ashabon (Abehabo, Anshobron, or Aushabec) from Pokemouche, Claude Astonash (Athanase) from Shediac, and Jeannot Peguidalouet of Cape Breton.[340] Lieutenant Governor Jonathan Belcher, who previously had been chief justice for the colony, ensured that the treaty-signing event was accompanied by pomp and ceremony. Peguidalouet gave a speech airing his attachment to the British Crown, and Belcher responded by promising to extend the protection of British law like a "hedge" around Mi'kmaw rights "as long as the Sun and Moon shall endure."[341]

Two more chiefs from the northeastern sector of the colony, Joseph Claude of Listuguj and Jean Nowell of Pictou, came to Halifax and signed on 12 October 1761, while the last Mi'kmaw leader to sign, François Mius of La Have, reluctantly put his signature on the treaty document on 9 November 1761.[342] Mius feared that in the event of another war the Mi'kmaw would have to adhere to strict neutrality, despite threats to their cherished interests. Evidence exists that Maillard may have contravened British treaty-making protocols by assuring Mius that, should such threats arise, the Mi'kmaq might once again take up arms.[343] One cannot help but wonder if the missionary offered similar illicit enticements to Argimault, to persuade the Siknikt leader to sign.

The Mi'kmaw Bid for a Homeland, and Belcher's Proclamation of 1762

Neither the 1760 treaty nor the official speeches that went with their signing made any mention of lands set aside and protected under British law for the Mi'kmaq. Belcher soon showed that he was as eager to settle the province quickly as Lawrence had been before him, and he was especially anxious to place New Englanders and British immigrants in areas vacated by the Acadians. It was not long before clashes occurred between the Mi'kmaq and settlers along the coast. Because the Mi'kmaq well remembered that Belcher in 1760 and 1761 promised them protection for their interests under British law, the lieutenant governor soon faced a bevy of Mi'kmaw requests for government intervention where the newcomers had taken over crucial Aboriginal weirsites and competed with the Mi'kmaq on hunting and trapping grounds. Like his predecessor Lawrence, Belcher relied on Father Germain, who was paid an annual stipend of fifty pounds, to keep the peace among the Malecite.[344] He also praised Maillard's work, though he feared Manach encouraged disgruntled Acadians to oppose the claims of the new settlers. As his suspicions escalated, on 9 April 1761 he had Abbé Manach apprehended and deported aboard the H.M.S. *Fowley* for England, to be delivered to the Lords of Trade and Plantations "for their disposal."[345]

Maillard tried as best he could to prevent violence between Mi'kmaq and settlers, especially around Lunenburg and in the Petitcodiac River region, and owing to his interventions no major incidents occurred.[346] Yet the settlers, drawn mostly from the New England colonies after 1759, pressed inland from the coast, carving new clearings beyond the bounds of the older Acadian communities. Oblivious to Mi'kmaw needs, they took over riverine fisheries, burned the forest for fields, and logged vast tracts to construct homes, barns, mills, wharves, and other wooden structures.[347] Faced with this new challenge, the Mi'kmaq, given the promises made to them by Belcher, naturally expected the executive council to treat their grievances seriously and afford them legal protection for their land and resource claims.

From their participation in Eastern Wabanaki Confederacy councils, Mi'kmaw leaders knew that the British periodically reinforced agreements made with Haudenosaunee or Six Nations chiefs to the west of them by giving presents and exchanging wampum belts bearing mnemonic beadwork designs. Similar protocols characterized diplomatic exchanges within the Eastern Wabanaki Confederacy, yet this fact was not recognized by Nova Scotian administrators. Still, the Mi'kmaq expected that the new pact they had signed would uphold the 1726 treaty's stipulation that the British could not establish new settlements without their consultation.[348] They also expected their rights to fish, hunt, and plant on their traditional lands to be protected under the panoply of British law, and that they would exercise an ongoing voice in the negotiating forum. The text of the 1760 treaty may have steered away from defining tracts for exclusive Aboriginal use, but the chiefs and their missionary and spokesperson, Maillard, saw this mainly as a flaw to be rectified in future rounds of diplomatic talks.[349]

Belcher knew that having lands they could call their own was extremely important to the leaders of the Mi'kmaw nation. He also was well familiar with the Aboriginal buffer zone concept, since his father, Jonathon Belcher Sr., while a member of the Massachusetts Council in 1720 had joined with Samuel Sewell and Edmund Quincy in recommending that a boundary line be drawn along the Kennebec River so that the Eastern Abenaki "might have some lands of their own" in the Northeast.[350] The subject of Indigenous homelands in the Northeast, moreover, had arisen in the context of the 1750–1 boundary commission convened in Paris, France.[351] With Maillard's assistance, Belcher devised a scheme to placate the Mi'kmaw leadership so that they would reject appeals from refugee Acadians anxious to resuscitate a Mi'kmaw militia in the colony. He also listened to Mi'kmaw chiefs who came to him with grievances about settler trespasses on their lands and promised to help them. While he did not have any ready solutions to such conflicts, he was prepared to defend the Mi'kmaq's right to bring their contentions forward and have the trespasses of which they complained examined in the court of law. He also sanctioned periodic present distributions, even though in 1760 General Jeffrey Amherst, commander-in-chief of the British forces in North America, argued that gifts were no longer necessary to "purchase" Indigenous friendship.[352] Belcher lacked Amherst's confidence in British military prowess to keep Mi'kmaw anger in check if Indigenous grievances were not addressed. He further worried that discontented Mi'kmaq and Acadians might join together to attack settlements throughout the province.

His fears were not unfounded. A series of incidents after February 1762 raised alarms at Halifax and Lunenburg that a French invasion might be imminent. In the midst of this crisis Belcher reached out to Maillard and the Mi'kmaw chiefs for help in formulating a plan to keep the Indigenous community loyal. The result was a resuscitation of the Mi'kmaw campaign for a homeland that had lain dormant since 1755. As this movement gained renewed momentum, Mi'kmaw leaders, acting together in councils, tailored the nature of the scheme to suit changed

circumstances. Being well versed in British jurisprudence, Belcher defended the Mi'kmaq's right to land and resources by referring to the doctrine of prior occupation, a simple concept holding that the claims of the earliest inhabitants of a region should take precedence over those of later comers.[353]

In 1755 Joseph Argimault and Paul Laurent had been the primary advocates of the scheme, which despite Le Loutre's earlier involvement in it remained Mi'kmaw inspired and Mi'kmaw directed. Just prior to the treaty signings of 1760 and 1761, Maillard informed the Mi'kmaq that, through shrewd negotiation, their proposal for a homeland might be recognized by the British regime, a thread of hope he kept alive to motivate the Mi'kmaq to sign treaty. Yet the missionary, despite being paid by the British for his services, seemed also to genuinely support the Mi'kmaw initiative, which to him seemed an avenue to preserve and protect cherished Mi'kmaw rights and interests. The fact that the bid for a Mi'kmaw homeland remained strong even after New France's fall, the British razing of the Shubenacadie mission, and Le Loutre's final disappearance from the colony testifies to the extent to which the campaign had taken root in Mi'kmaw consciousness, wholly independent of the sway of French territorial designs. The British no longer had to fear Le Loutre's stratagems, French control of Canso, or concerns about French shipping proceeding unhindered along the Northumberland Strait to and from Quebec. If the British had tended to view Joseph Argimault and Paul Laurent as mere dupes of a calculating missionary, they no longer had reason to do so.[354]

As Belcher's fears escalated, so did the strength of the Mi'kmaq's negotiating position. Their chiefs continued to submit suggestions to the lieutenant governor until, on 4 May 1762, Belcher signed a royal proclamation delineating a vast tract – larger than the one outlined in 1755 – that would remain Mi'kmaw territory, although the exact legal nature of the Indigenous tenure was left unclear. The final clause of the proclamation read:

> And, whereas claims have been laid before me in behalf of the Indians for Fronsac Passage and from thence to Nartigonneich [Antigonish], and from Nartigonneich to Pihtouk [Pictou], and from thence to Cape Jeanne [Cape John], from thence to Emchih, from thence to Kagi Pontouch [Tatamagouche], from thence to Jediack [Shediac], from thence to Cape Rommentie [Cape

Tormentine], from thence to Mirimichy [Miramichi], and from thence to Bay de Chaleurs, and the environs of Canso, from thence to Mushkoodabout, and from thence to Meshpatagan,[355] and so along the coast, as the claims and actual possessions of the said Indians, for the more special purpose of hunting, fowling and Fishing, I do hereby strictly enjoin and caution all persons to avoid all molestation of the said Indians in their said claims, till His Majesty's pleasure In this behalf shall be signified. AND, if any person or persons have possessed themselves of any part of the same to the prejudice of the said Indians in their Claims before specified or without lawful Authority, they are hereby required forthwith to remove, as they will otherwise be prosecuted with the utmost rigour of the law.[356]

Belcher probably meant for these terms to specifically protect Mi'kmaw claims to certain coastal locales that they had used for generations principally for fishing. Interestingly, the inclusion of the place name "Meshpatagan" ("Ashmutogun" or "Aspotagan"), which refers to the region of what today is termed "Aspotogan," implies that the Mi'kmaq did not consider Musquodoboit or even Chebucto (Halifax) as the southern coastal boundary of the tract they desired. Instead, they extended it south beyond Halifax to the Aspotogan Peninsula, lying between St. Margaret's Bay and Mahone Bay. This suggests that Aspotogan traditionally formed the southern boundary of the *Eskikwa'kik* Mi'kmaw district, which lay along Nova Scotia's Eastern Shore, long before influxes of Europeans settled the coastal lands from Musquodoboit southward. Indigenous politicized views of the land thus evidently remained unaffected by Halifax's rise and the imposition on the landscape of European territorial boundaries.

The proclamation also did not refer, as Argimault's and Laurent's 1755 earlier proposal had done, to mission lands in the interior, lying along the middle reaches of the Shubenacadie River, as part of the Mi'kmaq's "claims and actual possessions." Nor was there any indication that these Mi'kmaw claims would exclude European settlement altogether, since numerous Acadian settlements had existed in the delineated region and it was Belcher's intention to have these sites populated by British subjects.[357] There also was an expedient ring to the lieutenant governor's proclamation. An order-in-council dated 9 December 1761 that he received from London had required him to settle all land disputes with the Mi'kmaq. This

proved a challenging task. In a letter to the Lords of Trade and Plantations, Belcher stressed that the chiefs made and "still do continue to make great Complaints, that Settlements have been made, and possessions taken, of Lands, the properties of which they have by treaties reserved to themselves." Though he gave no names, he continued that certain settlers had usurped the "said lands under pretense of Deeds of Sale and Conveyance, illegally, fraudulently, and surreptitiously obtained of said Indians." Belcher concluded by expressing his satisfaction that the king had chosen to take "this Matter into his Royal consideration," especially as a "fatal effect ... would attend a Discontent among the Indians in the present Situation of Affairs." His proclamation was meant to "protect said Indians in their just rights [and] possessions and to keep inviolable the Treaties" that recently had been entered into with them.[358]

The situation surrounding the drafting of Belcher's proclamation, which until recently has tended to be glossed over by historians as a curious aberration in an otherwise straightforward progression of treaty making and policy formulation, warrants more attention. For one, the tract presented in the proclamation was much larger in size than the one earlier described by Argimault and Laurent, which suggests that chiefs living between Chignecto and Restigouche were responsible for modifications to the original scheme. Their lands had been part of New France and now fell under British suzerainty, a change that warranted the forging of ties with the new European power that exercised legal jurisdiction in their area. For another, the proclamation's emphasis on preserving Mi'kmaw claims to the coast posed one of the greatest challenges to settler appropriation of riverine sites. It is highly doubtful that the lieutenant governor, without Maillard's and the chiefs' input, would ever have advocated such a stance, since it constituted a substantial challenge to Belcher's own intentions to settle the northeastern region quickly and easily.[359] Joshua Mauger, appointed in April 1762 as the Halifax assembly's agent in London, had no compunction about revealing Maillard to the Lords of Trade and Plantations as the driving force behind the issuance of Belcher's proclamation.[360]

In some respects, Belcher's proclamation foreshadowed provisions found in the Royal Proclamation of 1763 that, also drawing on the principle of prior occupation, reserved large areas of land in North America for Indigenous use and set out a process for the protection and cession of Aboriginal land. Belcher would have been familiar with ideas, at the time formative, circulating in British legal circles concerning peaceful ways of interacting with Indigenous nations in North America following Pontiac's resistance movement of 1760 in the Ohio Valley. Belcher's proclamation differs substantially from the later 1763 proclamation, however, since it incorporated no provisions for land surrenders and focused exclusively on the Mi'kmaq. Maillard may have been moved by high-minded legal principles, but it appears that Belcher, though a jurist, was motivated at least as much by expediency. The lieutenant governor's fears that the Mi'kmaq and disgruntled Acadians might join together during a state of crisis, prevailing throughout the spring of 1762, to resist British rule compelled him to listen to Maillard and the chiefs. He knew his proclamation might prevent the Mi'kmaq from jeopardizing their cherished dream of a homeland, central to his document, by uniting with the French.[361]

As soon as they received it, Joshua Maugher and the Board of Trade opposed the proclamation, yet they presciently waited until the crisis was over and the French, who had occupied St. John's, Newfoundland, during the summer of 1762, had left before expressing their displeasure. On 3 December they collectively expressed "astonishment" at the lieutenant governor's course of action and sharply pointed out the compromising situation in which it placed British settlement aspirations, agricultural goals, and the fishery at Canso. Rather than casting their arguments in a legalistic frame, as Belcher had done, they adhered to an expedient and utilitarian theme. They "were of the opinion that the encouraging of the Indians to put in any claim whatever to Lands in the Province of Acadia and afterwards countenancing, and in some degree establishing, that claim by the Proclamation of 4th of May 1762, was imprudent and not warranted by His Majesty's Order in Council of the 9th of December 1761." To them, the king's instructions only referred to such claims of the Indigenous people "as had been heretofore of long usage, admitted and allowed on the part of the Government and confirmed by them by solemn Compacts." Prior occupation was not enough; there also had to be prior British recognition. The London Board of Trade particularly objected to the fact that the "Description of Lands reserved by the Lieutenant Governor's Proclamation" appeared to exclude British subjects from settling and carrying on the fishery. To this they retorted that Belcher was simply passing over the east coast fishery to illicit New England interests. The Mi'kmaq, they continued, should not be allowed to live along the coast, which they considered more appropriate for British settlement, "but rather [dwell on] the Lands amongst the woods and Lakes where the wild Beasts resort and are found in plenty."[362]

In the face of this barrage of denunciation, Belcher tried to defend his actions. But in so doing he jettisoned his former arguments based on the doctrine of prior occupation and, despite his training as a jurist, adopted a line of reasoning punctuated with inconsistencies and contradictions. In a letter to London written on 9 December, he began strongly by refuting the Lords of Trade and Plantations' contention that the Mi'kmaq were entirely an interior people. He pointed out that coastal resources were so important to them that settler trespasses elicited grave resentment. So many chiefs had complained to him about unprovoked settler hostilities towards their people on their riverine fishing and fowling grounds that he had issued his proclamation with the intent of "reserving a common right to the Mi'kmaq to an extent of sea coast, without disturbance." Otherwise, he cautioned, the Mi'kmaq "might have been incited by the disaffected Acadians and others to have made extravagant and unwarrantable demands, to the disquiet and perplexity of the new settlements in the Province." Treaties had promised that British law would protect Indigenous interests, but it was easier to allot the Mi'kmaq rights to land than to try cases of trespass in the courts, or to convict the settlers who committed the infractions. Not only was it difficult to apprehend perpetrators, but attempts to accommodate Mi'kmaq's grievances "in a private way in the courts" too often turned against the Mi'kmaw claimants "for want of sufficient Evidence or otherwise." In short, the British justice system was failing the Aboriginal populace it was supposed to protect, a situation the lieutenant governor feared would culminate in a "disagreeable consequence in the present Situation of Affairs."[363]

Despite this strong beginning, Belcher, evidently cowed by his superiors' stinging criticisms, ended his missive on a penitent, almost sycophantic note. By retracting his earlier reliance on the doctrine of prior right, he also waded into murky legalistic waters. "Your Lordships will permit me humbly to remark," he began, "that no other claim can be made by the Indians in this Province, either by Treaties or long possession (the rule, by which the determination of their claims is to be made, by virtue of His Majesty's instructions) since the French derived their title from the Indians and the French ceded their Title to the English under the Treaty of Utrecht." This last proposition was erroneous, since the Mi'kmaq had made no treaties with the French and had surrendered no land. There were thus no legal instruments under which Aboriginal prior right might have been negated. Belcher further assured the Board of Trade that his proclamation had not been widely circulated. This suggested that the Indigenous population remained unaware of its contents and would not retaliate if the suggestions contained in it were withdrawn.[364] In this, he was being evasive rather than honest. Maillard and the Mi'kmaq certainly would have known of Belcher's intentions to issue the proclamation, since the missionary had held meetings on the subject with chiefs throughout the province. Casting around for persons other than British subjects on which to pin blame for angering the Mi'kmaq, the lieutenant governor made scapegoats of the Acadians, whom he distrusted. The interruptions the Mi'kmaq encountered on "their hunting Grounds, the Governor upon inquiry had the satisfaction of finding was [*sic*, were] committed by some Acadians and not the inhabitants of this Province."[365]

Joseph Argimault's Mysterious Disappearance

Belcher provided neither a bulwark against settler intrusions on Mi'kmaw lands nor in the end any legal justification for the existence of Indigenous land and resource rights. His lack of sympathy with their land campaign and his fearful, hostile attitude towards the Acadians angered the Mi'kmaq.[366] Their negotiating position with the executive council worsened in July 1762 when Abbé Maillard fell ill and had to remain under the care of Louis-Benjamin Petitpas. The Mi'kmaq's missionary, interpreter, avenue of communication with British officialdom, and perhaps beacon of hope died on 12 August 1762.[367] Henry Schomberg's articles, confirmed by Edward Whitmore in 1758, had promised the Indigenous people freedom to practise their Roman Catholic religion, so after Maillard's death they called for the appointment of another missionary. In July 1763 the Mi'kmaq approached Belcher's successor, Montague

Wilmot, asking for the services of a Roman Catholic cleric, but they received no response.[368] Wilmot had no interest in addressing Mi'kmaw religious aspirations and land claims. He arrived in Nova Scotia just in time to receive a copy of the Royal Proclamation of 1763, which, after promising to read and circulate it, he promptly shelved.[369]

The Indigenous appeals grew in size and in intensity. In August, a large assemblage of leaders from southwestern Nova Scotia, including François Mius and Paul Laurent, pressed Wilmot once again for a missionary.[370] Their need, they stressed, was great. In 1763 Father Germain had retired to Quebec, so to obtain the Roman Catholic sacraments they had to go to Quebec or embark on a lengthy sea voyage to the French Îles of Saint Pierre and Miquelon.[371] Yet despite their growing frustration and anger, Wilmot steadfastly refused to entertain their petitions.[372]

At Chignecto, Joseph Argimault became deeply involved in the Mi'kmaw campaign to secure missionaries and gain rights to land, for on 30 September 1763 an official memo claimed that "Joseph Shickakett, Captain of the Tribe of Cumberland" and "John Baptiste of Cape Sable" had received a passport from the British authorities at Halifax to "depart from thence for England, Ireland by any conveyance that may offer."[373] "Joseph Shickakett" was Joseph Argimault, since Argimault was chief at the time of the Cumberland County Mi'kmaq. "Shickakett" was a version of the Mi'kmaw word for Chignecto – *Siknikt*. John Baptist of Cape Sable was Jean-Baptiste Philippe Tecouramart, who lived near Joseph Argimault at Baie Verte from 1753 to 1755. The men were close in age; Argimault was sixty-two and Tecouramart was sixty-three.[374] The memo makes no mention of what the two leaders planned to do once they reached Britain. Perhaps they hoped to gain an audience at the court of King George III and present a petition to the British monarch outlining their people's grievances regarding lands, resources, and religion.[375] In the end, one can only surmise their fate as they embarked on their voyage across the Atlantic Ocean at the onset of storm season. Whatever befell them, their names do not appear again in the documentary record.[376]

Taking Up the Torch

Baptiste Argimault, almost certainly Chief Joseph Argimault's son, succeeded his father as the Chignecto district leader.[377] Though Baptiste must have been upset with the British officials who refused his people rights to their lands, there are no reports of any member of the Argimault family committing acts of violence following the close of the Seven Years' War. Baptiste remained neutral during the American Revolution, even though several neighbouring Mi'kmaq, Penobscot, and Malecite chiefs leaned, at least briefly, towards the rebel cause. In May 1775 the Massachusetts Provincial Congress addressed a letter to the "Eastern Indians," promising them a truckhouse at Machias, Maine, that would offer necessities whose prices undercut those of goods offered by the British trading firm of Simonds and White on the Saint John River. The letter concluded by inviting them to join the rebel cause.[378] One of Baptiste Argimault's associates, Chief Jean-Battiste from Cape Maringouin on the Cumberland Basin, joined a delegation of ten Mi'kmaw and Malecite chiefs who travelled to Waterdown, the headquarters of the Massachusetts government during the British occupation of Boston, and signed a treaty with the rebel government on 19 July 1776.[379]

When Jean-Battiste later the same year discovered that by signing this document he was agreeing to raise an Indigenous militia corps to join the rebel army, the chief did a sudden about-face and claimed he had been misled by the rebel party's translators at Waterdown. What he had heard was that the Mi'kmaq could remain neutral in any upcoming conflict, and he refused to be drawn into supporting the revolutionary cause.[380] Baptiste Argimault sided with him. In September 1776 Baptiste Argimault, Jean-Noel Arguimon (Argimault), Joseph Sapsarouch[381] of Miramichi, Jean-Baptist Alymph and Augustine Michel (or Michel Augustine) of Richibucto, Thomas Athanage (Athanase) and Jerome Athanage of Shediac, and Charles Alexis of Cape Sable met at "Coquen" (Cocagne, just north of Shediac, present-day New Brunswick) and drafted a polite letter to George Washington declining to go to war. Their numbers were too small for such an exhausting undertaking, they claimed, and trusted that their stance would not give offence.[382]

Their document was given to John Allan, a rebel emissary, to deliver to Washington. Baptiste Argimault and his associates remained true to their promise to remain neutral by refusing to take part in Jonathon Eddy's unsuccessful siege of Fort Cumberland from 10 to 29 November 1776.[383] Just under two years later, Baptiste Argimault travelled to the mouth of the Saint John River to sign the Treaty of Fort Howe on 24 September 1778.[384] At the newly erected British fort, perched atop an escarpment overlooking what is now the city of Saint John, each chief submitted a string of wampum and promised to keep the peace, after which they received presents from James White, the deputy to Michael Francklin, who was now superintendent of Indian affairs.[385]

Baptiste Argimault never wavered from his promises of 1778 that he would remain neutral in the face of provocation, despite attempts by the rebels to divert him towards their cause.[386] It is even possible that Michael Francklin, admiring Baptiste's actions during the American Revolution, since they conformed to the terms and spirit of the early peace and friendship treaties, promised the chief a grant of land on the Petitcodiac River. But as Francklin died suddenly in November 1782, any paperwork relating to this grant would never have been completed. After the war, Argimault's people were confronted by incoming settlers on every side. They remained peaceful, but this was not the case for Mi'kmaq and Malecite living to the north of them. Regular soldiers stationed at Fredericton on the Saint John River deterred any major outbreaks of violence along the coast, although threats of Indigenous unrest nearly led to the abandonment of the first settlement in the Madawaska area owing to sporadic outbreaks of Indigenous violence in that district; after 1784 New Brunswick's newly appointed lieutenant governor, Thomas Carleton, had to borrow the 6th Regiment from Quebec in order to protect the first British settlers.[387] Yet the majority of Mi'kmaq remained quiescent. According to historian L.F.S. Upton, "It is surprising there was not more resistance. There was no attempt at any orderly transfer of … [Aboriginal] lands to the whites; everything belonged outright to the Crown. No government agents came … [to the Mi'kmaw leaders] bearing gifts and annuities and parchment treaties as they had in that other Loyalist colony being founded along the shore of Lake Ontario at the same time."[388]

Minor clashes between traders and trappers in the same area occurred when unscrupulous traders tried to rob the Mi'kmaq and Malecite of their furs. When the government ensured more honest practices, however, the local fur trade became profitable and Mi'kmaq could put their debt on credit to be carried over to their next hunting season. To stem the fur heists, a captain and lieutenant from Madawaska's

Acadian militia were appointed to enforce regulatory policing policies on the fur commerce.[389] Since settlement along the Petitcodiac Valley occurred slowly, the volatility that characterized Indigenous-settler relations in the Madawaska district did not spread to lands along the lower Petitcodiac River. Several Pennsylvania Dutch (also known as Pennsylvania German) families immigrated into the Petitcodiac area in the early 1760s, and oral traditions still circulating among both the Mi'kmaw and descendants of these settlers indicate that initial relationships between settlers and Baptist Argimault's band were peaceful.[390]

Baptiste Argimault died around 1780 and was succeeded as Chignecto chief by François Argimault (c.1760–c.1835).[391] The new chief was determined to secure a land grant that Baptiste Argimault had supposedly been awarded during the Revolutionary War. By the early summer of 1784, furthermore, he and his band faced a number of land developers operating on land along the Petitcodiac River that the Mi'kmaq claimed as their own. On 19 July George Henry Monk, Nova Scotia's Indian commissioner, noted that twenty Mi'kmaw families under the leadership of "Captain Francis Argemo" complained that "Mr. Baker, Mr. Guy, Mr. Delesdernier, Mr. Whidden and others" were making settlements on lands formerly granted to them.[392] Mr. Baker even threatened to have the local Mi'kmaq "distressed by Mohawk Indians" if François Argimault and his people tried to oppose the settlements he was making in the area.[393]

While Baker and his associates staked and surveyed plots in readiness for the numerous Loyalists that were arriving from south of the border, François stuck to his story that his band had received land in the area from the government. The chief was so certain his claim had validity that he called upon an early settler, Edward Barron, to represent his people's cause. Of pre-Loyalist stock, Barron had acquired a licence to trade with the Mi'kmaq at Chignecto in 1765.[394] François urged Barron to write to Richard Bulkeley.[395] The Mi'kmaw leader hoped that the aged Bulkeley, who had held the same office since Cornwallis's day and had signed just about every official document pertaining to the Mi'kmaw people, including the treaties of 1760 and 1761, might be able to confirm his claims.

Despite his best attempts, the chief ended up disappointed. Bulkeley failed to respond to Barron's letter, and no one else had the depth of knowledge regarding Indigenous affairs in the Chignecto region.

The Mi'kmaq argued that they had been given a written confirmation to their land but had left the paper in the care of Mr. Gildart, who could not be located. On hearing this, Charles Baker immediately denounced the Mi'kmaq's claim to have such a paper as mere myth. While he searched in vain for copies of Indigenous land petitions or land grants in the Petitcodiac region, Monk wrote a letter to Barron pressing him to reveal any particulars he might possess on Mi'kmaw land grants in the district. Barron handed Monk's letter to him around for others' comment, and on 12 August 1784 apprised Monk that the majority of settlers agreed with him that the Mi'kmaq had no basis for making any land claim. He also branded the elderly Jean Battiste, chief of forty families at Cape Maringouin, as a "troublesome fellow" who supported Argimault in his "groundless" assertions.[396] The Petitcodiac group claimed that they had exclusive rights to lands, above the flowing of the tides. "[H]ow far this may be true," Barron retorted, was a question that would best be ignored, or "the country can never be settled."[397] Baker added that it was possible Gildart had fabricated "bogus" Mi'kmaw claims for his own ends.[398] During his own research, Commissioner Monk grew so nonplussed that the Chignecto Mi'kmaq had no land to call their own that he declared that if no parcels had hitherto had been set aside, he personally would make an application for a tract on behalf of François Argimault's people. Faced by hostility from the land developers, however, Monk soon retracted this promise. His position as Indian commissioner, furthermore, was abruptly terminated once the province of New Brunswick came into being.[399]

Driven from the Petitcodiac region, two others of the Argimault famly, Louis Argimault and Newel Argimault, as well as eleven others of their band petitioned Sir John Wentworth in 1808 for 150 acres of land on the north cape of the River Philip, Pictou County, where they already had farms. Wentworth ordered Stephen Tuttle, the deputy surveyor at Ramsheg (Remsheg, now Wallace), to lay out a tract for them, but the grant was never confirmed, as Stephen Seaman, a local settler, claimed the land. The following year, Louis and his associates again approached Wentworth's successor as lieutenant governor, Sir George Prevost, to acquire a parcel on the north cape, but their campaign to secure their farming plots ultimately proved unsuccessful.[400]

In the fall of 1831 Louis Francis Algimou, along with Piel Jacques (also known as Peter Sark), Oliver

Thomas, Peter Toney, and Michael Mitchell, campaigned to acquire land for the Mi'kmaq on Prince Edward Island, known as *Epexiwitk* (also *Abegweit* or *Epekwitk*, meaning "lying in the water like a heavily laden canoe").[401] Prince Edward Island in 1767 had been parcelled out to absentee proprietors with no thought given to Mi'kmaw claims to the soil and local resources. Though Mi'kmaq from throughout the Chignecto district gathered each 26 July, St. Anne's Day, to attend ceremonies at St. Anne's Church on Lennox Island, in the northern part of Prince Edward Island, their claims to live and hold festivities on Lennox Island remained tenuous.[402] Following an appeal made to the Assembly in April 1831 by Thomas Irwin, an Irish immigrant sympathetic to Mi'kmaw individuals who wanted to attain land for agricultural purposes, Louis Francis Argimault drafted a petition to present before a special committee, set up to consider various issues that Irwin had raised.[403] The petition was read on 7 January 1832 by Oliver Thomas, who began by comparing the generosity of the French to the deceitfulness of the British, who had extended protection to the Mi'kmaq and their lands but so far had furnished neither. The speech concluded with the words "Fathers, we are poor – do not forsake us – remember the promises your fathers made to ours."[404]

This petition echoed words spoken by the shaman Philippe Argimault to Abbé Maillard in 1742, since both speeches held that prior to the coming of the Europeans, the Mi'kmaq enjoyed an abundance of resources that were later taken from them.[405] What had happened to British promises to secure these lands and resources, made to the Mi'kmaq at the time of the treaties? Memories within the Argimault family ran deep.

Emable Argimault succeeded François Argimault as district chief of Chignecto around 1835.[406] When Loyalists and Acadians established Monckton, some families moved north to Madawaska, or over to Prince Edward Island, yet most continued to range over countryside their ancestors had occupied since time immemorial. In 1860 Emable revived François Argimault's campaign for a grant of land along the Petitcodiac River, though his appeals seem to have received little sympathetic response from the government or the public.[407] As far as the new settlers were concerned, the land Emable wanted was now permanently granted to others.[408] In the 1860s officials, the public, and the press were far more attracted by exotic legends about persons named Argimault who lived in the distant past than by the trials and tribulations of Argimaults who lived among them.[409]

Legends, a Legacy, and an Unsolved Mystery

Memory of the Argimault chiefs remained entrenched in the public consciousness owing to information recounted about them by Moses Perley, New Brunswick's Indian commissioner from 1841 to 1848, and to a legend published by Silus Tertius Rand, a Baptist missionary in Nova Scotia. Perley apprised Samuel Douglas Smith Huyghue, a novelist of Danish ancestry born in Prince Edward Island, of a noted leader named "Argimou" (Argimault) who lived along the Petitcodiac River during the mid 1750s. From this information Huyghue, employing the nom de plume "Eugene," wove an intriguing but purely fictitious tale in 1841 that he entitled *Argimou: A Legend of the Micmac*. Huyghue supplied his leading character, "Argimou," with a father named "Pasconaway" – a name he derived from a noted New England chief – and a lady love whose father he called "Modockwando." In real life, Modockwando was a seventeenth-century Etchemin (Penobscot or Malecite) leader, whose daughter married the aristocratic French trader and military officer Jean-Vincent d'Abbadie de Saint-Castin (1652–1707). Huyghue's *Argimou* thus consists of fantastical elements drawn at random from history.

In the tale, a British military officer and a Mi'kmaw chief aid each other in securing personally cherished goals. With the assistance of the Petitcodiac Aboriginal leader Argimou, who acts as a guide and counsellor, Edward Molesworth retrieves his fiancée, earlier captured in a Malecite raid.[410] Here, "Argimou" appears as a heroic intermediary and peacemaker who favoured the British during the Seven Years' War – an unlikely scenario, but not an ineffective one, since one of Huyghue's intentions in writing the story was to muster public sympathy for the southeastern New Brunswick Mi'kmaq, deprived by 1841 of most of their land and resources.

Of more interest to historians and anthropologists is a legend that Thomas Boonis (or Bonis) told in 1857 to Silus Tertius Rand, the Baptist missionary to the Mi'kmaq. This story, which Rand titled "The history of the Celebrated Chief, Ulgĭmoo," told of a Chignecto chief who fought against foreigners, or "Kwĕdĕches," who penetrated the Petitcodiac River region and pressed into southwestern Nova Scotia. Ulgĭmoo reputedly drove them upriver as far as

Montreal, and then established an encampment near present-day Salisbury on the Petitcodiac River where he erected an earthen mound memorializing his final victory over his foes.[411] The story that Rand collected endowed Ulgĭmoo with extraordinary powers, not the least being an ability to draw on the hidden powers of the cosmos simply by smoking his pipe, always kept supplied with tobacco by his spirit tutelary, or *teomul*, Kioonek (or Kiunik), the Otter.[412] Regarded by all as a powerful shaman, he displayed an uncanny ability to transform himself into a youthful man at will, and even return from the dead. After his first death, at 103 years of age, Ulgĭmoo's body was laid on a scaffold during the ensuing winter, and when he revived in the spring the right side of his face showed a gruesome mark where a marten had gnawed at one of his cheeks. Lying on his second deathbed, at 104 years of age, he asked to be interred in a shallow pit in the ground near Amherst Hill in Cumberland County, from which in the future, as a peal of thunder rolled across a clear sky, he would arise again.[413] Boonis stressed that his community were anxious about having a person capable of exercising such unpredictable powers resurrect once again, so they buried his remains in a grave deep under a large pile of rocks from which he has not since arisen.

Fitting this legend into a historical time frame is impossible. *K'wedech* is the Mi'kmaw term ethnohistorians use today to refer to the St. Lawrence Iroquois, an Iroquoian-speaking people whom Jacques Cartier met in 1534 residing along the upper reaches of the St. Lawrence River Valley but who had mysteriously disappeared by the time Champlain visited the same region seventy-four years later. Any chief who faced down the St. Lawrence Iroquois would have lived at too early a date to have been Joseph Argimault's grandfather, Pierre Argim8, born in 1616. There is also the matter of Ulgĭmoo's brother and successor, a man called Mĕjĕlabĕgădăsĭch, or "Tied in a Hard Knot," who while mentioned in the legend does not appear anywhere else in the documentary record. As well, Ulgĭmoo supposedly had only one child, a daughter who married a man who lived in what is now the township of Horton.[414] Possibly the K'wedech referred to by Boonis were Mohawk rather than the Saint Lawrence Iroquois, as the Mohawk prior to 1701 waged war with the Mi'kmaq in the Saint John River Valley. What the legend does make clear is the geographical scope of the Chignecto chief's traditional territorial prerogatives, which extended from

Amherst in Cumberland County far up the Petitcodiac River and into the Madawaska district.

The history of the Argimault family has also interested linguists. In recent years several Mi'kmaw translations of the "Frenchified" name "Argimault" have been given. One intriguing one is *L'kimu*, meaning "he sends," and implying associations with shamanic power and traditional political acumen.[415] It has been further suggested that the surname "Argimault" derives from the same Mi'kmaw name as "Argomartin," which arose during the late eighteenth century among the Mi'kmaq of Remsheg (now Wallace in Pictou County) and at Cape Sable and Gold River on Nova Scotia's South Shore.[416] This contention remains controversial. The surname "Argimault" had died out in New Brunswick by the early nineteenth century and on Prince Edward Island in the 1870s, though there are members of the Sark family of Prince Edward Island, the Augustine family of Elsipogtog on the Richibucto River, and the La Bauve family of Prince Edward Island and northeastern New Brunswick, who state that they can trace their ancestry to Argimault forebears.

What finally happened to Joseph Argimault and his movement for a Mi'kmaw homeland in the Northeast remains a mystery. When the Colonial Office rejected the chief's land scheme and reneged on its promises to supply a Roman Catholic cleric, the Chignecto chief presumably sailed to Britain to lay his people's grievances before the British monarch. While his name does not appear again in the documentary record, his determined spirit fueled successive campaigns launched by his heirs.[417] While the historical tapestry woven from accounts of the activities of Joseph Argimault and his successors is shot through with cords of bravery, diplomacy, courage, and even mystery, there are also darker threads of tragedy running through the mix arising from land loss, colonial government inaction and betrayal, and a general disrespect for Indigenous land and resource rights.

– Janet E. Chute, assisted by Greg Solomon
and Sherise Williams

Acknowledgments: I extend thanks to Gregory Solomon, Vernon Cope, and James Howe of Sheet Harbour for their help with fieldwork and research. Sherise Willis, a student in the Canadian Studies program at Mount Saint Vincent University in 2009–10, also prepared a valuable research report entitled "A Favourite Mi'kmaw Son, Argimault."

Jean-Battiste Bouta: Founder of the Paq'tnket Community of Antigonish County

The Origin of the Surname "Bouta"

Jean-Battiste Bouta (or Jean-Battiste, or Jean-Baptiste, Momcharret *dit* Bouta),[1] who was born in the spring of 1726 and baptized at Annapolis Royal on 20 June of the same year, in 1801 was living along Nova Scotia's Eastern Shore with his wife, five sons, and three daughters.[2] Well respected within the local fur-trading community for his sobriety and industriousness, Jean-Battiste and his family moved from the Eastern Shore in 1815 to take up lands reserved for them by the government at Pomquet, or *Paq'tnket* in the Mi'kmaw language, near the town of Antigonish. Here Jean-Battiste founded a semi-permanent settlement on traditional Mi'kmaw planting, hunting and eeling grounds which would become the precursor of the *Paq'tnket* First Nation. When at least one of his daughters married into the family of Grand Chief Michel Thoma Denny Jr. of Eskasoni, Cape Breton, Jean-Battiste became increasing involved in political and social issues that involved the Mi'kmaw nation as a whole. Until his death around 1830, Bouta frequently played host to Chief Denny and other visitors from Eskasoni, a practice that his son and successor as *Paq'tnket* chief, Peter Battiste, continued until the 1850s.

Historians have given two explanations for the rise of the surname "Bouta" among the Mi'kmaq. The first is that it originated from "Boutin." Joseph Boutin and his wife, Mary Lejeune *dit* Briart (or Briard) were Acadians who resided at La Hève (now

La Have) along Nova Scotia's South Shore in the early eighteenth century. Offspring of this couple forged kin linkages with the family of Paul Guedry (or Guidry) *dit* Labrador, who operated a trading station at Merliguèche (now Lunenburg), as well as satellite posts on Cape Breton Island. In 1754 twenty-five persons, several with the surname "Boutin," returned to Merliguèche from Louisbourg where they had been trading. Hearing rumours of a possible war between France and England, they petitioned to be able to stay in Merliguèche where they hoped to find refuge, since they were related to "Old [Paul Guedry *dit*] Labrador."[3] The Acadian-*métis* population of Merliguèche, however, was ousted from this area in 1762 when Colonel Patrick Sutherland confiscated the "Labrador farm," as Guedry's establishment was called. Many of the Acadians were deported by the British, though Guedry *dit* Labrador himself and some of his *métis* kin fled into the woods with the Mi'kmaq.

There are problems with this first explanation, however, since "Boutin" does not readily convert linguistically over time into "Bouta." Instead, "Bouta" more likely derives from the surname "Boitou." A French nominal census of Acadians and Mi'kmaq living at Port Royal in 1708 lists a widow, Marie Cellier Momcharret, who had two unmarried sons, one twenty-one years old and the other sixteen, both with the same baptismal name, "Pierre."[4] While both boys used "Momcharret" (Anecouraret, Anquarret,

Charett, Charet, Quaret, Memcharet) as a surname – which was the name of their Mi'kmaw father – the younger of the two Pierres around 1720 began to distinguish himself from his older brother by adopting the designation "Pierre Charett, *surnommé* Boitou."[5] "Pierre Charett *dit* Boitou" (or Pierre Momcharret *dit* Bouta, 1692–c.1760) and his wife Marie Magdeleine Oujamindeiche had a son "Baptiste Charett," baptized at Annapolis Royal on 20 June 1726 who undoubtedly was Jean-Battiste Bouta.[6] As a youth Jean-Battiste entered the fur trade and after many years plying the water routes of eastern Nova Scotia and Cape Breton, hunting, fishing, and trading, he eventually settled in the Mi'kmaw community of *Paq'tnket,* Antigonish County, where he died at the age of 104.

Several of his youngest sons joined him at *Paq'tnket,* but others choose to remain closer to the trading centres with which they were most familiar. From 1769 onwards Mi'kmaw persons bearing the surname "Bouta" or "Boutou" appear in church registers throughout the Maritimes, suggesting that members of this family had advanced to the rank of fur-trade middlemen, since they ranged so widely.[7] By the early 1800s, however, settler overhunting and other pressures on the land and its natural resources had caused the fur trade to collapse. In the spring of 1801 Joseph Renshaw, a trader at Torbay on the eastern coast of Nova Scotia, sent an account to Halifax of supplies he had furnished the previous winter to "Jean-Baptiste Bouta" and several related head men and their families, in response to Bouta's hard-hitting appeals. Renshaw added that the Mi'kmaq, owing to lack of game and fur-bearing animals in the region, were near starvation. Bouta's band numbered twenty-three persons, including women and children. All were considered Mi'kmaq rather than Acadian *métis.* Though sympathetic to the Bouta family's plight, Renshaw knew that dealing too openly and intimately with this group would arouse concerns among Halifax's officialdom, ever suspicious of Mi'kmaw motives and actions in the years leading up to the War of 1812. For this reason, Renshaw in October informed the local justice of the peace, Richard Cunningham[8] of Antigonish, that he was detaining Louis Bouta, who was probably one of Jean-Battiste Bouta's adult sons, long enough to thoroughly question him about his loyalties and activities. Renshaw promised Cunningham he would relay the results of his investigation to him as soon as possible.

Cunningham, whose older brother John Cunningham was a former provincial Indian superintendent, must have sent a favourable report to Halifax on the Boutas on the strength of what Renshaw relayed to him. After Renshaw's meeting with Louis Bouta official suspicions diminished, and Bouta family fortunes changed for the better. Jean-Battiste Bouta's call in 1815 for land on which his group could settle reached Bishop Plessis of Quebec, who the same year asked Lieutenant Governor Sir John Coape Sherbrooke, as well as the Roman Catholic vicar apostolic of Nova Scotia, Bishop Edmund Burke, to look into the matter.[9] By this time Jean Battiste had become the leader of a small but high-profile band. He prevailed on John Wentworth, then surveyor of the king's forests, to carve out a 1,000-acre tract, in two sections, for his group at Pomquet, east of Antigonish. The larger part, of 880 acres, lay within a former British naval forest reserve. The remaining 120 acres, known as both "Pomquet Forks" and "Indian Gardens," flanked both sides of the mouth of the Pomquet River and was the site of an ancient Mi'kmaw eeling ground and weir fishery.

The *Paq'tnket* region area had rich soil, good pine timber, animals to hunt and trap, eeling grounds, ancient riverine weir sites, and good coastal fisheries. The younger generation of Boutas regularly visited Cape Breton and married into the Denny, Toney, and Prosper families.[10] Jean-Battiste Bouta's group, who had learned some carpentry skills and numbered about 150 persons in 1820 planted potatoes, oats, barley, and corn, and set to work building fences, small outbuildings and enclosing their gardens. During the winter they logged in the woods. Their labours drew admiration from the Roman Catholic clergy and from government officials. It appeared that the *Paq'tnket* community would soon become self-sufficient economically, and so stand as a model to encourage similar initiative in other Mi'kmaw groups who still had to be weaned off annual infusions of government relief.

Yet the very characteristics of the reserve that made it palatable to the Mi'kmaq also drew covetous Scottish and Irish settlers. Its pine forest drew loggers who harnessed the Pomquet River to provide water power for sawmills. Pressured by the Antigonish County Land Board headed by Richard Cunningham's brother John Cunningham, the Crown Lands Department, instead of evicting individuals who trespassed on the reserve, allowed such persons to remain and even granted some men title to some of the plots upon which they had encroached. One farmer in particular, Peter McChesney, on 8 November 1827 obtained 250 acres in the middle of the 880-acre tract, which reduced the *Paq'tnket* reserve drastically in size and diminished its agricultural value.[11] Neighbouring farmers usurped prime lands and fisheries along the forks at Indian Gardens. Jean-Battiste Bouta and his son Peter Battiste repeatedly complained to the government about these trespasses, but to no avail; the Crown Lands Department refused to force evictions. The chief's close ties with Father Vincent de Paul, a Trappist missionary at Tracadie, for a while provided an avenue for Mi'kmaw grievances, but again, nothing was done at Halifax. When Peter Battiste in 1848 complained about timber poachers on the reserve and the erection of a sawmill on his people's land to deputy surveyor Alexander Campbell, who was involved in laying out the lines for the new sawmill, Campbell reported to Halifax that Battiste, with the concurrence of Reverend Colin McKinnon and Bishop William Frazer, had signed a twenty-two-year lease with the parties.[12]

What Campbell failed to relate was that the Mi'kmaq actually had little control over the disposition of their land, since earlier, in 1820, the entire *Paq'tnket* reserve was placed in trust with Bishop Edmond Burke. This reserve remained in the possession of the Roman Catholic Church even after Burke's death, with Burke's successor, the Right Reverend William Fraser, taking over the reserve's underlying title. Whatever was left from the reserve's original thousand acres was not turned over to the provincial Crown Lands Department until after Bishop Fraser's death in 1852.[13] With Confederation in 1867, this land passed to the federal government. The *Paq'tnket* community ever since has fought an uphill battle trying to gain Ottawa's support in order to recoup their land and resource losses through legal action.

At 101 years of age, Jean-Battiste Bouta turned over his leadership duties in 1827 to his son Peter Battiste and retired from the stresses and strains of combating ongoing settler trespasses at *Paq'tnket*. He died three years later. A colourful character, with a grandfather who was undoubtedly Mi'kmaq and a grandmother, Marie Cellier, who was likely Acadian, he displayed a range of talents in the trading, negotiating and community leadership fields. Jean-Battiste during his long life participated in the fur trade, experienced the fall of the French regime, suffered destitution with his family at the turn of the eighteenth century when moose and other big game declined, for several years was pursued and interrogated by a suspicious British regime, and finally became chief of a community that, despite being constantly subject to encroachment by outsiders, thrives today. His life, though hard, was filled with activities that accorded him honour and satisfaction. He was associated with the Mi'kmaw Grand Council, upheld Mi'kmaw land and resource rights, and proved a hard-working, honest, and devoted Roman Catholic, for which he was held in high esteem by others, both Indigenous and non-Indigenous. Although his son Peter Battiste continued to reside at *Paq'tnket* and succeeded him as chief, many of Jean-Battiste Bouta's descendants later left Antigonish County to settle at Eskasoni or Chapel Island in Cape Breton.[14]

– Janet E. Chute, assisted by Natalie McConnell

Acknowledgments: Special thanks are extended to Dr. Marie Battiste, a descendant of Jean-Baptiste Bouta, for her willingness to share genealogical material.

Donald Joseph Daniel Sanipass, Mi'kmaw Tribal Leader, Basketmaker, Photographer

A Traditional Trailbreaker

Donald Sanipass was the most traditional of modern Mi'kmaw tribal leaders. People respected him because of his natural dignity, moral authority, unassuming generosity, and quiet self-confidence. An inspiring man, he embodied the qualities of a *meski'k mkamlamu* or "great heart" – a true *sakom*, or respected group leader[1] – who leads by example and community consensus, not by force, manipulation, or political wrangling.

Sanipass served two terms as chief of the Aroostook Band of Mi'kmaq, gained national fame as one of the finest Mi'kmaw basketmakers, gave countless demonstrations on Mi'kmaw crafts and culture in schools and other public forums, served as the first president of the highly successful Maine Indian Basketmakers Alliance, and appeared in numerous books, magazines, newspapers, and films chronicling American Indian politics, art, and culture. In addition, Sanipass documented the lives of his people in photographs published in various media and presented in museum exhibitions.

Considering the lasting impact of his life, it's clear that "passing on" has a double meaning when applied to Donald Sanipass: it includes the wealth of cultural knowledge he passed on to others before passing on to the Spirit World. His was a life well lived.

Born on 26 October 1928, Donald was the oldest of David and Margarite Labobe Sanipass's three sons.

His father came from Big Cove Reserve in New Brunswick and his mother from Lennox Island Reserve on the north shore of Prince Edward Island. But, like most Mi'kmaq of the day, they moved about, following seasonal work opportunities. So Donald, like his brothers, Harry and Wilfred ("Wolf"), was born in Shediac, New Brunswick, overlooking Northumberland Strait. Situated fifty miles south of Big Cove and about thirty miles west of Prince Edward Island, Shediac was an ancient Mi'kmaw campsite, a fishing cove that to this day remains rich with shellfish, especially lobsters and oysters.

Donald grew up in tough times, during the Depression. In Shediac, his father supported the family by fishing, carving ax handles, making furniture, and providing raw materials for Margarite's wood-splint baskets. Donald remembered his dad heading out on his dogsled to barter the couple's handiwork for pork, flour, molasses, and other groceries.

In 1935, when Donald was seven years old, his mother died of pneumonia. His father could not both work and care for the boys on his own, so he sent Donald and Harry to the Indian Residential School at Shubenacadie in central Nova Scotia, some one hundred miles from Shediac. Wolf, just three at the time, went to live with his grandparents at Big Cove. Established in 1929, "Shubie" was notorious for teachers who focused at least as much on crushing Mi'kmaw language and culture as they did teaching the 3 R's in English.

By the time Donald was fifteen and ready to leave Shubenacadie, his widowed father had moved to Saint John, New Brunswick, to work dry dock construction. He had married again – a non-Indigenous woman named Mercedes Barry – and Donald's little brother Wolf was living with the newlyweds. Donald moved in with them and found a job in the war plant building parts for the mosquito bomber, a combat aircraft made largely of birch plywood. He worked there until the war's end in 1945. During that time, he took up boxing, and at age seventeen he became New Brunswick's lightweight champion – a title he remained proud of throughout his life.

In 1948, after working from one construction job to the next, Donald began doing seasonal work in Gouldsboro on the Maine coast – cutting pulp wood and harvesting young spruce limbs used to make lobster traps. His father and uncles had worked often in Maine doing river driving and other seasonal jobs. Like other Mi'kmaq, they paid little heed to the international border created by European newcomers and slicing right through ancient Mi'kmaw territory. Their ancestors had hunted, traded, and fought battles on both sides of the border long before it was drawn.[2]

One weekend in 1952, Donald met Mary Lafford, a beautiful sixteen-year-old Mi'kmaw who worked as a cook at a Maine sporting camp. They crossed paths when she visited Gouldsboro to see her brothers, who were also doing seasonal work there. Mary's family hailed from Afton reservation in Nova Scotia. Like Donald, she went to Shubenacadie Residential School – but she had arrived there at age eight in 1943, just after Donald's departure.

In the fall of 1953, Donald and Mary ventured northward to pick potatoes in Aroostook County, Maine. Mary was pregnant and they wanted to get married, but her parents wouldn't consent, thinking she was too young. So, after the harvest, the lovestruck couple eloped, leaving for Boston. It was the beginning of a devoted partnership that would continue until Donald's death more than fifty years later.

In the years that followed, Donald and Mary had four children together – Marlene (1954), Donna (1955), David (1958), and Roldena (1966). They also raised a niece, Cheryl Lafford. Donald and Mary worked closely together, cutting pulp, picking blueberries, and working for various potato farmers, cutting seed, harvesting, and packaging. They also made big wood-splint "potato baskets" used to collect the crop in northern Maine well into the 1980s. In 1967, after years of moving about, they established a secluded home in an old lumberjack camp on the edge of the vast woods near Presque Isle, Maine. In the years that followed they added on to the rustic cottage, and for long stretches of time Don and Mary's siblings lived next to them in adjacent camps, turning the place into an extended family compound.

During the 1970s Donald and Mary gradually decreased their potato work, devoting more and more time to basketry and other traditional crafts. By 1982 they were full-time basketmakers, producing a wide variety of utility baskets as well as some fancy ones. All children in the Sanipass household learned basketry and other traditional skills from their parents.

The Sanipass children also learned about civic responsibility from Donald, a founding board member of the Association of Aroostook Indians (AAI), an off-reservation organization founded in 1969. Based in Houlton, it served the needs of Mi'kmaq, Maliseets, and other Indigenous families living across the county, as well as migrant Indian laborers from across the Canadian border. Moreover, it was the northern base for an Indigenous rights movement involving all four of Maine's tribes: the Maliseet, Mi'kmaq, Passamaquoddy, and Penobscot.

In 1980, Maine's tribes won a major land claim settlement. However, Aroostook Mi'kmaq were left out because historical and anthropological research documenting their long-time presence there had not yet been carried out. Over the next ten years, Donald played a key leadership role in reversing this exclusion. As with the AAI, he was a founding board member of the Aroostook Band of Micmacs (ABM) and served two terms as chief during its federal recognition campaign.

Personifying the struggle for Mi'kmaw rights in Maine, Donald was selected as the lead figure and narrator for the documentary film *Our Lives in Our Hands*, which profiled the basketmaking skills and economic struggles of Mi'kmaq in Maine.[3] When the film debuted at the American Indian Film Festival held at the American Natural History Museum in New York City, he travelled there on the first plane ride of his life in order to help introduce it. The documentary played a central role in reshaping the political landscape in northern Maine and helped Mi'kmaq to dramatically improve their own position there. With its debut, wood-splint baskets became the symbol for the Aroostook Band's federal recognition and land claim effort – and Donald became a key spokesperson for the cause.[4] When the Aroostook Band of Micmacs Settlement Act was finally signed into federal law in 1991, *National Geographic* marked the accomplishment in July 1993 with a photograph of Donald making a basket handle while his son and his dog Wastou (Mi'kmaw for "Snow") look on.[5]

Since this landmark Indigenous rights case, the Aroostook Band now run its own affairs from a new administration headquarters on newly purchased reservation lands near Presque Isle. Several dozen Mi'kmaw families, including some of the Sanipasses, have relocated there, within easy reach of a new tribal health clinic, school, and museum. Having the reservation as a gathering place has enabled the Aroostook Mi'kmaq to rekindle shared cultural practices. Several times they have hosted the Mi'kmaw *Mawiomi* (the meeting of the Mi'kmaw Grand Council), drawing Mi'kmaq from near and far to celebrate traditions and strengthen ties.

Donald Sanipass has been photographed countless times – and he himself has taken countless photographs. From the mid-1970s until the mid-1980s, he photographed for *Wabanaki Alliance*, a statewide inter-tribal newspaper that chronicled the all-important years before and after the 1980 Maine Indian Claims Settlement. Perhaps his most lasting and far-reaching photographic achievement is the work he did for a book and travelling exhibition about contemporary Mi'kmaw artisans. Given the same title as the documentary *Our Lives in Our Hands*, the book and the show grew out of the Aroostook Band's desire to gather and document its own museum-quality collection of work by contemporary Mi'kmaw artisans. Donald and several of his family members are among those profiled.

Well known for his basketry skills, Donald became an early mentor in the Maine Arts Commission Traditional Arts Apprenticeship Program, established in 1990. Soon thereafter, his peers in the newly formed Maine Indian Basketmakers Alliance chose him as their first president His work has been shown in numerous venues, from the Sioux Indian Museum in Rapid City, South Dakota, to the Smithsonian Natural History Museum, University of Pennsylvania Anthropology Museum, Peary-Macmillian Arctic Museum at Bowdoin College, Hudson Museum at University of Maine, Orono, University of Maine in Presque Isle, and the Abbe Museum in Bar Harbor.

In 2003, Donald jointly with his wife Mary received the Community Spirit Award from the First People's Fund. This prestigious five-thousand-dollar national award, established in 1995, honours Indigenous artists "who have worked selflessly throughout their lives to weave their cultural knowledge and ancestral gifts into their communities."[6]

Widely recognized as a traditional culture keeper, Indigenous community leader, and inspiring teacher, Donald received an honorary doctorate from the University of Maine in June 2008, a year after his death. His wife Mary also received an honorary doctorate that day, and their granddaughter Tanya participated in the commencement exercises as a graduating senior. Tanya also performed for the occasion, drumming and singing the traditional Mi'kmaw Honour Song for Donald. At the first beat, Mary stood and all followed in respect for this *meski'k mkamlamu.*

– Bunny McBride and Harald E.L. Prins

Plate 1 *Left to right*: Janet Chute, Richard Denny, and Marjorie Gould meet at Eskasoni, Cape Breton, to discuss Denny family history in the early spring of 2005.
Source: Photograph in possession of Janet E. Chute.

Plate 2 Principal investigator Janet Chute and three involved Mi'kmaw students meet in early spring 2009 with officers of the Social Sciences and Research Council of Canada (SSHRC) at its headquarters in Ottawa. Craig McNaughton, director of Aboriginal Strategic Programs, is seated fifth from the left. Student Courtney Brooks-Monteith, wearing a black top, is seated behind Dr. McNaughton; a second student, Brittany Pennel, is seated on Courtney's right, Janet Chute on Brittany's right, and a third student, Mary Wells, on Janet's right (partially hidden from view behind a SSHRC officer). Discussion focused on documentary and oral sources pertaining to the Gold River, New Germany, the Shubenacadie River Valley, Cape Breton, and Newfoundland Mi'kmaw communities.
Source: Photograph in possession of Janet E. Chute.

Plate 3 A large V-shaped stone fish weir spanning the Quinan River, Yarmouth County, NS. Stone weirs like this were built by Mi'kmaq on the Tusket and Quinan rivers and were later maintained by local Acadians. Large stone weirs were banned on the Tusket River by 1811 to allow logs to proceed downstream unimpeded.
Source: Photograph courtesy of Richard Haugen.

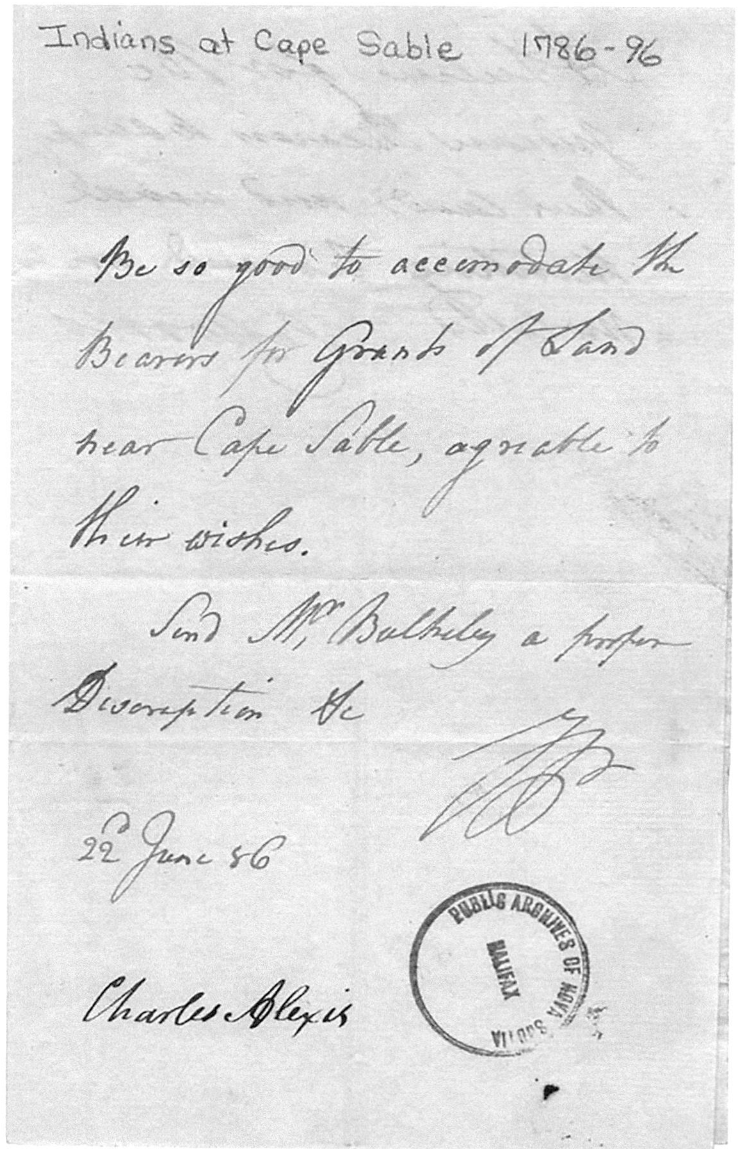

Plate 4 Surveyor General Charles Morris's order for a survey to include land given under a licence of occupation to Charles Alexis near Cape Sable Mi'kmaq at Eel Brook, near present-day Ste. Anne du Ruisseau. The provincial secretary, Richard Bulkeley, was to receive a "proper description" of the tract.
Source: NSARM, RG 20, series A, vol. 17, "Indians at Cape Sable, 1786–96," microfilm reel 15,691.

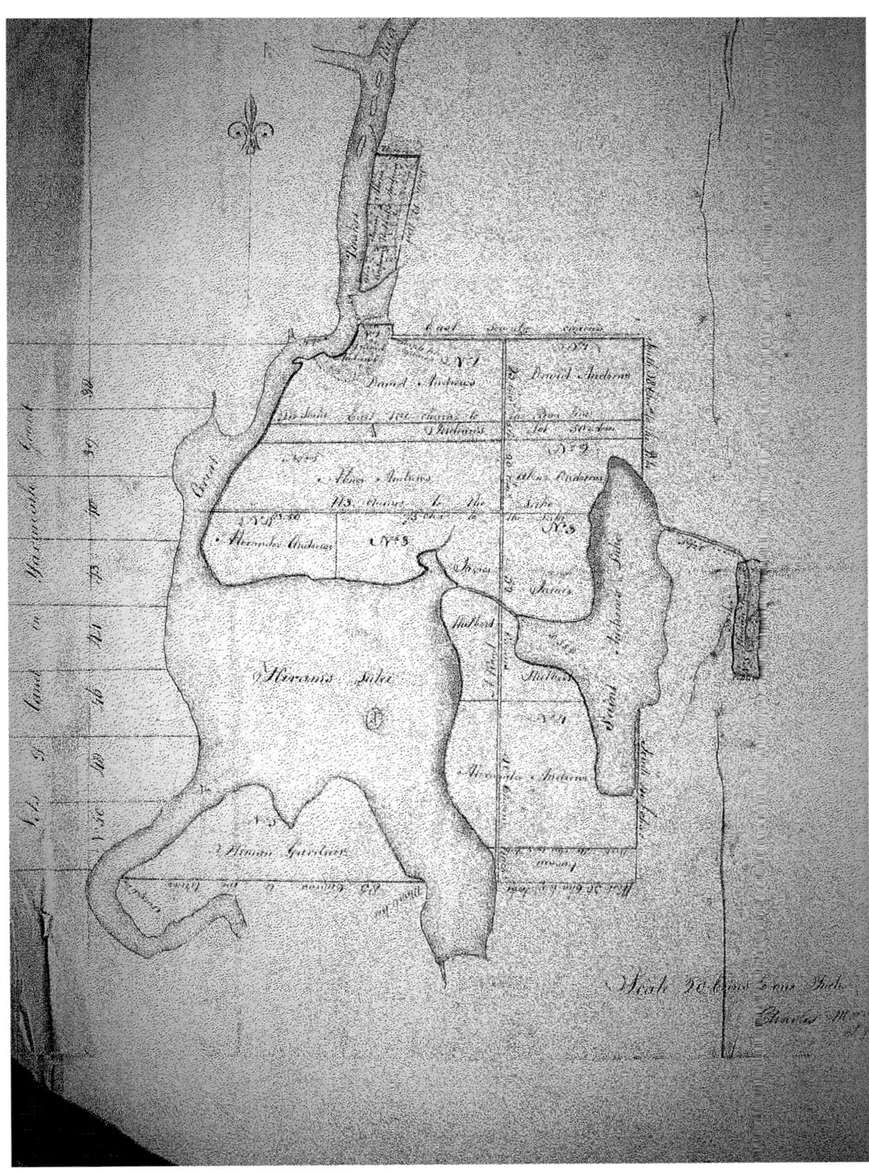

Plate 5 Survey plan signed by Surveyor-General Charles Morris that includes a narrow fifty-acre grant accorded the Alexis family on the east side of the upper Tusket River at what is now Kemptville, Yarmouth County, Nova Scotia. The allotment lies above Hiram's Lake (now Pearl Lake), which forms a widening in the Tusket River.
Source: NSARM, Micro. Places: Nova Scotia, Land Grants, microfilm reel 86, Letter Book L, 24, "Abner Andrews, David Andrews et al, 1824."

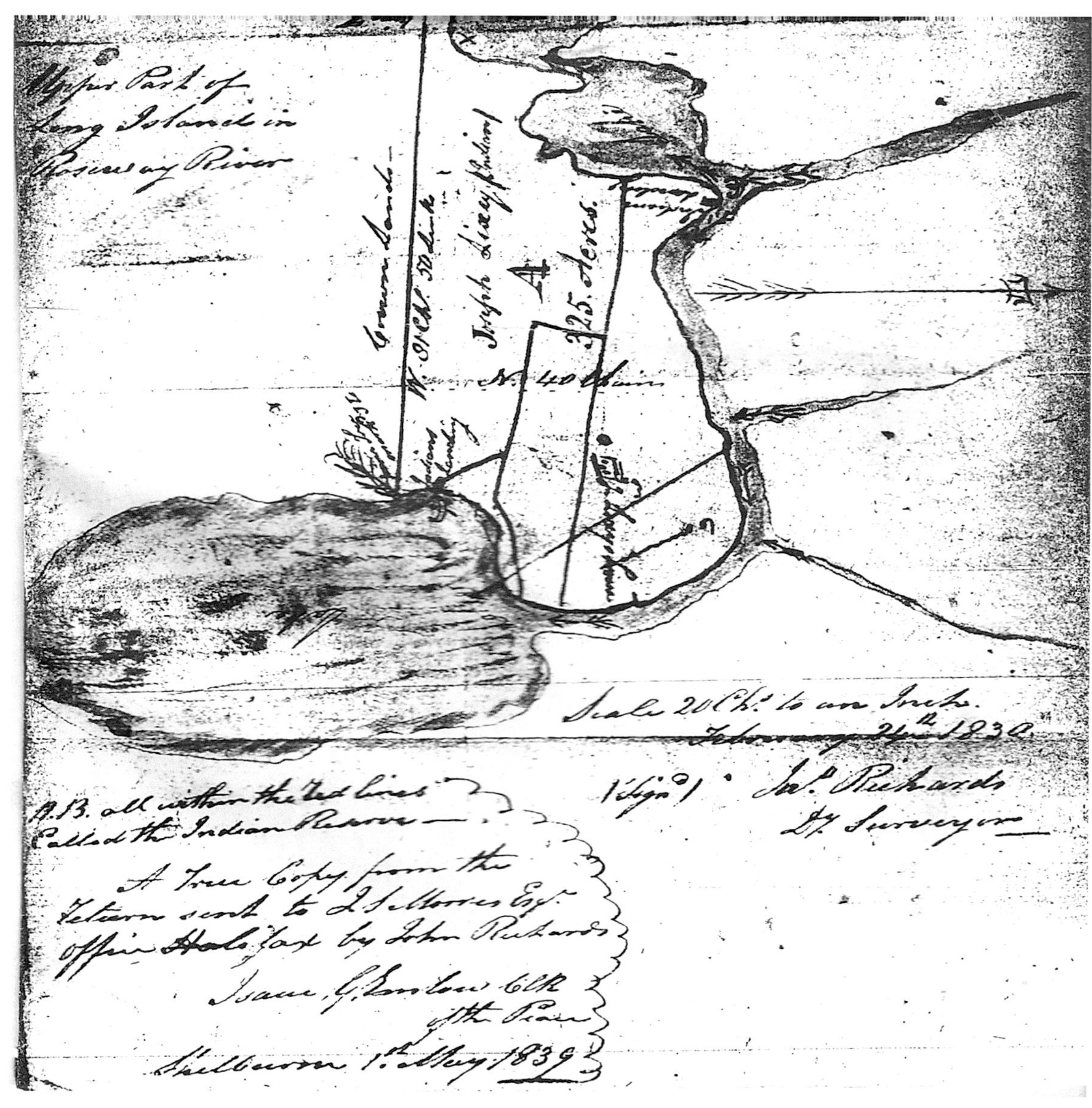

Plate 6   Deputy Land Surveyor James Richard's survey plan of Joseph Alexis's 325-acre tract on Long Island in the Roseway River, Shelburne County, May 1839. The site of Louis Alexis' house is also depicted. *Source*: LAC, RG 10, vol. 460, folder 11, no. 13, 295, "Indian Reserve, Long Island."

Plate 7 This Mi'kmaw woman, wearing a traditional peaked woman's headdress, was probably Cary Anne Alexis, a sister of Lewis Luxey Sr. of Shelburne. Though she wed Joseph Francis of Great Pubnico Lake around 1835, she retained her own name after her marriage. The artist likely was Amelia FitzClarence Carey, wife of Lucius Bentinck Cary, 10th Viscount Falkland, who was lieutenant governor of Nova Scotia between 1840 and 1846.
Source: LAC, C-116277, Viscountess Falkland Album, 82, "Anne Alexis, 1845."

Plate 8 This watercolour sketch of Peter Toney by Lady Falkland may represent the Merigomish chief of this name who in 1849 accompanied nine other chiefs to Halifax to petition the lieutenant governor.
Source: LAC, Viscountess Falkland Album, C-116273, "Peter Toney."

Plate 9 Lewis Alexis (Luxey) Jr., grandson of Chief Joseph Alexis of Long Island, Shelburne County, in the 1920s after he moved to Yarmouth.
Source: NSM, William Dennis Collection, MP0678, Ref. no. P113/73.180.609/N-14,767.

Plate 10   Étienne Alexis, also known as "Eggy" or "Heggie Luxey," a grandson of Joseph Alexis of Long Island, Shelburne County, with a client, Cyrus Ryan, c.1930 on a fishing expedition near Paradise, Annapolis County, Nova Scotia. *Source*: NSM, Collection of Evelyn Ryan McLeod, MP0663, Ref. no. P113/N-14,745.

Plate 11 Chief Stephen Bartholomew-Alexis *dit* Wisow Jr. at Yarmouth around 1900.
Source: NSM, MP0386, Ref. no. P112/17.46 (4578). This photograph was given to the Nova Scotia Museum by Chief Wisow's nephew, Jeremiah Bartholomew-Alexis.

Plate 12 Jeremiah Bartholomew-Alexis, or Jerry Lonecloud, posing in Halifax in 1920 with a birchbark cross ornamented with porcupine quills made by Adelaide (or Madeleine) Williams to be sent to Lucy Hardy in Dover, England, as a memorial to Major-General Campbell Hardy, who died on 11 April 1919. Lonecloud wears a coat and sash belonging to Big Peter Peminout Paul, as well as a George III silver medal once worn by Chief Jacques-Pierre Peminout Paul. *Source*: NSM, MP0572, Ref. no. P113/20.35 (4924)/N-5492.

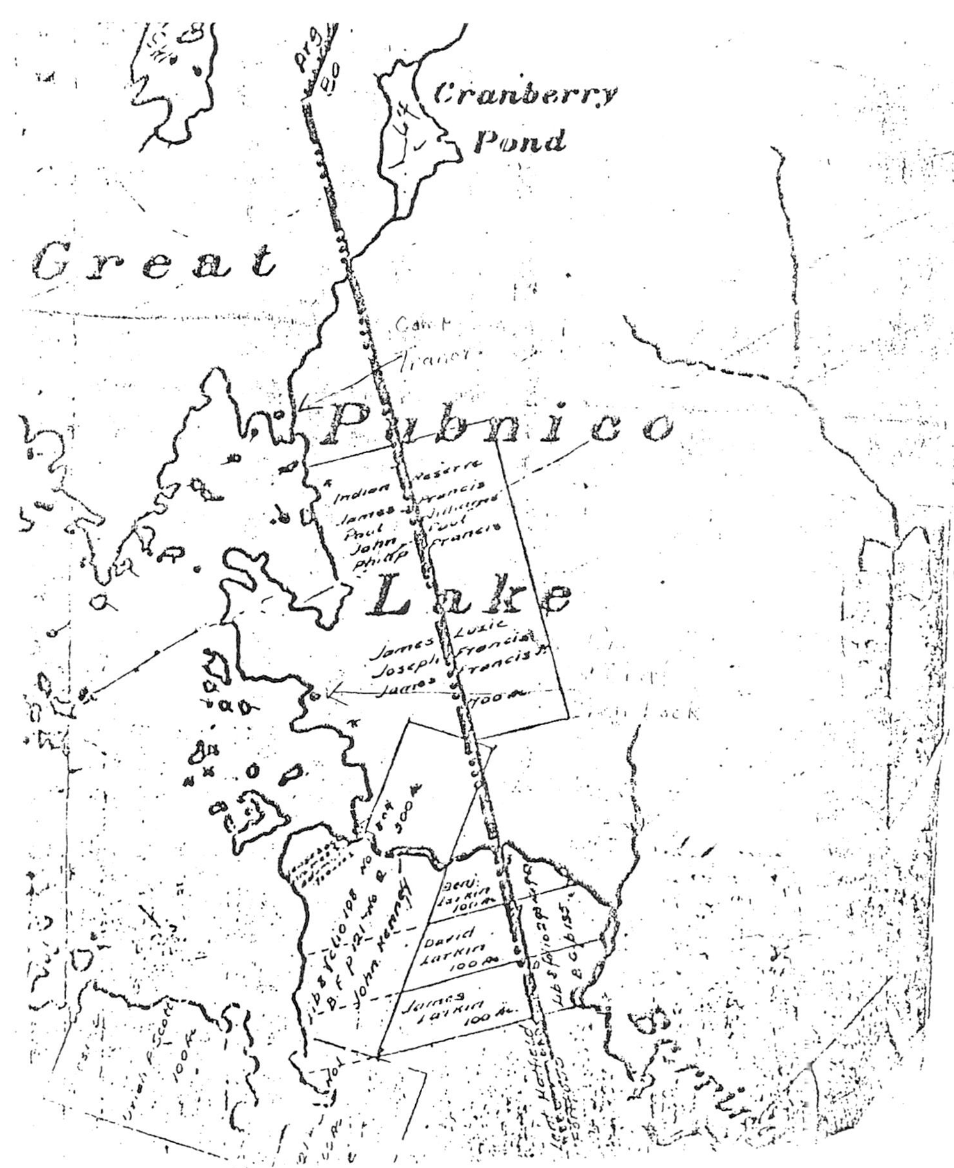

Plate 13 Survey plan of a seven-hundred-acre tract at Great Pubnico Lake laid out for seven Mi'kmaw family heads, James Francis, Paul Williams, John Paul, Phillip Francis, James Luxie (Luxey), Joseph Francis and James Francis Jr., by order of Joseph Howe in 1843. The survey of the tract was made by order of Indian Commissioner Joseph Howe, but Howe failed to confirm the tract as a reserve. For this reason, it is not considered a reserve today.
Source: NSARM, Miscellaneous "I" Indian Lands Records, on microfilm, extracted from the files of the Nova Scotia Department of Crown Lands.

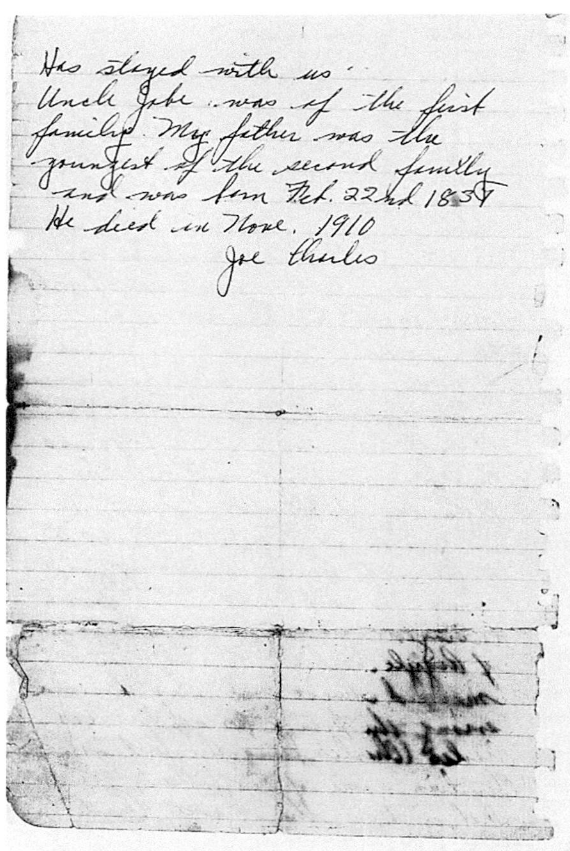

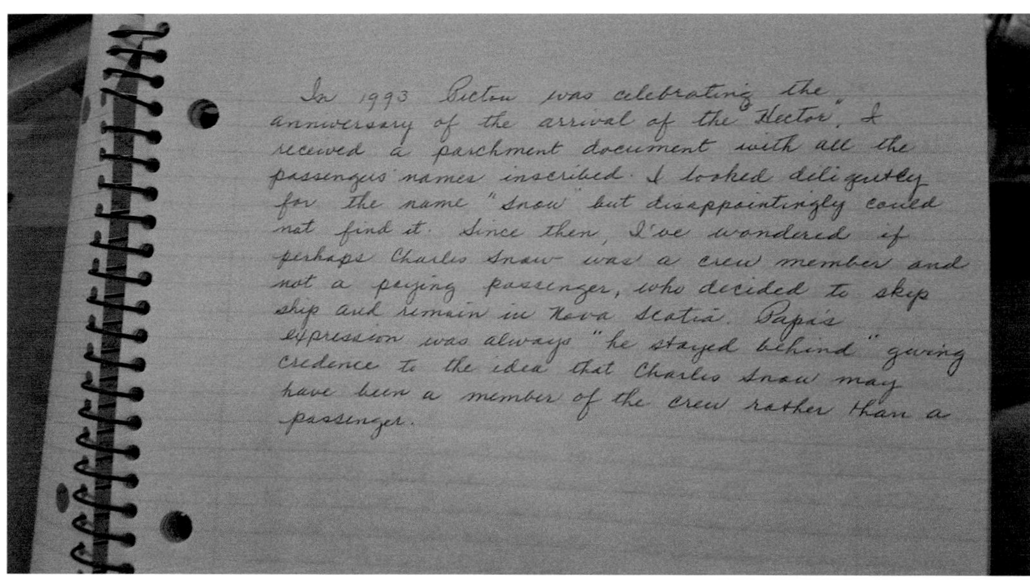

Plate 14 Joseph Charles's history of the Mi'kmaw Charles family of Clare, Digby County, as well as Elsie Charles Basque's thoughts on her family genealogy. When Elsie could not find Charles Snow's name on the *Hector*'s passenger list, she wondered if Snow in 1773 might have been a crewman on that vessel and not a paying passenger.
Source: Both manuscripts from the collection of Elsie Charles Basque, reproduced courtesy of her daughter Marcelle Basque Simon.

Plate 15 John Charles Sulno and his family and friends sitting in front of Sulno's shingled frame home near Lake Annis, Yarmouth County, Nova Scotia, around 1900. *Front row, left to right*: Margaret Labrador Charles, wife of Joseph Charles and later the mother of Lucy and Elsie Charles; Fannie Pictou of Bear River; John Charles and his wife Mahalia Franck. *Back row*: Will Carty, who was one of John Charles's friends from the Great Pubnico Lake Road area of West Pubnico, is flanked on the right by three grandchildren of John Charles's daughter, Clara Pictou.

Source: From the collection of Elsie Charles Basque, reproduced courtesy of Marcelle Basque Simon. There are also copies of this image in the MAAP-O Amerindian files and at NSM.

Plate 16 Mary Rose Charles Bartlett, wife of James Bartlett, with her daughters Frances Viola, born 6 January 1898, and Louise Mamie Bartlett, born 31 May 1903, at Yarmouth about 1904. The photographer, H. Lemire, at the time had a studio on Main Street in Yarmouth.
Source: YCMA, Yarmouth, Nova Scotia, neg. no. PH-34-9.

Plate 17 Margaret ("Maggie") Labrador Charles in 1917 with her daughters Lucy and Elsie Charles. *Source*: From the collection of Elsie Charles Basque, reproduced courtesy of Marcelle Basque Simon.

Plate 18 Elsie Charles and two of her young companions wearing white dresses in front of the Shubenacadie residential school during May Procession Sunday, 23 May 1931. Elsie Charles stands on the far left.
Source: From the collection of Elsie Charles Basque, reproduced courtesy of Marcelle Basque Simon. There is also a copy of this image at NSM, MP1250, Ref. no. P113/2000, 02/N-23,975.

Plate 19 Pencil sketch of Jacques or "Jack" Glode of Lequille by Ensign James Wandesford Butler of the 85th Regiment. *Source*: LAC, C-030966, "Jack Glode, A sketch from nature of an Indian chief – October 1837."

Plate 20 An idealized depiction of General's Bridge, Annapolis County, Nova Scotia, from a drawing by William H. Bartlett, portraying in the foreground what likely was the fishing camp of Chief Jack Glode's group, c.1838. *Source*: Engraved by J.C. Bentley under the direction of the Literary Department of N.P. Willis for *Canadian Scenery Illustrated* (London, 1842) from a drawing by William H. Bartlett. NSARM, Accession 1979-147, no. 57.

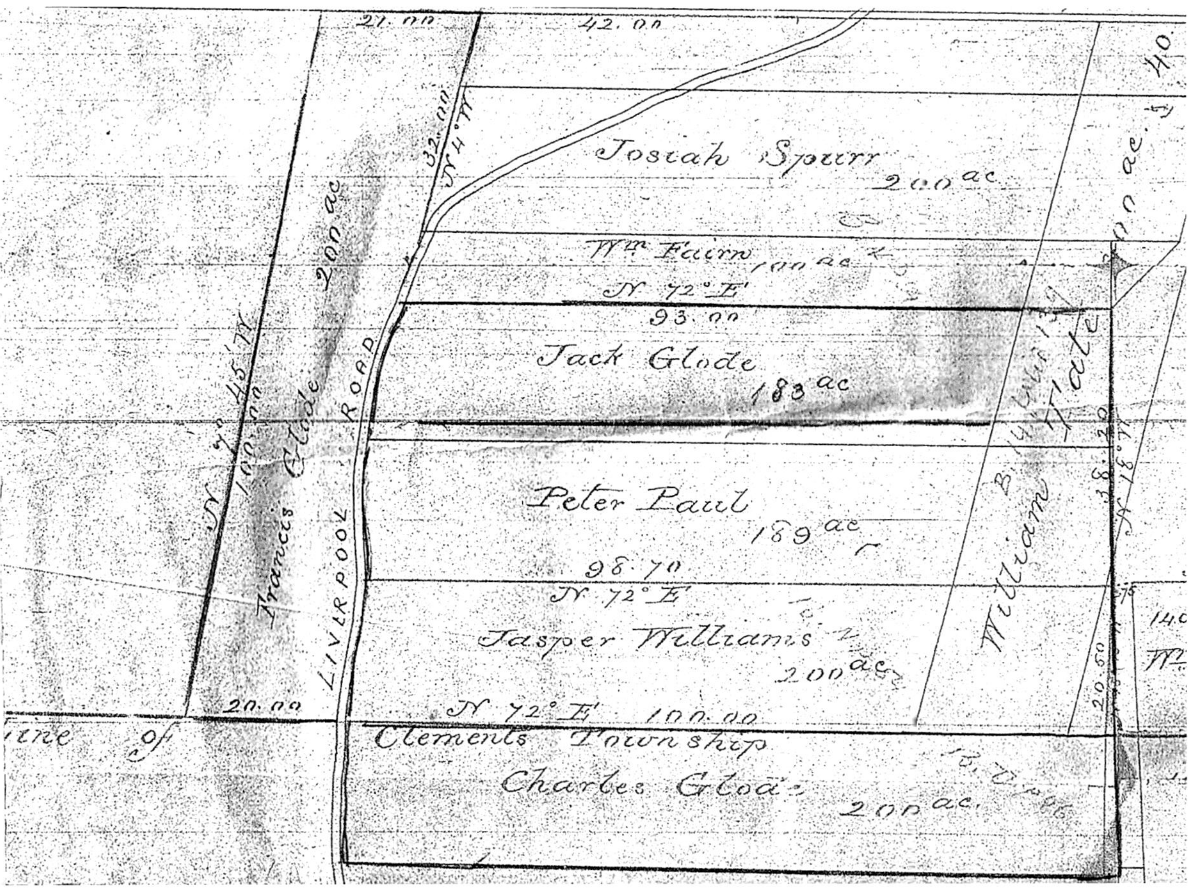

Plate 21 Plan of the Glode settlement, c.1827, showing five lots of land laid out for Mi'kmaw farmers, containing in all 1,000 acres situated on New Liverpool Road, Annapolis County. Charles Glode's 200-acre parcel lay to the east of Jaspar Williams's lot, while Peter Paul's 189-acre parcel and Jack Glode's 183-acre tract lay west of Williams's lot. Francis Glode's 200-acre lot was situated on the west side of the Liverpool-Annapolis Road.

Source: NSARM, Misc. "I" Indian Land Documents on microfilm, Reel 14,011, Package 10, 'Plan of Reserve No. 2." A later plan appears in NSARM, Nova Scotia Places: Land Papers, NS, Book U, 46. The second plan is signed by John Spry Morris and dated 1840.

Plate 22 Charles Glode and his daughter seated inside their log-sided, bark-roofed lodge at the Glode Settlement near present-day Millford, Annapolis County, Nova Scotia.
Source: LAC C-30968, Pencil sketch by Ensign James Wandesford Butler, "Charles Glode's camp on ye Road from Annapolis to Liverpool – October 1837."

Plate 23 Chief Andrew James Meuse Jr., his wife, Glyd Meuse, and others on St. Anne's Day at Bear River, Digby County, c.1907. *Left to right*: Mrs. Mary Tony, Glyd Meuse, Chief James Meuse, Mrs. Madeleine Paul with a child, and Mrs. (Fanny) Noel Pictou. Chief Meuse died in April 1912.
Source: Photograph by R.N. Harris, Alexander Leighton Collection, NSM, MP0451, Ref no. P113/N-6685.

Plate 24 Chief Ben Pictou, Jack Glode's successor as Annapolis district chief, standing in front of his two-storey house at Lequille, holding a wooden club and wearing a traditional coat with sash and a feathered headdress, c.1940.
Source: NSM, William Dennis Collection, MP0668, Ref. no. P113/73.180.599/N-14,766.

Plate 25 The noted Mi'kmaw guide James Glode holding a gun and wearing a ceremonial coat, leggings, moccasins, and headdress on St. Anne's Day at Shubenacadie, c.1890. Glode was approaching sixty years of age when he posed for this photograph.
Source: NSM, MP0265, William Dennis Collection, Ref. no. P113/73.180.581/N-14,795.

Plate 26 First World War hero Samuel Freeman Glode of Milton, Queens County, photographed between 1920 and 1930, wearing the Distinguished Conduct Medal, the British War Medal, and the Victory Medal.
Source: NSM, MP0265, Ref. no. P113/73.180.612c, detail N-14,761.

Plate 27 Thomas William Gloade, age fifty-seven, on Merigomish Island, Pictou County, Nova Scotia, in 1930. *Source*: Courtesy of NMAI, Washington, DC, Ref. no. N19825.

Plate 28 Young Johnny Glode of the Great Pubnico Lake Road settlement with Helen (Crowell) Goodwin, a local schoolteacher, following a successful deer-hunting expedition, c.1939.
Source: Collection of Kenneth and Doris Peters, who borrowed the photograph from Gilbert Goodwin of West Pubnico. ATCHA, Photo accession no. P1989: 4239.

Plate 29 Three of Young Johnny Glode and Marguerite Anne Robbins's children appear in this photograph taken outside the schoolhouse at Pubnico Head, near the Great Pubnico Lake Road community in Yarmouth County, c.1940. Samuel Glode stands third from the right in the back row, next to his sister Blanche. George Glode is third from the right in the second row.
Source: ATCHA, P1989: 39.

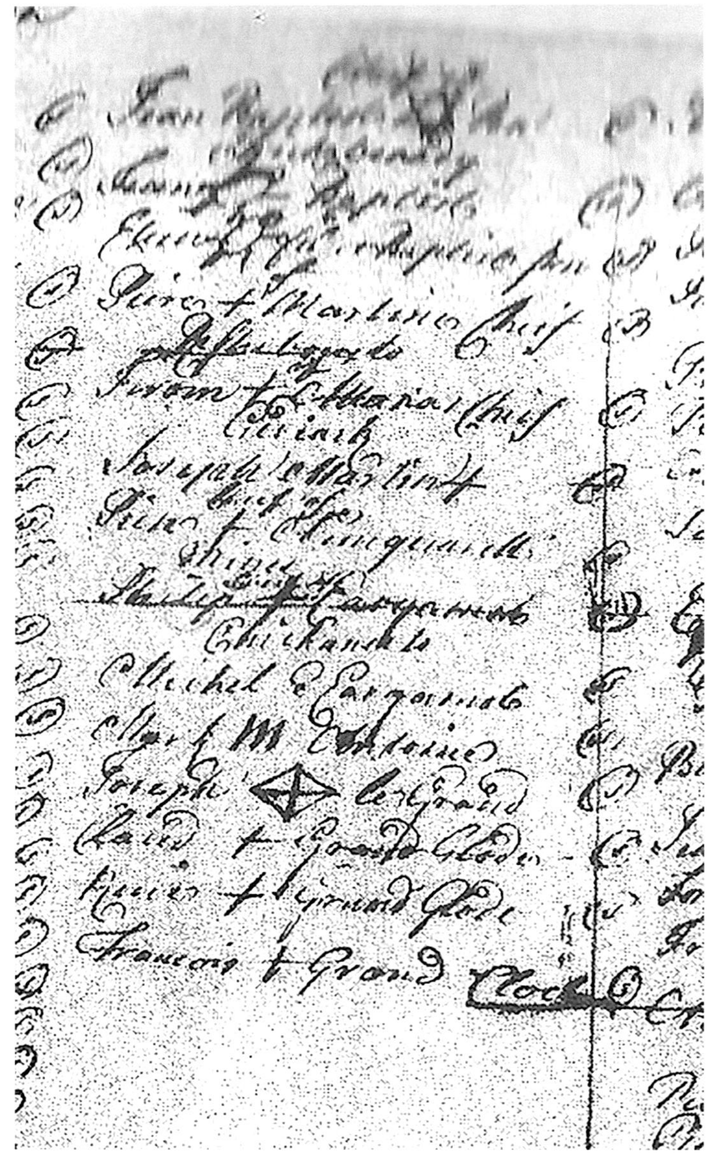

Plate 30 A close-up of some of the Mi'kmaw names forming the second column of Indigenous signatures on the 4 June 1726 ratification at Annapolis Royal of the treaty signed at Boston the previous year between the English and the Eastern Abenaki. The name of Jehan Grand Claude's son, Joseph Le Grand (Claude), appears fourth from the bottom, along with Joseph's unique designating mark, a diamond with a cross inside. The names "Philip Eargomot [Argimault], Chief of Chickanicto [Chignecto]" and "Pierre Amquarett [Momcharrett], Chief of Minis [Minas]" also appear in the same column.
Source: NSARM, CO 217/38/117.

Copy
of the Brevet de Commission of the Indian chief.

Nous Jean-Baptiste Louis Le Prevost
Chevalier Seigneur Duquesnel Capitaine de Vaisseau
du Roy Chev. de l'Ordre Royal & Militaire de S.t Louis
Commandant pour Sa Majesté a l'Isle Royale Isle
S.t Jean & autres adjacentes.

Estant necessaire pour le bien du Service de Sa
Majesté & pour la tranquillité du village Sauvage
Mikmak de Mirligueche en l'Acadie dependant
de ce gouvernement, de pourvoir à l'établissement d'un
Chef dont l'experience pour la guerre & la bonne
conduite Soit connue, & Sous le bon & louable rapport
qui nous a été fait de la personne du nommé
Francois Mious de Sa capacité pour la guerre
& de Son Zele & attachement à la France Nous
n'avons cru faire un meilleur choix que de Sa personne
pour Commander ledit village de Mirligueche; Et en
consequence l'avons commis & établi par ces presentes
pour le mettre à la tête de tous les Sauvages com-
posant ledit village afin de leur faire executer les
ordres que nous lui donnerons. Ordonnons à tous
lesdits Sauvages de le reconnoître & lui obeir en tout
ce qu'il leur commandera pour le Service du Roy.
Pour raison de quoi Nous lui avons donné les
Presentes & à icelle fait apposer le cachet de nos
Armes. Fait à Louisbourg ce vingt cinquieme Juillet
Mil Sept cent quarante deux   (Signé) Duquesnel

(L.S.)   N.B. The Son of Said Francis Mious, possessor of the original
hath besides a Medal of Louis XV. which he wears when he
appears at Church. He is now in a decrepit old age.

Plate 31 Copy of Francois Mius's commission naming him "Chef de Mikmaq de Mirliguèche," presented to him on 25 July 1742 by the governor at Louisbourg, Jean-Baptiste Louis Le Prevost, Chevalier Seigneur Duquesnel.
Source: NSARM, RG 1, microfilm reel 23.776. vol. 430, doc. 20.

Plate 32 John Williams and his wife Adelaide (or Madeleine) Thomas, a daughter of Louis Thomas and Mary Morris, about 1886. This photograph, by E.F. Heffler, was published as a postcard and read: "78881/E.F. Heffler, Hfx, N.S./M.J. Co. Mtl [Montreal] No. 916." John and Madeleine reputedly had fourteen children, but all, except for a daughter named Ruby, died before reaching adulthood.
Source: NSM MP0259, Ref. no. N-1030.

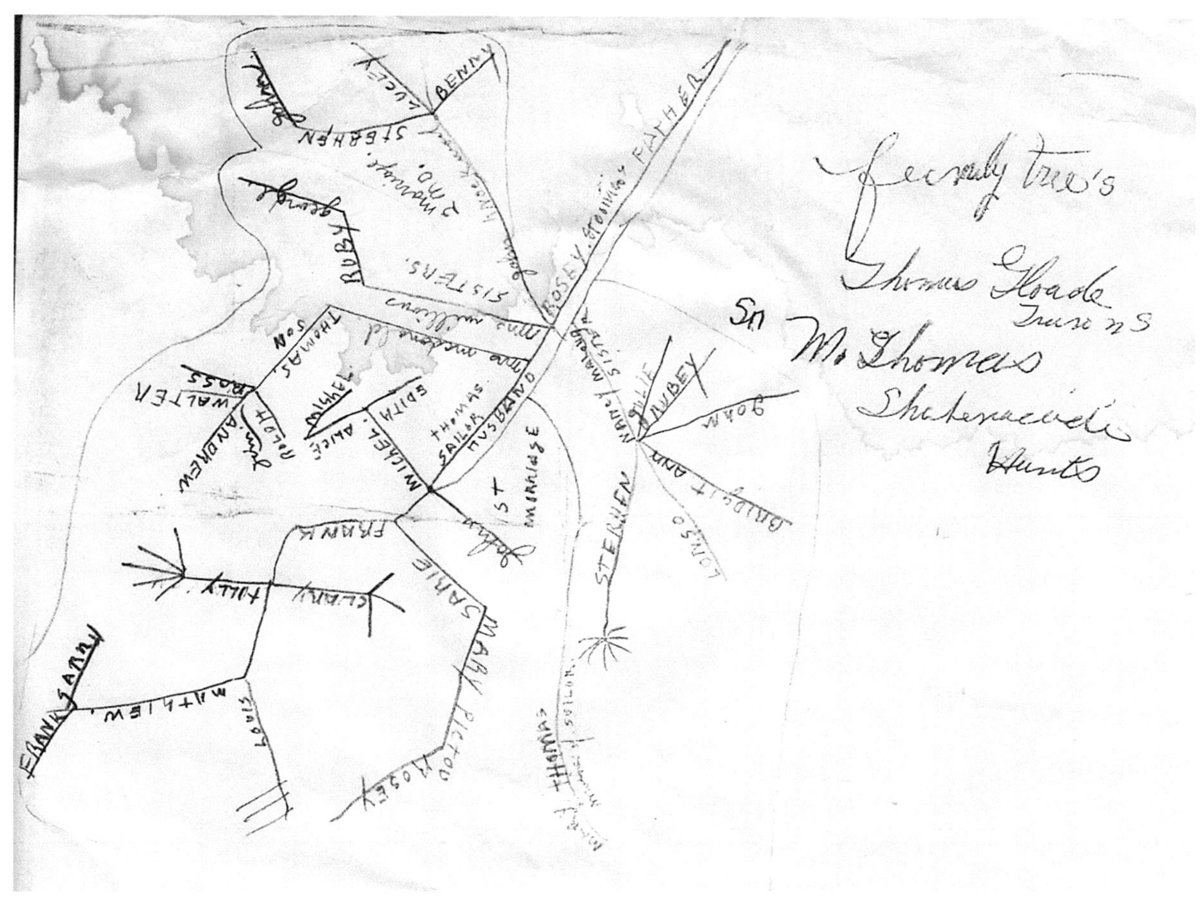

Plate 33 Edith Thomas's genealogical chart with "Thomas Sailor" inscribed in the middle of the page, near lines drawn to "Mrs. [John] Williams (nee Adelaide Thomas) and Ruby [Williams]" and to "Michael [Thomas], Edith and Alice." Edith correctly considers "Thomas, Sailor" to be the apical ancestor of the Mi'kmaw Thomas family, and depicts Mrs. Williams (Adelaide Thomas), the wife of John Williams, as one of Thomas's descendants. Edith, however, radically telescopes generations, as Chief Jean-Baptist Thoma died around 1770.
Source: Drawn by Edith Thomas, c.1960. Provided courtesy of Stephen and Carrie Gloade of Millbrook.

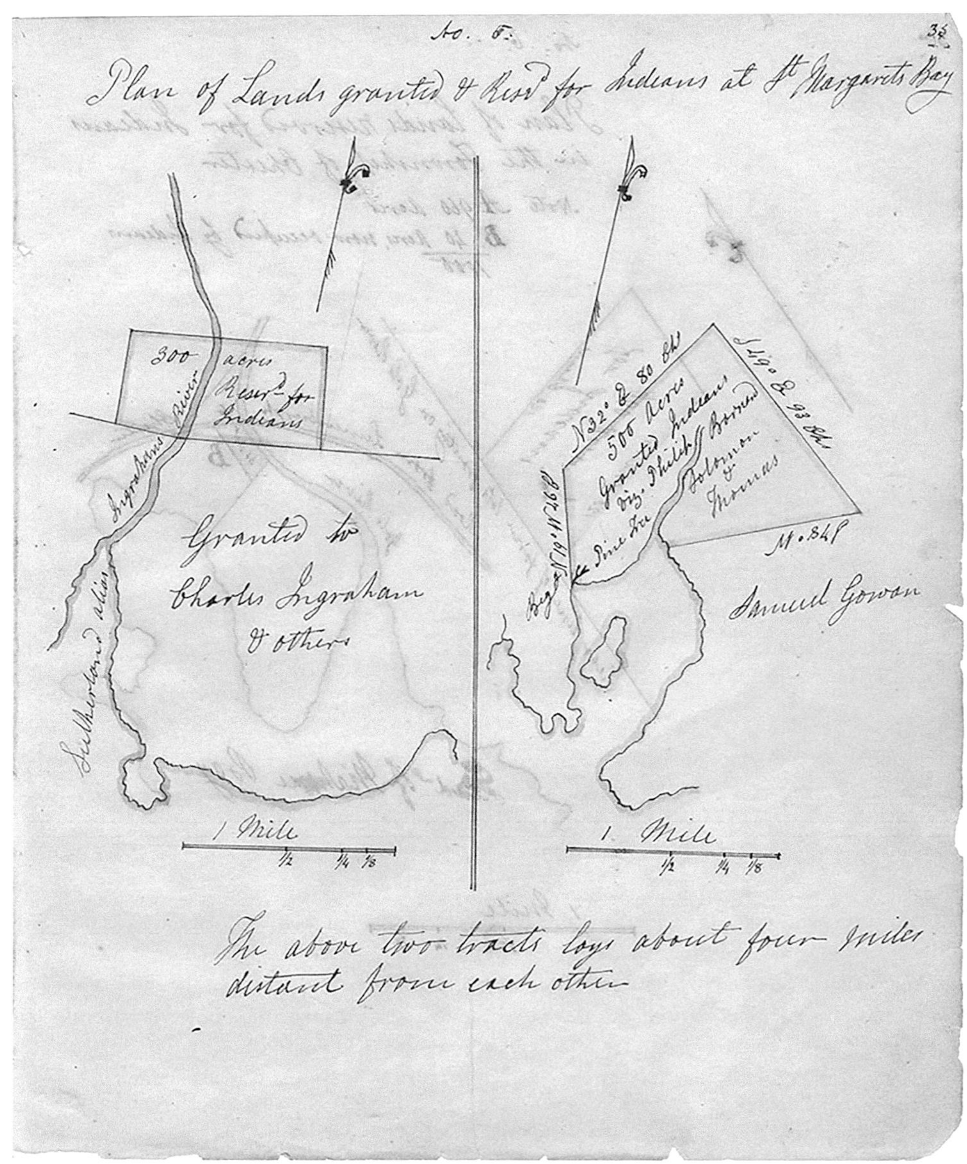

Plate 34 Plan no. 8 of part of the Indian Lands in Nova Scotia – Halifax County, St. Margaret's Bay, showing the three-hundred-acre reserve at Ingram's River and the five hundred acres accorded to Chief Philip Bernard at the Head of St. Margaret's Bay in 1786. This was one of nine plans of reserves signed by John Spry Morris, and dated 20 May 1842, that Joseph Howe carried with him during his "Western Tour" of southwestern Nova Scotia.
Source: NSARM, RG 1, microfilm reel no. 14011, vol. 432, 35.

Plate 35 Thomas Hammond (1886–1916), a descendant of Magdalene Pennel and the *métis* deserter Thomas Hammond, was born at Scarsdale near New Germany, Lunenburg County. In 1915 he joined the 26th New Brunswick Battalion of the Canadian Expeditionary Force as a private, and in 1916, at age twenty-nine, was killed in action during the Somme offensive at the Battle of Flers-Courcelette in northern France.
Source: NSM, Collection of Lena Paul Pictou, MP1187, Ref. no. P113/2000.4.58/N-17,311.

Plate 36 During the 1920s and 1930s, Joe Pennel (or Penall) of Lequille, Nova Scotia, was a celebrated fiddle player at events throughout southwestern Nova Scotia. The son of James Penall and Mary Anne Toney of Gold River, Joe stands, violin in hand, at the door of Evangeline Francis Pictou's house at Lequille. Joe married Mary Christine Pictou, a daughter of Chief Ben Pictou and Madeline Paul, in 1905.
Source: Collection of Evangeline Francis Pictou and Irene Sexton, NSM, MP1155, Ref. no. P113/2000.4.26/N-18,088.

Plate 37 Portrait of Michael Francklin painted in 1762 by the colonial artist John Singleton Copely (1738–1815). As Indian commissioner of Nova Scotia between 1766 and 1782, Francklin came into close contact with chiefs Peminout Paul and Charles Alexis.
Source: NSM, photographic collection. The original oil is housed at the Uniacke Estate Museum at Mount Uniacke, Nova Scotia.

Plate 38 *Left to right*: Unknown man, Judge Peminout Paul, Chief Jacques-Pierre Peminout Paul, and John Noel. The three women in front are unidentified. This image, taken by F.W. Jonson, may commemorate the installation of Jacques-Pierre Peminout (Peminuit) Paul as *Sipekne'katik* district chief at St. Mary's Cathedral in Halifax on 15 September 1856. *Source*: NSARM photographic collection, photograph by F.W. Jonson, c.1856.

Plate 39 Christianne Paul Morris (1814–84), who likely was a granddaughter of Chief Peminout Paul, seated in 1858 in Mayor William Caldwell's garden in Halifax. This unsigned 14.85 x 11- inch oil painting was photographed in 1917 by G.A. Gauvin of Halifax at the request of the Nova Scotia Museum.
Source: MSN, MP0189, Ref. no. P113/18.8 (4603)/N-5576.

Plate 40 Chief Jacques-Pierre Peminout Paul (*left*) embraces his cousin Judge Christopher Peminout Paul in 1878 during festivities associated with the installation of Lord Lorne as governor-general.
Source: LAC, Ref no. C-12800, e010999661.

Plate 41 Chef Jacques-Pierre Peminout Paul, Judge Christopher Peminout Paul, and other Mi'kmaw leaders meet in Halifax with Governor-General Lord Lorne in the Council Chamber of Province House on 26 November 1878, not long after Lorne's installation at governor-general. The artist is probably H.A. Ogden, who made at least two sketches of this occasion for presentation in *Frank Leslie's Illustrated Newspaper*, a New York publication.
Source: LAC, Ref. no. C-002295

Plate 42 Judge Christopher Peminout Paul of Shubenacadie, his wife Margaret Babaire, who hailed from Bear River, and a "daughter," who more likely was a grandchild.
Source: NSM, MP0409, Ref. no. P113/N-10,524.

Plate 43 Image from a glass negative by photographer George A. Gavin of St. Anne's Day, Shubenacadie, c.1905. *Left to right*: Father Pacifique, Big Peter Paul, Catherine Sack Maloney, Judge Christopher Paul, Mary Jerome Jadis (seated), and Newell Loulan (or Lulan). Image taken from a glass negative by photographer George A. Gavin.
Source: NSM, MP0427, Ref. no. P113/13.15 (4004)/N-7074.

Plate 44 Isaac Paul, the only son of Big Peter Peminout Paul, at Morris Lake, Cole Harbour, Nova Scotia, in 1891. Isaac died around 1898 of tuberculosis. This portrait is signed in the lower right-hand corner "Joe Cope, Photographer." It remains the only known remaining example of Joe Cope's photographic work.
Source: NSM, MP0287, Ref. no. P113/18.2 (4586)/N-5007.

Plate 45 John Noel in 1910. Noel's widowed mother married Chief Jacques-Pierre Peminout Paul. Raised as the chief's adopted son, John Noel became the *Sipekne'katik* district chief after Paul's death in 1895. John Noel's second wife was Marie-Antoinette Thomas, a descendant of Chief Jean-Baptist Thoma of Panuke, Hants County.
Source: NSM, MP0457, Ref. no. P113/10.5a (3565)/N-5574.

Plate 46 *Left to right*: Chief William Peminout Paul (Daoi Paul, son of Joseph Peminout Paul), Martin Sack, Ben Knockwood, and John Knockwood at Indian Brook, Shubencadie, Nova Scotia in 1948, recording Mi'kmaw stories for Halifax folklorist Helen Creighton.
Source: NSARM, Helen Creighton Collection, Accession no. 1987-178, Album 14, no. 120.

Plate 47 John W. Johnson in his later years.
Source: W. Whidden Johnson, "Fate Led Kidnapped Saco Boy Back Home, 20 Years After," *Sunday Telegram*, Portland, Maine, 16 December 1934.

Plate 48 Chief Peter Wilmot, photographed at Pictou in 1923.
Source: NSM, MP0610, Ref. no. P113/24/10.17a (5428)/N-15,086.

Plate 49 This photo engraving, based on a photograph of Second Red Bridge taken from Miller's Mountain, Dartmouth, by W.H. Stevens around 1890, shows Peter Cope's frame house standing to the right of the road. This image once belonged to the Dartmouth Chamber of Commerce but is now in the public domain.

Source: Reproduced in John Patrick Martin, *The Story of Dartmouth* (Dartmouth: Printed by author, 1957), 442.

Plate 50 This grainy newspaper photograph of Joseph Charles Cope appears with his obituary. Cope died at age ninety-three in early March of 1951. He was described as a son of Peter Cope "who conferred with Queen Victoria before Confederation," a "Prospector, photographer, and one of Nova Scotia's best-known citizens."
Source: "Obituary of Joseph Cope," *Chronicle Herald*, 9 March 1951, in NSARM, Nova Scotia Archives Photo Drawer – Indians – Cope, Joseph C.

Plate 51 Joseph Paul of East Quoddy, c.1866.
Photograph courtesy of Daniel N. Paul of Truro, Nova Scotia.

Plate 52 Henry Cope and his sister Elizabeth Cope at Truro in 1902 surrounded by their nieces and nephews, the children of Sandy Cope Sr. *Front row*: Joseph Cope (age six), Henry Cope (twenty-four), Frank Cope (eight), and Elizabeth Cope or "Aunt Libby" (nineteen). *Back row*: Bridget Cope (age eleven, who later became Joseph Julien's wife), Margaret or "Meggie" (fifteen, who later wed Charles Phillips), and Susan Jane Cope (thirteen, who later became Mrs. Bill Duncan).
Source: NSM, Collection of Redmond Cope and Candice Cope Kennard, MP0410, Ref. no. P113/N-18,738.

Plate 53 Men's choir singers at the funeral of Peter Wilmot held at Millbrook in December 1932. *Left to right*: Chief Matthew Francis of Pictou Landing, Pictou County, Nova Scotia; three of Chief Francis's brothers, Tom, John, and Stephen; Chief William Peminout Paul (Daoi Paul) of Shubenacadie; Joseph Julien; and Alex Cope Sr., whose right shoulder is all that is visible. Joseph Julien wears a headdress that once belonged to Chief Wilmot.
Source: NSM, William Dennis Collection, MP0853, Ref. no. P113/73.180.683/N-14,769.

Plate 54 Chief Joseph Julien making axe handles at Millbrook in 1946. This photograph, taken under the auspices of the N.S. Bureau of Information, was made into a postcard, several copies of which have been retained by members of the Julien family.
Source: Photograph courtesy of Madelene Julien of Millbrook. A copy of this image is also housed in the NSARM photographic collection.

Plate 55 Donald Sanipass, a leader of the Aroostook Band of Mi'kmaq of Maine and well-known basket maker, taken in the 1990s. Mr. Sanipass stands in front of several baskets he has manufactured.
Source: Photograph courtesy of Harald E.L. Prins.

Plate 56 Members of the Prisk and Gray families worked together as guides in the 1930s at Pabineau Falls Sporting Camp on the lower reaches of the Nepisiguit River. *Left to right*: George Gray, Paul Prisk Sr., Joseph Prisk, and Albert Gray, with his arm around J. Vinneau, the camp cook, 1936.
Source: BHS, photographic collection.

Plate 57 Grand Chief John Denny Jr. of Eskasoni, Cape Breton.
Source: Photograph courtesy of Trevor Sanipass, Chief Denny's great-great grandson.

Plate 58 Chief Joseph Lewis (or Louis) Mitchell of Prince Edward Island. In the spring of 1885 Grand Chief John Denny Jr. complained to Ottawa that Joseph Lewis Mitchell had been ousted from lands on Prince Edward Island he had cultivated for over thirty years.
Source: Prince Edward Island Public Archives and Records Office, Accession no. 2702/93, "Chief Louis."

Plate 59 Andrew Alex in 1930 displaying two wampum belts and an unidentified artifact. Chapel Island church stands in the background. Andrew Alex wears a purple wampum belt with white geometric designs across his chest, and holds a long white wampum belt worked with purple rectangles enclosing white crosses in his left hand. The wampum belts were read each year at the St. Anne's Day ceremonies.
Source: NSM, MP0694, William Dennis Collection, Ref. no. P113/73.180.624/N-6107.

Plate 60 Grand Chief Gabriel Sylliboy at Chapel Island in 1930 seated by a French cannon, mounted in its original cradle, which reputedly was taken from Fortress Louisbourg. The cradle was later lost when some boys hurled the cannon and its cradle into the nearby lake to test their strength. Only the cannon was recovered.
Source: NSM, MP0729, William Dennis Collection, Ref. no. P113/73.180.659/N-18,733.

Part Four

Kespek (Gespe'g) – Northeastern New Brunswick and Southern Quebec

16

Nicholas Prisk II Ouiouche: Community Rebuilder

Nicholas Prisk II Ouiouche rebuilt the Nepisiguit band after the original Mi'kmaw population of the Nepisiguit River region of northeastern New Brunswick dispersed following the Battle of Restigouche of 1760.[1] He was born in 1769 to Nicholas Prisk I Ouiouche and Hélène Caitenne in the Mi'kmaw village of Listuguj, from which the Restigouche River gets its name. His surname "Ouiouche," which means "meat" or "flesh" in Mi'kmaq, was likely his grandfather's name.[2] Nicholas Prisk II left Listuguj in the late 1780s before he reached the age of twenty, and by 1812 was chief of a growing Mi'kmaw community along the Nepisiguit River, in the district of *Kespek* (or *Gespe'g*).[3]

A tenacious defender of his people's land and resource rights once he became chief around 1805, Nicholas Prisk II at a young age joined forces with a British adventurer named John Young (c.1735–c.1828), who in 1802 became his father-in-law.[4] During the late 1750s, Prisk's father would have joined French and Indigenous fighters in opposing British expansionism and the removal of Acadians and French Canadians from around the Bay of Chaleur. Nicholas Prisk II knew many Mi'kmaw war veterans who had fought the British in the Battle of Restigouche, yet he welcomed British incomers to Nepisiguit, and several married into his group. Historian William Mark Landry recently has argued that until the mid-nineteenth century, the *Kespek* and *Siknikt* Mi'kmaq, as a whole, were still attached to France.[5] During the

Seven Years' War (1756–63) the French relied on Mi'kmaw warriors to defend France's presence in the region and provided gifts and honorifics to win them to the French cause. That the Mi'kmaq remained far more attached to the French-speaking than the English-speaking community following the late 1790s, however, when William Walker and his Roman Catholic Scots and English employees entered the area, may prove a controversial claim and perhaps should be revised for the Nepisiguit area. With the departure of the French administration after 1763, the Nepisiguit Mi'kmaq began to weigh their options and for the most part tried to remain independent of both French and English policymakers. Meanwhile, through intermarriage to outsiders of various ethnic persuasions, the Mi'kmaw community not only increased in size but its leadership, in resisting threats to its land and resources, combined with and drew upon the ideas and skills of a broad Mi'kmaw, *métis*, French Canadian, and British constituency.

Newcomers to Nepisiguit

Following the close of the Seven Years' War and the signing of the Peace of Paris in 1763, Acadian refugees, French Canadians, disbanded French soldiers who had seen action in the Battle of Restigouche, and a few Mi'kmaq from Listuguj entered the Nepisiguit River region.[6] In the 1770s only three Mi'kmaw families were at Nepisiguit, two from southwest Miramichi and the third being the Ouiouche family from Listuguj. Though Nicholas Ouiouche Prisk I did not stay long in the Nepisiguit River region, two of his sons, Nicholas and Mathieu, in their youth camped for extended periods along the Nepisiguit River – where they struck up an acquaintanceship with John Young Sr.[7] Young, who committed an undisclosed offence or felony in his home country and then fled to North America, spoke Mi'kmaw, French, and English, possessed a rudimentary education, and wrote with a fine cursive hand.[8] Around 1829 Robert Cooney, a New Brunswick Methodist clergyman and historian, encountered a ninety-four-year-old Nepisiguit resident named James Robertson (1736–c.1836), born in Morayshire, Scotland, who informed him that he and John Young Sr., deceased by 1829, had been employed by a naval war veteran named George Walker who at various times had been a privateer sea captain, merchant, and administrator and from 1768 to 1777 operated a fishing and trading station on Nepisiguit Harbour.[9] The main trading post lay on the harbour's north shore at Point-aux-Pères, where there was a wooden chapel dedicated to St. Mary. During the summer Walker lived at a splendidly furnished resort on Alston Point that he called Youghal Park.[10] This second establishment was surrounded by a fine lawn and an immense garden, and had five large storehouses and a gun battery located at the entrance to the basin.[11] Across from Alston Point, at the mouth of the harbour, lay Caron Point, which had been a seasonally occupied Mi'kmaw encampment ground for over six hundred years.[12]

Walker maintained a fishing station on the Restigouche River under the supervision of one of his employees named William Smith, who was married to a Mi'kmaw woman.[13] He also operated fisheries at Belledune, on the Jacquet River, at Paspebiac, and near the mouth of the Nepisiguit River. As the only justice of the peace in the district, he settled community disputes and in the absence of a priest, conducted baptisms, marriages and burials. Exports from Nepisiguit included fish, furs, moose hides, walrus tusk ivory and sea mammal blubber. His employees included coopers and carpenters who made barrels for the fish trade to the Mediterranean and Caribbean. They also built fishing shallops, although in 1776 Walker commissioned Alexis Landry, an Acadian boat-builder from Caraquet, to construct a larger vessel for sale on the London market. Among other duties, John Young, since he had a knowledge

of elementary mathematics, was responsible "for handling receipts with orders either coming or going to the Antilles" which suggested he managed the "shipping part of the business for Walker."[14]

Mi'kmaq who traded at Walker's post camped at the mouth of the Nepisiguit River. In June 1772 a member of the Miramichi band, François Julien, or Julian (1729–1830), and his wife Magdeleine David (1734–1819) brought their son Michel to be baptized at St. Mary's Chapel at Point-aux-Pères before returning to *Metepenagiag*, or Redbank, at the junction of the Northwest and the Little Southwest Miramichi River.[15] A decade later, François-André Julien, who was likely François Julien's grandson, moved permanently to Nepisiguit, where he and his wife Marie-Anne Chrisostome raised several daughters and one son.[16]

From 1772 until the onset of the American Revolution in 1775, the developing Nepisiguit Indigenous community, which included not only Mi'kmaq but also British, French Canadians, and Acadian *métis,* grew increasingly socially integrated and thrived economically, with all members finding a steady market for their products at Walker's establishment. Yet this unique milieu did not last longer than nine years. After American privateers threatened his Alton Point establishment, Walker left for London, probably in May 1777, hoping to secure at least one gunboat to protect his holdings. Just before his projected return to Nepisiguit later in the year, however, he died suddenly of a stroke at Seething Lane, Tower Street, in London on 20 September 1777.[17] In his absence American privateers plundered and burned his trading station and fledgling settlement to the ground. At first set adrift, John Young and James Robertson soon set up an independent trading post at Listuguj, where Young married a local woman, Magdeleine Dedam (1754–1804).[18] According to an oral tradition still circulating within the Nepisiguit Mi'kmaw community, Young continued trading at Restigouche until he could send three canoe-loads of furs to England to purchase an official pardon for a misdemeanour – probably desertion from the British navy – he earlier committed against the British Crown.[19]

John Young acted as a translator for English-speaking officials, for Nepisiguit had evolved into a British port community where French and Mi'kmaq dominated as languages of trade while English was the language of the colonial administration. Young, Robertson, their Mi'kmaw spouses, François-André

Julien and Marie-Anne Chrisostome, a young Nicholas Prisk II, and a family surnamed Paul lived during the summers at an encampment on Elno Minigo, or "Indian Island," located just east of the mouth of the Nepisiguit River.[20] Although Young and Robertson, along with several other former employees of Walker's establishment, built substantial wooden houses on a hill back of Nepisiguit Harbour, they also erected small log cabins on the island, while their Mi'kmaw associates lived in conical bark wigwams. Elno Minigo afforded access to ocean fish, riverine eels, and salmon runs. Migrating water fowl in the spring and fall flocked to headlands near the mouths of the Little River and Tetagouche River to the west.[21] Shellfish were abundant along the littoral, and hunters in canoes could pursue seals, porpoise, walrus, and other sea mammals. In the fall, Mi'kmaw families left their island community to weir fish along the Nepisiguit River at Oinpegitjoig, a stretch of rapids between Rough Waters and present-day Pabineau Falls, and afterwards dispersed inland to their winter territories where they hunted woodland caribou, moose, bear, beaver, and smaller fur bearers for both meat and furs. Each season brought a surplus that could tide a family over economically until the next phase of the subsistence cycle.

The Nepisiguit band was a small and occupationally diverse Mi'kmaw group. John Young's fluency in Mi'kmaq and familiarity with the local terrain in 1783 made him valuable to local officials as an interpreter, guide, and river pilot. Young travelled with survey teams, at which times Nicholas Prisk II, who was around fourteen years old, likely accompanied him as a camp boy.[22] Since François-André Julien, his siblings,[23] and the Paul family were reticent about openly engaging with British officialdom, they turned to Young, whom they felt to be an intelligent, educated, articulate, sympathetic, and well-connected intermediary, to intercede on their behalf in the corridors of colonial power.

John Young's Land Petition and Six Recommendations for Ensuring Good Relations between the Mi'kmaq and Incoming Loyalists

Only six heads of Mi'kmaw families, including John Young and James Morrison, lived permanently at Nepisiguit. At the insistence of this small group, in the spring of 1783 Young travelled to Windsor to meet with George Henry Monk, the newly appointed commissioner of Indian affairs for Nova Scotia. Young's instructions from the band were to acquire a large parcel of land for the Mi'kmaq around the ancient Indigenous weir fishery at Oinpegitjoig, and including the French and *métis* settlement at Rough Waters.[24] At Windsor, Monk courteously received Young into his office and the two men exchanged pleasantries. Young promised to give the commissioner a copy of a Mi'kmaw grammar he had in his possession and provide statistical data on "seven [Mi'kmaw] tribes" residing between Bay Verte and Restigouche. However, during his visit he did not secure a land grant.[25] So, upon returning to Nepisiguit, Young wrote Monk a letter on 7 September 1783 reminding the commissioner of the tract he had requested on behalf of his people and offering six ways of ensuring good relations between the Nepisiguit Mi'kmaq and incoming Loyalist settlers.[26]

Young stressed that the Mi'kmaq's reserve should be laid out prior to lands being given to Loyalists, and claimed that his six policy recommendations, once the influxes of Loyalists began to arrive, would resolve the raw frontier into a harmonious interplay of Mi'kmaw, French-speaking, and English-speaking communities. Young began his letter by stating that every Mi'kmaw person should be enumerated and associated with a "Respective place or River." The resulting master list, he continued, would facilitate the tracking down of Mi'kmaw miscreants who committed crimes, and thus prevent suspicion from being cast on the entire Mi'kmaw community. Second, while he knew Mi'kmaw individuals who responsibly consumed and distributed alcoholic beverages, liquor should be banned to all others.[27] Third, Young claimed that Mi'kmaw dog owners should be advised to leave their animals at home when visiting settler communities, since unruly dog behaviour had "been the cause of many disputes." His fourth point concerned the salmon fishery. Laws that prevented settlers or commercial interests from blocking a channel so that fish could not ascend upstream needed to be publicly advertised and more strictly enforced. Otherwise, such blockages would adversely affect salmon stocks and those upstream would not get an "equal share of the fishing." Fifth, Young stressed that British law had failed to defend Mi'kmaw property interests, unlike the case with "other Good Subjects." It was mandatory that boundaries be recognized immediately, for "the country will be full of people" and "Good Regulations" would "Be [a] plesure [*sic,* pleasure to have] on bouth sides …" Young's sixth and final recommendation included a detailed description of the tract the Mi'kmaq wanted as a reserve. In addition to Elno Minigo, they desired a parcel still "ungranted by the Crown lying "three miles + half Northwest from the harbour of Nepisiguit in the Bay Chaleur." Young specified: "It is called the North Brook. I whant [*sic*, want] from this brook to a brook called the third brook witch [*sic*, which] is three miles Northwest and + one mile Back from the Water's edge Southwest. This Sopt [*sic*, Spot] of land is very Risky [hilly and near rapids][28] + no harbour: But a good place for hunting." The proposed reserve encompassed not only the fishery at the rapids but the Rough Waters community lying closer to the harbour.

Young stressed that he was not interested in the land for himself. He identified himself as a Mi'kmaq by choice and argued he was acting wholly on behalf of his group and the good of the broader Nepisiguit community. "It is not for Self interest, Sir, that I trouble my Self in these affairs: But the Good Satisfaction it will Be to all people in that Quarter of the province." "My tribe," he continued, "consists of six families … their Great Granfathers [*sic*, Grandfathers] lived on this Spot of Land: from them to my families Down to this Day without Interruption."[29] Young concluded by asking Monk to reply to his requests in a letter addressed to Janvae Pellerin[30] at Birch Cove, located on the Bedford Road between Halifax and Fort Sackville. George Henry Monk, whose brother Charles maintained an estate at Birch Cove,[31] could easily ensure the letter got to Pellerin, who in turn would see it reached Young at Nepisiguit.[32]

Young's description of the tract the Nepisiguit Mi'kmaq wanted, along with a drawing, was put on file at Windsor and in 1784 transferred to the new Crown Lands Office in Fredericton, New Brunswick. Nothing would be done until six years later, in 1809, when at Chief Nicholas Prisk II Ouiouche's insistence a plot four square miles in extent was surveyed by Anthony DeGrace under orders from Fredericton. During the intervening years, action on the land issue was repeatedly delayed owing to the Nepisiguit band's lack of political credibility in the eyes of the British establishment. No chief from Nepisiguit ever signed a treaty with the British during either the Seven Years' War or the American Revolution, and this led one historian to regard the Nepisiguit group as merely a political appendage of neighbouring Mi'kmaw groups within the *Kespek* district, most notably the Miramichi and Listuguj communities.[33] According to this line of thought, the British failed to invite Nepisiguit leaders to treaty-making forums because of their band's small size and minimal political significance. Yet John Young's assertion in 1783 that ancestors of his group had lived for generations "without interruption" along the Nepisiguit River contradicts these assumptions.[34] And early historical evidence reveals that Nepisiguit was once home to an important Mi'kmaw band organization that retained its political and economic independence from other groups within the Kespek district.

The Nepisiguit Band from 1620 to 1800

Accounts of early French missionaries and fur traders confirm the presence of a large, distinctive band entity at Nepisiguit for 140 years, from 1620 to 1760. Word that an influential Mi'kmaw community resided along the Nepisiguit River led Recollect missionary Sebastian Bernardin to relocate his mission station from Miscou to Nepisiguit in 1620.[35] Though Bernardin died before he converted any Mi'kmaq at Nepisiguit,[36] Andrew Richard and Martin de Lyonne, two Jesuit missionaries later stationed at Miscou, encouraged the Nepisiguit chief Jariet and his wife to adopt the Christian faith. Both came to Miscou where they accepted baptism on 30 July 1645 and received the names "Denys" and "Marguerite."[37]

Fathers Richard and de Lyonne persuaded the Abbé de la Magdelaine, canon of Sainte Chappelle at Paris, and members of the Company of Miscou to send funds for the construction of a chapel and priest's residence among Chief Jariet's people, dedicated to St. Mary. The site they selected on the west side of Bathurst Harbour became known as Point-aux-Pères, or "Point of the Missionary Fathers." So insistent were Jariet and his people about having a mission established among them that even before the completion of the priests' residence, the Jesuits felt compelled to dwell in makeshift quarters and hold regular services.[38] The Mi'kmaq also wanted to avail themselves of any special powers the priests might wield on their behalf. When Father André, or Andrew, Richard told his Mi'kmaw congregation about the transforming influence of Divine Blessing, they suggested a practical application for such a valuable ritual undertaking. "Father," they implored, "our river is very bad, in the strong and dangerous current; it is perhaps because it has not been baptized."[39] Blessing the Nepisiguit River was one of the first duties the priests performed at their new mission station.

Yet while the Mi'kmaq at Nepisiguit welcomed Roman Catholic missionaries, they proved formidable foes to traders and settlers whom they distrusted. Jean-Jacques Enaud, a wealthy Basque trader married to a Mohawk woman, after establishing the first European settlement at Nepisiguit in 1638 was killed by his wife's brother. Oral traditions, later recorded by poet and historian Charles G.D. Roberts, held that during the Iroquois Wars Nepisiguit lay in a war zone that forced the Mi'kmaq to be vigilant for signs of Mohawk encroachment on their territory. Enaud's associations with the Mohawk disquieted the local band who, once they made their displeasure known, caused the settlers to flee in fear from their farms at the mouth of the Nepisiguit River to Île Saint Jean (Prince Edward Island).[40]

This series of events tarnished relations between the Mi'kmaq and their missionaries. Father Andrew Richard's successor, a Capuchin named Father Balthazar who arrived at Nepisiguit in 1648 and stayed six years, reputedly converted twenty Mi'kmaw families to Christianity. He failed, however, to identify Mi'kmaw leaders, and neither did Nicolas Denys, a French official and merchant who moved his headquarters to Point-aux-Pères in 1669 after a fire destroyed his post at Saint Pierre, Cape Breton.[41] Perhaps Denys, being seventy years old when he retired to Nepisiguit, retreated somewhat from the society about him, for his *The Description and Natural History of the Coasts of North America* that he wrote during these years gives no indication that he interacted with any Mi'kmaw individuals on a close personal basis.[42]

Sources other than Denys's work provide insights, if not on chiefs, then on the importance of the Nepisiguit group politically in relation to others within the *Kespek* district. The Recollect Chrestien Le Clercq, who in September 1676 travelled to Nepisiguit from his mission headquarters on the Restigouche River, grew so enamoured with the people and scenic geography of Nepisiguit that he approached Nicolas Denys's son, Sieur Richard Denys de Fronsac, at his trading station on Beaubears Island at the forks of the Miramichi River,[43] for a land concession in the area.[44] Though the missionary did not find that the Nepisiguit group distinguished itself from those around it by a specific mark, such as the salmon designation used at Listuguj or the cross employed by the Miramichi people, he regarded the Nepisiguit band as important enough to consider establishing a mission centre in its midst.[45] He even anticipated drawing Mi'kmaq from Restigouche and Miramichi to Nepisiguit for this purpose, but his hopes proved short lived. Facing serious financial troubles, Denys refused to commit either land or funds, and when the Quebec seminary also voiced opposition to the scheme Le Clercq had to abandon the project.[46]

Le Clercq remained on good terms with the Mi'kmaq, but this cannot be said of the settlers whom the missionary befriended. For a nominal rent Richard Denys de Fronsac granted Philip Henaut[47] (also known as Sieur Philip Henaut, or Enaud, de Barbanconnes) title to a land concession fronting on the Nepisiguit River, not far from where Jean-Jacques Enaud established his earlier settlement.[48] Henaut, who arrived at Nepisiguit in Denys's employ,[49] soon became Le Clercq's travelling companion.[50] In the early 1680s Le Clercq praised the way Nepisiguit under Henaut's auspices had become a bucolic port settlement; with the hills surrounding the basin crowned with wheat fields sown by Henaut's followers.[51] Yet following Le Clercq's departure in 1687, a disgruntled Mi'kmaw leader, Halion (Hilarion or Lalio) and his warriors launched an unexpected raid on Henaud's community in 1692, killing several of the French and driving the rest away. Though little is known of the motivating factors behind the Mi'kmaq's actions, it has been suggested that William Phips and his New England filibusters incited Halion to attack the French.[52] Philip Henaut fled for his life to Shippegan, but several of his sons and daughters who had married Mi'kmaw spouses remained behind and became absorbed into the Nepisiguit band.[53]

In subsequent years a number of Acadians and French Canadians who had cultivated a spirit of mutual intimacy and confidence with the Mi'kmaw population married Mi'kmaw spouses, although they did not necessarily join Mi'kmaw band society.[54] In response, the Mi'kmaq in the mid-eighteenth century took aggressive measures to prevent the British from deporting their French-speaking kin. Many of these French and *métis* kin clustered around Miscou and Caraquet, the headquarters of Roman Catholic mission activity for the surrounding area, including Nepisiguit. An Acadian patriarch of the Bas-Caraquet community, Gabriel Giraud *dit* Saint-Jean, married a Mi'kmaw woman, Madeleine

Angèlique, around 1731 and the two raised a large *métis* family. Giraud's presence at Bas-Caraquet encouraged Alexis Landry, the merchant and boat-builder known to George Walker, to lead Acadians fleeing deportation after 1755 to found homesteads, fishing stations, and boat-building establishments at nearby Saint-Anne-du Bocage.[55] Within six years, Captain Antoine-Charles Denys de Saint-Simon, a veteran of the Battle of Restigouche, accompanied by other French military survivors of the 1760 conflict, joined their ranks.[56] These French soon experienced the sting of betrayal, for after they agreed to be enumerated by Pierre du Calvert, who was working under British orders, Captain Roderick MacKenzie used Calvert's census to locate Acadian and French refugees, and in October 1761 set out to capture and deport them.[57] When MacKenzie arrived at Nepisiguit, bearing orders from Lieutenant Governor Jonathon Belcher to take Acadian captives, the local Mi'kmaq armed for action. Despite Mi'kmaw resistance, MacKenzie's men still seized 180 Acadian prisoners, so Chief Joseph Claude of Listuguj was immediately ordered to send warriors for a full-scale attack should any British have the temerity to return to Nepisiguit.

At this time one English ship captain, as soon as he heard that the Nepisiguit band planned to attack any English men who dared set foot on their territory, immediately hauled anchor and fled Nepisiguit Harbour, leaving his employer, Gamaliel Smethurst, abandoned on the shore. Smethurst, a merchant, had little choice but to approach the local Mi'kmaq for help, though their chief, whom he called "Captain Andrews" (or André),[58] viewed him with suspicion and refused to transport him to Caraquet.[59] Fortunately for Smethurst, he found more agreeable company in the crew of an Acadian skiff who took him to Bas-Caraquet where he was hospitably received by Gabriel Giraud *dit* Saint-Jean and his wife Madeleine-Angèlique. This couple assisted the merchant as best they could, by sending him with a small retinue bound for Fort Cumberland at Chignecto.[60] After enduring an arduous late fall journey by canoe and on foot, Smethurst, on reaching Chignecto, realized how close he had come to facing serious danger and possibly death. If the Mi'kmaq had "thought I had been in any way involved with Capt. Mckenzie [Mackenzie]," he reflected, "they would have cut me to pieces."[61]

Smethurst's journalistic account made it clear why the Nepisiguit group in 1760 and 1761 refused to meet with British authorities to take part in treaty-signing proceedings. Fearing British reprisals for their chief's actions in September 1761, the former Nepisiguit group within two years dispersed northward to Listuguj, where its members became incorporated into Joseph Claude's band. Listuguj provided a much-needed refuge, since in 1760 Chief Claude signed a peace and friendship treaty with the British and refused to take up arms in 1761.[62] Since missionaries only sporadically visited Nepisiguit after 1692, members of the former Nepisiguit band also appreciated the continuous spiritual solace they received at the Parish of Sainte-Anne de Restigouche, furnished after 1759 with missionaries from Quebec. Many Acadians and French who had escaped the British in 1761 returned to the vicinity of Miscou and Caraquet by 1766, though a few went to the Nepisiguit region.[63] The Vinneau family from Quebec, for example, at first lived twenty kilometres northwest of the Nepisiguit basin at Petit-Rocher and later settled on the lower reaches of the Nepisiguit River, where they became the pioneers of the Rough Waters community.

During the early 1770s, Commodore George Walker's establishment drew a few Mi'kmaq back to Nepisiguit, as did the arrival in 1773 of Abbé Joseph-Mathurin Bourg, an itinerant Spiritan missionary born in Acadia whose family had suffered deportation by the British.[64] The new missionary was assisted by Magdeleine David, François Julien's wife, who lived at Neguac at this time, spoke French, and had prior experience interpreting for priests at Caraquet and Burnt Church.[65] Travelling from his headquarters at Tracadièche (now Carleton, Quebec), Bourg, aided by Magdeleine, offered services and sacraments at the wooden chapel dedicated to St. Mary at Point-aux-Pères, until this chapel was destroyed by American privateers around 1777.[66] Firm in his demands for loyalty to the British Crown, Bourg gradually quelled whatever antipathy towards Britain lingered within the Nepisiguit Mi'kmaw community.

Resentment against the British still lingered among bands further to the south, however. A Mi'kmaw party at Miramichi raided British traders and settlers between 1775 and 1778, while denouncing other Mi'kmaq who supported the British.[67] Informed that a council of chiefs would be meeting at Bartibog to plot further attacks, Augustus Harvey, captain of *HMS Viper*, arrived at the mouth of the Miramichi River in July 1779.[68] Harvey sent a long-boat, deceptively flying French colours, to a local

Mi'kmaw encampment where its crew invited the rebel supporters to come aboard their vessel. Once on deck, however, the Mi'kmaq realized they had been tricked and, after mounting a brief but futile fight, sixteen were captured and stowed in the *Viper's* hold.[69] François Julien's elder brother, John Julian (or Julien), received praise for his "forbearance" during this incident, and on 28 July 1779 Harvey and Julien entered into a peace treaty that elevated Julien in the estimation of the British to the status of "king" of the entire Miramichi River region.[70]

These raids were only partially fuelled by sympathies for the rebel cause; attacks also occurred when settlers appropriated crucial Mi'kmaw resource areas. For example, two Scotsmen, John Cort and William Davidson, after acquiring one hundred thousand acres along the Miramichi River in 1765, encouraged local settlers to appropriate the best salmon fisheries.[71] In 1811 Chief François Julien explained to New Brunswick's provincial secretary, Jonathan Odell, that when the Scots first arrived his people welcomed them and often protected them from danger, yet the newcomers responded to their kindness only with a rapacious greed for local resources.[72] John Young, living at Nepisiguit during the Miramichi troubles, heard these complaints along with disturbing stories of earlier Mi'kmaw attacks on settlers waged in 1692 and 1761, all of which strengthened Young's resolve in 1783 to prevent future rifts between the Mi'kmaq and their English- and French-speaking neighbours.[73]

John Young doubtless shared his views with Mi'kmaw individuals who were close to him, among them the young Nicholas Prisk II. When Young wrote Commissioner Monk requesting that the Mi'kmaq be equipped to play an integral role within the province's ongoing development, Nicholas Prisk II was just a youth and, with his kin from Listuguj, camped at Nepisiguit only during summers. In 1783 Young became inspector of the king's woods for the Nepisiguit region, with a duty to seek out timber suited for mast-building for the British navy, a position he held until shortly before his death around 1828, at approximately seventy-two years of age.[74] In 1785, owing to his popularity among the Mi'kmaw people, knowledge of the *Kespek* countryside, and fluency in Mi'kmaq and French, he was invited to join a survey expedition led by the deputy surveyor of the Gaspé district, William Vondenveldon, to the upper reaches of the Restigouche River.[75] On 14 September 1785, Young was contracted for ten shillings a day to pilot the expedition's boat up the Restigouche River. He also was instructed to obtain the services of a Mi'kmaq guide who knew the country well and could handle a canoe. Along with pay and provisions, Young and his Mi'kmaw companion could keep any of the furs of animals they might "accidently kill on the journey."[76]

By this time Nicholas Prisk II was sixteen years old, so it is possible that he was the Mi'kmaw youth chosen by Young to accompany him in 1785. Young's own children, born between 1771 and 1785, were still too young to join him. Since childhood, Nicholas had travelled widely throughout the *Kespek* and, as he matured, met people of all backgrounds. One oral tradition suggests that in 1785 the young Nicholas Prisk even attracted the attentions of an English woman, Charlotte Taylor, who was fourteen years his senior. Charlotte at age twenty had fled from an upper-class country home with her family's Black butler to Jamaica, where her fiancé, the butler, died of yellow fever. Soon afterwards she made her way to Nepisiguit with the help of Commodore George Walker, where she took refuge in 1775 with the local Mi'kmaq. Although she married three times, first to one of Walker's employees named Captain John Blake, and had numerous children, she met a Mi'kmaq named "Wioche" with whom she corresponded for many years. Following her husband Blake's death, she and Wioche were even rumoured to have travelled together on snowshoes to Fredericton to address issues relating to Charlotte's late husband's estate.[77]

Nicolas Prisk II's activities at age sixteen cannot be linked definitively either to Young and Vondenveldon's fall surveying expedition, or to Charlotte Taylor's winter trek, made in search of an estate settlement.[78] John Young's duties involved timber cruising throughout the countryside, and during his absences Nicholas settled near John Young's family and cultivated a potato garden.[79] Young and his wife Magdeleine had two dwellings, a frame house located on a hill back of the harbour and a summer log cabin at Rough Waters. When he was not travelling, Young kept company with the six or seven other Mi'kmaw heads of families that composed the small Nepisiguit band. The forests along the Nepisiguit River provided space to live in ways they cherished: fishing for eel and salmon, hunting big game, trapping fur bearers, collecting medicines, protecting sacred spaces, making wooden implements for personal use and sale, and clearing grounds for special ceremonies. He carefully transcribed copies of hieroglyphic religious texts that members of the Indigenous community had retained in their possession since the late 1750s, when Abbé Pierre Maillard visited the Miramichi district. Maillard, who had developed the hieroglyphic script from Mi'kmaw prototypes, wintered with a number of refugee Acadians among the Miramichi Mi'kmaq following the second fall of Louisbourg.[80] One wonders if the grammar Young sent to George Henry Monk in 1783 was one used by Maillard.

Young worked as a government translator and, following Abbé Bourg's retirement from the Bay de Chaleur mission field in 1795, also translated for local Roman Catholic clergy when Magdeleine David was not present.[81] The Mi'kmaq relied on Young to translate what Bourg's French-speaking successors were saying to them into their own language.[82] From 1795 to 1799, Mi'kmaw family groups set out each year for Restigouche or Burnt Church to celebrate St. Anne's Day on 26 July.[83] Families reached the Restigouche mission by ascending the Nepisiguit River and then following the Upsalquitch River, which discharged into the Restigouche River. To get to Burnt Church, the Mi'kmaq either followed a trail from Nepisiguit to the Little Northwest River and then descended to the coast or traced an ancient inland portage route terminating near Néguac.[84]

The observance of St. Anne's Day, which was cherished by the Mi'kmaq, began at Nepisiguit after the construction of Église Sainte-Famille (or Holy Family Church) in 1800, the first religious edifice to be built in the area since St. Mary's chapel was destroyed at Point-aux-Pères around 1777.[85] Beginning with Abbé L.J. Desjardins in 1798, Roman Catholic clergy maintained parish registers of births, baptisms, and deaths, and some came to know members of the small Mi'kmaw community personally, even though many clerics only stayed a few years.[86] In July 1811 the bishop of Quebec, Joseph-Octave Plessis, visited Nepisiguit, and in addition to bestowing the name "Sainte-Famille" upon the parish, noted with some satisfaction that several new Mi'kmaw families recently had joined the Roman Catholic community.[87] At the core of the new parish lay the small, picturesque French village of St. Pierre, which flanked the hill crowned by the "neat little chapel [of Sainte-Famille] and two or three rustic windmills."[88] Bishop Plessis did not stay in Nepisiguit until 26 July, although earlier in the month he noted that Mi'kmaq were assembling in numbers from all parts

of *Kespek* to attend confession and participate in sacraments, in readiness for the upcoming St. Anne's Day festivities.[89]

Core Members of the Nepisiguit Band, 1783–1812

In 1783 the Mi'kmaq wanted their reserve to embrace the fertile meadows where they and close relatives of diverse cultural backgrounds farmed at Rough Waters, on the east side of the Nepisiguit River.[90] Though the band to which John Young Sr. belonged was originally composed of only six families, including his own, by 1790 three other families had joined the group; the Louis and Francis families and the Paul family, whose male head reputedly descended from Chief Paul Peminout of Stewiacke, Nova Scotia.[91] In 1832 Robert Cooney claimed that only six houses stood at Rough Waters, belonging to the pioneer Boucher, Lavigne, Vienneau, and Young families, though the settlement grew fairly rapidly owing to natural increase.[92] In time, the surrounding population included not only Mi'kmaq and *métis* but also Acadians, French Canadians, English, Scots, and Irish, some of who intermarried with the local Mi'kmaq and adopted their lifestyle and outlook. In addition to members of the earliest families, there were persons with the surnames "Adams," "Burns," "Chamberlain," "Doucet," "Ferguson," "Gray," "Haché," "Lagacé," "LeBlanc," "Morrison," "Patterson," "Prisk," "Pitre," and "Roy." They and their multilingual, multicultural descendants remained on friendly terms with both the Mi'kmaw community and the non-Indigenous settlers, so the Rough Waters community and the settlement on the front harbour, formed mainly of former employees of Walker's establishment, in their early years approximated the peaceful and harmonious interplay of diverse cultures that Young envisioned in 1783.

John Young Sr. and his wife Magdeleine raised four sons and a daughter: Noel (c.1780–c.1803), Philippe (c.1788–c.1882),[93] John Jr. (c.1785–c.1810),[94] Étienne (1786–c.1850), and Marie-Françoise, born around 1782. They may also have been the parents of two older sons, Levi and Michel Young, who lived in their later years at Richibucto.[95] Étienne, Noel, and Philippe, who were just boys in the mid-1780s, assisted their father operate a small fur trading post and produce farm at Rough Waters. John Jr. seems to have been the only one of the seven to be baptized. Born on 25 March 1785, he was baptized at Nepisiguit on 21 May 1786 by Antoine Girouard, an itinerant priest from Caraquet. James Robertson was John Jr.'s godfather.[96]

John Young – from 1783 onwards regarded as the Nepisiguit band's head chief – may have taught his older children Levi, Michel, and Noel to read, write, and master elementary mathematics, but Philippe, John Jr. and Étienne Young remained illiterate, signing their names, whenever needed, with an "x." In 1795, seventeen-year-old Philippe Young and his brother John, who was only ten, set their sights on acquiring land on Nepisiguit's front harbour. They were influenced to do so by John's godfather, James Robertson, who applied for land in the same area. The lots Philippe and John wanted were long strips of land, running back from narrow frontages on the harbour.[97] Many of the parcels near the harbour shore were already occupied by former employees of Walker's establishment, who had built homesteads on them between ten and twenty years before.[98] Upon receiving no response to their appeal for land, the two Youngs on 3 March 1801 applied for two of seventeen lots laid out in 1788 in central Nepisiguit by Major Thomas Millidge, the provincial deputy surveyor.[99] Later, realizing that these were the same parcels for which Robertson was applying, they retracted their petitions.[100]

The Nepisiguit band grew in size and became more culturally diversified. In 1801 Nicholas Prisk II Ouiouche was second chief of the Nepisiguit band, thirty-two years old, and still unwed. He ceased his adventurous roving and became a stable fixture in the community to whom others turned for direction and advice.[101] John Young relied heavily upon Nicholas to help him with band affairs, since his two eldest sons, Levi and Michel, were at Richibucto and Noel likely died around 1799.[102] In 1798 Marie-Françoise Young wed Noel Peminout Paul,[103] but this union was struck by tragedy: Noel died within a year, at age twenty-eight. His funeral was held at Sainte-Famille parish cemetery on 5 August 1799 – the same day Noel Young's child's remains were interred – so the occasion was a doubly poignant one for the Young family.[104]

Marie-Françoise Young, pregnant at the time of her husband Noel Paul's death, gave birth to a daughter, Marie Paul, in December 1799. The Young family's closest associates, André-François Julien and his wife Marie-Anne Chrisostome, stood as the child's godparents.[105] With a new infant requiring care,

Marie-Françoise needed a male companion, so not long after her husband's death she moved into Nicholas Prisk II Ouiouche's dwelling, an arrangement sanctioned by band custom.[106] After the birth of their first son John, Marie-Françoise and Nicholas were married at Sainte-Famille Church on 4 May 1802 while the bride's father, John Young Sr., and François Frigault looked on as witnesses.[107] François Frigault's family were long-standing residents of the Bay de Chaleur area. His father, Pierre Frigault, had fought with Captain St.-Simon at the Battle of Restigouche while his grandmother, Angèlique Bouteiller (Bouthillier), was a daughter of the Bas-Caraquet patriarch Gabriel Giraud *dit* Saint-Jean and his Mi'kmaw wife, Madeleine-Angèlique.[108]

Marie-Françoise's marriage was one of the few times John Young Sr. attended a public event at Nepisiguit. As inspector of the king's woods, Young was often absent from his community for extended periods of time. His wife Magdeleine Dedam died in 1804, although her funeral was not held at Sainte-Famille Church until eight years later, on 10 May 1812. She may have been away from Nepisiguit at the time of her death, perhaps travelling with her husband or visiting relatives at Listuguj, and her remains were temporarily interred in a shallow grave and later unearthed and carried to Nepisiguit for burial in ground consecrated by Roman Catholic rite. The entry pertaining to her funeral in the Sainte-Famille parish registers, however, suggests she died at or near Nepisiguit and was first accorded a burial in accordance with Mi'kmaw customary rite.[109] Magdeleine's funeral service in 1812 proved to be a bittersweet occasion for the Youngs, for on the same day Philippe and his wife, Marie-Elisabeth Grand-Louis, presented their infant son, Stanislaus, for baptism.[110]

Following his wife's funeral John Young Sr. withdrew from his duties as leader of the Nepisiguit band to devote more time to his responsibilities as a timber inspector. Philippe Young, John Young Jr., Étienne Young, the Juliens, the Pauls, and the heads of the Louis family then selected Nicolas Prisk II as their new chief. Philippe assumed the office of second chief, while Étienne became the band's first captain. Finally, after John Young Sr.'s death around 1828, the band's nodal core – a group entity found at the heart of Algonquian social organization throughout northeastern North America, to which Indigenous families originally external to the band attached themselves by marriage or adoption – irrevocably changed. A historic era closed and a new one began for the band, for no longer was a male member of the Young family, regarded by clerics, government officials, and local settlers as Mi'kmaq rather than *métis*,[111] at the centre of Indigenous life at Nepisiguit. From 1830 until Confederation in 1867, when the federal Department of Indian Affairs arose and sought to control band membership, Nicolas Prisk II and Marie-Françoise Young's children, and those related to them by consanguineal and affinal links, functioned as the core unit. Nicholas Prisk's brothers-in-law Philippe, John Jr., and Étienne may have declined to contend for their group's chiefship, but they continued to act in influential roles on band's council, as did many of their descendants.

After Philippe Young Sr. had given up the idea of becoming a landowner in his own right, he and his younger brother John temporarily lived in their parents' house overlooking the front harbour. Both men also hunted, fished, trapped, and planted at Rough Waters. Philippe had met his wife, Marie-Elizabeth Grand-Louis, at Listuguj, and the pair often camped and travelled with François-André Julien and Marie-Anne Chrisostome. The two couples often stood for each other at baptisms, marriages, and funerals for their respective family members.[112] Philippe Young Sr. and his wife Marie-Elizabeth had ten children: Philippe Jr., who died at a young age; Magdeleine; Denis; Stanislaus; Marie; Anne; Noel; Jean, who apparently died at an early age; a second Jean; and a second Philippe Jr.[113] In the early 1800s, when they were not camped on Elno Miningo, or "Indian Island," located at the mouth of the Nepisiguit River, or hunting and fishing inland, Philippe, his brother Étienne, his sister Marie-Françoise, and his brother-in-law Nicholas Prisk II dwelt in a concentric constellation of wooden cabins at Rough Waters. Philippe Young Sr. and Marie-Elizabeth's youngest son, Philippe Young Jr., married Madeleine Courniche of Burnt Church and had a large family. Philippe Jr. remained a member of the Nepisiguit band until his death around 1900.[114]

When Philippe Young Sr. married, John Young Jr. moved into his godfather James Robertson's house on the front harbour in Central Nepisiguit, where he learned coopering, carpentry, and how to make and mend shoes. On reaching the age of maturity, John Jr. rather ingeniously secured a witnessed statement from his betrothed, Cecile Pitre, dated 18 January 1803, by which she promised to wait for him until a priest or justice of the peace arrived to perform their marriage ceremony or, if she demurred, pay him twenty pounds British currency.[115] With that significant sum undoubtedly somewhat weighting her decision, Cecile married John Young Jr. at Sainte-Famille Church on 18 June 1803.[116] Rather than following in his brothers' wake by becoming a hunter or farmer, John Young Jr. became a cobbler, making shoes for Nepisiguit's growing population.[117] He was only married to Cecile for seven years when he died around 1810, after which Cecile wed François Le Breton. Though Le Breton had close relatives who joined the Nepisiguit band, he and his wife moved to Tracadie, Le Breton's parental home, where their descendants still live.[118]

Land Holding, Social Organizational Change, and the Persistence of Memory at Rough Waters

During the early nineteenth century, Rough Waters was a culturally and linguistically diversified community, composed of Mi'kmaq, *métis*, Acadians from the Bay de Chaleur and Gaspé, Acadian refugees from peninsular Nova Scotia with roots in the early French fur and fishing trade, French more recently arrived from Quebec, and British once associated with Walker's establishment. Despite having different backgrounds, the inhabitants of Rough Waters formed a close-knit group. Many were trilingual, speaking French, Mi'kmaq, and English to communicate with their neighbours, participate in the fur trade, and negotiate with colonial officials.

One of the pioneers of this settlement, Jean-Baptiste Vienneau (11 January 1754–9 August 1808), had Quebec parentage,[119] while his wife, Magdeleine-Louise Le Jeune *dit* Briard, traced her ancestry to Nova Scotia prior to the deportation of the Acadians in the mid-1750s.[120] The Vienneau household thus blended Quebec cultural elements with Acadian traits dating back to the early eighteenth century. Jean-Baptist and Magdeleine-Louise knew the Youngs and Prisks well and in 1806 agreed to stand as the godparents of Nicholas Prisk II and Marie-Françoise Young's daughter Françoise.[121] One of Jean-Baptiste Vienneau's daughters, Judith, in 1808 married Michel-Joseph Boucher, whose parents, Joseph Boucher and Rosalie-Isabelle Martin, moved to Nepisiguit from Kamouraska, Quebec. Both the Vienneaus and the Bouchers settled at Petit-Rocher before moving to Rough Waters. A third pioneer family was headed by Jean Lavigne Sr., born around 1722, and Isabelle Boiselle (or Baudville), whose parents hailed from Saint-Thomas-de-Montmagny near Nicolet in Quebec.[122] Jean and Isabelle's daughter Marie-Thérèse Lavigne wed John Young Sr.'s son Étienne Young at Sainte-Famille Church on 13 October 1812. Étienne, born in 1786, was an Indigenous hunter, trapper, and marginal farmer who spent the spring planting and harvest seasons at Rough Waters. Étienne and Marie-Thérèse had consorted for a decade before their wedding and by the fall of 1812 already had three children, Joseph-Athanase (Sr.) in 1803, Sebastian in 1807, and Marguerite on 23 May 1812. Following their marriage, they had Celeste in 7 March 1815 and Jean-Athanase on 20 September 1818.[123]

Étienne Young, unlike his older brother Philippe who eschewed land holding and relied on hunting and fishing for his livelihood, encouraged his eldest son, Joseph-Athanase Young Sr. (1803–84), to apply for land as soon as an opportunity arose. Joseph-Athanase Sr. married Marie Chamberlain on 14 February 1827 – Valentine's Day being a popular day for weddings in the Rough Waters community – and the couple had eight children: Joseph-Anathase Jr., Oliver, Abraham, Marie, William, John, Marguerite, and Louisa.[124] As survey teams were working in the vicinity of Rough Waters in 1827, Joseph-Anathase Sr. immediately applied for a Crown grant. Within a year he received one hundred acres, marked as Lot No. 7 on an official grid plan of the Nepisiguit community, which in 1826 was renamed "Bathurst" in honour of the Third Earl of Bathurst, the secretary of state for the colonies. Finding by 1838 that he could not cultivate this entire acreage, "Tenass Young" (Joseph-Athanase Young) subdivided his property in two and sold fifty acres to François Vienneau.[125] A decade later his younger brother, Jean-Athanase Young (1819-c.1885), acquired eighty-seven acres, designated as Lot No. 21, lying between Rough Waters and the reserve. Jean-Athanase and his wife, Mary – whose surname remains unknown – raised ten children on this parcel.[126]

The Youngs, Lavignes, Bouchers, and Vinneaus were closely knit by marital bonds based on brother-sister exchange as well as second cousin marriage.[127] During the winter, this constellation of families joined the Mi'kmaw band to fish, hunt, and trap, either on the reserve or on hunting territories in the interior ascribed to them by the Nepisiguit chief and council. Spring found them fishing at the Nepisiguit rapids, after which they planted potatoes and root vegetables and participated in Mi'kmaw ceremonies. During the summer they travelled along the coast, visiting and trading, until harvest time saw them back at Rough Waters, accompanied by many of their Mi'kmaw kin who camped on their properties and helped them harvest their crops. People were close and helped one another when in need, since farming at Rough Waters proved challenging, especially when severe crop failures during the mid-1840s necessitated reaching out to kin who relied on fishing, hunting, and trapping for provisions.

Though brother-sister exchanges were common among the Mi'kmaq, since they forged multi-stranded social bonds between families, marriage between cousins traditionally was rare.[128] By the nineteenth century, however, cousin marriage occurred within Indigenous society when persons treated land parcels they received as private possessions, and the practice gave rise over time to land-based collectivities. Though many traditional Mi'kmaw norms still operated at Rough Waters in the mid-1800s, landholding promoted a trend towards lineality. Joseph-Athanase Young Sr. presided as patriarch over three generations of his descendants who lived on Lot No. 7, and shortly before his death on 15 May 1884 at eighty-one years of age accorded portions of this parcel to four of his children who remained landless: Oliver, William, Abraham, and Mary, his son Joseph Athanase Jr. already being a land owner.[129] Mary, who cared for her aging father in her home, shared her parcel with her husband Pierre Boucher, who then purchased all parts of Lot No. 7 that were not otherwise distributed to heirs or assigns.[130] A tributary of the Nepisiguit River that runs through these lands is still known today as "Boucher's Brook."

Mi'kmaw families like the Youngs drew upon a diverse pool of cultural traits derived from their shared Mi'kmaw, Acadian, French Canadian, and British heritages and adopted those kinship mechanisms that best suited their long-term goals.[131]

Cousin marriage altered but did not take much away from the Mi'kmaw character of Etienne Young's descendants. Instead, it allowed for members of closely related families living on contingent land parcels to trace their relationship back to Étienne Young and, ultimately, to Étienne's brother-in-law, Nicholas Prisk II.[132] At Rough Waters, certain family heads continued to consider themselves as band members, with Chief Nicholas Prisk II as their chief, since Étienne Young was Mi'kmaq. They followed their chief and council's lead when they stayed on Elno Minigo, now better known as "Prisk Island," and when fishing and hunting on the reserve. They participated in Mi'kmaw rituals and ceremonies, including St. Anne's Day festivities. They also joined in band council discussions. where they tendered ideas and suggested lines of action, particularly when it came to the protection of Indigenous lands and resources.

Final Years of Nicholas Prisk II's Leadership: 1840–1857

Nicholas Prisk II was a persuasive orator and negotiator, but in order to address issues within his diverse constituency, he relied heavily for counsel on his head men, Philippe and Étienne Young, and Étienne's son Joseph-Athanase Young, whose social contacts penetrated deep into the Rough Waters community. As far as the chief was concerned, his territorial aegis extended inland over all the countryside drained by the Nepisiguit River.

When he was not hunting, fishing, or trapping, Nicholas farmed on his brother-in-law Étienne's property at Rough Waters, since the soil on the reserve was notoriously barren. After he received a land grant at Rough Waters, Étienne's eldest son Joseph-Athanase continued this practice of allowing his Mi'kmaw relatives to use his acreage. The chief's family was large. In addition to Marie Paul (who was Marie-Francois Young's daughter by her first husband Noel Paul), Nicholas Prisk II and his wife raised ten children: John, born in 1801; Marie in 1803; Françoise in 1806;[133] Noel in 1807;[134] Genevieve in 1808;[135] William around 1809; Philippe, who was often a witness at baptisms but whose own birth and baptism remained unregistered; Michel;[136] Jeanne-Monique in 1814;[137] and Jacques Prisk, who appears on a 1838 census of the Nepisiguit band. Names of persons standing as godparents at baptisms of Prisk children show how closely integrated the Prisks were with other members of the Rough Waters community.[138] In 1840, Nicholas Prisk II and Marie-Françoise's thirty-nine-year-old son John wed a Mi'kmaw woman named Margaret Francis and had three sons, William about 1842, John in 1855, and Michel in 1859.[139] John Prisk built a cabin close to Nicholas Prisk's farm at Rough Waters and cared for Nicholas and his wife as they aged.

The local reserve, four miles square and intended to enclose 1,000 acres, was used by the Mi'kmaq mostly for fishing, hunting camps, and ceremonies. Nicholas Prisk knew that it was a far cry from the parcel requested by John Young in 1783. It excluded the Rough Waters settlement that Young's tract had included, and remained unsurveyed until 1809, when at John Young Sr. and Nicholas Prisk II's insistence its lines were run by provincial deputy surveyor Anthony DeGracé. Degracé claimed that the tract, which at the time could only be informally designated "Indian land" since it was not confirmed by council as a reserve, covered 1,060 acres. And long after, provincial officials forgot where the lines lay and confusion set in.[140] In consequence, Prisk sent two petitions demanding its confirmation by order-in-council as a reserve, which eventually occurred on 28 March 1841. Deputy Surveyor Alex McNeil, who surveyed the parcel the same year, claimed it embraced 1,100 acres, with 600 acres situated on the west bank of the Nepisiguit River and 500 acres south of the community of Rough Waters.[141]

During the months leading up to the confirmation and second survey of the reserve, the chief counselled his people not to reveal any information about the size of their group to provincial commissioners, evidently because he feared that if Fredericton ever found out how small a Mi'kmaw body they were dealing with, their land base might be adversely affected. The best way, he felt, was to keep provincial officials guessing as to the size and strength of his band, and not make oneself or one's group readily available until a suitable deal was struck.[142] Prisk was canny. If colonial officialdom refused to act appropriately on his people's behalf, he counselled his group to withdraw from the negotiating table until the province agreed to sit down in a forum promotive of two-way discussion. He also compiled and maintained an archival record of past land transactions and agreements, since Fredericton's land agents proved remiss in keeping such documents or were hesitant to produce those they had, when asked, for the chief's perusal.

Land disputes between Chief Prisk and incoming logging interests also punctuated the years between 1830 and the early 1850s. Since these confrontations could turn violent, the chief made importunate appeals to Fredericton, until the deputy of Crown lands in 1835 eventually seized between one hundred and two hundred tons of timber illegally taken from the

Nepisiguit reserve.[143] While no part of the extra duties levied on timber companies as penalties for trespass seems to have gone into a band fund, the fact that the offenders were ejected from Mi'kmaw territory and fined constituted a major victory.

In another bid to avoid being categorized in ways that might affect their negotiating potential, Prisk in the spring of 1841 led his entire band temporarily "some 60 or 80 miles below Bathurst" to the outskirts of Tracadie (now Tracadie-Sheila). On 14 June Thomas N. DeBlois, one of the two Indian commissioners for Gloucester County, wrote dispiritedly of his chances of obtaining census data directly from Prisk's group, and added that he would do better to approach the local missionary for material. "[One] can only get incorrect information from the Indians, from what cause we know not," he recounted, "[since they] are very reluctant in giving information about their means of support" or concerning "any lands upon which they may be located." DeBlois suspected that Prisk was trying to outfox provincial authorities by keeping his band numbers secret until his group grew larger and politically feisty enough to make a distinct mark. He also noted that the band "generally claim a greater quantity [of land] from the government than the government has reserved [for them]."[144] As the Mi'kmaq had made few efforts to garden either on the reserve or on Indian Island, DeBlois, who had been counselled by his superiors to encourage agriculture among the Mi'kmaq by seed distributions, glumly observed that, while some families planted, he could find little evidence of farming within the bounds of the lands the government had allocated to the Mi'kmaq.

Since the reserve, spanning both banks of the river, had not yet suffered serious encroachment from timber interests, it retained its abundant salmon fishery and supplied large game and fur bearers for hunting and trapping. According to Moses Perley, the New Brunswick Indian commissioner, the reserve in 1844 retained its original acreage, which he estimated to be 1,053 acres.[145] Its survival depended equally on Chief Prisk's ejection of trespassers and its formidable natural terrain, which was an impediment to settlement. Rapids, turbulent cataracts, and rock-flanked gorges that twisted and turned as they cut through the countryside between Grand Falls and Rough Waters also discouraged penetration of the interior by timber interests.

Several band members at Rough Waters came to view the logging industry as a source of valuable monetary income at a time when barter was being replaced by the money economy. Since loggers needed river frontage for temporary camps and storage yards, they were willing to pay for the privilege of using others' land for such purposes. At the same time, they rarely prevented canoes from beaching or their occupants from fishing in the waters off their lumber yards. Having a lease meant access to a small but steady annual income that could be used to purchase seed and fishing and farming equipment. On 26 June 1836 Joseph-Athanase Young asked Hugh Munroe, the local magistrate and land officer, to register an agreement whereby he would lease a half an acre of his property along the river to two loggers, Henry Albee and Benjamin D. Smith, for ninety years at an annual rent of "one pound of lawful money."[146] Monetary returns often were not large, but contacts within the logging industry fostered by such transactions helped the Youngs and their associates secure employment during the winter as cutters and in the spring as log drivers. To secure additional funds, in 1838 Joseph-Athanase placed the whole of his lot, except for the lien to the logging interests, under mortgage to John Reid, a Bathurst merchant, until he amassed the means to redeem the whole in 1858.[147]

By the time a logging road was built in 1845 from Bathurst to Grand Falls and roller dams were constructed on cataracts along the fall zone,[148] the chief knew most of the timber bosses working on the river and had worked out deals with them palatable to both sides. Mi'kmaq began to be hired as guides, cutters, river drivers, and teamsters. Owing to Prisk's skills at negotiating, until Confederation in 1867 loggers and commercial sports fishers could only operate on Mi'kmaw land with the cooperation of the chief and his council.

Though there still were times of economic hardship, reliance on hunting, fishing, trapping, marginal farming, and employment with the logging companies had advantages when alternatives failed.[149] When a severe potato blight in 1846 and 1847 destroyed crops at Rough Waters, the Nepisiguit band were far less affected economically than Mi'kmaq elsewhere, who had come to rely heavily on potatoes for food.[150] The chief's success in protecting his people's lands against trespass also buffered them in 1844 from the consequences of a provincial policy that called for the sale of portions of reserves appropriated by settlers or industrial interests, especially where the intruders "improved" their plots agriculturally or commercially.[151] Monies from these sales were to be placed in an Indian land fund, supposedly to benefit the bands that lost their land. Knowing the turmoil this policy had wreaked on other Indigenous groups in the province, Commissioner Perley commended Prisk for his vigilance in ensuring that none of the Nepisiguit reserve would be leased or sold by government agents.[152] Perley denounced the view of reserves held by officials within the Crown Lands Department and the Provincial Secretary's Office, and especially opposed continuation of the 1844 policy. Proceeds from the sales of land to trespassers had been negligible and the benefits to the Mi'kmaw population correspondingly minimal. The entire system established by provincial fiat was so flawed, he proclaimed, that the Mi'kmaq "don't get the slightest benefit."[153]

During the 1840s and 1850s Chief Nicholas Prisk II and his band council retained their traditional territorial prerogatives by continuing to have a say in who might share in harvesting the tract's resources, be it fish, furs, big game, or wood. The preservation of Mi'kmaw rights to land and resources along the Nepisiguit River, coupled with the chief's maintenance of good relationships within the South Bathurst constituency, caused Indigenous individuals from elsewhere to seek to join his group. With the end of the logging disputes in the late 1840s, numbers soared. By the early 1850s the chief presided over a host of relationships with persons throughout the surrounding non-Indigenous community who, in many cases, shared affinal ties with those who belonged to the local band.

Chief Noel Prisk: Defender against Settler Trespass

On 21 July 1828, at the age of twenty-one, Nicholas Prisk and Marie-François Young's son Noel Prisk (1807–c.1872) wed Marie Labauve.[154] The two would have eleven children: Peter in 1834 – who became a noted guide[155] – Pierre-Noel in 1835, Paul about 1836, Marie-Angelique in 1837,[156] the "twins Prisk" – Nicholas and Joseph Prisk – in 1843,[157] "Ally" (Alexander) in December 1845, Ellen in 1846,[158] Louis in 1849, Andrew in 1851, and Mary in 1854.[159] As Nicholas Prisk II aged, Noel began to act in his father's stead at meetings with colonial officials, and with increasing physical infirmity, Nicholas finally asked Noel to shoulder his responsibilities as chief.[160] For many years Noel

Prisk had served as political "understudy" for his father, who enjoyed good health into the mid-1850s. He now was eager to take up the torch and continue his father's accomplishments as group builder and advocate. Once its members understood Nicholas Prisk's fragility, the band council in February of 1857 granted Noel leave to go to Fredericton and ask to be officially recognized as the new leader of the Nepisiguit Mi'kmaw community.

One of the most successful farmers and hunters within the Mi'kmaw community at Rough Waters, Noel Prisk was fifty years old when he assumed his father responsibilities in 1857.[161] And he had aspirations. He inquired about a policy initiated by Moses Perley in the early 1840s where a chief might obtain a parcel "to the extent of fifty acres" if he showed a willingness to farm.[162] He also continued his father's campaign to protect Prisk Island and lands on the northwest side of the Nepisiguit River "between Pabineau and Strong Waters [Rough Waters]" from trespass.[163] The perils of allowing non-Indigenous interests onto Mi'kmaw territory became all too clear to him during the 1840s when Lieutenant Governor William Colebrooke's administration ventured to sell all Aboriginal lands leased to or settled by non-Indigenous interests. But most important, he wanted tangible confirmation from the lieutenant governor's office that a vital connection existed between his group and the British Crown.

To secure this end, Noel directed a memorial to Lieutenant Governor John Henry Manners-Sutton on 2 March 1857. The band council, the petition contended, had installed Noel as leader in place of his father, who was "very feeble." Noel added that he, under the land initiative set up by Moses Perley in the 1840s, wanted fifty acres "on the southwest side of the river" adjoining the reserve where he had cleared and planted eight acres "to help support his large family."[164] This parcel lay in the neighbourhood of camps and gardens of other band members residing along the widening logging trail that had become known as the Big River Road.

Fredericton was six months in replying, and when a response did arrive in August it evoked shock and disappointment. Noel was informed that the New Brunswick government no longer had "any authority to grant land or to appoint Indian chiefs."[165] It was a devastating setback given his previously sanguine hopes. Since for many years he had been encouraging farming along with more traditional occupations, he expected gratitude rather than censure from the colonial capital. His father in the early 1840s had been chastised by Indian Commissioner Thomas Deblois for not promoting agriculture.[166] Noel felt he had set a good example to his people in the face of these earlier criticisms.

He sent a second petition, dated 25 October 1859, to Lieutenant Governor Manners-Sutton in which he emphasized the necessity, now that his father had stepped down, of having his rank as head chief, as well as that of his second chief and councillors, officially recognized by Queen Victoria's representative. Noel launched a persuasive campaign to have his group allied with the Crown and to stand as a self-determining entity. He felt he had to spell things out very clearly. "It is a very old custom of the Indians to be under the control of a chief," his petition began. "We want one of our own people over us to be placed by the authority of your Excellency as the Representative of the Queen. Chief Nicholas Prisque has been our chief or King as long as most of us can remember. He is now nearly 90 years old and not able to stand up and wishes to resign." It concluded by stressing that "Noel Prisque his son is a sober Indian and tills and cultivates some fields, and so sets a good example for a chief ... We are good subjects."[167] Noel signed this petition first, followed by 19 family heads constituting the 40 "Nepisiguit Indians [of] the I.R. at Big River on the De Blois River in Bathurst Basin."[168] The signees included Noel's older brother Jacques (John Prisk), Philippe Young Sr., Young Philip Young, Noel's son-in-law Thomas Narvy who had married his daughter Marie-Angelique, John Louis, and Étienne Damond (Étienne Young).[169]

Nicholas Prisk II Ouiouche died late in the fall of 1859, at ninety years of age. Indigenous leadership succession in the Northeast still followed ancient protocols; fifty-two-year-old Noel's first duty was to notify neighbouring leaders of his father's death, including members of the Mi'kmaw Grand Council and representatives of the Eastern Wabanaki Confederacy.[170] These persons would be invited to funeral ceremonies. He next asked Lieutenant Governor Manners-Sutton for a parchment commission denoting his new leadership status, additional commissions and belts for his councillors, and a British flag.

Bestowal of these honorifics, Noel trusted, would help the band leadership shed its ambiguous, marginalized status within the colonial structure of the province. As further grounds for a workable reciprocal relationship with New Brunswick's colonial administrators, Chief Prisk invoked protocols that in the past had recognized his people as military allies first of the French regime and later the British Crown. We are "willing to help the English in war as loyal and devoted allies," he proclaimed, "[and] to protect the colours from invading foes."[171] There were few wars threatening British North America at the time – unless one included a short-lived attempt by the District of Madawaska to declare itself independent, or the more amusing than dire Northwest Coast boundary fiasco known as the "Pig War."[172] Prisk's promises of military service and his campaign to have commissions and belts bestowed on his councillors raised no little consternation in the House of Assembly or the Provincial Secretary's Office, which had grown unaccustomed to responding to such requests.[173] Eventually, some members of the House vaguely recollected that the "mode of issuing commissions during the time when the Honourable William F. Odell was Provincial Secretary was to issue a paper, under the Lieutenant-Governor's seal, in order to mark the secondary rank [of the Mi'kmaw councillors] to the commissioners, with the Great Seal issued to the chief on parchment."[174] After considerable deliberation, the Provincial Secretary's Office formally presented Noel Prisk with a parchment commission and a number of ornamental belts, an outcome that the chief jubilantly heralded as a major coup, since no longer could his councillors, vested with their authentic marks of office, be ignored by colonial authorities as they had been in times past.[175]

During his years in office Noel Prisk focused on preventing further trespasses on his band lands and, like his father, proved successful in his campaigns. Not until Confederation in 1867 would he face the greatest challenge of his career, the appropriation of his and his councillors' control over band membership by the federal Department of Indian Affairs. The immediate result was a drastic reduction in the number of band numbers, caused by Ottawa officials dropping names from the band list. Prior to Confederation, census records gave only a vague cross-section of the band population and its compositional changes over time. In 1838 the group was reported as having only twenty-nine members.[176] Chief Prisk and Philippe Young were listed, but whether or not their relatives appeared on the census was subject to the idiosyncrasies of the census taker. A band member who owned property was not necessarily excluded, since Joseph-Anathase Young's name appeared on the roll. Yet the name of Joseph-Anathase's twenty-one-year-old brother John Young Jr. was omitted. Francois-André Julien, an elderly man by 1838, had four persons in his household, as had Noel Le Breton, a relative of François Le Breton who married Cecile Pitre, John Young Jr.'s widow. A single female family head, Susan Francis, appeared along with one child, while Joseph Faris, the final entrant, was an itinerant New England petty merchant who also visited mainland Nova Scotia. As Faris traded in peltry, in 1838 the fur trade must have been still fairly lucrative in the region. In many ways the 1838 census raised more questions than it answered, since a large number of younger band members were left off the list.[177]

It was the beginning of a population decline. The presence of the ancestors of these persons, whose predecessors had moved almost seamlessly between the French, Mi'kmaq, and even English-speaking worlds and swelled local Indigenous rank. Rigidly categorized as "White," "English," "French-speaking," or "Indian" in the mid-nineteenth century, these persons have been described by one historian as "colonial ghosts" who once lived vibrant lives in an Indigenous milieu, and as being "at the interstices of empire in the Atlantic World."[178]

In 1847 the band number declined further, to twenty-seven, though the following year it jumped to fifty-five. Possibly a new spirit of band cooperation with census takers arose in 1848, since such a radical increase within one year could not be solely due to natural increase.[179] While outbreaks of smallpox and cholera in the province in 1849 again temporarily reduced numbers, disease had no major long-term effect on population size.[180] Prior to 1867, group size at Nepisiguit depended on the chief's success in maintaining a stable social, economic, and political milieu, even though this was difficult to sustain within the framework of colonialism.[181]

According to the New Brunswick census of 1861, the core families in the band were still the Prisks and the Youngs. Chief Noel Prisk's household in 1861, which included his wife Mary Labauve, it formed the centre of a concentric ring of residences occupied by his sons and daughters and their spouses: John Prisk and his wife,[182] Pierre-Noel Prisk and his wife, Jane Dedam;[183] Angelique Prisk and her husband, Thomas Narvy;[184] and Ellen Prisk and her husband Peter Smith. Pierre-Noel Prisk's household in 1861

included his two unmarried brothers Nicholas and Joseph Prisk, both eighteen.[185] This residence arrangement obtained whether the band was located at their summer occupation site on Indian Island or at their fall camps and gardens located along Big River Road.

Philippe Young Sr., who was erroneously listed on the 1861 census as aged ninety (he was born around 1788, so in 1861 he would have been around seventy-three), lived with his son Philippe Young Jr., his daughter-in-law Madeleine Courniche, and a grandchild, Noel Young.[186] There had been some new arrivals. Cain (or Étienne) Bernard-Julien, upon marrying Philippe Young's daughter Madeleine, brought his fifty-year-old brother Andrew Bernard-Julien into the band.[187] Peter Bear, a man of the same age as Andrew Bernard-Julien who was born into the Malecite nation, and his wife Christy were newcomers, as were forty-year-old Francis Peters and his wife Mary.[188] Some, such as eighteen-year-old Alexander Wisehold, thirty-year-old Alexander Dieyer and his family, and twenty-four-year-old Peter Culanet, were likely transients. In all, fifty persons belonged to the Bathurst group in 1861.[189]

In 1871, four years after Confederation, the Bathurst Mi'kmaw population suddenly dropped to thirty-seven. Federal agents had removed the names of those who farmed or lived most of the time off reserve, which included Etienne Young's descendants.[190] Chief Noel Prisk's own family meanwhile had expanded slightly, since it was his duty to care for two orphans: Michael Prisk, the twelve-year-old son of his older brother John, who had died around 1865, and a two-year-old simply listed as "Mary A."[191] The loss of the control he and his council once had wielded over group membership doubtless weighed heavily on the sixty-four-year-old leader, who was listed as "ill" on the 1871 census. He died soon after.[192]

Though none of Noel's sons succeeded him as chief, Peter and Joseph earned reputations as excellent hunting and fishing guides. Angler and author Arthur P. Silver wrote an engaging account of a fishing trip he took with Peter and Joseph in late September 1886. Each evening, when their bark canoe was laid up on the beach and salmon steaks were sizzling on the fire, Joe Prisk would regale Silver with stories about his narrow escapes from dangers deep in the forest, and about his great-grandfather, John Young Sr. One tale told how Joe and Peter, lost in a blizzard in 1859 while out hunting moose, had been found and sheltered by inmates of a logging camp.[193] From their accounts, Silver came to understand that the winter wilds could be as perilous in the nineteenth century as they were in 1623, when Father Sebastian Bernardin perished on his winter journey from Nepisiguit to the Saint John River.

Leadership Succession, Community Growth, and Land Transactions

Noel Prisk was the last traditional life chief of the community, and was assisted in his duties during his later years by his eldest son, Peter. However, neither Peter nor John Prisk's eldest son, William Prisk (c.1842–c.1900), exhibited any interest in becoming chief. William had wed Marie Roy at Sainte-Famille Church on 23 May 1863 and raised four sons, Nicholas-Pierre (1862–1930),[194] Alexander (1865–1938), William Jr. (1874–c.1910), and John (b.1901).[195] After Noel Prisk's death in September 1895, the Mi'kmaq sent a petition to the Department of Indian Affairs, dated 31 March 1898, stating that Alexander Prisk, William's twenty-three-year-old son, had been unanimously selected as their next chief.[196] But perhaps owing to Alex's young age, Indian Affairs rejected the petitioners' choice of leader and instead imposed the triennial electoral system on the Mi'kmaw community. Peter Sewell (c.1850–1921) became the first chief elected at Bathurst under the provisions of the 1880 Indian Act, an office he retained until 1910. Sewell, whose surname is said to have been an Anglicization of a Mi'kmaw name, "Souel," was born at the mission of Ste. Anne de Restigouche, but joined the Nepisiguit Mi'kmaw community upon his marriage in 1872 to Sarah Roy, Marie Roy's sister.[197] Peter Sewell's sister Suzanne also entered the Nepisiguit band, by marrying William Prisk's son, Alex Prisk, at Sacré-Coeur Church in October 1893. Built in 1881, Sacré-Coeur Church stood on Bathurst's east side, making it more accessible to the Indigenous community than the older Sainte-Famille Church. Sacré-Coeur's parishioners included Mi'kmaq, *métis*, Acadians, French Canadians, and Scots who lived along the Big River Road, running through Rough Waters towards the reserve. One of the first marriages to take place in the new church edifice was that of William Gray Jr. and Jane (or Genné) Roy, a sister of Marie and Sarah Roy. Through their marriages to the Roy sisters, William Gray, William Prisk, and Peter Sewell

became brothers-in-law, and within the Mi'kmaw generational kinship system brothers-in-law "shared with each other, helped each other, [and] worked together."[198]

William Gray Jr. was of Indigenous ancestry, since he descended from a Scotsman named Richard Gray and a Mi'kmaw woman whom Gray met at Listiguj around 1770. An oral tradition tells how one winter Gray's pregnant wife became separated from her husband and gave birth to a child who afterwards died in the woods. A courageous and resourceful woman, she buried her infant's body in a river bank, and trapped, hunted, and fished until spring, when she was able to make it out to the coast and back to her husband.[199] In the late nineteenth century, Richard Gray's great-grandson, William Gray Jr., supervised logging camps along the Nepisiguit and Upsalquitch Rivers. With a flair for promoting wilderness adventure, William Jr. later became involved with the commercial angling trade, at one time owning or tending to no fewer than five fishing lodges along the Nepisiguit River Valley. Gray hired his brothers-in-law's sons and nephews to work as guides, and these youths addressed him respectfully as their "uncle," a practice passed down through the generations. Owing to the nature of early Prisk kin ties with the Grays and Roys, William Prisk Jr.'s grandchildren referred to William Gray Jr. and Jane Roy, as their "uncle and aunt."[200]

William Gray Jr. settled on the west side of the Nepisiguit River, close to the reserve and near Lazare Roy.[201] Both the Roy and Gray parcels lay within the boundaries of the tract petitioned for by John Young Sr. in 1783. Chief Nicholas Prisk II Ouiouche also had wanted the Roy and Gray properties to fall within the reserve. In the end, however, both the Roys and Grays acquired crown grants. The Crown Land Index for Bathurst shows Lot 32, of 103 acres, belonging to Frederick J. Roy Jr., a son of Lazare Roy, with a neighbouring plot, Lot 27, of 106 acres, in the possession of William Gray, Jr.[202] During the middle to late nineteenth century, the Roys and the Grays lived basically the same lifestyle as their Mi'kmaw neighbours, hunting and trapping in the winter, selling skins, logging on the river, river driving, planting gardens of potatoes and corn, and fishing and eeling in the fall and spring. And, like Etienne Young's sons, they participated in numerous property transactions relating to their grants without alienating any of their land permanently.[203]

Alex Prisk as Chief

William Prisk's second-eldest son, Alex Prisk, who had already been selected for his leadership capabilities by his community in 1898, was elected chief in 1910 and retained this office for several terms until shortly before his death from pneumonia in 1938.[204] He became known for his work to benefit his people and was also well liked by the Acadian and French at Bathurst.[205] Alex married Suzanne Sewell at Sacré-Coeur Church on 9 October 1893, and they had five children: Mary Elizabeth born in 1900, Peter in 1902, Helen in 1903 (who died as an infant), Joseph in 1904, and Christine in 1906. They also adopted a son, Joseph Pitre, born in 1885.[206]

One of the most formidable challenges the chief faced was the government's intervention in the way new members could enter his group. During his great-grandfather Nicholas Prisk II Ouiouche's time, in-marrying persons of both sexes could bring close relatives, especially their siblings, into the band. Chief Prisk, his wife, and persons closely related to them formed a "nodal core group" or "stem kindred," to which others attached themselves through marriage.[207] This pattern persisted when the leader at the centre of the nodal core group exercised territorial jurisdiction over sufficient resources to make joining his group a palatable option for others.[208]

For many generations the nodal core kin group within the Nepisiguit band welcomed outsiders in through marriage and adoption.[209] In this manner, the Narvy and Sewell families – who originally were adhesions to the Prisk-Young core group – grew increasingly central to the Bathurst band. In 1906, Monique Patlass, the only daughter of Ellen Prisk and her second husband, Joseph Patlass, wed Noel Peter-Paul and had three children, John, Elizabeth, and Sock (Jacques). John Peter-Paul later reinforced his linkages to the band by marrying Christine Prisk, one of Chief Alex Prisk's daughters.[210]

John Peter-Paul, a Second World War veteran, and his wife Christine raised several sons and daughters who would become leaders of the Pabineau group. One of these, Norman Peter-Paul, who married Hilda Sewell, later exhibited community-mindedness in organizing and sponsoring athletic endeavours. Now there were representatives of three leadership families living along the Nepisiguit River: the Prisks of Nepisiguit, the Sewells originally of Restigouche, and the Peter-Pauls, originally of Richibucto but later of the Miramichi district.

The arrival of the in-marrying Sewells and Peter-Pauls initially provided political clout for Chief Alex Prisk's policies. Yet, owing to the new elective system, factions arose within the band's power base, accompanied by the eventual wrenching away of exclusive power from the Prisk family, since the Prisks were now numerically in the minority. Election results began to favour members of the large Sewell and Peter-Paul families, and heads of these families were quick to demonstrate their leadership acumen. Peter Sewell, Alex Prisk's successor as chief, launched a trenchant campaign for land reclamation, which resulted in the federal government in November 1895 recognizing Indian Island as a reserve. After Peter Sewell's death, Alex Prisk was returned to power, only to wrestle with new challenges accompanying Bathurst's rapid industrialization. Prisk retained his composure under fire and won praise for his efforts. A local Roman Catholic priest, Father J. Mersereau, remembered him as an "outstanding Indian Chief in the late 1930s, greatly revered by all who knew him. He had all the manly qualities and had a reputation for integrity and strong character."[211]

Industrialization brought opportunities as well as challenges. Earlier merchants, such as Hugh Munroe, who dominated the Bathurst timber and fishing spheres in the late eighteenth century, were well known to the Mi'kmaq, for they also functioned as local magistrates and politicians.[212] By contrast, industrialization, as a consequence of the Intercolonial Railway's arrival in Bathurst in 1876,[213] lacked a human face with which Indigenous leaders in Bathurst, Pokemouche, and other points along the coast could identify, and called for skilled workers in the forestry and mining sectors. Many of those whose families had in the past relied primarily on the traditional Mi'kmaw economy left their communities to intermarry elsewhere or to seek wage work.[214] Lack of requisite schooling precluded the majority of the Nepisiguit River Mi'kmaw population from entering these new trades, though they were permitted to ride for free on the train to destinations where they could sell baskets or work in the fields during the berry and potato harvests. This helped stem outmigration. Especially important, the railway brought hunters and anglers from all over Canada, the United States, and Europe looking for Mi'kmaw guides. The Nepisiguit and Upsalquitch Rivers were touted as two of the best salmon fishing locales in the world, and by 1800 Noel Prisk's sons Peter (Pierre-Noel) and Joseph

Prisk emerged as noted guides. Meanwhile, the large population of moose encouraged Mi'kmaq from other parts of New Brunswick to join the Nepisiguit group. Caribou, however, declined rapidly owing to overhunting, and in the early twentieth century disappeared from northeastern New Brunswick.

Bathurst was incorporated as a town in 1912,[215] and by 1923 it was transformed by the paper industry and zinc and iron mining.[216] John P. Leger, a lumber magnate, in the early 1900s erected a hydro-electric dam on the Nepisiguit River to power a new mill belonging to the Bathurst Power and Paper Company. The mill opened in 1914, began producing paper in 1923, and during subsequent years employed over seven hundred men – as many as the entire population of Bathurst in 1871. Between twelve hundred and fifteen hundred more workers were hired seasonally to cut pulpwood on licensed wood reserves in the interior. At first all these changes proved hard on the Mi'kmaq. During the winters some found work in the woods, but for the rest of the year they were excluded from the employment opportunities available to others.

To worsen matters, this economic transformation occurred when Chief Alex Prisk and his two councillors – which actually exceeded the maximum number of councillors allowed the Bathurst band owing to its small population, although eventually all councillors were retained[217] – were struggling with an alien elective political system imposed on them by Ottawa. Mi'kmaw political mechanisms, which ensured a broad-based arena for the discussion of ideas, were ignored by the federal government, which aligned with business interests bent on developing the Bathurst waterfront. In consequence, the Department of Indian Affairs came down hard on and eventually persuaded the Bathurst chief and council to cede Indian Island in 1928.[218] Most residents did not want to surrender their island, since life on the island retained value for them. Much of their income came from fishing and basket making. Home owners in southeast Bathurst who purchased baskets often addressed the women who sold them as "Sister." They also gave the peddlers refreshments and small gifts, as it was considered "unlucky to let them go empty-handed."[219] Prior to 1928, island dwellers needing medical attention received visits from a community doctor, B.G. Duncan, whose services were paid by Indian Affairs. Residents also felt they could call upon local police and magistrates to intervene in local disputes.[220] For these persons, the loss of their island was a severe blow.

The band was politically vulnerable in 1928. Its members needed money to buy food and clothing, since the price of furs had dropped, and the government promised to distribute funds if a sale occurred. The Mi'kmaq also faced severe environmental degradation. The waters surrounding their island were filled with logging booms and debris from lumber mills. Pollution made shellfish unsafe for consumption and disrupted communal weir fishing. Without consulting the Mi'kmaq, Ottawa after the First World War sold fishing licences to sections of the river that ran across a reserve, and though the anglers' annual lease payments increased band funds, their activities interfered with Mi'kmaw weirsites.[221] The chief and council, reduced by government fiat to only three individuals, lacked the broadly based authority it needed to protect land held under its auspices. In the past, decisions involving land or resources required the sanction of all heads of families. Only when a consensus was reached would participants place their signatory marks on a document of surrender. The cession of 1928, by contrast, required only the signatures of the chief and two councillors, although the number of family heads within the band at the time numbered at least ten.

The sale of the island, which netted the band a minimal amount of money, occurred under extreme pressure from Ottawa and the industrial community of Bathurst.[222] It did not prompt a wholesale removal onto the reserve, as Indian Affairs wished. Instead, families lived during the summer in off-reserve camps located along the Big River Road, and only occupied the reserve in the fall and winter. As the chief could no longer ensure that enough resources existed within his band's traditional territories to sustain its population, he encouraged his people to get educated, take steady jobs in the mills, and send their children to school.[223] With time, scattered camps gave way to log houses and frame dwellings. Local historian Florence Gray-Godin, a descendant of William Gray Jr., held that by the 1930s "[i]t would be difficult to find a Mi'kmaq that did not live in a frame house."[224]

Several of Chief Alex Prisk's family guided visiting anglers and hunters, as well as parties of local company employees, along the river. Among these were Paul Prisk Sr. and Chief Alex Prisk's son, Joseph Prisk, who usually travelled with two members of the Gray family, George and Albert Gray. It was employment that fitted well with hunting and trapping and that, once fur prices rebounded, still brought in money. Under the direction of industrialist Angus McLean, the Bathurst Paper Company began to erect and maintain sporting camps along the Nepisiguit River, which drew fishing parties from Canada, the United States, and England. William Gray Jr. had been a supervisor since the late nineteenth century for several logging camps that employed Mi'kmaq.[225] In the twentieth century his descendants managed sporting locales, including the Pabineau Falls Sporting Camp, a choice trout-fishing locale built and maintained by the Bathurst Paper Company mainly for its employees. This camp had a sizeable and comfortable lodge erected on the east side of the Pabineau River, directly above the Pabineau Falls.

The Bathurst band's desire to improve their education and gain employment in the woods and in the mills led to almost every family having children in school. Gradually, after three decades of marginalization, Mi'kmaq attained responsible positions as paper mill workers, in the mines, as guides at fishing camps, and as participants in community offerings such as athletic tournaments. By the 1960s Chief Alex Prisk's grandson, Hector Prisk, a hoist man at the Wedge Mines and, later, at the Brunswick Mines, won awards for his angling prowess,[226] while his son-in-law, Norman Peter-Paul, not only coached softball but between 1975 and 1980 founded, owned, and managed the Pabineau Braves team within the South Bathurst and Pabineau Softball League.[227] He also sponsored the Pabineau Arrows, members of the Ladies' City Dart League.[228] Like the Pabineau Braves, the Arrows embraced players of all backgrounds from Pabineau and South Bathurst. When this community-minded man died on 8 August 1981, a journalist friend of his, Harvey Aubie, wrote a glowing testament in the local newspaper, *The Northern Light*, to Norman's many achievements.[229]

When, at age seventy-four in March 1938, the widely respected Chief Alex Prisk succumbed to pneumonia, his death made front page news in the *Gloucester Northern Light*.[230] To fill the leadership void left by his demise, Alex Prisk and Suzanne Sewell's second-eldest son Joseph first assumed the role of acting chief, and then served for eleven terms as the community's elected chief.[231] During Joseph's time in office from 1939 to 1972, the Bathurst Mi'kmaq were able to make headway on several major projects, among them

gaining compensation from the Canadian National Railway for land expropriated for the railroad right-of-way cutting across their reserve.[232] Joseph Prisk was in turn succeeded in 1972 by his son Hector Prisk, who remained chief for four consecutive terms in office, until 1980. By this time the Pabineau leadership was exhibiting a new dynamism that embraced participation in national and international issues affecting Indigenous communities across Canada. One exceptional leader on both the community and national fronts, Norman Peter-Paul, had travelled to London, England, in the summer of 1979 to take part in constitutional discussions, and shortly before his death had assumed the position of community health advisor with the Union of New Brunswick Indians.[233]

Norman Peter-Paul, as acting chief of Pabineau in 1979, worked closely with Gilbert Sewell, a grandson of Chief Peter Sewell and Sarah Roy.[234] Gilbert, in addition to being a welfare officer for a time with the Department of Indian Affairs, was on the board of directors of the Union of New Brunswick Indians. As acting chief for several years, he presided over pow-wows, athletic events, and organizations such as the Nepisiguit Woodcarvers Association – of which he was president – and sponsored community festivities and fundraisers. In 1972, he received a Ford Foundation fellowship to study Mi'kmaw folklore throughout Canada and the United States. Fluent in the Mi'kmaw language and with an interest in history and linguistics, Gilbert was already a prominent figure within the Bathurst community when he was elected to succeed Hector Prisk as chief on 24 April 1980. During the following winter, Chief Sewell helped draft the Aboriginal Declaration of the First Nations on Self-Government and Self-Determination, later presented to Governor General Edward Schreyer in Ottawa.[235]

Preserving a Diverse and Progressive Community

During the 1980s, descendants of persons who were once members of the Nepisiguit band but whose names later were dropped from the band list were invited to join in religious ceremonies on the reserve, as well as participate in community dinners and dances. In 1938, when the Roman Catholic bishop Patrice Chiasson moved his headquarters from Chatham to Bathurst and raised Sacré-Coeur Church to the status of a cathedral, the Roman Catholic community of South Bathurst and Pabineau erected its own local church, Our Lady of Grace, on Pabineau Road. Until a fire gutted the church in 1981,[236] the congregation regularly numbered around 125 Mi'kmaw and non-Indigenous families.[237]

By the mid-1980s, in addition to Prisks, several members of the Sewell and Peter-Paul families assumed high-profile leadership offices.[238] In 1984, Benjamin (or "Benoit") Peter-Paul (John Peter-Paul and Christine Prisk's son) was elected chief, with Yvonne Prisk (Hector Prisk's wife) and David Peter-Paul (Benjamin Peter-Paul's son) voted in as councillors.[239] The occasion was memorialized by Christine Prisk performing a traditional dance of welcome for the new chief, although in 1986 a schism appeared in the leadership ranks. Some of the Sewells claimed that the distribution of power and assets within the community's leadership organization was biased towards one family rather than embracing a representative cross-section of the Mi'kmaw constituency. This situation was rectified extraordinarily quickly, however, for within two years the Pabineau First Nation achieved a remarkable spirit of community consensus under the first woman to be elected as chief, Hilda Peter-Paul, who turned to all families for input on major issues.[240] This led Chief Benjamin Peter-Paul, Hilda Peter-Paul's successor, to target the fact that mechanisms ensuring community consensus were conspicuously lacking during negotiations prior to the cession of Indian Island, as only three persons signed the surrender. Under Chief Benjamin Peter-Paul's direction, the Pabineau First Nation later launched a campaign to have Indian Island returned to the Mi'kmaw community – a claim that is ongoing.[241]

Chiefs and councils have challenged the sale of Indian Island, complained about substandard Indigenous housing, and lobbied for better structures and focused on resource conservation. They have campaigned for Indigenous rights and self-determination in national and international forums, pushed for high-quality education for Mi'kmaw youth, and opened avenues for young people to contribute to both the Bathurst community and Canadian society at large.[242] Dedication to these quests built on the feistiness and determination to succeed shown by Chief Nicholas Prisk II Ouiouche and his son Noel Prisk during the nineteenth century. This drive is now cloaked in a new professionalism, since Pabineau First Nation members have entered the fields of business administration, social work, and nursing and have become politicians, conservationists, activists, educators, writers, filmmakers, archivists, historians, linguists, artists, and musicians.

The story of Chief Nicholas Prisk II Ouiouche and his group, which later developed into the Pabineau First Nation, illustrates intriguing facets of northeastern New Brunswick history. There are many threads to the history of Pabineau, Listuguj, Caraquet, Tabusintac, the Miramichi River area, and Richibucto, and further research undoubtedly will reveal even more complex layers of historical legacy, as the Bathurst region was a refuge for those who suffered and survived disease, war, threat of deportation, and raids by American privateers. The collapse of George Walker's trading establishment in 1777 led footloose British bachelors like John Young Jr. and James Robertson to marry into the Mi'kmaw community, where they had to learn to speak the Mi'kmaw language and interact with an understanding and sympathetic French Canadian and Acadian community, many of whose members still felt some sense of obligation to the Mi'kmaq who had sheltered them in times of crisis during the Seven Years' War.

The result was an internally diverse but unified Indigenous constituency at Bathurst, which embraced persons living at Rough Waters, on the Pabineau reserve, and along Big River Road. This somewhat dispersed community struggled to survive the fragmentation imposed on it by government land allocations and surveying policies and the drawing of fictitious and divisive ethnic boundaries. Despite the fact that the Roman Catholic clergy, let alone most members of the Nepisiguit community at large, regarded all descendants of John Young Sr. as "Mi'kmaq," government agents began deleting the names of persons descended from Young from band lists even though they were known to be landholders at Rough Waters. This often occurred without John Young's descendants realizing it was taking place. The situation was exacerbated between 1880 and 1986, when Mi'kmaq women lost their Indigenous status if they married persons whom the federal government considered to be non-status, even if they were direct descendants of Young and Nicholas Prisk II Ouiouche. Yet numerous marriages occurred between members of the Pabineau First Nation and non-status residents of Rough Waters, and they continue today. Until 1928 community members at Rough Waters planted crops in May and early June on their small farms rather than fishing on Indian Island, where census takers in the spring often collected information on Mi'kmaw numbers.[243] Yet come fall, persons from Rough Waters joined their Mi'kmaw kin in weir fishing, eeling, hunting, trapping, guiding, working in the woods for logging companies, and participating on spring river drives. For this reason, many off-reserve members of the original Nepisiguit Mi'kmaw community, though sharing a common ancestry and the same rich history as their on-reserve relatives, were shunted to the sidelines by government agencies when they tried to exercise their Indigenous rights and make claims to their rightful heritage. Only when all components of this multifaceted Indigenous constituency reunite and demand a more well-rounded portrayal of their past will the legacy of Chief Nicholas Prisk II Ouiouche and his descendants – whose actions rebuilt and sustained the Nepisiguit Mi'kmaw nation after the American Revolution – finally be fulfilled.

– Janet E. Chute, assisted by Carrie Gloade and Joseph-Nicholas Prisk

Part Five

Unama'ki aqq K'Taqmkuk – Cape Breton and Newfoundland

17

Capisto

Capisto (c.1600–c.1658) was a mid-seventeenth century Mi'kmaw leader living in Cape Breton, known as *Unama'ki* by the Mi'kmaq. The Jesuit Father Hierosme Lallemant, Superior of the Missions of the Society of Jesus in New France, claimed that Capisto and his brother were introduced to Christianity by Father Andrew Richard, a Jesuit missionary who arrived in Cape Breton from the Acadian mainland in 1653. Lallemant's report for 1659–60, which is included in volume 60 of *The Jesuit Relations*,[1] described Capisto as "a former Captain" of the Cape Breton Mi'kmaq, who apparently died just prior to 1659. Capisto had held fast to his people's traditional religion despite the presence of the missionaries in his people's midst.

His beliefs included the idea that contentious unseen spirits could wrestle with a man by making him look like he was being dragged violently from side to side. A shaman could be employed to intervene at such times, to use skills to wrestle on another's behalf. Lallemant also noted that Capisto's brother, whom the Jesuit left unnamed, had become "much loved by the French" and was connected with Nicolas Deny's trading settlement on Cape Breton. Capisto's brother, as well as his brother's wife and sister, accepted baptism by Father Richard. Lallemant's account is our only source for information on both Capisto and his brother.

– Janet E. Chute

18

Isidore

Isidore was a chief of *Unama'ki*, the Mi'kmaw name for Cape Breton, who lived into the first quarter of the eighteenth century. His life reflected many aspects of Mi'kmaw traditions and customs. Born around 1664, Isidore was about four years old when Nicolas Deny's trading establishment at *Salpo'lku'jk* (Saint Pierre or St. Peter's in present-day Richmond County, Cape Breton) burned during the winter of 1668–69.[1] From 1663 to 1667, Denys had been a prominent French entrepreneur, deeply involved in the *Unama'ki* fur trade. His trading centre at St. Peter's had been a principal point of contact between Mi'kmaq and European. Afterwards, Isidore's encounters with Europeans were for several years largely limited to seasonal meetings with French and Basque fishermen using the island's harbours, where the fishermen offered useful goods in exchange for furs. It was a pattern of life that, after 1713, would change dramatically.

Throughout most of the seventeenth century England and France had made competing imperial claims to the northeastern maritime region, with each power paying scant attention to the rights of the area's Indigenous population. In 1713 the Treaty of Utrecht provided a major realignment of these imperial claims for the next half century, when the French confirmed English claims to an undefined "Acadia" and to most of Newfoundland. France would retain Île Royal, or Cape Breton, and Île St. Jean, now Prince Edward Island. As a result, French officials from Placentia, Newfoundland, held a *prise de possession* ceremony at English Harbour, soon to be renamed Louisbourg, on the east coast of Cape Breton Island in September 1713. The French subsequently established the new colony of Île Royale, which embraced Île Royale, *Epekwitk* or Île St. Jean, and the Îles de la Madeleine or Magdalen Islands.

Enumerated on a nominal census of Mi'kmaq taken in November of 1708, Isidore was identified solely by his baptismal name.[2] This contrasted with almost all the other names of male family heads listed, where there was a Mi'kmaw surname noted as well. Isidore in 1708 was fifty-two years of age, married to Madeleine, with three sons, Claude, Philipe (or Philippe), and Paul, and two daughters, Louise and Marie. His two oldest sons later appeared as male heads of families in Île Royale on Father Courtin's 1727 census. His daughter Marie subsequently married Michel Michau, another prominent Mi'kmaw individual living on *Unama'ki*.

The founding of the French colony in 1713 presented new opportunities as well as exerting pressures on Mi'kmaw traditional life on *Unama'ki*. At this time, Isidore and other members of the *Unama'ki* band made only modest use of European goods. In 1716 Mi'kmaq visiting the new French establishment at Louisbourg still dressed in clothing made from furs and skins, but within a generation French missionary Abbé Pierre Maillard noted the Mi'kmaq primarily using cloth to make their garments.

The economy of the new French colony focused largely on the production of dried salt cod, with most French inhabitants living along the Atlantic coast of Cape Breton Island. As with the dyked marshland agriculture of the Acadians, this economic orientation minimized French encroachments on the lands most utilized by the Mi'kmaq, thereby lessening the potential for conflict between the two peoples.

French officials hoped to use their long friendship with the Mi'kmaq to help contain British expansion on mainland Nova Scotia. Drawing on over a century of good relations with the Mi'kmaq, the French used missionaries and annual ceremonies to cement their connection with the Mi'kmaw population. Not all efforts to influence the Mi'kmaq met with success, however. For example, few mainland Mi'kmaq answered French calls to relocate to Île Royale. Similarly, French efforts to encourage the Mi'kmaq to adopt a more sedentary lifestyle at missions established first at *Malikewe'jk* (Malagawatch) and later at *Potlotek* (Chapel Island) enjoyed only limited and largely seasonal success.[3]

Isidore, along with a leader named Miguel, were the chiefs of the Mi'kmaq of *Unama'ki* in 1716. No documentary confirmation exists that Chief Isidore was in any way related to another Mi'kmaq man, also named Isidore, at Musquodoboit in 1708 who had auspicious descendants who continued to reside along Nova Scotia's eastern shore until fairly recent times. Chief Isidore's family seems to have been primarily associated with Île Royale. While certain recorded twentieth-century oral traditions may suggest a kin connection between the two Isidores,[4] one must exercise caution owing to insufficient eighteenth-century evidence connecting the two men.

Because omissions occurred in eighteenth-century French censuses of the Mi'kmaq population, *Unama'ki's* other chief, Miguel, did not appear on the 1708 census at all, although his son, François, was listed. Chief Isidore was at Louisbourg in July of that year and later, in August, at the ceremony to renew their relationship with the French held at *Mjekati'jk* (Port Dauphin or today's Englishtown). A French naval officer observing the ceremonies described Isidore as baptized, shrewd, and speaking French.[5] An ability to make oneself understood in French was not common among the Mi'kmaq at the time, as the French maintained official interpreters to facilitate communication with them. Aware of his importance to the diplomatic milieu, the chief also could at times challenge France's hegemony over what were once his own people's lands. In 1716, for instance, the Frenchman Louis de Chancel de Lagrange reported that Isidore stated in a public forum that he suffered "the presence of the French on the island only because of the annual gifts he receives."[6]

Isidore's linguistic ability likely granted him prominence in both the Mi'kmaw and French communities. The nature of interaction between the two cultural groups vested Mi'kmaw individuals who could communicate with and receive the confidence of the French with special prestige.[7] Similarly, French missionaries, soldiers, and others who spoke Mi'kmaq gained standing among the French.

Isidore was a chief of *Unama'ki* during the critical period surrounding the establishment of a new French colony. Under his leadership, as well as guidance from the Elders of his people, the Mi'kmaq reached an accommodation with the French that lasted throughout the colony's existence.

– Berton A. Balcom

19

François N'8gin'tok

François N'8gin'tok[1] was a Mi'kmaw leader of *Unama'ki* between 1730 and 1740. He was also a reader of Mi'kmaw hieroglyphics and a well-known prayer leader. Since the conversion of Chief Membertou at Port Royal in 1610,[2] Roman Catholicism has played an important role in the spiritual life of the Mi'kmaq. By the mid-eighteenth century, Roman Catholicism was widely practised throughout *Mi'kma'ki* – the Mi'kmaw traditional homeland. French missionaries remained the driving force behind proselytization, yet *Mi'kma'ki* was large and the missionaries were few in number and were not always present. Episodes in the life of François N'8gin'tok provide insights into Mi'kmaw spirituality during the 1730s and 1740s.

Without the writings of Abbé Pierre Maillard we would know little, if anything, of the life experiences of François N'8gin'tok.[3] Maillard records N'8gin'tok's involvement in two incidents during the 1730s and 1740s.[4] These episodes touch on how important aspects of Mi'kmaw religious life at this time give historical significance to N'8gintok's life.

N'8gin'tok was fluent in the hieroglyphic writing style used by the Mi'kmaq. This hieroglyphic language was the first Indigenous written language developed north of Mexico, and predated that of the better-known Cherokee syllabic script by at least 120 years, if not much longer.[5] Missionaries used prayer books written in the hieroglyphic script in teaching the Christian religion and to facilitate observances. In the absence of the missionaries, Mi'kmaw prayer leaders, known in the Mi'kmaw language as *nuji-alasutma'jik*, led services.

The first episode occurred when Edward How, then an important British merchant and justice of the peace at Canso,[6] came to Port Toulouse in 1740. How attended a service at the small birch bark chapel customarily established some eight hundred paces from the fort for the annual gift-giving ceremonies. As the missionary was not there at the time, a Mi'kmaw prayer leader led the service. Intrigued by the use of the Mi'kmaw language and the beautiful singing, How arranged a discussion with the prayer leader and several Elders.

The ensuing meeting was held in a room at the fort with Barthèlemy Petitpas, the translator, present. The Mi'kmaw prayer leader recited the service and Petitpas translated it for How. The accuracy of the service was ensured by reference to a prayer book. Afterwards, How asked a question concerning the service, to which François N'8gin'tok responded "in the name of all" the Mi'kmaq present.[7] N'8gin'tok's position among the Mi'kmaq is not fully clear. In his account, Maillard seemed to distinguish between the anonymous prayer leader and N'8gin'tok. N'8gin'tok's role as spokesperson, however, suggested he may well have been an Elder, or at least someone well trusted by the Elders.

While the discussion began well, several disturbing elements later changed the tone of the meeting. In his answers, N'8gin'tok stated that he had heard that the English at Canso had criticized his people hundreds of times, and claimed that Canso residents at times had even ridiculed the Mi'kmaq to their faces.[8] Moreover, the Mi'kmaq orator began to think back on a similar but less happy meeting held earlier with an Englishman at the Saint-Martin family household at *Mekaqanji'tk*, now Petit Dégrat in Cape Breton. There, the attitude conveyed by the Englishman was so annoying that one Mi'kmaq man present at the time wished to kill him. It was only the friendship that N'8gin'tok's father and Saint-Martin held for each other that prevented a serious outbreak of hostilities. To spare his friend Saint-Martin embarrassment and possible harm, N'8gin'tok's father had calmed the Mi'kmaq's anger sufficiently to be able to lead them peaceably from Saint-Martin's house.

Barthèlemy Petitpas was certain Edward How had been the Englishman involved in both incidents. The Mi'kmaq's uncertainty stemmed from How's being dressed differently and being fuller in the face the second time they saw him. Petitpas grew concerned that the Mi'kmaq would eventually recognize How, so he arranged a ruse to get How out of the room and back on board his vessel. It appeared that Petitpas's fears were not without foundation. When Petitpas later explained to the Mi'kmaq that How suddenly had been called back to Canso but would return, they said they knew that they had been tricked but would wait for another time to exact revenge. Maillard argued that these incidents provided the motivation for How's killing under a flag of truce near Fort Beauséjour in 1751. The circumstances and motivations for How's death nevertheless remain contested.

While suggestions concerning possible links between these earlier incidents and How's later death may provide drama on the historical stage, they are even more important for the insights they offered into Mi'kmaw religious practices in the early to middle eighteenth century. There had been rumours that How ridiculed the Mi'kmaq's religious services, which would have bred deep anger with the British official. These religious services had been ritualized to a high degree, and many Mi'kmaq treated such ceremonies with great respect. Prayers books written in hieroglyphic script were widespread among the Mi'kmaw population and were used regularly. The role of Mi'kmaw prayer leaders capable of conducting services in the priest's absence was also significant and continued long after this period. The meeting with How at which N'8gin'tok spoke stressed the value of holding services in the Mi'kmaw language and underscored the value placed upon singing and chanting at these events. All of these were factors that contributed importantly to the strong attachment to Roman Catholicism that N'8gin'tok and other Mi'kmaq demonstrated in their meetings with How.

Yet religious syncretism flourished as well. Despite this strong attachment to Roman Catholicism, traditional beliefs also remained strong among many Mi'kmaq at this time, and not all were converted to Roman Catholicism. The missionary, Maillard, once criticized some Mi'kmaq for using the lengthy pilgrimage to the shrine at Ste.-Anne-de-Beaupré as an opportunity to remove themselves from the teachings of their missionary. Maillard also noted that certain Mi'kmaq mocked for him his efforts, or tried to reason with him by citing major differences between their traditional religious views and Roman Catholicism. The missionary was particularly scornful of shamans and dismissively referred to them as "tricksters." In reports to his superiors back in France, Maillard always described situations that showed shamans in a negative light.[9] Men like N'8gin'tok, however, were seen by him as shining beacons in the midst of an often nebulous ideological sea.

– Berton A. Balcom

20

Jacques Padanuques

Jacques Padanuques was a mid-eighteenth century chief of the Mi'kmaq of *Unama'ki* (also known as Île Royale or Cape Breton Island) who was killed by the English in Boston, Massachusetts, after April 1745. Micheline Johnson depended solely on an account by Abbé Pierre Maillard for her biography of this chief.[1] According to Maillard, in May 1744 an English privateer named Danao or David used the strategy of flying a French flag and the services of a renegade French interpreter to capture the Mi'kmaw chief at the Strait of Canso. Padanuques and his family were subsequently taken as captives to Boston where the chief was eventually killed. His son was retained as a prisoner even though the Mi'kmaq released captives for his exchange.[2]

Additional documentation now confirms much of Maillard's account. Most significantly, "Jacques Padanke" (Padanuques) headed a French nominal census of the Mi'kmaw male heads of families on Île Royale.[3] Given French practices of ranking such lists at this time, Padanuques's ordinal position likely reflected a high status in the band.

The person Maillard identified as Padanuques's captor – "Danao" or "David" – was David Donahew, captain of the *Resolution*. This vessel, with Donahew in command, had been a privateer during the fall of 1744 and then was leased the following year to the colony of Massachusetts as one of the armed vessels in the expedition against Louisbourg.[4] Donahew was an active commander throughout this campaign and

was instrumental in stopping Paul Marin de la Malgue's relief force, destined for Louisbourg, at Tatamagouche along the Northumberland Strait.

During the early stages of the Louisbourg campaign, Donahew captured two small parties of Mi'kmaq in separate occasions. The first capture of three Mi'kmaq was made in early April near the expedition's staging area at Canso. A New Englander noted Donahew's strategy in effecting this capture was to hoist French colours on his own sloop, and French colours over English ones on a sloop accompanying him. This made the two vessels appear like a French privateer with a prize. When the Mi'kmaq came on board to trade "they were immediately clap'd in irons."[5] Two of the captives were sent to Boston, while William Pepperrell, the New England expedition's leader, retained the third "in hopes of his being serviceable."[6] This Mi'kmaw individual subsequently agreed to act as a pilot but only on condition that he would not have to fight.[7]

On 24 April 1745, Chief Jacques Padanuques was among a party of Mi'kmaq on the shores of the Strait of Canso scrutinizing the approach of an unknown sloop.[8] His wife and son were with him, as was a chief from Acadia with his wife and child and another Mi'kmaw couple. The vessel flew French colours, but the Mi'kmaq knew from experience that the vessel was from New England. Since the outbreak of fighting the year before, the Mi'kmaq had taken part in attacks on Canso, Annapolis Royal, and Placentia, and they

354

viewed the vessel with caution.[9] An officer spoke with them in French assuring them that it was a recent French prize and inviting them on board. Once they boarded, however, the New England crew took them prisoner. Captain Donahue took Padanuques's paper and his medal, which Donahew wore around his own neck.[10] Donahew brought the Mi'kmaq to Canso, where they were held prisoner on board a vessel in the harbour. While some New Englanders regarded the prisoners with interest and some sensitivity, to others they were a provocation.[11] The vessel's acting captain was sent back in irons to his original vessel for firing a shot at the sentry guarding the prisoners.[12] A week after the New England landing at Louisbourg on 11 May 1745 Donahew was back in Canso and foiled a plot by the French and Mi'kmaq prisoners to seize the vessels.[13] The prisoners were divided and placed on two vessels and subsequently sent to Boston.

The New Englanders regularly held Indigenous prisoners hostage to influence the actions of their peoples, and this seems to have been the fate of Chief Padanuques and the other Mi'kmaw captives. Maillard asserted that Padanuques was killed after boarding the vessel that was to return him to Cape Breton, and his son remained a prisoner in Boston despite the Mi'kmaw release of prisoners for his redemption. While documents have not been found to support Maillard's claims, the details the missionary provided of Padanuques's capture appear plausible.

Warfare in northeastern North America involved the Indigenous peoples as well as the French and English. All parties took prisoners for a variety of reasons, including political ones. In some instances, as in the case of Chief Padanuques and his son, redemption was a long and difficult process and sometimes was not accomplished at all.

In an ironic twist of fate, David Donahew was killed in a *ruse de guerre* not far from where he had captured Chief Padanuques. On 9 July 1745 Donahew's sloop was in the Strait of Canso area when he saw a small party of Indigenous warriors on the shore. Donahew and eleven of his men went ashore in a boat only to be overwhelmed by the Indigenous and French force under Paul Marin. Donahew and about half his men were killed and the other half taken prisoner.[14]

– Berton A. Balcom

21

Jean Michau

Jean Michau (Michaux, Michault, Michaud) was chief of the Mi'kmaq of *Unama'ki* (Île Royale or Cape Breton Island) in the first quarter of the eighteenth century. Chief Michau was the first of three members of the Michau family who became prominent *Unama'ki* leaders. In 1722 he was chief of the Île Royale band, which numbered 107 members.[1] This total contrasted with the 196 Mi'kmaq on *Unama'ki* noted in a nominal French census of 1708.[2] Fluctuations in French census figures for individual bands, as well for as the Mi'kmaw nation as a whole, reflected not only increases and decreases through births and deaths, but also demographic changes stemming from movements of individuals and families. Although the French had difficulty gathering accurate information, the long association of French missionaries with the Mi'kmaq, and the continued French interest in Indigenous military strength, suggests that an overall reliability may be ascribed to the census figures.

As they did with other bands they noted on mainland Nova Scotia, the French census-takers described Jean Michau's band as a "village." This would have been a misnomer of sorts, since the seasonal round of the Mi'kmaq meant that they did not live in large year-round villages but moved about to take advantage of food supplies. Many bands, however, did have large annual encampments held seasonally at traditional locations. The French seemed to have described these large seasonal encampments as "*villages fixes.*" Unlike the majority of Mi'kmaq bands, the Mi'kmaq of *Unama'ki* were not identified by the 1722 census as having a "*village fixé.*"

Jean Michau became chief of the Île Royale band sometime after 1716, as his name does not appear on an earlier 1708 nominal French census of Mi'kmaw families on the island. Eight years later, in 1716, a French naval officer identified two chiefs; Isidore and Miguel, as the chiefs of *Unama'ki.*[3]

If Jean Michau came to Île Royale sometime between 1708 and 1722, his arrival may well have been linked to the French establishment of the new colony of Île Royale in 1713. With the creation of their new colony, the French appealed to the Mi'kmaq on the mainland to move to the island. They also hoped to attract Acadians, Maliseet, and Abenakis, though they had little success in winning many newcomers from any of these groups.

Another more pressing reason to move arose in 1722, with the outbreak of war between the British and a loose semi-political assemblage of northeastern nations known later as the Eastern Wabanaki Confederacy and including the Mi'kmaq. Wartime pressures encouraged the French to move the missionary Father Gaulin's mission from *Nalkitgoniash* (Antigonish) to Île Royale. French officials noted a number of Mi'kmaq associated with the older Antigonish mission who wanted to move to *Unama'ki.*[4] Mi'kmaw elders and chiefs subsequently chose the new mission site at *Malikewe'jk*

(Malagawatch) on the Bras d'Or lakes for its suitability for growing corn.

It was at this time that Jean Michau figured in an episode illustrating the struggle between the French and English for the support of the Mi'kmaq. One day in 1722, members of the Petitpas family (most likely Claude Petitpas and his eldest son, Barthélemy) induced Jean Michau to make statements denying the French governor of Canada's support for the Wabanaki Confederacy in its war with the English. Claude Petitpas was accused as early as 1698 of harbouring pro-English sentiments.[5] French officials reported the Mi'kmaq to be outraged by the Petitpas' behaviour and demanding their arrest. Some Mi'kmaq even wanted permission to kill the two Petitpas men in reprisal for the deaths of several Mi'kmaq by the English.[6] The Petitpas family nevertheless weathered this storm, and Barthèlemy went on to become a Mi'kmaw interpreter for the French.[7]

Abbé Courtin's 1727 nominal census of Mi'kmaq family heads for Île Royale and Antigonish offers an explanation for the movement of the Michau family.[8] Numbered among the Île Royale band was "Jean Michaux," who headed a large family group of seven men bearing arms and three women and children. His name was presented as the second of such family heads, coming immediately after that of "Jacques Padanke" (Padanuques), who also became a Mi'kmaw leader. Padanuques was described as a chief of *Unama'ki* when he was captured by New Englanders at the strait of Canso in 1745. The 1722 census also recorded "Petit Jean Michaux" as residing with the Antigonish band. "Jean Michaux" by this time had likely moved to *Unama'ki* via Antigonish, while his namesake remained there.

Jean Michau's experiences reflected two aspects of Mi'kmaw life during the first half of the eighteenth century. First, there was a need to deal with recurring pressures from both the English and the French on a variety of fronts – military, political, religious, economic, and even social. Second, there were the movements, sometimes intertwined with these pressures and sometimes not, of individuals and families between bands and areas.

– Berton A. Balcom

22

Michel Michau

During the first half of the eighteenth century, linkages between the Mi'kmaq of *Unama'ki* and the French of Île Royale occurred on numerous levels. The marriage of Michel Michau (Michaux, Michault, Michaud; c.1700–c.1750) and Marie Isidore circa 1728 marked not only the joining of two prominent *Unama'ki* Mi'kmaw families, but also the creation of a Mi'kmaw family with strong ties to the new French colony on the island. Marie Isidore was a daughter of Isidore, who had been recorded by the French as chief of *Unama'ki* in 1716. Michel Michau was a relative of Jean Michau, the head chief of *Unama'ki* in 1722, although the exact nature of Jean's and Michel's relationship remains unknown. Besides both coming from high-ranking social backgrounds in the Mi'kmaw community, Michel Michau and Marie Isidore also forged a relationship with pronounced social links to the French colony.

While language, lifestyle, and culture frequently separated the Mi'kmaq and the French, kinship and friendship provided links between the two. Abbé Maillard wrote of a Mi'kmaw individual staying for several days in the home of a Louisbourg resident and taking part in the family's evening entertainment. In another instance, a small group of Mi'kmaq paid a visit to a French household at Petit Dégrat when a dispute with another guest, an Englishman, threatened to turn violent. One of the Mi'kmaq party, François N'8gin'tok, calmed the situation because of his friendship with the French family.

On 17 August 1729 Michel Michau and Marie Isidore had their four-day-old son, Jacques Ange, baptized at the parish church in Louisbourg.[1] Five years later, on 28 October 1734, the couple had another son, three-day-old François, baptized in the same church.[2] These baptisms stand out in the Louisbourg parish records, as Mi'kmaq rarely had their children baptized in the French settlement. Only five other baptisms of Mi'kmaw children are noted among the more than two thousand entries in the town's parish records.[3] The rarity suggests a special link between the couple and the French.

As noted above, Marie Isidore's father was a chief of *Unama'ki* in 1716. A French observer to a French gift-giving ceremony held at Port Dauphin in that year noted that Isidore had been baptized, was shrewd in his dealings, and spoke French.[4] Isidore's ability to speak French was relatively uncommon among the Mi'kmaq, as the French maintained official Mi'kmaq interpreters. The 1708 census reveals that Isidore, then fifty-two, was married with three sons, Claude, Philippe, and Paul, and two daughters, Louise and Marie. In 1716, a French observer, Chancel de Lagrange, who commented favourably on Isidore's appearance, also remarked on the attractiveness of his daughters, whereas he had been critical of Mi'kmaq he had seen earlier at Louisbourg. Louise and Marie at the time would have been twenty and fourteen years old respectively.

The family connections of Michel Michau are less certain. His surname "Michau" indicated a relationship with both Jean and Denis Michau, who were both chiefs of *Unama'ki*. Jean Michel Michau was listed as *Unama'ki* chief in a French census in 1722 and appeared again as a male family head in a 1727 census. (The 1727 census did not identify who was then chief.) Denis Michau's name first appeared in the French documentary record in the 1740s, and by 1750 he was chief of *Unama'ki*. He died of disease the following year, with the French beforehand expending a sizeable sum in treatment to try to save his life. The French regarded him as so significant that in October 1751 King Louis XV was informed of his death.

Whether from their family connections or owing to their own social links, the godparents chosen for two of Michel Michau and Marie Isidore's children revealed a strong connection with the French. The godparents for their first son baptized at Louisbourg, Jacques Ange, were René Lambert DeGranges, an artillery officer in the garrison, and Dame Marie Courtiau, wife of the king's prosecutor. The godparents for their second son, François, were Joseph Duvivier, also an officer in the garrison, and Dame Angèlique Laureau de la Tour, the widow of a former captain in the garrison.

These French godparents were very respectable and socially more significant than the godparents presiding at the baptisms of other Indigenous children in Louisbourg. Yet not all similar baptismal arrangements signified that the Mi'kmaw parents were esteemed in the Indigenous community or by the French. One other baptism of an Indigenous child where the godparents were of high social standing but the parents were not was that of Claude-François in September 1729. Claude-François's mother was identified simply as "Marie-Josephe" while his father was unknown, suggesting that the mother may have been an Indigenous slave. The godparents of Claude-François were the children of Lieutenant de Laperelle. The children of prominent French families acted as godparents in some instances of slave baptism, as well as for children of less prominent families within the French community.

Relationships between the Mi'kmaq and the French were not driven solely by political, economic, military, or religious agendas. The two peoples also forged associations based on family and friendship. Both Michel Michau and Marie Isidore demonstrated that they exercised linkages with the French that were not only close, but also socially significant.

– Berton A. Balcom

23

Denis Michau

Denis Michau (Michaux, Michault, Michaud, c.1700–1751) was a noted chief of the Mi'kmaq of Cape Breton, known to the French at Îsle Royale and to the Mi'kmaq of Unama'ki. The relationship between the Mi'kmaq of Unama'ki and the French of Île Royale proved important to both peoples during the first half of the eighteenth century. Several Mi'kmaw chiefs were particularly prominent in maintaining this connection. Denis Michau was one such leader, and for his intermediary role received particular marks of esteem from the French.

Denis Michau gained special notice in 1744 when he received payment for a trip he made from *Salpo'lku'jk* (Port Toulouse or St. Peters) on behalf of the colony's government.[1] In the following years, the chief fought against the English during the War of the Austrian Succession. In 1750 he received three hundred livres towards the construction of the first house in *charpente et piquet* ever erected to lodge the chief of the Île Royale Mi'kmaq. This house was described as being part of a Mi'kmaw village on the Bras d'Or lakes;[2] it was likely at the mission centre at *Malikewe'jk* (Malagawatch) rather than a later mission site at Potlotek (Île de la Sainte Famille, or Chapel Island in today's Richmond County, Cape Breton). At both locales the French tried to influence the Mi'kmaq to adopt a more sedentary lifestyle, but ultimately the French colonial regime failed to achieve any major strides towards the hoped-for Mi'kmaw mission and farming settlement.

In November 1750 a number of Mi'kmaq came to Louisbourg to meet with the colony's commandant, Charles des Herbiers de La Ralière, who had come the year before with the French forces retaking possession of Louisbourg from the English.[3] According to the French records, the Mi'kmaw motivation was to assure des Herbiers of their population's faithfulness and attachment to King Louis XV. Des Herbiers in turn gave provisions to Chief Denis Michau for the feast traditionally held to commemorate such occasions.

Des Herbiers described Michau as a "bon" Mi'kmaq who was strongly attached to France. The commandant decorated Michau with one of the dozen medals sent to him for presentation to the Mi'kmaq and other Indigenous allies of the French. Des Herbiers considered the occasion a success with the exception of the unavoidable absence of Jeannot Peguidalouet, whom he hoped to be able to regard as a "major" – a rank below "chef" or chief – of the Unama'ki band. Peguidalouet had been recuperating at the mission centre from an illness.[4] Within two weeks, however, Peguidalouet had recovered sufficiently to arrive in Louisbourg bearing a letter from the French commander at Port Toulouse. Soon afterward, on 6 December 1750, des Herbiers noted he had given the major his commission and his medal.[5]

The roles played by prominent Mi'kmaq such as Michau and Peguidalouet were important to the functioning of Mi'kmaw-French relations. Intermediary leaders had to have the confidence of both parties. In consequence, these individuals derived part of their status in their own group from the confidence they received from the other party. Their prestige within Mi'kmaw society was reinforced by their ability to obtain gifts from the French that they then passed on to their own people. And such intermediary leaders were not found only on the Mi'kmaw side, for French officers, officials, and traders also increased their prestige and importance through positive responses they received from the Mi'kmaq.[6]

In 1751 Chief Denis Michau died from an unknown illness, probably at *Salpo'lku'jk* (St. Peters). Captain Gabriel Rousseau de Villejouin, the French commander at Port Toulouse, received 125 livres 12 sols for expenses incurred during Denis's illness.[7] It was a substantial sum at a time when a fisherman's yearly earnings might only be twice as much. Although the French colony's accounts noted payments for the general provision of medical services to the Mi'kmaq, this payment for a Mi'kmaw individual proved unique.

Depending on when he fell ill, Denis Michau prior to his death may have been among the Mi'kmaw chiefs from Unama'ki and the mainland who went to Louisbourg late in the summer of 1751. They had gone to welcome the new French governor, Comte de Raymond, in much the same fashion as they had met with des Herbiers the year before. Raymond had the chiefs shown a portrait of Louis XV, which reportedly made an "*impression singlière.*"[8]

Michau received his highest recognition from the French posthumously. In October 1751 his death, among other matters concerning the Mi'kmaq, was reported to Louis XV. Michau was eulogized as an excellent subject whose grandfather had rendered great services to the former king, Louis XIV. It was stated that he had even received Letters of Nobility as a reward. Since Michau left a widow and son, the widow was to receive help from the French, and Peguidalouet, the new chief, was to assume responsibility for raising the son.[9]

The reference linking Denis Michau to the French nobility probably explains a historical mystery concerning the Mi'kmaq and Louisbourg. In December 1737 the king's lieutenant and the *commissaire ordonnateur* noted the burial in Louisbourg a few days previously of the chief of Unama'ki. Although they did not give the name of the chief, the burial was still remarkable as one of a handful of Mi'kmaw interments[10] – only five Mi'kmaq numbered among the seven hundred or so burials recorded in over three decades

of parish records.[11] Even the more significant were the honours paid to the deceased, which included a military detachment under a sergeant present at the burial. The officials justified their actions by arguing that conferring such honours on a dead chief would encourage Mi'kmaw attachment to the French king. Yet such distinctions were so seldom accorded even at French burials that their provision at an interment of a Mi'kmaq merits further consideration. If the deceased had been a relative – perhaps even the father – of Chief Denis Michau, and also had claims to the French nobility, then the French actions are more easily understood.

Other than the reference at the time of Michau's death, no record of a Letter of Nobility granted to a Mi'kmaw person has survived. Yet it is possible Michau may have received his claim through the family of the famed French explorer Nicolas Denys.[12] Accompanying Isaac de Razilly to La Have in 1632, Denys was active throughout the early history of Acadia and held several important positions. At various times he was also involved with the French trading establishments at Port Rossignol (Liverpool), La Have, Chedabucto, St. Peters, and Tracadie.

Denys had received a seigneurial grant for his services, and although he died before all details were finalized, the grant was confirmed to his son Richard. Richard Denys had used the title "Sieur de Fronsac" during his father's lifetime, and it passed in turn to his own son, Nicolas. Richard Denys's first wife was a Mi'kmaq, Anne Parapego, by whom he had his son Nicolas. The son also married an Indigenous woman, Marie, who was likely a Mi'kmaq. They had at least three children, but reportedly all members of this family died in 1732.[13] Denys's title passed on the death of Nicolas back to the descendants of Richard Denys's second French wife, Françoise Cailleteau. That other unknown children of either Richard or Nicholas survived to gain prominence among their mother's people nevertheless remains an intriguing possibility.

Chief Denis Michau was one of a number of Mi'kmaw leaders who gained prominence from their association with the French during the first half of the eighteenth century. This was a period when the Mi'kmaw people came under great pressure during the imperial struggles between the English and the French. For many Mi'kmaw leaders, including Michau, accommodation often appeared to be more easily achieved with the French.

– Berton A. Balcom

24

Marie Josephe Le Borgne de Belisle

Marie Josephe Le Borgne de Belisle (1711–54) was the eldest daughter of Alexandre Le Borgne de Belisle (c.1679–1744) and Anastasie d'Abbadie de Saint-Castin. Marie Josephe married into Louisbourg elite society and became a successful businesswoman by defying cultural norms for women of the period, as well as colonial French prejudices regarding *métis*. The inventory taken of her possessions after her death was the richest female inventory taken in eighteenth-century Louisbourg.

Marie Josephe was the granddaughter of Jean-Vincent, Baron d'Abbadie de Saint-Castin, and Mathilde, daughter of the Abenaki chief Madock-awando. Saint-Castin and his sons achieved renown in New France and France for their roles as liaisons between the French and the Abenaki during years of tension between the English and French imperial claims. Saint-Castin's connection through marriage to the Abenaki, and the remote location of Pentagouët on what is now the Penobscot River, Maine, in relation to French and English authorities gave him, and his descendants, an influential position on the border of European claims in North America.[1] This esteem was not universal. In his nineteenth-century history of Acadia, Rameau de Saint-Père described Marie Josephe's mother as a "squaw" and Marie Josephe as a *métisse*.[2]

Marie Josephe's parents lived on the Belisle seigneurie near Port Royal until its final conquest by the British in 1710. They then resided in territory still claimed by the French near Anastasie's family in Pentagouët (Castine, Maine). Marie Josephe was born soon after their move. In speaking of their life in Pentagouët, Alexandre said he lived "avec sa famille dans le coin d'un Bois tout ce temps parmi les Nations Sauvages" (with his family in the corner of a wood all this time among the Indigenous nations).[3] Although Saint-Castin's establishment had regular contact and trade with both the English and the French, Marie Josephe grew up in an environment more familiar to her mother than her father, one that lay on the periphery of European claims and in regular contact with nearby Abenaki communities. The Le Borgnes afterwards moved to territory the French granted Saint-Castin on the Saint John River where, years later, Marie Josephe's younger sister Françoise continued the family tradition of mediating between Europeans and Indigenous peoples when she was chosen by the Malecite as their translator during treaty negotiations with the English in 1749.[4]

In the early 1720s Marie Josephe went to live with her aunt, Anne Le Borgne de Belisle, and her uncle, Jean-Baptiste Rodrigue, a *habitant pêcheur* and merchant in Louisbourg, the capital of the new French colony of Île Royale (Cape Breton). Acadian historian Clarence-J. d'Entremont wrote that Marie Josephe left her family as an infant, as the 1715 and 1716 censuses of Louisbourg indicated that a niece was living with the Rodrigue household. More probably those documents referred to another, older niece, Marie,

362

the then sixteen-year-old daughter of Anne's brother Emmanuel. In 1717 Marie Le Borgne de Belisle married Jean Bertrand, a *habitant pêcheur* at Baleine, a small fishing community near Louisbourg. For that year and 1720, the censuses recorded no niece with the Rodrigue household. In the censuses of 1724 and 1726, there was again a niece living with the Rodrigue household, and this time it was Marie Josephe.[5] Both Marie Josephe and her cousin learned the skills of a bourgeois household manager while helping their aunt with her busy household full of young children and with few servants.

Marie Josephe undoubtedly worked hard as she learned. Her aunt had five babies between 1724 and 1731, and there were already four children in the household when Marie Josephe first came to Louisbourg around 1724. Female servants were in demand in Louisbourg; there was never more than one in the Rodrigue home while Marie Josephe lived there. Most bourgeois Louisbourg homes, those of merchants, officials, or military officers, had two or three servants; in France the minimum standard for a bourgeois home was three.[6] In 1726 Madame Rodrigue engaged a female servant, Marguerite, a Mi'kmaw orphan. Marguerite, two years younger than Marie Josephe, was a servant with the Rodrigues for many years after.[7]

In 1733, at the age of twenty-two, Marie Josephe married the treasurer of the colony, Jacques Philippe Rondeau. He was about thirty years old at the time. Her marriage contract stipulated a two thousand livres dowry for her, and had no *dot*, or payment from her family, except a mutual gift of their possessions. It was a respectable bourgeois contract that favoured the bride's family in not requiring a *dot*.[8] The high male-to-female ratio in Louisbourg often resulted in advantageous marriages for women. Eight witnesses, all relatives from Marie Josephe's father's Acadian family and all members of Louisbourg's military and commercial elite, supported her by signing the marriage contract.[9] Marie Josephe had seven children between 1733 and the capture of Louisbourg in 1745 by a combined New England and British force.[10] The birth intervals of her children indicate that Marie Josephe rejected the upper-class French practice of employing a wet nurse and chose to nurse her own children.[11]

Rondeau, born in Trois Rivières, had been in Louisbourg since the early 1720s in the service of the civil administrator of the colony. He had been rewarded with increased responsibilities, and by 1733 he was the treasurer of the Marine.[12] As a Crown official, Rondeau was officially prohibited from engaging in trade;[13] nonetheless, like many French officials, he did trade a range of foodstuffs and other items, helped by his wife and her family connections. The governor of Louisbourg purchased veal, almost certainly originating in Acadia, from Madame Rondeau in 1742.[14] Acadia was an important source for fresh meat for Louisbourg. In 1743 Madame Rondeau also was at the sale of the assets of a bankrupt retail merchant and purchased significant amounts of dry goods, while in 1744 Monsieur Rondeau attended the estate sale of the governor and bought a large quantity of wine.[15] In each case the quantities purchased suggest they were for resale. An inventory of Rondeau's estate, taken in 1750, provided a record of their commercial activity.

When the population of Louisbourg was deported after the siege of 1745, the Rondeau household lived in La Rochelle, in the home of Rondeau's uncle. When Louisbourg was returned by treaty to the French in 1749, Marie Josephe, then a widow – her husband died between 1745 and 1749 – returned with four of her children and two servants, along with the rest of the deported population.[16] In the fall of 1750, as she was about to remarry, to an army officer, Joseph Dupont Duvivier, Marie Josephe requested an inventory of the community of goods from her previous marriage. This inventory not only shows commercial activity, but also Marie Josephe's role in it. Many of their customers were Acadians, and they had many female clients who sought cloth and dry goods. The net value of their enterprise in 1750 was about ten thousand livres.[17]

As well as recording commercial activity, the Rondeau inventory also provided evidence of Marie Josephe's political leanings and involvement. She requested that the notary at Louisbourg include in the tabulation of the Rondeau estate's debts an as-yet unknown amount owed to several Acadians for provisioning a detachment in 1745. During the war of the Austrian Succession (1744–48) many French and Acadians actively sought opportunities to retake Acadia. Marie Josephe's Acadian cousins led a campaign force from Louisbourg in 1744, and her sister Françoise, who resided on the Saint John River, provisioned and provided transport for a party of seventy Malecite warriors to aid the French at Annapolis.[18] Her brother Alexandre was killed while fighting at Annapolis in 1744.[19] The following year, Marie Josephe's own contribution to Paul Marin de la Malgue's Acadia campaign, which relied heavily for its military support on a large number of Indigenous fighters, demonstrated the presence of an important kinship network that encompassed Île Royale, the Acadians, and the Indigenous peoples in the region.[20]

Marie Josephe's second marriage in 1750 to Joseph Dupont Duvivier, an officer in the French army related to her through her mother and her father, tied her more closely than ever to a network of military/Acadian families in Louisbourg. It also documented both partners' commercial involvements, as each brought merchandise from existing businesses into the marriage, which each chose to keep out of the ensuing community of goods.[21] While married to Duvivier, Marie Josephe administered her own property that she had inherited from Rondeau. In 1753 she negotiated a contract with three Irish fishermen to rent her property at Gabarus for seven years. Although the property was hers, the contract stipulated that her husband had authorized her to enter into the contract, and that, without his permission, any contract she signed would be invalid. Although it was normal in French society for widows to continue to operate the business of their late husbands, it was unusual for a married woman to run her own business; her husband had to grant her the legal right to do so.[22] Yet the terms of the rental contract required specific developments and maintenance on the part of both parties, implying that Marie Josephe must have been involved in extensive negotiations.[23]

While she was married to Duvivier, Marie Josephe's commercial activities expanded. She operated a boutique and carried on business in cooperation with her aunt's cousin Madeleine d'Entremont, the widow Lafitte in Niganiche (Ingonish). Marie Josephe died in Louisbourg in 1753, at the age of forty-three. On her death an inventory was taken of her personal possessions and her business that revealed she had extensive goods for sale both in her own boutique and at Madame Lafitte's, as well as accounts recorded in five books. She shared ownership of a schooner with her cousin Antoine Rodrigue. She received goods from France for her business.[24] Her home had more porcelain and crystal than in 1750, and she had eleven *robes* (gowns of silk and stylish printed cotton, called *indienne* in French inventories). The average bourgeois woman of Louisbourg had between five and seven gowns. She also had fifty-nine chemises, the highest number in any Louisbourg woman's inventory.[25] The chemise, a linen undergarment, was a key element in an eighteenth-century woman's personal hygiene and appearance. Marie Josephe's wardrobe, the most valuable female wardrobe inventoried for a woman in Louisbourg, by French colonial standards reflected both wealth and refinement.[26]

In terms of social status in eighteenth-century Frenh society, Marie Josephe could claim a high social position based on her nobility and wealth. Yet her colonial birth, Abenaki heritage, and involvement in retail trade were factors that compromised her status by metropolitan French standards. Although the French had strong linkages with the Algonquian-speaking Abenaki peoples of the Northeast, they frequently disparaged Indigenous ways of living and expressed distrust in or discomfort with Indigenous North Americans in their writings.[27] Elite metropolitans also frequently disdained colonials, including Acadians, along with their tendency to be involved in trade. Retail trade was considered the lowest level of trading activity.[28] Marie Josephe avoided confronting these prejudices by marrying colonial-born men.

The records do not tell us whether Marie Josephe's Abenaki heritage was ever an issue in her life. Her mother's family did not appear in Louisbourg's documentary records. Her brother Alexandre was there to trade,[29] and she was able to act in common with her siblings in Acadia. Her Saint-Castin uncles continued their important role as borderland intermediaries and were in regular contact with the French administration in Quebec.[30] Perhaps she benefitted, as her uncles had, from support from the Crown based on her family's record of important service to France. There is evidence of persons of mixed Mi'kmaw/European parentage adapting without difficulty to Acadian society in the seventeenth century.[31] Yet the proceedings of the trial of Jules César Félix de la Noüe de Bogard in 1755 for insubordination for marrying Marguerite Guedry, a *métis* and a cousin of Marie Josephe, demonstrates the degree of French discomfort with *métissage* by the mid-eighteenth century.[32] It would be incorrect to assume that Marie Josephe concealed her heritage or that it did not matter, but we do know she managed her identity, although we do not know exactly how. All that is known is that she did so very successfully from the French colonial standpoint.

Marie Josephe Le Borgne de Belisle's family connections enabled her to make the transition from Pentagouët to the upper echelons of Louisbourg's colonial society. She combined advantageous marriages and business success to rise to the top of the French colonial community's economic hierarchy. Her possessions leave no doubt that she was a remarkably successful member of the community. Her business activity indicates that she was an unusual woman in eighteenth-century European society, set apart by her self-assertion in the economic world of men. Her experience, her family background, and perhaps her own ambition made her able to successfully transgress French behavioural cultural norms governing women of her class.

– Anne Marie Lane Jonah

25

Marguerite, Servant at Louisbourg

Marguerite (1713–sometime after 1745) was a Mi'kmaw orphan and servant at Louisbourg. The circumstances of her life were recorded in an extensive employment contract, which in conjunction with other records from Louisbourg provide a rare account of a life on the margins of colonial society.

In 1726 the royal notary at Louisbourg wrote the contract of engagement for the employment of a Mi'kmaw orphan named Marguerite. Marguerite was about thirteen years old at the time and had been in the care of Pierre Mansel since she was three years old. When Marguerite came into his care, Mansel was a beach master – a skilled fisheries worker – in Baleine, a small fishing village at the extreme eastern tip of Cape Breton. The contract of engagement concerning Marguerite stated that Mansel had raised and cared for her because she had been abandoned by her father and mother. Her parents were Mi'kmaq from Cape Breton – described as *"sauvages de cette isle"* on the contract – but the document did not say why they left their daughter or how Mansel came to be her guardian.

The terms of Marguerite's engagement were unusual in that initially she was employed for a trial period of six months, but after one and a half months she became subject to a formal contract. This was because her mistress, Anne Le Borgne de Belisle, Madame Jean-Baptiste Rodrigue, had become so attached to the girl that she wished to engage her indefinitely.[1] The engagement did not provide a wage for Marguerite, which was rare for very young servants, but it did allow for Marguerite to leave the Rodrigues eventually. Marguerite thus was neither a slave nor a paid servant, but something in between. The contract, as most contracts did, required that she be cared for and brought up as a Roman Catholic. It also stipulated that she would be educated.

Marguerite went into service with the Rodrigues after Mansel married one of the Rodrigues' servants. Mansel simply may have found that he could not support both his wife and Marguerite – which was likely, since he was bankrupt less than a year later. Though Marguerite no longer lived with Mansel, and she may even have been meant to replace the servant whom Mansel married, the terms of the engagement contract nevertheless continued to respect the parental role that Mansel had once played in Marguerite's life.[2]

In Louisbourg society Marguerite, an unpaid servant with no family, had no real freedom or options. Years later, after Madame Rodrigue had moved to France, Marguerite remained behind in the service of Michel Rodrigue, Madame Rodrigue's eldest son.[3] As a servant she had an endless round of tasks to perform to keep an eighteenth-century bourgeois household running. When she was thirteen her mistress had five young children; thirteen years later she was in the household of Michel Rodrigue and his new wife, who had five children between 1739 and 1744.[4] It is probable that wet-nursing was added to Marguerite's duties in the latter household;

upper-class French women often employed wet nurses in the early eighteenth century, and the young Madame Rodrigue's first three children were born at intervals that averaged fifteen months, implying the presence of a wet nurse.[5] Marguerite had borne and then lost a child in the same month as the birth of her mistress's first child, making her the ideal candidate for this task.

Marguerite's dead newborn was buried formally in 1739. The child's father, Thomas Stier *dit* la Françoise, a soldier in Captain Duvivier's company, attended the internment. Neither Marguerite nor Stier had the means to contravene or leave their respective social positions, marry, and start an independent life together, and their names do not appear in Louisbourg parish registers again. In 1745 the Rodrigue family, along with the entire population of Louisbourg, was deported to France after the successful siege of Louisbourg by a combined British and New England force. When the rest of the population returned to Louisbourg in 1749, Michel Rodrigue chose to remain in La Rochelle to direct his family's merchant business from there, and so his household remained with him. We do not know whether Marguerite was in La Rochelle with the Rodrigue family, but as most servants stayed with their employers during the deportation, she probably was in La Rochelle.[6] The few details that these records offer of Marguerite's life on the margins of a society alien to her people do not give a sense of an individual with choices or control. Perhaps she was cared for, but she was not free to make her own life in French society.

– Anne Marie Lane Jonah

26

The Diplomatic, Trade, and Emigration Policies of Unama'ki District Chief Jeannot Peguidalouet

Jeannot Peguidalouet Succeeds Chief Denis Michau as Unama'ki District Leader

In the summer of 1751 Jeannot Peguidalouet, at the time first captain of the Unama'ki council at *Malikew'jk* or Mirliguèche (present-day Malagawatch, Cape Breton), was thrust into the role of Unama'ki district chief following the death of Denis Michau, a high-profile Mi'kmaw leader with extensive contacts among the French. Peguidalouet's territorial prerogatives encompassed a sizeable geographical domain covering present-day Antigonish County, part of Guysborough County, Cape Breton Island, southwestern Newfoundland, and several islands in the Gulf of St. Lawrence, including Saint-Pierre and Miquelon.[1] Jeannot had already proven himself to be a courageous warrior and a sincere devotee of the Roman Catholicism associated with Abbé Antoine Gaulin, a missionary of the Société des Missions-Étrangères de Paris who established a mission at Mirliguèche in 1724.[2] And, like most of his Mi'kmaw associates, he could handle bark canoes and French shallops – open wooden clinker-built fishing boats that carried oars, one or two masts, and sails – with alacrity as he plied the waters of the Gulf of St. Lawrence.

Jeannot attracted the attention of Abbé Pierre Maillard, another graduate of the Société des Missions-Étrangères who, as soon as Jeannot became chief, prevailed on him to move his band to a site nearer Port Toulouse, known in Mi'kmaq as Potlotek.[3] Maillard, who arrived in Cape Breton from France in 1735, always referred to Jeannot as "Petit Jean."[4] Together, these two led the Mi'kmaq through the tumultuous times that followed the second fall of Fortress Louisbourg in 1758. After Maillard's death in 1762, the chief remained committed to the missionary's vision of upholding distinctive Mi'kmaq land and resource prerogatives, contingent on certain obligations to the new British regime and provided that the British respected and upheld Mi'kmaw rights. He saw the Mi'kmaq as integral to the new social order arising during the 1760s. Though Jeannot faced formidable obstacles in pursuing this quest, particularly with regard to his emigration and trade policies, he exhibited a rare sense of responsibility for the welfare of diverse groups, including *métis* and Acadian refugees who had been cast adrift following the shattering consequences of the British regime's Acadian deportation policy. To strengthen the Indigenous economy and address the spiritual needs of his people, he forged ties with traders and priests on the French islands of St. Pierre and Miquelon, though to do so was extremely risky: even though certain chiefs had signed treaties of peace and friendship with the British authorities in Halifax in 1760 and 1761, fears abounded in government circles that the Mi'kmaq, if in contact with French priests, might defect to the French cause should conflict between the French and British Crowns reoccur.[5]

Chief Jeannot Peguidalouet has gone down in history as a promoter of Mi'kmaw emigration to southwestern Newfoundland, yet his feats in the diplomatic and trade forums equal his accomplishments in the emigration sphere.[6] He opposed disaffected Indigenous leaders who targeted the British as betrayers of the Mi'kmaq whose perfidy should be avenged. Even in the heat of serious frays, he managed to keep the peace by warning that the diplomatic and trading ties he was fostering would collapse if the Mi'kmaq took up arms. Under his guidance, the Mi'kmaw Grand Council, as the guardian of Indigenous land and resource rights, became firmly rooted in Cape Breton, where it remains to this day. He frequently travelled to Newfoundland and encouraged others to not only to go but to stay, paving the way for the development of Newfoundland Mi'kmaw communities large enough to be recognized and eventually incorporated into the Canadian nation state.

Early Years

Jeannot Peguidalouet was born to Joseph Peguidalouet and Thérèse in 1705 and raised at Mirliguèche, an Indigenous encampment site on the shores of Bras D'Or Lake.[7] During Jeannot's early childhood, the Cape Breton regional band was headed by two chiefs, Isidore and Miguel. The territorial prerogatives of these leaders covered an extensive domain of land, water, and islands known as *Unima'ki* in Mi'kmaq.[8] They distributed hunting territories among families and monitored game and fish levels in accordance with long-standing cultural traditions regarding land and resource use.[9] Whenever human population pressure threatened the island's limited game reserves, the chiefs encouraged some families to hunt in Newfoundland or cross the Canso Strait to mainland Nova Scotia. Members of the *Unima'ki* group also regularly joined Mi'kmaq from the Northumberland Strait and Chignecto areas to hunt sea mammals on the Magdalene Islands, in Chaleur Bay and at Anticosti.[10]

Europeans settled in Cape Breton as early as the sixteenth century but later deserted the area. When Jeannot was only five years old a new influx of French and *métis* fled into the Bras d'Or region after the New England conquest of Port Royal in 1710. These incomers perceived Cape Breton, which they knew as "Île Royale," as a place of refuge, since the island remained French territory under the terms of the 1713 Treaty of Utrecht. Some settled in the environs of Port Toulouse, a military outpost built in 1714 at Saint-Pierre (now St. Peter's) – the same time as Fortress Louisbourg was established – while a few joined the Mi'kmaw community.

One of these incomers to Île Royale, Jean Denys Sr. (c.1680–c.1740), who spoke both Mi'kmaq and French, settled on the Atlantic coast near the Îles Michaud, a set of rocky ledges today known as the "Basque Islands" lying off the coast of present-day Richmond County. Though no record exists of his birth, Jean Denys was almost certainly the son of French naval commander Simon-Pierre Denys de Bonaventure (1659–1711) and a Mi'kmaw woman from Port Royal.[11] Either to conceal the particulars of his birth or simply to conform with Mi'kmaw naming practices while living with the Cape Breton band, Jean Denys apparently adopted "Michau" as his surname, as he resided near the Îles Michaud.[12] He may have arrived in Cape Breton with his paternal uncle, Louis Denys de Bonaventure, who from 1715 to 1720 served as commander of Port Toulouse. In 1722 Jean Michau was recognized as the Cape Breton chief, an office he retained until his death around 1737.[13] The fact that Louis Denys de Bonaventure presided over annual present distributions to the Mi'kmaq likely was a leading factor in Jean Denys's choice of place of residence.

Since Simon-Pierre Denys de Bonaventure was a naval hero and Louis Denys de Bonaventure commanded Port Toulouse, Jean Michau Sr. and his sons Jean Jr., Michel, and Denis were treated by the French as a form of "forest aristocracy."[14] Jean Jr. in the 1720s joined the Mi'kmaw community at Antigonish, but by the late 1740s lived at Port Toulouse. While en route to Île St. Jean (present-day Prince Edward Island), he conversed with Thomas Pichon, who would become secretary to Île Royale's governor. Pichon noted that Jean Jr. had approached Claude-Elisabeth Denys de Bonaventure, Jean Michau Sr.'s half-brother, about obtaining a land grant on Île St. Jean.[15] Jean Jr.'s brother Michel married Marie Isidore, a daughter of Chief Isidore, who in 1716 was one of two Cape Breton head chiefs. Michel and Marie's sons, Jacques-Angé, born in 1729, and François, born in 1734, were accorded the privilege of being baptized within the walls of Fortress Louisbourg. (Other Mi'kmaw infants were baptized at Mirliguèche.) After Jean Michau Sr.'s death around 1740, however, Michel left Cape Breton with his family, and his brother Denis assumed the office of Unama'ki head chief until he died in 1751.[16] At this time the Compte Raymond, the governor of Louisbourg, revealed that Denis Michau was descended from a French noblemen, whom he left unnamed but who almost certainly was Simon Denys de la Trinité, Simon-Pierre Denys's grandfather, who received letters of ennoblement from Louis XIV in 1668.[17]

Despite the inclusion of a French aristocratic element in their leadership ranks, the Unama'ki Mi'kmaq engaged in economic and trade practices that their ancestors had followed for generations. They interacted regularly, holding meetings and social festivities and performing customary rites of marriage and burial.[18] Cape Breton Island's natural carrying capacity rarely supported a human population of over 250 individuals for an extended period of time,[19] so when this number was surpassed, the district's leaders in council directed parties to hunt elsewhere, either on the adjoining mainland, in Newfoundland, or on nearby islands.[20] Yet the marriage universe required population numbers of at least 120 persons to sustain itself over time, since traditionally cousin marriage among the Mi'kmaq was proscribed until the third generation. This practice gave rise to exogamous extended family groups, with cores composed of brothers, sisters, and cousins who regarded and treated each other as siblings.[21] Circulation of population within the district allowed young persons to find mates who were marriageable and yet still associated socially and politically with their own regional band and its leaders.[22] It also facilitated the formation of brigades that could travel long distances to cement alliances and obtain exotic goods.[23]

The first decades of the seventeenth century brought major changes in Unama'ki's political and trading spheres. Prior to 1713 the headquarters of French power had lain distant from Cape Breton, so during colonial wars French agents travelled considerable distances to recruit Unama'ki warriors. Now, nearby Fortress Louisbourg stood as the French power base in the Northeast, and its satellite military station at St. Peter's, renamed Port Toulouse once Louis Denys de La Ronde assumed command of its fort, emerged as a bustling military and trading hub. Trade between Mi'kmaq and the French flourished. Traders from Louisbourg, as well as smaller Acadian communities at l'Ardoise, Arichat, Petit de Grat, and on Île Madam, eagerly exchanged manufactured goods for peltry, feathers, and sea mammal oil. *Métis*

traders belonging to the Guedry, Mius, and Ury families arrived from Pobomcoup, Merliguéche, and La Hève along Nova Scotia's South Shore and erected small posts, overwintering in the Bras D'Or region. These persons established kin and friendship as well as trading ties with the Unama'ki band.[24] Jeannot Peguidalouet's parents brought furs and oil to trade with the French and in return received cotton shirts, silken turbans, occasionally a shallop, ships' compasses, rope and rigging fittings, and ornaments, as well as a range of more utilitarian articles.[25] As he grew older, Jeannot travelled with them on trading expeditions to Quebec and Montreal.

Jeannot heard stories of the gifts bestowed by the French on noted Indigenous warriors during the late seventeenth-century colonial wars between the French and English Crowns. Prior to Peguidalouet's birth Simon-Pierre Denys de Bonaventure and Bernard-Anselme d'Abbadie de Saint-Casin had recruited Unama'ki Mi'kmaq to harass New England settlements and forts north of the Kennebec River. Warriors who responded were rewarded with provisions, clothing, guns, ammunition, luxury goods such as tobacco, and various honorifics.[26] But though they accepted French presents, they were not paid mercenaries. They exhibited a high degree of autonomy in choosing whether or not to enter a fray and fight, and if pressed in unwelcome ways they left for Newfoundland to escape the interference of colonial agents in their lives.

Eager to win his own accolades as a warrior both from his own people and from the French at Port Toulouse, Jeannot at age fifteen likely participated on 7 August 1720 in a raid with Acadians from Île Madam against the English fort at Canso. The Canso raid was one of the precipitating factors of Dummer's War, during which Jeannot undoubtedly joined more seasoned warriors from his community in skirmishes against the English and New Englanders until the spring of 1725.[27] After the war he also likely served as a delegate to Indigenous council forums in the Northeast, for the Mi'kmaq recently had joined six Algonquian nations as well as Iroquoian speakers from Caughnawaga (Kahnawake, near Montreal) in what, two centuries later, would be referred to as "The Eastern Algonkian Wabanaki Confederacy."[28] By this time the Mi'kmaq had subdivided their territory in the Northeast, known collectively as *Mi'kma'ki*, into seven districts, with at least two representatives from each district taking part in Eastern Wabanaki

Confederacy council forums. Communication with delegates from other nations allowed the Mi'kmaq to gain information and monitor what both the French and English were doing from year to year. Back in their communities they then could review their situation and options, based on the information brought back from the meetings by their delegates.

The Mirliguèche Mission

The French were unaware of how closely they were scrutinized by the Indigenous constituencies around them. After 1713 the French focused on making the Mi'kmaw population into sedentary farmers. It was believed that settling the Mi'kmaq in permanent villages would constitute a major coup for the French cause, since then able-bodied men could easily be located and recruited to fight, if need be, in colonial wars. Until that time, annual presents had to be the currency that cemented Mi'kmaw loyalty to the French Crown. Chiefs and head men who attended meetings convened by the French would receive, on behalf of their bands, provisions, cloth, grenadier muskets without bayonets, powder, shot, lead balls, and articles of clothing. Commissions, military clothing, and medals were extended to chiefs. To have a Roman Catholic mission in proximity to a present distribution point became a strategic necessity, not only to offer sacraments and otherwise attend to the spiritual needs of the Mi'kmaw assemblage, but to engage the incumbent missionary in dispensing provisions, cloth, and other practical items to families, while the governor or his representatives took care of bestowing luxury goods and honorifics.

The French policy of giving annual presents foundered at first, owing to the unsystematic manner in which it was conducted. The governor of Île Royale, Joseph Monbeton de Brouillan *dit* Saint-Ovide, dispensed goods and gifts at Port Toulouse in 1717, though the following year he held the distribution at Antigonish, a mission centre established in 1716, at the insistence of the French minister of marine, on the Nova Scotian mainland by Abbé Antoine Gaulin.[29] Gaulin had arrived in Acadia in 1698 to aid and finally replace Père Pierre Thury as missionary to the Abenaki at Pentagouët (Pemaquid), lying on the Penobscot River in present-day Maine. In 1702 Gaulin was appointed vicar general of Acadia, and by 1704 his jurisdiction extended over both Acadia and Plaisance in Newfoundland.[30]

In 1718 Port Toulouse won out over Antigonish as the centre for present distributions, owing to a flood of British complaints about the French meeting with a large assembly of Mi'kmaq outside of the French territories of Île Royale and Île St. Jean. Saint-Ovide arrived at Port Toulouse in June or July where, along with Louis Denys, he engaged in distribution ceremonies for two days before continuing on to meet with more Mi'kmaq at Port La Joye (now Charlottetown) on Île St. Jean. At both places the governor warned of the duplicity of the British while praising the generosity of the French king, their Father.

Equipped in 1722 with a new set of instructions from Jean-Frédéric Phélypeaux, the Comte de Maurapas, the French minister of marine, Abbé Gaulin, began searching for a site on the Bras d'Or Lake for a Mi'kmaw farming community that would eclipse his headquarters at Antigonish and relegate the latter to a satellite mission.[31] The parcel needed to be central enough to serve as a mustering point for Mi'kmaw guerrilla warriors during times of war, and be sheltered from British inducements that might weaken the Mi'kmaq's ties to France. To Maurapas and Saint-Ovide, the settlement would form a crucible in which the French would foster and shape Mi'kmaw antagonism towards the English while cloaking French intentions in a mantle of strict secrecy.[32] Before the year was up, Gaulin chose Mirliguèche, a peninsula on the west side of the Bras d'Or Lake, at the entrance of the River Denys basin about fifty-five kilometres from Port Toulouse. The site had two advantages: it had been a Mi'kmaw encampment ground for generations, and it was sufficiently removed from the Atlantic coast to shield it from British surveillance.[33]

In the spring of 1724 the Comte de Maurapas allocated twenty-five hundred livres for the construction of a church and presbytery of vertical log and half-timber construction and urged Gaulin to attract Mi'kmaq to the new mission station. The work took longer and cost more than expected, so by the time the two buildings were finished in 1726 their cost had soared to thirty-nine hundred livres.[34] Gaulin was told to recruit as many Mi'kmaq as he could to the new mission, something he was expected to do on his itinerant travels while serving the Mi'kmaq at Shubenacadie and the Indigenous communities along the Atlantic coast, from Cape Sable to Chignecto.[35] In 1725, finding the distances too arduous to travel, Gaulin left Mirliguèche permanently for a mission he had established in 1722 at Shubenacadie. His successor, Abbé Michel Courtin, focused on facilitating a Mi'kmaw summer hunt for walrus and seals on the Magdalen Islands as well as attaining a French grant for an island, later known as "Courtin's Island," in break Malpeque Bay for the use of the Mi'kmaq. He secured the grant of the island, but in 1732, before he had convinced Saint-Ovide to provide additional shallops and vats to render down walrus and seal fat, he drowned in a canoe accident on Prince Edward Island and the mission field fell vacant for two years.[36]

Abbé de Saint-Vincent, who joined the mission late in 1734, spoke Mi'kmaq well enough to teach it to Abbé Pierre Maillard, another graduate of the Société des m*issions étrangères de Paris* who had disembarked from the ship *Rubis* at Louisbourg on 13 August 1735. Within a year Maillard grasped enough of the Mi'kmaw language to devise a hieroglyphic system, using hieroglyphs already in circulation among the Mi'kmaq, which he used to set down formulas for prayers and responses of the catechism.[37] Maillard, however, failed to establish Mirliguèche as a Mi'kmaw agricultural centre. While families followed the missionary's directives by sowing small gardens of corn, squash, beans, potatoes, and wheat, they left soon afterwards to fish migrating salmon in the Rivière St. Marguerite (Margaree River).[38] Following the distribution of presents at Port Toulouse in the early summer, many set out on long-distance journeys to other parts of the Northeast for trading purposes or to participate in all-Indigenous councils. Once they had harvested their crops in the fall, they hunted migrating seabirds and pursued sea mammals on islands off the Atlantic coast. With the onset of winter, families left for their hunting and trapping territories. Much of the time only a few elderly women and men were left at the mission at such times to care for persons who were infirm or sick, for whom travel proved onerous.

During these years Maillard received little support for his agricultural endeavours from Saint-Ovide, who drew a storm of complaints from his superiors and the Mi'kmaq alike for focusing mainly on amassing large profits from illicit trading activities. The governor's trading practices undermined his political credibility and made it difficult for Unama'ki leaders to maintain close ties with him or Louisbourg's elite. He was absent in France when Jean Michau died in the fall of 1737. In Maillard's stead, François le Coutre de Bourville, the *lieutenant de roi* and acting governor, insisted that the chief's body be interred with military honours at Louisbourg, to strengthen Mi'kmaw attachment to the French king.[39]

Jeannot Climbs the Leadership Ranks

Following Jean Michau's death, Denis Michau became the Unama'ki chief. Jeannot Peguidalouet was an ambitious man, but the Michauds' entrenchment in the upper echelons of *Unima'ki*'s leadership hierarchy, bolstered by their French connections, frustrated his political aspirations for many years. In 1737 the French vested him with the commission of "major," after which he was regarded as a minor chief.[40] In contrast to Denis Michaud, whose connections with the French regime guided and stabilized his actions, Peguidalouet was less inclined to accommodate the wishes of Louisbourg's officialdom. In 1738 he caused a minor scandal when he encouraged a soldier stationed at Port Toulouse to desert in order to marry one of Peguidalouet's daughters. For this insubordinate act, de Bourville temporarily stripped Peguidalouet of his commission. That a soldier might desert and then move to a remote part of Newfoundland where he would be hard to trace was anathema to De Bourville; if not suppressed at once, the lovers' tryst could prompt similar desertions from the French ranks. The unnamed soldier was apprehended, imprisoned, punished, and returned to the barracks at Port Toulouse.[41] Since Peguidalouet was a valuable warrior in French eyes, his commission as major was later restored.[42]

This incident may have prompted Maillard in 1739 to decide it was time to ensure greater order within the mission community. He and Abbé Jean-Louis Le Loutre, a graduate of the Société des m*issions étrangères de Paris* who had arrived in Cape Breton the preceding year, devised a set of règlements, or rules, to guide the behaviour of the Mi'kmaq living at the mission stations of Mirliguèche, Antigonish, and Shubenacadie. Infractions of these rules courted severe punishment.[43] At the same time, the Unama'ki Mi'kmaq had their own complaints about the disorderly conduct of French officials during present distributions. Isaac-Louis de Forant, Saint-Ovide's successor, alerted the minister of marine to a host of Mi'kmaw concerns, one being a novel practice of changing the post commander at Port Toulouse annually.[44] The Mi'kmaq felt that this change undermined protocols and the spirit of continuity that had pervaded present distributions during the days when Louis Denys de Bonaventure presided over the gift giving, with Chief Jean Michau by his side.[45] The French governor made a concerted effort to address these complaints, beginning with instructing the post commander to hold a formal council annually in his quarters at the fort to listen to Mi'kmaw complaints. The French official was expected to dress in regimentals, while chiefs were invited to wear their regalia of office.[46] De Forant expected mission centres to double as mustering points for warriors in times of war.[47] The French governor identified thirty-two Mi'kmaw chiefs throughout Acadia and Cape Breton and presented commissions to them.[48] He also framed an idealized system of fourteen Mi'kmaw "commands" to guide French-Indigenous relations.[49] Duties of a command leader included mustering warriors for raids and challenging the right of New England fishermen "to settle or cure fish" along the Atlantic coast.[50] De Forant prided himself on being able, by means of the command system, to collect at least six hundred Mi'kmaq to serve as guerrilla warriors.

Responsibility for maintaining missions throughout Acadia was split between Maillard and Le Loutre. Maillard's labours focused on Cape Breton and Antigonish, while Le Loutre, headquartered at Shubenacadie, served Mi'kmaw communities from Cape Sable to Beaubassin and in what is now Pictou County.[51] Mi'kmaq living at Chignecto and along the Northumberland Strait met French officials and their missionary annually at Malpeque on Île Ste. Jean, while those from Cape Sable to Cape Breton collected at Port Toulouse. The two missionaries were directed to inculcate a love for the French, and to monitor, address, and channel Mi'kmaw concerns, especially during the annual displays of pomp and ceremony surrounding present distributions. "I must incessantly excite them to the practice of religion," Maillard wrote, "and labour to render them tractable, sociable, and loyal to the king. But especially, I apply myself to make them live in good understanding with the French."[52]

By early 1739 Maillard began thinking of moving his mission headquarters to Vachelouacadie, or "the place of running water" or "place of running spirits,"[53] near Port Toulouse. The Mi'kmaq baulked at farming intensively at Mirliguèche, and the only times they collected at his mission in any numbers were at Easter and Whitsuntide.[54] The church and presbytery at Mirliguèche were also in need of repair, but the missionary hesitated to ask for funds for this purpose. Hoping perhaps that the presence of the French at Port Toulouse might spur his congregants to greater agricultural effort, the missionary

urged Chief Denis Michau to relocate his people to Vachelouacadie, but Michau refused to move. After several months at the Antigonish mission, Maillard in 1740 became vicar general for Île Royale and the following year relocated his chapel and presbytery to Vachelouacadie.[55] The mission site, called Île de la Sainte-Famille (Island of the Holy Family), eventually became known in English as "Chapel Island."

At the new mission, dedicated to St. Anne, Maillard established St. Anne's Day festivities among the Mi'kmaq as a national holiday of celebration and revitalization. Prior to the 1740s, band members congregated at the Mirliguèche mission at any time from April to late August. By instilling in the minds of his congregants that attendance at annual rites on 26 July, St. Anne's Day, testified to a high level of veneration for the revered saint, within a few years Maillard could count on his Mi'kmaw parishioners to be annually waiting for him in late July.[56] But St. Anne's Day, or *setonewimg*, as a yearly revitalization rite was not merely the result of a gradual and undirected syncretism of the Indigenous summer council meeting and Roman Catholic ritual. Maillard had an important role in promoting the timing and format of the celebration, while local Mi'kmaw leaders ensured that the summer rite also retained distinctly Mi'kmaw elements. St. Anne, held to be the grandmother of Jesus and called "Our Grandmother" by the Mi'kmaq, became imbued with additional symbolic meaning through association with the Mi'kmaw mythic figure of Bearwoman or Grandmother Bear," who was held to aid infants, the elderly, and mothers in childbirth.[57] The Unama'ki chief played a major role in the ceremonies, including directing a speech to the assembly. The festival, seen as a time when the spiritual realm drew close to the secular sphere and thus infused events with special power, came to influence the timing of French present distributions at Port Toulouse, which beforehand had occurred at any point in either June or July.[58] The two weeks surrounding St. Anne's Day also became the preferred time for choosing chiefs and councillors, settling internal disputes, baptizing infants, and performing marriages.

Maillard found much to appreciate in Mi'kmaw culture. He came to understand that the Mi'kmaq believed in an all-pervading spiritual power that invigorated mind and body. The Mi'kmaq traditionally had held an annual spring ceremony that actively invoked the regenerating aspect of this spiritual agency, and since this force was represented by the sun, Maillard included specialized references to the sun in his mission's rites. The monstrance, the vessel that holds the Host during Eucharistic rites, was often termed *soleil* (sun) rather than *ostensoir*, which reinforced a distinctly Mi'kmaw rather than Roman Catholic interpretation.[59]

But try all he might, Maillard failed to turn the Mi'kmaq into farmers. Denis Michau continued to refuse to go to Île de la Sainte Famille except for religious observances, and as long as their chief preferred living at Mirliguèche, other Mi'kmaq stayed with him. Ensconced at his new mission headquarters, Maillard became a respected, even beloved figure who was addressed as "Mosi Meial" (Mr. Maillard).[60] A large boulder on Île de la Sainte Famille is still revered as the site of his first sermons. By contrast, De Forant's gifts and system of commands failed to capture Mi'kmaw affections, and proved far from seamless since some chiefs traded with New Englanders rather than rebuffed them.[61] De Forant nevertheless worked tirelessly at implementing his scheme, and when he died suddenly in May 1740, his successor as governor, Jean-Baptiste-Louis Le Prevost Duquesnel, carried on his work.

With the outbreak of King George's War in the spring of 1744, the French began awarding medals on the grounds of personal merit, particularly for prowess in guerrilla warfare.[62] Lacking the troops to attack the British in 1744, Duquesnel also distributed special articles of clothing to Indigenous leaders to encourage them to follow his military directives. Late in May, Jeannot Peguidalouet received a *habit de munition* (a soldier's greatcoat), a hat – likely trimmed with gold or silver braid – and a *hausse-col*, or gorget, to wear around his neck.[63] Jeannot's receipt of these articles suggests he participated with valour earlier the same month in the siege of Port Toulouse, when the Mi'kmaq saved a valuable altarpiece from a New England force that razed the French settlement and desecrated the Mi'kmaw cemetery.[64] In July he probably joined Maillard in the first siege of Annapolis Royal, and took part in the unsuccessful siege launched by François Du Pont Duvivier later the same year.[65]

Jeannot Peguidalouet in April 1745 became second captain after a chief named Jacques Padanuques was captured by the crew of a New England vessel and taken to Boston, where he died.[66] Owing to his reputation for bravery and his devotion to the Roman Catholic religion, Jeannot rose in stature commensurate with the power vacuum created by Padanuques's departure. At the same time he grew close to Denis Michau, who may have been his brother-in-law. The two treated each other like siblings, and attended ceremonials together.

In June 1745 Jeannot braved a hail of musket balls fired by twenty Englishmen during the Battle of Petit Lorembec, which occurred during the 1745 siege of the Louisbourg fortress. Afterwards, he credited his survival to St. Anne, whom he claimed he had called upon to intercede for him during the heat of battle. "Regarde, mon Père," he declared to Maillard, "comme un vray miracle de ce que tu me vois icy" (Look, Father, it is truly a miracle that you see me here before you).[67] The balls had pierced his clothing "to the right and the left," but his body had remained unscathed. Chief Claude Réné, who led the Mi'kmaw contingent of fifty men as well as three Frenchmen in the fray, by contrast sustained serious injuries and had to be carried to the hospital at Louisbourg.[68] When Réné fell, Jeannot assumed charge of the field and protected the Acadian fishing port of Petit Lorembec by forcing the British force to surrender and disperse.[69] An anonymous Acadian habitant who was an eye witness at the Battle of Petit Lorembec afterwards mistook Jeannot's hale and hearty form for that of Chief Réné and declared he had seen a miracle – Réné having arisen from near death.[70]

Many other Mi'kmaq had already left the Louisbourg area, galled by the military incompetence of the French governor, Louis Du Pont Duchambon de Vergor.[71] After assuming office in October 1744, Duchambon prompted a mutiny in the garrison over poor pay and atrocious living conditions, and in the spring of 1745 discouraged soldiers from going outside the ramparts to fight for fear they might desert. Consequently, on 11 May 1745, except for the fire of Indigenous and Acadian militia fighters, the New England artillery, sheltered on the seaward side by the Royal Navy fleet commanded by Commodore Peter Warren, landed practically unopposed about five kilometres southwest of the fortress at Pointe Plate (or Flat Point) in Gabarus Bay.[72] Guerrilla tactics were of little use against the artillery once it was positioned and directed against the town, and after a siege of over six weeks the French capitulated on 28 June 1745.

Peguidalouet subsequently fought beside Maillard in various forays around Port Toulouse, until the missionary was taken prisoner late in 1745, taken to Boston, and then released to leave for France.

Around this time eighty Mi'kmaw individuals from the Mirliguèche and Port Toulouse area travelled to Miramichi to reconnoitre with Mi'kmaq from other mission centres, but it is not known if Jeannot Peguidalouet was among them.[73] By late September of 1746 Maillard was back in Acadia, having returned to Nova Scotia with the Duc d'Anville and his fleet. Jeannot may have been with the missionary at Grand Pré on 11 February 1747, when a French and Indigenous force led by Nicolas-Antoine Coulon de Villiers defeated Arthur Noble's men in a bloody battle waged in blizzard conditions.[74] Yet, given Jeannot's penchant for sailing across the Cabot Strait, a more likely location for him at this time was Newfoundland.

During the winter of 1746–47, forty Mi'kmaq from Île Royale captured twenty-three English inhabitants of an isolated community in southwestern Newfoundland and brought them to Nova Scotia. In April, a party of eight Mi'kmaq were transporting twelve of these settlers along the Saint John River to Quebec alive, in keeping with Maillard's repeated injunctions against undue cruelty to prisoners, when their wards overpowered and killed most of them; a Mi'kmaw woman and a few children escaped. Two days later, when the rest of the Mi'kmaq heard of the fate of their comrades, they killed the eleven other prisoners in their possession and carried their scalps to Quebec.[75] Unama'ki Mi'kmaq in July of 1748 also attacked an English colliery on an island at Burnt Head, not far from Cape North.[76]

In 1748 the Treaty of Aix-la-Chapelle returned Cape Breton to France, left Acadia in the hands of the English, and launched Acadia and Cape Breton into an era of uneasy peace. The London Board of Trade directed the new English governor, Edward Cornwallis, to make peace treaties with the Indigenous population in order to open up the province for settlement, agriculture, and industry, and to do all at the least possible cost. Cornwallis arrived at Chebucto (*Kjipuktuk*, meaning "big harbour" in Mi'kmaq) on 21 June 1749 with twenty-five hundred settlers to found Halifax. The new settlement was to serve as a counterweight to Louisbourg and aid in regulating the cod fishery. Ignoring the local Mi'kmaq altogether, Cornwallis appealed to Indigenous leaders living west of the Chignecto Isthmus to sign a peace treaty, to bolster the British presence in territory that had become contested ground between the British and French Crowns. In response, in August 1749 two Malecite, one Passamaquoddy, and a Mi'kmaq delegate from Chignecto signed a pact, similar to the treaty signed by Indigenous leaders at Annapolis Royal in 1726, aboard the warship *Beaufort* anchored in Halifax Harbour.[77]

The Mi'kmaq near Halifax were angry at not being consulted, but they at first adopted a "wait and see" policy and remained quiet. The French, however, were immediately incensed at these developments. Charles des Herbiers, Île Royale's governor following the colony's return to France, pressed the Mi'kmaq to oppose English expansion. Following a Mi'kmaw attack on an English vessel at Chignecto in early August 1749, Cornwallis blamed Abbé Le Loutre, since the missionary had left Shubenacadie and established his headquarters at Beaubassin.[78] The British governor also refused to consult with chiefs whose territorial prerogatives included Kjipuktuk and regarded any shows of Mi'kmaw opposition to his actions as infractions of the articles of the peace and friendship treaty ratified in 1726 at Annapolis Royal, to be treated as serious violations of British law.[79]

On 25 September 1749 a large assemblage of Mi'kmaw leaders, among them Denis Michau, Jeannot Peguidalouet, and Claude Réné, met at Port Toulouse and responded to Cornwallis with a tirade of exasperation and challenge. They called Abbé Maillard from his mission headquarters on Île Ste. Famille to draft a memorial declaring that they, not the British, were the rightful owners of the soil. "[T]his land of which you wish to make yourself now absolute master, this land belongs to me," they declared. "I have come from it as certainly as the grass."[80] Concluding that the Mi'kmaq meant war, Cornwallis embarked on a plan to divide and conquer by favouring the Malecite with presents and provisions while sending rangers to scout out Mi'kmaw encampments and kill the inhabitants.[81] Tensions reached a fever pitch after Captain Edward How, who spoke Mi'kmaq and often acted as a negotiator with Mi'kmaw leaders, was shot on 26 August 1750 outside the walls of Fort Lawrence.[82] In response, Cornwallis on 2 October 1749 issued a proclamation offering ten guineas for every Mi'kmaw person or scalp, an amount he raised to fifty guineas the following June.[83]

Despite these events the Mi'kmaq in council at Chignecto in November 1750 proposed that both the British and French recognize a large tract north of the Shubenacadie River for the Mi'kmaq's exclusive use.[84] Even though Fort Lawrence and Fort

Beausejour already glowered at each other from opposite banks of the Missiguash River, which cut across the Isthmus of Chignecto, the Mi'kmaq called for the dismantlement of these European strongholds. "Their demands," Cornwallis fumed on hearing their requests, "… are so preposterous and ridiculous that they cannot be in earnest, such as abandoning Chignecto, not making a Fort, giving them half the country."[85] The only concession the governor would grant was that if Mi'kmaw leaders swore allegiance to the British Crown and signed treaty, their band members would be exempt from being hunted down for scalp bounty. After he refused to consider their petitions, Mi'kmaw warriors and Acadian resistance fighters, many from Le Loutre's headquarters in the Chignecto area, launched at least six raids on Halifax and Dartmouth.[86]

The French in the fall of 1750 felt the time was ripe to honour the Unama'ki leadership by a special distribution of French beneficence.[87] In early November, Denis Michau was invited to lead members of a Mi'kmaw delegation to Louisbourg; the group, after proclaiming their continued attachment to King Louis XIV, were given provisions for a feast.[88] The French governor also issued a commission on 8 November appointing Jeannot Peguidalouet as first captain of the Cape Breton Mi'kmaq, but Jeannot, being unwell, could not travel to Louisbourg to attend the ceremonies.[89] He received his parchment and medal two weeks later when he arrived at the fortress carrying correspondence from the commander of Port Toulouse.[90]

Des Herbiers was succeeded late in the summer of 1751 by the Comte de Raymond. Raymond was welcomed by a display of pomp and ceremony on his arrival at Louisbourg that included meeting a delegation of Mi'kmaw leaders that undoubtedly included Peguidalouet.[91] Since 1748, when his kinsman Claude-Élisabeth Denys de Bonaventure was appointed commandant of Île Saint-Jean – a post he held until 1754 – most members of Denis Michau's immediate family had moved westward.[92] His brother Jean Michau Jr. left for Île Saint-Jean in 1750, and was likely joined there by his other brother Michel. A harsh winter in 1750–51 brought scarcity of game and a period of famine in the early spring at Mirliguèche.[93] When Maillard pressed Louisbourg to have supplies and presents sent to his Mi'kmaw congregants, instructions arrived for him to establish a sedentary farming community located near Port

Toulouse. The missionary was told that such a settlement allowed for closer French supervision of the Indigenous population, especially as some Mi'kmaq in 1750 had approached Halifax with overtures of peace. Denis Michau still resisted moving to Port Toulouse, however, and in March 1751 still wielded sufficient influence to have a half-timber and piquet house built for him, at the cost of three hundred livres, at Mirliguèche.[94]

This dwelling was the first such structure constructed on Cape Breton for a Mi'kmaw chief, but it was not occupied for long. Chief Denis Michau sickened early in the summer of 1751, and by July he was taken to the surgery at Port Toulouse and placed under French medical care.[95] He died later the same summer. Lacking his brothers and other close kinsmen beside him, he turned to his friend Jeannot Peguidalouet to oversee matters upon his death. According to the Comte de Raymond, Michau left a wife and a young son "dans la misère" (in misery).[96] The French provided goods and clothing to assist Michau's destitute widow, while Jeannot assumed responsibility for raising Michau's young son, who remained unnamed in the French correspondence.[97]

Jeannot as Unama'ki District Chief

After an appropriate hiatus of several months following Chief Michau's death, the Unama'ki Mi'kmaq in November met in council and appointed Jeannot Peguidalouet to be their next district chief. On 10 December 1751 the Comte de Raymond directed his secretary, Thomas Pichon, to prepare and sign a chief's commission for the new appointee. "On account of the many evidences of fidelity and attachment to the French given by Jannet Pequidoualouet [Jeannot Peguidalouet], as well as of his zeal for the religion and the service of the King," the commission read, "we have nominated and appointed … him by these presents chief" of the Mi'kmaq of Île Royale.[98]

Scarcities during the winters of 1751–52 and 1752–53 proved so severe that some Acadian traders who had for years regularly dealt with the Mi'kmaq left the island.[99] To make Maillard's congregants more self-sufficient, Raymond again pressed the missionary to consolidate the Mi'kmaw populace around Île de Famille and teach them to farm. The governor also promised Jeannot three hundred livres for a house, similar to the one built for Denis Michau, if the new chief moved closer to Port Toulouse.[100]

Jeannot soon accepted the offer, and had a half-timber and piquet dwelling erected for his household on Île Ste. Famille, close to the presbytery where Maillard lived.[101] Aside from Peguidalouet, his family, and Maillard, the only other residents on the island were Louis-Benjamin Petitpas, an interpreter and servant to Maillard until the missionary's death in 1762,[102] and Abbé Jean Manach, a graduate of the Séminaire des Missions-Étrangères in Paris who arrived in 1750 but soon left to join Abbé Jean-Louis Le Loutre at Beaubassin. The rest of the Mi'kmaq pitched their encampments across the channel from the island at a site they called *Potlotek*, a Mi'kmaw place name derived from the French "Port Toulouse."

Maillard and Jeannot worked together to make Île Ste. Famille the centre of a flourishing religious community dedicated to St. Anne. In 1754 the missionary became grand vicar of the Acadian missions with jurisdiction over the Recollects at Louisbourg, which undoubtedly raised him in the Mi'kmaq's and Acadians' estimation. As the organization of observations for the Holy Year fell under the grand vicar's auspices, he was able to introduce an elaborate St. Anne's Day procession on 26 July as an annual event, as well as an accompanying dispensation – relating only to the Mi'kmaw people – that the annual Eastertide duties incumbent on all Roman Catholics be reserved for the fortnight surrounding St. Anne's Day.

Despite Maillard's close attention to his missionary duties, the French authorities were not particularly supportive of his efforts. As far as they were concerned, the Mi'kmaq's value to the French hinged on their capacity to harass the British militarily, and not on their godliness.[103] The Comte de Raymond had a road built at enormous expense to facilitate the movement of troops from Louisbourg into the Bras d'Or region. Maillard meanwhile received little money from the French regime. He used his own funds to repair the chapel and presbytery on Île Ste. Famille, and to acquire a wooden image of St. Anne to be used in St. Anne's Day processions. (Not until March 1757 would Augustin de Boschenry de Drucour, Raymond's successor, arrange for the missionary to be reimbursed the three thousand livres Maillard paid out of his own pocket five years before.)[104] Maillard also faced another pressing problem: the Mi'kmaq resented his pressuring them to settle down. "Why should it be disapproved of for us to leave these lands to go and overwinter other places, where we cannot fail to find abundant things on which to subsist, and where our earnings from fur trapping will be well beyond that which we need to pay our debts?" they countered.[105]

When the British colonial executive council headed by Governor Peregrine Thomas Hopson and, after November of 1754, by Governor Charles Lawrence failed to address their calls for a vast reserve extending from the Shubenacadie River north to the Northumberland Strait, the Mi'kmaq at Chignecto delivered one last memorial to Halifax on the subject during January 1755. In response, the members of the executive council denounced any plan that would lead to the dismantling of Fort Lawrence, jeopardize the Canso fishery, and allow French shipping to proceed freely between Louisbourg and Quebec.[106] While it was not the last time that the Mi'kmaq would launch a claim to the northeastern part of the province, discussion of the matter was silenced by a series of traumatic events. Mi'kmaq and Acadian resistance fighters raided the new Lunenburg settlements and in response, on 14 May 1756, four days before the formal declaration of what would become the Seven Years' War (1756–63), Governor Lawrence issued a reward of thirty pounds for every male Mi'kmaw prisoner brought in alive, and twenty-five pounds for each Mi'kmaw scalp.[107] On 16 June 1755 the commander of Fort Beauséjour, Louis du Pont Duchambon de Vergor, capitulated to a British force led by Lieutenant Colonel Robert Monckton, causing Le Loutre to flee permanently to France. The British occupied Fort Beauséjour and renamed it Fort Cumberland.[108] In August they began deporting Acadians from Grand Pré.

Following the outbreak of war, Louisbourg's officialdom became more attentive to Maillard and his congregants. The French had not completely repaired the shattered ramparts of their fortress town after the siege of 1745, and knew they would have to depend heavily on Indigenous guerrilla fighters to weather another attack.[109] In accordance with the French governor's instructions, Maillard kept the Unama'ki Mi'kmaq in a state of war, though he worried lest his zeal for the French cause carry him beyond the bounds deemed appropriate for an abbot, sworn to a life of poverty, whose first duties to his congregants were of a religious nature. The French practice of paying high prices for English scalps also troubled him.[110] He realized that the Mi'kmaq feared encirclement within their own territories. This anxiety fuelled their peacemaking proposals, which the colonial authorities ignored.[111] The missionary was beginning to probe the essence of the Mi'kmaq's struggle, and to make it his own.

Events During and After the Final Fall of Louisbourg

In 1757 Chief Peguidalouet and other Unama'ki Mi'kmaq travelled with Abbé Maillard to an encampment site near the Mira River, north of Louisbourg, to await a call to defend the fortress should the British attack. Those that gathered at Mira were treated to presents and foodstuffs at great expense to the French.[112] Provisioning depots were also set up along the coast to supply Indigenous and Acadian militia contingents on watch for any approaching British. Mi'kmaq warriors from other parts of the province went to Miramichi where they joined the French partisan leader, Charles Deschamps, Sieur de Boishébert and Raffetot, who, along with Malecite, Eastern Abenaki, and Acadian resistance fighters, had been conducting raids on Halifax.[113] On Sunday, 10 July, the Unama'ki Mi'kmaq joined Boishébert's Indigenous contingent to stage an elaborate war dance in anticipation of a British attack that was supposed to happen later in the summer, but never did. During this ceremony some of the chiefs knelt at Boishébert's feet and prevailed on the French commander to raise them up.[114] This was not an act of abject obeisance but rather, according to northeastern Algonquian cultural tenets, was intended to make a person appear temporarily "empty of power," ready to be "filled" by French generosity.[115] When the summer was over with no sign of the English, the warriors simply dispersed to their respective territories.

When the British forces failed to appear by the fall of 1757, Boishébert became impatient and took the liberty of trading along the Miramichi River and then visiting Quebec for several months.[116] On hearing in the spring of 1758 that his services were needed, Boishébert mustered his Acadian and Indigenous militia and marched down to Mira, arriving on 13 July, only to find that the British expeditionary force had successfully landed five days before. By contrast, Chief Peguidalouet and his warriors, accompanied by Mi'kmaq from Le Loutre's former mission at Beaubassin, had been stationed at Gabarus Bay and other points along the Atlantic coast since late May. When the British first tried to come

ashore on 2 July, these warriors bravely faced them on their own and prevented the British from gaining a foothold along the coastline.[117] Peguidalouet was wounded in this early confrontation, and was still recuperating when Boishébert's force arrived.[118] Because the French and Indigenous defences had sustained injuries, Governor Drucourt and Maillard urged Boishébert to march immediately on the town and run the British blockade, but much to the governor's and the missionary's chagrin, Boishébert tarried at Mira another day.

Sheltered by Admiral Edward Boscawen's fleet on their seaward side, four companies of rangers under the command of Acting Major George Scott come ashore on 8 July 1758 to the west of Louisbourg at Anse de la Cormorandière, today known as Kennington Cove. Indigenous and Acadian militia continued firing at the advancing force until the rangers were supported by reinforcements led by Scott and Major General James Wolfe, at which point the militia, being outnumbered, had to retreat.[119] Wolfe's men, unopposed except for the fire of a few intrepid French and Indigenous soldiers, beached artillery pieces, while British divisions under Jeffery Amherst, their commander-in-chief, positioned artillery on the hills behind the fort and at Lighthouse Point, which they captured. Though Boishébert tried to rally his militia to conduct guerrilla operations against the British siege lines, his efforts proved ineffective because of the small size, poor physical condition, and flagging morale of his party, who were suffering from hunger.[120] Maillard, after conducting mass for the disgruntled and hungry Mi'kmaq, Malecite, and Acadian soldiers, reproached Boishébert for his inactivity and charged that if he had acted sooner, the course of events might have ended much differently.[121]

On 15 July Boishébert directed an attack against Captain Patrick Sutherland and a contingent of Rogers' Rangers posted at Northeast Harbour, but the British by this time were far too entrenched to be seriously concerned about the activities of Boishébert's men, and on 26 July 1758 Louisbourg capitulated. Pursued by British soldiers and rangers, Peguidalouet, Maillard, Boishébert, and the militia withdrew to the vicinity of Île de Ste. Famille in Bras d'Or Lake, where the Mi'kmaq and French were able to elude their pursuers. Accompanied by Acadians from Port Toulouse who feared being deported by the British, they then followed Boishébert to his headquarters on the Miramichi River, where all spent a cold, miserable winter with few provisions and the ever-present threat of disease.

In August 1759 Maillard was at Malagomich (present-day Merigomish in Pictou County). After Louisbourg's capitulation, a British party led by Joseph Downson burned the Île Ste. Famille mission to the ground, so Maillard conducted services on an island in Merigomish Bay that the Mi'kmaq regarded as a sacred site.[122] Recognizing in those uncertain days that illness or death might at any time end his labours among his congregants, Maillard appointed chiefs who, in the absence of a missionary, could conduct prayer meetings, organize ceremonials such as St. Anne's Day, and preside over baptisms, marriages, and burials.[123] One of these appointees was Jeannot Peguidalouet.

Over three hundred Mi'kmaq and Acadians followed the missionary to Merigomish. Some of the men set up a station, hidden from the sight of passing vessels, from which they darted out in shallops to harass British and New England ships sailing along the coast. The group possessed several open, clinker-built boats, with Acadians among their number who had the boat-building expertise to construct more. Their most pressing problem was lack of provisions. The Acadians, wrested from their former farmlands at Beaubassin, lacked meat and other foodstuffs. As fall approached, food supplies at Merigomish diminished, and even when the group amassed hides and furs by hunting and trapping, lack of trading opportunities made it difficult to secure cloth, tools, nets for fishing, or sailcloth for their vessels.

News of repeated raids on New England supply ships by what the British considered an elusive hive of troublemakers, if not outright pirates, caused Brigadier-General Edward Whitmore, the British commander at Louisbourg, to send Captain Henry Shomberg to flush out Maillard's Mi'kmaq and Acadian associates. When he located them, Shomberg at first hesitated, since they outnumbered his party, and then assumed a conciliatory stance.[124] Quebec, he declared, had fallen to the British. After speaking with Maillard about palatable grounds on which to begin peacemaking negotiations, Shomberg returned to his frigate in Merigomish Harbour, where on 26 October 1759 he drafted a memorial promising the Mi'kmaq retention of "all of your possessions, your liberty, property and the free exercise of your

religion." He further advised that an exchange of hostages take place as security so that Mi'kmaw and Acadians leaders could proceed safely to Louisbourg to negotiate a treaty.[125] At a formal truce ceremony in mid-November, Maillard and his assemblage agreed to Shomberg's terms. Two Englishmen remained at Merigomish, while seven chiefs and around thirty Acadians journeyed to Louisbourg with Shomberg to meet with Brigadier General Whitmore.[126]

Peacemaking negotiations between Whitmore and the Mi'kmaw leaders began in late November, and by the end of December a treaty was concluded. Other than Jeannot Peguidalouet, whom Whitmore identified as the chief of Cape Breton in his correspondence to Major General Amherst, no other Mi'kmaw leaders were named.[127] The chiefs afterwards requested presents, and Peguidalouet in particular called for clothing, guns, shot, and powder for four men.[128] Whitmore further averred that the Acadians signed an oath of allegiance to the British king, although no copy of this allegiance document, or the 1759 treaty with the Mi'kmaq, has survived.[129] Louisbourg's commander failed to send copies of either to Commander-in-Chief Jeffery Amherst, Governor Lawrence, or the Colonial Office.[130] Whitmore depicted the Mi'kmaw delegates as "good Subjects" of King George II, which suggests that, rather than the more conciliatory tone of Shomberg's promises, the treaty's provisions echoed the conservative format of the pact signed at Annapolis Royal in 1726 that saw the Mi'kmaq, first and foremost, as subjects of the Crown.[131] The fortress's commander, however, was not inclined to be generous, for in January 1760 he initiated court martial proceedings against Shomberg for spending too much money on Mi'kmaw presents prior to the treaty-making proceedings.[132]

Yet the somewhat nebulous treaty agreement of 1759 provided Jeannot Peguidalouet with enough assurances for him to uphold its peacemaking stipulations during the tumultuous decade that followed its signing. The Mi'kmaq likely saw the treaty as the beginning of a new arrangement with the British that with time would take on the shape and form of the earlier relationship they had held with the French. They anticipated it would elicit forums for discussion of important issues, such as trade and especially their ongoing campaign for distinctive rights to a large tract in northeastern Acadia.[133]

Maillard regarded the treaty signing in this light. On first receiving Shomberg's letter of 26 October

1759 outlining the terms on which a permanent peace might be made, Maillard had deemed the conditions "good and reasonable." He went to Louisbourg with Jeannot and the other chiefs to act as their interpreter, and Whitmore got to know him well enough to recommend him to Lawrence as a potentially valuable aid in securing more treaty signings.[134] Lawrence responded by encouraging Maillard to draw other chiefs to the negotiating table. Maillard then urged Abbé Jean Manach at Chaleur Bay and Père Joseph-Charles Germain, S.J., labouring among the Malecite and Eastern Abenaki, to have their congregants sign treaty.[135] Manach did not take much prompting, for he had already accepted peace proposals tendered on 26 October 1759 at Richibucto by Henry Shomberg on behalf of Acadians living near him. In late February 1760 he drew up a list of fourteen chiefs, including Jeannot Peguidalouet – all leaders of commands that Isaac-Louis de Forant had set up in the late 1730s – and in early March sent the document to Colonel Joseph Frye, commander of Fort Cumberland.[136]

Maillard spent the late winter and early spring of 1760 travelling from Miramichi to Pomquet, where he met with members of the former Antigonish mission and helped establish a small chapel for the Mi'kmaq and Acadians living near present-day Heatherton.[137] He then cut across country, following the St. Mary's River, to the eastern shore of Nova Scotia and proceeded south to Cape Sable. Along the way he encouraged Mi'kmaq he met to extend peace overtures to the British. Paul Laurent, a La Hève chief who prior to 1755 had been with Le Loutre at Beaubassin and later moved with Manach to Miramichi, welcomed the missionary. Laurent noted that Colonel Frye gave food to destitute Acadians who swore allegiance to King George II, so he and a Richibucto chief, Michael Augustin, approached Fort Cumberland to see if the Mi'kmaq might also obtain foodstuffs in exchange for extending peace overtures to the British.[138] Laurent also hoped that treaty making might open renewed discussions on the Mi'kmaw land and resource campaign in which he, five years previously, had invested so much time and energy.

Chiefs Laurent and Augustin contacted Claude Réné at Shubenacadie, who sent a four-man delegation led by Richard Morris to Halifax to enquire about initiating a peace. After Morris received assurances on 9 January that the chiefs would be received

cordially, Laurent and Augustin, carrying letters of introduction from Colonel Frye, joined Réné and met with the executive council on 29 February. The timing of their visit to Halifax proved propitious, for Lawrence, with an eye to neutralizing potential trouble spots on the colony's frontier, had recently signed a treaty with the Passamaquoddy and Malecite.[139] This pact was similar to that made at Annapolis Royal in 1726, except for two major differences: there were no references whatsoever to Mi'kmaw land and resource rights, and the Indigenous people had to confine their trade to government-sponsored truckhouses.[140] The Mi'kmaq, however, were invited to come to Halifax where they would be fed and accommodated by the government. Each chief had to sign the treaty separately from his associates, after which he would receive a parchment copy for his own keeping.[141] In February Governor Lawrence also appointed Benjamin Gerrish as commissary for the truckhouse system, and arranged for the truckmasters to be supplied exclusively from Gerrish's store.[142] Lawrence could exercise a fair degree of autonomy in shaping both the contents of the treaty and the organization of the truckhouse system, since sickness in executive council's ranks precluded the formation of a council quorum to review Lawrence's actions from 23 February to 10 March 1760.[143]

When council resumed sitting on 10 March, Laurent, Augustin, and Réné signed the treaty prepared for them and were given provisions and presents. The pact's seven terms were brief and to the point. The chiefs had to submit to King George II in a "perfect, ample and solemn manner." They and their people were not to molest any of His Majesty's subjects or entice any troops to desert. They had to submit to the operation of His Majesty's laws, release all prisoners in their possession, have no dealings with enemies of the king, and agree to tender hostages as security for their pledge.[144] The signees also received a written assurance that they were no longer subject to the provisions of Lawrence's scalp proclamation of 1756, but had the right to travel to their home territories free from British molestation. Maillard was grateful to Paul Laurent for his assistance, and Laurent repaid the missionary's trust by staying by his side and helping him in any way possible throughout 1761 and 1762. Maillard knew about Laurent's and Argimault's failed land and resource campaign of 1754 and 1755, and also recognized that Lawrence's new pact omitted references to Mi'kmaw land rights, since he corresponded with Acadian refugees whose grandparents had been at the treaty proceedings at Annapolis Royal in 1726.[145] But in May 1760 he had other pressing problems occupying his attention.

When he, Manach, and Germain[146] encouraged chiefs to treat with the British, Charles Deschamps de Boishébert denounced all three missionaries for what he branded their abject, precipitate submission to the British before the war was over.[147] The most biting invective issued from Jean-François Bourdon de Dombourg (1720–89), a government interpreter and captain of the French merchant marine who, like Boishébert, was stationed at Petit-Rochelle (now Pointe-a-la-Croix) at the mouth of the Restigouche River. Jean-François was a voice from the past. Jeanne Jannière, Simon-Pierre Denys de Bonaventure's wife, was his great-aunt, and Jannière and Bonaventure's son, Claude-Élisabeth Denys de Bonaventure, was his uncle. Bourdon de Domberg had come to Cape Breton in 1733 in Bonaventure's train, and by 1739 worked as a government interpreter at Port Toulouse, where he met Denis Michau and Jeannot Peguidal-ouet. In 1741 Bonaventure posted him to Maillard's mission in order to improve his knowledge of Mi'kmaq.[148] By the spring of 1760 he was in charge of a small garrison of disgruntled French regulars and caring for more than a thousand Acadian refugees, a situation that made him splenetic after he heard of the French missionaries going over to the British. When the French laid siege to Quebec in May, Jean-François Bourden de Domberg hoped that the for-mer French stronghold might be retaken. To prevent Maillard's "seditious" activities from undermining the Mi'kmaq's loyalty to France, he prepared a dos-sier for Pierre-François de Rigaud de Vaudreuil, the governor of Canada, accusing Maillard of treason.

Vaudreuil asked Captain François-Gabriel d'An-geac, who was already at Petit-Rochelle, to investigate Jean-François's allegations. D'Angeac was in charge of troops associated with a French flotilla, commanded by François Chenard de la Giraudais, that had sought sanctuary in the estuary of the Restigouche River to escape British warships. In mid-May 1760 Maillard penned an emotional letter, presumably to d'An-geac at Restigouche, stating that he had been cruelly misrepresented by Bourdon de Domberg, whom he had known for twenty years. The French barbs hurt deeply, he admitted, but he still resolved to remain on good terms with Britain. He added that he had little choice, since those under his charge had been abandoned by France. His only hope was to exact tolerance and understanding for their plight from the English regime. Maillard's letter failed to receive a reply, for following what later would be termed "The Battle of Restigouche," D'Angeac and Bourdon de Domberg both surrendered on 8 June to a British naval force commanded by Captain John Byron.[149]

Soon afterwards, Lawrence offered Maillard a sal-ary of £150 per annum to go to Halifax and continue assisting the British in their peacemaking efforts among the Mi'kmaq. Maillard hesitated, but when he was told he could exercise "great freedom" in holding Roman Catholic services in a barn-like structure on Halifax harbour, he accepted the position provided he could bring two assistants, Louis-Benjamin Pe-titpas and Jean-Baptiste Roma, from Cape Breton to live with him. On receiving an affirmation, the mis-sionary took up residence in his new oratory in early October 1760, only to hear of Governor Lawrence's unexpected death on the 19th of that month.[150]

In the early spring Maillard faced two unexpected events, one good and one bad. A positive was that Joseph Claude, chief of Listuguj on the Restigouche River, extended peace overtures to the British in Jan-uary 1761, despite the havoc the British had wreaked on the chapel at Listuguj the preceding June.[151] At the same time, the British deemed Maillard's associate, Abbé Jean Manach, unpredictable and deported him to England.[152] Joseph Gueguen, Manach's assistant and interpreter, remained for a while at Miramichi mission and then moved his large family to nearby Cocagne, where he entered the fur trade.[153] Since Gueguen espoused neutrality, spoke Mi'kmaq flu-ently, and as a trader travelled around to Mi'kmaw communities, Maillard urged him to encourage chiefs from the northern part of the province to come to Halifax.

In early spring 1761 Jeannot Peguidalouet likely lived at Miramichi with his son Bernard, Bernard's wife Marie-Anne Googoo, and his brother Louis Peguidalouet.[154] Jeannot had already entered into a peace agreement with the British late in 1759, but Maillard called upon him to tender his services to the British by persuading leaders in northeastern *Mi'kma'ki* (the Mi'kmaw term for the entirety of their territory) to sign treaty. Though the missionary had no presents with which to reward the Unama'ki chief for his help, Jeannot agreed to come to Halifax in August. Jeannot's faith remained of vital impor-tance to him. Since Maillard's departure to Halifax, he had become a catechist and prayer leader who ensured that St. Anne's Day festivities were celebrated each year at the site of the ruined chapel on Île St. Famille. The chief also was beginning to compile a small personal archive, for in addition to two French commissions he possessed several hieroglyphic texts containing prayers and responses that aided him in approximating the ritual format Maillard had upheld prior to 1759.[155]

Jeannot, Maillard, and the Treaty of 25 June 1761

Jeannot and his Mi'kmaw associates lacked food and manufactured goods, since the British prevented the Indigenous community from trading with private interests. As a result, many Mi'kmaq and Acadians suffered from hunger and cold during the winter of 1760–61.[156] The plight of refugee Acadians particularly troubled the Unama'ki chief, so he prepared a speech to deliver at upcoming treaty negotiations in June that would shed light on difficulties faced by both his own people and their Acadian neighbours. In mid-June he convinced three northeastern Mi'kmaw leaders, Claude Atouash of Shediac, Étienne Aushobron of Pokemouche, and Joseph Shabecholouet of Miramichi, to travel with him to Halifax. The chiefs, their families, and their political assistants were accommodated at Halifax at public expense.[157]

On 25 June 1761 Jonathan Belcher, Charles Lawrence's successor, arranged for tents with seating to be set up on the grounds of his Halifax estate, "The Governor's Farm," which lay on the south side of what is now Spring Garden Road, overlooking the harbour. Copies of the treaty, ready for signing, lay on a pedestal, while a short distance away the King's Colours waved in the wind, marking a hole dug to receive the ceremonial hatchet.[158] There were tables with food and drink for after the ceremony, and a military band played in the background. Abbé Maillard arrived with the four chiefs, each garbed in a decorative cloth coat cinched with a bright woven sash. Their cotton shirtfronts were bedecked with crosses and medallions of wood and silver, and most had either a silken turban or an ornate headdress, ornamented with a leather head band displaying a number of upright feathers. Leggings and beaded moccasins completed their attire. Some had painted their faces, and each carried a hatchet. They walked into the yard gravely, talked little, and kept their countenances solemn. Maillard stood nearby, ready to act as interpreter.[159]

Military notables attending the event included Rear-Admiral Lord Alexander Colville;[160] Colonel William Foster, the commanding officer of His Majesty's army regiments; and Major-General John Henry Bastide, a military engineer.[161] A detachment of soldiers accompanied Lieutenant Governor Belcher, while Richard Bulkeley, John Collier, Joseph Gerrish, and Alexander Grant represented the executive council. The assembly became even more colourful after the entrance of several of Halifax's principal residents, as persons in civilian dress strolled among the men in various military uniforms.

Belcher, flanked by Colville, Forster, and Bastide, opened the ceremonies by urging the chiefs not to listen to Britain's enemies, since only the British king had the power to protect them. "Protection and allegiance are fastened together by links," he continued, and "if a link is broken the chain will be loose." If the Mi'kmaw leaders preserved this chain by their fidelity and obedience to George III, who recently had ascended the throne, they would have "the security of his Royal Arm" to defend them. The treaty covenant, founded on the "unmovable rock of Sincerity and Truth," would free the Mi'kmaq "from the chains of Bondage" and place them in the "wide and fruitful Field of English liberty." While these pastoral allusions likely held little meaning for the chiefs, the lieutenant-governor's assurances that their religion would "not be rooted out of this Field," where their "patriarch" Maillard would continue "to nourish them in this Soil," doubtless rang out loud and clear.[162]

Belcher went on to promise that British laws would stand like a "great hedge about their rights and properties," words which must have reminded Jeannot Peguidalouet of Henry Shomberg's earlier promise that the Mi'kmaq would retain their possessions, liberty, property, and the free exercise of their religion. Should persons break through this hedge "to hurt and injure you," Belcher stressed, the "great weight" of British laws would fall upon the offenders and "punish them for their disobedience."[163]

The tenor of Belcher's speech then shifted, from assurances to admonishments that the British were being generous towards persons whose past actions during the colonial wars rarely warranted such magnanimity. The ability to ensure that the British continued to look upon the Mi'kmaq with such favour lay in their own hands. Coupled with this admonition was a thinly veiled threat. "You see the Christian spirit of the King's covenant, not only in burying the memory of a Broken Faith by some of your People, but in stretching out the hand of Love and Assistance to you," Belcher charged. "Leniency despised may not be found any more by your submissions, and like Razors set in oil will cut with the keener edge."[164] To blunt the darker purport of these last words, the lieutenant governor delivered articles of clothing to each chief and announced, "You may clothe yourself with Truth towards us, as you do these Garments." The chiefs were then directed to the pedestal, where each separately inscribed his mark of assent on the parchment before the four councilmen, Bulkeley, Collier, Gerrish, and Grant, who witnessed the transaction.[165]

Each Mi'kmaw leader received a copy of the treaty, identical in form and content to the agreement signed by chiefs Laurent, Augustin, and Réné in Halifax on 10 March of the preceding year.[166] By it, each leader was bound before 21 September 1760 to send "no less than two persons" to reside "as hostages at Fort Cumberland or elsewhere in Nova Scotia." After being beckoned to the site prepared for the ceremonial burying of the hatchet, the four chiefs solemnly filed in tandem under the shadow of the flag flying overhead, and each dropped the hatchet he was carrying into the hole. Up to this point no Mi'kmaw leader had spoken, but after dispensing with his hatchet, Jeannot Peguidalouet gravely faced the crowd and, with appropriate gestures and modulations of voice, began his carefully prepared oration.[167]

While Maillard interpreted, Jeannot announced that he spoke not only for himself but also on behalf of the other chiefs. Then, addressing himself to "His Brittanic [sic, Britannic] Majesty," he proclaimed: "My Lord and Father! We come here to assure you … that the propositions … sent to us in writing have been very acceptable to me and my Brethren." Recent British displays of kindness towards the refugee Acadians, moreover, elicited their praise and increased their trust. "Our not doubting your sincerity has chiefly been owing to your charitable, merciful and bountiful behaviour to the poor French wandering up and down the Sea Coasts and woods without any of the necessities of life," he explained. "Certain it is that they, as well as us, must have certainly perished, unless relieved by your humanity, for we were reduced to extremities more intollerable [sic, intolerable] than Death itself … Those good and noble

sentiments of yours towards us in our distressed and piteous circumstances have emboldened us to come out of the woods, our natural shelter, from which we had purposely resolved not to stir, till the Establishment of Peace between both Crowns, whatever hardship we might have suffered."[168]

Jeannot vested the Christian God with penetrating attributes accorded the Sun in the northeastern Algonquian thought system by stating: "I swear, for myself, Brethren and People, by the Almighty God who sees all things, Hears all things, and who has in His power all things, visible and invisible, that I sincerely comply with all and each of the Articles that you have proposed to be kept inviolably on both Sides. As long as the Sun and Moon shall endure; as long as the earth on which I dwell shall exist in the same State you this day see it, so long will I be your friend and ally, Submitting myself to the laws of your Government; faithful and obedient to the Crown."[169] Whatever the future might bring, he would remain immovable in this determination. The rationale behind his steadfastness arose not from fear of British domination but from his realization that the British, too, were Christian. In the presence of God, "to whom the most hidden thoughts of Men's Hearts are laid open," he thanked the lieutenant governor for allowing his people to freely practise their Roman Catholic religion, and repented for "imbruing my hands in the Blood of a people who were Christians as well as myself."[170] "Sir," he concluded, "we pray you most humbly … that you will be pleased to inform his Majesty, as soon as possible, of what you have this Day seen and heard from our people, whose Sentiments have now been declared unto the King by my mouth." Following these final remarks, the festivities commenced, which included Mi'kmaw drumming, singing, dancing, and the "drinking of His Majesty's Health under three vollies of Small arms."[171]

On 1 July 1761 Lieutenant Governor Belcher issued a proclamation warning that, as the Miramichi, Pokemouche, and Shediac chiefs had signed treaty, anyone committing a hostile act against a member of their bands would do so at "their Peril."[172] News spread quickly of the warm welcome and protection accorded these leaders and Jeannot in Halifax.[173] Just over two weeks later, on 8 July 1761, the Chignecto chief, Joseph Argimault, appeared at the Governor's Farm to sign the treaty.[174] His stay in Halifax was followed in July by an entourage of six Mi'kmaw leaders from the Chaleur Bay area, in October by Chief Jean

Newel of the Pictou district, and in early November by Chief François Mius of La Hève, the last person Maillard persuaded to sign the treaty.[175]

Broken Promises and Maillard's Death

After the final treaty signings, Belcher was guardedly optimistic about the prospects for peace in the Northeast. Yet he also realized that lands inland from Chaleur Bay to Pictou remained virtually terra incognita to his administration. He had to preserve peace on this frontier, especially as the Massachusetts Bay Colony was pressing Nova Scotia to enter into boundary negotiations.[176] After he dispatched cruisers to patrol the Northumberland Strait and flush out disaffected Acadians, on 1 January 1762 he assured his superiors in London that the coast was "well guarded … by His Majesty's Ships" and that both Mi'kmaq and Acadians had "made submission."[177]

The picture Maillard painted was less rosy. Many Mi'kmaw leaders feared they were in the grip of a vise that was gradually closing in on them. Realizing they lacked land rights, they had begun meeting in councils to discuss what steps they might take. In the fall of 1761 Étienne Aushobron, the Pokemouche chief who had accompanied Jeannot to Halifax the previous spring, called the British "deceivers," claiming they had not properly informed him of the status of the war. He had thought the conflict was over, but French sources later told him otherwise.[178] The missionary warned Belcher that he would have to address these Indigenous fears quickly if Mi'kmaq leaders like Aushobron were not to be driven into revolt.

Throughout the early spring of 1762, Maillard worked with Belcher to ensure that the peace forged between the British Crown and the Mi'kmaq would endure. The lieutenant governor reformed the truckhouse system by making it more honest and financially accountable.[179] He further agreed to Maillard's demands that he grant the Mi'kmaw people a measure of security with regard to their land and resource rights. He could not stem the tide of British settlement north of the Shubenacadie River, for by 1761 settlers had already established footholds in the townships of Cumberland, Amherst, Petitcodiac, and Shepody. But he felt that, with Maillard's help, he could rectify the lack of protection for Mi'kmaw land and resource prerogatives in the recent treaty by issuing a royal proclamation on the subject. On 4 May 1762 he did so, reintroducing the concept that the Mi'kmaq

held aegis over lands and resources that the British were required to recognize and protect from settler infringement. Belcher justified his actions by reference to a set of royal instructions, dated 9 December 1761, requiring him to remove settlers who "without lawful authority" had entered lands the Mi'kmaq "by treaty" had "reserved to themselves." The lands outlined in Belcher's royal proclamation followed the coastline of Nova Scotia (which at the time included present-day New Brunswick) from Chaleur Bay to Canso, and then extended down the Eastern Shore to a point near Halifax. Belcher warned, "I do strictly enjoin and caution all persons who have possessed themselves of any part of the same [land], to remove from thence, as they will otherwise be prosecuted with the utmost rigor of the law."[180]

The tract described by Belcher exhibited parallels with the vast reserve in the northeastern part of the province proposed by chiefs Argimault and Laurent in the mid-1750s, but with three significant differences. The royal proclamation of 1762 mentioned no forts, no references were made to inland sites or geographical features such as the Shubenacadie River, and the tract embraced a much longer stretch of coast than did Argimault and Laurent's reserve.[181] In 1762 the shoreline in question extended all the way to Chaleur Bay, whereas in 1755 the northern boundary of the Mi'kmaw claim ended at Baie Verte. Evidently the Mi'kmaw claim had changed in response to new circumstances. It has been argued that the Mi'kmaw land campaign constituted a "response to the extension of English settlement, not an expression of high strategic concerns," yet Belcher's own father, Jonathan Belcher Sr., as a member of the Boston council in 1720 had supported the idea of preserving a tract north of the line of settlement where the Eastern Abenaki could hunt free from molestation.[182] Maillard furnished Belcher with information on the Nova Scotia Mi'kmaw land claim and also kept in contact with the chiefs, whose interests he represented.[183]

In May 1762 the lieutenant governor tried to address the abbé's concerns, yet on 2 July 1762 he directed a communication to the London Board of Trade reneging on all the points he had earlier made in his proclamation. An uncreative, aloof, and inflexible individual, Belcher executed a complete volte face when faced by a flood of opposition to his proclamation launched by Joshua Mauger, the province's London agent.[184] To avoid his opponents' barbs, Belcher declared that he never intended to support the idea that the Mi'kmaq held prior rights to the Crown. The Mi'kmaq could make no claims, either by treaty or by long possession, "since the French derived their Title from the Indians, and the French ceded their Title to the English under the treaty of Utrecht."[185] While earlier he had mentioned treaties and rights, and warned that any settlers who encroached on Mi'kmaw land would court the "upmost rigor of the law," Belcher now granted the Mi'kmaq merely a common right of fishing along the coast with other subjects. The Mi'kmaw could no longer look to his office for protection for their property rights; instead, calls for adjustments for infringements must "be settled in a private way in [the] courts." The lieutenant governor also claimed he had not published his proclamation at large, for fear that if its contents were known it might incite "extravagant and unwarrantable demands."[186] Yet Maillard would have shared its contents with chiefs who aided him in shaping the claim.

On 3 December 1762 the Lords of Trade and Plantations in London wrote to Belcher, expressing "astonishment" that the king's representative in Nova Scotia had called upon the Mi'kmaq to tender claims, since no treaties had ever confirmed Mi'kmaw rights to land "by solemn Compact." Since the proclamation excluded "His Majesty's subjects from settling or carrying on the Fishing upon any part of the Coast from Muscadoboit [*sic*, Musquodoboit] to the River St. Lawrence," it had to be disallowed. If any land was to be reserved to the Mi'kmaq in the future, they concluded, it should not lie near the coast, but "amongst the woods and Lakes where the wild Beasts resort and are to be found in Plenty."[187]

During the final year of his life, Maillard found himself in an extraordinary position. After being abandoned by the French, he had served the British because he viewed the signing of treaties with the British as the only way for the Mi'kmaq to establish formal ties with the new regime. From the correspondence of Joshua Mauger in London, it is obvious that Maillard clandestinely pressed for a reintroduction, with certain significant changes, of the Mi'kmaq's land and resource campaign dating from the 1750s. In so doing, Maillard was transparent, devoid of the artifice he had shown while acting under the mandate of the French regime to keep the Mi'kmaq warlike.[188] His paramount concern in his final years lay with the welfare of the Mi'kmaq and refugee Acadians.[189] Fatigued by his arduous journeys about the countryside, and doubtless feeling betrayed by Belcher's abrupt change of position on the Mi'kmaw land and resource campaign, Maillard fell ill. In late July 1762, as St. Anne's day was approaching, Mi'kmaq congregated near Lunenburg to meet with their missionary, but he was unable to join them. Jean-Baptist Roma and Louis-Benjamin Petitpas tended to the bedridden missionary's needs as best they could, and were soon joined in their care-giving duties by the Reverend Thomas Wood, an Anglican missionary with the Society for the Propagation of the Gospel in Foreign Parts.[190] On 11 August Maillard requested that Wood read to him, in French, the visitation of the sick according to the Anglican form before a large crowd of Mi'kmaq and Acadians. That same day Paul Laurent obtained a government passport to travel to see Maillard in Halifax and afterwards spread the sad news among his people of their missionary's imminent demise.[191] Maillard died at Petitpas's house on 12 August. He received a state funeral in which Lieutenant Governor Jonathan Belcher and William Nesbitt, the speaker of the Assembly, acted as pallbearers, and his body was interred in the Old Burying Ground flanking the Governor's Farm on its north side.[192] A Mi'kmaw oral tradition, still in circulation in 1926, "told that when he died, bushes bearing beautiful flowers sprang up over his grave, testifying to his virtues and his worth."[193] The Old Burying ground was not to be Maillard's body's final resting place, for in the 1780s his remains, under Roman Catholic auspices, were disinterred, carried across Spring Garden Road, and placed in the ground near St. Mary's Cathedral, possibly under where the present-day St. Mary's Cathedral Basilica's parking lot now stands.[194]

Deprived of their spiritual advisor and advocate, the Mi'kmaq were frustrated with their lot.[195] The British refused to find a Roman Catholic replacement for Maillard; the truckhouse system offered only a narrow range of manufactured goods; and Maillard's attempts to persuade the lieutenant governor to support their land and resource campaign bore no fruit. Montague Wilmot, Belcher's successor, received a copy of George III's Royal Proclamation permitting alienation of Aboriginal territory only after negotiation and the Crown's payment of compensation; after promising to give it wide circulation, he shelved and ignored it.[196] When a Mi'kmaw delegation visited Wilmot in July 1763 asking for another missionary, the lieutenant governor suggested to London that three Roman Catholic priests might be sent "from the King's German Possessions."[197] But despite the colonial government's previous assurances that the Mi'kmaq would be sustained in their religion, the Lords of Trade and Plantations prohibited Roman Catholic missionaries from serving in the province, from fear that they might foster an attachment to France. Instead, the Board of Trade directed the Society for the Propagation of the Gospel in Foreign Parts (SPGFP) to convert the Mi'kmaw population to Anglicanism, though only two of the SPGFP, the Reverend Thomas Wood and the Reverend J.B. Moreau, were ever in a position to shoulder the task.[198] Despite struggling for five years as proselytizers for the Anglican cause, neither Wood nor Moreau made any significant headway in weaning the Mi'kmaq away from Roman Catholicism.[199] The Mi'kmaw call for Roman Catholic missionaries rose to a crescendo in September 1763 and was sustained at the same intensity until 1768, when the government finally abandoned London's policy of keeping Roman Catholic clerics out of the colony.[200]

In the interim, the Mi'kmaq met in large councils to determine what action to take. At first these assemblages were held at Chignecto, but after 1763 the largest meetings occurred on Isle Madame, in the southeastern corner of Cape Breton, in Chief Peguidalouet's territory. When Jeannot presided over these meetings, his prestige was enhanced by his former connection with Maillard on Île Ste. Famille. Those Mi'kmaq who appealed to him for direction usually joined his band, and in consequence his group grew rapidly in size. At the close of the Seven Years' War, the Cape Breton Mi'kmaw population was small, owing to removals both to the Miramichi area and to Newfoundland, but by 1765 many young single Mi'kmaw and *métis* men from elsewhere married Unama'ki women and recognized Peguidalouet as their chief.[201] Michel Thoma Denny (also known as Thom Thoma II), was one of these individuals. Denny, who was almost certainly a son of Denis Michau – and perhaps even the same person whom Jeannot had raised following Chief Michau's death in 1751 – returned from either Newfoundland or Cumberland County to join Jeannot, as did several *métis* and Acadians. New surnames, among them "Le Basque" (Basque), "Benoit" (Benwa), "Cremeaux" (Cremo), "Doucet" (Doujet or Doucett), "Le Blanc" (or White), and "Pierro" (Pierre), appeared among the Mi'kmaq in both Cape Breton

and Newfoundland.[202] The entry of Acadians and *métis* into the Unama'ki band meant the group acquired persons with new and valuable skills, since many, in addition to being agriculturalists, possessed knowledge of carpentry and boat-building.[203] Unama'ki band members might trade for canvas, rope, marine fittings, compasses and tools, and then construct their own shallops. But since the government truckhouse system did not carry such articles, Chief Peguidalouet's people did not even have sailcloth for their seagoing wooden vessels.

The chief consequently eyed alternative trading opportunities to the truckhouse system. After 1764 the Îles de Saint-Pierre and Miquelon provided options, as did John Robin, a merchant at Arichat on Isle Madam who spoke French and Mi'kmaq as well as English and employed Acadians on his vessels.[204] Robin provided a far greater array of items than the truckhouse at Canso, established in 1764 under Wilmot's orders. The Canso station only operated for three years before the entire truckhouse system collapsed, owing to its unprofitability and corruption within its ranks.[205] Locating new markets for Mi'kmaw furs, fish, feathers, and wooden manufacturers was a priority for Jeannot, but he also needed to find merchants and officials willing to act as spokespersons on behalf of his people's ongoing land campaign.[206] Members of Joseph Gueguen's family at Cocagne occasionally assumed this role, as undoubtedly did the family of "Otho Robichaud (1742–1824), a retail merchant and founder of Néguac who dealt with the Mi'kmaq,[207] since whenever Mi'kmaq in the northeastern region were forced inland by incoming settlers they trespassed on Malecite territory, with inevitable clashes arising between the two nations over hunting grounds.[208]

Jeannot diligently pursued stable linkages with merchants and colonial officials so that his people could pursue their activities in peace. When he found that under the Treaty of Paris, signed on 10 February 1763, Saint-Pierre and Miquelon, which fell under his own traditional territorial aegis, remained in French hands as bases for the French fishery, he sought out markets on these islands. And as soon as he heard of a British merchant named Joseph Broom pursuing a fishery on the Island of Codroy, he also steered a course in early summer 1763 for this small community. He assumed that since he had signed a peace treaty with the British at Halifax in 1761, he and his people would be welcomed by British traders operating along the southwestern coast of Newfoundland.

Jeannot's Trade and Emigration Strategies

Jeannot Peguidalouet and his family often overwintered along the southwestern Newfoundland coast and knew the Island of Codroy well. He presided over allotments of family hunting territories in the Codroy Valley, and felt his band would benefit from establishing trade ties with a British merchant in the area.[209] He never considered that by so doing he might be breaking any rules. In 1763 Thomas Graves, the lieutenant governor of Newfoundland, received instructions that specifically mentioned the utility of "establishing and carrying on a Commerce" with the Mi'kmaq who travelled to Newfoundland, Anticosti, the Magdalens, and "other small islands."[210] But when Jonathan Broom and his men, who were mostly recruited from Halifax, reacted to the chief's overtures with agitation and fear, Jeannot was taken aback. Not only did Broom refuse to trade, he afterwards contacted Lieutenant Governor Graves and asked for arms and ammunition to defend his fishery operations from possible Mi'kmaw attack.[211] Graves directed Samuel Thompson, captain of the warship *HMS Lark*, to investigate.

Once Thompson arrived in the Codroy area in September, "two chiefs, Jenot Piquid Oulat and Bernard," came aboard his vessel and declared that they wished to renew the treaty they had signed earlier with the English. Bernard, who was almost certainly Jeannot's son, explained that they had only wanted to trade at Codroy Island for a shallop, which they needed to sail to Saint-Pierre to confer with Roman Catholic clerics and check out alternative trading options. Jeannot then produced a copy of a treaty, which accordingly was read aloud and endorsed by the *Lark*'s captain.[212] That Thompson was a representative of the British Crown was of utmost importance to Jeannot, since he saw the treaty renewal as embodying an ongoing reciprocal relationship between his people and the British monarch. He had carefully prepared for the moment: not only had he brought his copy of the treaty with him, but he had also compiled a list of items he expected to be given to his party as presents following the ceremony. (In the Indigenous diplomatic domain, official transactions were always accompanied by an exchange of presents and services.) This inventory included

a ship's compass, enough sailcloth to make sails for two shallops, fishing lines and nets, a number of muskets, shot, and a hundred pounds of powder.[213] Other articles included shirts, hats, coarse blue cloth, kettles, and hatchets.[214] Once the warship's captain endorsed the treaty, Jeannot left the document with him to send to London. On Thompson's suggestion, the chief also agreed to delay the present distribution until word arrived back from the British Admiralty Office.[215]

There is no reason to suspect that Peguidalouet's motives in the late summer of 1763, in asking for a treaty renewal and gifts, were other than sincere. Both requests were part and parcel of traditional Mi'kmaw diplomatic protocols that the chief expected the British to know about and observe.[216] Trade with the French isles also appeared a necessity to him, since the British made so little effort to address his people's needs. Yet Britain had radically altered its attitude towards the Mi'kmaq and Acadians after the June 1762 Bay Bulls incident and France's acquisition of Saint-Pierre and Miquelon, changes of which the chief remained unaware.[217] Halifax began to view the two tiny, treeless French isles lying in the Gulf of St. Lawrence as a veritable hotbed of French conspiracies to undermine British imperial economic interests. Saint-Pierre and Miquelon, they maintained, traded directly with the New England colonies. The administration of the French islands also sought to control Mi'kmaw loyalties by offering them presents, smuggled goods via the Acadians, and maintained a large fishing fleet that carried out an illicit fishery south of Point Riche, the southernmost limit of Newfoundland's "French shore."[218]

Jeannot's request for presents compelled the colonial government to try to control his movements. On receiving Thompson's letter, the British Admiralty Office deliberated on the appropriateness of naval officers distributing presents to Mi'kmaq on the Crown's behalf and concluded that the Royal Navy should not get involved in gift-giving.[219] Peguidalouet's application for presents henceforth would fall under the purview of the lieutenant governor of Nova Scotia, who would consider his request only if he appeared in person in Halifax.[220] The Mi'kmaw leader learned of this outcome from several sources, since instructions were sent to naval captains as well as Jonathan Broom to inform the chief of the new policy as soon as they met him.[221]

Since going to Halifax meant travelling a long way for what might prove to be a fruitless errand, Jeannot disregarded their directives. Instead he returned to Cape Breton during the summer of 1763 and applied for provisions from Major Walton, the commander of the troops at Louisbourg, who refused his request. In October he set sail for Saint-Pierre, as he told Walton he would.[222] Jeannot's initial reception at Saint-Pierre was coolly restrained. The French isles' new governor, François-Gabriel d'Angeac – the same man to whom Maillard had directed his impassioned letter in 1760 – had recently received instructions officially forbidding him from receiving Indigenous parties from Cape Breton. The Mi'kmaq no longer were of use to French imperial designs, d'Angeac's superiors stressed, and to welcome them would upset the British.[223] The governor's reticence to recognize his Mi'kmaw visitors faded, however, when he saw the advantages to be gained in fostering ongoing trade linkages with Chief Peguidalouet's people. By the time the Mi'kmaq left shortly before Christmas for their hunting grounds they were well aware that they, with their bounty of furs, feathers and dried fish, would be warmly welcomed by the French the following spring.[224]

During his stay on the French isles, Jeannot wanted to revive the old Mi'kmaw-French protocols that had characterized alliances in the Northeast. This deeply troubled Nova Scotia's new governor, Montagu Wilmot, who learned late in December 1763 that Chief Peguidalouet had stayed on Saint-Pierre for over three months.[225] On being informed that Jeannot actively courted French trade, rather than the other way around, Wilmot admitted to the secretary of the Lords and Plantations that the chief was intelligent, wily, and persistent. But he also feared that such a persuasive leader might induce the Mi'kmaq of Nova Scotia to harken to French directives and seek to obstruct British settlement in the province:

The Cape Breton chief used to receive very frequently presents of clothing and Provisions from the French … [His band members] were under the necessity of submitting themselves to His Majesty, in consequence of which they have several times received gratuities of that kind … [The Mi'kmaw] chief of Cape Breton, having made an unsuccessful application at Louisburg for some supplies, he declared his necessity and Resolution of going immediately to the French at St. Peter's and Miquelon for that purpose … [The French]

may try to re-establish once more that interest with these people by which they so long and effectively obstructed the settlement of this country, and well knowing of what great consequence it would be to gain the heart of the Natives in it against any future enterprises.[226]

"The uses the French might make of these people to our disadvantage will be too obvious to your Lordships for me to remark," he continued, before suggesting that the British might curtail this troublesome attachment by according the Mi'kmaq a few gifts and supplies.[227]

The following spring Jeannot visited Louisbourg once again to ask for gifts. Although the fortress had been reduced to a pile of rubble to ensure that the French could not regain possession of it, a British garrison remained at the site until 1768. The deputy governor of Cape Breton, Major Walton, and Louisbourg's commanding officer, Lieutenant Colonel James Pringle, received the Mi'kmaq graciously enough, but again declined to give them presents.[228] Pringle, however, acting on new instructions from Wilmot, distributed passes in 1764 to Peguidalouet and many of his band members to permit them to cross over unhindered by any official constraints to Newfoundland for the purposes of trapping and commerce. This act brought Pallister's ire down on both Pringle's and Wilmot's heads. While the Lords of Trade and Plantations were sympathetic to Palliser's stance, they did not intervene. In July 1764 they responded to Wilmot's December 1763 communication regarding the need for presents by instructing the governor to draw £250 from contingency funds for inducements to wean the Mi'kmaq away from trading at Saint-Pierre and Miquelon.[229] But as both the members of the Board of Trade and Wilmot were to find, Peguidalouet was not so easily manipulated through the giving or withholding of presents as the British thought he might be.[230] Indian commissioner John Cunningham's sporadic distributions of presents did little to quell Jeannot's determination to visit Saint-Pierre and Miquelon regularly.

While Jeannot welcomed the settlement of the French isles, he at first remained unaware of the consternation his actions caused in British official circles.[231] He was acting as district chiefs before him had done for generations, exploring opportunities within Unama'ki and linking up his people with valuable resources, markets. and services. Wilmot meanwhile expressed extreme annoyance that Jeannot's group had linked up with refugee Acadians to travel to Saint-Pierre and Miquelon.[232] Though the governor continued to issue Jeannot passes, he admitted to his superiors that he felt "mortification" at discovering that the Mi'kmaw leader, upon being refused gifts at Louisbourg, had been fêted at Saint-Pierre. The welcome the chief received caused him to invite his entire band to join him on the French isles for the remainder of the summer.[233]

Operating between Contending Colonial Powers

Despite Wilmot's fear that Chief Peguidalouet was beginning to favour the French, the chief refused to choose sides. His task was to forge workable alliances with both the English and French agencies who occupied his traditional domain. This meant visiting the headquarters of each authority and observing British and French diplomatic protocols.[234] His renewal of the 1761 treaty and his journeys to Louisbourg and Saint-Pierre in 1763 were evidence of this, as was his determination to meet with Walton, Pringle, and Wilmot in the spring of 1764 to acquire new passports to travel to Newfoundland. The measure of his success in providing for the welfare of his people resided in his balancing his responsibilities to the British against those to the French, while remaining neutral. There is no record of him after 1763 ever referring to the French king as his "father," as did some of his band. As long as the British and French Crowns remained at peace, he would focus on initiating and maintaining what he hoped were mutually beneficial commercial exchanges with representatives of both colonial powers.[235]

Wilmot tried to dissuade the Mi'kmaq from visiting the French isles by erecting a truckhouse at Canso in 1764, and asking Charles Morris, the surveyor general, to determine what routes the Mi'kmaq used to reach Canso.[236] Wilmot hoped to determine where Mi'kmaq lived on the Bras d'Or Lake, and how they accessed the coast, to avoid clashes with incoming settlers. After learning that settlers were coming, Chief Jeannot encouraged the majority of his band to winter in Newfoundland, leaving behind a few families who continued to hunt and trap in Cape Breton. Jeannot also knew of the arrival of administrators, priests, and merchants on the French isles. François-Gabriel d'Angeac, who was appointed governor of Saint-Pierre and Miquelon in

1763, brought two Jesuit priests with him who began to baptize, wed, bury, grant absolution, and oversee the Mi'kmaq's Eastertide duties that Maillard had reserved for the week around St. Anne's Day.[237]

The chief remained unaware of the consternation his emigration strategies were causing the new governor of Newfoundland, Hugh Palliser, until one of Palliser's agents ordered Jeannot to hand over his government passport. Palliser then admonished Pringle for handing out passports and pressed him to issue no more.[238] Though cloaked with a thin veneer of politeness, the governor's words to the lieutenant colonel revealed his exasperation. He had voiced his opposition to the Mi'kmaq travelling to his colony, he complained, yet "Chief Jean Pegidawa Oulaut with a Tribe of over Two Hundred return'd with fresh Passes to come to this Country."[239] While Palliser knew that the Mi'kmaq engaged in clandestine trade with the French on Saint-Pierre and Miquelon, news that the French were shipping presents to Mi'kmaw communities escalated his anxiety. In August 1764 at least one French ship had landed gifts, including "Arms and Ammunition," for the Mi'kmaq living on the west coast of Cape Breton, and the governor was certain that similar distributions were occurring in Newfoundland.[240]

Early in the spring of 1765, Palliser launched a raid on what he deemed to be illicit Mi'kmaw and French communities on Bay d'Espoir and at Grand Jarvis Harbour, Rattling Brook, and Conne River. More French than Mi'kmaq were taken by Pallister's men because the Mi'kmaq scattered into the interior. Saint-Pierre and Miquelon were treeless; the French, despite the risks, harvested timber throughout the winter along Newfoundland's south coast in order to build their fishing boats. Thomas Sperin, one of the Frenchmen arrested by Palliser's men, attested that the 150 or so Mi'kmaq and the French living near them not only traded but worked together. Sperin's wood-cutting party included two Mi'kmaw men.[241]

As he did with all of the Newfoundland governor's policies to control Mi'kmaw movements, Chief Peguidalouet simply ignored Palliser's orders, and asked for more passports from Louisbourg. On 31 May 1765, he acquired a letter of introduction from Major Walton, the deputy governor of Cape Breton, addressed to Governor Wilmot, stating that the chief and his people had "always behaved themselves extremely well and traded very honestly."[242] As a further testimonial to his confidence in Jeannot as trustworthy and dependable, Walton entrusted the Mi'kmaw leader with a portfolio of administrative documents destined for the governor and executive council in Halifax. The chief resided near Halifax during May and June, during which time he met with Governor Wilmot and his council, who, much to Palliser's chagrin, agreed to sanction more passports. Throughout most of July, the chief attended Aboriginal council meetings in Pictou and Isle Madame, and then returned for two weeks to his encampment on East Bay.

On 16 August Chief Peguidalouet arrived in a shallop at Louisbourg in company with a Captain Machormak,[243] who had been with the chief at Isle Madame; Peguidalouet immediately presented Lieutenant Colonel Pringle with a letter from the provincial secretary, Richard Bulkeley, dated 22 July 1765. With it was a passport, also dated 22 July, granting him "permission to go to Cape Rayes [*sic*, Cape Ray] on his lawfull occasion of commerce without any interruption."[244] On learning of this latest issuance, Palliser wrote Pringle in the late fall, demanding that any passports already issued be revoked, which Wilmot, after questioning the legality of Palliser's request, refused to do.[245] In a carefully worded reply to Newfoundland's governor, Wilmot explained that back in May Chief Peguidalouet had framed his request for a passport "thro' a decent Submission to the Authority of Government" that would be difficult to deny, since no "Law … prevents any of the King's subjects passing from any part of this Dominion to the other." Better to issue passports, Wilmot confided, than to have the chief defiantly leave for Newfoundland, heedless of Louisbourg's views on the matter. "[Had] I refused my consent," the governor added, Jeannot would "have taken that liberty with impunity."[246]

Wilmot's and Pringle's willingness to supply passports to Chief Peguidalouet and his people has been viewed by several ethnohistorians as a ploy on Nova Scotia's part to dispose of a troublesome problem. From this perspective Peguidalouet emerges as the "ball" in a highly strategic game played between Wilmot and Palliser that, more often than not, lands in Palliser's court.[247] But this view underestimate Jeannot's decision-making skills and the breadth of his responsibility as a district chief who regarded Newfoundland as under his aegis.[248] More likely, Walton and Wilmot grasped some of the ecological reasons why the chief led his people to Newfoundland, and

confirmed their understanding in ways that gained the chief's respect. This connection was nurtured by gift-giving, since the Board of Trade permitted Wilmot to offer gifts to Indigenous leaders who were of "such rank and consideration as to render it prudent."[249] Jeannot did not remain in Newfoundland, but travelled back and forth across the Cabot Strait. Each spring he asked for and received fresh passes from Pringle, despite the lieutenant colonel's misgivings towards the chief's Roman Catholicism and rumoured associations with the French on Saint-Pierre and Miquelon.[250] Chief Peguidalouet had the foresight to protect his freedom to lead his people to Newfoundland, since few trading opportunities remained in Cape Breton and after 1765 settlers would deplete big game and fur bearers around the Bras d'Or Lake. Palliser remained a thorn in Jeannot's side, but certainly not an insurmountable one. The Newfoundland governor had little inkling of the Unama'ki Mi'kmaq's extensive knowledge of the Newfoundland interior and its resources. His campaigns to rid his colony of the Mi'kmaq foundered because Mi'kmaw families could easily evade patrolling agencies lacking the requisite knowledge of the countryside to locate their quarry. When hydrographers and surveyors, among them Captain James Cook, sought to learn about the interior of southwestern Newfoundland, they turned to the Mi'kmaq for information.[251]

By the end of 1765, Chief Peguidalouet had regularized his comings and goings between Cape Breton and Newfoundland. He stayed on his Newfoundland hunting grounds until mid-May, when he travelled with others of his band to trade at Saint-Pierre and Miquelon. While some of his band remained on the French isles, Jeannot by late July was back in Cape Breton to preside at St. Anne's Day ceremonies and conduct marriages, baptisms, and funerals amid the ruins on Île St. Famille. Later in the summer he moved to East Bay, where he held prayer meetings in accordance with the instructions Maillard had set down for Mi'kmaw catechists.[252] By late fall he was back in Newfoundland.[253]

Chief Peguidalouet as Peacekeeper

In addition to obtaining British passports in 1765, Jeannot also played a vital role as a peacekeeper at two major Mi'kmaw councils. Disgruntled chiefs in the northeastern part of the province denounced the

British for not supplying Roman Catholic clerics and refusing to turn a listening ear to their land and resource campaign. The British expected the Mi'kmaq to trap and trade furs, yet their hunting grounds were being threatened by incoming settlers.[254] Protestant planters had taken up lands in the Annapolis Valley, and rumours spread that the same would happen in Prince Edward Island and Cape Breton.[255] Samuel Johannes Holland, the surveyor general of the Northern Department, was surveying Prince Edward Island into lots and would soon begin similar work in the Bras d'Or area. In 1765, the Island of Cape Breton became a county, comprehending Isle Madam and Scatarie Island, with a quarter session, an inferior court, and two country members on the assembly – a sure sign that settlers would soon be on their way.[256] The British government also granted the Magdalen Islands, known to the Mi'kmaw population as *Menquit*, to a merchant named Richard Gridley, whose walrus-hunting industry by 1765 drove the Mi'kmaq from crucial sea mammal hunting grounds.[257] Mi'kmaq in the Pictou area felt hemmed in by incoming colonists, whose presence they challenged by burning several settlers' houses to the ground.[258]

When Jeannot's counsel was sought on such matters, he advised other leaders to exhibit discretion and patience. During the three and a half months between the chief's receiving his letter of introduction from Major Walton in late May and his arrival with Captain Machormak at Louisbourg in August, he had attended a council of around five hundred Mi'kmaq held at Arichat, on Isle Madame. Machormak testified that the Mi'kmaq held several large meetings in 1765 at various locales, among these Prince Edward Island, the Bay of Fundy region, and Isle Madame.[259] In July at Isle Madame, he averred, when a Mi'kmaw splinter group hoisted a white flag on a staff, by which action they symbolically exhibited their attachment to France,[260] Chief Peguidalouet immediately ordered it taken down and British colours raised in its stead. The sight of a white flag terrified local fisheries operators, although Jeannot assured them that the Mi'kmaq would do "no Mischief."[261] Walton and Pringle tried to extract the reasons for the Isle Madam council from the chief, who, though he repeatedly stressed that the majority of his people had no "Evil Intentions," refused to discuss the subject further.[262]

Samuel Holland, upon completing his survey of Prince Edward Island and returning to his home in Louisbourg, also heard about Chief Peguidalouet, the peace-making Mi'kmaw delegate. The Mi'kmaq, he noted, "sent Last Summer one of the Chiefs with a formal Deputation here to Lieut. Colo. Pringle, to beg his Assistance, and to Promise to be as Trusty to King George as they were to King Louis." Jeannot had stressed that his people needed "a [British] Father to Keep them in the Right way," since several leaders retained the "King of France's Bust on a Silver Medal which they hang on their necks." In return for the chief's show of courage at Isle Madame on behalf of the British cause, "Colonel Pringle made the Chief a Present of a Gorget, and British Collours [*sic*, Colours], with which he was much pleased."[263]

Governor Hugh Palliser meanwhile continued to denounce the Newfoundland Mi'kmaq as "foreign intruders" who posed a dangerous threat to the security of the island.[264] That Jeannot performed a major service for the British, in exercising a moderating influence on a situation that might have flared like a tinderbox under a less discreet leader, failed to move him. He instead lamented that at least 175 Mi'kmaq had gone to Saint-Pierre in 1765, and afterwards left for Bay d'Espoir, where they "dispers'd themselves about the country."[265] In a futile attempt to get rid of these Mi'kmaq, in October he decreed that "all people whatever from the Plantations whether Indians or others without Distinction that may be met with in this Country after the first day of November, shall Immediately retire to the Governments to which they respectively belong."[266] As usual, Chief Peguidalouet ignored the governor's fiat, and on 24 December 1765 arrived by shallop at Miquelon with several companions, requesting provisions and complaining bitterly to the French about the treatment they had received from Newfoundland's governor.[267]

Although Palliser exaggerated the Mi'kmaq's capability to devastate the Newfoundland fishery, in 1766 his grievances temporarily gained the ear of Michael Francklin, the acting governor of Nova Scotia. (Governor Montague Wilmot died on 23 May and Francklin, a member of Nova Scotia's merchant elite who sat on the Halifax council, assumed the governor's office until the arrival of Lord William Campbell in November.) Palliser confided to Francklin on 16 October that he feared the Mi'kmaq were secretly involved in a French plot to overthrow the entire British regime in the Northeast, and a letter he wrote five days later to the London Board of Trade bordered on the paranoic.[268] Certain Mi'kmaw leaders, he warned, could bring "Thousands of Nova Scotia & Canada Indians under French influence in that part of the Island [of Newfoundland], with all the disaffected Acadians … mix'd with them, disguis'd as Indians, which would have Accomplish'd the French Plan for rendering that part of the Coast useless to us, by frightening our People away." To counter this dire sequence of events, he had summoned the chiefs and "delivered to them my Orders to quit this Country."[269] Jeannot, convinced that his loyalty to the British Crown deserved better respect, again ignored Palliser's directives.

When Francklin became Nova Scotia's lieutenant governor in March 1766, although he did not receive his mandamus or final official appointment until 26 November 1766, he learned that a large Mi'kmaw council had been convened late the previous summer on Saint-Pierre, and like Palliser, he feared that French influences were operating behind at the scenes at this gathering.[270] Yet he knew far more than the Newfoundland governor about Mi'kmaw culture and customs. In 1754 he was captured by a Mi'kmaw party on the outskirts of Halifax and taken to the Gaspé, where he remained among a band long enough to learn the Mi'kmaw language.[271] He also spoke French fluently and sought to open up channels of communication between Halifax and the Acadians, which Peguidalouet and other chiefs who were close to the Acadians, countenanced.[272] As a member of the merchant elite, he knew a number of trading chiefs living in the Shubenacadie Valley and along the Saint John River.

Mi'kmaw leaders he met stressed that they had received British assurances that their Roman Catholic faith would be respected and nurtured, and asked repeatedly if the government had "meant to deceive them." They also warned that, owing to the government's broken promises, some of their young men threatened "to destroy outlying settlements," and opposed settlers coming to Pictou or "that part of the Coast of the Continent that lays [*sic*, lies] nearest St. Peter's [Île Saint-Pierre]." These disgruntled youths were restrained and dispersed only with difficulty by influential chiefs like Jeannot and several unnamed "Gentlemen sent by the Government Amongst them, and upon finding "themselves deceived in their expected support from the French."[273] Francklin addressed their religious concerns by asking a Canadian priest who frequented the Chaleur Bay area to visit them. He then began looking for a Roman

Catholic missionary to serve permanently among the Mi'kmaq and Acadians, while in the interim he would give gifts to chiefs to "keep them from a rupture."[274]

Land was a major issue. In response, Francklin promised to find ways of protecting their hunting and fishing grounds by government fiat. So fruitful were these discussions that as early as 10 November 1766, Francklin declared "We are at perfect Peace … [with the Mi'kmaw population] … [since] encouragement has been lately given them to fix their places of abode, and to turn their minds to Agriculture."[275] News of Francklin's willingness to broach land issues travelled quickly. In summer 1768, Samuel Holland and his surveying party met five Mi'kmaw families fishing salmon on an island in Collard's Bay, near Whycocomagh. The group declared that they "would be glad to have a Tract of Land along St. Patrick's Lake & Channel granted them by His Majesty for the Conveniency of Hunting, & in which they might not be molested by any European Settlers." Yet, since "Jannot their chief in this Island was not yet returned from Newfoundland, to which Place he went last Fall," according to Mi'kmaw custom no council could be convened in his absence wielding sufficient weight to deal with major land matters. The families at Collard's Bay "could not fix upon the Extent they would have, until they saw him."[276]

Holland claimed that members of this group "frequently spoke to our surveying party in the Lake" about getting a priest to serve among them. He also knew that the Mi'kmaq near Whycocomagh comprised only a small part of the Unama'ki regional band, which by 1768 numbered over three hundred individuals. Two other local bands, the first of 60 families and the second of 120 families, arrived while his party were surveying the Bras d'Or region. Holland praised the Mi'kmaq's congeniality and forbearance in the face of what he knew were difficult circumstances for them. Surveys meant land division, settlement, and resource alienation. To assuage their hardship, he suggested that they be allowed to hunt, fish, and trap over 808,000 acres left free on his chart from land division and settlement. This acreage he marked down as "Indian land."[277]

The Bras d'Or Mi'kmaq did not get a chance to resubmit a petition for territory for many years. Francklin did not visit the island before the onset of the Revolutionary War, and local authorities were reticent to raise the subject of Indigenous right to lands. In other respects 1768 was a year of many changes. The Mi'kmaq and Acadians received a missionary, Abbé Charles-François Bailly, among them for the first time in six years.[278] The Board of Trade dismantled the truckhouse system and briefly implemented a licencing system, where trade occurred at fixed locations, among them Canso. This system, mainly due to Francklin's opposition to it, was also jettisoned in favour of allowing the Mi'kmaq to trade freely with private merchants.[279] Hugh Palliser left Newfoundland for the last time in November of 1768, and with rare exceptions the Unama'ki Mi'kmaq ceased to be the target of patrols and quit orders.[280] Francklin also received an exasperated reply from the Board of Trade when he presented a bill for £3,394.10s.1d for "clothing, provisions and entertainment" for Indigenous chiefs.[281] It was the first of several warnings Francklin, first as lieutenant governor and later as commissioner of Indian Affairs, would receive from London to keep expenditures on presents to a minimum. Francklin disputed each admonition by citing the need for gifts to keep the Mi'kmaq loyal to Britain, immune to French influences and, after the onset of the American Revolution, resistant to the inducements of George Washington's emissaries.

Abbé Bailly did not venture to Cape Breton until the summer of 1771, when he stayed two weeks at Neireichak (now Arichat on Isle Madame, in present-day Richmond County, Cape Breton).[282] On 26 July, St. Anne's Day, he baptized thirty-one Mi'kmaw children, and on 6 August he confirmed the marriage of "Jean Amable Pekide8alvet" (Jean Emable Peguidalouet) and his wife, Marie-Joseph. Jeannot's younger brother Louis Peguidalouet also asked the priest to confirm his union with Marie-Marthe Googoo, a daughter of Bernard Googoo with whom he had a daughter, Rosalie.[283] Bailly identified Louis as a "veuf [widower]," so Marie-Marthe was Louis's second wife. Meanwhile Charles-Michel Sischao asked to wed Catherine-Charlotte Peguidalouet, Louis's daughter. The following day, Jeannot – whom Bailly called "Amable" – and Marie-Joseph had their daughter Catherine baptized, while Louis Peguidalouet and Marie-Marthe Googoo brought Rosalie to be baptized. On 8 August Bailly wed Agathe and Pierre Bernard Googoo, a son of Bernard Googoo. Five other Mi'kmaw couples also exchanged nuptial vows. After leaving Isle Madame, Bailly visited the *métis* and Acadian community of Petit Brador – now

Little Brador – as well as L'indienne (now Lingan) on the coast. On his return journey to Halifax, he briefly revisited Arichat on 22 October, as he had earlier promised, to marry Charles Michel Sischao and Marie-Charlotte Peguidalouet.[284] It was the last stop on his journey through Cape Breton. He did not return. The young priest soon after asked Bishop Briand to recall him, for he found the strongly Protestant leanings of Halifax society isolating and missed Quebec.[285]

After Bailly's departure, whenever game scarcities occurred in Cape Breton Louis Peguidalouet and his family hunted and trapped between Canso and Antigonish, while Jeannot until the outbreak of the American Revolution returned to Newfoundland to hunt and trap over the winter months, and trade at Saint-Pierre and Miquelon. The district chief represented a diverse population, formed not only of individuals like himself generally loyal to the British Crown but also of persons dissatisfied with British treatment and wishing to establish closer ties with the French. Several of these persons preferred allegiance to their "French Father, King Louis XV," who on Saint-Pierre and Miquelon amply rewarded their loyalty with presents and provisions.[286]

The Years of the American Revolution

Prior to the onset of the American Revolution (1775–83), Jeannot attended Indigenous council meetings throughout the province with his brother Louis. He also travelled with merchants he knew, and associated with Indigenous persons who knew the English language well enough to act as his interpreter. His son Bernard Peguidalouet, who had been with him during the treaty-renewing ceremony aboard the *Lark* in 1763, now lived on the Burgeo Islands in Newfoundland. Though Bernard visited Cape Breton on occasion for St. Anne's Day festivities or to join district councils, his preference for Newfoundland over Cape Breton had by 1775 begun to assume a political cast. He regarded himself as first and foremost a resident of Newfoundland, while retaining ties to the broader Unama'ki group.[287] By contrast, Jeannot's interests always embraced the entire Unama'ki Mi'kmaw community. Like Bernard, he visited Saint-Pierre and Miquelon, but he was careful to retain a neutral stance in the diplomatic forum on behalf of his people.[288] He accepted presents from both the English at Louisbourg and the French at Saint-Pierre without ever publicly declaring an attachment to either side.

Bernard's group relied economically on the French fur trade and French wage labour. As early as 1777, Mi'kmaq from the Burgeo Islands cut wood with French work teams operating near their community.[289] Owing to lack of trees on the French isles, Baron de l'Espérance successfully negotiated to have Britain pass an act in 1776 allowing the inhabitants of Saint-Pierre and Miquelon to remove wood from Newfoundland's southern coast. Knowing that the French sent gunpowder and arms to New England in return for timber, the British agreed with Baron de l'Espérance's request to cut wood in Newfoundland, hoping that the allowance would limit trade between Saint- Pierre and Miquelon and the Thirteen Colonies.[290]

Suspicious of French ties to New England, however, the British continued to closely monitor exchanges taking place on the French isles. They vainly tried to prevent Bernard Peguidalouet, one of Jeannot's sons, and other Newfoundland Mi'kmaq from going to Saint-Pierre and Miquelon to trade and receive sacraments.[291] Bernard and his family formed core components of the "Isles Berjaus" (Burgeo Islands) Mi'kmaw community.[292] In July 1778 a Spiritan abbé, Jean-Baptiste François Paradis, presided on St. Anne's Day over the marriage of Bernard's son Louis "Beguiddavalouet" to Janette Doujet (Doucet), who hailed originally from Prince Edward Island. Following this ceremony, Louis's sister Véronique married Janette's brother François.[293] Louis and Veronique's mother, Marie-Anne Googoo, was not present at the dual wedding because she had shortly beforehand perished in a rockslide in Newfoundland while "passing under a cape."[294] Following the two marriages and the completion of St. Anne's Day ceremonies, the Mi'kmaq left at midnight for Burgeo, as it was clear and calm for a crossing.[295]

Less than two months later, on 6 February 1778, delegates of the second Continental Congress met in Paris with representatives of King Louis VI to sign the Treaty of Amity and Commerce and the Treaty of Alliance that heralded France's entry into the revolutionary conflict on the side of the rebels. Merchants on the French isles began to transfer weapons to the Thirteen Colonies, and during late July, when Bernard and his group were visiting, a New England privateer anchored in Saint-Pierre's harbour for almost a week. In late summer five British warships under the command of Commodore John Evans sailed into Saint-Pierre's harbour. With only thirty-one soldiers and six cannon, Baron de l'Espérance could do little but capitulate on 13 September. In one fell swoop, the Newfoundland Mi'kmaq lost their French trading partners and their access to the Roman Catholic sacraments. The British evacuated the French population of nearly two thousand and destroyed their buildings, stores, shallops, and wharves.

This series of events temporarily economically crippled Bernard Peguidalouet's community at Burgeo.[296] Lacking French markets for their furs and employment as wood cutters, the Mi'kmaq, despite initial shows of hostility from settlers, began to trade more intensively with British merchants on Bay Despoir and Bonne Bay. Their families still lay scattered over the landscape. Only in the nineteenth century, when settlers became increasingly numerous in the Burgeo area, would Bernard Peguidalouet's descendants remove permanently to Conne River, on Bay d'Espoir.[297]

Jeannot Peguidalouet spent more time in Cape Breton than his son Bernard, assisting Michael Francklin patrol Cape Breton's coastline for rebel privateers and joining in council meetings the lieutenant governor convened with the Mi'kmaw population of the province.[298] When Francklin became Nova Scotia's Indian commissioner in 1777,[299] he held meetings on land he owned in Cumberland County with Mi'kmaw leaders from the Pictou area, Antigonish, and Cape Breton, and exhorted them not to join forces with the rebels.[300]

Yet even with the assistance of leaders like Jeannot, Francklin faced an uphill battle in 1777 in gaining support for the British cause or even in ensuring neutrality among chiefs living along the Northumberland Strait, at Miramichi, and in the borderlands between Nova Scotia and New England. The previous year rebel emissaries had circulated among the Mi'kmaq and Malecite, and on 19 July 1776 three Malecite and six Mi'kmaw leaders signed a treaty with George Washington at Watertown, Massachusetts.[301] In September of the same year, Joseph Gueguen acted as an interpreter for the rebel leader Colonel John Allan, who addressed a large body of Indigenous leaders at Cocagne, although Gueguen later renounced his rebel leanings and advised the Mi'kmaq to remain neutral.[302] In November a second rebel sympathizer, Captain Jonathan Eddy, incorporated a small number of Mi'kmaq and Malecite into his militia contingent, which launched an unsuccessful attack on Fort Cumberland in November 1776.[303]

The Board of Trade's reluctance to give Francklin money for Indigenous presents added to the challenges he confronted. Even after France joined the Revolutionary War on the American side in the spring of 1778 and the British captured Saint-Pierre and Miquelon, London still maintained the Indigenous people were not worth the expense of presents.[304] Despite assertions from Colonel Francis McLean, the commanding officer at Halifax, and George Germain, the British Secretary of State, that the Mi'kmaq appeared sufficiently satisfied with their lot enough to remain peaceful despite lack of presents, a band near Merigomish continued to harass settlers in Pictou County.[305] Not long after, Mi'kmaq at Miramichi attacked a British merchant, compelling the British to make sixteen arrests and necessitating a treaty renewal on 22 September 1779 with Mi'kmaw leaders from Miramichi, Richibucto, Pokemouche, Shediac, and Listuguj (Restigouche).[306] Two days later, by surreptitiously drawing on monies for presents from the king's stores and military contingency funds, Francklin and his deputy, James White, on 24 September hosted a second treaty renewal ceremony with several Malecite (Wolastoqiyik) leaders as well as chiefs from Miramichi, Chignecto, and Minas at Fort Howe, at the mouth of the Saint John River.[307]

Francklin's monetary situation briefly improved in April 1779 and then sank to an all-time low.[308] Despite Francklin's warnings that the offshore fishery would suffer if the Mi'kmaq grew disgruntled owing to lack of presents, Lord George Germain, the secretary of state for the colonies, ruled that Brigadier General Francis McLean's capture of "Penobscot" (Castine in present-day Maine) rendered the duties of Indian commissioner less crucial than in 1779.[309] Consequently, the imperial government in December 1779 made no provisions for "Indian expenses" other than Francklin's salary.[310] Francklin retorted that American privateers would threaten the Cape Breton coast if he did not provide rewards to deserving Unama'ki leaders like Jeannot Peguidalouet. "[W]ith a good deal of management and proper rewards, [the Unama'ki Mi'kmaq] could be brought to surprise some of the small privateers and whale boats that Infest and Plunder our sea coast," he wrote Germain in August. "I have already succeeded to induce a party of them to act in conjunction with some Inhabitants against a privateer."[311] The following

September Francklin sent an invoice to London for £29.5.9, relating to "Expenses incurred to Indians of Cape Breton regarding [their] spirited behaviour in beating off a rebel Privateer, who came to plunder the inhabitants."[312]

With wisdom born of his seventy-four years, Chief Peguidalouet undoubtedly contributed to this outcome. Michael Francklin recruited high-profile Mi'kmaw leaders as enforcers to bring other chiefs into the British camp. He sought out Quebec chiefs willing to dissuade Mi'kmaq and Malecite from joining the rebels, and called upon Jeannot for the same purpose.[313] By fall 1780, however, his present-giving had landed him deeply in debt, so he turned to allocations of land as rewards for persuasive chiefs loyal to the British cause whom he felt merited such recognition.[314] Since he spoke Mi'kmaq and communicated with chiefs on a regular basis, he realized that leaders like Jeannot viewed him not as a delegator of land, but as a protector of territory they regarded as having been under their territorial jurisdiction for generations.

In 1779 several prominent Mi'kmaw chiefs received land in mainland Nova Scotia in return for services they rendered the British during the American Revolution. Francklin also promised to set aside two locales, one in Cape Breton and the other in Newfoundland, that Jeannot wanted reserved in perpetuity for his people. The first lay around the chief's summer encampment ground at East Bay; the other was on St. George's Bay. No boundaries were ever set out for the Newfoundland tract, which lay outside of the commissioner's jurisdiction.[315] What Francklin ultimately had in mind regarding the Newfoundland grant will never be known, since on 8 November 1782 he suddenly collapsed and died, probably from a heart attack, while handing out blankets to Mi'kmaq in Halifax.[316]

That Jeannot may have served as an enforcer of British policy, who merited a return for his services, explains why Mi'kmaq from St. George's Bay attested in 1813 that one of their chiefs (unnamed) received a grant of land as a "reward for persuading another Micmac group not to join the French American side during the American Revolutionary War."[317] Edward Chappell, a royal navy lieutenant serving aboard the HMS *Rosamund* when the Mi'kmaw party came aboard at St. George's Bay to tell their story, later wrote that the land grant sponsored both a Mi'kmaw migration to Newfoundland and a peace pact, though no representatives of the Crown were present to witness the ceremony:

During our war with America between the years 1775 and 1782, the Micmac Indians, inhabiting the island of Cape Breton and the parts adjacent, were amongst the numbers of our most inveterate enemies; but at length one of our military commanders having concluded an amicable treaty with them, he selected one of the most sagacious of their chiefs to negotiate a peace … The old Indian ambassador succeeded … and received the grant of a sterile tract of land in St. Georges Bay, Newfoundland, together with permission to transport as many of his countrymen as might be willing … Accordingly the old Sachem left his native land, accompanied by a strong party … and boldly launching out to sea in their own crazy shallops or canoes, they eventually reached St. Georges Bay in safety [… where their first act] was to appoint the old Indian, who had conducted them thither, their Chief in perpetuity; and they next "buried the sword," as a symbol that war had forever ceased between their tribe and the English nation.[318]

Chappell's account makes it seem like Francklin's land allocation on St. George's Bay elicited a frenzied departure for Newfoundland under the chief's auspices, despite the fact that Jeannot and his people had been occupying land in southwestern Newfoundland for generations. Instead, rapid population growth, along with increasingly scarce resources in Cape Breton, likely prompted the chief to urge the movement across the Cabot Strait. From this perspective the grant, rather than opening up a virgin homeland during the American Revolution for the Cape Breton Mi'kmaq, would simply "have sanctioned an existing state of affairs."[319]

Archaeologist and ethnohistorian Charles A. Martijn admitted his uncertainty whether the recipient of the land on St. George's Bay was Chief Peguidalouet or his successor as chief, Tomma (Thoma Denny Sr.). Although Martijn recognized that Jeannot Peguidalouet frequently travelled to St. George's Bay, he also held that "Old Tomma now seems a likely candidate" since the bestowal of the grant "may have been the event which triggered a major migration in 1784."[320] Yet at age seventy-eight in 1783, Jeannot Peguidalouet enjoyed good health, was still district chief of Unama'ki, and lived for a number more years, apparently not dying until his mid-eighties.

In the spring of 1783 Jeannot negotiated with George Henry Monk, who on 8 March had been appointed Nova Scotia's Indian commissioner, for the parcel he had received from Francklin. "Emable Janet [or Jeannot]," Monk recorded, "solicits as Chief of the Indians on Cape Britain [sic, Breton] for a Grant of the Settlement made by them on the Bay of Port au Louis (St. David's Bay) + on the Great Lake called George's Lake with a right to hunt in the Country around + to fish in the Rivers + Lakes near their hunting grounds + particularly in the great Lake."[321] This tract on St. David's Bay (which in the early 1830s would become the Eskasoni community on East Bay) was accorded the Mi'kmaq under a licence of occupation.[322]

Then, after he spoke with Monk, Jeannot led a group of eleven families to Newfoundland. Monk reported in spring 1783 that the chief's group numbered thirty-one families, yet on the licence of occupation he drafted on 18 December Monk mentioned only twenty families, so in the interim eleven families must had left for Newfoundland.[323] Chief Peguidalouet, knowing that in 1784 Cape Breton would become a separate colony from Nova Scotia, wanted to ensure that his possession of territory in Cape Breton was officially registered prior to that date. As for his territory in Newfoundland, he would leave it up to the families who lived at St. George's Bay to stake their claims with the Newfoundland colonial government, which they eventually did in 1813.

The Post-Revolution Years

Following the close of the American Revolution, Peguidalouet wanted to find out what employment opportunities had returned on Saint-Pierre and Miquelon. By the Treaty of Versailles, which came into force in 1783, Saint-Pierre and Miquelon were returned to the French, repopulated, and their governor again granted the right to harvest wood along Newfoundland's south coast. With a Mi'kmaw youth named Louis Christopher acting as his interpreter, Jeannot forged an agreement with Scipion de Castries, the naval commander who repossessed the French isles, whereby the French would hire Mi'kmaq to cut firewood and lumber in Newfoundland and deliver it to coastal stations to be retrieved by French ships. De Castries considered the chief an "intelligent person who looked well after the interests of his nation." He also noted that Jeannot's interpreter "prided himself about being baptized and spoke French relatively well." Louis, he continued, was an informed man, who had "nothing of the savage [about him] except for the name and the clothing, was well familiar with all affairs … had much credit and exerted great influence on the chiefs."[324]

The Mi'kmaq at St. George's Bay and at Burgeo welcomed the new arrivals from Cape Breton. The increasing size of the Cape Breton Mi'kmaw population had been placing a strain on local resources, a situation that worsened once Cape Breton became a separate colony and settlers appeared in numbers. Confronted by these challenges, a number of family heads, including Christophe or Christopher (who was Louis Christopher's father), heeded Jeannot Peguidalouet's instructions to split from the Bras d'Or group and travel to southwestern Newfoundland – a pattern that had happened many times in the past. The decision to move proved a salutary one for these persons for at least a decade, since the St. George's Bay area provided caribou, moose, beaver, salmon, and a productive eel fishery.

There were Roman Catholic clergy and new trading establishments on the French isles to receive the émigrés. Baron L' Espérance, who was recalled in 1783 to serve as the isles' governor, in August 1784 invited fifteen Mi'kmaq to a meeting where he distributed gifts of provisions, guns, ammunition, nails, pitch, and compasses. Not surprisingly, some of the persons whom Chief Peguidalouet had encouraged to immigrate to St. George's Bay the preceding year wanted to remove to Bay d'Espoir, which was closer to Saint-Pierre and Miquelon.[325] L'Espérance initially made little secret of the fact that he was courting the Mi'kmaq as potential military allies, since he also planned to fortify the islands. This state of affairs alarmed British authorities in Cape Breton until they realized that French imperial policy was too fiscally conservative to support the grandiose venture L'Espérance envisioned. Yet, following L'Espérance's return to France in 1785, British officials continued to distrust the Newfoundland Mi'kmaw population, referring to them as "foreign Indians" even though they knew that most of the Mi'kmaq had long lived in the colony.[326]

Jeannot Peguidalouet died in his mid-eighties, around 1790. According to oral tradition, his death occurred at Eskasoni in Cape Breton and his body was carried to Île St. Famille for burial.[327] The demise of a man who had contributed so much to the establishment and maintenance of peace in the Northeast went unnoticed in British governmental circles. Cape Breton authorities remained fearful of the Unama'ki Mi'kmaq, owing to their connections with the French on Saint-Pierre and Miquelon.

Jeannot's Successors

In accord with Mi'kmaw cultural tenets regarding leadership succession, after an appropriate period the Unama'ki council met on St. Anne's Day and chose Michel Thoma Denny Sr. as their next district chief.[328] One of Denny's first acts was to join with François Bask (Basque) in November 1792 in prevailing on Cape Breton's lieutenant governor, William MacCarmick, to provide monies and materials to rebuild the chapel on Île de St. Famille.[329] Abbé François Lejamtel, who in 1786 went to Miquelon to escape the onset of the French Revolution, in 1792 took charge of the Arichat parish on Isle Madame, which included the missions at Île de St. Famille and Cheticamp.[330] The outbreak of war overseas and the British capture of the French isles had shaken the families who emigrated with Jeannot the previous year, and several wished to return. In late summer 1794 Michel Thoma Denny set up camp near the town of Sydney to await the arrival of Louis Christopher, Jeannot's former interpreter, who had left St. George's Bay in Newfoundland with nine families in tow and ten more expected to follow later. After the two men met in Sydney on 7 September, Christopher first went before the executive council to assure its members of his peaceful intentions and enquire about land. He and his associates then joined Denny in the interior of the colony lest, during the French Revolution, the British suspect them owing to their former intercourse with the French on Saint-Pierre and Miquelon.[331]

Cape Breton's new status as a separate colony did not affect the unity of the broader Mi'kmaw political constituency. In 1794 Charles Alexis of Cape Sable met with Mi'kmaw district representatives at Gaspereau Lake in Kings County, Nova Scotia, to discuss ways of addressing settlers' infringements on Indigenous lands and the increasing scarcity of game. John Basque was the Cape Breton representative, while Francis Emable Peguidalouet acted on behalf of the Mi'kmaq around Antigonish. George Henry Monk, Nova Scotia's Indian commissioner, missed speaking with Basque, who passed through Windsor in early February while Monk was away from his office. This annoyed the commissioner, since he wanted to ask questions about the meeting at Gaspereau Lake. But when Francis Emable appeared at his office door on the 26th, he saw a second opportunity to question a Mi'kmaw leader about the mysterious council in Kings County.

Francis "spoke English very easily" and liked to talk. He was a son of Louis Peguidalouet, Chief Jeannot's younger brother, and went by two surnames, "Jennot" and "Emable," but refused to mention the name "Peguidalouet" – perhaps because of a Mi'kmaw custom of avoiding use of a name belonging to persons who had died. Francis Emable was twenty-six years old, born in 1768, although he looked older, and was stout, well clothed, and muscular. He had two older brothers with large families at Antigonish, while he was single and took care of his aged mother. His mother had once told him that she and his father had met Monk many years before along the Gulf of St. Lawrence.[332] Francis had just come from Halifax, where he was told about Monk's office at Windsor. During the winter he had hunted in the woods between Canso and Antigonish and, lacking powder and shot, had to make do with traps and deadfalls.[333]

Francis asked if presents were to be distributed by the government and, if not, what were the Mi'kmaq going "to do to live?" Monk, fearful that French emissaries might be spreading ideas within the Mi'kmaw community that were detrimental to the British, questioned him about the meeting at Gaspereau Lake, but Francis artfully dodged his inquiries.[334] Instead, he produced a pipe and asked Monk to smoke with him. Once the men finished their pipe, the commissioner gave Francis two pounds of powder, eight pounds of shot, and one-quarter of a ration of flour as a parting gift. After hefting these articles, Francis thoughtfully commented, "I must give some of this to some poor Indians at Gaspero Lake," and took his leave.[335]

While Monk did not mention Francis Emable again, merchant requisitions in the 1790s indicate that he and others of his family continued to visit Halifax.[336] Francis and his brothers remained in the Antigonish area, and after 1815 lived at least part of the year on lands surveyed for the Mi'kmaq at Pomquet (present-day Paq'tnket). In 1817, a census of the Mi'kmaq of Antigonish County listed a "Captain Marble" (Emable) and several others bearing the "Marble" surname.[337] Early nineteenth-century church registers kept by Father Francis Vincent at Tracadie also show the persistence of the surname

"Janot" (Jeannot) in the Pomquet area. In 1897 Peter Marble was a head man at Pomquet.[338]

Louis Peguidalouet's children were the only ones who maintained the "Jeannot" or "Amable" (Marble) name. Jeannot's son Bernard Peguidalouet remained in Newfoundland, and his sons dropped the "Peguidalouet" surname in favour of "Bernard." All of Jeannot's heirs in Cape Breton were daughters, one of which possessed his French chief's commission of 1751.[339] In 1869 John George Bourinot the younger, a Cape Breton author and journalist, met a granddaughter of the chief named Rosalie Googoo, who lived at Eskasoni and was travelling on a steamboat across the Brad d'Or Lake.[340] Rosalie was an attractive, neatly dressed, and chatty middle-aged woman who "showed[,] whenever she spoke and laughed, rows of teeth of perfect whiteness." She was carrying the "well-thumbed" parchment chief's commission, given by Comte Raymond to her grandfather on 10 September 1751, which she kept folded in a quillwork box.[341] In her later years, Rosalie sold the commission to a Halifax newspaperman, who gave it to the Provincial Legislative Library in Halifax. Between 1888 and 1910, by some mysterious happenstance the brevet was retrieved from the Legislative Library and placed, along with Jeannot's captain's commission dated 8 November 1750, in the care of Grand Chief John Denny Jr. at Eskasoni, Cape Breton.[342]

At some point during the nineteenth century the grand chief and council came to regard Chief Peguidalouet as one of a line of grand chiefs of the Mi'kmaw nation dating back to the late 1740s.[343] To include Jeannot was undoubtedly useful, since his commissions upheld the dynasty's close connection to the French on Île Royale. Jeannot's posthumous induction into the Thoma Denny line raised controversy, however. Following Michel Thoma Denny Sr.'s death, a member of the Googoo family, likely married to one of Jeannot's daughters, vied for the leadership with the immediate family of the deceased. On 25 January 1834, a newspaper article claimed that "[t]he regal line of Gogoo [sic, Googoo], which was formerly in possession of the Throne has consequently been latterly debarred from the Crown, and which family it is reported is now in possession of one of the emblems of Royalty or symbols of authority, but which its enemies states it clandestinely obtained from a late King." The last remark doubtless referred to Peguidalouet's chief's commission of 1751.[344]

While the origins of the grand chief and council are beyond the purview of this essay, it might be tendered that the ideological underpinnings of John Denny Jr.'s right to the grand chiefship were developed after Jeannot Peguidalouet's death. A persuasive, hegemonic oral tradition that anthropologist Frank G. Speck learned of from Grand Chief Denny in 1914 claimed that the grand chiefs of the Mi'kmaw nation were all descended from Thoma Denny I, who moved from the Chignecto region to Cape Breton around 1749. This would have been shortly before Jeannot Peguidalouet became the Unama'ki district chief.[345]

Members of the Denny (Denys, Denis, or Thoma Denys) family, who arose as leaders in the Unama'ki council forum, regularly assisted those they regarded as relatives or friends.[346] In 1885 Grand Chief John Denny Jr. went to the defence of Louis Mitchell at Indian Cove, near Stratford, Prince Edward Island, when setters destroyed Mitchell's property.[347] Until the 1850s, district chiefs, often called grand chiefs, learned about colonial policies and honed their negotiating skills in Eastern Wabanaki Confederacy councils. They used wampum belts and strings to underscore their words, though their groups lacked the rigorous organizational protocols governing succession to office associated with the Iroquois Confederacy.[348] Unama'ki leaders, by bolstering their claims by reference to oral traditions and artefactual evidence, over time exhibited a fair degree of stability. But despite this, in the late 1800s there were Newfoundland Mi'kmaq leaders anxious to exercise a greater degree of autonomy apart from the grand chief and council in Cape Breton.[349]

Jeannot's Legacy

It is a testament to Jeannot Peguidalouet's foresight and organizing capabilities that many of those he encouraged to emigrate to Newfoundland found the necessary resources to establish permanent ties to their new environment. Yet forethought was only one of the chief's many abilities. He was a hunter, fisher, and trapper who provided for a household that included children, close kin, and orphans. He was a seafarer with a vast store of traditional knowledge about currents, seasonal weather conditions, and marine resources associated with the Gulf of St. Lawrence region. He allocated hunting territories in Cape Breton and Newfoundland and, when necessary, allocated

population over the Unama'ki landscape, relative to available resources. He was an orator who spoke persuasively on the importance of land, resources, treaty rights, and the need for forbearance. He participated in the Eastern Wabanaki Confederacy and played instrumental roles at smaller Mi'kmaw and Malecite councils throughout the Northeast. A devout Roman Catholic, he was faithful to the paramount goals of the mission established by Abbé Pierre Maillard by continuing after the abbé's death to hold St. Anne's Day festivities on Île St. Famille (Chapel Island). He tried to forge ongoing ties with colonial powers that would ensure his people a measure of future safety and stability, and negotiated for tracts of land for his people's use in Cape Breton and Newfoundland. Recognized as a courageous warrior, leader, and diplomat by the French, after 1760 he formed alliances and even close friendships with British officials and merchants through his honest approach to trade dealings, his forthrightness in his goals and aspirations, and his faith that at times transcended the limitations of denomination.

While Jeannot Peguidalouet during his lifetime probably never viewed himself as the grand chief of the Mi'kmaw nation, his successors, particularly Thoma Michel Denny Sr., built upon his leadership legacy to enhance the institutional and ceremonial framework of the grand chief and council, as it is known today. Jeannot relied on long-standing Mi'kmaw traditions in achieving his goals, but he also incorporated external traits, if they enhanced his people's cultural repertoire and encouraged them to be resilient in the face of new challenges.[350] Abbé Pacifique stated that the Mi'kmaq continued to honour Chief Peguidalouet by calling a site on Campbell's Cove in Whycocomagh Bay *Galnôteq*, or "Jeannot's place." It was a location, they stated, where in times past "landed their celebrated Captain Jeannot."[351]

Charles Martijn has written that Jeannot Peguidalouet "figures among the most remarkable Native personages in the history of eastern Canada. From a redoubtable warrior, he developed into an able political leader, astute negotiator and respected statesmen who providently saw to the interests of his people during a transition period occasioned by the mid-18th century changeover from French to British administration in the Maritimes."[352] In the midst of a changing and politically tumultuous era, the chief courageously preached caution and forbearance on all sides. Though best known for encouraging emigration to Newfoundland, he also stands as a founder of a distinctive Mi'kmaw polity with enduring ties to the province, the emerging nation state, and other Indigenous nations. Though Peguidalouet has not received the attention from historians that he deserves, some of his words have been quoted repeatedly, especially the phrase "As long as the Sun and Moon shall endure; as long as the earth on which I dwell shall exist in the same State you this day see it, so long will I be your friend and ally." Such words flowed from a heart filled with a sincere desire to ensure there would be room forever for his people to thrive and grow.[353]

– Janet E. Chute, assisted by Richard Denny, Vernon Cope, Marjorie Gould, Natalie McConnell, Mary Wells, Berton A. Balcom, and Charles A. Martijn

Thoma Denny

Thoma Denny (also known as Thoma Thoma I, c.1680–c.1782) was one of the most mysterious of the eighteenth century Mi'kmaw chiefs.[1] He supported the French cause, since he believed the French to be more sympathetic than the British to Indigenous aspirations to retain their hunting, fishing, and trapping grounds. In return for his military service, the French colonial government gave him gifts and, as one story goes, vested him with a *brevet de commission* recognizing him as paramount chief of the entire Mi'kmaw nation.[2] Mi'kmaw oral tradition holds that Denny resided for years at Beaubassin, but when Halifax was founded in 1749 he moved to the Bras d'Or Lake region of Cape Breton Island, where Abbé Pierre Maillard and French officials at Louisbourg continued to recognize him as the Mi'kmaw grand chief.[3] For this reason the headquarters of the grand chief became perpetually linked to Cape Breton Island, known in the French colonial era as Île Royale. Prior to this time Grand Council meetings had shifted geographically, depending on the issue under discussion in the council forum. There is also a story that shortly before his death, Thoma Denny arose as a peacemaker, for despite his formidable reputation as a warrior in the French interest during King George's War (1744–48), he negotiated with the British regime on behalf of Mi'kmaq living in British territory.[4]

After Thoma Denny migrated from Beaubassin to Unama'ki his reputation for sound leadership continued to grow; among the contemporary Cape Breton Mi'kmaq he is viewed as one of the greatest Mi'kmaw leaders of all time. His winter encampment lay near Eskasoni, on East Bay, and in 1914 his descendants could still point out where his hunting tract lay, at *Twi'denutck* or Little Channel between East Bay and the Sydney River.

Oral traditions stress the chiefs' resilience, prowess, and fortitude in the face of formidable odds. They depict him as an excellent hunter and more than likely a *kinap*, or a Mi'kmaw strong person endowed with shamanistic powers, for he reputedly dispatched seven bears single-handedly in one week. On another occasion he is said to have wrestled two bears at once before killing the creatures with his tomahawk while his hunting companion, in keeping with his chief's instructions, sat placidly smoking a pipe. Much of what is known about Thoma Denny has been gained from Mi'kmaq oral traditions recorded by University of Pennsylvania anthropologist Frank Gouldsmith Speck, although two obituary notices reporting on the funeral of his son, Michel Thoma Denny Sr., also briefly mention him. On 18 February 1834 *The Cape Bretonian* referred to Thoma Denny as "King Thoma Thoma I" and stated that he had lived to be 102 years old.[5] Memories of Thoma Denny lingered on within the Cape Breton community into the 1830s, since the obituary read, albeit convolutedly, "It will be within the knowledge of many of our readers that the Sovereignty over the Indians of Cape Breton is stated to have been conferred by a former King of France upon a particular individual of the tribe of Indians here, and by whom in virtue therefore, the sceptre was borne."[6]

Despite the fact that oral sources claim the French at Louisbourg esteemed the chief highly enough to present him with a "seal and pipe of exquisite workmanship," Thoma Denny's name does not appear in any eighteenth-century French or British documentary sources. Most of the information on him, as said above, comes from Speck's published and unpublished writings. Thoma Denny's great-grandson, Grand Chief John Denny Jr., told Speck in 1914 that Thoma Denny was the Mi'kmaw grand chief and that he once resided near Beaubassin in Cumberland County.[7] It has been surmised that Denis Michau and Thoma Denny (whose full baptismal name may have been Thoma Denis Michau) were one and the same man, since both were Cape Breton chiefs around the same time.[8] If this was so, however, Thoma Denny could not have been 102 years old at his death, since Denis Michau was born around 1700 and died in 1751. It is more likely that Thoma Denny was a couple of decades older than Michau, and yet lived longer than Michau, still having children in the late 1740s.[9]

While living at Beaubassin, Thoma Denny would have participated in councils with Chief Joseph Argimault, or Alkimou, who acted as a high-profile Mi'kmaw intermediary in the Chignecto Isthmus region for the Mi'kmaw nation after 1745 with both the British and French colonial powers. Denny and Argimault also would have participated in what Frank Speck termed the "Eastern Wabanaki Confederacy," an Indigenous political organization formed principally of representatives of Algonquian-speaking nations that existed from around 1720 to the early nineteenth century.[10] The Confederacy met twice a year to address problems associated with settler encroachments on Indigenous territories. At issue during the mid-eighteenth century was the Mi'kmaq's desire for exclusive use of a neutral buffer zone covering lands in northeastern Nova Scotia and eastern New Brunswick; from Restigouche in the north to Canso in the east, including lands extending southward in Nova Scotia to embrace the Shubenacadie River and the Musquodoboit River valleys. The Mi'kmaw leaders stipulated in their petitions that no forts should be built on this territory. The British ignored the Mi'kmaq's appeals, however, and in consequence many chiefs threw their military weight behind the French.[11]

Thoma Denny's religious perspective reflected a syncretistic blend of elements from the Mi'kmaw and Roman Catholic belief systems. He would have interacted closely with Abbé Pierre Antoine Simon Maillard, although the missionary does not mention him in his writings. This omission is puzzling, since Maillard wrote about several other chiefs, among them Claude René, Joseph Argimault, and Jeannot Peguidalouet.[12] The nature and scope of Thoma Denny's leadership activities thus remain mostly unknown. Some historians contend he was the prominent Unama'ki chief, unnamed in the British documentary record, who signed a Treaty of Peace and Friendship with the British at the Governor's Farm in Halifax on 25 June 1761. With Abbé Maillard interpreting his words, this leader declared to the assembled officials "[As] long as the Sun and Moon shall endure; as long as the earth on which I dwell shall exist in the same state you this day see, so long will I be your friend and Ally, submitting myself to the Laws of your Government."[13] While Chief Thoma I has been claimed to have remained the Mi'kmaw grand chief well past the year 1761, popular opinion today holds that the unnamed chief who participated in the June 1761 treaty proceedings in Halifax was not Thoma Denny but rather Jeannot Peguidalouet, a leader well known to the British (see chapter 26), who would obtain a licence of occupation on behalf of the Unama'ki Mi'kmaq to lands on the Bras d'Or Lake in 1783. Owing to insufficient documentary evidence, this debate about who signed treaty in 1761 is not likely to be settled any time soon.[14]

Maillard's marriage, baptismal, and death registers may have contained the names of Chief Denny's wife and children, but unfortunately the registers have not survived. It is also possible that several of the chief's older offspring and other of his relatives remained behind in Cumberland County and Prince Edward Island when he moved to Cape Breton. His successor as Cape Breton district chief was Jeannot Peguidalouet, who was followed as chief in turn by Michel Thoma Denny Sr., almost certainly one of Denis Michaud's sons.

Denny's age at death still remains controversial. If the chief had been around one hundred years old when he died, he would have been born in the late seventeenth century. This, plus Denny's esteemed position among the French, has given rise to speculation that the chief shared kin connections with the family of Nicolas Denys, a French trader who was at La Hève (present-day La Have in Lunenburg County) on Nova Scotia's South Shore and, later, at Cape Breton and Nepisiguit (present-day Bathurst, New Brunswick). Nicolas Denys had a son, Richard Denys de Fronsac, who married a Mi'kmaw woman, but it is highly unlikely that Thoma Denny was closely related to this man. A better candidate would be Simon-Pierre Denys de Bonaventure, Nicholas Denys's grand-nephew. Around the turn of the seventeenth century, Bonaventure carried on a series of illicit liaisons with Indigenous women at Port Royal that produced *métis* issue. Bonaventure may have been the father of Chief Jean Michau (or Michaud), the Île Royale paramount head chief in 1722 who in turn was likely the father of Denis Michau, who died in 1751.[15] This conjecture, however, cannot be confirmed using the oral and historical evidence currently at hand.

In his ethnographic monograph *Beothuk and Micmac*, Frank Speck claimed that around 1749 Thoma Denny founded a leadership dynasty, transmissible in the male line, at Eskasoni that persisted for over 170 years. Speck exaggerated the Mi'kmaq's reliance on lineality in leadership succession, since Mi'kmaq social organization on the whole tended to be bilateral and generational, rather than patrilineal, and selections for chiefly offices relied on lengthy council deliberations. But there can be no doubt that Thoma Denny's descendants were held in high enough esteem, first by the French and later by the Mi'kmaq themselves, that the office of grand chief of the nation continued to be passed down through those offspring to the fourth descending generation. This "dynasty" ended with the death of John Denny Jr., Thoma Denny's great-grandson, after which the Mi'kmaq opted for an electoral system for determining leadership succession.

Thoma Denny's legacy gave rise to a long line of grand chiefs. His immediate successor, Michel Thoma Denny Sr., was known as "Chief Tomma" by British administrators and "Thoma Thoma II" at the time of this death in 1834. He was succeeded briefly by Christmas Thoma Denny, another of Thoma Denny's sons and the patriarch of the Christmas family in Cape Breton. Though the first choice of his father, Christmas soon relinquished the leadership on the ground of his advanced age, and his younger brother Michel Thoma Denny Jr. took over. Francis Thoma Denny, probably another son of Michel Thoma Denny Sr., became the next grand chief in 1860. John Denny Sr. became grand chief in 1869, to be succeeded by his son, John Denny Jr., in 1881. In this way the office of grand chief continued to be passed down in the Thoma-Denny line until John Denny Jr.'s death in 1918, when Gabriel Sylliboy became the first elected grand chief.

– Janet E. Chute

28

Michel Thoma Denny Sr.

Michel Thoma Denny Sr. (also known as Thoma Thomas II, 1747–1834) was almost certainly the son of Thoma Denny, an eighteenth-century war leader and grand chief of the Mi'kmaq.[1] Michel Denny assumed the office of grand chief following the death of his father's successor, Jeannot Peguidalouet, around 1792. Anxious to be viewed as a diplomat and trustworthy proponent of peace rather than as a threat to the new British regime, even while still a minor chief in the 1770s he became an intermediary between his people and government officialdom. He also interacted closely with the Roman Catholic clergy who had returned to serve, at first itinerantly, at the St. Anne's Mission in Richmond County, Cape Breton, after being prohibited from labouring in the region for six years following the death of Abbé Pierre Maillard in 1762. During the forty-two years after 1792 that Michel Denny Sr. was grand chief, lands were surveyed by the government at various locales for the Unama'ki Mi'kmaq. These included 2,800 acres at Eskasoni in Cape Breton County, 1,281 acres at Chapel Island or *Poteleg* in Richmond County,[2] 4,504 acres at Wagamatcook in Victoria County,[3] 2,074 acres at Whycocomagh (*Waycobah* or *We'koqma'q*) in Inverness County,[4] 1,500 acres at Malagawatch (*Malikewe'jk*),[5] and 150 acres formed of smaller parcels granted from 1810 onwards to Mi'kmaw individuals in the Margaree River area.[6] Together comprising 12,309 acres, these reserves were confirmed by a Nova Scotia Executive Order-in-Council dated 7 May 1834.

Attainment of these lands provided only a brief victory for Denny and other Cape Breton Mi'kmaw leaders who had negotiated for them. Settlers encroached on many reserves soon after they were surveyed; other tracts were stripped by timber poachers and plundered for valuable mineral resources. Big game, smaller fur-bearing animals, and fish stocks already had diminished owing to settlers' overfishing and overhunting.[7] Since the 1780s, settlers had vied with the Mi'kmaq for prime riverine fishing locales, oyster beds, moose hides, and beaver pelts. One colonial administrator, Thomas Crawley, the surveyor-general of the colony of Cape Breton, noted that over nine hundred moose had been destroyed by settlers on Cape Breton Island in 1789 alone. For these reasons, Michel Thoma Denny's term as grand chief spanned some of the most difficult years for the Unama'ki Mi'kmaq in recorded history.

The disappearance of moose constituted a major challenge. Shortly before his death the Unama'ki district chief, Jeannot Peguidalouet, also known as "Amable Jannot," obtained a licence of occupation from the British Crown that recognized the right of thirty-one Mi'kmaw families to hunt and fish on St. David's Bay.[8] Within a few years these families were suffering from the effects of chronic game shortages. Moose stocks had depleted as well along Nova Scotia's eastern shore where Unama'ki hunters ventured to supplement winter meat supplies. Family hunting groups from Cape Breton traditionally temporarily pressed into what are now Guysborough and Antigonish Counties, or southeast towards Jeddore in present-day Halifax County, whenever moose numbers declined on their own hunting tracts. A system of complex contracts between these hunters and the mainland Mi'kmaq in the past ensured that both had access to a wide range of locales to compensate for the omnipresent vicissitudes of the hunting life. To find that mainland moose herds could no longer compensate for moose scarcities to the north dealt both of these groups a severe blow. Seeking game reserves and new markets, Cape Breton Mi'kmaq between 1763 and 1795 migrated to Newfoundland, stopping to rest on St. Paul's Island, part way across the Cabot Strait.

Mi'kmaw canoes had plied the Cabot Strait prior to European contact, but never before in such numbers. French priests on the Îles de Saint-Pierre and Miquelon conducted Roman Catholic sacraments that were not available in Cape Breton or on the Nova Scotian mainland between 1762 and 1768. After 1768 Abbé Charles-François Bailly only visited Cape Breton once, in July of 1771, so journeys to the French isles continued, as did visits to French priests in the province of Quebec. Watching the numerical strength of the Cape Breton Mi'kmaw population dwindle owing to outmigration, Michel Thoma Denny Sr. when he became grand chief sought incentives to encourage the former migrants to return. He negotiated with Cape Breton's colonial establishment – Cape Breton being a separate colony from Nova Scotia from 1784 to 1820 – for official assurances that Mi'kmaw returnees would not be molested by settlers. Having been successful in this quest, he then chose a locale for a Mi'kmaw encampment ground near Sydney, a growing town lying on the shores of Sydney Harbour, called *Cibou* by the Mi'kmaq.[9] One of Chief Thoma Denny's sons, Thomas Denny, acted on his father's behalf by traversing the Cabot Strait and prevailing on Mi'kmaw families he found in Newfoundland to journey back to Cape Breton with him. By 1794 he had persuaded nine families under the leadership of Louis Christopher to leave the Bay St. George region of southwestern Newfoundland and settle temporarily at *Cibou* (probably present-day Sydney River), before moving to the shores of the Bras d'Or Lake.

The grand chief allayed government fears that the incoming Mi'kmaq, even in the event of war between the British and French Crowns, would not hearken to French emissaries and lean towards the French interest, a perennial concern for colonial administrators at this time. To achieve a climate of trust, Denny claimed that he knew the "Father of Christopher well," and that Louis Christopher's family and close kin espoused political neutrality. Denny further stressed that the Cape Breton Mi'kmaq as a whole wished "to fold their arms in all Wars between England and France." In return for this pledge of peace and goodwill, the grand chief attempted to elicit a promise from the executive council at Sydney that the Mi'kmaq's long-standing hunting and fishing tracts would be left under their exclusive aegis. As one member of the executive council put it, the chief expressed a "Hope [that] none of the subjects of England would inhabit lands around Lake George, that is to say the Grand Lake Brador."[10]

To curtail further Mi'kmaq visits to priests on St. Pierre and Miquelon, as early as 1790 Michel Thoma Denny had persuaded Roman Catholic clergy to come and serve among the Cape Breton Mi'kmaq. His repeated petitions for assistance in having a mission chapel rebuilt on Île de Saint Famille, or the "Island of the Holy Family" (known today as Chapel Island), finally gained a positive response from Cape Breton's colonial administrators late in 1792. Abbé Maillard had performed services earlier in the eighteenth century at this site, and the Mi'kmaq cherished it as sacred ground. The executive council minutes for Cape Breton Island indicate that on 28 November 1792 leaders "Francis Bask [Basque] and Tomma Michael [Michel Thoma Denny] and others of the Native Indians of the Island of Cape Breton" acquired permission from the island's lieutenant governor, William McCormick, "to take possession of the Island de Saint Villemai [*sic*, Île de Saint Famille], situate and lying and being in the Bras dor Lake near to the Portage at Mount Grenville, for the purpose of erecting thereon a Chappel [*sic*, chapel] to be used and appropriated for performing Divine Service agreeable to the rites and ceremonies of the Roman Catholic Religion, to hold, occupy and possess the same during His Majesty's Pleasure."[11]

Though the grand chief and his council attained exclusive rights to Chapel Island for ceremonials and festivities associated with St. Anne's Day on 26 July, they were less successful in halting settler encroachments on tracts they wanted to retain around the Bras d'Or Lake. Denny optimistically hoped that government mandates would force the eviction of squatters and halt settler resource overexploitation. In November 1827 Michel Thoma Denny, along with his brother, Christmas Thoma Denny, petitioned for a grant to a large tract in the East Bay region, which later would become the Eskasoni reserve.[12] In response to the grand chief's memorial, and other petitions from local chiefs and head men, among them Christmas Paul, Francis Googoo, and Noel Andrew, the bounds of Cape Breton reserves were laid out in 1832 and 1833. Grand Chief Denny did not live long enough to see these reserves officially ratified. He died at age eighty-seven at Eskasoni early in January 1834, before the order-in-council securing the reserve lands was issued the following May. Born a year before Louisbourg was restored to the French in 1748 under the provisions of the Treaty of Aix-la-Chapelle, Michel Thoma Denny's life spanned a time of radical social, political, and economic changes for the Mi'kmaq, although memories still lingered among the Cape Breton Indigenous population of an era when Mi'kmaq played integral roles in intercolonial military conflicts, the fur trade, and French missionary activities.

The chief's death in 1834 prompted two successive obituary notices in *The Cape-Bretonian*. Both offered their readers tantalizing glimpses of events that punctuated Denny's long career as grand chief. The first notice, published on 25 January 1834 and bearing the title "Demise of a Native Sovereign and Consequent Interregnum," stated that the leader had received honorifics from Sir James Kempt on behalf of the British sovereign,[13] as well as from a representative of the pope in Rome:

> The last of this tribe, invested with the Kingly office here was his late Majesty King Tomah [Michel Thoma Denny Sr.], who notwithstanding the adverse and conflicting claims of others, finally ascended the Throne and was fully admitted to sovereign power over his Tribe several years since – his authority not being merely acquiesced in by his subjects, but reported to have been acknowledged by a Right Reverend Prelate on the part of the See of Rome, and by His Excellency Sir James Kempt on behalf of the Court of St. James.[14]

Despite its willingness to view the deceased chief as deserving of such high honours, this notice said nothing about his ongoing struggles to retain rights to his people's traditional lands. Instead, it focused on pledges of peaceful co-existence and goodwill that he had extended to incoming Scottish settlers. It also assured its readers that the chief's powers were "exercised in full subordination to the British Government and to the government of the colony."[15]

The initial obituary left its readers in doubt as to whom the deceased chief's successor might be, and noted that a power struggle was in the offing between a faction headed by a member of the Googoo family (who were almost certainly descendants of Jeannot Peguidalouet) and members of the Thoma-Denny line:

> The Royal line of Gogoo [*sic*, Googoo] which was formerly in possession of the Throne has consequently been latterly debarred from the Crown, and which family it is reported is now in possession of one of the emblems of Royalty or symbols of authority; but which its enemies state it clandestinely obtained from a late King in a manner somewhat similar to that by which we read in the history of England, Blund [*sic*, Colonel Thomas Blood] obtained the Crown from the Tower.[16] It is said that the late King a few hours before dying, expressed a wish that his brother Christmas should be his successor and left with him the Royal Archives; others state that his son-in-law Francis Gregoire was left in charge. Further rumour exists that the Gogoo family will be Candidates for the Crown … Some time will probably elapse before the vacancy to the Indian Throne will be filled, as we understand that the election of a Sovereign will not take place until July next [during the St. Anne's Day ceremonies]. We know not whether a Christmas, a Gregoire, a Googoo or who else will accept the sceptre.[17]

The second obituary notice, appearing three days later on 28 January 1834, was entitled "The Indians and Their King." References in it to the Googoo family's being eager to resume control over the office of grand chief either harked back to an era prior to 1750 when the Googoo line may have prevailed, or else considered it to reflect ongoing tensions between two large, interrelated groups that over time probably both contributed positively to the political vitality of the Grand Council forum. Its author remained hesitant to concede that Michel Thoma Denny Sr.'s authority had ever extended beyond Cape Breton Island and evinced a paternalistic slant in its reporting of funeral proceedings for Denny on the island "which supports the Chapel built under his auspices." Yet this journalist also provided information regarding rites of leadership succession that otherwise would have been lost to future generations. According to this account, the grand chief's body lay "in state" for four days, before being placed in a bier "formed out of a solid trunk of hemlock."[18] This narrow wooden shell was then laid athwart two canoes, positioned side by side and lashed together, and paddled over to Chapel Island by eight individuals. Three canoes bearing twelve of the chief's principal men and six women singers led the procession out into the lake, while the chief's eldest son, bearing his father's spear, tomahawk, and gun, paddled behind the craft bearing his father's bier.

Pleading advanced age, Michel Thoma Denny's brother Christmas Thoma declined the office of grand chief, favouring instead the duties of grand captain. His signature, along with his rank, appear on a series of petitions drafted between 1838 and 1841 requesting government assistance to rebuild the mission church and wharf at Île de St. Famille. In his stead, in July of 1834 Michel Denny Thoma Jr., or the "chief's eldest son" referred to in the second obituary notice, became both the head of the Unama'ki district and grand chief of the Mi'kmaw nation.

– Janet E. Chute

29

Michel Thoma Denny Jr.

Born in 1768 at Eskasoni on Cape Breton Island, Michel Thoma Denny Jr. was the son of Michel Thoma Denny Sr. In his youth, he and father attended St. Anne's Day ceremonies on Chapel Island and meetings of the Eastern Wabanaki Confederacy.[1] He also was an elder brother of John Denny Sr., the Mi'kmaw grand chief from 1868 to 1881.

Michel Thoma Denny Jr. became Mi'kmaw grand chief a year after his father's death in 1834, and retained this status until his own death in November 1852.[2] His time in office was plagued with problems. Overhunting by settlers drastically reduced game on the island, and when the Mi'kmaq, encouraged by their grand chief, began farming, crop failures in the summers of 1846 and 1847 ushered in winters of famine. To add insult to injury, following the devastation wrought by a virulent potato blight, opportunistic Scottish settlers encroached on Mi'kmaw fields, which, they argued, had fallen into disuse.[3] The commissioner of Crown lands, vested with jurisdiction over lands reserved for the Indigenous people, usually refused to intervene in these disputes, and when he did he often took the settlers' side.

When this happened, Chief Michel Denny Jr. felt abandoned and betrayed by the colonial administration. While his grandfather, Thoma Denny, had favoured the French cause during the Seven Years' War, the grandson tried to demonstrate to British authorities and members of the Roman Catholic clergy that his main goal was to preserve peace and stability.

In keeping with official instructions sent to him in the 1840s, he had urged his people to practise agriculture, a difficult task since most Mi'kmaq favoured the hunting, fishing, trapping, and gathering way of life. Even as an elderly man with declining health, he tried to set an example by continuing to plant hay and potatoes. A nominal census taken during in July 1841 at Chapel Island, Richmond County, describes "Michael Dennie, Chief" as seventy-three years of age, "elderly and infirm, yet capable of harvesting 10 tons of hay and 18 bushels of potatoes, with the potentiality for raising another 30 bushels, if given seed to do so." Accompanying the chief in his Sisyphean farming labours was his sixty-two-year-old wife Mary, whose surname is unknown.[4]

Despite setbacks, Chief Michel Denny Jr. refused to be discouraged. He continued farming at Eskasoni and acted as steward of the mission chapel and grounds on Chapel Island. In March 1841 he petitioned the House of Representatives for monies to repair the wooden chapel built under his father's auspices in 1792.[5] The structure had fallen into disrepair, making it unfit for St. Anne's festivities. His appeal elicited some meagre government assistance, so in 1838 the Mi'kmaq began repairs, only to have a September gale destroy their efforts. Receiving no further aid, the chief and his brother, Grand Captain Christmas Thoma Denny, called all the Mi'kmaw men attending St. Anne's ceremonials in July 1841 to begin restoring the chapel once again. At the same time the House of Representatives received a second memorial, signed by Grand Chief Denny, Grand Captain Christmas Thoma, First Captains Matthew Morris and John Googoo, Second Captain Julian Basque, Third Captain Francis Gregoire – Chief Denny's brother-in-law – and 121 other attendees of the St. Anne's festivities.[6] The petitioners stressed that despite their combined labour and effort, they had been unable to get their building into "a proper state to have the Ceremonies of their Church performed." Nine months later the House of Assembly granted the grand chief and his council thirty pounds for repairs.[7]

Michel Thoma Denny Jr.'s campaign to preserve the Roman Catholic mission brought him to the notice of all echelons of the Roman Catholic hierarchy in the province. His correspondents included Jean Couteau, a Cape Breton mission priest;[8] Father Vincent de Paul, a Trappist monk who after 1819 resided at Tracadie in Antigonish County; and during the 1850s, William Walsh, the Roman Catholic bishop in Halifax. He also corresponded on church matters and Mi'kmaw land rights with Joseph Howe, the political reformer.[9]

Yet, because of his many diverse attachments and loyalties, he often found himself torn between his people's aspirations to maintain their hunting and fishing way of life and the government and church's insistence that the Mi'kmaq give up hunting, settle, and begin farming. After he accommodated to government mandates that the Mi'kmaq grow potatoes, many local chiefs charged that he had neglected his duties as a grand chief in failing to press for Indigenous hunting and fishing rights. The years between 1846 and 1849 proved especially harsh, as famine and fear for the future bred tensions within the Cape Breton Mi'kmaq communities. When things became extremely stressful, the elderly grand chief would slip away to his hunting grounds, which according to anthropologist Frank G. Speck ran from the "River Denny basin westward."[10] Or else he would cross the

Canso Strait to visit with kin and friends on the Nova Scotian mainland. In his later years he and his family often lived for lengthy periods at Crow Harbour, near Pomquet (in present-day Antigonish County, Nova Scotia) with the family of the elderly *Paq'tnket* leader Jean-Battiste Bouta, and after Chief Bouta's death about 1830, with his son Peter Battiste.[11] Although the *Paq'tnket* group held St. Anne's Day separately from the Cape Breton Mi'kmaq Chief Peter Battiste and several *Paq'tnket* head men interacted closely with the grand council.

Even while absent from Cape Breton, Chief Denny thought about the welfare of the Roman Catholic mission church on Chapel Island. In 1851 he directed one of his sons to carry a letter to Father Vincent de Paul at Tracadie calling for funds to erect a new church. At the same time, he upheld Peter Battiste as leader of the *Paq'tnket* community.[12] The chief knew that Battiste needed protection from the wiles of covetous settlers who hoped that the Mi'kmaw leader, who was determined to combat numerous settler trespasses on the *Paq'tnket* reserve, would be deposed through some sort of governmental fiat. He began by mustering support for Battiste among the clergy, and on 4 October 1851 he wrote Bishop Walsh that, as he was " 86 years old and feeble" (though if he was born in 1768, he was closer to eighty-three years old), he appreciated Peter Battiste's aid in helping him craft petitions and his courage in protecting his people's lands. Denny described Battiste as a "good man and sound leader" whom he wished to be "continued as the chief of the Indians of Pomquet."[13] Unfailing in his support for his church, his friends, and his people, Michel Denny Jr. died on 30 November 1852 at eighty-four years of age. He was succeeded as grand chief by Francis Thoma Denny.[14]

– Janet E. Chute

Acknowledgment: Special thanks are extended to A. J.B. Johnston for his assistance in editing this chapter.

30

Francis Thoma Denny

Almost certainly a son of Grand Chief Michel Thoma Denny Sr., Francis Thoma Denny (c.1780–c.1868) succeeded his brother, Michel Thoma Deny Jr., as grand chief of the Mi'kmaw nation eight years after Michel Jr.'s death in November 1852. In 1834 while lying on his deathbed, Michel Thoma Denny Sr. had requested that his brother Christmas Thoma Deny succeed him, but owing to Christmas Thoma Denny's advanced age, Michel Thoma Denny Jr. became grand chief. When Michel Jr. died in November 1852, Francis Thoma Denny was then approached to assume the office of grand chief the following July,[1] but he chose instead to adopt a low profile until he learned more about the prevailing political situation concerning Mi'kmaw lands and resources. Francis assumed the duties of grand chief in 1860.

Between 1853 and 1860, the Grand Council faced grave difficulties in trying to interact with provincial agents who demonstrated an utter lack of interest in Mi'kmaw affairs or aspirations. The Grand Council directed several petitions to Halifax asking for a halt to settler encroachment on the Cape Breton reserves that had been established by order-in-council in 1834.[2] Certain local leaders, among them Chief Peter Googoo of Whycocomagh who in 1833 had assisted the government surveyor in laying out the lines of his group's reserve, the following year shouldered the brunt of the struggle to retain the integrity of these boundaries. The worst settler trespasses occurred at Whycocomagh

(*We'koqma'q or Waycobah*),[3] Wagamatcook (Middle River), and Margaree.[4] The Wagamatcook and Margaree tracts contained rich farmland and salmon fishing grounds, while Whycocomagh lay at a road and steamboat junction. A number of Scottish settlers, some of whom first rented land from the Mi'kmaq, sought to obtain fee simple title to the parcels on which they squatted.

The Googoo family at Whycocomagh prior to 1860 mounted a determined resistance campaign against these trespassers. In 1821 ten Mi'kmaw families at *We'koqma'q* received a grant to two thousand acres, which they had occupied for fishing and planting purposes prior to 1780.[5] Yet within thirty years, tensions between Mi'kmaq living on this tract and settler intruders had reached a fever pitch. An elderly Chief Peter Googoo protested to a local clergyman in November 1850 that, owing to squatter hostility, it was no longer safe for his people to walk down the road through the reserve. Worse, some trespassers threatened to shoot Mi'kmaw children, whom they argued stole their potatoes.[6]

On 24 January 1854 Peter Googoo, Stephen Googoo, John Googoo. and Francis Googoo, along with their close kin, apprised Lieutenant Governor John Gaspard Le Marchant that, owing to encroachments and political opposition from Henry Bishop, Donald McLean, and William McPherson, they were in danger of "losing their place."[7] On 11 July the same year Stephen Googoo visited Reverend H.W. Crawley and asked the priest to send a letter to Father

Jean Courteau, a missionary residing at L'Ardoise in Cape Breton, stating that two more Scots by the names of Morrison and McDonald had trespassed on the Whycocomagh tract. Crawley at first raised Mi'kmaw hopes by asserting that a provincial act had been in place since 1842 to evict trespassers from Indigenous lands. James McKeagney, a lawyer as well as a member of the House of Assembly, also evinced interest in instigating legal proceedings against the trespassers, should the Roman Catholic Church or the government prove willing to foot the bill.[8]

Any concern that Father Courteau expressed over the Mi'kmaq's plight, however, faltered when the priest was faced with the prospect of a fundraising campaign to retain a lawyer to force squatter evictions. By March 1857 the Googoos faced stiff opposition from a number of Whycocomagh villagers, among them three justices of the peace who had directed a petition to the House of Assembly demanding that the reserve at Whycocomagh be opened to non-Indigenous settlement.[9] The province, meanwhile, found it lacked any firm precedent on which to act. In 1854 the Crown lands commissioner, James B. Uniacke, recommended that the province gain control over the lands that were squatted upon, but did little else. By contrast, Uniacke's successor as commissioner of Crown lands, Samuel P. Fairbanks, acted quickly. He devised a simple solution: sell all the parcels occupied by the intruders at a fixed rate. An Act Concerning Indian Reserves, passed in 1859 under Fairbanks's direction, allowed these tracts to be sold regardless of Mi'kmaw opposition.[10] Interest from such sales was to accrue to fund Mi'kmaw relief and the promotion of farming settlement, but the province's enforcement of the Act was so poor that squatters rarely paid anything into government coffers.

By late 1859 the local Cape Breton chiefs felt that things had gone beyond the scope of their limited political capabilities, and in 1860 they called for a resurrected grand chief and Grand Council to intervene on their behalf. Unlike before, Francis Thoma Denny now was ready to confront the challenges of the times. He was already regarded as a respected religious leader, endowed with shaman-like attributes. One oral tradition claimed that in 1857 he demanded that a large rock submerged off the shoreline of Chapel Island be retrieved and placed near a pit in which a sacred fire was lit each year during St. Anne's Day festivities. This rock, later surmounted by a

cross, became a focal point during the St. Anne's Day procession, as it became the spot on which the statue of St. Anne was positioned so that the assemblage could pay homage to their patron saint by kissing the statue's foot.[11] The practice of erecting a cross on top of a boulder had early roots at this mission. A nearby, larger flat-topped rock that was used as a dais by the eighteenth-century French missionary Abbé Pierre Maillard when giving his first mass at Chapel Island was also surmounted by a cross.[12] While an account of St. Anne's Day rituals in 1923 did not mention what served as a pedestal for the statue of the Virgin during the ceremonies, it was noted that at one point the Virgin's statue was "set down to one side" of the boulder associated with Maillard's ministry so that parishioners could kiss its feet.[13]

Performance of this rite entailed a syncretistic blending of an ancient belief in Grandmother Bear – a figure held in esteem by northeastern Algonquian-speaking peoples – and the Roman Catholic reverence for St. Anne. Maillard wrote of an ancient fire ceremony, although the pre-Christian ceremony he observed was held among the Mi'kmaq in February rather than late in July. Francis Thoma Denny's association with this ritual suggests that he belonged among a group of older, traditional leaders who could remember and recount ancient tribal traditions.

Disappointed but not cowed by the lack of funds accruing from the sales of Indigenous land, Francis Thoma Denny sent a memorial in 1859 to Lieutenant Governor George Phipps, the Earl of Mulgrave, charging that the Mi'kmaq population numbers recorded on a recent census by Indian commissioner Moses Perley were skewed because so many of the Cape Breton Mi'kmaq were absent, temporarily visiting Newfoundland and Prince Edward Island. Perley's numbers, the chief contended, were far too low; in actuality the Unama'ki Mi'kmaq's numerical strength warranted serious consideration of their grievances. The "representative of her Majesty in Nova Scotia," he demanded, should take measures to secure the integrity of Mi'kmaw reserve lands, and set "compensation … in every case for the benefit of the tribe." The grand chief then called for a special commission to be convened to examine survey lines, estimate improvements, and determine "sums to be paid for trespass."[14]

It was evident that under the leadership of their grand chief, the Unama'ki Mi'kmaq's political voice was exhibiting a new edge, for they also began to place new emphasis on "treaties made in former days with their forefathers by the British Government." A second petition, directed to the lieutenant governor in 1860 by Francis Thoma Denny, Louis Adelaide Clement Bernard, and Michael Christmas, held "[t]hat from time immemorial certain lands in Cape Breton have been in the possession of the Cape Breton Indians, and to these lands their claims have at all times, by the Provincial Government, been distinctly recognized, their limits marked out and clearly defined, and all applications to the government hitherto by white men, for any part of these lands, refused.[15]

Francis Thoma Denny's words in 1860 harked back to an earlier time when the Mi'kmaq expected the grievances of their grand chief to meet with a listening ear in official ranks. Not so in 1860. In 1862 and 1863 the chief again petitioned the government several times complaining about land trespasses and calling for redress.[16] The Unama'ki Mi'kmaq needed a powerful voice to represent them during these years. In 1863 a special commission, led by Samuel Prescott Fairbanks, recently vested with the offices of both provincial Indian commissioner and lands commissioner, continued to arrange for reserve lands that had been squatted upon by settlers to be sold to the trespassing parties, similar to what had happened in 1859. By 1864 Francis Thoma Denny looked to other parties to sustain the momentum of his earlier appeals, for he was elderly, unable to travel far to speak on the Grand Council's behalf.

On 9 March 1864 three of Denny's captains, Paul Christmas, Michael Christmas, and Paul Andrew, travelled without the company of the grand chief to Antigonish to meet with Colin F. McKinnon, the bishop of Arichat, to have a petition drafted and sent to the House of Assembly. The resulting missive was short and to the point. With the "approval of their Chief, Francis Thoma," they had been "appointed delegates" to address the House of Assembly "for redress of the wrongs which in years past have been perpetrated against their Brethren by your people at Middle River and at Whycocomagh … in encroaching and squatting upon the lands which have been reserved in those counties for their Brethren." Should the government not be able to restore the lands, they concluded, then the Mi'kmaq should be granted an equivalent "and have justice done."[17]

In his final years Francis Thoma Denny focused his interest on religious affairs. In 1865 he and the Grand Council directed a petition, with numerous signatures, to the lieutenant governor to have the roads and bridge to Chapel Island repaired.[18] This was his last memorial, and it received no response. Four years later he prevented a party of Mi'kmaw youths at Chapel Island from shooting what they held to be *owwiscooks*, or "spies from Canada," at the 1869 St. Anne's Day ceremonies. Silus Tertius Rand, who reported the incident, claimed that "old Tooma" was not entirely successful, for a stranger was shot and killed by a Mi'kmaq.[19] Chief Francis Thoma Denny died soon after this incident, leaving as his legacy a newly revived Indigenous land and resource movement, which blended traditional knowledge with hard-hitting demands for compensation for wrongs committed by settler society. This campaign, along with the ongoing responsibility for maintaining the mission chapel, would in following years be spearheaded by a new voice, that of John Denny Sr. of Eskasoni.

– Janet E. Chute, assisted by Alison Lloy and Lillian Marshall

31

John Denny Sr.

John Denny Sr. (Denis, Dennis, Dennys, Denys; c.1810–1881) was a grandson of the noted eight-eenth-century head chief Thoma Denny, who moved from Beaubassin to Cape Breton Island around 1748. John Sr.'s father was Grand Chief Michel Thoma Denny Jr. Born at Eskasoni in Cape Breton around 1810, John Denny Sr. was grand chief from 1869 until his death in 1881. He and his wife Elizabeth Marshall (originally Marchal or Marachal) raised a large family at Eskasoni.[1]

Following Michel Thoma Denny Jr.'s death in 1852, the office of grand chief lay vacant for eight years before being assumed by Francis Thoma Denny, Michel Thoma Denny Jr.'s younger brother, in 1860. Francis Thoma Denny was a religious leader and experienced negotiator, qualities required by the Grand Council during the 1860s when it had to address thorny issues arising from Scottish Highlander incursions on Cape Breton reserves. Indigenous land concerns came to a head in 1863 when Samuel Prescott Fairbanks shouldered the dual offices of Indian commissioner and commissioner of Crown lands. Overburdened with work, Fairbanks chose a simple solution: allow squatters at Whycocomagh, Malagawatch, and Margaree to purchase the parcels of Indigenous land on which they had settled, regardless of how the Mi'kmaw population felt about the decision. From 1860 to 1868 the Grand Council's memorials denounced this lack of respect for the integrity of Mi'kmaw lands and resources.

John Denny Sr. became grand chief a year after his uncle Francis's death.[2] Even before he assumed this office in 1869, he was active in community affairs, ensuring widows and their dependent children received food, blankets, and clothing, and acting in a fatherly manner towards orphans, some of whom he invited to join his household. He reassured his people when dangers threatened, as when rumours spread that "strangers" (also locally referred to as "Mohawks") might disturb celebrations surrounding the St. Anne's Day celebrations.[3] He also sought to improve community infrastructure by demanding that roads and bridges be kept in good condition at Eskasoni and in 1865 calling for a sturdy wharf to be built on Chapel Island, capable of handling steamer traffic.[4] After monies arrived from Halifax for this wharf, he turned his attention to land issues.

Chief Peter Googoo of Whycocomagh had directed numerous petitions to Nova Scotia's Crown Lands Department and the provincial House of Representatives. Following Googoo's death in 1860, his political successors at Whycocomagh, stymied in their efforts to prompt government action in support of their interests, called for assistance from the grand chief, who they felt could broaden the Mi'kmaq's base of political support by appealing to the Roman Catholic clergy. For over a decade the Grand Council promoted diverse land campaigns launched by local chiefs. Denny broadened the Mi'kmaw land and resource campaign to include the entire province of

Nova Scotia. He also sent men from Cape Breton, ones he regarded as capable leaders who could serve his new land and resource movement well, to various parts of the country, though this policy brought him into conflict with local leaders, who charged him with interfering in their own territorial jurisdictions.[5]

Despite such opposition, John Denny Sr. excelled at this kind of political campaigning, and entrenched the worth and prestige of the Grand Council in the minds of many officials, scholars, and clergy. He endeavoured to disseminate correct information on Mi'kmaw social and political organizations and other aspects of northeastern Algonquian culture. During his time in office, the first printed descriptions appeared in print of the Mi'kmaq's socio-political system of seven districts, overarched politically by the grand chief and Grand Council. Silus Tertius Rand, a Baptist missionary, noted in 1875 that the chief of Cape Breton maintained paramount status within the relatively complex leadership hierarchy responsible for Mi'kmaw territorial affairs in the Northeast.[6] Rand likely learned about the seven districts from his Mi'kmaw assistant from Cape Breton, Benjamin Christmas,[7] though two years later George Patterson, the Pictou county historian, made similar observations.[8] Patterson almost certainly obtained his information directly from Grand Chief Denny, since the grand chief often resided with the Mi'kmaw community at Pomquet (*Paq'tnket*) near Antigonish, where he and his wife Elizabeth Marshall had close

kin. According to anthropologist Frank G. Speck, "old John Denis" spent the winters on a family hunting territory extending from Cow Bay (Port Morien) towards Louisbourg. At other times of the year the grand chief moved widely around the countryside, making himself available as a source of information.[9]

There can be no doubt that he was held in high regard by personnel in the Department of Indian Affairs in Ottawa, for the Department's *Annual Report* for 1877 stated that "[t]he Grand Chief, John Denny, is a man of most excellent character and intelligence. He has two subordinate Chiefs, called 'Captains' on each Reserve, and it is essential to their retention of office that they be honest and sober. On Chapel Island, in the County of Cape Breton [*sic*, Richmond County], councils are held twice a year by the Grand Chief and his Captains, whereat matters affecting the different Bands and Reserves are discussed."[10] John Denny Sr. became well enough known to officials, scholars, and members of the Roman Catholic hierarchy in the Maritime Provinces that when he died his eldest son, John Denny Jr., found much of the way paved for him to assume a similar intermediary role. John Denny Jr. became grand chief on his father's death in 1881.

– Janet E. Chute

Acknowledgment: The author is grateful to A.J.B. Johnston for assistance in editing this chapter.

32

John Denny Jr.

Born in 1841 to Grand Chief John Denny Sr. and Elizabeth Marshall at Eskasoni and baptized at the Roman Catholic chapel at Red Island on the Bras d'Or Lake, John Baptiste Denny Jr. served as grand chief of the Mi'kmaw nation from 1881 until his death in 1918.[1] He descended from a long line of chiefs.[2] Frank Gouldsmith Speck, an anthropologist from the University of Pennsylvania whom Denny in 1914 had encouraged to investigate Mi'kmaw family hunting territories, reported that Denny's great grandfather, Thoma Denny, fought on the French side in the Seven Years' War.[3]

John Denny was a tall, handsome man, intelligent, notably self-possessed, physically strong, a good hunter, and cunningly astute in negotiations. As a youth he cultivated friendships with local priests, who recognized that he possessed special linguistic abilities and encouraged him to learn to speak different languages.[4] Once he became grand chief, his roles as a religious spokesperson and political mediator and negotiator were enhanced by his fluency in Gaelic, French, English, and Passamaquoddy, in addition to Mi'kmaq. His intelligence and dedication to the welfare of his nation were admired by Father Pacifique, a Capuchin missionary at Restigouche, Quebec, and his name appears frequently in Pacifique's newspaper, *The Micmac Messenger*.[5] His duties included travelling throughout *Mi'kma'ki* to attend major Roman Catholic religious events that had relevance to his people. In 1904 he attended a high mass at Indian Brook in the district of *Sipekne'katik* (Shubenacadie) conducted by the bishop of Saint John and translated into Mi'kmaq by Father Pacifique, the last cleric in the Northeast to speak the Mi'kmaw language fluently.[6] In 1910 he took part in ceremonies at Restigouche (*Listuguj*) commemorating the three hundredth anniversary of Membertou's baptism.[7]

Though unable to write English or French, Denny mastered the hieroglyphic writing system developed by Abbé Pierre Maillard, and became a skilled decipherer and transcriber of the hieroglyphic texts.[8] Owing to his ability to read religious passages in hieroglyphics, he became a grand council prayer leader.[9] He also learned to decode messages that had been mnemonically incorporated into the weave of the Grand Council's wampum belts. This meant he could assist the grand council's record keeper, the *Pu'tus* (also spelled *Putu's* or *Bu'tus*), during ceremonies. Endowed with a strong, resonant baritone voice, he also became a chant leader and choir member. His special area of concern during the St. Anne's mission was the provision of food for the men, as men and women did not eat together at the main feast. His duties included tending pots of stew and arranging for tea, pork, and bread to be distributed to the male guests.[10]

The Department of Indian Affairs did not challenge the formidable leadership legacy associated with the Thoma Denny family, at least not until after John Denny Jr.'s death, and despite the implementation of a triennial system for electoral reform, in 1890 he was formally recognized by Ottawa as Cape Breton's "life chief."[11] Yet his role as grand chief of the Mi'kmaw nation drew opposition from Mi'kmaw political rivals, most notably John Noel at Shubenacadie. Noel, the adopted son of Chief Jacques-Pierre Peminout Paul, the district chief of *Sipekne'katik*,[12] undermined Denny's claim to the office of grand chief while endeavouring to raise himself in the estimation of the Mi'kmaw community at large. In response six of Denny's supporters – Jacob Brooks, Abraham Hood, Joseph Hood, Stephen Hood, Christopher Peminout Paul, and Peter Paul, living either at Shubenacadie or in the Annapolis Valley area – on 15 February 1883 wrote to Lieutenant Governor Adams George Archibald branding Noel as an upstart. In their memorial they hinted that they had recourse to items or materials that could place Denny's claims to the leadership beyond question. "[I]f proof of the above statements is required," they confided, "your petitioners are in a position to produce such as will no doubt meet with your entire satisfaction."[13]

When the memorialists received a letter from the lieutenant governor requesting more information on the subject, the first petition was followed by a second, signed by Christopher Peminout Paul, a Mi'kmaw judge who had been installed in his office the same year, and sixty other Mi'kmaw head men. The petitioners stressed that the office of grand chief had been passed down in the Denny family line for generations, a tradition they hoped would be upheld by the queen's representative: "[A]bout one hundred and thirty-four years ago the Chieftainship was placed in the family of Denas [*sic*, Denny] and it has continued to descend from the father to son, following the blood, until the present time, our John Denas being now the regular chief, he being a resident of the Island of Cape Breton."[14]

John Noel's political ambitions were curtailed because in 1883 he could only claim to be Shubenacadie's acting chief, not its district chief, who was Jacques-Pierre Peminout Paul. Jacques-Pierre did not die until January 1895 at the age of ninety-six, and like Denny he represented a long-standing leadership tradition dating back to the eighteenth century. Members of the Denny and Peminout families both participated in Eastern Wabanaki Confederacy councils, but John Denny, bolstered by the support he had recently received from his supporters throughout the province, pressed for new institutional changes. He realized that the Mi'kmaw Grand Council, which once had functioned powerfully within the Eastern Wabanaki Confederacy, had to develop new roles and strategies if it was to continue to function as a protector of Indigenous rights. Backed by a strong show of support in 1883, Denny felt a renewed sense of commitment to launching a major Indigenous land and resource campaign. In a great show of magnanimity, Denny also ignored the taunts of John Noel and devoted his time to serving the needs of his people. He would let the Mi'kmaw constituency decide who should be grand chief, a stance he had maintained since he first assumed leadership. Years later a Boston newspaper correspondent, remembering Denny's installation as chief in 1881, noted: "In the beginning John Dinny ... was very modest about accepting the position ... [He only] would take it for three years, saying, 'If I fail to please you, you can select a better man.'"[15]

Despite Denny's desire to maintain a low profile, John Noel's political jousting with him sparked a second confrontation between the two men in 1887, during an election for chief of the Cole Harbour reserve in Dartmouth. Though hesitant to ignite further tension within Mi'kmaw leadership circles, Denny decided to back a different candidate from Noel.[16] Noel favoured Joseph C. Cope, whose ancestors, including Major Jean-Baptiste Cope in the mid-1750s, had resided along the Atlantic coast between Musquodoboit and Sheet Harbour. By contrast, Denny supported Andrew Paul, a newcomer from Cape Breton who had arrived on Nova Scotia's Eastern Shore around 1868. Born in Whycocomagh in 1820, Andrew Paul in his younger years served as a Grand Council captain under John Denny Jr.'s uncle, Grand Chief Francis Thoma Denny, but around 1841 had moved to the Halifax-Dartmouth area. He remained a captain of the Grand Council, became a captain of the Shubenacadie Grand Council under Chief Jacques-Pierre Peminout Paul, and in 1860 was delegated to meet HRH Prince Edward during the Prince of Wales's visit to Halifax in 1860. Ottawa meanwhile held that both men were equally qualified, since both could read and write English and were planting crops and raising livestock.

When Denny publicly revealed his preference for Andrew Paul at a ceremony at Shubenacadie in 1887, John Noel immediately branded Paul as a worthless outsider who persisted in failing to contribute to Shubenacadie's mission church. Cope, Noel's candidate, denounced Denny for overstepping his political mandate. "Dear Sir," Cope complained to Lawrence Vankoughnet, the deputy superintendent of Indian Affairs, had the "Cape Breton chief any right to go inside of our Grand Chief James Paul's jurisdiction to appoint his own men to Rule, and is he not interfering with our old and recognized Chiefdom of Halifax, Hants + Kings Counties?"[17] When Ottawa refused to get involved in the affair, the Reverend Desmond O'Connor, the local Indian agent as well as a Roman Catholic priest at Enfield, claimed that the contest had grown so contentious that Ottawa's best policy would be to pronounce the election of either Cope or Paul as null and void. O'Connor's warning came too late, however, for what had begun as a political contest had developed into a feud between families. In early December Cope's supporters knocked down Andrew Paul's fences, and in consequence Paul fled up the Musquodoboit Valley to Stewiacke, taking his cattle in tow. Cope, molested in turn by Paul's supporters, first went to Windsor and then resided temporarily at Tuff's Cove on the Dartmouth side of Halifax Harbour.

This incident, which had been aggravated by the government's imposition of an electoral system on the Shubenacadie group, whose leadership was still guided by considerations of family rank and precedence, eventually was settled amicably by the Mi'kmaw themselves at a number of district councils held especially for the purpose. Andrew Paul's experience as a negotiator with the grand council may have enabled him to strike a workable middle ground with his rival, since both he and Cope later served together on the Shubenacadie band council.[18]

Throughout this ordeal, John Denny remained true to his duty as grand chief to mediate in disputes, whether concerning land dispossession or successions to political offices. On 24 February 1885 he petitioned Ottawa on behalf of Joseph Lewis, an elderly Mi'kmaq man who was ousted by a farmer from lands in Prince Edward Island that he had been cultivating for over thirty years.[19] Though the Indian Affairs Department refused to pursue Lewis's case, claiming that there was insufficient evidence to uphold Lewis's claim on the grounds of adverse possession, the incident enhanced Denny's reputation as a champion of Mi'kmaw interests. Soon local leaders began coming to him to seek his aid. One of the most prominent was Chief Joseph Glode, the head man of a Mi'kmaq group residing at Kejimkujik in southwestern Nova Scotia. Discouraged by crop failures and settlers who plundered the timber on his reserve, Glode turned to the grand chief to act on his community's behalf.

Denny broached the subject of Glode's predicament in a letter he directed to the deputy superintendent general of Indian Affairs on 11 March 1909;[20] he argued that Ottawa should offer protection to Glode's people and their lands. He further declared that as grand chief he possessed the right to encourage Cape Breton Mi'kmaq to travel to Kejimkujik and begin a logging and manufacturing industry in Queens County. Cut logs from the Kejimkujik reserve could be shipped by train from Caledonia to Indigenous communities at Pictou, near Antigonish, and in Cape Breton for manufacture by the Mi'kmaq into wooden articles for use in the mines:

> The use of timber for the various purposes into which we manufacture it is our chief source of living, and I hope that your government will not deprive us of any part of the supply of timber in any part of the province. We who live in Cape Breton would be glad to go to a western part of the province and manufacture the timber into marketable articles which are saleable in the eastern part of the province. We make pick handles and shafts for our mines in large quantities. We make butter tubs, axe handles, baskets, and various other small articles which help to secure for us the means for providing for us our living expenses. These markets are growing larger from year to year but our wood material is growing scarcer and scarcer and we must look to those more distant portions of our reserves to get our supply in the future. I am getting petitions signed by the Chiefs of our Bands and will have them forwarded to you as early as possible. In the meantime please stop any proceedings towards disposing of the property in question by lease or otherwise.
>
> John Denys, Grand Chief
> Rose MacMaster, witness[21]

As the first years of the twentieth century proved more prosperous than previous decades, Denny saw a potentially bright economic future for his people if certain opportunities were allowed them. First and foremost, in 1909 he saw avenues to promote a redistribution of people to available reserve resources throughout the Atlantic region. To this end he directed his Grand Council captains residing throughout Nova Scotia to petition the Department of Indian Affairs and protest any attempt to lease or otherwise sell timber off the Kejimkujik reserve, or other Indigenous lands in the province. In response, between 11 March and 24 April the Department of Indian Affairs received two more formal petitions, the first from Chief John Steavens of Pomquet (*Paq'tntket*) and the second from Chief Joseph Gould of Millbrook. There also were letters from four Cape Breton leaders, Captain Simon Paul of Middle River, Chief Solomon Morris of Sydney, Chief Thomas Marshall of Chapel Island, and Chief James Joe of Malagawatch.[22] Denny's efforts staved off land surrenders in the Kejimkujik region for almost a decade, though he failed to gain the funds and political backing from mainstream society needed to put his larger economic scheme into operation. When Grand Chief Denny died in April of 1918, Ottawa less than a month later obtained the cession of the Kejimkujik reserve. At the time most of the Kejimkujik Mi'kmaw community's male population was serving overseas and so could not register their vote on the surrender.[23]

Mainstream society knew little of Denny's political struggles, his generous expenditure of his time and material resources, or his economic aspirations for the future of his people during his final years. The press portrayed him as a colourful person representative of an interesting cultural group, but rarely as a Mi'kmaw economist and a shrewd politician. Journalists encountered him principally on July 26, at St. Anne's Day ceremonies on Chapel Island. On such occasions he spoke English to the press and dressed immaculately in Western garb, yet he discouraged journalists from becoming too forthright in their questioning. His ambivalence towards them manifested itself in his jokes that photographs of him could be taken only if they first provided him with a "toddie" (toddy) of rum. To him, gentle humour proved the best way of deflecting the probings of those who seemed to want to understand Mi'kmaq culture yet all too plainly showed they had little concept of the culture's complexity.[24]

Denny thus could play the trickster as well as be forceful in the negotiating forum. As a result, he gained a reputation as someone who embodied attributes both of a *kinap* – a Mi'kmaq person who could demonstrate exceptional physical strength – and a shaman –a more unpredictable person of power who, according to the Algonquian cosmological system, could be an unsettling character if crossed. This shamanic side of Denny's reputation appears in an article in *The Micmac Messenger* in

which Denny is reputed to have had a hand in a fire that ravaged Campbellton, New Brunswick, in 1920. Father Pacifique referred to the powers that Denny was held to have drawn upon, after the grand chief and his party were roughed up at the hands of a Campbellton resident shortly before the fire's outbreak, as the workings of "natural justice." Before his death, Denny combined the dual roles of Roman Catholic Christian religious leader and dispenser of ancient Algonquian shamanic wisdom; a formidable pairing in the eyes of both the clergy and the Indigenous community at large.[25]

Another duty he took seriously was enforcing certain behavioural tenets he viewed as necessary for the proper functioning of a Mi'kmaq community. For instance, individuals were expected to donate money and labour to their mission church, and contribute as well to the St. Anne's Day mission. Some of these requirements had their origin in a set of rules, or *reglèments*, transcribed into Mi'kmaw ideograms – also often called "hieroglyphics" – by Abbé Pierre Maillard in 1739.[26] The abbé also had vested leaders with authority to preside over Mi'kmaw baptisms, marriages, and funerals in the absence of an ordained priest, a right that, according to parish registers, Denny regularly exercised within the Eskasoni community. Denny's strictness in enforcing these community rules and regulations did not always meet with universal approval, and caused at least one major rift within the Eskasoni community. After a debate over who should contribute what and when towards repairing the Chapel Island church, a group of families, led by Paul Christmas, left Eskasoni for *Kun'tewiktuk*, a locale along the Kings Road, which led into the town of Sydney. The schism proved a temporary one. Christmas and Denny, who were distant relatives, soon reconciled.

As more Mi'kmaq, seeking wage labour, joined the Kings Road settlement, *Kun'tewiktuk* in 1882 became recognized as a reserve community, and in 1902 its residents opted for an elected chief and council, guided by the provisions of the 1885 Indian Act.[27] The local Sydney Indian agent, D.M. McAdam, advised that John Denny Jr. – who in 1890 was federally recognized as the Cape Breton chief, though not the grand chief of the Mi'kmaw nation – should be consulted before Ottawa took any further action.[28] Yet in the fall of 1909 when Denny strongly opposed implementation of the electoral system on the Sydney reserve, fears arose, including among the

Mi'kmaq, that a politically debilitating schism might arise within the Indigenous polity if Ottawa recognized two chiefs in Cape Breton with equal and independent jurisdictional powers.[29] "Do not grant an election at all; let there be no sub chief at all. I am the Grand Chief, and I can look after the [Sydney] reserve as well as this one," Denny proclaimed.[30] One suggestion was for Ottawa to recognize a head man, rather than a chief, at Sydney. Inspector J.A. McCrae of the Department of Indian Affairs, by contrast, argued that the two principal Cape Breton leaders, John Denny Jr. and Ben Christmas, if left to their own devises would work together harmoniously.

Time proved McCrae right. After being forced from *Kun'tewiktuk* in 1916 by an order of the Exchequer Court, the Sydney Mi'kmaq settled at nearby Membertou and appealed to Ottawa to continue with their own chief and council. By this time Denny knew full well that his intervention would be regarded as unwelcome by both Ottawa and the Mi'kmaw constituency. Elderly and ailing, he refused to be drawn into another confrontation with the Sydney leaders, who still retained close ties with his own community, Eskasoni. He stressed that his role was principally that of a mediator who heard and sought resolutions for disputes, both on Cape Breton Island and, when petitioned to do so, throughout *Mi'kma'ki*, and not one of a "chief-maker."[31] While Denny for many years privately continued to oppose implementation of the electoral process at Membertou, he eventually came to see value in the triennial electoral system for band governments. Denny's successor as grand chief, Gabriel Sylliboy, furthermore held that adoption of the electoral system might prove the best route to follow, so within a year of Denny's death in 1918, Membertou, bolstered by Sylliboy's support, elected a chief and two councillors.[32]

Grand Chief John Denny Jr. died on Church Island at Whycocomagh, Cape Breton, on 12 April 1918 at a time when many Mi'kmaw youths were away at war. He left behind a wife, a married sister who lived in Newfoundland, two sons, three daughters, eight grandchildren, and several great-grandchildren. His body was transported to Eskasoni for burial. Recipients of an announcement in Mi'kmaq directed at those who were expected to attend the chief's funeral on 15 April, and they were many, included chiefs throughout the Atlantic region.[33] Meanwhile, those who could not attend the service received the following notice several days after the funeral was held:

My friends, the message we are letting you know in all of the Mi'kmaq land, our late Chief, Our Lord has taken him from the midst of our body, my friends, our chief's life was gone on the 12th day of this month at 8 o'clock in the morning. He went peacefully after he received all of his sacraments that our Lord had left for those to die quietly. He was 77 years old, he was chief for 31 years … all of the people came, even the strongest chief Matthew Francis, he was the chief of Merigomish, and all of the most powerful men; and then Chief Francis Stevens, from Pomquet, he even came with all of his men, then there was Chief Joseph Gould from Truro; he came too, and his men came; then there was John Denny Paul, Chief of Halifax and all of his men; from Cape Breton, five communities and it could be said that all of the men and women came, some even brought their children along. It was a big wonder at the size of the gathering who came together, because they loved our chief so much … we ask you to pray for our chief, we beg God for our elder, and to open the doors of heaven and to give him rest in his kingdom.[34]

At the St. Anne's festivities on Chapel Island in 1918, the traditional *salite*, or charity auction, raised sufficient funds to provide support to surviving members of Denny's immediate family and to purchase a granite obelisk to be set over his grave at Eskasoni.[35] While lying on his deathbed, Denny had directed his son, Simon Denny, to relinquish his hereditary right to the grand chiefship in favour of opting for an election to determine the next grand chief. Wearied by the political turmoil he had faced, he wanted to see his son spared the problems he had encountered as grand chief – and simply may have come to view the adoption of an electoral system as a progressive step for his people. As a result, an election occurred in 1918 in the wake of his death. Six respected men were selected by the Grand Council to run, with Gabriel Sylliboy from *We'koqma'q* being elected by ballot during the St. Anne's mission.[36]

The granite obelisk was raised over Denny's grave. The stone's inscription, in English, reads: "In Loving Memory of Our Grand Chief, John Denny Jr., Chief for the Maritime Provinces: After 37 Years Noble Service, Died April 12, 1918, Aged 77 Years. Rest in Peace."[37]

– Janet E. Chute, assisted by Richard Denny,
Marjorie Gould, Alison Lloy, and Natalie
McConnell

33

Beloni Thoma

An obituary in the April 1849 issue of *The Times and Cape Breton* described the tragic death of "Beloni Toma" (c.1815–April 1849), a member of the Thoma-Denny family of Eskasoni, Cape Breton.[1] It reported that Beloni spent a bitterly cold night walking the streets of Sydney asking for food and shelter from various townsfolk, all of whom refused him assistance. The obituary gave no indication of his age, though he may have been in his thirties. During St. Anne's Day festivities in July 1841 he had joined with 120 other Mi'kmaw men, including Grand Chief Michel Denny Jr., who was likely his uncle,[2] in signing a petition asking for government monies to repair the mission chapel on Chapel Island in Richmond County.[3] The warm spirit of community that would have pervaded this 1841 event was a far cry from the dark, cold, and lonely bleakness that confronted Beloni eight years later. The winter of 1849 had been severe for Cape Bretoners. Since 1846 a series of crop failures had made people hesitant to share their meagre food supplies. Worse, Scottish immigrant farmers' encroachments on Mi'kmaq reserve lands at Whycocomagh, Margaree, and Middle River led to sporadic outbreaks of violence involving individuals from both the Mi'kmaw and settler communities.

Beloni was found dead, his body frozen, in the back porch of a townsperson's house. He presented a dishevelled appearance, since the evening before he had been drinking heavily. It was also suggested that he had been suffering from an unnamed disease, probably tuberculosis. During the autopsy it was found that his stomach contained no food in it whatsoever, causing the coroner D.N. McQueen to pronounce that the victim "had died from the effects of cold and lack of food acting on a system already diseased."[4] This incident undoubtedly struck a chord in the hearts of mainstream and Mi'kmaw readers alike, for it reflected the callousness that could afflict Sydney's townsfolk during difficult times.

Benoni Thoma's plight is particularly poignant because he was educated and wanted to help his people. He may have learned to read and write under the tutelage of Father Simon Lawlor, a Roman Catholic cleric who in the mid-1820s operated a small school for Mi'kmaq children at Eskasoni.[5] When in better health, Benoni would have hunted and fished on his family's hunting territory near Malagawatch.[6] Yet he also strove to be a literate voice for the grievances of his group. Only a year or so before his death, Benoni addressed a petition to the "Honourable Jim [James] Luniack [Uniacke], Commissioner of Crown Lands" regarding settler trespasses on Indigenous lands in Cape Breton.[7] The fact that a literate Mi'kmaw promoter of Indigenous land rights could meet with such a dismal end served as a sad indicator of the degree of social distance that in the late 1840s separated the Mi'kmaw community from most Sydney residents and settler society in Cape Breton in general.

– Janet E. Chute

Peter Googoo, Chief of Whycocomagh (Waycobah)

Peter Googoo (1780–c.1860) was a prominent politically active leader who lived at Whycocomagh (*We'koqma'q* or *Waycobah*), Cape Breton, in the nineteenth century.[1] His surname, "Googoo," derived from the Mi'kmaw term for "owl," *kukwis*.[2] His parents almost certainly were Pierre Gougaux, a son of Bernard Gougaux, and Agathe, who were married by Abbé Charles-François Bailly on 8 August 1771.[3] Peter Googoo reputedly married a daughter – or a granddaughter – of the noted Cape Breton district chief Jeannot Peguidalouet (1705–c.1790). He also may have been the father of Rosalie Googoo, who prided herself on being Peguidalouet's granddaughter. Rosalie kept a parchment commission, given to Jeannot by the French at Louisbourg in 1751, in a birchbark box she carried with her whenever she travelled between communities. If Rosalie was Peter Googoo's daughter, however, she must have retained her maiden name, if and when she married.[4]

Peter hunted with his three brothers, Francis, Stephen, and John, northwest of Bras d'Or Lake. In 1914, anthropologist Frank G. Speck reported that a family hunting territory once belonging to "Peter Kugu" lay between Whycocomagh Bay and Lake Ainslie.[5] The Googoos belonged to a local band composed of family heads with the surnames Adley (André), Bernard, Googoo, Meuse, Newel (or Noel), Poulette, and Solomon. Though related by marital ties to the Thoma Denny family and others living on East Bay, the Mi'kmaq at *We'koqma'q* formed a distinct socio-political entity from the Eskasoni group.[6] As soon as the Mi'kmaq heard in 1821 that Cape Breton had relinquished its status as a colony separate from Nova Scotia, ten families at *We'koqma'q* petitioned Halifax the same year, on 5 November, asking for two thousand acres on Whycocomagh Bay. Though they received their grant, they had to wait until 1833 to have it surveyed.[7]

Peter's Googoo's younger brother, Francis, already had petitioned the Cape Breton colonial government in 1810 for land, which he received in the Margaree River Valley, near a productive salmon fishery.[8] The only other Mi'kmaq who applied for a tract at this time was a man known to the colonial authorities as "Benwa, the Indian" who asked for land at the Gut of Little Bras d'Or.[9] It is not known whether Benwa (Benoit) received his plot, but in 1834 Googoo's acreage formed the Margaree reserve. Within a few years the latter parcel, however, was so overrun with squatters that Francis and Peter were forced to vacate it and return to *We'koqma'q*.[10] Despite the fact the Margaree tract was granted to the Mi'kmaq, in 1864 the province sold it without notifying its Mi'kmaw owners, an experience that strengthened Peter and Francis's resolve to fight for what lands remained to their people.[11]

Peter, who had assisted with the running of reserve lines in 1833, later struggled to retain the integrity of these boundaries. Between 1850 and 1855, he and his brother Francis directed a series of petitions to the executive council as well as to Roman Catholic clergy, appealing for help in preventing squatters from occupying the Whycocomagh reserve. What they found was that several Scots did not even realize they were trespassing on a Mi'kmaw land, since the Department of Crown Lands had accorded them location tickets to parcels that overlapped reserve boundaries. Though the consequences of official carelessness temporarily placed both Scots and Mi'kmaq in a quandary, the Googoos soon learned to adopt a forthright, feisty tone when it came to protecting their territory. On 11 July 1850 Francis's brother Stephen Googoo upbraided Cape Breton's commissioner of Crown lands, H.W. Crawley, for failing to stop two more Scots farmers, Hugh Morrison and Donald McDonald, from trespassing on the Whycocomagh reserve.[12] Googoo wanted to know how Morrison and McDonald gained access, since the Mi'kmaq had complained several times to Crown Lands about unwelcome Scots taking up land on their reserve.

Crawley passed along Googoo's petition to the local Roman Catholic priest, Reverend J. Couteau. As he did so, he added that Googoo had been to see a lawyer, James McKeagney, who also was a member of the House of Assembly. McKeagney agreed to represent Googoo's claims if Couteau agreed to support his work on behalf of the Mi'kmaq and, presumably, pay his fees. Couteau must have demurred on this last point, for nothing more was heard of the matter.

Worse, the government failed to address Mi'kmaw grievances when incidents of violence erupted between the *We'koqma'q* band members and opportunistic settlers. On 17 November 1850 Chief Peter Googoo warned Crawley that squatters threatened to shoot any Mi'kmaq children found walking across their potato fields, even though their crops were cultivated on Mi'kmaw land.[13] When no replied ensued, the first memorial was followed by a second, directed to Halifax in January 1851.[14] On 24 January 1854 the Googoo brothers, along with a younger man named John Googoo[15] and heads of the Adley, Meuse, Newel, and Solomon families, petitioned Lieutenant Governor John Gaspard Le Marchant, declaring

that the Mi'kmaq at Whycocomagh were in danger of "totally losing their place."[16] When this memorial again met with no response, Peter and his associates sent a fourth memorial on 1 February 1855, holding that it was the government's responsibility to protect their lands.[17] Finally, Peter Googoo learned in March 1857 that the squatters had engaged three justices of the peace to petition the House of Assembly asking for the Mi'kmaq to be removed from Whycocomagh and for their reserve to be parcelled out among immigrant farmers.[18] While this did not happen, Nova Scotia's Crown land commissioner, Samuel Prescott Fairbanks, used his influence to have An Act Concerning Indian Reserves passed in 1859, which allowed for most of the tracts in question to be sold to squatters regardless of Mi'kmaw opposition.[19] Fairbanks justified his actions by stating that capital accruing from such sales would fund Mi'kmaq relief and hasten the promotion of an Indigenous farming settlement, although in the end few squatters ever paid for their lots.

Doubtless the government's implementation of An Act Concerning Indian Reserves was extremely discouraging to the chief. Considering his determined campaigns to preserve his people's land, Peter Googoo near the end of his life must have struggled with feelings of frustration and failure. When he died around 1860, the *We'koqma'q* Mi'kmaq lost a powerful champion of their rights. Not long afterwards, the Mi'kmaw community in Cape Breton turned to Grand Chief Francis Thoma Denny and the Grand Council to intervene with the government on their behalf. With the appearance of this new Mi'kmaq political entity on the scene, the settlers ceased their violent threats of the kind Peter Googoo had faced in the 1850s. Yet neither Nova Scotia nor, following Confederation, the federal government did anything for over one hundred years to compensate the Mi'kmaq for the land they lost between 1830 and 1860. Only since the 1970s has the federal government taken serious steps to try to rectify the We'koqma'q Mi'kmaq's outstanding land claims.[20]

– Janet E. Chute

<h1 style="text-align:center">35</h1>

Andrew Alex, Record Keeper

Andrew Alex, known to the Mi'kmaq as *Sipayikewa'j* or "The Travelling Man" (1849-1939), a farmer and fisherman, was the *Pu'tus* (*Putu's*) or record keeper for the Mi'kmaw Grand Council, as well as a prayer leader at Chapel Island, Richmond County, Cape Breton.[1] As a community historian and "archivist," he testified as a witness in the Sylliboy case of 1928 when Grand Chief Gabriel Sylliboy was arrested for taking furs out of season. Tall, lean, wiry, and sporting a bushy moustache, Andrew Alex was the fourth of his family to hold the office of record keeper, which descended in the male line. Being the *Pu'tus* made him privy to a semi-sacred body of information handed down for well over two centuries within the Mi'kmaq Grand Council, or *Mi'kmaw Mawio'mi*, the traditional political body of his nation.

Andrew Alex inherited the office of *Pu'tus* in the late nineteenth century on the death of his father Tuma, or "Thomas," Alex (1826–c.1880), who held the office before him. According to oral traditions passed down in the Alex family, Tuma Alex was the grandson of a man named Alexander *Skajjmen* (Scotchman) McDonald, said to have been the original record-keeping Mi'kmaw delegate at a council fire held in 1749 at Ka'nawa'ki (Kahnawaki or Caughnawaga), a Mohawk community located on the south shore of the St. Lawrence River not far from Montreal.[2] The hosts of the 1749 meeting were Mohawk from Ka'nawa'ki and Oka, also near Montreal, who had been enemies of the Mi'kmaq until 1701, when peace

was made between the nations.[3] Subjects raised for discussion at the Ka'nawa'ki forum included ways of maintaining harmony among the council attendees, appropriate and effective responses to the entrenchment of British colonial power in the Northeast following the founding of Halifax, and land issues. In addition to the Mi'kmaw delegates, representatives of three other Algonquian-speaking nations, the Penobscot, the Passamaquoddy, and the Malecite, attended. The Central Algonquian nations were represented by the Ottawa (or Odawa).

The 1749 meeting set the precedent for "gatherings of the same type" throughout the Northeast. Anthropologist Frank G. Speck called the ensuing institutionalized council fire the "Eastern Wabanaki Confederacy." Of all the nations participating in these councils, the Mi'kmaq were said to have joined last, and only reluctantly.[4] Grand Chief John Denny Jr. informed Speck in 1914 that confederacy delegates met every three years at different locations to discuss European intrusion onto Indigenous territory. By the 1840s, when confederacy meetings had become infrequent, the *Mi'kmawey Mawio'mi* turned its attention to challenges faced exclusively by the Mi'kmaw nation.

At the time of Tuma Alex's death around 1880, the body of distinctive knowledge pertaining to treaties and other affairs of importance to the entire Mi'kmaw nation had been transmitted patrilineally down the generations in the McDonald-Scotchman-Alex family for 130 years.[5] Tuma groomed his son Andrew to be *Pu'tus* after him by teaching Andrew to read syllabic script, preside at prayer meetings, and interpret the messages worked mnemonically into the weave of beaded wampum belts in the possession of the Grand Council. Andrew never attended school, but he was highly respected for his grasp of traditional knowledge. Though not affluent, by the time he became *Pu'tus* Andrew was economically stable; he owned a fishing boat on Bras d'Or Lake from which he marketed the fish he caught, and maintained a farm at *Potlotek* (Chapel Island). In 1881 he had a small wooden house, which a federal census called a "shanty," similar to all other Mi'kmaw dwellings on Chapel Island at the time,[6] as well as a barn. He kept a horse and a few cows and other farm animals and was known for his generosity in sharing milk and cream with his neighbours. Members of his family farmed, logged, worked for wage labour on the railway, and travelled seasonally to Maine to find employment during the potato and blueberry harvests.

When he was seventy years of age, he was called upon on 4 July 1928 to testify at a trial at Port Hood, Cape Breton, after Grand Chief Gabriel Sylliboy was arrested for taking muskrat peltry and a fox skin out of season. In the face of increasingly restrictive game laws and an unsympathetic governmental attitude towards Mi'kmaw treaty rights, Alex joined with other members of the Grand Council to put pressure on the province of Nova Scotia to incorporate the treaties into future wildlife legislation.[7] At first, fearing that whatever he said might be misconstrued in court, Andrew Alex hesitated to speak at length other than emphasizing that he was a farmer and fisherman who rarely hunted. He claimed, however, that the Mi'kmaq had the right to catch and sell fish at all seasons of the year. The *Pu'tus* added that when he was younger, he went to Sydney with his father Tuma to get blankets, flour, coats, ammunition, and hide for moccasins from "an Indian agent named Todd" (likely E.N. Dodd, a Cape Breton Indian commissioner). These goods, he contended, were not given as a form of relief, but as part of a treaty obligation assumed by the British government following the signing of a peace treaty with the Mi'kmaq in 1752. His family always received seed for planting in the spring, and no one ever interfered with their hunting and fishing activities. He held, as did the grand chief, that the Mi'kmaq retained treaty rights

to hunt, fish, and plant unmolested by settlers or government agents.[8] This was enshrined in what he and Sylliboy called the "English treaty," an old parchment peace and friendship treaty, which had been signed by Chief Peguidalouet of Unama'ki (Cape Breton) and the British administration in Halifax in 1760. The two Grand Council members stressed that ever since 1760 the Mi'kmaq had respected and upheld its provisions, and that they expected the government to similarly abide by its terms.[9]

In 1930 a well-known Halifax journalist, Clara Archibald Dennis, took several photographs of the *Pu'tus* at *Potlotek* wearing his Grand Council regalia and carrying articles associated with his office. In one picture, he displays a large white wampum belt incorporating a row of seven purple beaded squares, each with a white cross inside, said to represent the seven nations that participated in the first Eastern Wabanaki Confederacy council of 1749.[10] Andrew Alex was the last one who could read the message contained in the wampum belt in its entirety. There were other items of ceremonial and historical significance he had to tend to as well. A smaller wampum belt, a set of beads known as *l'nops'kuk*, or *l'naps'kuk*, that were said to date from the time of the Mi'kmaw-Mohawk peace treaty in the early eighteenth century,[11] a beaded sash, a pipe, a gold medallion with a yellow neck ribbon, and a large prayer book written in Mi'kmaw syllabics were all in *Pu'tus*'s custody.[12] When Nova Scotia, with Ottawa's backing, sought in the late 1930s to concentrate the entire Cape Breton Mi'kmaw population at Eskasoni, Andrew Alex moved from Chapel Island to Eskasoni shortly before his death. After he died in 1939, his eldest son, Isaac Alex, who still lived at Chapel Island, was expected to assume the office of *Pu'tus* and care for all the material paraphernalia that went with his new role.

Succession to office followed ancient protocols. It was only partly hereditary, since the grand chief and Grand Council had the final say in the selection process. After Andrew Alex's death, Grand Chief Gabriel Sylliboy recognized Isaac Alex as a suitable *Pu'tus*, since Isaac was a prayer leader, could read Mi'kmaw syllabics, and knew the extensive body of traditional lore needed to function competently as the Grand Council's record keeper. But times were also changing. Isaac travelled frequently to New England to seek wage labour. He married twice, first to a woman surnamed Marshall and then to Esther (or Ester) Paul. On 22 July 1934 Esther, living at Barra

Head, Chapel Island, gave birth to a son, Victor Alex, who at age eight in 1942 moved with his parents to Eskasoni. When Isaac Alex died in 1956, the grand chief, accompanied by Levi Poulette, a respected prayer leader, visited the Alex household at Eskasoni. Following the holding of the traditional wake, these leaders vested Victor Alex with his father's insignia of office:

My father [Isaac Alex] died on November 29, 1956 after being ministered to [or had prayers read over] by Grand Captain Simon Denny.[13] The next evening, the wake began with Grand Chief Gabriel Sylliboy and Levi Poulette leading with chants and prayers. My mother was present at well.

After the prayers, the Grand Chief took me to the kitchen along with Levi Poulette. He asked me in Mi'kmaw, "L'naps'kuk weskweyajik?" I said "e'e" or yes. He said "Jukwa'l" (Bring them). I went upstairs and opened my father's trunk and took a large white bag that contained the L'napskuk [literally, "the people's pebbles," referring to the wampum belts and beaded strings]. I brought them down to the kitchen table where the Grand Chief opened the bag and inspected the contents. He took out a little box and opened it and took out an [sic] gold coloured medallion with a gold coloured chain. Holding the medallion in his hands, he said to me "qama'si!" (Stand up!). He hung the medallion around my neck and said "Na!, neke'ki ki'ki'l Putu's" (There! Now you are Putu's). The Grand Chief, Levi Poulette and my mother took turns shaking my hand and then the two gentlemen left. The bag contained two beaded belts, a pipe, strings of l'napskuk, matches, tobacco, a map of some kind [reputedly with writing in French, English, and Mi'kmaw], a large shell that can be blown like a trumpet, a smaller shell with strings of L'napskuk attached to it, two items that looked like small drum sticks about a foot long, covered in leather and beaded with l'napskuk[,] and a large prayer book in the Mi'kmaw characters ("kɔmkwejwikasik").[14]

Victor's father, Andrew Alex, "often showed the l'napskuk to different visitors in Eskasoni and explained that they were a peace Treaty with the Kwetej [Mohawk] and other Lnu'k [Mi'kmaq]."[15] He also stated "When I die, it [the string of "people's pebbles"] will be passed down to the oldest living son." But just ovher a decade following Victor Alex's investiture as *Pu'tus*, a serious mishap occurred. In 1967, while Victor Alex was working in the United States, his mother Ester loaned the *Pu'tus*'s regalia – belts, beads, and other ceremonial items – to Chief Charles A. Francis of Eskasoni, who had recently been elected to the Native Advisory Council and was involved in a series of events connected with Expo '67.[16] Chief Francis promised to return the items to Ester at the St. Anne's mission on Chapel Island the following July, but before he could do so the regalia, belts, and other paraphernalia went missing.[17] Rumours spread that they were lost while being transported to Montreal for a ceremonial at Expo '67.[18] Immediately after their disappearance, someone other than Victor Alex temporarily assumed the role of *Pu'tus*, although when Ben Sylliboy became grand chief, Victor was re-invested with the office held by his ancestors.[19] The sixth member of his family in a direct line to hold the office of *Pu'tus*, Victor Alex, until his death on 16 March 2017, sought to ensure that the office of *Pu'tus* was valued and preserved. Unfortunately, despite extensive searches undertaken during his lifetime, the whereabouts of the Grand Council's *l'nops'kuk*, wampum belts, medallion, pipe, and other ceremonial items remains a mystery.

– Janet E. Chute, assisted by Victor Alex and
Marjorie Gould

36

Isaac Gabriel Sylliboy

Born on 18 August 1874 at Whycocomagh in the Mi'kmaw community of *Waycobah* (*We'koqma'q*) to John Sylliboy (or Syliboy) and Mary Barrington, Isaac Gabriel Sylliboy (1874–1964)[1] rose to prominence as a religious leader, politician, hunter, fisherman, and storyteller. In July 1918, at the age of forty-four, he also became the first elected grand chief of the Mi'kmaw nation. He was baptized at St. John the Baptist Church at Brook Village near Whycocomagh and raised a devoted Roman Catholic by his parents; local priests writing about him stressed his dutiful service in support of the Chapel Island mission each St. Anne's Day, on the 26th of July. Sylliboy became a prayer leader, as well as a caretaker for the mission chapel near St. Peter's, at a relatively early age. Yet when mentioning Sylliboy's religious accomplishments, local Roman Catholic clerics studiously avoided any references to the forceful political role he played as grand chief in taking a highly controversial stand in support of Mi'kmaw resource rights in 1927 and 1928. This penchant on the part of the priesthood to view the grand chief wholly in passive or symbolic terms, rather than in a proactive – and more realistic – political light, for many years deprived Sylliboy of the recognition he deserved in mainstream society as a strong and courageous fighter for Mi'kmaw interests despite formidable political odds. Only recently has a direct link been traced between Sylliboy's actions in the late 1920s and the results of a much later legal case, *R. v. Simon*, which in 1985 was settled in

favour of the Mi'kmaq after the defence adopted the same legal premises that Sylliboy had espoused fifty-eight years earlier.[2]

Sylliboy was never one to give up when things became difficult. As a young man he manifested a quiet, hard-working, and determined attitude towards life. He travelled seasonally with his father, mother, siblings, and other near relatives, among them his half-brother Simon Basque (his mother's son by her first marriage to Benjamin Basque), to Little Narrows near his home settlement on the Bras d'Or Lake to rake oysters for sale to local merchants. At other times he and his family fished, picked berries, and after late October hunted over the family's hunting and trapping territory near Askilton, in Inverness County, Cape Breton. Respected for his competence as a hunter and trapper in the woods, as well as his wisdom and honesty in dealing with his peers, he became a captain of the Grand Council. At this time, he began learning the traditions of his people from his father John Sylliboy, his godfather Lewis Newell, and the widow of Chief Peter Googoo of Whycocomagh, who was his godmother.

Gabriel Sylliboy was respectful of tradition, and yet his manner of exercising leadership of the Mi'kmaq nation would break new ground. Prior to his election at age forty-four as grand chief, the office of the Mi'kmaw grand chief had been hereditary. Succession had fallen to a son or close male relative of a deceased grand chief, after which the new leader's appointment would be ratified by the Grand

Council. Prior grand chiefs in Cape Breton had all been descendants of a mid-eighteenth-century leader named Thoma Denny, and most had lived at Eskasoni. By contrast, Sylliboy's family hailed from the Whycocomagh area and were closely kin-related to local leaders with the surnames "Newell," "Googoo," "Basque," and "Bernard."[3]

The circumstances surrounding Sylliboy's election in early July 1918 were unusual. His predecessor as grand chief, John Denny Jr., as he lay on his deathbed had dissuaded his son Simon Denny from aspiring to the grand chieftainship. Possibly Denny felt that following a revision of the federal Indian Act in 1880, which sought to impose an electoral system on Indigenous communities across Canada, the elective process inevitably would supplant hereditary succession among the Mi'kmaq. To try to buck the tide would be a losing proposition; better that the next grand chief be elected. Yet Denny also may have foreseen problems in gaining consensus support within the Mi'kmaw nation for one of his sons, since a Mi'kmaw contingent already had hived off Eskasoni in the 1860s to form the Kings Road settlement near Sydney, Cape Breton, after disagreeing with Denny's community policies. This controversy threatened the likelihood of strongly unified support for one of Denny's own heirs, and any lack of unanimity bothered the grand chief. He felt that the office of grand chief by 1918 needed broad-based support in order to survive. Though several prominent elders, as well as representatives of the Roman Catholic Church, principally Reverend D. Gillis of Antigonish, upheld Grand Chief Denny's decision to opt for an election, the succession question became a hotly contested issue. It drew the attention of Mi'kmaw leaders from Halifax, Pictou, Antigonish County, and southern Quebec. Several local chiefs contended that the electoral model was an imposition on the Mi'kmaq by outside agencies, but the majority eventually agreed to host elections.

In the end, with regard to the selection of a new grand chief, a compromise was struck between the new and old ways. An anonymous Mi'kmaq reporter provided a detailed description of Gabriel Sylliboy's installation ceremony in the 6 August 1918 issue of the *Setaneoei* or *Micmac Messenger*, published in Quebec by the Capuchin priest Father Pacifique. To placate the more traditional local element, the pool of contenders had to come exclusively from Cape Breton. These, moreover, could not run of their own

accord, but had to be selected by the Grand Council. Six high-profile community leaders were chosen: Francis Gould from Eskasoni, Samuel Noel Joe from Malagawatch, Steven Paul from *Po'tlotek* or Chapel Island, Isidore Pierro from Wagmatcook, Joseph C. Marshall from *Kijikank* (the Kings Road community in Sydney), and Gabriel Sylliboy from *We'koqma'q*. All met together on 22 July, four days before the commencement of the St. Anne's Day mission ceremonies on Chapel Island. Votes were cast into a large hat and were then counted under the shadow of a *gtjioigoom*, a pole structure covered with birch bark and tar paper. The crowd in attendance represented all the Mi'kmaw communities in the Atlantic region, and only adult males were permitted to vote. The electoral proceedings took three days, with the voting continuing until 11 p.m. of the third day.

Simon Sylliboy, Gabriel Sylliboy's son, years later remembered the Grand Council's captains explaining to him how ballots were taken to ensure the development of a spirit of consensus rather than merely a majority decision. Sylliboy won on the first round, with a large enough plurality of votes (the official count was sixty-seven) that further ballots were deemed unnecessary. The remainder of the investiture ceremony exhibited a syncretistic blend of Indigenous and Roman Catholic protocols. Father Pacifique, a Capuchin missionary from Restigouche, conducted mass, after which an engraved chief's medal was hung about Sylliboy's neck as he knelt at the altar. Sylliboy also wore a large silver cross. After the investiture, Chief Matthew Francis of Merigomish relayed greetings from Indigenous leaders who were attending from throughout the Mi'kmaw territory. Sitting on a chair within a space cordoned off by rope, Sylliboy then received these leaders graciously, one by one, as they bent to kiss his silver crucifix.

The annual St. Anne's Day procession took place in the afternoon of the following day. In the early evening, prayers were offered around a sacred fire, lit amid an assemblage of almost two thousand people. A Mi'kmaw auction or *salite* (derived from the Mi'kmaw pronunciation of the French word for "charity") raised eleven dollars – a sizable sum in those days – to give to surviving members of John Denny Jr.'s family, while plans were laid to erect a headstone over the former grand chief's grave at Eskasoni. Past and present thus flowed together in a seamless tide of goodwill, an auspicious beginning for the career of the newly installed grand chief.

Several of Sylliboy's former political rivals during the election accepted positions on the Grand Council, which was convened under the new leader's auspices. Noel Denny, Frank Gould, Frank Pierro, and Joseph Stevens became captains, and Andrew Alex (or Alek) of Chapel Island assumed the duties of *Putu's*, the speaker and record keeper whose role at Grand Council meetings included reading sacred wampum belts and what treaty documents the Grand Council possessed. A large tent was set up in from of the mission church at Chapel Island before St. Anne's Day expressly for this purpose. Sylliboy's half-brother Simon Basque was installed as grand captain, an office ranked one step below that of grand chief in the Mi'kmaw leadership hierarchy. As the installation ceremonies drew to a close, Chief Matthew Francis rose and delivered a speech intended to capture the positive, healing qualities of the occasion.[4]

Gabriel Sylliboy's actions over the next forty-five years would attract considerable attention from both mainstream and Indigenous society, for he was a man who had vowed to take his duties as grand chief seriously and carry them out energetically. He was expected to keep harmony within the Mi'kmaw community at large and not intervene in local affairs unless invited to do so by a band. When local leaders asked him for assistance, he tried to monitor the situation and rectify problems, while shielding the communities from unwanted outside interference. He sought out, heard, and meted out punishments to persons who had committed infractions. He presided over marriages, becoming a godparent to many, and lent political support to local chiefs although, unlike his predecessor John Denny Jr., he did not get directly involved in chiefs' appointments. Instead, he allowed the electoral system to prevail in keeping with the stipulations laid down in successive Indian Acts. He also actively supported the preference for the electoral system voiced by the Mi'kmaq who resided along the Kings Road and later moved to Membertou. Several members of this community were loggers or in occupations involving heavy industry, such as trimming coal. Grand Chief Sylliboy thus had to represent diverse interests by attending to the concerns of the traditional hunting and fishing Mi'kmaw sector as well as the more urbanized Mi'kmaw community.

The office of grand chief changed over time by assuming new and complex duties, though the institution of the grand chief and Grand Council,

known as the *Mi'kmawey Mawio'mi*, was distinctly Mi'kmaq in character and may have predated 1740.[5] In 1739, Abbé Pierre Maillard drafted a set of rules, or *règlements*, to guide the activities of chiefs as well as their constituents.[6] Translated by the abbé into ideographic script, these *règlements* were intended to ensure community harmony and punish infractions. Maillard expected the grand chief, in particular, to monitor the behaviour of persons under his charge. He also devised protocols so that a Mi'kmaw leader could preside over baptisms, marriages, and funerals in a priest's absence. Chief Sylliboy, like his predecessors, attended to these long-standing moral obligations, although he altered things here and there to fit with the changing times. Most important, he began to press for a continuation of a vital Indigenous resource rights movement begun in the late nineteenth century by Grand Chief John Denny Jr., a campaign that fell far outside the realm of interest and support of the Roman Catholic clergy.

Sylliboy's predecessor, John Denny Jr., had endeavoured to consolidate Mi'kmaw land holdings throughout the Atlantic Provinces under the Grand Council's jurisdiction in order to protect them against settler infringements, to enable an effective, integrated use of resources from all reserve lands for the benefit of the entire Mi'kmaq nation. His hopes were dashed in 1911 when the Kejimkujik reserve he had sought to preserve from outside encroachment was leased to non-Indigenous individuals and groups by the government and the timber and other resources on it sold to outside agencies. Within ten years Mi'kmaq found themselves facing charges of transgressing game laws, already restrictive on the Nova Scotia mainland and by 1927 beginning to be rigidly enforced on Cape Breton Island.

In response, the Grand Council launched an investigation into the nature of the warnings and arrests, and several leading Mi'kmaq individuals in different parts of Nova Scotia deliberately hunted or fished out of season in order to elicit test cases for the validity of treaties signed between the British Crown and the Mi'kmaq in 1752, 1760, and 1761 that were supposed to form hedges against outside infringements on Mi'kmaq resource rights. In July 1927 William Labrador was tried and convicted before a magistrate in the Lunenburg County Court for fishing salmon at Bridgewater out of season.[7] In the fall of the same year, Grand Chief Gabriel Sylliboy was apprehended under the Nova Scotia Lands and Forest Act, on a charge of taking fourteen muskrat and one fox fur out of season on his family's long-standing hunting territory at Askilton, south of Whycocomagh. Much of this hunting territory in 1927 lay on private land, the farm of Alex Gillies, who objected to what he saw as Mi'kmaw intrusions onto his property. Both Labrador and Sylliboy argued that their arrests were in contravention of their treaty rights. Provision Four of the 1752 treaty, which granted its Mi'kmaw signers "free liberty of hunting and fishing as usual," they argued, was still in force. They knew the treaty well, since it was undoubtedly one of the treaty documents read publicly during the St. Anne's Day festivities each year on Chapel Island. The following March, a delegation of chiefs from throughout Mi'kma'ki descended on Ottawa to secure the Department of Indian Affairs' support for their cause, and Frank Pedley, the department's deputy secretary, proved sympathetic. Soon after meeting with the Mi'kmaw representatives, Pedley directed a letter on 24 March 1928 to Nova Scotia premier E.N. Rhodes stating that the delegates "informed me that the Indians have never been interfered with in taking game until recently, and it has occurred to me that possibly this persecution is due to the fact that some of the recently appointed game wardens may not be aware of the privileges that the Indians have always enjoyed under this Treaty."[8]

Grand Chief Sylliboy and his associates appealed their arrest for hunting out of season before Acting County Court Judge George Patterson in the courthouse at Port Hood, Inverness County, Cape Breton, on 4 July 1928. During the ensuing Sylliboy (or Syliboy) case, Patterson contended that the 1752 treaty, which, he acknowledged, granted the Mi'kmaq rights to fish and hunt, failed to extend to Cape Breton's Mi'kmaq because, he held, it was signed exclusively between the British and leaders of the Shubenacadie band. Any hunting and fishing rights would only pertain to the small Sipekne'katik Mi'kmaw group. The judge then convicted Chief Sylliboy and his associates for contravention of provincial game laws, claiming that Mi'kmaq individuals retained such a minor status under British law that any Mi'kmaq group must be seen as totally incompetent to sign binding pacts, especially as early as 1752.[9] Patterson's judgments on both counts subsequently were overturned in 1985 with the Supreme Court's recognition in *R. v. Simon* that the treaty of 1752 not only continues to hold legal weight but is not restricted solely to the Shubenacadie band.

William C. Wicken, in referring to the final ruling in *R. vs. Syliboy* (1929),[10] points out that Judge Patterson gathered oral testimonies from the grand chief and several Cape Breton community elders in 1928, and then tended to ignore what those interviewed were saying. Five elders testified: Andrew Alex, Andrew Bernard, Ben Christmas, Joe Christmas, and Francis Gould. Joseph Christmas, a man of seventy-four years of age who had been grand captain under Grand Chief John Denny Jr., and later chief of the North Sydney band, stated that the Mi'kmaq practised conservation in their hunting and used what they caught to support themselves. Captain Francis Gould, who was the same age as Christmas, further held that Mi'kmaw rights throughout the Maritimes were upheld by the 1752 treaty. Similar comments were made by *Pu'tus* Andrew Alex from St. Peter's and Andrew Bernard, both seventy-eight years of age. These Elders were supported in their claims by Joseph Christmas's son, Ben Christmas, the chief at Kings Road and later of Membertou.

Gabriel Sylliboy argued that he had hunted and fished for thirty-four years on his family hunting territory and had never been arrested in the past. He further emphasized that he was "sort of a king" among the Mi'kmaq, with six sub-chiefs under him, and was responsible for upholding and protecting Mi'kmaw rights. All the testifiers stressed that they had always perceived that the goods, gifts, and honorifics given to them in the past by various government agencies were a consequence of a treaty signing, most particularly the treaty signed at Halifax in 1752, and not mere forms of relief. They were proofs of an ongoing treaty connection between themselves, both as Grand Council members and Mi'kmaw community leaders, and the Crown.[11]

Sylliboy explained in his testimony that he had told the arresting officer he possessed a copy of the original Treaty of 1752, yet, strangely, the county court in 1928 made no attempt to have the Grand Council produce such intriguing evidence.[12] Halifax journalist Clara Archibald Dennis in the early 1940s claimed that the grand chief showed her an old treaty document, as well as a wampum belt and an ornamented pipe. "We get it [the treaty] from the King long ago and keep it and honour it and serve it and follow it," the chief at the time explained to Dennis.[13] This document was either an original copy of the 1752 treaty or the treaty document given by Lieutenant Governor Jonathan Belcher to Chief Jeannot Peguidalouet of Cape Breton on 25 June 1761.[14] All the members of the Grand Council firmly believed that their rights were enshrined in treaty, despite the court decision's claims to the contrary. Dennis also maintained that the grand chief possessed wampum that mnemonically depicted the nature of reciprocal responsibilities between the Grand Council and various Mi'kmaq communities throughout the Atlantic Provinces, for the grand chief's authority extended far beyond the borders of Cape Breton Island. "The wampum belt was of leather, thickly ornamented with white and coloured beads," she observed. "Every pattern on the belt, the chief said, represented an Indian reserve – Shubenacadie, Pictou, Kedgemakooge [*sic*, Kejimkujik], Sissiboo, Bear River, Shelburne, Melrose, St. Mary's Bay, and others. All were there in the beads."[15] It was said to have been made at the time of the resolution of a conflict between the "Mohawk and the Mi'kmaq" about sixty-nine years before.

Despite the disappointing court ruling on Mi'kmaw hunting rights, Sylliboy attempted to preserve the Mi'kmaq community's lands, resources, and sacred spaces from further encroachment. He discouraged non-Indigenous visitors from visiting St. Anne's Day festivities on Chapel Island, known in French colonial times as Île de Saint Famille. By the early 1930s many outsiders had come to regard St. Anne's Day as little more than an exotic spectacle. When droves of tourists began to upset the dignity of the occasion, the grand chief demanded that non-Indigenous parties first ask his permission to view the ceremonies. He solicited financial assistance to support the dignity of the mission, especially during the Depression years. A press release in 1932 stated that, prior to Bishop James Morrison sending Father Leo J. Keats, the local priest from St. Peter's, to the Mi'kmaq with funds and letters of moral support, Chief Sylliboy, Benjamin Christmas, and John Gould seriously thought of temporarily cancelling the mission owing to insufficient monetary resources.

While his faith in the Roman Catholic Church remained strong, Chief Sylliboy by 1944 had become increasingly suspicious of government policies involving the Mi'kmaq. And he had good reason to be cautious. In 1942 Ottawa implemented a centralization policy intended to remove the Mi'kmaq of Nova Scotia to two growth centres, Shubenacadie on the Nova Scotian mainland and Eskasoni in Cape Breton.[16] When Sylliboy and Grand Captain Simon Denny initially agreed to support the government's

stance despite opposition to the policy from many other Mi'kmaw community leaders, they soon found that the government's promises of assistance to the Mi'kmaw community were largely vacuous. The rationale behind centralization was the government's desire to encourage the Mi'kmaw to vacate lands wanted by the non-Indigenous community. There was no follow up to ensure that any long-term benefits would accrue to the affected Mi'kmaq. Chief Sylliboy, who had been one of the first to remove to Eskasoni in 1942, found that that overpopulation quickly depleted the resources upon which the isolated East Bay Mi'kmaw community formerly had relied. Members of the Sylliboy, Cremo, and Cape Breton Phillips families resisted moving and also were able to prevent the razing of the *Waycobah* community church. Meanwhile Eskasoni's population soared from 257 to 533 individuals in just two years. Work became scarce while community resources dwindled. Worse, when Sylliboy and his immediate family visited their former residence in Whycocomagh in 1944, they found that the government had burned down their house, as well as the homes of their neighbours. When approached for an interview by folklorist Helen Creighton in 1944, he was living in nearby Nyanza. After 1945 he lived at Eskasoni and Sydney.

Disillusionment with the federal government after 1944 compelled the grand chief to become highly protective of the communities under his aegis. Non-Mi'kmaw outsiders were screened and occasionally denied admittance to ceremonies. This was a far cry from the warm welcome Helen Creighton had received just two years previously. By 1949 even a graduate student in anthropology from the University of Pennsylvania named Sheila Steen was having a hard time gaining admittance to view the St. Anne's festivities.[17] It was only on the recommendation of Chief Ben Christmas of Membertou that Sylliboy eventually recanted and granted Steen permission to stay and watch.[18]

The grand chief's stance also influenced the activities of the local mission priest, who occasionally tried to prevent persons who were not Mi'kmaq and not Roman Catholic from coming to Chapel Island. Visitors only found their welcome secure if they first sought admittance from the grand chief. Those with close attachments to the Mi'kmaw community were also expected to act with decorum at St. Anne's Day ceremonies or risk expulsion from the vicinity of the mission by the grand chief and council. In one instance Sylliboy asked a drunken non-Indigenous man married to a Mi'kmaw woman to leave the island for a spell; upon his return in a sober state, the man had to endure lengthy chastisements from the grand chief and members of the Grand Council, who warned the repentant individual never again to appear on Chapel Island's sacred ground in an inebriated state.[19]

The grand chief throughout his life upheld the customary laws of the Mi'kmaq community. When Sylliboy met with a Mi'kmaq who had broken the law, he weighed the facts of the case carefully and delivered a judgment on the spot. He also distributed formal moral injunctions to listeners whenever large crowds gathered together, such as at the church door following Sunday services. His duties in this regard extended to speaking with the children, especially young boys, regarding individual responsibilities to their families and the community at large. When some teenage boys broke a window in a man's house, the grand chief made the boys not only replace the window but also provide firewood for all the community's elderly. In another instance, a couple drank heavily and failed to provide for their young children. After the two had repeatedly been warned about this behaviour by members of the Grand Council, the grand chief asked the local band constable to take the children away from the couple. The children were not pressured to leave the community, but were sent to reside temporarily with families of Grand Council members. This sanctioning was effective, for the couple stopped drinking and began to take their responsibilities as parents seriously. Only where there was a proven serious contravention of the law would the grand chief and Grand Council consider turning a perpetrator over to a federal policing agency.

Grand Chief Sylliboy fulfilled his duties with dedication to the traditional Mi'kmaq tenets that he cherished. Though he apparently never attended school – although this is not certain – he exhibited exceptional intellectual acumen and could communicate fluently in Mi'kmaq, as well as haltingly in three other languages, English, French, and Gaelic. His intellectual abilities, and the fact that he was curious and willing to engage in new things, gained him widespread admiration.[20] Throughout his term in office Sylliboy maintained the Grand Council as a valid political, religious, and social entity. In keeping

with distinctive Mi'kmaw values, he and his family made room in their home for the poor, the needy, the oppressed, and the orphaned. He became a godfather to many, non-Indigenous as well as Mi'kmaq; one of his godchildren, James MacDonald, became bishop of Charlottetown. He also compelled those who wronged others, no matter who they were, to make reparations to those they had injured. Sylliboy consequently was highly respected by young and old. He became a listening ear and wise advisor to many, and inspired deep respect and religious devotion in those who attended his lectures at the church door or on the podium on St. Anne's Day.[21] Warm humour also permeated his words whenever he ascended a dais to speak: "*E'he, muin toqjua'tl stepl a'*: the bear is climbing the stairs," he used to proclaim.[22]

Following Sylliboy's death on 4 March 1964, a heated controversy arose over whether or not the grand chieftainship should once again be guided by principles of hereditary succession, since, prior to Sylliboy's election in 1918, the Denny Thoma family had held the office for over two centuries. This dispute was eventually resolved in favour of electoral succession. The selection process for grand chiefs henceforth eschewed hereditary factors. Sylliboy left three sons and five daughters, but to succeed in the future to the grand chieftainship, their fitness for the office, like that of their competitors, would have to be decided by vote.[23] Sylliboy's successor, Donald Marshall Sr. (1925–91), a son of Joseph Marshall and grandson of Charles Marshall of Sydney, was elected grand chief in July 1964 and continued to uphold the values and goals Gabriel Sylliboy cherished among those carrying on Sylliboy's campaign for recognition of treaty rights.

Though discouraged by his failure to secure justice on the issue of Mi'kmaw hunting and fishing rights in his lifetime, Gabriel Sylliboy and his campaign for treaty rights set a lasting precedent for future legal action.[24] In 1985, as noted above, the Supreme Court of Canada confirmed the existence of Indigenous treaty rights on the same legal premises introduced in the courts by Grand Chief Sylliboy many years before. In February 2017 the grand chief received a posthumous pardon for the charges once unjustly laid against him, as well as a formal apology from Nova Scotia and the Queen's representative, the lieutenant governor, for the dismissive attitude towards treaty rights evinced by Canada's legal system in 1928.[25]

Despite formidable odds, Gabriel Sylliboy built on the work of earlier Indigenous leaders who devised creative land policies and presided over long-standing land and resource campaigns in different parts of the Northeast. Their drive consolidated a program of thought and action that eventually informed a Mi'kmaw hunting rights case brought by James Simon in 1985, which then escalated into a movement for fishing rights on unceded Indigenous lands spearheaded in August 1993 by Donald Marshall Jr. (1953–2009), the son of Grand Chief Donald Marshall Sr. Donald Marshall Jr.'s determination to test the field of legal interpretation and break new ground gave rise to the Marshall II ruling, allowing Mi'kmaq to harvest a moderate livelihood from local resources. This could never have happened without the strength of resolve shown by earlier Mi'kmaw leaders like Chief Sylliboy, whose impact on the Northeast eventually breached regional geographic boundaries and influenced the future of Indigenous rights across Canada.[26]

– Janet E. Chute, assisted by Mary-Ellen Googoo and Alison Lloy

Part Six

Mi'kmaw Worldview

Mi'kmaw Worldview

The notion of worldview is a vast one, but essentially it can be defined as the way members of a culture perceive and act; it pertains to their philosophy based on their own unique sensibility. Spiritual beliefs, social life and customs, cultural beliefs and values, all stem from a shared worldview. Much of this is connected to the whole complex of factors that influence the form and ability of a people to survive, in the case of the Mi'kmaq a hunting and migratory pattern of life. Mi'kmaw groups moved over the landscape depending on the seasonal distribution of resources within their land, *Mi'kma'ki.* There were places and seasons for hunting, spear fishing, taking water fowl, and eeling. "The Mi'kmaq's understanding of their natural context establishes the vantage point from which they construct their worldview, language, knowledge and order."[1] The relationship the Mi'kmaq have with the natural environment is the foundation on which their worldview, ways of knowing, and language are based.[2]

This worldview is closely tied to the topography of the land, the water that provides both food and a ready mode of travel, the sky and constellations for ease of navigation, the plants and animals with which they live and upon which they depend. Cultural habits gradually evolved that were, and still are, central to the way the Mi'kmaq lived on the land and that sharply delineated their attitude from that of the Europeans who would arrive later. The land and its resources were to be shared and to

be respected. According to Peter Christmas, "Our worldview determined our behaviour and the way we interacted with nature. A fundamental belief was that the creator was the giver and regulator of life."[3] The Mi'kmaq and Malecite progressively devised creative ways "to use nature's resources so that nothing was wasted."[4]

Along with the importance of respect for the land is the idea that resources are not limitless and need to be used judiciously. The Mi'kmaw word *netuku-limk* – "provisioning" – means one takes only what one needs from the natural world.[5] In that sense, the Mi'kmaq truly were in the vanguard of the contemporary environmental movement. Unlike Western ecological theory, however, the Mi'kmaq acted more from the premise that the animate and inanimate were all equal components of the greater whole, of nature. Leaving behind a resource for one's children's children is more a construct of Western thought; that a rock, stream, or forest is part of nature and must be protected for its own sake no less than the animal or the human is more closely tied to the Mi'kmaw worldview. As Mi'kmaw Elder Albert Marshall has said, "So this is what we truly believe. This is what reinforces our spiritualities: that no being is greater than the next, that we are part and parcel, we are equal, and that each one of us has a responsibility to the balance of the system."[6]

The concept of kinship, consanguinity, and especially the extended family is intrinsic to the Mi'kmaw view of the ordered universe. Leah Rosenberg has written in her book *Mikwite'lmanej Mikmaqi'k – Let Us Remember the Old Mi'kmaq* that "*nikmatut* expresses relationships of family and community – that which is related. Many of these relationships extend to distant places. For Mi'kmaq these relationships are not just biological, but cultural and spiritual. More than anything else, *nikmatut* – relationships between family and friends – define Mi'kma'ki."[7] So along with a connection to the environment is the connection to each other – a connection placed under significant stress in post-contact times by what has been aptly termed the "denial of the fundamental human significance of Aboriginal peoples."[8] Yet despite the influence of non-Indigenous society this closeness remains one of the chief markers of Mi'kmaw culture. The Mi'kmaq still drop everything to travel hundreds of miles to attend the funeral and *salite* (a feast and auction within the community that provides emotional and financial assistance to the bereaved)[9] and even to renew a tenuous family connection. This contrasts sharply with current North American trends where convenience and the pressures of the work schedule hold greater sway.

Among the Mi'kmaq certain rules of protocol apply without necessarily being verbalized. The principles of non-interference and teaching by example both imply respect for another person. Approved behaviours in the community are encouraged by social means rather than through punishment. This philosophy is connected to the ideals of balance, harmony, and respect that comprise the worldview.

A prime tenet of Mi'kmaw culture is the language. Language and religious experience are inextricably connected, and according to Mi'kmaw linguist Bernie Francis, the "greater part of [Mi'kmaw] spirituality is embedded in our language."[10] Angela Robinson in her study of Mi'kmaw religion *Ta'n Teli-ktlamsitasit* (*Ways of Believing*), undertaken at Eskasoni, cites language as a "source for reclaiming, retaining, and reconstructing original Mi'kmaw ideas and beliefs."[11] Mi'kmaq is a distinctive language within the Eastern Algonquian language group, which includes Maliseet and Passamaquoddy. It is holophrastic – a single Mi'kmaw word may mean an entire phrase in English, is verb rather than noun based, shows gender depending upon a noun's context, and distinguishes between animate and inanimate nouns and verbs. Everything is "more or less animate" and therefore may have "spirit and knowledge."[12] This again is

closely tied to the idea of the connecting thread that runs through the different elements in nature, which is so integral to the Mi'kmaw worldview. It is easier to form a bond with something that has "spirit," and to be responsible for something that has "knowledge," than to care deeply for that which is viewed as inanimate. If one sees a lake as a living entity, it becomes more difficult to pollute it. The Mi'kmaw language frames and identifies an understanding of this relationship, this connection.

This is evident in names given to certain places by the Mi'kmaq. The name could indicate something about a particular area's unique features or how the Mi'kmaq related to it. Falls near Fredericton, New Brunswick, were called *Chigunikpe* – "the roaring, destroying giant," while *Wagwak*, meaning "it ends; the utmost limit," was the Mi'kmaw name for Egmont Bay, Prince Edward Island.[13] Mi'kmaw place names are considered to be verbs rather than nouns and consequently can reflect a changing environment in a way Western, noun-based, and more static languages can't.[14]

Another significant component of the Mi'kmaw worldview is its concept of time. In Western thought time is linear – moving in a straight line – with the future a point somewhere ahead. In the Mi'kmaw world, and commonly among many Indigenous groups, time (rather like their verbs) is more flexible and evinces more fluidity. Certain activities may be postponed because the time *is not right*. As Leroy Little Bear so succinctly puts it, "Time is part of the constant flux but goes nowhere. Time just is."[15]

Perhaps the most pervasive aspect of the Mi'kmaw worldview is the sense of spirituality. The spiritual is part of everyday existence, with little differentiation between the natural and the supernatural.[16] The universe has a prevailing, animating spirit called *mntu*. In later years this would have pejorative associations. In his dictionary Albert De Blois defines the word *mntu* as "devil,"[17] but in pre-contact times *mntu* simply meant the spiritual life force and had no demonic connotations.[18] As the spiritual life force is dynamic and creative, Sákéj[19] Youngblood Henderson holds that *mntu* might be better thought of as a verb than a noun.[20]

In Mi'kmaw cosmology apparently contradictory views could be held simultaneously. When Roman Catholicism spread among the Mi'kmaw people after the baptism of Membertou in 1610, it was still common to maintain the old beliefs, especially with regard to supernatural beings. The two belief systems held synchronous positions. Based on her research at Eskasoni, Robinson maintains that "what is understood as Mi'kmaw spirituality or culture informs the way in which Roman Catholicism is believed and practiced … there are commonly and continually practiced elements of Mi'kmaw spirituality that are separate from the teachings and beliefs of the Roman Catholic Church. However, these Mi'kmaw spiritual and religious teachings do not necessarily negate those of the Church. There are both points of convergence and points of departure between Catholicism and non-Christian Mi'kmaw faith."[21] And though many aspects of traditional Mi'kmaw life are no longer part of the culture, other elements remain an essential part of it – among these language, hieroglyphics, and stories and legends.[22]

When we compare the apocryphal tales of Western society to Mi'kmaw legends, obvious differences between the two become apparent. Western tales can be moralistic or mainly entertaining. By contrast, Mi'kmaw stories are often etiological, meant to explain something in familiar terms, or euhemeristic, containing supernatural elements believed to be true.[23] In the nineteenth century the Baptist missionary to the Mi'kmaq, Reverend Silas Tertius Rand, collected many legends that remain part of Mi'kmaw culture. *Niskam*, the sun, represented by the east and the colour red, was associated with the "Great Creator" and is a constant in Mi'kmaw traditional stories.[24] Sky beings were thought to inhabit a world above the stars, and they were endowed with great powers. Other tales involved medicine men, some with unpredictable powers (such a medicine man is called a *puowin*), who had magical abilities to varying degrees, particularly in regard to visions and water divination. The most powerful among them manifested amazing longevity and could foretell the future. As such, the *puowin* who did not use his powers in fearsome or unpredictably ways, and who felt a responsibility towards the welfare of his people, was held in great esteem and his advice sought and followed.[25] A *kinap* was a person with a notable aptitude for a particular activity based on supernatural power. The *kinap* might demonstrate great prowess in running or hunting or be especially strong. Possession of such a marked talent was often hidden in the *kinap's* youth, as it was thought too great a show of power at a young age would lead to early death.

A key figure in a Mi'kmaw *atukwaqan* or story of ancient times was the larger-than-life culture hero *Klu'skap*. Though he was not the Creator, he was an immensely significant figure whose adventures featured prominently in etiological legends. He was often portrayed as a teacher, transformer of the landscape, prophet, and even as a trickster. His home was in caves at Cape Dauphin, on Kelly's Mountain, Cape Breton, where he lived with "Grandmother" and Little Marten, his younger brother. Many of the stories surrounding *Klu'skap* help to explain the geography of the surrounding land. In fact, according to legend, the profile of *Klu'skap's* grandmother can be seen in the rock formation at Cape Dauphin (also known as the "Fairy Hole"), and when this rock gets wet it presages severe rains. This area has long been considered sacred to the Mi'kmaq, and as such helped to fuel Mi'kmaw resistance to a proposed rock quarry on Kelly's Mountain in the 1990s.

As the twenty-first century progresses, a mix of both the modern and the traditional has surfaced in Mi'kmaw culture, and indeed, the emergence of what has been termed "neo-traditionalism" is incorporated into contemporary life. Current neo-traditional Mi'kmaw teachings hold that there are seven gifts associated with the seven stages of life, which are considered to be love, honesty, humility, respect, truth, patience, and wisdom. When someone displays all these attributes, that person is considered an Elder. There are four sacred colours, and according to Mi'kmaw Elder and educator Murdena Marshall, "colours contribute to approximately ninety per cent of our [Mi'kmaw] perception of life."[26] Each colour is associated with a direction. Black is west and the spiritual world; yellow is south, where warm breezes emanate from and where life is renewed through the cycles; red is east, signifying the rising sun and the new day; and white is north, reserved for Elders and children under seven years of age. All colours are verbs, so that the Mi'kmaw word for white, *wape'k*, means "in the process of being white" and resonates with the idea of movement, change, and fluidity.

For the Mi'kmaw person the spiritual life is essential to one's well-being. Ideally this is reflected in the way the Mi'kmaq govern themselves based on their worldview in which respect for the individual, society, and all of nature is a guiding principle. The force of the spiritual life enables the Mi'kmaw man or woman to care for the other, whether that other be a child, an adult, or the environment. Because the Mi'kmaq have retained their language, other Indigenous groups (such as the Bhutanese) look to them to see how they have been able to preserve so many traditions. As well, Western thought has at last moved in the direction of acceptance of and respect for Indigenous knowledge systems. Many university programs, in particular at Cape Breton University, integrate Western and Mi'kmaw scientific thought into a single educational model, each enhancing the other. The resilience, strength, and perseverance of the Mi'kmaw worldview, embodying flux and movement, has enabled the Mi'kmaq to adapt to changing times while holding on to the essence of what makes an ancient culture a living, breathing entity in a contemporary realm. James Sákéj Youngblood Henderson perhaps put it best when he wrote, "The Aboriginal worldview may be understood from four complementary perspectives: as a manifestation of Aboriginal language; as a specialized knowledge system; as a unity with many diverse consciousnesses; and as a mode of social order, law, and solidarity. Each perspective of the worldview is learned, not genetically or racially encoded."[27]

– Diane Chisholm

Afterword

This volume was written with multiple audiences in mind. It was designed to encourage Mi'kmaw university students to become involved in researching and writing their people's history, with the intent of informing others about the lives of notable Indigenous individuals from previous centuries. It offers detailed genealogical data for those wishing to trace their own family trees, and provides a long and up-to-date bibliography of sources readers can utilize to further their own studies. The notes were written to have maximum explanatory value for academic and non-academic alike, so that readers would have the knowledge necessary to access original documents should they wish to learn more. Notes include descriptions of encampments, hunting grounds, fishing locales, and ceremonial sites used by the Mi'kmaq over the years so that interested readers can travel to and tour the landscape with an eye to what transpired in the past. Some Indigenous students, whose ancestors were associated with certain sites, enjoyed this exercise and found it elicited new questions about their ancestors' way of life.

Some of the individuals selected for biographical treatment here have not previously been written about at any length, although major strides have been made in the last forty years towards producing well-researched Mi'kmaw personal histories. The *Dictionary of Canadian Biography* contains entries on Membertou, Jean-Baptist Arimph, Peter Toney Babey, Philip Bernard, John Noel Cope, Charles Glode, Gabriel Glode, Jerry Lonecloud, Peminuit (or Peminout) Paul, Jacques-Pierre Peminuit Paul, Mary Christianne Paul, and Peter Wilmot. Authors include Sandy Balcom, Father Clarence-J. d'Entremont, Anne Marie Lane Jonah, Bunny McBride, Virginia Miller, Dianne O'Neil, L.F.S. Upton, Ruth Whitehead, and William C. Wicken. Complementing these entries are autobiographical works by Mi'kmaw authors, among them Richard McEwan, Missel Joe, Daniel Paul, Victor Gloade, Isabelle Knockwood, Douglas Knockwood, and Dorothy Moore, to name just a few. Mi'kmaw film-makers furthermore have taken an interest in recording the activities of members of their communities.

The individuals selected here for biographical treatment were born between the late 1690s and the close of the nineteenth century. Several well-known traditional Mi'kmaw Elders, all born after 1916, assisted with this project, although their personal biographies are not included therein. Some shared poignant memories of the consequences of the insidious ideology that underlay the operation of the residential school system between 1930 and 1967. Others, living in Nova Scotia, recounted how their families, under the government centralization scheme, had to relocate to centres where population numbers soon outstripped resources. Following the collapse of centralization, the 1950s and 1960s saw the rise of a number of extraordinary women in the fields of business, politics, and education. Their ability to retain prominence within both Mi'kmaw and mainstream society testified to the sound principals, many of them Indigenous in origin, upon which they founded their careers. John Knockwood's wife at Shubenacadie, Theresa ("Tessa") Knockwood, was a skilled artisan; Alice Mitchell of Rocky Point, Prince Edward Island, in the late nineteenth century stood up for Indigenous land rights and promoted Mi'kmaw education; and Elsie Charles Basque was a crusader for Indigenous rights and an educationalist. Women active from the mid-twentieth century and into the twenty-first who immediately come to mind include Josie Augustine, Marie Battiste, Sarah Denny, Caroline Gould, Marjorie Gould, Margaret "Dr. Granny" Johnson, Cathy Martin, Madeline Martin, Lillian Marshall, Murdena Marshall, and Viola Robinson. Some of the older individuals have passed, but younger women are taking up the torch, making impacts in a range of fields. In the future their activities will warrant biographical treatment.

Historic events in this study were examined in the light of how they affected the lives of various individuals, an exercise that gave rise to new courses of enquiry. One such question focused on a resistance fighter known in the documentary record simply as "Labrador." Labrador, an Acadian or *métis* who spoke Mi'kmaq and wore Indigenous dress, after 1754 sought refuge from the British on coastal lands lying between Chester and the Aspotogan Peninsula on Nova Scotia's South Shore. From there, he joined raiding expeditions, among them one mustered on the Saint John River in the spring of 1756 by Charles Deschamps de Boishébert et de Raffatot. Yet Labrador also single-handedly and strategically attacked Lunenburg settlers. Why then, near the close of the Seven Years War, did he achieve the freedom to hunt and trade in Lunenburg County when other resistance fighters, such as those hailing from the Petitcodiack River Valley, or even members of his own close kin group, were rounded up and deported by the British? The fact that Labrador could reintegrate himself within Lunenburg society by divesting himself of "problematic" Acadian traits and allowing his name to be placed on a Mi'kmaw band list warrants more study. He must have played an active role in this transition, rather than submitting passively to colonial fiat that relegated him to membership within the "colonial ghost" constituency.[1]

Other perplexing findings were uncovered. One involved the inclusion of lineal (Acadian) social organizational traits by the early nineteenth century within traditionally generationally structured Mi'kmaw communities. Yet another stems from evidence that French and Acadians in the seventeenth and eighteenth centuries rarely penetrated to the headwaters of large salmon rivers. If Chief Joseph Claude of Listuguj, Quebec, speaking in 1786 to Sir Guy Carlton, is to be believed, the French from Nicolas Deny's time in the seventeenth century and onward relied to a great extent on the Mi'kmaq to furnish them with riverine fish for commercial purposes. In 1768 a British merchant, Commodore George Walker, entered this exchange system, leaving it fundamentally unchanged until the collapse in 1778 of his trading establishment at Nepisiguit. A second intriguing revelation showed that Acadians and Acadian *métis* in the Ste. Anne du Ruisseau region of Yarmouth County recognized Mi'kmaw prior rights to riverine fish, especially eels, and "paid" for the right to fish at certain locales.

More investigation also should focus on the degree of assistance the Mi'kmaq, following the close of the Seven Years War, rendered Acadian and British settlers experiencing hardship, among them the Deveau family of Digby County in the late eighteenth century and the New Ross settlers of Lunenburg County in the early nineteenth century. Mi'kmaw leaders guided the responsible management and sharing of resources that lay under their aegis. This practice conforms with the tenets of *Netukulimk*, a spiritual as well as practical perspective that focuses on proper ways of acknowledging, protecting, managing, and distributing the bounty provided by the Creator. It currently forms a guiding principle in Indigenous discussions of Indigenous sovereignty, but it is hundreds – if not thousands – of years old. From the seventeenth to the nineteenth century, Acadians and Acadian-*métis* residing in the vicinity of Ste. Anne du Ruisseau of present-day Yarmouth County, Nova Scotia, understood, heeded, and respected its tenets.

As this study demonstrates, Mi'kmaw individuals fought in colonial wars, signed treaties, participated in diplomatic councils, challenged settler intrusion on their lands, resisted the imposition of colonial policies deleterious to their people, and launched extensive land and resource campaigns. Mi'kmaw society was inclusive, and leaders could be recruited from a variety of backgrounds. Groups included prominent individuals who had been born French, Acadian, British, and occasionally Black. Other members were petty traders and military deserters who, after a period of "Indigenization" initiated by chiefs or head men, joined groups. There were also leaders who borrowed selected aspects of thought and material culture from settler life while firmly holding on to cherished Mi'kmaw traditions. Competent Mi'kmaw actors and spokespersons shaped events, and their stories contain instances of exemplary leadership that will remain an inspiration for others for many years to come.

Abbreviations

AAQ	Archives de l'Archevêché de Québec, Quebec
AC	Archives des Colonies, Paris, France
AFL	Archives of Fort Louisbourg Historic Park
ANOM	Archives de Nationales d'Outre Mer, Aix-en-Province, France
AR	British Admiralty Records, London, England
ATCHA	Argyle Township Court House Archives, Tusket, Nova Scotia
BHS	Bathurst Historical Society, Bathurst, New Brunswick
BMD	British Ministry of Defence, Whitehall, London
CLRCO	Nova Scotia Public Crown Lands Record Office
CO	British Colonial Office Records
CTG	Bibliothèque de la Comité Technique du Génie, Paris, France
HILA	Harriet Irving Library and Archives, University of New Brunswick, Fredericton
JLA	Journals of the Legislative Assembly
LAC	Library and Archives Canada, Ottawa
MAAP-O	Musée Acadien et Archives de Pubnico-Ouest, West Pubnico, Nova Scotia
MG	Manuscript Group
MRC, MCI	Mi'kmaq Resource Centre, Mi'kmaw College Institute, Cape Breton University
NMAI	National Museum of the American Indian, Washington, DC
NSARM	Nova Scotia Archives and Records Management, Halifax
NSM	Nova Scotia Museum of Natural History, Halifax
PANB	Public Archives of New Brunswick
PANL	Public Archives of Newfoundland
PAPEI	Public Archives of Prince Edward Island
RG	Record Group
TARR	Treaty and Aboriginal Rights Centre, Shubenacadie, Nova Scotia
UCB	University College of Cape Breton
YCMA	Yarmouth County Museum and Archives

Notes

PREFACE

1 Mercedes Peters, "The Future Is Mi'kmaq: Exploring the Merits of Nation-Based Histories as the Future of Indigenous History in Canada," *Acadiensis* 48, no. 2 (2019): 206–16. See also Sherry M. Pictou, "Small 't' Treaty Relationships without Borders: Bear River First Nation, Clam Harvesters, the Bay of Fundy Marine Resource Centre and the World Forum of Fisher Peoples," *Anthropologica* 57, no. 2 (2015): 457–67; Pictou, "Decolonizing Mi'kmaw Memory of Treaty: L'sitkuk's Learning with Allies in Struggle for Food and Lifeways" (PhD diss., Dalhousie University, 2017).

2 Father d'Entremont pioneered research into Acadian-Mi'kmaw unions and their descendants.

3 Academic and honorific designations are omitted from the above list of persons. Several of these individuals have had special titles, awards, and honours bestowed on them for their service to community and country.

4 The most accurate translation, provided courtesy of Elder Lillian Marshall of Chapel Island, is "like saying, 'Let's honour our late ancestors.'" Three other attendees of the Membertou meeting who assisted with this change of title – Mary-Ellen Googoo, Dr. Margaret Johnson ("Dr. Granny"), and Dr. Murdena Marshall – are all granddaughters of Grand Chief Gabriel Sylliboy (see chapter 35 of this volume).

5 Ruth Holmes Whitehead, *The Old Man Told Us: Excerpts from Mi'kmaw History, 1500–1950* (Halifax: Nimbus, 1991); Whitehead, *Niniskjamijinaqik/Ancestral Images: The Mi'kmaq in Art and Photography* (Halifax: Nimbus, 2015).

6 Darlene A. Ricker, *L'sitkuk: The Story of the Bear River Mi'kmaw Community* (Black Rock, NS: Fernwood, 1997).

7 When the principal investigator and her husband visited Aroostook, Maine, in 2010 she found that the local Mi'kmaq held Bunny McBride and Harald E.L. Prins in the highest esteem for their unstinting support in securing Washington's legal recognition for their community in 1991.

INTRODUCTION

1 The word *Mi'kmaq*, ending in *q*, is a noun that refers to the nation or people known at least since 1670 by that term. *Mi'kmaq* derives from a Mi'kmaw term that means "our relatives" and is the plural form of the singular *Mi'kmaw*, "relative." *Mi'kmaw* is used as an adjective, as in "Certain traits of the Mi'kmaw culture are very old." By contrast, *L'nu* is the ancient term the Mi'kmaq themselves used to refer to an individual of their nation. The plural term, meaning "the people," is *L'nuk*.

2 Biographical entries produced under the auspices of the *DCB* are available at http://www.biographi.ca/en/. The *DCB* arose from a collaboration between the University of Toronto and Université Laval, and its website is supported by the Government of Canada through the Department of Canadian Heritage.

3 One story, recounted by a member of the Oland family in Halifax, echoed a recollection shared by Chief Joseph

Julien's grandson Dr. Donald Julien at Millbrook. Information drawn from both oral traditions confirmed that Chief Julien and Colonel Sidney Oland shared a friendship based on the two men's mutual love of hockey.

4 William C. Wicken, *The Colonization of Mi'kmaw Memory and History, 1794–1928: The King v. Gabriel Sylliboy* (Toronto: University of Toronto Press, 2012), introduction.

5 Dr. Carol Ann (Bunny) McBride and Dr. Harald Prins, who currently live in Maine, have had long-standing and notable careers as authors and university teachers in the fields of ethnohistory and anthropology. Both have been involved in researching oral history, in community development projects with the Mi'kmaq of Maine, and in writing books and articles about the Indigenous peoples of the Northeast.

6 Dr. Marie Battiste soon afterwards took up a faculty position with the College of Education at the University of Saskatchewan, where for many years she was director of the Aboriginal Learning Knowledge Centre. She later became the founding academic director of the Aboriginal Education Research Centre at the University of Saskatchewan and founding board member of the Canadian Council on Learning.

7 The word *métis* written with a lowercase *m* denotes a person or group of Aboriginal and European ancestry. It was not a term used by missionaries or officials in the Northeast until the nineteenth century. By contrast, *Métis* with an uppercase *M* denotes the *Métis* New Nation of the West and is a politicized term that refers to a specific group. This distinction, accepted by the United Nations Working Group on Indigenous Populations in 1984 in Geneva, is clarified by Jacqueline Peterson and Jennifer S.H. Brown, eds., in *The New Peoples: Being and Becoming Métis in North America* (Winnipeg: University of Manitoba Press, 1985), 3–16. As regional groups of *métis* formed of individuals residing in the Northeast become politicized in an effort to gain rights under section 35 of the Canadian Constitution Act of 1982, their organizations adopt the capitalized form, *Métis*.

8 Fish from the St. Croix River, which drains westward out of Panuke Lake, anciently supported a large Mi'kmaw population at certain seasons of the year. Sara Halwas, "Where the Wild Things Grow: A Paleoethnobotanical Study of Late Woodland Plant Use at Clam Cove, Nova Scotia" (master's thesis, Memorial University of Newfoundland, 2006), 43–6.

9 Chapter 12 examines members of the Cope family and those who were called the "East Coast Pauls" of *Eskikewa'kik*, which translates into English as "skin

dresser's country" and is the Mi'kmaw name for Nova Scotia's Eastern Shore. In 1929 Chief Joseph C. Cope of Dartmouth referred to the East Coast Paul family as the *Eskekagoowak* (*Eskikagoowak*), or the "residents of *Eskikewa'kik*." Nova Scotia Museum, Halifax, Printed Matter File, "J.C. Cope to Harry Piers," 29 March 1926.

10 Trudy Sable and Bernie Francis, *The Language of This Land, Mi'kma'ki* (Sydney: Cape Breton University Press, 2012), 21.

11 The Northumberland Strait area was a hub of early European-Indigenous trade, as is evidenced by the discovery of two copper kettle burials near Lowden's Beach in Pictou County. J. Russell Harper, "Two Seventeenth-Century Copper-Kettle Burials," *Anthropologica* 4 (1955): 1–36; Ruth Holmes Whitehead, *Nova Scotia: The Protohistoric Period 1500–1635* (Halifax: Nova Scotia Museum, 1993), 45–70. Later, an eighteenth-century chief named Jean Newit or John Noel from Merigomish signed a peace treaty with the British on 15 October 1761. Colonel Frye, "Extract of a letter from Col. Frye to his excellency the governor of Nova Scotia, dated Fort Cumberland, Chignecto," 7 March 1760, *Massachusetts Historical Society Collections*, ser. 1, 10 (1809), 115–16. Beamish Murdoch refers to this person as "Janneoville Pectogawash (Jean, the man of Pictou)." Murdoch, *The History of Nova-Scotia, or Acadie* (Halifax: James Barnes, 1866), 2.407. The Pictou County historian George Patterson confused Jean Newit with Captain Anthony Ury. Patterson, *History of the County of Pictou* (Montreal: Dawson Brothers, 1870), 23, 42–3. The Northumberland Strait region during the 1750s became part of a tract that Joseph Argimault of Chignecto, Paul Laurent of La Have, and Abbé Le Loutre wanted the British to reserve for the exclusive use of the Mi'kmaq. When the Lords of Trade and Plantations in London rejected this scheme, the Pictou leaders felt betrayed. In 1765 this discontent fuelled the burning of a few settlers' houses. To assuage the Mi'kmaq, Michael Francklin, who became Nova Scotia's Indian commissioner in 1776, forged diplomatic ties backed by regular distributions of presents with Jeannot Peguidalouet of Unama'kik, Captain Toney of Remsheg, Paul Chachegonouet of Merigomish, and Paul Peminout of Stewiacke, who in turn encouraged leaders along the Northumberland Strait to remain quiescent. The historic journey of the Northumberland Strait Mi'kmaq from a state of creative policymaking to a sense of betrayal and anger and finally to a willingness to allow settlement warrants further study.

12 Paul Chachegonouet was also known as "Vieaux à Paul." "Vieaux" is a French name, so one has to be careful

about assuming that *vieaux* in this contest is an erroneous rendition of the French *vieux*, or "old." "Vieaux à Paul" means "Vieaux, the son of Paul." Library and Archives of Canada, Ottawa (henceforth LAC), MG 23, GII-19, Monk Papers, vol. 4, 1028.

13 In December 1783 Captain Anthony Ury, or "Captain Toney," received a licence of occupation from Indian Commissioner George Henry Monk to a tract on the west side of the Remsheg River, while Paul Chachegonouet was allotted a licence of occupation for the land around Merigomish. NSARM, RG 1, vol. 430, document package 23½, licences of occupation dated 18 December 1783; NAC, MG 23, GII-19, Monk Papers, vol. 4, p. 1034. Members of the Ury family were *métis* fur traders, and in 1754 several of them claimed to be near relatives of Paul Labrador of Merliguèche, now the town of Lunenburg. In August 1754 the provincial secretary, William Cotterell, drafted a letter to Lieutenant-Colonel Patrick Sutherland stating that a group that included two Urys wanted tools and land at Lunenburg. They claimed they were "formerly Inhabitants of this Country and were nearly related to Old Labrador." NSARM, RG 1, vol. 134, p. 242, "William Cotterell, Secretary's Office, to Lieutenant Colonel Patrick Sutherland," 24 August 1754. The heads of families were Paul Boutin, Julian Bourneuf, Charles Boutin, Francis Lucas, Sebastian Bourneuf, Joseph Gedri (Guédry), Pierre Gedri (Guédry), Pierre Erio (or Ury), and Claude Erot (Ury). "Ury" is a surname that hails from Alsace in France. Despite temporary assistance offered this group in 1754, many of the individuals returned to Piziquid – where they were deported by the British or, like Captain Toney, removed to the coast of the Northumberland Strait.

14 This biographical project originally had been slated to investigate the Sark family of Prince Edward Island, Anthony Ury of Remsheg, and Chief Matthew Francis of Merigomish. According to Captain John Joe Sark of the Mi'kmaw Grand Council, the Mi'kmaw surname "Sark" derives from "Jacques." The apical ancestor of the Sark family was an individual who during the late French regime went by the name of Jacques Lamorieux. The surnames "Sark" and "Lamorieux" appear in the church registers of St. Anne's Roman Catholic Parish, Lennox Island, Prince Edward Island, which dates back to 1818. Otherwise, early church records for Prince Edward Island and the Northumberland Strait area are limited, though a few Mi'kmaw names appear in the registers, beginning in 1818, kept by the Trappist father Vincent de Paul for the parishes of Pomquet, Tracadie, and Havre Boucher. Anthony Ury, also known as Captain

Toney, was an intriguing individual of Mi'kmaw and French ancestry who aided the British at Fort Howe in the 1770s. Toney had a large number of sons, several sporting curly hair and light-coloured eyes, who fanned out over peninsular Nova Scotia from Pomquet on the east to Bear River in the southwest. At least one, Lewis Toney, understood European diplomatic protocols and spoke Mi'kmaq, French, and English fluently enough to act as an interpreter for the *Sipekne'katik* leaders, as well as members of the British establishment. Two of Lewis Toney's sons, Dan and Peter, as well as a woman named Magdalene who was probably Lewis's daughter, went to Bear River, where Magdalene married Chief James Andrew Meuse. Peter became Bear River's second chief under James Andrew Meuse, and eventually served a term as the Bear River leader. Enough information exists on the Sark family, Captain Toney, and Chief Matthew Francis to do at least skeletal biographies of all three. Yet the sphere of Mi'kmaw activities along the entire Northumberland Strait coast warrants so much more attention that it was felt undertaking such biographies before more was known about the history itself might prove precipitate.

15 There were at least four Mi'kmaw leaders named Peter Toney: James Andrew Meuse's brother-in-law Peter Toney, Peter Toney Babey of Near River and Parrsboro (who also had a son Peter Toney), Peter Toney of Merigomish, and Peter Toney of Dartmouth. A man named Peter Toney, familiar with Merigomish area, told the Baptist missionary Silus Tertius Rand an oral tradition about a Mi'kmaw warrior named Toonäle (from the French *tonnerre*, thunder) who was able to forge a peace with the Kennebec peoples of Maine. Rand, *Legends of the Micmac*, ed. Helen L. Webster (New York: Longmans and Green, 1984), 179–82. Rand does not identify who this man was or where he came from. There is a fair amount of information on Chief Peter Toney Babey. NSARM, MG 15, vol. 4a, no 126, "Petition of Peter Paul Toney Babey, 17 February 1852"; NSARM, MG 15, vol. 6, no. 59, "Indians of Parrsboro, Peter Bobie, chief, and Peter Toney, 16 January 1858"; NSARM, RG 1, vol. 431, doc. 106, "Petition of Peter Fabial, Peter Toney and Joseph Paul of Parrsboro, on behalf of seven families, nd (1858)." See also L.F.S. Upton, "Babey, Peter Paul Toney," *DCB* online, vol. 8 (1851–60) and the brief online Wikipedia article on the same man, https://en.wikipedia.org/wiki/Peter_Paul_Toney_Babey. A masterly three-quarter view of a youthful man named Peter Toney smoking a pipe can be found in Lady Falkland's Travel Album, housed in the National Library and Archives in Ottawa.

This sketch was likely done by Lady Falkland herself while her artist friend Mary McKie portrayed the same man in profile. Melinda Reinhart, "Lady Falkland's Travel Album: Negotiating Colonial and Feminine Discourses" (master's thesis, Concordia University, 2005), pp. 73–4. Though both depictions are obviously of the same Mi'kmaw man, no consensus exists as to which Peter Toney out of the possible four is represented in the two women's portrayals. Lady Falkland's sketch has been used to illustrate a Wikipedia article on Peter Toney Babey as well as a discussion of Chief Peter Toney of Merigomish on page 43 of Ruth Holmes Whitehead's *Niniskamijinaqik/Ancestral Images: The Mi'kmaq in Art and Photography* (Halifax: Nimbus, 2015). To further confuse matters, John Patrick Martin claims that McKie's profile view depicts the Peter Toney who lived near Sullivan's Pond in Dartmouth. Martin, *The Story of Dartmouth*, foreword by Thomas H. Raddall (Dartmouth: printed by the author, 1957), p. 479. Though the debate continues as to which Peter Toney the viscountess and her friend used as a model, it appears that Chief Peter Toney of Merigomish was probably too old to be the man the two women sketched. In 1846 the 116 members of the Merigomish band, which had been growing wheat and potatoes on Merigomish Island, were faced with a serious disease epidemic and potato blight. As early as June of that year, sixty-eight Mi'kmaw individuals had died. NSARM, RG 1, vol. 431, Papers regarding Indians, 1832–1866, "Statement of the actual conditions of the Indians at Indian Cove, Pictou Harbour, taken from information from William James Anderson, Secretary of the Board of Health," 29 June 1846; ibid., "Anderson to Sir Rupert D. George, Provincial Secretary, 18 July 1846." Peter Toney, whose name appears on Anderson's 1846 list, was forty-nine years old, while the chief, Assem Paul, was eighty-six. Assem died in 1847. A local priest, Father O'Reilly, and William Anderson distributed blankets, food, and medicine, but when conditions did not substantially improve Peter Toney directed a petition, dated 27 January 1849, to Halifax. NSARM, MG 15, vol. 4a, no. 113; NSARM, RG 5, Series P (Assembly petitions), vol. 45, no. 144 (1849), "Petition of Peter Toney on behalf of himself and the Mi'kmaq residing at Merigomish, Pictou County, for relief from distress"; *Journals of the Legislative Assembly*, 20 (1849), 235, "Of Peter Toney, Indian Chief, Merrigomish." The following month Chief Toney persuaded the Honourable G.R. Young to introduce a petition into the Nova Scotia legislature calling for more government assistance. *Acadian Recorder*, Halifax, 10 February 1849. Toney persisted with his uphill battle to get aid, though of a band that once had numbered over 900 persons, only 125 individuals remained by the 1870s. These had survived years of neglect, disease, crop failures, and relocations owing to settlement. While Toney was chief, fifty acres of what was known as Fisher's Grant was purchased on the eve of Confederation from funds collected by the province from sale of Mi'kmaw lands in Cape Breton. After Confederation, the federal government began to allot additional parcels – for instance, eighty-nine acres in 1874, sixteen acres in 1876, and so on through to 1928 – until a reserve emerged that encompassed 1,158 acres. This tract today is known as Pictou Landing. In 1960 an additional thirty-five acres, including the island at Merigomish, became Merigomish Harbour Indian Reserve No. 31.

16 Ruth Holmes Whitehead, "Wilmot, Peter (1824–1932)," *DCB* online, vol. 16 (1931–40).

17 LAC, RG 2, RS8, "Commissioner William Spragge to the Commissioner of Crown Lands," 12 April 1865, including documents relating to an interview between Chief Claude and the British commission in 1786.

18 Prisk and John Young wanted to include their farms and riverine salmon fishery within a large reserve, though when a reserve was surveyed it included only poor soil surrounding a single fishing locale at Pabineau Falls. The Nepisiguit people nevertheless retained their traditional proprietary rights over fish at this locale for many years, since rapids and tortuous landscape along the lower Nepisiguit River precluded fishing and timber interests from penetrating far into the interior. When they finally did move upriver, the band suffered as others had elsewhere from damming, log booms, and water pollution. Some tried farming to compensate for the loss of their fishery, but most of these persons had their names struck from the band roll, while their siblings who had not taken out land remained on the list. The same happened around Yarmouth. The late Jerry Bartlett (Bartholomew-Alexis) in 1990 summed up the latter situation by remarking that Mi'kmaq with title to land "had problems being Indian, but when greedy interests took away their land titles, they were allowed to be Indians again." Discussion session held at Yarmouth in June 1990 between Jerry Bartlett, Janet Chute, and Doris Labradore.

19 Sigogne's racial bias is examined in some depth by Gérald C. Boudreau in "L'*Apostolat* du *missionnaire Jean-Mandé Sigogne* et les *Acadiens* du *sud-ouest* de la *Nouvelle-Écosse*" (doctoral diss., Université de Montréal, 1989).

20 This issue is contentious because there is a concern within the presently recognized Indigenous community

that legitimization of a (capital *M*) *Métis* Nation (or Nations) in the Northeast might be detrimental to the sovereignty of both Mi'kmaq and New Nation *Métis*.

21 Born at Hectanooga on 12 May 1916, Elsie Charles Basque died just shy of reaching one hundred years of age in Saulnierville, Digby County, on 11 April 2016. For a recent biography of this remarkable woman, see Allison Lawlor, "Mi'kmaq Teacher Elsie Basque Was a Revered Role Model," *Globe and Mail*, 8 May 2016.

CHAPTER 1

1 There are several spellings of the way the surname "Alexis" is spoken by a person whose first language is Mi'kmaq. These include "Laski," "Lexy," "Lixi," "Lucy," "Luxey," and "Luxy." Charles also at different times was accorded the surnames "Alexander," "Alexe," and "Alexi." The Acadians called him "Charles Caboche" (the "big head" or "the intelligent one").

2 Though identified in 1727 by a priest as Mi'kmaq, Charles Alexis's father, Jacques Alexis, may have been born into the Etchemin or Penobscot nation. "Alexis" was not a surname found among the Mi'kmaq during the first decade of the 1700s. Clarence-J. d'Entremont, *Histoire du Cap-Sable de l'an mil au traité de Paris (1763)* (Eunice, LA: Hébert, 1981), 4.1580. When Jacques brought his eldest son, François-Joseph Alexis, to Annapolis Royal to be baptized in the summer of 1727, the Sulpician priest René-Charles de Breslay referred to both Jacques and his wife Angelique as "Cape Sable Micmac." Nova Scotia Archives and Records Management, Halifax (henceforth NSARM), RG 1, vol. 26a, Registers of St. Jean-Baptiste Parish, Annapolis Royal, 1702–55, 4, "Baptism of François-Joseph Alexis, four months old, 11 June 1727." Yet François-Joseph Alexis's baptism occurred only one year after the signing of a treaty at Annapolis Royal between Mi'kmaq and Malecite leaders and the English, an event that owed a great deal to the diplomatic endeavours of a Penobscot leader named Loron Alexis. Loron already had played a major role in proceedings leading up to the signing of a peace treaty in Boston in 1725; the treaty signed at Annapolis Royal in 1726 was a ratification of the earlier pact. Loron Alexis visited Nova Scotia to urge the Mi'kmaq to sign the treaty, and it may be that Jacques Alexis, as one of Loron's extended family, tagged along. A French nominal census compiled in 1707–08 shows that the surname "Alexis" existed among the Penobscot, while no Mi'kmaq bore the surname at this early date. An individual named "Pierre Alexis," for

instance, resided at Pintaouet in "cabane 9." Library and Archives of Canada, Ottawa (henceforth LAC), MG 18, F18, typescript of a French census, dated 1708, of Native encampments among the Penobscot by Abbé Pierre La Chasse, including nominal census information on Native families, men, women, and children belonging to villages on mainland Nova Scotia and Cape Breton, *Recensement genal fait au mois de Nouembre mile Sept cent huit de tous les Sauvages de l'Acadie que resident dans la Coste de l'Est, et ceux de Pintagouet et de Canibecky, Famille par Famille Leurs ages – Celuy de Leurs Femmes et Enfants avec une Recapitulation a la fin de la quantité d'hommes et de garçons capable d'aler a La guerres, comme aussy Le recensement des francois Establis a La ditte Coste de l'Es, 1708*. The original handwritten census manuscript is vol. 4, no. 751 of the Edward E. Ayer Collection at the Newberry Library in Chicago. Father Clarence-Joseph d'Entremont maintains that this census, though dated 1708, was taken in 1707, a deduction he made when he compared the ages of children in this census with the ages of children given in other French censuses. D'Entremont, "Census of Port Royal, Acadia, 1678," *French Canadian and Acadian Genealogical Review* 7, no. 1 (1979): 66. There also is a letter written by Mathieu de Goutin to the minister, dated 23 December 1707, stating that Governor Subercase at Port Royal had recently sent him a copy of the census of Aboriginal families and individuals. Document housed in the Archives des Colonies, Paris, France (henceforth AC), accessible on microfilm at LAC, AC, Serie CIID, vol. 6, fol. 83. If Jacques Alexis was indeed of Penobscot birth, there may also be an alternative explanation for his appearance in Nova Scotia. He may have joined the combined Penobscot, Malecite, and Mi'kmaw military force commanded by Bernard-Anselm Saint-Castin, the son of Baron Jean-Vincent d'Abbadie de Saint-Castin and his Etchemin wife Marie-Marthe Pidiĕmiskoa. Saint-Castin moved from the Penobscot River Valley to the vicinity of Port Royal in 1710. Jacques Alexis, acting under Saint-Castin's orders, might have participated in 1711 in the ambush and devastation of a party of soldiers sent by the English commander Colonel Samuel Vetch to a place later named Bloody Creek, near present-day Annapolis Royal. Penobscot warriors led by Saint-Castin were involved in this attack. George Patterson, "Hon. Samuel Vetch, First English Governor of Nova Scotia," *Collections of the Nova Scotia Historical Society*, 4 (1885): 28–9. In 1727 René-Charles de Breslay would have known whether or not Jacques Alexis was a fairly recent arrival to Cape Sable.

3 According to Clarence-J. d'Entremont *caboche* means "head" or, "in a figurative sense, intelligence. Charles Alexis, who was given this name, married Anne Hébert. Anne, born 14 February 1741, was the youngest child of Antoine Hébert (son of Étienne) and Antoine's second wife Anne Orillon (daughter of Charles Orillon), from the Annapolis Upper River." Letter from C.-J. d'Entremont to J.E. Chute, 30 November 1990. On 20 January 1794 Nova Scotia's provincial Indian commissioner, George Henry Monk, also indirectly referred to Charles Alexis's intelligence as well as his shrewdness in a letter to Lieutenant Governor John Wentworth. LAC, MG 23, GII-19, Monk Papers, Letterbook, 1051–51, "Letter from George Henry Monk to Governor Wentworth," 23 January 1794. When Chief Alexis set out to call Mi'kmaw leaders together at Gaspereau Lake in the Annapolis Valley to discuss what course they should take following the radical diminution of their lands and resources due to Loyalist influxes into the province, Monk observed that the Mi'kmaq proved "more restless + dissatisfied with their situation than I have ever known them to be – some of the more intelligent among them make circuitous visits with the different Tribes and give false reasons for such long and unusual excurtions [*sic*, excursions]."

4 Antoine Hébert, also known as Antoine *le jeune*, was a son of Étienne Hébert (c.1630–c.1670) and Marie Gaudet of Port Royal. Born in 1669 or 1670, he was the youngest of ten children. Around 1691 he married Jeanne Corporon at Port Royal, and the couple had fifteen children. After Marie Gaudet's death Antoine *le jeune* wed a second time, in February 1737. His new bride was Anne Orillon, daughter of Charles Orillon of Port Royal. This couple had at least four children, including Anne Hébert, born in 1740, who married Charles Alexis. Two of Antoine's sons by Anne Orillon married into the Thibodeau and Hébert families, while a second daughter married into the Deveau family. Antoine Hébert *le jeune* over time acquired sons-in-law and daughters-in-law bearing the surnames "Aubois," "Deveau," "Duon," "Labauve," "Mius d'Azy," and "Comeau." Most of these persons retained close close associations with the Mi'kmaw community. They also were closely tied to the Mius family. Charles Hébert, Anne Hébert's half brother, wed Clair Mius *dit* d'Azy, while Charles Hébert's sister Marie-Marthe wed Claire Mius's brother Charles-Amand Mius *dit* d'Azy. Charles Hébert and Claire lived at Chebogue, while Charles-Amand and Marie-Marthe settled at Ministiguèsche, now Barrington Head. Both Claire Mius *dit* d'Azy and Charles-Amand-Mius *dit* d'Azy were children of Joseph I Mius *dit* d'Azy, whom

Father d'Entremont holds was the eldest son of Philippe II Mius *dit* d'Azy and Phillipe's second Mi'kmaw consort, Marie. Clarence d'Entremont, *Histoire du Cap-Sable*, 3.976–7, 993. Philippe II Mius *dit* d'Azy, in turn, was the youngest of three sons of Baron Philippe d'Entremont of Pobomcoup (or Poubomcoup) and his wife, Madeleine Hélie Tillet.

5 According to the burial registers of the Parish of Ste. Anne du Ruisseau, Anne Hébert, the widow of Charles Alexis, died on 20 September 1831 at the age of ninety-two. Yet the registers for the Parish of St. Jean-Baptiste, Port Royal, list her birth year as 1741, which would make her ninety when she died. Clarence-Joseph d'Entremont, *History of Quinan, Nova Scotia* (Meteghan River, Yarmouth County: L'imprimerie Lescarbot, 1984), 8–10. The Mi'kmaq called The Forks *Nigtoiag, gisna Neoptogoiag*, meaning "where the Tusket River goes through." *Nigtoiag* is sometimes written *Nictahk*, which stems from another Mi'kmaw word, *Niketaouksit*, from which "Tusket" derives. The French rendition of this place name is *Tousquechet*, which appears on a French map of 1656. What is today Quinan was once called "Tusket Forks." After the arrival of the Loyalists, the Mi'kmaq referred to the English settlement of Tusket on the lower Tusket River as *Aglaseawakade*, which means "the English settlement." The Mi'kmaq also gave Quinan another name, one found in Abbé Sigogne's church registers: *Machoudiak, Macloudiak*, or *Mactoudiak*, which means "where they meet." Another, more precise name was *Mawtookyak* or *Mawtookgac*, "a place where two rivers meet." In 1885 the name "The Forks" was changed to "Quinan" in memory of Father John L. Quinan, who served at the parish from 1860 to 1867. D'Entremont, *History of Quinan*, 8–10; *Yarmouth Vanguard*, 20 November 1990, "The Place Names of Quinan."

6 "Letter from Mons. de la Varenne to his friend at Rochelle, Louisbourg," 8 May 1756. This letter is included in Pierre Maillard, *An Account of the Customs and Manners of the Mickmakis and Maricheets, Savage Nations Now dependent on the Government of Cape Breton* (London: S. Hooper and A. Morley, 1758).

7 The fact that Commissioner Monk still knew of the couple's marriage as late as 1793 makes it improbable that any other such union took place at Cape Sable prior to the Seven Years' War. Monk regarded Charles and Anne's marriage as a pragmatic expediency, while De la Varenne cast it in a far more romantic light. Monk wrote that at the time of the Acadian removals, "This woman [Anne Hébert], being then among the Indians, married this Charles Alexander [Alexis]." The commissioner

thus implied that he considered Anne Hébert to have been placed in the position of marrying Charles Alexis by force of circumstances rather than by her own volition. This view recently has been echoed by William C. Wicken, *The Colonization of Mi'kmaw Memory and History, 1794–1928: The King v. Gabriel Sylliboy* (Toronto: University of Toronto Press, 2012), 107. By contrast, Father Clarence-Joseph d'Entremont, who has extensively studied interconnections among the Native population and the Mius family of Acadians of the Cape Sable region, simply noted that the marriage took place but did not ascribe any expedient purpose to its occurrence. "The reason why she married an Indian from the Cape Sable region," he averred, "could be because her family (or some members of) would have taken refuge here, and [were] deported to France in 1759." Letter from Father C.-J. d'Entremont to J.E. Chute, 30 November 1990. See also d'Entremont, *History of Quinan*, 8. Father d'Entremont in his history of Cape Sable to 1763 was one of the first to examine kin interrelations between the Acadians and Mi'kmaq, and he continued these investigations in his later works on Quinan, Tusket, and Wedgeport. Janet Chute had the pleasure of conducting research on the Cape Sable band with the assistance of Father d'Entremont during the summers of 1990 and 1991.

8 Anne Hébert was buried in the Ste. Anne du Ruisseau cemetery near Eel Brook. Parish of Ste. Anne du Ruisseau, Burial registers, 20 September 1831.

9 NSARM, RG 1, vol. 26a, Baptismal registers of St. Jean-Baptiste Parish, Annapolis Royal, 1702–55, 4, "Baptism of François-Joseph Alexis, four months old, 11 June 1727." "Previously baptized at sea by Guillaume Blanchard Jr., he is the son of Jacques Alexis of Cape Sable and Angelique his wife, Mi'kmaq of Cape Sable" (translated from the French by Janet Chute). The entry in the Ste. Anne du Ruisseau parish registers for Anne's death on 20 September 1831 confirms that she was born in 1741, but no corresponding documentary source exists concerning the death of her husband Charles. He was undoubtedly older than his wife, but not quite as old as his brother François-Joseph Alexis, who was born to Jacques Alexis and Angélique in March 1727. François-Joseph Alexis's baptismal entry is the only source that identifies his and his brother Charles's parents as Jacques Alexis and Angélique.

10 King George's War, which took place in North America, was part of the longer continental War of the Austrian Succession, which lasted from 1740 to 1748.

11 An accessible online source for Louis Hébert is Steven A. Cormier's "Acadians in Gray, Acadians who Found Refuge in Louisiana, February 1764–Early 1800s, with Appendices," 2007, http://www.acadiansingray.com/.

12 "Ouikmakagan" is a French approximation of the Mi'kmaw word *Wipkomagakum* or *Wiplomesgokum*, which means "Place of Eels." Abbé Antoine Gaulin, who was an itinerant missionary to the Mi'kmaq and Acadians at Cape Sable during the early to middle 1720s, wrote that Ouikmakagan lay between the mouth of the Tusket River and the barony of Pobomcoup in what is today East Pubnico. Though Father Clarence-J. d'Entremont notes that Ouikmakagan may have been located on the Lower Abuptic River, now the East River, he argues that it was probably closer to Eel Brook, part of the present-day Parish of Ste. Anne du Ruisseau. It was probably the site of a major confrontation in 1756 between Acadian resistance fighters and Jedediah Preble's men from New England. D'Entremont, *Histoire du Cap-Sable*, 4.1890, 1997. Five Acadian families originally settled at Ouikmakagan. Early household heads were François Viger and his wife Marie Mius; Jean Pitre and his wife Marie Pressley, Marc Pitre and his wife Jeanne, Marc Pitre's brother Jean Pitre and his *métis* wife Françoise Babin, François Amirault *dit* Tourangeau and his wife Marie Pitre, and Gabriel Moulaison and his wife Marie Aubois. François Viger around 1695 wed Marie Mius, a daughter of Philippe Mius *dit* d'Azy and d'Azy's first Mi'kmaw consort. This couple's son, François Viger *fils*, married Claire Le Jeune, daughter of Martin Le Jeune and Marie Gaudet of La Have. Marie Amirault, a daughter of François Amirault *dit* Tourangeau and Marie Pitre, married Joseph Mius dit d'Azy, the eldest son of Philippe Mius *dit* d'Azy and his second Indigenous wife, Marie. Marie Amirault is considered the "matriarch" of many Acadian families residing at both Ste. Anne du Ruisseau and Quinan today.

13 This refuge site lay north of present-day Lake Vaughan, at Reynardton, which lies in the Gavelton area.

14 John Roy Campbell, *A History of the County of Yarmouth, Nova Scotia* (Saint John: J. & A. MacMillan, 1876), 74. Eustache Corporan was the son of Jean Corporan and Marie Pinet, and by the early 1750s he resided at Ouikmakagan. D'Entremont, *Histoire du Cap-Sable*, 3.1031. He was a cousin of Anne Hébert's step-siblings.

15 *The Boston Weekly News-Letter*, 2 September 1756. See also d'Entremont, *Histoire du Cap-Sable*, 4.1950–1, 2067–8.

16 "To His Excellent Thomas Pownall, esq. and Honourable Council in Boston," 15 September 1758. In *Records of the Deportation and Le Grand Dérangement, 1714–1768, Nova Scotia Archives* I (Halifax: Charles Annand, 1869), 306–7.

17 The Acadian village of Cheggogin lay along the Cheggogin River just northeast of present-day Yarmouth, Yarmouth County.

18 For a readily accessible and readable source regarding this event, see Dianne Marshall, *Heroes of the Acadian Resistance: The Story of Joseph Beausoleil Broussard and Pierre II Surrete, 1702–1765* (Halifax: Formac, 2011), 166–8. A more controversial look at the subject is presented in Warren A. Perrin, *Acadian Redemption: From Beausoleil Broussard to the Queen's Royal Proclamation* (Opelousas, LA: Andrepont, 2005).

19 Isaiah W. Wilson, *Geography and History of Digby County* (Digby: printed by the author, 1893), 25–6. This account tells of a surprise attack on a Mi'kmaq encampment at Roger's Point (now Point Prim, Digby County) by Roger's Rangers in the fall of 1759, in which men – including the chief – women, and children were killed. The story as it is recounted is problematic because Roger's Rangers had left the province by the autumn of 1759, though an attack by another group of rangers might have occurred.

20 For a discussion of Mi'kmaw weir fishing on the Tusket and Quinan Rivers, see Janet E. Chute, "Mi'kmaq Fishing in the Maritimes: An Historical Overview," in *Earth, Water, Air and Fire: Studies in Canadian Ethnohistory*, ed. David T. McNab (Waterloo: Wilfrid Laurier University Press, 1998), 95–113.

21 Janet Chute heard about these pictoglyphs while she was visiting friends in the Acadian community at Quinan in the 1990s. A descendant of Jacques Alexis and Angelique who went by three names, Jerry Bartholomew-Alexis, Jerry Bartlett, and Jerry Lonecloud, knew of their location in the early 1900s, and in the late 1980s a party from the Nova Scotia Museum, drawing on Lonecloud's statements and description of the pictoglyphs, searched unsuccessfully for the rock inscriptions.

22 Michel and Joseph travelled with Charles Alexis in the 1790s. LAC, MG 23, GII, vol. 4, Indian Accounts, 1217, entry for 25 November 1796. There are no church records available early enough to confirm that the others were siblings of Michael and Joseph. Yet if they were not all siblings, they certainly were first cousins, as cousins among the Mi'kmaq are often treated similar to siblings.

23 When the government was extending peace overtures to the Mi'kmaq near the end of the Seven Years' War, while at the same time still holding the scalp bounty – levied in 1756 – over the heads of those who did not submit, Governor Lawrence issued a "Full and explicit Pass to Francois Shagwaough [Chegua]," who was Argomartin's political delegate. Chagua made "his submission to his Majesty's Government" and declared that his chief Michel Agoumartin (or Argomartin) also was willing to make peace. NSARM, RG 1, vol. 156, 53–4, "Pass to François Shagwaough of Cape Sable, along with a Petition from Shagwaough on behalf of his chief, Michel Agoumartin," 24 April 1760.

24 Great Pubnico Lake is also referred to as Sabine Lake.

25 "Pobomcoup" or "Poubomcoup" derives from a Mi'kmaw term for "cleared land" or "land from which the trees have been removed to make it fit for cultivation." Charles Bruce Fergusson, ed., *Place-Names and Places of Nova Scotia* (Halifax: Public Archives of Nova Scotia, 1967), 564–5.

26 "Port Roseway," the English name for Port Razoir, is a corruption of the French "*razoir.*"

27 Jerry Bartlett, alias Lonecloud, stated that there was a Mi'kmaw oral tradition about Abbé Pierre Maillard labouring among the Cape Sable Mi'kmaq in the seventeenth century. Ruth Holmes Whitehead, *Tracking Doctor Lonecloud: Showman to Legend Keeper* (Fredericton: Goose Lane Editions, 2002), 57.

28 *Kespukwitk* or *Gespogeitnag* was dominated by rivers draining east, south, and west from the Tobeatic watershed. From the mid-1700s to the mid-1800s each Mi'kmaw district, including *Kespukwitk* , sent at least two delegates to annual Wabanaki Confederacy meetings. Most of the year *Kespukwitk* had a scattered Indigenous population, residing along rivers draining west, east, and south from what is now the Tobeatic watershed.

29 Interview with Charles Paul ("Charlie" Paul) at Yarmouth, 10 June 1990; interview with Bernard Armiro of West Pubnico, 10 June 1990. Bernard was a close friend of Charlie and went hunting with him. Charlie, who was in a nursing home at the time of interview, was for many years a well-known hunting and fishing guide who knew the interior of Yarmouth County extremely well. He succeeded Charlie Labrador as chief of the Acadia First Nation.

30 The Salmon River was highly regarded by the Mi'kmaq for its rich salmon runs. Its Mi'kmaw name, *Poulamonsebou*, means "place where the salmon abounds." There were also copious wild berry patches in this part of the interior. Blueberries, raspberries, strawberries, and blackberries appeared in season. Meanwhile, the Mi'kmaw word *Hectanooga* has been accorded various meanings, none of them definite. The Deveau family of the French Shore state that it refers to a "tamed animal," while Bernie Francis, a Mi'kmaw linguist, alleges that it is very similar to a Mi'kmaw word meaning "Your dog's

on fire." "Mi'kmaq Atlas Reveals Secrets behind Nova Scotia Place Names," CBC, 19 October 2015, https://www.cbc.ca/news/canada/nova-scotia/mi-kmaq-atlas-place-names-nova-scotia-1.3277687. Finally, according to a report prepared for the Mainland Confederacy of Mi'kmaq, the Mi'kmaw place name *Hectanooga* means "a place where the blackberries are in abundance." Michael Cox, *Mi'kmaq Use of Oositookum* (*Digby Neck*), *Its Surrounding Waters, and the Mainland Shore of St. Mary's Bay*, report prepared for the Mainland Confederacy of Mi'kmaq, Truro, December 2005, 12.

31 It has been suggested that *Tebok* might have been the seventeenth-century encampment ground of Chief Henry Membertou (Membeltou) and his family, since Cape Forchu or "Forked Cape" at Cheboque was a site where Membertou's son Louis held a feast in 1613 for Father Massé. This information comes from local oral traditions, and is not mentioned in Lucien Campeau's biography of Membertou for the *Dictionary of Canadian Biography* online (hereafter cited as *DCB*), vol. 1 (1000–1700).

32 *Kespukwitk* (or *Gespogeitnag*) means "last land" and is similar in meaning to *Kespuk* (or *Gespe'gewa'gi*), the Mi'kmaw word for northeastern New Brunswick and the Gaspé region of Quebec. It refers both to the area around present-day Yarmouth and to the broader district that embraces the watersheds and drainage areas of the Sissaboo, Meteghan, Salmon, Tusket, Barrington, Clyde, and Roseway rivers (the latter earlier known as the Shelburne River). While the Sisaboo, Meteghan, and Salmon rivers drain into the Gulf of Maine, the others drain eastward into the Atlantic Ocean. All these rivers have their watershed in what is now known as the Tobeatic Wilderness Area of interior Shelburne, Yarmouth, and Digby counties and well as part of Queens County. (The interior boundaries of these four counties meet in this watershed region). The Cape Sable band also maintained hunting and fishing territories in Digby County along the Sissiboo and Salmon rivers, which drain into St. Mary's Bay. Further north, however, their territory overlaps with that belonging to the Annapolis band.

33 Helen Locke, a direct descendant of the original Locke family of Lockeport, maintained a diary in which she described and then drew a pencil sketch around 1920 of a Mi'kmaw encampment at Monkey Hollow, also known as Sam's Point after Samuel Locke, an original settler of Lockeport. This site, which originally was attractive, sheltered from the winds, and proximate to a large sandy beach, was doubtless used by generations of Mi'kmaq. Since the 1950s, however, it has been employed sequentially as a gravel pit, the town dump and, most recently, a base for a sewage treatment facility. Peter Partington of Lockeport shared this information after obtaining a copy of Helen Locke's diary from its owner, Fred Partridge, a nephew of Locke. The authors are grateful to both Peter and Fred for their generosity in sharing this unique and valuable resource.

34 Abbé Gaulin served the Mi'kmaq and Acadians of Cape Sable, Cobequid, Shubenacadie, and La Have. Douglas S. Ormond, *The Roman Catholic Church in Cobequid Acadie, 1692–1755, and Colchester County, Nova Scotia, 1825–1978: Also Savage Island and the Kavanaghs 1778–1830* (Truro, NS: self-pub., 1979), 5.

35 As Ouikmakagan's exact location was obliterated when the English razed the settlement in 1759, one can only postulate rather than confirm that the village lay close to Eel Brook. The English place name "Eel Brook," however, is a direct translation from the Mi'kmaw *Wiplomesgokum* or *Ouikamagan*. When Acadians began to return to the area in the 1780s, Eel Brook retained many of the functional characteristics of the old village of Ouikmakagan, despite the fact that much of the land was granted in the 1760s to British landlords. In the 1950s the designation "Eel Brook," which had been used by both English and Acadians since 1750, was changed to "Ste. Anne du Ruisseau" to reflect the name of the local Roman Catholic parish of Sainte-Anne.

36 Clarence-J. d'Entremont notes that a 1748 document, ascribed to Abbé Jean-Louis Le Loutre, placed Ouikmakagan somewhere along the coast between the Tusket River and Pobomcoup. Father d'Entremont admits that one possible site for this village could have been on the lower Abruptic River, now the East River, although he greatly favours Eel Brook also known to the English as Eel Creek. D'Entremont, *Histoire du Cap-Sable*, 3.1220–2.

37 Throughout the Northeast, eels were taken by spear or at weirs in the spring and fall. They could be dried and smoked to take on prolonged on canoe trips, and were preserved in quantity during the fall to carry groups through the winter months. An extended family harvested from a single weir to which rights of access lay with the head of the group. Chute, "Mi'kmaq Fishing in the Maritimes," 95–115. An informative discussion about the value of eels to the Mi'kmaq and their culture is found in Kerry Prosper and Mary Jane Paulette, "The Mi'kmaq Relation with Eat (American Eel)," Social Research for Sustainable Fisheries (SRSF), March 2002, 1, https://people.stfx.ca/rsg/srsf/researchreports1/FactSheets/Factsheet7.pdf. Another account, focusing specifically on the value of eeling to the Paq'tnkek First Nation in

Antigonish County, Nova Scotia, is Anthony Davis et al., "The Paq'tnkek Mi'kmaq and Ka't (American Eel): A Case Study of Cultural Relations, Meaning and Prospects," *Canadian Journal of Native Studies*, 24 (2004): 357–88.

38 The whole area was known as Baie d'Equille in early French documents.

39 Charles La Tour, born in France, was governor of Acadia from 1631 to 1642 and again, following the death in 1650 of his rival Charles de Menou d'Aulnay de Charnisay, from 1653 to 1657. La Tour died at Port La Tour, Cape Sable. It is known that his first wife, whom he married in the country fashion, was an Eastern Abenaki, and she may have been Mi'kmaq, but she could just as easily have been from the Penobscot River area, where La Tour had built a post to participate in the fur trade. It is possible that the chief whom he brought to France on a visit with him may have been his father-in-law. See M.A. MacDonald, *Fortune & La Tour: The Acadian Civil War* (Toronto: Methuen, 1983), chap. 1. In 1624 La Tour established Fort Lomeron, located near present-day Cheboque, Yarmouth County, with resources bequeathed him by Charles de Biencourt de Poutricourt. This post seems to have been dismantled in favour of a post on Cape Sable Island not long after the raids organized by the Kirke Brothers. La Tour also maintained trading forts on the Penobscot River and the Saint John River. The identities of the Mi'kmaq with whom La Tour traded are impossible to trace.

40 D'Entremont, *Histoire du Cap-Sable*, 4.1212. The English in 1757 and 1758 completely razed the manor house and surrounding buildings at what is now East Pubnico.

41 Interview with John Muise *dit* Le Dude of Lower Eel Brook, 25 August 1994.

42 There is a recent work on King Philip's War by Eric B. Schultz and Michael J. Tougias entitled *King Philip's War: The History and Legacy of America's Forgotten Conflict* (Woodstock, VT: Countryman, 2000). King Philip's War, also known as Metacom's War, lasted from 1675 to 1678 and pitted the Wampanoag followers of Metacom (or Metacomet), a leader who previously had adopted the English name "King Philip," against the northern New Englanders. Peace was established with the signing of the Treaty of Casco Bay of 1678. The idea of selling the Mi'kmaq from Cape Sable as slaves in the Azores did not originate with either Waldron or Lavadure, but Lavadure was responsible for much of the expedition's highly deceptive and manipulative character. William Waldron was a relative of Major Richard Waldron, who appointed Henry Lawton of Picataqua, Maine, to seize

any Aboriginal people he met along the Eastern seaboard. Lawton, in turn, hired William Waldron, Jean Lavadure, Francis Mason, and Edmund Cooke to assist him, and all set sail early in 1676 for Machias, where they captured nine Aboriginal men. They then set out northward for Cape Sable. Once they had anchored, three or four Mi'kmaq came on deck at Lavadure's urging, since he could speak their language. He took them below decks to visit the vessel's galley, and asserted that his party was simply intent on extending hospitality to their Mi'kmaw guests. In the evening the Cape Sable chief and his wife, along with several others, joined the crew, so that eventually there were seventeen Mi'kmaq aboard the vessel. At this point Henry Lawton hoisted the sails and set a course for the Azores, where he and his companions sold their human cargo. When the crew of two New England vessels anchored in the harbour at Faial Island saw what was taking place, they sent notices to the New England authorities, and the guilty were apprehended in Boston in the summer of 1676. Henry Lawton and William Waldron were jailed, but John Laverdure was set temporarily at liberty after his mother, Priscella Melanson, back in Acadia raised one hundred pounds pounds as bail. When the day of his trial arrived, Lavadure jumped bail and returned to Nova Scotia. His brothers, out of consternation over their brother's deed, then took their mother's surname, Melanson.

43 The vessel's owner, Simon Lynde, although he traded in slaves, may not have recognized the scope of Waldon and Melanson's slaving intentions at this time. This is explored in a recent work by one of Lynde's descendants, Grant Hayter-Menzies, entitled *The North Door: Echoes of Slavery in a New England Family* (Norwich, VT: Old Johnson Place, 2019). See also John Demont, "Author's Ancestor Traded in Slaves," *Chronicle Herald*, Halifax, 11 April 2019.

44 Jean Lavadure's older brother, Pierre Melanson *dit* Laverdure, married Marie-Marguerite Muis d'Éntremont, a daughter of Baron Philippe I Muis d'Éntremont and Madeleine Hélie of Pobomcoup. In the baron's later years Marie-Marguerite took care of her father, who probably died at her and her husband's residence at Grand Pré about 1700. H. Léander d'Entremont, *The Baronnie de Pombcoup and the Acadians: A History of the Ancient "Department of Cape Sable," Now Known as Yarmouth and Shelburne Counties, Nova Scotia* (Yarmouth, 1931).

45 MS 252, Edward E. Ayer Collection, Newberry Library, Chicago, Robert Roule's Deposition; James Axtell, "The Vengeful Women of Marblehead: Robert Roule's

Deposition of 1677," *William and Mary Quarterly* 3rd. Ser., 31 (October 1974): 650–2.

46 Pierre Chegua's father was Germain Chegoueo (or Chegua), who was born in 1656. Germain's forty-year-old wife was Marie Madelaine and his two eldest sons were Estienne, fifteen years old, and Pierre, eight. This Pierre became chief around 1724. Germain and his wife also had four daughters: Marie-Joseph, who was nineteen; Madelaine, thirteen; Margueritte, ten, and a second child called Margueritte, who was nine. There were ninety-seven members of the Cape Sable band ennumerated in 1707–08. LAC, MG 18, F 18, *Recensement genal fait au mois de Novembre mile Sept cent huit de tous les Sauvages de L'Acadie… 1708.*

47 Ibid. Thirteen of the surnames recorded in the French census of 1707–08 for Cape Sable – Anougimtes, Cenadagoucet, Chegoueo (Chegua), Chepcouchep, Chesdabaquemades, Medeshep (Medechese), Nectabot, Netadermet, Pitsenet (Pisnet), Ouegamine, Ouytau, Talgoumatique (later rendered "Argomartin"), and Tecouenemac (Tecouramart) – also reflected the band's membership as early as 1660, since each of these surnames belonged to a family head who was forty-five years of age or older. These surnames also may be used to trace kin linkages across band boundaries. Ibid.

48 Ibid. According to the French nominal census compiled by Abbe Gaulin, Paul Tecounemac (or Tecouramart) was around forty-five years old, while his wife Marie Agathe was fifty. Paul and Marie Agathe had a seventeen-year-old son, Guillaume, at the time, whose name does not appear again in the documentary record. Nor do those of their sons Anthoine or Antoine, who was fourteen, and Philipe (Jean-Baptiste Philippe), who was eight. They also had two daughters" Marie, eighteen, and Cecile, one year old. They later had Anathase and Eustache, who must have been born after 1708, since they do not appear in the 1708 census.

49 D'Entremont, *Histoire du Cap-Sable*, 4.1885, 1921.

50 In 1712 Charles Mius d'Entremont married Marguerite Landry, who was the daughter of Pierre Landry and Madeleine Robichaud. On 2 June 1751 Charles's brother-in-law, Pierre Landry, put his mark alongside Charles's and Joseph's on a contract that gave Eustache Tecouramart seventy livres to transfer his rights to a *nijagan* (or fish weir) to Jacques II d'Entremont, the son of Jacques I Mius d'Entremont and Anne La Tour, as well as to Chief François Mius *dit* d'Azy, the son of Philippe II Mius *dit* d'Azy and his second Mi'kmaw spouse, Marie. *Histoire du Cap-Sable*, 4.1885–6. Marie Alexis's marriage to Eustache Tecouramart likely occurred in the mid-1740s. See

NSARM, copy of old registers conserved at Caraquet, New Brunswick, 1768–73, 1786–96, microfilm; *Registre des actes de baptême, marriages, et sepultures faits en la nouvelle ecosse ou acadie commence le vingt unieme jour de juillet de l'annee mil sept cent soixante huit, par mons. Charles-François Bailly, pretre missionaire des sauvages et acadiens, sujets de sa majeste britannique,* entry for 21 September 1769 for Baie Sainte-Marie, "Baptism of Anne, daughter of Eustache Tecouramart and Marie Alexis." Anne's godfather is Amable Doucet, the son of Pierre Doucet and Marie-Josephe Robichaud.

51 By this time a patronymic surname system had been imposed on Cape Sable Mi'kmaw society by Roman Catholic priests, so that descendents of earlier leaders can often be traced through time in the male line. Medogsnel (Medosset or Doucet) in 1722 was recognized both by the missionary Abbé Antoine Gaulin and the French administration at Louisbourg as head chief of a Cape Sable. Born around 1680, he was the first chief also to be recognized by both the French and English. In 1722 Abbé Antoine Gaulin listed Jean-Baptiste Medogsnel as chief of the group of ninety-four persons residing at Cape Sable. LAC, microfilm copies of material in the Archives des Colonies (AC), Paris, France, CIIB, Correspondance général, l'Ile Royale, vol. 6, doc. 77, *Recensement des Sauvages dans l'isle Royalle et de la peninsule de l'acadie qui sont deservis par les Missionaires du Seminire des missions étrangeres Etablis a Quebec fait par M. Gaulin pretre Missionaire desc. Sauvages en 1722.* The English at Annapolis Royal specifically referred to Jean-Baptiste Medogsnel as "Chief of Cape Sable" on a ratification of a treaty of peace and friendship, signed at Annapolis Royal and dated 4 June 1726 (though there were several copies of this treaty made at various times during 1726). British Colonial Records from the British Records Office in London, England, on microfilm at LAC, 217/38/108. The surname "Medosset" was sometimes "Frenchified" to "Doucet." Jean-Baptiste was evidently a brother both to Germain Medosset of the Port Royal band and to Michelle Medosset, who in 1708 was the wife of Jehan Grand Claude, head chief of Port Royal area. Jean-Baptiste Medogsnel may have moved from Port Royal to Cape Sable around 1724, since neither "Medogsnel" nor "Medosset" appears on the French census of 1708 for Cape Sable. And though Germain Medosset of Port Royal in 1708 had an eight-year-old son named Jean-Baptiste, born in 1700, this person is much too young to have become the Cape Sable chief, who had a seventeen-year-old daughter in 1727. According to local Acadian oral tradition, a Cape Sable Mi'kmaw woman

named "Françoise Doucet" was said to have been the wife of a noted Cape Sable chief, who may even have been Jean-Baptiste Medogsnel. "Medogsnel," a Mi'kmaw rather than an Acadian name, is however sometimes written "Medosset," which in turn on occasion becomes "Dosset" or "Doucet." Frances Doucet was buried in 1771 at Belliveau Cove, Digby County. Her gravesite near the beach is presently marked by an upright slab of slate with the words "Francis Doucet, 1771" roughly inscribed on it.

52 NSARM, Registers of the Parish of St. Jean-Baptiste, Annapolis Royal, 1702–55. RG 1, vol. 26, 242, "Marriage of Pierre Chegneau (or Chegua), 27 years old, to Marguerite Baptiste, 17 years old, daughter of Chief Jean-Baptiste (Medosgsnel) and his wife Magdeleine of Cape Sable, 25 June 1727." The presiding priest was René Charles de Breslay. The witnesses were Pierre Charet (Momcharret) *dit* Bouta and his brother Pierre Charet *dit* Cellier. Pierre Chegua was the son of Germain Cheguouéo, born in 1646, and his wife Marie Madelaine. The name "Chegua" can be also be written "Chego," "Chegon," "Chegouéo," "Chegneau," "Chequa," "Chigan," "Chishaw," "Shagwaough," "Sheshaw," "Toton," "Toutou," and "Tutter."

53 According to the French nominal census compiled by Abbé Antoine Gaulin in 1707–08, Paul Tecouenemac (Tecouramart) was forty-five, married to Marie Agathe, fifty, with three sons – Guillaume, seventeen; Anthoine (or Antoine), fourteen; and Philipe (or Philippe), eight – and two daughters – Marie, eighteen; and Cecile, one year old. LAC, MG 18, F 18, *Recensement genal fait au mois de Novembre mile Sept cent huit, Cap-Sable*. One copy of the 1726 treaty document, of which there are several, all dated 4 June 1726, bears Aboriginal signatory marks and what seem to be totemic marks (though none of these designations were made by signatories of the Tecouramart family). LAC, CO 217/38. This copy of the treaty accompanied a despatch, dated 27 November 1726, that Lieutenant Governor Lawrence Armstrong sent to the British Colonial Office in London. William C. Wicken notes the presence of Paul, Antoine, and Philip Tecumart (Tecouramart] at the 1726 treaty signing in *Mi'kmaq Treaties on Trial: History, Land and Donald Marshall Junior* (Toronto: University of Toronto Press, 2002), 42.

54 Charles La Tour operated fur trade and fishing posts at Cape Sable, on the Saint John River, and on the Penobscot River. About 1620 La Tour married a Mi'kmaw woman by whom he had three daughters. M.A. MacDonald, *Fortune & La Tour*, 12–13, 43–4. Whether or not this woman hailed from Cape Sable remains unknown, though this would have been around the time La Tour resided at Chebogue, near present-day Yarmouth, where he established Fort Lomeron. This fort, also called St. Louis, was named after La Tour's leading supplier at Rochelle in France, David Lomeron, and remained the only French stronghold left in New France following the Kirke brothers' capture of Quebec in 1627. Interestingly, prior to the Second World War there was a heap of rocks along the right bank of the Chebogue River at what used to be called "Indian Point" and later "Crocker Hill" that were rumoured to be the remains of a monument built to an early Cape Sable chief. When the Canadian army used the site as a firing range, the feature disappeared. Probably at the urging of Charles La Tour's father, Claude La Tour, a Chief Segipt made a pact of friendship in 1629 on behalf of the southwestern Mi'kmaq with Sir William Alexander the Younger's company at Scotsfort. Segipt probably belonged to the Port Royal band, though this is not certain. His name does not appear again after 1629. Charles La Tour travelled to France in 1632, first to Rochelle and later to Paris, bringing with him two Mi'kmaw men, one of whom was a chief. MacDonald, *Fortune & La Tour*, 44–5. The passenger list drafted on 28 April 1633 for the return voyage of the *Renard Noir* bound for Cape Sable gives the names both of La Tour and La Tour's two Mi'kmaw companions. The first man listed, Quichetech, was identified as a *caquis* (*caïque* or chief). The second simply bore the name Menougy. This passenger list is housed in the Archives de la Charente-Maritime, Amirauté de la Rochelle, B5654. MacDonald, drawing on Marc Lescarbot's observations on Mi'kmaw customs, holds that Quichetech was a member of the Mi'kmaq nation, since an *ech* or *ach* at the end of a man's name indicated a "younger person" in the Mi'kmaw language. MacDonald, *Fortune & La Tour*, 205n5; see also Marc Lescarbot, *The History of New France*, trans. W.L. Grant (Toronto: Champlain Society, 1907), 3.81. The documentary record pertaining to the years of civil unrest surrounding La Tour's and de Charnisay's struggle for the control of Acadia rarely mentions the Mi'kmaw peoples involved in the fray. It has been suggested that members of the de Perisse (Jean de Perisse, Jeanperis, or Iamperiss) family of Port Royal were possibly descended "from a Port Royal Mi'kmaq named Semcoudech, who called himself 'Paris' after a visit to that city c. 1607." In the mid 1730s the de Perisse famiy became allied by kin ties with the Eptemec family of La Have. In 1707–08, Pierre Eptemec, the sixty-five-year-old head of the Eptemec family at La Have and his

wife Madelaine had a married son, Guillaume thirty years old and two daughters, Anne and Catherine, who were seventeen and twelve respectively. LAC, MG 18, F18, *Recensement genal fait au mois de Nouembre mile Sept cent huit, for La heue [La Hève].* Though the majority of the members of the Eptemec family remained at La Have, Guillaume Eptemec and Aimé's daughter Anne married Guilllaume de Perisse, son of Estienne Ianneperis (Jean de Perisse) of Port Royal and remained there, and on 25 August 1735 Guillaume de Perisse and Aime's son Charles de Perisse wed seventeen-year-old Marie Grand Claude (later Glode) of Port Royal. The "Mi'kmaw Gloade Family," *Newsletter*, Annapolis Historical Society (Spring 2011), 3–4. The Claude-Eptemec-de Perisse alliance was important to the Alexis family too. In 1753 François de Perisse of Annapolis, most likely the thirty-eight- or thirty-nine-year-old son of Estienne Ianneperis, would act as an advocate for a group of sixty Cape Sable Mi'kmaq with the British. Finally, when Joseph Howe, in his capacity as Indian commissioner for Nova Scotia in 1842, interviewed a Cape Sable family surnamed "Toutou" (Chegua), he found that they used "Charnisay" as one of their synonymous names. This caused Howe to jot down, in the margin of his daily journal, "La Tour's old rival." He could elicit no further information on this subject, prompting him to muse how much intriguing Cape Sable history had been lost in the two hundred years since the heyday of La Tour. NSARM, RG 1, vol. 432, Joseph Howe, 96, "Western Tour," 1842.

55 Although La Tour and this woman may not have been wed according to the tenets of the Roman Catholic Church, their union was probably sanctioned under Mi'kmaw custom.

56 In addition to running a trans-shipment station, Baron Philippe Mius d'Entremont assumed the rank of king's attorney from 1670 until his death in about 1700.

57 The Cape Sable group was involved in these activities from 1690 onward. For instance, Villebon included in his journal of events on 25 May 1692, "There arrived from Cape Breton, La Heve and Cape Sable 64 Micmac Indians to whom I had sent word in the autumn that they were to join the Kennebecs at Pentagoet. I provided them a feast and afterwards supplied them with powder and balls and a little tobacco that they might go to the rendezvous." John Clarence Webster, *Acadia at the End of the Seventeenth Century: Letters, Journals and Memoirs of Joseph Robineau de Villebon, Commandant in Acadia, 1690–1700* (Saint John: New Brunswick Museum, 1934), 38.

58 Marie-Marthe was also known as Marie Pidianski or Marie Pidiwammiskwa. The Etchemin group encountered by the French in the early seventeenth century later gave rise to the Penobscot nation of Maine and the Malecite nation of New Brunswick.

59 Bernard-Anselme d'Abbadie de Saint-Castin moved to the vicinity of Port Royal from the Pemaquid and recruited Penobscot, Malecite, and Eastern Abenaki from as far south as the Kennebec River area to attack the English. In 1707 he defended Port Royal at the head of his Native contingent so stoutly that French officialdom gave him leave in October of that year to marry Marie-Charlotte Damours, a daughter of the seigneur of Jemseg. Bernard-Anselm de Saint-Castin and his Indigenous warriors were absent from Port Royal when the formidable naval force led by Sir Francis Nicholson on 2 October 1710 wrested the fort away for the last time from the French. Acadians who remained around Port Royal at this time were expected to take the oath of allegiance to Queen Anne, but the military weakness of the Annapolis Royal garrison once Nicholson's companies were withdrawn made English control of Acadia, whose bounds were poorly delineated anyway, ineffectual. In June of 1711 Bernard-Anselm, along with the French missionary Abbé Antoine Gaulin, was the instigator of a Native ambush of a party of soldiers sent out in a whaleboat and two flatboats to collect wood for Governor Samuel Vetch. Sixteen men were killed, nine wounded, and the rest captured in this melee, which became known as the Battle of Bloody Creek.

60 Anonymous, "Letter from Annapolis Royal," *Boston Newsletter*, 19 March 1713; Massachusetts State Archives, Boston, "A Journal of a Voyage to Cape Britton on ye Kings account by Mr. Peter Capon … 1715." Similar intentions to establish trade ties with the English were voiced over the next four years by leaders of neighbouring Mi'kmaw villages along the eastern Atlantic coast.

61 Baron Saint-Castin's marriage took place at Pentagouet, now Oldtown, Maine, according to Indian custom around 1678. Georges Cerbelaud Salagnac, "Abbadie de Saint-Castin, Jean-Vincent d', Baron de Saint-Castin," *DCB* online, vol. 2 (1701–40). Not long afterwards Queen Anne's War (1702–13) broke out. This conflict was the North American component of the War of the Spanish Succession that occurred in Europe, and was the second in a series of conflicts known as the French and Indian Wars fought between France and England for control of the North American continent.

62 On 4 December 1707 Bernard-Anselm's sister, Thérèse Saint-Castin, married Philippe Mius d'Entremont

(b. 1682), the son of Jacques I Mius d'Entremont *dit* Pobomcoup and Anne La Tour. Philippe was a grandson of Baron Philippe I Mius d'Entremont and his wife, Madeleine Hélie Du Tillet, of Normandy, France. D'Entremont, *Histoire du Cap-Sable*, 3.919–20. It was a double marriage on a single day for the Saint-Castin family, since Thérèse's half-sister, Anasthasie Saint-Castin, on the same day married Alexandre Bourg de Belle-Isle at Port Royal. NSARM, RG 1, vol. 26, 286, Parish of St. Jean-Baptiste, Port Royal, "Marriage of Thérèse de St. Castin and Philippe de Pobomcoup, witnesses Vincent baron de St. Castin and Marie Pidiwammiskwa." Thérèse's husband Philippe later died on the Saint-Castin estate at Bearn in France. Jacques Mius d'Entremont became the baron of Pobomcoup when his elderly father, Philippe, bequeathed him his baronial estate and went to live at Grand Pré with his daughter, Marie-Marguerite Melanson, the wife of Pierre Melançon *dit* Lavadure. Pierre Melançon, in turn, was the brother of Jean Lavadure who took part in the plot to sell Cape Sable Mi'kmaq as slaves in the Azores.

63 Baron Philippe I Mius d'Entremont and his wife, Madeleine Hélie, had raised a large family with kin connections throughout Acadia. Their daughter Marie-Marguerite had come with them from Normandy to Acadia in 1651. Around 1665 Marie-Marguerite married Pierre Melancon *dit* La Verdure, while her younger sister Madeleine remained unmarried. The baron also had three sons. Two of them, Jacques Mius d'Entremont *dit* Pobomcoup, born in 1659, and Abraham de Pleinmarais (also Plemzais or Plemarch), born about 1661, married, respectively, Anne and Marguerite La Tour, daughters of Charles La Tour and Jeanne Motin, Charnisay's widow and La Tour's third wife.

64 Philippe II Mius *dit* d'Azy was born circa 1660. D'Entremont, *Histoire du Cap-Sable*, 3.944.

65 D'Entremont, *History of Quinan*, 84–5. Philippe Mius *dit* d'Azy and his Native spouse were the parents of Joseph I Mius *dit* d'Azy, who was the father of Jean Baptist I Mius *dit* d'Azy, who in turn was the father of Laurent Mius who married Marie Alexis.

66 Clarence d'Entremont lists the first group of Philippe's offspring as Joseph Mius, Marie Mius, Mathieu Mius, Maurice Mius, and Françoise Mius. Mathieu remained at Cape Sable and married a Mi'kmaw woman named Marie-Madeleine, while Maurice Mius and his Mi'kmaw wife Marguerite resided at Musquodoboit. Joseph, the eldest son, wed Marie Amirault, daughter of François Amirault *dit* Tourangeau and Marie Pitre o Ouikmakagan. D'Entremont. *Histoire du Cap-Sable*, 3.968–1010.

(Note the caveat about Joseph Mius *dit* d'Azy possibly being the son of Abraham Mius d'Entremont *dit* Pleinmarais. The weight of opinion, however, holds that Joseph was the son of Philippe II Mius *dit* d'Azy.) Philippe's children by his second Native spouse entered fur trade society. This second union produced eight offspring, of which four were daughters. Marie Mius wed Jean-Baptiste Thoma (or Thomas), who became a head chief at Annapolis and Piziquid (Windsor) around 1756, while her sister Madeleine married Jean-Baptiste Guidry of Merliguesche (now Lunenburg). Françoise married three times (first to an unknown man, second to René Grand Claude [Glode], and third to Pierre Charet, or Momcharret, *dit* Cellier). The youngest daughter, Anne, wed Paul Guidry of Merliguèshe. Of the four sons, Jacques, the eldest, who married a Mi'kmaw woman, was hanged in Boston in November 1726 along with his brother-in-law, Jean-Baptiste Guidry, for piracy on the high seas. Jacques's son, Antoine Mius, later would become a chief and join the followers of Abbé Le Loutre at Beaubassin prior to the onset of the Seven Years' War. Pierre Mius *dit* d'Azy had a wife named Marguerite Lapierre and moved back and forth between Grand Pré and the Saint John River. François Mius, born in 1700, became a trader as well as the captain or chief of the "command" of Merliguèshe, which was recognized by a commission extended to him by Governor Duquesnel at Fortress Louisbourg in 1742. He remained head chief of Merligueshe until the end of the Seven Years' War and in November of 1761 signed a peace and friendship treaty with the British on behalf of the La Have band. His son Jacques Mius married Brigit (or Brigitte) Alexis, who was likely one of Charles Alexis's sisters. Finally, little is known of Philippe III Mius, born in 1703, who may have died early in life. D'Entremont. *Histoire du Cap-Sable*, 3.1010–18; NSARM, RG 1, vol. 430, docs. 20 and 21, "Abbé Jean-Mandé Sigogne to Lieutenant-Governor Sir John C. Sherbrook," 5 May 1812, with the 1742 commission, 1761 treaty parchment, and medal Sigogne acquired from François Mius's son Jacques.

67 These meetings may have taken place within the framework of the Wabanaki Confederacy, which at this time would have been in its heyday. Confederacy members continued to meet until the mid 1840s. Frank G. Speck, "The Eastern Algonkian Wabanaki Confederacy," *American Anthropologist*, 17 (1945): 492–508.

68 LAC, CO 217/2, "Regarding the Cape Sable Mi'kmaq taking several fishing vessels, 1915. Extract of a letter from David Jeffries and Charles Shoprove at Boston to Captain Robert Moars," 4 July 1715.

69 Major events associated with Dummer's War and its aftermath are examined in Wicken, *Mi'kmaq Treaties on Trial*, 77–87.

70 "Governor Dummer to John Wentworth," 9 July 1725, in "Letters of Colonel Thomas Westbrook and Others," *New England Genealogical and Historical Register*, April 1893, 164. A Mi'kmaw negotiator, Joseph Nebon (or Nevin), who had been born at La Have but later moved to Cape Sable, was also prominent in negotiations surrounding this treaty signing. D'Entremont, *Histoire du Cap-Sable*, 4.1600.

71 Captain Majory received his commission in August of 1724. The commission is found in "Documents Relating to Marblehead," *Essex Institute Historical Collections*, 62 (1926): 116–17.

72 Circumstances around the time of the English conquest of Acadia and the Treaty of Utrecht in 1713 affecting Paul Tecouenemac's (or Tecouramart's) son Antoine are discussed by William Wicken in "Mi'kmaq Decisions: Antoine Tecouenemac, the Conquest, and the Treaty of Utrecht," in *The "Conquest" of Acadia, 1710: Imperial, Colonial and Aboriginal Constructions*, ed. John G. Reid et al. (Toronto: University of Toronto Press, 2004), 86–100. For the Tecouramarts and the treaty signing of 1726, see NSARM, CO 217/38. This copy of the treaty (of which there are at least four, all dated 4 June 1726 and housed in the Nova Scotia Archives and Records Management in Halifax) bears signatory marks that may have had a totemic-like inference, though none of the Tecouramart family used such designations. It accompanied a dispatch dated 27 November 1726 from Lieutenant Governor Lawrence to the British Colonial Office in London, England. Wicken mentions the presence of Paul, Antoine, and Philip "Tecumart" at the 1726 signing in *Mi'kmaq Treaties on Trial*, 42. The treaty concluded at Annapolis Royal in 1726 was a ratification of a treaty signed between the English and the Eastern Abenaki at Boston the previous year. The other names on the document of head men from Cape Sable were Étienne and Jacques Chegua, Jean and Pierre Pisnet, and Joseph Ounaginitish. These names are taken from all of the copies of the treaty. Interestingly, an "Estienne Checau" (Étienne Chegua) appears as an Acadian individual on the 1707–08 French census for Port Rasoire [*sic*, Port Razoire]. The Étienne Chegua who signed the 1726 treaty, however, was a relative of Pierre Chegua. LAC, RG 18, F 18; LAC, CO 217/38/117–18; LAC, CO 217/38/108 and LAC, CO 217/38/102–03. As late as 1842, Joseph Howe noted that the members of the Touton (Chegau) family considered their synonymous surname to be "Charnisay." NSARM, RG 1, vol. 432, 96.

73 Though *Xs* representing Mi'kmaw signatures were placed on a treaty document of 1726, it appears that a train of final proceedings in securing a lasting peace between the Eastern Abenaki peoples and the English dragged on until 1728 in both New England and Nova Scotia. Wicken, *Mi'kmaq Treaties on Trial*, 158–9.

74 The fishing vessel under Captain Samuel Doty anchored in Merliguèche harbour, near the fishing and fur-trading establishment belonging to the Guedry *dit* Labrador family. The reason for the heist seems to have been the reluctance of New England to release François Mius, the son of Philippe II Mius *dit* d'Azy and his Native wife, Marie. This incident is discussed more fully in the entry in this volume on Paul Guedry *dit* Labrador. A thorough examination of the trial in Boston and its consequences may be found in Bill Wicken, "26 August 1726: A Case Study in Mi'kmaq–New England Relations in the Early Eighteenth Century," *Acadiensis* 23, no. 1 (1993): 5–22. Also see Wicken, *Mi'kmaq Treaties on Trial*, 148–53.

75 In November 1727 Paul Tecouramart and his sons Antoine and Jean-Baptist were called upon to reveal whatever they knew about Mi'kmaw attacks on crews of New England vessels that had occurred at Liscomb Harbour and Jeddore, along the eastern Atlantic coast. LAC, CO 217/38/176–77, At a Council Held Tuesday, 7 November 1727, regarding Chief Paul Tecouramart and his two sons [Antoine and Jean-Baptist Philippe Tecouramart]. At the time Governor Armstrong had the articles of the 1726 treaty read to these men.

76 Antoine Tecouramart Sr. at this time was the head man of an encampment of fifteen families at Cheboque, not far from where La Tour's old Fort Lomeron had existed in the seventeenth century. Antoine Tecouramart only narrowly escaped being unfairly charged with stealing valuables, including a ring and gold chain that the woman found aboard the *Baltimore* said he had taken. A New Englander named George Ridge meanwhile stripped the vessel of all its rigging and only left the anchors. The Cape Sable head men were asked to give testimony. After extensive depositions taken from Antoine Tecouramart, Anasthase Tecouramart, and Pierre Chegua as well as Charles Mius d'Entremont *dit* Pobomcoup and George Mitchell – who brought the woman from Pobomcoup to Annapolis Royal – Lieutenant Governor Lawrence Armstrong began to suspect the woman's story. A missionary, a Mr. Chevereau, had just served the Cape Sable Mi'kmaq with the sacraments, and he assisted the Mi'kmaq with their depositions. LAC, CO 217/39/152–58; LAC, CO 217/39/160–63, Examination of Charles d'Entremont of Poubomcoup; Declaration

of Anthony Telgudmott [Tecouramart]; LAC, CO 217/39/191–94, Deposition of Susanna Buckler; Copy of George Mitchell's Deposition; NSARM, RG 1, vol 24, Minutes of HM Council at Annapolis Royal, 1720–40, in Brown Papers, 1881, vol. 24, regarding Anthony Tecouneart [Tecouramart], his wife, his brother Anuthuse (Anathase) and 2 children. The letter by Lawrence Armstrong to "Dear Chief Pierre [Chegua]," 17 May 1736, is found in Archibald MacMechan, ed., *A Calendar of Two Letter-Books and One Commission-Book in the Possession of the Government of Nova Scotia, 1713–1741*. Nova Scotia Archives II (Halifax: Herald Printing House, 1900), 102. (During the investigation Armstrong addressed Pierre Chegua as "Dear Chief Pierre." Chegua, who had been tracked down by Armstong's party at La Have to give testimony, replied that he had no idea about the woman's identity or what had happened on the vessel to the crew. One major goal of the investigatory committee set up at Annapolis Royal was to find out why "Dame Buckler" remained the sole occupant of a vessel. Since the brigantine's decks had been smeared with blood, lurid stories had begun to circulate about a mutiny aboard the vessel where the perpetrators, after killing the crew, fled in longboats. Thomas Chandler Haliburton, *An Historical and Statistical Acccount of Nova-Scotia* (Halifax: J. Howe, 1829), 1.106n. At this point, Chegua and the Tecouremarts chose reticience over further disclosure, for they feared they might still be punished for looting items the woman said they had stolen. In the midst of this temporary conspiracy of silence, the voice that held sway was that of "Dame Butler." Yet it was obvious the crew had not died from natural causes, as she had stated, for the brigantine's hold revealed ample provisions as well as liquor. The woman made things even more confusing by claiming not only French descent but also to be a *cousin germaine* to the La Tour family living at Louisbourg. This would have meant she was a daughter of Agathe La Tour, who in turn was a daughter of Charles La Tour. Agathe La Tour at the time lived in Kilkenny, Ireland, and for a while the familiar claim seemed plausible as the brigantine had left Dublin on 7 October 1735. All these statements, however, were completely discredited when the real wife of the vessel's captain was located in Boston. The woman found aboard the *Baltimore* was revealed to be a convict who probably had plotted the mutiny in concert with the other convicts. Chief Chequa lent pathos to what was already suspected concerning the fate of the vessel's crew by recounting having seen newly dug graves on an island he had passed while travelling back from La Have. Father Clarence-J.

d'Entremont suggests that this island might have been l'Isle-au-Massacre, known as Murder Island in English, one of the isles in Tusket Bay. Though the island may have gained its grisly name from this incident, there are several other alternative explanations for its name. D'Entremont, *Histoire du Cap-Sable*, 4.1660–1.

77 Wicken reviews Mi'kmaw population numbers for Cape Sable, as recorded in the 1735 French census, in "Mi'kmaq Land in Southwestern Nova Scotia, 1771–1823," in *Making Adjustments: Change and Continuity in Planter Nova Scotia, 1759–1800*, ed. Margaret Conrad, (Fredericton: Acadiensis, 1991), 115.

78 NSARM, RG 1, vol. 26a, 12, Registers of the Parish of St. Jean-Baptiste, Annapolis Royal, 1702–55, "Baptism of Antoine Tekonmak (Tecouramart), thirteen months old, 20 November 1727, son of Antoine Tekonmak and Marie Magdelaine Huronne." The child had been conditionally baptized in the absence of a priest by Francois Villatte of Cape Sable. The officiating priest was René Charles de Breslay and witnesses were Prudeau Robichaux and Anne Robichaux.

79 Charles Tecouramart was born on 18 February 1733 and baptized at Port Royal on 1 March 1733. He was earlier conditionally baptized (*été ondoyé*) at Cape Sable by Joseph Amirault. At some time in the 1750s he married Marie-Rose Mius and the couple had a daughter, Marie-Rose Tecouramart. On 1 September 1789 this daughter wed Mathias Taianneugche at the Mission des Huron, La Jeune Lorette, Province of Quebec. She is identified in the church register as "Marie Rose Découvemat [*sic*, Tecouramart or Tecounemate]," daughter of Charles Découvemat and Marie-Rose Mius *"de la baie de Chebouctou dans la Nouvelle-Ecosse."* D'Entremont, *Histoire du Cap-Sable*, 4.1618–19. The Indigenous residents of Loretteville were once called the Huron of Lorette, though "Wendake" is the present name for the *Huron*-Wendat reserve. *Loretteville lies within* La Haute-Saint-Charles borough *of Quebec*. The Nova Scotian Tecouramart family must have continued to retain close ties for many years with the Lorette Huron community, since Charles' Tecouramart's daughter, Rose, as late as the 1780s married a Huron man. Interestingly, the surname "Tecouramart," or a variation of it, "Tek8erimat," also appears among members of the Algonkin nation north of the St. Lawrence. In 1664 a drunken Algonkin man named Robert Hache had assaulted the wife of an inhabitant of Ile d'Orleans and had been brought to trial in Quebec. At the time a Christian Algonkin by the name of Noel Tek8erimat asked that the death penalty for rape not be invoked, as his people were not aware

of the severity of the French punishment for rape. *Jugements et délibérations du Conseil souverain de la Nouvelle France* (Québec, 1885) 1.129–30, 174–5. This incident is also mentioned on p. 18 of a manuscript by Olive Patricia Dickason entitled "Louisbourg and the Indians: A Study in Imperial Race Relations, 1713–1760." A copy of this ms, dated September 1972, is housed in the archives of Fortress of Louisbourg Historic Park. It was subsequently revised and published in monograph (Ottawa: DIAND, 1976).

80 NSARM, RG 1, vol. 430, docs. 20 and 21, "Sigogne to Sherbrooke, 5 May 1812, with enclosures." One of these enclosures is Mius's 1742 French commission.

81 LAC, CO 217/8/48 ½. Captain Peter Warren stated that the French had so riveted the Mi'kmaq to their interest that the Indigenous people would "not suffer an English man to settle or cure Fish in any of the Ports on the South side of Nova Scotia." During his relatively short life, Warren (1703–52), an Irishman who signed on with the British navy as an ordinary seaman, rose quickly through the ranks and, as Commodore Warren, commanded the naval forces in the attack on Louisbourg in 1745. The role he played in this expedition earned him a fortune, a knighthood, and promotion to the rank of Rear Admiral of the Blue. He spent the remainder of his life in pursuing philanthropic activities and then died suddenly of a "violent fever" at the age of forty-nine. Julian Gwyn, "Warren, Sir Peter," *DCB* online, vol. 3 (1748–70).

82 D'Entremont, *Histoire du Cap-Sable*, 4.1885–6.

83 The name of Françoise Mius's first husband is unknown. Her second marriage was to René Grand Claude, a Mi'kmaw chief of Annapolis, and upon his death she married a third time, to Pierre Charet [Momcharret] *dit* Cellier, a prominent Minas headman. D'Entremont, *Histoire du Cap-Sable*, 3.968–1019.

84 The Cape Sable group was involved in intercolonial wars between the English and French from 1690 onward.

85 French officialdom did not court the Mi'kmaq as either kin or friends. According to Olive Patricia Dickason, the French at Louisbourg "never really learned to like the Indians." Dickason, "Louisbourg and the Indians, 1713–1760," ms., September 1972, ix. By 1730 fur trade society was changing and being redirected towards Louisbourg, where the official line combined adherence to the French trade system with loyalty to the French monarch. Because of this, a far greater measure of social distance ensued than had previously existed between the elite French partners in this relationship and the Indigenous trappers who supplied the furs and filled the ranks of Indigenous recruits in time of war. The contractual

system of commissions and honorifics set down by Louisbourg's officialdom was a far cry from the closeness of kin ties that characterized the Atlantic seaboard's combined Acadian, *métis*, and Mi'kmaw community around 1700. Louis Du Pont Duchambon de Verger's marriage to Jeanne Mius d'Entremont drew little adverse attention when it occurred at Port Royal in 1709. Some minor difficulties arose afterward when Jeanne Mius d'Entremont, who could speak the Mi'kmaw language fluently, assumed the role of Native interpreter, but this was because the Mi'kmaq did not think her role a suitable one for a woman. *et l'Amérique publies par le Canada-François*, vol. 3 (Quebec, 1890), 165. At the time of their marriage on 11 February 1709, Louis Dupont was identified in the Port Royal parish register as a lieutenant of the French garrison and a son of Hugues Dupont and Dame Marie de Gourville of the parish of Dupont, diocese of Xaintes in Xaintonge, France. Jeanne Mius d'Entremont was presented as "damoiselle Jeanne Mius de Poubomkou, daughter of Jacques Mius de Poubomkou and Dame Anne de St. Etienne … seigneurs of Acadia." The presiding Recollect missionary was F. Justinian Durant, with Daniel d'Auger de Subercase, Simon-Pierre Denys de Bonaventure, Marie Mius, Charles Mius, and Anne Mius acting as witnesses. "Abstract from the [Port Royal] parish register," in *Report Concerning the Canadian Archives Branch for the Year 1904*, Appendix G, 303. Louis Dupont Duchambon (1680–1775] was commander at Louisbourg at the time of its fall in 1745. Duchambon had remained second in command at the fortress until Commandant Jean-Baptiste-Louis Le Prévost Duquesnel's sudden death in October 1744 thrust him to the helm, as king's lieutenant of Ile Royale. The person who originally had been slated to be Duquesnel's replacement, Antoine-Alexis Perier de Salvert, was unable to reach the fortress. Eleven years later, in 1755, the social divide between those of *métis* ancestry and Louisbourg's officialdom came to a head when an ensign with French aristocratic ancestry by the name of Ferdinant de Noyes married Anne Guedry, a daughter of Paul Guedry *dit* Labrador and his wife Anne Mius, who was a sister of François Mius, the head chief of Merliguesche. Noyes's superiors immediately sought to have his union with Anne Guedry annulled. LAC, AC, F3 50: 504v–524, Conseil superieur, 17 February 1755; LAC, AC G2 189: 279–360, Greffes des colonies, 1754–55. See also d'Entremont, *Histoire du Cap-Sable*, 3.1017–18. The marriage vows took place at Baie des Espagnoles, which is now Sydney, Cape Breton. La Noye was the son of Messire Toussaint Marie de La Noue, Chevalier au Parlement de Bretagne.

86 Marshall, *Heroes of the Acadian Resistance*, 65–7. The others outlawed by the English were Joseph Broussard *dit* Beausoleil, Joseph-Nicholas Gautier and his sons Joseph *fils* and Pierre, Armand Bigeau, Joseph Le Blanc *dit* Le Maigre, Pierre Guedry *dit* Labrador, Charles and François Raymond, and Charles and Philip LeRoy.

87 Mocodome has been renamed Country Harbour, which lies in Guysborough County.

88 Chief Thoma wed Marie Mius, one of Chief François Mius's sisters.

89 Antoine Tecouramart Sr.'s recruitment of spokesmen from the ranks of the Annapolis band may have also been based in the fear that his own long-standing position as a middleman in the French fur trade might undermine his people's plea for leniency and much-needed English supplies.

90 Beamish Murdoch, *A History of Nova-Scotia, or Acadie* (Halifax: James Barnes, 1865), 2.225–6.

91 This generosity did not spring from an on-the-spot decision; it was received policy. British colonial governors had been instructed "to be attentive to shew kindness and to give protection" to such Mi'kmaq "as profess an Amity for us." NSARM, RG 1, vol. 29, 25. On 16 November 1753, Chief Baptist Thomas and a delegate from Cape Sable, representing a band of sixty people with two chiefs, met with the governor and council in Halifax. The two men had voyaged by canoe to Lunenburg, and from there were taken by schooner to Halifax under the auspices of Colonel Sutherland. Once in Halifax, they claimed that they were well known in New England since they had always given New England "Vessels all the assistance they could when one of them happened to be drove on that part of the coast which they inhabit." Owing to the recent hostilities that had broken out they had been "deterred from going among the English." It had been five months since they visited the Fort of Annapolis, and since they never received any assistance either from the French or English "they were reduced to great extremities by want of both provisons and clothing." Their desire was for "some authentick instrument" that they could show upon any occasion when they looked for relief and assistance. But ultimately they left the decision on this head entirely "to the consideration of the Council, with whose determination they should be entirely satisfied." After hearing their pleas, the council decided to give them supplies. NSARM, RG 1, vol. 210, 5, "At a Council holden at the Governor's House, Halifax, on Tuesday, 16 November 1753." Chief Jean Baptist Thoma, in his larger capacity as a district chief for the whole of southwestern Nova Scotia, was urged to act

for the Cape Sable band. This chief gained a reputation for promoting peaceful relations between the British and the Mi'kmaq of Gespogeitnag even during the tumultuous years of the Seven Years' War, as the entry on him in this volume discusses. The identity of the second chief who sent Jean de Perisse to Halifax as his delegate was not mentioned in the council minutes, but it probably was either Pierre Chegua or Antoine Tecouramart.

92 Around twelve hundred beaver pelts were shipped from Halifax in 1753, and though returns from beaver exports fell during Le Loutre's War by 50 per cent – which suggests that most furs of this type were being taken to Beasejour or Louisbourg – trade in other furs increased, indicating a continued interest among middlemen in trading with the English. LAC, CO 217/14/185r-196v, "Sir Thomas Peregrine Hopson to the Lords of Trade, 23 1753"; LAC CO 5/886/218, "Shirley to Lords of Trade," 22 October 1753; LAC, CO 5/886/218.

93 NSARM, RG 1, vol. 210, 5. The council furnished provisions for only twenty individuals rather than the entire sixty people the delegates represented. Bread was given in generous amounts, but also included were "3 lbs pork, 20 blankets, 30 lbs powder, 60 lb shot, 50 lb tobacco, 1 grosse of pipes, 2 Hats Gold Laced for the two chiefs and 1 hat Silver Banded for the Deputy." The master of schooner who brought the Mi'kmaw delegates down to Lunenburg was also paid ten pounds.

94 Chief Antoine Mius's presence in the vicinity of Beausejour in the early 1750s is mentioned in John Clarence Webster, *Thomas Pichon, "the Spy of Beausejour": An Account of His Career in Europe and America* (Halifax: Public Archives of Nova Scotia, 1937), 82. Antoine Mius was probably a son of Jacques Mius, a son in turn of Philippe II Mius *dit* d'Azy. Jacques Mius was hanged in 1726 in Boston for robbery on the high seas. D'Entremont, *Histoire du Cap-Sable*, 3.1012.

95 Webster, *Thomas Pichon*, 82–3.

96 Paul Laurent was captured by New Englanders and held for a number of years in Boston, where he learned to speak English fluently. One might wonder if he was in Boston at the same time as François Mius. "Extract of a letter from Col. Frye to his excellency the governor of Nova Scotia, dated Fort Cumberland, Chignecto, 7 March 1760," *Massachusetts Historical Society Collections* (1809), ser. 1, 10.115–16.

97 "Lawrence to Robert Monckton, 16 February," in "Two Letters of Charles Lawrence," *Cahiers de la Société historique Acadienne* 3 (December, 1969), 175.

98 It was revealed that it was the murder of a Cape Sable man and his family by Englishmen at Mocodome that led

to the killing of the government ship's crew at Jeddore in 1753. Archives de Colonies, Paris, France, documents on microfilm at AC, CIIB 33: 181v–182v, "Comte Raymond to Antoine-Louis Rouillé, Comte de Jouy," 17 June 1753.

99 Early in 1754 the Cape Sable Mi'kmaq were described as peaceful, but later and through to the late 1750s parties resumed hostilities. NSARM, RG 1, vol. 36, 7.

100 James F. More, *The History of Queens County, N.S.* (Halifax: Nova Scotia Printing, 1873), 121.

101 Thomas Robertson, "History of Shelburne County," Akins Prize essay (Halifax: ms. and typescript at King's College University Library, 1873), 5, 8–9.

102 Manach's list of chiefs with Michel Argomartin's name on it accompanied a letter from Colonel Frye to the governor of Nova Scotia dated Fort Cumberland, Chignecto, 7 March 1760. Both are published in *Massachusetts Historical Society Collections*, Massachusetts Historical Society (Boston, 1809), 10.115. Like Pierre Chegua, Michel Argomartin had deep roots in the southwestern Mi'kmaw community, for he almost certainly was the Michel Talgomatique born in 1702 at Cape Sable to Louis Talgoumatique and Marie Agathe, a married couple whose names appear on the La Chasse census of 1708 for Cape Sable. LAC, MG 18, F18, *Recensement genal fait au mois de Nouembre mile Sept cent huit … 1708*, "17th family enumerated at Cape Sable." Born in 1702, Michel Talgoumatique may have been the father of Bernard Argomartin, who reputedly supported the British and became a chief at Gold River in Lunenburg County, Nova Scotia, as well as Pierre Argomartin, a misogynist who reputedly murdered three wives as well as a Black woman from Shelburne whom he killed near Clements Pond, on the road from Clyde River to Barrington. Pierre kept one wife from escaping her fate by drawing a sharp knife across the soles of her feet and then filling the cuts with hot ashes. As punishment for his hideous crimes, the Cape Sable group hamstrung him on a beach near the mouth of the Barrington River in Shelburne. He later fled to the Cambridge area near Kentville, Kings County. Robertson, "History of Shelburne County," 5. The political dynamics that persuaded Michel Argomartin and his son Bernard to side with the English at the latter end of the Seven Years' War are unclear, but it is possible that, like Joseph Argimault of Chignecto, he subscribed to the Mi'kmaw scheme to have the British reserve a vast tract north of the Shubenacadie River. After Michel's death two men named Gabriel and Jean-Denis Argomartin continued to live in Yarmouth County until the 1820s. See Abbé Jean-Mandé Sigogne's census of

the Cape Sable Native Population c.1822, "Familles des Sauvages, listing heads of families," published in *Cape Sable: Vital Records, 1799–1841 from Roman Catholic registers of Saint Anne of Eel Brook/Argyle, Saint Michel of Tusket/Argyle, and Saint Peter of Pubnico*, transcribed and edited by Leonard Smith (Clearwater, FL: self-pub., 1979 [1974]). Jerry Bartlett or Jerry Lonecloud recounted a second story about Pierre Argomartin: that Argomartin had been a chief from Milton in Queens County who was at the "French Landing to meet the French fleet [the Duc d'Anville's expedition in 1746]" and then went back to Milton. While there, he was killed for unspecified reasons and his body thrown into Milton Pond. Nova Scotia Museum (henceforth NSM), Piers Papers, "Jerry Lonecloud to Harry Piers," 2 October 1917.

103 François Chegua was Chief Pierre Chegua's nephew. Joseph Howe noted that the name "Tutter" (Toutou or Chegua) was associated with the name "Charnisé" among a Mi'kmaw group in Clare Township in 1842, a fact that perplexed him since "Charnisay" was the name of La Tour's rival. NSARM, RG 1, vol. 432, 96, Joseph Howe, "Western Tour," 1842. François Shagwaough (or Chegua) was the same person as the "François Chegouéo" listed on the French census of 1707–08 as being the only son of Jacques Chegouéo and his wife Catherine. François was only one year old when the census was taken. His uncle Pierre Chegua, born about 1702, was actually seven years his junior. LAC, MG 18, F18, *Recensement genal fait au mois de Nouembre mile Sept cent huit*. There is a fair amount recorded about the Chegua family. François, born in 1707, was as stated above the only son of Jacques Chegouéo and his wife Catherine. Jacques Chegouéo was the son of Germain Chegouéo, who was born in 1646. Germain and his wife Marie Madelaine had three sons – Jacques, who was twenty-three in 1708; Estienne, fifteen; and Pierre, eight; and four daughters – Marie-Joseph, nineteen; Madeline, thirteen; Margueritte, ten; and another daughter called Margueritte who was nine. Pierre Chegua, who was born in 1700, in 1727 married Marguerite Baptist, a daughter of the Cape Sable chief Jean Baptist Medesgnal. NSARM, RG 1, vol. 26, Registers of St. Jean-Baptiste Parish, Annapolis Royal, 1702–55, 242, "Marriage of Pierre Chegneau [Chegua], son of Germain Chegneau and Marie Madelaine, to Marguerite Baptist, daughter of Chief Jean Baptist of Cape Sable, 25 June 1726, Witnesses Pierre Charet (*dit* Cellier) and his brother Pierre Charet (*dit* Bouta)." These two Charet brothers appear earlier on the 1707–08 census for Port Royal. Under

"*veuves*" (widows) one finds that in 1707 a Port Royal chief named Memcharet had recently died, leaving a widow "Marie veuve de Memcharet" (Momcharet, Charet, or Coureat) and her sons, Pierre Sellier (Cellier), twenty-one, and his brother Pierre, sixteen. These men later would become influential Native leaders at Minas. François Chegua, born in 1706 or 1707, and his wife Cecile had a son François baptized at Port Royal on 14 April 1733. D'Entremont, *Histoire du Cap-Sable*, 3.1033. There also was an orphan, a young woman named Anne Chegouéo, living with her one-year-old daughter at Cape Sable in 1707–08. "Estienne Chicau," listed in 1707–08 as living alone among the Acadian families at Port Razoire, probably also belonged to the Chegua family. Several of this family moved east along the Atlantic coast, and about 1780 some descendents of a man named Paul Chego (Chegua), whose forebearers had intermarried with the Guedry and Le Jeune families, left for Cape Breton, northeastern New Brunswick, and Newfoundland. At Chezzetcook in the spring of 1770, for instance, Father Charles-François Bailly, who came as a missionary to the Mi'kmaq and Acadians in 1768, christened Elizabeth Chego (Chegua), daughter of Paul Chego (Chegua). Thomas "Neaukout" (Neocout or Knockwood) and Marie Neaukout acted as witnesses. Elizabeth Chego later wed Henri L'Official and the pair moved to southwestern Newfoundland, where they had a daughter Anne who married François Benoit, the patriarch of the Mi'kmaw Benoit family of Newfoundland.

104 In 1760, when the British government was extending peace overtures to the Mi'kmaq while at the same time still paying the scalp bounties, first levied in 1756, on Mi'kmaq who did not submit to British rule, Governor Charles Lawrence issued a "Full and explicit Pass to Francois Shagwaough [Chegua] of the Cape Sable Indians, who having been to Halifax to make his submission to his Majesty's Government and declaring that his chief Michael Agoumartin is disposed to life in peace and perfect amity with his Majesty's Subjects of this Province, and purposes speedily to appear in persons and ratify for himself and his People the Peace now making with the Several tribes of Mickmack Indians, I have thought proper to make him some presents as a Token of my regard in the mean time and to give him this Pass hereby forbidding all manner of Persons to hurt or molest him. Signed, Charles Lawrence, 24 April 1760." NSARM, RG 1, vol. 156, 53–4, "Pass to François Shagwaough of Cape Sable, along with a Petition from Shagwaough on behalf of his chief, Michel Agoumartin," 24 April 1760. No documentary evidence exists that confirms Michael Agoumartin (or Argomartin) ever did sign a treaty with the British after this event.

105 NSARM, RG 1, vol. 165, 54–5, "Passes to several Mi'kmaq given in 1760, including one to Francis Keehosgeith of Cape Sable."

106 Janet Chute has viewed the originals of two of these treaties in NSARM. The copy she saw, which was originally drafted for Paul Laurent's signature on 10 March 1760, lacks Laurent's signature. The date of Paul Laurent's actual signing of the document was taken from Murdoch, *History of Nova-Scotia*, 2.385.

107 NSARM, RG 1, vol. 165, 224–5, "By the Honorable Jonathan Belcher, A Proclamation, May, 1762." The final section of this proclamation read: "And, whereas claims have been laid before me in behalf of the Indians for Fronsac Passage and from thence to Nartigonneich [Antigonish], and from Nartigonneich to Pihtouk [Pictou], and from thence to Cape Jeanne [Cape John], from thence to Emchih, from thence to Kagi Pontouch [Tatamagouche], from thence to Jediack [Shediac], from thence to Cape Rommentie [Cape Tormentine], from thence to Mirimichy, and from thence to Bay de Chaleurs, and the environs of Canso, from thence to Mushkoodabout, and from thence to Meshpatagan [the Aspotogan Peninsula, south of Halifax], and so along the coast, as the claims and actual possessions of the said Indians, for the more special purpose of hunting, fowling and Fishing, I do hereby strictly enjoin and caution all persons to avoid all molestation of the said Indians in their said claims, till His Majesty's pleasure In this behalf shall be signified. AND if any person or persons have possessed themselves of any part of the same to the prejudice of the said Indians in their Claims before specified or without lawful Authority, they are hereby required forthwith to remove, as they will otherwise be prosecuted with the utmost rigour of the law."

108 NSARM, RG 1, vol. 31, no. 10, "Extract from the Minutes of the Proceedings of the Lords Commissioners for Trade and Plantations," 3 December 1762; LAC, Co 217/20: 202–04, "Joshua Mauger to the Lords of Trade and Plantations," 28 September 1763.

109 More, *History of Queens County Nova Scotia*, 136.

110 Campbell, *A History of Yarmouth*, 19–22; NSARM, RG 1, vol. 380, *Sketches of the Eastern and Northern Parts of the Province in the Years 1801 and 1802, with General Observations Therein … by Titus Smith Jr.*, 3rd ed. (Halifax, 1851), 116.

111 NSARM, RG 1, vol. 36, 7–24; NSARM, RG 1, vol. 37, doc. 13, "Cape Sable proprietors, 1758–1760"; Wicken, "Mi'kmaq Lands in Nova Scotia," 116; LAC, CO

217/19/149f; LAC, MG 11, micr. B-1028, "General Return of the Inhabitants in the Several Townships Settled at Cape Sables," June 1762.

112   Murdock, *History of Nova-Scotia*, 2.431.

113   According to Lunenburg County historian Mather Byles Desbrisay, "On August 22nd, 1762, Francois Mius, chief of the Indians at La Have, and four others waited on the Lieutenant-Governor and Council, and asked that they might have a priest, as they had been without one since M. Maillard's death. They were assured that their request would be complied with as soon as possible, and having received the usual presents they took their leave." Desbrisay, *History of the County of Lunenburg*, 2nd ed. (Toronto: William Briggs, 1895), 345.

114   LAC, CO 217/19/16–23.

115   NSARM, RG 1, vol. 165, 282, "Passes to Jean Baptist of Cape Sable and Joseph Shickakett, Chief of Cumberland," 30 September 1763. There can be no doubt that "Joseph Shickakett" refers to Chief Joseph Argomault, for not only was Argimault head chief of Cumberland or Chignecto at the time, but the Mi'kmaw term "Shickakett" also is simply a variant of the Mi'kmaw word for "Chignecto," which is *Siknikt* or *Schiknikt*. "Jean Baptist," moreover, almost certainly refers to Jean-Baptist Philippe Tecouremart, who had been closely allied politically with Chief Argimault while both lived at Beaubassin from 1753 to 1755. The two leaders also were close in age: in 1763 Argimault was sixty-two years old and Tecouramart was sixty-three. LAC, MG 18, F18, *Recensement genal fait au mois de Nouembre mile Sept cent huit de tous les Sauvages de l'Acadie que resident dans la Coste de l'Est … 1708*, focusing on families listed for Chignecto and Cape Sable. The outcome of the chief's projected expedition to Britain cannot be determined from the documentary record, except that both leaders' names disappear from all sources of official correspondence after September 1763. Neither does Argimault's or Jean-Baptist Tecouramart's name appear in existing Roman Catholic church registers from 1769 to 1772, though this is not true of the names of the sons of Jean-Baptist Tecouramart's brother, Antoine Tecouramart *père*.

116   Father Clarence-J. d'Entremont wrote the first author about Parc á Sheshaw in 1990, so she visited this site in 1994. François Chegua was the deputy of Michel Argomartin in 1760. He later rose to be a chief at Cape Sable, and was living at Eel Brook when the Acadians returned to Cape Sable in the late 1760s.

117   Janet Chute has researched and written two manuscripts touching on this subject, after conducting interviews with Acadian residents of the Ste. Anne du Ruisseau area in the early 1990s. The first one, completed in 1999 under the auspices of the Aboriginal Title Project organized by TARR (Treaty and Aboriginal Rights Research, based at Shubenacadie, Nova Scotia), is titled "Interpenetrating Realities: A New Perspective on Acadian and Mi'kmaw Land Use in Southwestern Nova Scotia," and the second, a manuscript of 120 pages completed in September 1994, is titled "A Good Day on the Aboiteau: An Ethnographic and Ethnohistorical Study of the Acadian Métis of Eel Brook and Quinan Areas, Municipality of Argyle, Nova Scotia." Most members of the Miuse family at Quinan today are descendants of Joseph I Mius *dit* d'Azy, a grandson of Baron Philippe I Mius d'Entremont. The view of many genealogists is that Joseph I Mius *dit* d'Azy was the son of Philippe II Mius *dit* d'Azy and his first Mi'kmaw country wife. Joseph I Mius *dit* d'Azy married Marie Amirault *dit* Tourangeau, and many of the Acadians who returned to Lower Eel Brook, near present-day Ste. Anne du Ruisseau, after being in exile owing to the Acadian deportation were their descendants. The Acadian spelling of the surname that derived from "Mius" is usually "Muise," and the Mi'kmaw spelling is "Meuse." In 1994 at Lower Eel Brook near Ste. Anne du Ruisseau, John Mius *dit* "The Dude" a direct descendant of Joseph I Mius *dit* d'Azy and Marie Amirault *dit* Tourangeau, told the first author that his grandfather, Eli Miuse, who spoke Mi'kmaq, annually presented the Cape Sable chief Bartlett Alexis with a bag of salt before Eli's family fished at Eel Creek. The recipient of the salt would have been Chief Stephen Bartlett of Yarmouth. John Miuse *dit* "The Dude" of Lower Eel River was the "batman" of the first author's uncle, Philip Partington, during the Second World War, and the two men remained close friends afterwards. This opened the door for interesting conversations. John Miuse, one of whose ancestors, Louis Miuse, fled in 1756 to join the Mi'kmaq on the Tusket River before being caught by the English in 1758, also respected the rights of the Mi'kmaq. He explained that many of the Miuse family living along the Tusket River, and related in the past through kinship to the Alexis family, employed the designation *Les Gaspereau*. This is because around 1780 Laurent Mius of Tusket Forks, a great-grandson of Philippe II Mius *dit* d'Azy, married one of Charles Alexis's daughters named Marie Alexis and this couple had a son, Jean-Baptiste Mius, who married Geneviève Moulaison and had a grandson Léon, born in 1840, who was known as Léon Miuse *dit* Gaspereau. D'Entremont, *History of Quinan*, 85. Eli

Miuse, who used to take his grandson John Muise with him to go eeling, would ask the chief if they could fish for eels near the Mi'kmaq encampment, a wish Chief Bartlett granted. John Miuse stated, "[The Mi'kmaq] have rights … Well I knew Sam Glode and Bartlett. The Indians used to settle all through the places. They were welcome … My grandfather could speak Mi'kmaq. He had learned [it] from the fellow from Tusket who used to come for dinner all the time. That was the Bartlett … I remember the chief came out and he had a great big hat. He was all alone … I can't remember his [first] name. My grandfather gave him something [like salt] in a bag." John Miuse *dit* La Dude, personal communication, 25 August 2004. The Mi'kmaq left permanent marks on the social landscape because certain of their rights to resources became respected in perpetuity at the local level. This was not in small part owing to the aid from the Acadians and Acadian-*métis*, and there is still much to discover regarding these protocols.

118 Breynton, a Welshman, who was associated in Britain with the Society for the Propagation of the Gospel in Foreign Parts (SPGFP), in 1754 assumed the rectorship of St. Paul's Church in Halifax.

119 NSARM, RG 1, vol. 168, doc. 155, microfilm reel 15281, "To Francis Alexis, Chief of the Cape Sable Indians, Greeting … From William Campbell," 22 June 1771.

120 The 1771 commission to François-Joseph Alexis ignored the fact that the Mi'kmaq had fished at Eel Brook for generations and that the Acadians had recognized the Mi'kmaq's right to fish at Eel Creek since the seventeenth century. In the past the vulnerable state of small Acadian outposts along the eastern seaboard had required the French to find ways of forging bonds of trust with the Mi'kmaq. By taking care not to impinge on Native resource locales and by providing gifts and other acknowledgments of Mi'kmaw prior right whenever access to resources under Native aegis became necessary, the Acadians ensured that a spirit of peaceful reciprocity persisted between the two communities. By contrast, the British made the Mi'kmaw people's retention of land and resource rights conditional on the pleasure of the English monarch, a concept doubtless poorly understood by the Mi'kmaq at the time. British unwillingness to admit that respect protocols ever existed within the Cape Sable transactional context blinded Halifax's officialdom to the interpretation that Chief François-Joseph Alexis and his brother Charles Alexis would later place upon the 1771 commission. The chiefs held that the commission recognized Mi'kmaw prior right to their fishery as well as protected their planting and hunting grounds under a form of land grant. The fact that the document furnished no areal boundaries and failed to refer to enforcement mechanisms against trespass to which the Mi'kmaq might resort soon led to problems.

121 Eel Brook, also sometimes known as Eel Creek, drains from Eel Lake, whose water levels in earlier times were controlled by an Acadian *aboiteau* near Ste. Anne de Ruisseau. The brook today runs through a passage beneath Route 3. The name "Eel Brook" is said to originate in a translation of the Mi'kmaq word *Wiplomesgokum*, which means "place of eels, but they were poor and lean." The parish of Ste. Anne de Ruisseau was not established until the arrival of Abbé Jean-Mandé Sigogne in 1799, so it was not in existence at the time Lord William Campbell granted François Alexis his commission. This commission was not a licence of occupation to land, but an unusual document, almost one of a kind, that fell somewhere between the French commissions awarded to chiefs prior to the fall of Louisbourg in 1758 and stipulations in the treaties of 1726 and 1760–61 that chiefs subject themselves in various ways to the English Crown. François Alexis's commission, however, differed from earlier ones bestowed by the French because the Mi'kmaq in 1771 were no longer as independent of colonial impositions as they had been prior to 1760. The British by 1771 could use the Mi'kmaq's interest in preserving their eel fishery at Eel Creek as a tool to force them to keep the peace by stating that otherwise their rights to fish would be revoked. The entire document reads, "To Francis Alexis, Chief of the Cape Sable Indians, Greeting, Whereas I [Lord William Campbell] am well satisfied with the fidelity, zeal and attachment which you, Francis Alexis, have shown the King's most excellent Majesty, I do therefore as a mark of approbation give and grant unto you the said Francis Alexis the honour to wear the Glorious Colours of our Gracious Sovereign King George the Third, and Command you to behave as a good, faithful Overseer over the families of Indians at Cape Sable – and Order them strictly to keep themselves always in subjection and obedience – and upon this condition I do grant unto you the said Francis Alexis leave to hunt, fish and Improve lands under the usual instructions, particularly in the Creek known as Eel Creek, without hindering or molesting any other subjects who may chuse [*sic*, choose] to fish there also." For additional discussion of the content and nature of this document, see Wicken, "Mi'kmaq Land in Nova Scotia," 116–18, and Gillian Allen, "Licenses of Occupation in Nova Scotia: A Reserve by Any Other Name Is Still a Reserve?," discussion paper prepared for

the National Research Directors Workshop for Specific Claims Organizations across Canada (NRDW), Ottawa, 8 November 2006, 6.

122 Wicken, "Mi'kmaq Land in Nova Scotia," 117.

123 Campbell, *A History of Yarmouth*, 47–9.

124 NSARM, RG 1, vol. 189, 104, Halifax Executive Council Minutes, 5 November 1773.

125 William Wicken noted that the memorial was deferred for "further consideration," probably owing to a prohibition placed upon the granting of land in April 1773 by the Board of Trade, the government body in England responsible for administering Nova Scotia. Wicken, "Mi'kmaq Land in Nova Scotia," 118.

126 Wicken, "Mi'kmaq Land in Nova Scotia," 118.

127 NSARM, RG 1, vol. 26a, Registers of St. Jean-Baptiste Parish, Annapolis Royal, 1702–55, 4, "Baptism of François-Joseph Alexis, four months old, 11 June 1727," who was first baptized at sea.

128 Should Jacques Alexis have been born into the Penobscot nation, Antoine Tecouramart may have been one of the first to welcome him and his family to Cape Sable.

129 Claude Galarneau, "Bailly de Messein, Charles-François," *DCB* online, vol. 4 (1771–1800).

130 Janet Chute, "Ceremony, Social Revitalization and Change: Micmac Leadership and the Annual Festival of St. Ann," in *Papers of the Twenty-Third Algonquian Conference*, ed. William Cowan (Ottawa: Carleton University, 1992), 54.

131 NSARM, copy of old registers conserved at Caraquet, New Brunswick, 1768–73, 1786–96, on microfilm, *Registre des actes de baptême, marriages, et sepultures faits en la nouvelle ecosse ou acadie …*, 14, entries made at Piziquid, 4 June 1769. Antoine and Cecile's children, both four years of age, were named Isidore and Marie Anne.

132 These two unions constitute an example of a brother-sister exchange frequently found among the Mi'kmaq. As Bridget and Pierre-Paul Alexis were born in the early 1740s, they would have to be the offspring of Jacques Alexis and Angèlique.

133 NSARM, copy of old registers conserved at Caraquet, New Brunswick, 1768–73, 1786–96, on microfilm, *Registre des actes de baptême, marriages, et sepultures faits en la nouvelle ecosse ou acadie …*, 15–16, entries made at Chezzetcook, 21 June 1769. Godparents for Marie Mius were Joseph Lauverste and Catherine Argimaux (Argimault), while the godparents for Marie Jeanne Mius were Thomas Alexis and Geneviève Alexis. Godparents for Pierre-Paul and Helen Mius's son Germain Alexis were Paul Alexis and Marie Bonis, the godparents for their son Hierome were Jerome Denis and Félicité Mius,

and the godparents for Noel Alexis were Charles d'Ekouminat (Tecouramart) and Angelique Mius.

134 Bailly's registers, dating from 1768 to 1772, provide glimpses of where Charles Alexis's siblings were living at the end of the Seven Years' War. François Mius's son Jacques Mius and his wife Brigit Alexis, as well as Brigit's brother Pierre-Paul Alexis, were all probably situated at La Have, and travelled eastward along the coast to visit the missionary Bailly at Chezzetcook. At this time La Have had a sizeable Native population, drawing its residents from descendents of Philippe I Mius *dit* d'Azy, the Bernard family of Minas, Paul Laurent's family, the Argomartin family of Cape Sable, the Jeremy family of the Eastern Atlantic coast, and Alexis incomers. Charles Tecouramart, since he was closely associated with Jacques Mius and Brigit Alexis in the entries in Bailly's registers, also seems to have been part of the La Have Native community at this time.

135 NSARM, on microfilm, copy of old registers of Charles-François Bailly, 17, entries made at Cape Sable, 6 August 1769.

136 Jacques Jaco could have been François-Joseph's elderly father who, after his first wife Angélique's death, married a much younger woman, but it is most probable that Jacques was either François-Joseph's brother or François-Joseph's son.

137 NSARM, on microfilm, copy of old registers of Charles-François Bailly, 17, entries made at Cape Sable, 6 August 1769. The godparents of François-Joseph Alexis's son Jean-Baptiste were Jacques Alexis and Isabell Belliveax (Belliveau). The godparents of Jacques's son Simon were Jacques Amirault and Agnes Gaudet, while Jerome's godparents were François Alexis and Marguerite d'Entremont.

138 Ibid., Entries made at Baie Sainte-Marie, 21 September 1769; d'Entremont, *Histoire du Cap-Sable*, 4.1886, 1921.

139 Other ways of spelling this word are "Macloudiak," "Macoudiak," and "Mawtookvac." D'Entremont, *History of Quinan*, 5.

140 The Tusket River takes its name from the Mi'kmaw word *Niketaouksit*, or *Nakataoukit*, which means "the great forked tidal river." D'Entremont, *History of Quinan*, 4. On pages 6 to 8 of this work, Father d'Entremont describes lakes, rivers, marshes, Native graveyards, and portages in the region between Pubnico Lake and The Forks (now Quinan).

141 Michael and Joseph are mentioned in the papers of Indian commissioner George Henry Monk. LAC, MG 23, GII-19, Monk Papers, 1748–1823, vol. 4, Letter Book of George Henry Monk, 1046–7, entry for 10 December 1793.

142 Abraham and Samuel may also have been sons of Francois-Joseph Alexis who joined Charles's family after the death of their father in 1773. It is most likely, however, that they were Charles's sons.

143 Laurent Mius was related to François Mius of Merliguèche, who was a son of Philippe Mius d'Azy and his second Mi'kmaw consort, Marie.

144 Father Clarence-J. d'Entremont traced descendants of Laurent Mius and Marie Alexis. D'Entremont, *History of Quinan*, 84–118. Laurent Mius and Marie Alexis's son Jean-Baptiste married Geneviève Moulaison at Church Point, District of Clare, on 7 September 1810, and the couple would have six children: Marie-Osithe or Mary-Esther, born in 1811; Anne-Elizabeth, born in 1812. Jean-Remi, born in 1814; Perpétue-Anatasie, born in 1816; Louis-Baptiste, born in 1819; and Cyrille-Baptiste *dit* Weegeegane, born in 1812. The Weegeegane is a small stick used to hold pigment while porcupine needles were being dyed. Wilson Wallis and Ruth Sawtell Wallis, *The Micmac Indians of Eastern Canada* (Minneapolis: University of Minnesota Press, 1955), 89. Father d'Entremont also looked at Jean-Baptiste's grandchildren. For instance, Jean Remi Mius and his wife Gertrude Mius had a son, Léon Mius, born in 1840, who became known as Léon *dit* Gaspereau. Léon is the ancestor of several families at Quinan today.

145 *Wolastoqiyik* means "the people of the beautiful river" – which refers to the Saint John River.

146 L.F.S. Upton, *Micmacs and Colonists: Indian-White Relations in the Maritimes, 1713–1867* (Vancouver: University of British Columbia Press, 1979), 73–5.

147 Ibid.

148 Frederic Kidder, ed., *Military Operations in Eastern Maine and Nova Scotia during the American Revolution, chiefly composed from the Journals and Letters of Colonel John Allan* (Albany: John Munsell, 1867), 60–1. The Mi'kmaq were fearful of British reprisals if they supported the American cause. The chiefs in council reported to Allan: "Our situation and Circumstances being such at present, Our natural inclination being Peace, only accustomed to hunt for the subsistence of our family, We could not Comply with the Terms – our numbers being not sufficient among other objections. And as it was not done by our authority & consent of the Difft Tribes we are necessitated to return it." The chiefs concluded with the hope that they would cause no offence in sending the treaty back, "Protesting at the same time that the Chain of Friendship is still subsisting between us on our side & that we hope for ever. A further Account of our situation will in our Name be delivered our brothers & Countrymen by John Allan Esq., Bearer of this – Our Love and friendship be with you all." This missive was drafted at "Coquen," or Cocagne, just north of Shediac, present-day New Brunswick, on 19 September 1776. The chiefs were Joseph Sapsarouch of Miramichi, Jean-Baptist Alymph of Richibucto, Augustan Michel of Richibucto, Thomas Athanage of Shediac and Cocagne, Jerome Athanage of Shediac, Baptist Arguimon (*sic*, Argimault) of Chignecto, and Charles Aleria (*sic*, Charles Alexis) of Cape Sable. Each chief made his mark, since none could write.

149 Queens County at this time stretched all the way from Liverpool to Yarmouth and embraced present-day Queens, Shelburne, and Yarmouth counties.

150 Jackson Ricker, *Historical Sketches of Glenwood and the Argyles, Yarmouth Co., NS* (1941, repr. Yarmouth, NS: Sentinel Printing, 1994), 22–3. MacKinnon at first led the 2nd Light Infantry Company of the 2nd Battalion. Then, as commander of the 84th Regiment of Foot, also known as the Royal Highland Emigrants, he led a surprise night attack in 1778 against American privateers who were harassing Sable Island. The incident became known as "The Raid of Sable Island."

151 NSARM, RG 1, vol. 189, Executive Council Minutes, 5 November 1773; NSARM, RG 20, Land Grants, vol. 2, "Grant of the Reverend John Breynton," 21 January 1785. Breynton and MacKinnon complained that the Mi'kmaq claimed an exclusive right to the river lot and demanded that the Native fishers be excluded so that their own claims could be paramount. Considering that long before 1750 the southwestern district Mi'kmaw chief had always demanded some sort of reparation from outsiders for use of the Eel Brook fishery, the Alexis's claims to the river lot are not surprising. Breynton's and MacKinnon's memorial was deferred for further consideration, possibly under a temporary injunction set up by the British Board of Trade in April 1773 against granting further lots in Nova Scotia. Yet when the granting of lands was resumed after the Loyalist influxes, the Executive Council favoured Breynton's claim over the Mi'kmaw one, and the rector in early January of 1785 received seven hundred acres of land adjoining Eel Lake, in the vicinity of Eel Brook.

152 Alexis likely asked Parr to negate Breynton's recent grant acquisition at Eel Brook and reallocate the seven hundred acres to the Mi'kmaq on the same footing as Chief Philip Bernard's grant, given in early February 1786. NSARM, Papers of the NS Public Crown Lands Record Office (PCLRCO), book 18, 24, "Crown Land Grant to Philip Bernard [or Barnar], Solomon and Taumagh, registered

10 March 1786." John Parr was appointed governor of Nova Scotia in July 1782 with the support of the Earl of Shelburne, and was commissioned lieutenant governor on the abolishment of the governorship of the province in 1786. He died at Halifax on 25 November 1791.

153 Alexis, while speaking some English, could not sign his own name. The handwriting of the signature is so similar to that of George Henry Monk, who became provincial commissioner of Indian Affairs in 1783, that it seems reasonable to suggest Monk also was present at this audience and signed the document for Chief Alexis.

154 On 22 June 1786 Governor John Parr had directed Charles Morris, the surveyor general, "to accommodate the [Mi'kmaw] bearers for grants near Cape Sable agreeable to their wishes." The lands were to be properly located and surveyed and, once this was done, Morris was to contact the provincial secretary, Richard Bulkeley, to have both grant and survey confirmed. Whether Parr intended the survey to accompany an actual freehold grant, such as Parr extended to Chief Philip Bernard of St. Margaret's Bay the same year, rather than a licence of occupation remains a moot point. NSARM, RG 20, Series A, Land Papers, vol. 17, microfilm reel 15681, "Indians of Cape Sable 1786–96, Land for Charles Alexis, document dated 22 June 1786." The document stated that Richard Bulkeley, the elderly provincial secretary, should be given a "proper Description" of the grant.

155 Ibid., "Undated statement by Charles Morris, framed as a license of occupation, accompanying Parr's instructions." Charles Morris had succeeded his father, Charles Morris Sr., to the rank of superintendent-general of Crown Lands upon his father's death in 1781, and he would retain this position until his own death in 1801. Ethel Crathorne, "The Morris Family –The Surveyors-General," *Nova Scotia Historical Quarterly* 6 (June 1976): 207–9.

156 NSARM, RG 20, Series A, Land Papers, vol. 17, "Indians of Cape Sable 1786–96, document dated 22 June 1786, with accompanying license drafted and signed by Charles Morris."

157 Abbé Pierre Maillard set up provisions for certain prominent Acadians and Native chiefs to administer sacraments in the absence of a priest. Before the Seven Years' War there was not a permanent Roman Catholic chapel at Eel Brook, though makeshift chapels would have been constructed whenever itinerant French missionaries visited the area.

158 Robertson argues that "after the arrival of the English settlers" the Mi'kmaq "were generally treated with respect." Robertson, "History of Shelburne County," 5.

159 The French arpent approximates an acre of land. In 1767 Lieutenant Governor Michael Franklin granted 80 arpents to the heads of eighteen Acadian families in the Cape Sable region, yet in the early years Acadians were not allowed to hold land freehold at either Eel Creek or Tusket. Jacques Amirault, Joseph Moulaison, Jean-Pierre Mius, and Charles Doucette settled at Tusket, while Pierre and Louis Mius, Jean Bourque, Joseph Babin, Dominique Pothier, Pierre Le Blanc, and Pierre Surette resided at Eel Brook. In 1773 the Reverend John Breynton, who sat in the legislative assembly at Halifax, gained the right to lease 1,193 arpents, extending from Eel Brook to the local marsh and including Rocco Point, for 999 years to Pierre and Louis Mius, Dominique Pothier, Pierre Le Blanc, and Pierre Surrette. Pierre and Louis Mius were sons of Joseph Mius *dit* d'Azy and Marie-Joseph Préjean, and grandsons of Joseph I *dit* d'Azy and Marie Amirault. D'Entremont, *Histoire du Cap-Sable*, 4.2039–40. Later, these Mius brothers moved temporarily to Wedgeport, though some of their descendents, including John Miuse *dit* "The Dude," returned to Ste. Anne du Ruisseau. In 1775 Ranald MacKinnon rented 236 arpents of land, extending from the Baie-à-Outardes to Eel Brook, to Jean Babin, Dominique Pothier, Jean Bourque, and Paul Surrette for eight Spanish dollars. This tract eventually was sold to these four Acadian heads of families for one hundred pounds. At this time the Acadian village retained the name "Eel Brook," though the name was later changed by Abbé Jean-Mandé Sigogne to "Ste. Anne du Ruisseau."

160 Laurent Mius was the fourth-eldest son of Jean-Baptiste I Mius and Marie-Josephe Surrette, which made him the grandson of Joseph I Mius dit d'Azy and Marie Amirault *dit* Tourangeau who had once lived at Ouikmakagan. Joseph I Mius, Laurent's great-grandfather, in turn was the eldest son of Philippe II Mius dit d'Azy and his first Mi'kmaw spouse. In 1758 Laurent Mius and his parents were deported by the English from the Reynardton region of Cape Sable to Massachusetts. While in exile Laurent, who was literate, proved to be a tireless negotiator. He sent several petitions to the Massachusetts government asking for leave for his parents and himself to move from Tewksburg to Salem. "[O]n ne peut imaginer en trou plus miserable" (One cannot imagine a more doleful hole), he wrote of his lodgings at Tewksburg. Massachusetts State Archives, Boston, vol. 24, folio 121; d'Entremont, *Histoire du Cap-Sable*, 4.2022, 2025–7. By the late 1770s Laurent and his parents had made their way back to southwestern Nova Scotia. Like so many returning Acadians, they had travelled back to Cape Sable by way of Barrington in

present-day Shelburne County. They located for a while at Pointe-des-Bens, now Miuse Point near Eel Brook, and then proceeded up the Tusket River to The Forks. It was probably near Eel Brook, rather than at The Forks, that Laurent first met his bride-to-be, since their marriage apparently occurred prior to his taking up residence on the middle reaches of the Tusket River. Laurent, who was born around 1739, would have been around forty at the time of his marriage to Marie Alexis. D'Entremont, *Histoire du Cap-Sable*, 3.997–8.

161 Their children, Jean-Baptiste, Marie-Osithe and Marguerite, as well as Marie their foster child, married into either the Acadian or the Mi'kmaw community. In 1810 Jean-Baptiste Mius wed Geneviève Moulaison at the Église Sainte-Marie de Clare; in 1813 Marie-Osithe wed Laurent Gilbeau, also of Clare; Marguerite married a Mi'kmaq man from Liverpool; and Marie married Olivier Frontain, the son of Julien Frontain and Anne Mius of The Forks.

162 Marie Alexis's name was entered in the burial registers of the Parish of Ste. Anne du Ruisseau as Marie Alexis *dit* Michaud, which suggests a close association with her eldest brother Michael, also known as Michael Alexis. Registers of Ste. Anne du Ruisseau, Eel Brook, Burial of Marie Alexis *dit* Michaud, 6 October 1807, Abbé Jean-Mandé Sigogne presiding. This entry states that Marie Alexis died in the middle of the woods. "Michaud" was employed as a Mi'kmaw surname in Cape Breton (see the entry on Jean Michaud in this volume), and it is possible that the Alexis family and the Michauds were distantly related in the eighteenth century. The position of Laurent Mius's eldest daughter, also called Marie, remains a little problematic, as she seems to be much older than Laurent Mius and Mary Alexis's other children. D'Entremont, "The Family of Laurent Mius and Marie Alexis," in *History of Quinan*, 84–7; d'Entremont, *Histoire du Cap-Sable*, 3.1023–24. Marie Mius certainly was raised by Laurent Mius, even if Laurent was not her biological father. If she was his biological daughter, she and her husband, Olivier Frontain, were both great-grandchildren of Joseph I Mius *dit* D'Azy, as they both fell within the French kin category of *cousins germains*. Father d'Entremont notes that several of Laurent and Marie's daughters were at their mother's funeral in 1811, though as they were not named their identities remain unknown. D'Entremont, *History of Quinan*, 997–8.

163 In 1812 Jean-Baptiste Mius and Geneviève Moulanson had a son named Cyrille-Baptiste Mius, known as Weegeegane, who married Anne-Rosalie Doucet. Léon Mius *dit* Gaspereau was the thirteenth child of Cyrille-Baptiste Mius and Anne-Rosalie Doucet. Jean-Baptiste

kept up his relations with the Alexis family, for in 1816 he brought a close relative, Hélène Alexis, down to Eel Brook for her first communion. Hélène, who is cited as being Mi'kmaq, is recorded as being the daughter of Jean Baptiste, but he most likely would have been her foster father. RG 1, vol. 2A3, 26, "Baptism of Mi'kmaw woman, Hélène Alexis, 1 November 1816."

164 Conversations with Dr. Sylvestre Muise of Quinan and his family in 1990, 1994, 1999, and 2011. A biologist who has taught at the Université Sainte-Anne at Pointe-de-l'Église (Church Point), and in retirement has maintained a fox farm at Quinan, Dr. Miuse is a descendant of Laurent Mius and Marie Alexis. He and his family maintain a lively interest in the history of Quinan, as well as in the southwestern Nova Scotian Acadian community as a whole.

165 Oral traditions state that the Cape Sable Mi'kmaq supplied the first settlers with eels and moosemeat during the first hard winters. Campbell, *A History of Yarmouth*, 19–22.

166 Wentworth also asked for two hundred pounds for relief for the Mi'kmaq in his letter to Henry Dundas, principal secretary of state for the British Home Department. NSARM, RG 1, vol. 50, Letter Books of Governor Wentworth, "Wentworth to Dundas, 3 May 1793," n.p.; Murdoch, *History of Nova-Scotia*, 3.110.

167 Wentworth may also have expressed his views on raising an Indigenous militia to Brigadier General James Oglivie and several others. His appeal for relief for the Mi'kmaq was later taken up by William Cottnam Tonge, who became a member of the House of Assembly and in 1800 was made a member of the Committee of His Majesty's House of Assembly appointed to administer Relief to the Native Indians of the Province. NSARM, RG 1, vol. 430, doc. 34, "Members of the Committee to Edward Irish and Timothy Hierlihy, Antigonish, Nova Scotia," 10 December 1800. Not long after Wentworth contacted Dundas, Ogilvie led a British naval expedition against French-occupied Saint Pierre and Miquelon, where the British seized several French fishing vessels and two American schooners bearing naval stores. Lieutenant Governor John Wentworth wanted the six hundred French prisoners taken during this expedition housed in quarters on Kavanagh's Island (now Melville Island, where the old stone prison building is now a core part of the Armdale Yacht Club), but Ogilvie preferred to send them to the Cornwallis Barracks in Halifax. In July 1793, when it was learned that a French squadron lay in the waters of the Chesapeake, Ogilvie took the lead in urging the mustering Mi'kmaw militia defences,

which would include "buying the services of the Indians by feeding and entertaining them." He further directed George Henry Monk to act as their leader, "and to 'modify them' without pay of salary, except such reasonable contingent expenses as unavoidably must be incurred." Murdoch, *History of Nova-Scotia*, 3.115. When fears of a French invasion ebbed by late summer, the idea of raising an Indigenous Native militia was dropped.

168 In 1772 Michael Francklin granted a large tract at Stewiacke to Chief Paul Peminout and a second sizeable parcel at Grand Lake along the Shubanacadie River system to Chief Peminout's son, Jacques Peminout Paul. The Peminout lands were treated as freehold grants that could be, and ultimately were, sold by their Mi'kmaw possessors. The majority of Mi'kmaw chiefs, however, between 1779 and 1783 were accorded licences of occupation that remained subject to the pleasure of the British monarch. Importunity, however, occasionally proved effective. Chief Philip Bernard, finding that a licence of occupation offered him by the government in 1782 was rendered null and void by the fact that the parcel had previously been granted to another, went to Halifax to complain of his situation to Governor Parr. Parr then granted Bernard a freehold grant of five hundred acres at the Head of St. Margaret's Bay. The Peminout and Bernard grants were surveyed and properly registered, whereas most of the lands held under licences of occupation remained unsurveyed and vulnerable to trespass. Chief Bernard's grants of land on St. Margaret's Bay are examined in greater detail in chapter 7 of this volume.

169 Alexis, like Chief Bernard, would have bypassed the intricacies of formally applying for a land grant by simply appearing with his son Michael at the lieutenant governor's office in Halifax with his demands, and then expecting the lieutenant governor to act on his behalf. In response, Parr charged Morris with providing the Cape Sable Mi'kmaq the lands they requested. But the licence of occupation Morris issued to the Cape Sable Mi'kmaq on 22 June proved an ambiguous statement if there ever was one. No mention was made in it of bounds, nor was there reference to how the government might set up barriers to trespass. The eel fishery would become common ground for all, and Morris made no effort to secure even the Mi'kmaq's gardens or their burial ground at Eel Brook for their exclusive use.

170 NSARM, RG 1, vol. 430, doc. 26½, Licenses of Occupation, 18 December 1783.

171 LAC, MG 23, GII-19, Monk Letterbooks, vol. 4, 1037, "Monk to Lieutenant-Governor Sir John Wentworth," 23 May 1793.

172 LAC, MG 23, GII-19, Monk Letterbooks, 1046–7, "Entry for 10 December 1793." For a reference to "Antoine Ebere [Antoine Hébert]" in 1727, see LAC, CO 217/38/117.

173 Monk, however, felt far less concern about this incident near Windsor than Wentworth and in the end dissuaded the lieutenant governor from incarcerating the Mi'kmaw perpetrators, including their families, at Fort Edward at Windsor. Monk felt that the Mi'kmaq's retention of a few stolen sheep was insufficient grounds for such harsh punitive measures, especially as the Mi'kmaw party in question were destitute.

174 LAC, MG 23, GII-19, Monk Papers, Letterbook of George Henry Monk, 1037–8, "Governor John Wentworth to Monk," 18 October 1793. An account of the crisis and Monk's intended role in it as a militia leader appears on pages 1038–9 of Monk's Letterbook. Monk knew so little about Charles Alexis that he first wrote down that the chief was "the son of Anthony Ury of Annapolis Royal" (1046). He later crossed out the erroneous statement. It nevertheless was an odd mistake, since Anthony Ury was associated with Remsheg in Pictou County, a fact Monk should have known since he allotted a licence of occupation to Anthony Ury (also known as Captain Tony) in 1783.

175 Ibid.

176 The meeting would take place at Gaspereau Lake, the headwaters of the Gaspereau River that take their rise on the South Mountain in Kings County. The Mi'kmaq of Minas had begun frequenting Gaspereau Lake in the seventeenth century. They had maintained an earlier village site and meeting ground at Melanson, south of Grand Pré in Kings County. John Erskine, a curator of the Nova Scotia Museum, noted the presence of the Melanson site as early as 957. Erskine, *Micmac Notes* (Halifax: Museum of Natural History, 1957), 2. The Melanson site was also the focus of an archaeological excavation in 1990. Ronald Nash and Frances L. Stewart, ed., *Melanson: A Large Micmac Village Site in Kings County, Nova Scotia* (Halifax: Nova Scotia Museum, 1990). Janet Chute's father, Walter J. Chute, who was born in 1914, was aware of the site as a boy and remembered collecting "lots of stone arrowheads" there. The Melanson site was abandoned by the Mi'kmaq when the Acadians expanded into the Gaspereau Valley.

177 When Charles Alexis hinted casually that he was on his way to Annapolis Royal to a meeting of Mi'kmaw leaders, several of whom were from Gaspereau Lake, Monk grew alarmed, for he had been apprised earlier of Mi'kmaq killing cattle and committing other depredations on settlers' lands. He wondered if the assembly to

which Alexis referred might prove a hotbed of conspiratorial activity against the government, but he gave no hint of his fears in front of his Mi'kmaw visitors. This is also discussed in Wicken, *Colonization of Mi'kmaw Memory*, 104–9.

178 LAC, MG 23, GII-19, Monk Papers, vol. 4, 1047, entry for 10 December 1793. By 1793 Charles Alexis probably felt both hemmed in and pushed off his land at The Forks by the expanding Acadian population.

179 Ibid. The entire passage reads: "[Chief Alexis stated that] all the Indians wish Gov. Wentworth to be made acquainted with their situation + with the treatment they have received since the English came among them, at first giving them everything they asked for + continuing to give them supplies till all their Land, Rivers and Hunting Places were taken up + settled in Townships and then stopping all supplies + leaving them deprived + destitute of every means of subsistence."

180 Ibid.

181 Ibid.

182 Ibid.

183 LAC, MG 23, GII-19, vol. 4, 1083–86, "Notes to be included in letter to Wentworth," undated (c.1797). If one discounts Monk's fears about Alexis getting together with Chief Bernard on the subject of land issues, there is really no logic behind Monk's remark on this head. Charles Alexis's party could have gone by way of St. Mary's Bay or, alternatively, past St. Margaret's Bay. Since Alexis and his associates were heading for Halifax in the fall of 1793 it would have been shorter to go by way of St. Mary's Bay.

184 Ibid., 1051–2, "Monk to Governor Wentworth," 23 January 1794.

185 Louis Hébert *dit* Baguette during Le Loutre's War had joined forces with Joseph Broussard *dit* Beausoleil and other Acadian resistance fighters.

186 LAC, MG 23, GII-19, vol. 4, 1049, entry of 12 January 1794.

187 Ibid., 1047–8. James Paul had muttered that Monk could give him "two loaves of bread" if he chose, an utterance the commissioner immediately recognized as an allusion to the two loaves of bread he had given the Cape Sable chief.

188 Ibid., 1067–9, entry for 20 February 1794.

189 Ibid., 1075–7, entry for 31 March 1794.

190 Ibid., 1076.

191 Ibid., 1058, 1171, "Regarding payment to Job Ross sent by the government to seek out suspected emissaries among the Mi'kmaq"; Upton, *Micmacs and Colonists*, 84. One encounter with the Peminouts had briefly caused

Monk some trepidation. John Paul Peminout charged the commissioner not only of being discriminatory in his allocation of supplies, but worse, of being extremely parsimonious, a Mi'kmaw "sin," worthy of rebuke. John then defiantly proclaimed that "if King George is so poor that he could give no more to [the] Indians – the Indians better take nothing." Though these words arose from the same sense of frustration felt earlier by Michel Alexis, Monk felt they were a red flag calling for redress. Consequently, on 31 March 1784, in front of Michael Francklin's widow, whose presence still elicited respect from the Peminouts since her husband had known the Peminouts well and had granted the family land, Monk prevailed upon John Peminout to confess the error of his ways and tender an apology for so impulsively denigrating King George III. LAC, MG 23, GII-19, vol. 4, 1050, entry of 12 January 1794.

192 Wicken, *Colonization of Mi'kmaw Memory*, 109.

193 Richard Salisbury, "Transactions or Transactors? An Economic Anthropologist's View," in *Transaction and Meaning: Directions in the Anthropology and Exchange and Symbolic Behaviour*, ed. B. Kapferer (Philadelphia: Institute for the Study of Human Issues, 1976), 41–59. When the Algonquian-speaking northern Ojibwa experienced hardship during the fur trade era they often turned to traders and government officials for respite. Similarly, the Mi'kmaq when facing scarcities resorted to customary ways of explaining their needs and addressing how they could be mitigated. In so doing, they employed symbolic language and behaviour with very different connotations from what their non-Indigenous listeners thought they were hearing. Mary Rose Black-Rogers, "Varieties of 'Starving': Semantics and Survival in the Subarctic Fur Trade, 1750–1850," *Ethnohistory* 33, no. 4 (1986): 353–83.

194 On departing from the commissioner's office in December of 1793, Chief Alexis stated that he would return early the following spring to furnish Monk "with such particulars as may enable me to state his case correctly to the present governor." LAC, MG 23, GII-19, vol. 4, "Letterbook," 1047, entry for 10 December 1793.

195 Ibid., 316, "Regarding Charles Alexis, George Deschamps to George Monk," 26 May 1794.

196 Ibid., 1051–5, "Petition of the Mickmack Indians to Lieutenant-Governor John Wentworth, 24 January 1794, enclosed in a letter sent by D. Rudolph." The previous day Monk had written Wentworth discussing the plight of the Mi'kmaq due to loss of hunting grounds and to settlers' depredations.

197 Ibid., 1053–4. Georges Deschamps, who had been a business associate of both Monk and Joshua Mauger

of Halifax, realized the seriousness of the problems the Mi'kmaq faced, as settlers had cut down their forests to plant crops and build roads and had appropriated their weirsites. According to Deschamps, the reason for the Mi'kmaq's meeting was embedded in their practical need for food and clothing, as well as their discouragement at the government's failure to honour past promises. Michael Francklin, as Indian commissioner, had provided for their needs when emergencies had arisen and had treated them as valuable and integral components of the developing provincial structure. Deschamps concluded that "[w]ant of subsistence is more the cause of any discontent that may be expressed or discovered among them, than the want of Inclination to remain on kindly terms with the Inhabitants and peaceable, if they could obtain relief by such supplies as have heretofore been allowed them, when they were better able to live by hunting.

198 Ibid., 1084, entry for 12 November 1797.

199 For instance, on 25 November 1796 Charles Alexis, Michael Alexis, Joseph Alexis, two women, and five infants received "clothing, provisions, ammunition and utensils" supplied by merchant Joseph Davis. LAC, MG 23, GII-19, vol. 4, "Accounts," 1198; 1217, "To Joseph Davis for Supplies issued to the Indians by order of … Sir John Wentworth."

200 Solomon Jeremy and his associates Michael Jeremy, Joseph Glode, and Peter Martin began petitioning as early as 1793. NSARM, RG 1, vol. 26½, "Memorial of John Christopher Rudolf on behalf of sundry families at La Have River," 1 May 1793; NSARM, RG 20, Department of Lands and Forests, land grant registration books, Ser. A – Geremy [Jeremy], Solomon, 1794, "Memorial of Solomon Geremy, a Mi'kmaq of the La Have Tribe who has settled on an ungranted and uninhabited spot of land to the rear of the English settlement of La Have and has made improvements, including a petition for a grant or a license of occupation to this land." Bulkeley, the provincial secretary, suggested a licence of occupation.

201 The first migration from La Have may have occurred owing to a serious smallpox outbreak along the South Shore in 1801. NSARM, RG 1, vol. 430, doc. 72½. Others remained in Lunenburg County, however. On 11 November 1829 Joseph "Soulnow" (Joseph Sulnow Jeremy) drafted a memorial to the lieutenant governor, Sir Peregrine Maitland, for a grant of land at New Germany that his family had occupied for generations. Sulnow argued that the land in question had been passed down to him and his brother from his great-grandfather and asked that his group be granted this land. Desbrisay, *History of the County of Lunenburg*, 348; 368–69. These

Sulnows (or Sulnos) lived at Church Hill, Lunenburg County, near New Germany Lake. John Adam Fiendel, who was born in 1800, noted in 1889 that the Sulnows and Jeremies of New Germany used to dip for salmon in the rivers and used shad and alewives for manure on their potato gardens. Many of the Lunenburg County Sulnows and their close relations, the Jeremys, later moved into Queens County, Nova Scotia.

202 References to Captain Torey in the James White Papers, housed in the New Brunswick Provincial Archives in Saint John, New Brunswick, reveal that Toney aided the British at Fort Howe, at the mouth of the Saint John River, during the Revolutionary War. In 1801 George Oxley stated that Captain Tony's son "Lui Tonie [Louis Toney] is the Person who has the most influence over the Indians in this Place – he can Speak the English Language very well – he likewise shows a disposition to Settle. He left Tatamagouche this spring on account of the smallpox and is planting in Remsheg." Until 1803 Louis, his son Daniel, and his six other children lived at Remsheg, Pictou County. NSARM, RG 1, vol. 430, "George Oxley to Michael Wallace," May 1801, doc. 70; NSARM, RG 1, vol. 430, doc. 127, "George Oxley to Michael Wallace," 4 February 1803. An outbreak of measles in 1803 at Remsheg led many of the Toney family to leave the area.

203 In 1793 Captain Toney, who had fifteen people associated with his immediate household, and two of his older sons, who in turn had ten children among them, requested a grant of six hundred acres near Remsheg and forty-five hundred acres at Merigomish. NSARM, RG 20 series A – land grant registration books series, "Vry or Ury – Tony & others," 1793. Captain Toney spoke French, English, and Mi'kmaq, as did his son Louis. Louis's linguistic abilities attracted the attention of the Reverend Mr. Burke, who eventually became vicar apostolic of Nova Scotia in 1817, and the Indian agent at Remsheg, George Oxley. Both sought Toney's assistance as an interpreter. In January of 1812 Louis Toney and "Peter Mouice" decided to leave the Remsheg area permanently, since the Native peoples there were in "dire distress." NSARM, RG 1, vol. 430, doc. 148. By 1812, Louis Toney's son Daniel was head man of a group of seventeen family heads living near Annapolis Royal. In 1812 Daniel and Peter Tom (Thomas) petitioned for a tract of land at the Gut of Annapolis. NSARM, RG 1, vol. 430, doc. 148½, "Daniel Tony and Peter Tom to the lieutenant-governor, Sir John Coape Sherbrooke," 1813. Not long afterwards Daniel moved to Bear River, where he impressed Abbé Jean-Mandé Sigogne with his leadership capabilities and his fine singing voice.

204 Magdalene's brother, Peter Toney, also joined the Bear River community and eventually served a term as the Bear River leader.

205 Sigogne arrived in Halifax on 12 June 1799 and spent the first two weeks with his immediate superior, James Jones, overseer of missions throughout the Maritime colonies.

206 "I demanded of him [Jacques Mius] his Father's credential letters, which he willingly delivered," Sigogne wrote to Sherbrook. The elderly Jacques also told Sigogne interesting particulars concerning his father's reticence in 1761 to make peace with the English until Abbé Pierre Maillard finally persuaded Mius to bury the hatchet and sign a treaty. NSARM, RG 1, vol. 430, docs. 20 and 21, "Sigogne to Sherbrooke, 5 May 1812, with enclosures."

207 Descendants of Andrew James today spell their surname "Meuse" rather than "Mius." André James Mius, who after 1820 became better known as Andrew James Meuse, was born to Jacques Mius and Bridget Alexis circa 1780. He died in 1850. He and his wife Magdalene Toney raised four boys and two girls. The chief was instrumental in establishing the Bear River reserve, made two travels overseas to meet with British royalty, and launched campaigns on behalf of the land and resource interests of his people. He was concerned that the settlers' herring fishery would compete with the local porpoise hunt. NSARM, RG 5, *Journal of the Legislative Assembly of Nova Scotia*, 1821, II, 36, "Petition, To the Hon. House of Assembly now convened at Halifax … from Andrew Mius, residing near the Gut of Annapolis," 16 January 1821. Mius defended porpoise hunting in the Gut of Annapolis against a lobby group that held that such a practice destroyed the herring fishery. By 1821 the Mi'kmaq had been engaged in the hunt for almost thirty years, and derived income from the sale of porpoise oil. Muis claimed that the "[h]erring are not the slightest bit affected" and added that he would be willing to come to Halifax to plead the Mi'kmaq's cause. Andrew Meuse sometimes imbibed too much, to the annoyance of Abbé Sigogne and Joseph Howe, who otherwise lauded his leadership qualities. The Anglican chaplain and missionary James West, while touring Nova Scotia in 1825, found that Meuse possessed a keen wit and a clear grasp of the fundamentals of the Roman Catholic religion. West, *A Journal of a Mission to the Indians of the British Provinces of New Brunswick and Nova Scotia* (London: Seeley, 1827), 246–7. In April 1832 in London Meuse met with King William VI and Queen Adelaide, who presented him with a medal. As he could speak English, he also conversed with the Reverend Peter Jones,

or Kahkewaquonaby, a Mississauga Ojibwa Methodist missionary from Upper Canada, who was also visiting Britain. Carolyn Thomas Foreman, *Indians Abroad: 1493–1938* (Oklahoma: University of Oklahoma Press, 1943), 154–5. The date of this audience with the king and queen is given in Donald B. Smith, *Sacred Feathers: The Reverend Peter Jones (Kahkewaquonaby) & the Mississauga Indians* (Toronto: University of Toronto Press, 1987), 138. More information on Andrew James Meuse may be obtained from NSARM, RG 10, vol. 432, 87–193, Howe, "Western Tour," 1842; L.F.S. Upton, "Meuse (Mius, Mause, Muse), Andrew James," *DCB* online, vol. 7 (1836–50); Wicken, *Colonization of Mi'kmaw Memory*, 114–18; Ruth Holmes Whitehead, *The Old Man Told Us: Excerpts from Mi'kmaw History, 1500–1950* (Halifax: Nimbus, 1991), 201–2; and Darlene A. Ricker, *L'sitkuk: The Story of the Bear River Mi'kmaw Community* (Lockeport, NS: Roseway, 1997), 67–71.

208 The numbers of Mi'kmaq living at Bear River in 1832 and 1842 are provided in Ricker, *The Story of Bear River*, 197–8.

209 Ralph Johnson, *The Forests of Nova Scotia* (Halifax: Department of Lands and Forests/Four East Publications, 1986), 60.

210 The desecrated forest no longer provided suitable habitat for ungulates such as moose and caribou. What moose that did remain lay west of La Have towards Cape Sable, which likely caused more Mi'kmaw migrations into the Cape Sable region. Among the settlers, beef became the meat most often served, where before moosemeat had been a dietary mainstay. NSARM, RG 1, vol. 380, 113–25, *Sketches of the Eastern and Northern Parts of the Province in the Years 1801 and 1802, with General Observations Therein … by Titus Smith Jr.*, 3rd ed., Halifax, 1851. Smith also noted that in the past a fair number of Mi'kmaw men had married Acadian women.

211 NSARM, RG 1, vol. 52, doc. 54, "Sir John Wentworth to the Duke of Portland," 24 April 1798.

212 Interview with Jerry Bartlett of Acadia, Yarmouth, 17 July 1990.

213 NSARM, Land Petitions, Luxey, Joseph, 1819, "Petition of the Indians of Shelburne County for a License of Occupation for 200 acres on Long Island."

214 Bartholomew Alexis seasonally resided on George Ring's property, which lay along the lower Salmon River. His campsite lay near where Highway 1 currently spans the Salmon River. The tote road cut through Ring's tract above Herring Lake, a water body formed by a widening of the Salmon River before it entered the ocean. The locale was a convenient one since Bartholomew

and his family simply followed the road to Digby, or in the opposite direction to Yarmouth or Tusket, to sell baskets and wooden manufactures. Bartholomew and his brother Joseph both stated in 1819 that they began farming in 1794. Joseph Alexis and those of his brothers who were still living in 1819 claimed in a petition to Lord Dalhousie that they had farmed at Long Island for "twenty five years as permanent inhabitants." NSARM, Land Papers, Luxey – Joseph, 1819, "Petition of Indians of Shelburne for a license of occupation, 200 acres, To Lieut.-Gov. Rt. Hon. George Earl of Dalhousie, 1819, from five Mi'kmaq living in the river Roseway in the township of Shelburne." In 1816 Bartholomew Alexis's camp was described as embracing seven acres of George Ring's property for "a long time past, say 24 years." Yarmouth, Registry of Deeds, Yarmouth County, Grant Book for 1816, 412, "Indenture and plan relating to the subdivision of Lot No. 40 following the death of George Ring."

215 At this time Yarmouth County had not yet been separated off from Shelburne County.

216 NSARM, RG 34–324, Records of Sessions, Yarmouth and Argyle District, County of Shelburne, 1789–1816, 89, April term 1800. Also see Wicken, "Mi'kmaq Land in Nova Scotia," 119.

217 This chapel built by Bourg is long gone, but a replica of what this chapel may have looked like has recently been reconstructed at Rocco Point. There are some burial mounds nearby, marked by small boulders, which oral traditions at Ste. Anne du Ruisseau claim may be Mi'kmaq. Bourg made only occasional visits to Clare and Argyle and apparently visited during the summers from 1781 to 1783. His last visit was in 1786, when he might have aided Charles Alexis with his petition to Halifax for land at Eel Brook. Bourg did not maintain a formal register, and Pierre Mius conducted certain sacraments at other times. Before Abbé Charles-François Bailly left Nova Scotia in 1772, he granted permission to certain leading Acadian men at Eel Brook to perform baptisms and marriages in the absence of a priest. His successor, Father Jean-Antoine Ledru, arrived in the summer of 1786, but owing to various problems left in 1789. He was succeeded by three Irish itinerant missionary priests, William Phelan (1789), Thomas Power (1790), and Thomas Grace (1790–91). These men laboured mainly among the Acadians, and none, except Grace for a brief while, resided in the Cape Sable area. When Abbé Jean-Mandé Sigogne, Grace's successor, first arrived at Eel Brook in 1799, he discovered the chapel that had been built at Rocco Point and realized

that near it the dead had been buried in a small piece of consecrated ground. In the 1990s archaeologists from St. Mary's University in Halifax and historians conducted investigations at the site. In 1999 a small wooden commemorative chapel was constructed to commemorate the two-hundredth anniversary of the Parish of Ste. Anne du Ruisseau.

218 Marie Mius was likely Laurent Mius's sister, although neither Marie's birthdate nor the date of her marriage to Michel Alexis appear in the documentary record. Michel Alexis and Marie Mius brought their infant son Michel to be baptized by Abbé Sigogne on 12 November 1799. Witnesses were Joseph Amirault "du canton de Poumekou" and Amirault's wife, Marguerite Surette. NSARM, RG 1, vol. SA1, 30.

219 Sigogne had sailed up to Eel Brook on a fishing vessel belonging to Basile Bourque and while sojourning at Eel Brook resided at the home of Joseph Bourque, Basile's brother. Clarence-J. d'Entremont, *Histoire de Sainte-Anne-du-Ruisseau, Belleville, Rivière-Abram, Nouvelle-Écosse* (West Pubnico: printed by author, 1995).

220 Bernard Pothier, "Sigogne, Jean-Mandé," *DCB* online, vol. 7 (1836–50).

221 Joan Bourque Campbell, *L'Histoire de la paroisse de Sainte-Anne-du-Ruisseau (Eel Brook), Yarmouth* (Yarmouth: Éditions Lescarbot, 1985), 13. Sigogne worked hard for the Ste. Anne du Ruisseau community. In 1809 he replaced the earlier, much smaller wooden chapel there with a sizeable wooden church, which burned down in 1900. Pubnico had its own church, St. Pierre, by 1815, and became a separate parish in 1835. Saint Michel at Wedgeport followed in 1822. Saint Ambrose church at Yarmouth was erected in 1845, and St. Vincent de Paul Church at Salmon River was completed in 1849. The church registers drawn upon for this study include those for Ste. Anne (1799–1849), Saint Pierre (1836–49), Saint Michel (1836–49), Saint Ambrose (1845–49), and St. Vincent de Paul (1849–1907).

222 The surname "Eptemec" (or "Eptemek") used by Pierre Alexis *père* is problematic, as it suggests the Alexis family may have had connections with La Hève. The French census of 1707–08 lists two Mi'kmaw family heads, Pierre and Guillaume Eptemec, living at La Hève. Pierre was sixty-five years old, and he and his wife Madelaine had two daughters, Anne seventeen, and Catherine, twelve. Guillaume Eptemec was thirty, so he may have been Pierre Eptemec's son. Guillaune had a son, François, who was fifteen, and a daughter, Françoise, who was two. LAC, MG 13, F18, *Recensement genal fait au mois de Nouembre mile Sept cent huit … La Hève.*

223 NSARM, RG 1, vol. SA1, 37, "Marriage of Pierre Alexis *dit* Eptemek and Marie-Agnès Antoine, 26 April 1800."

224 Magdalene married Francois Joseph Claude on 12 July 1832.

225 Fabien Alexis also was the stepfather or foster father of an infant named Pierre Alexis, the son of Magdelene Pierre, whose husband evidently had died. NSARM, RG 1, vol. SA1, 3, Registers of the Parish of Ste. Anne du Ruisseau, "Baptism of Magdelene Alexis, daughter of Pierre Alexis and Marie-Agnès Antoine (Tony), 8 July 1799"; "Baptism of Cecile Alexis, daughter of Pierre Alexis and Marie-Agnès Antoine, 12 July, 1799, godparents François Gilis and Rosalie Mius." NSARM, RG 1, vol. SA1, 4, "Baptisms of Christine Alexis and Anastasie Alexis, daughters of Pierre Alexis and Marie-Agnès Antoine, 12 July, 1799, godparent for Christiane Alexis, Cecile Amirault, wife of Pierre Mius; godparents for Anastasie Alexis, François Gilis, and Anne Dousset [Doucet]." Ibid., "Baptism of Marie-Charlotte Alexis, daughter of Pierre Alexis and Anne, 12 July 1799, godparents Pierre Thomas and Marie." Ibid., 3, "Baptism of Pierre Alexis, step-daughter of Fabien Alexis and son of Magdalene Pierre, 12 July 1799, godparents Pierre Thomas and Anastasie Cadop."

226 Jacques Alexis was born in 1805 and was baptized by Sigogne at Ste. Anne du Ruisseau on 24 February 1806. Pierre Alexis's sister Marie-Joseph Alexis and Jacques Maurice were his godparents. Jacques Alexis later lived with Chief Michel Alexis's successor, Chief Joseph Alexis, on Long Island in the Roseway River in Shelburne County. Jacques Alexis married a woman named Marguerite Barac and the couple had a son named Jean-Baptiste in August 1838. Registers of Ste. Anne du Ruisseau, 22 August 1838. When Sigogne visited Long Island in the Roseway River around 1824, he noted that Chief Joseph Alexis and Jacques Alexis were the only adult male heads of families residing there. Smith, Jr., *Cape Sable, Nova Scotia: Vital Records, 1799–1841*; Smith Jr., ed., *St. Mary's Bay 1818–1829 and St. Mary's Bay 1840–1844: Catalogue of Families, St. Mary's Bay Roman Catholic Parish, Clare, Digby County, Nova Scotia*, comp. Jean-Mandé *Sigogne, ed. Leonard H. Smith Jr.* (Clearwater, *FL: Owl Books, 1975*).

227 NSARM, RG 1, vol. SA1, 30, "Baptism of Anne Alexis, born September 1799, daughter of Jean-Baptiste Alexis and Marie Amquarette, 7 November 1799, godparents Pierre Doucet and Marie Colombe Frontain." Anne died soon afterward, on 11 December 1800, barely fifteen months old. NSARM, RG 1, vol. SA1, 43, witnesses at burial, Pierre Mailliau and Charles Le Blanc; Ibid., 92,

"Baptism on 30 March 1807 of Marie-Françoise Alexis, born December 1806, daughter of Jean-Baptiste Alexis and Marie Amquarette, 'daughter of François,' previously baptized by Pierre Mius, godparents Martin Claude [Glode] and Agnès, wife of Pierre Alexis"; NSARM, RG 1, vol. SA1, 93, "Marriage of François Alexis, son of Jean-Baptiste Alexis and Marie, and Isabelle Beliard, daughter of Martin Beliard, witnesses Charlotte Malich and Pierre Henard, 10 April 1807."

228 Paul Williams and Honore Luxey had a daughter, Molly Williams, who married Joseph Penaul (Bernard) Labrador at Prospect, south of Halifax, in 1826. Registers of Our Lady of Mount Carmel, Prospect, 1823–35, 55, "Marriage of Joseph Penaul Labrador and Molly Williams." One of Joseph Labrador and Molly's sons, named Francis Labrador, later would marry Anne Glode at Caledonia in 1871.

229 NSARM, RG 1, vol. SA1, 30, "Baptism of Michel Alexis *fils*, 12 November 1799."

230 NSARM, RG 1, vol. SA1, 74, "Baptism of Joseph Alexis, born 28 July 1803, son of Joseph Alexis and Marie-Joseph Muice, godparents Brigitte Alexis, 'daughter of Barthelemi,' and Antoine Charles from Isle St. Jean, 28 July 1805." Joseph Alexis Jr. later would marry Marie-Anne Muice and in 1830 have a daughter, Catherine. NSARM, RG 1, vol. SA5, 24, "Baptism of Catherine Alexis, born 6 April,1830, baptized 8 April 1830, godparents Anselme d'Entremont and Anne Catherine d'Entremont." Joseph Alexis *fils* was also known as Joseph *dit* Makaq.

231 NSARM, RG 1, vol. SA1, 44, "Baptism of Eusebe Chishaw (Chegua), born 14 December 1800, daughter of Pierre Chishaw and Agnès. Godparents Louis Mius and Anne Surette, wife of Dominque Pottier (Pothier)."

232 Even in 1769 François-Joseph Alexis had dominated the sphere of Mi'kmaw contacts with Bailly.

233 Jean-Baptist Alexis joined his first cousin Michel's group on the upper Tusket and was treated as Michel's sibling. Pierre-Paul Alexis *dit* Eptemec, the last of Jacques Alexis Sr. and Angelique's sons to remain alive by this time, also dwelt near Michel.

234 Gerald C. Boudreau has observed that while Abbé Jean-Mandé Sigogne recognized the existence of many marriages as well as cohabitations between Mi'kmaq and Acadians, the abbé subscribed to an ideological system that stressed the *sang pur* (pure blood) as being more beneficial to the physical and intellectual attributes of human beings than the *sang melée*, or so-called mixed-blood constitution of those who had both Mi'kmaw and Acadian ancestry. Boudreau, "L'apostolat du missionaire, Jean-Mandé Sigogne et les Acadiens du sud-ouest de la

Nouvelle-Ecosse" (PhD diss., Université de Montreal, 1989), 24. See also Bernard Pothier, "Sigogne, Jean-Mande," *DCB* online, vol. 7 (1836–50). This ideological bias espoused by authority figures like Sigogne encouraged many Acadians who knew they had Mi'kmaw ancestry to try to hide their genealogical past. William C. Wicken has argued that formal intermarriages between Mi'kmaq and Acadians were rare in the Port Royal and, later, Annapolis Royal area. Wicken, "Re-examining Mi'kmaq-Acadian Relations, 1635–1755," in *Vingt ans après, Habitants et marchands: Lectures de l'histoire des XVIIe et XVIIIe siècles canadiens*, ed. Sylvie Dépatie et al. (Montreal and Kingston: McGill-Queen's University Press, 1998), 10. The first author, however, suggests on the basis of documentary evidence she has examined as well as copious oral traditions told her by *métis* descendants of specific persons of both Mi'kmaq and Acadian genealogical and cultural background that much further research needs to be done in this area to clarify the record. Chute, "Interpenetrating Realities: A New Perspective on Mi'kmaq Land Use in Southwestern Nova Scotia," prepared under the auspices of the Nova Scotia Aboriginal Title Project, Treaty and Aboriginal Rights Research, Shubenacadie, Nova Scotia, summer 1999, 43; Chute, "A Good Day on the Aboiteau," 77.

235 This area was sometimes referred to as Ring's Creek or Melbourne. Campbell, *A History of Yarmouth*, 114.

236 The prominence of a Planter named Lemuel Bartlett (1744–91), who emigrated from Plymouth, Massachusetts, and in 1774 married a local woman, Hannah Tinkham, may have influenced the Mi'kmaq's choice to adopt "Bartlett" as a patronym. "Yarmouth N.S. Marriage Records," in *The Mayflower Descendant*, 9 (Boston, 1907): 42. By 1850, three distinct Bartlett families had arisen in the Yarmouth area, one belonging to Lemuel Bartlett, who established his homestead at Chebogue; one being a Black family from Shelburne; and the third the Mi'kmaw Bartlett family. The Planter Bartletts, to which group Lemuel Bartlett belonged, were joined in the Cheboque-Yarmouth and Tusket areas by other families having the surnames "Baker," "Boyd," "Bridgeo," "Brown," "Cleveland," "Crosby," "Curtis," "Gowen," "Raymond," "Robbins," "Vander Horne," and "Van Norden." Bartholomew Alexis's son and daughters, as well as his grandchildren and great-grandchildren, used "Bartlett" and "Bartholomew Alexis" interchangeably as surname choices at Salmon River. Yet when residing along the eastern Atlantic coast, especially in Shelburne County, with members of their larger Alexis kin group, they often dropped the "Bartholomew" altogether as a surname

and simply referred to themselves as members of the "Alexis" or "Luxey" (Laksi, Lucy, Luxy) family. Ruth Holmes Whitehead, "The Life of Jerry Lonecloud," in *Tracking Doctor Lonecloud*, 29.

237 A Mi'kmaw man surnamed "Tom" (or "Thomas") from the Bay St. Mary's region married an Acadian woman named Sarah Thibeault around 1800, and the couple acquired four hundred acres of land in the district of Clare around 1817. *NSARM, RG 20 Ser. A – Guiddery, Frederick & Others, 1819. Department of Lands and Forests, land registration books series.* After her husband's death Mrs. Thibeault in 1839 sold fifty acres of this property for fifty dollars.

238 Captain George Ring had emigrated from Kingston, Massachusetts, to Yarmouth Township around 1762 and raised a large family. He held property in Yarmouth and Digby counties. Campbell, *A History of Yarmouth*, 69–70. Joshua Frost, a local justice of the peace, belonged to a Planter family who hailed from Kittery in Maine. Because of their continued American connections, both Ring and Frost found themselves under the shadow of suspicion during the American Revolution and in 1775 were compelled to take an oath of allegiance to King George III. Perhaps it was lingering feelings of outsiderhood fostered at this time that later led them occasionally to form closer connections with the Cape Sable Mi'kmaq than with the Loyalist incomers who settled at Yarmouth and Tusket.

239 NSARM, RG 1, vol. 430, doc. 71, "Joshua Frost to Sir John Wentworth," n.d. (c.1801).

240 Michal Wallace served as a member of a Commission for Indian Relief set up with Monk as chair.

241 NSARM, RG 1, vol. 430, doc. 117, "Sir John Wentworth to Michael Wallace," 28 September 1802; Wicken, "Mi'kmaq Land in Nova Scotia," 119. What is now Yarmouth County, which was part of Shelburne County in 1784, did not become a county in its own right until 1836.

242 All available fishery locales in southwestern Nova Scotia had been exploited by the Cape Sable Mi'kmaq, with different portions of a river being occupied and fished at different seasons of the year. As early as Archaic times, three thousand years ago, Indigenous populations constructed large stone weirs in the Quinan area and along other rivers, as archaeological finds readily attest. Large stone weirs still exist on the Quinan River, often with a characteristic "W" shape, with openings at the points for gaspereau going upstream to spawn, as well as eels to push through into waiting eelpots as they travelled downstream. These are now maintained by the local

Acadian population. Brush eel pots, weirs or baskets seasonally would be lifted to allow fish such as alewife and salmon to ascend to the stream's headwaters to spawn. Catadromous eels that spawn in the ocean have a high calorific content and may be dried or smoked for later consumption. They constituted one of the most important Mi'kmaw winter food resources as well as having a ceremonial importance. Temporary tidal brush weirs at river mouths could be easily dismantled. With pressure on caribou, moose, and especially beaver populations due to fires, settlement, harsh winters, and overhunting by settlers, fishing eels, alewife, salmon, and gaspereau became more important to the Mi'kmaq. Under the 1771 commission accorded Francis-Joseph Alexis by Lord William Campbell and the 1786 licence of occupation given Charles Alexis, the Mi'kmaq theoretically retained a common right to fish in all the rivers and streams in the district, along with the settler population. Yet settlers who owned properties that abutted the stream were privileged in where they could fish, though by law they were prohibited from setting nets entirely across a river and blocking fish from proceeding upstream. Members of the County Court of the Quarter Sessions, composed of justices of the peace, devised fishery legislation based on the principles of English common law. Wicken, *Colonization of Mi'kmaw Memory*, 105. Bartholomew Alexis intended to attain simply a few acres near a fish weir in order to provision his relatives whenever they came to visit. In 1802 the Sessions promised to see if any landholder would give up part of his grant along the Salmon River for the Mi'kmaq's use, but in the end admitted no one was willing to relinquish a parcel for such a purpose. After this, Bartholomew found it difficult to have his grievances concerning trespassers on his traditional fishery taken seriously by the Sessions. A fishery management system had been instituted for the Salmon and Tusket Rivers in 1793, which in 1801 lay under the surveillance of a Tusket merchant and grist mill operator named John Van Norden, who was also the local fishery inspector, tasked with monitoring the system and enforcing the fishery regulations. One of his duties was enforcing regulations prohibiting nets or weirs that lay more than one-third across a river. Nets also had to be placed more than a hundred yards apart from each other, to allow anadromous fish access to the heads of streams, yet Bartholomew repeatedly found his fishing activities obstructed by other fishers downstream. NSARM, RG 24–324, Record of Sessions, Shelburne County, Yarmouth and Argyle District, 1789–1816, April term 1791, Fishery Regulations for the Tusket River.

243 NSARM, RG 34–324, Records of Sessions, Yarmouth and Argyle District, 114–25, April Term 1803.

244 NSARM, RG 1, vol. 48, no. 105, "Sir John Wentworth to Henry Dundas," 23 July 1792; Wicken, "Mi'kmaq Land in Nova Scotia,"120. Around 1807, when the threat of a second possible French invasion loomed, settlers still suspected the Mi'kmaq of Cape Sable of harbouring sympathies for the French. Wentworth began toying with ideas he first had considered during the earlier crisis of 1793 and then put aside. These included regularizing distributions of provisions, clothes, and arms to the Native people. There also would be a new administrative policy that would fall as a direct charge upon the province. The province would be divided into twelve districts, each having an agent responsible for monitoring Mi'kmaq activities in his area. L.F.S. Upton, "Indian Policy in Colonial Nova Scotia, 1783–1871," *Acadiensis* 5, no. 1 (1975): 9–10. One of the agents, Mr. Crowell in Shelburne, warned that the primarily Loyalist settlers in his district were "very apprehensive" of the Mi'kmaq. NSARM, RG 1, vol. 430, doc. 6, "Returns to circular letter, 1808."

245 When Alexis asked Wentworth in 1801 to grant his people five acres of land along the Salmon River as a permanent Mi'kmaw encampment ground and fishing locale, Frost later discovered that this plot had already been granted to Sir Henry Wilmot, and no other nearby tracts were available to be granted.

246 At the end of the Revolutionary War, Captain John Van Norden had recruited potential émigrés of Dutch extraction in the New York area. These he conveyed in the transport ship *Steady* and other private vessels to Port Roseway, from where they spread out to other places in southwestern Nova Scotia, particularly to Tusket. For more information regarding this facet of history, see the *Shelburne County Genealogical Society Newsletter*, vol. 15, no. 2 (2001).

247 Joshua Frost, born in 1740, was the son of a Congregationalist minister, the Reverend John Frost of Kittery, Maine, and later Yarmouth. His mother was Lydia Stackpole. Joshua Frost settled in Yarmouth before 1771, and during the American Revolution the entire Frost family became the butt of MacKinnon's hostility for what MacKinnon deemed their American sympathizing. Campbell, *A History of Yarmouth*, 69; Ranald MacKinnon's last will and testament, probated at Shelburne, 25 May 1805. A copy of this will is housed with the Shelburne County Genealogical Society, Shelburne, Nova Scotia.

248 Jane Alexis was probably one of Bartholomew Alexis Sr.'s daughters or granddaughters, since Mi'kmaw women

tended to keep their own names when they married. The person called upon to give testimony was probably Bartholomew Alexis Sr.

249 Wicken, *Colonization of Mi'kmaw Memory*, 113–14.

250 NSARM, RG 34–324, Record of Sessions, Yarmouth and Argle District, County of Shelburne, 1789–1816, 1, October term, 1807. Sixpence was the minimal fine. By contrast, in 1815 when John Oxley and two other men assaulted a Mi'kmaw woman, Molly Tommy, in Cumberland County, they were charged ten pounds and costs, just the same as for an assault on a settler. NSARM, RG 34–308, Cumberland County, Court of General Sessions, 1808–33, 2, "The King *versus* John W. Oxley and John C. Simmon," 31 October 1815.

251 Charles Alexis was succeeded by Mike Luxey, "who visited Halifax and while there dined with the governor. He drowned at the Hawk Inlet between Cape Sable and the main and Cape Sable Island." Robertson, "History of Shelburne County," 5. Michael drowned east of Clark's Harbour in the Hawk Channel, which lies between the point still called "The Hawk" and the thin sandy spit of land simply called "Cape Sable." The Mi'kmaq went to Cape Sable and the neighbouring Seal Rocks to take seals. While en route there Michael's canoe could have been caught up in the strong and sometimes unpredictable tidal currents associated with the Gulf of Maine.

252 "Parish – Paroisse St-Vincent-de-Paul (Salmon River, la Rivière-aux-Saumons)," https://claretownship.ca/parish-salmon-river/. According to this website, "Oral history says that the first mass at la Rivière-aux-Saumons (Salmon River) was held in 1813 at the home of Jean Deveau and his spouse Marie Maillet, officiated by Père Sigogne."

253 Whitehead, *Tracking Doctor Lonecloud*, 29. Ekien Sr. died prior to 1855, since his grandson, Jerry Bartlett, makes no mention of Ekien being alive at the time of his own birth in the mid-1850s. Jerry's information is confusing, however, since he also once claimed that Ekien lived to be over one hundred years of age. Philip Sayer, a foster child raised by Ekien who was born around 1824, was actually much younger than most of Ekien's other children, who were born between 1810 and 1820.

254 Yarmouth County Registry of Deeds, Grant Book for 1816, 412–15, with survey plan by Miner Huntington, deputy surveyor, dated 19 October 1816. The subdivision was not registered until 24 January 1826.

255 Also spelled "Wesow," "Wessow," "Wisa'u," "Wissow," or "Wissau."

256 Anthropologist Frank Goldsmith Speck, who in 1914 linked Stephen Bartlett *dit* Wisow with the Bear River band, wrote in his Nova Scotia field notes in 1914 that *Wisaw* meant "yellow green." The field notes are housed in the library of the American Philosophical Society in Washington. Copies microfilm may be found in the library of St. Francis Xavier University in Antigonish, Nova Scotia. See also Speck, *Beothuk and Micmac*, ed. F.W. Hodge (New York: Museum of the American Indian, Heye Foundation, 1922), 101. Nova Scotia Museum's Accession Book 3: 45, Ref. P113/17.46 (4578) refers to a photograph taken of Chief Stephen Bartlett about 1900 and obtained from the subject's nephew, Jeremiah Bartlett Alexis. The caption that accompanies this photograph reads: "Stephen Bartlett, alias Stephen Lexi, alias Wissow, Chief of Mi'kmaq Indians of Gravel Pit Indian Reservation, about 2 miles from Yarmouth, N.S., born at Salmon River, Yar. Co., N.S., in 1819; died at age of 83 (about 1902)." Stephen Bartlett was called Stephen Green, or "Wissow," because he wore green clothes, according to his nephew Jerry Lonecloud. He was born the "same year as Queen Victoria." Since Stephen's father also was called "Wisow," as was Abraham Bartlett at times, Lonecloud's words must be treated with caution.

257 "Green" appears as a Mi'kmaw surname in the church registers of the Parish of St. Vincent de Paul, Salmon River. For instance, George Green and Mary's twenty-three-year-old daughter Marguerite was baptized on 28 September 1866. The witnesses were François Labrador and Angelique Labrador. Leonard Smith has edited and published information from the Salmon River church registers in *Salmon River, Digby County, Nova Scotia – Vital Records 1849–1907, from Parish Registers of the Roman Catholic Parish of St. Vincent de Paul* (Clearwater, FL: Owl Books, 1977). See also NSM, Mi'kmaq Portraits Collection, Image information relating to a photograph of Stephen Bartlett [Bartholomew Alexis] Jr. dated c.1900, Yarmouth County, NSM Accession Book 3: 45, Ref. P113/17.46 (4578). For an early reference to "Green" as a Mi'kmaw name, see Ruth Holmes Whitehead, *The Micmac Ethnology Collection of the Nova Scotia Museum*, Curatorial Report No. 25, September 1974, 55.

258 Sigogne found Philippe Alexis, who would have been Ekien Wisow Sr.'s brother, living at Annapolis in the 1820s. Abbé Jean-Mandé Sigogne's census of the Cape Sable Native population, c.1824, entitled "Familles des Sauvages," lists the heads of families, where each family was living, numbers of disabled and adults, and numbers of boys and girls. Janet Chute obtained a typescript copy of Sigogne's "Cape Sable Vital Statistics Records, 1799–1841" from Father Clarence-J. d'Entremont, whose document is housed at the Musee d'Acadienne in West

Pubnico. Researchers may access a printed copy in Smith, *St. Mary's Bay 1818–1829: Catalogue of Families.* Philippe Bartlett-Alexis also appears in the Ste. Anne du Ruisseau registers on 1 July 1832 as the godfather of Felicité Labrador, daughter of Pierre Labrador and Felicité. NSARM, RG 1, vol. SA6, 29, "Baptism of two-year-old Felicité Labrador, 1 July 1832, godparents Philippe Alexis and Marie-Marguerite Muis, presiding priest Jean-Baptiste Morin."

259 Smith, *St. Mary's Bay 1818–1829: Catalogue of Families.*

260 Mahalia was also known as Marie Ella or Matilda Frank (sometimes written "Franck"). The Frank family came from New Germany, Lunenburg County, and also intermarried with the Mi'kmaw Hammond family of Gold River and Elmsdale.

261 Three different Moore families lived in Argyle, at least one of which as early as 1783 was threatened with land forfeiture. See NSARM, MG10, Ser. C, Crowell, F.E., information on three Moore families, Bk. 1, Gen. #368 (1st family), 267, Gen. #369 (2nd family), 267, Gen. #370 (3rd family), 280; Campbell, *A History of Yarmouth*, 92. "Mason's Moore's consort, Marie Crowell, was born in the town of Crowell, which broke off from Barrington Passage. There were four towns within a few miles of each other, all part of Barrington Township. Maria was illiterate and perhaps somewhat of a drifter." Information from Elsie Charles Basque's notebook provided courtesy of Travis Pinn, October 2016. Maria's daughter Emeline Moore (c.1859–1935), whose father was Mason Moore, married Tom Bartlett (1851–96) about 1879. NSARM, Historical Vital Statistics, Registration Year 1936, "Death of Emeline Bartlett, of throat cancer, on 8 June 1935." At times Emeline took the surname "Crowell," and also "Boyd," drawn from another of her mother's consorts. The 1871 census for Barrington Township reveals that Maria Crowell, forty years old at the time, was consorting with a seventy-year-old Irishman named Jacob Boyd. Emeline Moore and Tom Bartlett had eight children: James around 1880, Hannah in 1882, Henry in 1884, John Burbon in 1885, Simon Thomas in 1887, Mary Elizabeth in 1889, Mary Caroline in 1890, and Joseph in 1897. Their youngest, Joseph, died the year he was born and was buried in the cemetery at Ste. Anne du Ruisseau. In the 1890s these Bartletts resided either in the Tusket Lakes district or at Labraduce. Before that Tom and his family lived at Summerside (now Dayspring, in Lunenburg County. Simon Thomas Bartlett, born in 1920 either at Labraduce or West Green Harbour in Shelburne County, wed Eva Labrador, the half-sister of Travis Pinn's ancestor, Joseph Charles's wife Maggie Labrador, at Hectanooga in Digby County. NSARM, Historical Vital Statistics, Year 1920, Digby County Marriages, book 4, 700, "Marriage of Simon Bartlett, widower, to Eva Labrador."

262 Joseph Bartlett Jr. married a woman surnamed Pictou, not to be confused with Clara Pictou (née Charles), the sister of John Charles, who wed Joseph Pictou of Bear River. Travis Pinn, personal communication, June 2017.

263 According to the federal census of 1871, Joseph Bartlett Sr. was fifty-nine and so was born in 1812, though on the 1881 census he was listed as being sixty-seven. Such discrepancies in birthdates recorded on early census records are not unusual. Canada, Census of 1881, Nova Scotia, District 195, Lunenburg Sub-district B, Division 2, 82–3; Canada, Census of 1881, Nova Scotia, District No. 11, Summerside, District D, Township of Lunenburg, 58–9. Although he had been married previously, reputedly to a Meuse woman from Bear River, by 1871 Joseph Bartlett lived at Summerside, now Dayspring in Lunenburg County, with Mahalia Ella Frank (listed variously as "Frances K. Mahalia" or "Matilda Franck"). Mahalia was twenty-five in 1871 and of German ancestry. Living with this couple were Tom and Joseph Bartlett Jr., both married at the time. Tom was twenty-one years old and so born in 1851, and Joseph was eighteen, born in 1853. The parents of Mary E. Bartlett, who was eleven months, and the infant Agnes could not be definitely determined. Agnes may have been a foster child, as there also was a twelve-year-old girl of African ancestry named Esther Barton who, like Mahalia, was a member of the Church of England. The 1881 census also lists the names of two boys: George, thirteen and so born in 1868, and Stephen, who was ten and born in 1871. Since George was listed as German rather than Mi'kmaq in the census record, he probably was born to Mahalia Frank before she met Joseph. Mary Esther, Agnes, and George Bartlett do not appear again in the documentary record. Marie Ella Frank may have been the mother of Mary, George, and Stephen but not of Joseph's older children. In 1881 Joseph and Marie Ella were listed as "cohabiting together," and it appears that the couple never formally married. Tom around 1867 had married Emeline Moore from Argyle, who also called herself "Amelia Crowell" or "Emeline Boyd." Emeline's parents were Planters. There was also another younger man named "Joseph Bartlett," born in 1831, living at Bridgewater, Lunenburg County, whose father was named "John Bartlett" but who evidently did not belong to the Summerside Bartletts. This man was a widower in 1866, and on 11 June 1867 he married a second time, by banns, a Mi'kmaw woman named Anne Morris, the daughter of Thomas M. Morris, at St.

Stephen's Roman Catholic Church in Chester. Joseph Bartlett's father John Bartlett was likely a brother of Joseph Bartlett Sr. of Summerside.

264 Members of the Carver and Awalt families intermarried with Mi'kmaq from Gold River and the Western Shore in Lunenburg County.

265 John Charles was Elsie Charles Basque's grandfather.

266 Stephen Bartlett *dit* Wisow Jr.'s birthdate is uncertain. A range of birthdates spanning 1807 to 1819 have been posited. His death certificate, dated 1901, claims he was born in 1807, but this date may be too early.

267 This information appears on the church register entry for Philip Sayer's (Cyr or Siah) marriage to Elizabeth Holmes of Annapolis on 14 August, 1880. Registers of St. Jerome's Church, Caledonia, "Marriage of Philip Sayer, son of Bartlett Luxey and Susan Michaud, and Elizabeth Holmes, daughter of Charles Holmes and Elizabeth Holmes." This is an error, since information found online at NSARM, Historical Vital Statistics, holds that Elizabeth's parents were George and Jane Holmes and that Elizabeth and Philip's marriage took place in Liverpool. NSARM, Historical Vital Statistics, Queens County Marriages, Registration year 1880, book 1834, p. 87, No. 31, "Marriage of Philip Sayer, age 55, the son of Bartlett and Susan, to Elizabeth Holmes, daughter of George and Jane Holmes of Annapolis. The witnesses were James Bartlett and Margaret Bartlett." Philip Sayer, who was born at Bear River, would have been born in 1822 as he is listed as being fifty-eight at the time of his marriage.

Jerry Lonecloud, the best-known member of the Bartlett family and grandson of Ekien (Étienne) Bartlett Sr., spoke about Ekien Sr. and his family. Lonecloud once stated more than a little misleadingly to Harry Piers, curator of the Nova Scotia Museum, that Ekien Wisow Sr. was a "full blood Indian" and that Ekien's wife (whom he did not name) was "full blood French." In making this assertion Lonecloud either ignored or did not know (which is unlikely) that Charles Alexis had married an Acadian, Anne Hébert. The name "Bartlet (*sic*) Luxey Jr." appears on the 1816 deed of subdivision for the Ring property at Salmon River and may have referred to Jerry Lonecloud's grandfather, Ekien Bartlett Sr. Lonecloud also told a journalist, Clara Dennis, that "his father lived to be 104 years old." Since Lonecloud could not have been referring to his father Abraham Bartlett, who died in middle age in 1865, he must have meant his grandfather Ekien Sr., though this advanced age of death cannot be confirmed. NSARM, MG 1, vol. 2867, Clara Dennis Archives, Note Book No. 4. The name "Michaud" appears among the Mi'kmaq of Cape

Sable in other contexts too, for when Laurent Mius's wife Marie Alexis died at The Forks in 1807, she was referred to in the burial registers of Ste. Anne du Ruisseau as "Marie Alexis *dit* Michaud." Lonecloud added that his own father, Abraham Bartlett, had been born at Ohio, Shelburne County. NSM, Piers Papers, undated ms. containing information about Jerry Lonecloud's parentage and his early years relayed by Lonecloud to Piers around 1927.

268 The assumption that John Bartlett was the son of Stephen Wisow Jr. must remain tentative, since John's parents' names are not given on his death certificate. NSARM, Historical Vital Statistics, Lunenburg County Deaths, Registration Year 1937, book 301, 364. Dr. W.E. (or Earl) Pollett, the physician who recorded John Bartlett's death in 1937 at Elmsdale, was unable to ascertain who John's parents were, though he did obtain John's date of birth. Dr. Pollett was the first author's own doctor for many years, and was a person who would have tried to obtain as much information about John Bartlett as he could.

269 Information for this Bartlett genealogy was drawn mainly from census records, vital statistics for Yarmouth and Digby counties, and the church registers of Ste. Anne du Ruisseau, St. Michel's Church in West Pubnico, St. Croix Church at Plympton, St. Vincent de Paul Church of Salmon River, and St. Louis Church at Annapolis Royal.

270 Both of these women's husbands were sons of Francis Charles Sulno Sr. As a young man John Charles went to live near Kentville. Registers of the Parish of St. Joseph's Church, District of Cornwallis, Kentville, and Aylesford, "Baptism of Susan Charles, daughter of John Charles and Mary Anne Bartholomew-Alexis (Bartlett), 10 June 1855."

271 Registers of St. Vincent de Paul Church, Salmon River, 1849–1907, "Marriage of Frank Bernard, son of Joseph Bernard and Mary Bernard, on 2 September 1888 to Mary Anne Bartlett, widow of James Charles, witnesses Joseph Pictou and Joseph Glode."

272 Francis Alexis was a son of François-Joseph Alexis, who was a son of Chief Lewis Alexis Sr., better known to history as Lewis Luxey of Long Island, Shelburne County. Lewis, in turn, was a son of Chief Joseph Alexis of Long Island, a son of Charles Alexis. Anastasia's father, Stephen Bartlett Jr. *dit* Wisow, thus was a great-grandson of Charles Alexis, while Francis-Joseph's father, Lewis, was a grandson of Charles Alexis. Anastasia and Francis were married at Meteghan on 22 February 1871. Surprisingly, Nancy's name appears in the 1881 census

for Salmon River, though this must be a mistake since the burial registers of the Parish of St. Vincent de Paul record that she died and was buried in 1880 at thirty-five years of age. Stephen Wisow Jr. and his son Joseph were both present at Nancy's interment on 14 October 1880.

273 The surname "Bartlett" is misspelled as "Bartly" in these marriage entries. NSARM, Historical Vital Statistics, Yarmouth County Marriages, Registration Year 1876, book 839, p. 106, nos. 13 and 14.

274 LAC, Microfilm reel C-13172, Canada, Census of 1881, District of Salmon River.

275 In 1896, at the age of thirty-two, "Frank Bartlett … son of Steven" married fourteen-year-old Susan Jerome of Millbrook, Colchester County. NSARM, Historical Vital Statistics, Colchester County Marriages, Year 1896, book 1807, p. 109, no. 161.

276 Henriette Christina also used "Christiana." Rosalie Bartlett, Stephen Bartholomew-Alexis *dit* Wisow Jr.'s daughter, stood as a godparent for several of Joseph Bartlett and Julia Pictou's younger children. At the baptism of Joseph and Julia's daughter Hilaire in the Parish of St. Vincent de Paul, Salmon River, on 25 February 1866, the child's godparents were Étienne Barthelemy-Alexis (Stephen Bartlett *dit* Wisow Jr.) and Rosalie Barthelemy-Alexis. When a son Benjamin was born to Joseph and Julia fourteen years later, the infant's godparents at his baptism on 29 March 1880 were Henriette Christina Bartlett and Henry Melanson.

277 Stephen Bartlett married Mary Anne Lawley or Lowney of Bear River and had a daughter, Cathy, in 1860 and a second daughter, Mary Anne, in 1865. Cathy was baptized in 1860 at St. Louis Church in Annapolis Royal, while Mary Anne's birth and baptism are entered in the Registers of St. Jerome's Church, Caledonia, for 1865, 57. Stephen and Mary resided in Caledonia in Queens County, and later at Bear River. In 1860 Joseph Bartlett Sr. and his second wife, Catherine Peters, had twins, Joseph Jr. and Peter. Registers of St. Louis Church, Annapolis Royal, "Baptism of Joseph Luxi and Peter Luxi, sons of Joseph [Bartlett] Luxi and Catherine Petrie [*sic*, Peters or Pitre], 1860." Joseph married Julia Pictou around 1862; it appears that Joseph and Catherine's son Joseph M. Bartlett was raised by Julia Pictou and his father. Matthew Bartlett was born on 13 December 1863 and baptized in 1864. Registers of St. Croix Church, Plympton, "Baptism of [Joseph] Matthew Bartlett, son of Joseph Bartlett and Julia Pictou, 9 February 1864." Hilaire and Benjamin Bartlett were born at Salmon River. Registers of St. Vincent de Paul, Salmon River, "Baptism of Hilaire B. Alexis, child of Joseph B. Alexis

and Julia Pictou, 11 February 1866, sponsors Étienne B. [Bartlett] Alexis [Jr.] and Rosalie B. Alexis"; Registers of St. Ambrose Cathedral, Yarmouth, "Certificate of Baptism, dated 2 June 1867, for Henrietta Christine Bartlett, born 13 May 1867, daughter of Joseph Bartlett and Julia Pictou"; Registers of St. Vincent de Paul, Salmon River, "Baptism of Benjamin Bartlett, son of Joseph and Julia Pictou, 29 March 1880, sponsors Henry Melanson and Henrietta Christiana Bartlett"; Registers of Ste. Anne du Ruisseau, "Baptism of James Solin [Sullivan], son of Joseph Barclay and Julie Pieton [*sic*, Pictou], 20 February 1873, witnesses James Barclay and Eunice Melançon." James Sullivan Bartlett was listed as born at Ohio in Shelburne County on the birth certificate of his son, James Lee Bartlett, in 1911. NSARM, Historical Vital Statistics, Yarmouth County Births, Registration Year 1911, "Birth of James Lee Bartlett," p. 53000409, no. 53000409. Henriette (or Henrietta) Christiana (Christine) Bartlett was probably born at Salmon River. She later married Samuel Labrador and was the mother of Margaret, or "Maggie," Labrador. Samuel and Henrietta Labrador's other children were Stephen Francis Labrador (born 10 March 1889) and Samuel Francis Labrador ("Sammy"), born on 8 September 1894 and baptized at St. Ambrose Cathedral in Yarmouth. Maggie Labrador wed Joseph Charles and became the mother of Lucy and Elsie Charles. According to Travis Pinn, Elsie Charles Basque was named Josephine Henrietta Charles after her father, Joseph Charles, and her grandmother, Henrietta Christine Bartlett. There were doubtless other children born to Joseph and Julia in the intervening years, but their births and baptisms were not recorded in the church records from either Salmon River or Ste. Anne du Ruisseau.

278 Whitehead, *Tracking Doctor Lonecloud*, 22. The census of 1871 lists him as being sixty and so born in 1811, though the later date of 1819 is probably more accurate. Philippe, Joseph, James, and John Bartlett and their apparently numerous sisters could have been born at either Salmon Lake or Roseway.

279 Ibid., 32. Sarah Bartlett, Abram (or Abraham) Bartlett's daughter, was Abraham Michael's third wife. Abraham's first wives were Eleanor Knockwood, with whom he had James and Fanny, and Agnes Paul with whom he had Margaret or "Maggie." He and Sarah were married about 1874 and had Peter Newel in 1875, Mary E. in 1867, Susan in 1880, Abraham in 188, Joseph in 1889, and Lavinia Christine in 1897. The information on Mary E. Michael came from the Registers of St. Croix Church in Plympton. All the other information came from the Registers of St. Louis Church, Annapolis Royal. The first author

is indebted to Ian Lawrence for helping her with this branch of the Michael family genealogy.

280 "Dr. Lone Cloud [Jerry Bartholomew-Alexis]" was recorded in one of Harry Piers's memos as being born at Salmon River, but this is incorrect. He was born in 1854 in Belfast, Maine. NSM, Printed Matter File, "Harry Piers notes, n.d." Jerry was a member of what was known in the 1850s as the "Cicopoo" (Sissaboo River) band, which at the time numbered around fifty persons.

281 NSARM, Historical Vital Statistics, Marriages, Lunenburg County, Year 1867, book 1828, p. 25, no. 140, "Marriage of Joseph Bartlett and Anne Morris, 11 June 1867."

282 James Bartlett was noted as living at Great Pubnico Lake in 1894, when a major Mi'kmaw campaign arose to secure a reserve in the West Pubnico area.

283 Robertson, "History of Shelburne County," 5–6.

284 NSARM, RG 1, vol. 430, docs. 20 and 21, "Sigogne to Lord Sherbrooke," 5 May 1812, with enclosures. As late as 1812 Abbé Sigogne noted that Jacques Mius still proudly wore his father's French medal around his neck on Sundays to church.

285 In 1994 John Muise *dit* "The Dude" stated that oral traditions within his family had it that Sigogne bought the land on which to build the Church of Ste. Anne du Ruisseau from Louis Muise of Rocco Point.

286 In his early writings and correspondence Jean-Mandé Sigogne drew an ideological distinction between Mi'kmaq whom he considered to be *sang pur* (pure blood) and both Mi'kmaq and *métis* whom he regarded as *sang mellé* (mixed blood). He tended to consider the *sang mellé* as socially unpredictable and possessing less moral fibre than their "pure blood" counterparts. Gérald C. Boudreau, "L'apostolat du missionnaire, Jean-Mandé Sigogne et les Acadiens du sud-ouest de la Nouvelle-Ecosse" (PhD diss., University of Montreal, 1989), 24–5. (Boudreau's revised dissertation was published as Boudreau's revised dissertation was published as *Le Pere Sigogne et les Acadians du sud-ouest de la Nouvelle-Écosse* (St. Laurent, PQ: Éditions Bellarmin, 1992); Bernard Pothier, "Sigogne, Jean-Mande," *DCB* online, vol. 7 (1836–50). Despite his initial ideological bias against Native-Acadian marital unions, Sigogne never cast a derogatory light on either the Alexis or Mius families of Eel Brook, Salmon River, and Bear River, though he must have known through his conversations with them that they possessed both Mi'kmaw and Acadian ancestry. As a classical scholar as well as a missionary, he encouraged them to learn Latin, and sing Latin anthems in church. This tradition of service to the church, instilled by Sigogne in the Barthlomew Alexis family, continued

after Sigogne's death in 1844. Étienne Bartholomew Alexis Sr.'s son Abraham sang in the choir at Ste. Anne du Ruisseau, and probably later at the Church of St. Vincent de Paul. Abraham's son, Jerry Bartlett Alexis, also known as Jerry Lonecloud, in the 1920s stated to journalist Clara Dennis that Sigogne "taught Latin to my father [Abraham] and my uncle [Stephen]. My father and my uncle sang in church at Eel brook chapel, near Tusket." Whitehead, *Tracking Doctor Lone Cloud*, 50. Earliest registers of the Church of St. Vincent de Paul, dating from 1849 to 1907, have been transcribed, edited, and indexed in book form by Leonard H. Smith as *Cape Sable, Nova Scotia: Vital Records, 1799–1841*.

287 The site for the primary rendezvous changed from year to year. Favoured locales were Charley Point, South West Point, and Indian Brook on Cape Sable Island. An "elderly person" told historian Thomas Robertson around 1871 that once he had counted fifty canoes drawn up on the shore of Charley Point, which would have conveyed at least two hundred Mi'kmaw individuals to that site. Robertson, "History of Shelburne County," 5. Though the sites mentioned are not found on modern atlases, residents of the Barrington Passage area can still point them out to those interested.

288 Whitehead, *Tracking Doctor Lonecloud*, 50.

289 Sir George Prevost succeeded Wentworth as lieutenant governor, and in the summer of 1811 Sherbrooke replaced Prevost. NSARM, RG 1, vol. 430, doc. 155, "Letter from Bishop Plessis, in French, to Sherbrooke," August 1815.

290 NSARM, RG 1, vol. 430, doc. 151, microfilm 15,469, "Report of Surveyor-General Charles Morris addressing information received by Sherbrook from Sigogne, with a copy to Henry Cogswell," 7 March 1815. Charles Morris's father and predecessor as surveyor general of Crown lands was also named Charles Morris (Charles Morris II, 1731–1802). The elder Morris had sought to help the Mi'kmaq on 2 July 1782 by introducing a bill into the House to prevent the destruction of moose, beaver, and muskrats on Mi'kmaq hunting grounds, but the bill was defeated. Nova Scotia, *Journals of the Legislative Assembly*, 1775–182: 177–8. 180.

291 Donald Chard, "Morris, Charles, 1759–1831," *DCB* online, vol. 6 (1821–35). Much later, when Jesse Gray and William Mangrum, Loyalists from South Carolina, wanted a land grant on Morris Island they were told it was already granted to Charles Morris by the government in exchange for his work on laying out Loyalist grants. In consequence, they sought land at Kemptville in the interior. The grant of the island was eventually

registered in the name of John Morris (John Spry Morris, Charles Morris III's son). Fred Burnett, "More Information on the Prossers of Kempville NS: A Letter from Society Member Fred Burnett," *The Argus* (newsletter) 20, no. 2 (2008): 23.

292 NSARM, microfilm reel 15,469, RG 1, vol. 430, doc. 151, "Report of Surveyor-General Charles Morris," 7 March 1815.

293 Ibid.

294 Morris knew that several tracts formerly granted to the Mi'kmaq had been sold, and proved especially chagrined when a member Nova Scotia's legislative council, Richard John Uniacke, bought the well-situated fertile tract allocated to Jacques Peminout on Grand Lake, located along the Shubenacadie River system, for a mere sixty pounds.

295 NSARM, microfilm reel 15,469, RG 1, vol. 430, doc. 151, "Report of Surveyor-General Charles Morris," 7 March 1815. Charles Morris's exact words were: "The Indians put me to a lot of expense ... The land that the Revd. Mr. Sigogne alludes to in his letter to your Excellency on the 1st of this month, which the Indians he names were desirous of obtaining at Cape Sable, were actually granted and of course not attainable, and in consequence those Indians were recommended to apply for other situations." Morris held that the Mi'kmaq had an interior focus, and hence should be given lands away from the coast.

296 As late as 1870 it was also noted that one important stopping place for the Mi'kmaq was at "*Oo-ne-gun-sook* on the Clyde River, probably near Lyle's Falls, where in the spring, after descending the river at the close of the hunting season, they ... made a temporary stand." This may have been Labraduce. The Mi'kmaq then "proceeded down the harbor to Cape Negro, crossing *Kes-poog-witk* (their Land's End, and our peninsula of Blanche) and launch their canoes again on Port La Tour Harbour." Their next stopping place was at *Ex-and-dy-week-took* (the Beach) to feast on clams. They proceeded to the "smooth and land-locked Barrington Harbour" and to *Men-tu-gek-se-boo* (Barrington River). From there they went to *Cock-a-wick*, or Wood's Harbour, then went to "Pubnico, which they visited while sojourning at Lake Sabine [now Great Pubnico Lake] where they often spent the winter, before coming down river again in the spring." Edwin Crowell, *A History of Barrington Township and Vicinity, Shelburne County, Nova Scotia, 1604–1870* (Yarmouth, n.d., c.1871), 9–10.

297 Robertson, "History of Shelburne County," 6. Robertson writes that "[a]bout 1½ acres of land were reserved for Indians, as a landing place, by the proprietors of Barrington Township, on a point of land running into the Clyde, on the north west side of Lyle's bridge. It received the name of 'Rabraduce' or 'Labraduce,'" which was afterwards "applied to the barrens in that part of the township." Labraduce is not mentioned in any other local history, although the first author as a child heard the term used for the Clyde River area.

298 NSARM, RG 3, vol. 214 ½ A, 136–39, "Report on the Reservation of Reserve Lands for the Indians by the Surveyor-General, signed by Charles Morris," 8 May 1820. A copy of this document may be found in NSARM, Miscellaneous "I" Indian Lands Documents, Microfilm Reel 14,011. No such land was allocated for the Mi'kmaq living in what would become Yarmouth County, as at that time it was still included in the County of Shelburne. Bear River was seen as a land base serving the Mi'kmaq of Digby County and Annapolis County.

299 Ibid. "In this county are places of resort for the Indians, particularly at Eel Bay, near the Tusket River where they take Eels in great quantities," Morris noted, "but, as their lands are private property, although the Indians had the use and occupancy of them from a very antient date, it might be advisable to recommend that a law be passed to protect them in their burial grounds at the spot where the cross is placed." Morris also suggested that certain offshore islands should have "small isolated tracts" reserved on certain islands. Perhaps "an acre or two ... in each of the situations" would suffice "and not affect the rights of others." In 1842 when Joseph Howe visited Cape Sable in the capacity of provincial Indian commissioner, he copied out Morris's words on these points verbatim in his journal. NSARM, RG 1, vol. 432, 26–30.

300 In 1976 Emerson Frank Francis, whose ancestors hailed originally from Great Pubnico Lake and the vicinity of the Clyde River, averred that the Mi'kmaq held a large council in a natural stone amphitheatre near Middle Ohio around 1726. Treaty and Aboriginal Rights Research (TARR) records housed at Shubenacadie, Nova Scotia, Union of Nova Scotia Indians (UNSI) Collection, 92–1004–06–030, "Sharon Copage to the Union of Nova Scotia Indians (UNSI)," 17 June 1977, and "Emerson Frank Francis of Shelburne to UNSI," 10 January 1976.

301 NSARM, MG 1, vol. 1776, Lord Dalhousie Journals, vol. 1, Transcriptions of original manuscripts in the Scottish Record Office in Edinburgh, Scotland, GD 45/3/541, entry for 17 July 1817; Marjory Whitelaw, ed., *The Dalhousie Journals* (Ottawa: Oberon, 1978), 39, entry for 17 July 1817.

302 NSARM, MG 1, vol. 1776, Lord Dalhousie Journals, vol. 1, GD 45/3/541, entry for 17 July 1817; Whitelaw, *The Dalhousie Journals*, 39, entry for 17 July 1817.

303 NSARM, Land Petitions, Luxey, Joseph, 1819. "To Lieu. Gov. Rt. Hon. George, Earl of Dalhousie and Dalhousie Castle … from Chief Joseph Luxey and four other native Indians on the river Roseway in the Township of Shelburne," petition for a grant of two hundred acres.

304 NSARM, Miscellaneous "I" Indian documents from the Department of Crown Lands, package 73, regarding 225 acres on Roseway River.

305 NSARM, Land Petitions, "Luxey, Joseph," 1819.

306 In 1818 Welsh settlers from Carmarthen and Cardigan in Wales founded the first Welsh settlement in Canada on the west side of the Roseway River, near present-day Lower Ohio. It was first called New Cambria, and later Welshtown. Welshtown still exists as a community in Shelburne County, though descendants of the original Welsh settlers have spread widely throughout the surrounding area.

307 Fifteen more Mi'kmaw families, or sixty-nine persons, lived in Argyle, around Yarmouth and northward on the Salmon River. The Shelburne and Argyle groups, together forming twenty-five families, constituted the membership of the Cape Sable band. To the north, in Digby County, twenty more families, or eighty-five individuals, resided along the shores of St. Mary's Bay, but these retained their closest connections with Sigogne's mission at Church Point and Chief Meuse's community of Bear River. Sigogne around 1822 recorded seventy-six family heads *in toto* associated with his mission, but many of these were associated with the Annapolis group at Bear River, Annapolis Royal, and Lequille. Smith, *St. Mary's Bay 1818–1829: Catalogue of Families*.

308 Robertson, "History of Shelburne County," 5–6. It is possible that Joseph not long before his death married a young wife named Catherine and had a daughter, Marie Anne. Registers of Ste. Anne du Ruisseau, "Baptism of Marie Anne Alexis, 6 April 1830." The godparents of Marie Anne were Anselm d'Entremont and Anne Catherine. In 1840 the same couple had a son named John Noel. Rather than being Chief Joseph's children, however, Marie Anne and John Noel were probably Joseph Alexis Sr.'s offspring, or children of another close member of the Alexis family living on the Roseway River in the 1830s.

309 "Familles des Sauvages," in Smith, *St. Mary's Bay 1818–1829: Catalogue of Families*.

310 Government relief requisitions attest to the hardship that the Mi'kmaq experienced during winters in the late 1820s and early 1830s. NSARM, microfilm 15,106, MG 15, vol. 3, doc. no. 31, "Relief supplies to Roseway River, 1829" and "An Account of Sundries supplied Joseph Luxey for the uses of Indians on Roseway River,"

NSARM, MG 15, vol. 3, doc. no. 33, "Supplies including two guns, flints and bullets, 28 pounds of shot, large hunting jacket and 2 lbs of lead balls," 1829–32.

311 In the documentary record Chief Joseph Alexis is almost always referred to by the surname "Alexis" (or "Elexie"), while his son Lewis is given the surname "Luxey."

312 LAC, RG 10, vol. 460, 295. The tract was surveyed by Jonathon Richards, deputy surveyor, on 24 February 1839, and the survey plan was signed by Isaac G. Emlow, a clerk of the peace, on 1 May 1838. The survey plan is ambiguous since it shows Joseph Luxey's log house located at the head of the island, while the 325 acres set out on the plan crosses the island like a wide band, just below this house. Lewis Luxey, Joseph's son, later argued that the Mi'kmaq originally had proprietorial rights to the whole head of the island.

313 LAC, microfilm reel 13,329 RG 10, vol. 460, Package 13, 400, Indian Affairs, Shelburne, Nova Scotia, Petitions, returns, and accounts, "Regarding grant of 325 acres to Joseph Luxey, Schedule of Reserve on West Branch Roseway River – 325 acres'; LAC, RG 10, vol. 460, package 13, 295, "Map of the Roseway River Reserve by J. Richards," 24 February 1830. In 1867 Lewis Luxey, who continued to treat the parcel as a grant, sold the Roseway River tract, so no mention of it can be found in the official documentary record after this date. LAC, RG 10, vol. 260, 469, "Return of Indian Reserves by County, Locality and Area"; LAC RG 10, vol. 459, 5, "Schedule of Occupied Reserves, 1871."

314 NSARM, MG 15, vol. 18, no. 23, "Copy of a letter from John D. Pinkham to John Spry Morris, Surveyor General of Crown Lands, requesting permission to buy land occupied by Joseph Alexis on Long Island, Ohio, in Shelburne County," 25 April 1835. Pinkham realized that for thirteen months Joseph Alexis had "held a letter," or a licence of occupation to the land, but he denigrated the Mi'kmaq's agricultural efforts by describing their parcel on the island as nothing but barrens. He then asked the Crown Lands department to write him, with their reply, care of John Holmes, the representative for the Township of Barrington.

315 *NSARM, RG 20 Ser. A – Luxey, John; Joseph & Other Indians, 6 May 1823; Nova Scotia Department of Lands and Forest, land grant registration books, vol. 88, microfilm reel 61.*

316 One son of Francis Charles I, John Charles, born in 1836, was the father of Joseph Charles, born in 1873, who in turn was Lucy Charles's and Elsie Charles Basque's father. This work is dedicated to the memory of Elsie Charles Basque. John Charles married

several times but lived longest with Mary Jane Firth (Crowell). After Mary Jane's death, he wed Marie Ella or Mahalia Frank, who previously had consorted with Joseph Bartlett Sr. of Summerside, Lunenburg County, in the mid-1870s and early 1880s. Marriage certificate of "Jean Charles, son of Francis Charles and Madeleine Peters," and "Nellie Frank" (*sic*, Marie or Mahalia Frank), daughter of George Frank and Christine Williams, dated 26 October 1891, housed in the Argyle Courthouse Museum and Archives. Another of Francis Charles I's sons, Francis Charles II, went inland to Kejimkujik. See "Marriage of Francis Charles and Mary Anne or Molly Peters of Kejimkujik," 7 May 1842, Church Registers of St. Jerome's Roman Catholic Church, Caledonia, Queens County. According to Joseph Charles's death certificate his mother's surname was "Williams," although this is incorrect. This mistake was made by Elsie Charles, who acted as the informant at the time of her father's death. Joseph Charles's mother's name in fact was Mary Jane Firth. Information courtesy of Travis Pinn, who holds genealogical information given to him by Elsie Charles Basque, and from NSARM, Historical Vital Statistics, Registration Year 1940, Halifax County Deaths, "Death of Joseph Charles, 8 March 1940," book 189, 1199.

317 Some of the descendants of Bernard Argomartin, the chief who founded the Gold River Mi'kmaw community, returned to Cape Sable, and these Penauls (also Pennals or Pennels) are sometimes referred to as the Cophangs. Persons with this surname continued living at Cape Sable until the early twentieth century. While members of Pierre Chegua's (or Toutou's) family remained close to the Alexis family, others bearing the Chegua surname fled at the time of the Acadian deportations to Cape Breton. The Tecouramarts may have left the province by 1780, as the name "Tecouramart" does not appear in the documentary record after this date. Rose Tecouramart, a daughter of Charles Tecouramart, married a Huron man from Lorette and remained there. What happened to the descendants of Eustache Tecourmart and his wife Marie Alexis after 1769 is unknown.

318 A site known as Bloody Creek, located in the Argyle Municipal District, falls in this region. Though there are several explanations for its name, it may be the stream on which Eustache Corporan at the time of the Acadians deportations led the British into an ambush. It is not where Samuel Vetch's men fell ambush to an Indigenous force outside Annapolis Royal in 1711.

319 B.R. Hurlbert, "Kemptville, Yarmouth, Nova Scotia," "The Indians," http://grassroutes.com/yarmouth/history/

kempt1. Hulbert is a descendant of one of the earliest families to settle at Kempville.

320 G.W.T. Farish, "A Medical Biography of the Bond-Farish Family," *Canadian Medical Association Journal* 23 (1930), 696–8, http://yarmouth.org/villages/town/people/farish.htm. Dr. Joseph B. Bond, who received the artefacts of what appears to be a burial mound, was a doctor and surgeon who took over his father's practice at Yarmouth in 1839. Farish, "Medical Biography," 698.

321 *John (or Jean-Baptiste) stated that he and his associates were responsible for acting on behalf of twenty Mi'kmaw families.* William Wicken views Jean-Baptiste Alexis and his brothers as increasingly moving inland owing to settler expansion along the coast. Yet it is also true that the Alexis family tried to preserve the integrity of their vast network of coastal and inland travel routes and encampment sites, retaining parcels of land that were much closer to the coast than the parcel at Kemptville. Wicken, *Colonization of Mi'kmaw Memory*, 112–13.

322 NSARM, microfilm reel 61, RG 20, Series A, vol. 88, "Petition of John-Baptist Elexey to Sir James Kempt," 6 May 1823.

323 NSARM, Misc. Places, Nova Scotia, Land Grants, Letter Book L, 24–6, "Grant to Abner Andrews and David Andrews *et al*, 1824." The Mi'kmaq only received a fifty-acre grant. According to local historian Fred Burnett, Major Samuel Andrews, the father of David, Abner, and Alexander Andrews, was said to be "one of the highest ranking former army officers in the country, a foreman of juries." Burnett, "More Information on the Prossers," 20–1.

324 Yarmouth County Deeds, 1825, Book Q, 335–36, "Indenture made 24 May 1825 between David Andrews and Seth Tinkham," registered 12 November 1825. Andrews sold his parcel to Tinkham for fifty pounds.

325 Yarmouth County Deeds, Argyle Township Deeds, Book Q, 1826, 45–46, "Indenture made 7 April 1826 between Samuel Alexis and Joseph Alexis and Daniel Nickerson," registered 18 July 1826. The Alexis sold their property to Nickerson for five pounds.

326 Crowell, *History of Barrington Township*, 62.

327 The Acadians for years could offer only friendly moral support to the Mi'kmaq, for the English regime at first considered that Acadians had no place in provincial life. In 1791 this changed. Benoni d'Entremont (1744–1841), the son of the last seigneur of Pobomcoup, was appointed the first Acadian magistrate in 1818. Benoni had experienced a somewhat easier time in exile than many Acadians. "Tradition has it that Benoni's father met a mariner in Boston whose life and ship he had

saved some 35 years earlier. To repay him, the seafarer pleaded his case with Governor William Shirley; as a consequence, his family was granted food, clothing, and a degree of liberty unknown to most exiles … [After Benoni arrived back at Pubnico he] imitated his father by becoming a community leader, initially of his own people and later of the entire population of Argyle Township, which included New England settlers who had arrived after the deportation at the invitation of Charles Lawrence, former governor of Nova Scotia. D'Entremont's position as a community leader benefitted from his aristocratic family background and his ability to read and write in both French and English – both of which he acquired, surprisingly, while he was in exile. He also exhibited qualities which people admired and respected, for he became an important figure in his church and an assistant to the parish priest, Jean-Mandé Sigogne, by acting as a sort of envoy for villagers with specific requests to make of their pastor. The provincial authorities also recognized d'Entremont's leadership. After a law was passed in 1791 permitting Acadians to serve as public officials he was named first treasurer for Argyle and a justice of the peace." Neil J. Boucher, "Entremont, Benoni d," DCB online, vol. 7 (1836–50). At an early age Benoni's son Simon showed an interest in Mi'kmaw welfare and learned the Mi'kmaw language so he could more effectively assist the local Indigenous community. When Yarmouth County was carved out of Shelburne County in 1836, Simon d'Entremont was elected MPP for Argyle Township. Louis R. Comeau, "Entremont, Simon d," *DCB* online, vol. 6 (1881–90).

328 The shores of Great Pubnico Lake were also important moose-hunting grounds for the Cape Sable Mi'kmaq. As well, about ten families maintained gardens and orchards on the southeast side of the lake, near the outflow of the Barrington River. As late as 1860 Mi'kmaw from the Roseway and Clyde Rivers and from near Pubnico continued a well-established seasonal harvesting pattern by portaging east from West Pubnico along a tote road to Great Pubnico Lake, down the Barrington River to Barrington Head on Barrington Bay, and then to the Clyde River, the Roseway River, and Cape Negro. At the time the Mi'kmaw continued to use Mi'kmaw terms for the places they stayed, rather than English place names. Barrington was *Pipguenishe*, while Barrington Head was *Menstuget* (or, according to the early French settlers, *Ministiguèche*). NSARM, MG 20, vol. 67, #16, 3–4; Rev. Edwin Crowell, "Old Barrington Township," Nova Scotia Historical Society, unpublished papers, presented to the society 7 February 1919.

329 Honore Catherine Alexis, born about 1788, was the mother of John Williams, who became a well-known guide. Born on the north side of Great Pubnico Lake, John later moved to the Shubenacadie area where he married Ann Peminout Paul. By 1847 the couple lived on the Preston Road east of Dartmouth where John raised a son Francis and a stepson Noel. NSM, Printed Matter File, Harry Piers Papers, Mi'kmaw Ethnology, Genealogies, 37; NSARM, MG 15, vol. 4, no. 20, February 1847, and MG 15, vol. 5, no. 69. After Ann's death John married Adelaide (or Madeleine) Thomas of Panuke Lake, near Windsor, who was a descendant of Baptist Thoma, a late-eighteenth-century head chief born near Port Royal. The two lived at Nine Mile River and at Shubenacadie. NS Museum Library, Piers Papers, Ethnology, Genealogies, 1 October 1929; Canada, Census of 1881, Nine Mile River, East Hants County. Kate Alexis, who married Joseph Francis, was likely another of Lewis's sisters. Kate was a widow by 1866.

330 A local physician named Dr. Geddes who had vaccinated the Mi'kmaq living near West Pubnico in 1841 drew up a list that also included James Bartlett, Ekien or Étienne Francis, Francis Labrador, John Labrador, James Lewis, John Meuse, Peter Paul and John Pictou, and their dependants, "making 40 in all" living at Great Pubnico Lake. NSARM, RG 1, vol. 432, 93–4, Howe, "Western Tour, 1842." Mr. Geddes's list was obtained from Samuel Kimble of Barrington. Howe also obtained a description of the improvements each head of family had made on the lake. NSARM, RG 1, vol. 432, 70.

331 Ibid, 93–4.

332 Howe stated that he saw no Mi'kmaq camped on the Clyde River in 1842. Ibid. 93.

333 Ibid., 92.

334 Howe evidently did not know much about this branch of the Alexis family. He had been given a list with names of three adult males, Joseph, John, and Lewis Alexis, but did not distinguish whether the name "Joseph" on the list referred to the deceased father or to his son, Joseph Jr. Howe may have been referring to Joseph Jr. *dit* Makaq, who apparently had recently died. Joseph Alexis Jr. was born to Joseph Alexis Sr. and his wife Marie-Josephe Mius in 1803. NSARM, RG 1, vol. SA1, 74, "Baptism of Joseph Alexis born 28 July 1803, son of Joseph Alexis and Marie-Joseph Muice, with godparents Brigitte Alexis, daughter of Barthelemi [Alexis] and Antoine Charles from Isle St. Jean, 28 July 1805." Joseph Alexis Jr. later became known as Joseph *dit* Makaq. He married Marie-Anne Muice and in 1830 had a daughter Catherine. NSARM, RG 1, vol. SA5, 24, Registers of Ste.

Anne du Ruisseau, "Baptism of Catherine Alexis, born 6 April 1830, baptized 8 April 1830, godparents Anselme d'Entremont and Anne Catherine d'Entremont." No entries for Joseph Alexis Jr. and his wife Marie-Anne could be found in church records after 1840, however.

335 Howe, 92, "Western Tour, 1842."

336 NSARM, RG 1, vol. 432, 23, "Letter from Cornelius White to Joseph Howe," 1843.

337 NSARM, RG 1, vol. 432, 92.

338 Cecumgega Lake and Kejimkujik Lake are the same body of water, but the Mi'kmaw word that has been translated as "Fairy" became "Kejimkujik," presumably by accident. "Kejimkujik" is a term used by the Mi'kmaq, but not often in mixed company. It means "constricted flow" or "swollen body parts," which may refer to the uncomfortable position in which men sometimes had to sit while paddling in a canoe for long stretches of time across a lake's choppy waters.

339 NSARM, RG 1, vol. 432, 88.

340 LAC, vol. 460, doc. 309, file 13, doc. 329, "Letter signed 'C.L.' discussing the acquisition of Long Island in the Roseway River in 1834 by Joseph Luxey," dated 13 June 1849. This letter is attached to a letter from John Spry Morris entitled "To Messrs. Saml. Irwin, Robert Quinlan and Thomas Quinlan, Shelburne," dated 4 December 1859; LAC, RG 10, vol. 459, C-13, 329, Accounts, Petitions and Returns, indexed 1857–74, doc. 300, "Letter of reply written by Philip Bowers to an inquiry sent by Indian Affairs," undated (c.1858); NSARM, Miscellaneous "I" – Indian Land Records on microfilm, package 73, "Correspondence referring to the Roseway Indian Reserve of Shelburne County."

341 This would have been Vict. C. 16 passed in March 1842, *Statutes of Nova Scotia, 1836–1846*, 23–4.

342 Philip Bower added, "The subscriber will add that the whole transaction has been pursued in according with the instructions given by the Indian to his satisfaction." LAC, RG 10, vol. 460, file 13, doc. 300, "Philip Bower to Indian Affairs," 1842–3.

343 LAC, RG 10, vol. 460, file 13, doc. 298.

344 Survey plans for the Kejimkujik settlement may be found in NSARM, Miscellaneous "I" Indian Records from Crown Lands on microfilm, package 38, Indian Lands at Kedgemakooge Lake, Annapolis, and Queens Counties, 1843. After 1846, only a few Mi'kmaw families, among them Jim Charles and some Gloades, struggled on farming. The place was vacant, however by 1880. For the fate of this settlement see Janet E. Chute, "Frank G. Speck's Contributions to the Understanding of Mi'kmaq Land Use, Leadership and Land Management," *Ethnohistory* 46, no. 3 (1999): 480–540.

345 Nova Scotia, *JLA*, 1844, Appendix 50, 123–5, "Joseph Howe's Account of Fairy Lake Settlers." Sally Peters (née Alexis, c.1816–c.1895), mentioned in this report, was very likely Lewis Luxey's sister. Also see Whitehead, *The Old Man Told Us*, 226. Sally Alexis was born around 1816, as she was said to be fifty-five years old according to the 1871 federal census. She died at Bear River. The late Basil Peters, who was born at Bear River, stated that the Peters surname stemmed from a French trader named Pierre Rossignol, who traded during the French era along what is now the Mersey River in southwestern Nova Scotia, and whose family married with the Mi'kmaq. Other scholars argue it may derive from "Pitre," a French surname.

346 LAC, RG 10, vol. 460, 292.

347 NSARM, RG 1, vol. 431 (no doc. no.), "John Minard, carpenter, to provincial Indian Affairs commissioner," 8 May 1845. Minard wrote that John Jeremy, Lewis Luxey, and Joe Peter were in the process of cutting timber for their barns, and that John Luxey already had his barn up and framed. Both Lewis Luxey and Joe Peter had cut twenty-five hundred feet of timber and were expecting help from Minard to raise their barns. These barns' dimensions would be thirty by twenty-four feet.

348 In 1849 Joseph Bartlett and his family lived eight miles from Mill Village, Queens County. NSARM, RG 5, Series P, vol. 45, doc. 135, "Petition of Dr. James Forbes," 10 February 1849.

349 NSARM, microfilm reel 15,614, RG 5, Series P, vol. 44, no. 142, "Petition of Gabriel Anthony," 13 January 1846. The contents of this petition were also published in the *Halifax Morning Post* on 14 January 1846.

350 John Patrick Martin, *The Story of Dartmouth*, foreword by Thomas H. Raddall (Dartmouth: printed by the author, 1957), 341.

351 Speck, *Beothuk and Micmac*, 56; Beverley Diamond, "Santu Toney, a Transnational Beothuk Woman," in Fiona Polack, ed., *Tracing Ochre: Changing Perspectives on the Beothuk* (Toronto: University of Toronto Press, 2018), 247–68. Santu married twice, but she always remained close to the Toney family, and her second husband was a member of this family. Santu's life story, as gleaned in 1910 by Frank G. Speck from Santu's son Joseph Toney, recently has been re-examined to show that Indigenous persons born in Newfoundland and bearing Beothuk ancestry had by the late nineteenth century spread throughout the Northeast.

352 This Peter Toney may have been the head chief of Merigomish, but he also may have been Meuse's brother-in-law named Peter Toney, who lived at Bear River and

at times posed as Meuse's political rival during band elections. It is not certain that Chief Peter Toney of Merigomish ever came to Halifax. He may have had a member of the legislative assembly, G.R. Young, present his petitions for him in Halifax. Ruth Holmes Whitehead holds, however, that the Peter Toney mentioned in the petition of 1849 was the Merigomish chief, who, it is true, was very politically active around this time. *Acadian Recorder*, 10 February 1849; Ruth Holmes Whitehead, *Niniskamijimaqik/Ancestral Images: The Mi'kmaq in Art and Photography* (Halifax: Nimbus, 2015), 42–3. In early February 1849 Peter Toney of Merigomish presented a petition to the Nova Scotia legislature on behalf of the thirty-five families under his leadership, so he may have been in the neighbourhood of Halifax when the second petition was submitted a week later to Lieutenant Governor John Harvey.

353 *Acadian Recorder*, 24 February 1849, col. 3, Concerning the Application of Ten Mi'kmaw Chiefs to the Legislature for Assistance, "To His Excellency John Harvey … Lieut. Governor of Nova Scotia: The Petition of the undersigned Chiefs and Captains of the Micmac Indians of Nova Scotia, 8 February 1849." The ten chiefs were Pelancea (François) Paul (Peminout), Colum (Gorham) Paul (Peminout), Piel (Pierre or Peter) Toney, Louis Paul, Cobliel (Gabriel) Bonus, Saagaach (**Sákéj**) Meuse (James Meuse), Louis Luxie (Lewis Alexis), Sabatier (either Jean Baptiste or Xavier) Paul, Piel (Pierre) Morris, and Pelancea Paul. Each one had a symbol inscribed after their name, such as an arrow or a canoe, on the petition, but rather than being traditional totems these were likely designations ascribed by Gesner to attract public attention in the capital. Traditional totems tended to be associated with animals or plants, such as bear, lobster, or cedar. François Paul Peminout was considered the "high chief" of the Sipekne'katik (Shubenacadie) district, while Andrew James Meuse was the main southwestern chief. NSARM, microfilm reel 3533, Nova Scotia, *JLA*, 1848, 118, Appendix 24; Nova Scotia, *JLA*, 1848, n.p., Appendix 88, "Report of the Committee of Indian Affairs." In 1848 the committee favoured regulations protecting the interests of the net and sports-angling salmon fishery over the Mi'kmaw spear fishery, which it saw as potentially damaging to the other two sectors.

354 Lillian Pictou of Yarmouth, who married Lewis Luxey Sr.'s great-grandson John Pictou, held that at this time Lewis wielded considerable political weight within the Cape Sable community and was sometimes known as "Kji [Great] Luxey [Alexis]." Interview session involving Lillian Pictou, Doris Labradore, and Janet Chute held at Acadia First Nation, Yarmouth, 10 July 1990.

355 Charles Morris III, born in in 1759 in Massachusetts, was the eldest son of *Charles Morris* II and Elizabeth Bond Leggett, and the grandson of *Charles Morris* I, the first surveyor general of Nova Scotia. John Spry Morris succeeded his father on the latter's death in 1831 as surveyor general of Crown Lands.

356 LAC, RG 10, vol. 460, file 13, doc. 317, "Alex Hamilton to Department of Crown Lands," 2 December 1862; LAC, RG 10, vol. 460, folio 5, 303, "Report on 1,000-acre Brookfield Reserve, 1853." The subdivision of the Brookfield reserve, now known as the Wildcat reserve, into ten lots of one thousand acres each was undertaken by Whitman Freeman, deputy surveyor, in December 1843.

357 LAC, RG 10, vol. 460, file 13, doc. 309, "Whitman Freeman to John Spry Morris, Surveyor-General of Crown Lands," 15 June 1849.

358 NSARM, vol. 460, 317, "Alex Hamilton to Crown Lands," 2 December 1862.

359 When the first author and research assistant Carrie Gloade visited the Clyde River area in 2011, they were told that the the Bowers still remembered the Luxey family of Roseway River and Wildcat with respect and affection. The Quinlans and the Luxys also continued to communicate with one another, and in 1865 a wedding took place between the two families. Registers of St. Gregory's Parish, Liverpool, "Marriage of Levi Quinlan and Mary Ann Luxy, September 1865."

360 Ibid.; NSARM, RG 10, vol. 460, file 13, "To Messrs. Saml. Irwin, Robert Quinlan and Thomas Quinlan from John Spry Morris," 4 December 1857.

361 LAC, RG 10, vol. 460, "Regarding Petition No. 6021, 8 June 1863, sent to Samuel Fairbanks, Commissioner of Crown Lands"; Ibid., "Alexander Hamilton, D.S., to Crown Lands," 20 October 1863; NSARM, Crown Lands Grant Book 30, 251, Roseway River, "To Give and Grant unto Lewis Luxie of Brookfield in Queen's County, Farmer, one hundred acres in the County of Shelburne, 31 July 1863. Survey plan attached drawn up by Alexander Hamilton, Deputy Surveyor, dated 20 August 1863"; NSARM, RG 10, vol. 460, file 13, folder 1, 293–5, "Plan of Indian Reserve of 325 acres for Long Island, 1863. The lines run of the original parcel had been run in 1839, Plan of reserve, signed by John Spry Morris and dated 24 February 1839"; NSARM, Crown Land Grant Book 33, 71, "[To] Give and Grant unto Lewis Luxey … one hundred and fifteen acres between the Eastern and Western Branches of the Roseway River," 16 May 1865. This plot also was surveyed by Alexander Hamilton.

362 Nova Scotia, *JLA*, 1862, 3, Appendix no. 30, "Report of Committee on Indian Affairs." This committee in 1862 noted that Joseph Alexis had "occupied" the lot for upwards of thirty years, and that Joseph's son Lewis Alexis "considered it as an inheritance from his father." The group also stated that Lewis had been "trying for a long time to get a grant, but he had never succeeded. We recommend that the Government give him a lease of one hundred acres of land, so as to include all his improvements." Lewis Luxey obviously did not accede to this recommendation and continued to negotiate in private to sell and buy land that he argued had been granted bone fide to his father in 1834, and that he had inherited on his father's death shortly before 1842.

363 LAC, RG 10, vol. 460, file 13, doc. 317, "Hamilton to Crown Lands," 2 December 1862. Hamilton noted, "Joseph Elexie occupied the head of the Island a number of years prior to the survey of the Common + since his decease his son Lewis claims the whole of the reserve. There are 2 surviving heirs besides Lewis + 3 children of a sister (who is dead). About 7 years ago Lewis sold the reserve to Colin C. Bowers for £70 or £75, for the lot to be paid in installments (say) four or five pounds yearly, the balance to be paid on receiving his grant."

364 Joseph Luxey *dit* Makaq, who was born to Joseph Alexis and his wife in 1803 and in early adulthood lived at Roseway for many years, ceases to appear in the documentary record by this time.

365 NSARM, G 15, vol. 6, doc. 42, "Report by Henry D. Ruggles of death of Molly Alexis who died of hemorrhage, Annapolis, 1857."

366 Queens County Museum and Archives, Liverpool, "Francis Family Genealogy."

367 Dalhousie University Archives, Halifax, Raddall Papers, Research notes, Series 14, box 29.8, folder 8, "Sam Glode, Micmac Indian" (twenty-two pages), 5; Dalhousie Archives, Raddall Papers, Ms.2.202, Q.2.E.2, "Thomas Raddall notes on John Francis"; NSARM, microfilm 4783, "Obituary of John Noel Francis," written by Radddall, *Liverpool Advance*, 20 February 1947. The genealogical information pertaining to Lewis Luxey's family comes from church registers associated with St. Gregory's Roman Catholic Church in Liverpool, St. Jerome's Roman Catholic Church in Caledonia, St. Louis Roman Catholic Church in Annapolis Royal, and from census data and vital statistics. The authors are also indebted to Ian Lawrence of Annapolis Royal who generously shared the copious genealogical information he had gathered and compiled over the years regarding the Luxey and Bartholomew-Alexis (Bartlett) families.

Francis Luxey was probably Francis-Joseph Luxey, born in 1846 to Lewis Luxey and his second wife, Mary Ann Cobliel (Mary Ann Gabriel Glode). Furthermore, John Noel Francis, born in 1874 to Joseph Francis and Carey Ann Luxey, remembered as a boy accompanying elderly members of the Luxey family to sell baskets at Lunenburg. Each year in September these Luxeys left Lunenburg County and returned to the interior to hunt moose. These persons may even have been Lewis Luxey Sr. and his second wife, Mary Ann Cobliel.

368 While information could not be found on John, it is known that Joseph Luxey married three times. The registers of St. Louis Church at Annapolis Royal record Joseph married to Catherine Pitre and having two sons by the early 1860s, so presumably Catherine Pitre was Joseph's first wife. Joseph's second wife was Mary Labrador, and between 1863 and 1867 the couple had three children, Elizabeth or "Betsy," Joseph, and Mary Ann. Elizabeth was baptized at Annapolis Royal on 3 May 1863, Joseph was baptized on 30 April 1865, and Mary Ann was baptized on 13 October 1867. After Mary Labrador's death in 1871, Joseph married a third time to Margaret Francis, a widow and the forty-five-year-old daughter of Thomas Wallace and Mary Ann Phillips. Registers of St. Gregory's Church, Liverpool, "Marriage of Joseph Luxey and Margaret Francis, 9 February 1872." (By this time Joseph was in his early forties.) Eliza Rose Luxey married Alec Jeremy of Port Medway, Queens County, in 1855. Registers of St. Gregory's Church, Liverpool, "Marriage of Eliza Luxey and Alex Jeremy, 18 February 1855." The chief's and Elizabeth Glode's second daughter, Mary Luxey, first married John Charles, the brother of James or "Jim" Charles of Fairy Lake, at Kentville in 1855, and the couple had a daughter, Susan. After John's death, Mary then wed Matthew Pictou in 1859. Registers of St. Louis Catholic Church in Annapolis Royal, "Marriage of Mary Luxey and Matthew Pictou, 1 August 1859."

369 Lewis Luxey's second wife, Mary Ann Cobliel, was born in 1829 and lived to be eighty-eight years of age. She died at Milton, Queens County, in 1917. NSARM, Historical Vital Statistics, Registration Year 1917, book 46, p. 249, no. 582. The 1871 federal census erroneously lists her as being sixty years of age, born in 1811. This date is far too early. The date on her death certificate is likely correct.

370 Catherine or Kate Luxey married Joseph Jeremy of Brookfield in 1862. Registers of St. Jerome's Church, Caledonia, Queens County, 2 November 1862. The wedding is also mentioned in the *Liverpool Transcript* of 6 November 1862. (The authors are indebted to Ian Lawrence of Annapolis Royal for this reference.) François-Joseph

Luxey, according to Samuel Freeman Glode of Milton, lived with Mary Anne Paul in the 1880s though they may not have been formally married. François-Joseph is probably the one who earlier married a woman named Catherine and had a son, François Luxey, who married Anastasia Bartlett (c.1825–c.1900) at Meteghan on 22 February 1871. Anastasia was a daughter of Chief Stephen Bartlett and Mary Ellen Brooks of Salmon River and later Yarmouth. François Luxey, a cooper, and his wife Anastasia lived at Pubnico. His sister Mary Ann ("Molly") Luxey married James Pictou of Wildcat in 1871. NSARM, Historical Vital Statistics, Queens County Marriages, Registration Year 1871, book 1834, p. 32, no. 35. Mary Ann and James had one son, John Pictou, born in 1871, before she died at Liverpool the following year. Registers of St. Gregory's Church, Liverpool, Burial of Mary Ann Pictou, 12 August 1872. Lewis (or Louis) Luxey Jr. married Catherine Michael at Ste. Croix Roman Catholic Church in Plympton in July of 1875. The couple had eight children: Mary Margaret, baptized at Plympton in 1876; Sarah Ann, baptized at Annapolis Royal in 1878; Beloni or Benjamin, baptized at Annapolis Royal in 1880; John, baptized at Annapolis Royal in 1886 and who died young; Josephine, born at Bear River and baptized at Annapolis Royal in 1888; John, baptized at Annapolis Royal in 1890; Rachael, baptized at Annapolis Royal in 1893; and Mary Ann, baptized at Annapolis Royal in 1895. Josephine married twice. Her first husband, whom she married in 1906, was James Pictou, born at Jordan River, the son of John Pictou and Mary Meuse of West Pubnico. The two settled in Yarmouth and had three children: Mary Rose on 13 April 1909, John on 25 April 1910, and Clifford, birthdate unknown. NSARM, Historical Vital Statistics, Yarmouth County Births, Registration Year 1909, p. 5290037, no. 5290037; NSARM, Historical Vital Statistics, Yarmouth County Births, Registration year 1910, p. 52900956, no. 52900958. James Pictou died at Yarmouth on 2 January 1919 at age thirty-five of tuberculosis. Josephine's second husband was Wilfred Robinson, the son of Benjamin Robinson and Angela Cook of Chebogue. Josephine's brother John Luxey, who was the youngest child of Louis Luxey Sr. and Mary Ann Cobliel, was born about 1855. On the 1891 federal census he is listed as a twenty-eight-year-old widower living at Bear River with a two-year-old son. Registration Year 1943, book 202, 400. Frank died in 1887 at the age of three years and nine months in Lowell, Massachusetts. Massachusetts Vital Statistics, Lowell Deaths, vol. 383, p. 130, no. 340. Lena was baptized at St. Louis Church, Annapolis Royal on 11 September 1892, but nothing else concerning her could be learned. Margaret died a single woman at Paradise in 1930. NSARM, Historical Vital Statistics, Registration Year 1930, death of Margaret Luxie, book 135, 369. Eggy's son Stephen Luxey, born in 1892, remained a single, licensed guide and died at fifty-one in Middleton in 1943. St. Louis Church Registers, "Baptism of Stephen Luxie, 11 September 1892"; NSARM, Historical Vital Statistics, Annapolis County Deaths, "Death of Stephen Luxie, 4 October 1943." The informant regarding Stephen's death was his niece Martha Luxe of Halifax.

371 A survey was made under instructions from Samuel Fairbanks. LAC, RG 10, vol. 460, "Fairbanks to Austin," 31 December 1867.

372 James F. Moore warned that some "violence may be resorted to if the difficulties are not settled." LAC, RG 10, vol. 460, file 13, "Moore to Fairbanks," 12 July 1865. Moore was the son of a former tannery and mill operator at Milton who had been a business associate of Simeon Perkins at Liverpool. The Moore family and Samuel Fairbanks at Shelburne were also connected, since Fairbank's mother had been a daughter of Perkins. Today James F. Moore is best known as the county historian of Queens County.

373 Nova Scotia, *JLANS*, 1863, III: Appendix no. 16, "Samuel P. Fairbanks to Joseph Howe, Provincial Secretary," 25 February 1863. This was carelessness rather than ignorance, since Samuel Prescott Fairbanks (1795–1882) had been brought up in Halifax, Queens, and Shelburne counties and maintained a law office in Liverpool.

374 Shelburne County Land Deeds, book 18, 66–8, "Indenture made the 20 December 1866 between Lewie Luxie of Brookfield in the County of Queens in the province of Nova Scotia, yeoman, and Molly (or Mary Ann) Luxie, wife of the said Lewis Luxey on the one part, and Collin [*sic*, Colin] C. Bowers of the County of Shelburne, yeoman, on the other, 26 March 1866, Registered 8 July 1867 in front of Samuel H. Freeman, J.P., witness." Neither of these Luxeys could write so they each signed the document with a "X." Colin Bowers paid Luxey two hundred dollars for the two tracts, which lay north of land owned by Quinlan and Irvin.

375 LAC, RG 10, vol. 460, "Return for the distribution of seed potatoes to Mi'kmaq in Queens County," 1868.

376 His sons-in-law were Matthew Pictou, who in 1859 wed Luxey's daughter Mary, and Joseph Jeremy, who in 1862 married his daughter Kate Margaret. His son Joseph, who also lived near him at Wildcat, in 1871 married Margaret Francis (née Wallace). Another of Luxey's daughters, Mary Ann, in 1871 wed James Pictou, but she

died the following year, possibly in childbirth. NSARM, Historical Statistics, Queens County Marriages for 1871, book 1834, p. 32, no. 35; Registers of St. Gregory's Church, Burial of Mary Ann Pictou, 12 August 1872. Mary Ann also had a son, John Pictou, who died at fourteen months, and James Pictou died of consumption in 1873. NSARM, Historical Vital Statistics, Queens County Deaths, Registration Year 1873, book 1814, p. 58, no. 52, "Death of James Pictou, son of John Pictou and Mary Labrador, 12 May 1873."

377 Registers of St. Gregory's Church, Liverpool, "Marriage of Rose Luxey and Alex Jeremy, 18 February 1855"; Registers of St. Gregory's Church, Liverpool, "Marriage of Rose Jeremy and Noel Paul, 6 October 1872."

378 LAC, RG 10, vol. 460, "List of Blankets and Coats distributed in the autumn of 1869 by Samuel Fairbanks, Indian Commissioner and Commissioner of Crown Lands," 1 April 1869.

379 LAC, microfilm reel C-11,233, RG 10, vol. 2520, file 107,000X, Part 2, "Census of Indian Population in Canada for the Year 1871." The population that in the 1840s moved eastward by this date began to return to Cape Sable. The population of Cape Sable was still dispersed, but kin ties throughout the area remained strong. The scattered families at Cape Sable by 1871 embraced 48 individuals. In Shelburne there were 28 people; 2 persons were at Port La Tour, 11 at Carleton Village, 15 at Louis Head on the coast near Gunning Cove and across from the head of Shelburne Harbour, and none remained on the Roseway River. Twenty Mi'kmaq lived in Yarmouth County, 10 were in Yarmouth, only 1 person lived at Cheboque, 6 lived on the west side of the Tusket River, 2 at Tusket, and 1 at Eel Brook in Argyle. The census was apparently taken in the summer, when some Cape Sable Mi'kmaq were at the coast fishing. In Digby County, 7 individuals of the Bartlett family lived at Salmon River. Further north, 26 lived near Church Point, 22 at Belliveau Cove, 4 in Clare, 1 in Weymouth, 7 at Meteghan, 3 at St. Mary's Bay, and 153 at Bear River. Altogether, 216 persons lived in Digby County. When the 7 persons at Salmon River are added to the others from Cape Sable, the Cape Sable band increases in number to 55.

380 As opposed to a variant of the name "Solomon," as was the case with the Sulno Jeremys of La Have in the early nineteenth century.

381 NSARM, RG 15, vol. 6, doc. 73, "Petition of Chief Peter Charles (Sulno)," March 1866. The petition was directed to the lieutenant governor of Nova Scotia, who in 1866 was Sir William Fenwick Williams, 1st Baronet of Kars and a noted military commander.

382 Ibid., "List of family heads at Cape Sable with their children," March 1866. The core of the group was made up of Peter Charles's family at Carleton Lake on the Tusket River. The other heads of families, besides Chief Charles and two Bartletts –Stephen Bartlett Jr. *dit* Wisow (c.1807–1901) and his brother Joseph Bartlett (c.1820–c.1870) – were Charles Francis, Job Francis, Newell Francis Sr., Noel Francis Jr., Elizabeth Francis, Mary Katy Francis (née Alexis), Matthew Glode, James Miuce, and Matthew Pictou of Pubnico. James Toney and Peter Labrador lived along the lower Tusket River. Katy Alexis Francis, likely a sister of Lewis Alexis Sr., was also in the Tusket area. Margaret Kinney, a widow, lived nearby. She may have been related to Mary Anne Luxey, who married Levi Kinney and gave birth to Henry Kinney in 1865 and Barbara Ann Kinney in 1867. Registers of St. Gregory's Church, Liverpool.

383 By the 1860s Stephen Wisow Jr. maintained two residences, one at Salmon River and one near Chief Peter Charles Sulno at Carleton Lake.

384 Peter Charles Sulno's census made no reference to Joseph's twin boys born to his first wife in 1860, nor of Joseph Matthew, the son of Joseph's second wife.

385 Chief Sulno also noted that five family heads belonging to the Francis family lived at West Pubnico, including a widow named Katy Francis. NSARM, RG 15, vol. 6, doc. 73, "Petition of Chief Peter Charles," 1866. Matthew Glode, Matthew Pictou, and James Miuce (Meuse) lived on the road leading to Great Pubnico Lake. A second widow, Margaret Kinny or Kenney (who also went by the surname "King") lived in Argyle, probably around the Tusket Lakes. As noted above, the widow Kinney was likely related to members of the Alexis family, notably Mary Anne Luxey. James Toney as well as Peter Labrador, who a decade later would marry one of Chief Wisow Jr.'s daughters, also resided at Tusket.

386 Joseph Howe did not go upstream along the Tusket River, but instead noted in his journal, "I learned that some slight improvements have been made by four families up the Tusket River, but from their roving habits it is considered extremely doubtful whether I should find them if I visited the spot. By a statement furnished by John Ryder, Esq., of the Indians in the County of Yarmouth, it appears that (omitting those residing at Sabine Lake [or Great Pubnico Lake] in the County of Yarmouth, and Clyde River … there are Honestus or Nestus Peter (a woman and 3 children), and Philip Francis, [with a] wife and 2 children, James Peter, [with a] wife and 3 children, Francis Charles and 1 child, Peter Charles and his wife and 2 children, Joseph Tom, [with

a] wife and 2 children, John Williams [with a] wife and 1 child … Poor living by charity according to John Ryder." Howe added that Ryder recommended the government send coats and blankets to the care of Reverend R. Godeau. NSARM, RG 1, vol. 432, 95–6.

387 Travis Pinn described the contents of an intriguing letter Joseph Charles wrote on the history of the Charles family from 1778 to 1837. Joseph claimed that "Chief Charles Sulno" was actually a man named "Charles Snow," a Scot born before 1755, and that one of his sons, Francis Charles, fought in a naval battle off the coast of Argyle during the War of 1812. Despite this, there are no historical records pertaining to either Charles Snow's or Francis's role in the war and Joseph's letter is currently the only source of information in existence about Charles Snow. "Joe told his daughter Elsie that Charles Snow 'stayed behind,' and Elsie thought this meant that Charles Snow was a lowly crewman [on the vessel], whose arrival and stay could have gone unrecorded." Information courtesy of Travis Pinn, 2 October 2016. As late as the early 1900s, the fact that Joseph Charles had some Scottish ancestry may have been more widely known, and may have accounted for Joseph's father John's identification as "white" on his death certificate. Joseph married three times. His first wife was an Acadian named Maggie (surname unknown). When she died, he married twenty-one-year-old Rose B. Morton at Port Maitland on 8 August 1900. He was twenty-seven years of age and living at Meteghan in Digby County; Rose, born at Cheboque, was a daughter of George and Mary Morton of East Quinan. Rose "was an English Baptist from Quinan who married my great-great-grandfather Joe Charles in 1900 in Port Maitland. The marriage was very short lived (less than a year) and rare (Mi'kmaq doing a Baptist wedding), with Rose moving out and marrying someone else by 1901 – according to her descendants." Information courtesy of Travis Pinn, 10 October 2016; NSARM, Historical Vital Statistics, Yarmouth County Marriages, Registration Year 1900, book 1840, p. 556, no. 75, "Marriage of Joseph Charles and Rose B. Morton." In 1902 Joseph married Maggie Labrador, a daughter of Samuel Labrador and Henrietta Bartlett, who was the mother of Lucy and Elsie Charles. When Maggie left permanently for the United States after Elsie's birth, Joseph did not remarry. Information courtesy of Travis Pinn, 10 October 2016.

388 Abbé Jean-Mandé Sigogne met an elderly Jacques Mius and his band at Clare in 1812.

389 Joseph's brief history, which he penned in 1939, holds that the surname "Snow" became supplanted by "Sulno" because "Sulno" was easier for Mi'kmaq to pronounce. Charles Snow was said to have been a crewman who left his ship in Pictou County. He may have encountered Jacques Mius's group at La Have around 1794 and travelled with it as it moved to Clare. At the time Snow made a conscious decision to remain with his wife's people, though some of his older sons returned to "white" society. No official evidence has been found to confirm the veracity of this story, though the search for more information goes on. The story nevertheless carried enough weight to have been passed down for four generations within the Charles family. If it is a valid account of the past, it appears that members of the Charles family spread from Cape Sable by 1850 to Shubenacadie. Travis Pinn, one of the authors of this chapter who is also a descendent of the Charles family through his great-grandmother Lucy Charles, Elsie's sister, has made a list of Mi'kmaq Charles who so far do not fit into the prevailing genealogy of the Charles family. They include Stephen Charles, born about 1812; Louis Charles, born about 1824; Solomon Charles, born about 1858; Michael Charles, born about 1861, Magdalene Charles, and Ellen Charles. Mary Elizabeth Charles, a noted artisan who lived at West Pubnico in the 1890s and was known in her later years as the *La vieille gaigue*, was the wife of Étienne Carty and the mother of William Carty, a well-known member of the Pubnico Lake Road community of Yarmouth County. William Carty was a close friend of his cousin, Joseph Charles, the father of Elsie and Lucy Charles.

390 Travis wrote, "Historian Peter Crowell of Yarmouth claimed that there was no record of a Battle at Argyle during the War of 1812. In addition, no written record of any kind has been found of a Charles Snow in Clare, Pictou County or Scotland from the proposed period." Travis also cautioned that there is evidence suggesting Charles Sulno was not a Scot. He stated that "Harry Piers, Director of the Museum of Natural History in Halifax, wrote on 18 November 1916 that Jerry Lonecloud [Jerry Bartlett, or Bartholomew-Alexis] once described Peter Charles Sulno as the son of a former chief, who had a great store of old information about his tribe." Here Travis is referring to a 1916 manuscript penned by Harry Piers. See NSM, Printed Matter File, Harry Piers Papers, manuscript of 18 November 1916. Travis continued, "Lonecloud's claim that Peter knew the history of his tribe suggests that Jerry thought Peter's father Charles Sulno was Indigenous, probably Mi'kmaq, and not a Scot. Photographs of John Charles (son of Francis Charles and Magdalene Peters) show

Indigenous features, and DNA evidence from John's great-grandchild indicates that John passed on a lot of Indigenous DNA." Travis Pinn to Janet Chute, 27 July 2021. The definitive answer as to the origins of the Charles family therefore remains an intriguing subject for future research.

391 NSARM, RG 1, vol. SA1, Registers of Ste. Anne du Ruisseau, 74, "Baptism of Joseph Alexis, born 28 July 1803, son of Joseph Alexis and Marie-Joseph Muice, godparents Brigitte Alexis who was a 'daughter of Barthelemi [Bartholomew Alexis Sr.], and Antoine Charles from Isle St. Jean [Prince Edward Island],' 28 July 1805."

392 Two sons of Charles Snow or Sulnow (c.1755–1800), Peter Charles Sulno and Francis Charles I (or Sr.), lived in the Cape Sable district. Francis Charles I was born around 1794.

393 It is possible that Gabriel's Falls, Yarmouth County, derived its name from this man, though it has been argued that the falls were named after Gabriel Van Norden, who owned a mill at Chebogue, now Arcadia.

394 Drawing on documentary and oral data, Travis Pinn, who is a descendant of John Charles, constructed the following kinship diagram for the Charles family of Cape Sable. The apical figure on his chart is Charles Snow, also known as Charles Sulno, who lived for a number of years in the Cape Sable district with a Mi'kmaw woman. This couple had at least two sons, Francis Charles I (or Sr.) and Peter Charles Sulno. Francis Charles I in turn had 5 sons: Francis II, James (Jim), Joseph (Joe), Job, and John. Copious support exists for these assertions.

According to Travis, "historian Mike Parker published an interview with Mi'kmaw guide Henry Peters, who stated that Joe Charles was the brother of the famous Jim Charles (of "Jim Charles' gold" fame). In addition, Frank Parker Day interviewed a man named Glode who held that Francis Charles [II] was another of Jim's brothers." John Charles, Travis's ancestor, was a fourth brother. Joseph, one of John's sons, confirmed that "his father John Charles was the brother of Job and Joe Charles." Francis Charles I's brother Peter Charles Sulno and his wife, surnamed "Peters," had three children, as the following chart drawn by Travis Pinn shows:

Descendants of Charles Sulno and an "Indian girl of Clare," according to Travis Pinn

I. Francis Charles I, born in 1794, had two Mi'kmaw partners in succession. The name of his first wife is not known. Francis's second marriage was to Magdalene Peters and they had six children.

a. Francis Charles II (Jr.), born 1823, married Mary Anne Peters
    1. Katie
    2. James
    3. Maggie
    4. Stephen
    5. Jane
    6. Catherine

b. Jim Charles, born 1828. First married Mary Elizabeth Glode, then Madeline Bartlett.
    1. Malti
    2. William
    3. Hannah

c. Joseph Charles, born in the 1820s. Married MaryAnne Glode.

    1. Catherine Charles, who had two partners (Daniel Toney and Freeman Berry). Catherine's daughter, Mary Rose Charles, married James Sullivan Bartlett.
    2. Abraham Charles. Married Mary Pictou. Abraham and Mary had four children: Gabriel Charles, Mary Anne Charles (wed Angus Paul), Henry Charles (wed Mary Lillian Glode), and Peter Charles.
    3. Frank, married Mary Robbins.
    4. Mary Lydia ("Sally"), married John Paul.

d. Job Charles, born in the 1830s. Married "Mary."
    1. Charlotte
    2. Julia
    3. John
    4. Mary Elizabeth. Married married Étienne Carty. Mary and Étienne's son was Will Carty, who wed Mary Anne Glode.

e. John Charles, born 1836. Married four times, to Mary Anne Bartlett, Elizabeth Labrador, Mary Jane Firth, and Mahalia Frank.
    1. Joseph Charles, born in 1873, wed three partners: Maggie (an Acadian), Rose Morton, and Maggie Labrador, whose father was Samuel Labrador and mother was Henriette Christina Bartlett. Joseph and his third wife had two daughters, Lucy and Elsie. Lucy married twice, first to Carl Pinn and then to Walter Powers. Elsie Charles married Isaac Basque.
    2. Clara Charles married Joe Pictou and the couple had two daughters, Rachael and Clara
    3. Matthew Charles

II.   Peter Charles Sulno (c.1788–c.1875), and his wife, a Mi'kmaw woman surnamed "Peters," had three children: Gabriel (who married Magdalene Martin), Frank, and Louise. Peter Charles is said at one point to have lived with Sally Paul (née Charles), a granddaughter of Francis Charles Sr.

Travis further explained that there is "[a]nother version of the Charles family genealogy circulating within the Mi'kmaw community [that] refers to Francis Charles I at Tusket as Peter Charles Sulno's *son*. This version holds that Francis Charles II of Keji is either the son of Francis Charles I or [of] Peter Charles. But I have examined several lines of evidence that lead me to believe the Francis Charles I of Tusket is my direct ancestor and grandfather of Joe Charles. For one, Joe's parents' Shelburne marriage record holds that Joe's father's parents resided at Clyde River. So, probably much like his father, Joe grew up in the Clyde River, Pubnico, and Tusket areas. Second, Joe's father lived in the Tusket area when he was elderly. Third and finally, Joe and his father maintained a closer relationship with the Bartletts of Cape Sable than with the Charles [kin] living in the communities of Bear River and Keji."

395   Genealogical information about Ann and Mary Charles is housed in the Queens County Archives.

396   Maria Moore was also the mother of Mary Jane Firth. Mary Jane's father, Thomas Firth, was a cooper of Irish descent who lived at Jordan River, Shelburne County; he died when Mary Jane was young. Mary Jane Firth wed John Charles on 10 October 1871. Born in 1836, John was a thirty-five-year-old widower working as a cooper, while Mary Jane, whose parents Thomas Firth and Maria Crowell lived in the Roseway River area of Shelburne County, was only sixteen. NSARM, Historical Vital Statistics, Yarmouth County Marriages, Registration Year 1871, book 1836, p. 36, no. 77; NSARM, Parish Registers of St. Gregory's Roman Catholic Church in Liverpool (on microfilm), "Marriage of John Charles, son of Francis Charles [Sr.] and Magdalene Peters, to Mary Jane Firth, the daughter of Thomas Firth and Mary Crowell, at Bridgewater," 10 October 1871. John and Mary Jane had a son Joseph Charles, born at Barrington Passage, Shelburne County, on 18 March 1873; a daughter Clara born in 1875 at Lower Woods Harbour; and a son Matthew at Bear Point in 1878 who died at birth. Canada, Census of 1881, Nova Scotia, District No. 13, Shelburne County, Woods Harbour. Travis Pinn stated that his great-aunt Elsie Charles Basque (1916–2016) claimed that Joseph loved his mother "very dearly." Although illiterate, Mary Jane was intent on having her children educated, so

Joseph at seven was sent to a local school and encouraged to study hard. When his mother died before he reached ten years of age, however, he had to live much of the time on his own. His father married four times in succession, first to Mary Anne Bartlett, second to Elizabeth Labrador, third to Mary Jane Firth (1855–82), and fourth, in October of 1891, to Mahalia Frank. Mahalia, of Germanic ancestry, previously had lived with Joseph Bartlett Sr. of Summerside, Lunenburg County. A certificate confirming the marriage of "Jean Charles, Widower of Marie Jeanne Croul [*sic*, Mary Jane Firth] and Nellie Frank [*sic*, Mahalia Frank], daughter of George Frank and Christine Williams" is housed in the Argyle Court House Museum and Archives in Tusket. After 1900 John and Mahalia lived with Stephen Bartlett's family on the Tusket Lakes, where John died on 27 November 1910 at the age of seventy-four of pneumonia. Canada, Census of 1901, Enumeration district "S," lines 28 and 29; NSARM, Historical Vital Statistics, Yarmouth County Deaths, Registration Year 1910, book 10, p. 126, no. 766. His son Joseph Charles died on 25 March 1940 at age sixty-seven of colon cancer at Victoria General Hospital in Halifax. His daughter Elsie Charles, in acting as informant, erroneously identified Joseph's mother on the death certificate as "Mary Jane Williams" rather than Mary Jane Firth." "Williams" was a surname used at times by the mother of John Charles's fourth wife, Mahalia Frank. Joseph's body was transported to Hectanooga and then to Salmon River for burial at St. Vincent de Paul Church two days later. NSARM, Historical Vital Statistics, Registration Year 1940, Halifax County Deaths, book 189, 1199.

397   NSARM, Parish Registers of St. Gregory's Roman Catholic Church in Liverpool (on microfilm), "Marriage of John Charles, son of Francis Charles [Sr.] and Magdalene Peters, to Mary Jane Firth, the daughter of Thomas Firth and Mary Crowell, Bridgewater," 9 October 1871. John Charles died on 27 November 1910 at seventy-four years of age, so he was born in 1836. NSARM, Historical Vital Statistics, Registration Year 1910, Yarmouth County Deaths, p. 126, no. 766. His son Joseph died in Halifax in 1940. NSARM, Historical Vital Statistics, Halifax County Deaths, Registration Year 1940, book 189, 1199, "Death of Joseph Charles."

398   Excerpt from a letter written in the summer of 1939 by Joseph Charles to his cousin Mary Rose Bartlett. According to this missive, Joseph Charles, grandson of Francis Charles I, was born in 1873 and was the son of John Charles, born in 1836, and John's wife Mary Jane Firth (Crowell). A copy of this document is in the possession of Travis Pinn.

399 Information courtesy of Travis Pinn, 2 October 2016. While Travis admits that the document might contain some "misinformation," he also holds there is probably some "truth value in it" that likely will become more apparent with time.

400 Elsie Charles's father, Joseph Charles, once enigmatically stated to her that Charles Snow "had stayed behind" when his ship sailed.

401 Interview with Charlie Paul, Argyle, 10 June 1993.

402 This was a peculiar assertion since the 2,300,000 acres promised Alexander McNutt (1725–1811) by Governor Lawrence in 1759 had failed to be improved by McNutt according to the primary condition that accompanied it, that the vast tract be settled within four years. In consequence, others took out grants within its parameters as early as the mid-1760s.

403 NSARM, Miscellaneous Indian "I" document from the Crown Lands Records on microfilm, file 13, Great Pubnico Lake reserve, "William Law to James Austin," 8 June 1890.

404 NSARM, Miscellaneous "I" Indian document files from Crown Lands Records on microfilm, file 13, "Documents associated with James A. MacKay's resurveying of the Great Pubnico Lake tract; John I. Brand to William Law, Esq., MPP," 10 January 1891; "Brand to Law," 12 June 1891; "Law to James H. Austin," 8 June 1891.

405 Ibid., "Brand to Law," 10 January 1891.

406 Ibid.

407 NSARM, Miscellaneous Indian "I" files from Crown Lands Records, on microfilm, file 13, "James A. McKay to Austin," 18 September 1894; "Plan by James A. MacKay, D.S., of 700 acres at Pubnico Lake, Yarmouth County, 1874." In 1843 a local landowner by the name of Carland had accompanied the surveyor Herbert Huntington, but in 1894 neither Carland nor Huntington could be located to give information about the survey. Late in 1842 Howe had directed a letter to Samuel Kimble of Barrington asking that Kimble hire a surveyor to lay out the Great Pubnico Lake reserve. Huntington must have been the man Kimble hired. NSARM, RG 1, vol. 432, 69–70.

408 Ibid., "Law to Austin," 8 June 1891.

409 Campbell, *A History of Yarmouth*, 18.

410 One member of the Bowers family from Clyde River in 2012 pointed out to the first author where Indian Gardens was located. He stated that at least one member of the Francis family still used it as a summer recreational spot.

411 Lewis Luxey, for instance, was enumerated in 1856 by Indian commissioner William Chearnley in Queens County. Others with Luxey were Joseph Bartlett, Peter Glode, Rose Jeremy (Lewis's daughter), Stephen Labrador, Nelly (Molly?) Luxie, Joseph Michael, Jeremy Miuse, John Pictou, Noel Pictou, and Peter Toney. All of these persons resided most of the year in Queens County and only seasonally visited the Clyde River area. NSARM, MG 15, vol. 6, no. 3, doc. 26; NSARM, MG 15, vol. 6, doc. 43.

412 Queens County Registry of Deeds, book 27, 132, "Agreement at Liverpool between Lewis Luxey and Luxey's son John on the one hand, and Ephraim Hunt on the other, regarding disposal of softwood and hardwood from 300 acres of timberland at Wildcat," 26 October 1878.

413 Queens County Registry of Deeds, book 15, 405, "Agreement between Joseph Walter Glode, Joseph Michael and Alec Jeremy on the one part, and Samuel Freeman of Liverpool, merchant, on the other, to lease Freeman timber rights to the 400-acre Ponhook reserve in Queens County for 99 years for a consideration of £8." Dated 24 October 1854.

414 Members of the Bowers family of Ohio and the Clyde joined Chief Luxey on guiding trips and both had engaged in mutually beneficial timber and trading agreements over the years. Many of the Bowers spoke highly of the Luxey and Francis families, with whom they had dealt with over the years.

415 Stephen Wisow Jr.'s daughters, Mary and Magdeline Bartlett, married sons of Chief Peter Charles Sulno's brother, Francis Charles Sr. Mary Anne Bartlett married John Charles, and the couple lived at first in Kings County, though they later returned to Wildcat. In 1855 the couple had a daughter, Susan, at Cornwallis, Kings County. Registers of the Parish of St. Joseph's Church, District of Cornwallis, Kentville and Aylesford, "Baptism of Susan Charles, daughter of John Charles and Mary Anne Lucy Bartlett-Alexis, 10 June 1855." Magdalene Bartlett was the second wife of Jim Charles, who for a while lived at the Kejimkujik Lake farming settlement but settled at Wildcat in his final years.

416 By the 1880s Lewis Luxey Sr. was less pressed financially, though he certainly at no time achieved the affluence of Jim Charles at the height of the latter's prosperity. Luxey had a comfortable house at Brookfield, built in part by government funds. So when Charles subsequently fell on hard times, Luxey eased Charles's transition back into farming by allowing him to take over Lot 1 at Brookfield with the government-built house, while Luxey temporarily moved to Bear River. Joseph Jeremy, who had married Lewis Luxey Sr.'s daughter Kate, also became involved. It transpired that

Jeremy's son-in-law, David Lewis, who had married Joseph and Kate Jeremy's daughter Esther, hoped to recover Charles's claim by staking the lode in his own name as well as in that of Jim Charles, since Charles was encountering difficulties in so doing on his own. To get to the gold, David and Jim followed an old portage route from the Shelburne [Mersey] River over to the source of the Tusket at Oakland Lake. But when they arrived it was too late. The Kemptville Gold Mine was up and running. Killam Library, Dalhousie Archives, Raddall Papers, Halifax, MS 2.202.Q.7.F, Thomas Raddall, "Jim Charles and His Gold Mine," passim. From the proceeds of his earlier gold sales Jim Charles, who also was a guide and farmer as well as a panner for alluvial gold, purchased horses and a buggy and other comforts for his first wife and family. Parker, *Guides of the North Woods: Hunting and Fishing Tales from Nova Scotia, 1860 to 1960* (Halifax: Nimbus, 1990), 38–40. After he killed Hamilton, Charles fled from the law for well over a year to hide in the interior, his diet supplemented by occasional food parcels brought to him by his first wife, Lizzie Pictou, and her brother Malti. A merchant at Caledonia in Queens County named John B. Harlow, who was also a local magistrate, proved instrumental in restoring Charles's freedom. Lizzie afterwards died or deserted her husband, so in 1884 Charles wed Mary Ann Bartlett, who was probably a daughter of Ekien Bartlett Sr., and had a son, Philippe Charles. It seems that after losing all hope of ever attaining his mine, Charles went downhill and eventually had to rely on John and Andrew Francis of Milton, Queens County, for his sustenance and care. He died at Milton an impoverished man, after which the Francis brothers conveyed his body to St. Gregory's in Liverpool for burial. Mary Ann Bartlett in 1888 married a second time, to Frank Bernard. Registers of Ste. Anne du Ruisseau, "Marriage of Frank Bernard, son of Joseph Bernard and Mary Bernard, on 2 September 1888 to Mary Anne Bartlett, widow of James Charles, witnesses Joseph Pictou and Joseph Glode."

417 For a brief history of the mines of the Kemptville area, see "Kemptville's Gold Mines, 1881–1919," https://yarmouthhistory.ca/yarmouthhistory/LocalHistory/Entries/2015/7/1_Kemptvilles_Gold_Mines__18811919.html. An article on this subject also was published in *The Argus* 26, no. 2 (2014): 34–43. An interesting personal perspective on Kemptville's early settlement is found in Ethel A. (Reeves) Randall's "Kemptville, Data and Datum: An Historical Sketch," in *The Argus* 19, no. 4 (2007): 37–48. Ethel Reeves was the daughter of Charles

Reeves and the niece of James Reeves, who found the gold. Janet Chute and research assistant Carrie Gloade in 2012 had the pleasure of meeting and conversing with Ethel Reeves's daughter Ruth Randall Cann, a retired school teacher who lives in Kemptville. Ruth Cann generously shared her extensive historical knowledge of the place and also let us read the original manuscript of "Kemptville, Data and Datum." A companion piece to Reeves's personal history is Burnett's "More Information on the Prossers," 19–23.

418 NSARM, Historical Vital Statistics, Queens County Deaths, Year 1917, book 46, p. 249, no. 582. Mary Ann Cobliel Luxey died at Milton on 20 September 1917 at the age of eighty-eight.

419 Étienne Luxey married Margaret Brooks (c.1851–c.1900) of Annapolis Royal about 1867 and became a well-known guide around Paradise, Annapolis County. His grandson Charles Luxey claimed he was born on 24 December 1835 and died at Middleton in Annapolis County on 5 January 194_ – reputedly at the age of 105 years and 11 days. He was buried in Bridgetown. NSARM, Historical Vital Statistics, Annapolis County Deaths, Year 1941, book 276, 648. Eggy's alleged birthdate of 1835 is seriously open to question since he was listed as only twenty-one on the federal census of 1871. He probably was born in 1850, so he most likely was a son of Lewis Luxey Sr. and his second wife, Mary Ann Cobliel. Eggy and his wife Margaret had at least eight children: two sons and six daughters. Their eldest child, Mary, was born in 1868, followed by Euphemia, Susie in 1870, Frank, Rose in 1880, Lena in 1888, Margaret in 1892, and Stephen in 1893. Susie Luxey, the mother of Charles Luxey, died at age seventy in Middleton in 1940. NSARM, Vital Statistics, Annapolis County Deaths, Registration Year 1940, book 176, 617. His eldest son, Frank, died at three years of age while he and Margaret were living in Lowell, Massachusetts. Their second son, Stephen (1893–1943), a licensed guide, remained single and died in Middleton in 1943. NSARM, Historical Vital Statistics, Annapolis County Deaths, Registration Year 1943, book 202, 400, "Death of Stephen Luxey, single, at Middleton on 4 October, 1943, niece Martha Luxey informant." Mary, Euphemia, Susie, Rose, and Lena never married, though Susie had a son, Charles, whose name does not appear again in the documentary record after his mother's death. Charles Luxey apparently did not have any issue. Mary was listed on the 1871 federal census as born in 1868, but little more could be determined regarding her or her sister Lena, who was born on 14 May 1888 and baptized on 11 September

1892 at St. Louis Church, Annapolis Royal. Rose died of cancer in 1930. NSARM, Historical Vital Statistics, Registration Year 1930, book 115, 858, "Death of Rose Luxie, born 1880, died single of cancer at age 45 at Paradise on 17 August 1930." Margaret died at Halifax in 1930. NSARM, Historical Vital Statistics, Halifax County Deaths, book 135, 369, "Death of Margaret Luxey," 22 September 1930.

420 Registers of St. Croix Church, Plympton, "Marriage of Louis Luxey and Mary Lucy Michael, daughter of Joseph Michael and Mary Pictou, July 1875." Mary Lucy Michael Luxey died at the age of eighty-two years and nine months on the Gravel Pit reserve on 25 February 1938 and was buried at St. Ambrose Church's cemetery three days later. She was born at Bear River to Joseph Michael and Mary Pictou on 28 April 1855. She was outlived by her husband, Lewis Luxey Jr., who lived well into his nineties. NSARM, Historical Vital Statistics, Year 1938, Yarmouth County Deaths, book 184, 80. Over the years Lewis Luxey Jr. was featured in many stories told locally about the guides from Bear River. According to one account, in 1893 he, Noel Lewis, and Jim Meuse of Bear River were out with H.A.P. Smith, the provincial game warden and sheriff of Digby County, as well as two sportsmen, Carmen O'Dell and Gilbert Ellis, when his party met up with Major John Daley and Daley's Mi'kmaw guide, John Lewis. The trip proved to be a historic one, since Smith, O'Dell, and Ellis began discussing the idea of introducing white-tailed deer from New Brunswick into southwestern Nova Scotia to compensate for the demise of caribou; only scatterings of white-tailed deer were present in Nova Scotia at the time. Daley afterwards acted on the scheme, and in 1894 eleven deer were transported by boat from Saint John to Digby to begin an experiment intended to usher in a new era in Nova Scotian big game hunting. As a result, by the 1920s the white-tailed deer had become the dominant wild ungulate species in Nova Scotia. Parker, *Guides of the North Woods*, 10–11. The introduction and encouragement of yet more deer unfortunately brought the nematode parasite *Parelaphostrongylus tenuis*, which can be fatal to both moose and caribou. Denis A. Benson and Donald G. Dodds, *The Deer of Nova Scotia* (Halifax: Department of Lands, 1977), 34–5.

421 John Jeremy was head man of the Mi'kmaw Kejimkujik farming settlement visited by Joseph Howe in 1842. One of Jeremy's sons, Joseph, later married Kate Luxey, a daughter of Lewis Luxey Sr. and Lewis's second wife, Mary Ann Cobeliel. Joseph and Kate frequently travelled to New England. As long as there was sufficient birchbark along the way, shelters could be fashioned in the woods, though by 1880 reserves of birch had begun to fail. Even so, Kate continued to visit New York State, since in 1880 she was enumerated on an American census as residing with her sons Abram and Joseph at Winchester, New York, in company with five other Mi'kmaw adults of both sexes. A second Mi'kmaw party, headed by Josiah (Sire) Jeremy and his wife Elizabeth Paul, were encamped nearby. A member of this second group was a thirteen-year-old boy named Joseph Bartlett. U.S. Federal Census 1880, for Winchester, Westchester Co., New York. Several years late Kate Jeremy was reported living once again in southwestern Nova Scotia in a "clean cottage" belonging to a farm with oxen and a horse. Robert R. MacLeod, *Acadian Land: Nature Studies* (Boston: Bradlee Whidden, 1899), 154.

422 NSARM, MG 1, vol. 2867, Clara Dennis Archives, Notebook no. 4, Interview with Louis [Lewis] Luxey of Yarmouth, n.d. (between 1923 and 1929), 13. Lewis Luxey Jr. claimed to be seventy-four years of age when he spoke with Clara Dennis, which since he was born in 1854 would have made the year of the interview 1929. (It is possible that Luxey was not completely certain about his own age and that the interview occurred a few years earlier.) There is also a photograph of Lewis Luxey Jr., taken between 1920 and 1930 at Yarmouth, with a caption designating him as "Chief of Yarmouth," in the William Dennis Collection at the Nova Scotia Museum. NSM, Accession 41755; NSM, P113/73180.610, N-14, 765. This portrait is also described as "Louis Alexis at the Gravel Pit Reserve, Yarmouth County," with the claim that it was taken by Clara Dennis about 1932.

423 NSARM, Historical Vital Statistics, Registration Year 1930, Yarmouth County Deaths, p. 133, no. 1117, "Death of Ben Luxey, Starr's Road, Yarmouth, 26 November 1930." Ben was born on 10 February 1884 and was only forty-six years old at the time of his death.

424 In 1999, Mrs. John Pictou referred to Lewis Luxey Sr. as the "Great Luxey."

425 Thomas Chandler Haliburton, *A General Description of Nova Scotia: Illustrated by a New and Correct Map* (Halifax: Printed at the Royal Acadian School, 1823), 55.

426 Jerry Lonecloud confided to Harry Piers, curator of the Nova Scotia Museum in Halifax, that Chief Louis Luxey shot Tom Wallace at Wallace's Ridge, about "3 miles south of Wallace's Lake near Kempt, in [the] northeast part of Yarmouth Co." The skull was later found by Dan Bowers, who recognized it by its teeth, which had been worn a particular way by Wallace's pipe. In 1880 this skull was still in the Nova Scotia Museum, though it

forms no part of the present museum collection. Harry Piers speculated that Lewis Luxey shot Wallace around 1877, but the event must have taken place almost twenty-five years earlier than this, about 1852 or 1853. Nova Scotia Museum Library, Piers Papers, Ethnology: Genealogies, 33, Lonecloud to Piers, 24 June 192[7?]: the last digit of the year in which Lonecloud relayed this information has been torn off in the original ms.

427 Whitehead, *Tracking Doctor Lonecloud*, 22.

428 Tom Wallace and Mary Anne Phillips had several children prior to the late 1840s, one being a daughter named Margaret, said to have been born about 1827 but who was undoubtedly younger. She first married a man surnamed Francis from Pubnico, and after her first husband's death became the second wife of Chief Louis Luxey Sr.'s eldest son, Joseph Luxey. Joseph's first wife, Margaret Labrador, died in 1871, and the following year he married a second time to Margaret Francis. If Margaret really was forty-five at the time of her second marriage, as the church records contend, she would have had to have been born in 1827, which is probably too early a date. Her mother, Mary Ann Phillips, was still young enough to bear children in 1854. Registers of St. Gregory's Church, Liverpool, "Marriage of Joseph Luxey and Margaret Francis, 9 February 1872."

429 An alternative date of 1847, which appears more than once in Piers's papers, is not correct.

430 Whitehead, *Tracking Doctor Lonecloud*, 32. Sarah Bartlett, Abraham Bartlett's daughter, was Abraham Michael's third wife. Abraham's first wives were Eleanor Knockwood, by whom he had James and Fanny, and Agnes Paul. Abraham and Agnes had a daughter, Margaret, or "Maggie." Abraham Michael and Sarah were married in 1874, after which they had Peter Newel, born in 1875 (married Hannah Labrador in 1903), Margaret Phillips, in 1903; Mary E., born in 1877 (died young), Susan, born in 1880; Abraham, baptized at St. Louis Church in Annapolis Royal in January 1882; Mary, born in 1888; Joseph, baptized at St. Louis Church in December 1889 (not living with the family in 1891); and Lavinia Christine, born in 1897. Information on Mary E. Michael came from the registers of St. Croix Church in Plympton. Other information came from the registers of St. Louis Church, Annapolis Royal. The authors are indebted to Ian Lawrence for helping them with this branch of the Michael family genealogy.

431 NSARM, MG 1, vol. 7863, #1, Clara Dennis Archives, "Clara Dennis' interview with Alex Paul from Liverpool in 1923."

432 Copious information regarding Jerry Bartlett, alias Jerry Lonecloud, may be found in the Piers Papers housed in the Nova Scotia Museum of Natural History in Halifax and in the Clara Dennis notebooks at the Nova Scotia Archives and Records Management in Halifax. In 2002 Ruth Holmes Whitehead published *Tracking Doctor Lonecloud: Showman to Legend Keeper*, which contains the memoir of his life that Jerry recounted to Clara Dennis. Whitehead also provides valuable annotations to the memoir drawn from Dennis's interview notes, data from the Piers Papers, and her own extensive research into Lonecloud's life.

433 Whitehead, *Tracking Doctor Lonecloud*, 53–4. Also see information about the 1786 grant given Chief Philip Bernard at the Head of St. Margaret's Bay in chapter 7 of this volume.

434 Gabriel Toney (or Tony) died on Tony Street near Sullivan's Pond in Dartmouth in 1849. Martin, *The Story of Dartmouth*, 379. Étienne Bartholomew Alexis Sr. *dit* Wisow (or Ekien *dit* Wiscw Sr.) may have died around the same time. It has been argued that "Sulno" stemmed from the Mi'kmaw pronunciation of the word "Charles," though in 1794 Solomon Jeremy's name was often written "Sulno Jeremy" and his offspring who continued to reside in Lunenburg County were referred to as "Sulnos."

435 It is not certain why Jerry was not taken in on his return by one of his father's two brothers, although Stephen Bartlett Jr. *dit* Wisow and Joseph Bartlett may have faced too many responsibilities while raising their own large families to take an abiding interest in the youngster. In 1916 Jerry presented the Nova Scotia Museum with a fur cap he had fashioned according to a description of how to do so offered years before by Peter Charles Sulno. NSM, Piers Papers, Notes on Accession no. 4438, dated 30 November 1916. The cap was made from the bell, or loose neck skin, of a moose. Ruth Holmes Whitehead held that the date of Jerry's birth (1847) and that of Peter Charles Sulno's death (1867) given in the accession notes that accompany this item in the museum collection are wrong. Jerry most probably was born on 4 July 1854 and Peter Sulno likely died around 1870. See also Whitehead, *Tracking Doctor Lonecloud*, 56. When Jerry Lonecloud told Piers about Chief Peter Charles, whose father he claimed was also a chief, Piers jotted down "Peter Charles and his [Peter's] father was [*sic*] the first Indian of his locality [about Tusket River] who heard a musket fire, which was fired at him at Gabriel's Falls, Tusket Co., when the French came. Peter Charles' name is Sulnow. A very old Micmac who died about 1867 at a camp between Parrs and Ogdens Lakes, 4 miles north of Carleton. Lone Cloud lived with him around four years, he died and LC buried him in cemetery at Eel Brook,

Yarmouth, many miles to the south." Peter Charles Sulno also was said to be the son of a former chief. Chief Charles Sulno died nearer 1875 than 1867, since Jerry was still in the United States in 1865 and it took him at least a year to get back to Nova Scotia.

436 James Meuse was the son of Chief James Andrew Meuse, who died in 1850. James Meuse Jr. married Marguerite Peters and, like his father, was often referred to as "Governor Meuse." NSARM, RG 1, vol. 2867, no. 29, continuation of Notebook no. 3, Notes taken by Clara Dennis after interview in 1926 with James Meuse. The James Meuse referred to by Jerry Bartlett died in April 1912. NS Museum, Alexander Leighton Collection, Accession no. PN-6685, Photograph dated c.1910 of Chief James Meuse, his wife Glyd Meuse, Madelene Bunch, Mary Michael and child, and Magdalene Toney at Bear River.

437 James Meuse only stayed with Healey's show during the summers, in the winter returning to the Maritimes to cut pulpwood. "My speciality was fancy rifle shooting," he told journalist Clara Dennis, "shooting an apple or potato – shooting it while it was swaying." NSARM, MG 1, vol. 2867, no. 29, continuation of book no. 3.

438 Ruth Holmes Whitehead, "Lonecloud, Jerry," *DCB* online, vol. 15 (1921–39).

439 Years later, Jerry Lonecloud could point out sites in southwestern Nova Scotia of special important to the Mi'kmaq. For instance, he stated that a mermaid, or merman-type of being, was associated with a big rock three miles from Tusket Falls. NSARM, MG 1, vol. 2867, book 4, Notes from Clara Dennis's interview with Jerry Lonecloud, 1923.

440 NSARM, Register of Births, Marriages and Deaths in the County of Lunenburg, commencing May A.D. 1859, on microfilm, "Marriage of Jeremiah Lexy (Dr. Lone Cloud) and Elizabeth Paul, St. Joseph's Roman Catholic Church, Bridgewater, 18 June 1884, Witness Rosa Lexy." See also Whitehead, *Tracking Doctor Lonecloud*, 67.

441 The couple had eight children, but two died young. NSM, Ethnology Papers: Micmac Correspondence, Item 7, "Lonecloud to A.J. Boyd," 4 December 1917.

442 In 2013 the first author encountered a man surnamed Rudolf who worked for Liscomb Lodge, who stated that his grandfather once had worked for Jerry Lonecloud's guiding operation. Also see Whitehead, *Tracking Doctor Lonecloud*, 34–6.

443 Ibid., 45.

444 Roger Lewis, an archaeologist and curator at the Nova Scotia Museum, supplied information on his own family background. He claims ancestry on his father's side from a man of Mohawk descent named John Lewis or Louis (from the surname "St. Louis") from Caughawaga (Kahnawake), Quebec. Lewis married a Mi'kmaw woman, May Hannah Glode, at Bear River and became a noted guide. Roger Lewis to Janet Chute, personal communication, November 2016; Ellen Robinson to R.H. Whitehead, personal communication, 1987, quoted in NSM, Mi'kmaq Portraits Collection, Information from notes associated with Accession N-250, Photograph Album 43 no. 1, Photograph of guides Louis Peters, John Peters, John McEwan, John Louis (Lewis), John Labrador, Malti Pictou, and Eli Pictou.

445 Jerry Lonecloud had relatives on his mother's side at Elmsdale. Thomas Phillips had a brother Noel who had settled at Elmsdale with his Acadian wife, Martha Comeau, who originally hailed from Digby County.

446 Whitehead, *Tracking Doctor Lonecloud*, 41. Elizabeth took both Libby and Louis with her to Truro, where she died in 1961. Louis Abraham Bartlett, or Luxey, who was born in 1902, was an invalid as a youth and in 1931 at the age of twenty-nine succumbed to tuberculosis. NSARM, Historical Vital Statistics, Registration Year 1931, book 119, 155, "Death Certificate of Louis [Lewis] Luxey [Bartholomew Alexis]." Lonecloud in his later years companioned with a young woman named Annie Glode.

447 William C. Borren, *Down East: Another Cargo of Tales Told under the Old Town Clock* (Halifax: Imperial Press, 1945), 44–5.

448 NSARM, Historical Vital Statistics, Registration Year 1930, Death Certificate of Jeremiah Luxey, book 134, 1618.

449 Descendants of Sarah Bartlett, Jerry's sister, and her husband Abraham Michael continue to live around Bear River. But what happened to Jerry's son Jeremiah Bartlett Jr. remains unknown, although he was reputed to have descendants living in Nova Scotia. Whitehead, *Tracking Doctor Lonecloud*, 45.

450 Abraham Bartlett's age was given as six years old on the 1911 federal census for Subdistrict 18, Tusket, Yarmouth County.

451 Stephen Bartlett, the son of Joseph Bartlett Sr. of Summerside, Lunenburg County, was sixty-two years old at the time of his marriage to Rose Labrador, though he was listed as being sixty on the 1933 marriage certificate. Interestingly, Boston was given as Stephen's birthplace on his and Rose's marriage certificate. NSARM, Historical Vital Statistics, Yarmouth County Marriages, Registration Year 1933, book 70, 410. Travis Pinn, who researched records regarding Samuel's mother, found she was an Acadian by the name of Rose Bertrand (also known as Rose Muff or Maphre). Samuel Labrador's death certificate states he was born in Yarmouth County

on 5 April 1867. NSARM, Historical Vital Statistics, Yarmouth County Deaths, Registration Year 1921, book 66, 346. Samuel's grandfather was Francis Labrador who lived in Lunenburg in the early 1800s and at Kejimkujik by the mid-1800s. In 1842, Joseph Howe noted that Stephen Labrador, Francis's son, had petitioned for land at the Kejimkujik farming settlement.

452 One of these sons was Jacques, or James, Bartlett, a son of Étienne Bartlett and Mary Bartlett, who wed Marie Anne Labrador, a daughter of Jacques and Madeline Labrador of Shelburne County, at Ste. Anne du Ruisseau on 9 February 1876. The witnesses to the wedding were Pierre Labrador and Rose Bartlett.

453 Prominent among these was the chief's adopted daughter Fanny Pictou and her husband Joe Labrador.

454 The land was part Lot 29 of the original Yarmouth Township Division granted originally to Thomas Rogers and after his death inherited by his son, Cornelius Rogers. The records do not provide a clear record prior to 1825, but apparently the land was subdivided on 17 April 1817 and twelve acres of it (known as Lot 39) lying on Pitman's or Starr's Road was set off to Lydia Saunders, daughter of Cornelius Rogers and wife of Nathaniel Sanders. Lydia mortgaged this and other adjacent land to Benjamin Rogers, who eventually gained possession of the whole. Benjamin Rogers then sold this lot for thirty-five pounds to Heman Rogers on 22 August 1859. Registry of Deeds, Yarmouth County, book A.K., 654. Heman Rogers and his wife Emily sold the land, which was part marsh, to Thomas Willett on 1 January 1872 for $220. Registry of deeds, Yarmouth County, book A.N., 136. When Thomas Willett died, his property passed to his heirs, George and Annie Willett. This plot, of 21 3/16 acres, lay on the eastern side of Starr's Road and was bounded on its other sides by the estates of Joseph Bond, Benjamin Rogers, Israel Lovitt (or Lovett), and James Lambert, who had access rights to a cart road over the land. George and Annie Willett sold the land to the Indian Affairs Department on 14 December 1887.

455 It is impossible to give the exact date of Stephen Wisow Jr.'s birth, given the range of birth dates for him provided in the documentary record, though census records show he was born between 1807 and 1819.

456 Like his ancestor Charles Alexis, Chief Stephen Jr. *dit* Wisow received respect offerings each spring before certain French-speaking residents of Eel Brook began their annual eel fishing. For instance, John Muise *dit* "The Dude" stated that his grandfather Eli gave Chief Bartlett a bag of salt for this purpose. Conversation between John Muise and Janet Chute, Lower Eel Brook,

June 2004. And it is even possible that by continuing to exercise such respect protocols towards the Mi'kmaw head chief, who was seen as retaining distribution rights over eels, the Acadians were actually helping to conserve a vulnerable resource from overfishing. The eels at Eel Brook are catadromous, belonging to the species *Anguilla rostrata*, and have to go to the sea to spawn. Depletion of fish stocks from overfishing thus constitutes a threat. There are freshwater eels today in Yarmouth and Digby Counties, as well as in the estuary of the LaHave River, but they have been artificially introduced in recent years. Moreover, "catadromous eels are often present in freshwater upstream from obstacles which would constitute a barrier to the migration of other fish species." D.R. Alexander, J.J. Kerekes, and B.C. Sabean, "Description of Selected Lake Characteristics and Occurrence of Fish Species in 781 Nova Scotia Lakes," *Proceedings of the Nova Scotia Institute of Science* 36, part 2 (Halifax, 1986): 71.

457 Stansburg Hagar, "Micmac Magic and Medicine," *Journal of American Folklore* 9 no. 34 (1 July 1896): 175–7. According to Hagar, a ratting plant stood about eight inches high, had leaves similar to that of a poplar tree, and had a root the size of a man's fist. Its stem was surrounded by "numerous brownish yellow balls as large as buckshot." To see the plant, one first had to find a bird called the *coaasoonech*, or "dwelling in old logs," singing in an interval in the forest. The finder then must gather thirty sticks and lay them in a pile near the plant. Next, he must induce a beautiful girl to accompany him to the plant. Both must crawl towards the plant on their hands and knees. The plant was said to be inhabited by the spirit of the rattlesnake, which first appears and circles around the plant's stem. The finder must handle this serpent, which then disappears, and the finder can then divide the plant into four parts, and use three of them. A potion obtained by steeping these three parts can be used to heal sickness and as a "love compeller." Stephen Bartlett told Hagar he once had seen the plant and had buried some of the yellow balls, but the next morning they and the plant had disappeared. Since Bartlett added that he had not gone through the necessary rituals, Hagar concluded he was "considered a doubtful authority, even by himself."

458 James Sullivan Bartlett was the son of Joseph Bartlett and Julia Pictou and as a child lived for periods of time on the Roseway River in Shelburne County. He probably was born at Tusket in Yarmouth County, although other sources claim he was born at Ohio in Shelburne County. NSARM, Historical Vital Statistics, Yarmouth

County Births, Registration Year 1873, book 1823, p. 192, no. 164. The priest, Father Underwood, who baptized him on 24 May 1873 at Ste. Anne du Ruisseau Church incorrectly entered his name in the parish church register as "Barclay, James Solin." Witnesses to the ceremony were his brother James and Eunice Melançon." In 1894 he married Mary Rose Charles, the daughter of Kate Charles and Daniel Toney. Kin connections between the Bartlett and Charles families are many and complicated, and there is still copious research to be done on these interconnections. Travis Pinn graciously supplied information on the Firth, Crowell, Bartlett, and Charles families from his own extensive genealogical research, including information provided him by his great-aunt Elsie Charles Basque.

459 Canada, Census of 1891, Nova Scotia, District 46 Yarmouth, District No. 17 Argyle, household 193.

460 In the fall of 1893 Chief Stephen Bartlett Jr. *dit* Wisow's son, James Bartlett, was enumerated by a local Indian agent as residing at Yarmouth, though he was more frequently found at other seasons of the year at Tusket.

461 LAC, RG 10, vol. 6823, file 494–16–5, pt.1, "Report of Indian agent, C.P. Smith of the Yarmouth Agency, to the Superintendent General of Indian Affairs, 1 November 1893, regarding the Mi'kmaq of District 14, Yarmouth County." Smith noted that "[t]his Statement does not fix the residence of any permanently as they are continually on the move, seldom remaining in one place more than a year. Those living on the Reserve are permanent or nearly so." One addition to the reserve community since 1891 was a widow named Julia Toney.

462 Tom Bartlett was buried at West Pubnico on 24 August 1896. His son Joseph, born 3 May 1897, was baptized at Ste. Anne du Ruisseau on 26 June 1897. The child's godparents were John Smith and Julie Toney. Emeline was only forty years of age when her husband and youngest son Joseph died, and she never remarried.

463 Emeline is listed as being born in 1859 rather than 1857, as on the 1911 census. She is enumerated as "Emeline Boyd" (after Jacob Boyd, her mother's consort in 1871) rather than her mother's unmarried surname "Moore") and was working as a housekeeper at Tusket.

464 The church registers at Ste. Anne du Ruisseau hold that "Étienne Bartlett" (Chief Stephen Bartlett Jr. *dit* Wisow) died on 5 January 1901 at ninety-five years of age and was buried in the Roman Catholic cemetery at Eel Brook on 7 January. This would mean he was born in 1806, not in 1811 or 1819 as most other sources aver. Father Clarence-J. d'Entremont suggests, in a series of notes housed in the Musée Acadien in West Pubnico,

that the erroneous rumour about Chief Stephen Bartlett's death at the age of 108 years old was circulated in an article by Alexandre Deveau written for *Le Petit Courier*. The 1901 federal census also lists Emeline Bartlett as a widow of forty-two years of age. Her five unmarried children – Henry William, eighteen; John Burbon, fifteen; Simon, fourteen; Mary Caroline, twelve; and Caroline, ten – lived with her. In 1911 John Charles, born in 1835 and so sixty-five years old, and his wife Mahalia, born in 1840 and sixty years old, were lodgers in Tom's brother Stephen Bartlett's household. The Charles and Bartlett families were close. Abraham Charles, born in 1865, and likely a son of John Charles who dwelt with Stephen Bartlett, lived nearby with his wife Mary and their three-year-old daughter Frances. Stephen Bartlett, born about 1860, was the son of Joseph Bartlett of Summerside and Mahalia Frank. When Joseph Bartlett died, Mahalia married John Charles, a son of Francis Charles of Carleton Lake, Yarmouth County. Stephen Bartlett's wife, Christiana ("Christie") Toney, was born to James Toney and Clara Glode around 1860. The census of 1911 claims Stephen Bartlett was forty in 1911, born in 1870, but he was probably born around 1860 and nearer fifty years of age in 1911, since the 1901 federal census also lists Stephen as forty years old a decade earlier. When his wife Christie died of cancer at Bridgewater on 14 October 1932, she was reported to be seventy years old. She was buried on 22 March 1932. NSARM, Historical Vital Statistics, Lunenburg County Deaths, Year 1932, book 149, 454.

465 "Bartlett, Mi'kmaw Indian, Yarmouth," genealogy.com, "Reply to children of James Bartlett," 20 February 2002.

466 John Charles lived with Stephen Bartlett at Tusket. Stephen Bartlett wed Christie Anthony (Toney) at Ste. Anne du Ruisseau on 28 April 1890, and by 1901 the pair had two children, Rosanna, twelve, and Matthew, nine. James Glode and his wife Sarah Toney, who was a sister of Stephen Bartlett's wife Christie, along with their fifteen-year-old daughter Victoria and thirteen-year-old son, Stephen, lived close by. The person listed on the 1901 federal census as "Mary E. Williams" refers to Mahalia Frank, John Charles's fourth wife. Mahalia occasionally adopted her maternal grandmother Christine Williams's surname. A fifty-nine-year-old man, Lewis Williams, and his wife Matilda, aged sixty, who lived near Stephen Bartlett's household with their twenty-five-year-old daughter, Rachel Williams, when John Charles was living at Tusket do not seem to be in any way related to Mahalia Frank, who hailed from Lunenburg County. Canada, Census of 1901, Tusket, Yarmouth County.

Meanwhile, John Charles's third wife, Mary Jane Firth or Crowell, was a half-sister to Emeline Crowell, who wed Tom Bartlett. In 1891 Tom and Emeline lived in Argyle with five children, the youngest son being Simon Bartlett. Simon Bartlett wed Eva Labrador, a half-sister to Maggie Labrador who became Joseph Charles's third wife as well as Lucy and Elsie Charles's mother. Joseph was the eldest son of John Charles and Mary Jane Firth (or Crowell).

467 NSARM, Historical Vital Statistics, Yarmouth County Marriages, Registration Year 1936, book 84, 371, "Marriage of Herbert Goudey and Mary Elizabeth Bartlett, presiding priest A.L. Blanc, witnesses Lizzie and Connie Churchill." Herbert could not read, while Mary was literate.

468 Registers of St. Pierre de Pubnico, "Marriage of Stephen Glode, born 25 June 1887, to Mary Caroline Bartlett, born in 1889," 19 September 1909.

469 One son, Stephen Lawrence Glode, born in 1926, died of tuberculosis in 1943 at the age of seventeen. NSARM, Historical Vital Statistics, Year 1943, Yarmouth County Deaths, book 206, 321. A daughter, Mary Catherine Glode, died of pneumonia at one year and seven months old in 1933. NSARM, Historical Vital Statistics, Year 1933, book 156, 156. A second daughter, Dorothy Theresa, died of tuberculosis in 1944 at age eighteen. NSARM, Historical Vital Statistics, Year 1944, book 209, 740.

470 "No Trace of Missing Lad," *Yarmouth Herald*, 28 February 1933. Clarence and Gordon Glode were described as "scholars" (schoolboys) on their death certificates. NSARM, Historical Vital Statistics, Year 1933, Yarmouth County Deaths, book 156, 55; book 156, 54, "Deaths of Clarence and Gordon Glode."

471 NSARM, Historical Vital Statistics, Year 1948, Yarmouth County Deaths, book 1316, p. 948, "Death of Mary Glode"; NSARM, Historical Vital Statistics, Year 1957, Yarmouth County Deaths, book for 1957, 5210. Stephen Glode perished in a house fire on 1 October 1957.

472 Henry Bartlett's second-youngest son, John Burbon Bartlett, for instance, died in 1926 at the relatively young age of forty-two of tuberculosis. NSARM, Historical Vital Statistics, Yarmouth County Deaths, Year 1926, book 111, 1179. Henry Bartlett's death was reported by his brother-in-law, Herbert Goudey, since none of Henry's immediate family members remained alive by 1958. According to Goudey, Henry was born in Clermont, Annapolis County. Interestingly, Goudey also held that Henry's father, Tom Bartlett, was born in Saskatchewan, although it is anyone's guess how he arrived at such a notion. Saskatchewan as a province did not yet exist in 1851, the year Tom was born, though it is possible that Tom's father, Joseph Bartlett, travelled with his wife west of Lake Superior in the mid-nineteenth century. Henry's remains were interred in St. Ambrose Cemetery in Yarmouth on 25 June 1958. NSARM, Historical Vital Statistics, Yarmouth County Deaths, Year 1958, 4336.

473 Maggie Shaw Paul Bartlett and her two children lived at Milton, Queens County, during the early years of the First World War. Her son Dean died on 12 December 1915 at three years of age in Liverpool, Queens County, while Louise (or Louisa) died at five years of age on 20 July the following year. NSARM, Historical Vital Statistics, Queens County Deaths, Year 1915, book 46, p. 132, no. 309; NSARM, Historical Vital Statistics, Queens County Deaths, Year 1916, book 46, p. 181, no. 424. Maggie died of exposure on 2 March 1917 at only twenty-five years old. NSARM, Historical Vital Statistics, Queens County Deaths, Year 1917, book 46, p. 215, no. 492.

474 NSARM, Historical Vital Statistics, Registration Year 1932, Digby County Marriages, book 4, 700. Eva Labrador was the half-sister of Joseph Charles's wife Maggie Labrador.

475 Both children died very young. Joseph Bartlett, who was born on 12 July 1921, died at two years of age on 12 July 1923, while Frances Elizabeth Bartlett was born on 10 May 1924 and died on 14 July of the same year. NSARM, Historical Vital Statistics, Digby County Deaths, Registration Year 1923, book 57, 417, "Death of Joseph Bartlett"; NSARM, Historical Vital Statistics, Yarmouth County Deaths, Registration Year 1924, book 111, 501, "Death of Frances Elizabeth Bartlett at the age 2 months 4 days, 10 May 1924, Burial at Eel Brook," 16 July 1924. The doctor officiating in the death wrote that the baby was not expected to live as both her parents were suffering from tuberculosis at the time.

476 "Obituary of Simon Joseph Bartlett, Son of Simon Thomas and Eva Bartlett," *Halifax Herald*, 8 March 2008. In his later years, Simon Joseph Sr. lived with his common-law wife, Clara Marie Bernard, at Church Point, and his funeral took place at Meteghan Funeral Home. He and his first wife, Lydia Labrador, had a large family: Simon, Thomas, James, Patrick, Mary, and Anne, members of the Acadia First Nation who mostly reside near Saulnierville. The couple lost a son John as well as a son in infancy, and two daughters, Joyce and Florence; Simon Joseph's son and namesake, Simon Joseph Bartlett Jr. (b. 1949), a cabinet maker, died in 2011.

477 NSARM, Historical Vital Statistics, Kings County Deaths, "Death of Simon Joseph Bartlett," book 93, 1074, 4 September 1925.

478 The surname for James Bartlett is rendered either "Bartly" or "Bartley" in some vital statistics records. See, for instance, NSARM, Historic Vital Statistics, Year 1876, Yarmouth County Marriages, book 1839, p. 106, nos. 13 and 14.

479 James Bartlett, born in 1855 or 1856, reputedly afterwards went back to Salmon River and lived in the household of his father Chief Stephen Bartlett for a number of years before journeying with his father to Yarmouth and remarrying.

480 NSARM, Historical Vital Statistics, Year 1876, Shelburne County Births, book 1821, p. 167, no. 97, "Birth of John Bartley [sic, Bartlett]," 21 May 1876. Unfortunately, the child's parents are not listed.

481 The fact that both James Bartlett and John Bartlett's surnames are mistakingly rendered "Bartley" or "Bartly" in vital statistics records for Shelburne County suggests that James and John were closely related. There is no document, however, that can confirm this fact. John Bartlett may have been James Bartlett's son, though he could also have been James's cousin. John Bartlett and Julia Labrador lost at least four of their grown children to pulmonary tuberculosis. Julia Labrador had first been married to a man surnamed Labrador and had two sons named Albert and Henry. One of John and Julia's sons, Joseph George Bartlett, died at seven years of age in 1924 of tuberculosis in Shelburne. NSARM, Historical Vital Statistics, Year 1924, Shelburne County Deaths, book 103, 948. Another son, John William Bartlett, died a single man in 1935 at twenty-one years of age of tuberculosis at Yarmouth, where his parents had moved by 1928. NSARM, Historical Vital Statistics, Yarmouth County Deaths, Year 1936, book 156, 957. A daughter, Mary L. Bartlett, died in 1929 at Yarmouth at seventeen years of age from tuberculosis and malnutrition. NSARM, Historic Vital Statistics, Year 1927, Yarmouth County Deaths, book 133, 836. A second daughter, Marian Katheryn (or Kathryn), died a single woman of tuberculosis at twenty-four years of age in 1944. NSARM, Historical Vital Statistics, Yarmouth County Deaths, Year 1944, book 209, 629. John Bartlett and Julia Labrador's son Thomas Vincent Bartlett was only eighteen when he perished from exposure during a shipwreck in the early spring of 1944. NSARM, Historical Vital Statistics, Digby County Deaths, Year 1944, book 1946, 2118.

482 James Sullivan Bartlett, the son of Joseph Bartlett and Julia Pictou, as a child lived much of the time on the Roseway River in Shelburne County. He probably was born at Tusket on 20 February 1873, although other sources claim he was born at Ohio in Shelburne County. NSARM, Historical Vital Statistics, Yarmouth County Births, Registration Year 1873, book 1823, p. 192, no. 164. He was baptized on 24 May 1873 at Ste. Anne du Ruisseau Church by a Father Underwood, who entered James's name in the parish church register as "Barclay, James Solin." Witnesses to the ceremony were his brother James and Eunice Melançon. In 1894 James Sullivan married Mary Rose Charles, daughter of Kate Charles and Daniel Toney. Joseph Charles and Maggie Labrador's two daughters, Lucy born in 1905 and Elsie born in 1916, were cousins to James Sullivan and Mary Rose's daughters. To show how complicated (and confusing) kin relations were between these Charles and Bartletts, Travis Pinn wrote on 2 October 2016: "Louise Bartlett, the daughter of James Sullivan Bartlett, and Lucy and Elsie Charles were cousins on both their Bartlett and Charles sides. Mary Rose Charles [mother of Louise Bartlett and James Sullivan Bartlett's wife] was the daughter of Kate Charles and Daniel Toney and Kate was the daughter of Joseph ('Joe') Charles and Mary Anne Glode. Joseph Charles was the brother of John Charles, who was the grandfather of Lucy and Elsie Charles. James Sullivan Bartlett [father of Louise Bartlett] was the brother of Henriette Christina Bartlett, the grandmother of Lucy and Elsie Charles. That means Louise Bartlett and Lucy Charles are first cousins once removed, with Joseph Bartlett and Julia Pictou as their common ancestors." Lucy married twice, first to Carl Pinn and then to Walter Powers, while Elsie married Isaac Basque.

483 Birchbark became increasingly hard to secure, as large paper birch trees were rapidly dying of disease. Mi'kmaq occasionally steamed planks to construct canoes, or made canvas-hulled canoes for transportation in New Brunswick, Nova Scotia, and Maine. Harald E.L. Prins, "Tribal Network and Migrant Labor: Mi'kmaw Indians as Seasonal Workers in Aroostook's Potato Fields, 1870–1980," In *Native American and Wage Labor: Ethnohistorical Perspectives*, ed. Alice Littlefield and Martha Knack (Norman, OK: University of Oklahoma Press, 1996), 45–65; Bonnie McBride, *Our Lives in Our Hands: Micmac Indian Basketmakers* (Gardiner, ME: Tilbury House/Halifax: Nimbus, 1990), 15–17.

484 Joseph Elia Bartlett was born on 15 February 1895 and died the same year; the second Joseph was born on 24 February 1899 and died by 1901. James Henry or "James Hy" Bartlett (erroneously entered in the province's vital statistics record as "Henry Lee" Bartlett) was born on 26 February 1911 and died at the age of four years, seven months on 14 September 1915 of cholera. NSARM,

Historic Vital Statistics, Yarmouth County Births, Registration Year 1911, p. 5300409, no. 53000409; NSARM, Historic Vital Statistics, Yarmouth County Deaths, Year 1915, book 50, p. 165, no. 548. Another son, James L. Bartlett Jr., was born at Yarmouth in 1921 and died in 1922. The most the parents could do at such tragic times was to leave the deceased in the care of the local undertaker, A.A. VanHorne of Yarmouth, who arranged for their burials at St. Ambrose Cemetery, and go on with their lives as best possible despite the constant threats posed by disease and hunger.

485 Frances Viola Bartlett was born on 6 January 1898, Louise Mamie on 31 May 1903, Dorothy [Dot] May on 31 March 1906, Georgina on 13 August 1907, and Marguerite [Mag] Julia on 1 September 1913. Another son, James L. Bartlett, was born at Acadia in 1921, but like his younger brothers seems not to have survived into adulthood. A further son, Charles R. Bartlett, was born to James Sullivan and Mary Rose in the United States on 19 February 1925. Frances Viola as a single woman in 1922 also had a child, James Lawrence, who died of rickets at the age of seven months, which suggests the child suffered from acute malnutrition. NSARM, Historical Vital Statistics, Yarmouth County Deaths, Year 1922, book 110, 782. Copious genealogical records pertaining to James Sullivan Bartlett's family are housed in the Yarmouth County Museum and Archives; other information may be found online. Francis Viola, the only one of the sisters who wed a man of Indigenous extraction, eventually married a Penobscot man from Oldtown in Maine. A granddaughter of Francis Viola Bartlett, who goes by the pseudonym "Nancy Pine Beers," shares information about her branch of the Bartlett family on her website "Ring of Firelight: A Creative Perspective of Off-Reservation, Non-Status American Indian Poetry, Stories and History," http://ringoffirelight.blogspot.com/.

486 NSARM, Historical Vital Statistics, Yarmouth County Marriages, Year 1922, book 18, p. 367, "Marriage of Louisa M.M. Bartlett to James Michael Maher, 27 November 1922, St. Amboise Church, Yarmouth, W.E. Young, presiding priest." Dorothy Bartlett, Louisa's sister, acted as a witness.

487 Both James and Louisa were literate and soon took up a new life in the United States. Their positive experiences piqued the interest of Louisa's sixty-one-year-old father James Sullivan Bartlett and his wife Mary Rose who, with their daughters still living with or near them, in 1924 embarked at Yarmouth on the Boston Steamship Company's vessel *Prince George* for Boston with the intention of merely visiting their married daughter Louisa

in Hartford and then returning to Nova Scotia. But things did not turn out as planned. After their arrival in Boston on 1 July and their subsequent journey to Hartford, weeks away turned into months until the family decided to stay permanently in New England. Family members may have returned to Nova Scotia for brief visits, though this is not certain. James Sullivan Bartlett eventually bought land and built a house in North Kennebunkport, later renamed Arundel. He died in Arundel in 1938, while Mary Rose lived on in Maine until 1955. All of their daughters eventually married American citizens. Even James Maher, Louisa's husband, took out American citizenship. Their descendants have entered a variety of professions, as teachers, lawyers, and nurses, and several retain a lively interest in the Bartlett family history and its roots in Cape Sable.

488 A son, Charles R. Bartlett, was born to James Sullivan Bartlett and Mary Rose Charles on 19 February 1925 in the United States but lived only a few months, while the five daughters born in Yarmouth County survived into adulthood. Frances Viola Bartlett was born on Starr's Road on 6 January 1898 (d. 1944), Louisa Marguerite Mary ("Mamie") on 31 May 1903, Dorothy ("Dot") on 31 March 1906 (d. 1961), Georgina ("Gigi" or "Geigi") on 13 August 1907 (d. 1962), and Marguerite Julia ("Mag") Julia on 1 September 1913 (d. 2001). Frances Viola, a single woman in 1922, gave birth at Yarmouth to a son named James Lawrence who died of rickets at the age of seven months, which suggests the child suffered from malnutrition. NSARM, Historical Vital Statistics, Yarmouth County Deaths, Year 1922, book 110, p. 782. Genealogical information pertaining to James Sullivan Bartlett's family is housed in the Yarmouth County Museum and Archives, while other information may be found online. Frances Viola Bartlett wed a Penobscot man from Oldtown in Maine. One of her granddaughters, who goes by the pseudonym "Nancy Pine Beers," maintains an interesting website, "Ring of Firelight: A Creative Perspective of Off-Reservation, Non-Status American Indian Poetry, Stories and History," http://ringoffirelight.blogspot.com/.

489 In 1886 Samuel Labrador married Henriette Christina Bartlett, a daughter of Joseph Bartlett and Julia Pictou and sister of James Sullivan Bartlett. Samuel and Henriette Christina had a daughter Margaret, or "Maggie," who married Joseph Charles, the son of John Charles and Mary Jane Firth (or Crowell). Joseph Charles and Maggie Labrador had two daughters, Lucy and Elsie, and Travis Pinn, co-author of this chapter, is a descendent of Lucy Charles. After their marriage Joseph and Maggie went to Hectanooga, Digby County. When

Henriette Christina died, Samuel Labrador married Victoria Francis of West Pubnico in 1896, and when Victoria died he wed Frances Murree in 1911 at Yarmouth. NSARM, Historical Vital Statistics, Yarmouth County Marriages, Registration Year 1911, book 16, p. 73, "Marriage of Samuel Labrador, 37, son of Stephen Labrador and Rose Maffre, and Frances Murree, 20, daughter of Henry and Elizabeth Murree, at St. Ambroise Church, Yarmouth; witnesses Frank Meuse and Clara Duclair; officiating priest W.E. Young." Joseph Charles enjoyed writing letters to his maternal uncle James Sullivan Bartlett, Mary Rose Charles (who was also related to him), and James and Mary Rose's daughters in New England. Joseph was also close to his father-in-law, and after his marriage to Maggie he and Samuel Labrador guided and worked together at a youth camp.

490 NSARM, Historical Vital Statistics, Year 1935, book 156, p. 710.

491 The marriage took place at Ste. Anne du Ruisseau on 4 October 1933.

492 According to his death certificate, Samuel Labrador was born at Yarmouth on 5 April 1867 and died on 23 January 1921 at age fifty-four. This information is correct. (By contrast, Stephen Bartlett and Rose Labrador's marriage certificate states that Samuel Labrador, Rose's father, was born in Boston. As Samuel's father Stephen Labrador farmed at Kejimkujik Lake in the early 1840s and later moved to farm at Brookfield, it is unlikely that either Stephen or his son Samuel travelled far in the 1860s. NSARM, Historical Vital Statistics, Yarmouth County Marriages, Registration Year 1933, book 70, p. 400. Though Samuel Labrador's mother's name appears indistinctly on his death certificate of 1921, it is known she was an Acadian woman named Mary Rose Bertrand, also known as Mary Rose Maffre. Information courtesy of Travis Pinn, 2 October 2016. Samuel Labrador was buried in the cemetery at St. Vincent de Paul Church in Salmon River, Digby County. His son-in-law Joseph Charles informed the authorities of his passing. NSARM, Digby County Deaths, Registration Year 1921, book 66, p. 346. Travis Pinn and his family in 2021 erected a gravemarker for him at this site.

493 NSARM, Historical Vital Statistics, Yarmouth County Marriages, Registration Year 1930, book 59, 561, "Marriage of Abraham Bartlett and Ella Gertrude Murree, 19 August 1930, West Pubnico"; NSARM, Historical Vital Statistics, Year 1934, Yarmouth County Deaths, book 156, 316, "Death of Ella Gertude Murree."

494 NSARM, Historical Vital Statistics, Year 1936, Yarmouth County Marriages, book 84, p. 489, "Marriage of Abraham Bartlett and Annie Emily Pictou." Abraham Bartlett and Annie Emily Pictou in turn had a son Abraham born at Tusket who became a well-known basketmaker and canoe manufacturer in the Yarmouth Area. "Indian Basket-Maker Finds Ready Market for Products," *The Indian Missionary Record* (Ottawa), vol. 19, no. 8 (October 1956): 3. Some of the younger generations of the Tusket and Yarmouth Bartlett families have been involved in the lobster industry and occasional take part in the Mi'kmaw struggles to gain recognition under the 1999 Marshall decision. John Demont, "Lobster Wars Rock Maritimes," *MacLean's*, 11 October 1999, https://www.thecanadianencyclopedia.ca/en/article/lobster-wars-rock-maritimes.

495 D'Entremont, *History of Quinan*, 22. At least twenty-five French people settled in southwestern Nova Scotia between the 1780s and 1820s, either escaping the French Revolution or avoiding compulsory military service during the Napoleonic Wars. Thirteen individuals can be traced as coming from France in Yarmouth County alone, Jean-Marie Blanchard being one of them. Several of Blanchard's sons moved to The Forks, and their descendants are still found today at Quinan. "French People Who Settled in Yarmouth County during the French Revolution and Napoleonic Wars," *Yarmouth Vanguard*, 12 September 1989. The local Acadians at Pubnico had obtained grants from the government on Great Pubnico Lake. Cyrille Duon, Jacques d'Entremont, Dominique d'Entremont, and François d'Entremont held the grants on the lake that lay nearest the road. Across the lake, towards its northeast shore, additional allotments had been granted to Guillaume d'Entremont, Cyriacque d'Entremont, André d'Entremont, and Pierre Duon. To the north, around the two Madashack Lakes, lay land granted to Joseph d'Entremont. Most of the grants lying nearest the Mi'kmaw reserve, however, belonged to English speakers from Pubnico Head, among them John Larkin, John Carland, Jeremiah Murphy, Walter Larkin, James Larkin, David Larkin, Benjamin Larkin, Benjamin Goodwin, and Ben Hamilton. The seven hundred acres allocated to James Francis, Paul Williams, John Paul, Philip Francis, James Luxey, Joseph Francis, and James Francis Jr. lay wedged in between grants earlier laid out to David Larkin and Benjamin Goodwin on the north and a grant laid out for John Kenny on the south. NSARM, Miscellaneous "I" Indian Land Records on microfilm, Package 13, "Survey Plan of Pubnico Great Lake Reserve by James A. McKay, Deputy Surveyor for the County of Shelburne," 23 August 1894.

496 The period 1850 to mid-1870 was one of relative economic prosperity for this area, fueled by the need to build large numbers of wooden vessels to deliver the great quantities of fish traded to the United States under the free trade agreement. "They Tied Themselves to the Mast and the Steering Wheel So Not to Be Washed Overboard," *Yarmouth Vanguard*, 25 April 1989.

497 Travis Pinn explained that Mary Rose Charles, the wife of James Sullivan Bartlett, was a biological daughter of Kate Charles and Daniel Toney and that Kate sometimes adopted the surname "Toney" in addition to "Charles." James Sullivan and Mary Rose Charles wed in 1894.

498 Father Clarence-J. d'Entremont conducted extensive research on the community along the Pubnico Lake Road; his notes on the subject are housed in the Musée Acadien in West Pubnico. Another excellent source of information is the online site "Local Stories and Folklore: The Lake Road (*Le Chemin du Lac*)," https://museeacadien. ca/archives/OLD/argyle/html/ecomm09.htm.

499 Mary Elizabeth Murree's father, Joseph Murree, was the brother of John Murree Jr. who helped to survey the Pubnico Lake reserve in 1843. The first Glodes who settled at West Pubnico married into the Francis and Murree families.

500 John Newel Glode led sportsmen on hunting expeditions north of Great Pubnico Lake until the early 1950s. Another man, Matthew Francis, related to John Newel's grandmother Victoire Francis, had a son, John Francis, and a very beautiful daughter known as the "Lady of the Lake," who was said to have married a rich American.

501 Deborah Gloade of Yarmouth, who as of 2017 worked as an administrator for the Acadia First Nation, graciously supplied this information as well as a copy of John Newel Glode's guiding licence.

502 Joseph Pictou died in Yarmouth in 1958 at age eighty-two. NSARM, Historical Vital Statistics, Yarmouth County Deaths, Registration Year 1958, 5082, "Death of Joseph Pictou, single, born in 1876." John Newel Glode reported Pictou's death to the authorities. Though overgrown with brush, the outline of the cellars of the Pictou and Glode residences can still be traced on the east side of the road proceeding towards the lake. Marriages also occurred between the Pictou family and the Alexis family in this area.

503 One member of the Charles family whose descent from Charles Sulno could not be clearly determined is Maria Elizabeth Charles, the wife of an Englishman named Stephen Carty who lived along the Pubnico Lake Road. Maria Elizabeth in her later years was known as "La Vieille Gaigue." No English translation for this name could be found, other than that "Gaigue" refers to a town in County Longford, Province of Leinster, Ireland. Maria Elizabeth Charles and Stephen Carty had a son William James Carty who married Mary Catherine Glode, "daughter of Jean [John] Glode and Mary [Victoria Murree,] on 21 August 1886." William James Carty drowned in 1915 at age forty-six and was buried by John Glode. NSARM, Historical Vital Statistics, book 50, p. 153, no. 506. Mary Anne Glode, born on 2 May 1860 to Matthew Glode and Victoire Francis, married a brother of William Carty. She died on 16 March 1930 and was buried at West Pubnico by James Glode. NSARM, Historical Vital Statistics, Registration Year 1930, Yarmouth County Deaths, book 133 943. The younger members of the Carty family were all close to their grandmother, Maria Elizabeth Charles, who was a respected traditional healer and basketmaker in the West Pubnico area.

504 Joseph Charles's father John was a son of Francis Charles I, while Joseph's mother, Mary Jane Firth (or Crowell) descended from Planters from Cape Cod who settled around Barrington. As stated elsewhere in this chapter, John married four times to Mary Anne Bartlett, in 1860 to Elizabeth (Lizzy) C. Labrador from West Pubnico, in 1871 to Mary Jane Firth (also known as Jane Crowell), and finally to Mahalia Frank, widow of Joseph Bartlett of Summerside, Lunenburg County. John and Mahalia wed at Ste. Anne du Ruisseau on 26 October 1891. Travis Pinn located "Jean's" (John's) and Mahalia's marriage certificate in the Argyle Courthouse and Museum. Letter from Travis Pinn to Janet Chute, 18 October 2016. This document states that Jean Charles was the son of "François Charles (late) and Madeleine [Peters]," and that John's wife "Nellie [*sic*, Mahalia] Frank" was the daughter of George Frank and Christine Williams. Witnesses to the couple's wedding were Frank Labrador and Samuel Claude (Glode). (Mahalia was incorrectly identified on the 1891 marriage certificate as the "widow of Francis Bartlett," rather than the widow of Joseph Bartlett Sr. of Lunenburg County.) Joseph Bartlett Sr. died between 1881 and 1891, since Mahalia and Joseph Bartlett were still listed as living together, but not married, on the 1881 federal census.

505 Maggie Labrador was Joseph Charles's third wife.

506 Registers of the Parish of St. Vincent de Paul, "Marriage of Joseph Charles, son of John Charles, to Magie [*sic*, Maggie] Labrador, daughter of Sam Labrador and Henriette Bartlett, 12 August 1902; witnesses Henry Thibeau and Zoe Theriault." After his marriage to Maggie, Joseph Charles and his father-in-law, Samuel Labrador, guided and worked together at a youth camp.

Maggie's mother Henriette Christina Bartlett, a daughter of Joseph Bartlett and Julia Pictou, married Samuel Labrador, a son of Étienne Labrador and Rose Anne Mab or Maffre, in 1886; Henriette died a decade later, on 11 February 1896. Samuel Labrador next wed Victoria Francis, daughter of Matthew Francis and Marie-Anne Guillaume, at Ste. Anne du Ruisseau. Witnesses to the wedding were Athanase Dulin and Rosalie Lefevre from Quinan. When Victoria died, he married Frances Murree in 1911. NSARM, Historical Vital Statistics, Yarmouth County Marriages, Registration Year 1911, book 16, 73, "Marriage of Samuel Labrador, widower, 37, son of Stephen Labrador and Rose Maffre, to Frances Murree, 20, daughter of Henry and Elizabeth Murree, St. Ambrose Church, Yarmouth, officiating priest W.E. Young; witnesses Frank Meuse and Clara Duclair."

507 Travis Pinn wrote, "Elsie Charles Basque (1916–2016) was born on 12 May 1916 in Hectanooga, Digby County, the daughter of Joseph Charles and Margaret ('Maggie') Labrador. Elsie's baptismal name was Josephine Henrietta Charles – Josephine after her father and Henrietta after her maternal grandmother, Henrietta Christiana Bartlett-Alexis. 'Elsie' was not part of her baptismal name, but her parents added the Elsie part later." When Elsie was very young, her mother Maggie permanently left for Boston. It is not exactly clear why Maggie, along with one of her Mi'kmaw relatives, left in the spring of 1921 or why she afterwards stayed there. Maggie's employer in Yarmouth was a hard man, and brighter economic prospects south of the border may have beckoned her to leave Cape Sable. She also was experiencing tensions at home. She had an infant die in 1904, and bore a stillborn child in 1908, but since these tragedies had occurred, respectively, seventeen and thirteen years before she left Cape Sable, they could not have been the primary reasons for her removal to the United States. Maggie's father, however, had died from influenza shortly before she left. Moreover, Maggie, Joseph and Lucy had all contracted the Spanish influenza, but while Maggie and Lucy got better, Joe's bout of influenza was replaced by a very serious case of TB. Maggie left shortly after Joe's TB forced him to go the sanitarium in Kentville, even though many Hectanooga neighbors rallied resources [for his care at home] and Maggie received money for living expenses each month. But whatever caused Maggie's departure, it was [a] wrenching time for her two young children. Elsie remembered years afterward being left on the pier in Yarmouth at the age of five watching her mother's ship leave." Travis Pinn to Janet Chute, 5 May 2016 and 5 October 2016. In later years, Elsie proved a woman of exceptional intellectual fortitude and determination, as well as humour and humanity. She became the first Mi'kmaq in Nova Scotia to teach in a mainstream setting, and spent many years in Boston, Massachusetts, giving lectures on issues dealing with Indigenous culture and society. She continued to teach in various forums for most of her life. In 1997 she received an honorary doctorate from the Nova Scotia Teachers College in Truro, in 2005 she received an honorary doctorate in education from Université-Sainte Anne, and in 2009 she became a member of the Order of Canada. Most recently, in 2013, she was awarded an honorary doctorate by Acadia University. See http://www.danielnpaul.com/ElsieBasque-Educator.html; http://www.danielnpaul.com/Col/1995/ElsieBasque-MicmacPioneer.html. She always recognized those who had helped her during trying times. After her mother left when she was a child, she lived for a while with a Mrs. Corporan, and then with Edmond and Lizzie Deveau at Salmon River. She had warm memories of her Mi'kmaw and Acadian neighbours, which attest to the long-standing and close ties connecting the French and Mi'kmaq in the Hectanooga area. The nature of this relationship has been ignored by historians and anthropologists, although in the mid-1960s folklorist Horace P. Beck visited Hectanooga to collect Mi'kmaw stories; see his *Gluskap the Liar and Other Indian Tales* (Freeport, ME: B. Wheelright, 1966). Some of Elsie's early experiences in the Hectanooga area and later at Yarmouth, however, were far from pleasant. Travis wrote: "Elsie contended that it was very uncomfortable on the reserve. Lucy would try to bring food back from her domestic job to feed her little sister Elsie, but the wealthy employer did not let her … [It] was likely the Indian Agent, and perhaps neighbours in Hectanooga, among them St. Vincent de Paul's parishioners, who arranged for Elsie to enter the foster care system late in the winter of 1922." With regard to Elsie's sister, Lucy Charles, Travis provided an engaging online illustrated story of this branch of the Charles family, including his great-grandmother Lucy's marriage to Carl Pinn, called "Gigi: A Short Biography of a Mi'kmaw Woman, Lucy Marie Celeste Charles Pinn, aka Aunty Lou & Nana, 1905–1985" (site defunct; printout available from the first author). According to Travis, "Carl Pinn's parents hailed respectively from North Virginia and Washington, D.C. In the 19th century some of the Pinns of North Virginia were identified as 'Indian,' but more often they were recorded as 'Mulatto.' During the 20th century, Carl's immediate family identified as Black, although they also had Native

American ancestry as well as prominent European ancestry." Travis Pinn to Janet Chute, 19 July 2021. See also Pinn, "Ancestorbios, Joseph N. Charles," January 2020, https://ancestorbios.wordpress.com/2020/01/10/joseph-joe-charles/.

508 Travis Pinn to Janet Chute, 19 July 2021. Travis held that "Lucy's father may also have wished to delay Lucy's engagement to an older Mi'kmaw man named Phillip Paul by encouraging Lucy to go to Boston, though he didn't count on her getting married to Carl Pinn in the fall of 1922. Lucy, in moving, was not disappointed, for in Boston she soon found work in a chocolate factory. But Joseph wanted his wife, Maggie, to come back from Boston and might've sent Lucy to coax her back. Maggie and Louise Bartlett's departure for the United States had a major impact on those of their families who remained behind. Maggie Labrador sporadically kept in contact with her husband and daughters by letter, sent them occasional presents, and may even have come back to visit them at least once. And Louise Bartlett, once she married James Maher and moved to New England, successfully persuaded her entire family from Nova Scotia to join her in the United States. Later Elsie Charles, at her sister Lucy's urging, became involved with vital Indigenous issues at Jamaica Plains, Boston. After marrying Carl Pinn, she became an American citizen." Travis Pinn to Janet Chute, 5 May 2016.

509 "Joe had heard about the opening of the residential school from a newspaper article. This article convinced him that it would be a good opportunity for Elsie, so he sent her to the school himself in 1930. Of course, he later resented the policies and actions of the school, and in 1931 he confronted the school principal, Father Mackey, and subsequently Elsie was invited to attend high school in Meteghan." Travis Pinn to Janet Chute, 5 May 2016.

510 "Obituary, Elsie J. Basque (Charles), 18 May 1916–11 April 2016," Meteghan Funeral and Cremation Services, Meteghan, Nova Scotia.

511 Ottawa, *Annual Report of the Department of Indian Affairs for the Year Ending June 30, 1902* (1903), Doc. no. 27, Sessional Paper no. 27, 3 Edward VII (1903), 79, "Report of Agent W.H. Whalen concerning the Mi'kmaq of Yarmouth County to Frank Pedley, Deputy Superintendent of Indian Affairs"; Ottawa, *Annual Report of the Department of Indian Affairs to March 31, 1907*, Sessional Paper no. 27 (A 1908), 7–8 Edward VII, 68, "Report of Whalen to Pedley," 4 April 1907.

512 For instance, in the late nineteenth century John Harlow of Milton, Queens County, paid a salary of merely seventy-five dollars per annum, regularly toured the Mi'kmaw settlements from Gold River southward to the interior of Queens County and so became well known to the Native population. Canada, *Public Accounts of Canada for the Fiscal Year Ended 30th June 1878*, III: 215, "Indians of Nova Scotia, 1878." John's son Charles Harlow later followed his father's example in taking an interest in Mi'kmaw individuals and families, so much so that one branch of the Pictou family adopted "Harlow" as its surname: Louis Harlow was a guide and porpoise hunter at Bear River in the late nineteenth century. Victor Cardoza, "Louis Harlow, 88, and His Wife Madeline, 86, Are the Oldest Residents at Bear River," *Halifax Herald*, 23 July 1965, 15. Charles Harlow, a son of Louis Harlow and Elizabeth Michael born on 10 August 1905, became a well-known guide at Bear River.

513 LAC, RG 10, vol. 3220, "Inspector's Report to Dr. McGill, Indian Affairs, Ottawa," 20 June 1933.

514 For a thorough discussion of this subject, see Marilyn Elaine Thomson-Millward, "'Researching the Devils': A Study of Brokerage at the Indian Residential School, Shubenacadie, Nova Scotia" (PhD diss., Dalhousie University, 1997), chap. 7.

515 Lewis (or Louis) Luxey Jr married Mary Catherine Lucy Michael at Ste. Croix Roman Catholic Church in Plympton in July 1875. They would have eight children: Mary Margaret, baptized at Plympton in 1876; Sarah Ann, baptized at Annapolis Royal in 1878; Beloni or Benjamin, baptized at Annapolis Royal in 1880; John, who died in infancy, baptized at Annapolis Royal in 1886; Josephine, born at Bear River and baptized at Annapolis Royal in 1888; John, baptized at Annapolis Royal in 1890; Rachael, baptized at Annapolis Royal in 1893; and Mary Ann, baptized at Annapolis Royal in 1895.

516 In the early 1930s Lewis Luxey Jr. was still working in the woods during the winter and spring months to support his family and so was not always able to address pressing events. He was present at Yarmouth, however, when his wife Mary Lucy Michael died in February 1938. NSARM, Historical Vital Statistics, Registration Year 1930, Yarmouth County Deaths, book 133, 1117, "Death of Ben Luxey, a 46-year-old trapper, 3 March 1930"; NSARM, Historical Vital Statistics, Registration Year 1938, Yarmouth County Deaths, book 184, 80; "Death of Mary L. Luxey from a cerebral hemorrhage on 25 February 1938." Mary, the daughter of Joseph Michael of Bear River, was born at Bear River on 23 April 1855.

517 James Pictou, the son of John Pictou and Mary Meuse of Pubnico, was born on the Clyde River in 1881. James and Josephine settled in Yarmouth soon after their marriage, about 1901. Josephine Luxey, who triumphed over

adversity in many ways, was deaf and mute for 93 years. She celebrated her 101th birthday at Yarmouth shortly before her death in 1990.

518 James Pictou and Josephine Luxey's six children, born between 1901 and 1917, were Rachel, Clifford, Marguerite Levinie, Mary Rose, John, and Clarence. Rachel, who was born in 1901, married three times. She was thirty-four at the time of her first marriage on 28 May 1935 to Noel Gabriel Glode of Tusket, who was twenty-four and whose mother was Charlotte Glode. (His father's name does not appear on the marriage licence.) Witnesses to the couple's wedding ceremony, held in St. Ambrose's Church in Yarmouth on 28 May 1935, were Stephen Bartlett of Tusket and Stephen's second wife, Rose Labrador. NSARM, Historical Vital Statistics, Yarmouth County Marriages, Registration Year 1935, book 76, 331. Rachel's second marriage was to Louis Surrette and her third marriage to John Huggins. She died in 2003. Little information could be found about Clifford Pictou, as his name does not appear in the vital statistics record. Marguerite Levinie Pictou, born 28 August 1907, married Ray Hallet Turner at the United Baptist Parsonage at Hebron on 23 September 1929. NSARM, Historical Vital Statistics, Registration Year 1907, 99200939; NSARM, Historical Vital Statistics, Registration Year 1929, Yarmouth County Marriages, book 57, 386. Mary Rose Pictou, born 13 April 1909, married James Albert Labrador, the son of Julie Labrador, who lived in Shelburne County. NSARM, Historical Vital Statistics, Registration Year 1909, p. 52900337, no. 52900337, Births in Yarmouth County, Birth of Mary Rose Pictou, 9 July 1909. Her brother John Pictou was born on 25 April 1910. NSARM, Historical Vital Statistics, Registration Year 1910, p. 52900956, no. 52900958. Clarence Pictou, born in 1917, died at age one of pneumonia. NSARM, Historical Vital Statistics, Yarmouth County Deaths, Registration Year 1918, book 51, p. 77, no. 261, "Death of Clarence Pictou," 30 July 1918.

519 John Pictou and his wife Lillian ran a well-known basket-making business and gift shop at Arcadia in Yarmouth. The first author had the pleasure of speaking with Lillian Pictou in 1990 when she still maintained her shop, which was shaped like a wigwam and lay on the southwest side of Starr's Road. The reserve community has since then moved to acreage on the opposite side of Starr's Road, where modern buildings have been constructed.

520 James Pictou died in Yarmouth at age thirty-five of tuberculosis on 2 January 1919. NSARM, Historical Vital Statistics, Yarmouth County Deaths 1919, book 5, p. 153, no. 499, "Death of James Pictou." Josephine's second

husband was Wilfred Robinson, a son of Benjamin Robinson and Angela Cook of Chebogue (now Acadia). NSARM, Historical Vital Statistics, Yarmouth County Marriages, Registration Year 1923, book 18, 368, "Marriage of Josephine Pictou, widow, and Wilfred Robinson at St. Ambrose's Church in Yarmouth." The groom was forty years old, while the bride was thirty-five.

521 It is not certain whether Josephine Luxey was born in 1887 or 1888, although the day of her birth is considered to be 18 April. No birth certificate for her could be found, although her and Wilfred Robinson's marriage certificate, dated 1923, states she was thirty-five years old at the time of her marriage, which suggests she was born in 1888. A site on ancestry.ca, however, claims she was born at Bear River in April 1887 and died in Yarmouth Regional Hospital in 1990, which would make her 103 years of age at the time of her death. By contrast, a second site maintained by the Mi'kmaw Resource Centre at the University of Cape Breton claims she was born in April 1888, so the best one can deduce is that she was either 102 or 103 years old when she died. See https://www.ancestry.ca/genealogy/records/josephine-t-luxey-luxie-pictou-robinson-24-26bg92 and https://www.cbu.ca/indigenous-affairs/mikmaq-resource-centre/mikmaw-book-of-days/march/.

522 The chief of Bear River continued to be recognized as the district chief of Annapolis, Digby, Yarmouth, Shelburne, and Queens counties and about half of Lunenburg County until the mid-1920s, though the Shubenacadie chief sometimes also held that he was head chief of the entire peninsular mainland. NSM, Harry Piers Notes, Lithics (I), Relics of the Stone Age in Nova Scotia, 1891, "Piers' Interview with Chief John Noel." Joseph C. Cope of the Halifax band argued that the Shubenancadie chief had Lunenburg County under his jurisdiction. NSM, Piers Notes, "Information on Chiefs from Joe C. Cope," 14 January 1924. What constituted the scope of the Bear River chief's territorial jurisdiction could even pose a problem for local Indian agents. The Annapolis County agent found this out when he had to intervene to uphold the status of the Bear River chief in 1904. In that year a committee planning a festivity celebrating the tercentenary of Samuel Champlain's landing in the Maritimes suggested that Levi Pictou be regarded as "Governor of the County." But when Pictou asked to be elected to that position, the local Indian agent, John Lacey, stressed that James Meuse was already the Bear River chief, though Lacey went on to admit he did not really know the scope of

Meuse's jurisdiction. The tercentenary committee, for the sake of their pageant, then proposed that "if Meuse was Governor for all Nova Scotia, Pictou could come in as the sub-Governor for Annapolis County." Such exchanges among officials and the agents underlined the degree of ignorance in official circles about the realities of Mi'kmaw governance structures in southwestern Nova Scotia. Martha Elizabeth Walls, *No Need of a Chief for This Band: The Maritime Mi'kmaq and Federal Electoral Legislation, 1899–1951* (Vancouver: University of British Columbia Press, 2010), 74.

523 NSM, printed file, "Letter from Ward Fisher to the Honourable W.L. Hill, Department of Marine and Fisheries," 10 February 1927. After launching his test cast on the question of Mi'kmaw fishing rights in 1927 when he took salmon out of season at Bridgewater, William Labrador pleaded not guilty under the terms of the 1752 Peace and Friendship Treaty and, at the time, lost his case. This incident provided a precedent, however, for the better-known test case relating to Aboriginal hunting and fishing rights launched in 1928 by Mi'kmaw grand chief Gabriel Syliboy of Cape Breton. Many men's lives were like that of Frank Joseph Francis, who had been born either at Great Pubnico Lake or the Clyde River about 1874. Frank Joseph went to work in a lumber camp of the Jordan River in Shelburne in 1885 at the age of eleven. Throughout their lives, men moved from lumber camp to lumber camp and from mill to mill seeking employment in the woods. It was hard and risky work. In the early 1940s the Hilton Scott mill reopened near West Pubnico, which gave men work in that area work again for a few years. Union of Nova Scotia Indians (USNI) Collection, 92–1004–06–030, Sharon Copage to the Union, 17 June 1977; Mike Parker, *Woodchips and Beans: Life in the Early Lumber Woods of Nova Scotia* (Halifax: Nimbus, 1992), 54–7.

524 This subject is touched on in Wicken, *Colonization of Mi'kmaw Memory*, 148. According to table 6.5 on page 182 of Wicken's book, the populations of only four mainland Nova Scotian Native communities were recognized by Indian Affairs from 1871 to 1911, and the Yarmouth and Shelburne County populations were not mentioned at all in official documents.

525 Frank Gouldsmith Speck, "Micmac Hunting Allotments in Nova Scotia, Bear River Band," *Beothuk and Micmac* (New York: Museum of the American Indian/Heye Foundation, 1922), 100–1. Speck also identified Louis Luxey Sr.'s hunting territory as being on Ponhook Lake in Queens County and claimed that it later had been divided among Luxey's sons.

526 Born in 1925, Jeremiah (Jerry) Bartlett of Robinson Road, Yarmouth, was a congenial, knowledgeable, and engaging gentleman with a flair for the theatrical. He donned a feathered headdress while recounting his stories about the land campaigns of his ancestors. Jerry stressed it had been the aim of Bartholomew Alexis Sr. and his siblings to acquire secure title to property around Eel Brook, the Roseway River, and at Salmon River. Bartholomew Alexis's descendants had imbibed this spirit. It was this drive that fueled Chief Stephen Bartlett *dit* Wisow Jr.'s push for the creation of the Acadia reserve in 1887 and seven years later, in 1894, fostered the rise of the Mi'kmaw campaign for the return of the Great Pubnico Lake tract laid out by Joseph Howe in 1843. Jerry suggested that the first author pay attention to the many leases, grants, and purchases of small parcels of land in Shelburne, Yarmouth, and Digby counties that the Alexis family, the Bartletts, the Charleses, the Labradors, and others obtained over the years. Owing to his urgings, Janet Chute and Doris Labradore spent many hours in county land records offices, and indeed did find freehold properties owned by several Cape Sable families. Unfortunately, they could not fulfil Jerry's further stipulation to search New England land records as well; this has to be left to a future generation of scholars. Certain members of the Bartlett and Charles families presently are seeking to learn more about their ancestors' activities in Cape Sable and New England, and this torch is passed to them. Jeremiah Bartlett passed away at Acadia on 8 July 2007. Like many Bartletts before him, he was born in Shelburne County, the son of John Bartlett of Shelburne County and Marguerite Bartlett. "Obituary of Jeremiah Bartlett," *Halifax Herald*, 11 July 2007. Jerry's wife, Rose Marie Cecelia Bartlett (*née* Paul), was born in Weymouth in 1926, the daughter of Joseph Paul and Marie Francis. Rose Marie, a homemaker who enjoyed making baskets, passed away on 3 May 2008. Obituary, Rose Bartlett, 3 May 2008 https://memorials.sweenys-funeralhome.net/rose-bartlett/1512310/obituary.php. The couple's daughter and son live in the United States.

527 Bart McKinnon and D.R. Cassie, *Report on Field Interviews with the Micmacs of Nova Scotia and the Areas in Which They Reside and the Unoccupied Reserves of the Nova Scotia Mainland, 1957*, housed in the Treaty and Aboriginal Rights Research (TARR) Centre at Indianbrook, Shubenacadie, Nova Scotia, file 92–1004–09–018, 33.

528 Joseph Jeremy, born in 1872, was the son of Joseph Jeremy of Wildcat and Catherine (or Kate) Luxey or Alexis. The couple had six children: Margaret (b. 1863),

Abraham (b. 1866), Peter (b. 1869), John (b. 1872), Joseph (b. 1874), and Beatrice (b. 1909). Jeremy was the only person residing at Wildcat in 1957, where he lived all his life. His paternal grandfather and grandmother were John Jeremy and Sally Toney, both leading members of the Kejimkujik settlement in the early 1840s. His father Joseph Jeremy was born in 1845 and his mother, the daughter of Lewis Luxey Sr. and Elizabeth Glode, Lewis Luxey's first wife, was born in 1844. Joseph and Kate Luxey married at St. Jerome's Church in Caledonia, Queens County, in 1862. *Liverpool Transcript*, 6 November 1862. By the late 1950s, John Jeremy's son Frank had moved to Greenfield, while a daughter lived at Lequille back of Annapolis Royal. A third son, Lewis Jeremy, moved about seeking employment cutting pulpwood.

529 Louis Labrador and Francis Pictou at Clyde River in Shelburne also complained to MacKinnon and Cassie that it was hard to find employment in their locale. Louis Labrador, born in 1882, and his son John, born in 1907, cut pulpwood for a living. The Bowater Mersey Company had begun hiring Mi'kmaq, among them Fred Francis, to take out pulpwood. Francis maintained a summer camp on the Ponhook reserve in Queens County. Other Mi'kmaw men worked on road construction. George Labrador of Hebron, born in 1893, was the grandson of James Labrador and Madeline Meuse of Bear River, and a son of John Labrador and his second wife Hannah Noel. As such, he was the nephew of Peter Labrador, who married Rose Bartlett and lived at Tusket, since Peter Labrador and his father John were brothers. George made a living operating a mobile canteen at Hebron in Yarmouth County. Several of these Mi'kmaq expressed an interest in the status of a property along the Clyde River known as "Indian Fields," which they held the Mi'kmaq owned at one time. McKinnon and Cassie, *Report on Field Interviews with the Micmacs of Nova Scotia*, 33–5, 54–6. The first author and field assistant Doris Labrador had the pleasure of interviewing Frank Jeremy, the son of John Jeremy, at Wildcat in July 1990. Frank spoke of the challenges and risks of being a Mi'kmaw lumberman in the woods of Queens County during the early twentieth century.

530 The six reserve communities organized in 1958–59 as Indian Act bands under an act arising from McKinnon's and Cassie's earlier recommendations were Bear River, Afton, Annapolis Valley, Pictou Landing, Shubenacadie, and Truro.

531 The population of the Yarmouth reserve, and the smaller communities from Wildcat to Gold River noted on the general list, periodically were allowed to appoint a spokesperson to forward grievances to Ottawa. With the final disbandment of this general list, in 1967 the Acadia band (later Acadia First Nation) was officially developed under the Indian Act. Acadia First Nation regards itself as "a non-profit organization that strives for self-sufficiency, community and social development." It administers five communities spread out between Gold River, Lunenburg County, and the town of Yarmouth. Most recently, the Acadia First Nation has attained 4.9 hectares of land along the Hammonds Plains Road near Halifax, which it hopes to develop.

532 Some men found jobs laying railway track and as part of road-building crews.

533 As Emeline Moore's husband Tom Bartlett was a third cousin of Lewis Luxey Jr. (since Tom's great-grandfather Bartholomew Alexis and Lewis Luxey Jr.'s great-grandfather Joseph Alexis were both sons of the eighteenth-century chief Charles Alexis), Emeline Moore in 1930 still felt responsible for informing the authorities of the death of Lewis Luxey's son Ben, in the absence of Ben's father, who may have been away hunting or guiding at the time. Many other examples of this persistence of kinship ties throughout several generations may be found in the documentary record for the Cape Sable area.

534 Charlie Labrador had been raised mainly at Wildcat, since his mother, Beatrice Jeremy, had moved back to live with her Jeremy relatives in Queens County after her husband Louis Francis Labrador, a veteran of the Second World War, suddenly died. Beatrice's grandparents, Joseph Jeremy and Kate Luxey, had her father, Joseph Jeremy Jr., in 1874. Joseph married Lalia (or Lallia) Paul, the daughter of Abraham Paul and Rose Pictou of Lequille. Rose was a daughter of Chief Ben Pictou of Lequille. Baptismal registers of St. Gregory's Church, Liverpool, "Baptism of Joseph Jeremy, 6 November 1874"; St. Louis Church, Annapolis Royal, "Marriage of Joseph Jeremy and Lalia Paul, daughter of Abraham Paul and Rose Pictou, 28 May 1902." After Lalia's death, Joseph Jeremy Jr. married Estelle Evangeline Gio (or Gehue) at Annapolis Royal in May 1915. Beatrice Jeremy, who was born to Joseph Jeremy and Lalia Paul in 1909, married Louis Francis Labrador, son of Louis Labrador and Mary Arenburg, at St. Joseph's Church in Bridgewater on 4 June 1930.

535 Daniel N. Paul's biographies of Charles Labrador include "Chief Charles Labrador, 1932–2002," http://www.danielnpaul.com/InterestingPeopleAndEvents.html; "Chief Charles Labrador, Well-Respected Elder," *Halifax Herald*, 17 April 1998; and "Charlie Labrador: A Great Role Model," *Halifax Herald*, 8 August 2002. After assuming

In 2000 the late Chief Charles (Charlie) Labrador stated, "My mother's parents' names – her dad was Joe Jeremy. He was a relative of the Luxi's [*sic*, Luxeys] from Kedjie. Her mother was named Lallia, she was a Paul from Lequille and they are descendent [*sic*, descended] from Chief Ben Pictou, he was an old gentleman who was the Chief of Lequille at that time … Then Rosy was my great-great-grandmother. Rosy Paul." The ELDER Transcripts, History You Can't Get From a Book, "Charlie Labrador, Bear River, 13 December 2000, interviewer Chris Callaghan." Daniel N. Paul's biographies of Charles Labrador include "Chief Charles Labrador, 1932–2002," http://www.danielnpaul.com/ChiefCharlieLabrador.html; "Chief Charles Labrador, Well-Respected Elder," *Halifax Herald*, 17 April 1998; and "Charlie Labrador: A Great Role Model," *Halifax Herald*, 8 August 2002. After assuming office as chief, Charles Labrador could only hold his position for a couple of years owing to the need to support his family in the absence of government support for his office. To quote Daniel Paul: "In Acadia's case, the administration fund allotted by Indian Affairs was so 'generous' that the chief could only afford to make three long-distance phone calls per month to the Yarmouth reserve. If problems arose at Yarmouth or at Wildcat, he often had to dig into his own very limited resources to help people out. Charlie kept a souvenir from those days: the 'office equipment' Indian Affairs had given him in 1969, a stapler."

536 The Clyde tract is presently not permanently occupied, although members of the Francis family and others related to them occupy the land as a summer encampment ground each year. Today they more frequently set up tents or occupy recreational vehicles rather than rely for shelter on the frame cabins of the past.

537 Prior to 1986, Mi'kmaq who had attended university lost their Native legal status, as superior educational achievement did not jibe with government perceptions of what constituted "Indian status."

538 Robinsons who are descended from Josephine Luxey have distinguished themselves as local politicians and community builders. Josephine's second husband was Wilfred (or Wintfred) Robinson, a son of Benjamin Robinson and Angela Cook of Chebogue. The couple married at St. Ambrose Church, Yarmouth, in 1923, with Father W.E. Young officiating and Josephine's mother Mary Lucy Luxey (née Michael) and Ben Luxey acting as witnesses. NSARM, Historical Vital Statistics, Yarmouth County Marriages, book 18, 365, "Marriage of Wintfred Robinson and Josephine Pictou, a 35-year-old widow, 20 December 1923." Josephine and Wintfred had

three sons, Louis Bernard (29 May 1922–29 December 2008), James Albert, and Peter R. Louis Bernard Robinson married Viola Marie Hood and the couple had eight children. One daughter, Deborah Robinson, was elected chief of the Acadia First Nation in June 1988 and still holds this office. During the three decades she has been chief, the Yarmouth Mi'kmaw settlement has been transformed from a marginal assemblage of houses and small shops into a modern community containing the Acadia First Nation's headquarters. Her mother, Viola Robinson, ONS, LLB, OC, and others of her family assisted in compiling this biographical entry. Viola was a founder as well as president of the Native Council of Nova Scotia from 1975 to 1990, and ever since has been a tireless defender of Aboriginal women and their families facing racial discrimination. Involved in the fields of housing, health, education, and the establishment of the Made-in-Nova Scotia legal network, in 1990 she became president of the Native Council of Canada. She received an honorary doctor of laws from Dalhousie University in 1990 and earned her bachelor of laws degree from the same institution in 1998. She acted as one of seven commissioners to the Royal Commission on Aboriginal Peoples between 1990 and 1995. Her other awards include the Commemorative Medal for the 125th Anniversary of Confederation (1992), the Halifax YWCA Women's Recognition Award (1997), the Frances Fish Women Lawyers' Achievement Award in 2003, the Order of Nova Scotia (2009) and, in 2011, the Order of Canada for her service to the nation. She also worked for over fifteen years as a consultant and advisor to the Acadia First Nation. Most recently she was appointed lead negotiator for the Kwilmu'kw Maw-klusuaqn Negotiation Office. Louis Bernard Robinson's brother, James Albert Robinson, born on 1 February 1926, married Joan Lawrence and lived in the Annapolis Valley and at Cheboque. A veteran of the Second World War, he served in the merchant navy and worked in construction until his death on 31 December 2009. *Chronicle Herald/Mail Star*, 31 December 2009. The third Robinson brother, Peter R., married Mary Ellen Lewis, a daughter of Annie (Hood) Lewis and Joseph Lewis of Bear River. Mary Ellen, like Viola Robinson, has been the recipient of numerous awards. A highly knowledgeable and respected Elder, she was a co-founder along with Viola Robinson of the Native Council of Nova Scotia. She passed away on 16 May 2012 and is buried in the cemetery of St. Kateri Roman Catholic Church, Indian Brook, near Shubenacadie. "Obituary, Robinson, Mary Ellen," *Halifax Mail Star*, 18 May 2012.

539 Today, five reserves are associated with the Acadia First Nation. The Clyde River reserve of Shelburne County and the Gold River reserve of Lunenburg County were laid out under Charles Morris's auspices in 1820. The Ponhook Lake reserve of Queens County was set up by Joseph Howe in 1843. The Medway River reserve of Queens County was established in 1868, and the land for the Yarmouth reserve purchased, by the federal government in 1887 on Chief Stephen Bartlett *dit* Wisow Jr.'s recommendation. There were originally six member reserves in 1968, but the Horton community, established in 1907 and since 2001 known as Glooscap, split off from the Acadia First Nation in 1984. This was not a surprising development, as this community has much closer ties historically to the old Minas band than to the Cape Sable band. In 2016 the on-reserve population of the Kespukwit'newaq Acadia First Nation numbered 223, while the off-reserve population stood at around 1,288 and was growing. The population of the Yarmouth reserve is around 100.

540 In the early 1980s the Yarmouth reserve occupied swampy land on the perimeter of the town and the town dump lay near one end of it. In 1986, however, the band started negotiations to purchase land opposite this reserve, the price of which was reduced owing to the land's proximity to the airport.

541 The First Nation's band office today lies at one end of Luxey's Lane and forms the nucleus of the community, along with other offices that house health, child care, and educational services.

542 This parcel, comprising 1,174 hectares in the interior of Yarmouth County, was donated to the Acadia First Nation by John Cook, and offers the potential for numerous economic opportunities. It lies near Carleton Lake, where Chief Charles Sulno of Cape Sable once maintained his camp in the mid-nineteenth century. Interestingly, some members of the Yarmouth Cook family had kin connections with the Ring family of Salmon River, Digby County, on whose land Bartholomew Alexis Sr. camped in the early nineteenth century.

543 Stansbury Hagar, who interviewed Stephen Bartlett Jr. *dit* Wisow Jr. in the late nineteenth century, did not identify the chief with the Cape Sable band.

CHAPTER 2

1 "Glode" or "Gloade" stems from the Algonquian-speaking person's way of pronouncing "Claude." When French priests in the seventeenth century engrafted a patrilineal surname system onto the Mi'kmaq's traditionally bilateral kinship structure, offspring of Jehan Grand Claude of Port Royal went by the patronymic designation "Grand Claude" into the late 1700s. Many census takers in the Maritimes in the early twentieth century adopted the spelling "Gloade," although some members of the family today prefer to retain the older spelling "Glode." Not all Glodes in the Northeast are Mi'kmaq, or even Aboriginal: neighbouring First Nations have families named "Glode," and the surname is found in France and Germany. Jehan Grand Claude's family also must not be confused with descendants of a late-eighteenth-century Mi'kmaw head chief at *Listuguj* (or Restigouche in southern Quebec), Joseph Claude. In 1786 Chief Claude, bearing a French commission and medal bestowed upon him at Quebec by Governor Beauharnois on 8 April 1730, launched a campaign along with two sub-chiefs, Joseph Gagnon and Francis Ewit *dit* Condo, to restore his people's exclusive right to the Restigouche River salmon fishery, which they argued had been recognized by the French. University of New Brunswick, Fredericton, Harriet Irving Archives, Indian Documentation Collection compiled in 1982 under a St. Thomas University–sponsored project, microfilm MC 408. The documents in question were retrieved in 1982 from the Library and Archives of Canada, Ottawa (henceforth LAC), Indian Affairs Records (RG 10), Indian Affairs Correspondence, 1860–69: LAC, RG 10, RS 105, doc. 37, "Report of William Spragge, Deputy Superintendent of Indian Affairs," 12 April 1865, and doc. 38, "Report to Restigouche Mission from Quebec," 19 June 1786, 12 pp. In 1865 the *Listuguj* chief and council showed Deputy Indian Commissioner William Spragge all the correspondence in their possession relating to their fishery "going back to 1786," including a report of the council in which the elderly Chief Claude and his sub-chiefs met with New Brunswick's lieutenant governor Nicholas Cox over Mi'kmaw resource issues. Spragge, being from Upper Canada, expressed his confusion at how such a dispute over fisheries could possibly arise, since he held it was "universally recognized that the Crown assumes no Indian territory without a deed of cession and surrender has been executed … and compensation been agreed upon." The commissioner, however, failed to recognize that the terms of the Royal Proclamation of 1763 relating to the surrender of Aboriginal lands, to which he was referring, had been applied in parts of Ontario but not in the Atlantic Provinces. Descendants of Chief Joseph Claude still live in northern New Brunswick and southern Quebec.

The surname "Glode" also appears among the *Woolastook*, or Malecite, of New Brunswick, Quebec, and Maine as well as among other northeastern Algonquian-speaking groups. In 1760 Malecite chief Ballomy (Bartholomew) Glode came to Halifax in company with some Passamaquoddy representatives to renew British peace and friendship treaties made between the English and Mi'kmaw people in 1726 and 1749. L.F.S. Upton, *Micmacs and Colonists: Indian-White Relations in the Maritimes, 1713–1867* (Vancouver: University of British Columbia Press, 1979), 57. Finally, there are "Glode" descendants of a Frenchman named Jacques Poissant *dit* La Saline, or Poissant *dit* Claude, some of whom, upon taking the surname "Claude," became voyageurs to the Northwest. Claude Poissant's seventeenth-century ancestors included an Algonkin woman who lived in the Ottawa River Valley named Marie Miteouamegoukoue.

2   The place name "Lequille" is French. Samuel de Champlain named the locale after a small smelt-like fish that was found there in abundance in the early 1600s. Thomas J. Brown, *Place Names of Nova Scotia* (Halifax: Royal Print and Litho, 1922), 351.

3   The Mi'kmaq maintained an ancient encampment at Potamoc that was still occupied by Mi'kmaw families in the 1840s and lay on the west side of the Mersey River across from Milton in Queens County. Brian Purdy, a historian and member of the Acadia First Nation, explained that Potamoc became an early French trading centre, a claim confirmed by archaeologists who have discovered at this site, among other artefacts, golden glass trade beads. Lisa Francis, an Aborginal development officer who works at Milton while living on the Ponhook reserve on Lake Rossignol, is investigating late historic use of weirsites along the Mersey River by the related Gloade and Francis families, while Nova Scotia Museum archaeologist Roger Lewis is tracing a number of weir types in this area, dating back to Archaic times. Department of Aboriginal Affairs, "Archeologists Explore Mi'kmaq Heritage at Mersey River," 2 February 2005, https://novascotia.ca/news/release/?id=20050202003.

4   What the French designated the Port Royal band numbered 102 in 1708. LAC, MG 18, F18 (Typescript of a French census by Abbé Pierre La Chasse, dated 1708), *Recensement genal fait au mois de Nouembre mile Sept cent huit de tous les Sauvages de l'Acadie que resident dans la Coste de l'Est, et ceux de Pintagouet et de Canibecky, Famille par Famille, Leurs ages – Celuy de Leurs Femmes et Enfants avec une Recapitulation a la fin de la quantité d'hommes et de garçons capable d'aler a La*

guerres, comme aussy Le recensement des francois Establis a La ditte Coste de l'Es, 1708. The original census manuscript is found in vol. 4, no. 751 of the Edward E. Ayer Collection in the Newberry Library, Chicago.

5   The Mersey River drains into the Atlantic Ocean at Liverpool. From the late 1760s until the early twentieth century this watercourse was known as the Liverpool River, but during the French era it was called the Rossignol River, while Liverpool was known as Port Rossignol. Samuel de Champlain reputedly named Port Rossignol after the French sea captain and fur trader Pierre Rossignol, who traded along the Mersey River early in the seventeenth century. The Port Royal band's hunting territories lay on either side of the Mersey-Medway river system, whose headwaters begin near present-day Graywood, fifteen kilometres inland from Lequille, Annapolis County. Jehan Grand Claude's people supplied fur and fish to the French at Port Royal and La Have. Since Grand Claude had an extensive family, his group could maintain territorial aegis over a vast triangular swath of land, extending southward along the Atlantic coast from La Have to present-day Barrington, and inland to the the shores of the Annapolis Basin. These lands encompassed Kejimkujik Lake on the Queens County-Annapolis Country boundary. Jehan Grand Claude's earliest trading encounters would have been with French at Port Royal and Port Rossignol.

6   The place name "Ranque," also spelled Ranquette, may have stemmed from the French family surname "Ranquette."

7   One Mi'kmaw coastal encampment in Queens County today was located within the bounds of the Port l'Hebert Pocket Wilderness, part of the larger Tobeatic Park system. When Thomas Raddall, the Queens County author and novelist, worked for the Mersey Paper Company, he met with Samuel Freeman Glode of Milton who told him that the *Saakawachkik* – or the folk of the olden time – made use of such sites during their seasonal wanderings up and down the river and along the coast. Raddall, *In My Time: A Memoir* (Toronto: McClelland and Stewart, 1976). Bark canoes were also built at such locales for longer journeys.

8   Bearing orders from the French governor general, Jacques-René Brisay de Denonville, to report on the peoples and resources of Acadia, de Meulles prevailed on two Mi'kmaq from Port Royal to guide him through their district. The French party had difficulties getting over portages and down rapids to the Atlantic coast. De Muelles's handwritten report, "Relation du voyage de

Mr. De Muelles dans l'acadie par ordre de La Majesté commence l'uniéme octobre 1684 et finy Le Six Juillet 1786," outlines the intendant's experiences in Acadia. A printed version of this report appears in John William I. Morse, ed., *Acadiensia Nova* (London: Quaritch, 1935), 1.84–131.

9 LAC, MG 18, F18, La Chasse, *Recensement genal ... 1708*, 1. According to this census, Jehan Grand Claude was listed as born in 1640 and having a wife named Marie. In the early 1980s a debate arose regarding the identity of Claude's wife. Father Clarence-Joseph d'Entremont, lacking access La Chasse's census of 1708, suggested in 1981 that "Jackish" (also known as Jehan or Jean) Grand Claude became the second husband of Marie Sallé of Port Royal, widow of Martin Aucoin. Clarence-J. d'Entremont, *Histoire du Cap-Sable de l'an mil au traité de Paris (1763)* (Eunice, LA: Hébert, 1981), 3.1124–5. This would have linked Jehan Grand Claude through marriage to the Aucoin family in North America. This heralded the onset of a spritely debate in Acadian genealogical circles, though recent evidence from France has proven that Marie Sallé's second husband was Jean Claude Landry, not Jehan Grand Claude. See, for instance, William D. Gerrior, *France and Acadia*, vol. 1 of *Acadian Awakenings: Routes and Roots: International Links, an Acadian Family in Exile* (Halifax: Port Royal, 2003), 186–7.

10 D'Entremont, *Histoire du Cap-Sable*, 3.1123–5.

11 Oral traditions circulating within the Mi'kmaw community at Millbrook, near Truro, hold that Jean Baptist Thoma, a head chief at Annapolis Royal, was descended from an English sailor who came to live among the Mi'kmaq. Edith Thomas of Millbrook, a well-known basketmaker who operated a craft shop at Millbrook in the 1960s and 1970s, held this view. Interview with Edith Thomas, 10 May 2012. Other traditions suggest that Jehan Grand Claude was a descendant of Membertou, the chief who befriended the French at Port Royal from 1605 until his death in 1611, though there is no evidence to confirm this speculation. Yet it demonstrates that it is generally recognized that the antecedents of the Claude/Glode/Gloade family were long-time members of the Port Royal band.

Oral traditions circulating within the Mi'kmaw community at Millbrook, near Truro, hold that Jean Baptist Thoma, a head chief at Annapolis Royal, was descended from an English sailor who came to live among the Mi'kmaq. Edith Thomas of Millbrook, a well-known basketmaker who operated a craft shop at Millbrook in the 1960s and 1970s, held this view. Interview with Edith

Thomas, 10 May 2012. Other traditions suggest that Jehan Grand Claude was a descendant of Membertou, the chief who befriended the French at Port Royal from 1605 until his death in 1611, though there is no evidence to confirm this speculation. Yet it demonstrates that it is generally recognized that the antecedents of the Claude/Glode/Gloade family were long-time members of the Port Royal band.

12 LAC, MG 18, F 18, La Chase, *Recensement genal ... 1708*, 3; LAC, F-135, Archives des Colonies, Paris France (documents on microfilm, henceforth AC), CIIB, vol. 6, *Ile Royalle, Correspondance générale*, doc. no. 77, *Recensement des Sauvages tam de l'isle Royalle que de la peninsula de l'acadie qui sont deservis par Les Missionaires du Seminaire des Missions etrangeres Etablis à Quebec fait par Mr. Gaulin pretre Missionarie des Sauvages en 1722.*

13 A thorough discussion of the chain of events leading up to the Canso attack of 1720 may be found in Upton, *Micmacs and Colonists*, chap. 3, and William C. Wicken, *Mi'kmaq Treaties on Trial: History, Land and Donald Marshall Junior* (Toronto: University of Toronto Press, 2002), chap. 5.

14 LAC, microfilm copies of colonial records housed in the British Public Records Office, London, England (henceforth CO), 217/3/155–56, Antoine and Pierre Couaret [Momcharret] to Governor Richard Philipps, 2 October 1720. Upton's translation of the chief's petition is found in *Micmacs and Colonists*, 41. Father Pain was very active among the Mi'kmaw peoples in the Minas region in the 1720s. John Mack Faragher, *The Great and Noble Scheme: The Tragic Story of the Expulsion of the French Acadians from their American Homeland* (New York: W.W. Norton, 2005), 155–70. Chief Pierre Momcharret was one of two "Pierre Selliers *dit* Memcharet," the first born in 1687 and the second born in 1692, recorded in 1708 by Father Pierre LaChasse as living with their mother, the "veuve de Memcharet" (widow of Memcharet), among the Port Royal Mi'kmaq. Father Clarence d'Entremont suggests that this widow woman may have been an Acadian, surnamed Cellier, married to a Mi'kmaw named Memcharet. D'Entremont, *Histoire du Cap-Sable*, 3.1128–32.

15 Governor Philipps to James Craggs, Secretary of War, 28 May 1720, in Archibald M. MacMechan, ed., *A Calendar of Two Letter Books and One Commission Book in the Possession of the Government of Nova Scotia, 1713–1741*, ed. Nova Scotia Archives II (Halifax: Herald Printing House, 1900), 60–1. This man may have been a member of the Grand Claude family, although the person's name is not given. William Wicken provides a detailed

16 By 1722 Governor Richard Philipps often was conspicuously absent from council and, for that matter, Fort Anne. The British party sent out under Philipp's orders to capture Mi'kmaw hostages had found Grand Claude's wife, daughter, and son peaceably encamped in nearby woods, probably at Lequille.

17 Little is known about Jehan Grand Claude's initial reaction to the British assumption of power at Annapolis Royal after 1710. But references to Grand Claude appear in the Minutes of His Majesty's Council at Annapolis Royal from 19 October through to 12 November 1722. In these minutes, Grand Claude is referred to by one of his synonymous names, "Jackish." As Jackish had his sons Martin and Claude with him, it is clear that Jackish is the same man as Jehan Grand Claude mentioned in La Chasse's 1708 census.

18 Minutes of Council, 19 October 1722, *Original Minutes of His Majesty's Council at Annapolis Royal, 1720–1739, Nova Scotia Archives* III (Halifax: McAlpine, 1908), 36. The British feared a major Mi'kmaw attack on their garrison after three English youths, Charles Davis, Nicholas Hutton, and George Willis, who had been captured by Mi'kmaq along the eastern seaboard and later ransomed by the French at Minas and Piziquid (Windsor), warned that, if provoked, an Acadian force accompanied by six hundred Mi'kmaw warriors from Canada as well as military aid from Louisbourg would descend upon Annapolis Royal. In consequence, Philip Melançon from Minas was instructed to bring in the two Momcharrets, Pierre and Antoine, to be questioned. Since they also brought the letter with them calling for the British to leave Minas they were detained, though one of the brothers, after calling for the release of the Mi'kmaq imprisoned at Fort Anne, escaped. Beamish Murdoch, *A History of Nova-Scotia, or Acadie* (Halifax: James Barnes, 1865), 1.403–4.

19 Minutes of His Majesty's Council, 3 November 1722, *Original Minutes*, 36–7. The Annapolis Council in November of 1722 was composed of Lieutenant Governor John Doucet, Paul Mascarene, John Adams, Hibbert Newton, William Skeen, William Sheriff, and Peter Boudre.

20 Minutes of His Majesty's Council, 5 November 1722, *Original Minutes*, 37.

21 By the mid-eighteenth century, agents of the French Crown had come to exercise a paternal interest in the welfare of the Mi'kmaq. French presents and honorifics bolstered continuation of this relationship, which had only grown stronger after 1720 with the rise of the French establishment at Fortress Louisbourg. The French, for their part, expected the Mi'kmaq to provide warriors for combat in intercolonial conflicts.

22 This suggests that Jehan Grand Claude may have understood some French.

23 Minutes of His Majesty's Council, 3 November 1722, *Original Minutes*, 37.

24 Minutes of his Majesty's Council, 3 November 1722, 12 November 1722, 14 November 1722, *Original Minutes*, 36–7, 38–3, 41. Historian Thomas Peace holds that hostage-taking reached a crisis point in 1722, when it is estimated that about 10 per cent of the Mi'kmaw population of Kespukwitk's Indigenous population were confined. He further posits that the Kespukwitk Mi'kmaq were not united in wanting to attack the British, but since many were imprisoned by the British, some opted to make peace rather than continue to fight. Jackish, or Jehan Claude, only three days after the British declared war agreed to the terms of the British governor's proclamation by promising "never to do anything in prejudice to the Government & that he would give himself Information of any who might have any evil Designe against it." Minutes of His Majesty's Council, 19 October 1722, *Original Minutes*, 36. Jackish and his companions were mainly "focused on freeing family members, rather than a general peace. There is no indication that this agreement was made on behalf of a larger Mi'kmaw political body." The British, by contrast, perceived things in a more formal light. To them, Jackish and three leaders from near Annapolis had stated that they would act only as friends and allies of King George and all his subjects, would not carry out any acts of violence against the British and would notify British authorities of impending danger, would leave chiefs with the British as hostages, and "would not take up arms against the English in the event of war." Thomas Peace, "Two Conquests: Aboriginal Experiences of the Fall of New France and Acadia" (PhD diss., York University, 2011), 196, 207–8.

25 Both the English and the French recognized Jean Baptist Thoma as the Annapolis district chief. That Thoma was one of the leaders persuaded by Jehan Grand Claude to sign treaty is strongly suggested by an account of an incident that occurred in early autumn 1723. On 23 September Prudent Robichaud Sr. (1669–1756), a rent collector, trader, and justice of the peace for Port Royal's Acadian community, fell afoul of Fort Anne's authorities, who had been erroneously informed that Robichaud had been trading with "enemy Indians." Robichaud explained, however, that his dealings had only been

with Chief Thoma who "had the *Governor's* Passport" and was "under the Protection of the Government." When he added that some of Thoma's associates had expressed an interest in signing a treaty with the British, the charges against Robichaud were dismissed. Minutes of His Majesty's Council, 21 September 1723, *Original Minutes*, 47–8; Maurice Basque, *Des hommes de pouvoir: Histoire d'Otho Robichaud et de sa famille, notables acadiens de Port Royal et de Néguac* (Néguac: Société historique de Néguac, 1996). Chief Thoma was a district chief, with wide-ranging political ties. Probably owing to his influence, in November of 1723 the head chiefs of Miramichi, the Bay of Chaleur, Richibucto, Shediac, and Chignecto stated an interest in making peace overtures to the British. Thoma furthermore would remain consistently peaceable towards the British for the next thirty years. According to a French census compiled by Abbé Antoine Gaulin in 1722, Thomas was leader of a group of only ten families at Annapolis Royal by this time. The Annapolis band had shrunk dramatically in population following the British capture of Port Royal, while communities such as La Have on the coast had swelled in size as a consequence. LAC, F-135, AC, CIIB, vol. 6, *Ile Royalle, Correspondance générale*, doc. no. 77, *Recensement des Sauvages tam de l'isle Royalle que de la peninsula de l'acadie … 1722*. During the final years of the Seven Years' War Thoma travelled regularly between Annapolis Royal and Piziquid, and during the final years of his life became leader of the Ponhook (or Panuke) Lake Mi'kmaw community, near present-day Three Mile Plains on the St. Croix River system running southeast from Piziquid towards St. Margaret's Bay.

26 Jehan Grand Claude probably was alive in 1726 although, as he was eighty-six, he may have been reluctant to attend the treaty signing. It is thus probable that Joseph, although not the eldest of Jehan's sons, was asked by his father to lead the Grand Claude family delegation to Fort Anne to participate in the treaty proceedings. Joseph was the only son to ascribe a totemic designation to his name, and he dropped the "Grand Claude" surname in favour of "Le Grand" to distinguish himself from his brothers. To date, no analyses have been undertaken of the Mi'kmaw totemic marks that appear on the treaty of 1726, although it is probably safe to say that a totem was a weighty symbol of family status and cohesiveness. There were several copies of the peace treaty drafted, but only one copy has totemic markings on it and bears the signatures of Grand Claude's sons. The fact that the Grand Claudes did not sign the treaty until most others had signed suggests that they may have considered

themselves already at peace with the British by virtue of the 1722 treaty signed by their father. Chief Jean-Baptist Thoma also signed in 1726, however, so he may have been instrumental in getting the younger Grand Claudes to come to the treaty table. All copies of the treaty document, including the one with the totemic marks on it, were accorded the same date, 4 June 1726. British Colonial Office documents on microfilm (henceforth CO), 217/38, "Treaty of 1726."

27 This particular copy of the treaty accompanied a dispatch sent by Governor Lawrence Armstrong to London on 27 November 1726. LAC, CO 217/38, Copy of a treaty, with signature and marks, made at Annapolis Royal, 4 June 1726. The actual signatures and marks were probably placed on this document at a much later date than 4 June. Furthermore, one can compare this treaty document, with its distinctive totemic designations, with what appear to be earlier ones, despite all copies bearing the same date of 4 June. LAC, CO 217/217/4, ff. 99–103; 320–21.

28 Le Loutre's registers were lost or destroyed in 1755, so the record of births and deaths for Jehan's descendants between 1722 and 1755, when Le Loutre left the province, is incomplete.

29 Philippe Mius *dit* d'Anzy had two Mi'kmaw consorts in succession. Marie was the second of them.

30 Nova Scotia Archives and Records Management, Halifax (henceforth NSARM), RG 1, Registers of the Parish of St. Jean-Baptiste, Annapolis Royal, vol. 26, 141, "Marriage of Pierre Cellier, widower of Louise Innocente, and Françoise Myus, widow of the second time of the late René Grand Claude of La Have, 26 August 1735," presiding priest De St. Poncy de La Vernède, witnesses François Robichau (or Robichaud), Prudent Robichau, Domique Robichau, Jean-Baptiste Jeanson, and Françoise Bourgeois.

31 NSARM, RG 1, vol. 26a, 18, "Baptism of Denis Claude, born 2 February 1728 to Claude [Grand Claude] and Marie [Pierre], 7 February 1728, presiding priest René Charles de Breslay, witnesses St. Seine, surgeon major of Annapolis Royal, and Marie, widow of the late Jacques Tanacomtoch, Mi'kmaq of this river"; NSARM, RG 1, vol. 26a, 108, "Baptism of Charles Claude, born to Claude [Grand Claude] and Marie Madeleine [Pierre] in April 1732, baptized 4 January 1733 at Annapolis Royal, presiding priest St. Poncy de La Vernède, godparents Étienne Martin and Catherine Mikmak." Claude Grand Claude and Marie Madeleine Pierre also may have been the parents of Françoise Grand Claude, the wife of Samson Quoraret (Momcharret) who had a

daughter, Agathe, baptized at Annapolis Royal on 27 April 1734, as well as Anne Grand Claude who married Antoine Hebcobeau of Annapolis Royal and had a daughter Cecile in 1735. NSARM, RG 1, vol. 26a, 120, "Baptism of Agathe Quoraret [Momcharret], born 15 March 1734, daughter of Samson Quoraret [Momcharret] and Françoise Grand Claude, 27 April 1734, presiding priest de St. Poncy de La Vernède, witnesses Jean Lore and Madeleine Pelerin"; NSARM, vol. 26a, 152, "Baptism on 20 May 1736 of Cecile Hebcobeau, born December 1735, daughter of Antoine Hebcobeau and Anne Grand Claude, presiding priest de St. Poncy de La Vernède, godparents Pierre Charette [Momcharret] *dit* Boitou and Marie Pelerin."

32 The surname "Pierre" has been Anglicized to "Peters." In 2011 two brothers, Basil Peters and Henry Peters, tendered their views to the authors as to its origin. Basil held that the surname "Peters" arose in the seventeenth century when Captain Pierre Rossignol was trading with the Mi'kmaq along the Rossignol River, a contention echoed by his brother. Though there is no definite evidence that Rossignol, prior to his expulsion from Nova Scotia for illicit trading, had children by a Mi'kmaw woman, it certainly might have occurred and would have explained the presence by the 1680s of the "Pierre" surname at Port Royal. Interview with Basil Peters and Henry Peters, Millbrook, 11 June 2011; Mike Parker, *Guides of the North Woods: Hunting and Fishing Tales from Nova Scotia, 1860 to 1960* (Halifax: Nimbus, 1990), 96–7. Father Clarence-J. d'Entremont, however, believed that the name "Peters," like the name "Granger" among the Acadians, stemmed from an Englishman who came to live among the French. A third argument holds that the surname is a corruption of the French surname "Pitre." Notes on file written by Father Clarence-J. d'Entremont, Musée Acadien and Archives de Pubnico-Ouest, Yarmouth County. Claude Grand Claude and Marie Pierre's daughter Marie was married at Annapolis Royal. NSARM, RG 1, vol. 26a, 141, Registers of the Parish of St. Jean-Baptiste, Annapolis Royal, "Marriage at Annapolis Royal of Charles Perrisse, son of Guillaume Perrisse and Anne Eptemek, to Marie Grand Claude, daughter of Claude Grand Claude and Marie Pierre, 25 August 1735, presiding priest de St. Poncy de La Vernède, witnesses Jean Baptiste Jeanson and Dominque Robichaux." Guillaume Perrisse, Charles's father, was the son of Estienne "Ianneperis" (or Jean Perise). LAC, MG 18, F 16, *Recensement genal ... 1708*, 2.

33 Ian Lawrence, "The Mi'kmaw Gloade Family," Annapolis Heritage Society, *Newsletter* (Spring 2011), 3–4.

34 NSARM, RG 1, vol. 26, 260, Registers of the Parish of St. Jean-Baptiste, Annapolis Royal, "Marriage of Martin Grand Claude, son of Grand Claude and Marie Medechek (Medosset) to Marguerite Le Jeune, 17 years old, daughter of François Le Jeune and Marie Egighighes of La Have, presiding priest René Charles de Breslay, witnesses Prudent Robichaux, Pierre Golier, a Mikmak of this river, and Joseph Doucet, son of Claude Doucet." Marie Egighighes's father, Antoine "Ziziguesche" (or Egigihighes), was born in 1658, his son Claude was born in 1696 and Marie was born in 1699. Antoine Egighighes was not a La Have chief. This office later was assumed by "Claude, fils d'eouachinouitte," who in 1708 was still listed as an "Orphelin" of 22 years of age, and so not in any way related to the Egighighes family. This man, whose name is written "Claude Eouachinouit," was head chief of La Have in 1722. LAC, MG 18, F 18 (typescript), *Recensement genal...1708*, 5, 7; LAC, AC, F-135, CIIB, vol. 6, Ile Royale, Correspondence *générale,* doc. No. 77, *Recensement des Sauvages tam de l'isle Royalle...1722.*

35 Pierre Le Jeune came to La Have with Isaac de Razilly in 1632 and wed a Mi'kmaw woman. He and his wife had three children, Pierre *fils*, Martin, and Jeanne. Jeanne married François Joseph, who was either Mi'kmaq or a French *métis*, and in 1682 had a son, François Le Jeune, who later took his mother's surname. François married Marie Gisigash and the couple became the parents of Marguerite, later Martin Grand Claude's wife. Though Marie Gisigash's father, Antoine Gisigash, was not a chief in 1722, her brother, Claude Gisigash (also "Egighighes" or "Ziziguesche"), became a prominent figure at La Have. In April 1753 Claude, who styled himself "governor" of La Have, appeared before the British governor and council in Halifax to make a peace pact. D'Entremont, *Histoire du Cap-Sable*, 3.1120–4; Murdoch, *A History of Nova-Scotia*, 1.219.

36 NSARM, RG 1, vol. 26a, 140, "Baptism of Paul Grand Claude, son of Martin Grand Claude and Marguerite Le Jeune, 25 August 1735, presiding priest de St. Poncy de La Vernède, witnesses André Simon and Marguerite Doucet."

37 Paul, Martin Jr., and Nicholas Grand Claude are the ancestors of many of the Gloades living today in Queens, Shelburne, Lunenburg, Annapolis, and Colchester Counties.

38 François Grand Claude and his wife lived in the vicinity of Annapolis Royal, though after 1735, when they had their son François Grand Claude *fils* baptized, their names do not appear in the documentary record again.

NSARM, RG 1, vol. 26a, 136, "Baptism of François, son of François Grand Claude and Marie Cellier [*dit* Bouta], 2 June 1735, presiding priest de St. Poncy de La Vernède, witnesses Martin Grand Claude and Madelene Boytoux [Boitou or Bouta]." Marie Cellier was a daughter of Pierre *Momcharret dit* Cellier *dit* Bouta and a neice of Pierre Momcharret *dit* Cellier of Annapolis and Minas.

39 When Jehan Grand Claude first traded at La Have in the 1680s, Pierre Le Jeune *dit* Briard and his wife, Marie Thibideau, presided over community affairs in the coastal community. Pierre's sister Jeanne Le Jeune and her husband François Joseph had seven children, one of whom was François Le Jeune, François Grand Claude's wife, who was born about 1682.

40 Murdoch, *A History of Nova–Scotia*, 1.86, 94, 103, 113, 125, 165.

41 Perrot entertained a short-lived hope of obtaining a seigneury, starting at Port Rossignol and embracing La Have to the east. This aspiration, however, petered out in 1687 when Perrot was succeeded by Louis Alexandre des Friches de Meneval, who remained governor until 1690. Perrot, however, remained at Port Royal until 1690, when he had to flee to Minas during William Phips's invasion of Port Royal.

42 The French held that during King George's War no English would dry fish along the Atlantic coast for fear of being killed by Mi'kmaq. John Romeyn Broadhead, ed., *Documents relative to the colonial history of the state of New York*, Paris Documents, vol. 9 (Albany: Weed, Parsons, 1885), 1107. In the 1740s at least one English vessel, seeking water, was boarded at La Have and its crew killed.

43 LAC, AC, Serie CIIB, Correspondance générale, vol. 1, 385, "*Memoire sur des missions des sauvages Mikmaks et dans l'Acadie,*" n.d. (c.1739). After 1730 the French noticed population shifts in communities that they viewed as mustering grounds for Mi'kmaw warriors in the event of intercolonial conflict. The Mi'kmaq meanwhile wanted to have sacraments performed by Roman Catholic missionaries who annually visited the Atlantic coast because these clerics spoke Mi'kmaq, and were familiar with Mi'kmaw society and culture.

44 Chief Claude Egighighes was the brother of Claude Grand Claude's wife's mother, Marie Egighighes. Claude Egighighes's precedessor was "Claude Eosechinuoich," who was listed as chief of La Hève by Father Antoine Gaulin in 1722. LAC, AC, F-135, CIIB, vol. 6, Correspondance generale, No. *77, Recensement des Sauvages … fait que a M. Gaulin pretre Missionaire des Sauvages en 1722*. On 12 April 1753 Egighighes, styling himself

the "governor of La Have," appeared before the Halifax Council ready to sign a peace treaty with the British on the same terms as those made the preceding year with the Shubenacadie and eastern shore head chief, Major Jean Baptist Cope. Murdoch, *History of Nova-Scotia*, 1.219; Thomas Akins, "History of Halifax City," *Collections of the Nova Scotia Historical Society* (Halifax, 1895; repr. Halifax: Brook House, 2002), 40. Interestingly, Martin Grand Claude, by his marriage to Marguerite Le Jeune, was closely related to the Egighighes family. Ruth Holmes Whitehead, *The Old Man Told Us: Excerpts from Mi'kmaw History, 1500–1950* (Halifax: Nimbus, 1991), 129.

45 In 1742 Philippe Mius d'Azy's son François Mius emerged as head chief of Merliguèche and received a French commission as such. François, as had his father, maintained a trade depot on Second Peninsula near Merliguèche, and his family group had an encampment ground nearby. He had numerous sisters, many of whom married fur traders or Mi'kmaw chiefs. A reticulate web of marriage alliances with the Muis sisters at the core thus came to underlie trading relations in the southwestern part of the province. One sister, Françoise, who became the widow of René Grand Claude, later married Pierre Momcharret *dit* Cellier. Her sibling, Marie, married Chief Jean Baptist Thoma of Annapolis. Another sister, Madeleine, wed Jean Baptiste Guedry of Merliguèche, while Anne married Jean Baptiste Guedry's brother, Paul Guedry *dit* Labrador. Unlike Martin Grand Claude and Charles Egighighes, François Mius remained sceptical of the value of treating in any way with the British until persuaded to do so by Abbé Pierre Maillard late in 1761. Meanwhile Paul Guedry *dit* Labrador, who evidently did not want or never had the chance to reconcile with the British, fled for several years into the interior of Lunenburg County to avoid being deported by the British. Against this backdrop of allegiances and varying degrees of warmth or, conversely, hostility towards the British cause, Martin Grand Claude remained, at least overtly, consistent in his attachment to the terms of the 1726 peace treaty he had signed at Annapolis Royal. In 1760 his first cousin, Charles Grand Claude, received a government pass that enabled him to travel unmolested throughout the province. It was an important privilege accorded only to Mi'kmaq whom the British trusted, since Governor Charles Lawrence's 1756 scalp proclamation remained generally in effect until the last treaty was signed in 1761. Chief Jean Baptist Thoma, who also had a British passport, assumed a high profile within the British establishment when clergy belonging to the Church of England tried their best to

win him to Anglicanism. By contrast, Martin Grand Claude remained conspicuously absent from both the British religious and political forums. François Mius, Paul Labrador, and Jean Baptist Thoma are the subjects of biographical treatment in chapters 3, 5, and 7 of this volume.

François Mius and Paul Guedry *dit* Labrador had compelling reasons for opposing the British during King George's War and the succeeding Seven Years' War. Both were devout Catholics who heeded Le Loutre's instructions during the 1740s and early 1750s to resist British expansion. In 1748, moreover, the British established a trade blockade to prevent furs from Atlantic coastal communities travelling to East Pubnico or across the Bay of Fundy. The following year a party from Halifax under orders from Governor Edward Cornwallis razed François Mius's trading post and the Mi'kmaw village of Chichimichecady (located on what is now Second Peninsula, Lunenburg County), of which Mius was chief, and drove him and his band to seek refuge on the upper La Have River, from where he launched raids on the Lunenburg settlers. Paul Guedry *dit* Labrador, a trader who had been in Cape Breton in the early 1750s, returned in 1754 to find his trading and fishing station at Merliguèche confiscated by the British, after which he and his two youngest *métis* sons, to avoid deportation by the British, took up residence at Mushamush, near modern-day Blockhouse in Lunenburg County. From there the Labradors joined François Mius and his sons in attacking settlers in the vicinity of Lunenburg. Not surprisingly, Germanic and Huguenot settlers who built houses along the coast at Second Peninsula constructed very small windows on the side of their dwellings facing the forest, to enable shots to be fired at Mi'kmaw attackers while providing a degree of protection against Mi'kmaw fire.

46 Some members of the Le Jeune family fled to l'Indienne (now Lingan) on the Bras d'Or Lake, where persons bearing the Le Jeune surname still reside. Le Jeunes may also be found in the Bathurst region of northeastern New Brunswick. See NSARM, Registers of Father Charles-François Bailly on microfilm, Copy of old register conserved at Caraquet, New Brunswick, *Registre des acts de baptême, mariages, et sepultures faits en la nouvelle ecosse ou acadie commence le vingt unieme jour de juillet de l'annee mil sept cent soixante huit, par Mons. Charles-François Bailly, pretre missionaire des sauvages et acadiens, sujets de sa majeste britanique, 1768–1773*, entry for 7 February 1769 at L'Indienne. In this community Bailly met with Chystophie, Joseph, and Germain Le

Jeune *dit* Briard, Boniface Benoist (Benoit), Charles Roy, and members of the LeSonde and Boucher families, several of whom had Mi'kmaw wives.

47 NSARM, RG 1, vol. 165, doc. 54, "Submissions of Mi'kmaw leaders and allocation of passes to eight Mi'kmaw persons," 28 April 1760. Allocation of passports was necessary since it was not until the end of 1761 that the British considered that sufficient treaties had been signed with the Mi'kmaq to warrant repeal of the scalp bounty levied on "enemy Indians" by Governor Charles Lawrence in 1756.

48 In 1765 Perkins acquired a government licence to trade in furs and fish with the Mi'kmaq along the Rossignol River. NSARM, RG 1, vol. 165, doc. 40, "License to S. Perkins to enter the Native trade," 24 April 1765.

49 Chiefs Bernard Argomartin and Philip Bernard are discussed in chapters 6 and 7 of this volume.

50 Owing to a lack of Roman Catholic clergy for six years following Maillard's death, a gap occurs from the early to late 1760s in the Grand Claude family's genealogical record. Maillard's registers were lost around the time of his death in 1762, and after 1763 the British effectively banned Roman Catholicism from Nova Scotia until 1768. Not until Abbé Charles-François Bailly came to Nova Scotia was any new information recorded concerning Martin Grand Claude and Marguerite Le Jeune's offspring.

51 This man would have been Martin Grand Claude and Marguerite Le Jeune's son, since, despite some of the Claudes' tendency to longevity, the senior Martin Grand Claude in 1769 would have been seventy-six years old.

52 NSARM, Copy of old register conserved at Caraquet, New Brunswick, 1768–73, 1786–96, on microfilm. *Registre des actes de baptême, marriages, et sepultures faits en la nouvelle ecosse ou acadie*, entry of 21 June 1769 at Achegetkouk (Chezzetcook), east of Halifax, "Baptism of René, six years of age, son of Paul Grand Claude and Marie Anne Nebenne, godparents René Martin and Marie Joseph Cope." Marie Anne Nebenne was likely a granddaughter of the "Joseph Neben" whom Father Pierre La Chasse in 1708 recorded as living at La Have. Ibid., "Baptism of Joseph, four years of age, son of Paul Grand Claude and Anne Marie Nebenne, godparents Pierre Ketkimouesche and Magdalene"; "Baptism of Joseph Claude, son of Martin Grand Claude [Jr.] and Anne Marie, godparents Joseph Laureuse [possibly Laurent or Lauverste] and Marie Joseph"; "Baptism of Anne, daughter of Martin Grand Claude and Anne Marie, godparents Pierre-Paul Alexis and Marguerite Usses." Three other couples brought children the same day to

be baptized were Jacques Mius and Brigette Alexis, Paul Pictou and Marie Joachim, and Pierre Paul Alexis and Helen Mius. Jacques Mius stood as the witness at the wedding of Bartholomew Momcharret and his spouse, who, like Pictou's wife, was also called Marie Joachim.

53 NSARM, RG 20, Ser. A, microfilm reel 15,686 – Geremy (Jeremy), Solomon, "Memorial of Solomon Geremy, a Mi'kmaq of the La Have tribe,' 1784. A memo inscribed on this document claims that the Provincial Secretary, Richard Bulkeley, had overseen the granting of Solomon Jeremy, Joseph Claude and others of their group a licence of occupation to land on the upper La Have. The Mi'kmaq's land, however, lacked any government protection against outside trespass, and was soon overrun by settlers.

54 The "Grand Claude" surname refers to those who are descendants of Grand Claude.Members of the eastern Algonquian language family used to designate persons of special importance and status as "Gji" or "Kitche." Use of the surname "Grand Claude," however, was inconsistent in the government documentary record over time and apparently ended around 1800.

55 NSARM, RG 1, vol. 430, doc. 26 ½, "Memorial of John Christopher Rudolf of Lunenburg to Sir John Wentworth on behalf of Solomon Jeremiah (*sic*, Jeremy), Michael Jeremiah, Joseph Clod (*sic*, Claude), Peter Martin and sundry others…on the La Have River who find hunting of late much decreased by reason of the settlements made and are desirous of cultivating Lands and making Farms to support themselves," 1 May 1793. A notation later penned on this document stated that the Mi'kmaq's grant had been approved by Surveyor General Charles Morris who issued a warrant of survey to 500 acres near New Germany Lake. This site likely included the "knoll camp" near Bridgewater, where the road from Bridgewater to New Germany crosses the La Have River. An island there was used anciently by the Mi'kmaq as a salmon spearing locale. John S. Erskine, *Micmac Notes*, Halifax: Nova Scotia Museum, 1959, 3.

56 Simeon Perkins, *The Diary of Simeon Perkins1766–1780*, ed. with introduction and notes by Harold A. Innis (Toronto: Champlain Society, 1947), 1.297.

57 A comprehensive discussion of settler incursions on Mi'kmaq fur-trapping returns at this time may be found in Julian Gwyn, "The Mi'kmaq, Poor Settlers, and the Nova Scotia Fur Trade, 1783–1853," *Journal of the Canadian Historical Association* 14, no. 1 (2003): 65–91.

58 George Henry Monk was also distantly related by marriage to Sir John Wentworth.

59 This group was composed of Peter Martin, Peter Knockwood, Solomon Jeremy, Joseph Claude, Thomas Aslin, Gabriel Jeremy, and Philip Bernard along with several wives and children. Born in 1765, Joseph Claude, Paul Grand Claude's son, would have been thirty-one years old. LAC, MG 23, GII-19, Monk Papers, George Henry Monk Letter Book, 1211–17, entry for 18 November 1796, "Clothing, provisions, utensils and ammunition" supplied Peter Martin, Salias (Solomon) Jeremy, Joseph Clod (Claude), Peter Noge, Thos. Aslin, Galiel (*sic*, Gabriel) Jeremy, and Philip Pernam and 5 wives and 14 children." The cost of these supplies came to £62.3.6.

60 Ibid., 1216, 1220, 1223, Entry for 2 July 1797, for clothing, provisions, and ammunition supplies to "old Martin Claude," his wife and nine in family amounting to £17.2.6.

61 "Geram Cloud" (Jeremy Claude), who may have been Paul's son, and "Jas. Paul" from La Have accompanied Paul Grand Claude from La Have. NSARM, vol. 430, doc. 147½, "To Harthorn and Tremain from His Excellency Sir John Wentworth, Requisition received by G.H. Monk for articles furnished Paul Martyn Glode and others in 1807 and 1808"; NSARM, RG 1, vol. 430, doc. 6, "Distribution list entry prepared by Monk for Paul Martyn Grove and another Indian," 12 January 1808; LAC, MG 23 GII-19, vol. 4 (Papers, Letterbooks and Account books of George Henry Monk), 1216. Joseph Claude also used to come in to have his gun repaired. NSARM, RG 1, vol. 430, doc. 138, "Henry Watkey's requisition demanding payment for repairing guns for Joe Glued [*sic*, Claude] and others," 21 January1803

62 These two Josephs appear quite often in documents, though the two other persons, René and Anne Grand Claude, who underwent baptism by Bailly do not appear in the documentary record after 1769.

63 LAC, MG 23 GII-19, vol. 4, 1248, "To the Government for Sundries Supplied Twenty-Two Cape Sable Indians in March of 1798 by Order of His Excellency Sir John Wentworth," 23 March 1798. The cost to the government of these supplies was £13.1.2. When the government did not reimburse Walker right away he wrote Halifax again, asking for his money. Ibid., 256, "Thomas Walker at Annapolis to His Excellency Sir John Wentworth," 4 June 1798. Walker, who seemed to know the group relatively well, furnished four bushels of corn, ten bushels of potatoes, a barrel of flour, six gallons of molasses, two barrels of herring, and six wood axes and six hoes. To avoid the bureaucratic tangles and delays of sending a requisition through Monk's office, Walker wrote directly to Governor Sir John Wentworth and stressed that he had given the Mi'kmaq sufficient supplies to enable them to get

back to Cape Sable. He listed the Mi'kmaw applicants as "Paul Williams, Josiah [Joseph] Luxy [Alexis], Joseph Glode, Andrew Glode and Peter Aleomatimck [Argomartin]," along with their wives and children. Peter Aleomatimck or Algomartin, who was hamstrung by the Cape Sable band for his ill treatment and reputed murder of several women, nevertheless died a married man in Kings County around 1800. NSARM, RG 1, doc. 77, "Names of Indians belonging to Kings County, 1800 & 1801." Bartholomew Momcharret, aged sixty-four, was leader of this group.

64 Paul Williams would remain in the Barrington area until after 1842, when he requested that Joseph Howe, then provincial Indian commissioner, reserve seven hundred acres for his band on Great Pubnico Lake.

65 The severity of the forest fires about the upper La Have River had left so little viable habitat that the local big game population could not restore itself for a few years. By moving southwest, the Grand Claudes avoided the smallpox epidemic that ravaged Mi'kmaw communities in Halifax County and Lunenburg County. All the descendents of Jehan Grand Claude who assembled in 1801 were also descendents of Martin Grand Claude Sr. (1693–c.1770) and Marguerite Le Jeune of La Have. By this time, however, some of the youths belonging to this group traced their kin links to the family partriarch Jehan back three or four generations.

66 The Great Storm of 1798 laid great swathes of forest completely flat from Jeddore to Barrington and inland as far as Windsor. The fallen trees and hot summer weather later gave rise to forest fires so that large ungulates, their numbers already reduced by settlers' overhunting, became extremely scarce, as were beaver and other valuable fur bearers. According to Titus Smith, who conducted a survey across the southwestern part of the province in 1801 and 1802, these conditions forced many Mi'kmaq to move southward or even temporarily leave Nova Scotia for New Brunswick or Maine. During these harsh years, some Mi'kmaw grew to resent settler intrusions, at least until the incomers turned from consuming vast quantities of moosemeat to eating farm-raised beef, at which time the moose population gradually began to recover. NSARM, RG 1, vol. 380b, microfilm reel 15,441, Titus Smith Jr., *Sketches of the Eastern and Northern Parts of the Province in the years 1801 and 1802, with general observations thereon …*, 3rd ed. (Halifax, 1851), 131–2. An original published copy of this rare volume exists in NSARM, RG 1, vol. 380.

67 NSARM, RG 1, vol 430, doc. 96, "Census of Mi'kmaq of Lunenburg County," n.d (1801).

68 The John Williams mentioned in 1801 was probably a brother of Paul Williams. Paul and his wife Catherine Luxy had a son John who was not born until 1819, so he could not have been the person named on the census. John became a well-known guide who moved east to Halifax County, where at the age of fifty-five on 14 April 1874 he married his second wife, Adelaide Thomas, daughter of Michael and Mary Thomas. (Michael was a descendant of Chief Jean Baptist Thoma of Annapolis.) NSARM, Historical Vital Statistics, Halifax County Marriages, Registration Year 1874, book 1816, p. 58, no. 126. The younger John was still guiding in the 1880s. Ruth Holmes Whitehead, *The Old Man Told Us*, 255, 282.

69 This Molti Pictou would have been born in the 1780s.

70 NSARM, RG 1, vol. 430, no. 57, "An Account of Indians that Belong to Queens County," by William Barss (1801). This census was compiled in response to a government circular sent out on 23 January 1801. Barss spelled the Claude surname "Groad" while the present author retains the spelling "Claude." Men living with the Liverpool group in 1801 who were not Claudes were Paul Williams, John Williams, Molti Pictou, Lewey Pictou, Joseph Pictou, Paul Pictou, Newel, Peter Beatle (Peters), and Andrew Beatle. Barss also noted that Joseph Atley (André or Andrew) recently had died, leaving four children. Not all Claudes were present at the Liverpool reunion in 1801, however. Some, such as the elderly Paul Grand Claude, chose to stay at La Have, though their movements are difficult to trace since church records pertaining to the Roman Catholic poplation of Lunenburg and Queens County are scarce during early 1800s. The first Roman Catholic missionary after Abbé Bailly to serve among these Mi'kmaq was Abbé Jean-Mandé Sigogne, who arrived at Cape Sable in 1799 and established his headquarters in Clare Township, Digby County. Sigogone knew only a few of the Claudes personally, though he met them as congregants on St. Anne's Day and at other sacred events. Barss, who had asked Sigogne for assistance in compiling his 1801 census, referred to the abbé as the "Priest belonging to Sicabo" (*sic*, the Sissabo River region of Digby County). Ibid.

71 NSARM, Vol. 430, doc. 3 ½, Report of Committee, 1807. This committee raised fears concerning larger-than-usual gatherings of Mi'kmaq along the Shelburne coast, though some of those groups may have contained families pressing southward from the La Have region.

72 This site has yielded a wealth of artefacts dating from the French era to the late eighteenth century, including ochre-coloured tubular glass trade beards. Stone items – points, gouges, adzes, and axes – date back to

Archaic times, three thousand years ago. Henry Sorette of Bridgewater, NS, found an Archaic ceremonial ground slate point or bayonet when excavations were being made for a canal at Milton. The author is indebted to historian Brian Purdy, a member of the Acadia First Nation, who provided the information about the trade beads found at this site. Purdy's residence stands on a parcel of land once occupied by Perkins's trading post.

73 Joseph Martin Claude married Sarah Phillips, a daughter of Chief Philip Bernard of St. Margaret's Bay, and raised a large family at Caledonia. He also fished at Lequille during the spring and fall. Like other Mi'kmaq in the region, in the early 1800s he relied mainly on weir fishing, since game was so scarce.

74 To trace kin connections back to Paul Grand Claude, to Martin Grand Claude, or to one of these men's siblings is difficult given the paucity of documentary information. Presumably the cohort that camped near Liverpool in 1801 was formed of a mix of siblings and first cousins, and those cousins, as among the Mi'kmaq generally, were treated as siblings. Only rarely did an official correspondence or a birth, marriage, or burial record provide enough information to allow one to be more specific.

75 Upton, *Micmacs and Colonists*, 186. The reserve of 1,150 acres lies on the Wildcat River, west of Molega Lake and north of Ponhook Lake in Queens County.

76 Ibid., 113–16.

77 Mather B. Desbrisay, *History of the County of Lunenburg*, 2nd ed. (Toronto: James Bowes and Sons, 1895), 348, "To His Excelencye's (*sic*, Excellency's) Pleasure: Petition of Joseph Soulnow (Jeremy)," New Germany, 11 November 1829. Sulnouw asked, "what shall I do for the land that my Grate Granfather first oned [*sic*, owned] before anybody was in Nova Scotia [?]" After he died it was "given to my Granfather, from him to my father, then to myself and my brother, and, it is gave away, and now, what shall I do? … [It] was given me from our Governer (*sic*, Governor) long ago, and lyd out: and the Governer did sine my plan and me luse it, but we had cleared on it and planted appel trees and fenced a garden, had a sellar (*sic*, cellar), and now me want to farm and nother man don't let me." The Soulnows later lived at Church Hill, near New Germany Lake, but they received no compensation for the loss of their land. Such experiences did not sit well with elderly Mi'kmaq who actually may have had considerable experience planting, since they learned agricultural techniques from their Acadians neighbours prior to the mid-1750s. But the high risk of losing what land they had to settler avarice blighted any aspirations most Mi'kmaw had to farm. Charles Morris, the

surveyor general who in 1820 reported on the reserves laid out in Nova Scotia, was the son of the man who had surveyed the La Have reserve in 1794 but in his account made no mention of the land grant at La Have. Similarly, Joseph Howe, when he was Indian commissioner in 1842, omitted any reference to the La Have tract in his discussion of Mi'kmaw lands in the province. NSARM, Miscellaneous "I" Indian Land Documents, extracted from Crown Land Records, Charles Morris III, "Report of the Reservations of Lands for the Indians by the Surveyor General on the 7th May 1820"; NSARM, RG 1, vol. 430, doc. 191, Joseph Howe's "Report on Indian Affairs," 25 January 1843, 5. Joseph Howe considered the St. Margaret's Bay tract given to Philip Bernard to have been completedly sold, when it is likely that only a part of the parcel was transferred by purchase.

78 He is not on Barss's census of Queens County Mi'kmaq, nor was he listed on the Lunenburg County census of the same year. NSARM, RG 1, vol. 430, no. 57, "An account of Indians that belongs to Queens County" by William Barss (1801); NSARM, RG 1, vol 430, doc. 96, "Census of the Mi'kmaq of Lunenburg County" (1801). He was still alive, however, as his name appears on Indian Commissioner George Henry Monk's requisition lists from 1801 to 1808.

79 NSARM, Miscellaneous Indian documents on microfilm, taken from Nova Scotian Crown Lands Records, Document Package 25, Pennel [Reserve No. 19] Walabeck Lake (or Wallabeck Lake), Lunenburg County, "To Major General John Gaspard Le Marchant, Lieutenant Governor of Nova Scotia, Petition of Joe Pennaul of Gold River," circa 1855.

80 Chief Joseph Martin Claude, owing to his elevated status, also would have acted as a religious leader when a priest could not be present. As such he would have organized prayer sessions and presided over openings of council meetings. Most of the Claudes, if not all, regarded him as a sibling or a cousin, and owing to the generationally organized kinship system prevailing among the Mi'kmaq, his prominence would have affected them all personally.

81 Clara Dennis, *More about Nova Scotia, My Own, My Native Land* (Toronto: Ryerson, 1939), 409.

82 Ibid., 124. This child was probably a nephew of Chief Joseph Claude. His father was reputed to have been a man named Newel Glode who lived around Caledonia. An oral tradition passed down in the Foster family holds that Claude Le Jeune, possibly from La Hève, and his wife Geneviève from Pisiquid had a son, Cobliel Claude (Le Jeune) about 1749. This Cobliel later lived at Glode's

Island in Queens County and had one son, Newell, who allegedly was the father of Allan Foster. Newel is supposed to have died around 1780, though there is no evidence to support this contention. No documentary evidence could be found to support or disprove this geneology. Allan's mother was probably non-Mi'kmaq. On 24 May 1799, Allan married Lydia Morreau (or Munroe) and had six children: Mary Elizabeth, William, Samuel, Henry, James, and Lydia Marie. Henry Foster (1841–29 August 1894) was the father of Clara May Foster Anthony, who became interested in her family history and its connections with the Mi'kmaq. She related that Allan's father Newel lived at Glode's Falls on the lower Medway River. Allan Foster died in 1894. If one abides by the documentary record alone, there are few persons recorded in it who could fit the description of Allan's father. A man named Noel Cobliel (possibly surnamed "Glode") was interred at age ninety at Greenfield on 16 April 1872, and thus born in 1782; he would have been seventeen at the time of Allan's birth, though he apparently maintained no connection with Allan Foster. Registers of St. Gregory's Parish, Liverpool. Also see "Allan Foster" on ancestry.com. Yet the Fosters, who were Baptists, and other Glodes, who were Roman Cathoics, remained on friendly terms after Allan's birth. For instance, the Canadian federal census of 1891 shows a Mary Glode living near forty-three-year-old Milton Foster, a carriage builder living in Milton.

83 There are documents pertaining to John Mehlman Jr. in the Nova Scotia Archives and Records Management in Halifax. NSARM, RG 20, Series A – Mehlman, John and Others. Documents relating to John Mehlman Jr. Mehlman at the time was thirty-five and Mi'kmaq and had four children. He wrote his signature "Fosorunr Masimaun." The story that Charles Glode cohabited in his later years with a Mehlman woman who was possibly John Mehlman's daughter still circulates within the Milford community of Annapolis County.

84 Francis Glode and Madeline Knockwood were the parents of James Glode, better known as "Jim Glode" (1831–1936), who became a famous guide.

85 Joseph Martin Glode Jr. and Mary Ann Stephens's wedding was performed "in the presence of many Indians." Registers of the Parish of St. Jerome, Caledonia, "Marriage of Joseph Claude, son of Joseph Claude of Annapolis Royal and Sarah Phillips, and Mary Ann Stephens, daughter of Joseph Stephens and Hannah Simons, 16 June 1834."

86 NSARM, Historical Vital Statistics, Digby County Deaths, Registration Year 1910, "Death of Abram [*sic*, Abraham] Glode, of chronic bronchitis at age ninety-six, 8 August 1910." While the Canadian federal census records list 1821 as Abraham Gldoe Sr.'s birthdate, his death certificate states he was born in 1814. The latter date is more accurate, as Abraham and his first wife, Mary Ann Meuse, had a son Alex at Bear River in 1832. Late-nineteenth-century Canadian census records are often erroneous on the matter of Mi'kmaw birthdates.

87 Debra Gloade, a descendant of Matthew Glode, shared this information with the author and her assistant, Carrie Gloade, at Yarmouth in the summer of 2012. Census records hold that Matthew was born in 1830, though his death certificate states he was born at five years earlier.

88 Dalhousie Archives, Raddall Papers, "Caledonia, Queens County," MS 2.202 Q.7.F. See particularly the testimony of George Parker, born in 1863, and Henry A. Waterman to Raddall, 25 August 25 1945. Parker held that while settlers in the 1820s had encountered Chief Joseph Glode in the Caledonia region, this locale was not as heavily populated as points further east, such as Molega and Ponhook on the lower Medway. Caledonia served primarily as a rendezvouz site where Mi'kmaq met for councils and feasts.

89 James F. More, *The History of Queens County, N.S.* (Belleville, ON: Mika Studio, 1972 [1873]), 13.

90 St. Gregory's Chapel in Liverpool was built in 1829. Shortly thereafter it became a satellite mission of the newly established Parish of St. Jerome in West Caledonia, and remained subordinate to St. Jerome's parish until 1941. Though visited in its early years by the Mi'kmaq, the Caledonia mission did not have a proper church edifice until 1836, when St. Jerome's Roman Catholic Church was built in West Caledonia. Before his death in the 1840s Chief Joseph Martin Claude was recognized as the district chief of Queens County by Roman Catholic clergy at both Liverpool and Caledonia

91 NSARM, RG 1, vol. SA6, 30, Registers of Ste. Anne du Ruisseau, Yarmouth County, "Marriage of François-Joseph Claude to Magdaleine Alexis, 12 July 1832. Presiding priest Jean Baptiste Morin; witnesses Joseph-Marie [cousin of the groom], Athanase Surrette, Sylvain Surrette, and Jacques Alexis, brother of the bride." Magdaleine Alexis died in 1833.

92 NSARM, RG 1, vol. SA1, p. 92, Registers of Ste. Anne du Ruisseau, Yarmouth County, "Baptism of Paul Claude, son of Martin Claude and Geneviève à Louis, 31 March 1807, presiding abbé Jean-Mande Sigogne, godparents J.B. Alexis and Bridgette Alexis." Many years later he appears on the 1871 Canadian federal census as a seventy-year-old widower living in the Bristol District of

Caledonia, Queens County (though he was born in 1805, not in 1801).

93 NSARM, RG 1, vol. 431, no. 16, "Malti Gloade to Sir Colin Campbell," 17 November 1835. The document was probably drafted by James Barss, the MP at Liverpool, who along with James Gordon, MP, signed the petition.

94 NSARM, RG 1, vol. 431, doc. 23 (included with a petition from Martel Sappier from Pictou), "Petition for blankets from Malti Glode, Abraham Glode, Alex Davis, Mulloy [Malti] Jeremy, John Meuse, Francis Labrador, Stephen Knockwood, Abraham Peter, Francis Glode, Paul Martin, James Glode Jr., Peter Bobbiei, and James Toney," 29 January 1836.

95 More, *History of Queens County*, 134. The nature of the occasion suggests it may have been held for the installation of a new chief.

96 NSARM, RG 1, vol. 431, doc. 31, "Petition of Malti Glode, Joe Jeremy and others," 1837.

97 The oldest house in Annapolis, the de Gannes-Cosby House, throughout the mid-nineteenth century was owned by the Henkel and related Tobias families.

98 NSARM, RG 10, series A – Charles Glode and others, "Abbé Sigogne to Ritchie," December 6, 1822; NSARM, Abbé Sigogne Papers, "Judge Haliburton to Abbé Sigogne," 10 March 1827. MICRO: Biography, Sigogne, Abbé, Jean-Mandé, microfilm reel 11,002.

99 On 9 March 1827, Lieutenant Governor James Kempt claimed that each M'ikmaw family "shall have a separate portion of land" and "an ax, a hoe and a few Seeds." Nova Scotia House of Assembly, *Journals and Proceedings*, 1827, 74–5.

100 Frank G. Speck, *Beothuk and Micmac*, ed. F.W. Hodge (New York: Museum of the American Indian/Heye Foundation, 1922), 101. To get meat for food and maintain a trapline to obtain furs for trade, Charles and Jack originally shared a hunting territory. When anthropologist Frank Goldsmith Speck toured Annapolis and Queens Counties in the summer of 1912, he found that members of the Glode family from Lequille could pinpoint exactly where Jack's hunting territory had been located, "at the upper end of Liverpool lakes" around present-day Milford. One of Jack's sons, Peter, later claimed the area around Kejimkujik Lake as his hunting ground, while another, James, hunted towards Maitland. Francis later joined forces with Jack's son Peter to begin planting as well as hunting and trapping near Kejimkujik Lake. During the early nineteenth century Charles and Jack thus followed a traditional system of land allocation and management that had existed in the region for generations.

101 NSARM, RG 20, series A – Glode and Other Indians, "Petition of Charles Glode and others," 12 March 1823. At the time Charles Glode was recorded as having a wife and two children, while Jack lived alone with a wife. Francis Glode had a wife (Madeline Knockwood) and one daughter, while Malti Paul had a wife and one son. As mentioned above, Charles and Jack were brothers living near Lequille, while Francis – likely another brother – lived at Kejimkujik Lake. Francis's son Jim Glode, the famous late-nineteenth-century Bear River guide born in 1831, stated in 1929 to Clara Dennis that his father Francis Glode had hailed from Kejimkujik. NSARM, MG 1, vol. 2867, no. 6, Clara Dennis Archives, Notebook, "Interview with Jim Glode," 1929. Jim Glode also informed Dennis that his grandfather was Joseph Glode, undoubtedly the man who met the first settlers at Caledonia. Charles Glode was the only member of the Glode family that Abbé Sigogne identified with the Annapolis Royal area, though Jack Glode also would have been living at Lequille at the time. All the other Glodes were listed by Sigogne as living in the vicinity of Liverpool (at Milton and Mill Village in Queens County). St. Mary's Bay, Catalogue of Families [of] St. Mary's Bay Roman Catholic Parish, Clare, Digby County, Nova Scotia, 1818–29, compiled by Abbé Jean-Mande Sigogne. There is a typescript of this list, transcribed and edited by Leonard H. Smith, in the Musée Acadien in West Pubnico.

102 Archives of the Archdiocese of Halifax (AAH), Edmund Burke Papers, no. 39, "Thomas C. Haliburton to Sigogne," 10 March 1827.

103 This stream today is called Spurr's Meadow Brook, and the larger water bodies associated with it are Pitt's Lake and Sandy Bottom Lake. Sandy Bottom Lake lies at the apex of the Medway-Mersey river system. It was averred that a mix-up might have occurred when naming Sandy Bottom Lake, which lacks any sand whatsoever and may originally have been called Liverpool Head Lake, a name that captures its identity as the true watershed. The Mersey River, before the establishment of the Bowater Mersey Pulp and Paper Company in the 1920s, was called the Liverpool River, and before that the Rossignol River. What is known today as Sandy Bottom Lake, which extends along the Virginia Road towards Bear River, lies further up the watershed than another body of water that is presently known as Liverpool Head Lake. Both lakes, by a series of streams and portages, empty into Geier Lake, Boot Lake, and Fisher Lake, which in turn feed the Medway and Mersey river systems running towards the Atlantic coast.

104 NSARM, Miscellaneous "I" Indian Land Documents, on microfilm, reel 14,011, Package 10, "Plan of Reserve No. 2 showing five lots of land laid out for Indians, containing in all 1,000 acres situated on New Liverpool Road, Annapolis County." Charles Glode's 200-acre parcel lay on the east side of the road and flanked Jaspar Williams's lot, while Peter Paul's parcel, containing 189 acres and also on the east side of the road, lay along the lower boundary of Jasper Williams's lot. Jack Glode's 183-acre tract meanwhile shared a common boundary on the south with Peter Paul's lot. Francis Glode's rectangular 200-acre lot was situated on the west side of the Liverpool-Annapolis Road. Though roughly the same shape and dimensions as the others, it lay perpendicular to those on the other side of the road. Of the three Mi'kmaw properties surveyed on the northeast side of the road, Charles Glode's tract was the only one that fell in Clements Township. His property was flanked on its eastern boundary by woods and on its western boundary by Jasper Williams's wooded property and so stood alone from the others. Jaspar Williams, who dabbled in land speculation, did not improve his lot, and after 1835 none of the Mi'kmaq other than Charles Glode farmed their properties.

105 NSARM, RG 20, Ser. A (NS Department of Lands and Forests, Land grant registration books on microfilm), microfilm reel 15,761, "Glode, Charles & Other Indians, Petitions, warrants, surveyor's report and draft, and recommendations regarding Charles Glode and other Mi'kmaq, 1823–1840."

106 In the 1820s only two Mi'kmaw family heads named "Williams" visited Queens and Annapolis Counties, Paul Williams and his son John. Paul Williams lived most of the time at Great Pubnico Lake, in Yarmouth County, where in 1842 Joseph Howe had arranged for seven hundred acres to be set off for Williams's band, though Howe later forgot to confirm the tract as a reserve. By 1855 Paul's son John Williams had left southwestern Nova Scotia and lived at Shubenacadie. His first wife was Madeleine Thomas, a daughter of Louis Thomas and Mary-Antoinette Morris. (Adelaide Thomas, John's second wife whom he married in 1874, was a relative of his first wife.) John died at Shubenacadie around 1893. The man named Jaspar Williams whose property in the 1820s was surrounded by parcels belonging to the Glode settlement was not Mi'kmaq; he and his wife Sarah were settlers who lived at Milford. By 1820 they had already been involved in a number of land transactions. As early as 5 April 1804 Jaspar Williams's name appears on a land transaction made between "John Robinson Jr., yeoman, and Susannah his wife, and

Jasper Williams, yeoman, and Sarah his wife on the first part, and Samuel Vetch Bayard Esquire on the second part," by which Lot No. 53 in the Second Division of Annapolis Township was sold by Robinson and Williams to Bayard for £269. Annapolis County Deeds, book 13 (1804), 125. (Jaspar Williams was illiterate, since he signed this transaction with an "x.")

107 NSARM, MICRO: Biography, Sigogne, Abbé, Jean-Mandé, microfilm reel 11,002, Abbé Sigogne Papers, "Judge Haliburton to Abbé Sigogne," 10 March 1827.

108 Despite the fact that he did not read it, James Andrew Meuse was still acknowledged as the originator of the petition. *Journal and Proceedings* of the Nova Scotia House of Assembly, 1828, 208, "Petition of Andrew alias James Meuse, acting chief of the Indians, presented by leave of the House by Charles Glower [*sic*, Glode], one of the Chiefs of the Tribe." As a result of Glode's appeal to the House, the Assembly passed a law allowing local magistrates discretion in banning such sales. It remains doubtful, however, whether many magistrates used their discretionary powers and enforced the law, since liquor sales continued.

109 NSARM, MG 1, vol. 979, folder VIII, no. 14, "Sigogne to Peleg Wiswal," 20 June 1828.

110 *Acadian Recorder*, 16 February 1828, 2, col. 3.

111 Haliburton was a friend of both Abbé Jean-Mandé Sigogne and Joseph Howe. He also belonged to an amateur literary association known as "The Club" that contributed articles to Joseph Howe's newspaper the *Novascotian* between 1828 and 1831. Fred Cogswell, "Haliburton, Thomas Chandler," *Dictionary of Canadian Biography* (hereafter *DCB*) online, vol. 9 (1861–70) (Toronto: University of Toronto/Université Laval, 2003), http://www.biographi.ca/en/bio/haliburton_thomas_chandler_9E.html. For early nineteenth-century perspectives on Glode, see Nova Scotia House of Assembly, *Journals and Proceedings,* 1828, 208. In this source, however, Glode is mistakenly referred to as "Charles Glower." NSARM, MG 1, vol. 979, no. 11, "William Bowman to Peleg Wiswal," 20 January 1829; NSARM, MG 15, package 3, no. 89; Nova Scotia, *Acts*, 1829.

112 *Acadian Recorder*, 16 February 1828; *Novascotian or Colonial Herald*, 13 August 1830.

113 NSARM, MG 1, vol. 979 (Edmund Burke Papers), folder VIII, 8, no. 14, "Bowman to Wiswal," 20 January 1829.

114 Charles Glode was not the only Mi'kmaq in Annapolis and Queens Counties who knew how to farm. Paul Williams and his son John as well as Charles's nephew Francis Glode of Kejimkujik were all competent farmers. Their farming knowledge may have stemmed from

relationships that existed prior to 1900 between the Grand Claudes, Acadians, and others at La Have.

115 NSARM, MG 15, unnumbered docs, "Edward W. Cutler to Sir Rupert George," 20 March 1841.

116 L.F.S. Upton, "Glode, Charles," *DCB* online, vol. 8 (1851–60).

117 Stephen Labrador from Jordan River and James Lewey (Lewis) also sought to join this settlement.

118 NSARM, vol. 432, doc. 17, "Charles Glode, Chief of the Micmac Indians in the Western Part of the Province, along the Liverpool to Annapolis Road, for himself and John Glode, Molti Paul, John Jeremy, Louis Luxey and George Peter," 1835. Charles also requested five pounds in order to build a twenty-by-sixteen-foot house for his family.

119 LAC, CO/178/91. Sigogne elicited these numbers from Charles Glode in response to a circular from the Colonial Office requesting information on the numbers and condition of the Mi'kmaq sent on 29 October 1835. Joseph Howe had a copy made of Sigogne's note regarding Charles's population figures. NSARM, RG 1, vol. 432, 19.

120 NSARM, RG 1, vol. 431, unnumbered documents pertaining to Indian Affairs, "Charles Glode to His Excellency Lucius Bentinck Cary," 20 April 1841. In this document Glode identified the group for which he was responsible as "a tribe … settled on the new Line of Road from Annapolis Royal to Liverpool." He stated that the past growing season had been poor so his group needed more seed potatoes and oats. Their perseverance in farming, he added, was so the "benefits of civilized life may be realized." The seven he listed as needing seed were John (Jack) Glode (who farmed one acre), Joe Peter (a half acre). Joseph Glode (a half acre), Molly Knockwood, a widow (a half acre), Abraham Peters (three and a half acres), John Jeremy (two and a half acres), and Francis Charles (one and a half acres). While Charles implied these persons all lived along the Liverpool-Annapolis Road, most were settled at Kejimkujik Lake. NSARM, RG 1, vol. 432, 115–16, "Petition of Charles Glode, Indian Chief residing near Annapolis, to His Excellency Lucius Bentinck Cary, Viscount Falkland," 17 March 1842. With a preciseness characteristic of him, Charles also informed the lieutenant governor that results from an earlier government distribution of fifty bushels of seed potatoes had brought striking returns of "excellent quality." Charles had harvested ninety bushels of potatoes, John Jeremy one hundred bushels, Francis Charles eighty bushels, Peter Joe (Joseph Peters) seventy bushels, and Abraham Peters ninety bushels. All except Charles were farming near Kejimkujik Lake. NSARM,

RG 1, vol. 432, pp. 115–116, "Petition to Viscount Falkland from Charles Glode," 17 March 1842. Glode claimed that four additional persons wanted to join the Glode settlement, which held out "to the industrious settler no inconsiderable inducement." These men, whom Glode did not name, had "long relinquished their migratory habits, being fully persuaded that the cultivation of the soil promises something much more substantial than the precarious nature of the Chase." Charles also asked for hoes and spades to distribute. It was an appeal carefully tailored to its audience, likely drafted for Glode by Andrew Henderson.

121 Annapolis County Deeds, book 31 (1835), 398; book, 33 (1839), 400. Jaspar Williams, who was not Mi'kmaq, sold his 200-acre lot in 1835 for £25.

122 NSARM, RG 1, vol. 430, doc. 188, Index to Crown Land Grants – Charles Glade (*sic*, Glode); NSARM, Annapolis County Deeds (NSARM, RG 47, vol. 33, 400; ibid., vol. 38, 278; ibid., vol. 44, 166; ibid., vol. 45, 95–6. Glode continued to petition, unaware of the change made in his tenure. Another petition followed to Sir Colin Campbell on 21 April 1841, after the grant had been awarded. See NSARM, RG 1, vol. 430, doc. 188.

123 Crown Land Grants, book U, p. 46; NSARM, PRO on microfilm, CO 217/178: 91, reel 13,913, Dispatches, June–December 1841 – Charles Glode; NSARM, RG 1, vol. 430, no. 188; NSARM, RG 20 A – Glode, Charles 1840. The petition at first was minuted away with the caution that some designing settler might entice Glode to sell his land for a pittance. Upton, *Micmacs and Colonists*, 149.

124 NSARM, RG 1, vol. 431, Miscellaneous unnumbered documents, Charles Glode "To the Right Honourable Lucius Bentinck Cary, Viscount Falkland, Knight of the Grand Cross of the Guelphic Order, Member of His Majesty's Honourable Privy Council, Lieutenant Governor and Commander in Chief of the Province of Nova Scotia and its Dependencies," 20 April 1841.

125 NSARM, RG 1, vol. 432, 115–116, "Petition to Viscount Falkland from Charles Glode," 17 March 1842.

126 Peter Warren of the *Squirrel*, a warship out of Boston, on 9 July 1739 wrote about the chiefs of these "commands" who held commissions from the governor of Quebec or Cape Breton, and generally bore "the Title of Captain of the Port to which they belong." CO 217/8/48 ½.

127 Nova Scotia Museum, Halifax (henceforth NSM), printed matter file, "Jerry Lonecloud (or Jeremiah Bartlett-Alexis) to Harry Piers, 1910" included with an item with Accession no. 4438, 30 November 1910. Perter Charles Sulno, despite being over eighty years of age, in 1866 sent a petition to the Nova Scotia government

offering military help in the event of a Fenian raid on the province. NSARM, RG 15, vol. 6, doc. 73, "Petition of Chief Peter Charles [Sulno]," 1866.

128 L.F.S. Upton, "Meuse, Andrew James," *DCB* online, vol. 7 (1836–50).

129 NSARM, RG 1, vol. 432, 116–18, "Petition of Charles Glode to Viscount Falkland," 17 March 1842. Henderson wrote that he had met with Charles at General's Bridge near Lequille and had handed the Mi'kmaw leader a government requisition order for the potatoes he requested, as well as one hoe and spade apiece for John Jeremy, Francis Charles, Joe Peters, and Abraham Peters. Francis Meuse at Kejimkujik Lake and Jack Glode at Lequille also received eight bushels of seed potatoes.

130 NSARM, RG 1, vol. 432, 117–20, "Henderson to Howe," 27 May 1842.

131 Upton, "Glode, Charles," *DCB* online, vol. 8 (1851–60).

132 NSARM, RG 1, vol. 432, 117–20, "Henderson to Howe," 27 May 1842.

133 The Mi'kmaq still relied on birchbark canoes, a mode of warm weather transportation they used until the 1920s, when disease struck down the large paper birch trees (*Betula papifera*) needed for bark canoe construction. Snowshoes were worn during the winter months while hauling meat and personal effects on toboggans across frozen lake surfaces. In later years, heavy logging of forests changed the environment for white-barked birch species, making forest birch trees susceptible to birch dieback disease, birch scale, and the inroads of the bronze borer beetle. With the absence of birch bark, canoes, containers, and wigwams could not be manufactured from traditional materials.

134 Upton holds that the second man who visited Howe with Jeremy was James Andrew Meuse, but given the circumstances, it was more likely Charles Glode. Upton, "Glode, Charles," *DCB* online, vol. 8 (1851–60). Upton's notes regarding Charles Glode and this incident are housed in the Upton Papers at the University of British Columbia.

135 NSARM, RG 1, vol. 432, 120, "Henderson to Howe," 27 May 1842.

136 In 1838 Bartlett drew what was presumably Jack Glode's camp. It had a thoroughly romantic cast, since Bartlett also drew a second depiction of General's Bridge that clearly shows the mill but lacks the Mi'kmaw encampment. A photograph of the print is available at NSARM, Photographic Accession No. 1979–147, no. 57, "General's Bridge, with Mi'kmaw encampment in foreground, engraved by J.C. Bentley from a drawing made in 1838 by William H. Bartlett." Bentley produced the engraving for *Canadian Scenery Illustrated* (London, 1842). Ever since Sieur de Poutricourt erected the first water-driven grist mill in America at Lequille in 1607, mills of various descriptions had operated in the vicinity of Lequille. In 1745 Lequille was part of a large grant allocated to a Scot named John Easson, who came to Fort Anne as a master artificer in 1737 on condition that Easson maintain the mill at Lequille that once belonged to an Acadian merchant, miller, and French resistance fighter, Joseph-Nicolas Gautier *dit* Bellair (1689–1752). From 1740 onward Lequille was a place where townsfolk from Annapolis Royal as well as Mi'kmaq could purchase supplies and construction materials and find markets for their wares. The Easson grant precluded freehold tenure of land until the mid-nineteenth century, but Mi'kmaq into the 1850s continued to occupy land in the area unmolested. Bartlett's engraving of the General's Bridge in which the Mi'kmaw encampment appears has the largest sawmill hidden from view. Instead Bartlett focuses on four bark wigwams belonging to Jack Glode's encampment. Two women dressed in European finery according to Mi'kmaw tastes stand where the back part of the graveyard belonging to St Alban's Anglican Church lies today. As the Mi'kmaw inhabitants are few and since their wigwams are not symmetrically conical, this engraving likely depicts a fishing camp, as one can see fish drying near an open fire.

137 NSARM, RG 1, vol. 432, 102–4, Joseph Howe, "Western Tour, 1842."

138 Ibid., 104.

139 NSARM, RG 20, Ser. A – Glode, Charles and Others, 1840. Orders from Sir Colin Campbell to John Spry Morris, 26 February 1840 on microfilm reel no. 15761. A desultory note permeated the granting process, since on a single sheet of orders Campbell had managed to confuse matters by referring on one line to the grantee as "Charles Glode" and on the final line to the grantee as "Meuse." By 1840 Francis Meuse was planting on the shores of Kejimkujik Lake.

140 NSARM, RG 1, vol. 432, 104–5, Joseph Howe, "Western Tour, 1842."

141 Ibid., 104.

142 Ibid.

143 NSARM, RG 1, vol. 432, Letters to commissioner, 108–9, "Howe to Nicholls," 2 November 1842.

144 Ibid., 111–12, "Charles Glade (*sic*, Glode) to Howe," 12 November 1842.

145 In 1835 Charles had petitioned the government for £5 to buy materials to build a 20 X 15 foot house, but no monies ever arrived for him to do so. Charles actually may

have preferred his more traditional log lodge, but it was obvious that Howe looked askance at his dwelling and Charles wanted to curry favour with the commissioner.

146 Ibid.

147 Ibid., 221–2, "Henderson to Howe," 21 June 1843.

148 Ibid., 182–3, "Nicholls to Howe," 12 November 1842.

149 Ibid., 110–11, "Howe to Nicholls," 21 November 1842.

150 Ibid., 113–14, "Nicholls to Howe," 3 December 1842.

151 Ibid., 220, "Howe to Henderson," 8 May 1843.

152 Ibid.

153 Ibid., 221–2, "Henderson to Howe," 21 June 1843.

154 NSARM, RG 20, series A, vol. 131 – Glode, Charles, 1845, microfilm reel 15,763, "Petition to Viscount Falkland from Charles Glode," 15 August 1845.

155 A makeshift hospital was erected at Dartmouth. Several members of a family headed by a man named Thomas Glode, who was sixty years of age in 1847, were cured. These included Hannah Glode, aged seventy-six; Joe, aged twenty, and Nancy, twenty. There were also three children, Noel who was seven, Mary Ann, nine, and Peter, eight. These were likely Joe and Nancy's children. One child, Francis Glode, two and a half years old, already had died. NSARM, MG 15, vol. 4, doc. no. 25. A year later a destitute individual named "Ann Gloud" (Glode) became the subject of an investigation when her lifeless body was found, partially eaten by rats, in an abandoned house in Halifax. The woman had taken to drinking heavily, and even Chief Joseph Cope, who lived near Dartmouth and several times had tried to help her, could not wean her from her injurious and ultimately fatal proclivities. Foul play was not suspected. Ann had climbed into the derelict building through an unfastened window to escape the elements and, hungry and sick, lay down in a corner and died. NSARM, RG41, "C," vol. 22, 6A, "Inquisition or inquest on the body of Ann Gloud," 4 January 1848.

156 NSARM, MG 15, Misc, detached documents, "Robert Leslie's report on the condition and circumstances of Indians in Annapolis," 27 November 1846.

157 NSARM, MG 15, vol. 3, unnumbered file, "Spurr to Whitman," 21 December 1846.

158 To this day Charles Glode remains a profoundly perplexing individual because so little is known of his early years or his family life. He must have married Frances Tobias at a relatively young age, since by 1840 the couple were raising at least seven children. Only four offspring, Christine, Peter, Gabriel and Mary, however, can be traced in the documentary record. Surprisingly Joseph Howe and other government officials never mentioned Charles' wife in their reports, though they must have known about Frances. Charles adhered to Roman Catholicism, and while Frances Tobias would have been born an Anglican, she seemed content to have their children baptized in the Roman Catholic faith. Frances also accompanied her husband on his travels from Lequille to Liverpool and down the Atlantic coast to Prospect, east of Halifax. There were several small Mi'kmaw communities near Halifax where Mi'kmaw visitors could stay. One was located at Portuguese Cove near Chebucto Head, where two of the Glode family; Ann Glode who had married William Brooks, and William Glode had an encampment, another was on Chocolate Lake near the head of the Northwest Arm. The enigmatic character of Charles' life is compounded by the fact that the date of his birth, his birthplace, the birthdates of most of his seven children, and even the location of his burial site remain unknown. A small Bible, now in the possession of the Nova Scotia Archives and Records Management in Halifax, is said to have once belonged to him but contains no family information. After the death of his wife Frances, Charles may have taken up with a woman from the Mehlman settlement in Queens County with whom he spent the last six years of his life. Milford cherishes the idiosyncracies of its past, and this story is a popular one within that community.

159 Annapolis County Deeds, book 44, 106–7, "Court of Probate, regarding estate of Charles Gload, Judge George Millidge presiding, 8 April, 1852." Dollars and pounds sterling were both used in transactions at this time.

160 Annapolis County Deeds, book 454, 98, Indenture made between Edward W. Cutler and John Carter, 19 March 1853, registered 5 April 1853.

161 Annapolis County Deeds, book 109, 506; book 4, 655. The first transaction was registered on 1 October 1898 and the second on 4 July 1891. Albert Hubley died in a mill accident. Milford and Area History Group, *Through the Woods: A Collected History and Reflection of the Milford Area & Communities* (Halifax: MAHG, 2005). Charles Glode's land was then bought by Hamilton Matthews in 1865. It has since returned to Hubley hands.

162 LAC, RG 10, vol. 2004, file 7687, doc. 10131, "George Wells to Lawrence Vankoughnet," December 1883. The Department of Indian Affairs erroneously thought that the land was a reserve of one thousand acres, and Wells first had to set Ottawa straight on this point. Wells then emphasized that the Mi'kmaq held that "this land had been granted to their fathers and they tell me they would not give it back to the government." Soon afterwards surrounding settlers began using the land. Part of it later was appropriated by the Department of National

Defence, and at one time there was a store located near Charles's old property. Today the land is inpenetrable scrub. The author's fieldnotes record statements that persons at Graywood and Milford told her about the fate of Charles Glode's propery. One person stated, "I don't know if his farm was just north of Majorie Hubly's place, but there was a trail there once called Glode Road and it led through the woods to west of Spring Hill." The author was told that "there was an old road which began about a mile north of Donald Charlton's place and which looped down through the woods and came out in front of Donald's house. Perhaps that was part of Glode Road. The only piece of land on the map that belongs to Charles Glode is a two-hundred-acre piece just north of Marjorie Hubley's. The Mi'kmaq have gone to Lequille. There is Paul Pictou, Allan Pictou, and Irene Sexton's mother – all on the Lequille and Princedale Road. Those at General's Bridge are Sam and Julie Pictou, Evangeline Pictou – related to old Chief Ben Pictou – Abe and Lena Pictou, Joe Paul, Tom Paul, Agatha Francis, 'Aggie' Himmelman, Howard Pail, Francis Halliday, and David Pictou. They likely know something." Fieldnotes, 10 July 2011.

163 LAC, RG 10, vol. 638, "Petition of Francis Glode who asks for freedom from restrictions on Indian land in order to sell his lot," 16 March 1861; LAC, RG 10, vol. 461, folder 14, 1861–62, Land Petitions, "Petition of Francis, Jacob and Simon Glode regarding land on the Liverpool Road"; NSARM, MG 15, vol. 6, no. 64, "Petition of Simon Glode to the Earl of Mulgrave, Lieutenant Governor of Nova Scotia," 21 December 1861. Simon wanted to purchase one hundred acres of land in the Township of Dalhousie, Annapolis County, about two miles south of the Dalhousie Road, where he had already improved the land; NSARM, MG 15, vol. 6, no. 65, Dr. Robert Leslie's letter concerning Francis Glode's land. Leslie held that Francis went to Halifax and was denied access to the lieutenant governor. Francis's land was eventually placed under lease.

164 Annapolis County Deeds, book 63, 585. Lease of land to Richard Brown for ninety-nine years, 21 May 1967, registered 18 February 1870. Signed by Peter Glode and his heirs, John and Catherine Glode.

165 Annapolis County Deeds, book 100, 618. Lease of two hundred acres to William Meehan, a tailor from Granville, under a lease term of ninety-nine years. Registered on 4 May 1894.

166 The signatories included Peter Paul, his wife Fanny, and his five children Frank, Joseph, May Ann, Catherine, and Newel.

167 NSARM, MG 15, vol. 19, no. 3 and vol. 19, no. 4, "Field trip and notes on Mi'kmaw land holding at Lequille and surrounding area, including lands on the Liverpool Road. Lequille title searches, August 1–September 6, 1978." One of the signatories to the Liverpool Road surrender of 1926 was Chief Benjamin Pictou of General's Bridge.

168 Joseph was the son of Chief Joseph Martin Glode and Sarah Philips. In 1834 Joseph Jr. married Mary Ann Stephens at Caledonia, and the occasion was attended with "great ceremony in the presence of many Indians." Registers of the Parish of St. Gregory's, Liverpool, "Marriage of Joseph Claude, son of Joseph Claude and Sarah Philips of Annpolis Royal and May Ann Stephens, daughter of Joseph Stephens and Hannah Simons, 16 June 1834."

169 NSARM, RG 5, Series P, vol. 8, no. 85, microfilm reel 15,605, "Petition against moose snaring from John N. Smith *et al* of Newport," 1 February 1842; House of Assembly, *An Act for making Regulations relative to the setting of Snares for catching moose*, 6 Vic., c. 19 (1843).

170 These persons were D. Ruggles, George Millidge, Peter Boinett, James Wilson, James Balcom, James Runciman, Joseph Williams, Alvin Gilpin, Bernard Gilpin, Millidge Ruggles, and Elochim Bert.

171 House of Assembly, *An Act for the preservation of Moose*, 7 Vic., c. 73 (1844), s. 1; NSARM, microfilm reel 3,532, 102, *Journal of the Legislative Assembly of Nova Scotia* (henceforth *JLANS*) 1844, 26 March 1844.

172 Although Charles Glode signed this petition, he did not exercise as strong a protective stewardship over local land and resources. Because of this the Annapolis County Mi'kmaq preferred the type of leadership engaged in by Jack and Joseph Glode and drifted away from Charles.

173 The nature of the relationship between Timothy C. Tobias and the Annapolis Mi'kmaq, as well as the unusual positioning of his signature on the petition, are interesting in the light of Charles Glode's wife also having the surname "Tobias." Could T.C. Tobias have been Charles Glode's brother-in-law? Nothing could be found in the documentary record to solve this mystery.

174 This information is obtainable from census records, passenger lists, and civil service records retrievable on ancestors.com.

175 The names of individuals introduced briefly in the text here are included mainly for heuristic purposes, as reference points for future scholars to learn more about Glode/Gloade family history. Between 1800 and 1835 there are few records to rely upon concerning

kin relationships, although oral traditions can be of assistance.

176 NSARM, RG 5, Misc. A, Series P, vol. 8A, No. 93, microfilm reel 15,605, "Petition of Joseph Glode *et al* to close the March moose hunting season to whites," 26 March 1844; NSARM, microfilm reel 3,532, 175, *J LAN S*, 19 April 1844.

177 NSARM, microfilm reel 3,522, *J LANS*, 1848, Report of the Committee for Indian Affairs, Appendix 88.

178 This was particularly rankling to the Mi'kmaq, though some tried to redirect their anger into humour. For instance, one of Chief Joseph Glode's descendants told Clara Dennis that when a game warden once caught him with a fish, he chucked the salmon over a nearby dam. "Hey, what are you doing?" he [the warden] hollered. I say, I'm just helpin' the salmon over the dam!" Dennis, *More about Nova Scotia*, 409.

179 NSARM, RG 1, vol. 431, "Petition of John Glode of Annapolis," 26 June 1845. This petition was witnessed by Thomas Fletcher on 27 June. When the second petition was sent in October of the same year, Jack had three children living with him. NSARM, MG 15, vol. 3, "Petition of John Glode to Viscount Falkland," 2 October 1845.

180 NSARM, MG 15, vol. 3, "Petition of John Glode to Viscount Falkland," 2 October 1845.

181 Annapolis Deeds, book 38, p. 278, "Sale of part of mill site No. 5 at General's Bridge for £2. Elizabeth Ritchie, widow, to John Gload (or Jack Glode)," 10 November 1845. Registered 12 February 1846.

182 Information on these marriages was taken from the registers of St. Gregory's Church, Liverpool, and St. Jerome's Church, Caledonia.

183 More, *History of Queens County*, 125. According to Travis Pinn, a descendant of Charles Sulno (the patriarch of the Mi'kmaw Charles family), there is a story that the Mi'kmaw Charles family were partly Scottish. See chapter 1 on Charles Alexis for further information.

184 Thomas H. Raddall mentions that Peter Glode's farm in the 1860s lay near Jim Charles's lot. He also states that Peter Glode's testimony was important to Jim Charles's trial. Dalhousie University Archives, MS 2.202.Q.7.F., Raddall Papers, "Jim Charles and His Gold Mine." Chief Charles Sulno's petition of March 1866 is found in NSARM, MG 15, vol. 6, no. 73.

185 NSARM, RG 15, vol. 4a, doc. 120, "Report of Dr. Forbes, MD," 1851. Francis Glode was likely the individual whom William Barss at Liverpool in 1801 had described as an unmarried "young man." Francis fell ill in 1851 when he was in his late sixties, but recovered and lived to at least one hundred.

186 NSARM, Misc. "I" Indian Land Documents, Crown Lands documents on microfilm, Pkg. 16, "Kedgemakooge Reserve no. 9, Survey Plan and notes, Indian lands on Cecumcega Lake by Whitman Freeman, dated at Liverpool," 26 December 1843. Peter Glode's original allotment (No. 10) was forty-five acres, while Francis Glode's allotment (No. 9) was seventy acres.

187 John was born in 1848. Peter was baptized in 1851 and Francis on 27 June 1861. John's and Peter's baptisms are entered in the Registers of St. Louis, Annapolis, while Francis's baptism is found in the Registers of St. Gregory's Church in Liverpool. Most of John's descendants lived in Caledonia.

188 NSARM, MG 100, vol. 189, no. 9b. The following words were inscribed around 1919 on the bottom of the handbill, which was dated 1900 (Acc. No. 4822): "Printed Handbill for Indian Concert by Chief Peter Glode [Jr.], assisted by his wife and daughter. Peter Glode and his father were born at Kejimkujik, Queens Co., N.S., & Peter is now 68 years of age. For a few years before 1912 he gave these entertainments in various parts of eastern United States, including Coney Island." This handbill advertising music, dancing, songs, and a talk by "Chief Peter Glode" can be found in NSAMR.

189 NSARM, MG 15, vol. 18, doc. no. 17.

190 Dominion of Canada, *Sessional Papers*, 1885, 41–2, "Report of Thomas J. Butler to the Department of Indian Affairs," 25 August 1884.

191 "Joseph Claude of Annapolis Royal," who married Sarah Phillips, had a son Joseph around 1810 who married Mary Anne Stephens on 16 June 1834 "in the presence of many Indians." Marriage entry for 16 June 1834, Registers of St. Gregory's Church, Liverpool.

192 Silus Tertius Rand, *Legends of the Micmacs*, ed. Helen L. Webster (New York: Longmans and Green, 1894), 14–22, 30–3.

193 *Dominion of Canada Sessional Papers*, 1898, James Farrell, "Annual Report to Indian Affairs for the year ending June 30," 1898.

194 *Annapolis Spectator*, 11 April 1918. The flag had been a gift from the deputy superintendent of Indian Affairs. The flag raising occurred Easter Sunday morning, at which time many Mi'kmaq assembled in their traditional dress.

195 It was probably the lot earlier purchased by Chief Jack Glode.

196 Dominion of Canada, *Sessional Papers*, 1887, 37, "J.E. Beckwith, Kentville, to the Department of Indian Affairs," 10 August 1886.

197 A Molti Pictou who appears on Barss's 1801 census of the Mi'kmaq of Queens County is older than Benjamin's father and may have been Benjamin's grandfather. Benjamin Pictou's paternal uncle and namesake Benjamin Pictou (c.1816–c.1895) also married a member of the Glode family named Mary Theresa Glode, while one of this uncle's sons, named Molti or Matthew, about 1835 married Elizabeth Glode. These two Glode women may very well have come from the Glodes living on the lower Mersey, since Sam Glode, who was raised near Milton, held there was a kin connection between his family and Malti Pictou in the 1870s. Even though Chief Benjamin Pictou's marriage to Mary Ellen Glode was short lived, it probably brought him to the notice of the Annapolis band as a fitting successor to Chief Joseph Claude Jr. Benjamin Pictou became the first Mi'kmaw in over a century to challenge the leadership pre-eminence of the Glodes in the Lequille area.

198 One of the author's first cousins by marriage proudly stated that he, on his maternal side, is of Black Loyalist and Mi'kmaw descent from Lequille. Fred Morgan of the Waterville-Berwick region of Kings County, conversation with author, 10 June 2012.

199 Ruth T. Ritchie and Denis J. Rice, *Lequillle: Chronicles of a Community* (Annapolis Royal: Annapolis Heritage Society, 2011), 3–5. The Mi'kmaw encampment ground at Lequille was not laid out as a reserve until an investigation of Mi'kmaw occupancy took place in the 1970s. After this a small land base was surveyed for the Mi'kmaq at Lequille, which today is viewed jurisdictionally as a satellite of the Bear River reserve. It lies just east of the Nova Scotia Power Corportion canal on the Clementsville Road.

200 In recent articles and commentaries about him, Samuel Freeman Glode's surname is often spelled "Gloade," though the mid-nineteenth-century spelling "Glode," which is the spelling he would have recognized, is adhered to here. The surname "Gloade" is used in this chapter when referring to individuals born close to the turn of the nineteenth century who used this particular spelling of their surname.

201 As late as the mid-1820s, falls on the lower Mersey River supported an extensive salmon fishery. As well, at Potanoc Mi'kmaw weirsites existed at Indian Gardens on the Mersey River as one approached Lake Rossignol (near present-day Ponhook Indian Reserve No. 10), on the Pleasant River draining into Molega Lake and along the Wildcat River (near present-day Wildcat Indian Reserve No. 12), and at Greenfield below Ponhook Lake and above Bangs Falls on the Medway River (close to today's miniscule Indian Reserve No. 11). Fishing for salmon was an important seasonal activity at these locales for thousands of years. Ground-stone artefacts found near Milton date back at least three thousand years. There is ample evidence, moreover, that these sites were occupied on a seasonal basis continuously through time. Side-notched stone points from the Woodland era have been unearthed as well as later French trade beads. In early French times Potanoc had offered an ideal spot to erect a trading post, and, later, Simeon Perkins was known to have owned the same site. Merchants dealing in fish and furs continued to carry on a trade with Molti Glode's people until 1840, before mills completely enveloped the site and dams destroyed its formerly abundant salmon fishery. Today the mills have gone, but the salmon, despite the presence of a fish ladder, have not returned in any numbers. During work on the Mersey River system near Milton, Archaic era artefacts, particularly a ground-stone bayonet and ground-stone axes and adzes dating back over three thousand years, have been found at this site. An exhibit of archaeological artefacts, including many others discovered in 2004 along the Mersey River, was held at the Sipuke'l Gallery in the old Liverpool Town Hall in 2015. Elissa Bernard, "First Nations Debut Show Offers Artifacts, Current Work," *Chronical Herald*, 19 June 2015. Jillian Francis, who hails from the Francis family of Milton, is the curator of this gallery.

202 The only person who can definitely be identified as one of Molti and his wife Geneviéve's sons is Paul Glode, who was baptized at St. Ann du Ruisseau Church at Eel Brook in Yarmouth County in 1807. Paul Glode was still alive in 1871, living in the Bristol district of Caledonia. There were very few Glodes baptized at Ste. Anne du Ruisseau, however, and Roman Catholic Church records were not generated in Queens County before 1829. Francis Glode's grandson Samuel Freeman Glode, who shared knowledge of his family's genealogical connections with Nova Scotia historian and novelist Thomas Raddall, in 1944 did not reveal the name of his great grandfather. Ronald Caplan, "Sam Glode: Travels of a Micmac," *Cape Breton's Magazine*, 35 (1983), 21.

203 In 1945 Thomas Raddall interviewed Henry A. Waterman, who claimed that his father moose hunted with Francis Glode Jr., a son of Chief Francis Glode. Francis and his son along with Peter Bobbyeye (or Bobiei) camped along the Pleasant River flowing into Molega Lake, northeast of the Medway River. One of their favourite encampment sites lay on a level field "below the Mill Privilege on the east side of the river north of the

road to Bridgewater, sometimes down the river back of the Meeting House." According to Waterman, Francis Sr. "held court" at council meetings in this locale. Waterman's family also would invite these Mi'kmaq, who came to their house to sell baskets, to spend the night, but they never expected a bed. "They were given supper and lay on the floor before the big fireplace in the back kitchen ... and were off in the morning before we were up." Dalhousie Archives, Raddall Papers, MS 2.202.Q. 7.5, Henry A. Waterman to Raddall, 25 August 1945.

204 NSARM, RG, vol. 431, no. 16, "Petition of Malti Glode to Sir Colin Campbell, Liverpool, 17 November 1835. Signed by James Barss, MP, and James Gordon, MP."

205 This Francis Glode married Frances Sappier. Although information from church records suggests that Frances Sappier came from New Brunswick, "Sappier" (Jean-Pierre) is a Mi'kmaw surname usually associated with Pictou County. Francis and Frances had a daughter Mary Clara in 1844, who in turn had a son named Joseph about 1869 and a second son Abram, whose father was listed in the church registers of St. Jerome's parish as "Alfred Paul." Two more children followed, a son William in 1872, whose father was James Charles, and a daughter Magdalene in 1875, whose father was Abraham Labrador. All these births occurred prior to Mary Clara's marriage in 1876 to Philip Holden Paul. She was described as a thirty-two-year-old "spinster" at the time of her wedding, while Philip Holden Paul, who was listed as only nineteen years old, was a basket maker from Bridgewater. NSARM, Historical Vital Statistics, Lunenburg County Marriages, Registration Year 1876, book 1828, p. 119, no. 19.

206 François-Joseph Gloade, likely one of Molti Glode's sons, was only married to Madeline Alexis a year before she died in 1833.

207 Paul's name may be found on the 1871 census for Bristol District in Caledonia; the census holds that he was seventy years of age, though chuch records show he was born in 1807. Peter and Hannah Glode, as well as a man named Stephen Glode, lived near Paul, who was a widower by 1871.

208 According to the registers of St. Gregory's parish, Bridget was born on 21 July 1840 to Cobliel Glode and Mary Bobieye.

209 Mary Ann Cobliel, also known as Mary Ann Glode, was born in Annapolis County and died at Milton in 1917. NSARM, Historical Vital Statistics, Queens County Deaths, Registration Year 1917, book 46, p. 249, no. 582, " of Mary Ann [Cobliel Gloade] Luxey, widow of Lewis Luxey Sr., 2 September 1917, age eighty-eight."

210 L.F.S. Upton, "Glode, Gabriel," *DCB* online, vol. 8 (1851–60).

211 NSARM, RG 1, vol. 432, Howe, "Western Tour," 1842, 78–9.

212 As well as "Big Glode Island" and "Little Glode Island," situated in Ponhook Lake below the better-known Molega Lake, "Glode Lake" (or "Glode's Lake") and "Glode Meadow Brook" are found near Riverdale on the lower Medway River. *Nova Scotia Atlas*, Service Nova Scotia and Municipal Relations and the Geomatics Centre. (Halifax: Formac, 2001), 73, 79.

213 There is also an Indian Gardens on the Mersey River near the lower end of Lake Rossignol.

214 "Cegumcega" and "Lake Cegumcega Gawich" are the Mi'kmaw place names for present-day Kejimkujik Lake and Grafton Lake used on the survey plan of the area drawn up by Whitman Freeman on 26 December 1843. NSARM, Miscellaneous "I" Indian Land Documents taken from the Department of Crown Lands, on microfilm, reel 14,011. Kegemakooga Indian Reserve No. 9, Queens County, package no.16. The terms employed by Freeman derive from a Mi'kmaw word that means "fairy"; hence "Fairy Lake." Howe evidently continued to believe that the word used by the Mi'kmaq he was travelling with, probably including Cobliel Glode, also meant "Fairy Lake," but in fact it means something very different. Not often used by males in mixed company, the term *Kejimkujik* refers to the uncomfortable physical consequences of paddling over a lake whose water was usually choppy and could cause sore and "swollen private parts." It has been suggested that the Mi'kmaq were playing a private joke on the commissioner. The term Howe heard and recorded nevertheless has become the registered place name for the lake. NSM, Printed Matter File, Harry Piers notes, n.d. Also referred to in Ruth Whitehead, *The Old Man Told Us*, 242–3.

215 Howe regarded John Jeremy as the head man of the settlement and later made arrangements for the government to build Jeremy a house.

216 The next morning Howe made a list of all the male heads of families within the settlement. He discovered that Joe Peters and his brother Abraham shared a point of land, while Francis Meuse lived on a small island. Peter Glode and Francis Charles lived on jutting headlands like the Peters families, while John Pictou and Lewis Luxy lived on the mainland further back in the woods. It was an interesting coterie of individuals. The Peters and their descendents traced their ancestry back to a trader named Rossignol who had defied de

Monts's trade monopoly and left his mark on history by having his name stand as the Acadian designation for both Liverpool (Port Rossignol) and the Mersey River (the old Rivière Rossignol). Luxy was a descendent of a famous Cape Sable district chief named Charles Alexis who around 1755 had married Anne Hébert, a daughter of Antoine Hébert and his second wife, Anne Orilion. Meanwhile Francis Charles, the son of another Cape Sable chief, was the father of the notorious Jim Charles, born around 1830. Though only a boy in 1843, Jim Charles would discover placer gold in and around Kejimkujik Lake and temporarily live a backcountry version of the high life, until implicated in a murder charge. After that, he spent several years living in relative isolation in the bush until he was legally exonerated. The Jim Charles story has been examined and re-examined over the years by Thomas H. Raddall, Will R. Bird, Albert Bigelow Paine, Frank Parker Day, and Michael Parker, to name only a few.

217 Contract drawn up between Joseph Howe and with Jos. Minard, Millard Cole, and Barnabus Miles, 22 October 1842; "Howe to Whitman Freeman," 22 October 1842; NSARM, RG 1, vol. 432, Howe, "Western Tour" 1842, 87–90. Howe also arranged to have one hundred acres laid off for each of the Kedjimkujik settlers. The Mi'kmaq were to direct the surveyor Whitman Freeman, at the government's expense, where to set out lots.

218 NSARM, RG 1, vol. 431, misc. detached documents, "List of Mi'kmaq in Queens needing blankets, 1836–37"; NSARM, Misc. "I" Indian Lands Documents, from the NS Crown Lands Department, Pkgs. 17, 55 and 74, on microfilm. Plan and Survey Notes of Liverpool Ponhook Reserve (no. 10), by Whitman Freeman, 26 December 1843. It is possible the group originally was headed by Molti Glode. Today the Ponhook reserve is occupied mainly by members of the Francis family.

219 NS Legislative Council, *Journal and Proc.*, 1843, app. 7, 24.

220 NSARM, RG 1, vol. 432, Howe, "Western Tour, 1842," 86.

221 *Nova Scotian and Weekly Chronicle*, Halifax, 10 July 1903, p. 8, col. 3. L.F.S. Upton, claimed that the settler population never forgot this incident. Stories also circulated about how the Indian commissioner smoked one of the chief's pipes in friendship, and then made off with the pipe. Later Howe sent Cobliel a dollar but still kept the pipe. Upton, "Glode, Gabriel," *DCB* online, vol. 8 (1851–60).

222 The Greenfield Mi'kmaw community remained at Greenfield, and burials were still made in the graveyard there. See, for instance, Registers of St. Gregory's Church, Liverpool, death of Noel Cobliel, age ninety, interred at Greenfield, 16 April 1872.

223 NSARM, MG 15, no. 60, "Albert Quinan's petition for a lot 18 miles from Liverpool, allegedly belonging to Peter Toney," c. 1855.

224 NSARM, MG 15, vol. 6, no. 20, "Freeman Whitman to William Chereley [*sic*, Chearnley], Comr. of Indian Affairs, 28 January 1857, regarding a petition of 1 February 1857 from Cobdeal [*sic*, Cobiel] Glode asking for aid toward erecting a small dwelling. He has procured wood for building purposes."

225 NSARM, MG 15, 5, no. 77; MG 15, 6, nos. 19–20 and 48. L.F.S. Upton notes that this physician "was attained at considerable public expense." Upton, "Glode, Gabriel," *DCB* online, vol. 8 (1851–60); NSARM, MG 15, vol. 6, no. 67, list of Mi'kmaq of Queens County – 106 individuals, 12 February 1862. The list includes the following family heads: (1) Francis Glode with three children, (2) Cobleal Glode and wife, (3) a second Francis Glode with a wife and one child, (4) a third Francis Glode with his wife, (5) Newel Glode with his wife, and (6) Peter Glode. T.B. Smith notes that Newel Glode was referred to to as "Cobielle of Greenfield." NSARM, T.B. Smith Papers, vol. 835 – Newel Glode, microfilm reel 14,948.

226 Noel Cobliel Glode was born between 1838 and 1845. He was reported to be fifty-six on the 1901 census, which made him born in 1845, but according to St. Gregory's parish registers he died at Greenfield in 1901 at sixty-three years of age, which put his year of birth as 1838.

227 Dalhousie Archives, Raddall Papers, "Bon Mature," MS2.202.Q.7.F. Newel Glode was arrested for intoxication within a year of his daughter Madeline's wedding. The ruling against selling alcohol to Mi'kmaq, instigated by Charles Glode and Haliburton in 1828, remained in force in the 1880s, and on 6 January 1886 the following notice appeared in the *Liverpool Advance*: "Conviction for anyone who sold liquor to Newel Glode on 19th December last. Thomas J. Foutlier, P.P." NSARM, T.B. Smith Papers, vol. 835 – Newel Glode, microfilm reel 14,948.

228 Madeline was born in 1865, John in 1867, Anne in 1869, Joseph in 1871, James Solomon in 1873, Paul David in 1876, and Mary Charlotte in 1879. (Mary Charlotte, as a single woman, later had a son Louis.) Church Registers of St. Jerome's Church, Caledonia, Madeline born to Noel Glode and Mary Ann Molti on 23 December 1865, St. Gregory's Parish; NSARM, Historical Vital Statistics, book 1834, p. 112, no. 8, "Marriage of Madeline Glode and Abraham Glode, 18 January 1885." Abraham was a thirty-four-year-old widower working as a cooper.

Abraham Jr. and Madeline's marriage was one of several marriages that took place between cousins in this area, which was not surprising, given that only eighty-four Mi'kmaq lived in Queens County in the early 1870s and numbers would not have risen that much by the mid-1880s. More, *History of Queens County*, 125.

229 Some of these births are registered at St. Jerome's parish in Caledonia, while others appear on the federal census for 1891 for Greenfield, Queens County. Benjamin Glode married Minnie Carver and died of influenza at Bear River in 1918. Janie was killed at Tuft's Cove in the Halifax Explosion of December 1917. NSM, Printed Matter File, "Jeremiah Bartlett to Harry Piers," 31 December 1917 regarding Mi'kmaq killed in the disaster of December 1917. Jeremiah Bartlett, alias Jerry Lonecloud, had to go and identify the body. Elizabeth Glode, after her mother Madeline's death in 1912, married Molti Francis, who for years lived with his brother John Francis at Milton, near Samuel Freeman Glode. Molti raised an orphan boy, sometimes referred to as "Little Chief," who is reputed to have been born to Sam Glode and Elizabeth Glode prior to Elizabeth's marriage to Molti. A veteran of the First World War, Molti became mentally deranged. As mentioned, Elizabeth's mother Madeline in 1909 also had another son, Clarence. NSARM, Historical Vital Statistics, Queens County Births, Registration Year 1909, p. 53900166, no. 53900167, Birth of Clarence Glode, Greenfield, 15 March 1909. Bridget Glode, Madeline's daughter, informed the provincial authorities of Clarence's birth and helped her mother care for the child in his early years, since Madeline was a widow with no other assistance. (Bridget also acted as an informant when her maternal uncle Paul David Glode and his wife Nancy Tony had a daughter Clara born to them ten days later.) After his mother's death in 1912, Clarence was raised at Bear River by Malti Pictou. Debbie Gloade of Bear River, who is a descendant of Clarence Glode, provided some of this information. Debbie reported that Clarence was raised by Malti and later lived with his family at Gold River in the 1950s, where he manufactured mast hoops for the schooner fleet. Ottawa, Department of Indian Affairs, "Report on Field Interviews with Micmacs of Nova Scotia, 1957," Treaty and Aboriginal Rights Resource Centre (TARR), Shubenacadie, UNSI Collection 92-1004-09-018, p. 21. Madeline Glode died at age forty-seven in 1912. NSARM, Historical Vital Statistics, Digby County Deaths, Registration Year 1912, book 6, p. 195, no. 1166, "Death of Madaline [*sic*, Madeline] Glode at Bear River of a heart attack, 14 September 1912."

230 NSM photograph collection, Reference Number: P113/2000.4.21/N-18,427. Photograph of a youthful Sam Glode with his pet moose Niggly, vicinity of Milford House, pre-1915, collection of Marg Miller.

231 NSM, Printed Matter File, list of guides in the Kejimkujik area. See also Parker, *Guides of the North Woods*, 234–5.

232 The Nova Scotia Guides Association was not incorporated until 1920.

233 Sam Freeman Glode stated to Raddall that his mother had been Sarah Jane Labrador from Tusket Forks, Yarmouth County, Stephen Glode's second wife.

234 Raddall thought the nickname might have stemmed from an affair that occurred in the distant past between one of Francis's ancestors and an English person, but the name might just as well have arisen because the Glodes, since 1722, had remained on fairly cordial terms with the English at Annapolis Royal and elsewhere. Raddall's notes on his interviews with Sam Glode are found in the Dalhousie University Archives, Halifax, Raddall Papers, Research notes, Series 14, box 29.8, folder 8, "Sam Glode, Micmac Indian," 22 pages, "Notes made from several interviews made with Sam Glode at Raddall's house in Liverpool and at Sam's shanty at Milton." These notes were later published as Ronald Caplan, "Sam Glode: Travels of a Micmac," *Cape Breton's Magazine*, 35 (1983), 21–9. Many of Francis Glode's descendants are traceable in the registries of St. Gregory's Roman Catholic Church in Liverpool, St. Jerome's Roman Catholic Church in Caledonia, and available census records. Complementing these as sources of information are stories that Francis Glode's grandson Samuel Freeman Glode shared between 1944 and 1953 with Thomas H. Raddall and T.B. Smith. An excellent booklet, researched and compiled by Ian of Annapolis Royal and printed by the Annapolis County Historical Association, contains Lawrence's extensive genealogical research on Mi'kmaw families of southwestern Nova Scotia, including data on the Glode/Gloade family. A copy of this booklet is kept by the Annapolis Heritage Society at 138 St George St, Annapolis Royal.

235 Potanoc was a canoe-buiding site. Sam Glode stated that in the 1850s his grandfather and grandmother built a birch bark canoe to carry them and their family from Cowie's Falls near Milton, Queens County, "up the Mersey River to Lake Rossignol, then up the Shelburne River to Koofang Lake. There they carried across to Moosehide Lake and went down the Sissiboo River to Weymouth. They crossed the Bay of Fundy and coasted up to Saint. John. They ascended the Saint John River

to its headwaters, carried their canoe over the portage
to Riviere du Loup, and followed that river down to
the St. Lawrence River to Montreal. Outside Montreal
they camped with several other families in a wigwam.
The winter proved harsh and the group left early in the
spring to return to the Mersey River area." Caplan, "Sam
Glode: Travels," 21–2.

236 Sam Glode claimed that his grandfather "never had
a permanent habitation, but made camps mostly in
Queens, at Indian Gardens, Kedji, the Screecher, and
in Middle Ohio – as well as Milton." "The Screecher"
referred to a low spit of land separating Fourth Lake
from Rossignol Lake, with a stream flowing past its tip.
It was a camping ground, but it also contained Mi'kmaw
graves. Dalhousie Archives, Raddall Papers, "Along the
Shores of Rossignol," MS 2.202.Q.7.F. This was distinct
from the boggy area up beyond Indian Gardens on the
Mersey River, about Kempton, Long, and Eagle lakes,
where it was said an early Mi'kmaw burial site lay.
Scaffold burials were anciently erected at the foot of
Kempton Lake. Ghostly noises, and sometimes piercing
screeches, were reputed to have occurred there at night.
Dalhousie Archives, Raddall Papers, "Indian Devil
Country," MS2.202.Q.7.F. NSARM, T.B. Smith Papers,
No. 835 – Glode family, on microfilm, reel 17,948. Copies
are also found at the Simeon Perkins House Museum
and Archives in Liverpool. The author is also grateful
to Brian Purdy, former curator of the Simeon Perkins
House Museum, for information about the Milton
Gloade family as well as the archaeology of the area.
Brian is married to Beverley Lowe, the daughter of Maurine Genevieve Lowe, who was one of three daughters
born to Louis Glode, son of Samuel Glode and his wife
Minnie Carver. Brian's daughter-in-law Melanie Robinson of the Acadia First Nation, who is married to Brian
and Beverley's son Jeff, led the author to such a trove
of information. Samuel and Minnie had only one son,
Louis but three daughters, Gertrude Josephine (Betty),
LeJean Virginia, and Maurine Genevieve. The couple
also had one step-daughter, Geraldine, and one step-
son, Ronald Lowe. *Liverpool Advance*, 29 March 1959,
obituary of Lewis Walter Glode.

237 *Liverpool Advance*, 15 December 1909, obituary of Steven
Glode of Milton, aged sixty-four years. T.B. Smith was
one of the pallbearers at the funeral, which was well
attended.

238 Steven Francis was a son of Joseph Francis and Cary
Ann Luxey of Clyde River. Lisa Francis and staff of the
Simeon Perkins Museum Archives have compiled a
detailed genealogy of the Francis family of Yarmouth,

Shelburne and Queens counties that is housed in the
Queens County Archives n Liverpool.

239 Registers of St. Gregory's Parish, Liverpool. Frank Glode
died of consumption at age twenty-five and was interred
at the cemetery at Ponhock on 22 February 1871.

240 On the 1901 federal census for Bridgewater North in
Lunenburg County, Fanny Pennel was born in 1841 and
her husband Peter Glode, who was eleven years younger,
was born in 1852. The couple had two daughters, Julia
born in 1879 and Elizabeth born in 1891. Peter Glode
may also have had an uncle who lived in Lunenburg
County, since the 1901 census lists a James Glode living
at Lunenburg who was sixty-four, and so born in 1837.
In the 1920s Peter Glode Jr. was often referred to as a
"chief" by the Bridgewater townspeople, though he was
not recognized as a chief at either Gold River or New
Germany.

241 Joseph Pennel and Sophia Rafuse's marriage certificate
appears in NSARM, Historical Vital Statistics, Queeens
County Marriages, "Marriage at La Have of James Penall,
son of Joseph Penall and Sophia Rafuse, and Mary Ann
Glode, age twenty, daughter of Francis Glode and Mary
Anne [*sic*, Madeline] Molti, St. Gregory's Parish, 19 January 1870, witnesses James Labrador and Rosa Newel."

242 Joseph, James, Peter, and Francis Glode, who were all on
the Annapolis County band list for 1856, often hunted
around Kejimkujik Lake. NSARM, MG 15, vol. 6, no. 1,
List of Mi'kmaq of Annapolis, 1856.

243 Milford and Area History Group, *Through the Woods*,
64–5.

244 *The Tent Dwellers* (New York: Outing, 1908) begins
with a detailed descriptor of Milford House, which is
still in operation today. Paine was also Mark Twain's
biographer.

245 Stephen Francis Glode died on 9 December 1909 at Milton, aged sixty-four. NSARM, Historical Vital Statisitics,
Queens County deaths, Registration year 1909, book 15,
p. 11, no. 181.

246 James in later life moved to Dartmouth where he
married Anne LaFayette and raised two children, a
son Newel and a daughter whose name could not be
determined.

247 The first child of this union, Mary Anne Glode, was not
with Samuel's family in 1881. James Glode died of consumption at age four.

248 James Michael's birthdate is derived from CEF Attesta-
tion Papers, soldier detail. Prior to the war, James was a
lumberman.

249 Maria Katherine married John Francis, who became a
close friend of Sam Freeman Gloade. "Kate" and John

had several children, including a daughter Rosie May in 1910. NSARM, Historical Vital Statistics, Queens County Births, Registration Year 1910, p. 5300364, no. 53900366, Birth of Rosie May, 13 Febuary 1910.

250 This second Stephen Glode Jr. in his later years lived at Millbrook and died a single man in 1954 in Halifax. He was buried at Millbrook.

251 Sarah Ann Labrador died on 23 May 1904 at the age of forty-three, while her husband died in 1909. NSARM, Historical Vital Statistics, Queens County Deaths, book 15, p. 31, no. 181, "Death of Stephen Glode, 64, of bowel disease, 9 December 1909."

252 NSARM, Historical Vital Statistics, Queens County Marriages, book 66, p. 968, "Marriage at Liverpool of Michael Glode, age fifty-two, son of Stephen Glode and Sarah Jane Labrador, and Elizabeth Labrador, widow, daughter of James Carver and Elizabeth Dorey of Lunenburg, 27 August 1932." Elizabeth, or "Bessie," died and was buried at Liverpool on 17 December 1949. NSARM, Historical Vital Statistics, Queens County Deaths, Registration Year 1949, p. 6398. NSARM, Historical Vital Stistics, Registration Year 1932 Queens County Marriages, "Marriage of Michael Glode and Elizabeth Labrador (née Carver)." Harold Gloade mentions Michael in *From My Vantage Point* (Nepean, ON: Borealis, 1991), 9.

253 Halifax & South Western Railway, *Summer Resorts along the Road by the Sea* (tourist brochure) (Halifax, 1916), 11.

254 NSM, Printed Matter File, Harry Piers, unpublished notes, 11 and 18 March 1916. Piers referred to James as "a member of the old well-known Micmac family of Claude."

255 NSARM, Historical Vital Statistics, Halifax County Deaths, Registration Year 1954, 2817, "Death of Peter Newell Glode of cancer of the pancreas, April 18, 1954." Peter for a while was manager of a hunting lodge serving Crousetown and Petite Rivière in Lunenburg County. Robert M. Mennel, *Testimonies and Secrets: The Story of a Nova Scotian Family, 1844–1977* (Toronto: University of Toronto Press, 2013), 177.

256 During his later years Stephen Glode was cared for by Annie Stephens of Millbrook.

257 NSARM, Historical Vital Statistics, Halifax County marriages, book 1821, p. 162, no. 577, "Marriage of James A. Glode, son of Stephen Glode and Mary Jane Labrador, to Anastasia Lafford, daughter of William and Sarah Lafford of Londonderry," 28 October 1912; NSARM, Historical Vital Statistics, Halifax County Deaths, book 83, 832, "Death of Joseph Glode, the one-day-old son of James Albert Glode and Anastasia Lafford of asphyxia,"

1 July 1922. The child's body was buried in Dartmouth. NSARM, Historical Vital Statistics, book 84, 943. One of James and Anastasia Lafford's sons, Newel (or Noel) Benjamin Glode, in 1938 wed Anne Margaret Wilmot, a daughter of Peter Wilmot and Christine Sappier of Pictou Landing. NSARM, Historical Vital Statistics, County Marriages, Registration Year 1938, book 91, 872. By the time of his son Newel's marriage, James had died. He lived at Lake William with his brother Peter for two years before his death.

258 The Glodes were enumerated in Shelburne on the 1891 census.

259 Polly Labrador was identified as a medicine woman by Hilton Scott, a mill operator at Great Pubnico Lake. Mike Parker, *Woodchips & Beans: Life in the Early Lumber Woods of Nova Scotia* (Halifax: Nimbus, 1992), 56.

260 "Sam Glode, Micmac Indian," 5; Peter Duffy, "Aboriginal People & the First World War," *Mi'kmaq-Maliseet Nations News*, May 2014, p. 14.

261 NSARM, vol. 432, 93–96. The couple were married by Father Egan. For years, members of the Francis family moved between the Barrington River in Shelburne County and the Mersey River in Queens County. In 1843 Joseph Howe ordered an allotment of seven hundred acres in Shelburne County to be surveyed for Joseph Francis, Freeman Francis, John Paul, Molly Paul, and Paul Williams on Great Pubnico Lake, Yarmouth County, though this reserve was not transferred to Ottawa at Confederation. Some of the Francis family also took up residence at Milton.

262 It has been argued, however, that the deaf-mute boy nicknamed "Little Chief," who was raised by Molti (or Malti) Francis until Molti entered the mental hospital, was actually Sam's son, born out of wedlock to him and Elizabeth Glode. See Dalhousie Archives, Raddall Papers, box 298, folder 8, "Malti Went Crazy," 3 pages. Oral traditions circulating in Milton also aver that Molti Francis sufferedfrom dementia that was exacerbated by syphilis, which he contracted while overseas serving in the First World War. Molti died on 14 October 1956, aged sixty-six, at the Dartmouth Hospital in Cole Harbour from chronic schizophrenia. NSARM, Halifax County Deaths, Registration Year 1956, 5258, "Death of Malti (or Molti) Francis, October 1956." His death certificate stated he was born at Shubenacadie in 1890.

263 NSARM, T.B. Smith Papers, No. 835, microfilm reel 14,948, Glode family – Lewis Glode.

264 NSARM, Historical Vital Statistics, Queens County Marriages, book 6, p. 495, "Marriage of Louis Glode, lumberman, to Minnie Lowe (née Carver), widow,

daughter of Henry Carver and Catherine Cowie, 8 August 1921." One of Walter Louis Glode's descendents is Bev Purdy of the Acadia First Nation, who is also a descendent of Josephine Luxy of Yarmouth County. Bev and her husband Brian live on the site of Simeon Perkin's old trading post at Milton. Both Bev and her sister Cathy Conrad spoke out about recent misrepresentations in the press that stated Sam Glode was from Bear River or even Cape Breton. Samuel Freeman Glode's surname is sometimes spelled "Gloade" in recent articles, although he always used the spelling "Glode." Brittany W. Verge, "'Our Sam Gloade': First World War Mi'kmaq Veteran was from Queens County," *Digby County Courier*, 19 August 2014, https://www.saltwire.com/atlantic-canada/federal-election/our-sam-gloade-first-world-war-mikmaq-veteran-was-from-queens-county-38881/.

265 Members of the Glode/Gloade family buried in the Deer Lake Roman Catholic cemetery include James (1916–95), Mike, and Myrtle (1917–91).

266 There are members of the Glode/Gloade family today living in Deer Lake and Cornerbrook.

267 Fales, who also had an interest in theoretical physics, died in 1954. At Dalhousie University there is an endowment set up in his name called the Fales Visiting Professorship.

268 "Sam Glode, Micmac Indian," 13.

269 Caplan, "Sam Glode: Travels," 26.

270 Peter Duffy, "Aboriginal People and the First World War," *Mi'kmaq-Maliseet Nations News*, May 2014.

271 NSARM, T.B. Smith Papers, No. 835, microfilm reel 14,948. Glode family – Samuel Freeman Glode. Sam was considering making a secret escape with his men from the tunnel under cover of nightfall, when Scotty Forrest, a man serving under Glode, heard men digging through the soil and all realized that a party had been sent to rescue them and help was at hand.

272 "Sam Glode, Micmac Indian," 21.

273 Ibid., 21. In addition, Sam received the British War Medal, the Victory Medal, and the Medal for the Great War for Civilization, 1914–1919.

274 The Distinguished Conduct Medal (DCM) was instituted in 1854 during the Crimean War to recognize gallantry within the "other ranks," for which it was the equivalent of the Distinguished Service Order (DSO) awarded for bravery shown by commissioned officers. In 1993, after a committee reviewed the military honours system, the DCM and DSO were discontinued as they were rank-associated decorations. The Conspicuous Gallantry Cross (CGC) now serves as the second-level award below the Victoria Cross for gallantry across all ranks and within the entire armed forces.

275 The main lodge of Milford House burned down in 2000, was restored soon afterward as a wilderness retreat, then burned down again in 2014, and has again been rebuilt.

276 Dennis, *More about Nova Scotia*, 409.

277 The mystery of the two missing boys still haunts Mi'kmaw and non-Mi'kmaw communities alike in Queens County. On 7 December 1941 two sons of Murray and Lucy (née Zwicker) Laing went to tend rabbit snares on a family trapline northwest of Liverpool in countryside that they both knew well, Queens County woods. Floyd Laing was nearly fourteen and Victor Laing was nine. (Lucy had been wed previously and Floyd was the son of her first marriage while Victor was Murray and Lucy's biological son.) Neither boy was seen alive again. Search parties scoured the countryside for eighteen years before hunters in 1959 discovered the boys' rubber boots, their skulls, a jacket, and a hatchet in a thicket far inland from where the boys usually trapped. The two skulls and other items had been set down in a semi-ritual formation on the ground, so it was obvious that the boys had succumbed to foul play. No other bones than the skulls were located. Sam Glode, speaking in Mi'kmaq, asked the man suspected of the crime if he had anything to do with the children's disappearance. The man, old and ill by this time, refused to confirm or deny the suspicions about him, and simply turned away towards the wall. A daughter of the Mi'kmaw man suspected of committing the crime once told folklorist Dr. Helen Creighton that her father "had been a witch and could kill people with his evil eye." No concrete grounds, however, could ever be found to implicate him in the crime. Ruth Legge, "Little Boys Lost: The Disappearance of Two Brothers Had a Profound Effect on Queens County Family," *Halifax Chronicle*, 23 November 2008.

278 Obituary of Samuel Freeman Glode, *Liverpool Advance*, 31 October 1957; Armand F. Wigglesworth, "Guides Sam Glode, DCM, and John Francis Go to War," *Liverpool Advance*, 1 March 1995.

279 "Sam Glode, Micmac Indian," 21.

280 These geological and geographical distinctions gave rise in the past to two district Mi'kmaw bands in the far southwestern end of the Nova Scotian peninsula: the Annapolis band, which held territorial aegis over lands along the Mersey-Medway river system, and the Cape Sable band, whose lands covered Yarmouth County, part of Digby County, and extended eastwards to the Clyde River in Shelburne County.

281 The pioneering genealogical investigations into Acadian-Mi'kmaw relations undertaken by Father Clarence-J. d'Entremont of West Pubnico have been continued by historical genealogist Ian Lawrence of Annapolis Royal. D'Entremont accessed material in the Roman Catholic registers belonging to the parishes of Ste. Anne du Ruisseau, St. Pierre de Pubnico, and St. Croix at Plympton and St. Vincent de Paul at Salmon River, both in Digby County. In addition to these registers, Ian Lawrence included entries from St. Louis parish at Annapolis, St. Gregory's parish at Liverpool, and St. Jerome's parish in Caledonia. Lawrence's genealogical findings are available to the public in a booklet housed at the Annapolis Historical Museum and Archives at Annapolis Royal.

282 Jean Baptist Alexis was the son of Francis Alexis, the Cape Sable head chief in 1771, while Bartholomew Alexis was a son of Charles Alexis, a brother of Francis Alexis, and Francis's successor as Cape Sable district chief. Charles Alexis around 1754 married an Acadian woman named Anne Hébert, the daughter of Antoine Hébert and his second wife, Anne Orillion. D'Entremont, *Histoire de Cap-Sable*, 3.976–7; d'Entremont, *History of Quinan, Nova Scotia* (Metegan, Yarmouth County: L'imprimerie Lescarbot, 1984), 8; personal conversations with Father Clarence-J. d'Entremont. The Claudes/Glodes and Alexis families continued to intermarry. For instance, the registers of Ste. Anne du Ruisseau show that Francis-Joseph Glode married Magdalene Alexis in 1832, who died the year following her marriage, in 1833.

283 Chief Joseph Martin Claude had a large number of children. Francis Glode and Joseph Glode of Caledonia and Lequille were two of the eldest, while Abraham Glode Sr. of Bear River and Greenfield and (presumably) Matthew Glode and John Glode, who moved from Caledonia to the Barrington area, were younger sons.

284 Matthew Glode died in 1913. NSARM, Historical Vital Statistics, Yarmouth County Deaths, book 19, p. 282, no. 1664, "Death of Matthew Glaud, 30 April 1913, at eighty-eight years of age." Samuel, Matthew's son, informed the authorities of Matthew's death. (This death certificate is hard to locate since it is incorrectly filed under the name "Martha E.L. Glode" rather than "Matthew Glode"). Matthew's brother John died around 1890 and John's widow, Victoria Murree, died at eighty-four in 1918. NSARM, Historical Vital Statistics, Year 1918, book 51, 33. After Matthew and John Glode's deaths, some of their descendants who joined the Acadia First Nation continued to spell their surname "Glode" while others spelled it "Gloade."

285 NSM, Printed Matter File, Piers Notes, "Jeremiah Bartlett Alexis to Harry Piers," 29 April 1921.

286 This family continued to spell their surname "Glode" until the 1920s, although the spelling in most other parts of southwestern Nova Scotia had changed to "Gloade."

287 When Joseph Howe met these Mi'kmaq on his route through Barrington in 1842, they asked for 700 acres of land on Great Pubnico Lake. Many of the Francis family later left for the Milton area, but some continued up until the 1960s to maintain cottages on land in the Barrington and Clyde River area.

288 NSARM, RG 15, vol. 6, doc. 73, "Petition and census of Chief Peter Charles [Sulno]," March 1866.

289 This had been a grant to proprietor and Anglican cleric John Breyton, but owing to lack of improvements, it had been forfeited to the Crown.

290 NSARM, Misc. "I" Indian Land Documents from Dept., Pkg. 40. "James McKay to James H. Austin, September 18, 1894. With Plan and Field Notes, Great Pubnico Lake Reserve, by James A. McKay, Deputy Surveyor, August 23, 1894." As this tract had been surveyed under instructions from Joseph Howe in 1843, and locals remembered it as having been so laid out, it was surveyed a second time in 1894. But Ottawa finally concluded that as the land had not been transferred to the federal government at Confederation, the Mi'kmaq had no claim to it.

291 NSARM, Historical Vital Statistics, Yarmouth County Deaths, Registration Year 1957, number 5210, "Death of Stephen Glode, age 72 years 3 months, on 1 October 1957 by burning in his home on Starr's Road in Yarmouth." Informant was Ernest Glode. This certificate states that Stephen was born on 25 June 1885.

292 According to the census for 1911, Stephen Glode was twenty-three in that year (so born in 1888), and he and his wife Mary Caroline had an eight-year-old daughter named Lillian. Canada, Census of 1911, Nova Scotia, District 53 Yarmouth, Sub-District Sluice Point, Amirault Hill, Tusket Village and Pleasant Lake, household 279. Mary Caroline was thus only twelve years old when she had Lillian. (The information provided by the 1911 census also lists Mary Caroline's birthdate as July 1895 and her age in 1911 as sixteen. This is incorrect, as she could not have been eight years old when she had Lillian.) The census of 1891 lists Mary Caroline Bartlett as being six months old in that year. The page honouring Stephen Glode on the Wartime Heritage site claims his birth year was 1888 (not 1885) and he was married to Mary Caroline Bartlett, http://www.wartimeheritage.com/whawwithosewhoserved/whawwithosewhoserved_glode_stephen.htm.

293 "No Trace of Missing Lad," *Dartmouth Herald*, 28 February 1933. Clarence and Gordon were described as

"scholars," meaning students, on their death certificates. NSARM, Historical Vital Statistics, Yarmouth County Deaths, Registration Year 1933, book 156, p. 56 and book 154, p. 54, "Deaths of Clarence and Gordon Glode at Tusket, household 1."

294 NSARM, Historical Vital Statistics, Yarmouth County Marriages, Registration Year 1939, book 96, 243, "Marriage at Tusket of Evangeline A. Glode, daughter of Stephen Glode and Mary Caroline Bartlett, and Charles Alexander Daurie [or Dorey], son of Truman Dorey and Bessie Hallimore of Newburne, Lunenburg County, 7 November 1939, witnesses Rose, Mary, and Stephen Bartlett." Bessie Hallimore was a descendant of Thomas Cotton, who during the War of 1812 escaped from a press gang and afterwards took the surname "Hallimore." Cotton was a companion of another escapee who took the name "Thomas Hammond," and who later married into the Gold River band of Lunenburg County. See chapter 8.

295 Stephen Glode was born in Barrington on 25 June 1885. Wartime Heritage Association, Remembering World War I, Yarmouth Connections, Private Stephen Glode, http://www.wartimeheritage.com/whawwithosewho-served/whawwithosewhoserved_glode_stephen.htm; NSARM, Historical Vital Statistics, Yarmouth County Deaths, Registration Year 1948, p. 1316, "Death of Mary Caroline Glode"; NSARM, Historical Vital Statistics, Yarmouth County Deaths Registration Year 1957, no. 5210, "Death of Stephen Glode, seventy-two years of age."

296 NSARM, Historical Vital Statistics, Yarmouth County Deaths, book 156, 578, "Death of Samuel Glode, Pubnico, 14 February 1935."

297 Registers of Ste. Anne du Ruisseau, Eel Brook, Yarmouth County, "Baptism of Pierre, son of Matthew and Victoire Claude, 31 March 1963, witnesses Étienne Claude and Mary François." Pierre afterwards disappears from the documentary record.

298 Matthew Glode and Victoire Francis's sons Samuel and John William became well-known guides in the Pubnico region. Their daughter, Mary Ann Catherine married a member of the Carty family who also guided. Samuel Glode wed Molly Murree and had at least one son, John. Samuel Glode, who died in 1935. NSARM, Historical Vital Statistics, Year 1935, Yarmouth County Deaths, book 156, 575. His brother John William married Mary Elizabeth Murree, a daughter of John Murree and Sarah Frontain of Quinan, and the couple had a son, John Newel (1889–1960) and, in 1892, a daughter, Margaret. In 1909 John Newel wed Margaret Elizabeth Ann Robbins,

a daughter of Henry Robbins and Elizabeth Connolly *dit* Quinan. Registers of the Church of St. Pierre, West Pubnico; Canada, Census of 1911, Yarmouth. John Newel's mother, Mary Elizabeth Murree, died in 1944. NSARM, Historical Vital Statistics, Year 1944, Yarmouth County Deaths, book 209, 681, "Death of Mary Elizabeth Murree Glode, age eighty-three." John Newel continued guiding until the early 1950s and then moved to the town of Yarmouth. He and Margaret Elizabeth Ann Robbins had seven children: James, who moved to Saint John, New Brunswick; George; Katherine; Blanche, who married Stanley Surrette; Margery; Mary, who wed Harvey Nelson; and Frank. All but James remained in the Yarmouth area. Obituary, Mrs. Margaret Ann Glode, *Yarmouth Light*, 8 June 1966. Margaret (née Robbins) Glode's obituary reads in part: "She is survived by two sons, James, who lives in Saint John; George, Yarmouth; four daughters, Katherine, Yarmouth Blanche (Mrs. Stanley Surrette), Yarmouth; Margery Yarmouth; Mary or Marian (Mrs. Harvey Nelson), Yarmouth; three grandchildren and three great grandchildren." Margery was Katherine's daughter, raised by Margaret. There was another son, Samuel Elmer, who was born on 11 November 1925 and died on 4 November 1962. Samuel Elmer married Hilda Leona Gaudet in 1945. This couple's daughter, Deborah Dianne Gloade, is currently in charge of band membership at the Acadia First Nation in Yarmouth. The author is very grateful to Deborah for providing information regarding the Glode/Gloade family of the Pubnico Lake Road and Yarmouth from the 1920s to the present. There is, however, still much to learn about the early history of this family.

299 Queens County Museum and Archives, Liverpool, Francis Family Genealogy. While he lived with them at West Pubnico, Sam Gloade remembered watching his Yarmouth relatives spearing fish while poling their canoes up the Tusket River.

300 Claire Mius was the daughter of Charles Amand *dit* d'Azy and Marie Josette Mius of Argyle. Her grandfather, Charles Amand Sr., married Marie-Marthe Hebert, who was a half-sister to Anne Hébert, the wife of Charles Alexis, the Cape Sable head chief in the late 1700s.

301 Otherwise, as Father Clarence-J. d'Entremont has noted, his background remained mysterious. D'Entremont, *History of Quinan*, 21–3.

302 The residents of the Great Pubnico Lake Road faced major difficulties in getting title to their lots, and only a few managed to do so. The land around Great Pubnico Lake and towards Barrington had been granted to a mix of Acadian and Irish proprietors, while the countryside

from Woods Harbour eastward to the Clyde River had been taken up by sixteen proprietors. If the Mi'kmaq and others belonging to the Pubnico Lake Road community could not buy land, either because of its unavailibilty or because they lacked the monetary means, they simply squatted on Crown land.

303 Book JH, p. 36, Conveyance of land from John Glode to Ray Skinner, 17 April 1947. This transaction was not recorded at the deeds office until 12 September 1974. Deed Book for 1975, p. 431, doc. no. 501006389, Between May Nelson, Katie Deveau, Blanche Surette, George W. Glode, and Hilda Glode, Grantors, and George W. Glode and Mary M. Glode his wife, Grantee, 4 August 1975. The grantees received the tract for one dollar.

304 Yarmouth Deeds Office, Land Conveyance between John Newel Glode and Bourneuf Lovitt, registered 17 May 1929, doc. 225. This embraced the two-hundred-acre parcel.

305 Mike Parker, *Woodchips & Beans*, 56–7.

306 Ibid.

307 "A small rapid existed at Wabei … then it was smooth going to Big Falls above Barrington Lake, then there was Weir Falls, then Sorrow Falls, Island Falls, Chrissie's Falls and then Phil's Falls." Ibid., 56.

308 NSARM, Historical Vital Statistics, Yarmouth County Deaths, book 19, p. 282, no. 1663, "Death of Matthew Glode, eighty-eight years old, 30 April 1913." His death certificate states that Matthew was a hunter from Pubnico Head. See also notes on file written by Father Clarence-J. d'Entremont, Musée Acadien and Archives de Pubnico-Ouest, Yarmouth County. Though John Glode Sr.'s exact death date is unknown, oral traditions attest that he died in West Pubnico and his body was transferred to St. Ambroise cemetery in Yarmouth for burial.

309 St. Pierre de Pubnico parish registers, marriage of Willam James Carty, son of Étienne Carty and Maria Elizabeth Charles, to Mary Catherine Claude [Glode], daughter of James (John) Claude and Mary (*sic*, Victoria Murree), 28 August 1886; witnesses James Claude and Christine Claude. William James Carty drowned in 1915 at age forty-six, while his widow died at West Pubnico on 8 March 1930. NSARM, Historical Vital Statistics, Yarmouth County Deaths, Registration Year 1915, book 50, p. 153, no. 506, "Death of William James Carty." Mary Anne Glode-Carty, a daughter of Matthew Glode and Victoire Francis, married a brother (unnamed) of William James Carty. Mary Ann Carty was born in 1860, died on 8 March 1930, and was buried at West Pubnico by John Glode. NSARM, Historical Vital Statistics, Registration Year 1930, Yarmouth County Deaths, book 133, 943.

310 Information obtained from Father Clarence-J. d'Entremont in October 1997, as well as from notes housed in the Musée Acadienne at West Pubnico.

311 NSARM, Historical Vital Statistics, Yarmouth County Deaths, Registration Year 1915, book 50, p. 153, no. 50, "Death of William Carty, forty-six years old." The authorities were informed on 15 May 1915. Carty had been a hunter and guide. It has been said that the surname "Carty" belonged to an Irishman who in the eighteenth century lived among the Acadians, but according to William Carty's death certificate, his parents were "English."

312 Parker, *Woodchips & Beans*, 57.

313 NSARM, Historical Vital Statistics, Yarmouth County deaths, Registration Year 1918, book 51, p. 133, no. 434, "Death of Victoria Glode, widow of John Glode of Bear River and Pubnico Head, 27 December 1918, seventy-four years old." Victoire died of paralysis of the throat.

314 Nelson married John Newel's daughter Mary Marian Glode. Mary Marion, the last member of John Newell's immediate family, died on 4 June 2017. Her siblings Samuel, George, James, Catherine, and Blanche predeceased her. She was born to John Glode and Margaret Robbins on 7 January 1914 and grew up on the Pubnico Lake Road. A housewife, housekeeper at Yarmouth, and "mother figure" to her many nieces and nephews, she lived to be 103 years of age. She and her husband were well-known figures in the Pubnico Lake Road community. Her sister, Catherine or "Katie" Glode, who married George Deveau, died on 24 August 2010.

315 These are described in accordance with a map and a set of notes drawn up by Father Clarence-J. d'Entremont's uncle, Leander d'Entremont, and are presently housed in Les Archives Père Clarence d'Entremont, Musée Acadien, West Pubnico.

316 NSARM, Historical Vital Statistics, Yarmouth County Deaths, Registration Year 1960, no. 5696, "Death of John Newel Glode, 10 October 1960." Though several of John Newell's children and grandchildren moved to Ontario and others to the United States, a few still live in the Yarmouth area. Debra Gloade, one of John Newel's granddaughters who assisted immeasurably with this chapter, is a registration administrator at Yarmouth with the Acadia First Nation.

317 Captain Toney (Anthony Ury) appears as a supporter of the Britain cause between 1776 and 1783 in the James White Papers housed in the Provincial Archives of New Brunswick.

318 LAC, MG 23, GII-19, Monk Papers, George Henry Papers, Accounts, p. 11247, Supplies given Lewey Glode and his wife Sally Glode en route with John Muse and

others to visit the Roman Catholic priest in Cumberland County, 4 June 1797. Lewey Glode and Sally requested supplies again on their return trip to the Annapolis Basin region on 18 October 1797. NSARM, RG 1, vol. 430, doc. nos. 65 and 66, "George Oxley at River Philip regarding 85 Mi'kmaw persons living in Cumberland County," 16 April 1801, along with a requisition for supplies distributed to them, dated June 1801.

319 The Mi'kmaq from the Gut of Annapolis group seasonally crossed the Bay of Fundy to the Parrsboro Shore to hunt, and by the mid-1850s several Glodes originally from the Annapolis Basin area had settled permanently in Cumberland County. Abraham Glode was born on 1 April 1867 when his parents from Lequille were camping in New Brunswick. They later travelled with the band in Cumberland County, where Abraham on his parents' death in 1875 was left an orphan. He was raised by John Logan, a well-known Mi'kmaw head man living near Amherst. The Logan and Toney families for years had supplied responsible leaders to the Maccan (or *Nemcheboowek*, which means "going up rising ground") group near Amherst.

Abraham married twice. His first wife was a Mi'kmaw woman named Mary (surname unknown), and the couple travelled frequently to New Brunswick and Maine. His second wife was Annie Jane McGrath, the daughter of an Irishman named Michael McGrath and an Acadian woman, Katherine Doucet of Parrsboro. Abraham and Annie raised two daughters, Lena May and Annie Josephine, and two sons, James and George Dewey, on a small but thriving farm at Newville. Lena Glode married Stanley Albert Gilroy in 1930 and Annie wed Joseph Privell. Abraham died at Halfway River, Cumberland County, in 1932. His second wife, Annie Jane McGrath, who was born on 20 May 1874, died at Stanley at age eighty-eight on 9 February 1963. She was buried in Parrsboro. Canada, Census of 1881, Mill Village, Cumberland County Nova Scotia; Canada, Census of 1891, Parrsboro subdivision, Cumberland County; NSARM, Historical Vital Statistics, Cumberland County Deaths, book 143, p. 141, "Death of Abraham Glode at Halfway River"; NSARM, microfilm reel 2,877, *Springhill Record*, p. 5, "Obituary of Abram [*sic*, Abraham] Glode, 29 September 1932"; NSARM, Historical Vital Statistics, Cumberland County Deaths, Registration Year 1963, p. 19445, "Death of Annie Glode, 1963."

320 By the early 1900s members of the Glode family lived at Newville, Springhill, and Stanley in Cumberland County. Noel Glode from Cumberland County, whose mother was listed simply as "Charlotte" in the documentary record, in 1935 married Rachael Pictou, a daughter of Josephine Luxey and James Pictou of Yarmouth County. NSARM, Historical Vital Statistics, book 76, p. 331, "Marriage of Rachael Pictou and Noel Gloade." Before his marriage to Rachael, Noel had moved back from Cumberland County to Bear River. The couple had a son, Newel, born at Yarmouth in 1937 and who died the following year. NSARM, Historical Vital Statistics, Yarmouth County Deaths, book 6, p. 195, no. 1166. Rachael and Noel's marriage must have been short lived, however, since in 1939 Rachael wed Pius Louis Surette, a son of John Alcide Surette and Anita Doty.

321 Nancy Glode, born in 1805, the wife of John Glode, died at Bear River in 1913 at the age of ninety-eight years. NSARM, Historical Vital Statistics, Digby County Deaths, "Death of Nancy Glode, widow of John Glode," Registration Year 1913, book 12, 221. In its early years the Bear River Mi'kmaw community suffered from food scarcities owing to lack of sustained farming and continued scarcity of game, so the government arranged for corn, beans, and molasses to be distributed to Bear River families. It was noted during the 1829 distribution that John Glode had died the previous year and his widow had remarried. NSARM, RG 1, vol. 430, doc. 169a, "Account of 40 Bbls Corn, 3 Bbls Beans and 64 Gallons Molasses delivered to the Indians at the Bear River Settlement by Stewart and Burch [? indistinct] under the direction of Judge Wiswal, Digby, 7 January 1829."

322 NSARM, RG 1, vol. 430, docs. 164 ½ and 169 ½, "Account of 40 Hwt. Potatoes delivered to the Indians at the Bear River Settlement by Stewart Bruce by order of Judge Wiswall, May 1828; Acct. of 40 B. Corn and 3 Buls. Beans and 64 Gls. Molasses delivered to the Indians at the Bear River Settlement by Stewart Bruce," 7 January 1829.

323 NSARM, RG 1, vol. 432, 95.

324 Francis and his contemporaries did not always have the right to choose the location of their farms at Bear River. For instance, in 1842 Howe requested that a "fifth lot" adjoining that of Francis Paul be laid out for Newell Paul, though this tract does not appear later on the reserve's survey plan. NSARM, RG 1, vol.432, 114–115, "Nicholls to Howe," 3 December 1842.

325 NSARM, MG 15, vol. 3 no. 14, "Robert Leslie regarding Francis Glode of Bear River," 30 October 1846; letter of 11 November 1846.

326 NSARM, MG 15, vol. 3 no. 14, "Robert Leslie regarding Francis Glode," 30 October 1846. Leslie stated that the government should take notice of Francis Glode and his companion, James Meuse Jr., owing to their "generous

and disinterested conduct to their fellow sufferers." NSARM, MG 15, vol. 6, no. 65, "Leslie to John Hayter," 1846. Leslie was concerned about the way Francis had been treated in Halifax when he went to petition for his grant. In a letter to Captain Chearnley, Leslie held that Francis had been told the House was sitting and he could not approach the lieutenant governor.

327 Francis Glode and Magdalene Knockwood were the parents of James (Jim) Glode, the famous guide. Francis lived at Bear River in the 1840s, and according to James Glode his father was "Joseph." There also were several other Francis Glodes, though younger than Jim's father, who appeared in the documentrary record: William Francis Glode, born about 1800, who married Susan Labrador and resided in Digby County; Francis Glode, born about 1810, who wed Madeline Newel; and Francis Glode, born about 1804, who married Fanny LaPierre (or Sapierre, or "Jacques Pierre') and had Polly Glode baptized at St. Gregory's in 1842.

328 Many of these photographs are housed in the Nova Scotia Museum of Natural History in Halifax. A photograph exists of Jim Glode wearing ceremonial garb at a St. Anne's Day ceremony, c. 1891, as well as one in the William Dennis Collection at the Nova Scotia Museum of him taken later in life.

329 NSM, Printed Matter File, Isaac Sack to Harry Piers, 26 February 1921; Noel Lewis Macdonald to Piers, 28 April 1921; Jeremiah Bartlett-Alexis to Piers, 19 April 1921.

330 This trip was evidently unsuccessful, as they failed to take any large game.

331 Although Jerry Bartlett-Alexis and Isaac Sack both claim Jim went with Lord Dunraven, Piers tends to question this, stressing instead that Jim went to the Rocky Mountains with Charles Alexander and his brother, who came to North America to hunt for twenty-five years.

332 Jim Glode stated to Clara Dennis, a Halifax journalist, in 1929 that he had come to know the Alexander family well and mentioned that Charles Alexander had two brothers, Walter and Charles, who both had died by 1929.

333 The names of only three of Peter Glode's wives are known: Janet Prosper Toney, Jeannette Toney, and Annie Maloney Toney. His first wife may have been named "Mary Jane" but her surname is unknown. Peter married Anne Maloney Tony, a daughter of John Tony and Mary from Dorchester in New Brunswick, at Enfield in 1916. NSARM, Historical Vital Statistics, Hants County Marriages, book 1824, p. 179, no. 29.

334 NSARM, MG 1, vol. 2867, no. 6, Clara Dennis Notebooks, Interview with Jim Glode, Shubenacadie, 26 July 1929. Dennis held that Jim's birthday fell on 26 July 1831, St. Anne's Day, a celebratory festival for the Mi'kmaq, though he was actually born a day earlier: his death certificate reports him as born on 25 July 1831. NSARM, Historical Vital Statistics, Hants County Deaths, Registration Year 1936, book 146, p. 745, "Death of James Glode of acute bronchitis at the age of 104 years and 7 months." Jim was buried at Shubencadie on 2 March 1936.

335 Though Dennis might have been slightly taken aback by this remark that Jim's grandfather Joe Glode was a Frenchman from Liverpool, Jim was trying to convey that his grandfather, Chief Joseph Martin Claude, who came to Liverpool, was descended from Martin Grand Claude Sr. and Marguerite Le Jeune of La Have, and hence was an Acadian *métis.*

336 Joseph and Jim Glode appear to have been born in the same year. This would make Joseph a son of Francis Glode and Magdalene Knockwood. Francis and Magdalene had two other sons, James and Simeon or Simon. (No exact dates of birth or death could be found for these two sons.) It is also possible that Matthew Glode of West Pubnico, born in 1825, was another of Francis's sons, though Matthew was more likely a son of Francis's father, Chief Joseph Martin Claude.

337 Anthropologist Frank Goldsmith Speck located Joseph Glode's hunting territory north of Maitland in Queens County. Speck, *Beothuck and Micmac,* 101.

338 NSARM, Clara Dennis Notebooks, Interview with Joseph Glode, 1929. Joseph Glode, as mentioned above, was likely a grandson of Chief Joseph Martin Claude. Chief Claude, born in 1766, lived to around 1840 and so was about seventy-five years old when he died.

339 Dalhousie Archives, Raddall Papers, MS 2.202.Q&F, "The Indian Devil Country."

340 In 1861 Francis Glode's son Simon had petitioned the government for a land grant near Dalhousie Crossing, lying on the Mi'kmaw overland route from La Have to Annapolis Royal, but when he failed to receive it he moved back to Annapolis County. NSARM, MG 15, vol. 6, doc. 64, "Petition from Simon Glode to the Earl of Mulgrave," 21 December 1861. Simon wanted to purchase one hundred acres of land in the Township of Dalhousie, Annapolis County, lying twenty-one miles south of the town of Dalhousie "as he has already improved it."

341 NSARM, Clara Dennis Notebooks, Interview with Jim Glode, 26 July 1929.

342 Ibid.

343 Jim Glode is said to have accompanied the Earl of Dunraven to Colorado in 1872, although this is unlikely.

Lord Dunraven, the 4th Earl of Dunraven and Mount-Earl (1841–1926), avidly pursued hunting adventures around the world and visited the American West in 1872. Though the earl wrote about his expedition to Colorado, he did not once mention Jim Glode accompanying him as a guide. Windham Thomas Wyndham-Quin, Earl of Dunraven, "A Colorado Sketch," in *Canadian Nights: Being Sketches and Reminiscences of Life and Sport in the Rockies, the Prairies, and the Canadian Woods* (London: Smith, Elder, 1914), 20–51. A good source from which to gain information on Dunraven's and other British aristocrats' adventures in the American West is Peter Pagnamenta, *Prairie Fever: British Aristocrats in the American West, 1830–1890* (New York: W.W. Norton, 2012). Like other adventurers of this kind, Dunraven was no conservationist. On one expedition in southwestern Nova Scotia, where Jim may well have been present, he is reputed to have shot a whole herd of caribou and taken only their antlers.

344 Jim Glode married at least twice. The mother of the majority of his children was Mary Paul. Jim and Mary had Susan in 1868, Peter in 1870, Joseph in 1872, Louis in 1874, Rebecca in 1879, and Anne in 1882, as well as others, but as he said, only two of his children were still living in 1929. He told Clara Dennis that he once had ten children living with him, but eight of them had succumbed to various diseases. He was, however, reputed to have had twenty-six children throughout his lifetime. Ruth Homes Whitehead, "Glode, James," *DCB* online, vol. 16 (1931–40). When Jim began to go blind in both eyes he moved to Shubenacadie and was cared for by his son Peter and Peter's fourth wife, Anne Jane Maloney Tony. At this time he had only two children remaining, Peter and a daughter Mary who had struck out on her own. In 1922, Mary wed Freeman Henry Maracle, a Tyendinaga Mohawk from Marysville, Hastings County, Ontario. NSARM, Historical Vital Statistics, Hants County Marriages, Registration Year 1922, book 11, 35, "Marriage of Freeman Henry Maracle and Mary Paul, widow (née Glode)." Freeman Henry Maracle was the son of William Henry Maracle and Sarah Brant. Freeman and Mary's marriage certificate is erroneously listed under the surname "Marade." Jim's son Peter continued living at Shubenacadie until his death in 1951.

345 Harold's father name is spelled "Newel" rather than "Noel" in this chapter because that is the way Harold spells it in his book *From My Vantage Point*.

346 Gloade, *From My Vantage Point*, 67.

347 Max Basque, a neighbour of Jim Glode at Shubenacadie, related to Ruth Holmes Whitehead that Jim in his last years would kneel on his cot for hours and make movements as though he were paddling a canoe. "And then he'd get up and drag his cot across the room, get on it again, and paddle, paddle. He thought he was portaging the canoe, see?" Max Basque to Ruth Homes Whitehead, personal communication, July 1978; Ruth Holmes Whitehead, *Niniskamijinaqik/Ancestral Images: The Mi'kmaq in Art and Photography* (Halifax: Nimbus, 2015), 94. Jim Glode was buried at Shubenacadie on 2 March 1936. NSARM, Historical Vital Statistics, Hants County Deaths, book 146, 745, "Death of James Glode, age 104 years of age and 7 months."

348 The date given for Abraham Glode Sr.'s birth varies from source to source. Federal census records list his birthdate as 1821. Yet this is too late, as he had a son Alexander in 1832. His death certificate of 1910 states he was born in 1814 and lived to be ninety-six years old.

349 This marriage likely had been arranged between his father, Chief Joseph Martin Claude, and Chief Andrew James Meuse.

350 St. Gregory's Parish, Liverpool, Birth at Caledonia of Alexander, son of Abraham Glode and Mary Anne Glode, 5 May 1832. Although no birth record could be found for Newel Gloade, who according to his death certificate was born in 1836, this Newel was almost certainly a son of Abraham Gloade Sr. and Mary Ann Meuse. Newel left Lequille and Bear River at an early age, married Anatasia Vicaire, and spent his final days at Millbrook, near Truro. Harold Gloade, a grandson of Newel's brother Abraham Glode Jr., referred to him as his "uncle." Gloade, *From My Vantage Point*, 52. Louis was born in Digby in 1848. Registers of the Parish of St. Croix, Plympton, Digby County, "Baptism of Louis Glode, one week old, son of Abraham Glode and Mary Ann Meuse, 12 November 1848." Mary Ann must have died within a couple of years of Louis's birth, since Abraham Jr. was born in 1851 to Abraham Sr. and his second wife, Margaret Knockwood. Annie, a widow who cared for two young children, Joe and Annie Lafford, belonged to Newel's household at Londonderry, Colchester County, in 1901.

351 Abraham Glode Jr. and Nancy Jeremy had at least two sons, John born in 1868 and Newel born on 15 October 1871. John, three years of age, appears on the Canadian census of 1871.

352 Nancy Siah was a daughter of Solomon and Sally Siah of Bear River. According to Richard McEwan, Solomon Siah was a large man, physically very strong, who was also reputed to be a *ginap* or person with special power. Richard McEwan, *Memories of a Micmac Life*

(Fredericton: 1988), 2–4. McEwan knew Solomon personally since the latter was his grandmother Victoria Siah's brother. Interview with Richard McEwan, 18 June 1999. Abraham Glode Jr. and Nancy Siah had three children, James, born in 1879, Solomon (also called "Stephen") born in 1881, and Annie Jossie, born in 1883. All three children were baptized at St. Louis Church in Annapolis Royal.

353 NSARM, Historical Vital Statistics, Queens County Marriages, Registration Year 1885, book 1834, 112, "Marriage of Abraham Glode and Madeline Glode, 15 January 1885, presiding priest Rev. Thomas J. Butler, witnesses Newel Labrador and Mary Pictou." Abraham Glode Jr. and Madeline Glode had ten children; Abraham, Benjamin, Joseph, Mary Jane, Isaac, Bridget, Henry, Bonaparte, Janet, and Elizabeth. Joseph, who became a labourer at Windsor, in 1914 at age twenty-nine he, like his father, married a cousin: Martha Glode, daughter of Peter and Eliza Glode of Kentville. NSARM, Historical Vital Statistics, Hants County Marriages, Registration Year 1914, book 1824, p. 62, no. 7, "Marriage of Joseph Glode and Martha Glode." The Mi'kmaw culture traditionally forbade close cousin marriage, although fourth cousin marriage was permitted. Harold F. McGee, "The Case for Micmac Demes," in *Actes du huitième congrès des algonquiniste*, ed. William Cowan (Ottawa: University of Ottawa, 1977), 107–14.

354 Newel was living with his grandfather Abraham Sr. when he was twenty years of age according to the 1891 census. Meanwhile Stephen, a ten-year-old boy living in the same household, may have been a son of Abraham Glode Jr. and Nancy Siah. According to Harold Gloade, Newel wanted to live with his grandparents "because his father had remarried when his mother died and he never accepted his stepmother." Gloade, *From My Vantage Point*, 6. Newel adored his grandfather but could never bring himself to mention or write to his father Abraham Glode Jr.'s name, even to the priest responsible for filling out the marriage certificate when he married his second wife, Beatrice Rose McKay de Long (née Fiendel), in 1920. Instead, in 1920 he gave his father's name as "Joseph," while "Peter Glode and Mary Ann Glode" are listed as his parents on his death certificate when he died at Hantsport in 1966. One wonders if the "Peter Glode" referred to on his death certificate was the Peter Glode who was the son of the Annapolis district chief, Jack Glode. This Peter, whose wife Hannah was also called Mary Ann, died in 1884. NSARM, Vital Statistics, Annapolis County Marriages, book 1, 779, "Marriage of Noel Glode and Beatrice Rose McKay de Long,

8 May 1920"; NSARM, Vital Statistics, Hants County Deaths, Registration Year 1966, 2303, "Death of Newell Gloade (or Gloade), age ninety-five."

355 On the basis of ambiguous information contained in the marriage certificate that accompanied Newel's marriage to Mary Ann Peters, the nineteen-year-old daughter of John Peter and Helen Paul, it has been claimed that Newel was Abraham Glode Sr. and Nelly Peter's son and not the son of Abraham Gloade Jr. Although "Nellie" Peters was only thirty-one at the time of Newel's birth, she probably was not his mother. There are three reasons to believe this. First, the entry relating to Newel and Mary Ann's marriage of 1892 in the registers of St. Louis Church in Annapolis Royal states that Newel was the son of "Abraham Gload and Helena [*sic*, Nancy] Jeremy." Second, the marriage certificate for Newel and Rose Beatrice McKay's nuptials in 1920 lists "Nancy Jeremy" as Newel's mother, and this Nancy is definitely Abraham Jr.'s first wife. Finally, Harold Gloade, Newel's son, related that Newel as a boy went to live with his grandfather (though he does not give the grandfather's name), and this claim is borne out by census information.

356 NSARM, RG 1, vol. 430, 155, "Account of the Children that have attended school for the Quarter ending 28 February 1842." Enclosed with a letter from the Bear River schoolmaster, Mr. M. Godfrey, to Joseph Howe, "Godfrey to Howe," 28 February 1842; NSARM, RG 1, vol. 432, 6. Abraham Glode Jr. was listed among the students. Mi'kmaw children were also attending a school in 1842 at Bristal in Caledonia, Queens County. NSARM, RG 1, vol. 43, 157, "Names of Indian scholars in the District of Bristol, Caledonia, Queens County," 5 April 1843. The children at the Caledonia school included John Williams, Joseph Jeremy, and two of Peter and Hannah Glode's children, Peter and Joseph. Canadian census of 1921 for Lequille and Graywood, Annapolis County, prepared by the Indian agent, J. Nicholls.

357 Gloade, *From My Vantage Point*, 6.

358 Registers of St. Louis Roman Catholic Church, Annapolis Royal, "Marriage of Newel Glode to Mary Ellen Peters, daughter of John Peters and Helen Paul, 1892." The baptismal register at St. Croix Roman Catholic Church in Plympton, Digby County, shows that Mary Ann Peters was baptized on 10 December 1873.

359 Births and baptisms of these children are entered in the registers of St. Louis Church, Annapolis Royal. Nova Scotia Vital Statistics also shows the deaths of several children in Annapolis County whose father was Newel Glode, but does not give the mother's name. Joseph Martin Glode survived the rigours of fighting overseas

in World War I only to succumb to measles and pneumonia on his return. He died on 11 May 1916, reportedly at seventeen years of age, and was buried in the St. Ann's cemetery, Bear River. He was probably only fifteen. NSARM, Historical Vital Statistics, Digby County Deaths, book 33, p. 249, no. 640.

360 The census of 1891 lists Abraham Glode Sr. at Bear River with his third wife Helen (Nellie) Peters. This census gives Abraham's birth date as 1821, which is undoubtedly wrong. Nellie was forty in 1891 and Newel, who was still living with his grandfather, was twenty years old. Stephen, likely Abraham Glode Jr. and Nancy Siah's son, who was also part of the household, was ten.

361 *Liverpool Advance*, 28 September 1904. Considerable information on Abraham (or Abram) Glode Sr. can be found in newspapers, oral traditions recovered by T.B. Smith and Dennis, and Hagar's ethnographic work on the Mi'kmaq (see the following note).

362 An avid but essentially amateur New England ethnographer who later in life became a New York lawyer, Stansbury Hagar possessed the monetary resources to visit Digby frequently, backed by monies derived from his mother's kin who were associated with Tiffany's. Hagar stated that Abraham Sr. had received no formal schooling. He further considered the elderly man "a fine example of a full blood" Mi'kmaq, so obviously Abraham did not tell Hagar of his Acadian antecedents. Probably basing his estimate on federal census data, Hagar in 1895 argued that Abraham was seventy-three years old, and considered Newel, who was often with Abraham, as "somewhat younger." Hagar, "Micmac Customs and Traditions," *American Anthropologist* 8, no. 1 (1895): 31–41; Hagar, "Micmac Magic and Medicine," *Journal of American Folklore* 9, no. 34 (1896): 170–7. During the serpent dance "the circle of dancers moved first to the right three times around the head man. The dancers then turned their backs to the head man and repeated the revolution three times; next the two sets turned their backs to one another and again moved thrice around the circle; finally, in the same position, they reversed the direction of the motion and move backward around the circle three times. This figure was thus completed in four positions and 12 revolutions, and, according to Newel Glode, signified the rattlesnake waking from his winter sleep." The head man now left the circle through the space made for him, simulating a serpent coming from its hole; "he led the dancers around the field, making many snake-like twistings and turnings. In one hand he held a horn filled with shot or small pebbles; with this he rattled the time for the step and the song of the other

dancers. After they had advanced some distance, the last dancer remained stationary and the others moved around the leader in a constantly narrowing circle until all were closely coiled around him. The head man then reversed the direction of the motion and the dancers came out of the circle in line as before. This represented the coiling and uncoiling of the rattlesnake." Hagar, "Micmac Customs and Traditions," 37.

363 *Halifax Herald*, 28 September 1904. This article argues Abraham Glode Sr. was born in 1819 and was eighty-five years of age.

364 NSARM, Historical Vital Statistics, Digby County Deaths, book 6, p. 90, p. 519, no. 536, "Death of Abram (or Abraham) Glode Sr. of Bear River at age ninety-six of acute bronchitis, 8 August 1910."

365 NSARM, Historical Vital Statistics, Digby County Deaths, Registration Year 1911, book 6, 130, "Death of Mary Ellen (or Nellie) Glode, widow of Abraham Glode, 13 May 1911." Nellie was seventy-nine years old, born in 1837.

366 Newel's son Harold wrote engaging vignettes about his father's life from the 1880s to the early 1920s around Graywood, Lequille, and the Bear River in his book *From My Vantage Point*. As a young boy, Newel spent the summer seasons with his grandfather, who was an expert porpoise hunter. After sending a farmer's ox cart laden with camping supplies on ahead with Newel's parents, his grandparents, with Noel in tow, walked from Milford along the Virginia Road to Bear River, where they had a canoe cached. This they paddled out to and along the south shore of the Annapolis Basin past Digby to the "Racket" (or Raquet , where their summer camp lay. Noel's father Abraham Jr. and his stepmother arrived next by canoe. The equipment and provisions, travelling by lumbering ox cart, came in last, well after dark. Gloade, *From My Vantage Point*, 2.

367 Mary Ann Peters, Newel Gloade's first wife, died in 1917 of tuberculosis at the age of 43. NSARM, Historical Vital Statistics, Digby County Deaths, book 33, p. 329, no. 857, "Death of Mary Ann Glode, 5 January 1917." Three years later Newel married Rose Beatrice McKay at St. Louis Church in Annapolis Royal. NSARM, Registration Year 1920, book 1, p. 779, "Marriage of Noel Glode and Rose B. McKay, 8 March 1920, witnesses Sarah and Joseph Toney." Rose's mother's family, the Fiedells of New Germany, were descendants of an early German settler, John Fiedell. Desbrisay, *History of the County of Lunenburg*, 368–70. Members of the family helped Desbrisay write sections of his history of Lunenburg County. John Adams Fiendel (or Fiedell) also knew the Jeremy family near LaHave well.

368 Registers of St. Gregory's Church, Liverpool. Harold William Gloade, born to Noel (Newel) Gloade and Rose McKay on 11 September 1920 and baptized 4 October 1920. Because Rose was older at the time of her second marriage, Harold was the only child she bore who lived. The Canadian federal census of 1921 shows Newel and Rose living at Graywood, Annapolis County, with their children Michael, who was twelve, Alice, eight, and Harold, eight months old.

369 Harold Gloade spells this surname "Barnjam." Gloade, *From My Vantage Point*, 41. The usual spelling, however, is "Barnjman."

370 Gloade, *From My Vantage Point*, 28. Dennis Brooks, born in 1882, was a son of John Brooks and Mary Lucy Pictou of Lequille. Registers of St. Louis Church, Annapolis Royal. The Gloades and the Brooks had been closely associated through kin ties for many generations. According to Silus Tertius Rand, the surname "Brooks" only arose among the Mi'kmaq in the early 1800s. In 1846 Rand undertook the study of the Mi'kmaw language under the tutelage of Joseph Brooks of Digby, whom he described as "a Frenchman with a Micmac wife." Judith Fingard, "Rand, Silas Tertius," in *DCB* online, vol. 11 (1881–90), http://www.biographi.ca/en/bio/rand_silas_tertius_11E.html. Rand added that Joseph had once been called "Joseph Ruisseaux [Brook]," but because he had jumped ship illegally in Nova Scotia, he had translated his surname into the English "Brooks" in order to escape detection. Joseph Brooks must have been elderly in 1846. He would have to have had children born in the late 1700s in order for one Mi'kmaq man, William Brooks, to be married to Ann Gloade and have at least one child at Portuguese Cove near Halifax in 1823. Registers of Our Lady of Mount Carmel, Prospect. Yet it is possible that kin linkages between the Brooks and Gloade families were forged very early in the nineteenth century and that some of Joseph Brooks's children travelled with Gloade spouses from the Annapolis Valley region to the South Shore.

371 Milford and Area History History Group, *Through the Woods*, 13.

372 Gloade, *From My Vantage Point*, xiii.

373 Peter Glode and Mary Ann Toney raised their family near Springhill, Cumberland County. Their son Abraham died there at sixty-five years of age in 1932. NSARM, Historical Vital Statistics, Cumberland County Deaths, Registration Year 1932, book 143, 1318. Nancy Glode, widow, former wife of John Brooks, died at Kentville in 1913 at age ninety-eight. NSARM, Historical Vital Statistics, Kings County Deaths, book 12, p. 221, no. 1351.

The Annapolis Glodes and the Brooks family intermarried over generations. For instance, in 1870 James Glode, son of Joseph Glode and Nancy Brooks, married Mary Anne Glode, daughter of Benjamin and Mary Brooks. NSARM, Historical Vital Statistics, Kings County Marriages, book 1823, p. 39, no. 7.

374 The Mi'kmaq had always hunted sea mammals from canoes using harpoons, but beginning with the French at Louisbourg they had begun to hunt sea mammals commercially for their oil. The thriving but short-lived porpoise oil industry in the Annapolis Basin area developed during the early 1800s and ended in the first decades of the twentieth century as electric light became more common and better lubricants were developed. On the Mi'kmaw's hunting of sea mammals for oil during the French era, see Charles Martijn, "An Eastern Mi'kmaq Domain of Islands," in *Actes du vingtième congrès des algonquinistes/Proceedings of the Twentieth Algonquian Conference*, ed. William Cowan (Ottawa: Carleton University Press, 1989): 208–31. The porpoise hunt continued in the Annapolis Basin until the late 1930s. In 1936 Dr. Alexander Leighton, an American, made a film about the hunt that featured the Pictou family.

375 A humorous account of a guides' meet held at Lake William in Lunenburg in the 1930s may be found in found in Harold Gloade, *As I Remember: Hantsport in the 30s*, book 2 (Hansport: Hansport: Hantsport and Area Historical Society, 1988), 46.

376 Louis Peters, who guided for many years out of Bear River, was one such man who combined hunting acumen with showmanship. His son Basil Peters, who well into his eighties lived at Millbrook, in 2011 possessed a photograph of his father addressing a large audience at a guide meet in Cleveland, Ohio, in the early 1900s. The author is most grateful to Basil Peters for assisting with information from this important era in Bear River history. See also Darlene A. Ricker, *L'sitkuk: The Story of the Bear River M'ikmaw Community* (Black Rock, NS: Fernwood, 1997), 162.

377 When the disease epidemic spread to Dartmouth, in 1847 Thomas Glode, who was then sixty years of age, and Hannah Glode, who was seventy-six, convalesced at a makeshift hospital erected by Dr. Edward Jennings near Dartmouth (possibly located near Loon Lake along present-day Main Street in Dartmouth) to tend to the suffering. NSARM, MG 15, vol. 4, no. 25. Dr. Edward Jennings' Report, 15 February 1847. NSM, Printed Matter File, "A Short History of the Mic mac Indians in Halifax Co., Nova Scotia, since Confederation by J.C. Cope,

Enfield," 9 February 1926. Joseph Glode was still living on Preston Road in 1870.

378 Gloades living near Truro today are either descended from this man, from Chief Francis Glode and Magdalene Molti of Potanoc near Milton in Queens County, or from Abraham Glode Sr. (c.1814–1910), who was born at Lequille, lived at Bear River, and was a younger son of Chief Joseph Martin Claude.

379 NSM, Printed Matter file, "Joseph C. Cope to Harry Piers," 29 March 1926.

380 "Vicaire" is a surname from Restigouche, so Newel Gloade (who used the spelling "Gloade" most frequently) likely met Anastasia, or Nancy, while he was river driving in southern Quebec. Nancy, born on 1 January 1838, was known as "Nancy Bigears" – a nickname for some of the members of the Vicaire family, and she also used the name "Nancy Tony." Her parents, according to her death certificate, were Alexis (or Lexy) Vicaire and Nancy Ann Tony, so when she used the name "Tony" she was adopting her mother's surname. When her son, William Thomas Gloade, married Bridget Ann Sack on 22 June 1831, her name was listed on the marriage certificate as "Nancy Vicaire," but when William Thomas Gloade died her name was given on his death certificate as "Nancy Ann Toney, born in Nova Scotia." NSARM, Historical Vital Statistics, Hants County Marriages, Registration Year 1931, book 63, p. 192, "Marriage of William Thomas Gloade, son of Newel Gloade and Nancy Vicaire, widower, age sixty-two, and Ann Basque Sack, widow, age forty-four, daughter of Isaac Sack, at Shubenacadie on 22 June 1931, presiding priest Rev. J.P. McKay, witnesses Alex Cope and his wife"; Historical Vital Statistics, Hants County Deaths, Registration Year 1934, book 146, p. 432, "Death of William Thomas Gloade, son of Newel Gloade and Nancy Ann Tony, at Shubenacadie, 24 October 1934." Newel and Nancy had at least three sons, Louis, Tom, and James, and several daughters, among them Annie and Katherine. After Newel died, Nancy married a man surnamed Paul, and for this reason her name appears as "Nancy Paul" on her death certificate. NSARM, Historical Vital Statistics, Colchester County Deaths, Registration Year 1925, book 112, 693, "Death at eighty-seven years and four months on 15 May 1925 of Nancy Paul, daughter of Lexy Vicaire and Ann Tony." Nancy was buried at Truro. She should not be confused with "Anastasia Glode," a daughter of Newel Glode and Mary Ann (Peters) of Bear River. This Anastasia (or "Nancy") Glode married John Brooks of Kentville in 1872 and had a son named William Thomas Brooks. NSARM, Historical Vital Statistics, Kings County Marriages, book 1826, p. 59, no. 123. Anastasia Glode's father, Newel Gloade, married Rose Beatrice McKay in 1920. NSARM, Historical Vital Statistics, Annapolis County Marriages, Registration Year 1920, book 1, 177. Harold Gloade, the only son of Newel Gloade and Rose Beatrice McKay, referred to Tom Gloade as his "uncle" (Gloade, *From My Vantage Point*, 52), but he was actually Harold's father Newel's first cousin, as Harold's father's father Abraham Glode Jr. and Tom's father Newel were brothers, both sons of Abraham Glode Sr. of Bear River. Newel, as mentioned above, apparently did not like to admit his father was Abraham Glode Jr. When he married Rose Beatrice McKay (née Fiendel) in 1920 he gave his parents' names as "Joseph Glode and Nancy Geremy" rather than the actual names of his parents, which were Abraham Glode Jr. and Nancy Jeremy or Geremy.

381 Newel and Anastasia's first son, Louis, according to Louis's death certificate of 1929, was born in 1862 in Dartmouth. NSARM, Historical Vital Statistics, Colchester County Deaths, Registration Year 1929, p. 119. Their second son, William Thomas, was born in 1866 at Windsor, Hants County. NSARM, Historical Vital Statistics, Hants County Deaths, Registration Year 1934, book 146, 132, "Death of Thomas William Gloade." Their third son, James, was born on the shores of the Northwest Arm in 1871, probably at Chocolate Lake near the present-day Armdale Rotary. NSARM, Historical Vital Statistics, Halifax County Births, Registration Year 1871, book 1810, p. 112, no. 85, "Birth of James Glode, son of Noel Glode and Anastasia Tony, on the shores of the North West Arm," Halifax. The fact that Tom Gloade lived his early years in Halifax may account for his ability to take apprenticeship training and become a stonemason, plasterer, and bricklayer. During the First World War he joined the First Battalion of the Royal Highlanders headquartered in Truro, though he did not see action overseas. Tom married three times, first to Mary Cope, second to Christina Snow, and third to Bridget Ann Sack. He also was the only one of his immediate family to gain enough education to become, in company with his son Stephen Anthony Gloade, Millbrook's first storekeeper. Tom's siblings, in addition to Louis and James, included three sisters, Sarah, Annie, and Katherine. Newel Gloade and Nancy Vicaire also adopted an orphan girl named Helen Maccan.

By 1881 Newel Gloade and his family had joined a small Mi'kmaw community at Nine Mile River that included Newel's brother James and Paul Williams's son John, originally from Cape Sable, who was married to

Adelaide Thomas. James Glode was forty-four, his wife Mary was thirty-six, and the couple had four children: James, seventeen, John, fifteen, Peter, eleven, and Rebecca, four. Three members of Newel Gloade's immediate family were listed as literate: his wife Anastasia, Tom, and Tom's wife Mary Cope. Newel in 1881 was fifty-five, Anastasia was forty-seven, and their daughter Sarah, who still lived with them, was eighteen (though her name later disappears from the record). Louis Gloade was twenty-eight, Louis's wife Mary Noel was twenty-seven, Tom Gloade was twenty-three, and Tom's wife Mary Cope was nineteen. Canada, Census of 1881, District no. 18, Hants County, Nine Mile River. In 1884 Louis Gloade married Mary Noel, a daughter of John Noel and Charlotte Noel of Halifax County. Witnesses to their wedding in Halifax were Louis's brother James and Mary Sack. NSARM, Historical Vital Statistics, Halifax County Marriages, book 1817, p. 218, no. 330. A decade later Newel and his family were living at Londonderry Station, Colchester County. According to the 1891 Canadian federal census for Acadia Mines East, Colchester County, Newel Gloade was born in 1835 and his wife Anastasia was born in 1843. Their son Louis, however, is incorrectly listed on this census as born in Londonderry in 1861. Louis was living with his wife Mary Noel, a basketmaker born in 1861. Tom Gloade and Mary Cope, who had a one-year-old son, James, lived near Louis's household. There was also a widow, Annie Gloade, born in 1843 and living at Acadia Mines in 1891 with two children, Joseph Lafford, who was nine, and Annie Lafford, who was four. This Annie was probably a sister of Newel Gloade. By the time the federal census taker came round on 31 March 1901, Tom Gloade and his wife Mary were living in Millbrook. Their son James was eleven and their daughter Annie was nine. Canada, Census of 1901, Town of Truro, Colchester County, S-1, 29. Tom and Mary would have two more sons; Daniel Thomas Gloade in 1902 and Stephen Anthony Gloade in 1903.

382 "Maccan" likely refers to the place in Nova Scotia where she came from, rather than her surname, which remains unknown.

383 Information provided by Carrie Gloade of Millbrook.

384 No official reserve ever existed at Londonderry Station, though many Mi'kmaq commuted from a small Mi'kmaw community there to work at Acadia Mines. In 1956, K.L. Smith of Londonderry produced a typescript, dated 4 August 1956, entitled "Londonderry Letters" in which she described Louis's wife, Susan Bernard. "Many elder and former residents will remember Mrs. Susan Glode, wife of Louis who walked with his hand on his knee," Smith wrote. "They and Mrs. Thomas Glode [Gloade] and her family lived on an Indian Reservation at Londonderry Station. About the turn of the century they all went to live at the new reservation near Truro and often I have seen Susan in Truro. So now she is recuperating from an illness." There is no explanation offered as to why Louis walked with his hand on his knee. Perhaps he suffered from lameness in one leg and needed his hand to support his leg. Colchester Museum and Archives, Truro. K.L. Smith, "Londonderry Letters," typescript, 4 August 1956, 3.

385 On 12 October 1925 Noel Andrew Gloade married Mary A. Paul, a son of John Denny Paul, whose father, Andrew Paul, was born in Waycobah in Cape Breton in 1818. Noel Gloade was twenty-four at the time of his wedding, so he was born in 1901, not long after Louis and Susan's marriage. NSARM, Vital Statistics, Registration Year 1925, Colchester County Marriages, book 46, 43. The Paul family's ties with Millbrook became even stronger in 1934 when Mary Paul's brother, Andrew Paul Jr., married Irene Elizabeth Cope, a daughter of Sandy Cope Jr. and Matilda McDonald of Truro.

386 NSARM, Historical Vital Statistics, Colchester County Deaths, Registration Year 1925, book 112, 693, "Death at 87 years of age on 15 May 1925 of Nancy Paul, daughter of Lexy Vicaire and Ann Toney."

387 This Annie Gloade, born in 1843, was fifty-eight years old on the 1901 federal census for Millbrook. Joe and Annie Lafford became her special responsibility. It is possible Sarah Gloade died and her sister Annie fostered her children. In 1922, when Annie Lafford married William J. Stephens of Millbrook, her parents were listed as Frank Lafford and Sarah Gloade. NSARM, Historical Vital Statistics, Colchester County marriages, book 45, 451.

388 Annie Gloade in 1908 wed Michael Thomas on 18 November 1908 and became the mother of Edith Jane Thomas in 1911 and Clara Agnes Thomas in 1914. NSARM, Historical Vital Statistics, Colchester County Marriages, Registration Year 1908, book 1807, p. 265, no. 156.

389 Daniel Thomas Gloade married Levinia Brooks in 1925. At the time of his marriage he was listed as twenty-two years of age, born in Londonderry, Colchester County. (The actual year of his birth was 1902, not 1903.) NSARM, Historical Vital Statistics, Registration Year 1925, book 45, 924.

390 Obituary of Stephen Anthony Gloade, age fifty-nine, son of William Thomas Gloade and Mary Cope, *Halifax Herald*, 1 December 1962. Stephen and his wife Anastasia Glode, a daughter of Peter Glode of Shubenacadie, had

six children: three daughters, Mary, Theresa, and Muriel, and three sons, Thomas, Stephen, and Gordon.

391 In 1847 a Truro magistrate stated that after "diligent inquiry" he had failed to locate any Mi'kmaq who made their permanent home in Colchester County. NSARM, RG 1, vol. 432, Miscellaneous detached documents, "Report on the Mi'kmaq of Colchester sent to James Whidden by James Johnson, Clerk of the Peace, Truro," 15 January 1847. Few Mi'kmaw remained long in Colchester County, though groups seasonally fished along the Salmon River, now deflected underground below the town of Truro. The Millbrook reserve is not near the old fishing site on the Salmon River. That plot was sold in 1855 to the Nova Scotia School of Agriculture, and the Salmon River in the area was sunk beneath buildings belonging to the Truro Normal School. The Millbrook reserve emerged out of a series of talks between Chief Peter Wilmot (1824–1932), a son of Joseph Wilmot of Pictou Landing and Madeline Deneau of New Brunswick, and the provincial and federal governments. After Wilmot left for Cumberland County in 1885, a Mi'kmaw group encamped at Christmas Crossing, on King Street in Truro, then moved on 6 December 1886 to settle permanently on thirty-five acres of land given them at Hilden, near the railway. With the help of a local Indian agent, the Mi'kmaq by 1897 also acquired funds to construct Sacred Heart Church and an Indian day school at Millbrook, both of which were built with Mi'kmaw labour. Between 1904 and 1910 land was added to the reserve to accommodate Mi'kmaq who wanted to settle in the growing community.

392 NSARM, Historical Vital Statistics, Colchester County Deaths, book 4, p. 60, no. 359, "Death of Mary Cope of Sheet Harbour, 16 December 1909." Tom and Mary's last child was Stephen Anthony Gloade, born in 1903.

393 A contentious issue that evoked major discussion was the province's leasing of the Kejimkujik reserve from 1 May 1908 onward for twenty-five years to C.W. Mills of Halifax to accommodate a large hunting and fishing lodge. The rental fee, supposedly to be directed to the Mi'kmaq's benefit, was a mere thirty dollars per year. The province held that the enterprise would employ Mi'kmaw guides and discourage timber pillaging, but Denny baulked at the loss of Mi'kmaw control over their land and resources. Documents relating to this affair are found in LAC, RG 10, vol. 3113, file 320,110–1A.

394 Janet E. Chute, "Frank G. Speck's Contributions to the Understanding of Mi'kmaq Land Use, Leadership and Land Management," *Ethnohistory* 46, no. 3 (1999), 483–540. Peter and Hannah Gloade's son Peter had moved to the United States, but it is possible that Peter's younger brother John, whose name is inscribed with the date 1877 on a rock face at Fairy Lake, may have spread word throughout the Mi'kmaw community of the leasing affair.

395 LAC, RG 10, vol. 3113, file 320,110–1A, "Grand Chief John Denys to the Minister of the Interior," 11 March 1909.

396 It also introduced Speck to a pursuit that he continued in other parts of the Northeast for many years afterwards.

397 As a boy, Joseph Julien had lived with John Denny Jr. at Escasoni and had come to know the grand chief personally.

398 Frank G. Speck, "Trying to Reconstruct Micmac Family Divisions," *Sydney Record*, 14 July 1914, p. 1, col. 2.

399 This reserve infantry regiment originated in Truro in April 1871 as the Colchester and Hants Provisional Battalion of Royal Highlanders.

400 The Annapolis-Liverpool Road plots (also known as the Graywood parcels) and Lequille allotments had already come up for government review in the early 1880s, and at that time the Mi'kmaq strongly objected to any loss of Aboriginal control over these tracts. But not until after a unified tribal council was formed at Bear River in 1970, with enough political clout to initiate title searches at Lequille nine years later, was a title search initiated at Lequille reserve. Two small reserves had been established in Annapolis County in the 1960s. Bear River Reserve No. 6B, sixty acres (24.3 hectares) in size, was established on 1 October 1962. It emerged out of an exchange between Ottawa and the Nova Scotia Light and Power Corporation. In return for relinquishing control over what became Reserve No. 6B, the corporation received fifty-nine acres from another reserve, Bear River Reserve No. 6A, situated at Grand Lake, Annapolis County. Bear River Reserve No. 6A presently is just over thirty-one hectares in size. Lequille remained a "non-reserve community," even though it originally had been the Annapolis band's political headquarters. Its residents were completely cut off from the Allain River, where the Mi'kmaq for generations used to fish, by a canal and spillway constructed by the Light and Power Corporation. NSARM, vol. 19 (Papers from Indian Land Claims in Nova Scotia), no. 3, "Field Trip to Lequille and Title Searches, Note and Sketches," 1979; Interview with Dan Ramsey, 20 July 2012.

401 Throughout the war years of 1916 and 1917 Mi'kmaq met in numerous emergency councils to thwart the surrender of Mi'kmaw lands in Queens, Annapolis, Lunenburg, and Halifax counties. At the same time

there was a drive to raise monies to secure additional land at Millbrook for Mi'kmaw who might be displaced by government fiat. An elderly Mi'kmaw leader, Jerry Bartlett-Alexis, also known as "Jerry Lonecloud," who became a prominent spokesperson and messenger for this campaign, contacted Captain Tom Gloade to ensure Millbrook's leaders would attend. The Mi'kmaq also began to collect maps, documents, and oral testimonies to support their contentions, especially after the person who leased the Kejimkujik lands from Ottawa illicitly removed many thousands of board feet of timber. LAC, RG 10, vol. 3113, file 320, 110 – pt. 1, John Lacey, Indian Agent, to the Department of Indian Affairs, 21 February 1912. Most of the Gloades who retained a principal interest in protecting the forest at Kejimkujik, and probably would have arisen as negotiators during this campaign had they been consulted, were away at war.

402 Tom Gloade was on the band council when the Millbrook community became a crucible for new ideas originating mainly from Chief John Denny Jr. of Eskasoni, regarding Aboriginal territorial aegis and resource management, some of which still inform Mi'kmaw political forums today. In the early twentieth century the idea arose within the Mi'kmaw polity that the Mi'kmaq should enhance the lands reserved to them by increasing their aegis over local resources like game, fish, and timber. Associated with this scheme was a system whereby Mi'kmaq from more populated and undersupplied areas might be directed by the Grand Council to move to Mi'kmaw-controlled lands where resources were abundant and their services more needed. After Denny's death in 1918, his work was taken up by Joseph Julien, who left a leadership position at Kings Road, Sydney, to come to Millbrook. Father Pacifique, a Capuchin missionary to the Mi'kmaq stationed at Restigouche, kept abreast of Mi'kmaw movements from Halifax County towards Truro. NSM, Correspondence file A, "Harry Piers, regarding the usefulness of Joe Cope at Truro for addressing a historical enquiry from Father Pacifique," 21 October 1921. Chief Julien, along with Chief Ben Christmas of Membertou, later vehemently opposed the government-sponsored centralization policy.

403 Noel Andrew in 1925 married Mary A. Paul, a daughter of Chief John Denny Paul and Frances Denny. NSARM, Historical Vital Statistics, Colchester County Marriages, Registration Year 1925, book 46, 43, "Marriage of Noel Andrew Gloade and Mary A. Paul at Millbrook on 12 October 1925, presiding priest W.K. Kinsella, witnesses Edith Thomas and Edward Cope." Tom probably would have been present in 1916 at Tuft's Cove, Dartmouth, at the funeral for John Denny's father, Andrew Paul. NSM, Printed Mattter File, Harry Piers notes, 24 February 1916; NSARM, Historical Vital Statistics, Halifax County Deaths, book 34, p. 197, no. 658, "Death of Andrew Paul, 24 February 1916, at age ninety-eight." Andrew Paul was an associate of Grand Chief John Denny Jr., who had moved to Halifax County, with Denny's encouragement, in the late nineteenth century. NSM, printed matter file, Harry Piers notes, 24 February 1916.

404 Annie's father is known to have lived at Millbrook, though she was not Tom's daughter of the same name, as Tom's daughter married Michael Thomas. There are two photographs of Annie Gloade in the Mi'kmaq Portraits Collection at the Nova Scotia Museum. The first photograph, bearing the reference no. N-1028 and dated 1927, is of a young Annie standing alone in a traditional Mi'kmaw costume that was borrowed from the Nova Scotia Museum. Annie, a young woman from Millbrook, was probably related to Newel Gloade, Thomas Gloade's and Louis Gloade's father. Ethnohistorian Ruth Holmes Whitehead, who wrote the caption for this photograph in the Mi'kmaq Portraits Collection, could not provide the names of Annie's parents, though she does state that Max Basque told her in 1977 that when Annie died of tuberculosis in 1931, her body was taken from her father's house at Millbrook to the church on a sled. The second photograph, with the reference no. N-4179, was taken on the same day as the first and shows Annie seated in the same traditional costume, with Jerry Lonecloud standing next to her.

405 Some of these changes are discussed in Anita Maria Tobin, 'The Effect of Centralization on the Social and Political Systems of the Mainland Nova Scotia Mi'kmaq (Case Studies: Millbrook – 1916 & Indian Brook – 1941)" (master's thesis, Saint Mary's University, 1999). Also see Daniel N. Paul, *We Were Not the Savages: Collision between European and Native American Civilizations* (Halifax: Fernwood, 2008), 309.

406 Gloade, *From My Vantage Point*, 48.

407 NSARM, Historical Vital Statistics, Deaths in Colchester County, book 112, 823, "Death of Christiana Glode, daughter of John Snow of Canso and Nancy Noel, 25 November 1925." Christiana died at age fifty-nine of an intestinal obstruction.

408 Tom's son Daniel died just six years after his marriage to Lavinia Brooks, at the age of twenty-nine from tuberculosis on 18 July 1931. NSARM, Historical Vital Statistics, Colchester County Deaths, Registration Year 1931, book 119, 1456, "Death of Daniel Thomas Gloade, 18 July 1931." Another of Tom's sons, Stephen Anthony, a carpenter,

married Anastasia Gloade, a daughter of Peter Gloade and Jeanette (or Janet) Prosper Toney of Shubenacadie. Anastasia also was a granddaughter of Jim Gloade of Bear River, as well as a distant cousin of her husband. NSARM, Historical Vital Statistics, Colchester County Marriages, Registration Year 1927, 1909. Witnesses to Stephen and Anastasia's wedding were Edith Thomas and Edward Cope, Stephen's cousin. Stephen Anthony Gloade died in 1962. Obituary of Stephen Anthony Gloade, *Halifax Herald*, 1 December 1962.

409 NSARM, Historical Vital Statistics, Colchester County Marriages, book 50, 784, "Marriage of Stephen Anthony Gloade, son of William Thomas Gloade, to Anastasia Gloade, daughter of Peter Gloade and Jeanette Toney, 7 November 1927." Peter Gloade, Stephen Anthony Gloade's father-in-law, was born in 1870. Stephen Anthony died in 1962. NSARM, Historical Vital Statistics, Colchester County Deaths, Registration Year 1962, 6779, "Death of Stephen Anthony Gloade, born in Londonderry, Colchester County, on 30 November 1903; buried at Millbrook, 3 December 1962."

410 Gloade, *From My Vantage Point*, 52.

411 Ibid., 51–2. Tom Gloade helped Harold Gloade learn the Mi'kmaw language. Harold had a talent for learning languages, and in addition to Mi'kmaq he taught himself French.

412 This trait reputedly aided Newel Gloade whenever he needed to locate something. Ibid., 57–61.

413 Harold remembered that if one walked up the main road from "the Truro end, on the right-hand side, the first house was Sandy Cope's, then Frank Gould, then Alex Cope, son of Sandy, then Tom Gloade's. Tom Gloade's sister, Kate, was next, then there were the houses of Charlie Henry Brooks, Madeline Silliboy, Louis Gloade and Ben Knockwood. The pasture was next to that. The dirt road bent to the left, then to the right and you came to the house of Dan, son of Tom Gloade, and just a little beyond that lived Jochi Silliboy. There was a little hill beyond Jochi's house, and Michael Thomas lived there." And the house of "Noel [Andrew] Glode, Louis' son" stood where the highway turned towards Truro. Ibid., 47–8.

414 The author is grateful to Gordon Gloade of Millbrook for providing information about Tom's and Stephen Anthony's store. NSM, printed matter file, Members of Halifax band now at Truro to A.J. Boyd, 12 January 1920. Chief Joseph Julien mentioned Gloade's store as the reason Mi'kmaq in Truro did not have to go to town for supplies but were self-sufficient right where they were.

415 Gloade, *From My Vantage Point*, 53.

416 While working on these chimneys, Tom Gloade temporarily became part of a huge industrial enterprise. The mill had a pier large enough to accommodate ocean ships and was powered by hydroelectricity from a dam erected at Indian Gardens, thirty kilometres upstream from Liverpool. This dam created a reservoir, dubbed Lake Rossignol, along the Mersey River, which had formerly been known as the 'Rossignol River."

417 NSARM, Historical Vital Statistics, Colchester County Deaths, book 119, 931, "Death of Louis Gloade at age sixty-eight years of age of pneumonia, 23 October 1929." Louis had lived at Millbrook for thirty-one years. Louis's mother's name is written on this certificate as "Annie S. Vickers," rather than Vicaire. Louis was born on 11 July 1861. He and his second wife, Susan Bernard, had two sons, Noel Andrew, born in 1901, and Charles Louis, born in 1909. Charles Louis married Annie Jane Sylliboy from Pictou Landing in 1931. NSARM, Historical Vital Statistics, book 62, 890, "Marriage of Charles Lewis Glode to Annie Jane Sillboy, 11 August 1931." Annie Jane was fifteen. Tom Gloade also provided a home for a while for Mary Bella, Louis's daughter.

418 Bridget Anne Sack was the daughter of Isaac Sack (1855–1930) and Annie Cope. Annie, in turn, was a daughter of Frank Cope and Mary Anne Quigley of Sheet Harbour. Tom Gloade and Bridget Anne Sack's marriage certificate, dated 22 June 1931, states that Thomas was sixty-two years old, the son of Newel Gloade and Anastasia Vicaire. It also reveals that Newel, Tom's father, was born at Windsor and that Bridget Ann Sack's family had lived at Elmsdale before moving to Indian Brook, Shubenacadie. NSARM, Historical Vital Statistics, Hants County Marriages, Registration Year 1931, book 63, 192, "Marriage of William Thomas Gloade and Bridget Ann Sack, Shubenacadie, 22 June 1931." Alex Cope Sr., Annie Cope's brother, born at Sheet Harbour on 4 November 1853, acted as a witness to the wedding. Alex Cope also was related to Tom's sister Katherine Gloade by marriage. Like Tom, Bridget had wed twice before. She married Noel Thomas Nicholas in 1904 and Simon Basque in 1909. Bridget's paternal grandmother was Marie Antoinette Thomas, the wife of John Noel who had succeeded James Peminout Paul as the Shubenacadie district chief. Tom died on 24 October 1934 at Shubenacadie; his death certificate states that he was born on 13 June 1866 and that his parents were Newel Gloade and Nancy Ann Toney. His wife Bridget Ann informed the authorities of his death. NSARM, Vital Statistics, East Hants County Death Records, Registration Year 1934, book 146, 432.

419 Harold and his father Newel made the trip from Truro to Shubenacadie on the "Accommodation," a train that ran between Sydney and Halifax and stopped at points between. During Harold's visit with Jim Gloade the ground started shaking, and the elderly man, who was lying in bed, had called out "Giog, na … [and then translated:] That was an earthquake." Gloade, *From My Vantage Point*, 66.

420 John Francis shared this information with the author and her research assistance Carrie Gloade at a Guides Association meet near Caledonia during the summer of 2012.

421 Gloade, *From My Vantage Point*, 115.

422 Ibid., 91–110. Glooscap First Nation lies in Kings County, Nova Scotia, about 6.4 kilometres from the town of Hantsport.

423 Mary Nancy Gloade was born at Bear River in 1899.

424 John Jodrey died at Hantsport on 15 February 2012.

425 In 2016 Bruce Jodrey, John Jodrey's son, reminisced with the author about members of the Gloade family who lived near the Jodrey family's hardboard business in Hantsport. The cabins in which the Gloades lived were a distance from town.

426 Gloade, *From My Vantage Point*, 111.

427 NSARM, Historical Vital Statistics, Hants County Marriages, Registration Year 1938, book 89, 776, "Marriage at St. Bernard's Church, Enfield, of Harold William Gloade, age seventeen, son of Newel Gloade and Nancy Vicaire, and Irene Agnes MacDonald, age seventeen, daughter of Levi MacDonald and Julia Syllaboy of Cow Bay, presiding priest Rev. J.J. Devine, witnesses Mrs. G.M. Davis and John Edward MacDonald, 8 June 1938."

428 NSARM, Historical Vital Statistics, Hants County Deaths, Registration Year 1966, 2303, "Death of Newel Gloade, born on 15 October 1870, at ninety-six years, five months and nine days." Newel's son Michael-Joseph informed the authorities of his death. Both of Newel's wives, Mary Ann Peters and Beatrice Rose McKay, are mentioned on Newel's death certificate, though the same document gives "Peter Gloade" and "Mary Ann Gloade" as his parents rather than Abraham Gloade Jr., his biological father, and Nancy Jeremy, his mother.

429 Gloade, *From My Vantage Point*, xiv.

430 The author is grateful to Mike Gloade and his daughter Carrie Gloade, descendants of both William Thomas Gloade and Jim Glode – the guide from Bear River – for their assistance in securing historical information on the Gloades of Millbrook. Mike explained that William Thomas Gloade's son, Stephen Anthony Gloade, married Anatasia Glode, a granddaughter of Jim Glode, the famous Bear River guide, and the couple had a son Tom. Mike is Tom's son. Mike's daughter Carrie, after graduating from the Canadian Studies program at Mount Saint Vincent University, became a research assistant and writer for this biographical project in the spring of 2012. She later completed a degree in education, worked for a time with the Annapolis County School Board, and now lives in Millbrook. Muriel Barr (née Gloade), a daughter of Stephen Anthony Gloade, and Gordon Gloade, Muriel's brother, also provided invaluable assistance.

431 Gloade, *From My Vantage Point*, 150.

432 Ibid., 135.

433 Ibid., 150.

434 Ibid.

435 Interview with Gordon Gloade, Millbrook, 10 June 2012.

436 Martha Jodrey (née Donahue), who owned and taught at Miss Muphy's Business College in the 1960s in Halifax, remembered an excellent student named Ann Gloade from the Hantsport area who led her class. With Martha's support and blessing, Ann went on to assume a career in government administration. Information courtesy of Martha Jodrey, 15 June 2017. Today there are Gloades who are artists, politicians, electricians, carpenters, soldiers, historians, archivists, writers, social workers, educators, cartoonists, lawyers, businesspeople, and financial experts. Many, too, have moved away from Nova Scotia to pursue their careers in Central Canada and the United States.

437 Samuel Freeman Gloade of Milton, Abraham Gloade Sr. of Bear River, and Grand Council captain Harold W. Gloade were all storytellers. Mi'kmaw storytellers drew the attention of collectors of historical knowledge and cultural lore, including Clara Dennis, Stansbury Hagar, Thomas H. Raddall, and Frank Goldsmith Speck. Harold Gloade, in *From My Vantage Point*, provided an engaging portrayal of the joys and vicissitudes experienced by one branch of the Gloade family, which lived successively at Graywood near Milford in Annapolis County, Millbrook near Truro, and in Hants County. Harold Gloade died in 2001 at age eighty in Kitchener, Ontario. *Windsor Star*, Obituary for Harold W. Gloade, born in Nova Scotia, 11 September 1920, died at Waterloo, Ontario, 8 January 2001. Harold and his wife Irene McDonald had ten children: George, Tom, Lee, Ira, Donald, Harold, Fred, Patrick, Rose, and Steven. Rose and Steven predeceased their father. The author is most grateful to one of Harold's grandsons, Daniel A. Gloade, a lawyer practising in Kitchener, Ontario, for helping with this project, particularly for directing the author to

his knowledgeable father, George Gloade, a son of Harold Gloade.

438 Following the end of Captain Joseph Gloade's term serving on the Millbrook council under Chief Joseph Julien from 1916 to 1918, W.J. Gloade became a council member in 1919. Gerald Gloade was chief from 1950 to 1961, while Dennis Gloade acted as a councillor in 1961 and 1962. The present Millbrook chief, Bob Gloade, a descendant of Louis Gloade, served twelve consecutive terms as a councillor before being elected chief on 6 March 2012. He holds a bachelor of commerce degree, has experience in the banking industry, has worked in human resource management and industrial relations, and is owner of G & G Home Heating, which provides fuel delivery to the Truro area. In 2005 he received the Aboriginal Business of the Year Award for Nova Scotia.

439 Joan Glode, executive director of Mi'kmaw Family and Children's Services of Nova Scotia, has received many honours for her leadership in the field of social work, including the Order of Canada in 2009, the National Aboriginal Achievement Award the same year, and an honorary doctorate in 2012 from Mount Saint Vincent University in Halifax. A daughter of Frank Glode and Mary Paul of the Acadia First Nation, Joan, born in Halifax, was the first Mi'kmaq to graduate from the School of Social Work at Dalhousie University.

CHAPTER 3

1 Joviality must have been a Guédry family trait, as Paul's father Claude was known as Claude Guédry *dit Grivois* (called "the jovial"). But *grivois* can also mean "saucy" or "ribald," however, as in the case with some soldiers' behaviour when on leave. Paul Guédry became known by a number of synonymous names, including Paul Labrador, Paul Guidry *dit* Grivois, Paul Guidry *dit* Lavadure, Paul Gueddrie, Paul Gedri, Paul Gueddrey and Paul Jeddrie.

2 Mather Byles Desbrisay, *History of the County of Lunenburg*, 2nd ed. (Toronto: William Briggs, 1895), 18. The French used two spellings of the place name, Merliguèche or Mirliguèche, while the English settlers preferred "Merliguèche" or "Maligash."

3 Paul Guédry *dit* Labrador *fils* is the only one of Paul and Nanette's sons who appears in the documentary record as living at Mushamush as late as 1801.

4 "Wolastoqiyik" is the name the Indigenous people of the Saint John River family use for themselves. The word "Malecite" means "poor or bad speakers" and was ascribed to them by the Mi'kmaq.

5 Claude Guédry's exact birth date is unknown. He was born between 1648 and 1652 and died on 9 January, 1723.

6 The symbol "8" in "Kesk8a" refers to a sound in the Mi'kmaq language that the French held approaches a "w" but is not found in either the French or English language.

7 Elizabeth Mancke and John G. Reid, "Elites, States and the Imperial Contest for Acadia," in *The "Conquest" of Acadia, 1710: Imperial, Colonial, and Aboriginal Constructions*, ed. John G. Reid et al. (Toronto: University of Toronto Press, 2004), 25–48; Maurice Basque, "Family and Political Culture in Pre-Conquest Acadia," in *The "Conquest" of Acadia*, ed. Reid et al., 48–63.

8 Public awareness of the history and genealogy of the Guédry family has increased since the founding in 2004 of Les Guédry d'Asteur, a society under the presidency of historian Marty Guidry of Baton Rouge, Louisiana, that conducts extensive genealogical research on Guédry origins and interrelationships. The society maintains a free website at http:/freepages.genealogy.rootsweb. ancestry.com/~guedrylab nefamily/. Claude Guédry *dit* Lavadure (or La Verdure) the husband of Marguerite Petitpas, was at Merliguèche in 1686 and the next year in Port Royal, where he owned some cows and sheep. By 1699 he was back on the Atlantic coast at La Hève and by 1701 was at Merliguèche. Acadian genealogist Bona Arsenault argues that Claude probably arrived in Acadia with his father Charles in 1671 on *L'Oranger*. Bona Arsenault, *Éditions: Histoire et généalogie des Acadiens* (Montreal: Léméac, 1976), 6, 58–9, 2499–2502. An alternative contention is that Claude Guédry was born in Acadia, perhaps at La Hève, and later lived with an Indigenous consort with whom he had several *métis* children. François-Edme Rameau de Saint-Père, writing in the late nineteenth century, depicted Claude's father Charles as a rugged individualist who left Rochelle for Acadia, either in 1632 with Isaac de Razilly or earlier with Sieur de Poutrincourt. Rameau de Saint-Père, *Une colonie féodale en Amérique: L'Acadie (1604–1881)*, bk. 2 (Paris: Éditions Granger frères, 1889). Although Bona Arsenault's view is widely favoured, without additional evidence this controversy is a difficult one to resolve conclusively.

9 The official reason, to promote the "Frenchification" of the Indigenous population, never worked well, as many French men who married Mi'kmaw and Malecite women stayed with their wives' groups.

10 Archives of the Archbishopric of Quebec, Quebec, G1S 4R5 (1679–86), Registers of Notre-Dame-du-Bon-Secours de Beaubassin Catholic Church. On microfilm,

CEA F1030, Centre d'Etudes Acadiennes, University of Moncton, New Brunswick.

11 Jeanne La Tour married Martin d'Aprendestiguy, Sieur de Jemseg, and resided on the shore of the Saint John River across from Menagoneche (or Menogonech). For further information on Jeanne La Tour, see M.A. MacDonald, *Fortune & La Tour: The Civil War in Acadia* (Halifax: Nimbus, 2000), 13, 43–44, 83, 196. Charles Saint-Etienne de La Tour had two other *métis* daughters besides his eldest, Jeanne. The second oldest was Antoinette, who died at a convent at Tours. The name of the youngest *métis* daughter is unknown; her mother may have been a close relative of one or both of the Mi'kmaw men, Quichetech and Menougy, who accompanied La Tour to France in 1632. Olive Patricia Dickason discusses the role played by some *métis* leaders in "From 'One Nation' in the Northeast to 'New Nation' in the Northwest: A Look at the Emergence of the *Métis*," in *The New Peoples: Being and Becoming Métis in North America*, ed. Jacqueline Peterson and Jennifer S.H. Brown (Winnipeg: University of Manitoba Press, 1985), 19–36.

12 Clarence-J. d'Entremont, "Petitpas, Claude," *Dictionary of Canadian Biography* online, vol. 2 (1701–40).

13 Persons at Merliguèche included Claude Guédry *père* (or Sr.), Marguerite Petitpas, and an unidentified man surnamed "Petitpas" who was either Claude Petitpas Jr. or Claude Petitpas's brother Bernard Petitpas. Jacques Provost and his wife Jeanne Faveau, Jacques Petit, Jacques LeBat *dit* Marquis, Pierre Lejeune *dit* Briart (or Briard), and Pierre's wife Marie Tibodeau lived at Petit Rivière. Martin Lejeune *dit* Briart and his Mi'kmaq wife Jeanne were at Port Maltois, while Francois Michel and his wife Madeleine Germaine lived at La Hève. Joan Dawon, "Guédry-Merliguèche Reunion, August 7, 2004," https://freepages.rootsweb.com/~guedrylabinefamily/genealogy/joandawson7august2004.

14 Archives Nationales de France, Le Centre des Archives d'Outre Mer (ANOM), col. G1 466, no. 10, *Recensement fait par Monsieur De Meules [sic, de Meulles, Intendant of New France] … de tout les Peuples de Beaubassin, Riviere St. Jean, Port Royal, Isle percée et autres Costes de L'Acadie commencement de l'annee 1686.* There is a transcribed copy on microfilm at Library and Archives Canada (henceforth LAC), Ottawa: MG 1, Series G1, vol. 466, no. 10, microfilm reel C-2572.

Claude Petitpas, Sieur de LaFleur (1626–90), married Catherine Bugaret *dit* St. Martin and the couple had fifteen children. Clarence-J. D'Entremont, "Petitpas [Jr.]," *Dictionary of Canadian Biography* online, vol. 2 (1701–05). Among these were Bernard (b.1659); Marguerite (b.1661) – who first married Martin Dugas and after Dugas's death married Claude Guédry *père*; Claude Jr. (b.c.1663), who married a Mi'kmaw woman named Marie-Thérèse and had six children; Barthélémy; Judith; Paul; Marie; Jacques; and Françoise. After Marie-Thérèze's death Claude Petitpas Jr. wed Françoise Lavergne of Port Royal and had fourteen more children: Jean-Baptist; Louis Benjamin; Joseph; a second son named Joseph; Jean; Jacques, who married Geneviève Serreau *dit* St-Aubin; Marie (b.1669), who married Michel de Forest; Isabelle (b.c.1670), who first wed Olivier Boudreau and after his death wed Alexandre Richard; Henriette (1674–1756), who married Prudent Robichaud; Paul (b.c.1675); Charles (b. 1676); Martin (b.1677); Pierre (b.1681); and Anne (b.c.1681), who married Jacques Levron Girouard.

15 The Gargas census lists only one child, a son, living in the Guédry household, but this is misleading since Claude and Marguerite were raising five children at this time. The Gargas census of 1687–88 is reproduced in Andrew Hill Clark, *Acadia: The Geography of Early Nova Scotia to 1760* (Madison: University of Wisconsin Press, 1969), 124.

16 Massachusetts Archives (Secretary of the Commonwealth), vol. 2 (Colonial, Chapter 8, Nova Scotia and Canada from 1643 to 1719), folio 540, "Liste des Acadiens qui ont prete le serment d'allegeance au roi d'angleterre, 1695. Signed at Port Royal, 16 August 1695." Microfilm copy at LAC, vol. 2, folio 540, microfilm reel F-579. There is also a facsimile of this document in *Mémoires de la Société Généalogique Canadienne-Française* 6 (1955): 316–17.

17 Archives des Colonies (henceforth AC), Archives Nationales de France, Paris, France, AC col. G1 466, nos. 18–20, 29, Acadian census of 1689. A transcribed copy is housed in LAC, microfilm reel C-2572, MG 1, Series G1, vol. 466, nos. 18–20.

18 Marie Dugas married Joseph Guyon *dit* Dion at Port Royal in 1697 and two years later the couple moved to Merliguèche. Paul was baptized in the absence of a priest by Joseph Guyon *dit* Dion at Merliguèche soon after his birth in 1701. This baptism was later confirmed on 8 September 1705 at Merliguèche by the Recollect priest, Félix Pain, and recorded in the registers of the Parish of St. Jean-Baptiste, Port Royal, by a Recollect priest, Justinien Durand, on 27 October 1705. Nova Scotia Archives and Record Management, Halifax (henceforth NSARM), RG 1, vol. 26, 38, Registres des baptêmes, mariages, et sepultures de la paroisse de St. Jean-Baptiste du Port Royal, 1702–55, "Baptism of Paul Guédry, 27 October 1705."

19 Owing to the distance to the priest at Port Royal, respected individuals at Merliguèche, such as Joseph Guyon, retained dispensations to conduct certain sacraments. In this closely knit society, these men often presided over children's baptisms, which often were confirmed by a priest at a later date. Guyon conditionally baptized Paul Guédry in January 1701, while Jean-Baptist Guédry presided over the conditional baptism of his youngest sister Françoise in 1703. A more formal baptism of these children took place on 8 September 1705 when Felix Pain, the Recollect priest from Port Royal, visited the community. Jean-Baptist Guédry also acted as a sponsor the same month at the baptism of twin sons of Martin Le Jeune and Marie Godet (or Gaudet) from Port Maltois. NSARM, Registres des baptêmes, mariages et sepultures de la paroisse de St.-Jean Baptiste du Port Royal, 1702–28, "Baptism of twins Paul and Martin Je Jeune, sons of Martin Le Jeune and Marie Godet, 10 September 1705." In 1725 Paul's sister Françoise Guédry would marry Jean Le Jeune (1697–1759), a son of Pierre Lejeune and Marie Tibodeau (or Thibodeau), and move to La Hève.

20 There is considerable information online about these two brothers, but much of it is based on scanty oral tradition and not a little guesswork.

21 He later settled further east along the Nova Scotia coast at Isles Anglaises (now Gerard Island and Phoenix Island), which lay close to a productive cod fishery off present-day Pope's Harbour. Two brothers, Denis and Bernard Godet, sailing from Port Royal to Île Royal (Cape Breton), found Claude Petitpas Jr. and his family living at Isles Anglaises on 22 May 1714. Clarence-J. d'Entremont, *Histoire du Cap-Sable de l'an mil au traité de Paris (1763)* (Eunice, LA: Hébert, 1981), 3.1575–6.

22 Claude Petitpas *fils* and his son Barthélemy aided New England fishermen along the Atlantic coast. Bernard Pothier, "Petitpas, Barthélemy," *Dictionary of Canadian Biography* online, vol. 11 (1741–70). Claude Petitpas *fils* even once paid the ransom of a certain New England fishermen out of his own pocket. In return, the legislative council of Boston in 1720 granted Claude one hundred pounds and promised to pay the tuition fees of one of his sons to Harvard University. Claude continued to support the British and New England. Seven years after his marriage to Françoise Lavergne at Port Royal in 1721, while he and he second wife were living in Île Royale (Cape Breton), the governor of Louisbourg, Joseph Monbeton de Brouillan *dit* Saint-Ovide, found Claude encouraging Mi'kmaw youth to support the British. For this, Saint-Ovide banished him for two years to France,

but Claude later returned to Acadia to resume his life as a fisherman and Mi'kmaw interpreter. He died around 1731. Though his son Barthélemy also favoured the English camp, he was called to Louisbourg to act as an interpreter, at an annual stipend of three hundred *livres*, for the French colonial administration. In 1745 Barthélemy was captured as a French supporter by a New England privateer captain named David Donahew, and sometime between 1745 and 1750 was put to death in Boston.

23 Clarence-J. d'Entremont uses "d'Azy" or "d'Azt" to distinguish Philippe II Mius d'Entremont's sons and daughters from those of Philippe's brothers. While this device has recently come under criticism, it is still used here. D'Entremont, *Histoire du Cap-Sable*, 3.793. For an alternative view, see P. Earle Muise and Chester A. Muise, "Searching the Truth: A Critique of Existing Research in the Genealogy of the Mius Family, February 2004," http://les_mius.tripod.com/.

24 D'Entremont, *Histoire du Cap-Sable*, 3.901–62.

25 See Robert Le Blant, "Les trois mariages d'une Acadienne Anne d'Entremont (1694–1778)," *La Nouvelle France* 2 (1932): 211–29.

26 Phillippe II's first Mi'kmaw wife may have belonged to the Cape Sable band, and the second, named Marie, likely came from the Merliguèche-La Hève area.

27 In 1701 Simon Pierre Denys de Bonaventure, Nicolas Denys's great nephew, spoke of this area as Chichimiscadie. Joan Dawon, "Guédry-Merliguèche Reunion, August 7, 2004," http://www.freepages.rootsweb/com/~guedrey-labinefamily/genealogy/joan dawson7august 2004/html.

28 LAC, MG 18, F18, *Recensement genal fait au mois de Novembre mile Sept cent huit de tous les Sauvages de l'Acadie qui resident dans la coste de l'Est, et de ceux de Pintagouet et de Canibeky, famille par famille, Leur ages celuy de Leurs Hommes et Enfants avec une Recapitulation a la fin de la quantite d'hommes et de garcons capables d'aler a La guerre. Connue aussy Le recensement des francois Establis a La ditte Coste de L'Es*. Information for this census was gathered in 1707 and compiled by Père La Chasse in November of 1708. The copy in Ottawa is a typescript, transcribed from the original in the Edward E. Ayer Collection (Ayer MS 751) at the Newberry Library, Chicago. Merliguèche, Petit Rivière, and Port Maltois all were subsumed under the designation "La Hève" in the 1708 census. Distinctions between Indigenous and French shown on this census were doubtless far less marked to those living in this area year-round than they were to itinerant missionaries. Philippe II's youngest children were far better versed in the Mi'kmaw culture than they were in the French language and practices. Over the

next forty years many of Philippe and Marie's *métis* sons and daughters came to occupy prominent intermediary roles between the Mi'kmaw community and the French and British colonial administrations.

29 Members of this Tibodeau family later may have gone into hiding around Mushamush Lake, Lunenburg County, with Paul's family during the Seven Years' War. As late as 1819 "Frederick Guiddery," a close relation of Paul's brother Augustin Guédry, was looking out for a "Widow Thibaudeau," an elderly Mi'kmaw woman who possessed four hundred acres in Digby County. NSARM, RG 20, Nova Scotia Lands and Forests, Land Grant Registration Books, Series A – "Guiddery, Frederick & others."

30 Some genealogists aver that the ancestor of these Le Jeunes, Pierre Le Jeune I (c.1595–c.1676), came to La Hève in 1632 with Isaac de Razilly and brought a French wife with him. Others, less certain of the date of this man's arrival, argue that Pierre I likely came from France as a single man, consorted with a Mi'kmaw woman from the La Héve area, and that three of his descendants, Pierre II, Catherine, and Aimee, were *métis*. One of his sons, Pierre II, wed a Mi'kmaw woman surnamed "Doucet" who died around 1661, after which Pierre II wed Jean Teriot. (A Mi'kmaw family with the surname "Doucet" lived at Cape Sable, and there is a stone grave marker erected to a Mi'kmaw man at Belliveau Cove, Digby County, inscribed with the words and date "Francois Doucet, 1771." The surname "Doucet" among the Mi'kmaq may have originated from "Medosset," found at Port Royal prior to 1700.) Pierre II Le Jeune and his first wife, surnamed "Doucet," were the parents of Pierre Le Jeune *dit* Briard and Martin Le Jeune *dit* Briard. In all, Pierre II had seven children by his two wives, and most of them, following the collapse of de Razilly's settlement, chose to follow the fur trade. In 1664 they weathered relocation by the English to Port Rossignol (now Liverpool) and then to Boston, though following the Treaty of Breda in 1667 most were back in their old haunts in Nova Scotia. Clarence-J. d'Entremont holds that by 1700 almost all Le Jeunes were probably of *métis* extraction. D'Entremont, *Histoire du Cap-Sable*, 3.1121–5.

31 François Lejeune married Marie Egighighes on 25 February 1727 at Port Royal in the presence of Pierre Cellier and Martin Grand Claude. Chief Claude Egighighes (also known as Egigoishe, Eosechinuoich, Gagoishe, or Gisigash), who was orphaned early in life according to La Chasse's 1708 census, rose to become head chief of the La Hève district in 1722. LAC, Archives des Colonies, Paris, France, F-135, CIIB, vol. 6, *Correspondance*

générale, no. 77, *Recensement des Sauvages tam de lisle Royalle que de la peninsula del'acadie qui fait deservis par Les Missionaires du Seminair des Missions etrangeres Etablis a Quebec fait que a M. Gaulin pretre Missionaire des Sauvages en 1722.*

32 Only 2.5 arpents of land had been cultivated in the entire La Hève region by 1687. LAC, AC, CIIB, vol. 10, "Sur l'Acadie"; Gargas census of 1687–88.

33 Controversy surrounds Madeleine Margaret's identity, although most Acadian genealogists hold that she is most likely a granddaughter of Baron Philippe I Mius d'Entremont of Pobomcoup. D'Entremont, *Histoire du Cap-Sable*, 3.1013–14; Marty Guidry, "Survival of a Family: The Family of Jean-Baptiste Guédry & Madeleine Mius d'Azy," http://freepages.rootsweb.com/~guedrylabinefamily /genealogy/survivalofafamilyguedrydazy.html. Les Guidry d'Asteur Genealogy Committee in the United States recently have contended, however, that Jean-Baptiste's wife may have been Madeleine Marguerite Moise, a daughter of François *dit* Latrielle Moise and Madeline Vincent, and that Guédry and Moise were wed around 1715 at Port Royal. After Jean-Baptiste Guédry's death in 1726, his eldest son, Joseph, married Marie Benoit and moved in 1752 to Baie des Espagnols, Île Royale, where the British captured them and deported them to Maryland.

34 While no baptismal record could be found for a son of Jean-Baptiste Guédry called Paul, Jean-Baptiste speaks of a son by that name being held in Boston in 1726. *The Trials of Five Persons for Piracy, Felony and Robbery: Who were Found Guilty and Condemned, at a Court of Admiralty for the Trial of Piracies, Felonies and Robberies Committed on the High Seas, Held at the Court House in Boston within His Majesty's Province of the Massachusetts-Bay in New England on Tuesday the Fourth Day of October, Anno Domini, 1726, Boston*, printed by T. Fleet for S. Gerrish, 1726, 2–19. Marie also may have been Jean-Baptiste's daughter. Stephen A. White, *Dictionnaire généalogique des familles acadiennes, Première partie, 1636 à 1714* (Moncton: Centre d'études acadiennes, 1999), 773–4; Guidry, "Jean-Baptiste Guédry & Madeleine Mius d'Azy."

35 *Boston Newsletter*, 1 August 1715.

36 For more information regarding this organization see Frank G. Speck, "The Eastern Algonkian Wabanaki Confederacy," *American Anthropologist* 17 (1915): 492–508.

37 A Wabanaki letter directed to Governor Samuel Shute of Massachusetts in 1721 indicated that the Mi'kmaq at that time were merely allies but not full-fledged members of the Wabanaki Confederacy councils. UK

National Archives, CO5, 106–07. The transcription of this letter appears in the *Maine Historical Society Quarterly* 13 (Winter 1974): 179–83. Frank Goldsmith Speck also stressed that the Mi'kmaq were late joiners of the Confederacy.

38 Murdoch, *A History of Nova-Scotia, or Acadie* (Halifax: James Barnes, 1865), 1.401.

39 Massachusetts State Archives, "A Journal of a Voyage to Cape Britton on ye King's Account by Mr. Peter Capoon … [1715]," vol. 38A, 14.

40 LAC, AC, on microfilm, CIIB 6: 73–4.

41 This conflict, which lasted from 1722 to 1725, is referred to variously in New England as Dummer's War, Lovewell's War, Rasle's or Rale's War, and the Three Year War.

42 While the British at Annapolis Royal periodically remembered Claude Guédry *père's* past assistance in saving New England crews, Boston did not. Early in 1722 a vessel was sent from Boston captained by the same Captain Blin who had negotiated with the Merliguèche Mi'kmaq two years before.

43 The identity of this Philippe Guédry remains enigmatic. There is an outside possibility that he was one of Claude Guédry *père's* children whose name was not recorded in any church register or census record. A second possibility is that Philippe was born to Guédry and Kesk8a before 1680. The only other reference in the eighteeenth-century documentary record to a "Philippe [Guédry *dit*] Labrador" pertains to the father of a child named François Noel Labrador, baptized at Halifax in 1771 by Abbé Charles François-Bailly. This Philippe, however, would have been too young to be the person taken to Boston in 1722. NSARM, French registers on microfilm, *Registre des actes de baptême, mariages, et sepultures fails en la nouvelle ecosse ou acadie commence le vingt unieme jour de juillet de l'annee mil sept cent soixante huit, par mons. Charles Francois Bailly, pretre missionaire des sauvages et acadiens, sujets de sa majeste britannique,* Entry for 23 December 1770, Halifax, "Baptism of François Noel, son of Philippe Labrador and Marie Bisk8ne. Godparents Bernard Lishaute and Françoise."

44 From New Hampshire a man named Jacob Parker sent them to Boston even though Boston had a law at that time that forbade any foreigner to settle in the town. The Boston council got around this law by viewing the Acadian and *métis* party not as immigrants but as prisoners.

45 D'Entremont, *Histoire du Cap-Sable*, 3.1016. At age twenty-three on 13 November 1737, Judith Guédry wed Jean Cousin at Merliguèche. Witnesses to the ceremony were Antoine Duplessis, Germaine Lejeune, and Jean Hébert. Judith and Jean lived at Ministiguèshe, now Barrington

Head, Shelburne County, before leaving in 1751 with their four children for Baie des Espagnols, Île Royale.

46 Massachusetts State Archives, vol. 63, folio 416, "Declaration of Joseph Marjory," 18 December 1724. Jean-Baptiste Guédry and Madeleine are known to have had four children, Jean-Baptiste *fils*, Marie, Claude, and Joseph. It is possible they also had a son named Paul whose birth went unrecorded. It has been suggested that Paul may have been similar in age to François Mius, who was born in 1700. Jean-Baptiste and Madeleine's other children married into the Lejeune, Moyse, and Benoit families.

47 This treaty was a ratification of an important peace and friendship treaty the British conducted with the Eastern Abenaki the preceding year in Boston.

48 Bill Wicken, "26 August 1726: A Case Study in Mi'kmaq-New England Relations in the Early Eighteenth Century," *Acadiensis* 23, no. 1 (1993): 18–19; Marty Guidry, "Tragedy for the Guedry Family: An Act of Piracy on the High Seas," parts 1 and 2, *Generations* 5 (Winter 2007): 1. Part 1 of the transcript for the trial of Jean-Baptist Guédry and his son Jean-Baptist *fils* records what happened on Tuesday, 4 October 1726, while Part 2 records the trial proceedings, involving James Mius, Philippe Mius, and John Missel, on 5 October 1726.

49 Though Marsel had jumped overboard, Marsel's wife and two children must have proceeded on to Boston. Nothing is mentioned about them, however, in the trial transcripts. Governor Saint-Ovide immediately viewed the debacle as an opportunity to foment further hostilities between the Mi'kmaq and the British. LAC, Archives des Colonies (AC) CIIB, vol. 9, fol. 9v, "Saint-Ovide au ministre," 20 December 1727.

50 William Wicken notes that in his defending arguments, "Hughes declared that the Mi'kmaq men could not be found guilty of piracy, since at the time the offence took place, they thought themselves to be in 'a State of War with us, [and] what they have done, they may well justify, by the Laws of GOD, Nature, Nations and Arms.' Hughes admitted that a treaty had been ratified at Annapolis Royal in early June, and another on at Casco Bay two months later, but contended that only the later Treaty was applicable to the three defendants. He also contended that even though they were subject to the treaty's articles, the government should not expect them to have had a perfect acquaintance with it, they living in a far, remote and distant Place of another Government. And being but an inconsiderable Number of People, the Law will not, with Submission, presume a person be knowing of a thing, unless there appear some circumstances by which it may be reasonably concluded,

he cannot but know it." Wicken, *Mi'kmaq Treaties on Trial* (Toronto: University of Toronto Press, 2002), 150. Quotations by Hughes are taken from *The Trials of Five Persons for Piracy, Felony and Robbery*, 31. Hughes's arguments were nevertheless overruled by Robert Auchmuty, the colony's advocate general, who presented a case that the Indignous contingent, particularly the Guedrys, James Mius, John Missel, and Philippe Mius, were guilty of piracy on the high seas.

51 Wicken, *Mi'kmaq Treaties on Trial*, 152.

52 *Boston Newsletter*, 4 November 1726; "Hanging of Two Acadians and Three Indians at Boston," *Yarmouth Vangard*, 31 January 1989.

53 These may have been Merliguéche Mi'kmaq, who visited Cape Breton annually. They were probably in Cape Breton at the time the report was written and remained there for a while after the attack on the ship.

54 British Colonial Records in microfilm at NSARM (henceforth CO) 217/38/176–77, "At a Council Held Tuesday, 2 November 1727"; Murdoch, *A History of Nova-Scotia*, 1.445.

55 L.F.S. Upton, *Micmacs and Colonists: Indian-White Relations in the Maritimes, 1713–1867* (Vancouver: University of British Columbia Press, 1979), 54–5.

56 LAC, AC, CIIB, vol. 8, vol. 8, ff. 38–43, "St. Ovide to ministre," 13 September 1727; AC CIIB, vol. 9, ff. 15–16, "St. Ovide to ministre," 20 September 1727; CO 217/38/203–06, "St. Ovide to Lawence Armstrong," 3 October 1727; "Armstrong to St. Ovide," 13 November 1727.

57 LAC, CO 217/38: 176–77, "At a Council Held Tuesday," 2 November 1727.

58 LAC, AC, CIIB, vol. 10, fol. 5v, "Extrait de la letter Ecrite a Saint-Ovide le 10 juin 1727."

59 "Colonel Thomas Peregrine Hopson to the Lords of Trade," 26 May 1753, cited in Winthrop Pickard Bell, *The "Foreign Protestants" and the Settlement of Nova Scotia: The History of a Piece of Arrested British Colonial Policy in the Eighteenth Century* (Toronto: University of Toronto Press, 1962). 403. When Hopson visited the Merliguèche area in 1753, he found between three hundred and four hundred acres of cleared land.

60 Duquesnal styled himself on the document as "Commandant pour Sa Majeste a l'Isle Royal [et] l'Isle S. Jean." This *brevet* was obtained from François Mius's grandson in the early nineteenth century by Abbé Jean-Mandé Sigogne. NSARM, RG 1, vol. 430, docs. 20 and 21, "Abbé Sigogne to Lieutenant Governor Sir John Cope Sherbrook, with attachments," 5 May 1812.

61 Around 1720, Pierre Guédry *dit* Grivois *dit* LaBine (1697–1751) wed Marguerite Brassaud (or Brasseau) from Piziquid. The couple's children were Marie-Josephe born in 1722, Pierre *fils* in 1723, Jean Baptiste Augustin in 1725, Charles in 1726, Marguerite in 1727, Hélène, who lived from 1729 to 1812, Jean-Anselm in 1730, Joseph in 1732, Jean Fermilien in 1735, Augustin in 1740, and Agnes in 1742. Bona Arsenault, *Histoire et Genealogie des Acadiens* (Ottawa: Editions Lemeac, 1978), 589, 635; http://sites.rootsweb.com/guedrylabinefamily/history.html. Jean-Baptiste and Joseph were close in age and probably at times visited Merliguèche together. Joseph lived at Piziquid and traded along the Musquodoboit River Valley. He is reputed around 1747 to have married Marie Cope, a daughter of Chief Jean-Baptiste Cope, who in 1752 signed a peace and friendship treaty with the British at Halifax. His brother Jean, who farmed and traded furs at Piziquid, went by a number of names, including "Jean Grivois" *and* "John Labrador."

62 Quoted in Murdoch, *A History of Nova-Scotia*, 2.81. Bell cautions about the accuracy of this figure: "Presumably the 'eight settlers' were the settlement's adult males, not the total number of 'souls.'" Bell, *Foreign Protestants*, 403. In 1746 Abbé Le Loutre held there were twelve French families at "Misliguesh," and a 1748 description of the community, apparently drafted for the French governor, reported that twenty families lived at "Mioleguech." *Collection de documents inédits sur le Canada et l'Amérique publies par le Canada-François* (Quebec: L.J. Demers & Frère, 1888), 1.43, 47.

63 Murdoch, *History of Nova-Scotia*, 2.117. As well as Pierre and Joseph Guédry, the proclamation outlawed Charles LeRoy; Philip Le Roy; Joseph Le Blanc *dit* le Maigre ("the Lean"); Louis Gautier and two of his sons, Joseph and Pierre; Amand Bugeau; Charles and Francis Raymond; and George Hébert dit Baguette (whose half-sister Anne Hèbert married Chief Charles Alexis of Cape Sable in the mid-1750s). Thirty-year old Charles Le Roy (1717–c.1760) was married to Margaret Lejeune, a granddaughter of Martin Le Jeune and Marie-Jeanne Kagijonias. Mail travelling between Nova Scotia and Boston was slow, however, and Shirley's proclamation was not received at Annapolis Royal until 12 April the following year. By this time the Broussard and his companions had taken precautionary measures and gone into hiding. None of them was captured and turned in to the authorities.

64 Stephen A. White, *Dictionnaire généalogique*, 1.772.

65 Paul's nephew, Joseph *dit* Labrador, who was Pierre dit LaBine's son, led raids during the middle to late 1750s on outlying Lunenburg settlements.

66 The Guédry *dit* Labradors traded with the Mi'kmaq on the shores of La Bras d'Or Lake, in what is now

Cape Breton, and in consequence may have taken the surname "Labrador" or "Labradore" in keeping with Mi'kmaw naming practice.

67 João Fernandes Lavrador, a late-fifteenth-century Portuguese explorer, is said to have settled colonists on the shore of the Cape Breton lake that still bears his name. The landmass lying northwest of Newfoundland is also reputedly named after him.

68 "Lavradure" and "Labrador" are etymologically the same. "Lavradure" and "Labrador" are etymologically the same. Their common Latinate root *labrar*, meaning "to cultivate," originally referred exclusively to landowning farmers. "Labrador" took on a wider meaning, however. The designation "Bras d'Or" (an abbreviated form of "Labrador") stems from a sixteenth-century Portuguese settlement that lay on the shores of what is now Bras d'Or Lake.

69 The oral account of this incident, which had been circulating among the Acadian population at Piziquid for generations, was recorded in the early 1930s by Reverend W.B. Bezanson of Windsor. According to Bezanson the incident took place near the "Indian Orchard at the head of tide on or near a farm now owned by John Davenny of Windsor Forks." W.B. Bezanson, *Stories of Acadia* (Dartmouth: privately printed, 1933), 16. Although this information is now well over eighty years old, the approximate site of the incident probably can still be plotted from it. The Joseph Cope mentioned in the story almost certainly was a son of Chief Jean Baptist Cope and so the brother-in-law of Joseph Guédry *dit* Labrador, who married Chief Cope's daughter Marie.

70 Ibid., 16–24.

71 Since Paul Guédry was the best-known coast pilot in the area, and he had not yet returned to Merliguèche, Cornwallis, uncertain how to navigate the *Sphinx* past the rocky ledges that flanked the Atlantic coastline between Mahone Bay and Chebucto Harbour, hired twenty-year-old Pierre Benoit and two other Acadian youths as pilots. Benoit impressed the governor enough with his dependability that Cornwallis later sent the young man from Chebucto overland with letters to Mascarene at Annapolis Royal. The story of Benoit acting as a pilot aboard the *Sphinx* was told and retold within the Benoit family of Tracadie, Nova Scotia. D.J. Rankin, *A History of the County of Antigonish, Nova Scotia* (Toronto: Macmillan Co. of Canada, 1929), 377–8. Bell points out errors that he suggests arose in the transmission of this story, but still upheld the validity of the oral tradition as historical source. Bell, *Foreign Protestants*, 404–5n15a.

72 NSARM, MG 1, vol. 2612, Letters of the Governors of Nova Scotia, no. 4, "Edward Cornwallis to the Lords of Trade," 22 June 1749; also cited in Bell, *Foreign Protestants*, 403–4.

73 It is doubtful, however, that Guédry's promises included an unconditional oath of allegiance to the British Crown.

74 D'Entremont, *Histoire du Cap-Sable*, 3.1018.

75 A 1752 French census for Baie des Espagnols reported that the Guédrys had "a good deal of fallow land where they will sow seed this year." It also listed Paul Guédry *fils* as ten years of age, Jean Petit Jean as nine, and François as two, although François, baptized in 1749, would have been three. *Canadian Archives: Report Concerning Canadian Archives for the Year 1905* (Sessional Paper no. 18), "Tour of Inspection Made by Sieur de la Roque. Isle Royale Census of 1752" (Ottawa, 1906), II, Appendix A, 40.

76 Augustin Guédry and Jeanne Anne Hébert had Jean-Baptiste in 1728, Joseph in 1735, and Pierre in 1741. All three were born in the Cobequid area. The couple later had a fourth son, Augustin *fils*, who was born in Louisiana.

77 Charles Boutin's mother Marie-Margaret Le Jeune *dit* Briard was a daughter of Martin Le Jeune *dit* Briard and Jeanne-Marie Kayigonias of Port Maltois, now Port Medway, Queens County.

78 Marty Guidry, "New Research Reveals Guédry's [*sic*] Exiled to North Carolina," https://freepages.rootsweb.com/~guedrylabinefamily/genealogy/guidry_exiled_north_carolina.html.

79 Germain Le Jeune was a son of Pierre Le Jeune *dit* Briard and Marie Tibodeau.

80 *Canadian Archives*, "Isle Royale Census of 1752," 40. Fifty-two-year-old Charles Le Roy, who sometimes Anglicized his surname to "King," and his wife Marie Charlotte Chauvet had a daughter Marie-Joseph Le Roy who married Charles Lejeune, a grandson of Pierre Le Jeune *dit* Briard and Marie Tibodeau.

81 Nicolas Joseph Deschamps *dit* La Cloche (c.1710–c.1758), who was born in France, was the son of Jean Deschamps of St. Martin, Île de Re, Rochelle. He was living at Merliguèche in June 1753, but he and his family previously resided at Anse au Comte de Saint-Pierre on Île St. Jean (now Prince Edward Island) and at Piziquid. His wife Judith (Judique) Doiron was a daughter of Philippe Doiron and Marie-Josephe Guédry, Paul Guédry's sister. Nicolas Joseph thus was only a "nephew" of Paul Guédry by virtue of his marriage to Paul's biological niece. His eldest son, Philippe, did not accompany him to Merliguèche but remained on Île St. Jean following his marriage to Madeleine Trahan at Port-La-Joye on 12 February 1753. The names of his wife, four of his sons, and three of his daughters appear as numbers 1312–1320

on the British victualling list for 1755. As their names do not appear on the February 1756 such list, they either had left Lunenburg or, more likely, their names had been deleted from the list by the British authorities. NSARM, MG 1, vol. 113, 63, microfilm copy of fMS Can 76, "A List of Foreign & Other Settlers Victualled at Lunenburg Between 16 & 29 June 1755 both Days Included." The original list is housed in the Hyde Collection at Houghton Library, Harvard University in Cambridge, MA. Dr. Marty Guidry of Louisiana, a retired organic chemist and the principal genealogist for the Guédry/Guidry/LaBine family in North America, takes Lawrence's assertion that Joseph Deschamps *dit* Cloverwater is *métis* at its face value. As far as Guidry is concerned, this completely disqualifies La Cloche from being Cloverwater, since La Cloche was born in France to French parents. Guidry admits he sees how La Cloche might have called himself Paul's "nephew" by virtue of his marriage to Judith Doiron, but points to another man, Jean Deschamps, born about 1698, whose name he found in eighteenth-century Massachusetts documents, as the more likely candidate for Cloverwater. Guidry, "New Research Reveals Guédrys Exiled to North Carolina," *Generations* (newsletter of Les Guédry d'Asteur) 7, no. 1 (2009): 28–9. La Cloche, however, may deliberately have sought to mislead the British into believing that he was *métis* in order to increase his value as an informant who was familiar with the Mi'kmaw language and cultural mores. It is even possible that Jean Deschamps, who was deported to Massachusetts in 1755, was La Cloche's older brother. Interestingly, Jean and Jeanne had a daughter Nanette who married Joseph La Noüe, and Paul Guédry's daughter Marguerite in 1755 wed Chevalier Jules César Félix de la Noüe de Bogard, who was an ensign at Fortress Louisbourg. For additional information on Marguerite Guédry's marriage to De La Noüe, and its consequences, see chapter 4 of this volume.

82 "Letters to the Governor, Lunenburg, 16 June 1753," in Charles Lawrence, *Journal and Letters of Colonel Charles Lawrence*, ed. D.C. Harvey, Bulletin no. 10 (Halifax: Public Archives of Nova Scotia, 1953), 18.

83 "Letters to the Governor, Lunenburg, 2 July 1753"; Lawrence, *Journal and Letters*, 32.

84 Joseph Deschamps *dit* Cloverwater, listed in Governor Hopson's yearly estimates as "1 French Guide and Pilot," received £18.5 for his services to the British. "Estimate of Expenses for Lunenburg 1754," printed in Bell, *Foreign Protestants*, 446.

85 Ibid., 443n3a.

86 Ibid.

87 "Letters to the Governor, Lunenburg," 2 July 1753. In Lawrence, *Journal and Letters*, 32.

88 Bell, *Foreign Protestants*, 446.

89 NSARM, vol. 163, "Letter of 18 July 1753."

90 Jean-Baptiste Guédry's parents were Pierre Guédry *dit* LaBine (1689–1751) and Marguerite Brassaud (c.1700–c.1747) and his maternal grandparents were Pierre Brassaud and Gabrielle Forest.

91 NSARM, RG 1, vol. 134, 242, "William Cotterell, Secretary's Office, to Lieutenant Colonel Patrick Sutherland," 24 August 1754. In this letter William Cotterell, the provincial secretary, wrote to Patrick Sutherland, Lawrence's successor as commander at Lunenburg, that members of this group were "formerly Inhabitants of this Country and were nearly related to Old Labrador." Sutherland was a lieutenant colonel in the militia. His rank in the army until shortly before his retirement in 1762 was that of captain, and he retired as a major. At his retirement Sutherland was given a land grant that encompassed the Labrador Farm.

92 As he was still a youth, Pierre Guédry lived with Pierre Boutin's household.

93 Marty Guidry suggests that the surnames "Erio" and "Eriot" are variations of the French surname "Terriau." Guidry, "New Research," 22.

94 "Lawrence to Sutherland," 13 April 1755, cited in Bell, *Foreign Protestants*, 483.

95 Marty Guidry, "The Last Guédrys in Merliguèche" and "The Family of Augustin Guédry and Jeanne Hebért."

96 Murdoch, *A History of Nova-Scotia*, 2.71.

97 "Governor's Correspondence," 13 April 1755, cited in Bell, *Foreign Protestants*, 483 and note 28. Charles King (or Roy), born at Port Royal, was associated with Joseph Broussard *dit* Beausoliel during King George's War. Even before this, in 1738, Roy was arrested and then jumped bail at Annapolis, which led Lieutenant-Governor Armstrong to order the Acadian deputies and habitants of Piziquid to find and return him to Annapolis Royal. Archibald MacMechan, ed., *A Calendar of Two Letter-Books and One Commission-Book in the Possession of the Government of Nova Scotia, 1713–1741*, Nova Scotia Archives II (Halifax: Herald Printing House, 1900), 223; Bell, *Foreign Protestants*, 483n28 and 415n11a.

98 Bell, *Foreign Protestants*, 484n32.

99 Despite Lawrence's orders in April, most of their names remained on the victualling list until late June 1755.

100 A few Le Jeunes changed their surname to "Young," and in the late nineteenth century some of them migrated to *métis* settlements on the southwest coast of

Newfoundland. Considerable genealogical work has been conducted by descendants of these families living in both Cape Breton and Newfoundland. See, for example, Lark Szick, "LeJeunes in the Acadian Censuses," http://cbnsorg.cbns.ca/LeJ_CensusExtracts.htm.

101 NSARM, vol.163, "Letter of 18 July 1753."

102 "William Cotterell to Captain Murray," 21 September 1754, cited in Bell, *Foreign Protestants*, 484n30. The "Grivoir" mentioned is probably Jean Guédry. Bell assumes that "Grivoir" is Paul Guédry but does not explain why Paul would be prevented from returning to his own property. Like Paul, Jean Guédry often used "Grivois" as a sobriquet, and it is known that Jean had returned to Piziquid by this time.

103 Public Archives of Canada, *Report for 1905*, vol. 2, Appendix A, Part 2, 117–18. Over one thousand Acadians were deported from Piziquid in October 1755.

104 Jean Labrador (Jean-Baptiste Guédry), being illiterate, required others to write these petitions for him. Massachusetts State Archives, Boston, "Archives of Massachusetts, Nova Scotia and Canada," vol. 23, folio 576, and vol. 24, folio 582; Canadian Archives, *Report Concerning Canadian Archives for the Year 1905, in Three Volumes* (Ottawa: S.E. Dawson, 1906), vol. 2, appendix E, 91, 97, 117–18, 131–2; D'Entremont, *Histoire du Cap-Sable*, 3.1016 and 1851–6; Marty Guidry, "Survival of a Family: A continuing series of articles by Marty Guidry on the children of Claude Guédry and Marguerite Petitpas: The Family of Pierre Guédry dit LaBine & Marguerite Brasseau," *Generations* (newsletter of Les Guidry d'Asteur) 4, no. 1 (2006): 2–5. In addition to the two letters, prior to 1766 Jean Guédry sent a number of petitions to the Massachusetts government asking for an improvement in his family's living conditions.

105 Like his father Pierre Guédry *dit* LaBine, Jean-Baptiste Guédry occasionally used the surname "Labrador." Yet he cannot be numbered among those Guédrys who were ancestral to the Mi'kmaw Labrador family, since he remained in the province of Quebec after 1766. Some of the Mi'kmaw Labradors may have stemmed from Paul Guédry's three youngest children, Paul *fils*, Jean Petit-Jean, and Françis, and almost certainly one of Paul LaBine's sons, Joseph LaBine *dit* Labrador, who was born in 1732. Pierre's youngest son Augustin Guédry is not a candidate since he did not use the surname "Labrador" and after 1763 preferred the company of Acadians.

106 Paul Guédry had seen what had happened to his first cousin Bathélèlemy Petitpas, who while living at Port Toulouse and acting as a Mi'kmaw interpreter had been captured by the British, who tried to claim him as a hostage in return for English prisoners. He was detained indefinitely, however, as Governor William Shirley saw him as a traitor to the king's service, and he died in prison in Boston in 1747. Thomas Pichon, *Genuine Letters and Memoirs relating to the National, the Civil and the Commercial History of the Islands of Cape Breton and Saint John* (London: Nourse, 1760), 163.

107 François-Edme Rameau de Saint-Père, *Une colonie féodale en Amérique: L'Acadie (1604–1881)*, book 2 (Montreal: Éditions Granger frères, 1889), 2.376.

108 AC F3 50:504v–524, Conseil Supérior, 17 February 1755; AC G2 189:270–360, Greffes des Colonies, 1754–55. It has been posited that Bogard de la Noüe and Marguerite Guédry reunited after this ordeal, but no evidence could be found to support this contention. After her ill-fated marriage to de la Noüe, the documentary record, as far as is known, is silent about Marguerite Guédry's fate, though further research may reveal new leads. Some Guédrys who went to Cape Breton undoubtedly were deported, and their names so far have not been located in records in the United States or France.

109 This chart, listed among the King's Maps, is in the British Museum, London. Bell, *Foreign Protestants*, 432n13a.

110 NSARM, RG 1, vol. 204, "Sutherland Grant, Lunenburg Township," 1 July 1762.

111 For a photograph of the old Merliguèche cemetery, see Joan Dawson, *Nova Scotia's Lost Communities: The Early Settlements That Helped Build the Province* (Halifax: Nimbus, 2018), 20.

112 NSARM, RG 1, vol. 430, doc. 96, "Census of Native population at Mushamush,"1801. Descendants of both Pierre Guédry *dit* LaBine and Paul Guédry adopted the surname "Labrador."

113 To escape detection, the Labradors ascended the East River which joins the Canaan River inland, which extends to Timber Lake and Panuke Lake and then on to Piziquid. From this area, there was a canoe route to the St. Croix River, flowing into the Minas Basin.

114 Nova Scotia, *The Nova Scotia Atlas* (Halifax: Formac, 2001), map of Chester, 66

115 The first-hand accounts of John and Lewis Payzant are two of the rare captivity narratives from Nova Scotia. John Payzant's story of the attack on Covey's Island and his subsequent forced journey to Quebec may be found in Brian C. Cuthbertson, ed., *The Journal of the Reverend John Payzant (1749–1834)* (Hantsport, NS: Lancelot, 1981). Lewis Payzant's account is examined in Silas Tertius Rand, "Early Provincial Settlers," *The Provincial* 1, no. 8 (August 1852). Information about the attack was also compiled by Dr. Elias Payzant, a grandchild of

Lewis and Marie Anne Payzant. NSARM, MG1, vol. 747, Payzant Family Papers, no. 42.

116 Desbrisay, *History of the County of Lunenburg*, 2nd ed., 494–500. Desbrisay gives an account of this attack on Lewis Payzant's family on Rous's Island in Mahone Bay that is based on local settler oral traditions.

117 Bell, *Foreign Protestants*, 505.

118 A recent account of the raids and its victims has been presented by Linda G. Layton in *A Passion for Survival: The True Story of Marie Anne and Louis Payzant in Eighteenth-Century Nova Scotia* (Halifax: Nimbus, 2003).

119 B.C. Cuthbertson, "Payzant, John," *Dictionary of Canadian History* online, vol. 6 (1821–35).

120 Desbrisay, *History of the County of Lunenburg*, 2nd ed., 494–8.

121 Labrador would have worked alongside leaders like François Mius in planning and carrying out the attacks. These raids were the precipitating incidents that led Lieutenant Governor Charles Lawrence on 14 May 1756 to place a scalp bounty of twenty-five pounds on Mi'kmaw heads and offer thirty pounds for every Mi'kmaw man brought in alive.

122 Desbrisay, *History of the County of Lunenburg*, 2nd ed., 343–4. Interestingly, there are Labradors today who can still remember Labrador participation in these raids. A study might be conducted drawing on information gleaned from Labrador storytellers.

123 The possibility that Joseph Guédry *dit* LaBine was "Labrador" also gains support from Mi'kmaw oral tradition. Sandy Cope Sr., a Mi'kmaw hunter and storyteller who lived at Millbrook near Truro in the early 1920s, claimed that the individual who killed Lewis Payzant and Wagner was known both as Joseph Labrador and as *Wasagos Unskah*. He further claimed that this man wed Marie Cope, a daughter of Chief Jean-Baptiste Cope who signed a peace treaty in 1752 with the British. Don Awalt, whose ancestors hail from Lunenburg County, claims also to have heard stories about Labrador, since "Jo Labrador and Marie Cope are the great, great grandparents of Elizabeth Dory who married John Awalt and are my great grandparents." Don (Byrd) Awalt, "The Mi'kmaq and Point Pleasant Park, The Mi'kmaq and Amtoukati: An Historical Essay in Progress by Don Byrd Awalt" (Halifax: Native Friendship Centre, 2006), 6–9. Awalt drew on transcripts of interviews that Muriel Cottam Yorke conducted with Sandy Cope at Millbrook in 1922. Don Awalt, personal communication, 10 March 2009. Labrador, he attests, viewed himself as an avenger of wrongs committed against the Acadian-*métis* and Mi'kmaq. He shot a Halifax ferryman named John

Connor who participated in killing several Mi'kmaq in April 1753. The perpetrators of this crime later brought the scalps to Halifax to claim bounty money. "Records of the Council Chamber for 17 April 1753," in Haliburton, *An Historical and Statistical Account of Nova Scotia* (Halifax, 1829), 1.154. Enraged by such acts, Labrador attacked settlers and threatened Mi'kmaw leaders who advocated neutrality. He was even said to have pursued one such chief, Philip Paul from the Sipekne'katik (Shubenacadie) district, and shot and killed him. Certainly a deep rift developed in the 1750s between those within the Aboriginal community who supported the French cause and those who favoured the British. Chief Jean-Baptiste Thoma in fall 1757 hoped to meet with British authorities at Lunenburg and try his hand at mediating between the opposing sides. En route, however, he was fired upon by Lunenburg patrols; he fell to the ground and feigned death in order later to escape back to his settlement on Panuke Lake, Hants County. John Knox, *An Historical Journal of the Campaigns in North America for the Years 1757, 1758, 1759, and 1760* (Toronto: Champlain Society, 1914), 1.89–92, 145–6. It is very possible that the notorious "Labrador" was not biologically Mi'kmaq, a surmise that contradicts the view of two well-known nineteenth-century historians, Mather Byles Desbrisay and Winthrop P. Bell, who held Labrador to be Aboriginal. Desbrisay, *History of the County of Lunenburg* (1870), 343–4; Bell, *Foreign Protestants*, 483, 659. Joseph Labrador's descendants, however, were Mi'kmaq by virtue of their father's marriage to a Mi'kmaw woman. By the mid-nineteenth century these individuals were indistinguishable in the eyes of the British authorities from the rest of the Mi'kmaw population. But some Mi'kmaq continued to view the Labradors as persons "in between" the Indigenous and settler populations, or viewed them as "French" or "white." For instance, in 1853 Chief Joseph Pennel of Gold River and New Germany referred to his wife, Marian Louisa Labrador, as "white." NSARM, Miscellaneous "I" Indian Documents on microfilm, Document Package 25, Pennel Reserve No. 19, Wallabeck Lake, Lunenburg County, docs. 25 and 105, "To Major General John Gaspard Le Marchant, Lieutenant Governor of Nova Scotia, Petition of Joe Pennaul of Gold River, 1853."

124 NSARM, RG 1, vol. 430, doc. 21, "Copy of the Treaty of Treaty of Peace and Friendship with François Mius," 1761.

125 The tomahawk given to Tanner by Joseph Labrador eventually came into Desbrisay's possession. Desbrisay, *History of the County of Lunenburg*, 2nd ed., 344.

126 Of Paul Guédry's four sons born before 1742 – Jacques in 1724, Claude c.1726, Jean-Anselm in 1730, and Joseph-Thomas in 1733 – none was a good candidate for being Labrador. Jacques married Bridgette Le Jeune, a daughter of Pierre Le Jeune and Jeanne Benoit of Merliguèche and a granddaughter of Pierre Le Jeune *dit* Briart and Marie Tibodeau. He and Bridgette in 1749 settled at Bedeque, Île St. Jean, on land given them by Simon de Bonnaventure. Claude lived at Cobequid. (Both Jacques's and Claude's names disappear from the documentary record after 1752.) Jean-Anselm in 1755 fled from Baie des Espagnols, was caught by the British at Miramichi, and was confined to prison at Louisbourg for three years for aiding the Acadian resistance. Upon his release he and his wife, Marie Le Blanc, lived on the Îles de St. Pierre and Miquelon. Their son Jacques Guédry (1767–1801) remained on the Îles after his parents boarded *La Petite Fortune* in 1767 bound for Martin de Re, near Rochefort, France. Archives nationales d'outre mer, France (ANOM), COL G1 413/349, "Registres Paroissiaux de Saint-Pierre et Miquelon: 1763 à 1790–1791, Baptêmes, 01/06/1767"; Jacques Guédry, "Jacques Guédry: Presence Acadienne en Guyane: Sinnamary Recensement de mai 1767," *Le Messager de L'Atlantique*, Falaise Acadie Québec, annexe 1, no. 32, premier trimestre (1996), 21–8. In 1785 Jean-Anselm and his wife left Rochefort for Louisiana, where they met up with Jean-Anselm's younger brother, Joseph-Thomas Guédry (1733–c.1815). Joseph-Thomas, until he was captured and imprisoned at Halifax in 1762, fought alongside the well-known Acadian resistance fighter Joseph Broussard *dit* Beausoleil (c.1702–65). Beausoleil shortly before his death led a group of Acadians, including Joseph-Thomas Guédry, to the Attakapas region of Louisiana where they founded an Acadian farming settlement. After 1762, neither Jean-Anselm nor Joseph-Thomas ever returned to Nova Scotia. Marty Guidry, "Survival of a Family: The Family of Paul Guidry *dit* Jovial and Anne Mius d'Entremont d'Azit [d'Azy] de Pobomcoup," 1.

127 Pierre Guédry *dit* LaBine *dit* Labrador and Marguerite Brassaud had eight children: four daughters (Marie-Joseph, Marguerite, Hélène, and Agnes) and six sons (Pierre *fils*, Jean-Baptiste Augustin, Charles, Joseph, Jean Femilien, and Augustin). Pierre *fils* married Agnes Triel and until 1758 lived at D'Escousse, Île Madam. His eldest sister, Marie-Joseph, wed Charles-Benjamin Mius d'Entremont, a descendant of Philippe II Mius d'Entremont d'Azy and his first Mi'kmaw consort, and the couple lived for a while at Point La Jeunesse, Île Royale. Charles Guédry and his wife, Adelaide Madeleine Hébert, lived

nearby. Following Pierre Guédry *père's* death, Charles took in four of his unmarried siblings: Joseph, who was twenty years old; Jean Femilien, seventeen; Augustin, twelve; and Agnes, ten. It is twenty-year-old Joseph (1732–c.1798), still unwed in 1752, who best fits the criteria for being Labrador the resistance fighter. After 1753 he disappears from the documentary record, but he may have been travelling from Cape Breton to Merliguèche in 1754 in company with his younger brother Augustin Guédry *dit* LaBine (1740–c.1822) when their transport vessel – likely owned by Jean Cousin, the merchant mariner from Louisbourg who in 1737 wed Paul Guédry's eldest daughter Judith at Grand Pré – was overtaken by a British crew intent on taking captives. Bernard L. Geddry, "Guidry, Guédry, Geddry, Jedry – The Story of an Acadian Family" (unpublished ms., Norwood, MA, 1975), cited in Marty Guidry, "Ancestry of the Guedry Family of Clare, Nova Scotia (Jedry, Geddry)," ancestry.com/guedrylabine family/2008. Another of Pierre LaBine's sons, Jean-Baptiste Guédry, went to Piziquid. He married three times, first to Claire-Hélène Benoit who died in 1755, second to Marie-Marguerite Picot, and third, in 1799, to Marie-Angelique Marois. Deported from Piziquid in 1755, Jean-Baptiste lived in exile in Massachusetts for over six years and then moved to the province of Quebec. At Saint-Jacques, Quebec, he and Marie-Marguerite raised at least three sons, Jean, Charles, and Mathurin. Mathurin died while river driving at Lachine, and Charles left the family homestead and entered the northwest fur trade as a voyageur. Mark LaBine, "Charles Guildry [*sic*, Guidry or Guédry] *dit* Labine, Voyageur," *Generations* (newsletter of Les Guidry d'Asteur) 7, no. 1 (2009), 3–9. (Mark Labine is a great-great-great-great-great-grandson of Jean-Baptiste Guédry *dit* LaBine *dit* Labrador.) Joseph and Firmin LaBine were living at Saint-Joseph in the 1820s. Jean Lafleur, Gilles Paquet, and Jean-Pierre Wallot, "Quelques propos sur la variance du prix de la terre dans la région d'Assomption (1792–1835)," in *Marchés, migrations et logiques familiales dans les espaces français, canadien et suisse, 18e–20e siècles*, ed. Luigi Lorenzetto, Anne-Lise Head-König, and Joseph Goy (Bern, 2005), 314n10.

128 After emerging from the interior around 1763, Augustin within the next four years obtained a farm lot on Hobb's Hill, near Gilbert's Cove, St. Mary's Bay, Digby County. Augustin Guédry or Gueddery obtained the parcel from James Boutineau Francklin, a son of Michael Francklin, who was lieutenant governor of Nova Scotia from 1766 to 1776 and commissioner of Indian Affairs from 1777 to 1782. Francklin introduced a policy of allotting

lands in southwestern Nova Scotia to Acadians who had returned from exile. James S. MacDonald, "Memoir of Lieutenant-Governor Michael Francklin, 1752–1782," *Collections of the Nova Scotia Historical Society*, no. 16 (Halifax, 1912), 1–40. In 1767 Augustin married Marie-Françoise Jeanson and the following year the couple moved to Bear Cove, where their son Augustin *fils* in 1799 wed Marie Eagle. NSARM, microfilm reel 15726, excerpts from registers kept by Abbé Jean-Mandé Sigogne of St. Mary's Bay that were subsequently damaged by fire and transcribed by Placide Gaudet, "Marriage at Salmon River on 11 August 1799 of Augustin Gueddery [Guédry] Jr., born on 20 June 1771 and baptized on 14 October 1774, son of Augustin Guiddery Sr. and Marie Anne Jeanson, and Marie Eagle, 23, born 1776, daughter of Edward and Catherine Eagle, Digby County. Witness, Joseph Mieuce [*sic*, Miuce]." Marie Eagle was born a Protestant but abjured her Protestantism on her marriage. Ibid., "Abjuration of Marie Eagle." Augustin's descendants, who spell their surname "Gueddry," are the pioneer founders of the Acadian community of St. Alphonse.

129 Reverend John Seccombe, "The Diary of Rev. John Seccombe," in *Report of the Board of Trustees of the Public Archives of Nova Scotia for the Year 1959*, Halifax, Public Archives of Nova Scotia, Appendix B, 20–37. Seccombe acquired a large Crown grant embracing Gold River in Lunenburg County.

130 NSARM, CO, 217/19/16–23, "Jonathan Belcher to the Colonial Office, London," 17 July 1762.

131 Desbrisay, *History of the County of Lunenburg*, 2nd ed., 55.

132 NSARM, CO 217/19/122, "A report on the situation at Lunenburg," 21 July 1762. Abbé Maillard also had invited chiefs from La Have and Cape Sable to a council at Lunenburg, but the missionary fell ill and could not attend the meeting. The Mi'kmaq nevertheless convened, and during the talks a Mi'kmaw woman committed a theft. Laurent was called upon "to dispense justice in this delicate situation," which allayed the settlers' fears. Micheline D. Johnson, "Laurent, Paul," *Dictionary of Canadian Biography* online, vol. 3 (1741–70).

133 If Joseph Labrador was the son of Pierre Guédry *dit* LaBine (or *dit* Grivois *dit* Labrador), he would have been thirty-one years old in 1763, since he was twenty in 1752. His uncle Paul Guédry was sixty-three in 1763.

134 NSARM, *Registre des actes de baptême, marriages et sepultures faits en la nouvelle ecosse*, "Baptism at Halifax of Francois-Noel, son of Philippe Labrador and Mary Bisk8ne, godparents Bernard Lishaute and Françoise,

23 December 1770." François-Noel Labrador's baptism also appears in a published transcript, the *Registre de l'Abbe Charles-François Bailly, 1768 à 1773*, transcribed under direction of Stephen A. White (Moncton: Centre d'études acadiennes, Université de Moncton, 1978). Philippe Labrador's party travelled to Halifax in company with Pierre Thomas and his wife Marie. Pierre was the foster son of Chief Jean-Baptiste Thoma of Panuke Lake, Hants County.

135 Joseph Labrador was single and still living with his brother Charles Guédry *dit* LaBine in Cape Breton in 1752, so if he was Joseph's son, Philippe Labrador would have to have been born after this date. If born in 1753, for instance, he would have been eighteen when he came to Halifax with his wife and son in 1770.

136 LAC, MG 23, GII-19, Papers of George Henry Monk, vol. 4, Indian accounts, 1793–99, 1211.

137 LAC, MG 23, GII-19, 1215.

138 NSARM, RG 1, vol. 430, doc. 96, census of the Mi'kmaq living at Mushamush in 1801.

139 This younger man named Joseph Labrador appears in accounts kept by merchants dispensing government supplies between 1797 and 1808 to Mi'kmaq living along the Eastern Shore. NSARM, RG 1, vol. 430, doc. 55. James Fulton, a merchant at Stewiacke in central Nova Scotia, held that Captain Labrador exhibited "a good character." NSARM, RG 1, vol. 380, A and B.

140 Nanette Ann-Marie, born in 1705, would have been ninety-six in 1801. D'Entremont, *Histoire du Cap-Sable*, 3.1016.

141 NSARM, RG 1, vol. 430, doc. 55.

142 Desbrisay, *History of the County of Lunenburg*, 2nd ed., 345–6.

143 NSARM, RG 1, vol. 430, doc. 146, "List of Mi'kmaq in Lunenburg County, 1808–1809." Paul Labrador was living with Gabriel Bernard, "Cheremie [Jeremy]" and Jeremy's wife, Hannah Jeremy. This Paul very well may have been Paul Guédry *dit* Labrador's son Paul *fils* who, born in 1742, would have been sixty-six years old.

144 NSARM, RG 1, vol. 430, doc. 9, "Returns to the Committee from Liverpool by Mr. Atkins, and from Chester by Major Thompson, and from other agencies," 1808. Thomas Akins (1762–1832) was an insurance broker and merchant at Liverpool who married Margaret Ott Beamish. Thomas and Margaret's son, Thomas Beamish Atkins (1809–91), became a barrister who in 1857 was appointed commissioner of public records for Nova Scotia. Major Thompson may have been John Sparrow Thompson Sr., the father of John Sparrow David Thompson, who lived in Halifax.

145 NSARM, RG 1, vol. 430, doc. 57, "An Account of Indians that belong to Queens County," circa 1808.

146 See for instance NSARM, MG 15, vol. 3, doc. 23, "Petition of John Bolman for Mahone Bay Indians, for smallpox vaccination," 10 February 1817.

147 Others belonging to the Shelburne group were Pierre Louis, Pierre Tatum, and Francois Tonton. Family Heads in Argyle Township, Clare Township, Yarmouth Township, Shelburne Township, the Sissiboo region, Shelburne Township, Digby, Annapolis and Liverpool, extracted from a census made around 1820 by Abbé Jean-Mandé Sigogne. This census was transcribed by Leonard H. Smith. A copy is in the Tusket Historical Museum, Tusket, Nova Scotia.

148 All these Labradors stemmed from those who lived at Mushamush Lake from the mid-1750s to the early 1800s.

149 Penall (Bernard) Labrador Sr. lived at Mushamush in 1800–01 and then moved to Shelburne County. Penall came to Prospect in 1826 for the marriage of his son Penall Labrador Jr. to Molly Williams. Molly was a daughter of Paul Williams and Honore Luxy (Alexis) of Cape Sable. NSARM, Church Records on microfilm, Registers of Our Lady of Mount Carmel, Roman Catholic Church, Prospect Nova Scotia, 1823–35. Witnesses at the wedding in 1826 were Penall Labrador and Peter Cowie. Penall Labrador and his wife Molly had a daughter Isabelle baptized at Prospect in 1826. Others who visited Prospect were Francois Labrador, Prosper Labrador, and Mary Paul from the Chester area.

150 NSARM, RG 1, vol. 432, 90, Joseph Howe, "Western Tour," 1842. Though they had become part of the Mi'kmaw community, the Labradors still retained many *métis* traits. These included speaking French as well as the Mi'kmaw language and pursuing Acadian occupations. For instance, they readily took to fishing and salting codfish, something that Joseph Howe noted Mi'kmaq rarely did. Joseph Labrador and his brother François were both cod fishermen. The Labradors' slab camps also were a different shape from the camps of other Mi'kmaq, which probably stemmed from their Acadian ancestry.

151 François Labrador and Mary Ellen Luxey married in 1834 and lived at Jordan River, Shelburne County. François's older cousin, also named François, had lived in Argyle Township since 1820. This man wed Charlotte "Chichin" (Shishaw, Chegeo,or Chegau) and the two had Gabriel in 1829, Ozithe around 1830, and Pierre in 1831. Charles Paul Labrador married Marie Agnes Pictou around 1825. Joseph and Ann Luxey lived at Clyde River and had a daughter Anne who in 1872 married

Stephen Luxey, son of Joseph Luxey of Clyde River. This information was taken from registers of the Parish of Saint Anne du Ruisseau, the Parish of St. Pierre de Pubnico, and the Parish St. Gregory's Church in Liverpool. Between 1830 and 1850 one finds three couples, François Labrador and Charlotte Chichan, François Noel and Anne Labrador, and Joseph Labrador and Marie Jeanne, living at West Pubnico. An unusual union, and a second marriage for both partners. was that of Jean-François Labrador and Mary Anne Labrador, the "descendants of two brothers," which required a special dispensation from the Church of St. Pierre de Pubnico. Marie Anne Labrador died in 1866 at the age of seventy-one, so she was born in 1785. Jean-François's birth date is unknown.

152 NSARM, RG 1, vol. 432, 90–1, Joseph Howe, "Western Tour," 1842, 90–1.

153 Ibid., 92.

154 François Labrador married Nelly Paul at Sable River, and the couple had Mary Ellen in 1867 and Sally in 1869. François may have been the son of François Labrador, whom Joseph Howe met at Sable River in 1842. Selina Labrador, who on 24 May 1887 married William Wesley of Sable River, was undoubtedly of the same family. There also is a John Labrador married to Mary Paul who had a son John born in 1866 at Bridgewater. John and François Labrador may have been brothers. The authors are indebted to William Labrador, his wife Pat, and their daughter Cheyenne for sharing information on Labrador family history during a visit to the Gold River community in the spring of 1990. In April 2014 the first author also had the pleasure of meeting Marguerite Labrador (nee McKay), a charming ninety-year-old woman who looked much younger than her years. Marguerite, who lived at Eastern Passage in Dartmouth, had married the late Elmer Labrador, William Labrador's brother. Both William and Elmer Labrador, whose paternal father and grandfather were both named Stephen Labrador, descended from the Labradors of Sable River, Shelburne County.

155 NSARM, Historical Vital Statistics, Shelburne County Marriages, Registration Year 1898, book 1840, p. 36, no. 13, "Marriage of Alpha Babin and Maggie Labrador, daughter of Frank and Mary." Carino Island has since been renamed Morris Island.

156 NSARM, Historical Vital Statistics, Registration Year 1920, Shelburne County Marriages, book 19, 576; NSARM, Historical Vital Statistics, Shelburne County, Late Registry of Birth, Registration Year 1899, no. 991005. Anne Marion Labrador's parents Ben Labrador

and Mary Covey were from Port Joli. An undated, unsigned letter found in the registers of St. Joseph's Roman Catholic Church, Bridgewater, reads: "My father's name is Ben Labrador and my mother's name was Mary Clara Covey. My godfather was John Labrador and my godmother Louise Harbour [Harlow] of Bear River."

157 Information provided to the author by Father Clarence-J. d'Entremont of West Pubnico in 1996. In 1959 Father d'Entremont interviewed Frank Burbine at his trailor park on the subject of Burbine family history.

158 NSARM, Miscellaneous "I" Indian Documents from Nova Scotia Crown Lands Department on Microfilm, Document 149, "Lots 1–11 on Cegumcega Lake, amounting to 970 acres, 1843, with lot no. 1 to John Jeremy." Twelve Mi'kmaw family heads expressed an interest in farming. In addition to Jeremy, the others were Francis Charles, Francis Glode, Peter Glode, Stephen Labrador, James Lewie (Lewis), Lewie Luxy (Lewis Alexis), Francis Mews (Mius or Meuse), Abram Peale (Peter), Joe Peale (Peter), John Pictoe (Pictou), and Stephen Labrador. The majority held one hundred acres, although Francis Glode held seventy acres, Francis Mius had fifty-five acres, and Peter Glode only held fort-five acres. Stephen joined the settlement at a later date than the others.

159 NSARM, Miscellaneous "I" Indian Records from Crown Lands, on microfilm, "Documents relating to Kedgemakooge #9, including tracing by Whitman Freeman of Island of Kedgemakooge, Annapolis and Queens Counties," 26 December 1843.

160 NSARM, Miscellaneous "I" Indian records from Crown Lands, on microfilm, Documents pertaining to Wildcat and the Clyde River Reserve, "William Vankoughnet to James H. Austin," 3 March 1892; "Austin, Deputy Commissioner of Crown Lands to Hayter Reed, Ottawa," 27 November 1893. Vankoughnet demanded that Austin get a surveyor to run the lines of the reserve. It is surprising that Indian Affairs had forgotten about this tract, since Howe wrote about its survey in his *Annual Indian Affairs Report* for 1843. Howe also ordered the subdivision of the Wildcat reserve into ten tracts of one hundred acres each.

161 One of the first permanent Labrador residents in the Annapolis Valley area was John Labrador, who married Mary Anne Penall (or Pennel) in the early 1840s.

162 Mike Parker, *Guides of the North Woods: Hunting and Fishing Tales from Nova Scotia 1860–1960* (Halifax: Nimbus, 1990), appendices. A list of contestants entered in the 1934 guides' tournament included John and Peter Labrador, who guided around Lake Jolly.

163 Around 1849 Marian Louisa Labrador became the second wife of Chief Joseph Pennel of Gold River. In 1855 Francis Labrador, his wife, and one child were also living at Gold River. NSARM, MG 15, vol. 5, doc. 69, "William Chearnley, Indian Agent, Indian List for 1855." Louis Labrador, a guide living at Bear River, married Mary Penall (or Pennel) of Lequille, Annapolis County, and between 1865 and 1891 the couple had four children, Betsy, Thelma, Peter, and Dominic.

164 For instance, when Thomas Labrador, a son of Francis Labrador and Hannah Glode born at Bridgewater in 1851, wed Mary Penall (Pennel), a daughter of Joseph Penall and Sophia Rafuse of New Germany, the couple held their wedding in Milton, Queens County. NSARM, Historical Vital Statistics, Queens County Marriages, Registration Year 1868, book 1834, p. 16, no. 35.

165 Thomas J. Butler, Nova Scotia, Department of Indian Affairs, 28 August 1883, Dominion of Canada, *Parliamentary Sessional Papers*, 1884, 36–7.

166 Nova Scotia Museum, Halifax, Printed Matter File, "Jeremiah Bartlett Alexis to Chiefs, Shubenacadie, NS, including an invitation to Tom Labrador of the Indian Reservation, Bridgewater," 15 August 1916. The designation "Bridgewater Reserve" referred to a cluster of off-reserve families who regarded Tom Labrador as their chief, rather than to an actual reserve community. The only two reserves in Lunenburg County in 1916 were at Gold River and New Germany.

167 William Labrador (1877–1931) was the son of Tom Labrador and Mary Elizabeth Rafuse of Bridgewater. He married Elizabeth Carver of Milton in 1901 and the couple had a son Thomas William in 1908. NSARM, Historical Vital Statistics, Lunenburg County Marriages, book 1829, p. 255, no. 120.

168 Nova Scotia Museum, Halifax, Printed Matter File, "Letter from Ward Fisher to the Honourable W.L. Hill, Department of Marine and Fisheries," 10 February 1927. William died four years after his test case was thrown out by the court on the grounds that the British North America Act of 1867 nullified any Indigenous rights the Mi'kmaq may have exercised in the past. Arguments used in Labrador's test case, however, were later brought forward in *Simon v. The Queen*, [1985], 2 S.C.R. 387. James Matthew Simon, a member of the Shubenacadie Band (now the Sipekne'katik First Nation), was stopped by the RCMP and arrested for carrying a gun and shells out of season. Simon pleaded the existence of Mi'kmaw hunting rights under the terms of the Treaty of 1752, signed by Chief Jean-Baptiste Cope and Cope's associates, and won his case.

169 Frank G. Speck, *Beothuk and Micmac* (New York, 1922), 102. Speck lists Labrador's tract as No. 19 of the Annapolis Band's territories.

170 Joseph Jeremy's grandfather, John Jeremy, in the early 1840s persuaded the provincial government to survey several farm lots on Kejimkujik Lake for the Mi'kmaq. One of the farmers had been Stephen Labrador, who hailed from Shelburne County and probably was a son of Francis Labrador who in 1842s lived at Sable River. After a devastating potato blight struck the Kejimkujik area, however, John Jeremy moved to the tract on the Wildcat River, near Brookfield in Queens County. Though one thousand acres along the Wildcat River had been laid out for the Mi'kmaq in 1843 during Joseph Howe's term as provincial Indian commissioner, as late as 1892 its status as a reserve still lay in limbo. Provincial land agents could find no information in the country Land Records Office on the reserve. A similar situation pertained to the Clyde River reserve in Shelburne County, where Joseph Jeremy lived. Owing to Jeremy's and others' appeals to Ottawa, the Indian Affairs Department compelled the province the resurvey and confirm both the Clyde River and Wildcat reserves. The Wildcat reserve gave Louis Labrador's descendants a tract where they could settle without fear of being called squatters and driven off their lands. Attempts to have the reserve resurveyed at first became bogged down by contentions that a large grant made to Alexander McNutt's proprietors took up all the available land from the mouth of the Clyde River to Cape Sable. NSARM, Miscellaneous Indian Records from Nova Scotia Crown Lands Department on Microfilm, Document 72, Letters to Indian agent regarding Clyde River, "James H. Austin, Deputy Commissioner of Crown Lands to Hayter Reed," 2 November 1893.

171 Louis Francis Labrador, born in 1892 to Louis Labrador and Mary Arenburg of Bridgewater, married Beatrice Geraldine Jeremy in 1930 and the couple had Charlie Labrador in 1932. Although educated and technically skilled as a blacksmith, after a spell of depression brought on by chronic unemployment during the Great Depression, Louis tragically died in 1934 by shooting himself in the head. NSARM, Historical Vital Statistics, Lunenburg County Marriages, Registration Year 1930, book 60, 325; NSARM, Historical Vital Statistics, Lunenburg County Deaths, book 161, 275, "Death of Louis Labrador, 4 October 1934." Lewis's brother John, who married Beatrice Hubley in 1924, is Doris Labrador's grandfather. Beatrice Hubley was contacted at Greenfield and supplied information on the Labrador family.

Doris conducted research, interviewed, wrote sections of the text, and acted as an editor for this entry on the Labrador family.

172 Frank Pennel was apprehended after building a number of cottages at Gold River without getting permission from Ottawa to take the necessary wood, and Department of Indian Affairs demanded that the cottages be razed to the ground. Chief Charlie Paul, however, was able to find a middle ground between the opposing sides and negotiated a resolution to the problem. Personal information from Steve Pennel, Gold River, and Donald Julian director of the Mainland Confederacy, Millbrook, April 2008. Donald Julien was working for Indian Affairs at the time and remembers the incident well. Daniel Paul, who also worked with Indian Affairs in the late sixties and early seventies, was a close friend of Charlie Labrador. Daniel Paul, "Chief Charles Labrador Well Respected Elder," *Halifax Herald*, 17 April 1998.

173 Charlie's son, Todd Labrador, who is an expert birchbark canoe builder, currently builds on his father's vision by giving lectures on Mi'kmaw culture to tourists at Kejimkujik National Park and other public venues.

174 Emma Smith, "Mi'kmaq, Acadian History Honored at St. Norbert's [Lunenburg," *Lighthouse Now*, Bridgewater, 29 July 2015.

175 J. Bernard Gilpin, "Indians of Nova Scotia," *Proceedings and Transactions of the Nova Scotia Institute of Science*, no. 4 (1877), 250–81.

176 One recent study that includes new insights into the history of the Labrador family is an unpublished 2020 doctoral dissertation by Nicole Dannielle Gilhuis entitled "Colonial Ghosts: Mi'kmaq Adoption, Daily Practice and the Alternative Atlantic, 1600–1763," https://escholarship.org/uc/item 30c3v1cz. Gilhuis posits that descendants of certain Acadian families in the past were shaped by the racial and imperial wars of the eighteenth century. These people moved between the European and Indigenous worlds, yet they disappeared for many years from the colonial records to become "colonial ghosts" because of both "their absence from the Acadian villages and the limits of imperial reach in the Early Americas." In Gilhuis's own words, her research "revises Acadian historiography and especially models of family genealogy by valorizing lived experience and community belonging over ancestry for these Europeans." Colonial ghosts were "resurrected" by the English empire as "their descendants faced increasingly rigid racial politics as they were categorized as either 'White' or 'Indian.'" As "revenants" (the French term for "ghosts," which

translates to "the returned"), their descendants were classified as wholly Indigenous, "which belied their complex cultural and racial heritage." Gilhuis, "Colonial Ghosts: Mi'kmaq Adoption, Daily Practice and the Alternative Atlantic, 1600–1763" (PhD diss., University of California at Los Angeles, 2020), thesis abstract, n.p.

177 These last comments were voiced in 2021 by members of the Labrador family living at Gold River and Annapolis Royal.

CHAPTER 4

1 Clarence-J. d'Entremont, *Histoire du Cap-Sable de l'an mil au traité de Paris (1763)* (Eunice, LA: Hébert, 1981), 4.1595–7.

2 William C. Wicken, *Mi'kmaq Treaties on Trial: History, Land, and Donald Marshall Junior* (Toronto: University of Toronto Press, 2002), 148–9.

3 Stephen A. White, *Dictionnaire généalogique des familles acadiennes* (Moncton: Centre d'études acadiennes, Université de Moncton, 1999), 1.771–2.

4 Ottawa, Public Archives of Canada, *Report concerning Canadian Archives for the year 1905 in three volumes* (Ottawa: printed by S.E. Dawson, 1906), "Tour of Inspection made by the Sieur de la Roque."

5 Archives nationales d'outre mer, France (hereafter ANOM), G2, vol. 189, ff. 270–360, "Procedure relative au marriage de Jules Caesar Felix de la Noue 1754–1755." All details of the marriage and court proceedings are from this source.

6 Bernard G. Hoffman, "The Historical Ethnography of the Micmac of the Sixteenth and Seventeenth Centuries" (PhD diss., University of California at Berkeley, 1955), 287–94.

7 ANOM, G2, vol. 189, "La nommee guedry, fille du nomme Guedry dit Paul Grivois et d'une sauvagesse, sa femme, accadiens." Author's translation.

8 Ibid. Her aunt Françoise Guédry, her first cousin Elisabeth LeJeune, and Elisabeth's husband Olivier Trahan made no response to the description of Marguerite's parentage.

9 Ibid., f. 282. The witnesses were Joseph Guédry, Estienne Trahan, (illegible) Trahan, Jean Mius, Charles Trahan, La Deroute, and Francois Commer.

10 Examples of use of the term "Créole," as in *Il y a lui même élevé la créole qu'il pris pour femme* (He himself raised the Creole there, whom he took as his wife) may be found in Dossier personnel de Nicolas Albert; Thomas Pichon (regarding the wife of Prévost, Commissionaire Ordonnateur), *Lettres et memoires pour servir a l'histoire naturelle, civile et politique du Cap Breton* (London: Pierre Gosse, 1760; repr., S.R. Publishers, 1966), 149. Examples of use of the term "Acadian": Louis Franquet, "Rapport sur Îles Royale et St-Jean, 1751," Ls-A Proulx, *Rapport de L'Archiviste de Québec pour 1923–1924*, 134–5; ANOM, C11B, 13 November 1717, "St. Ovide au ministre" (Speaking of Acadians at Port Toulouse) "à l'exemple des sauvages ne restent que pour y trouver une oisive subsistence." For a discussion of the use of such terms see A.J.B. Johnston, "Un regard neuf sur les Acadiens de Île Royale: Acadiens dans le sud-est de l'île du Cap-Breton, 1752," *Les Cahiers de la Société historique acadienne* 32, no. 3 (2001): 155–72.

11 Hoffman, "Historical Ethnography of the Micmac," 151–86; Wicken, *Mi'kmaq Treaties on Trial*, 30–1; Colonial Archives d'Outre-mer, G2, 189.

12 Archives des Colonies, Paris, France (hereafter AC), C11B, vol. 34, F 49–51, 25 November 1754, "Drucourt au ministre"; COL D2C 2/fol. 94v, 20 February 1758.

13 See chap. 24 in this volume on Marie Josephe le Borgne de Belisle, and Anne Marie Lane Jonah and Elizabeth Tait, "Filles d'Acadie, Femmes de Louisbourg: Acadian Women and French Colonial Society in Eighteenth Century Louisbourg," *French Colonial History* 8 (Spring 2007): 23–51.

14 ANOM, G2, vol. 189, f. 270. The payment resembled the French practice of the bride's father paying a *dot*.

15 Registres Paroissiaux de saint-Pierre et Miquelon: 1763 à 1790–91. Baptêmes, 01/06/1767, "Jacques Guédry; Presence Acadienne en Guyane: Sinnamary Recensement de mai 1767," in *Le Messager de L'Atlantique*, Falaise Acadie Québec, Annexe 1, no. 32 (Premier Trimestre 1996), 21–8.

CHAPTER 5

1 Pierre's surname was also spelled "Anecouaret," "Anquarret, " "Charet, " "Charett, " "Couaret, " "Quaret, " "Quared, " "Memcharet," "Memcharett, " "Momcharett, " "Nimcharet," and "Nimquaret." He also went by the name of Peter Walker.

2 Library and Archives Canada (henceforth LAC), MG 18, F 18 (typescript, with a census of the Port Royal and Minas bands in 1708), 2, 8, *Recensement genal fait au mois de Novembre mile Sept cent huit de tous les Sauvages de l'Acadie que resident dans la Coste de l'est, Et ceux de Pintagouet de de Canibeky*, 1708. The original manuscript is found in vol. 4, no. 751 of the Edward E. Ayer Collection in the Newberry Library, Chicago. Pierre Momcharret

dit Cellier's band intermarried with members of another band in the Minas region led by an elderly leader named Jacques Neocout or Naucoute (now Knockwood). Jacques Neocout's hunting territories lay along the Kennetcook River and overlapped with lands under the jurisdiction of the Sipekne'katik (Shubenacadie) district band.

3   Clarence-J. d'Entremont, a Roman Catholic priest, genealogist, and historian from West Pubnico in Yarmouth County, Nova Scotia, held that Pierre Momcharret *dit* Cellier's mother, Marie Cellier, was likely the *métis* daughter of an Acadian surnamed Cellier, who wed a Mi'kmaw man named Momcharret at Port Royal around 1677. Momcharret died around 1706, and his widow died in 1727 and was buried in the parish cemetery of St. Jean-Baptiste. Nova Scotia Archives and Record Management, Halifax (henceforth NSARM), RG 1, vol. 26, 367, Registers of the Parish of St, Jean-Baptiste, Annapolis Royal, 1702–55, "Burial of Marie Cellier Charet, widow, 75 years of age, interred on 8 March 1727; presiding priest René Charles de Breslay; witnesses Jean Dupuy and Paul Savoie." Father d'Entremont argued that Marie Cellier probably descended from one of two related branches of the French Cellier family, the Acadian branch and a Mi'kmaw-*métis* branch. The first recorded Cellier to come to North America, Pierre Cellier, arrived in Montreal from France in 1659. A younger Acadian man, also named Pierre Cellier, lived most of his life near what is now Halfway River in Cumberland County, Nova Scotia, and died in 1710 at Grand Pré. This Acadian, who wed Marie Joseph Aimée, alias Marie Joseph Le Jeune, may have been a son of the man named Pierre Cellier living in Montreal. Pierre and Marie Joseph Aimée, who was *métis*, had numerous sons and daughters who later married into the Le Jeune, Doiron (or Douairon), Hébert, La Bauve, and Guénard families. D'Entremont, *Histoire du Cap-Sable de l'an mil au traité de Paris* (Eunice, LA: Hébert, 1981), 3.1125–32. It is even possible that the Pierre Cellier in what is now Cumberland Cunty was a brother of Marie Cellier, Momcharret's wife. The origins and activities of the Mi'kmaw Cellier family are worthy of more research. Intriguingly, as late as 1800 one finds a signature that looks like "Cellier" or "Cielier" in registers kept by Abbé Sigogne at Ste. Anne du Ruisseau, Cape Sable. This signature often is accompanied by that of Pierre Mius, an Acadian community leader at St. Anne du Ruisseau. Who this "Cellier" was remains an enigma.

4   Marie Cellier (1663–1727) had six sons. Her eldest sons Jean and Antoine were born in 1678 when she was fifteen years old. They left for Minas at a relatively early age. Jean, who according to the La Chasse census was thirty years old in 1708, was second chief of the Minas band. He had a wife Agathe who was twenty-two years old and three children: Jacques, nine; Marie-Joseph, four; and Marie, one. Antoine, also thirty in 1708, had a twenty-two-year-old wife, Catherine, and a one-year-old son, Jean-Baptiste. Marie Cellier's third son, Jacques (1683–c.1747), remained near Annapolis Royal. In 1708 Jacques was twenty-five years old with a wife Elizabeth and no children. Marie's fourth son, Pierre, born in 1687 (and who later took the name Pierre Momcharret *dit* Cellier or Pierre Cellier), became the Minas chief. In 1708 he had a nineteen-year-old wife named Elizabeth and a one-year-old daughter, Marie. La Chasse in 1708 listed Marie Cellier's two youngest sons who lived with her at Annapolis Royal as orphans who were both named "Pierre." The Pierre who became Pierre Cellier (1687–c.1745) was twenty-one years old and the other Pierre (1692–c.1760) was sixteen. Marie Cellier died on 7 March 1727 and was buried the following day in St.-Jean Baptiste parish cemetery at Annapolis Royal. NSARM, RG 1, vol. 26, 367, "Registers of the Parish of St. Jean-Baptiste, Annapolis Royal," 1702–55, "Burial of Marie Charet; presiding priest, René Charles de Bresley; witnesses Jean Dupuy and Paul Savoye." De Breslay held that Marie was seventy-five years old in 1727, yet according to the La Chasse census compiled nineteen years earlier, she was forty-five in 1708, which would have made her sixty-four at the time of her death. The Registers of the Parish of St. Jean-Baptiste at Annapolis Royal, 1702-55 are also found online at "An Acadian Parish Remembered," https://archives.novascotia.ca/acadian/.

5   Pierre Momcharret *dit* Bouta married Marie Magdeleine Oujamindeiche and the couple had a son, Jean Baptiste (or Battiste) Bouta, baptized at Annapolis Royal on 20 June 1726. NSARM, RG 1, vol. 26, 242, Registers of the Parish of St. Jean Baptiste, "Baptism of Jean-Baptiste Charet, son of Pierre Charet (*dit* Bouta) and Magdelaine," 20 June 1726; presiding priest René Charles de Breslay; godparents Marie, wife of François Mius [*dit* d'Azy], and Jean-Baptiste Mikmak [or Jean-Baptist Thoma, head chief of Annapolis Royal]." Momcharret *dit* Bouta in the 1740s left Annapolis Royal to become a fur trade middleman along the St. John River Valley. Jean-Baptiste Bouta in the early 1800s became a noted chief in Antigonish County, where he acquired land for the Paq'tnket Mi'kmaw community.

6   Pierre Momcharret *dit* Cellier's and Louise's daughter, Marie-Louise, died in 1717. NSARM, RG 1, vol. 26, 218,

"Burial of Marie Louise Charet, two years old, 29 April 1717, daughter of Pierre Charet *dit* le Selier and [Louise] Innocente; presiding priest René Charles de Breslay; witnesses Pierre Selier (*dit* Boitou) and Denis Nemkoeret." Despite his loss, Pierre Momcharret *dit* Cellier stood as a witness at a Mi'kmaw wedding in August of the same year. NSARM, vol. 26a, 108, "Marriage of René Nectabo and Catherine Anorgin, 24 August 1726, presiding priest Rene Charles de Breslay, witnesses Pierre Charet and Pierre Charet, Francois Germain, and [Jean] Baptiste Thomas, Chief of the [Annapolis] Mikmak." Both the Pierre Momcharrets usually acted together as witnesses at rites-of-passage ceremonies, though they did occasionally serve independently. Pierre Momcharret *dit* Bouta alone witnessed the baptism of Cecile Hebcobeau, born in December 1735 to Antoine Hebcobeau and Anne Grand Claude of Annapolis Royal. NSARM, RG 1, vol. 26a, 152, "Baptism of Cecile Hecobeau, 20 May 1735; presiding priest De St. Poncy de La Vernède; witnesses Pierre Charett *dit* Boiteau and Marie Pelerin." By the 1730s Pierre Momcharret *dit* Cellier was welcoming grandchildren. For instance, in 1734 Samson Quoraret (Momcharret), a son of Pierre Momcharret *dit* Cellier and Louise Innocente, brought a daughter Agathe to be baptized at Annapolis Royal. NSARM, RG 1, vol. 26a, 120, "Baptism on 26 August 1734 of Agathe Quoraret, born 15 March 1734, daughter of Samson Quoraret and Françoise Grand Claude; presiding priest De Poncy de La Vernède; witnesses Jean Lore and Marie Madeline Pelerin."

7   Pierre Momcharret *dit* Cellier of Annapolis Royal married Françoise Mius, his second wife, on 26 August 1733. NSARM, RG 1, vol. 26a, 141, "Marriage of Pierre, widower of Louise Innocent, a Mi'kmaq of this River, and Françoise Myus, a widow of the second time of the late René Grand Claude of La Have, 26 August 1735, presiding priest De Poncy de La Vernède, witnesses François Robichau, Prudent Robichau, Dominique Robichau, Jean-Baptiste Robichau and François Bourgeois." This was Françoise Mius's third marriage. She first wed an unknown Mi'kmaq man and then, on his death, married René Grand Claude of Annapolis Royal.

8   Pierre Momcharret *dit* Cellier of Minas likely used the name "Pierre Walker" while trading with New England merchants between 1715 and 1720. See "Letter dated from Piscataqua," 29 July 1715. He also is referred to as "Peter Walker" on page 30 of "Trials of Five Persons for Piracy, Felony and Robbery ... Held at the Court House in Boston, within His Majesty Province of Massachusetts-Bay in New England on Tuesday the Fourth Day of October, Boston, 1726." Reviewing papers associated with the trial in Boston on 4 October 1726, William Wicken agrees that the "Pierre Walker" in this statement is probably "Pierre Amquaret" (Momcharret). Wicken, *Mi'kmaw Treaties on Trial: Land, History and Donald Marshall Junior* (Toronto: University of Toronto Press, 2002), 269. James Muse (Jacques Muis), who was hanged in Boston in November 1726 after being found guilty of robbery on the high seas, would have spoken familiarly of Pierre Momcharret, whose brother "Pierre Charett" at Annapolis Royal wed James's sister, Françoise Mius.

9   *Boston Newsletter*, 1 August 1715.

10 LAC, British Colonial Office records on microfilm, CO, 217/3/155–6, "Lettre de Antoine Couaret and Pierre Couaret, Les Chefs des Mynes," 2 October 1720; LAC, CO 217/9/116; LAC, CO 217/4/42-44, "Memo of R. Philipps," 16 August 1721. The English translation is the author's. A slightly different English translation appears in L.F.S. Upton, *Micmacs and Colonists: Indian-White Relations in the Maritimes, 1713–1867* (Vancouver: University of British Columbia Press, 1979), 41. Upton's translation reads: "This land here that God has given to us and of which we can be accounted a part as the trees are born here cannot be disputed by person ... We are Masters independent of everyone and wish to have our country free." The original letter was probably drafted by Father Félix Pain, who was very active among the Mi'kmaq of the Minas region in the 1720s. John Mack Faragher, *The Great and Noble Scheme: The Tragic Story of the Expulsion of the French Acadians from Their American Homeland* (New York: W.W. Norton, 2005), 155–70.

11 See, for example, the phrase "comme une herbe" that appears in a Mi'kmaw declaration, dated 25 September 1749, that was drafted by Abbé Pierre Maillard and directed to the executive council in Halifax.

12 In 1720 they probably joined with members of the neighbouring Kennetcook River band in boarding John Alden's vessel. LAC, CO 217/3/151, "Appeal of John Alden for redress," 17 December 1720. Even after the signing of a treaty with the British in 1726, the Minas Mi'kmaq still robbed trading vessels. In 1742, however, when Samuel Trefry had the cables of his sloop cut and his vessel robbed, two Mi'kmaw captains, Jacques Momquaret (Momcharret) and Thomas Wouito, "caused satisfaction to be made." LAC, CO 217/38/355, "To Jacques Momquaret and Thomas Wouito, from Paul Mascarene," 13 April 1742; Beamish Murdoch, *A History of Nova-Scotia, or Acadie* (Halifax: James Barnes, 1865), 2.18. Jacques Momcharret was likely a son of Pierre Momcharret *dit* Cellier. A British proclamation levied severe penalties

on Acadians who assisted in such raids, or who bought articles that had been taken from a vessel, though the raids continued until the onset of King George's War in 1844.

13 Archibald M. MacMechan, *A Calendar of Two Letter Books and One Commission Book in the Possession of the Government of Nova Scotia, 1713–1741.* Nova Scotia Archives II (Halifax: Herald Printing House, 1900), 76–7, "R. Philipps to the Board of Trade," 18 August 1721.

14 On the 1726 treaty "Pierre Armquarett" is listed as "chief of Minas," while "Pierre Nemcharett" is identified as "chief of this River [the Annapolis River]." LAC, CO 217/38, copy of 1726 treaty showing Mi'kmaw "dodems," dated 4 June 1726 and sent to London in November 1726. The British evidently did not know in 1726 that they were dealing with brothers, or they would not have spelled their surnames differently.

15 Thomas B. Akins, ed., *Selections from the Public Documents of the Province of Nova Scotia* (Halifax: Annand, 1869), 97–8, 101, "Council Minutes, Annapolis Royal," 25 July 1732, as well as two letters on the subject of the Mi'kmaq: "Governor Lawrence Armstrong to Lord Newcastle," 15 November 1732, and "Armstrong to Newcastle," 9 October 1733.

16 LAC, CO 217/38/253–4, "Minutes of a Council held by authority of Lieutenant-Colonel Paul Mascarene at Annapolis Royal," 9 April 1742.

17 LAC, CO 217/38/353–4, "Minutes of a Council at Annapolis Royal," 9 April 1742; LAC, CO 217/38/355, "To Jacques Momquaret and Thomas Wouito from Governor Mascarene," 13 April 1742.

18 LAC, CO 217/39/ 94, "Minutes of a Council at Annapolis Royal," 10 October 1742.

19 "Abbe Manach's list of chiefs, acquired from Manach by Colonel Frye at Fort Cumberland, 1760." This list is printed in *Collections of the Massachusetts Historical Society*, 1809, 116. (First published in 1760 in *The Pennsylvania Gazette*). Bartélèmy, or Bartholomew, Momcharret was probably Chief Pierre Momcharret *dit* Cellier's son.

20 NSARM, RG 1, vol. 165, doc. 54, "Submissions of eight Mi'kmaw leaders and allocation of passes to eight Mi'kmaw persons," 28 April 1760.

21 Isaac Deschamps's list of Minas Mi'kmaq was drawn up at Fort Edward, Windsor, on 20 December 1763. It is reproduced in Henry Youle Hind, *An Early History of Windsor, Nova Scotia, with a Sketch of the Old Parish Burying Ground of Windsor Nova Scotia: With an Appeal for Its Protection, Ornamentation, and Preservation* (Windsor: Jas. J. Anslow, 1889), 32. A facsimile reproduction of Hind's work was published by Lancelot Press of Handsport, NS, in 1989.

22 "Baptisms of Marie Agnes and Marie Monique, daughters of Bartélèmy Charet and Marie Joachim, Piziquid, 28 August 1768; godparents Pierre Jacques and Anne Martin." NSARM, microfilm copy of registers of Father Charles-François Bailley, Copy of old register conserve à Caraquet, register on microfilm, *Registre des actes de baptême, marriages, et sepultures faits en la nouvelle ecosse ou acadie, commence le vingt unieme jour de juillet de l'annee mil sept cent soixante huit, par mons. Charles François Bailly pretre missonnaire des sauvages et acadiens, sujets de sa majeste br tanique*, 75.

23 LAC, MG 23, vol. 4, GII-1c, George Henry Monk Papers, Letter Book, 1046–7.

24 NSARM, RG 1, vol. 430, doc. 68, "Names of Indians belonging to Kings County, 1800 and 1801."

25 Peter Argomartin was banished from the Cape Sable band for his cruelty towards several women and spent his final years in Kings County with the Momcharrets. Pierre Argomartin appears on the list of members of Bartholomew Momcharret's group. The only other band in the area was a group under the headship of an elderly Francis Nogood (Noucout or Knockwood) who travelled with his son Joseph Nogood, Dan Toney, and John Wilmot. The younger men were both in their forties. Dan Toney was a son of Louis Toney, who in turn was a son of Chief Louis Toney of Remsheg in Pictou County.

26 Some of Bartholomew Momcharret's descendants, who adopted the surname "Bottomy," around 1830 moved to Lequille, Annapolis County, and by the mid-1850s lived with Chief Ben Pictou's group. NSARM, MG 15, vol. 6, docs. 10 and 11, "Census of Annapolis Band, 1856."

CHAPTER 6

1 François's surname is also spelled "Meuse," "Miuse," "Moose," "Muse," and "Myus."

2 D'Azy also is spelled "d'Az t" or "d'Assis."

3 Charles La Tour was governor of Acadia from 1631 to 1642, and again from 1653 to 1657.

4 Clarence-J. d'Entremont, *Histoire du Cape-Sable de l'an mil au traité de Paris (1763)* (Eunice, LA: Hébert, 1981), 3.968–1010. Marie-Marguerite was born in Normandy; the other four children were born on Acadian soil. Jacques and Abraham wed, respectively, Anne and Marguerite La Tour, daughters of Governor Charles de La Tour and Jeanne Motin. Before she became La Tour's

third wife, Jeanne Motin was the widow of Charles de Menou d'Aulnay, Sieur de Charnizay (or Charnissay), who died in a drowning accident in 1650. Philippe consorted in succession with two Mi'kmaw women. His elder sister, Marie-Marguerite, married Pierre Melanson *dit* La Verdure, while his second sister, Madeleine, remained unmarried.

5 This village would fall within the area that Simon Pierre Denys de Bonaventure in 1701 called Chichimiscadie.

6 Connections were retained with the Mi'kmaw community. For instance, Joseph Mius's son Charles-Amand I wed Marie-Marthe Hébert, a step-sibling of Anne Hébert who around 1754 married Chief Charles Alexis of Cape Sable.

7 Mathieu's and Maurice's names appear respectively on pages 4 and 9 of a typescript of a French census compiled in 1708 by Father Pierre La Chasse. Library and Archives of Canada, Ottawa, MG 18, F 18, French census return, 1708.

8 Little is known about Francois Mius's Mi'kmaw mother Marie, except that she belonged to the La Have band. A *Wikipedia* article on Baron Philippe I Mius d'Entremont states that according to Mi'kmaw oral tradition Philippe II d'Azy's second Mi'kmaw consort was "Marie Coyote Blanc." This name in English translation came to light when Don Awalt, a historian and genealogist, assessed Mi'kmaw oral traditions from the 1920s at Millbrook and along the South Shore. Awalt, "The Mi'kmaq and Point Pleasant Park, the Mi'kmaq and Amtoukati: An Historical Essay in Progress by Don Byrd Awalt" (Halifax: Native Friendship Centre, 2006).

9 D'Entremont, *Histoire du Cap-Sable*, 3.1010–19. Father d'Entremont calls Philippe and Marie's offspring the "deuxième groupe d'enfants" to separate them from the more culturally "Acadian" first group, though the women of the second group, especially Marguerite and Anne, prior to 1757 observed an Acadian way of life.

10 A chief named Antoine Mius was encountered at Beaubassin by Thomas Pichon, a French official who also operated as a spy for the English. Antoine told Pichon that his father had died in Boston. Ibid., 3.1011–12.

11 Acadians and other French speakers, such as Antoine Mius, would at this time still have referred to this place as La Hève. Even today both spellings are used, depending whether one is French or English speaking. Generally, however, the British used the term "La Have" once the Nova Scotian mainland became British territory after 1713.

12 On 20 June 1726 the name "Marie, femme de François Mieux" appears in the Parish of St. Jean-Baptiste registers at Annapolis Royal as the godmother of one-year-old Jean-Baptiste Momcharret, son of Pierre Momcharet *dit* Bouta and his wife Magdalene Oiuchemetetch. NSARM, RG 1, vol. 26, 242, "Baptism of Jean-Baptiste Charet, son of Pierre Charet [Pierre Momcharret *dit* Bouta] and Magdelaine, 20 June 1726, presiding priest René Charles de Breslay, godparents Marie, wife of François Mius [*dit* d'Azy] and Jean-Baptiste Mikmak [Jean-Baptist Thoma, head chief of Annapolis Royal]." In 1815 Jean-Baptiste Momcharret *dit* Bouta, who by this time used the name Jean-Battiste Bouta, secured land for what would become the Pomquet and Afton reserves of Antigonish County. Jean-Battiste is the ancestor of the Antigonish County and Cape Breton Battiste family.

13 In 1769 Francois and Marie's son Jacques Mius and his sister Hélène travelled to Chezzetcook, east of Halifax, to participate in sacraments performed by Abbé Charles-François Bailly, Abbé Pierre Maillard's successor. NSARM, copy of old registers conserved at Caraquet, New Brunswick, 1768–73, 1786–96, on microfilm. *Registre des actes de baptême, marriages, et sepultures faits en la nouvelle ecosse ou acadie commence le vingt unième jour de juillet de l'annee mil sept cent soixante huit, par mons. Charles-François Bailly, pretre missionaire*, 14, entries made at Piziquid, 29 June 1769.

14 Ibid., 1012–13. Jean Baptiste's wife Marie died in 1730 and was buried at Annapolis Royal on 9 February 1730. She was a widow at the time. NSARM, RG 1, vol. 26a, 48, burial of Marie, wife of Jean-Baptiste Mius of the Mi'kmaq Nation, presiding priest Noel Alexandre de Noinville. She may have been the mother of Josephte-Marie Mius who continued to live at Merliguèche.

15 Françoise Mius and Pierre Momcharret *dit* Cellier were both widowed at the time of their marriage; he was the widower of Louis Innocent. The two were married at Annapolis Royal. NSARN, RG 1, vol. 26a, 141, "Marriage of Pierre Charet, widower, to Françoise Myus, widow, 26 August 1735."

16 A biographical treatment of Paul Guedry *dit* Labrador is presented in chapter 3 of this volume.

17 For a detailed discussion of this marriage annulment, see chapter 4 of this volume.

18 Thomas G.M. Peace holds that most chiefs who signed the 1726 treaty were "local head men" and remained peaceful over the subsequent years. A second attempt at treaty signing, in September 1728, brought more leaders. Peace, "Two Conquests: Aboriginal Experiences of the

Fall of New France and Acadia" (PhD diss., York University, 2011), 198–200; Peace, "A Reluctant Engagement: Alliances and Social Networks in Early-18th-Century Kespukwitk and Port Royal," *Acadiensis* 49, no. 1 (2020): 5–38.

19 NSARM, RG 1, vol. 430, doc. 21, "Copy of the Treaty of Peace and Friendship with François Mius," 1761.

20 Since the 1730s, François Mius had travelled to Pobomcoup to trade, see his Acadian relations, and attend services whenever Le Loutre visited the Cape Sable district. Le Loutre served five chapels at Cape Sable, but only three, those at Pobomcoup, Tebok (Chebogue, now Acadia), and Abruptic (near present-day Ste. Anne du Ruisseau), were readily accessible to the Mi'kmaq. The missionary not only performed mass and conducted sacraments but also harangued the Mi'kmaq to molest the English. After Le Loutre in the early 1750s relocated his mission headquarters from Shubenacadie to the Beaubassin area, François Mius and several of his close family members camped on the Chignecto Isthmus to be near the missionary and avoid being deported along with their Acadian kinsfolk.

21 The author is grateful to members of the Veinotte family of Second Peninsula, who shared information about this aspect of early house construction in coastal Lunenburg County.

22 Jacques Mius, who was living in an encampment in the District of Clare, Digby County, in 1812, told Sigogne of this incident fifty-one years after it had happened. As a child, Jacques may have been an eye witness to what transpired between his father and Abbé Maillard during peace-making negotiations in November 1761. NSARM, RG 1, vol. 430, docs. 20 and 21, "Abbé Sigogne to Lieutenant-Governor Sir John C. Sherbrooke," 5 May 1812, with enclosures. Sigogne's letter to Sherbrook was accompanied by François Mius's 1742 French commission as chief of Mirliguèche and his copy of the peace and friendship treaty, dated 9 November 1761, that he signed with the British. The treaty, also signed by Jonathan Belcher, identifies Mius as chief of La Have.

23 Beamish Murdoch, *A History of Nova-Scotia, or Acadie* (Halifax: James Barnes, 1866), 2.431.

24 Following the death of Abbé Pierre Maillard in 1762, François Mius led a campaign to secure a Roman Catholic missionary for his people, to replace Maillard. NSARM, CO 215/20/354–9, "Governor Montague Wilmot to the Lords of Trade, 10 December 1763, along with 'The Reply of the Lords of Trade to Wilmot, 13 July 1764.'" On 22 August 1763 the chief and four other Mi'kmaq met with Lieutenant Governor Wilmot and his council in Halifax and demanded that a missionary be sent to them, as promised under the provisions of the treaties of 1760 and 1761. D'Entremont, *Histoire du Cape-Sable*, 3.1015; NSARM, CO 218/6/216–17, "John Pownall to the Rev. Dr. Daniel Burton, Society for the Propagation of the Gospel," 20 June 1764; CO 217/21/23–4, "Burton to the Lords of Trade," 13 July 1764. Montague Wilmot became governor of Nova Scotia in 1764.

25 *Journey of the Legislative Assembly of Nova Scotia*, 21 January 1821, 36; NSARM, RG 5, misc. A, series P, vol. 2, "Petition of Andrew James Meuse regarding preservation of the porpoise hunt," 1821; *Halifax Journal*, December 1824; *Halifax Morning Post*, 1 February 1842.

26 Carolyn Thomas Foreman, *Indians Abroad: 1493–1938* (Oklahoma City: University of Oklahoma Press, 1943), 154–5; L.F.S. Upton, "Meuse, Andrew James," *Dictionary of Canadian Biography* online, 7 (1836–50). Though Abbé Sigogne chastised Meuse for his occasional bouts of inebriation, the two remained in close contact. NSARM, Papers of the Archdiocese of Halifax, Edmund Burke papers, "Sigogne to Wiswall," 29 March 1831.

CHAPTER 7

1 According to Mi'kmaw professor and linguist Bernie Francis, "Panuke" derives from the Mi'kmaw term *panu'k*, which in English means "it opens out." Ruth Holmes Whitehead, *The Old Man Told Us: Excerpts from Mi'kmaw History, 1500–1950* (Halifax: Nova Scotia Museum, 1991), 147, 249–50. "Panuke" ("Ponhook," "Banook") also denotes the first lake in a series of lakes.

2 The St. Croix River area of Hants County seasonally supported a large Mi'kmaw population. Sara Halwas, "Where the Wild Things Grow: A Paleoethnobotanical Study of Late Woodland Plant Use at Clam Cove, Nova Scotia" (master's thesis, Memorial University of Newfoundland, 2006), 43–6.

3 Louis Thomas or Thoma was born too late to have been a son of Chief Thoma, who died around 1769. Since Louis's name does not appear anywhere in the documentary record, one has to rely entirely on Mi'kmaw oral information to connect him with Thoma and the Panuke Lake community. Louis's son Michael, by contrast, appears fairly frequently in historical accounts. Born at Panuke Lake around 1810, Michael lived at Rawdon in 1830 with his wife, Sarah Paul, where he joined Francis Toney and several others in petitioning Lieutenant Governor Colin Campbell for blankets during a particularly harsh

winter. Nova Scotia Archives and Records Management (henceforth NSARM), RG 1, vol. 431, unnumbered documents pertaining to Provincial Indian Affairs, "To His Excellency Major General Sir Colin Campbell … from Francis Toney, Francis Paul, Peter Tom, Michael Tom, and Ned Nolin, 26 December 1837, with a letter from David How, J.P. of Douglas, who drafted the petition, dated 30 January 1838." Peter Thomas was almost certainly the same person as Pierre Martyn Thomas (c.1760–c.1850), who was forty years older than Michael (1810–c.1874). In his eighties in 1842, Peter Thomas wed Marguerite (or Magdalene) Baul (Paul), the eighty-year-old widow of Chief Louis-Benjamin Peminout Paul of Shubenacadie, and the pair remained at Rawdon until Pierre's death around 1850. In 1851 Michael Thomas, his wife Sarah, and Peter Thomas's widow Marguerite Baul were living with Chief Francis Peminout Paul's group. NSARM, MG 15, vol. 4A, doc. 9, "F.R. Parker to Abraham Gesner regarding a petition for land and seed from Francis Paul, Christopher Paul, John Paul and others," 29 May 1851. Deeming Michael Thomas to be an intelligent and honest person, in 1855 the provincial Indian commissioner, William Chearnley, directed Thomas to buy and distribute seed potatoes to the Shubenacadie band. NSARM, RG 1, vol. 431, no. 86, "Letter from William Chearnley to John Crompton regarding relief money for seed potatoes for the Shubenacadie band," 1855. Chearnley instructed Crompton to give Michael ten pounds for the potatoes and accompany him to McNab's store in the town of Shubenacadie to pick them up. Michael, the commissioner assured Crompton, "is most trustworthy [and in] whose distribution of the money for the purposes mentioned we place the utmost confidence." Michael was also reputed to have been a skilful fiddle player. He and Sarah, as well as Peter Sack who had married Michael's sister Marie-Antoinette, remained for several years with Francis Peminout Paul's group before returning to Rawdon.

4   As the Thoma/Thomas family was small, its members met together within their restricted circle and shared stories about their past. One person who knew the oral tradition well was Max Basque. On two separate occasions, in 1977 and 1984, Max spoke with ethnohistorian Ruth Whitehead of the Nova Scotia Museum about Chief Thoma and how he was descended from him. Louis Thomas was Max's great-great grandfather. Max's mother, Annie Sack, was the daughter of Isaac Sack, who in turn was a son of Peter Sack, whose wife, Mary-Antoinette Thomas, was a daughter of Louis Thomas and Mary Morris. Max held that Louis was Chief Thoma's son. "Max Basque to R.H. Whitehead, personal communication, 1977," and "Max Basque to R.H. Whitehead, taped interview, March 1984," in Whitehead, *The Old Man Told Us*, 120, 146, respectively. Owing to chronology, however, Louis Thomas could not have been a son of Chief Thoma, as Max averred. Louis was probably Thoma's grandson.

5   Library and Archives of the Nova Scotia Museum of Natural History, Halifax (henceforth NSM), Printed Matter File, Harry Piers Papers, unpublished notes, "Death of Marie-Antoinette Noel, 1822–1915 (née Thomas) of Indian Reserve, Shubenacadie, wife of Chief John Noel, Thursday, 11 March 1915."

6   NSM, Printed Matter File, Piers Papers, "Isaac Sack to Harry Piers," 26 February 1921. In 1861, during a smallpox outbreak in Antigonish County, a number of persons with the surname "Thomas" collected at Pope's Harbour and Musquodoboit. These Thomases reputedly came from Antigonish County, though some, who were connected to the Cope and Paul families of Nova Scotia's Eastern Shore, may have been descendants of Chief Thoma of Panuke Lake. NSARM, MG 15, vol. 6, doc. package 63, "Regarding a smallpox outbreak in Antigonish, at Musquodoboit and Pope's Harbour, Reports of 24 December 1860, 4 January 1861 and 23 January 1861."

7   John Noel's first wife was a Penall from Gold River, near Chester, Nova Scotia, and the couple had one son, Michael, late in September of 1850.

8   There was a Madeleine Thomas who was about Adelaide's age, and who married a man surnamed Francis. Madeleine may have been Adelaide's sibling.

9   Abraham wed Marie Loolan (Lulan) of Pictou on 22 February 1865 at St. Ignatius Church in Bedford, near Halifax, and not long after his father Neil (c.1815–c.1880) and Mary Ann Toney also married at St. Ignatius. On 25 June of the same year, Neil's daughter Madeleine married James Cope, a son of Joseph Cope and Mary Phillips of Sheet Harbour. Adelaide's brother Frank, meanwhile, married Mary Cope, James Cope's sister, and lived in Dartmouth. They had a son John on 10 January 1866. NSARM, Historical Vital Statistics, Halifax County Marriages, Registration Year 1866 (though the marriage took place in 1865), Book 1815, p. 30, no. 24, "Marriage at Bedford of Abraham Thomas, 21, son of Neil Thomas and Mary Ann Toney, and Mary Loolan [Lulan or Roland], 20, daughter of Joseph Loolan and Sally, 22 February 1865, presiding priest Edward Kennedy, witnesses Neil Williams and Adelaide Thomas." NSARM, Historical Vital Statistics, Halifax County Births, Registration Year 1865, Book 1815, p. 24, no. 243, "Marriage of James

Cope, son of Jos. Cope and Mary Phillips, and Medeleine [*sic*, Madeleine] Thomas, daughter of N. Thomas and M.A. Toney, 25 June 1865, presiding priest J. Woods, witnesses C. Paul and S. (? indistinct)." NSARM, Historical Vital Statistics, Halifax County Births, Book 1809, p. 22, no. 219, "Birth of John Thomas, 10 January 1866, son of F. Thomas and Mary Cope." James Cope's marriage to Madeleine Thomas and his sister Mary Cope's union with Francis Thomas provide an example of brother-sister exchange, a fairly common practice among the Mi'kmaq.

10 Adelaide Thomas and others of her family often camped on the grounds of St. Ignatius Roman Catholic Church in Bedford. In 1977, Max Basque erred when telling Ruth Whitehead that Adelaide (whom he called "Madeleine Thomas") was Louis Thomas's daughter. Whitehead, *The Old Man Told Us*, 300. Adelaide and John Williams's marriage certificate states that she was the daughter of Louis's son Michael. John Williams married twice; his first wife was Betsy Paul, reputedly a daughter of Chief Francis Peminout Paul of Shubenacadie. Though his and Adelaide's marriage certificate of 1874 states he was fifty-five old at the time of his second marriage, he was probably closer to sixty. NSARM, Historical Vital Statistics (available online at the NSARM website), Halifax County Marriages, Registration Year 1974, Book 1816, p. 58, no. 126, "Marriage at Bedford of John Williams, son of Paul Williams and H … [indistinct; John's mother was Honore Luxey], a widower 55 years old, and Adelaide Thomas, 30, daughter of Michael Thomas and Mary [Jerome], 14 April 1874; presiding priest Thomas Butler; witness Mary Paul." The baptismal registers of St. Bernard's church, Enfield, show that the couple had Elizabeth baptized on 29 April 1876, Mary in 1879, John William Jr. on 24 October 1880, and Sarah on 21 January 1881. According to the 1881 federal census for Nine Mile River, Hants County, "Adelaide Williams," born in 1844, was living with her husband John, sixty-six years old, and three of their children: Frank, who was sixteen (born in 1865) and so probably was John's son by his first wife; Ellen, ten (who also would have been John's child by his first wife); and John Jr., who was eight months old. John Williams, who for years guided Lord Dunraven, and from whom he received a pension in his later years, was economically stable. But this did not prevent his children from dying from illness. He and Betsy had a daughter named Mary in 1865 who died around the same time as Betsy. By 1881 there was no mention of Elizabeth or Sarah, so they too presumably had died by this time. Canada, Census of

1881, District No. 18, Nine Mine River, County Polling District no. 10, household no. 196. Adelaide and John had numerous children, but all died before reaching adulthood except for their daughter Ruby. See Ruth Holmes Whitehead's caption accompanying one of the photographs of John Williams in "Mi'kmaq Portraits Collection." NSM, Photograph Reference Number: N-1030.

11 NSARM, Historical Vital Statistics, Halifax County Marriages, Book 1817, p. 257, no. 389, "Marriage of 28 October 1885 of Josiah Thomas, 23 years old, born in 1862 at Stewiacke, son of Michael Thomas and Mary Jeremy, and Rosie Gooley, 15, born at Shubenacadie, daughter of Philip Gooley Jeremy and Louisa, both of Shubenacadie, presiding priest Mgr. Power, witnesses Peter Glode and Mary Sack." Josiah and Rose had two sons, Michael Thomas and Frank Thomas.

12 Frank Thomas and Matilda Lena Sack in 1922 had a child, Joseph Patrick, who died at Windsor within fifteen days of his birth. NSARM, Historical Vital Statistics, Hants County Deaths, "Death of Joseph Patrick Thomas, born 19 March 1922, died 3 April 1922." Joseph Patrick's body was buried in the cemetery at Indian Brook, Shubenacadie.

13 Michael Thomas's first wife's (1857–1902) death entry in the vital statistics registers simply identified her as "Mrs. Michael Thomas, born in Truro, 45 years old, Roman Catholic, a basketmaker, and English." She died in Halifax County of uterine cancer in 1902. NSARM, Halifax County Deaths, Registration Year 1902, p. 296, 56. Michael Thomas died of bowel cancer at Millbrook in 1960, aged seventy-three. NSARM, Colchester County Deaths, Registration Year 1960, 4573.

14 Edith Jane Thomas's father was Michael Thomas, whose father in turn was Josiah Thomas. In 1980, at the time she applied for her birth to be registered with the bureau of vital statistics, she testified that her father Michael Thomas, born at Shubenacadie, moved to Truro with her mother, Annie Gloade, and "was deceased in 1960." She never knew her paternal grandparents, Josiah Thomas and Rose Gooley. Edith's father, Michael, was born on 29 May 1887 (though Michael's and Annie Gloade's marriage certificate of 1908 erroneously states that Michael was born in 1882). Annie, born in 1891, was a daughter of William Thomas Gloade and Mary Cope of Millbrook. She was Michael's second wife. NSARM, Historical Vital Statistics, Registration Year 1908, Colchester County Marriages, "Marriage of Anne Gload [*sic*, Gloade], 17, daughter of Thomas Gload, and Michael Thomas, 26, widower, son of John Thomas and Polly [*sic*, Josiah

Thomas and Rosie Gooley] of Indian Road, Hants County, 18 November 1908, officiating priest, Edward Kennedy, witnesses Maria MacDonald and Katie Sark." Michael and Annie had two daughters who later became prominent within the Millbrook community, Edith Jane Thomas born on 7 October 1911, and Clara Agnes born on 8 February 1914. NSARM, Historical Vital Statistics, Colchester County births, Registration Year 1911, p. 9900653, no. 9900653, application from Edith Jane Thomas Peters of Millbrook (1911–2004) to have her birth of 7 October 1911 properly registered, dated 19 August 1980, with birth certificate attached; NSARM, Historical Vital Statistics, Colchester County Births, Registration Year 1914, p. 4690067, no. 4690068, Birth of Clara Agnes Thomas, daughter of Michael Thomas and Annie Gloade. Following Annie's death, Michael Thomas married a third time, to a woman named Theresa. He died at Millbrook at age of 73 on 5 August 1960. NSARM, Colchester County Deaths, Registration Year 1960, 4573, "Death of Michael Thomas, age 73 years, son of Joseph Thomas and Rosie Goolay, 5 August 1960."

15 NSARM, Historical Vital Statistics, Colchester County Deaths, Book 42, p. 166, no. 1001, "Death of Mary Rose Thomas [a daughter of Michael's first marriage] , aged 16, on 5 September 1911 from cholera, informant Thomas Gloade"; NSARM, Historical Vital Statistics, Colchester County Deaths, Book 32, p. 86, no. 315, "Death of Charles Thomas, 14, on October 1918, informant Joseph Gould"; NSARM, Historical Vital Statistics, Colchester County Deaths, Book 31, p. 243, nos. 784 and 785, "Deaths of Flora Thomas, two years two months, and Benjamin, four months, on 20 April 1916, of tubercular meningitis, informant William Thomas Gloade"; NSARM, Historical Vital Statistics, Colchester County Deaths, Book 32, p. 87, no. 325, "Death of Adelaide Thomas, two and a half years old, on 17 October 1918, from pneumonia, informant Joseph Gould"; NSARM, Historical Vital Statistics, Colchester County Deaths, Book 112, 506, "Death of Annie Thomas, stillborn, 2 November 1924, informant Michael Thomas."

16 Excerpt from "Max Basque to R.H. Whitehead, taped interview, March 1984," in Whitehead, *The Old Man Told Us*, 120.

17 Ibid.; "Max Basque to R.H. Whitehead, personal communication, 1977," in Whitehead, *The Old Man Told Us*, 120, 146.

18 John Knox, *An Historical Journal of the Campaigns in North America*, ed. A.G. Doughty (Toronto: Champlain Society, 1914), 2.197. Knox's original journal manuscript is housed in the Andrew Brown Collection, Add.

MSS-19071, in the British Museum, London, England. There is also a microfilm copy in the Library and Archives of Canada, Ottawa (henceforth LAC), Canadian Papers, MM651A (from the Brown Collection of the British Museum, Add. MSS-19071).

19 When Max Basque's grandfather Isaac Sack told him about the "sailor" Thomas who deserted from the British navy, Max assumed that Thomas's defection occurred in 1749, when Halifax was founded. Max also knew that from the 1790s to the 1850s members of the Sack and Thomas families, who intermarried, travelled through the *Sipekne'katik* district by following the Shubenacadie River from the Dartmouth Lakes northwest to Elmsdale and beyond to Shubenacadie and Stewiacke. This may be why, when he heard the name "Panuke" spoken by his maternal grandfather, he assumed that what was meant was Lake Banook, the first lake lying between Dartmouth and Shubenacadie, rather than Panuke Lake near Windsor. Max could trace an unbroken line of descent from Louis Thomas to Marie-Antoinette Thomas to Isaac Sack to his mother Anna. Though, as Basque contended, Louis Thomas was not Chief Jean-Baptiste Thoma's son, he might have been Thoma's great-grandson. Thoma had a son Pierre, who in turn had a son Pierre, and the second Pierre was likely Louis's father.

20 Henry Louis Peters was born in 1912. NSARM, Historical Vital Statistics, Hants County Births, Registration Year 1912, p. 55700981, no. 58700981, "Birth at Shubenacadie of Henry Lewis Peters, son of Lewis Peters and 'Kate Slack' [*sic*, Charlotte or Catherine McCumber], 21 May 1912, informant Simon Maximus Basque"; NSARM, Colchester County Marriages, Registration Year 1939, Book 94, 10, "Marriage of Edith Jane Thomas, 26, daughter of Michael Thomas and Annie Gloade, and Henry L. Peters, 24 [*sic*, he was 26], sportsman and guide, son of Louis Peters and Charlotte McCumber, 21 August 1939, presiding priest M.K. Kinsella, witnesses Peter Paul and Alice Thomas."

21 Since Edith knew that Adelaide Thomas, John Williams's wife, belonged to the Thomas family, she also penned in the names "Mrs. Williams" and "Ruby," Adelaide's daughter, on her genealogical chart.

22 Carrie Gloade, a researcher on this project and a descendant of William Thomas Gloade, Edith Thomas Peter's maternal grandfather, secured a copy of this chart, which she photographed and which appears as plate 33. Edith, as already stated, was a daughter of Michael Thomas (1887–1960) and Annie Gloade (1891–c.1950). NSARM, Historical Vital Statistics, Colchester County Births, Registration Year 1911, p. 99000653,

no. 99000653. This file is a document package, which includes Edith's application of 19 August 1980 for a late registry of her birth (she was born on 7 October 1911) as well as for her birth certificate. (In 1975, she retrieved information concerning her birth from Immaculate Conception Church in Truro.) Following her husband Henry Louis Peters's death, Edith became a companion of Henry's brother, Basil Peters, and the two of them worked together manufacturing baskets and operating a successful craft shop at Millbrook. Edith and Basil became known and honoured for their charitable activities. For instance, they annually donated baskets, often brightly painted with distinctive floral designs, free of charge to the Halifax Hospital Kermesse to raise money for sick children. Edith died at Millbrook early in 2004. "Obituary of Edith Jane (Thomas) Peters," *Halifax Herald*, 20 January 2004. Like Max Basque, Edith Jane Thomas Peters was a fifth- or sixth-generation descendant of Louis Thomas. Basil Peters stated in 2011 that Edith wanted to find out as much as she could about her connections to the "deserter story" but had trouble drawing a connection between her father Michael and Louis Thomas, whom Max Basque spoke about. Without recourse to official sources, she could not determine the identity of her paternal grandfather, Josiah Thomas, whom she never knew but who was Louis Thomas's grandson. Interview with Basil Peters, Millbrook, 10 June 2011.

23 LAC, MG 18, F 18, *Recensement genal fait au mois de Novembre mile Sept cent huit de tous les Sauvages de l'Acadie que resident dans la Coste de l'est, Et ceux de Pintagouet de Canibeky*, typescript of Pierre La Chasse's 1708 census of the Indigenous population of Port Royal, census of families and others, 2–3, 17. The original manuscript is housed in vol. 4, no. 751 of the Edward E. Ayer Collection in the Newberry Library, Chicago.

24 The Battle of Port Royal, by which England acquired Port Royal from the French in 1654, was the occasion of the first deployment of British regulars in North America. The force that took Port Royal, led by Colonel Robert Sedgwick acting under orders from Oliver Cromwell, comprised 200 professional soldiers and 100 New England volunteers. Since Port Royal was defended by a skeletal French garrison of only 130 soldiers, it readily fell to the English. After the battle the local Acadians were allowed to remain in the vicinity and practise their Roman Catholic religion. The English, however, destroyed Port Royal's monastery and church. Brenda Dunn, *A History of Port Royal, Annapolis Region: 1605–1800* (Halifax: Nimbus, 2004), 23–4.

25 Since his youngest orphaned child, Marcel, was only ten years old in 1708, Albiston may have died at Port Royal around 1700. La Chasse, though assisted in compiling material for the census by another French missionary, Abbé Antoine Gaulin, was inconsistent in his spelling of Mi'kmaw surnames, even when individuals were members of the same family. For this reason it is possible that "Estienne Albadoussine," age thirty-five, who lived at La Hève, was "Étienne Albison," another son of our hypothetical sailor and deserter.

26 LAC, microfilm copies of documents in the Archives des Colonies, Paris, France (AC), CIIB, Correspondance général, l'Ile Royale, vol. 6, doc. 77, *Recensement des Sauvages dans l'isle Royale et de la peninsule de l'acadie qui sont deservis par les Missionaires du Seminire des missions étrangères Establi a Quebec fait par M. Gaulin pretre … en 1722.*

27 Jehan Grand Claude, the patriarch of the Glode/Gloade family of southwestern Nova Scotia (who was also known as "Jackish" or "Little Jean"), Thoma, and three other Mi'kmaw leaders arrived at Annapolis Royal in early October 1722 "to surrender themselves" to the government upon terms set out in the Governor's Instructions earlier in the year. The Annapolis Council's board agreed that they had "Demean'd themselves Peaceably" during recent troubles associated with Dummer's War and should be "Admitted upon such Tarmes as aforesaid." The treaty was drawn up on 19 October 1722, and Jackish and his associates called in with two of his sons, "Claude & Martain who have their mother, A Brother and sister Hostages in the fort." Jackish's company were then ordered to remain at the fort until a few more Mi'kmaq arrived to sign as well. The terms were drafted on 5 November and the signing ceremony took place on 12 November. Archibald MacMechan, ed., *Original Minutes of His Majesty's Council at Annapolis Royal, 1720–1739*, Nova Scotia Archives III (Halifax, 1908), 36–8, "At a Council at Lieutenant-Governor John Doucett's House on 3 November 1722"; "At a Council at Lieutenant-Governor John Doucett's House on 5 November 1722"; and "At a Council held at the place aforesaid on 12 November 1722."

28 Thoma's name appears on the 1726 treaty as "Baptist Tomus, Chief of Annapolis Royale." LAC, British Colonial Office documents on microfilm (henceforth CO) 217/38/108, "Peace and friendship treaty, dated Annapolis Royal, 4 June 1726."

29 On 24 August 1726 Jean-Baptiste Thomas, "chef … de cette riviere," was a witness, along with Pierre Charret (Momcharret *dit* Cellier), Pierre Charret (Momcharret

dit Bouta) "de cette rivière," and François Germain, an Annapolis head man, at the wedding of Rene Nectab8 and Catherine Anorgin. NSARM, RG 1, vol. 26, 246, Registers of Baptisms, Marriages and Burials at the Parish of Saint Jean-Baptiste, Annapolis Royal, 1720–55, "Marriage of René Nectab8, 25 years old, son of Louis Nectab8 and Elizabeth of Cape Sable, to Catherine Anorgin, daughter of François Anorgin and Françoise Meodametch, 24 August 1726, officiating priest René Charles de Bresley, witnesses Pierre Charet, Pierre Charet [his brother], François Germain, and Baptiste Thomas."

30 Marie Mius, the youngest of Philippe Mius *dit* d'Azy's children, was born around 1710 when her Mi'kmaw mother Marie was nearly forty years of age. Marie therefore was around forty years younger than her husband Jean-Baptiste Thoma. Two dates, 24 August 1726 and 24 August 1727, have been suggested for Thoma and Marie's marriage at St. Jean-Baptiste chapel at Annapolis Royal. Priest, historian, and Acadian genealogist Clarence-J. d'Entremont gives 24 August 1726 as the day of their wedding, which corresponds to the date Thoma stood as a witness at René Nectab8's and Catherine Anorgin's marriage ceremony. D'Entremont, *Histoire du Cap-Sable de l'an mil au traité de Paris (1763)* (Eunice, LA: Hébert, 1981), 3.1013. A second date of 24 August 1727 appears on several online genealogical sites. No evidence exists in the St. Jean-Baptiste parish registers at Annapolis Royal that a Roman Catholic marriage ever took place between Thoma and Marie.

31 NSARM, RG 1, vol. 26a, 61, "Burial of Anne, 50 years old, born 1680, wife of Jean B. Thomas, chief of the Mikmak of this River, 29 April 1730, presiding priest René Charles de Bresley, witnesses Laurent Granger and Claude Granger."

32 Gabriel was born in November 1727 and baptized at Annapolis Royal on 29 March 1728; Clere, or Clare, was born in May 1732 and baptized on 5 April 1733. NSARM, RG 1, vol. 26a, 19, Registers of St. Jean-Baptiste Parish, "Baptism of Gabriel Thomas, son of Jean Baptiste Thomas and Marie Marie Muis, 29 March 1728 [born November 1727], presiding priest René Charles de Breslay, godparents Anne, daughter of said Thomas, and François Mius." Anne was a daughter of Thoma and his first wife, Catherine Anne. NSARM, RG1, vol. 26a, 107, "Baptism of Clere Thomas, daughter of Baptiste Thomas and Marie Mieux, 5 April 1733 [born May 1732], presiding priest De Poncy de Lavenède, godparents Charles Giroad and Magdeleine Robichaux."

33 Beamish Murdoch, *A History of Nova-Scotia or Acadie* (Halifax: J. Howe, 1865), 1.367; Archibald MacMechan, ed., *A Calendar of Two Letter-Books and One Commission-Book in the Possession of the Government of Nova Scotia* (Halifax: James Barnes, 1900), 60–1, "Philipps to Craggs [The Right Honourable James Craggs, Secretary of War]," 16 May 1719.

34 The first Port Royal stood on the Granville side of the Annapolis Basin, opposite Goat Island. The second Port Royal was built eight kilometres upriver on the site of present-day Fort Anne. The English thoroughly destroyed the French forts. By the mid-1700s no traces remained at Granville of the first French Port Royal, while remains of Scotchfort, built by the Scots and English in 1629, were visible on the Granville shore until the mid-1750s. Thomas Chandler Haliburton, *An Historical and Statistical History of Nova-Scotia* (Halifax: J. Howe, 1829), 1.45. The Copes, Momcharrets, and Grand Claudes had relied on the French trade prior to 1713, and moved after this date to access trade networks that still sent furs to France and received French goods in return. The patriarch of the Cope family was Paul Cope (or Cop), who with his wife Cecile in 1708 had four children: Jean-Baptiste, ten years old, Therese, eight, Marie, five, and Margueritte, one. LAC, MG 18, F 18, 1, "*Recensement genal …* 1708." The Momcharrets were descended from a late-seventeenth-century Mi'kmaw leader at Port Royal named Momcharret. Pierre Momcharret became the head chief of the Minas district, and between 1722 and 1728 at times acted as spokesperson for the *Kespu'kwit* district. Clarence-J. d'Entremont, *Histoire du Cap-Sable*, 3.1128–9. Several of the Grand Claude family moved to the Acadian-*métis* settlement of La Hève (now La Have).

35 LAC, AC, on microfilm, C11B, vol. 6, *Correspondance général*, doc. 77.

36 Philippe Mius *dit* d'Azy was the son of Baron Philippe Mius d'Entremont of Pobomcoup and his French wife Madeleine Helie. Philippe Mius d'Entremont came to Acadia in 1651, was awarded his barony by Charles La Tour in 1653, and was appointed procureur du roi of Acadia in 1670.

37 Philippe Mius *dit* d'Azy and his first Mi'maw consort had five children, Joseph, Marie, Mathieu, Maurice, and Françoise. Mathieu, who lived at Cape Sable, and Maurice, who lived at Musquodoboit, wed Indigenous wives, while their siblings married into the Acadian community. Chief Thoma's wife Marie Mius belonged to a second group of nine children born to Philippe Mius *dit* d'Azy and his second spouse, Marie: Jacques (or James), Jean-Baptiste, Pierre, Madeleine, Françoise,

Philippe, François, Anne, and Marie. Jacques was hanged in Boston in 1726 for robbery, along with his younger brother Philippe. Pierre traded along the Saint John River. Madeleine married Jean-Baptiste Guédry *dit* Labrador who, like James and Philippe Mius, was hanged in Boston in 1726. Françoise Mius, already a widow when she wed René Grand Claude, in 1735 after René's death married a third time to Pierre Momcharret *dit* Cellier of Annapolis Royal. Philippe d'Azy's youngest son, François Mius (1700–c.1765), maintained a trading post on Second Peninsula in Lunenburg County and was recognized as chief of Merliguèche by the French at Louisbourg in 1742. Anne Mius wed Jean-Baptiste Guédry's brother, Paul Guédry *dit* Labrador, who operated a fishery and trading establishment at Merliguèche (present-day Lunenburg). D'Entremont, *Histoire du Cap-Sable*, 3.968–1019, 1125–32.

38 Clarence d'Entremont provides information on these kin connections in his chapter on the children of Philippe II Mius d'Entremont *dit* d'azy. D'Entremont, *Histoire du Cap-Sable*, 3.968–1042.

39 The terms of this peace of 12 November 1722 were translated into French but not into the Mi'kmaw language. The Mi'kmaw leaders each received a copy of the document that they had signed as well as passports to ensure their safe passage through British territory. After this, three more Annapolis River Mi'kmaq came to embrace this peace and the protection of the British government. MacMechan, *Original Minutes*, 38–9, "At a Council held at Lieutenant Governor John Doucett's House on 14 November 1722." The British became extremely concerned in 1722 about rumours spread by three boys, Charles Davis, Nicholas Hutton, and George Willis, who had been captured by Mi'kmaq along the eastern coast and ransomed by a trader, James Blinn, from Acadians at Piziquid. These boys argued that the Acadians and Mi'kmaq might be joined by Indigenous warriors from Canada who together might attempt to burn Annapolis Royal during the winter of 1722–23, since it was rumoured abroad at Minas and Piziquid that the "English would Come" and destroy Minas. MacMechan, *Original Minutes*, 38, "At a Council at John Doucett's House," 12 November 1722.

40 MacMechan, *Original Minutes*, 36–8, "At a Council at Lieutenant-Governor John Doucett's House on 3 November 1722."

41 At least six Mi'kmaq men, including Jehan Grand Claude, Chief Thoma, and Germain of Annapolis Royal signed personal treaties with the British by 11 December 1722. Chief Thoma, as "Chief of the River Indians," likely make peace with the British around 1719, and so escaped having his family incarcerated at Fort Anne's dungeon three years later. MacMechan, *A Calendar*, 60–1, "Governor R. Philipps to James Craggs, Secretary at War," 26 May 1719. On 20 November the Mi'kmaq who had signed pacts with the British complained that they could not get any "provisions from the French Inhabitants, without an Order," a grievance that the board took "into Consideration." MacMechan, *Original Minutes*, 40–1, "At a Council at John Doucett's House," 20 November 1722.

42 MacMechan, *Original Minutes*, 46–8, "At a Council held at Lieutenant-Governor John Doucett's House on 20 September 1723."

43 Ibid.

44 On 2 October 1720, the two Momcharrets directed their French missionary priest, Antoine Gaulin, to draft a letter to the governor's council at Annapolis Royal and gave it to Phillip Melançon to deliver. This missive, signed by "Antoine and Pierre Couaret," demanded that all Mi'kmaw hostages held at Fort Anne immediately be freed. It then launched into the most powerful declaration of Aboriginal right to be expressed in Acadia up to that point. "This land here that God has given to us, of which we can be accounted a part as much as the trees are born here cannot be disputed by anyone," they proclaimed. "We are masters independent of everyone and wish to have our country free." LAC, microfilm copies of documents from the Public Records Office, London, England, Colonial Office Records (henceforth CO), 217/3/155–6; "Antoine and Pierre Couaret to Governor Richard Philipps," 2 October 1720; L.F.S. Upton, *Micmacs and Colonists: Indian-White Relations in the Maritimes, 1713–1867* (Vancouver: University of British Columbia Press, 1979), 41. The original letter drafted by Gaulin was in French. A translation into English may be found in Upton, *Micmacs and Colonists*, 199. This declaration indicates that the Minas Momcharrets, even before the outbreak of Dummer's War in 1722, had been involved in a widespread Mi'kmaw land and resource campaign against British encroachment on traditional lands and resources.

45 MacMechan, *Original Minutes*, 42–3, "At Councils at John Doucett's House on 3 December, 11 December and 13 December 1722."

46 Chiefs and their associates began assembling at Annapolis Royal in May 1726 to participate in the treaty proceedings. In early June the British released the last of the hostages kept at Fort Anne. Ibid., 114–17, "At a Council held at John Doucett's House," 4 June 1726. The treaty was drafted at this council and so is dated 4 June, but Mi'kmaw leaders' signatures were later collected over a

number of months. There are several copies of the 1726 treaty. The names of three Momcharrets appear on them: "Pierre Armquarett" is listed as "Chief of Minas," while "Piere Nimcharett" is regarded as belonging to the Annapolis band, and "Antoine Nimquarett" of Minas also signed the treaty. LAC, CO 217/38, "Copy of 1726 treaty, showing with some chiefs' symbolic identifying marks," dated 4 June 1726. Seven copies of the treaty are housed at NSARM in Halifax, but Lieutenant Governor Armstrong on 27 November 1726 sent a dispatch containing only one copy, the one with the few totemic-like symbols, to the Colonial Office in London. Each chief may have received a copy of the document, though this is doubtful. No parchment copies exist within the Mi'kmaw community. Chief Pierre Momcharret likely had raided traders at Minas before he signed treaty in 1726. He may even have been the "Pierre Numquadden" who, with eleven other Mi'kmaq, demanded fifty livres from John Alden for the liberty of trading at Minas. LAC, CO, 217/4/ no. 18 (xii), "Deposition of John Alden," 14 September 1720; LAC, CO 213/3/151. The British felt sure that the French missionaries were behind this and other such incidents, especially as some of the goods stolen from Alden's vessel ended up in a Roman Catholic chapel on the St. John River. LAC, CO 217/4/125-27, "Letter of John Doucett regarding Mons. Gaulin," 2 July 1722.

47 The Governor's Council had mulled over plans for military installations at Minas as early as 1713. MacMechan, *A Calendar*, 24–7, "Caulfield to Board of Trade," 1 November 1713.

48 Murdoch, *History of Nova-Scotia*, 1.481–3.

49 Chief Pierre Momcharret may have been the father of Antoine and Andreas, but this cannot be confirmed.

50 Ensign Cottnam was empowered by Annapolis Royal in 1734 to investigate and report on clandestine trade carried on with the Mi'kmaq at Minas and on the Saint John River. There were a fair number of traders of Indigenous extraction, who included Bently from Charlestown, Munier, a *métis* from New England, and Chatteneuf, a son-in-law of St. Castine of the Penobscot River. MacMechan, *Original Minutes*, 238–43, "Council at Annapolis Royal," 27 September 1734; ibid., 306–7; Murdoch, *History of Nova-Scotia*, 1.485–6.

51 Ensign Cottnam was empowered by Annapolis Royal in 1734 to investigate and report on clandestine trade carried on with the Mi'kmaq at Minas and on the Saint John River. There were a fair number of traders of Indigenous extraction, who included Bently from Charlestown, Munier, a *métis* from New England, and Chatteneuf, a son-in-law of St. Castine of the Penobscot

River. MacMechan, *Original Minutes*, 238–43, "Council at Annapolis Royal," 27 September 1734; ibid., 306–7; Murdoch, *History of Nova-Scotia*, 1.485–6.

52 MacMechan, *Original Minutes*, 238–43, "Deposition of Henry Cope, first given before Major Paul Mascarene and Council at Annapolis Royal, regarding the government's orders for building a magazine at Minas." This deposition was discussed in a council held at Lieutenant Governor Armstrong's house on 25 July 1732. Murdoch, *History of Nova-Scotia*, 1.485–6; Geoffrey Gilbert Plank, *An Unsettled Conquest: The British Campaign against the Peoples of Acadia* (Philadelphia: University of Pennsylvania Press, 2001), 84. The day after this incident about ten or twelve Mi'kmaq came to see Henry Cope and asked that the perpetrators of this deed be pardoned. Chief Pierre Momcharret was still alive and may have been among them, though his name does not appear in the documentary record at this time.

53 Thomas Akins, ed., *Selections from the Public Documents of the Province of Nova Scotia* (Halifax: Annand, 1869), 97–8, "Minutes of Council," 25 July 1732; ibid., 101, "Armstrong to the Duke of Newcastle," 15 November 1732. In June 1732 Henry Cope and his Boston associates had petitioned Council for permission to establish a colliery at Chignecto, Nova Scotia. MacMechan, *Original Minutes*, 224–8, "At a Council held by the order of Lieutenant Governor Lawrence Armstrong," 19 June 1723. Owing to Mi'kmaw opposition, the colliery only operated for a few years before it was abandoned. In the light of these events, in 1735 the Annapolis council suggested that steps be taken to approach the Mi'kmaw and get them to renew the 1726 treaty, though it seems this was never done. Murdoch, *History of Nova-Scotia*, 1.506.

54 NSARM, RG 1, vol. 24, "Minutes of Council from 12 October 1744 to 8 November 1748." The correspondence pertaining to May 1745 mentions "Old Surrette who either died or was killed by Indians." René LeBlanc was born in 1657 at Grand Pré and died on 3 January 1733. LeBlanc was the only Piziquid resident who overtly supported the British expansion scheme, and then likely from mercenary motives.

55 These words suggest that the Minas head chief may have died as early as 1737, his widow had remarried, and his son Bartholomew was being raised by his mother's new husband, possibly Thomas Wonito.

56 The Minas band discussed here is the group that gave rise to the Bernard family of St. Margaret's Bay and Philip Bernard's associate, "Biscaroon." Thomas Wonito seems to have been second in command to Pierre Momcharret and Pierre's brother Jacques. See NSARM, RG

1, vol. 24, "Regarding robbery of trader named William Trefry at Grand Pré in April 1742"; Murdoch, *History of Nova-Scotia*, 1.521.

57 Jones stated to Governor Armstrong that he had been robbed of goods to the value of at least eight hundred pounds, and also tendered a second claim for losses to his "Books of Accompts [*sic*, Accounts] valued at £700 more." Armstrong erroneously claimed that Barthelemy was Biscaroon's son, since Jones thought Barthelemy was the chief's wife's son, and therefore was Chief Thoma's foster son. Barthelemy was probably only in his teenage years at the time, and the fact he was now under Thoma's care and not that of a member of the Momcharret family suggests that his father had died and his mother had remarried Chief Thoma. By this time Armstrong realized that Mi'kmaw involvement in Jones's robbery drew on members of a kin and trade network involving Indigenous leaders from Chignecto, the St. John's River, and Cape Sable as well as Minas. Before this date it was easier to pin all such depredations on British and New England trade on the activities of French missionary priests. MacMechan, *A Calendar*, 112–14, "Armstrong to the St. John's Indians," 21 June 1727; "L. Armstrong to Father Daniloo, Missionary Priest at St. John River," 21 June 1727; Otho Hamilton, "Secretary of Council to the Deputies of Chignecto," 21 June 1737; Otho Hamilton, "to Charles D'Entremont," 1 June 1737.

58 "Honik" may have been an approximation of Jacques Momcharret's Mi'kmaw name, for throughout the 1740s and 1750s the position of the Momcharrets at Minas vis-à-vis the British remained ambiguous. Bruce Fergusson, ed., *Minutes of His Majesty's Council at Annapolis Royal, 1736–1749* (Halifax: Nova Scotia Archives, 1967), 14–17, "At a Council held at Lieutenant-Governor Lawrence Armstrong's House at Annapolis Royal, 10 June 1737'; NSARM, RG 1, vol. 24 [Brown Papers], "Minutes of Council for 10th to the 21st of June 1737." On 18 June 1737 Stephen Jones swore "to the truthfulness of his deposition" before the lieutenant governor and council, and his words were recorded by Otho Hamilton, the secretary of council. Armstrong was extremely upset by such an incident occurring at a time of "profound peace" and grew only more agitated when he found Jones was upping his losses to nine hundred pounds as well as books of accounts valued at seven hundred pounds more. The whole came to around £1,546. This incident led to circular letters being sent from Paul Mascarene at Annapolis Royal to the Acadian deputies at Minas and several chiefs, including the Momcharrets.

59 In early June 1726 the British were not yet familiar with the identities or relative ranks of the Mi'kmaw chiefs. For instance on some copies of the 1726 treaty, "John (or Jacques) Quarett (Momcharret)," rather than Pierre Momcharret, was listed as the head chief of Minas.

60 The raiders had cut Trefry's anchor cables, roughed him up, and after absconding with the contents of his hold, set his sloop adrift with him aboard. Fergusson, *Minutes of His Majesty's Council*, 37–9; NSARM, RG 1, vol. 24, Brown Papers, "Letter of April 1742'; Minutes of Council at Annapolis regarding letter from Abbé Louis-Joseph Le Loutre allegedly "written at the request of the Indians," 10 October 1743. Le Loutre claimed the traders were at fault, for by distributing whiskey they had encouraged a group of Minas Mi'kmaq to become intoxicated. Alexandre Bourg *dit* Belle-Humeur (1671–1760), an Acadian notary at Grand-Pré, and another Acadian deputy, François Mangeant, saved some of the ship's contents. Yet the British felt that Bourg, who had close contact with the Mi'kmaq as well as kin ties with the Mius family, should be suspended from his office as notary public, since he had failed to warn the British of the impending attack and done little to quash it once it was underway. When Trefry finally sailed into the harbour at Annapolis Royal, he asked to borrow anchors from the brigantine *Baltimore*, which had run aground in 1736 at Cheboque and been towed to Annapolis Royal. Murdoch, *History of Nova-Scotia*, 1.18–20.

61 NSARM, RG 1, vol. 24, Brown Papers, "Letter of Pierre Landry written at instance of the Indians," 24 August 1745. These Mi'kmaq petitioners seem to have been in earnest in their desire to renew a peace with the British as the country slipped into yet another intercolonial conflict, King George's War. Paul Mascarene also averred, on the word of Minas band member Joseph Dugas, that the Mi'kmaq "were inclined to come to a peace with the English if they could obtain it, since they could not pretend to live in the country without it and could not carry their families to Canada, besides they had no relations there." Statement of Paul Mascarene, ibid., 20 August 1745.

62 Upton, *Micmacs and Colonists*, 46.

63 This military expansion into Minas was part of a much larger plan developed in northern New England. Todd Scott, "Mi'kmaq Armed Resistance to British Expansion in Northern New England, 1676–1761," *Journal of the Royal Nova Scotia Historical Society*, 19 (2016): 1–18.

64 Pierre Chegua is not specifically mentioned, but he was the Cape Sable district chief at the time.

65 The "Baptiste Thomas" who, along with François Jean de Perisse, was involved in extending a peace overture to Halifax on behalf of the Cape Sable band was undoubtedly Jean-Baptiste Thomas Albiston, not Chief Jean-Baptiste Medosgnel, the Cape Sable chief from 1722 to 1728. LAC, CO 217/38/108. The chief who called upon Thoma and de Perisse to go to Halifax would have been Chief Pierre Chegua. In 1726, Medosgnel's seventeen-year-old daughter Marguerite wed Pierre Chegua, who around 1728 succeeded Medogsnel as Cape Sable district chief. NSARM, Registers of the Parish of St. Jean-Baptiste, Annapolis Royal, 1702–55, RG 1, vol. 26, 242, "Marriage of Pierre Cheguouéo [or Chegua], 27 years old, son of Germain Cheguouéo and Marie Madelaine, and Marguerite Baptiste, 17 years old, daughter of Chief Jean-Baptiste [Medosgnel] and Magdeleine of Cape Sable, 25 June 1727, presiding priest René Charles de Breslay, witnesses Pierre Charet [Momcharret] *dit* Bouta and Pierre Charet *dit* Cellier." In 1722 Abbé Antoine Gaulin recorded that Jean-Baptiste Medogsnel was chief of nineteen families, or ninety-four persons, living at Cape Sable. Chief Medosgnel was dead by 1753, and it would have been Chegua who contacted the elderly Jean-Baptiste Thoma to assist his group. NSARM, RG 1, vol. 210, 5, "At a council holden at the Governor's House, Halifax, on Friday 16 November 1753." The two Mi'kmaq spoke on behalf of sixty people at Cape Sable. (Thomas B. Akins in one of his works erroneously transcribed part of this document. Akins wrote that "Baptiste Thomas, one of their priests, was one of their chiefs," which makes no sense whatsoever. Chief Thoma was not a priest. Thomas Beamish Akins, *History of Halifax City* [Halifax: Collections of the Nova Scotia Historical Society, 1895], 41.) The original document reads "Baptiste Thomas is one of said chiefs, the other, François Jean de Perisse, was deputed by the other Chief."

66 The area around the headwaters of the St. Croix River was by this time one of the major refuges for the Mi'kmaq. In 1755 the British attested that "[t]he chief resorts of the ... Mickmacks are on the Eastern Shore between Halifax and Cape Breton; between Cumberland County and the northeast coast of the province towards the Bay de Chaleur; about the heads of Rivers running through Kings and Hants Counties, and between Cape Sable and Annapolis Royal." NSARM, RG 1, vol. 284, Brown Papers, doc. 2 (b), "The Province of Nova Scotia, drawn up by the Venerable Judge Deschamps for Dr. Brown, 1782," in "Transcripts of Documents made at the British Museum by order of the Government of Canada relating to the Province between the years 1750 and 1789–90."

67 Lawyer and ethnohistorian Gillian Allen directed me to a valuable historical source that discusses this water route. In the early 1950s Nova Scotian author and historian Thomas Raddall took part in a timber cruise for the Miller Lumber Company that extended from the St. Croix River through Panuke Lake and down to Atlantic coast. En route, Raddall listened to stories told by his associates Ralph Johnson and Raeburn Dauphinee, the head ranger for Mersey Paper, which was responsible for the cruise, about old Indigenous portages and trails. Dauphinee stated, "I have heard the old men say that the Indians went back and forth a good deal [along this route] in the olden times. They would come up the St. Croix [or Panuke] lake(s) to paddle down to the west end of Timber Lake [lying below Panuke Lake and situated over the Lunenburg County line], portage another mile to Connaught Lake, and then make their way down the Canaan branch of the East River to the sea. Doctor Cole of Chester now has a camp on an island in Timber Lake. He found on the shore a well-made stone gouge left by some Indian on this route long ago. But I have heard that sometimes they portaged from the end of St. Croix Lake to Westhaver Lake, then to Dauphinee Lake, and down Dauphinee Lake and stream to where Hubbards is now, on the sea. I suppose it depended entirely on whether they were heading for St. Margaret's Bay or Mahone Bay." Dalhousie Archives, T.H. Raddall Papers, MS2.202, Raddall, "A Timber Cruise on the St. Croix," unpublished document dated September 1952, 15. Dauphinee knew the route from Panuke Lake to Dauphinee's Beach at Hubbards. But a second water route, with more portages, branched off east of Panuke Lake and ran east through Long Lake and Bates Lake. A major portage led to the Muskrat Lakes and then to Big Indian Lake. From there one descended through Rafter Lake, Sandy Lake, Little Indian Lake, and Mill Lake to the Head of St. Margaret's Bay. Roger Lewis, an archaeologist with the Nova Scotia Museum of Natural History in Halifax, has examined many ancient Mi'kmaw sites along this route. Some of his findings, and those of William Jones, are presented in the introduction to Trudy Sable and Bernie Francis, *The Language of This Land: Mi'kma'ki* (Sydney: Cape Breton University Press, 2012), 21–3. Archaeological investigation of the Panuke Lake drainage system indicates that this water and portage route was used in the same way as the Shubenacadie River, to cut across the province from one coast to another, as well as to access the resources of the interior. Archaeologists

and historians are beginning to focus on the importance to the Aboriginal population of this drainage system, which up to now has been ignored in favour of the Shubenacadie River Valley. And, unlike the more open and exposed Shubenacadie River route, Panuke Lake and its riverine connections remained one of only three areas where Mi'kmaw communities temporarily felt safe from military and settler encroachment at the close of the Seven Years' War.

68 The French in the 1730s realized this fact. LAC, AC, Série CIIB, Correspondance générale, Ile Royale, 1.384–5, "Mémoire (circa 1739)." The French viewed the Mi'kmaq of "Port Royal" and Le Have as a single group entity, owing to the constant exchange of people that occurred between the two communities.

69 The Mi'kmaq accessed Panuke Lake from the Minas Basin by means of the St. Croix River. To reach the Atlantic coast, they canoed to the eastern end of Panuke Lake, then descended a system of lakes, rivers, and portages, whose lower reaches carved through a coastal fall zone of rocky hills before meeting the Atlantic Ocean. In the 1760s moose still grazed in numerous interior swamps and caribou roamed over lichen-covered barrens. Abundant seasonal salmon, alewife. and eel runs prompted residents of the Panuke Lake settlement to forge along the waterways and trails each spring and fall to build their stone and brush weirs on rivers running into the Atlantic Ocean.

70 NSARM, on microfilm, copy of old registers of Charles-François Bailly housed at Caraquet, New Brunswick. *Registre des actes de baptême, marriages, et sepultures, faits en la nouvelle ecosse ou acadie comme le vingt unième jour de juillet de l'annee mil sept cent soixante huit, par mons. Charles François Bailly, prêtre missionaire des sauvages et acadiens, sujets de sa majeste britanique, 1768-1773*, 5, "Piziquid, 28 août 1768, Joachim, 11 ans, fils de Jean Baptiste Thomas et Marie Mius." Joachim's godparents were François Levron and Theodore Boudrot. Thoma's son Jacques and his wife Marie-Thérèse also brought a son, Nicolas, to be baptized by Bailly on 28 August 1768. Nicolas's godparents were Pierre Thomas and Marianne. In 1768 Thoma and Jacques were travelling with François-Xavier Nancourt (Knockwood), a leading man of the Minas band, and his wife, Marie-Thérèse Abstiago. For Monk's description of Pierre Martyn Thomas, see LAC, MG 23, GII-19, Monk Papers, Letterbooks, 1061–2.

71 According to Isaac Deschamps (1722–1801), a judge and merchant who arrived at Windsor in 1754, two local bands occupied the Minas region and together formed the regional Minas band. The first band Deschamps called the "Necoute Tribe," after its most prominent family who held proprietary aegis over the Kennetcook River Valley, running through the present-day Newport Township, Hants County. The second group he called the "Amquaret Tribe," after the Momcharrets who for many years had supplied its leaders. The Amquarret group hunted and fished along the Gaspereau River Valley. Judge Deschamps described the bands in a report he wrote in 1763, but the two groups would have occupied the same areas prior to this date. Chief Joseph Bernard, whose name appears first on Deschamps's list of Amquaret band members in 1763, later became a prominent Minas leader during the American Revolution. NSARM, MG 1, vol. 258, Isaac Deschamps Papers, item 8, 8, 20–1; Isaac Deschamps, 1763, "Indian Tribe of Amquaret, now hunting between Cornwallis and the River between two plains on the Annapolis road – Summer Residence on the River Piziquid [Avon River] and Gaspero"; Isaac Deschamps, "Tribe of Nocout, now hunting on the Kenecoot [*sic*, Kennetcook] River in the Township of Newport; Summer residence there also"; NSARM, RG 1, vol. 284, doc. 2 (b), transcripts of documents made at the British Museum by order of the Government of Canada relating to the Province between the years 1750 and 1789–90, Doctor Brown Collection, "[Report on] The Province of Nova Scotia drawn up the Venerable Judge Deschamps for Dr. Brown, 1782"; LAC, MG 23, GII-19, George Henry Monk Papers, vol. 4, 1061, "Journal Entry for 11 February 1794." Deschamps in 1763 completely ignored the band led by Thoma at Panuke Lake, situated less than twelve kilometres inland from his Windsor estate. Though, traditionally, the land over which Thoma and his group hunted belonged under the jurisdiction of Minas regional band, Thoma considered it under his proprietorial auspices.

72 Gabriel Thomas was born in November of 1727, and Clare was born in May of 1732. Some of Thoma's children, among them Anselm and Louis, though mentioned in the documentary record, either were not baptized or their baptismal entries have not survived. Eleven-year-old Joachim, brought to Piziquid in August of 1768, may have been the chief's grandchild.

73 Knox, *An Historical Journal*, 1.89–90.

74 Sutherland held this office until 1758. Charles Bruce Fergusson, "Sutherland, Patrick," *Dictionary of Canadian Biography* online, vol. 3 (1741–70).

75 Knox, *An Historical Journal*, 1.89–90.

76 Ibid., 1.90.

77 Ibid., 2.169–70. The commanding officer at Fort Anne at first was told that the chief had been killed. At this point, he decided to retain Clare and Gabriel until a way could be found to send the pair to Halifax.

78 Ibid.

79 Even after the Seven Years' War, the Mi'kmaq's Acadian and *métis* kinsmen – who now displayed the customs and manners of those who sheltered them – remained with the Panuke Mi'kmaw settlement in order to escape the radical changes to the Minas countryside caused by the coming after 1759 of the New England Planters.

80 Gorham was succeeded in this office by Michael Francklin from 1777 to 1782 and George Henry Monk in 1783 and again from 1793 to 1808.

81 NSARM, RG 1, vol. 165, doc. 18. The actual documents are missing, but a government memo, dated 28 April 1760, states that "Passes of the same Tenor and Date as the above" were granted to "Beleban Quarrie" and six other Mi'kmaq who had appeared in Halifax and made their submissions to the British Crown. No evidence, however, could be found that Jean-Baptist Thoma signed a peace treaty with the British in 1760 or 1761, though he was heralded by the British establishment as "king" of the Mi'kmaq for several years after 1763.

82 Gorham, the only person other than the Reverend Thomas Wood who came to know Thoma personally, favoured him over all other chiefs in the Minas area.

83 Thoma doubtless temporarily lost face among his people when settlers shot at him after he had agreed to act as an advocate for peace with the British. He also would have grieved on learning of Clare's and Anselm's deaths in Halifax.

84 Wood was briefly with the garrison at Fort Anne in 1753, and twenty-five years later, in 1778, he died at Annapolis Royal. Arthur Wentworth Eaton, *Project Canterbury: The Church of England in Nova Scotia and the Tory Clergy of the Revolution* (New York: Thomas Whittaker, 1891), chap. 4.

85 LAC, MG 17 B1, Papers of the Society for the Propagation of the Gospel in Foreign Parts (SPGFP), box 1, file 6, series B.25, microfilm reel H-1994, 188–90, "Reverend Thomas Wood to Society," London, 15 October 1765.

86 Near the beginning of this service, a chief came forward and knelt down and prayed that Almighty God would bless His Majesty, King George III. He further appealed to providence that prosperity might rest upon His Majesty's province of Nova Scotia. He then rose and asked Wood to translate his prayer, which was given in Mi'kmaq, to the congregation. After Wood did so, the governor turned and bowed to the entire Mi'kmaw

assemblage. The Mi'kmaq closed the service with an anthem in Mi'kmaq, and then thanked God, the governor, and Mr. Wood for the opportunity of hearing prayers in their own language.

87 LAC, MG 17 B1, box 1, file 6, series B.25, Microfilm Reel H-1994, "Reverend Thomas Wood to Society, London," 15 October 1767; LAC, MG 17 B1, box 1, file 6, series B. 25, "Wood to the Society," 8 October 1767. Mary-Josephte Thoma was seventy years old. She was a daughter of Thoma and his first wife Ann Catherine. Ann, born in 1696, was older than Mary Josephte, but Mary was the oldest of the chief's daughters that Wood knew about. Pierre Jacques's age is not given, but it is assumed he was a widower.

88 Max Basque was the great-grandson of Peter Sack, who married Mary-Antoinette Thomas. Whitehead, "A Visit with Max Basque, Whycocomagh," *Cape Breton's Magazine*, 1 February 1989, 23.

89 NSARM, RG 1, vol. 430, docs. 20–1, including French commission given François Mius in 1742. Despite the complete destruction of his post by the British between 1749 and 1752, François reluctantly signed a peace treaty with the English Crown on behalf of the La Have Mi'kmaq in November 1761.

90 There also may have been influences stemming from Thoma's Mi'kmaw maternal side. Jean Baptiste Thoma Albiston stressed to the Reverend Thomas Wood that he descended from a line of chiefs that extended back several generations. He also relished being called "King of the Mi'kmaq," a title also accorded Chief Segipt, chosen by his people at Port Royal in 1629 to acknowledge the suzerainty of Charles I over New Scotland. Segipt and his wife and son were sent to England by Sir William Alexander the younger, where they became known as the "King, Queen and Prince." In February 1630 the Mi'kmaw party were hailed with great ceremony at the court of Charles I. Though Segipt lived a century and a half earlier than Thoma, it is possible that Thoma's mother descended from Segipt. The fact that Segipt sailed across the Atlantic to England might also have served to entrench the idea in his descendants' minds that they had a "sailor" in their background. See D.C. Harvey, "Segipt," *Dictionary of Canadian Biography* online, vol. 1 (1000–1700).

91 In 1768, the Thoma family were travelling with Francois-Xavier Nancourt (now Knockwood) and his wife, Marie-Thérèse Abstiago.

92 Abbé Charles-François Bailly was appointed in 1768 by Lieutenant Governor Michael Francklin. Since he was the first Roman Catholic missionary to serve the Mi'kmaq and Acadians since the death of Abbé Pierre

Maillard in 1762, many of the Mi'kmaw children he baptized were several years old. NSARM, microfilm reel 10,053, copy of old registers of Charles-François Bailly housed at Caraquet, New Brunswick, NSARM, on microfilm, *Registre des actes de baptême, marriages, et sepultures, faits en la nouvelle ecosse ou acadie …*, 4, "Baptême, Piziquid, 28 août 1768, Joachim, 11 ans, fils de Jean-Baptiste Thomas et Marie Mius." The same day, Thoma's son Jacques and his wife Marie-Thérèse asked Baily to baptize their son Nicholas. Nicolas's godparents were Pierre Thomas and Marianne. On 21 November 1770 at Halifax, Abbé Baily also baptized Pierre Thomas Jr., the son of Pierre Thomas and his wife Marie. Ibid., 77. (Pierre Thomas Sr. was Thoma's and his first wife Ann Catherine's son. Pierre and his sister, Mary-Josephe, both married into the Jacques [or Sack] family.) Pierre Thomas Jr.'s godparents were Bernard and Cecile. Chief Thoma may have died by this time.

93 Author conversations with Fred Phillips of Cambridge, NS, 13 October 2013.

94 One of Chief Philip Bernard's neighbours, Chief Bernard Argomartin (c.1722–1817) of Gold River, Lunenburg County, had a son, John Penall, who rescued a deserter during the War of 1812. Penall arranged for the family of George Frédéric Mason, one of the earliest settlers to St. Margaret's Bay area, to hide the deserter in their house until all was clear. The deserter later took the name "Thomas Hammond," married a daughter of John Penall, and joined the Gold River Band. Chief Argomartin's brother, Peter Argomartin, also had a daughter, Molly, who married one of Philip Bernard's sons, Joseph. Joseph Bernard and Molly Argomartin lived in Kings County in the early 1800s.

95 Barbara (Mason) Peart, *As the Last Leaf Fell: From Montebéliard to the Head of St. Margaret's Bay, An Illustrated History* (Tantallon, Halifax County: Department of Culture and Recreation/Four East, 2002), 51–2. The community at the Head of St. Margaret's Bay today extends from Upper Tantallon to Dauphinee's Cove. Barbara Peart, who still holds land in the vicinity of the Bernard grant, is the daughter of Asa Singleton Mason (1891–1976), a descendant of George Fréderic Mason.

96 NSARM, MG 1, vol. 258, item 8, 20–1.

97 Pierre Martyn Thomas was Chief Jean-Baptiste Thoma's foster son. LAC, MG 23, GII-19, vol. 4, George Henry Monk Papers, 1748–1823, 1061, "Entry for 11 February 1794." Pierre's father was "Andrew Martyn," whose identity is unclear. There was a chief by this name at Cobequid in the late 1740s, and an Andre Martin acted as an interpreter at a treaty-signing aboard the British

ship *Beaufort* anchored in Halifax Harbour in 1749. The Bernards who came to St. Margaret's Bay in the late eighteenth century were relatives of Captain Joseph Bernard, chief of the Amquarret (or Momcharret) band of the Gaspereau River area in the early 1760s.

98 M.B. DesBrisay, *History of the County of Lunenburg*, 2nd ed. (Toronto: William Briggs, 1895), 143. The fact that no documentary confirmation can be found for such an occurrence does not preclude the possibility that a former pirate may have been incorporated into Mi'kmaw families living in the vicinity of La Have.

99 NSARM, RG 20, Ser. A, Nova Scotia Department of Lands and Forests, Land Grant Registration Books series – Umlock, John. John Umlah Sr. (Umlach, Umloch, Harlow, Hemlow, 1726–1821) was born in Scotland and, after his retirement from the military, settled first at East Chester and then at Seabright on the east coast of St. Margaret's Bay. Doubtless the Mi'kmaq, who likely included Chief Bernard, gained the notice of the British authorities in Halifax for active loyalty to the British cause. One of Umlah's sons, John Umlah Jr., born in Philadelphia in 1758, went to sea for many years and, on his return, settled at St. Margaret's Bay. In 1810, he received a grant on Luke Island, lying off the coast of his mainland property. His younger brother William farmed a grant given him along the Old St. Margaret's Bay Coach Road, a corduroy road that prior to 1800 had been cut through from Portuguese Cove, at the head of the North West Arm, past present-day Goodwood, and emerged just below French Village. Some of Umlah's descendants still live at Goodwood, though William Umlah's original grant was expropriated by the Halifax Water Commission and its topography radically altered.

100 Peart, *As the Last Leaf Fell*, 49.

101 Solomon Bescoloon would have been a near relative of "Biscaroon" who participated in the raid on Stephen Jones's vessel at Minas in 1737, while Thomas Ambroise probably was of Acadian *métis* ancestry. Although numerous Mi'kmaw persons bear the surname "Ambroise," not all are related to one another. "Ambroise," for instance, is a surname found among the Malecite as well as the Mi'kmaq. Some Ambroises are descendants of Ambroise St. Aubin, who frequently used "Ambroise" as his surname. Some of Ambroise St. Aubin's Malecite descendants later adopted the name *Mui'n*, or "Bear." The surname "St. Aubin" derives from Jean Serreau de Saint-Aubin (1621– c.1705) who lived, along with the better-known Jean-Vincent d'Abbadie de Saint Castin (1652–1707), along the Penobscot River in present-day Maine. "Peter and Anastasia Ambroise" and an orphan

named "Alic Ambroise" appear on a list of Mi'kmaq attending St. Anne's Day ceremonies at Chapel Island in 1841. NSARM, MG 15, vol. 3, doc. 65, "An Account of the Indians within the County of Richmond ... 26 July 1841." The Thomas Ambroise who lived with Chief Philip Bernard's band in 1786 was probably Acadian, or French from Quebec. A French-speaking family surnamed "Ambroise" had kin ties with the Momcharrets of Minas, and later intermarried with a Scotsman who pursued the fur trade in New Brunswick. Author conversations in 2014 with Carmen McIntyre, whose ancestors included Ambroises who lived near present-day Campbellton, New Brunswick.

102 Though Chief Philip Bernard lived most of the time at St. Margaret's Bay, he retained his ties with the Minas band. He also was close to Chief John Baul (Paul) who between 1788 and 1793 received land from the government at East Chester. Baul had signed treaty with the British in 1760 and, like Bernard, favoured the English. NSARM, RG 1, vol. 156, doc. 54, "Pass to Jean Ball, a Mickmack Indian, and Eight Others who have appeared in Halifax and made his submission to his Majesty's Government," 28 April 1760. The East Chester tract was surveyed for the Mi'kmaq in 1788 by John Prescott, under warrant. The reserve was not established until 1793. NSARM, RG 20 "C," vol. 90, docs. 33 and 45; Crown Grants, Old Deed Book 20, no. 1, dated 3 September 1793, "Reserve [established] by order-in-council of lots 31 and 32 at the Bottom of Mahone Bay near the Eastern Boundary of the Township of Chester [East Chester] to John Baul [or Paul] *et al* and their families, 1793." John Baul's three sons John Jr., Joseph, and Thomas as well as a daughter, Suzanna Baul, inherited title to the East Chester reserve, which lacked surveyed boundaries and soon was trespassed upon by settlers for hay and wood. In 1816 certain settlers also cast covetous eyes on outcroppings of quarry stone. In the end, a few determined men managed to wrangle more than a third of the reserve from the Mi'kmaq. Joseph Baul also sold a portion of the reserve to Tobias Cook, for which portion the Mi'kmaq were never paid. In 1842 and 1843 Joseph Howe, with the help of Francis Peminout Paul and Peter Thomas, sorted out how much compensation had to be paid to John Baul Sr.'s heirs as the result of the land grab. All that Howe ultimately could extract for Cook's lot of sixty acres was £10, with each of the three heirs that Howe could locate receiving £2 5s 7d. NSARM, RG 1, vol. 432, 47–9, 52–5, 71–2. In 1793, the same year that John Baul received the East Chester tract, Paul Solomon (or Sulno) Jeremy and Joseph Glode of La Have also

petitioned and received land on the La Have River, at New Germany. This tract, too, was soon appropriated by settlers. "Petition of Joseph Sulnow, 11 November 1829," in Desbrisay, *History of the County of Lunenburg* (1895), 227, 347–8. For Chief Morris's licence of occupation in the Sambro area, see NSARM, RG 1, vol. 430, doc. package 26½, "Regarding Paul Morris' land at Pendant Bay," 17 June 1784. A very elderly Paul Morris lived along the Prospect Road in 1856. NSARM, MG 15, vol. 6, doc. 9, "Paul Morris and Indian Chief Francis Paul on eastern road in Dartmouth," 11 October 1856.

103 NSARM, MG 1, vol. 58, docs. 20–1, "Pass to Beleban Quarrie," 1760. Incoming settlers may have resented the once politically prominent Momcharrets and Noucouts who, prior to 1760, had slowed English expansion into the Minas region, and perhaps set out to extract revenge against Bartholomew Noucout and others. During the mid-1760s, for example, an inebriated Bartholomew was set upon by settlers' dogs, though he later was able to exact five pounds for physical injury done to his person during this altercation. NSARM, RG 34–316, PI, Court of General Sessions, Kings County, Proceedings, 1760–64; Charles S. Hamilton, "A History of Kings County," Akins Historical Prize Essay, 1867, King's College, Halifax.

104 Before the arrival of the Acadians, Melanson along the Gaspereau River had been a major meeting ground for Mi'kmaw peoples involved in widespread exchange networks in the Maritime region since ancient times. John Erskine, "Erskine's Micmac Notes, 1958," Nova Scotia Museum of Natural History, Halifax, Printed Matter File, unpublished manuscript, MS 754; Ronald J. Nash and Frances L. Stewart, *Melanson: A Large Micmac Village in Kings County, Nova Scotia*, Curatorial Report no. 67 (Halifax: Nova Scotia Museum, 1990). In 1763 Judge Isaac Deschamps of Windsor still referred to one of the Minas bands as the "Amquaret [Momcharret] Tribe," even though the group's chief was no longer a Momcharret. NSARM, MG 1, vol. 58, docs. 20–1, Deschamps's "1763 list of individuals belonging to the Amquaret and Nocout Tribes." Only two years previously, however, "Beleban Quarrie" (Batholomew Momcharret) had signed a treaty with the English. NSARM, RG 1, vol. 156, 54.

105 LAC, MG 23, GII-19, Monk Papers, 1048, "Entry for 12 January 1794." In 1794 Bartholomew Momcharret had his wife and five children with him.

106 LAC, MG 23, GII-19, Monk Papers, 1050.

107 On 25 June 1769, at a sacrament service held by Charles François Bailly at Chezzetcook, Bartholomew

Momcharret, the son of Bartholomew Momcharret who signed treaty in 1760, married his long-standing partner Marie Joachim, after which the couple requested baptism for their two young children, Marie Agnes and Marie Monique Momcharret. *Mariage a Chezzetcook, 25 Juin 1769. Registre des actes de baptême, mariages, et sepultures faits en La nouvelle ecosse ou acadie ….* Charles François Bailly, NSARM, microfilm reel 10,053. The same man appears as sixty-four-year-old "Bartholmew Amquaret," born in 1736, residing in Kings County in 1800 with his wife Mally Sally and three children, Louis, thirteen years old; Andrew, eight; and Susannah, two. Names of Indians belonging to Kings County, Jon. Crane's account, 1800, NSARM, RG 1, vol. 430, doc. 77. There were thirty-four members of this Kings County band. Deschamps notes the presence of father and son in the Windsor area in 1763, and the son, like his father, sometimes travelled with the sons of Paul Peminout of Stewiacke. NSARM, RG 1, vol. 430, doc. 125, "Court of Sessions, January term, regarding condition of the following Indians [affected by sickness], by James Fulton *et al*," 4 January 1803. By 1810 Momquarrets were no longer leaders at Minas. Peter Argomartin, who was either the brother or son of Chief Michael Argomartin who signed treaty with the British in 1760, had risen as a head man. Crane noted that Kings County had been this member of the Argomartin family's last resting place, and that his widow and some of his sons-in-law still lived in the vicinity of modern-day Cambridge. Thomas Robertson, "History of Shelburne County," Akins Prize Essay, 1871, King's College Library, Halifax; Upton, *Micmacs and Colonists*, 144. Meanwhile, some of Bartholomew Momcharret's descendants, who adopted the surname "Bottomy," around 1830 moved to Lequille, Annapolis County, and by the mid-1850s lived with Chief Ben Pictou's group. NSARM, MG 15, vol. 6, docs. 10 and 11, "Census of Annapolis Band, 1856."

108 NSARM, RG 1, vol. 430, doc. 66, "An Account of the Indians in the District of Colchester, by James Fulton," 3 March 1801. Peter Phillips was probably in his mid-twenties, since in 1800 his four children were all very young. In the spring of 1801 James Fulton reported that Peter Phillips was camped near Stewiacke, though "not expected to stay long there."

109 By 1795 some of Chief Philip Bernard's sons and daughters had left St. Margaret's Bay, though references to "Capt. Philip and Family" still appear in the government documentary record. On 31 November 1807, "Capt. Philip, Peter Morris, Penard [Bernard] Argamatin [or Argomartin], Francis Argomatin [or Argomartin], John

Penard and Jno. Muse" were supplied by "Hartshorne and Boggs, Merchants." NSARM, RG 1, vol. 430, doc. 146. On 23 April the following year, Philip Bernard, Peter Morris and Bernard Argomartin arrived in Halifax together. NSARM, RG 1, vol. 430, doc. 146. One of Captain Bernard's sons, Joseph Philip, received powder, shot and a gun on 14 April 1807, while in February of 1808 "Madlin Doodon [*sic*, Doodoo]" came in for supplies. Captain Philip, Joseph Philip and Thomas Philip received provisions from the government in December of the same year. NSARM, RG 1, vol. 430, doc. 147½. Captain Philip and John Paul were supplied with provisions on 2 January 1796. John Philip and John Basque came to Halifax on 28 May 1796, the same date as Isidore Cope and Peter Jeddore arrived from Musquodoboit. Mi'kmaw women could access government provisions in their own right, since Catherine Philip, from Kings County, secured supplies on 27 October 1796. William Philip obtained seed potatoes and farming utensils on 6 July 1797. Paul Philip and Paul Bonis arrived at Halifax the same time as "Jo Claude, Peter Noge [Knockwood] and Philip Pernart [Bernard]" came in for supplies on 21 November 1796. Paul Phillip acquired provisions on 1 June 1797, while Jo Philip and two of his brothers obtained supplies on 22 August 1797. LAC, MG 23, GII-19, vol. 4, Monk Papers, Indian Accounts, 1163–123, Accounts for 1781; 1793–99; and 1808 and 1809. Peter Thomas and John Barthott, a son of Bartholomew Momcharett, came for provisions on 15 September 1795. Philip Quarred (Momcharret), Louis Anthony (Toney) and John Williams arrived in Halifax on 18 December the same year, and "Bartholl Quarred" (Bartholomew Momcharret) came in for supplies on 29 June the following spring. Chief Bernard's son, "Joseph Philip," received powder, shot and a gun on 14 April 1807. On 23 April 1808 "Capt. Philip, Peter Morris and Bernard Argomartin" arrived together in Halifax for supplies, while on 31 November 1807 "Capt. Philip, Peter Morris, Penard [Bernard] Argamatin, Francis Argomatin, John Penard and Jno, Muse" visited the merchant house of Hartshorne and Boggs. NSARM, RG 1, vol. 430, doc. 146. In February of 1808 "Madlin Doodon (*Doodoo* or Phillips) acquired supplies in Halifax. "Captain Philip" and his two sons "Joseph and Thomas Philip" received provisions in December the same year. NSARM, RG 1, vol. 430, doc. 147½. In the 1850s, descendants of Bartholomew Momcharret, who adopted the surname "Bottomy," moved to Lequille, Annapolis County, and joined Chief Ben Pictou's group. NSARM, MG 15, vol. 6, docs. 10 and 11, "Census of Annapolis Band, 1856."

110 LAC, MG 23, GII-19, Monk Papers, vol. 4, Indian Accounts, 1167, "Joseph Davies Account. To Three Family [*sic*, Families] at St. Margaret's Bay on 6 May 1796 – £19/9s."

111 Ibid., 1198, 1213, "Account for provisions and ammunition for 7 February 1797." Joseph's father-in-law, Peter Argomartin, in the 1790s reputedly killed a Black woman from Burchtown (now Birchtown) in Shelburne County. He afterwards was hamstrung by his group and banned from the Cape Sable district. He eventually moved to Kings County with his third wife. Robertson, "History of Shelburne County," 5; Upton, *Micmacs and Colonists*, 144. In 1800, Joseph Phillips and Molly Argomartin had five children: Joseph, eighteen; Sally, sixteen; Hannah, fourteen; Peter, four; and Marie-Josephe, two. Joseph and his wife remained with the Momcharret Minas group. Molly's father, Peter Argomartin, was dead by 1800, though his widow was still alive at Minas. NSARM, RG 1, vol. 430, doc. 77, "Names of Indians belonging to Kings County in 1800, Jon. Crane's account."

112 This younger Joseph Phillips was likely Joseph Phillips Sr. and Molly Argomartin's son, who was eighteen years old on Crane's census of 1800. NSARM, RG 1, vol. 430, doc. 77.

113 Chearnley recounted many stories about this man's antics. For example, around election time in 1853 Joseph Phillips was out porcupine hunting with his associate Tall Peter Pennel (Argomartin) when the two shot a farmer's ox. Phillips advertised the meat for sale in Mahone Bay as moose meat, while he sold the ox hide to John Hammond from the Gold River area. Fearing that someone might discover their ruse, the men then shot a cow moose, blended the ox and moose meat together, and went about selling both as moose meat. Another time Joseph Phillips, Tall Peter Pennel, and Joseph Pennel went bear hunting and came across a female bear and her cubs. They only had one gun among the three of them, which misfired. Phillips shot his dog instead and turned in the dog's snout as a bear snout to obtain a county bounty placed on shooting bear. NSARM, MG 1, vol. 1464, doc. 49; NSARM, MG 1, vol. 1465, Harry Piers Papers, doc. 51," William Chearnley's notes," n.d. Joseph Pennel (Argomatin) of Gold River also told Chearnley that once a moose he had snared at Five Mile Lake, at the head of Gold River, broke the snare and escaped when he fired at it. The following winter Joseph Phillips shot the same moose. NSARM, MG 1, vol. 1506, "Chearnley papers," n.d.

114 This man was probably the Joseph Phillips who for few years maintained a small farm at Sherbrook until 1851,

then moved to Gold River the next year. NSARM, MG 15, vol. 42, no. 105, "Letter from John Creighton," n.d.

115 NSARM, MG 1, vol. 1464, doc. 49, Harry Piers Papers, "Mi'kmaq Hunters of the Nineteenth Century."

116 LAC, MG 23, GII-19, Monk Papers, vol. 4, Indian Accounts, 1198, 1213, "Joseph Davies Accounts, Account for provisions and ammunition for Thomas Philip and 7 papooses, February 1797." Since Joseph Davies referred to Thomas Phillips Sr.'s children as "papooses," they were still young.

117 A smallpox outbreak in 1800–1801 caused members of the Phillips family to split up and scatter. Yet even before this date there were Phillips in Antigonish County. NSARM, RG 1, vol. 430, doc. 45, "Return of the under-mentioned supplies distributed among distressed Indians at Antigonish in the winter of 1801, by Direction of Michael Wallace of Indian Affairs, drawn up by Edward Kirk"; NSARM, RG 1, vol. 430, doc. 37½, "List of names of families from Antigonish, Pomquet and Tracady, numbering 126, on behalf of the Committee for Indian Affairs, winter of 1801; NSARM, RG 1, vol. 430, doc. 109, "Return of Indian Meal, Blankets & Potatoes ... for the use of orphan Indians residing in the Eastern District of Nova Scotia between the 11th Day of January & 31th March (1802) included – William Nixon's Account." One of the persons to whom Edward Kirk distributed provisions was "Philip, an old Tracida Indian."

118 NSARM, Printed Matter File, Piers Papers, "Joseph C. Cope to Harry Piers," Joseph C. Cope to Harry Piers, 1926. Cope was unclear whether he restricted this identifying designation to Phillips living in Halifax and Hants Counties in late 1800s, or extended it to all of Chief Philip Bernard's descendants in the male line. Documentary evidence from the later 1700s, however, suggests that it was used by all of Chief Bernard's family members. 'Doodoo' sounds something like "Touton," the name sometimes accorded members of the Che-gua family of Cape Sable, though there probably is no connection.

119 Ibid.

120 Six Mi'kmaq were suffering from smallpox at Pope's Harbour in December 1860. While it is not certain that the Phillips listed among this number were descendants of Chief Philip Bernard, they may have been. Michael Phillips, aged sixty, and his wife Ann, sixty-four, fled to Pope's Harbour with three children, Newel, eleven, Ann, seven; and Mary, who was seven months old. NSARM, MG 15, vol. 6, doc. 63. These persons belonged to a group of twenty-eight Mi'kmaq who were vaccinated against further infection. NSARM, RG 15, vol. 6, doc. 63.

Three years previously a Joseph Phillips and his family dwelt at New Glasgow. NSARM, RG 1, vol. 6, doc 16, "Distribution of Blankets by Hugh Reilly, priest," 1857.

121 Chief John Noel of Shubenacadie told Harry Piers about 1927 that in the 1850s "Isabel Dodo" lived at the Chain Lakes, in what is now the regional municipality of Halifax, "on the northern side between the upper and lower lakes," and that the Mi'kmaq called the Chain Lakes "Isabel's Lakes." NSM, Piers Papers, Ethnology: History, Canadian Geographic Board, "Notes"; Nova Scotia Museum Library, Piers Papers, Ethnology; Genealogies, 7 and 31, "Regarding Isabel Dodo (Tutuis) at the Chain Lakes, Halifax County, n.d. (c.1927)." First Chain Lake is located west of Halifax in the vicinity of the modern Bayers Lake Shopping Complex, while Second Chain Lake lies near the intersection of Highways 102 and 103. See also Nova Scotia Museum Printed Matter File, Jerry Lonecloud to Piers, 22 July 1927; Whitehead, *The Old Man Told Us*, 274–75. Isabel Dodo was a traditional Mi'kmaw doctor and herbalist who lived both near the Northwest Arm, possibly at Chocolate Lake, and on the nearby Chain Lakes. Her family was said to be from St. Mary's in Guysborough County, and when she died she was buried in an ancient Mi'kmaw grave site on an island at the head of the tide in the St. Mary's River, by "Saulsman's, between Upper County Harbour and Cross Roads." The fact that her parents had an attachment to the St. Mary's River region is not surprising, since several of Chief Philip Bernard's descendants, particularly those of Newel Doodoo Phillips, lived in Guysborough County for spells of time.

122 John Umlah, a soldier during the Seven Years' War, afterwards received land, first at Chester and then on the eastern side of St. Margaret's Bay. He knew the local Mi'kmaq well, and may even have recommended Chief Bernard to Michael Francklin, the Indian commissioner at the time, for special consideration.

123 Michael Francklin (1733–82) lived part of the time in Windsor and also maintained a town house on Birmingham Street in Halifax. He spoke English, French, and Mi'kmaq. As a young man he learned Mi'kmaq after he was captured while out hunting around Shubenacadie in 1754 and stayed with the Mi'kmaq several months to learn their language. Francklin was lieutenant governor from 1766 to 1772 and Indian commissioner from 1777 until his death in November 1782. He died suddenly in Halifax, probably of a heart attack, while distributing blankets to the Mi'kmaq.

124 A concise history of Chief Philip Bernard's grant at the Head of St. Margaret's Bay, as well as information on some of the early members of the Phillips family, may be found in Nik Phillips, *Mik'wie'ttm Ta'n Kis Teliaq Aqq Ni'n Majukwattm Ta'n L'nui Wetapeksi* (Remembering the past and following my Mi'kmaq roots), *Mi'kmaq-Maliseet Nations News*, May 2014, 15–16. Phillips, one of the authors of this chapter, is a descendant of Chief Philip Bernard.

125 Sir Richard Hughes was lieutenant-governor of Nova Scotia from 1778 to 1781, and Sir Andrew Snape Hamond was lieutenant-governor from 1781 to 1782. The description of the tract bestowed on Chief Bernard by Hamond reads: "Beginning at the upper bound of Land Granted Benjamin Green Esquire on the East side St. Margaret's Bay, thence to run South thirty degrees East four hundred and Eighty Rods, thence North thirty eight degrees East two hundred and twenty four rods, thence North thirty degrees West till it comes to a Cove on St. Margaret's Bay, thence to be bounded by said Cove and the Shore of St. Margaret's Bay to the bound first mentioned, Containing in the whole Five hundred and fifty acres." NSARM, RG 20, Series C, vol. 95, 72–3, "Licence of Occupation to Philip Bernard, Solomon Bescoloon and Thomas Ambroise, St. Margaret's Bay, 24 June 1782, Signed A.S. Hamond, countersigned by Richard Bulkeley, Provincial Secretary." This licence was declared to be of the "usual tenor" of licences in the province, which meant there were conditions attached to it, such as the need to improve a certain amount of acreage within a given time allowance. This licence pertained to a tract smaller than many other licences of occupation allocated to Aboriginal groups in Nova Scotia in the following years, and it made no mention of any right to hunt in surrounding forests or fish in nearby waters. Instead of being given to ensure continuance of a traditional Aboriginal subsistence round, it may have been offered as an inducement for Chief Bernard's group to start farming. Gillian Allen, "Licenses of Occupation in Nova Scotia: Is a Reserve by Any Other Name Still a Reserve?" Discussion paper, Ottawa, 8 November 2006, 21; Gillian Allen, personal communication.

126 NSM, Library, Piers Papers: Burial Practices, 2, "Lone Cloud to Piers," 7 June 1913. At one of the last traditional burials in this ancient gravesite, the body of a chief who died in the woods near Liverpool was suspended and smoked until it dried and then brought by canoe and buried at the Indian Point cemetery near French Village. Lonecloud claimed that an elderly Mi'kmaw woman he knew still living in Halifax in 1913 had seen the body brought in for burial. One wonders if the chief might have been Chief Philip Bernard.

127 NSM, Printed Matter File, "Jerry Lone Cloud to Harry Piers," 7 June 1913 and 24 July, 1916; Whitehead, *The Old Man Told Us*, 96. Jerry Lonecloud claimed that St. Margaret's Bay was the place where a party of Mi'kmaq led by Chief El-go-mard-dinip (Argomartin) raided a Spanish ship and afterwards hid the treasure it carried.

128 NSARM, RG 20, Series C, vol. 95, Governor's Licence Book, 72–3. In 1782 Brook Watson, soldier, merchant, seaman, and politician, was commissary general to the army commanded in North America by Sir Guy Carlton. After this he returned to London, where he served for a while as MP for the City of London. He became Lord Major of London in 1796.

129 NSARM, RG 1, vol. 430, doc. 26½, "Memorial of Solomon and Taumaugh, Indians of St. Margaretts Bay [*sic*, St. Margaret's Bay] and Philip Bernard Chief of the Tribe, S.F. Blowers to the Provincial Secretary," 1 February 1786.

130 Nova Scotia, Crown Lands Record Office (PCLRCO), Book 18, 24, "Crown Land Grant to Philip Barnar [Bernard], Solomon and Taumagh, registered 10 March 1786."

131 Peart, *As the Last Leaf Fell*, 51–2. The community at the Head of St. Margaret's Bay today extends from Upper Tantallon to Dauphinee's Cove. Barbara Peart, who still holds land in the vicinity of the Bernard grant, is the daughter of Asa Singleton Mason (1891–1976), a descendant of George F. Mason.

132 There is a trove of artefacts dating back at least until Woodland times in this area. St. Marguerite's River, so named by Champlain on a 1612 map, became the Northeast River, and the name "St. Margaret " (or "St. Marguerite") was transferred at a much later date to the bay into which the river flowed. Ibid., xx.

133 Ibid., 1–2.

134 NSARM, RG 1, vol. 430, doc. package 26½, "Confirmation of Grant of 500 Acres unto Philip Bernard, Chief of the Tribe of Indians, and Solomon and Taumaugh, two of his said Tribe at the Head of Saint Margaret's Bay, County of Halifax, signed [John] Wentworth, Grant no. 436, dated 3 March 1786"; NS Public Crown Lands Record Office, book 18, 24, "Crown Land Grant to Philip Bernard, Solomon and Taumagh, registered 10 March 1786." On this grant, Chief Bernard's surname was written "Barnard. The original warrant to survey was obtained when Sir John Wentworth was still surveyor of the King's Woods, and not yet lieutenant governor of the province. The grant, being held in free and common soccage, had conditions attached that required its possessors to make agricultural improvements. Yet dues for paperwork behind the grant application, as well as survey costs, seem to have been waived by the government, which may be the reason why the grant fails to appear in indexes to grant books and deed books in the usual way.

135 In lieu of clearing land, proprietors were expected to place three head of "neat cattle" on each fifty acres allotted to them, or else they could drain three acres of swamp, fill in three acres of a marsh, or fulfil certain conditions regarding mining or quarrying on their property. These latter conditions would not have applied to the Mi'kmaq at the time, though they were included in the document. NSARM, RG 1, vol. 430, doc. 26½, "Conditions attached to a grant to Bernard, Solomon and Taughmaugh, signed by John Parr, countersigned by Richard Bulkeley on 10 March 1786."

136 Virginia Miller, "Bernard, Philip," *Dictionary of Canadian Biography* online, vol. 4 (1771–1800); see also "Philip Bernard," *Wikipedia*, https://en.wikipedia.org/wiki/Philip_Bernard.

137 NSARM, RG 1, vol.430, doc. 26½, "Permission to Occupy a Tract 'during pleasure' at Pendant Bay accorded Paul Morris," 17 June 1784.

138 Alewife, which in Nova Scotia are also called gaspereau or kayak, are a species of herring.

139 In 1820 Morris noted that the five-hundred-acre grant at the head of St. Margaret's Bay, marked "A" on his plan, contained a valuable alewife fishery that was "sought after with avidity by the German settlers." He further worried that these persons had "succeeded in part on the purchase of this Land ... and having thus acquired a Right to the soil – the Indians are at perpetual variance with them about the land and fishery." Had "this Land been granted in trust solely and exclusively," he complained, "the land would have continued to support the Mi'kmaq in their traditional livelihoods." NSARM, Miscellaneous "I" Indian Land documents on microfilm, "Charles Morris' Report of the Reservations of Lands for the Indians by the Surveyor-General, dated May 1820." Morris had expressed his fears to Lieutenant Governor Sherbrook as early as 1815. NSARM, RG 1, vol. 430, doc. 151, "Charles Morris to Sir John Coape Sherbrooke," 7 March 1815. Complaints of the same type continued to come from officials familiar with the St. Margaret's Bay tract. NSARM, microfilm reel 15,290, RG 1, vol. 193, 450–6; NSARM, microfilm reel 15,315, RG 1, vol. 214½; NSARM, microfilm reel 15,472, RG 1, vol. 432, 32.

140 The description of the Ingraham's River reserve reads: "Beginning on the Eastern side of said river on the North Western Angle of Ingram's [*sic*, Ingraham's] grant – so called, thence to run North eighty degrees

East along the Rear line of said land fifty two chains fifty links – thence North ten degrees West on ungranted land forty chains – thence South eighty degrees West seventy five chains, thence South ten degrees East thirty eight chains to the upper line of land formerly granted Robert McKorn – thence North eighty four degrees East along said line twenty five chains to the River, thence crossing the same to the place of beginning." Description of Land Reserved for the Indians in the Different Counties throughout the Province, County of Halifax, St. Margaret's Bay, 1820, NSARM, RG 1, vol. 430, doc. 53. There also is a survey plan drawn up by Charles Morris in 1820 on file in the Nova Scotia Archives, and a copy of the original can be found on microfilm in NSARM, microfilm reel 14,011, Miscellaneous "I" Indian Land Records.

141 In 1794 a bounty of two hundred pounds was granted to alleviate the distress of the Mi'kmaw population. NSARM, RG 1, vol. 22, doc. 67, "Henry Dundas to Lieutenant-Governor John Wentworth," July 1794.

142 NSARM, RG 1, vol. 431, unnumbered requisition, "J. Geo. Pike to Michael Hennesy," 1799.

143 NSARM, RG 1, vol. 380, 131–2, Titus Smith Jr., *Sketches of the Eastern and Northern Parts of the Province in the years 1801 and 1802, with general observations therein …*, 3rd ed. (Halifax, 1851). Smith noted that the hills lying between St. Margaret's Bay and Windsor, as well as extending westward from Falmouth to the Sissaboo River of Digby County, were a continuation of the hills that formed the South Mountain. Though the hills north of St. Margaret's Bay were very rocky and difficult to traverse, they contained good stands of timber in 1801.

144 NSARM, RG 1, vol. 430, doc. 72.

145 John Wooden to Michael Wallace, 6 March 1801, NSARM, RG 1, vol. 430, doc. 53. At first Wooden felt disinclined to help, and Chief Bernard had to approach him several times before he would write to the lieutenant governor.

146 There is no way to tabulate how many deaths from smallpox or from cold and hunger Chief Bernard's group experienced during the winter of 1800–1801. Tom and John Phillips may have fled together in 1801 and temporarily joined a group near Antigonish under the leadership of Captain Marble (or Emable). As their names do not appear on a census for the same band in 1802, they may have returned to the St. Margaret's Bay region by that time. NSARM, RG 1, vol. 430, doc. 108, "List supplied by Wm. Nixon, 1802."

147 In consequence of these road alterations, the road now ran "through a small Piece of low Intervale (*sic*, interval) Land formed by the River dividing into two Branches where the Proprietor of all the surrounding Land/ Philip an old Indian/ had a small Garden of Potatoes." NSARM, RG 1, vol. 430, doc. 155, "James Walker to H.H. Cogswell," 7 October 1815.

148 Walker underestimated the injury to "Captain Philip," as he felt Philip did not farm extensively and was remiss in not fencing his land and not widening his fields. Instead he concluded that "hearing this old Indian well spoken of induced me to think of making him some remuneration for the trifling injury the Road has done him. He has abundance of as good land as any in St. Margaret's Bay." NSARM, RG 1, vol. 430, doc. 156, "James Walker, Road Commissioner to H.H. Cogswell," 8 December 1815. The lands office, however, remained vigilant about settler trespasses on the reserve. For instance, see NSARM, RG 20, Ser. A – Dorey, George, 1815, Nova Scotia Department of Lands and Forests, Land grant registration book, "Request by George Dorey for a lot on west side of St. Margaret's Bay, not to interfere with Mi'kmaw claims."

149 NSARM, RG 1, vol. 430, doc. 157, "Philip Belnar [Bernard], An Indian, to the King, regarding a grant for a road and compensation for injury during road widening, dated 7 May 1816. Signed by Mary Josephe separately from her husband. Witnesses James Walker of Chester, commissioner for the road work, John Jacob Mackenzie, and James Conrad of St. Margaret's Bay." Bernard was paid his five pounds' compensation for loss of land on 27 May 1816. NSARM, RG 1, vol. 430, doc. 156½, "Received from the aforesaid James Walker Esq. the Sum of Five Pounds in full of the consideration money mentioned in the annexed Deed at St. Margaret's Bay this 27 May 1816. Signed Philip Belnar and Mary Josephe Belnar." The witnesses to this transaction were James Walker of Chester, commissioner for the road work; John Jacob Mackenzie; and James Conrad. Payment of the money confirmed that the Bernards rightfully warranted compensation for injury. On 13 January 1817 Walker encountered problems in surveying the Bauls' property at East Chester, since several settlers wanted tracts surveyed out of this property without any negotiations having taken place with the local Mi'kmaq.

150 LAC, RG 10, vol. 461, doc. 333, "Survey of Indian Reserve at Head of St. Margaret's Bay, 1818."

151 Peart, *As the Last Leaf Fell*, 51–5. Peart provides an early photograph of this structure before it was torn down to make way for the Prince of Wales Hotel. Built in the 1780s, it exhibited a simple "salt box" construction and lay three-eighths of a mile south of Indian River.

152 Halifax County Deeds, Deed Book 44, 279, "Deed relating to Philip Bernard *et ux* to George Mason, 29 September 1817, registered 13 November 1818 on the oath of Thomas Holland and Jacob Burgogne." The boundaries of this particular sixty-acre lot are ambiguous. In the deed of sale the acreage is described as "being in [*sic*, on] the West side of North River at the head of St. Margaret's Bay aforesaid containing Sixty Acres more or less, being part of a grant granted unto the said Philip Barnard and Solomon and Towmaugh in the Year of Our Lord One thousand Seven hundred and Eighty Six and is abutted and bounded by Several Marks already agreed upon by both parties." More recent deeds contain descriptions of bounds that are helpful in determining the lines of the lot that was sold to Mason. One such deed pertains to the sale in February 1821 of thirty acres, held by George Mason, to his son John Mason. This tract at the head of St. Margaret's Bay begins "at a Rock on the Shore of a small Inlet [or Rivulet]," then runs north nine degrees west "along the eastern side of Lands belonging to the late Jacob Slaunwite deceased until it comes to the western angle of Lands purchased by the said George Mason from Philip Barnard, Chief of the Indians, thence to run southeast along north side of lot of land sold by George Mason unto John Gowers until it comes to the shore of said Bay – thence by several courses back to place of beginning, containing 30 acres more or less"; witness Thomas Holland, Deed Book 46, 241. A second deed, dated as recently as 12 November 1974, conveys a tract for a dollar from A. Singleton Mason and his wife Nellie Maud Mason to Barbara Peart, and describes the property as "[b]eginning at the point on the northern boundary of the old Chester Road where said boundary is intersected by the southeast boundary of the Philip Barnard *et al* grant, thence west along the boundary of the Old Chester Road to the southeast boundary of land of the Estate of John Mason, thence northeasterly along the northeast boundary of the Philip Barnard *et al* grant to the place of beginning." Halifax County Deeds, Deed Book 2519, 697–701, and accompanying Tax Deed, 736.

153 Before his death in 1864, Thomas Phillips Jr. became "a well-known man who lived at the foot of Ponhook Lake, Hants County, N.S., where he had a sort of half-way house." (From Lonecloud's words, one might infer that Phillips, as a noted hunting and fishing guide, was trying to emulate George Fréderic Mason's practice in the late 1800s of providing accommodation for those he guided.) Lonecloud also held that Thomas Phillips Jr. was a *métis*, the son of a "Micmac man and a French woman." NSM, Printed Matter File, Piers Papers, "Jerry Bartlett-Alexis

[Jerry Lonecloud] to Harry Piers," 11 June 1914. Thomas Ambroise, who was a member with Thomas Phillips Sr. of the St. Margaret's Bay band in the 1780s, was also an Acadian or *métis* originally from Piziquid (now Windsor). One of his daughters probably wed Thomas Phillips Jr.'s father. This man, Thomas Phillips Sr., visited Halifax in 1797 along with his wife and seven children. LAC, MG 23, G-II, Monk Papers, Accounts, 1213, "Thomas Philips, wife and children, entry for 1 July 1797." The same man would have been Jerry's great-grandfather. Jerry held that his maternal grandfather, Thomas Phillips Jr., had been born just before 1800 "at the foot of Big Indian Lake, near Indian Hill at the Head of St. Margaret's Bay," but he failed to give his grandfather's parents' names. Thomas Phillips Jr. left St. Margaret's Bay around 1840 and joined the Panuke (or Ponhook) Lake Mi'kmaw settlement back of Windsor. In 1860 he accompanied Edward, Prince of Wales, on a hunting expedition through the Rawdon Hills. He died in 1864 at nearby Three Mile Plains.

154 NSM, Harry Piers Papers, Ethnology: Genealogy, 33, "Jerry Lonecloud to Piers, *Vide* 24 June 1922."

155 Jeremiah Bartholomew-Alexis, or Jerry Lonecloud, claimed that "Old Tumar" (Thomas Phillips Jr., c.1795–1864) was his maternal grandfather and that he knew something of Phillips's personal history. In 1922 Lonecloud informed Harry Piers, curator of the Nova Scotia Museum, that a century previously the "wife of Old Tumar of Indian River, at the Head of St. Margaret's Bay," had been shot by her son-in-law, a person Lonecloud described as a Mohawk called "Sunislars." Sunislars had told his mother-in-law he was taking his wife, Mary Ann Phillips Wallace, and their children away to live in the Cape Sable region. When "Tumar's wife" tried to prevent Wallace from leaving St. Margaret's Bay the two became embroiled in a heated argument, until Sunislars "fired over a fence at Tumar's wife and killed her." NSM, Harry Piers Papers, Ethnology: Genealogy, 33, "Jerry Lonecloud to Piers, *Vide* 24 June 1922."

Sunislars was first tried at Halifax and then by a man who may have been Chief Louis-Benjamin Peminout Paul (who died in early 1842), since Lonecloud seems to have equated him with the father of the Mi'kmaw judge Christopher Paul Peminout. The Mi'kmaw judge in question, however, may also have been Peter Peminout Paul, a brother of Louis-Benjamin Peminout Paul who was the official Shubenacadie-based Mi'kmaw judge before Christopher Peminout Paul "hearing all cases and settling all parts of Micmac Law." NSM, Printed Matter File, Harry Piers Notes, "Regarding Chief Francis and Peter Paul," n.d. Sunislars, the

so-called Mohawk, was Lonecloud's pseudonym for a
non-Indigenous settler from Yarmouth County named
Tom Wallace. Wallace and Mary Ann Phillips had wed
in the late 1830s, and the couple, then living at Chezzetcook, had a daughter Marguerite who later married
a Mi'kmaw man surnamed Francis. After shooting
Tom Phillips Jr's wife, Wallace first fled into the interior of Yarmouth County, where Lonecloud averred he
gave his name to "Wallace Lake" in the northeastern
sector of Yarmouth County. He was apprehended,
however, and tried at Halifax, released, and re-tried in
a Mi'kmaw forum. NSM, Printed Matter File, Harry
Piers Notes, "Regarding Chief Francis and Peter
Paul," n.d. In the 1870s Wallace was shot by another of
Lonecloud's relatives, Chief Louis Luxey (or Alexis).
According to Lonecloud, Thomas Phillips Jr. had some
kind of lien on Luxey to avenge the wrong done to him,
which Luxey eventually fulfilled by shooting Wallace.
"Dan Bowers later found his skull, identifiable by the
wear patterns on its teeth made by clenching a smoking
pipe, at Wallace Bridge, three miles south of Wallace
Lake, near Kempt." This skull "had shot holes in it."
NSM, Harry Piers Papers, Ethnology: Genealogy, 33,
"Jerry Lonecloud to Piers, *Vide* 24 June 1922." Entries
in the registers of St. Gregory's Parish, Liverpool add to
information found in Harry Piers's files. In an odd twist
of fate, after her first husband's death Tom Wallace and
Mary Ann's daughter Marguerite Wallace wed Louis
Luxey Sr's eldest son, Joseph Luxey. Moreover, after
Louis Luxey shot her husband Tom Wallace, Mary Ann
Phillips married Lonecloud's father, Abraham Luxey
(Alexis). Without this additional information from
church records, Lonecloud's account of what happened
to the wife of Old Tumar remains confusing.

156 Ruth Holmes Whitehead, *Tracking Dr. Lonecloud: Showman to Legend Keeper* (Fredericton: Goose Lane Editions, 2002), 30.

157 LAC, CO 218/2/150-52; 97, "Regarding Trial of Peter Paul
of Hammonds Plains, Supreme Court of Nova Scotia,
Brenton Halliburton, Judge of the Nova Scotia Court
Supreme presiding," 12 May 1830.

158 The transfer of the road allowance and the conveyance
of 60 acres to Mason meant that Bernard's grant, though
still in the vicinity of 430 acres in size, had lost most of
its arable land.

159 NSARM, Microfilm Reel 3535. Nova Scotia, *Journal of
the Legislative Assembly*, 1854, Appendix 26, part 2, 211,
William Chearnley, "Report of the Commissioner of
Indian Affairs for Nova Scotia." Chearnley argued that
occupants of such "grants" should be obliged to "shew

title to the lands in question (lengths of holding not being allowed as a plea to title)."

160 NSARM, RG 1, vol. 430, doc. 54, "Description of the
land received for the Indians in the different Counties
throughout the Province. by Charles Morris, Surveyor
General, 1820."

161 *Journal of the Legislative Assembly*, 1854, Appendix 26,
211–12, "William Chearnley to Joseph Howe," 4 March
1854.

162 NSM, Piers Papers, Burial Practices, 2, "Lone Cloud to
Piers," 7 June 1913. According to Jerry Lonecloud, in the
early nineteenth century a chief of the St. Margaret's
Bay area was given a traditional burial. He had died
in the woods near Liverpool. His body was suspended
and smoked until it had dried and then was brought by
canoe to the Indian Point cemetery near French Village.
It was the last interment made in this grave site. Lonecloud claimed that a very elderly Mi'kmaw woman he
knew, who was still alive in Halifax in 1913, actually saw
the body brought in for burial. One thus wonders if the
deceased might not have been Chief Philip Bernard.

163 Nineteenth-century census data indicate that not all
Mi'kmaw individuals having the surname "Phillips,"
"Philips," or "Philip" are descendants of Chief Philip
Bernard of St. Margaret's Bay. Phillips found in Halifax, Hants, Kings, and Annapolis counties were often
children or grandchildren of Chief Bernard. Several of
Chief Bernard's grandchildren lived at Rawdon, among
them Alexander and Joseph Phillips. These men are
identifiable because they travelled with a Wapanoag man
from Martha's Vineyard named John Occam. Others are
harder to identify. Jerry Lonecloud's mother, a daughter of Thomas Phillips, often called herself "Mary Ann
Thoma," rather than Mary Ann Phillips. Whitehead,
Tracking Doctor Lonecloud, 30. Certain Phillips residing
in Pictou and Guysborough Counties may have been
Bernard's descendants, although this is uncertain. By
contrast, at least one family of Mi'kmaw Phillips in Cape
Breton stem from a different ancestry. Phillips at Wayco-
bah, Cape Breton, hold that their surname arose from a
union between a European man surnamed "Phillips" and
a Mi'kmaq woman. A Mi'kmaw individual, Alexander
Phillips, was probably the "Old Alex Philips" residing at
Tuft's Cove around 1870. NSM, Printed Matter File, "A
Short History of the Mic Mac Indians in Halifax County,
Nova Scotia, since Confederation, by J.C. Cope, Enfield,
Hants County," 9 February 1926. In 1853 Joseph Phillips,
Mary Anne Phillips, Hannah Phillips, and Madeline
Phillips lived in Guysborough County. NSARM, RG
1, vol. 430, doc. 73, "List of Articles issued by William

Chearnley, Commissioner of Indian Affairs, with the names of the Indian Men & Women to whom the articles were issued, Halifax, 31 Dec. 1853." Another "Indian List" for 1855 shows a Joseph Phillips living with his wife and three children, as well as a Francis Philips with a wife and six children living in Pictou, along with John Occam's brother, Samuel Occam. The same year another Thomas Phillips lived with his wife and two children at Shubenacadie, Hants County. NSARM, MG 15, vol. 5, doc. 69, "William Chearnley, Indian Agent, Indian List for the Year 1855." Louis Phillips, who was a brother of Newel or Noel Phillips (c.1830–1916) of Elmsdale, lived in Halifax County in 1855. Newel was likely a cousin of the guide Thomas Phillips and so also may have been a grandson of Chief Bernard. The first provincial census that lists Mi'kmaw households, the census of 1871, unfortunately appears too late in time to enable one to draw firm connections between the Phillips living in the 1850s and those listed from 1871 onward. In 1871 a cooper named Michael Philip lived at New Glasgow along with his wife Sally Philip and four children, James, twenty, John, nineteen, and Donald and Michael, both four. Meanwhile Joseph Philips lived at Howley's Ferry in Cape Breton. He and his wife Mary had six children, Anne, twenty-seven, Harriet, twenty-four, Susan, twenty, Mary, seventeen, Will, fifteen, and Noel, six. In 1881, Joseph Phillips lived at Salmon River, Truro. Joseph, a forty-six-year-old hunter, was accompanied by sixty-four-year-old "Magdlin [*sic*, Magdeline] Philips" and a ten-year-old girl, "Annmagda [*sic*, Ann Magdeline]." Persons having the surname "Phillips" also lived in 1881 at Antigonish and New Glasgow. According to the 1881 census for Antigonish-Saint Joseph's District, Noel Phillips, a forty-seven-year-old cooper, lived with his wife Mary Ann, thirty-five, and six children, Levi, eighteen, Alex, sixteen, Sarah, twelve, Anne, ten, Frank, seven, and Joe, 4. At New Glasgow John Philip, aged twenty-five, had a wife Jennie who was twenty, and a son Philip, five. In 1912 two persons in Antigonish County named Noel Phillips died. The first Noel, said to be eighty years old, had been a cooper and was buried at St. Ann's, near Summerside, in December 1912. The second Noel Phillips, who was approximately the same age, died on 30 December 1912 and was buried at Pomquet. (These may even reflect a duplicated entry for the death of the same person – as occasionally happens when recorders are not sure of a person's exact date of birth.) NSARM, Historical Vital Statistics, Antigonish County Deaths, Registration Year 1912, Book 2, p. 159, no. 935, and Book 14, p. 355, no. 2129. According to the 1891 federal census, persons with the surname "Phillips" lived at Pictou Landing and North Sydney. There were two separate households at Pictou Landing. The first was headed by thirty-five-year-old John Phillips, who had a wife Jenny, thirty, and four children, Alex, twelve, Hannah, ten, Mary, five, and John, three. The second household was composed of twenty-seven-year-old Joseph Phillips, his wife Jennie, and a son, James, who was two. No Phillips lived at Whycocomagh in 1891 where a number of Phillips reside today, but at North Sydney, then known as "Howley's Ferry," Noel Phillips, twenty-seven, and his wife Annie, twenty-two, had a son Peter who was seven months old. Noel Phillips probably was a son of Joseph Phillips of Howley's Ferry. The Phillips of the Northumberland Strait area and Cape Breton are likely ancestral to the Mi'kmaw Phillips of Newfoundland. Oral traditions from Cape Breton also suggest that Phillips there were not descendants of Philip Bernard of St. Margaret's Bay.

164 NSARM, RG 1, vol. 430, doc. 72, "Account of Mi'kmaq at Horton and in Kings County," 1800. These Mi'kmaq visited Roman Catholic priests at Minudie and Memramcook. NSARM, RG 1, vol. 430, doc. 66, "George Oxley to James Brenton, Charles Morris and Michael Wallace," 10 April 1801.

165 LAC, RG 10, vol. 459, doc. 333, "Regarding 300 acres at St. Margaret's Bay, by Thomas Holland 11 July 1818." Holland became a son-in-law of George Mason.

166 Francis Caninic Paul married Catherine Pennel from Gold River.

167 Around 1834, Chief Bernard's granddaughter, "Rosy Phillips," married Christopher Paul of Ingraham's River, Halifax County, and in 1836 their son, Larry Phillips, was baptized at the Church of Our Lady of Mount Carmel in Prospect, south of Halifax. Registers for the Parish of Our Lady of Mount Carmel, Prospect, 1823–36, "Baptism of Larry Phillips, D. O'Connor, priest, officiating." From 1826 onward a number of grandsons and granddaughters of Chief Philip Bernard appear in the Our Lady of Mount Carmel registers. For instance, in 1826 "Joseph Phillip and Mary" appear with "Peter Tony and Sally Phillip" and "Tom Hammond and Mary Phillip." Francis Paul, who eventually joined Tom Phillips at Panuke Lake, had the nickname "Caninic," or "ugly crying face," because he had cried a fair deal as a child. He grew into a very tall and stocky man, standing six feet, two inches. In his younger days he hunted at Vinegar Lake, near Hubbards. "Vinegar" in this context is a corruption of the Mi'kmaw word "Caninic." Local settlers often said "Winick" for "Caninic." "Winick" in turn was pronounced "Vinick" in the German language

spoken around Hubbards, and eventually became "further corrupted into Vinegar." NSM, Printed Matter File, Piers Papers, Ethnology: History, Geography Board of Canada, Notes, "*Vide* Jerry Lone Cloud," 30 August 1918. Ruth Whitehead states that Christopher Paul and Francis Paul were brothers. Whitehead, *The Old Man Told Us*, 250. Francis Paul in his later years lived at Panuke Lake, and in 1902 died at the age of ninety-two years at nearby Ellershouse. Though Thomas Baul [Paul] of East Chester had two sons, Francis and Abraham, these men do not seem to have been closely related to Francis Caninic Paul. The Francis Paul associated with the East Chester Reserve died around 1843. NSARM, RG 20, "C," vol. 90, doc. 45.

168 NSARM, RG 1, vol. 432, 62–63, "Regarding Division of Reserve at Ingraham's River into Lots, as requested by Titus Smith, c.1852." John Spry Morris was surveyor general of Nova Scotia from 1831 to 1853. Though the Ingram's River reserve was roughly laid out in 1820, it was not formally surveyed until 1832, and, as mentioned, a second time in 1852.

169 The official 1852 survey, and the accompanying order-in-council, are found in LAC, RG 10, vol. 460, file 18, "Ingram's (or Ingraham's) River."

170 NSARM, RG 1, vol. 432, 60; 71–2, "Joseph Howe, Western Tour, 1842."

171 Peter Toney and Sally Phillips's names appear in the registers of the Church of Our Lady of Mount Carmel at Prospect.

172 NSARM, RG 1, vol. 432, doc. 60, "Memorandum of Joseph Howe regarding Ingraham's River Reserve," 1843. The watershed area around Newport was called *Nelegakumik* by the Mi'kmaq.

173 Ibid.

174 Ibid.

175 Documents regarding Francis Philips and Louis Paul's situation at Ingraham's River, NSARM, RG 1, vol. 432, docs. 47, 64–6, 70–7, 82. The reserve lay near a large grant of fifteen hundred acres accorded Charles Ingram et al. in 1765. NSARM, RG 1, vol. 430, doc. 72, "William Chearnley to Messrs. Webber and Company, Ingraham's River," 25 July 1853.

176 Information courtesy of Gillian Allen, senior research officer for the Kwilm'kw Maw-klusuaqn Negotiation Office, which operates in the field of Aboriginal rights and treaty rights research, negotiation, and litigation. Kwilm'kw Maw-klusuaqn takes its direction from the Assembly of Nova Scotia Mi'kmaw Chiefs in working with the province and the federal government on rights implementation.

177 LAC, RG 10, vol. 460, file 18, "Regarding Ingram's (or Ingraham's) River."

178 LAC, RG 10, vol. 459, "S.F. Fairbanks to J. M. Andrews, Bridgewater," December 1871. This inquiry arose in response to a request from the House of Commons for information on the number of "Indian grants in Nova Scotia" and for the names of the Indian commissioners who exercised jurisdiction over these tracts. LAC, RG 10, vol. 2004, file 7687.

179 That James Lane reported only salmon and trout could be found in 1886 along the sector of the river lying within the reserve may have meant that only salmonids of the landlocked variety were present by this time, and that anadromous and catadromous species of fish could no longer ascend and descend the river. This was not always the case. In 1843 Howe had met Francis Phillips and Louis Paul fishing for alewife and eels at weirs on the reserve. Lane's report, however, also may have played down the presence of eels and alewife, if they still existed, owing to the government's determination to acquire the land for other than Mi'kmaw subsistence purposes. LAC, RG 10, vol. 2130, file 25,584, "Report, James Lane to Desmond," 24 May 1886; "Desmond to Indian Affairs," 11 June 1886; "Desmond to Caleb F. Hubley," 18 February 1886.

180 LAC, RG 10, vol. 2130, file 25,584, "Report, James Lane to Father A.P. Desmond," 24 May 1886; "Desmond to Indian Affairs," 11 June 1886; "Desmond to Caleb F. Hubley," 18 February 1886.

181 When the issue was raised again in 1899, the only reason the province did not push through a surrender of the Ingraham's River reserve was that its agents could not locate enough Mi'kmaw persons connected with the tract, scattered as they were by this time throughout central Nova Scotia, to sign a cession. LAC, RG 10, vol. 2130, file 25,534, "James McNamera to J.D. McLean," 26 April 1899; "Memorandum to the Secretary of Indian Affairs," 27 April 1899.

182 For a broad examination of the conditions under which these surrenders were signed, see Anita Tobin, "The Effects of Centralization on the Social and Political Systems of the Mainland Nova Scotia Mi'kmaq: (case studies: Millbrook – 1916 & Indian Brook – 1941)" (master's thesis, Saint Mary's University, 1999), 28–33.

183 Conversation with Fred Phillips of Cambridge, 18 October 2013.

184 NSARM, RG 1, vol. 430, doc. 53, "Charles Morris' Description of land Reserved for the Indians in the different Counties throughout the Province, County of Halifax, St. Margaret's Bay, 1820." Morris ignores the fact that the tract was given to Bernard and his associates in

"free and common soccage" and instead writes about "Tract A, the Bernard *et al* grant" and "Tract B, the Reserve at Ingraham's River," as if both parcels of land were set out by order-in-council right from the beginning.

185 Joseph Howe, Nova Scotia's Indian commissioner in 1842 and 1843, accordingly filed plans and descriptions relating to this tract, and filed them among documents pertaining to reserves throughout the province. NSARM, RG 1, vol. 432, "Map and Notes of the Indian Lands at St. Margaret's Bay, including Map of Part of the Indian Lands in Nova Scotia, 1842 – St. Margaret's Bay." See also Nova Scotia, *Journal of the Legislative Assembly*, 1843, Joseph Howe, "Report on Indian Affairs," 25 January 1843, and Appendix 1, 3.

186 Peart, *As the Last Leaf Fell*, 49–50, 52–7.

187 LAC, RG 10, vol. 2130, file 25,584, "Memo regarding Bernard *et al* and Charles Glode grants," 22 March 1895; "Hayter Reed, Deputy Superintendent General of Indian Affairs, to James Austin, Chief Clerk, Crown Lands Department, Halifax," 26 March 1895; "Austin to Hayter Reed," 10 May 1895. Austin, who was misinformed, thought that the Head of St. Margaret's Bay grant had been set out by order-in-council. For this reason he included it in a list of reserves managed by the province until Confederation, after which the lands "passed to the control of the Dominion Government."

188 The unsold portion of this old grant seems to have reverted by some mysterious process to the province, as Crown land. The part sold in 1817 still remains in private hands, and has changed ownership only a few times since the original sale.

189 From a note handwritten in pencil by Harry Piers on pages 129–30 of a copy of volume 1 of Campbell Hardy's *Sporting Adventures in the New World; or Days and Nights of Moose-Hunting in the Pine Forests of Acadia* (London: Hurst and Blackett, 1855), housed in the library of the Nova Scotia Museum in Halifax.

190 Father Pacifique, who knew Lonecloud well, held that "Lake Tomaeg" (Lake Thomas) which lies west of Halifax and is currently the water reservoir for the community of Fall River," was named after Lonecloud's "great grandfather, Thomas Germain (Selmah)." In the 1850s Lake Thomas was part of the Shubenacadie Canal route. While Père Pacifique did not specify whether Thomas Germain was Lonecloud's maternal or paternal great-grandfather, it is possible that Thomas Phillips Sr.'s full name was Thomas Germain Phillips. Pacifique, "*Le Pays de Micmacs": Études historiques et géographiques* (Québec: Société de Géographie de Quebec, 1928), 276; Pacifique, *Le Pays des Micmacs* (Restigouche, QC: Ste.

Anne de Restigouche, 1935), 289. A fall zone once lay between Miller Lake and Thomas Lake, which accounts for the place name "Fall River." The Mi'kmaq had an encampment ground here and used the waterway and portage route to connect with the Shubenacadie Valley.

191 See Whitehead, *Tracking Doctor Lonecloud*, 32. Abraham (or Abram) Bartholomew-Alexis did not return, and was probably killed by persons who stole his prize money.

192 In about 1923 Lonecloud told Clara Archibald Dennis (1881–1954), a reporter for the *Halifax Herald*, "My mother was Mary Ann Tomah from Windsor, Nova Scotia. Mother told us about her home in Nova Scotia. She told us about her place at St. Margaret's Bay – where the hydro-electric land is now, where the mill is and the electric plant. Mother's father had bought it, and Mother was his only heir." NSARM, Clara Dennis Notebooks, interview with Lonecloud, c.1923; also quoted in Whitehead, *Tracking Doctor Lonecloud*, 53.

193 Tom Phillips of Panuke Lake was the father of both Newel Phillips and Jerry Lonecloud's mother Mary Ann Phillips.

194 Author conversation with Fred Phillips at Cambridge, 18 October 2013. Fred Phillips related this fact without any prior inquiries or prompting, so this knowledge is deeply entrenched in the oral tradition of his family.

195 From Harry Piers's notes on pages 129–30 of the Nova Scotia Museum's copy of Hardy, *Sporting Adventures in the New World*, 1.

196 NSM, Harry Piers Papers, Ethnology, n.d. (1919). See also information acquired by the Nova Scotia Museum from Jerry Lonecloud between 1910 and 1930; NSM, "Notes by Harry Piers from Conversations with Jerry Lonecloud," edited and annotated by Ruth Holmes Whitehead; Whitehead, *The Old Man Told Us*, 250. Ruth Whitehead and Deborah Trask searched the Old Windsor burying ground but "could find no trace of the memorial," which they thought might have fallen victim to the ravages of time or vandalism. Whitehead, however, makes no attempt to reconcile the fact that Phillips's death occurred in 1864 with uncontestable evidence that Thomas Chandler Haliburton retired to England in 1856, eight years before Phillips's demise.

197 There also is no evidence that Haliburton, after his departure to England in 1856, ever arranged while living overseas for the erection at Windsor of a stone over the guide's grave.

198 As always, caution is needed while tracing family ties: there were Phillips living at this time at St. Croix, Hants County, among them the family of Charles D. Phillips, who were not Mi'kmaq.

199 NSARM, RG 1, vol. 431, doc. 5, "Petition of Paul Joseph Stevens, Noel Morris, Charles Lewis, Peter Mews [Meuse], Thomas Phillips and John Simons, in all 38 persons. At Windsor there is a scarcity of animals and they need blankets for approaching winter," December 1834.

200 NSARM, RG 1, vol. 430, doc. 28, "Lewie McWilken regarding the state of the Mi'kmaq at Windsor," 30 December 1836.

201 The one hundred acres laid out in 1852 for Christopher Paul at Panuke Lake was listed on this survey plan as occupied by Christopher Francis, rather than Christopher Paul. Two adjoining parcels were recorded as having been laid out for "Jacob Francis" and "Noel Francis." At first glance, this suggests that Francis Caninic Paul, who lived during his final years at Panuke Lake, was Christopher Paul's father, and that Christopher on occasion took his father's first name "Francis" as his surname. Yet the chronology does not permit this assumption. Francis Caninic Paul died at age ninety-two at Ellershouse in 1902, which means he would have been born c.1810, and as Christopher Paul was married to Rosy Phillips in 1836, Christopher and Francis Caninic would have been about the same age. One can only assume that the surveyor Redden in 1852 confused Christopher and his brother Francis when ascribing Mi'kmaw names to the lots he laid out. Some of Francis's sons adopted the nickname "Caninic." In 1870 a "John Caninic" lived near Louis Phillips at a Mi'kmaw community of twenty-seven families at the forks of the Preston and Guysboro roads. NSM, Printed Matter File, "Joseph C. Cope to Harry Piers," 9 February 1926; ibid., J.C. Cope, "A Short History of the Mic Mac Indians in Halifax County, Nova Scotia, Since Confederation," 1926.

202 NSM, Printed Matter File, "Jeremiah Bartlett-Alexis [or Lonecloud] to Harry Piers," 11 June 1914. Lonecloud, who refers to Thomas Phillips as the son of a Mi'kmaw man and a "French woman," does not identify Phillips's mother by name. She likely was Acadian, since the Phillips family had contacts with Acadians at Windsor, Annapolis, and the French Shore. Newel Phillips, for instance, married an Acadian woman named Martha Comeau.

203 Albert Edward, Prince of Wales (1841–1910), became Edward VII in 1901.

204 NSM, Printed Matter File, "Lone Cloud to Piers," n.d.

205 Hardy, *Sporting Adventures in the New World*, 1.129.

206 Ibid., 132.

207 Ibid., 129.

208 Ibid., 133–55.

209 LAC, RG 10, vol. 460, doc. package 17, "Survey plan of Ponhook Lake Reserve, dated the 6th and 7th of February 1852, signed by John Redel, Dept. Surveyor;" ibid., "Plan of Ponhook Reserve, dated 25 October 1852." When originally surveyed, the reserve was supposed to flank the St. Croix River, but a mill site granted to James Mosher cut it off from the water. The Mi'kmaq had to cross this mill site to launch their canoes In 1959 the reserve, though reduced to only 263.3 acres, was described as existing "as an Indian Reserve long prior to Confederation." NSARM, Miscellaneous "I" Indian Land documents on microfilm, reel 14,011, "Reserves transferred to the federal government at Confederation, 1959." The Panuke reserve is also mentioned in 8 Eliz. II, chap. 3, 1959, 24.

210 NSM, Printed Matter File, "Joseph C. Cope to Harry Piers," 16 April 1926. Ben Morris, son of Sebmolie Mollise, had deep roots in the Halifax-Dartmouth region. His grandfather had camped at Morris Lake in Dartmouth, which still bears his name. Ben was born at "Shag Bay" (Shad Bay), next to Prospect Bay, and was a relative of Paul Morris of Sambro.

211 George Elliott Clarke discusses the multi-ethnic composition of the Three Mile Plains community in Ashok Mathur, Jonathan Dewar and Mike DeGagne, eds., "'Indigenous Blacks': An Irreconcilable Identity?" in *Cultivating Canada: Reconciliation through the Lens of Cultural Diversity* (Ottawa: Aboriginal Healing Foundation, 2011), 399–406. Clarke, who is a poet, writer, playwright, and professor, knows first-hand of this crucible, since he was born at Three Mile Plains in 1960.

212 Campbell Hardy, *Forest Life in Acadie: Sketches of Sport and Natural History in the Lower Provinces of the Canadian Dominion* (London: Chapman and Hall, 1869), 295.

213 Whitehead, *Tracking Doctor Lonecloud*, 32.

214 NSARM, Miscellaneous "I" Indian Land documents on microfilm (taken from Crown Lands Records), reel 14,011, packages 34, 74 and 77, "Letters, surveys and field notes regarding the St. Croix Indian Reserve No. 34 in Hants County, including A Sketch of John Todd's and John Starks adjacent lots of land on the south side of St. Croix River by Robert King Jr., surveyor, dated 11 December 1827"; "Plan of John Todd's and P. Scott's lands – each roughly of 200 acres, by Bray Smith, 26 November 1852, extracted from Land Book EE, 129 (P. Scott had taken over the Stark grant)"; "James Davidson's survey of 1870"; "James Davidson's account c.1870 of trespass on the reserve (of 263 acres)"; "Plan of Survey of Indian Reserve by R.W. McKenzie dated 15 July 1905 showing the tract claimed by the St. Croix Lumber Company within the Stark and Todd grants, included in application of

C. Henry Dimock"; "Letter from R.W. McKenzie to J.D. McLean, Secretary of the Department of Indian Affairs, Ottawa, 18 July 1905"; Deed Book 82, 162, "Minas Basin Pulp and Paper." The 1827 and 1852 survey plans showed an ungranted area large enough to encompass the reserve, which was laid out just above where the St. Croix River (still known in 1827 as the "Pirquid River" or Piziquid River) flowed out of Panuke Lake. The tract was accessed by a secondary road that crossed over the uppermost end of Panuke Lake on a wooden bridge. The lines of the Stark and Todd grants nevertheless were later found to penetrate the reserve. McKenzie in 1905 complained bitterly about the confusing state of overlapping grants in the area. Meanwhile, the Minas Basin Pulp and Paper Company, the successor to St. Croix Lumber Company, wishing to have some certainty about the boundaries of their tract, paid part of McKenzie's survey.

215 Ibid., "Report on Panuke Lake, regarding houses that existed on the reserve on 25 October 1852 on property surveyed by Mr. Redden the same year." Though the official date for the establishment of the Panuke Reserve No. 34 remains 3 March 1852, there are indications that surveys of land for the Mi'kmaq were made in 1827 and 1837. Four hundred acres of land apparently had been laid off for Tom Phillips and Christopher Francis Paul by John Spry Morris in December 1837. Originally, the reserve was comprised of four one hundred-acre lots that formed one large rectangular piece. By the time the large triangular chunk had been carved out of the reserve, one of these lots belonged to Christopher Francis, a second to Noel Francis, a third to Jacob Francis, and a fourth to Tom Phillips, who had died by this time. Ibid., file no. 17, package 4, "Undated report," c.1870; LAC, RG 10, vol. 459, doc. 25, "Letter from James Davidson to Samuel P. Fairbanks, Commissioner," 23 August 1870. Davidson noted that a man named Adolphus Von Guzman was cutting hemlock trees on the reserve for their bark. Guzman reputedly had entered into an arrangement with Christopher Francis "for all the timber he might require." Francis, who had temporarily gone to New Brunswick, expected Guzman to pay for the timber when he returned.

216 Scott Paper bought out the Minas Basin Pulp and Power Company, which in the 1950s acquired the operations held by the St. Croix Lumber Company. Hants County Deeds, Deed Book 82, 169, "Minas Basin Pulp & Power lands, from plan of survey, dated 15 February 1951"; "Deed and survey plan pertaining to lands owned by Minas Basin Pulp and Paper Company Limited dated 23 February 1951." The 1951 plan showed the reserve as being 268.5 acres. In 1974 John Covert of the Legal Surveys Division of the Department of Energy, Mines and Resources contacted H.B. Robertson, director of surveys at the Department of Lands and Forests, and asked for confirmation that the Land Office no longer had any "interest to the triangular jog cutting into the Reserve." "Covert to Robertson," 16 May 1974, and "F. Archibald to Wayne Cochrane, Solicitor, Department of the Attorney General," 27 May 1975, both in NSARM, Miscellaneous "I" Indian Land documents on microfilm, reel 14,011. While there have been repeated calls since 1975 for the restoration of the entire 400 acres, the reserve today stands at 311.8 acres.

217 Speck, *Beothuk and Micmac*, 102. Chief Philip Bernard's descendants, being members of the Annapolis band as well as the St. Margaret's Bay band, are listed by Speck, although by 1914 they have been joined by Frank Pennel (Penall) and John Hammond, who both belong to the Gold River band of Lunenburg County. There were other incomers too. Speck noted that Joseph Brooks hunted around Uniacke Lake, not far from Mount Uniacke, and that John Ferris (Faris) was the son of an Englishman who traded in the St. John Valley and then settled at Windsor, where he wed a daughter of Gorham Paul. John Jadis's first wife was a daughter of Lewis Morris of Shubenacadie, while his second wife was the widow of Michael Thomas of Panuke Lake and Shubenacadie. NSARM, Printed Matter File, "Louis Noel MacDonald to Harry Piers," 20 November 1923. Stephen Hood and Abram Hood held hunting territories on the Paradise Lakes and down the Sand River, while Aleck Morris hunted on Gaspereau Lake. Louis Labrador accessed his hunting grounds by way of the Upper La Have River.

218 Around this time young men had less opportunity to engage in economic activities that could support a family. With government control over the landscape, forests were being cut down, fisheries dammed, and the need to travel widely to find wage work was increasing. For a discussion of the toll caused by economic uncertainty, see William C. Wicken, *The Colonization of Mi'kmaq Memory and History, 1794–1926: The King v. Gabriel Sylliboy* (Toronto: University of Toronto Press, 2012), 174.

219 Newel Phillips must have been a young-looking man throughout most of his life, for enumerators made mistakes about his age by as much as twenty years. For instance, In 1881 Newel, born in 1830, would have been fifty-one, but on that year's census for Nova Scotia Newel's age is recorded as thirty, perhaps because he

had such a young wife (the same census lists Martha Comeau as being twenty-seven, which was probably close to her true age), but presumably he also looked much younger than his age. Ten years later, however, the enumerator for the 1891 census put down Newel as a fifty-year-old widower, which was at least closer to his real age, which was sixty-one. Canada, Census of 1881, Halifax County, Polling District No. 19, 11; Canada, Census of 1891, Halifax County District 34, Gays River Area, Polling District No. 19, 10.

220 Jacob Lewis Phillips of "Indian settlement," Shubenacadie, was baptized on 23 May 1880 at St. Bernard's Roman Catholic Church at Enfield. Thomas Barnaby and Jeannet Barnard were his godparents. Jacob remained at Shubenacadie for the rest of his life. The St. Bernard's Parish registers from 1857 onwards sporadically show the names of Newel Phillips's sister and brother, Mary Phillips and Louis Phillips. Other Phillips who appear include Margaret Phillips, daughter of Joseph Phillips (who was probably another grandson of Chief Philip Bernard) and Magdalene Tony, baptized at Elmsdale on 21 July 1880, with Peter Paul and Lucy Francis standing as sponsors.

221 In the early 1880s, Newel Phillips, Ann Phillips, and Noel Benard headed the only three Mi'kmaw households at Elmsdale. In 1881 Noel, who was thirty years old, and his wife Jeannet, who was twenty, were the youngest members of the settlement. Canada, Census of 1881 for Gays River. Ann Phillips wed a man surnamed Barnaby from Miramichi, and in 1881 was a forty-year-old widow. Mary, Joseph, and Louis Phillips were Newel's siblings. Margaret, a daughter of Joseph Phillips and Magdalene Toney, was baptized at St. Bernard's Roman Catholic Church on 21 July 1880, with Peter Paul and Lucy Francis acting as sponsors. Newel and wife Martha had an infant, Jacob Lewis Phillips, baptized on 23 May 1880 at Indian Settlement, Shubenacadie, with Thomas Barnaby and Jeannet Barnard acting as sponsors. As Jacob's name does not appear again in the documentary record, he may have died young. Joseph Louis Phillips, a son of Charles Phillips and Margaret Cope, was born on 2 May 1909 and baptized at St. Bernard's parish church on 20 May 1909.

222 Isaac's father-in-law, Francis E. Phillips, appears as "Frank Philip" on the 1891 federal census for the Polling District of Lawrencetown Lane, Annapolis County. He was forty-seven in 1891 and his wife, Mary Paul, was thirty-eight. The couple had three children, seventeen-year-old Elizabeth or "Lizzy," fifteen-year-old "Betsy," and John, who was six months old. Lizzy's

husband Isaac Phillips was also living with them, though Isaac was mistakenly listed on the census sheet as their son. Other members of the household were Francis's brother-in-law John Bennet, John Bennet's eight-year-old son John, and a forty-four-year-old widow, Harriet Phillips, who was either Francis's sister or his sister-in-law. Isaac and Elizabeth shared the surname "Phillips" prior to their marriage. Elizabeth Phillips's name is found in 1907 in the registers of St. Joseph's Parish, "Baptisms in the District of Cornwallis, Kentville and Aylesford, 1853 onward." She must have been a paternal cousin of her husband. These kin relationships are examined in Nik Phillips's comprehensive genealogy of the Phillips family of central Nova Scotia entitled *Mikwie'tt Ta'n Kis Teliaq Aqq Ni'n Majukwattm Ta'n L'nui Wetapeksi, Mik'wie'ttm Ta'n Kis Teliaq Aqq Ni'n Majukwattm Ta'n L'nui Wetapeksi* (Remembering the past and following my Mi'kmaq roots), *Mi'kmaq-Maliseet Nations News*, May 2014.

223 Canada, Census of 1891, Halifax County District 34, Gays River Area, Polling District no. 19, 10. Of Newel's three sons – Isaac, born in 1869; Jacob Lewis, born in 1881; and Charles Joseph, born 7 April 1882 – only Charles Joseph remained at Elmsdale in 1891. Newel Phillips's age on the 1891 census is given as fifty, although he was actually sixty.

224 Ibid. Joseph Jeremy, who was forty years old in 1891, and his wife Jane, forty-seven, had five children: Joseph, eight; Frank, seven; Mary J., six; Lena, four; and Douglas, eight months. Louis Peters, who was forty-five, hailed originally from Bear River. Louis had a wife, Susan, forty-four, and a daughter Ellen, three. Newel (or Noel) Hammond was thirty and his wife Jasmine was thirty-three. The men worked as coopers and basket makers. Isaac Phillips had left by this date to live with Francis Phillips at Cambridge, Kings County.

225 NSARM, Historical Vital Statistics, Kings County Marriages, Registry Year 1870, Book 1826, p. 39, no. 56, "Marriage of Francis E. Phillip and Mary Paul, 23 September 1870 at Kentville." Frank was twenty-seven and Mary was seventeen. Mary gave her address as "Berwick," while Frank gave his as "Everywhere." Frank's parents were "Francis and Margaret Phillips of Gold River," while Mary's parents were listed as "Joseph and Sally Paul from Kingston, Nova Scotia."

226 An alternative name for Morris Lake, which was named after the Mi'kmaw Morris family who used to camp there, was "Minister Lake." Upton, *Micmacs and Colonists*, 184.

227 According to the 1901 federal census, Isaac and Elizabeth Phillips were living at Elmsdale in that year. Isaac in

1901 was listed as born on 22 May 1868, Elizabeth on 22 February 1873, and "Tressa" (Theresa) on 1 May 1898. Their sole Mi'kmaw neighbours, Joseph Brooks Jr. and his wife Mary, both in their thirties, had a one-year-old son. Canada, Census of 1901, Enumeration District Gay's River, Colchester County, 14 (nos. 53 and 54). Isaac and Elizabeth moved back to the Annapolis Valley in 1907. The 1911 federal census for Cornwallis, Kings County, lists Isaac as born in February 1869, Elizabeth in December 1874, Theresa in June 1898, Thomas in July 1901, and Charles in August 1907. These are all incorrect enumerator "guesstimates." Thomas Phillips was ten years old on the 1911 census, so he was born in 1901. Canada, 1911 federal census, Kings County, Nova Scotia, Census of Cornwallis electoral district (this census is very faint and hard to read). Isaac's, Elizabeth's, and Theresa's correct birthdates were as listed on the 1901 federal census, and Charles was born at Cole Harbour on 4 June 1907 according to his baptismal certificate. Baptismal registers of St. Joseph's Church, Kentville, "Certificate of Baptism of Charles Phillips, born at Cole Harbour 4 June 1907, baptized at Kentville in July of 1907, son of Isaac and Elizabeth Phillips, sponsors Philip Paul and [? illegible] Francis." NSARM, Historical Vital Statistics, Registration Year 1907, 99200641, "Delayed Registration, dated 1972, of Charles Phillips, born at Cole Harbour on 4 June 1907, living in 1972 at Cambridge Station, Kings County." In 1911, Isaac, Elizabeth, Theresa, Thomas, and Charles were all living at Cambridge. Canada, Census of 1911, Cornwallis Enumeration District, no. 29, 2. Their neighbours were Joseph Brooks and Stephen Knockwood, both sixty-four years old, and Toney Francis, Joseph Pictou, Stephen Pictou, and Mary and Paul Phillips. Meanwhile, in 1901, Frank Phillips and his wife Mary Paul had moved from the Annapolis Valley to Hammonds Plains. Although Frank was listed on the 1901 census for Hammonds Plains as sixty years old, he was actually fifty-seven, while Mary Paul, listed as forty-nine, was forty-eight. Canada, Census of 1901, Halifax District No. 33, Hammonds Plains I, 14.

228 Kings County Deeds Office, Kentville, Deed Book 42, folio 601, "Cambridge Reserve, Registered 27 February 1880." The original reserve was only 9¾ acres, thirty-eight square rods. It was purchased by the Crown in February 1880 from Albert A. Webster and Margaret Jane Webster. Isaac and Elizabeth Phillips raised their children and grandchildren on the Cambridge reserve. After twenty-nine years in the same community, Elizabeth died at age sixty-six of tuberculosis at Cambridge in 1936. Her husband outlived her by five years. NSARM,

Historical Vital Statistics, Kings County Deaths, Registry Year 1936, Book 148, 911, "Death of Elizabeth Phillips. Elizabeth, daughter of Frank Phillips and Mary Paul." According to her death record (which is more likely to be accurate than federal census records) Elizabeth was born at Kingston in the Annapolis Valley on 25 September 1869. Her body was buried at Kingston on 13 June 1936.

229 Alex Cope, born c.1856, the son of Frank Cope of Beaver Dam near Sheet Harbour in Halifax County, was a well-known guide. In his early sixties he lived at Truro. NSM, Printed Matter File, Piers Papers, "Micmac Indian Hunters and Guides of the Old Days: According to Lewie Newell McDonald of Enfield, N.S., as told to Harry Piers, 28 April 1921." He trapped and hunted near Debert, Colchester County, where his daughter Bridget was born in 1870. NSARM, Historical Vital Statistics, Hants County Marriages, Registration year 1905, Book 1824, p. 80, no. 46, "Marriage at Enfield of Joseph Julien, 29, born at New Glasgow [actually at Thorburn or Heatherton, Pictou County], son of Noel and Madeleine, and Bridget Cope, 15, born at De Bert [sic, Debert], daughter of Alex Cope and Mary, 19 June 1905." In honour of this man a hiking trail, Sandy Cope's Trail, located near Earltown in Colchester County, was recently named.

230 Charles Joseph Phillips, the husband of Margaret Cope, is listed erroneously on the 1911 census as "Henry Phillips."

231 After the Phillips family, the next-largest Mi'kmaw family recorded on the federal census for Elmsdale in 1911 was that of the Jeremys, whose roots lay in an eighteenth-century Mi'kmaw settlement at La Have. The patriarch of the Jeremy household was Joseph Jeremy Sr., also known as Joseph Howe Sr., an elderly widower in 1911. Joseph Howe changed his surname from "Jeremy" to "Howe" in the mid-1850s. Near him were his son Joseph Howe Jr., Howe Jr.'s wife Lizzie, and two young children, Ernest and Irene. Albert and Elizabeth Jeremy, who were in their teens, lived with their grandfather. There was also a three-year old girl named Mary Hammond who was being fostered by the Jeremy family. Louis Tony, a thirty-five-year-old widower, lived next to the Jeremys with his seventeen-year-old daughter Annie and his nephew Richard Basque. Martin Sack, his wife Mary Jane, and their four young children Louis, Joseph, Clarence, and Alfreda lived nearby. Joseph Brooks, who was forty-four, and his wife (unnamed) had two daughters, Ann, eleven, and Sarah, eight, while Susan Peters, a widow, lived with her granddaughter Ellen Paul and Douglas Jeremy, her grandson. Peter Paul, twenty-eight, and his wife Lena had two young sons, William and Leo.

They lived next to "May Lonecloud," the twenty-one-year-old daughter of Jeremy Lonecloud and Elizabeth Paul.

232 NSM, Printed Matter File, "List of Supporters for Mr. Peter Paul, Shubenacadie Indian Reserve, 27 July 1912." In 1866 and 1867 large numbers of Mi'kmaq from southwestern Nova Scotia attended political meetings at James Cope's house, located at the junction of the Preston and Old Guysborough roads. Discussions focused on treaty rights and land issues, and attendees included Newel Phillips and his brother Louis.

233 The Mi'kmaw population of Halifax County between 1800 and 1838 rose from a few scattered families to 101 families or 265 individuals. NSARM, RG 1, vol. 430, doc. 25. Families included the Copes, Labradors, Lewises, Pauls, and Phillips.

234 In 1916, sheet no. 66 of a geological survey map showed the Elmsdale site clearly marked as an Indian reserve. When Jacob Gilby told the Phillips, Howes, and Simons to vacate his property in 1916, the local Indian agent tried to counter Gilby's eviction notices by referencing this map. Yet it soon became evident that the drafters of the survey map had mistakenly assumed a reserve was laid out, owing to the presence of the longstanding Mi'kmaq settlement there.

235 NSM, Printed Matter File, Piers Papers, Ethnology: Correspondence with the Department of Indian Affairs, Item 5, "Notes taken during a meeting held at Shubenacadie on 26 July, 1916, and relayed by Jerry Lonecloud to the Deputy Superintendent Indian Affairs, J.D. McLean, on 17 July 1916."

236 NSM, Piers Papers, Ethnology, Correspondence with Department of Indian Affairs, item 3, draft of letter by Harry Piers, "Statement regarding Deposition of Jacob Gilby, Jerry Lone Cloud to J. D. Maclean, Indian Affairs," 6 July 1916.

237 NSM, Piers Papers, "Statement regarding Deposition of Jacob Gilby …," 6 July 1916.

238 Newel Phillips died on 28 November 1916 of pneumonia and complications arising from kidney disease at Camp Hill Hospital, Halifax. His death was recorded twice, once in 1916 and again in 1917. The 1916 entry is inaccurate, since it states he died on 29 November 1916 in Victoria General Hospital of kidney disease at seventy-eight years old, which makes him eight years younger than he was. The second death entry records him dying at age eighty-six years of pneumonia and kidney disease on 28 November 1916. At the bottom of the second certificate the words "Same [person] as in number 1072" (the erroneous entry) are written. NSARM, Historical Vital

Statistics, Halifax County Deaths, Registration Year 1916, Book 34, 326, no. 1072; ibid., Registration Year 1917, Book 34, 355, no. 1155, "Death Certificate[s] for Noel Philips."

239 NSM, Printed Matter File, "Martin Sack to John Erskine," in Erskine, "Erskine's Micmac Notes, 1958," 15. On 18 January 1919 Sack held that both "Elewie Doodoo [or Louis Phillips], who died 38 years ago his age unknown, but he died from old age" and his "brother Newell Doodoo, who died 2–3 years ago at 84 (sic, 86 years) years" were long-time residents at Elmsdale, as was Joe Howe who was 74 years old. Louis Phillips also had resided at times at the forks of the Preston and Guysborough roads from 1867 until his death NSM, Printed Matter File, Joseph C. Cope, "A Short History of the Mic Mac Indians in Halifax Co., 1926." For Sack's involvement with the Elmsdale land claim, see NSM, Piers Papers, Ethnology, Correspondence with the Department of Indian Affairs, "Martin Sack's notes addressed to H.J. Bury Esquire," 18 January 1919.

240 Margaret Cope Phillips gave birth to ten children but only seven survived past childhood. James died, unwed, relatively young. Joseph Louis, born on 2 May 1909 (and baptized at Enfield on 20 May 1909), died of pulmonary tuberculosis on 28 March 1923 while still a schoolboy. Charles Alexander, born on 7 May 1912, died on the train tracks near Africville at age 44 in April 1956. Catherine, by contrast, was the longest lived. Born in 1913, she died at age ninety-four on 24 February 2007.

241 Birch Cove was an ancient encampment site, occupied by Mi'kmaq principally during the summers, but it likely was temporarily vacated by the Mi'kmaw for at least a decade following the disastrous Duc d'Anville expedition of 1746 when sickness brought by the French spread to the Mi'kmaw population. Sharon Ingalls and Wayne Ingalls, *Sweet Suburb: A History of Prince's Lodge, Birch Cover & Rockingham* (Tantallon, NS: Glenn Margaret, 2010), 1–19.

242 Barbara (Mason) Peart's *As the Last Leaf Fell* contains a photograph of Lonecloud and a young boy, whom she identifies at Alfred Ruben Cook (p. 3). According to Peart, the two had been hunting around Fairview in the early 1920s. The Nova Scotia Museum photographic collection has a much better print, from the same photographic plate, taken at Climo Studios in Halifax. Ruth Whitehead identifies the boy in the print as Lonecloud's son Louis. Whitehead, *Tracking Doctor Lonecloud*, 115.

243 William Chearnley in the mid-1850s gave only an approximate location of this encampment ground. When required to visit the camp of one Sally Paul, Chearnley asked for directions, only to be told that "you only pass

along the road to Birch Cove and the sarten [it is certain that] you Hear Children cry!!!" NSARM, MG 1, vol. 1506, "Chearnley Papers," n.d.

244 LAC, RG 10, vol. 9029, file 51/18-11, "Letter to Mr. Rice, Cole Harbour Reserve," 23 October 1950. Though the signature has been blacked out, there can be little doubt that the letter's author was Margaret Cope.

245 For a discussion why such arrests began to take place in greater numbers from 1927 into the 1950s, see Wicken, *Colonization of Mi'kmaq Memory*, 56–75.

246 NSARM, Historical Vital Statistics, Halifax County Deaths, Registration Year 1957, 2779, death certificate of Charles Joseph Phillips, seventy years of age, born at Elmsdale on 7 April 1882, died of pneumonia at Colwell Road, Cole Harbour, on 21 April 1957. Funeral service by Dartmouth Funeral Home, burial at Eastern Passage, Dartmouth.

247 NSARM, Historical Vital Statistics, Halifax County Deaths, Registration Year 1956, 2726, "Death of Charles Alexander Phillips, 43 years 11 months old, born at Elmsdale on 7 May 1912, died in Fairview, Halifax, on 28 April 1956." At the time of his death he lived at 47 West Street, Halifax. He was buried at Hillcrest Memorial Gardens. He was recorded as being "English" on his death certificate, and that was also the racial designation he chose to give to the authorities when he did a stint in the military in his early twenties. He struggled with his Mi'kmaw identity, despite his parents' obvious pride in being Mi'kmaq. He also identified his father as "English" and claimed that both his parents – and not just his mother Maggie Cope – hailed from Sheet Harbour.

248 Interview with Fred Phillips, son of Charles A. Phillips and Florence Mae Pippy, Cambridge, NS, 18 October 2013; informal conversations among Fred Phillips, Nik Phillips, and Janet Chute during fall 2013 and spring 2014.

249 C.I. Fairholm, "Memorandum to the Director of Indian Affairs, with attached 'Report on Field Interviews with Micmacs of Nova Scotia and the areas in which they Reside, and the Unoccupied Reserves of Nova Scotia Mainland, 1957,'" transcript and report prepared for the Department of Indian and Northern Affairs, Ottawa, 11 July 1957; Ottawa, Department of Indian Affairs, DINA File 201/1-1, Report of Bart Mckinnon and D.R. Cassie, "Summary of Interview with Micmacs living on the Cole Harbour Reserve … [where] The only resident was Mrs. Margaret Phillips," attached to "Report on Field Interviews with Micmacs of Nova Scotia and the areas in which they Reside and the Unoccupied Reserves of Nova Scotia Mainland, 1957." A copy of this document file is housed in the Treaty and Aboriginal Rights Research Centre (TARR), Indian Brook, Shubenacadie, file 92-1004-09-018, 43–4. Lisa Lynne Patterson discusses Meggie Cope's hostility to centralization in "Indian Affairs and the Nova Scotia Centralization Policy" (master's thesis, Dalhousie University, 1985), 13.

250 McKinnon and Cassie incorrectly surmised that Charles Phillips "probably came from the Digby area," since his mother was a Comeau from the French Shore of southwestern Nova Scotia.

251 Janet Chute remembers her father telling her that such a practice operated in the late nineteenth century along the Cornwallis River near the Chute family farm in Kings County, so she was not surprised when members of farming families currently at Cambridge and Berwick stated they had heard of a similar tradition. Cursory perusal of deeds books and lawbooks, however, gave no evidence of such a tradition ever being codified. It is an area of Mi'kmaw-settler relations that needs much further research.

252 NSARM, Historical Vital Statistics, Registration Year 1907, 99200641. According to the 1881 federal census, Newel, Martha, and twelve-year-old Isaac lived at Elmsdale.

253 For an accessible site, which states that *Kampalijek* is the Mi'kmaw name of the Annapolis Valley First Nation, also known as the Cambridge Station community, see "Mi'kmaq," https://en.wikipedia.org/wiki/Mi%27kmaq. Following the departure in 1950 of Mr. Rice, the last Indian agent at Cambridge, John Toney was elected chief the same year and a band council was created. Though in the 1940s a large segment of the Cambridge Station population moved from Annapolis to Indian Brook, members of the Phillips family had lived at both Cambridge and at Shubenacadie long prior to this date, and for years had travelled between the two communities. Charles Phillips was the first chief elected in the post-centralization era. During the 1960s a Mi'kmaq person named Wobay Kitpou or "White Eagle" (whose surname was Pictou), a member of the Bear River band, was close friends with the Phillips and the Knockwoods who lived at Cambridge before he moved to British Columbia. A photograph of Mrs. Charles Phillips, taken by Wobay Kitpou, is housed in the Photo Collection of NSARM. A number of newspaper clippings relating to Kitpou's activities during the 1960s also may be found in the Archives of Ontario in Toronto under the heading "Shaman Wobay Kitpou – Newspaper clippings, 1970–1978."

254 In 2013 Fred Phillips shared his memories of the centralization era with Nik Phillips and Janet Chute. "Peter

Poulette, Charlie Phillips's wife's brother," he stated, "asked Charlie to join their family potato picking in Maine. In the early 1940s Charles and his family went to Cape Breton, to Castle Bay, Eskasoni. It was the time of centralization and the government made promises to establish work opportunities at the two growth centres of Eskasoni and Shubenacadie. At the time they continued to go to Maine to pick potatoes. Charles Phillips and his family were only in Cape Breton five or six years before removing to Shubenacadie for a while. Charlie Phillips made baskets and sold them in Halifax. He selected ash and maple off neighbouring farms and would give the farmer, off whose land he got the wood, a basket in return." Chute and Phillips, interview with Fred Phillips, Cambridge, Kings County, 18 October 2013.

255 While many leasehold properties are used for hunting camps, large parcels of land along the lower reaches of the local lake and river system are occupied by Nova Scotia Light and Power (now Nova Scotia Power Incorporated), which since 1922 has operated an electric generating station in the St. Margaret's Bay area. Electricity generated at the St. Margaret's Bay power station is conveyed through high-tension power lines carried by a string of large pylons leading into Halifax.

256 There is a photograph of the Salmon Hole Dam opposite page 159 in Harry Bruce, *RA: The Story of R.A. Jodrey, Entreprenuer* (Toronto: McClelland and Stewart, 1981).

257 "Report on Field Interviews with Micmacs of Nova Scotia … 1957," 46. The comments made in this field report reveal an extremely narrow understanding, since Panuke Lake boasts a panoramic view and has sands beaches, clear water, and recovering forest resources. If provided with a proper road, with a bridge, it could be accessed in less than half an hour by car from Windsor.

258 Jeffrey L. McNairn, "Meaning and Markets: Hunting, Economic Development and British Imperialism in Maritime Travel Narratives to 1870," *Acadiensis* 34, no. 2 (2005): 14.

CHAPTER 8

1 Beamish Murdoch, *A History of Nova-Scotia, or Acadie* (Halifax: James Barnes, 1865), 2.372n4. Murdoch's meeting with John Pennel Sr. may have been serendipitous, since Murdoch did not begin collecting information for his three-volume historical work on Nova Scotia until the early 1860s. K.G. Pryke, "Murdoch, Beamish," *Dictionary of Canadian Biography* online, vol. 10 (1871–80); P.D. Clarke, "Beamish Murdoch: Nova Scotia's National Historian," *Acadiensis* 21, no. 1 (1991): 85–109. Beamish Murdoch had a relative living in Lunenburg County, Margaret Ott Beamish, who married Thomas Akins (1762–1832), for several years a part-time Indian agent at Liverpool; it is possible that Akins in his later years directed Murdoch to "Captain Penall." Captain Penall also was mentioned by Lunenburg County historian Mather Byles Desbrisay, who spelled the chief's surname "Agdamoncton." M.B. Desbrisay, *History of the County of Lunenburg* (Halifax: James Bowes and Sons, 1870), 154.

2 "Argomartin" appears in various sources as "Agamatec," "Agamatine," "Agdamoncton," "Agomartin," "Agoumartin," "Argamartin," and "Hagomartin." "Bernard" appears as "Pennel," "Penall," "Parnall," "Pahnel," and "Panhorne." While "Penall" was the most common spelling until the mid-twentieth century, this chapter adopts the more modern spelling "Pennel," which is the way many of Chief Argomartin's descendants spell their surname today. The surname "Pennel" bears no relationship, other than a phonetic resemblance, to the Isle of Jersey surname "Pennell." There are Planter families with the surname "Pennell," so one has to be careful that the person encountered in documents is indeed Mi'kmaq. For instance, in Lunenburg County Thomas Pennell, who had a wife named Abegail Crosby, was a Planter from Marblehead, Massachusetts. The surname "Pennell" derives from "Pinel," a Jersey surname that is still common at Marblehead. Matthew Pennell was appointed lighthouse keeper at Sambro near Halifax on 28 September 1754. NSARM, RG 5, series A, vol. 1b, No. 113, "Appointment of Matthew Pennell as lighthouse keeper at Sambro in 1772, with a salary of £100 per annum from the government." In 1768 Pennell and his family received a grant of six hundred acres at Sambro, and in 1801 he was succeeded in his office by his son. NSARM, Vertical File, Harry Piers, Biog.: Pennel family of Sambro. Captain Argomartin's descendants dropped the surname "Argomartin" as early as 1807, when the Gold River band fell under the auspices of an Indian agent, though the surname survived for a few more years in the Annapolis Valley region.

3 Murdoch, *History of Nova-Scotia*, 2.372n4.

4 Ibid.

5 Jerry Lonecloud, born Jeremiah Bartholomew-Alexis (1854–1930), was a son of Abraham Bartholomew-Alexis and Mary Ann Phillips of Salmon River, Digby County, and a descendant of the noted eighteenth-century Cape Sable chief Charles Alexis. "Jerry Lonecloud" was Jeremiah's stage name. He was also called "Jerry Bartlett." Nova Scotia Museum (henceforth NSM), Printed Matter

File, Piers Papers, "Jerry Lone Cloud to Harry Piers, Director of the Nova Scotia Museum of Natural History," 24 July 1916. There was a man named André Martin, belonging to the Cobequid band, who acted as an interpreter at treaty negotiations in 1749 between Governor Edward Cornwallis and representatives of the Mi'kmaw, Passamaquoddy, and Malecite nations held aboard the warship *Beaufort*, anchored in Chebucto Harbour. In 1760 André Martin received a pass from the colonial government allowing him to move freely throughout the province. NSARM, RG 1, NSARM, RG 1, vol. 209, Despatches from the Board of Trade and Plantations and Secretaries of State to the Governor of Nova Scotia, "Minutes of Council," 14 August 1749. NSARM, RG, vol. 36, doc. 48½, "Treaty signed aboard the ship *Beaufort* anchored in Chebucto Harbour," 15 August 1749; NSARM, RG 1, vol. 165, doc. 79a, "Pass to André Martin, one of the Cobequid band of Indians, freely to pass from and to any part of this Province," 26 August 1760. During the French regime the Marquis of Denonville bestowed the seigneury of Saint Matthieu upon Matthieu Martin of Port Royal in 1689. Douglas Ormond, *The Roman Catholic Church in Cobequid, Acadie, 1692–1755, and Colchester County, Nova Scotia, 1828 to 1978* (Truro, 1979). Matthieu's seigneury lay north of Cobequid Bay, and the surname "Martin" afterwards appeared among members of the Wakobeilk, or Cobequid, band. Andrew acted as an interpreter on occasion, and in 1752 an individual whose full name was Andrew (or André) Handley Martin, who may have been the same person mentioned above, was one of the signatories to a peace and friendship treaty between the Mi'kmaq and the British at Halifax. A "son of Andrew Martyn" also was identified in 1794 by provincial Indian commissioner George Henry Monk as hunting in the woods between Piziquid (Windsor) and St. Margaret's Bay. MG 23, GII-19, vol. 4, George Henry Monk Papers, 1748–1823, vol. 4, 1061, Entry for 11 February 1794, "Regarding the son of late Andrew Martyn."

6 Lonecloud told Piers that he first heard about the capture of the Spanish ship laden with gold from an elderly Mi'kmaw woman while he was living in the United States. The woman claimed she was a descendant of one of the Mi'kmaq involved in the taking of the ship. Years later Lonecloud heard a similar story from an elderly Mi'kmaw man living in Nova Scotia.

7 Ruth Holmes Whitehead, *The Old Man Told Us: Excerpts from Micmac History, 1500–1950* (Halifax: Nimbus, 1991), 85. Joseph Argimault was a late seventeenth-century chief, negotiator, and intermediary who lived in the Petitcodiack River region, near the Isthmus of Chignecto. He had a daughter Agnes and three sons, Étienne, François, and Philippe, who were baptized at Beaubassin between 1680 and 1685. Philippe and Agnes were, respectively, nine and ten years old at the time of their baptisms, while Étienne and François were in their twenties. NSARM, registers on microfilm, *Copie des Registres de l'Etat Civil de differents endroits de l'Acadie et de la Gaspesie, 1680–1757, de l'Archevêché de Québec, Registre des baptêmes, mariages, et sepultures à Beaubassin*. No definite kin linkages can be traced between Chief Argim8 and members of the Argomartin family, however. Moreover, Abbé Charles-François Bailly, who married and baptized members of both families between 1768 and 1772, always distinguishes in his missionary registers between those he identified as "Argimeau" and those he considered to be members of the "Argomatine" family.

8 LAC, MG 18, F18, "Cabane No. 17, "Cape Sable," 4, typescript of a French census, dated 1708, of Indigenous encampments among the Penobscot by Abbé Pierre La Chasse, including nominal census information on Indigenous families, men, women, and children, belonging to villages on mainland Nova Scotia and Cape Breton (Isle Royale) most likely gathered by Abbé Antoine Gaulin. *Recensement genal fait au mois de Nouembre mile Sept cent huit de tous les Sauvages de l'Acadie que resident dans la Coste de l'Est, Et ceux de Pintagouet et de Canibecky, Famille par Famille, Leurs ages – Celuy de Leurs Femmes et Enfants avec une Recapitulation a la fin de la quantité d'hommes et de garçons capable d'aler a La guerres, comme aussy Le recensement des francois Establis a La ditte Coste de l'Es, 1708*. The original of this manuscript, of forty folios, is found in vol. 4, no. 751 of the Edward E. Ayer Collection housed at the Newberry Library in Chicago.

9 While a relationship between Bernard Argomartin of Gold River and Michel Argomartin (or Agoumartin) of Cape Sable cannot be definitively established, Michel and Bernard may have shared an apical ancestor by virtue of the similarity of their surnames. Since Michel was older, he may even have been Bernard Argomartin's father, though this cannot be confirmed. In the 1750s, a number of persons bearing the surname "Argomartin" resided along the Atlantic coast between La Have and Cape Sable. Since François Shagwaough (or Chegua) was acting in a peace-making capacity, the authorities in Halifax issued him a passport that described him as an emissary of Chief Michel Agoumartin. NSARM, RG 1, vol. 156, 70; NSARM, RG 1, vol. 165, docs. 53–4, "Pass to François Shagwaough," 24 April 1760. There is

no record that Michel Argomartin ever signed a treaty with the British, although it's possible that he did and the treaty document was lost. Michel seems to have left Cape Sable soon afterwards and may have been the "Mich. Argomatec" who in the late 1790s lived with Captain John Minuiho's band at River Philip, Cumberland County. LAC, MG 25, GII-19, George Henry Monk Papers, Indian Accounts, 1793–99, entry for 21 March 1797; Monk Papers, Indian Accounts, 1189, 1190, 1204. Monk spelled Michel's name "Mitchell Argamore." Though it is possible that a family with the surname "Talgoumatique" at Cape Sable in the early 1700s later became known as "Argomartin," both surnames can appear on the same document. Pierre Argomartin, a member of the Cape Sable band in the 1770s and a son of Michel Argomartin, became notorious for brutally murdering three women, two of them his wives. As punishment he was hamstrung by a party of Mi'kmaq in Shelburne County in the 1790s. Pierre fled Cape Sable and lived out his final days in the Wolfville area. Thomas Robertson, "History of Shelburne County," Akins Prize Essay, 1871, typescript, King's College Library, Halifax, 5. "Peter, son of Argamartin of Cape Sable" was also mentioned in the Monk papers in the 1790s. LAC, RG 25, GII-19, Indian Accounts 1793–99, 1073. At the same time, Simon Argomartin, likely Pierre's brother, was described as elderly, destitute, and residing in Halifax County. LAC, MG 25, GII-19, George Henry Monk Papers, Indian Accounts, 1793–99, 1256, "Thomas Walker to His Excellency Sir John Wentworth," 4 June 1798.

10 Charles Bruce Ferguson, ed., *Place-Names and Places of Nova Scotia* (Halifax: Public Archives of Nova Scotia, 1967), 248. In 1842 Joseph Howe reported that the band took eight to ten barrels of eels for the winter. NSARM, RG 1, vol. 432, 71, Howe, "Western Tour, 1842."

11 "The Mi'kmaq had winter encampments in the Pockwock Lake area and would move down a path to the shores of the Bedford Basin for the summer season. It is estimated that this journey would take them about one day traveling non-stop. It is thought that their trail was close to where … Hammonds Plains Road is today … There is evidence that a footpath about 3.5 meters wide was created from Halifax (via the Windsor Road) to Lunenburg" in the early 1750s. Hammonds Plains Historical Society, *Newsletter*, February 2015–16, no. 3, 1–3.

12 On 28 June 1769 Abbé Bailly baptized "Joseph, the son of Bernard Argomatine and his wife Isabelle Angelique, the daughter of François Nankout and Marguerite Joseph." Joseph may have been the chief's youngest son. NSARM, Registers of Abbé Charles-François Bailly on microfilm, copy of old register conserved at Caraquet, New Brunswick, *Registre des actes de baptême, mariages, et sepultures faits en la nouvelle ecosse ou acadie commence le vingt unieme jour de juillet de l'annee mil sept cent soixante huit, par Mons. Charles-François Bailly, pretre missionaire des sauvages et acadiens, sujets de sa majeste britanique, 1768–1773.*

13 The names of John's and Francis's wives remain unknown. Both women, however, were living at the time of Joseph Howe's visit to Gold River in 1842.

14 George Henry Monk was Nova Scotia's Indian commissioner from 1793 to 1799 and again from 1807 to 1809. LAC, MG 25, GII-19, George Henry Monk Papers, Indian Accounts, 1217; LAC, MG 25, GII-19, George Henry Monk Papers, Indian Accounts, 1222 and 1244. On 10 November 1796 "Pahnel Agomartin" and seven young men, four boys, six women, and eight infants went to Monk's office in Windsor to acquire clothing, utensils, and ammunition worth £62.3.7. The chief returned the following November, this time with three women and three children, for more provisions and ammunition. At this time Chief Argomatin's name was written "Barnard Agomati."

15 According to historian L.F.S. Upton, British officials at this time saw the distribution of goods to the Mi'kmaq as a "temporary expedient" and those who accepted the articles as beggars. Upton, *Micmacs and Colonists: Indian-White Relations in the Maritimes, 1713–1867* (Vancouver: University of British Columbia Press, 1979), 82.

16 For instance, on 21 May 1797 "John Penall" obtained supplies for "his sons and their families in Gould River, 40 in number." Ibid., 1219.

17 NSARM, RG 1, vol. 430, doc. 146, "To Hartshorn and Boggs, Drs., for Sundries supplied the Indian by Order of His Excellency." Entry in Monk's requisition books for December 31, 1807, for "Captain Philip, Peter Morris, Penard Argamatin, Francis Penard, John Penard, and John Muse." This party annually visited a priest, "Father Poor" (Father Power), at Minudie in Cumberland County. LAC, MG 25, GII-19, George Henry Monk Papers, 1793–99, 1247.

18 NSARM, RG 1, vol. 430, doc. 96, "Names of Indians residing at Gold River, 1800." The camp of Chief Argomartin, along with his wife Isabelle Angelique Nankout, lay near the bark wigwams of the chief's sons John and Francis, who by this time were married and had children. Additional bark structures sheltered the families of two other men, Joseph Quarrett, or Momcharrett, who hailed from Minas, and Peter Docomaw.

19 One distributor of such necessities in 1801 was John Wooden at St. Margaret's Bay. NSARM, RG 1, vol. 430,

doc. 58, "John Wooden to Michael Wallace," 6 March 1801. The group had remained relatively economically independent until the smallpox epidemic. The abundance of salmon, gaspereau, and eels in the spring and fall at Gold River was usually sufficient for them, but their inability in 1801 to come down to the coast threatened their economic independence. A harvest of fish was crucial to the band, as it could be dried and then carried while Argomartin's people moved about the countryside exploiting a wide range of crucial and overlapping resource areas. Since the surrounding woods provided caribou, moose, beaver, and smaller fur-bearing animals, during the late fall and winter the Mi'kmaq hunted and trapped inland and, come spring, sold their furs and hides in Halifax. In the fall they took migrating water fowl and sea mammals; in the spring, they travelled to the Minas and Gaspereau River regions to visit, meet in councils, and engage in trade.

20 NSARM, RG 1, vol. 430, doc. 143, "George H. Monk's list of Districts, Limits and Correspondents," 20 October 1807; NSARM, RG 1, vol. 430, doc. 146, "To Hartshorn and Boggs … for Sundries supplied the Indians by Order of His Excellency John Wentworth, 1808–1809," entry for 31 December 1808, supplies for "Captain Philip, Peter Morris, Penard Argamatin, Francis Penard, John Penard, and Jno. [John] Muse [Meuse]." By this time the British considered government distribution of supplies necessary to placate the Mi'kmaq and keep them peaceful during the intensification of the Anglo-American crisis that led to the War of 1812. The 1786 grant allotted to Chief Philip Bernard, whose descendants became known as "Phillips," is discussed in chapter 7. It is likely that marital arrangements were made in the early 1800s between members of the Gold River group and the Phillips of St. Margaret's Bay as well as the Paul family of Chester.

21 Members of Chief Argomartin's band frequently camped with Philip Bernard's group at the Head of St. Margaret's Bay, so they knew about Chief Bernard's land grant. In 1782, Sir Richard Hughes and Sir Andrew Snape Hamond gave Chief Bernard a grant on St. Margaret's Bay that they later retracted because they found that the parcel already had been allotted in London, England, to Brooke Watson. Undeterred, Chief Bernard once again petitioned for land and was again successful, receiving a grant at the Head of St. Margaret's Bay. NSARM. RG 1, vol. 430, doc. 26½, "Memorial of Solomon and Taumaugh, Indians of St. Margaret's Bay and Philip Bernard, Chief of the Tribe," 1 February 1786. The second land grant, roughly the same size at the first, was confirmed on 6 March 1786 by Sir John Wentworth.

22 NSARM, Grant Book, 1765, "John Seccombe *et al*, 29,750 acres, Chester," 31/10/1765. Seccombe was an original proprietor of Chester Township and, from 1761 to 1783, pastor of Mather's New England Congregationalist Church in Halifax. Mather's Church is the precursor of what is now St. Matthew's United Church on Barrington Street in Halifax. Seccombe's church's glebe lands in Halifax, lying between South Street and the North West Arm, fell under government control after the American Revolution, partly because of Seccombe's alleged sympathies with the American cause, but mainly because he failed to improve the lands. The same fate may have befallen the land granted to Seccombe and his associates near Gold River. Whatever was the case, Seccombe's grant at Gold River was available for government distribution in 1814. S. Buggey, "Seccombe, John," *Dictionary of Canadian Biography* online, vol. 4 (1771–1800), http://www.biographi.ca/en/bio/seccombe_john_4E.html.

23 LAC, RG. 10, vol. 459, "Accounts, Petitions and Returns," indexed 1857–74, Package 3 Lunenburg (Penhall), "Charles Morris, Superintendent of Surveys to D. Crandle," 2 January 1810, and "Charles Morris to Surveyor Crandle," 10 June 1810. Morris, in drawing up an application for land to Sir George Prevost, referred to Chief Pennel Argomartin as "Penhorne."

24 NSARM, British Colonial Office Records on microfilm, CO 217/141/401, "Penhall and Thomas and 39 families of Mahone Bay want land on Gold River"; LAC, RG 10, vol. 459, folder 3, "Charles Morris, Deputy Surveyor General to Surveyors Crandle and Vaughan," 16 June 1810.

25 LAC, RG 10, vol. 459, microfilm reel C-13,324, folder or package no. 3, "Accounts, Petitions and Returns, Gold River," 18; ibid., "Charles Morris to Secretary Crandle," 16 June 1810.

26 London, Guildhall Library, "Petition of Shubenacadie band leaders to Sir John Cope Sherbrooke," 5 April 1814, press clipping housed in the New England Company Papers, MSS 7956.

27 Walter Bromley, *An appeal … in behalf of the Indians of North America* (Halifax: Ward, 1820), 40; Upton, *Micmacs and Colonists*, 165; Judith Fingard, "English Humanitarianism and the Colonial Mind: Walter Bromley in Nova Scotia, 1813–25," *Canadian Historical Review* 54 (1973): 123–51.

28 Lieutenant Governor Andrew Snape Hamond spelled his name with only one "m" although "Hammonds Plains," named after him, is spelled with a double "m."

29 To lend credence to this story, during the War of 1812 the American brig *Jane* of 224 tons, with David George as its master, was carrying a cargo of salt for the fishing

industry in northern New Brunswick and southern Quebec, and was captured by the British while en route from Liverpool to New Brunswick. It was later recaptured by the Americans on 9 November 1814. *Peabody Essex Museum* Collections, 36 (Salem, MA, 1911), 285, "American Vessels Captured by the British during the Revolution and War of 1812, from Records of the Vice Admiralty Court at Halifax, Nova Scotia."

30 NSARM, microfilm reel 4187, "History of Elmwood, written in 1944 by Mrs. R.D. Wentzell, and attached to a letter written by Mrs. Stanley Wentzell of Barss' Corners to Mr. Spidell, dated 10 May 1944." Both manuscripts were published on 20 June 1945 in a local newspaper, the *Nova Farm News*. Dwight Dorey and his sister Dora Jones directed the author's attention to this piece, which lists descendants of Tom Hammond, including Tom's son John Hammond, John Hammond's wife Susan Rafuse, and members of the Dorey family of New Germany. Dwight Dorey was national chief of the Indigenous Peoples' Assembly of Canada (formerly The Congress of Aboriginal Peoples) from 2000 to 2006 and again in 2015. He passed away on 24 May 2018. https://ottawacitizen. remembering.ca/obituary/dwight-dorey-1066149238; https://windspeaker.com/news/windspeaker-news/ former-national-chief-dwight-dorey-has-passed-away.

31 That Chief John Pennel (or Penall) Sr. spoke French indicates that he interacted with Acadians at Cobequid, Chezzetcook, or Cape Sable. It also suggests that the Pennels had some French ancestry.

32 NSARM, MG 4, vol. 98, "H," Canon Harris Papers, no. 14, "Statement of James Hammond to Canon Harris," circa 1925.

33 The family of George Mason is mentioned at greater length in chapter 7 of this volume.

34 NSARM, RG 1, vol. 432, 74, Howe, "Western Tour, 1842." Howe stated that Hammond had married Magdalene about 1817, twenty-five years before the commissioner arrived at Gold River in 1842.

35 Ibid., 72–5.

36 NSARM, MG 1, vol. 2809, Helen Creighton Collection (History 1947–59), "New Ross History, English, Irish & Scots, informant Captain Burt Ross, July 1949."

37 Joseph Howe stated that Chief Argomartin died at ninety-five years of age "about 25 years prior to 1842," or around 1817. NSARM, RG 1, vol. 432, 72–3, Howe, "Western Tour, 1842." Mather Byles Desbrisay, the nineteenth-century Lunenburg County historian, stated that the Mi'kmaq conveyed their dead to a traditional burial ground at Indian Point, Mahone Bay, so this is

undoubtedly where Chief Argomartin's body was laid to rest. Desbrisay further wrote that Chief Argomartin's son Francis Pennel Sr., who died about 1840, as well as two of Francis's sons, Newel and Peter, were buried at this site. Desbrisay, *History of the County of Lunenburg*, 153–4. The body would have been ceremonially transported in a bark shroud in the midst of a large procession of mourners.

38 NSARM, British Colonial Office Records on microfilm, 217/141/401, "Penhall and Thomas and 39 families of Mahone Bay want land on Gold River," 1818. The "Thomas" mentioned in this petition was Thomas Hammond, John Pennel's son-in-law.

39 Magdalene and Catherine remained at Gold River for at least twenty years, since both appear on a list of Mi'kmaq living at Gold River in 1855. NSARM, MG 15, vol. 5, doc. 69, "Indian List for the Year 1855 compiled by Indian Commissioner William Chearnley, Chester and Gold River District."

40 NSARM, MG 15, vol. 24, "Petition [of] Walter Bromley," 1817.

41 There are oral traditions about this woman and her activities, but her name could not be determined.

42 LAC, RG 10, vol. 459, microfilm reel C-13,324, folder or package no. 3, Accounts, Petitions and Returns, doc. 3, Gold River, 14, "Charles Morris, Superintendent General of Crown Lands to D. Crandle, 28 January 1818, regarding the petition from Penhall and Thomas on behalf of 39 families at Mahone Bay for land up the Gold River and for building materials." The Mi'kmaq, Morris added, claim they are "not interfering with the settlement at Sherbrook" and want land given to them in perpetuity at a rate of 30 acres per family or 210 acres for seven families. An 1852 report by J.S. Morris, who was then a deputy surveyor, claimed furthermore that the Mi'kmaq originally had been told there "was no free land on the west side of the Gold River at the disposal of the governor. If there ever was any in 1784, it is embraced in the Township grant." NSARM, RG 1, vol. 430, doc. 53, doc. 4, "Report of J.S. Morris," 3 September 1852; NSARM, RG 1, vol. 430, doc. 53, "Description of the lands reserved for the Indians in the different Counties throughout the Province, 1820." This last document reads: "Lunenburg 960 acres. Beginning on the Rear line of Farm lots fronting on Gold River, and on the South Eastern angle of lands Granted Althorp and Co., From thence to run North twenty three degrees West along the South boundary of said land One hundred and twenty chains – thence south on ungranted land eighty chains – thence South seventy three degrees East One hundred and twenty chains to the Rear line above mentioned – thence

North along the same eighty chains to the place of beginning – containing Nine hundred and sixty acres according to the Plan." This description, incidentally, contains no mention of Tom Hammond's fifty acres on the East Branch of the La Have River.

43 The Gold River reserve would remain unsurveyed for years. Though a rough plan was drawn up by the Crown Lands office in 1820, no formal survey of the reserve's actual bounds was undertaken until 1852, when one was run by provincial deputy surveyor John Spry Morris in response to Mi'kmaw demands that official limits be set to discourage trespassers.

44 NSARM, RG 1, vol. 432, 72, Howe, "Western Tour, 1842." Howe described the Gold River reserve as embracing "40 acres of land on the eastern side of the river," chiefly interval [between the river and the Atlantic coast], skirting the margin of the River from about a quarter of a Mile above and below the Bridge, over which the Post Road passes – also 960 acres on the western side of the River." The bridge to which Howe referred carried the old post road, which roughly followed the line of today's Trunk 3 Highway, across the Gold River. NSARM, RG 1, vol. 430, doc. 191, Joseph Howe, "Report on Indian Affairs, 1843."

45 NSARM, MG 15, vol. 18, doc. 12, "Names of the heads of the Indian Families who resided at Shubenacadie when the first attempt was made to form a settlement in 1816."

46 NSARM, RG 1, vol. 432, 72, Howe, "Western Tour, 1842."

47 Although members of Tom Hammond's family had lived at New Germany since the early 1830s, not until 1880 would the government finally survey a 953-acre tract as a reserve along the east branch of the La Have River, near Lake Peter. NSARM, Miscellaneous "I" microfilm, Indian Land Documents taken from Crown Lands Records, Document Package 26, New Germany Reserve 19A; NSARM, Miscellaneous "I" Indian Documents on microfilm, Document Package 6, "Reserves transferred to the Dominion Government by Prov. at Confederation, schedule dated 1959, Lunenburg County, New Germany Reserve."

48 NSARM, RG 1, vol. 432, 72–5, Howe, "Western Tour, 1842."

49 Ibid., 72–3.

50 Ibid.

51 Desbrisay, *History of the County of Lunenburg* (1870), 153–4.

52 NSARM, RG 1, vol. 432, 73, Howe, "Western Tour, 1842." Joseph was not "young." In 1842 he was forty-four years old, though he may have looked young to the commissioner.

53 Ibid.

54 NSARM, RG 1, vol. 432, 75, Howe, "Western Tour, 1842." When she became elderly, Mrs. Francis Pennel could not tidy and repair her homestead as easily as she could in her younger years. Howe wrote, "I slept and breakfasted at Old Mrs. Penall's, in which establishment there was a strange blending of the practices of the savage and civilized life." The dwelling's residents were "cheerful, obliging and hospitable and although not so scrupulously clean as one could have wished, no more negligent in this respect than some white families upon the shore."

55 NSARM, RG 1, vol. 432, 165–6, "Letter of Daniel Dimock of Chester to Joseph Howe reporting on the Mi'kmaq of Gold River, 1843."

56 NSARM, RG 1, vol. 432, 74–5, Howe, "Western Tour, 1842."

57 NSARM, RG 1, vol. 432, 54–8, "John Spry Morris to Joseph Howe," 23 March 1842. This is an instance of an allocation of land (in this case made in 1793) to the Mi'kmaq of Lunenburg County being taken away from Indigenous control in the early decades of the nineteenth century. Part of this small tract was allocated in November 1834 to George P. Zink for £110. The Indian Point referred to in this letter is not the site of an ancient Mi'kmaw graveyard near the town of Mahone Bay, but refers to a Mi'kmaw grant at East Chester.

58 Charles Churchill, *Memorials of Missionary Life in Nova Scotia* (Nottingham: W. Dexbdes, 1845), 186.

59 NSARM, RG 20, Series A, Land Grant Registration Books, A – Geremy [sic, Jeremy], Solomon, "Memorial of Solomon Geremy, of the La Have tribe, for a grant or license of occupation," 1784. Solomon Jeremy's descendants continued living at Church Hill near New Germany Lake into the late 1820s, when one of their number, Joseph Soulnow, sought a confirmation for the parcel supposedly allotted to Solomon Jeremy. Desbrisay, *History of the County of Lunenburg* (1895), 348, "Petition of Joseph Soulnow, New Germany, December the 11th, 1829." Members of the Glode, Labrador, Jeremy, Newel, Paul, Soulnow [Jeremy], and Toney families had by by 1840 left the vicinity of the La Have River and moved further south along the Atlantic coast.

60 The witnesses at Joseph Pennel and Sophia Rafuse's wedding were Jacob Jeremy and Marie Ann Phillips. Joseph was born to Chief John Pennel Sr. at Milton, Queens County, in 1814. See NSM, Printed Matter File, "Jeremiah Bartlett-Alexis to Harry Piers," 17 June 1919. He was listed as a "widower" at the time of his marriage to Sophia; his first wife may have been Sarah Swinemar, a daughter of Philip Swinemar and Hannah Catherine

Rafuse. NSARM, Willa J. Kaiser (née Rafuse), "Western Shore, Gold River and Martin's Point, Rafuse, Rchfus, Rayfuss, Rehfus," 27.

61 Johannes George Rafuse and Maria Elizabeth Louisa Kaiser, the daughter of Michael Keyser and Anna Marie Weiler, were married on 21 September 1818.

62 In June 1853, John Hammond and Susanna Rafuse brought their first child, Mary Ellen, to be baptized at La Have.

63 John Pennel Jr. (1811–87) and Marian Barbara Rafuse's marriage took place at Gold River on 19 December 1851. According to the church registers for St. Gregory's Parish, the witnesses to the ceremony were "[Chief] Joe Penaule and Maria Anne Phillips." Joseph Pennel was John's older brother, who died later, in 1859. John Pennel was a forty-year-old widower. Barbara was fourteen years old at the time of her marriage and fifteen in 1852 when she had her first child, Catherine. NSARM, Register of Births, Marriages and Deaths in the County of Lunenburg, on microfilm, "Conditional baptism of Catherine Penuale, daughter of Barbara Rafus, daughter of Daniel J. Rafus and Margaret Adams, and of John Penaule of Gold River, 1852." The two witnesses at Catherine's baptism were the same as for John and Barbara's wedding: Joseph Penaule and Marie Anne Phillips. Marian Barbara Rafuse was born in 1837 to Johannus Daniel Rafuse (1799–c.1870) of Martin's Point and Margaret Adams of Gold River. She would live to be eighty-one years old, dying at Gold River in 1918. At the time of her birth, Barbara's father was married to Catherine Elizabeth Demont, a daughter of J. Frederick Demont and Sophia Lohnes. Daniel and Catherine married on 28 January 1821, and the two lived together first at Martin's River and later at Gold River until Catherine's death in 1848. (Following his wife's death, Daniel moved to Centreville in Kings County.) Barbara therefore must have been illegitimate, although this fact is not explicitly stated in the documentary record. John Pennel Jr. and Barbara had eight children: Catherine in 1852, Francis (Frank) in 1853, Barbara in 1856, James in 1858, Joseph around 1860, William in 1863, John Lawrence in 1868, and Sarah in 1873. Several children's baptisms were recorded in the registers of St. Gregory's mission in Liverpool. For instance, witnesses at the baptism on 1 July 1856 of "Barbara Pennel, daughter of John Penaule and Barbara Rafuse," were James Dollement and Sophia Rafuse, the wife of John Jr.'s first cousin Joe Goose Pennel. At the time, St. Gregory's mission fell under the auspices of St. Jerome's Parish in West Caledonia, Queens County. (St. Gregory's did not became an independent parish until 1941.) After St. Jerome's Church was built in Caledonia in 1836, itinerant priests associated with it in its early days travelled throughout Queens and Lunenburg Counties. (By contrast, St. Norbert's, the oldest Roman Catholic church in Lunenburg County, built in 1839, served the town of Lunenburg and the settler population.) In the 1890s, priests associated with St. Joseph's Parish in Bridgewater occasionally visited Gold River. Roman Catholic church records for Gold River and New Germany, dating from the mid-1850s, are found in NSARM, "Register of Births, Marriages and Deaths for the County of Lunenburg, commencing in 1854 – and extending into the late 1870s," on microfilm. The original registers are housed in St. Joseph's Roman Catholic Church, Bridgewater. Though Marian Barbara Rafuse's parents were Anglican, she accepted Roman Catholicism upon her marriage to John. John and Barbara lived their entire lives in Francis Pennel's old frame house, built in 1818. Their sons Frank and William lived nearby. Frank married Mary Edna Veinotte, daughter of Zachariah Veinotte (mother unknown), while William Pennel married Catherine Eisenhauer, daughter of David and Susan Eisenhauer of Gold River. After Catherine's death, William wed Emma Zwicker Franck. William's second wife erected a gravestone in St. Augustine's Church cemetery, Chester, to commemorate her mother-in-law, Marian Barbara. Though the stone does not give birth or death dates, it does state that Barbara was eighty-one at the time of her death. Marian Barbara's sons Frank and William, despite being born a decade apart, both died in 1920. NSARM, Historical Vital Statistics, Lunenburg County Deaths 1920, book 95, p. 175, "Death of Frank Pennell"; NSARM, Historical Vital Statistics, Halifax County Deaths, book 95, p, 228, "Death of William Pennell." Frank's widow, Mary Edna (Veinotte) Pennel died in Halifax in 1965 at the age of eighty. NSARM, Historical Vital Statistics, Halifax County Deaths, Registration Year 1965, 301. Frank and William each farmed to a degree and cut timber around Gold River and Chester Basin in the early nineteenth century. Each brother had a profoundly different perception of their ethnic identity. Frank embraced his Mi'kmaw heritage, while William eschewed it. Frank's death certificate states he was a Mi'kmaq from Gold River. William's death certificate, by contrast, states he was "white," born at "Fall River Hole," Fall River, near Halifax. William, before his death, farmed acreage he purchased at Chester Basin. In 1940 one of Frank and Edna's daughters, Barbara, at age twenty-five married Thomas Harold Woods, a soldier in

the medical corps stationed at the Wellington Barracks in Halifax. NSARM, Historical Vital Statistics, Halifax County Marriages, Registration Year 1940, book 102, 35.

64 Johannes George Rafuse had property on the east side of the Gold River, while Johannes Daniel Rafuse lived at Martin's River until he moved to the Annapolis Valley. The brothers were grandsons of Johannes Rehfus (1720–98), who emigrated, aboard the *Alderney*, to Nova Scotia in 1750 from the Duchy of Württemberg, now part of southwestern Germany. During the Seven Years' War, Johannes Rehfus joined militia parties mustered to protect the settler community against Mi'kmaw raids. Around 1755 Johannes and his wife, Anna Catherina Elizabeth Rab, had a son named Johannes Rafuse Jr. (1755–1829). Johannes Jr. later wed Apollonia Berghaus (now Barkhouse) and the couple had at least twelve children, among them Johannes Daniel Rafuse and Johannes George Rafuse.

65 Jacob and Johannes petitioned in 1810 for a portion of the forfeited Seccombe grant on the west side of Gold River. NSARM, RG 20, Series C, vol. 90, doc 78, folder 1, "To His Excellency Sir George Prevost, a Petition for land from Lot Church, Jacob Rafuse, Francis Millett, Joseph Hardy, Valentine Rafuse, and Francis Meisner on the west side of Gold River containing 2,000 acres, 1810."

66 Author conversations with members of the Hatt and Kaiser families of Gold River, 2003–05; Luther Roth, *Acadie and the Acadians* (Philadelphia: Lutheran Publishing Society, 1890), 57–61.

67 After 1850 the Pennels and Hammonds at New Germany often entered into unions with persons of Germanic and Protestant background, including members of the Awalt (Avolt), Eisenor, Fredericks/Franck, Hatt, Kaiser, Meisner, and Whynaught families.

68 James Pennel, a son of Joe Goose and Sophia Rafuse, married Mary Glode and the two travelled regularly between New Germany and Queens County visiting kin. John Hammond and Susanna Rafuse journeyed to Wildcat River Reserve in Queens County where many of John's relatives lived. Joseph Hammond and his wife, Catherine Luxey, lived at Wildcat where they had a son, Joseph, in 1874. Others went to Queens County or penetrated the Cape Sable district. These included Thomas Labrador and Mary Pennel, who had Thomas in 1875; John Hammond and Elizabeth Payzant, who had Louis Timothy in 1876; James Paul Labrador and Cecelia Hammond, who had Thomas in 1882; William John Hammond and Flora Lowney, who had Catherine in 1878 and Susan Valeria in 1882; Lewis Hammond and Mary McDonald (of Jordan River), who had Romney

(?) in 1881 and Leoni in 1884; Joseph Jeremy and Jane Hammond, who had Francis in 1884; Newel Hammond and Elizabeth Tony, who had Mary in 1884; John Alfred Hammond and Amelia McDonald (of Jordan River), who had William in 1877 and Norbert Lewis in 1886; and Louis Labrador and Mary Pennel (a daughter of James Pennel and Mary Glode) of Milton, Queens County, who had Dominic in 1891. Meanwhile, Tom Hammond's youngest daughter, Selina, remained with Joseph Pennel Labrador in Shelburne County, where she gave birth to at least ten children. NSARM, Registers of St. Gregory Roman Catholic Church, Liverpool, Queens County, on microfilm.

69 LAC, RG 10, vol. 459, Package 3, Lunenburg (Penall), "Letter from E. Macdonald to Joseph Howe, Secretary of State," 4 July 1871.

70 LAC, RG 10, vol. 459, Package 3, Lunenburg (Penall), "Letter of Chief Joseph Penall to Captain William Chearnley, to be directed to the House of Assembly," 17 February 1853.

71 LAC, RG 10, vol. 459, Package 3 – Lunenburg (Penhall), "Report of W.S. Morris, Deputy Surveyor, 3 September 1852, taken from the file of A. Dingman." The letter is signed by J.S. Morris, commissioner of Crown Lands, 11 April 1857.

72 NSARM, RG 1, vol. 430, doc. 191, "Report on Indian Affairs, 1843, by Joseph Howe."

73 The Indian Department made errors, however. In 1895, the deputy minister read the document wrong and stated that one portion was 960 acres and the other was 81 acres rather than 41. LAC, RG 10, vol. 2130, file 25,584.

74 The Indian Point cemetery carried a deeply sacred significance for the Gold River Mi'kmaq. Francis, John Sr., Tall Peter, and Newel Pennel were all buried at this site. Bernard Argomartin undoubtedly also was buried there in 1817. Francis's son Newel was said to be the last Mi'kmaq interred in this graveyard. Desbrisay, *History of the County of Lunenburg* (1870), 153–4. Though the cemetery has been eroded away by the ocean, a spot near the shoreline where it lay has been designated a historic monument site. Desbrisay also stated that the Lunenburg County Mi'kmaq venerated a large wooden cross that stood at "Indian Gardens, near Cook's Falls, along the New Germany Road." When a trespasser once removed an inscription nailed to this cross, he quickly restored it after some Mi'kmaq threatened to shoot him. Desbrisay acquired his information on the Gold River Mi'kmaq in the late 1860s from Francis Pennel's sons, particularly John Pennel Jr. The data he gathered became part of a manuscript history of Lunenburg County that,

in 1868, garnered second place in the Akins competition for historical writing, held each year by Kings College. Desbrisay published the reworked manuscript in 1870 as *History of the County of Lunenburg* (republished, as a revised second edition, in 1895). The two versions are slightly different but both are informative, since they provide "a slice of Gold River Mi'kmaw life" in the late 1860s. Describing the Mi'kmaw cemetery at Indian Point, Desbrisay stated, "Thither, to rest in peace, were brought the remains of Francis, Newell and Peter, father and brothers of John Pennel, who still lives in a big house near Gold River and is one of the most expert fly salmon fishers in the country, while another brother Joseph, who died at Gold River, 'sleeps his last sleep' in the Roman Catholic burial ground at Chester." Desbrisay erred, however, in writing that "[t]he grandfather of these Penalls was Captain Penall, a Micmac who, at the age of fourteen years went with the British forces to the capture of Quebec." Their grandfather was Chief Bernard Argomartin. Desbrisay had read what Beamish Murdoch wrote concerning "Captain Penall," but as Murdoch did not clearly state who this man was, Desbrisay took him to be John Pennel Sr.'s father, rather than John Pennel Sr. himself. Chief Argomartin would have been too old to be the fourteen-year-old boy who went to Quebec: Joseph Howe asserted that Chief Argomartin died in 1817 at age ninety-five, which meant he was born in 1722, not 1745. NSARM, RG 1, vol. 432, Joseph Howe, 72–5, "Western Tour, 1842." Francis Pennel Sr.'s son Joseph (1798–1859) claimed in a petition that his grandfather Pennel Argomartin had settled at Gold River a century prior to 1853. NSARM, Miscellaneous "I" Indian Land Documents on microfilm, from Crown Lands Department, Document Package 25, doc. No. 25, Pennel Reserve No. 19, "Petition to Sir John Gaspard Le Marchant from Joseph Pennell, 1853." Desbrisay gives no indication that he knew that Chief Argomartin's son John Pennel Sr. even existed. This is not surprising, since John Pennel Sr. died around 1843, and John Sr.'s sons had moved to New Germany by 1865. Yet it does leave Desbrisay's readers with the impression that all the Mi'kmaq at Gold River were descended solely from Francis Pennel, and that Chief Argomartin occupied a more recent period in history than he actually did.

75 NSM, Printed Matter File, Jeremiah Bartlett Alexis to Harry Piers, 17 June 1919. Joseph's joke, at Nathan Hilton's expense, would have been one that Hilton, a strict Presbyterian, would not have appreciated.

76 NSM, Nova Scotia Museum Printed Matter File, "Statement of Old Lunenburg woman, who had attended the funeral of Joe Goose, or Joseph Pennell, as told to Harry Piers, n.d." This tragedy occurred in 1876, when St. Peter's cemetery was consecrated. The Mi'kmaq during the course of their movements visited Roman Catholic churches in Bridgewater, Chester, Prospect, La Have, Liverpool, and Annapolis Royal.

77 NSM, Nova Scotia Museum Printed Matter File, "Joseph C. Cope to Harry Piers," April 1926.

78 Howe wrote that at Gold River, "long celebrated for its Salmon fishery," the Mi'kmaq with their dressed flies "annually kill as many Salmon with the Rod as they formerly killed with the spear." Howe felt, however, that ultimately this industry must fail "as it had on other rivers," so the Mi'kmaq should devote their attentions to farming. NSARM, RG 1 vol. 432, Howe, 75, "Western Tour, 1842."

79 A well-known businessman belonging to this Piers family, Walter McLarren Piers (a neighbour of the author in Halifax, who died in Toronto in 2010 at nearly one hundred years of age), stated that his father William Harrington Piers remembered how members of the Piers family, often in association with Joseph Howe and William Chearnley, would in the 1850s fish with the Pennels along the Gold River. William Harrington's father was a Halifax merchant named George Piers who had married Emily Ann Harrington from Antigonish County in 1866. NSARM, Historical Vital Statistics, Halifax County Births, Registration Year 1866, book 1809, p. 88, no. 319. Walter further explained that George and his brother Henry joined mining prospectors, among them members of Daniel Dimock's family from Chester, in taking ore samples along the Gold River, so that the Piers were present at the inception of gold mining on the Gold River in the early 1860s. Before his death, Walter Piers presented the author with a gold velvet bag containing three mineral samples, composed of quartz with flecks of gold, collected by members of his family during these years. He also possessed several photographs of his ancestors fishing with the Pennels on the Gold River. The Piers had a residence called "Stanyan" on Windsor Street at the time, in addition to a summer place in Chester. Walter's great uncle Henry Piers, the father of Harry Piers who was born in 1870 and became a well-known curator of the Nova Scotia Museum, would have been among these sportsmen. Given Harry Piers's father's close relationships with the Pennels, it is not surprising that Harry himself early on developed an interest in Mi'kmaw culture. Not only was Harry's father a brother of Walter's grandfather George, but Harry mother, Janet Louisa Harrington, was a sister of George

Piers's wife, Emily Anne Harrington. Walter M. Piers, who became president of Brookfield Brothers Ltd., was an older brother of Admiral Desmond Piers of Halifax and Chester, so the Piers family continued to have connections with Lunenburg County until the late 1990s.

80 Conversation with Walter Piers and his daughter Jane Piers, who stated that Chearnley, the Piers brothers, and Howe all knew each other well.

81 Howe in 1842 reported that the Mi'kmaq made clearings and planted potatoes in the woods on the upper reaches of the Gold River. These potatoes were "dug and eaten in the hunting season." NSARM, RG 1, vol. 432, 75, Howe, "Western Tour, 1842."

82 As late as 1921, Chief Isaac Sack at Shubenacadie held that "Joe Penaul of Chester … [had been] capital in the woods," while in 1926 Chief Joseph C. Cope of the Halifax County Band stated that "Joe Pennall of Gold River" had been "a good guide for fishing." NSM, Printed Matter File, "Micmac Indian Guides (Good) According to Chief Isaac Sack," Isaac Sack to Harry Piers, 26 February 1921; NSM, Printed Matter File, Joseph C. Cope to Harry Piers, April 1926, "Micmac Indian Guides, according to Joe C. Cope, Indian."

83 In 1834 Joseph Penall (or Pennel, c.1805–59) and his wife Mary Alexis left Gold River to travel to the Roman Catholic church at Prospect to have their son Francis baptized. With them were two of Joseph's younger brothers, Peter (dates unknown) and John Jr. (1811–87). Peter and his wife Mary Toney brought a son, Thomas, to Prospect for baptism, while John and his wife Molly Ann Toney had a son, John, baptized. After the relatively stable years of the 1830s, the 1840s brought a host of vicissitudes of fortune, especially sickness, to the Pennel family. Mary Alexis, Joseph's wife, died around 1840 along with two of her children, Isabelle and Francis. By the early 1850s her only living child was a daughter, Mary, the wife of Peter Glode. John's first wife, Molly Ann Toney, died in the late 1840s, and in 1851 he wed Marian Barbara Rafuse.

84 After Chief John Pennel Sr.'s death around 1843, his sons moved to New Germany. John Sr.'s eldest son, John, lived at New Germany until 1889. His second-eldest son, Joseph, travelled the countryside with his wife, Sophia Rafuse, peddling baskets and wooden implements, while his youngest son, James, lived at New Germany until 1890. Tom Hammond also resided at New Germany; Indian commissioner Chearnley called him "Old Tom Hammond." In 1853 Tom's first wife, Magdalene, and his son Louis were recipients of government supplies. Seven of the Pennels, who also appear on the government

requisition list for 1853, were all Francis Pennel Sr.'s children, including Joseph, Francis Jr., Tall Peter, Anne, Newel, Michael, John, and James. Four adult Pennel women mentioned in 1853 – Margaret, Elizabeth, Mary Ann, and Molly (Mary) – also likely belonged to Francis's family. Elizabeth, who married John Newel, and two of John Pennel Sr.'s sons, Joseph and John Jr., who received muskets from the government, lived at Gold River. NSARM, RG 1, vol. 430, doc. 175, "List of Articles issued by William Chearnley, Commissioner of Indian Affairs, with the names of the Indian Men & Women to whom the articles were issued, Halifax Decr. 31st, 1853." Radical changes occurred at Gold River between 1853 and 1855. The only Pennels still living at Gold River in 1855 were Francis Pennel Sr.'s widow, "Old Mrs. Penall"; his son Joseph (1798–1859); Joseph's second wife, Marie Louisa Labrador, and her three young children; Francis Pennel Sr.'s son John (1811–87) with his wife Barbara Rafuse and two children; and Tom Hammond's son John. NSARM, MG 15, vol. 5, doc. 69. Until her death around 1845, Francis Pennel's widow, who likely was of Germanic or Acadian background, had her sons Joseph and John living with her. John and his family moved into her house when she died, and were still living in it in 1858. Meanwhile, her son Joseph, his wife Marian Louisa Labrador, and their two young sons Frank and James moved to Wallabeck Lake, while Joseph's only remaining adult daughter, Fanny, and her husband, Peter Glode, lived at Gold River. Four of Old Mrs. Penall's sons, Joseph, Peter, Newel, and Thomas, were dead by 1865. Two gravestones were erected, at different times, in St. Augustine's Church cemetery in Chester to commemorate the lives of Joseph Pennel and his brother John. Grave markers were also raised honouring John Pennel Jr.'s wife, Barbara Rafuse (her birth and death dates are not recorded on the stone, although it is known she was born in 1837 and lived to be eighty-one years old), and Catherine Pennel (5 October 1863–2 May 1896), the widow of John Pennel Jr.'s grandson William, born in 1864. Indian commissioner William Chearnley erected Joseph Pennel's memorial stone (the name on this stone is spelled "Joseph Penall") in 1859, while the other grave markers were set up in 1920 by William Pennel's second wife, Emma Zwicker.

85 Joseph Pennel directed two petitions to the lieutenant governor, Sir John Gaspard Le Marchant, in 1853. The first discusses clearing land near New Ross, building a log cabin, and the loss of most of his children, and the second states that he is fifty-five years old and that his grandfather, Pennel Argomartin, had settled at Gold

River nearly one hundred years before. NSARM, Miscellaneous "I" Indian Documents on microfilm, Document Package 25, Pennel Reserve No. 19, "To Major General John Gaspard Le Marchant, Lieutenant Governor of Nova Scotia, Petition of Joe Pennaul of Gold River, 1853."

86 Howe had taken steps to stop encroachment on reserves, and in 1843, during his time as Indian commissioner, a law was passed to eject trespassers. Enforcement was always the major problem.

87 Wallabeck Lake was also known as William's Bay Lake.

88 This trespass may have been encouraged by Mi'kmaw vulnerability: a potato blight struck crops in 1845 and 1846, followed by a virulent fever that plagued Mi'kmaw communities throughout southwestern Nova Scotia.

89 LAC, RG 10, vol. 459, doc. 17, "Joseph Penall to the lieutenant-governor of Nova Scotia," 17 February 1853.

90 NSARM, Miscellaneous "I" Indian Documents on microfilm, Document Package 25, doc. No. 25, Pennel Reserve No. 19, "Petition to Sir John Gaspard Le Marchant from Joseph Penaul, 1853." In this memorial Joseph states that he is fifty-five years old and that his grandfather, Penall Argomartin, had settled at Gold River nearly one hundred years before.

91 NSARM, Miscellaneous "I" Indian Documents on microfilm, Document Package 25, Pennel Reserve No. 19, Wallabeck Lake, Lunenburg County. This information is taken from notes penned, after Joseph Pennel's death in 1859, directly on the petition Pennel sent in 1853 to Sir John Gaspard De Marchant.

92 This suggests that Chief Bernard Argomartin had at least been aware of the government's allotment in 1765 of the Seccombe grant.

93 NSARM, Miscellaneous "I" Indian Documents on microfilm, Document Package 25, Pennel Reserve No. 19, Wallabeck Lake, Lunenburg County, docs. 25 and 105, "To Major General John Gaspard Le Marchant, Lieutenant Governor of Nova Scotia, Petition of Joe Pennaul of Gold River, 1853." Joseph referred to Marian Labrador as "white," which indicates that he knew some of her ancestors prior to 1760 included members of the Acadian trading family of Guedry *dit* Labrador at Merliguèche. (For the history of these Labradors, see chapter 3 of this volume.) Marian wanted her husband Joseph to adopt a "white" way by life by attaining land and holding down a permanent job; NSARM, RG 20, microfilm reel no. 15,700, Ser. A – Labradore [Benjamin Labradore] and Nowel [Newel Labradore], Grant Registration Book, "Petition for Land at Lunenburg from two Applicants living at Mush a Mush, 1809." The surveyor general of Crown lands, Charles Morris, noted that these men had

made "extensive improvements on the first division of their lots which entitles them to favourable consideration." Benjamin Labradore was almost certainly a grandson or great-grandson of Paul Guédry *dit* Labrador, who was ejected from his trading centre at Merliguéche (Lunenburg) in the early 1760s. Marian hailed from the Labradors of Sable River who farmed parcels of land, barrelled salt fish, and hunted, fished, and trapped. Her roots were Acadian as well as Mi'kmaq, and in the early 1850s she likely had been ruminating on past vicissitudes experienced by her Acadian and *métis* ancestors, the Guedrys *dit* Labrador. A century earlier the Labradors had maintained a profitable trading and fishing station at Merliguèche, later renamed "Lunenburg." When the British expropriated the "Labrador farm" during the Seven Years' War, a few *métis* members of the Guedry family, from which she herself descended, escaped deportation. Among these was Joseph Labrador, a resistance fighter who earned a fearsome reputation in the 1750s for leading Indigenous attacks on outlying British and foreign Protestant settlements. When war ceased, Joseph and his Labrador kin emerged from their wartime headquarters on Mushamush Lake, Lunenburg County, to try to assume peaceful and profitable occupations within the postwar milieu. For instance, in 1809 Benjamin Labrador, of Mushamush, applied for acreage near the town of Lunenburg that he intended to farm.

94 NSARM, Miscellaneous "I" Indian Documents on microfilm, "Plan of Pennel I.R. No. 19, approximately 100 acres, laid out for Joseph Pennall and family," n.d. Today this reserve is administered by the Acadia First Nation.

95 Debrisay, *History of the County of Lunenburg* (1870), 153.

96 NSARM, microfilm reel 4187, "History of Elmwood," written in 1944 by Mrs. R.D. Wentzell and printed in *Nova Farm News*, June 1945. The genealogical information contained in this piece was supplied to Mrs. Wentzell by Thomas I. Spidell of Medford, MA.

97 Ozias Beeler and Agnes's children were: Howard, born in 1894, who married Phoebe Hallamore (a descendent of the man who fled with Tom Hammond during the War of 1812), Bertha, Gerald, Findley, Charles, Susan, and Theophilus, who married Ellen Moffat.

98 Samuel Dorey of New Germany, son of Henry Benjamin Dorey and Lucy Ann Rafuse, and his wife Mary Ellen raised ten children: Arthur, May, Clarence, Vincent, Leo, Pius, Maggie, Annie, Agnes, and Theresa. May, born in 1877, married Hiram Nauss from Italy Cross, Lunenburg County, and several of her children kept the Dorey surname. Many of these births are registered in the church registers of St. Gregory's Church

in Liverpool. One of May's sons, Claude Dorey, born in 1903, married Katherine Meuse of Yarmouth County and had two children, Delmar and Claude Basil Jr., who remained living on their father's farmland at Elmwood. Claude Basil Jr. served overseas in World War II and in 1929 married sixteen-year-old Catherine Merlina Muise, daughter of Peter Miuse and Mary Ann Jadis of New Ross. The couple had nine children whose names all begin with the letter "D": Delmar, Dale, Dora, Darrel, Doyle, Dalton, Darleia, Dwight, and Deborah. For Claude and Merlina's marriage certificate, see NSARM, Historical Vital Statistics, Lunenburg County Marriages, Registration Year 1929, book 57, p. 826. Information was also graciously provided by Dwight Dorey and Dora Jones.

99 Teresa Hammond was born in 1854 at New Germany. She and her husband Abenago had twelve children between 1872 and 1904 – John, Edna, Patrick, Hazel, Hugh, Evangeline, Bridget, Eldon, Douglas, Eugenia, Ferne, and Dennis – as well as an adopted daughter, Madelyn.

100 NSARM, Historical Vital Statistics, Lunenburg County Deaths, Registration Year 1918, book 43, p. 16, no. 62, "Death of John Hammond, Indian Reserve."

101 This couple remained childless.

102 Lewis Phillips of Hants County was a descendant of Chief Philip Bernard of St. Margaret's Bay.

103 James Hammond's first wife may have belonged to the Peminout Paul family of Shubenacadie. After her death, he married a second time. He died at eighty-seven years of age at New Germany in 1935. NSARM, Historical Vital Statistics, Lunenburg County Deaths, Registration Year 1935, book 161, 411, "Death of James Hammond, widower." Margaret Hammond left New Germany, and her whereabouts remain unknown.

104 The Franck family of Lunenburg County maintained close relationships with the Mi'kmaq. Chapter 1 of this volume notes that Joseph Bartlett-Alexis consorted with Marie Ellen or Mahalia Frank from Lunenburg County in the 1870s and 1880s. After Joseph Bartlett's death, Mahalia wed John Charles in 1891. Elizabeth, Tom Hammond's second wife, and Mahalia Frank were doubtless related, and perhaps were sisters. In 1872 Selina Hammond wed James Pennel (or Bernard) Labrador, best known simply as "James Pennel," from Sable River in Shelburne County. Selina, who lived into her eighties, proved a colourful character, as she had several children out of wedlock by different men and simply incorporated them into the already large family she raised with James. NSARM, Historical Vital Statistics, Lunenburg County Marriages, book 1828, 70. (The groom is referred to as "James Penall" rather than "James Penall Labrador.") Salina's brother Henry died unmarried.

105 NSARM, microfilm reel 4187, "History of Elmwood."

106 NSARM, Miscellaneous "I" Indian Documents on microfilm, taken from Nova Scotian Crown Lands Records, Package 26, "Reserve no. 19A – New Germany Reserve, Lunenburg County."

107 John Hammond was the nephew of this James Pennel, as James's sister Magdalene married John's father Tom Hammond. Joseph and John frequently travelled together and, once they married wives from the New Germany area, stood as sponsors at the baptisms of each other's children.

108 NSARM, Register of Births, Marriages and Deaths for the County of Lunenburg, on microfilm, "Baptism of Anne, daughter of James Penaule and Mary Toni [Toney], at New Germany, 6 October 1856." The godparents were John Hammond and Susanna Rafuse, who had their daughter Teresa baptized on the same day, with James and Mary standing as Teresa's godparents.

109 John Hammond died in 1918, aged ninety-four. NSARM, Historical Vital Statistics, Lunenburg County deaths, book 43, p. 16, no. 62. Louis likely died about 1876. Though Tall Peter Pennel may have been the son of Francis Pennel Sr., he more likely was a grandson of John Pennel Sr. John Sr.'s son James Pennel and James's wife, Mary Anne Toney, may well have named one of their sons "Tall Peter."

110 Five families had moved up to the headwaters of the Gold River at New Ross. The family heads were John Hammond, James Hammond, Tall Peter (Penall), James Penall, and John Hammond Jr. LAC, RG 10, vol. 459, Package 3, Lunenburg (Penhall), "Report of Captain W. Chearnley on the New Ross Reserve," 9 July 1861.

111 Howe, during his time as Nova Scotia's Indian commissioner, had a law passed calling for the ejection of trespassers from reserves, but enforcement was always an issue.

112 NSARM, RG 1, vol. 431, doc. 134 ½, "William Chearnley to the Provincial Secretary of Nova Scotia regarding harassment by whites on reserves in Lunenburg," 3 March 1862. The New Germany tract would not be surveyed again until 1880, when the reserve was subdivided into farm plots.

113 James Hammond died, a widower, at New Germany in 1935 at age eighty-seven of heart failure. NSARM, Historical Vital Statistics, Lunenburg County Deaths, Registration Year 1935, book 161, 411.

114 NSARM, Miscellaneous "I" Indian Land Documents on microfilm, Plan of New Germany Reserve No. 19A, 1861.

In 1879, the area of the New Germany Reserve would incorrectly be given as one thousand acres. Ibid., "Robert Sinclair, Superintendent General of Indian Affairs, to James H. Austin, Assistant Commissioner of Crown Lands," 5 June 1870.

115 NSARM, microfilm reel 4187, "History of Elmwood, written in 1944 by Mrs. R.D. Wentzell," *Nova Farm News*, June 1945. James Hammond and Elizabeth Dorey had a son, Thomas, born in 1886, who was killed in action during the First World War. A second son, Angus, born in 1888, also served overseas in the First World War, and after his return married an Englishwoman and lived at Shubenacadie. A daughter, Ellen, married Joseph Paul from Lequille and the couple had twelve children, while another son, Lewis, born in 1868, died in infancy. James's sister Margaret in 1862 married James Stephen Charles and the couple had Anne in 1863, Newel in 1868, and Stephen in 1877.

116 Except for Joe Pennel, who lived at Lequille, all of James Pennel's sons and daughters were said to eventually succumb to tuberculosis. NSARM, microfilm reel 4187, "History of Elmwood," written in 1944 by Mrs. R.D. Wentzell and printed in *Nova Farm News*, June 1945. Mary, Peter, and Catherine Nancy, however, married and had children. Mary married Louis Labrador of Milton in Queens County and the couple had a son, Dominic, in 1891. Catherine Nancy Pennel, as mentioned, married Henry Carver of New Germany and the pair had two daughters, Josephine and Minnie Naomi. Josephine Carver wed Charles Oickle of Milton, Queens County, and her sister Minnie in 1920 wed Lloyd Lowe. NSARM, Historical Vital Statistics, Annapolis County Marriages, Registration Year 1920, book 3, 279. When Lloyd Lowe died suddenly of a massive stroke ("apoplexy") in April 1921, Minnie later the same year wed Louis Glode, the only son of Samuel Glode and Louisa Francis of Milton, Queens County. NSARM, Historical Vital Statistics, Queens County Deaths, book 101, 181; NSARM, Historical Vital Statistics, Queens County Marriages, Registration Year 1921, book 6, 495. Louis Glode, like his father Samuel, served overseas in the First World War.

117 James Pennel (c.1824–c.1890), the youngest son of John Pennel Sr., should not be confused with James Pennel who married Mary Glode, a daughter of Francis Glode and Marie Ann Molti of Queens County. The James who wed Mary Glode was a son of Joseph Pennel (Joe Goose) and Sophia Rafuse. NSARM, Church Records of the Parish of St. Gregory's Roman Catholic Church in Liverpool, Queens County, on microfilm, "Marriage of James Penall, son of Joseph Penall and Susan [*sic*, Sophia] Rafuse, to Mary Glode, daughter of Francis Glode and Mary Ann Molti, 19 May 1870." James Pennel and Mary Glode had a number of children, among them James in 1871 and Ellen in 1871. By contrast, James Pennel, the youngest son of the noted fishing guide Joseph Pennel (1798–1859), wed Mary Ann Toney (who was also known as "Hannah Paul") in the early 1860s and lived for several years on a farm plot at New Germany. After James vacated his plot at New Germany, it was farmed by Claude Dorey. This parcel could still be easily picked out by Claude Dorey's descendants in 2007. Dwight Dorey, personal communication, summer 2007. James Pennel and Mary Toney's son Joseph Pennel (11 January 1872–16 March 1950) married Mary Christine (or "Kate") Pictou, a daughter of Chief Ben Pictou and Magdelene Paul of Lequille, Annapolis County, at Plympton, Digby County, on 25 October 1905. NSARM, Historical Vital Statistics, Digby County Marriages, 1905, "Marriage of Mary Christine Pictou and Joseph Penall [or Pennel], 23 October 1905," book 1812, p. 279, no. 60. Joseph, born at Gold River in 1871, was thirty-four years old at the time and engaged in the lumbering business, while his bride was twenty-six. Joseph and Christine had three children: John, born in April 1901 (prior to the couple's marriage); Madeline, born in October 1909, and Mary Madeline or "Marteen," born on 28 December 1915. Marteen died on 26 March 1936. Her father, Joseph Pennel, died on 16 March 1950. Joseph's birth date of 11 January 1872 is taken from an inscription on a gravestone located in the cemetery of St. Louis Roman Catholic Church in Annapolis Royal. James Pennel and Mary Toney's descendants today live in Lunenburg, Queens, and Annapolis counties. For more information on Joseph Pennel's marriage to Christine Pictou, see Ian Lawrence, "Notable Personalities of the Past: Chief Benjamin Pictou," https://annapolisheritagesociety.com/community-history/notable-personalities-past/chief-benjamin-pictou/ (accessed 1 December 2022).

118 David Luther Roth, *Acadie and the Acadians* (Philadelphia: Lutheran Publishing Society, 1890), 59–60.

119 Ibid.

120 Ibid.

121 Information taken from St Joseph's Church, Bridgewater, Nova Scotia, *Parish Directory*, 1986.

122 Roth, *Acadie and the Acadians*, 60–1.

123 The minister completed his book before he left Nova Scotia in 1890, which meant this meeting with Jim Pennel could have occurred around 23 December 1889, the day of ceremonies marking the completion of the NSCR's new line. Roth admitted that his own excitement

over the railway's inauguration at first made him unaware of the solemnity of the Mi'kmaw gathering. "An idea occurred," he maintained. "There had been some excitement in the town from which they were coming, over the opening of a new railroad. So when I came near [the procession] I accosted them. 'Been over to see the railroad, Jim?' 'My brother is dead, sir.' It was a funeral." Ibid., 60.

124 Ibid., 52. Roth does not mention which of Jim's brothers had died. It would not have been John Pennel Jr's funeral, however, as John had died at seventy-six years of age on 29 March 1887. It was another of Jim Pennel's brothers, of which he had several.

125 Daniel Dimock and David Whitfield have been credited with discovering gold on the Gold River on 20 June 1861, though the presence of alluvial gold in the area had been recognized by placer miners years before. Desbrisay, *History of the County of Lunenburg* (1870), 334. Prospecting, sinking tunnels into the hard rock, and ore-crushing by stamp mills occurred in the early years until the establishment of the large Jumbo Mine in 1885, by which time several enterprises flanked the river. Mining continued in the area into the late 1920s. In 2014, Danny Hennigar, a grandson of one of the Chester miners, conducted public tours of an old mine site located off the Beech Hill Road, which cuts uphill from the highway through the Gold River Reserve, to raise funds for the Chester Municipal Heritage Society. Beverley Ware, "History Buff Mines for Charity Gold," *Chronicle Herald*, 27 October 2014, A4.

126 In 1989 Mary Wentzell, the ninety-eight-year-old daughter of the proprietor of a local general store at Indian Point, described how the Mi'kmaq used to come in to her father's store and trade salmon. "They came from the reserve at Gold River to trade salmon for tobacco and molasses. That was summer barter. The salmon was never weighed. It was just a swap." NSARM, microfilm reel 9364, *Bridgewater Bulletin*, 24, May 1989, 1.

127 Frank Pennel and Mary Edna Veniotte married in the late 1870s. By this time all that was left of John Sr.'s and Francis Sr.'s old houses were foundations, surrounded by the remains of kitchen gardens.

128 NSARM, Miscellaneous "I" Indian Land documents, "William Mosher to the Hon. J.W. Longley," 12 October 1895.

129 LAC, RG 10, vol. 2130, file 25,584, "Robert C. Stewart to Frank Pedley," 2 May 1912. The province carved out a 160-acre grant from what was popularly known as the "Althrope location," part of the original Seccombe et al. grant of 1765. A second location was laid out at the same time, covering the interval of 41 acres on the eastern bank of the river, to Amos Heisler and his heirs. Sutherland sold his parcel on the western shore to George Heisler and his close kin, who by 1909 were associated with the Kent Lumber Company of Halifax. The Heislers hailed originally from Tancook Island.

130 LAC, RG 10, vol. 459, microfilm reel C-13,324, folder or package no. 3, doc. 3, "Accounts, Petitions and Returns, Gold River," 12–14. The Mi'kmaq in 1820 had acquired the support of the "principal men in Chester," who petitioned on their behalf for the government to lay out a reserve. Within thirty years, however, persons representing business interests living in the Chester locality were contending that the Gold River reserve constituted an impediment to "manufacturing and industry." Although surveyor general John Spry Morris, who conducted the first proper survey of the reserve in August 1852, admitted the government in 1819 had promised the Mi'kmaq one thousand acres in the vicinity of the Lower Bridge at Gold River, he added that no "land had been laid out until August 1852." Moreover, a sawmill had been operating on what was known as "Gray's Grant" which had been laid out and occupied by the mill previous to Spry's 1852 survey. Ibid., 14, "Memo drafted by John Spry Morris," August 1852, printed in Indian Affairs Report for that date. LAC, RG 10, vol. 459, microfilm reel C-13,324, folder or package no. 3, doc. 3, "Accounts, Petitions and Returns, Gold River," 14, "Memo drafted by John Spry Morris," August 1852, printed in Indian Affairs Report for that date; NSARM, Gold River Reserve, Grant no. 21763, 728 acres, Grant Book RR, 486; LAC, RG 10, vol. 459, package no. 3, doc. 3, 13, "E. Macdonald to Joseph Howe," 4 July 1871. John Pennel and Joe Rafuse, who had accompanied Spry on the 1852 survey, pointed out where the stone piles lay that Spry had erected as boundary markers.

131 LAC, RG 10, vol. 459, package no. 3, doc. 3, 13, "E. Macdonald to Joseph Howe," 4 July 1871.

132 On 1 July 1902, the Halifax and South Western Railway purchased the Nova Scotia Central Railway's line from Mahone Bay to Bridgewater, which initiated the laying of track between Bridgewater and Halifax. This new rail line construction, part of which crossed the Gold River Reserve, was completed by 1904.

133 LAC, RG 10, vol. 2130, file 25,584, "Charles Starratt to Indian Affairs," 8 August 1902; ibid., "Charles Starratt to Indian Affairs," 23 April 1907.

134 LAC, RG 10, vol. 2130, file 25,584, "Charles Harlow to Indian Affairs," 30 March 1907. In 1910, Harlow claimed that there were two reserves in Lunenburg County, each

of one thousand acres. Ottawa, Department of Indian Affairs, Annual Report for 1910, 1 George V, 1910–11, 71, "Report of Charles Harlow to Ottawa," 11 June 1910.

135 LAC, RG 10, vol. 2130, file 25,584, "S. Bray, Memo to the Deputy Superintendant of Indian Affairs," 28 June 1907.

136 Mary Edna Veinotte was a daughter of Zachariah Veinotte (mother unknown). Frank Pennel and Mary Edna had Francis on 3 August 1909, Annie on 6 October 1911, Joseph on 20 June 1912 and Barbara on 12 October 1914. NSARM, Historical Vital Statistics, Lunenburg County Births, Registration Year 1909, p. 54500724, no. 54500724; NSARM, Historical Vital Statistics, Lunenburg County Births, Registration Year 1911, p. 45700435, no. 45700436; NSARM, Historical Vital Statistics, Lunenburg County Births, Registration Year 1912, p. 49300007, no. 49300008; NSARM, Historical Vital Statistics, Lunenburg County Births, Registration Year 1914, p. 43500754, no. 4350056.

137 William Pennel was twenty-six when he wed Catherine Eisnor (Eisenhauer), aged twenty-four, in the town of Mahone Bay on 5 December 1889. The Reverend Edmund Carmody officiated at the ceremony, while Willie Tobin and Sarah Jodrey acted as witnesses. NSARM, Registration Year 1889, Lunenburg County Marriages, book 95, p. 63, no. 203. (This marriage is incorrectly listed on the NSARM online site as occurring in 1898, rather than 1889.) Catherine was born at Gold River on 5 October 1863 to David Eisenhauer and Susan Kedd, and she died of cancer at thirty-two years of age on 2 May 1896. Her body was buried in the Roman Catholic cemetery in Chester. William's second wife, Emma Zwicker (1867–1964), was a daughter of Nelson Zwicker and Maria Swinemar. After William's death in 1920, Emma erected three gravestones in St. Augustine's graveyard in Chester to honour her husband, his first wife Catherine, and his parents, John and Barbara.

138 LAC, RG 10, vol. 2130, file 25,584, "Charles Starratt to Secretary of the Department of Indian Affairs," 7 June 1907.

139 LAC, RG 10, vol. 2130, file 25,584, "Report of V.J. Paton," 8 August 1912.

140 One of these slurs painted the Gold River reserve population as a "mongrel brood" – a cruel and ridiculous assertion, since every person on the reserve could easily trace direct linkages back to the first chief of the Gold River region.

141 LAC, RG 10, vol. 2130, file 25,584, "J.D. McLean to William Penall," 19 September 1910.

142 NSARM, Grant No. 18306, "William Pennel – 25 acres, Grant Sheet No. 2, Chester Basin, Lunenburg County."

143 LAC, RG 10, vol. 2130, file 25,584, "Report of V.J. Paton," 8 August 1912.

144 LAC, RG 10, vol. 2130, file 25,584, "Robert C. Stewart to Indian Affairs," 2 May 1912; "Robert C. Stewart to Indian Affairs," 30 April 1912. Stewart hoped to get Mi'kmaw backing for his claims, as George Heisler had sent him a summons for not paying the $150.

145 LAC, RG 10, vol. 2130, file 25,584, "Robert C. Stewart to Frank Pedley, Deputy Superintendent of Indian Affairs," 2 May 1912.

146 LAC, RG 10, vol. 2130, file 25, 584, "In the Supreme Court, *George A. Heisler, The Kent Lumber Company, Limited, and John Croft*, Writ of Summons," 10 December 1912.

147 LAC, RG 10, vol. 2130, file 25,584, "Arthur Roberts to the Deputy Minister of Justice, 21 December 1912"; *The King vs. William Pennel*, 22 March, 1913; "N.P. Freeman to the Assistant Deputy of Indian Affairs," 7 January 1913; "George A. Heisler to Indian Affairs," 14 April, 1913. Heisler argued that there were sworn surveys of his property made over one hundred years previously.

148 LAC, RG 10, vol. 2130, file 25,584, "George Hiseler [*sic*, Heisler] to J.D. McLean," 14 April 1913.

149 LAC, RG 10, vol. 2130, file 25,584, "Assistant Deputy of Indian Affairs to N.P. Freeman," 7 January 1913. Pennel was annoyed at the differential treatment the law meted out to him and to his associate and, concerned over the loss of a major source of income, complained that Gold River residents should be encouraged to cut and square timber for railway and building purposes, rather than being punished for pursuing new forms of local employment.

150 LAC, RG 10, vol. 2130, file 25,584, "J.D. McLean, to local Indian agent, N.P. Freeman," 10 March 1914. In the early twentieth century the Mi'kmaq grand chief John Denny Jr. at Eskasoni, Cape Breton, promoted the cutting and sale of wood on reserves as a new economic occupation for Mi'kmaq throughout the province.

151 LAC, RG 10, vol. 2130, file 25,584, "Henry J. Bury, Memo to the Deputy Minister of Indian Affairs," 27 February 1914.

152 LAC, RG 10, vol. 2130, file 25,584, "Arthur Roberts to J.D. McLean, regarding *The King vs. William Pennall*," 24 April 1913; "McLean to N.P. Freeman," 9 May 1913.

153 LAC, RG 10, vol. 2130, file 25,584, "RE: Judge Russell's decision in *The King vs. Heisler*," 27 August 1913. Benjamin Russell was a puisne judge of the Nova Scotia Supreme Court from 1904 to 1935. In the end, he favoured an interpretation derived from a formidable array of documentary evidence that George Heisler had assembled in order to retain the Sutherland location. Heisler,

for instance, had argued that his grant was based on one given 168 years previously to one Nicholas Bachierac, while the Amos Heisler property had been bought from the Nova Scotian government only 148 years before. LAC, RG 10, vol. 2130, file 25,584, "George Hiseler [*sic*, Heisler] to J.D. McLean," 14 April 1913. When Russell ruled that the miners owned the lands they occupied he may have felt he could do little else, given the plethora of contradictory affidavits issued by Ottawa and the province, the ambiguous nature of survey lines, and conflicting views on the size of the reserve. The loss of reserve land amounted to 225 acres if one held to a description of the size of the reserve prepared by Charles Morris in 1820, and considerably more if one accepted Howe's, Chearnley's, and Harlow's contention that the reserve covered 1,000 acres.

154 LAC, RG 10, vol. 2130, file 25,584, "H.J. Bury to the Deputy Minister," 17 February 1914; "J.D. McLean to Hiram Donkin," 27 March 1914. On the plan of the Gold River reserve, signed and dated by C.H. Starratt in November 1910, the following addition of 27 August 1913 appears: "By judgment of the court … the Heisler claim is not included in the Reserve." LAC, RG 10, vol. 2130, vol. 25,584, "Plan of Indian Land at Gold River, Showing the Halifax & South Western Railway, by C.H. Starratt, November 1910."

155 LAC, RG 10, vol. 2130, file 25,584, "N.P. Freeman to Indian Affairs," 9 April 1914; LAC, RG 10, vol. 2130, file 25,584, "William Penal [*sic*, Pennel], Chester Basin, to Indian Department," 6 March 1914; "W.A. Orr to William Penal." 10 March 1914.

156 LAC, RG 10, vol. 2130, file 25,584, "Reginald W. Petre, Consulting Mining Engineer, to the Commissioner of Crown Lands," 5 July 1913.

157 LAC, RG 10, vol. 2130, file 25,584, "N.P. Freeman to Indian Affairs," 27 January 1914.

158 LAC, RG 10, vol. 2130, file 25,584, "J.D. McLean to Hiram Donkin, N.S. Department of Public Works and Mines," 27 March 1914. The issue at large concerned permits granted by the province to cut timber at Gold River issued to a Mr. McKeen.

159 NSARM, Miscellaneous "I" Indian Documents on microfilm, Document Package 6, "Reserves transferred to the Dominion Government by Prov. at Confederation, schedule dated 1959, Lunenburg County, New Germany Reserve."

160 These events are still held despite the fact that many individuals who have bought property in Elmswood are not of Mi'kmaw heritage. Today the community, which has a school and small church and cemetery, is

being increasingly perceived by city and town dwellers as desirable cottage country. Conversation with Dwight Dorey, 20 June 2007.

161 NSARM, MG 15, vol. 19, no. 1, Papers from Indian Land Claims, Pennel Reserve No. 19, "A.F. MacKenzie to Harry Redden of the Gold River Pulp and Paper Company," 29 February 1932; "MacKenzie to Gold River Pulpwood Company," 19 January 1934; ibid., "T.R.L. MacInnes, Acting Secretary of Indian Affairs, to W.G. Ernst, on behalf of the Gold River Pulpwood Company," 19 May 1934. Meanwhile, a second timber interest, headed by Earl Meisner, also wanted to buy the reserve

162 Ibid., "MacKenzie to Gold River Pulpwood Company," 19 January 1934; LAC, RG 10, vol. 7756, file 27042 – 1, "H.J. Bury to Dr. McGill, Deputy Supervisor of Indian Affairs," 18 May 1934; NSARM, Miscellaneous Indian "I" Land Documents on microfilm, Package No. 25, Pennel Wallabeck Lake, Lunenburg County; ibid., Package 7, "Schedule of Reserves Transferred to Dominion by the Prov. at Confederation, dated 1959, Lunenburg County, Pennel Reserve." There is no mention in the 1959 schedule of the Pennel Reserve's near-sale by Ottawa in 1932 and 1933.

163 Gold mining ceased in 1940, but more recently test holes have been bored around the Gold River area to assess the value of deposits bearing lead and molybdenum.

164 NSARM, Miscellaneous "I" Indian Land Documents on microfilm, Package 6, "Schedule of Reserves Transferred to the Dominion by the Prov. at Confederation, Lunenburg County, Gold River" (which according to the 1910 survey was held to consist of nine hundred acres), schedule dated 1959. The history of the resource conflicts at Gold River is contained in ibid., Package 28, Gold River Reserve; ibid., Package 63, "Letter [of William Chearnley] to Attorney General re: a Mill Site Flooding Indian lands at Gold River, Lunenburg County [1852]"; and ibid., Package 81, "Correspondence re the boundaries of the Gold River Indian Reserve to determine possible encroachments, from 1850s onward."

165 NSARM, Historical Vital Statistics, Halifax County Deaths, Registration Year 1920, book 95, 22. Frank Pennel's son and namesake, Frank Pennel Jr., in the 1960s built a number of cottages at Gold River without getting permission from the Indian Affairs Department to take the necessary wood off the reserve for commercial purposes. In consequence, the department demanded that the cottages be razed to the ground, but Charlie Paul, chief of the newly formed Acadia First Nation, was able to find a middle ground between the opposing sides that

led to a resolution of the problem. Information from Steve Pennel, Gold River, and Donald Julian, director of the Mainland Confederacy, Millbrook, April 2008. Don Julien was working for Indian Affairs at the time and remembers the incident well.

166 Ottawa, Department of Indian Affairs, "Report on Field Interviews with Micmacs of Nova Scotia, Areas in Which They Reside and the Unoccupied Reserves of Nova Scotia Mainland, 1957," Treaty and Aboriginal Rights Research Centre (TARR Centre), Shubenacadie, UNSI Collection 92–1004–09–018, 21. Clarence Glode (or Gloade), who as a child was an orphan from Queens County, was later raised by Molti Pictou near Lequille, Annapolis County, and afterwards lived for a number of years in Shelburne County before coming to Gold River. Debora Gloade from Bear River, who assisted with this entry, is descended from Clarence Glode.

167 Ibid., 51–2.

168 The nearby New Ross Reserve, which was laid out in 1820, is administered today by the *Sipekne'katik* (Shubenacadie) First Nation.

169 When the research for this study began in the late 1980s, few non-Indigenous residents of Chester and its environs even knew that a reserve existed in Lunenburg County, despite the fact that during the mid-eighteenth century the La Have band, the parent group from which the Gold River band and Chief Philip Bernard's group at St. Margaret's Bay originally sprang, had been one of the largest Mi'kmaw bands in southwestern Nova Scotia. Both of these groups, in turn, had frequently communicated with a larger regional entity, the Minas district band located to the west of them.

CHAPTER 9

1 "Knockwood" emerged as a Mi'kmaw family surname in the mid-1830s. The Mi'kmaw name from which it was derived was spelled various ways: "Knoucout," "Nancoute," "Naucoute," "Necoot," "Necout," "Neocout," "Nicoute," "Nocket," "Nockwood," "Nogood," "Nokut," "Noocat," "Noucout," "Nuffcoat," "Nughquit," and "Numquodden."

2 "Obituary, Stephen Knockwood, Indian Guide Dead at Age of 104," *The Register*, Kentville, 26 October 1938. The inscription on Stephen Knockwood's gravestone in Holy Cross Cemetery, Kentville, also states he died at 104 years of age. Yet a range of birth dates for him appear in the documentary record. His birth year of 1834 on his gravestone does not match information given in the 1911 federal census, which lists him as 64 and hence born in 1847. (The same census gives his wife Sarah Ann Paul's age as 66.) As no birth certificate could be located confirming his date of birth, the best that can be said is that Stephen Knockwood Jr. was born between 1834 and 1847 to Stephen Knockwood Sr. at Sandy Cove, Digby County. His mother's name is unknown. (Stephen Knockwood Jr. also had a first cousin, born in 1837, named Stephen John Knockwood, who was a son of John Knockwood Sr. and Mary Ann Labrador of Kentville.)

3 The author was given this information by Mrs. Spurgeon Knockwood (née Frances Marie Corkum) during a visit she and Doris Labradore made to the New Ross Reserve in June 1990. Abraham Pineo Gesner's practice of hiring Mi'kmaw guides for his collecting expeditions is examined by David W. Black in "Pioneers of New Brunswick Archaeology II: Abraham Gesner," Department of Anthropology, University of New Brunswick, Fredericton, https://www.unb.ca/faculty-staff/directory/_resources/pdf/arts-fr/dwblack/gesner.pdf. For a fuller examination of Gesner's life, see Elizabeth V. Haigh, *Abraham Gesner: The Lure of the Rocks and a Burning Ambition* (Victoria: Tellwell Talent, 2019).

4 Kings County Registry of Deeds, Kentville, Book 40, 52–3, "Indenture No. 53 made 10 May 1877 between the Honourable Samuel Chipman of Cornwallis and Jessie Chipman, his wife, on the one part, and Stephen Nockwood [*sic*, Knockwood] of the other part. Sale of four acres of land to Knockwood on the north side of Old Tupper Road in the Pine Woods. Registered 10 May 1878." Samuel Chipman (1790–1891) in 1815 married Elizabeth Gesner, Abraham Gesner's sister. (After her death he married Jessie Hardy.) Chipman, for many years the representative in the Assembly for Kings County, later sat in the Legislative Council, and until three years before his death was registrar of deeds for the County of Kings. He lived to be 101 years old. Although Gesner's sister Elizabeth had died by the time Knockwood bought the land from Chipman, Gesner still retained close enough ties with his brother-in-law to assist in Knockwood's acquisition of the property on Brooklyn Street. Knockwood and Gesner were now neighbours, as Gesner in 1841 had purchased a farm from his father at Chipman Corner, not far from the site of Kentville's modern hospital.

5 A Black bachelor named Pryor James who lived in the Pine Woods area was known to the author's grandfather, John Manning Chute of Brooklyn Corner. In a singular tragedy, James, who manufactured illegal "moonshine,"

was shot dead through the door of his cabin during an altercation between him and an officer of the Royal North West Mounted Police (the Royal Canadian Mounted Police were not formed in Nova Scotia until 1920). No trial ensued following his death. After 1905 Mi'kmaq, Blacks, and *métis*, and several white families clustered into a community at the far eastern end of Brooklyn Road known as "Yoho."

6 John Knockwood Sr. and Mary Ann Labrador's daughter Elizabeth married James Paul, son of Joseph Paul and Mary Ann Meuse (or Paul) in 1870, the same year that their thirty-three-year-old son Stephen John Knockwood Jr., born in 1848 at Lawrencetown, Annapolis County, wed James's sister, sixteen-year-old Betsy Paul. Nova Scotia Archives and Records Management (henceforth NSARM), Historical Vital Statistics, Kings County Marriages, Registration Year 1870, Book 1826, 33, "Marriage of Stephen John Knockwood and Betsy Paul, 2 May 1870"; NSARM, Historical Vital Statistics, Kings County Marriages, Registration Year 1870, p. 40, no. 80, "Marriage of James Paul and Elizabeth Knockwood, 14 June 1870." After Betsy's death, Stephen John Knockwood Jr. married Mary Barss in Kentville on 15 August 1887 and the couple resided near Berwick. NSARM, Kings County Marriages, Registration Year 1887, Book 1826, p. 199, no. 80, "Marriage of Stephen John Knockwood, widower, aged 40, and Mary Barss, widow, aged 22, daughter of Matt[hew] and Mary Barss."

7 Peter A. Knockwood Sr. and Mary's son Peter Knockwood Jr. married Margaret Morris, daughter of Alex and Mary Morris, at Kentville on 27 February 1871. NSARM, Historical Vital Statistics, Kings County Marriages, Registration Year 1871, Book 1826, p. 46, no. 26.

8 Members of the Pine Woods community included Francis Toney and his wife Madeleine Francis; Noel Morris and his wife Fanny Bobbiei (Stephen Knockwood Jr. and Sarah Ann stood as godparents at baptisms of this couple's children); Alexander Bobbiei; Toney Bobbiei; Peter Baptiste and his family; Benjamin Brooks and his wife Anastasia Pennel; John Brooks and his wife Louise Morris; John Charles and his wife Mary Pictou; John David and his wife Maria Paul; Michael Hood and his wife Marie Sire (Siah or Cyr); Stephen Hood and his wife Mary Jeremy; John Labrador and his wife Mary Agnes Pennel; Louis Labrador; James Michael and his wife Eleanor Knockwood; John Pennel; and Michael Pennel. Members of the Hood, Pennel, and Thomas families had relatives living near Lequille, at Panuke near Windsor, and at Mahone Bay. There were also Knockwoods who had moved elsewhere in Nova Scotia or to Prince Edward Island or New Brunswick, but who returned to visit. As well, Ben Christmas, originally from Cape Breton, and his wife Susan McDonald periodically joined the group. As a young man in the 1850s Ben had been an assistant to the Baptist missionary Silus Tertius Rand, though he afterwards had his children baptized according to the tenets of the Roman Catholic faith. Mi'kmaq belonging to the Pine Woods community appear in the baptismal registers of Father Saulnier (1853–68) for St. Joseph Parish, which included the districts of Cornwallis, Kentville, Cambridge, and Aylesford. Families also brought children to be baptized at St. Louis Church, Annapolis Royal. The Pine Woods settlement grew during the late nineteenth century as new economic opportunities arose. The Mi'kmaw population of Cornwallis District rose from 74 in 1877 to 106 by 1883, despite an infectious illness brought back in 1882 by a few Mi'kmaw men who had temporarily gone away to seek work in Massachusetts. John Knockwood Sr., although seventy years old and temporarily sickly in 1882, raised six bushels of potatoes. Those who travelled seasonally to find work returned in the fall. Louis and John Labrador prospected for gold near Bridgewater. Others became professional guides. In 1883 John Knockwood Sr., Isaiah Pictou, and Joseph Brooks all engaged in some farming, although the local Indian agent, John Edward Beckwith, saw Stephen Knockwood Jr.'s establishment as the most promising. *Dominion of Canada Parliamentary Sessional Papers*, 1884: 36–7, "Beckwith to the Department of Indian Affairs," 12 August, 1883.

9 In 1904 the British army expropriated the tract of land on which the Pine Woods and Knockwood's farm stood in order to establish Camp Aldershot northwest of the Cornwallis River. Though reduced in geographical extent from its original size, the army training facility today continues to operate under Canada's Department of National Defence.

10 The author's grandfather, John Manning Chute, owned an apple farm along Brooklyn Street two properties to the west of the Knockwood farm and knew Stephen Knockwood personally. He also mentioned that there had been a small school in the Pine Woods area, which operated for only six months in 1870, too early for Knockwood Jr.'s children to take advantage of it. The author's grandmother, Jessie Dow, before her marriage to John Chute taught two of Stephen and Sarah's children at the one-room schoolhouse at Brooklyn Corner. From school registers in the archives of the Kings County Museum in Kentville, as well as school registers in the

possession of the author, it appears that some Knockwood children attended classes and a few were good students.

11 Sarah Ann Paul was born at Kentville on 18 August 1846.

12 *Dominion of Canada Parliamentary Sessional Papers*, 1884, 36–7, "Beckwith to the Department of Indian Affairs," 12 August 1883.

13 *Dominion of Canada Parliamentary Sessional Papers* (1887), 37, "Beckwith to the Department of Indian Affairs," 10 August 1886.

14 Eighty dollars was a high price for four acres of land in Cornwallis Township, especially for acreage with sandy soil in the Pine Woods. In later years Knockwood would sell over one hundred acres of arable land on the South Mountain for just twice that amount. Perhaps at the time it was the only land available for sale. The high cost of land in the Kentville area deterred Alex Morris, Knockwood's friend and neighbour, from similarly seeking title to a plot.

15 *Dominion of Canada Parliamentary Sessional Papers* (1882), 224–6, "J.E. Beckwith, Cornwallis, N.S. to the Department of Indian Affairs," 23 July 1881.

16 Ibid.

17 *Dominion of Canada Parliamentary Sessional Papers* (1883), 24, "Beckwith to the Department of Indian Affairs," 26 July 1882. John Knockwood's death certificate states that he was born 8 December 1878, and the United States Federal Census for 1920 lists Benjamin as born in 1879. Stephen's birth date is unknown. John's death certificate can be found in NSARM, Historical Vital Statistics, Colchester County Deaths, Registration Year 1951, 1518, "Death of John Knockwood, son of Steven Knockwood and Sarah Paul, of a cerebral hemorrhage."

18 Beckwith reported that the Knockwoods had six children in 1882. (Stephen) John Knockwood's death certificate states he was born on 8 December 1878. He died of a cerebral hemorrhage at Truro on 22 January 1951 at seventy-two years of age. NSARM, Historical Vital Statistics, Colchester County Deaths, Registration Year 1951, 1518.

19 Sarah Ann Paul was, as noted above, descended from Chief Paul Peminout of Stewiacke, Nova Scotia; she was likely a daughter or granddaughter of Paul Peminout's eldest son, Jacques Peminout Paul. Jacques moved into the Newport area from the Stewiacke River region about 1790.

20 This was land reserved by the government in 1880 for the Cambridge or Annapolis Valley Band No. 32.

21 "Church of Saint Bernardette," *MicMac News*, April 1973, 4; Kings County Registry of Deeds and Wills/Probate, Kentville, Probate Records relating to Stephen Knockwood Jr.

22 Sandy Cove, Digby County, was given as Stephen Knockwood Jr.'s birthplace on his son William's birth entry. NSARM, Historical Vital Statistics, Registration Year 1909, Book 5, p. 5490044, no. 5490044, "Birth of William Knockwood." William was born at Forest Home, Kings County, on 2 November 1909.

23 NSARM, RG 1, vol. 432, Joseph Howe, 97–9, 101, "Western Tour, 1842."

24 Ibid. In addition to Stephen Knockwood Sr., Joseph Howe encountered Francis Tutter, Peter Meuse, and an elderly man named Peter Tom in the District of Clare, Digby County. Francis Tutter stated he had a synonymous name, "Francis Charnisé" (*sic*, Charnisay), although Howe admitted he was at a loss to establish any connection between Sieur de Charnisay, Charles La Tour's rival in the mid-seventeenth century, and the Mi'kmaw man he met in 1842. He could only ruminate on the fact that the southwestern Mi'kmaw community had a very complex and mysterious history.

25 In 1842 Stephen Knockwood Sr. was allowing a neighbouring farmer to plant and harvest his plot at Bear River in return for a share of the crop. Howe, realizing that Knockwood was probably too elderly to be expected to farm, finally agreed to the arrangement. NSARM, RG 1, vol. 432, 184–5, "Letter from Joseph Howe to Mr. Nicholl, fall 1842, granting permission to the farmer to take crops off Steven Knockwood's land as long as he knows that by doing so he sets up no claims to the land."

26 "Indian Guide Dead at Age of 104," *The Register*, Kentville, 26 October 1938.

27 The meaning of this name could not be determined.

28 Port Toulouse is present-day St. Peter's, Cape Breton. Jacques Neocout's name appears on both a French nominal census of the Minas area dated 1708 and a 1722 census by another French missionary priest, Abbé Antoine Gaulin. Library and Archives Canada, Ottawa (henceforth LAC), MG 18, F 18, Typescript, 42, *Recensement genal fait au mois de Novembre mile Sept cent huit de tous les Sauvages de l'Acadie qui resident dans la coste de l'Est, et de ceux de Pintagouet et de Canibeky, famille par famille, Leur ages celuy de Leurs Hommes et Enfants avec une Recapitulation a la fin de la quantite d'hommes et de garcons capables d'aler a La guerre … 1708.*" The French original, compiled by Père Pierre La Chasse in November 1708, is housed in the Edward E. Ayer Collection (Ayer MS 751) at the Newberry Library in Chicago. Gaulin's census of 1722 is housed in the Archives des colonies, Paris (hereafter AC). A microfilm copy is in

Library and Archives Canada (LAC, AC) C11B, vol. 6, *Correspondance général*, doc. 77, "*Recensement des Sauvages tam de lisle Royalle que de la peninsula de l'acadie qui fons deserves par Les Missionnaries du Seminaire des Missions étrangères Etablis a Quebec fait que par Mn. Gaulin, pretre Missionaire des Sauvages en 1722.*"

29   In 1708 the group was composed of eleven heads of families with their wives, and five widows. The large number of young boys, thirteen in all, should have ensured the growth of the band in later years, yet it did not. Soon after the onset of the Mi'kmaw War (1722–25), which belonged to a larger forum of conflict known in the United States as Dummer's War or Lovewell's War, Neocout's band was reduced to forty-four individuals: eight male heads of families, eight women, four young men, seven boys, sixteen girls, and one widow. This preponderance of young women over young men, sixteen to merely four, indicates considerable mortality among young Mi'kmaw men suffered during the Mi'kmaw attack on Canso in the spring of 1720 and in the early months of Dummer's War. In 1722, Governor Shirley of Massachusetts declared war on the Eastern Abenaki – a body to whom the Mi'kmaq belonged – and the consequences for the band at Minas were swift and severe.

30   LAC, British Colonial Office Documents on Microfilm (henceforth CO), 217/3/155–6, "Antoine and Pierre Couaret to Governor Philipps," 2 October 1720.

31   The English favoured the few Mi'kmaw chiefs they knew from diplomatic encounters or with whom they had traded in the past. They knew Chief Pierre Momchareet (Momcharret) of Minas better than his neighbour Jacques Neocout, since Momcharret's people traded with the British at Fort Anne whereas Neocout's people associated with the French at Port La Joye, Île St. Jean (now Prince Edward Island), and after 1718 at Louisbourg on Île Royale (Cape Breton). The Momcharrets, who originally hailed from the Annapolis River region, also were relatively recent migrants into the Minas district. In 1726 the British invited Chief Pierre "Nimquarett" (Momcharret) and others of his family to ratify a treaty already signed between the English and other eastern Algonquian-speaking nations at Boston the previous year. NSARM, CO, 217/38, "Treaty of 1726." This copy of the treaty document, of which there are several all dated 4 June 1726, bears Aboriginal signatory marks and some totemic marks. It accompanied a dispatch, dated 27 November 1726, from Lieutenant Governor Lawrence Armstrong to the British Colonial Office.

32   In the 1720s, most southwestern Mi'kmaq proceeding to Abbé Antoine Gaulin's mission station on the Shubenacadie River had to pass through lands under Neocout's aegis.

33   Minutes of a Council at Annapolis Royal, 25 July 1732, in Thomas B. Aikens, ed., *Selections from the Public Documents of Nova Scotia* (Halifax, 1869), 97–8; ibid., 101, "Lieutenant-Governor Lawrence Armstrong to the Duke of Newcastle," 13 November 1732.

34   Joseph undoubtedly was one of Jacques Neocout's sons or grandsons, although his name does not appear on Pierre La Chasse's census of 1708. Paul Biscaroon and Jacques Ashe encouraged at least five boys to join in the raid, including Claude and François. Other youths involved were Biscaroon's son Paul, one of Jacques Ashe's sons, and "the chief's wife's son, Barthemy [Barthelemy Momcharret]." Following this incident, the British at Annapolis Royal sent a circular letter, dated 20 June 1737, to the heads of the Minas band.

35   NSARM, RG 1, vol. 24, "Minutes of the Council at Annapolis Royal," 10–15 June 1737. A disposition dated 8 June 1737 by Stephen Jones and sworn before the lieutenant governor and council on 18 June 1737 shows a lower amount, £800. *Minutes of His Majesty's Council at Annapolis Royal, 1736–1749*, ed. Bruce Fergusson (Halifax: Public Archives of Nova Scotia, 1967), 15–17. Among those involved were John Nuffcout (Neocout), Solomon Nuffcoat, and Joseph Cofse (Casse). See also NSARM, F 106 H19 D79, Thomas F. Draper, "Essay on the History of Hants County," prize-winning essay, King's College, 1881, 5.

36   Only youths at this time, Claude and François Neocout would have been sons of Chief Joseph Neocout, not of Jacques Neocout. For instance, "Francis [or François] Noucout, son of Joseph," was seventy-five in 1800 and so was born in 1725. NSARM, RG 1, vol. 430, doc. 68, "Names of Indians belonging to Kings County, 1800 and 1801."

37   *Minutes of His Majesty's Council*, ed. Fergusson, 37–9; NSARM, RG 1, vol. 24, Brown Papers, "Letter of April 1742."

38   In 1737, Peter Numquodden (or Neocout) of the Minas band participated in a raid on a vessel at Minas belonging to a trader named Samuel Trefry. NSARM, RG 1, vol. 24, "'Minutes of the Council at Annapolis Royal, April to June 1742"; Beamish Murdoch, *The History of Nova-Scotia, or Acadie* (Halifax: James Barnes, 1865–661), 521. "Wouito" or "Ouytau" appears on the La Chasse 1708 census as well as on the 1726 treaty signed at Annapolis Royal.

39   NSARM, RG 1, vol. 24, "Minutes of Council from 6 December 1744 to 25 January 1745." Bourg also was

chastised for failing to stop Acadians from trading with Louisbourg and Quebec.

40 NSARM, RG 1, vol. 24, "Minutes of Council from 12 October to 8 November 1748."

41 NSARM, RG 1, vol. 24, "Minutes of Council from 24 to 29 August 1745, concerning the letter of Pierre Landry." The lieutenant governor at this time was Paul Mascarene.

42 The original band list drafted at Windsor by Isaac Deschamps, who at the time was a forwarding agent for Joshua Mauger, a Halifax merchant, is housed in NSARM, MG 1, vol. 258, item 8, 20–1. On 20 December 1763 Deschamps listed "18 men, 19 women and 41 children" as belonging to the "Nocoot Tribe" of Minas. This list is reproduced in Henry Youle Hind, *An Early History of Windsor, N.S.* (facsimile reprint of *Sketch of the Old Parish Burying Ground of Windsor Nova Scotia: With an Appeal for Its Protection, Ornamentation, and Preservation*) (Windsor, 1889), 32. Deschamps listed ten male family heads with the "Nocoot" surname: Joseph, Thomas, Janvier, François, Claude, Charles, Reni, Jacques, Lewis, and Philippe. Other heads of families were Paul Biskarone (or Biscaroon), Francois Segona, Charles Segona, Michel Thoma, Joseph Thoma, and Louis Michel. Despite the fact that prior to 1763 the Nocoots or Neocouts dealt with the French and the Momcharrets (Couarets or Amquarrets) with the English, after the close of the Seven Years' War leaders of both bands worked together to press for their rights to land and resources in the diplomatic forum. The rarity of the Momcharret surname among men in the Kennetcook region suggests that women, after marriage, moved between bands, while males tended to remain with their natal group.

43 Charles Bruce Fergusson, *Place-Names and Places of Nova Scotia* (Halifax: Public Archives of Nova Scotia, 1967), 325.

44 As late as 1849 "Joseph Nokut" (Neocout or Knockwood), an elderly chief from Shediac, still possessed and on occasion wore a Louis V medal that he claimed his grandfather – undoubtedly Chief Joseph Neocout of Minas – had received from the French around 1755. This leader frequently visited the Northumberland Strait area and Prince Edward Island. *The Nova-Scotian*, Monday, 30 July 1849, 3

45 NSARM, RG 34–316, P, vol. 1, "Kings County Court of General Sessions," 17 August 1763; NSARM, Chipman Collection, MG 1, vol. 181, nos. 68–71. See also Judith A. Norton, "The Dark Side of Planter Life: Reported Cases of Domestic Violence," in *Intimate Relations, Family and Community in Planter Nova Scotia, 1759–1800*, ed. Margaret Conrad (Fredericton: Acadienesis, 1995), 186–7. Hammond tried to claim that Neocout's injuries were inflicted by some horses that ran over him as he lay inebriated in their path.

46 Isabelle Angelique Neocout's marriage to Chief Pennel Argomartin, who with his son John Pennel Sr. was said to have joined General James Wolfe's expedition to the Plains of Abraham in 1758, may have signalled that Neocout hostility towards the British was waning slightly by the late 1760s. By 1800 the couple had moved to Gold River, Lunenburg County. NSARM, RG 1, vol. 430, doc. 96, "Gold River," census of 1801.

47 Some of the children brought for baptism to Bailly in 1769 were several years old. NSARM, Registers of Abbé Charles-François Bailly on microfilm, copy of old register conserved at Caraquet, New Brunswick, *Registre des actes de baptême, mariages, et sepultures faits en la nouvelle ecosse ou acadie commence le vingt unieme jour de juillet de l'annee mil sept cent soixante huit, par Mons. Charles-François Bailly, pretre missionaire des sauvages et acadiens, sujets de sa majeste britanique, 1768–1773*. Between 1769 and 1772, when Abbé Bailly finally left Nova Scotia, these Mi'kmaq could also turn to the missionary for solace regarding their troubles with land and resources. Doubtless the Neocouts had been close in the early 1750s to Louis-Joseph Le Loutre and, until 1762, to Pierre Maillard. Before his death Maillard provided guidelines by which Mi'kmaw chiefs could perform baptisms, marriages, and funerals according to Roman Catholic tenets in the absence of a Roman Catholic priest.

48 François Neocout was a son of Chief Joseph Neocout. He was seventy-five in 1800, so he would have been born in 1725 and likely died around 1780. NSARM, RG 1, vol. 430, doc. 68, "Names of Indians belonging to Kings County, 1800 and 1801." "Francis Nogood" (Neocout) travelled in 1800 with his son "Joseph Nogood," John Wilmot, and Daniel Toney – a son of Chief Louis Toney who was born at Remsheg (now Wallace, Nova Scotia). The latter three were in their forties at this time.

49 NSARM, RG 1, vol. 156 p. 54, "Passes granted to eight men on 28 April 1760." These eight leaders were Beleban Quarrie (Bartholomew Couaret or Momcharret of the Minas area), Lewis Jacques, Bartholomew Michael, Charles Claude, Thomas Ball (or Paul), Joseph Ball, Jacques Le Blanc, and Blanchois Wyegawook (Francis Cope – a son or grandson of Jean-Baptist Cope from the Sheet Harbour area). It seemed the British in 1760 continued to regard the Couaret chiefs as the rightful

leaders of the entire Minas area, and again ignored the Neocout family, as Bartholomew Couaret was the only Minas chief appearing on lists in the British colonial officialdom's possession. See Father Manach's list of chiefs, 1760, recorded by Colonel Frye, *Collections of the Massachusetts Historical Society*, 1809, 116 (copied by a Dr. Stiles and first published in *The Pennsylvania Gazette*).

50 Fort Menagouèche was a French fort located on the site of a Malecite village at the mouth of the Saint John River. After being burned by Charles Deschamps de Boishébert following the fall of Fort Beauséjour, it was rebuilt as Fort Frederick by the British. Michael Francklin, however, who was Indian commissioner from 1777 until his death in 1782, in his supply lists still referred to Fort Frederick as "Fort Menagouèche," the name used by the Mi'kmaq and Malecite. Major Gilfred Studholme arrived at Saint John in 1777 with the 84th Regiment of Foot with orders to repair Fort Frederick on the Saint John River estuary, but because of the vulnerable, low-lying position of this stronghold, he decided to erect Fort Howe on the brow of the escarpment that overlooks Saint John. Both forts are mentioned in Francklin's accounts. Provincial Archives of New Brunswick, Saint John New Brunswick, James White Papers, Identification no. 53, C1-1, "Lists of supplies issued to Indians of the village of Menagashe near Fort Howe," along with comments on their activities. Charles Neocout's courage was rewarded by the British, who awarded him presents and supplies.

51 LAC, MG 23, GII-19, George Monk Papers, 1051, "Entry for 20 January 1784." This member of the Neocout family may have been the same person who, as a youth, had been assaulted by settler ruffians twenty-one years before.

52 Mi'kmaw genealogist Joseph Knockwood, who resides at Fort Folly, not far from Dorchester, traces his own ancestry to François Xavier Neocout (Nocoute or Knockwood Sr., c. 1755–1832), who was born in the mid-eighteenth century into the "Nocoot Tribe" of Minas. When his first wife, Marie-Thérèse Abstiago, died at Minas, François-Xavier Neocout married "Marie-Madeleine Piminuit" (or Marie-Madeleine Peminout Paul), a daughter of Chief Paul Peminout of Stewiacke, Nova Scotia, and moved with his new wife to New Brunswick about 1784 or 1785. "Knockwood Family Genealogy: Submitted by Joseph Knockwood (Nocoute)," Fort Folly First Nation, https://fortfolly.ca/geneology-trace. Many of François Xavier Neocout's descendants are members of the Fort Folly First Nation near Dorchester. (For instance, the federal census for 1901 for Dorchester, New

Brunswick, lists Israel Knockwood, his wife "Marry [Mary] A.," and the couple's two children Francis, three years old, and Charles W., one year old.) Others later moved to Halfway River in Parrsboro and Springhill, Cumberland County. and finally to Nova Scotia. Douglas Freeman Knockwood, ONS, PhD, stated that his forebearers hailed from near Dorchester, New Brunswick, and that he was a descendant of Francois-Xavier Neocout. Doug was the son of Freeman and Mary Ann Knockwood of Springhill, Nova Scotia, and a respected elder, fluent speaker of the Mi'kmaw language, advisor, author, writer, educationalist, and spiritual leader. He lived at Shubenacadie, dying there on 17 June 2018 at the age of eighty-eight. Author interviews with Douglas Knockwood at Shubenacadie, 1991, 1994. and 2014; John Demont, "Doug Knockwood Mourned, Celebrated," *The Chronicle Herald*, Halifax, Wednesday, 20 June 2018; Allison Lawlor, "Doug Knockwood, 88, Survived Rough Early Life and Became a Mi'kmaq Elder Who Helped People Beat Addictions," *Globe and Mail*, 8 July 2018, https://www.theglobeandmail.com/canada/article-doug-knockwood-88-survived-rough-early-life-to-become-a-mikmaq/; Doug Knockwood and Friends, *Doug Knockwood, Mi'kmaw Elder: Stories, Memories, Reflections* (Halifax: Roseway, 2018).

53 The St. Ann Church registers for Lennox Island, Prince Edward Island, show that members of the Neocout or Knockwood family formed part of the congregation there as early as 1812. Public Archives and Records Office, Charlottetown, Prince Edward Island, Accession # 3672/3, Microfilm Reel # 1, "Records of St. Anne's Roman Catholic Church, Lennox Island, 1812–1900." Thaddeus or "Thaddy" Knockwood, a veteran who was gassed overseas during the First World War, was a descendant of these Knockwoods. M. Olga McKenna, *Micmac by Choice: Elsie Sark – An Island Legend* (Halifax: Formac, 1990), 75.

54 NSARM, RG 1, vol. 430, doc. 58, "Report of Smallpox outbreak in 1801." Jonathan Crane stated in 1801 that no non-Aboriginal individual other than himself knew the Mi'kmaw language, and he had learned only a few words as a part-time fur trader. By the 1830s, the Paul family had settled near Horton and the Morris family in the Pine Woods behind Kentville. Members of both families eventually joined the Pine Woods community.

55 Thomas Neocout was almost certainly the "Thomas Nankaut" mentioned in NSARM, MG 15, "Papers associated with Henry Youle Hind, 1768–1770." These documents reveal that Chief Pennel Argomartin was the husband of "Isabelle Angelique Nankaut," who in turn

was the daughter of "François Nankaut [likely the chief] and Marguerite Joseph." They also reveal that Thomas Nankaut was born at Piziquid (now Windsor) in 1768 to Louis Nankaut and his wife Ann. René Nankaut was Thomas's godfather.

56 These persons included Francis Knockwood and Magdalene Knockwood, who married Francis Glode of the Annapolis district and became the mother of the famous nineteenth-century guide Jim Glode.

57 NSARM, RG 1, vol. 430, doc. 56, "Heads of Families, District of Colchester," 31 March 1801; NSARM, RG 1. vol. 430, doc. 25, "Heads of Families," 25 March 1808. Thomas Neocout, who was forty years old in 1808, had two children, Francis and Sabia. Others of his family took up residence along the Parrsboro Shore rather than seasonally migrating back and forth across the Bay of Fundy. During the late nineteenth century Benjamin "Nocuous" (Knockwood) and Benjamin Brooks served as elected councilors for the Parrsboro band, headed by Chief John Logan, for a term of three years – from 1 July 1899 to 1 July 1902. This group originally came from the Minas region, and according to the 1911 census contained two Knockwood family heads, John Knockwood and Samuel Knockwood. In the early 1920s Chief Isaiah Paul of Maccan, Nova Scotia, had persons belonging to his group named Knockwood with ties to Kentville, Halfway River, Springhill, Pictou County, and Memramcook, New Brunswick.

58 John Knockwood was at the St. Anne's Day festivities at Chapel Island in 1841. NSARM, MG 15, vol. 3, doc. no. 65, "An Account of the Indians within the County of Richmond, as taken on the 26th of July 1841, at the Indian Chapel Bras d'or Lake, being the Anniversary of St. Ann's Day."

59 Chief Joseph Nokut was interviewed at North River, near Charlottetown, Prince Edward Island, by a journalist for the Prince Edward Island newspaper *The Royal Gazette. The Nova-Scotian*, Monday, 30 July 1849, 3. (The *Nova-Scotian* contains that interview.) The *Royal Gazette* reporter reflected on the chief's sad commentary on the course of Indigenous-settler relations since the founding of Halifax exactly one hundred years before, and then focused on the esteem other Mi'kmaq accorded Nokut during a feast held in his honour not long after St. Anne's Day, on 26 July. Nokut, the reporter claimed, was one of the few who took his meal inside a ceremonial enclosure instead of outside on the surrounding lawn. At the time the chief had a French medal in his possession dating to the reign of Louis XV (1715–74).

60 Ruth Holmes Whitehead. *The Old Man Told Us: Excerpts from Micmac History, 1500–1950* (Halifax: Nimbus, 1991), 287. On the federal census of 1901 for Kings County, Sarah Ann Paul is recorded as living at Upper Dyke in the District of Cornwallis. The census taker left the marital status column opposite her name blank. Sarah had her hands full. She still cared for Benjamin, born in 1879; Madeline, born around 1882; Rachael, born in 1883; Harry, born in 1884; Henry, born in 1885; and a "grandchild" Charlotte, born on 5 March 1891. She also was raising a foster child, Kathleen Katie Tonbarge. Canada, Census of 1911, District No. 45, Cornwallis, Nova Scotia, p. 1. In 1911 Charlotte Knockwood was listed as her granddaughter, though she may have been her daughter, since none of Sarah Ann's children were old enough to have a twenty-year-old daughter. On 3 November 1909, at age twenty-five, Henry, the last of Sarah Ann's children to leave home, married eighteen-year-old Madeleine Gabriel. NSARM, Historical Vital Statistics, Kings County Marriages, Registration Year 1909, Book 1827, p. 137, no. 159. Henry died at age twenty-nine at Truro in 1914. NSARM, Historical Vital Statistics, Colchester County Deaths, Registration year 1914, Book 31, p. 1, no. 5. Stephen John Knockwood Sr. struggled to put food on the table for his mother, his siblings, and his own children Stephen John Jr., Benjamin, Mary (who died young), and Lucy. After the appropriation of the Pine Woods property in 1904, Sarah Anne Paul, her son Stephen John, and daughter-in-law Rosie Gooley first moved to Upper Dyke Village, the site of a pre-1755 Acadian community lying north of the Knockwood farm and bounded by the dyke lying furthest inland up the Canard River. Not long afterwards, however, they occupied a small frame house at the east end of Brooklyn Street, where Rosie succumbed to stomach cancer at age forty-five on 22 May 1915. Her death certificate records her as "Black" rather than Mi'kmaq. NSARM, Historical Vital Statistics, Kings County Deaths, Book 40, p. 97, no. 371, "Death of Rosie Knockwood." Stephen John Sr., who continued to live along "B" Street near Kentville, married Theresa Eunice (or "Tessa") Simons of Cambridge on 22 August 1917. NSARM, Historical Vital Statistics, Kings County Marriages, Book 33, 336, "Marriage of Stephen John Knockwood, son of Stephen Knockwood and Sarah Ann Paul, and Theresa Simons, daughter of Noel Simons and Mary Paul." (Stephen Knockwood Jr. did not attend the wedding. As his name does not appear on the 1901 federal census for Upper Dyke Village – which included eastern Brooklyn Street and the Pine Woods – or the 1911 federal census, he

must have completely abandoned the Kentville area.) After Sarah's death Stephen John continued to live on the "B" Street extension of Brooklyn Street until 1920; during that time he struck up a relationship with Michael Thomas from the Windsor-Rawdon area and Jerry Bartholomew-Alexis of Halifax County, who both regarded him as leader of the Kentville Mi'kmaw community. NSM, Printed Matter File, "Letter of 15 August 1916 from Jeremiah Bartlett-Alexis to Chief John Knockwood of the Indian Reserve, Kentville, to be present at a Grand Meeting of the Micmac Tribe to elect a Grand Chief for the Districts of Halifax, Lunenburg, Kings, Hants, Colchester, Cumberland, and Queens to be held at the Indian Chapel at Spring Brook [Shubenacadie] on Tuesday afternoon, the 22 of August 1916." (There was no "Kentville Reserve," however. The closest reserve was at Cambridge.)

61 General Register, Brooklyn Corner School No. 35, 1897, Teacher, Leora C. Webster. "Student No. 44, Henry Knockwood, age 11, was in Grade 2 and had attended 31 days," which meant he had lost 81 days of school time throughout the term. Though others had lost far more days, Henry would have to repeat Grade 2. Henry was the only Mi'kmaw student in 1897. At this time, Jessie Dow, the author's grandmother, was also a student along with the Knockwoods, though in a few years she would be a teacher at the same school. Her school registers are in the author's possession. Some of Stephen John Knockwood's children did well academically. In 1913 Freida Marjorie Porter was a teacher at Brooklyn Corner, at which time Stephen John Knockwood Sr. had moved from Pine Woods and was living on "B" Street. The schoolhouse held only eighteen students, two of which – Stephen John Knockwood Jr., erroneously reported as age nine (he actually was eleven), and Ben, who was seven – were Stephen John Sr.'s children with Rosie Gooley, whom he married at Kentville around 1900. Stephen John Jr. had one of the best attendance records of all the children and, as noted, did well academically. Ben, by contrast, missed a fair number of school days. Stephen John was born in 1902. NSARM, Historical Vital Statistics, Kings County Births, Book 1902, 99100478, "Birth of Steven J. Knockwood Jr. on 8 November 1902 at Kentville, son of Stephen John Knockwood and Rose Gooley. Affidavit by Madeline Martin, cousin of the applicant. Delayed registration, registered 4th August, 1964." His grandmother, Sarah Knockwood, was the midwife at his birth.

62 Canada, Census of 1911, Census District No. 45, Indian Reserve, Cornwallis, Nova Scotia, p. 1.

63 Registry of Deeds for Kings County, Kentville, Deed Book 160, 123, "Deed. Conveyance of Sarah Ann Lockhart, widow, to Stephen Knockwood. Recorded 8 November 1938." This transaction with Sarah Ann Lockhart was originally made on 4 November 1898. The Blue Mountain farm in Kings County was described as located fourteen miles (approximately twenty-three kilometres) from Kentville.

64 The daughter of John and Jane Paul, Laura was born in Halifax but later resided at Cornwallis. She was married in her teens to a man named Butler, who left her a widow several years later. On 15 July 1882, at the age of twenty-two, she married a second time by Baptist ceremony to Alfred Brooks, a farmer, the son of John and Mary Brooks of Cornwallis. NSARM, Historical Vital Statistics, Kings County Marriages, Registration Year 1882, Book 1826, p. 153, no. 57. Born in 1860, she would have been in her forties when she met Stephen Knockwood Jr. and thus would have been fifty-three years old when her eldest son Spurgeon was born in 1913. Whether she had children other than those she had with Knockwood is not known.

65 NSARM, Historical Vital Statistics, Kings County Births, Registration Year 1909, p. 54900444, no. 54900444, "Birth of William Knockwood at Forest Home, Kings County, on 15 October 1919." The names of the rest of Stephen's and Laura's sons and daughters were furnished by Florence May Knockwood, Spurgeon Leander Knockwood's wife. She related: "I remember the property at Aldershot being given to Stephen Knockwood who lived down on Brooklyn Street. It was called 'Knockwood Hill.' He already had several other sons, [Stephen] John, Ben and Henry. Spurgeon also had four sisters, Katia, Rachael, Charlotte and Madeleine. Eric Knockwood of New Ross is my son and I have a number of grandchildren. Spurgeon worked in the lumbering industry and he retired on lands near New Ross." Also see Whitehead, *The Old Man Told Us*, "Letter from Henry Knockwood to R.H. Whitehead" (1984), 287. Florence explained that Spurgeon (1913–88) was named after Fred Spurgeon Lockhart, a friend of his parents at Forest Home. Spurgeon always received guests to his home graciously. Mohamed Elkateb, a friend of the author and her family, remembered that when he was a travelling salesperson after arriving in Canada from Lebanon, he enjoyed stopping at the New Ross Reserve for a visit with Spurgeon, as he was always sure of a warm welcome. In 1991, when the author and Doris Labradore spoke with Florence, she and her grandchildren were very hospitable. Some of the younger Knockwoods even

provided a farewell motorcycle cavalcade that drove alongside their guest's car until the highway turn-off. Interview with Mrs. Spurgeon Knockwood, New Ross, Lunenburg County, Nova Scotia, 25 June 1990. Florence May Knockwood, born in 1922 to Percy and Annie (Weagle) Corkum, died eight years after this interview took place and was buried in the United Baptist Cemetery at New Ross, Lunenburg County. Obituary of Florence Knockwood, *Halifax Herald*, 9 July 1998.

66 Registry of Deeds for Kings County, Deed Book 77, 779; Deed Book 87, 294, "Regarding life lease from William Lockhart and wife to Watson O'Leary of Massachusetts, 7 August 1899; Lease from Watson O'Leary to Lily May Knockwood, 21 March 1906; and the Life Lease from Watson O'Leary to Stephen Knockwood, 17 April 1906." Registry of Deeds for Kings County, Deed Book 160, 123. The final transaction on this property occurred on 8 November 1938.

67 Registry of Deeds for Kings County, Deed Book 75, 684, "Deed 553 between Stephen Knockwood, Farmer of Blue Mountain, and James Lockhart, Farmer of Blue Mountain," 7 March 1901. Recorded 11 March 1901.

68 NSARM, Historical Vital Statistics, Kings County Births, Registration Year 1909, p. 5490044, no. 5490044, Birth of William Knockwood, 15 October 1909.

69 NSARM, Historical Vital Statistics, Kings County Marriages, Book 65, 638, "Marriage of Arthur William Dorey of Forest Home, age 42, son of Albert Dorey and Rebecca Roasl, and Anne Louise Knockwood, 24, daughter of Stephen Knockwood and Laura Butler, 10 February 1932, presiding Anglican clergyman A.M. Bent, witnesses Laura A. Bent and Catherine Pineo"; NSARM, Historical Vital Statistics, Kings County Marriages, Registration Year 1931, Book 63, 710, "Marriage of Lily May Knockwood, 27, to Hollis Clarence Dunham, 28, son of Harris Dunham and Catherine Bennett, at Waterville Baptist Church, 13 July 1931, presiding minister Rev. Luther E. Stiles, witnesses Freeman M. Lohnes and Pearl V. Lohnes." Dorey was Anglican while Dunham was a Baptist. In their later years Spurgeon and William Knockwood adhered to the Baptist faith. After Knockwood's death, Dorey contested the dispersal of Knockwood's assets by arguing that he was owed $249 for farm "work and labor done and performed … at the request of Stephen Knockwood deceased." Dorey's letter, dated 9 May 1940, may be found in Registry of Deeds, Kings County, Kentville, Wills/Probate. Stephen Knockwood, Blue Mountain, K78, WB 2/204, 1940/01/01. Dorey received his money, and by 9 August 1940 released the executor of the estate, Barry W. Roscoe, from any further suits of

this nature. "Arthur Dorey of South Alton, in Court of Probate in the Matter of the Estate of Stephen Knockwood," 9 May 1938.

70 Kings County Registry of Deeds, Deed Book 155, 405, "Regarding sale of 500 acres at Cornwallis to Willard Ells," dated 24 August 1925. Recorded 16 December 1935.

71 Kings County Registry of Deeds, "Deed, for land at Port Williams and Blue Mountain, to George A. Chase," 1 January 671, Deed Book 151, 671.

72 Kings County Registry of Deeds, "Regarding Stephen Knockwood's sale of 88 acres at Blue Mountain to Thomas Lockhart, recorded 23 May 1932. Witness H.M. Chase." (See Deed Book 151, 671).

73 Kings County Registry of Deeds, "Regarding sale of 500 acres at Cornwallis to Willard Ells, dated 24 August 1925. Recorded 16 December 1935," Deed Book 155, 405.

74 Kings County Registry of Deeds, Wills/Probate, "Stephen Knockwood, Blue Mountain," K78, WB 2/204, 1940/01/01.

75 Kings County Registry of Deeds, "Quit Claim Deed, William Knockwood and Spurgeon Knockwood, Laborers of South Alton, to Henry Angus Welton, recorded 6 November 1943 in Book 165, page 368." On 1 January 1943 Spurgeon and William also disposed of all remaining land once held by their father at Blue Mountain, Coldbrook, to Norman R. Ward by quit claim deed. Deed Book 165, 368.

76 The executor, Barry W. Roscoe, thought it best to send money orders of a dollar to each son, but was unsure of their whereabouts. After inquiries he found out that Benjamin and Joseph both resided at Franklin, about thirty miles north of Farmington, Maine. Kings County Registry of Deeds, Wills/Probate. Stephen Knockwood, Blue Mountain, K78, WB 2/204, 1940/01/01, "Stephen Knockwood, Last Will and Testament, 21 April 1936, witnessed by Helen E. Copeland and Barry W. Roscoe"; ibid., "Barry Roscoe to Kenneth A. Rollins, Attorney-at-Law, Farmington, Maine, 15 February 1939; K.A. Rollins to Roscoe, Cornwallis Street, Kentville, 17 February 1939; 1920 United States Federal Census for the State of Maine."

77 Stephen Knockwood Jr. had five hundred dollars in saved funds and roughly five hundred dollars' worth of real estate. Kings County Registry of Deeds, Wills/Probate. Stephen Knockwood, Blue Mountain, K78, WB 2/204, 1940/01/01, "Deposition signed by Barry W. Roscoe, dated 27 October 1938, to the Court of Probate, Kings County."

78 The actual check to the parish is included with Stephen Knockwood Jr.'s will and other probate papers.

79 The former manager of the line, Laurie Ells of Cornwallis, denoted the bell. The locomotive from which it had come was also known as "Blomidon." Church of Saint Bernardette, 9 April 1941, reprinted in *Micmac News*, April 1973, 4.

80 The government certainly took this view. Mi'kmaw who gained an education or succeeded in business could be unilaterally removed from band lists by government agents and deprived of their Aboriginal status until as late as 1985.

81 Interview with Florence Knockwood, New Ross, 20 June 1990.

82 Church registers of the United Baptist Cemetery, New Ross, Lunenburg County. Spurgeon Leander Knockwood remained a logger much of his life. Obituary of Florence May Knockwood, née Corkum, *Halifax Herald*, 9 July 1998.

83 NSARM, Historical Vital Statistics, Kings County Marriages, Book 63, 710, "Marriage of Lily May Knockwood to Hollis Dunham C. Durham of Halls Harbour, N.S., 13 July 1931"; NSARM, Historical Vital Statistics, Book 65, 638, "Marriage of Arthur W. Dorey to Annie Knockwood, 10 February 1932." Durham was Baptist and Dorey was Anglican.

84 The two men were likely connected, because Michael Thomas's mother was Rosie Gooley, a daughter of Phillip Gooley (Jeremy) and Louise of Shubenacadie, while Stephen John Knockwood's first wife was also named Rosie Gooley. It is even possible that Stephen John Knockwood married Michael's mother Rosie after Michael's father, Josiah Knockwood, died. Josiah wed Rosie Gooley in 1885 when she was only fifteen, so she would have been born in 1870, while Stephen John's wife Rosie Gooley, who died in 1915, was said to have been born in 1872 (but this could have been an error; she might have been born in 1870).

85 Martha Walls examines the development and implementation of this government policy in *No Need of a Chief for This Band: The Maritime Mi'kmaq and Federal Electoral Legislation, 1899–1951* (Vancouver: University of British Columbia Press, 2010).

86 In the spring of 1920, Stephen John and Theresa hoped to be given the opportunity to raise their family at Millbrook. LAC, RG 10, vol. 3220, file 536,764, "Petition of Michael Tom and Stephen [John] Knockwood," 21 April 1920. Stephen's brother Joseph Knockwood, like Michael Thomas, eventually did gain admittance to Millbrook. Yet, despite his attempts to secure educational opportunities for his offspring. Stephen John Sr. was unable to make educational arrangements of his own choosing for his and Theresa's children, and faced the insult of seeing Henry, Isabelle, and Noel Raymond taken away to the Shubenacadie residential school.

87 These terms were March 1945–March 1948, March 1948–March 1951, and April 1954–April 1956.

88 His daughter, Rose Knockwood Morris, still possesses one of his prayer books. In the late 1880s, Stephen John Knockwood (1878–1951), often referred to simply as "John Knockwood," attended the Brooklyn Road Schoolhouse for a few years and, being a lifelong learner, as an adult taught himself to improve his reading and writing skills. He eventually wrote short stories, one being about Glooscap. He and his first wife Rosie Gooley had four children: Stephen John (1902–57), Benjamin (b. c.1905), Mary (b. 1908), and Lucy. The 1911 federal census for Cornwallis states that Ben was born in April 1905 and Mary in June 1908. Sarah Ann Paul assisted as a midwife with these children's births. Following Rosie Gooley's death in 1915, Stephen John married Theresa Simons in 1917, with whom he had three girls, Mary Isabelle in 1922 (who only lived for two months), Rose Ann, and Isabelle; and three boys, Joseph, Henry, and Noel Raymond. NSARM, Historical Vital Statistics, Kings County Marriages, Year 1917, Book 33, 336, "Marriage at Kentville of Stephen J. Knockwood, 37, widower, son of Stephen Knockwood and Mary Ann Paul, and Theresa Simons, 23, of Cambridge, daughter of Noel Simons and Mary Paul, 22 August 1917, presiding priest Alphonsus R. Donahue, witnesses John Julian and Marie Elizabeth Pictou"; NSARM, NSARM, Registration Year 1922, Colchester County Deaths, Book 62, 393, "Death of Mary Isabelle Knockwood." Stephen John and Theresa's marriage certificate of 1917 gives his birth year as 1880, though he was born on 5 December 1878.

     Stephen John Sr. was not the only one of his immediate family with such traditional knowledge. His brother Joseph Martin Knockwood also attracted the attention of folklorist Helen Creighton, who recorded him in the 1940s reciting Mi'kmaw prayers. NSARM, Helen Creighton collection, Ac2141, "St. Anne's Day Prayer recited by John Knockwood, recorded by Helen Creighton at Dartmouth on 22 April 1944." "Mrs. Joe Knockwood [Madeleine Martin] of Kennetcook," from whom Creighton also recorded songs and stories, was Joseph's wife. Joseph died in 1956 at Millbrook. NSARM, Historical Vital Statistics, Colchester County Deaths, Registration Year 19565, 6758. In 1990, Stephen John's youngest son, Noel Raymond Knockwood, told the author that he could not remember his grandfather physically at all, despite being six years old when his grandfather died, though he heard a great deal about him. That a distance remained between Noel Raymond's father, Stephen John Knockwood Jr,. and grandfather, Stephen Knockwood Sr., is also evidenced by the fact that Stephen John listed his father as "deceased" on his and Theresa Simons's marriage certificate, even though Stephen Knockwood Jr. was still living in 1917.

89 Theresa Simons, Stephen John's second wife, was well known as a basketmaker throughout the Mi'kmaw community. The Nova Scotia Museum photograph collection houses a 1943 portrait of Theresa Simons, known in Mi'kmaq as "Deodis," holding one of her baskets. NSM, N-17,824. Following Stephen John Knockwood Sr.'s death, caused by a stroke in 1951, Theresa, then fifty-six years old, married Michael Thomas, one of Knockwood's long-time friends and political associates.

Two of Stephen John Knockwood's sons, Henry and Noel Raymond, served in the military, Henry as mentioned in World War II and Noel Raymond in the Korean War. Henry landed on Juno Beach in June 1944 when he was only twenty years old. He once stated that although he had exuded confidence as part of the Canadian contingent overseas, this confidence waned when he found, despite his service to Canada, that he still faced racism after his return home. Carl Fleming, "Veteran Still Carries Bittersweet Memories," *The Daily News*, Sunday, 8 May 2005. For his military service overseas, Noel Raymond received the Korean War Medal and the Canadian Voluntary Service Medal.

90 Isabelle Knockwood and Gillian Thomas, *Out of the Depths: The Experiences of Mi'kmaw Children at the Indian Residential School at Shubenacadie*, 4th ed. (Halifax: Fernwood, 2015; first published Lockport: Roseway, 1992). Beginning in the 1930s, Stephen John Knockwood Sr.'s youngest children were placed by government agents in the Shubenacadie residential school, a nightmare experience Isabelle Knockwood discusses in *Out of the Depths*. She held that her father's first wife was an orphan who was adopted by a couple on the Cambridge Reserve, and in consequence as an adult was especially kind to foster children.

91 Michael Lightstone and Mary Ellen Macintrye, "Mi'kmaq Elder Noel Knockwood Dies at 81," *Halifax Herald*, 11 April 2014.

CHAPTER 10

1 Variations of this Mi'kmaw surname include "Bemmewit," "Bemmineau," "Pemenoiet," "Peminouite," "Peminuit," "Pemmineweit," "Pemminurch," and "Pemminwicke." Ethnohistorian Ruth Holmes Whitehead, quoting a story that Jeremiah Bartlett-Alexis told to Harry Piers, curator of the Nova Scotia Museum in 1917, wrote: "As to the origin of the name Bemenuit, it is stated it arose in this way. In the early wars of the Micmacs, on one occasion the women of the tribe went away in a canoe, while the men stood to give battle. While the women were thus on their way to the head stream of the Shubenacadie River, one of the Indian women while in the canoe gave birth to a boy child. This child and his descendants were called Bemenuit, which means, in Micmac, 'Born on the way.' They were called Pauls by the English." Whitehead, *The Old Man Told Us: Excerpts from Mi'kmaw History 1500–1950* (Halifax: Nimbus, 1991), 81. The original, written down by Harry Piers, is housed in the Nova Scotia Museum, Halifax (henceforth NSM), Printed Matter File, Piers Papers, "Jeremiah Bartlett Alexis [or "Jerry Lonecloud"] to Harry Piers," 17 September 1917. Paul Peminout, however, was certainly not the first Algonquian-speaking person in the Northeast to use the Peminout surname. A French nominal census compiled in 1708 reveals that a Mi'kmaq named Charles "Peminouite," who was born in 1654, lived in the vicinity of Minas with his wife Marie, his two daughters Madeleine and Agnes, and a son, René. A Penobscot family living at the same time in what is now Maine also bore this surname, while in 1726 the surname appeared among members of the Passamaquoddy nation. For instance, "Jacques Pemerot [Peminout]" and "Louis Pemeroit" of the Passamaquoddy nation both came to Annapolis Royal in 1726 to sign a ratification of a peace and friendship treaty made between the British and the Eastern Abenaki in Boston the preceding year. British Records Office, London, England, British Colonial Office records on microfilm housed in Library and Archives Canada, Ottawa (henceforth LAC, CO) 217/38/116, "Treaty of Peace and Friendship, dated 4 June 1726, showing signatures." (There are three copies of this document dated the same day, but probably not drafted on the same day. See for instance LAC, CO 217/4/99–103, which varies from the above.) A Mi'kmaw oral tradition, which Sandy Cope Sr. of Millbrook told to Muriel Cottam Yorke of Debert in 1922, further claimed that one of the names Paul Peminout used at times was "Pierre Paul Neptune," and that Paul was the son of "Chief Neptune Pierre Paul," a Passamaquoddy emissary who in 1725 signed a treaty with the British at Boston. Don Byrd Awalt of Halifax graciously related to the author what he knew about this story, derived from notes taken in 1922

by Muriel Cottam Yorke (interview 10 February 2011). Also see Awalt, "The Mi'kmaq and Point Pleasant Park, The Mi'kmaq and Amtoukati: An Historical Essay in Progress by Don Byrd Awalt" (Halifax: Native Friendship Centre, 2006). The Passamaquoddy chief Neptune Pierre Paul, along with his son Pierre Beminout (Peminout), also signed a ratification of the Boston treaty in 1726 at Annapolis Royal. Nova Scotia Archives and Records Management, Halifax (henceforth NSARM), MG 15, vol. 18, doc. 8, "Ratification in 1726 at Annapolis Royal of Treaty made in Boston in 1725." The surname "Neptune" or "Neptan" also surfaces in Francklin's correspondence from Fort Howe, on the Saint John River, in 1778. Despite this resemblance of surnames, however, it seems most likely that Paul Peminout was in some way related to Charles Peminout, who was at Minas in 1708, and was born either at Minas or along the Shubenacadie Valley. Given the paucity of early documentary data, any claims that the Peminouts of Nova Scotia were related to members of the Passamaquoddy nation must remain conjectural.

2 The French referred to "Chicabenackady" in the seventeenth century as a verdant sector of the Acadian countryside where groundnuts, "comme truffles," grew. Archives des Colonies, Paris, records on microfilm at LAC, AC, Series CIID, Correspondance générale, Acadia, vol. 2, 1686–95, 442. Groundnuts, *Apios americana*, also called "wild potatoes," are members of the pea family. The parent vine grows along the edge of flowing water, and its dark, reddish-brown flowers are so tightly packed together that they have a ball-like appearance. The place name "Shubenacadie" derives from *Sipekne'katik*, "groundnut land." Today, "Sipekne'katik First Nation" is the official name of what used to be called the "Shubenacadie" or "Indian Brook" Band.

3 It is not known when Paul Peminout first encountered Michael Francklin. Their relationship must have developed prior to the end of the Seven Years' War, since Francklin was said to have encouraged Peminout to fight at Quebec with the British forces in 1759.

4 L.R. Fisher, "Francklin, Michael," *Dictionary of Canadian Biography* online, vol. 4 (1771–1800). Michael Francklin was acting governor of the colony on four different occasions when Governor William Campbell was away from the province: from May to late July 1766, from 1 October 1767 to 10 September 1768, from 4 November to 4 December 1768, and from 2 June to 10 July 1772.

5 Other Mi'kmaw individuals also were approached by British authorities at this time to fight for the British

cause. For instance, John Pennel Sr. of Gold River, Lunenburg County, stated that at the age of fourteen he had been encouraged to join Wolfe's contingent and fight for the British on the Plains of Abraham. Beamish Murdoch, *History of Nova-Scotia, or Acadie* (Halifax: James Barnes, 1865), 2.372.

6 Awalt, "The Mi'kmaq and Point Pleasant Park," 7. Mi'kmaq-British interactions were frequently fraught with tension following the Seven Years' War. General Jeffrey Amherst, commander-in-chief of the British forces in North America, refused to give most Mi'kmaw presents, although he may have made an exception in Pul Peminout's case. Amherst has also been charged with distributing smallpox-infected blankets to Indigenous groups, although if this actually happened, the act probably was not intentional. The oral tradition relating to Paul Peminout reveals that there were chiefs whom the British trusted and treated as allies, and the story of Peminout's relationship with Francklin demonstrates how little is actually known of the complexity of Mi'kmaw-British interrelations between 1763 and 1782.

7 NSARM, RG 1, vol. 24, "Minutes of Council at Annapolis Royal from 6 December 1744 to 25 January 1745, including a letter written by Pierre Landry at instance of the Indians [Mi'kmaq]," 14 August 1745. See also NSARM, RG 1, vol. 24, "Minutes of Council at Annapolis Royal from 12 October 1744 to 8 November 1748, regarding a Letter of Frances Coumaruse on behalf of the Indians."

8 NSARM, RG 1, vol. 29, doc. 25, "Regarding need for a fort at Minas to check French and Acadians supplying the French garrison at Chignecto," 4 March 1754; LAC, CO 217/205, ff. 205–205½, "Jn. Handfield to Cornwallis," 7 December 1749. The ranger commander John Gorham had a blockhouse named Fort Vieux Logis, built earlier at Annapolis Royal, dismantled and moved to the Grand Pré during the summer of 1749. In early December of the same year around three hundred Mi'kmaq and Malecite as well as a number of Acadians attacked this blockhouse and captured a patrol of twenty men led by Lieutenant John Hamilton. This foray temporarily curtailed British plans to plant settlers at the mouth of the Shubenacadie River and halted further fort building in the *Sipekne'katik* district until 1754.

9 Chiefs met in September 1749 at Port Toulouse to discuss possible responses to the founding of Halifax without consultation with the Mi'kmaq. They allowed the settlement of Port Royal, they contended, since the Mi'kmaq had played an integral role in the early development of that settlement. By contrast, Halifax was

imposed in a unilateral bid to gain control of the whole province, something the Mi'kmaq immediately recognized. The Mi'kmaq declared their opposition to what they considered an outrage against their territorial rights in a letter drafted by Abbé Pierre Maillard, who wrote their words down, using the Roman alphabet, in both French and Mi'kmaq and sent the document to Halifax. The original letter is housed in the Archives de Seminaire du Quebec; a copy of the declaration is printed in H.R. Casgrain, ed., *Collection de documents inédits sur le Canada et l'Amérique publiés par le Canada-Français, Documents sur l'Acadie* (Québec: Demers and Frère, 1888), 1.17–19.

10 British suspicions of Indigenous intrigues against New England and Nova Scotia were rampant in early 1749. See LAC, CO217/32/47–50, "Letter of Governor William Shirley of Massachusetts," 9 May 1749.

11 In August 1750 Edward How, a well-known trader and negotiator and a member of the executive council, was lured outside the walls of Fort Lawrence by a man waving a white flag. When How left the fort, he was shot dead. Cope for years afterwards was implicated in the deed, though historians today believe the shot to have been fired by another, Étienne Batârd.

12 LAC, CO 217/9/118, "Proclamation of Governor Edward Cornwallis, made at Halifax," 2 October 1749.

13 There were short-term practical concerns too. The winter of 1751–52 had been "uncommonly severe." NSARM, G1, vol. 35, doc. 67, "Edward Cornwallis to the Lords Commissioners for Trade and Plantations," 16 February 1752.

14 A district chief protected lands and resources under his aegis. Yet even at the local community level chiefs allotted lands to individual hunting group leaders. From then on those who trespassed and took resources off another's lands, for whatever reason, were expected to inform the territory's owner and pay him compensation. Long before Frank G. Speck began systematically examining the Mi'kmaw hunting territory system in 1914, Titus Smith in 1801 wrote, "At the close of the American War, a period when the game was much more numerous than it is now, the Indians had divided all the Hunting ground among their families, they did not kill more moose than was necessary to supply themselves with provisions as they considered them as their own property. An Indian travelling through the Hunting ground of another might kill any game he met with, if he was in want of provisions, and he usually informed the proprietor of what he had done and offered him the skin, which the proprietor usually refused as an acknowledgement

of his right." NSARM, RG 1, vol. 380, 116, *Sketches of the Eastern and Northern Parts of the Province in the years 1801 and 1802 with close observations thereon … by Titus Smith Jr. 3rd ed., 1857.* For Speck's analysis of the Mi'kmaw hunting territory system see Janet E. Chute, "Frank G. Speck's Contributions to the Understanding of Mi'kmaq Land Use, Leadership, and Land Management," *Ethnohistory* 46, no. 3 (1999): 481–540.

15 Jean-Baptiste Cope received his commission of "major" from the French at Louisbourg. The French gave Indigenous leaders who supported the French cause different commissions: captain, major, and the highest, chief. The traditional district chiefship, or *bun,* is discussed in Wilson D. Wallis and Ruth Sawtell Wallis, *The Micmac Indians of Eastern Canada* (Minneapolis: University of Minnesota Press, 1955), 176.

16 This mission was strategically placed to draw Mi'kmaq from the Stewiacke River area, Minas, Pictou, Piziquid, and the Musquodoboit River Valley. Moreover, the Shubenacadie River Valley was part of a navigable water route, running across the province from Cobequid Bay to the Atlantic coast. Even before the building of the Shubenacadie Canal in the mid-1850s, long stretches of the Shubenacadie River remained navigable by canoe, and there were portages at waterfalls and at shallows, where summer dry spells often caused a lowering of the water.

17 Buried in the heartland of Nova Scotia's peninsular mainland, five kilometres from the confluence of the Shubenacadie and Stewiack Rivers, this mission dedicated to St. Anne catered to temporal as well as spiritual matters. It furnished both a centre for religious ceremonies and a mustering point for Indigenous war parties from many quarters during times of conflict. Established in 1722, it operated for sixteen years under Abbé Gaulin, and from 1738 to 1749 under Abbé Jean-Louis Le Loutre who, like Gaulin, was a graduate of the Société des Missions Étrangères in Paris. Le Loutre erected a sizeable mission house and an attractive chapel, whose bell on a clear day could be heard as far away as Nova Scotia's Noel Shore. The site was also suitable for agriculture. As early as 1699, a Jesuit, Pierre Thury, regarded Shubenacadie as a possible site for a farming community, although he died at Musquodoboit Harbour before he could realize his vision. Gaulin later sought, with only limited success, to establish a Mi'kmaw agricultural settlement with around 150 Mi'kmaw families. LAC, CO 217/4/132–5, "Gaulin to Lieutenant Governor John Doucett," 13 March 1722, and "Doucett to Gaulin," 14 March 1722; LAC, AC, vol. 7, 29v, "Governor Saint-Ovide,

Louisbourg, au minister," 24 November 1724; NSARM, RG 1, vol. 23, "Proceedings of Hibbert Newton, and Captain John Bradstreet with Governor Saint-Ovide of Louisbourg," 30 August 1725. Abbé Pierre Maillard, another graduate of the Société des Missions Étrangères, visited the Shubenacadie mission on an itinerant basis between 1738 and 1750 and, like Gaulin and Le Loutre before him, found the Mi'kmaq hesitant to farm. When they left the mission for prolonged periods, he feared they were abandoning their religious observances and losing their faith. Documents from the Archives des Colonies, Paris, France, on microfilm at LAC (henceforth Maillard in 1738 LAC, AC) CIIB, vol. 20, Correspondence générale, Île Royale, 87, 3 October 1738; Bernard Gilbert Hoffman, "The Historical Ethnography of the Micmac of the Sixteenth and Seventeenth Centuries" (PhD diss., University of California, 1955), 533–6; William C. Wicken, "Encounters with Tall Sails and Tall Tales: Mi'kmaw Society, 1500–1760" (master's thesis, McGill University, 1994), 106–7. The mission chapel lay on a knoll along the riverbank that by the mid-nineteenth century became known as "Indian Hill."

18 Chiefs who heeded the French priests still felt compelled to forge linkages, by treaty if possible, with the British. Yet it remains doubtful that a wholehearted transference of support from the French to the British ever occurred at Shubenacadie in 1752, or at any other time prior to the second fall of Louisbourg in 1758. Mi'kmaw leaders wanted to be as informed as possible and keep all options open until the final "chips fell" at the close of the Seven Years' War. A division in band loyalties could also arise, as occurred among the Malecite during the American Revolution, where one leader, Pierre Thomas, was pro-British while the other, Ambroise St. Aubin, supported the American cause. L.F.S. Upton, *Micmacs and Colonists: Indian-White Relations in the Maritimes, 1713–1867* (Vancouver: University of British Columbia Press, 1979), 69–70.

19 In 1722 Joseph Bomehudetche, or Bemgaboudes, was listed on a French census as the Shubenacadie head chief, yet only four years later an individual named Chief Jean-Baptiste Bon signed a 1726 ratification of a Boston peace and friendship treaty at Annapolis Royal on behalf of the Shubenacadie group. Since Bomehudetche was forty-eight years old in 1708, he would have been sixty-two in 1722, so he possibly died before 1726, or stepped down in favour of Bon. LAC, MG 18, F 18 (typescript), *Recensement genal fait au mois de Novembre mile Sept cent huit de tous les Sauvages de l'Acadie que resident dans la Coste de l'est*, 1708; LAC, AC, MG

1, CIIB, vol. 6, doc. 77, Correspondance générale, Île Royale, *Recensement des Sauvages tam de l'isle Royalle que de la peninsula de l'acadie qui sont deservis par Les Missionaires de Seminaire des Missions etrangeres Etablis à Quebec fait par M. Gaulin, pretre Missionaire des Sauvages en 1722*. In 1744 the "Chickabenakady" chief, René Madogonouit, acting under orders from a French priest, had his son-in-law, Bernard Bernard, and two others of his group, La Martier and Martier's son-in-law, capture an English vessel and kill its crew members. It is possible Le Loutre encouraged the raid. The master of the vessel captured by Madogonouit and his party was named Rich and the ship's owner was named Larkin. (The ship's master was also likely the man of the same surname who was captured around the time the Mi'kmaq took a man named William Pote near Annapolis Royal in 1747, although unlike Pote, Rich was released soon afterwards.) Madogonouit was identified as the chief at Shubenacadie by an Acadian trader, Antoine Gibbard, at an investigation into the incident at Annapolis Royal. According to Gibbard, the Shubenacadie chief engraved "signs" (pictoglyphs?) on a stone at Jeddore warning of the dire fate of any Englishman who dared venture onto his territory. NSARM, RG 1, vol. 25, "From a transcription of the Minutes of the Council at Annapolis Royal made by Dr. Andrew Brown in years 1798 and 1799," Document Package no. 6, 1744, "Declaration of Antoine Giffart [Gibbard or Claremont] from Louisbourg and wintering at Grand Pré and the east coast at Jeddore, sworn before Paul Mascarene," 4 May 1744. Madogonouit must have perished politically – and likely also bodily - after this event, for eight years later the British hailed Jean-Baptiste Cope as the new Shubenacadie head chief.

20 It may have been his role as spokesman for the greater Mi'kmaw community rather than any personal preference for peace that motivated Cope in 1752 to approach Halifax. He may well have participated in the attack on the Grand Pré blockhouse and raids on Halifax and Dartmouth.

21 LAC, AN, AC C11B 32, 163r–v, "Prevost au minister, 10 septembre 1752."

22 Council Minutes, 14 and 16 September 1752. Thomas B. Akins, *Selections from the Public Documents of Nova Scotia* (Halifax: Annand, 1869), 682–5.

23 Despite British promises, a truckhouse was not built at Shubenacadie in the early 1750s.

24 LAC, CO 217/40/225, "Response of Governor and Council," 18 October 1752 and "Council Minutes, 22 November 1752"; Akins, *Selections from the Public Documents*, 682–5; NSARM, RG 1, vol. 430, doc. 2, "Treaty

proclamation by Governor by Thomas Peregrine Hopson," 24 November 1752; LAC, CO 217/13/305-06.

25 "Peregrine Thomas Hopson, Treaty of peace and friendship with Jean-Baptiste Cope, André Martin and two others, 1752," in Akins, *Selections from the Public Documents*, 683–5. There were about forty men in his group. Abbé Maillard had found seventy-five males of fifteen years of age or older at Shubenacadie in 1735, and about half of these came from Minas. LAC, AC G1 466, doc. 71, *Recensement fait cette presente année du nombre des sauvages Miquemaq portant les armes*, 1735; William Wicken, *Mi'kmaw Treaties on Trial* (Toronto: University of Toronto Press, 2002), 184. Cope's territorial aegis, however, particularly embraced the lower reaches of the Shubenacadie River, the Musquodoboit Valley, and lands extending from Chebucto east along the Atlantic coast at least as far as Sheet Harbour.

26 In April 1753 Chief Claude Gisigash (Gagoish or Egighighes) of La Hève (now La Have) signed a peace agreement in Halifax. Murdoch, *History of Nova-Scotia, or Acadie,* 2.219.

27 Jacques Prevost, the governor of Louisbourg, denounced Cope as a "mauvais sujet," while Le Loutre, after his return from France, upbraided the British for treating for peace with a man he derided as the "tail of the Indians." LAC, AC MG I, CIIB, Correspondence général, vol. 33, f. 159, "Prevost to the Minister of Marine," 12 May 1753. The most probable explanation for Cope's actions in 1753 relates to his deep feelings of betrayal. Edouard Richard and Henri Arles, *Acadie, Depuis la Paix D'Aix-La-Chapelle jusqu'à la Deportation* (Québec: A.K. LaFlamme/Marlier, 1916), 2.85–9. After dismissing the value of the treaty of 1752, Le Loutre promoted a new idea raised by the Chignecto Mi'kmaq's council, to reserve the northwestern part of the province exclusively for the Mi'kmaq. NSARM, RG 1, vol. 210, "Minutes of Council, Halifax, regarding letter of Abbé Le Loutre," 27 August 1754.

28 Despite the promise Cope had received that Mi'kmaw grievances would receive a fair legal hearing, the Halifax establishment believed a fabrication devised by Connors that he and Grace had acted as they had out of self-defence. Connors and Grace were guests of the Mi'kmaq prior to the attack. The two had experienced shipwreck and, in keeping with the terms of the recent treaty, the Mi'kmaq, finding the two men washed up on the beach and nearly dead, resuscitated them and trusted them to the care of a woman while the men went hunting. To add insult to injury, after dispatching the woman and her infant, Connors and his companion scalped their former caregivers, stole a canoe, and brought the scalps to Halifax to claim a reward under the terms of Cornwallis's scalp bounty.

29 British Museum, Andrew Brown MSS, Add. 19073, f. II, no. 23, "Anthony Casteel's Journal"; LAC, CO 217/14/199–202, "Disposition of Anthony Casteel, from the time of his being held Prisoner by the Indians till his return to Halifax, sworn before William Cotterell, Provincial Secretary of his Majesty's Council," 30 July 1753.

30 Neither the French authorities at Louisbourg nor the fiery missionary priest Le Loutre can be charged directly with influencing Cope's radical change of heart towards the British in 1753. Either he or another member of his group snatched the treaty document he had recently signed out of the hands of an Acadian man at Cobequid, with whom the document had been lodged since the preceding fall, and thrust the paper into the fire, exclaiming, "that was the way they made Peace with the English." The depth of his anger at the British was heightened by the fact that the Mi'kmaq who were killed lived on lands under his territorial aegis and may even have been his kin relations. At the same time, the British penchant to lay the blame for what they called Mi'kmaq "fickleness" on the activities of the French often caused them to close their eyes to their own diplomatic blunders. Following the Connors-Grace affair, Cope felt that the imperative to avenge the injuries to his people outweighed the peaceful tenets of the Chignecto council. By duping the British at Jeddore in 1753, Cope has even been viewed in some quarters as a heroic resistance fighter, given that the British ignored Mi'kmaw land prerogatives by settling foreign Protestants soon after in Lunenburg County and dispossessing *métis* and Acadians of their lands. Daniel N. Paul, "Mi'kmaq Remember Chief Kopit as True Hero," *Halifax Herald,* 19 April 1996, http://www.danielnpaul.com/Col/1996/Mi'kmaqChiefKopit-TrueHero.html. Paul suggests that Cope's name may have derived from *kopit*, the Mi'kmaw word for "beaver." Cope could speak French and presumably was sympathetic to Acadian interests.

31 Abbé Jean Manach, a missionary who stayed at Beaubassin after Le Loutre left for France in 1755, claimed in February 1760 that "Claude" was the Sipekne'katik leader. Claude René – doubtless the same person – signed a peace treaty with the British on 10 March the same year. Murdoch, *History of Nova-Scotia, or Acadie,* 2.384. Manach compiled his list of Mi'kmaw chiefs for Colonel Joseph Frye at Fort Cumberland. The list was first published in the *Pennsylvania Gazette* in 1760, and in 1809 re-published on page 116 of volume 10

of the *Collections of the Massachusetts Historical Society*. Before becoming the Sipekne'katik district chief, Claude René had lived at Antigonish, Cape Breton, and Chignecto, which bolsters the idea that a Mi'kmaw Grand Council was responsible for distributing leaders over the Mi'kmaki landscape. In 1760 he may have been "parachuted" into the Sipekne'katik district to play a leading role. Abbé Pierre Maillard regarded Claude René as a formidable warrior and devout "praying chief," whom he once observed "stripping for battle" in preparation for a foray against the British during King George's War (1744–48). Pierre (Antoine Simon) Maillard, "Lettre de M. l'abbé Maillard sur les missions de l'Acadie et particulièrement sur les missions micmaques, Lettre à Madame Drucourt," in *Les soirées canadiennes: Recueil de littérature nationale*, vol. 3, 289–426 (Québec: Brousseau Frères, 1863), 3.371. Chief René also fought for the French during the Seven Years' War but, after signing treaty with the British in 1760, was accorded a passport by Governor Lawrence. LAC, AC CIID, vol. 10, "Sur l'Acadie, 1748"; NSARM, RG 1, vol. 64, 45, "Pass to Claud Renee, given by Charles Lawrence," 1760.

Lettre de M. l'abbé Maillard sur les missions de l'Acadie et particulièrement sur les missions micmaques, Lettre à Madame Drucourt." In *Les soirées canadiennes: Recueil de littérature national*

32 NSARM, RG 1, vol. 29, no. 17, "Whitehall to Hopson," 28 March 1753; John C. Reid, "*Pax Britannia* or *Pax Indigena*? Planter Nova Scotia (1760–1782) and Competing Strategies of Pacification," *Canadian Historical Review* 85, no. 4 (2004): 674.

33 In 1752, for instance, Lieutenant Governor Peregrine Thomas Hopson was praised by his superiors in London for making a peace treaty with the Shubenacadie band, whose lands embraced pockets of soil favourable for the promotion of Mi'kmaw agriculture. NSARM, RG 1, vol. 36, 2, "Minutes of Council, Halifax, 29 December 1753."

34 Traces of the foundation of the old chapel could be found *in situ* as late as 1830.

35 Abbé Pierre Maillard remained in Nova Scotia after Le Loutre left the province, and from1758 to 1762 tried to facilitate a peaceful accommodation between the Mi'kmaq and the new British regime. In 1760 Maillard had his mission headquarters in a refurbished barnlike building, located in Halifax at what is NSM, Piers Papers, Ethnology: History, Geographic Board of Canada, "Notes by Harry Piers from data provided by Jerry Lone Cloud," 27 May 1914.

36 Since Mi'kmaw leaders had presided over traditional Mi'kmaw ceremonies and festivities before the missionaries arrived, Maillard's initiative restored a degree of their previous autonomy in the spiritual realm. Upton, *Micmacs and Colonists*, 154; Janet Elizabeth Chute, "Ceremony, Revitalization and Change: Micmac Leadership and the Annual Festival of St. Anne," *Papers of the Twenty-Third Algonquian Conference*, ed. William Cowan (Ottawa: Carleton University, 1992), 54. For many years Sipekne'katik chiefs held services and hosted feasts on the mission grounds, and even as late as 1912 parts of a traditional wedding ceremony could still be remembered. NSM, Piers Papers, Ethnology: Material Culture, "Polly Williams, sister of John Williams of Great Lake, Pubnico, Nova Scotia, to Harry Piers," 3 February 1912.

37 James S. Macdonald, "Memoir of Lieut.-Governor Michael Francklin, 1752–1782," in *Collections of the Nova Scotia Historical Society*, no. 16 (Halifax: W. McNab and Son, 1912), 8.

38 Ibid., 10. Francklin was captured in 1754, prior to the demolishment of the St. Anne mission. Since the British destruction of the mission would have shocked and infuriated the local Mi'kmaq, Francklin might not have fared so well had he been captured late in 1755. The mission house and chapel were still standing when Captain Anthony Floyer wrote about his survey expedition along the Shubenacadie River during the summer of 1754. Floyer's journal entry for 18 August stated: "About half past twelve we came to the Masshouse, which I think is the neatest in the country, tis Adorned with a Fine Lofty Steeple and a Weather Cock. The Parsonage House is the only Habitation here, the land is good & seems to be more so on the opposite side." http://www.northeastarch.com/sainte_anne.html. St. Anne's mission was razed by the British during the summer of 1755. A decade later, when Captain William Owen travelled down the Shubenacadie River, all that remained of the mission were ruins. William Owen, *Narrative of American Voyages and Travels of Captain William Owen, R.N.*, ed. Victor Hugo Paltsits (New York: New York Public Library, 1942), "Entry for October 1766."

39 Paul Peminout would have been in his early thirties during the Seven Years' War, so his sons would have been young. Awalt, "The Mi'kmaq and Point Pleasant Park," 8; NSM, Printed Matter File. The Mi'kmaw chiefs' meeting in the vicinity of Halifax was said to have taken place in the late 1750s on St. Aspinquid's Day, east of what is now Chain Rock Drive and within the boundaries of Point Pleasant Park. In 1782 there was a boulder called the Chain Rock that had an iron eye holding one end of a chain suspended across the Sandwich River (now the

North West Arm) to prevent French ships from entering the Arm. John W. Regan, *Sketches and Traditions of the North West Arm* (Willowdale, ON: Hounslow, 1978), 73. Directly across from this spot on the other side of the Northwest Arm lay a cove originally called "Indian Cove" because the Mi'kmaq frequented it seasonally for fishing and ceremonies.

40 NSM, Printed Matter File, "Maggie Paul to Jeremiah Bartlett-Alexis, alias Jerry Lone Cloud, and retold to Harry Piers," 5 April 1927; NSN, Printed Matter File, Piers Papers, "Jerry Lone Cloud to Harry Piers," 11 August 1922. Jerry Lonecloud claimed that his information came from two elders, Joseph Howe (Jeremy) and Maggie Paul. An alternative possible location for Cope's death was the Miramichi River district, as Cope was held to have been in that vicinity. Micheline D. Johnson, "Cope, Jean-Baptiste," *Dictionary of Canadian Biography* online, vol. 3 (1741–70).

41 LAC, CO 218/205-06, "Lords of Trade to Lieutenant Governor Wilmot," 8 May 1764; LAC, CO 217/22/4-5, "Michael Francklin to the Colonial Office," 10 November 1766. At this time Francklin wrote: "We are at perfect peace with the Indians of this Province." No settlement made is to the "injury of the Indians," he continued, "[but] that on the contrary due regard is always paid to their rights." This letter shows that the Colonial Office had made Francklin very aware of the Royal Proclamation, and expected him to follow it. It is interesting that Francklin, when he became Indian superintendent, reserved large tracts of land in trust for the Mi'kmaw people that were never formally recorded. The instructions he received earlier in 1766 were likely meant to guide negotiations during one of the earliest Indigenous land transactions that occurred in Nova Scotia (which at the time included what is now New Brunswick). This was a grant of islands and riverbank to the Malecite in 1767 at Aukpaque. As early as 1764, however, Richard Bulkeley, the provincial secretary, held that no grants could be made on the Saint John River "without His Majesty's order for such a purchase." LAC, CO 217/22/50, "Bulkeley to Colonial Office," 24 December 1764.

42 Francklin arranged for Abbé Charles-François Bailly to take up missionary work in Nova Scotia in 1768. NSARM, vol. 43, 38, "Michael Francklin to the Earl of Hillsborough," 10 July 1768. The other missionary was Father Joseph Mathurin Bourg, who in 1773 went to serve on the lower Saint John River among the Acadians, Malecite, and Mi'kmaq. A makeshift chapel stood on the St. Anne's site at this time. Oral traditions relate that the Mi'kmaq and Acadians, although lacking proper

construction materials, rebuilt a makeshift chapel soon after the original was razed by the British in 1755. After the St. Anne's mission site was included in 1763 in a 1,900-acre grant accorded to Lieutenant Colonel Frederick Hamilton, Michael Francklin built and furnished a second chapel on the parcel in 1770. When a local landlord began driving the Mi'kmaq away from the locale, however, the Shubenacadie Mi'kmaq launched a campaign in 1810 to acquire both the mission chapel and a nearby burial ground.

43 Francklin proposed transferring a tract on the Stewiacke River to Peminout prior to the onset of the American Revoution. There is a memo, dated 1772, allocating land at Stewiacke to "Paul Pemminwick," in NSARM, Miscellaneous "I" Indian land documents.

44 Francklin's correspondence during the American Revolution, and particularly his accounts of activities during 1778 at Fort Howe, a military compound with a blockhouse and barracks perched atop a rocky escarpment overlooking what is now Saint John city, give insights into his relationship with the Mi'kmaq and Malecite. He mentions sustaining ongoing relations with "Old Capt. Antony" (the ancestor of the Toney Mi'kmaw family), Charles "Nocout" (Knockwood), Paul "Neptan" (Neptune), Achmobish, Pierre Thomas, and Captain Anthony (Toney). New Brunswick Museum, Archives and Research Library, Saint John, New Brunswick, Official Papers, Indian Affairs, 1778–81, S 5-1, MS Collection, 1–3, James White Papers, "The Honorable Michael Francklin Esq., Superintendent of Indians, to Wm. Hazen, for Sundrys paid and Supplies furnished by his order for the use of the Indians assembled at Menaguashe near Fort Howe the 13th Septr. to 19th Octob. 1778." Paul Peminout's name does not appear in these documents, unless Paul Neptune *is* Paul Peminout, a claim one historian has made. That "Pierre Paul Neptune" and Paul Peminout were one and the same man is raised in a Mi'kmaw oral tradition told in 1922 by Sandy Cope of Millbrook to Muriel Cottam Yorke. Awalt, "The Mi'kmaq and Point Pleasant Park," 8. In the fall of 1778 Francklin directed Charles Nocout, Michel Neptan, and Paul Neptan, who were employed as couriers by Major Gilfred Studholme at Fort Howe, to go to Restgouche "after M. Bourg, the Priest." Francklin repeatedly reimbursed Indigenous leaders for the services they rendered, or for injuries they sustained. For instance, in 1778 he "paid Charles Nocout [Noucout or Knockwood] ten dollars by order to make up for an Englishman beating of him," while Charles Nocout and Achmobish were rewarded handsomely for "going after two deserters & their spirited

attempt to surprize a Rebell Whale Boat's crew." New Brunswick Museum, Archives and Research Library, James White Papers, S 5-1, MS Collection, 3, "The Honble Michael Francklin … to Wm. Hazen … 13th Jany. to 19th Octob. 1778."

45 Several interpretations have been given for this place name, among them "It oozed slowly out from still water," "Flowing out in small streams," or "Whimpering and whining as it goes." Thomas Brown, *Place Names of Nova Scotia* (Halifax, 1922), 146; Charles Bruce Fergusson, ed., *Place-Names and Places of Nova Scotia* (Halifax: Public Archives of Nova Scotia, 1967), 647; Fergusson, *The Boundaries of Nova Scotia and Its Counties* (Halifax: Public Archives of Nova Scotia, 1966), no. 22, 23. The south branch of the Stewiacke River runs northeast, while the main branch runs southwest. Derek S. Davis and Sue Browne, *Natural History of Nova Scotia,* vol. 2 (Halifax: Nova Scotia Museum, 1996): 100–5. The territory through which the northeast branch ran was known as "Colchester." Between 1780 and 1835 "Colchester" referred to a division of Halifax County, and did not become Colchester County until 1835. Much of the interior, which was accessible by water, was shrouded in a mixed forest of oak, beech, birch, and pine. Canoes could travel from the Cobequid Basin all the way along the Shubenacadie River to Shubenacadie Grand Lake, the Shubenacadie River's watershed in Halifax County. After crossing a low divide, one then proceeded through a river and lake system to the Dartmouth Lakes.

46 This grant of 704 acres at Aukpaque on the Saint John River was reissued in 1779. The original grant was given to the Malecites in 1767. Land Grants, Old Book 12, 106–7; Upton, *Micmacs and Colonists*, 75. The Grantee Index by Surname, housed in the Crown Land Records Office in Halifax, did not list the tract accorded on the Stewiacke River in 1779.

47 NSARM, RG 1, vol. 189, 454–5, "Minutes of the Executive Council," 28 June 1779. NSARM, RG 1, vol. 212, 363, "Official transcript regarding [Peminout] grant," n.d. In 1770 Lord Egmont had received a grant of three thousand acres on the Shubenacadie River that was later escheated. A memo entitled "Regarding a tract of land four miles square ordered to be granted to Mr. Francklin and Paul Pemmeyweete on the Stewiac River, 28 January 1779" may be found in NSARM, Miscellaneous "I" Indian Land Records, documents photocopied in the 1970s by Charles Bruce Fergusson, provincial archivist. These records, though unidentified as to provenance, likely derived from the Crown Lands Office and the Office of the Attorney General.

48 James S. Macdonald, "Memoir of Lieut.-Governor Francklin," 40.

49 Monk was Nova Scotia's superintendent of Indian Affairs from 1783 to 1799 and again from 1807 to 1809.

50 LAC, MG 23, G II-19 vol. 3, 1034, Monk Papers, George Henry Monk Letter Book, "Paul Bemeneaut [or Pemeneaut] prays for a Grant of the Land on the River Schudiack applied for him + his tribe by the late Superintendent Mr. Francklin," n.d. (1784).

51 These nine licences are recorded in NSARM, RG 10, vol. 430, package 23½.

52 Ibid., "License to Paul Pemmenwick," 17 December 1783.

53 While Monk temporarily deemed the Peminout holding to be merely a licence of occupation rather than a trust deed, the Peminouts later successfully treated their property as a freehold grant, which could be sold.

54 Paul Peminout's licence of occupation for land on the Stewiacke River and Jacques's licence of occupation for land along the Shubenacadie Valley were probably both copied out by Charles Morris, the surveyor general, but if so, he was unaware that he was writing about two men of the same family, for he spelled their surnames differently in each document.

55 Morris likely both wrote and signed this document, as the signature and the handwriting throughout the document as a whole are similar. It was Morris, not Monk, who was responsible for the allocation of land to Jacques Peminout. NSARM, RG 1, vo. 430, doc. 23½, "Licence to Jack or James Pemmenwick," 18 December 1783. The original draft left out the words "son of" before the words "Chief of Shubenaccadie," but they were later inserted in the margin on the copy signed by Morris. This leads one to think that Morris was not really certain of the relationship between Paul and Jacques until sometime later, when he went back and inserted the words "son of" on the page. Another change from the original draft is Morris's scratching out of the words "to be granted to them" in favour of the phrase "land sufficient for" them. Even so, the parcel was treated as a grant, as it was sold by the Peminout family in 1812. Strangely, a typescript in the Crown Lands Records Office in Halifax does not have the words "son of" inserted in the text.

56 According to one Mi'kmaw oral tradition, Paul Peminout married Jean-Baptiste Cope's sister, Marie Cope – an improbable claim since Marie Cope was born in 1703 and Chief Peminout was born around 1725. Awalt, "The Mi'kmaq and Point Pleasant Park," 8; LAC, MG 18, F 18 (typescript), 1, *Recensement genal fait au mois de Novembre mile Sept cent huit de tous les Sauvages de l'Acadie que resident dans la Coste de l'est.* Paul Peminout was still

fathering children in the 1760s and lived until around 1812. An Irishman named John Nowlan who traded in the 1770s near Torbay along Nova Scotia's Eastern Shore, however, married a Mi'kmaw woman who was probably Cope's granddaughter. Nowlan's son Edward (or "Ted") wed a daughter of Francis Paul, one of Jacques Peminout's sons.

57 Joseph Peminout Paul moved to Ekoupahag (Apohaqui or Studville) on the Saint John River, where on 26 October 1769 he stood as godfather at the baptism of Joseph Anquarret (Momquarret) and Frances Naukaut's (Knockwood's) daughter Marie Josephe Momquarret. NSARM, microfilm reel 10,053, *Registre des actes de baptême, marriages, et sepultures faits en la nouvelle écosse ou acadie, commence le vingt unième jour de juillet de l'année mil sept cent soixante huit, par mons. Charles-François Bailly, prêtre missionaire des sauvages et acadiens sujets de sa majeste britanique*, 18, "Baptemes à Ekoupahag de Marie Josephe, fils de Joseph Anquarret et Frances Naukaut; parraine Joseph Pemouet [Peminout], 26 octobre 1769." Marie Madeline Peminout, a granddaughter of Paul Peminout, wed François Xavier "Nocout" (Knockwood) at Bouctouche, New Brunswick, on 11 September 1815, and their descendants later moved to Memramcook and Fort Folly. "Simeon Pimenuit and Marie Charlotte Charles of Windsor" had a daughter, Magdeline, baptized at Memramcook on 30 May 1823, and "Claude Pemenuit" was born in the same area on 26 July 1830. Provincial Archives of New Brunswick, Fredericton, microfilm reel 1731, Registre de la paroisse St. Thomas de Memramcook, 1806–1870. The Peminouts also married Acadians, for an Acadian farmer at Richibucto named Noel Mecure and his wife Marie Agnes Peminout had a son, Hilarion Mecure, baptized on 3 August 1830. Registre de la mission St. Antoine de Richibucto, Baptêmes, mariages et sepultures, 1796–1870 (parents not mentioned). All these Peminouts would have been Paul Peminout's grandchildren or great-grandchildren rather than his sons or daughters.

58 Monk recorded Simon Peminout, who was blind, travelling with Chief Peminout in 1808.

59 Jacques Peminout was named frequently in George Henry Monk's Letterbooks and Accounts. LAC, MG 23, GII-19, George Henry Monk Papers, Indian Accounts, 1793–99.

60 Louis-Benjamin's birth date remains uncertain. A newspaper report stated that Louis-Benjamin was seventy-eight years old in 1840, according to which he would have been born in 1762. *The Novascotian*, 7 May 1841. By contrast, L.F.S. Upton suggested he was born around 1755. Upton, "Peminuit Paul, Louis-Benjamin," *Dictionary of Canadian Biography* online, vol. 7 (1836–50). Abbé Charles-François Bailly's register furthermore records the baptism at Halifax on 22 October 1770 of an infant named "Benjamin-Louis Paul," the son of "Paul and Marie Joseph." NSARM, microfilm reel 10,053, *Registre des actes de baptême, mariages, et sepultures faits en la nouvelle écosse ou acadie … par mons. Charles-françois Bailly, pretre missionaire des sauvages et acadiens, sujets de sa majeste britanique*. The child baptized by Bailly, however, was likely not Louis-Benjamin Peminout, but rather a member of the Paul family who lived along the Eastern Atlantic coast. In 1841 Louis-Benjamin referred to himself as an "old man," and if he were born in 1770 he would in 1841 have been only sixty-one years old.

61 Mary Christiana (or Christianne) Paul Morris was likely born along the Stewiacke River, although it has also been argued that she may have been born at Ship Harbour on the Eastern Shore. In the early 1840s she lived with her husband, Tom Morris, on McNab's island, on the Dartmouth side of Chebucto Harbour. Her father was identified as "Hobblewest Paul," which Ruth Holmes Whitehead suggests may stand for "Ambroise Paul." She and Tom lived on McNab's Island until 1855, when they moved to the west side of the North West Arm near Thomas Hosterman's grist mill, close by Chocolate Lake. In 1851 she petitioned the government for funds to begin a small farm, since her husband was ailing and unable to work, she was responsible for two orphan children, and she had only a few fowl left for food. In response she received £7 10 s., with which she built a small green frame house and outbuildings where she kept livestock and hens. NSARM, MG 15, vol. 6, doc. 11, "Petition of Christy Morris to the lieutenant governor for money to purchase supplies and livestock," 1851. Her circumstances improved and she became friends with William Chearnley, appointed provincial Indian commissioner in 1853. An eye-catching woman, she was sought out as a model by artists who portrayed her in pastel, watercolour, and oil, and she posed for a number of studio photographs. She came to make a respectable living for her family through her exquisite quillwork, beadwork, basketry, and leatherwork, and several of her pieces won prizes at provincial exhibitions. Being childless, she and her husband adopted two children; a girl named Charlotte, who also was her biological niece, and a boy named Joe. In 1857, when Charlotte married Louis Paul of Hants County, she hosted a party with flute and violin music and a table laden with wine and cheeses. Notable attendees included Chearnley and two mayors of

Halifax, Samuel and William Caldwell. Mary Christiana died in 1886 and her body was probably buried at Elmsdale in East Hants County. Ruth Holmes Whitehead, "Paul, Mary Christianne, c.1804–1886," *Dictionary of Canadian Biography* online, vol. 11 (1881–1890); Whitehead, *Niniskamijinaqik/Ancestral Images: The Mi'kmaq in Art and Phtotgraphy* (Halifax, 2015), 46–50. For additional information on this woman as an artist and artisan, see Whitehead, "Christiana Morris: Micmac Artist and Artists' Model," *Material History Bulletin*, Spring 1977, National Museum of Man, Ottawa, 1–14.

62 Pierre Peminout Paul Sr. and his father obtained goods from a number of merchants, including Joseph Davis, Charles Dickson, Jacob Hurd, and Robert Mullens. On 2 December 1794, "Pemenute Paul, Peter Paul and Peter Paul Jr." received ammunition from Joseph Davis. Other articles desired by the Pemimouts were "clothing, blankets, fishing lines and hooks, salt for pickling fish, provisions – mostly flour pease and potatoes – salmon nets and farming utensils." LAC, CO 217/67/177–78; 182–7. The Mi'kmaw community at Stewiacke fluctuated in size depending on the time of year, but in the late 1700s remained at between sixteen to twenty-two individuals.

63 Joseph Paul was baptized in Halifax by Abbé Charles-François Bailly on 14 November 1770, and his brother James was probably a year older. NSARM, microfilm reel 10,053, 76, *Registre des actes de baptême, mariages, et sepultures faits en la nouvelle écosse ou acadie,* "Baptism of Joseph, son of Pierre Perminout and Marie, 14 November 1770." Joseph Nancout and Marie were Joseph's godparents.

64 NSARM, RG 1, vol. 430, doc. 43½, "Set of instructions sent out as a circular to agents," 23 January 1801. The government circular was directed to Fulton by a commission headed by Charles Morris, Michael Wallace, James Brenton, and William Cottnam Tonge that had been convened to address incidents of Mi'kmaw hardship and promote Indigenous farming settlements. NSARM, RG 1, vol. 430, doc. 55, "James Fulton to members of the Indian Commission in Halifax," 3 March 1801. Pierre's eldest son, Pierre Jr., had left the Stewiacke region by 1801, and afterwards became the judge of the Si band. Pierre Sr.'s second eldest, Nestus, who was thirty-seven in 1801 and a cooper by trade, acted as a local community leader. Fulton considered Nestus hard working, honest, bright, and a good craftsman. His brothers Abluis, who was thirty-two, and Joseph, thirty-one, were also coopers. Since all three were intelligent and knew enough English to carry on trade transactions, Fulton lamented that they refused to allow

"well-meaning" settlers to educate their children. In the 1820s, after the Stewiacke grant was sold by the Peminouts, Pierre Sr.'s sons moved to Kings County. Pierre Sr., referred to as the "antient Inhabitant of Suiack," was still alive in 1821 when Joseph, then living at Horton Corner, wrote to the General Assembly asking for supplies on behalf of his "aged father." NSARM, RG 1, vol. 430, doc. 161½, "Petition of Joseph Paul to Sir James Kempt on behalf of his aged father Peter Paul, Indians residing at Horton Corner," n.d. (c.1821). Many of the Pauls living in the nineteenth century at Horton, Kentville, and Cambridge in Kings County were descendants of Pierre Sr. For instance, Stephen Knockwood Jr., a well-known guide and farmer at Kentville, married a Paul woman who was likely one of Pierre's descendants.

65 Fergusson, *Place-Names and Places of Nova Scotia*, 87.

66 The aging Roma conducted Roman Catholic services at Chezzetcook after Maillard's death in Halifax in 1762, and also sporadically visited the St. Anne's mission site along the Shubenacadie River. Chezzetcook remained a centre for religious ceremonies with a strongly Mi'kmaw character well into the late eighteenth century, a fact noted by clerics of various denominations, including Abbé Charles-François Bailly between 1768–72, Father Vincent de Paul in 1818, and a Presbyterian minister, Andrew Brown, in the 1790s. Brown obtained two of Abbé Maillard's original manuscripts from Jean-Baptist Roma at Chezzetcook. Sara J. Beanlands, "Annotated Edition of Rev. Dr. Andrew Brown's Manuscript: Removal of the French Inhabitants of Nova Scotia by Lieut.-Governor Lawrence & His Majesty's Council in October 1755" (master's thesis, Saint Mary's University, 2010), 189, f. 277. George Henry Monk's accounts mention Jacques and Roma. LAC, MG 23, GII-19, George Henry Monk Papers, "Indian Accounts, 1793–1799," 1158–60, 1165. One entry, dated 6 June 1796, that reads "Jean-B. Roma for Jacques Pemenoiet and others" indicates that Roma secured goods from merchants on behalf of Jacques and his family.

67 John, though very elderly, was alive in 1814, and his death date remains uncertain.

68 Jacques's eldest son, John, acted as his father's emissary, interpreter, and aide, while Gorham's name testifies to the Peminout family's associations with the Gorham family of Windsor during the late 1770s, when Gorham was born. Pierre became a Mi'kmaw judge in the Shubenacadie district, along with Louis Paul, a son of Louis-Benjamin. After Pierre's death around 1850, another of Louis-Benjamin's sons, Christopher Peminout Paul, succeeded to his office. Birth and death dates of Jacques's

sons Samuel, Thomas, Claude, Alexis, and Paul, are unknown, although these men lived into the mid-nineteenth century.

69 The nickname "Sam," used by Joseph Howe and other officials in the early 1800s, may have been a corruption of the way the Mi'kmaq pronounced the name "Louis-Benjamin."

70 NSARM, RG 1, vol. 430, doc. 55, "James Fulton to members of the Indian Commission in Halifax," 3 March 1801. The boy who appeared with Louis-Benjamin was likely his son Louis Paul.

71 NSARM, RG 1, vol. 430, doc. 55, "James Fulton to members of the Indian Commission in Halifax," 3 March 1801. Nestus, Peter, Joseph, and Abluis Paul killed fifteen bears in the District of Colchester in 1796. NSARM RG 47, Colchester County Registry of Deeds, Book 3B, unpaginated, "Return of Bairs Kill'd [*sic*]," 10 September 1796.

72 Monk's father died while he was young and the Monk family for years struggled with financial worries. Even in adulthood, George Henry Monk lacked the reserves of capital and land that had been available to Francklin. Since he was poorly remunerated as Indian commissioner, he had to rely extensively on financial assistance from his elder brother James Monk, then living in Quebec. As early as 1774, James Monk had won the confidence of Governor Francis Legge, Francklin's arch political rival.

73 Louis Toney's stay in Newport Township was temporary, for Mi'kmaq from Remsheg seasonally travelled to the Newport area in the past. He was back in Remsheg in February 1803, where he encouraged an agent, George Oxley, to send a petition to Charles Morris and Michael Wallace. NSARM, RG 1, vol. 430, doc. 127, "George Oxley to Charles Morris and Michael Wallace," 4 February 1803. One of Louis Toney's sons named Daniel, however, pressed onward towards Bear River, and his descendants joined that community.

74 Louis Toney could speak Mi'kmaq, French, and English. He hailed originally from Pictou County, and his father was Captain Anthony of Remsheg (now Wallace), whom Michael Francklin mentioned in his Fort Howe correspondences of 1778.

75 LAC, MG 23, GII-19, George Henry Monk Papers, Monk Letter Book, 1046–7.

76 The commissioner suspected that dangerous conspiracies might arise at the meetings of Mi'kmaw leaders. Jacques Peminout Paul, called "James" in 1794 by Indian commissioner George Monk, who liked to anglicize Mi'kmaw names, told Monk about an upcoming Mi'kmaw council to be held in the Gaspereau Lake region of the Annapolis Valley. To Monk, such assemblies might import seditious ideas from French or American sources – or from pockets of disaffected Acadians in the province. He felt his main duty was to protect the settler population from any shows of Indigenous discontent, and was especially fearful of the movements of Chief Charles Alexis, since he knew Alexis's father-in-law, Anthony Hebert of Annapolis, had resisted the Acadian removals in 1755. James Peminout Paul exercised great reticence in answering Monk's questions regarding Alexis's whereabouts.

77 LAC, MG 23, GII-19, George Henry Monk Papers, Monk Letter Book, 1050.

78 Ibid.

79 Ibid., 1057–8, 1065. Monk paid Ross ten dollars for eight days of work. Upton, *Micmacs and Colonists*, 84.

80 Between 1 February and 4 February 1794, a Mrs. Mary Canon, as well as Robert Alexander and John Macomber of Newport, Nova Scotia, informed Monk that the party who had visited Windsor on 12 January dwelt in wretched conditions. Assistant Deputy Commissary Officer Daniel Hammill also noted that some Mi'kmaq had dragged the carcass of a dead dog from Fort Edward's premises to their camp to eat, they were so hungry. LAC, MG 23, GII-19, George Henry Monk Papers, Monk Letter Book, 1056–9.

81 Ibid., 1055. While John formerly had been reticent to communicate to Monk in other than Mi'kmaq, the commissioner discovered on 7 February that, when he wanted, John could communicate "very freely in English." John claimed that his father Jacques had compelled him to speak as he did, and that he would not have spoken in such a way if left to his own devices. He also had a settler friend named Andrews write him a letter to show to Monk, to help him get back into Monk's good graces. Ibid., 1060–1. Francklin's widow, who remained living at Windsor after her husband's death, was the former Susannah Boutineau of Boston.

82 Ibid.

83 John Paul was refused provisions for his absent father on 26 February 1794. Ibid., 1069.

84 Ibid., 1071.

85 NSARM, MG 15, vo. 3, doc. 1, "Bill for supplies delivered by order of the Honourable Richard Bulkeley … to the Indians, 1780, 1781 and 1782" 1074.

86 LAC, MG 23, GII-19, George Henry Monk Papers, Monk Letter Book, 1075–7. These mittens attracted favourable attention at Halifax. Ibid., 1065.

87 See, for instance, LAC, MG 23, GII-19, George Henry Monk Papers, Indian Accounts, 1781–1792, "Sundry

supply receipts from T.M.F. Bulkeley to Charles Dickson for supplies to Louis Paul, Peter Paul, Nestus Paul, Joseph Paul and James Paul."

88 On 31 March 1794 the chief's son Pierre Paul signed the document relinquishing rights to the property sold to McClellan and Bonnell, rather than his father.

89 NSARM, microfilm reel no. 17,439, Colchester County Deeds, Book 3A, 47, "Deed of Sale, Pemmenwick Paul to Robert Kennedy, 200 acres for £7. Witnesses William Dickson and Charles Dickson."

90 NSARM, microfilm reel no. 17,439, Colchester Deeds, Book 3A, 47–9.

91 Joseph claimed that this particular parcel had been "laid out by John Harris Esq. for me and my brother Sappier [Jacques-Pierre] on the north side of the river." NSARM, microfilm reel no. 571,672, Colchester County Deeds, Book 4, 135, "Bond of Joseph Pemmewit of Stewiacke River," 31 May 1801. This document is hard to read. It probably refers to 150 acres of land, though the number written on it is indistinct.

92 NSARM, RG 1, vol. 430, doc. 55, "James Fulton to the Indian Commissioners, An Account of the Indians in the District of Colchester," 3 March 1801.

93 The Upper Stewiacke concession was awarded in 1783 to thirty-nine men. One of these, John Harris, did not take up his grant. Israel Longworth, "A History of the County of Colchester, Nova Scotia," part 2, ed. Sandra Creighton (Truro: Book Nook, 1989 [1886]), 120.

94 NSARM, microfilm reel 571,672, Colchester County Deeds, Book 4, 418, "Peter Paul to John Bonnell," registered 25 June 1805.

95 Even though Lieutenant Governor John Wentworth had given his approval to the 1794 sales, no reference was made in either 1794 or 1805 to the terms of the Royal Proclamation of 1763, which stipulated that Aboriginal relinquishment of land called for negotiation between Indigenous leaders and officials of the Crown.

96 James Paul, described as a "native of Stewiack" who died at age thirty-nine in 1851, was likely a member of the Peminout Paul family. *Novascotian*, "Obituary of James Paul," 25 March 1851, 95.

97 Canada, Royal Commission on Aboriginal Peoples, *Report of the Royal Commission on Aboriginal Peoples*," vol. 1 (Ottawa: Indian and Northern Affairs, 1996), appendix D, 720–25. For documentary sources concerning the relevance of the Royal Proclamation of 1763 to Nova Scotia, see NSARM, RG 1, vol. 189, 194–5, and NSARM, RG 1, vol. 212, 179–80. The last is a copy of expanded instructions on this matter, dated 7 April 1772, and entered into the Minutes of the Executive Council of Nova Scotia on 20 July 1773.

98 In 1801, the surveyor and naturalist Titus Smith recorded sighting abandoned summer wigwams or "camps" but few Mi'kmaq in the Shubenacadie region, which led him to think that "considerable numbers had left the province." NSARM, RG 1, vol. 380, 112–13, Titus Smith, "Sketches of the Eastern and Northern Parts of the Province in the years 1801 and 1802."

99 NSARM, RG 1, vol. 430, doc. 125, "James Fulton, Robt. Archibald, James Archibald, William Cutten, Danl. McCurdy, Samuel Tupper, L.G.W. Archibald, Justices of the Colchester Court of Sessions, January Term, 1803, to members of the Indian Commission," 4 January 1803. Jacques in 1803 had five in his household, his son John had four, his son Claude also had four, and his brother Peter Sr. had seven. Peter Sr.'s family also included Abluis, with four in his household; Joseph with six; and Nestus with five. Bartholomew Momquarret, who also lived at Stewaick in 1803, had four in his household.

100 Since at least the late seventeenth century, Mi'kmaq travelled to Quebec and Montreal to trade, attend meetings, and participate in religious observances.

101 NSARM, RG 1, vol. 430, doc. 139, "Commissioners J. Brenton, M. Wallace and C. Morris to James Archibald," 11 January 1803. Smallpox appeared among the Mi'kmaq at Stewicke in 1801, followed by an outbreak of whooping cough.

102 NSARM, Miscellaneous "I" Indian Land Documents, microfilm reel 14,011, "Plan, signed W. Smith D.S. 26th April 1808, of a lot of land at head of Shubenacadie Great Lake marked Indian Lewis Paul's Farm."

103 The deed of sale was registered on 13 July 1812. NSARM, RG 47, Microfilm reel 17,888, Halifax County Registry of Deeds, Book 40, 131–132, "Paul Pemmineu's relinquishment of right, title and interest to land on lower or north western end of Great Shubenacadie Lake," 6 June 1812; "Deed from Paul Pemmineu to Richard John Uniacke of land at Shubenacadie Grand Lake," 6 June 1812, recorded 13 July 1812. This sale pertains to the land given under licence of occupation to "Jacques Pemmenwick" on 19 December 1783. NSARM, RG 1, vol. 430, doc. 23½. The Francklins, the Uniackes, and the Delesdernier family were close, and it is possible that this fact made the Peminouts willing to sell so readily to the attorney general. Michael Francklin's son, James Boutineau Francklin, held land across the Shubenacadie River from Jacques's grant of 1783. And in 1830, James Boutineau Francklin's daughter, Elizabeth Gould Francklin, married the Reverend Robert Fitzgerald Uniacke, a son of Richard John Uniacke and Martha Maria Delesdernier, who later

served as rector of St. George's Church in Halifax. Macdonald, "Memoir of Lieut.-Governor Francklin," 38.

104 These seven proprietors were Alicia Uniacke, Crofton Uniacke, Richard John Uniacke the Younger, Dame Mary Mitchell, the Honourable Thomas Nicholson Jeffrey, Anne Delesdernier, and Denis Rehn." A lot marked by a letter "A" on the plan attached to the Uniacke grant was the "land laid out for Lewis Paul … to whom the proprietors paid £60 to give up his right, the same to be divided between them share & share alike." Nova Scotia Crown Lands Information Management Center, Book C, 21, "Crown Grant to Norman Fitzgerald Uniacke *et al*, Shubenacadie Great Lake, 14 August 1812." It is possible in 1812 that the Peminouts considered the parcel they sold to Uniacke to form only part of the land originally intended for Jacques Peminout Paul and his sons in 1783. Louis-Benjamin's decision to send his son to live with a settler family to learn how to farm, moreover, does not seem like the action of a man who expected his tenure in the region to be temporary. The grant's description simply stated that the Mi'kmaq held land rights on the "Northern side of the River Shubenacadie at the Point where the great Lake Discharges Itself, and extending on the Great Lake, and the said River." How far the grant extended along the lake or river thus remained ambiguous, though the 104 acres, surveyed in 1808 and sold in 1812, likely was less than the acreage the Mi'kmaq believed they could lay claim to twenty-five years before. This riverine tract, near runs of bass, gaspereau and salmon in the spring and eels in the fall, had been occupied seasonally by the Mi'kmaq for generations. According to the grant description of 1783, Jacques and his sons actually possessed proprietory rights to all the land forming a large triangle between the northwest bank of the Shubenacadie River and the east coast of Shubenacadie Grand Lake, including the small island called Paul's Island. The Mi'kmaq, moreover, did not abandon the area after 1812, but simply moved onto neighbouring lands at Elmsdale. These Mi'kmaq later would contend, against the claims of a settler named Jacob Gilby, that the ground at Elmsdale belonged to them by virtue of long occupation. Moreover, there is no record that Paul's Island, positioned directly opposite the mouth of Lewey's Brook (renamed Uniacke Brook in 1812), was sold by the Mi'kmaq in 1812.

105 The tract "they parted with … was a very valuable one and capable of growing a considerable supply of that food they most delight in, Indian corn," Morris lamented. It "was purchased of them by the Honble. Richd. Uniacke for the sum of £60." NSARM, RG 1, vol.

430, doc. 151, "Charles Morris to Sir John Coape Sherbrooke," 7 March 1815.

106 This was included in the Hants County descriptions. NSARM, RG 1, vol. 430, doc. 53, "Descriptions of Reserve Lands, Hants County, 2100 acres, 1820."

107 In 1807 Monk resumed the office of Indian superintendent for two years, with instructions to distribute presents should such be necessary to keep the Mi'kmaq neutral in the event of war. The same year, Indian agents were appointed in twelve administrative districts, with mandates to dispense relief to the Mi'kmaq when necessary and to encourage agriculture. NSARM, RG 1, vol. 430, doc. 143, "Circular written and signed by George H. Monk, requesting information on the Indian population, with a schedule of divisions and the agents appointed to each," 20 October 1807.

108 NSARM, RG 20, NS Land Papers, Series A, vol. 27–9, 1807, microfilm reel 23, "Petition of Samuel, Francis and Gorham Paul and eleven others to Sir John Wentworth," 1807.

109 NSARM, Miscellaneous Indian "I" Indian Lands Documents, Packages 1 and 2, Charles Morris, "Report on the Reservation of Lands for the Indians by the Surveyor General on the 7 May, 1820."

110 Joseph Howe, when he was provincial Indian commissioner in 1842, was surprised that flooding from this source continued unabated even after the reserve's boundaries were marked out in 1820.

111 Chief Peminout was said to have asked to be buried next to Major Cope's grave. This gesture was a bid to assuage any lingering animosities between his descendants and those of Jean-Baptiste Cope following a serious altercation around 1758 at a Mi'kmaw council meeting at Point Pleasant Park in which both Peminout's son Phillip and Cope himself were said to have died. Awalt, "The Mi'kmaq and Point Pleasant Park," 7. Some oral traditions also hold that none of Jean-Baptiste Cope's male offspring lived to have children of their own, and that the present-day Cope family stemmed from one of Cope's granddaughters marrying a trader, John Nowlan. This is a subject, however, that requires further research. Moreover, not all of John Nowlan's sons took the Cope surname; one son, Edward or Ted, kept the surname "Nowlan." Edward married Francis Paul Peminout's daughter, Marguerite (or Margaret) Paul.

112 Provincial Archives of New Brunswick, Fredericton (henceforth PNAB), File 1, MG H54, doc. no. 43, "Samuel Paul, Gorham Paul and Francis Paul to Major General George Stacey Smythe regarding their need for provisions to return to Nova Scotia after choosing a new

chief," 1 July 1813. In Records of Lt.-Gov. Smythe (PANB, RG 1, RS 344), documents extracted from the Records of the Lieutenant Governors of New Brunswick and placed in the Indian Documentation Collection (on microfilm reel 408 at the Harriet Irving Archives, University of New Brunswick, Fredericton), as part of a St. Thomas University–sponsored project in 1982.

113 PNAB, RG 1, RS 344, File 1, MG H54, doc. no. 44, "Lieut.-Col. Robertson to Smythe," 3 July 1813.

114 PNAB, RG 1, RS 344, File 1, MG H54, doc. no. 45, "Thomas Wetmore to Judge Chipman," 5 July 1813.

115 Even in the early decades of the nineteenth century, representatives of member nations of the Eastern Wabanaki Confederacy throughout the Northeast ratified the installation of a new chief, prior to the new leader being presented by his people to prelates of the Roman Catholic Church and representatives of the British Crown. In 1813 the Shubenacadie Mi'kmaq and at least one Malecite community appointed new chiefs.

116 NSARM, RG 1, vol. 430, doc. no. 149½, "Petition of Samuel Paul, John Paul and Joe Barss, Halifax," n.d. (c. April 1814).

117 NSM, Printed Matter File, "Copies of documents from New England Company Papers at Guildhall, London, England, including a press clipping (MSS 7956) regarding a Mi'kmaw Petition to Sir John Coape Sherbrooke, dated 5 April 1814." The Mi'kmaq also wanted Sigogne to request more land for them at Shubenacadie, not "back in the woods" like the 1,100 acres they recently received, but composed of bottomland, close to markets, and containing the St. Anne's mission site. Sigogne added that the petitioners were all good Catholics, and intimated that no further assistance from humanitarian sources was required, except possibly some help in transcribing some books.

118 In 1814 Lieutenant Governor Sherbrooke vested Louis-Benjamin Peminout Paul with a commission stating that the Mi'kmaq "have made choice of you, the said Louis-Benjamin Pominout, to be their chief." The framed, original commission, Item 31.24, "Commission to Louis Benjamin Peminout," 28 April 1814, is housed in the Nova Scotia Museum of Natural History in Halifax. Sherbrooke considered Louis-Benjamin as chief only of peninsular Nova Scotia, as in 1814 Cape Breton was still a separate colony. Many years later, Harry Piers, a curator of the Nova Museum in Halifax, on 1 May 1913 found the medal given to Louis-Benjamin Peminout in 1814 to measure 2.98 centimetres across.

119 For a comprehensive examination of Bromley's humanitarian work, see Judith Fingard, "Bromley, Walter," *Dictionary of Canadian Biography* online, vol. 7 (1836–50).

120 Morris suggested that Ellis should be approached to sell "50 acres around the mass house site." (Ellis later adamantly refused to consider Morris's proposal, however, and this land was never purchased.) In his letter to Cogwell Morris stated that "[t]hey also want a little provision to support them until they return [from Maine], but where this is to come from, I know not. I think however if it meet His Excellency's approbation, twenty or thirty dollars might be allowed from the Province's fund." When the plan to attain the mission site fell through, the surveyor general then switched his attention to settling Mi'kmaq at Shubenacadie Grand Lake. In May 1814 he informed Cogswell, "I have requests of these Indians to procure a list of those of their tribe who wish to join them, preparatory to an arrangement for their being provided with Lands on the East side of the Great Shubenacadie Lake – I hope to do this soon." NSARM, RG 1, vol. 430, doc. 150, "Morris to Cogswell," 18 May 1814.

121 The Roman Catholic Diocese of Halifax at the time lay under the Diocese of Quebec's jurisdiction.

122 J.-O. Plessis, *Journal des visites pastorals de 1815 et 1816, par Monseigneur Joseph-Octave Plessis, évêque de Québec* (Québec: Henri Têtu, 1903), 76.

123 Simon and Peter Paul, who were members of the Peminout Paul family, arrived from the Stewiacke River area, while Peter Lulan travelled from Pictou and David Occam came from Shubenacadie. Occam, who was of Wampanoag ancestry, had a relative named Samuel Occam living at Merigomish, Pictou County. NSARM, MG 15, vol. 18, doc. 12, "Names of the heads of the Indian Families who resided at Shubenacadie when the first attempt was made to form a settlement in 1816"; NSARM, RG 1, vol. 430, docs. 46 and 50, "Lists of Pictou Indians in 1800." Members of the Wampanoag nation, from Martha's Vineyard in Massachusetts, had joined Gorham's Rangers during the Seven Year War, and a few after 1763 remained in Nova Scotia.

124 NSARM, MG 15, vol. 3, doc. 24, "Walter Bromley on behalf of the Indians for a road to their new settlement on the River Shubenacadie," 1817; *Journal of the Legislative Assembly of Nova Scotia* (henceforth *JLANS*), 1817, 273.

125 Lord Dalhousie continued to furnish monetary aid to the Shubenacadie farming settlement in 1817. NSARM, MG 15, vol. 3, doc. 26, "Lord Dalhousie's order to Michael Wallace, Provincial Treasurer, to provide £50 to Walter Bromley for Shubenacadie Mi'kmaq"; NSARM, MG 15, vol. 3, doc. 27, "Lord. Dalhousie's order for £30 to

pay Thomas Roach for relief of Shubenacadie Mi'kmaq"; NSARM, MG 15, vol. 3, doc. 29, "Lord Dalhousie's order to pay Walter Bromley £12.17.5 for the relief of the Shubenacadie Mi'kmaq." By 27 February 1817 twenty-four families had collected at Shubenacadie.

126 LAC, CO 217/141/40; Walter Bromley, *An Appeal … in behalf of the Indians of North America* (Halifax: Ward, 1820), 46–8. For twenty more years the twelve families at Shubenacadie, following Louis-Benjamin's example, established small farms, using ploughs and axes and maintaining livestock provided by Bromley in 1817 and 1818. As they had been instructed to do by Bromley, they saved seed over the winter to sow in the spring. After spring planting, however, many families left a few elderly persons and children left behind to see to the animals, and travelled to Rocky Lake, Rockingham on the Bedford Basin, or to Dartmouth to sell their wooden manufactures, ornamental quillwork items, splint baskets, axe handles, brooms, butter boxes, and buckets.

127 In the eighteenth and early nineteenth century, many Mi'kmaw upheld and guarded the continuance of a distinctive form of Roman Catholic faith that they had come to regard as integral to Mi'kmaw group identity. L.F.S. Upton stated that "[the Mi'kmaq] preserved that faith because it had become part of themselves." Upton, *Micmacs and Colonists*, 170.

128 Archives of the Archdiocese of Quebec, "Bishop Plessis to Mignault," 26 March 1817; Father Vincent de Paul, *Memoir of Father Vincent de Paul*, trans. A.M. Pope (Charlottetown: Coombs, 1886), 18–19.

129 The Copes obtained a grant of land and licence of occupation later than the Peminouts. Under Charles Morris's auspices, Captain Francis Cope on 4 September 1783 received eleven thousand acres for his band at Wigawick, now Sheet Harbour. Cope's hunting territories extended inland along the Musquodoboit Valley. NSARM, RG 1, vol. 430, doc. 20½, "A License for the Indians To Occupy Land … on the Eastern Branch of Sheet Harbour, containing in the whole Eleven Thousand Five Hundred and Twenty acres, including salmon fishery. Signed Charles Morris, Chief Surveyor, 4 September 1783." Another spelling for the Mi'kmaw name for Sheet Harbour is "Weijooik," or "[water] flowing wildly." Fergusson, *Place-Names and Places of Nova Scotia*, 616; Campbell Hardy, *Sporting Adventures in the New World; or, Days and Nights of Moose-Hunting in the Pine Forests of Acadie* (London: Hurst and Blackett, 1855), 1.315. John Nowlan, a trader who set up a post at Quoddy Harbour in the 1770s, married a daughter of Jean-Baptiste Cope and raised sons who took the Cope surname. Although

he may have secured a grant of land near Quoddy in 1801, Nowlan's offspring hunted with the Peminouts. Ted Nowlan and his wife Margaret Paul lived at Rawdon for many years, and at Elmsdale in 1855. NSARM, MG 15, vol. 5, no. 69, "William Chearnley, Indian List of the Year 1855." John Nowlan began petitioning for land in 1793, though he may not have received the parcel he wanted, for there is no mention of a grant, and he and his son Edward travelled with the Peminouts in later years. LAC, vol. 4, MG 23, GII-19, Monk Letterbook, 1043; NSARM, RG 1, vol. 430, doc. 34½, "Petition of John Nowlan of Nicumquodie, eastward of Beaver Harbour, for provisions and a spot of land between Col. Hales' & Nicumteauce [Necum Teuch]" for agricultural purposes," 1801. Another principal family head in the Sheet Harbour region in the 1800s was Lewis Paul, whose sons Francis and Joseph Paul in 1848 petitioned the lieutenant governor and council for land at the mouth of a river flowing into Ship Harbour Lake, east of Musquodoboit.

130 L.F.S. Upton, "Peminuit (Pominout) Paul, Louis-Benjamin," *Dictionary of Canadian Biography* online, vol. 7 (1836–50).

131 NSARM, RG 5, series P, vol. 41, no. 94, "Petition of Gorham Paul," 16 March 1829.

132 The Anglican Parish of Christ Church was founded in 1788 by Bishop Inglis, who also designed and presided over the building of the first Anglican church in Windsor. The associated burial ground, though older, was consecrated in 1826. The original Christ Church stood for almost one hundred years years, from roughly 1790 to 1882, in what is now called the Old Parish Burying Ground, below King's College. After a new church was built in the town of Windsor in 1882, the burying ground by 1889 fell into poor condition. Henry Youle Hind, *An Early History of Windsor, Nova Scotia, with a Sketch of the old Parish Burying Ground of Windsor, Nova Scotia* (Windsor: Jas. J. Anslow, 1889), 65. The Mi'kmaq would not have camped on the burying ground, but would have been on glebe land, closer to the church.

133 NSAM, RG 1, vol. 430, doc. 179, "Petition of Louis-Benjamin Peminout to Sir Peregrine Maitland," 17 January 1831. The Reverend Mr. Morris personally carried this memorial to Halifax.

134 NSARM, RG 1, vol. 430, doc. 176, "The Reverend George E. William Morris to Sir Peregrine Maitland," 17 January 1831.

135 Upton, "Peminuit (Pominout) Paul, Louis-Benjamin."

136 During the harsh winters from 1831 to 1835, members of the Peminout family and their associates living in the

Windsor and Rawdon areas sent several petitions to Halifax asking for assistance. See, for example, NSARM, RG 1, vol. 431, doc. 9, "Petition of Peter Paul, Joseph Stevens, Noel Morris, Charles Lewis, Peter Morris, Thomas Phillips and John Simons to the Lieutenant-Governor, Sir Colin Campbell," 2 December 1834.

137 NSARM, MG 15, vol. 3, doc. 60, "Warrant from Sir Colin Campbell to Gorham Paul for £20 for building a chapel at Shubenacadie," 28 April 1839. Gorham eventually realized that it was futile to keep pressing for a return of the mission property where Abbé Antoine Gaulin built the first chapel and Abbé Jean-Louis Le Loutre had had the chapel rebuilt in 1739. The St. Anne's mission site became part of the Snide Farm, often called the "Mass House Farm." This property lay a short distance from where the residential school was later erected at Shubenacadie. F.H. Patterson, "Old Cobequid and Its Destruction," *Collections of the Nova Scotia Historical Society*, no. 33 (1934), 56.

138 NSARM, RG 1, vol. 431, "Gorham Paul and Louis Paul to Sir Colin Campbell," 28 April 1838. The two men received twenty pounds.

139 The Queen and Prince Albert's wedding took place in London on 10 February 1840. Louis-Benjamin was seventy-eight or seventy-nine years old in that year.

140 Louis-Benjamin's wife Madelaine, born around 1775, was almost certainly the daughter of Francis Ball of East Chester. There is a slight possibility, however, that Francis Ball's daughter was the wife of Jacques Peminout Paul's son, Samuel Paul, who died around the same time as Louis-Benjamin.

141 Contemporary press accounts described Mi'kmaw boys standing near the chief's carriage holding bows and arrows. *The Novascotian*, 7 May 1840; Charles Churchill, *Memorials of Missionary Life in Nova Scotia* (Nottingham: W. Dexbdes, 1845), 188–9. Churchill noted that the chief and his wife, riding in a gentleman's carriage, also participated in a parade held each 8 June in Halifax to celebrate Edward Cornwallis's landing of 1749. The Nova Scotia Philanthropic Society provided some of the funding for such events, though a sum of money – possibly though not necessarily donated by a charitable society – was misplaced or stolen the following year. *The Morning Herald* reported on 15 January 1841 that a Mi'kmaw person had lost a silk purse containing "four five pound Notes, and four one pound Province Notes, a 7½ d and one penny." A reward was offered for the purse's return.

142 *Acadian Recorder,* 11 April 1840; see also *Halifax Times,* 14 April 1840. The relevance of various forms of feasting in upholding class distinctions is examined by Bonnie Huskins in "From *Haute Cuisine* to Ox Roasts: Public Feasting and Negotiation of Class in Mid-19th-Century Saint John and Halifax," *Labour/Le Travail* 37 (1996): 14.

143 LAC, CO 217/179, 406–8, "Petition of Louis Benjamin Peminout, or Chief Paussamigh Pemmenauweet, to Queen Victoria. Stamped 'received' 25 January 1841."

144 This would have been sometime between 1791 and 1802, which were the years Prince Edward Augustus was in Halifax. The prince became Duke of Kent and Strathearn in 1799, the same year he was made commander-in-chief of British North America.

145 LAC, CO 217/179, 406–8, "Petition of Louis Benjamin Peminout, or Chief Paussamigh Pemmenauweet, to Queen Victoria, 25 January 1841."

146 The officials at the Colonial Office who read it assumed its content to be dictated in Mi'kmaq and then translated by a sensitive interpreter into English. Still, there are turns of phrase, such as "The white wampum tell …," that do not correspond with Mi'kmaw phraseology but seem to have been placed in the document because the content derived a special symbolic charge from the lyrical but imperfect flow of English.

147 This impression lingered despite the fact that some chiefs, among them Pennel Argomartin in the late 1750s and Chief Paul Peminout during the American Revolution, supported the British. In his 1820 petition, Gorham Paul clearly stated that the Peminouts helped the British in the Revolutionary War.

148 LAC, CO 217/178, ff. 78–88, "Anthony Blackwood, Observations upon Lord Falkland's dispatch of the 15th of July 1841"; LAC, CO 217/178/78–88, "Observations of A. Blackwood on Nova Scotia's Indian affairs," 12 January 1842. Regarding Blackwood's assertions, L.F.S. Upton has written, "As the Colonial Office's resident specialist on Indian affairs pointed out, the Micmacs, unlike the natives of Canada, had no 'military title' to assistance based on past services against France and the United States. And no one considered that the Royal Proclamation of 1763 afforded any protection to the natives of the old established British colony of Nova Scotia." Upton, "Indian Policy in Colonial Nova Scotia, 1783–1871," *Acadiensis* 5, no. 1 (1975): 4.

149 Howe's interest in Mi'kmaw agricultural communities had been piqued after John Jeremy, a head man from Kejimkujik Lake in Queens County, requested government support for farming in his community in 1842. Howe took the position of commissioner partly because he saw it as an opportunity to put some of his own ideas on the subject into operation.

150 Howe knew that at least as early as the 1730s chiefs had commissions from the French to protect harbours both

in their own and the French interest. He even referred to them as territorial "commands," a term used by Captain Peter Warren in 1739 when describing the nature of commissions the Mi'kmaw chiefs obtained from the French. The chiefs were expected to protect their coastlines from English and New England vessels. LAC, CO 2178/77, ff. 136–41, "Account of P. Warren of the warship *Squirrel*, Boston, 9 July 1739."

151 Howe, "Western Rambles," *The Novascotian or Colonial Herald*, 9 October 1828. See also Joseph Howe, *Eastern and Western Rambles: Travel Sketches of Nova Scotia*, ed. M.G. Parks (Toronto: University of Toronto Press, 1973), 208.

152 Howe likely knew the chief's full baptismal name, since Louis-Benjamin placed it, along with his Mi'kmaw name, on his 1841 petition to Queen Victoria, which was the document that prompted Falkland's appointment of Howe as Indian commissioner. There can be little doubt that the person Howe called "Sam" was Louis-Benjamin, since "Sam," a chief, was elderly, sick, and blind. The Sipekne'katik Mi'kmaw community would not have appointed an interim or acting chief to replace Louis-Benjamin although he was ill and unable to see. Jacques Peminout Paul's son Samuel, although he may have died around the same time as Louis-Benjamin, was not a chief. The sobriquet "Sam," as mentioned above, may have been a corruption of the way the Mi'kmaw pronounced the chief's name, "Louis-Ben."

153 NSARM, RG 1, vol. 431, doc. 191, "Report on Indian Affairs," 25 January 1843; Joseph Howe, "Indian Accounts and Accounts Current, Miscellaneous Expenses, March and April 1842, showing 5s 3d – Old Chief, Sam Paul (blind and bedridden)."

154 Lewis-Benjamin Peminout Paul probably died in May 1842, while Joseph Howe was still Indian commissioner. Since Howe's accounts give no mention of the leader's death, the chief's funeral expenses must have been borne by the Shubenacadie band.

155 Howe habitually referred to Louis-Benjamin's wife as "Margaret" although her name is given as "Madelaine" or "Magdalina" in other documentary sources.

156 NSARM, RG 1, vol. 165, doc. 54, "Pass to Jean Ball [Baul or Paul]." Jean Ball signed a "Submission to His Majesty's government" on 28 April 1760. NSARM, RG 1, vol. 165, doc. 54. This passport exempted Jean and his family from molestation under Governor Lawrence's scalp proclamation of 1756 – which remained in effect generally until 1761 – and allowed him to travel freely throughout the province. His surname "Ball" (if not an outright adoption of the British surname "Ball") likely derived from a Mi'kmaw pronunciation of "Paul." Jean Ball belonged to a group known as the "East Coast Pauls," distinct from the Peminout Paul family, although the two families intermarried.

157 NSARM, Old Grant Book 20, no. 7, 1793; NSARM, RG 432, 47–56, "Correspondence of Joseph Howe regarding Indian Point, East Chester, spring 1842."

158 NSARM, Deeds, RG 47, vol. 5, 24–5. This lease was registered on 25 March 1799 in the Lunenburg County Deeds Office.

159 NSARM, RG 432, 47–56, "Correspondence of Joseph Howe regarding Indian Point, East Chester, spring 1842."

160 Howe decided that John Ball Sr.'s three sons John Jr., Joseph, and Thomas should share equally in the money accruing from the sale of the Chester plot. As mentioned, Madeleine, a daughter of John Ball Jr.'s son Francis and the widow of Louis-Benjamin Peminout Paul, received one-third of this compensation money. Her sister Isabel also received one-third of the compensation money for the East Chester property. Madeleine's and Isabel's father had died by 1843. Of Tom Ball's five heirs – his three sons Aslin, Francis, and Joe and two daughters Nancy Ann and Molly – Howe could only locate Nancy Ann, who lived in Shelburne County. She, too, received one-third of the compensation money.

161 In 1855 Indian Commissioner William Chearnley recorded Madeleine (who also went by the name "Marguerite) Ball") as being eighty years and living at Rawdon.

162 NSARM, RG 1, vol. 431, microfilm reel 350, Indian Affairs, 1832–66. Correspondence, 1842–43. Chief Francis Paul "received of Joseph Howe £2 5/7, being the balance of thirty pounds received from Tobias Cook to fulfill the claims of Micmac family to the lands occupied by him at Indian Point, Chester. Signed Francis Paul, 1842."

163 NSARM, RG 432, 62, "Joseph Howe, Indian Journal," entry for 11 May 1842.

164 NSARM, RG 1, vol. 432, 8–9, Howe, "Correspondence of Joseph Howe, Indian Commissioner," May 1842.

165 NSARM, MG 15, vol. 3, nos. 78, 79, and 82. Construction on the house and thirty-six-by-twenty-six-foot barn continued throughout 1843 and 1844, as may be seen from three work vouchers.

166 NSARM, MG 15, vol. 3, no. 60, "Warrant from Sir Colin Campbell to Gorham Paul for £20 to build a chapel at Shubenacadie," 28 April 1839.

167 Howe unfortunately failed to record the Mi'kmaw terms for these leadership positions, but he was the first person from outside the Mi'kmaw community to identity the office of Mi'kmaw judge. "Judges," "advocates," record keepers, emissaries, and spokespersons were all part of

Mi'kmaw leadership hierarchies in the Northeast. In 1842 there were two judges, Louis and Pierre Paul, who were sons of Louis-Benjamin Peminout Paul. When Louis Paul died, his son Christopher Peminout Paul succeeded to his office.

168 NSARM, RG 1, vol. 432, 85–9, Howe, "Correspondence of Joseph Howe, Indian Commissioner," May 1842.

169 Until as late as 1892, however, uncertainty remained within Indian Affairs regarding the details of this subdivision. NSARM, Miscellaneous "I" Indian Land Records on microfilm, "Regarding William Faulkner's subdivision plan being returned to the late Mr. Howe, mentioned in a letter from Lawrence Vankoughnet, Deputy Superintendent General of Indian Affairs, to James Austin, Halifax, Deputy Commissioner of Crown Lands," 9 December 1892.

170 Gorham had no biological children but his Malecite wife, prior to her marriage to him, had a daughter, Mary Catherine, the mother of John Jadis. Jadis's father was a son of an English *métis* man named James Jadis, who in turn was the grandson of Charles Jadis, who in 1760 set up a trading post at Grimcross on the Saint John River. LAC, CO 217/48/90-3, "Memorial of Charles Jadis," 27 August 1771, included with a letter from "Governor William Campbell to Lord Hillsborough," 9 October 1771; Upton, *Micmacs and Colonists,* 70–1. After experiencing a tumultuous trading career among the Malecite, who resented his living so close to their village and set fire to his trading post several times, Charles Jadis died in New Brunswick. His son James moved around 1810 to Cornwallis Township, Kings County, Nova Scotia, where at Kentville he married Mary Catherine, the daughter of Gorham Peminout Paul's Malecite wife, and the couple had John in 1827. Not long afterwards, James Jadis died, and John was raised by his mother and Gorham, though Gorham was not Mary Catherine's biological father. John remained with the Shubenacadie band, married Catherine Morris, a daughter of Louis Morris and Mary, and on Catherine's death wed Mary Jeremy (or Jerome), the widow of Michael Thomas, a son of Louis Thomas and Mary Morris from the Windsor-Rawdon area. In 1923 John Jadis was ninety-six years old. NSM, Printed Matter File, Piers Papers, "Louis Noel McDonald to Harry Piers," 20 November 1923.

171 On a census of Mi'kmaq compiled by Indian Commissioner William Chearnley in 1853, Gorham is stated to be living with "Mrs. Paul, Mary Ann McHenery and John Jadis." NSARM, RG 1, vol.430, doc. 75, "List of articles issued by William Chearnley, Commissioner of Indian Affairs, with the names of the Indian men &

women to whom the articles were issued, Halifax, Dec. 31st 1853." Louis Paul, Louis-Benjamin's son, after his father's death often lived with Gorham's household.

172 See also Joseph Howe's account, *JLANS,* 1844, appendix 50, 122–3.

173 LAC, CO 247/178/101–03, "Gorham Paul to Viscount Falkland, Lieutenant-Governor of Nova Scotia," 15 July 1842. Gorham apparently still had the bottomlands along the river around the old St. Anne's mission site in mind when he dictated this request.

174 Until 15 February 1842, the vicariate of Nova Scotia lay under the auspices of the Archdiocese of Quebec. After the creation of the independent Archdiocese of Nova Scotia, Roman Catholic clergy encouraged the Mi'kmaq to participate in special observances at St. Mary's Roman Catholic Cathedral Basilica in Halifax. *The Cross,* 2 August 1845. Originally constructed of wood, the cathedral was replaced around 1820 by a stone structure and progressively expanded in size after 1869.

175 Abraham Gesner, who was appointed provincial Indian commissioner in 1847, expressed astonishment at the numbers of Mi'kmaq who afterwards sought relief from his office. "At Christmas and other seasons of the year," he reported, "hundreds collect about the confines of the city to attend to their religious observances, and the aged, infirm and destitute seem naturally to throw themselves upon the Metropolis. It has been to supply the extreme destitution of such that so many small charges appear in my accounts." NSARM, RG 1, vol. 431, doc. 62 ½, "Abraham Gesner to Joseph Howe, Provincial Secretary, Report on Indian Affairs," 4 March 1852.

176 Walsh was not yet a bishop in 1844. He became bishop of Halifax on 20 July 1845 and archbishop on 4 May 1852. David B. Flemming, "Walsh, William," *Dictionary of Canadian Biography* online, vol. 8 (1851–60).

177 Churchill, *Memorials of Missionary Life,* 188.

178 Francis's wife was said to have been a Mohawk woman, likely from the vicinity of Montreal. Ruth Holmes Whitehead, *Tracking Doctor Lonecloud: Showman to Legend Keeper* (Fredericton: Goose Lane Editions, 2002), 171n4.

179 NSARM, RG 5, Series P, vol. 41, no. 93, "Petition of Chief Francis Peminout Paul for support from the Legislative Assembly for Passage to London to consult with Queen Victoria," 24 February 1844.

180 NSARM, microfilm 3532, *JLANS,* 1844, "Report of the Committee for Indian Affairs," appendix no. 69, 165. The Mi'kmaq were informed by the Committee on Indian Affairs that they could expect no public aid to go to London, though their request might become a fit object for private subscribers.

181 NSARM, MG 15, vol. 5, no. 49, "Petition of Francis Paul at Shubenacadie for monies to supply Native visitors to Shubenacadie on Christmas Day," mistakenly dated "23 December 1835" – the correct date is 23 December 1845. See also NSARM, vol. 431, though the date on this document is very hard to read.

182 This petition shows all the protocols of a traditional northeastern Algonquian elicitation for care and protection from a greater power. For the same mode of soliciting aid among the Central Algonquian Ojibwa, see Mary Black-Rogers, "Varieties of 'Starving': Semantics and Survival in the Subarctic Fur Trade, 1750–1850," *Ethnohistory* 33, no. 4 (1986): 353–83. Another interesting point is Francis Peminout Paul's mention of his "late Father" as the person who acquired the Shubenacadie tract by petition. He may actually have meant to refer to his father Paul Peminout, but the person who petitioned for the Shubenacadie tract was his brother, Jacques Peminout Paul. Paul Peminout's land was at Stewiacke.

183 NSARM, MG 15, vol. 5, no. 93. Also found in NSARM, RG 1, vol. 431, "Francis Paul to Viscount Falkland," 31 January 1846. This petition gave a list of those requiring farm help. Seeds and tools were given over the following summer. NSARM, MG 15, no. 94. Bishop William Walsh was expected to verify that the proper distributions of implements and seeds had taken place. A number of families were listed in 1846 as engaging in farming, those of Francis Paul, Louis Paul, Michael Tom, Peter Sack, Christopher Paul, Louis Charles, Stephen Charles, Ablouis (or "Abluis," Pierre Peminout Paul's son), Charles, Thomas Paul, James Paul, John Prosper, Prospere Lewis, Francis Toney, Prospere Noel, Joseph Stevens, and Peter John. Nearby settlers as well as local Mi'kmaq were employed in construction or on roadwork.

184 This may have been an outbreak of typhus fever.

185 Dr. Edward Jennings in 1847 stated that Francis Paul was sixty-nine, which meant he was born in 1778. At that time Francis Paul was living at Shubenacadie with his wife Elizabeth, who was forty-three, and two children: Anna Mary, nine and a half years old, and John, six. Edward Nolan was thirty-nine and his wife Margaret, who was Francis Paul's daughter, was thirty-five. NSARM, MG 15, vol. 4, doc. 18, "Dr. Jennings' report of his visit to the Indians of the Shubenacadie Reserve, 15 February 1847." Jennings attached a nominal census to this report.

186 NSARM, RG 1, vol. 431, doc. 43, "Gesner to Sir Rupert George, Provincial Secretary," 29 September 1847; *JLANS*, 1849, appendix 24, A. Gesner, "Report," 119. Gesner, a surgeon, geologist, amateur ethnologist, and the inventor of kerosene, became Nova Scotia's Indian commissioner in the late summer of 1847. For further information on Gesner's promotion of agriculture among the Mi'kmaq, see Elizabeth Haigh, "They Must Cultivate the Land: Abraham Gesner as Indian Commissioner, 1847–1853," *Journal of the Nova Scotia Historical Society*, no. 3 (2000), 18–21; and Loris S. Russell, "Gesner, Abraham," *Dictionary of Canadian Biography* online, vol. 9 (1861–70).

187 NSARM, RG 1, vol. 431, doc. 50, "Regarding report of Dr. Lewis Johnson," 8 June 1849.

188 NSARM, Minutes of Council, 11 June 1847, vol. 214½; "Report on Indian Affairs," 21 December 1847, *JLANS*, 1847, 114–26, appendix 24.

189 *The Acadian Recorder*, Halifax, 24 February 1849, "To His Excellency John Harvey, Lieutenant Governor of Nova Scotia, Petition of Chief Pelancea [Francis] Paul and nine others, Gorham Paul, Peter Tony, Louis Paul, Gabriel Bonus, James Meuse, Louis Alexis [Luxey], Xavier Paul, Peter Morris and Francis Paul, Chebucto," 8 February 1849.

190 Each leader inscribed a distinct mark after his name on this petition. Chief Francis Paul drew an arrow, while his brother Gorham Paul drew a spear, and so on. Though these symbols have been called "totems," they are individualistic, and hence unlike the totemic group identifiers belonging to central Algonquians such as the Ojibwa or Odawa. Among the Ojibwa, as well as among Algonquian-speaking nations south of the Kennebec River in New England, a son has the same mark as his father. See Janet E. Chute, *The Legacy of Shingwaukonse: A Century of Native Leadership* (Toronto: University of Toronto Press, 1998), 9–10.

191 The others present were Peter Tony (or Toney); Gabriel Bonus; James Andrew Meuse of Bear River, Digby County; Louis Alexis (or Luxey) from Shelburne County; and Sabatier (either Jean Battiste or Xavier) Paul, Peter Morris, and Francis Paul. The last three were head men of the Halifax County band.

192 Dr. Peter Christmas of Membertou observed in his introduction (vix–x) to Whitehead's book *The Old Man Told Us: Excerpts from Micmac History, 1500–1950* (Halifax: Nimbus, 1991) that the 1849 petition emphasized the Mi'kmaq's determination to survive as a distinct people. Christmas is son of Chief Ben Christmas of Kings Road and Membertou in Cape Breton, and a grandson of Joseph Christmas, who in turn was a descendant of Christmas Thoma, the son of Chief Thoma Denny (Thoma Thoma I) of Cape Breton.

193 *The Acadian Recorder*, 24 February 1849.

194 The Mi'kmaw proposals, which include pleas for relief, access to wood, and requests for farming equipment, are found in the *Times & Courier*, 24 February 1849 and 27 February 1849, and the *Church Times*, 2 March 1849.

195 Rand wrote about his work among the Mi'kmaq in his "Reports of the Micmac Missionary Society," published from 1850 to 1857. Between 1853 and 1856, he also amassed 458 acres at Hantsport, Nova Scotia, for a school and industrial establishment that he called "Mount Mic-Mac." He gained interdenominational support for this endeavour until 1857, when his superiors in the Baptist Church abandoned him.

196 Reverend James Twining was an evangelical Anglican curate, a member of the Society for the Propagation of the Gospel in Foreign Parts, and a brother of the better-known Church of England minister the Reverend John Thomas Twining. Henry A. Renfree, *Heritage and Horizons: The Baptist Story in Canada* (Eugene, OR: Wipf & Stock, 1988), 111. When the Micmac Missionary Society was established in 1850, Twining became one of its greatest supporters.

197 LAC, CO 217/213/8–25, "Petition of Planswa Pwl [Francis Paul] *et al* to Queen Victoria," 25 July 1853.

198 NSARM, RG 1, vol. 430, doc. 66, "The Reverend Silus Tertius Rand to His Excellency Sir Gaspard Le Marchant," n.d. (Spring 1853).

199 LAC, CO 217/213/8-25, "Petition of Planswa Pwl [Francis Paul], Golum Pwl [Gorham Paul], Peel Pwl [Peter Paul], Lui Pwl [Louis Paul], Josep Koop [Joseph Cope], Peel [Peter], Planswa Toni [Francis Tony], Pwl Palpis [Paul Palpis], Gluspwl Pwl and others to Queen Victoria," 25 July 1853.

200 In the spring of 1760 Chief Claude René of Shubenacadie signed a treaty of peace and friendship with the British, an event remembered by the Shubenacadie leadership. Chief Francis Peminout Paul recounted, "we can neither disbelieve nor forget what we have heard from our fathers, that when peace was made between the Mi'kmaq and the British, and the sword and tomahawk were buried by mutual consent, by the terms of the treaty then entered into which was ratified by all the solemnities of an oath, it was stipulated that we should be left in the quiet and peaceable possession of far the greater portion of this Peninsula." LAC, CO 217/213/22, excerpt from "Petition of Planswa Pwl [Francis Paul] *et al* to Queen Victoria," 25 July 1853. One wonders if Francis Peminout Paul is also recalling Lieutenant Governor Jonathan Belcher's Proclamation of 4 May 1762, which stipulated that a vast tract in the northeastern part of the province, from north of the Chignecto Isthmus along the Northumberland Strait to Canso and inland to Shubenacadie was to remain reserved exclusively for the Mi'kmaq. LAC, CO 217/19/ 27; NSARM, RG 1, vol. 165, 224–5, "Proclamation by Jonathan Belcher," 4 May 1762. While it has been argued that Belcher's proclamation was not circulated among the leaders of the Mi'kmaw community, it seems difficult to imagine that Abbé Pierre Maillard, shortly before his death, did not apprise Mi'kmaq leaders of its imminent drafting. Whitehall subsequently rejected Belcher's 1762 proclamation on the grounds that, by it, the British would lose control of the Canso fishery and allow French shipping to proceed unimpeded along the coast between Louisbourg and Quebec. NSARM, vol. 32, doc. 10, "Response to Belcher's Proclamation from the Lords of Trade and Plantations," December 1762.

201 LAC, CO 217/213/22, 18, excerpt from "Petition of Planswa Pwl [Francis Paul] *et al* to Queen Victoria," 25 July 1853.

202 Ibid., 18–19.

203 NSARM, RG 1, vol. 430, doc. 66, "The Reverend Silus Tertius Rand to His Excellency Sir Gaspard Le Marchant," n.d. (1853). Rand added that any questions regarding the Mi'kmaq and their memorial should be addressed to him, since he "understood their tongue … well."

204 LAC, CO 217/213/23, "Certificate of the Reverend Silus Tertius Rand," 14 December 1853.

205 The Colonial Office in London questioned the document's authenticity, yet one aspect of the petition that made it distinctly Algonquian in orientation was the use of the Mi'kmaw word *N'kijenen* at the beginning of pertinent statements – a linguistic device that harked back to a traditional northeastern Algonquian form of formal customary address gauged to give words clout, and to draw the close attention of the audience to each major point. When translating the memorial into English, Rand exercised a degree of linguistic licence by substituting the Mi'kmaw protocol with the words "May it please your Majesty …" Among both Eastern and Central Algonquian speakers an introductory term similar to *N'kijenen*, often used to punctuate each major point, is *Me mink*, roughly translatable as "Another thing." Use of these Indigenous protocols in a document allows the reader to judge the authenticity of Mi'kmaw input into a series of statements.

206 The petition elicited a call for Lieutenant Governor John Le Marchant to be better informed of an act, passed in 1842, for the appointment of Indian commissioners and the eviction of settlers who trespassed on reserves.

Considering Rand was charged with fabricating the memorial, it seems odd that it also was felt the Mi'kmaq might reject the 1842 act because it treated them as "occupants and not owners of the reserves." Upton, *Micmacs and Colonists*, 90.

207 LAC, CO 217/213/1–4, "To the Duke of Newcastle," 4 January 1854. Also see *Christian Messenger*, 16 March 1854.

208 Fundraising goals the missionary sought to achieve in support of his mission likely suffered from the criticism he received from overseas in 1853 and 1854.

209 NSARM, RG 5, Series P, vol. 47, no. 35, "Petition of Francis Paul, Chief of Shubenacadie, and others," 21 February 1854.

210 NSARM, RG 5, Misc. B, Series P, vol. 47, no. 35, "Memorial of Francis Paul, Gorham Paul, Louis Paul and others to the Members of the Legislative Council, witness, Silus T. Rand, Micmac Missionary," 21 February 1854. The other signees to the memorial came from Pictou County and the Eastern Shore. They were Peter Paul, Joseph Cope, John Peter, Francis Toney, Gloaspail Paul, and Peter Palpis. In 1853 Peter Paul had petitioned the House of Assembly complaining about restrictions on Mi'kmaw fishing rights imposed by new provincial game laws. NSARM, RG 5, Series P, vol. 46, no. 202, "Petition to the House of Assembly by Peter Paul, one of the head men," 3 March 1853.

211 *James Simon v. The Queen* (1985). James Simon lived at Indian Brook, Shubenacadie.

212 NSARM, MG 15, vol. 4A, doc. 96, "Letter of F.R. Parker," 29 May 1851; NSARM, RG 15, doc. 98, "List of farmers, with Gorham Paul being held to be the best farmer." The other farmers were "Lewey Paul – likely the son of Louis-Benjamin; Christopher Paul, [who was] Lewey's son; Chief Francis Paul, Peter Paul (a very old man), Lewey Charles, Stephen Charles and John Paul." John Paul, a young man who had returned to the community after some years' absence for work purposes, complained that certain Mi'kmaw farmers had acquired large plots while others, like himself, had to be content with very little property.

213 NSARM, RG 5, Series P, vol. 47, no. 35, "Memorial of Francis Paul regarding a land dispute"; NSARM, RG 5, vol. 44, no. 93, "Francis Paul asks for assistance regarding land dispute."

214 Upton, *Micmacs and Colonists*, 95.

215 NSARM, RG 20 Series A, Lands Papers, vol. 58, "Marshall Land Papers and plan of sales," 10 April 1815. The plan showed the lands, lying within the Stewiacke grant, purchased by William Kennedy and John Bonnell from Paul Pemmenwick.

216 NSARM, RG 1, vol. 432, 153, "Samuel Creelman, Indian Agent, to Joseph Howe," 9 December 1842.

217 NSARM, RG 1, vol. 431, doc. 67, "Memo of Indian Reserves throughout the Province of Nova Scotia including Cape Breton," 7 April 1852.

218 NSARM, RG 20, Series C, Deputy Surveyors' Correspondence, vol. 17, "William Faulkner's Annual Report in relation to Colchester County," 22 January 1857.

219 LAC, RG 10, vol. 460, 258–63, "William Faulkner to Uniacke," 20 January 1857; NSARM, MG 15, vol.18, doc. 19, "W. Falkner's Report relating to Indian reserve, Stewiacke River, Recd. 27 Jany. 1857"; LAC, RG 10, vol. 460, 258–63, "Faulkner's map of Middle Stewiacke, 20 January 1857."

220 The worth of the combined lots stemming from the McClellan-Bonnell purchase was £6,950.

221 NSARM, RG 20, Series C, Deputy Surveyors' Correspondence, vol. 17, "Isaac Archibald to Samuel Fairbanks," 4 March 1861. Archibald was convinced he could run a more accurate line for the southern boundary of the Peminout grant, and so deviated from the south line that most settlers held to be suitable for their own purposes. The result was that settlers continued to have difficulties over their property lines in the years before Confederation in 1867. The map by Archibald, dated 25 March 1861, is found in LAC, RG 10, vol. 460, 28–31. A second map of Middle Stewiacke by Archibald dated 12 September 1867 and showing the grant is found in NSARM, RG 20, Series C, Deputy Surveyors' Correspondence, vol. 17.

222 NSARM, RG 20, Series A, Land Papers, vol. 56, "Petition of John Bonnell," 17 April 1815; NSARM, RG 20, Series A, Land Papers, vol. 66, "Petition of John Corbet for land in the Indian Grant at Middle Stewiacke."

223 NSARM, RG 5, Series P, vol. 18, no. 155, "Petition of James Meuse *et al* for restoration of the Middle Stewiacke Reserve to the Mi'kmaq, 1864." There are errors in this petition regarding to whom the original grant was made and when.

224 NSARM, MG 15, vol. 5, no. 56, "Petition of numerous settlers and supporters to the House of Assembly for a small annuity for Chief Francis Paul," 9 February 1855.

225 NSARM, RG 1, vol. 431, 128, "Correspondence of William Chearnley regarding Chief Francis Paul Peminout's death," 28 May 1861. See also NSM, Printed Matter File, Harry Piers Papers, unpublished notes, "Francis Paul." NSARM, MG 15, vol. 6, doc. 63. Francis Peminout may have succumbed to a pulmonary complaint that spread among the Mi'kmaq of the east coast, along with smallpox, in 1861.

226 The Nova Scotia Museum in Halifax houses a photograph of what appears to be Jacques-Pierre Paul Peminout's confirmation as chief by Bishop William Walsh in 1856. NSM, AC, 1856, N 7697.

227 Original confirmation is in the NSM, Printed Matter File, "Sir John Gaspard Le Marchant to James Paul," 15 September 1856. The document mentions that the Reverend Michael Hannan certified to the lieutenant governor that James Paul had been duly elected as chief. William Walsh, bishop at this time, would become archbishop in 1852. Hannon would become archbishop of the Archdiocese of Nova Scotia in 1877, until 1882.

228 NSARM, Vertical Ms. File, "Obituary for Chief James Paul [Jacques-Pierre Peminout Paul]," *Halifax News*, 10 January 1895. This article claimed Paul to be chief of 2,500 Mi'kmaq. See also "Obituary for Chief James Paul," *Liverpool Advance*, 16 January 1895, which notes that though the chief once had a large family, all had died before him.

229 Though there are no physical descriptions of Chief Peminout Paul, several of his descendants, among them Jacques-Pierre Paul and Louis-Benjamin's son Judge Christopher Peminout Paul, had long full beards, which suggests Chief Peminout had some European ancestry.

230 Lucy Pictou to Elsie Clews Parsons, in Parsons, "Micmac Folklore," *Journal of American Folklore* 38 (1925): 92–3.

231 "A Visit with Max Basque, Whycocomagh" (interview conducted by Ruth Homes Whitehead), *Cape Breton's Magazine*, no. 51, 1 February 1990, 24–5. Jacques-Pierre was said to be able to elongate the stem of his pipe so it would fit around his hat band, which gave him with a handy place to store his pipe when it was not in use.

232 NSARM, MG 15, vol. 4, no. 25, "Report of Dr. Edward Jennings on state of Mi'kmaq at South Maitland," 15 February 1847.

233 In 1856 Jacques-Pierre and Madeleine had three children living in their household, while two of Jacques-Pierre's brothers, Louis and John, camped nearby. The identities of these children remain unknown, although one likely was John Noel and the other two Madeleine's daughters. NSARM, vol. 431, unnumbered docs., "Distribution of blankets at Sackville, N.S.," 11 December 1856. John Peminout-Paul had a wife and three children living with him, while his brother Louis had one child and an orphan boy. Others of the group included Thomas Morris and his wife, Peter Joe and his wife, Thomas Toney and his wife, the widow Cope, Prosper Paul and his wife, and Prosper Noel, who had his one-hundred-year-old mother living with him.

234 John Noel was born at Port Harbour, Pictou County, on 3 May 1829 and died at Indian Brook, Shubenacadie, on 20 May 1911. Ruth Holmes Whitehead, "Peminuit Paul, Jacques-Pierre," *Dictionary of Canadian Biography* online, vol. 12 (1891–1900).

235 Mi'kmaw regularly hunted on the upper reaches of the Stewiacke River. Jacques-Pierre Paul and his family had a campground in this area in the nineteenth century, and Martin Sack, a captain and councillor at Shubenacadie in the early twentieth century, stated that his grandfather, Peter Sack, used to hunt along the Stewiacke River. John S. Erskine, *Micmac Notes, 1959* (Halifax: Nova Scotia Museum, 1959), 4. Jacques-Pierre travelled extensively, visiting relatives and political associates at Gaspereau, Windsor, Horton, Kentville, and Lequille. Gabriel Paul, a son of Pierre Paul Peminout Sr., lived at Horton, Kings County, and Chief Benjamin Pictou lived at Lequille in Annapolis County. Several Peminouts lived at Lequille and one, F. Abram Paul, married a daughter of Chief Ben Pictou. NSARM, MG 1, vol. 85, no. 24; Ian Lawrence, "Chief Benjamin Pictou," Annapolis Heritage Society, https://annapolisheritagesociety.com/community-history/notable-personalities-past/chief-benjamin-pictou/; "Mrs. Samuel Pictou Jr.," *Morning Chronicle*, 27 July 1923; Parsons, "Micmac Folklore," 92–3, "23. Chief James Peter (Sah Biel Sahmo) [James Peter Peminout Paul or Jacques-Pierre Peminout Paul]," as told by Lucy Pictou]. Lucy Pictou (née Gloade) married Ben Pictou's son, James Pictou.

236 NSARM, RG 2, no. 114, "Address to the Prince [Edward] Albert, the Prince of Wales, on behalf of James Paul, Chief of the MicMac Tribe of Shubenacadie by John Thomas Lane, Medicine Man and deputed Speaker, Halifax," 30 July 1860. After the speech the Mi'kmaq were invited at to a magical show at 6 p.m. at the local Temperance Hall, free of charge, presented by an entertainer known as "The Wizard Jacobs." *The Halifax Reporter*, 11 August 1860, 2, col. 6.

237 *The Halifax Reporter*, 26 July 1860, 3, col. 3.

238 NSM, Nova Scotia Museum Printed Matter File, "Lord Mulgrave to James Paul," 6 August 1860.

239 *The Halifax Reporter*, Halifax, 11 August 1860, 2, col. 2.

240 Jacques-Pierre and Joe Cope both lived in Newport Township in February and March 1861. Captain Cope petitioned for government relief for his group of thirty-two persons in late March. NSARM, RG 1, vol. 431, doc. 127, "To the Honorable House of Assembly from Joe Cope, Newport," 20 March 1861. This petition accompanied a letter, dated 25 March 1861, from James Hill of Newport, who had drafted the petition for Cope, though

Hill noted that Joseph could read and write. In 1842 Joseph Howe, as Indian commissioner, had provided monies for Joe Cope, "a son of Jean [John] Cope of Sheet Harbour," to attend St. Mary's seminary in Dartmouth for a few years to learn to read and write.

241 NSARM, RG 1, vol. 431, doc. 121, "To the Honorable the Representatives of the Province of Nova Scotia in General Assembly Convened, the petition of the under-signed James Paul, a chief of the Micmac Indians and others, drafted and witnessed by the Reverend John M. McLeod," 14 February 1861. Chief James (Jacques-Pierre) Paul, Louis Paul, Christopher Paul, John Paul, Noel Paul, Peter Barss, Ben Brooks, Noel Lewie, Samuel Noel, Andrew Stephens, and John Williams signed the petition first. Twenty others signed at a later date, including Gorham's foster son John Jadis and John Ferris.

242 Andrew Paul lived near the Brewery in Dartmouth prior to his death in 1916. He had two sons, Peter and John Denny Paul. In 1961 Stephen Paul, John Denny's son, donated a hieroglyphic Bible, then approximately 150 years old and that had been the Paul family for four generations, to the Tatamagouche Museum. That the Paul family possessed this Bible suggests that Andrew Paul may have been a prayer leader of some consequence.

243 And Howe, after talking with Cope, undoubtedly shed much of the misinformation he harboured in the 1840s about limited Mi'kmaw political knowledge and aspirations.

244 NSARM, Miscellaneous "I" Indian Land Records on microfilm, "W. A. Hendry, D.L. Surveyor, to Joseph Howe, Attorney General," 4 September 1878.

245 Jacques-Pierre, clearly recognizable by his long beard, appears in an illustration by Sydney Hall housed in the Library and Archives of Canada entitled "Micmac Indians waiting to be received by Lord Lorne in Halifax, 1878." LAC, picture collection, LAC C-12800. Another illustration, of the chief, John Noel, and Judge Christopher Paul standing inside Province House to meet Lorne, appeared in the *Illustrated London News* for 11 January 1879, 44. LAC, picture collection, reference C-2295.

246 Jacques-Pierre Peminout Paul may have been the first Mi'kmaw leader to invite Father Pacifique, a Capuchin missionary stationed at Restigouche, to preside over St. Anne's Day ceremonies at Indian Brook, an event marked by prayers, festivities, and games.

247 Joseph C. Cope who, at various times, lived along the Eastern Shore, in Dartmouth, on the Mossman Grant in Halifax County, and in Lunenburg County, regaled Harry Piers at the Nova Scotia Museum with stories that

Jacques-Pierre (or James) told Cope's father, Peter Cope Jr. (1816–1913), about sixteenth-century conflicts between the Mi'kmaq and the *Kwetejk* (or *Kwedech*, who in this context were St. Lawrence Iroquois). Joseph C. Cope called these oral traditions "James Paul's Unwritten History." According to Jacques-Pierre, the Mi'kmaw chased Iroquoian speakers into what is now the province of Quebec, where a Mi'kmaw chief, Mijilapegatasijk, killed a Mohawk chief named Masoow-ow. The chief's use of the term "Mohawk" is historically incorrect, since the St. Lawrence Iroquois preceded the Mohawk nation in the St. Lawrence Valley and mysteriously disappeared after being encountered by Jacques Cartier in 1534. NSM, Printed Matter File, "James Paul's Unwritten History, Joseph C. Cope to Harry Piers," 21 January 1924. Another story Peter Cope Jr. acquired from Jacques-Pierre was "Glooscap the Second." NSM, Printed Matter File, "Joseph C. Cope to Harry Piers," 21 January 1924.

248 "A Visit with Max Basque" (interview), 24–5.

249 John Denny Sr. in the late nineteenth century urged the Mi'kmaq to protect their lands from government expropriation and to develop resources on their reserves, in keeping with their economic and cultural proclivities. Andrew Paul, who was a close associate of John Denny Sr., moved to the Halifax area and became a captain on the Sipekne'katik band council as early as 1860, and remained a captain until his death in 1916 at Tufts Cove, Dartmouth. NSM, Printed Matter File, Harry Piers Unpublished Notes, "Obituary of Andrew Paul," 24 February 1916.

250 When Paul Peminout and his descendants established their leadership legacy in the 1770s, Cape Breton was part of mainland Nova Scotia, although from 1784 to 1820 Cape Breton formed a colony separate from Nova Scotia.

251 NSARM, RG 2, vol. 9, doc. 1815, "Petition of Jacob Brooks *et al.* to Lieutenant-Governor Adams George Archibald," 5 February 1833. The six men who signed this memorial signed Christopher Paul and Stephen Hood's petition as well.

252 Christopher Peminout Paul was appointed Shubenacadie band judge in 1883. Prior to this, two of Jacques-Pierres's brothers, Louis and Peter, were the judges for the Shubenacadie district. When Louis died at age ninety-three in 1883 he was succeeded by his son, Christopher Peminout Paul.

253 NSARM, RG 2, vol. 9, doc. 1820, "Petition of Christopher Paul, Stephen Hood and 59 others to Lieutenant Governor Adams George Archibald," 29 March 1883.

254 Henry Buisson d'Valigny, better known as "Father Pacifique," from 1894 onwards always referred to the grand

chief and council as the paramount heads of the entire Mi'kmaw nation. Pacifique's preferential treatment of Grand Chief John Denny Jr. ended any further rivalry between the Shubenacadie and Cape Breton leadership. Tim Bernard, ed., *Mi'kmaw Past and Present: A Resource Guide*, 4th ed. (Truro: Eastern Woodland Communications, 1997), 25–6. In 1904 both John Denny Jr. and John Noel attended a high mass at Shubenacadie conducted by Timothy Casey, the bishop of Saint John, with the assistance of Father Pacifique. Yet until his death Noel continued to claim that the Sipekne'katik district leader ranked above any other Mi'kmaq leader on the peninsular mainland.

255 "Death of James Paul," *Halifax Herald*, 12 January 1895; *Novascotian and Weekly Chronicle*, 19 January 1895. The Mi'kmaw community at Shubenacadie still retains the name "Indian Brook." Prior to 1870 it was known as the "Indian Road," and in the 1930s as the "Spring Brook Reserve."

256 Stephen Maloney, who was acting chief for two years, failed to win the election because he contended that the Shubenacadie leader should not have to function as both a political and a religious leader. Evidently the time was not ripe for a separation of the chief's office from the plethora of religious duties that had been associated with it since the 1760s, when Abbé Maillard instructed Mi'kmaw leaders to assume various religious duties in the absence of an ordained cleric.

257 Chief Noel married twice. His first wife was a Pennal woman from Gold River, who died soon after their wedding. His second wife was Marie-Antoinette Thomas, the widow of Peter Sack who had children from her first marriage. Since all of Jacques-Pierre Peminout Paul's biological children had died by 1861, Jacques-Pierre treated John Noel as his own flesh and blood, preparing Noel to be his successor as chief. This was not a example John Noel could follow, since he and Marie- Antoinette had no children.

258 A Notman photograph of John Noel and his wife at this unveiling may be found in the collections of the Nova Scotia Archives and Records Management in Halifax. NSARM, Notman studio photographs, 1897.

259 Lewis Noel McDonald Jr., an infant white child, was adopted on 14 March 1856 by a man belonging to the Halifax County band named Louis (Lewey or Lewis) Noel Sr., who died at Second Red Bridge in Dartmouth around 1920. "Lewie Noel McDonald Jr." hunted with his adoptive father during years when Louis Sr. acted as a guide for numerous clients, including Captain L'Estrange, Captain Chearnley, Captain Campbell Hardy,

Lieutenant Dashwood, and Lord Dunraven. NSM, Printed Matter File, "Louis Noel McDonald to Harry Piers," 28 April 1921.

260 After his election as chief in 1912, Big Peter Paul was regarded as holding jurisdictional aegis over Mi'kmaw communities in Halifax, Lunenburg, Kings, Hants, Colchester, and Cumberland. Big Peter's captains were Jerry Bartlett (Jerry Lonecloud or Jeremiah Bartholomew-Alexis), John McDonald, and Martin Sack. Big Peter Paul died on 3 March 1930. NSM, Printed Matter File, "Notes on Peter Paul being elected 15 March 1913."

261 NSM, Piers Papers, Ethnology: Genealogies, 52, "Information from Joe Cope on Big Peter Paul"; "Notes on Chief Peter Paul," 15 March 1930.

262 The museum was located on Spring Garden Road, not far from Dresden Row, on the other side of the street from St. Mary's Basilica. This museum was the precursor of the Nova Scotia Museum of Natural History, now located on Summer Street in Halifax.

263 The Nova Scotia Museum has a photograph that shows Father Pacifique, Big Peter Paul, Mrs. Steve Maloney, Judge Christopher Paul, and Newel Lolan at Shubenacadie in 1905. NSM, N-7073. (Others in the Nova Scotia Museum photograph include Isaac Sack, Martin Sack, Steve Maloney Jr., Elizabeth Lonecloud [née Paul], Jerry Lonecloud, and Marie Antoinette Noel, the widow of John Noel.) A second photograph of Big Peter, taken not long after he succeeded Chief John Noel, belongs to the Geological Survey of Canada and was taken at Oldham, Nova Scotia, in July 1913. See Nova Scotia Museum Library, Piers Papers, Ethnology: Genealogies, 52, "Peter Paul, 15 March 1913." Big Peter, born at Shubenacadie on 10 May 1850, died in 1930 at age seventy-nine. NSM, Printed Matter File, Piers Notes Obituary, "Death of Big Peter Paul, son of Judge Christopher Paul, 3 March 1930."

264 NSM Library, Piers Papers, Ethnology: Politics, 1, "Notes by Harry Piers," 12 April 1913; NSM Library, Piers Papers, Letter of Harry Piers on behalf of Chief Peter Paul to the Rev. Father Young, Yarmouth, Nova Scotia, 31 October 1915; NSM Library, Piers Papers, Ethnology: Politics, 30, "Letter written by Harry Piers confirming Jerry Lone Cloud's transference of three documents; the ratification of Louis-Benjamin Paul's election to chief in 1814, the ratification of James Paul's election to chief in 1856, and an acknowledgement of James Paul's address of 1860, sent to the Reverend Thomas E. Sweet of Enfield, Nova Scotia for copying. The documents are to be returned. Letter signed by Jerry Lone Cloud and dated 5 November 1925."

265 NSM, Library, Piers Papers, Ethnology: Politics, 12, "Lone Cloud to Harry Piers," n.d. (c.1912). "John Newel [or Noel], a son of Lewis [or Louis] Newel," was the captain in 1912 for Hants and Kings counties.

266 Until the late eighteenth century, a Mi'kmaw regional band ranged from Musquodoboit to Sherbrook Settlement, and inland to the headwaters of the Musqudoboit and St. Mary's Rivers. In 1820, Lord Dalhousie was surprised to find that his Mi'kmaw guide was leading his party away from a tract lying between Horton Corner and the Sherbrooke Settlement. When asked to continue on further into the interior, Dalhousie's guide demurred, stating it was the only hunting ground left to the Mi'kmaq in the province "& that he did not wish the English should find it." NSARM, MG 1, vol. 1776, typescript copy of the original ms, "Journal entry for 30 January 1820." See also Marjorie Whitelaw, ed., *The Dalhousie Journals* (Ottawa: Oberon Press, 1978), 1. Approximately 11,000 acres at Sheet Harbour was accorded under a licence of occupation in 1783 to Captain Francis Cope. It lay under the aegis of the Cope family for seventeen years before being radically whittled down in size. Held "at the pleasure" of the British monarch, this land ended up being distributed to settlers. Today, the Mi'kmaq retain a 77-acre reserve at Sheet Harbour composed of two distinct parcels, one of 57 acres on the west side of the bay and a smaller one, of 14.9 acres, on the east side of the bay. NSARM, Miscellaneous "I" Indian Land Records on microfilm, Plans of Indian Reserve Number 36 at Sheet Harbour, Halifax County, N.S, "Tie Between Lots 1 & 2, Sheet Harbour, Indian Reserve 36"; Department of Mines and Resources, Mines and Geology Branch, Map 521A, Tangier 1936; Sheet Harbour Indian Reserve No. 36, 6 February 1953. The Mi'kmaq kept up a drive to attain other lands along the coast, however. Thomas and James Paul, descendants of Lewis Paul who lived along the Eastern Shore in the early 1800s, in the mid-nineteenth century petitioned for and received 100 acres at Ship Harbour, which increased the total acreage belonging to the Halifax County Band to 350 acres. Since the Mi'kmaq were allowed no more than 24,000 acres throughout Nova Scotia, William Chearnley, the Indian commissioner at the time, in 1860 had to obtain a surrender of a reserve on the Shinimacas River in Cumberland County, to counterbalance the tract allocated at Ship Harbour. NSARM, Miscellaneous "I" Indian Land Records on microfilm, "Joseph Howe to Charles D. Roach, Esq.," December 1860. In 1866 Joseph Paul Jr., a hunting guide and farmer, asked for a grant at Quoddy, which he received in 1868. NSARM, Miscellaneous "I" Indian Land Records on microfilm, "Samuel Fairbanks to the Lieutenant Governor of Nova Scotia regarding petition of Joseph Paul for lease of island and additional one hundred acres of land at Quoddy," 9 November 1866; Daniel N. Paul, *We Were Not the Savages: A Mi'kmaq Perspective on the Collision between European and Native American Civilizations* (Halifax: Fernwood, 2000), 218. Mi'kmaq at Pendant Bay, near Sambro, were driven off their fishing grounds, while at Ingraham's (or Ingram's) River Lewis Paul and Francis Philips contended from 1853 to 1855 with a logging interest, Francis Webber and Company, which dammed the river, flooding their reserve, and ran logs without warning through their weir. In 1913 Ottawa pressured the Halifax County band to sell their timber on the Ship Harbour reserve to a logging interest, Marks Brothers, for $5,500 and assured the Mi'kmaq that they would receive the proceeds of the sale. The Mi'kmaq wanted the money to buy land at Sand Point, on Shubenacadie Grand Lake. Hearing nothing more from Ottawa on the matter, in March 1916 Big Peter Paul and his councillors petitioned the Department of Indian Affairs for information. NSM, Nova Scotia Museum Printed File, "Petition of chief and members of the Micmac Tribe of Halifax to S. Stewart, Department of Indian Affairs," 10 March 1916. In reply, they were informed that the land they wanted at Sand Point, on the eastern side of the lake, belonged to a man named King. It was not recognized as a Mi'kmaw occupation site, although in the 1750s when Abbé Pierre Maillard visited the area a Mi'kmaw village known as Tlagatig, or "the camping ground," stood on the lake's west side. Hoffman, "Historical Ethnography of the Micmac," 535. When no money appeared, Big Peter, Louis Paul, and Joseph C. Cope demanded that Ottawa immediately release the monies that had accrued since 1913, so they could purchase a new reserve at Sand Point. Sand Point, they argued, would provide a refuge for the Mi'kmaq being evicted from Elmsdale, around twenty-seven families displaced from the forks of the Preston and Old Guysborough Roads and around seven Mi'kmaw families at Tuft's Cove. Landowners regarded these Mi'kmaq as unwelcome "squatters."

267 An 1891 photograph of a Mi'kmaw camp at Elmsdale taken by E.R. Faribault of the Geological Survey of Canada can be found in the photo collection of Library and Archives Canada, PA 39852.

268 NSM, Printed Matter File, "Martin Sack to H.J. Bury, Department of Indian Affairs," 18 January 1919.

269 Big Peter Paul had one son, Isaac Paul, who was photographed by J.B. Cope around 1898 at Morris Lake, near

Cole Harbour, Nova Scotia. Photograph in the collection of the Nova Scotia Museum, N-5007. Isaac Paul died without issue.

270 Maximus Simon Basque for many years had travelled between Cape Breton and Shubenacadie seeking employment in farming, quarrying, and construction and by raking oysters in the Bras d'Or Lake to earn a livelihood for his family. He was a descendant of François Basque, who, along with Thoma Michel (Thoma Thoma II), proved instrumental in 1792 in having a Roman Catholic chapel built on Chapel Island, Cape Breton, after the British destroyed Maillard's mission chapel on the island in 1758. Max Basque traced his descent from his apical ancestor, Francis Basque, as follows: Francis Basque had a son Louis who had a son Benjamin. Benjamin Sack was the father of Peter Sack, who married Marie-Antoinette Thomas. Peter and Marie-Antoinette were the parents of Isaac Sack (1855–1930), Max's grandfather. Isaac Sack had a son Simon, who was Max's father. "A Visit with Max Basque" (interview), 22–3.

271 NSM, Printed Matter File, Harry Piers Papers, "Lone Cloud to Harry Piers, regarding election of Simon Basque as chief on 26 July 1915," 22 September 1915. Jerry Lonecloud (Bartholomew-Alexis) had been an assistant chief to Big Peter Paul, as well as the leader of the Halifax County band.

272 "Quoddy," or "Newdy Quoddy," derives from the Mi'kmaw word *Noodakwade*, meaning "seal hunting place." Fergusson, *Place-Names and Places of Nova Scotia,* 471.

273 Jeremiah Bartholomew-Alexis (or Jerry Lonecloud) appealed to Harry Piers, the curator of the Nova Scotia Museum, to write letters to Ottawa for him to ensure that Mi'kmaw tenure, wherever it existed by virtue of long occupation, grant, or licence of occupation, was recognized by the government. Mi'kmaw families and communities found that settlers trespassed on their land and plundered their resources. The problem was exacerbated when the big game population fell drastically in the 1920s and the guiding industry, once an important source of income, collapsed.

274 NSM, Printed Matter File, "John Denny Paul to the Department or Indian Affairs," 5 December 1916.

275 NSM Library, Piers Papers, Ethnology: Politics, 14, "Notes taken by Piers from conversation with Lone Cloud [Jeremiah Bartholomew-Alexis]," 22 September 1915.

276 NSM, Printed Matter File, Piers Papers, "Harry Piers notes accompanying a statement from Isaac Sack to Piers dated 26 February 1921." Isaac Sack had been born

and spent his childhood at a small Mi'kmaw community near Dartmouth located at the juncture of the Preston Road and the Old Cobequid Road.

277 Isaac Sack married Anne Cope, a daughter of Francis Cope and Mary Anne Quigley, originally from Sheet Harbour along the Eastern Shore. Isaac, before he joined John Noel's household, lived near Red Bridge on the Dartmouth Lakes.

278 These cessions also included a tract of seven hundred acres, surveyed as a reserve at Ship Harbour in 1904, and one hundred acres at Beaver Lake, Halifax County, surveyed in 1852 for Simon Francis. NSARM, Miscellaneous "I" Indian Land Records on microfilm, "Plan of Indian Reserve at the Head of Ship Harbour Great Lake, Halifax County, N.S., including burial ground, by H.W. Andrews, P.D.S., Berwick N.S.," 25 February 1904; NSARM, Miscellaneous "I" Indian Land Records, "Survey of Beaver Lake [Dam] Indian Reserve, Halifax Co., by Simon Fraser," 11 August 1852.

279 An early name for the Cole Harbour Reserve was "Minister's Lake Reserve." Minister's Lake is called Morris Lake. Upton, *Micmacs and Colonists*, 184.

280 NSARM, Miscellaneous "I" Indian Land Records on microfilm, "Schedule of Reserves, Nova Scotia, 1959."

281 Harold Gloade, who had a prodigious memory for things he observed at Millbrook from the age of nine, was later able to recount the exact location and occupants of each house. Gloade, *From My Vantage Point* (Nepean, ON: Borealis, 1991), 47–9.

282 LAC, RG 10, vol. 7758, file 27047, "Chief Julian to Ottawa," 30 July 1919.

283 LAC, RG 10, vol. 7758, file 27047, "Chief Julien to Timber Inspector H.J. Bury," 3 January 1920.

284 LAC, RG 10, vol. 7758, file 27047, "J. D. Maclean, Assistant Deputy Superintendent of Indian Affairs, to F.A. Harrison, Deputy Commissioner of Crown Lands," 28 January 1920; "Harrison to MacLean," 2 February 1920; "MacLean to A.G. Doughty, Dominion Archivist," 10 February 1920; "Maclean to Harrison," 12 February 1920; "McLean to Julian," 13 February 1920; LAC, RG 10, vol. 3160, file 363-717-1, "Petition from those seeking to reside at the Millbrook community, along with an official acceptance by Chief Joseph Julian," 18 August 1919. Despite the fact that Joseph Julien failed to prompt a thorough government investigation of the Stewiacke claim during his lifetime, he was an influential presence at Millbrook in other ways for the next twenty years. After the initial phase of the government centralization scheme passed in 1940, Shubenacadie community residents suffered from overpopulation and a lack of

services, despite the government's earlier promises to lure families to settle in the growth centre. Chief Julien sought to relieve these pressures by warmly welcoming incomers and pressing for additional land to accommodate Millbrook's growing population. Owing to his appeals, many Mi'kmaq from Halifax County moved to Millbrook, while their former lands on the Atlantic coast reverted to Crown Land status or passed into the hands of new buyers.

285 Mi'kmaq from Shubenacadie and Millbrook continued to hunt in the Stewiacke region into the twentieth century. Frank Paul, whom anthropologist Frank G. Speck recorded as maintaining a hunting territory along the Stewiacke Valley in the late nineteenth century, may have been a descendant of Chief Paul Peminout. Speck, *Beothuk and Micmac*, ed. F.W. Hodge (New York: Museum of the American Indian/Heye Foundation, 1922), 103. In 1981, Chief Stanley Johnson of Millbrook launched a claim to investigate if there were any unsold Mi'kmaw land still existing at Middle Stewiacke. Although initially Ottawa rejected the suit, on the grounds it constituted a pre-Confederation claim, the impetus behind it has grown in recent years and it remains before the courts.

286 NSM, Printed Matter File, Harry Piers Unpublished Notes, "Notes on William Paul Peminout, n.d."

287 The term of a chief's office was only supposed to be three years. However, William Paul seems to have stayed in office longer than usual during both of his terms. Anita Maria Tobin, "The Effects of Centralization on the Social and Political Systems of the Mainland Nova Scotia Mi'kmaq (Case Studies: Millbrook – 1916 & Indian Brook – 1941)" (master's thesis, St. Mary's University, Halifax, 1999), 98.

288 Gloade, *From My Vantage Point*, 63. "One travelled a few miles west of Mill Village and down the Indian Road, passed over a bridge, skirted Simon Basque's farm on the left, mounted the hill with the local church on its crest, continued past an alder grove and Tom Maloney's large house on the right, climbed a slight grade and proceeded a little to the right, to reach the dwelling of Mister Daoi Paul."

289 Ibid. William Paul was succeeded as Shubenacadie chief by John Marr.

290 NSARM has recently placed several of the sound recordings that William Peminout Paul made with Helen Creighton on the Internet, for public access. See, for instance, "Chief William Paul to Dr. Helen Creighton, Taped Interview, Shubenacadie, N.S.," https://archives .novascotia.ca/mikmaq/results/?Search=&TABLE2 =on&SearchList1=all&Start=1501. For a transcribed version, see Whitehead, *The Old Man Told Us*, 222–3. In 1932 Paul also agreed to an interview session with Nova Scotian author Thomas Head Raddall.

291 NSARM, MG 1, vol. 2803, no. 6, Helen Creighton Collection, "Moose calling." "I could call most all kinds of animals it was ever grown in to this province," he stated. "I could call even down to the muskrat and owls and also many other animals that I could make them come."

292 NSM, Photograph Collection, Clara Dennis Collection, 73.180.674, "Chief William Paul in the 1920s with Chief Matthew Francis of Pictou Landing, among others." A later photograph, dated 1944, depicts William Paul during his second term of office as Shubenacadie chief, with Benjamin Christmas and John Knockwood. NSM, Photograph Collection, 1944.

293 "A Visit with Max Basque," 22–3.

CHAPTER 11

1 John W. Johnson, *The Life of John W. Johnson Who Was Stolen by the Indians When Three Years of Age and Identified by His Father Tweny Years Afterwards, Related by Himself* (Portland, ME: n.p., 1861), author's notes on chap. 3, pp. 11–12; John W. Johnson, *Life of John W. Johnson* (New York: Arno Press, 1977). There is also publication entitled *Indian John Life of John W. Johnson*, copied by Edward Johnson Ladd from Johnson's 1861 book, ed. Mr. Freeman (Fort Payne, AL: 1962). This last work was accessed from a 1998 online source that is no longer available. All quotations in this entry are from Johnson's *The Life of John W. Johnson*, 1861. When this work was accessed online notes on each chapter were taken so that quotes could be identified as appearing on specific pages within each chapter. These notes are in the possession of Dr. O'Neill. Information for this entry was also derived from Nan Wolverton, "American Indian Baskets Made in New England," *The Magazine Antiques* (January 2004), 184–90.

2 John was the son of James Whitcomb Johnson and Jane Manson. John's father's three hired men would "hustle him to a room of a building in the town and there hold him prisoner" W. Whidden Johnson, "Fate Led Kidnapped Saco Boy Back Home, 20 Years After," *Portland Sunday Telegram*, 16 December 1934, Section D. Whidden reported that Johnson was "snatched by Indians" and "passed from tribe to tribe" before becoming a medicine man. This is incorrect; he was not

"snatched." Three-year-old John had been playing in the Maine woods in 1833 with his sister when his sister unexpectedly left for home, thinking John would meet up with his older brother Samuel later. John and his older brother never connected. The Mi'kmaq found Johnson wandering alone in the woods and went to his aid. His biological parents, when John did not return, assumed he had drowned in the Saco River.

3 For more information on the Newell Penobscot family, see "Newell Family History" in "Genealogy ramblings of a Mainer with roots in Newfoundland, Canada (French, Portugal and Scotland), England and Penobscot Native American," https://geneologymaine.wordpress.com/2015/12/30/7/, accessed 8 February 2023.

4 His sons were named James Valpole Johnson and John Howard Cuvier Johnson. His second marriage was short-lived, and Mary went on to wed Abner Huntley in 1884, by whom she had three children. John Wesley Johnson, Family Search, https://ancestors.familysearch.org/en/LTZ7-BTS/john-wesley-johnson-1829-1907.

5 He is buried in Greenwood Cemetery, Biddeford, York, Maine. https://ancestors.familysearch.org/en/LTZ7-BTS/john-wesley-johnson-1829-1907.

6 Johnson, *The Life of John W. Johnson*, chap. 11, p. 5.

7 Johnson's date of birth is uncertain. It was probably 7 October 1829, but there is a competing date, 10 July 1829.

8 Johnson, *The Life of John W. Johnson*, chap. 2, p. 2.

9 Ibid., chap. 2, p. 9.

10 Ibid.

11 Ibid., chap. 2, p. 6.

12 Ibid., chap. 2, p. 8

13 This place name is somewhat similar to the Mi'kmaw word for Antigonish, which is *Articougnesche*, meaning "where the bears tear branches off trees." Mi'kmaq used to canoe or sail from the Antigonish area across the Northumberland Strait to reach southeastern Prince Edward Island.

14 Ibid., chap. 3, p. 15.

15 Ibid.

16 Ibid., chap. 2, p. 8.

17 John J. McCusker, "Comparing the Purchasing Power of Money in the United States (or Colonies) from 1665 to 2005," *Economic History Services*, http://eh.net/hmit/ppwerusd, accessed 2006.

18 D.C. MacKay, "Valentine, William," *Dictionary of Canadian Biography* online, vol. 7 (1836–50).

19 *Novascotian*, Halifax, Nova Scotia, 9 March 1837. The value of the pound was about five dollars.

20 Johnson, *The Life of John W. Johnson*, chap. 8, p. 3.

21 Ibid., chap. 10, p. 9.

CHAPTER 12

1 Grand Chief John Denny Jr.'s land and resource use strategies during the early twentieth century are examined in detail in Janet E. Chute, "Frank G. Speck's Contributions to the Understanding of Mi'kmaq Land Use, Leadership, and Land Management," *Ethnohistory* 46, no. 3 (1999): 509–15.

2 This characteristic of Chief Julien's career is illuminated in Anita Maria Tobin, "The Effect of Centralization on the Social and Political Systems of the Mainland Nova Scotia Mi'kmaq (Case Studies: Millbrook – 1916 & Indian Brook – 1941)" (master's thesis, Saint Mary's University, 1999), 51, 69.

3 Information provided by Donald M. Julien, 20 June 2013; see also *Aknutmaqn*, Membertou community newsletter, 5 July 2013.

4 Public Records Office, London, England, British Colonial Office Documents on microfilm housed in Library and Archives of Canada (henceforth LAC, CO) 217/54/219–26; LAC CO 217/55/17–19. For additional information on the meeting with Michael Francklin at Windsor in September, see L.F.S. Upton, "Julien (Julian), John," *Dictionary of Canadian Biography* online, vol. 5 (1801–20). A number of documents pertaining to "King John Julian" were held by Georgina Barlow of Miramichi, the daughter of the last chief to inherit the documents; after her father's death, she placed the documents in the Provincial Archives of New Brunswick (PANB). Document Package Reference Code: CA PANB MC61. Since the late seventeenth century, Mi'kmaq from the district of Kespek (Gespe'gewa'gi or Kespukwitk, meaning the "last land") have been recorded as travelling east along the shore of the Northumberland Strait towards Cape Breton and attaching themselves temporarily to local bands they encountered on their journeys. The spellings of the surname "Julian" and "Julien" are not interchangeable: individuals and families adopted the spelling accorded their surname when their names were set down on band lists, and did not deviate from it. There are both Juliens and Julians living at Millbrook and Shubenacadie today.

5 L.F.S. Upton, *Micmacs and Colonists: Indian-White Relations in the Maritimes, 1713–1867* (Vancouver: University of British Columbia Press, 1979), 99.

6 In return for their allegiance to the British Crown, King John Julian and his people received a licence of occupation for twenty thousand acres along the Miramichi River that they had already hunted and fished over for generations. But, as was so often the case, with the arrival of

Loyalist settlers after 1783 and the lack of protection from trespass offered reserves by the New Brunswick colonial government, this reserve became so drastically reduced in size by 1808 that members had to travel widely to find sufficient hunting grounds to support their families. When big game on these tracts failed, they sought labouring work wherever they could find it – as axemen in the woods, as log drivers on New Brunswick, Nova Scotian, and Newfoundland rivers, as stevedores in the growing shipyards, as coopers and basketmakers near farming and fishing communities, and as manufacturers of wooden articles for the mining industry. Grand Chief John Denny Jr. often remarked that many of his group in Cape Breton made and sold wooden tubs, beams, staves, and pick handles to mining companies. He wanted to regularize this practice into a large-scale business and for that reason he set his sights on discovering tracts of relatively under-exploited forest so that the Mi'kmaq could access ongoing supplies of wood for such pursuits.

7 Père Chrétien Le Clercq in his account of Gaspesia described Mi'kmaq going back and forth in the 1670s from the Kespek district to Cape Breton. "Gaspé" in French, "Kespek" is the way the place name is currently spelled in mainland Nova Scotia, and "Gespe'gewa'gi" is the way it is spelled in New Brunswick and southern Quebec.

8 NSARM, MG 15, vol. 6, doc. no. 22. The Juliens may not have farmed, since there were no seed potatoes given in 1870 to anyone named Julien. LAC, RG 10, vol. 461, 470, "Distribution of seed potatoes to family heads living at Eskasoni, Whycocomagh, Baddeck and Antigonish," June 1870. From the documentary resources at her disposal, the author could not trace a clear genealogical connection between Noel Julien and the two eighteenth-century chiefs, though such links must have existed. W.D. Hamilton traces Julien family genealogical lines within New Brunswick. Hamilton, *The Julian Tribe* (Fredericton: Micmac-Malecite Institute/ Mi'kmaq-Wolastoqey Centre, 1984). At least three Juliens – who may have been brothers – arrived in Cape Breton early in the nineteenth century and joined local bands. For instance, Dan Julien was present when the Chapel Island Reserve near St. Peter's, Cape Breton, was surveyed on 16 January 1833 and remembered when the "land base was much larger." Nova Scotia Archives and Records Management, Halifax (henceforth NSARM), RG 1, vol. 431, doc. 2. On 26 July 1841, forty-five-year-old Thomas Julian, accompanied by his wife Ann and their children, and forty-seven-year-old Noel Julian and his wife assembled for St. Anne's Day ceremonies on Chapel Island on. These persons were likely relatives of Joseph

Julien's father, who was of a younger generation, and they likely had travelled a fair distance to participate in the St. Anne's Day religious festivities. NSARM, MG 15, vol. 3, doc. 65, "An Account of the Indians within the County of Richmond, as taken on the 26th July 1841, at the Indian Chapel, Bras d'or Lake, being the Anniversary of St. Ann's Day"; NSARM, MG 15, vol. 4a, doc. nos. 111–12, "List of Mi'kmaq at Sydney," 27 November 1851.

9 NSARM, MG 15, vol. 6, doc. 64, "List of Mi'kmaq residing at North Sydney," January 1862. The late Roddy J. Gould (or Gold; 1914–2003) of Waycobah First Nation stated that "John Gold" and his wife Susan were probably the ancestors of the Goulds of Cape Breton. The author initially speculated that the surname "Gould" among the Mi'kmaq might have been borrowed from "Arthur Gould," a member of the Fifth Legislative Assembly, also known as the "Long Parliament," that sat from 1770 to 1784. Roddy Gould was probably right that the surname arose in Cape Breton in the 1830s or 1840s, since until the 1850s John Gould was the only Gould appearing in the documentary record. NSARM, MG 15, vol. 42, docs. Nos. 109 and 112, "List of Mi'kmaq at North Sydney," 27 November 1851. Members of the Gould family appear in the Truro area around 1880, and Joseph Gould was acting chief of Millbrook prior to Joseph Julien's election in 1919.

10 NSARM, RG 5, Series GP, vol. 9, doc. no. 67, "Petition of John Denys [Denny] Sr. and Paul Christmas, along with Mikmaq signatories, to Lieutenant Governor Sir Richard Graves MacDonnell, dated 22 August 1865." This petition was drafted by Father F. Cocteau.

11 Madeline, a widow whose surname at the time of her marriage to Noel Julien was "Sylliboy" ("Sylliboy" evidently being the surname of her first husband), hailed from the Pomquet-Afton reserve near Heatherton, Antigonish County, a tract which was confirmed by Order-in-Council in 1820. It now is the land base of the Paq'tnkek First Nation. Madeline was said to be a young widow whose sister wed a man named Martin who travelled between Cape Breton and Newfoundland. Though it could not be confirmed, Madeline's birth surname may have been "Benoit."

12 Louise Googoo, "Story of Joseph Julien," unpublished ms transcribed by Donald Julien from his grandmother Louise Googoo's accounts. (A printed version appears in the *Mi'kmaq-Maliseet Nations News*, January 2012.) It is possible that this daughter's baptismal name was "Mary Anathasia Julien," and that she was named after Joseph Julien's sister Mary. Author conversation with Lillian Marshall, great-granddaughter of Mary Julien, 14 July 2011.

13 "Remembering a Leader ... Chief Joseph Julien," *Mi'kmaq-Maliseet Nations News*, January 2012, 9. The

circumstances surrounding Noel Julien's death by drowning in the Saint John River are not known, though river driving was an extremely risky undertaking. Noel may have been killed during the spring log drive of 1878.

14 Googoo, "Story of Joseph Julien," 1.

15 There was a school and teacher at Eskasoni on and off since 1824. The first teacher was a missionary named Simon Lawlor. NSARM, RG 1, vol. 4320, doc. 167, "Petition of Simon Lawlor, Missionary at Bras d'Or, 1828." Several members of the Christmas family at Eskasoni were educated, particularly Ben Christmas, who was the only Mi'kmaw assistant in the late 1840s and 1850s of the Baptist missionary Silus Tertius Rand, and Benoni Christmas, who wrote journal articles in the 1840s. Ben hailed from Eskasoni (his father may have been Paul Christmas, who at times lived in North Sydney). He married Theresa McAdams and the couple had several children; those born after 1860 were baptized at St. Bernard's Roman Catholic Church at Enfield. Their daughter Harriet, for example, was baptized on 26 February 1866. Registers of St. Bernard's Church, Enfield. Ben left the Baptist mission in 1860, having become ambivalent towards Protestantism, and died in Truro, where he is buried. He is mentioned in Judith Fingard, "Rand, Silus Tertius," *Dictionary of Canadian Biography* online, vol. 9 (1881–90).

16 One recent biographical article about Joseph Julian states that "unfortunately, people could not remember her first name. The young lady's married name before she married Joseph would have been Morris." "Remembering a Leader," 9.

17 In 1867 J.J.D. Oland opened the Army and Navy Brewery in North Dartmouth, and when Oland died in 1870 his widow, Susannah Oland, changed the firm's name to S. Oland, Sons & Company Ltd. When this business was absorbed in 1895 by Halifax Breweries Ltd., G.W.C. Oland served as general manager, assisted by his son Sidney C. Oland. Both G.W.C. Oland and Sidney C. Oland then left Halifax Breweries to organize a new brewery, Oland & Son Ltd., in Dartmouth not far from Tufts Cove. This brewery, where Joseph Julien worked, was subsequently destroyed by the Halifax Explosion in 1917, and was not rebuilt.

18 "Remembering a Leader," 9.

19 The late Commodore Bruce Oland, Colonel Sidney C. Oland's son, was one of the late Colonel Malcolm Turner's closest friends. Colonel Turner was the author's uncle, and over the years he often told how much he and Colonel Oland respected Mi'kmaw guiding skills, as well as Mi'kmaw dedication to Crown and country when in uniform as war veterans. Given the depth of this attitude, it is not surprising that Joseph Julien would find a compatible friend in the man he guided during the years he lived in Dartmouth.

20 Mary Jane Paul was the daughter of Joseph Paul and his wife Mary Ann Paul of Nyanza. Their grandson John Julian served in the Canadian Expeditionary Force from 14 April 1917 to 17 July 1919. Donald M. Julien, "Mi'kmaq Historical Perspective on Mi'kmaw Veterans of the First World War," manuscript, completed 30 March 2017, in possession of the author, 214–16.

21 Halifax County Deeds, Deed Book 223, 530–1, "Indenture made 20 August 1880 between Her Majesty the Queen, represented by the Superintendent-General of Indian Affairs, on the one part, and Thomas Ritchie of Halifax, Executor of the last will and testament of William Almon Johnstone, late of Windsor, Barrister-at-Law, on the other." Thomas Ritchie, who was a relative of Judge Johnstone as well as his executor, arranged the sale of the Cole Harbour property to the Crown for three hundred dollars. The description of the land base as given in the indenture suggests that lots along Caldwell Road within the parcel were previously farmed by settlers. Although it was an independent reserve when it was founded in 1880, by the 1950s the forty-five acres located near the eastern end of Morris Lake was administrated by the Millbrook band, near Truro. "Although the population fluctuated over the years, as many as twenty-seven families lived on the reserve at the same time. The native people living there made hockey sticks, ash axe handles, splint baskets, and quillwork, which they sold at the city market in Halifax or door to door." Men worked as farmhands and occasionally joined local farmers hunting or chopping wood. There was a chapel as well as a school. Harry Chapman, *Along the Cole Harbour Road: A Journey through 1765–2003* (Dartmouth: Cole Harbour Rural Heritage Society, 2003), 152.

22 NSARM, RG 1, vol. 431, Indian Affairs, Miscellaneous detached documents, "John Johnson to John Whidden, Esq.," 15 January 1847. Johnson, a justice of the peace for Colchester County, stated that there were no Mi'kmaq resident at Truro, though "occasionally there are some transient ones from Pictou."

23 The middle reaches of the Musquodoboit River were accessible by canoe, after which an array of interconnected water bodies and Indigenous trails extended northwest to the south branch of the Stewiacke River.

24 At first glance it appears that "Vieaux," when applied to Chief Chachegonout, was simply Indian Commissioner

George Monk's misspelling of the French word *vieux*, "old." Monk thus would have been referring to Chachegonout as "Old Paul." Yet "Vieaux" was also a French surname, and "Vieaux à Paul" actually means "Vieaux the son of Paul" – an intriguing subject for future consideration. Monk undoubtedly knew more about the Pictou leaders than he wrote down in his journals and letterbooks, for he must have realized that persons with the surname "Vieaux" lived in the Northeast. For instance, Jacques Joseph Vieaux, who served with the Northwest Company, and his wife Marie Ann St. Germain had a son, Jacques Joseph Vieaux, (1757–1852), at Côte-des-Neiges, near Montreal. As an adult, the younger Jacques Vieaux went to Chequamegon, southern Lake Superior, where he wed Angelique Roy, a daughter of Joseph Roy and Marguerite Oskinaotame, so his offspring were *mètis*. Jacques died in 1852 in Howard Township, Brown County, Wisconsin. *Green Bay Advocate*, "Obituary of Jacques Vieaux *dit* Jambo," 8 July 1852.

25 NSARM, RG1, vol. 430, doc. 23½. Even in the late eighteenth century the Pictou Mi'kmaq retained only minimal contact with Halifax. Chief Jenneoville Pectougawach (John Noel of Pictou) signed a peace and friendship treaty with the English near the close of the Seven Years' War, but many Mi'kmaq in the district remained attached to the French, whom they hoped would return. In 1765 they threatened to burn houses of English settlers who encroached on their hunting grounds. Fear of Mi'kmaw raids also arose among settlers during the American Revolution, which impelled Michael Francklin to hasten to Pictou with presents to wean local leaders from their suspected attachment to George Washington. By the late 1770s some Merigomish band members received some rent from settlers who used portions of their lands. For instance, Donald Fraser of McLellan's Brook paid "Lulan (Roland) Mercataeway, son of Francia," a bushel of wheat annually and "was accustomed to speak of him as his landlord." George Patterson, *History of the County of Pictou* (Montreal: Dawson Brothers, 1877), 42–50, 186–7; Upton, *Micmac and Colonists*, 77.

26 Indian Island retained ceremonial significance for Mi'kmaq throughout the Pictou district even before Abbé Pierre Maillard held services there in the mid-1750s. During the French era a small chapel adorned the site, and another frame chapel was built in 1835 for the annual St. Anne's Day mission. This structure was rebuilt in 1897. During the 1840s the Merigomish band was headed by Assem Paul, while a second, distinct group, led by Peter Toney, Captain Anthony Eury's son, lived at Remsheg (Wallace), near Tatamagouche. Members of the two Pictou bands intermarried, participated in ceremonies at Merigomish, and eventually joined to become the Pictou Landing First Nation. Assem Paul, Chachegonout's son and successor, and Peter Toney, a son of Captain Anthony Eury who sided with the British during the American Revolution, were the two Pictou leaders in 1835. NSARM, RG 1, vol. 431, docs. 14 and 35, "Regarding the chiefs at Merigomish and Arasaig," 11 June 1835 and 18 June 1837.

27 Registers of St. Bernard's Parish, Enfield, "Baptism of Sarah Jane, daughter of Peter Wilmot and Maria Landry. 1880." Peter Wilmot had at least nine children. Ruth Holmes Whitehead, "Wilmot, Peter," *Dictionary of Canadian Biography* online, vol. 16 (1931–40). Despite the fact that there was a colonial governor in the mid-1760s named Montague Wilmot, the surname "Wilmot" may have been an Anglicized version of "Ouinette," a Mi'kmaw surname appearing first in what is now northern New Brunswick. Hamilton, *The Julien Tribe*, 90–2. Peter's grandfather Francis Wilmot may originally have belonged to the Remsheg band, as in 1800 he visited Cobequid with his wife, three children, and "Lewie Toney" (Louis Toney), a son of Captain Anthony of Remsheg. NSARM, RG 1, vol. 431, Indian Affairs, Miscellaneous detached documents, "Amount of Provisions and Clothing Supplied the Undermentioned Familys of Indians at Truro by Thomas Pearson," 15 January 1800. Pearson in 1800 counted sixty Mi'kmaq at Truro, all suffering from hunger. The documentary record provides ample evidence of lean years among these Mi'kmaq. NSARM, vol. 430, doc. 62, "Return of Indians resident in the District of Pictou," 19 March 1801; NSARM, RG 1, vol. 430, doc. 66, "Names of Indians resident at Pictou by Edward Mortimer," March 1801; NSARM, vol. 430, doc. 37½ and doc. 128, "List of names of families at Antigonish, c.1801"; NSARM, vol. 430, doc. 50, "Edward Mortimer regarding the Pictou band," 19 March to 23 June 1801. During the early 1850s, Indian Commissioner William Chearnley noted that only two family heads, both surnamed "Wilmot," lived in Pictou County: thirty-nine-year-old Joseph Wilmot, with a wife and four children, and thirty-six-year-old Tom Wilmot, with a wife and six children. Joseph Wilmot, aged thirty-nine and so born in 1813, would have been too young to be Peter Wilmot's father, although Chearnley could easily have mistaken his birth date. Peter Wilmot in the early 1850s belonged to the Pictou Landing band, composed of persons from Merigomish who had moved to be near the town of Pictou, but he spent considerable time at Truro,

and his hunting territory lay between Pictou and Truro. NSARM, MG 15, vol. 5, doc, no. 69, "William Chearnley, Indian List for the Year 1855"; NSARM, MG 15, vol. 41, doc. 112, "Band list," 6 January 1852.

28 NSARM, RG 1, vol. 430, doc. 128. One of Wilmot's children was reputed to have died young. Ruth Holmes Whitehead, "Wilmot, Peter," *Dictionary of Canadian Biography* online, vol. 16 (1931–40).

29 The Pictou Mi'kmaq experienced a severe influenza-like epidemic in 1845 and 1846 that caused disruption within families for many years and may have led Wilmot later to leave the area. The site frequented by Wilmot along the Salmon River lay where the river today runs between the town and the village of Bible Hill – close to what was known as the "Archibald property." NSARM, RG 1, vol. 432, doc. 41.

30 NSARM, RG 15, vol. 6, no. 67, "Mi'kmaq at Truro," 26 February 1862. St. Mary's School was erected on this property at Christmas Crossing, which is now the site of the Colchester Historical Museum and Archives.

31 In 1905 the School of Agriculture became the Nova Scotia Agricultural College, which in 2012 joined with Dalhousie University to become the Dalhousie School of Agriculture.

32 The indenture for release of two mortgages, as well as the release of dower rights, comprise one docket. Colchester County Deeds, Book 79, 298–99, "Indenture made 6 December 1886 between John Waller Jr. and Her Majesty the Queen"; Colchester County Deeds, Book 79, folio 300–301, "Indenture made the 4 of December 1886 between George Campbell, executor for the estate of John P. Gorston, late of Truro, railway constructor, and John Waller Jr., son of the late Samuel Waller and Susan Ann Waller of Truro, regarding a mortgage made in 1877 (in consideration of the sum of $220.00, with interest) and a second mortgage made in 1880 (in consideration of the sum of $180.00 and subject to the considerations of the first mortgage) executed between Samuel Waller and his wife Susan Ann, on the one part, and George Campbell, on the second part." The two mortgages amounted to $400. In 1886, however, Campbell released John Waller Jr. from both mortgage agreements on the payment of the much lower sum of "$100.00 paid in hand." John Waller's mother, "Susan Ann Waller, wife of Samuel Waller deceased," then relinquished her dower rights to her son John Waller on 16 October 1886. The description of the parcel was as follows: "lying and being at the Arch Culvert, so called, in the Township of Truro, lying on the east side of the Intercolonial Railway and … Beginning at a post in the railway fence twelve chains

north of the point where the mill brook and the railway fence intersect at the Arch Culvert aforesaid; thence south seventy-eight degrees, east thirty-one chains and seventy-five links to a stake. Thence south seven degrees, west eleven chains and fifty links to a fir tree; thence north seventy-eight degrees, west thirty-one chains and seventy-five links, or until it strikes the brook and railway fence; thence by the same railway fence in a northerly direction twelve chains to the place of beginning, containing thirty-five acres, more or less." John Waller Jr. sold the rectangular parcel at Millbrook to the Crown for $350.00 on 6 December 1886, and the transaction of sale was recorded on 20 June 1887. The parcel was laid out by the Colchester County surveyor, William Faulkner, in November 1887.

33 After his election as Millbrook leader, Peter Wilmot met opposition to his land and resource policies from Indian agents. The Department of Indian Affairs recognized him as chief of Millbrook, although an Indian agent named D.H. Muir wrote Ottawa on 2 June 1891 that Wilmot was "recognized to be incompetent and left the County in 1889. The Indians did not appoint a successor … in order to avoid repeating the mistake." Wilmot spent around seven years in Cumberland County. He was elected chief of the Cumberland County Agency on 14 October 1895, though another Indian agent, F.A. Rand, held that Wilmot was "an irresponsible person, incapable of being chief" and suggested that Ottawa not recognize his election. Cape Breton University, Sydney, Beaton Institute, Archives of the Mi'kmaq Institute, Report #100 MRC 98-100-454, untitled – "Names of Chiefs, Various NS bands, 1906–1971," 1–12. It is uncertain why these Indian agents disparaged Wilmot to such a degree, unless, of course, he refused to follow their directives. In 1886 Wilmot left Cumberland County and returned to Pictou. The Pictou Landing band had been expanding on a campaign Wilmot had launched as their leader in the 1850s to secure a permanent land base near the town of Pictou. In 1864 the group acquired a reserve of fifty acres, and then set about attaining additional plots suitable for farming and logging. The Mi'kmaq paid for the first fifty acres out of their own band funds. After Confederation in 1867, adhesions to the original grant that occurred between 1876 and 1889 were the result of Ottawa's purchasing portions of a tract known as "Fisher's Grant." These purchases gave rise to reserve plots 24A, 24B, 24C, 24D, 24E, 24F, and 24G. Pictou County Deeds, Book 73, 135–6; Book 93, 114–17; Book 127, 399; Book 128, 315, "William Ives *et ux* (1874), James Gillis Sproule *et ux* (1876) and Robert Fraser *et ux*

(1889)." Ottawa later referred to these as "parcels A, B, C, D, E, F, and G." Purchases of larger parcels followed. Peter Wilmot likely shared in this process, with his ideas and advice being sought, as he was a respected elder. He never became an elected chief at Pictou Landing, however, since no elections took place in that community during his lifetime. (The first official election under the provisions of the Indian Act took place at Pictou Landing on 24 June 1959, when Louis J. Francis was elected chief.)

34 At Millbrook Wilmot is remembered as an esteemed traditional leader, an engaging storyteller, and an active member of the Mi'kmaw Grand Council. Nova Scotia Museum (hereafter NSM), Printed Matter File, Piers unpublished notes, "Harry Piers, 28 December 1932."

35 NSM, Printed Matter File, Piers Notes, "Jeremiah Bartlett-Alexis to Harry Piers," 7 April 1923. William Prosper was born at Bay of Islands, Newfoundland, and came to Whycocomagh c.1848. In 1860 he was invited to meet the Prince of Wales in Halifax. A cooper who sold barrels at the Halifax market, he lived near Farrell's Pond in Dartmouth. Around 1880 he moved to Millbrook where he died on 3 April 1923 at the age of 101.

36 Newel and Anastasia, before settling at Millbrook, had lived in New Brunswick, on the North West Arm in Halifax, and at Londonderry, Colchester County.

37 NSARM, Miscellaneous "I" Indian Land Records from Crown Lands, on microfilm, "Schedule of Indian reserves in Nova Scotia, 1959." The three additions to the original reserve were designated as lots 27A, 27B, and 27C. Lot 27A adjoined the southern limit of the Corporation of Truro; 27B adjoined lot 27A on its south side, while Lot 27C flanked lot 27B. Treaty and Aboriginal Rights Research Centre (TARR) Shubenacadie, UNSI file 92-1004-19-032, "Profile of Truro, Millbrook IR 27, 27A, 27B, 27C."

38 There were two Frank Copes living at Sheet Harbour around the same time. One, who was not Sandy Cope Sr.'s father, wed Jane Redmond on 5 July 1857. He and Jane had least four children: Ann in 1857, Alice Bridget in 1862, Emily in 1866, and Henry in 1871. Registers of the Parish of St. Peter and Missions, Sheet Harbour. Sandy Cope Sr.'s son Frank named one of his sons "Redmond Cope," so this Frank Cope and Sandy's family were closely related. Frank Cope, Sandy Cope's father, born in 1829, and Mary Ann Quigley married at St. Peter's Parish Church at Sheet Harbour on 16 November 1857. Registers of St. Peter's Parish, Baptisms, Marriages and Deaths, 1857–97. (The parish only extended to Sheet Harbour for marriages and baptisms in 1857.)

Frank Cope began living with Mary Ann Quigley in 1851 and the couple had eleven children. The eldest was Alexander or "Sandy Cope Sr." (1853–1930), who was baptized in 1858, following his parents' marriage the preceding year. The couple's other ten children were Catherine Annie (1860–1922), Alice Bridget (b. 1862), Frank (b. 1864), Nancy (1855–1933), Emily (1866–1947), Henry (1871–1914), Bridget Ellen (b. 1876), Margaret (b. 1878), Peter (b. 1882), and Elizabeth May or "Libby" (1888–1974). Frank Cope, died in 1912 at the age of eighty-four. NSARM, Historical Vital Statistics, Halifax County Deaths, Registration Year 1912, Book 9, p. 339, no. 2030, "Death of Frank Cope"; NSARM, Historical Vital Statistics, Registration Year 1904, No. 71401702, late registration of birth (1888). Sandy Cope Sr. lived until 1870 at Beaverdam Lake, where his father Frank had a cabin and hunting territory. He married three times, first in 1882 to Matilda Stevens, second around 1888 to Mary Paul of the "Quoddy Pauls," and third in 1915, at age fifty-eight, to Bella Nicholas, a forty-eight-year-old widow who was a daughter of Michael Nicholas and Mary Walsh of Bayfield, Antigonish County. NSARM, Historical Vital Statistics, Halifax County Marriages, Registration Year 1882, Book 1817, p. 140, no. 388, "Marriage of Alexander Cope, son of Frank Cope and Mary A., to Matilda Stevens, daughter of Peter Stevens and Sarah"; NSARM, Historical Vital Statistics, Colchester County Marriages, Year 1915, Book 43, 741, "Marriage of Sandy Cope and Bella Nicholas, 27 September 1915." Around 1880 Sandy Cope moved to the Truro area and became a hunting guide in the Cobequid region. Today, a 6.3-kilometre-long hiking trail, named the "Sandy Cope Loop Hiking Trail," passes through Cope's former hunting territory along the Colchester-Pictou County Boundary. This trail lies southeast of Earltown, north of Kemptown, and twenty-five kilometres north of Truro, and forms part of the Gully Lake Wilderness Preserve. Sandy Cope Sr. died in 1930. NSARM, Historical Vital Statistics, Colchester County Deaths, Registration Date 1930, Book 119, p. 1052, "Death of Alexander Cope, born on 4 November 1853 at Sheet Harbour, the son of Frank Cope and Mary Paul [sic, Mary Ann Quigley], died 15 March 1930 at Millbrook at the age of 76 years, 4 months and 10 days." Sandy Sr. and Matilda Stevens's son Sandy Cope Jr. married Matilda Noel in 1904. NSARM, Hants County Marriages, Registration Year 1904, Book 1824, p. 74, no. 88. Sandy Jr. and "Tillie" had only a small family, and one of their daughters Mary, died in 1924. NSARM, Historical Vital Statistics, Registration Year 1924, Colchester County Deaths, Book 112, 300. Sandy Cope Sr.'s younger brother Peter married Mary Rose Paul ("Rose") of the "Quoddy Pauls" and had two sons, Francis in 1859 and Isaac in 1860. Sandy Sr.'s sister, Catherine Annie, married Isaac Sack in 1877; the two lived in Elmsdale. Henry, Sandy Cope Sr.'s son, lived with Sandy Cope Jr. after his parents' death, and died a single man at age thirty-eight at Truro of spinal paralysis. NSARM, Historical Vital Statistics, Colchester County Deaths, Book 31, p. 4, no. 22. Henry's sister Elizabeth May, or "Libby," married C.M. Moore and lived in Edmonton.

39 "Major" would have been a rank conferred on Jean-Baptiste Cope by the French at Louisbourg prior to 1752. He also would have had a parchment French commission and a corresponding medal. Cope was born to Paul Cope and Cecille at Port Royal in 1698. French census of 1708 in the Ayer Collection of the Newberry Library in Chicago, *Recensement genal fait au mois de Novembre mile sept cens huit de tous les Sauvages de l'Acadie qui resident dans la cost de L'Est, et de ceux de Pintagouet et de Canibeky, famille par famille, leurs ages, celuy de leurs hommes et enfants avec une recapitulation a la fin de la quantite d'hommes et des garcons capables d'aler a la guerre.* A typescript of this census is housed at LAC, MG 18, F 18, 1. Cope had three sisters: Thereze who was eight, Marie who was five, and Marguerite who was one. After the British conquest of Port Royal in 1710 and the signing of the Treaty of Utrecht in 1713, which established British sovereignty over mainland Nova Scotia, Jean-Baptiste's parents joined a band of around fifty families living along the Shubenacadie and Musquodoboit Rivers. The Copes grew close to the Acadian community at Piziquid, and Jean-Baptiste was reputed to have spoken French fluently. When he arose as the Sipekne'katik district chief in 1752, he spearheaded the signing of a peace and friendship treaty. Yet after a party of Mi'kmaq were killed at Mocodome, now Country Harbour, along the Eastern Shore, he grew hostile towards the British. Cope did not sign a peace and friendship treaty made in 1726 at Annapolis Royal on behalf of the Shubenacadie group. The chief at this time was Jean-Baptiste Bon, patriarch of the Bonis or Bonice (*Bon-ech* or "Little Bon") family of Musquodoboit. William C. Wicken, *Mi'kmaq Treaties on Trial: History, Land, and Donald Marshall Jr.* (Toronto: University of Toronto Press, 2002), 22–3. The Shubenacadie band hunted inland to Stewiacke, and some members regularly pressed into the Cobequid Mountains area. In 1699 Père Pierre-Louis Thury headed a Roman Catholic mission along the Eastern Shore, though he died before the mission became well established. The compiler of the 1708 French census,

Père La Chasse, estimated there were 123 Mi'kmaq at Musquodoboit, a large enough group to warrant Abbé Antoine Gaulin's establishing a mission in 1722 along the Shubenacadie River, downstream and on the opposite side of the river from the mouth of the Stewiacke River. Though as many as twenty-two families assembled at the mission for religious festivities, much to Gaulin's chagrin they refused to stay long enough to form an agricultural settlement. Cope would have attended services presided over by Abbé Jean-Louis Le Loutre at the Shubenacadie mission prior to 1749, and in the early to middle 1750s regularly visited Le Loutre at Beaubassin. As mentioned above, after signing treaty, Cope participated in 1753 at Jeddore in the killing of crewmen belonging to a government schooner, in revenge for a party of Englishmen killing several Mi'kmaq at Mocodome, now County Harbour. NSARM, RG 1, document 23, "Copy of 'Antony Casteel's Journal.'" The original ms. (Brown Mss, Add. 19073, f. 11, no. 23) is housed in the British Museum in London, England. Casteel was the only member of the party sent under the command of Captain Bannerman to Jeddore in 1753 who escaped being killed by Cope's men in reprisal for Mi'kmaq killings at Mocodome. An oral tradition recounted by Sandy Cope Sr. in 1922 and recorded and transcribed by Muriel Cottam Yorke of Debert holds that Major Cope was killed by a man named Francis Paul in what is now Point Point Pleasant Park, Halifax. "Sandy Cope, Millbrook, to Muriel Cottam Yorke, Debert Settlement, c.1922," in Don (Byrd) Awalt, "The Mi'kmaq and Point Pleasant Park, The Mi'kmaq and Amtoukati: An Historical Essay in Progress by Don Byrd Awalt" (Halifax: Native Friendship Centre, 2006), 6–7. According to this story, Cope charged Bernard Argomartin, Saylen Paul (Peminout), and Paul Laurent with betraying their people by their willingness to extend peace overtures to the English. In response, François Peminout, a brother or young son of Saylen Paul, rushed at Cope and killed him and Chief René Martin. A similar story was told by Maggie Paul of Panuke Lake, near Windsor. NSM, Printed Matter File, Harry Piers Papers, "Maggie Paul to Jeremiah Bartlett-Alexis, who told the story to Harry Piers," 5 April 1927; Whitehead, *The Old Man Told Us: Excerpts from Mi'kmaw History, 1500–1950* (Halifax: Nimbus, 1991), 140. After 1758 Jean-Baptiste Cope's name does not appear in the documentary record again.

40 Isaac Sack was the son of Peter Sack and Marie-Antoinette Thomas.

41 Joseph Cope and Frank Cope were both married and living at Truro. Bridget Cope married Joseph Julien

and had a daughter Rachel, who later married Charles Marshall and became chief of the Millbrook community from 18 December 1969 to 18 December 1971. Rachel Marshall was the second woman to hold chiefly office among the Mi'kmaq. Bridget's sister, Margaret or "Meggie," married Charles Phillips and the couple maintained a farm on the Cole Harbour reserve. Her sister, Susan Jane, wed John Louis Noel McDonald. Following John's death, Susan Jane married Bill Duncan, a Mi'kmaw constable at Shubenacadie. Sandy Cope Jr. wed John Louis McDonald's sister, Matilda Noel (McDonald). The Copes, East Coast Pauls, Noels, and McDonalds were closely kin related and also had ties with the local settler population along the Eastern Shore. Early Cope marriages are found in the Parish Registers of Saint Peter and Missions, Sheet Harbour, Baptisms, Marriages and Deaths, 1800–97; Sheet Harbour Baptisms, Marriages and Deaths, 1857–80s.

42 Joseph Julien was temporarily working at this time as a labourer at Enfield. NSARM, Historical Vital Statistics, Registration Year 1905, Book 1824, p. 80, no. 46 (his surname is incorrectly spelled "Jubien" in the Vital Statistics index), "Marriage at St. Bernard's Church in Enfield of Joseph Julien, widower, 29, son of Noel Cope and Madeleine of New Glasgow, and Bridget Cope, 15, born at Debert, Colchester County, daughter of Alex Cope and Mary, 19 June 1905, presiding priest W.E. Young, witnesses Alex Cope and Annie Newell"; "Remembering a Leader," 9.

43 Alex Cope and his wife were living in Colchester County by 1890. When Joseph Julien married Bridget Cope at Elmsdale, Hants County, on 19 June 1905, the couple's marriage certificate stated that Bridget was born in 1890 at Debert, Colchester County. NSARM, Historical Vital Statistics, Hants County Marriages, "Marriage of Joseph Julian and Bridget Cope," 19 June 1905.

44 *Wyegawook* (also written *Weijooik*, *Wegiwaick*, or *Wigawick*) means "flowing wildly" or "running crazily." It is the Mi'kmaw place name for what is now Sheet Harbour, lying 114 kilometres east of Halifax. The name was changed to "Sheet Harbour" in 1818 owing to a white boulder that, to ships at sea, looked like a large white sheet lying at the harbour's entrance. Charles Bruce Fergusson, *Place-Names and Places of Nova Scotia*, Nova Scotia Series 3 (Halifax: Public Archives of Nova Scotia, 1967), 616.

45 An Acadian oral tradition holds that around 1747 "Joe Copee" (Joe Cope) had a dog that saved Paul Labrador's family during a flood at Piziquid. This incident took place near the "Indian Orchard at the head of tide on or near a farm now owned by John Davenny of Windsor Forks." W.B. Bezanson, *Stories of Acadia* (Dartmouth: privately printed, 1933), 16.

46 In 1801 John Nowlan petitioned the lieutenant governor's office for a land grant along the Eastern Shore. NSARM, RG 1, vol. 430, doc. 34½, "Petition of John Nowlan to His Excellency John Wentworth, Legis Legum Doctor, Lieutenant-Governor and Commander in Chief in and over His Majesty's Province of Nova Scotia and its Dependencies," 1801. Nowlan previously met Wentworth when, as surveyor of the king's woods, Wentworth visited the Saint Mary's River region. Nowlan had a house and trading post at Nicumquoddie (now Newdy Quoddy, near East Quoddy). His petition to Wentworth was drafted by John Lawson, a prominent Halifax merchant who was visiting Nowlan's household in 1801, perhaps to provide supplies for Nowlan's post. (By the time of his death in 1828, Lawson owned a whaling business and a sugar refinery and had a presiding interest in the Shubenacadie canal. Some of Lawson's descendants married with the Piers family of Halifax – the family to which Harry Piers, the museum curator who took such an interest in the Mi'kmaq, belonged.) In the petition Lawson explained that Nowlan's wife was "an Indian woman, with a large young family in poor circumstances, although neat and clean." The plot of land Nowland wanted lay between "Col. Hales' and Nicumteau [Nicum Teuch]." (*Necum Teuch* in Mi'kmaq means "soft sand place," while "Newdy Quoddy" is derived from the Mi'kmaw *Noodakwade*, "seal hunting place.") Fergusson, *Place-Names and Places*, 55, 471. Although Wentworth agreed to Nowlan's request, Charles Morris, the surveyor general, insisted that a warrant of survey had to be drawn up before the land could be laid out. This order evidently was not carried out, as it does not appear that John Nowlan ever received his grant. One of his sons, William Nowlan, was however granted 123 acres at the mouth of Quoddy Harbour in 1861. William's grant had one stringent condition: it would become "null and void if alienated to any but an Indian – without the express assent of the Government." NSARM, Crown Land Book 28, 181, "Crown Grant to William Nowlan, Micmac Indian," 10 May 1861. Interestingly, unlike a reserve, this parcel was not transferred to the federal government in 1867, and no other Crown grant was issued for the tract.

47 On 15 June 1797 John Nowlan had "12 in [his] family." LAC, MG 23, GII-19, vol. 4, Monk Papers, 1219, "Joseph Davies, Requisition for 1797."

48 The meaning of the name "Doadaran" could not be determined.

49 NSARM, RG 1, vol. 430, doc. 20½, "A Licence for the Indians to Occupy Land … on the Eastern Branch of Sheet Harbour, containing in the Whole Eleven Thousand Five Hundred and Twenty Acres, including Salmon Fishery, signed by Charles Morris, Chief Surveyor, plan attached," 4 September 1783. Jonathan Belcher's grant of 1773 appears in Halifax County Crown Grant Book 2, Book 10, folio 223 and Grants Book 2, Book 10, folio 157. The terms of this licence of occupation, as later recorded in the Governor's Licence Book, deleted any references to the Sheet Harbour Mi'kmaq's having a right to occupy the land in perpetuity. NSARM, RG 20, Series C, vol. 95, Governor's Licence Book, 114, "Registration of Licence of Occupation to Joseph Copp at Sheet Harbour," 1783. For a discussion of these points, see Gillian Allen, "Licenses of Occupation in Nova Scotia: A Reserve by Any Other Name Is Still a Reserve?" Discussion paper prepared for National Research Directors Workshop for Specific Claims Organizations across Canada (NRDW), Ottawa, 8 November 2006, 11–12.

50 LAC, MG 23, G11–19, George Henry Monk Papers, pp. 1033–4, "Monk to Governor John Parr regarding request for land from Francis Cope of Wigawick, undated memo" (spring, 1784). Many fishermen, Acadians, and petty traders along the Eastern Shore were viewed as squatters by the government. The first official settlement arose at Sheet Harbour during the summer of 1783. In 1784 land at Ship Harbour was allocated to Loyalists and disbanded soldiers, with most of the Loyalist families being of German descent from South Carolina. The disbanded soldiers of the Royal Nova Scotia Volunteers tended to move on, but about half of the Germanic Loyalist families remained at Ship Harbour.

51 Ruth Holmes Whitehead claims that *We'jitu* means "I found it." Thus it may relate to his vision. Whitehead, *The Old Man Told Us*, 87.

52 Isidore Cope had a camp on First Dartmouth Lake. NSM, Printed Matter File, "Joseph C. Cope to Harry Piers," 14 January 1914.

53 Though the Reverend Sprott in 1846 declared that all ten of Isidore's sons predeceased their father, at least one grandson, Ned Jeddore's son Noel Jeddore, moved to the Annapolis Valley where he married and had a family. Around 1833 Noel, accompanied by a companion, Handley Squegun (André or Andrew Stephens), succeeded in making a two-hundred-mile canoe trip to Saint John, New Brunswick, in a single day. Noel, who later resided at Cambridge in Kings County, lost his leg in an accident in the early 1850s. NSARM, MG 15, vol.

4a, doc. 123, "Petition of Newel (Noel) Jeddore for £3 because of his difficulties owing to his loss of a leg and the dimness of his sight," 11 February 1852. Several of Isidore Cope's other grandsons pressed along the eastern shore to Cape Breton, from where some travelled to southern Newfoundland.

54 LAC, MG 23, G11–19, Indian Accounts, 1167, "Joseph Davis' requisition entry for 28 May 1796"; LAC, MG 23, G11–19, 1223, "Accounts kept by Joseph Davis for 1796." Captain Paul Bonis was a descendant of a Shubenacadie chief named Jean-Baptiste Bon who signed a treaty with the British in 1726. The surname "Bonis" ("Bonice," "Bonico," "Boonis," "Bonus," "Bones") derived from the Mi'kmaw word *Bon-etch*, meaning "Little Bon" or "son of Bon," rather than from the British surname "Bonice." Molly, another person whose name appears in several requisitions around this time, meanwhile was a feisty woman who dickered with merchants. LAC, MG 23, G11–19, Indian Accounts, 1223, "Joseph Davis' requisition entry for 15 April 1797." Davis wrote "Clothing, provisions and ammunition delivered to Majr. Sutherland to issue to the Eastward Tribe." The value of these goods amounted to £12.19.3. Major Sutherland was the local justice of the peace.

55 Joseph Labrador, who originally came from Mushamush in Lunenburg County, dwelt near François Cope at Sheet Harbour and was, as said above, likely Cope's brother-in-law. François and Joseph visited merchants dispensing government supplies to the Mi'kmaq, although after the arrival of a local merchant named Peter McConachie, the Sheet Harbour band conducted most of its dealings with this man. James Fulton of Stewiacke, who acted as an unofficial informant on Mi'kmaw affairs at Musquodoboit, Truro, and Stewiacke, held in 1801 that Chief François Cope was fifty years old, which would make him born in 1750, and that Joseph Labrador was forty years old. Though he gave no reasons, Fulton distrusted Cope, whom he held to be "under a bad character." NSARM, RG 1, vol. 430, doc. 55. The members of the "Eastward Tribe" were considered by the government to be independent though poor. In 1808 Fulton was replaced by James Kent as agent for the Mi'kmaq who visited Colchester County. NSARM, RG 1, vol. 380, A and B.

56 John Sprott, "Editorial: The Indians," *Nova Scotian*, 6 April 1846, 110, col. 2 (originally published in *The Wigtownshire Free Press*). Sprott was an optimistic Christian, who believed in the possibility of a near Edenic world once everyone subscribed to the tenets of Protestant Christianity.

57 Ibid., 110.

58 Titus Smith's survey reports of 1801 and 1802 show a
drastic decline in big game and beaver in parts of the
province, along with a corresponding drop in Mi'kmaw
numbers. NSARM, RG 1, vol. 380, *Sketches of the Eastern and Northern Parts of the Province in the Years 1801
and 1802 with General Observations Therein ...* by Titus
Smith, 3rd ed. (Halifax, 1857), 7–10, 112–13. Yet Smith
also held that caribou herds still roamed scrublands between Ship Harbour and Sheet Harbour.

59 M.B. Desbrisay, *History of the County of Lunenburg*
(Halifax: James Bowes and Sons, 1870), 156. Cope had
been living near the Labrador's headquarters at Mushamush in Lunenburg County. He and his family may have
been trying to escape an outbreak of smallpox occurring
further east. The woman who stabbed him afterwards
fled to a house on the coast belonging to a man named
Boutelier, who sheltered her despite the direness of
her deed. Cope died of his wounds and was buried at a
Mi'kmaw cemetery on Mahone Bay. Two of Cope's sons,
Joseph and Thomas, tracked Labrador's wife to Boutelier's house but failed to apprehend the woman. Desbrisay claimed, on the basis of oral evidence, that Cope's
death occurred nearer 1820, yet government records
clearly show that the chief died during the summer of
1802. A "Census of the Eastward Tribe" compiled in
January 1802, when François Cope was still alive, listed
four Mi'kmaw families, or twenty-two persons, living
at Sheet Harbour. (The first household was headed by
"old Francis Cope" with his two grown-up sons Joseph
and Thomas. The head of the second family was "Louis
[or Lewis] Cope," who had a wife and eight children
and also took care of his eighty-year-old bedridden
grandmother – probably the wife of the deceased Chief
Joseph Cope. Elam Cope, the widow of Paul Cope who
died in 1800, was raising four children, while Peter
Cope Sr., who headed the fourth family, had a wife and
four children. Louis, Paul, Peter, Joseph, and Thomas
were probably all sons of Chief François Cope.) A later
census, dated November 1802, showed François Cope's
widow living alone with three orphaned children, and
that Penaul (Bernard) Cope lived near her. Penaul Cope
was almost certainly Francis Bernard Nowlan, better
known as Doadaran Cope. NSARM, RG 1, vol. 430, doc.
104, "Census of Sheet Harbour Mi'kmaw population
compiled by James Sutherland, J.P.," 2 January 1802;
NSARM, RG 1, vol. 430, doc. 120, "Census of Sheet
Harbour band," 15 November 1802. Doadoran Cope was
married in 1802 but as yet had no children. He may have
felt obligated to take care of his maternal uncle's widow.

Though there was another outbreak of smallpox in 1817
that caused families from the Eastern Shore to flee to
Lunenburg County, the weight of evidence indicates
that Cope's death occurred long before 1820. NSARM,
MG 15, vol. 3, doc. 232, "Report of Zwicker and Rudolf
regarding a camp located at a distance of ten miles from
Lunenburg," 10 February 1817. Nowlan seems to have retained his trading post at Newdy Quoddy until Loyalists
from south of the border moved into the Quoddy area
and displaced the younger members of his family inland.
There is a water body, known as "Nowlin Lake," inland
from Quoddy where "Bill Nowlan," a great-grandson
of John Nowlan, lived in the late nineteenth century.
Daughters of the Nowlan (or Nowlin) family married
local settlers, among them members of the Furlong and
Watt families. Information courtesy of Walter Warren of
East Quoddy and Gary Meagher of Senora, Nova Scotia.
In 2018 Walter Warren was ninety-nine years old and
retained a prodigious memory.

60 Louis and Peter Cope travelled together in 1796. LAC,
MG 23, GII-19, Monk Papers, vol. 4, 1169, "Joseph
Davies, Requisition for 1796."

61 Doadaran Cope assumed some of the responsibilities
formerly held by François Cope, and he likely fostered
some of François's children. When François died about
1854 he had four sons, Louis, Peter Sr., Joseph, and
Thomas, but the first two were too old to be fostered
by Doadaran. François Cope's name appears on a list
compiled of Mi'kmaw persons living along the Eastern
Shore in 1853, but only his widow's name appears on a
similar list compiled in 1855. NSARM, RG 1, vol. 430,
doc. 75, "List of Articles issued by William Chearnley,
Commissioner of Indian Affairs, with the names of Indian Men & Women to whom the articles were issued,
Halifax, Decr. 31 1853"; NSARM, MG 15, vol. 5, doc.
69, "Indian List for the Year 1855 compiled by William
Chearnley." Doadaran Cope, who was not much older
than François's oldest sons, married twice, the first time
shortly before 1800 and the second time around 1814.
The first union produced no issue. His second wife,
Mollie (1796–1900), who lived to be 104 years old, reputedly was the daughter of a white pioneer family from
Cumberland County. Mi'kmaw oral tradition attests
that, at the age of fourteen, Molly trekked across country
from Sheet Harbour with her fiancé to be married by
a priest at Pictou, all the while carrying a two-year-old
child belonging to another woman on her back to be
baptized. In 1916 Jeremiah Bartlett-Alexis maintained
that Chief François Cope had been left with no male descendants and that most Copes in the twentieth century

were Doadaran's progeny, although the documentary evidence contradicts this assertion. Bartlett-Alexis stated: "This old Cope family has died out now, and no male descendants are now left, most of them having no sons. The present Cope family is descended from Cope women, sisters and perhaps daughters of John-Baptiste Cope, with Irishmen as fathers, Murphys and Knowlens [*sic*, Nowlans], such as those about Fish Lake, and Murphyville, near Little River, Musquodoboit; the children taking the Indian mother's name, and so being called Cope." NSM, Printed Matter File, "Jeremiah Bartlett Alexis to Harry Piers," 17 July 1916. Bartholomew-Alexis knew that Doadaran Cope's biological father was an Irish trader by the name of "Knowlan [Nowlan]" and that his mother was a Cope. Not all of John Nowlan Sr.'s twelve or so children took the Cope surname. John Nolan Jr. married Mary Rosella Cope about 1800 and had five children: Jane, William, Abegail, Mary Elizabeth, and Edward ("Ted"), all of whom kept the Nowlan surname. It has been said that Mary Rosella was a daughter of Doadaran Cope by his first wife, though this cannot be definitely confirmed. There are also oral traditions that hold that Ted Nowlan was a foster child of John Nowlan Jr. Ted married Margaret Paul, a daughter of Chief Francis Peminout Paul. (A genealogical record housed in the Records of the Native Council of Nova Scotia Genealogy Department erroneously holds that Doadaran was a son of Chief Jean-Baptiste Cope, rather than of John Nowlan Sr. and his wife Mollie. Doadaran was the father of Peter Joe, Frank (Sandy Cope Sr.'s father), and John Noel Cope. He drowned c.1845 on Fish Lake (Lake Charlotte), back of Ship Harbour.

62 The Reverend Sprott held Isidore to be in his late eighties or early nineties, while Joseph C. Cope claimed he lived to be 113 years old. Sprott, "Editorial: The Indians"; NSM, Printed Matter File, Piers Papers, "Joseph C. Cope to Harry Piers," 14 January 1914. Yet both men were commenting on a person whose birth occurred years before they were born. Sprott only arrived in Nova Scotia from Scotland in 1822, while Cope was born in 1859. Cope stated that his father Peter Cope Jr. had "seen Wedge-it-do," which seems very plausible, since Joseph's grandfather Peter Cope Sr. had hunted with Isidore before Isidore's death around 1840. Also referred to as Jeddore Cope, Isidore appears frequently in late eighteenth-century merchants' requisitions submitted to Indian commissioner George Henry Monk. Joseph C. Cope held that Isidore had experienced a vision in his youth which gave him a *kinap's* powers of physical strength and also endowed his kin with athletic prowess.

NSM, Printed Matter File, Piers Papers, "Joseph C. Cope to Harry Piers," 14 January 1914.

63 Genealogical information provided by Peter Cope Sr.'s grandson, Joseph Charles Cope (1859–1950), for Peter Cope Jr.'s family is confusing. For example, Joseph told Harry Piers, curator of the Nova Scotia Museum, that Doadaran Cope's son, Peter Joe Cope Sr., was the "uncle" of his own father, Peter Cope Jr. Yet Peter Cope Jr. was the son of Peter Cope Sr., who likely was the son of Chief Francis Cope who died in 1802. Peter Cope Sr. and Doardaran Cope therefore would have been first cousins, and Peter Cope Jr. and Peter Joe Cope Sr. would have been second cousins. As a youth, Joseph Charles Cope associated closely with Doadaran Cope's sons and grandsons, whom he may have treated like his siblings. NSM, Printed Matter File, Piers Papers, "Joseph C. Cope to Harry Piers," April 1926." When Joseph Charles Cope wed Catherine Meuse, his second wife, at Annapolis Royal in 1910, the couple's marriage certificate stated correctly that Joseph Charles was the son of Peter Cope (Jr.) and Louisa Paul. Yet Joseph Charles's death certificate of 1951 holds that he was the son of Frank Cope and Mary Ann Quigley. This error is surprising, and must have been made by Joseph's second wife Catherine, who reported his death. Frank Cope was a brother of Peter Joe Cope Sr. NSARM, Historical Vital Statistics, Annapolis County Marriages, Registration Year 1910, Book O, 651; NSARM, Historical Vital Statistics, Hants County Deaths, Registration Year 1951, 2279. A genealogical chart drafted by Ruth Holmes Whitehead tries to make sense of these confusing assertions, though it makes John Nowlan younger than Peter Cope Sr. Whitehead, *The Micmac Ethnology Collection of the Nova Scotia Museum*, Curatorial Report no. 25 (Halifax: Nova Scotia Museum, 1974), 55. Doadaran Cope, who was around the same age as Peter Cope Sr., probably regarded him as a brother. The author is very grateful to Vernon Cope, a descendant of Joseph C. Cope, for sharing material he obtained from the late Ellen Robinson, a daughter of Joseph Lewis and Annie Hood of Bear River who passed away at eighty-five years of age on 18 May 2012. Among her many achievements, she was one of the founding members of the Native Council of Nova Scotia, which collected genealogical data on Mi'kmaw families, including the Copes.

64 Jeremiah Bartlett Alexis inferred that Peter Jr. Cope was biologically descended from John Nowlan because Peter's son Joseph C. Cope once told him that one of his father's synonymous names was "Nowlan." NSM, Printed Matter File, Piers Papers, "Jeremiah Bartlett-Alexis to

Harry Piers," 6 September 1918; NSM, Nova Scotia Museum Accession Book II, 4806. Yet to adopt synonymous names from persons whom one regarded as siblings, cousins, or even close friends was common practice for northeastern Algonquian-speaking peoples. Among the Mi'kmaq, in particular, even second cousins, as these men were, would have treated each other as siblings and so might well have shared synonymous names. They did not have to descend biologically from John Nowlan to do so. NSM, Printed Matter File, Piers Papers, "Jeremiah Bartlett-Alexis to Harry Piers," 6 September 1918. Peter Cope Jr. and his wife resided in the mid-1850s with Doadaran's widow Mollie's family at Sheet Harbour. NSARM, MG 15, vol. 5, doc. 69, "Indian List for the year 1855, Sheet Harbour Road." This may have been because of Peter's kin relations with Doadaran's sons, or it may have been because Peter's wife, Louisa Paul, was a daughter of Joseph Paul, Mollie's second husband. That Louisa was actually Joseph's daughter could not be confirmed, however.

65 Mollie likely belonged to the same family as Matthew Salome, who had a hunting territory at Big Liscomb Lake. Speck, *Beothuk and Micmac*, ed. F.W. Hodge (New York: Museum of the American Indian/Heye Foundation, 1922), 103. And Peter Cope Sr. was undoubtedly the Peter Cope who appeared with Isidore Cope during the 1790s in merchant requisitions. LAC, MG 23, GII-19, Monk Papers, vol. 4, 1163, "Entry for 28 October 1795, To Provision & [give] ammunition – Jedore and Peter Cope – £1.12.8, Requisition of Joseph Davies, 1795."

66 Joseph C. Cope knew only a few stories about his grandfather. In 1926 he told Harry Piers, NSM curator, about his grandfather once being attacked by a bear in the Sheet Harbour Woods. Being unarmed at the time, his grandfather grabbed the base of the bear's tongue and held it, smothering the animal. Afterwards his grandmother wrecked vengeance on the bear for mauling her husband by going to the spot where the struggle occurred, chopping up the bear carcass, and strewing it about. Bears customarily were treated with respect by northeastern Algonquian-speaking people, but this proved an exception, given its circumstances. She afterwards had to nurse her husband for three months. This story conveyed Joseph C. Cope's pride in having such a powerful, resourceful, and courageous ancestor. NSM, Printed Matter File, Piers Papers, "Joseph C. Cope to Harry Piers," 1926; Whitehead, *The Old Man Told Us*, 200–1.

67 The registers of St. Peter's Roman Catholic Church in Dartmouth for the early 1840s record the baptism of Louis Cope and Mary Thomas's daughter Anastastia as occurring on the same day as the baptism of Peter Sack and Marie-Antoinette Thomas's baptism of their infant daughter Catherine. John Patrick Martin, *The Story of Dartmouth*, foreword by Thomas H. Raddall (Dartmouth: printed by the author, 1957), 379. This suggests that Mary Thomas was a sister of Marie-Antoinette Thomas (born 1822), who wed Peter Sack. The couple's son Isaac Sack was adopted by John Noel after Peter Sack died and John Noel became Marie-Antoinette Thomas-Sack's second husband. Isaac Sack, in turn, married Mary Anne Cope, a daughter of Frank Cope and Mary Ann Quigley of Sheet Harbour. In 1877 Isaac Sack and Mary Anne had a daughter Mary born at Sheet Harbour. Registers of St. Peter's, Sheet Harbour.

68 NSARM, mss file, Indians – Cemeteries, Letter and sketches, "H.J. Coady, District Ranger, Sheet Harbour, Department of Lands and Forests, to C. Bruce Fergusson, Provincial Archivist," 2 March 1973. Coady stated that at along Highway no. 224 at Beaverdam (or Beaver Dam) Lake one could still see "two old basements" and noted that on Upper Caribou Lake near Governor Lake one could still see an old stone fireplace. He also enclosed map sketches of locales of Mi'kmaw burying grounds on the shore of Northwest Arm, Sheet Harbour; at Spry Harbour; and on the Halifax County-Guysborough County border at Long Lake, north of the Moser River.

69 Campbell Hardy, *Sporting Adventures in the New World; or, Days and Nights of Moose-Hunting in the Pine Forests of Acadia* (London: Hurst and Blackett, 1855), 1.178–9.

70 Frank Cope, born in 1828 and husband to Mary Ann Quigley, died of "apoplexy" at Beaverdam on 12 October 1912 at the age of eighty-four. NSARM, Historical Vital Statistics, Halifax County Deaths, Book 9, p. 339, no. 2030.

71 Peter Joe Cope Sr. was born on 6 March 1834 and died at Sheet Harbour in 1912 at the age of seventy-five. He married Frances Magdeline Paul (c.1833–1910), and the couple lived along the Sheet Harbour Road running between Upper Musquodoboit and Sheet Harbour. NSM, Printed Matter File, Piers Papers, "Joseph C. Cope to Harry Piers," April 1926 They had Peter Joe Jr. in 1857, Moses in 1861, Martha in 1863, James in 1872, Bridget in 1873, Ellen, Francis, Margaret, Paul (1883–1910), and Magdalene in 1880. Registers of St. Peter's Parish, Sheet Harbour. According to her death certificate, Magdeline Paul, "a widow," died on 18 July 1910 at age seventy-seven of smallpox. NSARM, Historical Vital Statistics, Halifax County Deaths, Book 9, p. 165, no. 984.

72 John Noel Cope was born in April of 1847 and he died, at age 71, at Upper Musquodoboit on 25 August 1918. Also referred to as "John Newall, John Nowlan, Bolmoltie or Bowlmawltie (Paul Martin?)," he was an expert hunter, despite the fact he had a crippled arm. He guided military officers on moose hunts and sold moose meat to local settlers and to mining camps. NSM, Printed Matter File, Piers Papers, "Jerry Lonecloud to Harry Piers, 6 September 1918;" NSM, Accession book 11, no. 4806; Registers of St. Peter's Parish, Sheet Harbour; NSM, Nova Scotia Museum Accession Book II, no. 4806; NSM, Printed Matter File, "Harry Piers notes," 10 January 1917; Ruth Holmes Whitehead, "COPE, JOHN NOEL," *Dictionary of Canadian Biography* online, vol. XIV (1911–1920). John Noel married Fanny Doucet from Cape Breton, and the couple had Mary Ann Francis Bell Noel in 1879, John in 1881, Abraham in 1882, Thomas in 1894 and Mary Jane in 1898. Thomas, the youngest son, died in 1917 from tuberculosis at age 23. NSARM, Historical Vital Statistics, Halifax County Deaths, Registration Year 1917, Book 34, p. 402, no. 1307. Abraham lived in Dartmouth, while his older brother, John, a cooper, moved to Kings Road in Sydney, Cape Breton, where in 1907 he wed Bridget Bernard, a daughter of John and Angelica Bernard of Eskasoni, Cape Breton. NSARM, Vital Statistics, Registration Year 1907, Cape Breton County Marriages, Book 1805, p. 23, no. 45. John Cope and Bridget had a daughter, Mary Louise, who died of tuberculosis at 14 months of age on 19 July 1910. NSARM, Vital Statistics, Registration Year 1910, Cape Breton County Deaths, Registration Year 1910, Book 3, p. 299, no. 1809; NSARM, Vital Statistics, Registration Year 1910, Cape Breton County Deaths, Registration Year 1910, Book 3, p. 306, no. 1850. There are two official death certificates for Mary Louise, the first stating she was an "Indian" who died of tuberculosis, and the second holding that she died of measles and was "white." Yet both certificates refer to a 14-month-old child at Sydney who was the daughter of John Cope and Bridget Bernard. After suffering from tuberculosis for six months, Bridget died at North Sydney on 1 January 1911. NSARM, Vital Statistics, Registration Year 1911, Cape Breton County Deaths, Registration Year 1910, Book 3, p. 411, no. 2481. John wed married a second time, to Christiana Louis and had three daughters; Anne, Nancy and Mary Jane. The federal census of 1891 for Sheet Harbour lists "John Cope, age 27; Mrs. Cope (Christiana), 30; Anne, four; and an infant, Nancy Cope." Mary Jane, born in 1898, the youngest child of John Noel Cope and Fanny Doucet, lived following her father's death with her brother John and his second wife. Mary Jane wed William John Stevens of Millbrook in 1917, her oldest sister, Mary Ann Francis Bell, acted as a witness at her wedding. NSARM, Historical Vital Statistics, Colchester County Marriages, Registration Year 1917, Book 44, 194. John O. Cope moved from Sheet Harbour to Millbrook around 1916, perhaps to be near his relative, Sandy Cope Sr., and he died at Millbrook on 2 September 1931 of heart disease. Both Sandy Cope Sr. and John O. Cope were grandsons of Doadoran Cope. NSARM, Historical Vital Statistics, Registration Year 1931, Colchester County Deaths, Book 119, 1507. John Noel Cope's wife, Fanny Doucet, died at Beaverdam Lake in 1923 at the age of seventy-four. Her death certificate claims that after her marriage she went by three surnames; "Newel," "Cope," and "Nolin" (or "Nowlan"). NSARM, Historical Vital Statistics, Halifax County Deaths, Registration Year 1923, Book 85, 1186. A notation associated with a photograph of John Noel Cope Sr. and Fanny Doucet housed in the Nova Scotia Museum's photograph collection identifies John Noel Cope, or "John Bowlmaltie," b. April 1843, d. Aug 1918 at Stewarts, Upper Musquodoboit, son of Doadaran Cope, [as] brother of Major J.B. Cope." NSM, Photograph Accession No. N-55763. This is incorrect, since John Noel Cope Sr., a son of Doadaran Cope, was a grandson of John Nowlan Sr. of Newdy Quoddy.

73 Susan Cope, daughter of Nancy Molly Cope and a man remembered simply as "Charles," consorted with a fisherman surnamed Wessel of Sober Island, and bore Anastatia, who was raised by another member of the Wessel family, John Wessel, and his wife Catherine Ellen Lawlor of Sober Island. Susan's baptismal entry at St. Peter's Church states she was the daughter of "Charles" and "Nancy Molly" of Sheet Harbour, though her descendants, among them Heather Sutherland who was involved with this biography project, state that she was a daughter of Molly Cope and Francis Doadaran Cope. Interestingly, a William Wessel of Salmon River and Beaver Harbour married a Kegan – possibly the sister of Jane Kegan who wed Joseph Paul of Quoddy – and had a son John Henry Wessel in 1870. This would indicate a close connection between the Wessel family and the local Mi'kmaq prior to 1870. See NSARM, Historical Vital Statistics, Halifax County Births, Registration Year 1870, Book 1810, p. 57, no. 1123. Anastatia Wessel, John Wessel's daughter, on 20 September 1903 married Percival Seymour Verge, who was born at Shad Bay in 1879 and would die in 1944. Percival's mother, Mary Jane Cope, was a daughter of James Cope and Margaret Paul. She was baptized on 7 July 1864; sponsors at her

baptism were Thomas Thomas and his wife Mary Nolan. Baptismal Registers of St. Peter's Roman Catholic
Church and Missions, Dartmouth, 1864. It is not known
what became of Mary Jane Cope after 1879. Percival's
father, Henry Verge, was born at St. Margaret's Bay but
became a fisherman on Sober Island along the Eastern
Shore. NSARM, NSARM Vital Statistics, Halifax County
Deaths, Registration Year 1944, Book 219, 632, "Death
of Percival Seymour Verge." Percival's mother being
single at the time of his birth, he was raised by Henry
Verge and the woman Henry Verge later married, Ellen
Westhaver.

74 NSM, Printed Matter File, Piers Papers, "Howard Cruikshank to Harry Piers," 24 February 1933, Nova Scotia
Musuem Printed Matter File. Cruikshank, a Truro taxidermist who also collected Mi'kmaw artefacts, gained
his information from Sandy Cope Sr.'s son, Sandy Jr.,
who attended Truro Academy and whom Cruikshank
considered intelligent and well informed. Sandy Jr.
relished talking about local history, and in 1933 regaled
Cruikshank with many stories about his ancestors as
well as items of interest, such as an old flintlock gun
that belonged to his father. Cruinkshank then obligingly
passed on this information to Harry Piers, the museum
curator, who recorded it for posterity.

75 Sprott, "Editorial. The Indians," 110, col. 2.

76 There were four Mi'kmaw camps along the Murchyville
Road, running between Elderbank and Murchyville in
the upper Musquodoboit Valley, that were abandoned
owning to a smallpox outbreak. Mary Cook, "History of
South Section #9," Musquodoboit Valley Bicentennial,
1783–1983, in loose-leaf binder in NSARM, F 5248 M988
M988.

77 Captain Paul Bonis travelled with his son Noel Bonis up
the Shubenacadie River to the foothills of the Cobequid
Mountains and then pressed into Cumberland County.
Several of his offspring en route branched off towards
the Annapolis Valley to reside along the Cornwallis
River. By 1849 one of his sons, Gabriel Bonis, became a
chief in Annapolis County. On 9 February 1849 Gabriel
Bonis joined nine other chiefs as well as Nova Scotia's
Indian commissioner, Abraham Gesner, in petitioning
the lieutenant governor for relief owing to crop failures
and disease. "Indians of Nova Scotia," *Acadian Recorder*,
24 February 1849, col. 2. Before he left Musquodoboit,
Captain Bonis left a positive mark on youths he assisted
with their hunting and tracking skills, among them John
Williams from Shelburne County, who became a famous
guide. When Williams was guiding Lieutenant Campbell
Hardy in the 1850s on a moose hunt in the Cumberland

Hills and stumbled upon the eighty-year-old "Captain
Bonus' camp," Williams proclaimed to Hardy that "Bo-
nus was his protector in his youth, in whose hunting
camps he had learnt all his science." Hardy described
Bonis as "one of the finest old Indians I ever saw." Paul
Bonis sent his two visitors on to the camp of his son
Noel Bonis, "which was located on a hardwood hill just
beyond the last settler's house." Campbell Hardy, *Forest
Life in Acadie: Sketches of Sport and Natural History in
the Lower Provinces of the Canadian Dominion* (London:
Chapman and Hall, 1869), 140–3. John Williams married
Adelaide (sometimes referred to as Madeleine) Thomas
of Ponhook Lake and moved to Shubenacadie.

78 Peter Joe Cope Jr. was the second eldest son of Peter
Joe Cope Sr. and Frances Madeline (or Magdeline)
Paul, born 14 July 1857 and christened on 16 November
1857 at St. Peters Catholic Church in Sheet Harbour.
He was twenty when he married Mary Alexandria Farnell. NSARM, Registration Year 1878, Halifax County
Marriages, Book 1816, p. 225, no. 131. Peter Joe Jr. was a
hunter and trapper all his life and died of tuberculosis
on 13 June 1917. NSARM, Registration Year 1917, Book
34, p. 420, no. 1384. As mentioned, the couple's daugh-
ter Mary Sarah in 1902 wed Thomas Logan, a fisherman from Sober Island, at the head of Sheet Harbour.
NSARM, Historical Vital Statistics, Halifax County
Marriages, Book 1816, p. 225, no. 131, "Marriage of Pe-
ter Joseph Cope, 20, son of Peter [Joe] Cope [Sr.] and
Magdalin, and Alexandra Farnell, 15, daughter of James
and Elizabeth Farnell, 10 May 1878, presiding priest
Jonathon Woods, witnesses Joseph Paul and Nancy
Maurice"; NSARM, Historical Vital Statistics, Halifax
County Marriages, Registration Year 1902, Book 1820,
p. 38, no. 556, "Marriage at Sheet Harbour of Thomas
E. Logan, 22, son of William and Bridget Logan, and
Mary S. Cope, 22, the daughter of Peter Cope and Lexie
(Alexandria), 12 December 1902, presiding priest Rev. C.
MacManus, witnesses Elizabeth Farnell [the bride's ma-
ternal grandmother] and Janet Nelligan." Thomas Logan
and Mary Sarah Cope in turn had a daughter, Kathleen
Logan, who married George Westhaver of Sober Island.
Peter Joe Sr. may have lived with a woman other than
Madeline, since according to the 1891 Canada Census for
District no. 25, Sheet Harbour, Peter Joe Cope Sr. in 1891
was sixty-three years old, born in 1828 (*sic*, 1834), with a
wife Christie who was fifty-four (born in 1840). Peter Joe
Jr. was thirty-six and there were three children, "Marie,"
twelve; Paul, eight; and May, five." It is very possible,
however, that the enumerator made a mistake and listed
the wrong name for Peter Cope Sr.'s wife. Also, Peter Joe

Jr.'s wife "Lexie" was not enumerated. Peter Joe Cope Jr. died at sixty years of age on 13 June 1917 and was buried at Sheet Harbour on 16 June 1917. NSARM, Historical Vital Statistics, Halifax County Deaths, Book 34, p. 420, no. 1384. Heather Sutherland, who assisted with study, is related to the Copes, Farnells, and Logans of Sheet Harbour.

79 By attending to Mi'kmaw oral traditions, anthropologist Frank G. Speck in 1914 was able to rough plot the boundaries of Peter Joe Cope Sr.'s tract. Speck, *Beothuk and Micmac*, 103. Peter Joe Sr.'s intimate knowledge of the land and its resources was a matter of deep personal pride to him, and he remained in the vicinity of Sheet Harbour until his parents died. Unlike John Williams, who guided outside of the Maritimes, Chief Francis Cope's and Doadaran Cope's sons rarely ventured far afield from their local hunting grounds, though dwindling numbers of big game eventually forced them to move away from the Sheet Harbour area to seek employment. In 1855 six family heads – Peter Cope Jr., Frank Cope. John Noel Cope, Joseph Paul (who was Molly Cope's second husband), Jim Morris, and Peter Francis (who had married one of Molly Cope's daughters) – were living together along the Sheet Harbour Road at Beaverdam Lake. NSARM, MG 15, vol. 5, doc. 69, "William Chearnley, Indian Commissioner, Indian List for the Year 1855." By 1865, however, Peter Joe Cope Sr. had joined the community at Red Bridge on the outskirts of Dartmouth. In 1914 Speck considered the Eastern Mi'kmaq to be leaderless and placed them under the jurisdiction of the Windsor Band. In the early 1920s, Louis Noel McDonald praised the guiding skills of "Peter Joe Cope [Sr.], Frank Cope and Newel [John Noel] Cope of Beaver Dam," as well as Sandy Cope Sr. of Millbrook. He further held that Peter Joe Cope Sr. was "one of the best moose callers in the province." NSM, Printed Matter File, Piers Papers, "Louis Noel McDonald to Harry Piers," 28 April 1921. Isaac Sack of Shubenacadie also stated that Frank and John Noel Cope were exceptional guides. NSM, Printed Matter File, Piers Papers, "Isaac Sack to Harry Piers," 26 February 1921.

80 Abraham (or Abram) Gould was born in North Sydney in 1825. He died at age eighty-six at Millbrook in 1911. His brother Joseph informed the authorities of his death. NSARM, Historical Vital Statistics, Colchester County Deaths, Registration Year 1911, Book 4, p. 129, no. 781.

81 Speck, *Beothuk and Micmac*, 103–4.

82 Hardy, *Forest Life in Acadie*, 101–3. This rock was also known as the Halfway Rock. A similar offering site was the Grandfather Rock on the Upper Musquodoboit River. Ruth Sawtell Wallis and Wilson D. Wallis, *The Micmac Indians of Eastern Canada* (Minneapolis: University of Minnesota Press, 1955), 154.

83 Joe Cope's wife Mary Phillips required a doctor's attendance for her condition until July. To board and teach the Cope's two boys, John and James, at the seminary in Halifax cost the government £49.10 s – quite a sizeable sum for the day. *Report of Indian Affairs for Nova Scotia*, 1843, 10, and "Account Current, Miscellaneous Charities," 12–13 of this report.

84 Joseph Howe related that James Cope not surprisingly at first rebelled at being taken away from his parents, though he stayed long enough to learn basic reading and writing. He then returned to his parents' home at Indian Point, where he became an invaluable assistant to his father on hunting and fishing expeditions. James died at Hantsport at age seventy-four in 1909. NSARM, Historical Vital Statistics, Hants County Deaths, Book 12, p. 40, no. 248.

85 In the mid-1850s Joseph and Peter Jr. guided Chearnley on a moose hunt to Lake Mooin (or Bear Lake) in Guysborough County. NSARM, MG 1, vol. 1464, Piers Papers, no. 43. The three, accompanied by Charles McDonald and a boy named Stephen, returned to the same area in 1857. NSARM, MG 1, vol. 1464, Piers Papers, no. 45. Joseph Cope also guided Campbell Hardy on hunting expeditions near Grand Lake, Petit Rivière on the South Shore, north of Musquodoboit, and, twice, on lands in Guysborough County. On one of his last hunts with Cope, Hardy went up to Shubenacadie Grand Lake find moose with him and James. Though Joseph was elderly, Hardy claimed that the guide's death soon after came as a surprise to him. Hardy, *Forest Life in Acadie*, 94, 101–3. Joseph died in 1868, just before Hardy's book *Forest Life in Acadie* was published in New York by D. Applewood and Co. In 1869, Hardy added a note to his London publication of the same work that stated: "Since this was written, poor Joe has for ever left the hunting grounds of Acadie, having shot his last moose but a few weeks before he rested from a life of singular adventure and toil. *Requiescat in pace*." Whitehead, *The Old Man Told Us*, 277. Hardy once called Joe Cope the "best hunter in the province" and a good man "to accompany the white sportsman." Hardy, *Sporting Adventures*, 1.176.

86 Hardy, *Forest Life in Acadie*, 91–3.

87 NSARM, RG 41 "C," vol. 22, no. 6A, "Inquest into death of Annie Cloud [Glode]," 11 January 1848.

88 NSARM, RG 1, vol. 431, doc. 127, "Petition of Joseph Cope," 1861; NSARM, RG 1, vol. 431, doc. 141, "Regarding injury to John Cope at Musquodoboit," 1862. John was a youth born in 1847.

89 Hardy, *Forest Life in Acadie*, 89–93.

90 James Cope and Margaret Paul had a daughter, Mary Jane, who was baptized on 7 July 1864. Witnesses to the child's baptism were Thomas Thomas and his wife Mary Nowlan. Margaret must have died during or soon after giving birth. At his wedding the following year to Madeline Thomas, his father Joseph Cope and mother Mary Phillips acted as witnesses. NSARM, Historical Vital Statistics, Halifax County Marriages, Book 1815, p. 24, no. 213, "Marriage of James Cope and Medeline [*sic*, Madeline] Thomas in Dartmouth, 25 June 1865."

91 NSARM, Historical Vital Statistics, Halifax County Births, Registration Year 1869, Book 1809, p. 232, no. 890, "Birth of Joseph O. Cope, Ship Harbour, Halifax County," 12 July 1869, parents James Cope and Madeline Thomas. The baptismal registers of St. John's Roman Catholic Church in Windsor recorded the "Baptism of Josephum Cope, born July 12, son of Jacobi Cope and Madeline Thomas," on 22 October 1869.

92 James Cope was with Peter Wilmot's family at Truro early in the spring of 1862. NSARM, RG 15, vol. 6, no. 67, "Mi'kmaq at Truro on 26 February 1862." His son Joseph O. Cope also hunted in the Cobequid Hills.

93 After purchasing James Cope's explorer's rights, in 1887 Clarence Dimock, Gould Northrup, and others formed the Northrup-Dimock Company to mine the lode that James had found. The company erected a ten-stamp mill in 1888 and began crushing in August of that year. The next year 2,358 ounces of gold were retrieved from 375 tons of ore. The Central Rawdon Mining Company and the Northrup-Dimock Company were then incorporated in 1912, and the Northrup-Dimock Company continued mining the Cope lode. Five shafts were sunk on the Cope lode, the deepest of which was 405 feet in 1897. Malcolm Wyatt and E.R. Faribault, "The Gold Fields of Nova Scotia," *Geological Survey of Canada Memoir 20* (Ottawa: Department of Mines, 1912), 130–1.

94 NSARM, Historical Vital Statistics, Hants County Marriages, Registration Year 1865, Book 1815, p. 24, no. 243.

95 Joseph O. Cope and Sarah Tracey had their first child, Charles, in 1897, before they were officially married. Charles was baptized in 1899. Their second child, James Henry, was born in 1899 after their marriage. Baptismal Registers of the Parish Church of St. Francis of Assisi, Wolfville, "Baptism of James Henry Cope, 26 February 1899."

96 These nine children, born between 1890 and 1913, were Charles, James Henry, John, Rachel, Mary Agnes (born in 1906 but died soon afterwards), William, Matilda, Mary Agnes born in 1911, and Leo born in 1913. Baptismal registers of St. Francis of Assisi Church, Wolfville, and St. John's Church, Windsor, NSARM, Historical Vital Statistics, Kings County Births, Registration Year 1913, p. 55100058, no. 55100060, Certificate of Leo Cope's birth, dated 22 January 1913. The same certificate states that Joseph O. Cope, Leo's father, was born at Carr's Brook in Cumberland County. Joseph and Sarah had two more children after 1913, both of whom died in infancy.

97 Cathy Martin discusses the extensive research on Joseph and Sarah's family conducted by Ken Martin and Ben Martin in "In Memory of James Cope," *Mi'kmaq and Maliseet Nations News*, vol. 11, no. 11 (November 2002), 1, 9. See also Glen Parker, "Luck, Research, Bring War Heroes' Story to Light," http://www.danielnpaul.com/BenandKenMartin.html.

98 Another son, Leo Cope, was killed in World War II, in France in 1944.

99 NSARM, Historical Vital Statistics, Registration Year 1918, Halifax County Deaths, Book 35, p. 140, no. 465.

100 Chearnley jotted down a paragraph on James Cope, his son, and their branch of the Cope family. He stated that "Jim Cope had been born circa 1824 [in 1835 according to Jim's death certificate] at Indian Point, Ship Harbour, and was a member of the old Indian Cope family at that place. He died about 1912 [he died in 1909] at the Micmac Indian settlement about 3 miles back of Hantsport. He was 90 years of age when he died [Chearnley's calculations would make him 88 years old, although he is recorded as dying at 74 years of age on his death certificate]. He discovered the central Rawdon Gold Mines. He was paid about $6,000 for his rights ... He could write and was pretty well educated. Jim had a son, Joe Cope [Joseph O. Cope]. Joe had 2 sons, both went in the Great War, one of which was killed, the other wounded ... [One son] who served was awarded the military cross or some such medal. Signed Col. Wm. Chearnley, Dublin, Ireland, 1930." NSARM, MG 1, vol. 1464, no. 4. James Cope (1835–1909) died at Hantsport at seventy-four years of age on 18 September 1909. NSARM, Historical Vital Statistics, Kings County Deaths, Book 12, p. 40, no. 248. Chearnley mentioned that James's son Joseph O. Cope, while inebriated one night, was hit by a train on the railway tracks and in consequence lost an arm.

101 NSARM, Historical Vital Statistics, Colchester County Marriages, Registration Year 1931, Book 64, 153.

102 Conversation with Donald Julien, Joseph Julien's grandson, July 2014. Information also was provided by Cathy Martin, a filmmaker, artist, composer, writer, singer, and professor as well as a granddaughter of Michael

George Martin and Mary Agnes Cope. Donald Julien was not certain if Madeline Benoit was his great-grandmother's sister, cousin, or an in-law, but knew only that the two were related in some way. Michael's father, John Martin, hailed originally from Cape Breton and married Madeline Benoit in Newfoundland when she was fifteen. The couple left for Nova Scotia with expectations to continue on to Maine, but they had trouble crossing the international border. Boarder authorities argued they could not cross under the terms of the Jay Treaty since Madeline looked "white." At that point Madeline remembered her kin connections to Joseph Julien and suggested they go instead to Truro and settle at Millbrook. Their son, Michael George Martin, became a member of the Millbrook Band Council. Michael and Mary Agnes's son, Bennett Michael Martin (1932–2013), wed Jean Sophia Johnson. He began as a hunting guide, worked with the U.S. Marine Corps, and joined the military police, culminating in his providing security services for President Dwight Eisenhower and physicist Albert Einstein. He later worked as a building contractor in both Boston and Nova Scotia, became involved in the treatment of drug and alcohol abuse, and became the first executive director of the Eagle Nest Treatment and Recovery Centre at Indian Brook, Sipekne'katik First Nation. "Bennett Michael 'Ben' Martin: In Memoriam," http://www.inmemoriam.ca/view-announcement -347970-bennett-michael-ben-martin.html.

103 Joseph O. Cope died on 29 April 1936 of "cerebral apoplexy" at Gold River. NSARM, Historical Vital Statistics, Lunenburg County Deaths, Registration Year 1936, Book 164, 340. His daughter Rachael, from Maitland, informed the authorities of his death.

104 In a sister-brother exchange, the Cope brothers wed two daughters of John Jadis and Catherine Morris of Shubenacadie. Jadis was the grandson of a fur trader who in the late eighteenth century had a trading post on the Saint John River, and afterwards moved to Windsor where he married a daughter of Gorham Peminout Paul. Joseph Charles Cope married Rebecca Jadis in Dartmouth on 21 October 1881. His brother Isaac married Rebecca's sister, Annie Jadis. NSARM, Historical Vital Statistics, Halifax County Marriages, Book 1817, p. 102, no. 379, "Marriage of Joseph C. Cope, age 23, son of Peter Cope and Louisa [Paul], and Rebecca Judees [*sic*, Jadis], age 16, daughter of John Jadis and Catherine, 21 October 1881, presiding priest Jno. Woods, witnesses Richard Sack and Mary Maurice." Annie Jadis Cope's death certificate incorrectly lists her as the daughter of "Annie Morris" rather than Catherine Morris. NSARM,

Historical Vital Statistics, Colchester County Deaths, Book 212, 89, "Death of Annie Cope at age 73 at Millbrook in 1943." Isaac and Annie's son Louis Francis Cope died at age fourteen from the effects of shock in the Halifax Explosion of 1917. His body was sent by train from Halifax to Windsor Junction. NSARM, Historical Vital Statistics, Halifax County Deaths, Registration Year 1917, p. 45, no. 289, "Death of Louis Francis Cope," 6 December 1917. Another of Annie Jadis's sisters, Marie Jadis, wed Louis Noel McDonald of Second Red Bridge. (The two had a daughter Matilda Marie McDonald who in 1904 married Sandy Cope Jr., Joseph Julien's brother-in-law.) NSARM, Historical Vital Statistics, Hants County Marriages, Registration Year 1904, Book 1824, p. 74, no. 88; NSM, Printed Matter File, Piers Notes, "Louis Noel McDonald to Harry Piers," 20 November 1923. Harry Piers wrote around 1920 that the father of "Mrs. Joe Cope, the wife of [Joseph C. Cope] a well-known, educated Indian of Enfield, but lately of Lunenburg," was Louis Jeekouse (or Louis Noel), "who had reached the great age of 89 years before he died." NSM, Printed Matter File, Harry Piers, unpublished notes, c.1920. This was a mistake on Piers's part. Joseph C. Cope's first wife was Rebecca Jadis and his second wife was Catherine Muise. Piers must have confused Joseph C. Cope with Sandy Cope Jr., since Sandy wed Matilda McDonald, a daughter of Louis Noel McDonald. Yet Piers held that Louis Jeekouse died in 1920 and Louis Noel McDonald, Matilda's father, was alive and well in 1921. The word "Jeekouse" or, more accurately, *kjiku's*, meaning "the month of the great moon" (December), is often used by the Mi'kmaq as synonymous with "Christmas" or "Noel." Whitehead, *The Old Man Told Us*, 314. Isaac Cope died at Shubenacadie in 1949 at the age of eighty-six. NSARM, Historical Vital Statistics, Hants County Deaths, Registration Year 1949, 1726. Isaac and Joseph's mother Louisa Cope died in 1905 at the age of seventy-four. Her death certificate does not provide the names of her parents or her husband, though it does indicate that her husband was a "trapper." NSARM, Vital Statistics, Registration Year 1905, p. 66, no. 71.

105 Peter Cope Jr. hunted with Chearnley in the mid-1860s. Hardy, *Forest Life in Acadie*, 362–3.

106 Second Red Bridge lay across what is today known as Red Bridge Pond, about half a mile from the junction of the Waverly Road, now Highway 318, and the old Preston Road, now replaced by the Micmac Rotary and Highway 7 East. There was a mill on the pond in the past. A narrow causeway divided the pond from the main Darmouth Lakes system, and there was a bridge,

originally constructed of reddish-coloured wood, under which small craft could pass; hence the name "Red Bridge." The mill has long since gone, and part of the pond has been infilled. The most recent mill was operated by Scott Weeks and Company. A modern Irving service station stands on the site today.

107 There is a photographic engraving by W.H. Stevens dated about 1890 of Peter Cope Jr.'s house in Martin, *The Story of Dartmouth*, 442. His was apparently the first frame house to be erected by a Mi'kmaq person in the Dartmouth area, though Cope might have had help building it from the East Coast Paul family, especially Francis Paul of Ship Harbour, who was a good carpenter as well as a boat builder and cooper. Louisa Paul, Sandy Cope Sr.'s wife, may have been Francis Paul's daughter.

108 A member of the Second Red Bridge community, Louis Noel Sr. (1808–98), was a well-known guide who hailed from the St. Mary's River area. Nicknamed *Jeekouse*, which refers to the moon of December, as well as to Christmastide (or Noel), he may originally have come from Cape Breton. He also was known as Louis *Plowetch* or *Plowetchooti*. As an adult, he moved around, living in Antigonish County and later at Martinique Beach, Ship Harbour, and Cole Harbour in Halifax County. *Evening Mail*, "Obituary of Louis Noel," 4 July 1898; NSM, Printed Matter File, Harry Piers Papers, "Louis Noel McDonald to Harry Piers," 28 April 1921. Louis Noel Sr. lived in the Red Bridge community with Captain Peter Cope Jr. for many years before moving in 1880 to the Cole Harbour reserve, where he died at age ninety. He adopted a white child, Louis Noel McDonald, who was born on 14 March in 1856, and raised him to be a Mi'kmaw hunter as well as a farmer. Louis Noel, who married Marie Madeline Geddes of Shubenacadie in 1878, became Sandy Cope Jr.'s father-in-law. His son Louis Noel McDonald Jr. held that his parents came from Pomquet, Antigonish County. Louis Noel Sr. meanwhile had a brother, Francis Noel, and Francis's son Andrew Francis Noel wed Magdalene Ogden of Sheet Harbour; the couple had two children, Ella in 1881 and Louis in 1883. Francis Noel guided in Nova Scotia and Newfoundland; his clients included William Chearnley, Lord Dunraven, Lieutenant Dashwood, the Honourable Charles Alexander and Prince Arthur. Jeremiah Bartlett-Alexis, or Jerry Lonecloud, claimed that Francis Noel gave Francis Nose (Noel) Island in Musquodoboit Harbour its name. Lonecloud's assertion is controversial, however, since in 1970 John Erskine, then curator of the Nova Scotia Museum, suggested that the island was named after Francis Knowles, a trader and settler who lived in the area. The island was the site of an early French fort and trading post built by Mathieu de Goutin, who was granted a seigneury at Musquodoboit in 1691. It also contained a cemetery and chapel maintained until 1699 by the Jesuit father Louis-Pierre Thury. Francis Knowles was likely an older son of John Nowlan, the trader living at Newdy Quoddy in the late eighteenth century whose name often appears as "Knowles" in the documentary record. NSM, Printed Matter File, Piers Papers, "Jerry Bartlett-Alexis to Harry Piers," 27 July 1926; Whitehead, *The Old Man Told Us*, 253; Mike Sanders, "Francis Nose Archaeological Project, Preliminary Report," typescript, 10 October 2000, Heritage Permit A 1999NS 49, Nova Scotia Museum; John Erskine, "A Superficial Survey of Pre-Expulsion Acadie as It Remains Today," unpublished ms, Nova Scotia Museum archaeological report files; personal communication with David Christianson, curator of archaeology, Nova Scotia Museum (in 2014). Mi'kmaw cemeteries have been located at Sheet Harbour, on the shores of Upper Caribou Lake near Governor Lake, on the shore of Long Lake north of Mosher River, and at Senora. NSM, Printed Matter File, "H.J. Coady, District Ranger, to C. Bruce Fergusson, Provincial Archivist," 2 March 1973. In 1926 Joseph C. Cope stated that *Tgo'pechg* was the nickname associated with Louis and Francis Noel's family. *Tgo'pechg, Et-hoo-bay-etsh* or *Et-hoo-bay-eech* refers to "twins," so it may be that Louis and Francis Noel were twins. NSM, Printed Matter File, Piers Papers, "Cope to Harry Piers," 29 March 1926. On 19 October 1904, Sandy Cope Jr. married Matilda Mary Noel McDonald, while on the same day John Louis Noel McDonald, a son of "Louis Noel [McDonald] and Marie," married Susan Jane Cope, Sandy Cope Jr.'s fifteen-year-old sister, in a "brother-sister exchange." NSARM, Historical Vital Statistics, Hants County Marriages, Book 1824, p. 74, no. 88; NSARM, Historical Vital Statistics, Hants County Marriages, Book 1824, p. 75, no. 91. Other notable persons at Red Bridge were Isaac Paul, the son of Chief Jacques-Pierre Peminout Paul, and Louis Benjamin Brooks, a grandson of Jacques-Pierre's predecessor, Chief Louis-Benjamin Peminout Paul. NSM, Printed Matter File, Piers Papers, Joseph C. Cope, "A Short History of the Mic Mac Indians of Halifax Co. Nova Scotia Since Confederation, dated 9 February 1926, written for Harry Piers."

109 According to Joseph C. Cope, Queen Victoria assuaged these fears by stating that for as long as a Mi'kmaq remained a "True Ward of the English Government, so long His Treaty Rights would be respected and adhered to, to Hunt, fish and Camp wherever and whenever He

likes." NSM, Printed Matter File, Piers Papers, "Joe C. Cope, Indian, to Harry Piers," 9 February 1926. The issue that would later emerge regarding "wardship" versus "enfranchisement," when it came to the retention of treaty right, had not yet arisen in 1867. Queen Victoria's assurances of protection for treaty rights would ring hollow in the face of increasingly stringent game laws that prevented Mi'kmaq from hunting for subsistence in all seasons – but in the late 1860s the queen's words sufficed to ward off immediate fears.

110 John Nowlan and his sons, among them Peter and Joseph Nowlan (or Knowlan), in the 1790s came to Halifax to get supplies with other members of the Eastward Tribe. See, for instance, LAC, MG-23, GII-19, Monk Papers, Requisitions, "Entry for 3 June 1797, To [*sic*, For] clothing, provisions, seed potatoes – Pier Paul – John Nowlan, 12 in family – £15.4.0. Requisition signed Joseph Davies, Merchant, 1797."

111 LAC, RG 10, vol. 2520, file 107,000X, Part 2, microfilm reel C-11,233, Census of the Indian Population in Canada for the Year 1871, for Halifax County. There were 96 Mi'kmaw individuals recorded as living in Halifax County in 1871, though the total was more like 115, as there were 14 persons living along the North West Arm; 27 in the Musquodoboit area (16 at Upper Musquodoboit, which included Beaverdam Lake, and 11 at Middle Musquodoboit, which embraced Joe and Francis Paul's Ship Harbour settlement); 5 at Piers Mills; 4 at Little River; only 3 at Salmon River just east of Dartmouth; and 62 within the environs of Dartmouth. The census left out Mi'kmaq living at Wellington Station and at Shubenacadie Grand Lake, as well as those living along the border of Halifax and Hants counties at Elmsdale and Enfield.

112 Alexander Cope Sr.'s death certificate incorrectly states that his wife was Mary Paul. Mary Paul was Alexander Cope Sr.'s wife, while his mother was Mary Ann Quigley. NSARM, Historical Vital Statistics, Cochester County Deaths, Registration Year 1930, Book 119, 1052, "Death of Alexander Cope, age 76, at Millbrook, 15 March 1930." Mary Paul's father Joseph wed her mother Johanna (later Jane) Kachen (or Kauchen) at St. Peter's Church, Sheet Harbour, on 21 June 1865 (although some oral sources claim Johanna was a daughter of "Joseph Keegan" – rather than a man named Kachen – and a woman named Elizabeth Baldwin). NSARM, Historical Vital Statistics, Halifax County Marriages, Book 1815, p. 25, no. 268, "Marriage of Joseph Paul, son of Fr. Paul and Nobokt Paul of Sheet Harbour, and Jane Kachen." Jane's parents were not listed in her death certificate,

although it states that she was born in Cape Breton in October 1846. The presiding priest at the couple's wedding was the "Rev. Mart. Maas" and the witnesses were M. O'Leary and Jane Redmond.

113 Nova Scotia Museum, Printed Matter File, Piers Papers, "Joseph C. Cope to Harry Piers," 29 March 1926. *Sogun* or *Jogun* is the original Mi'kmaw name for a person of the East Coast Paul family. *Eskekagooah* stems from *Eski'kewag* – which originally may have meant "skin dressers' territory" (though this is not certain). The region extends from Halifax to Canso and constitutes the Eastern Shore District of the seven districts of Mi'kma'ki.

114 These Pauls likely were Jean Ball (Paul) and Joseph Ball who signed a treaty with the English, along with Chief François Cope, on 28 April 1760. While three of Jean Paul's sons in 1793 remained in the Chester vicinity, other members of the same Paul family moved eastward along the Atlantic coast, marrying into families at Hubbards, St. Margaret's Bay, and Musquodoboit.

115 NSARM, MG 15, vol. 5, doc. 69, "William Chearnley, Indian Agent, Indian List for 1855."

116 NSARM, RG 1, vol. 432, doc. no. 187, Joseph Howe, "Report on Indian Affairs," 25 January 1842.

117 This allowable acreage varied between 22,000 and 24,000 acres, depending on which report one reads. But Gesner knew he would have to ensure the surrender of one parcel in the province in order to secure a second of roughly the same size.

118 John Logan's name before he took the Logan surname may have been "John Nicholas." Peter Bobie (or Bobieye) late in 1857 took over the duties of chief of the Parrsboro band from him, and in January 1858 petitioned the government to have the Francklin Manor reserve divided into equal portions. NSARM, MG 15, vol. 6, doc. no. 59. (Heather Sutherland, whose ancestors are from Sober Island, at the head of Sheet Harbour, and who knows a fair deal about local Mi'kmaw and settler traditions, notes that a "James Logan," born in Scotland about 1770, settled at Sober Island and married a woman identified simply as "Dorothy, a Micmac." Heather, wondering if James Logan later might have gone to Parrsboro and joined the band there, tenders this possibility for further research.)

119 Nova Scotia's provincial secretary, Joseph Howe, later drew up a memorandum in which he traced the fate of the Shinimicas reserve. LAC, RG 10, vol. 460, 338–9, "Memorandum, Shinimicas Lands," 3 February 1862.

120 NSARM, RG 1, vol. 431, doc. 47, "Regarding Petition of Francis Paul and Joseph Paul of Musquodoboit for 500 to 1000 acres at Ship Harbour, and a reserve to

be created once land in Cumberland is exchanged for land at Ship Harbour Lake, which is their old resort"; NSARM, RG 1, vol. 431, doc 62½, "Report by Abraham Gesner concerning the Fish Lake reserve, Musquodoboit area, to be established in exchange for part of a reserve in Cumberland, 1851–1852"; NSARM, RG 1, vol. 431, doc. 114; NSARM, MG 15, vol. 4a, no. 130, "Report of Abraham Gesner of 4 March 1852 regarding cession of the Shinimicas Reserve and its division for sale." Gesner referred to the "rapid decline of the Micmac tribe" and the need to give them land as they fell further in numbers. In the mid-1840s Gesner fully expected the Mi'kmaq to be extinct as an ethnic entity within a few decades.

121 LAC, RG 10, vol. 461, folder 2, "Survey Plan of Great Lake Ship Harbour, Reserve No.18, c.1852." Abraham Gesner, who feared the Mi'kmaq might disappear altogether – since their population fell to its nadir in 1846 – was instrumental in having the Ingraham's (Ingram's) River reserve in Halifax County and the Panuke Lake reserve near Windsor confirmed the same year. Further information on Ship Harbour Reserve No. 18 can be found in NSARM, Miscellaneous "I" Indian Land Records from Crown Lands, on microfilm, docs. 102 and 103.

122 NSARM, MG 15, vol. 5, doc. 69, "William Chearnley, Indian Agent, Indian List for 1855." Louis likely was the same man who, with Francis Phillips, petitioned in 1852 and 1853 for redress against settler trespasses on the Mi'kmaw fishery at Ingram River, Halifax County. For information on the fishing dispute in which Louis Paul was involved, see NSARM, vol. 431, doc. 65.

123 James Paul married Mary Lewis and the couple had a daughter Isabella in 1859.

124 Louis Brooks's son Francis married Louisa Paul and the two had a son Benjamin in 1872.

125 Speck, *Beothuk and Micmac*, 103–4. F.G. Speck mentions an area around Grassy Lake north of the Killag River that "was supposed to have belonged to the Pauls" and was hunted over by Andrew Paul, who had moved from Cape Breton to Halifax by 1860. This indicated that Andrew Paul's family held a hunting territory close to hunting tracts belonging to the East Coast Pauls. Francis and Joseph Paul did not hold land on the shoreline, but occupied parcels that lay inland, back of a large waterfront lot known as the Waterman Grant.

126 By 1860 Champagne L'Estrange had been promoted to a captain. "Captain L'Estrange to A. Heatherington," 27 October 1867, in Alexander Heatherington, *A Practical Guide for Tourists, Miners and Investors, and All Interested in the Development of the Gold Fields of Nova Scotia* (Montreal: John Lovell, 1868), 25. *Plowitch*

was Lieutenant L'Estrange's spelling of Louis Noel Sr.'s Mi'kmaw name. Joseph C. Cope wrote it as *Plowetchooti*. NSM, Printed Matter File, Piers Papers, "J.C. Cope to Harry Piers," 29 March 1926.

127 "Mr. Pusiver's Statement," in Heatherington, *A Practical Guide*, 26–8.

128 Ottawa, *Geological Survey Memoir* 385 (Ottawa: The Survey, 1929), 2–4. Some years later, in 1880, Peter Paul, a Mi'kmaw farmer from Port Dufferin, Halifax County (who later resided at Beaverdam Lake), found a heavy boulder containing gold while out looking for his ox. He told two men about it, Kent Archibald and a man named Captain Brown, with Archibald beating out Brown in securing a claim. Paul probably received a payment for information relating to his discovery from both men. NSARM, "Men in the Mines: A History of Mining Activity in Nova Scotia, 1720–1992," https://archives.novascotia.ca/meninmines/.

129 NSARM, MG 15, vol. 6, doc. 36, Francis Paul, "A Prayer to the Sympathising," 12 March 1857. Francis Paul and his family began to suffer financially after the fire destroyed his business. NSARM, MH 15, vol. 6, doc. No. 14, "Petition of Daniel Curry residing at Ship Harbour," Halifax, 21 January 1858. Francis may have been the father of Jonas Paul, born at Sheet Harbour in 1854, a guide who died in 1918 at age sixty-four while living along the Herring Cove Road in Halifax. NSARM, Historical Vital Statistics, Halifax County Deaths, Book 35, p. 119, no. 403.

130 From the St. Peter's Parish registers for Sheet Harbour, one finds several large Mi'kmaw families still living at Ship Harbour and Sheet Harbour, despite the inroads of disease. At Beaverdam Lake settlement, Francis Paul and Rosanna Louis had Suzanne in 1864, and Francis Brooks married Louise Paul in 1872. Isaac Sack and Mary Ann Cope were living at Sheet Harbour in the mid-1870s and had a daughter Mary there in 1877. There were other East Coast Pauls living at Sheet Harbour who could not be readily identified. For instance, according to the St. Peter's Church registers for Sheet Harbour, Simon Joseph Googoo and his wife Mary Jane Paul had Henry Googoo at Sheet Harbour in 1875, and Francis Cope and Mary Bowden had Mary Cope in 1874. A few members of the East Coast Paul and Cope families remained living on land plots between Sheet Harbour and Liscomb well into the twentieth century.

131 NSARM, MG 15, vol. 6, doc. 14. Joseph Paul Sr. and his brother Francis Paul may have been sons of Matthew Paul, mentioned in government requisition lists in the 1790s. Both were having problems making a livelihood

at Ship Harbour in 1857, even though Francis, a cooper, had also learned the trade of boatbuilding: as noted above, a fire destroyed Francis's work shed and all its contents. They were, however, fortunate in not being laid low by epidemics that surfaced in later years. In the fall and spring of 1860–61 they escaped the effects of a smallpox epidemic that appeared at Pope's Harbour in January and March 1861. NSARM, MG 15, vol. 6, doc. 63. What appears to be a bout of influenza caused Peter Joe Cope and Peter Cope Sr. to become ill, but apparently not the Pauls. Peter Joe and Peter Cope, however, soon returned to their former life of hunting, fishing, and guiding. Peter Joe, Louis Noel and John Williams, with John Jadis as camp boy, guided Prince Arthur around Liscomb in 1869. NSM, Printed Matter File, Piers Papers, "Jeremiah Bartlett-Alexis to Harry Piers," 1 February 1926.

132 For mention of smallpox at Pope's Harbour in 1861 see NSARM, MG 15, vol. 6, doc. 63.

133 NSM, Printed Matter File, Piers Papers, "Jeremiah Bartlett-Alexis to Harry Piers," 29 April 1921 Whitehead, *The Old Man Told Us*, 319. Bartlett-Alexis stated that Joseph Sr. died around 1916, when a "very old man." He had a hunting camp at Dreadnaught Dam to the east of Hunting Lake, on the Liscomb River, along the Eastern Shore. This is the area where he lost his eye while out guiding Lord Dunraven. As late as 1921 one could still find the ashes of his campfire at his hunting camp One problem with dates, however, is that Mollie, Doadaran's widow whom he married, was born between 1798 and 1800. If Joseph died in 1916 he would have to have been born between 1800 and 1810 (and possibly was around 116 years old when he died) if he was close in age to Mollie.

134 Joseph in 1868 received a licence of occupation for 100 acres on the east side of "Newdiquoddy" and the island, comprising six acres of land, "at the mouth of the Newdiquoddy River." Crown Land Information Centre, Halifax, Book 1, record no. 500, "Licence of Occupation to Joseph Paul," 5 September 1868. (A second piece of property, marked out for "Indians" appears at the tip of Shiers Cove, east of the Paul's land, although when the survey of this second plot occurred remains unclear.) The actual licence of occupation is housed in the Crown Lands Information Management Centre, Department of Lands and Forestry, Founders Square Building, 1701 Hollis St. in Halifax, rather than at NSARM. The cryptic "Record 500" found in the Crown Lands Index is the document number, while the call number is Book 1, no. 500. Gillian Allen, senior legal and historical researcher, Kwilmu'kw Maw'klusuagn (Mi'kmaq Rights Initiative),

personal communication. Long-term leases were often for 999 years, and Daniel N. Paul suggests that this lease was for 1,000 years. Daniel N. Paul, "Joseph Paul: Mi'kmaq Land recipient," We Were Not the Savages, http://www.danielnpaul.com/GreatGrandfather-JosephPaul.html.

135 Joseph and his wife Jane remained at East Quoddy until 1881, when they removed for ten years to Sheet Harbour. The federal census for 1891 lists Joseph Paul (sixty-five), "Mrs. Paul" (forty-five), John (twenty-one), Anne (fifteen), Bridget (thirteen), Lillie (eleven), Maggie (eight), Susan (six), and Kate (three) at Sheet Harbour. When Joseph died at East Quoddy around 1910, Jane continued to live on the farm until she died of "apoplexy" (a stroke) at nearby Mooseland in 1928. Her daughter Susan, who wed John T. Lawlor of Sheet Harbour, reported her mother's death to the authorities. NSARM, Historical Vital Statistics, Halifax County Deaths, Registration Year 1928, Book 85, 786. Joseph and Jane's eldest son, Frank Thomas, wed Emily Cope, a daughter of Frank Cope and Mary Ann Quigley from Sheet Harbour. This couple lived along the Sheet Harbour Road and had eleven children; Ellen (b.1887), John William (1889–1939), Daniel (b.1891), Peter Joseph (b.1893), Cassie Mary (b.1896), Michael (b.1898), Francis Neal (b.1901), Margaret Ann (b.c.1902), Elizabeth Jean (?), Mary (?), and George A. (b. c.1912). John Edward Paul Sr., the third eldest of Joseph and Jane's sons, also had a wife named Emily (b.1873, surname unknown). John and Emily raised fourteen children, among them Susan (b.1895), William Gabriel (b.1896), and John Edward Jr. (b.1900). William Gabriel married Agnes Noel, and the well-known historian and author Daniel N. Paul is their son.

136 See, for instance, NSARM, Miscellaneous "I" Indian Land Records from Crown Lands, "Letter from Jane Kegan [Mrs. Joseph Paul] to J.D. Maclean, Deputy-Superintendent of Indian Affairs," 16 February 1921.

137 There was little consistency in the way the province classified Mi'kmaw land. The Pauls had farmed their land on Joseph Paul's Island since 1852, and as mentioned, until the early 1920s sent petitions to the government calling for its protection from intrusion.

138 Canada, Census records for 1901 and 1911, Sheet Harbour, Nova Scotia.

139 In 1930 Peter Paul received a land grant that became the core of the present-day Beaverdam Lake Reserve. NSARM, Places, Nova Scotia, Lands Grants, Peter Paul, 10 a, Beaver Dam Lake, Halifax, 1930, Book 81, 48. At some time around 1930 the Beaverdam Mi'kmaq lost their shoreline lands along Beaverdam Lake through a

sale to outsiders. The lakeshore now has cottages along it. The Beaverdam community still exists, but it lies on the other side of the highway from the lake.

140 Blueprint Sketch of Sheet Harbour, I.R. 36, Halifax County, from sketch on file 27052–4, dated 1910. The original survey gave the Mi'kmaq approximately 200 acres. In 1936 the reserve was considered to be 77 acres. Map 521 A, Tangier, Department of Mines and Resources, Nova Scotia, 1936. By 1953 this acreage had been cut down still further. Only 58.4 acres of land were surveyed between Sheet Harbour and Grand Lake to form "Lot 1," while 14.9 acres formed "Lot 2" on the harbour near Church Point. Nova Scotia, Administration Plan, Sheet Harbour Indian Reserve No. 36, Lot 1, Surveyed by the Department of Lands and Forests, 16 February 1953, signed Ernest Boehk, Provincial Land Surveyor; Lot 2 of Sheet Harbour, Indian Reserve No. 36, Surveyed by the Department of Lands and Forests, 6 February 1953, signed Ernest Boehk, Provincial Land Surveyor. The description given of both lots in 1953 was bleak. The harbour shoreline on Lot 1 was steep and rocky, and had the provincial highway going along it. There was a steep bank on the inland side of the highway where gravel may have been taken. The forest also had been culled of its best timber. Albert Howe Sr. – who likely stopped at Cole Harbour en route from Elmsdale – had a clearing on Lot 2 in 1953, which was mostly covered with second-growth scrub. A highway ran along the shoreline and any land on the water side belonged to the local church. On the opposite side of the road Howe kept a house, a shed, a log cabin, and three cultivated patches. There were no Pauls or Copes living on the tract. Alvin Boutelier, who lived in a small house in the southwestern corner of the reserve, was the only other resident. More recently the acreage the Mi'kmaq held in 1936 has been restored, so the reserve is currently seventy-seven acres in size.

141 In 1901 the price of timber land was forty dollars per one hundred acres, and it cost forty cents per acre per term to lease timber land for cutting purposes. NSARM, Miscellaneous "I" Indian Land Records from Crown Lands, "Timber Lands, General Provisions," n.d.

142 "Daniel Paul," *The Canadian Encyclopedia*, https://www.thecanadianencyclopedia.ca/en/article/daniel-paul; Daniel N. Paul, *We Were Not the Savages: A Mi'kmaq Perspective on the Collision between European and Native American Civilizations* (Halifax: Fernwood, 2000), 252.

143 Joseph Paul and Jane's great-grandson Daniel N. Paul, born in December 1938 at Indian Brook to William Gabriel Paul and Sarah Agnes Noel, related what his parents experienced after first moving to Millbrook. "My mother's parents, John MacDonald (Noel) and Jane, née Cope," he explained, "moved their children to Millbrook. That is where my father William met my mother Sarah Noel. After they wed they lived at Millbrook for some time, then they and many other Nova Scotia Mi'kmaq moved to New Brunswick where they worked in the lumber trade … Because of the land deal [which resulted in the sale of the Halifax County reserves and provided money to expand the Millbrook community], when they got married they were both members of the Millbrook Band … Around 1935 my parents were living in Saint John when my father got laid off and had to go on city social assistance. Some of the citizens objected to the municipality "feeding Indians," and they were put on a train and sent to Indian Brook, a place neither one had seen before. My siblings John, Robert, Violet, Rhoda, and Lawrence were born in NB. My sisters Jane, Mary, Sylvia, Rebecca and Rosalita and me were born in Indian Brook. Three siblings died when they were under ten. I have no idea where they were born, perhaps in Millbrook or NB." Letter from Daniel N. Paul to Janet E. Chute, 21 January 2019. Lawrence Alexander (23 July 1934–28 May 2014) and Daniel later returned to Millbrook, where both became prominent members of the Millbrook First Nation. As their parents formerly had been members of that band, they did not have to be voted back in. Lawrence was chief at Millbrook from 1984 to 2012 and during this time was instrumental in the development of a major business park in his community. Daniel, the recipient of many awards and honours, has been a building contractor in Truro, worked for the Department of Indian Affairs, and was a founder and then executive director of the Mainland Confederacy of Mi'kmaq from 1986 to 1994. He participated at Annapolis Royal in a well-known theatrical reconstruction depicting early Mi'kmaw life. He is a dedicated Indigenous rights activist and has assisted Mi'kmaw communities, among them Afton and Pictou Landing, in regaining their land and treaty rights. He has initiated fundraising efforts for Mi'kmaw community infrastructure throughout Nova Scotia, served on the Human Rights Commission, and worked with the Department of Justice. He founded and published the *Micmac/Maliseet Nations News* and wrote *We Were Not the Savages: A Mi'kmaq Perspective on the Collision between European and Native American Civilizations* (Halifax: Fernwood, 2000) as well as many articles and newspaper columns on subjects pertaining to social justice, Mi'kmaw history, and biography. He is the subject

of a recent biography by Jon Tattrie entitled *Daniel Paul, Mi'kmaw Elder* (Lawrencetown Beach, NS: Pottersfield, 2017).

144 Despite Cope's words, Andrew Paul, who originally came from Whycocomagh in Cape Breton around 1830, had been living in the Dartmouth region for years and by 1860 had risen as a sub-chief in the ranks of the Shubenacadie leadership. Furthermore, that he held a hunting territory after 1860 in the Sheet Harbour area indicates that he had been incorporated into the Sheet Harbour band before 1880. Louisa Paul, Joseph C. Cope's mother, died at Enfield in 1905 at the age of 74. NSARM, Historical Vital Statistics, Halifax County Deaths, Registration Year 1905, p. 66, no. 71.

145 Sebmolie Maurice, the grandfather of the three Morris brothers Louis, Ben, and John, camped for many years at the outlet of Morris Lake, near Dartmouth, which still bears his family's surname. NSM, Printed Matter File, Piers Papers, unpublished notes, "Harry Piers on Morris family," n.d., "Louis Noel McDonald to Harry Piers," 20 November 1923. Sebmolie, who lived at Shubenacadie in the 1880s, was also the maternal grandfather of Joseph C. Cope's wife, Rebecca Jadis, as John Jadis had married Catherine Morris. James Jadis was Rebecca's paternal grandfather and Charles Jadis of Grimcross was her great grandfather. Ben Morris, born around 1818, grew totally blind while he was living at Cole Harbour. He was a close friend of Joseph C. Cope and came with Cope to Cole Harbour in 1880. However, he left Cole Harbour in 1888 and went to Three Mile Plains, near Panuke Lake, where he died. All of the Morris brothers were also distantly related to Paul Morris, who received a reserve at Sambro in the late eighteenth century. NSM, Printed Matter File, Piers Papers, "Ben Morris' information provided to Jeremiah Barlett-Alexis (Jerry Lonecloud), who then conveyed it to Harry Piers," 20 December 1915.

146 NSARM, MG 15, vol. 7, doc. no. 11, "Regarding Relief for Christy Morris," 3 May 1856; MSARM, MG 15, vol. 6, doc. no. 10, "Regarding Old Morris on Prospect Road," 11 October 1856.

147 Toney Street formed part of what became Hawthorne Street, near Sullivan's Pond in Dartmouth. In the 1880s the Toney family of Dartmouth extended back three generations. The Anthonys (or Toneys) of Nova Scotia were descendants of Chief Anthony (Eury) of Remsheg, now Wallace, in Pictou County. "Captain Tony" was well known to Michael Francklin when he was lieutenant governor of Nova Scotia, and the captain continued to interact with Francklin at Fort Howe when Francklin was Indian commissioner during the American Revolution. The James White Papers in the New Brunswick Provincial Archives in Saint John, NB, mention the activities of Captain Toney during the American Revolution. He had a large family, some of whom spread eastward along the Northumberland Strait while others entered the Annapolis Valley, where descendants still live at Cambridge. Captain Toney's son Louis, who spoke English proficiently, became a spokesperson for Jacques Peminout Paul of Newport when Paul visited Indian commissioner George Henry Monk at Windsor in the late 1790s. Louis's son, Dan Toney, travelled to Bear River where he settled. Dan was reputed to have a magnificent voice, and Abbé Sigogne taught him to sing in church in Latin. Magdalene Toney of Bear River, who was either Dan Toney's sister or his daughter, became Chief James Andrew Meuse's first wife, while her brother Peter Tony became Bear River's second chief. Gabriel Anthony, after travelling widely from Cape Breton to the New England States, resided for a spell at Weymouth where by 1844 he claimed to be the district chief of southwestern Nova Scotia. Early in 1846 he journeyed to Halifax to direct a petition to the House of Assembly praying for his recognition as a chief as well as help for his people. *Halifax Morning Post*, 14 January 1846. He died soon afterwards in Dartmouth, probably among kin on Toney Street. Martin, *The Story of Dartmouth*, 379. Another of his claims to fame concerned his wife Santu, who reputedly had a Beothuk father. Speck, *Beothuk and Micmac*, 55–70. The first Toneys of Toney Street in the 1840s had pushed southwest into the Annapolis Valley from Pictou County and then turned eastward in the 1790s to come to the Atlantic coast, where they married into the Pennel, Gloade, Phillips, Morris, Wilmot, Cope, and Eastern Paul families. A local head man named Peter Toney, who won canoe races on Lake Banook, lived on this street in the mid-1840s.

148 Canada, Federal Census of 1881, Sheet 34, District 31D, compiled 14 April 1891, lists Peter Cope Jr. (sixty-seven) and Louise Paul (fifty-eight), and Joseph C. Cope (thirty-three), his wife Rebecca Jadis (twenty-five), and four children: Francis (eight), Paul (six), Lewis (four), and Elizabeth (one).

149 LAC, RG 10, 92-1004-06-004, Halifax County – General Documents from Indian Affairs. Copies of these documents are housed at the Treaty and Aboriginal Rights Research Centre, Shubenacadie (henceforth TARR), Indian Affairs fonds, Halifax County, File 10.838 – old, Halifax County, "Joseph Cope, Windsor Junction, to Indian Affairs," July 1892.

150 LAC, RG 10, vol. 2233, file 45,093, Halifax County Agency, "Correspondence regarding the election of a chief of the Cole Harbour reserve, 1883–1888." Another person contacted in 1883 was the Reverend Charles Underwood, parish priest, of Dartmouth.

151 Desmond stated that Cope had told his constituency he could "obtain favours for them by writing directly to the Department." TARR, Indian Affairs fonds, Halifax County, doc. 47957, "Desmond to Vankoughnet," 1 May 1888.

152 Internal land disputes proved chronic at Cole Harbour. TARR Indian Affairs fonds, Halifax County, doc. 47821, "Desmond to Vankoughnet," 26 April 1888. When Cope left Cole Harbour for a period of time, he found on his return that another member of the "Eastern Tribe," John Paul, had occupied his house and was planting his fields. Cope wanted Paul removed at once. If Cope faced a problem, he was doggedly persistent in attempting to solve it: for six straight years he berated Indian Affairs and the local agent for failing to attend to the numerous tasks he set out for them. In 1894 he was still arguing that in 1880 each head of family was allotted only three acres "and no more," but without any external supervision some persons were appropriating far more than their fair share. TARR Indian Affairs fonds, Halifax County, doc. 114430, "Joseph Cope to Indian Affairs," 16 May 1894.

153 Halifax County Deeds, Deed Book 223, 530–1, "Indenture made 20 August 1880 between Her Majesty the Queen, represented by the Superintendent General of Indian Affairs, on the one part, and Thomas Ritchie of Halifax, Executor of the last will and testament of William Almon Johnstone, late of Windsor, Barrister-at-Law, on the other."

154 For instance, in 1899 Reverend Desmond succeeded in temporarily stalling the cession of the Ingraham's River reserve after the government had deemed its continued protection of the Mi'kmaq's local weir fishery little more than a chronic nuisance. Desmond's predecessor D.C. O'Connor had recommended keeping the reserves, though he felt they were comparatively valueless as far as timber or soil was concerned. O'Connor also argued that the Sheet Harbour area had been vacated by the Mi'kmaq. TARR Indian Affairs fonds, Halifax County, doc. 23686, "O'Connor to L. Vankoughnet," 20 September 1880.

155 It is probably owing to Cope's persistence, however, that a school was built in the later 1880s, along with a chapel. Around 1900 the teacher at the school was Kate Giles, the wife of a Cole Harbour farmer named William Giles. Harry Chapman, *Along the Cole Harbour Road,* 152.

156 TARR Indian Affairs fonds, Halifax County, doc. 10838, "Department of Indian Affairs to Chief Joseph Cope," n.d. (1888).

157 TARR Indian Affairs fonds, Halifax County, doc. 46574, "Joseph Cope, Chief, to Indian Affairs," 7 May 1888. Cope also stressed that he and his brother Isaac, Francis Brooks from Ship Harbour, Joe Brooks, Elisha Jadis, John Morris, and Francis Syer were all entitled to one hundred feet of lumber as well as shingles. He later included his friend Ben Brooks in this number.

158 TARR Indian Affairs fonds, doc. 17824, "Rev. A.P. Desmond, Enfield, to Vankoughnet, Deputy Superintendent of Indian Affairs," 26 April 1888; and doc.10838, "Indian Affairs to Chief Cope," 19 March 1888.

159 TARR Indian Affairs fonds, Halifax County, doc. 53669, "Andrew Paul to Vankoughnet," 17 December 1888.

160 TARR Indian Affairs fonds, Halifax County, doc. 46574, Joseph Cope, Chief, to Indian Affairs, May 7, 1888. Cope also stressed at this time that there were eight families expecting lumber from the government. On 26 March 1888 he further stressed that "we will do all we can to induce friends to come into our reserve and to send their children to schools for I do really have faith in it and wish every ... child to know how to read and write." TARR Indian Affairs fonds, doc. 47821, "Cope to Vankoughnet," 26 April 1888.

161 TARR Indian Affairs fonds, Halifax County, doc. 47957, "Desmond to Vankoughnet," 1 May 1888.

162 This church, dedicated to Saint Catherine, is now named "Saint Kateri Tekawitha."

163 TARR Indian Affairs fonds, Halifax County, doc. 47957, "Desmond to Vankoughnet," 1 May 1888. Desmond also conveyed these statements to Thomas Ritchie, the lawyer who had participated in securing the reserve in 1880.

164 These petitions held that the grand chief's claims rested on sound historical evidence. NSARM, RG 2, vol. 9, doc. 1815, "Petition of Jacob Brooks *et al.* to Lieutenant-Governor Adams George Archibald," 5 February 1883; NSARM, RG 2, vol. 9, doc. 1820, "Petition of Christopher Paul, Stephen Hood and 59 others to Lieutenant-Governor Adams George Archibald," 29 March 1883.

165 In 1894 Cope stated that all his relatives and associates had left Cole Harbour "excepting me + blind Ben Morris." He got in one last jab at Andrew Paul for not regulating internal land boundaries properly: "poor blind friend Ben's [in] danger of losing half of his property." Cope declared he planned to move from Windsor Junction to Shubenacadie within the year. TARR Indian Affairs fonds, Halifax County, doc. 114430, "Joseph Cope to Indian Affairs," 16 May 1894. Ben Morris later left for

Three Mile Plains to live with his son. Joseph C. Cope's son Joseph would marry Josephine Howe, daughter of Joe Howe and Rose Mahoney Basque, while Frank would marry Susan Marble of Pictou Landing. (The name "Mahoney" among the Mi'kmaq seems to have derived from the Irish word "Mahone," a word that can mean "pirate," as in the meaning of "Mahone Bay." The surname "Mahone," rather than Mahoney, appears on a list of Mi'kmaq residing at Truro in 1800.) See NSARM, RG 1, vol. 430, doc. 55. Later, in the 1840s, Mi'kmaw persons with the surname "Mahone" appear on the East Coast of Nova Scotia and at Enfield. Frank Cope's wife's family, the Marbles (from the French *emable*, "congenial") lived at Pictou Landing, though in the early 1800s they lived at Antigonish, and may have been descendants of Emable Peguidalouet. Frank and Susan Marble had four children, two boys and two girls. In 1938 Frank, by then a widower, married a second time at Amherst to Susan Hood of Maccan, the thirty-three-old daughter of Stephen Hood and Mary Ann Paul. NSARM, Historical Vital Statistics, Cumberland County Marriages, Registration Year 1938, Book 88, 796. (This marriage certificate incorrectly lists Frank's mother as Elizabeth Jadis rather than Rebecca Jadis.) One of Frank's sons, Noel Michael Cope, moved back to Halifax from Pictou, married Mary Symington, and apprenticed as a garage mechanic. He worked and lived on Cunard Street. NSARM, Historical Vital Statistics, Pictou County Births (Delayed Registration 1971), Registration Year 1906, 99200323, "Birth Registration of Noel Michael Cope, born to Frank Cope and Susan Marble on 19 December 1906 at Pictou Landing." Noel Michael's son, Vernon, currently in the employ of Via Rail, admitted that as a boy he felt he lacked close relatives in Halifax. His parents Noel and Mary (Symington, née Brazil-Gorman) used to take him skating in the winter near Pockwock Lake, but he had no cousins with whom to enjoy these outings. His mother encouraged her children to acquire a solid knowledge of history, art, and Western culture in general, but not necessarily Mi'kmaw culture. Consequently, Vernon has a comprehensive knowledge of Western art – from modern works to iconographic religious art – and also of antiques. His younger half-brother, Leonard Paul, is an internationally known artist, author, and educator who incorporates Mi'kmaw themes into his work. Information drawn from Vital Statistics, from Leonard Paul's website, http://www.leonardpaulfoxtraileditions.com/about.html, and from conversations with Vernon Cope.

166 Between 1888 and 1892 Joseph C. Cope clashed with both Andrew Paul and Grand Chief John Denny Jr. If Cope had not been so consumed by his own political losses at Cole Harbour, he might have realized that the grand chief's main goal was not to replace existing leaders, but to ensure that incumbents set their sights on new challenges, including the potential loss of reserve land under the tenets of government centralization policy. Soon after his installation as grand chief in 1887, John Denny Jr. sent out instructions to certain leaders to prevent the government's taking reserve land, as well to instigate viable economic practices on existing reserves. His actions were based on Grand Council precedents set down during the French regime. Since the eighteenth century, the grand chief and council presided over special leadership appointments in areas outside of Île Royale (Cape Breton) whenever crises occurred or important leadership offices fell vacant. Though the system that gave rise to this practice has been regarded by historians as an invention of French authorities at Quebec and Louisbourg after 1715, it more likely arose out of a combination of French geopolitical aspirations and traditional Mi'kmaw hunting territory allocation practices. The Indigenous practice was gauged to ensure that the number of humans remained in equilibrium with the available land and resource base, whether with respect to trapping or hunting big game for subsistence or to maintaining the most appropriate form of leadership to administer and defend the allocation system. John Denny Jr.'s father, Grand Chief John Denny Sr., long after the conquest of the French at Louisbourg revived the earlier practice in 1880 by encouraging Andrew Paul to attain land at Cole Harbour to accommodate the growing Mi'kmaw population about Dartmouth. The grand chief also personally oversaw the training and appointment of Mi'kmaw prayer leaders and resource specialists. After 1887 John Denny Jr. promoted a land and resource campaign that drew upon distinctly Mi'kmaw ideological, political, and ecological expertise, and interwove this expertise with ideas pertaining to recent economic developments, particularly railway transport, that he drew from the Canadian mainstream. This new body of ideas, he felt, would help the Mi'kmaq respond to changes and challenges they faced at the turn of the nineteenth century. By contrast, Joseph C. Cope worried that "parachuting" in new leaders from elsewhere would disturb what continuity existed. His father had looked to enhanced interpretations of the treaties to ensure legal and constitutional recognition for Mi'kmaw hunting and fishing rights, a strategy Denny's successor as grand chief, Gabriel Sylliboy, would turn to in 1827 and 1828 when he pressed for Mi'kmaq individuals throughout the Atlantic Provinces

to hunt and fish out of season and then test the validity of Mi'kmaw treaty rights in the courts. Sylliboy himself was arrested and tried for hunting muskrat out of season. Joseph C. Cope doubtless would have understood that thrust of Sylliboy's campaign well, as his father had been a firm upholder of treaty rights. Yet he appeared lost as to what was going on at Cole Harbour, except insofar as he knew that his own leadership aspirations with regard to that place were doomed. He often transferred his stream of invective from Andrew Paul to Grand Chief John Denny Jr., whom he blamed for infiltrating Eastern Shore politics with specially picked men from Cape Breton. The Cape Breton Mi'kmaq, he felt, were of a different political cast from the original eastern shore population, and this led to endless disputes at Cole Harbour with Andrew Paul, who had the ear of the newcomers. "Both claim to be the right[ful] owners of the Reserve," he declared. "Of course today the Cape Breton man [Andrew Paul] Rules the Reserve to his heart's content, appointed by the Grand Chief John Dennie of Cape Breton, who last summer kindly paid a short visit to the reserve to perform the imposing ceremony of appointing a Ruler. [He] stated hereafter Andrew Paul (Cape Breton subject) should Rule and be recognized as [the] Indian Chief of Cole Harbour Indian Reserve. But the Halifax Co. Indians have not yet united to uphold and to satisfy the above. Dear Sir – had [the] Cape Breton Chief any right to go inside of Grand Chief James [Jacques-Pierre Peminout] Paul's jurisdiction to appoint his own men to Rule? Is he not interfering with our old and recognized Chiefdom of Halifax, Hants + Kings Counties? Who are the right[ful] owners of Cole Harbour Reserve? Would Halifax Co. Indians have any hopes of getting one of their own – to avoid the sad friction with others from other parts?" TARR, Indian Affairs (RG 10) fonds, Halifax County, file 10.838 – old, "Joseph Cope to Indian Affairs," July 1892, 511–15.

167   Andrew Paul died shortly afterwards in 1916. "Harry Piers' Obituary for Andrew Paul," 24 February 1916, Piers Notes, NSM, Printed Matter File.

168   TARR Indian Affairs fonds, Halifax County, File 10.838 – old, "Joseph Cope to Indian Affairs," July 1892.

169   NSM, Printed Matter File, "Chieftainships according to Joe Cope, aged 65 years," n.d. (c.1924).

170   NSARM, Historical Vital Statistics, Annapolis County Marriages, Registration Year 1910, Book O, 651. The ceremony took place at the Roman Catholic Church of St. Louis, Annapolis Royal, the Reverend Thomas T. Grace officiating, witnesses Sylvie Pictou and Rachel Pictou. Sylvie (or Levi) Pictou was the chief of the Kejimkujik

Reserve just before its surrender in 1918. Catherine Muise, whose parents hailed from Folleigh (or Folly) Village in Colchester County, was living at Windsor before her marriage, while Joseph Cope was living at Round Hill, Annapolis County.

171   Joseph C. Cope claimed that his father died at ninety-seven in 1913. NSM, Printed Matter File, Piers Papers, "Piers (vide Joe C. Cope)," April 1926. Joseph's mother, Louisa Paul Cope, born in 1831, died at the age of seventy-four in 1905. Though her husband had been a captain of the Shubenacadie council as well as a delegate meeting with Queen Victoria around the time of Confederation, his occupation was listed on her death certificate only as "trapper." NSARM, Historical Vital Statistics, Halifax County Deaths, Registration Year 1905, p. 66, no. 71.

172   The Glooscap Heritage Centre at Millbrook displays, under the heading "*Wi'kikaqnn Elapskita'sikl*" (Mi'kmaw Petroglyph), a quartzite boulder with an inscription on it that reads "Jos. Cope, June 22, 1876." Two single-mast sailing ships are carved into the rock face below the name and date. The boulder was "quarried from Miller's Mountain sometime in the past and placed along the highway that extends along the east shore of Lake Mi'kmaq." Miller's Mountain, which is more of a steep hill, rises behind Second Red Bridge. Edward J. Lenik, *Picture Rocks: American Indian Rock Art in the Northeast Woodlands* (Lebanon, NH: University Press of New England, 2003), 32. Born in 1859, Joseph C. Cope would have been only seventeen years old when he carved his name and drew the ships, which are similar to petroglyphs of sailing ships at McGowan Lake and Kejimkujik National Park in Queens County. An artistic man, the young Cope in carving the designs perhaps was trying to reconnect in some way with his ancestral roots.

173   Harry Piers's ancestor Lewis Piers came to Halifax with Cornwallis in 1749 and was descended from a knight-baronet of Nova Scotia who received his status from Sir William Alexander in 1624. By the 1900s the Piers family had set up a family merchant business and "ropewalk" (a long, straight, narrow lane where hemp strands were laid before being twisted into rope) in North End Halifax. Through intermarriage with the Brookfield family the Piers acquired a large part of the construction firm established by Samuel Brookfield of Halifax. In the 1840s and 1850s the Piers were friends of Joseph Howe and William Chearnley. They often hunted and fished with Chearnley at Gold River in Lunenburg County, with members of the Pennel family as their guides. Information drawn from conversations with the

late Walter Piers, Halifax, 2004 and 2005. According to Walter Piers, Harry Piers, who never married, found Mi'kmaw history and culture fascinating and enjoyed conversing with his Mi'kmaw friends and acquaintances.

174 Joseph C. Cope took the only existing photograph of Isaac Paul, Chief James Peminout Paul's biological son (John Noel was his adopted son) (see Plate 44). This photograph, taken at Morris Lake, Cole Harbour, Nova Scotia in 1891, is housed in the Nova Scotia Museum's Mi'kmaw Portraits Collection Isaac, who had a brown mustache, was nattily dressed in a suit for this occasion. He died around 1898 of tuberculosis. In its lower right-hand corner, his studio portrait bears the words "Joe Cope, Photographer." It remains the only known example of Joe Cope's photographic work. NSM, MP0287, Ref. no. P113/ 18.2 (4586)/ N-5007.

175 NSM, Printed Matter File, Piers Papers, "Joe C. Cope's device for directing aerial bombs onto their targets, Mossman's Grant, Lunenburg Co., to Mr. Piers," 7 March 1916; ibid., "Reply to Joe C. Cope from E.E.F. Goold Adams, Comptroller of Munitions and Inventions, Ministry of Munitions, London, England"; Upton, *Micmac and Colonists*, 173.

176 Among these stories were accounts of Mohawk spies told to Cope by Louis Noel McDonald of Sheet Harbour and Cole Harbour and Chief Jacques-Pierre Peminout Paul of Shubenacadie. NSM, Printed Matter File, Piers Papers, "A Short Unwritten History About Awiskookak, the Mohawk Indian Spies, by Joe C. Cope, Micmac Indian, Enfield, N.S"; ibid., "Glooscap the second, by J.C. Cope"; ibid., "Joseph C. Cope to Harry Piers," 31 January 1924. Another story concerned a Mi'kmaw chief named Mijilapegatasijk who drove out the Mohawk from the Maritime Provinces. NSM, Printed Matter File, Piers Papers, "Joseph C. Cope to Harry Piers," 21 January 1924. At the time the Nova Scotia Museum of Natural History where Piers was employed was located on Spring Garden Road.

177 NSM, Printed Matter file, Piers Papers, "Joseph C. Cope, *Sesep Obsquooch,* Enfield, to Harry Piers," 29 March 1929.

178 NSM, Printed Matter File, Piers Notes, "Cope to Harry Piers," 31 January 1924.

179 NSARM, Historical Vital Statistics, Hants County Deaths, Registration Year 1949, 1726. NSARM, Historical Vital Statistics, Hants County Deaths, Registration Year 1917, p. 48, no. 289.

180 According to the *Halifax Chronicle*, ninety-three-year-old Joseph C. Cope had been a "Prospector, photographer and one of Nova Scotia's best-known citizens."

"Obituary of Joseph C. Cope," *Halifax Morning Chronicle*, 9 March 1951, 1.

181 MSN, Printed Matter File, Harry Piers notes, "Information from John Noel, 1896."

182 LAC, RG 10, vol. 2130, file 25,584, "Father A.P. Desmond to Indian Affairs," 11 June 1886; ibid., "Reply to Joe C. Cope from E.E.F. Goold Adams, Comptroller of Munitions and Invention"; ibid., "Desmond to Caleb F. Hubley," 18 February 1886. And in fact the province did not push through a surrender of the Ingraham's River reserve in 1899 because its agents could not locate enough Mi'kmaw persons connected with the tract, scattered as they were by this time throughout central Nova Scotia. LAC, RG 10, vol. 2130, file 25,534, "James McNamera to J.D. McLean," 26 April 1899; LAC, RG 10, vol. 2130, file 25,534, "Memorandum to the Secretary of Indian Affairs," 27 April 1899.

183 Seven Mi'kmaw leaders, including Chief John Denny Jr., wrote petitions to Indian Affairs in the spring of 1909. These petitions are all contained in a single file in Ottawa: LAC, RG 10, vol. 3113, file 320, 110-pt. 1-A, "Documents pertaining to the surrender of the Kejimkujik or Fairy Lake Reserve, 1909–1918." These petitions include "To the Honourable Minister of the Interior [Frank Oliver] from John Denys, Grand Chief, Witness Rose McMaster, Eskasoni, Cape Breton, 11 March 1909"; "Chief Joseph Gould, Truro, to the Department of Indian Affairs, with signatures," 12 March 1909; "Chief John Steaven, Pomquet, to the Department of Indian Affairs, with signatures," 12 March 1909; "Captain Simon Paul, Middle River, to the Department of Indian Affairs, with signatures," 12 March 1909; "Chief Solomon Morris, Sydney, to the Department of Indian Affairs, with signatures," 12 March 1909; "Mr. James Joe of Malagawatch, Cape Breton, to the Department of Indian Affairs, with signatures," 12 March, 1909; and "Tom Marshall, Chapel Island, St. Peter's, to the Department of Indian Affairs," 27 March 1909. Despite the Grand Council's best efforts, the Fairy Lake reserve was ceded in 1918. LAC, RG 10, vol. 3113, file 320, 110-pt. 1-A, "Surrender of Fairy Lake Reserve, signed by Stephen Pictou and twenty others," 11 April 1918. The import of these petitions is explored further in Janet E. Chute, "Frank G. Speck's Contributions," 111–15. An incisive discussion of the Kings Road affair may be found in William C. Wicken, *The Colonization of Mi'kmaw Memory and History, 1794–1928: The King v. Gabriel Sylliboy* (Toronto: University of Toronto Press, 2012), chap. 7.

184 His interest in historical matters provided him with valuable information and insights into the past of one

major constituency, the Eastward Tribe, for whom he would one day assume responsibility.

185 Gillies argued that the Kings Road community suffered from frequent outbreaks of diphtheria, measles, and tuberculosis owing to crowded, unsanitary conditions. These assertions were found to be mostly unjustified at the Exchequer Court hearing and motivated by personal considerations. Tuberculosis, however, did take a toll. Certainly it touched the life of John Cope Jr., a son of John Noel Cope and a grandson of Francis Doadaran Cope, who in 1906 sold his shanty at Elmsdale to a settler named Andrew Roulston and, at the age of twenty-seven, settled on the Kings Road reserve. He wed Bridget Bernard from Eskasoni, but from the first year of their marriage tuberculosis haunted the young couple. Their fourteen-month-old daughter Mary Louise died of tuberculosis in 1910, and Bridget, after suffering from the same affliction for six months, died in 1911. NSARM, Historical Vital Statistics, Cape Breton County Deaths, Book 3, p. 299, no. 1809; ibid., Book 3, p. 41, no. 2481 (there are two death certificates for Mary Louise Cope); NSARM, Historical Vital Statistics, Cape Breton County Deaths, Book 3, p. 41, no. 2481. John's sale of his shanty to Roulston later became a bone of contention, since a Mrs. Joseph Howe (whose husband, originally surnamed "Jeremy," had at some point adopted the name of the non-Indigenous politician and former Indian superintendent Joseph Howe) felt it should have passed to her. NSM, Printed File, Piers Notes, Micmac Correspondence with Indian Affairs, "Jerry Lonecloud to Indian Affairs," 30 December 1915.

186 "Interview with Annie Louise Googoo conducted between 1973 and 1975 by Lillian Marshall of Potlotek." ("Potlotek" is Mi'kmaq for "Port Toulouse," also known today as Chapel Island, near St. Peter's in Cape Breton.) Lillian Marshall's great-grandmother was Mary Julien, Joseph Julien's sister, who after 1877 was raised at Burnt Church. Mary married John Alex (McDonald) of Potlotek. According to Lillian, Annie Louise Googoo still could remember her husband's tender solicitude for her feelings when she was an inexperienced young bride of sixteen. One example of this gentleness occurred when she was expected to provide kettle bread for the St. Anne's Day feast at Chapel Island. It was her first time baking such bread, and when she asked for instructions she was told to leave the dough in the covered kettle for a certain number of minutes. Louise, who in her early years could not tell time, left the bread cooking far too long, until it came out "very hard like cheese." Joseph, however, diplomatically accepted her loaves and took them with him to the mission banquet. Afterwards he cheerfully informed his new bride that "they loved your bread." Lillian Marshall of Chapel Island in conversation with Annie Louise Googoo, typescript transcription from the archives of the Confederacy of Mainland Mi'kmaq, Millbrook, Truro, 10. Joseph Julien knew how to sing the leader's *nesk-ko-wet*, or welcoming song, at occasions such as the annual mission, a song now lost. Lillian, elder and educationalist, with characteristic cordiality wrote the author early in August 2014, "Genealogists would say that Don [Julien, Joseph's grandson] and my dad were first cousins once removed. Also, Cathy Martin's grandfather, Michael Martin, would fall in the same category. Michael's father was a half brother to Joe and Mary Julian (my great grandmother)." Cathy Martin, who is an off-reserve member of the Millbrook community, is a well-known filmmaker, author, educationalist, singer, and composer.

187 *In the Matter of the Reference Respecting the Expediency of the Removal of the Indians from the Reserve at the City of Sydney, Cape Breton, in the Province of Nova Scotia,* (1916), 17 Ex. C.R. 517; Wicken, *The Colonization of Mi'kmaw Memory*, 221.

188 "Remembering a Leader," 9. Overcrowding was a major problem. In 1915, 120 Mi'kmaw residents occupied twenty-seven shanties, none of which, owing to space constraints, stood on a properly defined lot.

189 Ibid.

190 1–2 George V Cap 14, s. 2. "An Act to amend the Indian Act," 19 May 1911. From 1912 to 1917 the minister of the interior, who was also the superintendent general of Indian Affairs, was Dr. William James Roche.

191 In 1916 the Mi'kmaq moved of their own accord to land of their choice in Sydney where, in 1919, twenty-three-year-old Ben Christmas became chief of the fledging settlement that would eventually be officially renamed "Membertou." Mi'kmaw tenure to this tract remained tenuous until the early 1920s, since immediately after the close of the First World War Ottawa lacked the funds to purchase any new reserves. In 1921 the federal government briefly negotiated for land for the Sydney band from J.A. Gillies's widow, but the parcel lay outside city limits and the Mi'kmaq refused to abandon their prevailing surroundings. In 1926 the Department of Indian Affairs finally purchased the tract the Mi'kmaq wanted on St. Joseph's Road in Sydney from a local doctor, Arthur Kendall. The Mi'kmaq never forgot their earlier Kings Road settlement, however, and late in 2015 they successfully negotiated with Ottawa for a return of this parcel. Membertou Communications, *Kings Road*

Reserve 100 Years Later, The Journey On … The History of Membertou's Reconciliation, October 2016, https://www.membertou.ca/wp-content/uploads/2019/05/kings-road-reserve.pdf.

192 Ben Christmas was the son of Joe Christmas and Madeline Richards. Born in Port Morien on the eastern seacoast of Cape Breton on 14 July 1896, he was active in Mi'kmaw politics from an early age. For several years he participated in the Micmac Community Development Program (MCDP), set up by the Extension Department of St. Francis Xavier University at Antigonish from 1899 to 1951, although the range of his political interests and activities reached far beyond the policy strictures set up by the MCDP. Martha Walls, "Mi'kmaw Politicism and the Origins of the Micmac Community Development Program, 1899–1951," *Journals of the Royal Nova Scotia Historical Society* 20 (2017): 2–3. Ben died at Amherst, Cumberland County, Nova Scotia, on 28 March 1966. He was a prayer leader, a choir leader, and a member of the Grand Council as well as a band chief. He married Jane Denny and had several children, one of whom, Peter Christmas, is an educator, administrator, and former director of the Mi'kmaw Cultural Association. The late Helen Martin, Peter's sister, who died in 1993, was involved with Native women's rights and was one of the founders of the Nova Scotia Native Women's Association.

193 NSM, Piers Notes, April 1918, "Obituary of John Denny, who died on 12 April 1918 at 74 years of age." At the time of his death John Denny Jr. was living at Whycocomagh.

194 Sandy Julien married Martha Francis and raised Joseph Julian, Joe B. Marshall, Keith Julien, Derrick Julien, Angeline Paul, and Janet Bernard.

195 "Remembering a Leader," 9.

196 Ibid., 10; Googoo, "Story of Joseph Julien," 3.

197 Despite much correspondence from Indian Affairs between 1919 and 1957 referring to Joseph Julien as "chief of Millbrook," the first chief of Millbrook to be officially recognized by Ottawa was Gerald Gloade, who was elected on 23 June 1959. Throughout his lifetime, however, Joseph Julien remained the leader of the Millbrook community, a status informally recognized by Ottawa as well as Millbrook community residents. "Remembering a Leader," 9; Anita Maria Tobin, "The Effect of Centralization," 104.

198 Martin Sack, the spokesperson for the Elmsdale Mi'kmaw community, was a nephew of Isaac Sack, who married Bridget Ann Cope, one of Sandy Cope Sr.'s sisters. Martin also was a grandson of Peter Sack, whose widow, Marie-Antoinette Thomas, married John Noel, the Shubenacadie head chief. Jeremiah Bartholomew-Alexis, also known as "Jerry Lonecloud," was a spokesperson for the Halifax County Band.

199 LAC, RG 10, vol. 3119, file 327–352, "Petition to H.P. Bury from the Elmsdale Mi'kmaw community," 21 August 1919.

200 LAC, RG 10, vol. 3160, file 363–417–1, "Local Agent Daniel Chisholm to Superintendent Duncan Campbell Scott regarding residents' arrangement with A.P. King," 30 September 1918.

201 NSM, Printed Matter File, Piers Papers, Ethnology, Correspondence with the Department of Indian Affairs, "Petition of Members of the Micmac Tribe of Indians of Halifax County to S. Stewart, Department of Indian Affairs," 10 March, 1916. Edward Marks from Musquodoboit married Margaret Murchy, the great-granddaughter of a Scot named James Murchy Sr. who had emigrated from Aberdeen. James Murchy Sr. had a son James born in 1826, who later married Elizabeth Annand and ran a grist and carding mill at Elderbank. Margaret was the daughter of this man's son, James Murchy, born around 1850, and Elizabeth Cruikshank, his wife. Margaret's father had an older sawmill at Murchyville that he let his son-in-law Edward Marks run. Edward eventually replaced it with a modern sawmill that he operated himself. Margaret's brother Lewis Murchy meanwhile married Elizabeth Howe of Elderbank, who was a daughter of Edward Howe, a granddaughter of Joseph Howe, the political reformer, so the family were well connected. Edward Marks and his wife Margaret around 1900 moved to Ship Harbour, where Edward set up a lumbering business with his son Lawrence. By 1913, when Edward began to cut on the reserve, his business was known as the Marks Lumbering Company. See Jennie Reid, *Musquodoboit Pioneers: A Record of Seventy Families, Their Homesteads and Genealogies, 1780–1980,* 2 vols. (Musquodoboit, NS: Musquodoboit Enterprises Historical Committee, 1980), 1.2.

202 NSM, Printed Matter File, Piers Papers, Ethnology, "Petition from Tufts Cove Mi'kmaw residents," 20 March 1917; ibid., "Second Petition of Tufts Cove Residents," 9 April 1917. These Mi'kmaq argued that as prices for provisions were rising at Tufts Cove and they needed to be settled at their new locale early enough to plant crops, the government should turn over their funds as soon as possible. The four families responsible for this second petition were Frank Brooks, Joe Brooks, John Brooks, and Jerry Lonecloud. When no funds appeared, the community complained that owing to the excessive cost of meat and other foodstuffs they would have to kill

"moose out of season" in order to survive. Ibid., "Petition of 11 October 1917."

203 NSM, Printed Matter File, Piers Papers, Ethnology, Correspondence with Department of Indian Affairs, "Lewis Paul, Acting Chief, to J.D. MacLean," 27 April 1916. Louis Paul later moved to Truro and in 1920 assumed a place along with Chief Joseph Julien on the Colchester County Band Council. Lewis was educated enough to sign his name, but he prevailed on Harry Piers of the Nova Scotia Museum to write letters and petitions for him. In 1916 John Denny Paul, Louis Paul, and Peter Paul were living at Enfield near Joseph C. Cope. John Denny Paul died in 1924 at the age of sixty-three, making his birth year 1861. NSARM, Historical Vital Statistics, Halifax County Deaths, Registration Year 1924, Book 84, 401. John Denny and Peter and Louis Paul were all sons of Abram Paul, a son of Annie Morris and Andrew Paul of Cape Breton (1818–1916). Andrew Paul was born at Whycocomagh and left Cape Breton around 1830. He lived for a number of years in Guysborough County and died at Tufts Cove in 1916. NSARM, Historical Vital Statistics, Halifax County Deaths, Registration Year 1916, Book 34, p. 197, no. 658. Abram Paul, born in Guysborough County in 1840, married Ellen Morris, and died at Cole Harbour in Dartmouth in 1912. NSARM, Historical Vital Statistics, Halifax County Marriages, Registration Year 1883, Book 1817, p. 202, no. 83. John Paul, Abram Paul's brother, was twenty-five years old and living at Eastern Passage when he wed Teresa Murphy of Chezzetcook in 1883, making his year of birth 1858. Witnesses to the wedding were Abram Paul and Annie Morris. NSARM, Historical Vital Statistics, Halifax County Marriages, Registration Year 1883, Book 1817, p. 102, no. 392. (Another John Paul, a forty-year-old widower from Cape Breton born in 1844 and who married Mary Denny in 1884, was probably of the same family.) Jerry Lonecloud held that Peter Paul of Truro, a brother of John Denny and Louis Paul, was born at Morris Lake, Dartmouth, in 1870. NSM, Printed Matter File, Piers Papers, unpublished notes, "Harry Piers notes," 1 December 1924. Yet according to his death certificate, Peter was born on 5 April 1868; he died on 18 July 1944. NSARM, Historical Vital Statistics, Halifax County Deaths, Registration Year 1944, Book 212, 514.

204 NSM, Printed Matter File, Piers Papers, Ethnology, Correspondence with the Department of Indian Affairs, "Jeremiah Bartlett-Alexis to Indian Affairs," 27 November 1917.

205 NSM, Printed Matter File, Piers Papers, Ethnology, Correspondence with the Department of Indian Affairs, "Petition of John Denny Paul to A.P. Boyd, River Bourgeois, N.S.," 6 November 1916.

206 John Denny Paul explained to Ottawa that he was eastern sub-chief of the broader Shubenacadie Council, headed at the time by Big Peter Paul of Shubenacadie. NSM, Printed Matter File, Piers Papers, Ethnology, Correspondence with the Department of Indian Affairs, "Denny Paul, Enfield, to the Secretary of the Department of Indian Affairs," 5 December 1916. Big Peter Paul, who was the first chief to be elected after the death of John Noel on 20 May 1911, held the office of head chief at Shubenacadie in 1912 and again in 1916. The elections he won, however, were not recognized by Ottawa. Born on 10 May 1850, he was the son of Chief James Peminout Paul's brother, Christopher Peminout Paul, who was a Mi'kmaw judge, and was a captain under the headship of Chief James Peminout Paul. He was given the nickname "Big Peter" to distinguish him from Peter Paul, John Denny Paul's brother in Dartmouth. NSM, Printed Matter File, "Piers notes," 15 March 1913; NSM, Printed Matter File, Piers Notes, "Information from Jerry Lonecloud," 8 June 1921. Big Peter Paul was defeated in an election in 1913 by Simon Basque, a relative of Isaac Sack and Martin Sack. John Denny Paul's brother, Peter Paul, who lived near the Oland's brewery in Dartmouth, was elected as a captain in 1913. All of Abram Paul's three sons would assume increasingly important roles within the leadership of the Halifax County Band. Later they and their families would heed the call of Chief Joseph Julien and move to Millbrook. Big Peter Paul meanwhile remained at Shubenacadie, where he died on 3 March 1930.

207 NSM, Printed Matter File, "Jeremiah Bartlett-Alexis, election platform for 192_," 18 June 1921.

208 NSM, Printed Matter File, Piers Notes of 31 December 1917, "Micmac Indians and the Halifax Disaster of 6 December 1917."

209 Among others, Isaac Cope's son Louis died and Jeremiah Bartlett-Alexis lost two daughters. Whitehead, *The Old Man Told Us*, 34.

210 LAC, RG 10, vol. 3160, file 363-417-1, "Colchester County Band Council Resolution to accept Members of the Halifax County band," 18 June 1919.

211 William John Stevens, born to John Stevens (or Stephens) and Mary McDonald in 1896, was originally from Point Tupper, Cape Breton, and moved to Truro after 1915. He first married nineteen-year-old Mary Jane Cope on 23 July 1917 in Truro. A witness to their marriage was Mary Jane's aunt, Mary Bell Cope. NSARM, Historical Vital Statistics, Colchester County Marriages,

Registration Year 1917, Book 44, 194. The couple had one son, John Joseph Stevens. Mary Jane Cope was the daughter of Christiana Toney and John Cope Jr., a son in turn of John Noel Cope and Fanny Doucet of Sheet Harbour. When Mary Jane Cope died shortly after John Joseph was born, William Stevens married Annie Gloade and had three more children. William died in his early thirties. The author is indebted to Mary Jane Stevens of the Mainland Confederacy of Mi'kmaq at Millbrook for this information.

212 LAC, RG 10, vol. 3220, file 536-764-1, "Bury to Indian Affairs," 1 May 1919; ibid., "Bury to Indian Affairs," 30 May 1919. Bury's letter of 1 May 1919 contains a recommendation to centralize the Mi'kmaq. Documents pertaining to Millbrook's land base are housed in TARR Centre, UNSI, 92-1004-19-032, "Profile of Truro – Millbrook IR 27, 27A, 27B and 27C" (TARR Centre, File 92-1004-19-033 also contains a profile of the Millbrook reserve); LAC, RG 10, vol. 3220, file 536-764-1, "Correspondence between Chief Julien, H.P. Bury and the department of Indian Affairs, Ottawa, regarding purchase of the Creelman property."

213 One member of this family was Samuel Creelman (1808–91), a farmer and justice of the peace from Upper Stewiacke. Although he and his wife, Elizabeth Elliott Ellis, had no children, he would have been a relative, probably an uncle, of Henry Creelman of Truro. His paternal grandfather, who came from Ireland, was the patriarch of a fairly large Creelman clan. A staunch Presbyterian, Samuel Creelman advocated temperance and education and was on the board of trustees for the Truro Academy. He became involved in mining and writing historical studies in addition to farming, and was a prominent shareholder in two woollen mills, the Mulgrave Woolen Mills at Newton Mills and the Hopewell Woolen Mills. Bonnie Huskins, "Creelman, Samuel," *Dictionary of Canadian Biography online*, vol. 12 (1891–1900). In 1842 Joseph Howe contacted Creelman to search out a good spot for a Mi'kmaw settlement near Truro, to which Creelman replied that there was land in Colchester County between Stewiacke and Pictou that would be suitable. NSARM, RG 1, vol. 432, 153–5, "Samuel Creelman to Joseph Howe," 9 December 1842. This area lies south of the tract where Sandy Cope Sr. had his hunting territory, once he settled at Millbrook. The Mi'kmaq must have felt comfortable pitching their dwellings on Creelman land, for in 1888 wigwams were set up on a Creelman property at what is now 5 Braemar Drive, Dartmouth.

214 LAC, RG 10, vol. 3220, file 536-764-1, "Bury to J.D. McLean," 11 August 1919.

215 NSARM, RG1, vol. 430, doc. 26½. This licence of occupation was given, and signed, by provincial secretary Richard Bulkeley on 17 June 1784.

216 See, for instance, LAC, RG 10, vol. 3160, file 363-471-1, "Petition of Lewis Paul and others for monies from Ship Harbour reserve," 21 June 1916. The same file also contains "A response dated 20 April 1918 from A.P. Boyd to John D. [Denny] Paul and Louis Paul of Grand Lake Reserve relating to a release of funds from this source." Indian Affairs' ability to gain Mi'kmaw agreement with both a land purchase and a land cession on the same day testifies to the degree of preparation and strategic manoeuvring the government undertook in the weeks prior to the 18 June 1919 meeting.

217 Martin Sack may have been willing to sign because the Sack family had only slight interest in the Ship Harbour, Sambro, or Ingraham's River reserves. Martin's father, Louis Sack, was born at Panuke Lake, spent time on Prince Edward Island (where Martin was born), and lived for a while in Cumberland County, where Martin's brother Joseph Sack was born. Martin's mother, Matilda Morris, came from Panuke Lake. According to federal census lists for 1891 and 1921, Martin was born in 1876 and his wife, Mary Jane Howe, in 1886. Mary Jane was a daughter of Joseph H. Howe Sr. The federal census of 1921 listed Martin and Mary Jane Howe as having ten children: Louis (b.1903), Alfreda (b.1906), Freeman (b.1908), Isaac (b.1909), Josie (b.1910), Clarence (b.1913), Peter (b.1915), Leo (b.1917), Mary (b.1920), and Harvie (b.1914). Martin rarely visited Sheet Harbour where his in-laws lived, though his uncle Isaac Sack lived for a few years at Sheet Harbour after marrying Bridget Anne Cope, a daughter of Frank Cope and Mary Ann Quigley.

218 Daniel N. Paul provides a critique of these cessions in *We Were Not the Savages*, 230–3. In 2004 Daniel Paul's brother, Chief Lawrence Paul of Millbrook, spearheaded a surrender claim under Canada's specific claims policy with regard to these lands. A specific claim pertaining to these lands is still outstanding with Ottawa.

219 LAC, RG 10, vol. 3160, file 363–417-1, "Acceptance by Chief Joseph Julien of 15 families, or between 53 and 55 individuals, belonging to the Halifax County band onto the Colchester Reserve," 18 August 1919.

220 An examination of the consequences of the triennial electoral system on the Nova Scotia Mi'kmaq, as well as the reasons for the grand chief's exemption from it, is provided in Martha Elizabeth Walls, *No Need of a Chief for This Band: The Maritime Mi'kmaq and Federal Electoral Legislation, 1899–1951* (Vancouver: University of British Columbia Press, 2011).

221 NSM, Printed Matter File, Piers Papers, Ethnology, Correspondence with the Department of Indian Affairs, "Draft petition by Harry Piers, Mi'kmaw Response to the Deposition of Jacob Gilby;" Ibid., "Jerry Lone Cloud to MacLean, Indian Affairs," 6 July 1916. The Mi'kmaq argued that they had occupied the Elmsdale site along the Shubenacadie River for at least 100 years, and that oral testimonies collected between 1916 and 1919 from elderly residents, particularly Noel Phillips and Joseph Howe Sr., could prove it. NSM, Printed Matter File, Piers Papers, Ethnology, Correspondence with the Department of Indian Affairs, "Lone Cloud to MacLean, Deputy Superintendent of Indian Affairs," 17 July 1916; "Martin Sack to H.J. Bury," 18 January 1919. They also claimed that maps dated as early as 1818, as well as Geological Survey Map No. 66, designated the spot as a reserve, though Ottawa later determined the information in these maps to be erroneous. LAC, RG 10, vol. 3119, file 327–352, "Indian Affairs' response to Martin Sack *et al.*, 1916." When their bid to long possession failed, in June of 1919 the Elmsdale Mi'kmaq petitioned H. P. Bury on 21 June 1919 to encourage Ottawa to purchase the lot. LAC, RG 10, vol. 3119, file 3278, 352. Among the petitioners were Joseph Howe Sr., Newel Phillips, Louis Peters and Noel Hammond. NSM, Printed Matter File, Piers Papers, Correspondence with the Department of Indian Affairs, "Martin Sack to Bury,"18 January 1919. Jeremiah Bartlett-Alexis (Jerry Lonecloud) then petitioned Ottawa to intervene to keep the Tufts Cove settlement secure in the Mi'kmaq's possession, on the grounds of the Mi'kmaq's long occupation of the harbour site. NSM, Printed Matter File, Piers Papers, Ethnology, Correspondence with the Department of Indian Affairs, "Regarding Mr. Farnell's claim to Tuft's Cove land," 27 November 1917; "Jerry Lone Cloud to Indian Affairs, n.d.'; "MacLean to Bury regarding Musgrave's claim to have timber damaged on his property by Mi'kmaq and the need to compensate him for injury," 5 March 1918; LAC, RG 10, vol. 3160, file 363-417-1, "F.A. Trueman's inquiry about leasing or purchasing the Sambro reserve in the spring of 1919;" LAC, RG 10, vol. 3160, file 363-417-1, "Memorandum, Indian Affairs," 28 March 1918; NSM, Printed Matter File, Piers Papers, "Lone Cloud to MacLean, Deputy Superintendent of Indian Affairs," 3 June 1919. As early as 1886 the province had turned covetous eyes on what it deemed "unoccupied reserves," but the Halifax County Indian agent at the time, the Reverend A.P. Desmond, had responded that lands in Halifax County still furnished fish for Mi'kmaw weirs, though perhaps in drastically reduced numbers, and that local

forests provided wood for making baskets and wooden implements. But when buyers again appeared on the horizon after the war, no agent championed the retention of the reserves. In 1918 235 Mi'kmaq were enumerated in Halifax County, and 86 of these were listed as living off-reserve as "squatters" on private property. These numbers suggest that 149 Mi'kmaq still lived on reserves in Halifax County – an exceedingly high number given the government's determination to rid itself of these reserves. In the end, Bury cared little for such figures anyway, since he came to hold that monies from the sale of yet more reserves could be placed at the disposal of Indian Affairs administrators, who then would oversee the shepherding of Mi'kmaw groups onto two or, at the most, three locales. By 1929 Bury stipulated that he felt only three reserves, Millbrook, Shubenacadie and Whycocomagh, had enough farmland to allow this to happen effectively. LAC, RG 10, vol. 3220, file 536-764-1.

222 Tobin, "The Effect of Centralization," 34, 55. Tobin notes that Chief Julien retained a strong discriminatory control over band membership, allowing numbers to rise only as the land base was able demographically to sustain them without difficulty. In another ten years even Bury admired the way the Truro community had developed, and thought if such could be done at Millbrook, why not at other growth centres? Bury's motives, however, were far different from those of Chief Julien, who placed the interests of his people above financial or, at times, even personal considerations.

223 Ibid., 55.

224 Paul, *We Were Not the Savages*, 309.

225 NSARM, RG 10, vol. 3220, 536-764-1, "Bury to Indian Affairs," 2 January 1924.

226 The Rockingham group had a stable population during the summer months, but as it was largely composed of transient peddlers who met in the Bedford-Rockingham area to sell baskets and other wooden wares, its population dissipated before winter set in. Meanwhile, Millbrook in 1921 was held to contain 126 individuals. LAC, RG 10, vol. 2520, File 10,000, Part 7, microfilm reel C-11,233, "Census of Mi'kmaq in Nova Scotia in 1921, broken down by county and totalling 1943 persons."

227 Martin Sack (1876–1962) was the son of Louis Sack and Matilda Morris. Louis Sack in turn was a son of Peter Sack and Marie-Antoinette Thomas, who lived with Peter Cope Jr.'s group at Red Bridge in the 1860s. NSARM, Vital Statistics, Halifax County Deaths, Registration Year 1962, 5318. Martin Sack and his brother-in-law Bert Howe initially wanted to purchase their own plots of land in fee simple, to which Ottawa would agree only if

they accepted enfranchisement. Unwilling to lose their legal Aboriginal status, Sack and Howe remained at Elmsdale until the government forced them to relocate to Shubenacadie. LAC, RG 10, vol. 3119, file 327-352, "MacLean to Boyd," 6 July 1926; ibid., "Boyd regarding Elmsdale Mi'kmaq," 16 November 1926; ibid., "Report of local Indian Agent Maxner," 12 July 1930; ibid., "Departmental Memorandum of 16 July 1930"; ibid., "Maxner to Indian Affairs," 29 September 1930. Martin Sack became a councillor of the Shubenacadie band under Chief John Maloney on 28 August 1933, and again on 28 March 1945 during the administration of Chief Stephen Knockwood.

228 Bert Howe Sr., born in 1898 to Joseph Howe Sr. (christened with the name Joseph Jeremy) and Emma (or Mary Jane) Hammond, was the great-grandson of Chief John Jeremy of Queens County. In 1841 Chief Jeremy was head man of a Mi'kmaw settlement at Kejimkujik Lake, Queens County. He petitioned Indian superintendent Joseph Howe for land at Kejimkujik for a reserve, which he received in 1843. His first wife was Sally Toney and the couple had a son, John Jeremy Jr., and a daughter, Marie Oceola (or Usule). *Journals of the Legislative Assembly of Nova Scotia*, 1844, Appendix 50, "Report on Indian Affairs by Joseph Howe," 123–8. John Jeremy Jr. stayed in Queens County after his father left the region around 1850 to move to Elmsdale. John Jeremy Sr.'s second wife was simply known as "Mary." One of this couple's daughters, Mary Jeremy born around 1848, in 1876 wed John Jadis, a son of James Jadis of Windsor and Mary Paul. Mary was a widow in her late thirties when she became Jadis's second wife. NSARM, Historical Vital Statistics, Halifax County Marriages, Registration Year 1876, Book 1823, p. 101, no. 95. John Jeremy Sr. also had children by a third wife, Susie Phillips, a granddaughter of Chief Philip Bernard of St. Margaret's Bay. After the Kejimkujik Lake Mi'kmaw farming community dispersed, one of John Jeremy and Susie's sons, Joseph (c.1844–1936), moved with his parents to Elmsdale and was given the name "Joseph Howe" because his father admired Joseph Howe, the politician and journalist. This man, who became known as "Joseph Howe Sr.," married three times. He and his first wife "Katie" had a son named Abram Jeremy Howe who married Harriet Paul in 1894. NSARM, Historical Vital Statistics, Queens County Marriages, Registration Year 1894, Book 1834, p. 169, no. 2. His second wife was Emma (Mary Jane) Hammond from New Germany, and the couple had six children: Joseph Howe Jr. (1881–1958), born at Port Williams on 24 November 1881; Francis at Elmsdale in 1883; Elizabeth in 1894; Mary Jane in 1895; Lena in 1887; and Albert Noel in 1898. The 1891 federal

census lists "Joseph H. Jerime" as forty years old, living at Elmsdale with his wife (Mary) Jane (Hammond) who was twenty-seven. According to his death certificate, Joseph Howe Sr. died at age ninety-four at Millbrook on 27 November 1936. Although this implies he was born in 1842, he may have been born a few years later, since his father John Jeremy was still married to Sarah Toney in 1842 and Joseph's mother's name is listed as "Susie Phillips." The 1891 federal census, which states that he was born in 1851, is probably more accurate. His death certificate states that he married "Lucy M. Howe," who would have been his third wife. NSARM, Historical Vital Statistics, Colchester County Deaths, Registration Year 1936, Book 157, 1533. His son, Joseph Howe Jr., born in Lunenburg County in 1881, wed Elizabeth or "Lizzy" Cope and lived at New Germany and Petit Rivière. They had two children, Joseph and Irene, before Joseph Jr. died at Shubenacadie on 26 April 1958. NSARM, Historical Vital Statistics, Hants County Deaths, Registration Year 1958, 2940. His son Joseph, who continued to live at Shubenacadie, wed Rose Mahoney Basque and had a son, Everett John Howe, on 2 August 1908, as well as a daughter, Josephine. Both children married in 1934; Everett John wed Bridget Ann Maloney of Shubenacadie, and Josephine married Joseph Cope, a son of Frank Cope and Susan Marble of Halifax County who also was a grandson of Joseph Charles Cope of Enfield. NSARM, Historical Vital Statistics, Hants County Marriages, Registration Year 1934, Book 71, 80; Registers of St. Bernard's Church, Enfield.

Mary Jane Howe, Joseph Howe Sr.'s daughter born in 1895, married Martin Sack, the son of Louis Sack and Matilda Morris. In 1908 Martin Sack and Mary Jane baptized a son, Joseph Sack, at St. Bernard's Church in Enfield. The sponsors were Louis Newel (or Noel) and Elizabeth Jeremy. Baptismal Registers of St. Bernard's Church, Enfield. Elizabeth Jeremy (who later became Mrs. Elizabeth Cope) died at Shubenacadie in 1933 at age thirty-nine. NSARM, Historical Vital Statistics, Halifax County (Elmsdale) Deaths, Registration Year 1933, Book 146, 219. Her brother, Noel Albert ("Bert") Howe, who married Mary Paul, moved to Sheet Harbour in 1930. The couple owned a frame house, a log cabin, a barn, a horse, and a plough and cultivated potatoes, corn, beans, squash, and hay on the north side of Sheet Harbour below Church Point. In the winters Bert worked as a lumberman. Mi'kmaw families often set up camps on a hill on his property and harvested wood to make baskets and wooden items. By the mid-1940s Bert and Mary had fourteen children. In 2014 one of Bert's sons, James Howe, and his wife Florella recounted to the author that "Albert Noel Howe and Mary

Paul had four boys and 10 girls, Annie, Flossie, Pauline, Douglas, Donnie, Albert Michael Jr., Blanche, Dorothy, Marlene, Roxie, James, Laverne Cecelia [who died at ten years of age in 1954], and two others whose names we don't know." Interview with James and Florella Howe, Sheet Harbour Reserve No. 36, 15 June 2014. It also was said that Bert Howe discouraged the younger generation from learning the Mi'kmaw language and stressed schooling and hard work, though his descendants continued to express an interest in learning about Mi'kmaw history. There are some interesting parallels that can be drawn between the experiences of Charles Phillips and Meggie Cope on the Cole Harbour reserve and the situation Bert Howe Jr. and Mary Paul faced at Sheet Harbour. Both families farmed, both resisted going to Shubenacadie during the Centralization Era, both proved feisty enough to prevent the loss of their reserve lands, and both, as a somewhat unforeseen consequence of their feistiness, ended up after 1958 on the band list for Millbrook rather than on the list for Shubenacadie. Bert Howe's son Douglas wed Eleanor Henderson. See NSARM, Historical Vital Statistics, Halifax County (Sheet Harbour) Deaths, Registration Year 1958, 5303, "Death of infant Gordon Howe, son of Douglas Howe and Eleanor Henderson," 29 September 1958. And two of Bert's daughters married sons of Thomas Henry Asprey. Asprey, born in Halifax shortly after his parents' arrival from England, wed Helen Gerrier and had twenty-three children. Among them were John Asprey, who married Blanche Howe, and Ronnie Asprey, who wed Blanche's sister Roxie. Blanche and her husband lived on the south side of Sheet Harbour, although several of their children later moved to Beaverdam along the Sheet Harbour Road (Route 224). Today the Beaverdam settlement encompasses several houses lining the north side of the Sheet Harbour Road. The lake side of the highway has been ceded. The author is indebted to Carla Asprey of the Native Council of Nova Scotia, and a resident of Beaverdam, for this information.

229 H.P. Bury claimed that twelve families had moved to Truro from Windsor Junction before 1935. Some of these were likely Joseph Cope and Sarah Tracey's offspring. LAC, RG 10, vol. 3220, file 536-764-1, "General Report from H.J. Bury to Dr. McGill," 18 June 1935.

230 LAC, RG 10, vol. 3119, file 327-352, "Memo of 1919."

231 LAC, RG 10, vol. 3160, file 363-417-1, "Census of Mi'kmaq Relocating," 9 July 1919.

232 Tobin, "The Effect of Centralization," 72.

233 William G. Paul, "Oral Tradition," in *Mi'kmaq Past and Present: A Resource Guide*, Session 5 (Halifax: Department of Education, 1993), 18.

234 LAC, RG 10, vol. 3160, file 363-417-1, "Regarding acceptance of Peter Googoo and family," 21 June 1920; ibid., "Letter from J.D. MacLean regarding Peter Googoo's residency on old part of reserve," 2 July 1920.

235 Information courtesy of Gary Meagher of Senora. This Mi'kmaw cemetery was bulldozed.

236 LAC, RG 10, vol. 3220, file 536,764, "Petition of Michael Tom and Stephen [John] Knockwood," 21 April 1920.

237 The late Edith Jane Thomas, a daughter of Michael Thomas of Millbrook, ran a craft store and basket shop at Millbrook with the late Basil Peters. Carrie Gloade and Janet Chute in conversation with Basil Peters, Millbrook, July 1911; Kluscap/Glooscap Heritage Centre newsletter, Millbrook, Truro, July 2012.

238 These terms were from March 1945 to March 1948; from March 1948 to March 1951; and from April 1954 to April 1956.

239 NSARM, RG 1, vol. 189, 454–5, "Minutes of the Executive Council," 28 June 1779. Official transcript in NSARM, RG 1, vol. 212, 563. In 1770 Lord Egmont had received a grant of three thousand acres on the Shubenacadie River that was later escheated. There is also a reference to this application entitled "Regarding a tract of land four miles square ordered to be granted to Mr. Francklin and Paul Pemmeyweete on the Stewiac [*sic*, Stewiacke] River, 28 January 1779" in Miscellaneous "I" Indian Land Records, photocopied in the 1970s under the auspices of Dr. Bruce Fergusson, provincial archivist. These records, though unidentified as to provenance, come from the Office of the Attorney General and the Department of Crown Lands.

240 NSARM, RG 1, vol. 430, doc. 26½.

241 LAC, RG 10, vol. 7758, file 27047, "Chief Julien to Crown Lands Department," Ottawa, 30 July 1919. The surveyor, Isaac Archibald, was convinced in 1861 that he could run a more accurate line for the southern boundary of the Peminout grant that existed on prior survey maps of the grant, and so he deviated from the south line that most of the settlers occupying the tract believed was best suited to their purposes. There consequently were many settler disputes over property lines in the years before Confederation. The original survey map by Archibald, dated 25 March 1861, is found in LAC, RG 10, vol. 460, 28–31. A second map of Middle Stewiacke by Archibald dated 12 September 1867 and showing the grant is in NSARM RG 20, Series C, "Deputy Surveyors' Correspondence," vol. 17.

242 LAC, RG 10, vol. 7758, file 27047, "Joseph Julien to H.R. Bury, Timber Inspector for Indian Affairs," 3 January 1920.

243 LAC, RG 10, vol. 7758, file 27047, "J.D. MacLean, Assistant Deputy Superintendent of Indian Affairs, to F.A. Harrison, Deputy Commissioner of Crown Lands," 28 January 1920; ibid., "Harrison to MacLean," 2 February 1920; ibid., "MacLean to A.G. Doughty, Dominion Archivist," 10 February 1920; ibid., "Maclean to Harrison," 12 February 1920; ibid., "MacLean to Joseph Julien," 13 February 1920; NSARM, MG 15, vol.18, doc. 19, "W. Falkner's Report relating to Indian reserve, Stewiacke River, Recd. 27 Jany. 1857'; LAC, RG 10, vol. 460, 258–63, "Faulkner's map of Middle Stewiacke, 20 January 1857"; LAC RG 10, vol. 460, 258–63, "William Faulkner to Uniacke," 20 January 1857.

244 Since Mi'kmaq from Shubenacadie and Millbrook, some of them descended from Peminout Paul, hunted in the Stewiacke region into the twentieth century, information concerning the fate of the Stewiacke grant lingered in oral traditions. Joseph Julien certainly would have heard these stories. In 1981 Chief Stanley Johnson of Millbrook, drawing on Julien's earlier research, submitted a claim for the Middle Stewiacke land for consideration by the Department of Indian and Northern Affairs. In 2010 this claim was denied by Ottawa, partly on the grounds that it constituted a pre-Confederation claim, although interest in it remains within the Millbrook community.

245 John Denny Paul's son Stephen later would give two Mi'kmaw Bibles, one written in hieroglyphics that was around 150 years old, and a second about 50 years old that belonged to John Denny Paul's grandfather Andrew Paul, to the Tatamagouche Museum in Pictou County. NSARM, Mics. Files, "Micmac: Writing."

246 See table 3.9 in Tobin, "The Effect of Centralization," 104.

247 This information was taken from NAC, RG 10, vol. 7934, file 32-471, Records from the Colchester County Agency, comprising Truro and Millbrook Reserves, as well as from records housed in the Beaton Institute, Cape Breton University, Sydney, Cape Breton, Report #100 MRC 98-100-454, entitle, "Names of Chiefs, Various N.S. Bands, 1906–1971."

248 Harold Gloade refers to Chief Julien's living in the Creelman house at Millbrook in 1927. Harold Gloade, *From My Vantage Point* (Napean, ON: Borealis, 1991), 48.

249 Gloade, *From My Vantage Point*, 48.

250 The final change came in 1889. Towards the end of February of that year the Chebucto hockey team went to Montreal to play two games and lost both. As the Montreal (or Canadian) rules were different from those in the Maritimes, one half of each game was played under Maritime rules. After the return of the Chebuctos, the hockey game was changed to conform to the Canadian style. The rubber puck was introduced, and Mi'kmaq began making a stick handle with square edges instead of a rounded handle. Brian Cuthbertson, "The Starr Manufacturing Company, State Exporter for the World," *Journal of the Royal Nova Scotia Historical Society* 89 (2005): 60–3; Martin, *The Story of Dartmouth*, 427.

251 Conversation with Donald Julien, July 2014. Hockey stick manufacturing became industrialized around 1930, at which time "Mic Mac Sticks" were no longer made or sold. But memories of earlier days lingered. Don Julien stated that, even after his grandfather's death in 1957, Oland trucks would drive past the Julien house on the Creelman property and honk their horns in greeting to resident family members. Joseph C. Cope, who resided briefly at Millbrook in the early 1940s, promoted ice hockey as a distinctly Mi'kmaw invention. In a letter he sent to the *Halifax Herald* from Millbrook in 1943 in which he identified himself as "Old Joseph Cope, boxer, musician and hockey stick carver," he claimed that long before Europeans came to North America, the Mi'kmaq had a game known as *oochamlunutk* that could be played either on ice or on a field. Cope knew that hockey teams from the Royal Military College and Queens University in Kingston had vied against one another since 1879, and he referred to the modern form of ice hockey they played as *Achamadyuk*. Cope then stressed that hockey did not begin in Kingston, but rather among his own people, who played the game on ice with a ball. Garth Vaughan, www.birthplaceofhockey.com, 1999; Patrick Robertson, "The First Hockey on Ice," in *Robertson's Book of Firsts: Who Did What for the First Time* (London: Bloomsbury, 2011), entries arranged alphabetically. Although the Mi'kmaw author of the 1943 letter identified himself only by his surname, Joseph C. Cope was almost certainly the author, since the only other candidate, Joseph Cope, the husband of Sarah Tracey, died in 1936. NSARM, Historical Vital Statistics, Halifax County Deaths, Book 164, no. 340. Raymond Cope, a son of Alex Cope Jr. and Matilda Noel, and Sandy Julien, Joseph Julien's son born in 1917, were of roughly the same age and both good hockey players. They played for McClures Mills Hockey Team in the 1950s and later with the Truro Bearcats, representing the town of Truro with the Senior Hockey League. Most of the younger generation of Juliens and Copes, as well as many others from the Millbrook community, still regularly play hockey. Sandy Julien died at ninety-five years of age on 29 September 2012. Among his many recognitions and honours, Sandy Julien was made an honorary member of the Windsor Hockey Heritage Society.

252 Googoo, "Story of Joseph Julian," 6. The first trophy was for the Nova Scotia Indian Hockey Playoffs, while the second was for the Mainland Nova Scotia Indian Hockey Playoff Champs.

253 Noel Gloade and Rose Beatrice McKay married in Annapolis County in 1920. NSARM, Historical Vital Statistics, Annapolis County Marriages, Registration Year 1920, Book 1, 779. Noel was forty-eight at the time. His father, Abraham Glode Jr., and William Thomas Gloade's father, also Noel Gloade, were related. Noel Gloade's father married Nancy Jeremy and Tom's father married Anastasia Vicaire. Harold Gloade, who worked in the construction industry most of his life, travelled from Windsor, Ontario, to Texas and back. He later wrote two books of memories from his younger years and became the Grand Council captain for Horton, known as Glooscap or Pesikitk. He died at Port Hope, Ontario, in 2010.

254 Sandy Cope Sr. died at Truro at age seventy-six on 15 March 1930. NSARM, Historical Vital Statistics, Colchester County Deaths, Registration Year 1930, Book 119, 1052.

255 Harold Gloade, *From My Vantage Point*, 47–8.

256 Ibid., 48.

257 Ibid., 49.

258 Tobin, "The Effect of Centralization," 34.

259 John Denny Paul, who served as chief of the Halifax County band in 1916, died of stomach cancer while visiting Halifax in 1924. NSARM, Historical Vital Statistics, Halifax County Deaths, Registration Year 1924, Book 84, 401; NSARM, Historical Vital Statistics, Colchester County Deaths, Registration Year 1944, Book 212, 514.

260 Bridget Ann Sack was a daughter of Isaac Sack and Annie Cope; she married three times. She first wed Noel Thomas Nicholas, who was born in Eskasoni, in 1904. Peter J. Wilmot and Mary Clark were witnesses at their wedding. NSARM, Historical Vital Statistics, Hants County Marriages, Registration Year 1904, Book 1824, p. 74, no. 89. In 1909, a twenty-one-year-old widow, she wed Simon Basque and had several children, among them Max Basque who was interviewed by ethnohistorian Ruth Holmes Whitehead during the 1970s and 1980s. NSARM, Historical Vital Statistics, Hants County Marriages, Registration Year 1909, Book 1821, p. 11, no. 21. Her third husband was William Thomas Gloade of Millbrook. Tom Gloade was sixty-two and Bridget Sack was forty-four at the time of their wedding, which took place on 22 June 1931 at Indian Brook, Shubenacadie. NSARM, Historical Vital Statistics, Hants County Marriages, Registration Year 1931, Book 63, 192. Tom Gloade lived with Bridget at Indian Brook until his death in 1934. NSARM, Historical Vital Statistics, Hants County Deaths, Registration Year 1934, Book 146, 432. Bridget's mother, Anne Cope, was a descendant of Doadaran Cope and Molly, and her father, Isaac Sack, was a son of Peter Sack and Marie-Antoinette Thomas. Isaac died in 1930. NSARM, Historical Vital Statistics, Hants County Deaths, Registration Year 1930, Book 124, 948.

261 Googoo, "Story of Joseph Julien," 4. Church of the Sacred Heart belongs to the Parish of the Immaculate Conception.

262 Peter Wilmot died at age 108 at his son Charles Wilmot's home at Millbrook on 27 December 1932 (although journalist Clara Archibald Dennis claimed incorrectly that he was 106 years old at his death). *Halifax Herald*, 27 October 1932, 3; NSM, Printed Matter File, Piers unpublished notes, "Handwritten obituary of Ex-Chief Peter Wilmot by Harry Piers," 23 December 1932; NSARM, Historical Vital Statistics, Colchester County Deaths, Registration Year 1932, Book 157, 304; Ruth Holmes Whitehead, "Wilmot, Peter," *Dictionary of Canadian Biography* online, vol. 16 (1931–40).

263 There is a photograph of this group at Wilmot's funeral service in the Dennis Collection, accession no. 73.186.674, in the Nova Scotia Museum, Halifax.

264 Googoo, "Story of Joseph Julien," 4.

265 Emma Battell Lowman and Adam J. Barker, *Settler: Identity and Colonialism in 21st Century Canada*. (Halifax: Fernwood, 2015), 48.

266 Lisa Lynne Patterson, "Indian Affairs and the Nova Scotia Centralization Policy" (master's thesis, Dalhousie University, 1985), chap. 2.

267 W.S. Arneil, *Investigative Report on Indian Reserves and Indian Administration, Province of Nova Scotia, Indian Affairs Branch* (Ottawa: Department of Mines and Resources, August 1941), 4; Fred Wien (assisted by Donald Julien), *Rebuilding the Economic Base of Indian Communities: The Micmac in Nova Scotia* (Montreal: Institute for Research on Public Policy, 1986), 31–3.

268 Paul, *We Were Not the Savages*, 282.

269 Michael Isaac Sack also harkened to Chief Joseph Julien's call to join Millbrook in 1919. Michael married Mary Elizabeth Silliboy at Millbrook in 1934. NSARM, Historical Vital Statistics, Registration Year 1934, Colchester County Marriages, Book 75, 980. Henry Sack in turn was the son of Isaac Sack and Ann Cope and the grandson of Peter Sack and Marie-Antoinette Thomas. Martin Sack (1876–1962), Isaac Sack's nephew, was the son of Louis Sack and Matilda Morris. Louis also had a son, Joseph Russell Sack (1879–1954). NSARM, Historical Vital Statistics, Registration Year 1934, 99000134.

270 Googoo, "Story of Joseph Julien," 5; Patterson, "Indian Affairs and the Nova Scotia Centralization Policy," 100.

271 Daniel Paul, referring to his early days as a boy at Shubenacadie living in one of these houses, wrote that on cold winter nights he remembered "a considerable frost build-up around where my nose was sticking out of the blankets." Paul, *We Were Not the Savages*, 280.

272 Patterson notes that Joseph C. Cope denounced the centralization policy in a letter he wrote to the Department of Indian Affairs on 29 January 1943. Cope was joined by angry Mi'kmaw voices from Cumberland County, Pictou Landing, Cambridge in Kings County, and especially Ben Christmas at Membertou and Margaret Phillips at Cole Harbour. Patterson, "Indian Affairs and the Nova Scotia Centralization Policy," 65.

273 Ibid., 66–74; LAC, RG 10, vol. 7625, file 17050 (1); LAC, RG 10, vol. 7625, file 17051; LAC, RG 10, vol. 7758, file 27,050-pt 2. Also see Paul, *We Were Not the Savages*, 280–81.

274 In 1942 Wilfred Burchell maintained his own law office. The present law firm of Burchell MacDougall was founded in Truro, Nova Scotia, in 1944 by Wilfred Burchell and R. Lorne MacDougall. In 1984 the firm opened its office in Halifax. Wilfred Burchell probably came to know Joseph Julien well through the local hockey scene, as both men enjoyed hockey.

275 "To the Honourable Thomas Alexander Crerar, Minister of Mines and Resources, Ottawa from W. Burchell," 4 July 1942. Draft copy of letter housed in the archives of the Confederacy of Mainland Mi'kmaq, Millbrook, Truro.

276 Ibid., 2.

277 Government officials held that at the height of the economic depression, 24 families at Millbrook were on relief. Yet the centralization program had not worked either, for 271 out of Shubenacadie's 816 families were also on relief. Paul, *We Were Not the Savages*, 287–8.

278 Millbrook with its tradition of sound leadership "bounced back after the long hard struggle with hard times." Gloade, *From My Vantage Point*, 150. The military services and the army base at Debert built during the war offered employment, while new positions arose in Truro as the younger generation gained new skills.

279 "Remembering a Leader," 10.

280 Ibid.

281 LAC, RG 14, D 4, Records of Parliament, House of Commons, Commission on Indian Affairs, 1946; LAC, RG 14, D 4, Records of Parliament, House of Commons, Commission on Indian Affairs, 1949, "Letter to the Commission from Chief Joseph Julien and Council, Millbrook," 1949; Tobin, "The Effect of Centralization on the Social and Political Systems of the Mainland Nova Scotia," 106.

282 LAC, RG 10, vol. 8494, file 50 (3–5), TARR Centre, Shubenacadie, UNSI (copies of files from the Union of Nova Scotia Indians housed at TARR) file 92-1004-09-010; Tobin, "The Effect of Centralization," 68.

283 The populations of Cole Harbour, Sheet Harbour, and Beaverdam reserves apparently approached Millbrook to administer their programs and services. Cole Harbour reserve is located on Caldwell Road in Dartmouth, near Eastern Passage. Sheet Harbour and Beaverdam are situated about fifty kilometres east of Musquodoboit. These reserves, along with the Millbrook lands proper in Truro, make up the Millbrook First Nation administration district.

284 Information on the railway allowance and the attainment of the 625.48-acre rifle range may be found at the TARR Centre, Shubenacadie, in UNSI, 92-1004-19-032, 9.

285 Ibid., 9; "Remembering a Leader," 10; Tobin, "The Effect of Centralization," 51.

286 NSARM, Historical Vital Statistics, Colchester County Deaths, Registration Year 1957, 1837. Funeral arrangements were presided over by Mattatall Funeral Home in Truro.

287 Rachel Marshall was the second woman to become a Mi'kmaw First Nation community chief in Nova Scotia. She was chief of Millbrook from 18 December 1969 to 18 December 1971.

288 The Annapolis Valley band later split into the Annapolis band and Horton band (now Glooscap First Nation), making twelve bands, while the General List evolved in 1968 into the Acadia band (now Acadia First Nation), making thirteen bands.

289 Two of William Gabriel Paul and Agnes Noel's sons, Lawrence Alexander Paul, who excelled in business and community development, and Daniel N. Paul, who is an author, administrator, contractor, historian, and educationalist, made Truro their home. Daniel Paul for many years was director of the Mainland Confederacy of Mi'kmaq. His brother Lawrence sat on the Shubenacadie band council prior to 1960, but in December 1969 became a councillor at Millbrook along with Joseph Julien's son Sandy. Lawrence later served twenty-eight years as Millbrook's chief. He died at seventy-nine years of age on 28 May 2014. "Obituary of Lawrence Alexander Paul," *Truro Daily News*, 29 May 2014.

290 "Aboriginal Business, Nova Scotia First Nations Rising to New Levels of Prosperity," *Chronicle Herald*, 23 August 2014, B10. This article focuses on recent business successes at Millbrook and Membertou, which coped with formidable challenges in the twentieth century to rise to prominence in the twenty-first.

correspondence were from Minas, La Have, and Cape Breton.

20 William Inglis Morse, ed., "Sojourn of *Gargas* in Acadie, 1687–1688," in *Acadiensia Nova (1598–1779)*, vol. 1, ed. William Inglis Morse, chap. 4 (London: Bernard Quartich, 1935), 1:181. The size of the Chignecto band fluctuated depending on the time of year the census takers arrived and whether there was a war in progress. The band had 80 members around 1650, a mere 21 in 1688 at the outset of the War of the League of Augsburg, 100 in 1708, and 86 in 1722. Band numbers rose as high as 152 in 1735. William C. Wicken, "Encounters with Tall Sails and Tall Tales: Mi'kmaq Society, 1500–1760" (PhD diss., McGill University, 1994), table 2.1. In 1708, the band was composed of twenty-two men, nine boys of fifteen years or older, twenty women, six elderly persons, twenty boys under fifteen years of age, and twenty-three girls, for a total of one hundred persons. Adult males and youths were categorized according to their ability to bear arms. The number of men and women between 1708 and 1722 (twenty-two men in 1708 and twenty-one men in 1722, and twenty women for both years) remain fairly steady, but the number of youths able to bear arms dropped between those years, evidently owing to casualties during the Mi'kmaw War from 1722 to 1725. In 1722 Gaulin enumerated twenty-one men, twenty women, thirteen boys of twelve years or older, sixteen boys under twelve, fourteen girls, and two elderly persons, for a total of eighty-six. Despite such variations, one can regard the Chignecto band as being of medium size, with the largest bands having over 150 individuals and the smallest around forty. With the onset of peace after 1725, the Mi'kmaw population at Chignecto began to grow. Documents from the Archives des colonies, Paris, France, on microfilm at LAC, AC CIIB 6: 77r, "Recensement des sauvages dans l'isle Royale," 27 December 1722; AN AC G1466, doc. 71, "Recensement fait cette presente année, 1735." It is difficult to determine the size of the Chignecto Mi'kmaw band in the early 1750s, however, since chiefs and their band members from Shubenacadie and southwestern Nova Scotia joined the ranks of Abbé Le Loutre's Mi'kmaw contingent at Beaubassin.

21 In 1701, the French at Montreal invited representatives of Iroquois-speaking and Algonquian-speaking nations to Montreal where a peace treaty was signed, ending the Iroquois Wars.

22 Chief Argim8's people resided at a crucial location along the major Mi'kmaw trade route that penetrated the interior by means of the Petitcodiac and Saint John rivers. Middlemen traders, both Indigenous and French, flocked to Beaubassin for furs. Furs were carried from the Quebec region (called "Canada" at the time) to Petitcodiac, across the Bay of Fundy, and along the coast of southwestern Nova Scotia to Pobomcoup, now East Pubnico, where the baron had his manor and trading centre. The baron presided over the shipment of furs and fish to France and the distribution of trade goods from his French suppliers to the French, Mi'kmaq, and *métis* involved in the trade. The fur-trading community was closely knit by kinship ties. Two of Baron Philippe d'Entremont's sons married daughters of Charles La Tour. His third son, Philippe II Mius d'Azy, consorted with two Mi'kmaw women in succession, with whom he had a large number of children. Several of these became commercial and political associates of Chief Argim8's grandson, Joseph Argimault.

23 Honorius Provost, "Baudoin, Jean," *Dictionary of Canadian Biography* online, vol. 1 (1000–1700).

24 Basing his thesis partly on comments made by La Valliere's father-in-law, Nicolas Denys, Alfred Goldsworthy Bailey in the 1930s argued that by 1700 the Mi'kmaq could no longer survive without European trade goods; their society became wholly dependent on the acquisition of such articles. Denys noted that the Mi'kmaq by 1670 used iron knives and spear points rather than bones ones, preferred copper kettles to cauldrons of hollowed-out tree trunks, ate many European foods, obtained guns and ammunition, and adopted items of European clothing such as cloth coats, hats, turbans, and skirts. Nicolas Denys, *The Description and Natural History of the Coast of North America (Acadia)*, ed. W.F. Ganong (Toronto: Champlain Society, 1908), 67–8; Alfred G. Bailey, *The Conflict of European and Eastern Algonquian Cultures, 1504–1700* (Toronto: University of Toronto Press, 1969), 54. The Chignecto band may not have fitted the dependency model well, however, since Chief Philippe Argimault made it clear to the French missionary Abbé Maillard that the Mi'kmaq retained enough aspects of their traditional skills and technology in the 1740s that they could exist, if necessary, without European trade goods.

25 LAC, MG 18, F18, typescript, 16.

26 Philippe Argimault was recognized as one of two chiefs at Beaubassin by 1722. This fact was confirmed by an entry in the birth registers at Beaubassin of one of his grandchildren. LAC, MG 9 B8, 1:19–21, "Baptism de Pierre Arghimont, fils de Joseph Arghimont, fils de Philippe Arghimont, chef des Sauvages de Beaubassin, et Marie sa femme," 1 May 1722. Abbé Antoine Gaulin, however, did not list Philippe as Beaubassin's head chief

in 1722, but instead accorded this status to Philippe's fellow chief, sixty-four-year-old Joseph Pedoujaeolet. LAC, MG 17, CIIB, vol. 6, doc. 77, Correspondance générale, Île Royale, *Recensement des Sauvages tam de l'isle Royalle que de la peninsula de l'acadie qui sont deserves par Les Missionaires de Seminaire des Missions etrangeres Etablis a Quebec fait par M. Gaulin, pretre Missionaire des Sauvages en 1722.* Joseph Pedoujaeolet in 1708 was fifty years old, with a wife, Françoise, who was fifty-one and two children, Louise who was fourteen and Jean who was seven. LAC, MG 18, F18, typescript, 16.

27 Frank G. Speck, "The Eastern Algonkian Wabanaki Confederacy," *American Anthropologist* 17 (1915): 498.

28 Olive Patricia Dickason, "Louisbourg and the Indians: A Study in Imperial Race Relations, 1713–1760," ms., archives of Fortress of Louisbourg Historic Park, 1972.

29 "Minutes of a Council held at Annapolis Royal," 5 January 1724, in Archibald MacMechan, ed., *Original Minutes of His Majesty's Council at Annapolis Royal, 1720–1739* (Halifax: McAlpine, 1908), 89–90.

30 British Records Office, London, England, Colonial Office Documents, on microfilm at Library and Archives Canada, Ottawa (henceforth LAC, CO) 217/4: 118, "Journal of Hibbert Newton" (a member of the Council at Annapolis Royal), 16 June 1722; LAC, CO 217/4: 119, "Journal of George Lapham," 26 June 1722.

31 Robert, *A Compendious History of the Southern Part of the Province of New Brunswick and the District of Gaspe, in Lower Canada* (Halifax: Printed by Joseph Howe, 1832), 136–7. "Argimoosh the Great Witch" is also mentioned in Bernard G. Hoffman, "The Historical Ethnography of the Micmac of the Sixteenth and Seventeenth Centuries" (PhD diss., University of California, 1955), 672.

32 This pact was a ratification made at Annapolis Royal of a treaty signed in Boston with the Eastern Abenaki the previous year. Joseph Pedoujaeolet was not present at the treaty signing. At sixty-eight years of age in 1726, he simply may not have wanted to make the long journey to Annapolis Royal, although he also may have died during the Mi'kmaw War.

33 According to an oral tradition circulating within the Elsipogtog (or Eel Ground) First Nation, *Siknikt* was assigned in a Mi'kmaw council to the "clan" of Argimault. This tradition also holds that in the eighteenth century "Misel Alguimou" was baptized as "Michel Augustine Argimault." Michel later dropped the Argimault surname and became "Michel Augustine." In 1761 he signed a peace and friendship treaty with the British on behalf of the Richibucto River band. See the Wikipedia article

on the Elsipogtog First Nation, https://en.wikipedia.org/wiki/Elsipogtog_First_Nation. The Mi'kmaw name for the Richibucto River, *L'sipuktuk* (or *Elsipotog*), of the *Siknikt* district approaches the meaning "River of Fire," although it is not a direct translation into English. The Richibucto reserve, large when established in 1802, has since been whittled away by settler encroachments.

34 Earle Lockerby, "Ancient Mi'kmaq Customs: A Shaman's Revelations," *Canadian Journal of Native Studies* 24 (2004): 403–20. Maillard wrote in French, and Lockerby's article presents an English translation of Arguimaut's (Argimault's) words to Maillard. See also Ruth Holmes Whitehead, *The Old Man Told Us: Excerpts from Micmac History 1500–1950* (Halifax: Nimbus, 1991), 10. Maillard assiduously wrote down Chief Philippe Argimault's descriptions, word for word, of how to manufacture moose skin canoes, fashion sandstone pots, knap stone arrowpoints, and deflect ravenous sharks while at sea in a canoe – making his account the earliest in which the reader can actually "hear" the voice of the Mi'kmaw speaker. Its passages have resonated with ethnographers, anthropologists, and archaeologists, as they cast revealing perspectives on Mi'kmaw life in an era before the Mi'kmaw population came to rely extensively on European trade goods or had their lands taken from them.

35 Pierre Maillard, "Lettre de M. L'Abbé Maillard sur les missions d'Acadie et particulierement sur les missions micmaques, Lettre à Madame de Drucourt," in *Les Soirees Canadiennes: Recueil de littérature nationale* (Quebec: Brousseau Frères, 1863), 3.300–6.

36 Janet E. Chute, "Ceremony, Social Revitalization and Change: Micmac Leadership and the Annual Festival of St. Anne," in *Papers of the 23rd Algonquian Conference,* ed. William Cowan (Ottawa: Carleton University Press, 1992), 141–61.

37 D. Wilson Wallis and Ruth Sawtell Wallis, *The Micmac Indians of Eastern Canada* (Minneapolis: University of Minnesota Press, 1955), 145.

38 Maillard, "Lettre de M. L'Abbé Maillard, 3.304.

39 This is a very ancient origin legend in the Northeast. In the early 1600s Samuel de Champlain noted the existence of a similar legend among the Northeast Algonquian, though not of the Mi'kmaq exclusively, which told of a ritual uniting of the sun and earth, and how the grass, trees, and people emerged from this union. Later, in the 1670s, while travelling among the Montagnais (southern Innu), Chretien Le Clercq recorded a similar story about the sun creating human beings. Chretien Le Clercq, *New Relation of Gaspesia,* ed. and trans. W.F. Ganong (Toronto: Champlain Society, 1910), 84–5.

40 LAC, MG 18, E29, Charlevoix Papers, "Discours des savages de l'acadie du governeur de l'Île Royale," 1720. For a discussion of this event, see William C. Wicken, *Mi'kmaq Treaties on Trial: History, Land and Donald Marshall Junior* (Toronto: University of Toronto Press, 2002), 125–6.

41 LAC, CO 217/3/155r–v, "Antoine et Pierre Couaret á Philipps, 2 octobre 1720."

42 Maillard had also heard another elderly *sagamow*, or chief, invoke the Sun Spirit just before the Mi'kmaq were heading out to battle, with these words: "[I]t is plain we are thy children, for we can know no origin but that which thy rays have given us, when first marrying efficaciously with the earth we inhabit, they impregnated its womb and caused to grow out of it like the herbs of the field and the trees of the forest, of which thou art equally the common father." Pierre Maillard, *An Account of the Customs and Manners of the Micmakis and Maricheets, Savage Nations ... Published and Written by a French Abbott* (London: S. Hooper and A. Morley, 1758), 25–8. This document was not signed, so Maillard is the *assumed* author.

43 Hoffman, "Historical Ethnography," 556.

44 A readable account of the development of this resistance movement under Joseph Broussard and Pierre II Surrette is found in Dianne Marshall, *Heroes of the Acadian Resistance: The Story of Joseph Beausoleil Broussard and Pierre II Surette, 1702–1765* (Halifax: Formac, 2011). The reference to the Capon-Gaudet incident is found on pages 10–11.

45 Marshall, *Heroes of the Acadian Resistance*, 30.

46 Le Loutre at first failed to obtain a licence from the English at Annapolis Royal for his mission, though this omission was rectified by 1743.

47 After 1744, French authorities distinguished between priests administering to Acadian parishes and those serving the Indigenous community. The former were to remain and to preach the need to be neutral, while the other were expected to support the governor at Louisbourg and encourage Aboriginal warriors to make forays into British areas. Gérald Finn, "Le Loutre, Jean-Louis," *Dictionary of Canadian Biography* online, vol. 4 (1771–1800).

48 King George's War in North America formed part of the longer conflict in Europe known as the War of the Austrian Succession, which lasted from 1740 to 1748.

49 The French and their Indigenous associates at Canso captured a small garrison of the 40th Regiment of Foot.

50 Marshall, *Heroes of the Acadian Resistance*, 37.

51 Paul Mascarene immediately rejected Duvivier's surrender demand and replied that New England naval reinforcements were on the way. He further stated that if the French and their Indigenous allies surrendered they would receive benign treatment. Duvivier then gave Mascarene twenty-four hours before he warned he would attack at noon on 8 September 1744. He began the siege on 9 September. French troops and Mi'kmaq attacked the wall of the fort each night and conducted daily raids round the ramparts. On 15 September Duvivier again unsuccessfully asked Mascarene to surrender and the siege continued, with British who left the protection of the ramparts being fired upon. The mortality rate was not high, though on 25 September a British sergeant was killed and a private was wounded.

52 On 26 September 1744 New England ranger John Gorham disembarked with approximately 50 Mohawk rangers and ten Wampanoag, which brought the manpower of the Fort Anne garrison up to about 270. As Grand Pré proven to be a mustering ground for the French and Mi'kmaq sieges of Annapolis Royal, Gorham demanded to take control of and acquired command of Grand Pré after the first siege of 1744. Soon after his arrival in Acadia, Gorham also led his Indigenous rangers on a surprise raid on a nearby Mi'kmaq encampment where they killed and mutilated not only men but also women and children. The Mi'kmaq withdrew, and Duvivier was forced to retreat back to Grand Pré on 5 October. The following year, Mi'kmaq from the Minas area sought revenge on Gorham's Rangers by torturing the rangers they took prisoner in 1744 during the siege of Annapolis Royal.

53 For some time before this expedition Commodore Peter Warren had been with the Royal Navy's West Indies' station. After the fall of Louisbourg in 1745, he was promoted to the rank of rear admiral and Pepperrell was made a baronet by King George II.

54 These Mi'kmaq were probably congregants of Le Loutre's old Shubenacadie mission before Le Loutre left for Chignecto. In the spring of 1744, the governor's council at Annapolis Royal noted that a "great body" of Mi'kmaq had congregated at Minas and Chignecto, along with a number of Acadians. There was some concern that these Mi'kmaq might try to attack the garrison at Fort Anne. In the state of crisis that followed the English suspended the Acadian deputy, Alexander Bourg, from office. Bourg was chastised for failing to report suspicious acts among the Mi'kmaq and Acadians, and René Le Blanc was installed in his place. By mid-June, there were three hundred Canadians and three hundred Indigenous warriors camped at Minas, along with Beausoleil, Pierre II Surrette, Le Loutre, and Maillard. Their siege

of Annapolis Royal was, as we saw above, unsuccessful because Joseph Du Pont Duvivier did not bring reinforcements from Île St. Jean (Prince Edward Island) in the early summer, and news circulated of reinforcements on the way from New England. Though Duvivier did finally appear in mid-August, Mi'kmaq from Minas and Cobequid had already begun to consider making a peace overture to the British. At the time this involved only an isolated group of chiefs, mostly from Minas and Piziquid,. Meanwhile a force of Mi'kmaw warriors mainly from Cape Breton under Abbé Maillard raided a vessel belonging to Commodore Peter Warren and General Pepperrell at Tatamagouche before proceeding on to Cobequid. NSARM, RG 1, vol. 25, "Minutes of the Governor's Council from 6 December 1744 to 5 January 1745." Mi'kmaq encamped at Cobequid Mines, who may even have included some of the Cape Breton leaders, stated to council member Paul Mascarene they were "inclined to come to a peace with the English, if they could obtain it, since they could not pretend to live in this county without it and could not carry their families to Canada, and besides they had no relations there." Ibid., "Minutes of the Governor's Council for 20 August, 1745." A formal peace overture from the Minas and Cobequid Mi'kmaq was drafted in August of 1745 and sent to the British at Annapolis Royal through the auspices of Pierre Landry at Piziquid (Windsor). NSARM, RG 1, vol. 24, "Letter from Pierre Landry written at the instance of the Indians," 24 August 1745.

55 NSARM, RG 1, vol. 24, "Council Minutes," 8 November 1745.

56 Similar instructions were issued in 1711 from what is now Castine, Maine, to Bernard-Anselme d'Abbadie de Saint-Castin (1689–1720), son of Baron Jean-Vincent d'Abbadie de Saint Castin and Pidianske, a daughter of Chief Mokodawando of the Penobscot nation. Bernard-Anselme's brother Joseph also was an Acadian military leader.

57 After the fall of Louisbourg in June 1745, Maillard in Cape Breton continued to encourage the Mi'kmaq to mount raids against the British.

58 Chiefs could not coerce their young men to go to war. They might persuade, but if none wished to go there was little they could do. Le Loutre was only too aware of this, and by 1745 grew worried about the growing reluctance in some Mi'kmaw quarters to continue their guerilla fighting. He secured greater material inducements by persuading the French government to send more guns and ammunition, knives, provisions, and medals for presents, and often paid the Mi'kmaq premiums for British scalps and ships captured as prizes.

59 Marshall gives an account of these preparations in *Heroes of the Acadian Resistance*, 56–7.

60 To accomplish his reconnaissance activities, Boishébert paddled in a bark canoe with a few men directly across the Northumberland Strait to Port-La-Joye on Prince Edward Island, rather than taking the safer route by Cape Tormentine. Ramezay expressed amazement at the short time it took Boishébert to complete his information gathering.

61 During this attack, Indigenous warriors and Acadian fighters killed thirty-four British troops (twenty-seven soldiers and seven sailors) and imprisoned the rest. The members of the 29th Regiment were unarmed and making hay in a field on the banks of the Hillsborough River when de Montesson and his party caught them by surprise. Fired upon by British ships offshore, the attackers eventually retreated, but not before de Montesson returned to de Ramezay at Chignecto on 23 July 1746 with two Acadian prisoners taken previously by the New Englanders, numerous English prisoners, and an Acadian pilot. The English, in response, took local Acadians, whom they ransomed in September to the commander of the Duc D'Anville expedition. For more information on De Montesson, see Malcolm Macleod, "Legardeur de Croisille et de Montesson, Joseph-Michel," *Dictionary of Canadian Biography* online, vol. 4 (1771–1800).

62 Thomas Chandler Haliburton recounted that a third of the population of Nova Scotia died of typhus after their peoples' contact with members of the Duc d'Anville fleet. Haliburton, *An Historical and Statistical Account of Nova-Scotia* (Halifax: J. Howe, 1829), 1.128.

63 Finn, "Le Loutre, Jean-Louis."

64 On 21 January 1747 the French party began a winter march from Beaubassin to Minas on snowshoes. Its members crossed to Baie Verte, followed the coastline of the Northumberland Strait to Tatamagouche, and then crossed over to Cobequid, near present-day Truro. In early February they reached the Shubenacadie River and braved a crossing on treacherous ice. En route, the party was joined by additional Acadian militia and Mi'kmaw warriors and was sheltered and fed by Acadian families. After crossing the Kennetcook River, the men sheltered at the Acadian Village of Piziquid (Pisiguit), now Windsor. On 10 February the troops marched through a blinding blizzard to Melanson Village in the Gaspereau valley, where they joined Acadian guides who led them straight to the ten houses in Grand Pré where the New England militia were billeted. The continuation of the snowstorm into the night provided the French party with an element of surprise, especially since most of the

New Englanders were asleep, with only a few sentries on duty. The next morning the New Englanders capitulated. Sixty-seven New Englanders, including Noble, were killed in the attack, with around forty taken prisoner. The attacking party's losses were fifty-three. Ramezay planned the attack, although he was too ill to participate. Afterwards, de Villiers and La Corne both were awarded the Order of St. Louis from the French king for their participation in this engagement.

65 Le Loutre had persuaded Mi'kmaw and Acadian resistance fighters to join the Grand Pré expedition in 1747, but he may not have joined it himself. Maillard was there, and presided over a blessing held at a mass just before the attack.

66 Led by Joseph Marin De La Malgue, with Maillard as attending chaplain, Mi'kmaw parties in 1748 attacked English coal-mining operations in Cape Breton. LAC, AC CIIA 91, 126–128vm, "La Gallissonnière a Maurepas," 6 September 1748.

67 Des Herbiers reached Louisbourg on 29 June 1749, where he replaced the temporary British commandant, Thomas Peregrine Hopson. Le Loutre meanwhile proceeded to Beaubassin.

68 John Clarence Webster, *The Career of the Abbé Le Loutre in Nova Scotia, with a Translation of His Autobiography* (Shediac: privately printed, 1933), 33, 35–8.

69 The Reverend William Tutty of the Society for the Propagation of the Gospel in Foreign Parts noted that upon landing, the British were welcomed by the Mi'kmaq. "William Tutty to the Society of the Propagation of the Gospel in Foreign Parts," 20 September 1749, in "Letters and Other Papers Relating to the Early History of the Church of England in Nova Scotia," *Collections of the Nova Scotia Historical Society*, no. 8 (1889–91), 97.

70 These were Hopson's and Warburton's regiments.

71 Thomas Beamish Akins, "History of Halifax City," in *Collections of the Nova Scotia Historical Society*, vol. 8 (Halifax, 1895), 16; L.F.S. Upton, *Micmacs and Colonists: Indian-White Relations in the Maritimes, 1713–1867* (Vancouver: University of British Columbia Press, 1979), 48–51.

72 Wicken, *Mi'kmaq Treaties on Trial*, 115.

73 The Missiguash River, which likely means "marsh river" in Mi'kmaq, flows across the Isthmus of Chignecto from the Missiguash Bog, through the Tantramar Marshes, and into the Cumberland Basin. Today it forms part of the boundary between southern New Brunswick and Nova Scotia. In the mid-eighteenth century it delineated the northern boundary of the English domain of Acadia and the disputed territory to the north, claimed by France.

74 Johannes Pedousaghtigh possibly was related to "Jean Pedoujaelet," a son of Joseph Pedoujaelet who was reported by Abbé Antoine Gaulin's census to be head chief of Chignecto in 1722.

75 Jean Battiste Maddouanhook was probably a relative of Chief Charles Maniduphize, who ratified a version of the Annapolis Royal Treaty on behalf of the Malecite in 1728, two years after the treaty's initial signing at Fort Anne by other chiefs.

76 Cornwallis noted that the Malecite present were delegates rather than chiefs, and this also may have been the case with the Chignecto representative who was present. LAC, CO 217/40/118, "Cornwallis to the Colonial Office," 20 August 1749.

77 NSARM, RG 1, vol. 209, Council Minutes, 2, "Copy of signed treaty aboard ship *Beaufort* in Halifax Harbour," 14 August 1749. André, the Indigenous delegates' interpreter, and a man named Martin from Minas interpreted the treaty.

78 The treaty signed on 15 August 1749 is included in a large folio of papers, some dated as late as 1760. NSARM, RG 1, vol. 36, no. 48½, "Treaty of Peace and Friendship concluded with the Delegates of the St. John's and Passamaquoddy Tribes of Indians at Halifax, along with Articles of Submission and Agreement signed in Boston, 15 December 1725, and the Renewal of Boston Submission Agreement with Chignecto, St. John's and Passamaquoddy Delegates. Done in Chibucto Harbour the 15th day of August, 1749." François Arondawish, Simon Sactawino, and Jean Battiste Maddouanhook drew totemic devices by their signatures, while the signature of Pedousaghtigh has a seal attached next to it. Also included in the folio is the ratification of the August 15 treaty signed later by Malecite chiefs from the mouth of the Saint John River on 4 September 1749. Edward How officiated at this ceremony on the Saint John River and Madam de Bellisle was the interpreter.

79 Mary Pedley, "Map Wars: The Role of Maps in the Nova Scotia/Acadia Boundary Dispute of 1750," *Imago Mundi* 50 (1998): 96.

80 The French had carried over eight hundred Acadians to Prince Edward Island by August 1750.

81 The Mi'kmaq were expecting the vessels and when they appeared immediately sought to seize them. Captain Tom Daniel of one of the vessels was killed, as were the two unnamed chiefs. Some of the sons of François Mius, the chief of Merliguèche, also were killed. LAC, AC CIIB 28: 37 r–v, "M. Bigot au minister," 5 October 1750; NSARM, RG 1, vol. 186, 20–1, "Minutes of the Nova Scotia Council," 18 September 1749.

82 John Salusbury, *Expeditions of Honour: The Journal of John Salusbury in Halifax, Nova Scotia, 1749–1753*, ed. Edward Romkey (Newark, DE: University of Delaware Press, 1982), 65, "Entry of 18 September 1749." This second affair, however, was held to arose more from a private pique than from anti-British sentiment.

83 Webster, *The Career of the Abbé Le Loutre*, 39–42.

84 The English seized the French sloop *London*, which in addition to having just unloaded arms for the Mi'kmaq, was found to be carrying letters that showed Le Loutre was acting as a war leader of the Indigenous population under orders from Quebec. CO 217/10, "Cornwallis to the Lords of Trade and Plantations, 19 August 1750, along with Extract[s] of some letters found in the sloop *London* taken in Baie Verte by Captain Le Cras." Also see Murdoch, *History of Nova-Scotia*, 2.188.

85 C.J. Russ, "La Corne, Louis-Luc," *Dictionary of Canadian Biography* online, vol. 3 (1741–70).

86 Le Loutre and Maillard remained the only non-Indigenous individuals truly aware of the complexity of the Mi'kmaw campaign. Their Mi'kmaw congregants told them what was transpiring within their own communities and within Eastern Wabanaki groups to the south in New England. Instead of the French missionaries being solely fomenters of Indigenous discontent and warfare, it seems evident that these men had to keep abreast of matters within the Mi'kmaw communities and to constantly rely on the chiefs for clarification regarding concepts that were unfamiliar to their own French culture. Maillard, in particular, sought to translate Mi'kmaw speeches into French without losing their forcefulness and poetic charge.

87 Le Loutre had a twofold plan. He would encourage the Mi'kmaq and the Acadian resistance fighters to launch raids against the English until the English either were willing to capitulate to the bounds of Acadia as set out by the French or until another territorial scheme might be devised that proved palatable to all parties, including the Mi'kmaq.

88 Washington, DC, Library of Congress, "Massachusetts Council Records," 2 September 1720; Kenneth M. Morrison, "The People of the Dawn: The Abenaki and Their Relations with New England and New France, 1600–1727" (PhD dissertation, University of Maine, 1975), 351–2, 390–5.

89 Leaders from throughout *Mi'kma'ki* joined this council at Port Toulouse to discuss how to proceed in the face of English territorial expansion. *Le Canada-Français* (1888), 1.19. The Mi'kmaw declaration was written down by Maillard on 24 September 1749, five days before Saint Michel's Day. A prominent leader named Thoma Denny (or Denys) at this time moved permanently from the Chignecto district to Eskasoni, Cape Breton, which later became the seat of the Mi'kmaw Grand Council. It was a seminal moment in the history of the Mi'kmaw nation. In 1883, a Shubenacadie Mi'kmaw customary judge, Christopher Paul, and his associates cited an oral tradition relating to Chief Denny in order to uphold the claims of John Denny Jr., a descendant of Thoma Denny, as grand chief in opposition to the claims of Chief John Noel of Shubenacadie. NSARM, RG 2, vol. 9, doc. 1820, "Petition of Christopher Paul, Stephen Hood and 59 others to Lieutenant Governor Adams George Archibald," 29 March 1883. Moreover, one of Chief Denny's ancestors had been ennobled by the French. LAC, AC CIIC 15: 257–257v, "Dispatch from Governor Raymond at Louisbourg regarding of Chief [Thoma] Denys, dated November 1751." The Mi'kmaq obviously knew about this, since an oral tradition collected by anthropologist Frank G. Speck in Cape Breton in the early twentieth century held that Denny's grandfather was an ennobled French man. Frank Goldsmith Speck, *Beothuk and Micmac* (New York, 1922), 111; see also Dickason, *Louisbourg and the Indians*, 160. This evidence suggests that Denny's grandfather may have been Nicolas Denys's brother, Simon Denys de la Trinité (1599–1678), who after moving from Acadia to Canada in 1651 was ennobled in 1668 by Louis XIV. Jean Lunn, "Denys, Simon De La Trinité," *Dictionary of Canadian Biography* online, vol. 1 (1000–1700).

90 The Mi'kmaw proclamation is printed, in both Mi'kmaq and French, in its entirety in *Collection de documents inédits sur le Canada Amérique publiés par le Canada-Français* (Quebec: L.J. Demers & Frère, 1888), 1.17–19. It appears under the heading "Déclaration de Guerre des Micmacs aux Anglais s'ils refusent d'Abandonner Kchibouktouk (Halifax)," transcribed from a letter from Abbé Maillard to the Abbé du Fau, superior of the Séminaire des Missions Éntrangères at Paris, enclosed with a letter from Louisbourg by Maillard, dated 3 October 1749. The heading was not penned by Maillard, but constituted a later addition. An original copy of the document, in both French and Mi'kmaq, is housed in the Archives of the Seminary of Quebec, Quebec City. The English translation of it that appeared under the heading "A letter said to be sent by the Indian Prince of Nova Scotia, to the English governor of Chebucto" in the *Gentleman's Magazine and Historical Chronicle*, 20 (December–January 1749–50), page 8, was probably translated by a settler in Acadia, Otis Little, and sent to Sylvanus Urban, the *Gentleman's Magazine's* editor

in London, since Little and Urban were regular correspondents. Abbé Maillard, reminiscing on the declaration years after he wrote it, stated that the Mi'kmaq in 1749 were alarmed by the way the British were appropriating their land and that they could not be suspected of any "connivance." Maillard, *Customs and Manners of the Micmakis and Maricheets*. For further discussion on the Mi'kmaq's declaration of 1749, see A.J.B. Johnston, *Endgame: The Promise, the Glory and the Despair of Louisbourg's Last Decade* (Lincoln: University of Nebraska Press, 2007), 37–8.

91 "Maillard to the Abbé Du Fau, 18 October 1749," in *Collection de documents inédits sur le Canada et l'Amérique publiés par le Canada-Français* (Quebec: L.J. Demers & Frère, 1888), 1.17–19.

    "The worm which creeps knows how to defend itself when attacked," the declaration stated. "Surely I, called *elnoüi* [*El'nu*, Mi'kmaw person], as I am, am better than a worm, and must know how to defend myself, when attacked." Excerpted from the Mi'kmaw proclamation accompanying "Maillard to the Abbé Du Fau, 18 October 1749," 1.17–19.

92 "The worm which creeps knows how to defend itself when attacked," the declaration stated. "Surely I, called *elnoüi* [*El'nu*, Mi'kmaw person], as I am, am better than a worm, and must know how to defend myself, when attacked." Excerpted from the Mi'kmaw proclamation accompanying "Maillard to the Abbé Du Fau, 18 October 1749," 1.17–19.

93 "Maillard to the Abbé Du Fau, 18 October 1749," with a copy of the Mi'kmaw proclamation, 1.17–19.

94 Ibid.

95 Abbé Maillard was not as militant or as manipulative as Le Loutre. In mid-August 1749 he had helped Joseph Gorham, John Gorham's younger brother, and twenty of his men obtain a release from Louisbourg after their party was captured by Mi'kmaq while out haying at Canso. At the time Maillard assured Gorham that the Mi'kmaq associated with the Shubenacadie mission were committed to keeping the peace. Salusbury, *Expeditions of Honour*, 61, "Entry of 23 August 1749"; LAC, CO 217/9/117r–118r, "Cornwallis to the Lords of Trade and Plantations," 11 September 1749; LAC, MG 5, B1, Archives du minister des affaires étrangéres: Memoires et documents, 1749–53, vol. 9, 156–8, "Île Royale, remis le 3 novembre 1749, par M. Rouille." Wicken suggests that the raid on Gorham's men at Canso was a revenge attack, since the English earlier had killed twenty Mi'kmaq in Newfoundland. Wicken, *Mi'kmaq Treaties on Trial*, 179.

96 As quoted in Johnston, "Maillard, Pierre," *Dictionary of Canadian Biography* online, vol. 3 (1741–70).

97 John Grenier, *The Far Reaches of Empire: War in Nova Scotia, 1710–1760*, ed. Gregory J.W. Urwin (Norman: University of Oklahoma Press, 2008), 150.

98 Salusbury, *Expeditions of Honour*, 67, "Entry of 30 September 1749."

99 LAC, CO 217/40/142–44, "Cornwallis to the Duke of Bedford," 17 October 1749; NSARM, RG 1, vol. 209, "Proclamation arising from a council held on the *Beaufort*," 1 October 1749.

100 LAC, CO 217/40/142–44, "Cornwallis to the Duke of Bedford," 17 October 1749; Upton, *Micmacs and Colonists*, 52; Wicken, *Mi'kmaq Treaties on Trial*, 81. Though it was a draconian measure, the tactic previously had been employed in New England, and the bounty compared favourably with what the French often offered the Mi'kmaq and Acadians for British scalps. Cornwallis's bounty was raised in 1750 and stayed on the books until the early summer of 1752.

101 Salusbury, *Expeditions of Honour*, 68, "Entry of 2 October 1749."

102 These lesser amounts of provisions were to be sent to the Cape Sable band in Nova Scotia, who traded with groups along the Saint John River valley.

103 LAC, CO 217/9/188–94, "Cornwallis to the Lords of Trade and Plantations," 19 March 1750.

104 For more on this expedition against Fort Vieux Logis, see Marshall, *Heroes of the Acadian Resistance*, 84.

105 LAC, CO 217/9/202, "Nous les Sauvages Micmacs, Mariches, Cinabres, Hurons, Abenaquis, Esquimaux" (a call to defend Minas), dated Piziquid, December 1749. Although the originator of this blanket summons remained unnamed, it undoubtedly was Le Loutre.

106 Hamilton actually enjoyed Le Loutre's company and, in a strange twist of fate, retained a sense of obligation to the abbé "for his civilities." Murdoch, *History of Nova-Scotia*, 2.235. Le Loutre shouldered Hamilton's ransom himself, for in 1753 he complained to the interpreter Anthony Casteel about the English failing to remunerate him for paying Hamilton's ransom out of his own pocket. "Anthony Casteel's journal," in *Collection de documents inédits sur le Canada et l'Amérique publiés par le Canada-Français* (Quebec, 1889), 2.126 (the original of Casteel's journal is housed in the British Museum in the Brown MSS Collection, Add. 19073, f. II, no. 23. A copy is also on microfilm at NSARM); Grenier, *Far Reaches of Empire*, 153; Marshall, *Heroes of the Acadian Resistance*, 84. Fort Vieux Logis stood on the site of the present-day Acadian Cross monument in Hortonville,

Nova Scotia. In the fall of 1749, as it was too late in the year to build barracks, the fort consisted of three large houses formerly built and occupied by Acadians, where one hundred were stationed under the command of Captain John Handfield. The houses were surrounded by a triangular yard of pickets, equipped with three half bastions. The Acadians at Minas and Grand Pré feared reprisals from the Mi'kmaq if they swore an unconditional oath of allegiance to the English Crown. Instead, they wanted to swear a conditional oath, similar to an earlier one they had sworn to Colonel Mascarene and Governor Philipps, under which they did not have to bear arms. Cornwallis reacted to their hesitancy by preventing them from leaving Minas and threatening to use them to perform labour for the English government.

107 John Reid, "Amerindian Power in the Early Modern Northeast: A Reappraisal," in *Essays on Northeastern North America: Seventeenth and Eighteenth Centuries* (Toronto: University of Toronto Press, 2008); Grenier, *Far Reaches of Empire*, 154–5.

108 Fort Edward, whose first commandant was John Gorham, was built on a point of land where the St. Croix River met the Piziquid (Pisiquit or Avon) River.

109 W.A.B. Douglas, "Rous, John," *Dictionary of Canadian Biography* online, vol. 3 (1740–70).

110 Upton, *Micmac and Colonists*, 50–1.

111 The Mi'kmaq and even some French continued to refer to Fort Lawrence after it was built as Mejagouech. La Corne did not stay at long at Chignecto after the September engagement with Lawrence. Within a month the French officer was recalled from Acadia and replaced at Beaubassin by Pierre-Roch de Saint-Ours Deschaillons.

112 "Journal de ce qui s'est passé à Chinectou et autre parties des frontiers de l'acadie depuis le 15 septembre 1750 jusqu'au 28 juillet 1751," in Appendix N. 325, Placide Gaudet, *Report Concerning Canadian Archives for the Year 1905* (Ottawa: Canadian Archives, 1906); Grenier, *Far Reaches of Empire*, 159.

113 Charles Lawrence, "Journal of Charles Lawrence 1750," in John Clarence Webster, ed., *The Building of Fort Lawrence in Chignecto* (Saint John, 1941), 9.

114 How was lured outside the walls of Fort Lawrence under a flag of truce by a Mi'kmaw individual dressed as a French official who indicated he wished to discuss an exchange of prisoners and the subject of peacemaking with the Mi'kmaq. C. Alexander Pincombe, "How, Edward," *Dictionary of Canadian Biography* online, vol. 3 (1747–70). The only witness to the event, Captain Louis Vallière, was not able to identify the sniper. Louis le Neuf de la Valliére, "Journal of events in Chignecto and

Other Parts of the Frontiers of Acadie from Sept. 15, 1750 to July 28, 1750," in John Clarence Webster, *The Forts of Chignecto: A Study of the Eighteenth Century Conflict between France and Great Britain in America* (Shediac, NB: privately printed, 1930), 135–6. Maillard later held that Étienne Bâtârd shot How because years before at Port Toulouse the English officer had insulted a statue of the Virgin Mary within Bâtârd's earshot. Maillard, "Lettre de M. l'abbé Maillard," 3.388–407; Upton, *Micmacs and Colonists*, 50. Micheline D. Johnson, on the basis of research conducted by Albert David, also contends that Bâtârd was the shooter, but she questions David's exoneration of Le Loutre, whom she believes played a role in the ambush. Johnson, "Bâtârd, Étienne," *Dictionary of Canadian Biography* online, vol. 3 (1741–70); Johnson, *Apôtres ou agitateurs: La France missionaire en Acadie* (Trois Rivières: Boreal Express, 1970).

115 Captain How may have been targeted because he was a provisioner for the French. Since arrivals of French supply ships had become unpredictable, the intendant of Canada allowed the commissary at Louisbourg to treat with English merchants for peas, Indian corn, and other provisions. This was a practice that Le Loutre, who wanted the supply trade to remain in French hands, considered an anathema. How, who was a merchant as well as a military officer, had been contacted to supply French posts along the Saint John River. It was rumoured that, on hearing this news, Le Loutre took steps to lure How to his death.

116 LAC, CO 217/11/1–6 ½, "Edward Cornwallis to Colonial Office," 27 November 1750.

117 Phyllis R. Blakeley, "Morris, Charles," *Dictionary of Canadian Biography* online, vol. 4 (1771–1800); Upton, *Micmacs and Colonists*, 48–50; Jeffers Lennox, "An Empire on Paper: The Founding of Halifax and Conceptions of Imperial Space, 1744–1755," *Canadian Historical Review* 88, no. 3 (2007): 372–412. Charles Morris's 1749 map "Draught of Northern English Colonies," which is housed in Dalhousie University's Special Collections, was prepared with an eye to Protestant settlement of the Shepody, Memramcook, and Petitcodiac river areas. In 1751 Morris noted that the French had to go to considerable expense to send provision vessels to aid the fledgling Acadian settlements. He also stated that one could proceed from the Acadian Three Rivers district up the Petitcodiac River, which was navigable for six miles inland, and portage to the Saint John River, from which one could reach Quebec in seven days. Almost all Acadian adults in the district had travelled this route to receive confirmation from the bishop of Quebec. A

passage also lay open to Shediac on the Atlantic coast, and there was constant intercourse between Shediac and the Gaspé. Morris further estimated that there were around two hundred French regular troops at Chignecto, and with about two hundred Mi'kmaq, three hundred other Indigenous warriors from the Saint John River area and Canada, and one thousand Acadian inhabitants, the French would be able to muster a force of about fifteen hundred men.

118 NSARM, RG 1, vol. 284 (Transcripts of Documents made at the British Museum by order of the Government of Canada and relating to the Province between the years 1750 and 1789–90), Brown Collection, doc. no. 1, "Representation of the relative state of the French and English in Nova Scotia transmitted by Surveyor Morris to Governor Shirley, who was leaving for England, 1750–51"; Brown Collection, doc. no. 2, "Judge Morris' Paper on the Causes of the War of 1755 and the History of the Acadians."

119 Le Loutre provided Acadians with monetary and other incentives, such as supplies for three years, to move to Three Rivers. When many Acadians refused to leave the British domain, he resorted to coercion. He threatened them with Indigenous reprisals if they failed to settle on lands west of the Missiguash River; he withheld sacraments and offered highly dubious religious arguments as to why they should eschew any relationship with the British. A man of zeal rather than breadth of vision, Le Loutre was often oblivious to the hardships his militancy inflicted on the Acadians. Like many over-zealous schemes, his exhibited a narrowing of focus and revealed a sinister, manipulative side.

120 In 1748 approximately 2,700 people resided at Piziquid (or Pisiguit) and another 2,400 in the Grand Pré and Canard areas. English policy and threats of Indigenous violence, in some part fostered by Le Loutre, led many Acadians, particularly those along the Cobequid shore, to migrate to Chignecto and Île Saint-Jean. By 1755, there were only about 1,400 Acadians left at Minas and Piziquid.

121 Thomas Pichon, *Genuine Letters and Memoirs relating to the Natural, Civil, and Commercial History of the Islands of Cape Breton and Saint John* (London: Nourse, 1760), 164.

122 Few particulars are known about this incident, despite the fact that How lived for five days after the shooting. The Chevalier de Johnstone argued that Le Loutre dressed a Mi'kmaw man, Jean-Baptiste Cope, in an officer's uniform and asked Cope to beckon to Howe to come to him with a wave of a white handkerchief.

The two men conversed, though How soon became distressed since he realized that, while the other man spoke perfect French, his distinctive hand gestures were Mi'kmaq. "Extract from a document entitled Short account of what passed at Cape Breton from the beginning of the last War until the taking of Louisbourg in 1758, by a French officer. From a manuscript drafted by a person who served at Louisbourg from 1750 to 1758," in Murdoch, *History of Nova-Scotia*, 2.192–3. Historian Geoffrey Plank also asserts that Cope was involved, since "[l]ooking back on the incident years later, Cope claimed credit for killing the British officer." Plank, "The Two Majors Cope: The Boundaries of Nationality in Mid-18th Century Nova Scotia," *Acadiensis* 25, no. 2 (1996): 18–40; Plank, *An Unsettled Conquest: The British Campaign against the Peoples of Acadia* (Philadelphia: University of Pennsylvania Press, 2001), 131.

123 Cornwallis wrote on 24 June 1751 of the night raid on Dartmouth in which four settlers, six soldiers, and six Indigenous people were killed. See Mrs. William Lawson, *History of the Townships of Dartmouth, Preston and Lawrencetown* (Halifax: Morton and Co., 1893), 14; Grenier, *Far Reaches of Empire*, 160; Marshall, *Heroes of the Acadian Resistance*, 98–9.

124 A few soldiers taken hostage by the Chignecto band in the fall of 1751 were ransomed back to the English within two years. Grenier, *Far Reaches of Empire*, 35.

125 To free Le Loutre for the arduous task of dyke building, Abbé Manach took over the Beaubassin mission and also served at Cobequid, Père Desenclaves assumed Le Loutre's work at Cape Sable and Hénri Daudin ministered to the Mi'kmaq and Acadians remaining at Minas. These missions were extensions of the Shubenacadie mission, which was serviced itinerantly by Maillard.

126 Rouillé, as minister of marine, succeeded the well-known Jean-Frédéric Phélypeaux, Count de Maurepas, who played a major role in Louisbourg's earlier history. Le Loutre amassed the large sum for dyke building on the promise that he would make the Three Rivers community self-supporting within four years. At the same time Rouillé and the missionary stated in their report that the line of demarcation between the French and English Acadia should run from Cobequid to Canso. Canso, they averred, should remain neutral territory, though France would retain exclusive fishing rights there. Le Loutre added a detailed commentary on lands the Acadians might occupy and called for government aid for the refugee Acadians. Rouillé and Le Loutre then submitted their report in spring 1753 to Michel Barrin de La Galissonière, who was in charge of negotiating the

frontiers of North America. The boundary commissioners' report was not published until three years later; see Boundary Commission. *The memorials of the English and French commissaries concerning the limits of Nova Scotia or Acadie*, vol. 1 (London, 1755). In the end, Le Loutre failed to achieve anything with his submissions to the commission. The boundary issue would only be resolved under the terms of the Treaty of Paris in 1763, by which time Britain reigned supreme in North America.

127 Most Mi'kmaq raids took place from early spring to early fall, after which the Mi'kmaq departed inland for winter hunting grounds. Grenier, *Far Reaches of Empire*, 159–60.

128 Cornwallis reported that for nine months after the attack on Dartmouth in 1751, no raids occurred on Halifax or Dartmouth. NSARM, RG 1, vol. 35, no. 67, "Edward Cornwallis to the Lords Commissioners for Trade and Plantations," 16 February 1752. At this time Cornwallis was still fearful of sending foreign Protestants to outlying districts.

129 Le Loutre must have experienced attacks of conscience over depriving persons of the sacraments in order to fulfil French goals, since he brought the subject up with his religious superiors while in Paris. Finn, "Le Loutre, Jean-Louis."

130 NSARM, RG 1, vol. 35, no. 67, "Cornwallis to the Lords of Trade and Plantations," 16 February 1752. Cornwallis noted that in spring 1752 the Mi'kmaq may not have come in to make peace, but they also had not committed any acts of hostility since the attack on Dartmouth nine months earlier. The winter, he added, had been "uncommonly severe."

131 Anthony Casteel, "Anthony Casteel's journal," 2.120.

132 NSARM, Beaubassin registers on microfilm, "Baptism of Pierre Arghimont, fils de Jospeph Arghimont … et Marie sa femme," 1 May 1722. The names of the other sons appear throughout the English documentary record.

133 "Anthony Casteel's journal," 2.120; Murdoch, *History of Nova-Scotia*, 1.222–3.

134 LAC, CO 217/18/164. This report, dated 15 April 1761, also held that lands at Maccan, Memramcook, Petitcodiac, and Shepody could be settled by Protestants.

135 Jean-Baptiste Cope was born to "Paul Cop" and Cecilia near Port Royal in 1698, the same year as Joseph Argimault was born. LAC, MG 18, F18, 1, typescript of 1708 census by Father Pierre La Chasse, Port Royal, 1. In 1708, Jean-Baptiste, Paul Cop's oldest child, had three siblings; Therese, eight, Margueritte, five, and Marie, one. His parents moved to the Shubenacadie district

after the English conquest of Acadia in 1710. Though the "Cope" surname may stem from the Mi'kmaw word *ko-pit*, meaning beaver, the Mi'kmaw Copes also may have chosen to Anglicize their surname to "Cope" after interacting with English and New England traders. (Henry Cope, for instance, was a Boston merchant who set up a colliery at Minas in the early 1730s.) Although a Shubenacadie chief named Jean-Baptist Pon signed treaty with the English at Annapolis Royal in 1726, Cope by the 1740s exercised territorial prerogatives over lands flanking the Shubenacadie River, as well as a large tract on Nova Scotia's Eastern Shore that included the Chebucto peninsula. His military prowess attracted the attention of French officialdom, which vested him with a French commission of "major." The French dispensed three orders of commissions, "chef," "major," and "captaine." Dickason, *Louisbourg and the Indians*, 29–39, 155–6.

136 The French also held that Cope had an impulsive streak and could be sly and unpredictable, which caused at least one French officer to implicate him in the murder of Captain How. "Extract from a document entitled Short account of what passed at Cape Breton from the beginning of the last War until the taking of Louisbourg in 1758, by a French officer. From a ms. by a person who served at Louisbourg from 1750 to 1758," in Murdoch, *History of Nova-Scotia*, 2.193.

137 Claude Gagiosh (or Egighighes) was the son of "Anthoine Zizigueshche" and his wife, Barbe. In 1708 Claude had an older brother François, twenty-two, and a younger brother Guillaume, who was only one. He also had three sisters, Margueritte, fifteen, Marie, nine, and Cecille, six. Born in 1696, Claude was two years older than Argimault and Cope. In 1722, at the age of twenty-six, "Claude Eauchiaich [Gagiosh]" was regarded by Abbé Antoine Gaulin as chief of the La Have band, although his father "Antoine Egigish" signed the 1726 treaty as "Chief of La Have." LAC, AC F-135, CIIB, vol. 6, correspondance générale, no. 77; LAC, CO 217/38/108, "Treaty of 4 June 1726." Claude's sister Marie married François Joseph Le Jeune, the son of a Mi'kmaq man named François Joseph and Jeanne Le Jeune, the sister of a well-known Acadian trader, Martin Le Jeune of Port Maltois (now Port Medway, Queens County). Some historians aver that Martin and Jeanne Le Jeune's grandfather, Pierre Le Jeune, came to Acadia in 1632 with Isaac de Razilly and brought a French wife with him, while others, less certain of the date of Pierre's arrival, argue that he consorted with a Mi'kmaw woman, probably from La Have, and that his descendants were thus *métis*. Pierre's son Pierre II and his wife, a Mi'kmaw woman surnamed Doucet, were the

parents of Jeanne Le Jeune. (A Mi'kmaw family with the surname Doucet lived in the eighteenth century near Belliveau Cove, Digby Country, where there is an upright stone said to be the grave of a Mi'kmaq with "Francois Doucet, 1771" inscribed on it.) Owing to their ties to the Mi'kmaq, members of the Le Jeune family resisted removal to Port Royal following the collapse of de Razilly's settlement, preferring instead to follow the fur trade. Some weathered removal by the English to Port Rossignol and even Boston in 1664, but following the Treaty of Breda in 1667 they were back in their old haunts. Clarence-J. d'Entremont, *Histoire du Cap-Sable de l'an mil au traité de Paris (1763)* (Eunice, LA: Hébert, 1981), 3.1121–5. Jeanne and her husband François Joseph had a daughter Marguerite who in turn wed Martin Grand Claude on 25 February 1727. Marguerite and Martin were both members of Claude Gagiosh's band. In 1752 Claude was fifty-six years old. He had been chief of the La Have group for over twenty years, and had widespread kinship, trading, and political ties with the Acadian and Mi'kmaw communities. Since he was a middleman trader, the English embargo on Indigenous and French trade along the eastern Atlantic coast and Cornwallis's destruction in 1749 of François Mius's village and trading post near Merliguèche hurt him economically. By 1752 he espoused a neutral stance, likely fostered by a desire to have his group escape the fate of Mius's nearby village. Paul Laurent, who was probably Claude Gagiosh's son-in-law, succeeded Gagiosh as chief of La Have. Micheline Johnson states that Paul Laurent was a captain in Chief François Mius's band, but Paul Laurent signed treaty in his own right in Halifax before his paternal uncle François Mius did so. Micheline D. Johnson, "Laurent, Paul," *Dictionary of Canadian Biography* online, vol. 3 (1741–70).

138 The French regarded Cope as the "captaine" of a specific territorial "command." As early as 1739 Captain Peter Warren, a naval officer who took part in the first siege of Louisbourg, wrote that the French granted a chief "a commission from the Governor of Canada, or Cape Breton, to command a particular District ... [and who] generally bears the title of Captain of the Port to which they belong." LAC, CO 218/8/48½–49½, "P. Warren, captain of the *Squirrel*, Boston, to the British Colonial Office," 9 July 1739. Cope's lands encompassed the Shubenacadie River Valley, the crucial communication route across the province to the Minas Basin. Cope likely hoped that a treaty with the English would rid him of unwanted fishermen and traders who robbed and molested his people along the coast during spring fishing and fowling season.

139 This position aligns with one held by William Wicken, that Cope was acting in concert with others of his nation. Wicken, *Mi'kmaq Treaties on Trial*, chap. 8. Wicken's position has been criticized by Steven Patterson, who argues that Cope was politically isolated in 1752. Patterson, "Indian-White Relations in Nova Scotia, 1749–61: A Study in Political Interaction," *Acadiensis* 23, no. 1 (1993): 42–5.

140 Paul Laurent (Mius?) was almost certainly a grandson of Philippe II Mius d'Azy and a great-grandson of Baron Philippe I Mius d'Entremont, the first seigneur of Pobomcoup. His father was likely Jacques Mius d'Entremont. Chief François Mius, a son of Philippe's II Mius *dit* d'Azy and thus a brother of Jacques, moved first to La Have in 1750 and later to the Chignecto Isthmus with Paul Laurent after Governor Cornwallis razed the main Mi'kmaw village near Merliguèche, in what is now Lunenburg County, in 1749.

141 Laurent's statements cannot be confirmed, since he did not give the date of Jacques Mius d'Azy's hanging. He and Antoine Mius were likely both sons of Jacques Mius, who was born to Philippe II Mius d'Azy and his wife Marie in 1688. Jacques was thirty-eight years old when he was hanged in Boston, at which time Laurent would have been a young boy. Jacques Mius (referred to by the Anglicized "James" at his trial) was convicted of piracy after taking over a fishing vessel in Merliguèche Harbour with several of his close kin, including his brother Philippe, who died along with him. *The Trials of Five Persons for Piracy, Felony and Robbery... Held at the Court House in Boston, within His Majesty's Province of the Massachusett.-Bay in New England on Tuesday the Fourth Day of October, Anno Domini, 1726* (Boston, 1726), https://quod.lib.umich.edu/e/evans/n02375.0001.001/21?page=root;size=100;view=text; William Wicken, "26 August 1726: A Case Study in Mi'kmaq-New England Relations," *Acadiensis* 23, no. 1 (1993): 5–22; d'Entremont, *Histoire du Cap-Sable*, 4.1012; 1618–19. The hanging of Jacques Mius and his companions attracted considerable press attention in New England. *Boston Newsletter*, 4 November 1726.

142 For Pichon's mention of Antoine Mius, see John Clarence Webster, ed., *Thomas Pichon, "The Spy of Beausejour": An Account of His Career in Europe and America* (Halifax: Public Archives of Nova Scotia, 1937), 82.

143 John Salusbury, *Expeditions of Honour*, 61, "Entry of 23 August 1749."

144 LAC, AC CIIB 31, "Raymond à Rouillé," 19 November 1751.

145 Louis Le Neuf de la Valliére, "Journal of events in Chignecto and Other Parts of the Frontiers of Acadie from

Sept. 15, 1750 to July 28, 1750," in Webster, *Forts of Chignecto*, 135.

146 LAC, AC CIIB, vol. 31, 106–106v, "Raymond à Rouillé," 12 December 1751.

147 Cherished among the memories of the older generation of Mi'kmaw, *métis*, and Acadian middlemen and merchants was a time before 1720, when brigades could journey with relative ease to Boston and exchange furs and fish for sundry necessities. Claude Petitpas Jr. had been one such man. In 1719 Petitpas even accepted a payment of two thousand livres from Boston to win the Mi'kmaw and Malecite over to the English cause. LAC, AC CIIB 4: 64–5, "Lettre de Saint-Ovide, 20 septembre 1719, dans les délibérations du Conseil," 21 November 1719. In the early to middle 1700s the French administration lacked the ideological artillery to elevate French policies above local ones, and even to influence the missionaries wielding control over their congregants by putting men in mortal fear for their souls by threatening to deny them the sacraments. Instead, kin ties held people together, and communities could tolerate a degree of diversity of opinion within their parameters. French officialdom had not yet tightened its grip on what persons were supposed to think and feel. Claude Petitpas Sr. had not yet been shunned by his community for his activities with the British. One of his sons, Louis-Benjamin Petitpas, worked as an interpreter at Port Toulouse and later became an assistant and friend to Abbé Maillard during the years when the Mi'kmaw land and resource campaign had its apogee under the missionary, then working as an agent for the British.

148 LAC, CO 218/4, "Lords of Trade and Plantations to Cornwallis," 6 March 1752; LAC, CO 13, 38v, "P. Hopson to the Lords of Trade and Plantations," 6 December 1752; LAC, CO 218/4/221v, "Lords of Trade and Plantations to Hopson," 28 March 1753. John Gorham had maintained an extravagant expense account. Grenier, *Far Reaches of Empire*, 162. When Gorham died in London of smallpox in 1751 his brother Joseph took over as ranger leader.

149 LAC, CO 217/13, 292, "George Scott to P. Hopson," 17 August 1752.

150 Murdoch, *History of Nova-Scotia*, 2.165.

151 During the fall of 1751 Paul Mascarene, who had negotiated the 1726 treaty and represented Nova Scotia at conferences held between New England and the Eastern Abenaki, reported to Cornwallis that one of the Malecite chiefs, Monsarrett, not only promised to sign peace with the British but also stated he would try to bring the Mi'kmaq to Halifax. Though the Malecite leader did not come to Halifax with any Mi'kmaq, the anticipation his

words engendered temporarily buoyed confidence in British ranks that the Mi'kmaq might appear. Patterson, "Indian-White Relations," 35–6.

152 NSARM, RG 1, vol. 186, "Minutes of Council for 17 July 1752"; Patterson, "Indian-White Relations," 36.

153 "Anthony Casteel's Journal," 2.123. Casteel's assertion regarding Cope's involvement in the negotiations was made well after the fact. In 1753, when he relayed this information to Raymond, Casteel was a prisoner at Louisbourg, having been captured by Mi'kmaq at Jeddore, east of Halifax, earlier in the year.

154 On 8 April 1751 Piggot received a licence to open a coffee house and inn in Halifax. Akins, *History of Halifax City*, 30.

155 LAC, AC CIIB 32: 163r–v, "Prevost au ministre, 10 septembre 1752"; Wicken, *Mi'kmaq Treaties on Trial*, 183. Cornwallis felt the spring and early summer were the best times to pursue this task, since Mi'kmaw families were situated along the coast rather than inland hunting or away at other villages. Wicken suggests that Piggott met Cope at the annual St. Anne's Day celebrations at Port Toulouse.

156 LAC, AC CIIB, vol. 32, 163r–v, "Prévost au minister, 18 septembre 1752."

157 The Mi'kmaq seized two fishing schooners near Canso before they took Piggott's vessel in French waters, and sailed all three to Petit de Grat. LAC, CO 217/13, "Hopson à Raymond, 10 août 1753"; LAC, CO 217/13, "Raymond to Hopson," 30 August 1752; "Hopson to the Lord of Trade and Plantations," 16 October 1752; AC CIIB, 33, 163r–v, "Prévost au ministre, 10 septembre 1752."

158 "Anthony Casteel's journal," 2.116. Cope undoubtedly knew the Mi'kmaq who had taken Piggott's vessel, and may even have been with the party when they seized the boat.

159 It would have been an unseemly breach of protocol for a northeastern Algonquian leader to consider making peace with the English without first consulting other chiefs from the Mi'kmaw community in council, and probably also extending news of his intention to representatives of the Wabanaki Confederacy. In the absence of such consultations, the consequences if things went awry might prove too grave for the political fabric of the Indigenous constituency.

160 NSARM, RG 1, vol. 186, 214, "Nova Scotia Council Minutes," 14 September 1752; Thomas B. Akins, ed., *Selections from the Public Documents of Nova Scotia* (Halifax: Annand, 1869), 762–4; LAC, CO 217/40/ 371–7, "Minutes of Council," 16 September 1752.

161 Cope's perspective on the need for separate jurisdictions is discussed by William Wicken, who also noted that the

English hedged at defining what lands would remain under Mi'kmaw aegis. Wicken, *Mi'kmaq Treaties on Trial*, 184–5.

162 The Martin family travelled from Cape Breton to Cobequid and down the Shubenacadie River Valley to Halifax and Musquodoboit. Descendants of another delegate, François Jeremy, still live near Shubenacadie and at Sheet Harbour. The Jeremy family occupied the Sipekne'katik district and maintained hunting territories inland from the Eastern Shore. Many stayed in central Nova Scotia, although others migrated south to Lunenburg and Queens counties. John Jeremy was a chief in the late 1830s at Kejimkujik Lake, Queens County. Joseph Jeremy Jr., born in the early nineteenth century at Elmsdale in the Shubenacadie River Valley, changed his surname around 1854 from "Jeremy" to "Howe" by adopting the surname of well-known journalist and reform politician Joseph Howe. Some of John Jeremy's descendants today live on the Wildcat reserve in Queens County. Interview with Frank Jeremy, 12 June 1991; interview with James Howe, Sheet Harbour, 12 August 2014.

163 Since there are no transcripts of discussions between Cope and Governor Hopson in Halifax, one can only surmise why Cope took so long to sign. When compared to the length of time that elapsed between the chief's initial expression of interest in making a treaty and his signing on 22 November, the second signing event with the Martins and Jeremy was over quickly. Anthony Casteel, who likely acted in 1752 as the government's interpreter, may have made the treaty's terms sound palatable enough to Cope's principal men that they signed without hesitation.

164 NSARM, RG 15, vol. 18, "Newspaper clipping regarding the Treaty of 1752, signed below Fort Needham," *Sunday Leader*, 22 March 1928. Jeremiah Bartlett-Alexis, alias "Jerry Lonecloud," told Harry Piers, curator of the Nova Scotia Museum in 1922, that these items were buried close to a willow that stood by a brook running down past Richmond, now Mulgrave Park, in Halifax. Lonecloud obtained this information from an elderly woman at Ponhook Lake, near Windsor, named Maggie Paul. Nova Scotia Museum (henceforth NSM), Printed Matter File, Piers Papers, "Lone Cloud to Piers," 1922. Lonecloud heard an account of the treaty signing from Joseph Howe, the first of the Mi'kmaw Jeremy family to adopt Joseph Howe's surname. According to Lonecloud, many Mi'kmaw were camped in Halifax in 1752, but not all them agreed to sign the treaty parchment. Cope and his band camped at Richmond, and the treaty was signed

on a large knoll, later known as Fort Needham Hill. An associated story holds that Cope shot an English sentry whose frequent calls disturbed Cope's camp at Richmond, though because of heavy fog the evening the deed was committed no charges could be laid. Howe stated that this second account was told to him by his mother, who heard it in turn from Franklin Brooks. Howe's father was probably a descendant of "Francis Jeremiah" who signed the treaty with Cope. NSM, Printed Matter File, Piers Papers, unpublished notes, "Lone Cloud to Piers," 17 July 1916; Whitehead, *The Old Man Told Us*, 127–8.

165 Akins, *History of Halifax City*, 33–4.

166 This was a phrase appearing in the 1726 treaty. To the Mi'kmaq, who viewed it from the northeastern Algonquian perspective, it meant that English territorial expansion, and in particular the establishment of new settlements, would occur only after consultation with and payment to the Indigenous groups affected.

167 In 1752 the British adopted some French protocols. In September 1752 Hopson gave provisions for six months to the ninety persons of Cope's band as "the French have always done." NSARM, RG , vol. 35, doc. 77; NSARM, RG 1, vol. 186, 214, "Minutes of the Council of Nova Scotia," 22 November 1752; Akins, *Selections from Public Documents*, 783–5.

168 LAC, CO 217/13/384–88, "Hopson to the Lords of Trade and Plantations," 6 December 1752; PANS, RG 1, vol. 186, "Minutes of the Governor's Council," 24 November 1752.

169 Dickason, *Louisbourg and the Indians*, 108.

170 NSARM, RG 1, vol. 29, 1748–99, no. 17, Dispatches from the Board of Trade and Plantations and Secretaries of State to Governors of Nova Scotia, "Trade and Plantations to Hopson," 28 March, 753.

171 LAC, CO 217/13/ 384, "Hopson to the Lords of Trade and Plantations," 6 December 1752.

172 NSARM, RG 1, vol. 35, no. 78 "Hopson to Lords of Trade and Plantations," 4 January 1753.

173 Salusbury, *Expeditions of Honour*, 128, "Entry for 24 October 1752."

174 NSARM, RG 1, vol. 35, no. 77, "Hopson to Lords of Trade and Plantations," 6 December 1752.

175 "Morris to Cornwallis in England," 16 April 1753, prefixed to "Anthony Casteel's journal," 2.112.

176 LAC, AC CIIB, correspondance générale, vol. 32, 163–6, "Prévost à Rouillé, 10 septembre 1752"; LAC, AC CIIB, vol. 33, 159 ff, "Prévost à Rouillé, 12 mai 1753." Prévost reassured his colleagues that any Mi'kmaq who followed Cope's lead were simply taking advantage of an opportunity to go to Halifax and demand presents.

177 LAC, AC CIIB 33, 181v–182v, "Prévost a Rouillé, 17 juin 1753."

178 "Raymond au ministre, 24 novémbre 1752," in Gaston de Bosq de Beaumont, *Les derniers jours de l'Acadie* (Paris: Lechevalier, Librairie Historique des Provinces, 1899), 72. Raymond averred that Cope was a drunkard and that others of his nation had disowned him. His sources were suspect, since he also held that Cope was being detained in prison for some unspecified crime, which may simply have been wishful thinking on his part. He feared that more Mi'kmaw leaders would take advantage of Cope's treaty to solicit presents from the British. To encourage Maillard to take strong action against Cope, he promised the missionary a new church and presbytery.

179 LAC, AC CIIB, vol. 33, 159 ff, "Prévost à Rouillé, 12 mai 1753"; LAC, AC CIIB, vol. 33, 159 ff, "Prévost au minister, 17 juin 1753"; LAC, AC B 97, 313 [289], "Rouillé à Raymond, 17 juillet 1753."

180 Prévost held that ten men were killed and that the ship had been burned at Jeddore.

181 Mocodome, or Country Harbour, was the closest recognizable inlet on maps at the time. The incident actually happened at an unmarked site on the coast between Country Harbour and Tor Bay, probably on the shoreline of a little harbour west of Torbay called Martingo. Also see Whitehead, *The Old Man Told Us*, 136–9; Murdoch, *History of Nova-Scotia*, 1.410.

182 "Records of the Council Chamber for 17 April 1753," in Haliburton, *Historical and Statistical Account of Nova Scotia*, 1.154.

183 Ibid., "Records of the Council Chamber for 16 April 1753."

184 "Anthony Casteel's journal," 2.118.

185 Letter prefixed to "Anthony Casteel's journal," 2.121–2, "Charles Morris to Lord Cornwallis in England," 16 April 1753.

186 Murdoch, *History of Nova-Scotia*, 2.220.

187 LAC, CO 217/14/177–78, "Hopson to the Lords of Trade and Plantations," 29 May 1753; Murdoch, *History of Nova-Scotia*, 2.221.

188 Grenier, *Far Reaches of Empire*, 164. Even though Le Loutre was still in Paris at this time, Cope almost certainly had been refused the sacraments by other missionaries who ministered to the Mi'kmaq, among them Henri Daudin, a Spiritan cleric at Annapolis Royal and Minas who supported Le Loutre's policies. The Spiritan order was founded in Paris in 1703 to prepare missionaries for labours in both Christian and non-Christian countries. Maillard, Le Loutre, and Daudin had all been trained at the Séminaire du Saint-Esprit in Paris, although the latter two were also graduates of the Séminaire des Missions Étrangères. During the eighteenth century, French missionaries in the Northeast could be harsh to those they saw as contravening tenets they believed were necessary for the common good. They operated according to a strict system of rules, or *règlements*, under which perpetrators of a crime could be shamed, ostracized, or even killed. In the late 1730s, a slate of *règlements* was drawn up by a council of Mi'kmaq and French following complaints from Maillard and Le Loutre that their labours were being undermined by chiefs who would not punish crime. Once the notion of publicly shaming a "recalcitrant" took root, punishment could occur spontaneously, as soon as a decision was made in an Indigenous council, even though a missionary might not be present. David L. Schmidt and B.A. Balcom, "The Règlements of 1739: A Note on Micmac Law and Literacy," *Acadiensis* 23, no. 1 (1993): 110–27. As late as 1818, Father Vincent noted that Mi'kmaq at Chezzetcook, along Nova Scotia's Eastern Shore, threatened to kill the Shubenacadie head chief, Louis Benjamin Peminout Paul, because Paul had courted the attentions of a Protestant humanitarian, Walter Bromley. To win back his people's trust and so have his chiefly rank restored, Paul publically professed his loyalty to the tenets of Roman Catholic Church before Vincent's Mi'kmaw congregants. Vincent de Paul, *Memoir of Father Vincent de Paul*, translated by A.M. Pope (Charlottetown: Coombs, 1886), 18–19.

189 "Anthony Casteel's journal," 2.113. Cope wanted to go to Halifax with his family.

190 Ibid.

191 LAC, AC CIIB, Correspondance générale, vol. 33, 159 ff, "Prévost au ministre, 12 mai 1753" and "Prévost au ministre, 17 juin 1753." Prévost held that ten Englishmen were killed and their ship was burned at Jeddore. Also see Whitehead, *The Old Man Told Us*, 136–59.

192 This might not have been pure fabrication on Casteel's part. He may have been baptized as a child into the Roman Catholic faith, since the surname "Casteel" is Spanish in origin. He evinced no hesitation in kissing the ornamental cross suspended from the chief's neck. Cope likely put in a bid to spare Casteel, since the chief regarded the interpreter, whom he met during treaty negotiations in Halifax, as a friend and confidante. Casteel spoke both French and Mi'kmaq fluently, and may have been engaged in his youth in the fur trade.

193 "Anthony Casteel's journal," 2.118. This man's father-in-law expressed discouragement at the British having broken their peacekeeping promises so soon after the treaty was signed.

194 "Anthony Casteel's journal," 2.117; LAC, CO 217/19/200. The man who burned Cope's copy of the treaty was unnamed, and was not necessarily Chief Cope himself, as one historian has averred. Upton, *Micmacs and Colonists*, 55.

195 "Anthony Casteel's journal," 2.121–2. Casteel adds that afterwards those Mi'kmaq who were closest to him "went out of the house and shoved Paul Laurent out before them and used him very ill," possibly for what they saw on Laurent's part as a self-interested design to obtain scalp money. Laurent later attracted considerable attention from the French and British, since he acted as a negotiator and courier for the Mi'kmaw community. LAC, MG 11, Nova Scotia B, (7) 57, 64; (8) 2–7; (9) 47, 166–7; (10) 2, 13–20, 26–42, 49, 148, 160, 166, 171, 182, 184–5, 217, 220, 230, 236, 278, 282, 288; (12) 6, 47, 129, 134, 139, 145, 153, 158, 176, 178, 188–9, 198–9, 209; (13) 95, 188, 216; (14) 13, 15, 107, 170, 181; Upton, *Micmacs and Colonists*, 111–26; Murdoch, *History of Nova-Scotia*, 2.222, 257, 407, 419, 431; Albert David, "L'apôtre des Micmacs," *Revue de l'université d'Ottawa* 5 (1935): 49–82, 425–52; 6 (1936): 22–40; R.O. MacFarlane, "British Indian Policy in Nova Scotia to 1760," *Canadian Historical Review* 19 (1938): 154–67.

196 Le Loutre was elevated by the bishop of Quebec to grand vicar of Acadia in 1752. Murdoch, *History of Nova-Scotia*, 2.214.

197 The antipathy was mutual. Cornwallis once referred to Le Loutre as "a good for nothing ... scoundrel as ever lived." Ibid., 164.

198 "Anthony Casteel's journal," 2.124.

199 "Morris to Cornwallis in England," 16 April 1753, prefixed to "Anthony Casteel's journal," 2.112.

200 Murdoch, *History of Nova-Scotia*, 2.219.

201 NSARM, RG 1, vol. 210, 5, "At a Council holden at the Governor's House," 16 November 1753. The master of the schooner that brought these leaders down from Halifax was paid ten pounds. Murdoch, *History of Nova-Scotia*, 2.225. The delegates received bread, pork, blankets, powder, shot, fifty pounds of tobacco, a gross of smoking pipes, and two gold-laced hats for the chiefs and one hat with a silver band for the deputy, Jean La Perisse. "Chief Thomas" (although a negotiator for the Cape Sable band) was far more likely to be Jean-Baptiste Thoma of Annapolis and Panuke, near Piziquid, than to be Jean-Baptiste Philippe Tecouramart.

202 Several historians have portrayed Chief Cope as a master of ruse and subterfuge. Yet first and foremost he was a war leader who gained prestige with the Mi'kmaq and French (whose language he could speak) through participating in raids on British settlements. He remained a warrior rather than a peacemaker for the rest of his life. He may have appeared erratic and unpredictable in 1753, before his efforts to reinstate himself with the Baie Verte Mi'kmaw community succeeded, but he later associated closely with Joseph Broussard *dit* Beausoleil and the Acadian resistance movement. Doubtless Broussard appreciated his help, for he was a daring guerrilla fighter. His forays also often paid off, for Le Loutre began paying premiums for British scalps. In August 1753 Le Loutre offered Mi'kmaw warriors eighteen hundred livres for eighteen English scalps brought to Fort Beauséjour. LAC, AC CIIB 33: 197–201, "Prévost à Rouillé, 16 août 1753." Some incidents attracted international attention. Early in 1754 it was reported in England that the captain of an English sloop was killed by Mi'kmaq while en route from Louisbourg to Halifax. *Whitehall Evening Post or London Intelligencer*, 1–3 January 1754. Following the onset of the Seven Years' War, Jean-Baptiste Cope emerged exclusively as a war leader. (While war was not officially declared between the French and British Crowns until spring 1756, conflict between the English and French in North America had been going on for years previously. The French captured an English encampment in the Ohio Valley in 1754, Major General Edward Braddock launched an unsuccessful offensive against Fort Duquesne in the same area in June of 1755, and the same month the English in Acadia laid siege to and, afterwards, destroyed Fort Beauséjour. During these years Cope, rather than being shunned by his people, was recognized and rewarded by parties hostile to the English as a leader of men. When Admiral Boscawen captured the *Alcide* and the *Lys* off Cape Race, Newfoundland, on 8 June 1755, he found that the two French ships were carrying ten thousand scalping knives for distribution to, among others, Jean-Baptiste Cope and Joseph Broussard *dit* Beausoleil. The following year Cope received sixty livres for two scalps, presumably of English settlers, according to Louisbourg accounts. Because of raids launched against them by Mi'kmaq and Acadian resistance fighters, settlements in Lunenburg County out of necessity stood in the shadow of blockhouses. As early as December 1753, three hundred German settlers, unnerved by these forays, holed up in a blockhouse and declared their intention "to throw off the yoke of British subjection," so the Mi'kmaq would distinguish them as a people apart from the English and spare them from attack. The English branded this incident as a form of mutiny. Murdoch, *History of Nova-Scotia*, 2.227–9. Seven major raids occurred in the

Lunenburg area between 1753 and 1759. In 1756, follow-ing the onset of the Seven Years' War, Joseph Broussard *dit* Beausoleil led Acadian resistance fighters from Three Rivers and Mi'kmaw and Malecite warriors from Baye Verte in a major attack on the Lunenburg settlers. The war party was joined in southwestern Nova Scotia by disgruntled members of the Mius *dit* d'Azy and Guedry *dit* Labrador families, who had been displaced from their lands.

203 French officials during the late seventeenth century encouraged the Mi'kmaq to regard the French king as their "father" who, in return for protection and honour, demanded military service. They also vested warriors with quasi-military rank and continued to pay for Brit-ish scalps, which led to scalps being traded within the Indigenous community as a kind of gristly currency. LAC, AC CIIA 122, 10–42, "Lettre anonyme de Québec, 30 septembre 1705"; LAC, AC CIIB 36, 231–42, "Bor-dereau, 20 décembre 1756." British settlers, too, were paid for Mi'kmaw scalps under the terms of British scalp proclamations, whose principal goal was to eliminate the Mi'kmaq as a threat to British territorial aspirations. Thomas Raddall, *Halifax: Warden of the North* (Halifax: Nimbus, 1993 [1948]), 45.

204 For a discussion of the complexities underlying Mi'kmaw-French and Mi'kmaw-Acadian relations at this time, see Thomas Peace, "A Reluctant Engagement: Alliances and Social Networks in Early-18th-Century Kespukwitk and Port-Royal," *Acadiensis* 49, no. 1 (2020): 5–38.

205 Lawrence paid special attention to Beauséjour, Petitco-diac, Shepody, Memramcook, Shediac, Remsheg, and Cape Sable, which he viewed as locales from which Mi'kmaq and French attacked the Lunenburg County settlements. NSARM, RG 1, vol. 36, 7, "Statement of Charles Lawrence," Minutes of Council, 1 August, 1754; NSARM, RG 1, vol. 39, "Minutes of Council," 26 Decem-ber 1758.

206 NSARM, RG 1, vol. 29, no. 25, "Lords of Trade and Plan-tations to Col. Lawrence," 4 March 1754. Plans were be-ing laid for the removal of the Acadians from Grand Pré, the Three Rivers area, and the Saint John River Valley. NSARM, RG 1, vol. 30, no. 13, "Letter from Secretary of State," 10 March 1757. As late as 1756 the secretary of state admitted that little was known about the location of In-digenous settlements or the nature of Indigenous activi-ties. NSARM, RG 1, vol. 30, no. 5, "Letter to Lawrence," 8 July 1756.

207 Murdoch, *History of Nova-Scotia*, 2.210, 230. In 1752 Charles Morris had visited this area, lying between Cole

Harbour and Chezzekcook, and reported on the lay of the land. He also discovered a spot on the Dartmouth side, opposite McNab's Island, that had been cleared by the Mi'kmaq and Acadian *métis* and used as an encamp-ment ground during their raids on Dartmouth.

208 Lawrence tried two years later to resettle Lawencetown, but when attacks resumed on the settlement during the Seven Years' War, the scenario of 1754 repeated itself. The governor did not try to resettle Lawrencetown a third time. The settlement that finally developed in this area arose after the Seven Years' War.

209 "Letter no. 24, Thomas Pichon to Captain Hussey, 13 Jan-uary 1755," in John Clarence Webster, *Pichon, "The Spy of Beausejour,"* 81–2.

210 In New England, Penobscot diplomats had stressed that two New England forts, Fort Georges and Fort Rich-mond, both built in 1720 on the west bank of the Ken-nebec River by the Massachusetts Bay Colony and a land company known as the Pejepscot Proprietors, be razed to ensure the neutrality of the region. They further pro-posed that the Kennebec River be regarded as the south-ern boundary of a buffer zone that would extend all the way north to the southern limits of Acadia. In this they were echoing an idea put forward by members of the Massachusetts Council, among them Jonathan Belcher Sr., the father of Jonathan Belcher Jr., Nova Scotia's lieutenant governor who in 1762 presented Argimault's proposals to his superiors in England.

211 James S. Macdonald, "Memoir. Lieut.-Governor Michael Francklin, 1752–1782," in *Collections of the Nova Scotia Historical Society* 16 (Halifax: W. McNab and Son, 1912): 10. In 1754 Francklin was a well-known Halifax mer-chant who spoke fluent French. He was hunting between Halifax and Grand Lake, in the Shubenacadie River Val-ley, with two Mi'kmaw guides when he was overtaken by a Malecite party who marched him to Beauséjour and had plans to send him on to Canada. At Chignecto, however, a Mi'kmaq man intervened on his behalf and allowed him to remain with the man's family for three months. After his release, Francklin was in no hurry to go home, and his new Mi'kmaw associates, who by this time were living at Gaspé, accommodated his wishes. Francklin asked that money be sent to him at Gaspé so he could remain long enough to learn the Mi'kmaw lan-guage. He felt quite safe, for Abbé Le Loutre respected the Mi'kmaw decision to hold a ceasefire, at least until such time as peacemaking negotiations could be opened with the British. (Interestingly, when Francklin first ar-rived in Halifax in 1752 he asked Captain John Connor, the same man later implicated in the robbery at Jeddore

and the murders at Mocodome, what profession he should enter in the new town. Connor told him to open a rum shop.)

212 In the 1860s, historian and lawyer Beamish Murdoch, in holding that Le Loutre used Hamilton for his own purposes, failed to appreciate that Hamilton had come to value aspects of Mi'kmaw culture. "Le Loutre seems to have thought it expedient to endeavour to open some negotiations with the English on behalf of his Mi'kmaw followers," Murdoch wrote, "and he availed himself of Hamilton's gratitude and good opinion to make him the channel of intercourse." To Murdoch, Hamilton since 1749 "retained a sense of obligation to [Le Loutre] for his civilities." Murdoch, *History of Nova-Scotia*, 2.235.

213 "William Cotterrell to John Hamilton at Annapolis," 3 June 1754, quoted in ibid., 2.235.

214 NSARM, RG 1, vol. 187, 85–97, "Le Loutre to Governor Lawrence," 27 August 1754.

215 Murdoch, *History of Nova-Scotia*, 2.235–6.

216 Pichon left a secretarial post under the Compte de Raymond at Louisbourg in November 1753 to become a scribe and chief clerk responsible for stores for the French commandants at Fort Beauséjour.

217 Thomas Pichon, *Genuine Letters and Memoirs*, 119.

218 The commission's findings, published belatedly in 1755, were immediately made redundant by the onset of the Seven Years' War.

219 NSARM, RG 1, vol. 187, 85–97, "Le Loutre to Governor Lawrence and Council," 27 August 1754, included in "Minutes of Council for 9 September 1754." (Translation from the French by the author.)

220 For further information on this surveying expedition, see Mathew Floyer, *Captain Mathew Floyer's Survey Report: Journal of the March by the River Shebenaccadia* (Halifax: Public Archives of Nova Scotia, 1958), 17.

221 Some Acadian refugees resented Le Loutre's interference in their lives. To duck his directives, a party of French refugees from Chignecto in 1753, while Jean-Baptiste Mutigny de Vassan was commandant at Beauséjour, approached Halifax and stated they were willing to swear a conditional oath to the British king as long as they did not have to take up arms against the English, French, or Mi'kmaq. They also did not want to be compelled against their will into acting as pilots or guides and wanted to have free exercise of their Roman Catholic religion. Murdoch, *History of Nova-Scotia*, 2.223.

222 This man was probably Étienne Bâtârd.

223 NSARM, RG 1, vol. 187, 85–97, "Le Loutre to Governor Lawrence and Council," 27 August 1754. The missionary was criticized by his French superiors for employing

Mi'kmaq to control Acadian movements. Although the governor general of Canada, Michel-Ange Duquesne de Menneville, the Marquis Duquesne, lauded Le Loutre's policy of striking fear into the hearts of the British settlers by encouraging Mi'kmaw attacks, the bishop of Quebec, Le Loutre's religious superior, denounced the priest's actions in threatening the refugee Acadians with Indigenous reprisals and manipulating the sacraments for purely temporal purposes. When he heard that some refugee Acadians had appealed to Governor Lawrence for protection from Le Loutre's harassment, the bishop cautioned Le Loutre, "There you are, my dear sir, in the embarrassment which I foresaw and told you of beforehand." Quoted in Murdoch, *History of Nova-Scotia*, 2.253.

224 Le Loutre to Governor Lawrence and Council," 27 August 1754.

225 Ibid.

226 Ibid.

227 Ibid.

228 NSARM, RG 1, vol. 187, 97, "Governor Charles Lawrence's reply of 9 September 1754 to Le Loutre's letter of 27 August 1754."

229 Webster, *Pichon, "The Spy of Beauséjour,"* 81–2, letter no. 24, "Thomas Pichon to Captain Hussey," 13 January 1755; letter no. 25, "Le Loutre to Hussey," 15 January 1755.

230 Paul Laurent spoke French, but Hussey was not fluent in that language. Pichon was giving Hussey language lessons and correcting his letters written in French.

231 Ibid., 82, letter no. 26, "Hussey to Le Loutre," 15 January 1755.

232 Ibid., 83, letter no. 27, "Hussey to Mi'kmaw chiefs," 18 January 1755.

233 Ibid., 84, letter no. 28, "Chief Alkimou to Hussey," 19 January 1755.

234 Ibid., 85, letter no. 30, "Hussey to Lawrence," 20 January 1755. Hussey adhered to Pichon's view that Le Loutre was the real instigator of the peace proposals drafted by the Mi'kmaq, and during his half-hour interview with the chiefs did his best to make them see what he called "Le Loutre's drift" in making peace. The chiefs remained unimpressed by these warnings.

235 Ibid., 84, letter no. 29, "Hussey to Alkimou," 20 January 1755. This is almost identical to the words Hussey sent to the Mi'kmaw chiefs on 18 January when he wrote: "and I am certain if they [the chiefs] go well-disposed toward peace, they shall have all they can reasonably ask, because the General desires nothing so much as a firm and solid peace with them, and wishes to give them all the satisfaction possible with this end in view." Ibid.,

83, letter no. 27, "Hussey to Mi'kmaw chiefs," 18 January 1755.

236 Ibid., 85, letter no. 30, "Hussey to Lawrence," 20 January 1755.

237 The best information Pichon could acquire regarding the Mi'kmaq's military strength was from Madelaine le Songuer, the wife of Chief Jean-Baptiste Philippe de Conoumak (Tecouramart) of Cape Sable, one of Argimault's confidants. Madelaine spoke French well. Pichon learned from her that around 20 warriors lived at Tatamagouche, 50 at Pictou, 20 at Shediac, 17 at Richibucto, 150 at Miramichi, 120 from the Baye de Chaleurs, 120 from Remickik near the Bay de Chaleur, and 57 from Gaspereau. He knew these numbers may have been high, but he was sure that at any time the Mi'kmaq might muster at least "449 men or youths." Ibid., 81–2, letter no. 24, "Pichon to Hussey," 13 January 1755. According to Pichon, the two chiefs at Gaspereau were "Arguimault" and "François," the latter probably Argimault's son.

238 Webster, *Pichon, "The Spy of Beauséjour,"* 85–6, letter no. 31, "Pichon to Hussey," 24 January 1755.

239 Ibid., letter no. 33, "Pichon to Hussey," 3 February 1755. It is doubtful if Pichon and Hussey met face to face, though tentative arrangements for such a meeting were made on 31 January 1755. The two would get together at the Chignecto residence of Captain Sylvanus Cobb, who at the time was supplying goods to Fort Lawrence. The courier that Hussey used to convey messages to Fort Lawrence remains unnamed, although it is mentioned he was a surgeon's mate. The courier had to go by way of Butte à Roger, where Indigenous spies were less numerous than at the Buot bridge. Pichon had finally won Hussey's trust, as it was obvious Pichon had little love for the French officers at Fort Beauséjour and especially the commandant, de Chambon de Vergor, whom Pichon felt was lining his pockets from trade in wood and furs, thinking he had "authority to plunder." Though Vergor was a descendant of La Tour and well connected socially within the colony, Pichon regarded him as incompetent, noting wryly to Hussey that the commandant was "scarcely able to sign his name." H.R. Casgrain, ed., *Collection de documents inédits sur le Canada et l'Amérique publiés par le Canada-Français* (Quebec: Demers and Frère, 1889), 2.134, "Letter LXXXIX, Critique on Pychon by Captain Hussey," 11 November 1754. Hussey wote, "The inconsistence, the fear of guilt, make the guilty consult absurdities ruinous to themselves. Traitors are never cordially believed. They have broken the holiest obligations, how is it possible to bind them by ordinary

ties!" Hussey changed his opinion of Pichon, who later took the surname "Tirel" or "Tyrell," and came to rely heavily on his correspondence, especially as Pichon sent survey plans and other pertinent information regarding Fort Beauséjour's vulnerabilities to British attack. Webster, *Pichon, "The Spy of Beauséjour,"* 89–90, "Letter no. 33, Pichon to Hussey," 3 February 1755.

240 Paul Laurent, as the only remaining spokesperson, probably lacked sufficient authority to negotiate on behalf of his people.

241 NSARM, RG 1, vol. 210, 109, "Minutes of Council," 12 February 1755.

242 Mary Rose Black-Rogers, "The Ojibwa Power-Belief System," in *The Anthropology of Power*, ed. F.D. Fogelson and R.N. Adams (New York: Academic Press, 1977), 141–51.

243 "Minutes of the Governor-in-Council, 12 February 1755," in NSARM, RG 1, vol. 210, 109–11 and NSARM, RG 1, vol. 187, 184–6.

244 The British considered, as they had before, the demands preposterous for a number of sound strategic and military reasons, not in the least being the obvious advantages they brought to the French, who could sail unobstructed along the Northumberland Strait from Louisbourg to Quebec. Other reasons were the fact that Le Loutre wanted Canso to be neutral but for the French to have exclusive fishing rights there, and that there was no mention of the French forts on the Chignecto Isthmus being in any way demilitarized once Fort Lawrence was dismantled. This last was especially worrisome to the British, since Le Loutre in 1752 in Paris had originally seen the British restricted to southwestern Nova Scotia by a ring of French forts, and the Indigenous scheme required that though neither French nor British forts could be present within the desired tract, Fort Beauséjour would remain on its northwestern periphery.

245 Lawrence to Robert Monckton, 16 February, in "Two Letters of Charles Lawrence," *Cahiers de la Société historique Acadienne* 3 (December 1969): 175.

246 NSARM, RG 1, vol. 210, 111–12, "Minutes of Council," 13 February 1755.

247 Webster, *Pichon, "The Spy of Beauséjour,"* 88–9, Letter no. 33, "Pichon to Hussey, 3 February 1755." Le Loutre was not alone in holding these views on the problems faced by the Mi'kmaq. A Monsieur de La Varenne at Louisbourg in 1756 averred that the British settlers burned vast tracts well into the interior of the province that scared away game. La Varenne felt the British had ruined their chances of establishing cordial relations with the Indigenous peoples early on. If the British,

he contended, instead "of seeking to exterminate" the Mi'kmaq by "dint of power," had "behaved with more tenderness to them, and conciliated their affection by humoring them properly and distributing a few presents, they might easily have made useful ... Whereas disgusted with their haughtiness, and scared of the menaces and arbitrary encroachments of the English, they are now their most virulent and scarce reconcilable enemies." "A Letter from Louisbourg, 1756, written by Monsieur de La Varenne to a friend at La Rochelle, dated 8 May 1756, with an introduction by Ken Donovan," in *Acadiensis* 10, no. 1 (1980): 119.

248 Webster, *Pichon, "The Spy of Beauséjour,"* 89–90, Letter no. 33, "Pichon to Hussey," 3 February 1755. Since 1710 the British unilaterally had expropriated resources for themselves by erecting fish weirs to which they reserved exclusive access, and clearing uplands for agriculture that depleted the wild animal population, with no thought of compensating those injured by their actions. In 1756 Pichon was certainly not as sympathetic as the missionary – perhaps because he did not understand as much as Le Loutre did regarding Mi'kmaw problems over land. Instead, Pichon held that there was enough land left in Nova Scotia for both Mi'kmaq and British to share, and he had a hard time fathoming the deep attachment chiefs like Argimault had to a land scheme in which, according to Pichon's estimation, the missionary held such a determining share. Pichon held a jaundiced perspective on Le Loutre's reasons for upholding the Mi'kmaq's scheme, and argued that the abbé had been skimming off supplies and presents given him for dispersal to the Mi'kmaq for years, and thus "imposing, with the greatest effrontery on the poor people."

249 When Pichon told Hussey on 31 January 1755 that the missionary said the commander of Fort Lawrence had "gone too far," Hussey wanted Pichon to explain the meaning of Le Loutre's cryptic comment. Pichon replied that Le Loutre feared Hussey might acquiesce to some of the Indigenous proposals rather than denounce them outright, which would blunt the poignancy of a rejection, and hence their anger. Le Loutre thought that "you promised them to abandon Mejagouech [Fort Lawrence]," and hoped "that their visit to Halifax would result in a rude awakening." Ibid., 85–6, Letter no. 32, "Pichon to Hussey," 31 January 1755.

250 Ibid., 85, Letter no. 31, "Pichon to Hussey," 24 January 1755.

251 Wicken, who focuses on reinterpretations of the 1726 treaties from both the Mi'kmaw and British points of view, argues forcefully that, as the British were encroaching on Mi'kmaw lands, Laurent wanted to "renegotiate the 1726 treaty" to safeguard Mi'kmaw fishing and hunting grounds against "the enlarged British presence." Wicken, *Mi'kmaq Treaties on Trial,* 169, 190. Argimault would certainly have known about the 1726 treaty, since his father and brother had signed it, and a copy of the treaty might even have been in his possession. By contrast, Dickason argues that each treaty setting was viewed by the Mi'kmaq as a novel forum for discussion. Dickason, *Louisbourg and the Indians,* 105. Doubtless the Mi'kmaq, however, retained in their collective memory parts of the 1726 treaty that best suited their interests.

252 Wicken, *Mi'kmaq Treaties on Trial,* 190. Wicken notes that in 1755 "any hope that the Nova Scotia Council might accept Laurent's suggestions died a quick death through association with Le Loutre."

253 The campaign revived five years later with Maillard as its main spokesperson. As the Mi'kmaq had stated at Port Toulouse on 24 September 1749, their campaign dealt with a customary right, given to them by the Great Spirit, to lands and resources.

254 In fall 1754 Governor Shirley of Massachusetts called on Lieutenant Colonel Robert Monckton and Captain George Scott for assistance in mounting a secret naval expedition out of Boston to take the French forts on the Isthmus of Chignecto. Though the French had spies in Boston, their reports back to Chignecto proved sketchy as to details, so throughout the summer of 1754 and spring of 1755 Vergor was barraged by vague alarms of war that kept him on edge, without providing him with any firm course of action.

255 Webster, *Pichon, "The Spy of Beauséjour,"* 86–8, "Letter no. 32, Pichon to Hussey," 31 January 1755.

256 The commandant of Fort Beauséjour, Vergor, was said to have been awakened by a messenger of this event at two o'clock in the morning.

257 Murdoch, *History of Nova-Scotia,* 2.269.

258 "Journal of Louis de Courville," in John Clarence Webster, ed., *Journals of Beauséjour* (Halifax: Public Archives of Nova Scotia, 1937), 47–50; Murdoch, *History of Nova-Scotia,* 2.273. Historian Olive Patricia Dickson has written that the form of "total war" with its highly destructive technology, as waged at Beauséjour and Louisbourg in the 1750s, was nothing like the conflicts the Mi'kmaq or Malecite had ever waged in pre-contact days. By the mid-1750s war to the Mi'kmaq became less ritualized and more of a "desperate attempt to save something" of the Mi'kmaw way of life. Dickason, *Louisbourg and the Indians,* 149.

259 "Marquis de Vaudreuil au minister," 24 juillet 1755, in Placide Godet, *Acadian Genealogy and Notes*, Report Concerning the Canadian Archives for the Year 1905 (Ottawa: S.E. Dawson Printer, 1906), vol. 2, pt. 2, 344; E.B. Callaghan, ed., *Documents Relating to the Colonial History of New York* (Albany: Weed, Parsons and Co. Printers, 1858), 10.15; Webster, *Journals of Beauséjour*, 23; John Clarence Webster, ed., *Charles des Champs de Boishébert: A Canadian Solider in Acadia* (Shediac: privately printed, 1931), 15; Grenier, *Far Reaches of Empire*, 197.

260 LAC, AC CIIB 25, 59–61v, "Drucour et Prévost au minister, 11 novembre 1755"; LAC, AC CIIB 35, 59–61v, "Journal du siège du Louisbourg, 1758"; Dickason, *Louisbourg and the Indians*, 145. For many years Maillard's mission had been located at Malagowatch, Cape Breton, but in 1754 he moved his mission to Chapel Island.

261 Callaghan, *Documents Relating to the Colonial History of New York*, 10.15.

262 Cope was reported to be at Miramichi with Joseph Broussard *dit* Beausoleil after 1755. Murdoch, *History of Nova-Scotia*, 2.193.

263 After the fall of Fort Beauséjour to the British, Governor Lawrence regarded the presence of Acadian irregulars involved in the defence of Fort Beauséjour as an infraction of Acadian neutrality and used this fact to compel Acadian inhabitants to swear an unconditional oath of allegiance to the British Crown. As they had before, the majority of Acadians refused to comply. On 10 August, under Lawrence's directive, Monckton rounded up four hundred Acadian men and imprisoned them at Fort Cumberland to await deportation. This deportation action was extended to other settlements over the next few months, and in all around seven thousand Acadians were taken.

264 A major expedition of two hundred men led by Major Joseph Frye set out on 28 August 1755. "Diary of John Thomas," in Webster, *Journals of Beauséjour* (Halifax, 1937), 23; Grenier, *Far Reaches of Empire*, 197. Over eleven hundred Acadians were captured or otherwise affected by such British incursions along the Petitcodiac River. Two hundred troops under Major Joseph Frye destroyed the settlement of Three Rivers, beginning with Shepody. Acadian resistance fighters, along with Mi'kmaq and Malecite directed by Boishébert, counter-attacked, and it has been suggested that there were as many as twenty-three British casualties. After Frye abandoned his campaign, Boishébert evacuated the Shepody region and moved a number of Acadians to Shediac. Broussard led raids against British vessels sailing into the Bay of Fundy, which provoked George Scott, now a lieutenant colonel, to root out any Acadians remaining in the Shepody region, where some tenacious Acadians had started rebuilding homes. Boishébert's forces ambushed Scott's party, killing two of Scott's men.

265 About 1,066 people from Piziguit Windsor were boarded on four vessels on 13 October 1755, and on 20 October they left port to meet with other transports leaving Grand Pré on the Minas Basin, and from the Cumberland Basin, to sail in convoy to New England, Maryland, and other areas in the Thirteen Colonies.

266 Resistance guerillas were forever on guard to resist these burnings. It took Jeremiah Preble, Benjamin Goldthwait, and four hundred men to burn a single village outside Fort Monckton. Grenier, *Far Reaches of Empire*, 183.

267 Marshall, *Heroes of the Acadian Resistance*, chaps. 8 and 9. In 1756 Charles Boishébert returned for a time to the Saint John River before leaving for Shediac. Resistance fighters sometimes made daring escapes. For example, Joseph Broussard *dit* Beausoleil, who had been captured and held in captivity at Fort Lawrence, escaped with eighty-six others by digging a tunnel underneath the fort's wall and escaping to the woods on 1 October 1755.

268 They numbered about six hundred individuals.

269 French provisioning ships appeared sporadically, and as Le Loutre had not completed his *aboiteau* project, population exceeded the carrying capacity of the resource base.

270 The Marquis Duquesne built a string of forts between Lake Erie and the Ohio Valley to contain British expansion into Ohio country by the Ohio Company, an association of Virginian and British merchants and traders. Duquesne's actions invited British reprisals. In the spring of 1754 the governor of Virginia, Robert Dinwiddie, directed George Washington to respond militarily to what the he considered to be French aggression in the Ohio country. As a result Washington's men, finding themselves penned within an incomplete British entrenchment dubbed "Fort Necessity" near the Monongahela River, were defeated on 28 May 1754 by a French force under the command of Joseph Coulon de Villiers, Sieur de Jumonville (said to be the brother of Nicholas-Antoine Coulon de Villiers who had led the attack on Arthur Noble's troops at Grand Pré in 1747). This clash, in which Jumonville lost his life, ignited a series of attacks and counter-attacks between French and British in the Ohio region, as well as elsewhere in the Northeast. This North American conflict – usually known to American historians as the "Fourth French and Indian War" – rapidly escalated until eclipsed in 1756 by the onset of the Seven Years' War on the world stage.

271 The resistance forces were very canny. In February 1756 Lawrence sent a vessel disguised under French colours to the Saint John River, but the Acadians and Malecite saw through the ruse and set fire to the ship. Not long after, Captain George Scott set out to Chignecto to find Boishébert; he was ambushed from the rear by the man he was looking for and lost two of his regulars. Fort Cumberland was under siege on April 26 and 27 during which time nine British soldiers were killed and scalped. On April 26 Lieutenant Bowan of Fort Monckton, along with a party of thirty men, was attacked while out getting wood. George Scott responded by offering his rangers twenty-five pounds for each male Mi'kmaw prisoner above sixteen years old. Murdoch, *History of Nova-Scotia*, 2.304–6.

272 See Mather Byles Desbrisay, *History of the County of Lunenburg*, 2nd ed. (Toronto: William Briggs, 1895), 498; Winthrop Pickard Bell, *The "Foreign Protestants" and the Settlement of Nova Scotia* (Toronto: University of Toronto Press, 1961), 510. In 1755 relatives of Paul Guedry *dit* Labrador at Merligueshe had been taken off the provisioning list by the British. On 24 August 1754 nine of Labrador's relatives had asked for land and provisions from the British, and an agreement was made for the duration of only one year with William Cotterell. Anger within this family grew when Paul Labrador's land was confiscated and given to Colonel Sutherland. NSARM, RG 1, vol. 134, 242, "Letter of Secretary William Cotterell," 24 August, 1754; NSARM, RG 1, vol 204, 51, "Seven acres belonging to Paul Labrador confiscated and given to Col. Sutherland at Lunenburg."

273 Five of the remaining settlers – Marie Anne Payzant, whose husband Louis had been killed, and her four young children – were taken prisoner and sent to Quebec.

274 LAC, CO A 60, "Regarding proclamation of 14 May 1756, Lawrence to the Lord of Trade and Plantations," 25 May 1756. A copy of this proclamation can also be found in Murdoch, *History of Nova-Scotia*, 2.308.

275 Murdoch, *History of Nova-Scotia*, 319.

276 These Acadians had already removed from around Beaubassin and had limited resources, with no crops, no houses, and no farm animals. The years from 1756 to 1758 thus were an time of extreme poverty for these people.

277 Paris, Archives de la Marine, Série B4, Article 76, 41, "Mémoire concernant les Savages Mikcmacs, malechites et Cannibas rassembler dur la côte de L'ile Royale en 1757, de Emmanuel-Auguste de Cahideuc, Comte du Bois de la Motte, lieutenant général des armées navales."

278 Hearing about Lord Loudoun's plan to attack Louisbourg by sea and land, France in January began to send squadrons from Brest and Toulon to reinforce the squadron at Louisbourg. Comte du Bois de La Motte commanded one of the squadrons at Louisbourg, which was joined by another from Saint-Dominque and two frigates from Toulon. Although Admiral Holburne was aware of the arrival of these French reinforcements, his expedition only set sail in early August. By mid-August he was patrolling off Louisbourg, while La Motte continued to stay in the harbour. Finally, after several weeks, the storm season set in, and on 24 September 1757 the British fleet was scattered by a gale. Compte du Bois de La Motte returned to Brest, with typhus aboard his fleet, on 30 October.

279 This attack occurred near the same site where a force of Acadians and Mi'kmaq ambushed a troop of soldiers sent out from Annapolis Royal by Colonel Vetch in 1711. It still retains the name "Bloody Creek."

280 Boishébert alone was said to have mustered five hundred Indigenous warriors and Acadians in 1758. LAC, AC CIIA 103, 140–1, "Vaudreuil au ministre, 3 août 1758."

281 LAC, AC CIIC 16, "pièce 13," 1757.

282 For information on provisioning and preparing around seven hundred Indigenous militia, see the following Louisbourg accounts: LAC, AC CIIB 36, 209v, 29 November 1756; LAC, AC CIIB 37, 278v, 30 September 1757.

283 Maillard contended that the Mi'kmaq became "disgusted with the idea of remaining in camp where nothing was done by sleeping, and eating the livestock of the inhabitants. There was a failure in discipline and all decided to retreat." Quoted in Webster, *Charles des Champs de Boishébert*, 15. See also Grenier, *Far Reaches of Empire*, 197.

284 During an early foray a French officer died and the Mi'kmaq lost one of their chiefs and several warriors, so at first the Mi'kmaq and the French tried to resist the English landing. Murdoch, *History of Nova-Scotia*, 2.339.

285 Micheline D. Johnson, "Maillard, Pierre," *Dictionary of Canadian Biography* online, vol. 3 (1741–70). Maillard had pressed Boishébert to march on the town with his Indigenous and Acadian militia and then run the blockade that was being set up by the British and New Englanders.

286 The British had mustered a formidable force. Pitt assigned the high-ranking duties to Major General Jeffrey Amherst, whose brigadiers were Charles Lawrence, James Wolfe, and Edward Whitmore. Command of the navy was placed under Admiral Edward Boscawen. John Henry Bastide, the expedition's engineer, was at the first siege of Louisbourg.

287 Charles Lawrence complained to the Colonial Office that the Mi'kmaq still harassed the "promising settlement at Lunenburg" and on 26 December 1758 attacked a whole family. LAC, CO 217/116/305–307½. Amherst in his reply blamed the Mius family. Several of "The wild, the Gay, the sportive [Mius] D'Entremonts with their Indian blood," he observed cynically, had fled the English and kept up raids on the settlers. *Collection de documents inédits sur le Canada et l'Amérique*, 2.140, "Extract from a letter from General Amherst to Brigadier-General Lawrence," 29 May 1759.

288 Murdoch, *History of Nova-Scotia*, 2.350.

289 Marshall, *Heroes of the Acadian Resistance*, 164. Rangers led by Benoni Danks and Joseph Gorham focused on hunting down Acadians who had sought refuge in the Petitcodiac River region. As early as 21 March 1758, Gorham's rangers attacked Shepody, since they heard that Acadians had rebuilt farms there. They found only women and children. The men had left for Fort Cumberland, where they attacked a schooner. Danks also began to focus on taking the Acadian resistance leaders. He claimed that the scalps he took were Mi'kmaq and received payments for them, though they may have been Acadian scalps. Grenier, *Far Reaches of Empire*, 165, 197.

290 In the past, Maillard may have offered rewards for English scalps, but it is doubtful he ever manipulated the sacraments.

291 This proclamation is published in Marshall, *Heroes of the Acadian Resistance*, 172; for another, later proclamation see Murdoch, *History of Nova-Scotia*, 2.259–60.

292 In October 1758 Governor Lawrence optimistically proclaimed that the Acadian's lands were ready for advertisement to potential settlers from New England, though the continued campaigns of Indigenous and Acadian resistance fighters would prevent such lands being taken up for another two years. Some Acadian refugees from the Petitcodiac River campaign went to the Penobscot River area. Governor Thomas Pownall of Massachusetts had claimed control of this region since 1752. Although Pownall was sympathetic to the Acadians, his council was not, and early in 1759 there was a movement afoot to send out Jedidiah Preble to seek and get rid of the Acadians in the Penobscot River territory.

293 The site of Burnt Church on the Miramichi area was originally a Mi'kmaq encampment but became an Acadian settlement; today it forms the core of the Mi'kmaw community of Burnt Church. There was an Acadian village located in the area as early as 1727.

294 Murdoch, *History of Nova-Scotia*, 2.306. The following year the hostilities and destruction only escalated. In

1759 Moses Hazen ordered villages along the Saint John River destroyed, including the levelling and burning of Sainte-Anne-de-Pays-Bas, the Acadian village that stood on the site of present-day Fredericton. The hostilities involved numbers of Acadian women and children as well as men. With Lawrence's scalp proclamation still in effect, soldiers and rangers often scalped both Mi'kmaw and Acadian fighters who resisted them, and usually received bounties for both. Back in 1756, the commander at Fort Cumberland, George Scott, actually proposed placing bounties on both Acadian and Mi'kmaq scalps, as well as on individuals from both communities brought in alive. To Scott, the two peoples deserved equal punishment since they acted in conjunction in resisting the government in ways that were practically indistinguishable. He was, however, prevented from carrying out his plan by Governor Lawrence, who feared reprisals from the Lords of Trade and Plantations. Yet despite the official prohibition on taking Acadian scalps, by 1758 rangers frequently collected them for monetary gain from as many sources as they could access on the field of battle.

295 Though the Mi'kmaq still trapped, there were no trading posts operating in the late 1750s on the Petitcodiac or Saint John Rivers to receive the furs. To travel in pursuit of the traditional seasonal economic round proved extremely risky, owing to Lawrence's bounty proclamation still being in effect and parties of scalp-hungry rangers scouring the countryside until late into the season.

296 Marshall, *Heroes of the Acadian Resistance*, 174.

297 Ibid., 172–3.

298 Ibid., 175–6; Murdoch, *History of Nova-Scotia*, 2.366.

299 Ibid., 2.367.

300 Ibid.

301 Brown, *Place Names*, 92. *Malagomich*, or *Mallegomichk*, has been given several translations, one of which, provided by the Reverend Silus Tertius Rand, means "place of merrymaking." This, if correct, likely refers more to the annual celebration of revitalization ceremonies on Malagomich Island than to bouts of unrestrained revelry. Another translation is "hardwood grove" and yet another "punctuated or divided by coves," so there is diversity of opinion about its meaning. In the mid-eighteenth century the area was dominated by majestic pine forests, which although forming shelter from roving bands of rangers, did not provide good browse for game animals and so the area's carrying capacity remained limited. Since the 1720s, Mi'kmaq in the area had been encouraged by missionaries to engage in some horticulture, and possibly the Mi'kmaq at Malagomich in 1758

continued this practice to supplement their returns from the woods, rivers, and sea. For other supplies, including ammunition, the group resorted to raiding British shipping passing up Northumberland Strait. They released the crews but confiscated the cargos for their own purposes. *Boston Gazette*, 10 September 1759; Wicken, *Mi'kmaq Treaties on Trial*, 193.

302 Whitmore later wrote Amherst, "In the Month of August I was informed that Several vessells [*sic*, vessels] were taken, among Others One or Two Traded with, Necessary for the army of this Garrison & Cattle for the army before Quebec by a small Privateer fitted out from Pictou, a French & Indian settlement within the Gutt [*sic*, Gut] of Canso … There being none of his Majesty's ships here, nor any where upon the Coast, I thought it Necessary, after Repeated accounts of Vesells taken (and I believe in the whole there was [*sic*] about twenty some of Them of great value, to fit out some small vessels in Order to Destroy the Enemy's Vessells." British War Office Records, copies on microfilm at Library and Archives of Canada (henceforth LAC, WO) 24/17, "Whitmore to Amherst," 22 January 1760.

303 One interesting oral tradition derived from Acadian sources recounts that on 29 September 1759 Henry Schomberg threatened the Malagomich community with famine and death by the sword. See www.acadian-home.org/chezzetcook.html. This story does not correlate well with his conciliatory attitude in October, though he may have suffered from a mental disability that made him subject to rapid mood changes, as Whitmore later suggested. If this was so, the provisions in the pact, which promised to uphold the continuance of the Roman Catholic religion, probably issued directly from Maillard rather than from Schomberg, who may simply have agreed to them when they were presented to him in a logical way by the missionary.

304 In December 1759 Henry Schomberg lost the confidence of his superiors by behaviour that brought him, on 2 January 1760, to the brink of a regimental court martial. He would probably have endured the punishment, had not the court martial process been stayed by a charge that Schomberg was mentally disordered. Schomberg first ran into difficulties because he promised the Mi'kmaq expensive presents, which contravened British policy. Amherst refused to countenance the giving of presents in 1760 and 1761. LAC, CO 60/27–28, "General Amherst at New York to the Colonial Office," 12 December 1760. Brigadier-General Edward Whitmore was one of the first persons to charge Schomberg with strange behaviour. Although he was paid and thanked for his services

in 1759, Schomberg went on call himself the "Agent for Indian Affairs" and referred to the Mi'kmaq as "his Indians." Whitmore noted he also behaved insubordinately in a "Ridicolous [*sic*, ridiculous] and Ostentatious Manner." It also appears that Schomberg asked for money to provide presents to the Mi'kmaq, but ended up taking extravagant liberties in what he expended. Worse, he "laid claim to all the vessels that were taken" by the French and Mi'kmaq. LAC WO 24/17, "Whitmore to Amherst," 22 January 1760. The charges against Schomberg, however, did not negate the efficacy of the terms of truce agreed to at Merigomish in the fall of 1759.

305 LAC, WO 24/17, "Whitmore to Amherst," 22 January 1760.

306 *Boston Gazette*, 10 December 1759.

307 LAC, AC CIIA 105, 50v, "Henry Schomberg à Maillard," 26 October 1759. For Schomberg's expression of a similar attitude towards those who supported the French interest, see AC CIIA 105, 50r, "Schomberg à Capitaine Le Blanc, 23 novembre 1759."

308 Except for the head chief of Cape Breton, Jeannot Peguidalouet, the Mi'kmaw representatives were not identified by name in British correspondences. It also is likely that more than seven Mi'kmaq were present at the conference with Whitmore. It is recorded that thirty Acadians also departed with Schomberg for Louisbourg.

309 Murdoch, *History of Nova-Scotia*, 2.382.

310 Julian Gwyn, "Whitmore, Edward," *Dictionary of Canadian Biography* online, vol. 3 (1741–70).

311 For a detailed examination of this negotiation and treaty-making process in 1759, see Wicken, *Treaties on Trial*, 193–7.

312 Quoted in Johnson, "Maillard, Pierre."

313 At his mission on the Isle de la Sainte-Famille, Isle Royale, Maillard encouraged the Mi'kmaq to assume a state of war until 1758. Later, Maillard devised his own resettlement plans. He sought a refuge for Mi'kmaq and Acadians on Prince Edward Island and by late 1758 on the mainland along the shores of Northumberland Strait. By 1760 he was considered a spiritual leader not only by Acadians in Nova Scotia but by many dispersed Acadians.

314 Louis-Benjamin Petitipas (c.1726–?) was almost certainly the son of Claude Petitpas Jr. and Claude's second wife, Françoise Lavergne. His paternal grandfather, Claude Petitpas Sr., had been a principal notary at Port Royal. Claude Petitpas Jr.'s first wife was Mi'kmaq and his second wife French. For many years he resided at Musquodoboit, and his children spoke the Mi'kmaw language. Louis-Benjamin also lived at Port Toulouse,

Chezzetcook, and Halifax. He operated a trading vessel called *The Longsplice* between Halifax and Boston and, owing to difficulties he encountered with the British colonial government, mostly over his trading ventures, near the end of his life he became an American citizen. "The First Acadian to Become an American Citizen," *Yarmouth Vangard*, 26 September 1989. Jean-Baptist Roma, whose family came from Île St. Jean, was a servant associated with Maillard's mission, and like Petitpas he tended to Maillard's needs during the missionary's final years.

315 The waterfront area has since been infilled, but at the time this building stood near a battery on the Halifax waterfront across from St. George's Island.

316 In 1754 Maillard became vicar general of Acadia, although this status ceased formally to exist after 1760, following the fall of Montreal. Before 1754, he had shared the vicar generalship of Île Royale with the Recollects at Louisbourg. J.E. Burns, "The Abbé Maillard and Halifax," *Canadian Church History Annual Report, 1936–37*, 13–22; N.M. Rogers, "Apostle to the Micmacs," *Dalhousie Review* 6 (1926–27): 166–76; Albert David, "Messire Pierre Maillard, apôtre des Micmacs," *Bulletin des recherches historiques* 35 (1929): 365–75; David, "Une autobiographie de l'abbé Le Loutre," *Nova Francia* 6 (1931): 1–34.

317 "Germain à Vaudreuil, 26 février 1760," in Placide Gaudet, *Acadian Genealogy and Notes* (Ottawa: Queen's Printer, 1906), 196. The Malecite had been at odds with Boishébert since 1757, and ever since were disposed to weaken their ties with New France. Father Germain, who had been away from his mission on the Saint John River, returned in early November 1759 to be present at the negotiations at Fort Frederick with the British on the 12th and 13th of the same month.

318 Murdoch, *History of Nova-Scotia*, 2.384–5; Wicken, *Mi'kmaq Treaties on Trial*, 200–6. Talks between the British and the Malecite and Passamaquoddy nations occurred in Halifax in January 1760 and then resumed on 22 February. The treaty made on 23 February 1760 with the Passamaquoddy chief, Michel Neptune, and the Malecite leader, Ballomy (Bartholomew) Glode, followed the tenor, if not always the wording, of the 1726 treaty. A novel clause, however, confined the Saint John River trade in furs to a government truckhouse, to be operated out of Fort Frederick. Leading men of the two Eastern Abenaki nations assisted in setting a schedule of prices for furs to be exchanged under the truckhouse system, to be managed throughout the province by Benjamin Gerrish.

319 "Excerpts from Halifax Council Minutes, 13 January 1760," cited in Murdoch, *History of Nova-Scotia*, 2.384.

320 "Excerpts from Halifax Council Minutes, 9 January 1760," cited in Murdoch, *History of Nova-Scotia*, 2.383.

321 During King George's War, Maillard relates how Chief René, on seeing the British approach, stripped himself for battle, wearing only his French medal. Claude René was known to Bigot and Duchambon, and for this reason he was able to gain admittance to Louisbourg's hospital when he was wounded in battle. Maillard, "Lettre de M. l'abbé Maillard," 3.372, 377. See also Dickason, *Louisbourg and the Indians*, 159–61; Murdoch, *History of Nova-Scotia*, 2.384. Chief René was also close to the French missionaries, as he was called a "praying chief" by Maillard. Maillard, *Lettre sur les missions de l'acadie*, 371; AC CIID, vol. 10, "Sur l'Acadie, 1748." After he signed treaty with the British in 1760, he was given a pass so he could travel safely through the province. NSARM, RG 1, vol. 64, 45, "Pass to Claud Renee given by Charles Lawrence, 1760."

322 "Excerpts from Halifax Council Minutes, 13 January 1760," cited in Murdoch, *History of Nova-Scotia*, 2.384.

323 Michel Augustine reputedly was Joseph Argimault's brother.

324 Grenier, *Far Reaches of Empire*, 205. Manach by this time had assumed missionary responsibilities for the Mi'kmaw communities of Miramichi, Richibucto, and Buctouche. William Wicken suggests there was a pattern of relationship among these two leaders; working together, they represented two sectors of *Mi'kma'ki*, roughly separated by the Shubenacadie River Valley. Paul Laurent, he holds, represented the southwestern sector of *Mi'kma'ki*, while Michel Augustine represented the northeastern part. Wicken, *Treaties on Trial*, 201–2. This is an interesting observation, though it tends to overlook the leaders coming in January and February 1760 from Minas and the Annapolis Royal area. LAC, CO 217/145, "Regarding Michel Augustine signing on behalf of Richibucto," 10 March 1760; NSARM RG 1, vol. 188, 137, "Treaty with Shubenacadie and Musquodoboit." Minor dialectical and other cultural differences between the northeastern and southwestern spheres of *Mi'kma'ki* have been detected by linguists and anthropologists, so the division, though not great, is rooted deep in the past.

325 Almost immediately afterwards, two more chiefs, who remained unnamed, came to Frye and were given the same instructions. Exasperated by these leaders' requests thrust upon him so unexpectedly, Frye said to Manach that he hoped his dealings with the Mi'kmaq would

soon end, to which the missionary responded that they were only just beginning.

326 "Extract of a letter from Col. Frye to his excellency the governor of Nova Scotia, dated Fort Cumberland, Chignecto," 7 March 1760, *Massachusetts Historical Society Collections*, ser. 1, vol. 10 (1809): 115–16. The list of chiefs was first printed in the *Pennsylvania Gazette* in 1760, from which it was copied and later published with the MHS Collections. Versions of Frye's letter can be found in the *Annual Register*, 1760, 90, and *The London Magazine*, 1760, 377. The letter, erroneously identified as addressed to "The governor of New England," is also discussed in Murdoch, *History of Nova-Scotia*, 2.396.

327 The eleven chiefs from north of the Shubenacadie River were Joseph Argimault, Claude Athanase of Shediac, Étienne Abehabo of Pokemouche, Louis Francis of Miramichi, Augustine Michel of Richibucto, Dennis Winemowet of Tabusintac, John Newell of Pictou, Baptist La Morue from Prince Edward Island, René La Morue from Antigonish, Claude (René) of Shubenacadie, and Jeannot Peguidalouet of Cape Breton. Paul Laurent, Bartholomew Aunqualett (Momcharret) of Minas, and "Michael Algoumartin" (Michel Argomartin) of Cape Sable were the only leaders listed from southwestern Nova Scotia. On 7 March 1760 Frye sent a letter by courier to Lawrence enclosing Manach's list of chiefs, Paul Laurent's and Augustine Michel's written submissions, and similar declarations by two chiefs who arrived later. No submissions or treaty documents exist with the names of Dennis Winemowet, Louis Francis, Baptist La Morue, or René La Morue on them, though documents may have been lost. Beamish Murdoch refers to John Nowell (also Newit or Noel) as "Janneoville Pectougawash, chief of the Indians of Pictouck and Malagonich, who signed treaty on 9 October 1761." Murdoch, *History of Nova-Scotia*, 2.407. Murdoch likely derived his information from minutes of councils held on 12 and 15 October 1761, though the chief's name given in the council's minutes for 12 October was "Jannovit Peetongawash," meaning "Jean of Pictou." NSARM, RG 1, vol. 188, 282–3, "Minutes of the Halifax Council of 12 October 1761." Many chiefs from southwestern Nova Scotia signed treaty whose names were not on Manach's list. One chief, Jean-Baptiste Thoma of Windsor, already held a British passport and trading privileges with the British at Annapolis Royal and Halifax. Though he may have benefitted from his unique status, most trading chiefs suffered. Bands had their trade destroyed by the British embargo, though certain band members continued going to Quebec or engaged in unregulated and

risky trade with New Eng and fishermen. Roger Morris, who came to Halifax with three Frenchmen from Pictou, is mentioned in Murdoch. *History of Nova-Scotia*, 2.383. Morris may have been with Maillard's encampment at Malagomich, and may even have had kin connections to the trading family of Maurice de Vigneau, who in turn had ties with Vergor at Chignecto. In later years, one member of this family, Jacques Maurice de Vigneau, secured passes for deported Acadians from the governor of Georgia so they could cross safely into South Carolina. Geoffrey Plank provides an interesting account of Jacques Maurice Vigneau's life, looking at his childhood at Port Royal, his adult life at Chignecto, and his embarkation with his family for South Carolina. Geoffrey Plank, *An Unsettled Conquest*, 9, 23, 64, 98–9, 103, 113–14, 130–1, 135–6, 141–4, and especially 152–3; see also John Mack Faragher, *The Great and Noble Scheme: The Tragic Story of the Expulsion of the French Acadians from Their American Homeland* (New York: W.W. Norton, 2005), 110–12. Several members of the Maurice Vigneau family, around the time of the deportations, disappeared from the record and may have joined the Mi'kmaq. Morris Lake in Dartmouth is named after the Mi'kmaw Morris family. NSM, Printed Matter File, Piers Notes, "Material taken from Lone Cloud," 27 May 1914. Jerry Lonecloud stated that "Sebmolie Mollise" was the grandfather of "old blind Ben Morris who died at Three Mile Plains on 19 February 1918, aged 95 years." Ben Morris was born at Shag Bay, south of Halifax, around 1823, so his grandfather could have been a son or grandson of Roger Morris.

328 In September 1760 Fortress Louisbourg was mined and blown up, its *glacis* levelled and its ditches filled in, leaving nothing but piles of rubble. Much of the fine Portland stone was carried to Halifax to be used in construction projects in that town. Murdoch, *History of Nova-Scotia*, 2.394.

329 Chief Michel Argomartin of Cape Sable sent a delegate, François Shagwaough (or Chegua), who arrived in Halifax on 24 April, anxious to make peace, establish trading ties, and gain a passport from the government in order to avoid the dangers of Lawrence's scalp bounty. A second Cape Sable leader, Francis Keehosgeith, a day or two later signed a submission and received a passport for his safe passage through the province. Murdoch, *History of Nova-Scotia*, 2.385; NSARM, RG 1, vol. 156, 53, "Pass to François Shagwaough of Cape Sable, along with a Petition from Shagwaough on behalf of his chief, Michel Agoumartin," 24 April 1760. Lawrence's pass to Shagwaough read: "A Full and explicit Pass to Francois

Shagwaough of the Cape Sable Indians, who having been to Halifax to make his submission to his Majesty's Government and declaring that his chief Michael Agoumartin is disposed to life in peace and perfect amity with his Majesty's Subjects of this Province, and purposes speedily to appear in person and ratify for himself and his People the Peace now making with the Several tribes of Mickmack Indians, I have thought proper to make him some presents as a Token of my regard in the mean time, and to give him this Pass hereby forbidding all manner of Persons to hurt or molest him. Signed, Charles Lawrence, 24 April 1760." It is not known if Michel Argomartin ever came to Halifax to sign treaty, although it is likely that Francis Keehosgeith did, and the treaty has been lost. NSARM, RG 1, vol. 165, 54–55, "Passes to several Mi'kmaq, including one to Francis Keehosgeith of Cape Sable."

330 NSARM, RG 1, vol. 165, 53–4, "Pass to Jean Ball by Governor Charles Lawrence, he having appeared here [in Halifax] and made his submission or acknowledgement to be loyal to King George II, and Passes of the same tenor to be given to Lewis Jacques, Bartholomew Michael, Charles Claude, Joseph Ball, Jacques Le Blanc, Blanchois Wyegawook, and Beleban Quarrie (Bartholomew Momcharret of Minas)," dated 28 April 1760. Though these passes may refer to treaty signings that occurred in Halifax on 28 April 1760, the treaty documents have been lost.

331 François Cope went by the name "Blanchois Wyegawook." The Mi'kmaq often called a person by the name of the place where they lived. François also may have used the name "Wyegawook" rather than "Cope" to avoid repercussions from what happened between Jean-Baptiste Cope and the British in the early 1750s. While one historian has argued that Jean-Baptiste Cope may have died at Boishébert's camp along the Miramichi, Cope probably left Chignecto in 1758 to return to the vicinity of Wyegawook, or Sheet Harbour, and died soon after. A Mi'kmaw oral tradition holds that Cope participated in either 1758 or 1759 in a council held in Point Pleasant Park. When a few chiefs, among them Paul Peminout of Shubenacadie, spoke out in favour of making a peace overture, Cope took the opposite view. A conflict erupted between partisans and Cope reputedly was killed in the fray. He was said to have been buried in Point Pleasant Park, eastward of the Martello Tower. This tradition was discussed in a series of interviews held in 1922 between Sandy Cope of Millbrook and Muriel Cottam Yorke of Debert, Nova Scotia. Don Byrd Awalt, "The Mi'kmaq and Point Pleasant Park, The

Mi'kmaq and Amtoukati: An Historical Essay in Progress by Don Byrd Awalt" (Halifax: Native Friendship Centre, 2006). In the 1920s, Maggie Paul (Peminout) of Ponhook Lake, Hants County, claimed that Cope was killed in Halifax by François Peminout, a son of Paul Peminout from Stewiacke. NSM, Printed Matter File, "Maggie Paul to Jeremiah Bartlett-Alexis, alias Jerry Lone Cloud, and retold to Harry Piers, 5 April 1927; NSM, Printed Matter File, Piers Papers, "Jerry Lone Cloud to Harry Piers, Curator of the Nova Scotia Museum in Halifax," 11 August 1922; Micheline D. Johnson, "Cope, Jean-Baptiste," *Canadian Dictionary of Biography online*, vol. 3 (1741–70). Jerry Lonecloud argued that individuals who subsequently held the Cope surname were all offspring of John Nowlan, who wed one of Cope's daughters. Nowlan was an Irish trader who had established a trading post in the late eighteenth century near Torbay. In an ironic twist of fate, his son, Edward Anthony (or Ted) Nowlan, was said to have married one of Chief Francis Peminout's daughters. NSARM, RG 1, vol 430, doc. 34½, "Petition of John Nowlan of Nicumquodie [now Quoddy Harbour], eastward of Beaver Harbour, for provisions and a spot of land between Col. Hales' & Nicumteauce [Necum Teuch] for agricultural purposes, 1801." Nowlan began petitioning for land in 1793. LAC, vol. 4, MG 23, GII-19, 1043; Whitehead, *The Old Man Told Us*, 141, 213. That Cope did not have any descendants in the male line is wrong, however. François Cope Wyegawook, who was Jean-Baptiste Cope's son or grandson, had sons who lived alongside Nolan's descendants in the Sheet Harbour area. In 1783, François Cope obtained a licence of occupation to 11,500 acres at Wyegawook or Sheet Harbour. LAC, MG 23, GII-19, 1033–4; NSARM, RG 1, vol. 430, doc. 26½. The Sheet Harbour parcel was reduced radically in size, and now exists as a seventy-seven-acre parcel spanning both sides of Sheet Harbour. Upton, *Micmacs and Colonists*, 186; NSARM, Miscellaneous Indian "I" Land Papers, "Sheet Harbour." Chief François Cope died in the early 1800s while intervening in a fight between two women at Clearland, Lunenburg County, and was buried in the Mi'kmaw graveyard at Indian Point, Mahone Bay. M.B. Desbrisay, *History of the County of Lunenburg* (Halifax: James Bowes and Sons, 1870), 158.

332 Chief Laurent travelled at the government's expense on a schooner from La Have to Lunenburg to meet with Colonel Sutherland. Following the treaty signing, on 24 March he was given a passport and free schooner passage back to La Have. NSARM, RG 1, vol. 284, no. 17, "Peace and Friendship Treaty concluded by the

Government with Paul Laurent, Chief of the La Have Tribe of Indians, 10 March 1760," in "Transcripts of Documents made at the British Museum by order of the Government of Canada relating to the Province between the years 1750 and 1789–90," Dr. Brown Collection, made under the direction of the Commissioners of Public Records. A copy of the treaty can be found in NSARM, RG 1, vol. 156, 41. This second copy is a template, dated March 1760, and it does not bear Paul Laurent's signature.

333 The government schedule of prices for furs, agreed upon mainly by the Saint John River chiefs on 16 February 1760, is printed in Murdoch, *History of Nova-Scotia*, 2.395.

334 There is a template of the treaty with Paul Laurent, which gives the month but not the day in 1760 when the treaty was signed, in NSARM, RG 1, vol. 156, 41. A signed copy of this treaty is housed in the British Museum, Andrew Brown Collection, ms no. 19071, "Regarding the signing with Laurent on behalf of La Hève."

335 British naval commander Byron got to Restigouche on 24 June 1760 and was met with firepower from batteries managed by 250 French soldiers, 700 Acadian fighters, and 800 Indigenous warriors. Murdoch, *History of Nova-Scotia*, 2.389.

336 Ibid., 2.376. There originally were 190 Acadians with Joseph Broussard *dit* Beausoleil and his brother Alexandre, and what happened to the others is unclear. On 17 November three more Acadian deputies arrived, representing seven hundred persons in dire need at Miramichi, Richibucto, and Buctouche. Other Acadians hiding at a camp Boishébert had established at Petit-Rochelle, near present-day Pointe-à-la-Croix, Quebec, were all taken by the British. After the Battle of Restigouche, the Broussard brothers and Pierre II Surette and his family also were taken captive, brought to Halifax, and placed in confinement on St. George's Island. In October 1761 Lawrence's successor, Lieutenant Governor Jonathan Belcher, sent soldiers to the Bay de Chaleur under the command of Captain Mackenzie of the Montgomery's Highlanders. Mackenzie and his men returned to Halifax with 335 Acadian prisoners, among them the aging privateer owner Joseph-Nicholas II Gautier, who originally came from Lequille, near Annapolis Royal. Belcher remained very anxious the entire time the leaders of the Acadian resistance movement were impounded on St. George's Island. Marshall, *Heroes of the Acadian Resistance*, 181–99. Joseph Broussard *dit* Beausoleil died at age sixty-three in the Attakapas region of Louisiana, where his descendants still reside.

337 George II died at Kensington Palace in London on 25 October 1760. Despite the fact that Argimault's 1761 speech was referred to in the 1840s as the "Great Talk" by New Brunswick Indian commissioner Moses Perley, it was not recorded for posterity.

338 Governor Lawrence died suddenly in November 1760.

339 NSARM, RG 1, vol. 188, 254–5, "Executive Council Minutes concerning the Missiguash (Chignecto) Treaty, 8 July 1761," in transcript form on microfilm reel no. 15,288. The officials present at this council included the Honourable Jonathan Belcher, president, and councillors John Collier, Richard Bulkeley, Joseph Gerrish, and Alexander Garret.

340 NSARM, RG 1, vol. 37, doc. 14, "Treaties of Peace and Friendship," 25 June 1761; NSARM, RG 165, 160–6, "Treaties of Peace and Friendship with Etienne Ashobon, chief of Pokemoche, Claude Astonash, Chief of Shediac, 25 June 1761, including a copy of the Mirimichi Treaty, a pass for Augusten Gerounue et al., and a Proclamation regarding the Miramichi, Jedicack, Pogimmuch, & Mesiguash Treaties, 25 June to 8 July 1761"; NSARM, RG 1, vol. 165, 162, "Treaty of Peace and Friendship concluded by the Honourable Jonathan Belcher Esquire and His Majesty's Council with Joseph Shabecholouet, chief of the Miramichi district, 25 June 1761." On 1 July Belcher issued a proclamation repealing Charles Lawrence's 1756 bounty, insofar as it formerly related to these bands. NSARM, vol. 165, doc. 160, "A Proclamation by the Honourable Jonathan Belcher regarding Treaties made between Tribes of Indians of Miramichi, Jedeach and Poginouch, stating that all of his Majesty's subjects ... do forbear all acts of Hostility against the aforesaid Tribes of Indians," 1 July 1761. Joseph Claude of Restigouche probably signed treaty on 1 July 1761, but all that survived was the pass he was given after his visit to Halifax. NSARM, RG 1, vol. 165, 160–6, "To Suffer Augusten Gerounue, Aiene, Noel Joplief [Noel Joseph] and Glaude [Claude], Indians, to pass without let or molestation to Fort Cumberland in order to proceed to their own Country, having made Peace with this Government, and you are to give them all Aid and A*f*sistance by nece*f*sary Provisions or other ways to help them on their Journey. Given under my Hand and Seal at Halifax this First day of July 1761. Jonathan Belcher."

341 S. Buggey, "Belcher, Jonathan," *Dictionary of Canadian Biography* online, vol. 4 (1771–1800). The official governor of Nova Scotia, Henry Ellis, being absent from the province, Jonathon Belcher (1710–76) often assumed the duties of provincial governor. LAC, CO 217/18/277–84.

The treaties from 25 June to November 1761 took place on the governor's farm, located on Spring Garden Road where the courthouse now stands. Members of the executive council and military officials were always in attendance. On 25 June the Cape Breton district chief delivered a lengthy address to the assemblage, declaring his newfound allegiance to the British Crown. In 1761 "Treaties of the above Tenor … were signed by the Chief of Each tribe separately," even though originally the idea was to have a general treaty-gathering afterwards at Chignecto. In 1761 the British made no mention of Indigenous rights to land and resources. Authorities at Halifax linked Mi'kmaw fur trapping to the workings of the provincial economy and remained untroubled by the fact that the new treaties failed to set boundaries between British and Mi'kmaw lands. By 1761, only 3,580 new settlers had arrived in Nova Scotia, so they felt there was ample room for the Mi'kmaw people to continue hunting and trapping. At the earlier treaty signing of 1726, John Doucet, the lieutenant governor of *Annapolis Royal*, made a number of reciprocal promises to the Mi'kmaq, one of which was that English settlement would proceed "lawfully." This, the Mi'kmaq thought, meant they would be consulted before British expansion took place. Mi'kmaw oral traditions kept the memory of Doucet's promises alive within the Mi'kmaw community. Believing the 1726 treaty still to be in force, the Mi'kmaq in 1761 also expected their "hunting, fishing and planting grounds," as well as their other "Lawfull activities" to be protected under the British system of jurisprudence, until events began to prove otherwise. Wicken, *Mi'kmaq Treaties on Trial*, 205–8.

342 LAC, WO 12, 95r–v, "Mackenzie to Chief Joseph Claude," 23 February 1760; NSARM, RG 1, vol. 188, 149, "Nova Scotia Council Minutes, 5 June 1760"; LAC, WO 34/12 90r, "Joseph Claude to Roderick Mackenzie," 7 January 1761; LAC, CO 5/61, Part II, 24r–6r, "Robert Elliot to Jeffrey Amherst," 24 January 1761. As early as June 1760, Chief Joseph Claude of Listiguj had made tentative peace overtures, but because members of his group joined the resistance fighters, no treaty was signed until a year later, on 1 July 1761. Jean Nowell (Noel) of Pictou signed on 12 October, and François Mius signed on 9 November. It took all of Maillard's persuasive skills to get Mius to sign, for – in addition to the chief's fears that if he signed and things did not pan out with the British as Maillard had promised, he might face difficulties in taking up the hatchet again to defend his people's rights – Mius was still angry at the destruction of his village of Chichimichecady in 1749 and, later, the deportation of

his Acadian kin. NSARM, RG 1, vol. 188, 288; NSARM, RG 1, vol. 430, docs. 20 and 21. In 1761 Paul Laurent was the La Have leader, but as Mius had lost his village, the British made the expedient decision to recognize Mius as a second La Have chief.

343 In the nineteenth century, Abbé Sigogne wrote a letter, based on Mi'kmaw oral traditions regarding this incident with Mius, that stated that Maillard did offer the La Have chief such assurances. NSARM, RG-1, vol. 430, doc, 21.

344 Murdoch, *History of Nova-Scotia*, 2.407.

345 British Colonial Office records on microfilm housed at LAC, CO 217/18/170, "Belcher to the Lords of Trade and Plantations," 9 April 1761. On 11 June 1760 Governor Lawrence had accepted Manach's declaration of loyalty to the British Crown and allowed him to stay on at his mission station at Miramichi, but Belcher demanded his immediate deportation. Murdoch, *History of Nova-Scotia*, 2.390. Abbé Jean Manach was also referred to as Abbé Jean de Miniac or Ménac. "De Miniac" was a Maltese surname.

346 The British had reason to remain nervous from 1763 to 1765 in all areas outside those originally settled by the Acadians, for the Mi'kmaq could still muster six hundred fighting men.

347 LAC, CO 217/22/ 211v, "Michael Francklin, Regarding General Heads to Explain," 26 May 1768.

348 Wicken, *Mi'kmaq Treaties on Trial*, 209.

349 Unlike in the 1726 treaty, in the 1760 and 1761 treaties British settlements were no longer "lawfully to be made" but simply "to be hereafter made," a rewording that reflected a major change in British policy over time.

350 Washington, Library of Congress, Records of the States of the United States, ed. W.S. Jenkins, Massachusetts Council Records (microfilm compilation), "Minutes of the Massachusetts Council," 2 September 1720. The suggestion of a buffer zone arose two years before the outbreak of Dummer's War, known in Nova Scotia as the Mi'kmaw War.

351 Lennox, *Homelands and Empires*, 193–4.

352 LAC, CO/60/27–8, "General Amherst at New York to Colonial Office," 12 December 1760. Though Amherst ruled that the Indigenous people were to be kept in a state of awe of British military might, Belcher countenanced an extension of presents to the Malecite and Penobscot during a temporary crisis in 1762, since some members of these two nations still regarded the French king as their father. NSARM, RG 1, vol. 31, no. 10.

353 Belcher, unlike other British officials (with the exception of Michael Francklin), knew how important it was to

the chiefs to have rights to lands they could call their own. Most other officials only had vague notions of the number of chiefs in the colony and gave little thought to Indigenous territorial jurisdictions. This may be the reason why bands from Nepisiguit (now Bathurst, New Brunswick), Prince Edward Island, and Antigonish evidently were not invited to sign treaty in 1760 and 1761, although some bands may have had neighbouring chiefs sign for them; Chief David Pierre-Paul of Pabineau, near Bathurst, has suggested that the members of the Nepisiguit band may have agreed in 1760 to let Michel Augustine of Richibucto sign on their behalf. Conversation between David Pierre-Paul, Janet Chute, and Carrie Gloade, Pabineau, July 2012.

354 NSARM, RG 1, vol. 165, 196, "Orders and Instructions for Mr. John Cunningham, Agent for Indian Commerce," 3 December 1761; NSARM, RG 1, vol. 165, 207, "A Proclamation by J. Belcher, Lieutenant Governor," 1 January 1762.

355 "Meshpatagan" replicates the place name "Aspotogan," but if the Aspotogan Peninsula in present-day Lunenburg County was included in the proclamation, it would mean lands were being referred to in that document that lay quite far south of Halifax. The meaning of "Aspotogan" is unclear. It may derive from a Mi'kmaw word meaning either "where they block the passage way" or "where the seals go in and out." Public Archives of Nova Scotia, *Place Names and Places of Nova Scotia* (Halifax: Public Archives of Nova Scotia 1967), 22.

356 NSARM, RG 1, vol. 165, 224–5, "By the Honorable Jonathan Belcher, A Proclamation, 4 May, 1762."

357 It is even possible that Belcher hoped that Mi'kmaw claims to this tract would completely obliterate any lingering Acadian claims within the same region.

358 LAC, CO 217/19, 27, "Regarding the Proclamation signed by the Honorable Jonathon Belcher, dated 9 December 1762."

359 Though no transcriptions of these negotiations survive, various Mi'kmaw orators – including Argimault and Laurent – doubtless would have presented their arguments directly to the lieutenant governor, while Maillard shaped their ideas into a unified policy statement.

360 LAC, CO 217/20/202–4, "Joshua Mauger to the Lords of Trade," 28 September 1763; NSARM, MG 1, vol. 258, 24–5, Isaac Deschamps Papers, 24 September 1763.

361 This crisis involved a series of events leading up to the French landing at Bay Bulls and the French conquest of St. John's, Newfoundland. On 24 June 1762, Admiral d'Arsac de Ternay landed a force of seven hundred men at Bay Bulls and marched to St. John's, which was

captured and held for a period of months. When news of the successful French attack on Newfoundland reached Halifax, Belcher, urged on by the legislature, the council of war, and his own fears of the Acadians, on 30 July ordered all Acadian prisoners of war held at Halifax to be deported to Boston.

362 NSARM, RG 1, vol. 31, no. 0, "Extract from the Minutes of the Proceedings of the Lords Commissioners for Trade and Plantations," 3 December 1762; LAC, CO 217/20/202–4, "Joshua Mauger to the Lords of Trade and Plantations," 28 September 1763.

363 LAC, CO 217/19/ 22, "Belcher to the Lords of Trade and Plantations," 9 December 1762.

364 LAC, CO 217/19/22–6, "Belcher to the Lords of Trade and Plantations," 2 July 1762.

365 Ibid.

366 Belcher in 1761 felt that the numbers of Acadians were increasing in Cumberland County, on the Mirimichi, and at Restigouche. A warship was sent to these areas, and by the fall of 1762 Belcher had deported an additional thirteen hundred Acadians to Boston, where the Massachusetts government forbade their landing and sent them back to Halifax. Belcher also strengthened the powers of the militia. LAC, CO 217/19/70–8, "Regarding the militia bill," 1762. On 16 July 1762 Mi'kmaw leaders appeared at a session of the Lunenburg Council held at the governor's house and made what Belcher called "insolent" demands. For more on this incident see LAC, CO 217/19/94–5 and LAC, CO 217/19/80–1, "Minutes of the Halifax Council," 8 July 1762; LAC, CO 217/19/117–19, Belcher regarding apprehensions at Lunenburg, 15 July 1762; LAC, CO 217/19/108, "Minutes of the Halifax Council," 10 August 1762; LAC, CO 217/19/126–9, "Regarding Belcher's fears concerning subversive activities by French partisans, 1762."

367 In July 1762 Abbé Pierre Maillard, as the government agent to the Mi'kmaq appointed by Lawrence and Whitmore, set up a forum for negotiations between the British authorities and Mi'kmaq leaders from the Lunenburg region and Cape Sable, but severe illness prevented him from being present at the events. At his death on 12 August 1762 Maillard was attended by Petitpas, an Anglican clergyman named Thomas Wood whom he had asked to be present, and many of his Mi'kmaw and Acadian parishioners. LAC, MG 17, BI, vol. 1 (SPGFG), 104, "Thomas Wood to Society for the Propagation of the Gospel in Foreign Parts," 27 October 1762. He was accorded a state funeral by Belcher, and his pallbearers included the president of the Halifax Council

and the speaker of the Assembly. His body is buried in an unmarked grave in Saint Paul's Anglican burial ground in Halifax.

368 LAC, CO 217/20/354–9, "Wilmot to the Lords of Trade and Plantations," 10 December 1763. Belcher was replaced as lieutenant governor on 26 September 1763 by Wilmot. Henry Ellis, the governor of Nova Scotia, did not live in the province and in 1764 was succeeded as governor by Wilmot.

369 LAC, CO 217/21/7–8, "Montagu to the Lords of Trade and Plantations," 28 January 1764; Upton, *Micmacs and Colonists*, 62.

370 Paul Laurent gained prestige in July 1762 when Maillard was too sick to attend a meeting at Lunenburg between the government and the Mi'kmaq, and he was called upon to officiate. During the talks a Mi'kmaw woman committed a theft and, lacking a missionary to intervene in the situation, the British authorities turned to Paul Laurent to dispense justice. After this, Laurent probably "accompanied the chiefs from La Hève, including Francis [François] Mius, when they appeared before the governor and council on 22 August 1763 to obtain the appointment of a successor to Maillard." Michelle Johnson, "Laurent, Paul," *Dictionary of Canadian Biography* online, vol. 3 (1741–70).

371 LAC, CO 217/2/342, "Michael Francklin to Colonial Office," 3 September 1766.

372 When Michael Francklin became lieutenant governor three years later, he reported that during the early 1760s, when the new settlements were opening, both the Mi'kmaq and Malecite solicited the services of a Roman Catholic cleric. Though they had received governmental assurances that they could practise their Roman Catholic faith, these promises had not been honoured, and consequently in 1763 and 1764 many chiefs "openly declared that we meant to deceive them." When matters reached a crisis in 1765, Francklin continued, "the whole body of Mi'kmaq were collected from every part of the province and assembled on the Island called Isle Madam [near Port Toulouse] and declared they were to meet the French forces and threatened to destroy the outlying settlements, when they should return." Several government officials sent from Halifax with difficulty dispersed this assemblage, who by that time argued that they had been "deceived in the expected support from the French." Though the French threat continued, Francklin's assurances that the Roman Catholic religion would be secure in the province mollified the Mi'kmaq and allayed the crisis. In 1766 Francklin must have spread the word that missionaries were coming, and begun to put aside large

tracts for Mi'kmaw occupation, for he wrote, "We are at perfect Peace with the Indians of this Province. No settlements have been made to the injury of the Indians, but on the contrary, due regard is always paid to their rights. And encouragement has lately been given them to fix their places of abode and to turn their minds to agriculture." LAC, CO 217/22/4–5, "Michael Francklin to the Colonial Office," 10 November 1766. In 1768 Francklin appointed two Roman Catholic missionaries, François-Charles Bailly and Joseph-Mathurin Bourg. Bailly served in southwestern Nova Scotia, in Cape Breton, and among the Malecite, while Bourg remained with the Acadian and Mi'kmaw communities in the northeast of the colony. Bourg eventually became vicar general.

373 NSARM, RG 1, vol. 165, 282, "Passes to Jean Baptist and Joseph Shickakett," 30 September 1763.

374 This calculation of their ages was done by referring to the La Chasse census of 1708.

375 Through his connections with the Eastern Wabanaki Confederacy, Joseph Argimault doubtless knew of Pontiac's resistance campaign in 1760, but one wonders if the chief also was aware of the provisions regarding Mi'kmaw lands set out in King George III's Royal Proclamation of 1763, issued on 7 October 1763.

376 Topics concerning the Mi'kmaw peoples of North America appeared in the *Gentleman's Magazine* in September and October 1763. See, for example, Peter Collinson, "Two Proposals for Establishing a Lasting Peace and Friendship with the Indians of North America," *Gentleman's Magazine*, no. 33 (London, 1763), 419. The October issue printed portions of the Royal Proclamation of 1763 pertaining to Mi'kmaw lands. Yet no mention was made in the fall of 1763 of Argimault's party having arrived in London, even though the magazine generally kept abreast of such events.

377 It is possible, though not likely, that Baptiste was instead one of Joseph's younger brothers.

378 Frederic Kidder, ed., *Military Operations in Eastern Maine and Nova Scotia during the American Revolution, chiefly composed from the Journals and Letters of Colonel John Allan* (Albany, 1867), 51–5. One of those invited was Ambroise St. Aubin, who took his name from, or may even have been related to, a descendant of Serreau de Saint-Aubin, whose family intermarried with the Baron de St. Castine family of the Penobscot River area. Richard I. Hunt, "De Saint-Aubin, Serreau," *Dictionary of Canadian Biography* online, vol. 2 (1701–40). The name occurs in eighteenth-century documents as "St. Aubin" or "St. Obin" among the Malecite, and has been replaced by the surname "Bear."

379 Most Mi'kmaq remained neutral in 1775, but Jean-Battiste, whose territorial prerogatives extended over Minudie and Maccan in Nova Scotia, responded positively to the Massachusetts Congress's call. A pro-revolutionary Malecite party at Aukpaque led by Ambroise St. Aubin, and several Penobscot leaders, also accepted the invitation.

380 Resolves of the General Assembly of the Colony of Massachusetts-Bay, 29 May–13 January 1776, Boston, 1776, 57; Kidder, *Military Operations*, 60–1; 166–79.

381 The English were not good at rendering Mi'kmaw names phonetically, and so spellings varied widely from document to document. The Miramichi chief was Joseph Shabecholouet, who signed a treaty of peace and friendship on behalf of his group with the British on 25 June 1761. NSARM, RG 1, vol. 165, 160–2.

382 "Indians Decline to Go to War," Kidder, *Military Operations*, 57–8.

383 G.A. Rawlyk, "Eddy, Jonathan," *Dictionary of Canadian Biography* online, vol. 5 (1801–20).

384 W.O. Raymond, *The River St. John* (Saint John: J.A. Bowes, 1910), 456–62; LAC, CO, 217/54/46–7, "Sir Guy Carleton to Admiral Marriott Arbuthnot," 23 February 1778.

385 Gifts were also sent to Aukpaque and to the Bay of Chaleur, "to Mr. Mathurin Bourgue [or Bourg], priest, for distribution to encourage loyalty to the British crown." NSARM, RG 1, vol. 364, nos. 46 and 79, "Regarding Aukpaque," 18 June 1777; "Decision of the Council Chamber on 6 November 1778 to send presents to Abbé Bourg."

386 In the fall of 1778, the Malecite chief Ambroise St. Aubin, the Restigouche district leader Joseph Claude, and several other chiefs received copies of a proclamation issued in late fall 1778 by Admiral d'Estaing calling on them to join a general uprising "among the old possessions of France on the Atlantic coast." The chiefs thought over the offer, and eventually rejected it. NSARM, RG 1, vol. 364, doc. 78, "Manuscripts relating to the American Revolution." Only one of the proclamation documents circulating at this time and distributed through the rebel agent John Allan still exists, that which belonged to Chief Joseph Claude of Restigouche. See *Revue d'Histoire de la Gaspésie* 2, no. 4 (1964): 219–21; Upton, *Micmacs and Colonists*, 77.

387 "Lord Dorchester to Lt.-Gov. Thomas Carleton," 3 January 1787, in W.O. Raymond, ed., *Winslow Papers* (Saint John: New Brunswick Historical Society, 1901), 338–9.

388 Upton, *Micmac and Colonists*, 98–9.

389 LAC, CO 188/4/325, "Thomas Carleton to Lord Dorchester," 1 October 1790.

390 According to oral traditions in the Stief (Steeves) family, who hailed originally from Germany via Pennsylvania, the Mi'kmaq helped the first settlers, even though they were Roman Catholic and the Pennsylvania Dutch were mostly Lutheran. Since the settlers suffered from hunger the first winter, the Mi'kmaq brought them meat and fish and taught them which local roots were edible. An oral tradition passed down through one branch of the Steeves family tells of a young Mi'kmaq boy who was adopted into the Steeves's family of Hillsborough, on the Petitcodiac River. Shalyla Steeves, personal communication, 14 March 2013.

391 The dates pertaining to François Argimault are drawn from the facts that he was married twice and that his second wife was born in 1770. He and his first wife, Cecile, had a year-old daughter, Therese-Agnes, baptized at St. Basile Church in Madawaska on 21 June 1793. The child's godparents were "Étienne et Thérèse." François and Cecile also had a nine-month-old son, François, baptized on 20 August 1794 at the same church, with Joseph Pimouet and Marie Geneviévè acting as godparents. After Cecile's death, François wed Judith Denis on 22 June 1818. Judith may have been of Malecite ancestry. When she died at age fifty her funeral, held on 6 October 1820, was attended by "tout les sauvages du village." Registers of Ste. Anne, Fredericton, New Brunswick for the year 1818, "Marriage of François Argimault and Judith Denis, presiding priest A. Lagarde, witnesses Louis Bert and Jean Nicholas Bert." Judith Denis was the widow of Noel Bert when she married François Argimault.

392 There were powerful people involved in land transactions in the Petitcodiac region. Richard John Uniacke, who became provincial attorney general in 1797, had formed a partnership as early as 1774 with Moses Delesdernier, who was a trader and an agent for proprietors wishing to settle in Hopewel Township on the Petiticodiac River. Soon after arriving at Hopewell Township in 1775, Uniacke met and married Delesdernier's twelve-year-old daughter, Martha Maria Delesdernier. B.C. Cuthbertson, "Uniacke, Richard John," *Dictionary of Canadian Biography* online, vol. 6 (1821–35).

393 LAC, Monk Papers, MG 23, GII-19, vol. 3, pt. 4, Letter Book of George Henry Monk, 1794, 1029–30, "Letter from Monk to Edward Barron," 19 July 1784.

394 NSARM, RG 1, vol. 165, 390, "License to Trade for Edward Barron," 4 September 1765. Benoni Danks had also acquired a similar licence to trade in the same area around the same time. Ibid., 365. His licence extended over the Cumberland region. Danks, leader of a ranger company

that had terrorized the Petitcodiac region, was one of the first Englishmen to settle in Cumberland County, take out a trading licence, and facilitate settlement. He joined Eddy's Rebellion and died soon after at Windsor.

395 LAC, Monk Papers, MG 23, GII-19, vol. 3, pt. 4, 1029–30.

396 Monk refers to John Baptist as "Chief at Point Maringouin," now Cape Margouine, on the west side of Chignecto Bay, now in New Brunswick. Ibid., 1028.

397 Ibid., 1030–1, "Letter from Edward Barron to Monk," 12 August 1784.

398 Ibid., 1032–3, "Letter from Charles Baker to Monk," 7 August 1784.

399 Ibid.

400 NSARM, RG 20, Nova Scotia Department of Lands and Forests, Land grant registration books series, Ser. A – "Argimaeu, Lewis, Newel and others," 1809.

401 Janet E. Chute, "Riders in the Cradle on the Waves: An Ethnohistory of the Mi'kmaq of Epekwitk (Prince Edward Island)," prepared for the Epekwitk Assembly of Councils (EAC), December 2021, 75–9.

402 Lennox Island, Prince Edward Island, in the 1800s was occupied for much of the year by Mi'kmaq with the surnames "Bernard," "Dominick," "Francis," "Mitchell," "Toney," "La Bauve," and "LaMorue" (or "Lamoreaux," later changed to "Sark"). Captain John Joe Sark, Lennox Island, personal communication, June 2003. Chief Oliver La Bauve and Michel Argimault sat on the local church council as early as 1812. Provincial Archives of Prince Edward Island, Church Registers of Sainte Anne, Lennox Island, on microfilm, "Council of 30 June 1812, as well as notes regarding the minutes, written on the back page of the registers." Families also camped on Malpeque Bay, feeding on clams, oysters, lobster, and other shellfish before embarking on their early winter sea-mammal hunting. The old Mi'kmaw name for Prince Edward Island was *Inoi menigog*, as contrasted with *gigtjisipig*, a name recorded by Silus Tertius Rand in the 1850s. Père Pacifique (Henri-Joseph-Louis Buisson de Valigny), *The Micmac Messenger*, no. 388 (Restigouche mission), August 1919. (The *Micmac Messenger*, or *Setaneoei, migmaoi solnaltjitj*, was a small publication prepared monthly by Pacifique in Mi'kmaq.) The term *Epexiwit* (also *Epekwitk* or *Abeqweit*) refers to Prince Edward Island as an "island floating like a canoe." This evidently harks back to an origin story related by William Peminout Paul (or William Benoit Paul) and recorded in 1933 on Prince Edward Island by Thomas H. "Randall" (*sic*, Raddall), in which the island was created from soil and rock carried by a melting vessel made of ice. John Joe Sark, Russel L. Barsh, and Chantelle P. Marlor, *Mi'kmaq and the Crown:*

Understanding the Treaties in Maritime Canadian History, with Special Reference to Prince Edward Island (n.p.: privately printed, 2000), 3. Prince Edward Island, along with the mainland territory of Piktuk across the Northumberland Strait from it, forms the Mi'kmaw district of *Epexiwitk aqq Piktuk*. During the winter months some *Epexiwit* Mi'kmaq moved to *Piktuk* on the mainland to hunt but each spring returned to attend the new mission church of St. Anne built by Abbé de Calonne in 1806. Others remained on the island all year around. Yet the Mi'kmaq's right to live on Lennox Island and hold festivities there remained precarious for years. As early as 1804 the proprietor of Lennox Island, Sir James Montgomery, wanted to sell his holdings to the government for three hundred pounds, but the House of Assembly refused to grant the requisite funds. Louis Francis Argimault's petition of 1832 elicited public sympathy for the Mi'kmaq, but not until 1838, when a relative of Louis Francis Argimault named Chief Oliver Thomas Le Bone (LaBauve, LaBob, or Bartibog) sent a petition for land to the Colonial Office, would a humanitarian named Theophilus Stewart be able to get the London-based Aborigines' Protection Society to begin raising monies to purchase Lennox Island. *Journal of the Legislative Assembly of Prince Edward Island*, 1840, Appendix N, "Petition of Oliver Thomas Le Bone," August 1838. (Lieutenant Governor Fitzroy, who forwarded the petition to the Colonial Office, recommended buying Lennox Island in his covering letter.) The purchase of Lennox Island did not occur until 1870.

403 *Journal of the Legislative Assembly of Prince Edward Island*, 1831, 20–2, "Appeal of Thomas Irwin on behalf of land for Mi'kmaw agriculture."

404 Ibid., 1832, 11–12, "Appeal to committee from Louis Francis Algimou and others," 7 January 1832. The main body of Algimault's petition read:
Fathers:
When your fathers came and drove away our French fathers we were left alone – our people were sorry, but they were brave – they raised the war cry – and took up the tomahawk against your fathers. Then your fathers spoke to us – they said, put up the axe – we will protect you – we will become your Fathers. Our fathers and your fathers had long talks around the Council fire – the hatchets were buried – and we became friends.
Fathers:
They promised to leave us some of our land – but they did not – they drove us from place to place like wild beasts – and that was not just ... Fathers, you may soon see not one drop of Indian blood in this Island, once our own – where is now our land? – we have none.

405 By the 1830s traders, priests, officials, and merchants could no longer speak Mi'kmaq. Though some Mi'kmaw persons spoke French, most had to communicate imperfectly in the English tongue. This was a radical change from the 1750s, when Mi'kmaq was the language of negotiation and trade at Port-la-Joye, Baie Verte, and Port Toulouse.

406 Since for six years after 1762 there were no Roman Catholic missionaries serving in Nova Scotia, at least one member of the Argimault family made a long journey to the French islands of Saint-Pierre and Miquelon to partake in the sacraments. "Magdeleine Argimou," who died and was buried on the Island of St. Pierre in 1790, was born in 1714 and probably was a sibling of Chief Joseph Argimault. Those who appear later in the record may be Joseph's children. François, Joseph Jr., and Noel Argimault, who had children around the same time, were probably brothers. Joseph Argimault Jr. and his wife Agnes had a daughter, Marie-Josephte, baptized at St. Basile, Madawaska, on 27 June 1792, in front of "François [Argimault?] et Marie sauagesse" who acted as witnesses, while Noel Argimault and Marie Pierre Jean had a son, Jacques Argimault, baptized on 21 November 1817 in the parish church of St. Thomas de Memramcook. Witnesses to this ceremony were Joseph Prejean, Marguerite Babin, Baptiste Cormier, and Pauline LeBlanc. Registers of the Parish of St. Thomas de Memramcook, 1806–70. During the early years of the nineteenth century, members of the Argimault family at Remsheg, now Wallace, and River Philip, now Pugwash, visited a priest named Father Poor (Power) at Minudie on the Cumberland Basin. In 1808, when Nova Scotia was divided into eight districts for the purposes of "administering" the Indigenous people, Mr. Knapp, an Indian agent in Cumberland County, noted that there were only two or three families left at Shepody, six to eight at Bay Verte, and about twenty more at River Philip and Remsheg. Chief François Argimault remained at Petitcodiac. He had a sister, Marie Argimault, who married Thomas La Bone or La Bauve. Thomas and Marie brought two of their children, Joseph Thomas and Germain Gregoire, on 12 March 1769 to be baptized by Abbé Charles-François Bailly. NSARM, on microfilm, copy of old registers of Charles François Bailly housed at Caraquet, New Brunswick. *Registre des actes de baptême, marriages, et sepultures, faits en la nouvelle ecosse ou acadie comme le vingt unième jour de juillet de l'annee mil sept cent soixante huit, par mons. Charles François Bailly, prêtre missionaire des sauvages et acadiens, sujets de sa majeste britanique, 1768–1773*, 12. In an older register kept by Bailly, included in the above register, which begins in July 1768, an entry for 27 March 1768 shows Thomas and Marie standing as witnesses for the baptism of one-year-old Marie, a daughter of Paul Porteus and Marie Louise of Petitcodiac. Ibid., 12. Thomas and Marie first lived at Petitcodiac but later moved to Prince Edward Island, where Thomas was born. Bailly's registers for Nova Scotia end in 1772, and not until the 1790s are baptismal entries for the Argimault family found once more, at Madawaska, Fredericton, and Buctouche and on Prince Edward Island. What they show is that François Argimault and his first wife had at least four sons, Joseph Jr., Thomas, Pierre-Jacques, and Noel, and possibly another, named Michael, since a man named Michael Argimault attended the first church assembly of the Parish of St. Anne on Lennox Island on 30 June 1812. Provincial Archives of Prince Edward Island, Charlottetown, Registers of Baptisms of St. Anne, Lennox Island, on microfilm. (There are notations inscribed on the final page of the register identifying the participants at the 1812 meeting. A copy of this microfilm is in the possession of the author.) On 4 October 1816 Thomas Argimault married Marie, a daughter of "Pierre and the late Marie Joseph" at Buctouche. Pierre-Jacques Argimault, the groom's brother, and Oliver La Bauve, the groom's cousin, were witnesses to the marriage ceremony.

407 NSARM, RG 1, vol. 431, 115.

408 Evidence may exist pertaining to this claim, however, that has not yet been recovered and examined. Memories of it remained. In 1848 Moses Perley, the New Brunswick Indian commissioner, wrote that the Chignecto Mi'kmaq had been driven away from their critical resource sites and left to hunt on others' property. He also failed to understand why the Malecite acquired seven hundred acres at the mouth of the Madawaska River but the Mi'kmaq on the Petitcodiac River received nothing. Moses Perley, *Report for Indian Affairs in New Brunswick of 3 March 1848* (Fredericton: Department of Indian Affairs of New Brunswick, 1843), 5–6.

409 Given the persistent spirit that other members of his family manifested throughout the years, it seems unlikely that Emable Argimault simply fell silent. There may be evidence regarding this claim that has yet to be recovered; as with many events and activities involving the Argimault family, there is copious room for future research.

410 Samuel Douglas Smith Huyghue, *Argimou: A Legend of the Micmac*, 2nd ed. (Sackville, NB: Mount Allison University, 1977). The story originally appeared as a serial in a Saint John literary periodical, *The Amaranth*,

from May to September 1842, and was first published in book form in 1847 by the *Morning Courier Office*, Halifax. Gwendolyn Davies, in her introduction to the 1977 reprint, states that Huyghue likely learned what he knew of the Mi'kmaw past from George Perley. Perley and Huyghue hosted a show of Mi'kmaw and other Indigenous artefacts at a Mechanic's Institute's grand bazaar in Saint John in 1842.

411 "The history of the Celebrated Chief, Ulgĭmoo," as related by Thomas Boonis, in Silus Tertius Rand, *Legends of the Micmacs* (New York: Longmans, Green, 1894), 294–7.

412 An excerpt from this story may be found in Whitehead, *The Old Man Told Us*, 84.

413 This was the site of Fort Lawrence.

414 Intermarriage occurred in the late eighteenth century between the Argimault and Knockwood families.

415 This translation was provided by Professor Bernie Francis, a Mi'kmaw linguist at Cape Breton University. Whitehead, *The Old Man Told Us*, 84–5. Another translation, suggested by Samuel Huyghue in the 1840s, is "black eagle." "Black" in the Mi'kmaw language is *maqtewék*, while "eagle" is *gitpu* or *kitpu*. The name thus would be *Maqtewékgitpu* – although doubtless some elision would occur.

416 Ruth Holmes Whitehead suggests this was a possibility. Whitehead, *The Old Man Told Us*, 84.

417 Archival research in the Atlantic Provinces so far has revealed nothing about what happened to the chief after he obtained his passport from Halifax and presumably left for Britain. However, as no evidence has been found confirming that Joseph Argimault died in 1763, information needed to solve this mystery may emerge from British sources.

CHAPTER 14

1 Other renderings of this man's name include Jean-Baptiste Bouta (Boitteaux, Bouteille, Boutteau, Bouteaux) and Jean-Baptiste Amquaret (Charet, Charett, Coureat, Memcharet).

2 NSARM, RG 1, vol. 430, doc. 34, "Copy of a letter from the Committee of His Majesty's Council to Edward Irish and Timothy Hierlihy," Sydney County, Nova Scotia, 10 December 1800; NSARM, RG 1, vol. 430, doc. 50, "Joseph Renshaw to Indian Commissioner Richard Cunningham, June 1801, with account of supplies given Bouta's group, accompanied by statement regarding Louis Bouta," 20 October 1801. Louis Bouta was likely Jean-Battiste's brother.

3 NSARM, RG 1, vol. 134, folio 242, "Petition of Paul Boutin, Charles Boutin, Julian Bourneuf, Joseph Gedri [Guedry *dit* Labrador] *et al*," 24 August 1754.

4 LAC, MG 18, F 18 (typescript), *Recensement genal fait au mois de Novembre mile sept cent huit de tous les sauvages de l'Acadie que resident dans la coste de l'est, et ceux de Pintagouet de de Canibeky*, 1708. The original manuscript is found in vol. 4, no. 751 of the Edward E. Ayer Collection in the Newberry Library, Chicago.

5 Clarence-J. d'Entremont, *l'Histoire du Cap-Sable de l'an mil au traité de Paris (1763)* (Eunice, LA: Hébert, 1982), 3.1125–32. Father d'Entremont suggests that a marriage, or at least a country union, took place between a Mi'kmaw man named Momcharret and an Acadian woman, Mary Cellier, who used both the surname "Cellier" (or "Selier") and "Bouta" (or "Bouteau"). One of their sons, named Pierre, adopted "Bouta" as his surname while a second son, also named Pierre, habitually used "Cellier." Mary, who wed Momcharet around 1680, almost certainly was the mother of Pierre Momcharet *dit* Bouta as well as the grandmother of Jean-Battiste Bouta. Clarence-J. d'Entremont, *Histoire du Cap-Sable de l'an mil au traité de Paris (1763)* (Eunice, LA: Hébert, 1981), 3.1125–32.

6 Around 1725, Pierre Cellier Momcharret *dit* Bouta married Magdeleine Oujamindeiche (Ouaüamintetces, Ouaiamintetches, Ouaijamintetch, Oujaminveiche, Ouiamixtciche) and within a decade became the head of a large family. The couple's son Jean-Battiste (or Jean-Baptiste) Momcharret *dit* Bouta was born in June 1726. NSARM, RG 1, vol. 26, 242, Registers of the Parish of St. Jean Baptiste, "Baptism of Jean Baptiste Charet, son of Pierre Charet (*dit* Bouta) and Magdelaine, 20 June 1726"; the presiding priest was René Charles de Breslay, and godparents were "Marie, wife of François Mius (*dit* d'Azy) and Jean-Baptiste Mikmak" (Jean-Baptist Thoma, the head chief of Annapolis Royal). Jean Baptiste Momcharret *dit* Bouta had a younger brother Amable, born in 1734. NSARM, RG 1, vol. 26a, 128, "Baptism of Amable Charet (*dit* Bouta), son of Pierre Charet (*dit* Bouta) and Madelene Oujaminveiche, 27 October 1734"; presiding priest De St. Poncy de La Vernède, godparents Jean Baptiste Landry and Madeleine Charet. One of Pierre Momcharret *dit* Bouta and Marie Oujamindeiche's daughters, named "Marie le Celier (*dit* Bouta)," married François Grand Claude Sr. of Annapolis Royal and was the mother of François Grand Claude *fils*. NSARM, RG 1, vol. 26a, 136, "Baptism of François Grand Claude, son of François Grand Claude and Marie Celier (Cellier *dit* Bouta), 2 June 1735,

presiding priest De St. Poncy de La Vernède, witnesses Martin Grand Claude and Madeleine Boytoux (Bouta)." One of Pierre Momcharret *dit* Bouta and Marie's sons, Gregoire, was buried at Annapolis Royal in 1730. NSARM, RG 1, vol. 26a, p. 57, "Burial of Gregoire Charet (*dit* Bouta), son of Pierre Charet (*dit* Bouta) and Magdelaine Ouaïjamintetch, 18 April 1730," presiding priest René Charles de Breslay; witnesses Pierre Charet (*dit* Cellier *dit* Bouta) and Pierre Lavergne, de Breslay's servant. In 1727, Jean Baptiste Bouta's grandmother, Marie Cellier Sr., the widow of Momcharret, died at age seventy-eight at Annapolis Royal. NSARM, RG 1, vol. 26, 367. Moreover, the first wife of Pierre Bouta's brother Pierre, named Louise Innocent, died about 1733, and Pierre Cellier on 26 August 1735 married a second wife, Françoise Grand Claude, the sister of François Grand Claude who had wed Pierre Bouta's daughter Marie (see chap. 5). NSARM, RG 1, vol. 26, 368. Over time the Momcharret and Grand Claude families became tightly knit together by marriage alliances. Pierre Momcharret *dit* Bouta also often stood as witness or godparent at baptisms and weddings at Annapolis Royal. For instance, he witnessed the baptism of Cecile Hebcobeau, a daughter born in December 1735 to Antoine Hebcobeau and Anne Grand Claude of Annapolis Royal. NSARM, RG 1, vol. 26a, 152, "Baptism of Cecile Hecobeau, 20 May 1735, presiding priest De St. Poncy de La Vernède, witnesses Pierre Charett *dit* Boiteau and Marie Pelerin."

7 After 1726, the surname "Bouta," "Boitou," or "Boiteux" appears in missionary registers in the St. John River region. In 1769, thirty-three years after Jean-Battiste Bouta's birth at Annapolis Royal, l'Abbé Charles-François Bailly baptized several Mi'kmaw visitors to Ekpahoc along the St. John River, among them "Étienne Boitteaux, son of Pierre Boitteaux mikmak and Marie Joseph, his wife." Étienne's father, Pierre Boitteaux, was almost certainly "Pierre Charett, *surnommé* Boitou." Étienne thus would have been one of Jean-Battiste Bouta's brothers.

8 Richard Cunningham served as a member of the Legislative Assembly of Nova Scotia for Antigonish County from 1779 to 1783.

9 See, for instance, NSARM, RG 1, vol. 430, doc. 153, "Bishop Plessis to Sir John Coape Sherbrooke," 27 July 1815.

10 Jean-Battiste Bouta and his wife Marie Anne at this time had at least four children, Peter, André, Jean-Battiste Jr., and Anne.

11 Nova Scotia, Crown Lands Office, Halifax, Grant Book M, 48, "Grant of Crown Land to John McDonald, Peter McChesney *et al.*, made 8 November 1827 and registered 23 November 1827."

12 NSARM, RG 1, vol. 430, doc, 23, "Request of Peter Baptiste, Pomquet for investigation into the Peter McChesney intrusion, communicated by Thomas Trotter to William Hill, Deputy Provincial Secretary," 1825; NSARM, RG 5, Series P, vol. 41, no. 1, Petition 94, "Petition of Jean Baptiste Bouta, Chief of the Indians, drafted by Father J. Vincent, missionary at Antigonish," 26 February 1829; NSARM, RG 5, Series P, vol. 41, no. 1, "Robert Henry to Legislative Assembly, 26 February 1829, with accompanying letter from Father Vincent de Paul, Trappist missionary at Tracadie"; NSARM, RG 1, vol. 430, no. 194, "Letter of Alexander Campbell, Deputy Surveyor, to John S. Murray, discussing taking of timber from, and a sawmill erected on, Peter Battiste's land," 4 November 1848.

13 NSARM, RG 3, vol. 24 1/2G, p. 23, "Minutes of the Executive Council of Nova Scotia," 13 April 1852.

14 Descendants of Jean-Battiste Bouta took the surname "Battiste" rather than "Baptiste." Jean-Battiste Bouta's immediate descendants married into the Denny, Philip, Prosper, and Toney families. Peter Battiste married a Denny woman, possibly a daughter of Grand Chief Michel Thoma Denny Jr. André Bouteille (or Bouta) wed Marie Philip (who belonged to the Mi'kmaw Philip family of Cape Breton and Antigonish, and not the Phillip family of St. Margaret's Bay), Jean-Battiste Bouta Jr. married Marie Prosper, and Anne Bouta married Thomas Marc Antoine (or Toney). Original church registers of Farther Vincent de Paul and his successors, St. Peter's Church, Tracadie. The Prospers regularly visited Prince Edward Island. One of Jean-Battiste's descendants, Andrew Battiste who was probably his great grandson, moved back and forth between the Nova Scotian mainland, Prince Edward Island and the Island of Cape Breton during the first decades of the twentieth century before settling permanently at Eskasoni in the 1940s. Andrew Battiste, "Interview regarding government centralization and Eskasoni, interview and notes, c.1972," Treaty and Aboriginal Rights Centre, Shubenacadie, Union of Nova Scotia Indians (UNSI) Collection, 92-1004-09-005. Members of the Battiste-Bouta family had always been great travellers who traded along the New England coast as well as in Cape Breton. Andrew Battiste, mentioned above, married Isabel Nicholas and had a son Thomas Battiste who wed Bridget Stevens. Thomas and Bridget, in turn, had a son John Battiste who married Annie Lewis and had Marie, Geraldine, and Thomas Battiste. "The Battiste Genealogy," compiled

by Professor Marie Battiste. By the late nineteenth century, members of the Battiste family travelled seasonally to Maine to participate in the potato harvest. For an account of a Battiste family's ties to the Aroostook (*Ulustuk*) River region of Maine, see Marie Battiste, "Annie Battiste: A Mi'kmaq Family History," *Cape Breton's Magazine*, vol. 64 (August 1993), 23–42.

CHAPTER 15

1   *Sakom* is a term used more frequently by the Passamaquoddy and Malecite than the Mi'kmaq of peninsular Nova Scotia and New Brunswick.

2   Harald E.L. Prins, *The Mi'kmaq: Resistance, Accommodation and Cultural Survival* (New York: Harcourt Brace, 1995); Kathleen Mundell, *North by Northeast* (Gardiner, ME: Tilbury House, 2008).

3   Bunny McBride, *Our Lives in Our Hands: Micmac Indian Basketmakers*, photographs by Donald Sanipass (Gardiner, ME: Tilbury House/Halifax: Nimbus, 1990); Harald E.L. Prins, and Karen Carter, dirs., *Our Lives in Our Hands*, documentary, produced by Harald E.L. Prins, 1985.

4   Mary Sanipass and Donald Sanipass, *Baskedagen: Basketmaking Step by Step*, photographs by Donald Sanipass (Madawaska, ME: St. John, 1990).

5   *National Geographic*, vol. 184, no. 1 (July 1993), photograph by Pete Souza.

6   First Peoples Fund, "Community Spirit Award," https://www.firstpeoplesfund.org/community-spirit-award.

CHAPTER 16

1   Nicholas Prisk II Ouiouche was also known as Nicholas Brisk (Presque, Prisque) and Nicholas Weyaoush (Wioche, Wiouche).

2   "Ouiouche" is not an unusual name for a hunter among Algonquian speakers. The author encountered an Anishinabe person in the Lake Huron region with the name "Weyaus," which means "meat or "flesh" in Ojibwa. The word for "meat" is so similar in both Eeastern Algonquian and Central Algonquian, its linguistic root must have considerable antiquity in the Northeast. To have a name associated with "meat" and "the provision thereof" was regarded as an asset among the Mi'kmaq. The author thanks Chief David Pierre-Paul of the Pabineau First Nation in Bathurst for sharing his thoughts on the subject during the summer of 2012. The name

of Nicholas Prisk I Ouiouche's father was probably "Prisk Ouiouche." He was born around 1740 and by the mid-1760s lived at Listuguj. He married Hélène Caitenne and had at least three sons, Nicholas Prisk II "Ouiouche," François Prisk "Wioche," and Mathieu Prisk "Wiouche." The parish registers for Carleton and Ste. Anne de Restigouche give insights into Prisk family kin connections at Listuguj during the late-eighteenth and early nineteenth centuries. François Prisk, listed as born in 1769 and therefore likely Nicholas II Prisk's twin, married Hélène Larocque and died, aged eighty-four, in 1853 at Listuguj. Mathieu Prisk, born around 1770, married Marie Chrisostome (or Chrysostome) and moved with his older brother Nicholas to Nepisiguit, where he had three sons, Oliver, Mathieu II, and Alexis, and two daughters, Geneviève and Elizabeth. The Prisk Ouiouche family intermarried with the Morrisons, who were Scots *métis* traders, as well as the Juliens (Julians) from the Miramichi River area. François-André Julien, with his wife Anne Chrisostome, moved to Nepisiguit around 1805 and in 1813 had a daughter, Marie-Ursule Julien, who married William Morrison. (Mathieu Prisk's wife Marie and François-André Julien's wife Anne were sisters). François-André's brother Joseph-André Julien meanwhile wed Mathieu Wiouche's daughter Geneviève, while Elizabeth Wiouche, Geneviève's sister, wed John Morrison. Registers de Ste. Anne de Restigouche, "Burial of Elizabeth Wiouche, twenty eight years old, daughter of Mathieu Wioiche and Marie Chrisostome, and wife of John Morrison [who was a son of Isabelle Morrison, James Robertson's mother-in-law]," 16 July 1845; Registers of Ste. Famille, Bathurst, 1798–1859, "Baptism of Marie-Ursule Julien, six months old, daughter of François Julien and Anne [Chrisostome], 21 March 1813"; Registers of Ste. Anne de Restigouche, "Baptism of Magdelaine Julien, daughter of Joseph-André Julien and Genevieve Wiouche, 26 August 1848." (In the Ste. Anne de Restigouche church registers at Listuguj, the surname "Ouiouche" is usually spelled "Wiouche" or "Wyouche," and "Prisk" occasionally appears as "Brisk.") Two of Mathieu Wioiche and Marie Chrisostome's sons, Mathieu II and Oliver Wiouche, died in 1848, and before their untimely deaths they themselves lost several children to sickness. Register of Ste. Anne de Restigouche, "Burial of Marguerite Wiouche, aged 2 years, daughter of Oliver Wiouche and Agnés Lamkouine, 8 November 1842"; "Burial of Marie Wiouche, aged 14 months, daughter of Mathieu [II] Wiouche and Charlotte-Anastasie Labauve, 8 November 1842." These deaths were followed by births of children. Ibid., "Baptism of Marie, recently born, daughter of Oliver Wiouche and Agnés Lamkouine, 4 June 1843"; "Birth of Jean Nicholas, son of Mathieu Wiouche and Charlotte Labauve, born on 23 January 1848 after his father's death." Mathieu I Prisk's third son, Mathieu II Wiouche, married Anne Agoune in the early 1850s. Ibid., "Baptism of Hélène, 2 weeks old, daughter of Mathieu Wiouche and Anne Agoune, 4 June 1843."

3 The Mi'kmaw district name, *Kespek* or *Gespe'g*, gave rise to the place names "Gaspé," "Gaspésie," and "Gaspé Peninsula" in southern Quebec. The Mi'kmaw district of *Kespek* extends from southern Quebec to the Miramichi River Valley.

4 New Brunswick historian Robert Cooney contended on the basis of what James Robertson, one of Young's acquaintances, told him around 1829 that John Young was English. "Young," however, is often a Scottish name, and an oral tradition passed down for generations within the Young family at Bathurst claims that John Young was indeed Scottish. Young came to North America in the late 1760s in a merchant vessel with George Walker, who hailed from northern Scotland, and went first with Walker to Halifax and then about 1769 to Nepisiguit. Daniel P. Young, "History of the Youngs of Nipisiguit," http://johnyoung334.wordpress.com/2016/11/16/history-of-the-youngs-of-nipisiguit/. (The spellings "Nepisiguit" and "Nipisiguit" often appear interchangeably.) Young errs, however, in stating that John Young Jr. was born in 1749; he was born and baptized in 1785.

5 See Nicholas Landry, *La Cadie frontier du Canada: Micmacs et Euro-Canadiens au Nord-Est du Nouveau-Brunswick, 1620–1850* (Quebec: Septentrion, 2013).

6 From 1760 onward, the population of Listuguj fluctuated as refugees joined it and then went elsewhere. According to a 1760 British census, the village's population was around 100, although a contemporary French census placed it at 350. When French missionaries and priests visited the community, numbers soared. A 1765 British census listed 87 individuals belonging to the local band on the Restigouche River. L.F.S. Upton, "Claude, Joseph," *Dictionary of Canadian Biography* online (henceforth *DCB*), vol. 4 (1771–1800).

7 John Young Sr. was a close associate of James Robertson, so one can assume that John and James were approximately the same age.

8 Young was in his mid-thirties when he came to the Nepisiguit area, so he may have committed a crime such as deserting from a British man-of-war during the Seven Years' War. He gave no evidence of criminal behaviour while he was living at Nepisiguit.

9 Cooney claimed that Walker arrived at Nepisiguit "attended by several adherents, among whom were a Mr. John Young, an Englishman, and Mr. Robertson, a native of Morayshire, in Scotland." Robert Cooney, *A Compendious History of the Northern Part of the Province of New Brunswick and of the District of Gaspé, in Lower Canada* (Halifax: printed by Joseph Howe, 1832), 171. Cooney interviewed James Robertson in 1829 while Cooney was working for the Chatham *Gleaner* and gathering information for *A Compendious History*.

10 Point aux Pères, later known as Ferguson's Point, is currently the property of the Gowan Brae Golf Club. Although Walker was Scottish, he named his residence at Alston Point "Youghal Park" after Youghal, an Irish seaport in County Cork. Why he did so remains a mystery. "Youghal" in Gaelic means "Place of the Yew Trees," and there were no yews at Nepisiguit. Alston Point is sometimes spelled "Allston Point."

11 Cooney, *A Compendious History*, 171.

12 Alice R. Kelly, "Ground Penetrating Radar and the Search for Commodore Walker's 18th Century Occupation," paper presented at the 42nd Annual Meeting of the Geological Society of America, Northeastern Section, 12–14 March 2007. The city of Bathurst and the University of Maine sponsored the ground penetrating radar survey of the site in 2003. Patricia Allen, "Commodore George Walker at Nepisiguit: Protecting and Preserving an Extraordinary Fragment of 18th Century Maritime History," paper presented at meeting of Canadian Archaeological Association, Ottawa, 2002.

13 Cooney, *A Compendious History*, 172. There were actually two William Smiths trading in the Bay Chaleur area at the time. The second man set up at a post at Bonaventure on the Gaspé Peninsula and owned a trading vessel called the *Bonaventure*.

14 Young, "History of the Youngs of Nipisiguit."

15 On 21 June 1772 François Julien and his wife Magdeleine David brought their four-year-old son Michel (or Mitchel) to be baptized at Nepisiguit. Registers de la Paroisse St. Pierre-aux-Liens de Caraquet, 1772–96, on microfilm, "Julien, Michel, mikmak, baptisé le 21 juin 1772 à Nipisiquid en Nouvell Ecosse, âgé de 4 ans, fils de François Julien et de Magdeleine David." Gabriel Gadoux from Nipisiquit and his Mi'kmaw wife Marie-Magdeleine Barnabé (Julien) also had a son, François Eauve Gadoux, baptized the same day. In 1779 this François Julien, born in 1729, became second chief of the Miramichi River district under his brother, "King John Julien," and later rose as a head chief of the Red Bank community in his own right. His wife Magdeleine

David, born in 1734, was bilingual in Mi'kmaq and French and often interpreted prayers and parts of services given by French-speaking Roman Catholic priests into Mi'kmaq for Indigenous congregants. Magdeleine David died at Néguac in 1819 at age eighty-five. Parish Registers of St. Bernard de Néguac, 1796–1846, on microfilm, "Burial of Madeleine Julien (née David), 24 July 1819, wife of Chief François Julien." Néguac, an ancient Mi'kmaw encampment site located on a portage route to territories inland drained by the Tabusintac River, later became an Acadian village. At nearby Burnt Church, Colonel Murray's soldiers in September 1758 burned a large Acadian stone chapel to the ground; hence the village's name. Chief François Julien died at the age of 101 years and was buried at Bartibog, New Brunswick, on 27 April 1830. W.D. Hamilton, *The Julian Tribe* (Fredericton: Micmac-Malecite Institute/Mi'kmaq-Wolastoqey Centre, 1984), 79.

16 François-André Julien (or Julian) and Marie-Anne Chrisostome had at least nine children: Marie in 1799, Marguerite in 1806, Jeanne in 1808, Marie-Anne in 1810, Marie-Ursule in 1812, André in 1815, Marie-Luce in 1817, Pierre in 1819 (who died at one month of age), and Pierre Noel in 1821. Pierre Noel died at five years of age and was buried at Listuguj on 7 May 1826. Only one son, André Julien, survived to adulthood. Hamilton, *The Julian Tribe*, 11–15. Their first child, Marie, was baptized in 1799 at Néguac, where the local priest wrote in the baptismal entry that Marie's parents were "of this [Néguac] mission." *Registre des mariages, baptêmes et sepultures de la paroisse de St. Bernard de Nigawech* [*sic*, Néguac], 1796–1846, "Baptism of Marie-Anne, daughter of André Julien and Marie of this mission, 1799." François-André Julien was a son of Pierre-André Julien and Marie-Anne, identified in a baptismal entry in the registers of Saint-Famille parish for 29 March 1807 as the "grandparents of Marguerite Julien," François-André and Marie-Anne's seven-year-old daughter. An older André Julien, who with his wife Marie-Étienne Jacqueline baptized a daughter named Marie Madeline at Caraquet in 1796, was probably Chief Andrew (or André) Julien of the Northwest Miramichi. Des Registers de la Paroisse St. Pierre-aux-Liens de Caraquet, "Baptism at Nepisiguit of Marie Madeline Julien, daughter of André Julien and Marie-Étienne Jacqueline, 11 September 1796"; Hamilton, *The Julian Tribe*, 80.

17 Patricia Allen, *Commodore George Walker at Alston Point, Nepisiguit, 1768–1777*, New Brunswick Manuscripts in Archaeology 31 (Fredericton: Culture and Sport Secretariat, Archaeology Services, 2003), 11;

Patricia Allen, AR. Kelley, F.L. Stewart, and D. Bérubé, *In Search of Commodore Walker* (Toronto: Canadian Archaeological Association, 2006).

18 Around the same time, Robertson wed the daughter of a Scottish trader named William Morrison, who had a Mi'kmaw wife, Isabelle.

19 While two brothers, Joe Prisk and Peter Noel Prisk, were guiding author and angler Arthur P. Silver on a fishing expedition along the Nepisiguit River late in the summer of 1886, Joe stated that his ancestry extended three generations back to John Young and a Mi'kmaw woman. He added that Young, "an adventurer from England, where his life was forfeited by the Crown, made his escape and arrived here in a trading ship. He later married an Indian woman and became 'a great sachem.' He lived to a ripe old age, but before his death he sent home to His Majesty in England three canoe-loads of bear, otter, and beaver skins WITH A PETITION FOR A GRANT OF LAND FOR THE INDIANS, AND THIS WAS GRANTED." Silver mused that "though Newgate had lost a victim for the noose, Bathurst had gained a useful citizen." Arthur P. Silver, *Farm, Cottage, Camp and Canoe in Maritime Canada* (London, 1907), 237–8. Young's friend and business associate James Robertson always avoided speaking of Young's altercation with the law, possibly in an attempt to protect Young from local criticism.

20 Through the years Elno Minigo has been accorded a string of names; including Indian Island, Prisk Island, Peter's Island, and Goulais Island. The resources at this site were as important as the weir salmon fishery at Rough Waters to the Mi'kmaw economic round. It also was the place where families erected base camps before pushing further into the interior to hunt and trap. During the spring salmon run on the Nepisiguit River, hundreds of fish could be taken by a single person simply using a leister spear. While bark wigwams were used, many fishing camp dwellings tended to be rectangular and made of logs, with pole and bark roofs. Potatoes were planted in the spring in clearings among the trees around a camp and harvested in late summer. Trout pools lay above the rapids and were accessible throughout the year, yet few band members lived on the riverine tract during the summer months. The soil was rocky and in many places barren, unfit for planting. During the 1840s, many Nepisiguit band members lived in the community of Rough Waters or on pockets of good ground elsewhere between the harbour and the rapids.

21 In the 1670s these birds were present in such numbers that the prominent French official, merchant, and trader

Nicholas Denys complained their cries kept him awake at night.

22 One such contract involving John Young reads: "Engagement d'Indien et d'acadiens par Felson pour explorer la rivière Risitigouche, 1785. Contract avec John Young, indien [et] Contract avec Benjamin Le Blanc, *père* et *fils*, d'Etienne Bergeron de Louis Laviolette, dans le meme but. Copies 3 feuilles." Young, "History of the Youngs of Nipisiguit." It also appears in PANB, David F. Johnson's New Brunswick Newspaper Vital Statistics, vol. 39, number 1489, newspaper clipping taken from the *Daily Telegraph*, Saint John, New Brunswick, dated 3 October 1826.

23 The names of Pierre-André Julien, who married Marie Catherine, and Joseph-André Julien, who wed Marie Christy, appear in the Nepisiguit registers around 1800. They were probably François-André Julien's brothers.

24 *Oinpegitjoig*, also spelled *oinpegitjoitjitg* or *winpegijawik*, meaning "troubled, bad, rough, or foaming waters," gave rise to the place name "Nepisiguit." Cooney spelt this word *Winkapiguwick* and held that it referred solely to the lower reaches of the Nepisiguit River. Cooney, *A Compendious History*, 189–90. "Winnipeg" in western Canada derives from the same ancient Algonquian root word. *Oinpegitjoitjitg* specifically designated a locale along the Nepisiguit River today known as Grant's Brook.

25 It would be very interesting to know to which Mi'kmaw grammar Young was referring in 1783 as well as to determine the source from which he acquired it.

26 Library and Archives of Canada (henceforth LAC), MG 23 G II 19, vol. 4, George Henry Monk Papers, Indian Affairs Letter Book, 1783–97, 231, "John Young to George Henry Monk at Windsor, Nova Scotia," 7 September 1783. Monk was Indian commissioner from 1783 to 1799 and again during 1807 and 1808. From this letter, it is obvious that Young wanted to revive some semblance of the social and economic integration that had characterized the Mi'kmaw and settler communities during Commodore Walker's time at Nepisiguit.

27 Ibid. Young's choice of words studiously avoided any hackneyed references to Mi'kmaw drinking practices. He may have penned his words only after consultation with the local Mi'kmaw council, and as far as they were concerned alcoholic beverages did not exist before they were introduced by Europeans. In 2014, Nicholas Prisk of Pabineau, a descendant of Nicholas Prisk II, stressed that "[p]rior to contact, when natives gathered for celebrations among themselves or with other groups, they celebrated by eating, dancing, and consuming whatever non-alcoholic beverages were available. We did not want to offend the host by not indulging in their hospitality. After contact this practice may be why some Mi'kmaq indulged in drinking to excess – so not to be rude to their host. However, nobody knew how this would negatively impact their lives and actions." And, regarding dissentions, the counsellor adds, "Natives may have quarreled about territory or personal wrongs done to them, but I don't believe we ever quarreled about the Great Spirit. We never fought any Holy Wars. We respected other religious views, including Christianity. We did not pursue the 'one true church' concept we hear so much about today." The author is grateful to Prisk for these comments.

28 This refers to the rapids at Rough Waters.

29 LAC, MG 23 G II 19, vol. 4 231.

30 "Janvae Pellerin" is what is written, but no information on this individual could be found, which is odd, since there is extensive genealogical material on the Pellerin family.

31 Charles Monk and his wife Elspeth received their grant at Birch Cove in 1775.

32 Bruce Fergusson, ed., *Place Names and Places of Nova Scotia* (Halifax, 1967), 66. The site was once called Block House Cove. "Birch Cove" was the name William Donaldson gave in the late eighteenth century to his large Bedford Basin estate at Rockingham, located along the route of the old highway from Halifax to Fort Sackville. Until the 1920s, the Mi'kmaq had an encampment and fishing ground where the Sackville River empties into Bedford Basin. Some Acadians also lived in this area. Archaeologists have found traces of an Acadian village and cemetery, and when construction work was being done on the Kearney Lake Road in 1874 and 1890, gravesites were found with the remains of French soldiers who died in the tragic Duc d'Anville expedition of 1746.

33 L.F.S. Upton wrote, "The Restigouche Indians, whose territory included the coast from the Baie de Cascapédia (Que.) to the Miramichi River (N.B.) and all the land drained by the rivers between, were the survivors of the Gaspesian branch of the Micmac people." Upton, "Claude (Glaude), Joseph," *DCB*, vol. 4 (1771–1800). The Nepisiguit group belonged to a sociopolitical district known as *Kespek* (or *Cesgapegiag*), meaning the "Last Land," as it was the last tract to be wrested by the Mi'kmaq from the St. Lawrence Iroquois in the late sixteenth century. Anthropologists Ruth Sawtell Wallis and Wilson D. Wallis noted that a district Mi'kmaw leader was known as a *bun* in the Mi'kmaw language. Wallis

and Wallis, *The Micmac Indians of Eastern Canada* (Minneapolis: University of Minnesota Press, 1955), 174–6. The Wallises' claim that the Burnt Church or Tabusintac River chief was also head chief of the Mi'kmaq of the entirety of northern New Brunswick is unsubstantiated, however, and for a different view see Hamilton, *The Julian Tribe*, 47n8. During the early 1800s, when Miramichi, Tabusintac, Pokemouche, Buctouche, and Richibucto chiefs met in council, representatives from Nepisiguit were conspicuously absent, yet archaeological evidence has demonstrated that at periods in the past the natural carrying capacity of the area sustained a sizable Indigenous population.

34 LAC, MG 23 G II 19, vol. 4, George Henry Monk Papers, Indian Affairs Letter Book, 1783–97, 231, "Young to Monk," 7 September 1783.

35 The name of this mission, translated into English, was Our Lady of Consolation. Wallis and Wallis, *Micmac Indians of Eastern Canada*, 112.

36 Father Bernardin perished in the winter woods en route from Miscou to the Saint John River in 1623. "Mount Bernardin," located at the headwaters of the Nepisiguit River, was named by historian W.F. Ganong in honour of this Recollect missionary.

37 Nicolas Denys and his wife Marguerite Lafite were at Miscou in 1647 and seem to have inspired the names given to the Nipisiguit chief and his wife. Reuben Gold Thwaites, ed., *Jesuit Relations and Allied Documents* (Cleveland: Burrows Brothers, 1896), chap. 12, 23; Rev. C.J. Mersereau, "Early Missions along Bay Chaleur," in Canadian Church History Association (CCHA), *Report*, 17 (1950): 24. Denys married Marguerite in 1642, and one of his daughters married Sieur La Vallière of Beaubassin.

38 W.F. Ganong, *History of Miscou and Shippegan* (Saint John: New Brunswick Museum, 1946), 30.

39 Mersereau, "Early Missions," 25. Following Father Richard's blessing of the waters, it was said the river no longer caused loss of life.

40 Cooney, *A Compendious History*, 168–9. Cooney states that after 1638 Enaud maintained a sizable residence at Ashaboo, or Coal Point, on the highest stretch of land lying at the mouth of the Nepisiguit River. In 1832 the main Bathurst hotel stood on the spot. Enaud also built a large grist mill at a site taken over by Arthur Goold (or Gould) and later owned by a Mr. Deblois.

41 Denys's Nepisiguit post included a large residence built of a red sandstone, with stores and other outbuildings, all surrounded by a stockade with four gun bastions. It was located near the missionary station at Point aux Pères. In 1653 he purchased rights from the Compagnie de La Nouvelle-France to the coast and islands of the Gulf of St. Lawrence from Cap Canso to Cap des Rosiers on the Gaspé. Not long thereafter he was appointed governor and lieutenant general of this territory, at which time he made Jean Bourdon de Romanville his lieutenant at Nepisiguit. George MacBeath, "Denys, Nicolas," *DCB*, vol. 1 (1000–1700).

42 Denys wrote another book in which he included information on Mi'kmaw customs and culture, although he did not specifically mention any Nepisiguit Mi'kmaw individuals. The first edition of this work, published in 1672 in two volumes, was entitled *Histoire naturelle des peuples, des animaux, des arbres & plantes de l'Amérique septentrionale, & de ses divers climats: Avec une description exacte de la pesche des molûes, tant sur le Grand Banc qu'à la coste; & de tout ce qui s'y pratique de plus particulier*. This later was shortened to *Description géographique et historique des costes de l'Amérique septentrionale: Avec l'histoire naturelle du païs*. The title given to the 1908 English translation of Denys's book was the shortest of the three: *The Description and Natural History of the Coasts of North America*, edited and translated by William F. Ganong (Toronto: Champlain Society, 1908). In 1687, a year before his death, Denys's grant was revoked and the right to a large seigneury, "later to be chosen," was issued to his son, Sieur Richard Denys de Fronsac, who lived mainly on Beaubears Isand in the Miramichi River. This was the place where during the Seven Years' War French and Mi'kmaw resistance fighters retreated in 1757 with a large assemblage of Acadian refugees who feared being deported by the British. MacBeath, "Denys, Nicolas." Even though Richard had married a Mi'kmaw woman, Denys did not interact extensively with the Mi'kmaq by the late 1670s. Instead, he worried about exhibitions of Mi'kmaw drunkenness near his post and felt that Mi'kmaw reliance on European trade goods was undermining Mi'kmaw culture. Owing to the strategic assets of the locale where Denys had placed his post, a British merchant, George Walker, just over one century later built his trading station on the same site.

43 W.F. Ganong, "Additions and Corrections to Monographs on the Place-Nomenclature, Cartography, Historic Sites, Boundaries and Settlement-Origins of the Province of New Brunswick," Contributions to the History of New Brunswick, no. 7, Royal Society of Canada, *Proceedings*, Section 2 (1906): 125.

44 After Nicolas Denys's death in 1688, his son Richard Denys successfully petitioned to have his late father's rights

as French governor of the Gaspesian district conferred upon him. He also inherited a seigneury, fifteen leagues square, at Miramichi, on the north bank of the river near Beaubears (now Boishébert) Island. Alfred G. Bailly, "Denys de Fronsac, Richard," *DCB*, vol. 1 (1000–1700). Richard's title "Sieur de Fronsac" referred not only to the Fronsac region of southwestern France, but echoed the early French name for the Canso Strait, which was the "Passage de Fronsac."

45 Chrétien Le Clercq, *New Relation of Gaspesia* (Toronto: Champlain Society, 1910), 192–3.

46 Mersereau, "Early Missions," 27–8. Mersereau noted that historian Robert Cooney wrote that the Mi'kmaq "chased the French out of Nepisiguit, but this is not certain," since it seems some of Enaud's children remained. French missionaries who served in the Nepisiguit area included Michel Brulé (1706–20), Gelase (1728–48), Lue (1630), and Ambroise (1727–68).

47 Philip Henaut (Enaud) and Jean-Jacques Enaud may have been kin related, and future genealogical research may establish this. Robert Cooney held that Jean-Jacques Enaud was "nearly related to the governor of Quebec" and built his settlement at Coal Point, at the mouth of the Nepisiguit River. He also stated that Enaud probably was "liberally paid" by the French administration to contract a marriage with a Mi'kmaw spouse. Cooney, *A Compendious History*, 169–70.

48 Ibid., 170.

49 Ganong, "Additions and Corrections to Monographs," 139.

50 Enaud travelled with Le Clercq from Nepisiguit to Miramichi.

51 Le Clercq, *Gaspesia*, 160–1. According to Intendant des Meulles, Enaud was thirty-five years old in 1686, with a Mi'kmaw wife and three or four servants. De Meulles, "Census of La Rivière de Miramichy, de Chedabouchtou, de Nepisigny, et de l'Isle Persée [Isle Percé]," 1686, http://139.103.17.56/cea/livres/doc.cfm?ident=R0231&cform=T.

52 In 1688 France declared war on England. In response to the onset of the War of the League of Augsburg (also called the War of the Grand Alliance or the Nine Years War), New France's Governor Denonville launched a series of Indigenous raids across the northeastern frontier in 1689 and early 1690. The provisional government of Massachusetts responded to these attacks, and in the spring of 1690 Phipps, with seven ships and around seven hundred men, was appointed to move against the French in Acadia, which evidently included the Nepisiguit region. Nearby Percé was attacked in 1690. It is not certain how Phipps might have influenced Halion to side with the British adventurers. Robert Cooney contended that the English persuaded the Mi'kmaq to force the French departure, although C.J. Mersereau argued that Phipps's men directly attacked the French settlement in 1692. Cooney, *A Compendious History*, 170; Mersereau, "Early Missions," 28.

53 C.J. Mersereau wrote that a Bathurst lawyer named George Gilbert in the late 1920s had an elderly Tom Narvey, a member of the Bathurst band, invite him to speak with a Mi'kmaw woman, originally from Caraquet and said to be nearly 100 years old, on the subject of the rout of Jean-Jacques Enaud's settlers. In response to Narvey's questionings about the fate of the non-Native population at the time, the unnamed woman replied "all white people killed." Typescript entitled "Article written by Rev. Father J. Merseau," n d. (circa 1992), housed in the Bathurst Heritage Centre. Mersereau held that the attack on settlers at Nepisiguit in 1692 depleted missionary vigour in the area until at least 1755.

54 Charlotte Taylor noted this spirit of mutual respect in her diary writings, excerpts of which are cited in Sally Armstrong, *The Nine Lives of Charlotte Taylor: The First Woman Settler on the Miramichi* (Toronto: Random House, 2007), 388–92.

55 As early as 1762, Bourdages Raymond founded a fishing station at Caraquet, but it was attacked by American privateers in 1776 and molested by Mi'kmaw parties in 1779.

56 The Battle of Restigouche occurred after a French fleet, trying to run the British blockage in the Gulf of St. Lawrence, was cornered in the estuary of the Restigouche River by a British squadron. After a battle, in July 1760 the French scuttled the two vessels remaining of their fleet, the *Machault* and the *Bienfaisant* – although they were able to preserve the third – the *Marquis-de-Malauz*, a merchant ship – and fled to Listuguj.

57 Captain MacKenzie captured 20 persons out of an Acadian and *métis* community of 174 at Caraquet at this time. The Acadians who escaped fled temporarily to Miscou Island or Bonaventure in Quebec, or sought refuge among the Mi'kmaq.

58 This man would have been considerably older than André-François Julien, who lived at Nepisiguit in the 1770s.

59 As he was carrying trade goods, Smethurst used these articles to pay Mi'kmaw and Acadian individuals he met to convey him safely from Nepisiguit to Caraquet, then to Pokemouche, and finally to the Miramichi River area. However, he had to retrace part of his path to find the way to Fort Cumberland, his final destination. Gamaliel

Smethurst, *A Narrative of an Extraordinary Escape Out of the Hands of the Indians, in the Gulph of St. Lawrence*, in *Collections of the New Brunswick Historical Society*, 2, ed. W.F. Ganong (Saint John: New Brunswick Historical Society, 1905), 366, 380.

60 Ibid., 363–90. Smethurst first received a licence from Governor Murray in Quebec to pursue the cod fishery and had hoped to expand his enterprise by trading with the French and Mi'kmaq of the Bay Chaleur region. On 22 November 1763 he obtained a grant in the Township of Cumberland, on Bay Verte. After working as a merchant, customs official, and deputy surveyor, he was elected as the representative from Cumberland County to the Nova Scotia legislature. W.F. Ganong suggests that MacKenzie's sudden attack on the Acadian inhabitants at Nepisiguit, as Smethurst portrayed it, was based on mere rumours of Acadians from the area attacking British vessels, when in fact the Nepisiguit population may not have been involved in these activities at all. As a result of such depredations on their Acadian friends, the Mi'kmaq were "no friends at all to the English." Ibid., 363–6. While en route, Smethurst also learned that the Mi'kmaq feared the prospect of being overwhelmed numerically by British settlers with an alien culture and interests. At Pokemouche, which he reached in early November, he found five or six dwellings and about twenty people. The head chief, "Aikon Aushabuc" (Étienne Aushobron), using a combination of words and elaborate hand gestures, explained to him how the British were seeking to surround and crush his people. He and his council associates were "exceedingly shrewd" in their remarks. "When they wanted to inform me that the French and themselves are of one interest, they said they were so (pointing the same way with the forefinger of the right and left hands and holding them parallel); and when, that the English and Indians were in opposite interest, this they described by crossing their forefingers. The chief made almost a circle with his forefinger and thumb, and pointing at the end of his forefinger, said there was Quebec, the middle joint of his finger was Montreal, and the joint next to the hand was New York, the joint of the thumb next the hand was Boston, the middle joint of the thumb was Halifax, the interval between his finger and thumb was Pookmoush, so that the Indians would soon be surrounded, which he signified by closing his finger and thumb." Ibid., 372. The head chief at Miramichi that Smethurst met in 1761 was Louis François, and the "chief of Saint John" (Île Saint Jean, now Prince Edward Island) was Louis Lamoureau (or La Morue). Lamoureau was a son or grandson of Jacques

La Morue, the ancestor of the present-day Sark family of Prince Edward Island.

61 Ibid., 383.

62 The British government expected Father Bourg to exhort the Mi'kmaq living along the Miramichi and Restigouche Rivers, as well as the Malecite of the Saint John River Valley, to remain loyal to Britain throughout the American Revolution. Michael Francklin, lieutenant governor of Nova Scotia from 1766 to 1776, and commissioner of Indian affairs for Nova Scotia from 1777 until his death in 1782, listened to prominent chiefs and awarded licences of occupation in keeping with the depth of their loyalty to Britain. Extenuating circumstances associated with the American Revolution induced Francklin to provide the Mi'kmaq, led by King John Julien, with a twenty-thousand-acre grant to be held "at the pleasure of his Majesty," extending along both shores of the Miramichi river system where their major fisheries were located. Because the Miramichi land parcel secured important Mi'kmaw salmon fisheries to Chief Julien's people, this tract may have followed the outline of a resource area in which Mi'kmaw rights to salmon had been recognized and respected by the earlier French regime. But though the Julien chiefs of the Miramichi area in 1779 had been treated fairly generously by British administrators in this respect, other groups were not so fortunate. The end of the American Revolution correlated with Britain's radical diminishment of interest in parcelling out licences of occupation to chiefs unless they could furnish very convincing reasons for doing so. This was especially evident at the summer village of Tjigog, an ancient encampment site of the Listuguj Mi'kmaq lying near the mouth of the Restigouche River. Though he was likely approaching one hundred years of age at the time, Chief Joseph Claude contended that the French had respected an inherent prior right of the Mi'kmaq to salmon fisheries extending along both sides of the Restigouche River. As confirmation of his prerogative right, in 1786 he produced a French medal bestowed on him by Governor Beauharnois at Quebec on 8 April 1730. To placate Chief Claude and his people so that settlement could proceed uninterrupted, Nicholas Cox, the lieutenant governor of Gaspé. John Collins, deputy surveyor general of Quebec, and Abbé Joseph-Mathurin Bourg formed a commission to investigate the chief's claims. The commissioners spent from 29 June to 1 July 1786 interviewing Claude and other Listuguj leaders, after which Cox proclaimed Chief Claude's claims to be mere "pretensions," unsupported by law, historical evidence, or customary French

practice. HILA, Indian Affairs Records, RG 2, RS8, documents extracted from LAC, RG 10 (Indian Affairs), "Commissioner William Spragge to the Commissioner of Crown Lands, 12 April 1865, including with document concerning interview with Chief Claude and the commissioners in 1786." When Chief Claude complained that two settlers, Edward Isaac Mann and Robert Adams, were indiscriminately using seine nets to damage the salmon fishery for others, Cox replied that the lands and fisheries previous to 1760 had been part of French seigneuries that, through the exercise of reversionary right, now belonged to the British Crown. All the Mi'kmaq could hope for was "a trifling land concession lying between the Rivière Nouvelle and Point Macquache" – now Pointe à la Croix – the site of the mission of St. Anne de Restigouche, up to a boundary line marking a division between Mi'kmaw and settler holdings. As for the salmon fishery, Cox continued, "your pretensions as Natives of the Country" would be reported to the governor, Sir Guy Carleton, Lord Dorchester. Seeing no alternative, the elderly Claude, Gagnon who would become his successor. and François Est *dit* Condo signed the concession agreement. Around this time the Listuguj community, which during the years surrounding the Battle of Restigouche had been on the New Brunswick side of the river, moved onto the site at Pointe á la Croix in Quebec. Cox was uninformed regarding Listuguj history, for during the French regime reciprocal exchanges of small gifts, tributes, or honorifics for the privilege of fishing in waters known to lie under the territorial prerogative of a head chief like Claude had occurred at Listuguj, as in peninsular Acadia. As Claude and others were to find, a thread of hypocrisy underlay British peace agreements. They proclaimed that the Mi'kmaq could retain access to traditional natural resource areas while ignoring past cultural protocols and failing to establish specific territorial boundaries to limit expansion of British settlement. L.F.S. Upton, "Claude (Glaude), Joseph," *DCB*, vol. 4 (1771–1800).

63 Those who went to Caraquet later received land. In 1784 François Gionet travelled to Halifax and obtained what has been called "The Great Grant," which secured land for thirty-four families.

64 Joseph-Mathurin Bourg was a Spiritan priest who became vicar general of Nova Scotia. He was born in 1744 at Rivière-aux-Canards, in Nova Scotia, the eldest son of Michel Bourg and Anne Hébert and grandson of Alexandre Bourg *dit* Belle-Humeur. C.-J. D'Entremont, "Bourg, Alexandre *dit* Belle-Humeur," *DCB*, vol. 3 (1741–70). Along with his family, Bourg was deported from Nova Scotia in 1755 and may have been sent to Virginia. In 1756 he was in England. He crossed to France seven years later, where he resided at Saint-Suliac before moving to Saint-Servan in 1766. In 1767 he went to study philosophy at the Séminaire du Saint-Esprit in Paris. He was appointed vicar general of Nova Scotia in 1773 or 1774. Éloi Degrâce, "Bourg, Joseph-Mathurin," *DCB*, vol. 4 (1771–1800).

65 Hamilton, *The Julian Tribe*, 79. Early baptismal entries for the Parish of Caraquet indicate that Magdeleine David and her husband lived at Nepisiguit during the early 1770s. See Registers de la Paroisse St. Pierre-aux-Liens de Caraquet, 1772–96, on microfilm, "Baptism of Michel, four-year old son of François Julien and Magdeleine David, 21 June 1772." Itinerant priests from Quebec – and between 1768 and 1772 a missionary appointed under the auspices of Nova Scotia's lieutenant governor, Michael Francklin, named Charles-François Bailly de Messien – visited Nepisiguit sporadically. Their early church registers provide little data on genealogical connections within the Nepisiguit community. Mersereau, "Early Missions," 28. Magdeleine David assisted missionaries who were not fluent in Mi'kmaq. Her fluency in French was remarked upon by Bishop Plessis in 1812, who regarded her as an invaluable aid to the priest at Burnt Church in interpreting Mi'kmaw confessions. She also was opposed the consumption of spirituous liquors. When François Julien and Magdeleine left Nepisiguit, they lived for many years in a sturdy log house at Red Bank, on the Little Southwest Miramichi River. *The Julian Tribe*, 12.

66 Degrâce, "Bourg, Joseph-Mathurin," *DCB*, vol. 4 (1771–1800).

67 In June 1775 parties of Mi'kmaq from the Miramichi area, despite the fact that one of their chiefs, Joseph Sabecholouet, had signed a peace treaty with the British on 25 June 1761, plundered the stores of a Scottish land grantee and trader named John Cort and burned the houses of several other British settlers. Cooney, A *Compendious History,* 53; W.O. Raymond, "The North Shore (Incidents in the Early History of Eastern and Northern New Brunswick)," *Collections of the New Brunswick Historical Society*, 2 (Saint John, 1899): 94; Hamilton, *The Julian Tribe*, 7–8; L.F.S Upton, *Micmacs and Colonists: Indian-White Relations in the Maritimes 1713–1867* (Vancouver: University of British Columbia Press, 1979), 77–8; Stephen Patterson, "Eighteenth-Century Treaties: The Mi'kmaq, Maliseet, and Passamaquoddy Experience," *Native Studies Review* 18, no. 1 (2009): 25–52.

68 A man surnamed Ross from Percé on the Gaspé coast contacted Harvey and informed him of the seriousness

of the situation at Miramichi. At the time Harvey possessed French colours. These may have been found when his party captured an American privateer, the *Lafayette*, which Harvey towed behind the *Viper* en route to Miramichi.

69 One Mi'kmaq man, Martin, died after an intense struggle; a chief named Caiffe (or Cive) fled, and sixteen warriors were captured. These Mi'kmaw captives were first carried to Quebec and later brought to Halifax. In response, John and François Julien mustered an eight-person Mi'kmaw delegation, which included Chief Michel Augustine and François-Joseph Arimph of Richibucto, to go to Halifax to plead for the captives' release. Michael Francklin, the commissioner of Indian affairs for Nova Scotia, deflected this party towards his residence at Windsor, Nova Scotia, where he had the chiefs sign a treaty by which they promised to protect British traders and settlers from molestation. None of these delegates hailed from the Nepisiguit region. Then, once the Mi'kmaw captives in Halifax signed an oath of allegiance to the British Crown, all but two ringleaders were released to return to their people. In 1777 Lieutenant Governor Mariot Arbuthnot contacted Governor Guy Carleton, asking that the bishop of Quebec, Jean-Olivier Briand, send Abbé Bourg to Halifax. From there Bourg, accompanied by Michael Francklin and Gilfred Studholme, Fort Howe's commander, travelled to Fort Menagouèche to meet with an assembly of Malecite and Mi'kmaw leaders on 24 September 1778. Bourg showed the Indigenous delegates a letter from Bishop Briand that threatened rebel supporters with excommunication, after which the Indigenous leaders swore to remain neutral and signed a treaty. François-Joseph Arimph was either a brother or cousin of Jean-Baptist Arimph, the second chief of Richibucto who, along with others, was temporarily influenced by rebel promises to sign a document committing him and his associates to provide six hundred men for the rebel cause. Virginia P. Miller, *Canadian Dictionary of Biography* online, "Arimph, Jean-Baptist," vol. 4 (1771–1800).

70 LAC, British Library documents on microfilm, B II9, BM 21, 779, 37–42, Haldimand Papers, "Miramichi Treaty of 28 July 1779." This new treaty was based on a copy of an earlier treaty, signed on 10 March 1760 between the British and Chief Michael Augustine of Richibucto, that Augustus Harvey had in his possession. Hamilton, *The Julian Tribe*, 7.

71 Davidson and Cort's grant covered part of an earlier claim made by a man from Quebec called Banfield who was said to have purchased three French seigneuries; the

first at Miramichi, which included the site of Richard Denys's establishment, the second at Nepisiguit, and the third at Restigouche. Banfield's proprietary rights, as they were based on French precedents, were considered void by the British government. Later, in 1785, the Davidson and Cort grant was also examined critically because the proprietors had focused on riverine fishing and so had failed to bring in sufficient numbers of settlers. Harriet Irving Library Archives, University of New Brunswick, Fredericton (henceforth HILA), RG 10, RG 105, Surveyor General's Correspondence, 1785–1839, State of Indian land claims with Davidson and Cort's land grants along NW Miramichi, 20 August 1785.

72 HILA, Indian Affairs Records, MGH 54, Item 36, "Francis Julian and others to Provincial Secretary Jonathon Odell," 4 April 1811. It is even possible that competition between Mi'kmaq and settlers for scarce salmon resources prompted François Julien's temporary retreat to Nepisiguit around 1772. By 1789 the tract of 20,000 acres accorded "King John Julien" in 1779 along the Little Northwest Miramichi had been slashed to 3,033 acres, with further reductions to come in 1794. Meanwhile the elderly *Listiguj* chief Joseph Claude had trouble retaining even a fraction of the vast territory once under his aegis. Hamilton, *The Julian Tribe*, 9–11. In 1810 François Julien's ambivalence towards the English manifested itself when Chief John Julien's son, Andrew Julien, contracted the construction of a new church at Burnt Church to an English builder instead of a French or Indigenous one. If a British builder was used, François declared, he and his family would burn the edifice to the ground. Though François never had the opportunity to carry out his threat, since Andrew Julien applied to the Court of Quarter sessions to stay François's hand, this incident does show that prominent members of the Miramichi Mi'kmaw community harboured deep resentments against British incomers. Until his death in 1836 at the age of 101 years of age, François Julian, along with his sons Michel and Barnabé, never ceased to press for the British authorities to recognize and honour some measure of the reciprocal intent that had existed in the past between members of the French regime and the Mi'kmaq living in northeastern New Brunswick. Hamilton, *The Julian Tribe*, 15.

73 Oral traditions regarding the 1692 incident lingered at Nepisiguit until the early 1830s. Historian Robert Cooney stated, "I have been told by several of the oldest, and most intelligent Indians that this gentleman's stores were all demolished by their ancestors, and that he himself was driven from Nepisiguit, where he had his

permanent residence." Cooney, *A Compendious History*, 31.

74 Between 1783 and 1807 the Crown, in reserving large stands of forest for the exclusive use of the British navy, secured its own land titles and appointed its own timber inspectors. The office of inspector of the naval reserves, or king's forest, was a fairly prestigious one. For instance, Sir John Wentworth, who later became lieutenant governor of Nova Scotia, held such a position between 1783 and 1791.

75 Vondenveldon's official title was "deputy surveyor for the Gaspé district of Chaleur Bay, in the province of Quebec."

76 Archives of the Université de Moncton, Moncton, New Brunswick, Archives Acadiennes, document 1.32–6, "A copy of Orders for John Yong [*sic*, Young] to join William Vondenveldon, 14 September 1785, signed by Wm. Vondenveldon, Deputy Surveyor and John Young. Witnesses, F.L. Kemp and William Powell." Young was to meet Vondenveldon at New Carlisle and from there pilot the surveyor and his crew in a shallop as far upriver as navigation permitted, after which he was to furnish a canoe to penetrate still further into the interior of the Restigouche River region.

77 Other than Nicholas Prisk II Ouiouche's father or his brother Mathieu, it is difficult to think what other person by the name "Wioche" would be living in this particular area in 1785. Charlotte's life story has been woven into an intriguing work entitled *The Nine Lives of Charlotte Taylor: The First Woman Settler on the Miramichi*, by journalist Sally Armstrong. Armstrong, a descendant of Taylor, holds that stories pertaining to her ancestor still circulate at Tabusintac, New Brunswick, where Charlotte died and was buried in 1841. Armstrong – who on her mother's side is Charlotte's great-great-great-granddaughter – also states that her interest in Wioche, who became Charlotte's lifelong friend, began when she as a girl stayed at her family's summer cottage on Bathurst Harbour. She approached Mi'kmaw storytellers in Bathurst, Néguac, and Tabusintac, and these people related tales that had been passed down regarding Charlotte. "Every summer of my youth," she recounts, "we would travel from the family cottage at Youghall Beach to visit my mother's extended clan in Tabusintac near the Miramichi River. And at every gathering, just as much as there would be chickens to chase and newly cut hay to leap in, so there would be an ample serving of stories about Charlotte Taylor." Armstrong also sought assistance in her researches from Gilbert Sewell, an elder and former chief of the Pabineau First Nation.

Armstrong, *The Nine Lives of Charlotte Taylor*, 388–92. A journalist and biographer of Charlotte Taylor, Mary Lynn Smith, on her *website* "The Charlotte Taylor Story," chapter 3, believes Taylor to be one of the first settlers of Lepreau, Charlotte County, New Brunswick. Smith also argues that Taylor married her second husband, William Wishart, immediately following Blake's death in 1785, though no record of the date of her second marriage can be found. http://charlottetaylor.ca/wishart-period/.

78 Young may have not wanted to continue working on the survey project. The survey lines Vondenveldon ran caused dissension between the colonial administration and the Listuguj leadership in 1787, since one survey carried out on behalf of the settler population carved deeply into a tract the Listuguj Mi'kmaq wished to retain.

79 During this time the settlement on the cove later known as Bathurst Harbour, where Young's family lived during the winters, was called St. Peter's.

80 Abbé Pierre Maillard likely developed the script for this purpose with the aid of references to an earlier hieroglyphic system worked on by Father Le Clercq. Before his death in 1762, Maillard instructed these men to read the hieroglyphic religious texts to their family members, and conduct regular prayer services in the absence of a priest. Micheline D. Johnson, "Maillard, Pierre," *DCB*, vol. 2 (1741–70).

81 Abbé Bourg after 1785 served in a Quebec parish, though his name is mentioned in parish registers at Caraquet from 1791 to 1795, so he may have visited infrequently in his later years. He died in Quebec in 1797.

82 Abbés Jean-Baptist-Marie Castanet and Louis-Joseph Desjardins *dit* Desplantes, who replaced Bourg in 1795 as itinerant priests, were solely French speaking. Degrâce, "Bourg, Joseph-Mathurin," *DCB*, vol. 4 (1771–1800).

83 Janet E. Chute, "Ceremony, Social Revitalization and Change; Micmac Leadership and the Annual Festival of St. Anne," in *Proceedings of the Twenty-Third Algonquian Conference*, ed. William Cowan (Ottawa, 1992): 45–62.

84 After Jean Savoie and his family arrived in 1757, Néguac became a sizable Acadian settlement, but its origins indicate it was originally a major Mi'kmaw encampment site. The Mi'kmaw population after 1760 removed to establish the community of Burnt Church, which lay nearer to the mouth of the Tabusintac River. Prior to 1760 this was the site of an Acadian village with a sizeable stone church. This church was burnt by the British during the era of Acadian removals following the fall of Louisbourg.

85 Although the date of the erection of the church remains uncertain, Charles Doucet ceded land for both the

church and cemetery around 1795. The original edifice, with some architectural modifications, remained standing until 10 August 1880 when a stray spark from the local sawmill ignited a conflagration that destroyed it.

86 Mersereau, "Early Missions," 29. Desjardins had fled the persecution of the French Revolution and joined ranks with Bourg. He maintained regular register entries, as did his successors, though many did not stay at Nepisiguit for long. Father Delavairvre also had been an assistant for Bourg's mission, and resided for only a few years after 1800. Father Joyer remained until 1806, Father B. Orfray served from 1806 to 1810, and Father François Huot from 1810 to 1813.

87 Ibid., 29–30; Philip K. Bock, *The Micmac Indians of Restigouche: History and Contemporary Description*, Bulletin no. 213 (Ottawa: National Museum of Canada, 1966), 14–21; Père Pacifique (Henri J.-L. Buisson de Valigny), "Ristigouche: Métropole des Micmacs, théâtre du 'dernier effort de la France au Canada,'" Société de géographie de Québec, Bulletin no. 19 (Québec, 1925): 129–62.

88 Cooney, *A Compendious History*, 190.

89 Mgr. Joseph-Octave Plessis, "Deux voyages dans le Golfe Saint-Laurent et les provinces d'en bas, en 1811 et 1812," *Le Foyer Canadien* (Québec, 1865).

90 A survey of the Pabineau reserve by W.D. McClellan in 1963 showed five hundred acres on both sides of the river (rather than there being six hundred acres on the Pabineau side). Most members of the Nepisiguit band possessed Mi'kmaq and European ancestry, but the category "*métis*" was not officially recognized in the Maritime Provinces. The term "Mi'kmaq" conveniently became a catch-all for persons designated as "Mi'kmaq" in official correspondence of the time, including John Young Sr. – even though John Young was biologically British. Since the surname "Presque" (altered over time to "Prisk") was French and, as mentioned above, means "almost" or "nearly," it is probable that Nicholas Prisk I and Nicholas Prisk II shared Mi'kmaq and French Canadian or Acadian heritage. Though not an Acadian surname, "Presque" may refer to a local peninsula, with the placename Presque-Île, on which Nicholas Prisk I once lived. For instance, the Presque-Île River crosses the New Brunswick–Maine border.

91 There are two distinct Paul families at Nepisiguit. Members of the earliest Paul family spring from Peminout Pauls who came to New Brunswick after the American Revolution. Others, who arrived at Nepisiguit around 1800, were descendants of Chief Pierre-Paul Athanase (or Tenass) of Richibucto. Their surname "Pierre-Paul" is often Anglicized into "Peter-Paul" or shortened to "Paul."

92 Cooney, *A Compendious History*, 189–91.

93 On the 1861 census for Bathurst, Phillipe Young Sr.'s age is listed as ninety, which would make him born in 1771, though he was actually born around 1788.

94 Registres de la Paroise St. Pierre-aux-Liens de Caraquet, "Baptism at Nepisiguit of Jean [John] Young, 21 May 1786, son of John Young and Magdeleine Dedam." John Young Jr. was likely born in the spring of 1786, as John Young Sr. was away much of 1785 with a survey expedition to the Restigouche River.

95 Levi and Michel Young, born between 1777 and 1779, followed a Mi'kmaw lifestyle and eventually joined the Richibucto band. That they were John Young Sr.'s sons remains a tentative assertion, however; one has to be careful about the provenance of the surname "Young.". Probably they were of Scots extraction and hailed from Prince Edward Island. Scotsmen with the surname "Young" entered northeastern New Brunswick as traders by 1840. For instance, Indian Affairs commissioners in New Brunswick noted that a man named Gilbert Young came in 1825 from Prince Edward Island and settled in the Miramichi district. He paid the local chief one pound per year rent for twenty-three rods of riverine land until 2 September 1841, when he was reported as being very poor and supporting a large number of children. LAC, RG 10 (Indian Affairs records), vol. 2693, file 121,698–2, part 0. Michael Young leased land at Richibucto from the wife of Pierre Joseph Augustine and over time not only turned his hogs loose on his neighbours' fields but physically abused Augustine's wife. Brian Cuthbertson, *Stubborn Resistance: New Brunswick Maliseet and Mi'kmaq in Defence of Their Lands* (Halifax: Nimbus, 2015), 91–2.

96 Registres de la Paroise St. Pierre-aux-Liens de Caraquet, "Baptism at Nepisiguit of Jean [John] Young … 21 May 1786."

97 This land division arrangement derived from the French *rang* system found in Quebec along the St. Lawrence river valley. It also was a characteristic of *métis* communities in the early 1800s in the Upper Great Lakes region.

98 James Robertson applied in 1795 for a tract on which he, ten years before, had erected a "house thirty-three feet by twenty one" feet, a barn "thirty seven by twenty one" feet, and a "good grist mill." He also maintained "sixteen head of cattle, four sheep," and had cleared "twenty acres of land." When Philippe and John Young retracted their interest in obtaining land on the harbour, Robertson immediately sent a memorial to Governor Carleton requesting that the two parcels formerly requested by the Young brothers be granted instead to Isabelle Morrison,

Robertson's Mi'kmaw mother-in-law, and two of Isabelle's sons. But not until 1807, when a memorial was directed to Fredericton by a leading Acadian member of the Nepisiguit community, Pierre Doucet, and twenty-seven of Doucet's associates, would James Robertson finally secured a lot of 250 acres, known as Crown Grant Lot No. 5. Provincial Archives of New Brunswick (henceforth PANB), Crown Lands, Folio D, 113, "Grant # 447 to Pierrre Doucet and 27 others, County Northumberland, 20/02/1807. Source: Gabriel G. Ludlaw, President of Council at Fredericton, microfilm reel F16303." Robertson's son, James Robertson Jr., obtained Lot No. 2, of 234 acres, while Isabelle Morrison received Lot No. 4, containing 281 acres. Isabelle Morrison was a Mi'kmaw widow from Restigouche whose Scottish husband, surnamed Morrison, was "lost on the River St. Lawrence." Since Morrison is a surname found today among the Listuguj Mi'kmaq, Isabelle and her husband may have had children before coming to Nepisiguit. In 1788 Major Millidge claimed that the petitioners for plots on the harbour, who included several *métis* persons, originally wanted their lands to be granted in common "with the wish of making their own subdivisions as they improved all together." Millidge nevertheless in 1788 ran lines for seventeen lots, although no grants of land were confirmed at the time. George Sproule, the surveyor general for New Brunswick, noted twelve years later that two lots mentioned in Robertson's memorial of 1795 referred to land "applied for by John Young Junr. and Philip Young" on 3 March 1801. Though the two Young brothers renewed their petition for land on 24 July 1801, they withdrew their applications, as mentioned, upon learning that Robertson's petition preceded their own. Service New Brunswick/*Nouveau Brunswick,* Bathurst. Land, Property and Maps, Crown Land Index Sheet. As early as 25 February 1799 Saul Lee of the Crown Lands Department in Fredericton certified that Robertson and Morrison had been given the two lots for which they asked. NSARM, Biography File, "Robertson, James," 1795, "Memorial of James Robertson on behalf of himself, Isabelle Morrison and two of Morrison's sons for 400 acres that they have settled upon at Nepisiguit." (The docket includes comments written at different times by Crown Land officials.).

99 Evelyn de Blois Crossman, U.E.L. (United Empire Loyalist), *Millidge Ancestors* (Winnipeg, privately printed, 1908), 49. The author is a descendant of Thomas Millidge through her maternal grandmother, Sarah Helen Jean Millidge, who was born in Millidgeville, Saint John, NB.

100 PANB, Fredericton, microfilm reel F-506, Executive Council Records, "Minutes of Proceedings of the Committee on land, Petition of John and Philippe Young for a lot at Nipisighuit adjoining a lot belonging to Pierre Doucet," 17 March 1806.

101 Around 1812, Philippe Young Sr. became second chief of the band, while François-André Julien remained a head man. François-André treated Philippe like his brother. Since François-André did not share the same prejudices against the British as his grandfather Chief François Julien, he probably was one of those who in 1783 urged John Young Sr. to contact George Henry Monk. François-Andre and his wife Marie-Anne also were closely associated with the Morrisons at Nepisiguit and Restigouche. For instance, one of François's daughters, Marie-Ursule Julien, born in 1813, married William Morrison in 1848 and lived at Listuguj after her marriage. William Morrison would have been a grandson or great-grandson of Isabelle Morrison, James Robertson's mother-in-law.

102 Noel Young wed a Mi'kmaw woman named Marie-Françoise and the couple had a son, Philippe, who died at an early age. On 5 August 1799, Noel and Marie-Françoise brought the body of Philippe, who had been dead two and a half years, to Sainte-Famille parish cemetery for burial. Registers of the Parish of Sainte-Famille, Bathurst, 1798–1859, "Burial of Philippe Young, son of Noel Young and Marie-Françoise, on 5 August 1799." The lapse of time that occurred between this child's death and the Roman Catholic burial ceremony was not unusual. Deaths often occurred far away from a settlement having a church and clergy, so temporary internments were performed until an opportunity arose to recover the remains and have them placed in consecrated ground. Noel Young attended to his sister's needs after her husband Noel Paul died, but since Noel Young's name does not appear again in the documentary record after 1799, he may have later moved away from Nepisiguit, or died.

103 According to Mi'kmaw oral tradition, Noel Paul descended from the influential Peminout Paul family of mainland Nova Scotia.

104 Registers of the Parish of Sainte-Famille, "Burial of Noel Paul, about 28 years old, husband of Marie-Françoise Young, 5 August 1799, witnesses [André] François Julien and Gabriel Labauve." André François Julien and Gabriel Labauve were also witnesses at the interment of Noel Young and Marie-Françoise's son Philippe the same day.

105 Registers of the Parish of Sainte-Famille, "Baptism of Marie Noel, 5 months old, daughter of Noel [Paul] and Marie Françoise Young, 12 April 1800."

106 The couple were regarded as married by Mi'kmaw custom for over a year before their union was sanctioned

by Roman Catholic rite. This union may have been arranged between John Young Sr. and Prisk, as arranged marriages within the Mi'kmaw community were not unusual. A Mi'kmaw suitor usually waited a year before marrying, but with a widow the case might well be different, especially if there was an infant to be cared for. At the time of their wedding, Nicholas Prisk II was described in the church register as born at Restigouche, the eldest son of "Nicholas Ouiousse and Hélène." Marie-Françoise was the "veuve [widow] de Noël Paul." Registers of the Parish of Sainte-Famille, "Wedding of Nicholas Priske and Marie-Françoise Young," 4 May 1802. The newly wedded pair's son, John Prisk, who would have been a year old by this time, was never baptized.

107 Persons with the surname "Prisk" who belong to the Pabineau First Nation are descendants of Nicholas Prisk II Ouiouche and Marie-Françoise Young.

108 After the Battle of Restigouche in July 1760, an engagement with the British that lasted twelve days, Francois Frigault's father, Pierre Frigault, escaped in a rowboat with several others and his captain, St.-Simon, into a cove on the Restigouche River that later would be named in honour of St.-Simon. After a brief stay in Quebec, Pierre Frigault settled near Captain St.-Simon at Caraquet, where he married Josette Bouteiller. Josette was a daughter of Angèlique Giraud and a granddaughter of Gabriel Giraud *dit* St.-Jean, who assisted Gabriel Smethurst at Caraquet in 1761. According to Jean-Guy Frigault, the genealogist of the Frigault family, there were two sons named François belonging to Pierre's family; Joseph François and Francois. (The "Frigault Organization," from which this information was obtained, is a genealogical group dedicated to learning more about the Frigault family in British North America.) The younger François married Hélène Chaisson at Caraquet in 1810, so it probably was Joseph-Francois Frigault who stood at Nicholas Prisk II and Marie-Françoise Young's wedding. François Frigault's maternal grandmother, Angèlique Giraud *dit* St.-Jean, married twice, first to Joseph Bouteiller and second to Pierre Gallien. She died at eighty-five years of age and was buried at Caraquet in 1805. Registers of the Parish of St. Pierre-aux-Liens du Caraquet, 1771–96, "Burial of Angèlique Giraud," 7 February 1805.

109 Registers of the Parish of Sainte-Famille, "Burial of Madelaine, femme de Jean Young, inspecteur de bois à Népisiguit, décédée il a huit ans, âgée de 50 years, sepulture le 10 mai 1812," witnesses Pierre Arseneau and Romain Doucet.

110 Ibid., "Baptism of Stanislaus Young, born 3 May 1812, baptised 10 May 1812, son of Philippe Young [Sr.] and Marie-Elisabeth [Grand-Louis]." This child died within a year of his birth. Marie-Elisabeth may have been Mi'kmaq, but her surname, Grand-Louis, suggests that her parents were Mohawk from Caughnawaga (Kanawake).

111 In registering baptisms, births, and deaths for the Young family, the Roman Catholic clergy listed John Young Sr. and Magdeleine Dedam's descendants as "sauvauge." The "in-between" classification, *métis,* was not ascribed by clerics to individuals at Nepisiguit.

112 Owing to this continued connection with the Juliens /Julians, on 14 July 1843 Philippe Young Sr. and Marie-Elisabeth's daughter Madeleine wed Cain Bernard Julien, a great-grandson of Chief François Julien of Redbank. Though they were kin related, in keeping with Mi'kmaw kinship rules that prohibited close cousin marriage the spouses were at least four degrees of consanguinity distant from one another. Cain (the Mi'kmaw pronunciation of "Étienne") was the son of Bernard Julien, a son of Chief Barnaby Julien, who in turn was the son of Chief François Julien (1729–1830) and Magdeleine David. Madeleine and Cain's first child, Peter Julien, was born in May 1843, before their marriage of 14 July the same year, and baptized on 22 June 1843. The child's godparents were André Bernard Julien and Marie Prisk, the daughter – born in 1803 – of Chief Nicholas Prisk II and Marie-Françoise Young.

113 Information on these ten children is derived from church and census records. Parish of Sainte-Famille, "Baptism of Magdeleine Young, 22 May 1808"; ibid., "Baptism of Philippe Young [Jr.], 4½ months, son of Philippe Young and Marie-Elisabeth, 13 January 1811, godparents François Julien and Marie-Anne Chrisistome"; ibid., "Burial of Philippe Young, dead for ten days, aged eight months, 4 May 1811." Madeleine was born on 24 March 1808, Denis (or Dennis) in 1811 (1811 being the birth year reported on the 1861 New Brunswick census, although the 1881 federal census lists him as born in 1821), and Stanislaus on 3 May 1812. Marie's birthdate remains unknown, but she is known to have later married Paul Clairmont of Restigouche. Anne was born in 1815, Jean (or John) on 29 June 1818, Noel in 1820, a second Jean around 1830, and a second Philippe Jr. in 1831. See, for instance, Registers of the Parish of Sainte-Famille, "Baptism of Anne Young; presiding priest P. Parent, godparents Charles Doucet and Marie-Josephe, 18 June 1815." (Anne was born at Nepisiguit in early June 1815.) Denis Young, who lived near his

father at Nepisiguit in 1871, by 1881 was working as a stonemason in New Brandon. His sister Marie married Paul Clairmont, but when she died at a relatively young age, Clairmont wed "Louise Condeau" (Condo) of Listuguj. Noel married Angelique Caplan in 1843 and moved to Listuguj where the couple had three sons, William, Stephen, and Thomas. William, born 20 August 1844, was baptized at St. Joseph's mission at Nash Creek, Restigouche County, seven days later. Their second son, Stephen, on 16 November 1873 married Mary Ferlotte (Farlatte, Firlotte, Furlotte, 1850–1937), the daughter of Pierre Ferlotte and Marie Adee Allain of Jacquet River, and lived in Campbellton and Durham. They had seven children: Margaret Ann on 19 October 1874, Mary Elizabeth on 29 October 1875. William Stephen on 9 July 1877, Bridget Ann on 20 July 1881, Peter Gilbert on 30 August 1882, Helen Agnes on 12 July 1885, and Joseph Daniel on 18 May 1887. Registers of St. Joseph's mission church, Nash Creek, Restigouche County. Noel Young Sr. and Angelique's third son, Thomas, married a woman named Mary, and the couple's children were William Dempsey Young, baptized at St. Joseph's Church on 2 March 1878, and Joseph Young. Joseph wed Sara Arseneault around 1910 and the couple had Mary Malvina Young, who was baptized at Notre Dame de Lourds, Atholville, in June 1911; presiding priest E. Wallace, witnesses William Boucher and Ellen Young. (Two other children – Alexander, an infant who died on 8 March 1919, and Denis Young, buried at Atholville at three months of age on 22 May 1914 – likely also were children of Joseph and Sara.) When Noel Young's first wife Angelique died around 1844, he wed Margaret Marchand, and on 22 February 1846 Noel and Margaret had a son, James Young, baptized at St. Joseph's Church at Nash Creek, Restigouche County.

114	There is no mention of Philippe Young Jr.'s birth in the Parish of Sainte-Famille baptismal registers, but he was listed as aged thirty on the 1861 New Brunswick census, so he probably was born around 1831. Philippe Jr. acted on the band council with his father before becoming a councillor in his own right. In 1859, "Young Philippe Young" joined with "Philippe Young" and eight other head men, "Jacques Prisque, Thomas Narvy, John Louis, Étienne Damond, André Bernard and Peter Bear," in petitioning Fredericton to ensure that that, in accordance with the elderly Nicholas Prisk II's wishes, Prisk would be recognized as their new chief. Fredericton, University of New Brunswick, Harriet Irving Library and Archives (henceforth HILA), Indian Documentation Collection of Microfilm, MC

408 (project sponsored by St. Thomas University, 1982), RG 1, RS 347, Records of Lieutenant Governor Manners-Sutton, "Petition of Nepisiguit Indians," 23 July 1859. Philippe Young Jr. married Madeleine Courniche of Burnt Church around 1846 and the couple had seven children: Peter in 1848, Noel in 1850, Joseph in 1852, François-Pierre in 1856, Thomas in 1868, Jane in 1863, and Mary in 1872. Madeleine Courniche appears in register entries for the Parish of Sainte-Famille under six surnames: Bernard, Berry, Courniche, Courniviere, Neville, and Young. See, for example, Registers of the Parish of Sainte-Familille, "Baptism of Peter Young, 5 days old, son of Philippe Young and Madeleine Courniche, 26 September 1848, godparents Peter Young and Rosalie Bigears [Vicaire]"; ibid., "Baptism of Noel Young, 15 days old, son of Philippe Young and Madeline Courniviere, 22 June 1850, godparents John Louis and Madeleine Young"; ibid., "Baptism of Joseph Young, 1 month old, 20 October 1852, son of Philippe Young and Madeleine Bernard, godparents Noel Prisque and Mary Labauve"; ibid., "Baptism of François-Pierre Young, 2 weeks old, 5 July 1856, son of Philippe Young and Madeleine Neville, godparents Peter-Noel Prisk and Jenny Dedam"; ibid., "Thomas Young, two days old, baptised 7 January 1868, son of Philippe Young and Madeleine Berry, godparents Thomas Morrison from Restigouche and Marie Labauve." Philippe Young Jr. and Madeleine's youngest daughters, Jane and Mary, appear on the 1881 federal census. Philippe and his wife remained core members of the Nepisiguit group, although they also had close ties with Néguac, Burnt Church, Redbank, and Listuguj. The *Registre des mariages, baptêmes et sepultures de la paroisse de St. Bernard de Nigawech* (*sic*, Néguac) shows Philippe Young Jr. standing as a witness at the marriage of Thomas Cloud and Molly Gabriel at Burnt Church on 29 July 1844. Jane Young married Joseph Ginnish of Tabusintac around 1886 and had six children: Agnes in 1887, Thomas in 1891, John in 1892, Lucy in 1894, Louis in 1893, and Mary-Helen in 1900. Joseph Ginnish was a descendant of the well-known chief Thomas Kenout *dit* Ganiche (Ginnish) and his wife Henrietta Athanase. See *Registre des mariages, baptêmes et sepultures de la paroisse de St. Bernard de Nigawech*, 1796–1846, "Marriage of Thomas Kenout and Henrietta Athanase, 29 July 1796." In 1861 Philippe Young Jr. and Madeleine were caring for Philippe Jr.'s elderly father, who according to the New Brunswick census for that year was ninety years old. (This is incorrect; Philippe Young Sr., being born c.1778, would have been around eighty-three.) Philippe Young Jr., who was

115 According to an article in *the Daily Telegraph* of 3 October 1876, this security turned up in papers belonging to the estate of Hugh Munro, the first permanent magistrate in the Bathurst area following the demise of George Walker's establishment. It reads: "This Present Certifies – That I, Cicile PETRE daughter of Mary PETRE of Nipisiquit, Bay Chaleur, Do by these Presents before God and the witness hereunto Promise to Marry John YOUNG, Cordweaner [shoemaker or cobbler] of said Nipisiquit and Do by the True Christian faith Promise to perform this obligation of Marriage by the first Opportunity when any of his Majesties Justices of the Pease (*sic*, Peace) come to this Settlement. In failure of this Obligation I Cicile PETRE do hereby bind my Self Under the penalty of Twenty pounds to be paid to John Young and Do hereby set my hand and Seal this Eighteenth Day of January in the Year of Our Lord One Thousand Eight hundred and three (1803) – Signed in the Presence of Francis COMMEAUX Jr., [and] James SUTHERLAND."

116 Cecile Pitre, the daughter of Michel Pitre and Marie-Joseph Orillon *dit* Champagne, was born in Nicolet, Quebec, on 28 May 1779. John Young Jr. and Cecile had three daughters: Marie, born in October 1805, Adelaide, born in May 1807, and Elizabeth, born in June 1809. They also had an infant son in 1804 who died before 20 May 1804.

117 Peter Young, listed on the 1881 federal census as sixty-three years of age, was a shoemaker working in Bathurst. He was likely a son of John Young Jr. and Mary-Cecile Pitre. Peter Young and his wife Lucy had six children.

118 Marie-Cecile Pitre died at Tracadie on 31 October 1859. François Le Breton was the son of François Le Breton Sr. and Margaret Gionet. In turn, François Le Breton Sr. was a son or grandson of François Le Breton *dit* Robert, who around 1777 fled the perils the American Revolution by living with the Mi'kmaq for several years. Le Breton *dit* Robert married twice in succession, both times to Acadian women, first on Cape Breton to Marie Le Mordant and second to Marie-Thérèse Boissel of Tracadie.

119 Jean-Baptiste Vienneau (11 January 1754–9 August 1808) was a son of Michel Vienneau *dit* Michaud and Thérèse Bauvé (Baude or Bashault) of Quebec. Jean-Baptiste married Magdeleine-Louise Le Jeune and settled at Petit-Rocher prior to moving to Rough Waters, and died at Pokemouche at age fifty-four. Jean-Baptiste and Magdeleine's daughter Judith, who married Michel-Joseph Boucher, was born around 1784.

120 Magdeleine-Louise's father, Eustache Le Jeune, was a son of Martin Le Jeune *dit* Briard (or Briart, 1661–1750), a noted fish and fur trader at Port Maltois (now Port Medway), Queens County, in Nova Scotia, and Le Jeune's second wife, Anne-Marie Gaudet (or Godet). Martin Le Jeune *dit* Briard's first wife was a Mi'kmaw woman named Jeanne Kaygayonais, while Anne-Marie Gaudet was French. After Anne-Marie's death, Martin in 1729 married Marie Reynard.

121 Registers of the Parish of Sainte-Famille, "Baptism of Françoise Prisk, 13 April 1806."

122 Registers of the Parish of Sainte-Famille, "Mariage de Étienne Young, fils de Jean Young inspecteur de bois et de defunct Magdeleine, et Marie Lavigne, fille de Jean Lavigne [*père*] et Isabelle Baudville," 13 October 1812. Marie-Therese Lavigne was born on 23 April 1784 at Tracadie, Gloucester County, New Brunswick, and died at Bathurst at age 108 on 20 September 1892. Her father, Jean Lavigne, was born around 1722, either in France or at Port Royal, to Nicholas Lavigne and Anne Clemenceau, and he wed Isabelle "Baudville" (Boiselle) around 1753. (Isabelle's surname is spelled four different ways: "Baude," "Baudville," "Boiselle," and "Boudreaux"). Isabelle's grandparents were François Beaudry and Madeleine Boiselle from Quebec. By 1812 Jean Lavigne and Isabelle were among the most elderly residents of Rough Waters. Jean saw service with the French during the Seven Years' War and later worked for Commodore George Walker's establishment. He died at Nepisiguit at around age 110 on 20 August 1822. His wife Isabelle, born in 1746, died in 1849 at 103 years of age. *Miramichi Gleaner*, Chatham, NB, 14 August 1849, "Obituary of Mrs. Jean Lavigne."

123 Étienne Young and Marie-Therese's Lavigne's two elder sons, Joseph-Athanase and Sebastian, were born before Étienne and Marie were married by banns and finally by Roman Catholic rite at Sainte-Famille Church on 13 October 1812. Joseph-Athanase was born on 29 July 1803 and baptized on 16 October the same year at Sainte-Famille Church. His godfather was Athanase Boudreau. He married Marie Chamberlain at Sainte-Famille Church on 14 February 1827. Marie was born at Rough Waters, but her parents were French from Quebec. Her father, Jean-Baptiste Chamberlain, born in 1753 on Île-aux-Grues in the St. Lawrence River, married Michelle Pitre and settled in the late 1800s at St. Pierre, or French Village, in what is today West Bathurst. Joseph-Athanase and Marie's eldest son, Joseph-Jean Athanase Young Jr. (or *fils*), was born on 28 December 1827. As an adult he did not secure a Crown grant, though he did acquire

land through his marriage to Marguerite Bennett Boucher. Sebastian Young, born 8 July 1807, married Olive Doucet, born in 1813, at Saint-Famille Church on 25 July 1831 (the day prior to St. Anne's day, which was a popular day for weddings within the Mi'kmaw community). Olive's parents were Laurent Doucet and Marie Le Jeune *dit* Briand. Sebastian and Olive Doucet had a son John-Athanase Young in 1849 who became a farmer at Rough Waters. This John-Athanase married a woman named Mary and had two children, Frederick, born in 1878, and Mary Jane, born in 1880. Étienne Young and Marie-Thérèse Lavigne also had two daughters, Marguerite, born on 23 May 1812 and baptized on 18 July of that year, and Celeste, born on 7 March 1815 and baptized at Sainte-Famille Church on 30 March of that year by Père P. Parent; her godparents were John Pitre and Angélique Lavigne. She later wed a widower, Benjamin Theriault, on 29 May 1834. Étienne and Mary's youngest son Jean- (John-) Athanase, born on 20 September 1818 and baptized on 29 October 1818, married a woman named Mary (surname unknown).

124 Joseph-Athanase Young Sr. (incorrectly listed as aged sixty-five on the 1861 census) and Marie Chamberlain had Lawrence around 1827, John-Anathase Jr. around 1828, Oliver on 7 September 1830, Abraham around 1833, Marie in June 1836 (though she is held to be born in 1843 on the 1861 census), William around 1838, and Louis around 1848. Abraham married Isabella Watson and had five children: Mary-Ann in 1860, John in 1862, Caroline in 1867, Elizabeth in 1871, and George in 1879. When Abraham's wife Isabella died around 1880, he wed Sophia Lavigne. In 1861, Oliver Young and his wife Marie had a son, John, who was eleven months old. John's birth date here comes from the 1861 census, which must be treated with caution, although the names of Lawrence, Abraham, Marie, and John appear on land deeds and census records, while Oliver's and Marie's births appear in baptismal registers. Registers of the Parish of Sainte-Famille, "Baptism of Oliver Young, born 7 September 1830, son of Joseph-Athanase Lejeune [*sic*, Young] and Marie Chamberlain [also Chamberland], baptised 12 September 1830." Lawrence or "Larry" Young, listed as forty-five years of age on the 1871 federal census, had a wife Nora and three children: Larry, seventeen, Joseph, fifteen, and Philomene, one. Abraham Young and Isabella Watson's youngest son, George Young, eventually married Mary Pitre and had at least one child, Leonard. Land documents pertaining to Lot 7 show the names of "Sophia Young, née Lavigne" and "Abraham Young." It is most likely that this Abraham Young was

Joseph-Athanase's son, who first wed Isabella Watson and then Sophie Lavigne, and not a member of the Le Jeune *dit* Briard family, whose ancestors arrived in the Bathust area following the Acadian deportations in the 1750s. Over time certain members of the Le Jeune *dit* Briand family, however, did marry descendants of John Young Sr. and Madeleine Dedam. Further confusion is elicited by the presence of an immigrant couple who hailed directly from Scotland, Frederick Young and his wife Martha Gordon, who arrived in West Bathurst and had at least one child, J.B. Young. These Scottish Youngs are not related to either the Youngs at Rough Waters or the Le Jeunes. A study of the available land records for lots around Lot 7 helps clarify matters, since documents show that kin-related families tended to live close together. Surnames on local land transactions relating to Lot No. 7, beside Young and Boucher, include Lavigne, Chamberlain, Smith, and Bourque.

According to the New Brunswick census for Bathurst in 1861, five of Joseph-Anathase Young Sr. and Mary Chamberlain's children were still unmarried: William, twenty-three; John and his twin sister Marie, both twenty; Margaret, eighteen; and Louisa, thirteen. In 1863 Mary Young married Pierre Boucher. In 1859 Joseph-Athanase Sr.'s eldest son, Joseph-Anathase Young Jr., wed Margaret Bennett Boucher. Oliver, born around 1841 (although the 1861 census states he was born in 1831, which is too early since his father, born in 1819, would have been only twelve in that year) had a wife named Mary and, in 1861, a three-month-old son John. Abraham, reportedly born in 1832 – though again, this would have been too early – also had a wife named Mary and three children, Mary Ann born in 1860, John in 1862, and Caroline in 1867. After Mary died, Abraham married Elizabeth or Isabelle Ann Watson and had Elizabeth in May 1871, George in 1875, and Helen in 1882. Canada, federal census for Bathurst, New Brunswick, 1871.

125 Lot No. 7 was divided lengthwise into what was called "an eastern and western moiety." In 1858 Joseph Athanase Sr. conveyed portions of one moiety to his sons William, John, Oliver, and Abraham "of the Big River [Nepisiguit River]." By this time the other moiety had been sold to the Vienneau family.

126 Jean [-Athanase] Young, Étienne Young's youngest son, was born in 1819. Registers of the Parish of Sainte-Famille, "Baptism of John Young, son of Étienne Young and Marie Lavigne, 20 October 1819." John and his wife Marie (or Mary) had ten children: Marie in 1846, Margaret in 1848, John around 1850, William around 1852, Joseph around 1854, James around 1857,

Ellen in 1859, Elizabeth in 1861, Stephen in 1864, and Lawrence in 1866. The federal census of 1881 lists John A. Young as seventy-three years old, although he was eleven years younger and a widower who lived alone. His lot, in the name of "John A. Young," appears on the Crown Land Index Sheet for the Bathurst area. A blueprint copy of this index is available at Service New Brunswick/*Nouveau Brunswick,* Land, Property and Maps, Bathurst. According to this index sheet, to the immediate east of "John-A. Young's" Lot No. 21 of eighty-seven acres lay a lot belonging to John Ferguson, Lot No. 20 of ninety-four acres. Pierre Boucher's Lot No. 19 of ninety-four acres flanked Ferguson's lot on the east, and next to Boucher's property was Joseph Lavigne Jr.'s Lot No. 18. Gloucester Junction, following the survey and construction of the Intercolonial Railway through the reserve between 1870 and 1876, was situated near these properties. Joseph-Athanase Young Sr. lived on Lot No. 7, located at a short distance from the others.

127 Jean Lavigne Jr., a brother of Étienne Young's wife Marie-Thérèse, was the father of Cèleste-Louise Lavigne. Cèleste-Louise in turn became the wife of Firmin Boucher – a son in turn of Michel-Joseph Boucher and Judith Vienneau. Younger members of the Boucher, Lavigne, and Young families practised both brother-sister exchange and cousin marriage. Marie-Thérèse Lavigne (Étienne Young's wife) and Jean Lavigne Jr. were siblings, so Joseph-Athanase Young Sr. (Étienne Young's son) and Cèleste-Louise Lavigne (Jean Lavigne Jr.'s daughter) were first cousins. Celeste-Louise married Firmin Boucher. When Joseph-Athanase Young Sr.'s son Joseph-Athanase Jr. wed Firmin and Celeste-Louise's daughter Marguerite-Bennett Boucher,

he married his second cousin. (And in 1863, when Joseph-Athanase's sister Marie Young at age thirty-two married Pierre Boucher, Marguerite-Bennett Boucher's younger brother, another second cousin marriage occurred within the same families. The following chart traces the relationship between second cousins Joseph-Athanase Young Jr. and Marguerite Bennet Boucher.

128 Another case of second cousin marriage occurred at Rough Waters, again involving the Young and Boucher families. Joseph-Athanase Young Jr. and Marguerite Bennet Boucher had a daughter, Marguerite Young, born in 1856, who wed Alexander P. Doucet. Alexander Doucet and Marguerite in turn had a daughter, Winnifred Doucet, who married Jean-Albert Boucher *dit* Hébert, her second cousin. Winnifred and Jean Albert Boucher *dit* Hébert were second cousins because one of Joseph-Anathase Young Sr.'s daughters, named Mary Young, married Pierre Boucher, Marguerite-Bennett Boucher's brother. (They also shared a common great-grandparent, Joseph-Athanase Sr.) Mary and Pierre Boucher had a son, Albert Boucher, who on 2 November 1887 wed Mary-Elisabeth Roy, born in 1865 (a daughter of Alexander Roy and Catherine Mary Cowan). And Albert Boucher and Mary-Elizabeth Roy were the parents of Jean-Albert Boucher *dit* Hebert, who married Winnifred Doucet.

Cousin marriage, as long as not between first cousins, is permitted by the Roman Catholic Church, but it is looked at askance by the Mi'kmaq, who traditionally restricted marriage to fourth cousins. Cousin marriage, however, allows rights to land to be passed down through the generations within a restricted number of

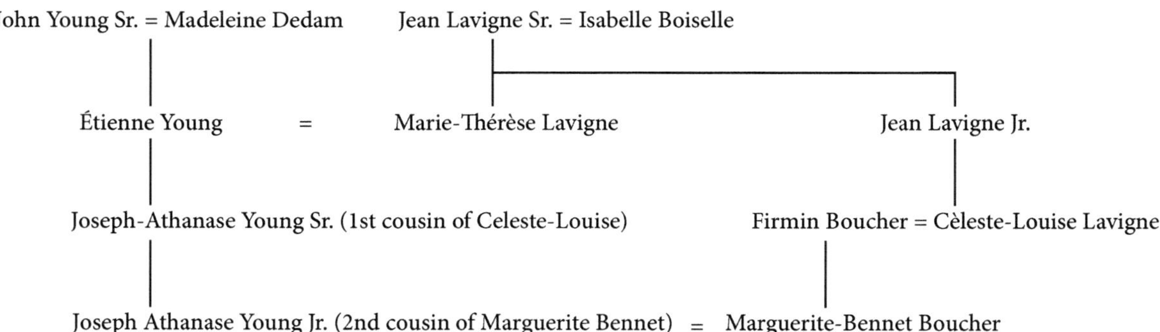

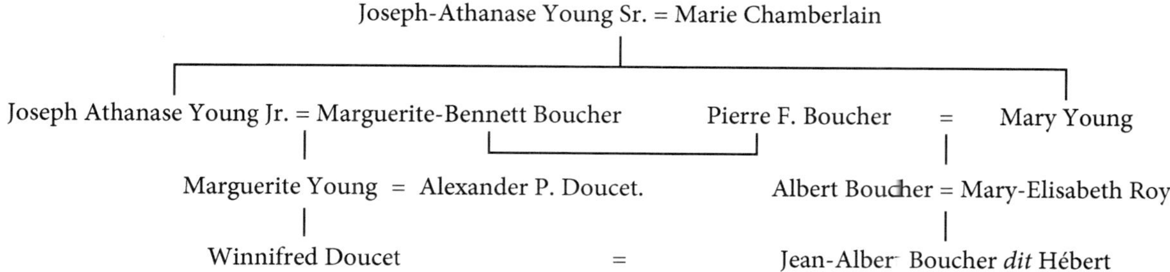

families. Owing to this fact, large blocks of the original grants at Rough Waters still remain in the possession of Étienne Young and Jean Lavigne Sr.'s descendants. For a theoretical examination of changes that occur in marriage patterns when members belonging to a bilateral group, such as the *métis* Youngs, evolve into a landed group that exercises property rights over time, see Ward H. Goodnough, *Cooperation in Change* (New York: Russell Sage Foundation, 1963). Mi'kmaw social organization, unlike that of Central Algonquian-speakers – who allowed cousin marriage – exhibited a generational bias that precluded close cousin marriage. Research into land-owning among certain Mi'kmaq revealed that an organizational shift among the Mi'kmaq away from bilaterality and generationality towards lineality is still in its infancy. Yet despite cousin marriage being frowned upon by the Mi'kmaq, such unions occurred in the mid-nineteenth century among Mi'kmaw families in northeastern New Brunswick and southwestern Nova Scotia. Owing to a drop in the Mi'kmaw population during these years, marital partners proved difficult to find and groups became influenced by French and Acadian social organizational norms.

129 A scholarly examination of the relationships between descendants and collateral kin of Étienne Young and his older brother Philippe Young Sr. might cast novel light on the unique sphere of intercommunity interaction at Rough Waters, which began in the early nineteenth century and continues to the present day. These Indigenous community interrelationships are interesting for three reasons. First, from the perspective of identity, the Youngs at Nepisiguit considered themselves Mi'kmaq rather than *métis*. They thus differed from the *métis* at Sault Ste. Marie, Canada West,

removed by government fiat in 1859 onto an Ojibwa reserve. The second and third generations of Youngs of Rough Waters did not "become Mi'kmaq" with time; they were born Mi'kmaq, bound by kinship and obligational ties to a Mi'kmaw chief, while interacting with Acadians and other settlers about them in ways that more closely approximated the French. Alan Knight and Janet E. Chute, "In the Shadow of the Thumping Drum: The Sault *Métis* – The People In-Between," in *Lines Drawn Upon the Water: First Nations and the Great Lakes Borders and Borderlands*, ed. Karl S. Hele (London, ON: Wilfrid University Press, 2005), 85–113. Census takers listed the Youngs as "Indian." As early as 1751, *métis* members of the Le Jeune *dit* Briard family from southwestern Nova Scotia moved to Cape Breton, Newfoundland, or Prince Edward Island, and by 1800 some lived at Nepisiguit region and contributed to the region's ethnic diversity. One anticipates new and fruitful approaches and models being developed in the future to address issues of group identity, diversity, and historic change within the Bathurst Indigenous community, particularly by scholars emerging from within that community itself. For instance, Daniel Young, a French-speaking descendant of Étienne Young, examines oral traditions circulating within his family. His work shows how fruitful such lines of inquiry can be, although he also reflects on his frustration in not being recognized as having Indigenous ancestry. "I got an ill feeling at first to see in brackets '(sauvage)' beside my ancestors' names," he writes, "but deep inside I always had a feeling that we were descendants of First Nation people … [and] I can imagine the life in [Nepisiguit in] those days when there was plenty of forest and little population in the area." Young, "History of the Youngs of Nipisiguit."

130 The deed books and electronic files at Service New Brunswick/Nouveau Brunswick, Land, Property and Maps in Bathurst shed light on a number of property transactions relating to Lot No. 7 between 1836 and 1853. In 1883 Joseph-Athanase Young Sr. conveyed the property on which he lived to his son-in-law Peter F. Boucher for $230. Deed Book, 30/51/Deed/28, "John Young and [Joseph] Athenase Young [Sr.] and Peter F. Boucher," 2 June 1883. Peter Boucher received "the eastern section of Lot No. 7 [about twenty-five acres] on the south side of the Nepisiguit River originally granted to said Athanase Young," with one quarter conveyed already to "John and William Young as tenants in common." Mary Young, Boucher's husband, was consulted apart from her husband respecting the transaction by the land registrar, Moses M. McGinley.

131 Joseph-Athanase Young Sr.'s daughter, Mary Young, and her husband, Pierre Boucher had a daughter, Ignatia Agnes Boucher, who wed Jerome Lavigne, a distant relative of Étienne Young's wife, Marie-Thérèse Lavigne. Jerome Lavigne's father, Pierre Lavigne, was the son of Michel Lavigne and Angelique Pitre. The important fact here is that three families; the Youngs, Lavignes and Bouchers, remained closely linked for generations, while also maintaining close ties, socially, culturally and economically with the Mi'kmaw band. A degree of confusion arises in the documentary record, because the recording priest translated Mary Young's name into French as "Marie LeJeune" and did not record the identity of her parents. In consequence, some researchers contend that "Marie LeJeune" was actually a member of the Le Jeune *dit* Briand family, rather than a descendant of John Young Sr. Mary Young (1836–1906) and Pierre F. Boucher were married at Sainte-Famille Church on 4 August 1863. Not all Bouchers living in Bathurst are closely related to the Bouchers of Rough Waters. Another intriguing branch of the Boucher family stems from Pierre Boucher, born about 1688 in St. Nicholas, Quebec and his wife Helene Gaudry. This couple's son, Pierre Boucher *fils*, moved to Acadia where Pierre married Anne Hébert, a daughter of Étienne Hebert and Jeanne Comeau of Port Royal, and had a son named Honoré Boucher *dit* Villedieu (1716–66). In 1743 Honoré married Marie La Sonde at Port Toulouse, now St. Peter's, Cape Breton and several of this couple's descendants moved to northeastern New Brunswick around 1758, where they interacted closely with the Mi'kmaq during the last years of the Seven Years' War. Marie La Sonde would have been the daughter of Marc La Sonde and Judith Petitpas, who held land at St. Peter's,

Cape Breton in 1752. (Interestingly, Chief Jean Baptiste Philippe Tecouramart of Cape Sable, who travelled regularly to Cape Breton and Chignecto, in the early 1750s had a wife named Madelaine de Songeur [or de Soude], who spoke French fluently, and could very well have been a daughter of Marc La Sonde and Judith Petitpas. John Clarence Webster, ed., *Thomas Pichon, The Spy of Beauséjour: An Account of his Career in Europe and America*, (Halifax, 1937), 81–82, Letter no. 24, "Pichon to Hussey," 13 January 1755.

132 The persistence today of a constellation of interrelated families at Rough Waters, speaking both French and English and, in some quarters, some Mi'kmaq and holding much of the land their ancestors held, is remarkable. On scanning an old land grant map, Daniel P. Young, who belongs to this group of families, stated: "Now that I look at [the map] closely I can see that it [one of the parcels on the map] belongs to [Joseph-] Athanase Young [Etienne's son] and it's the parcel where my father lives at the present time except it's much bigger than it is now. Close to it the viewer can see the lot of Frances Vienot who is our old neighbour Frances Vienneau – also a few lots over we can see the lot of Firmin Boucher." Young, "History of the Youngs of Nipisiguit." The author Janet Chute met several other people who were similarly conversant with lands and events at Rough Waters more than 180 years ago.

133 Registers of the Parish of Sainte-Famille, "Baptism of Françoise Prisk, 13 April 1806." Godparents Magdeleine-Louise Le Jeune and Jean-Baptist Vienneau. Françoise Prisk married Jean-Laurent Dedam, son of Louis Dedam and Marie Quartre Patte, on 14 May 1821. Witnesses were Louis Haché and Philippe Ouiyouche (Ouiouche).

134 Noel was born at Nepisiguit on 29 December 1807 but was not baptized at Sainte-Famille Church until 1 January 1809. Pierre Doucet and Monique were Noel's godparents. Registers of the Parish of Sainte-Famille, 1809.

135 Genevieve Prisk, born in 1808, died at fifteen years of age and was buried at Sainte-Famille Church on 13 November 1824.

136 Michel Prisk married Mary Patlass at Sacred Heart in February 1883.

137 Registers of the Parish of Sainte-Famille, "Baptism of Jeanne-Monique Prisk, born towards the end of March and baptized on 15 May 1814." The godparents were Jean Lavigne and Marie Lavigne Young, Étienne Young's wife. Jeanne-Monique married André Pominville (or Pomerville), a son of Charles

Pomerville and Marie Thomas, around 1832. See Registers of Parish of Ste.-Famille, "Baptism of Marie Pomerville, daughter of André Pomerville and Monique Prisk, 12 February 1833." Jeanne-Monique was one of the first of her family to marry; she and her husband had a daughter, Marie, in 1833. Ibid., "Baptism of Marie Pominville, daughter of André Pominville and Monique Prisque [Prisk], baptised 12 February 1833 at eight days of age."

138 One daughter, Françoise, had as her godmother Magdeleine-Louise Le Jeune, the second wife of Jean-Baptist Vienneau, who lived for a while at Petit-Rocher. Magdeleine-Louise's ancestral roots extended back to Nova Scotia's South Shore prior to the British deportation of the Acadians. Her father was Eustache Le Jeune (1715–60) and her mother was Marie-Anne Roy. Eustache was a son of Martin Le Jeune *dit* Briart (or Briard, 1663–1719), an inhabitant of the eighteenth-century Acadian-*métis* fur trade and fishing community of Port Maltois (now Port Medway, Queens County, Nova Scotia), and Martin's second wife, Marie Gaudet. Some of Eustache's descendants travelled in the early 1750s to Cape Breton, Prince Edward Island, and Newfoundland, while others went to the Chignecto area and northeastern New Brunswick. Bona Arsenault, *Histoire et généalogie des Acadiens*, 3rd ed. (Montreal: Léméac, 1978).

139 John Prisk married late in life to a Mi'kmaw woman named Margaret (c.1811–c.1889) and had three sons, William (c.1842–c.1900), John Jr. (1855–?), and Michael (c.1859–c.1885). William Prisk became a head man at Nepisiguit, known for his woods skills and medicinal knowledge; John died young; and Michael was born when his mother was over forty years of age and lived with her after she became a widow. Elders in the Mi'kmaw community were respected, and children often cared for their parents as they aged. On the Gloucester County, Holy Family Parish, census of 1881, one finds Michael Prisk, at age twenty-two, residing with his seventy-eight-year-old mother. After her death Michel wed Mary Patlass at Sacred Heart Church in February 1883.

140 HILA, File 1, MG H54, Indian Affairs in New Brunswick, 1788–1844, Doc. 62, "Gloucester County Surveys." The survey only stated that "1,000 a. [acres, had been surveyed on the] NW. Side of Nepisiguit River between Pabineau River and Strong Waters [now Rough Waters]."

141 HILA, RS 108, 1841, "Journal of Proceedings on Land, Petition of Nepisiguit Indians for a reserve, 26 March 1841, approved in council 28 March 1841"; "Petition from Nepisiguit group to Sir John Harvey," 31 March 1841;

HILA, RS 105, Records of the Department of Natural Resources, New Brunswick, Indian Affairs Correspondence, 1860–69, "Bathurst Reserve, 20 December 1861."

142 HILA, RG 2, RS 578, Records of the Executive Council, 1784–1837, Report of M. DeBlois, Indian Commissioner for Gloucester County, to W. Odell, 14 June 1841.

143 HILA, File 1, MG H54, Indian Affairs, New Brunswick, Doc. 67, "Indians of Gloucester County, Report of Thomas M. DeBlois and A. Barbarie, c.1831"; British Colonial Office Records, London, England, on microfilm at LAC (henceforth LAC CO) 188/64/160. The commissioners felt such trespasses would prevent the band from engaging in "industrious improvement."

144 Ibid. This missive was written near the end of DeBlois's term as commissioner, for on 1 September 1841 Adam Ferguson and John Fraser were appointed commissioners for Restigouche and Gloucester Counties respectively. It was obvious a distinct reluctance had surfaced among the Nepisiguit Mi'kmaq by 1841 regarding giving names of band members to census takers, possibly a legacy that went back to Pierre Calvert's census-taking of 1761, which led to the deportation of many members of the Acadian community later the same year.

145 Estimations of the reserve's size differed by fifty to one hundred acres. The tract reported on by Perley in 1844 formed the land base for today's Oinpegitjoig L'Noeigati, or Pabineau First Nation No. 11.

146 Deed Book for 1836, Bathurst, no. 177. Indenture made between Atenas (*sic*, Athanase) Young, Parish of Bathurst, farmer, and Henry Albee and Benjamin D. Smith, lumberers, 29 June 1836. William Napier, JP., witnessed the transaction, which was registered by Hugh Munro on 1 July 1836. A similar lease was signed between Albee and Smith and Athanase Young's neighbour Francis Vienneau four days later.

147 Young could not write, so signed his name with an "x." Registry of Deeds, Bathurst, Deed Book for 1838, 384, "Mortgage between Joseph-Athanase Young, farmer, on one part and Joseph Read, merchant, on the other, relating to 50 acres of Lot No. 7 on the southerly shore of Nepisiguit River. Witnesses Charles McManus and John Brown." Young redeemed his land by completing payments for the full amount of £130 to Read in 1858. He and his family also continued farming the land throughout the term of the mortgage.

148 These roller dams, which allowed logs to pass unharmed over the falls, were built on the Nepisiguit and nearby Tetagouche rivers.

149 The commissioners suggested that a supply of provisions and clothing be sent to the band in 1838. HILA,

University of New Brunswick Archives and Special Collections, Indian Affairs Documents, MG H54, doc. 67, "Thomas DeBlois and A. Barbarie, Letter of 6 September 1838."

150 HILA, RS 345, "Report of Peter Mazerolle, Indian Commissioner for the County of Kent," 18 March 1848. Famine caused by crop failures from 1846 to 1849 led to ill health. A cholera-like disease and smallpox from weakened immunity struck groups more agriculturally inclined. See, for instance, HILA, RG 2, RS 578, Records of the Executive Council, 1833–67, "Petition of Thomas Bernard at Dorchester, NB, to Lieutenant Governor Colebrooke," 20 February 1847. A severe cholera outbreak occurred along the St. Lawrence Valley in 1849.

151 HILA, RS 578, Records of the Executive Council of New Brunswick, 1833–65, "Report of the Committee of Council upon the Correspondence relative to the Act to regulate the management and disposal of the Indian Reserves in the Province of New Brunswick, 25 July 1844, as approved in Council." Perley traced the development of this policy from 1838 to 1848. HILA, RS 345, "Letter from Moses Perley regarding the disposal of Indian Reserves," 3 April 1848; HILA, RG 2, RS 578, doc. 269, "Report, dated 20 January 1844, of the Committee of Council upon correspondence in relation to the *Act to Regulate the Management and Disposal of Indian Reserves in the Province of New Brunswick*."

152 Perley derived this information from a report prepared by Samuel L. Bishop, a local Indian agent in Gloucester County. Bishop also held that the reserve at the junction of the Nepisisguit and Pabineau Rivers was 1,060 acres rather than 1,000 acres. HILA, RG 1, RS 345, "Report on Indian Reserves," 6 May 1847; HILA, RG 1, RS 345, Records of the Lieutenant Governors of New Brunswick, Records of Lieutenant Governor William Macbean Colebrooke, microfilm reel F-8872, "Report of Reserves, by County, compiled by Moses Perley from information drawn from local Indian agents, including Samuel L. Bishop, Commissioner for the Bathurst Region, May 1847." The situation at Nepisiguit was in stark contrast to reports for other reserves, where large portions had been marked for sale under the 1844 policy, which allowed for almost automatic subdivision and sale of Mi'kmaw land in New Brunswick.

153 HILA, RG 1, RS 345, "Moses Perley to Lieutenant Governor William MacBean Colebrooke," 3 April 1848.

154 Marie Labauve, a daughter of Thomas Labauve and Angelique Caplan, was born on 30 October 1812. Her father was the son of Gabriel Labauve, the man who on 5 August 1799 witnessed the burials of both Noel Paul (Marie-Françoise Young's first husband) and Noel Young's son Philippe. The priest at Noel Prisk and Marie Labauve's wedding at Sainte-Famille Church on 27 July 1818 noted that the couple were fourth cousins. Noel and Mary likely were related through kin at Listuguj. "Labauve," like "Le Jeune," was a surname that harked back to the early fur-trading days on the South Shore of Nova Scotia. Prior to 1708, Rene Labauve, the son of Noel Labauve and a *métis* woman named Jeanne Rembault, married Anne Le Jeune, a daughter of Martin Le Jeune of Port Maltois and his first wife, a Mi'kmaw woman named Marie-Jeanne Kayigonias. Descendants of this couple moved into the Petitcodiac area under the direction of Abbé Jean-Louis Le Loutre in the 1740s, and later, to avoid deportation by the British, fled to Prince Edward Island and northern New Brunswick. Thomas Labauve *dit* Eskimo, born around 1728, was probably a grandson of Rene Labauve. He fled to Chignecto and then to Prince Edward Island, where he married Marie LaMorue around 1745. Gabriel, their son, wed Genevieve Pominville at Restigouche on 1 November 1759. Marie Labauve, Noel's wife, was the daughter of Gabriel's son, Thomas Labauve, and Angèlique Caplan.

155 This was probably the Peter Prisk who at Redbank married Harriet Peter-Paul, daughter of Étienne Peter-Paul and Mary Jane Bernard in 1889. When Peter Prisk died, Harriet then wed his younger brother, Paul Prisk, in 1915. Harriet Peter-Paul, born around 1834, died at Eel Ground in 1937.

156 Marie-Angelique was born in October 1837. Around 1854 she married Thomas Narvy and the couple had eight children: Eliza in 1855, Elisabeth in 1856, Mary in 1859, Agnes in 1865, Noel in 1869, Anne in 1872, William in 1875, and Margaret in 1877. Thomas had a brother, Joseph Narvy, who married Mary Bernard at Sainte-Famille Church in 1846.

157 Nicholas Prisk (oddly, sometimes referred to as "Prisk Prisk") married Molly Aoset (or Aosset) from Listuguj in 1861. Registers of the Parish of Sainte-Famille, "Marriage of Nicholas Prisk and Molly Aosset, 23 September 1861." Joseph Prisk married Mary Pigeon around 1870 and the couple had a son, Peter, on 17 October 1871. Registers of Parish of Sainte-Famille, "Baptism of Peter Prisque, son of Joseph Prisque and Mary Piggeon [*sic*, Pigeon], 20 October 1871"; godparents Peter Smith and Ellen Prisque. (The surname "Pigeon" is used interchangeably with "Patrick" and "Patlass.") Joseph and Mary Patlass also two daughters, Rose on 2 March 1877 and Mary Madeleine on 15 August 1880.

158 Registers of the Parish of Sainte-Famille. Ellen Prisk was born 26 October 1846 and died 16 May 1919 in Bathurst. Ellen's first husband was Peter Smith and the couple had four children. Following Peter's death around 1877, Ellen married Joseph Patless (Patrick) in 1879. Joseph Patlass, also known as "Joe Pigeon" (1831–1914), was born in Bathurst and was said to be an "illegitimate son" of Pierre Patrick and Marie Jarden. He was forty years old and a widower at the time of his marriage to Ellen Prisk. Registers of the Church of Sacré-Coeur, West Bathurst, "Marriage of Ellen Prisk and Joseph Patlass, 16 June 1879"; witnesses were Joseph Prisk and Elizabeth Roy. Ellen and Joseph had a daughter, Monique Patlass, born in 1880, who married Noel Peter-Paul, a son of Noel Peter-Paul and Elizabeth Francis of Burnt Church. In 1938, Noel Peter-Paul and Monique's daughter Elizabeth Ann wed Paul Prisk, a great-grandson of John Prisk, Nicholas Prisk II's son. (John Prisk's son William was the father of Nicholas-Peter Prisk, who in turn was the father of Paul Prisk.) Paul Prisk and Elizabeth Ann Peter-Paul were distant cousins, since John Prisk, born in 1801, and Noel Prisk, born in 1807, were brothers, and John Prisk was Paul Prisk's paternal great-grandparent, while Noel Prisk was Elizabeth Ann's maternal great-grandparent.

159 Pierre-Noel Prisk, or "Peter Prisk," and his younger brother Joseph Prisk guided Arthur P. Silver on a hunting expedition along the Nepisiguit River in 1886. In 1853 Peter married Marcelline Pomerville and, after Marcelline's death around 1855, wed Jane Dedam from Listuguj. He and Jane had three sons: Louis Thomas Prisk, who was baptized at Sainte-Famille Church on 1 April 1857; Michel, born in 1858; and Alex, born in 1859.

160 The chief's eldest son, John, who was fifty-six years old at the time, supported his father's decision and stepped aside to allow his younger brother to assume leadership.

161 The 1861 Gloucester County census incorrectly lists Noel Prisk's age as sixty-six, which would make him born in 1795 (an error of twelve years, since church registers state he was born in 1807). Noel was fifty-four in 1861 and sixty-four in 1871, even though the 1871 census lists his age as seventy-nine. Noel, as chief, took responsibility for John Prisk's orphaned son Michael, who was twelve, as well as a child named Mary, aged two. By 1871, Michael Prisk, now twenty-two, was taking care of his seventy-eight-year-old widowed mother, Margaret.

162 HILA, RG 1, RS 345, "Petition of Mi'kmaq of Eel Ground and elsewhere for 50 acres," 23 October 1846. This initiative was instigated by Moses Perley a decade before.

163 HILA, Survey Records for Gloucester County, Indian Affairs Records, New Brunswick, 1788–1802, File 1, MG H54, Doc. No. 62, 1836.

164 HILA, Microfilm reel F 8873, "Petition of Noel Prisque, Chief of the Nepisiguit Mi'cmac, to Lieutenant Governor Henry Manners-Sutton," 2 March 1857. Prisk may have been partially literate, since he signed his own name.

165 HILA, Microfilm reel F 8873, "Reply to Petition of Noel Prisque," August 1857.

166 The commissioner held that, consequently, distributions of relief were sometimes necessary, particularly during hard winters. HILA, RG 2, RS 578, Records of the Executive Council, 1784–1837, "Report of M. DeBlois, Indian Commissioner for Gloucester County, to W. Odell," 14 June 1841.

167 HILA, RG 1, RS 237, "Petition to Lieutenant-Governor Henry Manners-Sutton," 25 October 1859. A statement dated 2 July 1859 that mentions Nicholas Prisk's death is attached to this document.

168 Ibid. When compared to a fairly complete census return for the band drafted around 1832, numbers had remained remarkably stable. The earlier return showed eighteen male heads, sixteen women, and twenty-one children for a total of 55 individuals. HILA, RG 3, RS 557, Indian Affairs Records, no date, Bathurst Return for "Big Nepisguit-Pabino."

169 One signee, Peter Bear, was a Malecite who joined the Nepisiguit group. Peter previously lived along the Southwest Miramichi and at Burnt Church before permanently joining the Nepisiguit group. The Awasos family (also called the Bear family) and the Malecite St. Aubin family were closely kin related. Ambroise St. Aubin, a Malecite head chief, died in 1841. The surname "St. Aubin" among the Malecite likely derives from Jean Serrreau de St. Aubin, a French trader operating along the Saint John River and in the Penobscot River region in the late seventeenth century.

170 There are several references to the Grand Council in the New Brunswick Indian Affairs documents at this time. See for instance HILA, RS 347, "Petition to Lieutenant-Governor Manners-Sutton from Joseph Francis and Joseph Gull, Ambassadors to the Grand Council to be held at Caughnawaga on 1 July 1855, on behalf of Francis Toma, Chief." Francis and Gull were Malecite representatives of the Wabanaki Confederacy.

171 HILA, RG 3, RS 557/A, Indian Affairs Records, "Petition to Lieutenant-Governor John Henry Manners-Sutton, Viscount Canterbury, for commission and belts for Nepisiguit band, from Noel Prisk, First Chief, 1861"; HILA RG 10, RS 105, Records of the Department of Natural

Resources, Indian Affairs Correspondence, 1860–69, "Petition of Nepisiguit Band for belts and medals," 10 December 1861.

172 This incident between British North America and the United States arose on the Northwest Coast in 1859 after British authorities threatened to arrest an American citizen living on San Juan Island – which at that time belonged to Oregon – for shooting a pig belonging to the Hudson's Bay Company. The affair led to sensationalized press reports from as far away as New Brunswick claiming that a dead pig had plunged the United States and Britain into a boundary dispute that bordered on war; hence the name "Pig War."

173 Neither had balked at Chief Prisk's request, but there was confusion since commissions of office had not been awarded to the Mi'kmaq for some time.

174 HILA, RG 3, RS 557/A, Indian Affairs Records, "Letter to G.M. Campbell, 1859, from the House of Assembly," 5 March 1859. William Francklin Odell (1774–1844) was provincial secretary of New Brunswick for thirty-two years, from the time of his father Jonathan Odell's retirement from the office in 1812 to his own death in 1844. HILA, Loyalist Collection, Jonathon Odell Family Papers, 1766–1919 (two micro. reels), MIC-Loyalist FCLFR.03F3P3.

175 Only one of these belts of office – or at least a buckle of a belt – still exists. It was carried to western Canada by one of Alex Prisk's descendants.

176 HILA, File 1, MG H54, Indian Affairs in New Brunswick, 1788–1844, Doc. 66, "Schedule showing number of Mi'kmaq residing in County of Gloucester, 6 September 1838. Signed William Ferguson, J. P., and Deputy Surveyor." Band membership is hard to determine from this census, since only family heads are named and many young persons were not enumerated. Chief Nicholas Prisk II Ouiouche's household included his wife Marie Françoise Young and two other persons. Noel Prisk was listed with his wife and 3 children, while his brother John Prisk was listed as residing alone with his wife. (John's three sons must have been visiting elsewhere). Philippe Young Sr.'s household was one of the largest, consisting of 6 individuals, while his brother Étienne Young was recorded as living alone. (Étienne's situation in 1838 poses a mystery since he and Marie-Thérèse Lavigne should have had several children living at home). Étienne Young's son, Joseph-Athanase Young, was also listed as living alone with his wife, Marie Chamberlain.

177 The 1838 enumeration took place during years when the Mi'kmaq were reluctant to share census data, which probably accounts for the census' skewed findings.

178 Nicole Dannielle Gilhuis, "Colonial Ghosts: Mi'kmaq Adoption, Daily Practice and the Alternative Atlantic, 1600–1763" (PhD diss., University of California at Los Angeles, 2020).

179 HILA, RG 3, RS 557, Records of Indian Affairs for New Brunswick, 1847–48, "Comparative Numbers of the Indian Population in the Province for 1847–1848." In 1847 there were nine men, eleven women, four boys, and four girls, for a total of twenty-eight persons, whereas fifteen men, sixteen women, nineteen boys, and eleven girls were recorded in 1848, for a total of sixty-one persons – an increase of thirty-three individuals in one year.

180 This outbreak elicited a vaccination program on reserves that helped stem further epidemics. In 1870 the band numbered exactly the same as it did in 1848. There were eighteen men, sixteen women, and twenty-one children, for a total of fifty-five individuals. HILA, RG 3, RS 557/A, Records of Indian Affairs for New Brunswick, no date, "Return of Indians of Bathurst, Big Nepisiguit–Pabineau, Gloucester County, circa 1870."

181 Patricia Kathleen Nietfeld, "Determinants of Aboriginal Micmac Political Structure" (PhD diss., University of New Mexico, 1981), 547–9.

182 John Prisk was alive in 1861, and is listed on the 1861 census as being sixty years of age.

183 Pierre-Noel Prisk was born in 1835. Registers de Caraquet, 1806–53, "Baptism of Pierre-Noel Prisque [Prisk], son of Noel Prisque and Mary Labauve of Nepisiguit, 1 November 1835." Pierre-Noel married Jane Dedam and by 1861 had two children: Mitchell, who was three in 1861, and Alexander, who was two. Pierre's unmarried brothers, Nicholas and Joseph, both in their early twenties, lived with him at the time.

184 Thomas Narvy, like Noel Prisk, was a hunter. Thomas, who was thirty-three in 1861, and his wife, who was twenty-seven, had only one child, four-year-old Eliza Narvy, living with them at the time of the census.

185 According to the 1861 census, Nicholas Prisk Jr. was twenty-two years old and his brother Joseph was twenty. Neither age is correct. Nicholas and Joseph were twins and, born in 1843, would have been eighteen years old. By 1881 Joseph had married Mary Patlass, also known as Mary Patrick or "Pigeon," and had at least two children: Peter, ten, and Mary Jane, seven. Nicholas wed Mary Aosets from Restigouche and in 1881 had four sons: Peter, nineteen, Alexander, seventeen, and William, six. A son named Mitchell, a year older than Alexander, apparently died young. Interestingly, two of Nicholas's sons, Peter and Alex Prisk, were listed as farmers, and not hunters like their father.

186 In 1881 Philippe Young Jr. was fifty-seven, his wife "Magollen," or Madeleine, was forty, and the couple had two children living with them, Jane, eighteen, and Mary, nine.

187 Other members of the Bernard-Julien family joined the Bathurst group because of earlier kinship ties made with the Bathurst band. Mary Bernard at the time of the taking of the 1871 federal census is listed as living alone, but only because her husband was away visiting, along with her children Elizabeth, fifteen, Mary-Frances, twelve, Susan-Frances, six, and Nancy B., who was one month old.

188 In 1861 Peter Bear and his wife Christy, who was twenty years old, had three children: John, nine, Peter, six, and Ann, three. Noel Ginnish and his wife Christy were Peter's neighbours. Francis Peters, who often had his name reversed to read "Peter Francis," and his wife Mary, who was twenty-two, had only one child, Christy. Francis's sister Ann Peters lived in his household.

189 Many Youngs moved away from Bathurst. In 1861, Philippe Young Sr.'s fifty-year-old son Dennis Young lived with his wife Margaret near his father and his brother Philippe Young Jr.; by 1881 Dennis was working as a stonemason in New Brandon. Others stayed. Frank Young, who married Minnie Patlass at Sacred Heart Church, Bathurst, on 9 July 1904, with Philippe Young Jr. and Monique Patlass as witnesses, probably belonged to Philippe Young Jr.'s family. On the other hand, Samuel Young who married Mary Noel on 8 November 1899, before witnesses Millidge Boucher and Helen Young, was likely a descendant of Philippe Young Sr.'s brother Étienne.

190 Étienne Young's sons and daughters were not enumerated with the band because they lived off reserve on their own farms and wed members of the French and Acadian community rather than Mi'kmaw persons.

191 There also were deaths and remarriages. In 1871 Ellen Prisk was living with her first husband, Peter Smith, and three children. By 1881 Peter had died and Ellen had wed Joseph Patlass, a forty-year-old widower. Joseph's household shows Ellen's children from her previous marriage and a one-year-old girl, Monique Patlass, who was Joseph and Ellen's daughter.

192 Noel Prisk died before 1881, and the 1901 census shows his widow, Mary Labauve, then sixty-three years old, living with her son William, her daughter-in-law Roseanne Condo, and an infant granddaughter, Mary Jane. After Prisk's death the band's population continued to decline. In 1881 only twenty-four persons were enumerated, although by 1901 the number had risen to thirty-six.

By 1901 most members of the original core group had died, although Noel Prisk's widow was still alive. Joseph Patlass, who was sixty-eight in 1901, and his wife Ellen Prisk had their two-year-old grandson living with them, as well as a seventeen-year-old boy they had adopted named Edward,. Ellen's daughter Maryanne Smith headed a family consisting of her daughter, Mary Smith. Another member of the Patlass family, Mary, was listed as a female family head with four children: Mary-Eunis, eighteen; Millie, fourteen; May, six; and Gilbert, one. Mary's household, situated on the Big River Road, also contained a lodger, Nancy Dedam.

193 Silver, *Farm, Cottage, Camp and Canoe*, 238.

194 In 1884 Nicholas-Pierre Prisk married Mary-Monique Connors from New Mills, Restigouche County, at Sacré-Coeur Church, erected in 1881 in East Bathurst. Mary-Monique was either an Irish or Mi'kmaw woman who was adopted by a family named McAllaster or McMaster. She used two surnames, "Connors" and "McAllaster." Nicholas-Pierre and Marie-Monique had two children, Jane (1888–1919) and Paul (1891–1971). In 1904 Jane married her fourth cousin, William G. Narvy, a son of Thomas Narvy and Noel Prisk's daughter Angélique. A Scottish mill owner at Restigouche named Robert Hervie (1797–1889) sometimes spelled his surname "Narvy," and one wonders if the Mi'kmaw surname was Anglicized to conform to the name of this businessman. Jane's brother, Paul Prisk, wed twice, first to Angélique Thomas with whom he had two children, Paul Jr., born 7 August 1929 – and who later moved to western Canada and married Dorothy May Jorgenson – and Peter Paul, born on 9 July 1833, who died at two months. After Angélique's death on 15 July 1933, Paul Prisk married a second time, to Elizabeth Anne Pierre-Paul on 2 June 1938. Elizabeth Ann was born on 26 July 1909 at Jacquet River, Restigouche County, to Noel Peter-Paul and Monique Patless. (Monique Patlass was a granddaughter of Chief Noel Prisk.) Paul and Elizabeth Ann had two children, Paul, Lawrence in 1948 and Joseph-Nicholas in 1951. Lawrence left Bathurst to find work elsewhere, making only sporadic returns to Bathurst to visit family. His younger brother Joseph-Nicolas, who now works as a social work councillor for the Pabineau First Nation, was of inestimable help to the author and her field assistant, Carrie Gloade, by providing insights into the history of the Bathurst Indigenous community.

195 William Jr., married Rosalie Condo from Restigouche, while John wed Lydia Chamberlain from Rough Waters.

196 LAC, RG 10, vol. 2603, file 21–698–2, Petition of Bathurst Band, 31 March 1897.

197 Registers of the Parish of Sainte-Famille, "Marriage of Peter Sewell and Sarah Roy, 25 November 1872." Peter was born around 1850 and Sarah was born in 1854. Before the establishment of band rolls monitored by the federal government owing to their centrality to the operation of the band electoral system, spouses and in-laws of band members, with the sanction of the chief and council, could join a group relatively easily. Such was the case when Peter Sewell married Sarah Roy, the sister of William Prisk's wife Marie.

198 Marie and Jane Roy were daughters of Lazare Roy, a woodsman born at Nepisiguit in 1803 to Acadian parents. A tributary of the Nepisiguit River, "Lazare's Brook," still bears his name. Lazare's grandparents were Acadian-*métis*, who before the Seven Years' War lived at Piziquid, now Windsor, and his parents were Thomas Felicien Roy and Marie-Josephte Godin. Born in 1803, Lazarre married twice, to Marie Lagracé and in 1828 to Lucille Boudreau, and had fourteen children: Raphael, Virginia, Lazarre Jr., Honoré, Timothy, Angélique, Joseph, Romuald, Sara (who married Peter Sewell), Susan, Tharsille, Étienne, Mary, and Frank.

199 Conversation with Florence Gray-Godin, August 2012. Florence, a researcher for the Bathurst Heritage Trust Commission and a founding member of the Bathurst Genealogy Association, compiled a number of writings and documents under the title "Pabineau First Nation" (c.2011). She wrote several entries herself. Her great-grandfather, William Gray Jr. of Bathurst, was a descendant of Richard Gray and his Mi'kmaw woman. Richard Gray lived on the Restigouche River in the late eighteenth century, and several of his descendants remained at Listuguj, among them James Gray who married Marie Capland in 1844. Register of Saint-Joseph de Carleton, "Marriage of James Gray and Marie Caplan, widow of Antoine Caplan, 15 October 1844, witnesses, Thomas Labauve and François Labauve."

200 Florence Gray-Godin wrote, "I remember hearing Polly Prisk, Hector Prisk, Hector's parents and his sister Rebecca, Theresa Paul and Norman Paul, all calling my grandfather and grandmother 'Aunt Ida' and 'Uncle Jimmy.' I could never figure out why. Later on I learned that one of my grandfather's aunts, Mary Roy, married William Prisk, and the other sister, Sarah Roy, married into the Sewell family. Although they were not their uncle and aunt, they were well liked and trusted by the natives." "The Mi'kmaq of Gloucester Co. and the Pabineau Reservation," in Gray-Godin, "Pabineau First Nation."

201 This land lay on the other side of the river from Rough Waters.

202 When the survey of the reserve took place in the 1840s, Lazare Roy's lot and the second parcel occupied by Thomas Gray were excluded from the areal extent of the reserve. An oral tradition holds that Chief Nicholas Prisk II allotted lands to the Grays and Roys on what he thought was the reserve, but later found that the reserve boundaries enclosed far less acreage than he had believed.

203 William Gray Jr. – listed in census records as a trapper – participated in several land transactions. On 6 July 1886, he and his wife Genné (Jane) Gray (née Roy) mortgaged Lot No. 27 of one hundred acres to Ivers W. Adams of the Boston for $125. Service New Brunswick/Nouveau Brunswick, Land, Property and Maps, Bathurst. Bathurst Deed Book for 1885, No. 321, 440–1. Shortly before his death, William Gray Jr. obtained a second Crown grant, Grant No. 27896 for Lot No. 28 of one hundred acres, on 28 October 1919. This lot lay close to his earlier Crown grant. Lot no. 27 was conveyed by inheritance to William Gray Jr.'s son James Gray who with his wife Ida in turn conveyed it, for one dollar, on 30 October 1954 to their son William Gordon Gray on condition that William Gordon maintain James and Ida for the rest "of their natural days." Bathurst Deed Book 133, Indenture No. 290, 464–5. William Gordon was to pay his parents $5,000 should he break the contact. James Gray, who could not sign his name, marked the document with an "x" in the presence of George Gilbert, the land registrar.

204 In 1901 Alexander Prisk was thirty-six years old and living with his wife Susan Sewell and a daughter, Mary Elizabeth, who was one year old. Their household included a sixteen-year-old youth named Joseph Pitre who was adopted. Nearby stood the residence of Joseph Ginnish, who was forty-seven years old, his wife Agnes, and their six children: Agnes, thirteen; Thomas, ten; John, eight; Lucy, six; Louis, two; and Lena, one.

205 LAC, RG 10, vol. 7935, file 32–55, pt. 2, "P.J. Veniet to Department of Indian Affairs," 7 December 1932. Veniot, the MP for Bathurst, remarked in 1932 that Chief Alex Prisk devoted a great deal of his time to looking after the interests of the local Mi'kmaq.

206 Joseph Prisk married Elizabeth Windsor of New Mills, Restigouche County, on 1 July 1924. Joseph became chief upon Alex Prisk's death on 19 March 1938. He and Elizabeth had two children, Hector and Rebecca; Hector, who married Yvonne Caplan of Eel Bar, succeeded Joseph as chief. He and his wife adopted a daughter, Sherry. Hector died on 28 February 1983, Yvonne on 28 August 1987.

207 See Harold F. McGee Jr., "The Case for Micmac Demes," *Actes du Huitième Congrés des Algonquinistes*, ed.

William Cowan (Ottawa: University of Ottawa, 1977), 107–14. McGee holds that the concept of a "deme" - a "marriage universe" involving a high percentage of marriages occurring within a bounded regional group - applies to the Mi'kmaq. The *Kespek* district would constitute a deme. The Mi'kmaq, although they have a generational cousin system, exhibit a bifurcate collateral kinship system on the first ascending generation (in that one's mother and father are distinguished terminologically from one's aunts and uncles). And despite the generational bias, in the Mi'kmaw kinshp system siblings are distinguished terminologically by age, older siblings being accorded a different kin term from younger ones. Father Chrestien Le Clercq noted that the *Kespek* Mi'kmaq regarded close cousin marriage as incest. The same prohibition on cousin marriage was observed by Marc Lescarbot, a lawyer at Sieur de Poutricourt's Port Royal settlement in the early 1600s. Chrestien LeClercq, *New Relation of Gaspesia*, ed. and trans. William F. Ganong (Toronto; Champlain Society, 1910), 238. Lescarbot stated that to the third degree of consanguinity, marriage remained prohibited, "after which, they may marry." LeClercq also identified a kin term the Mi'kmaq used interchangeably for siblings and cousins.

208 Janet E. Chute, *The Legacy of Shingwaukonse, A Century of Native Leadership* (Toronto, 1998), 12–13; J. G. E. Smith, "Leadership among the Indians of the Northern Woodlands," in Robert Hinshaw, ed., *Currents in Anthropology, Essays in Honour of Sol Tax*, The Hague: Mouton, 1979, 306–24; Edward S. Rogers, "Leadership among the Indians of Eastern Subarctic Canada," *Anthropologica* 7 (1965): 263–84.

209 The Mi'kmaq traditionally banned close cousin marriage, whereas central Algonquian speakers such as the Anishinaabe of the Great Lakes area viewed cousin marriage as an important integrating mechanism. The Mi'kmaw proscription on cousin marriage until the third descending generation is central to their generational kinship system. Cousins and siblings are treated almost identically – a behavioural trait observed by French writers three hundred years ago and that still prevails today. However, descendants of Étienne Young, though recognized as Mi'kmaw, resorted to second and third cousin marriage to prevent their land base from being subdivided and to forge strong linkages within a constellation of families having ties to the Nepisiguit chief.

210 Ellen Prisk's daughter, Monique (or Monica) Patlass, was born in 1880 and died in 1917. Monique was likely married young, and her first husband died. After having a son, Joseph Patless, at eighteen years of age, Monique married Noel Pierre-Paul a son of Noel Pierre-Paul Sr. and Elizabeth Francis of Redbank) and had John Pierre-Paul in 1906, Elizabeth-Ann Pierre-Paul in 1909, and Sock Pierre-Paul in 1910. Noel Pierre-Paul was descended from a late-eighteenth-century chief named Pierre-Paul Athanase (or Tenass) from St. Antoine, Richibucto. (The surname "Pierre-Paul" - or "Peter-Paul" - appears in documents as "Pier Paul," "Pearpol," and "Purpole.") A grandson of Pierre-Paul Athanase named Étienne Pierre-Paul moved around 1850 to Redbank on the Miramichi River, where he married Mary-Jane Bernard. Étienne's and Mary Jane's daughter Harriet Pierre-Paul married Peter Prisk and, after Peter's death, Paul Prisk. Meanwhile, Étienne and Mary Jane's son Noel Peter-Paul wed Elizabeth Francis. This couple's son, Noel Pierre-Paul Jr., married Ellen Prisk's daughter Monique Patlass. Thus, by 1900 there were kin connections between Étienne Pierre-Paul's family and the Prisks of Bathurst. Another linkage developed when Paul Prisk, a grandson of William Prisk and great-great-grandson of Nicholas Prisk II Ouiouche, married Elizabeth-Ann Pierre-Paul, Noel Pierre-Paul Jr. and Monique's daughter on 2 June 1938. And yet another connection arose when Christiana Prisk, Chief Alex Prisk's daughter, married Elizabeth-Ann's brother, John Peter-Paul. These linkages developed in the late nineteenth and early twentieth centuries, but one also can find earlier connections between the Pierre-Paul family and the South Bathurst community. For instance, a "Louis Peter-Paul ' born 1831, and his wife Elizabeth Wilmot (Anglicized from the Mi'kmaw name "Ouinette") had a son Mitchell Peter-Paul who married a Bathurst woman surnamed Chamberlain (Chamberland). Hamilton, *The Julier Tribe*, 90–2. Kinship ties also can be traced between the Prisk/Brisk family of Restigouche and the Peter-Pauls. Lemuel Peter-Paul, son of Étienne [or Stephen Peter-Paul – a chief man of Redbank – married Christiana Jones, half-sister to John Ginnish of Eel Ground. This couple had eight children, one of whom, Michael Peter-Paul, married Mary Eunice Brisk (Prisk) from Restigouche.

211 Rev. Father J. Mersereau, article in Gray-Godin, "Pabineau First Nation."

212 Hugh Munroe, who had settled at Nepisiguit in the early 1790s, was a magistrate, fish and lumber merchant, and the political representative in the provincial assembly for the Nepisiguit area. Around 1798 he built a large mansion known as Somerset Vale on the Tetagouche River, behind the row of properties earlier allotted around 1788 to James Robertson and his associates.

213 At first, transmission of influence and power within the Bathurst entrepreneurial community occurred on a fairly personal level. Munroe's estate of Somerset Vale was passed down through a number of local entrepreneurs, beginning with Francis Ferguson who married one of Munroe's daughters in 1836 and lived there periodically until Munroe's death in 1846. It became the property of William Carr-Harris in the late nineteenth century, and was bought in the twentieth century by industrialist Sir James Dunn, who liked fishing on the Nigadoo River. Carr-Harris established a large sawmill on the west side of Bathurst Harbour, which eventually became incorporated into the Bathurst Lumber Company. The need for wood to feed such mills as well as to provide for shipbuilding under men like Joseph Cunard in the 1830s and, later, James Dunn's father led to new employment opportunities in the woods for Mi'kmaw wood cutters and river drivers. The building of the Intercolonial Railway boosted the timber industry and zinc mining in the area, though it would be many years before the Mi'kmaq were reimbursed for the land expropriated from their reserve by the railway.

214 This situation was especially apparent at Pokemouche, which went in a few years from a vibrant traditional community to unoccupied land. Mark William Landry, "Pokemouche Mi'kmaq and the Colonial Regimes" (master's thesis, St. Mary's University, 2010).

215 Bathurst was not granted city status until 1966.

216 Bill Parenteau, "The Woods Transformed: The Emergence of the Pulp and Paper Industry in New Brunswick, 1918–1931," *Acadiensis* 22, no. 1 (1992): 5–43; "The Bathurst Pulp and Paper Industry: A Tale to Tell," Bathurst Heritage Centre, https://www.communitystories.ca/v1/pm_v2.php?id=exhibit_home&fl=0&lg=English&ex=00000429&pg=3.

217 In 1934, Ottawa informed P.J. Veniot, then the Indian agent at Bathurst, that the Pabineau band could not have a chief, owing to the fact that its population was only twenty. Veniot countered this departmental contention strenuously, stating that the Bathurst Mi'kmaq had exercised their right to have a chief for many years, and won his point. Alexander Prisk remained chief until his death in 1938. LAC, RG 10, vol. 7935, file 32–55–2, pt. 1, "Veniot to Indian Deputy Superientendant General of Indian Affairs," 1 March 1934.

218 The Mi'kmaq's difficulties at this time were compounded by Ottawa's imposed elective band system, which, being new to them, hindered them from mounting a strong campaign against government policies that advocated the sale of Indian Island. In the first decades after the First World War, Ottawa ignored the band's call to have their people's traditional checks and balances respected. Chief Alex Prisk struggled to uphold his people's traditional reciprocal responsibilities towards the land and its resources, but he could gain no ground against Ottawa's policies, which focused on alienating Aboriginal land required for industrial use and achieving the Mi'kmaq's assimilation into mainstream Canadian society. After 1923 the Department of Indian Affairs applied strong pressure on Chief Prisk to sell Indian Island in the interests of local industrial development, and to consolidate his band on the reserve. The island's purchaser in 1928 was the Gammon family of Bathurst. *The Northern Light*, 14 October 1992, "Move Made to Reclaim Indian Island. Pabineau Chief Sends Letter to Indian Affairs."

219 Rev. Father J. Mersereau, article in Gray-Godin, "Pabineau First Nation."

220 B.G. Duncan's medical office records, which include his visits to the Indian Island community in 1899 and 1900, were given to the Bathurst Heritage Society and are presently housed in the Bathurst Heritage Museum and Archives. These records mention a "Joseph Martin" and a "Mrs. Cook" living on Indian Island. Island dwellers also sought assistance from local police and magistrates whom they knew personally, although at times their chief took care of matters himself. After a drunken mother severely beat her adopted child, Alex Prisk brought the child to town for medical assistance. *The Northern Light*, 22 May, 1924, "Two Months in Jail for Abusing Child."

221 Prices were not set, but became open to tender. Consequently, these licences may not have commanded the same price as those on Crown Land, but many still cost several hundred dollars per annum, which at the time was a hefty sum. Purchasers tended to be wealthy men, especially industrialists, or company interests. See, for example, "Tenders for Fishing Privileges for the Nipisinquit [Nepisiguit] Indian Reserve for five years at an annual rental payable in advance. Signed Duncan C. Scott, Deputy Superintendent General of Indian Affairs," 17 November 1919. This document is included in Gray-Godin, "Pabineau First Nation."

222 This surrender was highly irregular, since elsewhere in the Maritime Provinces, the Department of Indian Affairs required the signatures of all family heads to make a cession legal.

223 The author is indebted to Joseph Nicholas Prisk of Pabineau First Nation for sharing his ideas on what life would have been like on the Pabineau Reserve in the mid-twentieth century. Mi'kmaw families still lived

at Rough Waters and along the main road main road going towards Bathurst. They travelled to town to sell their wares in Bathurst markets, and several sent their children to an English-speaking school. Conversation between Joseph Prisk, Carrie Gloade, and Janet Chute, June 2013.

224 "The Mi'kmaq of Gloucester Co. and the Pabineau Reservation," in Gray-Godin, "Pabineau First Nation."

225 Ibid.

226 *The Northern Light*, 7 July 1966, "Contest Winners, the Prizes for the Biggest Catch in the Brunswick Employees Association's Annual Fishing Contest. Hector Prisk, First Prize Winner."

227 Harvey Aubie, a journalist with *The Northern Light*, was a personal friend of Noel Peter-Paul and wrote about Noel's participation with the South Bathurst and Pabineau Softball League. *The Northern Light*, 7 June 1978, "Season Launched with Colourful Ceremonies"; *The Northern Light*, 20 September 1978, "Pabineau Braves Win Championship." Noel Peter-Paul in 1979 was owner and general manager of the team, which embraced players from all backgrounds and walks of life from South Bathurst, not only those of Indigenous ancestry. *The Northern Light*, 7 November 1979, "South Wind, The Pabineau Braves."

228 *The Northern Light*, 2 June 1980, "Pabineau Arrows Champions in Ladies' City Dart League."

229 *The Northern Light*, 12 August 1981, "South Wind, a Tribute to a Great Sport & Friend, by Harvey Aubie."

230 *Gloucester Northern Light*, 24 March 1938, 1, "Respected Indian Chief Is Dead."

231 When Alex Prisk died his son Joseph stressed that his father had been the last life chief at Bathurst. Moreover, Joseph related, "his ancestors were life chief[s], as far as four generations backward." LAC, RG 10, vol. 7935, file 32-55-2, pt. 1, "Joseph Prisk to Indian Affairs, 25 November 1938."

232 *The Northern Light*, 24 February 1964, "Indian Dispute Still Unsettled." The Pabineau group received $13,474, including interest, for the seventeen acres expropriated.

233 *The Northern Light*, 8 July 1979, "Reports on Indian Mission to England"; *The Northern Light*, 24 September 1980, "Elected by Pabineau Band, Daniel Sewell." Daniel Sewell was elected to fill Norman Peter-Paul's office when Norman left to sit on the Union of New Brunswick Indians. Daniel (1932–2011) obtained his schooling in Maine and worked for the Bathurst Pulp and Paper Company and as a boatman on the Nepisiguit River. He also was a river and hunting guide, a member of the Princess Patricia Light Infantry, and a radio operator.

234 Peter Sewell and Sarah Roy had a son, Lemmy (Emmanuel) Sewell, who married twice, first to Aurelia Vicaire from Restigouche, born c. 1876, and second to Angelique Peter-Paul of Redbank, who was born around 1880. Lemmy and Aurelia had a son Peter (1910–83) who in 1931 married Catherine Peter-Paul of Redbank. This couple had seven children: Daniel, born in 1932; Stella, in 1936; Hilda, in 1937; Gilbert, in 1939; Phyllis, in 1941; Jean Eunice, in 1943; and Catherine, in 1947. Hilda Sewell married Noel Peter-Paul, and after his death in 1981 she married George Spence. Lemmy Sewell and his second wife, Angelique Peter-Paul, had a daughter, Bertha, and a son, Lemmy Sewell Jr., who married Florence Chamberlain of South Bathurst.

235 *The Northern Light*, 2 August 1972, "Gilbert Sewell Receives Ford Fellowship"; *The Northern Light*, 7 June 1978, "Season Launched with Colourful Ceremonies"; *The Northern Light*, 26 March 1980, "Gilbert Sewell: Pabineau Chief Elects New Chief"; *The Northern Light*, 10 December 1980, "Pabineau Chief Meets with Ottawa Delegation."

236 *The Northern Light*, 25 March 1981, "Flames Gut Pabineau Church."

237 The church served as a meeting place for on- and off-reserve descendants of Chief Nicholas Prisk II who were interested in their history. Knowledge still existed of past hunting and fishing practices, yet anthropologists Frank G. Speck, Wilson D. Wallis, and Ruth Wallis ignored hunting territory systems in northeastern New Brunswick, other than to state that each fall chiefs allocated grounds. Despite a common pool of knowledge existing throughout the Mi'kmaw community in northeastern New Brunswick regarding lands and resources, individuals who married French and Acadians or held property off the reserve jeopardized their legal Aboriginal status. Today, however, members of the Young, Boucher, Lavigne, Chamberlain, Morrison, Robertson, Roy, and Gray families are treated similarly to other participants at events on the reserve, despite their lack of legal status. Injustices still prevail where persons were cut from the band roll simply because they lived on the fringes of rather than on the reserve.

238 No Prisk men were elected chief or sat on council. In the 1980s most sought work in western Canada or the eastern United States. For instance, Paul Prisk, a son of Paul Prisk Sr. and Angelique Thomas (and grandson of Nicholas Peter Prisk and Mary Monique Connors), moved to Edmonton and became a high steel worker. Following a spell in hospital after an operation, thirty-four-year-old Paul visited Bathurst with his wife, the former Dorothy

May Jorgensen, and attracted attention by donning Plains Indigenous dress during Jubilee week. *The Northern Light*, July 1962, "Jubilee Visitors Include Costumed Indian."

239 *The Northern Light*, 25 March 1984, "New Chief and Council for Pabineau Band." John Peter-Paul and Christine Prisk raised a large family of eleven children. Mary Rita was born in 1924, Mary Elizabeth or "Bertha" in 1927 (and was later adopted by William Narvy), Lawrence Peter in 1928 (he died in a house fire in 1931), Mary Helen in 1932, Norman in 1934, Benjamin or "Benoit" in 1936, Theresa in 1939, Dorothy in 1943 (she married Edward Gray, a son of Frederick Gray and Bernadette Young), Gloria Jean in 1945, John Henry in 1946, and Gilbert in 1950. Norman, Benjamin, and John Henry all took turns either as chief or on council. Benjamin's son, David Peter-Paul, was chief of Pabineau First Nation No. 11 from 2004 until 2020.

240 *The Northern Light*, 15 April 1987, "Rift in Pabineau Grows, Chief Looks for Guidance."

241 *The Northern Light*, 14 October 1992, "Move Made to Reclaim Indian Island, Pabineau Chief Sends Letter to Indian Affairs."

242 Many on-reserve Mi'kmaw youth speak Mi'kmaq as their first language, English as their second language, and French as their third. For many years, the local community college supplied courses only in French, to the disservice of many Aboriginals not only at Pabineau but across the province. In consequence, the Bathurst campus of the New Brunswick Community College was directed by the Pabineau First Nation to provide courses in both English and French, so that Mi'kmaw youth speaking English could have equal access with their French-speaking peers to skilled trades. *The Northern Light*, 18 December 1991, "Pabineau Chief Supports Bid for English Courses at Local NBCC"; *The Northern Light*, 1 March 1992, "National Chief Supports Bid for English Courses"; *The Northern Light*, 1 April 1992, "English-Language Course Issue: Atlantic Chief Says Support Is There for NBCC Lobby Group." Participation in salmon and eel studies granted young people first-hand opportunities to learn about scientific conservation management. *The Northern Light*, 19 August 1992, "The Nepisiguit Salmon Project Is a Joint Effort with Indians." Pabineau's leadership also addressed the need to provide future generations with the knowledge and skills to rise to economic challenges, such as the 2005 Bathurst paper mill shutdown and closures of mines in the Bathurst region. Successful campaigns to provide employment opportunities, as well as a welcoming learning milieu for Indigenous students, has resulted in increased band numbers. The number of eligible voters at elections has risen steeply in recent years, and this upward trend promises to continue. In 1980 there were only twenty-one eligible voters. *The Northern Light*, 26 March 1980, "Pabineau Band Elects New Chief." Twelve years later, when Ben Peter-Paul was re-elected Pabineau Band chief, forty-four votes were cast – the number of voters had more than doubled. In 2018 the status population stood at between 280 and 285 persons.

243 The Prisks, like other Mi'kmaq in the area, in the 1920s and 1930s farmed on lands off the reserve, as the soil on the reserve was shallow and poor.

CHAPTER 17

1 "Third Letter of the Acadian Missions by Reverend Father Hierosme Lallemant, Superior of the Missions of the Same Society in the New World, 1659–1660," in R.G. Thwaites, ed., *The Jesuit Relations and Allied Documents*, vol. 60 (Cleveland, 1890), 271.

CHAPTER 18

1 George MacBreath, "Denys, Nicholas," *Dictionary of Canadian Biography*, vol. 1 (1000–1700).

2 Ayer Collection, Newberry Library, Chicago, vol. 4, no. 751, *Recensement genal fait au mois de Novembre mile sept cent huit de tous les Sauvages de l'Acadie que resident dans la Coste de l'Est, et ceux de Pintagouet et de Canibecky, Famille par Famille, Leurs ages – Celuy de Leurs Femmes et Enfants avec une Recapitulation a la fin de la quantité d'hommes et de garçons capable d'aler a La guerres, comme aussy Le recensement des françois Establis a La ditte Coste de l'Es, 1708.*

3 B.A. Balcom and A.J.B. Johnston, "Missions to the Mi'kmaq: Malagawatch and Chapel Island in the 18th Century," *Journal of the Nova Scotia Historical Society* 9 (Fall 2006): 115–40.

4 Ruth Holmes Whitehead, *The Old Man Told Us: Excerpts from Micmac History, 1500–1950* (Halifax: Nimbus, 1991), 86–8.

5 L.A. Vigneras, "L'Isle Royale en 1716," *Revue Historique de l'Amerique Française* 13, no. 3 (1959): 427.

6 Chancels de Lagrange, "Voyage Made to Isle Royale or Cape Breton Island in Canada in 1716 aboard the Frigate Atalante Commanded by M. de Courbon St. Leger," *Revue d'Histoire de l'Amerique Française* 13, no. 3 (1959): 424.

7 For a description of these intermediary leaders in vicinity of the Great Lakes see Richard White, *The Middle Ground: Indians, Empires and Republics in the Great Lakes Region, 1650–1815* (Cambridge, 1991), 176–85.

CHAPTER 19

1 The "8" stands in for the way the French at the time represented a sound not found in their own language.

2 Lucien Campeau, "Membertou, Henri," *Dictionary of Canadian Biography* online, vol. 1 (1000–1700).

3 For the life of Abbé Maillard see Micheline D. Johnstone, "Maillard (Maillart, Mayard, Mayar), Pierre," *Dictionary of Canadian Biography* online, vol. 3 (1741–70).

4 Abbé Maillard, "Lettre de M. Abbé Maillard sur les missions de l'Acadie et particulièrement sur les missions Micmaques," *Les Soirées Canadiennes* (Quebec, 1863), 394.

5 The origins of this writing style and the role French missionaries had in its development have been the subject of historical debate. Schmidt and Marshall have convincingly argued for the Mi'kmaq playing the more important role in its development. See David L. Schmidt and Murdena Marshall, eds. and trans., *Mi'kmaq Hieroglyphic Prayers: Readings in North America's First Indigenous Script* (Halifax: Nimbus, 1995).

6 C. Alexander Pincombe, "How, Edward," *Dictionary of Canadian Biography* online, vol. 3 (1741–70).

7 Maillard's exact wording was "*au nom de tous.*" Maillard, "Lettre de M. Abbé Maillard sur les missions de l'Acadie," 394.

8 Maillard quoted N8gin'tok as saying "*entendu cent et cent fois*"; ibid., 398.

9 Maillard's exact word was "*jongleur*"; ibid.

CHAPTER 20

1 Micheline Johnson, "Padanugues, Jacques," *Dictionary of Canadian Biography*, vol. 3, 1741–70; Pierre Maillard, "Lettre de M. l'abbé Mailllard sur les missions de l'Acadie et particulièrement sur les missions micmaques." In *Les soirées canadiennes: Recueil de littérature nationale*, vol. 3 (Quebec: Brousseau Frères, 1863), 289–426.

2 Gaston du Bosq de Beaumont, *Les derniers jours de l'Acadie 1748-1755.* (Repr., Geneva, 1975; first published Paris, 1899), 249.

3 Archives des Nationales d'Outre Mer, Aix-en-Provence, France (ANOM), G1, vol. 466, no.72, "Recensement des Sauvages de l'Isle Royalle et Artigonech." This census document is anonymous and undated, but its totals match exactly the abstrac of one prepared by Father Courtin for the two band in 1727. French interest in Mi'kmaw military strength was the probable cause for the disproportionate number of males recorded.

4 Howard M. Chapin, "Privateering in King George's War 1739–1748," *Providence* (1928), 46–53.

5 "Journal of Rev. Joseph Emerson," *Massachusetts Historical Society Proceedings,* October 1910, 72. See also "First Journal – Anonymous," in *Louisbourg Journals*, ed. L.F. de Forest (New York: Society of Colonial Wars in the State of New York, 1932), . The *Boston Weekly News-Letter* of 25 April 1745 mistakenly identified all three captives as women.

6 *Collections of the Massachusetts Historical Society*, vol. 1, 15, "Pepperrell to Shirley," Canso, 10 April 1745 (OS).

7 University of Michigan, Clements Library, Louisbourg Papers, "W. Waldron to R. Waldron," Canso, 18 April 1745 (OS).

8 "First Journal – Anonymous," in L.F. de Forest, *Louisbourg Journals*, 7; "Fifth Journal – Anonymous," in ibid.., 73; Louis Effingham de Forest, ed., *Journals of Seth Pomeroy, sometime general in the colonial service* (New York: Society of Colonial Wars in the State of New York, 1926), 58.

9 For Canso and Annapolis Royal see Geoffrey Plank, *An Unsettled Conquest: The British Campaign against the Peoples of Acadia* (Philadelphia: University of Pennsylvania Press, 2001). For Placentia see *The Boston Weekly News-Letter*, 12 July 1744 (OS).

10 Clements Library, University of Michigan, Louisbourg Papers, "W. Waldron to R. Waldron," Canso, April 18, 1745 (OS).

11 For a sympathetic New England view see Daniel Giddings, "Journal Kept by Leut. Daniel Giddings of Ipswich During the Expedition against Cape Breton in 1744–45," in *Historical Collections of the Essex Institute*, vol. 48, October 1912, no. 4, 296.

12 *Massachusetts Historical Society Collections*, X, Pepperrell Papers, 10, Council of War, Canso, 23 April 1745 (OS).

13 Ibid., 156–7, "Cutter to Pepperrell," Canso, 8 May 1745 (OS).

14 See accounts in de Forest *Louisbourg Journals*, "W. Waldron to R. Waldron," Canso, April 18, 1745 (OS); Clements Library, University of Michigan, Louisbourg Papers, "First Journal," 33; "Dudley Bradstreet's Journal" in *Massachusetts Historical Society Proceedings*, June, 1897, 438, and *Massachusetts Historical Society Collections*, X,

Pepperrell Papers, Cutter to Pepperrell, 7 July 1745 (OS), 324.

CHAPTER 21

1   Archives Nationales, Paris, France (AC) C11B, vol. 6, fol.7, *Recensement des Sauvages dans l'Isle Royalle et de la peninsule de l'acadie … 1722.*

2   Ayer Collection, Newberry Library, Chicago, vol. 4, no. 751, *Recensement General fait au mois de Novembre mil sept cents huit de tous les Sauvages de l'Acadie … 1708.*

3   L.A. Vigneras, "L'Isle Royale en 1716," *Revue Historique de l'Amerique Française* 13 (December 1759): 427.

4   AC C11B, vol. 6, 107v–8, "Bourville au Ministre, 28 décembre 1722."

5   Clarence d'Entremont, "Petitpas, Claude," *Dictionary of Canadian Biography,* vol. 2, 1700–40.

6   AC CIIB, vol. 6, 107v–8, "Bourville au Ministre, 28 décembre 1722."

7   Clarence d'Entremont, "Petitpas, Barthélemy," *Dictionary of Canadian Biography*, vol. 3, 1740–70.

8   Archives des Nationales d'OutreMer, Aix-en-Provence, France (ANOM), G1, vol. 466, no.72, "Recensement des Sauvages de l'Isle Royale et Artigonech." This census, which is anonymous and undated, was prepared by Abbé Courtin to show the military strength of the two bands in 1727.

CHAPTER 22

1   Archives des Nationales d'Outre Mer, Aix-en-Provence (ANOM), G1, vol. 406, régistre 4, fol. 15, "Acte de baptême de Jacques Ange, 13 aout 1729." Jacques Ange's father was identified as Michel and his mother as Marie Isidore, so he was Michel Michau's son.

2   ANOM, G1, vol. 406, régistre 4, fol. 53v, "Acte de baptême de François, le 25 octobre 1734."

3   ANOM, G1, vol. 406, fol. 11v, "Acte de baptême de Jean François, le 26 mars 1725"; ANOM, G1, vol. 406, régistre 4, fol. 15, "Acte de baptême de Claude François, le 19 septembre 1729"; ANOM, G1, vol. 407, régistre 1, fol. 26v; ANOM, "Acte de baptême de Elie François, le 1 mai 1739"; ANOM, G1, vol. 407, régistre 2, fol. 41v, "Acte de baptême de Augustin Pierre, le 1 septembre 1744"; ANOM, G1, vol. 407, régistre 2, fol. 54, "Acte de baptême d'Antoine, le 15 juillet 1745."

4   L.A. Vigneras, "L'Isle Royale en 1716," *Revue Historique de l'Amérique Française* 13, no. 3 (1959): 427.

CHAPTER 23

1   Archives des Colonies, Paris, France (AC), C11B, vol. 26, fol. 177, "Bordereaux … pour les Despenses Extraordinaires 1744."

2   AC, C11C, vol. 13, fol. 148v, "Bordereaux … 1750, 13 novembre 1753."

3   John Fortier, "Des Herbiers de La Raliere (La Ratière), Charles," *Dictionary of Canadian Biography*, vol. 3 (1741–70).

4   AC, C11B, vol. 29, ff. 62–63v, "Desherbiers au ministre, Louisbourg, le 23 novembre 1750."

5   AC, C11B, vol. 29, ff. 66–71v, "Desherbiers au ministre, Louisbourg, le 6 décembre 1750." Although Peguidalouet's name is not given in des Herbier's correspondence, the dating and grantor of the commission indicate it was Peguidalouet.

6   For a description of these intermediary leaders in the Great Lakes Region see Richard White, *The Middle Ground: Indians, Empires and Republics in the Great Lakes Region, 1650–1815* (Cambridge: Cambridge University Press, 1991), 176–85.

7   AC, C11C, vol. 13, fol. 180v, "Bordereaux des despenses 1750, le 13 novembre 1753."

8   AC. C11C, vol. 15, no. 257, "Feuilles au Roy, Octobre 1750." A marginal note recorded that the note had been carried before the king.

9   Ibid. The new chief is not named in this document but is in the following one. See AC, C11B, vol. 29, fol. 136, "Raymonde au Ministre, Louisbourg, 4 novembre 1751."

10 AC, C11B, vol. 19, ff. 56v–7, "Bourville et Le Normant au ministre, Louisbourg, le 22 décembre 1737."

11 Archives de la France d'Outre Mer (ANOM), G1, vol. 408, régistre 1, fol. 154v, "Acte de sepulture de Adrien Sauvage, le 16 mai 1750"; ANOM, G1, vol. 406, régistre 3, fol. 1, "Décès de deux filles sauvages, le 29 mars 1723"; ANOM, G1 vol. 406, régistre 3, fol. 1., "Enterrement de la fille de Paul Sauvage, le 2 mai 1723." The 1737 burial of the Mi'kmaq chief does not appear to have been recorded in the parish records.

12 Nicholas Denys's brother, Pierre Denys de La Ronde, and La Ronde's son, Simon-Pierre Denys de Bonaventure, at times were both in Cape Breton.

13 Richard de Fronsac (1655–91) is identified as marrying Anne Parapego in 1682 and his cousin Françoise Cailleteau in 1689. His oldest son, Nicolas, married Marie Savagesse and had three children, François Denys de Fronsac (1708), Gabrielle (1716), and Jacques Denys de Fronsac (1717). They are all reported to have died in 1732. Alfred G. Bailey, "Denys de Fronsac,

Richard," *Dictionary of Canadian Biography*, vol. 1, (1000–1700), University of Toronto/Université Laval, 2003–, http://www.biographi.ca/en/bio/denys_de_fronsac_richard_1E.html. See also Yves Drolet, "Histoire généalogique de la famille Denys," ms., Montreal, 2016, housed in the Bibliothèque et archives du Quebec (BAnQ), Université du Québec à Montréal, https://numerique.banq.qc.ca/patrimoine/details/52327/2518395.

CHAPTER 24

1 Owen Stanwood, "Unlikely Imperialist: The Baron of Saint-Castin and the Transformation of the Northeastern Borderlands," *French Colonial History*, 5 (2004): 43–62; Clarence-J. d'Entremont, *Histoire du Cap-Sable de l'an mil au traité de Paris (1763)* (Eunice, LA: Hébert, 1981), 4.1606–7. The First Nations of Pentagouët also functioned as intermediaries, bringing the Mi'kmaq of Pobomcoup (now Pubnico in southwestern Nova Scotia) to accept a peace accord with the English in 1727. The baron's son and heir, Bernard-Anselme de Saint-Castine, died circa 1720. Stephen White, *Dictionnaire généalogique des familles acadiennes: Première partie, 1636 à 1714* (Moncton: Centre d'études acadiennes, University of Moncton, 1999), 6. His younger brothers continued the role. See Archives des Colonies, Paris, France, on microfilm at Library and Archives Canada, Ottawa (hereafter AC) C11A 124, fol. 489–490, "Délibération du Conseil de Marine et décision du régent sur une lettre de Vaudreuil qui a reçu du père Lauverjat des nouvelles du sieur de Saint-Castin et des otages abénaquis qui sont à Boston, 17 janvier 1722"; AC C11A 61, fol. 28–29v, "Lettre de Beauharnois et Hocquart au ministre – bonne conduite des sieurs de Saint-Castin et des Indiens de Panaouamské (députation venue à Québec), 5 octobre 1734"; AC C11A 77, ff. 130–2, "Lettre de Beauharnois au ministre au sujet d'une conférence tenue l'été dernier entre les Anglais et les Abénaquis de l'Acadie qui sont descendus avec Saint-Castin, octobre 6 1742"; AC, Colonial B, vol. 35, pp. 228–31, "Pontchartrain to St. Ovide," 10 avril 1713.

2 Edmé Rameau de Saint-Père, *Une colonie féodale en Amérique, l'Acadie (1604–1881)*, bk. 2 (Paris: Éditions Granger frères, 1889), 349–50.

3 D'Entremont, *Histoire du Cap-Sable*, 4.1546.

4 Olive Patricia Dickason, "Amerindians between French and English in Nova Scotia, 1713–1763," *American Indian Culture and Research Journal* 10, no. 4 (1986): 40.

5 D'Entremont, *Histoire du Cap-Sable*, 4.1546; Archives Nationales de France, Le Centre des Archives d'Outre Mer (ANOM), G1, 466, nos. 51, 52, 53, 55, 62, 67, 68, census for Île Royale for 1715-17, 1720, 1724, 1726. Also see White, *Dictionnaire généalogique*, 1.1029.

6 Jean-Pierre Gutton, *Domestiques et serviteurs dans la France de l'ancien régime* (Paris: Éditions Aubier Montaigne, 1981), 7–8.

7 See chap. 25, "Marguerite Servant at Louisbourg."

8 Peter Moogk, *La Nouvelle France: The Making of French Canada, A Cultural History* (East Lansing: Michigan State University Press, 2000). See pages 164–5 for a comparison of the status of grooms and the values of *douaires*.

9 ANOM, G3, 2038-2, 74, 16 avril 1733, "contrat de mariage de Jacques Philippe Rondeau and Marie Josephe le Borgne de Belisle."

10 ANOM, G1, vol. 406, reg. 4, 45v, and "Jacques Philippe Rondeau and Marie Josephe LeBorgne de Belisle," Family Reconstitution File, prepared by Barbara Schmeisser, Fortress of Louisbourg, National Historic Site of Canada (NHSC).

11 Louisbourg Family Reconstitution File, Rondeau; the average birth interval was twenty months. See discussion of birth intervals in Gisa Hynes, "Some Aspects of the Demography of Port Royal, 1650–1755," *Acadiensis* 3, no. 1 (1973): 15.

12 T.A. Crowley, "Rondeau, Jacques-Philippe-Urbain," *Dictionary of Canadian Biography* online, vol. 2 (1741–70).

13 Sophie White, "A Baser Commerce: Retailing, Class, and Gender in French Colonial New Orleans," *William and Mary Quarterly*, 3rd ser., 63, no. 3 (2006): 517–50, particularly 543–4. Since 1685 French colonial nobles could engage in either wholesale or retail trade without losing their nobility, but for metropolitan nobles the law only applied to wholesale trade, not retail. French Crown officials were still prohibited from engaging in trade.

14 ANOM, G2, vol. 199, dossier 189, "payements faits a la ducharge de la succession du feu M. Duquesnel Gouverneur de ce L'isle Royale."

15 ANOM, G2, 198, 180, "Succession of Jacques Rolland, 1743"; AC G2, 199, 189, Succession of Duquesnel, 1744.

16 ANOM, G1, vol. 466, no. 76, 1749–50.

17 ANOM, G3, 2047-1, 115, 30 octobre 1750.

18 Bernard Pothier, *Course à l'Acadie: Journal de campagne de François Du Pont Duvivier en 1744* (Moncton: Éditions d'Acadie, 1982), 173–5.

19 Maurice Basque and Josette Brun, "La neutralité à l'épreuve: Des Acadiennes a la defense de leurs interets en Nouvelle-Écosse du 18ᵉ siècle," in *Entre le quotidien et le politique: Facettes de l'histoire des femmes francophones en milieu minoritaire*, ed. Monique Hebert, Nathalie

Kermoal, and Phyllis Leblanc (Gloucester, ON: Reseau national d'action education femmes, 1997), 120n76.

20 AC C11A, vol. 84, fol. 147–150v. See also Donald Chaput, "Marin De La Malgue, Joseph," *Dictionary of Canadian Biography*, vol. 4 (1771–1800). I thank B.A. (Sandy) Balcom for this reference to the Marin campaign.

21 ANOM, G3, 2041–1, 23, Contrat de mariage entre Joseph Dupont, écuyer chevalier Duvivier, capitaine d'Infanterie, et Dame Marie-Joseph Leborgne, veuve de feu sieur Jacques-Philippe-Urbain Rondeau, trésorier de la marine, 2 novembre 1750. Her merchandise was unspecified, but the Rondeau estate was worth 10,000 livres while his merchandise was worth 640 livres.

22 AC, C11A, vol. 67, C-2392, pp. 40–62, "détail de toute la colonie par l'intendant Hocquart, 1737." Hocquart remarked that *les Canadiennes* had a certain "disposition pour les affaires." Cited in Josette Brun, "Le veuvage en Nouvelle-France: Genre, dynamique familiale et stratégies de survie dans deux villes coloniales du XVIIIe siècle, Québec et Louisbourg" (PhD diss., University of Montreal, 2000), 102–3.

23 ANOM, G3, 2041–2, 1753, 30 janvier.

24 ANOM, G3, 2042, 21 juin 1754.

25 Elizabeth Tait, costume curator, Fortress of Louisbourg, NHSC, provided this information on Louisbourg inventories, 2006.

26 Anne Marie Lane Jonah and Elizabeth Tait, "Filles d'Acadie, Femmes de Louisbourg: Acadian Woman and French Colonial Society in Eighteenth Century Louisbourg," *French Colonial History* 8 (Spring 2007): 25. See also Lane Jonah, "Unequal Transitions: Two *Métis* Women in Eighteenth-Century Île Royale," *French Colonial History* 11, no. 1 (2010): 109–29.

27 Olive Patricia Dickason, *Louisbourg et les Indiens: Une étude des relations raciales de la France 1713–1760* (Ottawa: Parks Canada, 1979).

28 White, "A Baser Commerce"; Lane Jonah and Tait, "Filles d'Acadie, Femmes de Louisbourg"; and Élisabeth Bégon, *Lettres au cher fils: Correspondance d'Élisabeth Bégon avec son gendre (1748–1753)* (Montreal: Boréal, 1994), Introduction.

29 ANOM, G3, 2046–1, 63, "6 juin 1738, vente de goélette, le Moineau."

30 AC C11A 77/fol. 115–120v and AC C11A 77/fol. 277–284v, 1742; AC C11A 85/fol. 197–199v, 202–203v, 1746.

31 Naomi Griffiths, "Mating and Marriage in Early Acadia," *Renaissance and Early Modern Studies* 35 (1992): 109–27.

32 See chap. 4 on Marguerite Guedry, and ANOM, G2, vol. 189, ff. 270–360, "procédure relative au mariage de Jules Caesar Foelix de la Noue, 1754–5." See also a mention

of Marie Joseph le Borgne de Belisle in Béatrice Craig, *Women and Business Since 1500: Invisible Presences in Europe and North America?* (London: Palgrave Macmillan, 2016), 76.

CHAPTER 25

1 Archives des Nationales d'Outre-Mer, Aix-en-Provence (ANOM), G3, 2058–2, 1726, 29 avril, contrat d'engagement de Marguerite. "…comme il a reconnu que la d. demoiselle a un soin particulier de la dite fille Il consent par ses presents qu'elle la garde avec elle tant si longtemps qu'elle voudra y demeurer."

2 ANOM, G1, vol. 406, reg. 2, fol. 8, 1726, "19 Mars, Mariage de Pierre Mansel et Charlotte La Musique," and G3 2058, 59, 1726, "5 novembre, contrat de vente d'un habitation … par Pierre Mansel."

3 ANOM, G1, 407, reg. 1, 27v, "27 mai 1739, enterrement de fils de Marguerite, sauvagesse."

4 ANOM, G1, 407, reg. 1, fol. 26v, 5 mai 1739; fol. 46, 12 avril 1740; fol. 72v, 22 juin 1741; Reg. 2, fol. 11v, 10 février 1743; fol. 36v, 22 juillet 1744.

5 Gisa Hynes, "Some Aspects of the Demography of Port Royal, 1650–1755," *Acadiensis* 3, no. 1 (1973): 15.

6 ANOM, G1, 466, 76, 1749–50.

CHAPTER 26

1 In a seminal article published in 1989, Charles A. Martijn explored how Cape Breton Island, southern Newfoundland, the Magdalenes, and the islands of St. Pierre and Miquelon constituted a single domain recognized and used by the Mi'kmaq over an extensive period of time. Martijn, "An Eastern Micmac Domain of Islands," in *Actes du vingtième congrès des Algonquinistes/Proceedings of the Twentieth Algonquian Conference*, ed. William Cowan (Ottawa: Carleton University Press, 1989), 208–13.

2 Mirliguèche, Cape Breton, which is also spelled "Merliguèche," "Marigaoueche," and "Maligaouèche" in French documents, is presently known as Malagawatch. "Mirliguèche" means "milky bay" and refers to the look of wave scud on the water's surface on a gusty day. "Merliguèche" also was the name given to an Acadian fishing and fur-trading community on Nova Scotia's South Shore that by 1762 was incorporated into the town of Lunenburg.

3 A synonymous Mi'kmaw place name is "Salpo'lku'jk," which is the way "Saint Peter's" is pronounced in

Mi'kmaq. "Salpo'lku'jk" described both the French fort of Port Toulouse and the nearby Acadian settlement of St. Pierre (St. Peter's). After 1722 most missionaries serving in Cape Breton were graduates of the Société des Missions étrangères *de* Paris (The Foreign Mission Society of Paris).

4   Jeannot Peguidalouet appears in the documentary record as "Janat Pequidaouaret," "Jeanot Beguiddavalouet," "Jeannot Peguid Aulat," "Jeannot Pekitaulit," "Jeannot Peguid Oulat," and "Jeannot Pequidawa Oulat." He also had two nicknames, "Amable (or Emable) Jeannot" and "Petit Jean," both of which appear sporadically in the documentary record. Abbé Pierre Maillard called Jeannot "Petit Jean," just as he referred to his servant and associate Louis-Benjamin Petitpas as "Petit Louis." In 1771 Charles-François Bailly knew him as "Emable Janat," as did George Henry Monk, Nova Scotia's Indian commissioner, in the 1790s. In the early twentieth century the Capuchin missionary at Restigouche, Father Pacifique de Valigny, held that "Pégitoaloet" ([Peguidalouet) meant "the one with the long beard." Ruth Holmes Whitehead disputed this interpretation, however, and proposed instead that "Pekitaulet" or "Pégitoaloet" means "he carries (something) on his back a long time." Whitehead, *The Old Man Told Us: Excerpts from Mi'kmaw History, 1500–1950* (Halifax: Nimbus, 1991), 86. Mi'kmaw speakers helping with this project suggested two other translations for the name: "he who is wounded or burdened" and "he who is marked by a special speaking ability." As the surname "Peguidalouet" was Jeannot's father's surname, it would have belonged first to an individual living in the mid-seventeenth century, with Jeannot acquiring it because missionaries like Père La Chasse and Abbé Antoine Gaulin imposed a patrilineal surname system on Mi'kmaw society in the early eighteenth century.

5   Not all Mi'kmaw leaders signed a treaty with the British in 1760 and 1761. For instance, the chief of the Nepisiguit band did not sign any pact.

6   Martijn, "Eastern Micmac Domain of Islands," 213.

7   Joseph Peguidarouaret (or Peguidalouet), born in 1680, and his wife Thérèse, born in 1682, had two sons, Jeannot and Charles, the latter born in 1707. Charles's name does not appear again in the documentary record. Newberry Library, Chicago, Edward E. Ayer Collection, Ayer MS 751, Nominal French census compiled in 1708 by Père Pierre La Chasse, 42, "Family no. 6, Cap Breton, *Recensement genal fait au mois de Novembre mile Sept cent huit de tous les Sauvages de l'Acadie qui resident dans la coste de l'Est, Et de ceux de Pintagouet*

et de Canibeky, famille par famille, Leur ages celuy de Leurs Hommes et Enfants avec une Recapitulation a la fin de la quantite d'hommes et de garcons capables d'aler a La guerre. Connue aussy Le recensement des françois Establis a La ditte Coste de L'Es. A typescript of this census is housed in Library and Archives of Canada, Ottawa (henceforth LAC), MG 18, F18, 13. Jeannot also had a second brother, Louis, born shortly after 1708, who appears in the registers of Abbé François-Charles Bailly, a missionary who visited Arichat, Cape Breton, in 1771. Louis was likely the father of Francis Emable, who in 1794 was thirty years old and called himself Jeannot's "nephew." LAC, MG 23, GII-19, vol. 4, George Henry Monk Papers, Letterbooks, 1067–8. In 1955 Bernard G. Hoffman argued that Jeannot had a third sibling named "Claud Peguidawalwet" who in 1760 was chief of "Chigabennakadik" (Shubenacadie or *Sipekne'katitk*). Hoffman erred, however, in transcribing a list of fourteen chiefs compiled by Abbé Jean Manach in 1760 for Colonel Joseph Frye at Fort Cumberland. Manach listed the Shubenacadie chief as "Claud": this individual was undoubtedly Claude René, the chief who signed a treaty with the British in 1760 on behalf of the Sipekne'katik band. Hoffman, "The Historical Ethnography of the Micmac of the Sixteenth and Seventeenth Centuries," PhD diss., University of California at Berkeley, 1955, 518; Robert Cooney, *A Compendious History of the Northern Part of the Province of New Brunswick and of the District of Gaspé in Lower Canada* (Halifax: printed by Joseph Howe, 1832), 37–8. Manach's list of chiefs appeared in print in 1760 in the *Pennsylvania Gazette*, and forty-nine years later a "Dr. Stiles" published it in *Collections of the Massachusetts Historical Society* 10 (1809):116.

8   In the early twentieth century, Father Pacifique held that "Unama'ki" meant "foggy land," since *u'n* is the Mi'kmaw word for "fog." More recently, however, Mi'kmaw language specialists Lillian Marshall and Bernie Francis have contended that Unama'ki is a variant of the word *Mi'kma'ki*, simply meaning "Mi'kmaw territory." Author conversation with Lillian Marshall, Potlotek First Nation, 12 June 2007. Trudy Sable and Bernie Francis also mention this point in *The Language of This Land, Mi'kma'ki* (Sydney: Cape Breton University Press, 2012), 21.

9   According to the La Chasse census, Chief Isidore of Cape Breton was fifty-two years old in 1708. Miguel must have been absent from the Bras d'Or area in 1708, since La Chasse only enumerated Miguel's son, François Miguel. According to a French naval officer, both Isidore and Miguel were still chiefs in 1716. L.A. Vigneras,

"L'Isle Royale en 1716," *Revue Historique de l'Amérique Française*, 13 (December 1959): 427. Isidore died before 1722, and Jean Michau became the Cape Breton head chief.

10   Charles A. Martijn and Ingeborg Marshall examined archaeological and historical evidence to determine if Mi'kmaw seagoing canoes, equipped with raised gunwales amidships, journeyed to the *Îles de* Saint-Pierre and Miquelon prior to European contact. They concluded that the Mi'kmaq had the technical ability, star charts, and knowledge of winds and currents to cross the Cabot Strait to Newfoundland on clear, calm nights. Martijn, "Eastern Micmac Domain of Islands," 208–13; Martijn, "Early Mi'kmaq Presence in Southern Newfoundland: An Ethnohistorical Perspective, c. 1500–1763," *Newfoundland Studies* 19, no. 1 (2003): 44–102; Marshall, "Le canot de haute mer des Micmacs," in *Les Micmacs et la mer*, ed. Martijn (Montreal: Recherches Amérindiennes au Québec, 1986), 29–48; Marshall, "and Micmac: Re-examining Relationships," *Acadiensis* 17, no. 2 (1988): 52–82. Frank G. Speck, who estimated that around three hundred Mi'kmaq lived in Newfoundland in 1911, wrote that Mi'kmaw parties travelled by canoe from Cap Nord (Cape North), the extreme northern point of Cape Breton Island, to Cape Ray, a distance of 105 kilometres. The journey took two days. The first goal was to reach St. Paul's Island, lying 24 kilometres off the northern point of Cape Breton Island, where the parties rested while three physically powerful men paddled the remaining 80 kilometres to Cape Ray. Once the paddlers reached Newfoundland, they lit a large bonfire on the shore to guide the others across on the second day. Speck also recorded oral traditions about "the ancients … earlier Micmac colonists from the mainland, whose numbers were few and whose isolation rendered them distinct in some respect in culture and possibly in dialect [from those of Cape Breton]." These permanent settlers kept up sporadic contact with their Cape Breton parent group and blended with later Mi'kmaw arrivals. Speck, *Beothuk and Micmac* (New York: Museum of the American Indian/Heye Foundation, 1922), 119–20, 123. To prove that Mi'kmaw seagoing vessels could cross large stretches of ocean, in 1996 the Wiawpukek First Nation at Conne River, Newfoundland, constructed a twenty-six-foot canoe and paddled it to Île Miquelon. Gerald Penny, "An Ocean-Going Canoe from Conne River," *Newfoundland Quarterly* 90, no. 4 (1997): 2–3. Catherine Martin, a filmmaker and descendant of a Mi'kmaq-Innu individual named Jean Martin, produced and directed a documentary film entitled *Spirit Wind* focusing on Chief Mi'sel Joe's journey with several of his companions in a canoe from Conne River to Cape Breton. In 2001 Martin's film won the Andres Slapinsh Memorial Award, given annually by the Smithsonian Institution, and was named Best Documentary of 2003 at the Reel Island Film Festival on Prince Edward Island.

11   Evidence strongly suggests that Jean Michau was the son of Simon-Pierre Denys de Bonaventure (or Bonnaventure) and an Indigenous consort. Before Simon-Pierre's marriage in 1693, at age thirty-four, to a Frenchwoman named Jeanne Jannière, he had two sons, Jean Denys and Pierre Denys, with an Indigenous woman. Yves Drolet, *Histoire généalogique de la famille Denys* (Montreal, 2016), housed at Bibliotheque et Archives nationales du Quebec, https://numerique.banq.qc.ca/patrimoine/details/52327/2518395. In 1696 Simon-Pierre, in company with Pierre Le Moyne d'Iberville and a Quebec force, and Baron Jean-Vincent d'Abbadie de St. Castin and his Abenaki warriors led a party of thirty Mi'kmaq from Baie d' Espagnols (present-day Sydney Harbour, Cape Breton) in the capture of Fort William Henry at Pemaquid (now Bristol, Lincoln County, Maine). But despite his courage, Simon-Pierre proved unpredictable. He traded with the English and was disloyal to his French wife. His taking of Louise Guyon (Mme. Damours de Freneuse) as his mistress and his rakish behaviour with various Indigenous women cost him a chance at promotion to commander of Port Royal in 1705, following the death of Jacques-François de Monbeton de Brouillan. A.J.E. Lunn, "Denys de Bonaventure, Simon-Pierre," *Dictionary of Canadian Biography* online, vol. 2 (1701–40). He continued to run afoul of his superiors for illicit trading forays to Boston and "misbehaving himself with Indian women." John Clarence Webster, *Acadia at the End of the Seventeenth Century: Letters, Journals and Memoirs of Joseph Robineau de Villebon, Commandant in Acadia, 1690–1700, and Other Contemporary Documents* (Saint John: New Brunswick Museum, 1934), 165–6; Beamish Murdoch, *A History of Nova-Scotia, or Acadie* (Halifax: James Barnes, 1865), 1.217; P.F.X. Charlevoix, *History and General Description of New France* (New York, 1900), 3.233. Jean Denys, Simon-Pierre's son, wed Geneviève Pelleren in 1704, but he also had a Mi'kmaw consort named Cecile with whom he had two daughters, Marie-Anne and Marie-Louise. On 26 September 1706 Jean and Cecile brought Marie-Anne, aged two, to Justinien Durand, the Recollect Father at Port Royal, for baptism. Witnesses to the ceremony were De Boulais le Faillon, an ensign of the company at Port Royal, and Damoiselle Françoise de

la Bate, the wife of Sieur de la Bate. (At the time of her birth on 11 May 1704 Marie-Anne was conditionally baptized by Thomas Le Fauve.) Marie-Louise Denys, born on 23 April 1707, was baptized by Father Durand the following day. Marie-Louise's godparents were Louis Corbi *dit* Pridemouche, a soldier, and Geneviève Pellerin, "la femme de Jean Denis, le père" (the wife of Jean Denis, the father). Pellerin did not accompany him to Cape Breton. Nova Scotia Archives and Records Management (henceforth NSARM), Registers of the Parish of St. Jean-Baptiste, Port Royal and Annapolis Royal, 1702–55, RG 1, vol. 26, 53 and 58. After the French capitulated to the British on 13 October 1710, Simon-Pierre Denys de Bonaventure left Port Royal. He died at Rochefort, France, in 1711.

12 "Michau," or "Michaud," is a French surname as well as a place name in Cape Breton. Jean Denys settled near Point Michaud, which, flanked by Michaud Cove and Michaud Beach, is the closest point on the Cape Breton mainland to the Îles Michaud, lying twenty-one kilometres southeast of St. Peter's. The name "Îles Michaud" predates 1650. In the 1660s the ledges were identified as "Les Insulae Michaelis," and Nicholas Denys, a French official and trader, referred to them as "Les Isles Michau." In the mid-eighteenth century Thomas Pichon, Comte Raymond's secretary at Louisbourg, called them "les Isles de Michault." Since it is an Eastern Algonquian custom to refer to persons by the places in which they live, the Mi'kmaq likely addressed Jean Denys as "Jean Michau." The contention that the name "Michau" was borrowed from a geographical feature is further bolstered by the fact that "Michau" was not a surname found at St. Peter's or at l'Ardoise, a community that grew to around sixty families lying close to Point Michaud. Local French surnames included "Briand," "Coste," "Gracie," "LaBille," "Landry," "Longuepee," "Martel," "Mombourquette," "Pitre," "Prejean," and "Samson," but not "Michau."

13 In 1722, Abbé Antoine Gaulin listed "Jean Michaud" as chief of the Île Royale band of 107 persons. LAC, Documents from the Archives des Colonies, Paris, on microfilm (henceforth AC), CIIB, vol. 6, f. 77, Correspondance générale, Île Royale, "Recensement des Sauvages … 1722."

14 Simon-Pierre Denys de Bonaventure was born at Trois Rivières in 1659 to Pierre Denys de La Ronde and Catherine Leneuf. La Ronde's father was Simon Denys (later known as Simon Denys de La Trinité), who with his brother Nicolas Denys established the first French trading post at St. Peter's (St. Pierre's), Cape Breton, in 1650.

(The name "St. Pierre's" or "St. Peter's" derived from the Portuguese "San Pedro," as the site was settled by Portuguese in the sixteenth century and then deserted.) When the Denys brothers first arrived in Acadia, the Aboriginal people were referred to by the French as "Souriquois" or "Tarrentines." The first European to use the term "Micmac" (Mi'kmaq) was a French businessman, Charles Aubert de la Chesnaye, in 1676. Wilson Wallis and Ruth Sawtell Wallis, *The Micmac Indians of Eastern Canada* (Minneapolis: University of Minnesota Press, 1955), 15. Simon Denys set up a trading post at nearby Sainte-Anne (present-day Englishtown), although he left soon afterwards for Quebec, where the Jesuits, the seigneurs of Notre-Dame-des-Anges, granted him a concession in August 1752 called the "ferme de la Trinité" (farm of the Trinity). Nicolas Denys stayed at St. Peter's, despite challenges posed by his political and commercial rivals, until his post was destroyed by fire during the winter of 1668–69, when he left Cape Breton permanently for Nepisigui (now Bathurst, New Brunswick). St. Peter's remained vacant until 1713, when the French built Port Toulouse on the charred ruins of the Deny brothers' earlier post. Louis Denys de La Ronde (1675–1741), Simon-Pierre Denys de Bonaventure's brother, commanded Port Toulouse from 1715 to 1720. Bernard Pothier and Donald J. Norton wrote that Louis Denys "noted with some emotion the vestiges of the pioneering efforts of his grandfather, Simon Denys de La Trinité, who over 60 years before had built a trading post at Sainte-Anne (Englishtown)." Louis in the mid-1720s engaged in an unsuccessful copper mining venture on Lake Superior and in 1727 became commandant of Fort Chequamegon, on the south shore of Lake Superior near present-day Ashland, Wisconsin. Pothier and Norton, "Denys de la Ronde, Louis," *Dictionary of Canadian Biography* online, vol. 3 (1741–70).

15 While travelling in 1750 through the Fronsac Passage (the present-day Strait of Canso between the Nova Scotia mainland and Cape Breton), Thomas Pichon encountered a "habitant du Port Toulouse" named "Jean Michaud [Michau]," who had recently approached "le Sieur Bonnaventure" for permission to seek resources and land at "la Pointe Prime de l'Isle St. Jean" (or Prince Edward Island). Thomas Pichon, *Lettres et Memoirs pour servir à l'Histoire Naturelle, Civile et Politique Du Cap Breton depuis sa établissement jusqu'à lareprise de cette Isle par les Anglois en 1758* (La Haye et Londres, 1760), 227. "Sieur Bonnaventure" was Simon-Pierre Denys de Bonaventure's son, Claude-Elisabeth Denys de Bonaventure, who in 1750 was acting mayor and commandant

of Île St. Jean (Prince Edward Island). Though Pichon does not mention any relationship, kin or otherwise, between Jean Michau and Bonaventure, Jean Michau Jr. was the son of Jean Michau Sr., Claude-Elisabeth Denys de Bonaventure's half brother. Although he had travelled widely as a youth in mainland Nova Scotia, after 1749 he wanted, with Bonaventure's help, to settle permanently on Prince Edward Island. An anonymous and undated French census, "Recensement des Sauvages de l'Isle Royale et Artigonech," compiled around 1727, lists "Jean Michaux [Michau Jr.]" living at Antigonish. A second nominal census, also dated 1727, by Abbé Michel Courtin shows "Chief Jean Michaud [Sr.]" of Cape Breton heading a group "of seven men, capable of bearing arms," and three women, with their children. ANOM, G1, vol. 466, no. 72, "Recensement des Sauvages de l'Isle Royale et Artigonech," n.d. (c.1727); Public Archives of Nova Scotia, *Place Names and Places of Nova Scotia*, with an introduction by Bruce Fergusson (Halifax, 1967), 537; 598–99; Clarence-J. d'Entremont, *Nicholas Denys, sa vie et son oeuvre* (Yarmouth, 1982), 345. Thomas Pichon, *Lettres et Memoirs pour servir à l'Histoire Naturelle, Civile et Politique Du Cap Breton depuis sa établissement jusqu'à lareprise de cette Isle par les Anglois en 1758* (La Haye et Londres, 1760), 227.

16 Jacques-Angé was baptized at Louisbourg on 17 August 1729, and François was baptized at Louisbourg on 28 October 1734. The high status of their French godparents testified to their father Michel's connection with the upper echelons of Louisbourg society. Jacques-Angé's godfather was René Lambert DeGranges, an artillery officer, and his godmother was Dame Marie Courtiau, wife of the king's prosecutor. François's godfather was Joseph Duvivier, an officer of the garrison, and his godmother, born at Port Royal, was Dame Angèlique Laureau de la Tour (c.1680–1762), the widow of Charles de la Tour Jr., son of Charles de Saint Etienne de La Tour and Jeanne Motin. (Jeanne was the widow of Charles de Menou d'Aulnay). Angélique's husband, a captain in the Louisbourg garrison, died in 1731. Les Archives nationales d'outre-mer, France (henceforth ANOM), on microfilm and file cards in the archives at Fortress Louisbourg Historical Park, Louisbourg, Cape Breton. Archives nationales d'outre-mer, France (ANOM, which is the old AFO used by archives at Park Louisbourg), G-1, 406, register IV, f. 144, "Acte de baptême de Jacques-Angé, fils de Michel [Michaud] et Marie Isidore, 17 aôut 1729" (born 13 August 1729); ANOM, G-1, 406, registre IV, f. 530, "Acte de baptême de François, fils de Michel Michau et Marie Isidore, 28 octobre 1734" (born 25 October 1734).

17 On Denis Michau's death in 1751, the Compte de Raymond, the governor of Île Royale, observed that Michau descended from a man ennobled for his past services to the French Crown. "C'etait un excellent subject, dont le grand-père [actually his great-great grandfather] avoit rendu de si grand services que le feu Roy lui avoit accordé Des Lettres de noblesse," he wrote to the French minister of marine. As far as Raymond was concerned, the "lettres of noblesses" cinched Michau's claim to aristocratic ancestry. LAC, AC, AIIC, vol. 15, 257–257v, "Raymond à Rouille, octobre 1751"; LAC, AC CIIC, vol. 15: 257–257v, "Raymond à Antoine-Louis, Secrétaire d'État de la Marine, octobre 1751." During his lifetime Denis Michau received tokens of French esteem, among them a chief's medal and a house worth three hundred livres at Mirliguèche. His medical expenses prior to his death also were paid by the French government. LAC, AC CIIC, vol. 13, 148v, "Raymond à Rouillé, 13 mars 1751." Recognizing that Michau belonged to a different category than the ordinary Mi'kmaw medal recipient, historian Olive Patricia Dickason sifted through "23 letters, confirmations and justifications of ennoblement recorded for persons living in New France until 1733" until she found a confirmation of enoblement, registered on 12 March 1680 (though originally awarded by Louis XIV in 1668), to Simon Denys de La Trinité (1599–1678), Simon-Pierre Denys de Bonaventure's grandfather. Dickason, *Louisbourg and the Indians: A Study in Imperial Race Relations, 1713–1760* (Ottawa: Government of Canada, 1976), 114. In 1668 Jean Talon, Comte d'Orsainville, the first intendant of New France, recommended Simon Denys for ennoblement by King Louis XIV, after which Simon took the name "Simon Denys de La Trinité." Lunn, "Denys de Bonaventure, Simon-Pierre"; B.A. Balcom and A.J.B. Johnston, "Missions to the Mi'kmaq: Malagawatch and Chapel Island in the 18th Century," *Journal of the Royal Nova Scotia Historical Society* 9 (2006): 120l. Simon Denys de Trinité was almost certainly Jean (Denys) Michau Sr.'s grandfather and Denis Michau's great-grandfather. Interestingly, a French surgeon named Dièreville encountered a Mi'kmaw man at Port Royal in 1699–1700 who claimed his grandfather had been ennobled by Henri IV of France. Sieur de Dièreville, *Relation of the Voyage to Port Royal in Acadia or New France*, ed. J.C. Webster, trans. Alice Webster (Toronto: Champlain Society, 1933), no. 20, 150. This person also may have been one of Simon-Pierre Denys de Bonaventure's sons by an Indigenous consort, since Bonaventure's great-grandfather, Jacques Denys de la Thibaudière (1561–1631), was ennobled by Henry III

(rather than Henri IV, though Jacques Denys served in the French army during the first part of Henry IV's reign). He may even have been Jean Denys – later to become Jean Michau Sr., though if he was the same man, Jean would have to be born earlier than c.1680, the birth date ascribed to him by most historians.

18 It has been argued on the basis of historical archaeological evidence that Delorey Island, also known as Tracadie Big Island, which lies north of Monastery, Antigonish County, contained an ancient Mi'kmaw meeting ground similar to the prehistoric Melanson site along the Gaspereau River in the Annapolis Valley. Personal communication, Ronald J. Nash, Department of Archaeology and Anthropology, St. Francis Xavier University, Antigonish, 1999.

19 Dickason, "Louisbourg and the Indians: A Study in Imperial Race Relations, 1713–1760," ms., Fortress Louisbourg National Park archives, September 1972, 92.

20 In 1708 the Mi'kmaw population of Cape Breton stood at 196 individuals, but this number fell to 107 in 1722, when Jean Michau was chief. LAC, AC, MG 17, Série CIIB, vol. 6, f. 77, Correspondance générale, Île Royale, "Recensement des Sauvages tam de l'isle Royalle que de la peninsula de l'acadie qui sont deserves par Les Missionaires de Seminaire des Missions etrangeres Etablis a Quebec fait par M. Gaulin, pretre Missionaire des Sauvages en 1722." The district chiefs and council in Cape Breton were responsible in the spring and fall for allocating hunting and trapping territories to Mi'kmaw families. Mi'kmaq also independently assembled on what is now Prince Edward to prepare for late fall sea mammal hunting expeditions to the Magdalene Islands in the Gulf of St. Lawrence. Smaller groups also journeyed to the Islands of Saint-Pierre and Miquelon, lying twenty-five kilometres south of Newfoundland's Burin Peninsula. Prehistoric archaeological evidence from the Magdalenes Islands and Saint-Pierre and Miquelon suggests that these strategies of resource exploitation existed prior to the coming of Europeans. Tim Rast, M.A.P. Renouf, and Trevor Bell, "Patterns of Precontext Site Location on the Southwest Coast of Newfoundland," *Northeast Anthropology* 68 (Fall 2004): 41–55; Moira T. McCaffrey, "Inventaire des sites archéologiques préhistoriques des îles-de-la-Madeleine, Bilan: Phase 1 (1988), Phase 2 (1989), Phase 3 (1990)," *Report* (Québec: Ministère de la Culture et des Communications, 1988). The Mi'kmaq early on incorporated features of the Newfoundland landscape into their oral traditions, since the cultural hero Gluscap (or Kluscap) counted Newfoundland among his hunting territories. Speck, *Beothuk and*

Micmac, 109; Martijn, "Early Mi'kmaq Presence," 48. In the modern discipline of cultural ecology, this is known as employing an "alternative foraging strategy." Martijn, "Early Mi'kmaq Presence," 52–5. The strategy came into play whenever big game or fur-bearing animals became overhunted. Nicholas Denys in 1672 was the first to note that when moose were scarce the Mi'kmaq vacated the island to allow the animals to recover. Denys, *The Description of the Natural History of the Coasts of North America (Acadia) by Nicholas Denys*, ed. William F. Ganong (Toronto: Champlain Society, 1908), 186–7. After the French established a fort at Plaisance, Newfoundland, in 1662, officials there observed the same pattern. In 1705 Daniel d'Auger de Subercase, governor of Plaisance (now Placentia, Newfoundland), reported that around twenty-five families had crossed over to his part of the island to allow moose to repopulate the lands they had just left. The same year, during the War of the Spanish Succession, Subercase recruited forty Mi'kmaw warriors to fight the English on the Avalon Peninsula. He requested presents for them from the French king and nominated Sieur de Rouville to be their military commander. LAC, AC CIIC, vol. 4, "Subercase au minister de la Marine, 22 octobre 1705" (transcription), 280–366. The following year an additional twenty families travelled from Cape Breton to Saint Pierre where they were provided by the French with ammunition and supplies. These Mi'kmaq obviously were already familiar with food resources available in the region. After Subercase left for Port Royal to become governor of Acadia, Philippe Pastour de Costebelle, his successor in Newfoundland, considered the Mi'kmaq intractable and devised various stratagems to get them to return to Cape Breton. Martijn, "Early Mi'kmaq Presence," 52–5, 73–4.

21 The Mi'kmaq differed organizationally from their Algonquian-speaking neighbours by treating cousins like siblings, a generational bias noted by Nicholas Denys as early as 1670 that precluded marriage among close kin. Denys, *The Description and Natural History of the Coasts of North America*, ed. William Ganong (Toronto: Champlain Society, 1908), 410. The taboo on cousin marriage extended the range of the incest taboo and facilitated co-ordination within large same-sex task groups, as there were fewer inter-group disputes and cousins could act together harmoniously, as siblings do; for example, they came together to construct fish weirs or hunt sea mammals. It also linked distant cousins together across space and so encouraged long-distance travel among kin. The boundaries of Mi'kmaw *demes*, or marriage universes within which roughly 60 per cent of marriages

occurred, coincided closely with the boundaries of districts. The peripatetic nature of Mi'kmaw society was a source of chagrin to colonial administrators, who drew unsavoury comparisons between the Mi'kmaq and their Algonquian-speaking neighbours who practised cross-cousin marriage and so could find spouses close at hand. Virginia Miller, "Social and Political Complexity on the East Coast: The Micmac Case," in *The Evolution of Maritime Cultures on the Northeast and the Northwest Coasts of America*, ed. R.I. Nash (Burnaby, BC: Department of Archaeology, Simon Fraser University, 1983), 41–55; Harold F. McGee, "The Case for Micmac Demes," in *Actes du huitième congrès des algonquinistes*, ed. William Cowan (Ottawa: University of Ottawa, 1977), 107–14; Janet E. Chute, "The Concept of Tribe as a Useful Tool for Examining Micmac Organization and Leadership," in *Papers of the Twenty-Fourth Algonquian Conference*, ed. William Cowan (Ottawa: Carleton University, 1993), 17–31. The Mi'kmaq rank structure evidenced institutional aspects separate from the norms of kinship. A chief's retinue of young men often were not related to him, and he could practise ritual adoption to recruit new members into his band. The Wabanaki Confederacy introduced a purpose for the district, known as a *bun*, since each district came to form a sociopolitical unit from which representatives to Eastern Wabanaki Confederacy Councils were drawn. The seven Mi'kmaw districts were Unama'ki, Kespek (the Gaspé Peninsula and the northern Miramichi River region), Sikepne'katik (the Shubenacadie River Valley), Siknikt (the Chignecto Isthmus area), Epexiwitk Agg Piktuk (Prince Edward Island and the region about Pictou across the Northumberland Strait), Eskikewa'kik (roughly the eastern coast of Nova Scotia), and Kesputkitk (southwestern Nova Scotia). In 1875, a Baptist missionary, Silus Tertius Rand, published information on these districts in his *A First Reading Book in the Micmac Language …* (Halifax, 1875), 78–81. Two years later George Patterson, the Pictou County historian, referred to the Mi'kmaw districts as Gaspé, Memramcook, Restigouche, Eskegawage, Sigunikt, Kespoogwit, Cape Breton, and an area encompassing both Pictou and Prince Edward Island. Patterson, *History of the County of Pictou* (Montreal: Dawson Brothers, 1877), 26. Rand restricted Unama'ki to Cape Breton Island, which is inaccurate since the term denoted a region extending across the Cabot Strait to Newfoundland. Some districts were recognizable to Europeans in the late seventeenth century. Chrestien Le Clercq, a Recollect missionary at Miramichi, held that his Mi'kmaw congregants belonged to Gaspesia (*Kespek*). Le Clercq, *New*

22 *Relation of Gaspesia*, ed. W.F. Ganong (Toronto: Champlain Society, 1910), 310–15.

Martijn recognized two levels of organizational integration for the Cape Breton Mi'kmaq: the "extended family" and the "local group." He further argued that parties broke away from the "local group" and dwelt for years in Newfoundland. Martijn, "Early Mi'kmaq Presence," 50, 54–5. Yet after 1751 Jeannot Peguidalouet became chief of a district or regional entity rather than a local group. His local band approximated the "census band," a French creation that focused on the number of warriors capable of being mustered by the Louisbourg regime if war broke out. Strong ties held the larger Unama'ki regional group together even when its members lived for long periods of time in Newfoundland or south of the Strait of Canso. The Mi'kmaw grand chief and council, or the *santa mawitomi*, with their headquarters in Cape Breton, continued to be recognized and respected by Mi'kmaq living in Newfoundland well into the twentieth century. Unama'ki was one of seven original Mi'kmaw sociopolitical territorial districts, and it is possible that district *demes* (or marriage universes) preceded the rise of these districts. District organization likely occurred within the context of the Eastern Wabanaki Confederacy around 1720. Frank G. Speck, "The Eastern Algonkian Wabanaki Confederacy," *American Anthropologist* n.s. 17 (1915): 492–508. In the mid-eighteenth century Newfoundland still belonged to the Unama'ki district. It was only during the twentieth century that Newfoundland became an independent district, known as *Taqamkuk* (*Ktaqamkuk* or *K'Taqmkuk*), meaning "the land across the water." B. Lawrence, "Reclaiming Ktaqamkuk: Land and Mi'kmaq Identity in Newfoundland," in J. Agyeman, P. Cole, R. Haluza-DeLay, and P. O'Riley, eds., *Speaking for Ourselves: Environmental Justice in Canada* (Vancouver: UBC Press, 2009), 42–64.

23 The nature of trade among Indigenous groups living around the Gulf of Maine was altered radically by the introduction of European goods into Indigenous trading systems. By the mid-seventeenth century, similar changes were occurring in the Gulf of St. Lawrence area, as all trading systems within the Maritime region were interconnected. Bruce Bourque and Ruth Holmes Whitehead, "Tarrantines and the Introduction of European Trade Goods in the Gulf of Maine," *Ethnohistory* 23 (1985): 327–41.

24 The Unama'ki Mi'kmaq watched over and protected these *métis* traders. In 1727, after members of the Mius and Guedry families were hanged in Boston on a charge of piracy, thirty Mi'kmaq and *métis* went to Cape

Breton, seized an English vessel at Port aux Basques, and sailed it back to Mirliguèche, Cape Breton. The hanged individuals, who lived at Merliguèche on the South Shore, had captured a fishing sloop and released several of its crew to sail to New England and call for the release of Mi'kmaw prisoners being held in Boston. Their kin and trade associates, on hearing of their hanging, sought to avenge their deaths. LAC, AC, Série CIIB, vol. 9, ff. 15–16, "Saint-Ovide au ministre, 20 septembre 1727"; LAC, British Colonial Records on microfilm at the National Archives of Canada, Ottawa (henceforth LAC, CO), 217/39/205–206, "Lieutenant-Governor Armstrong to Governor Saint-Ovide," 13 November 1727. L.F.S. Upton wrote of the French response to the 1727 incident, "Anxious to remove any English suspicions of his complicity, [French governor] St. Ovide … told the boat's owner where he might pick it up. His caution was understandable, for the attack had been carried out under French colours." L.F.S. Upton, *Micmacs and Colonists: Indian-White Relations in the Maritimes, 1713–1867* (Vancouver: University of British Columbia Press, 1979), 44–5.

25 LAC, AC B, vol. 35, f. 3, 188–9, "Jérôme Phélypeaux, Comte de Pontchartrain au Baron de St. Castin, 8 avril 1713"; LAC, AC B, vol. 35, f. 1, 228–31, "Pontchartrain à Saint-Ovide, 10 avril 1713."

26 As commander of the French warship *Soleil d'Afrique*, Simon-Pierre Denys de Bonaventure in 1691 conveyed Joseph Robinau de Villebon (1655–1700), the newly appointed governor of Acadia, to Port Royal via Quebec. Villebon established two headquarters in succession on the Saint John River, first at Jemseg and then at Nashwaak. From these vantage points he dispatched emissaries throughout Acadia, including Cape Breton, to recruit Indigenous warriors to harass the British during the War of the League of Augsburg (1688–97). During the War of the Spanish Succession (1701–14), Governor Subercase made a *métis* lieutenant, Bernard-Anselme d'Abbadie de Saint-Castin, responsible for the command of the Indigenous forces in Acadia, and recruited warriors from Cape Breton to fight under Saint-Castin until the fall of Port Royal to the English in 1710. Georges Cerbelaud Salagnac, "Abbadie De Saint-Castin, Bernard-Anselme, D," *Dictionary of Canadian Biography* online, vol. 2 (1701–40).

27 Canso does not lie far from the Bras d'Or Lakes, and the Mi'kmaq could reach the English fort overland as well as by travelling canoe routes between islands. On 7 August 1720 between sixty and seventy-five Mi'kmaq joined forces with French fishermen from Petit de Grat on Isle Madam and attacked the English fort, which was still being constructed. The Mi'kmaq killed three men and wounded four more, while the New England force stationed at Canso took twenty-one Indigenous prisoners whom they transported to Annapolis Royal. Two years later a Mi'kmaw warrior named Laimable (L'Amable), known to both the English and French, captured two boats in the Bay of Fundy in 1722 and threatened Port Royal with an attack, but this was not Jeannot, even though he went by the nickname "L'Amable," or the "Congenial One." Jeannot was only seventeen years old in 1722. LAC, CO, 217/3/155–59, "Governor Richard Philipps to the Lords of Trade," 27 September 1720; LAC, AC, Series B, vol. 35, f. 1, 228–31, "Le Normant de Mézy au minister," 7 August 1722; Upton, *Micmacs and Colonists*, 43.

28 Frank G. Speck, "Eastern Algonkian Wabanaki Confederacy," 492–508. The Algonquian-speaking participants in the Confederacy were the Mi'kmaq, Malecite, Penobscot, Passamaquoddy, Penacook, Eastern Abenaki and Ottawa. Councils were organized by the Aboriginal peoples themselves, without French interference. This distinguished the Wabnaki Confederacy from what had been termed the Indigenous -French "middle ground." Despite the middle ground's adoption of Indigenous protocols, it was designed primarily to be responsive to French needs. It provided commissions and material incentives to chiefs so they would muster warriors to defend French colonial interests. This alleviated some of France's burden of sustaining its hegemony in North America, although the costs of the system soared in the mid 1740s and remained high until the fall of the French regime. By contrast, the Wabanaki Confederacy, which functioned from the early 1700s to the mid 1800s, was an autonomous forum for reviewing French and English colonial policies and their impacts on the Indigenous population. To ensure freedom from colonial interference, it was kept secret from authorities of both colonial powers and the location of its council meetings was changed from year to year. Two representatives from a Mi'kmaw district, called a *bun*, attended an Eastern Wabanaki Confederacy meeting, whether it was held among the Penobscot, in the Atlantic Provinces, or at Kahnawake. A chief attended these meetings or sent delegates on their behalf who reported back to him. In this way, leaders became informed on a range of matters affecting peoples throughout the Northeast. For further information on the *bun*, see Wallis and Wallis, *Micmac Indians of Eastern Canada*, 176.

29 The French minister of marine at the time was Jerome Phélypeaux, Comte de Pontchartrain. LAC, MG1, series

2, Série B, transcripts, no. 35, 3, 58–69, "Jerome Phélypeaux, Comte de Pontchartrain, to Governor Philippe Rigaud de Vaudreuil, 29 mars 1713"; ibid., "Pontchartrain to Abbé Gaulin, 29 mars 1713."

30 Abbé Antoine Gaulin (1674–1740), like his predecessor Père Louis-Pierre Thury SJ, who died in 1699, began his missionary labours at Pemaquid but later followed French mandates to establish mission farming settlements further north. In 1704 he joined a Mi'kmaw party who offered to transport him in their bark canoe across the Cabot Strait to Plaisance. It was a fortunate choice on his part, since the nine crew members of a French bark who had earlier offered to take him to Plaisance – an offer he declined – all perished when their vessel sank en route.

31 LAC, AC B 47, 1263–4 (279), "Lettre de Jean-Frédéric Phélypeaux, Comte Maurepas, Ministère de la Marine, juin 1724"; Dickason, "Louisbourg and the Indians" (1972), 89. Antoine Louis Rouillé became Maurepas's successor as French secretary of state for the marine on 30 April 1749.

32 LAC, AC CIIB, vol.6, 75–77v, "Jacques-Ange Le Normant de Mézy au conseil de la Marine, 27 octobre 1722"; Bernard Pothier, "Menbeton de Brouillan, Saint-Ovide, Joseph de," *Dictionary of Canadian Biography* online, vol. 3 (1741–70).

33 Gaulin conferred with the Unama'ki leadership to find out if the Mi'kmaq would be willing to live in a farming settlement operating under the abbé's auspices. In the end, Jean Michau agreed to leave Point Michaud permanently and plant gardens at Mirliguèche. He doubtless felt that Gaulin, in addition to providing religious services to his peoples, would prove useful since he could direct missives to Louisbourg and other points in Acadia and Quebec on behalf of Mi'kmaw interests.

34 Acadian carpenters living in the vicinity of Port Toulouse were hired to do the construction, while the chapel's ornaments were ordered from France. Despite the chapel's measuring only forty-three by thirty-two feet in size, and the presbytery being only thirty-two by twenty-two feet, the construction of the two buildings, having gone over budget, forced Louisbourg's officialdom to dip into funds earlier set aside to assist Acadians relocating to Île Royale. Balcom and Johnston, "Missions to the Mi'kmaq," 124.

35 The Antigonish mission was established in 1717 and the Shubenacadie mission in 1722. LAC, AC, Série CIIB, 6, 73, "de Mézy au Conseil, 10 décembre 1722"; LAC, AC Série B, vol. 47, 1263–4 (279), "Letter of Jean-Frédéric Phélypeaux, Comte de Maurepas, 26 juin 1724";

Dickason, "Louisbourg and the Indians" (1972), 89; Upton, *Micmacs and Colonists*, 34.

36 LAC, AC, Série B, vol. 35/3, 239, "Pontchartrain à Saint-Ovide, 20 mars 1713"; LAC, AC Série CIIB 8, 50v–51, "Saint-Ovide à Maurepas, 18 novembre 1726"; AC Série CIIB 14, 14v–15v, "Conseil, 9 février 1733." In the beginning, Courtin only took the office of missionary at Mirliguèche on a part-time basis, and in 1726 asked for and received a young priest to aid him. This second man, however, left for the Shubenacadie mission to assist Gaulin at Shubenacadie, after which Courtin was appointed Gaulin's official successor in 1731. Courtin drowned in 1732 when his canoe overturned while crossing Malpeque Bay on Île St. Jean. LAC, AC, Série CIIB 14, 96, "Saint-Ovide à Maurepas, 1 septembre 1733." He was succeeded a year and a half later by an Irish priest named Abbé Byrne, who, finding the post uncongenial, only stayed a year before returning to France. Byrne was succeeded at the Mirliguèche mission by Father Vincent, who stayed four years and learned the Mi'kmaw language. He returned to France in 1738. A.A. Johnson, *A History of the Catholic Church in Eastern Nova Scotia* (Antigonish: St. Francis Xavier University Press, 1960), 1.64–5.

37 During the late seventeenth century in the Gaspé district, Father Chrestien Le Clercq also devised a system of hieroglyphics in his religious teachings to the Mi'kmaq. It is commonly thought that Le Clercq's system of hieroglyphic writing remained in use to be rediscovered by Maillard (though Maillard never acknowledged any contribution to his own system from LeClercq's work), and that this system served as the basis for eighteenth-century Mi'kmaw hieroglyphic writing. Marie Battiste argues that the fundamentals of both missionaries' hieroglyphic systems were probably based on distinctly Mi'kmaw prototypes. Battiste, "An Historical Investigation of the Social and Cultural Consequences of Micmac Literacy Education"(PhD diss., Stanford University, 1984).

38 Wheat grew well when Nicolas Denys maintained his trading fort at St. Peter's many years before.

39 LAC, AC, Série CIIB, 56v–57, "Bourville à Maurepas," 27 December 1737. Although Jean Michau's name is not mentioned directly in Bourville's correpondance, Michau was the only chief at the time warranting such marks of French esteem, and his name does not appear in the documentary record after his death in 1737.

40 LAC, G1, vol. 466, no. 72, n.d. (c.1738), "Census of Micmacs of Isle Royale and Artigonech." Jeannot Peguidalouet was listed as a Cape Breton "chef" (chief) on this census.

41 LAC, AC, Série CIIB, vol. 20, ff. 85–6; 87–87v; 88–90v, "Gouverneur de Bourville et Petit Jean [Jeannot Peguidalouet], 3 octobre 1738." In the 1730s the English also were well aware that French deserters often fled to the coast of southwestern Newfoundland. Captain William Taverner in 1733 asked for controls to be exercised on the settlement of the Port aux Basques region by French deserters, as well as Mi'kmaq from Cape Breton. See Dorothy Anger, *Nogwa'mkisk (Where the Sand Blows ...): Vignettes of Bay St. George Micmacs* (Port au Port East, NF: Bay St. George Regional Band Council, 1988), 66.

42 The fact that Jeannot had a daughter of marriageable age in 1738, when he was only thirty-three, testifies to his prowess as a provider at an early age, since Maillard claimed that most Mi'kmaw men waited until they were thirty years of age before they married. Even if the daughter in question was but fifteen when she caught the soldier's eye, Jeannot could not have been much older than eighteen when he became her father. Pierre Maillard, "An account of the customs and manners of the Micmakis and Maricheets, savage nations, now dependent on the government of Cape-Breton: from an original French manuscript-letter, never published, written by a french abbot, who resided many years, in quality of missionary, amongst them" (London: S. Hooper and A. Morley, 1758). This letter, dated 27 March 1755, was unsigned but, judging by its contents, was undoubtedly written by Pierre Maillard.

43 This agreement codifying criminal acts and their prescribed punishments was dated at Port Toulouse on 9 July 1739. Maillard copied this document and sent it to France along with a "Tableau des Hirogliphs des Savages du Cap-Breton ou Isle Royal, 1739." Head chiefs of each mission community, as well as the French governor, received a copy of the *regléments* written in both French and Mi'kmaq, rendered in alphabetic script and in Mi'kmaw syllabics. As an example of a punishment, a man charged with rape had to kneel at the door of the chapel for nine days, during which time entrants to the sanctuary could beat the accused with a rod. Carrying messages for the English, meanwhile, was viewed as tantamount to betraying the French king and was severely punished. LAC, AC, Serie CIIB, vol. 22, ff. 118–24, "De Bourville à Maurepas, 26 octobre 1740"; David L. Schmidt and B.A. Balcom, "The Réglements of 1739: A Note on Micmac Law and Literacy," *Acadiensis* 23, no. 1 (1993): 110–29.

44 LAC, AC, Série CIIB, vol. 21, f. 60, "De Forant au ministre, 14 novembre 1739."

45 Louis de la Ronde commanded the detachment at Port Toulouse intermittently from November 1715 to the spring of 1720, but he usually attended the distributions of Indigenous presents.

46 Maillard wrote, "[I]l est necessaire que nous nous assemblions, c'est toujours chez le commandant du Port Toulouse avec de chef decore de sa medaille." "Lettre de M. Maillard sur les missions de l'Acadie et particulièrement sur les missions micmaques, Lettre à Madame Drucourt," in *Les soirées canadiennes: Recueil de littérature nationale* (Quebec: Brousseau Frères, 1863), 3.370–1.

47 De Forant was not governor of Île Royale for long, since he died of an inflammation of the lungs on 10 May 1740. Before his death he ensured that a gunsmith and a surgeon were stationed at Port Toulouse to assist the Mi'kmaq.

48 LAC, AC, Série CIIB, Correspondance générale, Isle Royale, vol. 1, "Mémoire sur les missions des savages mikmaks et de l'Acadie (sans date, 1739)," 384–97. The word "village" in this document is used interchangeably with the term for "command," though in fact a command was not a village at all. It was a hub where chiefs were expected to assemble their band members to receive French officials and missionaries, or muster men for war. In southwestern Nova Scotia there were only three commands, Cape Sable, Merliguèche, and Port Royal, with La Héve and Port Royal "formant qu'un village [i.e., command]." Ibid., "Mémoire sur les missions," 385. The responsibilities of Louisbourg's officialdom did not include chiefs who lived in the Gaspé region, where leaders acquired their commissions and medals from Quebec. LAC, AC, Série CIIB, vol. 12, 254, "Saint-Ovide quant à Port Toulouse, 14 novembre 1733."

49 Some of these commands were large and combined sites that were far apart.

50 LAC, CO 217/8/48½, "Communication of P. [Peter] Warren of *The Squirrel*," Boston, 9 July 1739.

51 These included combined métis and Acadian communities at Merigomish, Remsheg, Tatamagouche, Beaubassin, Shediac, and Richibucto, although the French scheme omitted many other sites shown on late seventeenth-century and eighteenth-century French maps where Mi'kmaw groups were known to reside. LAC, AC, Acadie, 1603–85, Série C 11o, Correspondance générale, "Acadie, description du Pays, Côtes et Isles Voisines."

52 Maillard, "An account of the customs and manners of the Micmakis and Maricheets," https://www.gutenberg.org/cache/epub/15567/pg15567-images.html.

53 Other Mi'kmaw names for the island were simply *Mniku*, "the island," and *Pastukopajitkewe'kati*, which translates to "sea cow hunting place."

54 The Mi'kmaq were often away from the area, even after they agreed to follow Maillard to the new site in 1751, and this trend continued until the second fall of Louisbourg in 1758. The Mi'kmaq were not enumerated at all on a census compiled by Sieur de la Roque in 1752, but their frequent absences from the mission were noted in the late 1750s by a visiting French engineer, François-Claude Grillot de Poilly. Sieur La Roque, "Recensement du Sieur de la Roque," in *Rapport concernant les Archives Canadiennes pour l'année 1905*, vol. 2, document no. 18A and Appendice A, 1ère partie (Ottawa: King's Printer, 1906), 1–168. François-Claude Grillot de Poilly kept two diaries, and both are housed at the Bibliothèque of the Comité technique du Génie (CTG) in Paris, France. CTG, mss in f. 210f (diary of 1757); CTG, mss in vol. 4, 66, ff. 3–129 (diary of 1758). See also A.J.B. Johnston, *Storied Shores: St. Peter's, Isle Madame and Chapel Island in the 17th & 18th Centuries* (Sydney: University College of Cape Breton Press, 2004), 108–10.

55 Being vicar general granted him additional powers and status, though it brought him temporarily into conflict with the Recollects at Louisbourg. Micheline D. Johnson, "Maillard, Pierre," *Dictionary of Canadian Biography* online, vol. 3 (1741–70); LAC, AC CIIC, vol. 12, f. 97. A *certificat ordonnance*, or set of instructions, ordered Charles Boucher to construct a church "en charpente de bois de pin" and a "maison pour server au missionnaire … a Vauchetouakie." Boucher began work in 1741, since François Bigot, the financial administrator at Louisbourg, stated in October of that year that he had paid 770 livres to a carpenter for erecting the church and presbytery. Johnston, *Storied Shores*, 106–10.

56 Reverence for St. Anne among the Algonquian-speaking nations of the far Northeast generally was instilled by Father Barthélèmy Vimont SJ in the early seventeenth century, but it was Maillard who developed special calendrical ceremonies associated with St. Anne's Day among the Mi'kmaq. Janet Chute, "Ceremony, Social Revitalization and Change: Micmac Leadership and the Annual Festival of St. Anne," in *Papers of the Twenty-Third Algonquian Conference*, ed. William Cowan (Ottawa, 1992), 51–5; Rand, *A First Reading Book in the Micmac Language*, 334–45.

57 A legend tells of an elderly bear person who regains her sight in time to catch and chastise her companion for cheating her of her provisions. Bearwoman's capacities, which underline the need to respect the potential for healing and renewal in even the old and incapacitated, bears close associations with the protective, revitalizing

powers ascribed by the Mi'kmaq to St. Anne. Harold F. McGee, personal communication, spring 1992.

58 LAC, AC, Série CIIB, vol. 1, 380, "Mémoire sur les missions."

59 As late as the 1930s, the Capuchin Father Pacifique at St. Anne-du-Restigouche observed that Mi'kmaw attitudes towards the monstrance were more than a little unorthodox. Maillard, "An account of the customs and manners of the Micmakis and Maricheets," 104–5; Wallis and Wallis, *Micmac Indians of Eastern Canada*, 145.

60 Johnson, *History of the Catholic Church*, 1.65. Just before the outbreak of King George's War in 1744, Maillard took the time to converse deeply with certain Mi'kmaw leaders, among them Joseph Argimault of Chignecto, who shared with him valuable insights into Mi'kmaq cosmology.

61 NSARM, RG 1, vol. 24 (Brown Papers), "Letter of Pierre Landry, written at instance of the Indians," 24 August 1745. The French viewed the Mi'kmaq as valuable in war, whereas the British tended to treat the Indigenous people as dangerous obstructions to settlement and industry. Yet the Mi'kmaq petitioners seem to have been in earnest in their desire to renew a peace with the British just before the country slipped into yet another intercolonial conflict, called King George's War. Under the direction of Paul Mascarene, a military officer and classical scholar with patrician tastes who was appointed lieutenant governor of the Annapolis Royal garrison (rather than of Acadia as a whole), Mi'kmaw unrest subsided. Some chiefs began assisting the English in the recovery of stolen boats and their contents. Mascarene even drafted a letter of thanks to two chiefs for their help. Mascarene hoped that the English and Indigenous populations might eventually live together in peace, a sentiment that he circulated among the Acadian deputies to send to chiefs, and that may have fostered a climate for the extension of the peace overture written on the Mi'kmaq's behalf by Pierre Landry.

62 King George's War, which lasted from 1744 to 1748, was part of the War of the Austrian Succession, which began overseas in Europe in 1740. King George's War was declared in March 1744, but news of it did not reach Louisbourg until May 3.

63 A gorget was a flat piece of metal shaped like a half moon and often embossed with a crest or insignia that was worn, end points upward, on a sash around the neck. It was a relic of the days of medieval armour when the gorget was used to protect the front of the throat and upper breastbone. By the 1700s it was both an honorific and a designator of rank.

64 Port Toulouse housed twenty-three soldiers of the Compagnies Franches de la Marine, and was surrounded by earthenworks and a wooden palisade. The first time William Pepperell sent Jeremiah Moulton to capture the fort, Moulton's party was repelled by French soldiers aided by Acadian and Mi'kmaw fighters. Eight days later, the New Englanders returned with a force four times the size of the original attacking party, and the fort fell on 10 May 1745. Moulton's men demolished the fort, burned surrounding houses, stores, and outbuildings, and desecrated the Mi'kmaw graveyard at Île de St. Famille, much to Maillard's dismay. They left the mission buildings standing, however. Moulton's men then proceeded to attack Petit de Grat and Arichat on Isle Madame. The altar that was saved was recently returned to the Mi'kmaq of Potlotek. Peggy MacDonald, "Chapel Island First Nation Celebrates Return of Historic Altar," CBC News, 20 July 2015, https://www.cbc.ca/news/canada /nova-scotia/chapel-island-first-nation-celebrates -return-of-historic-altar-1.3160315; Lillian Marshall. personal communication. Lillian Marshall's research into the history of the subject and her unstinting campaign in support of the Potlotek Mi'kmaq's gaining ownership of the alter were instrumental in the altar's return to Chapel Island.

65 One event rekindled the Mi'kmaq's determination to keep the English behind their garrison's walls. After placing an embargo on Mi'kmaw trade in the Minas Basin, Mascarene imported Pigwackets and Mohawks "and other men fit for ranging the woods" under the command of Captain John Gorham, who raided Mi'kmaw encampments in the interior as well as along the coast. NSARM, RG 1, vol. 25, "Minutes of His Majesty's Council," 8 December 1745; John David Krugler, "Gorham, John," *Dictionary of Canadian Biography* online, vol. 3 (1741–70).

66 B.A. Balcom, "Jacques Padanuques," chap. 20 in this volume; Micheline D. Johnson, "Padanuques, Jacques," *Dictionary of Canadian Biography*, vol. 3 (1741–70) (University of Toronto/Université Laval, 2003–), accessed 10 December 2022, http://www.biographi.ca/en/bio /padanuques_jacques_3E.html. A former New England privateer owner, David Donahew, whose vessel was leased to the colony of Massachusetts during the New England expedition against Louisbourg, lured Jacques Padanuques and his son onto his vessel, which was flying French colours. Donahew then set sail for Boston, from which place neither Mi'kmaq ever returned. Donahew also captured two other Mi'kmaw parties, the first at Canso and the second along the Cape Breton coast,

placed them in irons, and took them to Boston. Later in 1745 Donahew prevented relief supplies from reaching Louisbourg by engaging the provisioner, Paul Marin de la Malgue, and his crew in a sea battle at Tatamagouche along the Northumberland Strait.

67 Maillard, "Lettre de M. l'abbé Maillard sur les missions," 3.379–82.

68 Ibid., 3.371–2, 337. Claude Réné, who travelled between the missions at Antigonish and Shubenacadie, was a zealous warrior. At the first siege of Louisbourg, he stripped down and pushed forward in pursuit, wearing only his French medal. After being wounded, he remained in the hospital at Louisbourg at French expense, until the French capitulated to the English. Ibid., 159–61.

69 The French fishing village of Petit Lorembec, founded in 1714 after Louisbourg, by 1753 became the most populous community in the colony of Île Royale. The confrontation that occurred there in 1745 is also known as the "Battle of Little Lorraine."

70 The French habitant saw Claude Réné shot in the chest and lingering near death; when a healthy Jeannot Peguidalouet, who looked like Réné, turned up three days later, the habitant thought he had witnessed an instance of miraculous healing. Anonymous, *Louisbourg in 1745: The anonymous Lettre d'un habitant de Louisbourg Cape Breton: Containing a narrative by an eye-witness of the siege in 1745, from original data*, ed. George M. Wrong (Toronto: University of Toronto Press, 1897).

71 Louis Dupont Duchambon married Jeanne Mius d'Entremont, a daughter of Jacques I Mius d'Entremont and Anne Saint-Étienne de la Tour, at Port Royal in 1709. Jacques I Mius, who became baron of Pobomcoup following his father's death, was the brother of Chief François Mius's father, Philippe Mius d'Azy. Duchambon had his wife, who spoke fluent Mi'kmaw, interpret what was said during meetings with the Mi'kmaq at Louisbourg and Port Toulouse. The Mi'kmaw leaders were not used to having a woman interpreting their words and complained about her acting in such a role. Olive Patricia Dickason, "From 'One Nation' in the Northeast to 'New Nation' in the Northwest: A Look at the Emergence of the Métis," in *The New Peoples: Being and Becoming Métis in North America*, ed. Jacqueline Peterson and Jennifer S.H. Brown (Winnipeg: University of Manitoba Press, 1985), 26.

72 In 1739 Peter Warren, as captain of the warship *Squirrel*, warned of the French's development of the Mi'kmaw "command" system throughout Acadia.

73 After the siege of Port Toulouse in the spring, the fall of Fortress Louisbourg on 28 June 1745, and the capture of

Maillard late in the same year, the Mi'kmaq, now temporarily without a missionary, left briefly for the Miramichi area. About eighty Mi'kmaq from Mirliguèsche and Antigonish joined two hundred Mi'kmaq belonging to Le Loutre's mission to meet up with Mi'kmaq from Father La Corne's mission at Miramichi. A group from Father Lestage's Restigouche mission was also present. "François de Beauharnois et Gilles Hoquart à Maurepas, Québec, septembre 1745," in *Documents Relative to the Colonial History of New-York*, ed. E.B. Callaghan (Albany: Weed, Parsons and Co. Printers, 1858), 15.

74 Murdoch, *History of Nova-Scotia*, 1.104–14. The much-vaunted French fleet commanded by the Duc D'Anville, sent from France to retake Louisbourg and free the mainland from English rule, met with storms and entered the Chebucto narrows in 1746 with sickness and death assailing its ranks. The disease turned out to be a highly contagious plague, probably typhus fever, from which Maillard was spared during his passage across the Atlantic. From this point onward it is doubtful whether or not the Mi'kmaq ever again placed a firm reliance on French military acumen. Instead, they would rely more on their own assessments of how to contain the increasingly formidable English presence. When the odds favoured the French, and French presents flowed freely, the Mi'kmaq would fight. In January 1747 they joined Commandant Jean-Baptist-Nicholas-Roch de Ramezay and a large French and Indigenous company in a surprise night attack against an expedition from Boston of 470 soldiers under Colonel Arthur Noble quartered among the habitants of Grand Pré. Louisbourg sensed a mercurial aspect to the Mi'kmaq's loyalties to the French Crown after 1746 and hastened to provide even more presents. From 1741 to the end of the war, except for his brief absence overseas, Maillard moved from Mirliguèche to join Le Loutre at Beaubassin in the Chignecto Isthmus.

75 *Colonial History of the State of New-York*, 10.174–5. Intelligence about this incident was sent to Abbé Maillard.

76 The colliery lay north of present-day Neil's Harbour. The English built a blockhouse at Cape North to protect the mines, but it proved of little avail in 1748. John George Holland and Samuel Goldfrap, "A Plan of the Sea Coast from Gage Point to Cumberland Cape, with the Coal Mines in that Extent," in *The Mapmaker's Eye: Nova Scotia through Early Maps*, by Joan Dawson (Halifax: Nimbus/Nova Scotia Museum, 1988), 66–7. The nearby Acadian fishing, trading, and provisioning depôt of Ingonish was important to the Mi'kmaq since it was where they acquired equipment and supplies before setting out for Newfoundland from Cape North. Ingonish once was home to a Portuguese fishing community, but all traces of this earlier settlement had disappeared by the time the French took over the site in 1713. In 1726 Ingonish was the second-largest French settlement in Cape Breton after Louisbourg. It survived King George's War, though in 1763 at the close of the Seven Years' War it was burned by the French to prevent the English from capturing it.

77 These Indigenous representations, along with eight other associates, met with Cornwallis and members of the executive council aboard the warship for a preliminary discussion on 14 August, and the following day signed what was essentially a renewal of the 1726 treaty. LAC, CO 217/9/73r, "Cornwallis to the Board of Trade," 24 July 1749; LAC, CO 217/9/82r, "Cornwallis to the Board of Trade," 20 August 1749; LAC, CO 217/40/118–21, "Cornwallis to the Duke of Bedford," 1749. The delegates brought their own interpreter, Andrew Martin, from Cobequid, and there was a second Acadian interpreter present as well. The August 1749 treaty was ratified in early September 1749 by other Malecite and Passamaquoddy leaders at a meeting on the banks of the Saint John River presided over by Captain Edward How. Murdoch, *History of Nova-Scotia*, 2.54–5.

78 Cornwallis received his first intimation that the Mi'kmaq and French were determined to prevent English expansion after several Acadian deputies stated that their people's rights should not be contingent upon swearing an unconditional oath of allegiance to the British king. Should they be forced to agree to a binding oath, they warned, the Mi'kmaq would attack English communities. Governor Shirley of Massachusetts urged Cornwallis to remain uncompromising and force the Acadians and Mi'kmaq to acknowledge English hegemonic rule. This unbending stance on the part of the English made it easy for French missionaries to urge their Indigenous congregations to resist English "pretensions" to sovereignty over the Acadian soil. Murdoch, *History of Nova-Scotia*, 2.157.

79 William Wicken, *Mi'kmaq Treaties on Trial: History, Land and Donald Marshall Junior* (Toronto: University of Toronto Press, 2002), chap. 8.

80 LAC, CO 217/9 /116r–118r, "Tous les Savages de l'Ilse Royal et de Nalhukonneich [Antigonish] au Port Toulous au Edward Cornwallis." The letter was dated five days before the feast of St. Michel, which is held on 29 September, so the meeting likely was held five days earlier, on 24 September. The English translation of the French original is similar to that found in Upton, *Micmacs and Colonists*, 201n26. Repercussions from

the establishment of Halifax quickly filtered back to the Mirligueshe mission, where Maillard arose as the central interpretative figure shaping Mi'kmaw consternation into terms that the British could understand. The Mi'kmaq, Maillard stressed, felt a kinship with the natural universe and, "comme la herbe" (like the grass), felt they had sprung up from and belonged to the land. The ensuing document drafted by Maillard has been referred to as a Mi'kmaw declaration of war, yet it might better be described as the opening phase of a new, edgy, and resounding campaign for Aboriginal land and resource rights. Peguidalouet likely would have been among the Mi'kmaw assemblage present when Maillard prepared the declaration. At the time the Mi'kmaw were ready to harass the English to contain further English expansion and to be sure their complaints were heard. As historian Olive Patricia Dickason notes, "When Halifax was founded in 1749 on favourite hunting grounds, again without consultation with the Indians, the result was years of raids and harassment." Dickason, "Louisbourg and the Indians" (1972), 28. The agreement signed with the English earlier in 1749 on the *Beaumont* became a major point of contention with the Comte de Raymond when he assumed charge of Louisbourg in 1751. In a letter to Maurapas's successor, Antoine-Louis Rouillé, Comte de Jouy, he stated that one of his first actions after taking office was to call for Réné and promise the Antigonish chief a reward if he would go among the Saint John River and Eastern Abenaki groups to break up the treaty. LAC, AC CIIB 31: 62–3, "Raymond à Antoine Louis Rouillé, Comte de Jouy, Secrétaire d'État à la Marine, 19 novembre 1751."

81 Despite English fears, that the Mi'kmaq meant unconditionally to declare war in 1749 remains doubtful. They wanted to contain English expansion and, by threats and raids, pressure Halifax's officialdom to listen to and eventually respect their demands. A.J.B. Johnston, *Endgame: The Promise, the Glory and the Despair of Louisbourg's Last Decade* (Lincoln: University of Nebraska Press, 2007), 37–8; Rosalie Marie Francis, "The Mi'kmaq Nation and the Embodiment of Political Ideologies: Ni'kmaq, Protocol and Treaty Negotiations of the Eighteenth Century" (master's thesis, Atlantic Studies Programme, Saint Mary's University, 2003).

82 Edward Howe fell prey to a trap. Recently appointed as commissary officer at Fort Lawrence, he was lured out into a clearing by an Indigenous or *métis* man dressed as a Frenchman and waving a white flag, who announced that he wished to discuss an exchange of prisoners. A bullet struck Howe as he approached the trickster-like

decoy, whose identity, though the subject of considerable debate over the years, has never fully been determined. Thomas Pichon held that the man who acted as decoy could have been Jean-Baptiste Cope, a Shubenacadie chief. See Thomas B. Akins, ed., *Selections from the Public Documents of the Province of Nova Scotia* (Halifax: Annand, 1869), 195–6. By contrast, M. de la Valière, captain of the troops at Île Royale at the time, stated that the decoy was a Mi'kmaq named Étienne Batârd. John Clarence Webster, *The Forts of Chignecto: A Study of the Eighteenth Century Conflict between France and Great Britain in America* (Shediac, NB: privately printed by author, 1930), 136.

83 LAC, CO 217/40/142–44, "Cornwallis to the Duke of Bedford, 17 October 1749, with enclosures," including "A Proclamation, 2 October 1749"; NSARM, RG 1, vol. 163, 41, "Commissions and Instructions, Proclamation of Edward Cornwallis," 21 June 1750; Gustave Lancetot, *Documents Relating to Currency, Exchange and Finance in Nova Scotia ... 1675–1758* (Ottawa: King's Printer, 1933), 281–2.

84 The Mi'kmaq described a tract covering the northeastern part of the province where they could reside in peace and pursue their cherished way of life. Since this scheme required the compliance of both the English and the French, negotiations with agents of both colonial powers were necessary. Le Loutre supported the plan, since it would provide a buffer zone for an Acadian farming settlement he was establishing in the Petitcodiac River region, but the scheme also owed much to discussions within Eastern Wabanaki Confederacy councils. Mi'kmaw leaders remembered a proposal, made in 1720 in the Boston council by Samuel Sewell, Edmund Quincey, and Jonathan Belcher Sr., for a buffer zone to be established between the frontiers of New England and Acadia. No forts were to be erected on the tract, and the southern boundary of the buffer zone was the allowable northward extension of New England settlement. Excerpts from Minutes of the Massachusetts Council, 2 September 1720, referred to in Kenneth M. Morrison, "The People of the Dawn: The Abnaki and Their Relations with New England and New France, 1600–1727," PhD diss., University of Maine, 1975, 351–2. Another topic under discussion in Mi'kmaw councils was the meaning of an article appearing in the treaty signed at Annapolis Royal in 1726 that referred to "Settlements ... Lawfully to be made." The Mi'kmaq interpreted this article to mean that English expansion would only occur after the English initiated "lawful" discussions with the Indigenous groups who occupied the land. LAC, CO 217/5/3v–5v.

85 LAC, CO 217/11/1r–6v, "Cornwallis to the Lords of Trade," 27 November 1750.

86 As mentioned above, Halifax was founded on Mi'kmaw hunting grounds without consultation with the Mi'kmaq, and the result was a number of serious attacks on the ramparts of the town and Dartmouth, across the harbour, by Indigenous parties and Acadian resistance fighters. The Mi'kmaq, however, continued after 1749 to hunt in the Halifax area. In 1751 Le Loutre wrote Governor Desherbiers that "150 Iroquois, Abénaquis and Micmacs sont allés fair un tour de chasse á Chibouctouk." LAC, AC CIIB, vol. 30, f. 104v, "Le Loutre à Desherbiers, 8 mai 1751." The Iroquois were probably from Caughnawaga (now Kahnawake) and may have been visiting Acadia to attend a Wabanaki Council gathering.

87 Britain's sparing use of gifts to secure specific ends from the Mi'kmaq contrasted sharply with France's seemingly open-handed generosity, and conspired against any forum developing for close Mi'kmaw-British understanding prior to the onset of the Seven Years' War. When the French began distributing copious gifts at Louisbourg, Fort Beauséjour, and a new French stronghold on Baie Verte called Fort Gaspereau, Britain embarked on a deliberate policy of overwhelming the Mi'kmaw population by building forts and importing German Protestants, Planters, and retinues from disbanded regiments who could be settled en bloc on lands frequented by the Mi'kmaq. Yet the hard line favoured by Cornwallis also had a gentler side, focusing on the construction and maintenance of government-sponsored truckhouses. In 1749, the offer of truckhouses had received a fairly enthusiastic reception from groups living on the Saint John River, which prompted certain officials to try to promote them as well among the Mi'kmaq, but the results proved disappointing.

88 LAC, AC CIIB, vol. 29, ff. 62–63v, "Desherbiers au ministre, 23 novembre 1750."

89 Maillard, "Lettre de M. l'abbé Maillard sur les missions," 379–81. Peguidalouet's career as a warrior and commission-holder also was of great interest to Father Pacifique, a Capuchin missionary who for many years laboured at the mission of Saint-Anne-de-Ristigouche (or Restigouche) in southern Quebec. Pacifique wrote about Peguidaoulet from the turn of the nineteenth century to the early 1930s. Père Pacifique, *Setaneoei/The Micmac Messenger/Le Messager Micmac*, no. 283 (Québec: Sainte-Anne de Restigouche [published at Rimouski], 1910), 136; Pacifique, "Le Pays des Micmacs," *Études Historiques et Géographiques* (Québec: Société de géographie de Quebec, 1928), 262; Pacifique, "Le Pays des Micmacs: Cap Breton," *Bulletin de la Société de géographie de Quebec* 27, no. 1 (1933): 34, 48; Pacifique, "Le Pays des Micmacs: Esgigeoagig-Acadie," *Bulletin de la Société de géographie de Quebec* 27, no. 1 (1933): 62; Pacifique, "Traité théorique et practique de la langue micmaque," in *Annales de l'Association Canadienne-Françoise pour l'Advancement des Sciences*, 4 (Montreal, 1938), 250.

90 Desherbiers in November 1750 decorated Denis Michau at Louisbourg with one of a dozen medals sent to honour chiefs who demonstrated close attachment to France, and had been unwavering in their opposition to the English. Desherbiers initiated the practice in 1749. LAC, AC CIIB, vol. 28, ff. 372–372v, "au Conseil, mai 1750." Jeannot was awarded the commission of first captain on 8 November 1750 but did not receive it on that date. On 6 December 1750, Desherbiers reported that a Mi'kmaq bearing the commission of major had arrived at Louisbourg with a letter, dated 22 November, from the commander at Port Toulouse, which had been restored after the French reoccupation of Louisbourg. The French governor vested the man, whose name he does not reveal, with a commission and a medal. This man was almost certainly Jeannot Peguidalouet. Peguidalouet had already attained a major's commission by 1738, so Desherbiers's reference to the commission being that of major, rather than captain, was doubtless a mistake on the governor's part. The commission, signed by Desherbiers on 8 November 1750, was definitely for that of first captain. LAC, AC CIIB, vol. 29, ff 62–63v, "Desherbiers au minister, 23 novembre 1750"; LAC, AC CIIB, vol. 29, ff. 66–71v, "Desherbiers au minister, 6 décembre 1750"; LAC, AC C11B, vol. 29, ff. 62–63v, "Desherbiers au ministre, 23 novembre 1750"; LAC, AC C11B, vol. 29, ff. 62–63v; B.A. Balcom and Charles A. Martijn, "A Chronological Note on the Mi'kmaq Chief, Jeannot Peguidalouet, and His Family," dated 8 September 1996.

91 LAC, AC CIIC, vol. 15, fol. 257, "Feuilles au Roy, octobre 1751." John Fortier, "Des Herbiers de la Ralière (la Ratière), Charles," *Dictionary of Canadian Biography* online, vol. 3 (1741–70). In November 1751 Raymond sent Chief Claude Réné, now fully recovered from his wounds, to the Saint John River to break up the treaty signed in August 1749 between the English and Malecite, Passamaquoddy, and Mi'kmaw delegates from west of the Isthmus of Chignecto. LAC, AC CIIB, vol. 31, fol. 62, "Raymond á Rouillé, 19 novembre 1751."

92 Andrew Rodger, "Denys de Bonnaventure, Claude-Élisabeth," *Dictionary of Canadian Biography* online, vol. 3 (1741–70). After 1754 he became the king's lieutenant at Louisbourg. Although extremely corpulent and unwell,

which restricted the range of his duties, he remained at the fortress town in this capacity until its final fall in 1758.

93 The spate of cold winters began in 1750–51. Governor Cornwallis described the winter of 1751–52 as "uncommonly severe." NSARM, RG 1, vol. 35, doc. 67, "Cornwallis to the Lords Commissioners for Trade and Plantations," 16 February 1752.

94 LAC, AC CIIC, vol. 13, fol. 148v, "Bordereau, Correspondence, 13 [or 15] mars 1751." The house was described as "baty en bois de charpente et de piquet" (built of timbers and vertical wooden pickets). It would have had a board or bark roof. H.P. Thibault, "Charpente Houses (The Timber House)," in Historians, Preliminary Architectural Studies, vol. 1, unpublished report HG 02, Fortress of Louisbourg, 1972, report no. H G 02 01 02.

95 LAC, AC CIIC, vol. 13, fol. 150v, "Raymond á Rouillé, 11 octobre 1751."

96 Raymond reported in October 1751 that Chief Michaud died of a critical illness during the summer and that his medical bills while he remained at the surgery at Port Toulouse were paid by the French government. LAC, AC CIIC, vol. 15, ff. 257–257v, "Raymond à Rouillé, Feuilles au Roy, octobre 1751."

97 LAC, AC CIIC, vol. 15, fol. 257–257v, "Raymond à Rouillé, Feuilles au Roy, octobre 1751."

98 Ibid. A marginal note attests that the French king, Louis VX, was informed of this appointment, though the recipient of the commission is not named. Comte Raymond mentions Jeannot by name in November 1751. LAC, AC CIIB, vol. 29, fol. 136, "Raymond à Rouillé, 4 novembre 1751." Raymond's secretary, Thomas Pichon, drafted the chief's commission. Jeannot's commissions as both first captain and as chief still existed in 1910: on 16 December 1932 Father Pacifique de Valigny wrote Harry Piers, curator of the Nova Scotia Museum in Halifax that he had seen both commissions at Eskasoni, Cape Breton. Pacifique's exact words were, "Now, in 1910, I saw myself in Cape Breton (in the care of the Grand Chief of Escasoni) – two certificates on 2 sheets relating to Jeannot Peguidalouet – one signed by Desherbiers, 8th November 1750, appointing him captain of the Indian troop + the other by Count Raymond, dated 10 September 1751, written by [Thomas] Pichon, appointing him chief + this didn't seem to be a copy." Nova Scotia Museum, Halifax (henceforth NSM), Printed Matter File, genealogy 8-A-B, "Father Pacifique, Capuchin Order, Monastère des Frères-Mineurs Capuchin près Montreal, to Harry Piers, Thursday, 9:30 am, 16 December 1932." Pacifique examined the *brevets de commission* long enough to make copies of them and translate their contents into the Mi'kmaq language, and published them both in *Setaneoei*, or the *Micmac Messager/Le Messager Micmac*, no. 283 (Québec, 1910), 136; Pacifique, "Le Pays des Micmacs: Esgigeoagig-Acadie," *Bulletin de la Société de géographie de Quebec* 27, no. 1 (1933): 62–3. While Pacifique held that Grand Chief John Denny Jr. held the commissions in 1910, in the late 1860s the chief's brevet was in the possession of Chief Peguidalouet's granddaughter, Rosalie Googoo. Author and journalist John George Bourinot the younger, while travelling on a steamer on the Bras d'Or Lake, met Rosalie, who was carrying "a small quill box and old piece of parchment, well thumbed and greasy." The document in question was Jeannot's commission "as chief of the Isle Royale Mi'kmaq, dated 17 [*sic*, 10] September 1751." Bourinot transcribed Peguidalouet's commission and published it in both French and English. Bourinot Jr., "The Island of Cape Breton: Its History, Scenery and Resources," *Stewart's Literary Quarterly Magazine* 3, no. 4 (1870): 351–2. In her later years, Rosalie sold the commission to a Halifax journalist who placed it in the Legislative Library in Halifax. In 1888 Marcisse-Henri-Édouard Faucher de Saint-Maurice, a travelling author, journalist, army officer, and politician, wrote, "Dans la bibliothèque [du Conseil législative] qui n'est pas trés considerable, on montre un brevet signé il y a cent vingt quatre ans par le comte de Raymond, commandant les troupes françaises de Louisbourg, et nommant un indien chef de tribu. Pendant plus d'un siècle, ce précieux parchemin a été porté au fond des bois par ses différents propriétaires jusqu'au jour où il fut acheté à une vieille sauvagesse par un journaliste d'Halifax." (In the library [of the Legislative Assembly], which is not very large, one finds a certificate signed one hundred and twenty four years ago by comte de Raymond, commander of the French forces at Louisbourg, appointing an Indian chief of the tribe. For over a century, this precious manuscript was held deep in the woods by the different owners until one day it was purchased from an elderly Mi'kmaw woman by a Halifax newspaper man.) Faucher de Saint-Maurice, *En route sept jours dans les provinces maritimes* (Québec: Imprimerie Générale A. Coté et Cie, 1888), 51. (Saint-Maurice erred as to the document's date: if 124 years old it would have been drafted in 1764, whereas it dated from 1751.) The Halifax newspaperman who bought the commission may have been Senator William Dennis (1856–1920), who might have temporarily placed it in the Legislative Library for safe keeping. The mystery is how Chief Peguidalouet's

commission was taken from the Legislative Library and, by 1910, returned to the Grand Chief in Cape Breton.

99 NSARM, RG 1, vol. 35, doc. 67, "Edward Cornwallis to the Lords of Trade and Plantations," 16 February 1752; NSARM, RG 1, vol. 134, doc. 242, "William Cotterell, Secretary's Office, to Lieutenant Colonel Patrick Sutherland," 24 August 1754. A number of traders, most of them with ties to Merliguèche on the South Shore, applied to Patrick Sutherland in 1753 for land and provisions at the new community of Lunenburg. The heads of families were "Paul Boutin, Julian Bourneuf, Charles Boutin, Francis Lucas, Sebastian Bourneuf, Joseph Gedri [Guedry], Pierre Gedri [Guedry], Pierre Erio [Eury or Ury] and Claude Erot [Ury]." Despite Sutherland's providing initial assistance, Governor Lawrence issued instructions the following April to have them struck off the provisioning list, citing what he held to be their incorrigible "sloth and idleness." Some went to Piziquid, where they were deported with other Acadians to Pennsylvania and Maryland in 1755. Marty Guidry, "The Last Guedrys in Merliguèche, or the Labrador and the Guedry Family," 1, https://freepages.rootsweb.com/~guedrylabinefamily/genealogy/guedry_merligueche_labrador.html. Others went to Pictou or retured to Cape Breton, where a few were captured and taken to France after the fall of Louisbourg in 1758. And a few Acadian-*métis* settled at Petit Bras d'Or, now Grand Narrows, Cape Breton, where the majority escaped deportation by the British.

100 LAC, AC CIIB, vol. 31, fol. 59, "Raymond à Rouillé, 4 novembre 1751." Denis Michau's son may have been Michel Thoma Denny (Michau) Sr. (1747–1834), who would have been only four years old at the time of his father's death.

101 Peguidalouet would only receive three hundred livres necessary to build a house similar to the one erected at Mirliguèche for Denis Michaud if he and his people moved to the Port Toulouse area. Ibid.

102 Louis-Benjamin Petitpas was born in 1726 at Port Toulouse, the son of Claude Petitpas and his second wife, Françoise Lavergne. From 1749 onward he served Maillard, and was at Maillard's bedside in Halifax in 1762 when the missionary died. Rev. John E. Burns, "The Abbé Maillard and Halifax," *Canadian Catholic Historical Association (CCHA) Report*, 1936–37, 13–22.

103 Dickason, "Louisbourg and the Indians," 158. A major problem for the missionaries "was one of political necessity versus religious idealism." The thrust was towards development, maintenance, and control over an Indigenous guerrilla force, though the elements of this basically coercive polity were embedded in pageantry and protocol. Ibid., 68.

104 Johnson, *History of the Catholic Church*, 1.66. C.W. Vernon also described an old carved altarpiece that bore the date 1717, and likely came from the old French fort at Port Toulouse. The Mi'kmaq allowed the priest at the Church of the Sacred Heart at Red Islands, Cape Breton, to keep it for safety's sake, since in 1758 the English had destroyed the chapel, presbytery, and fort at Port Toulouse. NSARM, Places – F 108 V59.

105 Maillard, "Lettre de M. l'Abbé Maillard sur les missions," 366. The English translation of Maillard's words approximates that found in Martijn, "Early Mi'kmaq Presence," 55.

106 Charles Lawrence assumed the office of president of the council in July 1753, in Governor Peregrine Thomas Hopson's absence, and in July 1756 became governor of Nova Scotia. NSARM, RG 1, vol. 187, 184–6, "Minutes of His Majesty's Council," 12 February 1755. On 21 February 1755 John Hussey, the British commander at Fort Lawrence, wrote Lawrence that the two major promoters of the buffer zone scheme, Joseph Argimault and Paul Laurent, wanted to know the outcome of the executive council's deliberations regarding their second petition. When Hussey received a reply from Halifax, he invited the Mi'kmaw leaders to a meeting and told them that the council had found their request "unreasonable." He was being tactful. In actuality, the executive council branded the Mi'kmawclaim "so extremely exorbitant that it failed to warrant serious reply." NSARM, RG 1, vol. 210, 111–12, "Reply to a Communication from Paul Laurent, by Charles Lawrence and council at Government House," 12 February 1755; NSARM, RG 1, vol. 187, 187–9, "Minutes of his Majesty's Council," 13 February 1755.

107 Murdoch, *History of Nova-Scotia*, 1.308.

108 Louis Du Pont Duchambon de Vergor, the son of Louis Du Pont Duchambon and Jeanne Mius d'Entremont, was as militarily incompetent as his father.

109 Costs of reconstruction soared while available monies were in short supply, so Louisbourg's walls never were fully strengthened before the outbreak of the Seven Years' War.

110 Dickason also held that Mi'kmaq society was experiencing stress since chiefs had to reconcile their desire for French gifts with cultural traditions that placed the welfare of the group before that of the individual. Dickason blamed French Machiavellian manipulations for this outcome, stated that "the French genius lay in recognizing the potential usefulness of the Native peoples and

capitalizing on it, rather than in sweeping them aside or in marching over them." By 1757 French payments to suppliers for articles to be used as gifts for the Mi'kmaq had soared, especially as the British threatened to counter French gift giving with presents of their own. Dickason, *Louisbourg and the Indians* (1976), 99–113.

111 Micheline D. Johnson, "Maillard, Pierre." In an anonymous report entitled *Motifs des sauvages mikmaques et marichites de continuer la guerre contre les Anglais depuis la dernier paix* (Motives of the Mi'kmaq and Malecite for continuing the war against the English since the last peace), Maillard alerted Raymond to the real reasons the Mi'kmaq continued fighting. They needed land to survive and were going to keep putting obstacles in the path of British settlement until the British were willing to discuss their scheme for a vast reservation for their exclusive use. In a letter to the Abbé Du Fau, one of the directors of the Séminaire des Missions Étrangères, Maillard commented, "The Indians are really forced to defend themselves as they can and to prevent the British from becoming entirely the masters of the interior of Acadia." Johnson, "Maillard, Pierre." Maillard also penned an apologia for what he suspected was Le Loutre's hand in the assassination of Edward How in 1750. Howe, he claimed, once had insulted a statue of the Virgin Mary. Maillard, "Lettre de M. l'abbé Maillard sur les missions," 404–7.

112 Gaston du Boscq de Beaumont, *Les derniers jours de l'Acadie* (Paris: Lechevalier, Librairie Historique des Provinces, 1899), 71–2.

113 Boishébert in January 1757 went to the Miramichi River area where he set up a temporary headquarters to act as a refuge for Acadians who had escaped deportation. With Père Charles Germain, who laboured among the Malecite, he tried to sustain both the Acadians' and the Malecite's opposition to the British.

114 LAC, MG2, B4, article 76, 41, "Mémoire concernant les Savages Mikmacs, malechites et Cannibas rassembler sur la cote de L'ile Royale en 1757, de Emmanuel-Auguste Cahideuc, comte du Bois et La Motte, lieutenant-générale des armées navales."

115 In a less obvious way, the same behaviour was observed by fur traders among the Algonquian-speaking Anishinaabe or Ojibwa of the Upper Great Lakes area, where trapping party leaders declared they were starving, even if they were not, so they would get presents and provisions from the trading posts. Mary Rose Black-Rogers, "Varieties of 'Starving': Semantics and Survival in the Sub-Arctic Fur Trade, 1750–1850," *Ethnohistory* 33, no. 4 (1986): 353–83.

116 It is likely that Peguidalouet did not stay in the Mira region of Cape Breton during the winter of 1757–58, and may even have slipped away to southern Newfoundland to hunt, trap, and fish. Despite British embargos placed since 1749 on the Saint John River trade to Quebec in furs, hides, and feathers, the Mi'kmaq and neighbouring Algonquian nations – the Malecite, Penobscot, Penacook, Passamaquoddy, and Canibas (who hailed from the Kennebec River area of present-day Maine) – still went on trapping expeditions and engaged in middleman trade. Owing to the embargo, however, they stockpiled their furs until near the close of the Seven Years' War, as they could find few markets for them. Then, in 1760 1,300 pelts were shipped from Halifax, to be followed by an astonishing 11,104 pelts in 1761. Bob Beal, "Nurturing the Pine Tree – Sovereigns, Governments, Indians, Treaties: Relationships in the North American Treaty Process, 1610 to 1930," unpublished ms., 1 April 1998, copy in the possession of the author courtesy of Bob Beal.

117 Acadian and Mi'kmaw militias from Cape Breton and the Northumberland Strait area arrived as early as 7 May 1758 to defend Louisbourg from the British. By the end of the month, thirty Mi'kmaw warriors from Île Saint-Jean and the Miramichi had joined them. Boishébert arrived in Cape Breton in early June with seventy more Acadians from Île Saint-Jean and sixty Mi'kmaw militiamen. Not until 15 July, however, did Boishébert have his forces attack Captain Patrick Sutherland, who had led a contingent of Rogers' Rangers to Northeast Harbour. By this time the British were too entrenched in the area, and the Acadians and Mi'kmaq had to retreat. When British reinforcements arrived under Scott and Wolfe, one hundred rangers were sent to track down the Mi'kmaq and Acadians, though the militias were extremely elusive and the rangers captured only one Mi'kmaw man.

118 Pacifique, "Le Pays de Micmac: Cap Breton," *Bulletin de la Société de géographie de Québec* 27, no. 1 (1933): 34, 48.

119 Lieutenant-Colonel Charles Lawrence led a brigade to Point Platte (now Simon Point), the same site where the New England army landed during the first siege in 1745, while Whitmore moved in to White Point, closer to the fortress. The Mi'kmaw and Acadian militia killed one hundred British, while fifty Indigenous and Acadian militiamen were killed and scalped by the British and seventy were captured. Fifty Mi'kmaw fighters also returned to Kennington Cove on June 15 and took five British seamen captive.

120 The influence of Boishébert and his men during the siege proved minimal, since in their initial foray they

killed only one British soldier, took one British prisoner, and burned a guardhouse. They also were a nuisance, since when they finally arrived they helped themselves liberally to the food and other supplies held in French depots along the coast. This led to severe shortages among the French, since the British embargo made re-stocking these caches from Louisbourg difficult.

121 Johnson, "Maillard, Pierre."

122 The Mi'kmaw name for this island is Maligomish, and it is now part of the Pictou Landing First Nation reserve. During 2007 and 2008 it was the focus of archaeological work conducted under the direction of Michelle Lelièvre, who at the time was a doctoral candidate in anthropology at the University of Chicago and is currently on faculty at the College of William and Mary in Williamsburg, Virginia.

123 Upton, *Micmacs and Colonists*, 154; Chute, "Ceremony, Social Revitalization and Change," 54; Johnston, *Storied Shores*, 110–11.

124 Wicken, *Treaties on Trial*, 193–6.

125 LAC, AC, CIIA, vol. 105, 50r–50v, "Shomberg à Maillard," 26 October 1759; Canada, *Sessional Papers*, 40, 7, part 2, 186.

126 LAC, AC CIIA, vol. 105, 50r, "Shomberg à Capitaine Le Blanc," 23 November 1759. Shomberg wrote in a letter to the British Treasury Department that seven chiefs, one being Jeannot Peguidalouet and another hailing from the Saint John River area, had attended the signing. No other chiefs were identified. LAC, British Public Records Office, Treasury Records, vol. 1/458, "Henry Shomberg to Lords Commissioners of the Treasury," n.d. (c.1760); Wicken, *Mi'kmaq Treaties on Trial*, 194.

127 LAC, British Public Records Office, War Office Records (RG 34), vol. 17, Amherst Papers, "Whitmore to Amherst," 1 December 1759.

128 LAC, RG 34, vol. 17, fol. 98, "Whitmore to Amherst," 14 November 1760.

129 Presumably the Acadians took some sort of oath of allegiance to the British king at this time. LAC, WO, RG 34, vol. 17, "Whitmore to Amherst," 14 November 1760; LAC, RG 34, vol. 17, "Whitmore to Amherst," 22 January 1760.

130 Chief Peguidalouet went to Louisbourg with six other unnamed Mi'kmaw leaders and agreed to some sort of peacemaking arrangement, though no copy of this document exists today as, strangely, no copies seem to have been forwarded either to Amherst or to London. Later, in 1763, Peguidalouet had a copy of a treaty on his person when he urged some British naval officers to renew the treaty. This document may have been the treaty he signed with the British at Halifax on 25 June 1761, rather than the treaty he signed in 1759.

131 Wicken, *Mi'kmaq Treaties on Trial*, 194–6.

132 LAC, RG 34, vol. 17, 53–54v, "Whitmore to Amherst," 22 January 1760. Shomberg's experience at the court martial in the spring of 1760 demonstrated just how mercurial official attitudes could be, as they were usually driven by financial considerations and fears of superiors' reprisals than by any understanding of the actual conditions at hand. Shomberg had addressed the conditions "on the ground" at Merigomish in the fall of 1759, and for this he was severely punished for generosity and forthrightness. Though he exhibited signs of minor mental instability after the allegations, he did not have to suffer Whitmore's indictments long. On 11 December 1761 Whitmore was swept overboard and drowned on a voyage from Louisbourg to Boston, and his body was buried in Boston.

133 Trade was an important topic of discussion at Louisbourg in 1759. William Wicken notes that a nineteen-year-old soldier at Louisbourg named Jonathan Proctor wrote in his diary on 29 November 1759: "Lt. Shobrey [*sic*, Shomberg] in from Pigto and has Come to a Cap [capitulation] with the french and the Ingens and some of them Com [*sic*, Come] Down with him to Conferme their Peace that they May have liberty to Trade." Jonathan Proctor, "Diary Kept at Louisbourg, 1759–1760," in *The Essex Institute Historical Collections*, vol. 70 (1934), 32. Wicken holds that the French's defeat on Île Royale and at Quebec forced the Mi'kmaq by 1759 to seek out new trading partners. Wicken, *Mi'kmaq Treaties on Trial*, 195.

134 Murdoch, *History of Nova-Scotia*, 1.390.

135 Johnson, "Maillard, Pierre."

136 This list was later included with a letter Frye sent to Governor Lawrence. Both the letter and the list were first published in the *Philadelphia Gazette* and later reprinted in 1809 in the collections of the Massachusetts Historical Society. "Extract of a letter from Col. Frye to His Excellency the governor of Nova Scotia, dated Fort Cumberland, Chignecto," 7 March 1760, *Massachusetts Historical Society Collections*, ser. 1, 10 (1809): 115–16.

137 As late as the turn of the nineteenth century, oral traditions about Maillard appearing in the southwestern part of Nova Scotia could still be recounted by Mi'kmaw storytellers like Jeremiah Bartlett-Alexis, also known as "Jerry Lonecloud." Ruth Homes Whitehead, "Memoir of Jerry Lonecloud," in *Tracking Doctor Lonecloud: Showman to Legend Keeper* (Halifax: Goose Lane Editions, 2002), 56–7, 58–9. Lonecloud reported he had heard

stories of Maillard from Chief Peter Charles, with whom he had lived at Carleton Lake, Yarmouth County, Nova Scotia, when a youth.

138 After Maillard pressed him to assist the British, Manach encouraged the Acadian resistance fighter Joseph Broussard *dit* Beausoleil to request assistance from the British at Fort Cumberland. So, under a flag of truce on 16 November 1759, Beausoleil and three of his associates came to Fort Cumberland seeking provisions for around 190 Acadian refugees under their care. Murdoch, *History of Nova-Scotia*, 1.376. When Chief Paul Laurent, who had been wintering near Manach's mission, saw that Colonel Joseph Frye, the commanding officer at Fort Cumberland, provisioned these destitute Acadians after they swore allegiance to George II, he and his associate, Chief Michel Augustin of Richibucto, proceeded to Fort Cumberland looking for assistance for their people. Laurent spoke English fluently; he had learned the language while a prisoner in Boston in the house of one Henshaw, a blacksmith, and became one of the most avid promoters of the Indigenous land and resource campaign launched in the Beaubassin region in 1754 and 1755. Laurent's account of his stay in Boston first appeared on page 98 of the *Annual Register* for 1760 and page 377 of the *London Magazine* for 1760. See also Murdoch, *History of Nova-Scotia*, 1.396.

139 LAC, CO 217/18/28v–29v, "Treaty of Peace and Friendship Concluded with the Delegates of the St. Johns and Passamaquoddy Tribes of Indians at Halifax," 23 February 1760; NSARM, RG 1, vol. 36, doc, 48½, "Treaty at Halifax with St. John's and Passamaquoddy Tribes," 23 February 1760.

140 Lawrence omitted clause 3 of the treaty made between the Eastern Abenaki and the British at Boston in 1725 (and ratified at Annapolis Royal by the Mi'kmaq and chiefs of neighbouring nations in 1726), which referred to "settlements … lawfully to be made." The Mi'kmaq had come to regard clause 3 as containing a safeguard that the British would not form any new settlements without first obtaining the consent of their people. Wicken, *Mi'kmaq Treaties on Trial*, 118–19. Joseph Chigaguisht from Cape Breton had signed the treaty at Annapolis Royal in 1726, so Jeannot Peguidalouet would have been well aware of clause 3. Chigaguisht seems to have been a late-comer to the treaty proceedings in 1726, since his name does not appear on early draftings of the treaty (though all copies of the treaty bear the same date, 4 June 1726). The copy signed by Chigaguisht contains identifying marks of certain Mi'kmaw leaders, though no symbol for the Cape Breton chief. LAC, CO

217/5/3r–5r. Another treaty, signed between the British and Shubenacadie band in 1752, promised signees that, in addition to retaining their usual haunts for hunting, fishing, planting, and fowling, a truckhouse would be built to facilitate trade and that gifts would be distributed on 1 October for as long as the pact remained inviolate. NSARM, RG 1, vol. 186, 250–4, "Nova Scotia Council Minutes," 22 October 1752; Murdoch, *History of Nova-Scotia*, 1.385.

141 By closely monitoring proceedings, Lawrence wanted to prevent any repetition of "aberrancies" that arose in the fall of 1759 as a result of Captain Shomberg's participation in the treaty-making process. Yet the entire range of chiefs who signed treaty remains unknown. For instance, François Shagwaough (or Chequa) from Cape Sable approached the executive council on 24 April enquiring about the likelihood of his chief, "Michel Argoumartin" (or Argomatin), making a treaty later in the spring. NSARM, RG 1, vol. 165, 53–4, "Petition of François Shagwaough," 24 April 1760. Despite Argomartin's being one of the fourteen chiefs whose name was on Manach's list of 1760, there is no evidence that he ever signed treaty, although evidence that a pass (or passport) was given to a Mi'kmaw individual usually indicated that a "submission" also was made. NSARM, RG 1, vol. 165, 54–5, 74.

142 Lawrence viewed the exclusion of private trade through the imposition of a government-sponsored truckhouse system as a way to control the movements of the Indigenous population, as well as to curtail injustices that had arisen where the prices of European goods had not been fixed over time. NSARM, RG 1, vol. 37, doc. 16, "An Act to prevent any private Trade or Commerce with the Indians,1760"; NSARM, vol. 430, doc. 19, "An Act for Continuing an Act entitled 'An Act to prevent any private Trade or Commerce with the Indians,1761'"; NSARM, RG 1, vol. 164, doc. 85, "Appointment of Benjamin Gerrish as commissary," 7 February 1760; LAC, CO 217/21/148–49½, "Instructions from Governor Lawrence to Benjamin Gerrish," 11 February 1760. The instructions stated that spirituous liquors would be prohibited from trade and that truckmasters will "only receive goods from you." Truckmasters were appointed between this date and the end of June the same year, among them Henry Green, Moses Delescernier, Isaac Deschamps, Philip Knaught, and Joshua Winslow. NSARM, RG 1, vol. 124, doc. 87, "Appointment of Henry Green as truckmaster at Fort Frederick," 3 February 1760; NSARM, RG 1, vol. 124, doc. 100, "Appointment of Moses Delesdernier as truckmaster at Fort Edward [Piziquid]," 9 April

1760; NSARM, RG 1, vol. 165, doc. 67, "Appointment of Joshua Winslow as commissary for Native commerce at Fort Cumberland," 8 May 1760; NSARM, RG 1, vol. 124, doc.108, "Appointment of Isaac Deschamps as truckmaster at Piziquid," 12 June 1760; NSARM, RG 1, vol. 124, doc. 107, "Appointment of Philip Knaught as truckmaster at Lunenburg," 3 June 1760. John Dogget was appointed truckmaster at Liverpool in May 1761. Murdoch, *History of Nova-Scotia*, 2.406. Gerrish was head of what was essentially a government monopoly. The government assumed all risk, paid Gerrish's subordinates, and guaranteed him a percentage of proceeds from all sales and purchases. He furthermore was able to retain his business as a private merchant and provide goods for the Indigenous trade from his own store. Not surprisingly, until he became embroiled in a scandal over his dealings with the trade, Gerrish profited greatly from his appointment. Upton, *Micmacs and Colonists*, 63; Wicken, *Treaties on Trial*, 198–200.

143 Murdoch, *History of Nova-Scotia*, 1.383.

144 NSARM, vol. 164, doc. 41, "Treaty between Paul Laurent, Chief of La Have, and His Excellency Charles Lawrence," March 1760 (unsigned, undated copy); Murdoch, *History of Nova-Scotia*, 1.385; Wicken, *Mi'kmaq Treaties on Trial*, 277n41; LAC, CO 217/145, "Treaty with Michel Augustine of Richibucto," 10 March 1760; NSARM, RG 1, vol. 188, doc. 137, "Treaty with Claude Réné of Shubenacadie and Musquodoboit," 10 March 1760.

145 When Maillard was confirmed in 1760 as vicar general for Nova Scotia, he began to view himself as the spiritual leader of the Acadian people, no matter where they resided. He communicated with Louis Robichaud, who resided at Salem, Massachusetts, concerning marriage practices. Louis was a descendant of Prudent Robichaud Sr., who had been instrumental to the British at the time of the 1726 treaty signing. Wicken, *Mi'kmaw Treaties on Trial*, 90. Though one of Maillard's biographers holds that his communications with Robichaud did not begin until 1761, it is possible that Maillard was receiving information at an earlier date from other persons who remembered events surrounding the signing of the 1726 treaty. Johnson, "Maillard, Pierre."

146 Père Germain, S.J., assisted the English only when he felt the French cause was reaching its nadir. As late as the early spring of 1760 he believed the French might recover from their losses. Micheline D. Johnson, "Germain, Charles," *Dictionary of Canadian Biography*, vol. 4 (1771–1800) (University of Toronto/Université Laval, 2003–), accessed 10 December 2022, http://www.biographi.ca/en/bio/germain_charles_4E.html.

147 Murdoch, *History of Nova-Scotia*, 1.383.

148 Jean-François Bourdon de Dombourg, born in 1647, died at La Rochelle in France in1690; his widow, Jeanne Jannière, went to Acadia and in 1693 married Simon-Pierre Denys de Bonaventure. (This Jean-François Boudon was the son of Jean Bourdon, a Quebec seigneur and engineer-surveyor, and Jacquelin Potel.) Jean Hamelin, "Bourdon de Dombourg, Jean-François (1647–1690)," *Dictionary of Canadian Biography* online, vol. 1 (1000–1700). The Jean-François Bourdon de Dombourg who became an interpreter at Port Toulouse was a great-grandson of Jean Bourdon the engineer, and regarded Simon-Pierre Denys de Bonaventure as his "uncle." He was a son of Jean-François Bourdon de Dombourg and Madeline Poirel. In 1739, at age nineteen, he shattered his left hand at Port Toulouse while proofing guns destined to be distributed to the Mi'kmaq. Though he lost his left hand, he fought the British during King George's War and the Seven Years' War. In 1752 at Port-la-Joye, he rose to the rank of lieutenant and married Marguerite Gautier, a daughter of Joseph-Nicolas Gautier, an Acadian merchant whose early years were spent at Lequille, near Port Royal. Lieutenant de Dombergserved on Île Saint-Jean and at Port Toulouse before being posted to Louisbourg. Not long before Louisbourg's capitulation to the British on 26 July 1758, he was ordered to join Charles Deschamps de Boishébert's force of Indigenous militia, French regulars, and Acadians. Jean-Francois's brother-in-law, Pierre Gautier, an Acadian resistance fighter, led Mi'kmaw parties from Cape Breton in 1757 on three separate raids against Halifax. During the last of these forays, in September 1757, Gautier and four Mi'kmaq killed and scalped two British men at the foot of Citadel Hill. He may also have participated in a raid in July 1759 in which five British were killed in Dartmouth, opposite McNabb's Island. Pierre's brother Joseph-Nicolas Gautier married a daughter of another Acadian resistance fighter, Joseph Le Blanc *dit* Le Maigre. Pierre and Joseph-Nicolas Gautier eventually settled on the Island of Miquelon. Bernard Pothier, "Gauthier, *dit* Belair, Joseph Nicolas," *Dictionary of Canadian Biography* online, vol. 3 (1741–70).

149 Abbé Manach intercepted Bourdon's letter but did not keep its contents quiet, and as they became known the Mi'kmaw and Acadian communities suffered a major schism. Dissension arose over whether to abandon attachment to the missionaries and join Bourdon at Restigouche. Bourdon fought in a confrontation that occurred when the English fleet under Captain Byron laid siege to the French convoy that had sought refuge

in an estuary to avoid meeting English warships nearer Quebec. François-Gabriel d'Angeac had taken command of Bourdon's post and, with the French convoy's commander, François Chenard de La Giraudais, had erected defences in anticipation of a British assault. Several prominent chiefs decided to isolate themselves from the increasing tense situation. As early as 29 February 1760 Chief Paul Laurent had given his assurances to Colonel Joseph Frye at Fort Cumberland that he and his people would remain on peaceful terms with the British, and proved his willingness by signing a treaty with the British on 10 March 1760. Laurent and his people remained quiet in June 1760, though other Mi'kmaq moved northward to fight alongside the Acadian militia at Restigouche. Between 27 May and 8 June of that year, when the English set fire to the French frigate *Michault*, which prompted a rout of the French troops, the Mi'kmaq and Acadians held their position. After Major Robert Elliot arrived at Restigouche in late October and presided over formal surrender, Bourdon was permitted to depart for La Rochelle in France, where his wife Marguerite Gautier and his children joined him four years later.

150 The Reverend John E. Burns undertook a study of locales where Maillard might have based his oratory and finally decided that none of the four batteries on Halifax harbour were large enough to conduct Roman Catholic services. Instead, Burns suggested that Maillard may have occupied a barn-like structure owned by John Murphy that lay near the foot of present-day Tobin Street and stood behind one of the batteries. Burns, "The Abbé Maillard and Halifax," *Canadian Church History Annual Report* (1936–37), 13–22. See also Dominick Graham, "Lawrence, Charles," *Dictionary of Canadian Biography* online, vol. 3 (1741–70). Maillard became an employee of the British colonial government around the time of Governor Lawrence's death on 19 October 1760. On Saturday, 11 October, Lawrence took a sudden chill and died eight days later. Murdoch, *History of Nova-Scotia*, 1.395. Lawrence's death was a blow to Maillard at first, although Lawrence's successor, Jonathan Belcher, welcomed the missionary and agreed to work with him.

151 LAC, RG 34/12/90r–91r, "Joseph Claude to Roderick McKenzie," 7 January 1761.

152 During summer 1760 Abbé Manach received a passport from the British government granting him the "freedom to pass … to any part of the Province, and also for his Domesticks [*sic*, Domestics]." NSARM, RG 1, vol. 165, 79b. Yet early in 1761 General Amherst wrote the London Board of Trade blaming Manach for British problems in negotiating treaties in the north part of the province where the Mi'kmaq "had not yet wholly made their submission to His Majesty." LAC, CO 5/60/240, "Amherst to the Board of Trade," March 1761; LAC, CO 217/18/170, "Belcher to the Lords of Trade and Plantations," 9 April 1761. Manach drank to the health of The Pretender, James Stuart, and encouraged the Acadians to renew their sympathies for France. Lawrence's successor, Jonathan Belcher, had him arrested, sent to New York, and then conveyed to England. From there he went to Paris, where he wrote several letters to the Acadians at Miramichi, vainly asking them to use their influence with the government to sponsor his return. Jacques Robin, a Jersey merchant situated at Miramichi, heard about Manach's letters from local Acadians. LAC, CO 217/20/366–7, "Letter of Jacques Robbins [*sic*, Robin]," 21 May 1763; LAC, CO 217/20/354–9, "Montague Wilmot to the Lords of Trade and Plantations," June 1763. Robin wanted to settle refugee Acadians at Miramichi but was discouraged from doing so by the government. LAC, CO/217/353–8, "Wilmot to the Lords of Trade and Plantations," 10 December 1763; Murdoch, *History of Nova-Scotia*, 2.436–7.

153 Gueguen was born in Bretagne, France, and came to Acadia in 1753 with Le Loutre. He trained as a theologian and mathematician and also excelled in languages and business. He is regarded as one of the founders of Cocagne, where he was a merchant and justice of the peace. By three wives he had at least fourteen children. In 1790 he was Acadia's wealthiest trader, though in 1818 he claimed the Mi'kmaq still owed him £5,709 for goods he had supplied them before 1800. He acquired most of Manach's library as well as manuscripts pertaining to Mi'kmaw subjects given to him by Maillard. Régis Brun, "Gueguen, Joseph," *Dictionary of Canadian Biography* online, vol. 6 (1821–35).

154 Jeannot's granddaughter Véronique, who was Bernard Beuiddavalouet's (Peguidalouet's) daughter, married François Doujet (or Doucet), from Île St. Jean at Miquelon on 26 July 1778. She had been baptized in what is now New Brunswick, likely at Miramichi, in spring 1761. Charles A. Martijn, "Mi'kmaq in the Parish Registers of the Islands of Saint-Pierre and Miquelon, 1764–1848," unpublished ms, September 1996, 27–30. (The copy of this work examined by the author was graciously supplied by Dr. Martijn.) In 1794, moreover, Louis's son Francis Peguidalouet stated that his parents occasionally visited the Gulf of Saint Lawrence area.

155 Peguidalouet and Joseph Gueguen knew one another and may have had discussions on the content of these texts, since Maillard supplied both men with literary

materials and Peguidalouet undoubtedly could read hieroglyphics.

156 When Saint-Luc de la Corne, a French squire, merchant, and interpreter, was shipwrecked off Cape Breton in 1761, he was brought down by some of his old French acquaintances to Antigonish where they encountered five camps of Mi'kmaq who were suffering severely from hunger. Saint-Luc de la Corne, *Journal du voyage de M. Saint-Luc de La Corne, ecuyer, dans le navire l'Auguste, en l'an 1761* (Montreal: Chez Fleury Mesplet imprimeur, 1778), 33.

157 Upton states that from 1763 to 1766 Mi'kmaw parties accommodated at public expense proved "big business" for at least one inn owner, William Fury. Around 3,040 Mi'kmaw visitors came to Halifax during those years. Upton, *Micmacs and Colonists*, 64–5.

158 The Governor's Farm was located in the area where the Halifax Provincial Courthouse and the School of Architecture now stand. The grounds extended to the lot now occupied by the recently erected modern municipal library. According to one oral tradition, the treaty-signing ceremony took place where the front of the courthouse now stands, and the cornerstone of the Halifax Provincial Courthouse marks the spot of the hatchet's burial. See "Burying the Hatchet Ceremony (Nova Scotia)," Wikipedia, https://en.wikipedia.org/wiki/Burying_the_Hatchet_ceremony_(Nova_Scotia).

159 NSARM, RG 1, vol. 37, doc. 14, and NSARM, vol. 165, doc. 162, "Treaty of Peace and Friendship concluded by the Honourable Jonathan Belcher, Esquire, President of His Majesty's Council," 25 June 1761.

160 In August 1762 Rear Admiral Colville embarked to re-take St. John's, following its capture by the French.

161 Major-General Bastide was the engineer responsible for ensuring Fortress Louisbourg's final reduction to rubble. In 1761 he was constructing military fortifications around Halifax, including at the citadel.

162 NSARM, vol. 165, doc. 162, "Treaty of Peace and Friendship concluded by the Honourable Jonathan Belcher," 25 June 1761. King George III ascended to the British throne on 25 October 1760, following the death of his father King George II, but he did not participate in a formal coronation ceremony until 22 September 1761.

163 Ibid.

164 Ibid.

165 Ibid.

166 Copies of these treaties are found in several archival repositories. See NSARM, RG 1, vol. 37, doc. 14, and NSARM, RG 1, vol. 165, doc. 66, "Treaties of Peace and Friendship concluded by Jonathan Belcher with chiefs of the Miramichi, Sediack, Pogmouch and Cape Breton tribes," 25 June 1761"; LAC, CO 217/18/ 277–283r, "Ceremonials at Concluding a Peace," 25 June 1761; NSARM, vol. 165, doc. 162; Fredericton, University of New Brunswick, Harriet Irving Archives, New Brunswick Indian Documents on microfilm, "Treaty made with Claude Atouash of the Sediac [Shediac] Tribe, 25 June 1761"; NSARM, RG 1, vol. 165, doc. 162, "Treaty made with Joseph Shabecholouet of the Miramichi Tribe, 25 June 1761"; LAC, CO 217/18/277r, "Treaty of the foregoing Date as concluded with Étienne Ashobron [or Aikon Ashabuc], Chief of the Pogmouch [Pokemouche] Tribe of Indians, 25 June 1761."

167 Once the treaties had been "subscribed and sealed, and upon them being delivered and the Hatchets buried," the chief of the Cape Breton Mi'kmaq, "in the name of the rest, addressing himself to His Brittanic [*sic*, Britannic] Majesty – spoke as follows – which was likewise interpreted by Mr. Maillard." NSARM, RG 1, vol. 37, doc. 14, "Ceremonials at concluding a peace, 25 June 1761." See also LAC, CO 217/18/ 277–283r, "Ceremonials at Concluding a Peace," 25 June 1761; NSARM, RG 1, vol. 165, doc. 66. A large extract from Peguidalouet's speech also appears in Whitehead, *The Old Man Told Us*, 158–60. In the original descriptions of the treaty-signing event there is no mention of war paint on the chiefs' faces being ceremonially washed off after the burial of the hatchets, as one recent account has contended, although such a ritual would not have been out of line with northeastern Algonquian custom. See "Burying the Hatchet Ceremony (Nova Scotia)," Wikipedia, https://en.wikipedia.org/wiki/Burying_the_Hatchet_ceremony_(Nova_Scotia), which states: "At the same time the hatchet was being buried, the Chiefs went through the ceremony of washing the paint from their bodies in token of hostilities being ended."

168 NSARM, vol. 165, doc. 162, "Treaty of Peace and Friendship concluded by the Honourable Jonathan Belcher, 25 June 1761."

169 Ibid.

170 Ibid. "I own that I long doubted that you were of this Faith," Peguidalouet admitted. "I declare moreover that I did not believe you was [*sic*] baptized; I therefore am overwhelmed with great Sorrow and repentance that I have too long given a deaf ear to my Spiritual Director [Maillard] touching that Matter, for often has he told me to forbear imbruing my hands in the Blood of a people who were Christians as well as myself."

171 Ibid.

172 NSARM, RG 1, vol. 165, 160, "By the Honorable Jonathan Belcher, A Proclamation," 1 July 1761.

173 Oddly, Chief Peguidalouet and his band were not mentioned in this document, which suggests Belcher assumed that the earlier 1759 treaty that the Cape Breton chief signed at Louisbourg offered Jeannot and his people protection against molestation.

174 NSARM, microfilm reel 15,288, RG 1, vol. 188 (transcript), 254–5, "Executive Council Minutes concerning a Treaty made with Joseph Argimault of the Chignecto and Missiquash [Missaguash] tribe, 8 July 1761." The assemblage Argimault faced was similar to those who had met with Peguidalouet and his companions on 25 June. While Abbé Maillard interpreted, Argimault stated that although he had formerly supported the French king, he now acknowledged the British monarch as "his only lawful Sovereign" whom he would always esteem "as his good Father and Protector." After signing the treaty, he laid his hatchet in the ground in front of the lieutenant governor, at which point bottles and glasses appeared, the assemblage drank to the king's health, and all raised three loud cheers. In the late 1840s Abraham Gesner, Nova Scotia's Indian commissioner, would refer to Argimault's oration as the "*great* talk," and added that following this speech and the burial of the hatchet, a ceremonial calumet was smoked, several bands played the national anthem, "and the garrison and men-of war fired royal salutes." Gesner, *New Brunswick with Notes for Emigrants* (London: Simmonds and Ward, 1847), 46–7. Gesner also named several other chiefs whom he argued signed the treaty in 1761, including Louis Francis of Miramichi, Dennis Winemowet of Taboguntik (now Tabusintac), and Baptist Lamourne (Baptist La Morue or Lamoreaux, said to be one of the ancestors of the Prince Edward Island Sark or Jacques family). One wonders, however, if Gesner simply extracted these names from the list of fourteen chiefs that Abbé Manach gave Colonel Frye in 1760. There is no documentary proof that treaties were signed with all these leaders.

175 NSARM, RG 1, vol. 188, 255; NSARM, vol. 165, doc. 161, "Passes to Augusten, Gerounue [Jeremy?], Aiene, Noel, Joseph and Glaude, in order to pass without molestation to Fort Cumberland having made peace with the Government," July 1761; NSARM, RG 1, vol. 188, doc. 282, "Treaty made at Pictou and Malagomich with John Noel," 12 October 1761; Murdoch, *History of Nova-Scotia*, 2.407; NSARM, RG 1, vol. 188, doc. 288, and NSARM RG 1, vol. 430, docs. 20 and 21, "Treaty made at La Hève with François Mius," 9 November 1761, along with Abbé Jean-Mandé Sigogone's commentary on the difficulties Maillard faced in getting Mius to sign. Beamish Murdoch in the mid-1860s referred to the chief of "Pictouck

and Malagonich [*sic*, Malagomich]" as "Janneoville Pectougawash," or "the man of Pictou." Murdoch, *History of Nova-Scotia*, 2.407. George Patterson in 1877 held that Janneoville might be Captain Anthony (or Tony/Toney) of Pictou who "became a high chief" and who spoke French and English as well as Mi'kmaq. The captain dined at the governor's table in 1762, and "ancestors of Tony assert that the treaty was made by him in the name of the whole tribe ... at a ceremony where a tomahawk [was] buried in a grave on the citadel hill [the Governor's Farm]." Patterson, *History of the County of Pictou*, 42–3. Information contained in the James White Papers, housed in the Provincial Archives of New Brunswick, suggested that Captain Anthony of Remsheg, also known as Anthony Eury, was younger than Chief Noel because Eury actively supported the British cause during the American Revolution. In 1783 he received a licence of occupation to land at Remsheg. The author, as a child at a summer cottage at Toney River, Pictou County, heard stories about Anthony Eury, reputedly a French trader who intermarried with the Mi'kmaq and lived at Remsheg, now Wallace, in Pictou County. In 1753, members of Eury's family, driven out of Cape Breton by famine, tried to secure township lots at Lunenburg.

176 This spirit of guarded optimism contrasted with his glum attitude the preceding spring. In 1760, fired by anger at British expansion into the Falmouth region of the Annapolis Valley, Mi'kmaw warriors had donned war paint, causing consternation among the settlers. Belcher also feared that disaffected Acadians in the northeastern part of the colony would fit out armed privateers to harass British and New England provisioning vessels. In November 1760 when Colonel Frye and other New England officers left for Boston, taking their troops with them, Belcher fretted over the weak state of the colony's fortifications, given the presence at least six hundred Mi'kmaw warriors in the province and the fact that he had but a single man-of-war at his command. Colonel Frye was replaced in November by Captain McKenzie of the 62nd Regiment. NSARM, RG 1, vol. 165, doc. 97, "Orders and Instructions to Captain McKenzie," 12 November 1760; NSARM, RG 1, vol. 37, 6, "Acadians in northeastern part of province, by Jonathon Belcher," 14 April 1761; LAC, CO/43/18,5–6, "Regarding Restigouche fitting out vessels to prey on British shipping," spring 1761; NSARM, vol. 36, doc. 13¾, "A Description of the several towns in the Province of Nova Scotia, by Jonathan Belcher," 11 January 1762. Lands bordering the Gulf of St. Lawrence were "little known to the British" and "formed a retreat of French Acadians." Belcher judged

there were around 250 Acadian families, totalling about 1,540 Acadian refugees, in the northeastern part of the colony. At the same time he felt inadequate to deal with the boundary negotiations being conducted with the Massachusetts Bay Colony, and on 3 May 1762 he transferred all decision-making on this matter to the imperial government in London. Murdoch, *History of Nova-Scotia*, 2.412.

177 NSARM, RG 1, vol. 36, doc. 133, "A Description of the Several Townships in the Province of Nova Scotia," 11 January 1762. In the spring of 1762 the members of the executive council also congratulated themselves that they had "subdued the Rebellious Acadians and made peace with several tribes." LAC, CO 217/21/34, "Alex Grant to the Lords of Trade and Plantations," spring 1762.

178 Étienne Aushobron, the head chief of Pokemouche who had signed treaty with Jeannot in 1761, retained such fears, which in November 1761he graphically conveyed by voice and hand signals to a licenced trader named Gamaliel Smethurst. Smethurst was impressed by the chief's extensive knowledge of continental geography and politics. He stated that "Aikon Aushabuc [Étienne Aushabron] made almost a circle with his forefinger and thumb, and pointing to the end of his forefinger, said there was Quebec, the middle joint of his finger was Montreal, the joint next the hand was New York, the joint of the thumb next to the hand was Boston, the middle joint of thumb was Halifax, the interval betwixt his finger and thumb was Pookmoosh [*sic*, Pokemouche], so that the Indians would soon be surrounded, which he signified by closing his finger and thumb." Smethurst, *A Narrative of an Extraordinary Escape out of the Hands of the Indians in the Gulf of St. Lawrence*, ed. W.F. Ganong, in *Collections of the New Brunswick Historical Society* (Saint John, 1905), 2.372n2. In 1765 Smethurst was elected to represent Cumberland County in the Nova Scotia Assembly, a position he held briefly before he returned to England.

179 Belcher tried to ensure that the Mi'kmaq would be treated kindly and respectfully by public officials. On 3 December 1761 he directed John Cunningham, who recently had been appointed to curb Benjamin Gerrish's exorbitant expenditures from the public purse, to make sure that all truckmasters dealt "fairly and honestly" with the Indigenous population. This was a departure from the cold, calculating manner in which Lawrence had allowed the truckhouse system to operate. On 23 March 1762 the lieutenant governor further announced that, since private interests were banned from the trade,

officers faced a unique opportunity to fulfil the Crown's duty to the Mi'kmaq by offering them justice, "protection, integrity and Friendship." To prevent dishonesty and irregularity, he worked with chiefs to set up a schedule of fixed prices and rates to govern exchanges (where, for instance, two pounds of spring beaver would equal the value of one large woollen blanket), and no trade was permitted "except upon the terms set out in these tariffs." LAC, CO 217/18/ 295–6, "An act for the preventing of a private Trade and Commerce with the Indians," 18 July 1762; LAC, CO 217/19/31–2, "Message from the Lieutenant-Governor to the Members of His Majesty's Council and House of Representatives, with a schedule of tariffs attached," 23 March 1762; NSARM, RG 1, vol. 165, doc. 196, "Instructions for John Cunningham, Indian commissioner and agent for the Indian commerce," 3 December 1761. After Lawrence's death in fall 1760, Belcher had tried to turn the money-losing government monopoly over to a private contractor, and later awarded the supply contract to Alexander Grant. Gerrish, however, was permitted to retain the nominal title of "Indian commissary," even though the truckhouse system continued to haemorrhage public money and Gerrish held that the province owed him £2,500. John Cunningham meanwhile was given the title of "Indian commissioner."

180 Belcher stated that "[c]laims have been laid before me [on behalf of the Mi'kmaq] for Fronsac Passage, from thence to Nartigonneich [Antigonish], from Nartigonneich to Piktouk, and from thence to Cape Jeanne, from thence to Emchich, from thence to Ragi [Tagi] Pougouch [Tatamagouche], from thence to Jediack [Shediak], from thence to Cape Tommentie [Cape Tormentine], from thence to Merrimichy, and from thence to the Bay de Chaleurs, and the environs of Canso, from thence to Mushkoodabroet [Musquodoboit], and from thence to Meshpatagan Aspotagan Peninsula, and so along the Coast, as the Claims and Possessions of the said Indians, for the more especial purpose of hunting, fowling and fishing." LAC, CO 217/19/ 27; NSARM, RG 1, vol. 165, doc. 207, "A Proclamation by Jonathan Belcher," 4 May 1762. Historians have tended to dismiss this proclamation as an irrelevant aberration of history, but for an insightful legal as well historical perspective on its value, in relation to both eighteenth-century events and the modern Indigenous claims context, see Eric Adams, "Ghosts in Court: Jonathan Belcher and the Proclamation of 1762," *Dalhousie Law Journal* (Fall 2004): 321–45. By the words "and so along the Coast," Belcher left it ambiguous how much coastline he was

willing to recognize as falling under Mi'kmaw aegis. "Meshpatagan" is similar to the word "Ashmutogun" (Aspotogan), meaning in Mi'kmaq "to block the passageway." The Aspotogan Peninsula lies south of Halifax. Public Archives of Nova Scotia, *Place-Names and Places of Nova Scotia*, introduction by Charles Bruce Fergusson (Halifax: Public Archives of Nova Scotia, 1967), 22. It is possible that Maillard and the Mi'kmaq were eyeing their prospects of gaining a foothold south of Halifax at Aspotogan, a locale that in 1762 colonists had not yet entered.

181 Maillard likely avoided references to the site of the old Shubenacadie mission, which was still associated in British minds with Abbé Le Loutre. Le Loutre's association with the Mi'kmaq's first proposal had caused the British to jettison it in 1755, and Maillard evidently was taking no chances. The fall of French power in the Northeast also rendered one of the 1755 stipulations, that British and French military establishments both be eliminated from the northeastern sector of the colony, superfluous in 1762. The fact that Fort Cumberland and other British forts still stood within the area outlined in the royal proclamation was not addressed.

182 Morrison, "People of the Dawn," 390; Upton, *Micmacs and Colonists*, 53. The tenor of Belcher's proclamation of May 1762 was forceful and assured, and implied the presence of entrenched legal principles without actually describing them. Belcher had more knowledge than most people about Indigenous land issues in the province, owing to his father's interest in the subject and his association with the provincial secretary, Richard Bulkeley, who dealt with the Mi'kmaq. Yet his motives in issuing his proclamation in the end seem to have been expedient, limited ones. He likely sought to placate Maillard, win Mi'kmaw compliance with the British peacemaking process, and secure hunting and fishing grounds for the Mi'kmaq so they could furnish furs, feathers, and meat to the government-sponsored truckhouses. As Belcher was a man of the law, however, it remains puzzling why he left the nature of the Mi'kmaw rights that he mentioned in his proclamation so poorly defined. Perhaps in May 1762 he saw the Mi'kmaq as having prerogatives that would compel incomers to consult with them before establishing new settlements along the coast, although he failed to state this clearly.

183 The man who saw Maillard's hand influencing Belcher's actions in May 1762 was Joshua Mauger, Nova Scotia's London-based agent and Belcher's political rival. Mauger appeared before the Board of Trade in 1762 and 1763 to demand Belcher's removal from office. Donald F.

Chard, "Mauger, Joshua," *Dictionary of Canadian Biography* online, vol. 4 (1771–1800); LAC, CO 217/20/ 202–4, "Joshua Mauger to the Lords of Trade," 28 September 1763; NSARM, MG 1, vol. 258, 24–5, "Isaac Deschamps notes and papers," 24 September 1763. Historians have tended to be dismissive of Belcher's 1762 proclamation, yet Maillard undoubtedly worked closely with the lieutenant governor as well as the Aboriginal community on it.

184 Belcher even initiated an Acadian deportation scheme, by sending a group of Acadians to Boston. S. Buggy, "Belcher, Jonathan," *Dictionary of Canadian Biography* online, vol. 4 (1771–1800). With regard to the Lunenburg disturbances in July, after a surprise capture of St. John's by the French, see LAC, CO 217/19/116–23, "S. Zouberbuhler, J. Creighton, and L. C. Rudolph to Belcher," 15 and 21 July 1762. One disturbance at Lunenburg in July turned out to be a private matter between individuals. A woman from the town had stolen a keg of rum from a Mi'kmaw canoe, after which the Mi'kmaw owner of the keg followed the woman to her house and "used her ill." Many Lunenburg settlers in consequence grew fearful, and several families deserted outlying farms. They worried about the intentions of a sizeable Mi'kmaq group composed of fifteen persons from Cape Sable and thirty from La Hève, who it later turned out had assembled at Lunenburg to wait for Maillard, as it was approaching St. Anne's Day. Maillard, who was too sick at the time to come to them, sent down Benjamin Petitpas to intervene and assess the seriousness of the disruption, while Belcher called on Paul Laurent, who agreed to seek legal means by which to punish the Indigenous perpetrator of the assault. Settler tensions remained high well into 1763, however, owing to concern about repercussions within the local Mi'kmaw and Malecite communities from Chief Pontiac's resistance during that year in the Detroit region. Among other things, Pontiac and his Indigenous allies were protesting the cessation of British present distributions under General Amherst's orders. Amherst in 1761 and 1762 declared that there was no longer a need to give gifts to purchase Indigenous neutrality or military assistance. His goal instead was to make the Indigenous population aware of British might and keep them in awe. British Public Records Office, CO 5/60/27–8, Amherst Papers, "Letter of Amherst, New York, 12 December 1760." At this time, Colonel Forster was asked to send troops to protect outlying Nova Scotian settlements. Murdoch, *History of Nova-Scotia*, 2.415–19, 429–30, 435. While Belcher hoped it would be less politically damaging to him if he backtracked on his former promises

to the Mi'kmaq, Mauger's dogged opposition to him facilitated Montague Wilmot's appointment as lieutenant governor in Belcher's stead on 14 March 1763. And once Henry Ellis resigned, Wilmot became governor of Nova Scotia in May 1764. Phyllis R. Blakeley, "Wilmot, Montague," *Dictionary of Canadian Biography* online, vol. 3 (1741–70). Belcher, who dealt extensively in land, also may have been warned by his fellow land speculators that drawing a boundary between British and Indigenous lands would hinder their common aspirations for the future. Wicken, *Mi'kmaq Treaties on Trial*, 207–8. Another reason for Belcher's sudden change of heart stemmed from his fears, bordering at times on chronic paranoia, that disaffected Acadians and Mi'kmaq during the Bay Bulls incident in July 1762 would band together to raid British settlements and launch exaggerated claims to lands. The entire scope of Belcher's motives from May to July 1762, however, remains enigmatic and calls for further research.

185 Belcher continued that his rationale in drafting his proclamation had nothing to do with prior Indigenous rights to land and resources, but was simply to stop the Mi'kmaq from joining with disaffected Acadians and making extravagant demands "to the disquiet and perplexity of the new settlements in the Province." Once the crisis associated with the Bay Bulls incident passed, so did Belcher's sense of expediency that had driven his drafting of the proclamation. Meanwhile, the refugee Acadians made convenient scapegoats. He claimed he had discovered that it was a party of these Acadians, rather than the Mi'kmaq, who had damaged some personal property and that those who had suffered from the depredations "would be accommodated in a private way in the courts." He wanted the alleged Acadian perpetrators deported. LAC, CO 217/19/22, "Belcher to the Lords of Trade and Plantations," 9 December 1762. Although he probably knew that the French prior to 1713 had not made treaties with the Indigenous people, Belcher still claimed that all group rights in Nova Scotia sprang from the provisions of the Treaty of Utrecht. William Wicken has noted that the Mi'kmaq "in theory retained a right to the soil after 1713, since they had not surrendered or sold lands to the French." Wicken, *Mi'kmaq Treaties on Trial*, 130.

186 LAC, CO 217/19/ 22–26, "Belcher to the Lords of Trade and Plantations," 2 July 1762.

187 NSARM, RG 1, vol. 30, doc. 10, "Extract of the Minutes of Proceedings of the Lords Commissioners for Trade and Plantations," 3 December 1762. The Board of Trade obviously did not bother to look at the bounds set out in the proclamation, since it included Aspotogan, and they only recognized it as extending as far as down the coast in the direction of Halifax as Musquodoboit. Their statement to Belcher undoubtedly was made on the advice of Joshua Mauger, who later claimed in writing that the Mi'kmaq should be kept in the interior. Mauger focused on a spate of disturbances along the northeastern and southern Atlantic coasts to try to kill the terms of Belcher's proclamation once and for all. LAC, CO 217/20/202–4, "Joshua Mauger to the Lords of Trade," 28 September 1763; Murdoch, *History of Nova-Scotia*, 2.429. Murdoch's statements show that by the 1860s historians did not really understand what Belcher's proclamation had been all about.

188 Maxime Morin, "Le Rôle Politique des Abbés Pierre Maillard, Jean-Louis Le Loutre et François Piquet dans les Relations Franco-Amérindiennes à la fin du Régime Français (1734–1763)" (master's thesis, Laval University, 2009), 71–5.

189 Maillard's motives both in peacemaking and in seeking to enshrine Mi'kmaw land and resource issues in the proclamation were undoubtedly consistent and sincere. Belcher, with Maillard's help, must have grasped to some degree the great importance the Mi'kmaq placed on having sufficient hunting and fishing grounds to survive as well as to continue the fur trade. During a brief window between fall 1760 and May 1762, a member of the British colonial administration had been willing to listen to what an advocate of Mi'kmaw interests had to say, even though the same official would later retract the statements he and Maillard had framed together. At Maillard's funeral, officials praised the service the missionary had rendered in pacifying the Mi'kmaq, but no mention was made of his endeavours to promote Mi'kmaw land and resource claims. Daniel N. Paul, in a discussion titled "Abbé Pierre Antoine Simon Maillard, Apostle to the Mi'kmaq," dated 27 January 2009, questions Maillard's sincerity towards the Mi'kmaq; the discussion includes Deveau's reply of 11 February 2009. http://www.danielnpaul.com/AbbePierreAntoineSimonMaillard-ApostleToTheMi'kmaq.html. Paul challenged the view that Maillard was sincere in his efforts by stating that if Maillard really had acted in the Mi'kmaq's best interests "he would have negotiated a peace that would have assured the inclusion of the Mi'kmaq in the Province's prosperity and left them with a country – not landless and excluded to the point that they came close to extinction." In reply, Leo Deveau justifies Maillard's support for the British treaty-making process by arguing that it prevented much bloodshed.

Deveau also recapitulated that the missionary not only calmed British paranoia towards the Mi'kmaq, but also aided the Mi'kmaq's continuation as a distinct people by elevating St. Anne's Day to a national Mi'kmaw festivity and appointing Mi'kmaw catechists who could perform certain sacraments in the absence of priests. Deveau concludes that Maillard "knew his peace-making efforts would be his final legacy to the Mi'kmaq and he had to make do with what was possible amidst frightening consequences. It was his love of the Mi'kmaq and his Christian faith that kept him going. As to what would come later he knew he had no control or influence over [it]." Paul, however, presents a more positive view of Maillard's actions in chap. 9 of *We Were Not the Savages: A Mi'kmaq Perspective on the Collision between European and Native American Civilizations* (Halifax: Fernwood, 1993). Neither Paul nor Deveau touched on Maillard's behind-the-scenes role in drafting the proclamation of 4 May 1762

190   Wood was also the House of Assembly's Anglican chaplain.

191   LAC, MG 17, B1, vol. 1, Papers of the Society for the Propagation of the Gospel in Foreign Parts (SPGFG), doc. no. 40, 104, "The Reverend Thomas Wood to the Society," 27 October 1762; NSARM, RG 1, vol. 165, doc. 226, "The bearer Paul Laurent and the Indian with him have the Lieutenant-Governor's liberty to depart for Halifax," 11 August 1762.

192   This cemetery, lying at the intersection of Spring Garden Road and Pleasant Street (now Barrington Street) on the harbour side of the Governor's Farm, was known both as St. Paul's Graveyard and the Old Burying Ground. Founded in 1749 as a place of interment for all Haligonians, the burial ground was originally non-denominational, although it fell under the auspices of St. Paul's Anglican Church in 1793.

193   Norman McLeod Rogers, "Apostle to the Micmacs," *Dalhousie Review* 6, no. 2 (1926): 176.

194   Maillard's final resting place is unmarked, although there is a plaque to him on a wall inside St. Mary's Cathedral Basilica.

195   Following Maillard's death, the Mi'kmaq awaited news of the fate of their land and resource proposal. Though Belcher tried to claim that his proclamation had not been circulated widely, Maillard, as mentioned above, almost certainly would have informed certain chiefs about the document's contents. The obvious correspondence of the provisions of the proclamation with the goals of the earlier Indigenous movement of the 1750s testified to the importance the Mi'kmaq still vested in their campaign

seven years later. Though any official support for the proclamation had been shattered by the Bay of Bulls incident and the document's subsequent disallowance in London, Maillard likely died before the Mi'kmaq were fully apprised of these facts.

196   LAC, CO 217/21/ 7–8, "Governor Wilmot to the Lords of Trade and Plantations," 28 January 1764.

197   LAC, CO 217/20/354–59, "Wilmot to the Lords of Trade," 10 December 1763.

198   When the Mi'kmaq appealed for a Roman Catholic cleric to replace Maillard, John Pownall, secretary of the Board of Trade in London, stated that Nova Scotia should "establish pious and discreet Protestant missionaries among them," drawn from the Anglican SPGFP. Three or four Protestant missionaries, Pownall held, should be sufficient to "to wean them from French prejudices." LAC, CO 218/6/ 216–17, "Pownall to Dr. Burton, Secretary of the SPGFP," 20 June 1764.

199   Jean-Baptiste Roma and Louis-Benjamin Petitpas devised their own way of keeping the Mi'kmaw population loyal to Maillard's teachings by distributing copies of a letter said to have been written by Jesus Christ to the bishop of Luca, promising eternal bliss to those who remained loyal to the Roman Catholic religion and damnation to those who did not. LAC, MG 11, Lambeth MSS, A78, 108–11, "Minutes of a General Meeting of the SPGFP," 19 December 1766. Letters of the same ilk had been circulating among the Mi'kmaq since 1761, as Gamaliel Smethurst mentioned one. The British regime tried to counter these campaigns. Michael Francklin late in 1766 hired Roma at public expense to teach the Reverend Thomas Wood the Mi'kmaw language. LAC, MG 11, Lambeth MSS, A78, 108–11, "Minutes of a General Meeting of the SPGFP," 19 December 1766; LAC, MG 17 (SPGFP), B1, vol. 1, doc. 129, 267–9, "Francklin to the Society," 29 December 1766; Upton, *Micmacs and Colonists*, 62, 66. John Cunningham, commissary of Indian trade from 1762 to 1768 and commissioner of Indian affairs from 1769 to 1774, allocated gifts and honorariums to win Indigenous compliance with Protestantism. Yet he also paid Père Germain two hundred pounds to quell unrest among the Malecite in the Saint John River region around the time of the Bay Bulls incident, though not long afterwards the priest retired to Quebec. Murdoch, *History of Nova-Scotia*, 2.422.

200   Chief Joseph Argimault of Chignecto and a Cape Sable chief named Jean Baptist considered going to present their complaints in Great Britain, for on 30 September 1763 "John Baptiste Joseph Shickakett [Chignecto], Captain of the Tribe of Cumberland" received a pass

"to depart from hence for England or Ireland by any conveyance that may offer." NSARM, RG 1, vol. 164, doc. 282.

201 Michel Thoma Denny's great grandson, John Denny Jr., recounted that when Thoma Denny returned to Unama'ki from the Chignecto region, the "population of Cape Breton was inconsiderable" although the chief had been able to enlarge his formerly small band after 1749. Speck, *Beothuk and Micmac*, 107–8. In 1883 a large Mi'kmaw contingent at Shubenacadie also claimed that heirs of Thoma Denny held the office of grand chief of the Mi'kmaw nation for 134 years. They ignored the fact, however, that Jeannot Peguidalouet was district chief of Unama'ki from 1752 to 1783. NSARM, RG 2, vol. 9, doc. 1820, "Petition of Christopher Paul, Stephen Hood and 59 others to Lieutenant Governor Adams George Archibald," 29 March 1883.

202 There were persons surnamed "Le Blanc" among the Mi'kmaq as early as 1760. NSARM, RG 1, vol. 165, 54–5, "Passes to Jacques Le Blanc, Bartholomew Michel and Lewis Jacques," 28 April 1760. By the 1790s four Mi'kmaq bore the Basque surname: Francis, Jean, Joseph, and Noel. Francis Bask and Michel Thoma Denny restored the chapel on Île Ste. Famille in 1792. Jean or John Bask appeared at Indian commissioner George Henry Monk's residence in February 1794 and Monk thought, erroneously, that this man was a son of "Blaze Argomartin" who had taken his father's first name. LAC, MG 23, GII-19 (Monk Papers), 1067, 1070. Additional references to Basques from Unama'ki appear in the church registers of the islands of Saint Pierre and Miquelon. For instance, Noel Basque and his wife Marie Anne Peter (or Pierro) brought their one-year-old daughter Marie to be baptized on the Island of Miquelon on 1 May 1825. Denis Michaud was the head chief of Unama'ki in 1749. Interestingly, Stephen A. White, a lawyer and Acadian genealogist, has noted that members of the Dorien, Dupuis, and Le Blanc families took the English names "Gold," "Wells," and "White" while residing in Maryland. White, "Acadian Family Names of the 18th Century," http://www.acadian-home.org/names-acadian.html. These Acadian families, White argues, were in Maryland. The fact that "Gold" (the name initially used by the Mi'kmaw Gould family in Cape Breton), as well as "Wells" and "White," are surnames found within the Unama'ki Mi'kmaw group is intriguing. Though it may never be confirmed, could it be possible that a few members of the Acadian Dorien, Dupuis, and Le Blanc families, who changed their names while in exile, later joined the Mi'kmaq? More research is needed in this area. In 1994 Roddy Gould, a well-known elder living at Whycocomagh, thought his surname may have had English roots, but could not go back further in time than his grandfather.

203 George Patterson noted that a man named Beetle (Peter) John built a shallop on Big Island at Merigomish. Patterson, *History of the County of Pictou*, 191.

204 John and Charles Robin were younger brothers of Jacques Robin, who in the early 1760s received a land grant at Miramichi where he set up a trading post. John after 1765 traded at Arichat on Isle Madame, while Charles established a trading station on the Gaspé Peninsula. The Robins brothers' main interest was codfish, although they did trade in furs. David Lee, "Robin, Charles," *Dictionary of Canadian Biography* online, vol. 6 (1821–35); David Lee, *The Robins in Gaspe, 1766 to 1925* (Markham: Fitzhenry and Whiteside, 1984). In the early twentieth century, Robin family merchant establishments included stores at Arichat, Cheticamp, Inverness, and Musquodoboit Harbour.

205 Before the Canso truckhouse was established in 1764, the government expected the Cape Breton Mi'kmaq to travel to Fort Cumberland or Lunenburg, both long distances away. The truckhouse system was struck down in London in 1768, but not before it collapsed of its own accord in Nova Scotia. Benjamin Gerrish, who had been allowed to retain the post of commissary, not only provided goods from "his own store at high prices plus a commission three times what he had contracted for; his accounts were confusing and irregular." Upton, *Micmacs and Colonists*, 63. Since the system, as originally proposed by George Scott in the early 1750s, was devised principally to wrest Mi'kmaw trade away from the French, little consideration was paid to how the system was going to sustain itself economically, except from increasing increments of public monies, or how it would affect the welfare of the Mi'kmaw people themselves. LAC, CO 217/13/ 29½, "George Scott to Colonial Office," 17 August 1752. The London-based Board of Trade, which had never fully supported the system, scrapped it in 1768 in favour of a freer, licenced trade. It also laid the onus for management of Indian Affairs henceforth wholly on the colony. Elizabeth Ann Hutton, "Indian Affairs in Nova Scotia, 1770–1834," *Collections of the Nova Scotia Historical Society* 23 (1963): 39–41. Hutton's article is reprinted in H.F. McGee, *The Native Peoples of Atlantic Canada: A Reader in Regional Ethnic Relations* (Toronto: McClelland and Stewart, 1973).

206 Upton, *Micmacs and Colonists*, 68; Dennis A. Bartels and Olaf Uwe Janzen, "Micmac Migration to Western

Newfoundland," *Canadian Journal of Native Studies* 10, no. 1 (1990): 74–7.

207 Maurice Basque, *Des hommes de pouvoir: Historic d'Otho Robichaud et de sa famille, notables Acadiens de Port-Royal et de Néguac* (Néguac: Société historique de Néguac, 1996).

208 That Mi'kmaq in the northeastern sector of the province lacked "back country" was stated clearly in a report by Indian commissioner George Henry Monk in April 1808. LAC, CO 217/82/ 202–5, "Indian Commissioner Monk regarding the division of Nova Scotia into twelve Native administrative districts," 23 April 1808; University of New Brunswick, Harriet Irving Archives (HIA), Documents pertaining to Indian Affairs in New Brunswick (reel 508 micro.), RS 345, 310–15, "Letter of Moses Perley to Assembly regarding History and Dispersal of Indian Reserves in New Brunswick," 3 April 1848; HIA, MC 508, MG H 54, file 1, nos. 6, 7, and 9, "Joseph Gueguen regarding settlers occupying Richibucto Band lands," 2 September 1800. The Gueguen family was probably the reason the Mi'kmaq had one hundred acres on Cocagne Island by 1791. HIA, MC 508, RG 2, R 568, doc. 20, "Regarding Indian Land on Cocagne Island," 8 October 1851. By 1832 the Richibucto head chief, Paul Atenass (Athanase) *dit* Cobege (Copage) made land agreements on his own with settlers like Joseph Ward. HIA, MC 508, MG H 54, RG 3, RS 557/A. doc. 1, "Agreement between Paul Copege and Joseph Ward, 1832." Cocagne Island was an ancient Mi'kmaw encampment ground, known as *Wijulmacadie*. The Acadians renamed it "Cockaigne," after a mythical paradise appearing in medieval French literature.

209 During the late fall and winter most bands split up into family groupings dispersed over the landscape. These extended families came together in the spring to participate in celebrations, rituals, and councils. The larger groups were led by chiefs chosen from a number of influential family heads who exhibited leadership abilities and who embodied cherished cultural values. District chiefs traditionally assigned hunting and fishing territories using their hunting experience and knowledge of the power-holding forces of the universe, seen and unseen, to determine the most appropriate divisions. Marc Lescarbot, *History of New France* (Toronto: Champlain Society, 1914), 3.205. In the district extending north from the Miramichi River to the Restigouche River during the late seventeenth century, it was the chief's prerogative to distribute hunting territories to individuals who had to stay within the limits set. Le Clercq, *New Relation of Gaspesia*, 237. Discussion and assignment took place

before the chief in assemblies of elders that were held each spring and autumn. Chiefs had to provide opportunities for hunting, fishing, and trade for their people. They offered religious direction, executed wise judgments at councils, and were oratorically skilled to present a group consensus in terms all could understand. Leaders had to act on behalf of those for whom they were responsible, including the ill, the needy, widows, and orphans. The late Alex Denny, *Kji Keptin* (grand captain) of the Mi'kmaw Grand Council, once remarked, however, that district chiefs could on occasion cause redistributions of population over a landscape lying outside the borders of their immediate district, through forming agreements with leaders of neighbouring bands. If there was not enough land for a band, more had to be obtained by their chief. District borders often proved indistinct, and overlapped. If neighbours "hemmed them in" then there were protocols to enquire of neighbouring groups whether persons from another group could hunt on their lands for a season. Alex Denny, personal communication, Eskasoni, June 2009.

210 Public Archives of Newfoundland (henceforth PANL), British Public Records Office, documents on microfilm, LAC, CO 195/9/164–216, "Draft of Instructions to Thomas Graves as Governor and Commander-in-Chief," 29 March 1763; Martijn, "Early Mi'kmaq Presence," 82.

211 British Public Records Office, London, England, Admiralty Records (henceforth PRO, AR), series 52, vol. 1316, no. 2, "Master's log, *HMS Lark*, 1763"; Bartels and Janzen, "Micmac Migration," 87.

212 Although Thompson did not give the date of this document, it likely was a copy of the 25 June 1761 treaty signed at Halifax. PRO, AR, 1/2590, no. 4, "Samuel Thompson to Admiralty Secretary, Philip Stephens," 16 April 1764. Thompson took this treaty, which would have been the only copy Chief Peguidalouet possessed, and sent it overseas with his letter to Stephens. The treaty document subsequently was detached from Thompson's letter and was lost.

213 Many of the gifts requested were gauged to help the Mi'kmaq bolster their navigational skills and increase the seaworthiness of their seagoing wooden vessels. The request for fishing nets further suggests that the chief was addressing the wants of Acadians, *métis*, and others of his group who wanted to pursue a commercial fishery.

214 Thompson stated that "2 Indian chiefs of Cape Breton begged to him to return and bring them the items mentioned in aforesaid letter." LAC, CO 217/20/318–21, "Captain S. Thompson to the Admiralty Office, with inventory of articles requested included," 21 April 1764;

LAC, CO 217/20, part 2, 322, "Samuel Thompson to the Board of Trade," 28 April 1764; National Maritime Museum (NMM), Greenwich, England, Graves Papers, vol. 105, "Remarks" of Captain Samuel Thompson, *HMS Lark*; NMM, Graves Papers, "Draft of Graves' comments to Secretary Stephens," 20 October 1763. John Pownall, secretary of the Board of Trade, concluded that "delivery of Presents to the Micmacs through any other channel than the Governor of the Colony may be attended with inconveniences." LAC, CO 218/6, ff. 204–6, "Pownall to Philip Stephens, Secretary of the Admiralty," 1 May 1764; Provincial Archives of Newfoundland (henceforth PANL, CO [British Colonial Office Records on microfilm]) 194/27/257–264v, "Palliser to Stephens, Secretary of the Admiralty," 25 August 1766.

215 Thomspon obligingly read through the 1761 treaty and then received Peguidalouet's list of presents. On 25 June 1761 Peguidalouet had promised to "sharpen his weapons" against Britain's enemies should war ever arise, and in return for this promise of military assistance he anticipated presents. Captain Thompson stated that he had no presents on hand to give, and was unsure about the appropriateness of a naval officer giving presents; he told Peguidalouet he would contact his superiors at the British Admiralty Office for instructions about how to proceed. The chief then agreed to wait until the proper channels were established through which he expected annual presents to flow.

216 John G. Reid, "Empire, the Maritime Colonies, and the Supplanting of Mi'kma'ki/Wulstukwik, 1780–1820," *Acadiensis* 38, no. 2 (2009): 78–97. The British throughout the Northeast tended to furnish presents only when there was a likelihood of an imminent attack by a hostile power and Indigenous warriors were needed to aid in boundary defence. In the Upper Great Lakes area, where sporadic threats arose from American sources until the mid-1800s, British present-giving continued until the 1850s. Janet E. Chute, *The Legacy of Shingwaukonse: A Century of Native Leadership* (Toronto: University of Toronto Press, 1998), 146–8.

217 It took Peguidalouet a while to catch on to the British policies that led to the implementation of the truckhouse system, denied the Mi'kmaq Roman Catholic priests and tried to substitute Protestant missionaries, and considered confining the Mi'kmaq to the interior of the colony. These were all strategies gauged to keep the Indigenous population away from French influences. None of them, however, ever offered the least benefit to the Unama'ki Mi'kmaq. No missionaries associated with the Society for the Propagation for the Gospel in Foreign Parts ever found their way north past the Gut of Canso, and the truckhouse system did not extend into Cape Breton. The Unama'ki people also relied on maritime resources and could not be forced to dwell in the interior. Acadians, however, became subject to a policy to keep them in the interior. In 1764 lands at Falmouth, Lunenburg, and Halifax were assigned to the French "distant from the sea shore," to prevent them from having any intercourse with Saint-Pierre and Miquelon. LAC, CO 217/21/99–99½.

218 The French shore, along which the French could fish under the terms of the Treaty of Paris of 1763, ran south down the west side of Newfoundland's northern panhandle, from Cape Bonavista to Point Riche. Yet despite Point Riche's setting a boundary, French and British fishery interests constantly clashed. English operators contended for grounds lying north of Point Riche on which they had fished prior to 1763, while French fishermen argued that their limits had always extended as far south as Cape Ray. To settle disputes on the water, Newfoundland's governors policed the fishery with naval cruisers, an expensive and time-consuming but necessary task. Following Pequidalouet's visit to Saint-Pierre and Miquelon, the need to monitor Mi'kmaw activities vis-à-vis the French was added to the *Lark's* and its sister ships' agendas. Brandon Morris, "'Those Two Insignificant Islands': Saint-Pierre and Miquelon, and Social and Cultural Continuity in Northeastern North America, 1763–1793" (master's thesis, University of Saskatchewan, 2012), 56–76.

219 NMM, Graves Papers, vol. 105, no. 46, "Answers to Heads of Inquiry, and Remarks and Answers of Captain Samuel Thompson, 1763"; NMM, Graves Papers, vol. 106, "Letter from Commodore Graves to the Admiralty," 22 October 1763.

220 Captains of Royal Navy ships were authorized to inform Peguidalouet of this decision. PRO, Admiralty Records (AR) 3/72, 6, "Meeting of the Lords of the Admiralty," 2 May 1764; Bartels and Janzen, "Micmac Migration," 80.

221 PANL, GN 2/1A/3, p. 235, "Hugh Pallister to Jonathan Broom," 29 July 1764.

222 NSARM, RG 1, vol. 37/14, doc. 89; LAC, CO 217/43/183–6, "Wilmot to Lords of Trade and Plantations," 10 December 1763. These Mi'kmaq, Wilmot observed, have "for three months past been cordially received by the French."

223 LAC, AC, CI2, 1 fol. 3v, "Mémoire du Roy pour server d'instruction au Sr Dangeac nomeé au government des Isles St. Pierre et de Miquelon," 23 February 1763. D'Angeac waited until Captain James Cook had first surveyed

the French islands before taking possession of them for France on 15 June 1763.

224 Bartels and Janzen noted, "Though the official French position was to discourage the Micmac from coming to St. Pierre for fear of antagonizing the English, such visits began almost immediately and seem never to have been discouraged. On the contrary, the visits were frequent and open, and numerous baptisms, marriages, and deaths were officially recorded." Bartels and Janzen, "Micmac Migration," 78.

225 LAC, CO 217/43/183–6, "Wilmot to Lords of Trade and Plantations," 10 December 1763. Wilmot had been appointed lieutenant governor of Nova Scotia on 14 March 1763, succeeding Jonathan Belcher, but did not arrive at Halifax from Quebec until September of that year. In the fall of 1763 Henry Ellis resigned the governorship of Nova Scotia, and in May 1764 Wilmot assumed the office of governor in his place. The province was suffering from heavy debts and deficits when he became governor, for almost the whole British naval and military establishment had been withdrawn from Halifax, and with it the revenue from duties on the sale of liquor. Wilmot supported the idea of present distributions to the Indigenous people to keep them peaceful while settlement occurred, but as the province was so deeply in debt, there was no money to spare for presents or even additional military protection. Phyllis R. Blakeley, "Wilmot, Montague."

226 LAC, CO 217/20/354–8, "Wilmot, letter of June 1764, to Lords of Trade and Plantations regarding Cape Breton Mi'kmaq, Canso fishery and Jacques Robin's letter of 21st May 1763."

227 Ibid. Also see LAC CO 217/20/360, "Letter of Jacques Robbins [sic, Robin]," 21 May 1763; AC, CO 217/21/96–8, "Regarding Robbin's land granted at Miramichi, his trade at Louisbourg and his attitude towards new trade laws," 5 November 1764. Jacques Robin suggested getting a Roman Catholic missionary for the Miramichi area where his trading station lay.

228 Major Walton was deputy governor of Cape Breton under Wilmot, the governor of Nova Scotia. In August 1764 Wilmot explained to the Lords of Trade and Plantations that "the same Indian chief [Chief Jeannot] mentioned by your lordships had ineffectually applied to the officer [Major Walton] commanding the troops at Louisbourg for some small allowance of provisions, and other necessaries, and the declarations he then made, of being obliged, on the refusal he met with, to have recourse to the Island of St. Peter, and I have lately had the mortification to find that he was not only well received

there, but that he has continued on that Island ever since with his whole tribe." LAC, CO 217/21/216, "Wilmot to the Lords of Trade," 17 September 1764. In many respects the substance of this letter echoes the contents of one he wrote earlier to the Lords of Trade on 29 August 1764.

229 LAC, CO 218/6/224–7, "Lords of Trade to Wilmot," 13 July 1764; LAC, CO 218/6/ 238–9, "Lords of Trade to Wilmot," 24 June 1765.

230 In 1764 Jeannot quickly dealt with any tarnishing of his status as a successful district chief caused by the British rejection of his requests for presents by enjoying the respect and gifts accorded to him on the French islands. British colonial administrators under instructions from General Amherst, who deemed presents an unnecessary expense, dispensed with the regular gift-giving that Mi'kmaq held to be an essential component of any ongoing peace. The Mi'kmaw still had a degree of power, and to some extent the return of the French to the Northeast under the terms of the Treaty of Paris of 1763 enabled the Mi'kmaq to play off the English against the French. Yet even then, the British resorted to present-giving only when crises demanded that the Mi'kmaq be placated sufficiently to halt their going over to an enemy cause. Jeannot would have realized how important recognition for his role as a district chief would be to the functioning of the domains both of Mi'kmaw-French and Mi'kmaq-British interrelations. A Mi'kmaw chief's ability to pass on gifts to his people reinforced his prestige within Mi'kmaw society. And such intermediary leaders were not found only on the Mi'kmaw side, for French officers, officials, and traders also increased their own prestige and importance through positive responses they received from the Mi'kmaq. The pockets of illicit French settlement that popped up after 1763 in Baie d'Espoir, Cape Ray, and on Codroy Island thrived to some extent because of their members' amiable relations with the Mi'kmaq, who knew the landscape and resources well.

231 Newfoundland's governor, Thomas Graves, failed in 1763 to act as consistently as his successor Hugh Palliser had in trying to eject the Mi'kmaq from the southwest coast. Yet he also complained about the Mi'kmaq's occupying lands under his aegis and even asked whether, if the administration of Cape Breton would "not confine them at Home, would it not be better to extirpate them from off this Island?" LAC, CO 194/15/108, "Graves to the Board of Trade," 20 October 1763.

232 Families of Acadians regularly left for Saint-Pierre and Miquelon without the permission of the Nova Scotia government. This migration in part was spurred by the

Board of Trade's refusal to provide either the Acadians or Mi'kmaq with Roman Catholic priests. So incensed was Père Germain about the British exclusively espousing Anglicanism that, when he retired to Quebec in 1764, he asked his Malecite followers to burn their chapel on the St. John River. Murdoch, *History of Nova-Scotia*, 2.444–5.

233　LAC, CO 217/21/7–8, "Wilmot to Lords of Trade," 20 January 1764; LAC, CO 217/21/91–2, "Wilmot to Lords of Trade," 29 August 1764; LAC, CO 217/21/216, "Wilmot to the Lords of Trade," 17 September 1764. In August 1764, 150 Acadians applied to Wilmot for leave to remove to Saint-Pierre, but many others simply left for the French islands without notifying British officialdom. LAC, RG 1, vol. 39, 95, "Regarding Acadians applying to go to Saint Pierre," 29 August 1764.

234　Bartels and Janzen claim they can follow Peguidalouet's movements over time from entries in documents that record his meetings with various officials. It was possible "to trace the movements of Chief Jeannot from Louisbourg in 1759, to Codroy in 1763, back to Louisbourg in 1763–64, to St. Pierre in 1763–64, back to Nova Scotia in 1765, and again to Newfoundland in 1767 and 1768 [when some of Peguidalouet's band members in Cape Breton stated to surveyor Samuel Holland that the chief was still in Newfoundland]." Bartels and Janzen, "Micmac Migration," 83.

235　The Mi'kmaq forged a commercial exchange relationship with the French on Saint-Pierre and Miquelon, similar to what had prevailed in Cape Breton and elsewhere before 1759, but without the same stress on Mi'kmaw military service, and presumably to the exclusion of English trade. Morris, "Those Two Insignificant Islands," 56–7.

236　Wilmot raised the issue of a survey of Prince Edward Island and Cape Breton in June 1764. LAC, CO 217/21/183, "Wilmot to the Lords of Trade and Plantations," 24 June 1764. While Morris was conducting the survey of the Cape Breton and Canso coastline, he recorded that many Mi'kmaq reached Canso by canoeing to Chedabucto Bay, following a trail overland to White Head, and then embarking once again in canoes to circumnavigate various islands to get to Canso. He also noted that St. Peter's, which was devastated in 1759, had by 1764 a population of fifty families, making it "one of the largest settlements in Cape Breton." LAC, CO 217/21/103–18, "Observations and Remarks on the Survey made by Order of His Excellency according to Instructions of 26th Day of June last, in the Eastern Coasts and Nova Scotia and the Western Parts of Cape Breton, by Charles Morris, autumn 1764." Charles Morris (1711–1881) had been instructed to survey Cape Breton and St. John's Island (Prince Edward Island) during the summer and autumn of 1764, but inclement weather confined his labours to Cape Breton and Canso.

237　In 1763 Père Joseph-Pierre de Bonnécamps arrived as curate for the parish of Saint-Pierre, while Père François-Paul Ardilliers served on Miquelon. As early as 14 March 1764, Bonnécamps baptized a Mi'kmaw boy named "Pierre," although this child appears to have been the son of an Indigenous domestic rather than a member of the Unama'ki group. Pierre's mother was recorded as "Marieanne or Marianna La Savagese [*sic*]." His father's name was not given. His godfather was a Frenchman, Pierre Texier. Five years later Marianna died in Saint-Pierre, "apparently without any relatives present[,] and may have been employed as a family servant." Between 1763 and 1848, there would be forty-two entries in the registers of the parishes of Saint-Pierre and Miquelon relating to the Indigenous people. With the exception of Pierre's baptism and Marianna's burial, until the British takeover of the French isles in 1778, all took place on the island of Miquelon. After the return of the French settlement in 1783, baptisms, marriages, and burials occurred on both Miquelon and St. Pierre. Martijn, "Mi'kmaq in the Parish Registers of Saint-Pierre and Miquelon," 5–6, 8. As more baptisms occurred, however, Mi'kmaw parents who had connections with the former French regime on Île Royale often chose French or Acadian godparents for their children. Morris, "Those Two Insignificant Islands," 89.

238　Palliser, who succeeded Thomas Graves as Newfoundland's governor in April 1764, complained that the Louisbourg authorities' practice of giving passports to Mi'kmaq desiring to go to Newfoundland "was very Inconsiderate in those who granted them." He had demanded that Pringle "recant these passes … and to Issue no more." LAC, CO 194/16/308v, "Palliser to Francklin," 16 October 1766.

239　PANL, GN 2/1, vol. 3, "Palliser to Pringle," 22 October 1765.

240　LAC, MG 11, CO 194/16/34–7, "Palliser to Lord Halifax, President of the Board of Trade," 9 October 1764. Both the Mi'kmaq and the French were "old hands" at this trade. Before 1758, when the French possessed both Île Royal and Saint-Pierre and Miquelon, trade frequently occurred between the French isles and the Mi'kmaq residing along the Gulf of St. Lawrence from Canso to Chaleur Bay. The Mi'kmaq exchanged furs for a range of French manufactured commodities, including luxury goods such as brandy and wine. LAC, CO 217/49/30–2, "Lord William Campbell to Lord Dartmouth," 26 April 1773. Palliser's actions had much in common with the activities of an earlier official named Captain William Taverner, whom Britain commissioned in 1713 to open avenues of trade with the Newfoundland Mi'kmaq, but who ended up declaring that the Mi'kmaq should be removed from the colony. Taverner promoted trade with the Mi'kmaq in a lethargic, perfunctory fashion, and relinquished the quest entirely after his Canadian interpreter at Placentia Bay was apparently drowned in a shipwreck. Instead, he came to hold that the British migratory fishery and trapping industry suffered on account of the Mi'kmaw presence. Owing to Taverner's influence, in 1733 controls were placed on the use and settlement of land in the Port aux Basques region by Mi'kmaq from Cape Breton. PANL, CO 194/23/ 180–182v, "Taverner to the Board of Trade," 2 February 1734. Within the mercantile communities along Newfoundland's southwest coast, memories of confrontations with the Mi'kmaq during past colonial wars still fuelled settler fears. Stories of Mi'kmaq capturing fur trappers at White Bay during the winter of 1745–46, taking prisoners and then killing them en route to Quebec in 1747, and proceeding through the Codroy Valley to Deer Lake in order to attack British sealing parties during the late French regime all fell into this category. Martijn, "Early Mi'kmaq Presence," 75–9. To Jeannot, looking at the post-war milieu from a Mi'kmaw perspective, the signing of treaties and the onset of peace in 1763 should have wiped the slate clean. After a conflict, northeastern Algonquian leaders performed rituals that were thought to remove the taint of war in favour of peaceful co-existence with the other power holders. For this reason the chief, in the absence of British gifts, welcomed the delivery of French presents from Saint-Pierre and Miquelon to members of his band who remained in Cape Breton.

241 LAC, CO 194/27/72–75v, "Testimonials of French residents of Saint-Pierre to Palliser, including the testimony of Thomas Sperin," 20–25 June 1765. Olaf Janzen, "'Une Grande Liaison': French Fishermen from Île Royal on the Coast of Southwestern Newfoundland, 1714–1766 – A Preliminary Survey," *Newfoundland Studies* 3, no. 2 (1987): 183–200; Olaf U. Janzen, "The Royal Navy and the Interdiction of Aboriginal Migration to Newfoundland, 1763–1766," *International Journal of Naval History* 7, no. 2 (2008), https://www.ijnhonline.org/wp-content/uploads/2012/01/Janzen.pdf.

242 William L. Clements Library, University of Michigan, Ann Arbor, Thomas Gage Papers, vol. 37, Major Walker Correspondence, "Major Walton, at Louisbourg, to Colonel Montague Wilmot, at Halifax," 31 May 1765.

243 Captain Machormak (or MacCormick) is no relation of William Macarmick (1742–1815), lieutenant governor of Cape Breton from 1787 to 1815, who, though captain of the British 75th Regiment of Foot in 1765, remained in Britain until shortly before appearing in Cape Breton twenty-two years later.

244 NSARM, RG 1, vol. 165, doc. 385, "Pass to John Pegedowa Oulaut," 22 July 1765.

245 NSARM, RG 1, vol. 136, 72–3, "Wilmot to Pringle," 12 December 1765. Also cited in R.T. Pastore, "Micmac Colonization and Newfoundland," unpublished ms, 1977, 13. A copy of Pastore's ms. is housed in NSARM, accession F 80 C16a P214 #1. See also LAC, CO 217/21/216, "Wilmot to the Lords of Trade and Plantations," 17 September 1764; Janzen, *War and Trade in Eighteenth-Century Newfoundland*, Research in Maritime History no. 52 (St. John's: International Maritime Economic History Association, 2013), 188–9.

246 NSARM RG 1, vol. 136, 72–3, "Wilmot to Pringle," 12 December 1765. The legality of Palliser's arbitrary efforts to prohibit the eastern Mi'kmaq, who were British subjects, from crossing over to Newfoundland was questioned not just questioned by Wilmot. Though the Board of Trade backed Palliser's decisions in 1765, a party of aggrieved traders launched a lawsuit based on the fact that Pallister's actions with respect to the Mi'kmaq and other British subjects had never received parliamentary sanction. Palliser lost the suit. William H. Whiteley, "The Establishment of the Moravian Mission in Labrador and British Policy, 1763–83," *Canadian Historical Review* 45, no. 1 (1964): 29–50.

247 Virginia Miller, Ralph T. Pastore, and Doug Jackson each suggest that Wilmot encouraged Peguidalouet and his people to migrate to Newfoundland to rid the Nova Scotia administration of a thorny problem. Miller, "The Decline of Nova Scotia Micmac Population, A.D. 1600–1850," *Culture* 2, no. 3 (1982): 110; Pastore, *Indian Summer: Newfoundland Micmac in the Nineteenth Century* (Ottawa: Canadian Ethnology Service, National Museum of Man, 1978), 167–78; Jackson, *On the Country: The Micmac of Newfoundland* (St. John: Harry Cuff, 1993), 26.

248 By spring 1765 Peguidalouet was regularly crossing to Newfoundland "with as many as 200 followers, who spread themselves from Fortune Bay and Bay d'Espoir on the south coast to St. George's Bay and all the way up the west coast to Port au Choix. Initially, many maintained the seasonal practice of crossing back to Cape

Breton, but over time these people became increasingly sedentary. More and more families decided to remain in Newfoundland and to mingle with the members of a small floating population, the Say'ewedkik or 'Ancients,' who were already established there." Martijn, "Early Mi'kmaq Presence," 81.

249 LAC, CO 218/3/205–6, "Board of Trade to Wilmot," 8 May 1764. Wilmot in the spring may even have over-reached the budgetary restraints set on his spending in this regard, since by July the Board of Trade was cautioning him to cut back on giving presents and instead encourage the Mi'kmaq to become self-sufficient through their fur commerce. The Board of Trade at the time also held to its view that honouring treaty promises by providing Roman Catholic priests for the Mi'kmaq would "confirm their prejudices in that Religion … so they can never be united in Interest and Affection to the British Government." LAC, CO 218/6/224–7, "Board of Trade to Wilmot," 13 July 1764.

250 Wilmot faced numerous stressors. He realized his colony was defended by only "one Regiment consisting only of five hundred men, who are dispersed," while the number of Indigenous men capable of bearing arms exceeded six hundred fighting men. Even a small disaffected Mi'kmaw party, he held, could "carry terror and devastation through the country." LAC, CO 217/21, ff. 118–204, "Wilmot to the Lords of Trade and Plantations," 24 June 1764. The Board of Trade proved sympathetic as long as Wilmot did not spend much on gifts. The Indigenous people, they stressed, must gain the commodities they needed by means of their own industry. One missive Wilmot received from Lord Hillsborough, president of the Board of Trade, stated that expenses incurred in the "Indian service" were "properly the object of the provincial government." Though Hillsborough signed his letter "Your very loving friend," Wilmot felt that the odds against his functioning adequately in the "Indian service" were becoming overwhelming. LAC, CO 218/6/238–9, "Hillsborough to Wilmot," 24 June 1765; LAC, CO 218/6/224–7, 238–9, "Lords of Trade and Plantations to Wilmot," 24 June 1765.

251 Captain James Cook encountered a "Tribe of Mickmak Indians" in Bay St. George while conducting his survey of the southwest coast of Newfoundland in 1767, but he failed to find Mi'kmaw settlements or encampments between Burgeo and Bay St. George. LAC, CO 194/16/305–305v; British Public Records Office, London, England, Adm. 52/1263, 233, "Master's Log, *Grenville* 20 May 1767." Martijn states that Cook's 1768 map had a note inscribed across the northeastern interior that read,

"This river and Lake Mickmack are laid down by Cook from the authority of the Micmack Indians." A similar note is written on the 1770 chart of Newfoundland by Lieutenant William Parker. Ibid., 47–8. Palliser expected that Cook's charts would extend the range of the British fishery, since he ordered Cook in 1764 to record "likely harbours and beaches for the creation of new fishing rooms," especially in areas where the British encountered French rivalry. In 1765 he also ordered Cook to chart the coastline near Saint-Pierre and Miquelon in order to assist his squadron's patrols. Palliser obtained the admiralty's permission for Cook to publish his charts, and in August 1766 he reported that the British fishery in consequence was likely to expand quickly. William H. Whiteley, "Palliser, Sir Hugh," *Dictionary of Canadian Biography* online, vol. 4 (1771–1800).

252 Chief John Denny Jr., a descendant of Chief Thoma Deny, maintained a house on a point of land at Eskasoni. Richard Denny, who counts John Denny Jr. as one of his ancestors, and who still lives on Chief Denny's parcel of land, graciously showed the author where he had heard that Jeannot Peguidalouet's residence lay, on the coast of East Bay just eastward of John Denny Jr.'s property.

253 As district chief, Peguidaloulet had to ensure three things for his people. First, he was responsible for locating hunting, fishing, and trapping grounds for their subsistence and the continuation of their trade. Second, he had to establish linkages with various European agencies interested in preserving Mi'kmaw culture, as Maillard had in the past. It was necessary to seek out priests who could serve, if at all possible, as interpreters with colonial authorities and to preside over the sacraments. (Though Mi'kmaw leaders and catechists could perform necessary roles on St. Anne's day and at marriages, baptisms, and funerals, many Mi'kmaq wanted these baptisms and marriages later confirmed by a priest.) Third, he had to ensure that a system of ongoing structured relationships would be established with British colonial authorities. This was usually done through accepting British presents, with the Mi'kmaq responding that they would provide military assistance if needed. Mi'kmaw chiefs framed their willingness to serve the British in these terms well into the early twentieth century.

254 It took at least twenty persons to maintain a winter hunting group in the Northeast, and such a group needed a large tract to support it. In Newfoundland, where hunting and trapping continued to produce much of a family's annual income well into the twentieth century, Mi'kmaw hunting territories could be a thousand or more square miles in size (or over twenty-five

hundred square kilometres). At the height of the fur trade, at least fifty thousand square miles probably would have been needed to support the Mi'kmaw population. During the historic era the northeastern Mi'kmaq had to expand their lands in Newfoundland at various times. In 1640, after both moose and fur bearers were overhunted on Cape Breton Island, the Mi'kmaq left Cape Breton. Reuban Gold Thwaites, ed., *The Jesuit Relations and Allied Documents* (Cleveland: Burrows Brothers, 1888), 32.35. Another influx of Mi'kmaq into Newfoundland happened after 1760, when not only did the big game stocks in Cape Breton become depleted, but the only relatively accessible markets supplying guns, ammunition, and other needed goods were on Saint-Pierre and Miquelon, so groups travelled across the Cabot Strait. This ecological perspective shows why the Mi'kmaq were so adamant about encroachment on their nation's land base in the 1760s, for, in short, they needed occupation of a vast tract to survive. Martijn, "Early Mi'kmaq Presence," 52–6; Virginia Miller, "Aboriginal Micmac Population: A Review of the Evidence," *Ethnohistory* 21 (1976): 117–26.

255 John A. Reid, "Pax Brittanica or Pax Indignena? Planter Nova Scotia (1760–1782) and Competing Strategies of Pacification," *Canadian Historical Review* 85, no. 4 (2004): 669–92.

256 Murdoch, *History of Nova-Scotia*, 2.454.

257 The Mi'kmaq suffered greatly after Gridley set up his walrus-hunting station. Prior to 1758, licenced French merchants on the Magdalene Islands had not deprived the Mi'kmaq of their sea mammal hunting grounds. Martijn, "Early Mi'kmaq Presence," 80. In 1765, Samuel Holland was also surveying lots on Prince Edward Island according to instructions that within two years would allocate that entire colony to absentee landlords and leave no territory that the Mi'kmaq could call their own. Upton, *Micmacs and Colonists*, 113.

258 Patterson, *History of the County of Pictou*, 187. These house burnings continued for two years, during 1765 and 1766. The Mi'kmaq around Merigomish complained that the gardens they sowed with corn, potatoes, and wheat and fertilized with fish offal were being taken from them without any form of compensation, although a few settlers in the area eventually paid rent for the lands they occupied.

259 Meetings were held at Baie Verte, Pokemouche, Isle Madam and Saint-Pierre. LAC, CO 217, vol. 51, 171r-174r; LAC, CO 217/21/179–80, "Wilmot to the Board of Trade," 9 October 1765. According to Wilmot, Mi'kmaq came "from all parts to a place called Baie Verte to meet a French priest to celebrate marriages and baptisms and to receive absolution, the performance of which ceremonies they have been without for more than three years. They will always have recourse to a French priest on these occasions." Wilmot instead held that they needed a priest in which "the government may confide." They had become impatient "without the exercise of the religion which they had been promised…[and] any attempt to convert them by a Protestant missionary will not only prove unsuccessful but will greatly exasperate them, the consequences of which may prove very fatal to the settlements in this province while they are in their infancy."

260 Since the early seventeenth century France's royal standard had been a white flag, seen as a symbol of purity, and sometimes marked by fleurs-de-lis when flown in the presence of the king. It was also used as a symbol of military command by the commanding officer of a French army. It further could be featured on a white scarf attached to the regimental flag to distinguish French units from foreign ones, and thus avoid "friendly fire" incidents. During the American Revolutionary Wars years, French troops participating in this conflict fought under the white flag. French naval vessels also used the plain white ensign for ships of the line, while commercial and private ships were forbidden to fly the white ensign. The French flag bore no symbolic resemblance to the Mi'kmaw flag, which may have been designed later, though both had white fields. The white field of the Mi'kmaw flag denoted the extensiveness of *Mi'kma'ki*; the red cross set upon this field represented the church; and the star or sun symbol, *Wasoo*, near the figure of the new moon in the upper right-hand quadrant "designated the source of animating power in the universe" and signified the persistence of traditional Mi'kmaw beliefs concerning power and revitalization. Chute, "Ceremony, Social Revitalization and Change," 50.

261 General Thomas Gage, who oversaw the British response to Pontiac's resistance of 1763, noted two years later that "[t]he People employed in the Fisherys were terrified at these Appearances, but they [the Mi'kmaq] had done no Mischief." University of Michigan, Ann Arbor, William L. Clements Library, Thomas Gage Papers, vol. 5, "General Thomas Gage to Seymour Conway," 12 October 1765. By 1766 Peguidalouet had ceased to vacillate. His mind was made up: he would continue to support the British cause.

262 William L. Clements Library, Ann Arbor, Thomas Gage Papers, vol. 41, "Lieutenant-Colonel James Pringle, at Louisbourg, to General Thomas Gage, in New York," 18 August 1765. Peguidalouet and MacCormick evidently

were expected by others at the council to meet with British officials at Louisbourg and assuage any concerns they might have concerning the meetings. While disaffected Indigenous and Acadian men voiced threats, and there were several incidents of settler house burnings in Pictou country, Jeannot stressed that the troublemakers were in the minority.

263 Samuel J. Holland, *Holland's Description of Cape Breton Island and Other Documents*, ed. Daniel C. Harvey (Halifax: Public Archives of Nova Scotia, 1935), 39–41, including "Letter to [John] Pownall, Secretary of the Lord Commissioners for Trade and Plantations, dated 24 November, 1765." Holland suggested that the British should strike medals with the king's likeness and distribute them to chiefs to replace the French ones.

264 PANL GN/1A/3, fol. 343, "Pallister to Pringle," 22 October 1765. On 30 October 1765 Palliser proclaimed to the Board of Trade, "In my Dispatches to His Majesty's Secretary of State I have offer'd my Apprehensions of ye danger of permitting any Indians getting footing in this Country, as thereby the Fisherys will be in the same Precarious State as when the French and their Indians possess'd Placentia and the South Coast." LAC, CO 194/16/173–173v, "Pallister to the Board of Trade," 30 October 1765; British PRO, Admiralty Office (AADM) 50/19, Admiral's Journal, "Order from Pallister to Lieutenant Stanford," 16 August 1767; LAC, CO 194/27/320–1, "Palliser to Earl of Shelburne," 5 December 1767; LAC, CO 194/27B, 461–5 (transcription), "Palliser to the Earl of Shelburne," 15 December 1767.

265 LAC, CO 194/16/302v, "Palliser to the Board of Trade," 21 October 1766.

266 PANL, CO 194/27/144–144v, "Order and Pass, 22 October 1765." See also PANL, CO 194/27/132–35v, "Palliser to the Board of Trade," 30 October 1765.

267 Baron Charles-Gabriel-Sébastien de l'Espérance, who was posted on the French isles, noted that a shallop of Mi'kmaq arrived at Miquelon on 24 December 1765 asking for food and complaining about the treatment they had received from the English. Chief Peguidalouet undoubtedly was among their number. LAC, MG-1, série C-12, vol. 2, Correspondence générale Saint Pierre et Miquelon, ff. 22–22v, "Baron de l'Espérance au ministre," 28 April 1766. De l'Espérance came with his uncle, François-Gabriel d'Angeac, to Saint-Pierre in 1763 and succeded his uncle to the governorship of the French isles in 1773.

268 LAC, CO 194/16/308v, "Palliser to Francklin," 16 October 1766.

269 LAC, CO 194/16/302v, "Palliser to the Board of Trade," 21 October 1766. See also PANL, CO 194/27/ 257–264v,

"Palliser to Stephens, Secretary of the Admiralty," 25 August 1766. The large Mi'kmaw meeting on Isle Madam in the summer of 1765 caused Palliser to renew his drive to force the Mi'kmaq to quit Newfoundland altogether. Though he included the Mi'kmaq along with other British subjects in his proclamation that after the first day of November each year all British subjects had to leave the southwest coast, his deeper intention was to discourage the Cape Breton Mi'kmaq from travelling over to Newfoundland in the first place.

270 Francklin wrote Palliser asking him to employ his patrol vessels to prevent Mi'kmaw trade and intercourse with Saint-Pierre. LAC, CO 194/16/307–307v, "Francklin to Palliser," 11 September 1766. From 1767 onwards both Francklin and his immediate superior, Governor William Campbell, opposed the annual Mi'kmaw migrations to Saint-Pierre and Miquelon. LAC, CO 217/44/164v–165, "William Petty, Earl of Shelburne, to Governor William Campbell," 19 February 1767. If France and Britain went to war, owing to the continuous "encouragements given by St. Peter's and Miquelon" to the Mi'kmaq, "I make no doubt they would break with us," Francklin stated. LAC, CO 217/45/161–164v, "Francklin to the Earl of Hillsborough, regarding circular letter of 20 July 1768." By 1769 Governor Campbell also was concerned about the lack of military protection for outlying posts and the possibility that the Mi'kmaq might be aware of the settlers' defencelessness. He therefore recommended distributions of provisions and presents to reduce pockets of Mi'kmaq discontent. LAC, CO 217/46/24–6. Francklin became lieutenant governor in March 1766, but his mandamus did not reach Nova Scotia until 22 August. In September he became acting governor. Francklin also served as acting governor, in Campbell's absence, on three other occasions; from 1 October 1767 to 10 September 1768, 4 November to 4 December 1768, and 2 June to 10 July 1772.

271 James A. Macdonald, "Memoir of Lieut.-Governor Michael Francklin, 1752–1782," *Collections of the Nova Scotia Historical Society* 16 (Halifax, 1912), 9–10.

272 Francklin became influential among the Acadians. He allowed those who had returned following the expulsion to settle around Minas Basin and in the southwestern part of the province, as well as giving guarantees that there would not be a second deportation. He also permitted the practice of the Roman Catholic religion and, though "not specifically empowered under the Board of Trade to give these guarantees, he managed to convince the Board that these policies were wise, and they were eventually ratified by that body." L.R. Fisher, "Francklin

(Franklin), Michael," *Dictionary of Canadian Biography online*, vol. 4 (1771–1800).

273 LAC, CO 217/21/ 342, "Francklin to the Board of Trade," 3 September 1766.

274 Ibid.; LAC, CO 217/44/89, "Francklin to Lords of Trade," 13 September 1766; CO 217/45, fol. 272. Francklin at the time warned that a "small number of Indians could bring fire and destruction to the very entrance of the Dominion."

275 LAC, CO 217/22/4–5, "Francklin to the Board of Trade," 10 November 1766. Francklin later allocated a land grant in 1768 to the Malecite at Aukpaque along the Saint John River, a second grant in 1772 (reissued in 1779) to Paul Peminout at Stewiacke and, in association with Lord William Campbell, a licence of occupation in 1771 to the Cape Sable head chief, François Alexis.

276 LAC, CO 5/70, 14–45, "A description of the Island of Cape Breton," 1 November 1768. This report is published in Holland, *Holland's Description of Cape Breton Island*, 68. These families may have been kin to Bernard Googoo, who in the late 1760s lived at Whycocomagh. During the summers they camped on the "North West point of the Bay," and in winter moved all around the lake "for the Conveniency of Hunting." By 1768 they averred that Europeans had discovered "all their private Haunts." They also revered an elderly man who was deemed "upwards of one hundred & twenty years old, quite decripit with Age and Disease who resides constantly on the Island … [who] they say is the Eldest of their Tribe; & upon his Counsel & advice they set great Value." One wonders if this elderly man might have been a patriarch of the Googoo family. In addition to land matters, the Mi'kmaq told Holland of traders who made them drunk and took their goods at half their value.

277 Ibid. Chief Peguidalouet had left for Newfoundland by the time Holland and his surveying party turned up in the fall near Whycocomagh. About twenty individuals, just enough people to allow survival without hardship, had opted to remain on Cape Breton during the fall and late winter, all the others having departed for Newfoundland and possibly for lands between Canso and Antigonish.

278 On 20 July Francklin informed the Board of Trade that Abbé Bailly, the person whom he and Lord Campbell had recommended as a replacement for Maillard, had arrived from Quebec and was staying in Halifax with the Reverend John Breyton, the rector of St. Paul's Anglican Church. LAC, CO 217/25/165–6, "Francklin to the Board of Trade," 20 July 1768; LAC, CO 217/45/161–164v, "Francklin to the Earl of Hillsborough, regarding

circular letter of 20 July 1768." Bailly travelled throughout the mission field left vacant by Maillard's death in 1762. Upton, *Micmacs and Colonists*, 67–8. Montreal born, he was a tall, handsome man with an aristocratic demeanour. He left for Nova Scotia soon after his ordination to the priesthood by the Grand Séminaire de Québec in March 1767. When appointed vicar general of Nova Scotia "and parts adjacent" by Bishop Briand of Quebec, he initially entertained grandiose plans for a mission headquarters he would establish at Restigouche, and satellite missions on Cape Breton, Prince Edward Island, and the Magdalen Islands. This ebullient vision faded as he found himself for over a year living off the charity of the Mi'kmaq and Malecite, since the province failed to pay him his promised stipend of one hundred pounds per annum until 1769. He finally established his mission on the outskirts of Halifax and made itinerant visits to Indigenous and Acadian groups throughout the province.

279 The idea of a licencing system was raised as early as 1764 as part of a "Plan for the Future Management of Indian Affairs, 1764." The plan appears in *The Documentary History of the State of New York*, vol. 7, ed. E.B. O'Callaghan (Albany, 1850), 637. Francklin pressed for the dismantling of the licencing system because it was isolating to the Indigenous people to confine their trade to a few persons by licence. The Mi'kmaq and Malecite, he stated, have "nothing but the peltries to pay for what they want, and this becomes a service to the inhabitants and has a very great tendency to create an attachment, and even an affection." LAC, CO 217/45/164½, "Francklin to the Earl of Hillsborough," 20 July 1768.

280 NMM, Duff Papers, DUF 13, fol. 204, "Instructions to Governor Robert Duff," 1775. After being harassed by the Newfoundland government for many years, the Mi'kmaw people were mostly ignored. Bartels and Janzen, "Micmac Migration," 84.

281 Murdoch, *History of Nova-Scotia*, 2.454. The following year Lord Hillsborough warned Campbell that Francklin was overzealous in his spending on the Mi'kmaq and that "Governors are not allowed to incur any expense whatever with regard to the Indians." LAC, CO 217/46/38–39½, "Board of Trade to Campbell," March 1769.

282 The place name "Neireichak," "Neliksak," or "Neliksaak" derives from a Mi'kmaw word meaning "a camping ground' or "worn spit or shivered rocks." Fergusson, ed., *Place-Names and Places of Nova Scotia*, 18.

283 Besides Jeannot, these individuals were André Bernard, Jean-Baptiste Marc Antoine, Bernard Googoux

(Googoo), Gabriel Googoux, who probably was Bernard Googoo's son, and six other men, identified as Louis Jerome, Gregoire, François, Guillaume, Charles, and Sischao. One Mi'kmaw child went by the surname "Bonaventure."

284 Bailly's registers give some idea of the composition of the Cape Breton band at the time. On 7 August 1771 the missionary baptized Therese, the daughter of Charles and his wife Jeanne Emchikp; Pelagie, daughter of François (possibly François Googoo) and his wife Marianne; Anne-Marie, daughter of Paul Piect8 (Pictou?) and Angelique Guillaume; Suzanne, daughter of Gregoire and Marie Jean; Marie Madelaine, daughter of Thomas (possibly Michel Thoma Denny) and Marie Charles; Genevieve, daughter of Victor Arkit and Marie Anne, with Thomas as witness; Ursula, daughter of Jean-Baptiste Arkit and his wife Catherine; Marie Françoise, daughter of Jean-Baptiste and Catherine Pierre; and Marguerite, daughter of François and Marie. *Registre des actes de baptême, mariages, et sepultures fails en la nouvelle ecosse ou acadie commence le vingt unième jour de juillet de l'année mil sept cent soixante huit, par mons. Charles François Bailly, prêtre missionaire des sauvages et acadiens, sujets de sa majesté britannique, 79–80.* Since Louis Peguidalouet and Marie-Marthe's daughter was named "Rosalie," it is possible that Jeannot's granddaughter, Rosalie Googoo, who for many years kept the chief's 1751 French commission in a birchbark box, was named after her great aunt. Bailly spent 6 and 7 August 1771 confirming marriages and renewing marriage vows. Louis Jerome renewed vows with his wife Agathe, and Gabriel Googou did the same with his wife Marie Guillaume. Entries in Bailly's register confirm that the Peguidalouet and Googoo families were interconnected by numerous kin ties. Bailly conducted Louis Peguidalouet and Marie-Marthe Googoo's wedding, and Marie-Marie's father Bernard Googoo was a witness at Catherine Peguidalouet's baptismal ceremony. Jeannot's younger brother Louis and Jeannot's son Bernard both married Googoo women. Bailly promised he would marry Sischao's son, Charles-Michel Sischao, and Louis's daughter, Catherine-Charlotte Peguidalouet, later on his return journey to Halifax. After burying a two-year-old child named Cyriaque on 18 August, Bailly travelled northeast to the small *métis* and Acadian community of Petit Brador where he met with the community's leader, Boniface Benoit. He next visited L'indienne on the coast, where he met with members of the Bouché, Lejeune *dit* Briard, Galand, and Roy families, many of whom had fled from their fur trade and fishing communities on the Nova Scotia mainland at the time of the Acadian deportations. *Registre des actes de baptême, mariages, et sepultures … par mons. Charles François Bailly,* 89–90.

285 Claude Galarneau, "Bailly de Messein, Charles-François," *Dictionary of Canadian Biography* online, vol. 4 (1771–1800). By 1772 Bailly was teaching rhetoric and belles-lettres at Quebec's Petit Séminaire.

286 LAC, AC, C12 vol. 2, 22–22v, microfilm reel F-568, "Baron de L'Espérance à ministre," 28 April 1766. This source refers to the Mi'kmaw group, which may have included Chief Peguidalouet, who came to Miquelon in 1765 to complain about the treatment they had received from the English. In 1769 another shallop arrived with Mi'kmaq who enquired about the French king's health and assured the French authorities of their continued attachment to the French Crown. Additional visits by smaller family groups occurred in 1777 and 1778. Jean-Yves Ribault, "La population des îles Saint-Pierre et Miquelon de 1763 à 1793," *Revue française d'histoire d'outre-mer* 53, no. 190 (1966): 35. Nine years later, not long before the expulsion of the French from Saint-Pierre and Miquelon, seven members of a Mi'kmaw family came to Saint-Pierre to enquire about "la Santé du Roy de france leur Père." LAC, MG1-C12, vol. 5, fol. 5, "L'Espérance à ministre, 21 février 1778." Finally, during the summer of 1784, after the French had returned to the isles under the terms of the second Treaty of Paris, a Mi'kmaw group of eighty men, women, and children from Cape Breton went to Saint-Pierre, where fifteen expressed a desire to settle in the "Baye de Desespoir" (Baie d'Espoir) to be close to the French. The French "Baye de Desespoir" given in this document is a direct translation from the English "Bay of Despair," though the correct French place name is "Baie d'Espoir" or "Bay of Hope." LAC, MG 1-C12, vol. 8, fol. 28, "L'Espérance à ministre, 26 août 1784." The French nurtured such loyalty by distributing presents of guns, tobacco, hatchets, and provisions as well as sailcloth, which were all strong inducements to the Mi'kmaq to voice their fidelity to the French King. LAC, MG-1-C12, vol. 8, ff. 72v–73v, "L'Espérance à ministre, 20 août 1784."

287 Some historians argue that Mi'kmaq like Bernard Peguidalouet, who stayed in southwestern Newfoundland, had begun to exhibit a slightly different political cast from their parent group in Cape Breton. These scholars hold that the continuation after 1763 of a French-Mi'kmaw middle ground on the Islands of Saint-Pierre and Miquelon hastened the development of distinct political camps, with one camp willing to put down roots in Newfoundland, while others, who only visited

Newfoundland for short periods, "chose to remain in the former French colonies of Acadia and Île Royal." Morris, "Those Two Insignificant Islands," 14–15; Martijn, "Eastern Micmac Domain of Islands," 208–31. The French-Indigenous arena of diplomatic protocols in the Great Lakes area has been designated "the middle ground" by Richard White in his *The Middle Ground: Indians, Empires, and Republics in the Great Lakes Region, 1650–1815* (Cambridge: Cambridge University Press, 1991). While it cannot be disputed that bands in northeastern Nova Scotia, Cape Breton, and southwestern Newfoundland differed from groups living south of the Shubenacadie River owing to the former's distinctive ecological responses to the environment of the Gulf of St. Lawrence, one must be cautious in assuming a sharp political divide as early as the later 1760s between those who went to Newfoundland and those who chose to return to the Cape Breton mainland. One distinctive feature of all Mi'kmaw groups flanking the Gulf of St. Lawrence was their high degree of interaction with Acadian refugees. Wicken, "Encounters with Tall Sails and Tall Tales: Mi'kmaq Society, 1500–1760" (PhD diss., McGill University, 1994), 252.

288 Jeannot Peguidalouet's name does not appear in the Saint-Pierre and Miquelon registers.

289 Scipion de Castries, *Souvenirs maritimes* (Paris: Éditions Mercure de France, 1992), 303–4.

290 Rear Admiral Robert Duff, after being appointed governor of Newfoundland in 1775, learned that the French isles traded with New England in return for provisions and construction materials. LAC, MG1-C12, vol. 4, 88–9, "Governor Robert Duff to Baron de l'Espérance," 19 October 1775. Thomas Graves, a naval commander in Boston, reported the same year that Baron de l' Espérance also obtained armaments from New England. LAC, MG1-C12, vol. 4, 55–6, "Extrait de la lettre de Monsieur le Baron de l'Espérance et Beaudeduiet, 29 septembre 1775." Instructions from London, which allowed the French to cut wood in Newfoundland if they stopped trading with the rebels, reached Duff's successor as governor, Vice Admiral John Montagu, in March 1776. LAC, MG 11, CO 194/33/2v–3, "Instructions to Governor Montagu," 9 March 1776. Montagu's term in office coincided with the American Revolutionary War, during which time he assumed control of Saint-Pierre and Miquelon as well as defended Newfoundland from French and American privateers. He was succeeded as Newfoundland's governor in 1778 by Richard Edwards.

291 Abbé Jean-Baptiste-François Paradis and his Spiritan associates, abbés Julien-François Becquet and J.-J.

Bouguet, conducted sacraments with the Mi'kmaq after 1767, when graduates of the Séminaire du Saint-Esprit of Paris replaced the Jesuit fathers on Saint-Pierre and Miquelon. The Spiritans remained on the islands until ejected by the British in September 1778, during the American Revolution. On 20 April 1773 Bernard Pegidalouet and his wife brought their one-year-old daughter, Anne-Marie, to Miquelon to be baptized by Abbé Paradis. According to Paradis, Anne-Marie was born at "St. Michel" on 25 September 1772. (St. Michel was either a locale on the Bras d'Or Lake or a small French farming community by that name on the outskirts of Montreal, since the Mi'kmaq visited Montreal to trade and meet with priests. The French regime bestowed saints' names on many sites in Cape Breton, although most of these were not used by the British after 1763. For instance, Eskasoni stands on the shores of what was once called the "Baie de Saint-Louis," now East Bay, a place name Chief Pegui dalouet would have known well, although it does not appear on British maps after 1763. See, for instance, Cape Breton University, Sydney, Beaton Institute, "N. Bellin Map of L'Isle Royale," 1764, Map 707.) Anne-Marie was likely the youngest child of her parents, since one of Bernard and Marie Anne's sons, Gabriel, was born in 1743. Her godparents were Jerome Barthelemi and Marie Barthelemi, while Jacob Abamou, a Mi'kmaw catechist from Bay d'Espoir, acted as a witness at her baptism. Martijn notes that Paradis did not give Anne-Marie's father's surname, perhaps because Paradis had trouble spelling it, but simply registered her as the "daughter of Bernard." Martijn, "Mi'kmaq in the Parish Registers of Saint-Pierre and Miquelon," 27–8.

292 Bernard Peguidalouet's family also associated with Louis Googoo, a head man and catechist, as well as a prominent leader named Michel (Mitchell) Agathe, also known in British circles as "King Agathe." Chief Agathe travelled between the Bonne Bay and St. George's Bay. By contrast, Bernard and his family remained mainly in the Burgeo region, close to the French isles. The Googoos eventually moved to Conne River, where Louis Googoo became a head man in the St. George's Bay region. In 1794 Major Peregrine Fraser Thorne, the British commanding officer on Saint-Pierre just prior to the return of the island to the French, noted that Louis Googoo was the spokesman of two Mi'kmaw families of eleven persons who came to Saint-Pierre to have their children baptized by Abbé Jean Longueville. PANL, CO 194/41/81–81v, "Major Peregrine Fras. Thorne to the Right Hon. Henry Dundas," 26 May 1794. Louis Googoo was a Roman Catholic catechist, as was his brother,

Gabriel Googoo, since Gabriel administered conditional baptism to Jean-Baptist Pikeuaruel. (Jean-Baptist, born at Codroy on 1 January 1778, was the son of Gabriel Pikeuaruel and Marie Douject.) Confusingly, the certificate associated with Jean-Baptiste's conditional baptism identified Gabriel Googoo as a "Catholic Irishman named Gabriel Gugoo." Martijn, "Mi'kmaq in the Parish Registers of Saint-Pierre and Miquelon," 32–4, 39. Gabriel, however, was most certainly of Mi'kmaq origin. A "Gabriel Googoux," who may have been a son of Bernard Googoo of Cape Breton, was mentioned in Bally's registers in 1771 and may have been the same man as "Gabriel Gugoo." In the fall of 1822 William Epps Cormack helped himself to provisions in a cache erected by Emanuel Gontgont (Googoo), whom Cormack stated was a leading man of the St. George's Bay Mi'kmaw community. James P. Howley, *The Beothucks or Red Indians: The Aboriginal Inhabitants of Newfoundland* (Cambridge: Cambridge University Press, 1915), 159. The surname "Googoo" may derive from the Mi'kmaw word for barred owl (*Strix varia*), *ku'ku'wes*. (A shorter word, *kukwes* – most certainly not the origin of the Googoo surname – referred in Mi'kmaw folklore to a man-eating ogre.) St. George's Bay, Codroy, Burgeo, and Bonne Bay were all areas frequented by the Mi'kmaq by this time. By 1783 the Mi'kmaq had penetrated north to Port aux Choix, south into St. John's Bay, across to White Bear Bay, and inland to the headwaters of the Exploits River, where they came in contact with the Beothuk. These encounters were stressful for both parties, though instances of outright hostility seem fairly rare, and there are at least two instances where a Mi'kmaq man took a Beothuk woman as wife. Ingelborg Marshall, "Beothuk and Micmac: Re-examining Relationships," *Acadiensis* 17, no. 2 (1988): 52–82; Speck, *Beothuk and Micmac*, 56; Jackson, *On the Country*, 44.

293 "Mariage de François Doujet et Veronique Beguiddavalouet, 26 juillet 1778." Véronique, born in 1761, was baptized by Abbé Bonaventure at Miramichi, while Francois Doujet, born about 1752, was baptized at Port-La Joye, Prince Edward Island, by Abbé Jacques Girard. Bernard Beguiddavalouet (Peguidalouet), Gabriel Beguiddavalouet, and Janette's parents were witnesses at the marriage ceremony. Martijn, "Mi'kmaq in the Parish Registers of Saint-Pierre and Miquelon," 27–8, 29–30.

294 Martijn, "Mi'kmaq in the Parish Registers of Saint-Pierre and Miquelon," 33–4. In 1778 Abbé Paradis at Miquelon was suffering from the initial stages of dementia and wrote rambling entries in his registers, which nevertheless contained ethnohistorical information

omitted from the succinct entries of other clerics. (In 1786, following the French repopulation of Saint-Pierre and Miquelon, Paradis's mental state worsened and he was recalled to France.) Ibid., 27. Paradis performed one baptism and two marriages pertaining to Bernard Pequidalouet's family, which is significant considering that from 1764 to 1848 only twenty-five Mi'kmaw baptisms, six Mi'kmaw marriages, and eleven Mi'kmaw burials appear in the registers of Saint-Pierre and Miquelon. All of the Mi'kmaq originally came from Cape Breton or Prince Edward Island. The Pikteuaruel family of Codroy, headed by Gabriel Pikteuaruel and his wife Marie Doujet as well as Gabriel's brother Louis, were formerly "habitants de Louisbourg" and were related to the Peguidalouets through the Doujets. Ibid., 38–9. Louis, aged twenty-seven, was baptized by Maillard in Cape Breton around 1751. His bride Janette, a daughter of Guillaume Doujet and Marie-Magdeleine Pegilahadesclez, was baptized in 1758 by Abbé Pierre Cassiet at the "northeast parish of St. Louis" on Prince Edward Island. The witnesses to Louis and Janette's wedding were Pépin Richard *dit* Menouche, Paradis's interpreter; Pepin's brother George; and Pierre Gobersz. Bernard Peguidalouet and his sons Louis and Gabriel were part of the group of twenty-one Mi'kmaq observed landing at Miquelon by Baron de l'Espérance on 22 July 1778. They arrived close to St. Anne's Day, for the performance of their Eastertide duties. LAC, AC, MG-1, série C-12, Correspondence générale, Îles de Saint-Pierre et Miquelon, vol. 5, ff. 70–73v, microfilm reel F-560, "Baron de l'Espérance au minister, 22 juillet 1778." Googoos were also important to the social fabric of the Bay St. George population. The oldest member of the Googoo family in southwestern Newfoundland was André Googoo, who died shortly before 1786. André and his wife Anne Etiennehuit had a daughter named Anne-Marie Googoo who married Joseph Guillaume on Île de Saint-Pierre on 12 September 1785. (Joseph Guillaume was the son of Bernard Guillaume and Marie Poucecoupé.) Paradis travelled to Île de Miquelon to preside over Anne-Marie Googoo and Joseph Guillaume's marriage ceremony. (Anne-Marie Googoo died shortly following her marriage to Joseph, after which Joseph married Julienne Andress, who bore him a daughter Anne in 1786.) Anne-Marie Googoo's brother Louis was the husband of Marie-Marthe Guillaume, and Marie-Marthe was a sister of Joseph Guillaume, who wed Anne-Marie, another example of brother-sister exchanges, which were common among the Mi'kmaq. Both Louis and Anne-Marie Googoo were children of André Googoo. Louis Googoo and Marie-Marthe later became the parents of Rosalie Googoo who wed Julien Etiennehuit, a son of Grégoire Etiennehuit and Marie Mocoquenich, on Saint-Pierre on 6 September 1790. The officiating priest at Rosalie and Julien's wedding was Abbé Jean Longueville. Louis and Marie-Marthe also had a daughter, Julienne Googoo, born in 1787 and baptized on Île Saint Pierre on 8 September 1790. Julienne Andress, Joseph Guillaume's second wife, stood as witness at this baptismal ceremony.

295 Jean-Yves Ribault, *Les Iles Saint-Pierre et Miquelon* (Saint-Pierre: L'Imprimerie au Gouvernement Saint-Pierre, 1986), 320–31; Whitehead, *The Old Man Told Us*, 174.

296 The Treaty of Amity also promised American support for France in future French wars until 1800, though this part of the pact was annulled in 1793 by George Washington's pronouncement that the United States would remain neutral during the French Revolution. LAC, MG1-C12, CO 194/5/ 30–1, "Lloyd à de l'Espérance," 12 July 1778; William F. Rannie, *Saint-Pierre and Miquelon* (Beansville, ON: Rannie Publications, 1972), 36. LAC, CO 194/34/36–7, "John Evans to Montagu," 17 September 1778; T.A. Crowley, "L'Espérance, Charles-Gabriel-Sébastien de," *Dictionary of Canadian Biography* online, vol. 4 (1771–1800).

297 J.D. Rogers, *Historical Geography of the British Colonies – Newfoundland* (Oxford, 1911), 164; PANL, MG 482, B-3-1, microfilm reel E8, Newman Papers, "Little Bay Ledger, 1790–1791, Newman and Hunt Company, 1790." The Newman Company was headed by several generations of the Newman family from Devon who plied the Newfoundland fish trade. In 1735 their firm went by the name of the Hunt, Roope and Newman Company. In 1779, following the death of one of the partners, John Newman, the firm became Robert Newman and Company. The Newman's organization probably had little to do with the Mi'kmaq prior to the 1780s, when the Mi'kmaq of Newfoundland traded mainly with the French on St. Pierre and Miquelon. In December 1767 Pallister reported 175 Mi'kmaq at Bay D'Espoir trading with French merchants. LAC, CO 194/27, ff. 320–1, "Palliser to the Earl of Shelburne," 5 December 1767.

298 In late September 1776 a rebel privateer crew, commanded by John Paul Jones, pillaged John Robin's establishment on Isle Madame and the nearby community of Petit-de-Grat. This raid was followed by other privateer raids that damaged property and destroyed vessels.

299 In 1776, Francklin's political rival Francis Legge became Lord William Campbell's successor as governor of Nova Scotia and recommended to his cousin, the

Duke of Dartmouth, that Francklin be relieved of his office as lieutenant governor. Francklin, citing his trade relationship with the Indigenous people and his ability to speak Mi'kmaq and French, in 1777 applied for and obtained the position of Indian commissioner. Legge left the province in 1776, although he remained governor of Nova Scotia until 1782. Murdoch, *History of Nova-Scotia*, 2.571. On Legge's recommendation, Marriot Arbuthnot replaced Francklin as lieutenant governor in May 1776, with Francklin remaining as president of council. Arbuthnot was succeeded in turn in 1779 by Sir Richard Hughes. Ibid., 599; Macdonald, "Memoir of Lieut.-Governor Michael Francklin," 28–32. John Cunningham was commissioner of Indian affairs from 1769 to 1774, while Francklin served in the same capacity throughout most of the American Revolution. LAC, CO 217/45/5–5v, "John Cunningham to the Lords of Trade and Plantations," 14 December 1767. After Francklin's death in November 1782, Cunningham briefly resumed office as Indian commissioner, though his position was taken over in 1783 by George Henry Monk, who was superintendent of Indian affairs from 1783 to 1799 and again from 1807 to 1809.

300 While he was lieutenant governor, Francklin settled émigrés from Yorkshire as well as Acadians on some of his lands in Cumberland County. One parcel, known as "Francklin Manor," eventually became a Mi'kmaw reserve. See James S. Macdonald, "Memoir of Lieutenant-Governor Michael Francklin, 1752–1782," in *Collections of the Nova Scotia Historical Society*, no. 16 (Halifax: W. McNab and Son, 1912), 1–40.

301 On 16 January 1779, Lieutenant Governor Richard Hughes sent a copy of the Watertown Treaty, which was dated 19 July 1776, to Lord Germain, president of the Board of Trade. The pact was made only fifteen days after the signing of the Declaration of Independence. None of the Indigenous delegates whose names appeared on the document belonged to the Unama'ki district. Three Malecite chiefs – Ambrius Var (Ambroise St. Aubin), Newell Wallis, and Francis – and six Mi'kmaq leaders – Pierre André, John Battis, Charles, Joseph Denequara, Sabbattis Netcbcobroit, and Mattahui Ontane – agreed to recognize the United States as an independent nation and promised to send warriors to aid the rebels. LAC, CO 217/54, ff. 151–2, "Hughes to Germain," 16 January 1779; LAC, CO 217/54, fol. 153, "Treaty of Alliance and Friendship entered into and Concluded by and between the Governors of the State of Massachusetts Bay and the delegates of the St. John's and Micmack Tribes of Indians," 19 July 1776. The signing of this treaty had

a significant and enduring consequence. Because of the Treaty of Watertown, all Mi'kmaw citizens are allowed to join the United States armed forces regardless of their nation of birth. After becoming Indian superintendent, Francklin set out to counter the influence of the rebels. In 1779 Germain praised Francklin for hosting the Treaty of Fort Howe with Malecite from the Saint John River area and Mi'kmaq from Miramichi, Chignecto and Minas. LAC, CO 217/54, ff. 178–178v, "Germain to Francklin," 3 May 1779; Murdoch, *History of Nova-Scotia*, 2.597–9; Frederic Kidder, ed., *Military Operations in Eastern Maine and Nova Scotia during the American Revolution* (New York: John Munsell, 1867; repr., New York: Kraus, 1971), 193; Upton, *Micmac and Colonists*, 76. The chiefs Pierre Tomah and Francois Xavier, along with four Malecite captains and eight principal Malecite men, were delegates to the Fort Howe Treaty, while twelve Mi'kmaw leaders were present. Jean-Baptist Arimph acted on behalf of the Richibucto band and Charles Alexis represented the Cape Sable group, but there is no mention of Jeannot Peguidalouet.

302 Allan and his rebel associates were angered by Gueguen's change of heart and in reprisal "stole goods, money, and a schooner from him." Régis Brun, "Gueguen (Gouguen), Joseph," *Dictionary of Canadian Biography* online, vol. 6 (1821–35).

303 Captain Jonathan Eddy (1724–1804) and Colonel John Allan (1746–1805) both had associations with Cumberland County, Nova Scotia. Eddy was born in Norton, Massachusetts, but moved to Nova Scotia in 1763, where he became deputy provost marshal of Cumberland County. From 1770 to 1775 he served as Cumberland County's representative in the House of Assembly. After joining the rebel cause in 1776, he gained the support of a Malecite chief, Ambroise Saint Aubin, from Aukpaque on the Saint John River. In 1776 Eddy raised a small militia force of around eighty persons, which included four Mi'kmaq and fifteen Malecites, and, as mentioned, launched an unsuccessful attack on Fort Cumberland. The next year Eddy defended Machias, in present-day Maine, against the British. His younger friend and associate, John Allan, was born in Edinburgh Castle in Scotland and came to Nova Scotia with his parents in his youth. In his early years Allan traded with the Mi'kmaq. He later became a justice of the peace, a clerk of the Nova Scotia Supreme Court, and in 1775–76 a representative for Cumberland County in the House of Assembly. In January 1777 the Continental Congress directed him to establish a militia station at Machias and assume a commission as superintendent of the eastern Indians.

He commanded an expedition to the Saint John region in June and July of 1777, though the outcome of this venture was hardly more successful than Eddy's attempt to take Fort Cumberland the previous year. LAC, CO 217/53/38–41, "Extract of a Journal, the Proceedings of Fort Cumberland," 4 January 1777; LAC, CO 217/53/101, "Mario Arbuthnot regarding River St. John settlers having repented of assisting rebels about Fort Cumberland," 12 March 1777.

304 Francklin warned that the Treaty of Alliance had increased Indigenous regard for the French and Americans, but Francis McLean, the commanding officer at Halifax, disagreed. As far as he could see, McLean retorted, the Mi'kmaq appeared to be satisfied. LAC, CO 5/97/79, "Colonel McLean to General Henry Clinton, Commander-in-Chief of the Forces of British North America," 28 December 1778.

305 In 1779 a large gathering of Mi'kmaq occurred at Fraser's Point in Pictou, after which sixteen Mi'kmaw individuals, who had been involved in plundering Pictou inhabitants, were seized by a British warship and brought to Halifax. This incident incited a large gathering of Mi'kmaq in Pictou County, which nevertheless dispersed peaceably. Patterson, *History of the County of Pictou*, 106.

306 LAC, CO 217/54/206–7, "Francklin to Germain regarding having to send HMS *Viper* to [the Miramichi area] to capture 17 Mi'kmaq, 8 September 1779"; LAC, CO 217/54/219–26, "Francklin to Lords with articles of treaty between Chief John Julien [or Julian] and his captains and other representatives from Pokemouche, Miramichy, Restigouche, Richebucto and Shediac, 26 September 1779." Those who signed from Miramichi were Chief John Julien, First Captain Antoine Arneau, and Miramichi councillors Francis Julien (John Julien's brother) and Thomas Demagonishe, who stated their willingness to "ratify all former treaties." The Richibucto, Pokemouche, and Restigouche bands had authorized to act for them Chief Michel Augustin (or Augustine) of Richibucto, along with two Richibucto captains, Louis Augustine Cabaise (Caboche) and Francis Joseph Arimph, and two Richibucto councillors, Antoines (Antoine) and Guiaume (Guillaume) Gabelier. Thomas Tanas (Anathanse), "the son and representative of the chief of Jediac [Shediac]" also signed the treaty renewal. The only veteran of the 1760–61 treaty signings was Michel Augustin, who in 1761 had signed treaty with the British on behalf of the Richibucto band. In 1779 the British kept Jean-Baptiste Arimph, who earlier had signed the Treaty of Fort Howe, and Michel Arimph as hostages for

the good behaviour of the Richibucto band. Murdoch, *History of Nova-Scotia*, 2.601.

307 Upton, *Micmacs and Colonists*, 76. Francklin and James White, one of Francklin's deputies, distributed strings of wampum on 24 September 1778 to seal the alliance at Fort Howe. This is interesting, because Speck noted that strings of wampum were part of the archival assemblage kept in Cape Breton belonging to the Mi'kmaw Grand Council. Grand Chief John Denny Jr., however, argued that at least some of the wampum strings in the Grand Council's possession stemmed from either a peace with the Mohawk or meetings of the Eastern Wabanaki Confederacy. "Draft Manuscript of Micmac Field Notes," Frank Gouldsmith Speck Collection, Library of American Philosophical Society, Philadelphia. A microfilm copy of these field notes is housed in the library at St. Francis Xavier University, Antigonish. James White, the Indian commissioner who presided with Francklin over the treaty renewal negotiations at Fort Howe in 1778, is the maternal great-grandfather of the author. White spoke Mi'kmaq and Malecite. Both Francklin and White travelled to Indigenous communities in the central and northeastern parts of the province with Abbé Joseph Mathurin Bourg, a Spiritan born in Nova Scotia and educated in Quebec, whom Lieutenant-Governor Arbuthnot asked Bishop Briand to send to Halifax in 1778. Éloi Degrâce, "Bourg, Joseph-Mathurin," *Dictionary of Canadian Biography* online, vol. 4 (1771–1800). Bourg was engaged by the British government on a stipend of one hundred pounds per year, and in August of 1778 Francklin received one hundred pounds for presents from the executive council in Halifax. LAC, CO 217/84/142–5, "At a Council Holden at Halifax," 21 August 1778; LAC, CO 217/54/151, "Francklin to the Board of Trade," 16 January 1779. In the spring of 1778, a Malecite and Mi'kmaw delegation bypassed the "gift-poor" Francklin by journeying to Quebec to meet with Sir Guy Carleton, who distributed presents lavishly while advising the Indigenous leaders to remain quiet. LAC, CO 217/54/46–7, "Carleton to Arbuthnot," 23 February 1778.

308 Throughout 1778 and 1779 Francklin encouraged Jeannot and other chiefs to support the British cause, while riding herd over their indecisive or recalcitrant counterparts. At first, his efforts were rewarded with only small, unpredictable monetary allowances from Halifax. It was not until April 1779, when rumours of a possible French attack on Nova Scotia compelled an unnamed but influential resident of Halifax to press the Board of Trade to provide Francklin with more money, that Lord Germain, the secretary of state for the colonies, ordered the British Treasury to advance Francklin five hundred pounds for presents. At the time, Germain informed Francklin that as the Malecite and Mi'kmaq needed to be "neutralized … in anticipation of a French descent on Nova Scotia, … the operation of your dept. is of great importance, as you have given so strong a proof of your influence over them.' LAC, CO 217/54/178–178½, "Germain to Francklin, with promise to send £500 for purchase of presents," 5 May 1779; West Yorkshire Archives, Ramsden Family Papers, vol. 2, part 2, "John Wentworth to Lord Rockingham," 21 October 1778. The unnamed influential individual was described as a "judicious man, an officer, intimately acquainted thro'out the province, has all his estate in it." Bartels and Janzen, "Micmac Migration," 94n54. This substantial sum allocated by the Board of Trade soon was spent, however, and by the summer of 1779 Francklin was complaining that "[f]or want of proper funds I cannot hire anyone, can't get necessary victuals … from the King's stores [unless] contingent expenses could be defrayed out of the military monies and that the necessary provisions be supplied from the King's stores. Otherwise it will not be in my power to keep the Indians in any decent humor." LAC, CO 217/54/202–4, "Francklin to the Lords of Trade and Plantations," 3 August 1779. Francklin had to appeal to General Henry Clinton, the commander-in-chief of Britain's North American forces, and the London Board of Trade for money and presents, since the military commander at Halifax, Colonel Francis McLean, was hesitant to release either. Though the commissioner constantly cast about for additional sources of revenue, he met unsympathetic responses on every side. Despite the fact that Germain in 1779 had praised him highly for keeping the Indigenous community neutral, he rarely could count on goods he needed to accomplish his ends arriving on time. Late in 1780, he still was complaining that a shipment of presents, shipped via Newport, had not arrived. LAC, CO 217/54/ 71, "Francklin to Clinton," 2 August 1779; LAC, CO 5 230/88–9; Bartels and Janzen, "Micmac Migration," 85; Murdoch, *History of Nova-Scotia*, 2.611.

309 Francklin held that a good understanding had to be maintained with the Indigenous constituency for the sake of the Atlantic fishery. LAC, CO 217/54/202–3, "Francklin to the Lords of Trade and Plantations," August 1779; LAC, CO 5/230/88–9, "Francklin to Lord Hillsborough," 4 May 1780.

310 LAC, CO 219/54/237, "Germain to Francklin," 4 December 1779; LAC, CO 217/55/169, "Germain to Francklin," 7 July 1779. Germain had already written to General

Francis McLean on this subject. LAC, CO 217/55/ 44–5, "Germain to McLean," 5 July 1780; LAC, CO 217/55/169, "Germain to Francklin," 7 July 1780. Francklin was told that Parliament had not set up provisions for defraying expenses connected with his duties towards the Indigenous population other than his annual salary of three hundred pounds, news to which he responded with alarm. "I perceive," he wrote Germain, "that there will be no provision made for the Expenses of Indian Affairs in Nova Scotia, and the charges already incurred will meet with difficulty in payment … It will be an expense hard for me to suffer, when the expense had been unavoidable." LAC, CO 217/55/109–109v, "Francklin to the Board of Trade," 18 May 1780.

311   LAC, CO 217/54/202–4, "Francklin to Germain," 3 August 1779.

312   LAC, CO 217/54/225–6, "Francklin to Board of Trade, Expenses incurred from May 4 to September 4, 1779." The Mi'kmaq kept on cordial terms with British sailors. The following year, in 1780, a company of the 84th Regiment of Foot were shipwrecked off Cape Breton, and three families of Mi'kmaq supplied them with clothing and food and helped them get to Halifax. The ragtag soldier survivors promised their rescuers some golden guineas as a reward, though whether the Mi'kmaq received the money remains unknown. *The Naval Chronicle*, vol. 14, ed. James Stanier Clarke, Stephen Jones, and John Jones (London: I. Gold, July–December 1805), 40–3.

313   In the late summer of 1780 Francklin thanked General Haldimand, the governor and commanding officer at Quebec, for prevailing upon Indigenous leaders in Quebec to persuade Maritime groups from joining the rebels. London, British Library, Add. Ms. 21,809, fol. 101, "Francklin to Haldimand," 7 September 1780. While Jeannot did not sign any treaty during the American Revolutionary War, he may have participated in events behind the scenes, especially as the Miramichi, Pokemouche, and Shediac groups who did sign treaty represented the same bands on whose behalf Jeannot had spoken on 25 June 1761. Bartels and Janzen also contend that a study of the attitudes and activities of naval personnel towards the Mi'kmaq in Newfoundland during the late eighteenth and early nineteenth centuries might provide new insights into what occurred in both Cape Breton and St. George's Bay during the American Revolution. Bartels and Janzen, "Micmac Migration," 87.

314   Francklin wrote to Lord Germain on 21 November 1780 reflecting on the fact that things were peaceful compared to 27 June 1779, when three hundred warriors, as well as women and children, congregated along the Saint John River with representatives of the Ottawa, Huron, Algonkin, and Abenaki nations. At that time he feared that Indigenous parties might go to Machias, where he knew they would receive gifts, including wampum belts and medals, as well as have access to the services of a Roman Catholic priest. He added he was nine hundred pounds in debt on account of supplies and gifts he supplied to the Mi'kmaq people to keep them allied to Britain. Murdoch, *History of Nova-Scotia*, 2.610–11.

315   Since evidence of the St. George's Bay land allocation stems wholly from Mi'kmaw oral tradition, it is open to dispute, yet it hard to believe that a promise or bestowal of land did not occur in the last years of the American Revolution, as the timing and circumstances of the allotment are so similar to those surrounding the 1779 Paul Peminout grant. Peminout, of Stewiacke, Nova Scotia, appealed to Francklin in spring 1779 for a land grant similar to one given to the Malecite in 1767. NSARM, RG 1, vol. 189, 454–5, "Minutes of the Executive Council," 28 June 1779; NSARM, RG 1, vol. 212, 363, "Official transcript regarding Peminout grant"; NSARM, Miscellaneous "I" Indian Land Records, Documents photocopied in the 1970s under the auspices of Charles Bruce Fergusson, provincial archivist, "Memo. Regarding a tract of land four miles square ordered to be granted to Mr. Francklin and Paul Pemmeyweete on the Stewiac River," 28 January 1779. In 1767 Francklin approved a grant of 704 acres to the Malecite of Aukpaque. Not properly registered the first time, this grant was reissued in 1779. NSARM, Land Grants, Old Book 12, 106–7. Other land allocations promised to chiefs around 1779 include one at the Head of St. Margaret's Bay to Chief Philip Bernard and a second to Francis Alexis at Eel Brook in Yarmouth County. Although Francklin appears to have promised land to a number of chiefs, his promises left a poor paper trail, if any at all. Some may have been allocated during a state of emergency or in the heat of expediency. The grant he accorded Jeannot Peguidalouet in southwestern Newfoundland was not even his to give, since Newfoundland, being a separate colony from Nova Scotia, lay outside of his jurisdiction. Bartels and Janzen, "Micmac Migration," 85.

316   Macdonald, "Memoir of Lieut.-Governor Michael Francklin," 40.

317   Edward Chappell, *Voyage of Her Majesty's Ship Rosamund to Newfoundland and the Southern Coast of Labrador* (London: J. Mawman, 1818), 76–8; Speck, *Beothuk and Micmac*, 124–5. The observation that Jeannot may

have been regarded as an enforcer by the British appears first in Bartels and Janzen, "Micmac Migration," 84.

318 Chappell, *Voyage of Her Majesty's Ship*, 76–8.

319 Bartels and Janzen, "Micmac Migration," 85. Following the close of the American Revolution, settlers entered Cape Breton in numbers and by 1787 had indiscriminately slaughtered a record number of moose, so the Mi'kmaq had sound reasons for emigrating to Newfoundland. Julian Gwyn, "The Mi'kmaq, Poor Settlers, and the Nova Scotia Fur Trade, 1783–1853," *Journal of the Canadian Historical Association* 14, no. 1 (2003): 74.

320 Martijn, "Eastern Micmac Domain of Islands," 224; Martijn, "Early Mi'kmaq Presence," 85. "Old Tomma," in his late thirties in the mid-1780s, was hardly "old" in chronological years, so the designation "old' given him in the documentary record likely reflected the respect he commanded within his group.

321 LAC, MG 23, vol. 4, Monk Papers, 1034, "Report to Governor Parr," 1783.

322 Ibid.

323 NSARM, RG 1, vol. 430, doc. 23½, "License of occupation to Emable Janot to lands on St. David's Bay," 18 December 1783. Monk did not furnish any reasons why the Cape Breton band numbered only twenty families by December.

324 De Castries referred to Jeannot's interpreter only by his first name, "Louis." Scipion de Castries, *Souvenirs maritimes*, 303–5; Martijn, "Early Mi'kmaq Presence," 83n33, 85. The arrangement made between Jeannot and De Castries, however, did not take Mi'kmaw hunting practices adequately into consideration. When the French failed to pick up the wood until the late fall, the Mi'kmaq were reluctant to stay and guard the stacks, as they wished to move inland to their hunting grounds.

325 According to Baron de l' Espérance, a group of eighty individuals of all ages and both sexes visited Miquelon for three weeks. Twelve men and three women of this company left for Saint-Pierre where they received gifts, though the others, owing to rumours circulating of a smallpox outbreak on Saint-Pierre, were afraid to cross over from Miquelon. Most stated that they were heading for Bay d'Espoir, where they intended to settle. The presents given on Saint-Pierre in 1784 were drawn from the King's Stores and cost forty livres. They included eighteen old guns, one hundred gunflints, one hundred pounds of powder, two hundred pounds of shot, ten quarts of flour each of which weighed 180 pounds, butter, molasses, fresh bread, one hundred pounds of leaf tobacco, six small hatchets, lengths of cord and canvass for sails and rigging, and pitch, nails, and compasses.

The French proved prescient about distinctive Mi'kmaw needs since certain items were indispensable to shallop owners. LAC, microfilm reel F-571, AC, Série C-12, Correspondance générale Saint-Pierre et Miquelon, vol. 8, fol. 73, "Etat des vivres et autres effects du Magasin du Roi livrès aux Sauvages à titre d'hospitalité par order de M. le baron de l'Espérance, Gouverneur des isles St. Pierre et Miquelon," 16 August 1784; LAC, microfilm reel F-571, AC, Série C-12, Correspondance générale Saint-Pierre et Miquelon, vol. 8 ff. 72v–73, doc. 54, "Lettre du baron de l' Espérance et Malherbe au minister, 26 aôut 1784."

326 While not all of the Mi'kmaq Jeannot encouraged in 1783 to go to Newfoundland remained in that colony, many families who earlier occupied the southwestern and south coasts remained and formed permanent settlements. The efforts of Palliser and Francklin to stop migrations of Mi'kmaq to Newfoundland accomplished absolutely nothing, especially as Jeannot Peguidalouet was determined to reap the benefits for his people on both sides of the Cabot Strait. Despite the fact that even in the late 1780s some British authorities still wished the Mi'kmaq gone, the number of Newfoundland Mi'kmaw encampment sites and settlements continued to spread as population increased, with numerous intermarriages taking place between the colony's Indigenous and non-Indigenous inhabitants. By 1787 the Mi'kmaq occupied a number of small communities, from St. George's Bay north to Port au Choix, and from Burgeo south around the coast to Ferole and St. John's Bay. British Ministry of Defence, Whitehall, London, Hydrographic Department Records, Misc. Papers, Ab3k, vol.34, 568–570, "Log of HMS *Echo*, maintained by Lieut Robert Carthew Reynolds," 1787; LAC, CO 194/38/54, "Report of Native and Foreign Indians...who visited parts of the French shore," by Lt Robert Carthew Reynolds of HMS Sloop *Echo*, 1787; LAC, CO 194/21, vol. 1, fol. 172, "Captain Reynolds to Governor John Elliot enclosing Report of Native and Foreign Indians," 1788. In 1797, Ambrose Crofton, captain of *HMS Pluto*, held that the Mi'kmaq at St. George's Bay annually travelled overland with their furs to Fortune Bay, where they received "Powder, Shot and Blanketing, in lieu of their Furs." Crofton added that the "great part of them...removed from Cape Britton [*sic*, Breton] in consequence of being informed that Deer [caribou] was more abundant in Newfoundland." Most of them remained "near to their Harbour during the Winter, to eel fish that are found in Flat Bay near St. George's Harbour, and all along the South Shore from Cape Anguille." PANL, CO 194/40/19–20, "Ambrose

Crofton, *HMS Pluto*, to Vice-Admiral William Walde-
grave," 10 January 1798.

327 No stone or other memorial marks the spot where Jeannot is buried.

328 The word order of Michel Thoma Denny Sr.'s name is
often reversed to read "Thoma Michael." NSARM, RG 1,
vol. 320, 35–7, "Minutes of the Cape Breton Council," 9
September 1794 (regarding Denis Michel's involvement
with the mission church).

329 Samuel Holland suggested years before that if Cape
Breton were to become an independent of Nova Scotia,
its shipbuilding industry would grow. Cape Breton remained a colony separate from Nova Scotia from 1784 to
1820. William MacCarmick, who assumed office in 1787,
was the colony's second lieutenant governor. The first
lieutenant governor was Joseph Frederick Wallet Des-
Barres, who interacted little with the Mi'kmaq.

330 According to the executive council minutes for Cape
Breton Island for 28 November 1792, "Francis Bask
[Basque], Tomma Michael [Michel Thoma Denny Jr,]
and others of the Native Indians of the Island of Cape
Breton" acquired permission from Lieutenant Governor MacCarmick "to take possession of the Island de
Saint Villemai [*sic*, Île de Saint Famille], situate and lying and being in the Bras dor Lake near to the Portage
at Mount Grenville, for the purpose of erecting thereon
a Chappel [*sic*, chapel] to be used and appropriated for
performing Divine Service agreeable to the rites and
ceremonies of the Roman Catholic Religion, to hold,
occupy and possess the same during His Majesty's
Pleasure." University of Cape Breton, Sydney, Beaton
Institute, Copies of Cape Breton Executive Council
Records on microfilm, Cape Breton B series, Minutes
of the Executive Council of Cape Breton, 1785–92,
182–5, "At a Council held at Government House, Island
of Cape Breton the 28th of November 1792." A later
reference to this event can be found in NSARM, MG
100, vol. 184, Scrap Book no. 2, 4, "Undated clipping
from *Boston Herald* about Chapel Island being granted
to 2 chiefs, Bask and Tomma, in 1792." Peguidalouet did
not have the opportunity to have the chapel restored,
although it probably remained a goal close to his heart.
During his later years, no Roman Catholic cleric was
availed to serve the Mi'kmaq, so the chief himself presided over services in a makeshift chapel erected on
the ruins of Maillard's old mission on Île de St. Famille.
Abbé Lejamtel assumed responsibility for the St. Anne's
mission in 1792, around two years after Jeannot's death.
Until 1814, Lejamtel was the only Catholic cleric serving in Cape Breton.

331 A member of the Cape Breton executive council noted,
"One Louis Christoph[e] who seemed to be a principal
Person amongst them said that he was a Native Indian
of Cape Breton – that he left the island Ten Years ago
that two Years since his Father died on this Island – that
he is now returned in Company with Nine Families
consisting of Sixty persons, Seventeen of whom are
Men grown that they have brought with them some Dry
fish, Furs and Feathers to sell that it is their intention to
become residents on this Island [Cape Breton] and they
pray for such assistance as the Governor may be pleased
to grant them to enable them to begin their Hunting.
He farther says that they are descended from the Native
Indians of this Island, that their place of residence in
Newfoundland was the Bay St. George – And that there
are ten other Families relations of the Indians of this Island intending to come here next Spring." NSARM, RG
1, vol. 320, 35–7, "Minutes of the Cape Breton Council,
A.C. Dod to David Matthews," 9 September 1794. Michel
Thoma Denny Sr. had sent one of his sons, Joseph
Denny, to Newfoundland to persuade Louis Christopher
and eight other family heads to return to Cape Breton.
When these Mi'kmaq camped near Sydney, the lieutenant governor and the inhabitants of the town caused a
watch and ward to be set up, since Christopher had been
in contact with officials on Saint-Pierre and Miquelon.
Not all British administrators, however, were as fearful
of the Newfoundland Mi'kmaw as Lieutenant Governor
MacCarmick. Peregrine Fraser Thorne, who was governor of the French isles from 19 November 1793 to 15
September 1749, after the British captured the isles from
the French in May 1793, was interested in the Mi'kmaq.
He estimated that around 150 Mi'kmaq resided at Conne
River (Miaqpukek), where they fished eels. Members
of this community had traded furs at Saint-Pierre for
many years. LAC, CO 194/43/261–4, "Major P.H. Thorne
to John Sullivan, with enclosure," 25 June 1793. Thorne
also met an "old Englishman named Dennis" among the
Mi'kmaq who stated that he had lived on Newfoundland
for 80 years and claimed to be 104 years old. Dennis may
have self-identified as "English" for diplomatic reasons,
however, since he was born in 1689 and was probably
originally French or *métis*. He may even have been one
of Jean (Denys) Michau's sons. LAC, CO 194/41/80–81v,
"Governor Percy Thorne to Secretary of State Henry
Dundas," 26 May 1794. The British regime on Saint-
Pierre and Miquelon in the 1790s did not last long, since
a French force led by Rear Admiral Joseph de Richery
forced the British to abandon the isles. Michel Thoma
Denny Sr. and Louis Christopher tried to alleviate

British fears. Christopher spoke English, and in 1791 his name was recorded in the ledgers of a British trading establishment at Bay d'Espoir in Newfoundland. Nine other persons – Jacob Abamou, Joseph Andress, Michael Argimault, William Bernard, Bernard Googoo, Julien Gregoire, John Helie, Michael Martin, and Jean-Baptiste Sekaquet – were with Christopher in 1791. PANL, Newman Papers, Newman Little Bay Ledgers, 1790–91 (on microfilm), "Mi'kmaw Hunters of Bay Despoir Region Listed in Newman Little Bay Ledgers (1790–91)." After 1794, Louis Christopher and his family settled permanently in Cape Breton. In 1852 members of the Christopher family were present at St. Anne's Day celebrations at Île de St. Famille. NSARM, RG 15, vol. 3, doc. 64, "An Account of the Indians within the County of Richmond Bras d'Or Lake being the Anniversary of Saint Ann's day," 26 July 1852.

332 This may have been in the Antigonish area in 1783 when Monk was trying to find out sufficient information about Mi'kmaw land use to draft a licence of occupation for the Antigonish Mi'kmaq.

333 LAC, MG 23, G II-19, Monk Papers, 1067–71. Monk jotted down in his journal: "he says he is nephew to old Gennet but says he does not know what his uncle's other name was – he says his Father and Uncle are both dead – that he has no wife or child but has the care of an aged mother – that he has two Brothers who have large Families – he has been hunting most of the Season in the depth of the woods back of the eastern settlements from Canso towards Antigonish."

334 Monk asked if any "Mohawks" had been seen, to which Francis replied that there had been a Mohawk man around the preceding year, "but he had not seen him." ("Mohawk" was a word often used interchangeably with "spy."). The commissioner then peppered him with questions concerning the location and numbers of Mi'kmaq throughout the province, "to all which he was realy [*sic*, really] or affected to be much a stranger." LAC, MG 23, G II-19, Monk Papers, 1069.

335 This brief comment confirmed that Francis was on his way to the council at Gaspereau Lake, though Monk learned little from his Mi'kmaw visitor about the council's nature or purpose.

336 A family of nine, composed of "Emable Jenet," three women, and five children, visited Joseph Davis's merchant establishment for provisions on 26 November 1796. LAC, MG 23, GII-19, Monk Papers, Indian Accounts 1793–99, 1196, "Entry for 26 November 1796."

337 NSARM, RG 1, vol. 445, no. 33, "A Return of Indians in the County of Sydney, the 24th day of October 1817."

The 1817 document listed Captain John Marble, John Marble Sr., Michael Marble, and Thomas Marble. The Antigonish band at this time numbered 112 persons. The Marble family remained in the Antigonish area well into the twentieth century. Vernon Cope, who helped immeasurably with this essay, stated that in the late nineteenth century his grandfather, Frank Cope, wed Susan Marble of Antigonish. Susan Marble was the mother of Noel Cope. NSARM, Historical Vital Statistics, Halifax County Marriages, Registration Year 1937, Book 85, 396, "Marriage of Noel Cope, son of Frank Cope [a son in turn of Joseph Charles Cope] and Susan Marble of Antigonish, to Hazel Syminson [or Gorman]."

338 Church registers dating from 1820 to around 1850 and maintained by Father Francis Vincent and his clerical successors are housed at Holy Cross Church (Église Ste.-Croix) at Pomquet, Antigonish County, Nova Scotia. Vincent had responsibility for the parishes of Tracadie, Havre au Boucher, and Pomquette (now Pomquet in Antigonish County). His early register entries were examined by the author during summer 2003 courtesy of Father Peter Baccadax. In 1897, a land dispute broke out between the Mi'kmaq and settlers from the nearby community of Heatherton in which Peter Marble, Peter Lewis, and Chief Joseph Salome played prominent roles. Salome had taken over from Lewis as chief, who in turn succeeded Peter Battiste. (The first chief of the Pomquet settlement was Jean-Battiste Bouta, Peter Battiste's father, and descendants of Peter Battiste moved to Cape Breton.) LAC, microfilm reel C-11165, RG 10, vol. 2134, file 27–046–1.

339 Abbé François-Charles Bailly's register of 1778 lists female children in Cape Breton who have the surname "Amable' or "Petit Jean," both names used by Jeannot. These were Anne Petit Jean, Annese Petit Jean, Catherine Petit Jean, and Louise Amable. At the same time, Jeannot's brother Louis had two daughters, Catherine-Charlotte and Rosalie. Bailly, *Registre des actes de baptême, marriages, et sepultures … par mons. Charles François Bailly*, 89–90. Descendants of Jeannot's son Bernard Peguidalouet eventually took the surname "Bernard." Julien William Bernard, Andrew Bernard, and Francis Bernard, in company with Jean Mitchell Agathe and Louis and Francis Googoo, traded during the 1840s at Bonne Bay. Memorial University of Newfoundland, St. John's, Maritime History Archives, vol. 69, microfilm reel 108, "T. Street Bird & J. Bird Account Letter Books, Bird Manuscript Collection, Bonne Bay Ledgers, 1839–1844."

340 It is not known whether Rosalie was a Googoo by birth or whether "Googoo" was her married name. Mi'kmaw

women still went by their maiden names in the late nineteenth century, even if they were married and fluent in English. Louis Peguidalouet, Jeannot's brother, had a daughter Rosalie, and perhaps Rosalie Googoo from Eskasoni was named after her great aunt.

341 Bourinot, "The Island of Cape Breton," 351–2. Rosalie also told Bourinot that she had shown the commission to a French admiral who was visiting Sydney, who had given her a handful of louis d'or, French francs, and a few small presents. She shared these with others in her encampment, who spent them on "finery and feasts." Rosalie's encounter with the generous French admiral would have occurred prior to 1870, the year Bourinot published his article. Several French naval officers came to Sydney in the nineteenth century. In 1884 a French frigate named the *Flor* visited Sydney with an admiral aboard at the time of the Canadian Nile expedition. Roy MacLaren, *Canadians on the Nile, 1882–1898* (Vancouver: University of British Columbia Press, 2011), 66.

342 Author and army officer Narcisse-Henri-Édouard Faucher de Saint-Maurice saw Jeannot's chief's commission in the late 1880s at the Legislative Library in Halifax. Faucher de Saint-Maurice, *En route sept jours*, 51. In 1910 the Capuchin abbot Father Pacifique de Valigny, for many years associated with the mission of Saint-Anne-de-Restigouche mission in Quebec, viewed the same commission in Cape Breton. It was accompanied by Jeannot's commission as first captain dated 8 November 1750. Both documents were in the possession of the grand chief, John Denny Jr. of Eskasoni. NSM, Printed Matter File, genealogy 8-A-B, politics, "Father Pacifique, Capuchin Order, *Monastère des Frères-Mineurs Capuchin près Montreal*, to Harry Piers," 16 December 1932.

343 By raising Denis Michau's son in his own household, Peguidalouet became viewed as an integral part of the Thoma-Denny line. He also may have had affinal ties with the Michau family.

344 *The Cape-Bretonian*, Sydney, "Demise of a Native Sovereign and Consequent Interregnum," 25 January 1834. An article that appeared three days later revealed that Michel Denny Thoma Sr. had left "insignia of office," although not commissions, in the care of his son-in-law, Francis Gregoire. On St. Anne's Day 1834, the Unama'ki council installed Michel Thoma Denny Jr. as grand chief. At the same time, Christmas Thoma Deny was selected as grand captain, Matthew Morris and John Googoo became first captains, Julian Basque became second captain, and Francis Gregoire was appointed third captain. *The Cape Bretonian*, "The Indians and Their King," 28 January 1834 (repr., *The Colonial Patriot*, Pictou, NS,

18 February 1834; *The Hants and Kings County Gazette*, Windsor, NS, 10 March 1834. Grand chiefs were not elected by vote prior to 1918, and succession did not always follow unilineal principles, although sons of former grand chiefs often were favoured. A candidate had to "be worthy to become chief; otherwise, some other male in the same family group would receive the title." Peter Joseph Christmas, *Wejkwapniaq* (Sydney: Micmac Association of Cultural Studies, 1977), 4.

345 The same contentions were stated in a Mi'kmaw petition drafted in 1883. NSARM, RG 2, vol. 9, doc. 1820, "Petition of Christopher Paul, Stephen Hood and 59 others to Lieutenant Governor Adams George Archibald," 29 March 1883; Speck, *Beothuk and Micmac*, 108. The memorial read, "[A]bout one hundred and thirty four years ago," at the time of the founding of Halifax in 1749, the grand chieftainship was placed "in the family of Denas [Denny or Dennis] and it has continued to descend from father to son, following the blood until the present time – one John Denas [*sic*, Denny] being now the regular chief – he being a resident of the County of Cape Breton." Chief John Denny Sr. was grand chief from 1881 to 1918. He lived at Eskasoni, on the tract Jeannot obtained from Monk in 1783. "Eskasoni" or "Escasoni" derives from the Mi'kmaw word *We'kwistoqnik*, which means "where the fir trees are plentiful." When the Eskasoni tract was first surveyed in 1832 and confirmed as a reserve in 1834, only a few scattered families, including the family of Michel Thoma Denny Sr., lived on it.

346 Taqamkuk Saqama'q (Chiefs of Newfoundland), http://oocities.org/pilip/saqamaq.htm.

347 Frank Powell echoes a suggestion first raised by Charles Martijn, that Denis Michau's son raised by Jeannot later married in Newfoundland and that one of his sons may have been "King Agathe" (Michel or Mitchell Agathe). "Who Was Mattie Mitchell?" https://www.vcn.bc.ca/~fgp/who.htm. Another view holds that the boy raised by Jeannot may have been Michel Thoma Denny Sr., who in his younger years may very well have married in Newfoundland and had children, among them a son named Mitchell Agathe. Agathe may have been the patriarch of the Mitchell family of Unama'ki, particularly in Newfoundland, although Mitchells also lived in Prince Edward Island. In 1885, John Denny Jr. aided Louis Mitchell in resisting settler trespasses at Indian Cove, near Stratford, Prince Edward Island. LAC, RG 10, vol. 2104, file 18,903, "Grand Chief John Denny in Charlottetown complaining of encroachment made by whites on lands of the Micmac Indians at Indian Cove, Prince Edward Island," 5 March 1885. (Today Stratford

and Charlottetown are joined by the Hillsborough River Bridge.) One intriguing hypothesis, which deserves greater attention, is that the Mi'kmaw Mitchell family of Newfoundland and the Mi'kmaw Mitchell family of Prince Edward Island were consanguinally related. For information on the Newfoundland leader Mattie Mitchell, see Wikipedia, "Mattie Mitchell," https://en.wikipedia.org/wiki/Mattie_Mitchell. Mattie Mitchell is recognized as the discoverer of the lode that led to the opening of the Buchans Mine. J. Geoffrey Thurlow, "Great Mining Camps of Canada 3: The History and Geology of the Buchans Mine, Newfoundland and Labrador," https://journals.lib.unb.ca/index.php/gc/article/view/18540/20101.

348 Morrison, "People of the Dawn," 40–2; Speck, "Eastern Algonkian Wabanaki Confederacy," 492–508. The seven socio-political districts were distinctly Mi'kmaq. The system bore no resemblance to the twelve districts set up in 1808 for the administration of Indian Affairs in Nova Scotia, nor a later administrative scheme incorporating seven districts proposed by Joseph Howe in 1871. LAC, CO 188/82/196–205, "George Monk to His Excellency Sir George Prevost," 23 April 1808; LAC, RG 10, vol. 459, 380–2, "Joseph Howe to Samuel P. Fairbanks," 19 May 1871. To function within the broader context of the Northeast, each chief maintained a corporate memory of events happening within his district and intervened in disputes on a number of subjects. In 1847 Abraham Gesner, Nova Scotia's Indian commissioner, noted that "Grand Chiefs" (here meaning district chiefs) adopted measures "to prevent collision in hunting and fishing." Gesner, quoted in Wallis and Wallis, *Micmac Indians of Eastern Canada*, 223. Moses Perley, New Brunswick's Indian commissioner, in 1848 further claimed that after the fall of Quebec "whole districts of the country were assigned to the Indians, and treaties were made by which the English settlers were restricted to certain bounds." LAC, CO/188/104/383–8, "By authority of Indian Affairs in New Brunswick, Supplemental Report of M.H. Perley," 3 April 1848; Janet Chute, "Frank G. Speck's Contributions to the Understanding of Mi'kmaq Land Use, Leadership, and Land Management," *Ethnohistory* 46, no. 3 (1999): 514–15. Though the Eastern Wabanaki Confederacy continued to function in the early 1800s, it became less effective with time. Instead, the Mi'kmaq convened councils like the one held at Gaspereau Lake in 1794.

349 Jackson, *On the Country*, 120. Over the next sixty years, the Mi'kmaq of southwestern Newfoundland, who had intermarried with the southern Innu, separated from the rest of Unama'ki to form a distinct political constituency. They no longer sent representatives to councils held on the island of Cape Breton. In 1973 the settlement at Conne River was officially recognized as an Aboriginal community under a federal-provincial joint agreement, and in 1987 became the Samiaji Miawpukek First Nation of Conne River. The jurisdiction of the Qalipu Mi'kmaq First Nation of Newfoundland was created by order-in-council in 2011. Owing to considerable intermarriage with European settlers over the years, it has grown to become the second-largest First Nation in Canada (without even counting the over one hundred thousand applicants who still want to join the group). Joe Friesen, "Surge in Newfoundland Native Band Has Ottawa Stunned, Skeptical," *Globe and Mail*, 14 April 2014, https://www.theglobeandmail.com/news/politics/ottawa-moves-to-tighten-aboriginal-membership-criteria/article17954032/. Jeannot doubtless would have been pleased by the long-range success of his Mi'kmaw emigration policy.

350 It may have been Jeannot who adopted rituals belonging to the *Say'ewedkik*, or "Ancients," within the grand council forum, since in the late nineteenth-century the festival of St. Anne incorporated "the *wigubaltimk* and *neskouwadijik*, the feast and mystic dance of the *sajawachkik* [*Say'ewedkik*]." Helen Webster, "The Manners, Customs, Language, and Literature of the Micmac Indians," in *Legends of the Micmacs*, by Silus Tertius Rand (New York: Longmans, Green, 1896), xxx–xlvi. The chief who danced the *neskouwadijik* to welcome noted guests to St. Anne's Day ceremonies was said to be impervious to projectiles or musket balls shot at him. "Such traditions underscored the fact that the presiding chief ought to be respected and his *neskawe* or song of welcome be taken in good faith." Chute, "Ceremony, Social Revitalization and Change," 51.

351 Jeannot on this occasion may have been on his way to Whycocomagh or Malagawatch. Pacifique, "Le Pays des Micmacs: Cap Breton," *Bulletin de la Société de géographie de Québec* 27, no. 1 (1933): 48. There is also a second Campbell's Cove located near Red Islands.

352 Martijn, "Early Mi'kmaq Presence," 91n28.

353 NSARM, vol. 165, doc. 162 "Treaty of Peace and Friendship concluded by the Honourable Jonathan Belcher," 25 June 1761.

CHAPTER 27

1 Thoma Denny's surname also appears as "Denis" and "Denys."

2 This French *brevet de commission* no longer exits.

3 The rank of grand chief was not contingent on French recognition, but almost certainly arose in the context of the wholly Indigenous-devised Eastern Wabanaki Confederacy. The French, however, sought to embellish the office by making it integral to gift distributions and St. Anne's Day ceremonies on Cape Breton Island. Frank Gouldsmith Speck, *Beothuk and Micmac*, ed. F.W. Hodge (New York: Museum of the American Indian/Heye Foundation, 1922), 111; Washington, DC, American Philosophical Society, Speck Papers, unpublished notes on Mi'kmaq of Cape Breton, 1914 (there are copies of these on microfilm at St. Francis Xavier University in Antigonish); NSARM, RG 2, vol. 9, 1815, "To His Honor the Honorable Adams George Archibald, C.M.G., Lieutenant Governor of Nova Scotia, from Jacob Brooks and others," 5 February 1888; NSARM, RG 2, vol. 9, 1820, "To His Honor the Honorable Adams G. Archibald, C.M.G., Lieutenant Governor of Nova Scotia, from Christopher Paul and 60 others," 29 March 1888. Grand Chief John Denny Jr.'s supporters at Shubenacadie held that he was a direct descendant of Thoma Denny, who became grand chief of the Mi'kmaq in 1749.

4 No documentary evidence has been found that confirms this story.

5 *The Cape Bretonian*, 28 January 1834, "The Indians and Their King"; reprinted in Pictou in *The Colonial Patriot*, 18 February 1834, and in Windsor in the *Hants and Kings County Gazette*, 10 March 1834.

6 Ibid.

7 Speck, *Beothuk and Micmac*, 111–12.

8 It is possible that Denis (or Denny) Michaud's full name was "Thomas (or Thoma) Denny Michaud."

9 It is possible that Thoma Denny was the elderly chief whom Samuel Holland heard about when he was surveying around Whycocomagh on Cape Breton Island, although the old man was more likely a patriarch of the Googoo family. Holland wrote in 1768 that the Mi'kmaq revered an elderly man who was deemed "upwards of one hundred & twenty years old, quite decripit [*sic*, decrepit] with Age and Disease who resides constantly on the Island … [who] they say is the Eldest of their Tribe; & upon his Counsel & advice they set great Value." LAC, CO 5/70, 14–45, "A description of the Island of Cape Breton," 1 November 1768. This report is published in Holland, *Holland's Description of Cape Breton Island and Other Documents*, ed. Daniel C. Harvey, Publication no. 2 (Halifax: Public Archives of Nova Scotia, 1935), 68.

10 Frank G. Speck, "The Eastern Algonkian Wabanaki Confederacy," *American Anthropologist* 17 (1915): 492–508.

11 John Webster, ed., *Life of Thomas Pichon* (Halifax, 1937), 84, letter no. 28, "Chief Alkimou at (Gaspereau, Nova Scotia) to Captain Hussey," 19 January 1755.

12 Before 1750 Maillard's endeavours focused mainly on the Cape Breton Mi'kmaq, but near the end of the Seven Years' War he, with the permission of the British authorities, moved his mission headquarters to Halifax.

13 One can imagine Maillard, prior to the ceremony, wending his way on foot uphill from his mission station – a barnlike structure located at what is now the base of Tobin Street – to the Governor's Farm where the treaty was to be signed. NSARM, RG 1, vol. 37, no. 14, "Ceremonials at Concluding a Peace with several Districts of the General Mickmack Nation of Indians in His Majesty's Province of Nova Scotia and a Copy of the Treaty, 25 June 1761"; Abraham Gesner, *New Brunswick with Notes for Emigrants* (London: Simmonds and Ward, 1847), 46–7. Historian L.S.F. Upton simply relates that the "Chief of the Cape Breton Indians gave the speech," since the chief's name is not mentioned in the documentary record. Upton, *Micmac and Colonists: Indian-White Relations in the Maritimes, 1713–1867* (Vancouver: University of British Columbia Press, 1979), 57. The offices of the Cape Breton district chief and the grand chief of the Mi'kmaw nation became one around 1745.

14 Chief Jeannot Peguidalouet was a devoted follower of Abbé Maillard. In the author's view he, rather than Thoma Denny, was probably the one who joined the missionary in Halifax and spoke so eloquently at the Governor's Farm in 1761. Marie Ann Battiste, "A History of the Grand Council to 1800," typescript, report #10 MRC 98-10-364, Mi'kmaq Resource Centre, Cape Breton University. At least one other source confidently proclaims he was the chief who signed treaty in 1761. See Wikipedia, "Burying the Hatchet ceremony (Nova Scotia)," https://en.wikipedia.org/wiki/Burying_the_Hatchet_ceremony_(Nova_Scotia), accessed 18 February 2023.

15 Olive Patricia Dickason, *Louisbourg and the Indians: A Study in Imperial Race Relations, 1713–1760* (Ottawa: Government of Canada, 1976), 114.

CHAPTER 28

1 Michel's surname also is written "Denis," "Denys," and "Tomma." As Thoma Denny, Michel's father, was likely

the Chief Denis Michaud who died in 1751, Michel Denny Sr. would have been only four years old when his father died.

2 *Poteleg* derives from the way the Mi'kmaq pronounced the French place name "Port Toulouse."

3 *Wagmatcook* translates as "clean wave" and refers to the waters of the Wagmatcook River, also known as Middle River.

4 *Waycobah* or *We'koqma'q* means "head of the waters."

5 The Mi'kmaw place name *Malikewe'jk* may mean "the place of Mary [*Mali*]," since Malagawatch was the site of a Christian mission before Abbé Maillard moved the Mi'kmaq under the leadership of Jeannot Peguidaoulet to Chapel Island in 1751.

6 There also was acreage accorded the Benoit family at the Cut of Little Bras d'Or, but it was not included in the reserve lands. NSARM, RG 20, series B, vol. 3 (Cape Breton Land Papers, 1810), no. 550, "Report by H. Crawley, Superintendent of Surveys, on Benwa's [or Benoit's] grant of 140 acres at the Cut of Little Bras d'Or, 1810"; no. 563; "Petition of Francis Coogu [Googoo] and two other families at Margaree to Brigadier General Napean, President of the Council and Commander in Chief, 1810"; NSARM, RG 20, Cape Breton Land Books, 1835, book 9, 205.

7 R. Montgomery Martin, *A History of Nova Scotia, Cape Breton, Sable Island, New Brunswick, Prince Edward Island, the Bermudas, Newfoundland etc.* (London: Whittaker, 1837), 100.

8 LAC, MG 23 GII-19 (George Henry Monk, Indian Commissioner), Letterbook 1783–97, 1034; NSARM, RG 1, vol. 430, doc. 23½, "License of Occupation to Amable Jannot and 31 families, St. David's Bay," 18 December 1783.

9 *Cibou* means "inlet" in the Mi'kmaw language.

10 NSARM, RG 1, vol. 320, Minutes of the Executive Council of the Island of Cape Breton, from 10 April 1794 to 9 August 1798, 35–7, "Minutes of the Executive Council for 9th September 1794."

11 University of Cape Breton, Beaton Institute, Executive Council Records, Cape Breton "B" series, Minutes of the Executive Council of Cape Breton, 1785–92 (on microfilm), 182–5, "At a Council held the Government House, Island of Cape Breton the 28th of November 1792."

12 NSARM, RG1, vol. 430, doc. 163, "Petition of Michel Tomma, Christmas Tomma and others to His Majesty the King," 20 November 1827. Chief Peguidalouet had obtained a licence of occupation to a tract on East Bay in 1783, but the government made no attempts to prevent settler trespass on this land.

13 Sir James Kempt was lieutenant governor of Nova Scotia from 1820 to 1828.

14 NSARM, Newspapers, "Demise of a Native Sovereign and Consequent Interregnum," *The Cape-Bretonian*, 25 January 1834.

15 Ibid.

16 In 1671 Colonel Thomas Blood made an unsuccessful attempt to steal the British Crown jewels from the Tower of London.

17 Ibid.

18 NSARM, Newspapers "The Indians and Their King," *The Cape-Bretonian*, 28 January 1834.

CHAPTER 29

1 Frank Gouldsmith Speck, *Beothuk and Micmac*, ed. F.W. Hodge (New York: Museum of the American Indian/Heye Foundation, 1922), 111; Speck, "The Eastern Algonkian Wabanaki Confederacy," *American Anthropologist* 17 (1945): 492–508. Michael Thoma Denny's name appears in the documentary record as "Michel Denis," "Michel Deny," "Michel Dinney," and "Michel Thoma Deny."

2 He likely was installed as grand chief in 1835, as a year usually elapsed between the death of a grand chief and the appointment of a chiefly successor.

3 NSARM, RG1, vol. 431, doc. 36, "Trespassers at Wagamatcook, from Rupert D George, Provincial Secretary," 1837; Ottawa, Indian Affairs, documents pertaining to the Whycocomagh reserve, 1868–1976, file B8260-104, copies housed at NSARM.

4 NSARM, RG 15, vol. 3, no. 64, "A nominal census of the Mi'kmaw attendees at St. Ann's in 1841," attached to "An Account of the Indians of the County of Richmond as taken on the 26th July 1841, at the Indian Chapel Bras d'or Lake, being the Anniversary of Saint Ann's Day."

5 NSARM, RG 5, Series P, vol. 43, no. 100, Petition No. 233, "Petition of [Grand Chief Michel] Dinney and Others to the House of Representatives," 13 March 1841.

6 NSARM, RG 15, vol. 3, no. 64, "An Account of the Indians of the County of Richmond as taken on the 26th July 1841, at the Indian Chapel Bras d'or Lake, being the Anniversary of Saint Ann's Day."

7 NSARM, J104 K3 1842, Nova Scotia, *Journal of the Assembly*, 7 March 1842, 308

8 NSARM, RG 5, misc. B, Series P, vol. 44, no. 4, "Petition of J. Courteau, Indian Missionary," 8 January 1842.

9 NSARM, MG 15, vol. 49, no. 101, "Denny Michael, Chief of the Mic Mack Indians, to the Honourable Joseph Howe," 1851.

10 Speck, *Beothuk and Micmac*, 111.

11 See, for early interactions, the church registers of Father de Vincent Paul, dating to 1820, Holy Cross Parish, Pomquet, Antigonish County.

12 NSARM, MG 15, vol. 3, doc. 65, "Petition from Michel Denny on behalf of Peter Battiste of Pomquet," 6 October 1851.

13 NSARM, Biog.: William Walsh, microfilm reel 3, vol. 2 (207-h), "Petition of Denis, Chief of the Indians of the Bras d'or," 4 October 1851.

14 Richard Denny, "Grand Chief John Denny Jr.," *Micmac Maliseet Nations News* (September 1997), 20. Richard Denny contends that Michel Thomas Denny Jr. died in 1852 at age ninety. But if he was seventy-three in July 1841, as one census states, he would have been born in 1768 and been eighty-four years old at his death. And if he was eighty-six in 1851, as he himself stated in his petition to Bishop Walsh, he would have been eighty-seven when he died.

CHAPTER 30

1 NSARM, MG 15, vol. 4a, "Regarding the election of Francis Thoma," 12 January 1853.

2 Oral traditions regarding these petitions remain, but the actual documents have been lost.

3 *Waycobah* or *We'koqma'q* is Mi'kmaq for what is now Whycocomagh. The Mi'kmaw name means "head of the waters."

4 Harold F. McGee, "White Encroachments on Micmac Reserve Lands, 1836–1867," *Man in the Northeast* 8 (1974): 154–67; L.F.S. Upton, *Micmacs and Colonists: Indian-White Relations in the Maritimes, 1713–1867* (Vancouver: University of British Columbia Press, 1979), chap. 6, "The Micmacs and the Government: Nova Scotia"; NSARM, Miscellaneous "I" Indian Lands Records, from the Crown Lands Office, on microfilm, Whycocomagh.

5 NSARM, RG 1, vol. 430, doc. 158, "Petition of ten Mi'kmaw families at Whycocomagh for 2,000 acres," 5 November 1821.

6 NSARM, MG 15, vol. 4, doc. 87, "Peter Gougou *et al.* to H.W. Crawley," 17 November 1850.

7 LAC, RG 10, vol. 460, folder 19, "Chief Googoo *et al.* to Crawley," 24 January 1851.

8 NSARM, RG 5, Petitions, Series P, vol. 15, no. 9, "Petition of Chief Peter Googoo and others at Whycocomagh regarding settlers taking over their lands," 1 February 1855.

9 NSARM, RG 5, Series P, vol. 15, no. 47, "To the House of Assembly, Petition of Undersigned Inhabitants of Whycocomagh regarding lands granted to Indians, signed by L.M. McDougall, J.P., J. McLeod, J.P., Samuel Beaton, J.P., and 73 others," 16 April 1857.

10 Upton, *Micmac and Colonists*, 95–6.

11 "New Indian Chief, Gabriel Sylliboy of Whycocomagh, in Micmac and English," in *Setaneoei*, or *Micmac Messenger* (September 1918), ed. Father Pacifique, Rimouski, Quebec.

12 Lillian Marshall, a well-known Elder and historian residing at *Potlotek*, remarked: "[T]he rock is still there. I remember when it had an engraving and the name of the Grand Chief Francis Thoma Denny and the year engraved on it. There was also a cross imbedded in the rock … I don't remember what was written on it." When the cross came loose, it was secured with cement, which "covered the engraving." Information courtesy of Lillian Marshall, 18 February 2017.

13 L. Marshall and L.C. Boudreau, "St. Ann's Day Mission, Chapel Island, featuring an interview with Grand Captain Noel Marshall held in July 1983, with information on the ceremonies in 1923 provided by Clews Parsons and Sarah Denny," *Cape Breton's Magazine*, no. 40 (August 1983), 36. The rock recovered by Grand Chief Francis Thoma Denny in 1857 was not the same boulder on which Abbé Maillard delivered his first mass on Chapel Island. This statement contravenes another story, that the English force which razed the Chapel Island mission in 1758, seeing a boulder with cross surmounted on it which had been used in Roman Catholic rites, hurled the stone into the water, after which Grand Chief Denny in 1857 retrieved the rock and restored it to its rightful place.

14 Nova Scotia, *Journal of the House of Assembly*, 1860, "Appendix – Indians," 322–8, including Grand Chief Francis Thoma Denny's petition, "To His Excellency the Lieutenant Governor and Commander-in-Chief of the Province of Nova Scotia, signed by Francis Thomas [Francis Thoma Denny], witness J. Couteau, P.P.," 29 July 1859.

15 NSARM, J104 K3, Nova Scotia, *Journal of the House of Assembly*, 1860, Appendix "Petition of Indians of Cape Breton," 1860, 323.

16 NSARM, vol. 431, doc. 135, "Petition of Francis Thoma *et al.*," 1862; Nova Scotia, *Journal of the House of Assembly*, 1862, Appendix No. 30, "Report of Committee on Indian Affairs," 3–5; Nova Scotia, *Journal of the House of Assembly*, 1863, Appendix No. 16, "Indian Affairs"; NSARM, RG 5, series P, vol. 8, no.167, "Petition regarding Middle River," 1864.

17 NSARM, RG 5, Series P, vol. 18, no. 167, "To the Honourable House of Assembly of her Majesty's Province of Nova Scotia in Parliament Assembled, 9 March 1864, a petition signed on behalf of Chief Francis Thoma by Paul Christmas, Paul Andrew and Michael Christmas, to be directed to the House of Assembly by Bishop Colin F. Mackinnon, Bishop of Arichat, Cape Breton."

18 NSARM, RG 5, Series GP, vol. 9 [roads], no. 67, "Petition of the Grand Chief and Mi'kmaq of Chapel Island for Better Roads and Bridges to their Chapel, with signatures," 1865; NSARM, RG 1, vol. 431, doc, 142, "Petition of Lewis Joe and others, Chapel Island," 1865.

19 Silus Tertius Rand, *Legends of the Micmacs* (New York: Longmans, Green, 1894), 244. There were twelve strangers feared to be "spies" on Chapel Island in 1869.

CHAPTER 31

1 Elizabeth Marshall was a daughter of Charles Marchal, now pronounced "Mar-shall." Lillian Marshall, a historian and educator from Chapel Island, wrote the author on 4 April 2017 that "Grand Chief John Denny Sr's wife was actually a Marshall … she was the daughter of my great-grandfather, Charles Marchal. (That's the old spelling of the surname)." "Marchal" is a French surname, though its origin is Germanic and means "a steward who care for horses" (from Old High German: *marah*, "horse" and *scalc*, "servant").

2 Richard Denny, "John Denny Jr.," *Micmac-Maliseet Nations News*, September 1997, 20; *Micmac Hymnal*, Mi'kmaw Association of Cultural Studies (MACS), Sydney, NS, 1983.

3 At the tercentenary celebration of the baptism of Membertou held at the mission of Ste. Anne de Restigouche in Quebec in 1910, Grand Chief Denny addressed representatives of the Mi'kmaw nation, among them leaders from Pictou in Nova Scotia, Lennox Island on Prince Edward Island, and Big Cove in New Brunswick. At the time a story was circulating that Mohawk from Quebec might get hold of some physical measurements that anthropologists Wilson D. Wallis and Ruth Sawtell Wallis had taken of Malecite persons from New Brunswick. By means of witchcraft, these Mohawk were said to be able to make statutes of Eastern Abenaki persons that could assist them in sweeping down and exterminating the Micmac. Denny, in response, made a speech in which he stated that these stories could only have been invented by *Gjimento*, the Big Liar, and that the Mi'kmaq must not let such rumours disturb their minds. Wallis and

Wallis, *The Micmac Indians of Eastern Canada* (Minneapolis: University of Minnesota Press, 1955), 190, 208–9. By stating this, Chief Denny was following the lead of one of his predecessor chiefs, Thoma, who prevented young men from taking up guns to seek out *owwiscooks* (Mohawk spies), rumoured to have come to Cape Breton Island to harass the Mi'kmaq at their St. Anne's Day festivities. Silus Tertius Rand, *Legends of the Micmac* (New York: Longmans, Green, 1894), 244.

4 NSARM, RG 5, Series GP, vol. 9 (roads), no. 67, "Petition of John Denny and others to the Lieutenant-Governor for assistance to build a better road, a bridge and a dock at Chapel Island, with signatures," 1865.

5 Under John Denny Sr. it became Grand Council policy that Mi'kmaw lands should be preserved secure from threats of government expropriation. Denny had encouraged Andrew Paul to work with the Shubenacadie district chief, Jacques-Pierre Peminout Paul, on land matters as early as 1860.

6 Silus Tertius Rand, *A First Reading Book in the Micmac Language* (Halifax: Nova Scotia Printing Company, 1875), 81.

7 For Rand's work among the Mi'kmaq see Judith Fingard, "Rand, Silus Tertius," *Dictionary of Canadian Biography* online, vol. 11 (1881–90).

8 George Patterson, *History of the County of Pictou* (Montreal: Dawson Brothers, 1877), 26. Other scholars who later developed an interest, undoubtedly piqued in part by Rand's and Patterson's mentions of Mi'kmaw districts in the late nineteenth century, were Harry Piers, a curator at the Nova Scotia Museum of Natural History, and Père Pacifique at Restigouche. Piers, "Brief Account of the Micmac Indians of Nova Scotia and Their Remains," *Transactions of the Nova Scotia Institute of Science* 13, no. 2 (1911–12): 104; Père Pacifique, "Les Pays des Micmacs – the Micmac County," *Bulletin de la société de géographie de Québec* 28, nos. 1–2 (1934)" 177. Though Piers in the early twentieth century relied on John Denny Jr. to explain Grand Council matters, in the nineteenth century initial releases of information to scholars and other interested non-Indigenous parties on the subject of the Grand Council and the seven Mi'kmaw districts owed much to the activities of John Denny Jr.'s father, John Denny Sr.

9 St. Francis Xavier University Library, Antigonish, Frank G. Speck Papers, on microfilm, "Handwritten Micmac Notes, Hunting Territories of Cape Breton." There also was a traditional hunting territory belonging to the Denny-Thoma family extending "from East Bay to Sydney River." Speck, *Beothuk and Micmac*, ed F.W. Hodge

(New York: Museum of the American Indian/Heye Foundation, 1922), 111.

10 Department of the Interior, *Report of the Deputy Superintendent General of Indian Affairs* (Ottawa: Department of the Interior, 1877), 12.

CHAPTER 32

1 John Denny's surname also appears as "Denas," "Denis," "Dennis," "Dennys," "Denys," and "Dinney."

2 Leslie Jane McMillan, "'*Mi'kma.wey Mawio'mi*': Changing Roles of the Mi'kmaq Grand Council from the Early Twentieth Century to the Present" (master's thesis, Dalhousie University, 1996).

3 Frank Gouldsmith Speck, *Beothuk and Micmac*, ed. F.W. Hodge (New York: Museum of the American Indian/Heye Foundation, 1922), 111. Denny recruited Speck to look into the distribution of family hunting territories among the Mi'kmaq in order to further his own land and resource campaigns.

4 Richard Denny, "Grand Chief John Denny Jr.," *Micmac Maliseet Nations News* (September 1997), 20. On becoming grand chief, John Denny Jr. followed his father's and grandfather's lead by cultivating relationships with representatives of the Roman Catholic Church. See, for example, NSM, Harry Piers Papers, "Letter from James Morrison, Bishop of Antigonish, to Chief John Denys, Grand Chief of the Micmac Indians at Eskasoni," 5 November 1912. John Denny Jr. regularly corresponded with members of the clergy. This was a tradition begun by Grand Chief Michel Thoma Denny, who had been on good terms with Trappist Father Vincent de Paul and Father Christian Kauder. Kauder, who had become disenchanted with the Redemptorist faith, joined the Trappist monastery at Tracadie, Antigonish County, for a few years before moving his missionary headquarters to Merigomish in Pictou County. John Denny Jr.'s uncle Francis Thoma Denny may have assisted Christian Kauder with his translations of religious tracts into hieroglyphic script, though Kauder apparently worked more closely with Jacques Prosper at *Paq'tnkek*, near the Acadian village of Pomquet, Nova Scotia. For an analysis of the role of Roman Catholic missionaries among the Mi'kmaq into the 1860s, see Carlo J. Krieger, "Ethnogenesis or Cultural Interference? Catholic Missionaries and the Micmac," *Proceedings of the Twentieth Algonquian Conference*, ed. William Cowan (Ottawa: Carleton University, 1989), 193–200; and Nicholas N. Smith, "Politics and Western Religion Shape the Wabanaki World,"

Papers of the Forty-First Algonquian Conference, 2009, ed. Karl S. Hele and J. Randolph Valentine (Albany: University of New York Press, 2013), 280–99.

5 *Micmac Hymnal*, Micmac Association of Cultural Studies (MACS), Sydney, NS, 1983, 48.

6 Bernie Francis and John Hewson, eds., "Introduction," in *The Mi'kmaw Grammar of Father Pacifique*, translated, edited, and updated by Bernie Francis and John Hewson (Sydney: University of Cape Breton Press, 2012).

7 *Micmac Hymnal*, 48.

8 Maillard attended Les Missions étrangères de Paris and soon after his graduation arrived in Louisbourg, Cape Breton, in the summer of 1735. The hieroglyphic script he developed had its origin in Mi'kmaw prototypical hieroglyphic forms. As early as 1670, Chrestien LeClercq, a Recollect priest at Miramichi, organized the Mi'kmaw prototypes into a script, but it appears Maillard developed his hieroglyphic writing system independently of LeClercq's earlier work.

9 Janet E. Chute, "Frank G. Speck's Contributions to the Understanding of Mi'kmaq Land Use, Leadership and Land Management," *Ethnohistory* 46 (3): 480–540; Chute, "Ceremony, Social Revitalization and Change: Micmac Leadership and the Annual Festival of St. Anne," *Papers of the Twenty-Third Algonquian Conference*, ed. William Cowan (Ottawa: Carleton University Press, 1992): 45–61.

10 "Gabriel Sylliboy Becomes Grand Chief, 1918," *Cape Breton's Magazine*, no. 71 (1996), 63–7, in Mi'kmaq and English with an introduction by Helen Sylliboy and David L. Schmidt.

11 Nine years after his installation as grand chief, Denny was also formally recognized by Ottawa on 7 August 1890 as head chief of the Cape Breton Mi'kmaq. Though under the provisions of the 1880 Indian Act chiefs were to serve for a term of only three years, annual Department of Indian Affairs' reports described Denny's office as being of "indefinite" duration." Ottawa, *Report of the Deputy Superintendent General of Indian Affairs* (Canada: Department of Indian Affairs, 1899), https://library-archives.canada.ca/eng/collection/research-help/indigenous-heritage/Pages/indian-affairs-annual-reports.aspx.

12 John Noel was born in Pictou County to Lewis and Mary Noel. Following his father's death, his mother married Chief Jacques-Pierre Peminout Paul, who adopted Noel as his son, though Noel retained his biological father's surname. The marriage was Peminout Paul's second; he was first married to a woman named

Sally by whom he had at least three sons and a daughter. Despite his having sons by his first marriage, in a society where sons of a high-ranking chief often succeeded to their father's status, in 1895 Jon Noel became Paul's only successor to the office of Shubenacadie head chief. Ruth Holmes Whitehead, "Peminuit Paul, Jacques-Pierre," *Dictionary of Canadian Biography* online, vol. 12 (1891–1900). John Noel valued his attachment to the Peminout Pauls highly. Jacques-Pierre Peminout Paul was installed as Shubenacadie grand chief in 1856 at a ceremony conducted by William Walsh at St. Mary's Basilica in Halifax. Noel also associated himself with the legacy of his adoptive grandfather, Louis-Benjamin Peminout Paul, who in 1814 was given a commission by Lieutenant Governor Sir John Coape Sherbrooke designating him "Chief of the Micmac Tribe of Indians [in] This Province." NSM, item 31.24, Commission of Louis Benjamin Peminout Paul, "Commission signed by H.H. Cogswell, Provincial Secretary, on behalf of Sir John Coape Sherbrooke," 28 April 1814. The Peminout Pauls traditionally wielded territorial aegis over lands along the Shbenacadie and Stewiacke River Valleys, as well as eastward towards the Dartmouth Lakes. Many members of this family became advocates of Indigenous rights. For instance, in 1841 Louis-Benjamin Peminout Paul, also known as Paussamigh Pemmeenauweet, petitioned Queen Victoria complaining of settler encroachments on Mi'kmaw land in the *Sipekne'katik* (Shubenacadie) district. LAC, CO 217/179, ff. 406–08, "Petition of Chief Pemmeenauweet, received at the British Colonial Office, London, on 25 January 1841." The Peminout Pauls, like the Denny-Thoma family, had exercised leadership prerogatives in the Northeast for generations, and no member of either family, as far as is known, ever signed a peace treaty with the British between 1726 and 1761. See, for instance, LAC, CO 217/4/99-103 (British Colonial Office Records), "Treaty of 1726, made at Annapolis Royal, 4 June 1726, with signatures."

13 NSARM, RG 2, vol. 9, 1815, "To His Honor the Honorable Adams George Archibald, C.M.G., Lieutenant Governor of Nova Scotia, from Jacob Brooks and five others," 5 February 1883; NSARM, RG 2, vol. 9, 1820, "To His Honor the Honorable Adams G. Archibald, C.M.G., Lieutenant Governor of Nova Scotia, from Christopher Paul, Stephen Hood, Peter Paul, John Paul, Abraham Hood and 56 others," 29 March 1883. John Noel contended that John Denny Jr., being from Cape Breton, lived too far away from the province's capital to make a strong mark on the canvas of Mi'kmaw politics, but time proved him wrong.

14 NSARM, RG 2, vol. 9, 1815, "To His Honor the Honorable Adams George Archibald, C.M.G., Lieutenant Governor of Nova Scotia, from Jacob Brooks and five others," 5 February 1883.

15 *Boston Herald*, 20 August 1900.

16 Denny intervened in the election because at the time the chief of the Cole Harbour reserve would have had access to valuable timber revenue.

17 LAC, Indian Affairs Records, RG 10, copies in possession of the Treaty and Aboriginal Rights Research Centre (TARR), Shubenacadie, Nova Scotia, "Joseph C. Cope to L. Vankoughnet," March 26, 1888; "A.P. Demour to Indian Affairs," 1 May 1888; "Cope to Deputy Superintendent of Indian Affairs," 16 May 1888; "Rev. D. O'Connor to L. Vankoughnet [Deputy Superintendent of Indian Affairs]," 30 September 1888; "Cope to A. Austin," 7 November 1888; "Andrew Paul to L. Vankoughnet," 17 December 1888; "Cope to D. O'Connor," July 1990; "Joseph Cope to Deputy Superintendent of Indian Affairs," 16 May 1894."

18 Andrew Paul died in the Dartmouth area in 1916. NSM, Printed Matter File, Harry Piers's unpublished notes, "Obituary of Andrew Paul," 24 February 1916.

19 LAC, RG 10, vol. 2104, file 18,930, Documents pertaining to the claims of Joseph Lewis, including "Petition of Grand Chief John Denny, Charlottetown, P.E.I., complaining of encroachments being made by certain whites on the lands of the Micmac Inds. at P.E.I. at Indian Cove," 24 February 1885.

20 Chute, "Frank G. Speck's Contributions."

21 LAC, RG 10, vol. 3113, file 320, 110-pt. 1-A, "To the Honourable Minister of the Interior [Frank Oliver, who was also superintendent general of Indian Affairs] from John Denys, Grand Chief, Witness Rose McMaster, Eskasoni, Cape Breton," 11 March 1909.

22 LAC, RG 10, vol. 3113, file 320, 110-pt. 1-A, Documents pertaining to the surrender of the Kejimkujik or the Fairy Lake Reserve, 1909–18; "Secretary of the Department of Indian Affairs to Chief Solomon Morris," 27 March 1909; "Chief John Steaven, Pomquet, to the Department of Indian Affairs, with signatures," 12 March 1909; "Chief Joseph Gould, Truro, to the Department of Indian Affairs, with signatures," 12 March 1909; "Captain Simon Paul, Middle River, to the Department of Indian Affairs, with signatures," 12 March 1909; "Chief Solomon Morris, Sydney, to the Department of Indian Affairs, with signatures," 12 March 1909; "Mr. James Joe of Malagawatch, Cape Breton, to the Department of Indian Affairs, with signatures," 12 March, 1909; "Tom Marshall, Chapel Island, St. Peter's, to the Department of Indian

Affairs," 24 April 1909; LAC, RG 10, vol. 4743, file 274/8-10-11-5, pt. 1, "Petition of John Denny, Grand Chief of the Micmac Tribe, signed by Matthew Francis, Chief of the Merigomish Tribe; John Stephen, Chief of the Heatherton Mission [Pomquet]; Simon Basque, Head Captain; Simon Paul, Captain; Francis Bernard, Captain; Thomas Marshall, Captain; James Louis, Captain, and 27 others to the Superintendent of Indian Affairs," undated.

23 LAC, RG 10, vol. 3113, file 320, 110-pt. 1-A, "Surrender of Fairy Lake Reserve, signed by Stephen Pictou and twenty others," 11 April 1918.

24 Nova Scotia Museum (NSM), item NS. S71.698, newspaper clipping, "St. Anne's Day Among the Micmacs," by John H. Wilson, 1896; NSARM, MG 100, vol. 184, no. 9, Scrapbook no. 2, p. 4; New Brunswick Museum, St. John, New Brunswick, Ganong Scrapbooks; NSM, Nova Scotia Museum Printed File, Harry Piers, unpublished notes, 24 February 1916.

25 New Brunswick Museum, Ganong Scrapbooks.

26 B.A. Balcom and David L. Schmidt, "The Règlements of 1739: A Note on Micmac Law and Literacy," *Acadiensis* 23, no. 1 (1993): 110–27.

27 Many residents of the Kings Road Mi'kmaw community were born in Eskasoni and had come to Sydney looking for wage work.

28 LAC, RG 10, vol. 7936, file 32-61, pt. 1, "D.M. MacAdam to J.D. MacLean," 30 June 1902. Local Indian agents and Ottawa officialdom refused to regard Denny as the grand chief of the Mi'kmaw nation, although they were willing to recognize him as the chief of Cape Breton.

29 Denny argued that the implementation of an electoral system at Sydney would only worsen an already strained situation. Ibid., "John Denny Jr. to J.D. MacLean," 16 September 1909.

30 LAC, RG 10, vol. 7936, file 32–61, pt. 1, "A.J. Boyd to Mr. Scott," 19 August 1919.

31 Ibid. Boyd claimed that the duties of the grand chief with regard to dispute resolution were so effective that litigation was "an unheard occurrence among Indians in Nova Scotia." The grand chief thus was not only useful "but necessary."

32 Martha Walls, *No Need of a Chief for This Band: The Maritime Mi'kmaq and Federal Electoral Legislation, 1899–1951* (Vancouver: University of British Columbia Press, 2010), 85, 99–102.

33 The first message that was circulated among the Mi'kmaw communities gave the location and time of the funeral. Written in Mi'kmaq, it began: "No'kmatutk, wla aknutmaqniwtuk kinua'tulek ta'n telki'k Mi'kma'ki mawi lnui aqmaminua Kisu'lkw weji wksua'lata mekwaye'k ntininenaq, no'kmatut, ksaqmaminuaq tujiw kaqia'q wmimajuaqnemek 12 te'suknitaq wla tepknuset, asukuom atjietek eksitpu'kek." The message was signed "A.O. aqq T.M."

34 "Message on the Death of Chief John Denny, Sa'n Patis [John Baptiste] Tenio'q, Saqmawaq Alasutmelsewanej Eskisoqnik: Unama'kik, Penatmuiku's 5 tesukna'q [5 April] 1918," https://www.cbu.ca/indigenous-affairs/mikmaq-resource-centre/miscellany/message-on-the-death-of-chief-john-denny/, accessed 24 February 2023; *Mi'kmaw Maliseet Nations News*, https://www.mmnn.ca/2014/05/grand-chief-john-denny/, accessed 22 February 2023. English translation by Helen Sylliboy, 2003. In July 2014 descendants of John Denny Jr. gathered at Eskasoni to honour him as well as other past grand chiefs. "Denny Descendants Remember Former Grand Chiefs," *Cape Breton Post*, 19 July 2014.

35 A *salite* accompanies a Mi'kmaw funeral to provide funds for the bereaved. Likely derived from the French word *solliciter*, a *salite* focuses on "soliciting for charity."

36 A hundred years after Grand Chief John Denny Jr.'s death, some of his descendants are calling for restoration of the office of grand chief as hereditary in the Denny line. Wendy Martin, "After 100 Years a Mi'kmaw Family Wants the Role of Hereditary Grand Chief Restored," https://www.cbc.ca/news/canada/nova-scotia/mi-kmaq-hereditary-grand-chief-denny-family-john-denny-junior-1.4619014, CBC News, 13 April 2018. These persons maintain that substitution of an electoral system for the traditional form of hereditary succession was meant to be temporary.

37 These words were transcribed directly from the inscription on Denny's grave obelisk at Eskasoni.

CHAPTER 33

1 Beloni Thoma Denny's name also is written "Beloni Toma," "Beloni Tomi," and "Benoni Toma." "Beloni" may be a corruption of "Bartélèmy," or "Bartholomew."

2 Chief Michel Thoma Denny Jr. was too young to have been Beloni's father, though Beloni may have been a younger brother of the grand chief.

3 NSARM, RG 5, Series P, vol. 43, no. 100, petition 233, "Petition of Dinney and Others to the House of Representatives," 13 March 1841.

4 NSARM, newspapers (microfilm reel 1249), *The Times and Cape Breton*, April 1849, "Obituary of Beloni Toma."

5 See, for example, NSARM, RG 1, vol. 430, doc. 163, "Reverend Simon Lawlor, Bras d'Or, to Lawrence Kavanagh,"

7 August 1827; NSARM, RG 1, vol. 430, doc.167, "Petition of Simon Lawlor," 1828.

6 Richard Denny, Eskasoni, 11 December 2006, personal communication.

7 "Obituary of Beloni Toma."

CHAPTER 34

1 The origin of the place name "Whycocomagh" is controversial. Some argue that it derives from the Scottish Gaelic *Why-cog-ho-mah or Hogamah*, while others claim it is a corruption of the Mi'kmaw term *We'koqma̓q*, which means "head of the waters."

2 Variant spellings of Peter Googoo's surname include "Cogo," "Cooko," "Gaugaay," "Gogoo," "Gougaux," "Gougou," and "Ku'gu."

3 "Marriage of Pierre Gougaux, son of Bernard Gougaux, and Agathe, 8 August 1771," NSARM, microfilm reel 10,053, copies of registers of Abbé Charles-François Bailly, 1768–73, 81, *Registre des actes de baptême, marriages, et sepultures faits en La Nouvelle Ecosse ou Acadie, commence le vingt unième jour de juillet de l'année mil sept cent soixante huit, par mons. Charles-François Bailly, prêtre missionaire des sauvages et acadiens, sujets de sa majesté britanique.* The Peguidalouet and Googoo families were related by numerous kin ties. In 1771, Jeannot Peguidalouet's brother "Louis Pekid8al8et" wed Pierre Gougaux's sister "Marthe, fille de Bernard [Gougaux]." Ibid., 80. Also, Abbé Pierre Maillard married Jeannot's son Bernard Peguidalouet and Marie-Anne Gougou at Chapel Island in 1755. Jean-Yves Ribault, *Les Iles Saint-Pierre et Miquelon: Des origines à 1814* (Saint-Pierre: L'Imprimerie au Gouvernement Saint-Pierre, 1962), 30–2.

4 George Bourinot Jr. "The Island of Cape Breton, Its History, Scenery and Resources," in *Stewart's Literary Quarterly Magazine* 3, no. 4 (1870), 351–2. It is not known whether Rosalie was a Googoo by birth, or whether "Googoo" was her married surname. She may have been Peter Googoo's daughter, though she could have been his wife. She eventually sold Jeannot Peguidalouet's commission to a Halifax journalist.

5 Frank Gouldsmith Speck, *Beothuk and Micmac*, ed. F.W. Hodge (New York: Museum of the American Indian/ Heye Foundation, 1922), 11–12.

6 Jeannot Peguidalouet obtained a licence of occupation for land on East Bay in 1783, but he also resided for lengthy periods with kin at Whycocomagh.

7 NSARM, RG 1, vol. 430, doc. 158, "Petition of ten Mi'kmaw families at Whycocomagh for 2,000 acres,"

5 November 1821; NSARM, RG 1, vol. 430, doc. 158, "F. Cranwell to Mr. George," November 1821.

8 NSARM, RG 20, series 3, vol. B (Cape Breton Land Papers, 1810), No. 563, "Petition of Francis Coogu [Googoo] and two other families at Margaree, Cape Breton, to Brigadier General Napean, President of the Council and Commander in Chief, 1810."

9 NSARM, RG 20, series 3, vol. B (Cape Breton Land Papers. 1810), no. 550, "Report of Cape Breton's Surveyor General, H. Crawley, regarding the petition of Benwa, the Indian, who wishes to attain one hundred and forty acres near the western entrance of the Gut in Little Bras D'Or, Sydney, 22 January 1810." Benwa had occupied this land for many years prior to 1810.

10 Lands surveyed for the Mi.kmaq of Cape Breton in 1833 were confirmed under an executive order-in-council dated 7 May 1834.

11 A Scottish oral tradition relates that Peter Googoo, on first meeting James and Hector McNeil who in 1804 were intending to settle near Whycocomagh at Grand Narrows, threatened to kill the Scotsmen for trespassing on Mi'kmaw land, but when one of the McNeils made the sign of the cross, Googoo recanted and said he would recognize him as his "brudder." The Googoos called these Scots *saskatbaymit*, or "flatheads," because they wore "flat bonnets," or Scottish tams. Mary L. Francis, *Folklore of Nova Scotia* (N.p.: published by author, n.d. [1940s?]), 10. Francis's account portrays Peter Googoo in an unflattering light, as impulsive and somewhat uncouth. Googoo was neither. His petitions show him to be an intelligent, thoughtful man dedicated to the welfare of his people. W.H. Crawley, the Cape Breton commissioner of Crown lands who also acted as the island's Indian commissioner in 1849, wrote a report that included valuable information on the *We'koqma̓q* Mi'kmaq. Nova Scotia, *Journal of the Legislative Assembly of Nova Scotia*, 1849, Appendix 49, 354–8, "Report of W.H. Crawley."

12 LAC, RG 10, vol. 460: 675, "H.W. Crawley to Reverend J. Couteau, regarding the petition of Stephen Googou," 11 July 1850.

13 NSARM, MG 15, vol. 4, doc. 87, "Inhabitants of Indian River to Crawley," 27 August 1850, and "Peter Gougou *et al.* to Crawley," 17 November 1850.

14 LAC, RG 10, vol. 460, folder 19, "Peter Gougou *et al* to Crawley," 24 January 1851.

15 John Googoo was likely Peter's brother but could have been his son. John later became a prominent leader at *We'koqma̓q* in his own right.

16 LAC, RG 10, vol. 460, 465, "Petition to Sir John Gaspard Le Marchant from Chief Peter Gogoo, Stephen Gogoo *et al.*," 24 January 1854.

17 NSARM, RG 1, vol. 431, "Petition of Chief Peter Gogoo and others at Whycocomagh regarding settlers taking over their lands," 1 February 1855.

18 NSARM, RG 1, series P, vol. 15, no. 47, "To the House of Assembly, Petition of the Undersigned Inhabitants of Whycocomagh regarding lands granted to Indians," 16 April 1857, signed by L.M. McDougall, J.P., J. McLeod, J.P., Samuel Beaton, J P., and 73 others. See also LAC, RG 10, vol. 461, "Widow McKenzie to Samuel P. Fairbanks," 10 December 1858; LAC, RG 10, vol. 460, folder 10, "Quarrie McQuarrie to Fairbanks," 27 December 1858; LAC, RG 10, vol. 460, folder 8, "Donald McLean to Fairbanks," 30 September 1864; LAC, RG 10, vol. 461, 730, "L. McDougall to Fairbanks," 10 June 1870.

19 L.F.S. Upton, *Micmacs and Colonists: Indian-White Relations in the Maritimes, 1713–1867* (Vancouver: University of British Columbia Press, 1979), 95.

20 George Bourinot Jr.'s article was written in 1870 before the *Flor*, a French frigate with a French admiral aboard, visited Sydney at the time of the Canadian Nile expedition in 1884, so Rosalie must have met a French admiral who visited Cape Breton earlier in the nineteenth century. For information on the *Flor* and the Canadian Nile expedition, which included some Indigenous recruits, see Roy MacLaren, *Canadians on the Nile, 1882–1898* (Vancouver: University of British Columbia Press, 2011), 66. Nothing more could be found on the encounter between Rosalie and the French officer, other than, according to Bourinot, that Rosalie Googoo shared her good fortune she obtained from the admiral before 1870 with others who came to her encampment, who in turn spent it on "finery and feasts."

CHAPTER 35

1 Andrew Alex also went by the name "Andrew Macdonald."

2 Typescript statement of Victor Bosco Alex, dated at Eskasoni, 16 December 1999. Witnessed by Gregory U. Johnson, a commissioner of the Supreme Court of Canada. Data relating to the Alex family genealogy presented in this typescript bear a fairly close resemblance to evidence from the documentary record, although the generations are compressed in the typescript. A census of Mi'kmaq attending St. Anne's Day festival on Chapel Island in 1841 lists a seventy-year-old widower named Peter (Alex) Scotchman, born in 1771, who almost certainly was a younger son of Alexander *Skajjmen*, or "Scotchman," who attended the council held at Ka'nawa'ki in 1749. Born around 1720, Alexander *Skajjmen* was likely a Scottish military deserter named Alexander McDonald who joined the Mi'kmaq in Cape Breton just before or during the War of the Austrian Succession (1740–48). In 1841 Peter Alex, a Scots *métis*, had three sons: Alic (Alex) Scotchman, forty (1801–c.1881); Paul Scotchman, thirty-five; and Francis Scotchman, twenty-five. Alic Scotsman was the father of Thomas Scotchman, but since Thomas was only fifteen at the time his name does not appear on the 1841 census. A second census, compiled in 1858 by Indian agent Moses Perley, showing names of attendees at Chapel Island on St. Anne's Day, lists Thomas (Alex) McDonald, born in 1826, as a married man with a wife named Marie. Thomas and Marie were the parents of Andrew Alex. NSARM, RG 15, vol. 3, doc. 64, "An Account of the Indians within the County of Richmond, taken on the 26th July 1841, at an Indian Chapel Bras dor [*sic*, d'Or] Lake, being the Anniversary of Saint Ann's Day." (The printed version of this census that appears in Ruth Holmes Whitehead, *The Old Man Told Us: Excerpts from Micmac History, 1500–1950* (Halifax: Nimbus, 1991), 219–20, omits Peter Scotchman's name, though it is present on the original document. Nova Scotia, *Journal of the House of Assembly*, 1860, appendix, 326, "An enumeration of the Micmac Indians of Cape Breton, made at Chapel Island, Great Bras d'Or Lake, July, 1859, by M.H. Perley.") The later anatomy of the Alex-Scotchman-McDonald family may be traced by referring to the federal censuses of 1871, 1881, and 1891.

3 The 1749 occasion was said to have been the first council meeting of the Eastern Wabanaki Confederacy, convened to discuss British expansionism and its effect on Indigenous land issues following the 1748 Treaty of Aix-la-Chapelle, which gave Louisbourg back to the French and set the stage for the founding of Halifax the following year. Author conversation with Victor Alex and Dr. Marjorie Gould at Eskasoni, December 2007. Though Iroquoian-speaking and Algonquian-speaking nations in the Northeast had been enemies during the Iroquois Wars, a peace pact between the two was made in 1701 under the aegis of a former governor of Montreal, Louis-Hector de Callière. This treaty, signed at Montreal on 4 August 1701, became known as the Great Peace of Montreal and included over thirty Indigenous nations, including the Mi'kmaq, residing between the Atlantic coast and the headwaters of the Mississippi. There was

little discussion about Indigenous sovereignty over land on this occasion, but the nations were told to lay any grievances before the governor of New France. The 1749 Eastern Wabanaki meeting, by contrast, was convened without French or English intervention. William C. Wicken refers to the Iroquoian-speaking members who attended the Wabanaki Councils and made peace with the Mi'kmaq as Haudenosaunee (Six Nations), while the Mi'kmaq, even today, refer to them as "Mohawk." Wicken, *The Colonization of Mi'kmaw Memory and History 1794–1928: The King v. Gabriel Sylliboy* (Toronto: University of Toronto Press, 2012), 79–80.

4 Frank G. Speck, "The Eastern Algonkian Wabanaki Confederacy," *American Anthropologist* 17 (1915): 492–08. Speck gained his information on this confederacy from Grand Chief John Denny Jr. at Eskasoni, and not the *Pu'tus*, Andrew Alex, at Chapel Island, Cape Breton.

5 The original Alex *Skajjmen* McDonald was either a military deserter from the British forces during the colonial war era or a trader who joined the Mi'kmaq. It is interesting that he was living among the Mi'kmaq during the French era. Whatever the case, oral traditions in Cape Berton hold that a descendant of this man, who retained the surname "McDonald," moved from Cape Breton to Shubenacadie in the nineteenth century and became the patriarch of the McDonalds associated with Shubenacadie. Meanwhile, oral traditions from the Shubenacadie area attest that Louis Noel of Halifax County adopted a "white child" named "Lewey" who became "Lewey Noel McDonald" and later moved to Shubenacadie. The child was probably Scots *métis*, for the surname "McDonald" is fairly old among the Mi'kmaq. In the 1850s, Indigenous persons bearing this surname lived in Pictou and Antigonish Counties, as well as well as in southern Newfoundland.

6 Wicken, *Colonization of Mi'kmaw Memory*, 137–9.

7 Ibid., 76–92. Wicken examines the appeal, as well as Andrew Alex's role in it, in considerable detail.

8 *R. v. Sylliboy* (1928), 50, c.c.c.; William C. Wicken, "'Heard It from Our Grandfathers': Mi'kmaq Treaty Tradition and the Sylliboy Case of 1928," *New Brunswick Law Journal* 44 (1995): 145–59.

9 NSARM, MG 1/2868, #2, Clara Dennis Notebook, no. 2. Chief Sylliboy and Andrew Alex explained this to journalist Clara Dennis while they were showing her the parchment treaty. The only other time that the Grand Council showed the treaty to the Mi'kmaw community was on a table in a large tent during the annual St. Anne's Day celebrations.

10 Two of these photographs taken by Clara Dennis in 1930 are well known. The first is a photograph of Andrew Alex, with the Chapel Island mission church in the background, standing in a field of flowers holding a large wampum belt, a smaller belt, and another ceremonial item, possibly a pipe. NSM, William Dennis Collection, P113 113. This photograph of Andrew Alex as *Pu'tus* appears in Marie Battiste, ed., *Living Treaties: Narrating Mi'kmaw Treaty Relations* (Sydney/Halifax: University of Cape Breton Press/Nimbus, 2012), 2. The second photograph is of Andrew Alex at Chapel Island wearing the white wampum belt, bandolier-fashion, across his chest. NSM, P113/73.180.62/N-14,74.

11 In 1983, Grand Captain Noel Marshall stated that the *l'nops'kuk* was brought back from the Mi'kmaw-Mohawk treaty forum by his great grandfather. He recalled that the beads were always read by the *Budu's* (*Pu'tus*) in council before the St. Anne's Day procession. M. Marshall and L.C. Boudreau, "St. Ann's Day Mission, Chapel Island," *Cape Breton's Magazine*, no. 40 (August 1983), 31–44.

12 While the antiquity of the medal or wampum could not be determined, it seems plausible that at least one of the wampum belts dates to the eighteenth century, while another was said to be sixty-nine years old.

13 Grand Captain Simon Denny was a son of Sylliboy's predecessor as grand chief, John Denny Jr.

14 Typescript statement of Victor Bosco Alex, dated at Eskasoni 16 December 1995. Witnessed by Gregory U. Johnson, commissioner of the Supreme Court of Canada.

15 Janet Chute and Marjorie Gould, conversation with Victor Alex, Eskasoni, spring 2011.

16 See, for instance, *The Indian News* 8, no. 2 (Ottawa, July 1965), 1, "Advisory Councils Elected, Indian Voice to Government."

17 Marie Battiste refers to the loss of this traditional insignia and other ritual paraphernalia in "Introduction – Linking the Past to the Future," in *Living Treaties: Narrating Mi'kmaw Treaty Relations*, ed. Marie Battiste (Sydney/Halifax: University of Cape Breton Press/Nimbus, 2016), 3.

18 One story was that the belts and other articles were being conveyed down the St. Lawrence River en route to Expo '67 in a bark canoe that upset in choppy water, and the items were swept away.

19 On 7 July 2012 Victor Bosco Alex Sr., as Grand Council *Pu'tus*, along with Grand Chief Ben Sylliboy and Grand Captain Andrew Denny, drafted a petition at the *Mi'kmawey mawio'mi* of 7 January 2012 asking for

protection for Indigenous rights in the face of new federal legislation that they felt could injure those rights. Victor Alex conducted religious ceremonies and, as a highly respected Elder, stood as a role model for youth. In 2015–16 he was presented with a Role Model of the Year plaque by teachers and students at Allison Bernard Memorial High School in Eskasoni. Born to *Pu'tus* Isaac Alex and Esther Paul on 22 July 1934 at Barra Head, Cape Breton, he moved to Eskasoni, where he wed Leona Prosper. He passed away in Cape Breton Regional Hospital at age eighty-two on 16 March 2017. Canada Obituaries, https://necrocanada.com/obituaries/victor-bosco-alex-july-22-1934-march-16-2017.

CHAPTER 36

1   Sylliboy's surname is also spelled "Syliboy," "Syllibye," "Syliboye," and "Sylipay." "Sylliboy" is the Mi'kmaw way of pronouncing "Levi." Author conversation with Caroline Gould, Whycocomagh, Cape Breton, 14 June 1998.

2   William C. Wicken, "'Heard It from Our Grandfathers': Mi'kmaq Treaty Tradition and the Syliboy Case of 1928," *UNB law Journal* 44 (1995): 145–59; Wicken, *The Colonization of Mi'kmaw Memory and History, 1794–1928, The King v. Gabriel Sylliboy* (Toronto: University of Toronto Press, 2012); Daniel P. Strouthes, "Change in the Real Property Law of a Cape Breton Island Micmac Band," vol. 1 (PhD diss., Yale University, 1994).

3   Chief Sylliboy's grandfather likely was Sylliboy Newell of Whycocomagh, a man whose name appears on early nineteenth-century census records. LAC, RG 10, vol. 461, 471, "Return of Indians at Whycocomagh, to S.P. Fairbanks," 9 June 1870. Several of the Whycocomagh families, particularly the Googoos, Newells, Bernards and Sylliboys, were related to the late eighteenth-century Cape Breton district chief Jeannot Peguidalouet.

4   Père Pacifique, "New Indian Chief Gabriel Sylliboy of Whycocomagh, in Micmac and English," in *Setaneoei*, or *The Micmac Messenger/Le Messager Micmac* (September 1918), Rimouski, Quebec; University of Cape Breton, Mi'kmaq College Institute, Mi'kmaq Resource Centre, Article no. 244, MRC, "Gabriel Sylliboy Becomes Grand Chief, 1918," in Mi'kmaq and English with an introduction by Helen Sylliboy and David L. Schmidt; Albert DeBlois, "Remembering: A Micmac Story Told by the Grand Chief Gabriel Sylliboy," *Recherches amérindiennes du québec* 22, nos. 2–3 (1992): 11–18; Micmac Association of Cultural Studies (MACS), *Micmac Hymnal* (Sydney: MACS, 1983); NSARM, Helen Creighton Collection,

Ref. A 5108.5114, "Sound Recording of Chief Silliboy of Nyanza regarding the Coming of the Scottish People," 1944.

5   Leslie Jane McMillan, "*Mi'kmawey Mawio'mi*: Changing Roles of the Mi'kmaq Grand Council from the Early Seventeenth Century to the Present" (MA thesis, Dalhousie University, 1996).

6   David L. Schmidt and B.A. Balcom, "The Règlements of 1739: A Note on Micmac Law and Literacy," *Acadiensis* 23, no. 1 (1993): 110–27.

7   Labrador deliberately took salmon out of season at Bridgewater to test the status of Indigenous fishing rights, and was charged under the game laws. NSM, Printed File, "Copy of Rights of the Indians, Ward Fisher, Chief Inspector of the Eastern Fisheries, to Hon. W.L. Hall," 10 February 1927.

8   LAC, RG 10, vol. 4743, file 420-7, "Frank Pedley, Deputy Superintendent of Indian Affairs to Premier E.N. Rhodes," 24 March 1928.

9   R. v. Syliboy [1929] 1 DLR 307. The earlier appeal was also reported in the same docket: R. v. Syliboy (1928), 50 CCC 389, Nova Scotia County Court, G. Patterson, Acting Inverness County Court Judge, 10 September 1928.

10 R. v. Sylliboy (1928), 50 CCC 389.

11 William C. Wicken, "Heard It from Our Grandfathers," 145–59. See also Walls, *No Need of a Chief for This Band: The Maritime Mi'kmaq and Federal Electoral Legislation, 1899–1951* Vancouver: University of British Columbia Press, 2010), 102–5.

12 R. v. Sylliboy (1928), 50 CCC 889 at 390–1; synopsis of proceeding at Port Hood, 4 July 1928, Decision of Acting County Court Judge, District 6, G. Patterson, in case of *King & Sylyboy* [*sic, Syliboy* or *Sylliboy*], Port Hood, Cape Breton, July 1928, including Judge G. Patterson's rough notes; Wicken, *Colonization of Mi'kmaw Memory*, 132; "Max Basque to R.H. Whitehead and Ronald Caplan, 9 March 1984," in *Cape Breton's Magazine*, no. 51 (1989), 18–19; Ruth Holmes Whitehead, *The Old Man Told Us: Excerpts from Micmac History, 1500–1950* (Halifax: Nimbus, 1991), 318, 327–36.

13 Clara Dennis, *Cape Breton Over* (Toronto: Ryerson, 1942), 48–54.

14 Unfortunately, Dennis recorded neither this treaty's contents nor its date, and the document is now lost. It may have been a 1761 treaty parchment preserved by Chief Peguidalouet's descendants. NSARM, vol. 165, doc. 162, "Treaty of Peace and Friendship concluded by the Honourable Jonathan Belcher, 25 June 1761." If it was a copy of the 1752 treaty with the Mi'kmaq, however, this means that a treaty signing often regarded as being localized to

the Shubenacadie district did in fact reach Cape Breton and was still in the possession of the Grand Council in 1927–28, when Chief Sylliboy launched his Indigenous resource right claim. The Grand Council for years maintained an archive of important documents and artefacts. One string of stone beads in its possession was said to have stemmed from a peace between the Mohawk and the Mi'kmaq in the early eighteenth century. Elder, historian, and educator Lillian Marshall of Potlotek noted on 4 April 2017 that according to oral tradition, the "Treaty Beads the chief had were from the Mohawks and not the British." The author is grateful to Lillian Marshall for supplying this and other information.

15 Dennis, *Cape Breton Over*, 48–54.

16 LAC, RG 10, vol. 7758, file 270 50-2 pt. (1), "Gabriel Sylliboy and Whycocomagh, 1942–1944"; LAC, RG 10, vol. 9022, file 23–4 (1), "G. Sylliboy and S. Denny to T. Crerar, Indian Affairs," 9 March 1944. See also Lisa Lynne Patterson, "Indian Affairs and the Nova Scotian Centralization Policy" (MA thesis, Dalhousie University, 1985); Patterson, "Centralization in Nova Scotia: An Adventure in Canadian Indian Policy," paper presented at the Learned Societies Conference, University of Manitoba, Winnipeg, June 1986.

17 This happened during Sheila Steen's fieldwork for her master's thesis in anthropology for the University of Pennsylvania, entitled "The Psychological Consequences of Acculturation among the Cape Breton Micmac" (University of Pennsylvania, 1951).

18 Born at Port Morien, Cape Breton, to Joseph Christmas (Christmas Denny Thoma) and his wife Madeleine Richards on 14 July 1896, Benjamin Edmond Christmas, a distant relative of Grand Chief John Denny Jr., became chief at Kings Road at the age of twenty-three in 1919, a year after Gabriel Sylliboy's election as grand chief. He continued on after 1926 as the chief of the new community established at Membertou. His early years were spent at Port Morien and on the Kings Road. A devoted Roman Catholic, he was a member of the Grand Council, a prayer leader, and a choir member, could read hieroglyphics and act as an interpreter, and throughout his lifetime was extremely politically active both locally and internationally. He was president of the North American Indian Brotherhood. Most important, he vehemently resisted government centralization policy and was able to encourage others, among them Joseph Julien of Millbrook, Noel Marshall of Chapel Island, and Margaret (Maggie) Phillips of Cole Harbour to support his opposition campaign. He and his wife, Jane Denny, a daughter of Peter-Paul Denny of Eskasoni, raised twelve children, of whom nine – Victor, Patrick, Augustus, Raymond, Peter Joseph, step-son Alex, Madeline, Mary, and Helen – were living when Ben Christmas died suddenly on 28 March 1966 while attending a Regional Advisory Council meeting in Amherst. Peter Joseph Christmas was an educator in Queens County and later became head of the Mi'kmaq Cultural Association in Sydney. Helen Martin (née Christmas) became a human rights activist. "Indian Chief Ben Christmas Dies, March 28, 1966, *"Micmac News*, Sydney, 2 March, 1966, 1–3; Daniel N. Paul, "Chief Ben Christmas: A Centennial Salute to a Hero," *Halifax Herald*, 26 July 1996.

19 *Cape Breton's Magazine*, no. 71 (1997), 63–7; "St. Anne's Day Mission, Chapel Island," *Cape Breton's Magazine*, no. 40 (1984), 31–43; *Halifax Herald*, 28 July 1932, 2, and 2 August 1932, 3.

20 In 1936, for instance, Chief Sylliboy agreed to contribute a blood sample for research undertaken by Dr. Phillip Smith, a professor of pathology at Dalhousie University who was a co-investigator in a larger study examining racial "admixture" in Cape Breton. A particular research focus was the consequences of past unions between Mi'kmaq and Europeans. It was thought that if members of a Mi'kmaw family all exhibited blood type O they were of "purer Indian racial stock" than families in which some members exhibited blood type A. Chief Sylliboy had type O, but his brother and sister both had type A blood – hardly a surprising finding given that Sylliboy's mother, Mary Barrington, was an Englishwoman. William C. Wicken, *Colonization of Mi'kmaw Memory*, 229–32.

21 For a discussion of village etiquette surrounding St. Anne's Day ceremonies on Chapel Island, see L. Marshall and L.C. Boudreau, "St. Anne's Day Mission, Chapel Island," featuring an interview with Grand Captain Noel Marshall held July 1983, and additional information from Elsie Clews Parsons and Sarah Denny, *Cape Breton's Magazine*, no. 40 (August 1983), 31–44. See also "A Talk with Grand Captain Alex Denny," *Cape Breton's Magazine*, no. 40 (August 1983), 45–8.

22 For reference to the grand chief's words as he ascended the church steps on St. Anne's Day, see Ruth Homes Whitehead's explanatory text accompanying a photograph of Gabriel Sylliboy, taken in 1930 by Clara Dennis (NSM, William Dennis Collection, Ref. no. P113/73.180.659/N-18,733, MP0729), which appears on the Nova Scotia Museum's website "The Mi'kmaq Portraits Collection," https://novascotia. ca/museum/mikmaq/?section=image&id=426&results=search&page=1&keywords=Gabriel%20Sylliboy.

Mention of Gabriel Sylliboy calling himself a bear also appears in Whitehead, *Niniskjamijinaqik/Ancestral Images: The Mi'kmaq in Art and Photography* (Halifax: Nimbus, 2015), 100.

23 "Obituary of Gabriel Sylliboy," *Chronicle Herald*, 6 March 1964, 15.

24 Donald Marshall, Sr., Alexander Denny, and Simon Marshall, "The Covenant Chain," in *Drumbeat: Anger and Renewal in Indian Country*, ed. Boyce Richardson (Toronto: Summerhill, 1989), 73–104; Geoffrey York, *The Dispossessed: Life and Death in Native Canada* (Toronto: Lester & Orpen Dennys, 1989), chap. 3, "Inside the Reserves."

25 Andrea Gunn, "Former Grand Chief Sylliboy to Receive Pardon," *Herald News*, 15 February 2017; Aly Thomson, "Nova Scotia Pardons Sylliboy," *Chronicle Herald*, 17 February 2017.

26 Several photographs were taken in 1930 of Gabriel Sylliboy by journalist Clara Dennis. See NSM, 73.180.672, "Chief Gabriel Sylliboy, Indian Island," taken in 1930 by Clara Dennis, William Dennis collection; NSM. 73.180.650 N-6104, "Procession at Chapel Island, St. Anne's Day, showing Father Pacifique and Chief Gabriel Sylliboy, third from left, photo by Clara Dennis, taken 26 July 1930"; NSM, P113/73.180.659.N-18,733, "Gabriel Sylliboy with a miniature cannon, St. Anne's Day, 26 July, Chapel Island, N.S."

CHAPTER 37

1 James "Sákéj" Youngblood Henderson, "Ayukpachi: Empowering Aboriginal Thought," in *Reclaiming Aboriginal Voice and Vision*, ed. Marie Battiste (Vancouver: University of British Columbia Press, 2000), 257.

2 Trudy Sable and Bernie Francis, *The Language of This Land, Mi'kma'ki* (Sydney: Cape Breton University Press, 2012), chap. 1; Trudy Sable, "Another Look in the Mirror: Research into the Foundation for Developing an Alternative Science Curriculum for Mi'kmaw Children" (master's thesis, St. Mary's University, 1996).

3 Peter Joseph Christmas, *Wejkwapniag* (Sydney: Micmac Association of Cultural Studies, 1977), 23. For many years Dr. Christmas, who passed away on 31 January 2023, was director of the Mi'kmaq Association for Cultural Studies.

4 Vivian Grey and Mora Dianne O'Neill, *Pe'l A'tukeway: Let Me Tell a Story* (Halifax: Art Gallery of Nova Scotia, 1993), vi.

5 William Hipwell, "Taking Charge of the Bras d'Or: Ecological Politics in the 'Land of Fog'" (PhD diss., Carlton University, 2001), 275.

6 Albert Marshall, quoted in ibid., 275.

7 Leah Rosenberg, *Mikwite'lmanej Mikmaqi'k – Let Us Remember the Old Mi'kmaq* (Halifax: Nimbus, 2001), 13.

8 Jennifer Reid, *Myth, Symbol, and Colonial Encounter: British and Mi'kmaq in Acadia, 1700–1867* (Ottawa: University of Ottawa Press, 1995), 73.

9 *Salite* is a borrowed word in the Mi'kmaw language, derived from the French *soliciter*, "to solicit [for charity]."

10 Bernie Francis, quoted in Isabelle Knockwood, *Out of the Depths: The Experiences of Mi'kmaw Children at the Indian Residential School at Shubenacadie* (Lockport: Roseway, 1992), 3.

11 Angela Robinson, *Ta'n Teli-ktlamsitasit (Ways of Believing): Mi'kmaw Religion in Eskasoni, Nova Scotia* (Toronto: Pearson, 2005), 45.

12 Leroy Little Bear, "Jagged Worldviews Colliding," in *Reclaiming Aboriginal Voice and Vision*, ed. Marie Battiste (Vancouver, 2000), 78.

13 William P. Anderson, *Micmac Place Names in the Maritime Provinces and Gaspe Peninsula Recorded between 1852 and 1890 by Rev. S.T. Rand* (Ottawa: Surveyor General's Office, 1919), 21, 83.

14 Dan Moonhawk Alford, "Manifesting Worldviews in Language," Report no. 137, Mi'kmaq Resource Centre, Cape Breton University, 1992.

15 Little Bear, "Jagged Worldviews Colliding," 78.

16 Harald E.L. Prins, *The Mi'kmaq: Resistance, Accommodation, and Cultural Survival* (Fort Worth, TX: Harcourt Brace, 1996), 36–7.

17 Albert D. DeBlois, *Micmac Dictionary* (Hull: Canadian Museum of Civilization, 1996).

18 Robinson, *Ta'n Teli-ktlamsitasit*, 23.

19 "Sákéj" translates as "Jacques" or "James."

20 Henderson, "Ayukpachi: Empowering Aboriginal Thought," 257.

21 Robinson, *Ta'n Teli-ktlamsitasit*, 23–4.

22 Anne-Christine Homberg, *A Landscape of Left-Overs: Changing Conceptions of Time and Place among the Mi'kmaq Indians of Eastern Canada*, Lund Studies in the History of Religions, 14 (Lund, Sweden: Almqvist & Wiskell, 2001), 217.

23 "Euhemeristic" refers to an interpretative approach that presumes mythological accounts to have originated in real historical events and personages.

24 Bernard Hoffman, "The Historical Ethnography of the Micmac of the Sixteenth and Seventeenth Centuries" (PhD diss., University of California at Berkeley, 1955), 380, 347–9; Wilson D. Wallis and Ruth Sawtell Wallis, *The Micmac Indians of Eastern Canada* (Minneapolis: University of Minnesota, 1955), 321–481.

25 Prins, *Mi'kmaq: Resistance, Accommodation, and Survival*, 36.
26 Murdena Marshall, "Sacred Colours: A View into the World of Mi'kmaq Tribal Consciousness," unpublished ms (Report no. 236, Mi'kmaq Resource Centre, Cape Breton University, 1997); Marshall, "Mi'kmaq Sacred Teachings: 7 Stages of Life with the 7 Gifts (with a chart)," unpublished ms, n.d.
27 Henderson, "Ayukpachi: Empowering Aboriginal Thought," 261.

AFTERWORD

1 Nicole Dannielle Gilhuis, "Colonial Ghosts: Mi'kmaq Adoption, Daily Practice, and the Alternate Atlantic, 1600–1763" (PhD diss., University of California, Los Angeles, 2020).

Bibliography

The following bibliography contains many entries from the *Dictionary of Canadian Biography*. To conserve space, the relevant URL is not included within each entry. Instead, readers are referred to the *DCB*'s home page (http://www.biographi.ca/en/welcome.html), where the site's search function will readily provide access to the desired individual biographies.

Primary Archival Sources

Archdiocese of Halifax

Bishop Burke Papers

Archives de l'Archevêché de Québec

I-5 "Rev. James Jones to Bishop Inglis," 23 April 1787
VI-3 "Rev. Wm. Phelan to the Vice General of Quebec," August 1787
VG 1, 40 "Rev. James Jones regarding Benjamin Petitpas," 22 October 1787

Archives de la Charente-Maritime, La Rochelle, France

Amirauté de la Rochelle, B5654

Archives des Colonies (AC), Paris, France

Série CIIA, Correspondance générale, Canada
Série CIIB, Correspondance général, l'Ile Royale, 1712–63
Série CIIB, vol. 6, 77 f, *Recensement des Sauvages dans l'isle Royalle et de la peninsule de l'acadie qui sont deservis par les Missionaires du Seminire des missions étrangeres Etablis a Quebec fat par M. Gaulin pretre Missionaire desd. Sauvages en 1722*Série CIID, Correspondance générale, Acadie, 160388
F3 50, 504v–524, Conseil superieur, 17 February 1755
G2 189, 279–360
Greffes des colonies, 1754–55

Archives des Nationales d'Outre-Mer, Aix-en-Provence, France (ANOM)

Records pertaining to Fortress Louisbourg, Île Royale

Archives of Fortress Louisbourg Historic Park (AFL)

AC, Série CIIB, vol. 1, 1739, fols. 249–54
Archives de la France d'Outre Mer (AFO, now ANOM), G1, fols. 406 and 530. Births and baptisms of members of the Mi'kmaw Michau family of Cape Breton
Family Reconstition File, prepared by Barbara Schmeisser, Fortress of Louisbourg, NHSC, "Jacques Philippe Rondeau and Marie Josephe LeBorgne de Belisle"

Archives of the American Philosophical Society, Philadelphia

Frank Gouldsmith Speck Papers (microfilm copies of these documents are in the library of St. Francis Xavier University in Antigonish, Nova Scotia)

Ayer Collection, Newberry Library, Chicago

Ayer Collection, vol. 4, no. 751, in 40 folios, *Recensement genal fait au mois de Novembre mile sept cent huit de tous les Sauvages de l'Acadie que resident dans la Coste de l'Est, et ceux de Pintagouet et de Canibecky, Famille par Famille, Leurs ages – Celuy de Leurs Femmes et Enfants avec une Recapitulation a la fin de la quantité d'hommes et de garçons capable d'aler a La guerres, comme aussy Le recensement des françois Establis a La ditte Coste de l'Es, 1708* (General census made in the month of November seventeen hundred and eight of all the Native people of Acadia who reside on the East Coast, and at Pintagouet [in the Penobscot River area of Maine] and at Kennebec [near the present-day Kennebec River of Maine], family by family, their ages – also their wives and children with a recapitulation at the end of the number of men and boys capable of bearing arms, as well also of the French [Acadians] residing along the same coast, 1708)
MS 252, Edward E. Ayer Collection, Robert Roule's Deposition

Bibliothèque de la Comité Technique du Génie (or CTG), Paris, France

CTG, mss in fol. 210f (diary of François-Claude Grillot de Poilly for 1757); CTG, ms, vol. 4, 66, fols. 3–129 (diary of François-Claude Grillot de Poilly for 1758)

British Admiralty Records, London, England

AR, 1/2590, no. 4, "Captain Samuel Thompson of HMS *Lark* to Philip Stevens, Secretary of the Admiralty," 16 April 1764

British Library, London

Add. Ms. 21,809, fol. 101, "Francklin to Haldimand," 7 September 1780

British Ministry of Defence, Whitehall, London

Hydrographic Department Records, Misc. Papers, Ab3k, vol. 34, 568–70, "Log of HMS *Echo*, maintained by Lieut. Robert Carthew Reynolds," 1787

British Museum

Casteel, Anthony, "Anthony Casteel's journal," Andrew Brown MSS, Add. 19073, f. II, no. 23.

British Public Records Office, London

Adm. 52/1263, 233, "Master's Log, *Grenville*, 20 May 1767"
British Colonial Office Records (CO)

Canadian Museum of History, Gatineau, Hull, Quebec

Edward Sapir Correspondence
Frank Gouldsmith Speck Papers

Dalhousie University

Dalhousie University Archives, Copy of Andrew Brown ms BL, Add. mss 19069-7); DAL, MS-1–1,
    C-1 (Dalhousie College, letter-book, 1818–20), 13–30
Killam Library, Special Collections
Thomas Raddall Papers
Silus Tertius Rand's published writings

Deeds Offices, Nova Scotia

Annapolis County Deeds Office
Cumberland County Deeds Office
Halifax County Deeds Office
Kings County Deeds Office
Queens County Deeds Office
Shelburne County Deeds Office
Yarmouth County Deeds Office

Deeds Offices, New Brunswick

Gloucester County Deeds Office

Harriet Irving Archives, University of New Brunswick, Fredericton

MG H54 (Indian Affairs, New Brunswick)
MC 408 Indian document collection on microfilm, St. Thomas University project, 1982

Legislative Library, Province House, Halifax

Legislative Assembly of Nova Scotia Journals (*LANSJ*), 1800–66

Library and Archives Canada, Ottawa (LAC)

CO (British Colonial Records), on microfilm from British Records Office, London

MANUSCRIPT GROUPS
MG 1, France, Archives des Colonies, Série B, 1663–1774 (194 microfilm reels) MG 9 B8, 1:
    19–21, *Copie des Registres de l'Etat Civil de differents endroits de l'Acadie et de La Ga[s]pesie,*
    1680–1757

MG 11, micr. B-1028, "General Return of the Inhabitants in the Several Townships Settled at Cape Sables," June 1762

MG 15, Ethnic Groups

MG 17 B1, C series, box 2, Nova Scotia, 1752–58 (Microfilm Reel A-170)

MG 17 B1, vol. 1, Society for the Propagation of the Gospel in Foreign Parts (SPGFP), B 25 Nova Scotia, 1760–86 (folder), 1–313

MG 18 F18, Typescript of a French census, dated 1708, of encampments among the Penobscot by Abbé Pierre La Chasse, including nominal census information on Mi'kmaw families, men, women and children, belonging to villages on mainland Nova Scotia and Cape Breton (Île Royale) most likely gathered by Abbé Antoine Gaulin. The original ms, of 40 folios, is housed in vol. 4, no. 751 of the Edward E. Ayer Collection in the Newberry Library in Chicago.

MG 23, GII-19, George Henry Monk Papers and Letterbooks, vols. 3 and 4. Letterbook, Indian Affairs, 1783–97; 1808; Accounts

MG 100, vol. 189, no.10, "Regarding regalia of chief presented to Captain Henry O'Halloran at Miramichi"

RECORD GROUPS

Canada, *Sessional Papers*, Department of Indian Affairs Reports and Appendices

Canada, Federal Census Records, Census records for 1871, 1881, 1891, 1901, 1911, and 1921

RG 2, RS8, "Commissioner William Spragge to the Commissioner of Crown Lands, 12 April 1865, including documents relating to an interview that took place between Chief Joseph Claude of the Restigouche River area and the British commission in 1786."

RG 10, (Indian Affairs)

RG 34, British Public Records Office, War Office Records (WO)

Massachusetts Historical Society Collections

Collections of the Massachusetts Historical Society, vols. 1–10, 1809. First published 1760 in *The Pennsylvania Gazette*.

Massachusetts Historical Society Collections (1809), ser. 1, vol. 10, 115–16, Colonel Frye, "Extract of a letter from Col. Frye to His Excellency the governor of Nova Scotia, dated Fort Cumberland, Chignecto," 7 March 1760

Massachusetts State Archives, Boston

"Archives of Massachusetts, Nova Scotia and Canada," vols. 23 and 24

Capon, Peter. "A Journall of a Voyage to Cape Britton on ye King's Account by Mr. Peter Capon, 1715." Massachusetts State Archives, 38A:15

French Neutrals, 1758–1769, vol. 24, f. 121, "Laurent Mius to Massachusetts Legislature, 1758"

Memorial University of Newfoundland, St. John's

Maritime History Archives, Memorial University of Newfoundland, vol. 69, microfilm reel 108, "T. Street Bird & J. Bird Account Letter Books, Bird Manuscript Collection, Bonne Bay Ledgers, 1839–1844"

Musée des Acadiens des Pubnicos et Centre de recherché, West Pubnico, Nova Scotia

Father Clarence-J. d'Entremont, Collection of Documents

Land Papers

Maps

National Maritime Museum, Greenwich, London

Graves Papers

New Brunswick, Department of Natural Resources

Land Grants IV and Grants Book B

New Brunswick Museum

W.F. Ganong Scrapbooks

Nova Scotia Archives and Records Management, Halifax (NSARM)

Acadian French Records (five reels of microfilm)
Annapolis Royal: Parish of Saint Jean-Baptiste, Burials, Marriages, Deaths: 1702–28 (copied from
    RG 1, vol. 26), 1727–55 (Reels 1, 3, and 4)
Beaubassin: Baptisms, Marriages, Deaths, 1712–23, 1732–35, 1740–48 (Reel 1)
Copy of register kept by Charles-François Bailly, 1768–73, 1786–96, housed at Caraquet, New
    Brunswick. On microfilm at NSARM. *Registre des actes de baptême, mariages, et sepultures faits*
    en la nouvelle ecosse ou acadie commence Le vingt unième jour De juillet de L'année mil sept cent
    soixante huit, par mons. Charles-François Bailly, prêtre missionaire des Sauvages et acadiens, sujets
    de sa majesté britannique.
Grand Pré: Parish of St. Charles des Mines. Baptisms 1707–13, 1717–41, 1709–48; Deaths 1709–48
    (Reels 1 and 5)
H.R.S. Prince Arthur
Index to Land Grants
Indians: Land
Land Grants, Book 3A, 47–50 on Peminout grant
Land Grants, Book 4, 135, 418 on sale of Peminout grant
Land Grants, Book G
Land Grants (on microfilm), New Books 31 and 33
Land Grants (on microfilm), Old Books 6, 9, 12, 18, and 20
Map Collection – Map of Acadia by Governor Denys, 1672
Miscellaneous Indian "I" Land Papers for Nova Scotia, from Crown Lands Department files
NS Public Crown Lands Record Office (PCLRO)
Papers relating to the Acadian French, 1714–55
Registers of Acadie and Gaspé, 1679–86, 1751–58 (one reel)
Vertical Manuscript File
V/F 281 no. 6, "A History of Anderson's Mountain, Black Point, Boat Harbour, Chance Harbour, Kings
    Head, Little Harbour and Woodburn," by Mary Cullen, Shirley Aikins, and Margaret Forbes. Little
    Harbour Community Center, 1964

MANUSCRIPT GROUPS
Box 47, no. 24
MG 1, vol. 85, "Paul," T.B. Smith's Collection of Queens County names
MG 1, vols. 979–80, Peleg Wiswall Papers
MG 1, vol. 1189a, John Payzant's Journal
MG 1, vol. 2005, no. 12, Rev. J. Couteau on behalf of Chapel Island Mi'kmaq, 1839
MG, vol. 2806, nos. 8 and 21, Helen Creighton Collection

MG 1, vol. 2809, Helen Creighton Collection

MG 1, vols. 2865–9, Clara Dennis Archives: Papers, Notebooks, Scrapbooks, Photographs

MG 4, vol. 98 "G," Canon Harris Notes, no. 14, Tom Hammond and John Penall

MG 15, vols. 3–6 (Aboriginal Peoples and ethnic groups)

MG 100, grants

Bishop Burke Papers

Bishop Walsh Papers

Brown Manuscripts, BL, Add. MSS 19071, on microfilm from British Library, London

Dalhousie Journals, manuscripts

Smith, T.B., Collection

RECORD GROUPS

Journals and Proceedings of Nova Scotia House of Assembly, microfilm reel 3529

RG 1, vol. 9, 284, 363 Andrew Brown Papers (from British Museum)

RG 1, vols. 22–35, Minutes of H.M. Council at Annapolis Royal, 1720–40

RG 1, vol. 23, a manuscript copy of "Anthony Casteel's Journal" housed in the British Museum, (Brown MSS, Add. 19073, F II, no. 23). Prefixed to this document is a letter from Charles Morris to Lord Edward Cornwallis.

RG 1, vol. 26a, Registers of St. Jean-Baptiste Parish, Annapolis Royal, 1702–55

RG 1, vols. 29–34, 129, Original and duplicate dispatches of the Board of Trade and the Secretary of State to the Governors of Nova Scotia, 1749–99, commonly known as the "Whitehall Dispatches"

RG 1, vol. 37, no. 14, Ceremonials at Concluding a Peace with the Several Districts of the General Mickmack Nation of Indians in His Majesty's Province of Nova Scotia, with a Copy of Treaty dated 25 June 1761

RG 1, vol. 50, Letterbooks of Governor Wentworth

RG 1, vols. 60–71, Original dispatches from the Secretary of State to the Governors of Nova Scotia, 1800–33

RG 1, vol. 134, Provincial Secretary's Correspondence. NSARM, RG 1, vol. 134, 242, "William Cotterell, Provincial Secretary's Office, to Lieutenant Colonel Patrick Sutherland," 24 August 1754

RG 1, vol.135, correspondence, some treaties, and passes given to Mi'kmaq

RG 1, vol. 189, Halifax Executive Council Minutes

RG 1, vol. 320, 35–7, Minutes of the Executive of Cape Breton, 9 September 1794

RG 1, vol. 380, *Sketches of the Eastern and Northern Parts of the Province in the Years 1801 and 1802, with general observations thereon. Also a survey of the land between Sackville (Bedford) and Shubenacadie, and* observations on the Western Parts of the Province with a list of trees, shrubs, grasses and plants. By Titus Smith Jr. 3rd edition. Halifax, 1857.

RG 1, vols. 430–2 (Indian Affairs, Nova Scotia). Vol. 432 contains Joseph Howe's "Western Tour" of 1842 and Howe's papers and letterbooks, 1842–43.

RG 2, vol. 9. Petition of Jacob Brooks et al., Amherst, 5 February 1883, and Petition of Christopher Brooks et al., 29 March 1883

RG 3, vol. 1, no. 166, Commr. James D. Fraser and purchase of land for Mi'kmaq in Pictou County, 1863

RG 5, series A

RG 5, series P (Assembly petitions)

RG 20, series A, Records of the Commissioner of Crown Lands

RG 41, C, vol. 22, 6A, Inquest into the Death of Anne Cloud (Gloade)

Registers of baptisms, marriages and deaths in the Parish of Baye Ste. Marie, 1799–1811

Registers of the L'Eglise Saint François Xavier, Bear River

Registers of the Parish of Saint-Anne-du-Ruisseau, 1799–1841. Early parish records are available on the NSARM-sponsored website "An Acadian Parish Reborn," https://archives.novascotia.ca/acadian/reborn/.

Registers of the Paris of St. Jean-Baptiste, Annapolis Royal, 1705–1722, NSARM, RG 1, vols. 26 and 26a. These parish records are available on the NSARM-sponsored website "An Acadian Parish Remembered: The Registers of St. Jean-Baptiste, Annapolis Royal, 1702–1755," https://www.splitgraph.com/novascotia-ca/an-acadian-parish-remembered-the-registers-of-st-szq9-zgre/-/overview.

Registre des baptêmes, mariages, et sepultures à Beaubassin. *Copie des registres de l'etat civil de differents endroits de l'Acadie et de la Gaspesie, 1680–1757, de Archevêché de Québec,* on microfilm

Nova Scotia Museum (NSM)

Harry Piers Papers

"Mi'kmaq Portraits Collection," https://novascotia.ca/museum/mikmaq/. Database of more than 700 portraits

NSM, Ethnology Papers, Micmac Correspondence. (Ruth Holmes Whitehead has compiled copies of Harry Piers' original Ethnology Papers within three volumes)

NSM, Harry Piers Papers, History VII, A, corresp. E – general, Glace Bay, 20–21 December c.1920? Albert Almon's correspondence with Harry Piers regarding "old Indian altar, bearing date 1704"

NSM Photograph Collection

Provincial Archives of New Brunswick (PANB), Saint John

Journals of the Legislative Assembly of New Brunswick (JLANB)

MC1 family histories

MC80/1619, André Vienneau's "Vienneau family"

MC89 local histories

MC408, Indian Documentation Collection, Inventory

PANB, Genealogical collection

Parish of Sainte-Famille, Bathurst, 1798–1921 (F9368)

Parish of Belledune, Saint Jean L'Evangeliste (F9371)

Parish of Saint Pierre aux Liens, Gloucester County 1852–78 (F9372)

Perley, Moses. "Report on the Indian Settlements." Annexed to *the Journal of the House of Assembly* for 1844.

Roman Catholic Church Registers, New Brunswick

RS 636 Land Grants, New Brunswick

MANUSCRIPT GROUP

James White Papers

RECORD GROUPS

RG 1, Records of Lieutenant Governors of New Brunswick

RG 2, RS6, Minutes of the Executive Council

RG 2, RS7, Executive Council Minutes, Aboriginal peoples

RG 3, Records of the Provincial Secretary

RG 4, RS 24, Assembly Papers

RG 9, Records of the Department of Justice

RG 10, Records of the Department of Natural Resources and the Surveyor General

Provincial Archives of Newfoundland (PANL), St. John's

Newman Papers, Newman Little Bay Ledgers, 1790–91 (on microfilm), "Mi'kmaw Hunters of Bay Despoir Region Listed in Newman Little Bay Ledgers (1790–1791)"

Provincial Archives of Prince Edward Island

Legislative Assembly of Prince Edward Island Journals (*LAPEIJ*), 1832, 11, "Petition of Louis Francis Alguimou, Piel Jacques, Oliver Thoma, Peter Tony and Michael Mitchell"

Queens County Museum and Archives, Liverpool, Nova Scotia

"Francis Family Genealogy"

Registries of Deeds, Nova Scotia

Registry of Deeds, Annapolis Royal
Registry of Deeds, Halifax
Registry of Deeds, Kentville
Registry of Deeds, Yarmouth

Registries of Deeds, New Brunswick

Registry of Deeds, Bathurst, New Brunswick

Roman Catholic Parish Registers, New Brunswick
Registers of Sacré-Couer Church, Bathurst
Registers of Our Lady of Grace Church, Bathurst
Ste. Famille (Holy Family) Parish, Bathurst

Roman Catholic Parish Registers, Nova Scotia
Holy Cross Church, Pomquet, registers of Father Vincent de Paul
Mission of Ste. Ann, Indian Island, Diocese of Antigonish
Register of Father Vincent St. Paul, at Holy Cross Church, Pomquet, Nova Scotia
St. Ambrose Parish, Yarmouth, Nova Scotia
St. Ann's Parish, Thorburn, Antigonish County, Nova Scotia, 1884–1988
St. Anselm's Mission, 1799–1845, 1845– 63, 1866
St. Bernard's Roman Catholic Church, Enfield, beginning in 1857
St. Gregory's Parish, Liverpool, Queens County
St. Jerome's Roman Catholic Parish and missions, Caledonia, beginning in 1840
St. John's Parish, Windsor
St. Joseph's Parish, Bridgewater
St. Joseph's Roman Catholic Church, Kentville, Nova Scotia
St. Louis Parish, Annapolis Royal
St. Peter's Church, Tracadie, Nova Scotia
St. Peter's Parish, Dartmouth and Eastern Shore, 1800–97
St. Thomas Parish, Annapolis Royal
St. Vincent de Paul, Salmon River, Digby County, Nova Scotia
Ste. Anne du Ruisseau, Argyle Township, Yarmouth County
Stella Maris Church, Pictou

Roman Catholic Parish Registers, Prince Edward Island

St. Anne's Roman Catholic Church, Lennox Island, registers on microfilm

Treaty and Aboriginal Rights Research (TARR) Centre, Shubenacadie, Nova Scotia

Union of Nova Scotia Indians (UNSI) Collection, 92-1004-06-030, "Sharon Copage to the Union of Nova Scotia Indians (UNSI)," 17 June 1977, and "Emerson Frank Francis of Shelburne to UNSI," 10 January 1976

University of Cape Breton, Sydney

Beaton Institute, Copies of Executive Council Records on microfilm, Cape Breton "B" series, Minutes of the Executive Council of Cape Breton, 1785–92 (CB B7), 183–85, "At a Council held at the Government House, Island of Cape Breton the 28th of November 1792, before His Excellency the Lieutenant Governor, The Honourable David Matthews" (From British Colonial Office Records, CO/220)
Mi'kmaq College Institute, Mi'kmaq Resource Centre, Article no. 244, MRC, "Gabriel Sylliboy Becomes Grand Chief, 1918," in Mi'kmaq and English with an introduction by Helen Sylliboy and David L. Schmidt. This article appeared in Mi'kmaq and English with an introduction by Helen Sylliboy and David L. Schmidt in *Cape Breton's Magazine*, no. 71 (1996), 63–7

Université de Moncton, Moncton, New Brunswick

Archives of the Université de Moncton, Archives Acadiennes. Document 1.32-36, "A copy of Orders for John Yong [*sic*, Young] to join William Vondenveldon, 14 September 1785, signed by Wm. Vondenveldon, Deputy Surveyor and John Young. Witnesses, F.L. Kemp and William Powell"

University of Michigan, William L. Clements Library, Ann Arbor

Louisbourg Papers
Massachusetts Council Records
Thomas Gage Papers
Washington, DC, Library of Congress

West Yorkshire Archives

Ramsden Family Papers, vol. 2, part 2, "John Wentworth to Lord Rockingham," 21 October 1778

Newspapers

Acadian Recorder, Halifax
Aknutmanq, Membertou newsletter
The Advance, Liverpool
Berwick Register
Boston Weekly News-Letter
Bridgewater Bulletin
Cape Bretonian, Sydney
Cape Breton's Magazine
Cape Breton Post

The Casket, Antigonish
Christian Messenger, New York City
Chronicle Herald, Halifax
Church Times, Halifax
Colonial Patriot, Pictou
The Cross, Roman Catholic weekly, Halifax
Globe and Mail, Toronto
Green Bay Advocate, Michigan
Halifax Morning Post
Hants and Kings County Gazette
Indian Missionary Record, Ottawa, vol. 19, 8 October 1956
London Illustrated News, London, England
London Magazine or *Gentleman's Monthly Intelligencer*, London, England
Maclean's
The Micmac Messenger, Restigouche and Rimouski, Quebec (see *Setaneoni*)
Mi'kmaq-Maliseet Nations News
Miramichi Gleaner, Chatham, NB
Morning Herald, Halifax
The Northern Light, Bathurst, New Brunswick
Nova Farm News, Bridgewater
Nova Scotia Almanac
Nova Scotian and Weekly Chronicle, Halifax
Novascotian or Colonial Herald, Halifax
Parrsboro Record
Portland Sunday Telegram, Portland, Maine
The Register, Kentville, Nova Scotia
Royal Gazette, Charlottetown, Prince Edward Island
Setaneoni/Le Messager Micmac/The Micmac Messenger, no. 283, Rimouski, 1910
Sydney Record
The Times and Cape Breton, Sydney
Times and Courier, Halifax
Truro Daily News
Wabanaki Alliance, Orono, Maine
Whitehall Evening Post or the *London Intelligencer*, London, England
Yarmouth Herald
Yarmouth Vanguard

Primary Sources

"Abstract from the [Port Royal] parish register." In *Report Concerning the Canadian Archives Branch for the Year 1904*, 4–6 Edward VII, Sessional Paper No. 18, A 1905, Arthur G. Doughty, Archivist. Appendix G, 303. Ottawa: S.E. Dawson, Queen's Printer, 1905.

Akins, Thomas B., ed. *Selections from the Public Documents of the Province of Nova Scotia*. Halifax: Annand, 1869.

Akins, Thomas Beamish. "History of Halifax City." In *Collections of the Nova Scotia Historical Society*, vol. 8. Halifax: Morning Herald Printing and Publishing, 1895. Reprinted in book form, Halifax: Brook House, 2002.

Alline, Henry. *Henry Alline: Selected Writings*. Edited by George A. Rawlyk. Magwah, NJ: Paulist Press, 1987.

Anonymous. *Louisbourg in 1745: The anonymous Lettre d'un habitant de Louisbourg, Cape Breton: Containing a narrative by an eye-witness of the siege in 1745, from original data.* Edited by George M. Wrong. Toronto: University of Toronto Press, 1897.

Arneil, W.S. *Investigative Report on Indian Reserves and Indian Administration, Province of Nova Scotia, Indian Affairs Branch.* Ottawa: Department of Mines and Resources, August 1941.

Baxter, James Phinney, ed. *Baxter Manuscripts: Documentary History of the State of Maine.* 24 vols. Portland: Maine Historical Society, 1869–1916.

Beaumont, Gaston du Bosq de. *Les derniers jours de l'Acadie.* Paris: Lechevalier, Librairie Historique des Provinces, 1899.

Bégon, Élisabeth. *Lettres au cher fils: Correspondance d'Élisabeth Bégon avec son gendre (1748–1753).* Montreal: Boréal, 1994.

Bigger, H.P. *A Collection of Documents Relating to Jacques Cartier and Sieur de Roberval.* Ottawa: Public Archives of Canada, 1930.

– *The Works of Samuel de Champlain.* 6 vols. Toronto: Champlain Society, 1922–36.

Boundary Commission. *The memorials of the English and French commissaries concerning the limits of Nova Scotia or Acadie.* Vol. 1. London, 1755. First published 1755 by Imprimerie Royale, Paris.

Broadhead, John Romeyn, ed. *Documents Relative to the Colonial History of the State of New York.* Paris Documents, vol. 9. Albany: Weed, Parsons, 1885.

Bromley, Walter Henry. *An Account of the Aborigines of Nova Scotia Called the Micmac Indians.* London: Luke Hansard and Sons, 1822.

– *Address on the Deplorable State of the Indians.* Halifax: Recorder Office, 1814.

– *An Appeal to the Virtue and Good Sense of the Inhabitants of Great Britain, &c. in Behalf of the Indians of North America.* Halifax: Ward, 1820.

– *Two Addresses on the Deplorable State of the Indians.* London: T. Hamilton, 1815.

Casgrain, H.R., ed. *Collection de documents inédits sur le Canada et l'Amérique publiés par le Canada-Français.* 3 vols. Quebec: Demers and Frère, 1888–90.

Casteel, Anthony. "Anthony Casteel's Journal." In *Collection de documents inédits sur le Canada et l'Amérique publiés par le Canada-Français.* Quebec, 1889. Original housed in the British Museum, Brown MSS, Add. 19073, F II, no. 23.

Chappell, Edward. *Voyage of Her Majesty's Ship Rosamund to Newfoundland and the Southern Coast of Labrador.* London: J. Mawman, 1818.

Charlevoix, P.F.X. *History and General Description of New France.* Vol. 3. New York: F.P. Harper, 1900.

Cuthbertson, Brian C., ed. *The Journal of the Reverend John Payzant (1749–1834).* Hantsport, NS: Lancelot, 1981.

David, Albert. "Une autobiographie de l'abbé Le Loutre." *Nova Francia* (1931): 1–34.

de Forest, Louis Effingham, ed. *Journals of Seth Pomeroy, sometime general in the colonial service.* Publication no. 38. New York: Society of Colonial Wars in the State of New York, 1926.

– ed. *Louisbourg Journals, 1745.* New York: Society of Colonial Wars in the State of New York, 1932.

De Lagrange, Chancels. "Voyage Made to Isle Royale or Cape Breton Island in Canada in 1716 Aboard the Frigate Atalante Commanded by M. de Courbon St. Leger." *Revue d'Histoire de l'Amerique Française* 13, no. 3 (1959): 424.

Denys, Nicolas. *The Description and Natural History of the Coasts of North America (Acadia).* Translated and edited by William F. Ganong. Toronto: Champlain Society, 1903.

Department of the Interior. *Report of the Deputy Superintendent General of Indian Affairs.* Ottawa: Department of the Interior, 1877.

de Paul, Vincent. *Memoir of Father Vincent de Paul.* Translated by A.M. Pope. Charlottetown: Coombs, 1886.

Dièreville, Sieur de. *Relation of the Voyage to Port Royal in Acadia or New France.* Edited by J.C. Webster. Translated by Alice Webster. Toronto: Champlain Society, 1933.

The Documentary History of the State of New York. Vol. 7, edited by E.B. O'Callaghan. Albany: Weed, Parsons, 1856.

Documents Relative to the Colonial History of the State of New York, procured in Holland, England and France, edited by E.B. Callaghan. Vol. 10. Albany: Weed, Parsons, 1858.

Essex Museum Collections (formerly *Essex Institute Historical Collections*). "American Vessels Captured by the British during the Revolution and War of 1812, from Records of the Vice Admiralty Court at Halifax, Nova Scotia." Salem, MA, 36, 1911, 285. (In 2009, these records were compiled and published in book form by Cornell University, Ithaca, NY.)

– "Documents Relating to Marblehead." Salem, MA, 1926, 116–17.

Fergusson, Bruce, ed. *Minutes of His Majesty's Council at Annapolis Royal, 1736–1749*. Halifax: Nova Scotia Archives, 1967.

Floyer, Mathew. *Captain Mathew Floyer's Survey Report: Journal of the March by the River Shebenaccadia*. Halifax: Public Archives of Nova Scotia, 1958.

"François de Beauharnois et Gilles Hoquart à Maurepas, Québec, septembre 1745." In *Documents Relative to the Colonial History of New-York*, edited by E.B. Callaghan, 15. Albany: Weed, Parsons, 1858.

Ganong, William F. "Richard Denys, Sieur de Fronsac, and His Settlements in Northern New Brunswick." New Brunswick Historical Society, *Collections* 7 (1907): 7–54.

Gentleman's Magazine and Historical Chronicle, no. 20 (December–January 1749–50): 8. "A letter said to be sent by the Indian Prince of Nova Scotia, to the English governor of Chebucto." London: Edward Cave at St. John's Gate, Printer, 1750.

Hardy, Campbell. *Forest Life in Acadie: Sketches of Sport and Natural History in the Lower Provinces of the Canadian Dominion*. London: Chapman and Hall, 1869.

– *Sporting Adventures in the New World; or, Days and Nights of Moose-Hunting in the Pine Forests of Acadia*. Vols. 1 and 2. London: Hurst and Blackett, 1855.

Hind, Henry Youle. *Narrative of the Canadian Red River exploring expedition of 1857 and of the Assiniboine Saskatchewan exploring expedition of 1858*. London: Longman and Green, 1860.

Holland, Samuel J. *Holland's Description of Cape Breton Island and Other Documents*. Edited by Daniel C. Harvey. Publication no. 2. Halifax: Public Archives of Nova Scotia, 1935.

Howe, Joseph. *Eastern and Western Rambles: Travel Sketches of Nova Scotia*. Edited by M.G. Parks. Toronto: University of Toronto Press, 1973.

Johnson, W. John. *Life of John W. Johnson*. New York: Arno Press, 1977.

– *The Life of John W. Johnson Who Was Stolen by the Indians When Three Years of Age and identified by his Father twenty years afterwards, Related by Himself*. Biddeford, ME: Brown Thurston, 1861.

Jugements et délibérations du Conseil souverain de la Nouvelle-France. 6 vols. Quebec: Imprimerie Coté et Cie, 1885–91.

Kauder, Christian. *Sapeoig Oigatigen tan teli Gômgoetjoigasigel Alasotmaganel, Ginamatineoel ag Getapefiemgeoel; Manuel de Prières, instructions et 28erver28 sacrés en Hieroglyphes micmacs; Manual of Prayers, Instructions, Psalms & Hymns in Micmac Ideograms*. Ristigouche, Quebec: The Micmac Messenger, 1921. First published 1866.

Kidder, Frederic, ed., *Military Operations in Eastern Maine and Nova Scotia during the Revolution, chiefly composed from the Journals and Letters of Colonel John Allan*. New York: John Munsell, 1867; reprint, New York: Kraus, 1971.

Knox, John. *An Historical Journal of the Campaigns in North America for the Years 1757, 1758, 1759, and 1760*. Edited by Arthur G. Doughty. 2 vols. Toronto: Champlain Society, 1914.

La Corne, Saint-Luc de. *Journal du voyage de M. Saint-Luc de La Corne, ecuyer, dans le navire l'Auguste, en l'an 1761*. Montreal: Chez Fleury Mesplet imprimeur, 1778.

La Roque, Sieur. "Recensement du Sieur de la Roque." In *Rapport concernant les Archives Canadiennes pour l'année 1905*, vol. 2, document no. 18A and Appendix A, 1ère partie, 1–168. Ottawa: King's Printer, 1906.

La Varenne. "Letter from Mons. De la Varenne to his friend at Rochelle, Louisbourg, 8 May 1756." In Pierre Maillard, *An Account of the Customs and Manners of the Mickmakis and Maricheets, Savage Nations Now Dependent on the Government of Cape Breton* ... London: S. Hooper and A. Morley, 1758. https://www.gutenberg.org/cache/epub/15567/pg15567-images.html.

Lawrence, Charles. *Journal and Letters of Colonel Charles Lawrence.* Edited by D.C. Harvey. Bulletin no. 10. Halifax: Public Archives of Nova Scotia, 1953.

"Lawrence to Robert Monckton, 16 February." In "Two Letters of Charles Lawrence," *Cahiers de la Société historique Acadienne,* 25ième cahier, vol. 3, no. 5 (Moncton, December 1969), 174–7.

Le Clercq, Chrestien. *New Relation of Gaspesia.* Edited and translated by W.F. Ganong. Toronto: Champlain Society, 1910.

Lescarbot, Marc. *The History of New France.* Translated by W.L. Grant with an introduction by H.P. Biggar. Vol. 3. Toronto: Champlain Society, 1907.

Lettres et memoires pour servir à l'histoire naturelle, civile et politique du Cap Breton. La Hague, France : Pierre Gosse, 1760. Reprint, Andhra Pradesh, India, S.R. Publishers, 1966.

Longworth, Israel. "A History of the County of Colchester, Nova Scotia." Part 2, edited by Sandra Creighton. Truro, NS: Book Nook, 1989. Original ms c.1886.

MacMechan, Archibald, ed. *A Calendar of Two Letter-Books and One Commission-Book in the Possession of the Government of Nova Scotia.* Nova Scotia Archives II. Halifax: Herald Printing House, 1900.

– ed. *Original Minutes of His Majesty's Council at Annapolis Royal, 1720–1739.* Nova Scotia Archives III. Halifax: McAlpine, 1908.

Maillard, Pierre. *An Account of the Customs and Manners of the Micmakis and Maricheets, Savage Nations, now dependent on the government of Cape-Breton, from an original French manuscript-letter, never published, written by a French abbot, who resided many years, in quality of missionary, amongst them.* London: S. Hooper and A. Morley, 1758. https://www.gutenberg.org/cache/epub/15567/pg15567-images.html.

– "Lettre de M. l'abbé Maillard sur les missions de l'Acadie et particulièrement sur les missions micmaques, Lettre à Madame Drucour." In *Les soirées canadiennes: Recueil de ittérature nationale,* vol. 3, 289–426. Quebec: Brousseau Frères, 1863.

Manach, Jean. "Manach's list of chiefs that accompanied a letter from Colonel Frye to the Governor of Nova Scotia, dated Fort Cumberland, Chignecto, 7 March 1760." Both letter and list are published in *Massachusetts Historical Society Collections,* Boston. Massachusetts Historical Society, 1809, first ser., 10: 115.

Massachusetts Historical Society Proceedings. October 1910. "Journal of Rev. Joseph Emerson."

Massachusetts Society of Mayflower Descendants. "Yarmouth N.S. Marriage Records." In *The Mayflower Descendant,* vol. 9. Boston: Massachusetts Society of Mayflower Descendants, 1907.

Massachusetts State Archives (MSA), vol. 63, folio 416, "Declaration of Joseph Marjory," 18 December 1724.

Mémoires de la Société Généalogique Canadienne-Française 6 (1955): 316–17.

Morse, William Inglis, ed. *Acadiensia Nova (1598–1779),* vol. 1: *New and Unpublished Documents and Other Data Relating to Acadie (Nova Scotia, New Brunswick, Maine, etc.).* London: Bernard Quaritch, 1935.

– "Sojourn of Gargas in Acadie, 1687–1688." In Morse, *Acadiensia Nova (1598–1779),* vol. 1, chap. 4.

The Naval Chronicle. Edited by James Stanier Clarke, Stephen Jones, and John Jones. Vol. 14. London: I. Gold, July–December 1805.

New England Genealogical and Historical Register. "Letters of Colonel Thomas Westbrook and Others," April 1893, 164.

Ninth Annual Report of the Committee of the Micmac Missionary Society, 16 November 1858. Halifax: Printed at the Wesleyan Conference Steam Press, 1858.

Original Minutes of His Majesty's Council at Annapolis Royal, 1720–1739. Nova Scotia Archives III. Halifax: McAlpine, 1908.

Ottawa, Canada Public Archives. *Report concerning Canadian Archives for the year 1905 in three volumes*, Sessional Paper no. 18, vol. 2, edited by Arthur G. Doughty, Dominion Archivist. Ottawa: S.E. Dawson, 1906. (Vol. 2 includes "Recensement effectué par le Sieur de La Roque, 1752/Tour of Inspection made by the Sieur de la Roque, December 5, 1752." De la Roque's original manuscript, "Recensement fait par le Sieur de la Roque, arpenteur du Roi des habitants de tous les ports, havres, ances, rivières d l'Île Royale et de l'Île St-Jean, commencé le 5 fevrier 1752 par ordre de M. le Comte de Raymond," is housed in the Archives Nationales d'Outre-Mer, vol. G1 466, vol. 81, pieces A, B, C, D, E.)

Owen, William. *Narrative of American Voyages and Travels of Captain William Owen, R.N.* Edited by Victor Hugo Paltsits. New York: New York Public Library, 1942.

Perkins, Simeon. *The Diary of Simeon Perkins 1766–1780*. Edited with introduction and notes by Harold A. Innis. 5 vols. Toronto: Champlain Society, 1948.

Perley, Moses. *Report for Indian Affairs in New Brunswick of 3 March 1848*. Fredericton: Department of Indian Affairs of New Brunswick, 1848.

Pichon, Thomas. *Genuine Letters and Memoirs relating to the Natural, Civil, and Commercial History of the Islands of Cape Breton and Saint John.* London: Nourse, 1760.

– *Lettres et Mémoirs pour server à l'histoire naturelle, civile et politique du Cap Breton: Depuis sa établissement jusqu'à la reprise de cette isle par les Anglois en 1758.* La Haye: Pierre Gosse/London: Jean Nourse, 1760.

"Plan for the Future Management of Indian Affairs, 1764." In *Documents Relative to the Colonial History of the State of New York, procured in Holland, England and France*, edited by E.B. Callaghan, 7.637. Albany: Weed, Parsons, 1856.

Plessis, Joseph-Octave. "Deux voyages dans le Golfe Saint-Laurent et les provinces d'en bas, en 1811 et 1812." *Le Foyer Canadien*, 1865.

– *Journal des visites pastorals de 1815 et 1816, par Monseigneur Joseph-Octave Plessis, évêque de Québec.* Quebec: Henri Têtu, 1903.

Proctor, Jonathan. "Diary Kept at Louisbourg, 1759–1760." In *The Essex Institute Historical Collections*, vol. 70 (1934).

Proulx, Ls.-A. *Rapport de l'archiviste de Québec pour 1923–1924.* Quebec: Imprimeur de Sa Majesty le Roi, 1924.

Rameau de Saint-Père, Edmé. *Une colonie féodale en Amérique: L'Acadie (1604–1881).* Book 2. Paris: Éditions Granger frères, 1889.

Rand, Silus Tertius. "Early Provincial Settlers." *The Provincial* 1, no. 8 (1852).

– *The Epistles and Revelation translated into Micmac.* Halifax: n.p., 1874. (Copy in NSARM.)

– *A First Reading Book in the Micmac Language.* Halifax: Nova Scotia Printing Company, 1875.

– *Legends of the Micmacs.* New York: Longmans, Green, 1894.

– *Report of the Micmac Mission for the Year ending December 1866.* Halifax: J. Chamberlain, 1867.

Raymond, W.O., ed. *Winslow Papers.* Saint John: New Brunswick Historical Society, 1901.

Records of the Deportation and Le Grand Dérangement, 1714–1768. Nova Scotia Archives I, Halifax: Charles Annand, 1869, 306–7, "To His Excellency Thomas Pownall, Esq. and Honourable Council in Boston," 5 September 1758.

Registre de l'Abbe Charles-François Bailly, 1768 à 1773. Transcribed under the direction of Stephen A. White. Moncton: Centre d'études acadiennes, Université de Moncton, 1978.

Resolves of the General Assembly of the Colony of Massachusetts-Bay, 29 May–13 January 1776. Boston, 1776.

Salusbury, John. *Expeditions of Honour: The Journal of John Salusbury in Halifax, Nova Scotia, 1749–1753.* Edited by Edward Romkey. Newark: University of Delaware Press, 1982.

Seccombe, John. "The Diary of Rev. John Seccombe." In *Report of the Board of Trustees of the Public Archives of Nova Scotia for the Year 1959*, Appendix B, 20–37. Halifax: Public Archives of Nova Scotia.

Sigogne, Jean-Mandé, Abbé. Census of the Cape Sable Native Population c. 1822, "Familles des Sauvages." In *Cape Sable Vital Records, 1799–1841*, trans. by Leonard Smith. Florida: Clearwater Press, 1979.

Smethurst, Gamaliel. *A Narrative of an Extraordinary Escape out of the Hands of the Indians in the Gulf of St. Lawrence*. In *Collections of the New Brunswick Historical Society*, edited by W.F. Ganong, vol. 2, 358–90. Saint John: New Brunswick Historical Society, 1905. First published 1764 by the author, London.

Smith, Leonard H., Jr., ed. *Cape Sable, Nova Scotia: Vital Records, 1799–1841 from Roman Catholic Registers of Saint Anne of Eel Brook/Argyle, Saint Michel of Tusket/Argyle, Saint Peter of Pubnico*. Clearwater, FL: Owl Books, 1979.

– ed. *Salmon River, Digby County, Nova Scotia – Vital Records 1849–1907, from Registers of the Roman Catholic Parish of St. Vincent de Paul*. Clearwater, FL: Owl Books, 1974.

– ed. *St. Mary's Bay, 1818–1829* and *St. Mary's Bay 1840–1844: Catalogue of Families, St. Mary's Bay Roman Catholic Parish, Clare, Digby County, Nova Scotia*. Compiled by Father Jean-Mandé Sigogne. Transcribed, edited, and indexed by Leonard H. Smith Jr. Clearwater, FL: Owl Books, 1975.

Thwaites, Reuban Gold, ed. *The Jesuit Relations and Allied Documents*. 73 vols. Cleveland: Burrows Brothers, 1886–91.

The trials of five persons for piracy, felony and robbery: who were found guilty and condemned, at a Court of Admiralty for the trial of piracies, felonies and robberies committed on the high seas, held at the court-house in Boston within His Majesty's province of the Massachusetts-Bay in New England on Tuesday the fourth day of October, anno domini, 1726, Boston. Printed by T. Fleet for S. Gerrish, 1726. https://quod.lib.umich.edu/e/evans/n02375.0001.001/21?page=root;size=100;view=text.

Tutty, William. "First Letter, From on board ye Beaufort in ye Harbour of Chebuctou, September 29th, 1749." In "Letters and Other Papers Relating to the Early History of the Church of England in Nova Scotia." In *Collections of the Nova Scotia Historical Society*, no. 7, 89–127. Halifax: Morning Herald Printing and Publishing, 1891.

– "Letter to the Society of the Propagation of the Gospel in Foreign Parts," 20 September 1749. In "Letters and Other Papers Relating to the Early History of the Church of England in Nova Scotia," *Collections of the Nova Scotia Historical Society*, no. 8, 93. Halifax: Morning Herald Printing and Publishing, 1891.

Uniacke, Richard J. *Uniacke's Sketches of Cape Breton, 1862–1865*. Edited by Bruce C. Fergusson. Halifax: Public Archives of Nova Scotia, 1958.

Washington, Library of Congress. Records of the States of the United States, Massachusetts Council Records, edited by W.S. Jenkins, microfilm.

Webster, John Clarence, ed. *Acadia at the End of the Seventeenth Century: Letters, Journals and Memoirs of Joseph Robineau de Villebon, Commandant in Acadia, 1690–1700, and Other Contemporary Documents*. Monographic series no. 1. St. John: New Brunswick Museum, 1934.

– *The Career of the Abbé Le Loutre in Nova Scotia, with a Translation of His Autobiography*. Shediac: privately printed, 1933.

– ed. *Charles des Champs de Boishébert: A Canadian Solider in Acadia*. Shediac: privately printed, 1931.

– ed. *Journals of Beausejour*. Halifax: Public Archives of Nova Scotia, 1937.

– ed. *Thomas Pichon, "The Spy of Beausejour": An Account of His Career in Europe and America*. Halifax: Public Archives of Nova Scotia, 1937.

West, John. *A Journal of a Mission to the Indians of the British Provinces of New Brunswick and Nova Scotia, and the Mohawks on the Ouse or Grand River, Upper Canada.* London: Seeley, 1827.

Wyndham-Quin, Windham Thomas, Earl of Dunraven, "A Colorado Sketch." In *Canadian Nights: Being Sketches and Reminiscences of Life and Sport in the Rockies, the Prairies, and the Canadian Woods,* 20–51. London: Smith, Elder, 1914.

Unpublished Reports, Essays, and Dissertations

Allen, Gillian. "Licenses of Occupation in Nova Scotia: Is a Reserve by Any Other Name Still a Reserve?" Discussion paper prepared for National Research Directors Workshop for Specific Claims Organizations across Canada (NRDW), Ottawa, 8 November 2006.

Allen, Patricia. "Commodore George Walker at Nepisiguit: Protecting and Preserving an Extraordinary Fragment of 18th Century Maritime History." Paper presented at meeting of the Canadian Archaeological Association, Ottawa, May 2002.

Anger, Dorothy. *Nogwa'mkisk (Where the Sand Blows ...): Vignettes of Bay St. George Micmacs.* Port au Port East, NF: Bay St. George Regional Band Council, 1988.

Awalt, Don Byrd. "The Mi'kmaq and Point Pleasant Park, The Mi'kmaq and Amtoukati: An Historical Essay in Progress by Don Byrd Awalt." Halifax: Native Friendship Centre, 2006.

Balcom, B.A., and Charles A. Martijn. "A Chronological Note on the Mi'kmaq Chief, Jeannot Peguidalouet, and His Family," 8 September 1996.

Battiste, Marie. "An Historical Investigation of the Social and Cultural Consequences of Micmac Literacy Education." PhD dissertation, Stanford University, 1984.

Beal, Bob. "Nurturing the Pine Tree – Sovereigns, Governments, Indians, Treaties: Relationships in the North American Treaty Process, 1610 to 1930." Unpublished ms., 1 April 1998.

Beanlands, Sara J. "Annotated edition of Rev. Dr. Andrew Brown's manuscript: 'Removal of the French inhabitants of Nova Scotia by Lieut. Governor Lawrence & His Majesty's Council in October 1755.'" Master's thesis, Saint Mary's University, 2010.

Bennett, Ella. "We Had Something Good and Sacred Here: Restoring *A's'ek* with Pictou Landing First Nation." Master's thesis, Dalhousie University, 2013.

Boudreau, Gérald C. "L'Apostolat du missionnaire Jean-Mandé Sigogne et les Acadiens du sud-ouest de la Nouvelle-Écosse." PhD diss., University of Montreal, 1989.

Brennan, Sharon. "Revisiting the Proverbial Tin Cup: A Study of Political Resistance of the Mi'kmaq of Nova Scotia, 1900–1969." Master's thesis, Saint Mary's University, 2000.

Brun, Josette. "Le veuvage en Nouvelle-France: Genre, dynamique familiale et stratégies de survie dans deux villes coloniales du XVIIIe siècle, Québec et Louisbourg." PhD diss., University of Montreal, 2000.

Chute, Janet E. "A Comparative Study of Bark, Bone, Wood and Hide Items Made by the Historic Micmac, Montagnais-Nascapi [Innu] and Beothuk Nations." Master's thesis, Memorial University of Newfoundland, 1976.

– "A Good Day on the Aboiteau: An Ethnographic and Ethnohistorical Study of the Acadian *Métis* of Eel Brook and Quinan Areas, Municipality of Argyle, Nova Scotia." September 2004.

– "Interpenetrating Realities: A New Perspective on Acadian and Mi'kmaw Land Use in Southwestern Nova Scotia." Ms, 1999.

– "The Long Road Back: Origins of the Nova Scotia Mi'kmaq Land and Resource Campaign." Shubenacadie: Aboriginal Title Project, 1999.

– "Report on Paq'tnlet First Nation Claim." Ms, August 2004. Ottawa, Indian Affairs.

– "Riders in the Cradle on the Waves: An Ethnohistory of the Mi'kmaq of Epekwitk (Prince Edward Island)." Paper prepared for the Epekwitk Assembly of Councils (EAC), December 2021.

Coffin, Michelle. "United They Stood, Divided They Didn't Fall: Culture and Politics in Mi'kmaq Nova Scotia, 1969–1988." Master's thesis, Saint Mary's University, 2003.

Cook, Mary. "History of South Section #9." Musquodoboit Valley Bicentennial, 1733–1983. In loose leaf binder in NSARM, F 5248 M988 M988.

Cox, Michael. *Mi'kmaq Use of Oositookum (Digby Neck), Its Surrounding Waters, and the Mainland Shore of St. Mary's Bay.* Report prepared for the Mainland Confederacy of Mi'kmaq, Truro, NS, December 2005.

Cuthbertson, Brian. *Stubborn Resistance: New Brunswick Maliseet and Mi'kmaq in Defense of Their Lands.* Halifax: Nimbus, 2015.

De LaFleche, Solange Richer. "Who I Am: An Examination of My Aboriginal ancestry" (essay examining the Nevin Family). Mount Saint Vincent University, Spring 2015.

Department of Indian Affairs, Ottawa. DINA File 201/1–1. Bart Mckinnon and D.R. Cassie, "Report on Field Interviews with Micmacs of Nova Scotia and the areas in which they Reside and the Unoccupied Reserves of Nova Scotia Mainland." 1957.

Desbrisay, M.B., "History of the County of Lunenburg." Atkins Prize Essay for 1868. Manuscript in King's College University Library, Halifax.

Dickason, Olive Patricia. "Louisbourg and the Indians: A Study in Imperial Race Relations, 1713–1760." Ms, Fortress Louisbourg National Park archives, September 1972. Rev. ed. published in monograph, Ottawa: DIAND, 1976.

Draper, Thomas F. "Essay on the History of Hants County." Prize-winning essay, King's College, 1881. Copy in NSARM, F 106 H19 D79.

Drolet, Yves. "Histoire généalogique de la famille Denys." Montreal: Bibliothèque et Archives nationales du Québec, 2016. https://numerique.banq.qc.ca/patrimoine/details/52327/2518395. Accessed 16 March 2023.

Duguay, Hermel, and Donald J. Morrison. "Extraits de Documents Microfilm, Micmak Indien ou Sauvage." Typescript, n.d.

Erskine, John. "Erskine's Micmac Notes, 1958." Nova Scotia Museum of Natural History, Printed Matter File, ms, MS 754.

– "A Superficial Survey of Pre-Expulsion Acadie as It Remains Today." Ms, dated 1970, in Nova Scotia Museum archaeological report files.

Ferguson, Robert S.O. "Archaeological Sites in Kejimkujik Park, Nova Scotia." Nova Scotia Museum, 1986.

Francis, Rosalie Marie. "The Mi'kmaq Nation and the Embodiment of Political Ideologies: Ni'kmaq, Protocol and Treaty Negotiations of the Eighteenth Century." Master's thesis, Saint Mary's University, 2003.

Gilhuis, Nicole Dannielle. "Colonial Ghosts: Mi'kmaq Adoption, Daily Practice, and the Alternate Atlantic, 1600–1763." PhD diss., University of California, Los Angeles, 2020.

Gray Godin, Florence, comp. "The Mi'kmaq of Gloucester Co. and the Pabineau Reservation." Unpublished pamphlet, part of a collection of papers and documents compiled by Florence Gray Godin.

– "Pabineau First Nation." Undated typescript, c.2011, researched, compiled, and written by Florence Gray Godin. Bathurst Heritage Trust Commission.

Halwas, Sara. "Where the Wild Things Grow: A Paleoethnobotanical Study of Late Woodland Plant Use at Clam Cove, Nova Scotia." Master's thesis, Memorial University of Newfoundland, 2006.

Hamilton, Charles S. "A History of Kings County." Akins Historical Prize Essay, 1867, King's College, Halifax.

Hipwell, William. "Taking Charge of the Bras d'Or: Ecological Politics in the 'Land of Fog.'" PhD diss., Carlton University, 2001.

Hoffman, Bernard G. "The Historical Ethnography of the Micmac of the Sixteenth and Seventeenth Centuries." PhD diss., University of California at Berkeley, 1955.

Indian and Northern Affairs Canada. "Middle Stewiacke Specific Claim." File no. B8260–674.

Johnson, Eleanor. "Mi'kmaq Tribal Consciousness." Master's thesis, Saint Mary's University, 1992 (in Mi'kmaq).

Julien, Donald M. "Story of Joseph Julien." Unpublished ms based on stories recorded and transcribed by Donald Julien from his grandmother, Louise Googoo. A printed version appears in the *Mi'kmaq-Maliseet Nations News*, January 2012.

Kelly, Alice R. "Ground Penetrating Radar and the Search for Commodore Walker's 18th Century Occupation." Paper presented at the 42nd annual meeting of the Geological Society of America, Northeastern Section, 12–14 March 2007.

Landry, Mark William. "Pokemouche Mi'kmaq and the Colonial Regimes." Master's thesis, Saint Mary's University,
2010.

Lawrence, Ian. "Mi'kmaw Families of Southwestern Nova Scotia." c. 2011. Copy in possession of Janet Chute.

Locke, Helen. "Diary." c.1920–22. Helen Locke, a direct descendant of Samuel Locke, an original settler of Lockeport, Nova Scotia, maintained a diary in which she described and drew a pencil sketch of a Mi'kmaw encampment at Monkey Hollow, also known as Sam's Point. The diary is currently in the possession of Helen's nephew, Fred Partridge.

MacDonald, Lindiwe. "The Process of Mi'kmaq Community-Based Development: A Case Study of the Bear River Mi'kmaq *Npisunewawti* (Medicine Trail) Project." Master's thesis, Dalhousie University, 2000.

Marshall, Murdena. "Sacred Colours: A View into the World of Mi'kmaq Tribal Consciousness." Unpublished report no. 236, Mi'kmaw Resource Center, Cape Breton University, 1997.

Martjin, Charles A. "Mi'kmaq in the Parish Registers of the Islands of Saint-Pierre and Miquelon, 1764–1848." Unpublished ms, September 1996.

McGee, Harold F. "Ethnic Boundaries and Strategies of Ethnic Interaction: A History of Micmac-White Relations in Nova Scotia." PhD diss., Southern Illinois University, 1973.

McMillan, Leslie Jane, "Mi'kmatwey Mawio'mi: Changing Roles of the Mi'kmaq Grand Council from the Early Seventeenth Century to the Present." Master's thesis, Dalhousie University, 1996.

Mi'kmawey Mawio'mi. Petition of 7 January 2012 signed by Grand Chief Ben Sylliboy, *Kji Keptin* Andrew Denny, and Grand Council *Pu'tus* Victor Alex. Photocopy of original in possession of Janet E. Chute.

Morin, Maxime. "Le 43ole politique des Abbés Pierre Maillard, Jean-Louis Le Loutre et François Piquet dans les relations Franco-Amérindiennes à la fin du régime français (1734–1763)." Master's thesis, Laval University, 2009.

Morris, Brandon Robert. "'Those Two Insignificant Islands': Saint-Pierre and Miquelon, and Social-Cultural Continuity in Northeastern North America, 1763–1793." Master's thesis, University of Saskatchewan, 2012.

Morrison, Donald. "Family Charts Line of Peter Paul." Typescript, 2005.

– "Family Tree of Joseph Nicholas Prisk." Typescript, 2005.

Morrison, Kenneth M. "The People of the Dawn: The Abnaki and Their Relations with New England and New France, 1600–1727." PhD diss., University of Maine, 1975.

Mullen, Eric. "The Story of Jim Charles." Ms on file at Kejimkujik National Park, n.d.

Nietfeld, Patricia Kathleen. "Determinants of Aboriginal Micmac Political Structure." PhD diss., University of New Mexico, 1981.

Pastore, R.T. "Micmac Colonization and Newfoundland." Ms. n.d. (1977?). Copy in NSARM, accession F 80 C16a P214 #1.

Patterson, Lisa Lynne. "Centralization in Nova Scotia: An Adventure in Canadian Indian Policy." Paper presented at Learned Societies Conference, University of Manitoba, Winnipeg, June 1986.

– "Indian Affairs and the Nova Scotia Centralization Policy." Master's thesis, Dalhousie University, 1985.

Peace, Thomas. "Two Conquests: Aboriginal Experiences of the Fall of New France and Acadia." PhD diss., York University, 2011.

Phillips, Nik. *Mikwie'tt Ta'n Kis Teliaq Aqq Ni'n Majukwattm Ta'n L'nui Wetapeksi* (Remembering the past and following my Mi'kmaq roots). *Mi'kmaq-Maliseet Nations News*, May 2014.

Pictou, Sherry M. "Decolonizing Mi'kmaw Memory of Treaty: L'sitkuk's Learning with Allies in Struggle for Food and Lifeways." PhD diss., Dalhousie University, 2017.

"Registres Paroissiaux de Saint-Pierre et Miquelon: 1763 à 1790–1791, Baptêmes, 01/06/1767." *Le Messager de l'Atlantique*, Falaise Acadie Québec, annexe 1, no. 32 (Premier Trimestre 1996).

Reinhart, Melinda. "Lady Falkland's Travel Album: Negotiating Colonial and Feminine Discourses." Master's thesis, Concordia University, 2005.

Robertson, Thomas. "History of Digby County." Akins Prize essay, 1873. Ms, King's College University Library, Halifax.

– "History of Shelburne County." Akins Prize Essay, 1871. Ms, King's College University Library, Halifax.

Robineau de Villebon, Joseph. "Journal of Acadia from November 11, 1692, to August 7, 1693. Villebon to Count Ponchartrain." In *Acadia at the End of the Seventeenth Century: Letters, Journals and Memoirs of Joseph Robineau de Villebon, Commandant in Acadia, 1690–1700, and Other Contemporary Documents*, edited by John Clarence Webster, 44–8. Saint John, NB: Tribune, 1934.

Sanders, Mike. "Francis Nose Archaeological Project, Preliminary Report." Typescript, 10 October 2000. Heritage Permit A 1999NS 49, Nova Scotia Museum.

Stein, Sheila. "The Psychological Consequences of Acculturation among the Cape Breton Micmac." Master's thesis, University of Pennsylvania, 1951.

Strouthes, Daniel P. "Change in the Real Property Law of a Cape Breton Island Micmac Band." 2 vols. Includes census material. PhD diss., Yale University, 1994.

Thomas, Rebecca. "Guarded Borders: Colonially Induced Boundaries and Mi'kmaq Peoplehood." Master's thesis, Dalhousie University, 2012.

Thomson-Millward, Marilyn Elaine, "'Researching the Devils': A Study of Brokerage at the Indian Residential School, Shubenacadie, Nova Scotia." PhD diss., Dalhousie University, 1997.

Tobin, Anita Maria. "The Effect of Centralization on the Social and Political Systems of the Mainland Nova Scotia Mi'kmaq (Case Studies: Millbrook – 1916 & Indian Brook – 1941)." Master's thesis, Saint Mary's University, 1999.

Wicken, William C. "Encounters with Tall Sails and Tall Tales: Mi'kmaq Society, 500–1760." PhD diss., McGill University, 1994.

Willis, Sherise. "A Favourite Mi'kmaw Son, Argimault." Essay written for undergraduate course in Canadian Studies program, Mount St. Vincent University, Halifax, 2009–10.

Secondary Sources

Abler, Thomas S. "A Mi'kmaq Missionary among the Mohawk: Silus T. Rand and His Attitudes towards Race and 'Progress.'" In *With Good Intentions: Euro-Canadian & Aboriginal Relations in Colonial Canada*, edited by Celia Haig-Brown and David A. Nock, 72–86. Vancouver: University of British Columbia Press, 2006.

Adams, Eric. "Ghosts in Court: Jonathan Belcher and the Proclamation of 1762." *Dalhousie Law Journal* (Fall 2004): 321–45.

Alexander, D.R., J.J. Kerekes, and B.C. Sabean. "Description of Selected Lake Characteristics and Occurrence of Fish Species in 781 Nova Scotia Lakes." *Proceedings of the Nova Scotia Institute of Science* 36, pt. 2 (1986): 71.

Allen, Patricia. *Commodore George Walker at Alston Point, Nepisiguit, 1768–1777*. New Brunswick Manuscripts in Archaeology 31. Fredericton: Culture and Sport Secretariat, Archaeology Services, 2003.

– "The Oxbow Site: An Archaeological Framework for Northeastern New Brunswick." In *Approaches to Algonquian Archaeology: Proceedings of the Thirteenth Annual Conference*, edited by Margaret G. Hanna and Brian Kooyman, 119–33. Calgary: Department of Archaeology, University of Calgary, 1982.

Allen, Patricia, R. Kelley, F.L. Stewart, and D. Bérubé. *In Search of Commodore Walker*. Toronto: Canadian Archaeological Association, 2006.

Anderson, William P. *Micmac Place Names in the Maritime Provinces and Gaspé Peninsula Recorded between 1852 and 1890 by Rev. S.T. Rand*. Ottawa: Surveyor General's Office, 1919.

Armstrong, Sally. *The Nine Lives of Charlotte Taylor: The First Woman Settler on the Miramichi*. Toronto: Random House, 2007.

Arsenault, Bona. *Éditions: Histoire et généalogie des Acadiens*. 3rd ed. Montreal: Léméac, 1976–78.

Atkinson, Christopher W. *A Historical and Statistical Account of New Brunswick, B.N.A., with Advice to Emigrants*. 3rd ed. Edinburgh: Anderson and Bryce, 1844.

Augustine, Stephen. *Mi'kmaq and Malecite Cultural Ancestral Material: National Collections from the Canadian Museum of Civilization*. Gatineau, QC: Canadian Museum of Civilization, 2005.

Axtell, James. "The Vengeful Women of Marblehead: Robert Roule's Deposition of 1677." *William and Mary Quarterly*, 3rd. ser., 31 (October 1974): 650–2.

Bailey, Alfred G. *The Conflict of European and Eastern Algonquian Cultures, 1504–1700*. 2nd ed. Toronto: University of Toronto Press, 1969. First published 1937 by New Brunswick Museum, Saint John.

– "Denys de Fronsac, Richard." *Dictionary of Canadian Biography* online, vol. 1 (1000–1700).

Baker, Emerson W. "'A Scratch with a Bear's Paw': Anglo-Indian Land Deeds in Early Maine." *Ethnohistory* 36 (1989) 3:235–56.

Bakker, Peter. "Basque Pidgin Vocabulary in European-Algonquian Trade Contacts." In *Papers of the Nineteenth Algonquian Conference*, edited by William Cowan, 7–15. Ottawa: Carleton University, 1988.

Balcom, B.A., and A.J.B. Johnston. "Missions to the Mi'kmaq: Malagawatch and Chapel Island in the 18th Century." *Journal of the Nova Scotia Historical Society* 9 (Fall 2006): 115–40.

Bannon, Richard V. "Antoine Gaulin 1674–1730: An Apostle of Early Acadie." In *Report*, Canadian Catholic Historical Association, no. 19 (1952), 49–59.

Bartels, Dennis A. "Time Immemorial? A Research Note on Micmacs in Newfoundland." *Newfoundland Quarterly* 75, no. 3 (1979): 6–9.

Bartels, Dennis A., and Olaf Uwe Janzen. "Micmac Migration to Western Newfoundland." *Canadian Journal of Native Studies* 10, no. 1 (1990): 74–7.

Basque, Maurice. *Des hommes de pouvoir: Histoire d'Otho Robichaud et de sa famille, notables Acadiens de Port-Royal et de Néguac*. Néguac: Société historique de Néguac, 1996.

– "Family and Political Culture in Pre-Conquest Acadia." In *The Conquest of Acadia, 1710: Imperial, Colonial and Aboriginal Constructions*, by John Reid, Maurice Basque, Elizabeth Mancke, Barry Moody, Geoffrey Plank, and William Wicken, 48–63. Toronto: University of Toronto Press, 2004.

Basque, Maurice, and Josette Brun. "La neutralité à l'épreuve: des Acadiennes à la défense de leurs intérêts en Nouvelle-Écosse du 18ᵉ siècle." In *Entre le quotidien et le politique: Facettes de l'historie des femmes francophones en milieu minoritaire*, edited by Monique Hebert, Nathalie Kermoal, and Phyllis Leblanc, 107–22. Gloucester, ON: Réseau national d'Action éducation Femmes, 1997.

Battiste, Marie, ed. "Annie Battiste: A Mi'kmaq Family History." *Cape Breton's Magazine*, no. 64 (August 1993), 23–42.

– "A History of the Grand Council to 1800." Typescript, Report no. 10, MRC 98-10-364, Mi'kmaq Resource Centre, Cape Breton University.

– ed. *Living Treaties: Narrating Mi'kmaw Treaty Relations*. Sydney/Halifax: University of Cape Breton Press/Nimbus, 2012.

– *Reclaiming Aboriginal Voice and Vision*. Vancouver: University of British Columbia Press, 2000.

– ed. *Visioning a Mi'kmaw Humanities: Indigenizing the Academy*. Sydney: Cape Breton University Press, 2016.

Baudry, René. "Moireau (Moreau), Claude." *Dictionary of Canadian Biography* online, vol. 2 (1701–40).

Beaudry, R. "Thury, Louis-Pierre." *Dictionary of Canadian Biography* online, vol. 1 (1000–1700).

Beck, Horace P. *Gluskap the Liar and Other Indian Tales*. Freeport, ME: B. Wheelright, 1966.

Beck, J. Murray, *Politics of Nova Scotia*. 2 vols. Tantallon, NS: Four East, 1988.

Bell, Winthrop Pickard. *The "Foreign Protestants" and the Settlement of Nova Scotia: The History of a Piece of Arrested British Colonial Policy in the Eighteenth Century*. Toronto: University of Toronto Press, 1961.

Benson, Denis A., and Donald G. Dodds. *The Deer of Nova Scotia*. Halifax: Department of Lands, 1977.

Berkhofer, Robert J., Jr. "Review of *The Middle Ground: Indians, Empires, and Republics in the Great Lakes Region, 1650–1815*, by Richard White." *Journal of American History* 79 (1992): 1134–5.

Bernard, Tim, ed. *Mi'kmaw Past and Present: A Resource Guide*. 4th ed. Truro: Eastern Woodland Communications, 1997.

Bezanson, W.B. *Stories of Acadia*. Part 3. Kentville, NS: Kentville Publishing, 1935.

Biggar, H.P., ed. *The Early Trading Companies of New France: A Contribution to the History of Commerce and Discovery in North America*. Toronto: University of Toronto Library, 1901.

– *The Voyages of Jacques Cartier*. National Archives of Canada Publications no. 11. Ottawa: NAC, 1924.

Black-Rogers, Mary Rose. "The Ojibwa Power-Belief System." In *The Anthropology of Power*, edited by F.D. Fogelson and R.N. Adams, 141–51. New York: Academic Press, 1977.

– "Varieties of 'Starving': Semantics and Survival in the Sub-Arctic Fur Trade, 1750–1850." *Ethnohistory* 33, no. 4 (1986): 353–83.

Blakeley, Phyllis R. "Morris, Charles." *Dictionary of Canadian Biography* online, vol. 4 (1771–1800).

– "Wilmot, Montague." *Dictionary of Canadian Biography* online, vol. 3 (1741–70).

Bock, Philip K. "Micmac." In *Handbook of North American Indians*, vol. 15: *Northeast,* edited by Bruce G. Trigger, 109–122. Washington, DC: Smithsonian Institution, 1978.

– *The Micmac Indians of Restigouche: History and Contemporary Description*. Bulletin no. 213. Ottawa: National Museum of Canada, 1966.

Borren, William C. *Down East: Another Cargo of Tales Told under the Old Town Clock*. Halifax: Imperial, 1945.

Boucher, Neil J. "Entremont, Benoni d'." *Dictionary of Canadian Biography* online, vol. 7 (1836–50).

Boudreau, Gérald C. *Le père Sigogne et les Acadiens du sud-ouest de la Nouvelle-Écosse*. Montreal: Bellarmin, 1992.

Bourinot, George Jr. "The Island of Cape Breton: Its History, Scenery and Resources." *Stewart's Literary Quarterly Magazine* 3, no. 4 (1870): 351–2.

Bourque, Bruce J. "Ethnicity on the Maritime Peninsula, 1600–1759." *Ethnohistory* 36 (1989): 257–84.

Bourque, Bruce J., and Ruth Holmes Whitehead. "Tarrantines and the Introduction of European Trade Goods in the Gulf of Maine." *Ethnohistory* 32 (1985): 327–41.

Brebner, J.B. *New England's Outpost: Acadia before the Conquest of Canada*. Columbia University Studies in History, Economics, and Public Law no. 193. New York: Columbia University Press, 1927.

– "Subsidized Intermarriage with the Indians." *Canadian Historical Association* 5 (1925): 33–4.

Brown, D. *From the Traditional Mi'kmaq Government to Now: Changing Those Who Did Not Need to Be Changed (at Paqtatek)*. Halifax: Garamond, 1991.

Brown, Richard. *A History of the Island of Cape Breton, with some of the Discovery and Settlement of Canada, Nova Scotia and Newfoundland.* London: Sampson Low, Son, and Marston, 1869.

Brown, Thomas. *Place-Names of the Province of Nova Scotia.* Halifax: Royal Print and Litho, 1922.

Bruce, Harry. *RA: The Story of R.A. Jodrey, Entrepreneur.* Toronto: McClelland and Stewart, 1981.

Brun, Régis. "Gueguen, Joseph." *Dictionary of Canadian Biography* online, vol. 4 (1821–35).

Buckner, Phillip A., and John G. Reid, eds. *The Atlantic Region to Confederation: A History.* Toronto: University of Toronto Press, 1994.

Buggey, S. "Belcher, Jonathan." *Dictionary of Canadian Biography* online, vol. 4 (1771–1800).

Burley, David B. "Cultural Complexity and Evolution in the Development of Coastal Adaptations among the Micmac and Coast Salish." In *The Evolution of Maritime Cultures on the Northeast and the Northwest Coasts of America*, edited by Ronald J. Nash, 157–72. Burnaby, BC: Simon Fraser University Press, 1983.

Burnett, Fred. "More Information on the Prossers of Kemptville, NS: A Letter from Society Member Fred Burnett." In *The Argus* (newsletter of the Argyle Municipality Historical and Genealogical Society), 20, no. 2 (2007), 19–23.

Burns, John E. "The Abbé Maillard and Halifax." *Canadian Church History Annual Report*, 1936–37, 13–22.

Calnek, W.A., and A.W. Savary. *History of the County of Annapolis.* Toronto: William Briggs, 1897.

Campbell, Joan Bourque. *L'Histoire de la paroisse de Sainte-Anne-du-Ruisseau (Eel Brook), Yarmouth.* Yarmouth: Éditions Lescarbot, 1985.

Campbell, John Roy. *A History of the County of Yarmouth, Nova Scotia.* Saint John: J. & A. MacMillan, 1876.

Campeau, Lucien. "Membertou." *Dictionary of Canadian Biography* online, vol. 1 (1000–1700).

Canada, Royal Commission on Aboriginal Peoples. *Report of the Royal Commission on Aboriginal Peoples.* Vol. 1. Ottawa: Indian and Northern Affairs, 1996.

Canadian Archives. *Report Concerning Canadian Archives for the Year 1905, in Three Volumes.* Ottawa: S.E. Dawson, 1906.

Caplan, Ronald. "Sam Glode: Travels of a Micmac." *Cape Breton's Magazine*, no. 35 (1983), 21.

Caplan, Ronald, and Alex Denny. "A Talk with Grand Captain Alex Denny." *Cape Breton's Magazine*, no. 40 (August 1983), 45–8.

Casgrain, Henri-Raymond. *Les Sulpiciens et les prêtres des missions-étrangeres en Acadie (1670–1762).* Québec: Librairie Montmorency-Laval, 1897.

Chapin, Howard M. "Privateering in King George's War 1739–1748." *Providence* (1928), 46–53.

Chapman, Harry. *Along the Cole Harbour Road: A Journey through 1765–2003.* Dartmouth: Cole Harbour Rural Heritage Society, 2003.

Chaput, Donald. "Marin de la Malgue, Joseph." *Dictionary of Canadian Biography* online, vol. 4 (1771–1800).

Chard, Donald F. "Mauger, Joshua." *Dictionary of Canadian Biography* online, vol. 4 (1771–1800).

– "Morris, Charles, 1759–1831." *Dictionary of Canadian Biography* online, vol. 6 (1821–35).

Christmas, Peter Joseph. *Wejkwapniag.* Sydney: Micmac Association of Cultural Studies, 1977.

Churchill, Charles. *Memorials of Missionary Life in Nova Scotia.* London: John Mason, 1845.

Chute, Janet E. "Ceremony, Social Revitalization and Change: Micmac Leadership and the Annual Festival of St. Anne." In *Papers of the Twenty-Third Algonquian Conference*, edited by William Cowan, 45–61. Ottawa: Carleton University Press, 1992.

– "The Concept of Tribe as a Useful Tool in Examining Micmac Social Organization." In *Papers of the Twenty-Fourth Algonquian Conference*, edited by William Cowan, 17–31. Ottawa: Carleton University, 1993.

– "Frank G. Speck's Contributions to the Understanding of Mi'kmaq Land Use, Leadership and Land Management." *Ethnohistory* 46, no. 3 (1999): 480–540.

– *The Legacy of Shingwaukonse: A Century of Native Leadership*. Toronto: University of Toronto Press, 1998.

– "Mi'kmaq Fishing in the Maritimes: An Historical Overview." In *Earth, Water, Air and Fire: Studies in Canadian Ethnohistory*, edited by David T. McNab, 95–113. Waterloo: Wilfrid Laurier University Press, 1998.

Clark, Andrew Hill. *Acadia: The Geography of Early Nova Scotia to 1760*. Madison: University of Wisconsin Press, 1969.

– *Three Centuries and the Island: A Historical Geography of Settlement and Agriculture in Prince Edward Island*. Toronto: University of Toronto Press, 1959.

Clarke, George Elliott. "'Indigenous Blacks': An Irreconcilable Identity?" In *Cultivating Canada: Reconciliation through the Lens of Cultural Diversity*, edited by Ashok Mathur, Jonathan Dewar, and Mike Gagné, 399–406. Ottawa: Aboriginal Healing Foundation, 2011.

Clarke, P.D. "Beamish Murdoch: Nova Scotia's National Historian." *Acadiensis* 21, no. 1 (1991): 85–109.

Comeau, J.-Roger. "Leneuf, de la Vallière de Beaubassin, Michel." *Dictionary of Canadian Biography* online, vol. 2 (1701–40).

Comeau, Louis R. "Entremont, Simon d'." *Dictionary of Canadian Biography* online, vol. 6 (1881–90).

Confederacy of Mainland Mi'kmaq. *Mikwite'lmanej Mikmaqi'k: Let Us Remember the Old Mi'kmaq*. Halifax: Nimbus, 2001.

Cooney, Robert. *A Compendious History of the Southern Part of the Province of New Brunswick and the District of Gaspe in Lower Canada*. Halifax: Printed by Joseph Howe, 1832.

Craig, Béatrice. *Women and Business since 1500: Invisible Presences in Europe and North America?* London: Palgrave Macmillan, 2016.

Crathorne, Ethel. "The Morris Family – The Surveyors-General." *Nova Scotia Historical Quarterly* 6 (2 June 1976): 207–9.

Crossman, Evelyn de Blois. *Millidge Ancestors*. Winnipeg: privately printed, 1908.

Crowell, Edwin. *A History of Barrington Township and Vicinity, Shelburne County, Nova Scotia, 1604–1870, with an introduction to the Native and French era by Professor Arnold Doane*. Yarmouth, NS, n.d. (c.1871).

Crowley, T.A. "L'Espérance, Charles-Gabriel-Sébastien de." *Dictionary of Canadian Biography* online, vol. 4 (1771–1800).

Cuthbertson, B.C. "Payzant, John." *Dictionary of Canadian Biography* online, vol. 6 (1821–35).

– "The Starr Manufacturing Company, State Exporter for the World." *Journal of the Royal Nova Scotia Historical Society* 89 (2005): 60–3.

– "Uniacke, Richard John." *Dictionary of Canadian Biography* online, vol. 6 (1821–35).

David, Albert. "L'apôtre des Micmacs." *La Revue de l'Universite d'Ottawa* 5 (1935): 49–82, 425–52.

– "Messire Pierre Maillard, apôtre des Micmacs." *Bulletin des recherches historiques* (1929): 365–75.

Davis, Anthony, Mary Jane Paulette, Kerry Prosper, and John Wagner. "The Paqtnkek Mi'kmaq and Ka't (American Eel): A Case Study of Cultural Relations, Meaning and Prospects." *Canadian Journal of Native Studies* 24 (2004): 357–88.

Davis, Derek S., and Sue Browne. *Natural History of Nova Scotia*. Vol. 2. Halifax: Nova Scotia Museum, 1996.

Dawson, Joan. *The Mapmaker's Eye: Nova Scotia through Early Maps*. Halifax: Nimbus/Nova Scotia Museum, 1988.

– *Nova Scotia's Lost Communities: The Early Settlements That Helped Build the Province*. Halifax: Nimbus, 2018.

Dawson, Samuel Edward. *North America*, vol. 1: *Canada and Newfoundland*. London: Edward Stanford, 1897.

DeBlois, Albert D. *Micmac Dictionary*. Mercury Series Paper 131. Hull: Canadian Museum of Civilization, 1996.

– "Remembering: A Micmac Story Told by the Grand Chief Gabriel Sylliboy." *Recherches amérindiennes du québec* 22, nos. 2–3 (1992): 11–18.

de Bonnaventure, Guy. *Les Denys – en Canada*. Tours, 1989.

de Castries, Scipion. *Souvenirs maritimes*. Paris: Éditions Mercure de France, 1992.

Degrâce, Éloi. "Bourg, Joseph-Mathurin." *Dictionary of Canadian Biography* online, vol. 6 (1771–1800).

Dennis, Clara Archibald. *Cape Breton Over*. Toronto: Ryerson, 1942.

– *More about Nova Scotia, My Own, My Native Land*. Toronto: Ryerson, 1937.

Denny, Richard. "Grand Chief John Denny Jr." *Micmac-Maliseet Nations News*, September 1997, 20.

d'Entremont, Clarence-J. "Broussard, Beausoleil." *Dictionary of Canadian Biography* online, vol. 3 (1741–70).

– "Census of Port Royal, Acadia, 1678." *French Canadian and Acadian Genealogical Review*, 7, no. 1: 47–66.

– *Histoire de Saint-Anne-Du-Ruisseau, Belleville, Rivière – Abram (Nouvelle-Écosse)*. West Pubnico: Printed by the author, 1995.

– *Histoire du Cap-Sable de l'an mil au traité de Paris (1763)*. 5 vols. Eunice, LA: Hébert, 1981.

– *History of Quinan, Nova Scotia*. Meteghan River, Yarmouth County: L'Imprimerie Lescarbot, 1984.

– *Histoire religieuse de Pubnico, Nouvelle-Écosse*. West Pubnico, NS: Éditions Lescarbot, 1992.

– *Nicolas Denys: Da vie et son œuvre*. Yarmouth: L'Imprimerie Lescarbot, 1982.

– "Petitpas, Claude." *Dictionary of Canadian Biography* online, vol. 2 (1701–40).

– "Petitpas, Barthélemy." *Dictionary of Canadian Biography* online, vol. 3 (1740–70).

– *Wedgeport de 1767 à nos jours*. Sous la direction e Blair Boudreau. 2nd ed. Wedgeport: Les Éditions Lescarbot, 1995.

d'Entremont, H. Léander. *The Baronnie de Pombcoup and the Acadians: A History of the Ancient Department of Cape Sable, Now Known as Yarmouth and Shelburne Counties, Nova Scotia*. Yarmouth: Herald-Telegram Press, 1931.

Desbrisay, Mather B. *History of the County of Lunenburg*. Halifax: James Bowes and Sons, 1870. 2nd ed., Toronto: William Briggs, 1895.

Diamond, Beverley. "Santu Toney, a Transnational Beothuk Woman." In *Tracing Ochre: Changing Perspectives on the Beothuk*, edited by Fiona Polack, 247–68. Toronto: University of Toronto Press, 2018.

Dickason, Olive Patricia. "Amerindians between French and English in Nova Scotia, 1713–1763." *American Indian Culture and Research Journal* 10, no. 4 (1986): 31–56.

– "From 'One Nation' in the Northeast to 'New Nation' in the Northwest: A Look at the Emergence of the Métis." In *The New Peoples: Being and Becoming Métis in North America*, edited by Jacqueline Peterson and Jennifer S.H. Brown, 19–36. Winnipeg: University of Manitoba Press, 1985.

– *Louisbourg and the Indians: A Study in Imperial Race Relations, 1713–1760*. Ottawa: Government of Canada, 1976.

– *Louisbourg et les Indiens: Une étude des relations raciales de la France 1713–1760*. Ottawa: Parks Canada, 1979.

Douglas, W.A.B. "Rous, John." *Dictionary of Canadian Biography* online, vol. 3 (1740–70).

Dumas, G.-M. "Leclercq, Chrestien." *Dictionary of Canadian Biography* online, vol. 3 (1740–70).

Dunn, Brenda. *A History of Port Royal, Annapolis Region: 1605–1800*. Halifax: Nimbus, 2004.

Earl of Dunraven. "A Colorado Sketch." In *The Nineteenth Century*, September 1889. https://books.google.ca/books?id=IsDUr-Sl75gC&pg=PA445&source=gbs_toc_r&cad=3#v=onepage&q&f=false.

Eaton, Arthur Wentworth. *Project Canterbury: The Church of England in Nova Scotia and the Tory Clergy of the Revolution*. New York: Thomas Whittaker, 1891.

Erskine, John. *Micmac Notes, 1957*. Halifax: Nova Scotia Museum, 1957.

– *Micmac Notes, 1959*. Halifax: Nova Scotia Museum, 1959.

Fancher de Saint-Maurice, Marcisse-Henri-Édouard. *En route: Sept jours dans les provinces maritimes*. Quebec: Imprimerie Générale A. Coté et Cie, 1888.

Faragher, John Mack. *The Great and Noble Scheme: The Tragic Story of the Expulsion of the French Acadians from Their American Homeland*. New York: W.W. Norton, 2005.

Farish, G.W.T. "A Medical Biography of the Bond-Farish Family." *Canadian Medical Association Journal* 23 (1930): 698.

Ferguson, Robert. "An Archaeological Investigation of Jim Charles' Cabin Site in Kejimkujik National Park." In *Archaeology in Nova Scotia 1987 and 1988*, edited by Stephen A. Davis, Charles Lindsay, Robert Oglivie, and Brian Preston, 227–47. Halifax: Nova Scotia Museum, 1991.

Fergusson, Charles Bruce. *The Boundaries of Nova Scotia and Its Counties*. Bulletin 22. Halifax: Public Archives of Nova Scotia, 1966.

– ed. *Minutes of His Majesty's Council at Annapolis Royal, 1736–1749*. Halifax: Public /Archives of Nova Scotia, 1967.

– *Place-Names and Places of Nova Scotia*. Nova Scotia Series 3. Halifax: Public Archives of Nova Scotia, 1967.

– "Sutherland, Patrick." *Dictionary of Canadian Biography* online, vol. 3 (1741–70).

Fingard, Judith. "Bromley, Walter." *Dictionary of Canadian Biography* online, vol. 7 (1836–50).

– "English Humanitarianism and the Colonial Mind: Walter Bromley in Nova Scotia, 1913–1825." *Canadian Historical Review* 54 (1973): 29–42.

– "Rand, Silus Tertius." *Dictionary of Canadian Biography* online, vol. 11 (1881–90).

Finn, Gérald. "Le Loutre, Jean-Louis." *Dictionary of Canadian Biography* online, vol. 4 (1771–1800).

Flemming, David B. "Walsh, William." *Dictionary of Canadian Biography* online, vol. 8 (1851–60).

Foran, Thomas George. "Early History of Antigonish." *The Xavierian* (St. Francis Xavier College, Antigonish) 23, no. 3 (1920): 7–15.

Foreman, Carolyn Thomas. *Indians Abroad: 1493–1938*. Norman: University of Oklahoma Press, 1943.

Fortier, John. "Des Herbiers de la Ralière (La Ratière), Charles." *Dictionary of Canadian Biography* online, vol. 3 (1741–70).

Francis, Bernie, and John Hewson. "Introduction." In *The Mi'kmaw Grammar of Father Pacifique*, translated, edited, and updated by Bernie Francis and John Hewson. Sydney: University of Cape Breton Press, 2012.

Francis, Jesse, and A.J.B. Johnston. *Ni'n na L'Nu: The Mi'kmaq of Prince Edward Island*. Charlottetown: Acorn, 2013.

Francis, Mary L. *Folklore of Nova Scotia*. N.p.: published by author, n.d. (1940s?).

Fisher, L.R. "Francklin (Franklin), Michael." *Dictionary of Canadian Biography* online, vol. 4, 1771–1800.

Freeman, Mr., ed. "Indian John: Life of John W. Johnson." Copied by Edward Johnson Ladd from Johnson's 1861 original autobiography, *The Life of John W. Johnson*. Fort Payne, AL: printed by Freeman, 1962.

Galarneau, Claude. "Bailly de Messein, Charles-François." *Dictionary of Canadian Biography* online, vol. 4 (1771–1800).

Ganong, William F. "Additions and Corrections to Monographs on the Place-Nomenclature, Cartography, Historic Sites, Boundaries and Settlement-Origins of the Province of New Brunswick." Contributions to the History of New Brunswick no. 7, Royal Society of Canada, *Proceedings*, sec. 2 (1906), 125.

– *History of Miscou and Shippegan*. Saint John: New Brunswick Museum, 1946.

– "A Monograph of the Place-Nomenclature of the Province of New Brunswick." *Transactions of the Royal Society of Canada*, 2nd ser., 2, sec. 2 (1896), 261.

Gaudet, Placide. *Acadian Genealogy and Notes.* **Ottawa: Queen's Printer, 1906.**

– *Report Concerning Canadian Archives for the Year 1905.* Ottawa: Canadian Archives, 1906.

Gerrior, William D. *France and Acadie.* Vol. 1 of *Acadian Awakenings: Routes and Roots, International Links, an Acadian Family in Exile.* Halifax: Port Royal, 2003.

Gesner, Abraham. *New Brunswick; with Notes for Emigrants.* London: Simmonds and Ward, 1847.

Gespe'gewa'gi Mi'gmawei Mawiomi. *Nta'tugwaqanminen: Our Story: Evolution of the Gespe'gewa'gi Migmaq.* Halifax: Fernwood, 2016.

Giddings, Daniel. "Journal Kept by Lieut. Daniel Giddings of Ipswich during the Expedition against Cape Breton in 1744–45." In *Historical Collections of the Essex Institute*, vol. 48, October 1912, no. 4.

Gilpin, J. Bernard. "Indians of Nova Scotia." *Proceedings and Transactions of the Nova Scotia Institute of Natural Science*, no. 4 (1877): 250–81.

Gloade, Harold. *As I Remember: Hantsport in the 30's.* Hansport, NS: Hantsport and Area Historical Society, 1988.

– *From My Vantage Point.* Nepean, ON: Borealis, 1991.

Goodnough, Ward H. *Cooperation in Change.* New York: Russell Sage Foundation, 1963.

Graham, Dominick. "Lawrence, Charles." *Dictionary of Canadian Biography* online, vol. 3 (1741–70).

Grenier, John. *The Far Reaches of Empire: War in Nova Scotia, 1710–1760.* Edited by Gregory J.W. Urwin. Norman: University of Oklahoma Press, 2008.

Grey, Vivian, and Mora Dianne O'Neill. *Pe'l A'tukwey: Let Me … Tell a Story: Recent Works by Mi'kmaq and Maliseet Artists.* Halifax: Art Gallery of Nova Scotia, 1993.

Griffiths, Noami E.S. *From Migrant to Acadian: A North American Border People, 1604–1755.* Montreal: McGill-Queens University Press, 2004.

– "Mating and Marriage in Early Acadia." *Renaissance and Early Modern Studies* 35 (1992): 109–27.

Guidry, Marty. "New Research Reveals Guedry Exiled to North Carolina." *Generations* (newsletter of Les Guédry d'Asteur) 7, no. 1 (Winter 2009): 12–39 (not including unpaginated references at end of article).

– "Survival of a Family: A Continuing Series of Articles by Marty Guidry on the Children of Claude Guedry and Marguerite Petitpas: The Family of Pierre Guedry dit LaBine & Marguerite Brasseau." *Generations* (newsletter of Les Guédry d'Asteur) 4, no. 1 (2006), 1–2, 7.

– "Tragedy for the Guedry Family: An Act of Piracy on the High Seas." Parts 1 and 2. *Generations* 5 (Winter 2007): 1.

Gutton, Jean-Pierre. *Domestiques et serviteurs dans la France de l'ancien régime.* Paris: Éditions Aubier Montaigne, 1981.

Gwyn, Julian. "The Mi'kmaq, Poor Settlers, and the Nova Scotia Fur Trade, 1783–1853." *Journal of the Canadian Historical Association* 14, no. 1 (2003): 65–91.

– "Warren, Sir Peter." *Dictionary of Canadian Biography* online, vol. 3 (1748–70).

– "Whitmore, Edward." *Dictionary of Canadian Biography* online, vol. 3 (1741–70).

Hagar, Stansbury. "Micmac Customs and Traditions." *American Anthropologist* 8, no. 1 (1895): 31–42.

– "Micmac Magic and Medicine." *Journal of American Folklore* 9, no. 34 (1896): 170–7.

Haigh, Elizabeth V. *Abraham Gesner: The Lure of the Rocks and a Burning Ambition.* Victoria: Tellwell Talent, 2019.

– "They Must Cultivate the Land: Abraham Gesner as Indian Commissioner, 1847–1853." *Journals of the Nova Scotia Historical Society*, no. 3 (2000): 18–21.

Haliburton, Thomas Chandler. *A General Description of Nova Scotia: Illustrated by a New and Correct Map.* Halifax: Printed at the Royal Acadian School, 1823.

– *An Historical and Statistical Account of Nova-Scotia, in Two Volumes*. Vol. 1. Halifax: Joseph Howe, 1829.

Halifax & South Western Railway. *Summer Resorts along the Road by the Sea*. Tourist brochure. Halifax, 1916.

Hamelin, Jean. "Bourdon de Dombourg, Jean-François." *Dictionary of Canadian Biography* online, vol. 1 (1000–1700).

Hamilton, W.D. *The Julian Tribe*. Fredericton: Micmac-Malecite Institute/Mi'kmaq-Wolastoqey Centre, 1984.

Hardy, Campbell. *Forest Life in Acadie: Sketches of Sport and Natural History in the Lower Provinces of the Canadian Dominion*. New York: D. Appleton, 1868. Reprint, London: Chapman and Hall, 1869.

– *Sporting Adventures in the New World; or, Days and Nights of Moose-Hunting in the Pine Forests of Acadia*. Vol. 1. London: Hurst and Blackett, 1855.

Harper, J. Russell. "Two Seventeenth-Century Copper-Kettle Burials." *Anthropologica* 4 (1955): 1–36.

Hayter-Menzies, Grant. *The North Door: Echoes of Slavery in a New England Family*. Foreword by Lora-Ellen McKenna. Afterword by Daryl D'Angelo. Norwich, VT: Old Johnson Place, 2019.

Heatherington, Alexander. *A Practical Guide for Tourists, Miners and Investors, and All Interested in the Development of the Gold Fields of Nova Scotia*. Montreal: John Lovell, 1868.

Henderson, James (Sakej) Youngblood. "Ayukpachi: Empowering Aboriginal Thought." In *Reclaiming Aboriginal Voice and Vision*, edited by Marie Battiste, 248–63. Vancouver: University of British Columbia Press, 2000.

Hind, Henry Youle. *An Early History of Windsor, Nova Scotia, with a Sketch of the Old Parish Burying Ground of Windsor Nova Scotia: With an Appeal for Its Protection, Ornamentation, and Preservation*. Windsor: Jas. J. Anslow, 1889. Facsimile reproduction, Handsport, NS: Lancelot Press, 1989.

Holland, John George, and Samuel Goldfrap. "A Plan of the Sea Coast from Gage Point to Cumberland Cape, with the Coal Mines in That Extent." In *The Mapmaker's Eye: Nova Scotia through Early Maps*, by Joan Dawson, 66–7. Halifax: Nimbus/Nova Scotia Museum, 1988.

Homberg, Anne-Christine. *A Landscape of Left-Overs: Changing Conceptions of Time and Place among the Mi'kmaq Indians of Eastern Canada*. Lund Studies in the History of Religions no. 14. Lund, Sweden: Almqvist & Wiskell, 2001.

Howley, James P. *The Beothucks or Red Indians: The Aboriginal Inhabitants of Newfoundland*. Cambridge: Cambridge University Press, 1915.

Hunt, Richard I. "De Saint-Aubun, Serreau." *Dictionary of Canadian Biography* online, vol. 2 (1701–40).

Huskins, Bonnie. "Creelman, Samuel." *Dictionary of Canadian Biography* online, vol. 12 (1891–1900).

– "From *Haute Cuisine* to Ox Roasts: Public Feasting and Negotiation of Class in Mid-19th-Century Saint John and Halifax." *Labour/Le Travail* 37 (1996): 9–36.

Hutton, Elizabeth. "Indian Affairs in Nova Scotia, 1760–1834." *Collections of the Royal Nova Scotia Historical Society* 23 (1963): 33–54.

Huyghue, Samuel Douglas Smith. *Argimou: A Legend of the Micmac*. 2nd ed. Sackville, NB: Mount Allison University Press, 1977 [1847].

Hynes, Gisa. "Some Aspects of the Demography of Port Royal, 1650–1755." *Acadiensis* 3, no. 1 (1973): 1–17.

Ingalls, Sharon, and Wayne Ingalls. *Sweet Suburb: A History of Prince's Lodge, Birch Cove & Rockingham*. Tantallon, NS: Glenn Margaret, 2010.

Jackson, Doug. *On the Country: The Micmac of Newfoundland*. Edited by Gerald Penny. St. John: Harry Cuff, 1993.

"Jacques Guédry: Presence Acadienne en Guyane: Sinnamary Recensement de mai 1767." *Le Messager de L'Atlantique*, Falaise Acadie Québec, annexe 1, no. 32 (Premier Trimestre 1996): 21–8.

Janzen, Olaf. "The Royal Navy and the Interdiction of Aboriginal Migration to Newfoundland, 1763–1766." *International Journal of Naval History* 7, no. 2 (2008). https://www.ijnhonline.org/wp-content/uploads/2012/01/Janzen.pdf.

– "'Une Grande Liason': French Fishermen from Île Royal on the Coast of Southwestern Newfoundland, 1714–1766 – A Preliminary Survey." *Newfoundland Studies* 3, no. 2 (1987): 183–200.

– *War and Trade in Eighteenth-Century Newfoundland.* Research in Maritime History no. 52. St. John's: International Maritime Economic History Association, 2013.

Jobb, Dean. *The Acadians: A People's Story of Exile and Triumph.* New York: John Wiley & Sons, 2005.

Johnson, A.A. *A History of the Catholic Church in Eastern Nova Scotia.* 2 vols. Antigonish: St. Francis Xavier University Press, 1960.

Johnson, Micheline D. *Apôtres ou agitateurs: La France missionaire en Acadie.* Trois Rivières: Boreal Express, 1970.

– "Bâtârd, Étienne." *Dictionary of Canadian Biography* online, vol. 3 (1741–70).

– "Germain, Charles." *Dictionary of Canadian Biography* online, vol. 4 (1771–1800).

– "Maillard, Pierre." *Dictionary of Canadian Biography* online, vol. 3 (1741–70).

– "Padanuques, Jacques." *Dictionary of Canadian Biography* online, vol. 3 (1741–70).

Johnson, Ralph. *The Forests of Nova Scotia.* Halifax: Department of Lands and Forests/Four East, 1986.

Johnston, A.J.B. *Endgame, 1758: The Promise, the Glory and the Despair of Louisbourg's Last Decade.* Lincoln: University of Nebraska Press, 2007.

– *Storied Shores: St. Peter's, Isle Madame and Chapel Island in the 17th and 18th Centuries.* Sydney: University College of Cape Breton Press, 2004.

– "Un regard neuf sur les Acadiens de l'Île Royale: Acadiens dans le sud-est de l'île du Cap-Breton, 1752." *Les Cahiers de la Société historique acadienne* 32, no. 3 (2001): 155–72.

Johnston, A.J.B., and Jesse Francis. *Ni'n na L'nu: The Mi'kmaq of Prince Edward Island.* Charlottetown: Acorn, 2013.

Jones, Elizabeth. *Gentlemen and Jesuits: Quests for Glory and Adventure in the Early Days of New France.* Toronto: University of Toronto Press, 1986.

Kennedy, Gregory, Thomas Peace, and Stephanie Pettigrew. "Social Networks across Chignecto: Applying Social Network Analysis to Acadie, Mi'kma'ki, and Nova Scotia, 1670–1751." *Acadiensis* 47, no. 1 (2018): 8–40. https://journals.lib.unb.ca/index.php/Acadiensis/article/view/26239.

Kerr, W.P. *Port-Royal Habitation: The Story of the French and Mi'kmaq at Port Royal, 1604–1613.* Halifax: Nimbus, 2005.

Kidder, Frederic, ed. *Military Operations in Eastern Maine and Nova Scotia during the American Revolution.* Albany, NY: J. Munsell, 1867.

Knight, Alan, and Janet E. Chute. "In the Shadow of the Thumping Drum: The Sault *Métis* – The People In-Between." In *Lines Drawn Upon the Water: First Nations and the Great Lakes Borders and Borderland*s, edited by Karl S. Hele, 85–113. London, ON: Wilfrid Laurier University Press, 2005.

Knockwood, Doug, & Friends. *Mi'kmaw Elder: Stories, Memories, Reflections.* Halifax: Roseway, 2018.

Knockwood, Isabelle. *Out of the Depths: The Experiences of Mi'kmaw Children at the Indian Residential School at Shubenacadie.* 4th ed. Halifax: Fernwood, 2015. First published 1992 by Roseway, Lockeport, NS.

Krieger, Carlo J. "Ethnogenesis or Cultural Interference? Catholic Missionaries and the Micmac." *Papers of the Twentieth Algonquian Conference*, edited by William Cowan, 193–200. Ottawa: Carleton University, 1989.

Krugler, John David. "Gorham, John." *Dictionary of Canadian Biography* online, vol. 3 (1741–70).

LaBine, Mark. "Charles Guildry [*sic*, Guidry or Guédry] *dit* Labine, Voyageur." *Generations* (newsletter of Les Guédry d'Asteur) 7, no. 1 (2009), 3–9.

Ladd, Edward Johnson. *Indian John: Life of John W. Johnson*. Edited by Mr. Freeman. Fort Payne, AL: privately printed, 1962.

Lafleur, Jean, Gilles Paquet, and Jean-Pierre Wallot. "Quelques propos sur la variance du prix de la terre dans la région d'Assomption (1792–1835)." In *Marchés, migrations et logiques familiales dans les espaces français, canadien et suisse, 18e–20e siècles*, edited by Luigi Lorenzetto, Anne-Lise Head-König, and Joseph Goy, 303–17. Bern: Peter Lang, 2005.

Lanctot, Gustave, ed. *Documents Relating to Currency, Exchange and Finance in Nova Scotia with Prefatory Documents 1675–1758*. Ottawa: King's Printer, 1933.

Landry, Nicolas. *La Cadie frontière du Canada: Micmacs et Euro-Canadiens au Nord-Est du Nouveau-Brunswick, 1620–1850*. Quebec: Septentrion, 2013.

Landry, Peter. *The Lion and the Lily: Nova Scotia between 1600–1760*. Bloomington: Trafford, 2007.

– *Settlement, Revolution & War*. Bloomington: Trafford, 2009.

Lane Jonah, Anne Marie. "Unequal Transitions: Two Métis Women in Eighteenth-Century Île Royale." *French Colonial History* 11, no. 1 (2010): 109–29.

Lane Jonah, Anne Marie, and Elizabeth Tait. "Filles d'Acadie, Femmes de Louisbourg: Acadian Women and French Colonial Society in Eighteenth-Century Louisbourg." *French Colonial History* 8 (Spring 2007): 23–51.

LaPlante, Corinne. "Bastarache, dit Basque, Michel." *Dictionary of Canadian Biography* online, vol. 5 (1801–20).

Larracey, Edward. *A Story of the Chocolate River: Petitcodiac River*. Hantsport, NS: Lancelot, 1985.

Lawrence, B. "Reclaiming Ktaqamkuk: Land and Mi'kmaq Identity in Newfoundland." In *Speaking for Ourselves: Environmental Justice in Canada*, edited by J. Agyeman, P. Cole, R. Haluza-DeLay, and P. O'Riley, 42–64. Vancouver: University of British Columbia Press, 2009.

Lawrence, Ian. "The Mi'kmaw Gloade Family." In newsletter of the Annapolis Heritage Society (Spring 2011), 3–4.

Lawson, Mrs. William. *History of the Townships of Dartmouth, Preston and Lawrencetown*. Halifax: Morton and Co., 1893.

Layton, Linda G. *A Passion for Survival: The True Story of Marie Anne and Louis Payzant in Eighteenth-Century Nova Scotia*. Halifax: Nimbus, 2003.

Le Blant, Robert. "Les trois mariages d'une Acadienne Anne d'Entremont (1694–1778)." *La Nouvelle France* 2 (1932): 211–29.

Lee, David. "Gaulin, Antoine." *Dictionary of Canadian Biography* online, vol. 2 (1701–40).

– "Robin, Charles." *Dictionary of Canadian Biography* online, vol. 4 (1821–35).

– *The Robins in Gaspé, 1766 to 1925*. Markham: Fitzhenry and Whiteside, 1984.

LeLiévre, Michelle A. *Unsettling Mobility: Mediating Mi'kmaw Sovereignty in Post-Contact Nova Scotia*. Tucson: University of Arizona Press, 2017.

Lenhart, John. *History relating to Manual of prayers, instructions, psalms and hymns in Micmac Ideograms used by Micmac Indians of Eastern Canada and Newfoundland*. Sydney: Cameron Print, 1932.

Lenik, Edward J. *Picture Rocks: American Indian Rock Art in the Northeast Woodlands*. Lebanon, NH: University Press of New England, 2003.

Lennox, Jeffers. "An Empire on Paper: The Founding of Halifax and Conceptions of Imperial Space, 1744–1755." *Canadian Historical Review* 88, no. 3 (2007): 372–412.

– *Homelands and Empires: Indigenous Spaces, Imperial Fictions, and Competition for Territory in Northeastern North America, 1690–1763*. Toronto: University of Toronto Press, 2017.

Little Bear, Leroy. "Jagged Worldviews Colliding." In *Reclaiming Aboriginal Voice and Vision*, edited by Marie Battiste, 177–85. Vancouver: University of British Columbia Press, 2000.

Lockerby, Earle. "Ancient Mi'kmaq Customs: A Shaman's Revelations." *Canadian Journal of Native Studies* 24 (2004): 403–20.

Lorenzetto, Luigi, Anne-Lise Head-König, and Joseph Goy, eds. *Marchés, migrations et logiques familiales dans les espaces français, canadien et suisse,18e–20e siècles*. Bern: Peter Lang, 2005.

Lowman, Emma Battell, and Adam J. Barker. *Settler: Identity and Colonialism in 21st Century Canada*. Halifax: Fernwood, 2015.

Lunn, A.G.E. "Denys de Bonaventure, Simon Pierre." *Dictionary of Canadian Biography* online, vol. 2 (1701–40).

Lunn, Jean. "Deny (Denis) de la Trinité, Simon." *Dictionary of Canadian Biography* online, vol. 1 (1000–1700).

MacBeath, George. "Denys, Nicolas." *Dictionary of Canadian Biography* online, vol. 1 (1000–1700).

– "Saint-Étienne de la Tour, Charles de." *Dictionary of Canadian Biography* online, vol. 1 (1000–1700).

Macdonald, James S. "Memoir of Lieutenant-Governor Michael Francklin, 1752–1782." In *Collections of the Nova Scotia Historical Society*, no. 16, 1–40. Halifax: Wm. McNab and Son, 1912.

MacDonald, M.A. *Fortune & La Tour: The Acadian Civil War*. Toronto: Methuen, 1983. Reprint, Halifax: Nimbus, 2000.

MacFarlane, R.O. "British Indian Policy in Nova Scotia to 1760." *Canadian Historical Review*, 19 (1938): 154–67.

MacKay, D.C. "Valentine, William." *Dictionary of Canadian Biography* online, vol. 7 (1836–50).

MacLaren, Roy. *Canadians on the Nile, 1882–1898*. Vancouver: University of British Columbia Press, 2011.

MacLeod, Robert R. *Acadian Land: Nature Studies*. Boston: Bradlee Whidden, 1899.

Mancke, Elizabeth, and John Reid. "Elites, States and the Imperial Contest for Acadia." In *The "Conquest" of Acadia, 1710: Imperial, Colonial, and Aboriginal Constructions*, by John G. Reid, Maurice Basque, Elizabeth Mancke, Barry Moody, Geoffrey Plank, and William Wicken, 48–63. Toronto: University of Toronto Press, 2004.

Marsden, Joshua. *The Narrative of a Mission to Nova Scotia, New Brunswick, etc. (1800)*. 2nd ed. London: J. Kershaw, 1827.

Marshall, Dianne. *Heroes of the Acadian Resistance: The Story of Joseph Beausoleil Broussard and Pierre II Surrete, 1702–1765*. Halifax: Formac, 2011.

Marshall, Donald, Sr., Alexander Denny, and Simon Marshall. "The Covenant Chain." In *Drumbeat: Anger and Renewal in Indian Country*, edited by Boyce Richardson, 73–104. Toronto: Summerhill, 1989.

Marshall, Ingelborg. "Beothuk and Micmac: Re-examining Relationships." *Acadiensis* 17, no. 2 (1988): 52–82.

– "Le canot de haute mer des Micmacs." In *Les Micmacs et la mer*, Collection signes des Amériques no. 5, edited by Charles A. Martijn, 29–48. Montreal: Recherches Amérindiennes au Québec, 1986.

Marshall, M., and L.C. Boudreau. "St. Ann's Day Mission, Chapel Island." Includes interview with Grand Captain Noel Marshall, July 1983, with additional information from Elsie Clews Parsons and Sarah Denny. *Cape Breton's Magazine*, no. 40 (August 1983), 31–44.

Martijn, Charles A. "Early Mi'kmaq Presence in Southern Newfoundland: An Ethnohistorical Perspective, c. 1500–1763." *Newfoundland and Labrador Studies* 19, no. 1 (2003): 44–102.

– "An Eastern Micmac Domain of Islands." In *Actes du vingtième congrès des algonquinistes/Papers of the Twentieth Algonquian Conference*, edited by William Cowan, 208–31. Ottawa: Carleton University Press, 1989.

– "Les Micmacs aux îles de la Madeleine: Visions fugitives et glanures ethnohistoriques." In *Les Micmacs et la mer*, edited by Charles A. Martijn, 163–94. Montreal: Recherches Amérindiennes au Québec, 1986.

– ed. *Les Micmacs et la mer*. Montreal: Recherches Amérindiennes au Québec, 1986.

Martin, John Patrick, *Our Storied Harbour: The Haven of Halifax*. Halifax: Department of Tourists and Travel, 1948.

– *The Story of Dartmouth*. Foreword by Thomas H. Raddall. Dartmouth: printed by author, 1957.

Martin, R. Montgomery. *A History of Nova Scotia, Cape Breton, Sable Island, New Brunswick, Prince Edward Island, the Bermudas, Newfoundland etc.* London: Whittaker, 1837.

McBride, Bunny. *Our Lives in Our Hands: Micmac Indian Basketmakers*. Photographs by Donald Sanipass. Gardiner, ME: Tilbury House/Halifax: Nimbus, 1990.

– *Women of the Dawn*. Lincoln: University of Nebraska Press, 2009.

McBride, Bunny, and Harald E.L. Prins. *Indians in Eden: Wabanakis and Rusticators on Maine's Mount Desert Island, 1840s–1920s*. East Peoria, IL: Down East Books/Versa, 2009.

McCaffrey, Moira T. *Inventaire des sites archéologiques préhistoriques des îles-de-la-Madeleine, Bilan: Phase 1 (1988), Phase 2 (1989), Phase 3 (1990)*. Quebec: Ministère de la Culture et des Communications, 1988.

McCusker, John J. "Comparing the Purchasing Power of Money in the United States (or Colonies) from 1665 to 2005." *Economic History Services*, http://eh.net/hmit/ppwerusd, site now defunct, accessed 2006.

McEwan, Richard. *Memories of a Micmac Life*. Edited by W.D. Hamilton. Fredericton: Micmac-Malecite Institute, 1988.

McGee, Harold F. "The Case for Micmac Demes." In *Actes du huitième congrès des algonquiniste*, edited by William Cowan, 107–14. Ottawa: University of Ottawa, 1977.

– *The Native Peoples of Atlantic Canada: A Reader in Regional Ethnic Relations*. Carleton Library Series no. 72. Toronto: McClelland and Stewart, 1974.

– "White Encroachments on Micmac Reserve Lands, 1836–1867." *Man in the Northeast* 8 (1974): 154–67.

McKenna, Olga M. *Micmac by Choice: Elsie Sark – An Island Legend*. Halifax: Formac, 1990.

McLellan, J.S. *Louisbourg from Its Foundation to Its Fall, 1713–1758*. Sydney: Fortress, 1969.

McNairn, Jeffrey L. "Meaning and Markets: Hunting, Economic Development and British Imperialism in Maritime Travel Narratives to 1870." *Acadiensis* 34, no. 2 (2005): 3–25. https://journals.lib.unb.ca/index.php/Acadiensis/article/download/10633/11273?inline=1.

Membertou Communications. *Kings Road Reserve 100 Years Later, The Journey On … The Story of Membertou's Reconciliation*. October 2016. https://www.membertou.ca/wp-content/uploads/2019/05/kings-road-reserve.pdf.

Mennel, Robert M. *Testimonies and Secrets: The Story of a Nova Scotian Family, 1844–1977*. Toronto: University of Toronto Press, 2013.

Mersereau, Rev. C.J. "Early Missions along Bay Chaleur." In Report no. 17 of the Canadian Church History Association (CCHA), 1950, 21–30.

Micmac Association of Cultural Studies (MACS). *Micmac Hymnal*. Sydney: MACS, 1983.

Mi'kmaq Grand Council. "Mi'kmaw Past and Present: A Resource Guide." n.d. (c.2005).

Milford and Area History Group. *Through the Woods: A Collected History and Reflection of the Milford Area & Communities*. Halifax: MAHG, 2005.

Millais, J.G. *Newfoundland and Its Untrodden Ways*. London: Longmans, Green, 1907.

Miller, Virginia P. "Aboriginal Micmac Population: A Review of the Evidence." *Ethnohistory* 21 (1976): 117–26.

– "Arimph, Jean-Baptist." *Dictionary of Canadian Biography* online, vol. 4 (1771–1800).

– "Bernard, Philip." *Dictionary of Canadian Biography* online, vol. 4 (1771–1800).

– "The Decline of Nova Scotia Micmac Population, A.D. 1600–1850." *Culture* 2, no. 3 (1982): 107–20.

- "Social and Political Complexity on the East Coast: The Micmac Case." In *The Evolution of Maritime Cultures on the Northeast and the Northwest Coasts of America*, edited by R.I. Nash, 41–55. Burnaby, BC: Department of Archaeology, Simon Fraser University, 1983.

Moogk, Pierre. *La Nouvelle France: The Making of French Canada, A Cultural History*. East Lansing: Michigan State University Press, 2000.

More, James F. *The History of Queens County, N.S.* Halifax: Nova Scotia Printing, 1873. Reprint, Belleville, ON: Mika Studio, 1972; Milton, ON: Global Heritage Press, 2003.

Morrison, James, and Lawrence Friend. *'We Have Our Own': The Western Interior of Nova Scotia, 1800–1940*. History and Archaeology Branch Report no. 47. Ottawa: National Parks and Sites Branch, 1981.

Morrison, Kenneth. *The Embattled Northeast: The Illusive Ideal of Allegiance in Abenaki-Euramerican Relations*. Berkeley: University of California Press, 1984.

Mundell, Kathleen. 2008. *North by Northeast*. Gardiner, ME: Tilbury House, 2008.

Murdoch, Beamish. *A History of Nova-Scotia, or Acadie*. 3 vols. Halifax: James Barnes, 1865–66.

Nash, Ronald J., and Francis L. Stewart. *Melanson: A Large Micmac Village in Kings County, Nova Scotia*. Curatorial Report no. 67. Halifax: Nova Scotia Museum, 1990.

Nash, Ronald J., F. Stewart, and M. Deal. *Melanson: A Central Place in Southwestern Nova Scotia*. In *Prehistoric Archaeology in the Maritime Provinces: Past and Present Research*, Reports in Archaeology no. 8, edited by M. Deal and S. Blair, 213–20. Halifax: Council of Maritime Premiers, 1991.

National Geographic Magazine staff. "A Brighter Future Ahead for Maine's Micmac." Photograph by Pete Souza. *National Geographic Magazine* 184, no. 1 (July 1993), https://wldwind.com/natg.htm (excerpt).

Norton, Judith A. "The Dark Side of Planter Life: Reported Cases of Domestic Violence." In *Intimate Relations: Family and Community in Planter Nova Scotia, 1759–1800*, edited by Margaret Conrad, 182–9. Fredericton: Acadiensis, 1995.

Nova Scotia. *The Nova Scotia Atlas*. 5th rev. ed. Prepared by Service Nova Scotia and Municipal Relations, Nova Scotia Geomatics Centre. Halifax: Formac, 2001.

O'Neill, Mora Dianne. *At the Great Harbour: 250 Years on the Halifax Waterfront*. Halifax: Formac, 1999.

- *Legend Drawings by Leonard Paul*. Exhibition catalogue. Halifax: Mount Saint Vincent University, May 2005.

Ormond, Douglas S. *The Roman Catholic Church in Cobequid, Acadie, 1692–1755, and Colchester County, Nova Scotia, 1825–1978: Also Savage Island and the Kavanaghs 1778–1830*. Truro: published by author, 1979.

Ottawa. *Geological Survey Memoir 385*. Ottawa: The Survey, 1929.

Pacifique, Père (Henri-Joseph-Louis Buisson de Valigny). "Le Pays de Micmac: Cap Breton" and "Le Pays des Micmacs: Esgigeoagig-Acadie." *Bulletin de la Société de géographie de Quebec* 27, no. 1, 34–64. Quebec: Société de géographie de Québec, January 1933.

- *Le Pays des Micmacs*. Ste. Anne de Restigouche: chez l'auteur, 1935.

- "Le Pays des Micmacs." *Études historiques et géographiques*, no. 25, 96–106. Quebec: Société de géographie de Québec, 1931.

- "Le Pays des Micmacs." *Études historiques et géographiques*, no. 24, 135–8. Quebec: Société de géographie de Québec, 1930.

- "Le Pays des Micmacs." *Études historiques et géographiques*, no. 23, 37–45. Quebec: Société de géographie de Québec, 1929.

- "Le Pays des Micmacs." *Études historiques et géographiques*, no. 22, 43–55, 140–5, 270–7. Quebec: Société de géographie de Québec, 1928.

- "Le Pays des Micmacs." *Études historiques et géographiques*, no. 21, 111–17, 165–854. Quebec: Société de géographie de Québec, 1927.

– "Les Pays des Micmacs – the Micmac County." *Bulletin de la Société de géographie de Québec* 28, nos. 1–2. Quebec: Société de géographie de Québec, January 1934.

– ed. "New Indian Chief Gabriel Sylliboy of Whycocomagh, in Micmac and English." In *Setaneoei, or The Micmac Messenger/Le Messager Micmac* (September 1918), Rimouski, QC.

– "Quelques traits caractéristiques de la tribu des Micmacs," *Proceedings of the International Congress of Americanists* 15, no. 1, 315–28. Quebec, 1906.

– "Ristigouche: Métropole des Micmacs, théâtre du 'dernier effort de la France au Canada.'" Bulletin 19, 129–62. Quebec: Société de géographie de Québec, 1925.

– *Setaneoei, or The Micmac Messenger/Le Messager Micmac.* No. 283. Quebec: Sainte-Anne de Restigouche (published at Rimouski, QC), 1910.

– "Traité théorique et practique de la langue micmaque." In *Annales de l'Association canadienne-françoise pour l'Advancement des Sciences*, no. 4, 250. Montreal: Association canadienne-française pour l'Advancement des Sciences (ACFAS), 1938.

Pagnamenta, Peter. *Prairie Fever: British Aristocrats in the American West, 1830–1890.* New York: W.W. Norton, 2012.

Paine, Albert Bigelow. *The Tent Dwellers.* New York: Outing, 1908.

Parker, Mike. *Guides of the North Woods: Hunting and Fishing Tales from Nova Scotia 1860–1960.* Halifax: Nimbus, 1990.

– *Woodchips and Beans: Life in the Early Lumber Woods of Nova Scotia.* Halifax: Nimbus, 1992.

Parnaby, Andrew. "The Cultural Economy of Survival: The Mi'kmaq of Cape Breton in the Mid-19th Century." *Labour/Le Travail* 61 (Spring 2008): 69–98.

Parsons, Elsie Clews. "Micmac Folklore." *Journal of American Folklore* 38 (1925): 55–133.

Pastore, R.T. *Indian Summer: Newfoundland Micmac in the Nineteenth Century*, Mercury Series no. 40. Ottawa: Canadian Ethnology Service, National Museum of Man, 1978.

– "Native History in the Atlantic Region during the Colonial Period." *Acadiensis* 20, no. 1 (1990): 200–25.

Patterson, F.H. "Old Cobequid and Its Destruction." In *Collections of the Nova Scotia Historical Society*, no. 23, 49–80. Halifax, 1934.

Patterson, George. *History of the County of Pictou.* Montreal: Dawson Brothers, 1877.

– "Hon. Samuel Vetch, First English Governor of Nova Scotia." *Collections of the Nova Scotia Historical Society*, no. 4, 28–9. Halifax: William McNab, 1884.

Patterson, Stephen E. "Eighteenth-Century Treaties: The Mi'kmaq, Maliseet, and Passamaquoddy Experience." *Native Studies Review* 18, no. 1 (2009): 25–52.

– "Indian-White Relations in Nova Scotia, 1749–61: A Study in Political Interaction." *Acadiensis* 23, no. 1 (1993): 23–59.

Paul, Daniel N. *We Were Not the Savages: A Mi'kmaq Perspective on the Collision between European and Native American Civilizations.* Halifax: Fernwood, 2000.

Paul, William G. "Oral Tradition." In *Mi'kmaq Past and Present: A Resource Guide*. Session 5, p. 18. Halifax: Department of Education, 1993.

Peace, Thomas. "A Reluctant Engagement: Alliances and Social Networks in Early-18th-Century Kespukwitk and Port-Royal." *Acadiensis* 49, no. 1 (2020): 5–38.

Peart, Barbara (Mason). *As the Last Leaf Fell: From Montebéliard to the Head of St. Margaret's Bay, An Illustrated History.* Tantallon, Halifax County: published by author, with assistance from Department of Culture and Recreation/Four East, 2002.

Pedley, Mary. "Map Wars: The Role of Maps in the Nova Scotia/Acadia Boundary Dispute of 1750." *Imago Mundi* 50, no. 1 (1998): 96–104.

Penny, Gerald. "An Ocean-Going Canoe from Conne River." *Newfoundland Quarterly* 90, no. 4 (1997): 2–3.

Perrin, Warren A. *Acadian Redemption: From Beausoleil Broussard to the Queen's Royal Proclamation.* Opelousas, LA: Andrepont, 2005.

Peters, Mercedes. "The Future is Mi'kmaq: Exploring the Merits of Nation-Based Histories as the Future of Indigenous History in Canada." *Acadiensis* 48, no. 2 (2019): 206–16.

Peterson, Jacqueline, and Jennifer S.H. Brown, eds. *The New Peoples: Being and Becoming Métis in North America*. Winnipeg: University of Manitoba Press, 1985.

– "Small 't' Treaty Relationships without Borders: Bear River First Nation, Clam Harvesters, the Bay of Fundy Marine Resource Centre and the World Forum of Fisher Peoples." *Anthropologica* 57, no. 2 (2015): 457–67.

Piers, Harry. "Brief Account of the Micmac Indians of Nova Scotia and Their Remains." *Transactions of the Nova Scotia Institute of Science* 13, no. 2 (1911–12): 99–125.

Pincombe, C. Alexander. "How, Edward." *Dictionary of Canadian Biography* online, vol. 3 (1741–70).

Plank, Geoffrey Gilbert. "The Two Majors Cope: The Boundaries of Nationality in Mid-18th Century Nova Scotia." *Acadiensis* 25, no. 2 (1996): 18–40.

– *An Unsettled Conquest: The British Campaign against the Peoples of Acadia*. Philadelphia: University of Pennsylvania Press, 2001.

Pothier, Bernard. *Course à l'Acadie: Journal de campagne de François Du Pont Duvivier en 1744*. Moncton: Éditions d'Acadie, 1982.

– "Gauthier, *dit* Belair, Joseph Nicholas." Dictionary of Canadian Biography online, vol. 3 (1741–70).

– "Menbeton de Brouillan, dit Saint-Ovide, Joseph de." *Dictionary of Canadian Biography* online, vol. 3 (1741–70).

– "Sigogne, Jean-Mandé." *Dictionary of Canadian Biography* online, vol. 7 (1836–50).

Pothier, Bernard, and Donald J. Norton. "Denys de la Ronde, Louis." *Dictionary of Canadian Biography* online, vol. 3 (1741–70).

Pothier, Yvonne M. *The Pothiers/Pottiers of Lower Eel Brook and Belleville*. Yarmouth County, NS: Yvonne M. Pothier, 2004.

Prins, Harold E.L. *The Mi'kmaq: Resistance, Accommodation and Cultural Survival*. New York: Harcourt Brace, 1995.

– "Tribal Network and Migrant Labor – Mi'kmaw Indians as Seasonal Workers in Aroostook's Potato Fields, 1870–1980." In *Native Americans and Wage Labor: Ethnohistorical Perspectives*, edited by Alice Littlefield and Martha Knack, 45–65. Norman: University of Oklahoma Press, 1996.

Prins, Harald E.L., and Karen Carter, dirs. *Our Lives in Our Hands*. Documentary. Produced by Harald E.L. Prins. 49 mins. 1985.

Prins, Harald E.L., and Bunny McBride. *Asticou's Domain: Wabanaki Peoples at Mount Desert Island*. Ethnographic Program, 2 vols. Washington, DC: National Park Service, US Department of the Interior, 2007.

Provost, Honorius. "Baudoin, Jean." *Dictionary of Canadian Biography* online, vol. 1 (1000–1700).

Pryke, K.G. "Murdoch, Beamish." *Dictionary of Canadian Biography* online, vol. 10 (1871–80).

Public Archives of Nova Scotia. *Place-Names and Places of Nova Scotia*. Introduction by Charles Bruce Fergusson. Nova Scotia Series 3. Halifax: Public Archives of Nova Scotia, 1967.

Quinn, David B. "The Voyage of Etienne Bellenger to the Maritimes in 1683: A New Document." *Canadian Historical Review* 43 (1962): 328–43.

Raddall, Thomas H. *Halifax: Warden of the North*. Halifax: Nimbus, 1993 [1948].

– *In My Time: A Memoir*. Toronto: McClelland and Stewart, 1976.

"The Lost Gold at Kejimkujik." In *Footsteps on Old Floors: True Tales of Mystery*, 195–218. New York: Doubleday, 1968.

Rand, Silus Tertius. *A First Reading Book in the Micmac Language Comprising the Micmac Numerals, the Names of the Different Kinds of Beasts, Birds, Fishes, Trees, &c. of the Maritime Provinces of Canada*. Halifax. Nova Scotia Print Co., 1875.

– *Legends of the Micmac*. Edited by Helen L. Webster. New York: Longmans and Green, 1894.

Randall (Reeves), Ethel A. "Kemptville, Data and Datum: An Historical Sketch." *The Argus* 19, no. 4 (2007): 37–48.

Rankin, D.J. *A History of the County of Antigonish, Nova Scotia.* Toronto: Macmillan, 1929.

Rannie, William F. *Saint-Pierre and Miquelon.* 4th ed. Beansville, ON: Rannie, 1972.

Rast, Tim, M.A.P. Renouf, and Trevor Bell. "Patterns of Precontext Site Location on the Southwest Coast of Newfoundland." *Northeast Anthropology* 68 (Fall 2004): 41–55.

Rawlyk, G.A. "Eddy, Jonathan." *Dictionary of Canadian Biography* online, vol. 5 (1801–20).

Rayburn, Alan. *Geographical Names of New Brunswick.* Ottawa: Department of Energy, Mines and Resources, 1975.

Raymond, W.O. "The North Shore (Incidents in the Early History of Eastern and Northern New Brunswick)." In *Collections of the New Brunswick Historical Society*, no. 2, 81–134. Saint John, NB: Daily Telegraph Steam Book and Job Print, 1899.

– *The River St. John.* Saint John: J.A. Bowes, 1910.

Regan, John W. *Sketches and Traditions of the North West Arm.* Willowdale, ON: Hounslow, 1978 [1908].

Reid, Jennie. *Musquodoboit Pioneers: A Record of Seventy Families, Their Homesteads and Genealogies, 1780–1980.* 2 vols. Musquodoboit, NS: Musquodoboit Enterprises Historical Committee, 1980.

Reid, Jennifer. *Myth, Symbol, and Colonial Encounter: British and Mi'kmaq in Acadia, 1700–1867.* Ottawa: University of Ottawa Press, 1995.

Reid, John G. "Amerindian Power in the Early Modern Northeast: A Reappraisal." In *Essays on Northeastern North America: Seventeenth and Eighteenth Centuries*, 77–106. Toronto: University of Toronto Press, 2008.

– "Empire, the Maritime Colonies, and the Supplanting of Mi'kma'ki/Wulstukwik, 1780–1820." *Acadiensis* 38, no. 2 (2009): 78–97.

– "Immigration to Atlantic Canada: Historical Reflections." *Journal of the Royal Nova Scotia Historical Society* 19 (2016): 38–53.

– "Imperial-Aboriginal Friendship in Eighteenth-Century Mi'kma'ki/Wulstukwik." In *The Loyal Atlantic: Remaking the British Atlantic in the Revolutionary Era*, edited by Jerry Bannister and Liam Riordan, 75–102. Toronto: University of Toronto Press, 2012.

– "*Pax Britannica* or *Pax Indigena*? Planter Nova Scotia (1760–1782) and Competing Strategies on Pacification." *Canadian Historical Review* 85, no. 4 (2004): 669–92.

– "Scots in Mi'kma'ki, 1760–1820." *Nashwaak Review* 22–23, no. 1 (2009): 527–57.

– "1686–1720: Imperial Intrusions." In *The Atlantic Region to Confederation: A History*, edited by Phillip A. Buckner and John G. Reid, 78–103. Toronto: University of Toronto Press, 1994.

– "The Three Lives of Edward Cornwallis." *Journal of the Royal Nova Scotia Historical Society* 16 (2013): 19–45.

Reid, John G., Maurice Basque, Elizabeth Mancke, Barry Moody, Geoffrey Plank, and William Wicken. *The "Conquest of Acadia," 1710: Imperial, Colonial and Aboriginal Constructions.* Toronto: University of Toronto Press, 2004.

Reid, John G., and Phillip Buckner, eds. *Revisiting 1759: The Conquest of Canada in Historical Perspective.* Toronto: University of Toronto Press, 2012.

Reid, John G., and Thomas Peace. "Colonies of Settlement and Settler Colonialism in Northeastern North America, 1450–1850." In *The Routledge Handbook of the History of Settler Colonialism*, edited by Edward Cavanagh and Lorenzo Veracini, 79–94. Abingdon, UK: Routledge, 2017.

"Remembering a Leader ... Chief Joseph Julien." *Mi'kmaq-Maliseet Nations News*, January 2012, 9.

Renfree, Henry A. *Heritage and Horizons: The Baptist Story in Canada.* Eugene, OR: Wipf & Stock, 1988.

Rex v. Syliboy (1928), 50 CCC 389, 390–1, Nova Scotia County Court, G. Patterson, Acting Inverness County Court Judge, 10 September 1928. Includes synopsis of proceedings at Port Hood, 4 July

1928, with decision of Acting County Court Judge, District 6, G. Patterson, in case of *King &* *Sylyboy* [sic, *Syliboy* or *Sylliboy*], Port Hood Cape Breton, July 1928.

Rex v. Syliboy [1929] 1 D.L.R. 307.

Ribault, Jean-Yves. "La population des îles Saint-Pierre et Miquelon de 1763 à 1793." *Revue française d'histoire d'outre-mer* 53, no. 190 (1966): 5–66.

– *Les Iles Saint-Pierre et Miquelon: Des origins à 1814*. Saint-Pierre: L'Imprimerie au Gouvernement Saint-Pierre, 1962.

Richard, Edouard, and Henri d'Arles. *Acadie: Reconstitution d'un chapitre perdu de l'histoire d'Amérique*. In two volumes, Quebec: A.K. LaFlamme/Marlier, 1916.

Richardson, Boyce, ed. *Drumbeat: Anger and Renewal in Indian Country*. Toronto: Summerhill, 1989.

Ricker, Darlene A. *L'sitkuk: The Story of the Bear River Mi'kmaw Community*. Black Rock, NS: Fernwood, 1997.

Ricker, Jackson. *Historical Sketches of Glenwood and the Argyles, Yarmouth Co., NS*. Truro: Truro Printing and Publishing, 1941; reprint, Yarmouth, NS: Sentinel Printing, 1994.

Ritchie, Ruth T., and Denis J. Rice. *Lequille: Chronicles of a Community*. Annapolis Royal: Annapolis Heritage Society, 2011.

Roberts, Charles George Douglas. *The Canadian Guide-Book: The Tourist's and Sportman's Guide to Eastern Canada and Newfoundland*. New York: D. Appleton, 1891.

Robertson, Patrick. *Robertson's Book of Firsts: Who Did What for the First Time*. London: Bloomsbury, 2011.

Robinson, Angela. *Ta'n Teli-ktlamsitasit (Ways of Believing): Mi'kmaw Religion in Eskasoni, Nova Scotia*. Toronto: Pearson, 2005.

Rodger, Andrew. "Bourdon de Dombourg, Jean-François (1720–1789)." *Dictionary of Canadian Biography* online, vol. 6 (1771–1800).

– "Denys de Bonnaventure, Claude-Élisabeth." *Dictionary of Canadian Biography* online, vol. 3 (1741–70).

Rogers, Edward S. "Leadership among the Indians of Eastern Subarctic Canada." *Anthropologica* 7 (1965): 263–84.

Rogers, J.D. *Historical Geography of the British Colonies – Newfoundland*. Oxford: Clarendon, 1911.

Rogers, N.M. "Apostle to the Micmacs." *Dalhousie Review* 6, no. 2 (1926–27): 166–76.

Rosenberg, Leah. *Mikwite'lmanej Mikmaqi'k – Let Us Remember the Old Mi'kmaq*. Halifax: Nimbus, 2001.

Ross, Sally, and Alphonse Deveau. *The Acadians of Nova Scotia, Past and Present*. Halifax: Nimbus, 1992.

Roth, David Luther. *Acadie and the Acadians*. Philadelphia: Lutheran Publishing Society, 1890. 2nd and 3rd eds., L.C. Childs and Son, 1891.

Russ, C.J. "La Corne, Louis-Luc." *Dictionary of Canadian Biography* online, vol. 3 (1741–70).

Sable, Trudy, and Bernie Francis. *The Language of This Land, Mi'kma'ki*. Foreword by Leroy Little Bear. Sydney: Cape Breton University Press, 2012.

Salagnac, Georges Cerbelaud. "Abbadie De Saint-Castin, Jean-Vincent d'." *Dictionary of Canadian Biography* online, vol. 2 (1701–40).

Salisbury, Richard. "Transactions or Transactors? An Economic Anthropologist's View." In *Transaction and Meaning: Directions in the Anthropology of Exchange and Symbolic Behaviour*, edited by B. Kapferer, 41–59. Philadelphia: Institute for the Study of Human Issues, 1976.

Sanipass, Mary, and Donald Sanipass. *Baskedagen: Basketmaking Step by Step*. Photographs by Donald Sanipass. Madawaska, ME: St. John, 1990.

Sark, John Joe (*keptin* of the Grand Council), ed., assisted by Russel L. Barsh and Chantelle P. Marlor. *Mi'kmaq and the Crown: Understanding the Treaties in Maritime Canadian History, with Special Reference to Prince Edward Island*. N.p.: privately printed, 2000.

Sayres, William C., ed. *Sammy Louis: The Life History of a Young Micmac*. New Haven, CT: Compass, 1956. (Sammy was a Lewis from Bear River, Nova Scotia.)

Schmidt, David L., and B.A. Balcom. "The Règlements of 1739: A Note on Micmac Law and Literacy." *Acadiensis* 23, no. 1 (1993): 110–27.

Schmidt, David L., and Murdena Marshall, ed. and trans. *Mi'kmaq Hieroglyphic Prayers: Readings in North America's First Indigenous Script*. Halifax: Nimbus, 1995.

Schultz, Eric B., and Michael J. Tougias. *King Philip's War: The History and Legacy of America's Forgotten Conflict*. Woodstock, VT: Countryman, 2000.

Scott, Tod. "Mi'kmaq Armed Resistance to British Expansion in Northern New England, 1676–1761." *Journal of the Royal Nova Scotia Historical Society* 19 (2016): 1–18.

Shane, Gwendolyn Vaughan. *Historic Hants County*. Halifax: Petheric, 1979.

Shelburne County Genealogical Society newsletter 15, no. 2 (2001), n.p.

Silver, Arthur P. *Farm, Cottage, Camp and Canoe in Maritime Canada*. London: G. Routledge & Sons, 1907.

Smith, Donald B. *Sacred Feathers: The Reverend Peter Jones (Kahkewaquonaby) and the Mississauga Indians*. Toronto: University of Toronto Press, 1987.

Smith, James G.E. "Leadership among the Indians of the Northern Woodlands." In *Currents in Anthropology: Essays in Honour of Sol Tax*, edited by Robert Hinshaw, 306–24. The Hague: Mouton, 1979.

– *Salmon River, Digby County, Nova Scotia – Vital Records, 1849–1907, from the Registers of the Roman Catholic Parish of St. Vincent de Paul*. Clearwater, FL: Owl Books, n.d. (c.1977–78).

Smith, Nicholas. "Politics and Western Religion Shape the Wabanaki World." *Papers of the Forty-First Algonquian* Conference, edited by Karl S. Hele and J. Randoph Valentine, 280–99. Albany: University of New York Press, 2013.

Speck, Frank Gouldsmith. *Beothuk and Micmac*. Edited by F.W. Hodge. New York: Museum of the American Indian/Heye Foundation, 1922.

– "The Eastern Algonkian Wabanaki Confederacy." *American Anthropologist*, n.s. 17 (1945): 492–508.

– "Micmac Hunting Allotments in Nova Scotia, Bear River Band." In *Beothuk and Micmac*, by Frank Gouldsmith Speck, edited by F.W. Hodge, 100–1. New York: Museum of the American Indian/Heye Foundation, 1922.

Stanwood, Owen. "Unlikely Imperialist: The Baron of Saint-Castin and the Transformation of the Northeastern Borderlands." *French Colonial History* 5 (2004): 43–62.

Surette, L.L. "The Abbé Jean-Mandé Sigogne, from 1763 to 1844." In *Collections of the Nova Scotia Historical Society*, no. 25, 175–94. Halifax, 1942.

Surette, Roland F. *Métis/Acadian Heritage, 1604 to 2004*. Yarmouth: published by author, 2004.

Tattrie, Jon. *Daniel Paul, Mi'kmaw Elder*. Foreword by Wanda Thomas Bernard. Lawrencetown Beach, NS: Pottersfield, 2017.

Tennyson, Brian, ed. *Impressions of Cape Breton*. Sydney: University College of Cape Breton Press, 1986.

Trottier, Maxine, Dozay Christmas, and Helen Sylliboy. *Loon Rock: Pkwima Wkuntem*. Sydney: Cape Breton University Press, 1996.

Upton, L.F.S. "Babey, Peter Toney." *Dictionary of Canadian Biography* online, vol. 8 (1851–60).

– "Glode, Charles." *Dictionary of Canadian Biography* online, vol. 8 (1851–60).

– "Glode, Gabriel." *Dictionary of Canadian Biography* online, vol. 8 (1851–60).

– "Indian Policy in Colonial Nova Scotia, 1783–1871." *Acadiensis* 5, no. 1 (1975): 3–31.

– "Julien (Julian), John." *Dictionary of Canadian Biography* online, vol. 5 (1801–20).

– *Micmacs and Colonists: Indian-White Relations in the Maritimes, 1713–1867*. Vancouver: University of British Columbia Press, 1979.

– "Peminuit Paul, Jacques-Pierre." *Dictionary of Canadian Biography* online, vol. 12 (1891–1900).

– "Peminuit (Pominout) Paul, Louis-Benjamin." *Dictionary of Canadian Biography* online, vol. 7 (1836–50).

Vernon, C.W. "Indians of Saint John Island." *Acadiensis* 3 (1903): 110–15.

Vigneras, L.A. "L'Isle Royale en 1716." *Revue d'histoire de l'Amerique française* 13, no. 3 (1959): 422–34.

Wallace, Anthony F.C. "The Value of the Speck Papers for Ethnohistory." In "*The American Indian*": *A Conference in the American Philosophical Society,*" APS Library Publication no. 2, 20–6. Philadelphia: APS, 1968.

Wallis, Wilson D., and Ruth Sawtell Wallis. *The Micmac Indians of Eastern Canada.* Minneapolis: University of Press, 1955.

Walls, Martha. "Mi'kmaw Politicism in the Origins of the Micmac Community Development Program, 1899–1951." *Journals of the Royal Nova Scotia Historical Society* 20 (2017): 1–11.

– *No Need of a Chief for This Band: The Maritime Mi'kmaq and Federal Electoral Legislation, 1899–1951.* Vancouver: University of British Columbia Press, 2010.

Webster, Helen. *The Building of Fort Lawrence in Chignecto.* Historical Studies no. 3. Saint John: New Brunswick Museum, 1941.

– *Charles des Champs de Boishébert: A Canadian Soldier in Acadia.* Shediac: privately printed, 1931.

– *The Forts of Chignecto: A Study of the Eighteenth-Century Conflict between France and Great Britain in America.* Shediac, NB: published by author, 1930.

– ed. *Journals of Beausejour.* Halifax: Public Archives of Nova Scotia, 1937.

– "The Manners, Customs, Language, and Literature of the Micmac Indians." In Silus Tertius Rand, *Legends of the Micmacs,* xxx–xlvi. New York: Longmans, Green, 1894.

– *Thomas Pichon, "The Spy of Beausejour": An Account of his Career in Europe and America.* Halifax: Public Archives of Nova Scotia, 1937.

West, John. *A Journal of a Mission to the Indians of the British Provinces of New Brunswick and Nova Scotia.* London: Seeley, 1827.

White, Richard. *The Middle Ground: Indians, Empires and Republics in the Great Lakes Region, 1650–1815.* Cambridge: Cambridge University Press, 1991.

White, Sophie. "A Baser Commerce: Retailing, Class, and Gender in French Colonial New Orleans." *William and Mary Quarterly,* 3rd ser., 63, no. 3 (2006): 517–50.

White, Stephen A. *Dictionnaire généalogique des familles acadiennes: Première partie, 1636 à 1714.* Moncton: Centre d'études acadiennes, University of Moncton, 1999.

Whitehead, Ruth Holmes. "Christiana Morris: Micmac Artist and Artists' Model." *Material History Bulletin,* Spring 1977, National Museum of Man, Ottawa, 1–14.

– "Cope, John Noel." *Dictionary of Canadian Biography* online, vol. 14 (1911–21).

– *Elitekey: Micmac Culture from 1600 A.D. to the Present.* Halifax: Nova Scotia Museum, 1980.

– "The Life of Jerry Lonecloud." In *Tracking Doctor Lonecloud: Showman to Legend Keeper.* Introduction by Donald Julien. Fredericton: Goose Lane Editions, 2002.

– "Lonecloud, Jerry." *Dictionary of Canadian Biography* online, vol. 15 (1921–39).

– "Memoir of Jerry Lonecloud." In *Tracking Doctor Lonecloud: Showman to Legend Keeper.* Fredericton: Goose Lane Editions, 2002.

– *The Micmac Ethnology Collection of the Nova Scotia Museum.* Curatorial Report No. 25. Halifax: Nova Scotia Museum, September 1974.

– *Micmac Quillwork: Micmac Indian Techniques of Porcupine Quill Decoration, 1600–1950.* Halifax: Nimbus, 1982.

– *Niniskamijinaqik/Ancestral Images: The Mi'kmaq in Art and Photography.* Halifax: Nimbus, 2015.

– *Nova Scotia: The Protohistoric Period 1500–1635.* Halifax: Nova Scotia Museum, 1993.

– *The Old Man Told Us: Excerpts from Mi'kmaw History, 1500–1950.* Halifax: Nimbus, 1991.

- "Paul, Mary Christianne." *Dictionary of Canadian Biography* online, vol. 11 (1881–90).
- "Peminuit Paul, Jacques-Pierre." *Dictionary of Canadian Biography* online, vol. 12 (1891–1900).
- *Stories from the Six Worlds: Micmac Legends.* Halifax: Nimbus, 1988.
- *Tracking Doctor Lonecloud: Showman to Legend Keeper.* Fredericton: Goose Lane Editions, 2002.
- "A Visit with Max Basque, Whycocomagh" (interview). *Cape Breton's Magazine*, no. 51, 1 February 1989.
- "Wilmot, Peter." *Dictionary of Canadian Biography* online, vol. 16 (1931–40).

Whitelaw, Marjory, ed. *The Dalhousie Journals.* Vol. 1. Ottawa: Oberon, 1978.

Whiteley, William H. "The Establishment of the Moravian Mission in Labrador and British Policy, 1763–83." *Canadian Historical Review* 45, no. 1 (1964): 29–50.
- "Pallister, Sir Hugh." *Dictionary of Canadian Biography* online, vol. 4 (1771–1800).

Wicken, Bill. "26 August 1726: A Case Study in Mi'kmaq-New England Relations in the Early Eighteenth Century." *Acadiensis* 23, no. 1 (1993): 5–22.

Wicken, William C. *The Colonization of Mi'kmaw Memory and History, 1794–1928: The King v. Gabriel Sylliboy.* Toronto: University of Toronto Press, 2012.
- "'Heard It from Our Grandfathers': Mi'kmaq Treaty Tradition and the *Sylliboy* Case of 1928." *UNB Law Journal* 44 (1995): 145–61.
- "Mi'kmaq Decisions: Antoine Tecouenemac, the Conquest, and the Treaty of Utrecht." In *The "Conquest of Acadia," 1710: Imperial, Colonial and Aboriginal Constructions,* by John G. Reid, Maurice Basque, Elizabeth Mancke, Barry Moody, Geoffrey Plank, and William Wicken, 86–100. Toronto: University of Toronto Press, 2004.
- "Mi'kmaq Land in Southwestern Nova Scotia, 1771–1823." In *Making Adjustments: Change and Continuity in Planter Nova Scotia, 1759–1800*, edited by Margaret Conrad, 113–22. Fredericton: Acadiensis, 1991.
- *Mi'kmaq Treaties on Trial: History, Land and Donald Marshall Junior.* Toronto: University of Toronto Press, 2002.
- "Re-examining Mi'kmaq-Acadian Relations, 1635–1755." In *Vingt ans après, Habitants et marchands: Lectures de l'histoire des XVIIe et XVIIIe siècles canadiens*, edited by Sylvie Dépatie, Catherine Desbarats, Danielle Gauvreau, Mario Lalancette, and Thomas Wien, 93–114. Montreal and Kingston: McGill-Queen's University Press, 1998.

Wien, Fred. *Rebuilding the Economic Base of Indian Communities: The Micmac in Nova Scotia.* Montreal: Institute for Research on Public Policy, 1986.

Wilson, Isaiah W. *Geography and History of Digby County.* Digby: printed by author, 1893.

Wolverton, Nan. "American Indian Baskets Made in New England." *The Magazine Antiques*, January 2004, 184–90.

Wyatt, Malcolm, and E.R. Faribault. "The Gold Fields of Nova Scotia." *Geological Survey of Canada Memoir 20.* Ottawa: Department of Mines, Geological Survey, 1912.

York, Geoffrey. *The Dispossessed: Life and Death in Native Canada.* Toronto: Lester & Orpen Dennys, 1989.

Personal Diaries

Janet Chute, "A Southwestern Tour," June and July 1990
- "Visit to Antigonish," May 1990
- "Trip to Cape Breton," June 1991
- "St. Anne's Day Celebrations, St. Peter's, Cape Breton," July 1991
- "Fieldwork Notes from Southwestern Nova Scotia," 1991–2016
- "Visit to the Sanipass Family of Maine," 2010

Carrie A. Gloade, "Fieldwork Notes on the Gloade Family," 2012

Natalie McConnell, "Lost in Cape Breton, a Diary," 1991

Online Resources

Acadians at Malagomich: www.acadian-home.org/chezzetcook.html (concerning Henry Schomberg threatening the Malagomich Indigenous and Acadian community).

Bartlett family: Nancy Pine Beers, *Ring of Firelight: A Creative Perspective of Off-Reservation, Non-Status American Indian Poetry, Stories and History* (blog), http://ringoffirelight.blogspot.com/; and "Bartlett, Mi'kmaw Indian, Yarmouth," genealogy.com, "In reply to: Re: Children of James Bartlett," 20 February 2002. https://www.genealogy.com/forum/surnames/topics/bartlett/3316/.

Benoit First Nation. http://www.benoitfirstnation.ca/. Accessed 3/16/2023.

Black, David W. "Pioneers of New Brunswick Archaeology II: Abraham Gesner." Department of Anthropology, University of New Brunswick, Fredericton. https://www.unb.ca/faculty-staff/directory/_resources/pdf/arts-fr/dwblack/gesner.pdf. Accessed 16 March 2023.

Bras d'Or First Nation. https://www.crwflags.com/fotw/flags/xa-braso.html. Accessed 16 March 2023.

"Burying the Hatchet Ceremony (Nova Scotia)." Wikipedia. https://en.wikipedia.org/wiki/Burying_the_Hatchet_ceremony_(Nova_Scotia).

Cape Breton University. "Ethnographies" (continuing Mi'kmaw student project examining the history and description of Mi'kmaw communities in Nova Scotia).

Cormier, Steven A. "Acadians in Gray: Acadians Who Found Refuge in Louisiana, February 1764–early 1800s," with appendices, 2007. Information from this source is accessible at https://www.lazeut.com/genweb2/showsource.php?sourceID=S658&tree=arbre1.

"Descendants of Francois-Xavier Neocout": http://www.nekg-vt.com/DTM/picard/francois/d1.htm.

Drolet, Yves. *Histoire généalogue de la famille Denys*. Montreal, 2016. https://numerique.banq.qc.ca/patrimoine/details/52327/2518395.

"Genealogy Trace: Fort Folly First Nation." https://fortfolly.ca/geneology-trace.

Guidry, Marty. Information from "Ancestry of the Guedry Family of Clare, Nova Scotia (Jedry, Geddry)," "The Last Guedrys in Merliguèche, or the Labrador and Guedry Families," "Survival of a Family: The Family of Augustin Guidry and Jeanne Hebert," "Survival of Family: The Family of Jean-Baptiste Guédry & Madeleine Mius d'Azy," and "Survival of a Family: The Family of Paul Guidry *dit* Jovial and Anne Mius d'Entremont d'Azit [d'Azy] de Pobomcoup," which were formerly online as individual articles, is now found at https://freepages.rootsweb.com/~guedrylabinefamily/genealogy/history.html.

"History of the Saqmawaq of Ktaqmkuk (Chiefs of Newfoundland)." http://www.oocities.org/pilip/saqamaq.htm?20188. Accessed 26 July 2005.

Hurlburt, B.R., "Grassroutes, Kemptville, Yarmouth." http://yarmouth.org/villages/kemptvil/history/.

"Kemptville's Gold Mines, 1881–1919." https://yarmouthhistory.ca/yarmouthhistory/LocalHistory/Entries/2015/7/1_Kemptvilles_Gold_Mines__18811919.html.

Lane Jonah, Anne Marie. "The Acadians of Cape Breton," 2004. http://www.krausehouse.ca/krause/FortressOfLouisbourgResearchWeb/Search/AcadiaPaperE.html.

MacDonald, Peggy. "Chapel Island First Nation Celebrates Return of Historic Altar." CBC News. https://www.cbc.ca/news/canada/nova-scotia/chapel-island-first-nation-celebrates-return-of-historic-altar-1.3160315.

Muise, Earl, and Chester A. Muise. "Searching the Truth: A Critique of Existing Research in the Genealogy of the Mius Family, February 2004." http://les_mius.tripod.com/.

Musée des Acadiens des Pubnicos et Centre de recherche. "Local Stories and Folklore: The Lake Road (*Le Chemin du Lac*)." https://museeacadien.ca/archives/OLD/argyle/html/ecomm09.htm.

– "Port Lomeron or Chebogue." https://museeacadien.ca/en/port-lomeron-or-chebogue/.

Newell genealogy page: "Newell Family History," in "Genealogy ramblings of a Mainer with roots in Newfoundland, Canada (French, Portugal, and Scotland), England, and Penobscot Native American." https://geneologymaine.wordpress.com/2015/12/30/7/.

NSARM. "An Acadian Parish Remembered." (St. Jean Baptiste Parish, Annapolis Loyal, 1705–1722). https://archives.novascotia.ca/acadian/results/?Search=Bourg&fieldSelect=last&Language=.

NSARM. "An Acadian Parish Reborn: Post-Deportation Argyle – First 50 Years of Catholic Parish Records 1799–1849." (Parish of St. Anne du Ruisseau, Argyle, Yarmouth County). https://archives.novascotia.ca/acadian/reborn/catholic/.

NSARM. Historical Vital Statistics online (births, marriages, and deaths). https://archives.novascotia.ca/vital-statistics/

NSARM. "Men in the Mines: A History of Mining Activity in Nova Scotia, 1720–1992." https://archives.novascotia.ca/meninmines/.

NSM. "Mi'kmaq Portraits Collection." Organized and captioned by Ruth Holmes Whitehead. https://novascotia.ca/museum/mikmaq/default.asp.

Paulette, Jane. "The Mi'kmaq Relation with Kat (American Eel)." Social Research for Sustainable Fisheries (SRSF), March 2002. https://people.stfx.ca/rsg/srsf/researchreports1/FactSheets/Factsheet7.pdf.

Pike, Dwayne. "A Partial List of Account Holders in the Bird Ledgers for Bonne Bay (1839–1841)." https://sites.rootsweb.com/~cannf/npbb_birdpartial.htm.

Pinn, Travis. "Gigi: A Short Photo *Biography* of a Mi'kmaw Woman, Lucy Marie Celeste Charles Pinn, Northern Lights, Aka Aunty Loo & Nana (1905–1985)." In possession of Janet E. Chute.

Powell, Frank. "Who Was Mattie Mitchell?" https://www.vcn.bc.ca/~fgp/who.htm. Accessed 10 October 2005.

Saint Matthew's Church, Halifax. "St. Matthew's United Church, History." https://www.stmatts.ns.ca/about/history/. Accessed 13 March 2023.

Sylliboy, Helen. Translation of *Sa'n Patis* [John Baptiste] *Tenio'q, Saqmawaq Alasutmelsewanej Eskisoqnik: Unama'kik, Penatmuiku's 5 tesukna'q,* 1918 (Grand Chief John Denny Jr.'s funeral notice). https://www.cbu.ca/indigenous-affairs/mikmaq-resource-centre/miscellany/message-on-the-death-of-chief-john-denny/. Accessed 16 March 2023.

Szick, Lark. "LeJeunes in the Acadian Censuses." http://cbnsorg.cbns.ca/LeJ_CensusExtracts.htm/. Accessed 13 March 2023.

White, Stephen A. "Acadian Family Names of the 18th Century." http://www.acacian-home.org/names-acadian.html.

Vaughan, Garth. "Birthplace of Hockey," 1999. https://birthplaceofhockey.com/hockey-history/research/#:~:text=The%20origin%20of%20the%20history,by%20author%20historian%20Garth%20Vaughan.

Young, Daniel P. "History of the Youngs of Nipisiguit." Posted online by djdannyazz on 16 November 2016. https://johnyoung334.wordpress.com/2016/11/16/history-of-the-youngs-of-nipisiguit/.

Interviews, 1990–1991

Bernard Amiro, West Pubnico

Jeremy Bartlett, Yarmouth

David Brooks, Shubenacadie

Alex Denny, Eskasoni

Mrs. Rose (Barney) Francis, Yarmouth and Prince Edward Island

David Gehue, Shubenacadie

Frank Jeremy, Wildcat, Queens County

Donald M. Julien, Millbrook and Truro

Doug Knockwood, Shubenacadie

Henry Knockwood, Dartmouth

Noel Knockwood, Halifax

Mrs. Spurgeon Knockwood, New Ross
William Labrador, Gold River
Donald Marshall, Jr., Halifax
Donald Marshall, Sr., Halifax and Eskasoni
Murdena Marshall, Eskasoni
Greg McEwan, Bear River
Richard McEwan, Bear River
John Muise *dit* Le Dude, Lower Eel Brook
Sylvestre Miuse, Quinan
Charles (Charlie) Paul, Yarmouth
Lillian Pictou, Yarmouth
John Joe Sark, Lennox Island, Prince Edward Island
Patrick Wilmot, Shubenacadie
Max Zinc, Gold River

Interviews, 1992–2023

Jean Babin, Ste. Anne du Ruisseau
Muriel Barr, Truro
Elsie Charles Basque, Yarmouth
Marie Ann Battiste, Eskasoni, Cape Breton
Kevin Boucher, Bathurst
Walter Commeau, Halifax
Vernon Cope, Halifax
Richard Denny, Eskasoni
Sarah Denny, Eskasoni
Debbie Gloade, Bear River
Debra Gloade, Yarmouth
Gordon Gloade, Millbrook
Mike Gloade, Millbrook
Frances Godin-Grey, Bathurst
Caroline Gould, Waycobah, Whycocomagh
Roddy Gould, Waycobah
Joseph Howe, Sheet Harbour
Donald Julien, Millbrook
Sandy Julien Jr., Millbrook
Henry Knockwood, Dartmouth
Noel Knockwood, Halifax
Mrs. Spurgeon Knockwood (née Florence May Corkum), New Ross
Marguerite Labrador, Cole Harbour
Mrs. John Labrador (née Bent), Kentville
Lillian Marshall, Potoleg
John Muise *dit* Le Dude, Lower Eel Brook
Sylvestre Muise, Quinan
Peter Partington, Lockeport
Philip Partington, Lockeport
David Peter-Paul, Bathurst
Basil Peters, Millbrook
Fred Phillips, Cambridge, Annapolis County
Joseph Nicholas Prisk, Bathurst

Nicholas Prisk, Bathurst
Brian Purdy, Liverpool
Linda Rafuse, Liverpool
Dan Ramsay, Lequille
Viola Robinson, Yarmouth, Truro, and Halifax
Mary Jane Stevens, Millbrook

Index

Peguidalouet, Catherine-Charlotte (daughter of Louis Peguidalouet; wife of Charles-Michel Sischao), 393

Peguidalouet, Francis. *See* Emable, Francis

Peguidalouet, Jeannot or Janot (son of Joseph Peguidalouet and Thérèse; known as "Petit Jean"; husband of Marie-Joseph), 25, 307, 360–1, 368–9, 372–84; trade and emigration strategies, 386–400, 402, 404, 406, 421, 424

Peguidalouet, Joseph (father of Jeannot Peguidalouet; husband of Thérèse), 369

Peguidalouet, Louis (son of Bernard Peguidalouet and Ann-Marie; husband of Janette Doucet), 394, 804n294

Peguidalouet, Louis (younger brother of Jeannot Peguidalouet; second wife Marie-Marthe Googoo, daughter of Bernard Googoo; father of Rosalie), 381, 393

Peguidalouet, Rosalie (daughter of Louis Peguidalouet and Marie-Marthe Googoo), 393

Peguidalouet, Véronique (daughter of Bernard Peguidalouet and Marie-Anne; wife of François Doucet), 394

Pejepscot Proprietors, 710n210

Pekide8alvet. *See* Peguidalouet

Pellerin, Janvae, 328

Peminout, Paul (district chief living at Stewicke, Nova Scotia), 190, 203; land grant on Stewiacke River, 206–8, 213, 224, 231, 332

Peminoute, Agnes, 631n1

Peminouite, Charles, 631n1

Peminouite, Madeleine, 631n1

Peminouite, René, 631n1Peminout Paul, Ablius (son of Pierre Pemonout Paul Sr.), 208

Peminout Paul, Alexis (son of Jacques-Pierre Peminout Paul), 208, 213

Peminout Paul, Betsy Ann (wife of John Williams), 38

Peminout Paul, "Big Peter" (Stephen Peter Paul; son of Christopher Peminout Paul and Margaret Barbaire), 165, 228–9; regalia and medals missing during instalment ceremonies as chief, 228

Peminout Paul, Christopher (husband of Margaret Barbaire; Mi'kmaw judge), 221, 227, 251, 416

Peminout Paul, Claude (son of Jacques-Pierre Peminout Paul), 208

Peminout Paul, Francis (son of Jacques-Pierre Peminout Paul; wife is Mohawk), 208, 215–21; memorial drafted by Silus Tertius Rand, 214–15, 222–5, 231

Peminout Paul, François (son of Paul Peminout), 207

Peminout Paul, Gorham (son of Jacques-Pierre Peminout Paul; wife is Malecite), 119, 213–21, 223

Peminout Paul, Hobblewes- (possibily "Ambroise"; father of Mary Christiana Peminout Paul), 207

Peminout Paul, Isaac (son of "Big Peter" Peminout Paul), 655–6n269

Peminout Paul, Jacques (or James; son of Pierre Peminout Paul Sr.), 153, 207–8, 214

Peminout Paul, Jacques-Pierre (or James, son of Paul Peminout), 104, 153, 207–9; licence for Jacques for tract at Shubenacade Grand Lake, 207; visits Monk's office in January 1784, 208–14, 218; requests support for farming, 220, 221, 227, 246

Peminout Paul, Jacques Pierre (son of Louis-Benjamin Peminout Paul; first wife Sally; second wife Madeleine Pictou), 208; Sipekne'katik district chief, 225–8, 231, 249, 416

Peminout Paul, James (son of Jacques-Pierre Peminout Paul), 208

Peminout Paul, Jean Lucien, or John (son of Jacques-Pierre Peminout Paul) 208, 213

Peminout Paul, Joseph (son of Paul Peminout), 207, 211

Peminout Paul, Joseph (son of Pierre Peminout Paul Sr.), 208, 221

Peminout Paul, Louis (son of Louis-Benjamin Peminout Paul and Madleine Ball), 208, 215–16, 221, 223

Peminout Paul, Louis-Benjamin (Mi'kmaw name "Pausaumigh Pemmenauweet"; husband of Madelaine Ball), 207–8; Sipekne'katik district chief, 213–16; petition to Queen Victoria, 216–18; attends Eastern Wabanaki Confederacy meeting, 213, 217–18, 220, 231

Peminout Paul, Marie-Madeleine (wife of François-Xavier Neocout), 194

Peminout Paul, Mary Christiana (wife of Tom Morris). *See* Morris, Mary Christiana or Christianne

Peminout Paul, Nestus (son of Pierre Pemonout Paul Sr.), 208

Peminout Paul, Peter (son of Jacques-Pierre Peminout Paul), 208

Peminout Paul, Phillip (son of Paul Peminout), 207

Peminout Paul, Pierre Jr. (son of Pierre Peminout Paul Sr.), 208, 214

Peminout Paul, Pierre Sr. (son of Paul Peminout; husband of Marie), 207–8, 224–5

Peminout Paul, Samuel (son of Jacques-Pierre Peminout Paul), 208, 213–14, 210

Peminout Paul, Sarah Ann (wife of Stephen Knockwood Jr.), 190–1

Peminout Paul, Simon (son of Paul Peminout), 207

Peminout Paul, Stephen Peter. *See* Peminout Paul, "Big Peter"

Author Biographies

Berton A. ("Sandy") Balcolm was for many years a senior historian at the Fortress of Louisbourg Historic Park. His interests range widely, and include the history of the North Atlantic fishery, eighteenth-century French costume design, Cape Breton missions, Mi'kmaw biography, and Mi'kmaw hieroglyphic script.

Diane Chisholm was coordinator of the Mi'kmaq Resource Centre at Cape Breton University, Sydney, and is now enjoying her retirement. She retains her longtime interest in Mi'kmaw education, spirituality, and biography.

Janet E. Chute's interests include resource campaigns launched by Anishinaabe leaders north of Lakes Huron and Superior, and the lives of Mi'kmaw men and women from the eighteenth century to the late 1960s. For many years she has taught anthropology, Indigenous studies, Canadian studies, and ethnohistory at Dalhousie University and Mount Saint Vincent University in Halifax, and in years past was an adjunct of Dalhousie's School of Resource and Environmental Studies. She is the principal investigator for the SSHRC project that gave rise to this collection of Mi'kmaw biographies.

Carrie Gloade holds a degree in education from Mount Saint Vincent University. She was employed as the Mi'kmaw education consultant at Annapolis Valley Regional School Board and is presently working in the educational field at Millbrook, near Truro, Nova Scotia.

Anne Marie Lane Jonah was a senior historian with the Fortress of Louisbourg Historic Park and is currently with Parks Canada in Halifax. She has written on gender, commerce, culture, and cuisine, and in this volume provides biographical insights into the lives of eighteenth-century Mi'kmaw women on both the Acadian mainland and Île Royale (Cape Breton).

Donald M. Julien, CM, ONS, DCL, DHum, is a peace-time veteran of the Canadian army and has won many accolades as an educator, historian, writer, and administrator. From

1994 to 2022 he was director of the Mainland Confederacy of Mi'kmaq and has served as an honorary lieutenant-colonel since 2011.

Doris Labradore, a graduate of Dalhousie University, conducts historical research on subjects pertaining to the Mi'kmaq and Acadians of southwestern Nova Scotia.

Bunnie McBride is an anthropologist with extensive experience in journalism, cultural ecology, Indigenous biography, and social activism. She and her husband, Harald E.L. Prins, have a special interest in the Mi'kmaq and were instrumental in securing legal status for the Aroostook Band of Mi'kmaq in Maine.

Mora Dianne O'Neill has since 1997 been associate curator, Historical Prints and Drawings, Art Gallery of Nova Scotia. She has prepared two exhibitions annually for installation in the John and Norma Oyler Gallery of Early Canadian Prints and Drawings at that gallery. She was co-curator with Viviane Gray, director of the Indigenous Art Centre in Ottawa, of a touring exhibition of work by contemporary Mi'kmaw artists in 1993, and was guest curator of *At the Great Harbour: 250 Years on the Halifax Waterfront*, installed at the AGNS in 1999.

Nicholas ("Nik") Phillips was a student in the Sociology and Anthropology Department at Mount Saint Vincent University in Halifax when he joined this biographical project. He subsequently graduated with a master's degree in child and youth studies from the Mount and is currently director of early childhood education at Millbrook, near Truro, Nova Scotia.

Travis Pinn has been exploring his genealogical roots, which lie deep in the Indigenous history of the Cape Sable district of southwestern Nova Scotia. A descendant of Lucy Charles, Travis is currently pursuing a master's degree in sociocultural anthropology at Northern Arizona University. His research interests include examining the intersections of history, space, place, and power in multicultural settings. His current research applies an Indigenous framework that addresses institutional obstacles Indigenous students face at a predominantly white public university in the southwest United States.

Harald E.L. Prins, a noted anthropologist, photographer, filmmaker, and Indigenous rights activist, has taught at Bowdoin and Colby colleges and recently retired as a Distinguished Professor at Kansas State University. His many works on the Eastern Wabanaki include *The Mi'kmaq: Resistance, Accommodation, and Cultural Survival*. He and his wife, Bunny McBride, live in Maine.

Heather Sutherland, whose interests embrace nineteenth-century Mi'kmaw communities along Nova Scotia's eastern coast, has recently completed her master's degree in Atlantic Canada studies at Saint Mary's University in Halifax.